ISBN 978-1-5282-4157-1
PIBN 10920020

English
Français
Deutsche
Italiano
Español
Português

www.forgottenbooks.com

Mythology Photography **Fiction**
Fishing Christianity **Art** Cooking
Essays Buddhism Freemasonry
Medicine **Biology** Music **Ancient
Egypt** Evolution Carpentry Physics
Dance Geology **Mathematics** Fitness
Shakespeare **Folklore** Yoga Marketing
Confidence Immortality Biographies
Poetry **Psychology** Witchcraft
Electronics Chemistry History **Law**
Accounting **Philosophy** Anthropology
Alchemy Drama Quantum Mechanics
Atheism Sexual Health **Ancient History**
Entrepreneurship Languages Sport
Paleontology Needlework Islam
Metaphysics Investment Archaeology
Parenting Statistics Criminology
Motivational

APPLETONS'

ANNUAL CYCLOPÆDIA

AND

REGISTER OF IMPORTANT EVENTS

OF THE YEAR

1887.

EMBRACING POLITICAL, MILITARY, AND ECCLESIASTICAL AFFAIRS; PUBLIC
DOCUMENTS; BIOGRAPHY, STATISTICS, COMMERCE, FINANCE, LITERA-
TURE, SCIENCE, AGRICULTURE, AND MECHANICAL INDUSTRY.

NEW SERIES, VOL. XII.

WHOLE SERIES, VOL. XXVII.

NEW YORK:
D. APPLETON AND COMPANY,
1, 3, AND 5 BOND STREET.
1889.

´PREFACE.

ONE of the most notable features in this volume of the ANNUAL CYCLOPÆDIA is to be found in the group of patriotic articles—the Grand Army of the Republic, the Loyal Legion, the United States Medal of Honor, and Memorial Day. The article on the Medal of Honor is especially valuable from the fact that it presents lists (not accessible elsewhere) of the soldiers and sailors who have received the medal. These articles are illustrated with a brilliant colored plate. Another illustrated article of special interest is that on Modern Houses, which shows the wonderful progress in American domestic architecture, with views of some of the finest residences that have been erected in recent years. At the other end of the social scale we find the remarkable series of Strikes, which are classified and set forth in a way to be convenient for ready reference. The Disasters and other Events of the year are also recorded briefly in chronological order. Among the articles that will be found timely this year are those on the laws, customs, and theories of Elections, on the Fisheries and treaties relating thereto, and on the Interstate Commerce Law, the last named being from the pen of Hon. Thomas M. Cooley, chairman of the Commission. Closely related to these is the learned article on Treaty-making Power of the United States. In relation to education, we have the articles on Industrial Education, Indian Education, Mind-Reading, Physical Training, and Volapük. Among the organizations treated are the Law-and-Order League, the Ancient Order of United Workmen, Mutual Aid Societies, and the White Cross Society. The scientific articles include that on Astronomical Progress and Discovery, by Prof. Harkness, of the Naval Observatory at Washington; Chemistry and Metallurgy, by Dr. William J. Youmans, editor of "The Popular Science Monthly"; those on Emery-Wheels and Engineering, by Col. Charles L. Norton; that on utilizing the power of Niagara Falls; and the description of the new Croton Aqueduct. Among the industrial topics treated are those on Photo-Engraving, Porpoise-Hunting, Postal Facilities, Salt-Mining, and Tree-Planting. The special articles, on subjects not treated every year, include those on Domesticated Buffalo, Guns for Coast Defense, Library Laws, Polo, Records of the Turf, and Prison Reform. Besides the usual general article on Patents, some of the inventions of popular interest are treated, including Mechanical Carriers, Naphtha Motors, and the mysterious Keely Motor. The necrology of the year includes Henry Ward

Beecher, the greatest of pulpit orators; Alvan Clark, the most successful tele-
scope-maker; Spencer F. Baird, Secretary of the Smithsonian Institution; James
B. Eads, the eminent civil engineer; Gen. William B. Hazen, head of the
Weather Bureau; Roswell D. Hitchcock and Mark Hopkins, the eminent
scholars; Jenny Lind, the greatest singer of her time; Lord Lyons, the British
diplomatist; Ulysses Mercur and William B. Woods, jurists; John Roach, the
greatest of American ship-builders; James Speed, of President Lincoln's Cabinet; Emma Lazarus, John G. Saxe, and Benjamin F. Taylor, poets; William A.
Wheeler, ex-Vice-President; Bishops Lee and Potter, Catherine L. Wolfe, Elihu
B. Washburne, and Edward L. Youmans. Portraits of all these and others will
be found in the volume, and an unusually large number of brief sketches of those
who passed away during the year. The three portraits on copper—of Henry
Ward Beecher, President Sadi-Carnot, and the new Emperor of Germany—were
etched by Valerian Gribayedoff. The portraits in the text were drawn by
Jacques Reich, whose fine work has been so noticeable in the new "Cyclopædia
of American Biography."

The article on Recent Growth of American Cities is continued from last year,
and the numerous regular topics that are treated every year have been carefully
and fully discussed by competent writers, most of whom are regular contributors,
and keep track of the subjects from year to year. An Index for this volume
will be found at the end, and a combined Index for the twelve volumes of the
series is issued separately.

NEW YORK, *April 2, 1888.*

CONTRIBUTORS.

Among the Contributors to this Volume of the "Annual Cyclopædia" are the following:

Lyman Abbott, D. D.,
Editor of the Christian Union.
BEECHER, HENRY WARD.

Phineas T. Barnum.
LIND, JENNY.

Marcus Benjamin,
Fellow of the London Chemical Society.
BAIRD, SPENCER FULLERTON,
HAYDEN, FERDINAND VANDEVEER,
PHARMACY,
and other articles.

John Paul Bocock.
KEELY MOTOR.

J. H. A. Bone,
Editor of the Cleveland (O.) Plaindealer.
OHIO.

Charles Rollin Brainard.
MUTUAL AID SOCIETIES,
POSTAL FACILITIES.

James P. Carey,
Financial Editor of the Journal of Commerce.
FINANCIAL REVIEW OF 1887.

Gen. Charles A. Carleton, U. S. V.,
Recorder of the New York Commandery, Loyal
Legion.
LOYAL LEGION.

Henry Chadwick,
Of Editorial staff of Outing.
POLO.

John D. Champlin, Jr.,
Editor of Cyclopedia of Painters and Paintings.
FINE ARTS IN 1887.

Hon. Thomas M. Cooley,
Chairman of Interstate Commerce Commission.
INTERSTATE COMMERCE LAW.

Henry Dalby,
Editor of the Montreal Star.
CANADIAN ARTICLES.

Eaton S. Drone.
TREATY-MAKING POWER.

Maurice F. Egan,
Editor of the Freeman's Journal.
ROMAN CATHOLIC CHURCH.

Rev. William E. Griffis, D. D.,
Author of "The Mikado's Empire."
JAPAN.

George J. Hagar,
Of Newark (N. J.) Public Library.
ARTICLES IN AMERICAN OBITUARIES.

William Harkness,
Professor of Mathematics in the U. S. Navy.
ASTRONOMICAL PROGRESS AND DISCOVERY.

Frank Huntington, Ph. D.
FRANCE,
GREAT BRITAIN,
ZANZIBAR,
and other articles.

A. S. Isaacs, Ph. D.,
Editor of the Jewish Messenger.
JEWS.

Charles Kirchhoff.
CENTRAL AND SOUTH AMERICAN ARTICLES.

William H. Larrabee.
ANGLICAN CHURCHES,
ARCHÆOLOGY,
METHODISTS,
and other articles.

William F. MacLennan,
Of U. S. Treasury Department.
UNITED STATES, FINANCES OF THE.

Montague Marks,
Editor of the Art Amateur.
LAZARUS, EMMA.

Frederic G. Mather.
MIND-READING,
NIAGARA FALLS, UTILIZING POWER OF,
SALT-MINING,
and other articles.

Charles Alexander Nelson,
Of the Astor Library.
LIBRARY LAWS.

Col. Charles Ledyard Norton.
CARRIERS, MECHANICAL,
ENGINEERING,
GRAND ARMY OF THE REPUBLIC,
and other articles.

Frank H. Norton.
INDIAN EDUCATION,
PHOTO-ENGRAVING,
SAMOAN ISLANDS,
and other articles.

Rev. S. E. Ochsenford.
LUTHERANS.

Evangeline M. O'Connor.
GEOGRAPHICAL PROGRESS AND DISCOVERY.

William M. F. Round,
Secretary of Prison Association of New York.
PRISON REFORM.

Charles H. Saltmarsh.
UNITED WORKMEN, ANCIENT ORDER OF.

George W. Sheldon,
Author of "Artistic Country Seats."
HOUSES, MODERN.

T. O'Conor Sloane, Ph. D.
ASSOCIATIONS FOR ADVANCEMENT OF SCIENCE,
PATENTS.

Helen Ainslie Smith.
EDUCATION, INDUSTRIAL.

William Christopher Smith.
ARTICLES ON THE STATES AND TERRITORIES.

Rev. Jesse A. Spencer, D. D.
LITERATURE, CONTINENTAL,
PROTESTANT EPISCOPAL CHURCH.

Charles E. Sprague,
Author of "Hand-Book of Volapük."
VOLAPÜK.

Arthur Dudley Vinton.
ELECTIONS, LAWS, CUSTOMS, AND THEORIES OF,
STRIKES,
and other articles.

Louis von Eltz.
MUSIC IN 1887.

Zebulon L. White.
TURF, RECENT RECORDS OF.

Gen. George W. Wingate,
President of the National Rifle Association.
RIFLES, REPEATING.

Mrs. Annie Gibson Yates.
CRAIK, DINAH MARIA MULOCK,
LIBERIA.

William J. Youmans, M. D.
CHEMISTRY,
METALLURGY,
METEOROLOGY,
PHYSIOLOGY.

ILLUSTRATIONS.

PORTRAITS ETCHED ON COPPER.

BY VALERIAN GRIBAYEDOFF.

PAGE

THE CROWN-PRINCE (NOW EMPEROR) OF GERMANY . . . . . *Frontispiece*
HENRY WARD BEECHER 64
PRESIDENT CARNOT 288

PORTRAITS IN THE TEXT.

DRAWN BY JACQUES REICH.

PAGE

	PAGE		PAGE
SPENCER F. BAIRD	54	EMMA LAZARUS	414
LADY BRASSEY	70	JENNY LIND	421
ALVAN CLARK	137	LORD LYONS	451
DINAH M. MULOCK CRAIK . . .	212	ULYSSES MERCUR	479
DONALD M. DICKINSON . . .	776	HORATIO POTTER	604
JAMES B. EADS	229	JOHN ROACH	716
CHARLES S. FAIRCHILD . . .	776	JOHN G. SAXE	733
CROWN-PRINCE OF GERMANY AND HIS SON	321	JAMES SPEED	741
FERDINAND V. HAYDEN . . .	856	BENJAMIN F. TAYLOR . . .	757
WILLIAM B. HAZEN	858	ELIHU B. WASHBURNE . . .	799
ROSWELL D. HITCHCOCK . . .	359	WILLIAM A. WHEELER . . .	804
MARK HOPKINS	360	CATHERINE L. WOLFE . . .	807
ROBERT M. T. HUNTER . . .	371	WILLIAM B. WOODS	621
GUSTAV R. KIRCHHOFF . . .	412	EDWARD L. YOUMANS . . .	809

FULL-PAGE ILLUSTRATIONS.

COLORED PLATE—BADGES OF GRAND ARMY AND LOYAL LEGION, AND MEDAL OF HONOR . 329
MAP OF NEW HEBRIDES ISLANDS 538

ILLUSTRATIONS IN THE TEXT.

	PAGE		PAGE
TEMPLE OF BUBASTIS	20	COL. ANDREWS'S HOUSE . . .	362
JAR DISCOVERED AT L'ARGAR . .	23	LODGE OF FREDERICK L. AMES .	363
MECHANICAL CARRIERS (18 illustrations)	95–99	INTERIOR OF SEASIDE COTTAGE .	364
GOVERNMENT BUILDING AT ERIE .	120	G. N. BLACK'S HOUSE . . .	366
BANK IN TORONTO	131	JOSEPH H. CHOATE'S HOUSE .	367
BRIDGE AT POUGHKEEPSIE . .	253	WILLIAM SIMPSON JR.'S HOUSE .	369
LIFTING BRIDGE AT TARANTO . .	254	TRAVIS C. VAN BUREN'S HOUSE .	370
STIFFENED SUSPENSION BRIDGE (2 illus-		THE KEELY MOTOR (3 illustrations) .	408, 409
trations)	254, 255	NAPHTHA ENGINE	525
SECTIONS OF GREAT DAMS . . .	256	NEW CROTON AQUEDUCT (4 illustrations)	556–560
CROTON WATER-SHED . . .	256	RECENT INVENTIONS (12 illustrations)	651–656
THE GREAT RAFT	257	A PORPOISE	681
CAP FOR ARTESIAN WELL . . .	259	REPEATING RIFLES (4 illustrations) .	714, 715
HARBOR OF CEARÁ	260	A TARPON	756

THE

ANNUAL CYCLOPÆDIA.

A

ABYSSINIA, a monarchy in Eastern Africa, having an area of about 200,000 square miles, and a population estimated at 4,000,000 souls. The monarch, who is called the Negus, is Johannis, or John, formerly prince of the province of Tigré, who, after a period of civil warfare following the British invasion of 1868, was proclaimed king in 1872.

Treaty with England.—During the operations for the withdrawal of the Egyptian garrisons from the Soudan in the early part of 1884, concessions were offered to the Abyssinian Negus for the removal of the long-standing differences between him and the Egyptian Khedive. A formal delimitation of the frontier was offered, which would restore to him the territory of Bogos; also free transit for all goods, including arms and ammunition, through the port of Massowah, under British protection. It was further agreed that all difficulties in the matter of supplying an Aboona, or high-priest, for Abyssinia from one of the Coptic churches of Egypt should be removed. For these concessions King Johannis agreed to facilitate the retreat through his territory of the Egyptians at Kassala and other posts in the neighboring parts of the Soudan. All future disputes between Abyssinia and Egypt were to be referred to the British Government for arbitration. A treaty containing these provisions was concluded by Admiral Sir William Hewett as special British envoy. The Abyssinians subsequently more than redeemed their promises, not merely granting passage to the garrisons of Gallabat and Ghirra, but actively intervening for their rescue, and making a brave attempt to succor the Egyptians at Kassala.

The Italians at Massowah.—The port of Massowah, which had formerly been an object of dispute between the rulers of Abyssinia and the Khedive of Egypt, was taken possession of by Italy, with the concurrence of Great Britain, when the Egyptian garrisons were withdrawn from the Soudan, the Italians undertaking to carry out the British agreement

respecting the transit of merchandise. The Abyssinians did not desire to possess Massowah, not being able to hold so distant a post, and were willing that it should remain in the possession of Great Britain, but grew jealous when it was handed over to the Italians, whom they immediately suspected of aggressive designs on their territory. Their suspicions increased when the Italians established friendly relations with the Habab tribe, which was in rebellion against the Abyssinians, and when they occupied places in the surrounding country for the troops that had been in dispute between the Abyssinians and Egyptians, but which the latter had never gone so far as to take possession of. King John sent a letter to the Queen of England, complaining of these acts, and asserting that the Italians obstructed the transit of goods. The Italian Government dispatched an imposing mission, in the beginning of 1886, to confer with King Johannis, and conclude a treaty similar to that made by the English. The Italians were willing to increase the concessions already granted, and desired in return to extend their settlements so as to include healthful quarters for their soldiers in the district of Keren, situated in the uplands near Massowah. The English Government determined on sending an envoy to accompany the Italian officers for the purpose of making explanations that would help to bring about a good understanding between the Italians and the Negus, and also of conveying presents and expressions of gratitude for the aid given by the Abyssinians in extricating the Egyptian garrisons. The Italian envoys were recalled, when it became evident that they would not be cordially received. The Englishman proceeded alone, and at Asmara, the first Abyssinian village, met Ras Aloula, the King's general, who was incensed at reports of Italian encroachments, and threatened to attack their advanced positions. The envoy found the Negus also annoyed. No steps were taken by the Italians, after their rebuff, to remove the coolness, or to allay the suspicions, which were fomented by Frenchmen and Greeks in Abyssinia, and by the Arab sheiks whose territory lies between Abyssinia and the sea.

Attack on Italian Troops.—The post of Saati was occupied by bashi-bazouks when the Italians took possession of Massowah. The Abyssinians complained of the occupation, but at length connived at it, because the bashi-bazouks gave protection to their caravans. In January, 1887, Gen. Gene, the commander of the Italian forces in Africa, made arrangements to forward European troops to Saati. Ras Aloula collected an army without the knowledge of the Italians, and marched upon Keren. Gen. Gene, in his dispatches giving intelligence of the hostile movement, said that he had means more than sufficient to repel any force that the Abyssinians could send against him. In a later dispatch he asked for a re-enforcement of 600 men, in order, if necessary, to make a military demonstration. The Ras sent a messenger to warn the Italian commander to evacuate the advanced forts, and to limit the occupation to Massowah, threatening to throw into chains Count Salimbeni, the leader of a scientific expedition to Abyssinia, if this were not done. On January 19 the Abyssinians attacked the Italian outposts at Monkullo. In a combat lasting four hours, more than half of their force, which numbered 300, were slain. Of the Italians five were killed, and three made prisoners. One of the prisoners was sent back with a letter saying, that if the Italians wished peace they must remain in Massowah. The commandant replied that peace was not desired on such conditions.

A day or two afterward a force of 1,500 men of all arms was sent out from Monkullo to succor Saati, and prevent that post from falling into the hands of the Abyssinians. Near Dogali the column, which was commanded by Col. Decristoforis, was attacked on January 24 by Ras Aloula's entire force. The Italians could not work their machine-guns, and sent back to Monkullo for more men and mitrailleuses. One of the two companies forming the garrison was dispatched under the command of Capt. Tanturi, but, before the re-enforcements came up, Col. Decristoforis's three companies were utterly routed. The bashi-bazouks fled in the beginning of the engagement. The Italian soldiers formed into a hollow square, and defended themselves as long as their ammunition lasted. The Abyssinians, who were said to number 20,000 men, had many Remington and Martini rifles. After the rout of the Italians, they withdrew to the hills. The Italian losses on the 25th and 26th were 23 officers and 407 men killed, and one officer and 81 soldiers wounded. Ras Aloula is said to have made the attack without the sanction of the Negus. A letter was dispatched, on January 26, by King Johannis, who said: "In the first place you took Wuaa, and now you have come to Saati to erect a fortress. What object have

you? Is not this country mine? Evacuate my country if you have come by orders. Why erect fortresses? You bring what is abundant with you—cannon, muskets, and soldiers." Ras Aloula, after the battle, returned with his troops to Asmara, whence he sent one of his prisoners, Maj. Piano, with a letter, saying: "What has happened was caused by your tricks. Let us now be friends, as in the past. Remain in your own country. All the region between Massowah and here belongs to the Negus."

The Conquest of Harrar.—Simultaneously with Ras Aloula's movement, King Menelek, of Shoa, led his army against Harrar, which had been restored to the hereditary ruler by the English, and was an object of Italian aspirations. The Emir's troops were met near the frontier and put to flight. When Menelek encamped before the city, the inhabitants sent an Italian merchant with an offer of surrender, and prayers for clemency. The Abyssinians thereupon entered the town and took possession without pillage or bloodshed. King Menelek remained in Harrar several weeks, and when he departed left a garrison of 4,000 men. The Negus and his son, with large bodies of soldiers, attempted the conquest of other parts of the Soudan.

The Dispatch of Re-enforcements.—In response to Gen. Gene's first request for re-enforcements, 800 men were sent from Italy, with 120 Gatling guns. They landed at Massowah on February 15. The Italians had raised a force of 1,000 bashi-bazouks, and had distributed arms among the inhabitants. With the new troops from Italy the strength of the garrison was about 2,500 Europeans and 1,500 natives. The news of the reverse at Dogali was communicated to the Italian Chamber on February 1, and a credit of 5,000,000 lire was voted for the dispatch of fresh troops. The second detachment of 2,000 soldiers reached Massowah on February 22. The credit was granted only on the understanding that there should be no extension of operations beyond the occupied posts. On March 12 another detachment, numbering 666 officers and men, was sent out.

Negotiations with Ras Aloula.—Maj. Piano returned to the Abyssinian camp to treat especially for the release of Salimbeni and his party. Count Salimbeni himself was allowed to go to Massowah to arrange for the payment of a ransom. Ras Aloula sent word, in the latter part of February, that he would not attack the Italians provided they remained at Massowah, Monkullo, and Arkiko. In March, Gen. Gene agreed to the conditions demanded for the release of the Italian prisoners, which were the delivery of 1,000 rifles that had been seized as contraband by the customs authorities, and the surrender of five Arabs belonging to a tribe friendly to the Italians. The Arabs were executed by the Ras, and the tribesmen were incensed against the Italians. All the members of the scientific party were released, with the exception of Count Savoiroux, who was detained by Ras Aloula to act as his physician.

The Change of Commanders.—The Italian Government ordered Gen. Gene to establish an effective blockade, with the object of preventing the importation of arms into Abyssinia. Count Robilant sent a dispatch severely censuring the commandant for purchasing the freedom of the prisoners by the surrender of arms and fugitives, and soon afterward sent Gen. Saletta, the first commander of the Italian troops in East Africa, to relieve him of his post. An Abyssinian bishop, the head of the Order of Jerusalem, while returning from a pilgrimage to the holy city, was detained by Gen. Gene as a hostage for the safety of Maj. Savoiroix. Letters from the Negus and his general to the French consul, M. Saumagne, proved that he had carried on a hostile intrigue, though he had been formally instructed by his Government to facilitate their settlement at Massowah. In consequence of this revelation, he was removed from his post. Gen. Saletta arrived at Massowah in the middle of April, and took over the command on April 23. He notified the merchants in Massowah to recall all their agents in Abyssinia, as he intended to declare a blockade by sea and land. On May 2 he proclaimed martial law, and on the following day announced the blockade of the coast from the Bay of Hamfila on the south to the point opposite the Difnen Islands on the north. A prize court was instituted at Massowah to deal with vessels breaking the blockade. The Negus appointed Ras Aloula governor-general of the Taocaze country as far as the Red Sea, excepting the province of Makalle. Rifles of an improved pattern were distributed among the soldiers of the Ras, and all commerce with the Italians was prohibited on pain of death. On July 11 the Italians lost about 600,000 francs' worth of ammunition by the explosion of their powder-magazine, which was supposed to have been set on fire by Abyssinians to avenge one of their countrymen who was shot as a spy. There were 10 persons killed and 75 wounded by the explosion.

Offer of Mediation.—On July 12 the British Government communicated its readiness to act as mediator between Italy and Abyssinia, and the Italian Government accepted the principle of British mediation in its answer, given before the end of the month. No movement was undertaken by either side during the summer; but in August the Italian Government chartered steamers for the dispatch, if necessary, of 10,000 troops in the autumn. The Mohammedans on the coast were generally willing to join the Italians against the Abyssinians, and treaties were made by Gen. Saletta with several Arab tribes.

ADVENTISTS, SEVENTH-DAY. The following is a summary of the statistics of the Seventh-Day Adventist denomination, by Conferences, as given in the "Seventh-Day Adventist Year-Book" for 1887:

CONFERENCES.	Ministers.	Churches.	Members.
California	14	85	1,750
Canada	1	5	187
Colorado	2	5	200
Dakota	6	22	594
Denmark	4	9	177
Illinois	8	30	784
Indiana	8	40	1,004
Iowa	14	61	1,550
Kansas	18	45	1,701
Kentucky	5	6	128
Maine	4	21	430
Michigan	28	122	4,067
Minnesota	15	68	1,584
Missouri	7	20	707
Nebraska	8	31	650
New England	8	24	658
New York	10	30	820
North Pacific	1	13	801
Ohio	9	48	1,090
Pennsylvania	7	35	748
Switzerland	8	15	800
Sweden	2	10	250
Tennessee	8	6	127
Texas	1	12	390
Upper Columbia	4	9	240
Vermont	7	17	470
Virginia	3	5	120
Wisconsin	12	49	1,522
MISSIONS.			
British	5	8	122
General Southern	5	..	820
Scandinavian	3	8	175
Total	218	796	23,111

Besides the ministers, 166 licentiates were returned. The whole amount of Conference funds was $146,936. The reports show increase from the previous year of 27 ministers, 15 licentiates, 57 churches, 2,564 members, and $24,295 in Conference funds.

The International Tract and Missionary Society reported 12,512 members, 247 cities entered by Bible workers and colporteurs, $59,166 received on account of the tract and missionary fund, $27,551 received on account of periodicals, $6,315 on account of the tract and missionary reserve fund, $28,579 pledged and $20,965 paid for home work, $67,851 pledged and $18,981 paid to other enterprises, and an excess of $62,356 of resources over liabilities. City missions in 36 cities and towns employed 102 "experienced workers." The General Sabbath-School Association, at its anniversary meeting, adopted a form of constitution for State Associations. The American Health and Temperance Association had on its rolls the names of nearly 15,000 members. The Central Seventh-Day Advent Publishing Association returned a net gain from business during the year of $11,849, and a present valuation of $166,520. Its accounts were balanced at $343,588. The Pacific Seventh-Day Advent Publishing Association returned a capital of $49,692, and total assets valued at $175,741. The Seventh-Day Adventist Educational Society reported the present value of its property and resources as $56,156. About 175 students of the college were attending Biblical lectures. Healdsburg College returned an excess of $15,889 of assets over liabilities. The net resources of the Health Reform Institute were returned at $178,014. The average number of patients had exceeded 200. A "Rural Health Retreat" was also sustained at St. Helena, Cal. A the meeting of the European Missionary Council, held in Great Grimsby, England, in September and October, 1886, reports were made of the condition of the denominational work in the Scandinavian countries, in all three of which were 22 churches, 602 members, 809 Sabbath-keepers, 288 Sabbath-school members, 9 ministers, and 16 colporteurs; and $1,293 had been realized from tithes and donations. Tent-work had been carried on in England—not so successfully as in the previous year—and in France and Italy.

General Conference.—The twenty-fifth General Conference of Seventh-Day Adventists met at Battle Creek, Mich., Nov. 18, 1886. Elder George I. Butler presided, and presented at the opening session, reports on the work of the denomination in the United States and foreign countries. Besides missions in various parts of the United States, special accounts were given of missions in Australia, South Africa, England, Scandinavia, and other parts of Europe. Attention was invited to the Maoris of New Zealand as a suitable people among whom to establish a mission, and to the expediency of publishing a paper in their language. The reports were accepted by the Conference as indicating a more rapid spread of "The Third Angel's Message" than had ever been known before, and, with the "persecutions to which the Seventh-Day people were subjected," of the approaching culmination of the Adventists' work. The hearty Christian sympathy of the Conference was tendered to the brethren who were suffering persecution, and they were urged, with "others upon whom the same things may come, to be in nothing terrified by the adversaries." It was resolved to begin labor among the Hollanders in the United States, and the publication of a paper in the Dutch language was advised. The publication of a book of plans for buildings for church societies was directed. Resolutions were adopted recommending to persons in charge of city missions, to introduce foreign departments into their work; that all persons connecting themselves with missions, "should, before going, bring their wearing apparel into harmony with the teachings of the Bible, and the testimonies on the subject"; that at each camp-meeting at least one session should be devoted to the subject of education, and special effort should be made to induce youths to attend the denominational schools; directing the establishment of a Labor Bureau at Battle Creek; advising the opening of missions in South Africa, South America, and British Honduras, and calling for $100,000 during the year, in addition to pledges already made, for missionary operations; recommending the institution, at the denominational schools and academies, of special courses for young ministers and persons engaged in evangelistic labors; especially

insisting upon the importance of the health and temperance branches of the denominational work; relating to the appointment of reporters of the proceedings of camp-meetings, and other meetings, with reference to securing the critical correctness of translations of denominational writings into foreign languages; declaring the rebaptism of persons who have been "properly baptized" before "embracing the message," not to be necessary; and approving a publication called the "Chart of the Week," as "an incontrovertible testimony to the unbroken continuity of the creation week, an unanswerable argument to the Sunday theory, and a positive proof of the perpetuity of the Seventh-Day Sabbath, showing, that out of more than one hundred and fifty languages and dialects, the large majority recognize Saturday as the Sabbath."

AFGHANISTAN, a monarchy in Central Asia. The ruler, called the Ameer, is Abdurrahman Khan, who was placed on the throne by the English after their conquest of the country in 1879. He receives a regular subsidy of about $50,000 a month from the Indian treasury, and is under a treaty engagement to follow the advice of the Viceroy in his relations with foreign powers, while the British Government is under obligation to give him military assistance in case of an unprovoked aggression on his territory.

The Ghilzai Revolt.—Abdurrahman has made use of the money and arms given him by the English in an endeavor to establish a firm authority over his immediate subjects, the turbulent and independent Afghan tribes. The Ameer, a man of stern and resolute disposition, was guided in his policy by the conviction that Afghanistan would lose its national existence in the conflict between Russia and England unless the tribes were united and controlled by a single autocratic will. The tribes have never been subservient to a central authority, and are unwilling to pay taxes, or to recognize any master superior to their own chiefs. The Ameer imposed a tax of ten rupees on every marriage of a daughter and every son born, and five rupees on every widow married, every girl born, and every man migrating to India for employment. The attempt to exact imposts stirred a section of the Ghilzais—the strongest and most independent of the Afghan tribes—into rebellion. Some of the southern Ghilzais expelled the Ameer's officers, and rose in arms in the autumn of 1886. The Afghan commander-in-chief, Gholam Hyder Charkhi, marched against the insurgents, and was successful to the extent of securing the safety of the road between Cabul and Candahar. During the winter, military operations could not be carried on; but in the spring of 1887, the revolt broke out afresh, and extended to most of the Ghilzai tribes south of Ghuzni.

The Ameer, who already possessed a good disciplined army, well armed and drilled, provided with artillery, and commanded by faithful lieutenants, whose fortunes were bound up in his own, prepared in the early spring for a vigorous campaign against the insurgents, and for the defense of his frontier against any sudden movement of Russia. He raised new regiments, mostly among the Duranis of the Candahar province, called on all his subjects over eighteen years of age to enlist in the army, and issued a manifesto, which was at first reported to contain the proclamation of a Jehad, or holy war, but which was really a statement of the dangers arising to Afghanistan from the rivalries of European powers, and a patriotic and religious appeal for union and loyal submission in face of the national peril.

The disturbances were begun again near the close of March by the Hotak section of the Ghilzais, holding the country about Khelat-i-Ghilzai, who seized some officers sent from Candahar to levy fines, and killed the governor of Maraf who was leading a force against them. Sikundar Khan marched from Candahar with a large force for the purpose of occupying the hilly district of Attaghar, where the defiance to the Ameer's authority occurred. It is situated about one hundred miles east of Candahar, and the same distance north of Quetta. The Ghilzais in the neighborhood of Ghuzni also rose in great force about the 1st of April, and held the road between Cabul and Candahar. Gholam Hyder Orakzai moved out from Ghuzni against these insurgents, who were assembled at Mukur, about a third of the distance between Ghuzni and Candahar. The Andak and Tarak tribes fell upon Gholam Hyder Khan, who was in pursuit of a rebel chief, and killed him and 200 horsemen. To avenge his death, Purwana Khan, who, though not a soldier by profession, was held to be the ablest of the Ameer's generals, was sent with 3,000 men, and was defeated at Nani, a short distance to the south of Ghuzni. The force led by Gholam Hyder Orakzai had an encounter with the rebels, who were driven back upon the hills, leaving the road to Candahar free again; but the general was afraid to pursue, and, fearing that they would return to the attack, intrenched himself in the plain. Sikundar Khan was attacked by the Hotaks on April 12, and compelled to retire from the Ghilzai district, and go into intrenchments near Maruf, so as to maintain his communications with Candahar through the Durani country. The Ameer's troops were beaten at first, and some of them fled to Khelat-i-Ghilzai; but the rest finally made a stand, forming a breastwork of their camels. All the sections of the Ghilzai tribe south of Shutargardan Pass joined in the rebellion, as well as the Jaowri Hazaras. The Hotaks and Andaris took the lead, but the movement spread to the Tarakhis and the Tokhis. Troops were withdrawn from the Jelalabad district to be sent against the southern insurgents, and presently the Shinwarris, who had been uneasy for some time, and whom the Ameer's commander-in-chief was trying to

pacify, broke into open revolt when the Ameer's officials attempted to enforce the payment of taxes. Abdurrahman, who is afflicted with an organic disease, fell ill about this time. Secret intelligence passed between the insurgents and various pretenders to the throne, especially Ayub Khan, who was interned in Persia. About the end of April a defeat was inflicted on the royal troops by the Shinwarris near Jelalabad. Two other attacks were made, and some damage inflicted by the rebels on the forces in the south. On the 15th of May Gholam Hyder Orakzai effected a junction with Sikundar Khan, and their combined forces, estimated at 4,500 infantry and cavalry, with 8 guns, encamped at Karez-i-Ahu, at some distance from Attaghar, where they were confronted by 4,000 Ghilzais. The opposing forces remained for several weeks in their respective camps. The Ameer's troops made raids through the Hotak country, burning villages, and even destroying the fruit and almond orchards, which are the main source of wealth of the inhabitants. Finally, Gholam Hyder Orakzai moved northward to prevent a junction between the Tarakhis, who were gathering in large numbers, and the Hotaks. When he had gone, the rebels plundered the Durani villages of Maruf. Gholam Hyder went first to Shinkhai to reopen communications with Ghuzni, and on June 11 moved eastward to disperse the gatherings of Tarakhis, Tokhis, and Nasiris in the plain north of Lake Abistada. On the 13th he met them at a fortified position called Katalkhan, and was repelled. Three days later he marched against a force of Tarakhis and Nasiris, and defeated them, killing 300. In June a Ghilzai chief named Tamar Shah, who was second in command, led a mutiny in the garrison of Herat. A regiment of Ghilzais attempted to kill the governor and seize the town. The mutiny of other troops was arranged, but the governor attacked the regiment that took the lead, and drove them from the town, after the mutineers had provided themselves with breech-loading rifles and cartridges from the arsenal. A detachment was sent from Candahar to intercept them, but they succeeded in joining the main body of the rebels at Nawai Tarakhi. Their leader fled toward Persia, but was captured and sent to Cabul. There were many encounters between the Ameer's forces and the rebels. The latter ventured several times to attack the troops on the plains, but lost heavily. The Ameer had proclaimed them outlaws, and the heads of the slain were sent by the hundred to Cabul. The troops dared not attack them in the hills, and were kept busy marching and countermarching to defend the points that were successively threatened. Gholam Hyder attempted to cut off the Andari mutineers when they moved southward from Nawabi-Tarakhi to join the Hotaks and Nasiris at Attaghar. A combat took place on July 25 at the pass of Kotal-i-Ab, by which the road from Khelat-i-Ghilzai crosses the Sura mountains. The rebels had fortified the pass, and were there in considerable force, but were outnumbered and gave way before re-enforcements arrived, after inflicting heavy losses on the royal troops. There was another fight on August 8, in which the Ameer's general was worsted and forced to retire to Khelat. A large part of Abdurrahman's army was composed of Andari Ghilzais, and military discipline was not strong enough to overcome the spirit of the clan. No Ghilzai troops were sent against the rebels. After the mutiny of the Andari regiment, the other Cabuli troops in Herat were sent out of the town. The ringleaders of the mutiny were captured and sent to Cabul, but the Ameer did not dare punish them, for fear of provoking a general mutiny of their fellow-tribesmen, with the exception of Taimar Shah and two other officers, who were executed for holding treasonable correspondence with Ayub Khan. The Herat garrison was recruited from the neighboring peoples, who can not be relied on for soldierly qualities, nor for loyalty to the Ameer of Cabul. The attempt of the Ameer to awaken a religious spirit in the northern Afghan country with the help of the mollahs was a failure, for his despotic rule was thoroughly unpopular, and the friends of the pretenders drew an effective contrast between his and Shere Ali's reign. The Duranis of the Candahar province had thus far escaped the Ameer's exactions, and were still faithful; yet the attempt to raise fresh regiments among them was not successful, because they are averse to a military life. The bulk of the Ameer's army remained in the north, where, notwithstanding the re-enforcements sent to the southern garrisons, Gholam Hyder Khan had about 20,000 regular troops, while the forces under Hyder Orakzai and Sikundar Khan numbered about 7,000 men, and the garrisons of Ghuzni and Candahar, 5,000. The Shinwarris, led by the Sirdar Nur Mohammed Khan, who, after first gaining possession of the Khost district, joined them with a large body of recruits, held their own country against the forces sent against them from Jelalabad by Hyder Gholam Khan.

The British Strategic Railways.—The rails of the Sibi and Quetta sections of the Sind-Pishin Railroad via the Harnai route were joined on March 14, 1887. The alternative Bolan road was still far from complete. The line over the Harnai Pass is a superior engineering work, comparable, except in the point of length of tunnel, with any of the mountain railroads of Europe. The highest point is 7,000 feet above the sea. By means of the Quetta Railroad the Indian Government is enabled to place all the supplies for an army of 100,000 men within one hundred miles of Candahar. Surveys have been made for a military road from Dera Ghazi Khan through the Bori valley to Pishin. A short line of railroad from Peshawur to Jamrud on the Afghan frontier, at the entrance of

the Kaiber Pass, is in progress. Two branches of the Quetta line extend across the Pishin valley to Gulistan and Kiela Abdula, at the foot respectively of the Gwajja and Khojak Passes in the Khojah Amran range. The expenditure on the Harnai and Bolan lines, from 1885 to the close of the financial year 1886–'87, was about $19,000,000. Surveys for the extension of the line beyond the Khojah Amran mountains have been made. The route over the Khojak Pass is the more direct one, while the Gwajja Pass presents fewer engineering difficulties. To extend the road into the country of the Afghans, the British must be prepared to carry out a military occupation, which they are not likely to undertake until a crisis in Afghan affairs renders it necessary. The Duranis attacked their stations and survey parties several times in the early part of 1887. The Ameer appointed khans in that district who would be favorable to the English, but he has no power to facilitate the entrance of their railroad into Afghanistan, and only incurs the contempt of the Afghans by his subservience. On January 8 the Duranis, with the concurrence of the Governor of Candahar, attacked the post of Kiela Abdula, with the intention of killing the British political officer and the engineer of the railroad. They did not find those officers, but destroyed the telegraph, and killed the local khan and one hundred railroad laborers. When work was begun on the extension of the road from Gulistan to Chaman Chauki, the head of the Khojak Pass, every one from Quetta was required by the Governor of Candahar to find security for his future conduct.

The Trans-Caspian Railway.—The strategic railroad from the Caspian Sea across the Turkomanian desert, which was begun in 1880, was completed as far as the Oxus in the spring of 1887. It is to be continued thence to Samarcand, a total distance of 1,335 versts from the coast. The island of Usun Ada, twelve miles to the west of Mikhailovsk, was selected as the starting-point, neither Krasnovodsk nor Mikhailovsk being suitable on account of the steep hills surrounding the one and the shallow harbor of the other. Usun Ada harbor has twelve feet of water. It is eighteen to twenty hours by steamboat from Baku. The foundation for portions of the road running across the shifting sands between the coast and Kizil Arvat, about two hundred versts, was made by watering the sand with sea-water, and laying over it clay dug from the steppes. There were as many as 5,000 Russians and 20,000 Asiatics employed on the work at one time. The naphtha-springs, which are as numerous and productive on the eastern shore of the Caspian as in the Baku district, supply an abundance of astatki for heating the locomotives. A line of rails runs from the station of Bala Ishem to the petroleum-springs, from which the fuel is brought, only thirty-five versts away. There are five wells opened, yielding 5,000 poods of naphtha daily. Between the oases of Akhal and Merv the road passes through a level country, which, notwithstanding some strips of desert, presented no serious engineering difficulties; but between Merv and Chardjui it had to be laid across a waterless desert, a length of 232 versts. At Dushakh, where the line turns eastward toward the river Tejend, a branch line to Herat, by way of Sarakhs, will be constructed some day. The Oxus at Chardjui is one and a half verst wide, and is crossed by a steam ferry-boat.

Beyond Chardjui a steppe, twenty versts across, required large quantities of water, taken from the Oxus, to fix the deep, shifting sands. Through Bokhara the line is traced along the edge of the cultivated country, so as not to interfere with the irrigation-works. The time required for the journey from Tiflis to Samarcand will be about three days and a quarter. The railroad already constructed enables the Russians to transport troops and war material from Odessa or any other point in Southern Russia to the Tejend in five days, and thus reach Herat sooner than could the English, even after extending the Indus Railroad to Candahar.

The Council of the Empire appropriated the money for the extension of the railroad to Samarcand. Gen. Annenkoff went to Asia in July, 1887, to prepare for the construction of the last part of the line, which could not be begun before autumn, but will be completed before the summer of 1888. The portion of the line running through Bokharan territory is 300 versts; and that in Russian Turkistan beyond, eighty-five versts. Before this last section of the railroad was begun, the military center of Asiatic Russia was transferred from Tashkend to Samarcand.

Russian Occupation of Kerki.—The town of Kerki, situated on the left bank of the Oxus, on the main road between Bokhara and Herat, was occupied by a Russian detachment under Gen. Ozan Tora, commander of the Samarcand army in May, 1887. This fresh advance of the Russians caused much disquiet in England, and increased the difficulties of the Ameer's position in Afghanistan. Yet no question of an encroachment on Afghan territory could be raised, because the Afghans, who succeeded in extending their sway over Maimena and Andkhoi, never held Kerki, nor brought under their rule the Ersari Turkomans inhabiting the district, which formed a part of the outlying dominions of the Emir of Bokhara. The Russians did not proceed to occupy the place without the latter's consent. Kerki is an important strategical position, and brings the Russians in contact with the discontented Turkoman and Uzbeck subjects of the Ameer. The British Government was informed of the intended occupation a month before it was carried out, the Russian Foreign Office declaring that it was done in order to protect the flank of the Asiatic Railroad.

Ayub Khan.—When Yakub Khan, the son and successor of Shere Ali, abdicated in 1879, after the murder of Sir Louis Cavagnari, his brother Ayub declared himself the enemy of the English and of his cousin Abdurrahman whom they set upon the throne. He led the Afghans, defeated Gen. Burrows on July 27, 1880, and besieged his forces in Candahar until, on Sept. 1, he was in turn defeated by Gen. Roberts. For a year thereafter he kept up a rival government at Herat, but was finally driven out by Abdurrahman, and fled to Persia, where he was arrested at the instance of the English, and kept interned at Teheran, the British Government paying $60,000 a year for his maintenance. The surveillance grew less strict, as Russian influence gained the upper hand in Persia. He has kept himself in communication with the exiles from Afghanistan and the discontented sections of Abdurrahman's subjects. In August, 1887, Ayub made his escape from Teheran. The Shah issued orders for his apprehension to the local officials between the capital and Afghanistan, but he fled in another direction, and arrived in safety within Russian dominions. In October he was heard of in the neighborhood of the Russo-Afghan frontier, and was supposed to be engaged in fomenting a revolt against his cousin in the Herat province and Afghan-Turkistan. Another influential agent for stirring up rebellion in Herat is Iskender Khan, who was appointed governor of Penjdeh in the spring of 1887.

Dhuleep Singh.—The Russians found a new ally, who may be put forward at a convenient juncture as an Indo-Afghan pretender, in the person of the mediatized hereditary Maharajah of Lahore, whose ancient dominions embraced a large part of Afghanistan as well as the entire Punjaub. When the Punjaub was annexed to British India in 1849, the enormous private treasure of the Maharajah was confiscated. Dhuleep Singh, who was an infant at that time, has several times appealed to the British Government to make restitution of the fortune, but has been told that the allowance of £40,000 a year on which he was induced to live in England was sufficient for the wants of a private individual. He settled on an estate in Norfolk, abandoned the customs and religion of his forefathers, and became thoroughly Anglicized and a popular country squire; but his expenses exceeded his income, and, when he had run deeply in debt, he petitioned to have his allowance increased. The rejection of his suit impelled him to assume a political rôle and become an instrument of Russia in stirring up disaffection among the Sikhs in Northern India. He left England in 1885, for India, but was not permitted to land. Returning to Europe, he was joined in Paris by an Irish revolutionist named Patrick Casey, passed through Berlin under the latter's name, lest English machinations should thwart his purpose, and arrived in June at Moscow, where he took counsel with the editor Katkoff, and was warmly received by the Panslavists.

The Frontier Negotiation. — The advance of Russian troops up the Heri Rud to Pul-i-Khatun, and up the Murghab to its junction with the Kushk, defeated the expectation of the English to draw the frontier line of Afghanistan as far north as Sarakhs and Sari Yazi. When, by the battle of Pul-i-Khisti, the possession of Penjdeh passed into the hands of Russia, the contention for an ethnographic frontier was more nearly realized. The interrupted negotiations were resumed after the Ameer had publicly declared that the place was not worth fighting for; and when the Zulfikar difficulty was arranged to the satisfaction of the Russian Cabinet, Sir Peter Lumsden was recalled, and the British boundary commission was divested of its imposing political and military character. Col. Ridgeway and Col. Kuhlberg, the newly-appointed Russian commissioner, proceeded to survey and mark out the frontier on principles that had been settled upon in London. There were differences of opinion regarding the Kaissar pasture-lands in the Maimena district, but no serious disagreement arose until after the commissioners had reached Andkhoi. Between there and the Oxus Col. Kuhlberg contended that the line should be drawn to the mound of the saint called Ziarat Khoja Saleh, whereas Sir West Ridgeway claimed for the Ameer all the country south of Kham-i-Ab. The difficulty was referred, as had been arranged for cases of divergence on questions of principle, to the home governments, and, the surveys having been completed, the commissioners returned to Europe in the autumn of 1886. The negotiations were continued in St. Petersburg in the spring and summer of 1887. Sir West Ridgeway, after receiving full instructions from his Government, proceeded thither early in April. The principal negotiator on the Russian side was M. Zinovieff, the head of the Asiatic Department in the Russian Bureau of Foreign Affairs. Col. Kuhlberg and M. Lessar also took part in the conferences on behalf of Russia, while Captains Barrow and De Laessoe assisted Col. Ridgeway. The conferences began on April 23. At the earlier meetings both parties adhered firmly to their claims in respect to Kham-i-Ab. The Russians were the less disposed to give way, because the progress of the Ghilzai rebellion raised doubts as to whether Abdurrahman would remain on the throne to receive the benefit of their concessions. The negotiations were interrupted in May, and the English commissioner, after references to the British Foreign Office, and informal discussions with the Russian representatives, returned to London in the beginning of June, to communicate the Russian views and ascertain the maximum concession that his Government was prepared to make. He returned to St. Petersburg with a proposition to compensate Russia for the relinquishment of her claims to Khoja Saleh and the district on the Oxus, which the Ameer, who had it in actual possession, insisted on retaining, by ceding a tract of pasture-land that was much desired by the Saryk Turkomans of Penjdeh, situated in the Kushk and Kashan valleys. They formerly possessed this district, but were ousted in 1886, notwithstanding the protest of the Russian commissioner, because the London protocol of June 5, 1885, assigned the territory to the Ameer. The St. Petersburg Government accepted the offered arrangement, and conceded to the Ameer the territory around Khojah Saleh, which, by a strict interpretation of the agreement of 1873, would have fallen to Russia, but which was occupied by Afghan Uzbecks, receiving in return the restoration of lands necessary for the sustenance of the Saryks and the development of the town of Penjdeh. The extent of the land restored to the Turkomans is 825 square miles, bringing the Russians 11½ miles nearer to Herat. The extent of the disputed Kham-i-Ab district is 770 square miles, but it is at present more productive than the lands between the Kushk and the Murghab conceded to Russia. The final protocol was signed at St. Petersburg on July 22, and ratified on August 2. The southern limit of Russian territory on the Oxus is Bosaga. The frontier delimitation extended over three years. The boundary-line, 855 miles in length, was drawn through a wild and previously unknown region. The first portion running from Zulfikar to Maruchak is 120 miles, and the other, reaching to the Oxus, 235 miles. There are no natural boundaries for any part of the distance, yet both Afghans and Turkomans are said to have respected the pillars erected by the British and Russian officers.

ALABAMA. State Government.—The following were the State officers during the year: Governor, Thomas Seay, Democrat; Secretary of State, C. C. Langdon; Treasurer, Frederick H. Smith; Auditor, Malcolm C. Burke; Attorney-General, Thomas N. McClellan; Superintendent of Public Instruction, Solomon Palmer; Railroad Commissioners, H. C. Shorter, W. C. Tunstall, L. W. Lawler; Chief-Justice of the Supreme Court, George W. Stone; Associates, David Clopton, H. M. Somerville.

Legislation.—The Legislature, which met Nov. 9, 1886, concluded its session on the last day of February, 1887, when it expired by limitation. Perhaps its most important act was an amendment to the law regulating the rights and estates of married women, which aims to rescue from almost hopeless entanglement a large part of the property of the State. The old law was characterized by the Governor in his inaugural as "a means of fraud to the wicked and a snare to the unwary. It is the result of the work of different epochs, and is largely patchwork." By the amendment, all property of the wife held by her previous to the marriage, or to which she may become entitled after the marriage, is the separate property of the wife, and is not subject to the liabilities of the husband. The earnings of the wife are her separate estate; but the written consent of her husband is necessary to allow her to contract in writing, or to alienate her property. Husband and wife may contract with each other, and the wife with the consent of the husband may carry on business as if sole. Further, the husband is not liable for the debts or engagements of the wife, contracted or entered into after marriage, or for her torts, in the commission of which he does not participate; but the wife is liable for such debts or engagements entered into with the consent of the husband in writing, or for her torts, and is suable therefor as if she were sole.

The former Legislature having provided for the appointment of a commission to codify the State laws, the results of its labors were reported at this session and adopted, and provision was made for publication of the new code.

Provision was made also for the establishment and endowment of Alabama University for colored people, and Montgomery was chosen by the trustees as the site of the new institution. The sum of $25,000 was also appropriated for a separate institution for the colored insane. A similar sum was voted for a separate asylum for the blind.

For the relief of maimed and disabled Confederate soldiers, $30,000 was appropriated.

The State was redivided into four chancery divisions (instead of three as before), and the time and place for the sessions of the several chancery courts were fixed.

Another important act was the reduction of the tax-rate from 60 cents on the $100 to 55 cents, to take effect Oct. 1, 1888, and a further reduction to 50 cents for Oct. 1, 1889. It was estimated that the rapid increase in values in the State would offset this reduction; so that the revenue would not be diminished. Other acts were:

To provide for the sale of the swamp and overflowed lands of this State, and for the sale of the indemnity land scrip issued to this State in lieu of such lands disposed of by the United States.

To prosecute and secure to the State the benefits resulting from all claims of the State of Alabama against the United States for or on account of swamp and overflowed lands, other public land in Alabama sold or otherwise disposed of by the Federal Government, and all other claims the State has under existing laws or may have under laws hereafter enacted.

To prohibit the employment of minors to sell liquors in this State.

To incorporate Lafayette College.

To authorize the Mayor and Aldermen of Birmingham to issue bonds for the funding of the floating debt of the city.

To exempt cotton and other agricultural products in the hands of the producer from taxation.

To authorize street railroads to purchase and condemn property for the purpose of constructing and maintaining and operating street railroads in the same manner as now provided by law for taking private property for railroads and other public uses.

To provide for holding a teachers' institute for a period of not less than one week in each congressional district.

To enable women to hold the office of notary public.

Requiring all insurance companies, whether chartered by the State or admitted from other States, to have an actual cash capital fully paid up of not less than $100,000, and to require such companies to make annual statements to the Auditor.

To require locomotive-engineers to be examined and licensed by a board to be appointed by the Governor.

To prevent the compelling of women and children, or the permitting of children under fourteen years of age, to labor in a mechanical or manufacturing business more than eight hours on any day.

For prevention and suppression of infectious or contagious diseases of horses and other animals.

To incorporate the Alabama State Agricultural Society.

The session was noteworthy for the amount of work accomplished—568 bills and resolutions being passed, or 115 more than at the preceding session. The members were nearly all Democrats.

Finances.—The following table shows the condition of the State treasury at the beginning of the year:

Balance in treasury on Oct. 1, 1886	$340,811 88
Receipts from Oct. 1, 1886, to Dec. 81, 1886, inclusive	120,887 97
	$461,699 85
Disbursements from Oct. 1, 1886, to Dec. 81, 1886	818,236 57
Balance in treasury at close of business on Dec. 81, 1886	$143,803 28
Amount in treasury on Dec. 81, 1884	$98,862 65
Amount in treasury on Dec. 81, 1885	122,574 90

Of the bonded debt which amounts to $9,198,900, the greater part is already funded at 4 per cent. interest, but $954,000 of bonds bearing 6 per cent. interest still remained at the beginning of the year. The Legislature authorized the funding of these at 3½ per cent., a lower rate than the State had before ventured to offer.

Prohibition.—The sale of liquor becomes more restricted with every session of the Legislature. Prohibition is granted, and has been obtained, in the greater part of the State, on petition of the inhabitants of each locality. The Legislature this year added in the same way Butler County and Montgomery, outside the police jurisdiction of the city, to the prohibitory column. It adopted also a local-option law applying to a large part of the State, by which "no license" is likely to be still further extended. At the same time, the license-tax is increasing yearly. In 1884 it was $50 for retail dealers; the Legislature of that year increased it to $100; this year it was fixed at from $125 to $250, according to the population of the locality.

Confederate Monument.—Strong pressure was brought upon the Legislature to aid in the erection of a monument to the Confederate soldiers of the State, which had already been begun at Montgomery. A bill appropriating $5,000 for this purpose passed the lower house, but failed in the Senate on a close vote. Private subscriptions have since forwarded the work. Before the close of the year the shaft had been carried up to the height of eighty feet, and only the figures at the top and at the base were wanting to render the memorial complete.

Miscellaneous.—An improvement in the treatment of the State convicts was made this year by the passage of an act establishing a reformatory system for them, but the practice of hiring them out still leaves much room for improvement, especially in the case of county convicts. Of these the State Inspector says: "They are scattered over the State in such a way as to make it almost impossible to properly inspect them and ascertain their real condition. It seems probable that this state of affairs is going to become worse, as new contracts are being made by many of the counties, and some of these are in exceedingly inaccessible localities."

Early in the year ex-State Treasurer Vincent, who, in 1883, embezzled $225,000 of the State funds, was brought back, tried, convicted, and sentenced.

The burning of the building occupied by the State Agricultural and Mechanical College, on June 24, caused a loss of $100,000 to the State, and the destruction of valuable cabinets and apparatus.

Development.—The following statement shows the increase of assessments and taxes on railroads in the State for this year, as compared with last, also the increase of mileage:

Total value for 1887	$27,989,771 26
Total value for 1886	23,638,431 01
Increased assessment	$4,251,340 25
Tax on $27,989,771.26 at 55 cents on $100	$153,668 74
Tax on $23,638,431.01 at 60 cents on the $100	142,180 58
Increase of taxes	$11,588 16
Miles reported in 1886	2,068 94
Miles reported in 1887	2,185 82

The towns and cities of the mineral belt have advanced rapidly, while the agricultural districts remain stationary. In Jefferson County, which contains the city of Birmingham, the valuations were fixed by the assessors for this year at $30,000,000, an increase of $17,500,000, or more than 100 per cent. over 1886. The iron industry has grown so rapidly that the pig-iron production of the State has increased from 130,000 tons in 1880 to nearly 400,000 tons in 1887. The production of cotton during this time shows comparatively little change. The movements of the population, and the change at work upon them, are noteworthy. "Already many of the planters of the Black Belt have taken all the money they have heretofore invested in cotton-raising and have invested it in real estate and industries in Birmingham. The chief danger in the impending change is in the fact that the lands are falling into the hands of men who will be inclined to consolidate it in large holdings, and that the poor man will not get a chance for a small farm. All the mineral lands are now owned by corporations, and wherever there is a sign of speculative value land companies have been formed."

ANGLICAN CHURCHES. The "Year-Book" of the Church of England for 1887, being the fifth number of that publication, embodies information furnished by 11.500 of the nearly 14,000 clergymen of the Church. In 80 per cent. of the parishes, 1,182,000 communicants were returned on Easter of 1885. The churches provided 3,000,665 free and 1,000,497 paid sittings. The amount of voluntary offerings during the year was given as £5,000,000 : in addition to which, £1,000,000 were raised in the educational department, £16,000 for theological schools, and £10,000 for public schools.

Report of the Ecclesiastical Commissioners.—The report of the Ecclesiastical Commissioners gives the following summary of the work accomplished by the commissioners in the augmentation and endowment of benefices during a period of forty-six years, from 1840 (when the common fund was first created), to the 31st of October, 1886 : number of benefices endowed, 5,400; amount of grants made in the augmentation and endowment of these benefices, about £754,000 per annum in perpetuity, or in capital value about £22,624,000. The benefactions by private donors, consisting of stock, cash, land, tithes, and other property, received by or conveyed to the commissioners or to the incumbents of benefices, amount to about £4,620,000, and are equivalent to a permanent increase of the endowments of benefices of about £154,000 per annum. There is, moreover, a sum of about £26,000 per annum contributed by benefactors to meet the commissioners' grants for curates in mining districts. The total increase in the incomes of benefices from the augmentation and endowments made by the commissioners, or through their instrumentality, amounted, therefore, up to the 31st of October, 1886, to about £934,000 per annum, and may be taken to represent the income which would be derived from a capital sum of about £28,024,000.

Convocation of Canterbury.—The Convocation of Canterbury met on Feb. 8. The subject of a union of the two convocations was considered in both houses. The lower house having requested the president (archbishop) "to direct the appointment of a committee to consider and report on the relations subsisting between the convocations of Canterbury and York, with a view to their common action," the archbishop said that it was not desirable that there should be a mere fusion or union of the two convocations. Each should preserve its integrity. A conference of the two bodies would be very serviceable; and in such a case nothing would be gained by the separation of the bishops into one and the presbyters into another conference, but the conference ought to be held in one combined house. A committee was appointed to consider the subject. In response to a request that an effort be made to secure a reduction of the rate of interest on loans by the Queen Anne's Bounty Office, the committee reported its opinion to be that the loans could not be made at a lower rate than at present without endangering in some degree the absolute safety of the money and the certainty of making the annual payments that were due. Resolutions were adopted by the lower house, asking for such legislation as would make the collection of tithe-rent charges more easy; requesting the bishops to use all their power to prohibit and suppress the preaching by clergymen of the Church of England in dissenting chapels—a practice which was declared not only to be contrary to the principles and laws of the Church, but also to tend rather to hinder than promote the unity of the Christian people; and deprecating the use in the celebration of the holy communion of wine other than the juice of the grape. A canonical amendment was approved which should make the hours during which marriages may be celebrated from eight o'clock in the forenoon till three o'clock in the afternoon, and should contain a provision that, "in case of the marriage of minors, the parents or governors should signify their consent." The house requested that a committee be appointed to consider the working of the Incumbents' Resignation Act, and that the committee on occasional services be reappointed. The Earl of Selborne was re-elected president of the House of Laymen. This house recommended that a summary and inexpensive tribunal be appointed with power to deal with criminous clerks; declared it desirable to repeal or greatly modify all the legislative enactments which prevent a deacon from engaging in secular occupations; suggested that the law relating to tithe-rent charges should be strengthened and amended; and expressed cordial satisfaction at the scheme of the "Church House" "as a means of extending and strengthening the action of the Church."

The houses of convocation met again May 10. The upper house approved a scheme for the enlarged representation of the clergy in convocation, for which the sanction of the crown is to be asked. A committee report was adopted adverse to the "Deacons' (Church of England) Bill," then pending in the House of Commons, as contemplating a departure which it was not expedient to make, from the long-continued practice of the Church. The bill provided for the modification of the acts precluding deacons from following secular occupations so that they need not apply to deacons who may hereafter be ordained after they are thirty years of age. The report declared that the resolution passed by Convocation in 1884 approving the ordination to the office of deacon of men possessing other means of living who are willing to serve the clergy gratuitously — which involved no change in the law—marked the extreme extent to which it was at present advisable to go in the premises. By this resolution, deacons seeking ordination to the priesthood, besides being subject to all the regular examinations, would first have

to devote their whole time for four years to spiritual labor. On the subject of clergymen of the Church of England preaching in the houses of worship of denominations not in communion with it, the Lower House requested the bishops to take such steps as might be in their power to suppress the innovation. The upper house declared on this subject that, in its opinion, "it is contrary to the principles of the Catholic Church as maintained at the English Reformation, that clergymen should take part in the public religious services of those who are not in full communion with the Church of England, and it is desirable that the bishops should use their authority and influence to induce the clergy of their respective dioceses to abstain from the practice. Nevertheless, the house deeply sympathizes with the desire to bring all Christians into sincere communion with each other through a union with the great Head of the Church, and recognizes the fact that there are many ways of maintaining kindly intercourse with non-conformists, which are not open to reasonable objection." On the report of the committee appointed to deal with proposed additions to the Catechism, a form of answer to the question, "What is meant by the Church?" was approved by the lower house, as follows: "I mean the body of which Christ is the head and of which I was made a member by baptism; of this body part is militant here on earth and part at rest in paradise awaiting the resurrection." A modification of the marriage act was recommended for the benefit of seafaring men who are not able to fulfill the conditions of residence required by the existing acts. Concerning the case of the Rev. James Bell Cox, of the diocese of Liverpool, who was suffering imprisonment for contempt of court in not obeying a sentence of suspension for ritualistic practices, the lower house expressed its judgment that "such imprisonment is entirely inappropriate to questions of ritual observances, causes the greatest distress to many devout members of the Church, and ought, in accordance with the resolution of the Royal Commission on Ecclesiastical Courts, to be abolished." The upper house concurred in the action, and requested the archbishop to seek to obtain a conference on the subject between the bishops and archbishops of the two provinces. The House of Laymen declared itself, by resolution, in favor of the abolition of imprisonment of clergymen as a means of enforcing the judgments of ecclesiastical courts.

The convocation met again in July. The resolution of the Convocation of York on the subject of the canons of the hours of marriage was adopted. Various questions were considered concerning the Additional Rubrics Bill, the proposed amendments to the Church Catechism, and the report of the Royal Commission on Ecclesiastical Courts. A joint committee of the three houses was appointed to consider on the Draft Rubrics and Additional Services Bill.

Deputation to the Queen.—A deputation representing the upper and lower houses of the Convocation of Canterbury was received by the Queen at Windsor Castle, March 8, to present an address from the members of the two houses congratulating Her Majesty on her accession to the fiftieth year of her reign. The address, after the words of congratulation, related that during the year that had elapsed since the convocation had last had the privilege of approaching the Throne, ample evidence had been afforded of " the steady progress of the Church of England in her works of duty and love, and a constant strengthening of attachment to her communion. Some measure (though an inadequate one) of that attachment appears in the vast amount of free-will offerings devoted to the work of the Church of England and Wales. There is no part of the country which is not yielding abundant signs of this progress and this devotion. One event there has been in our own history fruitful (as we trust) of good counsels and good works. An elective House of Laymen is invited to deliberate, not as a part of the constitutional convocation, but as a body of advisers at its side. The experience and judgment of many distinguished men thus become readily available for the service of the Church."

The Queen, in her reply, said : " I rejoice with you in observing the substantial progress of the Church of England and the increasing zeal manifested alike by clergy and laity. The willingness of the laity to organize a voluntary representative body to assist with their counsel and advice, when required, the deliberations of the House of Convocation, is much to be commended."

Convocation of York. — The Convocation of York met February 15. The archbishop, in his opening address, spoke concerning a projected fusion of the two convocations, which, he said, should be viewed with regard to its bearings on the question of disestablishment. The establishment of the Church of England as a national church was expressed by a few elements. They were, the power of the Crown to summon convocation, the nomination of bishops, the visitational power of the Crown, appeal from ecclesiastical courts to the Crown, the fact that no change could take place in the doctrine or worship of the Church without the consent of the Crown expressed by Parliament, and the power of modifying the regulations of the Church by means of statutes. There remained for consideration the plan of a delegation of each convocation to meet together to discuss all convocation business. The combined influence of the delegations, and of convocation, would be great, and it was also conceivable that, by the method suggested, convocation might be altered from assemblies for discussion to bodies where serious business would be considered and accomplished.

A discussion took place between the two houses with reference to the procedure in debating the scheme which was thus brought forward. The lower house desired to meet with the upper house in considering the question, then to retire and debate, and vote upon the matter in separate session. The President of the upper house did not feel free to grant this request, and thought it best for each house to proceed with business, the upper house, as usual, sending down information to the lower house as occasion might arise. The proposition for the joint meeting of the two Convocations by delegations, as approved by the upper house, provides that all the members of that house shall be its delegation, while the delegation of the lower house shall consist of the prolocutor and 85 members, chosen by a committee of selection ; that the rights and privileges of the delegates of either house shall apply to the meetings of the delegates in like manner as to the sessions of the Houses themselves ; that the York delegation shall vote separately, if any four members of either house shall demand it ; and that the joint delegations shall have power to discuss any business which may be submitted by the president of either Convocation, and may pass resolutions thereon, provided that such resolutions are to be considered as recommendations only, which the whole Convocation may afterward discuss and adopt, if they shall think fit. The lower house resolved that " it is greatly to be desired that there should be a joint meeting annually of the Convocations of Canterbury and York," and approved of provisions for the nominating of delegates to attend it. The president said, with reference to obtaining a right of access of the Convocation to the Throne, that he had made an effort in that direction some years ago, and had obtained from the Home Office a distinct refusal. A resolution was passed by the lower house in February, 1886, but he did not consider that he should again go to the Crown to receive the same reply, without some new matter in the form of an address of the house, or the like. A suggestion had been made that in this jubilee year a new attempt should be made to obtain a place for presenting their address in person. The lower house passed a declaration in favor of the revival of diocesan synods, and recommended that advantage be taken of this year of jubilee to form a fund for augmenting the stipends of poorer benefices, and the relief of impoverished clergymen.

Church Missionary Society. — The anniversary of the Church Missionary Society was held in London, May 3. Sir John Kennaway presided. The ordinary income of the society had been £207,793, or £6,555 in excess of the ordinary income of the previous year, which was the largest that had then been returned in the history of the society. The total amount of the receipts on all accounts, had been £284,689. Eighteen young men, university graduates, and four young women, had been accepted for missionary work, and twelve young men were in training. Among the special features of the missionary work mentioned in the report, was the contemplated sending out, in the fall, of a special mission to India, for the purpose of holding services for the native Christians akin to those of the parochial missions at home. The society returns 230 ordained and 58 other European missionaries, 11 ordained Eurasian and 250 ordained native missionaries, 25 Eurasian teachers, 3,789 native helpers and teachers, 42,717 communicants, and 185,878 adherents.

A review of the work of the society during the past fifty years, embodied in the report, showed that during that period more than 900 missionaries had been sent out, 855 native clergymen had been ordained, and 80,000 adult converts, and tens of thousands of their children, had been baptized.

Society for the Propagation of the Gospel.—The annual meeting of the Society for the Propagation of the Gospel in Foreign Parts was held on Feb. 19. The Lord Bishop of Rochester presided. The receipts of the society for the year had been £105,712, of which £86,966 had been for the general fund, and £18,743 for special funds. A further sum of £1,678 had been received for certain invested trust funds. The society employed 595 ordained missionaries, of whom 128 were natives of the countries in which they were laboring, and 1,700 lay agents, the majority of whom were natives, at 461 stations, situated in 75 colonial dioceses. The missions of this society are directed to the Christian subjects of the British colonies as well as to the Mohammedan and heathen subjects of the empire, and nearly half of its income is devoted to missions in India.

The Liberation Society.—The annual meeting of the Society for the Liberation of Religion from the Patronage and Control of the State, was held on May 4. Mr. G. Osborne Morgan, M. P., presided, and in his address urged vigorous agitation of the principle of disestablishment, whether a "practical question" be offered or not, and invited special attention to the movement for disestablishment in Wales. The annual report of the society said that the year had not been a favorable one for its agitation.

The Case of Mr. Bell Cox.—The case of Mr. Bell Cox, to which reference is made in the proceedings of the Convocation of Canterbury, had been before the courts for nearly two years, and originated in a process for ritualism instituted against him by a gentleman not of his parish. At any early stage in the proceedings, a series of monitions had been addressed to him by Lord Penzance, directing him to discontinue the practices complained of. He paid no attention to them, and in June, 1886, an order was issued suspending him from his office for six months. This he likewise disregarded. Then, in August, Lord Penzance declared him contumacious, when a complication arose, based upon the fact that the order of suspension had been issued, not by Lord Penzance himself, but by his surrogate in York. Mr. Bell Cox therefore applied to the Queen's Bench Division to prohibit the issue of the writ *de contumacio capiendo*, resting upon this informality. The case was decided against him, by both the court of first instance and the court of appeal. In the mean time, however, the order of suspension had run out, and it was no longer possible for him to be contumacious. Nevertheless he was imprisoned. Upon the ground, however, as shown, that the cause of action against him had already expired when the order for his imprisonment actually took effect, an order for his release was issued on the 20th of May, and he was at once discharged.

The Church Congress.—The twenty-seventh Church Congress met at Wolverhampton, October 8, and was opened with a sermon by the Bishop of Durham. The Bishop of Lichfield presided over the sessions, and in his inaugural address reviewed what the twenty years that had elapsed since the Congress had previously met at Wolverhampton had done for the Church, and what lessons they had left behind them. The Education Act, which, it had been feared, would work disastrously to the schools of the Church, had had an opposite effect, in quickening its zeal in behalf of religious education. The Burials Act had not resulted in the prevalence of irregularities, which had been apprehended. The period had been signalized by the meeting of the Lambeth or Pan-Anglican Conference, at which one hundred bishops had assembled from all parts of the world, under the presidency of the Primate of England. Five new bishoprics had been created within the Church of England, "an event without parallel during the last three centuries." Ancient churches, such as those of Assyria, Armenia, and Egypt, were beginning to come into relations with the English Church. The revision of the Holy Scriptures had been begun and completed. The discussion of the relations of the Bible and science, which had gone on unceasingly, was continued, but with changed character and under changing conditions. The time of loud assertion and of angry controversy was passing. Timid minds were still staggered by the discoveries of science, but they were beginning to remember that all truth is of God. The honest doubter was no longer regarded as a criminal, but as an invalid. It was even admitted that there might be a considerable religious element in doubt. The Archbishop of Canterbury followed with an address on the influence of the Church upon society. The first subject for formal discussion was "The Church and History," which was considered under the three heads—"The Evangelization of England," by the Rev. H. Hensley Henson; "The Relations of the English Church with Rome in the Middle Ages," by the Rev. Canon Creighton and the Rev. J. D. C. Cox; and "The Reformation Settlement," by the Rev. Canon Curteis. On the general topic of "The Adaptation of Spiritual Agencies to Modern Needs," the agency of "Preaching Orders" was treated of by Mr. G. S. S. Vidal; "Itinerating Missions," by the Rev. S. J. W. Sanders; and "Teaching Missions," by the Rev. Canon F. E. Carter. The Bishop of Ossory and Mr. G. C. E. Maline, with voluntary speakers, spoke on "The Priesthood of the Laity: its Responsibilities and Privileges." The subject of "Elasticity of Worship" was introduced in papers by Archdeacon Watkins and the Rev. Prebendary Dumbleton, who were followed by Earl Beauchamp, the Rev. J. E. C. Welldon, and other speakers. The question of "Tithes" was discussed by Mr. P. Vernon Smith, Mr. Jasper Most, M. P., and Prebendary Grier. On the question of "The Use of the Influence and Organization of the Church for the purpose of Alleviating Distress and giving a more Intelligent Direction to the Movements of the Population, and by the Systematic Promotion of Emigration and Colonization," the Rev. Prebendary Billing considered the evil of the migration of people from the rural districts to the large towns; Mr. James Rankin, M. P., spoke on emigration; and the Earl of Meath advocated colonization by the Church; "The Relations of the Church of England to Eastern Churches — the Armenian, Assyrian, Coptic, and Native Indian Churches," were discussed by the Rev. Dr. E. L. Cutts, Mr. Athelstan Riley, the Rev. E. A. B. Owen, and Bishop Blyth, of Jerusalem. Regarding "The Church in Africa," papers were read on "Early Churches," by Prof. G. T. Stokes; "Mohammedanism," by Canon Isaac Taylor; and "Modern Missionary Advances and Hindrances," by Archdeacon Hamilton and Prebendary W.J.Edwards. At evening and other special meetings were considered the subjects of "Hindrances to Religion in Common Life," by the Bishops of Carlisle and others; "The Sunday-School in its Relation to the Church," by Canon Bowley; "The Home Duties and Domestic Relations of Educated Women"; "Child-Life in our Great Cities," by the Bishop of Bedford and other speakers; "Christian Socialism," by Mr. H. T. Davenport, M. P., the Bishop of Manchester, and others; "Socialism and Christianity," by the Bishop of Derry, Mr. H. H. Champion, and Mr. Stanley Leighton, M. P.; and "The Devotional Life of the Church as illustrated by Religious Societies of the Eighteenth Century, by Guilds and Associations for Communicants, for Prayer and Bible Reading, etc., and by Retreats and Quiet Days," by the Rev. W. H. Barlow, the Rev. R. S. Hassard, Prof. Stokes, and other speakers.

ARCHÆOLOGY. (American.) Data for American Prehistoric Chronology.—Dr. Daniel G. Brinton delivered an address as its chairman before the Section of Anthropology of the American Association, on the "Prehistoric Chronology of America." The means at our command, he

said, for reconstructing the history of the peoples who inhabited America during the prehistoric period could be divided into six classes:

First were the legends or traditions of the various tribes. The resemblance which many of them bore to Semitic or Oriental myths must be regarded as coincidences only. In the case of the savage tribes, ignorant of writing, it is probable that the lapse of five generations, or say two centuries, completely obliterates all recollection of historic occurrences. The case is not much better with the semi-civilized nations—the Mayas and Nahuas, or the Quichuas of Peru. The chronicles of Mexico proper contain no fixed date prior to that of the founding of Tenochtitlan, A. D. 1325. When we turn to the monumental data, we find it doubtful whether the edifices of the Pueblo Indians, or any of the great structures of Mexico, Yucatan, and Peru supply prehistoric dates of excessive antiquity. The pueblos of New Mexico and Arizona were constructed by the ancestors of the tribes who still inhabit the region, and at no distant day. There is every reason to suppose that the same is true of all the stone and brick edifices of Mexico and Central America. The majority of them were occupied at the period of the conquest; others were in process of building, and of others the record of their construction was clearly in memory. There were, indeed, some once fine cities fallen to ruins, and sunk into oblivion, such as Palenque and T'Ho, on the site of the present city of Merida. But tradition, and the present condition of the sites, unite in the probability that they do not antedate the conquest more than a few centuries. A more ancient class of monuments are the artificial shell-heaps along the shores of both oceans, and of many rivers of North and South America. They differ widely in antiquity. Those of Maine contain bones of the great auk, which now exists only in the Arctic regions. Of great antiquity, also, are the shell-heaps of Costa Rica, estimated by Dr. Earle Flint to be 20,000 years old, and the Sambaquis of Brazil, which were coeval with a race different from that which occupied the country when it was discovered by the white man. This class of monuments, therefore, supply us with data that prove man's existence in America in the Diluvial, Quaternary, or Pleistocene epoch, which was characterized by extinct species.

Of the third class, or industrial evidences, the oldest shell-heaps hitherto examined in Brazil, Guiana, Costa Rica, and Florida, supply fragments of pottery, of polished stone, and compound implements occur even from the lowest strata; but, venerable though they are, they furnish no date older than what in Europe would be regarded as of the Neolithic period. The arrow-heads found in the lake-beds of Nebraska, and the net-sinkers and celts from the gold-bearing gravels of California, prove by their form and finish that the tribes who fashioned them had already taken long strides beyond the culture of the earlier Palæolithic age. The only station in America that has furnished an ample line of really and exclusively primitive specimens, is that of the Trenton gravels, in New Jersey. They were of a date much earlier than the extinction of the native American horse and the mastodon. There is nothing unlikely, therefore, in the reported discoveries of man's pointed flints and his bones in place along with the remains of these quadrupeds. There is no *a priori* argument against mastodon mounds and pipes, but their authenticity is merely a question of evidence. The material of which implements are made supplies us data. All of the oldest implements are manufactured from rocks of the locality. When, therefore, we find a weapon of a material not obtainable in the locality, as the obsidian of the Yellowstone Park in Ohio, and the black slate of Vancouver's Island in Delaware, we have a sure indication that it belongs to a period of development considerably later than the earliest. The extension of cultivated plants, as of maize and tobacco—plants of Southern Mexico, which were cultivated from Canada to Patagonia—is also evidence of considerable development.

Another source of evidence is in the consideration of languages, of which there are about eighty stocks in North and one hundred in South America, some of them having scores of dialects spoken over wide areas. Nothing less than a vast antiquity, stretching back tens of thousands of years, can explain this exceeding diversity of languages and their dialects.

More attention has been paid to the physical than to the linguistic data of the native Americans, but with not more satisfactory results. The most accurate examinations of their physical characteristics show that, with a great diversity in details, essentially the same type prevails over the whole of both continents, and Prof. J. Kollmann, of Basle, has concluded, from analysis of the cranioscopic formulas of the most ancient American skulls, that the physical identity of the American race is as extended in time as it is in space; and we may declare that throughout the whole continent, and from its earliest appearance in time, it is and has been one, as distinct in type as any other race, and from its isolation probably the purest in all its racial traits.

The geological evidences are such that no one who examines them will now deny that man lived in both North and South America immediately after the Glacial epoch, and that he was the contemporary of many species now extinct. Some discoveries are said to place the human species in America previous to the appearance of the glaciers; but they have not been of a character to convince the archæologist. In the light of present knowledge we can not assume any immigration from Africa or Southwestern Europe, or Polynesia; and zoölogists hesitate, from the lack of other types near enough to him in development, to consider man

an autochthon in the New World. From the theories of man's origin at a primal center, which is the one most agreeable to anthropologists, the earliest Americans must have made their advent on this continent as immigrants. But we can not assign the position of the immigration on the scale of geologic time, till we have more complete discoveries.

Work of the Bureau of Ethnology.—The Bureau of Ethnology of the Smithsonian Institution having undertaken an exploration of the mounds in the United States on an extensive scale, has so far made a prominent feature of its plan the search for and study of the various forms and types of the works and minor vestiges of art, and the marking out of the different archæological districts as disclosed by investigation. Operations have been carried on in Southwestern Wisconsin and the adjoining districts of Minnesota, Iowa, and Illinois, the northeastern part of Missouri, the western part of Southern Illinois, Southeastern Missouri, the eastern part of Arkansas, certain points in Northern and Western Mississippi, the Kanawha valley of West Virginia, East Tennessee, Western North Carolina, Northern Georgia, and a few points in Northern Florida. Some work has also been done in New York, Ohio, Kentucky, West Tennessee, Alabama, and Southwestern Georgia. Hundreds of groups have been examined, and in most cases surveyed, platted, and described. More than 2,000 mounds have been explored, including almost every known type as to form, and not less than 38,000 specimens have been obtained. Some singular and unexpected discoveries have been made of objects in relatively modern styles. Some of these things clearly pertained to intrusive burials, but a large portion of them appear to have been placed in the mounds at the time they were constructed, and in connection with the original interment. From the data so far obtained by the bureau and other workers in the same field, the conclusions are drawn, according to the report of Dr. Cyrus Thomas, that the mound-builders of the area designated consisted of a number of tribes or peoples bearing about the same relations to one another and occupying about the same status in culture as the Indian tribes that inhabited the country when it was first visited by Europeans; that the archæological districts, as determined by the investigations, conform to a certain extent to the localities of the tribes or groups of cognate Indians at the time of the discovery; and that the theory is not justified by trustworthy discoveries that the builders belonged to a highly-civilized race, or that they were people who had attained a higher status in culture than the Indians. It also appears that each tribe adopted several different methods of burial, at which often some kind of a religious or superstitious ceremony was performed, in which fire played a conspicuous part; but there is no evidence that human sacrifices were offered. The custom of removing the flesh before the final burial prevailed more or less extensively. The large flat-topped mounds in the southern districts are thought to have been occupied, as a general rule, by the council-houses and the residences of the chiefs and principal personages of the tribes; and it seems to have been a common custom when deaths occurred in dwellings standing on low mounds, to bury in the floors of the dwellings, burn the houses, and heap mounds over them before they were entirely consumed or while the embers were yet smoldering. The links that have been discovered connecting the Indians and mound-builders are held to be numerous and well established. The statements of the early navigators and explorers concerning the habits, customs, circumstances, etc., of the Indians when first visited by Europeans are largely confirmed by what has been discovered in these works. This is declared to be especially true as to Arkansas, Georgia, and other Southern States, where the discoveries made by the assistants of the bureau bear out even to details the statements of the chroniclers of De Soto's expedition and of the early French explorers. The testimony of the mounds is regarded as decidedly against the theory that the mound-builders were Mayas or Mexicans who were afterward driven south, and as equally against Morgan's theory that relates them to the Pueblos of New Mexico. From evidences of contact with European civilization, which have been already referred to, which can not be attributed to intrusive burial, it is believed that a goodly number of the mounds were built subsequently to the discovery of the continent by Europeans.

Funeral Rites of Certain Mound-Builders.—In the explorations in the valley of the Little Miami river, Ohio, by F. W. Putnam, in behalf of the Peabody Museum of American Archæology and Ethnology, two mounds in Brown County bore evidence in their interior of fire having been kept up on the spot for a long time. Marks of post-holes around the ash-beds in both of these mounds showed that structures had been erected over them, and the charcoal contained in the post-holes of one of the mounds indicated that the posts had been burned. Dr. Putnam offers as an interpretation of the history of this mound: "Apparently there was originally here a wooden structure which was burned, and this was followed by a long-continued fire until the immense bed of compact ashes had been formed. On this, in some places, clay had been placed and burned hard. Over this bed of ashes clay mixed with ashes, either from the edges of the bed or from some other fire, had been placed, and over all the thick layer of clay, making a mound of at least 60 feet in diameter by at least 8 in height." For the origin of the mounds and the fires, the explanation is offered that they commemorated ceremonies connected with the dead. In the search among the burial-places near Madisonville, a considerable number of graves were opened which had

been carefully constructed of stones, and in which the skeletons lay at full length on the back. In many of these graves the bones of the hand held spool-shaped ornaments made of hammered copper, which the explorations had proved to be ear-ornaments. Such ornaments had previously been found in various parts of Ohio and west to the Mississippi in Illinois and Tennessee, but not in the stone-graves of the Cumberland valley, or among the graves associated with the ash-pits in the cemeteries of the Little Miami valley, or with the skeletons buried in the stone-mounds or in the simple burial-mounds of Ohio. They seemed to be particularly associated with a people with whom cremation of the dead, while a rite, was not general, and who built the great earthworks of the Miami valley. Cremation and inhumation were everywhere found to have been connected with the mortuary rites of the people whose graves these were.

Decipherment of Mexican Manuscripts.—Mrs. Zelia Nuttall, who is familiar with the Nahuatl language of Mexico, has found, by a translation into that language of the phonetic symbols of the ancient Mexican documents known as the Vienna Codex and the Selden and Bodleian manuscripts, that these entire codices are composed of signs representing parts of speech forming in combination words and sentences, and has discovered determinative signs making the interpretation of the writing certain. She is satisfied that the documents in question are records of lands, tributes, tithes, and taxes; and she is convinced by a partial decipherment of portions of them, that the Borgian, Vatican, and Fejeroary codices do not relate, as has been supposed and maintained, to astrological and exclusively religious matters, but deal with the details of a commercial form of government.

Assyrian and Babylonian Antiquity of the Cuneiform Characters.—Mr. A. H. Sayce has called attention to the fact, as presented by a comparison of the older and the later cuneiform inscriptions of Assyria and Babylonia, which are particularly illustrated in the "Tableau comparé des Écritures Babylonienne et Assyrienne" of Messrs. A. Amiand and L. Méchineau, that "in most instances the oldest form of a character which we know is as widely different from the original picture represented by it, as are the latest forms met with in Babylonian and Assyrian texts. Not only is the character already cuneiform, the primitive curves and connected lines having become angular and broken, but it is generally impossible to tell any longer what is the object intended to be depicted. The hieratic characters of Egypt have departed less widely from their primitive pictorial forms than have the earliest specimens of cuneiform writing with which we are acquainted. And yet the monuments of Telloh (see "Annual Cyclopædia" for 1882), upon which these degenerated hieroglyphs occur, go back to the fourth millennium before our era, and still preserve reminiscences of the vertical direction in which Chaldean writing, like that of China, originally ran. It is true that in some cases we can trace the lineaments of the primitive hieroglyphs, and thus learn, for instance, that the inventors of the writing were a circumcised race who worshiped the stars, regarded destiny as a flying bird, and symbolized the act of walking by the human leg; but, as a general rule, the almost entire obliteration of the original picture is complete.

Minor Assyrian Documents.—Mr. S. Alden Smith, an American Assyriologist, studying in the British Museum, has made a special work of examining the collection of small tablets on which are recorded the dispatches, letters, and minor documents of the court and camp life of the empire. The nature of the writings is described by the compiler by saying that the perusal of them is "as if some one, 2,500 years hence, studying and deciphering the annals of Great Britain, would find some short letters from Yorkshire, Lancashire, Scotland, Wales, and Ireland, written by the chief of police, or some revenue or tax collector, whose grammar would not be regular, or style faultless." Written in the popular dialects, these tablets teach much regarding the manners and customs of the people, and the composition and etiquette of the court, and give views of various classes of Assyrian society. They are of both private and official character, the official papers being the most numerous. One series of the documents relate to the affairs of Babylonia after its capture by Tiglath-Pileser II, and depict an active agitation in favor of the restoration of Babylonian autonomy, continuing under the leadership of Merodach Baladan II, and those who came after him, during the reign of Tiglath-Pileser II and Sennacherib. The agitation was marked by rebellious disturbances and intrigues, which are clearly revealed, and illustrate how, in ancient as in modern times, apparently trivial circumstances may be the beginning of great political movements. They are also of much interest to the student of Oriental literature and manners, in that they show how many expressions and forms of address still current in the East have come down from extremely ancient times.

Inscriptions from Abu-Habba.—A private collector in England has obtained a large number of inscribed tablets and cylinders that were collected by Arab antiquity-hunters from the mound of Abu-Habba, which represents the ancient city of Sippara, after Mr. Rassam had discontinued his work there. The majority of the tablets relate to the collection of the revenues of the temple (the great Temple of the Sun-god), which were derived from tithes and dues on corn and dates, and from contributions from pious donors. In addition to these sources of revenue, large grants of land had been made from time to time by kings and others, and were farmed like the Wakouf estates of the Turkish mosques or the glebe-lands of

the English Church. Thus, in the twelfth century b. c., the king gave to the temple "a farm adjoining the city of Al-Essa (New Town), which is within Babylon, and placed it in charge of Ekur-sum-ibassi, a priest." Similar grants were made by other kings. The collection affords very clear indications of the wealth of the land of Chaldea in the seventh and sixth centuries before the Christian era; such as four thousand sheep given as sheep-dues in one year; ten thousand measures as tithes of corn in the third year of Nabonidus, B. C. 553; in another year, five hundred measures from one man. Receipts are also found for quantities of barley, dates, and other fruits, oils, and honey—all collected from farmers, boatmen, scribes, weavers, the master of the camels, and tax-paying women. The tablets further mention the receipt of various material for the repairs or adornment of the temple; of wood and stone in the eighth year of Nabopalassar, B. C. 616; of wood, furniture, and bricks, in the seventh year of Nebuchadnezzar II, B. C. 547; of straw and reeds for building; of five minæ worth of cedar and cypress-wood in the first year of Cambyses, B. C. 529; and of fifty-four shekels of gold in the reign of Darius. One of the most interesting features of the tablets is the care with which the accounts are kept. The names of the payers are entered in full, and sometimes the name of the father and the trade are given. The amount is entered in ruled columns, with total summed up at the foot, and the whole sometimes countersigned by witnesses. Some of the tablets are of great historical value as connecting links in the chain of documents on which Babylonian and Assyrian chronology are based. Every one of the tablets is dated in the month, day, and regnal year of the king's reign in which the transaction took place, and they are therefore a valuable aid in fixing the chronology of the period. Among the new names is that of Sui-sar-iskun, as one of the claimants to succeed Assurbanipal; a name which, in the abbreviated form of Sariskun, bears a resemblance to the Saracus, given in the list of Berosus as the name of the last king of Assyria. Another tablet is of the tenth year of Kindalanu, the Kinladinus of the Canon of Ptolemy, B. C. 637. Among the relics from the most ancient period of the mounds of Tello, M. Berthelot has identified a vase as made of metallic antimony, a substance which was supposed to have been unknown till the fifteenth century.

Cyprus. The Succession of Five Kings.—Importance is attached to a Phœnician inscription on a marble slab, consisting of one hundred and thirty letters in one line, which has been discovered by Herr Richter, near Dali, in Cyprus, because it contains the name of Baalram, the son of Azbaal, the son of Baalmelek; Baalram being known to have been the father of Melikeathon, this name establishes the line of succession of the Phœnician kings of Kition from Baalmelek to Pamiathon (five lives in all; from about 450 to 800 B. C.). The list in lineal descent is as follows:

Baalmelek, B. C. circa	450–420
Azbaal	" "	420–400
Baalram	" "	400–880
Melikiathon	" "	880–860
Pamlathon	" "	850–800

The inscription is dated in the third year of the reign of Azbaal, and records the dedication of the monument, with an invocation. It is mutilated in both ends of the line, and shows traces of a short second line, the restitution of which is hopeless.

Egypt. The Sphinx and Neighboring Tombs.— The work of clearing away the sand from around the Great Sphinx, which was begun under M. Maspero, has been going on intermittently under his successor, M. Grébaut, for several months. At the beginning of 1887, the entire fore-part of the figure had been laid bare, exposing the chest, the paws, the space between the paws, the altar in front of them, and the plateau on which they stand. A space had been cleared between the Sphinx and the edge of the Pyramid plateau, by which the flight of steps forty feet in width, described by Pliny and uncovered by Caviglia in 1817, leading down to the Sphinx, was again exposed to view. A second flight of steps and two Roman buildings, also discovered by Caviglia, are yet to be brought out. A further excavation in the direction of the granite temple to the south, which was in progress, is expected to solve the question whether the Sphinx stood in the midst of a huge amphitheatre hewn out of the solid rock. The whole height of the figure may now be measured from the level of the area below the flight of steps as it rises one hundred feet above. The space between the paws is thirty-five feet long and ten feet wide. It was anciently converted into a small sanctuary lined with votive tablets. One of these—the *stela* of Thothmes IV—still remains *in situ*. It records a dream of the king, in which the even then venerable image exhorted him to clear away the sand in which it was nearly buried. A part of the fourteenth line of this inscription, containing the name of Khafra, or Cephren, has scaled off since the last copy was made. The stone on which it is written appears to have been appropriated by Thothmes from the neighboring Temple of Khafra. The paws of the Sphinx, as they now appear, are a restoration of Roman date, and the facing of the breast, also apparently Roman, has been repaired again. The paws are covered with the Greek *graffiti* of early travelers, which M. Maspero has undertaken to translate. M. Grébaut has worked his excavations to the face of the Libyan cliff bounding the Pyramid plateau on the west, and has discovered several interesting tombs in the neighborhood of the Great Pyramid. In two of the rock-cut tombs in the face of the cliff, the walled-up recesses, or *serdabs*, constructed for the safe-keeping of funerary portrait-statues, were still intact, with their contents. One contained a monolithic group of four figures representing the deceased, his wife, his brother, and a child. An alabaster altar, sculptured in bas-relief, with the likeness of one Ra-ur, was found in another; and on the walls of another tomb occurred the name of Aseska-f, the successor of Menkara (Menkeres or Mycerinus), of the fourth dynasty. Another tomb proved to be the sepulchre of a *sutenes*, or royal son, named Kuhfu-Kha f (the glory of Kuhfu), who was probably the son of the builder of the Great Pyramid. The doorway of the inner chamber of this tomb is decorated with the earliest representation of a column yet discovered, with base, shaft, torus, and capital complete, the whole showing that, as an architectual feature, the column with all its members was already fully developed at the time of the fourth dynasty.

The Cemeteries of Tell el Yehoodieh.—The excavation of the mound Tell el Yehoodieh (mound of the Jew), twenty-two miles northeast of Cairo, on the Suez Railway, has raised some interesting questions. The mound, on account of its name and of the correspondence of its distance from Memphis with that given by Josephus, was identified by Sir Gardner Wilkinson forty years ago, as probably marking the site of the city of Onia, which, according to Josephus, was founded in the latter half of the second century B. C., by Onias, a Jewish fugitive from the persecutions of Antiochus Epiphanes, King of Syria, and in founding it assumed to be fulfilling the prophecy of Isaiah (xix), that there should be "an altar to the Lord in the midst of the land of Egypt." A magnificent building, richly decorated, had been discovered here in 1870, in which were found a statue of Rameses II, a statue of Meneptah, his successor, two black basalt statues of the cat headed goddess Bast, and ovals of Rameses III. The statues of Bast are in harmony with Josephus's identification of an ancient building at this place with the name of Bast, or Diana, and with the mention in the letter of authorization issued by Ptolemy and Cleopatra to Onias, of "that temple which has fallen down," and which he was permitted to purge, as "named from the country Bubastis." The Tell consisted of two artificial hills, in appearance like the two towers of a pylon, from the top of which could be distinctly traced the plan of what looked like a Roman military settlement, bounded on one side by the desert, and on the other by the cultivated land, very regularly laid out in two large parallel streets. The excavations were conducted by M. Naville and Mr. F. Llewellen Griffith, who first endeavored to find in the mound some record of the ancient name of the city and temple before the occupation by Onias. Failing in this, they turned their attention to the necropolis, where they found the tombs cut in the rock very close to one another, and all designed on nearly the same plan. Two or three steps led to a small door, which opened on a square chamber, on all sides of which were horizontal niches of the size of a coffin, sometimes in two rows, one above the other. Nearly all the tombs had been rifled in ancient times. They were regarded as certainly Greek and Roman, and the corpses had not been mummified. Some of the names on the tombs were apparently Hebrew. Such were Nethaneus, Eleazar (ελεΑ ΖΑΡε), Barchias (ΒΑΡΧΙΑΣ ΒΑΡΧΙΟΥ), and others which might be Greek or Jewish. Thus, out of a small number of tablets discovered, one half contain names which are decidedly Jewish; and M. Naville "can not help concluding that the tradition which makes Tell el Yeboodieh a Jewish settlement rests on an historic basis." Further in the desert was another necropolis, containing a great number of terra-cottà coffins, generally hidden in brick chambers. They had nearly all been rifled. The coffins had urns placed at the head and feet. They were painted with Egyptian patterns and hieroglyphics in imitation of the Egyptian style, but in designs which appeared to have no other meaning. M. Naville was not able to agree with Brugsch's supposition that the city was the city of Heliopolis, rebuilt after the Hyksos invasion, but came to the conclusion that it was of more recent origin, and did not come into importance till under the Ptolemaic rulers; that the site was probably that of the city given to the Israelites by Ptolemy Philopater. Mr. F. Llewellen Griffith made more extensive examinations of the further cemetery, from which he qualifiedly ascribed the graves to the period of the Ramesside dynasties. So far as the relics—the statues, the porcelain images of cats and of Bast, porcelain lion-amulets, scarabei, and fragments of pottery of twelfth and thirteenth dynasty types, and a single inscription on a granite altar of Thoth-Uper Se-Bast Mer-Amen, a hitherto unknown king, probably of the twenty-second dynasty—throw any light on the history of the old city, it appears to have been as ancient as the time of the thirteenth dynasty; to have been embellished by Rameses II and Meneptah; to have received additions to the temple under Rameses III, and to have been still a flourishing city when Bast was worshiped under the Bubastic kings, or in the tenth century B. C. But in the time of Ptolemy Philopater it had long been deserted, and given up, according to Josephus, to the "sacred animals," or cats.

A few miles from this place, at Tukh-el-Karmûs, M. Naville and Mr. Griffith explored a singular group of buildings surrounded by a wall measuring about a mile each way, with a smaller inclosure containing the sites of two temples, of all of which only two foundations could be traced. Rich collections of small objects, including some Phœnician figures, were found in a part of the excavations, with a plaque bearing the prenomen of Philip Arideus B. C. 323 to 317.

The Great Temple of Bubastis.—The attention of M. Edouard Naville was drawn to Tel Basta, the site of the ancient Bubastis, by the thought that no remains of the eighteenth dynasty had yet been found in the Delta. It having been reported during the winter that some tombs had been opened at this place, in which scarabs were found bearing the name of Amenhotep III, he visited the place in April, in hopes that he might find other monuments of that king's dynasty, "more conclusive than scarabs." The site is about half a mile from the station of Zagazig, on the railroad between Cairo and Ismailia, but although it marked the position of one of the finest of the ancient Egyptian cities —the Bubastis of the Greeks, the Pi Beseth of the Bible, and the Pi Bast of the Egyptians, the seat of the worship of the goddess Pasht and her sacred animal the cat—it was regarded as a place from which all things of interest had disappeared. M. Naville found that the rumors about the tombs were false; but a few of the scarabs mentioned had been found at the Tell. He, however, decided to sink some pits in the bed of the great central depression which marks the area of the ancient temple. The topography of the depression, surrounded by high banks of rubbish on all sides, corresponds almost exactly with the description given by Herodotus (book ii, chap. cxxviii) of a temple which was looked down upon by the encircling buildings that stood upon the embankments high above it. The results of the excavations were unexpectedly satisfactory, and encouraged an active prosecution of operations as long as the season would permit. The plan of the temple was uncovered in three different parts, to which M. Naville gave the names of the Festive Hall, the Hypostyle Hall, and the Ptolemaic Hall. The general effect was to remind him of the great Temple of Sân. The Festive Hall, a large building without columns, was "peopled by a crowd of statues in red and black granite," all of which bore the name of Rameses II, but many of which were probably usurped by that king. In this hall were also found a standing statue of a governor of Ethiopia; a limestone group of a priest and priestess of the twenty-sixth dynasty, engraved with an interesting geographical inscription; a small statue with the name of Achoris, of the twenty-ninth dynasty, whose monuments are very rare; and a squatting statue in black granite of a son of Rameses II, wearing the side-lock of youth, which was evidently usurped from the work of an earlier (the thirteenth) dynasty. The most interesting objects were a large number of sculptured blocks, which once constituted a single tableau, representing a great festival of King Osorkon II, of the twenty-second dynasty. Though they are in confusion, it is possible to gather some outline of the design. It pictured processions of priests bearing standards and offerings; other priests, two and two, carrying shrines and sacred boats, supported by long poles upon their shoulders; frequently repeated representations of Osorkon wearing sometimes the crown of Upper, sometimes of Lower Egypt, generally with the cat-headed goddess

LOTUS COLUMNS, GREAT TEMPLE OF BUBASTIS.

Pasht by his side; sometimes offering incense and libations to various gods, or himself worshiped by the priests; sometimes in company with his queen, Karoama; and religious dances executed by the priests, some of whom make fantastic gestures, while others lie flat on the ground. A fragment of an inscription makes record of a festival which took place every fifty years. The entire hall was constructed of red granite, with the sculptured surfaces unpolished. A stone was found bearing an inscription with the cartouch of Pepi I, of the sixth dynasty, the reputed founder of the Temple of Denderah. The "Hypostyle Hall" contained a colonnade, which is declared to justify the judgment of Herodotus in saying that the Temple of Bubastis was one of the finest in Egypt. It consisted of magnificent monolithic columns in red granite, with capitals in the form of lotus-buds, or palm-leaves, or the head of Hathor, with two long locks. Though they bore the name of Rameses II, or of Osorkon II, they were evidently of an older dynasty, and were attributed to the twelfth dynasty; and a stone was found which bore the name of Usertesen III, of this dynasty. In the western extremity

of the pile, behind the sanctuary, in what M. Naville calls the Ptolemaic Hall, occurs the name of Nekhthorheb, or Nectanebo I. of the thirtieth dynasty, as the author of additions. The history of the temple is thus written by intervals for a period, according to Brugsch's chronology, of about 3,200 years, or from the sixth to the thirtieth dynasty. On this point M. Naville remarks that it is a singular fact that "at Bubastis, as at Tanis, we find traces first of the sixth dynasty, then of the twelfth dynasty, and then occurs a gap which carries us down to the nineteenth dynasty. No name belonging to the eighteenth dynasty has yet appeared, though some may yet be discovered. Scarabs, bearing the name of Amenhotep III, have, it is true, been found from time to time in tombs at Bubastis; but, so long as we fail to discover any trace of the eighteenth dynasty in the ruins of the temple. we are compelled to believe that the Pharaohs of that line ruled only in Upper Egypt, and that the Delta must still have been in the possession of the Hyksos." According to this view, the strength of the foreign element was not finally broken till in the nineteenth dynasty, and Seti I may have been the first king who once again actually reigned over both Upper and Lower Egypt. The absence of any mention of Shashank or Shishak, the founder of the Bubastic dynasty, who is supposed to have been a native of Bubastis, is remarked upon. The tenor of the evidence afforded by this temple is to indicate that Osorkon II, of whom little has been hitherto known, was the most powerful monarch of the Bubastic line. The condition of ruins indicates that the temple was destroyed by some great convulsion, either an earthquake or a revolution or military assault of extraordinary violence.

Early Christian Cemetery at Alexandria.—An early Christian cemetery has been discovered near Alexandria, on the Ramleh Railway line, between Alexandria and Mustapha Pasha stations, and near the site of the Augustan city and camp of Nicopolis. It is composed of tombs excavated in the rock which underlies the region. In the first tomb discovered, a doorway cut into the solid rock gave entrance to a crypt, surrounded by thirty-eight rock-cut *loculi* measuring about nine feet in length by from four feet to six feet in width, ranged one above another in two and sometimes three tiers. In each recess were found ten skeletons, all apparently skeletons of men, the bones being very large, and the teeth in all sound and white, and firmly fixed in their sockets. Two other excavations were discovered also with *loculi* and interments; and the discoveries make it seem probable that the whole area inclosed by the Roman wall, which is one of the marks of the place, is one vast cemetery. Terra-cotta lamps were found with a few of the skeletons, some impressed with an eight-pointed cross, some with a priestl figure in the attitude of benediction, and some with I. H. S. Over one niche was painted a palm-branch ornament, and other half-obliterated Christian ornaments were here and there painted on the ceilings of the galleries. The only inscription found by Count d'Hulst, who directed the excavations, is too fragmentary for translation.

The Hyksos.—Mr. H. Flinders Petrie exhibited at the meeting of the British Association a collection of casts and photographs of the ethnic types depicted on the Egyptian monuments. Among them were representations of the Hyksos chieftains, or shepherd kings. Dr. Isaac Taylor remarks in the features of these portraits, as he considers them—which are distinguished by "high cheek-bones, and broad, flat, dumpy noses"—evidence that the Hyksos were not Semites, but Mongols or Tartars; and that "the story of the conquest of Egypt by the Hyksos is the story of the conquests of the Huns under Attila, and of the Moguls under Genghis-Khan." Portraits of Hittite chieftains also indicate to Dr. Taylor that the royal race of that nation "belonged to the Mongolic Hyksos type, somewhat softened by intermarriage, while the race over whom they ruled presents an ethnic type of quite another character.

It would seem," he adds, "that in their career of conquest, the Mongolic invaders subdued Syria as well as Egypt; and that their dominion, after it had been overthrown in Egypt by the Ramessides, endured yet awhile in Northern Syria."

The Throne of Queen Hatasu, of the eighteenth dynasty, was placed in view of the public at the exhibition in Manchester. This queen was one of the most famous sovereigns of her dynasty. She was a daughter of Thothmes I, and the queen of Thothmes II, who reigned as his successor for many years. She was distinguished by the erection of some grand buildings, including the great Temple of Dayr-el-Baharee, in Western Thebes, and obelisks at Karnak; and by the expedition which she dispatched to the "Land of Punt," or the eastern coast of Africa—on the oldest voyage of discovery known in history—which returned laden with precious goods and novelties. The throne is made of a hard and heavy wood, of a rich dark color, resembling rose-wood. The legs are carved in the shape of the legs of a hoofed animal, and each ornamented in front with two royal basilisks in gold. The arms are made of the same dark wood, are of curious shape, and finished with basilisks of lighter-colored wood. The seat and back have disappeared, and have had to be restored. The whole was richly plated, trimmed with silver, while the nails by which the parts of the chair were connected, were round-headed, and plated with gold. A part of one of the royal ovals remains; it is nine or ten inches long, is carved on both sides, and contains about one fourth of the field of the cartouch. On it are identified, on one side, the throne-name, "Ra-mo-ka," and on the other side the family-name, "Amen Knum-Hatshepsn," of the queen. The wood of this cartouch, like that of the basilisks on the arms, is very hard and close-grained, and of a tawny-yellow hue, like box-wood.

The throne, and other objects associated with it, are the property of Mr. Jesse Haworth.

Grecian. The Temple of Jupiter Olympius.—Mr. E. P. Penrose has described to the British Archæological School in Athens his discoveries in the Temple of Jupiter Olympius, where he has been excavating on behalf of the Society of Dilettanti. Various massive foundations were come upon, which were in all probability the work of Pisistratus, together with three distinct beds intended for the pavement of different parts of his temple, which were found at levels varying from about nine feet to eleven feet below the floor of the later *naos*. Some drums, about seven and a half feet in diameter, remain of the columns prepared by Pisistratus. The most important result of the excavations was that of settling the question that the temple was octastyle, instead of being decastyle, as had been generally supposed. The probable position of the statue had been ascertained, and the disposition of the foundations corroborated Mr. Fergusson's view of the hypœthrum and general system of lighting connected with this temple, as published in that author's work, "The Parthenon." The foundations had been found of one wall, apparently belonging to even a more ancient structure than that of Pisistratus, which the author called, for convenience, the work of Deucalion, to whom the original foundation of the temple was assigned by a tradition which Pausanias records.

Contemplated Excavations at Delphi. — An arrangement has been made between the Greek and French Governments, by which the latter is conceded the exclusive privilege of excavating at Delphi for five years. The ruins of the city are situated under the modern village of Kastri, and this is to be removed, the Greek Government paying the expense of extinguishing the titles to the property, while the French will bear the cost of the excavations. All objects recovered will remain the property of Greece, while the French will have the exclusive right of reproduction, publication, and multiplication of the objects found for five years after the discovery of each. Two previous experiments in investigating this interesting site were that of Karl Ottfried Müller at the southern wall of the terrace on which the Temple of the Pythian Apollo stood, who found fifty-two inscriptions, and that of the École d'Athènes about twenty years ago, in continuation of Müller's work, the fruits of which are embodied in a considerable volume of Delphic inscriptions that are regarded as of great value for the history of the Amphictyonic League and the city of Delphi.

Ruins at Thasos. — Mr. J. Theodore Bent, excavating in the island of Thasos in behalf of the Hellenic Society and the British Archæological Association, has recovered a number of interesting marbles and about forty inscriptions. The most important relics brought to light were a Roman arch and the theatre. The Roman arch appears to have been erected by the Thasiotes to the honor of the imperial family, and to commemorate the victories over the barbarians. It was fifty-four feet in length, and consisted of three entrances, the central one being twenty feet wide. Of the columns one of the inner ones was intact, and stood nine feet nine inches high, with a scroll-pattern running down one angle. Capitals decorated on two sides only, with floral devices in very high relief, and an egg and tongue pattern below, had adorned these columns. Fragments of six of these capitals were found. Above the capitals appears to have run, both behind the arch and in front, a rich frieze, two feet six inches wide, in blocks of marble from seven to ten feet in length, below which in front ran the inscription in two lines in Greek letters, embodying the legend, "The reverend and great city of Thasos to the greatest and most divine emperor, Marcus Aurelius Antoninus, well deserving of his country, great Bretannikos, great Germanikos. The city of Thasos to Julia Domna. The city of Thasos to the God L.

Septimius Severus and to Pertinax." Above the frieze was a projecting cornice, and on the top of this had rested a large statue of a man struggling with a lion, fragments of which were found beneath the *débris* of the arch. In front of the two central columns of the arch stood four pedestals, carrying statues, and with inscriptions, and in front of the columns nearest the city stood a pedestal, the inscription of which told that the statue it bore was erected by the senate "to their mother Phloneibia Sabina, the most worthy arch-priestess of incomparable ancestors, the first and only lady who had ever received equal honors to those who were in the Senate." The statue was found, almost entirely preserved, representing a young and handsome woman gracefully robed. In the same neighborhood were found fragmentary remains of a Doric building of much earlier date, on one stone of which was an inscription to Ceraunian Zeus, with a thunderbolt underneath it. Of the theatre, which was situated about five hundred feet above the level of the town, the lines of the seats, the semicircle of the orchestra, and the colonnade behind the stage erections, alone were visible. The seats were separated from the orchestra by a wall of twenty-seven large marble blocks, on each of which had been inscribed two large letters, the purpose of which is supposed to have been to indicate the number of the seats. Along the top of this wall ran iron railings to protect the seats. Letters, names, and initials were found to have been cut on all the seats.

In the southern part of the island, at a spot called Alki, were found the remains of a town of considerable size, which had been built upon an isthmus, and was joined to the capital of the island by a road built of irregular blocks of marble, parts of which could still be seen intact. Of the many buildings found, the most interesting was a large Temple of Apollo, with part of an archaic statue of the god and votive tablets offered by mariners to various gods. Pedestals of other statues were found, including one of Athena, and also a small altar to Dionysus. While the temple was probably dedicated to Apollo in the first place, it seems to have become in later times the recognized shrine of many gods.

Tomb of a Lady. — In digging a trench in the Great Varda Street, Thessalonica, at a depth of two and a half metres, a marble sarcophagus of the pre-Christian Roman period was discovered, which seems to have contained the body of a lady of rank. Handsome ear-rings, rings, a gold chain, a brooch, and other articles, were found near it. The sarcophagus was covered in every part with fine and well-preserved reliefs.

Contemplated Excavation of Sybaris. — The Italian Government has determined upon the excavation of Sybaris, which was famed in ancient times as one of the most splendid and luxurious cities of Magna Græcia, and has placed the work under the charge of Prof. Viola. The fact that it was suddenly destroyed at the moment of its highest prosperity, B. C. 510, coupled with the soft alluvial character of the deposit, like that of Olympia, with which it is buried, encourages the hope that its treasures may be found in a well-preserved condition.

Spain and France. Ancient Sepulchres of l'Argar and Fuente Alamo.—The MM. Siret, of Brussels, in their books, "Les Premiers Ages du Metal dans le Sud-est de l'Espagne," describe some thirty prehistoric stations, furnishing relics of the ages of stone, copper, and bronze of which about twelve thousand objects have been collected. The sepultures present some very interesting characteristics; among them are examples of inhumation in jars and in cists constructed of blocks of stone. The arms, tools, and vessels of the deceased were usually placed with him in the tomb; if a man, his hatchet; if a woman, her poignard and bodkin; and jewelry with both sexes, but most abundantly with the female. The jars containing the dead were deposited in a horizontal position with the mouth closed by a stone. In the jar represented in the figure, which was found at l'Argar, were found near the skull three spiral ear-pendants, two of which are of bronze and three of copper. Pieces of linen cloth were still adhering to them; a ring was upon one of the fingers of the skeleton, and beside it lay a bodkin indicating its sex. At the station of Fuente Alamo, of the same age as l'Argar, the burial-places were made of slabs of stone. One of them was 0·82 metre long, 0·55 m. broad, and 0·50 m. deep, and contained the bodies of a man and a woman. Among the *débris* under the skull of

the woman was found a fillet of silver. Upon the bones of the other skeleton lay a flat bronze sword studded with rivets. Beautiful pieces of pottery, which had been made without the aid of the wheel, and footless vases, were deposited in the tomb. In another instance, a silver diadem, somewhat like the one just mentioned, but complete, was found upon the head of the skeleton. It was a simple fillet of metal, with an appendage made of a thin plate of silver, occupying a curious position which suggests that some accident must have happened to disturb it during or after burial. Ear-buckles to a round shape, and beads of bone or stone, completed the list of ornaments found in this tomb.

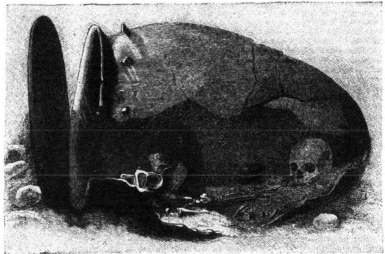

JAR DISCOVERED AT L'ARGAR, SPAIN.

In another tomb was found a bracelet. weighing 114 grains, made of rolled golden wire.

Roman Necropolis at Carmona.—The existence of a Roman necropolis at Carmona, near Seville, has been known for several years. The site is marked by mounds which have proved to be tumuli of a prehistoric age. Around these mounds the Romans had hewed small chambers out of the rock to serve as family tombs. They are from four to five yards square, and of the height of a man. In the walls are small cavities or niches for the cinerary urns, each of which generally contains, besides the ashes of the dead, a coin, a mirror, a lachrymary, needles, a stylus and tabula. and a signet-ring. The walls are mostly painted in fresco or distemper in the Pompeiian style, with representations of birds, dolphins, ,and wreaths of flowers. Near the entrance of each tomb is the crematorium, an oven, also hewed out of the rock, on the sides of all of which signs of fire are still visible. The 320 tombs which have so far been discovered are disposed in groups, around the tumuli, near the Roman quarry, and on both sides of the Roman roads. The excavations during the past year have been carried on under the direction of the Spanish Government and the Royal Academies of History and the Fine Arts of Madrid. They have brought to light near the Roman roads, a columbarium and three large triclinia for the funeral banquets, in each of which a deep channel is provided, into which the guests threw the libations. The largest of the triclinia contains three tables with their couches, the one for winter use being in a hall, another in the sun, and the third, for the summer, in the shade. Besides these were found an altar, a tomb with its cinerary urns, a kitchen, a bath, a well, and a sanctuary in which is a stone statue. About three thousand objects of interest were found, and some of considerable value.

Neolithic Polishing-Stones at Nemours.—Several stones, on which the neolithic men polished their implements, have been observed near Nemours, in France. They are a fine-grained sandstone with calcareous cementing material, and are marked by depressions of various shapes and sizes; some, narrow, deep, and pointed at either end, appear to be the grooves in which the hatchet-edges were sharpened; others, broader and nearly hemispherical, were adapted to the polishing of arms broadside. There are about a dozen of these stones at the Gué du Beaumoulin, on the right bank of the Loing river, bearing some fifty grooves and twenty-five cup-shaped depressions, and suggesting that a considerable business was carried on at the place. The site is not more than a metre above the present level of the river, a fact that shows that the waters did not at that time rise much, if any, higher than now. Another polishing-stone, in the wood of Laveau, has eight parallel grooves from 60 to 80 centimetres long, together with several plain or slightly concave places, which have been worn down by the rubbing of the sides of the hatchets. Another polisher, a megalith, near the mouth of the Loing, has but one groove and one cup, but is remarkable for being of the same stone as the larger polisher of Beaumoulin, and evidently came from the same spot. Another stone, called the Devil's Rock, is associated in popular belief with a curious legend of the devil playing at quoits.

Syria and Palestine; Syrian School of Archæology.—Arrangements have been made for the establishment of a "School of Biblical Archæology and Philology" in connection with the Syrian Protestant College at Beirut. Its purpose will be to afford students the opportunity of studying the Bible in the country where it was written; to promote the study of all the Semite languages, and to afford facilities for research among the ruins and antique relics of the country. It was intended to open the school in October, 1887.

The Rock-cut Tombs of Sidon.—Some quarrymen working in March, about a mile northeast of Sidon, discovered a shaft, open at the top, about 30 feet square and 35 or 40 feet deep. When this was cleared out, doors were found in each of the perpendicular walls, leading to four chambers, in addition to which other chambers were afterward discovered. The walls of the shaft were perfectly oriented. The whole was excavated out of the white limestone; but the walls separating the chambers from the main shaft were built up. The excavation and examination of the chambers were conducted under the direction of Hamdi Bey, of the Imperial Museum at Constantinople. In the southeast chamber lay a large sarcophagus, with a conically gable-roofed lid, of the same shape with seven sarcophagi which had been previously discovered at different times in the province of Lycia. This sarcophagus was decorated with elaborate and artistic sculptures of two winged sphinxes on the rear pediment; a pair of centaurs at either end, the one pair quarreling over a captured stag, and the other pair pouring jugs of water over each other; on the sides, four-horse chariots driven by Amazons, and a boar-hunt. In the east chamber were two sarcophagi, the principal one of which is in the form of a Greek temple, with a gable-roofed cover. Its sculptures include groups of female mourners on the pediments; a hunting-scene on the panel that skirts the base, in which are portrayed wild boars, panthers, lions, bears, bucks, and hyenas; a representation of the funeral scene on the panels extending along the upper edge of the sides; Doric pilasters at the corners, and Ionic columns around the whole, between which are mourning damsels, eighteen in all, each differing from all the others in pose, features, and expression. The north chamber contained two white-marble sarcophagi in the Egyptian style, of the shape known as anthropoidal sarcophagi, having all the variations in the contour of the human form represented. Two other chambers opened out from this one at a lower level, the northwestern of which contained four sarcophagi, only one of which was sculptured. This bore figures dressed in the Assyrian style, with a funeral scene, in which the deceased, stretched upon a funeral-couch, wears an Assyrian tiara. He is guarded by servants, and watched by his wife, and food and drink are offered to him. The west chamber contained one mummy-cased sarcophagus. The southwest chamber, more remote from the entrance, was larger, richer in contents, and more elaborately arranged than the others. It contained in the hither side three white-marble sarcophagi, of the Greek temple shape, covered with rich cornices, and ornamented with a tracery of yellow-leaved vines upon a purple background. Beyond there was a fourth sarcophagus, which is described as being one of the most remarkable specimens of ancient art yet brought to notice anywhere. It is 3·30 metre long, 1·70 metre wide, and 1·40 metre high, with a cover .80 metre high, and walls nearly ·40 metre thick. On one side and end is portrayed a battle between Greeks and Persians, and on the other side and end a chase, in which the recent combatants unite. The Greeks are nude, wearing only a helmet, and carrying a great round grooved shield. The Persians are completely clothed, wearing the head-dress called the mitre, and long trousers. One of the principal Greek characters in the battle wears a head-dress made of a lion's skin, and may have been intended to refer to Alexander the Great. The chase-scene gives a representation of a lion attacking a horse, whose rider has pierced the assailant with his spear. The figures stand out in a bold relief, and the whole is colored in various shades, in which combinations of Tyrian purple prevail. These sarcophagi, all apparently Greek, are supposed to belong to different ages, according to their several styles; but no clew to the dates of any of them was found, unless it be contained in some coins found near the last one that bore the stamp of Alexander Bala, 149 to 144 B. C. Two Phœnician sarcophagi of black marble were also found. One was found in the east chamber, under the sarcophagus of the eighteen female mourners, and contained a skull with long black hair, in good preservation, and the skeleton of a woman with remnants of bandages, articles of ornament, etc. The second was found in a separate shaft, in which at first only two bronze candelabra were discovered. The floor of this chamber was formed of great blocks of stone, below which were two other layers still thicker, and beneath this a monolith of ten cubic metres, covering a pit cut in the solid rock. In this pit la an anthropoidal sarcophagus, which has been pompared with the sarcophagus of Ashmanezer in the Louvre, from which, however, it presents some striking differences. The carvings consist of a head, a winged globe, a kneeling female figure, two erect Egyptian idols, eleven vertical lines of hieroglyphics, and seven and a half lines of Phœnician letters. The sarcophagus was nearly filled with water, and within it lay the body of a young man, with the flesh, except where it had not been covered with water, still tender and firm, but of a bluish tint, with the internal organs intact. Several translations or paraphrases of the Phœnician inscription on this sarcophagus have been offered, all of which are in substantial agreement. The one given by Baltaji Bey, Director of Antiquities at Smyrna, reads: "I Tabnith, priest of Astarte, and king of Sidon, son of Ashmanezer, priest of Astarte and king of Sidon, lying in this tomb, say: 'Do not open my tomb, for there is in it no gold, nor silver, nor treasures. He who opens this tomb shall have no prosperity under the sun, and shall not find rest in his own sepulchre.'"

The City of Tiberias.—Herr Schumaker has traced the whole wall of Herod's City of Tiberias, on the Lake of Tiberias. It is three miles in length, and is in shape an oblong, the long side of which is presented to the lake. At its southwest corner rises a hillock five hundred feet in height, crowned with ruins which were noticed, but not examined, by Col. Kitchener at the time of his survey. The ancient wall of Tiberias ran up, and was connected with a strong wall round this hill. Within the wall are ruins, probably of Herod's palace, certainly of a fort. This is then adjudged to have been the Acropolis of Tiberias, which is now proved to have been in the time of Jesus no mean village, but a considerable city, dominated and guarded by a stronghold situated on an elevation of five hundred feet.

The Hittite (Hamath) Inscription.—Capt. C. R. Conder has published in the book, "Altaic Hieroglyphs and Hittite Inscriptions," the results of his studies of the inscriptions of the class formerly called Hamathite, and at a later period, Hittite inscriptions. These inscriptions had been found at Hamath, Aleppo, Carchemish, and through Asia Minor, and had for many years furnished one of the most interesting questions of Oriental archæology. For a long time their origin was in deep doubt, and it was only after evidence had accumulated from the frequent mentions of them in Egyptian and Assyrian inscriptions that the Hittites were a more important people than had been supposed, that the consensus of a considerable number of Oriental scholars accredited them to that nation. Even then they remained undecipherable, because the language in which they were written was unknown. Capt. Conder claims, or hopes, that he has found a key to the reading of this writing, which he calls the Altaic system, which may be accepted by Orientalists as simple and demonstrable, and to have identified the language as belonging to the family of Ugro-Altaic dialects; and he presents in his book the evidence on which his belief rests. He was led to the special investigation by the detection of resemblances of certain of the characters in the texts with particular characters in the Cypriote syllabary, and by the observation of a connection between certain combinations and Accadian word-roots. The symbols appear to have been originally ideographic — or representing objects; but to have lost their original ideographic meaning, and to have become "representative of certain distinct sounds articularly connected in definite grammatical structure." Capt. Conder's conclusion is, that the characters are connected with the Cypriote characters, and that the vocabulary and grammar of the language are Accadian, or nearly related to it. Upon these bases, he has deciphered and published tentative translations of ten of the principal inscriptions. These he finds to be religious in their character, being mostly invocations. None of them are historical. Paleographists are generally agreed with Capt. Conder in supposing a connection between the Altaic and the Cypriote characters. But his identification of the language with the Accadian stock, and the correctness of his translations, are questioned.

ARGENTINE REPUBLIC, an independent republic of South America. (For details of area, population, etc., see "Annual Cyclopædia" for 1883.)

Government.—The President is Dr. Juarez Celman, whose term of office will expire on Oct. 12, 1892. The Vice-President is Señor Cárlos Pellegrini. The Cabinet was composed of the following ministers: Interior, Dr. Eduardo Wilde; Foreign Affairs, Q. Costa; Finance, Dr. Pacheco; Justice, F. Posse; War and Navy, General Racedo. The Argentine Minister at Washington is Señor Quesada, and the Consul at New York, Señor Adolfo G. Calvo. The American Minister-Resident and Consul-General at Buenos Ayres is Hon. Bayless W. Hanna.

Army and Navy.—The army of the republic, exclusive of the National Guard, according to latest official returns, was 7,324 strong, comprising 3,550 infantry, 2,844 cavalry, and 930 artillery. The National Guard was 347,653 strong.

On March 15 a decree reorganized the infantry, which in future is to be composed of twelve regiments of three battalions, each regiment to have one battalion of troops of the line, and two of National Guards, the battalions to number 250 rank and file in times of peace, and 500 in war-time.

The navy consists of 37 vessels, mounting 72 guns, of a total tonnage of 16,112, with 12,855 indicated horse-power, manned by 1,926 sailors. There are three iron-clads, four gunboats, seven torpedo-boats, three steam transports, four cruisers, and sixteen smaller steam and sailing craft. The Minister of the Navy decreed in March the formation of a squadron of evolutions. The manœuvres lasted from April 20 to April 30 at Punta Lara, whence the squadron went to sea.

Finances.—In May, 1887, the foreign indebtedness of the republic amounted to $93,882,962, and the home debt to $53,792,820; total, $147,675,282. The income in 1886 was $46,634,000, and the expenditures $46,615,000.

During the summer of 1887 the Government resolved to convert certain outstanding bonds; these were $3,582,315 9 per cent. treasury bonds of 1875, $458,106 of the 1858 foreign loan, and $874,251 1868 bonds of the home debt. For the treasury bonds the Government gave 5 per cent. foreign bonds with 1 per cent. annually set aside for the sinking fund thereof, receiving the treasury bonds in payment at 108¼ per cent. The Government furthermore succeeded in floating among German bankers a 5 per cent gold loan to the amount of $10,291,000 at 90, to be refunded when due at the rate of 4 marks (96 cents) per dollar. This was the first Argentine loan ever placed in Germany, yet it was subscribed for eight times over.

The Argentine Government also found a market in Europe for the "cédulas," or mortgage-bonds of the Banco Nacional Hipotecario, bearing 7 per cent. interest, and guaranteed by the Argentine Republic, $20,000,000 having been issued thereof under provisions of the law of Sept. 24, 1886, with 1 per cent. per annum drawn for their gradual extinguishment. During the first six months of 1887, the customs' revenue collected at Buenos Ayres produced the following amounts: January, $2,877,695; February, $2,584,692; March, $3,727,911; April, $3,240,882; May, $2,890,100; June, $2,413,309; total, $17,734,589. Between January 1 and August 3, the amount collected was $21,059,780, against $17,042,900 during the corresponding period of 1886.

The suspension of specie payment decreed in 1885, which expired on Jan. 9, 1887, was prolonged for two years. The share capital of the National Bank was increased during the summer of 1887 to $47,273,400. The vote of November, 1886, approving the budget estimate for 1887, fixed the allowance to members of Congress, both senators and deputies, at $8,400.

Railroads.—The extension of the railway system has been as rapid as the increase in commerce. In 1884 there were fewer than 2,500 miles in operation; in 1885 there were 4,947; and on Jan. 1, 1887, 6,161 miles constructed at a total cost of $175,000,000 in gold. The Andine Railroad extends from Buenos Ayres to the boundary-line of Chili, and there has been a hope that the Government of that republic would either build up to it or permit some private corporation to do so. But the recent action of the Congress of Chili indicates that the gap of 140 miles between the two oceans, west of the Cordilleras, would remain. There appears to be a decided opposition in Chili to the construction of this road, on the supposition that it would cause much of the merchandise now shipped around through the Straits of Magellan to enter at the port of Buenos Ayres, and thus rob Valparaiso of its commercial prestige. The Argentine Government has granted a concession to a company to to construct another transcontinental line from Bahia Blanca, a port 200 miles south of Buenos Ayres to the port of Talcahuano on the Pacific coast, where are extensive coal-mines. The Argentine Government guarantees a dividend of 6 per cent. on the actual cost of the road for twenty years, and gives a generous grant of the public domain. This road would make a large part of the pampas accessible, and give the Argentines a chance at the fuel-deposits of Chili. At present all the coal used in the Argentine Republic, or by ships entering the harbor, has either to be brought around through the Straits of Magellan or from Europe. But it is apprehended that the Government of Chili will refuse to concur in the concession, even to the extent of refusing permission for the construction of the road, for the same reason that it objects to the other transcontinental line. The Argentine Congress, during its last session in 1886, passed a bill ordering surveys for the lowing projected railroads: Extension of Northern Central *via* Jujuy, between the eza del Buey, Santa Rosa, and the southern emity of the Lerma valley, through Salta; i Chumbicha to Tinogasta, Fuerte de An-ala, *via* Punta del Negro or Quebrada de la; from Mendoza to San Rafael, *via* San ite, Lujan, Tupungato, and San Cárlos; San Juan to Jachal, and from Albardon ncete; from Cajamarca to the Northern al Junction *via* the Totoral; and finally, Rioja to Santa Rosa or Cholo. Concession en applied for for the construction of a d from the Paraná river at a point op-the city of Corrientes to Tartagal on the n frontier *via* Oran, the Government to ee 5 per cent. interest and make the y a land-grant of 360 square leagues in ng lots, with a two-league frontage on es of the line.

il the railroad company that is build-illa Maria-Rofino (Pacific) Railway ap-he Government for authority to ex-Bahia Blanca, the southern port of mise. Another important project is at is to connect by rail Buenos Ayres evideo. From Buenos Ayres, Las ould be reached over the Northern ilroad. The total cost of this line l at $12,500,000 in gold. One third m Argentine territory, and the re-Uruguayan.

er Lines.—Under the auspices of ie Government two new lines of ips for European traffic are to be and the projects were submitted in July. One is to ply between s and Bordeaux, carying the mails vernment guaranteeing the 5 per for a term of twenty years, and annual net profit of the company r cent., such surplus to accrue ment till it shall have recouped nterest disbursements. Another a to be called "La Argentina," of eight first-class steamships carrying the Argentine flag. are to be furnished with re-nbers for the conveyance of o carry immigrants from Ligu-mbardy, the Romagna, Tyrol, . The Government to have a suitable compensation to s transports in time of war. receive a suitable bonus for brings into the country be-y.

lines in operation in 1886 erated as follows:

(OTH IN KILOMETRES.			Offices.	Em-ployés.
lles.	Wire.	Cable.		
177	29,634	72	428	1,263
655	9,428	68	197	271
832	39,057	185	626	1,764

There were in course of construction 800 kilo-metres of state lines. At the close of the year 1886 a consolidation of telephone companies took place at Buenos Ayres, and the new company immediately raised its rates so much that a good many subscribers withdrew, and a movement was set on foot to establish a co-operative telephone company in opposition.

Commerce.—The foreign trade of the Argentine Republic for five years has been:

YEARS.	Imports.	Export.
1882	$61,246,000	$60,389,000
1883	80,435,000	60,207,000
1884	94,056,000	68,029,000
1885	92,221,000	83,879,000
1886	94,370,000	69,090,000

The Argentine foreign trade was distributed in 1885 as follows (in thousands of dollars):

COUNTRIES.	Import.	Export.
England	85,375	11,227
France	14,545	24,165
Belgium	7,463	14,888
Germany	7,268	8,512
Italy	4,207	2,448
Spain	8,189	2,243
Holland	545	67
United States	7,007	5,584
Brazil	2,907	2,170
Uruguay	4,343	3,366
Chili	46	2,494
Paraguay	1,471	180
West Indies	78	1,438
Other countries	4,584	5,146
Total	92,231	83,879

The goods shipped were: Wool, tons, 128,393; hides, number, 2,742,771; sheep-skins, tons, 31,337; horse-hides, number, 373,365; other skins, value, $1,986,000; tallow, tons, 23,260; horse-hair, tons, 2,009; jerked beef, tons, 32,-056; cattle, head, 159,664; minerals, value, $1,682,000; bones, tons, 85,424; linseed, tons, 69,426; wheat, tons, 78,493; Indian corn, tons, 197,860; horns, tons, 1,261; ostrich-feathers, kilograms, 34,710. During the wool-clip of 1886–'87 the export from Buenos Ayres from Oct. 1, 1886, to July 31, 1887, was 226,614 bales, against 262,116 the previous season. During the first quarter of 1887 the import into the Argentine Republic amounted to $30,-322,467, including $2,765,716 specie, against, respectively, $30,642,681 and $6,455,495 during the corresponding period of 1886. The export reached $27,580,500, inclusive of $1,000,327 specie, as compared with, respectively, $36,-124,758, and $5,133,871 the previous year. The American trade with the Argentine Republic is shown in the following table:

CALENDAR YEAR.	Import into the United States.	Domestic exports to the Argentine Republic.
1886	$4,354,880	$5,020,825
1885	4,775,616	3,984,190

Education.—In 1886 there were 2,415 schools, 1,804 of them being primary public schools, and 611 private; 180,768 pupils were attending them, and the number of teachers was

5,348, the increase since 1885 being 63 public schools, with 12,390 pupils and 612 teachers. The national territorial educational establishments had an increase of pupils, in 1886, of 262, as compared with the previous year. The national capital counts 54 educational establishments, 40 of which, ready to receive 22.-000 children, were opened on Oct. 3, 1886. During the year $3,500,000 were spent on the schools, which is an average of about $1 to each inhabitant of the country.

Immigration. — The number of immigrants landed at Buenos Ayres in 1886 was 93,116, and 19,293 cabin-passengers; total, 112,409. During the thirty years from 1857 to 1886, 1,098,220 immigrants arrived. During the past seventeen years, 1870 to 1886, there landed from Europe 605,533 immigrants, and from Montevideo 328,003. It has been decided to build eleven hotels for the reception of new-comers, each to have a capacity for boarding and lodging from 500 to 1,000 individuals; one to be located in the suburbs of Buenos Ayres; two in the province of Buenos Ayres; and two in each of the provinces of Córdoba, Santa Fé, Entre-Rios, and Corrientes. The Argentine immigration law secures the newcomer, during the first days after landing, board and lodging. But the Bureau of Labor immediately busies itself about procuring them work on the spot, dispatching them to a colony, on the Government, if able to utilize their labor anywhere, causes them to be conveyed thither at its own expense. In the new colonies the Government makes the first twenty-five families a land-grant of thirty hectares each. More land is at the disposal of such families at $2 per hectare, and advances up to $1,000 are made to each family, if desired, in the shape of provisions, seed for the first crop, animals, tools, and agricutural implements. The liberal credit of ten years is allowed settlers on such land purchases and advances, within which to refund the Government, but a title is given them after two years of cultivation.

New Industries. — The Argentine Congress passed a bill in 1886 incorporating the sugar-refinery to be founded by Messrs. Ernest Tornquist & Co., at Rosario, and guaranteeing for the term of fifteen years 7 per cent. per annum interest on the actual capital to be invested therein, subject to work none but domestic cane-sugar, the capacity of the refinery to be at the least 15,000 tons annually of refined sugar. All machinery and material to be admitted duty free, and the refinery to enjoy immunity from any kind of taxation. The new refinery is expected to be in full operation within two years. The production of cane-sugar in the republic has reached 40,000 tons per annum. The Provincial Government of Buenos Ayres in April sold to Lorenzo Pascual Cortada a large plot of land, at the low price of thirty centimes the square yard, on which he is to erect a factory for the weaving of wool, silk, linen, and cotton, at a cost of

$500,000, the factory to be finished within twelve months. The exportation to Europe of carcasses of sheep, on board refrigerator steamers, has become an important item of trade. In 1883, 17,160 carcasses were shipped; in 1884, 108,800; in 1885, 190,600; and in 1886, 361,200. A company was formed at Buenos Ayres in the summer, with a capital of $2,000,000, incorporated for a term of thirty years, for the purpose of exporting live cattle, chiefly to Europe. Another company was in the course of formation, with a capital of $2,000,000, having for its object the export of frozen meat. It proposes to acquire from three to four leagues of grazing-land of superior quality, seed 1,500 cuadras, thereof with clover, and buy cattle enough to have at all times a ready supply of 20,000 head for slaughtering. A similar stock of sheep is to be kept, and the slaughtering is to take place not far from the harbor of Buenos Ayres, so as to facilitate the rapid transfer of meat to be shipped to the -re frigerator steamers. A project is on foot in the province of Córdoba, to create an experimental viticultural station, combined with a model establishment for wine-making, under the superintendence of practical viticulturists, who engage to superintend the building of cellars and to furnish all that is necessary for the manufacture of wine in accordance with the most approved modern Bordelais style, the station to be called the Château Córdoba. The province makes them a land-grant covering an area of fifty hectares, thirty-four of which are to be planted with vines; eight hectares are to be set aside for the instruction of apprentices intending to become viticulturists. The Provincial Government will, at its own expense, erect the school-buildings adjoining the station.

Coal and Oil. — Under an offer of a prize of $25,000, scientific men have been scouring the country for deposits of coal, and are said to have found large beds in the northern part of the republic. The Department of Public Works, which has had the direction of the explorations, is so well satisfied with the genuineness of the discovery that the prize has been awarded, and operations to develop the mine have been begun.

Petroleum. — Petroleum-wells have been discovered thirty-two miles from Mendoza in the Cachenta mountain district.

ARIZONA. Territorial Government. — The following were the officers of the Territory during the year: Governor, C. Meyer Zulick; Secretary, James A. Bayard; Treasurer, C. B. Foster; Auditor, John J. Hawkins; Superintendent of Public Instruction, Charles M. Strauss; Commissioner of Immigration, Cameron H. King. Chief-Justice of Supreme Court, James H. Wright; Associate Justices, William W. Porter, Willliam H. Barnes.

Legislation. — The fourteenth Territorial Legislature convened January 10, and was in session till March 11. One of its first acts was to create a code commission to collate and perfect

:e Territorial laws, and much of the time of
e session was given to changing or enlarging
a fundamental law, as the following captions
acts will indicate: Trial of title to real prop-
ty. Concerning juries and jurors. Forci-
entry and detainer. Trial of right of per-
al property in certain cases. Abolishing
distinction between sealed and unsealed
ruments. Attachments and garnishments.
cerning frauds and fraudulent convey-
s. Concerning bills, notes, and other writ-
nstruments. Concerning registration. Re-
rs and their duties. Concerning husband
wife. Concerning executions. Concern-
artnerships. Concerning evidence. Lim-
ns of actions. Concerning wills, descent,
stribution of real property. Concerning
pals and sureties. Concerning home-
Concerning judgments and liens. A
'nal code and a code of civil procedure
lso adopted.
license law passed at this session repeals
ises for general merchandising, and im-
donble tax on saloons. Persons hold-
holesale liquor license are forbidden to
the same license. The retail tax was
$200 a year. The following are cap-
other acts:

u telegraph tax law.
and distribution of public moneys.
arantine.
do funds for carrying out the provisions of
otect domestic animals.
d brands.
own-sites.
ounty indebtedness.
'.
ige the destruction of wild animals.
ing election laws.
ower to the Governor to veto sections in
ion bill.
prison and county jails.
mines.
injuries resulting in death.
unding act.

nture was composed of twenty-five
id eleven Republicans, both houses
ratic.
—From the report of the Super-
'ublicSchools, made at the begin-
ir, it appears that there was an
enrolment and average attend-
a preceding year. Twelve school
created, making a total of 130,
idditional school - houses were
rere maintained in the Terri-
aar and 125 primary schools.
t open on an average only 124
year. The Normal School at
opa County, has been in oper-
year, and a Territorial Univer-
Pima County, is in process of

wth.—According to the report
for 1887, there has been a
> the population of the Terri-
L0,440 in 1880. and may now
000. The aggregate assessed

valuation for 1887 is $26,818,500, which shows
an increase in one year of nearly $6,000,000,
notwithstanding the fact that by the present
system of assessment and taxation much of the
real and personal property is undervalued, and
a large portion of the personal property is not
listed for taxation. The last legislative assembly created a Territorial Board of Equalization
with power to revise the assessments of the
different counties.

There are 1,050·04 miles of railroad in the
Territory. Two trunk lines, the Southern Pacific and the Atlantic and Pacific, traverse the
Territory from east to west, the former representing 883 miles and the latter 392 miles.
During the past year 137.8 miles of the new
road have been built—the Maricopa and Phœnix, connecting Phœnix, the county seat of
Maricopa County, via Tempe, with the Southern Pacific road, at or near Maricopa station,
84·5; the Prescott and Arizona Central, connecting Prescott, the capital of the Territory,
with Prescott Junction, on the Atlantic and
Pacific road, 73.8 miles, and 30 miles of the
Mineral Belt road.

The United States Land Office certifies that
there are 2,000,000 acres of arable land in the
valleys of the Colorado, Salt, and Gila rivers.
Irrigation alone is needed to reclaim these
tracts, and a beginning has been made in the
construction of canals. There are now about
400 miles of these canals in Arizona, representing a cost of over $1,000,000, and reclaim-
ing about 215,000 acres. Most of the stock in
these is owned by the holders of the lands
under them. The farmer pays for the number
of inches he uses to produce his crop, the
amount used varying from three eighths to one
half an inch per acre.

The product of Arizona in precious metals
for 1886 was $6,103,378. It would be safe to
add at least 20 per cent. for chlorides and ores
shipped for treatment in Colorado and San
Francisco, which are constantly being transported and not reported.

The Mogollon forest, near the center of the
Territory, is nearly 200 miles in length, and its
average width is about 50 miles, making 10,000
square miles, or 6,400,000 acres. Outside of
the pineries of Michigan, Wisconsin, and Washington Territory, there are few portions of the
republic that contain such an extensive body
of timber. The Arizona Lumber Company, at
Flagstaff, sawed in the past year 5,976,493
feet, and shipped 8,305,093 feet of lumber.

Indians.—The principal tribes of Indians in
Arizona are the Apaches, the Pimas and Mari-
copas, the Papagos, the Yumas, the Mohaves,
the Moquis, the Navajos, and the Hualapais.
The Navajos are most prosperous, intelligent,
and enterprising, and doubtless the wealthiest
tribe in the United States. They number 15,-
000 and are increasing. It is estimated that
the tribe owns at least 20,000 horses and
1,000,000 sheep. They occupy the Navajo reservation, in the extreme northeast corner of

the Territory, which also takes in a portion of New Mexico and covers about 5,000 square miles. All the other tribes, except the Apaches, are peaceable, and chiefly engaged in agriculture. The latter are lazy, murderous, thievish, and seemingly incapable of civilization.

ARKANSAS. State Government.—The following were the State officers during the year: Governor, Simon P. Hughes, Democrat; Secretary of State, Elias B. Moore; Treasurer, William E. Woodruff; Auditor, William R. Miller; Attorney-General. Daniel W. Jones; State Land Commissioner, Paul M. Cobbs; Superintendent of Public Instruction, Wood E. Thompson; Chief Justice of the Supreme Court, Sterling R. Cockrill; Associate Justices, W. W. Smith, B. B. Battle.

Railroads.—The Legislature, which was in session from January 10 till March 31, devoted much attention to railroad problems, and passed several acts restricting the power of railroad corporations, and protecting the public from possible injustice at their hands. After the rejection of a measure that involved the creation of a special State railroad commission, a bill known as the Smith railroad bill, was adopted. The leading provisions of this are:

That no railroad shall consolidate with, or lease or purchase, or in any way control, any other railroad owning or having under its control a parallel or competing line, nor shall any officer of such railroad act as an officer of any other railroad owning or having control of a parallel or competing line; that no discrimination in charges or facilities for transportation shall be made between transportation companies and individuals, or in favor of either by abatement, drawback, or otherwise, and no railroad shall make any preferences in furnishing cars of motive power; that it shall be unlawful for any railroad in this State to enter into any combination with any other parallel or competing line of railroad for pooling of freight, by dividing between them the gross or net earnings of such railroads, or by dividing the property or passengers carried by said railroads; that all railroad corporations in this State shall keep posted up at every depot freight-office under the control of any such railroad corporation printed schedules showing the rates of fare, and the kinds and classes of property carried.

Another act regulates the rate of charge per mile for the carriage of passengers. Still another prohibits any State officer, whether executive, legislative, or judicial, from accepting a free pass on any railroad in the State, or any railroad from issuing such. A fourth provides that no foreign corporation shall be permitted to lease, build, maintain, or operate any railroad within the State. Doubts were raised regarding the constitutionality of this last act, on the ground that it did not accord to citizens of another State the privileges and immunities of citizens of Arkansas; but the Attorney-General has interpreted it to mean, in accordance with the probable purpose of the Legislature in passing it, but scarcely in harmony with its letter, that all railroad corporations owning property in the State shall *ipso facto* be considered citizens of the State, amenable to its laws, and subject to its taxes. The measure was framed to prevent any further claims by certain large railroads whose lines ran into the State, that they could not be legally taxed as its citizens.

In 1884 the property of all the railroads in the State, other than lands not connected with the roads, was valued at $6,352,985; in 1885 at $9,612,778; in 1886, at $13,704,688; and in 1887, at $15,323,472.

State Debt.—The Governor in his annual message says:

The bonded debt of the State amounts to $5,102,563, including interest to the first day of October, 1886. Of this $22,000 are State bank bonds, and bear 5 per cent. interest; $2,057,000 are real-estate bank bonds, bearing 6 per cent. interest; $1,000 are a Loughborough bond, bearing 6 per cent., and $100 are a Brooks-Baxter war-bond bearing 10 per cent. interest; but upon the two last named interest has ceased to run. Of the whole amount of the State debt $2,080,100 are principal, and $3,023,463 accrued interest.

For meeting this long-standing debt the following measure was passed by the Legislature:

First, it was provided that in order to create a "sinking fund" with which to liquidate the valid and undisputed bonded indebtedness of the State, there shall be levied and collected, and paid into the treasury annually a tax of one mill on the dollar on all taxable property, to be denominated "sinking-fund" tax; second, a State-debt board, consisting of the Governor, Secretary of State, and Auditor, was created to superintend the debt settlement. This board was authorized whenever there should be in the treasury, to the credit of the sinking fund, the sum of $25,000 or more, to advertise for proposals for the sale to the State of any of the State bonds with accrued interest, and to accept any such proposals at its discretion, and to pay the amount so agreed upon to the bondholders on surrender of the bonds. For this purpose of purchasing bonds during the two years next ensuing, the sum of $800,000 was appropriated out of the sinking fund. Provision was also made to enable holders of bonds to exchange them for certificates of indebtedness receivable for certain taxes. Under this act bids were made and accepted in July for the sale of bonds at prices ranging from 71½ to 72 cents on the dollar.

Legislation.—Among the acts passed by the Legislature were the following:

To provide for the reorganization of the Arkansas Industrial University.

To abolish public executions.

To regulate the practice of dentistry.

To provide for allowance for widows and children out of estate of deceased persons.

To provide for the collection of overdue taxes from corporations doing business in this State.

To fix the time for holding elections in cities of the second class.

To give effect to the constitutional provision against usury.

To prevent minors from playing cards or pool in dram-shops or other public places.

Fixing the price of State lands at $1.25 an acre.

To authorize the several counties of the State to issue bonds in lieu of their indebtedness existing prior to 1874.

To make appropriations for the support and maintenance of the Branch Normal College at Pine Bluff.

To limit the time of bringing suits on mortgages.

To provide for the assessment and collection of a public highway tax from corporations, companies, and individuals running sleeping-cars over railroads in this State, and for other purposes. The rate fixed is $3 per mile for each car per annum.

To submit to the people of the State the question of holding a convention to frame a new constitution.

To encourage sheep-raising by providing against the ravages of dogs.

To provide for the donation of forfeited lands.

To compel railroad companies to build and maintain depots, and to stop their trains within certain limits of cities and incorporated towns.

To amend the law relative to Sabbath-breaking, allowing "Seventh-day Adventists," and other sects observing as the Sabbath another day than Sunday to labor, but not to keep open shop on that day.

To protect employés and other persons against railroad companies giving such employés a lien for services and material furnished.

There were 78 Democrats in the lower house, 14 Republicans, 4 members of a semi-political organization, known as the Agricultural Wheel, 1 Independent, and 1 Greenbacker; the Senate was composed of 29 Democrats and 2 Republicans.

Education.—For the year ending June 30, 1885, $1,199,005.82 were received from all sources for school purposes, and of this sum $729,168.81 were expended in maintaining the free schools of the State. For the year ending June 30, 1886, $1,327,710 were received, and $866,892.45 paid out for school purposes. A large number of school-houses have been built in the State within the past two years, and many of them cost from $3,000 to $20,000 each.

Finances.—The annual expenses of the State government, including charitable institutions, are about $300,000, this being about one third of the total amount raised by State taxation. In 1887 the sum of $815,408 was apportioned from the State treasury among the counties for the use of the common schools. As the whole school population numbers 358,000 the amount per capita would be $0.88. A poll-tax of $1 is also applied to school purposes, besides the tax of about 5 mills levied by each school district for its own purposes of education.

In the case of the State vs. ex-State Treasurer Churchill, the Supreme Court on appeal sustained the decision of Chancellor Carroll rendered at the beginning of last year, by which the sureties of the treasurer's first and third bonds were discharged, but found their liability on the second bond to be $26,000 instead of $3,000, and the entire liability of Churchill to the State was adjudged to be $115,000. As the expenses of litigation will equal the amount of judgment rendered against the sureties, the State will practically lose the whole sum originally misapplied.

ASSOCIATIONS FOR THE ADVANCEMENT OF SCIENCE. American.—The thirty-sixth annual meeting of the American Association for the Advancement of Science was held in the buildings of Columbia College, New York, beginning Aug. 10, and adjourning Aug. 16, 1887. The following were the officers of the meeting: President, Samuel P. Langley, of Washington. Vice-Presidents: Section A, Mathematics and Astronomy, John R. Eastman, U. S. Navy, elected in place of Prof. William Ferrel, of Washington, who was unable to be present. Section B, Physics, William B. Anthony, of Ithaca, N. Y. Section C, Chemistry, Albert B. Prescott, of Ann Arbor, Mich. Section D, Mechanical Science, Eckley B. Coxe, of Drifton,

Pa. Section E, Geology and Geography, Grove K. Gilbert, of Washington, D. C. Section F, Biology, William G. Farlow, of Cambridge, Mass. Section H, Anthropology, Daniel G. Brinton, of Media, Pa. Section I, Economic Science and Statistics, Henry E. Alvord, of Amherst, Mass. Permanent Secretary, Frederick W. Putnam, of Salem, Mass. General Secretary, W. H. Pettee, Ann Arbor. Assistant General Secretary, J. C. Arthur, Geneva, N. Y. Treasurer, William Lilly, of Mauch Chunk, Pa. The meeting derived additional importance from the fact that it was held in the metropolis. The Buffalo meeting of 1886 had been attended by a comparatively small number, and it was felt that something should be done to increase the attendance. The selection of New York had the desired effect, and 711 members registered as being present. The high character of the officers of the meeting guaranteed an important series of papers, and this promise was well carried out.

Opening Proceedings. — On August 9, the Standing Committee met for the transaction of routine business, and during its sessions three hundred and fifteen new members were elected, including many well-known names.

The meeting formally opened on Wednesday, August 10, at 10 A. M. The meeting in general session in Library Hall organized, and was called to order by the retiring president, Prof. Edward S. Morse, of Salem. The public had been invited to attend the meeting, and had responded so that the large room was crowded with auditors. On the stage with Prof. Morse sat President F. A. P. Barnard, of Columbia College; Prof. Langley, the new president of the Association; Prof. Pettee, the general secretary; and Bishop Potter. Pres. Barnard addressed the meeting, reviewing the list of distinguished deceased members of the Association who had done good work in the scientific field. Bache, Henry, Agassiz, Torrey, Pierce, Mitchell, Hare, and other illustrious names were cited. He ended his address by welcoming the Association as representative of the trustees of the college.

Prof. Langley gave a short address in reply. In it he described the mission of the society, and while saying that too much indulgence should not be exercised in admitting every one to membership and a hearing, yet pleaded for liberality in these regards. Truth sometimes comes to us in an unfamiliar dress, and a large tolerance of errors of speculation should be indulged in, where accompanied by a faithful original study of facts. As a short exposition of the true scope of the society the address was as timely as eloquent, and it met with much appreciation.

The members then left the Library Hall, and at half-past two assembled in the different section-rooms to hear the addresses of the vice-presidents of the sections.

Vice-Presidents' Addresses. — Owing to the change of vice-president there was no address in Section A. In Section B, devoted to physics, the address was delivered by Prof. William A. Anthony on "The Importance to the Advance of Physical Science of the Teaching of Physics in the Public Schools." The title indicates the general tendency of the address. The utilitarian tendency of modern thought was deprecated, the plea being made that science pursued from purely scientific motives was sure to lead eventually to remunerative results. The fact was also referred to that many of the foremost scientific workers have not given freely of all their work to the scientific world. He proposed that science should be studied in the primary departments, beginning when children are but ten or twelve years old. The object of this teaching would be to graduate from the schools an army of workers fitted to carry on in some shape original investigation.

In Section C, devoted to chemistry, the address was delivered by Prof. Albert B. Prescott, on "The Chemistry of Nitrogen as disclosed in the Constitution of the Alkaloids." Much of the address was strictly technical, hardly admitting of an abstract. The abundance of nitrogen in the free state, its comparative rarity in the combined, settling in its combinations the value of supplies for the nourishment of life, and its paradoxical character in the two-fold *rôle* thus outlined was developed. After a lengthy consideration of its position in the chemical scale, the structure of the chief alkaloids of plants was considered, and the progress of alkaloidal synthesis was described. Morphine is now convertible into codeine, and efforts that promise well are now being made to convert strychnine into brucine and cinchonine into quinine. Some good medical alkaloids are now being made in the laboratory, and the identical alkaloids of nature may yet be made by art. Prof. Prescott's character as a worker in organic analysis increased the value of his address by the authority it conferred upon it.

In Section D, devoted to mechanical science, the address was delivered by Eckley B. Coxe on "The Necessity of Scientific Training for Engineers." The speaker spoke of the peculiarity of his position as an engineer who was really a business man presiding over a meeting of engineers. The divisions of the profession into civil, mining, and other branches, was alluded to. The indebtedness of the working engineer to the scientists who have determined and deduced the many data needed in his work was described. The great success of the early engineers, graduates of the workshop, was achieved in spite of, not on account of, their defective training. The young student of the present day should decide at the start as to the branch of engineering he wishes to follow, whether scientific, consulting, or business. To the proposed course his studies should be adapted.

In Section E, devoted to geology and geog-

raphy, the address was delivered by Grove K. Gilbert on "The Work of the International Congress of Geologists." This topic, in view of the active work of the congress during the past seasons, was a peculiarly timely one, and the address won well-merited recognition for its ability. It was made the subject for general discussion for the whole session of Section E on August 12. He reviewed the history of the congress, tracing its origin to the 1876 meeting of the American Association for the Advancement of Science and Art held in Buffalo. The first convention of the congress was held in Paris, in 1878; the second, in Bologna, in 1881; the third, in Berlin, in 1885. The next meeting is set for London, in 1888, and the fifth meeting, it is to be hoped, will be held in the United States. The work of the congress in unifying geological nomenclature, classification, and conventions, as of map-colors and similar points, was described. The great map of Europe, in forty-nine sheets, in preparation by the congress, was spoken of. A long account of the basis for the scheme of classification followed—the divisions of groups, systems, series, and stages being described and defined.

In Section F, devoted to biology, the address was delivered by Prof. William G. Farlow on "Vegetable Parasites and Evolution." His address was devoted to the application of the Darwinian theory to the parasitical forms of plant-life. The two classes "saprophytes," or those living on dead matter, and the true "parasites" growing on living matter, were described. Thus the mold on bread is a saprophyte, and the potato-rot fungus the true parasite. Most parasites belong to the fungi. The various views of the evolutionists as to their origin were stated, and left open for adoption. The speaker evidently felt that no fixed conclusion could be reached in the light of present knowledge.

In Section G, devoted to anthropology, the address was by Prof. Daniel G. Brinton, "A Review of the Data for the Study of the Prehistoric Chronology of America." An exhaustive classification and statement of the material at our disposal for building up the prehistoric annals of this country was given. Six sources of information are at our disposal; Legends, Monuments, Industries, Language, Physical Sources, Ethnology, and Geology comprise our sources of information. When these various data have been sufficiently studied a large increase in our knowledge of the early history of our continent may be anticipated. A field for much thought and work was outlined, and a precision of result at least foreshadowed in this address.

In Section I, devoted to economic science and statistics, the address was by Prof. Henry E. Alvord on "Economy in the Management of the Soil." The speaker stated that the visible wealth of the country could be traced principally to the soil, which has been hitherto drawn upon with reckless prodigality, no systematic effort being made to prevent absolute deterioration or exhaustion. Land excepted, the value of the possessions of the people does not equal the sum total of three years' production of our industries. Food, clothing, shelter, and fuel are almost entirely derived from or dependent on the soil. For twenty years agricultural products have constituted three quarters of our exports. This involves a heavy drain upon the nitrogen, phosphoric acid, and potash of the soil. Hence we should witness with feelings of congratulation the increase of interest in agricultural studies and the number of men of ability who are making them their life's work.

Other Papers.—Prof. Edward S. Morse delivered his address as retiring president on "What American Zoölogists have done for Evolution." It was a very able presentation of the present aspect of the Darwinian theory. The speaker appeared as a strong partisan of and advocate for the doctrine of evolution, and appealed to the standing of American naturalists on the subject, as well as to observed facts in natural history in support of his arguments. His address was very long, and gave a full presentation of the subject. It referred more particularly to the work done for the establishment of the theory during the last ten years.—Prof. Lucien I. Blake, of Terre Haute, spoke on "A Method of Telephonic Communication at Sea." It described the use of the sea-water as a sound-bearing medium, and gave an account of some of the author's experiments in sound-transmission by water without the aid of a telephone. These were performed in 1883–'85, and were believed to antedate all attempts at devising telephonic methods. Drs. Michelson and Morley excited much attention, and received quite an ovation for the researches on "A Method for making the Wave-Length of Sodium Light the Actual and Practical Standard of Length." This proposal amounted to fixing a definite natural standard for measurements of all kinds, something that has never yet been obtained. The metre was only an unsuccessful effort to obtain such a standard. The society immediately voted to recommend the council to appropriate money to continue the investigation in order that a new unit might be produced, to be known as the American Association unit. This would be a worthy rival to the British Association or B. A. units. Prof. Lewis M. Norton spoke on "The Fatty Acids of the Drying Oils," treating of linoleic acid, the characteristic of linseed-oil and ricinoleic acid (of castor-oil). Prof. Arthur L. Green, of Purdue University, presented a scheme of analysis entitled "A Process for the Separation of Alkaloidal Poisons for Students' Use." An interesting paper was presented by Prof. Robert H. Thurston, of Cornell, on "The Strength of Nicaraguan Woods." It embodied the results of a research by Rufus Flint, a native of Nicaragua. It proved that in that country there exist most valuable varieties of wood. The present im-

pending wood-famine may, the speaker said, be averted by the use of tropical timber. "The American System of Water Purification," and notes on a recent outburst of typhoid fever, its cause and cure, were given by Prof. Albert R. Leeds, of Stevens Institute. Rev. Dr. William M. Beauchamp discussed "Aboriginal Villages in New York State." This gave a vivid picture of the old forts, stockades, and long houses of the Iroquois Indians, and alluded to the tenure of land among the aborigines. Prof. Wilber O. Atwater gave papers on "The Economy of Food" and "Food of Workingmen and its Relations to Work done." In these the question was brought down to the most practical basis of cost and nutritive value. The American workman, he said, eats one half more than the German; his daily food represents 6,776 foot tons of potential energy. A description of the Boston cooking-schools, by Mrs. Ellen H. Richards, appropriately followed Prof. Atwater's laborious and practical papers. Later, the Panama Canal and the rival plans for crossing the Isthmus were treated by several essayists. Commander Taylor, U. S. N., in his paper on "The General Question of Isthmian Transit," and Civil Engineer R. E. Peary, U. S. N., in his paper on "The Engineering Features of the Nicaragua Canal," presented two aspects of the problem, while Mr. J. W. Miller, of the Nicaragua Steamship Company, on "Historical and Geographic Notes concerning the Nicaragua Canal Route," and Surgeon J. F. Bransford, U. S. N., on "Climatic and Sanitary Notes on the Nicaragua Canal Route," gave some practical views of the case. Prof. George F. Barker read two papers by Thomas A. Edison on a direct conversion of heat into electricity effected by "The Pyro-Magnetic Dynamo" and on "A Magnetic Bridge or Balance for Measuring Magnetic Conductivity." These can not well be described here, but both mark an important advance in electrical science.

Many entertainments and visits to places of interest filled up the leisure hours, and finally on Monday, Aug. 16, the Association adjourned.

Committees, Etc.—President Langley appointed Professors E. D. Cope, J. R. Eastman, and G. K. Gilbert, a committee to devise methods of obtaining from Congress a reduction of the tariff on scientific books. Miss Alice C. Fletcher and Mrs. T. Stephenson were appointed a committee to petition Congress to take the necessary steps to preserve the archæological monuments on the public lands of the United States.

A resolution was passed recommending the publication by the Government of an index to the literature of meteorology, now being prepared by the Chief Signal-Service officer, Cleveland Abbe. Another resolution urged President Cleveland to appoint at once a permanent superintendent of the United States Coast and Geodetic Survey. A third petitioned Congress to provide a Bureau of Standards, by which accurate standards of measure should be established for electricity, heat, and light, and arrangements made for the issue of authenticated copies of the same.

Election.—The following officers for the next meeting were elected: President, Major John W. Powell, of Washington; Vice-Presidents, by sections: Mathematics and Astronomy, Prof. Ormand Stone, of the University of Virginia; Physics, Prof. Albert A. Michelson, of Cleveland, Ohio; Chemistry, Prof. C. E. Monroe, of the U. S Navy, Newport, R. I.; Mechanical Science, Prof. C. W. Woodward, of the Washington University, St. Louis; Geology and Geography, Prof. G. H. Cook, New Brunswick, N. J.; Biology, Prof. C. V. Riley, Washington; Anthropology, Prof. Charles C. Abbott, Trenton, N. J.; Economic Science and Statistics, O. W. Smiley, Washington; Permanent Secretary, Prof. F. W. Putnam, Cambridge; General Secretary, Prof. J. C. Arthur, Lafayette, Ind.; Secretary of the Council, Prof. C. Leo Mees, Athens, Ohio; Treasurer, William Lilly, Mauch Chunk; Secretaries of sections, in order, Prof. C. L. Doolittle, Bethlehem, Penn.; Dr. A. L. Kimball, Johns Hopkins University; Prof. W. L. Dudley, Nashville; Prof. George H. Williams, Johns Hopkins University; Prof. Arthur Beardsley, Swarthmore College; Dr. N. L. Britton, Columbia College; Prof. Frank Baker, Smithsonian Institution; and Prof. C. S. Hill, Washington.

The place for the next meeting is Cleveland, and the date the fourth Wednesday in August, 1888.

British.—The British Association for the Advancement of Science held its fifty-seventh annual meeting in Manchester beginning August 31, 1887. Great preparations were made to insure the success of the third Manchester meeting of the Association. Owens College was selected as the place of meeting. Nearly every distinguished man of science abroad it is said had a letter of invitation to attend the meeting. The total attendance amounted to nearly 4,000. Among those Americans who accepted may be noted the following: Prof. C. V. Riley, Washington, D. C.; Prof. H. A. Rowland, of Baltimore, Md.; Asa Gray, of Cambridge, Mass.; Charles A. Young, of Princeton, N. J.; Frank W. Clarke, of Washington, D. C.; John W. Langley, of Ann Arbor, Mich.; Cleveland Abbe, of Washington, D. C.

President's Address.—The inaugural address by the president, Sir Henry E. Roscoe, treated of the progress of science during the last fifty years. The speaker uttered a plea for the acceptance of the elements as final constituents of matter, at least for the present, seeming inclined rather to resist Crooke's recent generalizations. He traced the history of chemical and physical science through the line of workers of the past five decades, and ended by a brilliant allusion to the delights of seeking truth and acquiring knowledge.

Section Presidents' Addresses.—In Section A, devoted to mathematical and physical science, the president, Sir Robert Ball, Astronomer Royal of Ireland, spoke on "A Dynamicable Parable," the theory of screws. This gave a review of its subject in the form of a disputation between a number of fictitious characters, such as Mr. Helix, Mr. Querulous, Mr. Anharmonic, etc. The address reads well, and is probably *sui generis* as far as the annals of the Association are concerned.

In Section B, devoted to chemical science the address was delivered by Dr. Edward Schunck. The speaker first described the chemistry of fifty years ago as he first studied it, contrasting it with that of the present day. Then, with this as a basis, he endeavored to outline what the chemistry of the future would be. The address, from so old a representative of science, possessed a peculiar interest, and will repay careful perusal.

In Section C, devoted to geology, the address was delivered by Sir Henry Woodward. He treated of the world's work in geology. He referred to Sir William Dawson's ideas as to a a Federal Union of Geologists with great approval. The International Congress of Geologists was then spoken of with special reference to the 1888 London meeting thereof. Finally, the work of the world's geologists was described briefly, each authority being cited by name, and a valuable *résumé* of the work now going on being thus presented.

In Section D, devoted to biology, the address was delivered by Prof. A. Newton. It was largely devoted to the Darwinian theory, of which the speaker appeared as an eager advocate. He spoke of the fauna of the British colonies, and lamented their rapid extinction, affirming that from them biologists might draw their most valuable lessons.

In Section E, devoted to geography, the address was given by Maj.-Gen. Sir Charles Warren. It was local in its scope, the speaker dwelling upon the importance to the English nation of the dissemination of geographical knowledge among its people.

In Section F, devoted to economic science and statistics, Dr. Robert Giffen, on "The Recent Rate of Material Progress in England." This, too, was of local character, applying to England only.

In Section G, devoted to mechanical science, the address was delivered by Prof. Osborne Reynolds. It was devoted to the progress of the steam-engine toward theoretically perfect results. The lecturer took for a starting point the labors of Clausius, Carnot, Regnault, and the other great students of thermodynamics, and traced the progress from them to the practical results of the present day.

In Section H, devoted to anthropology, the address was delivered by Prof. A. H. Sayce, on the evidence to be obtained from a study of language as to the history and development of mankind.

Other Papers.—Among the papers presented by Americans may be noted those by Prof. C.

V. Riley, of Washington, on the hop aphis, the *Phorodon humuli*, and one by Prof. Charles A. Young, of Princeton, on the work done by his party in observing the eclipse of the sun at a station in Russia. Sir William Thompson read a paper on the Vortex Theory of the Luminiferous Ether. This showed mathematically that a perfect fluid completely enwrapped in minute vortices would do everything that the luminiferous ether was called on to do. The paper had its origin in the theory proposed by Prof. Fitzgerald, of Dublin. It is regarded as one of the events of the meeting, and as marking the nearest approach yet made to the mathematical conception of the ether.

Several committee reports were read on solar radiation, magnetic observations, electrolysis, and other subjects.

Various public lectures were given. Prof. H. B. Dixon spoke on "The Rate of Explosions"; Prof. George Forbes gave a workingmen's lecture on "Electricity"; Sir Francis de Winton spoke on "Exploration in Central Africa."

In connection with Section H, an anthropometric laboratory has been established. Many of the members of the Association were here weighed, measured, and subjected to various tests to obtain data as to the statistics of the cultivated class to compare with those gathered from all classes, by Mr. Francis Galton, of South Kensington.

Grants.—The total grants for researches made by the Association amounted to £2,025, ranging from £5 to £200 each, and divided among all the branches.

ASTRONOMICAL PROGRESS AND PHENOMENA.—During 1887 the usual steady advance was made in all departments of astronomy, but attention was specially concentrated upon celestial photography and the total solar eclipse of August 19. Among the notable events of the year was the twelfth meeting of the International Astronomische Gesellschaft, which was held at Kiel, from August 29 to August 31, under the presidency of Dr. Auwers.

Instruments and Methods.—In volume xvii of the "Annals" of the Harvard College Observatory, S. C. Chandler has published a description and theory of his "almucantar," and a reduction and discussion of a long series of observations made with it in 1884-'85. The instrument, which belongs to the equal-altitude class, consists of a telescope mounted upon a base floating in mercury, and the observations are made by noting the times when stars cross the horizontal circle defined by the wire system of the telescope. In the hands of the inventor this instrument has given most excellent results; but experience alone can decide whether it will prove superior to the ordinary zenith telescope in the hands of other persons. Be that as it may, equal-altitude instruments enjoy such a remarkable immunity from systematic errors, that astronomers must ultimately have recourse to them in order to eliminate the small systematic errors inseparable from meridian work.

M. Loewy, of the Paris Observatory, has proposed a method of determining the constant of aberration from differential measurements of the changes in the distances of suitably-chosen pairs of stars. In all the pairs the two constituents must be separated by nearly the same interval—say about 90°—and the changes in the distance of each pair are to be measured in the field of an equatorial into which the stars have been reflected by a double mirror, formed by silvering two surfaces of a glass prism. The method is explained at length in several papers printed in the "Comptes Rendus," volumes civ and cv. M. Houzeau claims that in 1871 he suggested the principle upon which this method depends. Sir Howard Grubb has written an elaborate paper on the best forms of instruments for astronomical photography, and has made some experiments with a new object-glass, suggested by Prof. Stokes, which can be changed at pleasure from an ordinary visual objective to a properly corrected photographic lens. The change is effected by merely separating the lenses, but for photographic purposes the field of view is rather small. Prof. Abbe has called attention to a heretofore neglected correction in the computation of refraction, arising from the circumstance that the reading of the barometer does not give the true weight of the air until it has been corrected for the variation of gravity due to the latitude of the observer. By applying this correction to the Pulkowa refraction-tables, Prof. Abbe finds that at the equator the correction amounts to 0·2″ for a zenith distance of 45°, and increases with the tangent of the zenith distance. The omission of the correction may, perhaps, explain some of the small systematic differences now existing in star catalogues. Prof. J. M. Schaeberle, of the Ann Arbor Observatory, has recently published a short method of computing refractions for all zenith distances, but his formulæ scarcely differ from those given in the Pulkowa refraction-tables.

Astronomical Photography.—Nothing is more remarkable than the way in which the world at large will neglect an important invention or discovery for years, and then suddenly take it up with the wildest enthusiasm. This was well illustrated by the recent electrical craze, during which many persons actually believed that gas-lighting antedated electrical lighting; and now photography is having its turn. The old bromo-iodized daguerreotype plates were not as sensitive as the best wet collodion plates, but they would have borne as long exposure as a modern dry plate, and much of what is now done with gelatine plates might have been accomplished with them. They were inferior to gelatine plates in convenience of working, in extreme sensitiveness, and in the impossibility of printing paper positives from them; but they were superior in the security which they afforded against the images being disturbed by slipping of the film. The daguerreotype process was made public in 1839, and in March, 1840, prior to the introduction of bromine for increasing the sensitiveness of the plates, Dr. John W. Draper, of New York, took some daguerreotypes of the moon about one inch in diameter, with an exposure of twenty minutes. Daguerreotypes were taken of the total solar eclipse of July 8, 1842, by Prof. Majocchi, at Milan, and of the total solar eclipse of July 28, 1851, by Father Secchi, at Rome, and by Dr. Busch, at Königsberg, Dr. Busch's pictures being the first that showed the corona. The first eclipse photographed on collodion plates was that of Sept. 7, 1858, some negatives of the partial phases being made by Liais in South America. All the pictures thus far mentioned were made with ordinary astronomical telescopes, corrected for visual rays, and it was not till the total eclipse of July 18, 1860, that De la Rue introduced the use of equatorial cameras, having lenses specially corrected for photography, the particular instrument employed being one that had been constructed under his direction in 1855–'56 for the Kew Observatory. Since then all solar eclipses have been observed with what may be called modern instruments. The first daguerreotype of the uneclipsed sun was made in 1845 by Fizeau and Foucault. After Draper's daguerreotypes of the moon, it is not known that any more were made until 1850, when the Bonds took up the subject, and with the Cambridge 15-inch telescope produced daguerreotypes of such excellence that they attracted marked attention in the Great Exposition held in London in 1851. These pictures incited De la Rue to take up photography, and toward the end of 1852 he made some beautiful negatives of the moon, which were remarkable as being the first astronomical pictures taken on collodion. Since that time photographs of the moon have been made by many persons, but those produced by Lewis M. Rutherfurd and Dr. Henry Draper are unrivaled. On July 17, 1850, the Bonds, aided by Messrs. Whipple and Black, of Boston, daguerreotyped a Lyræ by means of the Cambridge 15-inch telescope, and this was the first stellar photograph ever made. The double star Castor was subsequently daguerreotyped, but the experiments were soon abandoned on account of the length of the exposures—indeed, for some reason hard to comprehend at the present day, they were unable to obtain any impression whatever from Polaris, no matter how long the exposures were continued. In 1857 the Bonds again reverted to the subject, and on April 27 of that year, they made collodion negatives of ζ and g Ursæ Majoris; and the former being a double star, they measured the position, angle, and distance of its components from the negatives, in the manner now in vogue. During 1857 they succeeded in photographing stars of the sixth to seventh magnitudes in less than a hundred seconds,

and they inferred that stars of the ninth magnitude could be photographed in ten minutes. At that time they also made some negatives of Saturn. The next person to take up the subject was Lewis M. Rutherfurd, of New York. In 1857–'58 he worked with an ordinary achromatic telescope; in 1859–'60 he used the same telescope with correcting lenses applied between the objective and the eye-piece; in 1861 he used a silver-on-glass reflector; and having found all these unsatisfactory, in 1864 he constructed a telescopic objective of 11¼ inches aperture, specially corrected for photography. With that instrument he obtained photographs of ninth magnitude stars upon wet collodion plates, after an exposure of about three minutes; and thus modern stellar photography came into being. Nevertheless, for twenty years it made little progress, and it is only recently that astronomers seem to have realized its importance. As frequently happens with new processes, there is now a tendency to exaggerate its capabilities, but in due time that will be corrected, and much of the secondary work hitherto done by meridian circles will fall to the photographic camera. The adoption of the new method will doubtless be hastened by the action of the Paris International Congress, an account of which is given below. Photography affords special facilities for the detection of small planets or stars having large proper motion, and it has been successfully used for both these purposes during the past year. By its aid Mr. Roberts determined the position of the asteroid Sappho (80), which is not known to have been observed since 1872, except by Dr. Gill in 1882. The asteroid was of about the eleventh magnitude, and with an exposure of an hour it showed a distinct trail upon the plate. As an instance of the detection of a star's proper motion by the aid of photography, the case reported by Herr von Gothard, in the "Astronomische Nachrichten," may be cited. On examining a photograph of the cluster No. 4440, Herschel's "General Catalogue," taken at the Herény Observatory, he found that a small star of the eleventh magnitude had changed its position relatively to the other stars since Vogel's measurement of the cluster in 1867–'69. The proper motion thus detected amounts to about 2·3″ per annum. Prof. Pritchard, of the Oxford University Observatory, has published some results, which he regards as provisional only, of his photographic investigation of the parallax of the well-known double star 61 Cygni. The measurement of 330 plates, obtained on 89 nights, gives:

Parallax of 61¹ Cygni = 0·4389″
Parallax of 61² Cygni = 0·4358

For comparison we may cite the following results obtained by other astronomers working with equatorials and heliometers in the usual way:

Bessel in 1840	0·348″
Auwers in 1863	0·564
Ball in 1878	0·468
Hall in 1880	0·261

Prof. Pritchard lays stress upon the fact that each plate must be considered as carrying with it its own scale; and, due regard being paid to the unavoidable though slight variations of scale in the different plates, he is of opinion that in this delicate class of work photography will give as accurate results as any other known method. The nebula No. 1180 of Herschel's "General Catalogue" has been photographed by Mr. Roberts in England, and by the Henry Brothers in Paris. The latter made their negative on Jan. 27, 1887, giving it an exposure of two hours, and obtaining an image extending 25' from east to west, and 15' from north to south, with a nebulous star, or condensation, a little detached toward the south. During such long exposures as this it is necessary to guard against displacements of the images upon the sensitive plate, arising from changes in the refraction due to the earth's diurnal motion. Dr. Dryer has investigated the magnitude of these displacements, and finds that in latitude 50° north, with a perfect clock, and an accurately adjusted instrument, they will not exceed 0·5″ (and may therefore be neglected) in the case of an equatorial star moving from 27ᵐ east to 27ᵐ west of the meridian, or in the case of a star of +25° declination moving from 39ᵐ east to 39ᵐ west of the meridian.

Prof. E. C. Pickering has recently published his first annual report on the photographic study of stellar spectra at the Harvard College Observatory, made with funds provided by Mrs. Draper as a memorial to her husband, the late Dr. Henry Draper. The results already obtained are so encouraging that Mrs. Draper has decided to extend the original plan of the work sufficiently to embrace a complete discussion of the constitution and conditions of the stars as revealed by their spectra, so far as present scientific methods permit. In order to reach all parts of the sky, it is expected that a station will be established in the southern hemisphere. The investigations already undertaken extend only to declination −24°, and include a catalogue of the spectra of all stars of the sixth magnitude and brighter, a more extensive catalogue of spectra of stars brighter than the eighth magnitude, and a detailed study of the spectra of the bright stars. Three telescopes have been used in the work: an 8-inch Voigtländer photographic lens refigured by Alvan Clark & Sons, Dr. Draper's 11-inch photographic lens, and the 15-inch refractor of the Harvard Observatory. The spectra have been produced by returning to Fraunhofer's method of placing a large prism in front of the object-glass. The spectrum of a star formed in that way is extremely narrow when the telescope is driven by clock-work in the usual manner, but it may be broadened as much as is desired by giving the telescope a speed slightly different from that of the earth. The negatives were subsequently enlarged; and a specimen print is given of part of the spectrum of Pollux on a scale that would separate H and K by nine-tenths of an inch. In a comparatively short space it shows nearly 150 lines with remarkable clearness. Several points of interest have been already brought out by Prof. Pickering's work. A photograph of α Cygni, taken Nov. 26, 1886, shows the H line double, its two components having a difference in wave-length of about one ten-millionth of a millimetre. A photograph of ο Ceti shows the lines G and h bright, as are also four of the ultra-violet lines characteristic of spectra of the first type. The H and K lines in this spectrum are dark, showing that they probably do not belong to that series of lines. The star near χ^1 Orionis, discovered by Gore in December, 1885, gives a similar spectrum, which affords additional evidence that it is a variable of the same class as ο Ceti. Spectra of Sirius show a large number of faint lines, besides the well-known broad lines. Progress is reported in the various investigations that are contemplated, namely: 1. Catalogue of spectra of bright stars. 2. Catalogue of spectra of faint stars. 3. Detailed study of the spectra of the brighter stars. 4. Faint stellar spectra. 5. Absorption spectra. 6. Wave-lengths. Mrs. Draper has decided to send to Cambridge a 28-inch reflector and its mounting, and the remarkably perfect 15-inch mirror constructed by Dr. Draper and used by him in making his photograph of the moon.

The literature respecting the use of photography in astronomy has recently been enriched by articles written by Mr. A. A. Common; Dr. David Gill, Astronomer Royal at the Cape of Good Hope; Prof. E. S. Holden, Director of the Lick Observatory; Admiral Mouchez, Director of the Paris Observatory; M. G. Rayet, Director of the Bordeaux Observatory; Otto Struve, Director of the Pulkowa Observatory; and Prof. C. A. Young, of the Princeton Observatory. Some of these articles are mainly historical, others are theoretical and practical, and still others are of a more popular character. Among the historical articles those by M. Rayet, in the "Bulletin Astronomique," are particularly noteworthy on account of their completeness and accuracy.

The Paris International Astrophotographic Congress.—In compliance with the request of Admiral Mouchez, an International Congress of Astronomers was called in April by the French Academy of Sciences, to take steps to obtain a photographic chart of the heavens upon the co-operative plan so successfully carried out by the German Astronomische Gesellschaft in their zone observations. The Congress was opened at the Paris Observatory on April 16, by M. Flourens, Minister of Foreign Affairs of the French Government, and addresses were made by M. Bertrand, the eminent mathematician, by Admiral Mouchez, Director of the Paris Observatory, and by Prof. Struve, Director of the Pulkowa Observatory. Admiral Mouchez was chosen honorary president; Struve, president; Auwers, Christie and Faye, vice-presidents; Bakhuyzen and Tisserand, secretaries; and Dunér and Trépied, assistant secretaries. At the first meeting a committee of nineteen was appointed to consider and report upon the size and construction of the instruments to be employed, and upon the limit of star-magnitudes to be included in the photographs. This committee reported on April 19, and after some discussion it was decided to divide the Congress into two sections—one to deal with purely astronomical questions, and the other with those involving photography. Each section drew up a series of resolutions, which were further discussed and amended by the Congress in full session, and were finally adopted in the following form:

1. The progress made in astronomical photography demands that astronomers of the present day should unite in undertaking a description of the heavens by photographic means.

2. This work shall be carried out at selected stations, and the instruments shall be identical in their essential parts.

3. The principal objects shall be:

a. To prepare a general photographic chart of the heavens for the present epoch, and to obtain data which shall enable us to determine the positions and magnitudes of all stars down to a certain magnitude, with the greatest possible accuracy (magnitudes being understood in a photographic sense to be defined later).

b. To be able to utilize in the best way, both in the present and in the future, the data obtained by photographic means.

4. The instruments employed shall be exclusively refractors.

5. The stars shall be photographed as far as the fourteenth magnitude, inclusive; this magnitude being indicated provisionally by the scale actually in use in France, and with the reservation that its photographic value shall be definitely fixed afterward.

6. The aperture of the object-glasses shall be 0·33 metre (13·0 inches), and the focal length about 3·43 metres (11¼ feet), so that a minute of arc shall be represented approximately by 0·001 metre.

7. The directors of observatories shall be at liberty to have the object-glasses made where they desire, provided they fulfill the general conditions laid down by the Congress.

8. The aplanatism and achromatism of the objectives shall be calculated for radiations near the Fraunhofer ray G.

9. All the plates shall be prepared according to the same formula; this formula to be subsequently agreed upon.

10. A permanent control of these plates from the point of view of their relative sensibility to the different radiations shall be instituted.

11. Questions in regard to the preservation and reproduction of the negatives can not at present be settled, and shall be referred to a special committee.

12. The same conclusions are adopted in regard to the photographic magnitudes of the stars.

13. Resolution 8 above, in regard to the aplanatism and achromatism of the object-glasses, shall be understood in the sense that the minimum focal distance shall be that of a ray near G, so as to attain the maximum sensibility of the photographic plates.

14. The object-glasses shall be constructed in such a manner that the field to be measured shall extend at least 1° from the center.

15. In order to eliminate fictitious stars, and to avoid inconvenience from minute specks which may exist upon the plates, two series of negatives shall be made for the whole sky.

16. The two series of negatives shall be so made that the image of a star, situated in the corner of a plate of the first series, shall be found as nearly as possible in the center of a plate of the second series.

17. Besides the two negatives giving the stars down to the fourteenth magnitude, another series shall be made with shorter exposures, to assure a greater precision in the micrometrical measurement of the fundamental stars, and render possible the construction of a catalogue.

18. The supplementary negatives, destined for the construction of the catalogue, shall contain all the stars down to the eleventh magnitude approximately. The Executive Committee shall determine the steps to be taken to insure the fulfillment of this condition.

19. Each photographic plate to be used in the formation of the catalogue shall be accompanied by all the data necessary to obtain the orientation and the value of its scale; and, as far as possible, these data shall be written on the plate itself. Each plate of this kind shall show a well-centered copy of a system of cross-wires for the purpose of eliminating errors which may be produced by a subsequent deformation of the photographic film. Further details of this nature shall be determined by the Executive Committee.

20. In the negatives intended for the map, the number of cross-wires to be used in their control and reduction shall be reduced to a minimum.

21. The tubes of the photographic instruments shall be constructed of the metal most likely to give an invariable focal plane, and shall carry a graduation for the determination and regulation of the position of the plate.

22. The Executive Committee shall choose the reference stars to be used.

23. The question of the methods of measurement, and the conversion of the numbers obtained into right ascensions and declinations for the equinox of 1900, is left to the Executive Committee. That committee shall first occupy itself with the study and methods of use of measuring-instruments, giving either rectangular or polar co-ordinates, and based upon the simultaneous use of scales for the larger distances, and micrometer screws for scale subdivisions.

24. The connection of the plates will be effected in conformity with resolution No. 16.

At the last general session, April 25, the Congress elected a permanent committee of eleven, consisting of Christie, Dunér, Gill, Paul Henry, Janssen, Loewy, Pickering, Struve, Tacchini, Vogel, and Weiss, and it was decided that all directors of observatories actually taking part in the work of forming the map should, by virtue of that circumstance, become members of this committee. The observatories of Algiers, Bordeaux, Buenos Ayres, Paris, Rio de Janeiro, and Toulouse, were announced as now ready to undertake their share in the new work, and Trépied, Rayet, Beuf, Mouchez, Orula, and Baillaud were thus added to the committee. An Executive Bureau of this committee was elected, consisting of Mouchez, president; Christie, Dunér, Janssen, Struve, and Tacchini, members; and Gill, Loewy, and Vogel, secretaries. A special committee was also elected by the Congress to occupy itself with the application of photography to astronomy, other than the construction of the map, having regard to the importance of all these applications, and to the relations that it is desirable to establish between these different kinds of work. Common and Janssen were requested to take charge of this matter. It is intended that the Executive Committee shall meet every year at one of the observatories engaged in the photographic work, and reports of these meetings will be published.

Observatories in the United States.—At the Naval Observatory in Washington the 26-inch equatorial has been used by Prof. Hall in observations for stellar parallax, and also in observations of satellites, of double stars, and of Saturn. The transit-circle work has been continued as in former years, and comets and asteroids have been observed with the 9·6-inch equatorial. Prof. Frisby has been engaged upon a revision of Yarnall's catalogue. The facilities for testing chronometers have been improved, and the time-service has recently been considerably extended. About 200 "Gardner clocks" are automatically corrected daily by a signal from the observatory, and time-balls are dropped at New York, Philadelphia, Baltimore, Washington, Hampton Roads, Savannah, and New Orleans. For the erection of a new observatory upon the site near Washington purchased in 1880, Congress has appropriated $100,000, with the provision that the cost of the whole work shall not exceed $400,000. The plans for the new buildings are now being prepared.

The latest report of the Director of the Harvard College Observatory, at present available, was submitted to the visiting committee Dec. 7, 1886. The extensive series of photometric observations has been continued, with gratifying success. Stellar photography is now receiving considerable attention, and interesting results have been obtained, to which reference has elsewhere been made. The financial resources have recently been greatly increased. The Paine bequest, half of which, about $164,-000, is now available, has been added to the endowment of the observatory; and the Boyden fund of over $230,000—which was left for the purpose of making observations "at such an elevation as to be free, so far as practicable, from the hindrances to accurate observations, which occur in the observatories now existing, owing to atmospheric influences "—has been transferred to the President and Fellows of Harvard College, so that the researches Mr. Boyden had in view may be carried out under the administration of the observatory. Prof. Pickering has already occupied, during the past summer, a high station in Colorado for experimental purposes, and intends eventually to establish an observatory in the southern hemisphere, where a series of photographic observations will be carried on supplementary to similar work at Cambridge.

The report of the Dearborn Observatory of Chicago for 1885 and 1886 has lately been issued. It contains a list of nebulæ discovered there by Prof. T. H. Safford in 1866-'68; papers on the motion of the lunar apsides, and on the companion of Sirius by Prof. E. Colbert; and an illustrated paper on the physical aspect of Jupiter, a catalogue of 209 new double stars, and a description of a printing chronograph, by Prof. G. W. Hough. The lawsuit respecting the ownership of the instruments has been decided in favor of the observatory.

The first of the publications of the Morrison Observatory, Glasgow, Mo., is a well-printed volume of 111 pages, giving an account of the founding of the observatory, with a full description of the building and instruments, and the observations in detail. The instruments consist, chiefly, of a 12½-inch Clark equatorial, and a 6-inch Troughton and Simms meridian circle, similar in plan to the meridian circle of the Harvard Observatory. Observations of double stars, of planets, comets, and occultations by the moon have been made by the director, Prof. C. W. Pritchett, assisted by Prof. H. S. Pritchett and C. W. Pritchett, Jr.; and as a preliminary work the geographical co-ordinates of the meridian circle were determined. The volume contains several drawings of the observatory, and sketches of Saturn and of comets.

Prof. Stone has devoted the 26-inch refractor of the McCormick Observatory mainly to the study of nebulæ; an especial feature of his work being the determination of accurate positions of all the nebulæ north of 30° south declination, which are condensed at the center and as bright as the fourteenth magnitude. The great nebula of Orion has been repeatedly examined, for the purpose of determining the relative brightness of the various condensations composing it, and thus of furnishing means of detecting any change that may take place in them. Prof. Stone speaks highly of the electric illumination, which he has applied to the equatorial.

The Washburn Observatory, which was left without a director upon Prof. Holden's resignation in the winter of 1885, was placed temporarily under the charge of Prof. John E. Davies, on July 1, 1886, and Prof. Davies has now been succeeded by Prof. G. C. Comstock, who served as assistant in the observatory to both Prof. Holden and his predecessor, Prof. Watson. The fifth volume of publications, giving an account of the work accomplished down to April 1, 1887, has been issued by Prof. Davies. With the meridian circle a series of observations has been made for the determination of the latitude, and a discussion of that co-ordinate is given by Mr. Updegraff. A list of stars has also been observed in declination, with this instrument. The 15½-inch equatorial has been used for measuring double stars and for observations of Sappho (80) and of comet 1887 II. Miss Lamb contributes a useful index to certain stars contained in various Greenwich catalogues.

The 36-inch lenses of the great refractor of the Lick Observatory were safely transported across the continent, and were deposited in the vaults of the Lick Observatory on Dec. 27, 1886. The safe transportation was a matter of great moment to· the trustees. The lenses were wrapped separately in fifteen or twenty thicknesses of soft cotton cloth, and were put into separate wooden boxes lined with felt. No nails were used near the glasses, and the boxes were made to fit the latter in shape. These boxes were inclosed in two others of steel, each nearly cubical, and packed with hair. Each steel box was then inclosed in another steel box, the inner sides of which were covered with spiral springs, and both boxes were made air-tight and water-tight and placed in outer chests packed with asbestus to render them fire-proof. They were then suspended by pivots in strong wooden frames, with means for turning one-quarter round every day during the journey. This was in order to prevent any molecular disarrangement in the glasses, and to avoid the danger of polarization, through the jarring of the train. The great 75-foot dome is in place and works well. It revolves with a longitudinal pressure of 225 pounds, so that the hydraulic machinery provided is almost unnecessary. Work upon the mounting, which is still in the hands of Messrs. Warner and Swasey, is progressing favorably.

The new observatory of Bucknell University, Lewisburg, Pa., was finished early in 1887. It is provided with a 10-inch Clark equatorial, and a 8-inch transit instrument. Creighton College, at Omaha, also has a new observatory, with a 5-inch equatorial and a 3-inch transit. An exchange of longitude-signals was made with the Naval Observatory, Washington, in August, 1887.

The Solar Parallax.—The report of the committee appointed to superintend the arrangements for the British expeditions to observe the transit of Venus in 1882, together with the report of Mr. Stone, who had charge of the reductions, has recently been published as a Treasury document. Expeditions were sent from England to Jamaica, Barbadoes, Bermuda, Cape of Good Hope, Madagascar, New Zealand, and Brisbane, Australia; and the observers were successful at all these stations except Brisbane, where the sky was cloudy. The British committee were not satisfied with their photographic work in 1874, and for various reasons they decided to rely entirely upon contact observations in 1882. From the observations of external contact at ingress, Mr. Stone has obtained a parallax of 8·760″ ± 0·122″; from those of internal contact at ingress, 8·823″ ± 0·028″; from those of internal contact at egress, 8·855″ ± 0·086″; and from those of external contact at egress, 8·953″ ± 0·048″. The most probable combined result he considers to be 8·832″ ± 0·024″, which corresponds to a mean distance of 92,560,000 ± 250,000 miles between the earth and the sun.

The commissions of the United States and France trusted principally to photography in their schemes for observing the transit of 1882. Of the negatives obtained under the auspices of the United States Commission, after the rejection of all imperfect ones, there remained 1,571 which have been measured, and Prof. Harkness believes that the value of the solar parallax deducible from them will be obtained early in 1888. The French Commission have

measured 1,019 of their negatives, and in February, 1887, M. Bouquet de la Grye announced to the Academy of Sciences that the computations necessary for their reduction were half finished, and would probably be completed about the end of 1887.

The German Commission trusted principally to heliometers in the observations made under their direction, and Dr. Auwers has recently published a large volume containing investigations of the constants of the instruments employed; but it is not known when the resulting parallax will be obtained.

The Sun.—During 1886 sun-spots were confined almost entirely to the southern hemisphere of the sun, and there was a decided decrease in their size and number, relieved only by outbursts in March and May. Faculæ and eruptions seemed to follow the spots. The prominences diminished in height and mean extent, but they were nearly equally divided between the two solar hemispheres, and the decrease was not so rapid as in the case of the spots. The Greenwich photographs, supplemented by those from Dehra Dún in India, show that for the thirty-eight days beginning Oct. 31 and ending Dec. 7, 1886, there were only seven days on which even a single spot was shown. For a rotation and a half the sun was practically free from spots. Riccò, on searching the Palermo records, finds a similar case in 1875, five years after the maximum of 1870, and nearly eight years after the minimum of 1867. He predicts that the true minimum of the eleven-year period will fall in 1890. Wolf's observations at Zürich show that the variations in the spots and in magnetic phenomena kept together in 1886 as in previous years.

An exhaustive discussion of the sun's horizontal and vertical diameters, with special reference to the alleged variations in its mean annual diameter following the period of the sun-spot cycle, has been made by Dr. Auwers from the Greenwich, Washington, Oxford, and Neufchâtel meridian observations. He concludes that there is no valid reason for supposing the sun's diameter to vary, and that the apparent changes arise from insufficiently determined personal equations. He also points out that meridian observations are quite unsuited for determination of any possible ellipticity in the sun's disk, and that there is no reason to conclude from these results that such ellipticity exists. The several mean values of the sun's (assumed circular) diameter are: Greenwich, 32′ 02·37″; Washington, 32′ 02·51″; Oxford, 32′ 02·19″; Neufchâtel, 32′ 03·27″, the discordances of which are to be ascribed to instrumental or uneliminated personal peculiarities. In a second paper, Dr. Auwers discusses the apparent changes of both the horizontal and vertical diameter during the course of a year deduced from meridian observations, and he concludes that the periodic variations in the monthly value of the diameters result not from physical changes in the sun, but from the effect of temperature on the instruments, and from difference in the quality of the telescopic images at opposite seasons of the year. Another discussion of the horizontal diameter of the sun has been made by Prof. di Legge from meridian transits of the sun observed at Campidoglio from 1874 to 1883. The mean horizontal diameter at mean distance deduced from 5,796 transits by four observers on 2,218 days is 32' 02·38". From May, 1876, the sun's transit has been observed by projection, thus enabling two or more persons to observe simultaneously, and thereby affording exceptionally favorable opportunities for the determination of personal equation.

Prof. John Trowbridge and Mr. C. C. Hutchins have recently investigated the solar spectrum with very powerful apparatus, and they find that the alleged bright bands, upon which Dr. Henry Draper based his so-called discovery of oxygen in the sun, do not exist. They have also examined Prof. J. C. Draper's hypothesis of the coincidence of certain dark lines in the solar spectrum with the lines in the spectrum of oxygen, and find it equally destitute of any physical basis.

Total Solar Eclipse of August 19, 1887.—This eclipse excited the greatest interest throughout Europe, and will be memorable as the first during which attempts were made to observe and photograph the corona from balloons. At Berlin the totality began at 5·05 A. M., and as there were few favorable points for observation within the city, the people flocked by tens of thousands out into the open country, whither they were conveyed by special trains, steamboats, and vehicles innumerable. The principal streets of the city were more thronged from 2 to 4 A. M. than they usually are at midday, and the Tempelhof field never held a larger crowd during a grand review than at daybreak on the morning of the eclipse. Most of the people obtained only momentary glimpses of the partial phases; but those at Hoppegarten, ten miles east of Berlin, were more highly favored. There the totality was concealed only by a thin veil of clouds, through which both the chromosphere and the corona were visible; but unfortunately no skilled observers were present. While totality lasted, the darkness was so great that it was hardly possible to recognize faces at a yard's distance.

In Russia, quite unprecedented preparations were made for the occasion, and, had the weather been favorable, this eclipse would have been observed and investigated there in the most thorough manner. An intelligent taste for scientific work is very widely spread among educated Russians, and their enthusiasm on this occasion may be imagined from the sale in Moscow alone of 145,000 glasses and 400,000 descriptive pamphlets. Enlightened by this surprising quantity of popular literature, the Russians of all classes flocked in great numbers to many points of observation. For the first time in Russia, an excellent service of cheap excursion-trains was organized, with traveling comforts such as are only to be had on the great trunk-lines. Even the Grand Duke Constantine, who selected Tver as his point of view, did not disdain to travel by a special train of this class on the Nicholas Railway. During the night preceding the eclipse, about 300 persons went to Klin from St. Petersburg, and about 600 more from Moscow. The Physical Society of St. Petersburg distributed papers, with directions for amateur observations, to all passengers in the special train on the Moscow line, but the weather turned out so badly that probably not one of the blanks was filled out by the disappointed enthusiasts. Among the visitors to Russia were many distinguished foreign astronomers, all of whom were received with the utmost kindness, and assisted in every possible way.

The central line of the eclipse first struck the earth at a point 58 miles west-northwest of Leipsic, in latitude 51° 38' north, longitude 11° 16' east of Greenwich, where the sun was just rising. From there the line of totality, which was about 185 miles wide, sped across Germany, Russia, Siberia, China, and Japan, and finally left the earth at a point in the Pacific Ocean, in latitude 24° 27' north, longitude 178° 30' east., where the sun was just setting. The actual distance traveled by the shadow was about 7,960 miles, and the time occupied was $2^h 42^m 12^s$, whence the average rate of motion was 49 miles a minute, say fifty times that of an express train, or twice that of a shot from a modern, high-powered, rifled gun—but the speed was considerably less near the middle of the path, and greater toward its ends. The entire duration of the partial phase of the eclipse upon the earth's surface was $4^h 53^m 24^s$. In Germany the sun was too low during totality for advantageous photographic and spectroscopic work, and for such observations it was necessary to go farther east. The best localities were in Eastern Siberia, about latitude 50° 30' north, longitude 112° east, but, as it was practically impossible to transport heavy instruments beyond the Ural mountains, and in the immediate neighborhood of these mountains the meteorologists thought it likely to be cloudy, nearly all the best equipped parties were concentrated between Moscow and St. Petersburg. This proved most unfortunate, for speaking generally, during the eclipse, the sky westward of the Ural mountains was overcast, while eastward it was beautifully clear. The neighborhood of Moscow and Tver, of which the meteorologists spoke highly as regards the chances of fine weather, was shrouded in clouds and mist, while Yekaterinburg, which they had comparatively condemned, was rejoicing in a clear sky. And, whereas the early morning hours, in which the eclipse took place, are more generally fine than the corresponding evening hours, it so happened that in the evening of the 19th the eclipse could have been observed most successfully.

In Germany, the Berlin Observatory established six stations on the central line of the eclipse, together with some others near the northern and southern boundaries of the total zone, and many additional points were occupied by well-known astronomers; but fog, rain, and clouds prevailed to such an extent that only at Nordhausen and Eisleben were even partially successful observations obtained. In Russia, west of the Ural Mountains, at least thirty different points were occupied by about one hundred and fifty thoroughly-equipped astronomers and physicists, many of whom had traveled far to see the eclipse, but the weather was so unpropitious that the corona was visible at only five of their stations. In Siberia, where the sky was perfectly clear, only four parties are known to have been located, and their equipment was not of the first order. A party from the United States was stationed in Japan, but there again the weather was bad.

The Satellites of Saturn.—Prof. Hall has published, in Appendix I to the "Washington Observations for 1888," a discussion of the orbits of the six inner satellites of Saturn, his main object being to determine, if possible, the motions of the perisaturnia, and the mass of the ring. The observations of the satellites he has discussed were made by Prof. Newcomb and himself with the 26-inch Washington refractor, in 1874, and following years. Prof. Hall finds from these observations that Rhea, Dione, Tethys, Mimas, and Enceladus, move in orbits sensibly circular—a result which, of course, sets aside any consideration of the motion of their lines of apsides. From the elements of Titan Rhea, Dione, and Tethys, the mean result for the mass of Saturn is $\frac{1}{3473 \cdot 7 \pm 1 \cdot 10}$, the mass of the sun being taken as unity.

Asteroids.—Six of these little bodies were added to the list during 1887, making the total number now known 270. The following table gives their numbers and names, the names of the discoverers, the dates of discovery, and the principal elements of the orbits, together with the names of the computers:

No.	Name.	Discoverer.	Date of discovery—1887.	Longitude of node.	Inclination.	Eccentricity.	Mean distance.	Computer.
265	Anna	Palisa, at Vienna	February 25	385° 27′	25° 47′	0·261	2·49	Knopf.
266	Aline	Palisa, at Vienna	May 17	286 18	18 20	0·157	2·81	Lange.
267	Tirza	Charlois, at Nice	May 27	74 5	7 19	0·047	2·89	Charlois.
268		Borrelly, at Marseilles	June 9	121 58	2 25	0·129	3·06	Lange.
269		Palisa, at Vienna	September 21					
270		Peters, at Clinton	October 8					

An asteroid, detected by Dr. Luther on April 11, and independently by Coggia on April 16, proved to be Hesperia (69), which had been looked for in vain in 1882, 1885, and in March, 1887. The rapid motion in right ascension of (265) would seem to indicate that it approaches quite near the earth, and is, therefore, suitable for determining a new value of the solar parallax. Of the asteroids "unnamed" in last year's article (256) has been called Walpurga, (261) Prymno, (262) Valda, (263) Dresda, (264) Libussa: (269) was the sixtieth asteroid discovered by Palisa. Dr. de Ball has made a careful discussion of all the observations of Eucharis (181) obtained since its discovery in 1878. He has taken into account the perturbations due to Jupiter and Saturn; and those due to Jupiter seem likely to afford an accurate means of determining that planet's mass.

Comets of 1887.—Including the periodic comet of Olbers, six comets have thus far (October 1) been discovered during the year. As it is now possible to give to the new comets their permanent designations, we record them in the order of perihelion passage:

Comet 1886 VIII, the third comet discovered in 1887, was found by E. E. Barnard, of the Vanderbilt Observatory, Nashville, Tenn., on Jan. 23, or the morning of Jan. 24, civil reckoning, in the constellation Cygnus. A preliminary computation of the elements showed that the comet had passed perihelion in the preceding November, hence it is catalogued with the comets of 1886. Although a faint object when discovered, and growing fainter as it receded from both the sun and earth, observations were obtained as late as the end of April.

Comet 1887 I, known as the "Great Southern Comet," was detected by Dr. Thome, Director of the Cordoba Observatory in South America, on Jan. 18, 1887. On the same evening it was seen at a village near Cape Town, South Africa, and a day or two later at several places in Australia, but it does not seem to have become visible in the northern hemisphere. Dr. Thome describes the comet as a beautiful sight to the naked eye—a narrow, straight, sharply-defined, graceful tail, over 40° long, shining with a soft, starry light against the dark sky; beginning apparently without a head, and gradually widening and fading as it extended upward. Unfortunately, neither a well-defined nucleus nor even the slightest condensation upon which to point could be made out at any of the observatories where the comet was visible, and we are thus without means of determining the orbit with any degree of precision. In its physical appearance the new comet bore a considerable resemblance to the great comets of 1843, 1880, and 1882, and it certainly passed within a few thousand miles of the sun's surface.

Comet 1887 II was discovered by W. R. Brooks, of Phelps, N. Y., on the evening of Jan. 22, 1887, in the constellation Draco. It increased gradually in brightness till about the middle of February, when it was described as a bright telescopic object, about 3′ in diameter, with well-marked central condensation of the tenth magnitude. The last observation published was made at Geneva on April 30.

Comet 1887 III was discovered by Mr. Barnard on the night of February 16, a very faint nebulous object with a rapid motion toward the north and west. In physical appearance it presented no marked variation from the ordinary telescopic comet during the four or five weeks it was under observation.

Comet 1887 IV. A third comet was discovered by Mr. Barnard on the night of May 12, its position then being R. A. = 15ʰ 11ᵐ; decl. = —30° 36'. On May 18 it was described by Prof. Boss as having a starlike nucleus of the 11·5 magnitude; it increased somewhat in brightness till about the middle of June, without, however, changing its general appearance. Mr. Chandler has combined all the observations at present available into four normal places, and finds that they are rather more satisfactorily represented by an ellipse than by a parabola.

Comet 1887 V is Olbers's periodic comet, rediscovered by Mr. Brooks on Aug. 24, 1887. This comet was originally discovered by Olbers at Bremen, on March 6, 1815, and in 1816 Bessel predicted that it would return to perihelion about Feb. 9, 1887. In 1881 Dr. Ginzel, of Vienna, published an elaborate rediscussion of the orbit, using 346 observations from 14 observatories, and taking account of perturbations. He obtained a period of about 74 years, with an uncertainty of 1·5 years, and gave Dec. 16, 1886, as the most probable date of perihelion passage. An extensive sweeping ephemeris was prepared by him, and for months a search for the comet was kept up by several astronomers, resulting in its discovery by

Mr. Brooks, who was also the first to detect Pons's comet at its return in 1883-'84. Especial interest attaches to Olbers's comet as the third member of the group of comets having a period of about 75 years (Halley's, Pons's, and Olbers's) which has returned to perihelion in conformity with prediction. Early in September the comet showed some slight traces of a tail, in spite of its considerable distance from the earth. The nucleus was quite well defined, its brightness being from the eighth to the tenth magnitude.

Dr. Krueger's corrected orbit of the comet discovered by Mr. Finlay on Sept. 26, 1886 (1886 VII), shows that it can no longer be regarded as identical with De Vico's lost comet of 1844. However, Finlay's comet is moving in an ellipse whose period is about 6·7 years, and as it passed its perihelion on Nov. 29, 1886, another return will be due in the summer of 1893.

The approximate elements of the new comets' are as follows, the dates being in Greenwich mean time:

Designation.	Perihelion passage T.	Ω	ω	i	q	Discovery.	Synonym.	
1886, VIII..	1886, Nov., 28·33	259° 19'	81° 58'	85° 85'	1·480	1887, Jan. 28, by Barnard.	1887 c	
1887, I	1887, Jan., 11·41	339 52	64 40	138 2	0·005	1887, Jan. 18, by Thome ..	1887 a	
II	1887, Mar., 17·08	279 51	159 11	104 17	1·628	1887, Jan. 22, by Brooks..	1887 b	
III....	1887, Mar., 23·45	135 27	36 26	129 47	1·007	1887, Feb. 16, by Barnard.	1887 d	
IV	1887, June, 16·66	245 13	15 8	17 33	1·894	1887, May 12, by Barnard.	1887 e	Periodic.
V	1887, Oct., 8·50	34 31	65 17	44 34	1·200	1887, Aug. 24, by Brooks..	1887 f	Olbers.

Prof. Daniel Kirkwood has suggested the probability that certain comets of short period may have originated within the solar system. For example: before its last near approach to Jupiter, Wolf's comet, 1884 III, had an eccentricity of 0·28, which is exceeded by twelve known asteroids, and a period of revolution of 3,619 days, or five sixths that of Jupiter. It was then an asteroid too distant to be seen even at perihelion. Again: the orbit of Tempel's comet, 1867 II, lies between Mars and Jupiter, and its elements do not differ greatly from those of an eccentric asteroid.

Dr. Bredichin has made a study of Fabry's comet, and of Barnard's two comets of 1886, with respect to their bearing upon his new theory of comets' tails. The tail of Fabry's comet belongs undoubtedly to type II, and the principal tail of Barnard's first comet (1886 II) to the same type. The secondary tail of this comet, noticed by Backhouse, seems to have been merely an elongation of the head, a phenomenon observed in other comets. Barnard's second comet (1886 IX) had two tails distinctly visible for a month, which belonged respectively to types I and III, and after passing perihelion it furnished further confirmation of Bredichin's theory by throwing out a third tail belonging to type II.

Stellar Photometry.—From a comparison of the star-magnitudes of the Oxford Uranometry with those of Wolff's second catalogue, and with those of the Harvard Photometry, Prof. Pickering has found that the Oxford magnitudes are, on the average, less than the Harvard magnitudes for stars down to the third magnitude, but greater for the fourth and fifth, and less again for stars below the sixth. The Harvard catalogue differs less from those of Wolff and Pritchard than the two latter do from each

other. The "wedge photometer," constructed under the direction of Prof. Pritchard for Prof. Pickering, has been submitted to a careful examination by Profs. Langley, Young, and Pickering, and it appears from Prof. Langley's observations of the wedge by means of his bolometer, that there is a selective absorption of light throughout the wedge; feeble in the more luminous portion of the spectrum, but of such a character that, broadly speaking, the transmissibility always increases from the violet toward the red, increasing very greatly in the infra-red. These results have been confirmed by Prof. Pickering's experiments, and they emphasize the danger, already recognized by Prof. Pritchard, of employing an instrument of this kind in the observation of deeply-colored stars.

The magnitudes of the standard stars of the British, French, German, Spanish, and American nautical almanacs, have been rediscussed by Prof. Pickering, and his results will probably be adopted in future issues of the French, Spanish, and American works. The plan proposed was, that the magnitude adopted for each star should be the mean of those derived from the Harvard photometry, the photometric observations of Wolff, the Uranometria Oxoniensis, and the Uranometria Argentina. The list published by Prof. Pickering embraces 800 stars, and of these the magnitudes of all but 64 depend upon at least two and generally upon three authorities; 182 stars being common to all four of the adopted standard catalogues of brightness.

Variable Stars.—Several new variable stars have been detected by Chandler, Sawyer, Espin, and others, and among them are two of more than ordinary interest, as they apparently belong to the well-known "Algol" type.

The first was discovered by Mr. Chandler in the constellation Cygnus, R. A. = 20ʰ 47·5ᵐ, decl. = + 34° 14′ (DM. + 34°, 4181). Its light varies from 7·1 magnitude to about 7·9 magnitude, and the period is some aliquot part of 5·997 days, which can not be exactly determined until further observations are obtained. The second star referred to was discovered by Mr. E. F. Sawyer, in March, 1887, in the constellation Canis Major, and as it is the first undoubted variable found in that constellation, it will probably be known as R Canis Majoris. Its position for 1887 is R. A. = 7ʰ 14·4ᵐ; decl. = —16° 11′. The minimum observed by Mr. Sawyer was 6·8 magnitude, and the period is probably about twenty-seven hours.

The new variable discovered by Mr. Gore on Dec. 18, 1885, has continued to receive careful attention at the hands of several observers. From a series of observations with the Zöllner photometer of the Potsdam Observatory, Dr. Müller found that the star attained its maximum (6·20 magnitude) on Dec. 12, 1886, which would give it a period of 864 days. In substantial agreement with this result is Mr. Sawyer's maximum of the 6 6 magnitude, observed on Dec. 13, 1886.

For the past four years the observatory of Harvard College has published an annual statement of the number of observations made during the previous year upon each variable star. In the fifth of these publications, to appear during 1888, Prof. Pickering proposes to give a statement of the number of dates of observation of each variable star during each year since its discovery, and he requests all who are interested in this department of astronomy to cooperate by contributing any information that will assist him in making this index as complete as possible.

Double and Binary Stars.—The following table contains the results of computations of the orbits of binary stars. The star δ Equulei is of especial interest, as the period of eleven years and a half assigned to it is the shortest known. Wrublewsky's orbit gives for 1887·24, position angle = 204·9°; distance = 0·48″. Further observations are very desirable:

STAR.	δ Equulei.	Σ 1757.	Σ 948.	¹⁴ (¹) Orionis.
Time of periastron T	1892 08	1791 98	1716·0	1959·05
Position of node Ω .	24·05°	87° 86′	166° 80′	99° 85′
Position of periastron λ............	26·61	185 28	98 86	802 42
Inclination i........	81·75	40 56	46 8	44 57
Eccentricity e......	0·2011	0·4498	0·229	0·2465
Semi-axis major α..	0·406″	2·05″	1·64″	1·22″
Mean motion μ	....	+1·80°	-0·741°	-1·89°
Period in years P...	11·473	276·92	485·8	190·48
Computer	Wrublewsky	Gore.	Gore.	Gore.

Prof. G. W. Hough, of the Dearborn Observatory, Chicago, has published a valuable catalogue of 209 new double stars discovered and measured by himself, with the 18½-inch Clark refractor of that institution.

A short list of thirteen new double stars, discovered by Messrs. Leavenworth and Muller

with the 26-inch McCormick refractor, is published in No. 156 of the "Astronomical Journal."

Pleiades.—The details of Dr. Elkin's determination of the relative positions of the principal stars in the Pleiades have been published as Part I of the first volume of "Transactions" of the Astronomical Observatory of Yale University. This is, we believe, the first heliometer-work done in this country. Dr. Elkin has included all the stars in the "Durchmusterung" down to the 9·2 magnitude, which may reasonably be said to fall within the group. One of the stars used by Bessel in his celebrated work with the Königsberg heliometer was omitted on account of its faintness, but Dr. Elkin has added seventeen stars to Bessel's list of fifty-three, so that he has taken sixty-nine stars in all.

With the filar micrometer of the Washington 26-inch telescope, Prof. Hall has measured the positions of sixty-three small stars in the Pleiades relatively to the brighter stars determined by Bessel and Elkin; thus furnishing data for testing in the future whether or not there is any proper motion of the brighter stars relatively to the fainter ones.

Star - Catalogues. — Argelander's " Durchmusterung," or survey of the northern heavens, has been extended from 2° south declination to 23° south declination, by Dr. Schönfeld, who has recently published his results as volume viii of the Bonn Observatory "Beobachtungen." This catalogue contains the places of 133,659 stars within the limits mentioned, together with an additional 1,173 stars falling beyond these limits, all referred to the epoch of Argelander's work, namely, 1855·0. In the atlas accompanying the volume each chart embraces one hour of right ascension, with an overlap of four minutes on either side, and 22° of declination, reaching from —1° to —23°. Dr. Thome, of Cordoba, is extending Schönfeld's work to the south pole, and has already gone over 10° of declination.

Among recent star-catalogues are Romberg's and Kam's compilations of the star-places scattered through the volumes of the "Astronomische Nachrichten," and Respighi's mean declinations of 1,004 naked-eye stars observed with the meridian circle of the Campidoglio Observatory during 1879, 1880, and 1881. An important list of 480 stars, to be used as fundamental points for zone observations between 20° and 80° south declination, is published by Dr. Auwers, in the June (1887) number of the "Monthly Notices of the Royal Astronomical Society."

Dr. C. H. F. Peters, Director of the Litchfield Observatory, Clinton, N. Y., has contributed two valuable papers to the third volume of the "Memoirs of the United States National Academy of Sciences." The first paper is a critical examination of all data bearing on Flamsteed's twenty-two "missing" stars, and in every case Dr. Peters has formulated a plausible explanation of the supposed disappearance of the star from the heavens. The second paper is a list of corrigenda to various star-catalogues.

Dr. Swift has published in the "Astronomische Nachrichten" his sixth catalogue of nebulæ, discovered at the Warner Observatory, Rochester, N. Y.

Astronomical Prizes.—The Lalande prize of the Paris Academy has been awarded to Dr. Backlund for his investigations on the motion of Encke's comet; the Valz prize to M. Bigourdan, chiefly for his inquiries into the effect of personality in the observation of double stars; and the Damoiseau prize to M. Souillart, for his revision of the theory of Jupiter's satellites. An *encouragement* of 1,000 francs from the Damoiseau fund has also been decreed to M. Obrecht. The gold medal of the Royal Astronomical Society has been awarded to Mr. G. W. Hill for his researches on the lunar theory. The Watson gold medal of the United States National Academy of Sciences and an *honorarium* of $100 were conferred on Dr. Gould at the spring meeting of the Academy in 1887, and the gold and silver medals of the American Academy, of Boston, were presented to Prof. Langley on May 11, 1887. The Warner prizes of $100 for each new comet discovered have been awarded to Messrs. Barnard and Brooks, the former having detected three and the latter two comets, including that of Olbers. On account of the importance of early observations of the latter comet, and the uncertainty existing in the computed period, a special prize had been offered for its detection.

Bibliography.—Among the recent books worthy of mention are: Houzeau and Lancaster's "Bibliographie générale de l'Astronomie," vol. i, Part I; Oppolzer's "Canon der Finsternisse"; and Schram's "Tafeln zur Berechnung der näheren Umstände der Sonnenfinsternisse"; Airy's "Numerical Lunar Theory"; Lockyer's "Chemistry of the Sun"; Braun's "Cosmogonie"; and also the second editions of Miss Clerke's "History of Astronomy during the Nineteenth Century"; and of Lancaster's "Liste générale des Observatoires et des Astronomes." We are glad to notice the reappearance of the "Astronomical Journal," which was started by Dr. Gould at Cambridge in 1849. The sixth volume was completed in 1861, and, after an intermission of twenty-five years, the first number of the seventh volume is dated Nov. 2, 1886.

AUSTRALASIA, a division of the globe, of which the chief inhabited portions are the British colonies of the Australian continent and the islands of New Zealand and Tasmania. The colonies of New South Wales, Victoria, Queensland, South Australia, Tasmania, and New Zealand possess responsible government. Western Australia has a representative system that is more under the control of the crown; and the Fiji and Rotumah islands, the Kermadec islands, and the Auckland islands, with the Carolines and many small islands, constitute crown colonies. The total

area of British Australasia is 3,268,366 square miles, with a population of 3,625,809 souls.

Naval Defense.—Most of the colonies have acquiesced, fully or in part, in the recommendations of the British Admiralty for co-operation in the naval defenses that were submitted to the Colonial Conference held in London early in 1887. The Admiralty adopted Admiral Tryon's suggestion of fast cruisers, but instead of favoring the "Scout" class, recommended the "Archer" class. These have a displacement of 1,630 tons, will steam 17 knots an hour, and carry six 6-inch breech-loading rifled guns, besides a torpedo armament. It is proposed to secure five of these and two fast torpedo-boats having a displacement of 430 tons, steaming 19 knots, and armed with three tubes for Whitehead torpedoes, one 8-inch breech-loading gun, four quick-firing 3-pounders, and two machine-guns. This fleet will be auxiliary to the vessels possessed by the separate colonies, and to the Australian squadron of the British navy.

New South Wales.—The Legislature consists of two branches, the Legislative Council and the Assembly, the former of which is composed of not less than 22 members, nominated by the Crown, and the latter of 122 members, elected by manhood suffrage and secret ballot. The Governor, who is appointed by the Crown, is Lord Carrington, who assumed office on Dec. 12, 1885. The Ministry, appointed on Jan 19, 1887, consists of the following members: Premier and Colonial Secretary, Sir Henry Parkes; Colonial Treasurer, John Fitzgerald Burns; Minister for Lands, Thomas Garrett; Minister for Public Works, John Sutherland; Attorney-General, W. J. Foster; Minister for Public Instruction, James Inglis; Minister for Justice, William Clarke; Postmaster-General, C. J. Roberts; Minister of Mines, Francis Abigail; The area of the colony is 310,700 square miles. The estimated population in 1885 was 957,985. The average net immigration during the five years 1880–'85, was 80,000 per annum. In 1885 the number of immigrants was 78,188, and of emigrants 30,455. The births in 1885 numbered 35,043, the deaths 15,382, and the marriages 7,618. The population comprised 662,635 Protestants, of whom 425,883 belonged to the Church of England, 92,542 to the Presbyterian, and 82,195 to the Methodist Church; 264,692 Roman Catholics; 4,215 Jews; 11,882 Pagans; and 18,776 of various beliefs. The state schools in 1885 had 181,573 scholars and 3,552 teachers. Sydney, the capital, contained at the end of 1886 about 280,000 inhabitants.

The value of imports in 1885, including specie and bullion, was £23,295,232; the value of exports, £16,541,745. The export of wool was valued at £7,678,247. The quantity of wool sent to Great Britain was 110,106,216 pounds, of the value of £4,958,759. The number of sheep in the colony in March, 1886, was 34,-551,662. The area leased for pastoral purposes in 1885 was 217,407 square miles. The area under cultivation was only 868,093 acres, producing besides other crops 2,768,330 bushels of wheat, 4,285,163 bushels of Indian corn, 41,359,360 pounds of sugar, and 555,470 gallons of wine. The next most important exports after wool were coal of the value of £966,663, and tin of the value of £728,969. The gold product in 1885 was £366,388.

The length of the state railroads in 1885 was 1,732 miles. Their capital cost was £24,962,-972, the earnings for the year £2,174,868, and the expenses £1,458,153. There were 19,864 miles of telegraph-wires. The number of paid messages was 2,625,992. The post-office transmitted 39,351,200 letters.

The public revenue in 1885 was £7,588,656; the expenditure, £7,544,594; the debt on Dec. 31, 1886, £41,064,259.

In the beginning of 1887 a difference on financial questions arose in the Cabinet, and the Premier, Sir Patrick Jennings, taking exceptions to certain statements of the colonial secretary, G. R. Dibbs, in connection with the deficit of 1880, requested the latter to resign. On his refusing, the entire ministry tendered their resignations on January 10. After several conferences with the Governor, a new ministry was formed under Sir Henry Parkes, who, in explaining his policy to the Legislative Assembly, announced that the Government would revert to the principle of pure free trade, and undertake a thorough reformation of the disorganized finances of the colony, stating that they would endeavor to obtain a larger revenue from lands, better management of the railroads, retrenchment in the civil service, and, if necessary, would resort to an equitable property tax. With this programme they appealed to the electorate, and obtained a working majority in a new parliament. In the financial statement the colonial treasurer proposed the repeal of the customs act of the last session, and announced a new tariff limited to twenty-four articles selected for revenue purposes only, including higher rates on spirits and an excise duty on domestic ales. With no other new taxes, the ministry expected an increased revenue, which, with the aid of savings, would enable them to extinguish the accumulated deficits, amounting to £2,600,000, within eight years. The estimates showed a reduction of £450,000 on the appropriations of 1886, and the ministry expected a surplus of £800,000 at the end of the year. There were some stormy sittings during the debates, and on May 21 a continuous session of forty-eight hours was ended by the application of the *clôture*. A bill was passed for protecting the colony from the influx of foreign criminals whose sentences have expired, containing, among other stringent provisions, one making persons who harbor such criminals liable to a year's imprisonment, and empowering the Governor to proclaim foreign penal settlements. Vessels bringing time-expired convicts are liable to forfeiture, and their captains to a sentence of five years in the penitentiary.

Victoria.—The legislative power is vested in the Legislative Council, composed of eighty-six members, elected under property and educational limitations, and the Legislative Assembly, elected by universal suffrage. The Governor is Sir Henry Brougham Loch, who assumed the government on July 15, 1884. The Cabinet is made up as follows: Premier, Minister of Mines and of Railways, Sir Duncan Gillies; Chief Secretary and Commissioner of Water-Supply, Alfred Deakin; Attorney-General, H. J. Wrixon; Commissioner of Public Works, J. Nimmo; Minister of Justice, Henry Cuthbert; Commissioner of Trade and Customs, W. F. Walker; Commissioner of Lands and Survey, J. L. Dow; Minister of Public Instruction, Charles H. Pearson; Minister of Defense, James Lorimer; Postmaster-General, F. T. Derham; Ministers without office, M. H. Davies and James Bell.

The area of Victoria is 87,884 square miles. The population was estimated on June 30, 1886, at 1,009,753, comprising 541,015 males and 468,738 females. The number of births in 1885 was 29,975; of deaths, 14,860; of marriages, 7,395. The capital city, Melbourne, had in 1886 about 365,000 inhabitants. The population was divided in respect to religion in 1885 into 352,087 Episcopalians, 149,849 Presbyterians, 122,504 Methodists, 74,669 other Protestants, 229,917 Roman Catholics, 4,894 Jews, 11,000 Pagans, and 30,100 others. There were in 1885 1,826 state schools, with 224,685 enrolled pupils, and 3,650 teachers. The immigration by sea in 1885 was 76,976, and the emigration 61,994.

The total value of the imports in 1885 was £18,044,604, and of the exports, £15,551,758. The export of wool was valued at £5,028,011; of gold and specie, £4,309,535; of live-stock, £900,801; of breadstuffs, £772,432. Of the wool export, amounting to 106,078,932 lbs., only about one half was the produce of the colony. The quantity of gold produced in 1885 was 735,218 ounces, valued at £2,940,872. There were 2,405,157 acres in cultivation in March, 1886, of which 215,994 were under wheat. The wheat-product was 9,170,538 bushels, or 9 bushels to the acre. The number of sheep in the colony was 10,681,837 in 1886; of cattle, 1,290,790 head.

The government railroad system had in June, 1886, a total length of 1,743 miles, besides 267 miles in process of construction. There were 3,949 miles of telegraph lines and 9,617 miles of wire at the close of 1885. The gross railway receipts in 1885-'86 were £2,329,126, and the net receipts £1,018,589, being a profit of 4·36 per cent. on the capital investment of £23,380,000, all but £2,400,000 of which was raised by loans. The number of letters forwarded in 1885 was 36,061,880; of telegraph dispatches in 1884, 1,594,296. The revenue from telegraphs in 1885 was £387,802. A parcel post was introduced in 1887.

The receipts of the treasury in the year ended June 30, 1886, were £6,416,405; the expenditures, £6,605,901. Of the revenue £2,633,510 came from taxes, and the rest from the railroads, telegraphs, crown lands, and similar sources. The expenses of the public debt amounted to £1,285,904, and £1,413,690 were expended on railways, £968,284 on other public works, and £549,671 on posts and telegraphs. The expenditure for public education amounted to £642,070. The public debt at the end of 1885–'86 amounted to £30,127,382. The average rate of interest paid is 4½ per cent. The revenue for 1886–'87 amounted to £6,783,000; that for 1887–'88 is estimated at £6,906,000, and the expenditure at £7,444,000. The receipts are to be increased by a duty of 3s. 6d. per cwt. on cane-sugar, and 6s. on beet-sugar, and by increased timber duties.

A centennial exhibition is arranged to be held in Melbourne, to begin on August 1, 1888, and remain open six months.

South Australia.—The Legislative Council, elected by limited suffrage, can not be dissolved by the executive. Each of the fifty-two members is elected by the entire colony, but the seats are apportioned among four districts.

The House of Assembly consists of fifty-two members, elected by universal manhood suffrage. The Governor, who received his appointment in November, 1882, is Sir William C. F. Robinson. The House of Assembly passed a vote of want of confidence in the government on June 8, 1887, and a new Cabinet was formed, composed as follows: T. Playford, Premier and Treasurer; James Gordon Ramsay, Chief Secretary; A. Cott, Commissioner of Public Works; C. C. Kingston, Attorney-General; and Mr. Johnson, Commissioner of Education.

The area of the colony is 903,425 square miles. The estimated population on Dec. 31, 1885, was 313,428 persons, of whom 163,641 were males and 149,782 females.

The value of imports in 1885 was £5,548,403; of exports, £5,636,255. The leading articles of export are wool, of the value of £1,417,245 in 1885; and wheat and flour, of the value of £2,162,513. The area of cultivated land is 2,785,490 acres, of which 1,942,453 are devoted to wheat, producing 14,621,755 bushels in 1884–'85. There are 226,180 square miles held under pastoral leases. The number of sheep in the colony in 1885 was 6,484,406.

The railroad mileage in 1885 was 1,063 miles of completed lines and 718 under construction. There were 1,063 miles of telegraph lines and 9,378 miles of wire.

The revenue for the year ended June 30, 1886, was £2,279,038; the expenditure, £2,383,289. The revenue for 1886–'87 was estimated at £2,318,124, and the expenditure at £2,214,563. The actual receipts, however, only amounted to £1,868,000, leaving an accumulated deficiency of £1,080,000. The public debt amounted to £17,020,900 on Dec. 31, 1885. The entire amount was raised for productive public works.

Queensland.—The members of the Legislative Council are nominated by the Crown for life, and those of the Legislative Assembly elected by the people without restriction of suffrage, holders of real estate having votes in the districts where their property is situated as well as in their places of residence. The Governor is Sir Anthony Musgrave, who was appointed in April, 1883. The ministry consists of the following members: Sir Samuel Walker Griffith, Premier, Chief Secretary, and Vice-President of the Executive Council; James Robert Dickson, Colonial Treasurer; Thomas MacDonald-Patterson, Postmaster-General; Arthur Rutledge, Attorney-General; William Miles, Secretary for Public Works; Berkeley Basil Moreton, Colonial Secretary and Secretary for Public Instruction; Charles Boydell Dutton, Secretary for Public Lands.

The colony has an area of 668,497 square miles and an estimated population on June 30, 1886, of 330,090 souls. The number of immigrants in 1885 was 34,834, including 679 Chinese and 1,929 Polynesians. The emigration was 22,768, including 1,238 Chinese and 1,903 Polynesians. The Chinese immigration in 1888 was 2,951, and the decline is caused by restrictive legislation. The number of births in 1885 was 11,672; of deaths, 6,235; of marriages, 2,842.

Of the total area of the colony, 7,728,568 acres, or less than 2 per cent., had been alienated by the Government up to the end of 1885. There were 307,290,880 acres leased for pastoral purposes in 1885, the number of runs being 9,292. The number of sheep in the colony was 8,994,322. Under the new land act of 1884 agricultural leases for not more than 1,280 acres will be granted for fifty years, and pastoral leases for a maximum of 20,000 acres to run thirty years.

The total value of imports in 1885 was £6,422,490; the value of exports, £5,243,404. The export of wool was valued at £1,779,682; of sugar, £720,921. The area devoted to the cultivation of sugar-cane in 1885 was 59,186 acres. The produce of 38,557 acres was valued at £1,075,235. The quantity of gold produced in 1885 was 310,941 ounces.

At the end of 1885 there were 1,434 miles of railroad, in which the Government had invested £9,484,654. There were 558 miles more in course of construction. The railroad receipts during 1885 amounted to £691,541, and the working expenses to £444,140. The number of letters sent through the post-office in 1895 was 9,776,407. The mileage of telegraph lines was 7,533 at the end of 1885; of wires, 12,290. The number of messages during the year was 1,082,183.

The revenue of the Government during 1885–'86 was £2,868,295; the expenditure, £3,090,160. The revenue for 1886–'87 was £2,870,000; the expenditure, £3,263,000. The public debt on Dec. 31, 1885, amounted to £19,320,850.

Western Australia.—The Governor is assisted by a Legislative Council, composed of eight nominated and sixteen elected members. The present Governor is Sir Frederick Napier Broome, appointed in December, 1882.

The area of the colony is estimated at 975,920 square miles. The population at the end of 1885 was estimated at 35,186. The net immigration during the year was 2,228; the number of births, 1,200; the number of deaths, 600. The value of imports in 1885 was £650,391; of exports, £446,692. There were 2,288 miles of telegraph and 76 of completed railroad, while 48 miles of railroad were building.

Tasmania.—The Legislative Council has 18 members, and the House of Assembly 36, all elected under property qualifications of different degrees for each house.

The Governor is Sir Robert G. C. Hamilton, appointed in January, 1887. The Cabinet resigned in March, 1887, and a new one was formed, composed of the following ministers: Premier and Chief Secretary, P. O. Fysh, who succeeded James W. Agnew; Treasurer, Mr. Bird, who succeeded William H. Burgess; Attorney-General, Mr. Clarke, successor to John S. Dodds; Minister of Lands, Mines, and Works, Mr. Braddon, successor to Nicholas J. Brown.

The area of the colony is estimated at 26,215 square miles. The population on Dec. 31, 1885, was estimated at 133,791 souls. The net immigration for the year was 649.

The imports in 1885 amounted to £1,757,486; the exports to £1,813,693. The chief articles of export are wool, gold, tin, timber, and preserved fruits. The revenue of the Government in 1885 amounted to £600,550, and the expenditure to £603,657.

New Zealand.—The Legislative Council is composed of 54 members, nominated for life by the Crown; the House of Representatives, of 95 members, elected by restricted suffrage for three years.

The Governor is Lieut.-Gen. Sir William Francis Jervois, appointed in November, 1882, in March, 1887.

The ministry is composed of the following members: Sir Julius Vogel, Colonial Treasurer, Postmaster-General, Commissioner of Telegraphs, and Commissioner of Stamp Duties and Customs; Sir Robert Stout, Premier, Attorney-General, and Minister of Education; Edward Richardson, Minister of Public Works; John Ballance, Native Minister, Minister of Defense, and Minister of Lands and Immigration; Joseph Augustus Tole, Minister of Justice; Patrick Alphonsus Buckley, Colonial Secretary; William J. M. Larnach, Minister of Mines and Minister of Marine; W. H. Reynolds, without office.

The area of New Zealand is estimated at 104,027 square miles. The North Island contains 44,736, the Middle Island 55,224, and Stewart's Island 1,800 square miles. The population in 1886, according to a census taken on March 28 was, exclusive of aborigines, 578,482, of which number 312,221 were males, and 266,261 females. The number of births was 19,693 in 1885; of deaths, 6,081; of marriages, 3,813. The number of immigrants was 16,199; of emigrants, 11,695. The Maori population in March, 1886, was 41,432, of which number 22,765 were males and 18,667 females. The number of Maoris in 1881 was 44,097.

The chief industries of the colony are agriculture, stock-raising, and gold-mining. Two thirds of the surface of the islands is fitted for agriculture or grazing. The total area of the colony is 66,710,320 acres, of which 18,305,594 had passed into the hands of private owners up to the close of 1885. The cultivated acreage in 1886 was 6,668,920, but of this 5,465,157 acres were under grass-crops. The production of wheat in 1886 was 4,242,285 bushels. The average yield of wheat per acre is 24·40 bushels; of oats, 26·11; of barley, 25·92. The number of sheep in the colony in March, 1886, was 16,580,388. The product of the gold-mines in 1885 was 222,732 ounces, valued at £890,056.

The total value of the imports in 1885 was £7,479,921; of the exports, £6,819,939. The export of wool was 86,507,431 pounds, valued at £3,205,275. Grain and flour were exported to the value of £627,865, and frozen meat of the value of £373,857. The value of the gold exported was £890,056.

On March 31, 1885, there were 1,654 miles of railroads in the colony. The capital investment up to March 31, 1886, amounted to £18,726,166. The net receipts for the year were £357,078, representing a profit of not quite 2½ per cent. The post-office in 1885 forwarded 37,149,788 letters and 14,283,878 newspapers. There were, on Jan. 1, 1886, 4,463 miles of telegraph lines and 10,981 miles of wire.

The revenue for the year ended March 31, 1886, was £3,746,945, of which £181,883 were derived from land sales, leases, and mining licenses. The public debt in March, 1886, amounted to £34,965,222, in part offset by a sinking fund amounting to £3,276,873. The revenue for 1886–'87 was £3,882,428, and the expenditure £4,012,598. To secure an equilibrium the Government proposed to increase the property tax to 1d. in the pound for all properties exceeding £2,500 in value. The ministry was defeated on a resolution declaring the budget unsatisfactory, and Parliament was dissolved in June, 1887, and new elections were appointed for August. Before the prorogation a bill was passed providing for the self-adjustment of parliamentary representation on the basis of population.

British New Guinea.—Great excitement was caused in Queensland by the massacre of Capt. Craig and the "Emily," while pearl-fishing off Jennet Island, New Guinea, in October, 1886. In the winter the British naval vessel "Diamond" was sent to punish the natives. They fied at the approach of the ship, but several of their villages were burned.

AUSTRIA - HUNGARY, an empire in Central Europe. The two states of which it is composed are united in the person of their sovereign, and have a common army, navy, and diplomacy. They are also joined in a customs-union, which with the fiscal arrangements for the defrayal of common expenses, is renewable every ten years. Appropriations for common purposes are obtained from the Delegations, a body of 120 members chosen one half from the Austrian and one half from the Hungarian Parliament, each upper house sending 20 and each lower house 40. The sovereignty in the Austrian or Cisleithan Empire, and in the Hungarian or Transleithan Kingdom is hereditary in the House of Hapsburg. The Emperor is Franz Josef I, born Aug. 18, 1830, who ascended the throne in 1848. The heir-apparent is the Archduke Rudolf, born Aug. 21, 1858. The Ministry for Common Affairs is composed as follows: Minister for Foreign Affairs and of the Imperial Household, Count G. Kálnoky de Köröspatak; Minister of War, Lieut. Field-Marshal Count Bylandt-Rheydt; Minister of Finance, Benjamin de Kállay.

Area and Population.—The area of the principal political divisions of the Austrian and Hungarian monarchies, and their estimated population at the end of 1885, are given in the following table:

PROVINCES.	Square miles.	Population.
EMPIRE OF AUSTRIA:		
Lower Austria	7,654	2,468,898
Upper Austria	4,631	767,779
Salzburg	2,767	166,925
Styria	8,670	1,241,651
Carinthia	4,005	358,485
Carniola	3,856	491,562
Coast Provinces...............	3,084	666,534
Tyrol and Vorarlberg..........	11,324	910,966
Bohemia.......................	20,060	5,697,888
Moravia	8,568	2,187,475
Silesia	1,987	561,977
Galicia	30,307	6,219,660
Bukowina......................	4,035	610,325
Dalmatia......................	4,940	508,695
Total Austria	115,908	22,868,995
KINGDOM OF HUNGARY:		
Hungary and Transylvania.....	106,258	14,841,276
Croatia and Slavonia.........	16,773	1,992,674
Town of Fiume.............. ...	8	21,736
Total Hungary	125,039	16,855,686
Total Austro-Hungarian Empire.................	240,942	39,724,511

The number of births in Austria in 1885 was returned as 885,201; deaths, 714,031; marriages, 175,233; excess of births over deaths, 171,170. The number of births in Hungary in 1884 was 758,652; deaths, 515,254; marriages, 167,404; natural increment of population, 238,398. The number of emigrants through the German free ports in 1885, was: Austrians, 20,558; Hungarians, 13,195. The population of Vienna, the Austrian capital, in 1880, was

1,103,857; that of Buda-Pesth, the capital of Hungary, in 1886, 422,557.

The Roman Catholics form 79·9 per cent. of the population of Austria proper; the Greek and Armenian Catholics, 11·5 per cent.; Protestants and other Christians, 1·8 per cent.; Byzantine Greeks, 2·3 per cent.; Jews, 4·5 per cent. In Hungary the proportions are 50 per cent. Roman Catholics, 9·7 per cent. Greek Catholics and Armenians, 20·6 per cent. Protestants, 15·6 per cent. Byzantine Greeks, and 4·1 per cent. Jews. In the whole empire 67·6 per cent. of the population are Roman Catholics, 10·6 per cent. Greek and Armenian Catholics, 9·6 per cent. Protestants, 7·9 per cent. of the Byzantine Greek Church, and 4·3 per cent. Jews. According to statistics 1880, the total illiterate class formed 32·59 per cent. of the male and 36·08 per cent. of the female population of Austria over six years of age. In the lands of the Hungarian Crown 31·6 per cent. of the population could neither read nor write. In 1883, 84·9 per cent. of the children of school-age were receiving instruction in Austria, while in Hungary 85·8 per cent. were attending school in 1885.

Finances.—The revenue in 1886 for common affairs amounted to 119,724,748 florins. The budget estimates for 1887 amounted to 123,855,414 florins, of which 102,055,440 florins were to be provided by the contributions from the two parts of the empire, 18,642,206 florins derived from customs, and the rest from the receipts of the ministries. The total expenditure for the diplomatic service was set down as 4,477,150 florins; the ordinary expenditure for the army as 99,950,528, and the extraordinary as 5,984,850 florins; the ordinary expenditure of the navy as 9,145,009, extraordinary as 2,171,080 and expenses of the Board of Control as 128,867 florins.

The Army.—The army law of 1886 created in addition to the Landwehr a Landsturm, or second line of reserves. The annual recruit of the regular army amounts to 94,000. The term of service in the active army is three years, in the regular army reserve four years, in the Landwehr five years, and in the Landsturm twelve years. Men who have served in the regular army are liable for service in the Landsturm as commissioned or non-commissioned officers up to the age of sixty. In time of war the Landsturm may be drawn on to complete the Landwehr regiments. The Landsturm is expected to add a million men to the war-effective, which will nearly double the numerical strength of the Austro-Hungarian army. Three army corps are to be provided with the new repeating-rifle by the beginning, and seven more before the end of 1888. The armament of the Landwehr is to be completed by 1891.

The common ministry, impelled by the precarious political situation in Europe, called an extraordinary session of the Delegations in the beginning of March, 1887, and obtained an extraordinary war credit of 52,500,000 florins,

Russia had concentrated a large force of cavalry on the frontier of Galicia, which caused a similar but less extensive movement of Austro-Hungarian troops, and hastened the carrying out of military measures already decided upon. Wooden barracks for cavalry were erected along the whole frontier of Galicia, and large numbers of workmen were employed in February and March in completing the fortress of Cracow, and on fortifications at Prezmysl.

The work on the strategic lines in Galicia was also pushed forward. The Austrian Reichsrath voted 12,011,655, and the Hungarian Diet 7,460,000 florins in February for the Landwehr and Landsturm, and arms were provided for the Austrian Landwehr and the Hungarian Honved, and uniforms purchased for the Landsturm of both countries. Following the example of France and Germany, the Austro-Hungarian Government prohibited the exportation of horses, making an exception in favor of Italy. The regulations for the organization of the Landsturm were not uniform in the two parts of the empire. In Austria every man below the age of forty-two, unless unfit even for ambulance service, and ex-officers up to the age of sixty are enrolled, while in Hungary those only are taken who have had military training, or are likely to make efficient soldiers. The Hungarian Government in order to satisfy the national craving for industrial independence of Austria granted valuable concessions to the firm of Nordenfeldt for the establishment of a factory for small-arms at Buda-Pesth, and contracted for a supply of 400,000 rifles within two years. Owing to the improved state of affairs in Bulgaria and Western Europe, the Imperial Government, after having spent 24,000,000 florins of the extraordinary appropriation, announced that they would require no more.

The Navy.—The Austro-Hungarian Government in 1886 possessed 10 armor-clad vessels of from 3,550 to 7,390 tons displacement, with armor ranging from 5 to 14 inches. Great attention has been paid to the torpedo-fleet. Three cruisers of 1,500 tons displacement, and capable of steaming 19 knots an hour, have recently been built. A new steel-plated turret-ship, the "Stéphanie," was launched at Trieste, April 14, 1887. The displacement is 5,100 tons, and the maximum thickness of the armor 9 inches.

Commerce.—The total value of the merchandise imports of the empire in 1885, including the annexed provinces but excluding Dalmatia, which lies outside of the imperial line of customs, was 557,948,324 florins, and the value of the exports 672,088,194 florins. The values of the leading articles of import were as follow: Vegetable fibers and manufactures, except cotton, 68,170,132 florins; silk and silk manufactures, 53,699,663 florins; clothing, etc., 27,452,800 florins; wool and woolen goods, 21,957,428 florins; cotton and manufactures thereof, 9,450,484 florins; vegetables and fruits, 48,465,-

518 florins: grain and pulse, 32,924,212 florins; sugar, coffee, etc., 27,586,642 florins; animals, 26,973,980 florins; fats and oils, 36,156,366 florins; furs, 16,551,260 florins; machinery and vehicles, 22,608,184 florins; wood and manufactures thereof, 15,937,841 florins; books and objects of art, 15,705,589 florins; gums and resins, 12,628,895 florins; salt, 12,788,321 florins; metals and metal manufactures, 11,839,-271 florins; pottery, 8,945,570 florins; fuel, 7,700,788 florins; wines and spirits, 7,545,645 florins; minerals, 6,062,106 florins. The leading articles of export and their values for 1885 were as follow: Grain, flour, and pulse, 96,-447,608 florins; fuel, 79,080,893 florins; sugar, 50,658,667 florins; instruments, watches, etc., 46,944,551 florins; wool and woolens, 40,004,-984 florins; cattle, 35,666,612 florins; animal products, 31,300,839 florins; wines and spirits, 28,528,588 florins; leather and leather manufactures, 21,445,100 florins; glass and glass wares, 19,896,943 florins; vegetable fibers and manufactures thereof, 18,779,181 florins; cotton manufactures, 16,604,457 florins; minerals, 12,481,218 florins; paper and paper manufactures, 11,465,173 florins; iron and iron manufactures, 11,120,839 florins; tobacco, 8,167,673 florins.

The imports of specie and bullion in 1885 amounted to 12,282,529, and the exports to 8,727,579 florins. Of the merchandise imports 837,495,617 florins, and of the exports 317,-319,252 florins passed over the German frontier, while 87,881,560 florins of imports and 95,002,077 florins of exports went through Trieste, and 81,748,124 florins of imports and 51,576,122 florins of exports through Fiume and the other sea-ports. The import trade with Roumania amounted to 40,047,688, and the export trade to 39,157,016 florins. The Russian imports were 21,390,116, and the exports to Russia 21,671,517 florins. The imports from Italy amounted to 19,176,409, from Servia to 14,162,174, from Switzerland to 5,477,370, and from Turkey and Montenegro to 569,316 florins, while the value of the exports to Italy was 47,-638,326, to Servia 13,991,139, to Switzerland 29,570,127, and to Turkey and Montenegro 157,618 florins. High protective tariffs have caused a decline in the import trade, which were valued in 1884 at $247,860,000, and in 1885 were only $295,990,000, while for 1886 they were estimated at $221,616,000. The Russian imports fell off most, but the decrease in those from Great Britain, Germany, and France were considerable. The customs dues have risen from 40 to 86 cents *per capita*, with a simultaneous increase in the consumption duties from 86 cents to $1.60. The estimated value of the exports in 1886 is $291,600,000.

Railroads and Telegraphs.—In January, 1886, the Austrian Government owned 2,299 miles of railroad and the joint-stock companies 6,023 miles, though of the latter 981 miles were operated by the state. The length of the Hungarian railroads in 1885 was 5,685 miles, of which

2,765 miles were operated by the Government. In 1885–'86 12,885,000 florins were appropriated for the construction of new lines in Austria.

The telegraph system of Austria in 1885 comprised 24,212 miles of lines and 62,447 miles of wires; that of Hungary, 10,872 miles of lines and 40,172 miles of wires. In Bosnia and Herzegovina there were 1,780 miles of lines. The number of dispatches in Austria in 1885 was 6,701,899, and in Hungary 3,636,830.

The Post-Office.—The Austrian post-office in 1885 transmitted 383,118,000 letters and postal-cards, 86,604,400 newspapers, 53,389,000 circulars and patterns, and 35,362,200 packages of goods. The receipts in 1884 were 20,020,-730, and the expenses 16,478,730 florins. The extent of the postal traffic in Hungary was 120,651,740 letters and cards, 47,031,820 journals, 15,721,814 circulars, etc., and 10,502,302 parcels. The receipts of the Hungarian post-office in 1884 were 8,801,264, and the expenses 7,215,917 florins.

Shipping and Navigation.—The Austro-Hungarian merchant-marine in 1886 numbered 61 steamers of 69,452 tons, in the foreign trade; 82 coasting steamers, of 14,491 tons; and 9,225 sailing-vessels of all descriptions, of which the tonnage was 228,044. In 1884 there were 62,-112 vessels, of 7,478,522 tons, entered; and 61,998 vessels, of 7,481,690 tons, cleared at Austro-Hungarian ports. Of the tonnage, 87 per cent. was Austrian.

The Occupied Provinces.—The provinces of Bosnia and Herzegovina were occupied by Austria-Hungary under the provisions of the treaty of Berlin, and have since been administered by imperial civil officials. The same instrument stipulated that the Austrian military should occupy the Sanjak of Novi-Bazar, but that the civil administration should continue to be Turkish. Bosnia has an area of 16,200 square miles, and contained 187,574 inhabitants in 1885. The area of Herzegovina is 3,540 square miles, and the population in 1885 was 1,148,517. Novi-Bazar, with an area of 3,592 square miles, had 168,000 inhabitants in 1879. The revenue of the occupied provinces for 1887 was estimated in the budget at 8,977,-890, and the expenditure at 8,920,616 florins. The cost of the army of occupation was estimated at 5,119,000 florins.

Secret Treaty with Russia.—In April, 1887, the German Government, through the semi-official press, revealed the existence of a secret treaty in which Russia agreed to an annexation of Bosnia and Herzegovina, as the price of Austrian neutrality, long before the Russo-Turkish war. The disclosure, which was intended to refute complaints of Russian journals that Germany had supported Austrian policy in antagonism to Russia, was embarrassing to Austro-Hungarian statesmen, and especially so to Tisza, the Hungarian Premier, who resigned when the occupation of the provinces was resolved upon by the Imperial Government, because his country-men, whose sympathies were with the Turks during the war, considered it a betrayal of Turkey. He withdrew his resignation, and obtained from Parliament the supplies for the occupation, but it was by representing Austria-Hungary's action as necessitated by the situation resulting from the war. The secret treaty was negotiated in 1876 during the meeting of the Austrian and Russian Emperors at Reichstadt, and was signed at Vienna on Jan. 15, 1877. When the Russian troops entered Bulgaria Count Andrassy did not proceed to the occupation of the provinces, and is said to have been driven from office by the pro-Russian party at court because he would not act in concert with Russia, and thus failed to obtain the absolute possession of the promised territory. The occupation finally took place by an arrangement arrived at after the cession of Cyprus to Great Britain, which Russia was precluded by the previous secret understanding from opposing. The Russian delegate at Berlin therefore acquiesced in the proposal of Great Britain to intrust Austria-Hungary with the pacification and administration of Bosnia and Herzegovina. M. Tisza, in an explanation to the Chamber on May 21, 1887, defended his statements made at the time by explaining that the conditions of the secret treaty were never fulfilled, and that the occupation was undertaken in obedience to the European mandate.

The Ausgleich.—A new ten-year treaty between the two states composing the empire was finally settled in May, 1887. The negotiations occupied an entire year, and on several occasions came to a stand-still. The difficulties which threatened to prevent a continuance of the customs league were not solved, but were simply waived or compromised for the sake of averting the external and internal dangers that would result from a breech of the fiscal union. Count Szapary broke off the negotiations in March, and refused to agree to a new basis suggested by M. Tisza, but in the Cabinet crisis that ensued was forced to resign his post as Hungarian Minister of Finances, and allow the Premier to conclude the arrangements. The Hungarians were desirous of formally incorporating in their kingdom the small strip of territory called the Militärgrenze, which is an integral part of Hungary, but is included in the old military boundaries of Austria. They assumed the share of this territory in the common expenditures, but, failing to obtain certain concessions, would not agree to a new apportionment of the burden which presses unequally on Austria, whose share in the common expenses for the ten years' period beginning Jan. 1, 1888, will be 68¼ per cent., while Hungary pays only 31¼ per cent.

Treaty Negotiations with Roumania.—There was a conference at Bucharest for the negotiation of a new commercial treaty with Roumania in March, 1887, but it led no nearer to a conclusion than the previous negotiations. The Roumanian delegates who met representatives of Austria-Hungary in Vienna in the winter of 1886–'87 proposed that inspection at the frontier should be abolished, and that herds consigned to Austria-Hungary should be examined only in the districts where the existence of disease was reasonably suspected. In the subsequent conferences the Roumanian Government modified its demand that the Roumanian cattle import should be admitted without quarantine, but insisted that it should be subjected only to the rules that are applied to the imports of Switzerland, Italy, and other treaty powers. An arrangement was about to be concluded on this basis, when the Hungarian Minister of Agriculture introduced conditions that were inconsistent with it, and inacceptable to the Roumanians, viz., that the Hungarian frontier should be closed to Roumanian cattle whenever Germany should prohibit the importation of cattle from Austria-Hungary, and that all cattle coming from Roumania should undergo a five days' quarantine at Steinbruch, near Buda-Pesth.

Austria.—The Austrian Parliament, called the Reichsrath, consists of two chambers—a House of Lords and a House of Deputies. The upper chamber was composed in 1886 of 18 princes of the blood royal, 53 hereditary peers, 10 archbishops, and 7 prince-bishops, and 105 life-members. The representative chamber consists of 353 members, elected partly directly and partly indirectly by all citizens of the age of twenty-four years or over possessed of a low property qualification. Important legislative powers are exercised by the Provincial Diets, seventeen in number, each of which consists of but one chamber composed of the heads of the Roman and Greek Churches, and chancellors of universities, and of representatives of land-owners, municipalities, boards of commerce, guilds, and of rural communes, the latter being voted for indirectly by all tax-payers. The head of the Austrian Cabinet is Count Edward Taafe, who, though his ancestors have lived in Austria for several generations, is an Irish nobleman, and a peer of the United Kingdom. He was appointed Minister of the Interior and President of the Council on Aug. 19, 1879. The Minister of Public Instruction and Ecclesiastical Affairs is Dr. Paul Gautsch von Frankenthurn, appointed Nov. 6, 1885; the Minister of Finance, Dr. J. Dunajewski; the Minister of Agriculture, Count Julius Falkenhayn; the Minister of Commerce and National Economy, Marquis von Becquehem; the Minister of National Defense, Maj.-Gen. Count S. von Welsersheimb; the Minister of Justice, A. Prazak. F. Ziemialkowski has a seat in the Council, but holds no portfolio.

Revenue and Expenditure.—The budget estimates for the year ending March 31. 1887, make the total receipts of the treasury 507,-833,841 florins, and the expenditures 516,625,-771 florins. The ordinary receipts are estimated at 491,927,845, and the ordinary expenditures at 470,059,347 florins. The indirect taxes, viz.: a land-tax, a house-tax, a tax on industrial establishments, and an income-tax, produce 99,052,000 florins of revenue. The yield of customs is 47,243,417, of excise duties 84,484,900, of the salt-tax 20,444,000, of the tobacco-tax 74,002,800, of stamp-duties 17,-800,000, of judicial fees 36,650,000, of the state lottery 20,224,000 florins, the total product of indirect taxation being 301,794,417 florins. The posts and telegraphs produce 27,299,050, and the railroads 47,171,917 florins. The chief items of expenditure are 117,975,054 florins for the service of the public debt, 93,578,071 florins for financial administration, and 86,888,-803 florins for common affairs. The public debt on July 1, 1886, amounted to 3,485,881,-310 florins, not including 412,000,000 florins of paper currency. About 50,000,000 florins of new paper *rente* were issued in the beginning of the financial year 1887–'88 to cover the financial requirements of the year.

The Language Question.—The German Liberals in the Austrian Chamber won a triumph over the Government in April, 1887, by carrying through a motion of ex-Minister von Schmerling, who is called the father of Austrian constitutionalism, providing for the appointment of a committee to consider the question of the use of other languages besides German in official documents and the pleadings of law courts. German has been acknowledged by the Government to be the official language of the empire, and the German party maintains that edicts that have been issued at various times authorizing the employment of the Czech, Polish, and Italian languages for judicial and administrative purposes are illegal. After the rejection of a resolution offered by Herr von Plener, the German leader in the Diet of Prague, all of his party threatened to take no part in the legislative proceedings until the Czech majority should agree to alter the law which makes the use of the Czech language sometimes compulsory in the law courts of German districts. In January, before closing its sessions, the Diet by a unanimous vote declared that the German abstainers had vacated their seats. In order to satisfy national or local ambitions the Government has in recent times established gymnasia in many country towns which are too poor to maintain them, and has in consequence been induced to aid the schools by annual grants. Dr. von Gautsch, the Minister of Education, declaring himself opposed to over-education and the multiplication of the intellectual proletariate, ordered in the summer that the least frequented of the schools should be closed. His decree resulted in the suppression of several Czech gymnasia, and brought upon the ministry the denunciations of the press of Bohemia.

Anarchist Trials. — Socialistic doctrines are more prevalent among the workingmen of Austria than in Germany or any other country. The socialists are much stronger in Vienna than in the other European capitals, and their theories are generally accepted also by the working-classes of Grätz, Klagenfurth, Brünn, and Reichenberg, and have taken deep root in Hungary, though their public expression is hindered by the new anti-socialist law of that country. The revolutionary socialists are not numerous in Austria, yet a band of desperate characters was organized among the industrial population of the suburbs of Vienna, with affiliated groups in other places, which the police detected just as some of their destructive plots were ripe for execution. In March, 1887, 15 anarchists were tried in Vienna before a special court of six judges without a jury, on the charge of preparing and secreting explosives. It was proved that they had entered into a conspiracy to fire several lumber-yards for the purpose of creating a panic, and that they had provided themselves with bombs and grenades charged with a powerful explosive. The ringleaders were a mason named Kaspari, and a weaver named Wawrunek. A tinsmith named Kratochwill had attempted to set fire to a lumber-yard, but the fuse would not burn. Two of the prisoners were acquitted, and the rest were sentenced to the penitentiary for terms ranging from six months to twenty years.

Hungary.—The Hungarian legislative authority is exercised by a Diet consisting of two branches. The upper house, called the House of Magnates, contains, under the law of 1885, all hereditary peers who pay a land-tax of 3,000 florins or over; archbishops, bishops, and certain other ecclesiastics of the Roman and Greek Catholic Churches, 39 altogether; 11 ecclesiastical and lay representatives of Protestant bodies; 50 life-peers who were elected by the house, but are to be hereafter nominated by the Crown; 16 high state and judicial dignitaries, who are members *ex-officio*; 1 delegate from Croatia and Slavonia; and the archdukes who are of full age. The House of Representatives in 1886 consisted of 453 members, of whom 40 were the delegates of Croatia and Slavonia. The ministry is composed of the following members: President of the Council, Koloman Tisza de Boros-Jenö, who in February, 1887, took over the Ministry of Finance on the resignation of Count Gyula Szapary; Minister of the Interior, Baron Bela Orczy, who succeeded the Prime Minister when the latter assumed charge of the finance department; Minister of Education and Worship, Dr. August Trefort; Minister of the Honved, otherwise called the Minister of National Defense, Baron Geza Fejérváry, appointed Oct. 28, 1884; Minister *ad latus*, Baron Orczy; Minister of Justice, Theophile Fabinyi, appointed May 17, 1886; Minister of Communications, Baron Orczy; Minister of Agriculture, Industry, and Commerce, Count Paul Széchényi; Minister for Croatia and Slavonia, Koloman de Bedekovich.

Revenue and Expenditure.—The total revenue in 1885 was 818,444,919 florins, and the ex-

penditure 358,645,446 florins. The estimated revenue for 1887 is 328,356,095 florins; the expenditure 350,400,091 florins, of which 111,-882,886 florins are applied to the national-debt account, 29,470,424 florins to the common expenses of the empire, besides 4,150,917 florins of extraordinary expenditure, 56,106,852 florins to financial administration, 27,295,000 florins to state railways, 17,907,680 florins to investments, and 11,799,008 florins to debts of guaranteed railroads taken over by the Government. The public debt in the beginning of 1886 amounted to 1,342,380,381 florins, besides Hungary's share in the common debt of the empire, on which the interest charge is 30,000,-000 florins per annum.

Parliamentary Elections.—The general election which began on June 17, was attended with the usual popular excitement, but with fewer disturbances than in former years. Notwithstanding the strong position of the Tisza Cabinet, corrupt inducements and administrative pressure were employed as usual to augment the Government majority. Count Albert Apponyi, the eloquent leader of the Moderate Opposition, made much of this practice of corruption in his arraignment of the Government, and summed up all the errors committed during Tisza's twelve years' premiership; yet the Government obtained a larger majority than ever. There were riots in five or six districts, in which many persons were killed and wounded. At Usbeck the troops were called out to quell a disturbance, during which 8 persons were killed and 30 injured. At Verbo the anti-Semites wrecked the polling-place, but the soldiery did not interfere. The result of the election was a majority for the Government of 103 to 56 in 1884. The Moderate Opposition, which numbered 67 members in 1878, was reduced to 44. The Independents, who had 70 seats in 1878, now secured 77, but the anti-Semites, who vote with them on general questions, lost a number of seats. The Nationalists also elected fewer members than in the last election.

Fires and Floods.—Hungary was visited during May and June with calamities of more than usual severity. Fires are of common occurrence in that country, and are shown by statistics to be particularly prevalent in the month of May. The unusual number of large fires in May, 1887, may have been the result, as is the case in Galicia, of the careless use of petroleum. The town of Toroczko in Transylvania was partially destroyed, and a day or two afterward the villages of Merenyo and Mezoecsueged were entirely consumed. On May 4 a fire broke out in the town of Arad which destroyed 150 houses and a large factory. In the mining town of Ruszkabanyi 111 houses were burned; and at Nagy Karolyi the family estate of the Counts Karolyi, including their mansion, 25 large workshops, and 225 other buildings, was destroyed. This was followed by a greater catastrophe at Eperies, the chief center of Protestantism in Hungary, where all the churches, Government buildings, schools, banks, and a great number of dwellings and workshops were burned to the ground.

About the same time floods did great damage in various parts of the country, and culminated in a destructive inundation that swept over the alluvial district around Szegedin. After the destruction of that town in 1879 it was rebuilt on high ground, and a system of embankments was constructed at a cost of 44,-000,000 florins for the purpose of securing the neighboring farming lands from the overflow of the Theiss. A sluice at Kistisza was badly constructed, and left in charge of a heedless or incapable inspector, with the consequence that on May 31 the river, which was swollen by rains but yet not within several feet of the high-water mark, carried away the dam and flooded 80,000 hectares of growing wheat, destroying many farmsteads, and reducing nearly 2,000 families to destitution.

Croatia.—The vigorous measures of Count Khûn-Hedervary, the Ban of Croatia, have broken up the National or Home-Rule party as an open political organization. The elections to the Croatian Diet, which took place a week before the Hungarian elections, resulted in the return of 86 Government candidates to only 19 of the Opposition. The Roman Catholic clergy head the Separatist movement in the Banat, but they are kept in check by the repressive means in the hands of the civil authorities. In August a clergyman was sentenced by the court at Agram to a year's imprisonment with hard labor for seditious language.

B

BAIRD, SPENCER FULLERTON, an American naturalist, born in Reading, Pa., Feb. 8, 1823; died in Wood's Holl, Mass., Aug. 19, 1887. He was graduated at Dickinson College in 1840, and in 1842 studied medicine at the College of Physicians and Surgeons in New York city, but was not graduated. Meanwhile, he devoted much time to long pedestrian excursions through Pennsylvania for the purpose of col-

SPENCER FULLERTON BAIRD.

lecting specimens in natural history, and his private cabinet ultimately became the nucleus of the museum connected with the Smithsonian Institution. In 1845 he was appointed, Professor of Natural History at Dickinson, also teaching chemistry, where he remained until 1850, when he was elected assistant secretary of the Smithsonian Institution. This office he held until May, 1878, when, on the death of Joseph Henry, he succeeded to the full secretaryship. The department of exploration was placed under his authority from its beginning, and his annual reports constitute the only systematic record of the National explorations ever prepared. During the decade of 1850–'60 he devoted much time to enlisting the sympathies of the leaders of Government expeditions in the objects of the Institution, supplying them with all the appliances for collecting, as well as with instructions for their use. In many instances he organized the natural-history parties, named the collectors, employed and supervised the artists in preparing the plates, and frequently edited the zoölogical portions of their reports. The specimens brought back to Washington were intrusted to his care. These, with his own collection and those obtained on the Wilkes exploring expedition during 1842, were the beginnings of the United States National Museum, which, under his administration, has developed until it is now unsurpassed throughout the United States. The system of international exchanges organized under the direction of the Smithsonian, is likewise due to his genius. In 1871 Prof. Baird was appointed Commissioner of Fish and Fisheries, an office which he held without salary until his death. This great work, organized by him, has grown until it includes: 1. The systematic investigation of the waters of the United States, and the biological and physical problems they present. 2. The investigation of the methods of fisheries, past and present, and the statistics of production and commerce of fishery products. 3. The introduction and multiplication of useful food-fishes throughout the country, especially in waters under the jurisdiction of the General Government, or those common to several States, none of which might feel willing to make expenditures for the benefit of others. In 1877, at the request of the United States Government, he was present at the Halifax Fishery Commission in the capacity of advisory counsel. His work on fisheries has been honored with awards of medals from the Acclimation Society of Melbourne in 1878, and from the Société d'acclimation de France, in 1879; the first honor prize from the International Fish Exhibition held in Berlin in 1880, and the order of St. Olaf from the King of Norway and Sweden. The degree of Doctor of Physical Science was conferred on him by Dickinson College in 1856, and that of LL.D. by Columbian University in 1875. For many years he was a trustee of the latter institution, and from 1878 filled a similar appointment to the Corcoran Gallery of Art in Washington. He was Permanent Secretary of the American Association for the Advancement of Science in 1850–'51, and edited the proceedings of the fourth, fifth, and sixth meetings. In addition to being a member of the leading scientific societies in the United States, he held foreign or honorary membership in many of the scientific societies in Europe and the British colonies, and became a member of the National Academy of Sciences in 1864. The nomenclature of zoölogy contains many memorials of his connection with its history. One genus of fishes was called in his honor by Prof. Theodore N. Gill, and over twenty-five species of mammals, birds, fishes, mollusks, and other forms of life bear his name, together with several fossil or extinct varieties. His literary work was very great, and a complete bibliography from 1843 till 1882, including 1,063 titles, was prepared by George Brown Goode, and issued as number twenty of the "Bulletins of the United States National Museum" (Washington, 1883). From 1870 till 1878 Prof. Baird was the scientific editor of Harper and Brothers' periodicals, including the "Annual Record of Science and Industry" (8 volumes, New York, 1871–'79). The various reports and annual volumes of the United States Commission of Fish and Fisheries were prepared by him, and also the annual "Reports of the Board of Regents of the Smithsonian Institution" from 1878. His other works include the translating and editing of the "Iconographic Encyclopædia" (4 volumes, New York, 1852); "Catalogue of North American Reptiles" (Washington, 1853); "Mammals of North America" (Philadelphia, 1859); "The Birds of North America," with John Cassin (1860); "Review of American Birds in the Museum of the Smithsonian Institution" (Washington, 1864–'66); and "The Distribution and Migrations of North American Birds" (1866). His latest work was a "History of North American Birds," prepared with Thomas M. Brewer and Robert Ridgway (5 volumes, Boston, 1874–'84). Prof. Baird's ornithological studies were placed by him, in 1887, in the hands of Robert Ridgway, and since his death have been published as "Manual of North American Birds" (Philadelphia, 1887).

BAPTISTS. I. Regular Baptists in the United States. The following is a summary of the statistics of the Regular Baptist churches in the United States, as given by States in the "American Baptist Year-Book" for 1887:

STATES AND TERRITORIES.	Associations.	Ordained ministers.	Churches.	Members.
Alabama	100	1,288	2,172	166,928
Arizona	1	5	6	140
Arkansas	59	802	1,442	76,060
California	8	185	130	6,499
Colorado	3	29	34	2,595
Connecticut	6	187	126	21,746
Dakota	5	55	86	2,664
Delaware	..	10	13	1,626
District of Columbia	3	45	36	10,561
Florida	28	248	586	27,702
Georgia	107	1,389	2,889	266,818
Idaho	1	6	10	257
Illinois	42	694	1,006	79,010
Indiana	31	381	545	114,478
Indian Territory	8	65	107	4,361
Iowa	28	317	494	24,583
Kansas	22	254	431	21,706
Kentucky	62	906	1,774	196,027
Louisiana	34	650	1,017	86,694
Maine	18	144	247	19,871
Maryland	1	47	57	12,445
Massachusetts	14	369	296	59,768
Michigan	19	326	381	80,056
Minnesota	10	187	191	10,799
Mississippi	79	1,106	2,099	170,814
Missouri	74	1,050	1,608	106,689
Montana	1	6	12	337
Nebraska	12	180	165	7,000
Nevada	..	2	1	46
New Hampshire	6	52	80	8,802
New Jersey	5	210	192	35,130
New Mexico	..	3	3	55
New York	48	828	864	119,888
North Carolina	81	1,051	2,265	226,767
Ohio	82	478	627	58,185
Oregon	6	60	74	3,709
Pennsylvania	28	491	605	72,512
Rhode Island	3	59	66	11,554
South Carolina	49	740	1,216	170,946
Tennessee	48	966	1,484	122,342
Texas	99	1,838	2,697	166,498
Utah	1	3	4	195
Vermont	7	96	115	9,146
Virginia	42	868	1,623	242,481
Washington	3	87	45	1,401
West Virginia	15	239	485	32,866
Wisconsin	15	128	194	12,526
Wyoming	..	2	2	150
Total	1,244	19,817	30,529	2,732,570

The whole number of Sunday-schools is given as 18,889, with 107,087 officers and teachers, and 1,011,585 pupils; number of additions to the churches by baptism, 155,878; value of church property, $42,558,794. Amount of contributions reported: for salaries and expenses, $5,549,563; for missions, $849,887; for education, $108,749; miscellaneous, $1,334,-881; aggregate, $7,843,081.

The "Year-Book" gives, of general statistics in North America (including the United States), 1,268 associations, 31,507 churches, 19,986 ministers, 160,173 baptisms during the year, and 2,844,491 members; for South America (Brazil), 5 churches, 12 ministers, 23 baptisms, and 168 members; for Europe, 67 associations, 3,500 churches, 6,642 ministers, 5,488 baptisms, and 883,971 members; for Asia, 8 associations, 933 churches, 560 ministers, 3,467 baptisms, and 65,657 members; for Africa, 3 associations, 82 churches, 56 ministers, 130 baptisms, and 3,212 members: and for Australasia, 6 associations, 159 churches, 118 ministers, and 15,527 members. Total, 1,352 associations, 36,186 churches, 27,868 ministers, 169,281 baptisms, and 3,813,026 members.

Seven theological institutions in the United States returned 48 instructors and 543 pupils; 27 universities and colleges, 251 instructors, and 3,660 pupils; 30 institutions for the education of young women exclusively, 281 instructors and 2,899 pupils; 43 seminaries and academies and institutions for both sexes, 258 instructors and 4,757 pupils; and 19 institutions for the colored race and Indians, 154 instructors and 3,776 pupils. In all, 126 educational institutions, 1,092 instructors, and 15,635 pupils.

American Baptist Home Mission Society.—The fifty-third anniversary of the American Baptist Home Mission Society was held in Minneapolis, Minn., May 30. Mr. Samuel Colgate presided. The total receipts of the society for the year had been $552,314, or $15,000 more than the receipts of the previous year. Of this sum $349,797 were returned as contributions from churches, Sunday-schools, and individuals; $158,257 from legacies; $17,599 as income from church-edifice loans and invested funds; and $19,987 from the schools of the society. The Executive Board in making appropriations had adhered to the rule of limiting them to the average of annual receipts of the three years preceding. The expenditures had been $290,887, of which $130,666 had been for ministers' salaries, $59,261 for teachers' salaries, $41,443 for special educational purposes, $29,296 in gifts for church-edifice work, and $31,855 for expenses of administration and agencies. In addition to these expenditures, the indebtedness of the previous year, $123,429, had been been paid off with the results of special offerings. A settlement had been effected with Mr. J. H. Deane, a former treasurer of the society, whose failure in business had involved the society in financial loss (see "Annual Cyclopædia" for 1886), by which he was to pay 50 per cent. of the deficiency in his accounts, or $66,000 in stated instalments. The summary of the missionary work showed that 678 laborers had been employed in the supply of 1,385 churches and out-stations having a total church membership of 28,398, with 673 Sunday-schools, returning a total attendance of 44,740 persons; also that 129 churches had been organized, and 3,800 members had been added by baptism. The amount of benevolent contributions reported from the mission churches was $28,539. Besides the stations among American populations, the society had assisted the German Baptist Convention among the Germans of Ontario; had aided the Scandinavian churches, particularly in Minnesota; had labored among the French in Maine, Massachusetts, Rhode Island, Connecticut, and Illinois; and among the colored people in various States of the South

and North; had sustained 12 missionaries to Indians in the Cherokee Nation, among the Delawares, and to Sacs and Foxes of the Indian Territory, and at the Pyramid Lake and Walker river reservations; had maintained missions among the Chinese in California and Oregon; and had supported missions in Mexico. In the church-edifice department, grants had been made to 62 churches in the shape of $10,818 in gifts and $13,325 in loans; while receipts were acknowledged to the Loan Fund of $7,051, and to the Benevolent Fund of $78,645. The Loan Fund amounted to $122,047, and was regarded as sufficiently large for all demands that were likely to be made upon it. The educational institutions of the society included 11 incorporated and 6 unincorporated institutions; with mission day-schools, largely supported by the Woman's American Baptist Home Mission Society of Boston, in Salt Lake City, the city of Mexico and Salinas, Apodaca, and Santa Rosa, Mexico, and Tahlequah, in the Indian Territory; and mission night-schools for the Chinese in Oakland, San Francisco, and Fresno, Cal. Fifteen schools for the colored people were supported wholly or in part by the society, while Leland University, New Orleans, with an endowment of nearly $100,000, had become self-supporting. These schools had employed 122 teachers, 28 of whom were colored, and returned 2,807 pupils. Ministerial training was provided for at several of these schools, industrial education in many of them, with appropriations from the "Slater Fund" at seven, and medical education in the Leonard Medical School, at Raleigh, N. C., and for women at Spelman Seminary, Atlanta, Ga.

American Baptist Publication Society.—The sixty-third anniversary of the American Baptist Publication Society was held in Minneapolis, Minn., May 25, 26, and 27. Mr. Edward Goodman, of Illinois, vice-president, presided. The total receipts and business of the society in all of its departments for the year had been $624,140. The business of the year had amounted to $481,997. The Board of Managers reported that a defalcation by two of the bookkeepers had caused a loss to the business department computed at the date of the meeting to amount to $24,156. One hundred and ninety-four new works had been published, of which 331,500 copies had been issued, and 737,300 copies of new additions of former publications had been printed; while the whole number of books, tracts, and periodicals printed during the year was 26,751,800. The gross receipts of the missionary department had been $8,084 less than in the previous year. The receipts for permanent investment funds in this department had been $8,500. The gross receipts in the Bible department had been $15,972. Seventy-eight missionaries had been employed, under whose labors 710 persons had been baptized, 43 churches constituted, 311 sunday-schools organized, 501 institutes held and addressed, and 1,822 Sunday-schools and

214 pastors and ministerial students had been aided with grants for their libraries. Grants had been made in the Bible department of Scriptures in 13 languages and 21 versions, to the number of 50,000 copies. Special reports were made respecting the mission to the Armenians in Turkey, which was begun at the request of converted Armenians to be appointed to work among their countrymen, after the American Baptist Missionary Union had declined to act in the matter, in 1883. The Missionary Union had been invited several times to take charge of the work, but had declined on each occasion. Other missionaries had been appointed, and the society had now four missionaries or colporteurs at Constantinople, Arabkir, Erzeroum, and some field to be selected; with 82 members at Constantinople, and two schools for girls with 40 pupils, a church attendance of 1,810, and a Sunday-school attendance of 1,612 at Erzeronm. Another report concerned the relations of the mission with the American Board, with whose Armenian missions the Baptist work appeared to many persons to be in rivalry. It maintained the right and duty of the society to continue and sustain the mission. Resolutions were adopted making this report the expression of the society, and again inviting the American Baptist Missionary Union to assume charge of the work among Armenians, appointing the present missionaries and accepting the money and pledges which had been gathered for their support. The Board of Managers was urged by resolution to publish tracts and treatises bearing upon the subject of temperance and in opposition to the traffic in intoxicating liquors for the purpose of use as beverages.

American Baptist Missionary Union.—The seventy-third anniversary of the American Baptist Missionary Union was held in Minneapolis, Minn., beginning May 27. The Rev. Edward Judson, D. D., presided. The receipts of the society for the year had been $406,689. The missions of the society to the heathen include the Burman, Karen, Shan, Kachin, Chin, Assamese, Garo, Naga, and Telugu missions in Burmah and India; the Chinese missions in Bangkok, Siam, and in China; the mission in Japan; and the African missions, on the west coast, in the Congo, and "at home." These returned altogether 54 stations and 974 out-stations, 248 European missionaries, 780 native preachers, 92 Bible-women, and 244 other native helpers—making a total missionary force of 1,359 persons; 624 churches, with 58,108 members, and 3,290 baptisms during the year, 216 Sunday-schools, with 11,841 pupils, and 778 day-schools, with 874 native teachers and 16,560 pupils. The missionary property at all these stations was valued at $492,077. The contributions of the mission stations were returned at $38,040. The European missions in Sweden, Germany, France, Spain, and Greece, returned 950 preachers, 641 churches, and 65,-422 members, with 6,052 baptisms during the

year. The Board of Managers had been applied to by the Bishop of Rangoon and the British and Foreign Bible Society, for permission to publish the Missionionary Union's translations of the Bible into the language of Burmah, substituting ordinary terms or the Greek words untranslated for the more specific terms relating to baptism used in these versions. The request had been declined. The Board of Managers was authorized to accept the direction of the missionary work in Armenia now carried on by the American Baptist Publication Society, such acceptance to be conditioned upon the favorable report of a specially-appointed committee of investigation. A resolution of protest was adopted against permitting the importation of strong drink into the newly-opened Congo Valley in Africa, and a committee was appointed to invoke such help as it might be possible to secure from the Government of the United States to prevent such importation.

Other Baptist Societies.—The American Baptist Historical Society, Philadelphia, has a permanent fund of $3,600.

The Woman's Baptist Foreign Missionary Society, having its office at Boston, returned its receipts, according to the "American Baptist Year-Book" for 1887, at $59,709. It sustained in Asia, Europe, Japan, and Africa 27 missionaries and 109 schools, with 4,049 pupils.

The Woman's Baptist Foreign Missionary Society of the West, having its central office at Chicago, reported an income of $31,595, 25 missionaries, 147 schools, 46 native teachers, and 1,656 pupils.

The receipts of the Woman's Baptist Home Mission Society, Chicago, were $43,240. It sustained 68 missionaries.

The Woman's American Baptist Home Mission Society of Boston, reported the receipt of $24,017, and employed 28 teachers.

German Baptists.—The triennial German Baptist General Conference includes five annual conferences, with which are connected, in all, 12,676 members.

Southern Baptist Convention.—The Southern Baptist Convention met in Louisville, Ky., May 6. The Rev. P. H. Mell, D. D., was chosen president. The Board of Home Missions presented a summary of its work during the year as follows: Number of missionaries, 251; of churches and stations, 822; of baptisms, 3,923; received by letter, 2,319; total additions, 6,242; Sunday-schools reported, 818; teachers and pupils, 18,081; churches constituted, 119; houses of worship built, 62; cost of houses and lots, $60,000.

The Choctaw Indians, under the direction of an agent of the Board, were endeavoring to establish a Baptist school within the nation, and had nearly completed a building for it at Atoka. Three churches had been constituted in Cuba, the oldest of which, at Havana, had 101 members. These churches also returned 6 candidates for the ministry, 4 Sunday-schools, with 17 teachers and 400 pupils, and 2 day-schools, with about 150 pupils. Report was made concerning co-operation in sustaining churches with the local organizations in various States, and of work among the colored people. The Woman's Missionary Societies had contributed $2,231 to the funds of the board, had supported three laborers in the field, and had given aid to the Levering-School in the Indian Territory.

The receipts of the Board of Foreign Missions had been $87,955, and its disbursements, $87,744. The financial exhibit was the best the board had ever been able to make. The missions—which are in Brazil, Mexico, Italy, Africa (Yoruba Mission, etc.), and China—returned, in all, 116 missionaries, native and foreign; 65 churches and stations; 1,551 members; 228 baptisms during the year; 25 schools, with 587 pupils; and $3,012 of contributions.

Colored Baptist Organizations.—The colored Baptists of the United States are represented in the American National Baptist Convention, and the Baptist General Association of the Western States and Territories.

The American Baptist National Convention of colored churches in the United States was organized at a meeting held in St. Louis, Mo., August 25, 1886, with William J. Simmons, of Louisville, Ky., as president. Seventeen States were represented by delegates and visitors. Papers were read and lectures delivered on subjects relating to colored Baptists and the interests of the Baptist Church, and an Executive Board was organized, to have its headquarters at Louisville, Ky.

The receipts of the Baptist General Association of the Western States and Territories were $5,163. The association had sent two missionaries to the Congo Valley in Africa. Steps were taken at its meeting in 1886, for consolidating its work with that of the American Baptist National Convention.

Baptist Congress.—The sixth annual session of the Baptist Congress was held in Indianapolis, Ind., November 15, 16, and 17. Mr. William S. Holman presided. The proceedings consisted in the discussion of the following subjects, in papers and brief addresses: "The Organic Union of Christendom," Rev. G. D. Boardman, D. D., Prof. Norman Fox, the Rev. Dr. Bulkley, and volunteer speakers; "Phases of the Labor Problem," "The Land Question," by the Hon. J. R. Doolittle, and the Hon. Allen Zollars; and "Profit Sharing," by Prof. Moncrief, of Franklin College; "The Proper Functions and the Influence of the Newspapers of To-day," R. J. Burdette, the Rev. Dr. G. W. Lasher, and the Rev. H. L. Wayland, D. D.; "Improvements in Methods of Theological Education," Rev. W. C. Wilkinson, D. D., and Rev. Dr. H. C. Mabie; "Woman's Work in the Church," Rev. Dr. W. M. Lawrence, Rev. M. Willmarth, and volunteer speakers; "The Proper Attitude of the Church toward Amuse-

ments," Rev. M. Watson, Rev. T. I. Eaton, D. D., Rev. Dr. E. A. Wood, and Rev. Kerr B. Tupper; and "The Sin of Covetousness," Prof. Stifler, the Rev. Dr. C. R. Henderson, and Rev. Dr. P. S. Henson.

II. Free-Will Baptist Church.—The "Free-Will Baptist Register and Year-Book" for 1887 gives in the summary of the statistics of forty-eight yearly meetings of the Free-Will Baptist Church, 194 quarterly meetings, 1,542 churches, 1,291 ordained preachers, 5,988 licensed preachers, and 82,323 members. Twelve new yearly meetings united with the General Conference at its last session (six of them mainly composed of colored people), the membership of which is about 6,500. They are all in the Western and Southern States.

The Free-Will Baptist Education Society received and disbursed in 1886, $3,226. Its funds were: Permanent fund, $1,000; Library fund, $2,235; E. True fund, $9,965. One hundred students were preparing for the ministry in the schools of the Church. The Free-Will Baptist Home Mission Society had received and expended $9,126, and returned a permanent fund of $10,355. The special appropriations to missions amounted to $7,449. The receipts of the Free-Will Baptist Foreign Mission Society had been $14,781. It returned a permanent fund of $9,283, a Bible-school fund of $18,136, and a Bible-school hall fund of $50. The mission, which is in India (Bengal and Orissa), returned 558 communicants; 16 additions by baptism; a native Christian community of 1,085 persons; 2,904 pupils in Sunday-schools; and 8,568 pupils in other schools. The native contributions amounted to 585 rupees. The educational institutions comprise five colleges (one, Storer College, at Harper's Ferry, W. Va., with a State Normal and Academic Department in operation, largely attended by freedmen), and five seminaries and academical schools. Other benevolent institutions are the Temperance Society, the Sunday-School Union, and the Woman's Mission Society.

III. Seventh-Day Baptist Church.—The position of the Seventh-Day Baptist Church is described by the Rev. A. H. Lewis, D. D., author of "Sabbath and Sunday," and the "Seventh-Day Baptist Handbook," as that of making a plea for the Sabbath (as distinguished from Sunday) "not on merely denominational grounds, nor as a sectarian peculiarity, but rather as a fundamental requirement of God's moral government. We plead for a return to the Sabbath as against the Sunday, because there is no scriptural warrant for the change, and because the verdict of history is, that the reason assigned for observing Sunday, and the method adopted for upholding it, have failed to create conscience toward God, and hence to make of it a sacred day."

Statistical reports to the General Conference from 75 of the 110 churches gave the number of members therein as 8,255. Seventy-nine Sabbath-schools returned 485 teachers, and 6,557 members. The contributions reported were: for the Tract Society, $4,216; for the Missionary Society, $4 860; for educational purposes, $44,687. The treasurer of the memorial fund reported that the total amount of assets in his hands on account of that enterprise was $80,683.

The receipts of the Seventh-Day Baptist Tract Society for the year, derived from sales and contributions, were $16,078. The society publishes one quarterly, one monthly, and two weekly journals in the English language, and monthly journals in the Swedish, Hebrew, and Dutch languages. The "Hebrew Journal," which is printed without points, has been well received by Jews in various parts of the world, particularly in Southern Russia and Asia Minor.

The total receipts of the Missionary Society were $11,588, and its expenditures were $10,-858. Four foreign missionaries and 20 home missionaries were employed. The mission in China returned 2 foreign and 8 native laborers, with 3 teachers and 54 pupils, and 1 church with 18 members. The medical mission at Shanghai had served 1,407 patients. The mission in Holland returned 55 Seventh-Day Baptists, at 12 different places. The 3 churches at Haarlem, Amsterdam, and Rotterdam included 32 members. Missionary work had been begun among the Jews. The Woman's Board returned receipts amounting to $5,001.

The Seventh-Day Baptist General Conference met in its seventy-third session at Shiloh, N. J., September 21. A. B. Prentice presided. A committee appointed to correspond with persons interested in the Sabbath cause reported that it was in correspondence with about 100 such persons. The committee on denominational history recommended the opening of a department on that subject in either the "Seventh-Day Baptist Quarterly," or the "Sabbath Recorder." A declaration was adopted in favor of the prohibition of the liquor traffic. A part of the time of the Conference was devoted to the discussion of special topics bearing on the interests of the denomination.

IV. Baptists in Great Britain.—According to the "Baptist Hand-Book" for 1887, there are in the British Isles 2,742 churches, 3,787 chapels, 1,192,274 chapel-seats, 302,615 members, 47,170 teachers, and 456,694 pupils in Sunday, schools, 4,041 local preachers, and 1,868 pastors in charge.

The "Spring Session" of the Baptist Union of Great Britain and Ireland was held in London, beginning April 25. The Rev. Dr. Culross, of the Bristol Baptist College, was instituted president for the year. The report of the council gave the amount of funds received during the year for all the purposes in which the Union is interested as £20,630. Good results were claimed from the visitation of the churches. It had been resolved to raise a Jubilee fund for the further extension and consolidation of the British and Irish Mission. The value of

the securities belonging to the Annuity fund was estimated to be upward of £117,000; and the number of beneficiary members on the books was 846. The council had applied to be heard before the special committee of the House of Commons in opposition to the bill before Parliament respecting the attendance of registrars at non-conformists' places of worship.

The annual meeting of the Baptist Missionary Society was held April 26. Sir Robert Phayse presided. The receipts of the year had been £69,252. the largest amount ever returned. The expenditures had, however, exceeded the resources of the society by £2,385, and had been £3,341 in excess of the expenditures of the previous year. The increase had been mainly in India, China, and Ceylon, and were incidental to the reinforcements of the missions in those countries, particularly in China, where, within the last few years, the mission staff had been increased from 2 to 21. Nineteen brethren had been accepted for missionary service, 8 of whom had been sent to China, 6 to the Congo, 3 to India, and 2 to Ceylon. The committee had had considerable anxiety in consequence of the transfer by the British Government of the Cameroons, including the Victoria settlements, to the Germans, without inquiring whether the Baptist missionaries were willing to become German subjects. After protracted but fruitless negotiations with the view of inducing the German Government to purchase the mission station and property, the latter had been sold on satisfactory terms to the Basle Mission. Another matter of general interest had been the application of Mr. Stanley to be allowed the use of the steamer "Peace" for the Emin Bey relief expedition. It was found impossible to grant the request without violation of the conditions laid down by Mr. Arthrington, the donor of the vessel, who refused to allow it to be employed in any way for military purposes. In India, numerous conversions were reported; forty new Christian schools had been established, and a large number of educated natives were preparing for the ministry and the work of teaching in the schools. In China, an institution had been started for the training of Chinese Christians and of parties of "self-supporting" congregations.

The missions of the society in India, Ceylon, China, Japan, Africa, the West Indies, and Jamaica, and parts of Europe, return 94 ordained and 48 other European missionaries, 66 native ordained missionaries, 300 evangelists, 366 teachers, 45,113 communicants, 26,679 pupils in Sunday-schools, and 16,351 pupils in day-schools.

The receipts of the Baptist Zenana Mission for the year had been £6,422, and the expenditure £6,920. The working-staff of the society in the mission fields consisted of 44 lady zenana visitors, 17 assistants, and 104 native Bible-women and teachers; 1,206 zenanas were regularly visited, 1,800 pupils were receiving daily instruction, 50 schools and 1,650 pupils were superintended by the mission, and 20,000 patients were cared for in the dispensaries. The work of the society is chiefly carried on in the large cities of India, including Calcutta, Delhi, and Agra.

The autumnal meetings of the Baptist Union were held in Sheffield, beginning October 8. The proceedings consisted chiefly of meetings in behalf of the societies connected with the Union, and addresses on subjects pertaining to the work and interests of the Baptist churches, among which were the address by the President, Rev. Dr. Culross, on "Belief on the Son of God"; "The Churches and the Coming Ministry," by the Rev. C. P. Gould; "The Work of the Church among the Young," by the Rev. S. R. Aldridge; "Christian Fellowship," by the Rev. E. Medley; "The Practical Aspect of Christian Fellowship," by the Rev. Dr. Landels, and addresses to workingmen.

The Rev. C. H. Spurgeon gave notice of his withdrawal from the Baptist Union, by publication in his journal, "The Sword and Trowel," for November, and in a letter to the secretary of the body, dated October 28. As a reason for taking this step, he affirmed that the Union was tolerating error, and permitting a "downward tendency" of ministers in points of doctrine, in that some persons were allowed to remain in it who make light of the atonement, deny the personality of the Holy Ghost, call the fall of man a fable, speak slightingly of justification by faith, refuse credence to the dogma of the plenary inspiration of the Holy Scriptures, and hold that there is another probation after death, with possibilities of a future retribution of the lost; while efforts to induce him to reconsider his decision were without avail, he declared that he remained as much a Baptist as ever, his denominationalism not being affected by his relations with the Union, a voluntary, unofficial body.

The Baptist Union of Scotland consists, according to the report made by the secretary to the annual meeting in October, of 85 churches, with 10,380 members. The number of baptisms during the year had been 928. There were connected with the Union 76 Sunday-schools, with 1,015 teachers, and 8,961 pupils.

General Baptists.—The annual meetings of the General Baptist Assembly were held in London, beginning May 31. The Missionary Society returned an income of £7,625, 8 ordained and 9 woman European missionaries, 24 native ministers, 1,286 communicants, and 3,366 adherents. The principal mission is in India.

BEECHER, HENRY WARD, an American clergyman, born in Litchfield, Conn., June 24, 1813; died in Brooklyn, N. Y., March 8, 1887. He was the eighth child of Lyman and Roxana Foote Beecher. His mother died when he was but three years old, and his stepmother was by birth and early education an Episcopalian. Thus the early influences that surrounded Mr. Beecher tended to that catholicity which was so characteristic of him. For both mother and stepmother he had a profound reverence, which showed itself in habitual reference in his public ministry to the sacredness of motherhood. His home education was of the severe New England type, alleviated by the irrepressible sense of humor in his father, and by the poetic and mystical influence of his stepmother. He was graduated at Amherst College in 1834. His college life was fruitful, though not in the ordinary sense studious; he made his mark chiefly outside the recitation-room, and yet he was a great reader, following the bent of his own inclination rather than the lines laid down by his instructors. He made even then a careful study of English literature, analyzing the elements of style in different writers and orators, submitted himself to a thorough course of training in elocution, took hold of phrenology—not, of course, a college study—with great zest, gave lectures upon it, and upon temperance, and participated in class-room meetings and religious labors in the neighboring country towns. The time was one of great religious ferment; reaction had already set in against the purely intellectual in theology, the literalism in Biblical interpretation, the hardness in spiritual thinking, and the lack of what we may call the humanities in religion, which characterized the early epoch of New England history. The Unitarian defection from the orthodox Congregational faith had already taken place; the first great missionary organization of the Puritan churches —the American Board—had just been formed, and incipient indications pointed to that bitter struggle between the New School and the Old School theology, in both Presbyterian and Congregational churches, which was the most eventful feature in church history during the early years of Mr. Beecher's manhood.

Mr. Beecher himself was thoroughly grounded in the intellectual elements of Congregational evangelical belief; for his father was an intensely polemical and orthodox though liberal divine. In Mr. Beecher's case, the reaction against the excessive intellectualism of a too rigorous Puritanical faith, took the form of a spiritual experience, as it must necessarily have done in one of his emotive temperament; an experience that transformed his entire being, and pervaded all his subsequent life. "I know not," he says, describing this experience, "what the tablets of eternity have written down; but I think that when I stand in Zion, and before God, the brightest thing which I shall look back upon, will be that blessed morning of May, when it pleased God to reveal to my wandering soul the idea that it was his nature to love a man in his sins, for the sake of helping him out of them; that he did not do it out of compliment to Christ, or to a law, or a plan of salvation, but from the fullness of his great heart; that he was a being not made mad by sin, but sorry; that he was not furious with wrath toward the sinner, but pitied him—in short, that he felt toward me, as my mother felt toward me, to whose eyes my wrong-doing brought tears, who never pressed me so close to her as when I had done wrong, and who would fain, with her yearning love, lift me out of trouble." From this eventful May morning dated his consecration to the Christian ministry, a self-consecration, which subsequent intellectual doubts and difficulties, though often serious, never induced him to abandon, even temporarily. He returned from college to his father, who had now moved to Cincinnati, to take the chair of Systematic Theology in Lane Seminary, and entered there upon his theological studies. The same variety of mood and largeness of sympathy that on the one hand had given breadth, but on the other had prevented discipline, in his college life, followed him into the seminary, where, while he pursued his theological studies, he did successful service as editor of a Cincinnati paper, in which he took occasion to give ardent expression to his anti-slavery views: and at the same time he assumed charge of a Bible-class, in the teaching of which he cleared, if he did not absolutely dissipate, his religious doubts, and settled finally, not only his own personal relation to Jesus Christ as a living friend and helper, but his own mission as a preacher of that Christ as the friend of each individual soul, and so the regenerator of society. In 1837 he began his ministry in the town of Lawrenceburg, Indiana, a small settlement on the Ohio river, which at one time had the ambition to be a rival of Cincinnati, but is now a comparatively insignificant village. The parish was not such a one as young men graduating from the seminary in our time are usually eager for. The church consisted of nineteen women and one man; the pastor acted as sexton, filled and lighted the lamps, swept the church, made the fires, opened the church before prayer-meetings and preaching, and looked it up afterward. His pastorate here was of short duration. In 1839 he was called to a Presbyterian church in Indianapolis, the capital of Indiana. Here he delivered his "Lectures to Young Men," which are still in print, and are a remarkable specimen of the power of graphic rhetoric. In them he depicts, as from a personal and practical knowledge, the dangers that threatened the young men of the capital, where all evil influences quickly gathered. With his peculiar skill in drawing men out, he made the acquaintance of one of the most noted gamblers in the city; from him elicited the secrets and methods of his trade, and utilized the knowledge in one of his Sunday evening lectures. His church was crowded, and among his most eager listeners were members of the Legislature, when it was in session. His library was small, and his income meager, but he made himself felt, not only in the city but throughout the State, through which he frequently made journeys, for the purpose of

conducting revival services, then far more common than in our time. He was wont to preach daily for weeks, and even for months at a time; and once this daily preaching lasted through eighteen consecutive months without the exception of a single day. For recreation he took to the study of horticulture, and agriculture, and to writing on those topics for the "Indiana Journal," the agricultural department of which he for a time edited.

In 1847 he accepted a call to Plymouth Congregational church then just organized in Brooklyn, N. Y., on the Heights. His first sermon was delivered on Sunday, Oct. 10, 1847, and contained an exposition of his views with regard to slavery, war, temperance, and other moral reforms, as well as in regard to theology, which in his thought and experience centered wholly about Christ as the revelation and disclosure of the true character of God. In the nearly forty years' pastorate in this church, which made up the rest of Mr. Beecher's life, he never varied from the platform of principles laid down in that opening sermon, except by broadening and extending it. Under his pastorate the church grew steadily both in numbers and in influence; it now contains, in round numbers, twenty-four hundred members. It has a creed, adopted in 1848, which is strictly evangelical; but since 1870 persons uniting with the church are not required to assent to this creed; they simply assent to a covenant of consecration to the service of God, and to acceptance of his Word as the rule of their life. While the additions to the church have been for the most part steady and gradual rather than intermittent and extraordinary, its life has been characterized by some notable revivals of religion; in one of which (1858) three hundred and thirty-five persons made profession of their faith. Except in the summer vacations, and four visits to Europe, Mr. Beecher was rarely absent from his pulpit, even for a single service, for he rarely exchanged; the church throughout the period of his ministry was always crowded, both morning and evening, and with two distinct congregations; for the pastor urged his people to remain away in the evening, and leave their pews vacant for strangers. The original church-building was destroyed by fire in 1849, and the present structure was erected in its place, with accommodations for about twenty-eight hundred persons, and with lecture-room, Sunday-school room, social parlors, and kitchen attached.

While Mr. Beecher's great work was that of a preacher, it was by no means confined to preaching. He began editorial work in Cincinnati, before he was licensed to preach, and retained an interest in journalism in some form throughout the greater part of his life. He was connected with Drs. Richard S. Storrs, Leonard Bacon, and Joseph P. Thompson in the New York "Independent," in the stormy anti-slavery times out of which it was born. He subsequently withdrew from the "Independent," and founded the "Christian Union," with which he remained connected as editor-in-chief, until 1881, when the pressure of other public duties and an increasing disinclination to the slow process of the pen led him to withdraw, and devote his energies exclusively to the pulpit and the platform. The catholicity, that in its birth, he imparted to the "Christian Union," was then wholly unknown in religious journalism. It was supposed to be necessary, to have a special church constituency behind each religious organ. Even the great reviews represented each a religious school, and such monthly symposia as the "Nineteenth Century," and the "Contemporary," in which atheists and Roman Catholic churchmen sit down at the same table, were not dreamed of in the public mind.

Mr. Beecher's work as a moral reformer and political instructor has been even more prominent than his work as either a theological thinker or a preacher. Living in the most exciting period of American history, he threw himself with ardor into the anti-slavery conflict, and from the day of his first occupancy of Plymouth pulpit took a front rank on a platform that abounded with orators, and in an epoch that evoked oratory such as has been heard in America at no other time in American history. No other single voice did more than his to arouse the North against the encroachments of the slave power, and the various devices under which its campaign was carried on. Against the abolition of the Missouri compromise, against "squatter sovereignty," against the fugitive slave law and the compromise measures of which it was a part, against the doctrine of secession and all yielding to it, against slavery itself, from which all these proceeded, his voice was heard in eloquent, indignant, continuous protest in pulpit and press and on the platform. Yet in this indignation, he never lost mental balance or a certain moral composure and self-restraint. Believing with the abolitionists that slavery was a crime against humanity and against God, he yet never joined them in either personal execration of the slaveholder or in condemnation of the Constitution or the union of the States, which that Constitution cemented and secured. He took an active part in several of the great presidential elections. In that in which Mr. Lincoln was elected for the second time (1864) he took an active part upon the stump, and his voice exerted a powerful influence in securing the election of Mr. Cleveland in the presidential canvass of 1884. But by far the most remarkable of his political addresses were those delivered by him in Great Britain in 1863 — in Manchester, Glasgow, Liverpool, and London, each address distinct, and prepared with special reference to the audience there gathered. The great danger to the national cause in our civil war was from intervention of European powers, England, especially. To these four addresses, more than to any

other one cause, America owes it that the public sentiment of the common people in England was changed from one of apathy or hostility to one of sympathy ; and it is not too much to say that Mr. Beecher, by at once instructing and giving voice to the silent moral sentiment of the democracy of Great Britain, not only prevented all danger of intervention, but cemented an alliance between England and America which has gained in strength from that day to this. Subsequent to the civil war and the consequent recession of the great moral issues, Mr. Beecher added to the work of the pulpit that of a popular lecturer; always, however, speaking on serious subjects, and for a serious purpose. His lecture agent is reported as saying, that, as the result of fourteen years of lecturing, he was paid $240,-000 over and above his traveling expenses, an indication not indeed of his moral power as an orator, but of his popularity.

A man so active, so intense, and so outspoken, in times of heated debate, could not but make many and bitter enemies. Throughout his half-century of public life Mr. Beecher was a target of innumerable attacks from men who either from self-interest feared, or from conservative considerations dreaded, the effect of his teaching. Of these attacks one only cast any shadow upon his name. He was accused of immoral relations with the wife of one of his church-members. The accusation at first was allowed to drift into the public press by piecemeal, but rumor at length resulted in definite charges, and finally in a public trial, in which the only evidence offered against him was that of alleged confessions, which he, under oath, explicitly denied, and of letters that were ambiguous in their meaning, to which he, under oath, gave an innocent construction. The jury disagreed ; standing nine for Mr. Beecher, against one for the plaintiff, while two voted variously on different ballots. This suit was never tried again ; a second suit involving the same issues was brought, but when pushed to trial by Mr. Beecher's counsel, was discontinued, the plaintiff paying all costs. The largest Congregational council ever convened, which included representative men from all sections of the country, and all schools of thought, after a week spent in thorough scrutinizing inquiry, in the course of which Mr. Beecher was himself submitted to a searching cross-fire of questions from the members of the council in an open session, extended to him, without a dissenting voice, the Christian fellowship and sympathy of the churches, and expressed the confidence of the entire council in his integrity. What is known as the great scandal has already drifted with other scandals into the past, and in the future will be no more remembered against the memory of Mr. Beecher than the somewhat analogous episode in the history of John Wesley.

In the spring of 1887, Mr. Beecher was

laboring with exceptional vigor even for himself, adding to his preaching the labors of literary work in the completion of his long-delayed "Life of Christ," which he purposed to follow with an autobiography. On the 2d of March he experienced what at first appeared to be a severe bilious attack, but proved to be apoplexy, under the effects of which he fell into a deep sleep, and so painlessly passed away, dying on Tuesday morning March 8, at half-past nine o'clock in the morning, without a struggle. His wife, three sons, and one daughter survive him. No death ever produced more wide-spread expressions of sorrow throughout the American nation. In pulpits representing every school of thought sermons on his career and character were delivered; in all sorts of organizations, religious and secular, resolutions to his memory were passed; in every kind of journal, from "Turf and Field," to the distinctively religious organs, there was some recognition of his services to this generation. The public exercises held in Plymouth Church the Sunday evening after his death, in which Unitarian, Presbyterian, Lutheran, Swedenborgian, Universalist, Methodist, Baptist, Jewish rabbi, Reformed Dutch, Episcopalian, Congregationalist, Roman Catholic, all took part, were typical of the universality of respect expressed throughout the country, transcending all bonds of sect and party.

Mr. Beecher's genius was distinctively that of an orator. He showed no power in executive or administrative functions. As an editor, he shaped and inspired the journals with which he was connected, but never administered them; as a preacher and pastor he filled his audience with his never-failing enthusiasm, but did not attempt to allot to them individual work; as a public reformer, he touched the hearts and consciences of the nation, but took no part in the administration of either political, moral, or missionary organizations. But as a preacher, whether measured by the power of his utterances, or by the variety of his pulpit themes, he was certainly without a peer in the American pulpit, and probably without a superior in the history of the Christian Church. He was an omnivorous reader. Whatever interested humanity interested him. His library of twenty-five hundred or three thousand volumes embraced representatives of every phase of literature, from technical treatises on medicine, theology, and the various arts, to rare editions of the best English classics; but he was a reader rather than a scholar, and on doubtful and debated points, was accustomed to take as conclusive the opinions of experts. At the same time, he familiarized himself with the great principles involved in the public discussions in which he took a part; and during the anti-slavery discussions "Kent's Commentaries," and "Curtis on the Constitution," stood side by side with the commentaries of Meyer and Alford on his library

shelves. Theologically he belonged to that broad school which is represented in England by the names of Erskine, Maurice, Robertson, Stanley. The truths on which he laid the greatest emphasis were, that God is the father of the whole human race; that he is manifested historically in the person of Jesus Christ; that he is immanent in the hearts and lives of all who will receive him; that the Bible is a record of an inspiration which has been by no means confined either to the epochs or to the people with which it deals; and that, under the direct and immediate influence of the spirit of God, the human race has from the beginning made, and still is making, steady progress toward that consummation of liberty and life, which is the kingdom of God, and which when God's purposes are accomplished will embrace the whole sentient universe. Several biographies have been given to the public since Mr. Beecher's death; the two that possess the largest measure of authority are one, the materials for which were gathered by the Rev. S. B. Halliday, the pastoral helper of Plymouth Church, which was published with Mr. Beecher's sanction during his lifetime; and one now in course of preparation, prepared by his widow, his son William C. Beecher, and his son-in-law, the Rev. Samuel Scoville, which will contain a large amount of autobiographical material gathered from his letters and his various addresses.

Mr Beecher's publications include: "Lectures to Young Men on Various Important Subjects" (Indianapolis, 1844, revised edition, New York, 1850); "Star Papers; or, Experiences of Art and Nature" (1855); "New Star Papers; or Views and Experiences of Religious Subjects" (1858); "Freedom and War: Discourses suggested by the Times" (Boston, 1863); "Eyes and Ears" (1864); "Aids to Prayer" (New York, 1864); "Norwood; or, Village Life in New England" (1867); "Overture of Angels" (1869), being an introductory installment of "Life of Jesus the Christ: Earlier Scenes" (1871); "Lecture-Room Talks: A Series of Familiar Discourses on Themes of Christian Experience" (1870); "Yale Lectures on Preaching" (3 volumes, 1872-'74); "A Summer Parish: Sermons and Morning Services of Prayer" (1874); "Evolution and Religion" (1885); Also, numerous addresses and separate sermons, such as "Army of the Republic" (1878); "The Strike and its Lessons" (1878); "Doctrinal Beliefs and Unbeliefs" (1882); "Commemorative Discourse on Wendell Phillips" (1884); "A Circuit of the Continent" (1884); and "Letter to the Soldiers and Sailors" (1866, reprinted with introduction, 1884). He has edited "Plymouth Collection of Hymns and Tunes" (New York, 1855), and "Revival Hymns" (Boston, 1858). Numerous compilations of his utterances have been prepared, among which are: "Life Thoughts," by Edna Dean Proctor (New York, 1859); "Notes from Plymouth Pulpit," by

Augusta Moore, (1859); "Pulpit Pungencies" (1866); "Royal Truths" (Boston, 1866), reprinted from a series of extracts prepared in England without his knowledge; "Prayers from Plymouth Pulpit" (New York, 1867); "Sermons by Henry Ward Beecher: Selected from Published and Unpublished Discourses," edited by Lyman Abbott (2 volumes, 1868); "Morning and Evening Devotional Exercises," edited by Lyman Abbott (1870); and "Comforting Thoughts" (1884), by Irene Ovington.

BELGIUM, a constitutional monarchy in Western Europe. The Legislature is composed of a Senate and a House of Representatives. The Chambers meet annually in November, and sit for at least forty days. The members of both Chambers are elected under a property qualification, which excludes twelve thirteenths of the citizens from the voting franchise. The House is composed of 138 members, elected for four years; the Senate of half that number, elected for eight years. The present ministry was appointed on Oct. 26, 1884, and is composed as follows: President of the Council and Minister of Finance, A. Beernaert; Minister of Justice, J. Devolder; Minister of the Interior and of Instruction, J. Thonissen; Minister of War, Gen. C. Pontus; Minister of Railways, Posts, and Telegraphs, J. H. P. Vandenpeereboom; Minister of Foreign Affairs, Prince de Chimay; Minister of Agriculture, Industry, and Public Works, Chevalier A. de Moreau.

Area and Population.—The area of the kingdom is 11,373 square miles. The population on Dec. 31, 1885, was estimated at 5,853,278 persons, of whom 2,923,902 were males and 2,929,376 females. The population of the principal cities at that date was as follows: Brussels, with suburbs, 416,659; Antwerp, 198,174; Ghent, 143,242; Liége, 135,371. The number of births in 1885 was 175,048; of deaths, 117,775; of marriages, 39,910; increase of population, 57,268. The net immigration during the year was 5,075.

The Army.—The army is recruited by conscription and voluntary enlistment. Every Belgian of the age of twenty is liable to service, but substitution is allowed. The legal period of service is eight years, but the men are not usually required to serve more than a third of that time. The peace effective provided for in the budget of 1887 is as follows:

DESCRIPTION OF TROOPS.	Officers.	Men.	Total.
Infantry	1,888	28,611	30,499
Cavalry	868	5,090	6,048
Artillery	509	7,861	8,370
Engineers	89	1,890	1,479
Administration troops	74	890	894
Total	2,928	44,362	47,290

The war strength of the army is 103,860 officers and men, 13,800 horses, and 240 guns. There is besides a civic guard, which in 1885 numbered 84,597 men, and the gendarmerie, consisting of 2,084 men with 1,379 horses.

Fortification of the Valley of the Meuse.—During the war panic in the early part of 1887, when it seemed probable that war would break out before long between France and Germany, the old question of frontier fortifications became an urgent one. Strong hints were received from England, when the sentiments of that country were probed in regard to defending the neutrality of Belgium, that the Belgians could not look for military assistance from that quarter, notwithstanding the international guarantee of the treaty of 1839. The ministry determined on fortifying the Meuse valley and increasing the army. A committee of the Chamber found Gens. Brialmont, Inspector-General of Fortresses, Nicaisse, Inspector-General of Artillery, Wouvermans, in charge of the works at Antwerp, Vandersmissen, Commander of the First Military Circumscription, and nine other general officers who were consulted, all in favor of a first line of fortifications in the valley of the Meuse. The Catholic majority opposed augmenting the army by the introduction of universal obligatory military service. Military authorities were found who asserted that the army was sufficiently numerous to man the new forts, proposed in the plan of Gen. Brialmont, and the central citadel at Antwerp with its chain of outlying forts, and still leave a considerable force to maneuver in the field. M. Frère-Orban, supported by other military experts, opposed, not the principle, but the expediency of the projected fortifications, and insisted on the importance of maintaining a large field army. The Government did not abandon the idea of a central fortress for the army to fall back upon, as provided in the plan of 1857, but proposed to strengthen the works in and around Antwerp. The fortification project was adopted by the Chamber on June 14 by a vote of 81 to 42. The forts will be able to resist the new explosives. Their cost was originally estimated at 24,000,000 francs, but it will exceed that figure. To arm and provision them will cost 5,500,000 francs. It was also decided to provide the infantry with a new rifle at an expense of 11,000,000 francs; also to complete the outlying defenses of Antwerp, consisting of a line of forts extending to the Nethe River on one side and to the Senne on the other, which will be a work of four years. The Meuse fortifications were begun, under the direction of Col. Kebers, on August 15, but are hardly expected to be in condition for effective defensive operations before the summer of 1889. Six large and six small forts are to be built at Liége, and five large and four small ones at Namur, while Huy is to be made a fortified post. The plan for the disposition of the available military forces is as follows: army of campaign, 67,782 men; Antwerp garrison, with a flying column 12,000 strong, 35,785; at Termonde, 4,796; at Diest, 2,594; at Liége, 6,997; at Namur, 5,124; at Huy, 541; depot troops and territorial gendarmerie, 5,422; total, 129,191 men. The ministry claim that they can mobilize 100,000 troops in the first

D. Appleton & Co.

line and a reserve of 30,000, while the opposition leader asserts that a mobilization would not produce more than 80,000 men. Of 26 bridges across the Meuse only seven remain unprotected by the new fortifications; and of 19 railroads only three, and two of these lead from Holland. With the protection of the *têtes-de-pont* of Liége and Namur, the Belgians expect to be able to reach without danger any point where an invading army should attempt to cross the river, and resist the passage or force the invaders to detach large forces and delay their march until troops could arrive from France or Germany.

Commerce.—The general commerce in 1884 amounted to 5,450,200,000 francs. The special commerce consisted of 1,425,700,000 francs of imports and 1,387,500,000 francs of exports. The chief articles of import were breadstuffs of the value of 275,007,000 francs; wool and woolens, 101,479,000 francs; metals and minerals, 99,636,000 francs; textile fabrics, 90,149,000 francs; hides and skins, 73,693,000 francs; live animals, 63,118,000 francs; oil-seeds, 47,666,000 francs; cotton, 52,743,000 francs; timber, 45,307,000 francs; coffee and sugar, 31,583,000 francs; chemicals, 38,076,000 francs; butter, 21,597,000 francs; flax and hemp, 16,227,000 francs. The chief exports were yarns, valued at 131,962,000 francs; breadstuffs, 105,157,000 francs; machinery, 80,353,000 francs; stones, 98,889,000 francs; coal, 76,581,000 francs; wool, 76,481,000 francs; textiles, 70,398,000 francs; hides, 63,368,000 francs; iron, 50,050,000 francs; glass, 48,406,000 francs; zinc, 41,022,000 francs.

France leads in the import trade with 276,858,000 francs, the Netherlands coming next with 187,530,000, and then Germany with 185,423,000, Great Britain with 184,856,000, the United States with 160,673,000, and Russia with 123,873,000 francs. Of the exports 411,964,000 francs went to France. 252,142,000 to Great Britain, 286,240,000 to Germany, 176,205,000 to the Netherlands, and 89,559,000 francs, the next largest amount, to the United States.

Railroads, Posts, and Telegraphs.—The railroads of Belgium have a total length of 4,410 kilometres, or 2,758 miles. There are 3,166 kilometres worked by the state and 1,244 kilometres by companies. The receipts of the state lines in 1885 were 119,772,557 francs, the expenses 70,097,356 francs; the receipts of the companies' lines 37,229,787 francs, the expenses 20,333,582 francs. The capital expended on the state lines up to 1886 was 929,697,462 francs, besides annuities of the capital value of 319,798,631 francs for the purchase of lines already constructed.

The post-office in 1885 transmitted 91,498,150 private letters, 13,917,560 official letters, 26,539,334 postal-cards, 51,473,000 circulars, etc., and 103,559,000 journals. The revenue amounted to 14,393,081 francs and the expenses to 8,609,871 francs.

The length of telegraph lines in 1885 was 3,800 miles, with 17,713 miles of wires; the number of dispatches, 6,807,772; the receipts, 2,666,736 francs; the expenditures, 3,587,659.

Navigation.—Belgium had on Jan. 1, 1885, a commercial navy numbering 64 vessels, of 80,592 tons, including 51 steamers, of 74,667 tons. There were 324 vessels, of 11,474 tons, employed in the fisheries. The aggregate tonnage of vessels entered at Belgian ports during 1884 was 4,072,987, and the total tonnage cleared 4,060,612.

Revenue and Expenditure.—The ordinary receipts of the treasury according to the budget estimates for 1886-'87 amount to 319,625,109 francs, of which 118,897,000 francs represent the railroad receipts, 39,128,000 francs the excise duties, 25,507,100 francs the customs duties, 28,860,000 francs the registration fees, 23,699,700 francs the land-taxes, 19,320,000 francs the succession duties, and 19,100,000 francs the personal taxes. The total ordinary expenditure was estimated at 316,663,411 francs, 102,582,547 francs being the interest on the public debt, 87,245,471 francs the expenses of the railways, posts, and telegraphs, 45,624,100 francs the military budget, and 22,005,421 francs the appropriation for public instruction, etc. The total revenue for 1887-'88 is estimated at 313,661,559, and the expenditure at 307,743,123 francs.

The public debt in 1887 amounted to 1,874,510,824 francs, besides annuities requiring the payment of 12,243,000 francs. The debt was mainly contracted for public works, and large as it is, representing a burden of $75 *per capita*, the revenue from the railroads alone is more than sufficient to pay the interest.

Cattle Duties.—The Clerical party brought forward in the Chamber a long contemplated protectionist measure imposing high duties on foreign cattle and meat. The Premier himself took strong grounds against the bill. While it was under discussion the price of meat rose 30 per cent. in the retail market. Although meat is too dear a luxury for most Belgian workingmen, the proposed law produced a ferment throughout the masses of the people, and when disturbances resulted, the Premier proposed the adjournment of the debate, on the ground that it would be improper to reject the bill as a concession to threats and outrages. The majority were not influenced by the popular excitement, and after adopting an amendment exempting cattle sent through Belgium for re-exportation, carried the bill on May 10 by a vote of 69 to 54, the Premier and the Minister of Railways voting with the minority against their own party. The measure increases the duties on cattle, sheep, and all fresh meat fifty or sixty per cent. The Senate passed it on June 1 by a vote of 36 to 23, after a declaration of the Minister of Agriculture that the ministry would demand the repeal of the duties if any considerable rise in the price of meat resulted. The Chambers also increased the import duty on vinegar, and abolished the stamp-tax on insurance policies.

Labor Strikes.—The vote of the Chamber was the signal for strikes among the workmen all over the country, which had for their object the redress of political grievances. By quitting work the laboring-class not only intended an imposing political demonstration, but expected to force their employers to join them in their demands. Chief among these was universal suffrage, or a wide extension of the franchise. This reform they wished to have immediately accomplished by the dissolution of the Chambers and the convocation of a Constituent Assembly. Another urgent demand was a general amnesty for all who were convicted for offenses connected with the labor disturbances of the year before. The abolition of substitution in the army was also desired, and an income tax instead of duties on consumption, the removal of the high property qualification for the Senate and other reforms were urged. The strikes began in the coalmines, and spread to the metal-workers of Louvain, Centre, Brussels, and other places, the carpenters, tailors, painters, and other mechanics of Brussels, the quarrymen at Tournai, and the iron-workers in the large foundries of the Seraing, Charleroi, and other districts. Collisions with the gendarmes occurred at La Croyère, where two miners were killed and several wounded; La Louvière, where dynamite was used by the strikers in an attempt to blow up a *café*, and against workmen who would not join them; and Brussels, where dynamite outrages occurred, and where several policemen and rioters were wounded. Later severe collisions between troops and strikers occurred in Ghent, and dynamite outrages were perpetrated in the Centre district and elsewhere. Many agitators, including a French anarchist named Jahn, were arrested. Troops were stationed at Seraing and other places, and two classes of reserves were called out. At Morlanwelz the coal-mine proprietors agreed to unite with their workmen in demanding the adjournment of the cattle-tax project by the Senate, the pardon of the convicted rioters of 1886, and the establishment of councils of conciliation and a laborer's benefit fund. French authorities closed the frontier within the Department of the Nord, and arrested and conducted to Paris the Belgian socialist leader, de Fuisseaux. Fauviaux, a noted socialist, was arrested at Quaregnon, and a leader named Loor in the mining districts. After two or three weeks the strikes subsided, and by the 1st of June nearly all had returned to work.

The Progressist and Radical associations in a congress at Brussels on May 29 adopted a programme embodying modification of the senatorial tax qualification, lay education, separation of Church and State, equal military burdens, an income-tax instead of taxes on consumption, responsibility of employers for accidents, councils of arbitration, professional syndicates,

an invalid fund for workmen, the democratic organization of credit, equality of the French and Flemish languages, and the right of voting for all who can read and write. In July the Chamber voted down a proposal for obligatory military service, upon which the Opposition moved a revision of the Constitution for the extension of the electoral franchise. The proposal, which is the third one of the kind since the Constitution was framed, was rejected by 83 votes against 33, all the Liberals voting for it, and all the Clericals in the negative.

Labor Legislation.—A new law for the suppression of drunkenness prescribes the punishment of fine and imprisonment for persons found drunk on the streets and for liquor-sellers who furnish drink to intoxicated persons or to children, and abolishes the right to recover debts incurred in a liquor-shop. An act regulating the payment of workmen's wages provides that two fifths of the pay of workingmen and of clerks' salaries, not exceeding 1,200 francs, are inalienable, and one fifth is exempt from seizure by legal process. The Chamber passed a bill, introduced by M. Frère-Orban, instituting councils of industry for the reconciliation of the interests of employers and laborers in cases of conflict. The truck system was abolished by a bill providing for the payment of wages in cash.

Fishery Riots.—Belgian fishermen have for years carried on a warfare against the English steam-trawlers by cutting their nets with grapnels. Finding that their better-equipped competitors were ousting them from their own market, they felt aggrieved because, while foreign fishermen have free access to the Belgian markets, they themselves must pay heavy duties in France, and are excluded from the London market by a combination of middlemen. A British cruiser which was stationed on the fishing-grounds to protect the English boats from piratic outrages was unable to capture the users of the submarine cutting-apparatus; but evidence was produced before Belgian tribunals on which some of the misdemeanants were convicted and fined, a result which further inflamed the minds of the fishing population. The British Government subsequently increased the naval force in the North Sea to five steamers and four sailing cruisers. On August 23, when the crew of three English smacks were landing their cargoes at Ostend a crowd gathered, destroyed a part of the fish, and broke the windows of a proprietor of English fishing-boats. The gendarmerie interfered, and were beaten off, but came again in greater force, and charged the rioters with their bayonets, wounding many of them and killing three. The civic guards were called out, but during the next day fishermen attacked some English smacks in row-boats, and would not leave them in obedience to a formal summons, whereupon the artillery fired, killing two and fatally injuring three. The women took an active part in the disturbances, and joined in attacks upon porters that were handling English fish.

BIBLE SOCIETIES.—The earliest society for the circulation of the Bible appears to have been the Canstein Bible Society, which was founded at Halle in 1710, by Karl Hillebrand, Marquis of Canstein. The Naval and Military Bible Society existed in London in 1787, for the purpose of furnishing the Scriptures to the navy and army of Great Britain. The Society for the Promotion of Christian Knowledge in London, in 1787, published several thousand copies of the Bible for distribution. A French Bible Society was instituted in London in 1792. The British and Foreign Bible Society was formed in 1804, with the purpose, as declared in its constitution, of adding its endeavors to those employed by other societies for circulating the Scriptures through the British dominions, and also of extending its influence to other countries, "whether Christian, Mohammedan, or Pagan."

American Bible Society.—The first Bible Society in the United States was instituted in Philadelphia, in 1808. The organization of other societies followed, at Hartford, Conn., in 1809, Boston, Mass., New York city, and Princeton, N. J., in the same year, until in 1816, the number of these organizations had risen to between fifty and sixty. The American Bible Society was formed in 1816 by the union of thirty-five of these local institutions, and in the course of the first year of its life added eighty-four societies as auxiliaries. The resolution of organization of this society, expressing the object of the convention at which it was effected, declared that "it is expedient to establish, without delay, a general Bible institution for the circulation of the Holy Scriptures without note or comment." The same provision is embodied in the first article of the constitution of the society, which declares that its "sole object shall be to encourage a wider circulation of the Holy Scriptures, without note or comment." To this, it is added, that "the only copies in the English language to be circulated by this society shall be of the version now in common use." By reason of this provision, the society is not at liberty to circulate the Revised Version of the Scriptures, which has been prepared under the direction of the Convocation of Canterbury. In pursuance of the purpose as further declared, of extending its influence to all countries, whether Christian, Pagan, or Mohammedan, the society publishes versions of the Scriptures in nearly two hundred languages, among which nations and tribes in all quarters of the earth are represented.

The seventy-first annual meeting of the American Bible Society was held in New York city, May 12. The Hon. E. L. Fancher presided. The year's cash receipts of the society for all purposes had been $493,358, of which $18,656 had been given for investment. The cash payments had been $554,490. The receipts were less by $80,552 than in the previous year. The invested, or trust funds, of which only the interest was at the disposal of the board of managers, amounted to $342,750, and had yielded an income of $11,964. The investments available for general purposes amounted to $164,691, and had yielded an income of $11,-246. Twenty-six Bible societies had been organized during the year, and recognized as auxiliaries. Progress was reported upon the translation of the Old Testament into the Ponape language; the Muskokee version of the New Testament, which had been completed; a version of the Psalms in Choctaw, which had been accepted and published; the Japanese version, in which all the books had been translated, but were waiting for a final revision; the translation of the Gospels into Kurdish; the revision of the Modern Syriac Old Testament, and typographical correction of the Ancient Syriac New Testament and Psalms; Spanish and Portuguese versions; and the Mandarin, Colloquial, and Classical or Wenli versions in China. The issues from the press in foreign countries had been very large, and included 68,200 Bibles and portions of the Bible in Turkey—in the Turkish, Armenian, and Arabic languages; 356,400 volumes in China; 1,500 copies of the Proverbs in Siam; 2,800 volumes in Japan; and editions at Honolulu, Bremen, and Dorpat (Russia). The whole number of issues for the year, at home and in foreign countries, had been 1,447,270 copies. The missionary and benevolent work of the society included the employment of colporteurs to carry the Bible into destitute neighborhoods, where it is never likely to be brought by the usual channels of trade, and distribution through benevolent societies, and, in foreign countries, through missionary societies. The work of the general supply of the United States had been continued, but not on a scale so extended as in some previous years. Of the auxiliary societies, 824 had made reports, of which 148 were engaged in the canvass of their fields and had employed 155 paid agents. One hundred and fifty-three colporteurs had sold 83,-478 copies, and given away 24,659 copies. The combined results of the work of the year were represented by the visitation by the society and its auxiliaries of 639,269 families, of which 71,-569 were found without the Scriptures, and 49,903 were supplied; in addition to which, 22,892 individuals were supplied. During the five years in which the work of resupply had been going on, every eighth family visited had been found without a Bible in their home; while nearly 400,000 families had received the book, 150,000 rejected it. The exact numbers were: families visited, 4,468,494; found without the Scriptures, 547,124; supplied, 384,-924; individuals supplied in addition, 217,261. The "Table of Foreign Distribution," gave the following summaries: Number of Bibles, Testaments, and portions printed abroad, 482,168; number purchased abroad, 103,360; number issued abroad, 469,665; number sent abroad,

51,691, making a total foreign circulation of 521,356 copies; cash remittances to foreign lands, $159,986; cash receipts from foreign lands, $41,611; number of agents and colporteurs employed in the distribution of the Scriptures in foreign lands, 410.   The lands in which this work is performed include American and European states, and every country in which Protestant American missionaries labor.

British and Foreign Bible Society.—The eighty-third annual meeting of the British and Foreign Bible Society was held in London, May 4. The Earl of Harrowby presided, and in his address—appropriately to the Queen's Jubilee—gave some comparative statistics respecting the progress of the society during the past fifty years. Fifty years before the income of the society had been £100,000, now it was £225,-000; then it had 2,370 auxiliary societies at home, now 5,800; then 260 auxiliary societies abroad, now 1,500. Fifty years ago the annual issues of publications were 600,000 copies, now they are 8,000,000; then the cheapest Bible cost 2 shillings, now it was only 6d.; then the cheapest New Testament cost 10d., now the cheapest was Lord Shaftesbury's 1d. Testament.   Fifty years ago the Scriptures were published in 136 languages, now in 280. The full income of the society for the year ending March 31, 1887, amounted to £116,764, and the sum received for Scriptures sold, at home and abroad, was £104,888. These sums, with £104 received on a special account, made a total of receipts of £221,754. The expenditures had been £231,776. The issues for the year had been 3,932,678 copies in Bibles, Testaments, and portions of Scripture. The whole number of issues by the society since its beginning had been 112,253,547. The Queen, at the request of Australian auxiliaries, had written a passage of Scripture—"On earth peace, good will toward men," with the royal autograph, to be placed in fac simile in the Testaments of the school-children of the Australian colonies, as a lasting memorial of the Jubilee year. The income of the society for the year had declined by £31,000.

BOLIVIA, an independent republic of South America. (For details relating to area, territorial divisions, population, etc., see "Annual Cyclopædia" for 1883 and 1886.)

Government.—The President of the Republic is Don Gregorio Pacheco. His Cabinet is composed of the following ministers: Foreign Relations, Don Juan Crisóstomo Carrillo, who combines with his office that of Minister of Justice, Public Worship, and Instruction; Finance, Señor Garcia; Interior, Dr. M. M. Dilledina; War, Brigadier-General Don Casto Arguedas.

On April 7 the Bolivian Minister at Washington was recalled, the legation being withdrawn for the present, while the American Minister at La Paz, Hon. William A. Seay, resigned on account of failing health. The Bolivian Consul-General at New York is Don Melchor Abarrio; the Consul at San Francisco,

Don Francisco Herrera, and at New Orleans, Don José P. Macheca; the American Vice-Consul-General at La Paz is Mr. S. Alexander.

Army.—The strength of the regular army is 2,000 men, with eight generals and 1,013 other officers, the annual outlay for the War Department being $2,000,000.

Finances.—The income of the Government in 1886 was $2,964,079, but the outlay exceeded it by $800,000. A concession was granted, near the close of 1886, for a bank at La Paz. The Banco Nacional de Bolivia experienced serious financial distress during the summer of 1887, not being able to pay at sight outstanding notes of its own circulation, even in small amounts. It suspended payment temporarily and telegraphed to Potosi for bar-silver.

Boundary Treaties.—During the autumn of 1886 a preliminary boundary treaty was signed at La Paz by the Peruvian Minister Plenipotentiary and the Bolivian Government, the chief clauses of which were: 1. The present acknowledged limits between the two countries are confirmed, except those southward from Lake Titicaca; 2. The two republics will undertake to negotiate with Chili, if possible, a modification of the treaty of Ancon, so far as it relates to the occupation for ten years of the provinces of Tacna and Arica; 3. Should Chili consent to such modification, Peru and Bolivia are to engage jointly to pay Chili the $10,000,000 indemnity, offering as a security the national revenues of both countries; 4. Peru agrees to cede to Bolivia the two provinces named against payment by the latter to the former of $5,000,000; 5. The war expenses of the war on the Pacific, which Peru advanced to Bolivia, are thereby waived by the former. This latter arrangement did away with the debt contracted by Bolivia in virtue of the Reyes Ortiz-Irigoyen protocol of April 15 and June 17, 1879, in which Bolivia bound herself to pay half of the cost of the war, together with the subsidies that Bolivia received from Peru during the Tarapacá and Tacna campaigns.

On Feb. 16, 1887, a treaty was signed between Bolivia and Paraguay, fixing the limits between the two republics on the one hand, and laying down the basis of an agreement facilitating Bolivian navigation down the Paraguay river to the Atlantic, on the other.

Education.—A college is to be founded in the city of Oruro, the number of students not to be fewer than 50, and the annual amount to be spent for instruction to be $11,180. Don Aniceto Arce undertook in the autumn of 1887 to found at La Paz a college on a grand scale.

The Fugitive Jesuits.—The Jesuits expelled from Peru found their way to La Paz, where they settled comfortably; but a strong opposition to their stay arose during the autumn of 1887, on the strength of a previous decree of expulsion issued in Bolivia by Marshal Sucre.

Railroads.—In November, 1886, Dr. Antonio Quijarro, ex-Minister of State in the Campero administration, returned to La Paz from Buenos

Ayres, whither he had gone in furtherance of the project for a railway from a port of Paraguay river *via* Oruro to the heart of Bolivia.

The Huanchaca Company of Bolivia acquired, in the spring, 1887, the Antofagasta railroad, paying the Nitrate Company $8,000,000 for it. This railroad from Antofagasta into the interior was completed during the summer as far as El Añil, while work was pushed as far as the Poruña mountains near Santa Bárbara.

The La Paz city authorities granted a concession to introduce a system of tramways.

Public Works.—The Committee on Roads and Telegraphs in the Department of La Paz was actively at work in the spring of 1887 to push to completion the Obrajes and Vizcachain bridges and the wagon-road from La Paz to Oruro, ready as far as Licasica.

New Route.—In May, 1886, the President issued a decree for the opening of a new route intended to give Bolivia an outlet toward the Atlantic down the Paraguay and La Plata rivers, so that when completed the time separating Sucre and Santa Cruz in the center of Bolivia from Buenos Ayres shall be reduced to a fortnight. The new route, beginning at Bahia Negra, traverses the northern Chaco of Bolivia to a place called Carumby, where it forks, and one of its branches penetrates to Santa Cruz and Port Higuerones in the Department of Beni, while the other puts in communication Sucre with Potosi, Huanchaca, Tarija, and Cochabamba. From Sucre to Cobija and Antofagasta the distance is 655 miles, and from Sucre to Puerto Pacheco, on the western bank of Paraguay river, the distance is 580 miles. The Atlantic route will be preferable to the Pacific, as the former does away with the long circuit *via* the Straits of Magellan or around Cape Horn, and besides, the Chaco route is destined to link the tributaries of the Amazon to the Rio de la Plata.

Telegraphs.—In November, 1886, it was resolved to lay a telegraph line between Huanchaca and Ascotan, ultimately to be extended to Calama and Antofagasta. Simultaneously telegraphic communication was opened between Camargo and Potosi. In September, 1887, communication was opened between Bolivia and Chili by means of the Huanchaca Company's line. Telephonic communication was opened at La Paz in May, 1887.

Agriculture.—Bolivia produces all the fruits and vegetables of Europe, while the sugar-cane flourishes on the banks of Paraguay river, and cotton in the Department of Santa Cruz. The coffee from Yungas in the Department of La Paz is celebrated for its flavor. Both tobacco and cocoa are raised. The export of coca-leaves is likely to fall off somewhat, since a beginning has been made with shipping crude cocaine instead to consuming countries. Handsome green coca-leaves were becoming scarce in Europe in consequence. In the Department of Beni, where grazing is also successfully carried on and cattle-farming is extensive, the

gathering and preparing of India-rubber has become an important pursuit, no fewer than eighteen establishments being devoted to it. The traveler, Edward R. Heath, who visited that region in 1881, and explored the Beni river to its junction with the Mamoré, reports that India-rubber trees abound on the banks of Beni river from the Madidi to the Madeira, there being from 500 to 1,000 trees to the square league, and at some points as many as 3,000. At some points toward the south the depth of forests containing rubber-trees is from one to three leagues from the river-banks inland. In the summer of 1887 an immense number of rubber-trees was reported to have been discovered beyond the Carabaya valley.

Cinchona-Bark.—Since 1876 quinquina plantations or "quinales" have steadily gained in extent in the eastern regions of the Andes, spreading over half a dozen districts—Yungas, Songo, Mapiri, Guanay, Camata, and Caupolican—there being, by latest accounts, 3,842,000 trees yielding bark in those districts, 3,000,000 of which are in the Mapiri district alone. Adding thereto the new plantations at Challana, the total in bearing may be set down at 4,000,000. Most of the trees are from five to ten years old, and represent in the aggregate an estimated value of $20,000,000. Europe and America are, however, receiving large amounts of quinine-bark from Ceylon, Java, Jamaica, Venezuela, Mexico, and Western Africa, and the value in the world's markets has been drooping of late, as shown by the import into England during the first seven months of 1887, which was 94,743 cwt., worth £455,951, against 87,043 of the value of £505,430 during the corresponding period of 1886, and 69,673 cwt., representing a value of £491,428, in 1885.

Precious Metals.—Bolivia holds the third rank among the silver-producing countries of the world, and its production is believed to be susceptible of a notable increase, so soon as railroads facilitate and cheapen the transportation of machinery and material. But in spite of obstacles in the way of transportation, the mining industry has made steady headway in Bolivia. Even while the war on the Pacific lasted $20,000,000 was invested in new mining enterprises, and all this money was raised in the country.

During the summer of 1887 two Americans, James Lynch and John Araya, discovered rich gold placer-mines on the banks of Cielo Agüiria river, in the Songo district. At the depth of a yard and a half the auriferous sand yields 2·35 grains per 12 quintals of sand. Machinery, etc., was to be conveyed thither to undertake gold-washing on a large scale.

Nitrate.—Extensive deposits of nitrate of soda were discovered in the spring of 1887 at Zapa, by an Italian, who forthwith went to Europe for the formation of a company.

Indian Troubles.—There have been repeated risings of Indians in several localities, at Izozo, San Lorenzo del Secure, and on the banks of the Blanco and Beni rivers. In June a picket-guard sent to the Department of Beni were cut off by them. The soldiers, who had packed their rifles in a cart drawn by Indians, were suddenly attacked and killed, with the exception of a few who reached a small chapel. Here they defended themselves for three days, and finally, when their ammunition was exhausted, endeavored to escape during the night, but were overtaken and clubbed to death. On receiving particulars of this disaster, the prefect sent seven missionaries to the Indians. Of these seven two joined the Indians, four were allowed to return after they had sworn to assist the insurrectionary cause, and the seventh was barbarously murdered. The Government later in the year sent a new prefect to Beni to endeavor to suppress the Indians, who continued in open revolt. Three more tribes joined the movement, and it was apprehended that if the Government did not display greater promptness and energy, all the settlements in Beni would be destroyed.

BRASSEY, Lady ANNIE, an English traveler and author, born in London about 1840, died at sea, Sept. 14, 1887. She was a daughter of John Allnutt, a man well known as a steeplechase rider, from whom she inherited a passion for riding and out-door sports. In 1860 she mar-

LADY ANNIE BRASSEY.

ried Thomas Brassey, who was one of the two sons of Thomas Brassey the railway-builder, and inherited half of his immense fortune. Mr. Brassey was a member of Parliament for Hastings, was knighted in 1881, and in 1886 was raised to the peerage as Baron Brassey. He is a Liberal in politics. For several years he has owned a whole fleet of yachts, which he is able to navigate himself, and he and his wife were fond of making long voyages. Her first printed work was "The Flight of the Meteor," an account of two cruises in the Mediterranean and travels in the East (for private distribution

only). In 1872 she published "A Voyage in the Eothen," which described their visit to the United States and Canada. In 1876–'77 they made a voyage round the world in their yacht "Sunbeam," crossing the Atlantic from the English Channel to the coast of Brazil, thence around South America, passing through the Straits of Magellan, across the Pacific to Japan, China, and India, and home again by way of the Suez Canal and the Mediterranean. Her account of this voyage, published in London in 1878, had an immediate success, was republished in New York, and seemed to bring her to the familiar acquaintance of large numbers of American readers. It has appeared in several editions, including one to be used as a school reader and one priced at sixpence, which had a very large circulation. In 1880 she published "Sunshine and Storm in the East—a cruise to Cyprus and Constantinople," and in 1888 "In the Trades, the Tropics, and the Roaring Forties." In 1885 Mr. Gladstone accompanied the Brasseys in a trip on board one of their yachts to the coast of Norway. The home of the Brasseys is Normanhurst Castle, near Hastings, Sussex, and Lady Brassey was prominent in many charitable undertakings there and in London. A personal friend writes: "Lady Brassey was a woman of extreme energy; there was nothing she disliked more than to have no immediate object of action before her. So long as she was in health she wished to be up and doing something tangible. She was an active member of the St. John's Ambulance Association, and assisted in forming sundry classes or centers thereof. She passed the South Kensington School of Cookery (scullery department and all), and took a first-class certificate therein; she was a Dame of the Order of St. John of Jerusalem in England. Few ladies of the fashionable world get through as much effort in a week as Lady Brassey often incurred in a single day. We have known her spend a day at Normanhurst thus (as a sample): Correct proof-sheets for printer and interview head servants as to orders for the day before breakfast; hunting with the local harriers for three hours, riding straight as a die over the stiff timber fences of Pevensey Marshes; home to a late luncheon; then drive a waggonette to show some visitors the beauties of the neighboring Ashburnham Park; after afternoon tea an overhauling of fancy costumes for an approaching fancy-dress ball; after dinner a rehearsal of some fancy-dress quadrilles with the various young ladies and gentlemen who were to form her party to the said ball on the morrow. Or, as an illustration of a day in the London season: Down to Chatham (or some such port) in the morning to launch a vessel; to the East End in the afternoon to distribute prizes at a training-ship, and to make a speech to the pupils; and in the evening a reception at her own house." Lord and Lady Brassey were on board the "Sunbeam" with their son and their daughters, sailing from Port Darwin, North Australia, for the Cape of Good Hope, when Lady Brassey died of a fever. They were a thousand miles from land, and her body was buried at sea.

BRAZIL. (For details relating to area, territorial divisions, population, etc., see "Annual Cyclopædia" for 1884.)

Government.—The Emperor is Dom Pedro II, born Dec. 2, 1825. The Emperor went to Europe on June 30 for his health, and his daughter, Donna Yzabel, Countess d'Eu, born July 29, 1846, was installed Princess-Regent during his absence. Her Cabinet is composed of the following ministers: President of the Council of Ministers and Minister of Foreign Affairs, Counsellor of State, Senator Baron de Cotegipe; Interior, Senator Baron de Mamoré; Finance, Senator Francisco Belisario Soares de Souza; Justice, Deputy Wallace McDowell; Navy, Deputy Carlos Frederico Castrioto; War, Senator Joaquin Delfino Ribeiro da Luz; Agriculture, Commerce, and Public Works, Rodrigo Augusto da Silva.

The Brazilian Minister at Washington is Baron de Itajubá. The Consul-General of Brazil at New York is Dr. Salvador Mendonça. The American Minister at Rio de Janeiro is Hon. Thomas J. Jarvis; the Consul-General, H. Clay Armstrong.

Finances.—The entire indebtedness of the Government up to March 31, 1887, for the home debt, and up to Dec. 31, 1886, for the foreign debt, was 987,391,610 milreis. Of this amount, 256,951,000 milreis, or £23,552,500, are under the head of gold loans, negotiated in London; 72,209,000 milreis under that of the two internal loans; and 882,608,000 milreis under that of internal consolidated indebtedness in currency, 91,286,000 being besides the floating debt, and 184,355,000 milreis paper money in circulation. The internal consolidated debt consists mainly of five-per-cent. "apolices," or bonds, of which 381,476,000 milreis are in circulation. Of the foreign debt, £6,430,000 represent the loan negotiated in 1886.

According to the report of the Minister of Finance, submitted to Parliament during the summer of 1887, the income during the fiscal year 1885-'86 was 124,328,000 milreis, and the outlay 149,774,000. Until then the budget covered the period from June 30 to July 1; but by the law of Oct. 16, 1886, the financial year is to run from Jan. 1 to Dec. 31. This being the case, 1887 will cover 18 months, and the budget estimate is 202,168,000 milreis revenue and 229,927,000 expenditure.

Army.—The parliamentary vote relating to the army in 1887 maintains its strength at 13,-500 men in time of peace. Should unforeseen events arise it may be increased to 30,000. There are 800 cadets in the various military schools. The army is recruited by voluntary enrolment. Besides a premium, those entering the military service are entitled to 109 square metres of public land.

Postal Service.—During the fiscal year 1885-'86 the receipts, reduced to American money, reached $950,000, against $875,000 in 1884-'85, being an increase of $75,000. The expenses exceeded the previous year by $45,000.

Telegraphs.—In 1887 there were in operation 10,610 kilometres of Government telegraphs, with 18,312 kilometres of wire, the service being done by 171 offices. The service includes 25 kilometres of cable.

Direct cable communication was established in 1887 between Pará and New York by the Pedro Segundo American Telegraph and Cable Company. The company entered into a combination with La Compagnie télégraphique des Antilles, a French corporation, the better to accomplish the objects for which the company was formed. In this manner the exclusive concession was obtained of laying a cable between Cayenne in French Guiana and Brazil, and an exclusive contract for the interchange of business with all the Brazilian land telegraph lines. The French Government guarantees the company a subsidy of $200,000 a year.

Lotteries.—The amount of money invested in lotteries by the people of Brazil in 1886 was $9,140,000, not including the province of Pará, from which returns have not yet been received. Out of this amount, $6,889,000 was paid to holders of lucky tickets, resulting in a loss to the gambling public of $2,251,000. This loss has been sustained almost wholly by the population of Rio de Janeiro, where not only the tickets of lotteries, authorized by the General Government are sold, but also those drawn in the remotest provinces. The concessions to hold lotteries are given for the benefit of public works and charities, but the profits of the *concessionnaires* in the provinces often largely exceed the money accruing to the institutions. Thus, in 1866, the profits made by *concessionnaires* amounted to $1,093,200, out of which the institutions to be benefited received only $670,400. This contrivance has at length provoked interference on the part of the Minister of Finance, who recommends that Parliament pass a law reforming completely the present system of granting lottery concessions.

Commerce.—On June 22, 1887, the Minister of Finance issued the decree giving effect to the new tariff to go into force on the 1st of July. The alterations from the tariff of 1879 are numerous, the valuations of the 1,104 articles having been revised, mostly in the direction of elevation, and the rates of the duties raised on most manufactured articles from 8 to 15 per cent.

The foreign trade movement in Brazil, including specie and bullion, in milreis, was as follows:

	Import.	Export.
1884-'85	178,481,000	226,260,654
1885-'86	197,501,500	194,961,619

and the home trade was, coastwise, import and export combined, as follows: 1884-'85, 137,552,500; 1885-'86, 136,796,600.

The value of exports from Brazil is represented by the following amounts in thousands of milreis:

ARTICLES	FISCAL YEARS.	
	1883-'84.	1884-'85.
Coffee	180,062·7	152,488·5
Sugar	89,131·6	80,022·7
India-rubber	9,459·5	10,628·0
Cotton	19·8	10,944·2
Tobacco	4,767·9	6,759·8
Hides	4,408·2	5,132·8
Cocoa	2,987·7	2,874·9
Brazil-nuts	1,385·4	1,300·8
Gold-dust	1,195·9	1,387·6
Horse-hair	943·8	896·2
Diamonds	1,287·6	643·8
Paraguay tea	884·8	688·5

Coffee shipments from the two leading Brazilian ports, Rio de Janeiro and Santos, were as follows, during the twelve months from July 1 to June 30:

TO—	1886-'87.	1885-'86.
	Bags.	Bags.
Europe	3,110,000	2,926,965
United States	2,648,000	2,924,818
Other countries	185,000	121,681
Total	5,898,000	5,972,862

The sugar and cotton exportation from Pernambuco have been as follows:

YEARS.	Sugar.	Cotton.
	Tons.	Tons.
1884	187,898	9,500
1885	118,959	10,595
1886	106,797	13,234

The export of cotton-seed amounted in 1886 to 2,175 tons. During the first six months of 1887 the export of India-rubber from Pará amounted to 6,331 tons, of which 2,810 tons went to Liverpool, 289 to Havre, and 3,232 to New York. The India-rubber crop of the fiscal year 1886-'87 yielded 13,390 tons, being 390 in excess of the previous fiscal year.

Maté Exportation.—The export of maté, or Paraguay tea, from Brazil, is assuming large proportions. The movement from these provinces was as follows:

FROM—	Kilogrammes.	Value in American money.
Paraná	16,600,000	$1,300,000
Santa Catharina	2,984,954	212,000
Rio Grande do Sul	604,147	48,000
Total	20,189,101	$1,560,000

The annual average export of the preceding three seasons was only 12,440,000 kilogrammes, worth $712,000.

The American trade with Brazil exhibits these figures:

FISCAL YEAR.	From the United States to Brazil.	From Brazil to the United States.
1885	$7,256,085	$45,268,660
1886	6,450,782	41,907,532
1887	8,071,658	52,958,176

Coffee.—In May, 1879, Dr. Martinho Prado bought a coffee-plantation at Ribeirão Preto, in the province of São Paulo, then only having 20,000 coffee-shrubs on it, and there organized free labor. In 1886 and 1887 the same estate produced between 900,000 and 1,600,000 kilogrammes of coffee per annum. The men employed number 1,000, and are for the most part Italians.

Trade-Marks.—During 1886 the "Junta Commercial," of Rio, registered 139 industrial and 72 commercial trade-marks, together 211, of which 126 were entered by Brazilians and 85 by foreigners. Of the latter 28 came from England, 27 from France, 8 from the United States, 4 from Germany, 3 from Italy, 3 from Portugal, and from Switzerland and Holland one each.

Railroads.—On May 1, 1887, there were in operation in Brazil 7,929 kilometres of railway, 1,832 kilometres thereof being the property of the Government. There were 1,631 kilometres building, and additional concessions for 3,656 kilometres had been granted. During the first four months of 1887, 260 kilometres were thrown open to traffic. The Brazilian railroad system is in part the property of the General Government, partially of provinces and partially of Brazilian and English companies, only one company being French. The Minister of Public Works has adopted and submitted to Parliament the plan of his predecessor in office to complete the Brazilian railroad system. As the latter exists at present, most of the lines run from the coast in a westerly direction inland. The Prado plan proposes to fill certain gaps from the north southward, and to use, wherever feasible, the navigable rivers, so that, when the extensions and branch lines shall have been built, there will be communication by rail and water between the northern and southern extremities of the empire.

The five tramway lines of the city of Rio conveyed in 1886 altogether 40,496,000 passengers, being at the rate of 111,000 a day, or about one third of the population of the capital. There are also three suburban lines which, in 1886, conveyed 155,000 passengers.

The apparatus and rolling-stock for an electric tramway is expected at Rio. The trials made with it at Brussels proved entirely successful. Accumulators of the Julien patent are used; the speed will be 18 kilometres an hour, and each car is to convey 50 passengers.

The Princess-Regent, on July 2, opened the exhibition of Brazilian railroads.

Steamer Lines.—The Government subsidizes 14 steamship lines, one of which plies between Rio de Janeiro and New York. The Government aid extended to the 14 lines named involved, in 1886, an expenditure of $719,000.

Lighthouses.—Brazil possessed, early in 1887, 59 lighthouses; one of them inland on the Amazon river. The finest of them is on Raza Island, at the entrance to the Bay of Rio de Janeiro, measuring 96 metres in height, and its light being visible at a distance of 24 miles. It has an electric light.

Emancipation.—The census completed throughout Brazil on March 30, 1887, showed that there are now fewer than 700,000 slaves in the whole empire. On March 31, 1873, 1,580,000 were still registered. Deputy Alfonso Celso consequently introduced, during the summer, a bill for immediate emancipation, the fate of which remains uncertain, there being considerable opposition to its passage among conservatives and slave-holders.

Immigration.—The number of immigrants landed in 1886 at Rio, was 22,286, of the following nationalities:

Italians	11,584	Poles	148
Portuguese	4,287	British subjects	98
Germans	1,718	Other nationalities	464
Spaniards	1,189		
Austrians	644	Total	22,286
Frenchmen	218		

There were 7,439 that remained at Rio permanently, while 14,847 left for the provinces. At the same time 7,503 third-class passengers went abroad, so that the net gain of population by immigration amounted to 16,975.

The Government made a contract for the introduction in 1887 of 5,000 immigrants from Northern Europe at reduced rates of passage from either Hamburg, Bremen, or Antwerp to either Rio or Santos, the maximum passage money for adults to be 60 marks; for children between the ages of 8 and 12, 30 marks; and 15 marks for children between 3 and 8 years. To certain immigrants the Government will grant a free passage. The steamers employed will enjoy all the privileges of mail-steamers.

Penal Settlement.—Brazilian convicts are sent to the island of Fernando de Noronha, in the province of Pernambuco, if condemned to hard labor. Besides the convicts there is a free population consisting of Government officers, soldiers, and their families. There were 3,955 inhabitants on the island in 1887, 1,434 of them being convicts.

Various Industries.—A coal-mine of considerable depth and extent was discovered early in 1887 in the municipality of Santa Clara, province of São Paulo. The chief coal-deposits in Brazil are those of Tubarão, in the province of Santa Catharina, and of the Arroyo dos Ratos, Rio Grande do Sul, the latter producing 6,000 tons a month, and being the property of an English company. Its product is consumed in the province. The company is extracting coal from two shafts and 32 galleries, and employs 100 miners, who, with the aid of powerful machinery, are capable of taking out 250 tons of coal a day. The "briquette" and washing-works are furnished with two steam-engines, of 120 horse-power each, and can turn out 60 tons of washed coal and 70 tons of brick-coal daily. A railroad of 17 kilometres connects the mine with the navigable Jacuhy river. A Brazilian company owns besides a large mine of bituminous peat at Taubaté in Parahyba, said to be very profitable.

There are in the province of Minas-Geraes 110 iron-works, occupying 1,100 workmen; an industry capable of considerable development, in view of the extensive iron-ore deposits in the Espinhaço mountains, estimated to contain 2,000,000,000 cubic metres of ore.

There were in operation in Brazil, in 1887, 62 cotton-spinneries and weaving-factories, with 5,084 horse-power, and 5,712 looms; the number of yards of cotton fabrics turned out being 48,175,000, representing a value of $8,400,000. Fourteen of the concerns were in Minas-Geraes, with a joint capital of $1,600,-000, 13 in São Paulo, 12 in Bahia, 9 in the province of Rio de Janeiro, and 6 in the city of Rio de Janeiro.

There are in operation in Brazil 52 central sugar-houses, 33 of which have the interest on their capital ($10,900,000) guaranteed by the Government. They are distributed very unequally, 22 of them, as follows: Pernambuco, 11; Bahia, 6, and Rio de Janeiro, 5. The guaranteed interest is 6 per cent. in most cases; a few receive 7 per cent. because the capital in each case amounts to $1,200,000.

English capitalists propose building flour-mills in Rio de Janeiro, and, under concessions from the Government, they intend to import wheat from the Argentine Republic free of duty. This would create a competition with American flour now so extensively consumed in the empire.

The province of Rio Grande do Sul has taken the necessary steps to introduce the growing of wheat on a large scale. A hundred families of wheat-growing peasants, procured in Europe, were landed at Pelotas. Ninety years ago wheat was cultivated successfully in the province, but when the rust appeared this branch of culture was abandoned.

The municipality of Itatiba, in the province of São Paulo, produced, in 1887, 160 pipes of wine, or 768 hectolitres, one of the viticulturists alone turning out 550 hectolitres. Viticulture is rapidly on the increase in the locality, giving returns as remunerative as coffee at present high prices, and requiring but half the number of field-hands.

The raising of cattle and breeding of horses is one of the principal pursuits in the province of Rio Grande do Sul. On a single *estancia*, that of the Curral das Pedras, there are 30,000 head of cattle, 4,500 mares, 2,000 stallions, and 3,000 sheep. The *estancia* is divided into seven farms. Vines and European fruits are also cultivated. Only whites and freedmen are employed, the number of hands being 75.

New Plants.—There grows abundantly and spontaneously in the province of Ceará a plant of the *Malva* kind, whose botanical name is *Orena lubata*, hitherto looked upon as a mere weed of no commercial value. It has recently been discovered that, with a very simple treatment, not involving much expense, it can be made to furnish a valuable textile fiber, having properties akin to those of the jute of British

India. European manufacturers have begun to order large quantities of the dried plant, one French firm alone receiving 890 bales of it.

Early in 1887 two valuable new plants were discovered in the municipality of Jaboticabal in the province of São Paulo. One belongs to the family of *Euphorbiaceæ*, and furnishes India-rubber; while the other belongs to the family of *Fraxineleæ*, the resinous secretions from which resemble the Italian manna.

Explorations.—Two Brazilian engineers, Dr. Paulo de Frontin and Dr. Julio Paranaguá, explored during the summer the Rio das Velhas, one of the chief tributaries of the San Francisco river, and its basin. The Rio das Velhas through the greater portion of its course is obstructed by waterfalls and rapids, 200 of which the explorers passed in a canoe during the nine days of their navigation to a point where the Velhas flows into the San Francisco. The object of the trip was to ascertain whether by means of a series of blastings these obstacles could not be removed. In March, 1887, the members of a German scientific exploring expedition arrived at Rio, intending to explore the Xingú river, a tributary of the Amazon. See "Brazil," by C. C. Andrews (New York, 1887).

BUFFALO, OR BISON, EXTERMINATION OF THE. At the conclusion of the civil war in 1865 the range of the bison, or buffalo, as they are more commonly named (*Bos Americanus*). extended from well within the British possessions on the north to the Staked Plains of Texas on the south. They were found as far east as Kansas, and westward to the Pacific slope, and their numbers were estimated at from six to ten million, an estimate which in the light of subsequent statistics does not appear to have been excessive. The general introduction of breech-loading firearms, and the opening of the Union Pacific Railway across the continent in 1869, began the most wantonly wasteful slaughter of valuable wild animals that has ever occurred through human agency. Sportsmen are responsible for but a small portion of this destruction, though they too should bear their share of the blame, since many of them killed merely for the sake of killing. The real exterminators of the bison were the fur-traders, who saw their opportunity of marketing countless hides at small initial outlay. They organized hunts on a large scale. The best hunters on the plains were engaged to kill as many and as rapidly as possible, and with the aid of repeating-rifles the slaughter was carried on during all the months when the hide was in a marketable condition. The hunters were systematically followed up by a corps of men with the necessary tools and wagons, who, with the aid of mules, literally pulled off the skin, which was at once salted and packed for transportation. In this way the skinners and packers could keep up with the hunters, who, mounted on fleet horses, hung upon the flanks of the great herds and kept up a ceaseless fusillade with the best of modern firearms.

The Union Pacific Railway divided the great continental herd of bison into sections, which were thereafter known respectively as the northern and southern herds. The former ranged over Montana, the town of Glendive marking about the center of the range, and the latter sought the Staked Plains of Texas. The completion of the Atchison, Topeka, and Santa Fé, and of the Kansas and Northern Pacific railroads opened the whole buffalo country, and enabled their enemies to attack the prey in flank and rear.

In 1872–'73 the Atchison, Topeka, and Santa Fé road transported 459,463 buffalo-hides, and the Kansas Pacific and Northern Pacific railroads probably transported each as many more —exact figures are lacking—making a total of more than a million and a quarter hides. Mr. T. W. Hornaday, of the Smithsonian Institution, says, that during these early years of the war of extermination, the hunters and packers were so careless that not more than one hide in three was delivered to the railroads. In other words, the total of buffaloes slaughtered numbered 4,000,000. From 1874 onward the hunters took more care with skins, since they were getting scarce, so that every 100 marketed represented only 125 dead buffaloes. Taking the lowest estimate for three years, 1872–'74, based on the hides actually shipped, it is found that the total number of buffaloes killed by the hide-hunters was 3,158,730. To this number must be added those buffaloes killed by the Indians during the same period. This number was about 1,215,000, making, when added to the white hunter's record, a grand total of 4,373,730 buffaloes killed in the Southwest in three years. The remnant of the southern herd fled to that great barren waste known as the Staked Plains, and thither a few hide-hunters followed them, until as late as 1880, when their numbers had decreased so that hunting them for profit ceased entirely.

In 1876 the northern herd greatly exceeded the southern herd alike in numbers and in the extent of its range. The traders of Miles City, Montana, estimated that there were at that time more than 500,000 buffaloes within 150 miles of that place, and that all told the northern herd numbered something like a million head. The Northern Pacific Railroad was opened for traffic eastward from Glendive in 1881. "I am told by the hide-buyers," says Mr. Hornaday, "that in that year it carried 160,000 buffalo-hides out of the country, and an equal number the year following. The number shipped by steamers on the Missouri river is at present unknown. In 1883 the number of hides shipped fell to 25,000 and the catch of the next season amounted to but one car-load of hides, which were shipped from Dickenson, Dakota. In 1885 not a single hide was in the market, and the buyers announced that the end had come."

"The northern herd, then, survived the extinction of the southern herd by about ten years, and its extermination is to-day so nearly complete as to be regarded as an accomplished fact. To-day what remains of the millions of twenty years ago? Two or three little bands of trembling, terror-stricken fugitives, vainly endeavoring to find shelter from blood-thirsty man in the wildest and most desolate country, pursued hither and thither, and shot at by every cow-boy whose glance falls upon them, and to be pursued with increasing vigor and recklessness until the last one falls. As the result of a careful investigation, I am convinced that there are now not more than 200 wild buffaloes alive in the United States territory, outside of Yellowstone Park. Of this number there are, as has been said, about 100 or fewer in the Panhandle of Texas, about 80 more in the country where our collecting was done (near Little Dry, Montana), and perhaps 75 more in the neighborhood of Bear's Paw mountain, Montana. Strange as it may seem, there are still half a dozen head in Southwestern Dakota, and I am told there are a few straggling bison in Clark's Fork region near the National Park. In the latter reservation there are between 100 and 125 head, and they are increasing at the rate of ten per cent. annually."

This statement is no doubt more recent than the report of the Park superintendent cited elsewhere, and it is to be hoped, though not as yet confidently affirmed, that it is the more correct of the two.

In 1886 the Smithsonian Institution awoke to the fact that the bison was nearly extinct, and the National Museum still without specimens. Mr. T. W. Hornaday, one of the most accomplished naturalists and taxidermists of the staff, was directed to organize an expedition which visited the Bad Lands of Montana, near Little Dry, 75 miles north of Miles City, Montana.

While the expedition was on its way toward the hunting-grounds, its members saw thousands of bleaching skeletons scattered over the prairie in every direction. After passing the Red Buttes they were hardly ever out of sight of these white memorials of man's short-sighted rapacity, and at times twenty or more were in sight at once. In one place seventeen skeletons were counted grouped together in a space of not more than two acres. The skeletons were often in a remarkable state of preservation, and eight absolutely perfect ones were secured, bleached to a snowy whiteness. The hunters remained in the Bad Lands till the blizzards of December warned them to retreat, and reached Washington early in 1887 with the fruits of what must be regarded as the last buffalo-hunt. They killed altogether twenty-five animals, but the hide of one of the finest was stolen by hostile Indians. A fine group has been set up in the National Museum at Washington under Mr. Hornaday's superintendence, representing six bison, from a calf of three months old to a magnificent bull nearly six feet high. When

it is remembered that these animals would no doubt have been wantonly shot, and perhaps left for the wolves to devour, their sacrifice to the interests of science is excusable. On its way back the expedition secured fifty-one perfect skulls from among the thousands upon the prairie, for now that the living buffalo is gone, even his bones have acquired a commercial value, and the more accessible portions of the "buffalo range" are stripped of everything that is worth carrying away.

It has been said that an effort is being made to preserve and protect the bison in the Yellowstone National Park. A troop of United States cavalry is permanently quartered there charged with protecting it; but fifty or sixty men, even with the best intentions, must needs find their hands full to guard 3,500 square miles of forest and mountain yearly invaded by tourists, and perpetually subject to the inroads of scarcely less predatory Indians and white marauders.

In his report for 1887, Mr. P. H. Conger, the Park superintendent, says: "A small number of buffaloes still remain in the Park; but after as careful and thorough an investigation as is practicable, I am unable to state their numbers with any approach to accuracy. My impression is that they have heretofore been somewhat over-estimated, and that at the present time they will not exceed one hundred in number. They are divided into three separate herds. One of these ranges between Hellroaring and Slough creeks; in summer well up on these streams in the mountains outside the Park limits, and in the winter, lower down on small tributaries of the Yellowstone, within the Park. If the reports made several years ago can be relied on, this herd has rapidly diminished, and it is doubtful if it now exceeds some twenty or thirty in number. Whether or not this decrease has been due to illegal killing by hunters, or to other causes, I am unable to say, though I do not believe that many have been killed within the past two years. Another herd ranges on Specimen mountain, and the waters of Pelican creek. The herd was seen by reliable parties several times last winter, and was variously estimated at from forty to eighty. A traveler on the Cook City road claimed to have counted fifty-four near the base of Specimen ridge. A scouting party which I sent out during the month of May found but twenty-seven head of this herd, with four young calves. It is possible that the herd at this time was broken up, and that but one portion of it was found. The third herd ranges along the Continental divide, and is much scattered. A band of nine or ten from this herd was seen several times this spring in the vicinity of the Upper Geyser Basin. It will take close observation for several years to determine with any certainty the number of these animals, or whether or not they are diminishing in numbers. It is practically certain that none have been killed within the Park limits within the last two years, and yet there is an equal certainty that the present numbers do not approach those of past estimates."

The Yellowstone Park buffaloes differ from those that formerly abounded on the Great Plains, and even from those known as the mountain buffalo, that ranged in the Colorado parks. It is probable that they are a cross between the two. They are described as somewhat smaller, of lighter color, less curly, and with horns smaller and less spreading. They have smaller shoulder-humps, and larger, darker brisket-wattles. It is said that they are more hardy, fleet, and intelligent than the larger variety of the plains, and their hides are more valuable, being covered with a softer quality of hair.

Besides these wild preserves there are scattered through the country several small private herds which confirm the universal testimony as to the possibility of domestication. In the British possessions an attempt in the same direction is making on a larger scale. In 1879, Mr. S. L. Bedson, warden of the Manitoba penitentiary, at Stony mountain, in that province, foreseeing the approaching extermination of the wild bison, secured a bull and four calves with a view to breeding pure stock as well as crossing with domestic cattle. The increase was so surprisingly rapid, that in a few years he had a considerable herd, and was a prime mover in the organization of "The Northwest Buffalo Breeding Company," having for its object the cultivation of buffalo grade-cattle. Mr. Bedson writes that there is seldom much difficulty in crossing the buffalo with the domestic cow. It has no particular breeding-season, calves being dropped at all times of the year, and with apparent impunity, even in the rigorous climate of Manitoba. Owing to the hereditary traits of the animal it needs but little care, requiring no housing, even in winter; and they forage a great deal of their own food at all times. At the date of writing the herd numbered eighty-two head, all told, of which fifty-two, namely twenty bulls and thirty-two cows—are pure-bred Manitoban buffalo. It is estimated, judging from Mr. Bedson's actual experience, that in five years, with average good fortune, the company will control a herd of near three hundred head.

The flesh of the buffalo is nearly equal to beef in its nutritious and savory qualities. The fresh hide is now worth $35, and there is every probability that a few years of training will make the wild ox of North America a tractable servant of man.

BULGARIA, a principality in Eastern Europe, created into an autonomous province, tributary to and under the suzerainty of the Sultan of Turkey, by the Treaty of Berlin. The legislative powers were committed to a single assembly, called the Sobranje, the members of which are elected directly by universal suffrage, in the proportion of one to every ten thousand of the population.

Eastern Roumelia by the same instrument was made an autonomous province of Turkey, remaining under the direct political and military authority of the Sultan. In the revolution of Sept. 17, 1885, the Governor-General was deposed, and the union of the province within Bulgaria proclaimed. Prince Alexander of Bulgaria immediately placed himself at the head of the revolution, and soon afterward issued a ukase for the assimilation of the civil, military, and judicial systems of the two provinces. A conference of the treaty powers was held in Constantinople toward the close of 1885, and in accordance with their suggestions, the Sultan, on Jan. 31, 1886, appointed Prince Alexander Governor-General of Eastern Roumelia, and issued a firman on April 6, 1886, recognizing a personal union of the provinces under the Prince of Bulgaria. The Mussulman districts of Kirjali and the Roupchous, or Rhodope, were to be receded to the Porte. The same firman provided for the revision of the organic statute by a Turco-Bulgarian commission, which met in Sofia, but did not conclude its labors, owing to the Bulgarian revolution of Aug. 20, 1886. The administrative union of the provinces had already been accomplished. The customs line of Bulgaria was extended to the Turkish frontier. A legislative union was also established by the admission of Roumelian delegates to the Sobranje.

Alexander I, who was elected Prince of Bulgaria by the Constituent Assembly on April 29, 1879, was seized by revolutionists on the night of Aug. 20, 1886, and conveyed across the frontier. He subsequently returned, and formally abdicated on Sept. 7, 1886, having first selected a regency to administer the government pending the election of his successor. The regents, who, in accordance with an amendment of the Constitution made in 1883, were three in number, were Karaveloff, Stambuloff, and Mutkuroff.

Area and Population.—The area of Bulgaria is 24,360 square miles, and its population in 1881 was 2,007,919. Eastern Roumelia has an area of 13,500 square miles, and had in 1885, according to a census taken Jan. 18, over 975,050 inhabitants, of whom 681,734 were Christian Bulgarians, 200,495 Moslem Bulgarians and Turks, 53,028 Greeks, 27,190 Gypsies, 6,982 Jews, 1,865 Armenians, and 3,733 foreigners. Sofia, the capital of the united provinces, had in 1881 a population of 20,501 souls. Philippopolis, the capital of Eastern Roumelia, has 33,442. The Mussulman population of Eastern Roumelia was reduced by the recession of the canton of Kirjali and twenty villages of the Rhodope to 160,000.

Commerce.—The value of imports into Bulgaria in 1884 was 46,351,280 leii, or francs; of exports, 48,867,235 leii. The leading articles of export are wheat and wool. The chief products of Eastern Roumelia are grain, wine, tobacco, wool, hides, timber, a coarse woolen cloth, and woolen braid, which are exported to Turkish countries, and timber, which is exported to Asia Minor. The total value of the imports in 1883 was 54,749,868 piasters, and of the exports, 64,099,964 piasters.

Railroads.—Bulgaria has a line of railroad running from Rustchuk to Varna, a distance of 140 miles. A line, 74 miles in length, is in process of construction from Vakarel to Tsaribrod, to connect with the Turkish system.

Finance.—The Bulgarian budget for 1886 estimated the receipts at 48,000,000 leii, and the expenditure at 35,780,324 leii. The revenue of Eastern Roumelia was reckoned by the European commission of 1879 at 800,000 Turkish pounds per annum, and the tribute to be paid to the Porte was fixed at three tenths of this sum, or 240,000 Turkish pounds. The actual revenue has not exceeded 600,000 Turkish pounds, and the Provincial Assembly in 1882 voted to reduce the tribute to 180,000 Turkish pounds. Since the overthrow of the Eastern Roumelian Government in 1885 no tribute has been paid. The Treaty of Berlin provided that Bulgaria's share in the public debt of Turkey and the annual tribute that she should pay should be fixed by agreement between the signatory powers, but the amounts have not yet been settled upon. The revenue of Eastern Roumelia in the budget of 1885-'86 was estimated at 672,550 Turkish pounds, and the expenditure at 676,650 pounds.

Diplomatic Negotiations.—The Russian Government, after proposing the Prince of Mingrelia as a candidate for the Bulgarian throne, sent a note to the powers complaining that the regency had summoned the Sobranje, contrary to its advice, and, instead of forming a coalition government, had introduced a more radical element. To this the regents replied early in January, 1887, pointing out that a proposition made to Zankoff to form a coalition ministry had been rejected by the counsel of Gen. Kaulbars. A suggestion was made that Russia should enter Bulgaria as the madatory of the powers, and compel the observance of the Treaty of Berlin, but the Czar declined to accept a European commission to intervene in the principality. Russia, before proposing another candidate, demanded the retirement of the regents and their supporters in the government, and the election of a new Sobranje for Bulgaria only. Negotiations on these bases were carried on between Russia, Austria, and the Porte, and between the Porte and Bulgaria. In January, Zankoff went to Constantinople, and submitted to the Grand Vizier the demands of his party, which included the portfolio of Foreign Affairs and the Interior, the appointment of a Russian as Minister of War, the election of the Prince of Mingrelia, a general political amnesty, and the disbandment of the existing army. The regency offered to resign if so advised by all the powers, and all of them except England approved this step. Grekoff and Stoiloff were sent to Constantinople as envoys of the Bulgarian Government, and the Porte discussed with them Zankoff's pro-

gramme, except the propositions for appointing a Russian Minister of War, disbanding the army, and recalling the exiled officers, and the points relating to the immediate resignation of the regency, the summoning of a new Great Sobranje, and the election of the Mingrelian prince to the vacant throne. When the Bulgarian delegates met Zankoff, the latter proposed that the ministerial offices should be divided between the party in power, the adherents of Karaveloff, and the Zankoffists. Finally, after Zankoff had made various impracticable propositions, the Porte, on Feb. 22, accused him of bad faith, and refused to treat with him longer. Dr. Vulkovich, the Bulgarian agent in Constantinople, agreed, on behalf of his Government, that the regency should resign, and a new one be appointed with one Zankoffist member; that a new Cabinet should be constituted, having two Zankoffist members and a Russian Minister of War, but the latter should be responsible to the Assembly, and no Russian officers should enter the Bulgarian army, except in the capacity of instructors; and, finally, that the Sobranje should be dissolved immediately, but on condition that a Great Sobranje should be convoked for the election of a prince within thirty days, and that some other candidate should be presented by the great powers besides the Prince of Mingrelia, and Prince George of Leuchtenberg, who had been more recently suggested for the place by the Russian Government.

Revolutionary Conspiracies.—While the diplomatic discussion was proceeding, a plot was laid for carrying out the Russian plan, as proposed by Zankoff, by means of a military revolution. Col. Nicolaieff, the Minister of War, and Major Popoff, commander of the 1st infantry regiment, received through a merchant named Papasoglou and his wife, offers of large bribes if they would join in the conspiracy. The woman went to Sofia to make the arrangements with Nicolaieff, who pretended to enter into the plot. She was arrested in the latter part of January, and in the judicial examination charged M. de Nelidoff, the Russian ambassador at Constantinople, with being the prime mover in the conspiracy.

After the final rejection of Zankoff's terms, a serious military outbreak occurred at Silistria and Rustchuk. The mutiny was planned from Roumania by Grueff, Bendereff, Dimitrieff, Dikoff, Kavaloff, and other cashiered and exiled officers of the Bulgarian army. The opposition leaders, Karaveloff, Zanoff, and Zankoff, were privy to the plot. At Silistria the revolt was headed by Col. Kristeff, the commander of the garrison.

The Government had taken precautions against a general insurrection of the Zankoffists, which had been planned for the 3d of March, the anniversary of the signing of the Treaty of San Stefano. The rising in Silistria was begun prematurely by Kristeff, on learning that messages from Bendereff had fallen into the hands of the Government. He summoned the troops on Feb. 26, announced that the regents had resigned, and proposed that Zankoff should be proclaimed regent. A part of the garrison marched away, and prepared under Capt. Krivandoff to resist the revolution, while the others followed their commander. In the evening an engagement was fought, in which the disloyal troops were successful. On the following afternoon, after the militia and others of the population had joined the troops who were faithful to the regency, he sallied from the fortress, but was driven back. He then cannonaded the town in order to awe the people, but only exasperated them. On Feb. 29, he marched his force into the town, and while he was away Krivandoff overpowered the guards that were left at the fortress, and took possession of it. Kristeff made an attempt to rouse the population against the Government, and, failing in that, left the town to escape the troops who were rapidly approaching from Rustchuk, Varna, and other places. After vainly seeking to gain adherents among the country population, the leader of the revolt returned, bearing a flag of truce, but was shot while riding through the streets. Several hundred persons were killed during the disturbances. The mutinous soldiers who were not killed fled into Roumania, and were arrested by the authorities of that country and sent to Bucharest.

During the absence of a great part of the Rustchuk garrison, a revolt was raised in that town. The officers who were implicated were in correspondence with Nabokoff, a Russian subject, who was the author of the revolt at Bourgas, and had since lived as a refugee in Constantinople. Two officers named Cardjeff and Panoff, rode through the city proclaiming the Metropolitan Clement as regent. The battalion of engineers stationed there in the night of March 2 attacked the troops of the line who took refuge in the barracks, and were about to surrender, when the militia and townspeople surrounded the mutinous troops. An engagement ensued which lasted from early morning till near evening, when the rebels fled and attempted to cross the Danube in boats, but were compelled by a heavy fire to leave their boats and take refuge on an island, where they were captured. Major Onzounoff and Col. Filoff, the leaders of the insurgents, were severely wounded. The participants were punished with exemplary severity. Numbers escaped into Roumania, where they were sent to Sugovista.

After the suppression of the uprising, Karaveloff, Nikisoroff, Zanoff, and twenty-two other prominent persons were placed under arrest. A court-martial condemned to death sixteen officers and civilians for having been the leaders in the revolt at Rustchuk. Of these nine were shot on March 6, while the sentences of the others were commuted. A captain of engineers named Bolmann, who

was a Russian subject, was handed over to the German consulate. Another court-martial tried the minor conspirators. The private soldiers of the mutinous battalion who were new recruits were pardoned, but 120 of them and 11 non-commissioned officers were sentenced to imprisonment with hard labor. One of the leaders of the insurrection, an editor named Staveneff, had previously supported the regency, and Ouzounoff was formerly a warm adherent of Prince Alexander. Nikisoroff complained that he was maltreated by his jailers, in a letter to the French diplomatic representative. The Bulgarian Government ordered an investigation, and reported that he refused to show any marks of ill-usage. It has, nevertheless, been credibly asserted, that he was severely flogged by a high military officer, and that many politicians of the Zankoffist party were subjected to the same treatment. The French chargé d'affaires at Constantinople joined M. de Nelidoff in protesting to the Grand Vizier against the military executions and the alleged cruel treatment of Karaveloff and other prisoners at Sofia. In a circular to the powers, Russia proposed an inquiry at Sofia, but most of them, including Turkey, declined to interfere in the internal affairs of Bulgaria. On March 12, Karaveloff, Zanoff, and Nikisoroff were released on bail. Shumla, Trn, Plevna, Varna, and other places, were placed under martial law. The Bulgarian Government complained of the supineness of the Roumanian authorities, in allowing the refugees to plan disturbances across the border. After the insurrection had been suppressed, Grueff, Bendereff, and other conspirators, as well as the fugitive insurgents, were arrested, and were subsequently expelled from Roumania, while no Bulgarian refugees were allowed longer to reside near the frontier. The Bulgarian authorities dismissed many officials, cashiered many officers in the army, while others resigned, and by their rigorous measures produced depression and discontent in the country. The leaders of the Opposition were re-arrested, and on April 3, were again admitted to bail, but were still kept under surveillance. Troops were sent to Widdin, Plevna, Vratza, and Tirnova, to disarm the reserves, who showed an insurrectionary spirit, but while those of Tirnova submitted, the reservists of the other districts resisted the order, and at Vratza, the troops sided with the mutineers. Refugees in Bucharest attempted to murder Mantoff, the prefect of Rustchuk, and Capt. Andreff, who had presided over the court-martial. The Roumanian Government, after those events, ordered all Bulgarians who were not domiciled or engaged in business, to leave the country.

Financial Difficulties.—The Zaribrod-Vakarel line was to be completed by Sept. 15, 1887, and for that and other purposes the Government found it necessary to seek a foreign loan. Until the Bulgarian branch of the Turkish junction lines should be completed, the Servian line, which was already finished, could not be opened to Salonica, because the Conférence à Quatre had decided that both railroads were to be opened for traffic simultaneously, in order that neither of them should have the commercial advantage of first getting into operation. When the delegates of the Sobranje visited England, in the latter part of 1886, they opened negotiations with a financial group for a loan of 25,000,000 francs, to be issued at 94, bearing interest at 6 per cent. English capitalists would not take the risk of lending to a Government which Russia refused to recognize, and in May, 1887, signified their final refusal. An Austrian bank offered to lend the sum at 6 per cent. with issue at 90, but this was considered usurious by the Bulgarians, who could have borrowed at 5 per cent. with issue at par before the deposition of Prince Alexander.

Mission of Riza Bey.—The mediatory negotiations of the Porte were transferred to Sofia in order that they might be governed by a better knowledge of the conditions in Bulgaria. Riza Bey, the Turkish commissioner, arrived just before the suppression of the insurrection. He advised the Bulgarian Government to refrain from retaliatory measures in order to preserve the good-will of the powers and avoid further bloodshed. He gave offense to the Government by proposing that an international commission should investigate the charges of cruelty to prisoners. The ministry refused to discuss longer the admission of Zankoffists into the regency and the Cabinet. M. de Nelidoff, in a confidential communication to the Porte, proposed that a Turkish army corps should occupy Eastern Roumelia, but the Turkish Government refused to proceed to such a measure. A proposition to appoint a regent and send a Russian and a Turkish commissioner to Bulgaria was likewise not entertained. Riza Bey's report was favorable to the regency. The Porte on May 21 sent a circular to the powers urging them to nominate one or two candidates for the post of prince, in order to put an end to the crisis. Informal proposals were made by Russia for a simultaneous intervention of the Turks in Eastern Roumelia and of the Russians in Bulgaria, but these overtures were repelled by the Turkish Government. When all efforts failed to induce Russia to abandon her obstructive attitude, or to bring about concerted action of the other powers in opposition to Russia, the Bulgarians were impelled to solve their difficulties by independent action. When the question of the election of a prince arose there were unequivocal manifestations all over the country in favor of the re-election of the Battenberg prince. There was much popular dissatisfaction with the Government, not alone on the part of the Opposition, the members of which had been arrested and grossly mishandled by the police officials during the recent crisis, but even in the Patriotic party. There

was jealousy between Radoslavoff, the Prime Minister and nominal leader of the party in power, and Stambuloff, who, with the support of his colleagues, Mutkuroff and Zukoff, the successor to Karaveloff, actually governed the country. Radoslavoff and Colonel Nicolaieff, the War Minister, were strong partisans of Prince Alexander. The regents toward the end of May decided, with the concurrence of a part of the ministry, on proposing Prince Ferdinand of Saxe-Coburg-Gotha for the throne, but the military party threatened to proclaim Alexander as sovereign, and were only restrained by that prince himself who conjured his friends not to persist in a policy that would bring ruin to Bulgaria. He did not, however, at once renounce his candidature, but proposed that Aleko Pasha or Goltz Pasha should be chosen regent, and thus keep the place open for him. The feeling in favor of his restoration grew stronger, and the army was only appeased by assurances that it was in the end inevitable. Quarrels between the members of the Government and the feverish political condition of the country at last constrained the regency to summon the Great Sobranje.

The Election of a Prince.—The Great Assembly was convoked for July 3. The members of the Government had been in communication with various possible candidates for the throne. The Bulgarian delegates to the courts of Europe had eight months before asked Prince Alexander of Coburg if he would accept, and he then made it conditional on the approval of Russia and Germany. Prince Oscar, of Sweden, was tendered the place in like manner, but by the command of his father declined. Prince Waldemar, of Denmark, was still spoken of, and Aleko Pasha was a candidate. Stambuloff was opposed to the recall of Alexander, and when compelled to yield to the popular sentiment was ready to acquiesce in a formal vote in favor of the late prince, but expected him to decline. Radoslavoff and the Radicals desired that Alexander should be elected, and that a new provisional government, with a single regent, should be formed until the favorable moment arrived for him to return. They had, for the event of his refusal, another candidate in the person of Prince Bernard, of Saxe-Weimar, while the regents had settled on the Coburg Prince. Besides Prince Bernard, Prince Frederick of Hohenzollern and Prince Ferdinand of Schleswig-Holstein-Sonderberg-Glücksberg were mentioned as nominees of Prince Alexander, whose election would not preclude his ultimate return. Stambuloff wrote a firm letter to Alexander, in which he submitted that it was necessary for the country to know what hopes could be built on the prince, who replied that his weak state of health would not permit his immediate acceptance, and that so long as he was opposed by the two most powerful men in Europe, meaning the Czar and Prince Bismarck, his restoration would bring disaster and loss of independence to Bulgaria. The Sobranje convened at Tirnova, the ancient capital, on July 4. The strength of the two factions in the Government was measured by the vote for president, Dr. Tontcheff, a candidate suddenly proposed by Stambuloff, receiving 275 votes, against 74 for the regular nominee of the ministry, and a like number for the candidate of the Opposition. On July 7, Prince Ferdinand of Saxe-Coburg-Gotha was elected Prince of Bulgaria by acclamation. After receiving Ferdinand's conditional acceptance, and choosing a deputation to make the formal tender to the prince-elect, the Sobranje adjourned on July 9.

Change of Ministers.—After the election of a Prince, the quarrel between members of the Cabinet and Stambuloff was brought to an issue by the latter's insisting that Nicolaieff, who objected to the regent's giving direct orders to the army, should resign. The whole Cabinet resigned, and a new one of moderate liberal character was constituted as follows: Stoiloff, President of the Council, Minister of Justice, and Minister of Finance *ad interim* ; Nachevich, Minister of Foreign Affairs ; Dr. Tchomakoff, Minister of Public Instruction ; Dr. Stransky, Minister of the Interior ; Major Petroff, Minister of War. The new Government at once directed that all persons under arrest for political reasons should be released. Dr. Stransky, the leader of the Eastern Roumelian revolution, was, when called into the Cabinet, diplomatic agent at Belgrade. Major Petroff was chief of staff during the Servo-Bulgarian war. Stoiloff and Nachevich were the conservative members of the late Cabinet.

Installation of the Prince.—Prince Ferdinand telegraphed his acceptance of the invitation of the Great Assembly, subject to the approval of the Porte and the great powers. To the deputation of the Sobranje which waited on him at Ebenthal, in Austria, on July 15, he said that he should hasten to Bulgaria if he followed the impulses of his heart, but that treaties must be respected, and he hoped by showing his respect for them to justify the confidence of the Porte, regain the good-will of Russia, to whom Bulgaria owed her emancipation, and secure the approval of the other great powers. He announced his conditional acceptance to the representatives of the powers in Vienna. The Porte sent a circular to the powers asking an expression of their views in regard to Prince Ferdinand's election, and all gave a qualified consent except Russia, which replied that, as the Assembly which elected him was an illegal one the St. Petersburg Cabinet could pay no attention to its acts. The Bulgarian deputies urged Prince Ferdinand to come at once to Tirnova and take the oath of office. He intended first to visit St. Petersburg, and enter Bulgaria if possible with the approval of the Czar, but the Russian Government informed him that his election could not be recognized on any pretext. After waiting till the patience of the Bulgarians was al-

most worn out, and finding the European Governments apathetic, he decided to go to Bulgaria without their consent, but not, perhaps, without secret intimations from controlling quarters. When he started, the St. Petersburg Government addressed a circular to the powers expressing the hope that they would not tolerate this infraction of the Berlin Treaty, and declaring that Russia could not constitute herself the sole guardian of its stipulations, now threatened with final subversion. On arriving at Widdin, August 11, the prince issued a proclamation promising to consecrate his life to the happiness of his dear people. He took the constitutional oath at Tirnova before the Sobranje, assembled in special session, on August 14. The proclamation with which he assumed the Government made no allusion to Russia, or to the suzerain power, or to international treaties, and ended with the words, " Long live Bulgaria, free and independent ! " The ministry resigned their portfolios into his hands, and the Sobranje was prorogued. On arriving at Widdin, Prince Ferdinand sent a telegram to the Sultan presenting his homage. The St. Petersburg Cabinet, in a dispatch to the Porte, formally protested against Prince Ferdinand's action, and Riza Bey was recalled from Sofia, yet diplomatic relations were not broken off, Artin Effendi receiving the nominal appointment of high commissioner to Bulgaria. In answer to a circular of the Porte, England and the other powers in an identical note expressed their sense of the illegality and impropriety of Prince Ferdinand's proceedings. Russia proposed to denounce the Berlin Treaty, and sounded the Turkish Government on the question of the occupation of Bulgaria by Russian and Eastern Roumelia by Ottoman troops. The Turkish occupation of the Balkans, accompanied with a peremptory demand that Prince Ferdinand should quit the country was then discussed ; also the sending of a Russian commissioner to Sofia, Gen. Ernroth being mentioned for the place, accompanied by Artin Effendi, who should act in the same capacity for Turkey. The latter plan was supported by France and Germany, but the Porte, following the counsels of the other powers, declined to take part in such a proceeding. When Prince Ferdinand arrived in Sofia, on August 22, none of the foreign diplomatic agents participated in his reception. Dr. Vulkovich, the Bulgarian political agent at Constantinople, attempted to explain away the declaration of Bulgarian independence contained in the Prince's manifesto. The Turkish Government in a dispatch to Prince Ferdinand informed him that the Porte and the powers considered his conduct illegal. Prince Ferdinand asked permission to go to Constantinople to do homage to the Sultan, but it was refused.

The New Cabinet.—There was much difficulty in the formation of a ministry, but on August 31 one was constituted at last, made up of the following members: Stambuloff, Prime Minister and Minister of the Interior; Dr. Stransky, Minister of Foreign Affairs; Nachevich, Minister of Finance; Mutkuroff, Minister of War; Zivkoff, Minister of Instruction; Stoiloff, Minister of Justice.

BURMAH, formerly the kingdom of Ava, in Farther India, now a province of the British Empire, administered by a Chief Commissioner under the Viceroy of India. Lower Burmah, hitherto known as British Burmah, comprises the provinces of Arakan, Irrawaddy, Tenasserim, and Pegu, the first three of which were conquered in 1824, and the last-named in 1852. Upper Burmah was formerly incorporated in the British Empire by the proclamation of the Viceroy, on Jan. 1, 1886, after the defeat of the King's forces on the Irrawaddy, the capture of the capital, Mandalay, and the deposition of Thebaw, the last King of Ava. The area of Lower Burmah is 87,220 square miles. Its population in 1881 was 8,786,771. Upper Burmah has an area of about 210,000 square miles, and in the neighborhood of 4,000,000 inhabitants.

The Subjugation of Burmah.—Only about 10,000 troops composed the expeditionary force that broke through Thebaw's river-defenses with ease, captured the capital, and led the King into captivity. The cost of the expedition did not exceed $750,000. For a month after the British were seated in Mandalay the country was tranquil, and the conquest was generally regarded with complacency, because it had rid the country of an incompetent and unpopular monarch. The absence of all central authority soon resulted in an increase of village robberies and dakoity. The disbanded soldiery of the King had no way of living except by plunder. The disturbance and devastation of the invasion had reduced many of the villagers to the same necessity. The Alaungpra princes, who had been released from confinement by the British, gathered small armies, and attempted to set up their rule in parts of the country that were not held by British troops, appointing civil governors and collecting taxes. The English civil commissioners, of whom three were left, each with a small military force, at different points on the Irrawaddy below Mandalay, were successful at first in introducing order in their districts and in securing the submission of the local Woons or governors; yet, as soon as the Alaungpra pretenders appeared in the field, the allegiance of the native officials was given to them, the British were everywhere attacked, and the rule of the district officers was circumscribed within the cantonments of their soldiers, who now vied with the Burmese marauders in ravaging the country. At this point the Ming-woon, or central council, was reinstated in authority at Mandalay, and instantly there was a cessation of disorder, but it soon broke out again when the British still delayed appointing a successor to Thebaw, the members of the Ming-woon themselves secretly embracing the cause of one

or the other of the pretenders. The policy of hesitation had the effect of dividing the allegiance of the Burmans between the different aspirants to the throne, each of whom hoped by gaining a large following and establishing his power over a wide district to induce the conquerors to select him for the succession. The abolition of their sacred monarchy, and the subjection to a foreign yoke, did not enter into the conception of the Burmans. When at last British sovereignty was proclaimed, the rival factions were unable to unite under the standard of any one prince, and the English were able to cope with the universal revolt by attacking the leaders in their separate districts, many of them weakened by intestine wars.

In the valley of the Irrawaddy, below Mandalay, a robber chief named Bo-Swe or Boshway, who had long been a source of annoyance to the British on the river and along the frontier, gathered the strongest body of insurgents. By the end of August, 1886, he held the entire country west of the Irrawaddy, except a small strip on the river. The deputy commissioner of the district, Mr. Phayre, was killed in action. East of the Irrawaddy, bands of robbers infested British as well as Upper Burmah. Naval launches on the Sittang river was attacked, villages were plundered, Englishmen killed, and even in the large trading town of Ningyan robberies were committed and houses burned almost under the eyes of the British soldiers. In the fertile and populous region between Yemethen and Mandalay, the Minzaing or Myentsein prince, a brother of Thebaw, unfurled his banner. Not only did the people in this district, which has been called the garden of Burmah, accept the rule of the youthful pretender, and pay him tribute, but insurgent leaders in other parts of the country fought in his name, and he even counted among his adherents members of the central council and the governors of many districts. The chief, Boh-cho, who received from the pretender the title of governor of Pagan, contested with the English deputy-commissioner the control of that district, which had at first been most submissive to the conquerors. He collected revenue from many villages, and burned those that were friendly to the English. A chief named Tokkyan, with a following of 2,000 men, carried his raids into the same district, in which also a marauder named Nga-kway, with a band of 1,500, also levied contributions, and another leader named Aung-din practiced dakoity. In the south of the district an area of 1,000 square miles was held by Waya-byin, a partisan leader, while on its borders hovered the Kanhle prince with 2,500 fighting men. North of Mandalay, in the country between the Chindwin and the Irrawaddy, the brigand Hla-oo held undisputed sway, except in some of the towns, like Mingin, where the captive employés of the Burmah and Bombay Trading Corporation were delivered up to the British by the Woon. In the same region a number of Alongpra princes who fled from Mandalay raised bands of adherents. The Bhamo district in the north was one of the least disturbed, though robberies were committed by wild Kachyens from Katran and by dakoits, who, in November, 1886, attacked the town and set fire to some buildings. The Sawbwa of Woontho, a Shan state west of Bhamo, who had been a loyal vassal of Thebaw, refused to recognize the rule of the British, although they offered to leave undisturbed the privileges he had hitherto enjoyed, and promised not to interfere in the internal administration of the state. The Shans farther north, where mines of jade and amber and India-rubber forests are found, manifested a friendly disposition.

On Oct. 1, 1886, the army of occupation consisted of 1,328 British infantry, 15,684 native infantry, 2,273 native cavalry, and 991 artillery. The measures adopted for the pacification of the country were the establishment of troops at various posts, and the formation of movable columns; the organization of a Burmese and Indian police; the establishment of armed steamers on the rivers; amnesty to all who would cease hostility and the general disarmament of the people; division of the country into administrative districts; freedom of trade and of religion; codification of the laws; moderate taxation; and improvement of communication, especially the extension of the railroad from Toungoo to Mandalay. For purposes of government, Upper Burmah was cut up into four main divisions, and subdivided into seventeen districts. The Indian code was extended to the conquered country, but with certain important limitations. The deputy-commissioners were given juridical powers, and could sentence criminals to imprisonment, and even to death, subject to an appeal to the commissioners. In most cases those who were caught in acts of hostility were shot as dakoits by their captors, without trial. The fierce Mohammedan troops struck terror into the hearts of the Burmans by their cruelty, not less than by their prowess. The so-called native police was composed of Sikhs and Ghoorkas, who cast off all restraints of discipline, and plundered at will. The fanatical Mohammedans, when they entered the monasteries, were accustomed to destroy the statues of Buddha. The climate was scarcely less trying to the Indian than to the European troops. During the year ending Oct. 31, 1886, 930 men died, not reckoning 91 who were killed, and 2,032 were taken sick.

When Sir Frederick Roberts, commander-in-chief of the Indian army, assumed command of the forces in Burmah in October, 1886, after the death of Sir Herbert MacPherson, the army of occupation was greatly strengthened for a vigorous winter campaign against the insurgents. When cold weather came there were more than 30,000 troops in the field. This force was increased by Sikh military police, who were to take the place of the soldiers

after the formidable bodies of rebels were overthrown. But, since the Sikhs were themselves unruly, and their behavior provocative of discontent, Sir Frederick Roberts pronounced in favor of organizing a Burmese police, and conceived the idea that the militant part of the population, from which were recruited the bands of the rebel leaders and the gangs of dakoits, would afford excellent material for a constabulary.

A successful campaign was prosecuted in 1886 against the most important of the Alaungpra pretenders, the Minzaing prince. His bands were successively routed, and he was driven from every post, until he had to take refuge with the Sawbwa of a small Shan state. Here he died in August, 1886, and his adherents, after quarrelling over the division of his property, and killing the Sawbwa who had given them an asylum, dispersed, and were not heard of more as an organized force.

Flying columns scoured the valley of the Irrawaddy, and the outposts were advanced into the interior after the rains had dried off the plains and cool weather set in. The regular troops were invariably successful in their encounters with the large bands of rebels, and when the latter attempted to make a stand in their stockades, they were driven out with ease and killed by hundreds. The smaller bands were not easily caught, and were often able to inflict losses on the columns of infantry, which could not protect their flanks while moving through the jungle, and were too much encumbered to be able to pursue their assailants. The most effective service was performed by the cavalry, which moved with impunity in the bush and through ravines, where the Burmese could have inflicted serious damage, but were restrained by their common dread of mounted troops, especially lancers.

A large detachment of the re-enforcements from India were sent against Boshway, while river-pirates were suppressed by the naval brigade in steam-launches. Columns of troops soon swept the low country west of the Irrawaddy of Boshway's bands, driving them and their leader back into the Arakan hills. In the Pugan district the agricultural and trading classes had, to a large extent, returned to their peaceful occupations before the beginning of the cold season. The English district officer was unable, however, to defend those who accepted British rule from the vengeance of the rebels, who murdered native officials, and sacked and burned friendly villages. Once Bo-cho surrounded the deputy commissioner and his guard with 900 men, and fired at them all day, without, however, inflicting any damage. When the troops took the field the district was soon cleared of hostile bands. Before the end of cold weather Bo-cho was a fugitive with only 30 followers. He raised a new band by uttering a prediction that the 16th of April, which is the end of the Burmese year, would terminate the British dominion, but could mustar only about 100 men, who were soon dispersed. Tok-kyan's large force was also crushed, and himself driven to flight with only 60 followers left. Nga-kway lost 200 of his 1,500 men in battle, 60 being slain in one fight, and after his band was broken up, offered to accept the promised amnesty. The Kanhle prince lost 200 men in a single combat, and was finally driven from his teak-stockade, and after collecting a fresh force, was again defeated, and compelled to flee from the district. The villagers in some cases beat off marauding bands without assistance from the troops, and sometimes dakoits were captured and sent in by the head men of the villages. Many of the robbers after surrendering were enlisted in the new Burmese police force, and their leaders were made officers. Waya-byin surrendered and delivered up his arms, and was restored to his former official position. Dakoits had formerly impoverished whole villages by driving off all the cattle and selling them for their hides and meat, and sometimes for their hides alone. Large numbers of draft-oxen were also taken for military purposes. The distress that was caused by robbery and the devastation of guerrilla warfare was, to some extent, relieved by giving the people labor at good wages on new roads, and on the Toungoo Railroad. The robbery of cattle was rendered unprofitable by preventing the exportation of hides.

In the north columns were placed in the field against Hla-oo as soon as the troops arrived from India. After numerous encounters, his forces were completely broken, and at length he offered to surrender on condition that he should not be banished, but the British would not agree to his remaining in the district. On April 15, when his band was reduced to 40 men, who were suffering for want of food, this insurgent chief was murdered in his hiding-place in the jungle, near Moneganee, in the Sagain district, by one of his own followers. In January an expedition was sent into the northern Shan country. The Sawbwa of Woontho had been accorded a year of grace in which to make his submission. When the troops appeared he fled northward, and his town was occupied by Gen. Cox. Other Sawbwas of the neighborhood submitted, and were confirmed in their offices by the British. The Woontho-Sawbwa afterward returned with a considerable force, and threatened the British. Re-enforcements were sent, and about the 1st of March, while the British were preparing an attack in force, he agreed to their terms, delivered up a quantity of arms, and after undertaking to pay a tribute of 30,000 rupees, received from them investiture as Sawbwa. A garrison was left in Woontho until the revenue should be paid in full, and other posts were held in Katha, on the north. The full amount of the tribute was paid by the Bombay and Burmah Trading Company for the Sawbwa, but his submission was only nominal, and he subsequently refused to meet the Commission-

er of Mandalay, and fired on British troops. The Sawbwa of Gouksouk, with the assistance of a number of chiefs who had been supporters of the Limbin prince, carried out an attack on a British column that was sent into the eastern Shan states in January, but was defeated. The Shan confederacy began to break up in March, and many of the followers of the Limbin prince deserted him. In May this prince, who was the last of the Alaungpra pretenders in the field, gave himself up, and was taken as a prisoner of state to Rangoon. Sekyamise, another prince of the royal family, raised his standard in the summer, but was joined only by inconsiderable bands, which were continually hunted and harassed by the mounted infantry and police. Still another Alaungpra prince plotted an insurrection in Mandalay, but was captured in a house in that city with 60 other conspirators.

Sir Frederick Roberts returned to India in February, being succeeded as commander-in-chief in Burmah by Gen. Arbuthnot. The most important service of Gen. Roberts for the pacification of Upper Burmah was securing the co-operation of the Buddhist priesthood by recognizing the ecclesiastical authority of the regular head of the hierarchy, whereas formerly in British Burmah preference was shown to a schismatic sect. Before leaving, the general made a tour in Lower Burmah with the Buddhist archbishop. A proclamation had been issued at Mandalay, signed by the archbishop, who counseled submission and obedience to British rule, and by the commander-in-chief, who offered a full pardon to all who should deliver up their arms before February 16, and promised work to those who submitted. Sir Charles Bernard, the civil commissioner, was recalled about this time, being succeeded by C. H. T. Crosthwaite, formerly commissioner at Rangoon. The separation of the two provinces had already ceased, Upper and Lower Burmah being placed under the same civil administration. The strength of the military garrison in Upper Burmah for the ensuing season was fixed at 16,000 men, with about the same number of the new police. The police force already organized consisted only of 5,000 Sikhs and others from Northern India and 3,500 Burmese, but until it could be brought up to the required strength enough soldiers were retained to supply the deficiency. When the military force was reduced to its summer strength Gen. Arbuthnot turned over the command to Maj.-Gen. White. In May it was decided to increase the military police to 23,000 men, of whom 6,000 should be Burmans. About 11,000 men had already been raised in the Punjaub. Some severe encounters took place in May and June between the troops and the Burmans in the district where Boshway was still at liberty. There were also fresh disturbances on the other side of the river along the frontier of British Burmah, but the civil officer was here able to cope with the insurgents, and removed the cause of trouble by giving the people work on the roads. There was a scarcity of rice, which rose to a very high price, but supplies were brought from Lower Burmah, and the large sums paid out in wages on the public works prevented a famine, except in some districts. The Shans, who refused to work, suffered great distress.

The Civil Administration. — Mr. Crosthwaite remedied certain evils that had existed under the administration of his predecessor. The Chinese had grievances which brought them into disputes with the authorities and threatened to increase the frontier difficulties. In January the deputy commissioner at Bhamo went so far as to impose fines on the Chinese community and imprison their head man. The new chief commissioner met a deputation of Chinamen at Mandalay on March 24, and agreed that the duty on jade should be paid at Mogoung, and that Chinese leases of the India-rubber forests should be recognized. The barbarous practice of decapitating dakoits and exhibiting their heads, which had been permitted as a means of inspiring terror, was discontinued by his orders, after the subject had been brought up in the British Parliament. In the beginning of March the Kubo valley, on the frontier of the Indian province of Munipoor, was annexed to the British possessions.

The Government revised the leases held by the Bombay and Burmah Corporation, for a supposed infraction of whose contract rights the war against Thebaw was begun. The leases were recognized, but instead of paying the yearly rental specified in the contract, the company will be required to pay a fixed price for every log of teak extracted.

In the spring and summer the claims against the late Burmese Government were considered. They amounted altogether to 64½ lakhs. The bulk of them were for articles furnished by merchants, mostly Frenchmen, to Thebaw. These were excluded under a decision that the Indian Government would not be responsible for the personal debts of the King, but only for the liabilities of his Government. This distinction, which was an entirely arbitrary one, and had never been recognized in Burmese jurisprudence, seemed particularly unjust, because the Indian Government had confiscated the contents of the King's palace and had sold for its own benefit many of the very articles for which payment was now refused.

The Ruby-Mines. — Northeast of Mandalay, at some distance back from the Irrawaddy river, is a ruby-producing tract, the only one known to exist. The mines were the property of the kings of Ava, who derived a considerable revenue from letting the right to dig for rubies. The last lease made by Thebaw expired in July, 1886. At the close of that year a military expedition was sent from Mandalay to take possession of the mines for the new Government. It set out on December 19, crossed a mountain pass, and descended upon Mogouk, the principal town of the mining district. Merchants and miners who were working the mines contributed their means to raise a military force to resist the British occupation, and secured the co-operation of the Shan Sawbwas of the region. Strong stockades were erected and formidable preparations were made to meet the invaders, but as soon as the troops approached, the Shans and Burmese birelings fled to the hills, after first robbing their employers of all their wealth. A garrison was left at the mines, but their possession was not secure because the Sawbwa of Mainlung and other Shan chiefs refused to submit to British authority. A column was sent against Mainlung, and was fired on when approaching the town, which was strongly stockaded. Sir Frederick Roberts visited the mines in January and arranged the disposition of garrisons and selected healthy quarters for troops during the hot season. Mr. Streeter, a junior member of a great London firm of jewelers, accompanied the original expedition to the mines, and was allowed to purchase rubies, thoroughly examine the mines, and make experiments in mining. After his inspection an offer of four lakhs of rupees per annum was made for a five years' lease of the mines. The Indian Government provisionally accepted this tender, but when the facts became known the secret bargain was denounced in Burmah, India, and Europe. Merchants of Bombay, Calcutta, and Rangoon asked permission to examine the mines, but the authorities refused to furnish them with an escort, or to allow them to visit the mines without an escort. A syndicate of Parisian jewelers, who were supposed to represent the banking-house of Rothschild, made an offer of twelve times the price proposed by Messrs. Streeter. Those who were acquainted with the subject asserted that the mines, with the aid of machinery and explosives, would pay a profit on a rent many times greater than the English jewelers offered to pay. Mr. Crosthwaite went to inspect the ruby-mines in April. While he was there the Sawbwas of Momeik and Mainlung offered their submission and agreed to pay tribute. Other Shan chiefs still held aloof. The Government finally decided to retain the monopoly of the mines in its own hands, throwing them open to be worked by the old methods, and exacting the usual duty of 80 per cent. of the value of every stone.

Petroleum Fields. — There are two places in Burmah where earth-oil has been produced in quantities for some years. At Akyab, on the coast of Arakan, in British Burmah, wells have been sunk and are worked by two English companies on the American system. The oil obtained here is light and clear, and has the advantage over American oil of being less explosive, though its illuminating power is less. The production, however, is so costly that the works have yielded no profit. The other oil-field is at Yenangyoung, on the Irrawaddy, in Upper Burmah. Here there are no bores. The oil is obtained by digging holes in the earth, and allowing it to ooze up and collect. It is a dark, heavy liquid, like the Baku product when the wells there were worked in the same way. There are other parts of Upper Burmah where oil of the same kind is obtained by the same process. Great expectations are enter-tained regarding the petroleum-fields of Upper Burmah, yet nothing is yet known of the depth of bore necessary to reach a flow of oil, of the strata of rock, of the probable productivity of the wells, or of the quality of the oil when obtained by scientific methods from below.

C

CALIFORNIA. State Government.—The following were the State officers at the beginning of the year: Governor, Washington Bartlett, Democrat; Lieutenant-Governor, R. W. Waterman, Republican; Secretary of State, W. C. Hendricks, Democrat; Treasurer. Adam Herold, Democrat; Comptroller, J. P. Dunn, Democrat; Attorney-General, G. A. Johnson, Democrat; Surveyor-General, Theodore Reichert, Republican; Superintendent of Public Instruction, Ira G. Hoitt, Republican; State Engineer, William H. Hall, Democrat; Railroad Commissioners, A. Abbott, P. J. White, J. W. Rea; Supreme Court: Chief-Justice, Robert F. Morrison; Associate Justices, E. W. McKinstry, J. D. Thornton, J. R. Sharpstein, Jackson Temple, T. B. McFarland, A. Van R. Patterson. The death of Chief-Justice Morrison in March, caused a vacancy on the supreme bench, which was filled by the appointment of Miles Searle. On Sept. 12, Governor Bartlett died, and the State government again came into the hands of the Republicans, by the promotion of Lieutenant-Governor Waterman.

Legislative Session.—The Legislature assembled Jan. 3, and adjourned March 12. One of its earliest acts was the election of George Hearst, Democrat, to be United States Senator for six years, by a vote of 65 against 52 for Henry Vrooman. The measures of prime importance discussed at this session related to the disposition of mining *débris*, and to irrigation. Legislation was had on the latter subject only. As the Supreme Court of the State had decided in favor of the ownership of the riparian proprietor in the streams of the State, the irrigation problem consisted in devising some means of permitting the withdrawal of water without violating that right. It was enacted that "whenever fifty or a majority of freeholders owning lands susceptible of one mode of irrigation, from a common source, and by the same system of works, desire to provide for the irrigation of the same, they may propose the organization of an irrigation district." An election shall then be held, in which the voters of the proposed district decide whether such district shall, in fact, be organized. If the proposal is favored, certain district officers and a board of directors are chosen for a term of two years. The board of directors shall have the right to acquire, either by purchase or by condemnation, according to law, all lands and waters and other property necessary for the construction, use, supply, repair, or improvement of canals, or other works needful for irriga-tion purposes. It shall have power to manage and conduct the business of the district, make all necessary contracts, take conveyances, maintain suits at law or in equity to carry out its powers, and generally to accomplish the purpose of the act by constructing canals, apportioning the flow of water, and otherwise. It may issue bonds of the district in payment for lands or waters purchased or taken. These bonds shall be paid by an annual assessment on the real property of the district. The use of all water required for irrigation in any such organized district, together with the rights of way for canals and other property required for the purpose of this act is declared to be a public use. Under this act several districts were created during the year, but no test of its constitutionality has yet been made.

Another important measure authorizes the annual levy of a tax of one cent on each $100 of property, for the exclusive support and improvement of the University of California, the money thus collected to be called the State University fund.

The insurance laws were extensively amended in matters of detail, and numerous changes made in the organization and regulation of the militia. The uniformed militia of the State is named the National Guard of California, and is not to exceed fifty companies.

An act regulating the hours of labor fixes eight hours as a day's work, unless otherwise stipulated by the parties. Twelve hours of labor, shall, however, constitute a day's work for drivers, conductors, and grip-men, on street-cars, and any contract for longer hours shall be void at the option of the employé.

Towns, cities, and municipal corporations, are permitted to issue bonds and incur indebtedness for extensive public improvements only when two thirds of the legislative branch of the town or city and the executive thereof approve and two thirds of the voters at a special election signify their assent.

The laws regulating government of counties and the duties of county officers were also thoroughly revised.

An appropriation of $5,000 was made for a monument to James W. Marshall, the discoverer of gold in California, to be erected at his grave in Coloma, Eldorado County. Other acts were as follow:

To prevent fraud and imposition in the matter of stamping and labeling produce and manufactured goods.
Appropriating $250,000 for the erection of additional buildings for the chronic insane.

To encourage and provide for the dissemination of a knowledge of the arts, sciences, and general literature, and the founding, maintaining, and perpetuating public libraries, museums, and galleries of art, and the receipt of donations and contributions thereto when established.

To prohibit the sophistication and adulteration of wine, and to prevent fraud in the manufacture and sale thereof.

To authorize certain officials of cities to levy taxes for the maintenance of public parks of over ten acres within their respective limits.

To provide for permanent improvements at the California Home for the care and training of feeble-minded children; also an act to provide for the government and management of said Home.

To grant to the United States certain tide-lands, belonging to the State of California, for the purpose of improving the harbor of Humboldt Bay.

To provide for the completion of all unfinished county, city, city and county, town, and township buildings in the several counties, cities, and counties, cities, and towns throughout the State.

To enlarge the county of San Benito, by including therein portions of the counties of Fresno and Merced; to redefine the boundaries of Del Norte and Siskiyou counties.

To protect life and property against the careless and malicious use or handling of dynamite and other explosives.

To authorize executors and administrators to make mortgages and leases of the real estate of decedents in certain ways.

For the better protection of settlers on the public land of the United States within the State of California, and for the protection and encouragement of persons desirous of settling thereon.

To amend the law relating to mechanics' liens. Regulating the use of trade-marks.

To regulate the vocation of fishing, and to provide therefrom revenue for the restoration and preservation of fish in the waters of the State, requiring every person engaged in such vocation on the public waters of the State, who shall use a boat and net, to obtain a license for such fishing.

Appropriating $10,000 to prevent the introduction of contagious and infectious diseases.

Providing for the incorporation of any church or other religious association.

Constitutional Amendments.—Three amendments to the State Constitution were submitted by this Legislature and voted upon by the people at an election held April 12. Two of these, relating to the Supreme Court of the State, failed of adoption. The third and successful amendment gives to cities containing a population of over 10,000 the same right to frame their own charter as that enjoyed under the Constitution by San Francisco and other cities of over 100,000 inhabitants. This right is exercised by the election of 15 freeholders of the city, who submit a draft of a charter, which must be approved by a majority of the voters of the city, voting at a general or special election, and by a majority of the State Legislature, before becoming law.

Finances.—In accordance with a provision of the Legislature of 1883, a portion of the State debt, represented by the State Capitol bonds of 1872, amounting to $250,000, and maturing July 1 of this year, was discharged at that time. This payment reduced the bonded indebtedness of the State to $2,703,500, of which the sum of $2,698,000 in funded-debt

bonds of 1873 is interest-bearing. These bonds, with the exception of $384,000 held by individuals, are all held in trust by the State treasurer for the support of the common schools and for the State University. They mature in 1893, and bear 6 per cent. interest.

The Controller's report shows that the State expenditures for the thirty-sixth and thirty-seventh fiscal years exceeded the two preceding years by $2,622,591.74, necessitating an increase in the rate of taxation from 45 2 cents in 1884, to 56 cents in 1886. Yet, even at this increased rate the disbursements for the last two fiscal years exceeded the receipts by $374,185.37. No less than fifty deficiency bills were passed by the Legislature of this year, as a result of this over-expenditure in various departments. The same body directed a levy of $9,800,000 by taxation for the thirty-ninth and fortieth fiscal years, as against $8,152,512 for two previous years.

The long-continued dispute between the State and the railroads, over the payment of taxes, is still unsettled. A test case, which was appealed to the United States Supreme Court in 1885 to determine the constitutionality of the assessment, was advanced upon the calendar, and heard in the latter part of that year. A decision adverse to the State was then given on a technical point raised by the defendants, leaving the main issues still to be decided. At the beginning of this year the State claimed from the Central and Southern Pacific roads and their branches, the sum of $2,347,618.59 in unpaid taxes. Of this sum $416,252.28 are due for the years 1880, 1881, and 1882; for 1883, $222,251.23 of the sum of $555,628.46 assessed are yet unpaid; for 1884 the assessment was $653,373.12, of which the sum of $323,852.49 is due; for 1885 and 1886 nothing has been paid, the taxes for these years being $720,703.31 and $664,559.18 respectively. A suit brought in the State Superior Court to collect the taxes for 1886 was decided in May against the State, on the ground that the provision of the State code prescribing a form of complaint to be used by the people to recover railroad taxes was unconstitutional. The railroads have thus far successfully evaded all attempts to force payment, and the State suffers great inconvenience and loss by this withholding of nearly 5 per cent. of her revenue.

Development.—The Governor, in his message at the beginning of the year, says: "The manifold industrial, mechanical, and commercial interests of the State are in a highly-prosperous condition; immigration is pouring in, property values are being enhanced, rich resources developed, and fields for labor are multiplying."

The following figures will show the condition of the chief industries: The product of wheat for 1886 is estimated at 1,070,000 tons; the total production of wool for 1886 was 47,225,160 pounds. This staple has shown some fluctuation in the last few years, the total for

1884 being 37,415,830 pounds, and for 1885 50,439,840 pounds.

The raisin industry has grown from a product of 180,000 pounds in 1881 to 14,060,000 pounds in 1886. Nearly all of this comes from three districts, the Fresno, the Riverside, and the Orange and Santa Ana. The total dried-fruit crop for 1886 was 20,745,000 pounds, against 5,070,000 pounds for 1883. In this total are included, besides raisins:

	Pounds.		Pounds.
Prunes	2,125,000	Pears	50,000
Apples	800,000	Grapes	175,000
Peaches	1,050,000	Apricots	600,000
Plums	585,000	Nectarines	50,000

Shipments of oranges from the State aggregated, in 1886, 25,966,830 pounds. Of this amount 21,513,880 pounds went from Los Angeles, 4,267,850 from Colton, 81,300 from Sacramento, and 43,800 from San Francisco.

The product of extracted honey for the same year amounts to 6,000,000 pounds, besides 800,000 pounds of comb, and 80,000 pounds of bees-wax.

The vintage of 1887 was 15,000,000 gallons, or nearly the same as in 1884. It reached 17,000,000 gallons in 1886.

The salt-water fisheries have flourished, but of the principal inland-fishing industry, the Commissioners of Fisheries say: "It is a matter of serious regret that our choicest and most valued fish, the Quinnat salmon, is annually decreasing, and the supply for exportation and home consumption is diminishing. On account of the small run, and decreased take of salmon, more than half of the canneries that were operated in 1883–'84 were closed in 1885–'86. The number of cases packed in 1885 was 90,000, as against 120,000 for 1883, and 200,000 for 1882. In 1882 nineteen canneries were in successful operation, while in 1885 only five or six were running."

By the report of July, 1882, made to the Bank Commissioners, the deposits of the savings-banks of San Francisco amounted to $46,869,-689.91. The report of the same banks for January, 1887, shows a deposit of $57,586,-741.31, a gain of $11,117,051.40, or of $2,779,-262.85 per year. The savings-banks outside this city gained in the same period $1,770,349.-36. The total gain for the whole State in four years was $12,887,400.76, and the total deposits at last report was $66,196,189.54. The population of California is put at a million, and the deposits in her savings-banks, which are largely the surplus earnings of her wage-workers, equal $66 to each man, woman, and child in the State.

The assessed value of railroad property is slightly over $7,000,000. There were operated in 1886 in the State 2,425 miles of broad-gauge, and 426 miles of narrow-gauge road. The total assessed valuation of the State was for 1885, $761,271,449; for 1886, $768,395,600.

Education.—The State supports a normal school at San José, and a branch normal school at Los Angeles, both of which are flourishing; the former having in 1886 an average of 430 pupils, and the latter 252. Provision was made by the Legislature of this year for the establishment of a second branch school in Northern California.

The public schools are supported by income from State bonds, by the State school fund, and by local taxation. In 1885 the Superintendent of Public Instruction apportioned to them from the State fund $1,845,883; in 1886, $2,012,235; in 1887, $1,528,641. The State University and the normal schools are supported by special appropriations. The school law forbids the use of the school fund for the support of any schools other than of the primary and grammar grades, but permits districts or municipalities to maintain high-schools by a local tax. An amendment to the State Constitution, adopted in 1884, created a State board to prepare a series of text-books to be exclusively used in the common schools of the State; and several elementary books, compiled by leading educators of the State, have been published. The present Legislature appropriated money for a continuation of the series, and directed that a suitable treatise on the injurious effect of alcoholic liquors should be included in it.

The total valuation of school property for 1886 was $8,920,984, a gain of $493,797 over 1885, and of $984,864 over 1886.

Mention has already been made of the generous provision of the Legislature for the State University. Higher education in the State will be still further advanced by the founding of Stanford University, the corner-stone of which was laid at Palo Alto, with appropriate ceremonies, on May 20. The founder, Senator Stanford, contemplates the establishment of an institution of the highest standard, richly equipped and endowed.

Charities and Prisons.—In the last two fiscal years the State expended for the orphan asylums, $448,526.33; for aged persons in indigent circumstances, $123,145.56; for the Veterans' Home, $20,913.60; and for the Home for Feeble-Minded Children, $87,139.44, making a total for charitable institutions of $624,-724.93.

It also supports a school for the deaf, dumb, and blind, at which 186 persons have received instruction during the last two years. A separate institution for the adult blind was provided for by the Legislature of 1885, but unfortunate management has partially defeated the purposes of the act.

There are two insane asylums, the one at Stockton having 1,486 patients in 1886, an increase of over 185 per year during the last two years. The asylum at Napa held in 1886 1,486 patients, and two years previous 1,819, showing an increase of 117, or less than half that of Stockton. An asylum for the chronic insane in Santa Clara County was completed in 1887.

The State Prison at San Quentin contained

at the close of the fiscal year, 1886, a total of 1,247 prisoners, or 85 more than in 1885. At Folsom there were 644 prisoners, an increase of over 80 in one year.

Southern California.—A recent writer says: "That California can much longer remain one State, is not probable. The project of a division has been widely discussed, and it is now conceded that the work of separation can not be delayed beyond a very few years. The reasons are based upon causes so deep-seated, and dependent upon geographical and topographical, as well as climatic differences so radical, that the union already works serious detriment to the southern portion of the State and retards its progress. Between the two lies a great transverse range of mountains, the lowest passes of which vary from 4,000 to 5,000 feet above the sea. It is this range, with the absolute division it makes in the lines of trade and travel, which, more than any other one cause, is forcing them apart."

The most wonderful growth of recent years in California is exhibited in and around Los Angeles. This place is a century old (it celebrated its centennial in 1881), and exhibits a curious combination of the ancient and the modern. It is from 350 to 500 feet above sea-level. In 1854 the population of the town was about 4,000, of whom only 500 were Americans; the population is now about 70,-000. Wine has been produced here for many years, and some fine samples were sent to President Buchanan in 1857. Now the county contains 22,000 acres devoted to grapes for wine-making, and produces 5,000,000 gallons yearly. Other fruits grown in abundance are oranges, lemons, figs, limes, almonds, peaches, apples, cherries, guavas, melons, olives, pomegranates, and quinces. The city owns the Los Angeles river, and sells the water for irrigation of orange-groves. It has cable street-railways, an opera-house, a crematory, twenty-nine churches, numerous schools and benevolent institutions, and a free public library. It is the seat of the University of Southern California, founded in 1880. There are eleven banks, nine iron-foundries, two flouring-mills, five planing-mills, a pottery, brick-yards, and establishments for the manufacture of soap, cigars, ice, brooms, artificial stone, mattresses, furniture, beer, pickles, candy, jewelry, hats, lithographs, leather, and street-cars. Fifteen lines of railway, either completed or in course of construction, pass into or through the city. There are two harbors, one thirteen and the other twenty miles distant. The assessed valuation of property in the city in 1887 was $40,000,000, the real value being over $100,-000,000.

Immense quantities of honey, wheat, and barley are produced in this part of the State, besides corn, castor-beans, English walnuts, and other crops. Most of the towns are growing rapidly, numerous health and pleasure resorts are being established, and there is a constant influx of settlers and capital. It is estimated that by 1890 Southern California will have 1,000,000 orange-trees of bearing age. In the production of grapes, the most important of which is the raisin-grape, the following is the acreage in the five counties comprising Southern California in the present year compared with that of last year:

COUNTIES.	Acreage, 1886.	Acreage, 1887.
Los Angeles	15,560	17,120
Santa Barbara	900	1,125
Ventura	880	456
San Diego	774	1.090
San Bernardino	3,470	4,080
Total	21,556	24,838

Improved land for the business of cultivating raisin-grapes is valued at from $100 to $500 per acre, the third year yielding $25 per acre, the fourth year $50 per acre, the fifth year $100 per acre, and when the vines are in full bearing, from $100 to $300 per acre. The vineyards of California yield from six to eight tons per acre in full bearing, while in Malaga, the yield is less than two and a half tons to the acre. Statistics show that California is furnishing for home consumption a little more than a third of the amount of raisins imported.

The petroleum and asphaltum supply of Southern California are among the largest and richest in the world. A single well in the Pico Cañon has produced within the past nine years about $1,000,000 worth of oil, and is still producing steadily. The peculiar feature of the oil-wells of this section is their permanence. Petroleum and asphaltum were discovered here by the first Spanish settlers more than a century ago, but no attention was paid to the oil, while asphaltum was melted and used as roofing. The oil region of Southern California extends from the northern part of Santa Barbara County, along the coast through that county, thence a few miles inland through Ventura and Los Angeles Counties, 160 miles. From the San Fernando wells the oil is carried in a pipe to Newhall station and refinery, on the Southern Pacific Railway, and also down the Santa Clara valley to the sea, at the ports of Hueneme and San Buenaventura. The oil from Santa Paula is conveyed in the same way to Newhall and to the sea. The amount of capital invested in the business of production and development is about $8,000,000. (See "California of the South," by Walter Lindley and J. P. Widney, New York, 1888.)

CANADA, DOMINION OF. The fifth Parliament of the Dominion was dissolved on Jan. 15, 1887, and in the elections that followed the government of Sir John Macdonald was sustained, but by a greatly reduced majority. The sixth Parliament met on April 18, elected Lt.-Col. Joseph Alderic Ouimet speaker, and was prorogued on June 24. The Government, when it met Parliament, was composed as follows: Premier, President of the Privy Council, and Superintendent-General of Indian Affairs, Rt. Hon. Sir John Macdonald, G. C. B.; Minister of Finance, Sir Charles Tupper; Postmaster-General, A. W. McLelan; Minister of Public Works, Sir Hector Langevin; Minister of Railways and Canals, J. H. Pope; Minister of Customs, Mackenzie Bowell; Minister of Militia, Sir Adolphe Caron; Minister of Marine and Fisheries, G. E. Foster; Minister of Agriculture, John Carling; Minister of Inland Revenue, John Costigan; Minister of the Interior, Thomas White; Minister of Justice, J. S. D. Thompson; Secretary of State, J. A. Chapleau; without portfolio, Frank Smith. Sir Charles Tupper resigned temporarily the office of Canadian High Commissioner in London, in order to become Minister of Finance. During the session, John J. C. Abbott, Mayor of Montreal, entered the Cabinet without portfolio and became the leader of the Senate, and Edward Blake resigned the leadership of the Opposition on account of failing health, being succeeded by Wilfrid Laurier. The sanction of Parliament was obtained for a radical reorganization of the Dominion Cabinet, but the carrying of the changes into effect was postponed. Provision was made for uniting the two departments of Customs and Inland Revenue, as the Department of Trade and Commerce. When the law comes into force, the offices of Minister of Customs and Minister of Inland Revenue will cease to exist, but each of the departments then united will still have a parliamentary head, who will hold office and retire with the Government, but will not necessarily or probably be a member of the Cabinet. The duties of these officers, who will be called, respectively, the Controller of Customs and the Controller of Inland Revenue, will be analogous to those of the Under Secretaries in the Government of Great Britain. Provision was also made for the appointment of a Solicitor-General, who will occupy a similar position in the Department of Justice.

Finances.—The ordinary revenue for the fiscal year ending June 30, 1886, was $33,177,040, and the ordinary expenditure $39,011,612, thus leaving a deficit of $5,834,572. The deficit is partly accounted for by payments during 1886 on account of the Northwest rebellion of 1885, amounting to $3,177,220. The ordinary revenue averaged $6.92 per head of the population, and the expenditure $8.13. The gross amount of taxation was $25,226,456, or $5.26 per head. The gross public debt on June 30, 1886, was $273,164,341, an increase during the year of $3,460,734. The net debt was $223,159,107, an increase of $26,751,415. The expenditure on public works since confederation has been as follows: Railways, $97,056,423; canals, $29,876,800; light-houses and navigation, $8,-284,580; acquisition and management of the Northwest Territories, $5,356,035; Government buildings and miscellaneous works, $13,-680,829; total, $154,254,667. Prior to confederation $52,944,175 had been expended on

railways and canals, and $10,690,917 on other public works.

Trade and Commerce.—The imports for the year ending June 30, 1886, amounted to $104,424,-561, and the exports to $85,251,814, a decrease in the imports from the previous year of $4,-516,925, and in the exports of $3,987,047. The commerce of the Dominion was thus distributed:

COUNTRIES.	IMPORTS.		EXPORTS.	
	Value.	Per-cent'ge.	Value.	Per-cent'ge.
United States........	$50,475,418	48·34	$36,578,760	42·91
Great Britain........	40,569,500	38·67	41,542,629	48·72
Germany.............	2,139,426	2·05	258,298	0·30
France..............	1,866,392	1·79	584,368	0·68
British West Indies..	993,422	0·95	1,256,549	1·47
Other West Indies...	1,511,412	1·45	865,021	1·01
Other British possessions...............	568,889	0·56	258,290	0·30
Japan...............	1,485,969	1·42	1,708	......
South America	1,052,496	1·00	1,012,306	1·19
China	908,429	0·87	61,415	0·07
Belgium.............	554,774	0·53	6,565	0·01
Newfoundland and Labrador...........	388,171	0·37	1,752,048	2·06
Spain	351,196	0·37	56,075	0·06
Holland.............	308,111	0·29	7,587	0·01
Switzerland.........	202,399	0·19	918	......
Turkey..............	168,988	0 16	48	......
Italy...............	105,565	0·10	108,601	0·12
Greece	98,925	0·09	......	......
Austria.............	67,577	0·07	8,089	......
Portugal	57,059	0·05	245,450	0·29
Norway and Sweden ..	29,513	0·03	71,747	0·08
Australasia.........	12,795	0·01	263,660	0·31
Russia	10,921	0·01	490	......
Denmark............	795	......	......	......
Other countries......	445,549	0·43	378,222	0·44
Total..........	$104,424,561	100·00	$85,251,814	100·00

Iron.—The most important legislation accomplished was the extension of the national policy with a view to fostering the manufacture of iron, and the new tariff was graded in proportion to the presumed value of the labor involved in producing iron in its various stages of manufacture in Canada. As a general principle, the rate of duty is about equal to two thirds of the amount of the duty payable in the United States. This principle was not adhered to in the case of the higher grades of steel manufactures, because it was thought that no amount of protection would insure the manufacture of these grades in Canada, nor in the case of locomotive tubes and boilerplates, because it was especially desired to encourage railway development in Canada. Nova Scotia and British Columbia are the only Canadian provinces in which iron and coal are found in close proximity, but the Government hope to see re-established under the new tariff the charcoal-iron manufactures, which were once the chief industries of Ontario and Quebec. The imports of iron and steel and manufactures thereof into the Dominion for home consumption in recent years have been: 1879, $7,962,295; 1880, $10,128,660; 1881, $12,-955,855; 1882, $17,199,488; 1883, $20,080,274; 1884, $14,790,727; 1885, $11,415,713; 1886, $11,053,865. The Dominion pays a bounty of $1.50 a ton on all pig-iron manufactured in

90 CANADA, DOMINION OF.

Canada, and this bounty will continue until June 30, 1889. From that date until June 30, 1892, the bounty will be $1 a ton. The amount of bounty paid during the fiscal year ending June 30, 1886, on pig-iron manufactured in Canada was $39,269.56. The amount paid for bounty between July 1, 1886, and May 1, 1887, was $32,667.65.

Treaty-Making Power.—Sir Charles Tupper, in his budget speech, announced that the Imperial Government had decided to allow the Dominion to negotiate its own commercial treaties with foreign countries; negotiations to be conducted conjointly by the representative of Canada and the minister representing Her Majesty's Government, the former being clothed with plenipotentiary powers and placed upon an equal footing with the latter. He quoted the following extract from a letter sent by the Foreign Office to the Colonial Office, dated July 26, 1884, and referring to proposed commercial negotiations between Canada and Spain:

If the Spanish Government are favorably disposed a full power for these negotiations will be given to Sir Robert Morrier (then British Ambassador at Madrid) and Sir Charles Tupper jointly. The actual negotiation would probably be conducted by Sir Charles Tupper, but the convention, if concluded, must be signed by both plenipotentiaries, and be entered into between Her Majesty and the King of Spain, with the special object of regulating Canadian trade with the Spanish territories specified in the convention.

Irish Home Rule.—The following resolutions were passed by the House of Commons on a division of 135 against 47:

That the Parliament of Canada in the year 1882 adopted a humble address to Her Most Gracious Majesty the Queen expressing the hope that a just measure of home rule would be granted to the people of Ireland; and

That in the year 1886, by resolution of the House of Commons, the sentiments of said address to Her Most Gracious Majesty were earnestly reiterated and the hope again expressed that such a measure of home rule would be passed by the Imperial Parliament; and

That such measure of home rule has not been granted to the Irish people, but, on the contrary, there has been introduced into the Imperial House of Commons by Her Majesty's Government a bill enacting the most stringent coercive measures for Ireland, by which the Irish people will be deprived of rights most dear to all British subjects.

That this house has learned with profound regret of the introduction into the Imperial House of Commons of the Coercion bill above mentioned, and earnestly hopes that a measure so subversive of the rights and liberties of Her Majesty's subjects in Ireland may not become law.

That this house again expresses the hope that there may speedily be granted to Ireland a substantial measure of home rule, which, while satisfying the national aspirations of the people of Ireland for self-government, shall also be consistent with the integrity of the Empire as a whole.

That the granting of home rule to Ireland will fittingly crown the already glorious reign of Her Most Gracious Majesty as a constitutional sovereign, will come with special appropriateness in this her Jubilee year, and, if possible, render Her Majesty more dear to the hearts of her already devoted and loyal subjects.

Inter-Provincial Conference.—In October, delegates duly accredited by the governments of Quebec, Ontario, Nova Scotia, New Brunswick, and Manitoba met at Quebec to consider propositions for the amendment of the British North America act of 1867, of the Imperial Parliament, which embodies the constitution of the Canadian Confederation. Since this act, which was based upon a series of resolutions formulated by a similar conference, was passed, difficulties have from time to time arisen between the Federal and provincial governments and legislatures as to its interpretation, necessitating appeals to the Privy Council in England to decide upon the constitutionality of acts of the Dominion Parliament and Legislatures. Most of the provincial governments of the present day belong to the Liberal party, while the Dominion Government is Conservative, and the issue between the advocates of provincial autonomy and the advocates of centralization of governing power at Ottawa has naturally assumed great importance. As a matter of fact, most of the resolutions adopted by the Conference were in favor of increasing the powers of the provincial authorities. The delegates were, for Ontario: Oliver Mowatt, Prime Minister; C. F. Fraser, Commissioner of Public Works; A. S. Hardy, Provincial Secretary; A. M. Ross, Provincial Treasurer; G. W. Ross, Minister of Education. For Quebec: Honoré Mercier, Prime Minister; D. A. Ross, Arthur Turcotte, Joseph Shehyn, Provincial Treasurer; C. A. E. Gagnon, Provincial Secretary; James McShane, Commissioner of Public Works; George Duhamel, Solicitor-General; F. G. Marchand, Speaker of the Legislative Assembly. For Nova Scotia: W. S. Fielding, Prime Minister; J. W. Longley, Attorney-General; A. MacGillivray. For New Brunswick: Andrew G. Blair, Prime Minister; and David McLellan, Provincial Secretary and Receiver-General. For Manitoba: J. Norquay, Prime Minister; and C. E. Hamilton, Attorney-General. Twenty-two resolutions were adopted (subject to the approval of the several provincial legislatures) as the basis upon which the British North America act should be amended. The resolutions provide for amendments to the following effect:

That the power of disallowing provincial statutes be taken away from the Dominion Government and placed in the hands of the Imperial Government, to be exercised in regard to provincial legislation upon the same principles now recognized in regard to Federal acts.

That, to prevent the Federal Parliament assuming powers belonging exclusively to the provincial legislatures, equal facilities be afforded to the Federal and provincial governments for testing the validity of Federal or provincial statutes. That constitutional provision be made for obtaining judicial determination on such acts, as well before as after they are enforced, the decisions to be subject to appeal as in other cases in order to obtain final adjudication.

That, to prevent uncertainty and litigation, the constitutionality of statutes should not be open to question by private litigants, except within a limited time (say two years) after their passing. After the lapse of that period the constitutionality of a statute to be questioned only at the instance of a government, and, if it is then declared unconstitutional, the act to be regarded as if originally enacted by and to be subject to amendment or repeal by the legislature or parliament having the jurisdiction to enact it.

That half the Senators of the Dominion be chosen by the provinces, and that all the Senators hold office for a limited term of years, not as now, for life.

That the British North America act should expressly declare the lieutenant-governor of each province to have the same executive authority as the governors and lieutenant-governors of other British colonies. Hitherto this right has been assumed, but it is deemed necessary to maintain it and place it beyond question by an express provision.

That the Federal authorities shall no longer have the power of withdrawing from provincial jurisdiction, local works (railways, for instance, situated entirely in one province), merely by declaring them " to be for the general advantage of Canada."

That the provincial legislatures should control the Dominion franchise; the electoral lists prepared for the elections to the legislative assemblies to be used in elections to the Dominion Parliament.

That all doubts be removed as to the right of the provincial authorities to appoint all magistrates and other officers under the control of the provincial legislatures.

That the provincial legislatures be authorized to legislate with regard to fees payable on legal proceedings, and to apply the revenue therefrom to provincial purposes.

That, to remove doubts now existing, it be expressly declared that lieutenant-governors have the power, subject to provincial statutes, to issue commissions to hold courts of assize and nisi prius, oyer and terminer, and general jail-delivery. At present the uncertainty is such that by arrangement between the Federal and provincial authorities independent commissions expressed in identical terms are issued by the governor-general and by the lieutenant-governor of each province.

That the provincial legislatures should have the same powers to define the privileges and immunities of their houses and of their members individually that are now enjoyed by the Dominion Parliament.

That Her Majesty may by proclamation abolish the legislative council of any province upon an address in favor of that step, concurred in by at least two thirds of the members of the House of Assembly of that province.

That the claim made by the Federal Government to all crown lands as to which there was no treaty with the Indians before confederation, be declared invalid.

That in the absence of a Dominion insolvency law each province be allowed to legislate upon the matter, subject to any future insolvency law that may be passed by the Parliament of Canada.

That the pardoning power for the infraction of provincial laws be reposed in the lieutenant-governor in council of each province.

That the boundaries between Ontario, Manitoba, and the remainder of the Dominion, as far as determined by the Privy Council, should be established by Imperial statute, and that the whole northern boundaries of Ontario and Quebec be determined without further delay.

That the annual subsidies payable by the Dominion to the provinces be increased, and the increased amount be declared by Imperial enactment to be final and absolute, and not within the power of the Federal Parliament to alter. The annual subsidies provided by the British North America act were as follow: Ontario, $80,000; Quebec, $70,000; Nova Scotia, $60,000; New Brunswick, $50,000, with a further annual grant equal to eighty cents a head of the population as ascertained by the census of 1861, with special provision for Nova Scotia and New Brunswick. The Conference suggests that the subsidies be

as follow: Where the population is under 150,000, $100,000; where the population is 150,000, but does not exceed 200,000, $150,000; where the population is 200,000, but does not exceed 400,000, $180,000; where the population is 400,000, but does not exceed 800,-000, $190,000; where the population is 800,000, but does not exceed 1,500,000, $220,000; where the population exceeds 1,500,000, $240,000, and an annual grant of eighty cents a head, to be based upon the population of each province as ascertained at each decennial census, until the population exceeds 2,500,000; and of sixty cents a head for so much of the population as exceeds 2,500,000. Special provision is made for British Columbia and Manitoba.

That the provincial legislatures should take steps to secure the enactment by the Imperial Parliament of amendments to the British North America act, in accordance with the resolutions embodying the foregoing suggestions.

The Conference also dealt with certain matters in respect whereof no amendments to the British North America act are required, passing resolutions making recommendations to the following effect:

That the provincial legislatures should enact that no action shall lie against any judge or officer for any act done under the supposed authority of any statute subsequently declared *ultra vires* of the parliament or legislature enacting it, provided the action would not lie if the statutory provision had been within such legislative jurisdiction.

That the laws of the several provinces for the enforcement of debts should be assimilated as far as may be consistent, with the different legal systems prevailing; and that such assimilation should include provisions against preferences by insolvent debtors; for the examination of debtors, and for taking speedy possession of an insolvent's estate for the benefit of his creditors, so far as these subjects can be dealt with by the provincial legislatures.

That legislative provision be made in all the provinces for rendering effectual in all of them probates and letters of administration granted in any one of them.

That similar laws be passed in all the provinces with respect to probates and letters of administration granted in the United Kingdom, to go into effect when probates and letters of administration granted in the Dominion are by Imperial legislation made effectual in the United Kingdom.

The foregoing resolutions were concurred in by all the delegates. A resolution condemning the disallowance by the Federal Government of the Red River Valley Railway charter was passed, the New Brunswick delegates dissenting. A resolution was also passed in favor of commercial union with the United States, but as this subject is not within the jurisdiction of the provinces, the chief importance of the resolution lies in the fact that it commits the Liberal party to the policy of commercial union so far as the party can be committed, by the formal declaration of so many of its chiefs. The Conference adjourned on October 28.

CAPE OF GOOD HOPE, a British colony in South Africa. The legislative authority is exercised by a Legislative Council, consisting of twenty-two members, elected for seven years, and a House of Assembly of seventy-four members, elected for five years. By a law passed in 1882, speeches in the Cape Parliament may be made in either English or Dutch. The Governor of the Cape of Good

Hope and High Commissioner for South Africa is Sir Hercules George Robert Robinson, appointed in 1880. The Prime Minister is Sir Gordon Sprigg.

Area and Population.—The area of Cape Colony proper is 199,406 square miles, and including its dependencies, 231,276 square miles. The population of Cape Colony proper in 1881 comprised 269,725 persons of European origin, and 541,725 others. The estimated population of the colonies and its dependencies in 1885 was 1,252,347. The dependencies are Griqualand West, with an area of 17,800 square miles, and 16,927 white and 32,174 colored inhabitants; the Transkei, area, 2,535 square miles, population 820 whites, and 118,782 others; Griqualand East, area, 7,480 square miles, population, 3,066 whites, and 93,114 others; and Tembuland, area, 8,320 square miles, population, 8,320 whites, and 114,318 others. The capital of the colony is Cape Town, which has about 60,000 inhabitants. A large proportion of the white people of the colony are descended from the original Dutch, French, and German settlers. The immigration in 1884 was 292.

Basutoland, with an area of 10,290 square miles, and 128,000 inhabitants; Bechuanaland, with 180,000 square miles, and 478,000 inhabitants; and Pondoland, with 200,000 inhabitants, are British possessions, directly under imperial jurisdiction.

Commerce.—The total value of imports in 1885 was £4,772,904, and of exports, £3,159,487, exclusive of specie and diamonds. The export of wool was valued at £1,426,108; ostrich-feathers, £585,278; hides and skins, £424,755; copper-ore, £395,675; Angora hair, £204,018; wine, £17,245. The value of diamonds exported was £2,489,659. Including gold and diamonds, the total value of exports was £5,811,444.

The railroad mileage at the close of 1885 was 1,599. The gross earnings for the year were £1,087,359, and the expenses, £672,489. The number of letters carried in the mails in 1885 was 6,244,169, and of newspapers, 3,986,124. The telegraph lines at the end of 1885 had a total length of 4,329 miles; the number of messages for the year was 798,468; the revenue, £52,458; the expenditures, £45,030.

Finances.—The revenue for the year ended June 30, 1887, was £3,155,000, which was balanced by the expenditure. The estimated revenue for 1887-'88 is £3,186,000, and the estimated expenditure £3,147,000 The finances of the colony are steadily improving.

Disfranchisement of Natives.—When responsible government was granted to Cape Colony in 1853, the Constitution was framed so as to secure equal political rights to whites and blacks. The idea of political equality of the races is obnoxious to the Afrikander population, although the natives have not abused the privilege of voting, have made scarcely any use of it, and are not able, if they should all vote, to influence the results of elections, except in a few constituencies. In 1887 the Cape Legislature passed a bill to deprive of the franchise all natives whose qualifications are derived from communal occupation, the effect of which will be to disfranchise nearly all natives who can now exercise the right of voting. A petition to have it disallowed by the Imperial Government was made through the English society for the protection of aborigines, but was not entertained.

Proposed Customs Union.—Cape Colony and Natal have entered into a competition with each other for the increased trade of the Dutch republics resulting from the gold discoveries in the Transvaal. The customs duties were almost entirely abolished by the two colonies, to the detriment of their revenues and the benefit of the Transvaal and the Orange Free State. A proposition for a conference to discuss a customs union of all the South African countries, and the question of railroad connections was favorably received in the republics, but the British colonies find it difficult to harmonize their reciprocal interests, since the free admission of sugar from Natal into Cape Colony would entail a heavy loss of revenue on Cape Colony, and the sacrifice of a profitable trade with Mauritius, without any resulting benefit. The Cape Government is extending the Kimberley railroad to the Vaal river, and railroads from the east coast into the Free State or the Transvaal are under discussion. In the mean time the Delagoa Bay Railroad project is being carried out by the South African Republic, which found a Belgian syndicate ready to take the concession.

Annexation of Zululand.—By a convention concluded on Oct. 22, 1886, between the British Government and the Boers who had established a new republic in Zululand on the borders of the Transvaal, and had proclaimed a protectorate over the entire Zulu nation, the partition of the country between the Zululand Republic and the Zulus was agreed to, the Boers, in return for the recognition of their republic, giving up all rights over Eastern Zululand, and surrendering a part of the territory that they had already occupied. A large proportion of the valuable lands in Zululand were included in the Zulu Reserve, over which a British protectorate had been established, and the greater part of those that were left were contained in the New Republic. Eastern Zululand, the section still retained for the possession of the natives, consisted to a large extent of marshes and fever-scourged areas, yet enough of good land remained, in the opinion of the British negotiators for the maintenance of the diminished Zulu nation. In the district of Kwamagaza, east of the boundary-line, 400 Boers had settled on 80 farms, and the British promised that their titles should be respected. Within the borders of the New Republic lived about 40,000 Zulus. The district of Umgojana, north of the Umkusi river, forming a wedge between Eastern Zululand and Swaziland, and another tract on the south, next to the Reserve, and jutting likewise into Eastern Zululand, were added to the bounds of the republic as a compensation for lands that were given back to the Zulus in the center. This arrangement was made for the sake of securing to the English the main trade-route. The Boers agreed to allow free passage for goods across the territory of the New Republic, without payment of license or transit dues, into the South African Republic or Zululand. The area of the New Republic is 2,700,000 acres, or about half of Zululand outside of the Reserve, leaving the Zulus one third of their former country, and not more than one fifth of its habitable portions. The Natal Legislative Council complained against being excluded from the negotiations. The people in Natal were as desirous of securing grazing-farms and collect a hut-tax in Zululand as the Boers. Resolutions were passed in favor of the immediate extension of British authority over the whole of Zululand, except the Boer republic, and proposing its annexation to Natal. When the demarkation was begun, on Dec. 14, 1886, Dinizulu, who pretended to be King of the Zulus, with other chiefs, instigated by their white friends, attempted to upset the convention and have the Boers either driven out of Zululand altogether, or deprived of a large slice of the territory that had been conceded to them. They were rebuked for their desire to reopen the question. The boundary survey and demarkation was completed on January 26, and on the 28th the British boundary commissioner, Mr. Osborn, summoned Dinizulu and the other chiefs to ratify the settlement. They were not permitted to bring any of their white advocates to the meeting, or to communicate with their friends in Natal. They had previously sent a deputation to Sir Arthur Havelock, but could only induce him to negotiate with the Boers for the preservation of the burial-ground of their kings at Makosini. The Zulu chiefs refused to concur in the boundary, in the alienation of any part of their country to the Boers, or in the proposed extension over the rest of it of British sovereignty, but were informed that the arrangements were final and could not be altered.

A British protectorate was first proclaimed over Eastern Zululand. Mr. Osborn, the Resident Commissioner, sent messages in February, 1887, to the chiefs. Umyamana, one of Cetewayo's former counselors, was the only one who returned an acquiescent answer. Dinizulu and the rest made no reply. Subsequently the demand for annexation grew so strong among the English, that Eastern Zululand and the Reserve were declared to be a British possession from the 19th of May, 1887. Sir Arthur E. Havelock was appointed Governor of Zululand, and given authority to establish courts and legislate by proclamation, with the assistance of an advisory council, composed of

delegated members of the Legislative Council of Natal. The Queen's sovereignty was formally proclaimed on June 21 by Mr. Osborn, at Ekowe. Dinizulu and other chiefs refused pensions from the British, and on August 24 the late King left Eastern Zululand to establish his residence in the Boer republic, but subsequently returned to his former home, and, on renewing his demands, was threatened with punishment.

Swaziland.—The convention between Great Britain and the Transvaal Republic contained a stipulation that the British should not interfere in Swaziland. The discoveries of gold in Swaziland and the neighboring parts of the Transvaal quickened the interest of the English in this remote region, and furnished a new motive for the annexation of Zululand. The Swazi King, Umbandine, had sold the lands where gold was found to Boer graziers, but the diggers who flocked in paid him for mining rights, and he accepted the British doctrine that he still controlled the minerals, though most of his people sided with the Boers, who claimed the minerals under the soil. Theophilus Shepstone was sent as confidential adviser and commissioner to Umbandine, and was installed on Feb. 18, 1887. The Boers threatened to send a commando into the country in the winter, but were not upheld by the Transvaal Government. Mr. Shepstone called on all the farmers and miners to have their claims registered, and established a tariff of £20 for every mineral concession, and £5 for every trading license.

Amatongaland.—Preliminary steps were taken for establishing a British protectorate over Amatongaland. The Tonga Queen was persuaded, through fear of Portuguese encroachments, to petition for British annexation. In July, a treaty was concluded by which she bound herself not to make any treaty or cede any territory to a foreign power without the consent of the British Government. The Portuguese had come into conflict with the Tongas by asserting their claims to the territory north of the Maputa river, and 26° 30′ south latitude, which was awarded to them by the President of the French Republic in the Delagoa Bay arbitration on July 24, 1875.

CARNOT, MARIE FRANÇOIS SADI, President of the French Republic, born in Limoges, Aug. 11, 1837. He is the grandson of Lazare Nicolas Carnot, Minister of War in the first republic from 1793 to 1797, whose genius and energy in raising and maintaining the army that repelled the allied enemies of the republic earned for him the title of the "Organizer of Victory." The son of the great Carnot, Lazare Hippolyte, inherited the instincts of republicanism. He became a St. Simonian, but turned from the socialists of that school when they adopted Enfantin's views of marriage. From 1839 till 1848 he was a deputy, and voted with the Extreme Left. Under the second republic he was Minister of Education, and after the fall of the empire acted with the Extreme Left. Since 1875 he has been a life-senator. His son, to whom he gave the Persian name Sadi while interested in the study of Oriental languages and literature, was educated as an engineer. He entered the École Polytechnique in 1857, passing fifth in his class, led the class in the École des Ponts et Chaussées, and completed his professional education in 1863. After being for some time assistant secretary to the council for roads and bridges, he was appointed engineer at Annecy in 1864. He introduced improvements in railroad and bridge construction, and planned, among other important works, the great bridge over the Rhône at Collonges, near the Swiss frontier, where he applied a new system of tubular foundation of his own invention. On Jan. 10, 1871, he was appointed prefect of the department of Seine-Inférieure, and at Havre organized the national defense in Normandy, being nominated commissary-extraordinary for the departments of Seine-Inférieure, Eure, and Calvados. On February 8 he was elected by 42,000 votes as the representative of the department of Côte d'Or in the National Assembly. He took his seat with the Left, was chosen secretary of the group of the Republican Left, and voted for all the measures tending to the definitive establishment of the republic and in favor of all the constitutional laws. He was a member of various special committees on public works and industry, and advocated the bill relating to explosives. In the general election of Feb. 20, 1876, he was a candidate for deputy in the second circonscription of the arrondissement of Beaune, and was elected by a large majority over the combined vote of his two competitors. He was chosen secretary in the new Chamber, and was also a member of the budget committee. He was re-elected over the official candidate in the election of Oct. 14, 1877, took a prominent part in all the discussions relating to public works, especially railroads and canals, was several times appointed on the budget committee, and in 1878 was chosen to report the budget of Public Works. On August 12 of that year he was appointed under-secretary of state in the Ministry of Public Works. In the Ferry Cabinet of 1880 he was the head of that ministry, and prosecuted important works, on the development of which he had been engaged while Secretary of State. He was for a time Minister of Finance in 1882. In 1885, M. de Freycinet again called him into the Cabinet. He first took the portfolio of Public Works, but, on the retirement of M. Clamegeran, became Minister of Finance. In that office he had the same trouble with the budget as his predecessors, and was unable to induce the budget committee of the Chamber to adopt his general recommendations. Among other propositions that were defeated was one that he made to allow the Panama Canal Company to issue lottery bonds. He gained much credit for refusing to refund 75,000 francs of stamp duties that

the banker Dreyfuss claimed were illegally exacted, retiring from the ministry in December, 1886, when President Grévy insisted on the restitution. On Oct. 4, 1885, he was again elected deputy for the Côte d'Or. Sadi-Carnot has hitherto made himself conspicuous only by his professional accomplishments, and has never been a political leader, but he has won exceptional esteem by reason of his unquestionable integrity. On the retirement of President Grévy, the two great Republican orators, Ferry and Freycinet, were the principal candidates for the succession. In the first trial ballot of the Republican senators and deputies on the morning of Dec. 3, 1887, the former received 200 and the latter 193 votes, Brisson coming next with 81, and then Sadi-Carnot with 69. The election of Ferry threatened to produce a popular disturbance, and Freycinet's supporters, when they saw that his chance was hopeless, decided to give their votes to Carnot. When the Congress met in the afternoon, Sadi-Carnot received on the first ballot 303 votes, Ferry 212, Gen. Saussier 148, Freycinet 76, Gen. Appert 72, Brisson 26, and other candidates 31. MM. de Freycinet and Ferry then withdrew in favor of Sadi-Carnot, who was elected on the second ballot by 616 votes, Gen. Saussier receiving from the Conservatives 186. President Carnot's wife is a daughter of Dupont White, who translated John Stuart Mill's works into French. Their family consists of four girls. M. Carnot has himself published a translation of Mill's essay on "The Revolution of 1848, and its Detractors" (Paris, 1875).

CARRIERS, MECHANICAL.—The term "store-service," first appeared in the Patent-Office "Gazette" in 1879, in connection with the invention of Joseph O. White, of New York, hereafter described, and two years afterward William S. Lamson, of Lowell, Mass., patented a "cash-carrier." Since that time about 300 patents have been issued in the United States alone bearing upon devices for the ready transmission of cash and small parcels in retail shops or other establishments where such service is required. At present one or another system is in use in a great many of the large mercantile houses where there is likely to be a rush of customers at certain hours or seasons. Almost every ingenious boy has at one time or another constructed some sort of rudimentary carrier, if only a match-box running upon a thread and pulled back and forth between the adjacent desks of school-room intimates. More complete structures are often seen stretching between the windows of neighboring houses in the country, and sometimes across city streets. But to Mr. Lamson apparently belongs the credit of having first brought skilled mechanical construction to bear upon the problem, and introduced cash-carriers as part of the necessary equipment of modern retail stores. Several companies now exist for the manufacture of these carriers, and the business is of such magnitude as to justify some account of the various systems.

Carriers as used in store-service naturally divide themselves into two classes—cash-carriers, which are intended merely to expedite the making of change, and parcel-carriers, which do double duty, carrying the money to the cashier and the goods purchased to an "inspector," who checks off the items of the purchase, and wraps the parcel for delivery. In large establishments, particularly in great cities, the advantage of such service is obvious, as it does away with the necessity of much running to and fro of messengers, which must necessarily interfere with the convenience of customers. The less costly systems are coming into use in small stores, and are found of almost equal advantage. The systems at present in use are, if not as numerous as the patents themselves, at least too many for description here; but the general mechanical principles involved are common to nearly all of them, the difference being in minor details of construction, which, however, are often of vital importance in enabling a merchant to de-

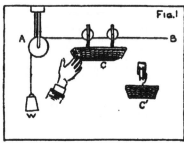

A PRIMITIVE CARRIER.

cide which system is best adapted to his special requirements. A large retail establishment in New York has lately spent about $15,000 in setting up a store-service system; and where such an amount of money is involved, great care is naturally exercised to adopt only the best and simplest devices.

The rudimentary type of carrier is the schoolboy contrivance already referred to, namely, a box or a basket sliding back and forth upon a horizontal cord. The first improvement is the substitution of a smooth wire for the cord, with the basket or car running upon wheels, and an arrangement for keeping the wire permanently tight. Such a system is indicated in Fig. 1. A B is the wire passing over a fixed pulley at A, and kept taut by the weight W. C is the car hanging on the wire ready for use, and C' an end view of the same showing the shape of the wheel attachment. Hand-power is used, a smart push or pull sufficing to send a properly-constructed car fifty or sixty feet. Such contrivances are used to advantage in

stores of moderate size where there is not apt to be an overwhelming rush of customers. The hand propulsion is, however, awkward and uncertain, and the next step is the introduction of the gravity-car, which appears in different forms and at frequent intervals throughout the Patent-Office reports. Fig. 2 shows it in one

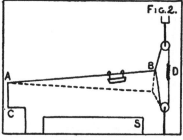

A REVERSIBLE GRADE.

of its simplest forms. A B is the wire, C the cashier's desk, and S the salesman's station. At B the main wire is attached to an endless band running over two pulleys, and provided with a tension-spring at O. Obviously, by revolving the band B D upon the pulleys, the point B can be raised or depressed as much as is necessary to change the angle of inclination of the wire and cause the car to run in either direction. In practice it is found that a rise of $\frac{1}{12}$ of an inch to each foot is enough to carry a properly-constructed car. Much ingenuity has been expended in devising methods of changing the level of wires. Fig. 3 shows one of the simplest and most effective (patent No. 271,-895). The triangles (which may be simply arms) are pivoted at O O, and wires A B are stretched from one to the other. By reversing

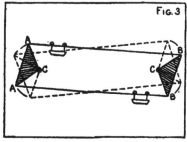

REVERSIBLE DOUBLE WIRE.

the position of the triangles or arms, the inclination of the wires is changed as indicated by the dotted lines.

In Fig. 4 (patent No. 304,585) the necessity of raising and lowering the car is recognized. The wire A B passes over a fixed pulley at O, and over a stationary rest at D. By pulling upon A the car E is raised almost vertically until it is high enough to clear D, when the angle of general inclination is reversed, and

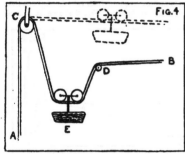

LOWERING, HOISTING, AND REVERSING.

the carrier moves toward B. By this or a similar arrangement, the main line from C to B may be kept high enough to be out of the way, while the carrier alone is lowered to the counter.

The engraving shows only the mechanical principle. In the different systems used there are many ingenious appliances to render the operation of hoisting and lowering certain and easy. (See Figs. 8 and 9.)

Fixed rails for the transit of gravity-cars in store-service were patented by Joseph C. White, of New York, in 1879 (patent No. 221,488), under the title "An apparatus for facilitating payments and delivery of goods." The principle of the invention is shown in Fig. 5, C being the cashier's desk, and S S S the stations of salesmen. The cars were of the usual easily detachable type, so that the salesman could lift his car off from the rails if he

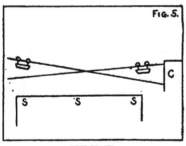

FIXED TRACKS.

saw it coming, but the necessity of making each car announce its arrival at its own particular station was at once apparent, and the inventor provided for it by means of projections upon the cars so placed and adjusted that each car

would ring a bell and derail itself at its own particular station. This was effected by setting the peg or projection at a different height on each car, and providing an inclined plane to correspond at each station. This is indicated in Fig. 6. A B is the inclined track, C and C' are cars, and the round black dots are the projections on each car. D and D' are small inclined planes fixed just below the main track. Car C in descending the incline will carry its projection clear of D', but will engage D,

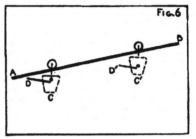

DERAILING DEVICE.

while car C will be stopped by D'. In this this way a considerable number of cars can be made to derail themselves, each falling into or against a suitable receiver. The inventor subsequently broadly claimed "Traveling carriers propelled along ways leading from store-counters to cashier's desk and back to counter through mechanism distinct from the carriers proper." The drawing in the Patent Office shows an endless belt running on suitable sup-

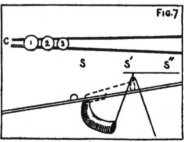

BALLS AND DIVERGENT RAILS.

ports in a horizontal plane, each car being hung upon the belt and detachable at pleasure. Under this patent the system of stoppages foreshadowed in the earlier claim was further elaborated.

Another phase of the gravity system was the early use of ball-carriers. This was the system adopted by Mr. Lamson before referred to, and alleged to have been the first actually in use. It contemplates in general the transmission of cash alone to and from the cashier's desk. Each carrier consists of two hollow hemispheres fastened together by any of the simple mechanical devices, and provided with interior springs which hold the coin and bills near the center of gravity after the two hemispheres are joined together. The balls are of as many different sizes as there are stations to be served, varying perhaps ¼ of an inch in their succcesive diameters. The railway consists in its simplest form of two slightly divergent rails (see Fig. 7) laid at a sufficient angle of inclination from the cashier's desk C, past the salesmen's stations S S' S''. Now, suppose the three balls to be started on the incline from the cashier's desk, number 3 will fall between the rails at S, number 2 will follow suit at S', and number 1 will go on to the end of the line. Under the rails at each station is a net or pocket into which the balls drop convenient to the salesman's hand. For the return of the balls to the cashier a set of parallel rails is provided, inclined in the contrary direction, and various devices are resorted to for hoisting the balls to the rails where they are out of reach. Several systems provide baskets of different kinds, which are hoisted by pulley into position, and release the balls through various mechanical devices. One system adopts a flexible tube, large enough to receive the balls. The loaded ball is dropped into the open end of this tube which is hoisted, until the ball rolls out upon the rails, and goes its way. (See dotted lines in lower section of Fig. 7.)

Another plan provides a system of tubes communicating with a main tube leading to the cashier's desk, which must usually be on

BALL-CARRIER SYSTEM.

the floor below the salesroom. The small tubes rise through the counter, and the salesman merely drops in the balls destined for the cashier. They are returned to the salesmen through a separate tube, or upon rails to which they are necessarily hoisted mechanically.

VOL. XXVII.—7 A

This is distinct from the pneumatic systems described farther on.

The best ball-carrier systems, as used at present, are either modifications of the divergent track, or use a parallel track with automatically-opening switches or traps, for the operation of which many most ingenious de-

GRAVITY PARCEL-CARRIER.

vices are employed. The fundamental idea of most of these is the impact of a moving ball against a trigger so placed that only a ball of a certain size can touch it. The trigger releases a catch, which allows a trap to fall open, or disengages a switch, like those of an ordinary railway, which turns the ball off upon a little side platform or cage that can be lowered to the counter if not within reach, or hoisted to the return track when desired. Fig. 8 shows a ball-carrier system in operation. The arrows indicate the direction of the balls going and returning. C is the cashier, and S the station with the automatic appliances for stopping the balls and lowering them to the counter.

Parcel-carriers have the advantage of doing double duty, since they serve as cash-carriers as well. A simple and effective one is shown in operation in Fig. 9. The hoisting-apparatus at the station S (similar to that shown in Fig. 4) raises the car to the wire, the wheels automatically adjusting themselves. Then the same apparatus hoists the wire itself till the grade is sufficiently changed. This system requires a separate wire for each salesman's station.

More elaborate systems use but a single fixed rail instead of a wire. Switches are provided at each station, and a simple hoisting-apparatus enables the salesman to lower the carrier or hoist it to either of the rails overhead. The switching devices used for carriers having wheels are similar to those described under ball-carriers, but are somewhat more direct and certain in operation. In Fig. 10, for instance, A is a frame set over the track, and B an attachment to a carrier. Each of these frames is pierced with holes, which register upon radii of the same circle. C is a pin, which can be set in any hole on the carrier, and D is a lever connected with the switch. C can be shifted to register with D wherever placed, and thus a large number of carriers can run upon a single track, each turning off at its proper station, leaving the track clear. A similar arrangement, with the adjustment bars straight instead of curved, may be employed though the number of possible switches is considerably reduced in that case, owing to the limitations of space, and the unavoidable oscillations of a single-track car. With a double track, as in a cable system (Fig. 11), a nicer adjustment is practicable. The ends of the carriers in a single-track system are shaped with reference to possible collisions and are provided with buffers so that only a momentary delay results from a chance encounter. The carrying capacity varies, of course, with the strength of construction, but the ordinary retail business, where many customers carry away their purchases, seldom calls for a capacity of more than twelve or fifteen pounds.

The carrier-systems thus far described have depended for motive power mainly upon the always available force of gravity, but gravity is too slow for modern ideas and other means have been adopted. First among these, because simplest, is the "Spring Carrier." It consists of a single taut wire beneath which a small cash-carrier is suspended arranged so as to be readily opened from below without detach-

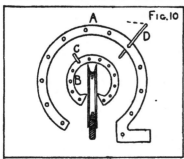

SWITCHING DEVICE.

ing the car from the wire. The wire stretches from a salesman's station to the cashier's desk, and at each end is a spring either of rubber or wire operated by a handle and a releasing-clutch. The carrier can be sent almost instantaneously from end to end of the wire up to a distance of 150 feet. The longest line in operation in New York is 180 feet. This system commends itself for inexpensiveness and simplicity, and is especially adapted for use in shops of moderate size.

One of the most elaborate of the modern cash-carriers is precisely similar in general construction to cable railways as described in the "Annual Cyclopædia" for 1886. The minor

details involving automatically-acting switches are different and merit a description.

The cable is simply an endless wire running over drums at the ends, and bearing upon sheaves wherever necessary in passing curves or the like. The cable runs between light rails

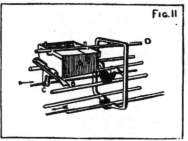

A CABLE-CARRIER.

upon which the carriers slide, and a guide-rod provides against accidental derailment in transit. In Fig. 11 the arrows show the direction of motion in the cable. A is the carrier, and B a lever acting upon the cable-grip C. The salesman has several of the carriers within reach, and when he wishes to send one to the cashier he raises the lever B, and sets the carrier upon the rails in a position it necessarily assumes. Placing his finger upon the lever B, he presses it downward; the grip C closes upon the moving cable, and the carrier disappears so swiftly that the eye can hardly follow, perhaps plunging down through an opening in the floor to the cashier's department, whence it is returned at a like rate of speed, and switches itself off upon a little platform at the proper station. The switching device is unlike any of those described, in that a thin curved piece of metal is fixed at each station in such a position that it engages projections set on top of the carrier and derails it at the proper point. First, however, the cable-grip is automatically released by an inclined fixture against which the lever B strikes just before reaching the switch. At the switch there is a break in the guide-rod D, so that the carrier is free to leave the rails and falls into a suitable receptacle. The whole structure of rails, guide-rods, and supports occupies very little space, and can be so disposed as not to be in the least unsightly or inconvenient. The motive power can be derived from any available source—steam, electricity, water, or the like.

It remains to notice the pneumatic systems which are operated through tubes of glass or metal, either by exhaust-engines or by means of compressed air. These systems necessitate a special tube for each salesman's station, all converging at the cashier's desk. The tubes are about two inches in diameter, and the carriers are cylindrical, fitting the tube loosely, but provided with an elastic attachment which fills the tube and prevents the passage of air. In the exhaust or vacuum systems the air is drawn from the tube in front of the carrier, and the motive force is derived from the natural atmospheric pressure of about fifteen pounds to the square inch. The air current has to be kept up constantly in order to afford a uniform and trustworthy service, and the circulation of air is an important consideration in a crowded establishment.

In the systems operated by compressed air the current is in motion only when actually required. In stores of moderate size, foot-power air-pumps are used, with highly satisfactory results. The fixtures at either end of such a line are shown in Figures 12 and 13, the tubes being carried under the counters or floors, or overhead if more convenient. A salesman (Fig. 13) is represented in the act of sending a carrier. After dropping the carrier into the receptacle he turns the small handle at the side, closing a valve within the tube, and then steps upon the air-pump lever. A slight pressure only is necessary to deliver the carrier in an instant at a distance of 150 feet. Releasing the handle, the valve opens automatically, and the tube is ready for the return carrier. If the valve at either end is closed, the operator at the other end is instantly aware, from the

large establishments a central air-compressor is worked by machinery, and no foot-power is required, the compressed air being furnished from a central receiver, and turned on by salesmen or cashier as required at each station.

Cash and parcel carriers are generally rented

FIG. 13

SALESMAN, PNEUMATIC SYSTEM.

out to merchants at so much a station, the price ranging from $15 to $30 per annum. Each station is supposed to be equivalent or superior in efficiency to the average cash-boy, without any of his mischievous propensities. The saving, therefore, in wages and responsibility is very considerable where a good store-service system is introduced.

CHEMISTRY. Chemical Philosophy.—The determination and graphic representation of the constitution of matter, is the subject of one of the most notable of recent papers in this department of chemical science. The article appeared in "Nature," and begins with the declaration that the growth of the science of organic chemistry is to be measured, not so much by the innumerable new compounds which it has brought to light, as by the unfolding of its doctrine of constitutional formulæ, this being the particular contribution which it has been able to make toward solving the central problem of all chemistry—the constitution of matter. That as a whole these formulæ

FIG. 12

CASHIER, PNEUMATIC SYSTEM.

resistance of the air-pump, that the tube is not clear. At the delivery end the carrier is shot out, falling upon a cushion, as shown in the engraving of the cashier's desk (Fig. 12). In

stand for representations of what is real is attested by the fact that the most successful experimenters of the day confess to having been guided by them at almost every step of their researches. A modern constitutional formula takes the various atoms of a compound in the proportions indicated by the empirical formula, and in the absolute number prescribed by the molecular weight, and arranges them in the way which, within the limits of the law of valency, will best account for the reactions of the compound. The doctrine of these formulæ originated in the difficulty of explaining isomerism under Dalton's law of atomic weights, and of indicating it by his empirical formulæ. The phenomena of isomerism did not militate against the theory of atoms, but really gave it support; for while they were incongruous with the other theories of matter, they were susceptible of explanation under the hypothesis that it consists of atoms variously arranged. From this point of view it was necessary to determine, so far as possible, the mode of arrangement of the atoms in the different compounds. The results of this attempt are embodied in the constitutional formulæ. The method resorted to in solving this problem was similar to that which had been employed in determining the ultimate composition of compounds. Just as when, after isolating from a compound, or introducing into a compound, some particular kind of elementary matter, chemists concluded that the compound actually contained that kind of matter, so when in a reaction a particular group of atoms was eliminated bodily from a compound, or introduced bodily into a compound, they concluded that this group existed as such in the compound. This conclusion, however, is not always so warrantable in the case of atomic groups as in the case of elements. The reaction, for example, by which an atomic group is eliminated from a compound involves the destruction of the parent compound, and in the process it is easy for the atomic groups to undergo rearrangement. The development of the idea of the molecule as distinct from that of the atom and the discovery of a means of determining the molecular weight of bodies, led to the division of isomerides into two classes—those in which the proportions of the various atoms were the same, though the number of atoms in the molecule was different, constituting cases of polymerism; and those in which both the proportions and the whole number of the atoms were the same, or isomeric bodies proper. The knowledge of the molecular weight aided in the construction of constitutional formulæ by determining the exact number of atoms in the molecule, and thus facilitating the task of arranging those atoms by stating precisely how many had to be arranged. The law of valency exercised an important influence by limiting the number of legitimate arrangements. The validity of a constitutional formula is attested by its correctly predicting reactions which

were not contemplated during its construction. It is not probable that there is anything like the constitutional formula—in the sense of its being a picture—in the molecule itself, but quite possibly there is something corresponding with it. A comparison of the physical properties of similarly-constituted compounds shows that in many cases very definite relations can be traced between constitution and physical properties. They are found in such features as the melting-point, boiling-point, specific gravity, behavior toward light, and molecular volumes at boiling-points.

Sir Henry E. Roscoe devoted his presidential address before the British Association at Manchester, chiefly to the general discussion of the present development and prospects of the science of chemistry. Dalton's theory of atoms had become established after fifty years of research, and that had been accomplished, at least to a certain extent, respecting it which he had declared impossible—the atoms had been measured. What are the exact relations between the atomic weights of the different elements—whether or not they are multiples of some ultimate unit—has still escaped painstaking investigation. But it appears to have been determined that "while the atomic weights are not exactly either multiples of the unit or of half the unit, many of the numbers expressing most accurately the weight of the atom, approximate so closely to a multiple of that of hydrogen, that we are constrained to admit that these approximations can not be a mere matter of chance, but that some reason must exist for them; what that reason is, and why a close approximation, and yet something short of absolute identity exists, is as yet hidden behind the veil." Another set of relationships between the elements and their atomic weights has engaged Lothar Meyer, Mendelejeff, and Carnelly in the investigation from which they have agreed in placing all the elementary bodies in a regular sequence, and thus bringing to light a periodic recurrence of analogous chemical and physical properties. Under this system chemists have ventured to predict the atomic weights and qualities of undiscovered elements, and in several cases—gallium, scandium, and germanium—these predictions have been fulfilled. Such results, although they by no means furnish a proof of the supposition that the elements are derived from a common source, clearly point in this direction. Evidence regarding this inquiry is furnished by the action of heat, and consists in the fact that distinct chemical individuals capable of existing at low temperatures, are incapable of existence at high ones, but split up into new materials possessing a less complicated structure than the original. Not only compound bodies have been decomposed by this method, but Victor Meyer has proved in the case of iodine, that the molecule—which the author defines as a more or less complicated aggregation of atoms — is broken into atoms, and J. J. Thomson has shown that this breaking up of the molecule can be effected by heat-vibrations, and by the electrical discharge at a comparatively low temperature. But none of our present atoms have been as yet split up. The spectrum has been thought at times to indicate something of the kind, but the phenomena so regarded may be more rationally referred to the presence of impurities or defect of observational power. So that neither the earth nor the stars have as yet given any evidence of a resolution of any element. Crookes has, however, added a remarkable contribution to the question of the possibility of decomposing the elements, in his observations of the peculiar and characteristic lines in the phosphorescent lights emitted by certain chemical compounds, especially the rare earths, under an electric discharge in a high vacuum; but the explanation of these phenomena does not necessitate atomic decomposition. Thermal chemistry is even yet in its infancy, but "an infant of sturdy growth, likely to do good in the world"; while great advance is promised in the region of electrical chemistry. By the theory of the constitution of matter by molecular arrangement, we are able not only to explain the differences in isomeric substances, but also to predict the number of distinct variations in which any given chemical compound can possibly exist. "This power of successful prediction constitutes a high-water mark of science, for it indicates that the theory upon which such a power is based is a true one." With this doctrine, associated with that of valency, organic chemistry has become synthetic, and Liebig and Wöhler's prediction fifty years ago, that sugar, morphia, and salicene would be artificially prepared, has been fulfilled. With the success achieved in this line of experimentation, "the belief in a special vital force has disappeared like an *ignis fatuus*, and no longer leads us in the wrong direction. We know now that the same laws regulate the formation of chemical compounds in both animate and inanimate Nature; and the chemist only asks for a knowledge of the constitution of any definite chemical compound found in the organic world, in order to be able to promise to prepare it artificially." Yet the barrier which exists between the organized and unorganized worlds is one which the chemist at present sees no chance of breaking down. "Protoplasm, with which the simplest manifestations of life are associated, is not a compound but a structure built up of compounds. The chemist may successfully synthetize any of its component molecules, but he has no more reason to look forward to the synthetic production of the structure than to imagine that the synthesis of gallic acid leads to the artificial production of gall-nuts." Liebig's classification of food-substances into those which serve for maintaining the heat of the body and those which are needed for repairing muscular waste, has not held good. The nitrogenous constituents of food do doubtless go to repair the waste of muscle, while the function of the non-nitrogenous food is not only to supply the animal heat, but also to furnish, by its oxidation, the muscular energy of the body. We thus come to the conclusion that it is the potential energy of the food which furnishes the actual energy of the body, expressed in terms either of heat or of mechanical work; and to this must be added the action of the mind or the body not yet accounted for. Liebig's assumption that plants derive their carbon mainly from the atmosphere rather than from the ground, has been confirmed by the forty-four years' experiments of Lawes and Gilbert; but his theory that the whole of the nitrogen required by the plant is derived from atmospheric ammonia, is shown by the same experiments to be inadequate. Some light is given upon the origin of this nitrogen by Berthelot, who has shown that under certain conditions the soil has the power of absorbing the nitrogen of the air and forming compounds which can subsequently be assimilated by the plant. The microscope has contributed to our knowledge of fermentative processes by showing, in contradiction to Liebig's purely chemical view, that they are produced by the growth of new organisms; but chemistry steps in again at this point with the discovery that these organisms act by developing definite chemical compounds, the nature of which, and their function in provoking disease, it is for that science to determine.

Investigations of the spectra of various rare earths have led Mr. William Crookes to declare that there are elements, the existence of which is revealed by the spectrum lines, but which still remain to be separated. This view is confirmed by his own fractional separation of the earths of yttrium and by the parallel researches of Dr. Auer von Welsbach, M. de Boisbaudran, and M. Demarçay. Under these researches, yttrium indicated that it was composed of five constituents, and the two elements into which the didymium had been separated appeared each to consist of several. Other researches, by Drs. Krüss and Nilson, upon rare earths in Scandinavian minerals, have yielded still more interesting results, the main outcome of which appears to be that, instead of holmium, erbium, thulium, didymium, and samarium, we must, if we follow these authors, recognize the existence of at least twenty-two new elements. If we add to these the results previously obtained by Mr. Crookes with respect to yttrium, instead of six, we shall find ourselves in the presence of twenty-seven elements, and realize a gain of at least twenty-one such bodies.

Dr. T. Sterry Hunt proposes a new theory of the process of chemical union or combination, which he defines as integration. It may take place either among unlike or like species, and is in the latter case a homogeneous integration, constituting what is called polymerization, while depolymerization is a homogeneous disintegration. These two forms of the chemical process are respectively metamorphosis by condensation and by expansion. As between unlike species they constitute heterogeneous integration and heterogeneous disintegration, or chemical metagenesis, and give rise to species differing in centesimal composition from the parents. The chemical species to those agencies which do not effect its disintegration, is a complete entity or integer. This, in the case of homogeneous integration of gases and vapors, is generated by the condensation into a single volume of two or more volumes of less condensed species ; as where the atoms $H+H$ became the molecule H^2. A number of substances are named which are double or dyad integers at normal temperatures, while others, tryad, tetrad, hexad, etc., at ordinary temperatures become dissociated by intense heating into equivalent numbers of dyads. As the specific gravity is known to vary with the equivalent weight in the case of gases and vapors, so a similar direct relation is indicated in liquids and in solids ; and the hardness and chemical indifference of solid species are in like manner functions of their atomic weights. Further, the author advances that the gas or vapor of a volatile body constitutes a species distinct from the same body in its liquid or solid state, the chemical formula of the latter being some multiple of the first ; and the liquid and solid species (probably always) constitute two distinct species of different atomic weights, whence it follows that all condensation of gases and vapors by cold or pressure, and all fusion, solidification, and vaporization, are chemical metamorphoses. This is in accordance with Henri Sainte-Claire Deville's views on dissociation. It is also in harmony with a suggestion by Prof. J. P. Cooke, that certain alloys are to be regarded in part as examples of a progressive series of isomorphous compounds of antimony and zinc of high equivalent, differing from each other nZn_2. This term is not to be considered a deviation from the law of definite proportions, but "only an expression of that law in a higher form."

Chemical Physics.—In his report on the subject of solution made to the meeting of the British Association, in 1885, Prof. W. A. Tilden particularly referred to the question whether the phenomena of that name are to be considered chemical or mechanical. At what point in the curve of the evolution of heat which takes place during the process of solution can we set up a distinction between the effect due to chemical combination and that due to other causes, such as the change of volume consequent on dilution, or the possible loss of energy from the adjustment of the motion of the molecules of the constituents to the conditions requisite for the formation of a homogeneous liquid, or the decomposition of the compound by the water? In the action of the solution of solids in water, the volume of the solution is always, with the exception of some ammonium salts, less than the sum of the volumes of the solid and its solvent. Similarly, the addition of water to a solution is followed by contraction, which may be due to mechanical fitting of the molecules of the one liquid into the interspaces between those of the other ; or to a readjustment of molecular motion. The heat evolved or absorbed during the admixture of any substance with water is a continuous function of the quantity of water added. Similarly, the contraction which ensues on diluting an aqueous solution proceeds continuously, and the molecular volume of a salt in solutions of different strengths is continuously greater the larger the amount of salt present. So that no indication is observed of the formation of compounds of definite composition distinguishable by characteristic properties. As to the question whether the solvent and the substance dissolved in it, or any portion thereof, exist independently of one another the view seems preferable that save, perhaps, in excessively dilute solutions, the dissolved substance is attached in some way to the whole of the water. As to what determines the solubility of a substance, the following propositions seem to be true : Nearly all salts which contain water of crystallization are soluble in water, and for the most part easily soluble ; insoluble salts are almost always destitute of water of crystallization, and rarely contain the elements of water. In a series of salts containing nearly allied metals, the solubility and capacity for uniting with water of crystallization generally diminish as the atomic weight increases. The fusibility of a substance has much to do with its solubility. Neither fusibility alone nor chemical constitution alone seems sufficient to determine whether a solid shall be soluble or not, but it may be taken as a rule that when there is a close connection in chemical constitution between a liquid and a solid, and the solid is at the same time easily fusible, it will also be easily soluble in that liquid. Salts containing water of crystallization may be considered as closely resembling water itself, and these are, for the most part, both easily fusible and easily soluble in water. No definite explanation of supersaturation has been generally accepted. In the opinion of the speaker it is identical with superfusion. The conclusion seems inevitable that chemical combination is not to be distinguished by any absolute criterion from mere physical or mechanical aggregation ; and probably chemical combination differs from mechanical combination—called cohesion or adhesion—chiefly in the fact that the atoms or molecules of the bodies concerned come relatively closer together, and the consequent loss of energy is greater.

From experiments on more than forty elements, Mr. James Blake supposes that the action of inorganic substances upon living matter depends on their isomorphic relations, and that all substances belonging to one and the same isomorphous group give rise approximately to the same physiological reactions. To this rule he has found only two exceptions—nitrogen and potassium. When the same element forms two classes of salts belonging to distinct iso-morphous groups, the physiological action of the salts in each class is different, but agrees with that of other substances of the group to which it belongs. In substances of the same isomorphous group the physiological action increases in intensity with the atomic weights of the elements present. A speciali-zation of the reactions for each isomorphous group is also observed. Thus the compounds of the alkali-metals act upon the internal ganglia of the heart; the compounds of phos-phorous, arsenic, and antimony act upon the splanchnic ganglia; the substances of the mag-nesian group act upon the center for vomiting; and in an analogous manner for other groups, it is by modifying the action of some nerve-center that their physiological action is shown. Isomorphous substances are found to give rise to the same physiological reactions when they have homologous spectra, but when in an isomorphous group there are found elements whose spectra do not resemble the spectra of other elements of the group, these elements with anomalous spectra give rise also to anoma-lous physiological reactions. The exceptional character of the action of nitrogen and potas-sium is indicated by the exceptional character of their spectra, which are homologous with no other; and nitrogen, with a very complex spectrum, reveals its presence by its action on the nerve-centers, and is sharply distinguished from all the other elements of the same group.

M. Konovaloff, in treating of contact-action phenomena, has thrown out the suggestion that the bombardment of the molecules on the solid matter might cause a transformation in part of their kinetic energy into intra-molecu-lar work, tending to bring about dissociation of the molecules. A. Irving has investigated that class of results which are observed when under the influence of heated spongy platinum, or platinized asbestos, or other porous or finely-divided bodies, combinations are brought about with the intervention of contact-action at much lower temperatures than are required without it. While we admit that the kinetic energy of a gas is proportional to its absolute temperature, and that the total resistance of a gas is the sum of the energies of motion of its constituent mole-cules, it does not follow that the energy of mo-tion is the same in all the molecules. The tem-perature indicated by the thermometer must rather be regarded as the mean of the tempera-tures (or energies of translation) of the mole-cules. Further, the atoms themselves must be regarded as carriers of dynamical energy, and there must be variations in atom temperatures along with variations in the energy of translation of the molecules. "Dissociation temperature," so far as individual molecules are concerned, may be taken to represent simply a sufficient increase in the vibratory motions of the atoms

to carry them beyond the range of the attrac-tion of affinity which holds them together in the molecule. Since both the energy of trans-lation of the molecule and the atom-tempera-ture may vary within wide limits, it follows that in a given mass of gas there must be some mole-cules which require a smaller accession of heat from without the system than is required by those which are in the condition of the mean dynamical intensity of the system, in order that they may be dissociated. This is what is known as the initial temperature of dissocia-tion. If the mean temperature of the system be maintained constant above that of the ini-tial temperature of dissociation, a certain per-centage of the gas will be dissociated. For the same temperature, other things being equal, the same percentage of the gas is dissociated, but not the same identical molecules. New molecules are continually undergoing dissocia-tion, while some of the previously dissociated atoms, owing to diminution in the intensity of their vibratory motion, enter again into molec-ular union, so that for complete dissociation either the removal from the system of the iso-lated atoms, or an enormous elevation of tem-perature of the whole system is required. When we have the intervention of a porous or finely-divided solid, the enormous increase of the solid surface must lead to a corresponding increase of the number of collisions in a given time between the individual molecules and that surface; and consequently internal work may be, and probably is, done among the atoms of the molecules by increasing the intensity of their vibratory action; and so far as the mole-cules thus affected are concerned, a smaller ac-cession of heat derived from without the sys-tem would most likely be necessary to bring about initial dissociation.

Landholt has made some researches on the velocity of movement of the molecules of fluids and solids. He found that fluids which react immediately upon one another in certain de-grees of concentration require more space for the process when dilute, in proportion to the degree of dilution. In his test experiment with a mixture of sulphurous and hydriodic acids resulting in the separation of iodine, other conditions being the same, the time in which the moment of reaction would take place could be foretold by the clock. A mixt-ure of one molecular part of the sulphur acid to 90,000 molecular parts of water and two of the iodine acid to the same quantity of water, with starch added, remained colorless for twen-ty seconds, when the change to deep blue took place at once. When the dilution was doubled, two minutes, when tripled, seven minutes elapsed before the sign of the reaction was given. If, instead of water the dilution was effected with a liquid of greater viscosity—glycerin, for example, was employed as a diluent—the time required for the reaction was prolonged, and the exhibition of the effect, or the appear-ance of the blue color, was gradual.

J. N. Buchanan has experimented upon the composition of the ice produced in saline solutions, and more particularly in sea-water. It has been a question whether the salt found to be retained in the ice is to be attributed to the solid matter of the ice or to the liquid mechanically adhering to it. The experiments in freezing showed that the composition of the saline contents of the ice formed was the same as that of the original water, and this was of itself regarded as almost conclusive that the salt is contained in adhering brine, and not as a solid constituent of the ice. Assuming this to be so, the amount of ice formed as deduced from the composition of the mother-liquor, agreed well with the amount deduced from the thermal exchange taking place during the freezing. It has been proved by Guthrie, Rüdorff, and others, that in solutions of the salts occurring in sea-water, ice separates at first, and continues to separate until the concentration has become many times greater than that of sea-water. Assuming that in sea-water all the chlorine is united to sodium, 87 per cent. of the water would have to be removed as ice; and if it contained nothing but sulphate of soda in the proportion corresponding to the sulphuric acid formed in it, over 90 per cent. of the water would have to go as ice, before the cryohydrate would be formed. In Mr. Buchanan's experiments about 15 per cent. of the weight of the water was frozen out as ice, causing a lowering of the freezing-point by $0.3°$ C. In Nature the ice forming at the actual freezing surface probably does so at an almost uniform temperature. In the interstices of the crystals there will be retained a weight of slightly concentrated sea-water at least as great as that of the ice-crystals. At the winter quarters of the Vega, brine was observed oozing out of sea-water ice and liquid at a temperature of $80°$ C. It was very rich in calcium and especially magnesium chlorides. In fact, it is probably quite impossible by any cold occurring in nature to solidify sea-water. As residual and unfreezable brine remains in considerable quantity when sea-water is frozen, it must also remain in greater or less quantity when fresh water is frozen. All natural waters, including rain-water, contain some foreign and in nearly all cases more or less saline ingredients.

Victor Meyer has found that magnesium melts at a temperature that can not fall far short of $800°$ C. As it is completely volatilized at a white heat the density of its vapor can not be determined. While the author was unsuccessful in his efforts to ascertain the densities of the vapors of antimony and germanium, he found that antimony could be completely, though slowly, volatilized at about $1,300°$ C.

Experiments by George Man, on the freezing of aërated water, gave the results that in a thin ice coating the upper or surface half contained barely a trace of eliminated air, while the under or bottom half contained 0.08 cubic inch of air in each pound of ice, and that a surface coating of ice $1\frac{1}{4}$ inch thick contained 0.15 cubic inch of air in each pound, while an entirely frozen mass contained 0.59 cubic inch of air in each pound weight. The freezing of a limited body of water which had first been frozen over and had the surface ice removed, pointed still more strikingly to the concentration of air in solution, for this contained 0.89 cubic inch of air in each pound weight.

Olzewski has continued his experiments in the study of liquefied and solidified gases with very interesting results. Liquid hydrofluoric acid is frozen at $-102.5°$ C. into a transparent crystalline mass, which at a lower temperature becomes white and opaque, and which melts at $-92.3°$ C. The glass tubes used in the experiments were protected from the action of the acid by a thin transparent coating of paraffine. Gaseous phosphoretted hydrogen was easily liquefied at $-90°$ C., and frozen at $-133.5°$ into a white crystalline mass, which melted again at $132.5°$ C. and boiled at $-85°$ C. Antimoniureted hydrogen was likewise liquefied and condensed into a white snow, which melted at $-91.5°$ C. into a colorless liquid. Ozone has been liquefied at the ordinary atmospheric pressure at a temperature of $-181.4°$ C. The liquid in very thin layers at this temperature is transparent, but in layers 2mm. thick it is nearly opaque. Its point of incipient boiling was fixed at $-109°$ C. with a thermometer containing carbon disulphide, which corresponds with $-106°$ C. on a hydrogen thermometer. Sealed in a glass tube the liquid becomes a blue gas, which may be again condensed by placing it in boiling ethylene. The author has been able, with boiling ethylene and pressure, to obtain from 18 to 15cc. of any desired gas in the liquid condition. The volume, mass, and density of the liquid can be very readily determined with his apparatus. The densities of methane, oxygen, and nitrogen, thus found, are, at the temperature of their boiling-points:

PRODUCT.	Density.	Boiling-points.
Methane........................	0·415	$-164.0°$
Oxygen.........................	1 124	-181.4
Nitrogen	0·885	-194.4

Experiments by Baker to determine the nature of the gas given up by charcoal on heating when it has absorbed oxygen, indicate that carbon monoxide is the chief product, and that the carbon is burned to this gas by the absorbed and firmly retained oxygen.

New Substances.—The new metal, germanium, is described by its discoverer, Clemens Winkler, as grayish white, having a brilliant metallic luster, and crystallizing in well-formed, regular octahedrons. It melts at a somewhat lower temperature than silver, $900°$ C., and volatilizes at a slightly higher one than this, expands on solidifying, and crystallizes. Before the blowpipe it fuses to a globule, which evolves white fumes and explodes, as does antimony. Its atomic weight is calculated at 72.320. Leooq de Boisbaudran estimated its atomic weight from two characteristic lines in the spectrum at 72·31 or 72·27. The position of germanium is that of ekasilicon in Mendelejeff's table, for which he predicted an atomic weight of 72 and specific gravity of 5·5. The specific gravity of germanium is 5·469. This position is more conclusively indicated by two of the compounds of germanium prepared by Dr. Winkler. The first is germanium-chloroform, GeHCl₃, analogous to the similar compounds of carbon and silicon, which is obtained by gently heating germanium in a stream of dry hydrochloric-acid gas. The second is germanium ethide, Ge $(C_2H_5)_4$, analogous to the ethides of silicon and tin, which is obtained by the action of two volumes of zinc ethide upon one volume of germanium tetrachloride. This disposes of all doubt that the gap in the periodic table must be occupied by germanium, for Dr. Mendelejeff predicted that the metal thus filling up this particular gap would be found to form, if discovered, a tetraethide of specific gravity about 0·96, and boiling at 160° —conditions which germanium ethide fulfils.

A fine series of new coloring-matters has been discovered by Dr. J. H. Siegler, by the employment of the hydrazine reaction upon amido-derivatives of triphenyl-methane. Rosaniline hydrochloride was first converted by nitrous acid into its diazo-derivative, and this was then reduced with 'tin and hydrochloric acid, yielding brilliant green crystals of a hydrazine salt. This new hydrazine, which the discoverer terms roshydrazine, is itself a coloring-matter of a somewhat bluer shade than fuchsine, and forms the nucleus of the series. By treatment with aldehyde, acetone, or benzophenone, condensation products are obtained possessing brilliant colors, varying from red to violet; benzaldehyde and aceto-acetic ether, yield beautiful blues; while grape-sugar forms with roshydrazine a dye of a greenish-blue tint. Numerous shades are further produced by the action of other reagents. The sulphoderivative of roshydrazine appears to form a second series of colored substances quite as numerous as those of the nucleus itself. These new colors are practically insoluble in water, and a fact of most vital importance about them is that they may be readily prepared in situ upon the fiber; for it is only necessary to immerse the material first in a bath of roshydrazine, and afterward in a second bath containing the condensing reagent.

Mr. Cary Lea has published a series of papers to show that chlorine, bromine, and iodine are capable of forming compounds with silver exhibiting varied and beautiful colors—peach-blossom, rose, purple, and black; that these compounds (except under the influence of light) possess great stability; that they may be obtained by purely chemical means, and in the entire absence of light; that of them the red chloride shows a tendency to the reproduction of colors. It is not improbable that the material of the infinitesimally thin films obtained by Becquerel, Niepce de St. Victor, Poitevin, and others, may be the red chloride; and that these substances, formed by purely chemical means, constitute the actual material of the latent invisible photographic image, which material may now be obtained in the laboratory without the aid of light and in any desired quantity. They also form part of the visible product resulting from the action of light on the silver haloids. The salts thus produced are called by the author photo-salts, because of their identity with the products of the action of light on the normal silver haloids. Mr. Lea concludes from the results of his experiments, that the latent photographic image consists neither of the normal silver haloid modified nor of a subsalt, but of a combination of normal salt and subsalt; that the salt loses in this way its weak resistance to reagents, and acquires stability, thus corresponding to the great stability of the latent image, which, though a reduction product, shows considerable resistance to even so powerful an oxidizer as nitric acid; further, that this combination of normal salt and subsalt, which constitutes the material of the latent image, can be obtained by chemical means, and wholly without the aid of light; that the forms of the photo-salts which correspond to the material of the latent image are colorless or nearly so, but that other forms, possessing beautiful and often intense coloration, also exist. With the chloride some of these brightly-colored forms show a ready tendency to reproduce color, in some cases with well-marked and beautiful tints. "So that we have here an approach to the solution of the problem of obtaining images of objects in their natural colors from a quite new direction, and probably with better hopes of an eventual complete success than by any of the older methods."

A new preparation, salol, or phenolsalicylic acid, offered by Professor Rencki as a substitute for the unpleasant specific salicylate of soda in rheumatic disorders, has found a ready market. The new compound is as valuable as an antiseptic and antipyretic as in its more special application. It is a white, crystalline powder, having a weak aromatic odor, but perfectly tasteless, insoluble in water, but easily soluble in alcohol and ether. The pure preparation melts at 42° or 43° C., and is not colored by chloride of iron, which stains its components, phenol or carbolic acid, and salicylic acid— deep bluish green or violet. It is prepared by heating molecular proportions of salicylate of soda and phenol-soda with chloride of phosphorus. Salol is perfectly harmless in its effects on the system, and is used in the same way as the salicylate of soda.

The theory that microbes are the primary sources of disease has been qualified by the discovery that certain alkaloids which act as violent poisons are the immediate result or accompaniment of bacterial fermentation. Brieger has isolated a well-characterized alkaloid, which he calls tetanine, from the liquid used for cultivating a bacillus which has been supposed to cause tetanus traumaticus in animals. His experiments raise the question whether the bacillus or the tetanine is the immediate cause of the disorder. It remains to be determined whether the alkaloid is a secretion or other product of the life of the bacillus, when the bacillus would be the primary cause and the tetanine the secondary or immediate cause of disease; or, whether it is a direct result of chemical action in the cultivating liquid.

About 300 cases of cheese-poisoning having occurred in Michigan in 1883-'84, all traceable to the eating of twelve different cheeses, Victor C. Vaughn examined specimens of all the cheeses, in order to detect the toxic agent. The cheeses were in good condition, with nothing in the taste or odor to excite suspicion; but from a freshly-cut surface there exuded numerous drops of a slightly opalescent fluid, which reddened litmus instantly and intensely. It was also observed that when samples of this cheese and of a good cheese were placed before a cat or a dog, the animal would invariably select the good cheese; while it would eat the poisonous cheese if no other were offered. From an alcoholic extract of the cheese a residue was collected which produced the symptoms of poisoning, but from which the poison itself could not be separated. The aqueous extract was also poisonous, but when evaporated at the boiling-point of water, carried off the poison with the vapor, proving the poison to be volatile. Distillation at a low temperature likewise seemed to cause a decomposition of the poison. It was, however, separated by spontaneous evaporation in needle-shaped crystals, having a penetrating, old-cheesy odor, like that which Husemann and Boehm have observed in poisonous sausage. If the crystals are allowed to stand exposed to the air at ordinary temperature, they decompose with the formation of an organic acid. The substance, which is called tyrotoxicon, is soluble in water, alcohol, chloroform, and ether. The smallness of the amounts obtained and the rapid decomposition have prevented definite analysis. The only certain test for the poisons is the physiological one. A few drops of an aqueous solution of the crystals placed upon the tongue produce the symptoms characteristic of poisonous cheese: dryness of the throat, nausea, vomiting, and diarrhea. The same poison recognized by its crystalline appearance and its physiological effects, was isolated from milk which had stood in a glass-stoppered bottle for about six months. Normal milk placed in perfectly clean bottles secured with glass-stoppers, developed the poison in about three months. In the case of the poisoning of a number of persons by ice-cream, the effect was traced to tyrotoxicon; and in this instance the poison was found to have been formed after exposure, under favorable bac-

teriological conditions, for only a few hours. It is known that milk, while undergoing the lactic-acid fermentation, does not possess any such poisonous properties as belong to tyrotoxicon; and there is no evidence that the poison is connected with the ordinary decomposition of milk. It is probably the product of a peculiar bacterial fermentation.

A new amorphous modification of arsenic has been obtained by Geuther, by slowly adding cold water to a mixture of arsenic trichloride and phosphorus trichloride, and heating the whole to boiling. It is brownish black in color, and has a specific gravity of 3·70; ordinary amorphous arsenic is black, and has a specific gravity of 4·71.

Mr. Fletcher has obtained a third crystalline form of carbon by treating an Australian meteoric iron with *aqua regia*. Bright opaque grayish-black crystals remained, having a metallic luster, and presenting forms belonging to the cubic system. The hardness is considerably greater than that of graphite, which the crystals otherwise resemble in density, color, and streak, but their sharply-defined cubic forms are quite different from the indistinct tabular crystals of graphite.

W. F. Hillebrand has described a new mineral from Tombstone, Arizona, which is called Emmonsite. It is yellowish green, translucent, and occurs in crystalline scales and patches in a brownish gangue, composed of lead-carbonate, quartz, and a brown substance containing iron, tellurium, and water. It is probably monoclinic, and slightly pleochroic. Its specific gravity is about 5. In composition it is a hydrated telluride of iron, usually containing a trace of selenium.

A new chlorobromide of silicon—chlorotribromide, $SiClBr_3$—has been isolated by Prof. Emerson Reynolds from crude silicon tetrabromide. It is a liquid which fumes in the air, and on addition of water is decomposed into a mixture of silicic, hydrobromic, and hydrochloric acids. It is of considerable theoretical interest, inasmuch as it completes a series of compounds in which chlorine and bromine mutually replace each other, and the end-members of which are formed by the tetrachloride and tetrabromide of silicon, respectively, as follow: $SiCl_4$, $SiCl_3Br$, $SiCl_2Br_2$, $SiClBr_3$, and $SiBr_4$. This series is now perfectly analogous to the one formed by the compounds of chlorine and bromine with carbon.

Gottig has described two new hydrates of potassium hydroxide, which were obtained from alcoholic solutions having different specific gravities. The hydrate from the stronger solution forms large prismatic crystals, and gives the formula $(KOH)_3 \cdot (H_2O)_2$. The other hydrate, $(KOH)_3 \cdot (H_2O)_5$, forms exceedingly long needles which split in drying into fine filaments, causing the mass to resemble cotton-wool; and on complete drying these unite again to form a hard, compact mass.

New Processes.—Mr. Castner's new process for

the production of metallic sodium and potassium, which has been mentioned in previous volumes of the "Annual Cyclopædia," has proved to be practicable and successful. A more detailed description of the process than we have hitherto given is the following: "The mineral known as 'purple ore,' an oxide of iron, is heated to a temperature of 500° C., and at the same time a mixture of carbonic oxide and hydrogen is poured over it. By this the oxide of iron is changed into metallic iron, which remains in the state of a fine powder. This powder is mixed with melted pitch, and the whole is allowed to cool. .It is next broken into lumps of about the size of bricks, and these are heated in large crucibles, and converted into coke. This coke is found to contain a definite quantity of iron and carbon, which can not be separated again by mechanical means. It is next powdered finely, and added in proper proportions to the hydrate of potash or soda, and the mixture is gently heated for about thirty minutes in a retort of cast-steel or cast-iron, whereby it is fused and made to give off large quantities of hydrogen gas. When the bulk of this gas has disappeared, the reaction proceeds with less violence; and the retort is then placed in a hotter furnace where the temperature rises to about 800° C. The sodium or potassium distills over very quickly, and in about ninety minutes the operation is complete. Great care is taken that no carbonic-acid gas should be produced during the distillation of the metal, because this gas is the cause of the formation of the explosive compound. This is practically possible without adopting any other precaution than that of using a quantity of the coke slightly less than the theoretical amount."

C. A. Crampton and T. C. Trescot describe a process for the estimation of carbonic acid in beer. The analysis is difficult in the case of beer in casks or kegs, on account of the impossibility of preventing the loss of carbonic acid in drawing the beer, but is easier with bottled beer. A champagne tap is used for drawing the gas. A difficulty arising from the stoppage of the tube by the accumulation of bubbles was obviated by connecting the champagne tap with an Eslenmeyer flask, in the broad bottom of which the bubbles are broken. This is connected with a U-tube filled with sulphuric acid, and this with a calcium-chloride tube and then a soda-lime tube to absorb the dried carbonic acid. The drawing of the gas through the tap is assisted by heating it to 80° C. after it has ceased to flow spontaneously. The gas is collected and absorbed in the soda-lime tube; and the increase in weight of the latter after the experiment gives the amount of carbonic acid in the beer.

H. B. Cornwall, analyzing butter for the detection of artificial coloring-matters, extracts annotto by the ethereal process. The dry, yellow, or slightly-orange residue of this substance turns blue or violet-blue with sulphuric acid, then quickly green, and finally brownish, or to a violet variable according to the purity of the extract. Saffron, which can be extracted in the same way, differs from annotto very decidedly; the most important difference is in the absence of the green coloration. Genuine butter, free from foreign coloring-matter, imparts at most a very pale-yellow color to the alkaline solution; but it is important to note that a mere green coloration of the dry residue on the addition of sulphuric acid is not a certain indication of annotto; for the author has obtained from genuine butter, free from foreign coloring-matter, a dirty-green coloration, but not preceded by any blue or violet-blue tint. Turmeric is easily identified by the brownish to reddish stratum that forms between the ethereal fat solution and the alkaline solution before they are intimately mixed. It may be better recognized by carefully bringing a very slightly alkaline solution of ammonia in alcohol beneath the fat solution, and then gently agitating the two for a moment.

The brothers O. and A. Brice, of Paris, obtain oxygen in quantities for economical use by utilizing the property of barium oxide, BaO, of absorbing oxygen from the atmosphere at a moderate heat, whereby the superoxide, BaO₂, is formed, and giving it out again when heated to a higher temperature. During the oxidating process the nitrogen is pumped into a second system of retorts containing a baryta coke, formed by mixing caustic baryta and charcoal-dust with tar, whereby a cyanide of barium is formed, and then converted by treatment with steam at 800° C. into ammonia, carbonic acid, and regenerated baryta. Baryta is obtained for this purpose by treatment of the nitrate by a patented process.

H. Moissan has isolated fluorine by exposing anhydrous hydrofluoric acid to a strong electric current, using platinum for the negative, and a mixture of nine parts of platinum and one part of iridium for the positive electrode, and re-enforcing the hydrofluoric acid at a certain moment with hydrofluorate of potash. Hydrogen appeared at the negative electrode, and at the positive, fluorine, as a colorless, strongly-smelling gas. In it, silicon burned with a bright glow, producing fluosilicic acid, as did also, likewise with light, and producing their respective fluorine compounds, boron, phosphorus, arsenic, antimony, sulphur, and iodine. Water was decomposed with the formation of hydrofluoric acid and ozone; iodine was separated from potassium iodide. The gas acted less vigorously upon the metals, probably because the resultant coating of fluoride protected the rest of the metallic substance; and was inert as to carbon. Many organic substances were strongly attacked, and some, including alcohol, ether, benzine, petroleum, and turpentine oil, with ignition. After some time, the fluorine and hydrogen again came in contact, when they were reunited, with detonation.

MM. Colson and Gauthier describe a new

quantitative reaction, by means of which any desired substitution of chlorine may be readily effected in a large number of hydrocarbons. It consists of heating in a sealed tube the calculated quantities of hydrocarbon and phosphorus pentachloride, when the pentachloride is dissociated into the trichloride and free chlorine. The value of this means of substitution lies in the fact that, instead of the uncertain results so frequently obtained by the graduated use of free chlorine, it now becomes possible to obtain a quantitative yield, in a form that is easily separable, of the particular chlorine derivative desired.

R. T. Thomson publishes two methods for the estimation of aluminum in the presence of a large proportion of iron. One is for use when but little, the other when a larger proportion of manganese is present. Both depend upon the reduction of the iron to a ferrous state and the precipitation of aluminum as a phosphate by means of ammonia and ammonium acetate.

Franke describes the preparation of manganic anhydride, MnO_3. To obtain it, dry potassium permanganate is added to well-cooled sulphuric acid; the green solution formed is either heated to 50° C., after addition of a little water, or better, allowed to flow, drop by drop, on to calcined soda. Violet vapors of manganic anhydride are evolved, and condense in the receiver to a dark amorphous mass. When heated at 50° it volatilizes in violet vapors, with partial decomposition into manganic dioxide and oxygen. If heated more strongly, it is completely decomposed into those substances. It dissolves only sparingly in water, imparting to it a deep-red color. It is also a most vigorous oxydizing agent.

Industrial Chemistry.—Mr. A. E. Fletcher, chief inspector under the Alkali Works Regulation Act, describing in the British Association the present position of the alkali manufacture, said that Leblanc's process had withstood the attacks of all rivals, and that, although the competition against it was fiercer than at any previous period, he thought that it would maintain its position for many a year to come. During the last ten years slight alterations had been proposed in the proportions to be used of the three ingredients forming the charge of the black-ash furnace—the coal, brimstone or chalk, and sulphate of soda—and in the method of throwing them in the furnace. The main process, however, of fusing these materials together, and, when cold, lixiviating the mixture for the extraction of carbonate of soda, is followed almost exactly as was proposed by Leblanc, now almost a century ago. It must be acknowledged that this process is seriously attacked by another, so far as the manufacture of carbonate of soda is concerned, and it would have been by this time completely driven out of the market by its rival, but for the importance of its by-product. Bleaching-powder had not as yet been made in connection with the ammonia process. Three methods were, however, proposed, and were on their trial for the attainment of that end. If bleaching-powder could be produced by either of them at a moderate cost, the older alkali process could no longer stand its ground.

Traube has made some new researches on the part taken by water in the combustion of carbonic oxide, which have a double interest in their bearing on the properties of water-gas, and of the peroxide of hydrogen. The peroxide of hydrogen is constantly finding increasing application, more or less diluted with water, as an oxidizing, bleaching, and disinfecting agent. It is used for the bleaching of bones and ivory, wool, silk, feathers, and hair; in housekeeping for removing wine and fruit spots from white cloths. It stops all kinds of fermentation, and is therefore a good preserving agent. Destroying all micro-organisms, it is valuable in the treatment of wounds and skin-diseases. To prevent decomposition, however, the solutions of this substance must be kept at a low temperature and protected from the light. According to Dixon's experiments, a perfectly dry mixture of oxygen and carbonic oxide can not be exploded by any ordinary means; and ignition will not take place until a certain quantity of the vapor of water is introduced. Traube has confirmed these important observations, and has found, further, that carbonic oxide already inflamed is immediately extinguished in a perfectly dry atmosphere. He found, further, that carbonic oxide, even at a high temperature, will not decompose water, so that no trace of carbonic acid or hydrogen is developed under those conditions. But hydrogen has a reducing action on carbonic acid at a red heat; and if we pass an electric spark through a mixture of the two substances, carbonic oxide and water are formed. Traube, therefore, concluded that water plays a similar part in the combustion of carbonic oxide at a red heat to that which it plays, according to his researches, in the slow combustion of the baser metals; that is, that in both cases it is decomposed with the formation of peroxide of hydrogen. Carbonic oxide, which alone can not decompose water, exerts this action with the aid of oxygen. In fact, direct experiments show that the flame of carbonic oxide when brought in contact with water gives off so much peroxide of hydrogen that very intense reactions are produced with potash permanganate or zinc iodide, and sulphate of iron, or with chromic acid and ether.

Cholesterin is a fat which occurs in the feathers of birds and other animal coverings, and is present in considerable proportions in wool. Because of its uncleanness and unpleasant smell, and of its containing 25 per cent. of free fatty acid, it has to be removed in the preparation of the fabric; while hitherto it has been regarded as of no value except as a combustible or as the raw material for illuminating gas. The clear fat arising from the combination of cholesterin with the fatty acids has been found, however, to possess some valuable properties. It is perfectl neutral, and not saponifiable with alkaline hydrates, while it is capable of taking up an equal weight of water, and forming an extremely pliant soft mass absorbable by the skin, which can be incorporated with various medicaments. Liebrich has closely studied this substance, which he calls "Lanolin," and having been manufactured commercially and introduced to the trade, it has in a short time come into quite general demand as a basis for salves and cosmetics.

Mr. C. O'Neill, in a British Association paper on "the extent to which calico-printing and the tinctorial arts have been affected by the introduction of modern colors," after remarking upon the continuing multiplication of the modern colors, said that none of them, except alizarene and its allied blue and orange derivatives, could be said to be fast colors upon cotton in the sense that madder and indigo are fast. At the same time many of them were fast enough for the purposes to which they were applied, and had contributed in calico-printing to give a variety of coloring which had no doubt extended the demand for printed goods. The idea that all new dyes were bad dyes was not warrantable. Whatever might be the true state of the case with regard to cotton fabrics, the author considered that the introduction of modern colors in the dyeing of fancy silk and woolen styles had proved of very great advantage.

The search for means for improving artificial lights of all kinds has led to the utilization of rare earths which, like lime and magnesia, have great light-emitting properties combined with permanent powers of resistance. Zirconia thus figures as the wick in Linneman's oxygenated gas-lamp, and in Auer's new incandescent gas-light, a combination of similar rare earths is said to be employed.

Dr. C. Fahlberg, of Johns Hopkins University, read a paper in the British Association on "Saccharine, the New Sweet Product from Coal-tar." The new extract, which was two hundred and fifty times sweeter than sugar, had become an article of commerce, and was manufactured in Germany. Experiments upon animals and men, and nine years' use by the author, had proved it to be entirely harmless.

Charles L. Bloxam describes the following as a characteristic and delicate test for indentifying strychnine: the alkaloid, on a glass slide or a porcelain crucible lid, is dissolved in a drop of dilute nitric acid, and gently heated; to the warm solution a very minute quantity of powdered potassium chlorate is added, which will produce an intense scarlet color; one or two drops of ammonia will change this to a brownish color, giving a brownish precipitate. The mixture is then evaporated to dryness, when it leaves a dark-green residue, dissolved by a drop of water into a green solution, changed to orange brown by potash, and becomes green again with nitric acid. These last changes of color may be repeated any number of times. None other of the commonly-colored alkaloids which were tried could be mistaken for strychnine by this test, but each of them exhibits some peculiarity when treated in the same way, which would give a clew to its identity. A convenient reagent for the detection of alkaloids can be made by mixing a weak solution of potassium chlorate with enough strong hydrochloric acid to turn it bright yellow, and enough water to make it very pale yellow. This *euchlorine* solution is added by degrees to the solution of the alkaloid in HCl, which is boiled after each addition. Strychnine gives a fine red color, bleached by excess and returning when boiled. Brucine gives a violet color in the cold, which is bleached by excess and restored by boiling. Narcotine gives a bright-yellow color in the cold, which becomes pink on boiling and adding more of the euchlorine solution. Quinine gives a faint yellowish pink on boiling. After cooling the solution weak ammonia is gradually added, when: Strychnine gives a yellow color unchanged by boiling. Brucine gives the same. Narcotine gives a dingy green, becoming brown on boiling. Quinine gives a bright green, becoming yellow on boiling. Morphine gives no reaction, but if, after boiling with the euchlorine solution, the liquid be cooled and allowed to remain in contact with zinc for a minute or two, it will give the characteristic pink reaction with ammonia.

William Crookes, observing the phosphorescence of alumina and its various forms under the influence of the electrical discharge *in vacuo*, has remarked the full red color which it presents. The spectrum of the glowing earth is marked by an intensely brilliant and sharp line, to which the color is due. Observations by M. de Boisbaudran led him to suppose that the presence of chromium is indispensable to the production of this color. Mr. Crookes having, in experiments directed expressly to this point, produced the red color with alumina freed from chromium, suggests four other possible explanations of the phenomenon: 1. The crimson line is due to alumina, but is capable of being suppressed by an accompanying earth which concentrates toward one end of the fractionations. 2. It is not due to alumina, but is due to an accompanying earth concentrating toward the other end of the fractionations. 3. It belongs to alumina, but its full development demands certain precautions to be observed in the time and intensity of ignition, degree of exhaustion, or its absolute freedom from alkaline and other bodies carried down by precipitated alumina; or, 4. The earth alumina is a compound molecule, one of the constituent molecules of which gives the crimson line. According to this hypothesis, alumina would be analogous to yttria.

Among the questions to which the Committee on Electrolysis of the British Association gave attention during the year, was whether the well-marked metallic alloy or *quasi*-compound could be in the slightest degree electro-lyzed by an exceedingly intense current. Un-til all such bodies as were open to experiment had been cautiously and strenuously examined, they were unable to say whether there was a hard and fast line between the modes of con-duction, or in what manner the graduation from one to the other occurred. Another im-portant question was whether the electric cur-rent actually decomposed or tore asunder the molecules of the liquid through which it passed, or whether it found a certain number of those torn asunder or dissociated into their atoms by chemical, or at any rate, non-electrical, means, and that these loose and wandering atoms sub-mitted to the guiding tendency of the electric slope, and joined one or the other of two pro-cessions toward either electrode, only offering resistance when brought into immediate prox-imity with the electrode.

Dr. Hans Molisch proposes as more delicate and speedy tests than have hitherto been used for distinguishing between animal and vegeta-ble fibers, two new sugar reactions which he has discovered and described in full in the "Transactions of the Imperial Academy of Sci-ences in Vienna." They are, the production by all sugars with alpha naphthol of a deep-violet coloration, and with thymol of a cinnabar-ru-by-carmine - red, flocculent precipitate. The same reactions are given indirectly by the car-bohydrates and glucosides, from which sugar is formed after treatment with sulphuric acid. Plant-fibers contain sugar or the substances convertible into sugar, and give the sugar-tests; animal fibers do not. A few silks give a weak, transient reaction, but it is so slight and con-tinues for so short a time that it need not de-ceive the careful observer. It is important, however, in applying the test, to remove all foreign vegetable matter that may be acciden-tally present, or left in the finishing. This may be done by boiling and washing.

Lecoq de Boisbaudran having asserted, con-tradictory to Becquerel's conclusions, that cal-cined alumina does not give a trace of fluores-cence when submitted to the electric discharge in vacuo, and that the red fluorescence of alumi-na seems to depend upon the presence of chro-mium, Becquerel has repeated his experiments, using for the purpose substances furnished by De Boisbaudran himself, and finds his previous conclusions confirmed. The fragments of albu-mina, when excited by the light of the elec-tric arc, emitted a red light, which, however, was much weaker than that given out, under the same circumstances, by alumina containing chromium. But, after calcination, this alumi-na became quite as luminous as alumina con-taining chromium, and of the same color. With alumina prepared by himself, the light emitted was the characteristic red light. The addition of chromium, then, does not change the color of the phosphorescent light, but sim-ply increases its intensity. Becquerel calls at-tention to the difference in the luminous phe-

nomena according as they are produced by the electric light in the phosphoroscope or by the electric discharge in vacuo; the former effects being simple, but not obtainable with all bod-ies. Crookes has also examined this subject, with a view of clearing up the discrepancies between the two observers. His results gen-erally corroborate Becquerel's observations.

A. Percy Smith says, in a note on " The Identification of Alkaloids and other Crystal-line Bodies by the Aid of the Microscope," that the number of cases in which such substances can be identified by this instrument alone is extremely limited; but, as a test of purity, mi-croscopic investigation has a very wide appli-cation. When we are dealing with a substance that, when pure, crystallizes in a definite form from any particular solvent, it is manifest that any departure from that form would lead to the suspicion of adulteration. Again, if we take such a substance as bark or opium, it is quite possible to distinguish from one another the various alkaloids which it contains. Be-sides the form assumed by the free base, it is of importance to convert it into a salt, as there is frequently a marked departure in the form of the crystals of the latter from that of the base. Some experience is necessary in selecting the most suitable solvent from which to crystallize an alkaloid, as the duration of the evaporation may have a marked effect upon the form of the crystals. In some cases, evaporation may be accelerated by the aid of heat; in others, such a proceeding is fatal to success. The ad-dition of alcohol to ether, and of water to al-cohol, appears to be the best means of retard-ing the process when necessary. The author always employs polarized light by which to view the crystals, either with or without the addition of a selenite plate. Here, again, the duration of evaporation has a marked effect, as also does the strength of the solution. If the substance is deposited in a thin film, it may be altogether invisible without polarized light. Thick crystals frequently produce color with-out the selenite, and those that are very thick may depolarize without any coloration. This being borne in mind, no difficulty whatever is experienced in practice, as it is easy to compare with an alkaloid of known purity crystallized under the same conditions.

J. Edward Whitfield has reported upon the analysis of natural borates, in which, instead of the inaccurate methods hitherto in use, boric acid has been determined by a method devised by Dr. F. A. Gorch. The minerals analyzed are Colemanite, from California; Priceite, from Oregon; Ulexite, from Nevada; Ludwig-ite, from the Banate, Hungary; Datolite, from Bergen Hill, N. J.; Danburite, from New York; and Axinite, from Cornwall and from Dau-phiny, France.

Atomic Weights.—Prof. Thorpe and Mr. A. P. Laurie have redetermined the atomic weight of gold from a preparation of the double bro-mide of potassium and gold. Taking Stas's value for oxygen at 15·96, the atomic weight of gold is fixed by the average result of their analyses at 196·85; but if, with Mendelejeff, we consider oxygen 16, the atomic weight of gold becomes 197·28. Mendelejeff considered the old value of gold, 196·2, to be too low, because there was no place in the periodic system for an element of that atomic weight having the properties of gold. Hence the result of the present determination has been to place gold in what seems to be its proper position in the periodic classification.

Gerhard Krüss has determined the atomic weight of gold by the analysis of neutral trichloride and of potassium gold bromide. The mean value derived from five methods was 196·669. The author regards 196·64 as most probably correct.

A. O. Cousins has observed, in studying the relations between gold, thallium, and mercury, that the atomic weight of mercury is the mean of those of gold and thallium; that its specific gravity in the liquid state is very nearly the mean of their atomic volumes; and that its own atomic volume is almost exactly the theoretical specific gravity of an alloy formed of equal weights of gold and thallium.

Prof. Carnelly, in a paper in the British Association on "The Antiseptic Properties of Metallic Salts in relation to their Chemical Composition," held that there was a relation between the atomic weights of various substances and their antiseptic properties, and suggested that there was a distinct relation between the power which these antiseptic bodies had upon animals and those which they produced upon micro-organisms.

Prof. Thorpe and Mr. J. W. Young have determined the atomic weight of silicon, from the tetra-bromide, which they prepared in considerable quantity, at 28·332.

Apparatus.—J. B. Mackintosh has devised an improved form of Elliott's gas-apparatus to obviate difficulties in the ordinary form of that apparatus, and prevent the liability of accidentally introducing some air during the operation. The essential feature of the apparatus is a three-way T-stopcock on the measuring burette, by which connection may be made between any two of the burettes to the complete isolation of the other. Another time-saving device is in the fixing of the zero-point of the graduations. In the measuring and explosion burettes the zero-point is taken at that point where the capillary-tube expands into the burette, and where the water will naturally remain when the excess drains to the bottom of the burette. This renders the adjustment to zero an automatic one, with no sacrifice of accuracy. The absorption-tube has a single gradation at 100cc.

A new form of spectroscope has been devised by G. Krüss, which is based upon the Bunsen and Kirchhoff instrument, but has received a number of modifications and additions adapted to make it available as a universal spectroscope.

With it, spectrum measurements may be made between two colors whose wave-lengths differ by only 0.000,000,000,015mm. The inventor thinks that the results obtained by this instrument when used as a spectro-photometer, are fully equal, if not superior, to those obtainable with polarizing instruments.

Charles W. Folkard has described a simple apparatus, made from ordinary laboratory appliances, for the bacteriological examination of water. Test-tubes, about 7 inches long and seven-eighths of an inch in diameter, are used to receive the nutrient jelly. They are closed by a plug of cotton-wool, which is tied by thread round a piece of glass tube bent at right angles and drawn off at one end. The bent tube has a capacity of 1cc., and serves for the introduction of the measured quantity of water for experiment. The whole is sterilized in the usual way. The water, of which a sample is to be examined, is allowed to run through a piece of three-eighths-inch India-rubber tube (pierced with a small hole in the middle, and furnished with a glass jet at the end) till all the germs on the tube have been washed away. The capillary end is passed through the hole in the India-rubber tube, and sufficient time is allowed for any germs on it to be washed off. The capillary end is then broken off by the fingers or by a pair of pliers, while it is inside the India-rubber tube. The water (which is of course running all the time) fills the bent tube, being assisted, if necessary, by partially stopping the glass jet for an instant. The bent tube is then withdrawn, the capillary end is sealed in the flame, and the 1cc. of water is transferred to the test-tube by shaking.

Schall has constructed a balance on which the ratio of the density of any given gas to that of hydrogen—and hence the molecular weight of this gas—may be read directly from the deflection.

Agricultural Chemistry.—Sir J. Lawes and Dr. Gilbert, reporting in the British Association on "The Present State of the Question of the Sources of Nitrogen in Vegetation," quoted the opinions of a number of writers on the cultivation of the soil, and said that the results at present are extremely conflicting as to whether free nitrogen comes into play in any way. The results quantitatively are most discrepant, and the explanations are almost as numerous as the observers; still there are many results which can only be explained in one of two ways: either error was at work or free nitrogen was brought into operation. The authors thought, however, that they must hold their opinions in abeyance for the present. They dwelt upon the experiments which had been made in the raising of various crops, and said it was shown that nitrogen was derived from the residue of crops previously taken from the soil. There was clear evidence of nitrification of the subsoil in certain cases. The evidence was at present inadequate to justify a definite conclusion upon the matter.

Warrington's experiments at Rothamstead, before referred to in the "Annual Cyclopædia," indicated that in "our clay soils the nitrifying organism is not uniformly distributed much below nine inches from the surface." In later experiments, in which rather more soil was placed in the solution to be nitrified, and a proportion of gypsum was added, the results were in many respects entirely different. No failure to produce nitrification was observed in samples of soil down to and including a depth of two feet from the surface; and in some instances nitrification took place at as great depths as four and six feet, but at seven and eight feet all the experiments failed.

Miscellaneous.—John Trowbridge and C. C. Hutchins have made new spectroscopic examinations to determine the question of the existence of oxygen in the sun's atmosphere, which is still a matter of doubt. Dr. Henry Draper was firmly persuaded from the apparent coincidences of lines of oxygen with certain bright spaces in his photographs of the sun's spectrum, that oxygen existed in the solar atmosphere; and his investigation was accepted by M. Faye. Prof. J. C. Draper also reasoned that oxygen existed in the sun from the coincidences of bright oxygen lines with dark oxygen lines in the spectrum. With the use of spectroscopes of much wider dispersion power than were at the command of these observers, and therefore giving more numerous and accurate data, the authors found that the "bright lines" of the sun's spectrum vanished at once, or no longer appeared as such, and all the apparent connections between them and the oxygen lines also disappeared. The hypothesis of Prof. J. C. Draper, that the dark lines occupying the bright bands of Dr. H. Draper's spectrum is rendered untenable by the lack of any systematic connection between the two.

Dr. Edward Schunk, President of the Chemical Section of the British Association, delineated the probable future of chemistry in his inaugural address. The question, he said, had frequently suggested itself to him, will chemical science go on expanding and developing during the next few generations, as it has done in the course of the last hundred years, or will there be limits to systematic chemistry—i. e., to the history and description of all possible combinations of the elements? He was inclined to take the latter view. He thought it probable that in the course of time, at the rate at which we are now progressing, nearly all possible compounds will have been prepared, all the most important chemical facts will have been discovered, and pure chemistry will be practically exhausted, and have arrived at the same condition as systematic botany and mineralogy, with only rarely a new plant or mineral to be determined, now are. But chemical science would not cease. It would continue to develop, but in other directions than those previously pursued. As the botanist has still a wide field of investigation in physiological

botany, so the chemist will find extensive opportunities for research in such investigations as those of the processes whereby the substances constituting the various organs of plants and their contents are formed, and those again to which the decomposition and decay of vegetable matter are due; subjects as to which our knowledge is quite elementary, but which, it seemed to him, admitted of an extension and development of which we have at present not the least conception. The very first steps of the process whereby organic or organized matter is formed in plants are hardly understood. Granted that we are able to trace the formation in a plant of a compound of simple constitution, such as oxalic or formic acid, how far would we still be from understanding the building up of such compounds as starch, albumen, or morphia? The syntheses so successfully and ingeniously carried out in our laboratories do not here assist us in the least. We know the steps by which alizarene is artificially produced from anthracene; but does any one suppose that the plant commences in the same way with anthracene, converting this into anthraquinine, and having acted on the latter first with acid, then with alkali, arrived at last at alizarene? Indeed, the plant never contains ready-formed alizarene at all. What we have observed from the beginning is a glucoside, a compound of alizarene and glucose, which, so far as we see, is not gradually built up, but springs into existence at once. With respect to the decomposition of organic and organized matters, the author was inclined to think that some of the younger chemists and physiologists of to-day might live to see the time when all the now mysterious and unaccountable processes going on in the organisms of plants and animals, including those of fermentation, will be found to occur in accordance with purely physical and chemical laws.

In a lecture on the rate of explosion in gases, delivered during the meeting of the British Association, Prof. Harold B. Dixon illustrated his subject by performing the experiment of filling a vessel full of hydrogen and allowing it to siphon itself out while the air penetrated into the vessel and mixed with the hydrogen. This experiment, the author said, exhibited the three divisions of gaseous explosions: the ordinary combustion; the vibratory movement, due, he believed, to the explosion of the air and hydrogen in unison with the mass of the gas in the tube; and the explosion of the whole mass. He believed there was some relation between what he might call the mean velocity of translation of the products of combustion and the bodies burned, which would be found to coincide with the actual rate of explosion. The study of explosions was of double interest—an interest attaching to the power which it offered in the hands of men, and a grander theoretical interest attaching to the play of the natural sources here shown in great intensity. In their ordinary questionings of nature we were accustomed to experiment only at an atmospheric pressure, a few pounds on the square inch, and at only a few hundred degrees removed from absolute cold. Under other conditions we had the temperatures of the suns and stars which might be measured by thousands of degrees; we had pressures in the center of the earth which might be measured by millions of atmospheres; and we had motions of masses of planetary matter which might be measured by hundreds of miles in a second. Without reaching these extreme limits, the study of explosives widened our range of experience, and as such it must lend some efficient aid to the advance of science.

CHILI, an independent republic of South America. (For details relating to area, see "Annual Cyclopædia" for 1884.) The population of Chili, according to the last census, taken on Nov. 26, 1885, is 2,524,476.

Government.—The President is Don Manuel Balmaceda, whose term of office will expire on Sept. 18, 1891. The Cabinet was composed in 1887 of the following ministers: Interior, Don Anibal Zañartu; Foreign Affairs, Don Miguel Lamunátegui; Justice. Don Pedro L. Cuadra; Treasurer, Don Agustin Edwards; War and Navy, Don Manuel García de la Fuente; and Public Works, Don Pedro Montt. The Chilian Minister to the United States is Don Domingo Gana. The Chilian Consul at New York is Don Justo R. de la Espriella; and the Consul-General at San Francisco, Don Juan de la Cruz Cerda. The United States Minister to Chili is Hon. William R. Roberts.

Army and Navy.—While the rank and file remained 5,541, the number of officers, toward the close of 1886, was reduced from 970 to 928, the National Guard being at the same time, for the three arms, fixed at 48,674 men.

The Minister of the Navy, Aug. 20, 1886, reported that the navy consisted of two ironclads, one monitor, three corvettes, two gunboats, three cruisers, one steam transport, four escampavais, six pontoons, and nine torpedoboats, the armament of the fleet being 75 guns; the joint tonnage 17,080, with 4,550 horsepower, manned by 1,481 sailors. Adding the officers, engineers, and garrison, the number of men serving in the fleet aggregated 2,478. In September, 1887, this number was increased by decree to 2,800, to be raised if need be to 6,000. The number of cadets in the naval schools was fixed at 150, volunteers, after serving their time, to be entitled to 108,900 square metres of Government land, and the premiums to be paid them as follows; $200 to those enlisting for the first time; $250 to those re-enlisting; and $300 to those serving a third term.

In August the Government ordered Don Enrique Simpson, Captain of the Navy, to draw up a project of fortification for the ports of Iquique, Antofagasta, Coquimbo, Valparaiso, Talcuhuano, Lota, Corral, and Ancud.

A commission of engineers was sent from

Valparaiso to Fiume, Austria, to study the construction of Whitehead torpedoes.

The French firm of George Chantiers, naval architects, made proposals to the Government in September, 1887, to build a steel-clad of 6,000 tons, furnished with all the latest improvements of naval warfare.

Finances.—In spite of the costly war with Peru and Bolivia, the public debt amounted on Jan. 1, 1886, to but $83,653,737, being composed as follows: Foreign indebtedness, payable in gold, $33,733,500; home indebtedness, bearing from 8 to 9 per cent. interest, $23,232,321; paper money in circulation, $26,687,916. Total, $83,653,737. On Jan. 1, 1887, the foreign debt stood, $34,601,270; and the internal debt, $49,223,429. Total, $83,824,699. The total increase consequently was, $170,962, the home debt having decreased $686,808, and the foreign debt increased $867,770. Toward the close of 1886 the Chilian Government succeeded in converting into £6,200,000 4½-per-cent. bonds, at 98½; £852,100 1858 4½-per-cent.; £1,244,800 1867 6-per-cent., and £3,696,800 1870, 1873, and 1875 5-percent. old outstanding bonds. The proceeds, while canceling the old bonds, left besides £315,000 for Peruvian bondholders. The report of the Chilian Minister of Finance, June 1, 1887, showed that in 1886 the amount of money received into the treasury was $65,764,588, which included the $14,652,331 surplus from 1885. The expenditure in 1886 was $49,413,775.

War Claims.—During 1887 negotiations continued between Chili and Germany with respect to fourteen claims presented by German subjects for losses suffered by them during the war in the Pacific. The Italian Government also holds heavy claims in behalf of Italians, and demands that at least 20 per cent. of the amount claimed shall be paid. The French Government, tired of the continuous disputes that have occurred in consequence of the French claims, has offered to accept a round sum of $1,000,000 in coin, which it would distribute among French neutral citizens who were sufferers by the war.

Commerce.—The foreign-trade movement in Chili has been as follows:

MOVEMENT.	1885.	1886.
Import	$41,218,725	$47,101,850
Export	51,490,286	58,581,641
Total	$92,709,011	$100,682,991
Increase		7,973,980

The chief exports of 1886 consisted of: Products of the mines, $40,264,840, showing a decrease, as compared with the previous year, of $1,785,831; agricultural products, $9,710,747, being $1,783,401 greater than in 1885; manufactures, $172,900, being $31,000 more; and specie and bullion, $644,416, being $8,138 less. The amount representing nitrate exportation was $1,424,075 less than in 1885; copper in bars showed $1,237,745 decrease, and silver in bars, $202,187, all due to the decline in values, and reduced quantities shipped, so far as copper is concerned. Products of agriculture, of the mills, and stock farms showed the following items of increase: Wheat, $917,514; wool, $425,816; barley. $124,668; oats, $127,398; flour, $37,907. During the first nine months of 1887, Chilian copper exportation did not exceed 22,872 tons, against 30,212 tons during the corresponding period of 1886. The Chilian exportation of nitrate of soda has been as follows:

DESTINATION.	1884.	1885.	1886.
	Quintals.	Quintals.	Quintals.
To Northern Europe	10,390,510	8,554,687	7,950,452
To the Mediterranean	156,576	41,930	168,092
To the United States on the Atlantic	1,211,714	827,296	1,436,189
To the United States on the Pacific...................	49,078	77,712	255,505
Total	11,838,178	9,501,625	9,805,288

The American trade with Chili has been as follows:

FISCAL YEAR.	Imports from Chili into the United States.	Domestic exports from the United States to Chili.
1883	$435,384	$2,887,551
1884..................	587,936	3,284,945
1885..................	604,525	2,192,674
1886..................	1,192,945	1,973,548
1887..........	2,863,238	2,062,507

In August, 1887, the Chilian Chambers passed a law exempting from import duties articles introduced for mining and other industrial purposes.

Merchant Marine.—There were afloat under the Chilian flag, on May 1, 1886, 37 steamers, with a joint tonnage of 18,525; 7 ships, with 8,461 tons; 88. barks, with 44,343 tons; 5 brigs, with 1,514; 7 schooner-brigs, with 2,148; 11 schooners, with 1,182; and 18 sloops with 1,112; together, 173 vessels, with 77,285 tons, being an increase for the year of 2 steamers and 5 sailing-vessels.

Railroads.—The Republic of Chili, which will soon be in intimate connection by transcontinental railways with the Argentine Republic, is rapidly developing its great resources. The geographical configuration of the country, long and narrow, with a great coast-line, and more than fifty seaports, makes it unusually independent of railroads as means of communication. But Chili was the first of the South American nations to introduce railroads and telegraphs, and while Brazil, Peru, and the Argentine Republic have a greater mileage, Chili, in proportion to population, still stands at the head, both in railways and telegraph lines. Of the latter she has 15,000 kilometres in operation; of railways, 2,500 in operation, and 3,000 more in process of construction. The Chilian Senate has unanimously voted a subsidy to be used in completing the gap of 140 miles to connect the Chilian system with that of the Argentine Republic. The Chilian Government has caused surveys to be made with a view to the extension of the Palmilla and San Fernando Railroad to the coast. It was found that the extension would have to be 85 kilometres long, and would cost 8,000,000, It is probable that the work will be taken up in sections, the first and most practicable of which, from Palmilla to Alcones, is fully half of the entire proposed extension, estimated not to exceed in cost $750,000.

In December, 1886, the Arauco Company was incorporated in London for the purpose of carrying out a concession granted by the Chilian Government in October, 1884, to build a railroad from Concepcion to Rios de Curanclahue, and undertake certain public works in the province of Arauco, and other portions of Chili.

In 1887 tramways were laid in the principal streets of Concepcion. The new viaduct between Concepcion and Curanclahue, in course of construction, will be the third highest in the world.

The Grace Contract.—The Chilian Government having taken umbrage at certain clauses of the Grace-Aranibar contract between Peru and her bondholders, the Peruvian Government abstained from carrying out the agreement. Chili based her objections on two of the principal clauses of that document. First, the implied assertion that she is responsible for half of the Peruvian foreign debt, as she has seized the property by which that obligation was guaranteed, whereas, by the treaty of peace she declared that she would hand over to the bondholders half of the net proceeds of the guano she might sell abroad, and the Peruvian debt was never alluded to. The second objection is based on the immigration of Europeans to Peru, proposed in the contract, and the large grants of land to be given to the Grace Company. Chili declared that this was nothing but handing over the independence of Peru to a foreign power, and that the Monroe doctrine, established by the United States, would forbid such concession.

Telephones.—Communication by telephone was opened during the summer between Santiago and Valparaiso.

Electric Light.—The city of Coquimbo adopted and received in 1887 the electric light for illuminating its thoroughfares.

New Lazaretto.—The Chamber of Deputies passed a bill, early in 1887, creating a lazaretto and provisioning station of infected vessels at the Islands of Juan Fernandez.

New Colony.—During the latter part of 1885 a colony was founded by agricultural immigrants at Ercilla, in Araucania, and in less than a year the village had all the appearance of a civilized community, and the adjoining farms were in a prosperous condition.

Cholera.—The cholera invaded Chili by land from the Argentine Republic toward the close of 1886, the sanitary cordon having been broken despite the severest quarantine measures. It ravaged Chili till the summer, and up to May 21 there had been 899 cases at Valparaiso, of which 628 proved fatal; at Quillota, out of 1,959 attacked. 1,002 died.

Mineral Resources.—The province of Coquimbo has become remarkable for the production and exportation of manganese. In 1885 the exportation reached 3,753 tons, and during the first half of 1886 it was 38,802 tons. Nearly the whole of this was shipped to England. A mine of good coal was discovered in the latter part of 1886, on the island of Chiloe, which has been bought and is worked by an English company. This discovery is the more important as Chili has so far been obliged to import coal from England and Australia. At Esmeralda a rich silver-mine was discovered toward the close of 1886, in addition to similar discoveries made in that locality three years previously. About $3,000,000 was taken out during the interval. A company was formed in New York in 1887, with a capital of $300,000, for the purpose of doing a general milling and smelting business in Chili. Important gold discoveries were made in 1886 at Condoriaco, in the province of Coquimbo.

Industries.—Chilian wines are so excellent that they begin to attract attention in France, prizes having been awarded them at the last exhibition in Bordeaux. The Argentine Republic is Chili's best market at present for her wines.

Oysters.—Viscount V. R. de Solminhac, a Frenchman, has applied to the Government for a concession to plant oyster-beds along the Chilian coast.

The export from Chili to France of the berries of the Chilian shrub *Aristotelia Magin*, of the *Tiliaceæ*, was begun in 1886. It is used in Chili for the purpose of coloring wines. Every portion of the plant is utilized; the leaves have medical qualities, the wood is used for cabinet-work, the bark for tying.

On Nov. 1, 1887, an international exhibition was opened at the Agricultural Experimental Garden in Santiago, of machines adapted to separating flax from the fiber, stem, and leaves of the flax-plant, a prize of $1,000 being offered for the machine that should be decided by the jury of award to be the one best fitted for the work.

It was resolved in the summer of 1887 to convert the large sugar-refinery of Julio Bernstein at Viña del Mar, near Valparaiso, into a stock company. As Chili has hitherto been dependent for the large amounts of refined sugar consumed in the country on importation from Europe and the United States, this industry has undoubtedly a promising future.

Large quantities of wool are being bought in Peru and Bolivia, and new factories are being erected in Chili. The Government has given an order for 18,000 woolen blankets and 21,000 yards of woolen cloth to be used in supplying the police and the army.

Education.—The state devotes $3,000,000 a year to public instruction, which is free in all grades, and the country has 1,500 primary schools, which are attended by more than 100,000 children.

CHINA, an empire in Eastern Asia. The Emperor is Hwangti, surnamed Kwang-seui, son of the Prince Ch'un, or Seventh Prince. He was born in 1871, succeeded to the throne by proclamation in 1875, and assumed the government of his dominions on attaining his majority Feb. 7, 1887; yet the Empress Regent still exercises, to a large extent, the royal prerogative. The Emperor's father, though precluded from holding any official post, has, for some years, been the leading statesman in China. The highest official body is the Neiko, consisting of four members, with two assistants from the Han-lin, who see that the acts of the ministry conform to the laws. Under the four ministers are the seven government boards, viz.: the Board of Civil Appointments; the Board of Revenue; the Board of Rites and Ceremonies; the Army Board; the Board of Public Works; the Tribunal of Criminal Jurisdiction; and the Admiralty Board. (For statistics of area and population, and the army, see "Annual Cyclopædia" for 1886.)

Finances.—The revenue of the Imperial Government is known only by estimates. A writer estimates the ordinary revenue for 1885 at 64,000,000 taels, or about $87,000,000, of which 20,000,000 taels represent the portion of the land-tax that is payable in money; 7,000,000 taels the rice tribute to Pekin, and the rice levy in the provinces; 9,500,000 taels, the salt-taxes; 13,000,000 taels the foreign customs; 5,000,000 taels the native maritime and inland taxes, and the new levy on opium; and 9,500,000 taels, levies on native opium, and on various other goods, native and foreign. The receipts from foreign customs are published regularly. They amounted, in 1885, to 14,472,766 taels. The larger expenditure is on the army, the cost of which is estimated to be about $75,000,000 per annum. The total foreign debt in 1887 amounted to about $25,000,000. A loan of 5,000,000 marks, bearing 5½ per cent. interest was contracted in Berlin in 1887, being eagerly taken at a premium. The Imperial customs department is managed by foreigners, with an Englishman at the head, under whom are a large staff of European, American, and Chinese subordinates. It is organized similarly to the British civil service.

In accordance with conventions concluded with foreign powers, the *likin* and barrier dues can be commuted by payment at the custom-house of 2½ per cent. ad valorem, on all imported goods. A transit-pass is then issued which protects the goods from all local dues between the port and the market. The consolidated tax is much less than the aggregate of the separate dues, but the Pekin Government agreed to it because the money goes into the Imperial treasury, whereas the *likin* tax was collected by the provincial authorities. The provincial administrations have, however, succeeded in evading the agreement, by assessing consumption duties on Chinese purchasers of foreign goods, asserting that they have the right to tax their own subjects.

The Navy.—Five new vessels left Europe in the autumn, under the command of Admiral Lang, a captain in the British Navy, who is commander of the North China fleet. Two of them are swift, protected cruisers, built in England, and named the "Chih Yuen" and the "Ching Yuen." Their displacement is 2,300 tons, the length 268 feet, the draught 16 feet. They are divided into water-tight compartments, and have double sets of engines and double bottoms. Their speed is 18½ knots. The armament consists of three 21-centimetre Krupp guns, two 6-inch Armstrongs, eight rapid-firing six-pounders, and six Gatlings. Two others are armored cruisers built at Stettin, named the "King Yuen" and the "Lai Yuen." They can steam 16 knots, and are armed with two 21-centimetre Krupp guns, mounted *en barbette*, and two 6-inch guns. The fifth vessel is a torpedo-boat, that has a maximum speed of 28 knots, and is armed with two torpedo-guns in the bows, one on deck, and Hotchkiss and Gatling guns.

Education.—Literary knowledge is the only passport to official station; and a large section of the people devote their lives to the study of Chinese literature and the difficult art of literary composition, forming a special lettered class. Examinations are held annually for literary degrees, and the successful candidates are eligible for vacant posts in the public service. Within a short period, schools have been established for instruction in European learning, especially the physical and mathematical sciences and technical branches. Many valuable works have been translated into Chinese. The principal seminary for Western science and literature is the Tong Weng College in Pekin, a Government institution, presided over by an American, Prof William A. P. Martin, in which European and American instructors teach mathematics, astronomy, meteorology, natural history, physiology, anatomy, chemistry, and the English. French, German, and Russian languages, and Chinese professors impart the standard Chinese education. There are a number of colleges at Shanghai under the direction of Roman Catholic and Protestant missionaries; also elementary schools at that and other seaboard cities, where ordinary branches of science and the English language are taught. Military and naval academies and torpedo-schools have recently been established in connection with the arsenals at Tientsin, Foochow, and Shanghai, in which European methods of warfare and Western languages and literature are taught by foreigners.

Commerce.—The total value of the imports in 1885 was 88,200,018 haikwan taels, or $114,-600,000; the value of the domestic exports,

65,005,711 haikwan taels, or $84,500,000. The chief imports were in value as follow:

IMPORTS.	Taels.	IMPORTS.	Taels.
Opium	25,488,914	Woolen goods	4,824,056
Cotton goods	31,498,828	Metals	5,508,416
Raw cotton	1,298,007	Coal	1,785,875

The leading exports in 1885 were valued at the following amounts:

EXPORTS.	Taels.	EXPORTS.	Taels.
Tea	32,262,040	Straw braid	1,574,804
Silk	20,001,175	Hides	941,118
Sugar	1,885,608	Paper, tinfoil, etc	505,752

The imports to and exports from the principal foreign countries in 1885, were of the following values in taels:

COUNTRIES.	Imports.	Exports.
Hong Kong	35,268,197	15,669,987
Great Britain	28,991,688	21,992,185
India	16,145,751	568,547
United States	3,515,402	8,297,782
Japan	5,268,918	1,491,296
Russia	194,668	4,852,360
Other European countries	2,518,847	7,804,370

During 1885 the number of vessels entered and cleared at Chinese ports was 23,440, of 18,068 tons; of which 18,691, of 17,012,930 tons. were steamers. Of the total tonnage, 11,842,255 tons represented British vessels, 2,261,750 American, 2,243,584 Chinese, 1,217,-685 German, 211,585 Japanese, and 73,855 French.

Railroad Construction.—The Government has authorized the construction of a line of railway north of the Peiho from Taku to Tientsin.

American Concessions.—An important charter was provisionally granted during the summer of 1887 to an American syndicate. The negotiations had been carried on for two years, on behalf of Wharton Barker, a banker of Philadelphia, and others, by the Count E. C. Mitkiewicz, an American citizen of Polish birth. The concessions embraced the privilege of establishing the American system of banking and coinage, and a scheme for introducing railroads of the American type; also a postal service, mining privileges, the construction of telephone lines, and the extension and operation of the telegraphs. The *concessionnaires* were to establish a mint for the coinage of silver on a system based partly on the American and partly on the Japanese coinage. They were to have the right to issue paper money on the plan of the American national banking system, and the refusal of Imperial loans. The syndicate proposed to construct first a railroad from Tientsin to Shanghai, a distance of 900 miles; then one from Shanghai to Nankin, and thence to Canton, 1,000 miles long; and afterward other lines, including one to the Russian frontier, and others designed to develop the working of the coal-fields and iron-deposits. It also intended to erect mills for making rails and rolling-stock, and to introduce both the long and the short telephone systems. The concessions were actively opposed by the English and Germans, but received diplomatic support from Russia. The negotiations were carried on with the Viceroy Li-Hung-Chang. After they had been concluded to the satisfaction of the Tsung-li-Yamen, the opposition was still continued, and the Imperial sanction was finally withheld.

New Policy Toward Christians.—The Chinese Government has carried into execution the policy that it announced after the Tonquin hostilities of no longer recognizing France as the protector of Catholic Christians in China. The negotiations for the removal of the Peh-tang Cathedral overlooking the garden of the Imperial palace at Pekin were conducted at the Vatican by John Dunn, an Englishman in the Chinese civil service. The Lazarist society, which constructed the cathedral over a century ago, and the Pope were entirely willing that the site should be changed, while the French at first resisted, but finally acquiesced. The Chinese Government gave the ground for the new cathedral and the money for its construction, stipulating that the edifice should not be over fifty feet high, which is thirty feet lower than the old one, and that the bell-tower should not be carried above the roof-ridge. Bishop Tagliabue and another missionary who aided in the negotiations, were made mandarins. The corner-stone of the new building was laid on May 30, 1887. The Pope was coerced by the French Government in 1886 into abandoning his intention of sending a legate to Pekin in accordance with the request of the Imperial Government, but a Chinese envoy was received at the Vatican, and Monsignor Agliardi, the Papal delegate to the East Indies, was authorized to treat with the Chinese Government, which in March, 1887, assented to this temporary arrangement, while reiterating its desire for the establishment of direct diplomatic relations. The Vatican is practically represented at Pekin by the Bishop of North China, Tagliabue. When the French consul in Canton interfered on behalf of some native Christians, Chang Chih-tung, the viceroy, denied in the strongest manner his right to make representations regarding Chinese subjects. In accordance with instructions from Pekin, the viceroys of the various provinces issued proclamations calling on the people to live at peace with the Christians, and explaining that the Christian religion teaches men to do right and aims to make them better citizens, and that the converts are not the less Chinamen because they are Christians, and have the same duties, and are entitled to the same protection as their neighbors. Formerly the French missionaries have obtained for their flocks, owing to the fears and ignorance of the local authorities, immunity from taxation and from the jurisdiction of the courts, claiming that they were under French protection. In the proclamations that were put forth by the governors the Christians were warned that they owed the same obedience to the laws as other Chinese, while all others were threatened with punishment if they committed unlawful acts against Christians, or disturbed their congregations. Anti-Christian riots took place in Chung-King in the province of Szechuen, in the course of which the house of a wealthy Christian named Lo was attacked. In defending themselves the inmates killed several of the assailants. The authorities arrested Lo, and on trial he was sentenced to death. At the solicitation of missionaries, M. Constans, the French minister, with some reluctance, represented to the Chinese Government the injustice of the sentence, with the result that Lo, who is said to have committed many previous offenses and escaped punishment through the protection of the missionaries, was immediately beheaded. Toward the close of April the Chinese Government ordered that all foreign missionaries must henceforth procure passports from their own Governments, as no others would be recognized. The German, Italian, and other Governments, had expressed their readiness to assume the protection of their own subjects, and had issued passports to Roman Catholic missionaries.

Treaties with France and Portugal.—The treaty that was concluded with France in the spring of 1886 was so distasteful that the French Government refused to ratify it; and, recalling M. Cogordan, sent out M. Constans to reopen negotiations and endeavor to secure better terms. The principal concession granted to France was the opening of two places for trade above Langson and Laokai, through which the French might carry on commerce with the provinces of Yunnan and Kwangsi. The import duties were made a little lower than at the treaty ports. The admission of a French agent in Yunnan was strenuously refused; yet the right of China to appoint consuls throughout Tonquin was accorded, though the English have persistently refused to allow Chinese official representatives to reside at Hong-Kong or Singapore. The French were greatly disappointed at not being permitted to import opium into China, for they expected to raise the poppy successfully in Tonquin, and soon compete with the Malwa and Patna product. After a year's negotiations, by showing complaisance in regard to the protection of Roman Catholics, exercised by France for thirty years, and by giving up the promontory of Paklung on the Tonquin frontier, which both parties claimed for strategic reasons, M. Constans obtained more favorable commercial conditions. He was unable to secure the right to import salt into China, because that article is an Imperial monopoly and the source of a considerable revenue, but inserted a clause that the salt-farmers may purchase their supplies in Tonquin. The prohibition of the opium import from Tonquin was withdrawn, allowing the French to grow the drug for the southern Chinese if they can with profit, or to bring it in the raw state from Yunnan and manufacture it in Tonquin for the Chinese market. Finally the Chinese Government agreed that four places should be opened on the frontier to

French trade, instead of two, and that the customs tariff, which by the previous treaty was one third less than at the coast-ports, should be further reduced.

A treaty of friendship between Portugal and China has been under discussion for twenty-five years, without a definite result, until a protocol was signed at Lisbon in March, 1887, and a treaty was concluded at Pekin in June. By this treaty the Chinese secured the co-operation of the Portuguese authorities in the suppression of opium-smuggling. In accordance with the provisional treaty, the Governor of Macao, on April 1, 1887, put into force the same measures in regard to the opium-trade that were established at Hong-Kong.

Retrocession of Port Hamilton.—In January, 1887, negotiations were concluded for the transfer of Port Hamilton, which the English had seized upon during the Russian war scare, to China, and shortly afterward the British naval commander formally surrendered the place to Chinese occupation.

Frontier Negotiations with Russia.—After the conclusion of the boundary treaty with Russia in relation to the Amoor region, on Nov. 4, 1860, the boundary was marked off, and since it followed the course of rivers for the most part, there have since arisen few difficulties. At the coast the bank of the river Tiumen formed the Russian boundary for seven miles, the opposite bank being Corean territory. The Russian Government requested recently a de-limitation of the frontier, and Chinese and Russian commissioners were appointed, and a protocol has been signed which, besides some trifling changes, declares the mouth of the Tiumen and the Gashkiavetch Gulf, which is an inlet of the estuary, to be Russian, and includes an arrangement for the navigation of the river, according to which vessels under the Chinese, Corean, and Russian flags have the exclusive right to ascend the river, unless the contracting powers agree to extend the right to other nations.

CHRISTIAN CHURCHES. The "Quadrennial Book" of the American Christian Convention gives as connected with that body 1,327 ordained and 209 unordained ministers, with 1,662 churches. The entire number of members is about 122,000. Eight colleges, institutes, and seminaries are under the charge of the Convention or of churches affiliated with it.

The Christian Church, a body in the Southern States, holding principles similar to those of the American Christian Convention, has 75 churches, 127 ministers, and 18,000 members.

The Christian Union Churches, which exist chiefly in Ohio and States west of it, comprise 15,000 churches, with 500 ministers and 120,-000 members.

A joint Committee on Union of the American Christian Convention and the Christian Union Churches met in Covington, Ohio, July 26th. Dr. N. Summerbell was elected chairman. The following report, drafted by a sub-committee appointed for the purpose, was unanimously adopted:

The Committee on Union from the "General Council of the Christian Union," and from the "American Christian Convention," met at Covington, Ohio, July 26, 1887. After full and frank discussion of the resolutions on union, passed by both bodies, it appeared plain to all that we in aim and spirit practically are one people; and we find no valid reason why we should be separate. In the discussion, and in this report, it is unanimously agreed that it is a fundamental principle of Protestantism, and a well-established questions of biblical interpretation, that "the Church and the State should be separate," and that true liberty and efficiency of service in the Church are best obtained by a congregational form of government; and, therefore, in the absolute independency of the local church that all matters of business, service, and worship, shall be decided by each local church for itself.

Therefore, your committees in joint session agree and recommend the union of the two bodies upon the following principles:

The Holy Bible our only rule of faith and practice.

Christ the only Head of the Church.

Christian character the only test of fellowship.

Individual interpretation of Scripture the privilege and duty of all.

The union of all the followers of Christ without controversy.

Each local church absolutely independent in government.

And, further, we agree and recommend that in the united body the individual believer be known as "a Christian"; that all the churches retain their present local names; conferences and councils be known hereafter as assemblies of Christians, and that the general body, head and representative of the union herein sought, shall be "The General Assembly of Christians in America."

And, lastly, we agree that this basis be presented to the various conferences and councils, and through them to the local churches for their ratification and adoption.

CITIES, AMERICAN, RECENT GROWTH OF. This subject is continued from the "Annual Cyclopædia" for 1886, and will be further continued, with other cities, in the volume for 1888.

Allentown, a city, and the capital of Lehigh County, Pa., on the west bank of Lehigh river, 18 miles above its confluence with the Delaware. In relation to the surrounding cities, it is almost the mathematical center, Wilkes-barre and Scranton lying 85 miles to the north, New York 90 miles to the east, Philadelphia 60 miles to the south, and Harrisburg 85 miles to the west. Transportation to the north, south, east, and west is amply afforded by the Lehigh Valley, the Lehigh and Susquehanna, the Philadelphia and Reading, and the Perkiomen railroads, and the Lehigh Coal and Navigation Company's canal. Allentown dates from the middle of the eighteenth century. The first house was erected by William Allen in 1753, and nine years later the town was founded by him upon a grant of 3,000 acres from Joseph Turner, to whom it had been assigned by Thomas Penn. In 1838 its former name, Northampton, was changed to Allen's Town, in honor of its founder. The population, numbering 25,000, is composed mainly of Pennsylvania Germans and natives of German and Irish descent. The Lutheran and Reformed denominations predominate. Allentown, although the center of a rich mineral and agricultural district, depends mainly upon its varied manufactures, the most important of which are of iron and iron products, silk, furniture, cigars, linen thread, boots and shoes, barbed wire, leather, hosiery, brick, and lime. Its public buildings are substantial and commodious. Muhlenberg College and Allentown Female College afford accommodation for higher education. Allentown enjoys many advantages, chief among which are its natural drainage, its water-supply, its proximity to limestone, iron, cement, and slate formations, and its rich agricultural surroundings.

Amsterdam, a city of Montgomery County, N. Y., on the north side of the Mohawk river, 33 miles west of Albany. The population in 1870 was 7,706; in 1880, 11,710; in 1888, 17,403. It is a thriving manufacturing center, and was incorporated as a city in 1885. The New York Central and Hudson River Railroad passes through, leaving 1,042 car-loads of freight, and receiving 600 car-loads monthly. It is touched on the south side of Mohawk river, at Port Jackson, by the West Shore Railroad and the Erie Canal. In 1882 a system of water-works was constructed at a cost of $271,221, which is one of the best in the country, having a pressure in the principal business center of 133 pounds to the square inch. In 1887 were laid 742 miles of sewers, under the separate system, at a cost of $80,000. The work will be continued until the city is completely sewered. Street-cars traverse the principal streets, and electric lights have been introduced. The free schools occupy four buildings, one erected in 1884 at a cost of $12,000. There are 13 religious societies, and 11 churches, 4 erected in 1887. Three lines of stages connect the city with outlying villages. There are 3 national banks, 1 private bank, 1 savings-bank, 3 daily newspapers, 5 weeklies, and 1 monthly, a Children's Home, a Young Men's Christian Association, and a Board of Trade. One carriage-spring manufactory employs 125 hands. There are also 1 burial-case manufactory, 2 planing-mills, 3 machine-shops and foundries, 1 paper-mill, 2 paper-box factories, and 2 dyeing establishments. The broom industry employs $300,000 capital and 600 hands, with a daily output of 15,000 brooms and broom-brushes. The Amsterdam Linseed-Oil Works, established at Galway in 1824, removed to Amsterdam in 1857, consume 750,000 bushels of flax-seed yearly, producing 1,700,000 gallons of oil, and 15,000 tons of oil-cake. The works employ 100 men. Carpet manufacturing employs 275 looms and 2,100 persons, with an annual output of 4,000,000 yards. In the manufacturing of knit goods there are 15 firms, with 112 sets of machinery, and 25,176 spindles, producing 2,980 dozens of garments daily, and employing 2,190 hands. The total value of manufactured products is $8,500,000. The total assessed valuation of the city is $7,000,000.

Atlantic City, a health-resort on the Southern New Jersey coast, about 65 miles southeast of Philadelphia, with which city it is connected by rail. Atlantic City is built on an island known as Absecom Beach, a ridge of sand about half a mile wide and ten miles long, five or six miles from the main-land. The population in 1880 was 5,477; in 1885, 7,942; in 1887, estimated at 10,000. Atlantic City is altogether a health-resort, having no manufacturing industries whatever. It is supplied with excellent water from the main-land, has a complete system of underground drainage, and has three banks and two newspapers. The streets are regularly laid out, lined with shade-trees, and graded and graveled. There are about one hundred hotels and boarding-houses, one third of which are open all the year. During Lent, Atlantic City is thronged with fashionable visitors from Philadelphia and New York. The city is governed by a Mayor and Common Council, has a Board of Health, a Board of Trade, a dozen churches, fifteen different secret societies, ten physicians, as many lawyers, and a public-school system that employs more than thirty teachers. The city is lighted with gas and electricity. A board walk, or elevated beach promenade, extends along the beach front a distance of about three miles, which at all seasons is a favorite resort for promenaders. Building operations are extensively carried on during the autumn and spring. Absecom Lighthouse is the only Government building. There are many cottages and summer residences.

Bradford, a city in McKean County, Pa., on Tuna creek, a tributary of Allegheny river, 125 miles by rail north by east from Pittsburg, and 62 miles south by east from Buffalo. The population in 1870 was 400; in 1880, 9,127; and in 1887, was estimated at 12,000. Four systems of railroad enter the city, one of which operates three diverging lines, and a horse-car railroad traverses the main streets, running to the suburb of Tarport. The manufacturing interests comprise three large oil and gas well supply-works, a large tooth-pick factory, and numerous smaller industries. The growth of the city has been remarkable, as it had a population of only 500 in 1875 when the petroleum development around it was begun. It is the center of the great Bradford oil-field, which contains 100,000 acres of productive territory, on which over 15,000 wells have been drilled, at a cost of $38,000,000. About 14,000 of these are still producing an aggregate of 22,000 barrels a day. The field has already produced nearly 145,000,000 barrels of oil, which has been sold for over $100,000,000. The transactions in the Bradford Oil Exchange since its organization in 1879, have averaged 1,500,000 barrels daily, and on one day reached an aggregate value of $3,000,000. The value of sawed lumber taken from the adjacent forests reaches $3,000,000 annually. Six newspapers—3 daily, 2 Sunday, and 1 weekly—are published, and a monthly magazine devoted to oil and natural gas. The city has been heated and lighted with natural gas since 1879, and was the first place where fuel-gas was systematically supplied and generally used. Two companies are piping gas to the city from the Kane district, 30 miles distant.

Chicopee, a township in Hampden County, Mass., incorporated as a town in 1848, when its territory was the north part of Springfield. It is about six miles square; its population numbers about 12,000. The assessed value of property is $5,844,065. Its railroad communication is by the Connecticut River road. A horse-railroad to connect with the Springfield line has been surveyed, and is to be built in 1888. Its leading manufacture is cotton. Two companies have a combined capital of $2,200,000, with 191,000 spindles and 4,673 looms; hands employed, 2,800; value of product, about $3,200,000, consisting of sheetings, shirtings, flannels, and fancy goods. The Ames Company manufactures general machinery, bicycles, tricycles, tools, and bronze statuary; capital, $500,000. The manufacture of agricultural tools is a large industry, with several shops. There are two shops for the making of society swords and military goods, including army swords. Other manufactures are pistols, rifles, shot-guns, knitting-machines, locks, factory reeds, and bobbins. There are three large brickyards, established within a few years. There are three Catholic churches and eleven Protestant congregations, a town hall costing $100,000, a free public library of 10,000 volumes, and two high-school buildings with philosophical apparatus; one national bank, and two savings-banks. There is a complete system of sewerage, with water-works for domestic and fire purposes. There are three post-offices —Chicopee, Chicopee Falls, and Willimansett.

Cohoes, a city in the northeast corner of Albany County, N. Y., at the junction of the Mohawk and Hudson rivers, nine miles north of Albany and three miles from Troy. Two railroads and two canals pass through the city, and three horse-railway lines lead to Troy, Lansingburg, and Waterford. The city has within three years expended $90,000 for additional water-works, consisting of a new reservoir, holding 70,000,000 gallons, new pumping apparatus, and street-mains. An electric-lighting plant, operated by water-power, was established in 1887. The hydraulic canals of the Cohoes Company, which supply power for all the mills, have recently been permanently improved by vertical stone embankments. The cotton-cloth mills operate 266,000 spindles, and produce 85,000,000 yards of cloth, valued at over $3,000,000, and consume 27,000 bales of cotton annually. The same mills in 1876 operated 258,000 spindles, and produced less

than 80,000,000 yards of cloth. Twenty-five mills, operating knitting machinery and employing the equivalent of 205 standard (40-inch) sets of woolen cards, produce annually knit underwear of the value of $4,600,000, and consume 16,450 bales of cotton and 3,860,000 pounds of scoured wool. In 1876 there were 17 knitting-mills, with 118 like sets of cards, and the annual production was valued at $3,426,000. A rolling-mill, which in 1876 turned out 6,900 tons of rolled iron, worth $355,800, has been enlarged so as to produce the past year 11,500 tons, worth $575,500 and tube-works, which ten years ago turned out annually steam, water, and gas wrought-iron piping, valued at $100,000, have been enlarged so as to produce the past year $750,000 worth. The manufacture of special knitting machinery has been nearly doubled in ten years, while that of axes and edge-tools has remained about the same. The population in 1875 was 17,482; in 1880, 19,416; in 1887, estimated at 22,000.

Erie, a city, port of entry, and county-seat of Erie County, Pa., on Presque Isle Bay, Lake Erie. It is 88 miles southwest of Buffalo, N. Y., 530 miles from New York city, and 450 miles northwest of Philadelphia. Population in 1870, 19,646; in 1880, 27,730; present population (estimate based on city census taken in 1885) 37,000. Erie is the terminus of the Philadelphia and Erie and the Erie and Pittsburg Railroads, and is traversed by the Lake Shore and Michigan Southern, and the New

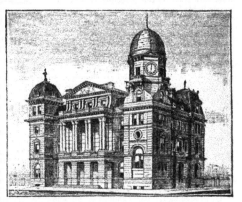

York, Chicago, and St. Louis Railroads. The streets are broad, and are laid out at right angles, and many of them are paved with asphalt. Horse-cars run through the principal streets. The manufactures are extensive and diversified, consisting of iron and brass, cars, stoves, boots and shoes, engines and boilers, machinery, pumps, organs, flour, sashes, blinds, woodenware, etc. The capital employed in

1886 was $7,814,000; number of men, 4,642; value of product, $10,585,000. There was a considerable increase of manufactures during 1887. The harbor is one of the finest on the lakes, being 5 miles long, 1½ miles wide, and land-locked. In 1887 nine vessels in the foreign trade entered and six cleared, with a total tonnage of 2,337. The coastwise arrivals were 832, with tonnage of 709,141; cleared, 845, with tonnage of 720,606. The principal receipts by lake are grain and iron-ore; the principal shipments, coal and general merchandise. The grain is handled by three large elevators. A new custom-house, court-house, and post-office building is nearly completed, at a cost of $250,000 (see illustration). A new city hall is also approaching completion and will cost $150,000. The State Soldiers' Home was recently completed at a cost of $240,000. St. Peter's (R. C.) Cathedral, nearly completed, is the finest church edifice in the State, and will cost $300,000. The city water-works were enlarged during the year, the present pumping capacity being 6,000,000 gallons daily, to a height of 287 feet in the reservoir, two miles from the lake. The city has recently been connected with the natural-gas wells of the oil region by a pipe-line about 70 miles long, and during the year gas very largely took the place of coal for fuel for domestic use and to some extent for manufacturing. Erie is itself on the edge of the natural-gas belt. It has had several wells for twenty-five years or more; but the pressure is light and the supply insufficient and uncertain. The city has 4 national banks, 1 savings-bank, 31 churches, 3 daily and 8 weekly newspapers, and 2 monthly publications. Two new railroad projects, which are likely to be consummated, are the Ohio River and Lake Erie road, of which Erie will be the northern terminus, and a short line connecting Erie with the New York, Pennsylvania, and Ohio Railroad.

Evansville, a city and port of entry of Vanderburgh County, Indiana, on the Ohio river, midway between Louisville, Ky., and Cairo, Ill. The population in 1870 was 21,300; in 1880, 29,248; in 1887, 46,800. Seven railroads radiate from it to Chicago, to Brazil, Ind. (in the block-coal field), to Peoria, Ill., to St. Louis, to Nashville, to Louisville, and to Princeton, Ky. The latter is intended to run to Memphis, Tenn., and Florence, Ala. There are three horse-car lines, a transfer railroad track through the city, and a belt railroad, and a suburban railroad to Newburgh, Ind., will be built in the spring of 1888. There are steamboat lines to Louisville, Cincinnati, Cairo, Nashville, Florence, Ala., Memphis, St. Louis, Vincennes, and Bowling Green. The city is one of the largest hard-lumber markets on the continent, and also a grain and leaf-tobacco market. It is situated over inexhaustible beds of bituminous coal, there being six mines within the city limits, employing 900 miners. The Government has a fine building for post-

office, customs, and court purposes, and a $500,000 county court-house is being erected. There are 17 public school-houses, 39 churches, and a handsome city hall. In 1887, 67 steamboats were registered here. There are 395 manufactories in the city, the principal products of which are: engines and boilers, mowers and reapers, sugar-mills, sorghum-evaporators, plows and stoves, chairs and furniture, bricks, drain-pipe, earthenware, cotton and woolen goods, bent-wood boxes, hames, horse-collars, iron-railing, wire-screens, doors, sash and interior house-fixtures, hard and soft lumber, flour, meal, hominy, and grits, barrels, brooms, carriages, wagons, burial-caskets, beer, wash-boards, wooden butter-dishes, segars, staves and heading, spokes and hubs, mattresses, monuments, artificial ice, hoes, ginger ale, crackers and cakes, overalls, blank books, architectural iron, and tin and galvanized-iron work. The total value of manufactured products for 1887 was $18,957,000. The amount of capital invested is $30,750,000, and the number of people employed in these industries is 10,800. Among the new manufacturing industries established during 1887, were fruit-canning works, malleable-iron works, veneer-mills and a hames factory.

Gloucester, a city and port of entry of Essex County, Mass., on the peninsula of Cape Ann, thirty miles north-northeast from Boston, to which it is connected by a branch of the Boston and Maine Railroad; there is also a line of steamers running to that port. It has a fine, safe harbor which is used as a refuge from the storms by the large fleet of fishermen and coastwise vessels. It is the largest fishing-port in the United States, employing 419 vessels and boats, aggregating 28,848·97 tons of the finest crafts afloat, most of them being fast sailors and able sea-boats. The number of men employed is 5,000. There are 43 fitting-out establishments. The city comprises eight distinct villages, viz.: Magnolia, East Gloucester, West Gloucester, Riverdale, Amesquam, Lanesville, and Bay View (the two last-named are extensively engaged in granite-quarrying, shipping large quantities of excellent stone), and lastly the "Harbor," which comprises the central wards. There is a fine city hall, a public library building, custom-house, water-works, electric lights and gas, with all the modern improvements. A new high-school building is in process of erection, and there are several fine churches, among which is the elegant St. Anne's Roman Catholic Church, built of Cape Ann granite, with a convent and parochial school attached. The last census, 1885, gave a population of 21,703; it will now exceed 23,000. Is a noted summer resort with fine hotels and boarding-houses near the sea; two large tracts of land, one at Eastern Point of 400 acres, and Willoughby Park at Coffin's Beach, West Gloucester, 150 acres, have recently been purchased and are being laid out for first-class summer company. Coffin's Beach is the finest on the coast, about 2 miles in length and 600 feet in width from high to low water mark, clear, hard sand. There are several manufactories, including anchor-works, a twine-factory, 3 fish-glue factories, 1 boot-and-shoe manufactory, several oil-clothing establishments, etc. There is a daily and weekly newspaper. The horse-car tracks extend to East Gloucester, and other extensions are soon to be made. The town has an extensive foreign commerce, mostly with the Provinces, and imports salt from Trapani, which is used largely in the fisheries. For the year ending Oct. 1, 1887, there were 17 vessels of an aggregate tonnage of 1,137·67 tons lost from this port, together with 123 men, leaving 25 widows and 59 fatherless children.

Grand Rapids, a city of Michigan, at the head of navigation on Grand river, thirty-two miles from Lake Michigan. It is the county-seat of Kent County. Nine railroad lines have their termini in or pass through the city, and prior to Jan. 1, 1887, $250,000 had been invested in real estate requisite for the erection of a $500,000 union depot. Two systems of street-railway, with nearly thirty miles of track, one of them a cable-road, connect the outlying districts with the factories and business center of the city. The State Soldiers' Home is one mile north of the city, on the river-bank, and the State Masonic Home, one mile east of the city, on Reed's Lake, a beautiful sheet of water, a favorite summer resort, especially since its selection as the regatta course of the Northwestern Regatta Association. Two raceways, one on either side of the river, furnish water-power for a score of factories and mills. The chief industries are furniture, pianos, flour, mill-machinery, carpet-sweepers, felt boots, leather, beer, bricks, plaster, stucco, wagons, carriages, sleighs, staves, brushes, wooden ware, clothes-pins, soap, barrels, coffins, and electric supplies. The value of manufactured products for 1887 was about $45,000,000, and the business of its wholesale and jobbing houses about $20,000,000. The city has a public library, a free law library, two electric-light, two water, and one gas company, twenty-three public schools, five national and two savings banks, with $2,800,000 capital stock and $5,500,000 deposits; sixty churches, ten private schools, thirty-five publications, and many benevolent and social organizations. The population in 1870 was 16,000; in 1880, 33,000; in 1884, 42,000. A new city hall, costing $300,000, was completed in 1887, and a site purchased for a $200,000 building for a county court-house and other county offices. The completion of several railroad lines has materially aided the rapid growth of the city during the past few years.

Hamilton, the second city, in respect of population, in the province of Ontario, Canada. It is beautifully situated on the southern shore of Hamilton Bay, the westerly arm of Lake Ontario, forty miles from Toronto and forty-three miles from Suspension Bridge. The population in 1861 was 19,096; in 1871, 26,716; in 1881, 35,961; and in October, 1887, 51,884. Three railroads enter the city, and two more, the Ontario Southern and Niagara Central, are in course of construction. A new building for a custom-house and post-office has recently been erected, together with several fine new schools. A new city hall is also being built. The chief manufactures are stoves, bridges, tools, agricultural implements, nails, boots and shoes, furniture, tobacco and cigars, carriage wood-work, engines and boilers, locomotives, hats, clothing, clocks, and glassware. It is the trade-center of the great fruit-growing district of Niagara, and fruit and vegetables are largely canned here. Hamilton does a large wholesale trade in groceries and clothing. The city is rapidly growing, and being admirably situated in respect of railroad and water communication, finds favor in the eyes of manufacturers. Hamilton beach, a narrow strip of land that separates the bay from Lake Ontario, is a noted summer resort, and is called the "Long Branch of Canada."

Hudson, a city of Columbia County, N. Y., on the eastern bank of Hudson river, 28 miles below Albany. It is on the line of the Hudson River Railroad, and is the terminus of the Chatham and Hudson branch of the Boston and Albany Railroad. During the navigation season four lines of steamboats touch daily each way. It was the third city incorporated in the State, receiving its charter April 2, 1785. In 1790 it was made a port of entry, and at that time had more shipping-tonnage than New York city, chiefly whalers. The population in 1880 was 8,670; it now (1888) exceeds 10,000. The city is one mile square, surrounded by thickly-settled villages and a rich farming and fruit growing country. The principal business is manufacturing and produce-shipping. Within the past six years four large knitting-mills have been erected. Among the other manufacturing industries are iron furnaces, steam fire-engines, paper car-wheels, bridge-works, planing-mills, sash-and-blind factory, box factories, etc. The city has one of the most perfect systems of water-supply in the State, the Hudson river being its source. A fine high-school building has just been completed at a cost of $30,000. Although the city for half a century advanced but little in population or business, it has taken a fresh start within the past ten years, and is now rapidly increasing.

Indianapolis, the capital of the State of Indiana, and the county-seat of Marion County, on the west fork of White river, almost exactly in the center of the State. Its population in 1870 was 48,244; in 1880, 75,056; and in 1887 was estimated at 110,000. It is the terminus of fifteen railways, and within a radius of two hundred miles has more railways and telegraph lines than any city of its size in the world. The most recently constructed roads are the Indianapolis, Decatur, and Western and the Louisville, New Albany, and Chicago. Its railroad facilities give it great advantage as a distributing center, and the Belt railroad system handles half of the 4,000 cars used daily, outside the city. All parts of the city are connected by a street-railway transfer system, and several cable-lines connecting suburbs are projected. The erection of a new State house, after ten years' labor, and at a cost of $2,000,000, and the Union Passenger Station, at a cost of $250,-000, indicate the recent growth of the city. The development of natural-gas fields in close proximity to the city has given manufacturing interests a prodigious impetus, and numerous concerns, employing millions of dollars of capital and thousands of persons, will probably move from other cities to Indianapolis if facilities for using the gas are effected. The tax duplicates show the value of the real and personal property to be in excess of $50,000,-000. The amount of capital invested in manufacturing is $16,000,000, employment is given to 15,000 persons, and annually $30,000,000 worth of goods is produced. The principal manufacturing interest is that of iron goods; but upholstered goods and furniture are also extensively manufactured. The grain-trade is mainly the growth of the past ten years, and the several elevators have an aggregate capacity of 1,000,000 bushels. The stock-yards have also been a recent growth, and transact a business of great magnitude. They have a capacity of 4,000 head of cattle and 35,000 hogs and sheep. The receipts annually are: Hogs, 1,068,-387; cattle, 961,698; sheep, 120,389; horses, 16,158. Half of these receipts are consumed by local packers.

Kingston, the shire town of Ulster County, N. Y., the tide-water terminus of the Delaware and Hudson Canal, the eastern terminus of the Ulster and Delaware Railroad, and the northern terminus of the Wallkill Valley Railroad. It is picturesquely situated at the foot of the Catskill mountains, on the west bank of Hudson river, 88 miles north of New York and 54 miles south of Albany. The West Shore Railroad passes through the city, which is a point of departure for the Catskills and the Stony Clove Notch. The streets are wide, well paved, and lighted by electricity and gas. The abundant water-supply is brought by gravity from the Catskills, seven miles distant. Horse-cars and a cheap cab system connect the most distant points of the place. The city is bounded by Esopus creek on the north, the Hudson on the east, and the Rondout on the south, and next to Albany is the most important shipping-point on the Hudson. The principal shipments are coal, cement, brick, bluestone, ice, lime, hoops, hides, woodenware, butter, milk, and fruit. Boat-building is carried on extensively, and large manufacturing interests are being established. The value of bluestone shipped in 1887 was $2,000,000, and 60,000,000 bricks were manufactured and shipped between the opening and close of navigation in 1887, and during the same period between 2,000,000 and 8,000,000 barrels of hydraulic cement were shipped. A new city hall has recently been erected. Kingston Academy, founded in 1784, Ulster Academy, Hillside Seminary, and several public schools are crowded with pupils. Nearly 500 buildings, principally private residences, have been erected since Jan. 1, 1887.

Knoxville, the third city in size in Tennessee, on the Tennessee river, in the center of the famous fertile valley of East Tennessee, 250 miles east of Nashville. The population in 1880 was 9,689; in August, 1887, by actual enumeration, it was 37,026. Since that time the population has increased at the rate of 1,000 a month, owing to the development of coal and iron mines, opening of marble quarries, erection of large manufactories, and the building of new railroads. In August, 1887, the city of Knoxville voted $500,000 to the stock of two new railroads—one, the Powell's Valley, to the Cumberland Gap coal-fields, where is found the finest coking coal; and the other the Knoxville Southern, southward through exhaustless beds of magnetic iron-ore. In October, 1887, the city voted another $100,-000 to the stock of the Carolina, Knoxville, and Western Railroad, a line from Knoxville to the sea at Port Royal. Railroads now come into Knoxville from eight directions, and the city is connected with all the railroad systems of the South. Knoxville is one of the principal wholesale trade-centers of the South, having an annual business of $86,000,000. In 1880 the capital invested in manufacturing was $886,-900, employing 881 hands. In 1887 the amount of capital in manufacturing was $5,783,000, and the number of hands employed 5,786. The principal manufactories are iron-mills, marble-mills, zinc-works, lumber-mills, cotton-mills, woolen-mills, car-wheel foundries, car-factories, soap-factories, furniture-factories, tanneries, stove-foundries, and wagon-factories. In all, Knoxville has 150 manufacturing establishments. In 1886 a new court-house was completed at a cost of $200,000; also the East Tennessee Hospital for the Insane,' at a cost of $275,000, an opera-house costing $60,000, and a public library costing $50.000. The United States Custom-House and Post-Office is built of East Tennessee marble, and cost $500,000.

Los Angeles, the county-seat of Los Angeles County, Cal., on the Los Angeles river, 482 miles from San Francisco, 13 miles from the ocean. The population in 1870 was 8,000; in 1880, 11,183; in 1887, estimated at 70,000. Six railroads have their terminal points in the city, besides several motor-roads, which run from five to fifteen miles into the suburban districts. Several other lines are making Los Angeles their objective point. Horse-car tracks are laid in the principal streets, and there are also two cable-roads and two electric roads, with several others building. Work has been begun on a complete system of cable-roads, to cost $1,500,000, which will be the most extensive possessed by any city in the world. Congress has appropriated $150,000 for a public building, the site of which has been purchased: $200,000 has been voted for a new court-house, work on which is begun; a new jail, costing $23,000, has just been completed, and work on a city hall, to cost $185,000, is well under way. At present (December, 1887), 1,200 houses are in course of erection within the city limits, many of them large blocks. The main streets are paved with granite blocks and asphaltum. The city has been lighted by electricity for five years. Water is supplied by three systems, all drawing from the river. There are 11 banks, with over $5,000,000 resources. The city has 6 parks. The headquarters of the Arizona military district are here. The public-school system is complete, and there is also a university. The exports of produce by rail from Los Angeles amounted last year to 79,158,407 pounds. The chief articles of export are citrus fruits, deciduous fruits (dried and green), raisins, wine, brandy, and wool. There were imported, by way of San Pedro, 125,543,000 feet of lumber and 118,536 tons of coal. The chief resource of Los Angeles consists in its climate and soil. The growth of citrus fruits, though still in its infancy, has assumed large proportions, and is constantly increasing. Almost every known agricultural and horticultural product can be grown in the Los Angeles valley. The health-giving climate, which is mild and salubrious all the year round, is attracting thousands of people from the East, who make their homes here. Costly and tasteful residences, embowered in orange-groves, are being built in every direction. Petroleum is found in great abundance, at convenient distances from the city. There are 5 foundries and iron-works, and the manufacture of iron water-pipe employs 10 establishments. There are 2 flouring-mills, 10 wineries, 8 distilleries, several canneries and fruit-evaporating works, 5 planing-mills, and a number of smaller manufacturing establishments. The city assessment for 1887 amounts to $41,696,812, against $16,482,435 for the previous year.

Lynchburg, the principal inland city of Virginia, on James river, 150 miles above Richmond, 174 miles by rail south-by-west of Washington, D. C. According to the revised census of 1880, the population of the city proper was 15,959, of which number 7,485 were whites and 8,474 negroes. Three lines of railroad cross at this point, and ground has been broken for a fourth, to connect the city with Durham, N. C., and place it within reach of a section famous for fine, bright tobaccos. Besides many handsome residences and business-houses, a custom-house is being built by the United States Government. The city is liberally provided with public-school buildings for both races; and there is a handsome orphan asylum, endowed by the late Samuel Miller with $350,000 besides real estate. Ample water-power is furnished by James river, which is 600 feet wide and has an average depth of 4 feet, a series of dams in and above the city affording a fall of 20 feet. The principal trade and manufacture of the city is tobacco, of which the sales in 1871 aggregated 17,425,589 lbs.; in 1886 they amounted to 49,332,050 lbs. unmanufactured leaf. Of this latter amount, 21,710,723 lbs. were exported, and the remaining 27,621,327 lbs. were manufactured in the city for home markets. There are 25 factories engaged in making chewing-tobacco, 9 making smoking-tobacco, 3 making cigarettes, 1 making snuff, 1 making tobacco-extract, and 1 making tobacco-fertilizer; besides 6 warehouses, 1 storage-warehouse, manufactures of boxes, machinery, etc. In 1868 the total values of the city in real, personal, and mixed property were $3,264,705, which in 1883 had increased to $12,695,874. The total bank-capital, surplus, and deposits had increased during the same period from $587,811.82 to $3,428,078.17. A growing industry is the manufacture of iron of all kinds, from native ores, which is represented by three furnace and rolling-mill companies. The city is well supplied with water, lighted by electricity, and traversed on its principal thoroughfares by street-car lines. Within the past five years several large wholesale houses have been opened in various lines of goods, and have met with most encouraging experience in building up a southern and local trade.

Manitou, a summer resort in El Paso County, Col., eighty miles south of Denver, and six miles from the Harvard Observatory, on the summit of Pike's Peak. The town contains 10 large hotels, 3 stone railroad station-houses, and a very large bath-house for mineral-water bathing. The streets and buildings are lighted by electricity. The chief natural attractions about Manitou are the "Garden of the Gods," Cheyenne and Manitou cañons, the "Cave of the Winds," "Grand Caverns," Rainbow Falls, Ute Pass, "Glen Eyrie," and Pike's Peak. The summit of Pike's Peak may be reached by trail from Manitou in four hours. There are 9 cold mineral springs at Manitou, 6 effervescent soda and 3 iron. The Navajo soda-spring flows 6,000,000 gallons annually. This water and the iron-waters are bottled for the market. Capital employed, $75,000. Manitou may be reached by rail from Denver or Pueblo. During 1887 two electric plants were put in operation in the town, a new railroad connection was made, a new stone city hall was built, and water-works with four miles of iron mains. The number of visitors in 1887 was estimated at 70,000. The industries are lime and stone quarrying. The present population is 1,050.

Montreal, the metropolis and chief port of the Dominion of Canada, on the island of Montreal, in the Province of Quebec, in latitude 45° 31' north, longitude 73° 35' west, at the head of ocean navigation, on the river St. Lawrence, and near the junction of that river with the Ottawa. The population, which, according to the Government census of 1880, was 140,747, is now, according to a civic census taken in 1887, 191,000, the increase being partly due to the annexation of suburban municipalities. About three fifths of the inhabitants are French Canadians, and the remainder are chiefly of British extraction. The most important public work undertaken for the benefit of Montreal is the deepening of the ship-channel between that port and Quebec. This work, begun in 1851, at which time no ships drawing more than eleven feet could pass through Lake St. Peter, was completed in lu 1887; the channel now being deepened to 27½ feet. This port is also the termination of the St. Lawrence system of canals. The completion in 1886 of the Canadian Pacific Railway has given a great impetus to the development of Montreal, which was already an important railway center. The boot and shoe, the tobacco, and the cotton factories, and the locomotive and car building works, are among the chief industries. At present building operations are going on at an unprecedented rate. In 1878 the assessed value of real estate in the city was $63,561,150; in 1885 it was $90,220,-475. Among the most conspicuous architectural additions in recent years are the City Hall, the Windsor Hotel, and St. Peter's (Roman Catholic) Cathedral. The latter building, which is approaching completion, is closely modeled after St. Peter's at Rome. A fine drill hall has recently been erected. The Canadian Pacific Railway has constructed a new cantilever bridge across the St. Lawrence at Lachine, near Montreal, and a grain-elevator in the harbor. Fine terminal stations are also in course of erection for the Grand Trunk and Canadian Pacific Railways. The universities of McGill College and Laval, and the schools of medicine of the universities of Bishop's College and Victoria, make Montreal the chief educational center of the Dominion. Laval University is now erecting a college which will be one of the finest buildings in Canada. Mount Royal was converted into a public park in 1874, the natural appearance of the mountain being preserved as much as is consistent with the convenience of visitors. Large sums have been spent in the construction of the roads. The commerce of the port is seriously affected by the annual closing of navigation. The last vessel generally leaves for sea between November 20 and the end of the month, and the first vessel from sea generally arrives about the end of April. During the season of 1885 there arrived 629 sea-going vessels, of 688,854 tonnage, and 5,003 inland vessels, of 724,975 tons. In 1875 the number of sea-going vessels was larger, 642,· but the tonnage was less, 386,112. The number of inland vessels in 1875 was 4,148, the tonnage 811,410. There

is a wide range of temperature in Montreal. In 1885, for instance, the maximum was 87·1° on July 17, and the minimum 21·3° below zero on January 22. Snow falls on about 85 days in the year, and the annual snowfall averages 122 inches. Montreal is most favorably situated for drainage, but maintains a somewhat high death-rate, partly through lack of sanitary education among the masses, and partly due to an abnormally high birth-rate among the French Canadians. A good system of main-sewers has lately been constructed, and Montreal was the first city on the continent to dispose of scavengering refuse and night-soil by cremation.

Newport, Campbell County, Ky., an incorporated city, on the south bank of the Ohio river, opposite Cincinnati, and immediately above the mouth of Licking river. The first settlement, where the city now stands, was made in 1791. The population in 1850 was 5,895; in 1860, 10,046; in 1870, 15,087; in 1880, 20,433; in 1887, about 27,000. The city is well laid out and handsomely built, on an elevated plane, rising somewhat as it recedes from the river. The many fine residences are embowered in trees. The suburbs, especially the district called the Highlands, a mile and a half from the center of the city, are noted for fine residences and picturesque grounds. Newport is largely occupied as a place of residence by persons whose business is in Cincinnati. The water-works, several miles above on the Ohio river, furnish an abundant supply of water remarkable for its purity and clearness. It is allowed to settle in immense reservoirs before it is run into the mains. The city is lighted with gas, and several fine roads radiate from it. Two large steam ferry-boats ply between Newport and Cincinnati; and there is also a magnificent iron bridge connecting the cities for ordinary travel, street-railways, and railroad trains. A new iron truss and pier bridge connects Newport and Covington, over which a street-railway passes through Covington to Cincinnati. A street-railway connects Newport and the suburban towns of Bellevue and Dayton. The Louisville, Cincinnati, and Lexington Railroad passes through, and the Elizabethtown, Lexington, and Big Sandy Railroad is now in process of construction through the city. There are four large and commodious school-houses and five smaller ones, one of which is devoted to the instruction of the colored children. Newport has a rolling-mill, employing 500 men; a nut and bolt works, employing 250; iron and pipe works, employing 500; stove-works, employing 150; a watch-case manufactory, with 750 employés, besides saw-mills, shoe-manufactories, and various other works. There are two national banks in the city, a United States arsenal and military post, and sixteen churches; a daily paper, a tri-weekly, and two weekly papers are published. The principal courts of the county are held in the fine new court-house.

Norristown, a borough and the county seat of Montgomery County, Pa., on Schuylkill river, seventeen miles by rail northwest of Philadelphia. It extends two miles along the left bank of the river, rising by a series of terraces to a height of 200 feet above the water. Its area is 2,300 acres. The population in 1870 was 10,753; in 1880, 13,063; in 1887, 18,736. The mortality, according to the census of 1880, was 12·74 per thousand. The town's funded debt is $73,000. The value of its taxable real estate, etc., is $7,551,541. Three railroads run through the borough, and two more at Bridgeport, on the opposite side of the Schuylkill, are of easy access. Two telegraph lines have offices in the town, and eighty telephones are in use. There are two street-railways with an aggregate trackage of seven miles, two electric-light companies, a board of trade with 800 members, and a land and improvement company. A project well under way contemplates the formation of a trust to provide capital for new manufactories brought to Norristown. All the streets are macadamized. The buildings are all of brick or stone, frame structures being prohibited in the thickly-settled parts of the town. In 1887 250 new dwellings were erected. The industries are varied : its 84 manufacturing establishments include 12 iron-works, 18 woolen, cotton, and carpet mills, 4 hosiery factories, 8 shirt factories, 5 flouring-mills, 5 brick-works, and a glass-works. The total number of persons employed in the town in manufactures is 3,511, and the total value of the property used for manufacturing purposes, $3,013,000. Among the public institutions are two opera-houses, a large marble court-house, built in 1854, at a cost of $150,000, 19 churches, a library of 2,300 volumes, and another of 6,000 volumes, 5 public schools, 372 business establishments, 7 building and loan associations, 45 secret, beneficial, and literary societies, 8 national banks, 1 private bank, and a trust, insurance, and safe-deposit company ; 5 weekly and 8 daily papers are published. The Hospital for the Insane of the Eastern District of Pennsylvania is on high ground in the northern part of Norristown. The institution comprises twenty massive brick buildings, and has 1,600 patients. The water-supply of Norristown is obtained from the Schuylkill (at a point where the river is 800 feet wide) by means of submerged pipes. The reservoir, 194 feet above the surface of the river, has a capacity of 110,000,000 gallons, the daily pumping capacity of the water-works machinery being 2,500,000 gallons. Over 21 miles of distribution-pipe are laid. The built-up portion of Norristown has been doubled in size within the past ten years, the greatest changes occurring within the four years previous to 1888, during which street-railways were built, electric lights introduced, a board of trade established, and a general impetus given to manufacture. Its proximity to Philadelphia and the low price of commutation

tickets have combined to make it the home of many men whose business is conducted in Philadelphia.

Oakland, a city of Alameda County, Cal., on the eastern shore of San Francisco Bay. The population in 1870 was 10,500 ; in 1880, 34,555 ; and in 1887 was estimated at 70,000. It is connected with the interior of the State by the Southern Pacific Company's system of railroads and the Sacramento and San Joaquin rivers. On account of its harbor facilities it is admirably adapted for commercial and manufacturing purposes. Woolen and cotton fabrics, jute bags, flour, nails, glass-ware, agricultural implements, files, tacks, boots and shoes, and furniture form the principal manufactured products. Being a suburb of San Francisco, it is a city of schools, churches, and homes. The streets are well kept, and the city presents a pleasant appearance on account of its fine residences and grounds. The climate is remarkable for its uniformity. The mean maximum temperature for the decade ending in 1885 was 91°, and the mean lowest temperature for the same period, 32°. Delicate plants, as the heliotrope, fuchsia, and geraniums, thrive out of doors during the winter months. The city is well supplied with cable and horse cars, and communication is regularly maintained with San Francisco — eight miles distant — by a system of steam cars and ferries running at intervals of fifteen minutes.

Pasadena, a city of Los Angeles County, Cal. In 1883 the population was about 1,200 ; in January, 1888, it was estimated at 12,000. It has 10 miles of graded streets ; 11 churches ; one of the finest school-buildings in California ; a free public library of 10,000 volumes in a fire-proof building that has also accommodations for natural history collections ; 4 banks ; good hotels ; and many beautiful villa residences. Twelve railway trains arrive and depart daily. The newly incorporated Salt Lake and Los Angeles Railroad will soon enter the city through one of the wildest passes of the Sierra Madre mountains. There is an open trail from the city to the summit of the range, where a hotel is to be built 4,000 feet above sea-level. The city is surrounded by immense fruit-ranches, and manufactures large quantities of wine.

Pawtucket, a city of Rhode Island, incorporated in 1886, four miles north of Providence, and at the head of navigation on Pawtucket river. The population in 1885 was 19,030, and in 1887 a little over 23,000. Three lines of railroads pass through the city, and horse-car tracks were laid in the principal streets in 1886. Water was introduced in 1878, and the cost of the present water-works is $1,333,000. In December, 1887, $150,000 was voted for a new pumping station. In 1887 there were received at this port 150,000 tons of coal, 5,000,000 feet of lumber, 1,800,000 bricks, 11,000 casks of cement, 4,000 casks of lime, 6,000 feet of North river stone, 1,200 bales of cotton, 250 tons of soda-ash, and 2,000,000 laths and shingles. Exported, 1,000 bales of cotton, 50 tons of scrap-iron, 110 tons of fertilizer, and 150 tons of bone. The industries are varied. There are over 600 establishments that employ labor, and the number of employés is about 15,000. The Conant Thread-Works, with a capital of $2,000,000, employs 2,200 hands; the Dunnell Print-Works, 450 hands; the Union Wadding-Works, 250; and D. Goff & Son's plush and braid mill, 300. The total number of cotton and woolen industries is 28. The first cotton-manufactory in the United States was established in Pawtucket by Samuel Slater.

Portland, the chief city of Oregon, on the Willamette river, twelve miles above the confluence of that stream with the Columbia, and 120 miles from the ocean. Portland was founded in 1847. It is the chief commercial city of the vast region drained by the Columbia river and its tributaries, and is the depot of a large mineral country including extensive gold and silver mines. It is the center of a large inland (steamboat) navigation system, the terminus of three transcontinental railroads, and the center of the railroad system of the Pacific Northwest. Ships ascend the Columbia and Willamette rivers to Portland from the sea, and the shipments of grain, flour, lumber, salmon, and wool are very large. The direct exports by sea to foreign countries of the products of Oregon and Washington Territory from Portland reached in 1887 nearly $20,000,000. The city does a wholesale and jobbing trade amounting to $45,000,000 a year. It contains twenty-six churches; its public and other schools are attended by 9,000 children, and with its suburb, East Portland, which lies just opposite, across the Willamette river, it contains 45,000 inhabitants.

Quebec, a city on the left bank of St. Lawrence river, which here receives the St. Charles, 400 miles from the mouth, 180 miles northeast of Montreal. The population in 1871 was 59,699; in 1881, 62,446. Five railways connect Quebec and the provinces, three of which have their terminus in Levis, a town of 13,000 inhabitants on the south side of the St. Lawrence opposite the city, while the other two enter the city. Ferries cross the river every fifteen minutes in summer, and every half-hour in winter, when there is no ice-bridge. Horse cars run through the principal streets. There are a parliament and departmental building costing $1,200,000, and a court-house costing $800,000. Graving-docks, situated at St. Joseph's, three miles below Quebec on the south shore, costing $500,000, have recently been built. A harbor is in course of construction which will cost $4,000,000. The lumbering interests of this ancient port have fallen off 50 per cent. within the past ten years. The number of arrivals from sea in 1876 was 987, and the clearances 976; in 1886, 501 entered, and 484 cleared. The manufacture of boots and shoes has increased to a large extent of late, and at present there are 18 factories employing 7,000 operatives, and 34 tanneries, employing 800. Capital to the amount of $18,000,000 is invested in these two industries. Gas and electricity have to some extent been substituted for steam-power. The city was lighted by electricity in 1887. The Quebec and Charlevoix Railway is in course of construction.

Quincy, the capital of Adams County, Ill., and the second city in size in the State. It is on a limestone bluff 180 feet high, on the eastern bank of the Mississippi, 160 miles north of St. Louis, and 264 miles south of Chicago. The streets are regularly laid out, three miles in length from north to south, and two and three quarter miles from east to west. In the business portion they are well paved and have numerous fine business blocks. In the residence portion many of the streets are bordered on each side by stately shade-trees. Handsome residences are numerous, surrounded by large, well-kept lawns. The streets are lighted by electricity. Water is supplied through 25 miles of mains from a reservoir with a capacity of 20,000,000 gallons at an elevation of 229 feet, giving an average pressure in the city of 40 pounds. The reservoir is supplied by two pumps 2½ miles from the reservoir, which draw their water from the channel of the Mississippi. Six miles of street-car line traverse the streets. The population, by the census of 1880, was 27,800. The present population is estimated at 37,000, about 7,000 of which are foreigners, the major part being Germans, and about 1,500 colored. Quincy has four parks, and two miles east of the city are the fair-grounds. Two miles north from the business center is the Illinois Soldier's and Sailor's Home, which has a fine wooded tract of 140 acres. This home, when completed according to present plans, will be one of the most beautiful in the country. The State has already appropriated $606,500. Seventeen buildings are now completed and others are in course of construction. All the buildings are connected by a tunnel 2,500 feet long with a ventilating shaft 135 feet high. The total number of inmates is 509. The capacity when all the buildings are completed will be 1,000. Quincy has a fine court-house of stone, surrounded by a beautiful park built at a cost of $300,000, a new Federal building just completed at a cost of $280,000, and there are in course of construction a city hall which will cost $100,000, and a hotel to cost $140,000. The city has an extensive trade which it distributes by seven lines of railroad and the Mississippi river. The commercial interests are represented by 1,813 different firms with a capital of $10,800,500. The more important manufactories are 6 stove-foundries with a capital of $1,000,000; 6 machine-shops, capital $800,000; 5 carriage and wagon factories, capital $400,000; 5 flouring-mills, capital $400,000; 9 ice-houses, capital $450,000; 27 cigar-manufactories, capital $500,-

000; 3 chewing - tobacco factories, capital $250,000; and 6 breweries, capital $800,000. Besides these there is a large paper-board mill, with a capital of $250,000, and the Gardner Steam Governor Works, capital $200,000. There are also manufactories of furniture, plows, plug tobacco, organs, soap, files, and matches, and planing and saw mills, giving employment to over 4,000 persons. Quincy has 9 public schools, 18 parochial schools, 2 literary, and 1 medical college. There is a free library and reading-room association which has over 6,000 volumes, and is erecting a building to cost $40,000. There are 32 churches, 2 hospitals, and 2 orphan asylums. There are published 5 daily newspapers, 8 weeklies, 1 bi-monthly, and 2 monthlies. Quincy was laid out in 1825, was organized as a city in 1839, and was the home of the first Governor of Illinois, Gov. Wood, to whose memory a bronze statue was erected in Washington Park in 1884.

Racine, a city on the west shore of Lake Michigan, in Racine County, Wis., at the mouth of Root river, which, with the government piers, makes a fine harbor. The city is 23 miles south of Milwaukee, and 62 miles north of Chicago. Two railroads and the lake afford excellent shipping facilities. It is on a plateau 40 feet above the lake-level, and 690 feet above sea-level. Racine was settled in 1836. The population in 1860 was 7,751; in 1870, 9,880; in 1880, 16,031; in 1885, 19,636; in 1887 estimated at 20,500. The valuation of real and personal property in 1887 was $8,552,090. The indebtedness of the city was less than $200,000. Manufacturing is the leading industry, employing 3,800 men and a capital of $5,000,000, the annual products being valued at $9,000,000. The principal articles made are thrashers, wagons, plows, harrows, fanning-mills, portable engines and boilers, and feed-cutters. The lumber and coal trade is large. The University of the Northwest is located here. The court-house and city hall are handsome structures, the latter completed in 1886 at a cost of $62,000. A street-railway line connects the depot and traverses the principal streets. There are three national banks. A system of water-works is just completed, with a stand-pipe capacity of 330,480 gallons. Water is obtained from a distance of one and a quarter mile at the lake.

Saint John, a city and port of entry of New Brunswick, Canada, on the Bay of Fundy, at the mouth of St. John river, occupying both banks. Portland adjoins it to the north, and the two cities have a common harbor, and supply of gas and water. The population of St. John in 1871 was 28,805; in 1881, 26,127; the decrease being due to the great fire of 1877, by which half the city, including almost the entire business portion, was destroyed. By this Portland gained in population from 12,520 in 1871 to 15,226 in 1881. Since the fire, St. John has been rebuilt in a substantial manner. Three railways touch the city, and

street-cars have just been added. The port has a large trade, mainly with England and the United States. St. John owns more ships than any other port in Canada, the registry at the close of 1886 showing 635 sailing-ships and steamers of 216,959 tons. In 1866, apart from the coasting-trade, 1,899 vessels, of 501,527 tons, were cleared. The exports, chiefly lumber, for the year ended June 30, 1886, were $3,901,495, and the imports $4,075,062, the customs duties collected being $861,002. The chief industries are lumber-mills, two cotton-mills, engine and car factories, nail-works, foundries, red-granite works, and a cordage-factory. The manufacture of lime is extensively carried on near the city, the product being largely shipped to the United States. St. John harbor, in which spring-tides have a rise of twenty-eight feet, has valuable fisheries of herring, shad, gaspereaux, and salmon. In 1886 was completed the fine steel cantilever railway-bridge across St. John river, a short distance above the city. St. John was incorporated by royal charter in 1785.

San Diego, a city and seaport of Southern California, the county-seat of San Diego County, 480 miles southeast of San Francisco. It is the Pacific terminus of the Atchison, Topeka, and Santa Fé Railway system. The present population (Jan. 1, 1888) is 30,000. In 1885 it was 4,000; in 1880, 2,637; in 1870, 2,300. Through railway connection with the Eastern States was established in 1885. Local lines connect the city with the interior of the county and with Los Angeles, San Bernardino, Riverside, and the principal Southern California towns. The Southern Pacific Railroad, connecting with the East as well as with San Francisco and Northern California and Oregon, is extending a branch from its main line to the city, and direct connection with Southern Nevada and Utah by another line will be made in the near future. The street-railroads, operated by electric, cable, and horse power, have an aggregate length of twenty-six miles, and the steam-motor railroads to suburban points have about thirty miles more. The city is lighted by electricity and gas. A complete sewer-system, embracing forty-seven and a half miles of pipe, is now being constructed. The ocean and coastwise traffic is considerable and is growing rapidly. It is the largest lumber importing port, next to San Francisco, on the Pacific coast. The salubrious climate of San Diego, which possesses the most equable temperature of the coast, makes it a popular health-resort. The city has numerous fine hotels and several daily newspapers. There are four national banks and two State banks. Coronado Beach, on the opposite side of the bay, is a city in itself, with a hotel costing $1,200,000, street-railways, electric lights, etc. Ferry service, with five-minute trips, connects the beach with the city proper. The water-supply of the city and Coronado Beach is obtained from the San Diego river, being pumped to reservoirs on the heights north of the town, and piped throughout the city and under the bay to the beach. A company is now building a large flume from the head-waters of San Diego river and other mountain sources, which will be completed in a few months, and, besides supplying a large area with irrigating facilities before reaching the municipal limits, will increase the city's supply to an extent adequate to the requirements of a population of 200,000.

Sandusky, a city of Erie County, Ohio, and a port of entry on Lake Erie. The population, by the last school-census, is 22,500. The city is on the northern division of the Lake Shore and Michigan Southern Railroad, and is the Lake Erie terminus of the Iudianapolis, Bloomington, and Western, the Baltimore and Ohio, the Lake Erie and Western, and the Sandusky, Ashland, and Ooshocton railways. Sandusky Bay is a landlocked harbor, eleven by three miles. It has the largest coastwise trade on the lakes, and is the largest fresh-water fish market in the world, its fish-business aggregating over $1,500,000 yearly. Here are manufactured over 2,000,000 gallons of wine annually, Sandusky being in the heart of the grape section of Ohio. In fresh fruits—principally peaches, pears, and apples—its business has reached over $1,000,000 in a year. It does a heavy trade in white and blue limestone and in lime, the country being underlaid with limestone. The Government locks at Sault Ste. Marie are built of Sandusky white limestone. Sandusky is largely engaged in the manufacture of carpenters' tools, and spokes, wheels, hubs, and buggy bodies, over 600 men being employed in these branches of manufacture. There are two large establishments, employing 350 men, turning out flouring-mill machinery, engines, boilers, and agricultural implements. There are four national banks. The streets are wide. The buildings, both private and public, are chiefly built of blue limestone. There are two establishments employing 250 men in the manufacture of tubs, pails, and fish-packages. The new Ohio State Soldiers' and Sailors' Home, to accommodate 1,500 men, is being built here. This institution is on the cottage plan, each cottage to accommodate fifty men, with central dining-hall, kitchen, laundry, bath-house, and administration building—in all, thirty-four buildings, of blue limestone and practically fire-proof, costing $585,000, exclusive of the ninety acres of ground, which were given by the city. The cost of maintaining the home will be $150,000 to $160,000 a year. There is a central high-school, four ward-school buildings, and a half-dozen smaller ones. There are three Catholic, two Episcopal, one Presbyterian, Methodist, Baptist, and Congregational, and nine German Protestant churches. The court-house is new, built of bluestone. There is a complete system of water-works. The stand-pipe, built of steel-plates, is 180 feet high and 25 feet in diameter, with another

VOL. XXVII.—9 A

stand-pipe 225 feet by three, for fire-purposes. Lake Erie furnishes the water-supply. The city is thoroughly sewered. Four newspapers are published here.

San José [San Hoza'y], the county-seat of Santa Clara County, Cal., 47 miles south of San Francisco, 6 miles southeast of San Francisco Bay, 28 miles from the Pacific Ocean. With its suburbs, it numbers 25,000 inhabitants, and the assessed valuation of property within its corporate limits is $12,000,000. San José is essentially a modern city, with broad streets, sidewalks of concrete and asphaltum, fine business buildings, and handsome residences. It is lighted mainly by electricity, has street-railroads, and an electric-motor road connects it with the town of Santa Clara, three miles distant. Three railroads connect this city with San Francisco, and two of these lines pass through the city to the Pacific Ocean. It is also connected by rail with the southern part of the State. The city owns two public parks, one containing 400 acres, six miles distant. This park is noted for its mineral-springs and its wild scenery. The State Normal School building, in the center of Washington Square of 28 acres, cost $150,000, and has 700 pupils. The court-house is a massive Corinthian structure, costing $200,000. The new city hall is a beautiful building, costing $75,000. There are ten churches and eight large school-houses, each surrounded by spacious grounds. The college of Notre Dame (Roman Catholic), for young ladies, has a fine building and extensive grounds valued at $600,000. There is a business college in the city. Between San José and Santa Clara is the University of the Pacific (Methodist), which owns sixteen acres and has five large buildings. The city has a public library of 7,000 volumes. Four daily and three weekly newspapers and a monthly periodical are published here. The city contains a woolen-mill, three foundries, three flouring-mills, three breweries, three distilleries, three fruit-canning establishments, two fruit-driers, two glove-factories, a silk-factory, three candy-factories, two furniture-factories, five carriage-factories, a tannery, a box-factory, several wineries, and various machine-shops, planing-mills, cigar-factories, etc. There are four banks, with a capital of $2,500,000. San José is rapidly increasing in population and wealth. Its position, in close proximity to Mt. Hamilton, the site of the great Lick Observatory on the east, and to the $20,000,000 Leland Stanford, Jr., University on the west, and its unrivaled climate, are great inducements for those looking for pleasant homes.

Schenectady, a city of Schenectady County, N. Y., in the Mohawk valley, on the New York Central Railroad, 17 miles west of Albany. Other railroads running into the city are the Troy and Schnectady, the Rensselaer and Saratoga, and the Delaware and Hudson Canal Company. The Erie Canal passes through the city. Its important industries are: locomotive works, employing 1,200 men; the Westinghouse Agricultural Works; and the Edison Machine-Works, which removed to Schenectady in 1886. These works occupy extensive buildings and employ 1,000 men. The Gilbert Car-Works is also a recent and important industry. There are also several knitting-mills, a shawl-factory, hay-wire factories, and other minor factories and mills. The city is supplied with water from Mohawk river by its own system of water-works. The streets are lighted with electricity, as are also the public buildings and many of the stores and private dwellings. Horse-cars run upon the main street. Union College is located here. A new depot of fine design has been erected by the New York Central Railroad, and a city hall has been built and given to the city by one of its residents. The city is very compactly built, and in the old part may still be found many traces of its Dutch origin. The population in 1880 was 18,675. Since that time its growth and improvement have been more marked than in any other period of its history, and its population is now estimated at 20,000.

Sherbrooke, a city of the province of Quebec, Canada, on the rivers Magog and St. Francis. It is the capital of the Eastern Townships, the designation given to that part of the province which lies south of the river St. Lawrence. It is 101 miles east of Montreal, and 121 miles southwest of Quebec. The population, about 9,000, is composed of English and French speaking races, the French largely predominating. It is the terminus of the International, Passumpsic, Waterloo and Magog, and Quebec Central Railways, and is connected both east and west by the Grand Trunk Railway. A new connection will shortly be made by the extension of the Canadian Pacific Railway through the city to the maritime provinces. Sherbrooke possesses magnificent water-power, derived from the fall of the river Magog, which here descends 120 feet, within half a mile, to the St. Francis. The city is the seat of a Roman Catholic bishop, and contains a cathedral and bishop's palace and two district churches of the same denomination, 2 Anglican churches, 1 Methodist, 1 Presbyterian, and 1 Congregational, and a Baptist church will soon be erected. All criminal and civic cases within the district of St. Francis are tried here. The main industry is the manufacture of woolen goods, one firm alone employing between 500 and 600 people and paying out annually in wages over $140,000. There are also saw-mills, iron-foundries, machine-shops, snath, bobbin, corset, and other factories. There are 13 hotels and 4 newspapers, two English and two French. The public schools are under the direction of two boards of trustees, one Protestant and the other Roman Catholic. There is a large Roman Catholic hospital here, and the land has been purchased for a similar institution by the Protestants. The export trade to

the United States is considerable, the entries made through the United States consulate amounting to about $1,000,000 a year, principally lumber, pulp, asbestos, and live-stock. The city is well supplied with gas and water, is the center of a good agricultural district, and is growing rapidly.

Stockton, the county-seat of San Joaquin County, Cal., on an arm of San Joaquin river, three miles from the main stream. It is 92 miles from San Francisco by rail, and 120 by water. Horse-car tracks are laid in the principal streets, and an electric-motor railroad will soon be in operation. A new agricultural pavilion, costing $60,000, was completed in September, 1887, and is the finest structure of its kind west of the Rocky Mountains. A granite court-house is in process of erection at a contract price of about $300,000. Stockton is emphatically a city of churches, the following denominations being represented by commodious and well-built edifices: Roman Catholic, 1; Episcopal, 1; Congregational, 2; Baptist, 2; Methodist Episcopal, 2; Methodist Episcopal (South), 1; Lutheran, 1; Presbyterian, 1; Cumberland Presbyterian, 1; German Reformed, 1; German Methodist, 1; Latter-Day Saints, 1; Christian, 1. The public schools are as good as any in the State, and the graduates of the high-school are admitted to the State University on the recommendation of the principal without examination. Stockton is one of the leading wheat-markets of the Pacific coast, and there are warehouses here having an aggregate capacity of over 100,000 tons. It is the natural commercial center of a fine agricultural district. Among the numerous manufactures are two flouring-mills, each having a daily capacity of 1,500 bbls., two combined harvester-works, a wheel-and-axle factory, a paper-mill, a woolen-mill, two carriage-factories, three foundries, and several planing mills. The population in 1880 was 10,287. In 1887 it was estimated at 18,000.

Toronto, a city, port of entry, and the capital of Ontario, Canada, county-seat of York County, on the north shore of Lake Ontario, 310 miles southwest of Montreal, and 528 miles northwest of New York. Latitude, 43° 39′ north; longitude, 79° 21′ west. Population in 1861, 44,821; 1871, 56,092; 1881, 77,034; 1886, 111,800; 1887, 118,408. The bay south of the city is formed by an island, and is about three miles long and two miles wide. The river Don, which falls into the bay on the east, is now being straightened and made navigable, so that it will form part of the harbor, at an expenditure of over $300,000. The corporation limits, which have been much extended by annexation of late, include 9,858 acres, or 15¼ square miles, as compared with 5,000 acres in 1871. The assessed value of real and personal property (not counting stocks in public companies) in 1875 was about $46,000,000; in 1885, $65,119,702; in 1886, $68,377,508; in 1887, $78,288,226; in 1888 (estimated), $93,-

889,754. The taxes in 1874 yielded $608,475. In 1886 the total revenue was $1,595,550, of which taxation at the rate of 16½ mills contributed $1,134,958. The imports for 1885-'86 valued $18,301,177, of which $7,332,156 were from the United States. The exports for the same year, as officially reported, were $3,095,-800, of which $2,189,414 went to the United States. The value of manufactures, according to the census of 1881, was $19,100,116, the chief items being boots and shoes, furniture, clothes, whisky, and ale. The amount of capital invested is $11,502,210; the number of hands employed, 12,708; the amount of yearly wages, $3,721,861. The total failures in To-

annually by a vote of the rate-payers. The city has a fire-alarm telegraph, telephonic system, paid fire-department, and street-railways. The water-work system is owned by the city; the revenue of this department in 1886 was $315,227, and the expenditure $196,495, exclusive of payments made on account of water-works' debt; the amount of the indebtedness of the department is $2,530,205, exclusive of $350,000 which the city has just decided (1887) to expend in improving the system. Surveys are being made at present with a view to securing water by a system of gravitation from lakes to the north of the city; this scheme, if carried out, will cost $5,000,000 or $6,000,000.

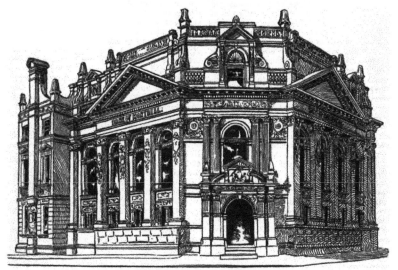

BRANCH OF MONTREAL BANK, TORONTO.

ronto in 1886 were 86, with estimated liabilities of $1,048,509 and assets of $528,859. The total number of letters delivered from the Toronto post-office in 1886 was 9,776,509, besides 2,592,380 newspapers; the total number of letters, books, post-cards, circulars, etc., posted at Toronto in the same year was 21,024,824. There are ten banks having headquarters in this city, and branches of four Quebec and Montreal banks. The branches of the Montreal Bank and Quebec Bank have recently erected new and handsome buildings; that of the first-named institution is one of the most complete and thoroughly equipped bank-buildings in the Dominion. The city is divided into twelve wards, each of which elects three aldermen and two school trustees. The aldermen are vested with legislative and executive powers, and can act as magistrates if possessed of legal property qualification. The mayor is elected

The city is abundantly supplied with educational institutions, many of which form also the principal public buildings. The University of Toronto, erected in 1859 for $900,000, is controlled by the Ontario Government, and has been conducted hitherto at a cost of about $13,000 annually. By an act passed at the last session of the Ontario Legislature it was arranged to federate with Toronto University Victoria University, Cobourg, a Methodist institution, as the first step in a contemplated complete scheme of university federation for the province. At the same time it was decided to establish a medical faculty in connection with the university. In consequence of the proposed extension of this institution by federation, the endowment will be increased from $78,000 to $100,000, $15,000 of the increase to come from the endowment fund of the Upper Canada College, another institution under the control of the Provincial Government; the college site is to be sold, and a new building to be erected for $100,000 of the proceeds, the remainder going to further swell the university endowment. Trinity University is an Anglican institution established in 1852, having about 60 resident and non-resident students, and a handsome building. McMaster Hall is a Baptist college, which in 1887 was converted into a university and received a bequest of $800,000 from the late Senator McMaster. Besides these universities there are in the city a Presbyterian college (Knox), an Anglican college (Wycliffe), Trinity Medical School, with 300 students; Woman's Medical College, College of Pharmacy, College of Physicians and Surgeons, Royal College of Dental Surgeons of Ontario, Veterinary College, etc. There are thirty public schools in the city, the total expenditure on their account in 1886 being $245,957, including $57,000 for new buildings; there are also sixteen separate schools, or Roman Catholic institutions, and several other institutions for higher education, both undenominational and Roman Catholic. The city has numerous charitable and benevolent institutions, including the Insane Asylum and the General Hospital, having a capacity respectively of 700 and 400. There are 26 organized and thoroughly equipped institutions of this nature. At the 1886-'87 session of the Ontario Legislature, the sum of $1,050,000 was appropriated for the erection of new legislative buildings in Queen's Park; they will be constructed of Credit valley red sandstone, in Neo-Greek architecture. The buildings were commenced in 1886. Plans are being prepared also for a combined police headquarters, court-house, and city-hall building, for which the City Council has appropriated $400,000. Construction will be commenced in 1888. A public library was opened March 6, 1884, and was considerably enlarged in 1887; it covers the ground-floor of a not very handsome building at the corner of Church and Adelaide Streets, and contained in 1887 about 48,000 volumes. There are several other libraries, free to the public with certain restrictions, chief among which are the Parliamentary and the Osgoode Hall. Other public buildings are Osgoode Hall, the seat of the principal law and equity courts of the province; Government House, the residence of the Lieutenant-Governor of Ontario; the customs house and the post-office; the Grand Opera-House and Jacobs' and Shaw's Opera-House, each having a capacity of about 1,500; the Central Prison; School of Practical Science; the Observatory; the Normal School buildings, the present city hall, court-house, police and legislative buildings. There are 105 churches in the city, exclusive of several organized congregations worshiping in public and other halls. The principal buildings are St. James's Cathedral (Anglican), costing $220,000, and having a spire of 316 feet; the Metropolitan (Methodist),

costing $100,000; St. Michael's Cathedral (Roman Catholic); St. Andrew's West (Presbyterian); and Jarvis Street Baptist Church. New and handsome churches are now being erected in every quarter of the city. There are three morning newspapers and three evening newspapers issued, besides sixty-three weekly, monthly, and quarterly publications, many of which are religious journals. The railway connections of the city are the Ontario divisions of the Canadian Pacific Railway, being the Credit Valley, the Toronto, Gray, and Bruce, and the Ontario and Quebec sections; the Grand Trunk, Midland, and Northern and Northwestern; and the Erie and Huron. There are two telegraph companies, the Canadian Pacific and the Great Northwestern of Canada; and one telephone company, the Bell. Toronto was founded in 1794 by Governor Simcoe, and became and remained until 1841 the seat of Government for Upper Canada. It bore the name of York until 1834, when it was incorporated as the city of Toronto. From 1849 to 1858 it alternated with Quebec as the seat of the united government, and at confederation (1867) became permanent capital of Ontario.

Trenton, the capital of New Jersey, at the head of navigation on Delaware river, on the main line of the Pennsylvania Railroad. 33 miles from Philadelphia, and 57 miles from New York. Its population by the State census of 1885 was 34,886; but this does not include the suburban municipalities of Chambersburg and Millham, which are mere outgrowths of the city, and would increase its population to over 50,000. Trenton is the seat of the largest pottery industry in the United States, of a large and rapidly growing rubber-manufacturing interest, rolling-mills, wire-rope works, woolen-mills, anvil-works, and a variety of other important industries. One of the largest and handsomest theatres in the country has lately been finished. There are two horse-railroad companies, with about ten miles of track. The Pennsylvania Railroad, the Belvidere Delaware Railroad, the Bound Brook Railroad, and the old Camden and Amboy Railroad, radiate from the city. It is also intersected by the Delaware and Raritan canal, which has several large basins in the city. There are two lines of steam-propellers. The water-supply is one of the best in the country. The works are owned by the city, and the rates are very low. The city is surrounded by a rich and beautiful agricultural country. The climate is salubrious, and the death-rate is only 16 in 1,000. Several miles of streets are paved with Belgian block, asphalt, and Telford. The capital invested in manufactures aggregates about $10,000,000, mainly in pottery, iron and steel, rubber, brick, and woolen goods.

Tucson, a city of Arizona, on Santa Cruz river, in the southeastern part of the Territory, and on the line of the Southern Pacific Railroad. It is 60 miles from the border of Mexico, and about 175 miles from the Gulf of California. In 1884 it had about 10,000 inhabitants, and in 1887 about 7,500. It is the county-seat of Pima County, and has the most expensive court-house in the Territory. It has a fine, large brick school-house, erected at a cost of $50,000, and there are now in course of erection a very large Catholic church, hospital, and convent, and a Territorial university. Congregationalists, Baptists, and Methodists have each a fine church-building. There are no manufactories, but arrangements for a tannery are being made. A root found in very large quantities in the surrounding country contains 96 per cent. of tannic acid. Two new railroads have been projected, one of which is now in course of construction. There are several large irrigating ditches in course of construction in the immediate neighborhood of this city, which, when finished, will place many thousands of acres under cultivation that are now of no value whatever. Tucson has gas-works, ice-works, and water-works. Two daily papers are published here, and one weekly in the Spanish language.

Virginia City, the largest town in Nevada, in Storey County, in the western part of the State, on the eastern slope of Mount Davidson, 6,100 feet above the level of the sea. It is 52 miles by rail from Reno, on the Central Pacific Railroad, with which it is connected by the Virginia and Truckee Railroad, Virginia City being the southern terminus. The town grew rapidly for several years following the uncovering of immense bodies of ore in the Comstock lode, in 1868-'69. From 1875 the ore-yield was much less. Deep mining proved unprofitable, and many people sought their fortunes in other directions. Houses were taken down and removed to other localities, or burned for fire-wood. Large bodies of low-grade ore had been left in the haste of extracting that of more value, and it having been found that this can be milled with profit to the mining companies, fresh bodies of ore being also found near the surface, a new impetus has been given to the town within the past two years. No new buildings have been erected for ten or twelve years, owing to the causes mentioned. The town's prosperity depends wholly on the mines, there being no business except such as is connected with them, and the furnishing of supplies for the people. The production of the mines varies largely; in some years it has been as high as $80,000,000, but it is now much less. It is supplied with water from Lake Marlette and its tributaries, distant 21 miles, by an extraordinary piece of hydraulic engineering, the flumes and pipes having been carried up and down the walls of 12 steep cañons, one of the depth of 1,540 feet. The town contains a fine court-house, school-houses, 5 churches, a few elegant private residences, and the largest and most complete hoisting-works over the mines that are to be found in the world. The

population is fluctuating, depending on the amount of milling and mining being done. In 1885 it was estimated at 10,000; but it is now, 1887, nearer 12,000.

Washington, the capital of the United States of America, in the District of Columbia, on the northeast bank of the Potomac river, 116½ miles above its mouth at Smith's Point, and 184½ miles from the Atlantic at the mouth of Chesapeake Bay, between the Anacostia or Eastern branch and Rock creek (which separates it from Georgetown on the west), 35 miles (direct) S. W. of Baltimore, and 205 miles S. W. of New York; latitude (Capitol) 38° 53′ 20·1″ N., longitude 77° 0′ 27·9″ W. of Greenwich; population in 1870, 109,199 (35,455 colored and 13,757 foreigners); in 1875, estimated at 133,-000; in 1880, 159,855; in 1887, estimated at 179,000, of whom nearly one third are colored. It covers a little more than 9½ square miles. The site is an undulating tract having a mean altitude of about 40 feet above the river. Beyond the limits is a circling range of wooded hills. The streets, with the exception of those designated as avenues, are laid out at right angles, running due north and south, and east and west. The north and south streets are designated by numbers, the east and west by letters. The width of the streets varies from 70 to 160 feet. There are 21 avenues, named after States of the Union, crossing the streets diagonally, the principal of which radiate from the Capitol, the White House, or Lincoln Square east of the Capitol. Of these 19 are from 120 to 160 feet wide, and 2 are 85 feet wide. Pennsylvania Avenue, the great business thoroughfare, extending across the city from Rock creek to the Eastern branch, is interrupted by the Capitol and the White House, between which it forms the main avenue of communication. There are several squares handsomely laid out and containing fountains, trees, shrubbery, and statues of naval and military heroes. Among the most noteworthy are Farragut Square, between Sixteen-and-a-half and Seventeenth and I and K Streets, with a heroic statue in bronze by Vinnie Ream Hoxie; Lafayette Square, between Vermont Avenue and Sixteen-and-a-half Street and Pennsylvania Avenue and H Street, containing an equestrian statue of Gen. Jackson, designed by the late Clark Mills; Washington Circle, at the intersection of Twenty-third Street and Pennsylvania Avenue; McPherson Square, at the intersection of Vermont Avenue and I Street; Scott Circle, Sixteenth Street and Massachusetts Avenue; Thomas Circle, Fourteenth Street and Massachusetts Avenue, all of which contain statues of the men after which they are named. The Mall, extending west from the Capitol Grounds, contains the Botanic Garden, the Smithsonian Institution, and the Department of Agriculture. The "Park" extends west from the Mall to the banks of the Potomac, and contains the recently finished Washington Monument, 555 feet high, and the Government Propagating Garden and Nursery. The Capitol is on the west brow of a plateau that forms the east portion of the city, and fronts the east. Its entire length is 751 feet 4 inches, and the greatest depth, including porticoes and steps, is 348 feet. Exclusive of court-yards, it covers a little over 8½ acres. The walls of the central building are of sandstone painted white ; the extensions are of white marble slightly variegated with blue. Outwardly the Capitol has various architectural adornments, with several groups of sculptures ; within it is profusely decorated with frescoes, sculptures, and paintings. From the center rises a cast-iron dome, 185½ feet in diameter, to a height of 287½ feet above the basement-floor of the building. The dome is surmounted by a bronze statue of Liberty by Crawford, 19½ feet high. The Capitol contains the Senate Chamber, the Hall of the House of Representatives, the Supreme Court, and Library of Congress. ·The Capitol Grounds comprise 51½ acres, handsomely laid out, and containing a great variety of trees. East of the Capitol is a colossal statue in marble of Washington, by Greenough. East of the Capitol Grounds is the site of the new Library of Congress, work on which was commenced in the summer of 1887. When completed it will be the largest building in the city except the Capitol, and will form a noble addition to the already numerous public buildings. The structure will cover 111,000 feet of space, 14,000 feet more than the British Museum Library. Its general architectural features will be in keeping with the Capitol, which it will face. The President's house, or Executive Mansion, is in the west part of the city, 1½ miles from the Capitol. It is 170 feet long and 86 feet deep, built of freestone, and painted white, from which circumstance it is popularly known as the "White House." The grounds comprise about 75 acres, of which about 20 are inclosed as the President's private grounds, are handsomely laid out, and contain a fountain. Other Government buildings are the Treasury Department, the recently completed edifice for the State, War, and Navy Departments, the Department of the Interior (containing the Patent-Office), the General Post-Office, and the Department of Justice and Court of Claims, all magnificent or imposing structures. In Judiciary Square is the Pension-Office, a big brick structure, completed in 1887 after designs by Gen. Meigs, U. S. Army, at a cost of $900,000. The U. S. Naval Observatory (latitude 38° 53' 38·8", longitude 77° 3' 1·8") occupies a commanding site on the bank of the Potomac in the west part of the city. By act of Congress the meridian of the Observatory is adopted as the American meridian for all astronomical purposes, and the meridian of Greenwich is adopted for all nautical purposes. The Army Medical Museum, the Ordnance Museum, and the Government Printing-Office are noteworthy. The Navy Yard is on the Anacostia. The Corcoran Art Gallery occu-

pies a fine building near the White House. The principal theatres are Albaugh's Opera-House and the National Theatre. The hotels of Washington are a prominent feature of the city. The principal are the Arlington, Ebbitt, Willard's, Riggs, Metropolitan, National, St. James, and St. Marc. There is a bridge across the Potomac known as the "Long" Bridge, for railroad and ordinary travel, and a free bridge at Georgetown built by the Government. Communication with the North is furnished by the Baltimore and Potomac Railroad ; with the West by the Baltimore and Ohio and Pennsylvania ; and with the South by the Alexandria and Washington, which crosses the Long Bridge, and the Richmond and Danville system. Washington and Georgetown are supplied with water from the great falls of the Potomac above by an aqueduct 12 miles long, which discharges into a distributing reservoir 2 miles from Rock creek and 4½ miles from the Capitol. Among the charitable institutions, many of which receive aid from the Government, are the Naval Hospital and the Washington Asylum, serving as an almshouse and work-house for the District. The Soldier's Home, 3 miles north of the Capitol and beyond the city limits, was established in 1851 for aged or disabled soldiers of the Regular Army. It occupies a beautiful site, and the grounds, comprising 500 acres, are handsomely laid out. The District Reform School for boys, with a farm of 150 acres, is northeast of the city. The Government Hospital for the Insane, with accommodations for 550 patients, is on the southeast bank of the Anacostia. It was opened in 1855, and is designed for the insane of the Army and Navy and the indigent insane of the District of Columbia. The Columbia Institution for the Deaf and Dumb, on the northeast border of the city, was chartered by Congress in 1857, and is designed for deaf-mute children of the District of Columbia, and those whose parents are in the Army or Navy. ⬤ collegiate department, the National Deaf-Mute College, was organized in 1864 ; it is open to students from all parts of the country. The public schools of Washington form part of the free-school system of the District. Separate accommodations are provided for colored children. Howard University is near the north border of the city, beyond the limits. Columbian University (Baptist), just northwest of the city, was incorporated as a college in 1821, and as a university in 1873. Its law and medical departments, the latter known as the National Medical College, are in the city. In 1875-'76 there were 12 instructors and 103 preparatory and 48 collegiate students. Near the Columbian University is Wayland Seminary, also under Baptist control, established in 1865 for the education of colored preachers and teachers. Gonzaga College, north of the Capitol, is under the control of the Jesuits. In the city are also the Law and Medical Departments of Georgetown College the National College of Pharmacy, and the Law Department of the National University. The last is the only department organized of a proposed university incorporated in 1870. The Louise Home was established and endowed by W. W. Corcoran, in memory of his wife and daughter; only gentlewomen in reduced circumstances are eligible for admission. The permanent seat of the Federal Government was fixed on the Potomac by an act of Congress, passed July 16, 1790; in 1791 the site was selected by Washington, and commissioners were appointed to lay out the city. The Government was established here in 1800, Congress assembling on November 17. On Aug. 24, 1814, the British took possession of the city, and burned the public buildings. In July, 1864, when it was defended by a circle of forts, it was for a few days threatened by the Confederates. Washington was under municipal government from 1802 to 1871, when its corporate existence was merged in the government organized for the entire District; but the territory formerly within the corporate limits continues to be known as the city of Washington.

Wilmington, a city of Hanover County, N. C., on Cape Fear river, twenty miles from the sea. The population in 1850 was 7,264; in 1860, 9,552; in 1870, 13,446; in 1887, estimated at nearly 25,000. There are 2 banks, and a savings-bank just established; 2 successful building and loan associations; a real-estate and investment company; 39 churches, 28 benevolent societies, a large number of academies and schools, and a library association. There are 4 daily and 7 weekly newspapers, rice-mills, 4 steam saw- and planing mills, turpentine distilleries, flouring-mills, an iron foundry, and sash and blind factories. There are 2 marine railways, with dry-docks 70 feet wide, with a keel support of 139 feet, which accommodate vessels of 1,000 tons. The capacity of the cotton-mills has been greatly increased during the past year The Hanover Knitting-Mill, a new venture, turns out hosiery, plain and in colors. The Carolina Oil and Creosote Company have a plant valued at $120,000, where annually from 5,000,000 to 7,000,000 feet of lumber are treated by a patent process. This is a method of extracting the sap and wood acids from lumber, and by a pressure of 125 pounds to the square inch forcing the hot creosoting oil into the open pores of the wood. This preserves the lumber from either the ravages of salt-water, insects, or from dry rot. The output of creosoting oil (extracted from the "fat" pine or "lightwood" of the old turpentine plantations) is 3,000 gallons daily. A new railroad 89½ miles long opens up a large territory to the trade of Wilmington. It runs from Chadbourn, N. C., to Conway, S. C. The town of Crowly, N. C., near Wilmington, laid out and owned by a Wilmington firm, is the site of the Acme Fertilizer Factory and the Acme Pine-Fiber Factory, the latter manufact-

uring fiber from the hair or leaves of the pine-tree by a patent process, and from the fiber, carpets. The factories are in the center of a pine forest. The Navassa Guano Company's factory is just above the city. The United States Government has recently purchased a valuable site, and made an appropriation for a public building. The United States has also a Marine Hospital in Wilmington. Carolina Beach, a new watering-place, opened in 1887, is 15 miles below the city. It was patronized by 25,000 visitors the first season. The city is lighted by electricity, and supplied with water-works. It has 8 steam fire-engines, and 1 hook and ladder company, and a fire-alarm system. The value of exports was $2,-250,000 more for the fiscal year of 1886-'87 than for the previous year. The principal exports are cotton, naval stores, and lumber and shingles. Over 70,000 bushels of peanuts are handled annually.

Woburn, the most populous town in Middlesex County, Mass., near the upper end of Mystic valley, ten miles northwest of Boston, in the midst of rural surroundings as picturesque as any in New England. It is on the Boston and Lowell Railroad. In point of freight and passenger business this is the most important station between Boston and Lowell. There are two recently built and admirably equipped street-railway lines in the town. The population of Woburn in 1870 was 8,560; in 1880, 10,991; on May 1, 1887, 12,750. It is now growing faster than ever, and an application for a city charter will soon be made. In the past ten years it has grown to be the largest leather-manufacturing town or city in New England. In capital invested, men employed, and value of products, it leads all other places engaged in the same business. There are over thirty leather-making establishments here which give employment to more than 2,000 workmen, to whom is annually paid in wages over $700,000. The capital invested in this industry is nearly $4,000,000; value of annual products, $6,000,000; cost of stock used, $4,-000,000. Besides leather-making, glue, chemicals, incandescent electric lamps, dynamos, tanners' machinery, steam-engines, and shoe-stock are manufactured on an extensive scale. There are foundries, machine-shops, and other mechanical establishments in town, while the mercantile business is large, prosperous, and steadily increasing.

Woonsocket, a town of Providence County, R. I., bordering on Massachusetts, 16 miles north of Providence and 26 miles south of Worcester. The town is the commercial and business center of the Blackstone valley; was incorporated in 1867; in 1890 it had a population of 16,052, and in January, 1886, of 18,852. Three railroads touch the town, and street-cars traverse the principal thoroughfares. Twenty-nine manufacturing establishments, with $6,633,482 invested, including $3,358,766 in machinery and tools, give employment to 6,877 operatives. These concerns pay $2,328,435 annually in wages, and expend $7,730,103 for materials, and their annual product is valued at $11,894,223. Eleven cotton-mills produce 35,833,982 yards of sheetings, shirtings, and twills, and 5,888,847 yards of prints, using 11,727,500 pounds of cotton. Six woolen-mills consume 3,191,068 pounds of native wool and 1,425,619 of foreign, producing 1,682,692 yards of cloth annually. The industrial classes have over $8,000,000 deposited in four local savings-banks. More than 500 new buildings, including a million-dollar mill, a railway-passenger station, a dozen business blocks, hospital buildings, two churches, and four school buildings, have been erected since 1880, and a model opera-house is under way. Among the new improvements are extensive public water-works, street-car service, electric fire-alarm, letter-carriers, exclusive electric street-lights, a paid fire department, and a cottage system of hospitals with park. A city charter has been asked from the Legislature, and a bill is before Congress for a public building.

Worcester, the second city in size in Massachusetts, midway between Boston and Springfield, on the Boston and Albany Railroad; population in 1860, 24,973; in 1870, 41,105; in 1880, 58,295; in 1887, estimated at 80,000. The railroad facilities now represent the Boston and Albany, Boston and Maine, and the Fitchburg, the Providence and Worcester, and the New York and New England. The city has a well-equipped street-car service. It has over 50 miles of sewers, 100 miles of water-service, and 200 miles of streets. The water-service, on the elevated storage-reservoir plan, gives a pressure that carries to the height of the tallest buildings. A post-office structure is at once to be erected. Many of the city blocks are costly and notable. The chief educational features of the city are the Worcester Polytechnic, founded in 1868; the College of the Holy Cross, 1843; Worcester Academy, 1835; Highland Military Academy, 1557; the Massachusetts State Normal School, 1871. Clark University, to the founding of which $2,000,000 have been devoted by Jonas S. Clark, Esq., has just been established. The manufacturing industries of Worcester are many and varied, the largest being the Washburn & Moen Manufacturing Company's Wire-Works, which give employment to about 3,500 men, with $6,000,000 product annually, or from 150 to 200 tons a day. Other large industries are Brussels carpets, of which 1,000,000 yards are made yearly; envelopes, of which, at three establishments, 8,000,000 are made daily; machinists' tools, an annual product of nearly $2,000,000, employing 800 men; two large loom-works, giving about the same figures as the last; fire-arms, wood-working machinery, woolen and worsted goods, wrenches, skates, steam-engines, folding-chairs, wool-cards, and agricultural machinery, all represent large cap-

ital and product. In boots and shoes 14 establishments give employment to 1,800 hands with an annual product of over $4,500,000, Worcester's prosperity has from the first been helped by a healthful and beautiful location. The city is the home of the American Antiquarian Society, with its vast library and collections. The Public Library is one of the best in the United States. The school system is excellent. The whole vicinity is filled with interest and attractions. Worcester is the shire town of one of the largest and wealthiest counties in New England.

York, the county-seat of York County, Penn., on both sides of Codorus creek, 94 miles west of Philadelphia, 57 miles north of Baltimore, 26 miles south of Harrisburg. In 1850 the census was 6.863; in 1860, 8,605; in 1870, 11,008; in 1880, 13,940. The last census, counting the suburbs, made the population nearly 15,000; but since then great accessions have been made in the south and west, as well as in the northeast parts of the city, so that now, adding the suburbs, the figure would be fully 20,000. The public buildings worthy of note are the court-house, built of granite, the jail, almshouse, Orphan's Home, opera-house, Collegiate Institute, and high-school. The Eastern, Western, and City Markets are also three fine buildings. There are 25 churches. The public schools number 50, employing more than 60 teachers. In this connection are also to be noted the Collegiate Institute, the York County Academy, and the Young Ladies' Seminary, besides private schools and business colleges. York is both a commercial and a manufacturing center. It is in the midst of one of the wealthiest and most fertile farm regions in the country. The city contains 12 good hotels and 10 banks, with an aggregate capital of $3,000,000. There are agricultural works, a furnace, foundries, machine-shops, car-works, boiler and engine works, planing-mills, chain-works, cigar-factories, candy-factories, scale, lock, and safe works, an organ-factory, shoe-factory, extensive brick-works, tanneries, a book-bindery, and numerous printing-offices. Five weekly papers and four dailies are issued. The following are the latest manufacturing statistics by the census reports of 1880: men employed in the shops, 2,055; annual wages, $456,616; capital invested, $1,282,-848; material consumed, $1,274,131; annual product, $2,285,890. The city has made such rapid strides in the past few years that the annual product of the factories and shops can not now be short of $3,500,000, with the other statistics correspondingly increased. York began to thrive about 1861. In 1884 the city was overwhelmed with a deluging flood that swept away all the bridges and wrecked stores and dwellings. Steady improvement immediately set in—the bridges were replaced with large iron structures, seven of which, and one of wood, now span the Codorus. The water-works have been enlarged and improved, the streets graded and macadamized, and nearly all of them are now lined with trees. There is a new street-railroad. The entire city is lighted by electricity, and telephone and telegraph wires connect with neighboring towns and distant cities. The water-supply is ample, though not without fault, as it is obtained from the Codorus.

CLARK, ALVAN, an American optician, born in Ashfield, Mass., March 8, 1808, died in Cambridge, Mass., Aug. 19, 1887. He was the son of a farmer, and obtained his education in public schools. At an early age he showed considerable artistic ability, which was put to practical use when he became an engraver for calicoes at the print-works in Lowell and elsewhere. This occupation he followed until 1835, when he settled in Boston, and there opened a studio on Tremont Street, where he continued his career as a portrait-painter for

ALVAN CLARK.

many years. His pictures of Robert Hare, Thomas Hill, and Daniel Webster, are well-known specimens of his skill. In 1846, in connection with his sons, Alvan G. and George B. Clark, he established the firm of Alvan Clark and Sons, which has since continued and become famous as the leading telescope-makers of the world. Its origin is due to the younger son, Alvan G. Clark, who is an accomplished astronomer, and who, being unable to secure suitable lenses, induced his father to establish the business. For ten years the subject of optics was carefully studied, and Mr. Clark spent some time in Europe making himself familiar with astronomy, before the reputation of the firm was fully established. His first order for a large telescope came from the University of Mississippi in 1860, the object-glass of which was to be 18½ inches, 3 inches larger than any that had hitherto been successfully used in the world. The civil war prevented the completion of the contract, and the instrument was purchased for the University of Chicago. Then followed the construction of two glasses of 26 inches each, one of which was made for the

University of Virginia, and the other for the U. S. Naval Observatory in Washington. These lenses required four years of labor, and cost $46,000. Many others of varying sizes, from 4 inches to 36 inches, have been made for observatories throughout the world. Some idea of the labor required may be formed from the fact that for a good 4-inch objective a month's constant work is required, and for an 8- or 10-inch glass a year is necessary. In 1870 the Russian Government contracted with Messrs. Clark & Sons for an enormous telescope to be placed in its observatory in Pulkowa, and in 1888 the instrument was completed. Otto N. von Struve, the distinguished astronomer, visited all of the well-known makers in the world before giving the order. The telescope was then the largest in existence, costing $33,000, having a clear aperture of 30 inches, a 45-foot focus, and weighing 418 pounds. It possessed a magnifying power of 2,000 diameters, and was capable of increasing the surface of the object viewed 2,500,000 times its natural size. Mr. Clark received a vote of thanks from the Imperial Academy of Science, and a gold medal from the Emperor of Russia. A few years since this firm undertook the construction of the 36-inch object-glass for the Lick Observatory on Mount Hamilton, Cal., which was completed and safely forwarded to its destination in the autumn of 1887. Mr. Clark invented numerous improvements in telescopes and their manufacture, including the double eye-piece and an ingenious method of measuring small celestial arcs. A list of the discoveries made by him with telescopes of his own construction is given in the " Proceedings of the Royal Astronomical Society" (London, vol. xvii). Mr. Clark received the honorary degree of A. M. from Amherst College in 1854, from Princeton in 1865, and from Harvard in 1874, and also the Rumford medal from the American Academy of Arts and Sciences.

COLOMBIA, an independent republic of South America, covering an area of 586,000 square miles, and having a population of 3,500,000. It has been decided that the capitals of departments are to be the following: Medellín, capital of Antioquía; Carthagena, of Bolívar; Tunja, of Boyacá; Popayan. of Cauca; Bogotá, of Cundinamarca; Santa Marta, of Magdalena; Panamá, of Panamá; Bucaramanga, of Santander; Tolima, of Ibagué. Each of these capitals is to be the seat of a superior court.

Government.—At Bogotá, on June 4, Dr. Rafael Nuñez, re-elected President for six years, from December, 1886, entered formally upon his office. Subsequently, he formed the following Cabinet: Minister of Government, Dr. Felipe F. Paul; Foreign Affairs, Dr. Cárlos Holguin; Treasury, Dr. Ontario Roldan; War, Don Felipe Angulo; Education, Dr. Domingo Ospina C; Auditor-General, Dr. Cárlos Martinez Silva; Public Works, Dr. Jesus Casas Rojas. Vice-President, Gen. Eliseo Payan.

The United States Minister at Bogotá is Hon.

Dabney H. Maury, and the Colombian Minister at Washington is Don Ricardo Becerra. The Colombian Consul at New York is Señor C. Calderon. The American Consul-General at Bogotá is John G. Walker.

A decree was issued in July, recalling the Colombian legations in France and Germany, and abolishing the consulates at London, Brussels, and San Francisco.

Army.—The strength of the army was fixed for 1887 at 6,500 on a peace footing, to be increased in time of war to any extent that may be deemed necessary.

Finance.—The public indebtedness in 1887 was represented by a foreign debt of $11,158,-000 and a home debt of $11,057,628. The national bank, founded in 1881, has besides issued $8,000,000 notes, still in circulation. A branch bank is to be established at Panama. The budget estimate for 1887–'88 fixes the income at $20,890,000, and the outlay at $22,893,-645. The product of the salines in the interior during the last four months of 1886 gave jointly a revenue of $483,874. Dating from Dec. 15, 1886, the Government established as a monopoly of its own the manufacture of sea-salt in the department of Panama; all salt consumed there will have to be purchased at the government offices.

Much trouble was experienced in Panama during the spring and summer respecting the circulating medium, and this led to a decree declaring legal tender, in the department of Panama, the national silver coins of 0·885 and 0·900 fineness, in dollar and fifty-cent pieces, and those of equal coinage of lower denominations, even should their fineness be inferior to that mentioned. Foreign gold and silver coins of 0.900 fineness, and national gold coins of the same quality, or of 0·666, coined in the Medellin Mint under decree 659 of 1885, and national and foreign bank-notes of all descriptions and denominations will be considered in the department of Panama to be merely objects of commerce. Meanwhile in Medellin, Cauca, in August, gold rose 20 per cent. in value, as compared with June prices, and drafts on foreign countries were at 80 per cent. premium; imported goods rose from 8 to 10 per cent. in price.

During the spring a law was passed abrogating all privileges and exemptions granted by prior legislation or government decrees in favor of banks doing business in Colombia.

Commerce.—The imports into Colombia in 1885–'86 were valued at $6,879,541, and the exports at $14,171,241. The United States' trade with Colombia in two years has been:

FISCAL YEAR.	Import.	Domestic export to Colombia.
1886	$8,006,921	$5,294,799
1887	8,950,958	5,973,965

The national legislative council determined in January that the law of Sept. 21 and 22, 1886, prohibiting the coasting-trade in sailing-vessels from Panama southward, should not comprise the port of Buenaventura.

The Panama Canal.—On July 21, a meeting of the Panama Canal Company was held in Paris. The aggregate expenditure, during the fiscal year 1885–'86, was 144,811,119 francs, and as, since the incorporation of the company, there had been spent 495,862,076 francs, the total amount reached the sum of 640,173,195 francs. But there is to be deducted from this the sum of 88,446,785 francs not yet paid, reducing the actual disbursements to 601,726,410 francs. Deducting the latter from the share capital of the company, the 250,000 5-per-cent. bonds, the 600,000 3-per-cent. bonds, and the 409,667 4-per-cent. bonds, together, 784,098,628 francs, there remained on June 30, 1886, an available capital of 132,372,218 francs.

While the U. S. steamer "Galena" lay at anchor off Colon early in March, 1887, Lieut. Rogers was assigned by the Navy Department to accompany M. Charles de Lesseps, vice-president of the canal, on his tour of inspection. The trip began on March 10, and lasted seventeen days. The report of Lieut. Rogers embraces the following passages: "Estimates of the total excavations necessary to complete the canal are now placed at 105,090,000 cubic metres. Out of this, up to date, the amount completed is 81,920,000 cubic metres, leaving 73,170,000 metres to be excavated. Up to the end of 1885, 18,417,318 cubic metres had been excavated. During 1886 11,727,000 cubic metres were added. I put down the time of the completion of the canal at seven years. That is, without there being any hitches, and everything working in perfect order. M. Ferdinand de Lesseps has quoted the most sanguine figures as to the possible output in the coming two years. To my mind, there will be no increase on the present output. In the first place, it is easy to see that the deeper the works get, the more difficult becomes the task of removing the rock and soil; and the difficulty of the Culebra mountain has not yet been solved. M. Charles de Lesseps was rather guarded on the subject, saying: 'In two years the canal will be completed from Colon to Kilometre Forty-four, and from La Boca to Paraiso. As to the Culebra, I leave you to form your own conclusions. It is a difficult work.' The serious question in the Culebra is, how to avoid the accumulation of sediment and the vast land-slides it is subject to. Last year 78,000 cubic metres of earth were washed away or fell into the bed of the canal, and, according to the rate of extraction of 1886, it must have taken the work of six weeks to make good the damage. The hill-side on the left is a mixture of sand, alluvium, and conglomerate. During the rainy season, the surface deposit becomes saturated with water, and the increased weight, coupled with the incline, causes the deposit to slide over the smooth surface of the clay into the canal excavation-works. The clay in turn contracts during the dry season, large fissures result, and hence another source of land-slides. The natural wash of the sides by the heavy rains is another cause of deposit. Worse than all this is the fact that, up to the present time, the mountain on the left side of the cut is found to be moving bodily toward the axis of the canal, at an annual rate of from twelve to eighteen inches, owing to the cutting away of its lower support."

The Government has resolved to build a large lighthouse at Colon for its own account, instead of granting a concession to private parties. At a distance of 430 metres from the Cape of Puerto Belillo, a second lighthouse was lighted in Sabanilla harbor, Aug. 1, 1887.

The sum of $200,000 has been voted toward building a breakwater at Carthagena.

Post-Office.—The British postal money-order system has been extended to the Isthmus.

Railroads.—The Government toward the close of 1886 granted a concession to Don Juan Gaulmin to build the following railroads: the Cauca line, the Antioquia line, and the one from Bogotá to the Magdalena river, *via* Tunja, Socorro and Bucaramanga. Much headway was made in 1887 toward completing the line of railway from Bolivar to Puerto Belillo, as well as toward finishing the wharf at the latter place. Capitalists of Bogotá have conceived the project of building a railway to Chapinero, afterward to be extended to Zipaquirá. Perhaps no other enterprise on the Isthmus has been a gainer to such an extent from M. de Lesseps's scheme of connecting the two oceans as the Panama Railroad. M. Lucien N. B. Wyse, in his late book entitled "Le Canal de Panama" (1886), says: "The railroad before the commencement of work on the interoceanic canal annually transported 27,000 passengers and 270,000 tons of merchandise sufficiently valuable to pay the exorbitant rates charged by the management. To-day, double the amount of freight is carried, including excavation materials, and the number of passengers transported exceeds 550,000, 94 per cent. of whom are workers on the canal." The road is 47 miles long, two miles longer than the proposed route of the canal, and the fare from Colon to Panama was until recently $25 in gold, which means $35 in Colombian currency. It has been reduced, however, to $4.80 gold, or $6.90 Colombian currency.

In January the exclusive privilege of providing the city of Carthagena with tramways was granted to the American engineer, Mr. J. E. Davies, for thirty years. Besides a track in the streets there will be branches to the Cabrero, the Isla de Manga, the Pié de la Popa, and the Turbaco district, four leagues.

Steamer Lines.—The Legislature of Colombia passed a bill in 1886 authorizing the Government to subsidize to the extent of $2,000 annually any ocean steamship line that will undertake to touch regularly every two months at Santa Marta and Riohacha. The Government was empowered in January, 1887, to renew its contract with the Pacific Steam Navigation Company, on condition of a lowering of freight rates on Colombian products, and also on merchandise that may be shipped from Panama, Buenaventura, and Tumaco. Authority was also given to advance $8,000 to any company establishing steam navigation between Buenaventura and the San Juan river. On September 5 there arrived at Panama from Antwerp the steamer "Costa Rica" of the Marqués de Campo's new Spanish Central American line of steamships, and on September 11 the "Nicaragua," belonging to the same line, both with cargo *via* the Straits of Magellan, each of a capacity of 4,000 tons and 2,000 horse-power, the trip *via* Buenos Ayres and Puerto Coronel having been made by both in 53½ days.

Telegraphs.—In July the new telegraph between Mompos and Magangue went into operation, as did also the branch line between Cármen de Santander and La Gloria, putting Carthagena and Barranquilla in connection with Bogotá, Medellin, Tunja, Popayan, Panama, and, through the cables from the Isthmus, with all parts of the world in which cables or land-lines exist.

The Colombian Government granted in July, to the Central and South American Telegraph Company, authority to establish and operate a telegraph line across the Isthmus of Panama, and to extend its cables from Colon along the Atlantic coast of South America. Concession has been granted to connect by cable Colon and Carthagena.

Don Rufino Guzman was granted a concession in April, 1887, to build a telegraph between Bogotá and Honda, with stations at Facatativa, Agualarga, Villeta, and Guaduas.

Electric Light.—The Government, toward the close of 1886, granted a concession to Gen. Ramon Santo Domingo Vila for lighting by electricity the districts and cities of Panama and Colon, in such localities as the Government and private citizens may desire.

The exclusive privilege for twenty years was granted to Don Emilio Viollet to manufacture, use, and sell an apparatus of his invention throughout Colombia for "aërial cable transportation."

Water-works.—The laying of pipes at Bogotá for the city water-works proceeded actively under a contract with Señor Jimenez during the summer. At the same time a company was formed at Panama for supplying that city with water-works, the company paying the Government $60,000 for the privilege, which is to last forty years, when the Government will become owner of the works. The work is to be finished in two years from the summer of 1887, the Government to cede the company for fifteen years the subvention it receives from the Panama Railroad in aid of the undertaking, which sums the company agrees to reimburse the Government for thirty years from date. United States Consul Vifquain reports to the

State Department on the subject of water-works to the following effect from Barran-quilla: " Within the next five years not less than one hundred cities of South America will establish water-works, and all the material for these will be furnished by England. Large works are now in process of construction at Bogotá, and all the material for them is landed at this port. It comes from England and is carried in English bottoms. Speaking to the contractor the other day while looking at the material being put on river steamers—steamers mostly built in England—I told him that the United States could furnish better pipes than those he shipped to Bogotá. 'I know it,' said he, 'but these are good enough for all pur-poses, and 35 per cent. cheaper than any I priced in the States. I would prefer to deal with your people, but business is business.' An English syndicate of iron-manufacturers—the same that had operated so extensively in Chili during the last few years—has just pur-chased a 200-mile railroad concession in this country. It might be as well to remember that if English capital controls the railroad system of this continent, as it is in a fair way of doing, the same capital will control all the commercial and industrial avenues of this vast and extremely rich country—second, in fact, to no other land in the world in natural re-sources of all sorts."

Coal and Phosphate Discoveries.—Señor Jorge Isaacs, in his explorations during the summer on the shores of the Gulf of Uraba, discovered some excellent coal-fields near the shores of the gulf, and valuable phosphates in large quantities on an island in the gulf.

Mining-Schools.—The Government has resolved to establish two mining-schools, one at Ibagué and another in the department of Antioquia. The sum of $10,000 each is set aside to build the schools, and $20,000 annually, each, toward assisting them.

Cinchona-Bark and India-Rubber.—Messrs. Nieto, Rocha & Co., of Baranquilla, informed the Gov ernment, in December, 1886, that their "qui-nal" or plantation of cinchona-trees, "El De-rado," in the chaparral district, Tolima, was then in a flourishing condition, there being 600,-000 trees in an advanced state of growth, to-gether with 130,000 India-rubber trees. The samples of bark sent to Europe proved richer in quinine than those sent from Jamaica, and there was every inducement to give impulse throughout Colombia to this pursuit. At the same time they offered the Government seed for gratuitous distribution among farmers.

New Textile Fiber.—A concession was granted to Don Wenceslao Campuzano for the extrac-tion and elaboration of the "fique" fiber, the contractor engaging to furnish the Govern-ment, within two years after his factory shall be in operation, 20,000 yards of fine carpet-tissue, 80 centimetres wide, of fast colors.

Chinese Immigration.—One of the laws passed by the Colombian Legislature prohibits the im-portation of Chinese workmen into Colombia. This law is not retroactive, and affects no con-tracts made with Chinamen prior to its passage.

Literary Property.—A treaty was concluded between Colombia and Spain on Nov. 28, 1885, mutually guaranteeing and securing literary property, and on Nov. 22, 1886, a decree was published at Bogotá promulgating the law.

Diseases.—The "Medical Bulletin" of Cali, Cauca, contained an article in its June issue on leprosy, of which many cases are to be found in the interior of Colombia. The writer be-lieves the disease can be acquired without con-tact, and cites the case of a man who had never been in a locality where the disease exists, and yet became afflicted with it through falling into a river while heated from a hard day's sport. "El Tiempo," of June 15, of San José de Cucuta, Santander, says that very few cases of yellow fever now occur there, and adds, that the doctors were about to make a report declaring that inoculation had been the con-queror in the struggle against yellow fever. About ten per cent of the inoculated patients were attacked but none of them died.

Claims of Foreigners.—Toward the close of 1886 a very important law was promulgated at Bogotá respecting the claims of foreigners who suffered losses during the late revolution. It provides that the Minister of Foreign Affairs shall receive all such claims and pronounce judgment on them; claimants will be allowed to appeal from such decisions to the Supreme Court; the nation will not hold itself responsi-ble for damage suffered at the hands of the revolutionists; all claimants must prove their nationality by duly authenticated documents; foreigners who have not remained neutral can not present claims under this law; no claim will be received after the expiration of one year from the time of the publication of this law, even should the claimants be children, women, or persons residing abroad, otherwise entitled to claim this law, and all contracts will be null and void which may have been made between revolutionists and foreigners.

COLORADO. State Government.—The State of-ficers during the year were as follows: Gov-ernor, Alva Adams, Republican; Lieutenant-Governor, Norman H. Meldrum; Secretary of State, James Rice; Treasurer, Peter W. Breene; Auditor, Darwin P. Kingsley; Attorney-Gen-eral, Alvin Marsh; Superintendent of Public Instruction, Leonidas S. Cornell; Railroad Commissioner, A. D. Wilson; Chief-Justice of the Supreme Court, William E. Beck; Associate Justices, Joseph C. Helm and S. H. Elbert.

Legislative Session.—The sixth biennial ses-sion of the General Assembly began on Janu-ary 5 and adjourned April 4. It adopted a conservative course, refusing the demands of those seeking radical legislation against cor-porations, especially the railroads. It changed the basis of representation for its own mem-bers, allowing one senator for every 9,881 in-habitants, and one representative for every

4,978, and redistricted the State accordingly. The danger of alien landlordism was provided against by a law prohibiting non-resident aliens from acquiring agricultural, arid, or range lands in the State, or any interest therein greater in value than $5,000, mines and mining property being excepted from the operation of the act. Real estate owned in violation of these provisions is forfeited to the State. A new code of civil procedure was adopted, which abolishes the distinction between actions at law and suits in equity, provides that a married woman may sue or be sued as if sole, and otherwise simplifies the common-law practice. Several measures tending to increase in the revenue available for maintaining the State Government were passed. By the constitution, mines and mining property were exempt from taxation for ten years subsequent to its adoption. That period having elapsed, a bill taxing this large class of property was passed at this session. It was also voted to submit to the people, at the next election for members of the General Assembly, in accordance with a provision of the Constitution, the following question: "Shall the rate of taxation on property for State purposes for the years 1889-'90 be increased to five mills on each dollar of valuation for each of those years?" The present rate is four mills. An amendment to the Constitution, to be voted upon at the same election, was proposed, modifying the clause that forbids a State debt. It provides that within certain limits, the State may contract debts to meet casual deficiencies in revenue, to erect public buildings for the State, to suppress insurrections, to defend the State, and in time of war to assist in defending the United States. Considerable changes were made in the government and methods of the public schools. The city of Denver obtained extensive amendments to its charter. Other acts of the session were:

To prevent and prohibit the sale of injurious or unwholesome articles of food or drink.
To establish agricultural-experiment stations in El Paso, Bent, and Delta Counties, and San Luis Valley.
To regulate the use of artesian wells, and to prevent the waste of subterranean waters.
To prohibit the black-listing or publishing of employés when they have been discharged.
To establish a bureau of labor statistics.
To provide for the sale of lots and lands given to the Territory of Colorado for the purpose of aiding in the erection of a capitol building.
To prohibit the employment of children under fourteen years of age in any underground works or mines, or in any smelter, mill, or factory.
To restore the right of trial by jury.
To prevent the hiring out of convicts by the State or its officers, and to prevent the importation of materials made by convicts for use on public improvements.
To provide for the formation of corporations for the purpose of warranting or insuring the title to real property.
To establish the county of Logan, and the county-seat thereof.
To establish the county of Washington, and the county-seat thereof.

To prevent cruelty to children.
To protect the food-fishes in the natural streams of the State.
Designating the first Monday in September of each year as a public holiday, to be known as "Labor day."
Regulating the lease, sale, and management of the State lands.
To prevent discrimination in the sale or delivery of news items, news dispatches, or press reports.
To prevent frauds in the nominating of public officers at primaries, or conventions, or otherwise.
To regulate the practice of pharmacy, licensing persons to carry on such practice, and providing for the appointment and defining the duties of a State board of pharmacists.
To straighten the channel of the Rio Grande river, and to build a levee along the same at Alamosa.
To provide for the study of the nature of alcoholic drinks and narcotics, and of their effects upon the human system, by the pupils in the public schools.
To set aside not less than six hundred and forty acres in that portion of Saguache County, which includes the Royal Arch and Echo mountains, for the purpose of a State park.

Education.—The value of public-school property in the State is about $2,500,000, an increase of 300 per cent. in five years. This is twice as much in proportion to the school population as New York holds in school property, and only slightly less in proportion than Massachusetts. The number of teachers has doubled in five years, while the enrollment shows a large increase. Of the higher institutions, the School of Mines and the Agricultural College are well attended, the latter having a total enrollment of 116 pupils in 1886. With reference to the State University at Boulder, the Governor says: "There is a general and well-founded feeling throughout the State that this institution is disappointing the expectations of its founders. It is supported by a dedicated tax of one fifth of one mill on the property in the State, which produces an income of about $22,000, and by a noble endowment of lands from the nation, which largely increases its resources. It has an excellent faculty of able and learned instructors; its funds are ample for its needs, and yet it lacks somewhere the vitalizing energy that insures success. There are but ten counties, besides the one in which it is situated, represented on its roll, and these ten by only fourteen scholars. The county in which it is situated sends one hundred scholars, and all other States and Territories only eighteen."

State Institutions.—The Legislature of 1887 provided for the establishment of a State Home and Industrial School for Girls, at or near Denver. The State Industrial School for Boys, at Golden, has been in existence for several years. At the close of 1886 it contained ninety pupils.

The total number of prisoners in the State Prison during the past two years was 682, the average number being 356. This is a large average in proportion to the population. The cost of maintaining the prison for the past two years, including betterments and every description of charge, has been $269,036; total earnings, exclusive of prison-labor, on real estate, $70,067, showing an increase over the previous term of $19,651. The total net charge above earnings was $198,968.

Valuations.—The total assessed valuation of the State for 1887 was $140,000,533, nearly one third of which, or $45,753, 685, is credited to the county of Arapahoe, which contains the city of Denver. The total valuation for 1885 was $115,420.193.90. In 1886 this amount was increased to $124,269,710.06.

In 1885 the assessed lands and improvements amounted to 3,926,782 acres, valued at $22,-504,768; in 1886 there were 4,534,938 acres, valued at $24,211,001. This is exclusive of town and city lots, which in 1885 were valued at $41,106,457; in 1886, at $43,779,068. The valuation of railroad property in 1886 was $23,506,367; in 1887 it was $23,696,666.

Corporations.—The Governor, in his message at the beginning of the year, says: "During the past two years 802 corporations have filed their certificates in the office of the Secretary of State. These nominally represent a capital of $361,000,000, the Denver and Rio Grande Railway alone representing $78,500,000 of the sum. It is incredible that the legitimate course of business can be healthfully promoted by any such inflated capitalization. There must be humbug, if not downright rascality, behind such a pretentious array of figures. It represents three times the total valuation of the State. I therefore recommend that you guard the good name of Colorado against a reputation for bombastical finances by considerably increasing the charge for every thousand dollars above one hundred thousand of capital stock."

Cereals.—The production of crops for 1886 is estimated as follows: Wheat, 2,100,000 bushels; oats, 600,000 bushels; barley, 250,000 bushels; and corn, 175,000 bushels. The season of 1887 has been favorable, and an increase over these figures is counted upon.

Irrigation.—As the constitution of the State declares all streams within its limits to be public property, Colorado avoids at the outset the difficulties that have hindered irrigation in California. The construction of canals has, therefore, progressed rapidly, especially in the past two years; but the system of ownership has developed tendencies opposed to agricultural interests. "A large percentage of the earlier canals were built on the co-operative plan, in which many farmers united, and through their joint credit and labor, built the canals to water their farms. This method was not suited to large enterprises, and capital was not slow to perceive that ditch enterprises offered a safe and lucrative field for investment, and, as a result, the majority of the canals constructed during the past two years, or now being projected, are owned by corporations merely as speculative enterprises." These corporations, holding no landed interests, have not hesitated to take advantage of the monopoly that from the nature of their business they must necessarily enjoy, to extort from the farmers excessive rates for the supply

of water. The Legislature has found it necessary to take the question in hand, and by several enactments of this year it gave enlarged powers to the county commissioners to fix the water-rates in any part of the county, on application of any person interested, and prohibited the exaction of more than the legal rate so established, either by means of royalty, bonus, premium, or otherwise. Any refusal to supply water at such rate is made punishable.

Stock-Raising.—Official reports show that the number of cattle in the State assessed in 1886 was 845,038, valued at $12,425,961. This is an increase over 1885 of 66,443 in number, and $1,132,987 in value. In 1884 there were shipped out of the State to various markets, 54,874 head; in 1885, 75,579 head; and in 1886, 122,678 head. During 1886 there were consumed within the State 66,300 head. Notwithstanding these increased shipments, the industry has not greatly prospered of late. The area of cattle-ranges is steadily lessening by the settlement of immigrants, the prices for beef have fallen, and the cost of transportation increased. Leading cattlemen, both outside and inside the State, appreciating these conditions, have organized an International Range Association. The second annual meeting of the association was held at Denver in February, 1887.

This year witnessed a practical abandonment of the custom of driving herds northward through Colorado to Wyoming and Montana, for the purpose of fattening them on the rich grasses of the northern plains. Immense herds of Texas cattle have in former years passed through the State over what is known as the "National Cattle-Trail," but so rapidly have settlements been made that herders now find their progress impeded by the fences and farms of pioneer settlers. In a few years these barriers will be entirely impassable, and Southern cattle owners will be compelled to ship their herds by rail to the North, or abandon the Northern prairies altogether.

Mining.—The product of metals for 1886 is estimated as follows: Silver, $16,450,921; lead, $5,123,296; gold, $5,087,901; copper, $132,-570; making a total of $26,794,688. This is an increase of $4,294,688 over the figures for 1885. The production of the Leadville mines alone aggregates $13,750,783, showing a gain over the previous year of $1,893,071. Colorado produced in 1886 over 65 per cent. of all the lead mined in the United States. The product of the Leadville and Red Cliff mines was nearly equal to half of the output of the country. Such is the prosperity of the Leadville district that at the close of 1887 it contained over 150 distinct producing mines, the yield from which during the year will reach nearly $16,000,000.

Increasing attention is being given to the rich coal deposits in the State. The productive and partially-developed coal-fields of Colorado embrace an aggregate area of over 1,000,000 acres, while the area of the coal-bearing formation is estimated by geologists to aggregate over

26,000,000 acres, consisting of three varieties— the lignites, bituminous and anthracite coals of various grades and qualities. These deposits underlie a great part of the plains near the foot-hills, extending from the northern part of the State to the Raton mountains, which lie along the border of New Mexico. Coal is also found in South Park, near Como; in the vicinity of Florence, above Pueblo; near Walsenburg, in Huerfano County; in inexhaustible quantities in the vicinity of Durango, near the extreme southwestern corner of the State; in the vicinity of Crested Butte, and other localities in Gunnison County, and it underlies almost the whole of northwestern Colorado. The production of the State for each of the past six years, is as follows:

YEARS.	Tons.	YEARS.	Tons.
1880	875,000	1884	1,130,024
1881	706,744	1885	1,398,796
1882	1,061,479	1886	1,436,911
1883	1,229,568		

The value of the product for 1886, at $2.35 a ton at the mines, is $3,875,095.

Oil has been struck at several places in these coal-fields, and in the vicinity of Florence, thirty miles west of Pueblo, are oil-wells that are producing about 700 barrels a day.

The Utes.—In the latter part of August the people of the State were alarmed by exaggerated accounts of an outbreak of the Ute Indians, headed by Chief Colorow. The Governor was induced to order out the State troops against them, and thought it necessary to hasten himself to the scene of disturbance in the western part of the State, not far from the town of Meeker. It was soon ascertained, however, that the whites were the aggressors, and that a sheriff's posse, sent to arrest several Indians on the charge of horse-stealing, had taken advantage of its authority to make brutal attacks upon a peaceable Indian camp. Colorow's party were taken entirely by surprise at the first attack, and after a short skirmish retreated toward their reservation, which was several days' journey distant. The whites followed, and just before the border of the reservation was reached fell upon them again, killing several of their number, and driving off their ponies and flocks. No excuse for these attacks can be found. When responsible officials reached the scene, the aggressors were restrained, and Colorow with his followers returned to their reservation. The Indian loss, besides a half-dozen or more of their own number killed, was estimated at over 600 horses, with 37 head of cattle, and 2,330 sheep and goats. For these animals restitution was made. On the other side three white men were killed, and the State was subjected to a needless expense of several hundred thousand dollars for support and payment of the troops called out. The bitter hatred felt by the settlers against the Indians was the chief cause of this unfortunate episode.

COMMERCE AND NAVIGATION OF THE UNITED STATES.—The aggregate volume of American foreign commerce for the year ended June 30, 1887, was $93,542,013 greater than for the preceding fiscal year. The imports of merchandise in 1887 were of the value of $692,819,768, as compared with $635,436,136 in 1886. The total value of the exports of merchandise in 1887 was $716,183,211, as against $679,524,830 in 1886. There was a surplus of exports over imports of $23,363,443 in 1887, as compared with $44,088,694 in 1886. The value of the exports of domestic merchandise in 1887 was $703,022,923, as compared with $665,964,529 in 1886; that of the exports of foreign merchandise $13,160,288, as compared with $13,560,301. The increase in the exports of domestic products was $37,058,394.

The imports of specie in 1887 amounted to $60,170,792, as against $38,598,656 in 1886; and the exports of specie to $35,997,691, as against $72,463,410, showing an excess of imports in 1887 of $24,173,101, as compared with an excess of exports in 1886 of the amount of $33,869,754.

Imports.—There was an increase in the value of merchandise imports in 1887, as compared with the total value in 1886, of $56,883,632, or 9 per cent. The increase in the importation of articles on the free list was $22,061,881, and in dutiable merchandise $34,821,797. The following imports of free merchandise show a material increase:

IMPORTS.	Increase.
Chemicals	$2,304,226
Coffee	13,574,688
India-rubber and gutta percha, crude	1,868,591
Silk, unmanufactured	1,365,561
Tin bars	1,058,944

The dutiable articles which showed the largest increase were as follow:

IMPORTS.	Increase.
Animals	$1,068,566
Art works	1,365,418
Fancy articles	1,388,890
Flax, hemp, jute, etc.:	
Unmanufactured	2,252,466
Manufactures	969,398
Fruits and nuts	2,447,372
Hops	2,959,680
Iron and steel:	
Ores	$812,824
Pig-iron	2,473,274
Scrap-iron	2,910,185
Railway-bars, steel	1,218,272
Ingots, etc.	3,598,490
Machinery	677,578
All other	507,127
	12,481,410
Precious stones	2,623,292
Silk manufactures	3,350,964
Wools:	
Combing	919,796
Carpet	1,973,295
Wool, manufactures	3,481,899

The largest decrease among the articles of the free list was in hides and skins, amounting to $2,480,212, and in seeds not medicinal. amounting to $937,125. The dutiable articles showing the largest decrease were the following:

IMPORTS.	Decrease.
Breadstuffs	$1,293,148
Cotton, manufactures	765,918
Leather	1,065,647
Seeds not medicinal	850,776
Sugar, molasses, and candy	2,698,529
Wools, clothing	3,219,698

Exports.—The values of the principal articles of domestic merchandise exported during the two years ended June 30, 1886 and 1887, were as follow:

ARTICLES.	1887.	1886.
Animals	$10,598,362	$12,518,660
Breadstuffs	165,768,662	125,846,558
Coal	4,526,825	4,188,580
Copper, and manufactures of	8,727,447	5,671,748
Cotton, and manufactures of	221,151,399	219,045,576
Furs and fur-skins	4,807,277	8,321,102
Iron and steel, and manufactures of ...	15,968,756	15,755,490
Leather, and manufactures of	10,486,188	8,787,662
Oil-cake and oil-cake meal	7,309,691	9,058,714
Oil, mineral	46,624,915	50,199,844
Provisions :		
Meat products	82,945,994	79,748,750
Dairy products	9,837,802	10,876,466
Sugar	11,442,387	10,977,759
Tobacco, and manufactures of....	29,230,672	30,424,908
Wood, and manufactures of	19,654,984	20,748,890
Total	$644,225,211	$605,010,177

The values enumerated in the above table constituted 91·6 per cent. of the total value of domestic exports for 1887, and 91·2 per cent. of the total value for 1886.

The values of exports of domestic merchandise during the year ended June 30, 1887, classified according to sources of production and the proportion of the total value represented by each group, were as follow:

GROUPS.	Value.	Per cent.
Products of agriculture	$528,073,798	74·41
Products of manufacture	136,785,105	19·45
Products of mining (including mineral oils)	11,758,662	1·67
Products of the forest	21,126,273	3·01
Products of the fisheries	5,155,775	0·73
Other products...............	5,173,810	0·73
Total	$708,092,923	100·00

The articles of domestic product in which there has been a material increase in the values exported in 1887, and the amount of the increase in each, were as follow:

EXPORTS.	Increase.
Wheat	$40,458,766
Wheat flour	18,507,127
Pork and meat products, except beef products ..	6,185,297
Leather, and manufactures of..............	1,698,456
Furs and fur-skins....................	1,486,175
Cotton, unmanufactured	1,186,415

The exports which show a material falling off in the values exported were the following:

EXPORTS.	Decrease.
Corn................................	$12,888,561
Mineral oils	8,374,929
Beef products	2,9~8,053
Spirits, distilled	1,944,411
Oats	1,765,188
Hops	1,659,518
Copper-ore	1,374,955
Tobacco, and manufactures of...	1,194,236
Fire-arms	1,114,407
Dairy products	1,089,164

Imports entered for Consumption.—The total value of imported merchandise entered for consumption in 1886–'87 was $683,418,981, exceeding the total of the preceding fiscal year by $58,110,167, or 9·3 per cent. The value of dutiable merchandise entered for consumption was $450,325,322, as compared with $413,-

778,055 in 1886; the value of merchandise free of duty, $233,093,659, as compared with $211,530,759. The amount of ordinary revenue collected on imports in 1887 was $212,-032,424, of which 61·3 per cent. was collected under specific, and 38·7 per cent. under ad-valorem rates. In 1886, on dutiable imports amounting to $413,778,055, the amount collected was $188,533,171, of which 60·5 per cent. represents specific, and 39·5 per cent. ad-valorem duties. In 1888, just before the change in the tariff, the dutiable merchandise taken out of bond amounted to $493,916,384, on which duties were collected to the amount of $209,650,699, of which specific duties formed 56, and ad-valorem duties 44 per cent. The increase of $23,653,627 in the amount of ordinary customs revenue in 1887 over 1886 took place in the following classes of imports:

CLASSES OF ARTICLES.	1886.	1887.	Increase.
Sugar. sugar-candy, and molasses. .	$51,778,948	$58,016,686	$6,237,738
Iron and steel, and manufactures of ..	14,631,576	20,713,234	6,081,858
Wool and manufactures of:			
Wools	5,126,108	5,899,517	773,709
Manufactures ...	27,278,528	29,729,717	2,451,189
Silk, manufactures of	13,988,097	15,540,801	1,602,204
Tobacco, and manufactures of	8,311,114	9,127,758	816,644
Glass and glassware.	3,694,924	4,510,812	815,868
Fruits, including nuts	3,498,569	4,210,099	711,580
All other articles	60,191,283	64,284,500	4,163,267
Total	$188,379,897	$212,082,424	$23,653,027

The increase of $58,110,167 in the total value of merchandise entered for consumption was principally in the following articles:

ARTICLES.	1886.	1887.	Increase.
Free of duty:			
Coffee	$42,675,600	$56,360,701	$13,685,101
Tin, in bars	5,873,773	6,927,710	1,058,937
Ores (emery, gold, and silver)	1,343,294	3,840,925	2,497,631
Dutiable:			
Iron and steel, and manufactures of:			
Ores	1,312,322	2,112,128	799,806
Pig iron	4,041,367	6,510,126	2,468,759
Scrap - iron and steel	557,402	3,723,471	3,166,069
Railroad-bars,iron and steel	274,878	1,000,329	725,451
Bars, billets, etc., of steel	1,859,827	5,529,704	3,669,877
All other	30,585,961	31,743,228	1,157,247
Total	$38,631,777	$50,618,986	$11,987,209
Wool and manufactures of:			
Wools	$13,794,213	$16,851,870	$2,557,157
Manufactures ...	40,586,509	44,285,944	3,698,735
Total	$54,380,722	$60,586,614	$6,255,892
Silk, manufactures of	$28,055,855	$31,264,277	$3,208,422
Jewelry and precious stones..	8,367,818	10,981,192	2,613,354
Flax, hemp, jute, and manufactures of	31,612,641	33,807,283	2,194,642
Fruits and nuts	12,973,309	15,088,074	2,114,766

The average ad-valorem rates of duty on articles paying a higher rate in 1887 than in 1882 were as follow:

ARTICLES.	1882.	1887.
Sugar and molasses	59·05	78·15
Cotton, manufactures of	39·08	40·17
Glass and glassware	56·94	59·01
Tobacco, and manufactures of	78·03	83·89
Liquors:		
Malt liquors	44·49	48·47
Spirits, distilled	142·79	154·01
Wines	49·69	54·90
Salt	45·62	49·92

The increase in the average duties ad valorem on sugar, molasses, malt liquors, spirits, and salt is mainly due to a decrease in the import prices of these articles, the rates of duty being specific, and in the case of tobacco and wines to increased tariff rates.

In the following articles there has been a decrease in the average rates of duty ad valorem:

ARTICLES.	1882.	1887.
Wools, raw	87·90	86·06
Wool, manufactures of	68·19	67·91
Iron and steel, and manufactures of	44·77	40·99
Silk, manufactures of	50·05	49·71
Fruits and nuts	27·90	24·58
Buttons and button materials	28·71	28·79
Paper, and manufactures of	34·69	31·89
Musical instruments	30·00	25·00
Rice	98·54	64·01

Foreign Carrying-Trade.—The following table shows the values of the imports and exports of the United States carried respectively in American vessels and in foreign vessels during each fiscal year, from 1856 to 1887 inclusive, with the percentage carried in American vessels:

Year ending June 30—	In American vessels.	In foreign vessels.	Per cent. carried in American vessels.
1856	$482,268,274	$159,836,576	75·2
1857	510,831,027	213,519,796	70·5
1858	447,191,804	160,066,267	73·7
1859	460,741,881	229,816,211	66·9
1860	507,247,757	255,040,793	66·5
1861	381,516,788	208,478,278	65·2
1862	217,695,418	218,015,296	50·0
1863	241,573,471	342,056,631	41·4
1864	184,061,486	485,798,343	27·5
1865	167,402,879	487,010,194	27·7
1866	325,711,961	685,224,691	32·2
1867	297,384,904	581,330,408	33·9
1868	297,981,578	550,546,074	35·1
1869	289,956,772	586,492,019	33·1
1870	352,969,401	638,927,488	35·6
1871	356,664,179	755,522,576	31·2
1872	345,831,101	839,846,362	29·5
1873	346,806,592	966,723,651	25·8
1874	350,451,994	989,206,106	26·7
1875	314,257,792	884,788,517	25·8
1876	311,076,171	813,854,967	33·1
1877	316,660,281	859,920,586	26·5
1878	318,050,906	876,991,129	26·9
1879	272,015,692	911,269,282	22·6
1880	256,346,577	1,224,265,484	17·18
1881	250,586,420	1,269,002,933	16·22
1882	227,229,745	1,212,978,769	15·40
1883	240,490,500	1,258,506,934	15·54
1884	233,609,085	1,127,796,199	16·60
1885	194,865,748	1,079,518,586	14·76
1886	197,349,508	1,073,911,118	15·01
1887	194,356,746	1,165,194,508	13·50

Of the exports and imports still carried under the American flag, less than one half are carried in steam-vessels.

CONGREGATIONALISTS. The following is a summary of the statistics of the Congregational churches in the United States, as they are given in the "Congregational Year-Book" for 1887:

STATES AND TERRITORIES.	Churches.	Ministers.	Church-members.
Alabama	20	14	1,261
Arizona	3	3	102
Arkansas	9	7	388
California	114	124	7,806
Colorado	31	25	1,872
Connecticut	297	398	55,104
Dakota	140	81	4,461
District of Columbia	4	13	1,119
Florida	29	25	584
Georgia	18	17	1,604
Idaho	1	1	14
Illinois	251	255	27,695
Indiana	33	23	2,009
Indian Territory	13	6	198
Iowa	261	229	19,917
Kansas	159	147	9,242
Kentucky	12	6	896
Louisiana	19	13	1,412
Maine	244	174	21,111
Maryland	2	2	272
Massachusetts	586	665	94,967
Michigan	282	251	19,882
Minnesota	145	118	10,248
Mississippi	8	4	168
Missouri	79	71	6,406
Montana	6	4	207
Nebraska	155	122	6,452
Nevada	1	1	45
New Hampshire	188	176	19,948
New Jersey	25	27	3,563
New Mexico	7	10	102
New York	361	362	37,501
North Carolina	16	10	1,004
Ohio	223	224	26,789
Oregon	27	26	1,116
Pennsylvania	90	72	8,150
Rhode Island	28	50	5,858
South Carolina	3	3	304
Tennessee	22	17	1,115
Texas	15	14	612
Utah	4	10	218
Vermont	198	199	19,755
Virginia	2	1	142
Washington Territory	51	33	1,196
West Virginia	2	2	145
Wisconsin	201	167	13,982
Wyoming	3	2	294
Total	4,277	4,090	486,879

Of the churches, 8,185 were recorded as "with pastors," and 1,092 as "vacant." Of the ministers, 2,852 were "in pastoral work," and 1,238 "not in pastoral work." The number of additions to the churches during the year by profession of faith was 27,166. The number of persons in Sunday-schools was 521,983; number of families represented in the churches, 245,068. The total amount of benevolent contributions reported by 3,485 churches was $1,677,210, and the amount of contributions for home expenditures returned by 2,938 churches was $3,909,225.

The seven theological seminaries—Andover (Mass.), Bangor (Me.), Chicago (Ill.), Hartford (Conn.), Oberlin (Ohio), Pacific (Oakland, Cal.), and Yale (New Haven, Conn.)—returned for 1886, 44 professors, 22 instructors or lecturers, 10 resident licentiates, 19 in advanced or graduate classes, and 398 students, of whom 86 were "special" students. Of the "special" students, 12 were in German, 13 in Dano-Norwegian, 26 in Swedish, and 4 in Slavic departments.

American College and Education Society.—The income of the American College and Education Society for the year 1885–'86, was $76,-641; of which $52,529 were contributed for colleges and paid to them, and $18,299 were paid to students fitting for the ministry. Two hundred and ninety-one young men had received assistance from the society during the financial year, and 7,170 had been aided by it since 1816. Twenty-three colleges and theological seminaries had been assisted since 1843; three of which had passed off the list of assisted institutions during the past year, while two others had been added to it. The society had a scholarship fund of $91,718, the income from which had been $4,983, and a secretary fund of $11,700, which had yielded an income of $774.

New West Education Commission.—The income of the New West Education Commission for the year 1885–'86 was $57,362, and its expenditures were $2,998. The receipts exceeded those of any previous year by $7,204. The commission had maintained 85 schools of all grades, with 63 teachers, and 2,560 pupils, of whom 764 were Mormons, 541 "Apostates," and 142 Mexicans. The Woman's Home Missionary Association, of Boston, was supporting 8 teachers in co-operation with the association, in Utah and New Mexico; and 10 State Woman's Missionary Unions were auxiliary to it.

The Sunday-School and Publishing Society sustains Sunday-school missionaries, and furnishes Sunday-school helps, libraries, and other literature to needy Sunday-schools. The National Council of the Congregational churches has recommended it as a worthy object for contributions to the extent of $100,000 a year.

American Home Missionary Society.—The sixty-first annual meeting of the American Home Missionary Society was held at Saratoga Springs, N. Y., June 7. The Rev. Julius Seelye, D. D., LL. D., presided. The Executive Committee reported that the entire resources of the society for the year had been $510,144, and the expenditures had been $512,741. Fifteen State auxiliary societies of women were organized and actively at work; the contributions to the Woman's Fund for Foreign Work had been $5,674; and the Ladies' Missionary Society, having its office in Boston, had furnished $1,-700 for the support of four teachers in Arkansas and the Indian Territory. Fifteen hundred and seventy-one missionaries had been employed, of whom 5 had preached to congregations of colored people, and 136 had preached in foreign languages; 29 to Welsh congregations, 40 to German, 88 to Scandinavian, 14 to Bohemian, 1 to Armenian, 1 to Spanish, 2 to Chinese, 1 to Indian, 7 to French, and 8 to Mexican congregations. They had had the

care of 2,188 Sunday-schools, 323 of which had been newly organized, comprising in all about 180,000 pupils. One hundred and thirty-five churches had been organized, 63 churches had become self-supporting, and 112 new houses of worship had been completed. The number of additions to the churches by confession of faith had been 6,469. The amount of contributions to benevolent objects, reported by 806 missionaries, was $36,809. The Executive Committee of the society having been instructed in 1886 "to take steps for the removal of any existing impediments which debar the society from holding its annual meetings wherever it may choose to direct," reported that the impediments could not be removed, and that the annual meeting must be held within the State of New York. A report on the Christianization of cities, adopted by the society, declared that that work could not be accomplished by mission chapels and evangelistic services, but demanded churches, composed of Christian families and promoting Christian family life. These churches would need to be helped in their support by their more prosperous neighbors, constituting the service "a foreign missionary work on home soil." It ought to be carried on undenominationally in spirit, but would have to be sustained by denominational methods and organizations; and that churches in each city should assume the responsibility for the evangelization of that city, while the society should assume only the responsibility of giving to them necessary aid, and as it is needed. The officers of the society having been requested to compile the statistics bearing on the subject of interference between denominations in the home missionary work, were given another year.

American Congregational Union.—The thirty-fourth annual meeting of the American Congregational Union was held in New York, May 12. The Rev. William M. Taylor, D. D., LL. D., presided. The income of the society for the year had been $120,597. The receipts on account of the parsonage loan fund had been, for the year, $7,543, and for the five years since the fund was instituted, $50,320. Toward a fund of $100,000, which the trustees were endeavoring to raise for work at large centers of population, $64,150 had been paid in. The Union had aided in the completion of 84 houses of worship, and 31 parsonages.

The Andover Cases.—The Board of Visitors of Andover Theological Seminary announced their decision in the cases of the professors who were charged with holding and teaching certain erroneous doctrines, particularly the doctrine of a future state of probation after death (see "Annual Cyclopædia" for 1886), on the 15th of June. These cases originated in charges presented to the Board of Visitors, July 23, 1886, by J. W. Wellman, D. D., a trustee of the seminary, Dr. H. M. Dexter, Dr. O. T. Lanphear, and Prof. J. J. Blaisdell, "Committee of Certain of the Alumni," against Profs.

Egbert C. Smyth, D. D., William J. Tucker, John W. Churchill, George Harris, and Edward Z. Hincks, all holding positions as instructors in the institution, of holding and teaching the doctrine mentioned. A preliminary hearing was granted by the Board of Visitors, Oct. 25, 1886, when an amended complaint was presented, setting forth four charges, with many specifications, upon which a trial was held during the last days of the year. In their decision, as announced in June, the board declared that they had found that Prof. Smyth, as professor, maintained and inculcated beliefs inconsistent with and repugnant to the creed of the institution and its statutes, in the following particulars, as charged in the amended complaint, viz. :

That the Bible is not "the only perfect rule of faith and practice, but is fallible and untrustworthy, even in some of its religious teachings.

"That no man has power or capacity to repent without knowledge of God in Christ.

"That there is and will be probation after death for all men who do not decisively reject Christ during the earthly life."

The board, therefore, "adjudged and decreed that Prof. Smyth be removed from his position, and that the office be declared vacant." In the case of Profs. Tucker, Churchill, Harris, and Hincks, the Rev. Mr. Eustis, a member of the board, declined to act with his associates, upon the ground that he was not present on the day of the hearing of the complaints, when the respondents severally appeared and made their statements in defense. Thereupon, the complaints as amended being taken up and severally considered, none of the charges contained in them were sustained. The Board of Visitors at the same meeting refused to approve of the election of the Rev. Frank E. Woodruff to the Associate Professorship of Sacred Literature in the Theological Seminary. Upon the announcement of the decision, the Board of Trustees of the Seminary expressed regret :

That the charges made against the professors were not prosecuted before the Board of Trustees, and denied the authority and jurisdiction of the Board of Visitors, asserting that the latter had only appellate power, and that the case should have been prosecuted before the trustees in the first instance.

They regretted all the more that this case was first prosecuted before the Visitors, because the matter had previously been brought to the attention of this board in a memorial presented by one of the Trustees, Jan. 12, 1886, referring to public reports and charges against the professors, and praying that the Board of Trustees would request the Board of Visitors to investigate the same. This the Board of Trustees declined to do, on the ground that if sufficient cause to consider them existed, it was the duty of this board to investigate the charges before they should go to the Board of Visitors.

In further regret, the circular continued :

That when proceedings had been initiated before the Visitors all effort of this board to secure a standing at the hearing failed. We felt that as a Board of Trustees especially charged with the administration of the seminary, we should have been recognized as a party in a trial which involved the best interests of the institution intrusted to our care.

The Trustees had carefully weighed all the evidence presented at the trial, and with all the other light they could gain, had come to the conclusion that the charges were not sustained, saying that—

In our opinion the teachings of the professors accused are either not correctly reported, or, when correctly represented, are not inconsistent with the creed which the professors have signed and are bound to sustain in all their utterances. . . . In our judgment the whole aim of the professors has been to enlarge and deepen the apprehension of Christian truth in its application to the problems of faith and the work of the Church in the world, and they have done this along the lines of the symbols of the seminary. And we think that they deserve for their industry, their zeal, their scholarship, and their piety, not the disfranchisement and suspicion of the friends of the seminary, and of sacred learning, but encouragement and sympathy. In conclusion, we can not refrain from expressing our deep conviction that no greater mistake can be made in endeavoring to promote the growth of Christ's kingdom than that of insisting that such differences on points in eschatology as exist between the accusers and the accused in this case should be made the occasion of accusations so grave, and a trial so momentous as that which these distinguished and high-minded professors have been called upon to face.

Professor Smyth, through his counsel, on the 1st day of November, entered an appeal in the Supreme Court of Essex County, Mass., against the finding of the Board of Visitors, to which it was agreed that the answer of the board should be filed by December 1. The appeal under the statute founding the seminary has to be argued before the full bench of the court sitting at law.

The American Board.—The American Board of Commissioners for Foreign Missions, the oldest of American foreign missionary societies, is a close corporation, consisting at present of about 200 corporate members, all of whom derive their right and title as such from the nine commissioners who were designated in the original act of incorporation by the Legislature of Massachusetts. As the area of the churches contributing to sustain the work of the board increased, additional members were voted in so as to give the new contributors representation. These corporate members constitute the body who transact the business and decide upon all questions at the annual meetings of the board, while honorary members and members by virtue of their contributions take part in the discussions, but do not vote. The Prudential Committee, to whom the management of affairs and the control of its policy is committed during the intervals between the annual meetings of the board, consists of five clergymen and five laymen living in Boston or its vicinity, and meets weekly. The three secretaries and the treasurer, who are elected by the board, are not members of this committee, but attend its meetings.

The seventy-eighth annual meeting of the Board was held in Springfield, Mass., beginning October 4. The President, the Rev. Mark Hopkins, D. D., having died since the last meeting of the board, Mr. E. W. Blatchford, Vice-President, presided. The ordinary receipts for the year had been $476,444; the total receipts, including what had been spent out of funds contributed for special work (in China, Japan, Central Africa, and Northern Mexico), had been $679,573; the expenditures had been $679,377. The grounds of the Home for Missionary Children at Auburndale, Mass., had been bought for the society. The Home had entertained during the year 32 missionary children and six families, and since its foundation, nineteen years previously, 111 children. In the "survey" of the missionary work, notice was taken, in connection with the missions in Turkey, of divisions caused by the proselyting efforts of agents belonging to another denomination, and of the prosperity of the Bulgarian mission. Four weekly newspapers were published in these missions, in as many different languages, having a circulation of 9,000 copies. In Japan there were 40 churches, with more than 4,000 members, and the Christian College had 300 students. In Africa, progress was reported in the organization of the two central missions and the removal of a serious obstacle at Bihé by the death of the hostile king. It had become expedient to resume missionary work to a certain extent in the Sandwich Islands, and to send new missionaries there. The Micronesian missions continued to advance rapidly, and included 46 wholly self-supporting churches, with 5,312 communicants. The mission in Ponape had been interrupted by the arrest by the Spanish Governor, of the Rev. Mr. Doane, on frivolous charges, and his deportation to Manila, in the Philippine Islands, for trial. But, on the representations of the Government of the United States, he had been released, and was to be restored to his work. The following is the General summary of the missions, in Mexico, Spain, Austria, India, Ceylon, Japan, China, Africa, the Sandwich Islands, and Micronesia:

MISSIONS.

Number of missions	22
Number of stations	89
Number of out-stations	891

LABORERS EMPLOYED.

Number of ordained missionaries (11 being physicians)	166	
Number of physicians not ordained, 8 men and 4 women	12	
Number of other male assistants	10	
Number of women (wives, 168; unmarried, besides physicians, 106)	269	
Whole number of laborers sent from this country		457
Number of native pastors	155	
Number of native preachers and catechists	898	
Number of native school-teachers	1,164	
Number of other native helpers	325	
Whole number of laborers connected with the missions	2,037	2,494

THE PRESS.

Pages printed, as nearly as can be learned 19,650,000

THE CHURCHES.

Number of churches	825
Number of church-members	28,043
Added during the year	2,906
Whole number from the first, as nearly as can be learned	101,089

Number of high-schools, theological seminaries, and station-classes	55
Number of pupils in the above	2,622
Number of boarding-schools for girls	41
Number of pupils in boarding-schools for girls....	2,318
Number of common schools	578
Number of pupils in common schools	34,417
Whole number under instruction	41,151

Doctrinal Tests for Missionaries.—The reports of the Prudential Committee contained a full account of its action on two matters which had been referred to it for consideration at the preceding meeting of the board. The first of these matters related to the expediency of referring questions respecting the doctrinal soundness of candidates for appointment as missionaries to councils of churches. The second matter related to representations which were made by the Congregational church of New Haven, to which the person in question belonged, in favor of the Rev. Mr. Hume, the missionary whom the committee had declined to reappoint to his post in the Marathi Mission because of his belief in the doctrine of probation after death. On this subject, the committee had been instructed to "seek to the utmost of its power an adjustment of its differences." After correspondence and several interviews, the committee had decided, on the 11th of February, that it understood—

That under the action of the board at its last annual meeting it had no option but to decline to send out as a missionary any person who has committed himself to the acceptance of the hypothesis of a probation after death. That action was in the following terms: "The board is constrained to look with grave apprehension upon certain tendencies of the doctrine of a probation after death, which has been recently broached and diligently propagated, that seems divisive and perversive, and dangerous to the churches at home and abroad. In view of those tendencies, they do heartily approve of the action of the Prudential Committee in carefully guarding the board from any committal to the approval of that doctrine, and advise a continuance of that caution in time to come." In the case of Rev. R. A. Hume, the report continued, "embarrassment and consequent delay have arisen from doubt as to his exact position on the subject. After several interviews and much correspondence, it appears that Mr. Hume regards the hypothesis in question as not forbidden by the Scriptures, and that some considerations favor it, while on the other hand he affirms that he has not in his past utterances committed himself, and that he does not now commit himself, to the acceptance of the hypothesis. It has been a question with the committee how far sympathy with this hypothesis, even where it is not accepted, would control one's thought and action; but it has not been unmindful of the fact that Mr. Hume is not a new applicant for missionary appointment. He has for eleven years rendered good service in the mission field, and the record of that service, as well as his recent statements, give reasonable assurance that he will work in the future, as in the past, as a loyal representative of the American Board, and in harmony with the wishes of his mission, as expressed in their letter of October 28, 1886: 'that he avoid the preaching or teaching of any speculation in favor of a future probation.' The committee therefore assents to the return of Mr. Hume to his cherished work in the Marathi mission."

In reply, Mr. Hume, acknowledging the receipt of the committee's assent to his return to his missionary work, said:

In deference to the wishes of many members of the board and members of my mission, I can again heartily assure you that I shall feel such restriction as ought to influence a Christian man who is accustomed to respect, so far as he conscientiously can, the wishes of his associates, and is accustomed to study the things that make for peace. That I am such a man my missionary brethren heartily testify. Moreover, I shall carefully bear in mind the divergent views of the constituency of the board and the solicitude of many, and shall do what I can to satisfy all. But I assume that you understand me as otherwise returning with such liberty of thought and speech as is enjoyed by evangelical ministers at home, and as free from pledges. Therefore, I gladly accept the opportunity to return to India to renew my work in the same spirit and devotion as in the past.

On the same day of the date of this letter, a communication was inserted in the newspapers by Mr. Hume, declaring his intention to return to India and reiterating the expressions of the letter. In view of these documents, the committee reaffirmed its action, which had been based on the fact that "Mr. Hume in letters and statements was understood by the committee to give reasonable assurances that he would work in harmony with the wishes of the Mission as expressed in their letter of October 28, 1886." The letter here referred to had been received from the members of the Marathi Mission at Ahmednuggar, India, and contained expressions of high regard for Mr. Hume, and testimony to the value and efficiency of his labors, with the intimation of a desire that he should return; to which was added:

We were, however, surprised and grieved at his utterances at Andover, which have been so widely published. We have no sympathy with the sentiments he there expressed. We believe that the teaching of a future probation here, even as a hypothesis, would be extremely harmful to our work. While, therefore, the question of his return must be decided by the Prudential Committee, we wish to say that we would gladly welcome brother Hume back to occupy the position he held before and to teach the same doctrines as before, provided that he avoid the preaching or teaching of any speculation in favor of a future probation.

Upon the action of the board at its meeting in 1886 approving the course of the Prudential Committee in acquainting itself in the doctrinal fitness of candidates for appointment as missionaries, the committee had adopted the following minute:

1. The question of appointing certain candidates whose applications for missionary service indicated that they accepted under some form of statement the hypothesis of a probation after death for those who have not had the gospel revelation of Christ during the earthly life, came before the committee last year, and the committee decided that it was not expedient at present to make the appointments.

2. This action of the committee was severely criticised in certain quarters, and was brought before the board at its last annual meeting, accompanied by a definite statement as to the course pursued by the committee, with the reasons for that course.

3. The board, after prolonged deliberation and discussion, voted with emphasis that they approved of the caution exercised by the committee on the matter under debate, and recommended the exercise of the same caution in the future.

4. The present committee therefore has no option on this matter, except to follow the instructions of the board and to decline to appoint candidates who hold these views.

In accordance with these principles, of 101 cases of applications which had come before the committee for decision, 71 had received appointment.

Of the 80 persons who did not receive appointment, the reasons relating to 23 had no connection with defective or erroneous doctrinal views. Of the remaining seven, one had been postponed in order that further time might be given for thought, particularly as to the scriptural teachings upon the conscious existence of the wicked after death; two had been declined on account of the avowal of their belief in universal salvation; one who particularly desired appointment as missionary teacher to Japan, had been declined on account of serious doubts as to the existence of a personal God, and three had expressed such views in relation to the hypothesis of probation after death that they seemed to the committee to be included in the class referred to in the action of the board and in the minute of the committee. The action of the committee in all these cases was, as usual, taken in view not only of the correspondence involved, but also in view of the reports of personal interviews with the candidates, which, of course, cover impressions and statements not reduced to writing.

The precise action of the committee in relation to the cases involving doctrine was given in full, together with the correspondence that had been had with the parties. Concluding its report, the committee said that it was its serious conviction, confirmed by many years' experience—

That the commonly received doctrines of the churches which sustain the missions of the board include the scriptural teaching of the decisive nature of the present earthly probation as related to final character and destiny. It has also been a recognized principle with the committee, that whenever any proposed action would, if adopted, be, in the judgment of the committee, contrary to the conscientious convictions of a large part of the constituency of the board, it was not expedient to recommend such action. These considerations, which directed the course of the committee during the preceding year, have continued to guide them during the year now under review, with the added emphasis of what they regarded as the decisive and helpful instructions of the board itself at its last annual meeting.

With regard to the question of the expediency of calling councils of the churches to determine upon the doctrinal fitness of candidates, the committee reported that the practice of seeking the advice of councils had been adopted in the early days of its organization, but had been abandoned because it had seemed to be needless, and also because it had been adopted without due regard to ecclesiastical regularity. Since then, the committee's discretion in the matter had not been questioned until the present issue arose. It was shown that while councils were Congregational institutions, the board was not exclusively Congregational, but included Presbyterians among its members, its missionaries, and the contributors to its funds. To make it a denominational and ecclesiastical body would be a breach of trust as toward these persons. Councils are not bodies of sufficiently extensive jurisdiction to assume the responsibility for the appointment of missionaries. Composed of local groups of churches, they did not and could not represent the whole Church; or in any way combine the diversified views and wants that exist within it. "No council limited, as is inevitable, can represent or act for the constituency of a body scattered over the whole territory of the United States, and which includes contributors in other lands also." Councils, moreover, were transient bodies, existing only for a few hours, and could not be held to a responsibility more abiding than their own ephemeral existence. They end their functions in the induction into the ministry of ministerial missionaries. The Prudential Committee had work to do in view of its entire make-up, and could not farm out any portion of its responsibility. After considering these and other like points in full, the report concluded:

The usual method, aimed at and pursued by the Prudential Committee the past year, still commends itself as the wisest and best. Should the method so long tested, and with satisfactory results, have the approval of the board and its friends, present embarrassments will, we believe, be removed, and further embarrassments will be averted more satisfactorily than in any other way. Seeing then that, by general consent and usage, such bodies as the American Board can not appropriately call ecclesiastical councils in any case; seeing that to call such councils only in doubtful cases turning upon doctrinal views of candidates would be open to very grave objections, and that to call them for all candidates would be superlatively cumbersome; seeing that councils, being local, ephemeral, and irresponsible, are inadequate for the purpose named; seeing that a mixed responsibility in the selection of candidates would produce friction and dissatisfaction; and seeing that unity of trust in the appointment of missionaries and in the administration of funds for their support has borne the test of long experience, and will secure a wider harmony than any other method—the Prudential Committee deem the measure inexpedient.

Majority and minority reports were brought in by the committee to whom the report of the Prudential Committee was referred. The majority report referred to a resolution which had been adopted by the board more than thirty years before, declaring that the contributors to the funds of the board would hold the Prudential Committee responsible "for seeing that no part of their contributions goes for the propagation of error, either in doctrine or practice," and said that the Prudential Committee had long been governed by this principle. It had considered the doctrine of future probation as erroneous and dangerous in its tendency. The action of the board itself at its last annual meeting, at Des Moines, indicated a coincidence with this view. The Prudential Committee had in its examinations of candidates manifested an earnest desire to secure the services of able and cultivated men, and deserved high commendation for its faithfulness in this part of the work; while in those cases in which the candidates failed to receive appointments, the result was the only one consistent with the action of the board concerning missionary appointments at its last annual meeting. To this report were appended resolutions declaring—

That the board adheres to the position taken at the last annual meeting at Des Moines concerning the doctrine of future probation, reaffirms its utterances made at that time, and accepts the interpretation of the Prudential Committee as the true interpretation of its action. And that we recommend to the Prudential Committee an unabated carefulness in guarding the board from any committal to the approval of that doctrine.

The minority report denied that the American Board was a representative body of the churches, or possessed of the functions of a synod, and held that it was not competent to fix the standards of doctrinal faith to which its missionaries should conform. "That is a work which must be done, if it is done at all, by ecclesiastical assemblies, authorized by the churches to undertake so difficult and responsible a work." The board, under its present constitution, should refrain from sending to the Prudential Committee specific doctrinal instructions either on one side or the other of existing doctrinal controversies. This report concluded with resolutions reaffirming the position that neither the board nor the Prudential Committee was in any sense a theological court to settle doctrinal points of belief; that the board would have its missionaries always remember that they are sent to preach and teach these essential truths of Christianity in which all evangelical bodies mainly agree; that—

The missionaries of this board shall have the same right of private judgment in the interpretation of God's word, and the same freedom of thought and of speech as are enjoyed by their ministerial brethren in this country. In the exercise of their rights they should have constant and careful regard to the work of their associates, and to the harmony and effectiveness of the missions in which they labor. And all persons, otherwise well qualified, are to be regarded as acceptable candidates for missionary appointment, who heartily receive the fundamental truths of the Gospel, held in common by the churches sustaining the board, and ascertained by their actual uses.

A full discussion was had of all the points involved in the controversy, at the end of which the majority report was adopted.

The Rev. R. S. Storrs, D. D., of Brooklyn, N. Y., was elected President of the Board, to succeed the Rev. Mark Hopkins, D. D., deceased.

Dr. Storrs accepted the office of president in a letter of the 31st of October, in which he said that the questions which had largely engrossed the attention of the board at its last two meetings appeared to him to be practically settled, so far as the board was concerned, certainly for a considerable time. The board had decided, by a majority so large that further opposition to the decision was not likely to be made, that it would continue to intrust the examination of candidates for its missionary service to its permanent committee, and that this committee was not to be guided as to the theological fitness of its candidates by the opinions of improvised councils. It had also decided, under circumstances of unusual impressiveness, that the theory of a probation after death offering opportunities beyond the grave to attain by repentance eternal life, is, at any rate, not a constituent part of the gospel of Christ, to be a portion of the message sent by this society to mankind. This question also must, therefore, be considered as practically retired from further debate at the annual sessions of the board, at least for years to come, and "remitted to that general and legitimate outside debate which never ceases in books, essays, articles, sermons, in church conferences, and local associations. . . . Nothing could be more conspicuously absurd than to expect the board, in its corporate action, to authorize a theory which most of its members thus far believe to be only an attractive, but a delusive, human speculation, with no basis in the Scriptures, and forming no part" of the Divine Message. It would not be wise, in the writer's judgment, "to allow altogether the same latitude of opinion among those representing all our churches in the missionary field, which is allowed, whether properly or not, by local churches in our own country to those who transiently minister in them." No further discussions of these questions in the board would be proper until the views of a majority of its members upon them should have been essentially modified.

American Missionary Association.—The forty-first annual meeting of the American Missionary Association was held in Portland, Me., beginning October 25.

The receipts of the association for the year had been $306,761, and its expenditures, $304,507, of which there had been applied to missionary work, in the South, $107,768; among the Chinese, $7,565; in the Indian missions and schools, $47,920; and for purposes of foreign missions, $5,120. Adding to the amount of receipts given above what had been contributed for special objects and the receipts of Berea College, Hampton Normal and Agricultural Institute, and Atlanta University, the entire amount of contributions for the general work in which the association is engaged was $426,589. A debt of $5,783 had been paid, and a credit balance of $2,193 had accrued. Fifty-four schools were sustained in the Southern States, having 246 instructors and 8,616 pupils. Six of them were chartered institutions, or colleges; 16 normal and training schools, and 32 common schools, distributed in nine States. Three new school buildings and two buildings for industrial training had been erected during the year. Industrial training occupied a place of growing importance, and included farming, tinning, blacksmithing, wagon-making, carpenter's work, painting, and the use of steam-power, for boys; and domestic work for girls. In the department of church work in the South were returned 127 churches, 103 missionaries, 7,896 church-members, and 15,109 pupils in Sunday-schools. The amount of contributions for church purposes and benevolence had been $18,337. The

"mountain work" included two fields; one in Kentucky, having for its base the Louisville and Nashville Railroad, and one along the Cumberland mountains in Tennessee, extending back from the Cincinnati Southern Railroad. In both districts were five schools and twelve churches. The Indian work of the association was chiefly in Nebraska and Dakota, and was represented by five churches, with 61 missionaries and teachers, and 370 members, and eighteen schools with 608 pupils. The "Chinese work" included seventeen missions, with 28 missionaries and an enrollment of 1,044 pupils. A foreign missionary society had been organized among the Chinese brethren in California; and a beginning of work had been made among the Japanese in that State. The association has ceased to be directly engaged in foreign mission work, but it contributes to the support of the Mendi Mission in Africa, which it formerly conducted, but which is now under the charge of the society of the United Brethren in Christ.

Congregational Union of England and Wales.—The annual meeting of the Congregational Union of England and Wales was held in London, beginning May 9. The Rev. Dr. Bruce, of Huddersfield, was elected chairman for the ensuing year. The report of the secretary said that the accounts of the Union showed an adverse balance for the year. The Jubilee fund now reached £400,000. The report further gave accounts of various matters that had been acted upon or were awaiting action. Among them were new plans for electing the chairman of the Union, and for insuring a better method of ministerial settlements; the examinations of young people in religious knowledge, which had not been taken up in the way that had been hoped, but in which another attempt was to be made, with a more limited number of subjects; a conference to be held with the Baptists in July concerning home mission work in England; the movement in behalf of social purity; the want of success in the effort to come to an agreement with the Presbyterians with reference to the De Foe Church at Tooting; the Marriage Registration Bill; the new hymnal, which was to be ready in June; and the ecclesiastical history by Dr. Dale, which was to be brought out on the author's own account, but for which the churches were asked to furnish exact statistics. A special committee on the election of a chairman had proposed a plan for the publication, at least fourteen days before the day for balloting, of the names of candidates approved by at least twenty members, but the Union decided not to interfere for the present with the existing method of electing the chairman. For facilitating the settlement of pastors the Union recommended that an educational tractate respecting the election of ministers be published, copies of which should be sent to vacant churches, and advised the appointment of confidential committees in aid of settlements by the country associations.

The judgment of the Assembly was expressed in favor of the formation of a young mens' guild in connection with the Congregational churches of the country, for the promotion of purity of life, and for other purposes connected with the moral welfare of the community and the prosperity of the churches; and the committee of the Union was instructed to appoint a special committee to draft a scheme for such guild, and report upon the subject to the autumnal meetings of the Union. A resolution was adopted against "coercion" in Ireland.

The autumnal meetings of the Congregational Union were held in Leeds, beginning October 11. The Rev. Alexander McKennal, D.D., presided, and delivered an opening address on "The Decay of Dogma" in the present time, for which he said a spiritual rather than a philosophical reason should be sought. Many of the doctrines professedly held in the churches a generation since had ceased to represent their real beliefs. An altered type of piety had come in which was simpler and more direct than it had been, franker in the utterance of personal experience and personal conviction, and building less on conviction and logic. The final report of the Jubilee fund showed that the total receipts on its account had been £430,000, while the payments had been about £4,800 less. The balance was almost exclusively appropriated as a reserve fund for the Church Aid Society. The amounts expended had been: For the liquidation of church debts, £246,225; for church aid and home mission work, £85,324; for Congregational church extension in London, £92,000; for various societies, £4,540; for colleges and schools, £20,218; for new churches and school-rooms, £22,370; for an old debt on the Memorial Hall, £1,000. The working expenses were £2,046; toward these the Congregational Union had voted £1,000, and the rest had been obtained from interest on investments, so that the contributors had the well-nigh unique privilege of knowing that every shilling they had subscribed had been devoted to the purpose desired. The Australian colonies had raised a Jubilee fund for similar purposes. New South Wales £40,000 for chapel debts. Victoria £20,300; and South Australia £14,430. The addition of these sums made a total of more than half a million pounds (£504,730) as the result of this special effort. Addresses were made and papers read during the sessions on "The Desirableness of County Conferences for the Revival of Faith, and Piety in the Churches," by Mr. Guest; "The Present Aspects of the Question of Church Comprehension," by the Rev. Samuel Pearson; "The Exposition and Enforcement of Free Church Principles" (a general discussion, embracing the subjects of "The Scriptural Ideal of Church Life," by the Rev. W. P. Clarkson; "The Congregational Idea of Church Life," by the Rev. R. H. Lovell, and "John Milton as a Free Churchman," by the Rev. Dr. Fairbairn); "The Great Need of Pastoral Oversight of the

Young," by the Rev. W. Spensley; "The Importance of Making Systematic Arrangements for the Scientific Study of Theology," by Prof. Wilkins; and "The Necessity for Maintaining the Christian Spirit in Political Conduct," by the Rev. Carvell Williams. Mr. R. S. Ashton, who was deputed to represent the Free Churches of France, informed the Union that there were now 88 of these churches, comprising more than 8,000 members. At the annual meeting of the Total Abstinence Association, which was held on the evening preceding the opening session of the Union, it was reported that of the Congregational ministers in England and Wales, the abstainers outnumber the non-abstainers by 400, and that of 875 students in Congregational colleges, 815 were abstainers.

Congregational Chapel - Building Society. — The report of the Congregational Chapel-Building Society, which was made in May, covered the work of 83 years. The total receipts during that time had been £169,577, and the total expenditures £161,842. The society had aided 667 churches and 88 manses, representing property valued at about £1,800,000, for the most part freehold, and to a large extent free from interest-bearing debt. The churches provided 300,000 sittings. The society was possessed of available funds, promissory notes, and investments, amounting to £20,000.

Church Aid and Home Mission Society.—The annual meeting of the Church Aid and Home Mission Society was held May 10. The receipts of the society for the year had been £34,978. Aid had been given to 706 churches and branch churches, and 419 mission stations, or 1125 congregations in all. These congregations were under the care of 513 pastors and 108 missionaries and pastor evangelists, and returned 85,908 attendants, of whom 32,842 were church-members, with 74,200 pupils in Sunday-schools. They had raised for ministerial support, etc., £50,000, had received from public funds £5,894, and had been aided by the society to the extent of £26,246.

London Missionary Society.—The ninety-third annual meeting of the London Missionary Society was held in London May 12. The year's income had been £105,380, of which £9,000 had been contributed by the native mission churches. The expenditure left a deficit of nearly £15,000. Besides the ordinary staff of missionaries, 1,150 ordained native workers and 6,000 catechists and preachers were employed in the service of the missions. The report noticed as events favorable to the missions the issue of an imperial edict in China, recognizing the status of Chinese Christians, and a movement in Bengal and Madras to form a native Christian Church.

Irish Congregational Union.—The fifty-eighth annual meeting of the Irish Congregational Union was held at Sligo in May. Nearly every church had made advance during the year. A scheme for the establishment of a Theological hall in Belfast was considered.

CONGRESS OF THE UNITED STATES. The second session of the Forty-ninth Congress convened Dec. 6, 1886, and President Cleveland sent in his second annual message, as follows:

To the Congress of the United States:

In discharge of a constitutional duty, and following a well-established precedent in the Executive office, I herewith transmit to the Congress at its reassembling, certain information concerning the state of the Union, together with such recommendations for legislative consideration as appear necessary and expedient.

Our Government has consistently maintained its relations of friendship toward all other powers, and of neighborly interest toward those whose possessions are contiguous to our own. Few questions have arisen during the past year with other governments, and none of those are beyond the reach of settlement in friendly counsel.

We are as yet without provision for the settlement of claims of citizens of the United States against Chili for injuries during the late war with Peru and Bolivia. The mixed commissions, organized under claims conventions, concluded by the Chilian Government with certain European states, have developed an amount of friction which we trust can be avoided in the convention which our representative at Santiago is authorized to negotiate.

The cruel treatment of inoffensive Chinese has, I regret to say, been repeated in some of the far Western States and Territories, and acts of violence against those people, beyond the power of the local constituted authorities to prevent, and difficult to punish, are reported even in distant Alaska. Much of this violence can be traced to race prejudice and competition of labor, which can not, however, justify the oppression of strangers whose safety is guaranteed by our treaty with China equally with the most favored nations.

In opening our vast domain to alien elements, the purpose of our lawgivers was to invite assimilation, and not to provide an arena for endless antagonisms. The paramount duty of maintaining public order and defending the interests of our own people may require the adoption of measures of restriction, but they should not tolerate the oppression of individuals of a special race. I am not without assurance that the Government of China, whose friendly disposition toward us I am most happy to recognize, will meet us half-way in devising a comprehensive remedy, by which an effective limitation of Chinese emigration, joined to protection of those Chinese subjects who remain in this country, may be secured.

Legislation is needed to execute the provisions of our Chinese convention of 1880 touching the opium-traffic.

While the good-will of the Colombian Government toward our country is manifest, the situation of American interests on the Isthmus of Panama has at times excited concern, and invited friendly action looking to the performance of the engagements of the two nations concerning the territory embraced in the interoceanic transit. With the subsidence of the Isthmian disturbances, and the erection of the State of Panama into a Federal district under the direct government of the constitutional administration of Bogotá, a new order of things has been inaugurated which, although as yet somewhat experimental and affording scope for arbitrary exercise of power by the delegates of the national authority, promises much improvement.

The sympathy between the people of the United States and France, born during our colonial struggle for independence and continuing to-day, has received a fresh impulse in the successful completion and dedication of the colossal statue of "Liberty Enlightening the World" in New York Harbor—the gift of Frenchmen to Americans.

A convention between the United States and certain other powers for the protection of submarine cables was signed at Paris on March 14, 1884, and has been duly ratified and proclaimed by this Government. By agreement between the high contracting parties this convention is to go into effect on the 1st of January next, but the legislation required for its execution in the United States has not yet been adopted. I earnestly recommend its enactment.

Cases have continued to occur in Germany giving rise to much correspondence in relation to the privilege of sojourn of our naturalized citizens of German origin revisiting the land of their birth, yet I am happy to state that our relations with that country have lost none of their accustomed cordiality.

The claims for interest upon the amount of tonnage dues illegally exacted from certain German steamship lines were favorably reported in both houses of Congress at the last session, and I trust will receive final and favorable action at an early day.

The recommendations contained in my last annual message in relation to a mode of settlement of the fishery rights in the waters of British North America—so long a subject of anxious difference between the United States and Great Britain—was met by an adverse vote of the Senate on April 13th last; and thereupon negotiations were instituted to obtain an agreement with Her Britannic Majesty's Government for the promulgation of such joint interpretation and definition of the article of the Convention of 1818, relating to the territorial waters and inshore fisheries of the British provinces, as should secure the Canadian rights from encroachment by United States fishermen, and, at the same time, insure the enjoyment by the latter of the privileges guaranteed to them by such convention.

The questions involved are of long standing, of grave consequence, and from time to time, for nearly three quarters of a century, have given rise to earnest international discussions, not unaccompanied by irritation.

Temporary arrangements by treaties have served to allay friction—which, however, has revived as each treaty was terminated. The last arrangement, under the treaty of 1871, was abrogated after due notice by the United States on June 30, 1885, but I was enabled to obtain for our fishermen for the remainder of that season enjoyment of the full privileges accorded by the terminated treaty.

The Joint High Commission by whom the treaty had been negotiated—although invested with plenary power to make a permanent settlement—were content with a temporary arrangement, after the termination of which the question was relegated to the stipulations of the Treaty of 1818, as to the first article of which no construction satisfactory to both countries has ever been agreed upon.

The progress of civilization and growth of population in the British provinces to which the fisheries in question are contiguous, and the expansion of commercial intercourse between them and the United States, present to-day a condition of affairs scarcely realizable at the date of the negotiations of 1818.

New and vast interests have been brought into existence; modes of intercourse between the respective countries have been invented and multiplied; the methods of conducting the fisheries have been wholly changed; and all this is necessarily entitled to candid and careful consideration in the adjustment of the terms and conditions of intercourse and commerce between the United States and their neighbors along a frontier of over 3,500 miles.

This propinquity, community of language and occupation, and similarity of political and social institutions indicate the practicability and obvious wisdom of maintaining mutually beneficial and friendly relations.

While I am unfeignedly desirous that such relations should exist between us and the inhabitants of Canada, yet the action of their officials during the past season toward our fishermen has been such as to seriously threaten their continuance.

Although disappointed in my efforts to secure a satisfactory settlement of the fishery question, negotiations are still pending, with reasonable hope that before the close of the present session of Congress announcement may be made that an acceptable conclusion has been reached.

As at an early day there may be laid before Congress the correspondence of the Department of State in relation to this important subject, so that the history of the past fishing season may be fully disclosed and the action and the attitude of the Administration clearly comprehended, a more extended reference is not deemed necessary in this communication.

The recommendation, submitted last year, that provision be made for a preliminary reconnaissance of the conventional boundary-line between Alaska and British Columbia is renewed.

I express my unhesitating conviction that the intimacy of our relations with Hawaii should be emphasized. As a result of the reciprocity treaty of 1875, those islands, on the highway of Oriental and Australasian traffic, are virtually an outpost of American commerce and a stepping-stone to the growing trade of the Pacific. The Polynesian island groups have been so absorbed by other and more powerful governments, that the Hawaiian Islands are left almost alone in the enjoyment of their autonomy, which it is important for us should be preserved. Our treaty is now terminable on one year's notice, but propositions to abrogate it would be, in my judgment, most ill-advised. The paramount influence we have there acquired, once relinquished, could only with difficulty be regained, and a valuable ground of vantage for ourselves might be converted into a stronghold for our commercial competitors. I earnestly recommend that the existing treaty stipulations be extended for a further term of seven years. A recently-signed treaty to this end is now before the Senate.

The importance of telegraphic communication between those islands and the United States should not be overlooked.

The question of a general revision of the treaties of Japan is again under discussion at Tokio. As the first to open relations with that empire, and as the nation in most direct commercial relation with Japan, the United States have lost no opportunity to testify their consistent friendship by supporting the just claims of Japan to autonomy and independence among nations.

A treaty of extradition between the United States and Japan, the first concluded by that empire, has been lately proclaimed.

The weakness of Liberia, and the difficulty of maintaining effective sovereignty over its outlying districts, have exposed that republic to encroachment. It can not be forgotten that this distant community is an offshoot of our own system, owing its origin to the associated benevolence of American citizens, whose praiseworthy efforts to create a nucleus of civilization in the dark continent have commanded respect and sympathy everywhere, especially in this country. Although a formal protectorate over Liberia is contrary to our traditional policy, the moral right and duty of the United States to assist in all proper ways in the maintenance of its integrity is obvious, and has been consistently announced during nearly half a century. I recommend that, in the reorganization of our navy, a small vessel, no longer found adequate to our needs, be presented to Liberia, to be employed by it in the protection of its coastwise revenues.

The encouraging development of beneficial and intimate relations between the United States and Mexico, which has been so marked within the past few years, is at once the occasion of congratulation and of friendly solicitude. I urgently renew my former representation of the need of speedy legislation by Congress to carry into effect the Reciprocity Commercial Convention of January 20, 1883.

Our commercial treaty of 1831 with Mexico was terminated, according to its provisions, in 1881, upon notification given by Mexico in pursuance of her announced policy of recasting all her commercial treaties. Mexico has since concluded with several foreign governments new treaties of commerce and navigation, defining alien rights of trade, property, and residence, treatment of shipping, consular privileges, and the like. Our yet unexecuted Reciprocity Convention of 1883 covers none of these points, the settlement of which is so necessary to good relationship. I propose to initiate with Mexico negotiations for a new and enlarged treaty of commerce and navigation.

In compliance with a resolution of the Senate, I communicated to that body on August 2 last, and also to the House of Representatives, the correspondence in the case of A. K. Cutting, an American citizen, then imprisoned in Mexico, charged with the commission of a penal offense in Texas, of which a Mexican citizen was the object.

After demand had been made for his release, the charge against him was amended so as to include a violation of Mexican law within Mexican territory.

This joinder of alleged offenses, one within and the other exterior to Mexico, induced me to order a special investigation of the case—pending which Mr. Cutting was released.

The incident has, however, disclosed a claim of jurisdiction by Mexico, novel in our history, whereby any offense, committed anywhere by a foreigner, penal in the place of its commission, and of which a Mexican is the object, may, if the offender be found in Mexico, be there tried and punished in conformity with Mexican laws.

This jurisdiction was sustained by the courts of Mexico in the Cutting case, and approved by the executive branch of that Government, upon the authority of a Mexican statute. The appellate court, in releasing Mr. Cutting, decided that the abandonment of the complaint by the Mexican citizen aggrieved by the alleged crime (a libelous publication), removed the basis of further prosecution, and also declared justice to have been satisfied by the enforcement of a small part of the original sentence.

The admission of such a pretension would be attended with serious results, invasive of the jurisdiction of this Government, and highly dangerous to our citizens in foreign lands; therefore I have denied it, and protested against its attempted exercise, as unwarranted by the principles of law and international usages.

A sovereign has jurisdiction of offenses which take effect within his territory, although concocted or commenced outside of it; but the right is denied of any foreign sovereign to punish a citizen of the United States for an offense consummated on our soil in violation of our laws, even though the offense be against a subject or citizen of such sovereign. The Mexican statute in question makes the claim broadly, and the principle, if conceded, would create a dual responsibility in the citizen, and lead to inextricable confusion, destructive of that certainty in the law which is an essential of liberty.

When citizens of the United States voluntarily go into a foreign country they must abide by the laws there in force, and will not be protected by their own Government from the consequences of an offense against those laws committed in such foreign country; but watchful care and interest of this Government over its citizens are not relinquished because they have gone abroad; and if charged with crime committed in the foreign land, a fair and open trial, conducted with decent regard for justice and humanity, will be demanded for them. With less than that this Government will not be content when the life or liberty of its citizens is at stake.

Whatever the degree to which extra-territorial criminal jurisdiction may have been formerly allowed by consent and reciprocal agreement among certain of the European states, no such doctrine or practice was ever known to the laws of this country, or of that from which our institutions have mainly been derived.

In the case of Mexico there are reasons especially strong for perfect harmony in the mutual exercise of jurisdiction. Nature has made us irrevocably neighbors, and wisdom and kind feeling should make us friends.

The overflow of capital and enterprise from the United States is a potent factor in assisting the development of the resources of Mexico, and in building up the prosperity of both countries.

To assist this good work all grounds of apprehension for the security of person and property should be removed; and I trust that in the interests of good neighborhood the statute referred to will be so modified as to eliminate the present possibilities of danger to the peace of the two countries.

The Government of the Netherlands has exhibited concern in relation to certain features of our tariff laws, which are supposed by them to be aimed at a class of tobacco produced in the Dutch East Indies. Comment would seem unnecessary upon the unwisdom of legislation appearing to have a special national discrimination for its object, which, although unintentional, may give rise to injurious retaliation.

The establishment, less than four years ago, of a legation at Teheran is bearing fruit in the interest exhibited by the Shah's Government in the industrial activity of the United States and the opportunities of beneficial interchanges.

Stable government is now happily restored in Peru by the election of a constitutional President, and a period of rehabilitation is entered upon. But the recovery is necessarily slow from the exhaustion caused by the late war, and civil disturbances. A convention to adjust, by arbitration, claims of our citizens has been proposed, and is under consideration.

The naval officer who bore to Siberia the testimonials bestowed by Congress in recognition of the aid given to the Jeannette survivors, has successfully accomplished his mission. His interesting report will be submitted. It is pleasant to know that this mark of appreciation has been welcomed by the Russian Government and people as befits the traditional friendship of the two countries.

Civil perturbations in the Samoan Islands have during the past few years been a source of considerable embarrassment to the three governments, Germany, Great Britain, and the United States, whose relations and extra-territorial rights in that important group are guaranteed by treaties. The weakness of the native administration and the conflict of opposing interests in the islands have led King Malietoa to seek alliance or protection in some one quarter, regardless of the distinct engagements whereby no one of the three treaty powers may acquire any paramount or exclusive interest. In May last Malietoa offered to place Samoa under the protection of the United States, and the late consul, without authority, assumed to grant it. The proceeding was promptly disavowed, and the over-zealous official recalled. Special agents of the three governments have been deputed to examine the situation in the islands. With a change in the representation of all three powers, and a harmonious understanding between them, the peace, prosperity, autonomous administration, and neutrality of Samoa can hardly fail to be secured.

It appearing that the Government of Spain did not extend to the flag of the United States in the Antilles the full measure of reciprocity requisite under our statute for the continuance of the suspension of discriminations against the Spanish flag in our ports, I was constrained in October last to rescind my predecessor's proclamation of Feb. 14, 1884, permitting such suspension. An arrangement was, however, speedily reached, and upon notification from the Government of Spain that all differential treatment of our vessels and their cargoes, from the United States or any foreign country, had been completely and absolutely relinquished, I availed myself of the discretion conferred by law, and issued on the 27th of October my proclamation, declaring reciprocal suspension in the United States. It is most gratifying to bear testimony to the earnest spirit in which the Government of the Queen Regent has met our efforts to avert the initiation of commercial discriminations and reprisals, which are ever disastrous to the material interests and the political good-will of the countries they may affect.

The profitable development of the large commercial exchanges between the United States and the Spanish Antilles is naturally an object of solicitude. Lying close at our doors, and finding here their main markets of supply and demand, the welfare of Cuba and Porto Rico, and their production and trade, are scarcely less important to us than to Spain. Their commercial and financial movements are so naturally a part of our system that no obstacle to fuller and freer intercourse should be permitted to exist. The standing instructions of our representatives at Madrid and Havana have for years been to leave no effort unessayed to further these ends; and at no time has the equal good desire of Spain been more hopefully manifested than now.

The Government of Spain, by removing the consular tonnage fees on cargoes shipped to the Antilles, and by reducing passport fees, has shown its recognition of the needs of less trammeled intercourse.

An effort has been made during the past year to remove the hindrances to the proclamation of the treaty of naturalization with the Sublime Porte, signed in 1874, which has remained inoperative owing to a disagreement of interpretation of the clauses relative to the effects of the return to and sojourn of a naturalized citizen in the land of origin. I trust soon to be able to announce a favorable settlement of the differences as to this interpretation.

It has been highly satisfactory to note the improved treatment of American missionaries in Turkey, as has been attested by their acknowledgments to our late minister to that Government of his successful exertions in their behalf.

The exchange of ratifications of the convention of Dec. 5, 1885, with Venezuela, for the reopening of the awards of the Caracas Commission under the Claims Convention of 1866, has not yet been effected, owing to the delay of the Executive of that republic in ratifying the measure. I trust that this postponement will be brief; but should it much longer continue, the delay may well be regarded as a rescission of the compact and a failure on the part of Venezuela to complete an arrangement so persistently sought by her during many years and assented to by this Government in a spirit of international fairness, although to the detriment of holders of bona-fide awards of the impugned commission.

I renew the recommendation of my last annual message, that existing legislation concerning citizenship and naturalization be revised. We have treaties with many states providing for the renunciation of citizenship by naturalized aliens, but no statute is found to give effect to such engagements, nor any which provides a needed central bureau for the registration of naturalized citizens.

Experience suggests that our statutes regulating extradition might be advantageously amended by a provision for the transit across our territory, now a convenient thoroughfare of travel from one foreign country to another, of fugitives surrendered by a foreign government to a third state. Such provisions are not unusual in the legislation of other countries, and tend to prevent the miscarriage of justice. It is also desirable, in order to remove present uncertainties, that authority should be conferred on the Secretary of State to issue a certificate in case of an arrest for the purpose of extradition, to the officer before whom the proceeding is pending, showing that a requisition for the surrender of the person charged has been duly made. Such a certificate, if required to be received before the prisoner's examination, would prevent a long and expensive judicial inquiry into a charge which the foreign government might not desire to press. I also recommend that express provision be made for the immediate discharge from custody of persons committed for extradition where the President is of opinion that surrender should not be made.

The drift of sentiment in civilized communities toward full recognition of the rights of property in the creations of the human intellect has brought about the adoption, by many important nations, of an International Copyright Convention, which was signed at Berne on the 18th of September, 1885.

Inasmuch as the Constitution gives to Congress the power "to promote the progress of science and useful arts by securing for limited times to authors and inventors the exclusive right to their respective writings and discoveries," this Government did not feel warranted in becoming a signatory pending the action of Congress upon measures of international copyright now before it, but the right of adhesion to the Berne Convention hereafter, has been reserved. I trust the subject will receive at your hands the attention it deserves, and that the just claims of authors, so urgently pressed, will be duly heeded.

Representations continue to be made to me of the injurious effect upon American artists studying abroad and having free access to the art collections of foreign countries, of maintaining a discriminating duty against the introduction of the works of their brother artists of other countries; and I am induced to repeat my recommendation for the abolition of that tax.

Pursuant to a provision of the diplomatic and consular appropriation act, approved July 1, 1886, the estimates submitted by the Secretary of State for the maintenance of the consular service have been recast, on the basis of salaries for all officers to whom such allowance is deemed advisable. Advantage has been taken of this to redistribute the salaries of the offices now appropriated for, in accordance with the work performed, the importance of the representative duties of the incumbent, and the cost of living at each post. The last consideration has been too often lost sight of in the allowances heretofore made. The compensation which may suffice for the decent maintenance of a worthy and capable officer in a position of onerous and representative trust at a post readily accessible, and where the necessaries of life are abundant and cheap, may prove an inadequate pittance in distant lands, where the better part of a year's pay is consumed in reaching the post of duty, and where the comforts of ordinary civilized existence can only be obtained with difficulty and at exorbitant cost. I trust that, in considering the submitted schedules, no mistaken theory of economy will perpetuate a system which in the past has virtually closed to deserving talent many offices where capacity and attainments of a high order are indispensable, and in not a few instances has brought discredit on our national character and entailed embarrassment and even suffering on those deputed to uphold our dignity and interests abroad.

In connection with this subject I earnestly reiterate the practical necessity of supplying some mode of trustworthy inspection and report of the manner in which the consulates are conducted. In the absence of such reliable information, efficiency can scarcely be rewarded, or its opposite corrected.

Increasing competition in trade has directed attention to the value of consular reports printed by the Department of State, and the efforts of the Government to extend the practical usefulness of these reports have created a wider demand for them at home and a spirit of emulation abroad. Constituting a record of the changes occurring in trade and of the progress of the arts and invention in foreign countries, they are much sought for by all interested in the subjects which they embrace.

The report of the Secretary of the Treasury exhibits in detail the condition of the public finances and of the several branches of the Government related to his department. I especially direct the attention of the Congress to the recommendations contained in this and the last preceding report of the Secretary, touching the simplification and amendment of the laws relating to the collection of our revenues; and in the interest of economy and justice to the Government, I hope they may be adopted by appropriate legislation.

The ordinary receipts of the Government for the fiscal year ended June 30, 1886, were $336,439,727 06. Of this amount $192,905,023.41 was received from customs and $116,805,936.48 from internal revenue. The total receipts, as here stated, were $13,749,020.68 greater than for the previous year, but the increase from customs was $11,434,084.10, and from internal revenue $4,407,310.94, making a gain in these items for the last year of $15,841,295.04—a falling off in other resources reducing the total increase to the smaller amount mentioned.

The expense, at the different custom-houses, of collecting this increased customs revenue was less than the expense attending the collection of such revenue for the preceding year by $490,608; and the increased receipts of internal revenue were collected at a cost to the Internal-Revenue Bureau $155,944.99 less than the expense of such collection for the previous year.

The total ordinary expenses of the Government for the fiscal year ended June 30, 1886, were $242,483,138.50, being less by $17,788,797 than such expenditures for the year preceding, and leaving a surplus in the Treasury at the close of the last fiscal year of $93,956,588.56 as against $63,463,771.27 at the close of the previous year, being an increase in such surplus of $30,492,817.29.

The expenditures are compared with those of the preceding fiscal year, and classified as follow:

OBJECT.	Year ending June 30, 1886.	Year ending June 30, 1885.
For civil expenses	$21,955,604 04	$23,826,942 11
For foreign intercourse	1,332,820 88	5,439,609 11
For Indians	6,099,158 17	6,552,494 63
For pensions	63,404,864 06	56,102,267 49
For the military, including river and harbor improvements and arsenals	34,324,152 74	42,670,578 47
For the navy, including vessels, machinery, and improvement of navy-yards	13,907,887 74	16,021,079 69
For interest on public debt	50,580,145 97	51,386,256 47
For the District of Columbia	2,892,321 59	3,499,650 95
Miscellaneous expenditures, including public buildings, lighthouses, and collecting the revenue	47,986,688 04	54,726,056 21

For the current year to end June 30, 1887, the ascertained receipts up to Oct. 1, 1886, with such receipts estimated for the remainder of the year, amount to $356,000,000.

The expenditures ascertained and estimated for the same period are $266,000,000, indicating an anticipated surplus at the close of the year of $90,000,000.

The total value of the exports from the United States to foreign countries during the fiscal year is stated and compared with the preceding year as follows:

EXPORTS.	For the year ending June 30, 1886.	For the year ending June 30, 1885.
Domestic merchandise	$665,964,529 00	$796,692,946 00
Foreign merchandise	18,560,801 00	15,504,809 00
Gold	42,952,191 00	8,477,892 00
Silver	29,511,219 00	33,753,633 00

The value of some of our leading exports during the last fiscal year, as compared with the value of the same for the year immediately preceding, is here given, and furnishes information both interesting and suggestive:

EXPORTS.	For the year ending June 30, 1886.	For the year ending June 30, 1885.
Cotton and cotton manufactures............	$219,045,576 00	$213,799,049 00
Tobacco and its manufactures...............	30,424,906 00	24,767,305 00
Breadstuffs.............	125,846,556 00	160,370,821 00
Provisions........	90,625,216 00	107,332,456 00

Our imports during the last fiscal year, as compared with the previous year, were as follow :

IMPORTS.	1886.	1885.
Merchandise..............	$635,426,136 00	$579,580,058 80
Gold....................	20,743,349 00	26,691,696 00
Silver...................	17,850,307 00	16,550,627 00

In my last annual message to the Congress attention was directed to the fact that the revenues of the Government exceeded its actual needs ; and it was suggested that legislative action should be taken to relieve the people from the unnecessary burden of taxation thus made apparent.

In view of the pressing importance of the subject I deem it my duty to again urge its consideration.

The income of the Government, by its increased volume and through economies in its collection, is now more than ever in excess of public necessities. The application of the surplus to the payment of such portion of the public debt as is now at our option subject to extinguishment, if continued at the rate which has lately prevailed, would retire that class of indebtedness within less than one year from this date. Thus a continuation of our present revenue system would soon result in the receipt of an annual income much greater than necessary to meet Government expenses, with no indebtedness upon which it could be applied. We should then be confronted with a vast quantity of money, the circulating medium of the people, hoarded in the Treasury when it should be in their hands, or we should be drawn into wasteful public extravagance with all the corrupting national demoralization which follows in its train.

But it is not the simple existence of this surplus and its threatened attendant evils, which furnish the strongest argument against our present scale of Federal taxation. Its worst phase is the exaction of such a surplus through a perversion of the relations between the people and their Government, and a dangerous departure from the rules which limit the right of Federal taxation.

Good government, and especially the government of which every American citizen boasts, has for its objects the protection of every person within its care in the greatest liberty consistent with the good order of society, and his perfect security in the enjoyment of his earnings, with the least possible diminution for public needs. When more of the people's substance is exacted through the form of taxation than is necessary to meet the just obligations of the Government and the expense of its economical administration, such exaction becomes ruthless extortion and a violation of the fundamental principles of a free government.

The indirect manner in which these exactions are made has a tendency to conceal their true character and their extent. But we have arrived at a stage of superfluous revenue which has aroused the people to a realization of the fact that the amount raised, professedly for the support of the Government, is paid by them as absolutely, if added to the price of the things which supply their daily wants, as if it was paid at fixed periods into the hand of the tax-gatherer.

Those who toil for daily wages are beginning to understand that capital, though sometimes vaunting its importance and clamoring for the protection and favor of the Government, is dull and sluggish, till, touched by the magical hand of labor, it springs into activity, furnishing an occasion for Federal taxation and gaining the value which enables it to bear its burden. And the laboring-man is thoughtfully inquiring whether in these circumstances, and considering the tribute he constantly pays into the public Treasury as he supplies his daily wants, he receives his fair share of advantages.

There is also a suspicion abroad that the surplus of our revenues indicates abnormal and exceptional business profits, which, under the system which produces such surplus, increase without corresponding benefit to the people at large, the vast accumulations of a few among our citizens whose fortunes, rivaling the wealth of the most favored in anti-democratic nations, are not the natural growth of a steady, plain, and industrious republic.

Our farmers too, and those engaged directly and indirectly in supplying the products of agriculture, see that day by day, and, as often as the daily wants of their households recur, they are forced to pay excessive and needless taxation, while their products struggle in foreign markets with the competition of nations, which, by allowing a freer exchange of productions than we permit, enable their people to sell for prices which distress the American farmer.

As every patriotic citizen rejoices in the constantly increasing pride of our people in American citizenship and in the glory of our national achievements and progress, a sentiment prevails that the leading-strings useful to a nation in its infancy may well be to a great extent discarded in the present stage of American ingenuity, courage, and fearless self-reliance. And for the privilege of indulging this sentiment with true American enthusiasm, our citizens are quite willing to forego an idle surplus in the public Treasury.

And all the people know that the average rate of Federal taxation upon imports is to-day, in time of peace, but little less, while upon some articles of necessary consumption it is actually more, than was imposed by the grievous burden willingly borne, at a time when the Government needed millions to maintain by war the safety and integrity of the Union.

It has been the policy of the Government to collect the principal part of its revenues by a tax upon imports ; and no change in this policy is desirable. But the present condition of affairs constrains our people to demand that, by a revision of our revenue laws, the receipts of the Government shall be reduced to the necessary expense of its economical administration ; and this demand should be recognized and obeyed by the people's representatives in the legislative branch of the Government.

In readjusting the burdens of Federal taxation, a sound public policy requires that such of our citizens as have built up large and important industries under present conditions, should not be suddenly and to their injury deprived of advantages to which they have adapted their business ; but if the public good requires it, they should be content with such consideration as shall deal fairly and cautiously with their interests, while the just demand of the people for relief from needless taxation is honestly answered.

A reasonable and timely submission to such a demand should certainly be possible without disastrous shock to any interest ; and a cheerful concession sometimes averts abrupt and heedless action, often the outgrowth of impatience and delayed justice.

Due regard should be also accorded in any proposed readjustment to the interests of American labor so far as they are involved. We congratulate ourselves that there is among us no laboring-class fixed within unyielding bounds, and doomed under all conditions to the inexorable fate of daily toil. We recognize in labor a chief factor in the wealth of the republic, and we treat those who have it in their keeping as citizens entitled to the most careful regard and thoughtful attention. This regard and attention should be awarded them, not only because labor is the capital of our workingmen, justly entitled to its share of Government favor, but for the further and not less important reason that the laboring-man, surrounded by his family in his humble home, as a consumer is vitally interested in all that cheapens the cost of living, and enables him to bring within his domestic circle additional comforts and advantages.

This relation of the workingman to the revenue laws of the country, and the manner in which it palpably influences the question of wages, should not be forgotten in the justifiable prominence given to the proper maintenance of the supply and protection of well-paid labor. And these considerations suggest such an arrangement of Government revenues as shall reduce the expense of living, while it does not curtail the opportunity for work nor reduce the compensation of American labor, and injuriously affect its condition and the dignified place it holds in the estimation of our people.

But our farmers and agriculturists—those who from the soil produce the things consumed by all—are, perhaps, more directly and plainly concerned than any other of our citizens in a just and careful system of Federal taxation. Those actually engaged in and more remotely connected with this kind of work, number nearly one half of our population. None labor harder or more continuously than they. No enactments limit their hours of toil, and no interposition of the Government enhances to any extent the value of their products. And yet for many of the necessaries and comforts of life, which the most scrupulous economy enables them to bring into their homes, and for their implements of husbandry, they are obliged to pay a price largely increased by an unnatural profit which, by the action of the Government, is given to the more favored manufacturer.

I recommend that, keeping in view all these considerations, the increasing and unnecessary surplus of national income annually accumulating be released to the people by an amendment to our revenue laws which shall cheapen the price of the necessaries of life, and give freer entrance to such imported materials as by American labor may be manufactured into marketable commodities.

Nothing can be accomplished, however, in the direction of this much-needed reform, unless the subject is approached in a patriotic spirit of devotion to the interests of the entire country, and with a willingness to yield something for the public good.

The sum paid upon the public debt during the fiscal year ended June 30, 1886, was $44,551,043.36.

During the twelve months ended Oct. 31, 1886, three-per-cent. bonds were called for redemption amounting to $127,283,100, of which $80,643,200 was so called to answer the requirements of the law relating to the sinking-fund, and $46,639,900 for the purpose of reducing the public debt by application of a part of the surplus in the Treasury to that object. Of the bonds thus called $102,269,450 became subject under such calls to redemption prior to Nov. 1, 1886. The remainder, amounting to $25,013,650, matured under the calls after that date.

In addition to the amount subject to payment and cancellation prior to November 1, there were also paid before that day certain of these bonds, with the interest thereon, amounting to $5,072,350, which were anticipated as to their maturity, of which $2,664,850 had not been called. Thus $107,341,800 had been actually applied prior to the 1st of November, 1886, to the extinguishment of our bonded and interest-bearing debt, leaving on that day still outstanding the sum of $1,153,443,112. Of this amount $86,848,700 were still represented by three-per-cent. bonds. They, however, have been, since November 1, or will at once be, further reduced by $22,606,150, being bonds which have been called, as already stated, but not redeemed and canceled before the latter date.

During the fiscal year ended June 30, 1886, there were coined, under the compulsory silver-coinage act of 1878, 29,838,905 silver dollars, and the cost of the silver used in such coinage was $23,448,960.01. There had been coined up to the close of the previous fiscal year under provisions of the law, 203,882,554 silver

dollars, and on the 1st day of December, 1886, the total amount of such coinage was $247,131,549.

The Director of the Mint reports that at the time of the passage of the law of 1878 directing this coinage the intrinsic value of the dollars thus coined was ninety-four and one fourth cents each, and that on the 31st day of July, 1886, the price of silver reached the lowest stage ever known, so that the intrinsic or bullion price of our standard silver dollar at that date was less than seventy-two cents. The price of silver on the 30th day of November last was such as to make these dollars intrinsically worth seventy-eight cents each.

These differences in value of the coins represent the fluctuations in the price of silver, and they certainly do not indicate that compulsory coinage by the Government enhances the price of that commodity or secures uniformity in its value.

Every fair and legal effort has been made by the Treasury Department to distribute this currency among the people. The withdrawal of the United States Treasury notes of small denominations, and the issuing of small silver certificates have been resorted to in the endeavor to accomplish this result, in obedience to the will and sentiments of the representatives of the people in the Congress. On the 27th day of November, 1886, the people held of these coins, or certificates representing them, the nominal sum of $166,873,041, and we still had $79,464,345 in the Treasury—as against about $142,894,055 so in the hands of the people, and $72,865,876 remaining in the Treasury one year ago. The Director of the Mint again urges the necessity of more vault-room for the purpose of storing those silver dollars which are not needed for circulation by the people.

I have seen no reason to change the views expressed in my last annual message on the subject of this compulsory coinage, and I again urge its suspension on the grounds contained in my former recommendation, re-enforced by the significant increase of our gold exportations during the last year, as appears by the comparative statement herewith presented, and for the further reasons that the more this currency is distributed among the people the greater becomes our duty to protect it from disaster; that we now have abundance for all our needs; and that there seems but little propriety in building vaults to store such currency when the only pretense for its coinage is the necessity of its use by the people as a circulating medium.

The great number of suits now pending in the United States courts for the Southern District of New York, growing out of the collection of customs revenue at the port of New York, and the number of such suits that are almost daily instituted, are certainly worthy the attention of the Congress. These legal controversies, based upon conflicting views by importers and the collector as to the interpretation of our present complex and indefinite revenue laws, might be largely obviated by an amendment of those laws.

But, pending such amendment, the present condition of this litigation should be relieved. There are now pending about twenty-five hundred of these suits. More than eleven hundred have been commenced within the past eighteen months, and many of the others have been at issue for more than twenty-five years. These delays subject the Government to loss of evidence, and prevent the preparation necessary to defeat unjust and fictitious claims, while constantly accruing interest threatens to double the demands involved.

In the present condition of the dockets of the courts, well filled with private suits, and of the force allowed the district attorney, no greater than is necessary for the ordinary and current business of his office, these revenue litigations can not be considered.

In default of the adoption by the Congress of a plan for the general reorganization of the Federal courts, as has been heretofore recommended, I urge the propriety of passing a law permitting the appointment of an additional Federal judge in the district where these Government suits have accumulated, so that by continuous sessions of the courts devoted to the trial of these cases they may be determined.

It is entirely plain that a great saving to the Government would be accomplished by such a remedy, and the suitors who have honest claims would not be denied justice through delay.

The report of the Secretary of War gives a detailed account of the administration of his department, and contains sundry recommendations for the improvement of the service, which I fully approve.

The army consisted at the date of the last consolidated return of 2,103 officers, and 24,946 enlisted men.

The expenses of the department for the last fiscal year were $36,990,903.38, including $6,294,305.43 for public works and river and harbor improvements.

I especially direct the attention of the Congress to the recommendation that officers be required to submit to an examination as a preliminary to their promotion. I see no objection, but many advantages, in adopting this feature, which has operated so beneficially in our Navy Department, as well as in some branches of the army.

The subject of coast defenses and fortifications has been fully and carefully treated by the Board on Fortifications, whose report was submitted at the last session of Congress; but no construction work of the kind recommended by the board has been possible during the last year, from the lack of appropriations for such purpose.

The defenseless condition of our sea-coast and lake frontier is perfectly palpable; the examinations made must convince us all that certain of our cities named in the report of the board should be fortified, and that work on the most important of these fortifications should be commenced at once; the work has been thoroughly considered and laid out, the Secretary of War reports, but all is delayed in default of congressional action.

The absolute necessity, judged by all standards of prudence and foresight, of our preparation for an effectual resistance against the armored ships and steel guns and mortars of modern construction which may threaten the cities on our coasts, is so apparent, that I hope effective steps will be taken in that direction immediately.

The valuable and suggestive treatment of this question by the Secretary of War is earnestly commended to the consideration of the Congress.

In September and October last the hostile Apaches who, under the leadership of Geronimo, had for eighteen months been on the war-path, and during that time had committed many murders, and been the cause of constant terror to the settlers of Arizona, surrendered to General Miles, the military commander who succeeded General Crook in the management and direction of their pursuit.

Under the terms of their surrender, as then reported, and in view of the understanding which these murderous savages seemed to entertain of the assurances given them, it was considered best to imprison them in such manner as to prevent their ever engaging in such outrages again, instead of trying them for murder. Fort Pickens having been selected as a safe place of confinement, all the adult males were sent thither, and will be closely guarded as prisoners. In the mean time the residue of the band, who, though still remaining upon the reservation, were regarded as unsafe, and suspected of furnishing aid to those on the war-path, had been removed to Fort Marion. The women and larger children of the hostiles were also taken there, and arrangements have been made for putting the children of proper age in Indian schools.

The report of the Secretary of the Navy contains a detailed exhibit of the condition of his department, with such a statement of the action needed to improve the same as should challenge the earnest attention of the Congress.

The present Navy of the United States, aside from the ships in course of construction, consists of—

First, fourteen single-turreted monitors, none of which are in commission, nor at the present time serviceable. The batteries of these ships are obsolete, and they can only be relied upon as auxiliary ships in harbor defense, and then after such an expenditure upon them as might not be deemed justifiable.

Second, five fourth-rate vessels of small tonnage, only one of which was designed as a war-vessel, and all of which are auxiliary merely.

Third, twenty-seven cruising-ships, three of which are built of iron, of small tonnage, and twenty-four of wood. Of these wooden vessels it is estimated by the Chief Constructor of the Navy that only three will be serviceable beyond a period of six years, at which time it may be said that of the present naval force nothing worthy the name will remain.

All the vessels heretofore authorized are under contract or in course of construction, except the armored ships, the torpedo and dynamite boats, and one cruiser. As to the last of these, the bids were in excess of the limit fixed by Congress. The production in the United States of armor and gun-steel is a question which it seems necessary to settle at an early day, if the armored war-vessels are to be completed with those materials of home manufacture. This has been the subject of investigation by two boards and by two special committees of Congress within the last three years. The report of the Gun Foundry Board in 1884, of the Board on Fortifications made in January last, and the reports of the select committees of the two houses made at the last session of Congress, have entirely exhausted the subject, so far as preliminary investigation is involved, and in their recommendations they are substantially agreed.

In the event that the present invitation of the department forbids to furnish such of this material as is now authorized shall fail to induce domestic manufacturers to undertake the large expenditures required to prepare for this new manufacture, and no other steps are taken by Congress at its coming session, the Secretary contemplates with dissatisfaction the necessity of obtaining abroad the armor and the gun-steel for the authorized ships. It would seem desirable that the wants of the army and the navy in this regard should be reasonably met, and that by uniting their contracts such inducement might be offered as would result in securing the domestication of these important interests.

The affairs of the postal service show marked and gratifying improvement during the past year. A particular account of its transactions and condition is given in the report of the Postmaster-General, which will be laid before you.

The reduction of the rate of letter-postage in 1883, rendering the postal revenues inadequate to sustain the expenditures, and business depression also contributing, resulted in an excess of cost for the fiscal year ended June 30, 1885, of eight and one third millions of dollars. An additional check upon receipts by doubling the measure of weight in rating sealed correspondence and diminishing one half of the charge for newspaper carriage, was imposed by legislation which took effect with the beginning of the past fiscal year; while the constant demand of our territorial development and growing population, for the extension and increase of mail facilities and machinery, necessitates steady annual advance in outlay; and the careful estimate of a year ago upon the rates of expenditure then existing contemplated the unavoidable augmentation of the deficiency in the last fiscal year by nearly two millions of dollars. The anticipated revenue for the last year failed of realization by about $64,000; but proper measures of economy have so satisfactorily limited the growth of expenditure that the total deficiency, in fact, fell below that of 1885; and at this time the increase of revenue is in a gaining ratio over the increase of cost, demonstrating the sufficiency of the present rates of postage ultimately to sustain the service. This is the more pleasing, because our people enjoy now both cheaper postage, proportionably to distances, and a vaster and more costly service than any other upon the globe.

Retrenchment has been effected in the cost of supplies, some expenditures unwarranted by law have ceased, and the outlays for mail-carriage have been subjected to beneficial scrutiny. At the close of the last fiscal year the expense of transportation on star routes stood at an annual rate of cost less by over $560,000 than at the close of the previous year; and steamboat and mail-messenger service at nearly $200,-000 less.

The service has been in the mean time enlarged and extended by the establishment of new offices, increase of routes of carriage, expansion of carrier-delivery conveniences, and additions to the railway-mail facilities, in accordance with the growing exigencies of the country and the long-established policy of the Government.

The Postmaster-General calls attention to the existing law for compensating railroads, and expresses the opinion that a method may be devised which will prove more just to the carriers and beneficial to the Government; and the subject appears worthy of your early consideration.

The differences which arose during the year with certain of the ocean-steamship companies have terminated by the acquiescence of all in the policy of the Government approved by the Congress in the postal appropriation at its last session; and the department now enjoys the utmost service afforded by all vessels which sail from our ports upon either ocean—a service generally adequate to the needs of our intercourse. Petitions have, however, been presented to the department by numerous merchants and manufacturers for the establishment of a direct service to the Argentine Republic and for semi-monthly dispatches to the Empire of Brazil; and the subject is commended to your consideration. It is an obvious duty to provide the means of postal communication which our commerce requires, and with prudent forecast of results the wise extension of it may lead to stimulating intercourse and become the harbinger of a profitable traffic, which will open new avenues for the disposition of the products of our industry. The circumstances of the countries at the far south of our continent are such as to invite our enterprise and afford the promise of sufficient advantages to justify an unusual effort to bring about the closer relations which greater freedom of communication would tend to establish.

I suggest that, as distinguished from a grant or subsidy for the mere benefit of any line of trade or travel, whatever outlay may be required to secure additional postal service, necessary and proper and not otherwise attainable, should be regarded as within the limit of legitimate compensation for such service.

The extension of the free-delivery service as suggested by the Postmaster-General has heretofore received my sanction, and it is to be hoped a suitable enactment may soon be agreed upon.

The request for an appropriation sufficient to enable the general inspection of fourth-class offices has my approbation.

I renew my approval of the recommendation of the Postmaster-General that another assistant be provided for the Post-Office Department; and I invite your attention to the several other recommendations in his report.

The conduct of the Department of Justice for the last fiscal year is fully detailed in the report of the Attorney-General, and I invite the earnest attention of the Congress to the same, and due consideration of the recommendations therein contained.

In the report submitted by this officer to the last session of the Congress he strongly recommended the erection of a penitentiary for the confinement of prisoners convicted and sentenced in the United States courts; and he repeats the recommendation in his report for the last year.

This is a matter of very great importance and sho[uld] at once receive congressional action. United St[ates] prisoners are now confined in more than thirty [dif]ferent State prisons and penitentiaries scattere[d] every part of the country. They are subjecte[d] nearly as many different modes of treatment [and] discipline, and are far too much removed from control and regulation of the Government. So as they are entitled to humane treatment and an portunity for improvement and reformation, the G[ov]ernment is responsible to them and society that t[he]se things are forthcoming. But this duty can scarce be discharged without more absolute control and [di]rection than is possible under the present system.

Many of our good citizens have interested the[m]selves, with the most beneficial results, in the qu[es]tion of prison reform. The General Governm[ent] should be in a situation, since there must be Un[ited] States prisoners, to furnish important aid in [this] movement, and should be able to illustrate what [may] be practically done in the direction of this refo[rm] and to present an example in the treatment and provement of its prisoners worthy of imitation.

With prisons under its own control, the Gove[rn]ment could deal with the somewhat vexed quest[ion] of convict-labor, so far as its convicts were concern[ed] according to a plan of its own adoption, and with [a] regard to the rights and interests of our laboring izens, instead of sometimes aiding in the operat[ion] of a system which causes among them irritation [and] discontent.

Upon consideration of this subject it might thought wise to erect more than one of these instituti[ons] located in such places as would best subserve the p[ur]poses of convenience and economy in transportati[on]. The considerable cost of maintaining these convi[cts] as at present, in State institutions, would be saved the adoption of the plan proposed; and by empl[oy]ing them in the manufacture of such articles as w[ere] needed for use by the Government, quite a large cuniary benefit would be realized in partial return our outlay.

I again urge a change in the Federal judicial s[ys]tem to meet the wants of the people and obviate delays necessarily attending the present condition affairs in our courts. All are agreed that someth[ing] should be done, and much favor is shown, by th[ose] well able to advise, to the plan suggested by the [At]torney-General at the last session of Congress a recommended in my last annual message. This r[ec]ommendation is here renewed, together with anoth[er] made at the same time, touching a change in the m[an]ner of compensating district attorneys and marsha[ls], and the latter subject is commended to the Congr[ess] for its action, in the interest of economy to the G[ov]ernment, and humanity, fairness, and justice to [the] people.

The report of the Secretary of the Interior prese[nts] a comprehensive summary of the work of the vari[ous] branches of the public service connected with [this] department; and the suggestions and recommen[da]tions which it contains for the improvement of [the] service should receive your careful consideration.

The exhibit made of the condition of our Indi[an] population, and the progress of the work for their e[n]lightenment, notwithstanding the many embarra[ss]ments which hinder the better administration of tl[is] important branch of the service, is a gratifying a[nd] hopeful one.

The funds appropriated for the Indian service the fiscal year just passed, with the available inco[me] from Indian land and trust moneys, amounting in to $7,850,775.12, were ample for the service und the conditions and restrictions of laws regulating th[eir] expenditure. There remained a balance on hand June 30, 1886, of $1,860,023.30, of which $1,337,768. are permanent funds for fulfillment of treaties, a[nd] other like purposes, and the remainder, $322,255.0[9] subject to be carried to the surplus fund as requir[ed] by law.

The estimates presented for appropriations for the ensuing fiscal year amount to $5,608,878.64, or $442,386.20 less than those laid before the Congress last year.

The present system of agencies, while absolutely necessary and well adapted for the management of our Indian affairs and for the ends in view, when it was adopted, is at the present stage of Indian management inadequate, standing alone, for the accomplishment of an object which has become pressing in its importance—the more rapid transition from tribal organizations to citizenship, of such portions of the Indians as are capable of civilized life.

When the existing system was adopted the Indian race was outside of the limits of organized States and Territories, and beyond the immediate reach and operation of civilization; and all efforts were mainly directed to the maintenance of friendly relations and the preservation of peace and quiet on the frontier. All this is now changed. There is no such thing as the Indian frontier. Civilization, with the busy hum of industry and the influences of Christianity, surrounds these people at every point. None of the tribes are outside of the bounds of organized government and society, except that the territorial system has not been extended over that portion of the country known as the Indian Territory. As a race the Indians are no longer hostile, but may be considered as submissive to the control of the Government; few of them only are troublesome. Except the fragments of several bands, all are now gathered upon reservations.

It is no longer possible for them to subsist by the chase and the spontaneous productions of the earth. With an abundance of land, if furnished with the means and implements for profitable husbandry, their life of entire dependence upon Government rations from day to day is no longer defensible. Their inclination, long fostered by a defective system of control, is to cling to the habits and customs of their ancestors, and struggle with persistence against the change of life which their altered circumstances press upon them. But barbarism and civilization can not live together. It is impossible that such incongruous conditions should coexist on the same soil.

They are a portion of our people, are under the authority of our Government, and have a peculiar claim upon and are entitled to the fostering care and protection of the nation. The Government can not relieve itself of this responsibility until they are so far trained and civilized as to be able wholly to manage and care for themselves. The paths in which they should walk must be clearly marked out for them, and they must be led or guided until they are familiar with the way and competent to assume the duties and responsibilities of our citizenship.

Progress in this great work will continue only at the present slow pace and at great expense, unless the system and methods of management are improved to meet the changed conditions and urgent demands of the service.

The agents having general charge and supervision in many cases of more than five thousand Indians, scattered over large reservations, and burdened with the details of accountability for funds and supplies, have time to look after the industrial training and improvement of a few Indians only; the many are neglected and remain idle and dependent—conditions not favorable for progress in civilization.

The compensation allowed these agents, and the conditions of the service, are not calculated to secure for the work men who are fitted by ability and skill to properly plan and intelligently direct the methods best adapted to produce the most speedy results and permanent benefits.

Hence the necessity for a supplemental agency or system, directed to the end of promoting the general and more rapid transition of the tribes from habits and customs of barbarism to the ways of civilization.

With an anxious desire to devise some plan of operation by which to secure the welfare of the Indians, and to relieve the Treasury as far as possible from the support of an idle and dependent population, I recommended in my previous annual message the passage of a law authorizing the appointment of a commission as an instrumentality auxiliary to those already established, for the care of the Indians. It was designed that this commission should be composed of six intelligent and capable persons—three to be detailed from the army—having practical ideas upon the subject of the treatment of Indians, and interested in their welfare; and that it should be charged, under the direction of the Secretary of the Interior, with the management of such matters of detail as can not with the present organization be properly and successfully conducted, and which present different phases, as the Indians themselves differ, in their progress, needs, disposition, and capacity for improvement or immediate self-support.

By the aid of such a commission much unwise and useless expenditure of money, waste of materials, and unavailing efforts might be avoided; and it is hoped that this or some measure which the wisdom of Congress may better devise, to supply the deficiency of the present system, may receive your consideration, and the appropriate legislation be provided.

The time is ripe for the work of such an agency.

There is less opposition to the education and training of the Indian youth, as shown by the increased attendance upon the schools, and there is a yielding tendency for the individual holding of lands. Development and advancement in these directions are essential, and should have every encouragement. As the rising generation are taught the language of civilization and trained in habits of industry, they should assume the duties, privileges, and responsibilities of citizenship.

No obstacle should hinder the location and settlement of any Indian willing to take land in severalty; on the contrary, the inclination to do so should be stimulated at all times when proper and expedient. But there is no authority of law for making allotments on some of the reservations, and on others the allotments provided for are so small, that the Indians, though ready and desiring to settle down, are not willing to accept such small areas, when their reservations contain ample lands to afford them homesteads of sufficient size to meet their present and future needs.

These inequalities of existing special laws and treaties should be corrected, and some general legislation on the subject should be provided, so that the more progressive members of the different tribes may be settled upon homesteads, and by their example lead others to follow, breaking away from tribal customs and substituting therefor the love of home, the interest of the family, and the rule of the state.

The Indian character and nature are such that they are not easily led while brooding over unadjusted wrongs. This is especially so regarding their lands. Matters arising from the construction and operation of railroads across some of the reservations, and claims of title and right of occupancy set up by white persons to some of the land within other reservations, require legislation for their final adjustment.

The settlement of these matters will remove many embarrassments to progress in the work of leading the Indians to the adoption of our institutions and bringing them under the operation, the influence, and the protection of the universal laws of our country.

The recommendations of the Secretary of the Interior and the Commissioner of the General Land-Office looking to the better protection of public lands and of the public surveys, the preservation of national forests, the adjudication of grants to States and corporations and of private land claims, and the increased efficiency of the public land service, are commended to the attention of Congress. To secure the widest distribution of public lands in limited quantities among settlers for residence and cultivation and thus make the greatest number of individual homes, was the primary object of the public land legislation in the early days of the republic. This system was a simple one. It commenced with an admirable scheme of public surveys, by which the humblest citizen could identify the tract upon which he wished to establish his home. The price of lands was placed within the reach of all the enterprising, industrious, and honest pioneer citizens of the country. It was soon, however, found that the object of the laws was perverted under the system of cash sales, from a distribution of land among the people to an accumulation of land capital by wealthy and speculative persons. To check this tendency a preference right of purchase was given to settlers on the land, a plan which culminated in the general pre-emption act of 1841. The foundation of this system was actual residence and cultivation. Twenty years later the homestead law was devised to more surely place actual homes in the possession of actual cultivators of the soil. The land was given without price, the sole conditions being residence, improvement, and cultivation. Other laws have followed, each designed to encourage the acquirement and use of land in limited individual quantities. But in later years these laws, through vicious administrative methods and under changed conditions of communication and transportation, have been so evaded and violated that their beneficent purpose is threatened with entire defeat. The methods of such evasions and violations are set forth in detail in the reports of the Secretary of the Interior and Commissioner of the General Land-Office. The rapid appropriation of our public lands without *bona-fide* settlements or cultivation, and not only without intention of residence, but for the purpose of their aggregation in large holdings, in many cases in the hands of foreigners, invites the serious and immediate attention of the Congress.

The energies of the land department have been devoted during the present administration to remedy defects and correct abuses in the public land service. The results of these efforts are so largely in the nature of reforms in the processes and methods of our land system as to prevent adequate estimate; but it appears by a compilation from the reports of the Commissioner of the General Land-Office that the immediate effect in leading cases which have come to a final termination has been the restoration to the mass of public lands of two million seven hundred and fifty thousand acres; that two million three hundred and seventy thousand acres are embraced in investigations now pending before the department or the courts, and that the action of Congress has been asked to effect the restoration of two million seven hundred and ninety thousand acres additional; besides which four million acres have been withheld from reservation, and the rights of entry thereon maintained.

I recommend the repeal of the pre-emption and timber-culture acts, and that the homestead laws be so amended as to better secure compliance with their requirements of residence, improvement, and cultivation for the period of five years from date of entry, without commutation or provision for speculative relinquishment. I also recommend the repeal of the desert-land laws unless it shall be the pleasure of the Congress to so amend these laws as to render them less liable to abuses. As the chief motive for an evasion of the laws, and the principal cause of their result in land accumulation instead of land distribution, is the facility with which transfers are made of the right intended to be secured to settlers, it may be deemed advisable to provide by legislation some guards and checks upon the alienation of homestead rights and lands covered thereby until patents issue.

Last year an executive proclamation was issued directing the removal of fences which inclosed the public domain. Many of these have been removed in obedience to such order; but much of the public land still remains within the lines of these unlawful fences. The ingenious methods resorted to in order to continue these trespasses, and the hardihood of the pre-

tenses by which in some cases such inclosure justified, are fully detailed in the report of the tary of the Interior.

The removal of the fences still remaining whi close public lands will be enforced with all t thority and means with which the executive b of the Government is or shall be invested by the gress for that purpose.

The report of the Commissioner of Pension tains a detailed and most satisfactory exhibit operations of the Pension Bureau during the last year. The amount of work done was the larg any year since the organization of the bureau; has been done at less cost than during the pre year in every division.

On the 30th day of June, 1886, there were 8 pensioners on the rolls of the bureau.

Since 1861 there have been 1,018,735 applic for pensions filed, of which 78,834 were based service in the War of 1812. There were 621, these applications allowed, including 60,178 t soldiers of 1812 and their widows.

The total amount paid for pensions since 18 $808,624,811.57.

The number of new pensions allowed durin year ended June 30, 1886, is 40,857—a larger n than has been allowed in any year save one 1861; the names of 2,299 pensioners which had previously dropped from the rolls, were restored ing the year, and after deducting those dropped in the same time for various causes, a net in remains for the year of 20,858 names.

From Jan. 1, 1861, to Dec. 1, 1885, 1,967 p pension acts had been passed. Since the last tioned date, and during the last session of the gress, 644 such acts became laws.

It seems to me that no one can examine our pe establishment and its operations, without being vinced that through its instrumentality justice c very nearly done to all who are entitled under ent laws to the pension bounty of the Govern but it is undeniable that cases exist, well entit relief, in which the Pension Bureau is powerl aid the really worthy. Cases of this class are su only lack by misfortune the kind or quality of which the law and regulations of the bureau re or which, though their merit is apparent, for other reason can not be justly dealt with through eral laws, and these conditions fully justify ap tion to Congress and special enactments; but t sort to Congress for a special pension act to ove the deliberate and careful determination of the sion Bureau on the merits is to secure favorable when it could not be expected under most l execution of the laws. It must be admitted tha opens the doors to the allowance of questio claims, and presents to the legislative and exec branches of the Government applications conce not within the law and plainly devoid of meri so surrounded by sentiment and patriotic feelin they are hard to resist. I suppose it will not t nied that many claims for pensions are made wi merit and that many have been allowed upon fr lent representations. This has been declared the Pension Bureau, not only in this, but in administrations.

The usefulness and the justice of any syste the distribution of pensions depend upon the eq and uniformity of its operation.

It will be seen from the report of the Commiss that there are now paid by the Government one dred and thirty-one different rates of pension.

He estimates from the best information he ca tain that nine thousand of those who have serv the Army and Navy of the United States are supported, in whole or in part, from public fun by organized charities, exclusive of those in sol homes under the direction and control of the Go ment. Only 13 per cent. of these are pensio while of the entire number of men furnished fo late war something like 90 per cent., including their widows and relatives, have been or now are in the receipt of pensions.

The American people, with a patriotic and grateful regard for our ex-soldiers—too broad and too sacred to be monopolized by any special advocates—are not only willing but anxious that equal and exact justice should be done to all honest claimants for pensions. In their sight the friendless and destitute soldier, dependent on public charity, if otherwise entitled, has precisely the same right to share in the provision made for those who fought their country's battles as those better able, through friends and influence, to push their claims. Every pension that is granted under our present plan upon any other grounds than actual service and injury or disease incurred in such service, and every instance of the many in which pensions are increased on other grounds than the merits of the claim, work an injustice to the brave and crippled, but poor and friendless soldier, who is entirely neglected, or who must be content with the smallest sum allowed under general laws.

There are far too many neighborhoods in which are found glaring cases of inequality of treatment in the matter of pensions; and they are largely due to a yielding in the Pension Bureau to importunity on the part of those, other than the pensioner, who are especially interested, or they arise from special acts passed for the benefit of individuals.

The men who fought side by side should stand side by side when they participate in a grateful nation's kind remembrance.

Every consideration of fairness and justice to our ex-soldiers and the protection of the patriotic instinct of our citizens from perversion and violation, point to the adoption of a pension system broad and comprehensive enough to cover every contingency, and which shall make unnecessary an objectionable volume of special legislation.

As long as we adhere to the principle of granting pensions for service, and disability as the result of the service, the allowance of pensions should be restricted to cases presenting these features.

Every patriotic heart responds to a tender consideration for those who, having served their country long and well, are reduced to destitution and dependence, not as an incident of their service, but with advancing age or through sickness or misfortune. We are all tempted by the contemplation of such a condition to supply relief, and are often impatient of the limitations of public duty. Yielding to no one in the desire to indulge this feeling of consideration, I can not rid myself of the conviction that if these ex-soldiers are to be relieved, they and their cause are entitled to the benefit of an enactment under which relief may be claimed as a right, and that such relief should be granted under the sanction of law, not in evasion of it; nor should such worthy objects of care, all equally entitled, be remitted to the unequal operation of sympathy, or the tender mercies of social and political influence with their unjust discriminations.

The discharged soldiers and sailors of the country are our fellow-citizens, and interested with us in the passage and faithful execution of wholesome laws. They can not be swerved from their duty of citizenship by artful appeals to their spirit of brotherhood born of common peril and suffering, nor will they exact as a test of devotion to their welfare a willingness to neglect public duty in their behalf.

On the 4th of March, 1885, the current business of the Patent-Office was, on an average, five and a half months in arrears, and, in several divisions more than twelve months behind. At the close of the last fiscal year such current work was but three months in arrears, and it is asserted and believed that in the next few months the delay in obtaining an examination of an application for a patent will be but nominal.

The number of applications for patents during the last fiscal year, including reissues, designs, trademarks, and labels, equals 40,678, which is considerably in excess of the number received during any preceding year.

The receipts of the Patent-Office during the year aggregate $1,205,167.80, enabling the office to turn into the Treasury a surplus revenue, over and above all expenditures, of about $163,710.30.

The number of patents granted during the last fiscal year, including reissues, trade-marks, designs, and labels, was 25,619—a number also quite largely in excess of that of any preceding year.

The report of the Commissioners shows the office to be in a prosperous condition, and constantly increasing in its business. No increase of force is asked for.

The amount estimated for the fiscal year ending June 30, 1886, was $890,760. The amount estimated for the year ending June 30, 1887, was $853,960. The amount estimated for the fiscal year ending June 30, 1888, is $778,770.

The Secretary of the Interior suggests a change in the plan for the payment of the indebtedness of the Pacific subsidized roads to the Government. His suggestion has the unanimous indorsement of the persons selected by the Government to act as directors of these roads and protect the interests of the United States in the board of direction. In considering the plan proposed, the sole matters which should be taken into account, in my opinion, are the situation of the Government as a creditor, and the surest way to secure the payment of the principal and interest of its debt.

By a recent decision of the Supreme Court of the United States it has been adjudged that the laws of the several States are inoperative to regulate rates of transportation upon railroads, if such regulation interferes with the rate of carriage from one State into another. This important field of control and regulation having been thus left entirely unoccupied, the expediency of Federal action upon the subject is worthy of consideration.

The relations of labor to capital and of laboring men to their employers are of the utmost concern to every patriotic citizen. When these are strained and distorted, unjustifiable claims are apt to be insisted upon by both interests, and in the controversy which results, the welfare of all and the prosperity of the country are jeopardized. Any intervention of the General Government, within the limits of its constitutional authority, to avert such a condition, should be willingly accorded.

In a special message transmitted to the Congress at its last session I suggested the enlargement of our present Labor Bureau and adding to its present functions the power of arbitration in cases where differences arise between employer and employed. When these differences reach such a stage as to result in the interruption of commerce between the States, the application of this remedy by the General Government might be regarded as entirely within its constitutional powers. And I think we might reasonably hope that such arbitrators, if carefully selected and if entitled to the confidence of the parties to be affected, would be voluntarily called to the settlement of controversies of less extent and not necessarily within the domain of Federal regulation.

I am of the opinion that this suggestion is worthy the attention of the Congress.

But after all has been done by the passage of laws either Federal or State to relieve a situation full of solicitude, much more remains to be accomplished by the reinstatement and cultivation of a true American sentiment which recognizes the equality of American citizenship. This, in the light of our traditions and in loyalty to the spirit of our institutions, would teach that a hearty co-operation on the part of all interests is the surest path to national greatness and the happiness of all our people, that capital should, in recognition of the brotherhood of our citizenship and in a spirit of American fairness, generously accord to labor its just compensation and consideration, and that contented labor is capital's best protection and faithful ally. It would teach, too, that the diverse situations of our people are inseparable from our civilization, that every citizen should, in his sphere, be a contributor to the general good, that capital does not necessarily tend to the oppression of labor, and that violent disturbances and disorders alienate from their promoters true American sympathy and kindly feeling.

The Department of Agriculture, representing the oldest and largest of our national industries, is subserving well the purposes of its organization. By the introduction of new subjects of farming enterprise, and by opening new sources of agricultural wealth and the dissemination of early information concerning production and prices, it has contributed largely to the country's prosperity. Through this agency, advanced thought and investigation touching the subjects it has in charge should, among other things, be practically applied to the home production at a low cost of articles of food which are now imported from abroad. Such an innovation will necessarily, of course, in the beginning, be within the domain of intelligent experiment; and the subject in every stage should receive all possible encouragement from the Government.

The interests of millions of our citizens engaged in agriculture are involved in an enlargement and improvement of the results of their labor; and a zealous regard for their welfare should be willing tribute to those whose productive returns are a main source of our progress and power.

The existence of pleuro-pneumonia among the cattle of various States has led to burdensome and in some cases disastrous restrictions in an important branch of our commerce, threatening to affect the quantity and quality of our food-supply. This is a matter of such importance and of such far-reaching consequence, that I hope it will engage the serious attention of the Congress, to the end that such a remedy may be applied as the limits of a constitutional delegation of power to the General Government will permit.

I commend to the consideration of the Congress the report of the Commissioner, and his suggestions concerning the interest intrusted to his care.

The continued operation of the law relating to our Civil Service has added the most convincing proofs of its necessity and usefulness. It is a fact worthy of note that every public officer who has a just idea of his duty to the people, testifies to the value of this reform. Its stanchest friends are found among those who understand it best, and its warmest supporters are those who are restrained and protected by its requirements.

The meaning of such restraint and protection is not appreciated by those who want places under the Government, regardless of merit and efficiency, nor by those who insist that the selection for such places should rest upon a proper credential showing active partisan work. They mean to public officers, if not their lives, the only opportunity afforded them to attend to public business, and they mean to the good people of the country the better performance of the work of their Government.

It is exceedingly strange that the scope and nature of this reform are so little understood, and that so many things not included within its plan are called by its name. When cavil yields more fully to examination the system will have large additions to the number of its friends.

Our Civil-Service reform may be imperfect in some of its details; it may be misunderstood and opposed; it may not always be faithfully applied; its designs may sometimes miscarry through mistake or willful intent; it may sometimes tremble under the assaults of its enemies or languish under the misguided zeal of impracticable friends; but if the people of this country ever submit to the banishment of its underlying principle from the operation of their Government, they will abandon the surest guarantee of the safety and success of American institutions.

I invoke for this reform the cheerful and ungrudging support of the Congress. I renew my recommendation made last year that the salaries of the Commissioners

be made equal to other officers of the Gover[n] having like duties and responsibilities, and I hop such reasonable appropriations may be made [a] enable them to increase the usefulness of the they have in charge.

I desire to call the attention of the Congres plain duty which the Government owes to the [c] itors in the Freedman's Savings and Trust Com

This company was chartered by the Congre the benefit of the most illiterate and humble [o] people, and with the intention of encouraging in industry and thrift. Most of its branches wer[e] sided over by officers holding the commission clothed in the uniform of the United States. [?] and other circumstances reasonably, I think, led simple people to suppose that the invitation to d their hard-earned savings in this institution in an undertaking on the part of their Governmen their money should be safely kept for them.

When this company failed it was liable in the of $2,939,925.22 to 61,131 depositors. Divi amounting in the aggregate to 62 per cent. have declared, and the sum called for and paid of such dends seems to be $1,648,181.72. This sum d[o] ed from the entire amount of deposits leaves $1 744.50 still unpaid. Past experience has show[n] quite a large part of this sum will not be calle There are assets still on hand amounting to the mated sum of $16,000.

I think the remaining 38 per cent. of such of deposits as have claimants should be paid by the ernment, upon principles of equity and fairnes

The report of the Commissioner, soon to be la[id] fore Congress, will give more satisfactory detai this subject.

The control of the affairs of the District of Colu having been placed in the hands of purely exec officers, while the Congress still retains all legis[l] authority relating to its government, it become duty to make known the most pressing needs o District and recommend their consideration.

The laws of the District appear to be in an u tain and unsatisfactory condition, and their cod tion or revision is much needed.

During the past year one of the bridges le[a] from the District to the State of Virginia becam fit for use, and travel upon it was forbidden. leads me to suggest that the improvement of al bridges crossing the Potomac and its branches, the city of Washington, is worthy of the attenti[on] Congress.

The Commissioners of the District represent the laws regulating the sale of liquor and gra licenses therefor should be at once amended, and legislation is needed to consolidate, define, an[d] large the scope and powers of charitable and [?] institutions within the District.

I suggest that the Commissioners be clothed the power to make, within fixed limitations, [?] regulations. I believe this power, granted and fully guarded, would tend to subserve the good [?] of the municipality.

It seems that trouble still exists growing out o occupation of the streets and avenues by certain roads having their termini in the city. It is ver[y] portant that such laws should be enacted upon subject as will secure to the railroads all the faci they require for the transaction of their business at the same time protect citizens from injury to persons or property.

The Commissioners again complain that the ac modations afforded them for the necessary office District business, and for the safe keeping of [?] able books and papers, are entirely insufficien recommend that this condition of affairs be rem[e] by the Congress, and that suitable quarters be nished for the needs of the District government.

In conclusion, I earnestly invoke such wise a on the part of the people's legislators, as will sub[serve] the public good and demonstrate during the re[s]

ing days of the Congress as at present organized, its ability and inclination to so meet the people's needs that it shall be gratefully remembered by an expectant constituency. GROVER CLEVELAND.
WASHINGTON, *December 6, 1886.*

Counting the Electoral Votes.—March 17, 1886, a bill to fix the day for the meeting of the electors of President and Vice-President, and to provide for and regulate the counting of the votes for President and Vice-President, and the decision of questions arising thereon, passed the Senate. December 7, the measure was reported with certain amendments to the House from a select committee to consider the subject. The following is the bill as reported, with the passages stricken out inclosed in brackets and those inserted printed in italics:

Be it enacted, etc., That the electors of each State shall meet and give their votes on the second Monday in January next following their appointment, at such place in each State as the Legislature of such State shall direct.

SEC. 2. That if any State shall have provided, by laws enacted prior to the day fixed for the appointment of the electors, for its final determination of any controversy or contest concerning the appointment of all or any of the electors of such State, by judicial or other methods or procedures, and such determination shall have been made at least six days before the time fixed for the meeting of the electors, such determination made pursuant to such law so existing on said day, and made at least six days prior to the said time of meeting of the electors, shall be conclusive, and shall govern in the counting of the electoral votes as provided in the Constitution, and as hereinafter regulated, so far as the ascertainment of the electors appointed by such State is concerned.

SEC. 3. That it shall be the duty of the Executive of each State, as soon as practicable after the conclusion of the appointment of electors in such State, by the final ascertainment under and in pursuance of the laws of such State providing for such ascertainment, to communicate, under the seal of the State, to the Secretary of State of the United States, a certificate of such ascertainment of the electors appointed, setting forth the names of such electors and the canvass or other ascertainment under the laws of such State of the number of votes given or cast for each person for whose appointment any and all votes have been given or cast; and it shall also thereupon be the duty of the Executive of each State to deliver to the electors of such State, on or before the day on which they are required by the preceding section to meet, the same certificate, in triplicate, under the seal of the State; and such certificate shall be inclosed and transmitted by the electors at the same time and in the same manner as is provided by law for transmitting by such electors to the seat of Government the lists of all persons voted for as President and of all persons voted for as Vice-President; and section 136 of the Revised Statutes is hereby repealed; and if there shall have been any final determination in a State of a controversy or contest as provided for in section 2 of this act, it shall be the duty of the Executive of such State, as soon as practicable after such determination, to communicate, under the seal of the State, to the Secretary of State of the United States, a certificate of such determination, in form and manner as the same shall have been made; and the Secretary of State of the United States, as soon as practicable after the receipt at the State Department of each of the certificates hereinbefore directed to be transmitted to the Secretary of State, shall publish, in such public newspaper as he shall designate, such certificates in full; and at the first meeting of Congress thereafter he shall transmit to the two Houses of Congress copies in full

of each and every such certificate so received theretofore at the State Department.

SEC. 4. That Congress shall be in session on the second Wednesday in February succeeding every meeting of the electors. The Senate and House of Representatives shall meet in the hall of the House of Representatives at the hour of one o'clock in the afternoon on that day, and the President of the Senate shall be their presiding officer. Two tellers shall be previously appointed on the part of the Senate and two on the part of the House of Representatives, to whom shall be handed, as they are opened by the President of the Senate, all the certificates and papers purporting to be certificates of the electoral votes, which certificates and papers shall be opened, presented, and acted upon in the alphabetical order of the States, beginning with the letter A; and said tellers, having then read the same in the presence and hearing of the two Houses, shall make a list of the votes as they shall appear from the said certificates; and the votes having been ascertained and counted in the manner and according to the rules in this act provided, the result of the same shall be delivered to the President of the Senate, who shall thereupon announce the state of the vote, and the names of the persons, if any, elected, which announcement shall be deemed a sufficient declaration of the persons, if any, elected President and Vice-President of the United States, and, together with a list of the votes, be entered on the journals of the two Houses. Upon such reading of any such certificate or paper, the President of the Senate shall call for objections, if any. Every objection shall be made in writing, and shall state clearly and concisely, and without argument, the ground thereof, and shall be signed by at least one Senator and one member of the House of Representatives before the same shall be received. When all objections so made to any vote or paper from a State shall have been received and read, the Senate shall thereupon withdraw, and such objections shall be submitted to the Senate for its decision; and the Speaker of the House of Representatives shall, in like manner, submit such objections to the House of Representatives for its decision; and no electoral vote or votes from any State from which but one *lawful* return has been received shall be rejected [except by the affirmative vote of both Houses]. If more than one return or paper purporting to be a return from a State shall have been received by the President of the Senate. those votes, and those only, shall be counted which shall have been regularly given by the electors who are shown by the determination mentioned in section 2 of this act to have been appointed, if the determination in said section provided for shall have been made, or by such successors or substitutes, in case of a vacancy in the board of electors so ascertained, as have been appointed to fill such vacancy in the mode provided by the laws of the State; but in case there shall arise the question which of two or more of such State authorities determining what electors have been appointed, as mentioned in section 2 of this act, is the lawful tribunal of such State, the votes regularly given of those electors, and those only, of such State shall be counted whose title as electors the two Houses, acting separately, shall concurrently decide is supported by the decision of such State so authorized by its laws; and in such case of more than one return or paper purporting to be a return from a State, if there shall have been no such determination of the question in the State aforesaid, then those votes, and those only, shall be counted which [the two Houses, acting separately, shall concurrently decide to be the lawful votes of the legally appointed electors of such State] *were cast by electors whose appointment shall have been duly certified under the seal of the State by the Executive thereof, in accordance with the laws of the State, unless the two Houses, acting separately, shall concurrently decide such votes not to be the lawful votes of the legally appointed electors of such State.* When the two Houses have voted, they shall immediately again meet, and the presiding officer shall then announce the decision of the question submitted. No votes or papers from any other State shall be acted upon until the objections previously made to the votes or papers from any State shall have been finally disposed of.

Sec. 5. That while the two Houses shall be in meeting as provided in this act the President of the Senate shall have power to preserve order; and no debate shall be allowed and no question shall be put by the presiding officer except to either House on a motion to withdraw.

Sec. 6. That when the two Houses separate to decide upon an objection that may have been made to the counting of any electoral vote or votes from any State, or other question arising in the matter, each Senator and Representative may speak to such objection or question five minutes, and not more than once; but after such debate shall have lasted two hours it shall be the duty of the presiding officer of each House to put the main question without further debate.

Sec. 7. That at such joint meeting of the two Houses, seats shall be provided as follows: For the President of the Senate, the Speaker's chair; for the Speaker, immediately upon his left; the Senators, in the body of the hall upon the right of the presiding officer; for the Representatives, in the body of the hall not provided for the Senators; for the tellers, Secretary of the Senate, and Clerk of the House of Representatives, at the Clerk's desk; for the other officers of the two Houses, in front of the Clerk's desk and upon each side of the Speaker's platform. Such joint meeting shall not be dissolved until the count of electoral votes shall be completed and the result declared; and no recess shall be taken unless a question shall have arisen in regard to counting any such votes, or otherwise under this act, in which case it shall be competent for either House, acting separately, in the manner hereinbefore provided, to direct a recess of such House not beyond the next calendar day, Sunday excepted, at the hour of ten o'clock in the forenoon. But if the counting of the electoral votes and the declaration of the result shall not have been completed before the fifth calendar day next after such first meeting of the two Houses, no further or other recess shall be taken by either House.

In explanation of the measure, Mr. Eden, of Illinois, said:

"The object of the bill of the Senate is to fix certain rules by which the two Houses shall be governed in counting the electoral vote.

"In case of but one return from a State, the Senate bill allows the vote to be rejected by the affirmative vote of both Houses.

"When there is more than one return from a State, and a tribunal of the State, according to section 2 of the bill, has determined who are the lawfully appointed electors of the State, the votes of such electors are to be counted without question.

"If a question arises as to which of two or more of such State authorities, acting under section 2 of the bill, is the lawful tribunal of the State, then the vote of such electors only shall be counted as the two Houses, acting separately, shall concurrently decide is supported by the decision of such State so acting under its laws.

"In case of more than one return from a State, if no determination has been made by a tribunal thereof as to which is the lawful return, then those votes only shall be counted

which the two Houses, acting separately, shall concurrently decide to be the lawful votes of the legally appointed electors of the State.

"It will thus be seen that under the Senate bill there are three contingencies in which the two Houses in counting the electoral vote may refuse to count the vote of the State.

"The House committee has undertaken to remedy this defect by a limitation of the power of the two Houses to reject the vote of a State. We propose to amend the bill so that where there is but one return, or paper purporting to be a return, from a State, and the vote was regularly given, and the credentials of the electors are in due form and in accordance with the laws of the State, and properly certified by the executive authority thereof, the vote shall be counted.

"We propose a further amendment, that where there are two or more returns from a State, and no tribunal thereof has determined who are the legally appointed electors from the State, the votes regularly given by electors, whose appointment shall have been duly certified under the seal of the State by the Executive thereof, in accordance with the laws of the State, shall be counted, unless the two Houses, acting separately, shall concurrently decide such votes not to be the lawful votes of the legally appointed electors of such State. If the amendments proposed by the House committee be agreed to, there will be but one contingency in which the vote of a State may be rejected. That contingency is the presentation of double returns from a State by opposing State authorities, disagreeing in the determination as to which set of electors are the legally appointed electors of the State. In that case no electoral vote of the State will be counted unless the two Houses, acting separately, shall concurrently decide that one of the opposing sets of electors are the duly appointed electors of the State.

"In case of more than one return from a State, where no State tribunal has determined the question as to which is the true and lawful return, the vote of those electors regularly given who bear the official certificate of the Governor under the seal of the State, showing that they were duly appointed in pursuance of the laws of the State, under our amendment are to be counted unless rejected by the concurrent vote of both Houses, acting separately. I am of opinion that with the adoption of the proposed amendments the Senate bill may be safely passed, and that no question will remain to be determined relative to the count of the electoral vote, when the two Houses meet for that purpose, that can not be rightfully determined in accordance with the terms of this bill. Under the bill as thus amended the States are left not only to appoint the electors, but to determine all disputes relative to their appointment.

"If no dispute arises relative to the appointment, and no contesting electors appear to demand a hearing, the bill as amended, should it become a law, absolutely requires the electoral vote of the State to be counted. If a dispute or contest has arisen relative to the appointment of electors, and the proper State authorities have determined who are the lawfully appointed electors, the bill as amended says the vote shall be counted. If more than one return of electoral votes is made from a State, and no determination has been made under its laws who, of the opposing forces, were lawfully appointed electors of the State, the bill as amended requires that the vote of those electors regularly given, who hold the certificate of the Governor under the seal of the State, showing that they were appointed according to the laws of the State, shall be counted, unless rejected by the concurrent vote of the two Houses, acting separately.

"In the one instance only, where a question arises as to which of two or more State authorities, acting under the second section of the bill, and having made conflicting decisions as to lawfully appointed electors from the State, is the concurrent action of both Houses required to decide as to the legally appointed electors from a State. In case no decision can be reached, of course the vote of the State will be lost; but that is an extreme case, and one not likely to arise except in revolutionary times."

Mr. Adams, of Illinois, in criticism of the measure, said:

"Whenever the two Houses of Congress agree that a certain alleged return is the legal vote of a State, their determination that that alleged return is the legal return is the counting of the vote of that State within the meaning of the Constitution; and whenever the two Houses of Congress agree that a certain alleged return does not represent the legal vote of the State, their concurrent determination that that alleged return is not the legal vote of the State is equivalent to a refusal to count the vote of that State within the meaning of the Constitution; hence, my judgment is that the entire scope of our power to legislate on this matter must be confined to the third contingency, namely, the case in which the two Houses of Congress neither concurrently vote 'yea' upon the proposition nor concurrently vote 'nay' upon it, but differ in opinion, and one decides one way and the other the other. The power of Congress to intervene in such a case arises, in my judgment, out of the necessity of the case, and the exercise of our legislative power to meet the contingency must be considered now to be in accordance with the meaning of the Constitution.

"There are several causes, Mr. Speaker, why it may be determined that an alleged vote of a State is not the real vote of the State.

"In the first place the persons claiming to be electors may not have been voted for by the people of their State according to the provisions of the Constitution and the laws enacted by the State.

"In the second place the persons assuming to have been elected as electors may have been ineligible to that office.

"In the third place, admitting that they were eligible and were duly elected, yet when they met to cast the electoral votes it may be that they did not cast them in accordance with the Constitution and the laws; and, fourthly, if in all their acts they complied with the Constitution and the law, and they are eligible to act as electors, and have been duly voted for as such, at the polls, yet the persons for whom they vote may not have been eligible to the office to which they assumed to elect them; and, in my judgment, notwithstanding the changes that have come over the character of Presidential elections in this country, these objections to the validity of an alleged electoral vote stand in full force to-day, and will so stand until the Constitution has been amended.

"I am aware that some of these cases of invalidity are not so important in our minds as they were in the minds of the framers of the Constitution. To us it may make little difference whether a person chosen as an elector is a Senator or Representative or person holding an office of profit and trust under the Government. To us it may appear to make little difference whether the electors vote by ballot as the law requires or not; or whether they cast their votes upon the day appointed by law or not.

"To us accustomed to the choice of a Presidential candidate by the convention of a political party, it may appear of less importance than it appeared to our fathers that the President elected should be a native-born citizen, or over thirty-five years of age. Yet all these provisions are still the provisions of the Constitution, and in my judgment it is not our duty to disregard them; it is our duty to observe them until in the wisdom of Congress and of the people it shall have been determined that the Constitution shall be changed.

"The reason why I refer to these different causes of invalidity is that, if the amendment proposed by the House committee is adopted, the only means which we have or can have for enforcing these provisions of the Constitution will have been done away forever. I know that when the two Houses of Congress meet here to count the electoral vote, the main question present to their minds and present to the minds of the people is the question which Presidential candidate the people appear to have preferred. And yet, so long as these provisions regarding the eligibility of electors, regarding the eligibility of a Presidential candidate, regarding the form and manner in which the electoral vote shall be cast, remain as portions of the Constitution, it is not only our bounden duty to observe and abide by them, but it is also the bounden duty of those two Houses of Congress, who have a duty imposed on them which is not imposed on us in passing upon this bill, the duty, namely, of sitting here in joint convention and deciding upon the electoral vote submitted to them by the President of the Senate.

"But, Mr. Speaker, the main objection I have to the amendment proposed by the House committee, namely, the proposed striking out of the words 'except by the affirmative vote of the two Houses,' the effect of which would be that a single return would have a conclusive presumption of validity in its favor—the main objection which I have to that provision is that I believe it possesses no legal and constitutional validity whatever. However wise it may seem to us, in attempting to legislate on this subject, that a single return shall be conclusively presumed to be valid, the real question will arise when the two Houses meet here to pass upon the electoral votes in the next Presidential election; and those Houses, in my judgment, when they meet here to discharge a duty which is expressly imposed upon them by the Constitution, will not be bound by the action of the Senate and House of the Forty-ninth Congress and the President, when he signs this bill, if it shall pass. It is their duty, conferred on them by the Constitution, to count the votes. If for any reason whatever a single return shall appear to both Houses of Congress to be an invalid return they have the right so to determine; and if they do so determine, that vote will not be counted, however many statutes we may pass like this."

Mr. Oates, of Alabama, moved to "amend section 4 by striking out of lines 20 and 21 the following words: 'and the names of the persons, if any, elected'; so that the provision, if amended, will read: 'who [the President of the Senate] shall thereupon announce the state of the vote; which announcement shall be deemed a sufficient declaration of the persons, if any, elected President and Vice-President of the United States.'" The amendment was adopted by a vote of 141 to 109. Mr. Eden, of Illinois, moved the following amendment, which was also adopted:

After the word "State," in line 37, of section 4, insert "which shall have been regularly given by electors whose appointment has been certified to according to section 3 of this act"; so that the clause will read as follows:

"And the Speaker of the House of Representatives shall, in like manner, submit such objections to the House of Representatives for its decision; and no electoral vote or votes from any State which shall have been regularly given by electors whose appointment has been certified to according to section 3 of this act, from which but one return has been received, shall be rejected."

The bill was then passed, December 9, without a division. The Senate non-concurred in the House amendments, and a conference committee was appointed which reported Jan. 14, 1887, as follows:

That the Senate agree to the amendments of the House numbered 1 and 2.

That the Senate agree to the amendment of the House numbered 3 with an amendment, to wit: On page 8, line 30, insert in the sentence proposed by the House to be inserted in the bill, after the "been," and before the word "certified," the "lawfully"; and that the House agree to the sa

That the Senate agree to the amendment o House numbered 4, with an amendment, to wi lieu of the words stricken out by the House inse following: "but the two Houses concurrently reject the vote or votes when they agree that vote or votes have not been so regularly give electors whose appointment has been so certifi and that the House agree to the same.

That the Senate agree to the amendment o House numbered 5, with an amendment, to wi lieu of the words proposed to be stricken out a be inserted insert as follows: "the two Houses concurrently decide were cast by lawful elector pointed in accordance with the laws of the State less the two Houses, acting separately, shall co rently decide such votes not to be the lawful of the legally appointed electors of such State. if the two Houses shall disagree in respect o counting of such votes, then, and in that case votes of the electors whose appointment shall been certified by the Executive of the State, unde seal thereof, shall be counted"; and that the H agree to the same.

Both Houses adopted the conference rep and the measure was approved by the Pr dent Feb. 3, 1887.

Polygamy.—Jan. 8, 1886, a bill passed Senate to amend an act entitled "An ac amend section 5352 of the Revised Statute the United States in reference to bigamy, for other purposes," approved March 22, 1 The Judiciary Committee of the House rep ed this measure Jan. 12, 1887, with a substit The substitute proposed by the committee slightly amended on motion of Mr. Tucker Virginia, and then passed without a divis January 13, the Senate non-concurred in House amendments, and a conference comm tee was appointed. February 15, the con ence committee reported recommending passage of the following measure:

SECTION 1. That in any proceeding or examina before a grand jury, a judge, justice, or a United St commissioner, or a court, in any prosecution for amy, polygamy, or unlawful cohabitation, under statute of the United States, the lawful husband wife of the person accused shall be a competent ness, and may be called, but shall not be compelle testify in such proceeding, examination, or prosecu without the consent of the husband or wife, as the c may be; and such witness shall not be permitted testify as to any statement or communication made either husband or wife to each other, during the ex ence of the marriage relation, deemed confidentia common law.

SEC. 2. That in any prosecution for bigamy, pol amy, or unlawful cohabitation, under any statute the United States, whether before a United St commissioner, justice, judge, a grand jury, or court, an attachment for any witness may be issu by the court, judge, or commissioner, without a p vious subpoena, compelling the immediate atten ance of such witness, when it shall appear by oath affirmation, to the commissioner, justice, judge, court, as the case may be, that there is reasona ground to believe that such witness will unlawfu fail to obey a subpoena issued and served in the us course in such cases; and in such case the usual w ness fee shall be paid to such witness so attache Provided, That the person so attached may at a time secure his or her discharge from custody by e cuting a recognizance, with sufficient surety, con tioned for the appearance of such person at the proper time, as a witness in the cause or proceeding wherein the attachment may be issued.

SEC. 3. That whoever commits adultery shall be punished by imprisonment in the penitentiary not exceeding three years; and when the act is committed between a married woman and a man who is unmarried, both parties to such act shall be deemed guilty of adultery; and when such act is committed between a married man and a woman who is unmarried, the man shall be deemed guilty of adultery.

SEC. 4. That if any person related to another person within and not including the fourth degree of consanguinity computed according to the rules of the civil law, shall marry or cohabit with, or have sexual intercourse with such other so related person, knowing her or him to be within said degree of relationship, the person so offending shall be deemed guilty of incest, and, on conviction thereof, shall be punished by imprisonment in the penitentiary not less than three years and not more than fifteen years.

SEC. 5. That if an unmarried man or woman commit fornication, each of them shall be punished by imprisonment not exceeding six months, or by fine not exceeding $100.

SEC. 6. That all laws of the Legislative Assembly of the Territory of Utah which provide that prosecutions for adultery can only be commenced on the complaint of the husband or wife are hereby disapproved and annulled; and all prosecutions for adultery may hereafter be instituted in the same way that prosecutions for other crimes are.

SEC. 7. That commissioners appointed by the Supreme Court and district courts in the Territory of Utah shall possess and may exercise all the powers and jurisdiction that are or may be possessed or exercised by justices of the peace in said Territory under the laws thereof, and the same powers conferred by law on commissioners appointed by circuit courts of the United States.

SEC. 8. That the Marshal of said Territory of Utah, and his deputies, shall possess and may exercise all the powers in executing the laws of the United States or of said Territory possessed and exercised by sheriffs, constables, and their deputies as peace officers; and each of them shall cause all offenders against the law, in his view, to enter into recognizance to keep the peace and to appear at the next term of the court having jurisdiction of the case, and to commit to jail in case of failure to give such recognizance. They shall quell and suppress assaults and batteries, riots, routs, affrays, and insurrections.

SEC. 9. That every ceremony of marriage, or in the nature of a marriage ceremony, of any kind, in any of the Territories of the United States, whether either or both or more of the parties to such ceremony be lawfully competent to be the subjects of such marriage or ceremony or not, shall be certified by a certificate stating the fact and nature of such ceremony, the full names of each of the parties concerned, and the full names of every officer, priest, and person, by whatever style or designation called or known, in any way taking part in the performance of such ceremony, which certificate shall be drawn up and signed by the parties to such ceremony and by every officer, priest, and person taking part in the performance of such ceremony, and shall be by the officer, priest, or other person solemnizing such marriage or ceremony filed in the office of the probate court, or, if there be none, in the office of the court having probate powers in the county or district in which such ceremony shall take place, for record, and shall be immediately recorded, and be at all times subject to inspection as other public records. Such certificate, or the record thereof, or a duly certified copy of such record, shall be *prima-facie* evidence of the facts required by this act to be stated therein, in any proceeding, civil or criminal, in which the matter shall be drawn in question. Any person who shall willfully violate any of the provisions of this section shall be deemed guilty of a misde-

meanor, and shall, on conviction thereof, be punished by a fine of not more than $1,000, or by imprisonment not longer than two years, or by both said punishments, in the discretion of the court.

SEC. 10. That nothing in this act shall be held to prevent the proof of marriages, whether lawful or unlawful, by any evidence now legally admissible for that purpose.

SEC. 11. That the laws enacted by the Legislative Assembly of the Territory of Utah which provide for or recognize the capacity of illegitimate children to inherit or to be entitled to any distributive share in the estate of the father of any such illegitimate child are hereby disapproved and annulled; and no illegitimate child shall hereafter be entitled to inherit from his or her father or to receive any distributive share in the estate of his or her father: *Provided*, That this section shall not apply to any illegitimate child born within twelve months after the passage of this act, nor to any child made legitimate by the seventh section of the act entitled "An act to amend section 5352 of the Revised Statutes of the United States, in reference to bigamy, and for other purposes," approved March 22, 1882.

SEC. 12. That the laws enacted by the Legislative Assembly of the Territory of Utah conferring jurisdiction upon probate courts, or the judges thereof, or any of them, in said Territory, other than in respect of the estates of deceased persons, and in respect of the guardianship of the persons and property of infants, and in respect of the persons and property of persons not of sound mind, are hereby disapproved and annulled; and no probate court or judge of probate shall exercise any jurisdiction other than in respect of the matters aforesaid, except as a member of a county court; and every such jurisdiction so by force of this act withdrawn from the said probate courts or judges shall be had and exercised by the district courts of said Territory, respectively.

SEC. 13. That it shall be the duty of the Attorney-General of the United States to institute and prosecute proceedings to forfeit and escheat to the United States the property of corporations obtained or held in violation of section 3 of the act of Congress approved the 1st day of July, 1862, entitled "An act to punish and prevent the practice of polygamy in the Territories of the United States and other places, and disapproving and annulling certain acts of the Legislative Assembly of the Territory of Utah," or in violation of section 1890 of the Revised Statutes of the United States; and all such property so forfeited and escheated to the United States shall be disposed of by the Secretary of the Interior, and the proceeds thereof applied to the use and benefit of the common schools in the Territory in which such property may be: *Provided*, That no building, or the grounds appurtenant thereto, which is held and occupied exclusively for purposes of the worship of God, or parsonage connected therewith, or burial-ground, shall be forfeited.

SEC. 14. That in any proceeding for the enforcement of the provisions of law against corporations or associations acquiring or holding property in any Territory of the United States in excess of the amount limited by law, the court before which such proceeding may be instituted shall have power in a summary way to compel the production of all books, records, papers, and documents of or belonging to any trustee or person holding or controlling or managing property in which such corporation may have any right, title, or interest whatever.

SEC. 15. That all laws of the Legislative Assembly of the Territory of Utah, or of the so-called government of the State of Deseret, creating, organizing, amending, or continuing the corporation or association called the Perpetual Emigrating Fund Company are hereby disapproved and annulled; and the said corporation, in so far as it may now have, or pretend to have, any legal existence, is hereby dissolved; and it shall not be lawful for the Legislative Assembly of the Territory of Utah to create, organize, or in any manner recognise any such corporation or association, or to pass any law for the purpose of or operating to accomplish the bringing of persons into the said Territory for any purpose whatsoever.

SEC. 16. That it shall be the duty of the Attorney-General of the United States to cause such proceedings to be taken in the Supreme Court of the Territory of Utah as shall be proper to carry into effect the provisions of the preceding section, and pay the debts and to dispose of the property and assets of said corporation according to law. Said property and assets, in excess of the debts and the amount of any lawful claims established by the court against the same, shall escheat to the United States, and shall be taken, invested, and disposed of by the Secretary of the Interior, under the direction of the President of the United States, for the benefit of common schools in said Territory.

SEC. 17. That the acts of the Legislative Assembly of the Territory of Utah, incorporating, continuing, or providing for the corporation known as the Church of Jesus Christ of Latter-Day Saints, and the ordinance of the so-called General Assembly of the State of Deseret incorporating the Church of Jesus Christ of Latter-Day Saints, so far as the same may now have legal force and validity, are hereby disapproved and annulled, and the said corporation, in so far as it may now have, or pretend to have, any legal existence, is hereby dissolved. That it shall be the duty of the Attorney-General of the United States to cause such proceedings to be taken in the Supreme Court of the Territory of Utah as shall be proper to execute the foregoing provisions of this section and to wind up the affairs of said corporation conformably to law; and in such proceedings the court shall have power, and it shall be its duty, to make such decree or decrees as shall be proper to effectuate the transfer of the title to real property now held and used by said corporation for places of worship, and parsonages connected therewith, and burial-grounds, and of the description mentioned in the proviso to section 13 of this act and in section 26 of this act, to the respective trustees mentioned in section 26 of this act; and for the purposes of this section said court shall have all the powers of a court of equity.

SEC. 18. (a) A widow shall be endowed of the third part of all the lands whereof her husband was seized of an estate of inheritance at any time during the marriage, unless she shall have lawfully released her right thereto.

(b) The widow of any alien who at the time of his death shall be entitled by law to hold any real estate, if she be an inhabitant of the Territory at the time of such death, shall be entitled to dower of such estate in the same manner as if such alien had been a native citizen.

(c) If a husband seized of an estate of inheritance in lands exchanges them for other lands, his widow shall not have dower of both, but shall make her election to be endowed of the lands given or of those taken in exchange; and if such election be not evinced by the commencement of proceedings to recover her dower of the lands given in exchange within one year after the death of her husband, she shall be deemed to have elected to take her dower of the lands received in exchange.

(d) When a person seized of an estate of inheritance in lands shall have executed a mortgage, or other conveyance in the nature of mortgage, of such estate, before marriage, his widow shall nevertheless be entitled to dower out of the lands mortgaged or so conveyed, as against every person except the mortgagee or grantee in such conveyance and those claiming under him.

(e) Where a husband shall purchase lands during coverture, and shall at the same time execute a mortgage, or other conveyance in the nature of mortgage, of his estate in such lands to secure the payment of the purchase-money, his widow shall not be entitled to dower out of such lands, as against the mortgagee or grantee in such conveyance or those claiming under him, although she shall not have united in

such mortgage; but she shall be entitled to her dower in such lands as against all other persons.

(f) Where in such case the mortgagee, or such grantee or those claiming under him, shall, after the death of the husband of such widow, cause the land mortgaged or so conveyed to be sold, either under a power of sale contained in the mortgage or such conveyance, or by virtue of the decree of a court, if any surplus shall remain after payment of the moneys due on such mortgage or such conveyance, and the costs and charges of the sale, such widow shall nevertheless be entitled to the interest or income of the one-third part of such surplus for her life as her dower.

(g) A widow shall not be endowed of lands conveyed to her husband by way of mortgage unless he acquire an absolute estate therein during the marriage period.

(h) In case of divorce dissolving the marriage contract for the misconduct of the wife, she shall not be endowed.

SEC. 19. That hereafter the judge of probate in each county within the Territory of Utah provided for by the existing laws thereof shall be appointed by the President of the United States, by and with the advice and consent of the Senate; and so much of the laws of said Territory as provide for the election of such judge by the Legislative Assembly are hereby disapproved and annulled.

SEC. 20. That it shall not be lawful for any female to vote at any election hereafter held in the Territory of Utah for any public purpose whatever, and no such vote shall be received or counted or given effect in any manner whatever; and any and every act of the Legislative Assembly of the Territory of Utah providing for or allowing the registration or voting by females is hereby annulled.

SEC. 21. That all laws of the Legislative Assembly of the Territory of Utah which provide for numbering or identifying the votes of the electors at any election in said Territory are hereby disapproved and annulled; but the foregoing provision shall not preclude the lawful registration of voters, or any other provisions for securing fair elections which do not involve the disclosure of the candidates for whom any particular elector shall have voted.

SEC. 22. That the existing election districts and apportionments of representation concerning the members of the Legislative Assembly of the Territory of Utah are hereby abolished; and it shall be the duty of the Governor, Territorial Secretary, and the Board of Commissioners mentioned in section 9 of the act of Congress approved March 22, 1882, entitled "An act to amend section 5352 of the Revised Statutes of the United States, in reference to bigamy, and for other purposes," in said Territory, forthwith to redistrict said Territory, and apportion representation in the same in such manner as to provide, as nearly as may be, for an equal representation of the people (excepting Indians not taxed), being citizens of the United States, according to numbers, in said Legislative Assembly, and to the number of members of the Council and House of Representatives, respectively, as now established by law; and a record of the establishment of such new districts and the apportionment of representation thereto shall be made in the office of the Secretary of said Territory, and such establishment and representation shall continue until Congress shall otherwise provide; and no persons other than citizens of the United States otherwise qualified shall be entitled to vote at any election in said Territory.

SEC. 23. That the provisions of section 9 of said act approved, March 22, 1882, in regard to registration and election of officers, and the registration of voters, and the conduct of elections, and the powers and duties of the board therein mentioned, shall continue and remain operative until the provisions and laws therein referred to, to be made and enacted by the Legislative Assembly of said Territory of Utah, shall have been made and enacted by said Assembly and shall have been approved by Congress.

SEC. 24. That every male person twenty-one years of age resident in the Territory of Utah shall, as a condition-precedent to his right to register or vote at any election in said Territory, take and subscribe an oath or affirmation, before the registration officer of his voting precinct, that he is over twenty-one years of age, and has resided in the Territory of Utah for six months then last passed and in the precinct for one month immediately preceding the date thereof, and that he is a native-born (or naturalized, as the case may be) citizen of the United States, and further state in such oath or affirmation his full name, with his age, place of business, his status, whether single or married, and, if married, the name of his lawful wife, and that he will support the Constitution of the United States and will faithfully obey the laws thereof, and especially will obey the act of Congress approved March 22, 1882, entitled "An act to amend section 5352 of the Revised Statutes of the United States, in reference to bigamy, and for other purposes," and will also obey this act in respect of the crimes in said act defined and forbidden, and that he will not, directly or indirectly, aid or abet, counsel or advise, any other person to commit any of said crimes. Such registration officer is authorized to administer said oath or affirmation; and all such oaths or affirmations shall be by him delivered to the clerk of the probate court of the proper county, and shall be deemed public records therein. But if any election shall occur in said Territory before the next revision of the registration lists as required by law, the said oath or affirmation shall be administered by the presiding judge of the election precinct on or before the day of election. As a condition-precedent to the right to hold office in or under said Territory, the officer, before entering on the duties of his office, shall take and subscribe an oath or affirmation declaring his full name, with his age, place of business, his status, whether married or single, and, if married, the name of his lawful wife, and that he will support the Constitution of the United States and will faithfully obey the laws thereof, and especially will obey the act of Congress approved March 22, 1882, entitled "An act to amend section 5352 of the Revised Statutes of the United States, in reference to bigamy, and for other purposes," and will also obey this act in respect of the crimes in said act defined and forbidden, and that he will not, directly or indirectly, aid or abet, counsel or advise, any other person to commit any of said crimes; which oath or affirmation shall be recorded in the proper office and indorsed on the commission or certificate of appointment. All grand and petit jurors in said Territory shall take the same oath or affirmation, to be administered, in writing or orally, in the proper court. No person shall be entitled to vote in any election in said Territory, or be capable of jury service, or hold any office of trust or emolument in said Territory who shall not have taken the oath or affirmation aforesaid. No person who shall have been convicted of any crime under this act, or under the act of Congress aforesaid approved March 22, 1882, or who shall be a polygamist, or who shall associate or cohabit polygamously with persons of the other sex, shall be entitled to vote in any election in said Territory, or be capable of jury service, or to hold any office of trust or emolument in said Territory.

SEC. 25. That the office of Territorial Superintendent of District Schools created by the laws of Utah is hereby abolished; and it shall be the duty of the Supreme Court of said Territory to appoint a Commissioner of Schools, who shall possess and exercise all the powers and duties heretofore imposed by the laws of said Territory upon the Territorial Superintendent of District Schools, and who shall receive the same salary and compensation, which shall be paid out of the treasury of said Territory; and the laws of the Territory of Utah providing for the method of election and appointment of such Territorial Superintendent of District Schools are hereby suspended until the further action of Congress shall be had in respect thereto. The said superintendent shall have power to prohibit the use in any district school of any book of a sectarian character or otherwise unsuitable. Said superintendent shall collect and classify statistics and other information respecting the district and other schools in said Territory, showing their progress, the whole number of children of school age, the number who attend school in each year in the respective counties, the average length of time of their attendance, the number of teachers and the compensation paid to the same, the number of teachers who are Mormons, the number who are so-called Gentiles, the number of children of Mormon parents and the number of children of so-called Gentile parents, and their respective average attendance at school; all of which statistics and information shall be annually reported to Congress, through the Governor of said Territory and the Department of the Interior.

SEC. 26. That all religious societies, sects, and congregations shall have the right to have and to hold, through trustees appointed by any court exercising probate powers in a Territory, only on the nomination of the authorities of such society, sect, or congregation, so much real property for the erection or use of houses of worship, and for such parsonages and burial-grounds as shall be necessary for the convenience and use of the several congregations of such religious society, sect, or congregation.

SEC. 27. That all laws passed by the so-called State of Deseret and by the Legislative Assembly of the Territory of Utah for the organization of the militia thereof or for the creation of the Nauvoo Legion are hereby annulled and declared of no effect; and the militia of Utah shall be organized and subjected in all respects to the laws of the United States regulating the militia in the Territories: *Provided, however,* That all general officers of the militia shall be appointed by the Governor of the Territory, by and with the advice and consent of the Council thereof. The Legislative Assembly of Utah shall have power to pass laws for organizing the militia thereof, subject to the approval of Congress.

February 17, the House adopted the report of the Conference Committee by the following vote:

YEAS—G. E. Adams, J. J. Adams, C. H. Allen, J. M. Allen, J. A. Anderson, Atkinson, Baker, Ballentine, Barksdale, Barry, Bayne, Belmont, Bingham, Blanchard, Bliss, Blount, Bound, Boutelle, C. R. Breckinridge, C. E. Brown, W. W. Brown, Buchanan, Buck, Bunnell, Burleigh, Burrows, Butterworth, Bynum, Caldwell, J. M. Campbell, J. E. Campbell, Cannon, Caswell, Catchings, Clements, Cobb, Comstock, Conger, Cooper, W. R. Cox, Crisp, Croxton, Cutcheon, A. C. Davidson, R. H. M. Davidson, Davis, Dawson, Dingley, Dockery, Dorsey, Dunham, Eldredge, Ely, Farquhar, Fisher, Fleeger, Forney, Fuller, Funston, Gallinger, Gay, Geddes, C. H. Gibson, Gilfillan, Glass, Goff, Grosvenor, Grout, Guenther, Halsell, Hammond, Harmer, Harris, Hatch, Hayden, Haynes, Heard, Hemphill, J. S. Henderson, T. J. Henderson, Henley, Hepburn, Hermann, Hiestand, Hires, Hiscock, Hitt, Holman, Holmes, Hopkins, Houk, Howard, Hutton, Jackson, James, F. A. Johnson, J. T. Johnston, T. D. Johnston, J. T. Jones, Laffoon, La Follette, Laird, Landes, Lanham, Lehlbach, Lindsley, Little, Louttit, Lyman, Mahoney, Matson, Maybury, McComas, McCreary, McKenna, McKinley, McMillin, McRae, Merriman, Millard, Moffatt, Morgan, Morrison, Morrow, Muller, Neal, Nelson, Oates, O'Donnell, O'Ferrall, Charles O'Neill, Osborne, Owen, Parker, Peel, Perkins, Peters, Pettibone, Plumb, Price, Randall, Reed, Reese, Richardson, Riggs, Robertson, Rogers, Romeis, Rowell, Ryan, Sawyer, Sayers, Seney, Sessions, Seymour, Shaw, Singleton, Smalls, Sowden, Spooner, Springer, Stahlnecker, Steele, Stephenson, J. W. Stewart, E. F. Stone, W. J. Stone of Kentucky, Storm, Strait, Struble, Swope, Symes, E. B. Taylor, I. H. Taylor, J. M.

Taylor. J. R. Thomas, O. B. Thomas, Thompson, Townshend, Van Eaton, Van Schaick, Viele, Wade, Wadsworth, Wait, Wakefield, J. H. Ward, William Warner, A. J. Weaver, J. B. Weaver, Weber, West, Wheeler, A. C. White, Milo White, Whiting, Wilkins, Willis, Winans, Wolford, Woodburn, Worthington—202.

NAYS—Barbour, Bennett, Bragg, Cabell, T. J. Campbell, Carleton, Clardy, Collins, Compton, Culberson, Daniel, Dargan, Dibble, Eden, Foran, Frederick, Hale, Hall, Hill, Irion, J. H. Jones, Kleiner, Le Fevre, Martin, Mills, Mitchell, Neece, O'Hara, J. J. O'Neill, Outhwaite, Perry, Reagan, Skinner, W. J. Stone of Missouri, Tarsney, Tillman, Turner, T. B. Ward, A. J. Warner, Wilson—40.

NOT VOTING — Aiken, C. M. Anderson, Bacon, Barnes, Bland, Boyle, Brady, W. C. P. Breckinridge, T. M. Browne, Brumm, Burnes, Felix Campbell, Candler, Cowles, S. S. Cox, Crain, Curtin, Davenport, Dougherty, Dunn, Ellsberry, Ermentrout, Evans, Everhart, Felton, Findlay, Ford, Eustace Gibson, Glover, Green, Hanbeck, D. B. Henderson, Herbert, Hudd, Kelley, Ketcham, King, Lawler, Libbey, Long, Lore, Lovering, Lowry, Markham, McAdoo, Miller, Milliken, Morrill, Murphy, Negley, Norwood, Payne, Payson, Phelps, Pidcock, Pindar, Ranney, Rice, Rockwell, Rusk, Sadler, Scott, Scranton, Snyder, Spriggs, Charles Stewart, St. Martin, Swinburne, Taulbee, Zachary Taylor, Throckmorton, Trigg, Tucker, Wallace, Wellborn, Wise—76.

The conference report came up for discussion in the Senate, February 18. In opposition to it Mr. Call, of Florida, said:

"This bill, in my opinion, is an anomaly on the statute-book of this country. It is the second step toward the establishment of religious persecution and intolerance. It is but a thin disguise for the acute lawyers who have prepared this bill, to assert that it is no violation of the Constitution of the United States or of the principles of civil liberty or religious tolerance upon which this Government is founded.

"Mr. President, every law has a policy, has a spirit. It is not to be determined by the letter of the law as it is sought to be justified here, and that is the very first thing a student of the law learns; and it is strange that in the Senate of the United States the very original and first principles of the profession in the interpretation of law which have been handed down for hundreds of years should be boldly violated and the Senate should declare to the professional opinion of the world that the cardinal principles of the profession have no force or effect. Why, sir, the great commentator upon law, when he teaches the student of the laws of England the manner of interpretation, cites the instance of the law in Venice, which said that he who lets blood in the streets of Venice shall be punished with death, and the example of the man who, falling in the streets with sudden illness, had his blood let by a surgeon, violating the letter of the law; but the commentator declares that the law was not violated, because its spirit must determine its interpretation. It was not violated because the spirit and the purpose of the law was to prevent the unlawful shedding of blood.

"The acute sophists who have written this bill do no credit to the intelligence of the age

or the faculty of reason when they declare in this bill that it is not violative of the Constitution, that it is not a law 'respecting an establishment of religion,' that it is not an intolerant proscription of religion, that it is not an unjust denial and discrimination between different citizens in their political rights, because the language of the bill carefully avoids the open statement of any or all these things.

"If the effect of a law—if its object and effect—accomplishes these results, then it is equally liable to the inhibition of the organic law, and of an honest and wise public policy, as if it reached these results by the use of plain and direct language.

"Now, take this act presented to the Senate, and I venture to assert that before any tribunal, impartial and rational, it can not be justified in any single provision. What shall we say of a law that undertakes to punish acts which a particular religion or sect of men worshiping God are prone to commit, violations of the laws which may, as this bill assumes, be the result of their religious belief, and that imposes penalties not demanded by the universal good of the people, but because they are committed by that particular sect of men, and imposes penalties in excess of those that are imposed for the rest of the community for the purpose of affecting that form of religious belief, with the effect by accumulated penalties of forcing that people to abandon that form of religious belief. Suppose you select some one act which your law makes a crime, which is prevalent among that people, but not peculiar to them, but which with them is a religious belief, and you impose on that act committed by them extraordinary penalties. You make the methods of trial partial, oppressive, and cruel. You make the processes of summons and arrest revoltingly harsh and arbitrary. You confiscate their church property. You interfere between parents and their children in their education, and yet you ask honorable men to believe that you think this is not legislating against a particular form of religion.

"Is that lawful? Can you extinguish by such legislation as that a form of religious belief, and yet put up the alleged plea that the letter of the law is complied with, that the Constitution is not violated? We punish all men alike, but we accumulate on that particular sect and the offenses they choose to commit penalty after penalty for the purpose of affecting that form of religious belief. Why, Mr. President, the subterfuge is unworthy of reasonable men, and can have no place in logic or in reason. 'The letter of the law killeth, but the spirit maketh alive,' said a great lawyer and an inspired man many centuries since, and from that day to this the intelligence of every age has sanctioned it. That to carry out the spirit and purpose of the law is to kill it, and to carry into effect its letter is to keep it alive; that when the letter of the law defeats its spirit and purpose you sustain the law by defeating its spirit and purpose and adhering to the letter—who believes this, Mr. President? No intelligent person. Yet the Senate Committee on the Judiciary so declare, and this bill so declares.

"Take this bill, which is the re-establishment of the Inquisition of old, which is religious persecution, which is a law respecting the establishment of religion, because these men have a form of belief and a practice which we disapprove. It is as much the establishment of a particular religion by law as if it declared it in particular terms."

Mr. Hoar, of Massachusetts, objected to the measure on one specific point, and Senators Blair, of New Hampshire, and Dolph, of Oregon, concurred in his objection:

"I have given sometimes somewhat reluctantly my assent to the policy of this bill and to most of its provisions; but I regard, for reasons which I have already stated, the abolition of the right of suffrage by women as not merely unjustifiable but as tyrannical. I think the Senators who have had the conduct of this bill have taken an advantage which they had no right to take to strike out something they did not like, although twenty-four Senators in this body have recently recorded their opinion in its favor, by the use of the power which the public disapprobation of polygamy put into their hands for an entirely different purpose. I voted against the bill for that reason before, and I shall vote against this conference report, which is in fact a bill not merely dealing with the matters in dispute, but the original bill in a new draught, for the same reason.

"The other provisions of the bill, as being the policy which the best judgment of the Senate has been able to agree on for the extirpation of this foul blot on our civilization, I expect to support when I have an opportunity to deal with them separately, although some of them march clear up to the boundary-line which divides reasonable police legislation aimed at crime and evil from legislation which interferes with the great principles and safeguards of personal liberty. I am not prepared to go quite so far in that line."

The Senate then adopted the measure as recommended by the conference committee, by the following vote:

YEAS—Allison, Bowen, Cameron, Cheney, Cockrell, Colquitt, Conger, Cullom, Dolph, Edmunds, Evarts, Farwell, Frye, George, Hale, Harrison, Hawley, Ingalls, Jones of Arkansas, Jones of Nevada, McMillan, McPherson, Mahone, Manderson, Maxey, Miller, Mitchell of Oregon, Morgan, Morrill, Platt, Pugh, Sabin, Sawyer, Walthall, Williams, Wilson of Iowa—37.

NAYS—Blackburn, Brown, Butler, Call, Coke, Gibson, Hampton, Harris, Hoar, Kenna, Ransom, Vance, Whitthorne—13.

ABSENT—Aldrich, Beck, Berry, Blair, Camden, Chace, Dawes, Eustis, Fair, Gorman, Gray, Jones of Florida, Mitchell of Pennsylvania, Palmer, Payne, Plumb, Riddleberger, Saulsbury, Sewell, Sherman, Stanford, Teller, Van Wyck, Vest, Voorhees, Wilson of Maryland—26.

The measure became a law without the approval of the President.

Interstate Commerce.—This session of Congress crowned years of apparently fruitless discussion by passing a measure regulating interstate commerce. May 12, 1886, by a vote of 46 yeas to 4 nays, the Senate passed a moderate bill for this purpose, and July 30, the House, by a vote of 180 yeas to 104 nays substituted for it the Reagan bill, and passed that measure by a vote of 190 yeas to 40 nays. July 31 the Senate non-concurred in the House amendment, and a conference committee was appointed. The report of the committee was made in the Senate, December 15, the following bill being recommended as a substitute for those passed by either House:

Be it enacted, &c., That the provisions of this act shall apply to any common carrier or carriers engaged in the transportation of passengers or property wholly by railroad, or partly by railroad and partly by water when both are used, under a common control, management, or arrangement, for a continuous carriage or shipment, from one State or Territory of the United States, or the District of Columbia, to any other State or Territory of the United States, or the District of Columbia, or from any place in the United States to an adjacent foreign country, or from any place in the United States through a foreign country to any other place in the United States, and also to the transportation in like manner of property shipped from any place in the United States to a foreign country and carried from such place to a port of transshipment, or shipped from a foreign country to any place in the United States and carried to such place from a port of entry either in the United States or an adjacent foreign country : *Provided, however*, That the provisions of this act shall not apply to the transportation of passengers or property, or to the receiving, delivering, storage, or handling of property, wholly within one State, and not shipped to or from a foreign country from or to any State or Territory as aforesaid.

The term "railroad" as used in this act shall include all bridges and ferries used or operated in connection with any railroad, and also all the road in use by any corporation operating a railroad, whether owned or operated under a contract, agreement, or lease ; and the term "transportation" shall include all instrumentalities of shipment or carriage.

All charges made for any service rendered or to be rendered in the transportation of passengers or property as aforesaid, or in connection therewith, or for the receiving, delivery, storage, or handling of such property, shall be reasonable and just, and every unjust, unreasonable charge for such service is prohibited and declared to be unlawful.

SEC. 2. That if any common carrier subject to the provisions of this act shall, directly or indirectly, by any special rate, rebate, drawback, or other device, charge, demand, collect, or receive from any person or persons a greater or less compensation for any service rendered, or to be rendered, in the transportation of passengers or property, subject to the provisions of this act, than it charges, demands, collects, or receives from any other person or persons for doing for him or them a like and contemporaneous service in the transportation of a like kind of traffic under substantially similar circumstances and conditions, such common carrier shall be deemed guilty of unjust discrimination, which is hereby prohibited and declared to be unlawful.

SEC. 3. That it shall be unlawful for any common carrier subject to the provisions of this act to make or give any undue or unreasonable preference or advantage to any particular person, company, firm, corporation, or locality, or any particular description of traffic, in any respect whatsoever, or to subject any particular person, company, firm, corporation, or locality, or any particular description of traffic, to any undue or unreasonable prejudice or disadvantage in any respect whatsoever.

Every common carrier subject to the provisions of this act shall, according to their respective powers, afford all reasonable, proper, and equal facilities for the interchange of traffic between their respective lines, and for the receiving, forwarding, and delivering of passengers and property to and from their several lines and those connecting therewith, and shall not discriminate in their rates and charges between such connecting lines; but this shall not be construed as requiring any such common carrier to give the use of its tracks or terminal facilities to another carrier engaged in like business.

SEC. 4. That it shall be unlawful for any common carrier subject to the provisions of this act to charge or receive any greater compensation in the aggregate for the transportation of passengers or of like kind of property, under substantially similar circumstances and conditions, for a shorter than for a longer distance over the same line, in the same direction, the shorter being included within the longer distance; but this shall not be construed as authorizing any common carrier within the terms of this act to charge and receive as great compensation for a shorter as for a longer distance : *Provided, however,* That upon application to the commission appointed under the provisions of this act such common carrier may, in special cases, after investigation by the commission, be authorized to charge less for longer than for shorter distances for the transportation of passengers or property; and the commission may from time to time prescribe the extent to which such designated common carrier may be relieved from the operation of this section of this act.

SEC. 5. That it shall be unlawful for any common carrier subject to the provisions of this act to enter into any contract, agreement, or combination with any other common carrier or carriers for the pooling of freights of different and competing railroads, or to divide between them the aggregate or net proceeds of the earnings of such railroads, or any portion thereof; and in any case of an agreement for the pooling of freights as aforesaid, each day of its continuance shall be deemed a separate offense.

SEC. 6. That every common carrier subject to the provisions of this act shall print and keep for public inspection schedules showing the rates and fares and charges for the transportation of passengers and property which any such common carrier has established and which are in force at the time upon its railroad, as defined by the first section of this act. The schedules printed as aforesaid by any such common carrier shall plainly state the places upon its railroad between which property and passengers will be carried, and shall contain the classification of freight in force upon such railroad, and shall also state separately the terminal charges and any rules or regulations which in any wise change, affect, or determine any part of the aggregate of such aforesaid rates and fares and charges. Such schedules shall be plainly printed in large type, of at least the size of ordinary pica, and copies for the use of the public shall be kept in every depot or station upon any such railroad, in such places and in such form that they can be conveniently inspected.

Any common carrier subject to the provisions of this act receiving freight in the United States to be carried through a foreign country to any place in the United States shall also in like manner print and keep for public inspection, at every depot where such freight is received for shipment, schedules showing the through rates established and charged by such common carrier to all points in the United States beyond the foreign country to which it accepts freight for shipment; and any freight shipped from the United States through a foreign country into the United States, the through rate on which shall not have been made public as required by this act, shall, before it is admitted into the

United States from said foreign country, be subject to customs duties as if said freight were of foreign production; and any law in conflict with this section is hereby repealed.

No advance shall be made in the rates, fares, and charges which have been established and published as aforesaid by any common carrier in compliance with the requirements of this section, except after ten days' public notice, which shall plainly state the changes proposed to be made in the schedule then in force, and the time when the increased rates, fares, or charges will go into effect; and the proposed changes shall be shown by printing new schedules, or shall be plainly indicated upon the schedules in force at the time and kept for public inspection. Reductions in such published rates, fares, or charges may be made without previous public notice; but whenever any such reduction is made, notice of the same shall immediately be publicly posted and the changes made shall immediately be made public by printing new schedules, or shall immediately be plainly indicated upon the schedules at the time in force and kept for public inspection.

And when any such common carrier shall have established and published its rates, fares, and charges in compliance with the provisions of this section, it shall be unlawful for such common carrier to charge, demand, collect, or receive from any person or persons a greater or less compensation for the transportation of passengers or property, or for any services in connection therewith, than is specified in such published schedule of rates, fares, and charges as may at the time be in force.

Every common carrier subject to the provisions of this act shall file with the commission hereinafter provided for copies of its schedules of rates, fares, and charges which have been established and published in compliance with the requirements of this section, and shall promptly notify said commission of all changes made in the same. Every such common carrier shall also file with said commission copies of all contracts, agreements, or arrangements with other common carriers in relation to any traffic affected by the provisions of this act to which it may be a party. And in cases where passengers and freight pass over continuous lines or routes operated by more than one common carrier, and the several common carriers operating such lines or routes establish joint tariffs of rates or fares or charges for such continuous lines or routes, copies of such joint tariffs shall also, in like manner, be filed with said commission. Such joint rates, fares, and charges on such continuous lines so filed as aforesaid shall be made public by such common carriers when directed by said commission, in so far as may, in the judgment of the commission, be deemed practicable; and said commission shall from time to time prescribe the measure of publicity which shall be given to such rates, fares, and charges, or to such part of them as it may deem it practicable for such common carriers to publish, and the places in which they shall be published; but no common carrier party to any such joint tariff shall be liable for the failure of any other common carrier party thereto to observe and adhere to the rates, fares, or charges thus made and published.

If any such common carrier shall neglect or refuse to file or publish its schedules or tariffs of rates, fares, and charges as provided in this section, or any part of the same, such common carrier shall, in addition to other penalties herein prescribed, be subject to a writ of mandamus, to be issued by any circuit court of the United States in the judicial district wherein the principal office of said common carrier is situated or wherein such offense may be committed, and if such common carrier be a foreign corporation, in the judicial circuit wherein such common carrier accepts traffic and has an agent to perform such service, to compel compliance with the aforesaid provisions of this section; and such writ shall issue in the name of the people of the United States, at the relation of the commissioners appointed under the provisions of this act; and failure to comply with its requirements shall be punishable as and for a contempt; and the said commissioners, as complainants, may also apply, in any such circuit court of the United States, for a writ of injunction against such common carrier, to restrain such common carrier from receiving or transporting property among the several States and Territories of the United States, or between the United States and adjacent foreign countries, or between ports of transshipment and of entry and the several States and Territories of the United States, as mentioned in the first section of this act, until such common carrier shall have complied with the aforesaid provisions of this section of this act.

SEC. 7. That it shall be unlawful for any common carrier subject to the provisions of this act to enter into any combination, contract, or agreement, expressed or implied, to prevent, by change of time schedule, carriage in different cars, or by other means or devices, the carriage of freights from being continuous from the place of shipment to the place of destination; and no break of bulk, stoppage, or interruption made by such common carrier shall prevent the carriage of freights from being and being treated as one continuous carriage from the place of shipment to the place of destination, unless such break, stoppage, or interruption was made in good faith for some necessary purpose, and without any intent to avoid or unnecessarily interrupt such continuous carriage or to evade any of the provisions of this act.

SEC. 8. That in case any common carrier subject to the provisions of this act shall do, cause to be done, or permit to be done any act, matter, or thing in this act prohibited or declared to be unlawful, or shall omit to do any act, matter, or thing in this act required to be done, such common carrier shall be liable to the person or persons injured thereby for the full amount of damages sustained in consequence of any such violation of the provisions of this act, together with a reasonable counsel or attorney's fee, to be fixed by the court in every case of recovery, which attorney's fee shall be taxed and collected as part of the costs in the case.

SEC. 9. That any person or persons claiming to be damaged by any common carrier subject to the provisions of this act may either make complaint to the commission as hereinafter provided for, or may bring suit in his or their own behalf for the recovery of the damages for which such common carrier may be liable under the provisions of this act, in any district or circuit court of the United States of competent jurisdiction; but such person or persons shall not have the right to pursue both of said remedies, and must in each case elect which one of the two methods of procedure herein provided for he or they will adopt. In any such action brought for the recovery of damages the court before which the same shall be pending may compel any director, officer, receiver, trustee, or agent of the corporation or company defendant in such suit to attend, appear, and testify in such case, and may compel the production of the books and papers of such corporation or company party to any such suit; the claim that any such testimony or 'evidence may tend to criminate the person giving such evidence shall not excuse such witness from testifying, but such evidence or testimony shall not be used against such person on the trial of any criminal proceeding.

SEC. 10. That any common carrier subject to the provisions of this act, or, whenever such common carrier is a corporation, any director or officer thereof, or any receiver, trustee, lessee, agent, or person acting for or employed by such corporation, who, alone or with any other corporation, company, person, or party, shall willfully do or cause to be done, or shall willingly suffer or permit to be done, any act, matter, or thing in this act prohibited or declared to be unlawful, or who shall aid or abet therein, or shall willfully omit or fail to do any act, matter, or thing in this act required to be done, or shall cause or willing-

ly suffer or permit any act, matter or thing so directed or required by this act to be done not to be so done, or shall aid or abet any such omission or failure, or shall be guilty of any infraction of this act, or shall aid or abet therein, shall be deemed guilty of a misdemeanor, and shall, upon conviction thereof in any district court of the United States within the jurisdiction of which such offense was committed, be subject to a fine of not to exceed $5,000 for each offense.

SEC. 11. That a commission is hereby created and established, to be known as the Interstate Commerce Commission, which shall be composed of five commissioners, who shall be appointed by the President, by and with the advice and consent of the Senate. The commissioners first appointed under this act shall continue in office for the term of two, three, four, five, and six years, respectively, from the 1st day of January, A. D. 1887, the term of each to be designated by the President; but their successors shall be appointed for terms of six years, except that any person chosen to fill a vacancy shall be appointed only for the unexpired term of the commissioner whom he shall succeed. Any commissioner may be removed by the President for inefficiency, neglect of duty, or malfeasance in office. Not more than three of the commissioners shall be appointed from the same political party. No person in the employ of, or holding any official relation to, any common carrier subject to the provisions of this act, or owning stock or bonds thereof, or who is in any way pecuniarily interested therein, shall enter upon the duties of or hold such office. Said commissioners shall not engage in any other business, vocation, or employment. No vacancy in the commission shall impair the right of the remaining commissioners to exercise all the powers of the commission.

SEC. 12. That the commission hereby created shall have authority to inquire into the management of the business of all common carriers subject to the provisions of this act, and shall keep itself informed as to the manner and method in which the same is conducted, and shall have the right to obtain from such common carriers full and complete information necessary to enable the commission to perform the duties and carry out the objects for which it was created; and for the purposes of this act the commission shall have power to require the attendance and testimony of witnesses and the production of all books, papers, tariffs, contracts, agreements, and documents relating to any matter under investigation, and to that end may invoke the aid of any court of the United States in requiring the attendance and testimony of witnesses and the production of books, papers, and documents under the provisions of this section.

And any of the circuit courts of the United States within the jurisdiction of which such inquiry is carried on may, in case of contumacy or refusal to obey a subpœna issued to any common carrier subject to the provisions of this act, or other person, issue an order requiring such common carrier or other person to appear before said commission (and produce books and papers if so ordered) and give evidence touching the matter in question; and any failure to obey such order of the court may be punished by such court as a contempt thereof. The claim that any such testimony or evidence may tend to criminate the person giving such evidence shall not excuse such witness from testifying; but such evidence or testimony shall not be used against such person on the trial of any criminal proceeding.

SEC. 13. That any person, firm, corporation, or association, or any mercantile, agricultural, or manufacturing society, or any body politic or municipal organization, complaining of anything done or omitted to be done by any common carrier subject to the provisions of this act in contravention of the provisions thereof, may apply to said commission by petition, which shall briefly state the facts; whereupon a statement of the charges thus made shall be forwarded by the commission to such common carrier, who shall be called upon to satisfy the complaint or to answer the same in writing within a reasonable time, to be specified by the commission. If such common carrier, within the time specified, shall make reparation for the injury alleged to have been done, said carrier shall be relieved of liability to the complainant only for the particular violation of law thus complained of. If such carrier shall not satisfy the complaint within the time specified, or there shall appear to be any reasonable ground for investigating said complaint, it shall be the duty of the commission to investigate the matters complained of in such manner and by such means as it shall deem proper.

Said commission shall in like manner investigate any complaint forwarded by the railroad commissioner or railroad commission of any State or Territory, at the request of such commissioner or commission, and may institute any inquiry on its own motion in the same manner and to the same effect as though complaint had been made.

No complaint shall at any time be dismissed because of the absence of direct damage to the complainant.

SEC. 14. That whenever an investigation shall be made by said commission, it shall be its duty to make a report in writing in respect thereto, which shall include the findings of fact upon which the conclusions of the commission are based, together with its recommendation as to what reparation, if any, should be made by the common carrier to any party or parties who may be found to have been injured; and such findings so made shall thereafter, in all judicial proceedings, be deemed *prima-facie* evidence as to each and every fact found.

All reports of investigations made by the commission shall be entered of record, and a copy thereof shall be furnished to the party who may have complained, and to any common carrier that may have been complained of.

SEC. 15. That if in any case in which an investigation shall be made by said commission it shall be made to appear to the satisfaction of the commission, either by the testimony of witnesses or other evidence, that anything has been done or omitted to be done in violation of the provisions of this act, or of any law cognizable by said commission, by any common carrier, or that any injury or damage has been sustained by the party or parties complaining, or by other parties aggrieved in consequence of any such violation, it shall be the duty of the commission to forthwith cause a copy of its report in respect thereto to be delivered to such common carrier, together with a notice to said common carrier to cease and desist from such violation, or to make reparation for the injury so found to have been done, or both, within a reasonable time, to be specified by the commission; and if, within the time specified, it shall be made to appear to the commission that such common carrier has ceased from such violation of law, and has made reparation for the injury found to have been done, in compliance with the report and notice of the commission, or to the satisfaction of the party complaining, a statement to that effect shall be entered of record by the commission, and the said common carrier shall thereupon be relieved from further liability or penalty for such particular violation of law.

SEC. 16. That whenever any common carrier, as defined in and subject to the provisions of this act, shall violate or refuse or neglect to obey any lawful order or requirement of the commission in this act named, it shall be the duty of the commission, and lawful for any company or person interested in such order or requirement, to apply, in a summary way, by petition, to the Circuit Court of the United States sitting in equity in the judicial district in which the common carrier complained of has its principal office, or in which the violation or disobedience of such order or requirement shall happen, alleging such violation or disobedience, as the case may be; and the said court shall have power to hear and determine the matter, on such short notice to the common carrier complained of as the court shall deem reasonable; and such notice may be served on such common carrier, his or its officers, agents, or servants, in such manner as the court shall direct; and said court shall proceed to hear and determine the matter speedily as a court of equity and without the formal pleadings and proceedings applicable to ordinary suits in equity, but in such manner as to do justice in the premises; and to this end such court shall have power, if it think fit, to direct and prosecute, in such mode and by such persons as it may appoint, all such inquiries as the court may think needful to enable it to form a just judgment in the matter of such petition; and on such hearing the report of said commission shall be *prima-facie* evidence of the matters therein stated; and if it be made to appear to such court, on such hearing or on report of any such person or persons, that the lawful order or requirement of said commission drawn in question has been violated or disobeyed, it shall be lawful for such court to issue a writ of injunction or other proper process, mandatory or otherwise, to restrain such common carrier from further continuing such violation or disobedience of such order or requirement of said commission, and enjoining obedience to the same; and in case of any disobedience of any such writ of injunction or other proper process, mandatory or otherwise, it shall be lawful for such court to issue writs of attachment, or any other process of said court incident or applicable to writs of injunction or other proper process, mandatory or otherwise, against such common carrier, and if a corporation, against one or more of the directors, officers, or agents of the same, or against any owner, lessee, trustee, receiver, or other person failing to obey such writ of injunction or other proper process, mandatory or otherwise; and said court may, if it shall think fit, make an order directing such common carrier or other person so disobeying such writ of injunction or other proper process, mandatory or otherwise, to pay such sum of money not exceeding for each carrier or person in default the sum of $500 for every day after a day to be named in the order that such carrier or other person shall fail to obey such injunction or other proper process, mandatory or otherwise; and such moneys shall be payable as the court shall direct, either to the party complaining, or into court to abide the ultimate decision of the court, or into the Treasury; and payment thereof may, without prejudice to any other mode of recovering the same, be enforced by attachment or order in the nature of a writ of execution, in like manner as if the same had been recovered by a final decree *in personam* in such court. When the subject in dispute shall be of the value of $2,000 or more, either party to such proceeding before said court may appeal to the Supreme Court of the United States, under the same regulations now provided by law in respect of security for such appeal; but such appeal shall not operate to stay or supersede the order of the court or the execution of any writ or process thereon; and such court may, in every such matter, order the payment of such costs and counsel fees as shall be deemed reasonable. Whenever any such petition shall be filed or presented by the commission it shall be the duty of the district attorney, under the direction of the Attorney-General of the United States, to prosecute the same; and the costs and expenses of such prosecution shall be paid out of the appropriation for the expenses of the courts of the United States. For the purposes of this act, excepting its penal provisions, the circuit courts of the United States shall be deemed to be always in session.

SEC. 17. That the commission may conduct its proceedings in such a manner as will best conduce to the proper dispatch of business and to the ends of justice. A majority of the commission shall constitute a quorum for the transaction of business, but no commissioner shall participate in any hearing or proceeding in which he has any pecuniary interest. Said commission may, from time to time, make or amend such general rules or orders as may be requisite for the order and regulation of proceedings before it, including forms of notices and the service thereof, which shall conform, as nearly as may be, to those in use in the courts of the United States. Any party may appear before said commission and be heard, in person or by attorney. Every vote and official act of the commission shall be entered of record, and its proceedings shall be public upon the request of either party interested. Said commission shall have an official seal, which shall be judicially noticed. Either of the members of the commission may administer oaths and affirmations.

SEC. 18. That each commissioner shall receive an annual salary of $7,500, payable in the same manner as the salaries of judges of the courts of the United States. The commission shall appoint a secretary, who shall receive an annual salary of $3,500, payable in like manner. The commission shall have authority to employ and fix the compensation of such other employés as it may find necessary to the proper performance of its duties, subject to the approval of the Secretary of the Interior.

The commission shall be furnished by the Secretary of the Interior with suitable offices and all necessary office supplies. Witnesses summoned before the commission shall be paid the same fees and mileage that are paid witnesses in the courts of the United States. All of the expenses of the commission, including all necessary expenses for transportation incurred by the commissioners, or by their employés under their orders, in making any investigation in any other places than in the city of Washington, shall be allowed and paid, on the presentation of itemized vouchers therefor approved by the chairman of the commission and the Secretary of the Interior.

SEC. 19. That the principal office of the commission shall be in the city of Washington, where its general sessions shall be held; but whenever the convenience of the public or of the parties may be promoted or delay or expense prevented thereby, the commission may hold special sessions in any part of the United States. It may, by one or more of the commissioners, prosecute any inquiry necessary to its duties, in any part of the United States, into any matter or question of fact pertaining to the business of any common carrier subject to the provisions of this act.

SEC. 20. That the commission is hereby authorized to require annual reports from all common carriers subject to the provisions of this act, to fix the time and prescribe the manner in which such reports shall be made, and to require from such carriers specific answers to all questions upon which the commission may need information. Such annual reports shall show in detail the amount of capital stock issued, the amounts paid therefor, and the manner of payment for the same; the dividends paid, the surplus fund, if any, and the number of stockholders; the funded and floating debts, and the interest paid thereon; the cost and value of the carrier's property, franchises, and equipment; the number of employés, and the salary paid each class; the amounts expended for improvements each year, how expended, and the character of such improvements; the earnings and receipts from each branch of business and from all sources; the operating and other expenses; the balances of profit and loss; and a complete exhibit of the financial operations of the carrier each year, including an annual balance-sheet. Such reports shall also contain such information in relation to rates or regulations, concerning fares or freights, or agreements, arrangements, or contracts with other common carriers, as the commission may require; and the said commission may, within its discretion, for the purpose of enabling it the better to carry out the purposes of this act, prescribe (if in the opinion of the commission it is practicable to prescribe such uniformity and methods of keeping accounts) a period of time within which all common carriers subject to the provisions of this

act shall have, as near as may be, a uniform system of accounts, and the manner in which such accounts shall be kept.

SEC. 21. That the commission shall, on or before the 1st day of December in each year, make a report to the Secretary of the Interior, which shall be by him transmitted to Congress, and copies of which shall be distributed as are the other reports issued from the Interior Department. This report shall contain such information and data collected by the commission as may be considered of value in the determination of questions connected with the regulation of commerce, together with such recommendations as to additional legislation relating thereto as the commission may deem necessary.

SEC. 22. That nothing in this act shall apply to the carriage, storage, or handling of property free or at reduced rates for the United States, State, or municipal governments, or for charitable purposes, or to or from fairs and expositions for exhibition thereat, or the issuance of mileage, excursion, or commutation passenger tickets; nothing in this act shall be construed to prohibit any common carrier from giving reduced rates to ministers of religion; nothing in this act shall be construed to prevent railroads from giving free carriage to their own officers and employés, or to prevent the principal officers of any railroad company or companies from exchanging passes or tickets with other railroad companies for their officers and employés; and nothing in this act contained shall in any way abridge or alter the remedies now existing at common law or by statute, but the provisions of this act are in addition to such remedies: *Provided,* That no pending litigation shall in any way be affected by this act.

SEC. 23. That the sum of $100,000 is hereby appropriated for the use and purposes of this act for the fiscal year ending June 30, A. D. 1888, and the intervening time anterior thereto.

SEC. 24. That the provisions of sections 11 and 18 of this act, relating to the appointment and organization of the commission herein provided for shall take effect immediately, and the remaining provisions of this act shall take effect sixty days after its passage.

After extended discussion, the Senate agreed to the Conference Committee's report, Jan. 14, 1887, by the following vote:

YEAS—Allison, Beck, Berry, Blackburn, Bowen, Cockrell, Coke, Colquitt, Conger, Cullom, Dolph, Edmunds, Eustis, Fair, Frye, George, Gibson, Gorman, Gray, Hale, Harris, Hawley, Ingalls, Jones of Arkansas, Jones of Nevada, McMillan, Manderson, Mitchell of Oregon, Palmer, Plumb, Pugh, Sabin, Saulsbury, Sawyer, Sewell, Sherman, Spooner, Teller, Vance, Vest Walthall, Whitthorne, Wilson of Iowa—43.

NAYS—Aldrich, Blair, Brown, Cameron, Chace, Cheney, Evarts, Hampton, Hoar, Mahone, Mitchell of Pennsylvania, Morrill, Payne, Platt, Williams—15.

ABSENT—Butler, Call, Camden, Dawes Harrison, Jones of Florida, Kenna, McPherson, Maxey, Miller, Morgan, Ransom, Riddleberger, Stanford, Van Wyck, Voorhees, Wilson of Maryland—17.

Just previous to the final vote, a motion to recommit was lost, as follows:

YEAS—Aldrich, Blair, Brown, Cameron, Chace, Cheney, Evarts, Frye, Gray, Hale, Hampton, Hawley, Hoar, Mahone, Mitchell of Oregon, Mitchell of Pennsylvania, Morgan, Morrill, Payne, Platt, Sawyer, Sewell, Sherman, Spooner, Williams—25.

NAYS—Allison, Beck, Berry, Blackburn, Bowen, Call, Cockrell, Coke, Colquitt, Conger, Cullom, Dolph, Edmunds, Eustis, Fair, George, Gibson, Gorman, Harris, Ingalls, Jones of Arkansas, Jones of Nevada, McMillan, Manderson, Palmer, Plumb, Pugh, Sabin, Saulsbury, Teller, Vance, Vest, Walthall, Whitthorne, Wilson of Iowa, Wilson of Maryland—36.

Absent—Butler, Camden, Dawes, Harrison, Jones of Florida, Kenna, McPherson, Maxey. Miller, Ransom, Riddleberger, Stanford, Van Wyck, Voorhees—14.

In the House, Jan. 21, 1887, the conference committee's report was agreed to by the following vote:

Yeas—G. E. Adams, J. J. Adams, J. M. Allen, J. A. Anderson, Baker, Ballentine, Barbour, Barksdale, Barnes, Barry, Bayne, Belmont, Bennett, Blanchard, Blount, Bound, Brady, C. R. Breckinridge, W. C. P. Breckinridge, C. E. Brown, W. W. Brown, Buck, Bunnell, Burnes, Burrows, Butterworth, Bynum, Cabell, Caldwell, Felix Campbell, J. M. Campbell, Cannon, Carleton, Catchings, Clements, Collins, Compton, Comstock, Conger, Cooper, Cowles, W. R. Cox, Crain, Crisp, Croxton, Culberson, Curtin, Cutcheon, Daniel, R. H. M. Davidson, Dawson, Dingley, Dockery, Dorsey, Dougherty, Dunham, Dunn, Eden, Eldredge, Ellsberry, Everhart, Farquhar, Fisher, Fleeger, Foran, Fuller, Funston, Gallinger, Geddes, C. H. Gibson, Glover, Goff, Green, Grout, Hale, Hall, Halsell, Hammond, Harmer, Harris, Hatch, Haynes, Heard, Hemphill, D. B. Henderson, J. S. Henderson, T. J. Henderson, Henley, Hepburn, Herbert, Hermann, Hiestand, Hires, Hitt, Holman, Holmes, Hopkins, Howard, Hudd, Irion, J. T. Johnston, T. D. Johnston, J. H. Jones, J. T. Jones, Laffoon, La Follette, Landes, Lanham, Lawler, Le Fevre, Lehlbach, Lindsley, Little, Lore, Louttit, Lovering, Lowry, Lyman, Mahoney, Matson, McAdoo, McComas, McCreary, McKinley, McMillin, McRae, Millard, Milliken, Mills, Moffatt, Morrill, Morrison, Muller, Murphy, Neal, Neece, Nelson, Norwood, O'Donnell, O'Ferrall, Osborne, Outhwaite, Owen, Parker, Payson, Peel, Perkins, Perry, Peters, Pettibone, Phelps, Pirce, Plumb, Randall, Richardson, Riggs, Robertson, Rockwell, Rogers, Romeis, Rowell, Rusk, Ryan, Sadler, Sawyer, Sayers, Scott, Scranton, Sessions, Shaw, Singleton, Skinner, Sowden, Spooner, Springer, Steele, Stephenson, Charles Stewart, W. J. Stone of Kentucky, W. J. Stone of Missouri, Storm, Strait, Struble, Swope, Symes, Tarsney, Taulbee, E. B. Taylor, I. H. Taylor, J. M. Taylor, Zachary Taylor, J. R. Thomas, O. B. Thomas, Thompson, Tillman, Townshend, Trigg, Tucker, Turner, Van Eaton, Van Schaick, Wade, Wakefield, Wallace, J. H. Ward, T. B. Ward, A. J. Warner, William Warner, Weber, Wellborn, Wheeler, Milo White, Wilkins, Willis, Wilson, Winans, Wolford, Woodburn, Worthington —219.

Nays—C. H. Allen, C. M. Anderson, Bliss, Boutelle, Boyle, Bragg, Brumm, J. E. Campbell, Caswell, Dibble, Ely, Evans, Felton, Findlay, Frederick, Gay, Gilfillan, Grosvenor, Hayden, Hill, F. A. Johnson, Kelley, Ketcham, Libbey, Long, Markham, Martin, McKenna, Miller, Morrow, Oates, Charles O'Neill, J. J. O'Neill, Ranney, Reed, Rice, Seymour, Wadsworth, Wait, J. B. Weaver A. C. White—41.

Not Voting—Aiken, Atkinson, Bacon, Bingham, Bland, T. M. Browne, Buchanan, Burleigh, T. J. Campbell, Chandler, Clardy, Cobb, S. S. Cox, Dargan, Davenport, A. C. Davidson, Davis, Ermentrout, Ford, Forney, Eustace Gibson, Glass, Guenther, Hanback, Hiscock, Houk, Hutton, Jackson, James, King, Kleiner, Laird, Maybury, Merriman, Mitchell, Morgan, Negley, O'Hara, Payne, Pidcock, Pindar, Reagan, Reese, Seney, Smalls, Snyder, Spriggs, Stahlnecker, J. W. Stewart, St. Martin, E. F. Stone, Swinburne, Throckmorton, Viele, A. J. Weaver, West, Whiting, Wise—58.

Feb. 4, 1887, the President approved of the measure.

Non-Intercourse.—Jan. 19, 1887, a bill was reported in the Senate from the Committee on Foreign Relations, "to authorize the President of the United States to protect and defend the rights of American fishing-vessels, American fishermen, American trading and other vessels in certain cases, and for other purposes." January 24 it passed the Senate by a vote of 46 to 1, the negative vote being cast by Senator Riddleberger, of Virginia. The measure is as follows:

Be it enacted, etc., That whenever the President of the United States shall be satisfied that American fishing-vessels or American fishermen, visiting or being in the waters or at any ports or places of the British dominions of North America, are or then lately have been denied or abridged in the enjoyment of any rights secured to them by treaty or law, or are or then lately have been unjustly vexed or harassed in the enjoyment of such rights, or subjected to unreasonable restrictions, regulations, or requirements in respect of such rights, or otherwise unjustly vexed or harassed in said waters, ports, or places; or whenever the President of the United States shall be satisfied that any such fishing-vessels or fishermen, having a permit under the laws of the United States to touch and trade at any port or ports, place or places in the British dominions of North America, are or then lately have been denied the privilege of entering such port or ports, place or places, in the same manner and under the same regulations as may exist therein applicable to trading-vessels of the most favored nation, or shall be unjustly vexed or harassed in respect thereof, or otherwise be unjustly vexed or harassed therein, or shall be prevented from purchasing such supplies as may there be lawfully sold to trading-vessels of the most favored nation; or whenever the President of the United States shall be satisfied that any other vessels of the United States, their masters or crews, so arriving at or being in such British waters or ports or places of the British dominions in North America, are or then lately have been denied any of the privileges therein accorded to the vessels, their masters or crews, of the most favored nation, or unjustly vexed or harassed in respect to the same, or unjustly vexed or harassed therein by the authorities thereof, then, and in either or all of such cases, it shall be lawful, and it shall be the duty of the President of the United States, in his discretion, by proclamation to that effect, to deny vessels, their masters and crews, of the British dominions of North America any entrance into the waters, ports, or places of or within the United States (with such exceptions in regard to vessels in distress, stress of weather, or needing supplies as to the President shall seem proper), whether such vessels have come directly from said dominions on such destined voyage or by way of some port or place in such destined voyage elsewhere; and also to deny entry into any port or place of the United States of fresh fish or salt fish or any other product of said dominions, or other goods coming from said dominions to the United States. The President may, in his discretion, apply such proclamation to any part or to all of the foregoing-named subjects, and revoke, qualify, limit and renew such proclamation from time to time as he may deem necessary to the full and just execution of the purposes of this act. Every violation of any such proclamation, or any part thereof, is hereby declared illegal, and all vessels and goods so coming or being within the waters, ports, or places of the United States contrary to such proclamation shall be forfeited to the United States; and such forfeitures shall be enforced and proceeded upon in the same manner and with the same effect as in the case of vessels or goods whose importation or coming to or being in the waters or ports of the United States contrary to law may now be enforced and proceeded upon. Every person who shall violate any of the provisions of this act, or such proclamation of the President made in pursuance hereof, shall be deemed guilty of a misdemeanor, and, on conviction thereof, shall be punished by a fine not exceeding $1,000, or by imprisonment for a term not exceeding two years, or by both said punishments, in the discretion of the court.

In explanation of the measure, Senator Edmunds, of Vermont, said: " This bill provides that if our vessels are mistreated in Canadian ports—pure fishing-vessels, I will stick to that now, for the time being—and are denied or embarrassed in the fair exercise of the rights that they have, the President of the United States may, as a countervailing operation, say that the Canadian fish, and the Canadian fisherman, and the Canadian trader, and the Canadian everybody else, shall not come into the waters of the United States at all. Suppose he says that; that is not war. Suppose it continues for ten years; it is a question of who can stand it best. I think the people of the United States can stand it best, and it will be a persuasion to those people to mitigate accordingly somewhat of the rough asperity of their manners and somewhat of the irregularity of their conduct. Suppose it does not. Then you have simply got non-intercourse between the British provinces and the United States. The question is, short of war, who can stand that the longest. I think there can be but one answer to that proposition.

" So the question whether we have got to fight to protect American fishermen in their rights that they are entitled to under the treaty alone, as I said before, is not a question at this present moment or this present year of any war, but it is a question of countervailing regulations which all nations have resorted to long before, and usually never coming to a war afterward, in respect of adjusting these rights.

" The very matter of these fisheries has been for a hundred years carried on in the same way. Her Majesty's Government have, from time to time, made their regulations or authorized them to be made, and they have been made and they have executed them, and the Congress of the United States has authorized the President, under our laws, to adjust his conduct accordingly as to whether they could come here or whether they could not. So it is no new thing; and it is not war. There may be war if, by-and-by, it is found that it is impossible for these countries to adjust this matter under clear and definite rights as they now exist, and one party or the other may go to war. The British Government may say, " If you do not choose to admit Dominion vessels into the United States which you are under no treaty obligation to do, we will go to war with you," as we might with China, because she will not admit American vessels into every one of her ports and places; but that is a very ultimate and a very far-off question."

Senator Ingalls, of Kansas, took a less pacific view of the controversy. He said: "It may be that the British Government, by these unwarranted seizures and atrocities, outrages and wrongs, admitted to be in violation of that treaty, have had no ulterior purpose except to compel us to accept their construction of that treaty, to subject us to duress and coercion to force the United States to admit their interpretations of the marine league, of the rights of the fishermen, of the rights of shelter, water, food, and fuel were such as they proposed to put upon them. But I do not read these transactions in that way; the American people do not read them in that way. There was some design and purpose other than to obtain a peaceful solution of the question of the construction or interpretation of doubtful provisions of the Treaty of 1818.

" Sir, England has always been the ruffian, the coward, and the bully among the nations of the earth; insolent to the weak, arrogant to the feeble, cringing and obsequious to the strong, her history for centuries has been a record of crimes against the human race. In Ireland, in Scotland and Wales, against the Roman Catholics, against the Boers of South Africa, against the Hindoos and the Chinese, against the Afghans, the Persians, and the Egyptians, wherever there has been a feeble and helpless people, Great Britain has appeared for the purpose of rapacity, plunder, and conquest.

" England bears no good-will to this country. The memory of defeat in two wars rankles, I have no doubt, in the breasts of Englishmen. When I say that Great Britain is not friendly to America, I mean that the ruling classes are not, and that they have never been.

" Their course toward us has uniformly been one of supercilious insolence and of outrage. They cheated the South with false hopes of recognition, and they outraged the North by violating the rights of neutrality. Their action in the Treaty of Washington was controlled solely by a fear of the consequences to their own commerce in the next war in which they might be engaged if they permitted the precedent that they had established to stand undenied.

" I believe that there is no special reciprocity and good-will on the part of America toward England. There are few Americans who do not regret Waterloo. There are few Americans who do not recognize the fact that the conduct of Great Britain toward this country has been characterized by jealousy and malevolence from the beginning of our national existence, and that she is our only enemy among the powers of the earth.

" If I read these transactions aright, there is no desire on the part of Great Britain to secure a peaceful solution, a pacific interpretation of the doubtful provisions of the Treaty of 1818, but a deliberate design to so far foment the irritation, the discontent that exists between the United States of America and the Dominion of Canada, as to prevent the pacific political affiliations of those two powers in the immediate future, which would be inevitable if it were left to the operation of the natural laws of politics, of trade, and of society.

" I think I discern very plainly what the purpose of Great Britain has been in this matter. She means to render it impossible for free, friendly, reciprocal relations, political and other, to exist between Canada and the United States."

Mr. Hoar, of Massachusetts, regarded the action of the Canadian authorities as shaped to procure a modification of American tariff laws. He said: "I do not think there will be any very great necessity for further argument in support of this bill to convince the minds of a majority of Senators of the expediency of the measure. But the State which I represent is more interested five times over than all the other communities together in the immediate controversy. Of the vessels which have experienced the outrages and annoyances recited in the report of the committee, twenty-five belong to the State of Massachusetts besides four whose port is not stated, and seven to the State of Maine, formerly a part of Massachusetts.

"I understand that the object of these annoyances and grievances which have been recited in the report of the committee is not principally or largely to assert the British or Canadian interpretation of the Treaty of 1818. A dispute is sought in regard to the terms of that treaty, not to protect the sources of the fisheries from an interference by Massachusetts or Maine competition, but it is to compel the people of the United States to change their laws in a matter of purely domestic concern. It is not that Canada may catch fish without molestation; it is that she may sell fish without the interference of the American tariff policy that these difficulties are fomented.

"I regard, in that point of view, the attempt by a foreign country by hostile interference with our ships on the high-seas, or in the neighborhood of their ports, or in their ports, to enforce upon us, against our will, a certain domestic policy as being one of the most emphatic and flagrant acts of hostility that can be committed without actual war. These seizures, with the exception, perhaps, of one or two instances, are seizures upon a pretense and without the reality of any interference either with treaty or with local regulation or law by the American vessels.

"This attempt on the part of Canada has received, as is apparent from the diplomatic correspondence, the full countenance of the mother-country, of which Canada is a dependent. It is said that in one instance there has been an expression of regret for the actual lowering of the American flag. I do not see that the lowering of the American flag is in substance an offense at all equal in rank, of which we have any more reason to complain, than the taking custody without actual right of American vessels and their masters and crews when they are about their lawful employment. It is an affront undoubtedly; it is an insult; but the substance of the offense is not the lowering of the flag, but is the seizure of the ship whose nationality the flag protects.

"The apology which has been conveyed to us is not the apology which is due for the out-

rage. There is no apology on the part of Great Britain, but a simple communication to us by the British minister of an expression of regret of the local dependency, with which we can have no diplomatic relations, and whose satisfaction or dissatisfaction with the act of the officer is of no sort of importance. The absence of any other expression of regret, either for the single action to which this relates or for a series of offenses or outrages of which that is but one, is a more significant matter, as it seems to me, than the single expression which has been communicated to our Secretary of State by the British representative to this country.

"I do not understand, with the Senator from Kansas, that the object of this measure is to bring about either a war on one side or new diplomacy or negotiation on the other. All that is to be done is that we say to Great Britain, and to the Dominion of Canada through her, that so far from accomplishing anything in the way of diminution, or lightening, or repeal of our customs duties by this course of conduct, so long as it continues you shall not be permitted to sell your fish or any other product of the offending district in the American market.

"The only answer to this measure which is to be expected, and all that will be expected, and which will be effectual, is a communication of Great Britain that she has given orders that this course of offensive proceeding shall stop. It requires no new treaty, and certainly, I think, requires no further exertion of force on the part of the American Government."

Senator Morgan, of Alabama, argued that the great issue is the interpretation of the Treaty of 1818. He said: "The committee in preparing the bill and bringing it forward in the Senate first took into consideration what was the actual condition of the treaty relations between the United States and Great Britain respecting the British provinces in North America, and a very close, narrow investigation of the whole field of inquiry satisfied us that we were entirely without treaty engagements with Great Britain in respect of our commerce with the Canadian Dominion. It is true that in the Treaty of Washington we have mutual stipulations in respect of transportation, liable to be suspended, I believe, upon two years' notice or upon the failure of either Government to carry out in good faith, according to the opinion of the other Government, the provisions of those mutual stipulations. But the Senate will do well to remember, in approaching this question and in deciding what is its duty in respect of it, that the United States have no commercial engagements with Great Britain with reference to our commerce with the Canadian provinces. Our engagements are limited to what I have already stated and to the Treaty of 1818 relating to the fisheries. The relations between the United States and the provinces of Canada depend entirely upon the statutes of the two countries, and not upon any treaty engagements; so that in legislating upon this question we have an open field in which we are permitted to exercise our own sweet will without question on the part of Great Britian. We can establish by act of Congress any of the ordinances that we see proper for the regulation of our commercial relations with those provinces, and so they can do the same thing.

"When two countries, thus neighbors to each other, are thus situated in respect of their treaty obligations and are left only to provide for their mutual interests by legislation, it is very clear that if the Dominion of Canada, backed by the Government of Great Britain, shall legislate in hostility to our trade, it becomes not only our duty but our only alternative to legislate in hostility to theirs, to legislate according to the principles of retrosion and of retaliation, if you please.

"If we had commercial treaties with Great Britain respecting our relations to the Canadian provinces, we should of course be attempting to understand whether the proposed legislation of the Committee on Foreign Relations was in any sense in conflict with those commercial regulations agreed upon by treaty; but having nothing of the kind, as I before observed, the field is entirely open to us, and we have no alternative but either to negotiate our first treaty of commerce with Great Britain in respect of the provinces, or to go on in the old line of legislating *pro* and *con* so as to balance up our interests and make them mutually agreeable.

"It is not a credit to these great English-speaking peoples on both sides of the Atlantic Ocean, who control so immensely the destinies of commerce and all other destinies of the inhabitants of this earth, that we should have been all this long time, more than a hundred years since our independence, without a treaty of commerce to regulate our relations with that part of the British possessions which lies next to us and upon this continent. But so it is, so it has been, and so it is likely to remain.

"The Senator from Kansas was anxious to know whether the committee proposed to go to war. About what should we go to war? Not certainly on account of the breach of any commercial treaty with Great Britain in respect of the Canadian provinces, for we have not got any. It would be a war of words, necessarily followed by a war of acts of a commercial character simply, if we should have a war, for there is to be no broken engagements brought to the attention of any government in consequence of the conduct either of Great Britain or of our Government upon these questions, unless it may be that some rights which have been guaranteed to our fishermen in the Treaty of 1818, not commercial rights, but fishery rights, shall have been violated by the Canadian Government or by ourselves.

"The Treaty of 1818 is the real point of dispute between us—the construction of it, the question of its proper enforcement, and the question of the responsibility of the British Government for the acts of the Dominion in regard to that treaty. That is the real bone of controversy between us to-day, and it is about that which we differ. We are undertaking to improve our condition in respect of our differences on that subject, and other commercial questions between us and Great Britain or the Canadian provinces, by the reformation of our statutes, so as to give to our own Government by the authority of Congress under the sanctions of law that degree of.power which is necessary to enable our Government to protect itself and to protect its people against aggressive acts on the part of the Canadian provinces or the Government of Great Britain, as you please. That is all of it."

February 23, the measure was reported to the House from the Committee on Foreign Affairs, with an amendment by way of substitute, the main point of which was that it provided for retaliation by stopping intercourse with Canada by land as well as by sea. This substitute was adopted by the House by the following vote:

Yeas—J. J. Adams, J. M. Allen, Ballentine, Barbour, Barksdale, Barnes, Barry, Belmont, Bennett, Blanchard, Bland, Bliss, Blount, Boyle, Bragg, C. R. Breckinridge, W. C. P. Breckinridge, Bynum, Cabell, J. M. Campbell, J. E. Campbell, Carleton, Catchings, Clements, Cobb, Compton, Comstock, Cowles, W. E. Cox, Crain, Crisp, Culberson, Daniel, Dargan, A. C. Davidson, R. H. M. Davidson, Dawson, Dibble, Dockery, Dougherty, Dunn, Eden, Ermentrout, Findlay, Fisher, Foran, Forney, Gay, Geddes, C. H. Gibson, Glass, Green, Hall, Halsell, Hammond, Harris, Hatch, Heard, Hemphill, J. S. Henderson, Herbert, Hill, Holman, Howard, Hudd, Hutton, Irion, T. D. Johnston, J. H. Jones, J. T. Jones, King, Kleiner, Laffoon, Landes, Lanham, Lawler, Le Fevre, Lovering, Martin, Matson Maybury, McCreary, McMillin, McRae, Merriman, Miller, Mills, Mitchell, Morgan, Morrison, Muller, Murphy, Neal, Neece, Norwood, Oates, O'Ferrall, J. J. O'Neill, Outhwaite, Peel, Perry, Randall, Reagan, Richardson, Riggs, Robertson, Rogers, Rusk, Sayers, Scott, Seymour, Shaw, Singleton, Snyder, Sowden, Spriggs, Springer, Stahlnecker, Storm, Swope, Tarsney, Taulbee, J. M. Taylor, Tillman, Townshend, Tucker, Turner, Van Eaton, T. B. Ward, A. J. Warner, William Warner, J. B. Weaver, Wilkins, Willis, Wilson, Wise, Worthington —137.

Nays—G. E. Adams, C. H. Allen, J. A. Anderson, Atkinson, Baker, Bayne, Bound, Brady, C. E. Brown, W. W. Brown, Brumm, Buck, Bunnell, Burleigh, Burrows, Butterworth, Cannon, Caswell, Conger, Cutcheon, Davis, Dingley, Dorsey, Dunham, Ely, Evans, Everhart, Farquhar, Felton, Floeger, Ford, Frederick, Fuller, Funston, Gallinger, Gilfillan, Goff, Grout, Guenther, Hale, Hanback, Harmer, Hayden, Haynes. D. B. Henderson, T. J. Henderson, Hepburn, Hermann, Hiestand, Hires, Hiscock, Hitt, Holmes, Hopkins, Houk, Jackson, James, F. A. Johnson, J. T. Johnston, Kelley, Ketcham, La Follette, Laird, Lehlbach, Libbey, Lindsley, Little, Long, Louttit, Lyman, Markham, McComas, McKenna, McKinley, Millard, Moffatt, Morrill, Morrow, Negley, Nelson, O'Donnell, O'Hara, Charles O'Neill, Osborne, Owen, Parker, Payne, Perkins, Peters, Plumb, Price, Rice, Rockwell, Romeis, Rowell, Ryan, Sawyer, Scranton, Sessions, Skinner, Smalls, Spooner, Steele, Stephenson, J.

W. Stewart, Strait, Struble, Swinburne, Symes, E. B. Taylor, I. H. Taylor, Zachary Taylor, J. R. Thomas, O. B. Thomas, Thompson, Wadsworth, Wait, Wakefield, A. J. Weaver, Weber, West, A. C. White, Milo White, Whiting—124.

Not Voting—Aiken, C. M. Anderson, Bacon, Bingham, Boutelle, T. M. Browne, Buchanan, Burnes, Caldwell, Felix Campbell, T. J. Campbell, Candler, Clardy, Collins, Cooper, S. S. Cox, Croxton, Curtin, Davenport, Eldredge, Ellsberry, Eustace Gibson, Glover, Grosvenor, Henley, Lore Lowry, Mahoney, McAdoo, Milliken, Payson, Pettibone, Phelps, Pidcock, Pindar, Ranney, Reed, Rouse, Sadler, Seney, Charles Stewart, St. Martin, E. F. Stone, W. J. Stone of Kentucky, W. J. Stone of Missouri, Throckmorton, Trigg, Viele, Van Schaick, Wade, Wallace, J. H. Ward, Wellborn, Wheeler, Winans, Wolford, Woodburn—57.

The measure was then passed by a vote of 256 yeas to one nay, Mr. Dougherty, of Florida, voting in the negative. The Senate non-concurred in the House amendment, and a conference committee was appointed which failed to come to an agreement. March 2, the subject came up in the House, and there was a hot debate as to whether that body should recede from its amendment and accede to the limited non-intercourse for which the Senate bill provided. It was determined by the following vote to yield the point:

Yeas—G. E. Adams, C. H. Allen, C. M. Anderson, J. A. Anderson, Atkinson, Baker, Barksdale, Bayne, Bingham, Bound, Boutelle, T. M. Browne, C. E. Brown, W. W. Brown, Brumm, Buchanan, Buck, Bunnell, Burleigh, Burrows, Butterworth, J. M. Campbell, Cannon, Caswell, Conger, Crain, Cutcheon, Dargan, Davis, Dingley, Dorsey, Dunham, Ely, Evans, Everhart, Farquhar, Felton, Findlay, Fleeger, Ford, Fuller, Funston, Geddes, Gilfillan, Goff, Grosvenor, Grout, Guenther, Hale, Hall, Harmer, Hayden, Haynes, T. J. Henderson, Hepburn, Hermann, Hiestand, Hires, Hiscock, Hitt, Holmes, Hopkins, Houk, Jackson, James, F. A. Johnson, J. T. Johnston, Kelley, Ketcham, Kleiner, La Follette, Laird, Lehlbach, Libbey, Lindsley, Little, Long, Lore, Lyman, Markham, Martin, McComas, McKenna, McKinley, Millard, Milliken, Mills, Moffatt, Morrill, Morrow, Negley, Nelson, O'Donnell, O'Ferrall, O'Hara, Charles O'Neill, J. J. O'Neill, Osborne, Owen, Parker, Payne, Payson, Perkins, Peters, Pettibone, Phelps, Plumb, Price, Reed, Rice, Riggs, Rockwell, Romeis, Rowell, Ryan, Sawyer, Scranton, Sessions, Skinner, Smalls, Spooner, Steele, Stephenson, J. W. Stewart, E. F. Stone, Strait, Struble, Swinburne, Symes, E. B. Taylor, I. H. Taylor, Zachary Taylor, J. R. Thomas, O. B. Thomas, Thompson, Van Eaton, Van Schaick, Wade, Wadsworth, Wakefield, William Warner, A. J. Weaver, Weber, West, A. C. White, Milo White, Woodburn, Worthington —148.

Nays—J. M. Allen, Bacon, Barbour, Barnes, Barry, Belmont, Bennett, Blanchard, Bliss, Blount, Boyle, C. R. Breckinridge, W. C. P. Breckinridge, Burnes, Bynum, Cabell, Caldwell, Felix Campbell, J. E. Campbell, T. J. Campbell, Candler, Carleton, Catchings, Clements, Cobb, Compton, Cowles, S. S. Cox, W. R. Cox, Crisp, Croxton, Culbertson, Daniel, A. C. Davidson, R. H. M. Davidson, Dawson, Dibble, Dockery, Dougherty, Dunn, Eden, Eldredge, Ermentrout, Fisher, Forney, Frederick, C. H. Gibson, Eustace Gibson, Glass, Green, Halsell, Hammond, Harris, Hatch, Heard, Hemphill, J. S. Henderson, Herbert, Hill, Holman, Howard, Hudd, Hutton, Irion, T. D. Johnston, J. H. Jones, King, Laffoon, Lanham, Lawler, Le Fevre, Lovering, Lowry, Mahoney, Matson, Maybury, McAdoo, McCreary, McMillin, McRae, Merriman, Miller, Mitchell, Morgan, Morrison, Murphy,

Neal, Neece, Norwood, Oates, Outhwaite, Page, Peel, Perry, Pindar, Randall, Ranney, Reagan, Richardson, Robertson, Rogers, Rusk, Sayers, Scott, Seney, Seymour, Shaw, Singleton, Sowden, Springer, Stahlnecker, St. Martin, W. J. Stone of Kentucky, W. J. Stone of Missouri, Storm, Swope, Tarsney, Taulbee, J. M. Taylor, Tillman, Townshend, Trigg, Tucker, Turner, Wallace, J. H. Ward, T. B. Ward, A. J. Warner, J. B. Weaver, Wellborn, Wheeler, Wilkins, Willis, Wilson, Wise, Wolford—136.

Not Voting—J. J. Adams, Aiken, Ballentine, Bland, Brady, Bragg, Clardy, Collins, Comstock, Cooper, Curtin, Davenport, Ellsberry, Foran, Gallinger, Gay, Glover, Hanback, D. B. Henderson, Henley, J. T. Jones, Landes, Louttit, Muller, Pidcock, Reese, Sadler, Snyder, Spriggs, Charles Stewart, Throckmorton, Viele, Wait, Whiting, Winans—35.

Mr. Dougherty, of Florida, in the course of the debate on the subject, deprecated all such legislation. He said:

"Mr. Speaker, upon this question no man can say what action this House will take, but in a few moments the position of the majority will be defined, because they must decide one way or the other. As far as I am concerned as an individual Representative, this matter is now just where I hope it will stop. I hope that this House will not recede, and I hope that the Senate will insist, and that this proposed legislation will die, where many a piece of legislation has died, in a committee of conference.

"During this whole discussion it has not been discovered that any American citizen has been deprived of any of his rights, because investigation will show, so far as I am advised, that each and every vessel that has been molested in Canadian waters has been taken up in pursuance of a law which is not in derogation of any treaty existing between the two Governments. It has not been claimed anywhere that there has been any violation of the existing treaty on the part of the English Government, and the laws of Canada, of which we complain, are in consonance with existing treaty, and when Americans violate them they do so at their own peril. No gentleman has claimed that such is not the case, and the difficulty with which we are brought face to face here is the difficulty which has come to us wherever we have had what is called diplomatic negotiation. Except, perhaps, in the instance when a treaty was negotiated with France during the Revolution, men have been appointed to represent this Government who have yielded everything that the representatives of the opposing government asked, and obtained nothing for us. Mr. Speaker, we are too fast in this matter. This pending bill, if it be carried out, if its provisions be put in force, is a virtual declaration of war against the British Government, a friendly power. I take no stock in this spread-eagle, bloody, and patriotic war-talk. The people of this country have had war enough, they do not want any more without good reason. I rely upon the good sense of the American people, and upon the good sense of the English people, to adjust all difficulties; and, as I have said, I take no stock in this patriotic war-talk. I yield to no man in my devotion to this country. Whenever I am called upon I am ready to take my stand for the maintenance of the sovereignty of the Government of the United States, and for the protection of our citizens in all their rights against every enemy, foreign or domestic. But what is the question presented here? It is a proposition for retaliatory legislation, although it has not been even charged—much less successfully maintained—that there has been any violation on the part of the British Government of any stipulation in any existing treaty; in fact, it is admitted that the opposite is the truth. Vessels not violating law have not been molested, and being seized and the law complied with they have been released.

"The true way to settle this question is through the diplomatic departments of the two Governments; or, failing a settlement there, let us have a new treaty, taking care to appoint as our representatives men who will have sense enough not to yield to the commissioners of the British Government all they may demand, and get no advantageous concessions in return. There is no necessity for this haste, and no danger of any war; it is merely a matter of business, and such legislation is simply an effort to bring about by legislation a remedy for difficulties which exist by virtue of the incompetence of what are called diplomats."

The President approved the bill March 3, 1887.

Pensions.—Jan. 10, 1887, there was reported from the House Committee on Invalid Pensions a bill for "the relief of dependent parents and honorably discharged soldiers and sailors who are now disabled and dependent on their labor for support." January 17, Mr. Matson, of Indiana, moved that the rules be suspended, and the measure passed. In support of the bill he said: "The first section provides simply that the rule of evidence in claims filed by dependent parents shall be changed so that hereafter those who make such claims shall be required to prove only a present dependence, instead of a dependence existing at the time of the death of the soldier. This section of the bill is an exact copy of one section of a bill passed under a suspension of the rules, on motion of the distinguished gentleman from Ohio (Mr. Warner), on the 21st day of April, 1884. That bill, in that form, passed the House and went to the Senate. It is in precise accord with the recommendations of the Secretary of the Interior, as contained in his last annual report, to be found on page 50 of that report.

"As to the second proposition, the more important one, I desire to call the attention of the House, in the first place, to the fact that this provision embraces honorably discharged soldiers of all the wars in which the United States has been engaged; it embraces those engaged in the Seminole, in the Black Hawk, in the Mexican, and in the last war. It is a broad measure, and not confined to the soldiers of any particular war. The gist of the proposition, Mr. Speaker, is to take from the poor-houses of the country the soldiers who have honorably served their country during any war. The proposition contained in this section of the bill is simply that every man who is totally unable to labor, and is in a dependent condition, shall be pensioned at the rate of $12 per month. There is no provision for pensioning any one who has a less disability than a total inability to labor; and in addition to that he must show that he is dependent upon his daily labor for his support, and has no property from which to derive an income. It is a charity measure.

"It will not be asserted by the friends or enemies of the bill, I apprehend, that there is anything in any contract made by the Government that would call for this legislation; but the legislation itself is the outgrowth of a sentiment that I believe prevails, throughout the length and breadth of this country, against permitting the men who have defended the Government to remain in the poor-houses to be supported by charity; and it is in obedience to that sentiment that the committee deem it proper to bring in a measure placing these men upon the honorable roll of pensioners of the United States.

"Now, as to the matter of cost: I desire to say that early in this Congress, in obedience to a suggestion made to the Commissioner of Pensions, when he was before the Committee on Invalid Pensions, and was being examined in connection with various matters relating to the pension laws, he wrote to the authorities in every county in the United States for the purpose of ascertaining how many soldiers and sailors who had been in the United States service were then objects of public or private charity throughout the land. He learned from 1,240 of the 2,583 counties in the United States that in the 1,240 counties there are 5,172 cases of soldiers and sailors who are now being supported in the public institutions of charity. So that it is estimated, inasmuch as these reports came in about equal proportions from all sections of the country, that there are an equal number in the remaining counties, not quite one half having been heard from, and so on that basis it is assumed that there are now in the United States a total of 10,344 persons dependent upon organized charities in the several States and Territories who would become pensioners under this bill.

"The report affords no exact information as to the inmates of soldiers' homes, both State and national, who may be entitled to the benefits of the bill, but we are clearly of opinion, from the best information obtainable, that the number will not exceed 3,000.

"The committee did not stop there. In addition to that, there has been added an estimate as to those who are not supported by public charity, but who are the recipients of private relief—the recipients of charity from those who are not legally bound for their support—and there has been added, because of that class, an average of five to each county, giving a total of 12,905 in all. That added to the other number makes a total of 26,249 probable pensioners in the event of the passage of this bill. That is the estimate of the committee. Then, in addition to that, the committee considered the further fact that there were pending in the Pension-Office claims of those who perhaps could bring themselves within the provisions of this bill, who were now receiving a small pension, and they added on that account a considerable number, 6,856 persons in all. So that the grand total of those who are to be benefited by the passage of this bill is estimated by the committee, from the best available sources, to be 33,105 persons at an annual expense of $144 each, or a total aggregate of $4,767,120 per annum.

"This estimate, Mr. Speaker, which I have given to the House, is based upon the number of soldiers in the last war. Now, in addition to that, the other soldiers of other wars must be taken into account. It will be liberal, I think, to say that not more than 10 per cent. would be added to it, and even if 15 per cent. more would be added under this section, it would still require less than six million dollars per annum to pay the expenses of all the pensions provided for in the bill.

"This, then, Mr. Speaker, is not only a broad and philanthropic measure, but it is a reasonable and conservative proposition. It is not wild and is not extravagant. It is in the line of action suggested by the Chief Executive in his last annual message."

In criticism of the measure Mr. Warner, of Ohio, said:

"While I may not vote against this bill, there are some features of it which I deem very objectionable, and I hope that at least in one particular an amendment will be allowed.

"There is no subject, Mr. Speaker, upon which Congress is called to legislate where it is more important to adhere to sound and consistent principles than in legislating upon the subject of pensions; and yet there is no subject on which we are so likely to be carried away by sentiment, by emotion, and, if I may say so, by demagogy, as on the question of pensions.

"The first section of this bill I heartily approve. I think it entirely sound in principle. There is every reason to suppose that a soldier who was killed in the war if he were living would extend now to his aged parents if in need. The question should not therefore be were they in need at the time of the soldier's death, but are they in need now? This bill differs very widely in principle, too, from the bill passed at the last session of Congress which I voted against, and if I ever cast a righteous vote I think that was one; I allude to the bill increasing the pensions of that small class who

were already receiving very large pensions. That bill to the few who had much gave more, and to those who had nothing it gave nothing.

"But, Mr. Speaker, the principal objection which I have to this bill is to the pauper feature of the second section. Indeed, the bill is made by this section rather a pauper bill than a pension bill. I do not like that feature of it. In 1818 a bill was passed not unlike this relating to the soldiers of the Revolutionary War; it was a bill granting pensions to those who were indigent or paupers, but it did not stand long. It was modified the next year, I believe, so as to include all who had not property of the value of $300. It never gave satisfaction, and led to frequent amendments, and finally was repealed entirely. The principle of this act was frequently condemned in the debates in Congress."

The rules were suspended, and the bill passed by the following vote:

YEAS—G. E. Adams, J. J. Adams, C. H. Allen, C. M. Anderson, J. A. Anderson, Atkinson, Bacon, Baker, Bayne, Bound, Boutelle, Boyle, Brady, C. E. Brown, W. W. Brown, Brumm, Buck, Bunnell, Burnes, Burrows, Butterworth, Bynum, J. M. Campbell, J. E. Campbell, Cannon, Carleton, Caswell, Clardy, Cobb, Conger, Cooper, Curtin, Cutcheon, Davenport, Davis, Dingley, Dorsey, Dougherty, Dunham, Eden, Eldredge, Ellsberry, Ely, Ermentrout, Evans, Everhart, Farquhar, Fisher, Fleeger, Foran, Ford, Frederick, Fuller, Funston, Gallinger, Gay, C. H. Gibson, Goff, Grosvenor, Grout, Guenther, Hale, Hall, Harmer, Hatch, Hayden, Haynes, D. B. Henderson, Henley, Hepburn, Hermann, Hiestand, Hill, Hitt, Holman, Holmes, Hopkins, Howard, F. A. Johnson, J. T. Johnston, Kelley, Ketcham, Kleiner, La Follette, Landes, Lawler, Le Fevre, Lehlbach, Libbey, Lindsley, Little, Long, Lore, Louttit, Lovering, Lowry, Lyman, Markham, Matson, McAdoo, McKenna, McKinley, Merriman, Millard, Milliken, Moffat, Morrill, Morrison, Morrow, Murphy, Neece, Negley, Nelson, O'Donnell, Charles O'Neill, J. J. O'Neill, Osborne, Outhwaite, Owen, Parker, Perkins, Peters, Pettibone, Phelps, Pindar, Pirce, Plumb, Randall, Ranney, Reed, Rice, Riggs, Rockwell, Romeis, Rowell, Rusk, Ryan, Sawyer, Scott, Scranton, Seney, Seymour, Shaw, Sowden, Spooner, Springer, Stahlnecker, Steele, Stephenson, E. F. Stone, W. J. Stone of Missouri, Strait, Struble, Swope, Taulbee, E. B. Taylor, I. H. Taylor, J. R. Thomas, O. B. Thomas, Thompson, Townshend, Van Schaick, Viele, Wade, Wadsworth, Wait, Wakefield, J. H. Ward, T. B. Ward, A. J. Warner, William Warner, J. B. Weaver, Weber, A. C. White, Milo White, Wilkins, Winans, Wolford, Woodburn, Worthington—180.

NAYS—J. M. Allen, Ballentine, Barbour, Barksdale, Barnes, Bennett, Blanchard, Bland, Blount, Bragg, C. R. Breckinridge, W. C. P. Breckinridge, Cabell, Caldwell, Catchings, Clements, Compton, Comstock, Cowles, W. R. Cox, Crisp, Croxton, Culberson, Dargan, A. C. Davidson, R. H. M. Davidson, Dawson, Dibble, Dunn, Glass, Glover, W. J. Green, Halsell, Hammond, Harris, Hemphill, J. S. Henderson, Herbert, Hutton, Irion, T. D. Johnston, J. H. Jones, J. T. Jones, Laffoon, Lanham, Martin, McCreary, McMillin, McRae, Miller, Mills, Neal, Oates, O'Ferrall, Peel, Perry, Richardson, Robertson, Rogers, Sadler, Sayers, Singleton, Skinner, Charles Stewart, Storm, J. M. Taylor, Throckmorton, Tillman, Trigg, Tucker, Turner, Van Eaton, Wellborn, Wheeler, Willis, Wise—76.

NOT VOTING—Aiken, Barry, Belmont, Bingham, Bliss, T. M. Browne, Buchanan, Burleigh, Felix Campbell, T. J. Campbell, Candler, Collins, S. S.

Cox, Crain, Daniel, Dockery, Felton, Findlay, Forney, Geddes, Eustace Gibson, Gilfillan, R. S. Green, Hanback, Heard, T. J. Henderson, Hires, Hiscock, Houk, Hudd, Jackson, James, King, Laird, Mahoney, Maybury, McComas, Mitchell, Morgan, Muller, Norwood, O'Hara, Payne, Payson, Pidcock, Reagan, Reese, Sessions, Smalls, Snyder, Spriggs, J. W. Stewart, St. Martin, W. J. Stone of Kentucky, Swinburne, Symes, Tarsney, Zachary Taylor, Wallace, A. J. Weaver, West, Whiting, Wilson—63.

The full text of the bill was as follows:

Be it enacted, etc., That in considering the pension claims of dependent parents, the fact and cause of death, and the fact that the soldier left no widow or minor children, having been shown as required by law, it shall be necessary only to show by competent and sufficient evidence that such parent or parents are without other present means of support than their own manual labor or the contributions of others not legally bound for their support: *Provided,* That no pension allowed under this act shall commence prior to its passage, and in case of applications hereafter made under this act the pension shall commence from the date of the filing of the application in the Pension-Office.

SEC. 2. That all persons who served three months or more in the military or naval service of the United States in any war in which the United States has been engaged, and who have been honorably discharged therefrom, and who are now or who may hereafter be suffering from mental or physical disability, not the result of their own vicious habits or gross carelessness, which incapacitates them for the performance of labor in such a degree as to render them unable to earn a support, and who are dependent upon their daily labor for support, shall, upon making due proof of the fact according to such rules and regulations as the Secretary of the Interior may provide in pursuance of this act, be placed on the list of invalid pensioners of the United States, and be entitled to receive, for such total inability to procure their subsistence by daily labor, $12 per month; and such pension shall commence from the date of the filing of the application in the Pension-Office, upon proof that the disability then existed, and continued during the existence of the same in the degree herein provided: *Provided,* That persons who are now receiving pensions under existing laws, or whose claims are pending in the Pension-Office, may, by application to the Commissioner of Pensions, in such forms as he may prescribe, receive the benefits of this act; but nothing herein contained shall be so construed as to allow more than one pension at the same time to the same person or pension to commence prior to the passage of this act: *And provided further,* That rank in the service shall not be considered in applications filed thereunder.

SEC. 3. That no agent, attorney, or other person instrumental in the presentation and prosecution of a claim under this act shall demand or receive for his services or instrumentality in presenting and prosecuting such claim a sum greater than $5, payable only upon the order of the Commissioner of Pensions, by the pension agent making payment of the pension allowed, except in cases heretofore prosecuted before the Pension-Office, when, in the discretion of the Commissioner of Pensions, a fee of $10 may be allowed in like manner to the agent or attorney of record in the case at the date of the passage of this act; and any agent, attorney, or other person instrumental in the prosecution of a claim under this act who shall demand or receive a sum greater than that herein provided for, for his services in the prosecution of the claim, shall be subject to the same penalties as prescribed in section 4 of the act of July 4, 1884, entitled "An act making appropriations for the payment of invalid and other pensions of the United States for the fiscal year ending June 30, 1885, and for other purposes.".

SEC. 4. That section 4716 of the Revised Statutes is hereby modified so that the same shall not apply to this act: *Provided,* That this act shall not apply to those persons under political disabilities. And no person shall be pensioned under this act for any disability incurred while engaged in the military service against the United States.

This measure differed from that passed by the Senate at the previous session of Congress in not limiting its provisions to soldiers who had served in the civil war. It came up for discussion in the Senate January 27, and passed that body without a division.

Feb. 11, 1887, the President sent in the following veto message:

To the House of Representatives:

I herewith return without my approval House bill 10,457, entitled "An act for the relief of dependent parents and honorably discharged soldiers and sailors who are now disabled and dependent upon their own labor for support."

This is the first general bill that has been sanctioned by the Congress since the close of the late civil war, permitting a pension to the soldiers and sailors who served in that war upon the ground of service and present disability alone, and in the entire absence of any injuries received by the casualties or incidents of such service.

While by almost constant legislation since the close of this war, there has been compensation awarded for every possible injury received as a result of military service in the Union Army, and while a great number of laws passed for that purpose have been administered with great liberality, and have been supplemented by numerous private acts to reach special cases, there has not, until now, been an avowed departure from the principle thus far adhered to respecting Union soldiers, that the bounty of the Government in the way of pensions is generously bestowed when granted to those who in this military service, and in the line of military duty have, to a greater or less extent, been disabled.

But it is a mistake to suppose that service pensions such as are permitted by the second section of the bill under consideration, are new to our legislation. In 1818, thirty-five years after the close of the Revolutionary War, they were granted to the soldiers engaged in that struggle, conditional upon service until the end of the war, or for a term not less than nine months, and requiring every beneficiary under the act to be one "who is, or hereafter by reason of his reduced circumstances in life shall be, in need of assistance from his country for support." Another law of a like character was passed in 1828, requiring service until the close of the Revolutionary War; and still another, passed in 1832, provided for those persons not included in the previous statute, but who served two years at some time during the war, and giving a proportionate sum to those who had served not less than six months.

A service pension law was passed for the benefit of the soldiers of 1812, in the year 1871—fifty-six years after the close of that war—which required only sixty days' service; and another was passed in 1878—sixty-three years after the war—requiring only fourteen days' service.

The service pension bill passed at this session of Congress, thirty-nine years after the close of the Mexican War, for the benefit of the soldiers of that war, requires either some degree of disability or dependency, or that the claimant under its provisions should be sixty-two years of age; and in either case that he should have served sixty days or been actually engaged in a battle.

It will be seen that the bill of 1818, and the Mexican pension bill being thus passed nearer the close of the wars in which its beneficiaries were engaged than the others—one thirty-five years and the other thirty-nine years after the termination of such wars—embraced persons who were quite advanced in age, assumed to be comparatively few in number, and whose circumstances, dependence, and disabilities were clearly defined, and could be quite easily fixed.

The other laws referred to, appear to have been passed at a time so remote from the military service of the persons which they embraced, that their extreme age alone was deemed to supply a presumption of dependency and need.

The number of enlistments in the Revolutionary War is stated to be 309,791, and in the War of 1812, 576,622; but it is estimated that on account of repeated re-enlistments the number of individuals engaged in these wars did not exceed one half of the number represented by these figures. In the war with Mexico, the number of enlistments is reported to be 112,230, which represents a greater proportion of individuals engaged than the reported enlistments in the two previous wars.

The number of pensions granted under all laws to soldiers of the Revolution, is given at 62,069 ; to soldiers of the War of 1812 and their widows, 60,178 ; and to soldiers of the Mexican War and their widows up to June 30, 1885, 7,619. The latter pensions were granted to the soldiers of a war involving much hardship, for disabilities incurred as a result of such service ; and it was not till within the last month that the few remaining survivors were awarded a service pension.

The War of the Rebellion terminated nearly twenty-two years ago ; the number of men furnished for its prosecution is stated to be 2,772,408. No corresponding number of statutes have ever been passed to cover every kind of injury or disability incurred in the military service of any war. Under these statutes, 561,576 pensions have been granted from the year 1861 to June 30, 1886, and more than 2,600 pensioners have been added to the rolls by private acts passed to meet cases, many of them of questionable merit, which the general laws did not cover.

On the 1st day of July, 1886, 365,763 pensioners of all classes were upon the pension-rolls, of whom, 305,605 were survivors of the war of the rebellion, and their widows and dependents. For the year ending June 30, 1887, $75,000,000 have been appropriated for the payment of pensions, and the amount expended for that purpose from 1861 to July 1, 1886, is $808,624,811.51.

While annually paying out such a vast sum for pensions already granted, it is now proposed, by the bill under consideration, to award a service pension to the soldiers of all wars in which the United States has been engaged, including, of course, the War of the Rebellion, and to pay those entitled to the benefits of the act the sum of $12 per month.

So far as it relates to the soldiers of the late Civil War, the bounty it affords them is given thirteen years earlier than it has been furnished to the soldiers of any other war, and before a large majority of its beneficiaries have advanced in age beyond the strength and vigor of the prime of life.

It exacts only a military or naval service of three months without any requirement of actual engagement with an enemy in battle, and without a subjection to any of the actual dangers of war.

The pension it awards is allowed to enlisted men who have not suffered the least injury, disability, loss, or damage of any kind, incurred in or in any degree referable to their military service, including those who never reached the front at all, and those discharged from rendezvous at the close of the war, if discharged three months after enlistment. Under the last call of the President for troops in December, 1864, 11,303 men were furnished who were thus discharged.

The section allowing this pension does, however, require, besides a service of three months and an honorable discharge, that those seeking the benefit of the act shall be such as "are now or may hereafter be suffering from mental or physical disability, not the result of their own vicious habits or gross carelessness, which incapacitates them for the performance of labor in such a degree as to render them unable to earn a support, and who are dependent upon their daily labor for support."

It provides further that such persons shall, upon making proof of the fact, "be placed on the list of invalid pensioners of the United States, and be entitled to receive for such total inability to procure their subsistence by daily labor, twelve dollars per month; and such pension shall commence from the date of the filing of the application in the Pension-Office, upon proof that the disability then existed, and continue during the existence of the same in the degree herein provided : *Provided*, That persons who are now receiving pensions under existing laws, or whose claims are pending in the Pension-Office, may, by application to the Commissioner of Pensions, in such form as he may prescribe, receive the benefit of this act."

It is manifestly of the utmost importance that statutes which like pension laws should be liberally administered as measures of benevolence in behalf of worthy beneficiaries, should admit of no uncertainty as to their general objects and consequences.

Upon a careful consideration of the language of the section of this bill above given, it seems to me to be so uncertain and liable to such conflicting constructions, and to be subject to such unjust and mischievous application, as to alone furnish sufficient ground for disapproving the proposed legislation.

Persons seeking to obtain the pension provided by this section must be now or hereafter—

1. "Suffering from mental or physical disability."

2. Such disability must not be "the result of their own vicious habits or gross carelessness."

3. Such disability must be such as "incapacitates them for the performance of labor in such a degree as to render them unable to earn a support."

4. They must be "dependent upon their daily labor for support."

5. Upon proof of these conditions they shall "be placed on the lists of invalid pensioners of the United States, and be entitled to receive for such total inability to procure their subsistence by daily labor twelve dollars per month."

It is not probable that the words last quoted, "such total inability to procure their subsistence by daily labor," at all qualify the conditions prescribed in the preceding language of the section. The "total inability" spoken of must be "such" inability—that is, the inability already described and constituted by the conditions already detailed in the previous parts of the section.

It thus becomes important to consider the meaning and the scope of these last-mentioned conditions.

The mental and physical disability spoken of has a distinct meaning in the practice of the Pension Bureau, and includes every impairment of bodily or mental strength and vigor. For such disabilities there are now paid one hundred and thirty-one different rates of pension, ranging from $1 to $100 per month.

The disability must not be the result of the applicant's "vicious habits or gross carelessness." Practically this provision is not important. The attempt of the Government to escape the payment of a pension on such a plea, would of course, in a very large majority of instances, and regardless of the merits of the case, prove a failure. There would be that strange but nearly universal willingness to help the individual as between him and the public treasury, which goes very far to insure a state of proof in favor of the claimant.

The disability of applicants must be such as to "incapacitate them for the performance of labor in such a degree as to render them unable to earn a support."

It will be observed that there is no limitation or definition of the incapacitating injury or ailment itself. It need only be such a degree of disability from any cause as renders the claimant unable to earn a support by labor. It seems to me that the "support" here mentioned as one which can not be earned, is a complete and entire support, with no diminution on account of the least impairment of physical or mental condition. If it had been intended to embrace only those who by disease or injury were totally unable to labor, it would have been very easy to express that idea, instead of recognizing as is done a "degree" of such inability.

What is a support? Who is to determine whether a man earns it or has it or has it not? Is the Government to enter the homes of claimants for pension, and after an examination of their surroundings and circumstances settle those questions? Shall the Government say to one man that his manner of subsistence by his earnings is a support, and to another that the things his earnings furnish are not a support? Any attempt, however honest, to administer this law in such a manner would necessarily produce more unfairness and unjust discrimination and give more scope for partisan partiality, and would result in more perversion of the Government's benevolent intentions, than the execution of any statute ought to permit.

If in the effort to carry out the proposed law, the degree of disability as related to earnings, be considered for the purpose of discovering if in any way it curtails the support which the applicant if entirely sound would earn, and to which he is entitled, we enter the broad field long occupied by the Pension Bureau, and we recognize as the only difference between the proposed legislation and previous laws passed for the benefit of the surviving soldiers of the civil war, the incurrence in one case of disabilities in military service, and in the other disabilities existing but in no way connected with or resulting from such service.

It must be borne in mind that in no case is there any grading of this proposed pension. Under the operation of the rule first suggested, if there is a lack in any degree, great or small, of the ability to earn such a support as the Government determines the claimant should have, and by the application of the rule secondly suggested, if there is a reduction in any degree of the support which he might earn if sound, he is entitled to a pension of $12.

In the latter case, and under the proviso of the proposed bill, permitting persons now receiving pensions to be admitted to the benefits of the act, I do not see how those now on the pension-roll for disabilities incurred in the service, and which diminish their earning capacity, can be denied the pension provided in this bill.

Of course none will apply who are now receiving $12 or more per month. But on the 30th day of June, 1886, there were on the pension-rolls 202,621 persons who were receiving fifty-eight different rates of pension from $1 to $11.75 per month. Of these, 23,-142 were receiving $2 per month; 63,116, $4 per month; 37,254, $6 per month; and 50,274, whose disabilities were rated as total, $8 per month.

As to the meaning of the section of the bill under consideration there appears to have been quite a difference of opinion among its advocates in the Congress. The chairman of the Committee on Pensions in the House of Representatives, who reported the bill, declared that there was in it no provision for pensioning any one who has a less disability than a total inability to labor, and that it was a charity measure. The chairman of the Committee on Pensions in the Senate, having charge of the bill in that body, dissented from the construction of the bill announced in the House of Representatives, and declared that it not only embraced all soldiers totally disabled, but in his judgment all who are disabled to any considerable extent; and such a construction was substantially given to the bill by another distinguished Senator who, as a former Secretary of the Interior, had imposed upon him the duty of executing pension laws and determining their intent and meaning.

Another condition required of claimants under this act is that they shall be "dependent upon their daily labor for support."

This language, which may be said to assume that there exists within the reach of the persons mentioned "labor," or the ability in some degree to work, is more aptly used in a statute describing those not wholly deprived of this ability, than in one which deals with those utterly unable to work.

I am of the opinion that it may fairly be contended that under the provisions of this section any soldier, whose faculties of mind or body have become impaired by accident, disease, or age, irrespective of his service in the army as a cause, and who by his labor only is left incapable of gaining the fair support he might with unimpaired powers have provided for himself, and who is not so well endowed with this world's goods as to live without work, may claim to participate in its bounty; that it is not required that he should be without property, but only that labor should be necessary to his support in some degree; nor is it required that he should be now receiving support from others.

Believing this to be the proper interpretation of the bill, I can not but remember that the soldiers of our civil war, in their pay and bounty, received such compensation for military service as has never been received by soldiers before, since mankind first went to war; that never before, on behalf of any soldiery, have so many and such generous laws been passed to relieve against the incidents of war; that statutes have been passed giving them a preference in all public employments; that the really needy and homeless Union soldiers of the rebellion have been, to a large extent, provided for at soldiers' homes, instituted and supported by the Government, where they are maintained together, free from the sense of degradation which attaches to the usual support of charity; and that never before in the history of the country has it been proposed to render Government aid toward the support of any of its soldiers based alone upon a military service so recent, and where age and circumstances appeared so little to demand such aid.

Hitherto such relief has been granted to surviving soldiers few in number, venerable in age, after a long lapse of time since their military service, and as a parting benefaction tendered by a grateful people.

I can not believe that the vast peaceful army of Union soldiers, who have contentedly resumed their places in the ordinary avocations of life cherish as sacred the memory of patriotic service, or, who having been disabled by the casualties of war justly regard the present pension-roll, on which appear their names, as a roll of honor, desire at this time and in the present exigency, to be confounded with those who through such a bill as this are willing to be objects of simple charity and to gain a place upon the pension-roll through alleged dependence.

Recent personal observation and experience constrain me to refer to another result which will inevitably follow the passage of this bill. It is sad but nevertheless true that already in the matter of procuring pensions there exists a wide-spread disregard of truth and good faith, stimulated by those who as agents undertake to establish claims for pensions, heedlessly entered upon by the expectant beneficiary, and encouraged or at least not condemned by those unwilling to obstruct a neighbor's plans.

In the execution of this proposed law under any interpretation, a wide field of inquiry would be opened for the establishment of facts largely within the knowledge of the claimants alone; and there can be no doubt that the race after the pensions offered by this bill would not only stimulate weakness and pretended incapacity for labor, but put a further premium on dishonesty and mendacity.

The effect of new invitations to apply for pensions, or of new advantages added to causes for pensions already existing, is sometimes startling.

Thus in March, 1879, large arrearages of pensions

were allowed to be added to all claims filed prior to July 1, 1880. For the year from July 1, 1879, to July 1, 1880, there were filed 110,673 claims, though in the year immediately previous there were but 36,-832 filed, and in the year following but 18,455.

While cost should not be set against a patriotic duty or the recognition of a right, still, when a measure proposed is based upon generosity or motives of charity, it is not amiss to meditate somewhat upon the expense which it involves. Experience has demonstrated, I believe, that all estimates concerning the probable future cost of a pension-list are uncertain and unreliable, and always fall far below actual realization.

The chairman of the House Committee on Pensions calculates that the number of pensioners under this bill would be 33,105, and the increased cost $4,767,-190; this is upon the theory that only those who are entirely unable to work would be its beneficiaries. Such was the principle of the Revolutionary pension law of 1818, much more clearly stated, it seems to me, than in this bill. When the law of 1818 was upon its passage in Congress the number of pension-ors to be benefited thereby was thought to be 374; but the number of applicants under the act was 22,-397, and the number of pensions actually allowed 20,485, costing, it is reported, for the first year, $1,-847,900, instead of $40,000, the estimated expense for that period.

A law was passed in 1853 for the benefit of the surviving widows of Revolutionary soldiers who were married after Jan. 1, 1800. It was estimated that they numbered 300 at the time of the passage of the act; but the number of pensions allowed was 3,742, and the amount paid for such pensions during the first year of the operation of the act was $180,000, instead of $24,000 as had been estimated.

I have made no search for other illustrations, and the above being at hand, are given as tending to show that estimates can not be relied upon in such cases.

If none should be pensioned under this bill except those utterly unable to work, I am satisfied that the cost stated in the estimate referred to would be many times multiplied, and with a constant increase from year to year; and if those partially unable to earn their support should be admitted to the privileges of this bill, the probable increase of expense would be almost appalling.

I think it may be said that at the close of the War of the Rebellion every Northern State and a great majority of Northern counties and cities, were burdened with taxation on account of the large bounties paid our soldiers; and the bonded debt thereby created still constitutes a large item in the account of the tax-gatherer against the people. Federal taxation, no less borne by the people than that directly levied upon their property, is still maintained at the rate made necessary by the exigencies of war. If this bill should become a law, with its tremendous addition to our pension obligation, I am thoroughly convinced that further efforts to reduce the Federal revenue and restore some part of it to our people, will and perhaps should be seriously questioned.

It has constantly been a cause of pride and congratulation to the American citizen that his country is not put to the charge of maintaining a large standing army in time of peace. Yet we are now living under a war-tax which has been tolerated in peaceful times to meet the obligations incurred in war. But for years past, in all parts of the country, the demand for the reduction of the burdens of taxation upon our labor and production has increased in volume and urgency.

I am not willing to approve a measure presenting the objections to which this bill is subject, and which, moreover, will have the effect of disappointing the expectation of the people and their desire and hope for relief from war-taxation in time of peace.

In my last annual message the following language was used:

" Every patriotic heart responds to a tender consideration for those who, having served their country long and well, are reduced to destitution and dependence, not as an incident of their service, but with advancing age or through sickness or misfortune. We are all tempted by the contemplation of such a condition to supply relief, and are often impatient of the limitations of public duty. Yielding to no one in the desire to indulge this feeling of consideration, I can not rid myself of the conviction that if these ex-soldiers are to be relieved, they and their cause are entitled to the benefit of an enactment under which relief may be claimed as a right, and that such relief should be granted under the sanction of law, not in evasion of it; nor should such worthy objects of care, all equally entitled, be remitted to the unequal operation of sympathy, or the tender mercies of social and political influence with their unjust discriminations."

I do not think that the objects, the conditions, and the limitations thus suggested, are contained in the bill under consideration.

I adhere to the sentiments thus heretofore expressed. But the evil threatened by this bill is, in my opinion, such that, charged with a great responsibility in behalf of the people, I can not do otherwise than to bring to the consideration of this measure my best efforts of thought and judgment, and perform my constitutional duty in relation thereto, regardless of all consequences, except such as appear to me to be related to the best and highest interests of the country.   GROVER CLEVELAND.

EXECUTIVE MANSION,
     Washington, Feb. 11, 1887.

February 24, the motion to reconsider and pass the bill came up for discussion in the House, and, after a long and heated debate, it failed, by the following vote—lacking the constitutional majority of two thirds requisite for overriding a veto:

YEAS—G. E. Adams, C. H. Allen, J. A. Anderson, Atkinson, Baker, Bayne, Bingham, Bliss, Bound, Boutelle, Brady, T. M. Browne, C. E. Brown, W. W. Brown, Brumm, Buck, Bunnell, Burleigh, Burrows, Butterworth, Bynum, J. M. Campbell, J. E. Campbell, Cannon, Carleton, Caswell, Conger, Cooper, Cutcheon, Davenport, Davis, Dingley, Dorsey, Dunham, Eldredge, Ely, Evans, Everhart, Farquhar, Felton, Fleeger, Ford, Frederick, Fuller, Funston, Gallinger, Geddes, Gilfillan, Goff, Grosvenor, Grout, Guenther, Hale, Hanback, Harmer, Hayden, Haynes, D. B. Henderson, T. J. Henderson, Hepburn, Hermann, Hiestand, Hires, Hiscock, Hitt, Holman, Holmes, Hopkins, Houk, Howard, Jackson, James, F. A. Johnson, J. T. Johnston, Kelley, Ketcham, Kleiner, La Follette, Laird, Landes, Lawler, Le Fevre, Lehlbach, Libbey, Lindsley Little, Long, Lore, Louttit, Lovering, Lyman, Mahoney, Markham, Matson, Maybury, McComas, McKenna, McKinley, Merriman, Millard, Milliken, Moffatt, Morrill, Morrow, Murphy, Neece, Negley, Nelson, O'Donnell, O'Hara, Charles O'Neill, J. J. O'Neill, Osborne, Owen, Parker, Payne, Payson, Perkins, Peters, Pettibone, Phelps, Pindar, Pirce, Plumb, Randall, Ranney, Rice, Riggs, Rockwell, Romeis, Rowell, Ryan, Sawyer, Scranton, Seney, Sessions, Smalls, Spooner, Sprigga, Steele, Stephenson, J. W. Stewart, E. F. Stone, Strait, Struble, Swinburne, Swope, Symes, Tarsney, Taulbee, E. B. Taylor, I. H. Taylor, Zachary Taylor, J. R. Thomas, O. B. Thomas, Thompson, Townshend, Van Schaick, Wade, Wadsworth, Wait, Wakefield, J. H. Ward, William Warner, A. J. Weaver, J. B. Weaver, Weber, West, A. C. White, Milo White, Whiting, Wilkins, Wolford, Woodburn, Worthington—175.

NAYS—J. J. Adams, J. M. Allen, Bacon, Ballentine, Barbour, Barksdale, Barnes, Barry, Belmont, Bennett, Blanchard, Bland, Blount, Boyle, Bragg, C. R. Breckinridge, W. C. P. Breckinridge, Burnes, Cabell, Caldwell, Felix Campbell, T. J. Campbell,

Catchings, Clements, Cobb, Collins, Compton, Comstock, Cowles, S. S. Cox, W. R. Cox, Crain, Crisp, Culberson, Curtin, Daniel, Dargan, A. C. Davidson, R. H. M. Davidson, Dawson, Dibble, Dockery, Dougherty, Dunn, Eden, Ermentrout, Findlay, Fisher, Forney, Gay, C. H. Gibson, Eustace Gibson, Glass, Green, Hall, Halsell, Hammond, Harris, Hatch, Heard, Hemphill, J. S. Henderson, Herbert, Hill, Hudd, Hutton, Irion, T. D. Johnston, J. H. Jones, J. T. Jones, King, Laffoon, Lanham, Martin, McAdoo, McCreary, McMillin, McRae, Miller, Mills, Mitchell, Morgan, Morrison, Muller, Neal, Norwood, Oates, O'Ferrall, Outhwaite, Peel, Perry, Reagan, Reese, Richardson, Robertson, Rogers, Sayers, Scott, Seymour, Shaw, Singleton, Skinner, Snyder, Sowden, Springer, Stahlnecker, Charles Stewart, St. Martin, W. J. Stone of Kentucky, W. J. Stone of Missouri, Storm, J. M. Taylor, Tillman, Trigg, Tucker, Turner, Van Eaton, Viele, T. B. Ward, A. J. Warner, Wellborn, Wheeler, Willis, Wilson, Wise—125.

Not Voting—Aiken, C. M. Anderson, Buchanan, Candler, Clardy, Croxton, Ellsberry, Foran, Glover, Henley, Lowry, Pidcock, Reed, Rusk, Sadler, Throckmorton, Wallace, Winans—18.

Jan. 17, 1887, Mr. Eldridge, of Michigan, from the House Committee on Pensions, reported back the bill granting pensions to soldiers and sailors of the Mexican War, and moved that the rules be suspended and the Senate amendments concurred in. The motion prevailed, by a vote of 247 yeas to 5 nays. The original House bill and the Senate substitute, which the House concurred in, were given in the "Annual Cyclopædia" for 1886, at page 238. February 1, Congress was notified that the President approved of the measure. Though containing an age limit, it virtually provides for pensioning everybody who served sixty days in the army or navy in the Mexican War, even though the time was passed at a frontier station, or en route to the seat of war.

Court of Claims and Circuit Courts.—Jan. 13, 1887, the House passed a bill to provide for the bringing of suits against the Government of the United States. In explanation of the measure, Mr. Tucker, of Virginia, who reported it from the Committee on the Judiciary, said:

"As to this bill I would say that it is one which was very carefully matured by the Committee on the Judiciary nearly a year ago. The committee took all the bills with this general object that had been referred to it, as well as one reported by the Judiciary Committee of the Senate, and from those bills matured this one, which was reported, I think, from the committee with entire unanimity. The object of the bill is this: It extends the jurisdiction of the Court of Claims beyond the mere contract obligations of the Government to obligations of all kinds, as well those that could be asserted in a court of law as those which could be asserted in a court of equity or in admiralty. The bill also gives concurrent jurisdiction to the Circuit Court of the United States in the locality where the claim originates or where the party plaintiff resides, to consider all claims concurrently with the Court of Claims up to the amount of $10,000. The Court of Claims has jurisdiction with the circuit courts as to all claims, and under this bill the circuit courts will have concurrent jurisdiction with the Court of Claims in all cases up to the amount of $10,000.

"The only cases not provided for are suits upon the use of a patent right by the Government and suits in reference to captured and abandoned property which are now barred by the statutes of limitations. This bill extends the jurisdiction of the Court of Claims to all cases which arise, not only ex contractu but ex delicto, and to cases in admiralty, so that it will take the whole mass of these claims away from Congress."

The Senate amended and passed the measure February 24. The House non-concurred in the Senate amendments, and a conference committee was appointed, which recommended the following measure, to which both Houses agreed on March 3:

Be it enacted, &c., That the Court of Claims shall have jurisdiction to hear and determine the following matters:

First. All claims founded upon the Constitution of the United States or any law of Congress, except for pensions, or upon any regulation of an Executive Department, or upon any contract, expressed or implied, with the Government of the United States, or for damages, liquidated or unliquidated, in cases not sounding in tort, in respect of which claims the party would be entitled to redress against the United States either in a court of law, equity, or admiralty if the United States were suable: Provided, however, That nothing in this section shall be construed as giving to either of the courts herein mentioned jurisdiction to hear and determine claims growing out of the late civil war and commonly known as "war claims," or to hear and determine other claims, which have heretofore been rejected, or reported on adversely, by any court, department, or commissioner authorized to hear and determine the same.

Second. All set-offs, counter-claims, claims for damages, whether liquidated or unliquidated, or other demands whatsoever on the part of the Government of the United States against any claimant against the Government in said court: Provided, That no suit against the Government of the United States shall be allowed under this act unless the same shall have been brought within six years after the right accrued for which the claim is made.

SEC. 2. That the district courts of the United States shall have concurrent jurisdiction with the Court of Claims as to all matters named in the preceding section where the amount of the claim does not exceed $1,000, and the circuit courts of the United States shall have such concurrent jurisdiction in all cases where the amount of such claim exceeds $1,000 and does not exceed $10,000. All causes brought and tried under the provisions of this act shall be tried by the court without a jury.

SEC. 3. That whenever any person shall present his petition to the Court of Claims, alleging that he is or has been indebted to the United States as an officer or agent thereof, or by virtue of any contract therewith, or that he is the guarantor, or surety, or personal representative of any officer, or agent, or contractor so indebted, or that he, or the person for whom he is such surety, guarantor, or personal representative, has held any office or agency under the United States, or entered into any contract therewith, under which it may be or has been claimed that an indebtedness to the United States has arisen and exists, and that he or the person he represents has applied to the proper department of the Government requesting that the account of such office, agency, or indebtedness may be adjusted and settled, and that three years have elapsed from the date of such application and said account still remains unsettled and unadjusted, and that no suit upon the same has been brought by the United States, said court shall, due notice first being given to the head of said department and to the Attorney-General of the United States, proceed to hear the parties and to ascertain the amount, if any, due the United States on said account. The Attorney-General shall represent the United States at the hearing of said cause. The court may postpone the same from time to time whenever justice shall require. The judgment of said court or of the Supreme Court of the United States, to which an appeal shall lie, as in other cases, as to the amount due, shall be binding and conclusive upon the parties. The payment of such amount so found due by the court shall discharge such obligation. An action shall accrue to the United States against such principal, or surety, or representative to recover the amount so found due, which may be brought at any time within three years after the final judgment of said court. Unless suit shall be brought within said time, such claim and the claim on the original indebtedness shall be forever barred.

Sec. 4. That the jurisdiction of the respective courts of the United States proceeding under this act, including the right of exception and appeal, shall be governed by the law now in force, in so far as the same is applicable and not inconsistent with the provisions of this act; and the course of procedure shall be in accordance with the established rules of said respective courts, and of such additions and modifications thereof as said courts may adopt.

Sec. 5. That the plaintiff in any suit brought under the provisions of the second section of this act shall file a petition, duly verified, with the clerk of the respective court having jurisdiction of the case, and in the district where the plaintiff resides. Such petition shall set forth the full name and residence of the plaintiff, the nature of his claim, and a succinct statement of the facts upon which the claim is based, the money or other thing claimed, or the damages sought to be recovered, and praying the court for a judgment or decree upon the facts and law.

Sec. 6. That the plaintiff shall cause a copy of his petition filed under the preceding section to be served upon the district attorney of the United States in the district wherein suit is brought, and shall mail a copy of the same, by registered letter, to the Attorney-General of the United States, and shall thereupon cause to be filed with the clerk of the court wherein suit is instituted an affidavit of such service and the mailing of such letter. It shall be the duty of the district attorney upon whom service of petition is made as aforesaid to appear and defend the interests of the Government in the suit, and within sixty days after the service of petition upon him, unless the time should be extended by order of the court made in the case, to file a plea, answer, or demurrer on the part of the Government, and to file a notice of any counter-claim, set-off, claim for damages, or other demand or defense whatsoever of the Government in the premises: Provided, That should the district attorney neglect or refuse to file the plea, answer, demurrer, or defense as required, the plaintiff may proceed with the case under such rules as the court may adopt in the premises; but the plaintiff shall not have judgment or decree for his claim, or any part thereof, unless he shall establish the same by proof satisfactory to the court.

Sec. 7. That it shall be the duty of the court to cause a written opinion to be filed in the cause, setting forth the specific findings by the court of the facts therein and the conclusions of the court upon all questions of law involved in the case, and to render judgment thereon. If the suit be in equity or admiralty, the court shall proceed with the same according to the rules of such courts.

Sec. 8. That in the trial of any suit brought under any of the provisions of this act, no person shall be excluded as a witness because he is a party to or interested in said suit; and any plaintiff or party in interest may be examined as a witness on the part of the Government.

Section 1079 of the Revised Statutes is hereby repealed. The provisions of section 1080 of the Revised Statutes shall apply to cases under this act.

Sec. 9. That the plaintiff or the United States, in any suit brought under the provisions of this act, shall have the same rights of appeal or writ of error as are now reserved in the statutes of the United States in that behalf made, and upon the conditions and limitations therein contained. The modes of procedure in claiming and perfecting an appeal or writ of error shall conform in all respects, and as near as may be, to the statutes and rules of court governing appeals and writs of error in like causes.

Sec. 10. That when the findings of fact and the law applicable thereto have been filed in any case as provided in section 6 of this act, and the judgment or decree is adverse to the Government, it shall be the duty of the district attorney to transmit to the Attorney-General of the United States certified copies of all the papers filed in the cause, with a transcript of the testimony taken, the written findings of the court, and his written opinion as to the same; whereupon the Attorney-General shall determine and direct whether an appeal or writ of error shall be taken or not; and when so directed the district attorney shall cause an appeal or writ of error to be perfected in accordance with the terms of the statutes and rules of practice governing the same: Provided, That no appeal or writ of error shall be allowed after six months from the judgment or decree in such suit. From the date of such final judgment or decree interest shall be computed thereon, at the rate of 4 per cent. per annum, until the time when an appropriation is made for the payment of the judgment or decree.

Sec. 11. That the Attorney-General shall report to Congress, and at the beginning of each session of Congress, the suits under this act in which a final judgment or decree has been rendered, giving the date of each, with a statement of the costs taxed in each case.

Sec. 12. That when any claim or matter may be pending in any of the Executive Departments which involves controverted questions of fact or law, the head of such department, with the consent of the claimant, may transmit the same, with the vouchers, papers, proofs, and documents pertaining thereto, to said Court of Claims, and the same shall be there proceeded in under such rules as the court may adopt. When the facts and conclusions of law shall have been found, the court shall report its findings to the department by which it was transmitted.

Sec. 13. That in every case which shall come before the Court of Claims or is now pending therein under the provisions of an act entitled "An act to afford assistance and relief to Congress and the Executive Departments in the investigation of claims and demands against the Government," approved March 3, 1883, if it shall appear to the satisfaction of the court, upon the facts established, that it has jurisdiction to render judgment or decree thereon under existing laws or under the provisions of this act, it shall proceed to do so, giving to either party such further opportunity for hearing as in its judgment justice shall require, and report its proceedings therein to either House of Congress or to the department by which the same was referred to said court.

Sec. 14. That whenever any bill, except for a pension, shall be pending in either House of Congress providing for the payment of a claim against the United States, legal or equitable, or for a grant, gift, or bounty to any person, the House in which such bill is pending may refer the same to the Court of Claims, who shall proceed with the same in accordance with the provisions of the act approved March 3, 1883, entitled "An act to afford assistance and relief to Congress and the Executive Departments in the investigation of claims and demands against the Government," and report to such House the facts in the case and the amount, where the same can be liquidated, including any facts bearing upon the question whether there has been delay or laches in presenting such claim or applying for such grant, gift, or bounty, and any facts bearing upon the question whether the bar of any statute of limitation should be removed, or which shall be claimed to excuse the claimant for not having resorted to any established legal remedy.

Sec. 15. If the Government of the United States shall put in issue the right of the plaintiff to recover, the court may, in its discretion, allow costs to the prevailing party from the time of joining such issue. Such costs, however, shall include only what is actually incurred for witnesses and for summoning the same and fees paid to the clerk of the court.

Sec. 16. That all laws and parts of laws inconsistent with this act are hereby repealed.

The bill was approved by the President the same day.

Jan. 13, 1887, the House passed a measure regulating the jurisdiction of the circuit courts of the United States, which, in substantially the same form, had been passed by the House in the three preceding Congresses. Mr. Culberson, of Texas, said, in explanation of the measure: "The object of the bill is to diminish the jurisdiction of the circuit courts and the Supreme Court of the United States, to promote the convenience of the people, and to lessen the burden and expense of litigation. The methods employed by the bill are, first, to raise the minimum amount giving the circuit courts jurisdiction from $500 to $2,000. In the second place, we propose to take away from the circuit courts of the United States all jurisdiction of controversies between the assignees of promissory notes and the makers thereof, unless suit could have been maintained in such courts had no assignment been made. In the next place, the bill proposes to take away wholly from the circuit courts the jurisdiction now exercised by them over controversies in which one of the parties is a corporation organized under the laws of one State and doing business in another State. We propose to provide that the circuit courts shall have no jurisdiction over controversies of that sort; that whenever a corporation organized under the laws of one State shall carry on its business in another State, the corporation shall, for judicial purposes, be considered as a citizen of the State in which it is carrying on business.

"There is another provision in the bill in relation to the removal of causes from State to Federal courts. The provisions of the bill take away all right on the part of the plaintiff in a suit to remove his cause from a State to a Federal court after he has elected the forum in which to bring suit. The bill further provides that wherever the cause of action arises under the Constitution of the United States, or a law or treaty thereof, the defendant who is sued in a State court upon such a cause of action may remove the cause to a Federal court, provided he shall make it appear to the court in which the case is pending that his defense depends upon a proper construction of the Constitution of the United States, or some law or treaty thereof.

"The bill does not propose to repeal the act of 1867, which authorized either the plaintiff or the defendant in a suit pending in a State court to remove the cause from that court into a Federal court upon the ground of prejudice. That act is re-enacted, with a provision to this effect: that the plaintiff or the defendant, before he can remove the cause from the State to the Federal court, must satisfy the judge or court having jurisdiction of the cause of the truth of the matters alleged in his application for removal.

"This embodies, substantially, all the changes in the act. The effect of these changes I beg to refer to for a moment. The minimum jurisdiction of $500 was placed in the original judiciary act in 1789, and it has been the law ever since. The population of the country then was 4,000,000, and now it is over 54,000,000. The amount of business of the country in the courts then and now sustain no comparison whatever.

"The next proposition is to deny the right of an assignee of a promissory note to bring suit in a Federal court. That was the law from 1789 until 1875. For ninety years the assignee of a promissory note, or any other chose in action, could not bring suit in a Federal court, unless a suit could have been maintained had no assignment been made.

"The increase of jurisdiction of the circuit courts of the United States, from that change of law in 1875, has multiplied the business in that court enormously, while it diminishes the business in the circuit courts, which are overloaded everywhere now. It also diminishes the business in the Supreme Court of the United States, which is three years behind on its docket.

"The withdrawal of the right to remove causes from State to Federal courts in the manner provided in this bill, after the plaintiff has selected his forum, will largely diminish the business in the circuit courts of the United States, and also the business in the Supreme Court of the United States in cases over $5,000.

"The other proposition is to take away from the circuit courts of the United States jurisdiction over controversies between corporations created by the laws of a State and which go into other States and open offices and carry on business. For judicial purposes we make such corporations citizens of that State, and compel them to sue in the forum or in the courts of the State in which they carry on their business. Over one third of the business now in circuit courts of the United States and in the Supreme Court of the United States springs from this very jurisdiction to which I call your attention.

"And we deprive such corporation of the right to transfer that case or change it from a State to a Federal court.

"There is another provision in the bill to which I wish to call attention, and that is, it repeals section 640 of the Revised Statutes, which empowers or authorizes a corporation created under an act of Congress, whenever sued in a State court, to remove the cause from such court to a Federal court upon a mere suggestion that the defense of such corporation to the cause of action arises under an act of Congress, or under the laws of Congress. We repeal that statute, and the bill provides whenever a corporation. or any one else, is sued in a State court and the defense of such corporation or individual depends upon a right construction of the laws of Congress, or of the Constitution of the United States, then such cause may be removed. And the bill does not attempt to interfere with the right of appeal in the last resort from the Supreme Court of a State to the Supreme Court of the United States."

March 2 the Senate amended and passed this measure, and reconsidered, amended, and repassed it March 3. The House non-concurred in the Senate amendments, but on conference receded from its non-concurrence; and March 3 the President approved the bill. It is as follows:

Be it enacted, etc., That the first section of an act entitled "An act to determine the jurisdiction of circuit courts of the United States, and to regulate the removal of causes from State courts, and for other purposes," approved March 3, 1875, be, and the same is hereby, amended so as to read as follows:

"That the circuit courts of the United States shall have original cognizance, concurrent with the courts of the several States, of all suits of a civil nature, at common law or in equity, where the matter in dispute exceeds, exclusive of interest and costs, the sum or value of $2,000, and arising under the Constitution or laws of the United States, or treaties made, or which shall be made, under their authority, or in which controversy the United States shall be plaintiffs or petitioners, or in which there shall be a controversy between citizens of different States, in which the matter in dispute exceeds, exclusive of interest and costs, the sum or value aforesaid, or a controversy between citizens of the same State claiming lands under grants of different States, or a controversy between citizens of a State and foreign states, citizens, or subjects, in which the matter in dispute exceeds, exclusive of interest and costs, the sum or value aforesaid, and shall have exclusive cognizance of all crimes and offenses cognizable under the authority of the United States, except as otherwise provided by law, and concurrent jurisdiction with the district courts of the crimes and offenses cognizable by them. But no person shall be arrested in one district for trial in another in any civil action before a circuit or district court; and no civil suit shall be brought before either of said courts against any person by any original process or proceeding in any other district than that whereof he is an inhabitant; but where the jurisdiction is founded only on the fact that the action is between citizens of different States, suit shall be brought only in the district of the residence of either the plaintiff or the defendant; nor shall any circuit or district court have cognizance of any suit, except upon foreign bills of exchange, to recover the contents of any promissory note or other chose in action in favor of any assignee, or of any subsequent holder if such instrument be payable to bearer and be not made by any corporation, unless such suit might have been prosecuted in such court to recover the said contents if no assignment or transfer had been made; and the circuit courts shall also have appellate jurisdiction from the district courts under the regulations and restrictions prescribed by law."

That the second section of said act be, and the same is hereby, amended so as to read as follows:

"Sec. 2. That any suit of a civil nature, at law or in equity, arising under the Constitution or laws of the United States, or treaties made, or which shall be made, under their authority, of which the circuit courts of the United States are given original jurisdiction by the preceding section, which may now be pending, or which may hereafter be brought, in any State court, may be removed by the defendant or defendants therein to the circuit court of the United States for the proper district. Any other suit of a civil nature, at law or in equity, of which the circuit courts of the United States are given jurisdiction by the preceding section, and which are now pending, or which may hereafter be brought, in any State court, may be removed into the circuit court of the United States for the proper district by the defendant or defendants therein being non-residents of that State." And when in any suit mentioned in this section there shall be a controversy which is wholly between citizens of different States, and which can be fully determined as between them, then either one or more of the defendants actually interested in such controversy may remove said suit into the circuit court of the United States for the proper district. And where a suit is now pending, or may be hereafter brought, in any State court, in which there is a controversy between a citizen of the State in which the suit is brought and a citizen of another State, any defendant, being such citizen of another State, may remove such suit into the circuit court of the United States for the proper district, at any time before the trial thereof, when it shall be made to appear to said circuit court that from prejudice or local influence he will not be able to obtain justice in such State court, or in any other State court to which the said defendant may under the laws of the State, have the right, on account of such prejudice or local influence, to remove said cause: *Provided*, That if it further appear that said suit can be fully and justly determined as to the other defendants in the State court, without being affected by such prejudice or local influence, and that no party to the suit will be prejudiced by a separation of the parties, said circuit court may direct the suit to be remanded, so far as relates to such other defendants, to the State court, to be proceeded with therein. At any time before the trial of any suit which is now pending in any circuit court or may hereafter be entered therein, and which has been removed to said court from a State court on the affidavit of any party plaintiff that he had reason to believe and did believe that, from prejudice or local influence, he was unable to obtain justice in said State court, the circuit court shall, on application of the other party, examine into the truth of said affidavit and the grounds thereof, and, unless it shall appear to the satisfaction of said court that said party will not be able to obtain justice in such State court, it shall cause the same to be remanded thereto. Whenever any cause shall be removed from any State court into any circuit court of the United States, and the circuit court shall decide that the cause was improperly removed, and order the same to be remanded to the State court from whence it came, such remand shall be immediately carried into execution, and no appeal or writ of error from the decision of the circuit court so remanding such cause shall be allowed.

That section 3 of said act be, and the same is hereby, amended so as to read as follows:

Sec. 3. That whenever any party entitled to remove any suit mentioned in the next preceding section, except in such cases as are provided for in the last clause of said section, may desire to remove such suit from a State court to the circuit court of the United States, he may make and file a petition in such suit in such State court at the time, or any time before the defendant is required by the laws of the State or the rule of the State court in which such suit is brought to answer or plead to the declaration or complaint of the plaintiff, for the removal of such suit into the circuit court to be held in the district where such suit is pending, and shall make and file therewith a bond, with good and sufficient surety, for his or their entering in such circuit court, on the first day of its then next session, a copy of the record in such suit, and for paying all costs that may be awarded by the said circuit court if said court shall hold that such suit was wrongfully or improperly removed thereto, and also for their appearing and entering special bail in such suit if special bail was originally requisite therein. It shall then be the duty of the State court to accept said petition and bond, and proceed no further in such suit, and the said copy being entered as aforesaid in said circuit court of the United States, the cause shall then proceed in the same manner as if it had been originally commenced in the said circuit court; and if in any action commenced in a State court the title of land be concerned, and the parties are citizens of the same State, and the matter in dispute exceed the sum or value of $2,000, exclusive of interest and costs, the sum or value being made to appear, one or more of the plaintiffs or defendants, before the trial, may state to the court, and make affidavit if the court require it, that he or they claim and shall rely upon a right or title to the land under a grant from a State, and produce the original grant, or an exemplification of it, except where the loss of public records shall put it out of his or their power, and shall move that any one or more of the adverse party inform the court whether he or they claim a right or title to the land under a grant from some other State, the party or parties so required shall give such information, or otherwise not be allowed to plead such grant or give it in evidence upon the trial; and if he or they inform that he or they do claim under such grant, any one or more of the party moving for such information may then, on petition and bond, as hereinbefore mentioned in this act, remove the cause for trial to the circuit court of the United States next to be holden in such district; and any one of either party removing the cause shall not be allowed to plead or give evidence of any other title than that by him or them stated as aforesaid as the ground of his or their claim.

Sec. 2. That whenever in any cause pending in any court of the United States there shall be a receiver or manager in possession of any property, such receiver or manager shall manage and operate such property according to the requirements of the valid laws of the State in which such property shall be situated, in the same manner that the owner or possessor thereof would be bound to do if in possession thereof. Any receiver or manager who shall willfully violate the provisions of this section shall be deemed guilty of a misdemeanor, and shall, on conviction thereof, be punished by a fine not exceeding $3,000, or by imprisonment not exceeding one year, or by both said punishments, in the discretion of the court.

Sec. 3. That every receiver or manager of any property appointed by any court of the United States may be sued in respect of any act or transaction of his in carrying on the business connected with such property, without the previous leave of the court in which such receiver or manager was appointed; but such suit shall be subject to the general equity jurisdiction of the court in which such receiver or manager was appointed, so far as the same shall be necessary to the ends of justice.

Sec. 4. That all national banking associations established under the laws of the United States shall, for the purposes of all actions by or against them, real, personal, or mixed, and all suits in equity, be deemed citizens of the States in which they are respectively located; and in such cases the circuit and district courts shall not have jurisdiction other than such as they would have in cases between individual citizens of the same State.

The provisions of this section shall not be held to affect the jurisdiction of the courts of the United States in cases commenced by the United States or by direction of any officer thereof, or cases for winding up the affairs of any such bank.

Sec. 5. That nothing in this act shall be held, deemed, or construed to repeal or affect any jurisdiction or right mentioned either in sections 641, or in 642, or in 643, or in 722, or in title 24 of the Revised Statutes of the United States, or mentioned in section 8 of the act of Congress of which this act is an amendment, or in the act of Congress approved March 1, 1875, entitled "An act to protect all citizens in their civil and legal rights."

Sec. 6. That the last paragraph of section 5 of the act of Congress approved March 3, 1875, entitled "An act to determine the jurisdiction of circuit courts of the United States and to regulate the removal of causes from State courts, and for other purposes," and section 640 of the Revised Statutes, and all laws and parts of laws in conflict with the provisions of this act, be and the same are hereby repealed: *Provided*, That this act shall not affect the jurisdiction over or disposition of any suit removed from the court of any State, or suit commenced in any court of the United States, before the passage hereof except as otherwise expressly provided in this act.

Sec. 7. That no person related to any justice or judge of any court of the United States by affinity or consanguinity, within the degree of first cousin, shall hereafter be appointed by such court or judge to, or employed by such court or judge in, any office or duty in any court of which such justice or judge may be a member.

The bill as first passed by the Senate had a section providing that the salaries of district court judges be $5,000 a year, but on reconsideration that section was dropped, as it was feared that the House would not consent to a conference if it were retained.

Pacific Railroad Investigation.—Jan. 18, 1887, the House passed a joint resolution authorizing an investigation of the books, accounts, and methods of the Pacific Railroads, which have received aid from the United States. The measure was referred to the Judiciary Committee of the Senate, which reported the following substitute, by way of amendment:

Be it enacted, etc., That the President of the United States, by and with the advice and consent of the Senate, be, and he is hereby, authorized to appoint three commissioners, whose compensation shall be $750 per month to each, and the necessary traveling expenses and board bills, for which proper vouchers shall be returned, to be approved by the Secretary of the Interior; and said commission may appoint a stenographer, if necessary, and fix his compensation; and the persons appointed on the said commission shall have power to examine all books, papers, and methods of the companies hereinafter named, employ experts, if necessary; and they shall at all times be under the immediate direction and control of the President of the United States, and may, at any time, be removed by him in his discretion.

Sec. 2. That the duty of said commission shall be to examine into the working and financial management of all of the railroads that have received aid from the Government in bonds; to ascertain whether they have observed all the obligations imposed upon them by the laws of the United States under which they received such aid, or which have been since passed in reference thereto, and complied with all other obligations to the United States; and whether their books and accounts are or have been so kept as to show the net earnings of the aided roads, and what said books and accounts actually show in regard thereto, and what have been in fact said net earnings; or whether there has been a diversion of earnings of aided roads to less productive branches, through constructive mileage allowances, or average mileage allowances between aided and non-aided roads or parts of roads, or otherwise; and also whether such system of constructive mileage allowances is fair and usual, and in practical operation has resulted adversely or otherwise to the aided roads and the interest of the United States; or whether there has been a diversion of earnings of aided roads to wrongful or improper purposes, and, if so, to what extent; whether there is a discrimination of rates in favor of unaided against aided roads; whether any, and if so, how much, money is due and owing to the United States on account of mistaken or erroneous accounts, reports or settlements made by said roads; whether any traffic or business which could or should be done on the aided lines of said companies has been diverted to the lines of any other company or to non-aided lines, and what amounts have been deducted from the gross earnings of any of said aided railroad companies, by their general freight and passenger agents or auditors, by way of rebate, percentage of business done, constructive mileage, monthly or other payments on any pooling or rate arrangement, contract, or agreement; and also to inquire into, ascertain, and report as to the kind, character, and amount of the assets of said companies, and what assets of each company are now subject to the lien of the Government, and the value thereof; and also whether any dividends have been unlawfully declared by the directors or paid to the stockholders of said companies, and, if so, to what extent, and whether the amount thereof may not be recovered from the directors unlawfully declaring the same or persons who have unlawfully received the same; whether the proceeds of any trust funds or lands loaned, advanced, or granted have been diverted from their lawful use; whether any new stock or bonds have been issued or any guarantees or pledges made contrary to or without authority of law; whether any of the directors, officers, or employés of said companies, respectively, have been or are now directly or indirectly interested, and to what amount or extent, in any other railroad, steamship, telegraph, express, mining, construction, or other business company or corporation, and with which any agreements, undertakings, or leases have been made or entered into; what amounts of money or credit have been or are now loaned by any of said companies to any person or corporation; what amounts of money or credit have been or are now borrowed by any of said companies, giving names of lenders and the purposes for which said sums have been or are now required; what amounts of money or other valuable consideration, such as stocks, bonds, passes, and so forth, have been expended or paid out by said companies, whether for lawful or unlawful purposes, but for which sufficient and detailed vouchers have not been given or filed with the records of said companies; and, further, to inquire and report whether said companies, or either of them, or their officers or agents, have paid any money or other valuable consideration, or done any other act or thing, for the purpose of influencing legislation; and to investigate and report all the facts relating to an alleged consolidation of the Union Pacific Railroad Company, the Kansas Pacific Railway Company, and the Denver Pacific Railway and Telegraph Company into an alleged corporation known as the Union Pacific Railway Company. Said investigation shall include the alleged sale of the stock of the Kansas Pacific Railroad Company to the Union Pacific Railroad Company, and all the circumstances and particulars pertaining to said alleged sale, and whether any of the Pacific Railroad corporations, which obtained bonds from the United States to aid in the construction of their railroads have expended any of their moneys or other assets in the construction, or to aid in the construction, of other railroads, or invested their moneys or other assets in the stocks or bonds of any manufacturing, mining, and com-

mercial companies or corporations, or of other railroad corporations; and if any such expenditures, or investments have been made, the extent and character thereof made by each of said corporations shall be inquired into, and also the present interest of any of said corporations in the railroads auxiliary to their respective railroads.

And said commission shall also ascertain and report the names of all the stockholders in each of said companies, from its organization to the date of the investigation herein provided for, as they appear on the books of said companies at the date of its annual meeting in each year; the amount of stock held by each; what consideration, if any, was paid by each stockholder to said company for his stock, and when and in what property such payment was made; the date when each stockholder so appearing on the books became such; and whether stock is now held or has heretofore been held in the name of any person in trust or for the benefit of any other, and the names of all such persons; the total amount of the stock in each company, and the dates and amount of any increase of such stock, and the reason for such increase; and the amount of the annual salaries or compensation that are now or at any prior time have been paid to any officer or employé of said company, when such salary or compensation amounts to $5,000 or more per annum, and the names of the persons now receiving or who have heretofore received such salaries or compensation, and all bonuses or donations which may have been given or paid to any such person; and all payments made under the head of legal expenses, to whom made, and the amount paid to each, and for what specific services such payments were made.

Said commissioners shall also consider and report whether the interests of the United States require any extension of the time for the performance of the obligations to the United States of said companies, or any of them, and the facts and circumstances upon which said opinion is based, including the security held by the United States for the performance of such obligations, and the value thereof, and the value of the property of such companies, and either of them, not included in such security, and what further security it is expedient that said companies shall be required to give; and if, in their opinion, such extension shall be required by the interests of the United States, they shall submit a scheme for such extension, which shall secure to the United States full payment of all debts due them from said companies, with a reasonable rate of interest, in such time as the commissioners shall propose, having due regard to the financial ability of said companies and the proper conduct of their business in such manner as shall afford efficient service to the public.

And the said commission shall report in full in regard to all such matters aforesaid, and in regard to any other matters which may be ascertained or come to their knowledge in regard to said companies, respectively, on or before Dec. 1, 1887, to the President of the United States, who shall forward said report to Congress, with such recommendations or comments as he may see fit to make in the premises.

That the commissioners hereby created, or either of them, shall have power to require the attendance and testimony of witnesses, and the production of all books, papers, contracts, agreements, and documents relating to the matter under investigation, and to administer oaths; and to that end may invoke the aid of any court of the United States in requiring the attendance and testimony of witnesses, and the production of books, papers, and documents under the provisions of this section. Any of the circuit or district courts of the United States within the jurisdiction of which such inquiry is carried on may, in case of contumacy or refusal to obey a subpœna issued to any person, issue an order requiring any such person to appear before said commissioners, or either of them, as the case may be, and produce books and papers if so ordered, and give evidence touching the matter in question; and any failure to obey such order of the court may be punished by such court as a contempt thereof.

The claim that any such testimony or evidence may tend to criminate the person giving such evidence shall not excuse such witness from testifying; but such evidence or testimony shall not be used against such person on the trial of any criminal proceeding.

SEC. 3. That the sum of $100,000, or so much thereof as may be necessary, is hereby appropriated, out of any money in the Treasury of the United States not otherwise appropriated, for the purposes of this investigation.

SEC. 4. That whenever, in the opinion of the President, it shall be deemed necessary, to the protection of the interests and the preservation of the security of the United States, in respect of its lien, mortgage, or other interest in any of the property or any or all of the several companies upon which a lien, mortgage, or other incumbrance paramount to the right, title, or interest of the United States for the same property, or any part of the same, may exist and be then lawfully liable to be enforced, the Secretary of the Treasury shall, under the direction of the President, redeem or otherwise clear off such paramount lien, mortgage, or other incumbrance by paying the sums lawfully due in respect thereof out of the Treasury; and the United States shall thereupon become and be subrogated to all rights and securities theretofore pertaining to the debt, mortgage, lien, or other incumbrance in respect of which such payment shall have been made. It shall be the duty of the Attorney-General, under the direction of the President, to take all such steps and proceedings, in the courts and otherwise, as shall be needful to redeem such lien, mortgage, or other incumbrance, and to protect and defend the rights and interests of the United States in respect of the matters in this section mentioned, and to take steps to foreclose any mortgages or liens of the United States on any such railroad property.

SEC. 5. That from and after the 1st day of July, 1887, there shall be charged to and collected from the Central Pacific Railroad Company, the Union Pacific Railway or Railroad Company, by whichever description it may be lawfully known, the Central Branch Union Pacific Railway Company, the Sioux City and Pacific Railroad Company, and the Kansas Pacific Railway Company, as all the same are described and known in the acts of Congress providing for issuing bonds in aid of the same, or acts in addition thereto, their successors and assigns, respectively, 40 per cent. of their respective annual net earnings, to be ascertained as provided in section 1 of the act of May 7, 1878, in lieu of the 25 per cent. provided for in said act, so far as the same respects the companies mentioned in said act, and as to the others herein mentioned absolutely; and to that end the said act of May 7, 1878, and any and all amendments or modifications thereof, be and the same are hereby extended to the Kansas Pacific Railway Company, to the Sioux City and Pacific Railroad Company, and to the Central Branch Union Pacific Railway Company; and said act, and all amendments thereto or modifications thereof, shall henceforth apply to the said respective corporations herein last named, as well as to the corporations named in said act.

SEC. 6. That the sinking-funds which are or may be held in the Treasury for the security of the indebtedness of either or all of said railroad companies may, in addition to the investments now authorized by law, be invested in any bonds of the United States heretofore issued for the benefit of either or all of said companies, or in any of the first-mortgage bonds of either of said companies which have been issued under the authority of any law of the United States and secured by mortgages of their roads and franchises, which by any law of the United States have been made prior and paramount to the mortgage, lien, or other security of the United States in respect

of its advances to either of said companies as provided by law.

February 25, the subject came up for discussion in the Senate, and, in Committee of the Whole, on motion of Mr. McPherson, of New Jersey, the fifth and sixth sections were struck out by a vote of 26 yeas to 14 nays. In explanation of the motion, he said: "Let me simply state the fact that while the 40 per cent. increase upon the basis of the net earnings of the Union and the Central Pacific Railroads for 1884 and 1885 would require the Union Pacific Railroad to pay into the public Treasury something over $2,600,000 annually, a sum of something like $600,000 in excess of the entire interest account paid by the Government, and $1,400,000 more than it now pays on account of net earnings and transportation account into the public Treasury, it would only compel the Central Pacific Railway Company to pay $129,000 additional, or a sum equal to $1,300,000 less than the Government pays annually upon its interest account. Hence you will see the inequality of the application of the 40 per cent. Therefore, as it is likely to provoke discussion, I shall ask the Senate to strike out everything in the shape of new legislation, and take the resolution of investigation pure and simple."

Subsequently the Senate, on considering the report of the Committee of the Whole, restored section 6, on motion of Mr. Edmunds, of Vermont, by a vote of 37 to 9, but refused to restore section 5 by a vote of 15 to 26. A motion by Mr. McPherson to strike out section 4 was defeated by a vote of 19 to 27. A motion was made by Mr. Riddleberger, of Virginia, to strike out the following clause of section 2:

The claim that any such testimony or evidence may tend to criminate the person giving such evidence shall not excuse such witness from testifying; but such evidence or testimony shall not be used against such person on the trial of any criminal proceeding.

It failed by a vote of 18 to 25. On motion of Mr. Stanford, of California, the following amendments were inserted in section 2:

The commissioners shall also ascertain the average cost per annum of Government transportation in the regions now traversed by the Pacific Railroads between the year 1850 and the completion of said roads, and also the average cost per annum since such completion, and what additional facilities have been furnished to the Government and the people by said roads.

Also to inquire what discount the Pacific Railroad and its several branches were forced to make in disposing of the bonds guaranteed by the Government to obtain the gold coin which was the currency of the country through which the greater part of said roads passed. Also to ascertain the comparative cost of construction of said roads as compared with what they would have cost with the prices of labor and commodities prevailing five years preceding or five years subsequent to the completion of said roads.

Also to inquire whether or not the Pacific Railroad was completed in less time than was allowed by law, and, if so, how much less time, and if the United States was benefited thereby. Also to inquire if either of the Pacific Railroad companies have been embarrassed and the earning capacity impaired by antagonistic local or State legislation. Also to inquire if the United States, since the Union and Central Pacific Railroad Companies accepted the terms proposed by Congress for the construction of the Pacific Railroad, has granted aid in land for building competing parallel roads to the said Pacific Railroad, and, if so, how many such roads, and to what extent such competing lines, have impaired the earning capacity of the Pacific Railroads.

Also to inquire if the United States have contracts with the branch roads controlled by either of said Pacific roads for carrying United States mails, and, if so, what service has been performed by them, and what money, if any, has been paid for said service, and what remains due and unpaid, and if the United States, by failing to pay for said mail service, has embarrassed said railroad companies or either of them in paying their indebtedness to the United States.

Also to inquire if the several Pacific Railroad companies have complied with the provisions of the act "to alter and amend an act entitled ' An act to aid in the construction of a railroad and telegraph line from the Missouri River to the Pacific Ocean, and to secure to the Government the use of the same for postal, military, and other purposes,' approved July 1, 1862; also to alter and amend an act of Congress approved July 2, 1864, in amendment of the said first-named act," commonly known as the Thurman act, and, if not, in what particulars they have failed to comply. Also to inquire what sums the Pacific Railroads and their branches can severally pay annually on account of their indebtedness to the United States without imposing such burdens upon the people, and particularly upon the localities through which the roads pass, as to retard the development of the country.

On motion of Mr. Plumb, of Kansas, the following clause was inserted in the same section :

Said commission shall also inquire into and report upon the relations of said railroads to the interests of the communities through which they pass, and all questions concerning the payment of taxes, especially upon lands granted by Congress, and the delay of said companies in taking out patents for such lands, the rates of fare and freight charged, discrimination, differential pools, and other devices, and the facilities and accommodations furnished to the patrons of such roads, and their report shall embrace a consideration of the interests and rights of said communities as effected by whatever plan of settlement the payment of the existing debt may be proposed.

In the course of the debate on the measure, Mr. Sherman, of Ohio, said of section 4 :

"This proposes to place in the hands of a President of the United States to be elected eight or ten years hence the enormous power of assuming the payment of $65,000.000 indebtedness. It does not invest him with the power to take the money from the Treasury, because the criticism made by the Senator from Massachusetts (Mr. Dawes) is perfectly just. You may impose a duty upon the President of the United States, whatever it may be, and yet he can not take one dollar from the Treasury, except in pursuance of an appropriation made by express law. That appropriation can only be expressed in such words as these, that so much money be appropriated out of any money in the Treasury not otherwise appropriated. Consequently, this is mere *brutum fulmen ;* it does not amount to anything, except that it confers, nominally at least, a very dangerous power long years in advance of the time for its exercise.

"The Senator from New Jersey suggested that these companies might default in their interest. They have never thought of such a thing. Such a thing is not to be conceived of as possible. That interest must be paid and is paid as promptly and as regularly as the interest on the bonds of the United States, because it is a primary lien on all these roads. That is, therefore, a contingency which need not be provided for by law.

"This is an intimation that these railroad companies intend to commit an act of bankruptcy, when there is no such disposition and no sign of such an act. It is to suggest a state of things that has not occurred to the mind of mortal man, because standing back of and behind these first-mortgage securities there is an immense interest, amounting to over $130,000,000 or $140,000,000. Therefore, the contingency of the companies failing to pay the interest on these bonds or their failure to pay the bonds on maturity is a thing not to be thought of, at least for ten years, and consequently it is a mere idle section threatening the credit of these companies to even suggest the possibility that the interest is not to be paid on these first-mortgage bonds, which are high in the market, equal to the bonds of the United States. Such a suggestion as this in a law of this kind, passed by both Houses of Congress, appears to be a mere effort, you may say, to bear down these bonds, to toss them into the market as discredited and suspected by the Congress of the United States."

Mr. Hoar, of Massachusetts, said in discussing the relations of the Pacific Railroads to the Government :

"There is not one single dollar due to this Government from any of these roads—not one, and will not be until the year 1897, or thereabout. The United States Government agreed, in consideration of the enormous risk of the original builders of this road, that they would lend them these Government bonds, and they should not be called upon to pay back either principal or annual interest till their maturity at the end of thirty years.

"What the Government did by the Thurman act was not to come in as a creditor who had made a bargain and break it, to repudiate their contract with these men—not at all. They said that under our supervising power as a government we will require you to pay into a sinking-fund a sum of money, so that there shall be some preparation toward the payment of your debt at maturity. Now, what is the result of that process? That sinking-fund is required by law at this moment to be invested in securities which pay only 2.2 per cent. annually of interest.

"As to the money expended on the road, the Senator from Mississippi says they buy everything on credit, and do not pay cash for anything. They find a road that has been built by somebody else with a bond and mortgage, and they buy the equity and pay for it, and have to pay the interest on those bonds, and they have a property which at the present rates at which it sells in the stock market, having a capital stock of $60,000,000, is worth $33,750,000—the Union Pacific Railroad alone at this moment—beyond all the debts that it owes, Government debts and everything else.

"If you will just pass a law: 'You shall do just what you have a mind to, and if you pay off our debt at maturity it is all that we will ask'; they can take advantage of a favorable condition in the money market and raise the money and pay every cent they owe you before 1897. We do not ask the Government to extend its debt. They will find a new creditor who will let them have money on fifty, sixty, or seventy-five years with 3 or 4 per cent. interest, and pay you, and pay the first-mortgage bonds, too.

"What you are doing by this 40-per-cent. business of yours is to say to this railroad company: 'You shall not use your money as you please, as you would let another debtor, as you would have to let him because you could not help yourself; you shall not put it where it serves the public and pays an income, as Mr. Adams shows in his report it does, of from 8 to 10 per cent., but you shall take this amount of money which you are getting 8 or 10 per cent. for now, and for twelve years lock it up where you can can get only 2 per cent., and put it into a sinking-fund; not that you can pay us anything that is due now, but that you can be ready to pay us in the year 1897.'

"Remember this is not a creditor laying his hand on the debtor's property. It is the guardian of the ward; it is the paternal Government or non-paternal Government saying, 'We propose only to make you manage your property reasonably, with reference to the fact that you have a debt coming due in twelve years.' That is the only assertion of authority under which this is vindicated at all, and I affirm, Mr. President, on my serious responsibility, that there never was a more wicked, unjust, monstrous proposition than this proposition is, if you strip it of the mistakes which have deceived honorable and just gentlemen on this floor and elsewhere, and come to understand it in all its relations.

"Here is a railroad that you said you would lend this money to, and they should not pay you until 1897, and now you come in twelve years before, when they have so managed their property that it is worth beyond all their debts, yours and every other, by the unerring test of the stock-market, $33,750,000, and you say, 'Take every single dollar that you want to occupy new territory with against rival lines, every single dollar that you want for an improvement over 4,600 miles of railroad territory, every single dollar that you want to secure increased safety with for passengers, for life and property and character; take every single dollar, and strip yourself of your credit which is necessary to carry on your road and have it hold up its head, and put your money out at 2 per cent. and lock it up for twelve years'; and Senators are going to be frightened into a performance of that kind by anonymous articles in irresponsible New York newspapers, if they do it at all."

Senator McPherson, of New Jersey, said in answer:

"I have been earnest, I have been persistent in demanding that this resolution be brought to the attention of the Senate. Sir, the conduct of Congress within the last six months has been the most humiliating in its history. Bills have been brought before the Senate and House of Representatives seeking a settlement with different Pacific railroads on terms which would grant to them, if passed, a larger subsidy than was ever heretofore given to them at any time. If the bill reported by the honorable Senator from Massachusetts, known as the funding bill —as to which I will here and now do him the credit to say that as soon as he discovered its character he immediately withdrew it from the attention of the Senate—if that bill had passed the Senate, the stock of the Union Pacific Railroad would have gone up 50 per cent. Why? It contemplated giving them a larger subsidy than the entire amount of the original subsidy bonds.

"That bill was reported by the Judiciary Committee, an honorable and intelligent committee, and now that same committee bring before the Senate as an addendum or as a rider to this resolution, which was simply a resolution of inquiry, what? An amendment which applies mainly to one line of railroad, to wit, the Union Pacific. If that amendment had been incorporated into this resolution, the stock of the Union Pacific Railroad in an hour would have fallen 50 per cent.

"Now, I want to know why the honorable Senator from Massachusetts charges newspapers in the city of New York with being stock-jobbing newspapers. There is no agency upon earth which has been so influential as the Judiciary Committee of the Senate to enable stock-jobbers to make money; in the first place, on the funding bill, and, in the next place, to bear the stock on the resolution now before the Senate. I have no sympathy with such talk.

"There are such things, of course, as stock-jobbing newspapers. Why not stock-jobbing newspapers as well as stock-jobbing men? But for the Senator from Massachusetts or myself to say that the great influential journals in the city of New York were engaged in a stock-jobbing scheme because they opposed the passage of the funding bill, is to my mind exceedingly unjust. I do not believe they were controlled by any such mercenary motive; and certainly if this resolution becomes a law and the investigation of these Pacific Railroads can be made under the resolution full, thorough, and sufficient, it will reveal to my mind a condition of corruption and extravagance never known before in the history of this country."

Mr. Edmunds, of Vermont, in arguing for an advance in the amount to be paid into the treasury annually by the Pacific Railroads from 25 per cent. to 40 per cent. of the net earnings, said:

"Now, let us see first where the United States stands as respects its securities for the advances that it made. I have here the statute itself of 1862, which is precisely like that of 1864 as far as these matters are concerned, except that by the act of 1864 the first-mortgage bonds, as they now are, of these two railway companies were then second-mortgage bonds, but they were transposed and advanced over the United States subsidy bonds by the act of 1864. But so far as it respects the mortgage, the lien, the right of the United States for security for the forty, or fifty, or sixty million dollars of its advance, the act of 1862 will answer my purpose, as I happen to have it before me.

"Let us see on what property the security of the United States rests as to the Union and the Central Pacific Railway Companies. I am speaking now chiefly of the Union Pacific because it is true, as the Senator from California has said, that the Central Pacific has at all times done everything that the statutes of the United States required it to do. Whether it had an offset or whatever, it obeyed the law and awaited its time to get the money that it might otherwise have applied back again. What does this act provide as to the security of the United States? The United States shall issue bonds, etc.:

The issue of said bonds and delivery to the company shall *ipso facto* constitute a first mortgage on the whole line of the railroad and telegraph, together with the rolling-stock, fixtures, and property of every kind and description, and in consideration of which said bonds may be issued; and on the refusal or failure of said company to redeem said bonds, or any part of them, when required so to do by the Secretary of the Treasury, in accordance with the provisions of this act the said road, with all the rights, functions, immunities and appurtenances thereunto belonging, and also all lands granted to the said company by the United States, which, at the time of said default, shall remain in the ownership of the said company, may be taken possession of by the Secretary of the Treasury for the use and benefit of the United States: *Provided*, This section shall not apply to that part of any road now constructed.

"It took in by provision some roads in some State, I believe. Now, then, the road which Congress authorized this company to build was, as it has turned out when it is planted on the face of the earth, a road from Omaha to Ogden—I am now speaking of the Union Pacific —and it was nothing else. The bonds of the United States, to the amount of the dollars that I may mention by-and-by, were issued upon the strength of that security and that rolling-stock and the fixtures that belonged to those 1,034 miles of road as now constructed.

"Then there was the Kansas Pacific branch, as it was called, which was part of the same system in this incorporation, on which for 365

miles, or whatever the distance was, bonds of the United States were also issued, which I will come to by-and-by. There was our security for this money advanced for the building of the road.

"Now the question is whether under the act of 1878, called the Thurman act, the 25 per cent. of net earnings is to be computed upon and taken out of the earnings and gains and profits and receipts of the Union Pacific Railroad Company and the Central Pacific Railroad Company for all the other lines in which they are interested besides these main lines."

Interrupting him, Mr. Morgan, of Alabama, said:
p
"I ask the Senator whether or not section 5 of the act of incorporation does not cover all the roads that may be in the ownership of this company at the time of the default made in the payment of the bonds, and whether this statutory mortgage does not extend over all the road that it may own at that time and subsequently acquired, being 'all the rights, functions, immunities, and appurtenances belonging . . . at the time of said default.'"

And Mr. Edmunds continued:

"I am extremely sorry to say that according to the decisions of the Supreme Court as I understand them—and I am afraid they are right in point of law—it does not, and I am extremely sorry to say for the interests of the tax-payers of the United States that so far as I know not a single one of what are called these branch roads and extensions belongs either to the Central Pacific or the Union Pacific Railroad corporation as such. They are separate corporations, the stock of which is held or controlled by these corporations of which they have perpetual leases so that the lien of the United States under this statutory mortgage, when you come to bring it down to judicial determination if the bonds were due yesterday and there was a foreclosure to-day, will be the right of the United States to foreclosure upon the line of road from Omaha to Ogden, to take the Union Pacific which is enough for my purpose to illustrate this matter, or if you take the Central Pacific from Ogden to Sacramento and perhaps taking in the Western Pacific with which it was consolidated going down toward and perhaps to San Francisco, but not the vast system of State railways that the Central Pacific got the control and real ownership and possession of which were not under the mortgage at all.

"That being the state of the case, let us see how much money was paid out and how much land was paid out on that kind of security. I have the report of the Railroad Commissioner, who stands impartial between the tax-payers and these corporations, for 1885, in my hands, and then I have later that of 1886, which does not state differently at all on this question of how the matter stands.

"We find by this report that in respect of

the Union Pacific Railroad Company the United States has issued its own bonds to the amount of $27,236,512; that interest accrued and not yet paid by the United States because the coupons have not been presented, amounts to $817,095.86; that the interest already paid by the United States to the 1st of July, 1885—and this report was made up to that date—was $27,409,136.49. Out of that is to be taken, according to this tabular statement, for transportation and cost of the 5 per cent. of the net earnings in the first place, $10,647,579.86, and the 5 per cent. of the net earnings reserved in the Treasury $283,162.99, making a balance of interest paid by the United States, besides the $817,095.86 of outstanding coupons yet to be paid, $16,478,394.14.

"So, as the Commissioner states it, the state of the accounts between the United States and the Union Pacific Railroad Company on the 1st of July, 1885, sums up in this way: The total debt of the Union Pacific, including the Kansas Pacific, is $33,539,512 of principal; accrued interest on the bonds that we are paying the interest on, $35,111,924.94, making on the 1st of July, 1885—there being still twelve years on an average of interest yet to be paid, which would make 72 per cent. of the original $33,000,000 of the debt—$68,651,436.94.

"There is twelve years of interest yet on $33,000,000, which would be, at 6 per cent., 72 per cent. on $33,000,000, which, in round numbers, is three quarters of that, which would be about $24,000,000 more, which added to your $68,000,000, leaving off the odd hundred thousands, would make $92,000,000, that within ten years from this date will be due to the United States from this corporation for actual cash that the United States will have paid out.

"Now, what else did it get? Let us see. The land question is stated in the same report. The net proceeds of land-sales, after deducting all expenses of management, commission, etc., to Dec. 31, 1884, were $25,668,806.65. Add that twenty-five million dollars to the ninety-odd millions that I had before and you have, in round numbers, just about $120,000,000 of cash that this company will have had from the United States.

"The estimated value of the unsold lands is $13,602,696.25.

"Take that to be a fair estimate of that value and add that to your $120,000,000, and you have $134,000,000 that the people of the United States have paid into this thousand miles of road from Omaha to Ogden."

After citing the Supreme Court decision to the effect that the 25-per-cent. payment from the Pacific Railroads on their net earnings under the provisions of the Thurman act was simply computed on the earning of the "aided" part of the lines, the Senator said:

"What became of the balance of the 75 per cent.? For some years after this act of Congress was passed, and which denounced penalties against any director or officer of the

company who, until they met the obligations of the United States and to the creditors by paying into the sinking-fund, should declare any dividend, the companies proceeded year after year to declare dividends, and to pay them, and but for this statute they might do it; it was 'net,' everything to carry on the road and keep it in the best possible condition was authorized to be drawn out before the 25 per cent. was computed, and it was drawn out, and then that being computed and the 25 per cent. paid in or not paid in, as it was not, the balance was divided among the stockholders; and I will assume that every stockholder was a widow, and that every other stockholder, to use a phrase which is exuberant, was an orphan and innocent, paid 200 per cent. to buy their stock, what of it?

"What right has a widow to wrong her creditors? What right has an orphan to wrong his creditors or her creditors? I do not understand it. I am in favor of the widow—not that I wish anybody's husband to die; I am in favor of orphans—not because I wish anybody's father or mother to die; but I do not quite understand on what principle it is that widows and orphans and all the other people who are supposed to be represented by Mr. Charles Francis Adams are entitled to be allowed by Congress to go on year by year as they are quite likely to do—and they have done it for many years—to take money that belongs to their creditors and put it in their own pockets."

Mr. Hoar, of Massachusetts, interrupting, said:

"The Senator said just now that if he made any misstatement he would be glad to be corrected, and I think he made unwittingly a misstatement in answer to the Senator from South Carolina, who asked if all above 25 per cent. now passed into the pockets of the stockholders, and the Senator said yes; and also when he stated—though he stated the fact with literal correctness—that there was a dividend year after year when they did not pay what was due. There has not been a dividend paid to the stockholders for several years. All the earnings have gone into the improvement of the property."

Mr. Edmunds continued:

"I did say that the 75 per cent. went into the pockets of the stockholders. Very likely I was incorrect about that, for a good many of the net earnings of corporations that are net earnings do not quite get into the pockets of the stockholders. It may be that I overstated that a little. I am not sure that it all went into the stockholders' pockets, but it was net earnings all the same.

"Year after year, I repeat, after the passage of the Thurman act, the Union Pacific Railroad Company did not obey it, and proceeded to declare dividends when the statutes of the United States said if they did they should suffer punishment, and the Administration—a Republican one, too—in some way or other failed to bring them to time, as I suppose this Congress is altogether likely to fail to do anything whatever, which is exactly what all these railroads want, and we shall go on again, year by year, without taking any single step in advance.

"At least three or four years ago the matter came to the knowledge of the Committee on the Judiciary that the Union Pacific was not obeying this statute, and had been for some one, two, three, four, five, or six years declaring and paying dividends; whether it paid all the 75 per cent. that was left or not, I do not know; and that committee was rather disposed, Republican though it was, to see if it was possible to have the laws of the United States obeyed by a great corporation, whose president was a very eminent man, and whose stockholders were widows and orphans. We made considerable of a stir on the subject in a quiet way, and the result was, without trying to do the almost impossible thing of getting the two Houses of Congress to do anything about it, that we got a little more than three quarters of a million of dollars paid into the Treasury, and it is there yet, I suppose, a part of the surplus or part of something. After that time it became to be a serious question whether it would be advisable for the directors of the Union Pacific Railroad Company to declare any more dividends.

"Now, what, since the time they stopped paying dividends, has become of the 75 per cent. clear net earnings, I confess I do not know. I assume that the directors have disposed of it, not having paid dividends, in some suitable and proper way. I have no suspicion to express, no inquiry to make. It is their affair, if they obey the law as far as it goes, what they did with the other 75 per cent.

"Why should not this corporation out of this net income of the aided part of its lines, and no other, do something more than appropriate 25 per cent. of the net earnings for the benefit of its creditors, and advance 15 per cent. to 40, leaving them still 60 either for dividends or for enterprises as they may please, and thus accumulate and not lose but save, to meet their inevitable obligations to become due in ten years, amounting to in round numbers $200,000,000; or are they to be left free to dispose of this clear net balance of cash in such a way as they please, and let the beast—I will not say that other individual, because nobody in the Senate would know who I meant—'take the hindmost?'

"My friend from Massachusetts says it would injure the credit of the company to be compelled to save its funds for the benefit of its creditors. That is not the way we understand it in the rural country where I live. We generally think that a man who saves his funds to pay his debts is rather benefiting his creditors, but it may be different in Massachusetts. I can not say."

The measure, as amended, passed the Senate without a division; the House non-concurred in the Senate amendments and a conference committee was appointed. It reported, March 2, in favor of the bill as passed by the Senate, with the following amendment:

Strike out, in the first and second lines, the words "by and with the advice and consent of the Senate," and add to the first section as follows:
The term of office of said commissioners shall not extend beyond the beginning of the next session of the Senate. If the Senate shall be convened after the 4th day of March, 1887, and before the 1st of December in said year, and the duties of said commissioner shall not then be completed, the President shall, by and with the advice and consent of the Senate, appoint three commissioners who shall perform and complete the duties prescribed in this act within the time therein specified.

The President approved of the measure March 3.

Chinese Affairs.—Jan. 6, 1887, the Senate passed, without a division, a bill to provide for the execution of Article II of the treaty concluded between the United States of America and the Emperor of China, Nov. 17, 1880, and proclaimed Oct. 5, 1881. The bill passed the House Feb. 8, 1887, without a division, and the President approved of it February 23. The text of it is as follows:

Be it enacted, &c. That the importation of opium into any of the ports of the United States by any subject of the Emperor of China is hereby prohibited. Every person guilty of a violation of the preceding provision shall be deemed guilty of a misdemeanor, and, on conviction thereof, shall be punished by a fine of not more than $500 nor less than $50, or by imprisonment for a period of not more than six months nor less than thirty days, or by both such fine and imprisonment, in the discretion of the court.

SEC. 2. That every package containing opium, either in whole or in part, imported into the United States by any subject of the Emperor of China, shall be deemed forfeited to the United States; and proceedings for the declaration and consequences of such forfeiture may be instituted in the courts of the United States as in other cases of the violation of the laws relating to other illegal importations.

SEC. 3. That no citizen of the United States shall import opium into any of the open ports of China, nor transport the same from one open port to any other open port, or buy or sell opium in any of such open ports of China, nor shall any vessel owned by citizens of the United States, or any vessel, whether foreign or otherwise, employed by any citizen of the United States, or owned by any citizen of the United States, either in whole or in part, and employed by persons not citizens of the United States, take or carry opium into any of such open ports of China, or transport the same from one open port to any other open port, or be engaged in any traffic therein between or in such open ports or any of them. Citizens of the United States offending against the provisions of this section shall be deemed guilty of a misdemeanor, and, upon conviction thereof, shall be punished by a fine not exceeding $500 nor less than $50, or by both such punishments, in the discretion of the court. The consular courts of the United States in China, concurrently with any district court of the United States in the district in which any offender may be found, shall have jurisdiction to hear, try, and determine all cases arising under the foregoing provisions of this section, subject to the general regulations provided by law. Every package of opium or package containing opium, either in whole or in part, brought, taken, or transported, trafficked, or dealt in contrary to the provisions of this section, shall be forfeited to the United States, for the benefit of the Emperor of China; and such forfeiture, and the declaration and consequences thereof, shall be made, had, determined, and executed by the proper authorities of the United States, exercising judicial powers within the Empire of China.

The treaty provision which this measure is designed to carry out was doubtless intended not only as a protection for China, but as a protest against the policy of Great Britain in forcing into China the Indian opium raised under government monopoly. Mr. Cox, of North Carolina, said in explanation of it:

"This bill, Mr. Speaker, does not interfere between the citizens of the United States and other governments, except with reference to China. By a treaty which was ratified in 1881 it was agreed that in the open ports of China, certain designated ports, they should not permit opium to be carried there by citizens of the United States, nor to be brought here and sold by United States citizens to the subjects of China.

"It is well known that one of the greatest social evils, probably, prevailing in China is the traffic in opium. By the treaty of 1841, made by Mr. Reed, it was restricted, and citizens of the United States in China violating the provisions of that treaty were punishable under the laws of China. The Burlingame treaty made no provision in reference to the subject, but there is a treaty which regulates the mode and method of punishment of United States citizens who reside in China and engage in this traffic. Now they are punishable under the laws of the United States, and this is expressly to prevent citizens of the United States in China from engaging in the traffic.

"By the treaty of 1844 there are five open ports provided for in China. and in these open ports the citizens of the United States have the right to obtain houses and places of business, etc. By the treaty of 1858, the number of these ports was increased, with the power to the citizens of the United States who may be there to reside with their families in the same, and to trade, and proceed from one port to another on business and pleasure. They shall not, however, use the privilege thus accorded them to carry on a clandestine or illegal trade along the coast, under such pains and penalties as may be prescribed by law. The treaty concluded November, 1880, contains the article which I will send to the Clerk's desk to be read."

The Clerk read as follows:

ARTICLE II. The Governments of China and of the United States mutually agree and undertake that Chinese subjects shall not be permitted to import opium into any of the ports of the United States ; and citizens of the United States shall not be permitted to import opium into any of the open ports of China ; to transport it from one open port to any other open port ; or to buy and sell opium in any of the open ports of China. This absolute prohibition, which extends to vessels owned by the citizens or subjects of either power, to foreign vessels employed by them, or to vessels owned by the citizens or subjects of either power and employed by other persons for the transportation of opium, shall be enforced by appropriate legislation on the part of China and the United

States ; and the benefits of the favored-nation clause in existing treaties shall not be claimed by the citizens or subjects of either power as against the provisions of this article.

"The President of the United States in May last communicated to Congress in special message the necessity for some legislation to carry into effect the provisions of this article. There are provisions in this treaty affecting our citizens in China which are provided for under this bill. A recent case has been called to the attention of the State Department by United States minister at Pekin concerning the right of an American citizen to lease to a British merchant a portion of his house for the opium business. The manifest intent of this treaty is to prevent American citizens in China from engaging in this opium-traffic, or in knowingly aiding others to do so. The treaty itself is not self-executing. Appropriate legislation is required to make it effective. The passage of this bill, it is believed, will accomplish the purpose, and if no gentleman desires to be heard on the subject, and no further explanation is required, I ask that it may be put upon its passage."

At the first session of this Congress, the Senate passed a bill to indemnify certain subjects of the Chinese Empire for losses sustained by the violence of a mob at Rock Springs, in the Territory of Wyoming, in September, 1885. The measure provided for the appointment of a commission to investigate the actual loss and damage, and report the testimony taken, and the findings, to the Secretary of State, the President being empowered to apportion to each person a just compensation for the injuries sustained, the aggregate sum so apportioned not to exceed $150,000, to be paid over to the Chinese minister at Washington, in full satisfaction of injuries inflicted upon the subjects of the empire. The House substituted for this measure the following, which was passed Feb. 8, 1887 :

Be it enacted, &c., That the sum of $147,748.74 be, and the same is hereby, appropriated, out of any moneys in the Treasury not otherwise appropriated, to be paid to the Chinese Government, in consideration of the losses unhappily sustained by certain Chinese subjects by mob violence at Rock Springs, in the Territory of Wyoming, Sept. 2, 1885 ; the said sum being intended for distribution among the sufferers and their legal representatives, in the discretion of the Chinese Government.

The President approved of this measure February 28.

Redemption of Trade-Dollars.—The old question in regard to the redemption of trade-dollars was settled in this session of Congress. Dec. 17, 1886, the Senate passed a bill providing for the redemption of these coins. Feb. 12, 1887, the House adopted and passed a substitute for this measure ; and the Senate nonconcurred in the House amendments. The main difference of opinion was, as to whether the redeemed trade-dollars should be regarded as part of the bullion to be purchased and coined under the act of Feb. 28, 1878. A

202   CONGRESS. (LAND-GRANT RAILROADS.)

conference committee was appointed, and recommended the following measure as a substitute:

"That for a period of six months after the passage of this act, United States trade-dollars, if not defaced, mutilated or stamped, shall be received at the office of the Treasurer or any assistant treasurer of the United States in exchange for a like amount, dollar for dollar, of standard silver dollars or of subsidiary coins of the United States.

"Sec. 2. That the trade-dollars received by, paid to, or deposited with the Treasurer or any assistant treasurer or national depositary of the United States, shall not be paid out or in any other manner issued, but, at the expense of the United States, shall be transmitted to the coinage mints, and recoined into standard silver dollars or subsidiary coin, at the discretion of the Secretary of the Treasury: *Provided*, That the trade-dollars recoined under this act shall not be counted as part of the silver bullion required to be purchased and coined into standard dollars as required by the act of Feb. 28, 1878."

February 19, both Senate and House agreed to the report of the conference committee, and the measure became a law without the approval of the President. In recommending the passage of this bill, Senator Beck, of Kentucky, introduced a statement of the merits of the question, from Dexter A. Hawkins, the following passages of which give a summary of the history and claims of the trade-dollars:

By Chapter CXXXI of the laws of 1873, page 424, Congress enacted as follows : ' Sec. 15. That the silver coins of the United States shall be a trade-dollar, a half-dollar or fifty-cent piece, a quarter-dollar or twenty-five-cent piece, a dime or ten-cent piece, and said coins shall be legal tender at their nominal value for any amount not exceeding $5 in any one payment.' The act of which this is a part was approved by the President, and became a law of the United States, Feb. 12, 1873. There is not a word in the statute to indicate any other or different use than that of the fifty-cent, twenty-five-cent, and ten-cent silver coins; hence the statement often made that they were coined only for export has no justification in the statute."

"Under said section 15 of said act, the United States Mint, between July 12, 1873, and Aug. 1, 1876, coined 15,631,000 of these trade-dollars. Every one of these 15,631,000 trade-dollars was 'a legal tender for any amount not exceeding $5 in any one payment,' and, like the small silver coins described in section 15, could be used to the extent of not exceeding $5 as a legal tender in any payment, public or private, in the United States."

"Under the act of 1873 the coinage of trade-dollars was, like the coinage of gold and the coinage of the standard dollar before said act, free and unlimited. Anybody was at liberty to bring to the mint any amount of silver bullion, and, on paying the coinage charge, have it, like gold bullion, coined into trade-dollars, and delivered to him for use as lawful money. If the Government can honestly repudiate these trade-dollars, it can repudiate every coin it issues.

"No statute has ever been enacted that in terms or by just implication takes away from the 15,631,000 trade-dollars coined before August, 1876, the legal-tender quality given to them by said section 15 of the act of July 12, 1873.

"But what has been done as to the trade-dollar, is, that on July 22, 1876, after said 15,631,000 trade-dollars had been coined and issued, Congress passed a joint resolution, the second section of which is as follows: ' Sec. 2. That the trade-dollar shall not hereafter be a legal tender, and the Secretary of the Treasury is hereby authorized to limit from time to time the coinage thereof to such an amount as he may deem sufficient to meet the export demand for the same.'

"This is a joint resolution, not a statute. It in terms, though awkwardly, seems to limit itself to the hereafter-issued trade-dollars, not the theretofore-issued trade-dollars. If the intention of the resolution was to repudiate the trade-dollars theretofore issued, to demonetize them, and to reduce them from money with limited legal-tender quality to merchandise with no legal-tender quality whatever, it would have omitted the word ' hereafter.' The word ' hereafter ' has no proper function or meaning in the resolution, except to indicate that Congress did not intend to affect or to change anything already done, or the trade-dollar already issued. When this section was inserted by the Senate, had any Senator suggested that it would cause repudiation, the Senate would probably have either withdrawn it, or so modified it as to preclude such a construction.

"The plain intention of the resolution of July 22, 1876, was that none should be coined after that date except for export. But right here the Government failed of its duty to the people. It paid no attention to the last clause of the resolution as to coining only for export, but let unlimited coinage of trade-dollars go on for fifteen months, or until October, 1877. From July, 1876, to and including October, 1877, it coined $15,079,400. This is as nearly as many as in the previous three years and five months.

"Then it did not stop the coinage. All it did was, on Oct. 15, 1877, to order at the Philadelphia Mint and the New York Assay-Office, and four days later at the other mints, ' That the receipt of deposits for silver for coinage into trade-dollars should be discontinued.'

"But twenty days later, Nov. 5, 1877, this order was modified so as ' to authorize deposits of silver bullion at the mint in San Francisco for returns in trade-dollars.'

"Under this modification, unlimited coinage of trade-dollars went on for seven months more, until May, 1878, when for the first time the coinage was actually and finally stopped. During this seven months 5,248,960 more trade-dollars were coined, making a total of $5,950,360.

"The official returns of exports of trade-dollars from the beginning of their coinage up to Oct. 31, 1879, show $27,039,817 ; and according to the statement of experts these no longer exist, but have in the Asiatic countries to which they were exported, been converted into their coin. (See statement of Director of Mint, 1879.) This would leave in this country $8,869,543, but the bullion dealers say that at least $2,000,000 have been melted up in this country for manufacturing purposes. That would leave about $7,000,000 still in existence. Of this $7,000,000 all that bear date previous to 1877 were legal-tender coin in this country, and common honesty and the practice of nations require the Government to redeem them. It must either do that or repudiate."

Land-Grant Railroads.—Feb. 28, 1887, the Senate took up the House bill to provide for the adjustment of land-grants made by Congress to aid in the construction of railroads within the State of Kansas, and for the forfeiture of unearned lands and for other purposes, and passed it with amendments, making also a change in its title. The result was a conference committee, which agreed upon the following measure:

Section 1. That the Secretary of the Interior be, and is hereby, authorized and directed to immediately adjust in accordance with the decisions of the Supreme Court each of the railroad land-grants made by Congress to aid in the construction of railroads and heretofore unadjusted.

SEC. 2. That if it shall appear, upon the completion of such adjustments respectively, or sooner, that lands have been, from any cause, heretofore erroneously certified or patented, by the United States, to or for the use or benefit of any company claiming by, through, or under grant from the United States, to aid in the construction of a railroad, it shall be the duty of the Secretary of the Interior to thereupon demand from such company a relinquishment or reconveyance to the United States of all such lands, whether within granted or indemnity limits; and if such company shall neglect or fail to so reconvey such lands to the United States within ninety days after the aforesaid demand shall have been made, it shall thereupon be the duty of the Attorney-General to commence and prosecute in the proper courts the necessary proceedings to cancel all patents, certification, or other evidence of title heretofore issued for such lands, and to restore the title thereof to the United States.

SEC. 3. That if, in the adjustment of said grants, it shall appear that the homestead or pre-emption entry of any *bona-fide* settler has been erroneously canceled on account of any railroad grant or the withdrawal of public lands from market, such settler, upon application, shall be reinstated in all his rights and allowed to perfect his entry by complying with the public-land laws: *Provided*, That he has not located another claim, or made an entry in lieu of the one so erroneously canceled: *And provided also*, That he did not voluntarily abandon such original entry: *And provided further*, That if any of said settlers do not renew their application to be reinstated within a reasonable time, to be fixed by the Secretary of the Interior, then all such unclaimed lands shall be disposed of under the public-land laws, with priority of right given to *bona-fide* purchasers of said unclaimed lands, if any, and if there be no such purchasers, then to *bona-fide* settlers residing thereon.

SEC. 4. That as to all lands, except those mentioned in the foregoing section, which have been so erroneously certified or patented as aforesaid and which have been sold by the grantee company to citizens of the United States, or to persons who have declared their intention to become such citizens, the person or persons so purchasing, in good faith, his heirs or assigns, shall be entitled to the land so purchased, upon making proof of the fact of such purchase at the proper land-office, within such time and under such rules as may be prescribed by the Secretary of the Interior, after the grants respectively shall have been adjusted; and patents of the United States shall issue therefor, and shall relate back to the date of the original certification or patenting: and the Secretary of the Interior, on behalf of the United States, shall demand payment from the company which has so disposed of such lands of an amount equal to the Government price of similar lands; and in case of neglect or refusal of such company to make payment as hereafter specified, within ninety days after the demand shall have been made, the Attorney-General shall cause suit or suits to be brought against such company for the said amount: *Provided*, That nothing in this act shall prevent any purchaser of lands erroneously withdrawn, certified, or patented as aforesaid from recovering the purchase-money therefor from the grantee company, less the amount paid to the United States by such company as by this act required: *And provided*, That a mortgage or pledge of said lands by the company shall not be considered as a sale for the purpose of this act, nor shall this act be construed as a declaration of forfeiture of any portion of any land-grant for conditions broken, or as authorizing an entry for the same, or as a waiver of any rights that the United States may have on account of any breach of said conditions.

SEC. 5. That where any said company shall have sold to citizens of the United States, or to persons who have declared their intention to become such citizens, as a part of its grant, lands not conveyed to or for the use of such company, said lands being the numbered sections prescribed in the grant, and being conterminous with the constructed parts of said road, and where the lands so sold are for any reason excepted from the operation of the grant to said company, it shall be lawful for the *bona-fide* purchaser thereof from said company to make payment to the United States for said lands at the ordinary Government price for like lands, and thereupon patents shall issue therefor to the said *bona-fide* purchaser, his heirs or assigns: *Provided*, That all lands shall be excepted from the provisions of this section which at the date of such sales were in the *bona-fide* occupation of adverse claimants under the pre-emption or homestead laws of the United States, and whose claims and occupation have not since been voluntarily abandoned, as to which excepted lands the said pre-emption and homestead claimants shall be permitted to perfect their proofs and entries and receive patents therefor: *Provided further*, That this section shall not apply to lands settled upon subsequent to the 1st day of December, 1882, by persons claiming to enter the same under the settlement laws of the United States, as to which lands the parties claiming the same as aforesaid shall be entitled to prove up and enter as in other like cases.

SEC. 6. That where any lands have been sold and conveyed, as the property of any railroad company, for State and county taxes thereon, and the grant to such company has been thereafter forfeited, the purchaser thereof shall have the prior right, which shall continue for one year from the approval of this act, and no longer, to purchase such lands from the United States at the Government price, and patents for such lands shall thereupon issue: *Provided*, That said lands were not, previous to or at the time of the taking effect of such grant, in the possession of or subject to the right of any actual settler.

SEC. 7. That no more lands shall be certified or conveyed to any State or to any corporation or individual, for the benefit of either of the companies herein mentioned, where it shall appear to the Secretary of the Interior that such transfers may create an excess over the quantity of lands to which such State, corporation, or individual would be rightfully entitled.

Both Houses agreed to the report of the Conference Committee March 3, and the President approved of the measure the same day.

Congress passed and the President approved a bill "to declare a forfeiture of lands granted to the New Orleans, Baton Rouge, and Vicksburg Railroad Company, to confirm title to certain lands, and for other purposes." The real purpose of the measure was to confirm title to the New Orleans Pacific Railroad Company in lands originally granted to the first-named railroad company, never earned by that corporation, but claimed by the last-named railroad company as its assignee.

Congress passed and the President approved a bill " for the relief of settlers and purchasers of lands on the public domain in the States of Kansas and Nebraska." The measure provides for the reimbursement of persons who in good faith took up lands within the grant made in 1866 to the Northern Kansas Railroad and Telegraph, and who afterward were obliged to make payment to that corporation for their holdings.

Miscellaneous.—The following measure, regulating proceedings in contested-election cases in the House, was passed, and approved by the President, March 3, 1887:

Be it enacted, etc., That section 127 of the Revised Statutes of the United States be so amended as to read as follows:

All officers taking testimony to be used in a contested-election case, whether by deposition or otherwise, shall, when the taking of the same is completed, and without unnecessary delay, certify and carefully seal and immediately forward the same, by mail or by express, addressed to the Clerk of the House of Representatives of the United States, Washington, D. C. ; and shall also indorse upon the envelope containing such deposition or testimony the name of the case in which it is taken, together with the name of the party in whose behalf it is taken, and shall subscribe such indorsement.

The Clerk of the House of Representatives, upon the receipt of such deposition or testimony, shall notify the contestant and the contestee, by registered letter through the mails, to appear before him at the Capitol, in person or by attorney, at a reasonable time to be named, not exceeding twenty days from the mailing of such letter, for the purpose of being present at the opening of the sealed packages of testimony and of agreeing upon the parts thereof to be printed. Upon the day appointed for such meeting the said Clerk shall proceed to open all the packages of testimony in the case, in the presence of the parties or their attorneys, and such portions of the testimony as the parties may agree to have printed shall be printed by the Public Printer, under the direction of the said Clerk, and in case of disagreement between the parties as to the printing of any portion of the testimony, the said Clerk shall determine whether such portion of the testimony shall be printed; and the said Clerk shall prepare a suitable index to be printed with the record. And the notice of contest and the answer of the sitting member shall also be printed with the record.

If either party, after having been duly notified, should fail to attend, by himself or by an attorney, the Clerk shall proceed to open the packages, and shall cause such portions of the testimony to be printed as he shall determine.

He shall carefully seal up and preserve the portions of the testimony not printed, as well as the other portions when returned from the Public Printer, and lay the same before the Committee on Elections at the earliest opportunity. As soon as the testimony in any case is printed, the Clerk shall forward by mail, if desired, two copies thereof to the contestant, and the same number to the contestee, and shall notify the contestant to file with the Clerk within thirty days a brief of the facts, and the authorities relied on to establish his case. The Clerk shall forward by mail two copies of the contestant's brief to the contestee with like notice.

Upon receipt of the contestee's brief the Clerk shall forward two copies thereof to the contestant, who may, if he desires, reply to new matter in the contestee's brief within like time. All briefs shall be printed at the expense of the parties respectively, and shall be of like folio as the printed record ; and sixty copies thereof shall be filed with the Clerk for the use of the Committee on Elections.

The following measure, to amend the law relating to patents, trade-marks, and copyrights, was passed, and approved by the President, Feb. 4, 1887:

Be it enacted, etc., That hereafter, during the term of letters patent for a design, it shall be unlawful for any person other than the owner of said letters patent, without the license of such owner, to apply the design secured by such letters patent, or any colorable imitation thereof, to any article of manufacture for the purpose of sale, or to sell or expose for sale any article of manufacture to which such design or colorable imitation shall, without the license of the owner, have been applied, knowing that the same has been so applied. Any person violating the provisions, or either of them, of this section, shall be liable in the amount of $250 ; and in case the total profit made by him from the manufacture or sale, as aforesaid, of the article or articles to which the design, or colorable imitation thereof, has been applied, exceeds the sum of $250, he shall be further liable for the excess of such profit over and above the sum of $250 ; and the full amount of such liability may be recovered by the owner of the letters patent, to his own use, in any circuit court of the United States having jurisdiction of the parties, either by action at law or upon a bill in equity for an injunction to restrain such infringement.

SEC. 2. That nothing in this act contained shall prevent, lessen, impeach, or avoid any remedy at law or in equity which any owner of letters patent for a design, aggrieved by the infringement of the same, might have had if this act had not been passed ; but such owner shall not twice recover the profit made from the infringement.

Its scope was explained by Mr. Morton, of Alabama, as follows :

"A man making carpet, or oil-cloth, or wall-paper, or anything of that kind, goes to an artist and gets him to furnish a design which he thinks will captivate the eye and fancy of the purchaser. The moment he gets a patent for that design there must be left in the Patent-Office a lithograph of it ; and that lithograph can be obtained by any one who wants it for a few cents. Those who infringe the patent purchase these lithographs of designs. They have a full description of the design and make an exact counterfeit, or imitation ; so exact hardly any man can see the difference between them.

"There is a law allowing a man a patent for his design. He has now two remedies: action on the case for damage for use of it, and relief by injunction to prevent the manufacture of the goods. Both of them, I will say, are practically useless and futile as means to be employed for preventing infringement. A design only lives for a year ; and how can you prevent a man making a carpet of a certain design without knowing he is engaged in making it? How do you know he is making it? It can not be known until the carpet is made and put upon the market. The remedy, when the carpet has been manufactured and put on the market, is by the action on the case. The patentee had another remedy by injunction. Every lawyer knows the remedy by injunction is a preventive remedy, and that in order to avail yourself of the benefit of it you must know of the contemplated injury in time to prevent the commission of it. So I say the remedy by injunction for a man who has a patent design amounts to nothing. What this bill seeks to correct is sufficient, of itself, to commend it to all men.

"We can not protect the man on his patent and in the possession of his patented rights unless we attach a penalty for the infringement of the same : and that is simply what the bill does."

The following bill, providing for the disposal of the famous Twiggs swords, was passed, and approved by the President March 3, 1887.

Be it enacted, etc., That the Secretary of the Treasury is hereby authorised and directed to deliver up the so-called "Twiggs swords," which are now in his custody, and which were captured or seized by General B. F. Butler, in 1862, to such person, or to the legal representatives of such person, as was owner thereof at the time they were captured or seized. For the purpose of determining who was such owner the Secretary of the Treasury shall send the petitions of all persons who may claim said swords to the Court of Claims. Said court shall thereupon examine such claimant or claimants, and such other legal evidence as may be offered in behalf of such claimant or claimants, and determine who was such owner and who is entitled to receive said swords under the provisions of this act. Said court shall certify their judgment to the Secretary of the Treasury: *Provided, however,* That all claims for said swords shall be filed with the Secretary of the Treasury within three months from the passage of this act.

Feb. 1, 1887, the following bill to effect a rearrangement of grades of office in the Adjutant-General's Department of the Army, passed the House without a division:

Be it enacted, etc., That the Adjutant-General's Department of the Army shall consist of one adjutant-general, with the rank, pay, and emoluments of brigadier-general; four assistant adjutants-general, with the rank, pay, and emoluments of colonel: six assistant adjutants-general, with the rank, pay, and emoluments of lieutenant-colonel; and six assistant adjutants-general, with the rank, pay, and emoluments of major: *Provided,* That the vacancies in the grade of colonel and lieutenant-colonel created by this act shall be filled by the promotion by seniority of the officers now in the Adjutant-General's Department.

Mr. Wheeler, of Alabama, said, in explanation of the measure:

"This bill I will state does not create any additional officers; it simply has the effect of increasing the rank of certain officers, already commissioned, in the Adjutant-General's Department.

"In all armies of the world the adjutant-general is the chief of staff, and generally has a rank higher than that of all other officers of the staff; but owing to the fact that in the United States Army promotion has been slower in the Adjutant-General's Department than in any other branch of the service, in nearly every case the Adjutant-General is inferior in rank to all the other officers of the staff of the commanding officer. Another reason for this is that it not infrequently happens that a junior officer is giving orders to a superior; and in addition the officer whose dignity and position is highest is compelled to accept a junior place in selecting quarters, and in all of the other emoluments conferred upon officers of the Army.

"The report in this case shows that the four officers who will be promoted to lieutenant-colonel from major have held the office of major for periods ranging from eighteen to twenty years."

The Senate passed the bill February 23, and the President approved of it February 28.

Congress passed and the President approved a bill for the allotment of land in severalty to Indians. The first two sections are as follows:

That in all cases where any tribe or band of Indians has been, or shall hereafter be, located upon any reservation created for their use, either by treaty stipulation or by virtue of an act of Congress or executive order setting apart the same for their use, the President of the United States be, and he hereby is, authorized, whenever in his opinion any reservation or any part thereof of such Indians is advantageous for agricultural and grazing purposes, to cause said reservation, or any part thereof, to be surveyed, or resurveyed if necessary, and to allot the lands in said reservation in severalty to any Indian located thereon, in quantities as follows:

"To each head of a family, one quarter of a section;

"To each single person over eighteen years of age, one eighth of a section:

"To each orphan child under eighteen years of age, one eighth section; and

"To each other single person under eighteen years now living, or who may be born prior to the date of the order of the President directing an allotment of the lands embraced in any reservation, one sixteenth of a section: *Provided,* That in case there is not sufficient land in any of said reservations to allot lands to each individual of the classes above named in quantities as above provided, the lands embraced in such reservation or reservations shall be allotted to each individual of each of said classes pro rata in accordance with the provisions of this act: *And provided further,* That where the treaty or act of Congress setting apart such reservation provides for the allotment of lands in severalty in quantities in excess of those herein provided, the President, in making allotments upon such reservation, shall allot the lands to each individual Indian belonging thereon in quantity as specified in such treaty or act: *And provided further,* That when the lands allotted are only valuable for grazing purposes, an additional allotment of such grazing-lands, in quantities as above provided, shall be made to each individual."

SEC. 2. That all allotments set apart under the provisions of this act shall be selected by the Indians, heads of families selecting for their minor children, and the agents shall select for each orphan child, and in such manner as to embrace the improvements of the Indians making the selection. Where the improvements of two or more Indians have been made on the same legal subdivision of land, unless they shall otherwise agree, a provisional line may be run dividing said lands between them, and the amount to which each is entitled shall be equalized in the assignment of the remainder of the land to which they are entitled under this act: *Provided,* That if any one entitled to an allotment shall fail to make a selection within four years after the President shall direct that allotments may be made on a particular reservation, the Secretary of the Interior may direct the agent of such tribe or band, if such there be, and if there be no agent, then a special agent appointed for that purpose, to make a selection for such Indian, which selection shall be allotted as in cases where selections are made by the Indians, and patents shall issue in like manner.

The other sections provide that the allotments shall be made by agents appointed by the President, for modes of procedure, for holding allotted lands in trust and issuing of patents, for allotments to Indians not on reservations. It also limits the application of the law, excluding certain tribes.

Dec. 15, 1886, the House passed a bill to amend sections 5191 and 5192 of the Revised Statutes which regulate the reserve to be held in the national banks of certain cities. March 3, 1887, the Senate amended and passed the measure; the House non-concurred; a Conference Committee was appointed, and reported the following, which both Houses agreed to:

That whenever three fourths in number of the national banks located in any city of the United States having a population of 50,000 people shall make application to the Comptroller of the Currency, in writing, asking that the name of the city in which such banks are located shall be added to the cities named in sections 5191 and 5192 of the Revised Statutes, the Comptroller shall have authority to grant such request, and every bank located in such city shall at all times thereafter have on hand, in lawful money of the United States, an amount equal to at least 25 per cent. of its deposits, as provided in sections 5191 and 5195 of the Revised Statutes.

SEC. 2. That whenever three fourths in number of the national banks located in any city of the United States having a population of 200,000 people shall make application to the Comptroller of the Currency, in writing, asking that such city may be a central reserve city, like the city of New York, in which one half of the lawful money reserve of the national banks located in other reserve cities may be deposited, as provided in section 5195 of the Revised Statutes, the Comptroller shall have authority, with the approval of the Secretary of the Treasury, to grant such request, and every bank located in such city shall at all times thereafter have on hand, in lawful money of the United States, 25 per cent. of its deposits, as provided in section 5191 of the Revised Statutes.

SEC. 3. That section 3 of the act of January 14, 1875. entitled "An act to provide for the resumption of specie payment," be, and the same is hereby, amended by adding, after the words "New York," the words, "and the city of San Francisco, Cal."

The measure was approved by the President March 3.

A bill was passed to enable the Commissioner of Agriculture to make a special distribution of seeds in the drought-stricken districts of Texas, and making an appropriation for that purpose; but the President vetoed the measure, saying:

I can find no warrant for such an appropriation in the Constitution; and I do not believe that the power and duty of the General Government ought to be extended to the relief of individual suffering which is in no manner properly related to the public service or benefit. A prevalent tendency to disregard the limited mission of this power and duty should, I think, be steadfastly resisted, to the end that the lesson should be constantly enforced that, though the people support the Government, the Government should not support the people.

The friendliness and charity of our countrymen can always be relied upon to relieve their fellow-citizens in misfortune. This has been repeatedly and quite lately demonstrated. Federal aid in such cases encourages the expectation of paternal care on the part of the Government and weakens the sturdiness of our national character, while it prevents the indulgence among our people of that kindly sentiment and conduct which strengthens the bonds of a common brotherhood.

The measure to restrict ownership of real estate in the Territories to American citizens was passed by Congress and approved by the President in this form:

That it shall be unlawful for any person or persons not citizens of the United States, or who have not lawfully declared their intention to become such citizens, or for any corporation not created by or under the laws of the United States or of some State or Territory of the United States, to hereafter acquire, hold, or own real estate so hereafter acquired, or any interest therein, in any of the Territories of the United States or in the District of Columbia, except such as may be acquired by inheritance or in good faith in the ordinary course of justice in the collection of debts heretofore created: *Provided*, That the prohibition of this section shall not apply to cases in which the right to hold or dispose of lands in the United States is secured by existing treaties to the citizens or subjects of foreign countries, which rights so far as they may exist by force of any such treaty, shall continue to exist so long as such treaties are in force, and no longer.

SEC. 2. That no corporation or association, more than 20 per cent. of the stock of which is or may be owned by any person or persons, corporation or corporations, association or associations, not citizens of the United States, shall hereafter acquire or hold or own any real estate hereafter acquired in any of the Territories of the United States or of the District of Columbia.

SEC. 3. That no corporation other than those organized for the construction or operation of railways, canals, or turnpikes shall acquire, hold, or own more than 5,000 acres of land in any of the Territories of the United States; and no railroad, canal, or turnpike corporation shall hereafter acquire, hold, or own lands in any Territory, other than as may be necessary for the proper operation of its railroad, canal, or turnpike, except such lands as may have been granted to it by act of Congress; but the prohibition of this section shall not affect the title to any lands now lawfully held by any such corporation.

SEC. 4. That all property acquired, held, or owned in violation of the provisions of this act shall be forfeited to the United States, and it shall be the duty of the Attorney-General to enforce every such forfeiture by bill in equity or other proper process. And in any suit or proceeding that may be commenced to enforce the provisions of this act, it shall be the duty of the court to determine the very right of the matter, without regard to matters of form, joinder of parties, multifariousness, or other matters not affecting the substantial rights either of the United States or of the parties concerned in any such proceeding arising out of the matters in this act mentioned.

There was passed by Congress, and approved by the President, a bill "to prohibit any officer, agent, or servant of the Government of the United States to hire or contract out the labor of prisoners incarcerated for violating the laws of the Government of the United States." It declares that it shall not be lawful for any officer, agent, or servant of the Government of the United States to contract with any person or corporation, or permit any warden, agent, or official of any State prison, penitentiary, jail, or house of correction where criminals of the United States may be incarcerated, to hire or contract out the labor of said criminals, or any part of them, who may hereafter be confined in any prison, jail, or other place of incarceration for violation of any laws of the Government of the United States of America.

A bill was passed by Congress and approved by the President, extending the free-delivery system to cities of over 10,000 inhabitants, according to the last general census taken by State or United States law, or to offices that had during the previous fiscal year a gross revenue of not less than $10,000. It also divided letter-carriers in cities of more than 75,-000 inhabitants and over into three classes, members of the first to receive a salary of $1,000, members of the second a salary of

$800, and the members of the third a salary of $600. In cities of less than 75,000 population, it divided the letter-carriers into two classes, those of the one class to receive a salary of $800, and those of the other a salary of $600.

Foreign Contract Labor.—A bill was passed by Congress and approved by the President, which added to the act to prohibit the importation and immigration of foreigners and aliens under contract or agreement to perform labor in the United States, its Territories, and the District of Columbia, approved Feb. 26, 1885, and to provide for the enforcement thereof, the following sections:

SEC. 6. That the Secretary of the Treasury is hereby charged with the duty of executing the provisions of this act; and for that purpose he shall have power to enter into contracts with such State commission, board, or officers as may be designated for that purpose by the Governor of any State to take charge of the local affairs of immigration in the ports within said State, under the rules and regulations to be prescribed by said Secretary; and it shall be the duty of such State commission, board or officers so designated to examine into the condition of passengers arriving at the ports within such State in any ship or vessel; and for that purpose all or any of such commissioners or officers, or such other person or persons as they shall appoint, shall be authorized to go on board of and through any such ship or vessel; and if in such examination there shall be found among such passengers any person included in the prohibition in this act, they shall report the same in writing to the collector of such port, and such persons shall be permitted to land.

SEC. 7. That the Secretary of the Treasury shall establish such regulations and rules, and issue from time to time such instructions, not inconsistent with law, as he shall deem best calculated for carrying out the provisions of this act; and he shall prescribe all forms of bonds, entries, and other papers to be used under and in the enforcement of the various provisions of this act.

SEC. 8. That all persons included in the prohibition in this act, upon arrival, shall be sent back to the nations to which they belong and from whence they came. The Secretary of the Treasury may designate the State Board of Charities of any State in which such board shall exist by law, or any commission in any State, or any person or persons in any State, whose duty it shall be to execute the provisions of this section, and said board or person shall be entitled to reasonable compensation therefor, to be fixed by regulation prescribed by the Secretary of the Treasury. The Secretary of the Treasury shall prescribe regulations for the return of the aforesaid persons to the countries from whence they came, and shall furnish instructions to the board, commission, or persons charged with the execution of the provisions of this section as to the time of procedure in respect thereto, and may change such instructions from time to time. The expense of such return of the aforesaid persons not permitted to land shall be borne by the owners of the vessels in which they came; and any vessel refusing to pay such expenses shall not thereafter be permitted to land at or clear from any port of the United States, and such expenses shall be a lien on said vessel. That the necessary expense in the execution of this act for the present fiscal year shall be paid out of any money in the Treasury not otherwise appropriated.

SEC. 9. That all acts and parts of acts inconsistent with this act are hereby repealed.

SEC. 10. That this act shall take effect at the expiration of thirty days after its passage.

In addition to the bills already noticed, those relating to appropriations and those giving pensions and relief to individuals, bills were passed as follows:

Providing for the erection of public buildings at Eastport, Me., Springfield, Mass., Worcester, Mass., Binghamton, N. Y., Camden, N. J., Wilmington, N. C., Charleston, S. C., Huntsville, Ala., Detroit, Mich., Owensborough, Ky., Chattanooga, Tenn., Houston, Tex., Fort Scott, Kan., San Francisco, Cal., and Los Angeles, Cal.; also increasing the appropriations for the public buildings at Brooklyn, N. Y., and Troy, N. Y., and authorizing the exchange of the property purchased at Abingdon, Va., as a site for a public building, for more suitable property.

Authorizing the construction of bridges as follows: Across the East River between the city of New York and Long Island; across the Great Kanawha River below the Falls; across the Eastern Branch of the Potomac River at the foot of Pennsylvania Avenue East; across the Tradewater River by the Ohio Valley Railroad Company; across the Coosa River by the East and West Railroad Company of Alabama, and across the same river by the Talladega and Coosa Valley Railroad Company of Alabama; across the Sunflower, Yazoo, and Tombigbee Rivers in Mississippi by the Georgia Pacific Railroad Company; across the Tombigbee River at or near Columbus, Miss., by the Tombigbee Railroad Company; across the Red River in Louisiana by the Louisiana North and South Railroad Company; across the Tennessee River at or near Sheffield, Ala., at or near Guntersville, Ala., at or near Chattanooga, Tenn., and at or near the foot of Muscle Shoals Canal; across the Cumberland River, by the county of Davidson, Tenn.; across the Red River of the North; across the St. Louis River at the most accessible point between the States of Minnesota and Wisconsin; across a part of the Mississippi and a certain island therein by the city of Winona, Minn.; across the Mississippi River at Fort Madison or Keokuk or between those points, at Grand Tower, Ill.; between East Dubuque, Ill., and Dubuque, Ia., and at St. Louis, Mo.; across the Missouri River between Omaha, Neb., and Council Bluffs, Ia., within five miles of Yankton, Dak., at Pierre, Dak., by the Duluth, Pierre, and Black Hills Railroad Company, and at the most accessible point between the city of Kansas and the town of Sibley, Mo.; and across Bayou Barnard, in Mississippi.

Granting right of way to railroads as follows: To the Annapolis and Baltimore Short Line Railroad Company across the Government farm connected with the Naval Academy at Annapolis, Md.; to the Ohio Central Railroad Company through United States lock and dam property in the Great Kanawha Valley, W. Va.; to the Chicago, Kansas, and Nebraska Railway through the Indian Territory; to the Fort Worth and Denver City Railroad Company through the Indian Territory; to the Fremont, Elk Horn, and Missouri Valley Railroad across the Fort Meade military reservation; to the Prescott and Arizona Central Railway Company across the Fort Whipple military reservation in Arizona; to the Maricopa and Phoenix Railway Company of Arizona through the Gila River Indian reservation; to the Utah Midland Railway Company through the Uncompahgre and Uintah reservations in the Territory of Utah; through certain public lands in the Territory of Utah, etc.; to the Rocky Fork and Cooke City Railway Company through a part of the Crow Indian Reservation in Montana Territory; and to the St. Paul, Minneapolis, and Manitoba Railway Company through the Indian reservations in Northern Montana and Northwestern Dakota.

To make Tampa, Fla., a port of entry and Hartford, Conn., in place of Middletown.

To provide for holding terms of United States courts at Vicksburg, Miss., and at Texarkana, Ark.; at Wilmington, N. C.; of the Circuit Court for the Eastern Judicial District of North Carolina; of the Circuit and District Courts of the United States for the Eastern District of Michigan at Bay City; providing an additional circuit judge in the second judicial circuit ; to amend section 536 of the Revised Statutes of the United States relating to the division of the State of Illinois into judicial districts, and to provide for holding terms of court of the Northern District at Peoria ; and to amend the act dividing the State of Missouri into two judicial districts, and to divide the eastern and western districts thereof into divisions, establish district and circuit courts of the United States therein, and provide for the times and places for holding such courts, and for other purposes.

For the relief of the sufferers by the wreck of the United States vessel Ashuelot.

For the construction of a military telegraph line from Sanford, Fla., to Point Jupiter, Fla., and the establishment of a signal-station.

To provide for the settlement of an account with the Vicksburg and Meridian Railroad Company for internal-revenue tax, and to refund the amount of said tax erroneously assessed and collected.

To establish agricultural experiment stations in connection with the colleges established in the several States under the provisions of an act approved July 2, 1862, and of the acts supplementary thereto.

To provide a school of instruction for cavalry and light artillery, and for the construction and completion of quarters, barracks, and stables at certain posts for the use of the Army of the United States.

To provide for the location and erection of a branch home for disabled volunteer soldiers west of the Rocky Mountains.

Making an appropriation for the establishment and erection of a military post near the city of Denver, in the State of Colorado.

To repeal certain provisions of the act approved March 3, 1875, relating to the purchase of arms for the use of the States.

For the relief of graduates of the United States Military Academy.

To amend an act entitled " An act to provide for the muster and pay of certain officers and enlisted men of the volunteer forces," approved June 3, 1884.

Authorizing the Secretary of War to accept certain lands, etc., near Chicago, Ill.

To amend the act entitled "An act to modify the postal money-order system, and for other purposes," approved March 3, 1883.

For the relief of the survivors of the exploring steamer " Jeannette," and the widows and children of those who perished in the retreat from the wreck of that vessel in the Arctic seas.

To grant certain seal-rocks to the city and county of San Francisco, State of California, in trust for the people of the United States.

To provide for the redemption and sale of the school-farm lands now held in Beaufort County, South Carolina, by the United States.

To provide for the appointment of hospital stewards in the United States Army, and to fix their pay and allowance.

Authorizing the employment of mail-messengers in the postal service.

To amend an act entitled "An act to amend the statutes in relation to the immediate transportation of dutiable goods, and for other purposes," approved June 10, 1880.

To provide for the adjustment of matters connected with certain judicial proceedings in Pennsylvania in which the United States was a party.

To amend the third section of an act entitled " An act to provide for the sale of the Sac and Fox and Iowa Indian reservations, in the States of Nebraska and Kansas, and for other purposes," approved March 3, 1885.

To authorize the city of Newport, R. I., to use the site of Fort Greene as a public park.

To release unto the city of San Antonio, Tex., for its use as a public thoroughfare, certain portions of the military reservation near said city.

To authorize the Secretary of War to improve and enlarge the barracks at Newport, Ky.

To convey to and confirm in the city of Aurora, in the county of Kane and State of Illinois, a small island in Fox River, located within the limits of said city.

To provide for the settlement of accounts with the Mobile and Ohio Railroad Company.

To define the boundaries of the collection districts of Miami and Sandusky, in the State of Ohio.

To authorize the Secretary of War to credit the Territory of Dakota with certain sums for ordnance and ordnance-stores issued to said Territory, and for other purposes.

Relating to the importing and landing of mackerel caught during the spawning-season.

For the allowance of certain claims reported by the accounting officers of the United States Treasury Department.

To amend section 1661 of the Revised Statutes, making an annual appropriation to provide arms and equipments for the militia.

To amend an act in relation to the immediate transportation of dutiable goods, and for other purposes, approved June 10, 1880.

To amend section 533 of the Revised Statutes of the United States.

To repeal certain sections of the Revised Statutes of the United States relating to the appointment of civil officers.

Providing for the sale of public documents.

To provide for grading and paving the approaches to the national cemetery near Danville, Va.

For the repair and preservation of the road, heretofore constructed by the Government, leading from Vicksburg to the national cemetery adjacent thereto.

To authorize the construction of a graveled road to the Richmond national cemetery, near Richmond, Va.

To authorize Frank W. Hunt to maintain a ferry across the Missouri River at the military reservation of Fort Buford, Dakota.

For the construction of a stable for the use of the horses and wagons for the use of the officers of the House of Representatives.

Extending the charter of " The President and Directors of the Firemen's Insurance Company of Washington and Georgetown," in the District of Columbia.

To regulate insurance in the District of Columbia.

For the further protection of property from fire, and safety of lives, in the District of Columbia.

To enable foreign executors and administrators to sue in the District of Columbia, and for other purposes.

For the relief of St. Dominic's Church, in the District of Columbia.

To authorize the Commissioners of the District of Columbia to permit the temporary occupation of streets by a railway for the purpose of transporting material to fill about the base of the Washington Monument.

To regulate steam-engineering in the District of Columbia.

To regulate the construction and operation of elevators within the District of Columbia, and for other purposes.

To quiet title to certain land in the city of Washington, D. C.

Relating to arrears of taxes in the District of Columbia.

Authorizing the Treasurer of the United States to credit the District of Columbia with certain moneys in lieu of investing the same in bonds.

CONNECTICUT. State Government. — The following were the State officers during the year : Governor, Phineas C. Lounsbury, Republican ; Lieutenant-Governor, James L. Howard ; Secretary of State, L. M. Hubbard ; Treasurer, Alexander Warner ; Comptroller, Thomas Clark ; Secretary of State Board of Education, Charles D. Hine ; Railroad Commissioners,

George M. Woodruff, W. H. Haywood, John W. Bacon succeeded by William O. Seymour; Chief Justice of Supreme Court, John D. Parks; Associate Justices, Elisha Carpenter, Dwight W. Pardee, Dwight Loomis, Miles T. Granger succeeded by Sidney B. Beardsley. The first five officers were elected by the Legislature in January, there being no choice by the people in the election of 1886.

Legislative Session.—The session of this year was the first under the biennial system established by a recent amendment to the constitution. It continued from January 5 till May 15. United States Senator Joseph R. Hawley, Republican, was re-elected early in the session by a vote of 128 to 98 for Charles R. Ingersoll, Democrat. The refunding of a part of the public debt was accomplished by an act authorizing the redemption of $1,080,000 of bonds issued in 1877 and bearing 5 per cent. interest on or before the 1st of August of this year. To enable the treasurer to do this, he was empowered to issue new bonds to the amount of $1,000,000 bearing 3½ per cent. interest from May 2, and payable May 1, 1897. The remaining $80,000 of bonds were to be paid out of funds already in the treasury. The new bonds were made exempt from taxation. Under this law the State treasurer, by advertising for bids, was able to sell the new bonds in June at a premium, one half of them at 108·27 and one half at 102·55.

The State tax for 1886 was 2 mills on the dollar, an increase over former years necessitated by extraordinary expenses for building new armories, and for the enlargement and improvement of the State prison. No such expenses being required for 1887 and 1888, the Legislature restored the former rate of 1¼ mills on the dollar.

The following resolutions were passed by the lower house:

Resolved, That the following be proposed as an amendment to the constitution of the State, which, when approved and adopted in the manner provided by the constitution, shall to all intents and purposes become a part thereof, viz.: The manufacture or compounding of, and sale or keeping for sale of, intoxicating liquors, excepting for sacramental, medicinal, scientific, mechanical, and art purposes, shall be and hereby are prohibited in this State; and it shall be the duty of the Legislature to pass laws for the enforcement of this article.

Resolved, that the foregoing proposed amendment to the constitution be continued to the next general assembly, and be published with the laws passed at the present session.

The principal sums voted for specific objects were, for the Statute Revision Commission, $18,000; for the Industrial School for Girls, $10,000; State Reform School, $30,500; for preserving the record of the Connecticut Volunteers, $25,000; Danbury Hospital, $6,000; Waterbury Hospital, $25,000; Fitch's Soldiers' Home, for the purchase of land, $8,000; School for Imbeciles, $5,000.

Other acts of the session were as follow:

To subject trust and investment companies to the supervision of the bank commissioners.

To punish false pretenses in obtaining the registration of cattle and other animals, and to punish giving false pedigrees.

Restricting railroad traffic on Sunday to cases of necessity or mercy, and providing that the highest regular fare shall be charged on that day; season, mileage, or commutation tickets not being receivable.

To punish desertions by husbands.

Raising the age of consent in females from ten to fourteen years.

To procure enforcement of the law requiring the attendance of children at school.

Regulating the rights and duties of electric companies, in placing their wires in public highways.

To punish blackmail.

Providing that no person shall practice dentistry unless he has a diploma from some duly authorized dental college; or has had eighteen months' experience in a dental office and attended a course of lectures; or, if from another State, a certificate from a board of dental examiners, or six years' practice.

To prevent discrimination by life-insurance companies against persons of color.

Prohibiting and punishing the employment of women or children under sixteen years of age more than ten hours a day in any manufacturing, mercantile, or mechanical establishment.

Providing for weekly payments of wages.

Enabling the agents of the Connecticut Humane Society to take charge of and care for animals neglected, abandoned, or cruelly treated, and to destroy diseased, disabled, or useless animals.

Providing that imitation butter shall not be sold or used unless the fact of such sale or use is plainly stated on a printed notice posted at the place of sale or use; that it shall only be sold in packages labeled to show the fact of such imitation, and appointing and creating a dairy commissioner to enforce these provisions.

To prevent the sale of liquors at agricultural fairs.

To regulate the sale of medicines and poisons.

Imposing a tax on the net earnings of any registered or enrolled sailing-vessel.

Revising the law regarding collection of taxes.

Providing for the punishment of incorrigible criminals.

To establish free public highways across the Connecticut river in Hartford County.

Requiring insurance agents to obtain a license from the insurance commissioner.

Enabling women to be eligible to any office connected with the management of the public schools.

Adopting the revision of the general statutes made by the commission appointed for that purpose.

Providing for the inspection of factories as to dangerous machinery, bad ventilation, etc.

Revising the methods of assessing the valuation of railroads, and imposing a tax of 1 per cent. on such valuation, and also on the amount of their funded or floating indebtedness.

That treasurers of savings-banks shall give new bonds at least once in six years.

That a druggist shall not make more than one sale on any liquor prescription.

That houses of persons who make a business of taking children under ten years to board, exceeding two at the same time, shall be under the supervision of the selectmen, and inspected monthly.

Amending the militia law so as to recognize the machine-gun platoons, and adding trumpeters to the militia.

That no cemetery association shall make any regulation prohibiting the erection of headstones provided by the State for the graves of soldiers, sailors and marines.

That $10,000 of bonds, mortgages, or money held by any church shall be exempt from tax, provided the revenue is used for church purposes, and provided the society's property, real and personal, exempt from taxation, does not exceed $20,000.

That no person not a citizen of the State shall be appointed a special constable, policeman, or deputy sheriff, excepting the Governor may appoint as special officer any regular employé of any railroad or steamboat company.

The Senate contained 14 Republicans and 10 Democrats; the House, 137 Republicans, 109 Democrats, and 2 Independents.

State Prison.—The remodeling of the State prison at Wethersfield, for which provision was made by the Legislature of 1886, was in progress during the year, and was nearly completed at its close. The improvements include not only additions to the former buildings, but the entire reconstruction of the cells and flooring, leaving only the stone walls of the old prison intact. When finished, the new structure will be one of the best-equipped institutions of its kind.

Railroads.—The Legislature of 1884 passed a law permitting the gradual removal of grade-crossings in the State, on petition of the railroad company or the local authorities to the board of railroad commissioners, the expense of such removal to be equally borne by the town and the railroad. Considerable anxiety was felt in the latter part of the year over the workings of this law, and petitions from more than forty towns were received by the Governor, urging him to call an extra session of the Legislature to secure its repeal. The danger apprehended arose from the intention of the New York, New Haven, and Hartford Railroad to abolish all its grade-crossings within two or three years, compelling the towns along the line to bear half of the expense. As the law contemplated only a gradual removal, and its execution rested entirely in the discretion of the commissioners, the Governor refused these petitions, believing that the board would carry out the spirit of the law and not impose too heavy a burden upon the towns by hastening removals.

COSTA RICA, one of the five Central American republics. The area is estimated at 19,980 square miles; and on Dec. 31, 1886, the population was 196,280.

Government.—The President of the Republic is Don Bernardo Soto, whose Cabinet is composed of the following ministers: Foreign Affairs, Finance, and Commerce, Don Mauro Fernandez; Interior, Public Works, Justice, Public Worship, and Charity, Don Cleto Gonzalez Viquez; War and Navy, Don A. de Jesus Soto. The United States Minister to the five Central American republics, resident at Guatemala, is Hon. H. C. Hall. The Costa Rican Consul-General at New York is Don José Maria Muñoz.

Treaties.—In September, 1887, the Costa Rican Congress ratified the extradition treaty with Guatemala. On July 26, 1887, the Presidents of Costa Rica and Nicaragua made a treaty at Managua, the principal provisions of which are the following: Confirmation of the boundary treaty as it stands; permission to dig a canal and conduct enough water from Colorado river for improving the navigation of San Juan river, Costa Rica to pay 25 per cent. of the expense involved in such work; free navigation for all time on San Juan river and Lake Nicarauga; acknowledgment of Costa Rica's right in the canal; settlement of all doubtful points in the treaty having reference thereto; Costa Rica to be consulted in all matters of granting concessions relating to the canal or transit; liberty to navigate in Nicarauga waters without exercising jurisdiction; fixing of a date when commissioners are to meet for determining the boundary-line.

Finance.—The report of the Minister of Finance, of June 8, 1887, shows that the national indebtedness stood as follows: Consolidated foreign debt, £2,000,000; home debt, $527,-819; paper money in circulation, $1,044,983. Of the latter, $25,000 were withdrawn and destroyed on January 22, and this canceling is to continue at the rate of $25,000 quarterly till extinguished. It had been estimated by him that the home debt would be reduced to $426,-828 on Dec. 31, 1887; but the Government resolved to pay this amount by anticipation, and did so on September 30, much to the benefit of Costa Rican finances, the two series of bonds advancing in London to 79¼ and 77¼, respectively, on the strength of the dispatch announcing the liquidation of the internal indebtedness of the republic. Another wise financial measure, sanctioned by the National Government on Dec. 31, 1886, was the renting of the Central and Atlantic sections of the Government railroad to the Costa Rica Railroad Company, a London corporation, undertaking to finish the line under the management of Minor Cooper Keith, the well-known financier and railroad contractor. From 1879 to 1887 the Government had incurred an annual loss of $48,000 on that portion of its railway, while it now ceded the management upon terms favorable to the national exchequer. The income of the nation in 1886-'87 was $2,888,752, being $176,188 in excess of the estimate; the actual outlay was $2,772,315.

At the instigation of the President, a "banco hipotecario" is to be established in the capital, with a capital of $1,000,000 in shares; the charter to extend over seventy years; to be a bank of deposits and issue; to do a general banking business, and advance, on first mortgage on long credits, money on real estate.

Army.—The actual strength of the active army in 1887 was 6,219 men; of the reserve, 1,067; national guard, 692; together, 7,978 men, commanded by 2,521 officers. There were 40,238 citizens capable of bearing arms.

Post-Office.—In 1886 there passed through the post-offices of the republic 2,437,639 items of mail matter, as follows: 664,910 letters; 325,-738 Government dispatches; 618 registered letters; 9,576 postal-cards; 1,411,602 newspapers, and 24,959 sample packages. The increase was 609,247 as compared with the previous year.

Telegraphs.—During the year 1886–'87 the national telegraph employed 27 offices, and 7 of them had been opened during the year. The income was $22,962, against $17,608 in 1885–'86, an increase of $5,359. Messages dispatched to the interior during the fiscal year 1886–'87, 69,885; sent abroad, 4,191. New lines laid during the year, 20,324 metres. The telephone service of the capital was improved in July, 1886, by building a central station, and uniting all the telephones in one system. In July, 1887, the Minister of Public Works of Costa Rica completed with Señor Cuenca Cruz, of Paris, a contract respecting cable communication. Under it Señor Cruz is granted permission to lay one or more submarine cables from Costa Rica to the West Indies and Venezuela, and to New York. Permission is also granted to run the cables to any points in Central or South America. The contractor binds himself to connect these cables with the Canary cable system in course of construction. Costa Rica guarantees the contractor receipts amounting to 35,000 francs a year. The first cable must be laid within two years.

Railroads.—The Costa Rica Railroad Company has been formed in London to finish and operate the Central and Atlantic sections of the Government railway under a lease, with a share capital of £3,055,000, £1,255,000 of which are set aside for finishing the railroad, the first £355,000 shares being placed on the London market and sold on June 24, 1886, at 92·10. The republic is a shareholder in the company to the extent of £600,000, and is also entitled to dividends in the net earnings, after the interest of 6 per cent. shall have been paid on the £1,255,000 named. The Pacific section of the railroad, which has remained under the Government's own management, showed net earnings of $19,798 in 1885–'86, and of $17,226 in 1886–'87. But this Government railway is in good running order, well equipped, and the workshops furnished with the best of machinery.

Steamer Lines.—During the summer of 1887 M. C. Keith completed arrangements for placing on the line from Port Limon to the United States eight steamers a month to convey plantains, such steamers to leave on Wednesday and Saturday of each week, the line to go into operation with the year 1888. The Government has extended to the end of 1887 the time which Don Rafael Montúfar has to perfect arrangements for the establishment of a line of steamers between Port Limon and New Orleans or New York.

Chinese Immigration.—On Jan. 27, 1887, the Minister of the Interior issued a circular directed to the captains of the ports of Puntarenas and Limon, saying that the Government will not, under any pretext whatever, allow the landing of individuals belonging to the Mongolian race arriving from China, whether they come on their own account or under contract with others.

New Industries.—The Government procured from abroad 25 cwt. of superior cotton-seed, for free distribution among planters, in order to encourage this branch of agriculture, and also 10,000 "ramie" plants.

Rosewood.—Until the spring of 1887, no Costa Rican rosewood had been exported from the Pacific coast. But this trade has now been established.

The manufacture of salt has been undertaken at Puntarenas—a new enterprise.

Goods admitted Duty Free.—In July, 1887, the Congress of Costa Rica continued for another year the law exempting from duty the following articles imported into Costa Rica through Port Limon: Linseed-oil, turpentine, plows, harrows, pitch, carts, wheelbarrows, nails, stills, hammers, chopping-knives, wooden houses in pieces, doors, windows, putty, spades, pitchforks, rakes, pickaxes, paints, slates, cartspokes and felloes, salt, seed of all descriptions, screws, glassware, bits, sacks, galvanized iron, and zinc in sheets. The right to import Indian corn, beans, and rice duty free into Limon was also extended for one year.

Commerce.—The imports into Costa Rica during the fiscal year 1886–'87 amounted to $4,562,727, as against $3,428,696 in 1885–'86; an increase of $1,134,081, from which $718,846 railroad material is to be deducted, leaving the increase $415,685. The exports were valued at $3,296,508 during the calender year 1885, but in 1886 they did not exceed $3,225,807, the decrease being $70,701. The various products shipped during 1886 were represented by the following amounts: Coffee, $2,259,262; bananas, $476,775; hides, $95,754; gold-dust, $27,340; cabinet and dye woods, $89,289; other products, $120,787. The amount of coin shipped was $246,650, against $229,351 in 1885. The American trade was as follows:

FISCAL YEAR.	Import into the United States.	Domestic export to Costa Rica.
1887	$1,609,516	$708,980
1886	896,045	548,215

The expansion of trade was due to the rise in coffee.

Education.—There were on Jan. 1, 1887, 138 primary public schools, attended by 14,478 pupils, who were taught by 278 teachers, the Government paying toward the expense involved in teachers' salaries the sum of $103,598. Early in 1887 a decree was issued that, at the expense of the public treasury, eight young men and two girls, Costa Ricans by birth, be sent either to Europe or the United States, after examination as to capacity; the former to study either mining, civil or mechanical engineering, or arts and manufactures, or the military or natural sciences, the latter artistic or any other suitable female pursuits, the monthly outlay for each pupil not to exceed $50, with free passage.

CRAIK, DINAH MARIA MULOCK, an English novelist and poet, born in Stoke-on-Trent, Staffordshire, England, in 1826; died in Shortlands, Kent, Oct. 12, 1887. She was the daughter of a clergyman of the Established Church, who died when she was young, and was soon followed by his widow. At her death, the small annuity on which the family had depended ceased, and the young girl was left to take care of her two brothers with the earnings of her pen. Her first published book was one for children, "How to Win Love, or Rhoda's Lesson." Her first novel, "The Ogilvies" (1849), contained subtile delineations of character and life-like scenes, and was well received by the public, giving her a fair start in the literary life. This was followed by "Olive," which proved equally popular, and in 1851 by

DINAH MARIA MULOCK CRAIK.

"The Head of the Family," a story of Scottish life in the middle classes, of one man's devotion to his family of younger brothers and sisters left dependent upon him by the death of his parents. Strange as it may seem, in a book whose title is simplicity itself, and whose plot is far from enigmatic, Mrs. Craik displayed qualities highly imaginative and dramatic. Soon after this story, appeared "Alice Learmont," a fairy tale. In 1852 followed "Agatha's Husband," "Avillon, and other Tales," and stories and books for young people.

In 1857 was published "John Halifax, Gentleman," her most popular novel. The author says of this book, that a goodly portion of it was written at an inn in the old town of Tewkesbury. Neither before nor since "John Halifax," has there been given to the world any such living portraiture of a gentleman, a Christian hero, a practical business man placed amid surroundings adverse to gentlemanliness, and in times full of corruption. This hero performs no deeds of sensational heroism, but leads an independently pure, strong life, which of itself is heroism when brought into contact with actual business life. Here is a man

anxious for a name such as he can build for himself, a man with great business capacity, and an inventor, a man who has solved the problem of capital and labor, and would accumulate a fortune in the ordinary course of events, making his natural instincts secondary to his religious convictions. Miss Mulock, herself prophetic, makes John Halifax say, "I nevertheless uphold a true aristocracy, the best men of the country. These ought to govern and will govern one day, whether their patent of nobility be birth and titles, or only honesty and brains." She has religious convictions and is forcible in their definition, but has no denominational feeling. Although the daughter of a churchman, she was not a churchwoman. In her earlier novels she frequently avows her belief in religious freedom of thought and action, "that every one's conscience is free, and that all men of blameless life ought to be protected by and allowed to serve the state, whatever be their religious opinions." This, a rare doctrine when Mrs. Craik wrote "John Halifax," has now come to be almost the popular voice.

Such books as "A Life for a Life," "The Woman's Kingdom," and "A Brave Lady," are good examples of the strong purpose around which Mrs. Craik drew her plot, as a wreath engraved in the glass encircles a goblet. The carving may be delicate and the cutting lend a shimmer of beauty to the glass, but its strength is not thereby enhanced.

The pure, tender, gentle woman, in her story of "My Mother and I," will long live as a perfect type of the holy estate of motherhood combined with that of true widowhood. In "A Noble Life" she represents a Scottish earl, the last of his line, heir to a wealthy estate, but a cripple, as the exemplification of the Christ principle humanly presented, developed in the soul and lived in a life of constant bodily suffering. In this hero we see a character of such intellectual breadth and spiritual depth that it can not be dwarfed or bound down by its environment, but illumines with divine light the lives of those about it. Her theme in this book might have been made surpassingly interesting, but not for the mere sake of tickling the fancy was Mrs. Craik ever tempted into the making of books. With the calm imperturbability born of her single, strong, moral purpose, she passes by openings into merely romantic or emotional fields of thought which would be entered with avidity by the ordinary novel-writer. She does not like the details of vice, but rather would shield the poor sinner in his shame, leaving the plague-spot to that dear Lord who can heal the miseries revealed to him. In addition to her novels she was also the author of several stories for girls, some volumes on social and domestic subjects, translations from the French, and innumerable magazine articles on a great variety of subjects. She took much interest in travel, especially in the Irish journey of

1886, which is the subject of a book published with illustrations by her young friend, Noel Paton, "An Unknown Country."

As a poet, Mrs. Craik won a lasting though somewhat humble place. Her verse is good, and the sentiment is invariably noble. Her words are full of cheer and comfort, and will linger in the memory when many a finer lyric has been forgotten. Her most pleasing lyrics are "Rothesay Bay," "By the Alma River," "Philip my King," "Douglas, Tender and True," "Plighted," and "The Unfinished Book." "Philip my King" was written for her god-son, who afterward became known as "the blind poet," Philip Bourke Marston.

Like several other noted writers of the last half-century, Mrs. Craik seemed to wish, as she grew older, to address herself more especially to youth, and she carried with her into old age the same child heart and its sparkling freshness and grace, winning, as in earlier days, the love of the children. Among the most popular of her juvenile stories are "The Adventures of a Brownie" and "The Little Lame Prince." In the former, a sprightly, good-natured family brownie in contradistinction to a "family ghost," becomes the means of teaching the most wholesome lessons of law, order, and unselfishness in a very palatable and amusing way, so that even a brownie may be a missionary if he belongs to a good family. In "The Little Lame Prince" we have a diminutive political allegory, well adapted to youthful minds, and the same wholesome truths with which she fills her books for older people are conveyed in one of the most delightful little fairy stories.

In 1864 a pension of £60 a year was conferred upon Miss Mulock. A personal friend of hers writes: "In 1864 her literary work received the appreciation of a pension from the civil list, and the next year her personal life was crowned by her marriage to George Lillie Craik, the younger. Mr. Craik, who is a member of the publishing firm of Macmillan & Co., was somewhat younger than his wife, but the marriage was most happy as she once had occasion to say to another lady who came to her in regard to a marriage under similar conditions." The home that Mr. and Mrs. Craik built for themselves was one of the most charming about London, across "the lovely Kentish meadows" at Shortlands, ten miles southeast of London. It stood in the pleasant English country, with a delightful garden stretching out from it, and outside the house toward the garden was a little recess called "Dorothy's Parlor," where Mrs. Craik was fond of taking her work or her writing on a summer's day. It was named for the little daughter they had adopted years ago, having no children of their own, who was the sunshine of the house up to the time of her foster-mother's death. Within the recess was the Latin motto "Deus hæc otia fecit" (God made this rest), which Mrs. Craik once said, she selected as the motto she would wish to build into a home of her own, should it ever be given to her to make one. In the house there was one charming room that served for library, music-room, and parlor, filled with books and choice pictures, but chiefly beautiful because of the presence of its mistress, as she brought her work-basket out for a quiet talk with her friends. Over the mantel of the dining-room was the motto "East or West, Hame is best," which pleasantly gave the spirit in which Mrs. Craik lived in her home, for she used to say that home-keeping was more to her than story-writing, and she often got only one hour a week for her pen. She was tall and stately in carriage, with a winning smile and a frank and quaint manner, which gave one the best kind of welcome, and her silver-gray hair crowned the comfortable age of a woman who had used her years, one could see and feel, always to the best purpose. In the spring of 1887 Hubert Herkomer painted Mrs. Craik's portrait. Frances Martin says of it that "he depicts all that the painter can render of the repose, the quiet dignity, and the beauty of her advancing age. All but the few who remember the elegance of her youthful figure, and the intent gaze of the youthful face, will be contented with such a portrait. It is true to her as she lived and as she died." Mrs. Craik's death was caused by failure of the heart's action. The passing away was as peaceful as any death she has described. It was like that of Catherine Ogilvie, and like the falling asleep in death of John Halifax, and as like a translation into the Heavenly Land as that of Ursula his wife. It was the death Mrs. Craik had always foreseen for herself. Her only desire was to live long enough to witness the marriage of her adopted daughter; when this could not be, she murmured, "No matter, no matter," a fitting remark from the lips of one who had once penned these words "whether we see it or not, all is well." The Sunday after her death, in the church she had attended at Shortlands, Mr. Wolley, in his sermon, introduced this stanza from one of her poems:

"And when I lie in the green kirkyard,
    With the mold upon my breast,
Say not that she did well—or ill,
    Only, 'She did her best.'"

Mrs. Craik was a conspicuous advocate of the legalization in England of marriage with a deceased wife's sister, in order that the law might be uniform at home and in the colonies, and not long before her death she offered, in promotion of this reform, to reissue her "Hannah," with a new preface dealing with the question. She always considered that the critics and the public were wrong in ranking her most famous work as her best. "A Life for a Life" she invariably maintained was her highest reach in fiction, an opinion shared by many of her literary friends.

There must be, however, in "John Halifax" a quality that appeals to the universal heart, a certain homeliness that causes it to be read and loved wherever English is spoken. Her last completed literary work was an article for "The Forum," published in New York, and at the time of her death she was at work upon another article for the same periodical, entitled "Nearing the End." She left an estate of about $85,000.

The following list of Mrs. Craik's works was made last year by her husband, with her co-operation, adding one or two that have since appeared. Novels: "The Ogilvies" (1849); "Olive" (1850); "The Head of the Family" (1857); "Agatha's Husband" (1853); "John Halifax, Gentleman " (1857); "Christian's Mistake" (1865); "A Noble Life" (1866); "Two Marriages" (1867); "The Woman's Kingdom" (1869); "A Brave Lady" (1870); "Hannah" (1871); "My Mother and I" (1874); "The Laurel Bush" (1876); "Young Mrs. Jardine" (1879); "His Little Mother" (1881); "Miss Tommy" (1884); "King Arthur" (1886). Miscellaneous works: "A villion and other Tales" (1853); "Nothing New" (1857); "A Woman's Thoughts about Woman" (1858); "Studies from Life" (1861); "The Unkind Word and other Stories" (1870); "Fair France" (1872); "Sermons out of Church" (1875); "A Legacy, being the Life and Remains of John Martin, Schoolmaster and Postmaster" (1878); "Plain Speaking" (1882); "An Unsentimental Journey Through Cornwall" (1884); "About Money and Other Things" (1886); "An Unknown Country" (1887). Poetry: "Poems" (1859), expanded into "Thirty Years' Poems, New and Old" (1881); "Children's Poetry" (1881); "Songs of Our Youth" (1875). Children's Books: "How to Win Love; or, Rhoda's Lesson" (1848); "Cola Monti" (1849); "Alice Learmont, a Fairy Tale" (1852); "A Hero" (1853); "Bread Upon the Waters" (1852); "The Little Lychetts" (1855); "Michael the Miner" (1846); "Our Year" (1862); "Little Sunshine's Holiday" (1875); "Adventures of a Brownie" (1872); "The Little Lame Prince" (1874). She also prepared the "Fairy Book" and "Is it True?" two volumes of old fairy tales translated from Mme. Guizot de Witt's "Motherless, or a Parisian Family," "A French Country Family," "The Cousin from India," and "Twenty Years Ago," and edited a series of books for girls.

CUBA, an island in the West Indies, belonging to Spain. (For statistics of area, population, etc., see "Annual Cyclopædia" for 1883.)

Army.—The Commander-in-Chief and Captain-General of the island is Don Saba Marin, and the Segundo Cabo, Señor Sanchez Mira. The strength of the Spanish forces in Cuba in 1887 was 19,000.

Finance.—The Cuban budget for 1887–'88 estimates the outlay at $22,862,541, being $3,097,-194 less than for 1886–'87. The income is estimated at $23,273,100, hence there would result a surplus of $410,559 in spite of the sup-

pression of the export duties on sugar, molasses, and rum, the reduction by 20 per cent. of the consumption tax, and the annual reductions fixed with reference to the traffic between Cuba and the Peninsula, such reductions being estimated to aggregate $2,721,625.

A highly creditable measure was the payment by anticipation of the custom-house bonds of 1878 still in circulation, and of the 6-per-cent. hypothecary bonds of 1880 at par, in Cuba, Madrid, Paris, and London, on July 1 and Oct. 1, 1887, respectively. The directors of the Spanish Bank declared on July 1 a semi-annual dividend of 4 per cent. gold; and the Bank of Commerce declared a semi-annual dividend of 8 per cent. A new bank is to be founded at Havana by tobacco-exporters, for the purpose of facilitating their dealings.

General Condition.—Cuba, being thinly populated, mountainous toward the east, and thickly wooded, with comparatively few railways and good high-roads, while lying within the tropics, is still suffering from the disorders resulting from a ten years' insurrection and the abolition of slavery. The daily press teemed in 1887 with accounts of highway robberies, the kidnapping of well-to-do farmers, and even children, held for a ransom, incendiarism, and even a few landings of filibusters. Soldiers, mounted police, and armed bands of citizens have been keeping up a lively warfare with those anarchical elements, but the task is difficult, and it may take some time yet ere the island is purged of those disorderly elements continually cropping up again in consequence of the deep demoralization which seems to exist in a portion of the lower stratum of society. To a considerable extent it also exists among merchants and Government officials, notably revenue officers; hence the Captain-General was compelled to take energetic measures to arrest gigantic frauds at the Havana Custom-House, the existence of which had been no secret for a long time. Small-pox and yellow-fever were exceptionally malignant in 1887 at Santiago de Cuba and elsewhere. Extensive and destructive inundations also occurred, and an earthquake visited Santiago September 23, but without doing much harm. Yet planters have borne these visitations with patience, as the great planting interest is evidently entering upon an era of comparative prosperity through the better organization of labor and the sugar industry, the gradual appreciation of the value of the staple, and several well-timed reforms, chiefly in the interest of the agricultural and mercantile classes.

Suspicions having been aroused that the treasury was systematically defrauded through the connivance of custom-house officials at Havana, the Captain-General, on Aug. 18, 1887, ordered the military seizure of the custom-house, all means of outlet to the wharves and warehouses having been closed, and guards established over every wharf and avenue. For several days following a committee of investigation was engaged in an examination of the recent operations of the custom-house, and the superior officers and many subordinates were suspended. Meanwhile, all other operations were paralyzed—the wharves were covered with goods, numbers of loaded lighters were not permitted to discharge their cargoes, while crowds of laborers were standing around idle. Several committees of importing merchants called upon the Captain-General, and, admitting that they were more or less compromised in the irregular way of doing custom-house business, begged to be allowed to correct their entries already made. But three days were allowed them, and during that time the ordinary receipts from customs duties were more than trebled. The Government at Madrid approved the acts of the Captain-General. The resignation of the Intendant-General of Finance was also accepted, and Don Anibal Arieste was put in charge of the custom-house as special delegate of the Captain-General.

Reforms.—The excise duty on fresh meat was reduced July 1 from 30 cents to 25 cents on each eight kilogrammes, and the collection was committed to the Spanish Bank according to an agreement made in Madrid between the governor of the bank and the Home Government. The amount to be collected is $1,000,000. Cigars manufactured for local consumption, and not packed in boxes, but simply wrapped in paper, it was decided by the Intendant General, are henceforth not to be subjected to the stamp duty. The following Spanish-colonial products are to be admitted duty free into Spain and the Balearic Isles, provided they are shipped thither direct under the Spanish flag: Sugar, molasses, rum, coffee, chocolate, and cocoa. Those shipped under a foreign flag are to be subject to the duties established by the law of June 30, 1882, which duties are gradually being reduced till the year 1890, with the difference that products under a foreign flag coming from the Philippine Islands are only to pay one fifth of the duty that Cuban products are subject to.

Emancipation.—A royal decree dated Oct. 7, 1886, abolished the "patronato" or semi-slavery in Cuba, which was a transitory form of servitude created by the Abolition Law of Feb. 13, 1880, thus doing away with the last vestige of slavery.

Immigration.—At the instigation of the Crédito Territorial Hipotecario de la Isla de Cuba, arrangements were made in March to set on foot a current of Italian immigrants of the laboring-class, sugar-planters being anxious to procure field-hands and other operatives from Southern Europe, such operatives to receive $15 a month the first half of the year, and $9 the latter half, together with board and lodging, if between the ages of eighteen and fifty.

Modus Vivendi Treaty.—On Sept. 21, 1887, the Department of State at Washington published the ensuing memorandum of an agreement between the Government of the United States and the Government of Spain for the reciprocal and complete suspension of all discriminating duties of tonnage or imposts in the United States and the islands of Cuba and Porto Rico and all other countries belonging to the Crown of Spain, upon vessels of the respective countries and their cargoes:

1. It is positively agreed that from this date an absolute equalization of tonnage dues and imposts shall at once be applied to the production of or articles proceeding from the United States or any other foreign country, when carried in vessels belonging to citizens of the United States and under the American flag, to the islands of Cuba, Porto Rico, and the Philippines, and also to all other countries belonging to the Crown of Spain, and that no higher or other tonnage dues or imposts shall be levied upon said vessels and the goods carried in them, as aforesaid, than are paid by Spanish vessels and their cargoes under similar circumstances.

2. On the above conditions the President of the United States shall at once issue a proclamation declaring that these discriminating tonnage dues and imposts in the United States are suspended and discontinued as regards Spanish vessels and produce, manufactures or merchandise imported into the United States proceeding from Spain, and from the aforesaid possessions and from the Philippine Islands, and also from all other countries belonging to the Crown of Spain, or from any foreign country.

This protocol of an agreement is offered by the Government of Spain and accepted by that of the United States as a full and satisfactory notification of the facts above recited.

3. The United States Minister at Madrid will be authorized to negotiate with the Minister for Foreign Affairs, either by an agreement or treaty, so as to place the commercial relations between the United States and Spain on a permanent footing advantageous to both countries.

Americans in Cuba.—About the middle of October the Government published at Havana some new regulations, according to which American citizens are now allowed to land at or depart from Cuban ports without being obliged to present a passport or other document signed by a Spanish consul. A simple certificate from the American consul at the port of entry henceforth suffices for the identification of any citizen of the United States, and enables him to travel all over Cuba, to remain on the island as long he pleases, and to leave whenever he wishes.

Railroads.—A concession was granted to Don Marcos Fial y Cabrizas to build in the province of Santiago de Cuba a railroad between Palma, Soriano and San Luis. A branch line has been built connecting Remedios with Rojas and the Zaza Railway. In February work was begun to extend the Western Railroad from Consolacion del sur to Pinar del Rio. A French company has taken the necessary steps to build a railroad from Holguin to Nipe. The Matanzas Railroad reduced, early in the year, the freight on new machinery 50 per cent., and on old machinery 65 per cent., coal to pay 70 cents a ton, and only 63 cents on quantities of 1,000 tons and upward. Application was made early in the year for a concession to construct a railway to connect Sagua la Grande with Manicaragua, where, next to that of the Vuelta Abajo, the best tobacco is grown in Cuba. The government of the island has resolved that a branch railway be built from Júcaro to Punta de Burro, in order to facilitate the export of cattle and wood from Moron and Ciego de Avila. During 1886 the Cerro, Jesus del Monte, Carmelo and Principe lines of tramway in the city of Havana, with the Vedado and Vibora branch lines, forwarded altogether 5,529,604 passengers paying fares, and 99,396 riding free; together, 5,629,000 passengers; the total fare collected being $766,795. Adding thereto $15,169 accruing from other sources of income, the total gross earnings reached $781,964; and deducting therefrom the expenses, $572,647, there were net earnings to the amount of $209,317 or 18 per cent. on the capital. The Minister of the Colonies at Madrid has decreed a general plan of high-road building for Cuba.

Telegraphs.—The Spanish Minister of the Colonies granted during the summer a concession to Don José Rafael, Vizarrondo to lay a cable between Cuba and Hayti. A cable was laid early in the year in the bay of Havana, connecting Forts el Morro, la Cabaña, and the city of Havana.

Steamship Lines.—The subsidy that the Spanish Government has agreed to pay the Spanish Transatlantic Steamship Line insures the following: Line between Spain, the Spanish West Indies, and Mexico, 36 voyages per annum; Philippine Island line, 13 voyages; La Plata, 6 voyages; Fernando-Po, 6 voyages; Morocco, 24 voyages. The company engages to establish branch lines for the traffic with the United States, Central America, the Marianne and Caroline Islands, China, and Japan.

Meteorological Observatory.—The Government intends establishing a meteorological observatory at Santiago, and has written to New York, London, and Paris for the purpose of procuring the latest and most approved instruments.

Farming.—The new sugar-making system known under the name of central plantations has given satisfactory results to all planters who have been able to adopt it. The number of plantations of this class increased notably in 1887, absorbing at the same time all the surrounding small cane. Land-owners of the demolished estates subdivide them among farmers and small planters, who sell their cane to the central factories at prices that are either paid in money or in manufactured sugar, $2.50 for 100 pounds centrifugal, as an average, being generally considered as the equivalent for 2,500 pounds of cane after grinding and marketing expenses are deducted. It has been estimated that from 35 to 40 per cent. of the 1887 crop has been manufactured under this system, and that, despite the disappearance of slavery and the financial difficulties under which a large number of planters have been laboring, sugar-crops above the average in size will be produced. In the Zaza Central sugar-house a new sugar-bagging machine, invented by Don Joaquin Bárbara, was introduced early in 1887, an apparatus evidently destined to do good service as a labor-saving machine. Señores Mendieta and Gorriti have introduced a new furnace for sugar-

houses, in which "leagasse," or expressed cane, is advantageously utilized as the only fuel. The Cuban sugar-crop, ended Dec. 1, 1886, was 637,-237 tons for export, besides 35,000 tons for home consumption; together, 672,237 tons, against 695,311 tons in 1885. The exports to Aug. 1, 1887, amounted to 391,506 tons, while the stock in the six ports on that date was 116-798 tons; total, 508,299 tons, against exports during the corresponding period in 1886 of 418,-764 and stock 174,845 tons; total, 593,609. These figures, showing a falling off of 85,310 tons in the crop up to August 1, indicated that the crop of 1887 would not exceed in yield 600,000 tons, which has since been confirmed. A fresh impulse is to be given to cocoa-planting, which had been allowed to go to decay, there being only twenty-five plantations in the island. Don José Antonio Barrera, Don Manuel Delgardo, and Don Manuel Carrera y Sterling of Remedios purchased early in 1887 the Itabo cocoa estate of Yaguajuay, in order to extend and replant it and revive this branch generally in the district.

Botanic Garden.—In the Campo de Marte the necessary transformation was taken in hand in May to lay out six lateral gardens, in which Philippine plants imported by Dr. Villarraza are to begin the creation of a botanic garden.

Iron-Mining.—In 1883 an American company bought a group of the iron-mines that had been claimed, and built a railway 16½ miles in length, and a large wharf. In 1884 the company exported to the United States 22,000 tons of ore; in 1885, 80,000 tons; and in 1886, 110,000 tons. But, so far, they have not begun to ship in proportion to the capacity of the mines; that they may do so they are building a line of steamers of their own under the English flag, two of which vessels are already running. When the ships are completed they expect to ship 1,000 tons of ore a day. There is no underground mining of this ore, but merely cutting down the hill-side, throwing away the incasing dirt and rock, and taking out the ore from the solid vein. Although some contracts have been lately made with people in the United States for manganese-mines, none of them have been worked.

Commerce.—The trade of the Spanish West Indies was distributed among leading commercial nations as follows:

NATION.	Imports.	Exports.	Total.
United States ..	$45,410,856	$10,575,865	$56,965,721
England........	4,798,886	10,892,727	15,626,113
France	2,608,158	1,157,959	8,766,147
Spain..........	9,473,588	18,610,573	28,064,106

The American trade with Cuba is shown in the following table:

FISCAL YEAR.	Import from Cuba into the United States.	Domestic export from the United States to Cuba.	Total trade.
1883...........	$65,544,584	$14,567,918	$80,112,452
1884...........	57,181,497	10,562,880	67,744,577
1885...........	42,306,098	8,719,195	51,025,298
1886....... ..	51,110,780	10,090,679	61,181,629
1887...........	49,515,484	10,188,980	59,654,864

Columbus's Remains.—The mortal remains of Christopher Columbus were removed from the cathedral of Havana, where they had hitherto found a resting-place, to the city of his birth, Genoa, on board the Italian man-of-war, Matteo Brazza, on July 2, in charge of Monsignore Cocio, the Papal Internuntius in Brazil, and buried with great ecclesiastical pomp.

D

DAKOTA. Territorial Government.—The following were the Territorial officers during the year: Governor, Gilbert A. Pierce, Republican, succeeded by Louis K. Church, Democrat; Secretary, M. L. McCormack; Treasurer, J. W. Raymond; Auditor, E. W. Caldwell, succeeded by James A. Ward; Superintendent of Public Instruction, A. S. Jones, succeeded by Eugene A. Dye; Attorney-General, George Rice, succeeded by C. F. Templeton; Commissioner of Immigration, Lauren Dunlap, succeeded by P. F. McClure; Chief-Justice of the Supreme Court, Bartlett Tripp; Associate-Justices, Charles M. Thomas, William H. Francis, William B. McConnell, Cornelius S. Palmer, Louis K. Church, succeeded by James Spencer.

Legislative Session.—The Seventeenth Territorial Assembly convened on January 11, and remained in session two months. One hundred and thirty-five new laws, and twelve joint resolutions, were passed. The most important measures were the appropriation bills, the local-option law, and the law submitting the question of division of the Territory to a vote of the people. In the matter of appropriations, the session has been criticised for its extravagance. The total appropriations were $1,580,718, as against $705,000 in 1885. The local-option bill provides that on petition of one third of the legal voters of any county, an election shall be held at the time of any general election, to determine whether prohibition or license shall prevail in that county. Under this law, at the November election, a large majority of the counties declared for prohibition. Another act of this Legislature authorizes the acceptance of the partially-constructed Capitol building at Bismarck. When the Territorial capital was removed to Bismarck, in 1883, that city gave 320 acres of land, and agreed to erect a suitable structure within that area; but as accepted, the building is without the north and south wings originally planned, and the Territory assumes about 70,000 of unpaid bills incurred in the construction. It is provided that these bills be paid by a sale of the adjoining lots given by the city. Other acts of the session were:

Creating two agricultural districts, and providing for a board of agriculture for each district. There had been one board for the whole Territory previously.

To provide for the construction and maintenance of artesian wells, appointing a well-commissioner for each county, and prescribing his duties and regulating the assessment and collection of taxes for such wells.

Creating the office of county auditor.

Authorizing incorporated boards of education or school districts to refund outstanding indebtedness; also giving cities and counties like authority.

Permitting cities and municipal corporations to issue bonds for erecting school and other public buildings, and for other public improvements.

Permitting the construction of bridges over navigable rivers, and providing the manner for paying for them.

To suppress and prevent the spread of contagious or infectious diseases among domestic animals, and creating the office of State Veterinary Surgeon.

To appropriate, for the support of fire departments of each city, town, or village a part of the tax paid by fire-insurance companies upon premiums received in any such town, city, or village.

Regulating the manner of ingress and egress of public buildings.

To allow the establishment of free libraries and reading-rooms by towns or cities, upon the approval of a majority of the electors voting upon the question, and authorizing a tax-levy for their support.

Increasing the annual license-fee for the sale of liquors, and fixing it at sums from $500 to $1,000. It was from $200 to $500 previously.

Protecting the use of irrigating ditches.

Declaring that woman shall retain the same legal existence and personality after as before marriage.

To regulate the practice of pharmacy, the licensing of persons to carry on such practice, and the sale of poisons in the Territory.

To create the office of public examiner, and dividing the Territory into two examiners' districts. These officials are directed to exercise a constant supervision over the books and financial accounts of the several public, educational, charitable, penal, and reformatory institutions of the Territory, and are invested with large powers to investigate the general management of the institutions.

To regulate grain-warehouses, and the inspection, weighing, and handling of grain, and defining the duties of the Railroad and Warehouse Commission in relation thereto.

Raising the age of consent from ten to fourteen years.

Providing the manner for assessing the stocks and shares of banks and bank associations, and collecting tax for the same.

Creating liens on the crops of persons buying seed on credit, and providing for filing and foreclosing the same.

Creating a new Capitol Commission, to have control of the Capitol and grounds, and to superintend the sale of certain lands given to the State and held for the benefit of the public-building fund.

To create Pierce and Church counties, and to define the boundaries of certain other counties.

Population.—The Territory has had another year of wonderful growth in population. The building westward, through the northern counties of Dakota, of the St. Paul, Minneapolis, and Manitoba Railroad, and the construction by this and the Northern Pacific Railway companies of numerous north and south feeders, has turned a great tide of immigration toward the agricultural and stock lands of the Mouse river, Turtle mountains, Devil's lake, and other regions. This, together with the largest crop ever harvested in many sections of Northern Dakota, have made it almost impossible to keep pace with the development going on in the districts named. A few of the more westerly counties, having scarcely a single inhabitant at the beginning of the year, are now well populated with thrifty farmers and residents of towns that have grown up in a day. According to the Federal census, in 1860 Dakota had a population of 4,837; in 1870, of 14,181; in 1880, of 135,177; in 1885, as shown by the Territorial census, 415,610. At the close of 1887, careful estimates show over 600,000.

Land Ownership.—The entire area of Dakota is 96,596,480 acres. Of this, 26,847,105 acres are contained within Indian reservations; about 7,000,000 acres were granted by the Government to aid in the construction of the Northern Pacific Railroad; 3,000,000 acres are set aside for support of schools; and, according to computations made from the records and plat-books of the several land districts, there had been disposed of, up to June 30, 1887, 35,937,-980 acres under the general land laws. leaving a vacant area open to settlement at this time (not deducting the small area of unsurveyed lands held by squatters) of 23,811,445 acres. As an area equal to 2,067,281 acres was taken up by the filing of entries during the year ending June 30, 1887, the time when all the vacant land will be settled can be computed.

Finances.—The total bonded indebtedness of the Territory is $1,098,800, bearing from 4 to 6 per cent. interest, all of it incurred in the construction of public institutions. Of this amount $530,100, or nearly half, was authorized and incurred by the Legislature of this year for improvements and additions to the already crowded benevolent and penal institutions. For the Insane Hospital at Yankton, $92,500 in bonds was authorized; for the Deaf-Mute School at Sioux Falls, $23,000; for the University of Grand Forks, $20,000; for the University of Vermilion, $30,000: for the Penitentiary at Sioux Falls, $14,300; for the Penitentiary at Bismarck, $29,000; for the Agricultural College at Brookings $54.500; for the Insane Hospital at Jamestown, $153,-000; for the Normal School at Madison, $35,-800; for the School of Mines at Rapid City, $23,000; for the Reform School at Plankinton, $30,000; and for the Normal School at Spearfish, $25,000. At the same time the 6-per-cent. 5-20 bonds of 1881, amounting to $90,000, were refunded at 4½ per cent. Bids for these bonds were received and opened May 30. The highest bid was par and 0·52 per cent. premium. Five sixths of the bonds issued and sold bore 4½ per cent. interest; the balance 5 per cent., most of them subject to an option clause, reserving the right to redeem in five and ten years. This is the first time in the history of the country that a Territorial bond has sold for less than 5 per cent.

The total assessment of property in the Territory in 1885 amounted to $106,499,549; in 1886, to $132,542,703; and in 1887, to $157,-084,365. The per cent. of increase in valua-

tion in 1887 was not as large as in previous years, owing to the assessments being made at a lower valuation; yet the increase in acreage was much larger, being nearly 40 per cent. This extraordinary increase is due in part to the rapid growth of the Territory, and in part to the assessment of several million acres of land owned by the railway corporations, which had heretofore escaped taxation. The Legislature of 1883 provided for the taxation of railroads upon their "gross earnings," and all property of such corporations has heretofore been held exempt under the "gross-earnings law." The average local levy for all purposes for 1885 was 3 mills, for 1886 it was 2·4 mills, and for 1887 it was 2·9 mills.

Railroads.—At the beginning of this year the total number of miles of road operated in the Territory was 3,491. During the year over 700 miles of new road were completed, making a total of about 4,200 miles. Of these new constructions, the most important are on the Northern Pacific from Grand Forks to Pembina, 95 miles, on the St. Paul, Minneapolis, and Manitoba from Minot, west 150 miles, and on the Chicago, Milwaukee, and St. Paul from Bristol to Lake Preston, 75 miles.

Education.—During 1879, only 25 per cent. of the school population were in regular attendance. The per cent. in 1883 increased to 37, while in 1887 there were 58 per cent. attending every day for the whole term of 112 days. In this respect Dakota leads nearly all of the States.

Taxation for the support of common schools is of four kinds: 1. The county clerk at the time of making the annual assessment, levies a tax of $1 upon each elector; 2. At the same time he levies an additional tax of two mills upon each dollar of taxable property in the county, and the fund raised by these two he divides among the townships in proportion to the children of school-age resident thereof; 3. A township tax not exceeding 3 per cent. of the taxable property of the township is levied by the township board for the support of the schools of the township; 4. The patrons of any given school may meet in what is known as a subdistrict meeting and vote an additional tax upon their own property for the support of the school of their own subdistrict. The law of 1887 has made considerable change in the organization and administration of the school system of the Territory. The general supervision and control of public instruction is vested in a Territorial Board of Education consisting of three members appointed by the Governor. The Territory has established two universities, one at Vermilion, having 193 students by the last report, and one at Grand Forks, recently established, having 75 pupils; a State normal school at Madison, having 174 pupils: a territorial normal school, with 104 pupils; an agricultural college, with 256 pupils; and a school of mines, opened this year. The private universities and academies are

Pierre University at Pierre, Yankton College, at Yankton, Dakota University at Mitchell, Sioux Falls University and All-Saints School at Sioux Falls, Jamestown College, Tower University, Groton College, Redmond College, and Augustana College. Over 600 students attend these institutions.

Charities and Prisons.—The Hospital for the Insane at Yankton has a capacity for 120 patients, but in September 160 inmates were reported. To relieve this crowded condition, the appropriation of the Legislature previously mentioned was made, but as charges of irregularity were preferred against a majority of the Board of Trustees of the institution, the Governor refused to sanction the expenditure of this appropriation under the direction of the present board. The North Dakota Hospital at Jamestown is in the third year of its existence, and had cared for 248 patients up to September of this year. There were then 147 inmates. The Legislature of 1883 located a reform school at Plankinton, Aurora County, but no appropriation for the erection of buildings or the maintenance of the school was made till 1887. The contract for the building was let August 9, and the work is now in progress. At the Sioux Falls Penitentiary there were 82 convicts in June, against 92 at the same time last year. At Bismarck there were 56, an increase of 4 over 1886.

Mining.—The Black Hills produce all the gold and silver mined in Dakota, and nearly the entire output is credited to but four mines. The total production of gold and silver since the settlement of this region in 1877, is $33,770,000. In 1886 the product was $3,125,000, a slight decrease from 1885. The whole country west of the Missouri river and a large part of the surface of North Dakota is underlaid with a deposit of lignite coal, which crops out in many places in veins 18 feet thick; at present, from lack of transportation facilities, only these outcroppings are worked, and generally for the supply of the neighborhood simply. But along the Northern Pacific Railway at Sims in Morton County, Dickinson in Stark County, and Little Missouri in Billings County, coal-mining is already carried on extensively, and thousands of tons are shipped as far east as Jamestown. It is estimated that during the winter of 1886-'87 10,000 tons were shipped into the city of Bismarck, where it is retailed at $3.50 a ton.

At Sioux Falls, Dell Rapids, and other points of Southeastern Dakota, along the Big Sioux River, there is an outcropping of the most remarkable deposit of quartzite (granite of jasper) ever discovered on the continent. Eight hundred car-loads of this granite were shipped last year from Dell Rapids alone.

In several sections of Dakota great interest is manifested in discoveries of natural gas, and companies have been formed at Blunt, Jamestown, and Fargo to utilize these discoveries.

Agriculture.—The season of 1886 was not altogether favorable to farming interests in the Northwest, although, owing to the opening of new farms, and the increased acreage sown, the yield in every instance was in excess of that of the previous season.

The season of 1887 was more favorable, and reports from the corn-crop show that it will reach 27,000,000 bushels, an increase over last season's yield of about 70 per cent. The area sown to wheat in 1887 is estimated at 3,899,389 acres, and the yield will approximate 60,000,000 bushels, or about one seventh of the entire wheat-crop of the United States last year.

Stock-Raising.—In 1885 the value of live-stock in the Territory was $40,528,897. At the beginning of this year the value had increased to $42,828,838, an amount nearly 50 per cent. greater than the value of the three principal farm products—wheat, corn, and oats—of the same year. In seven years the value of live-stock in Dakota has increased $36,365,065.

Militia.—The present militia of the Territory, designated as the Dakota National Guard, consists of 2 regiments of infantry of 9 companies each, one battalion of mounted infantry of 2 companies, and a battery of artillery of 2 guns. The maximum number of enlisted men to each company is 50 men and 3 commissioned officers.

The effective strength of this command is 1,031 enlisted men and 84 commissioned officers of the field, staff, and line. The general staff consists of 22 commissioned officers; total number, 1,136.

Indians.—Dakota leads all the States and Territories in the Union (excepting, of course, the Indian Territory) in the numbers of her Indian population and the extent of her reservations; nearly one fifth of her entire area is set apart for the use of 30,076 Indians. If the existing reservations were divided equally among them, there would be 892 acres for every man, woman, and child. The Great Sioux Indian reservation stretches from Missouri river on the east to the Black Hills on the west, from the Nebraska boundary on the south almost to the city of Bismarck, in Northern Dakota, and occupies nearly one fourth of the area of Dakota. It contains 22,010,048 acres, on which reside 23,093 Indians. This area includes a tract known as the Crow Creek and Winnebago reservation, which was thrown open to settlers by order of President Arthur. Early this year, however, by advice of the Attorney-General, President Cleveland revoked the order, and directed all white settlers to be driven out. This entailed severe hardship on innocent settlers under the first order, and was not obeyed until the military were brought into use.

Division.—By a law passed in March, it was provided that the people of the Territory should express their opinion, at an election in November, upon the question whether Dakota should be admitted as two States or as one, the division, if favored, to be on the seventh

220 DELAWARE.

standard parallel, an established line corresponding with the 46th parallel of latitude. Preliminary to the election, two divisionist conventions were held, one for South Dakota at Huron, July 13, and one for North Dakota at Fargo, July 23, at which a plan of campaign was adopted and resolutions favoring division passed. Among the resolutions of the Huron convention were these:

Resolved, That we reaffirm the declarations already many times made in constitutional conventions, legislative assemblies, and in memorials to Congress, that we are unalterably opposed to admission as a whole.

This convention declares for the division of this Territory into North Dakota and South Dakota, on the seventh standard parallel, and that we seek such division for the reason, among others, that good government, economical and well administered, will be more readily secured thereby for both sections than by admission as a whole. That thereby we shall have our proper and rightful representation in Congress, preserve that just balance of power to which a great population should be entitled. and secure the highest permanent good for both North and South Dakota.

That the convention affirms its conviction that it is the just and primary right and province of a people about to be admitted to the Union to designate their State boundaries, subject to be modified with their consent upon the proposal of Congress, for grave reasons only affecting the general welfare.

While we recognize the fact that the Constitution confers upon Congress a just discretion in the admission of now States, we protest against the unjust and tyrannous exercise of power by refusing to admit a new State into the Union upon an equal footing with other States, after having fulfilled the purposes of Territorial life.

At the November election the divisionists were in the majority. Southern Dakota voted generally in favor of division, and Northern Dakota against it.

DELAWARE. State Government.—The following State officers assumed or held office at the beginning of the year: Governor, Benjamin T. Biggs, Democrat; Secretary of State, John P. Saulsbury; Treasurer, William Herbert; Auditor, John H. Boyce; Attorney-General, John H. Paynter; Superintendent of Free Schools, Thomas N. Williams; Chief-Justice of the Supreme Court, Joseph P. Comegys; Associate Justices, Ignatius C. Grubb, John W. Houston, Edward Wootton; Chancellor, Willard Saulsbury. The office of Superintendent of Free Schools was abolished during the year by a legislative act. In March the death of Judge Wootton created a vacancy on the Supreme bench which was filled by the appointment of Attorney-General Paynter. The Assistant Attorney-General, John Biggs, son of the Governor, was then promoted by his father to the Attorney-Generalship.

Statistics.—Careful estimates show that the population increased from 146,000 in 1880 to about 170,000 in 1887. There are 110,000 people living in cities, towns, and villages, and 60,000 residing on farms and engaged in agricultural pursuits. One city has a population of 55,000, one city over 3,000, four towns over 2,000, ten towns over 1,000, seven towns over 500, fifteen villages over 300.

The farms of the State are now valued at $36,789,672, live-stock $4,000,000, valuation of cities and towns $60,000,000, annual products manufactured $40,000,000, agricultural products $10,000,000—$150,000,000 besides the personal property and investments.

Finances.—The State debt, at the beginning of the year, was composed of 4-per-cent. State bonds to the amount of $585,000, 6-per-cent. school-fund bonds valued at $156,750, and $88,000 of indebtedness to Delaware College bearing 6 per cent. interest. By an act of the Legislature in March authority was given the treasurer to refund $250,000 of the State bonds at 3 per cent. interest. The new bonds are payable in 10 to 30 years at the option of the State. There are assets in the State treasury more than sufficient to meet the whole State indebtedness.

The auditor estimates the total receipts of the State for 1887 at $203,277. Three fourths of this amount is composed of the following items: receipts from the Philadelphia, Wilmington, and Baltimore Railroad Company, $40,000; from the Baltimore and Ohio Railroad Company, $40,000; from licenses, $80,000. The first two items are in commutation of taxes. In the third item is included a State tax on manufacturers. The receipts from licenses in 1886 were $75,243, of which New Castle County contributed $57,577.85, Kent, $9,974, Sussex, $7,692.

Legislative Session.—The General Assembly was in session from January 4 to April 22. It re-elected United States Senator George Gray for the full term of six years. Among the acts of the session were the following:

Authorizing the levy court of Sussex to fund $30,000 of the county debt, at 4 per cent.

For the suppression of policy-gambling.

An act in relation to oysters, being a codification of most of the prior legislation on this subject, with some amendments.

To regulate the practice of medicine and surgery.

Reserving certain portions of the Delaware Bay for fishing and domestic oyster purposes.

Appropriating $2,500 to pay for the right of way of the proposed canal connecting the Delaware Bay with Assawoman Bay.

Providing for the care of the indigent insane.

For the preservation of the health of female employés.

For the protection of fisheries [prohibiting the use of explosives or poison in streams and ponds].

For the protection of property from fire.

For the protection of public health and to prevent the adulteration of dairy products [the oleomargarine bill.]

Relating to the revenues of the State [applying the State laws to the taxation of the Delaware Railroad, and empowering that road to commute for such State taxes by the payment of $3,000 per year].

To regulate the practice of pharmacy.

Amending chapter 562, volume 14 [providing that no exemption of real property from attachment shall be allowed for claims of $25 or less pertaining to wages for manual labor].

For the study of physiology and hygiene in the public schools, with special reference to the effects of stimulants and narcotics.

In relation to the education of colored children. Increasing the appropriation to $6,000, and making other changes.

Supplement to the charter of the Delaware Railroad Company [authorizing a consolidation with the Delaware, Maryland, and Virginia Railroad and with the Eastern Shore feeders, and the absorption of the link between Rodney and Wilmington, with power to build a branch between Dover and Milford].

Empowering the State treasurer to collect claims against the United States Government on a commission of 25 per cent. of his collections. There are three of these claims. One for $300,000, one for $175,000, and one for an amount undetermined.

Concerning presidential electors [constituting the Superior Court of Kent County a tribunal for the hearing of contests between electoral candidates].

Accepting grants of money by the General Government for the establishment of agricultural experiment stations.

For the protection of minors [to keep boys under eighteen out of pool-rooms and similar places].

Regulating the conduct of caucuses and other primary elections. It provides that every election held by any political party, for the purpose of nominating or selecting candidates by ballot to be voted for at any subsequent election, or for the purpose of selecting delegates or representatives to any political convention, shall be held by one presiding officer and two judges at each voting precinct. These officers, as well as the clerk of the meeting, shall take a prescribed oath to perform their duties impartially. The procedure at such meetings is determined, and heavy penalties for fraud in the balloting or the counting of votes are fixed. The act applies to Newcastle County, which includes half the population of the State, and is especially directed against frauds in the city of Wilmington.

Railroad Taxes.—A decision rendered by the State Supreme Court in March had the effect of invalidating all city and county taxation of railroads. The question at issue arose upon the interpretation of the act of 1873, which permitted the Philadelphia, Wilmington, and Baltimore Railroad to commute all taxes by the payment of $40,000 annually, the benefit of which had been extended by subsequent legislation to all railroads in the State. The court decided that this payment, under the words of the statute, was in commutation of all taxation, State, county, and city, on all classes of railroad property. As this result was not contemplated by the framers of the act, who had in view only commutation for State taxes, the Legislature nullified the future effect of the decision by an act permitting taxation by cities and counties of such property, the road-bed excepted. But all back taxes were lost.

Education.—A radical change was made in the public-school system of the State, by an act that vacates the offices of State superintendent and assistant superintendent of public schools, and substitutes therefor a superintendent for each county. These commissioners are to be appointed by the Governor, and to hold office for one year. By the same act the business of furnishing text-books for the schools was taken from the State, in whose hands it has proved a losing transaction.

The Delaware State College has been crippled in its work during the year by the hostility existing between its president and members of the faculty. The board of trustees has been unable to settle the difficulty, being itself nearly evenly divided between the friends and opponents of President Caldwell. At a meeting in July, the Caldwell faction succeeded in postponing action on the president's resignation till March, 1886. There is danger that this deep-seated quarrel may wreck the institution, which, at its best, has never had much prosperity.

The report of the State actuary of colored schools for the year ending July 1, shows that the work in these schools, though making little advance, is still equal to that of previous years. The total number of schools for the year was 70, an increase of one over the last report, and the total number of pupils 3,847.

Constitutional Convention.—The following is an extract from the bill passed by the Legislature on this subject:

Whereas, The subject of a convention to revise and amend the Constitution of this State has been agitated among the people; and, *whereas,* this General Assembly, without expressing any opinion as to the necessity of a convention, deems it to be right and proper to afford an opportunity to the people to make their sense known: *Therefore, be it enacted,* On the first Tuesday in November next a special election shall be held for the purpose of ascertaining the sense of the people of this State upon the question of calling a convention to change, alter, and amend the Constitution of the State.

The grounds of dissatisfaction with the present Constitution are numerous, the clauses giving each county, regardless of size, the same representation in the General Assembly, and providing that the whole county shall vote for all the Senators and Representatives nominated in each of its districts being especially objectionable. The election in November resulted in a vote of 14,450 in favor of the proposed convention, to 464 against; but, owing to a peculiar provision of the State Constitution, which requires that the vote to call a convention shall be a majority of the highest number of votes cast at any one of the last three preceding elections, the result was practically in favor of the anti-convention party. The negative vote was not a fine test of the strength of the latter party, as its members generally refrained from voting, in order to bring the total vote below the 15,640 votes required to make a decision possible. The present Constitution dates from 1830.

DENMARK, a constitutional monarchy in northern Europe. A new constitution was adopted on July 28, 1866. The representative and legislative assembly is called the Rigsdag, and consists of two chambers. The Landsthing is composed of 66 members, of whom 12 are appointed for life by the King, and the rest are elected for eight years by indirect suffrage. The city of Copenhagen has 7 representatives; Bornholm, 1; the Faroe Islands, 1; and the electoral districts of the towns and rural communes, 45. The Folkething has 102 members, all elected directly for three years. The reigning sovereign is Christian IX, born April 8, 1818, who ascended the throne in 1863. The heir-apparent is his son, Frederick, born June 3, 1843. The ministry is composed as follows: President of the Council and Minister of Finance, Jacob B. Scavenius Estrup, appointed June 11, 1875; Minister of Justice and for Iceland, J. V. M. Nellemann; Minister of Foreign Affairs, Baron O. D. Rosenorn-Lehn, appointed Oct. 11, 1875; Minister of Marine, Rear-Admiral N. F. Ravn, appointed Jan. 4, 1879; Minister of Worship and Public Instruction, J. F. Scavenius, appointed Aug. 24, 1880; Minister of War, Colonel J. J. Bahnsen, appointed Sept. 12, 1884; Minister of the Interior, H. P. Ingerslev, appointed Aug. 7, 1885.

Area and Population.—The kingdom of Denmark has an area of 38,302 square kilometres, or 14,124 square miles. The population in 1882 was estimated at 2,018,432. In 1880 the population was 1,980,259, of which number 515,758 inhabited the towns, and 1,453,281 the country districts. The foreign-born population comprised 38,152 Germans, of whom 22,007 were natives of Schleswig; 24,148 Swedes; 2,828 Norwegians; 454 English; 384 Russians; 182 Austrians; 188 French; and 1,702 of other nationalities. The population of the capital, Copenhagen, on Jan. 1, 1887, was 289,900, inclusive of the suburbs.

The great majority of the inhabitants of Denmark adhere to the Lutheran or state Church. Of other denominations the Baptists in 1880 counted 3,687 adherents; the Roman Catholics, 2,985; the Mormons, 1,722; the Reformed Church, 1,363; the Irvingites, 1,036. There were 8,946 Jews, and 1,074 persons who professed no belief.

In 1880 there were 5,667 emigrants; in 1881, 7,985; in 1882, 11,614; in 1883, 8,875; in 1884, 6,307; in 1885, 4,346; in 1886, 6,623. Nearly all the emigration is to the United States.

The natural movement of population for the last three years reported has been as follows:

YEARS.	Marriages.	Births.	Deaths.	Surplus of births.
1883	15,462	66,899	39,828	27,071
1884	15,970	70,272	39,529	30,743
1885	15,645	69,517	39,053	30,464

Legislation.—The Rigsdag met on October 8. The Left was not present, but held a meeting at which Berg's radical proposals were rejected and the views of the moderate wing in favor of negotiating with the Government were approved. No compromise was reached, however, and the finance law decreed by the Government was rejected by 68 votes against 25. The Government thereupon promulgated another provisional finance law under which it will collect the existing taxes and make necessary disbursements during the current year.

Finances.—The net receipts of the treasury from the various sources of revenue for the year ended March 31, 1886, were as follow: Domains, 570,177 kroner; forests, 200,437 kroner; reserve and invested funds of the state, 3,843,150 kroner; direct taxes, 9,517,682

kroner; indirect taxes, 34,272,258 kroner, of which 2,618,526 kroner were derived from stamped paper, 24,366,424 from customs, the tax on playing-cards, and the duty on beet-sugar, and 7,287,308 from various sources; the postal receipts, 224,548 kroner; telegraph receipts, 129,884 kroner; lottery, 884,622 kroner; receipts from the Faroe Isles, 63,206 kroner; other receipts, 4,271,366 kroner. The expenditure on the army amounted to 10,122,-161 kroner, not including 1,572,038 kroner of extraordinary expenditure; on the navy, 6,142,674 kroner, besides 766,642 kroner of extraordinary expenditure; on the public debt, 9,550,758 kroner; on the financial administration, 3,059,822 kroner; on the Department of Justice, 2,969,918 kroner; on the Interior Department, 2,749,883 kroner. The budget for 1888-'89 places the receipts at 54,000,000 kroner, inclusive of a balance of 1,500,000 kroner in the treasury, and the expenditures at 56,000,000 kroner. On March 31, 1886, the internal debt amounted to 180,929,771 kroner, and the total debt to 194,395,438 kroner. The debt has since been reduced by 1,600,000 kroner through the payment of the Amsterdam loans of 1764 and 1785 and the Antwerp loan of 1788. This is offset by assets consisting of investments and securities amounting to 103,-112,023 kroner, not including the capital of the Government railroads, telegraphs, and other reproductive public works.

The Army.—The regular army and reserve in 1887 numbered 1,201 officers and 41,749 men. The infantry mustered 801 officers and 33,192 men; the cavalry, 189 officers and 2,420 men; the artillery, 175 officers and 4,755 men; the engineers, 61 officers and 1,366 men. The second ban or extra reserve consisted of 294 officers and 16,318 men. The government asked in 1882 for an extraordinary credit of 72,000,000 kroner to be expended mainly in fortifying Copenhagen on the sea and land sides and in constructing fortresses and intrenched camps in other localities. The refusal of the Folkething to vote the supplies, and that of the ministry to resign in consequence of their defeat, led to a constitutional crisis, which is still pending.

The Navy.—The Danish war-fleet in 1886 consisted of 5 armor-clads of the first class, carrying 79 guns; 3 of the second class, carrying 28 guns; 7 cruisers, with 79 guns; 8 iron gunboats, with 36 guns; and 7 first-class and 9 second-class torpedo-boats. The largest iron-clad is the "Helgoland," completed in 1880, a vessel of 5,345 tons displacement, which has 12 inches of armor at the water-line, and is armed with one 36-ton and four 22-ton guns. The "Tordenskjöld," a large torpedo-vessel, is armed with a single 50-ton gun, a 14-inch Krupp breech-loader, besides four 6-inch Krupps, light guns, and appliances for shooting Whitehead torpedoes. The "Valkyrien," a cruiser of 2,900 tons displacement, and protected with 2½-inch steel deck-armor, was begun in 1886.

Commerce.—The total value of the imports in 1884 was 274,168,607 kroner; of the exports, 178,394,088 kroner. (The krone has an exchange value of about 15 cents). The commerce was divided among the following classes of commodities, the value being given in kroner:

CLASSES.	Imports.	Exports.
Articles of food	91,300,000	182,100,000
Raw materials	90,200,000	94,800,000
Manufactures	69,400,000	10,200,000
Machines, tools, and other means of production	22,800,000	11,800,000

The imports for 1885 are reported as 249,-200,000 kroner, and the exports as 162,800,000, divided among the classes in the following proportion:

CLASSES.	Imports.	Exports.
Articles of food	84,500,000	118,900,000
Raw materials	85,600,000	22,900,000
Manufactures	63,600,000	10,800,000
Machinery and plant	15,500,000	10,600,000

The leading articles of import and the values imported in 1884 were as follow: Textiles, 89,744,768 kroner; iron and steel manufactures, 19,574,743 kroner; timber and manufactures, 18,088,406 kroner; coal, 14,489,286 kroner; wheat, 9,666,253 kroner; rye, oats, barley, Indian corn, and other cereals and flour, 22,186,-402 kroner. The following are the values of the chief exports in 1884: butter, 81,570,879 kroner; hogs, 22,887,090 kroner; cattle, 21,-999,800 kroner; pork products, 13,287,790 kroner; wheat-flour, 7,850,852 kroner. In the total value of the imports in 1884 Germany is represented by 98,546,948 kroner; Great Britain by 62,662,078 kroner; Sweden and Norway by 40,070,370 kroner; Russia by 16,514,390 kroner; and the United States by 15,492,682 kroner. Of the total exports 68,-449,668 kroner went to Great Britain, 57,754,-682 kroner to Germany, 41.078,881 kroner to Sweden and Norway, and 3,590,195 kroner to the United States.

Navigation.—The Danish commercial marine consisted on Jan. 1, 1886, of 3,046 sailing-vessels, of 188,923 tons, and 281 steamers, of 89,-815 tons; total number of vessels, 3,327; total tonnage, 278,738. The movement of navigation at Danish ports in 1885 was as follows: sailing-vessels entered (exclusive of 15,258 coasters, of 183,229 tons), 16,427, of 754,400 tons; sailing-vessels in the foreign trade cleared, 15,886, of 126,415 tons; steamers entered (exclusive of 12,105 coasters, of 260,872 tons). 10,-871, of 1,004,609 tons; steamers cleared, 10,957, of 1,881,710 tons.

Railroads, Posts, and Telegraphs.—The railroad mileage in 1886 was 1,214. The Government lines had a total length of 1,000 miles, and cost up to March 31, 1886, 146,471,475 kroner. The receipts from the state railroads in 1885-'86 were 12,913,386 kroner, and the operating expenses 10,617,180 kroner.

In 1885 the number of letters sent through the mails was 86,724,663, including postal cards; circulars and printed matter, 8,423,862; journals, 41,385,557. The receipts in 1885-'86 were 4,278,209 kroner; the expenses 4,048,666.

The telegraph lines belonging to the Government had in 1885 a total length of 2,417 miles, with 6,757 miles of wire. There were 149 Government telegraph stations and 192 stations on the private telegraph lines belonging to the railroads. The number of paid messages forwarded on the state lines in 1885 was 1,261,468, of which 729,056 were domestic and 532,412 international. The receipts in 1885-'86 were 694,565 kroner; the expenses 824,399.

Iceland.—According to the Constitution of 1874, the lower chamber of the Legislature, called the Althing, consists of 24 members elected by the people, and the Landsthing, or upper chamber, of 6 elected members and 6 chosen by the King. By virtue of a clause in the Constitution the Legislature has changed the proportion, making the number in the Althing 21, and in the Landsthing 15, of which latter 9 are elected by the people and 6 nominated by the King. The Icelanders desire to have a resident ministry and an administration under the control of their Legislature, affirming that the minister for Iceland in Copenhagen, who directs the entire administration, is unable to understand the wishes of the people or to regulate the conduct of his subordinates. The area of the island is 39,756 square miles, but the inhabited portions contain only 16,180 square miles. The number of inhabitants in 1880 was 72,445, of whom 34,150 were males and 38,295 females. There has been distress in Iceland and considerable emigration in recent years.

Colonies.—The Danish West Indies are the only colonies of commercial importance. They have an area of only 118 square miles, but produce large quantities of rum and sugar. The portions of Greenland that are free from ice have an area of 88,800 square miles. On Dec. 31, 1885, Northern Greenland had 4,414 inhabitants, of whom 2,119 were of the male and 2,295 of the female sex; and Southern Greenland, 5,500 inhabitants, of whom 2,557 were males and 2,943 females.

DEPRÊTIS, AGOSTINO, Italian statesman, born in Stradella, Piedmont, in 1811; died there, July 29, 1887. After completing his studies at the University of Turin. he began the practice of law in his native town. He took part in the agitation against Austrian rule, and by that course injured his professional prospects, so that he was compelled to abandon legal practice, and took the management of the large estate of the Gazzaviga family. He participated in the unsuccessful rising at Milan, but afterward played no part in the military events of the Italian revolution. In 1850 he was elected to the Sardinian Parliament as deputy from Broni, and afterward sat for Stradella. Originally he was an opponent of Cavour, but became his supporter when the National movement had taken definite form. In 1859 he was appointed Civil Governor of Brescia, and in 1860 he went to Sicily as commissary-general and pro-dictator to carry into effect the union with Italy by proclamation of the statute. Garibaldi had requested his appointment to this post, but Cavour trusted him to check any dangerous revolutionary developments, and for that purpose provided him with a royal commission as governor-general. Although a member of the Radical party, and at various times the leader of the parliamentary Opposition against Cavour, he always maintained cordial personal relations with that statesman. In 1862 he entered the Ratazzi Cabinet as Minister of Public Works. In 1866 he was Minister of Marine in the Cabinet presided over by Ricasoli, and in 1867 Minister of Finance when that statesman was again at the head of the Cabinet. After the death of Ratazzi he became chief of the Opposition, and when the Minghetti Cabinet fell under the assaults of the Left, he was called, in March, 1876, to the head of the Government. He abolished the grist-tax, and carried through a bill prohibiting religious processions outside of churches, because such processions took the character of political manifestations. In March, 1878, his ministry was overthrown by a combination led by Cairoli, but that minister, who was singularly deficient in parliamentary management, soon succumbed to the tactics of Deprétis, who returned to power in the following December. The new Cabinet was a surprise to Parliament, and its composition indicated his desire to cut loose from the Radicals, and attach to himself the moderate members of both parties. He left out all the able and ambitious men of his party, and chose for his colleagues persons of no ministerial experience, and not identified with the aims of the Left. This was the beginning of the "transformism" with which his name was thereafter coupled, and which his enemies among the Radicals described as going in as Minister of the Left and governing as Minister of the Right. His Cabinet lasted only six months, but not long after its defeat he was again called to the helm, and after that he remained the "indispensable" prime minister. While alienating the extreme Radicals, and being as often opposed as he was supported by the various groups of the Left and their leaders, he preserved a shifting parliamentary majority, usually a large one, by his political sagacity and parliamentary tact. He was virulently abused by the extremists of both parties, but won the confidence of a great section of the voters, was supported by Minghetti and others of the old Conservatives, and by making concessions that did not involve the sacrifice of his patriotic aims, he governed almost as a dictator, shaping the foreign and domestic policy of the kingdom during a long and critical period. His political manifestoes, which he was accustomed to date from Stradella, were effective electioneering documents.

The legislation that he originated was not such as to gain him the reputation of a creative statesman, but he carried through reforms at a rate sufficient to satisfy the progressive spirit of the bulk of the nation. In 1882 he extended the franchise, established *scrutin de liste*, and secured the passage of a bill confirming the use of the parliamentary oath. In 1883, by a coalition with the Right, he carried through a repressive law against socialism. He differed with the other members of the Cabinet on the question of an education bill, and resigned, but formed a new ministry. In the early part of 1887 the disaster at Massowah led to the most violent recriminations in the Chamber, and the reconstruction of the Cabinet, into which Crispi, long an assailant and rival of Deprétis, was taken, possibly with a view to the succession, for the health of the "old man of Stradella," always vigorous up to this year, was now broken, and he wished to retire, but was persuaded by the King to remain in office. Deprétis was not a great orator, but was skillful in debate, and possessed the art of disarming his enemies by ready explanations, and warding off savage attacks with smooth and conciliatory phrases. He was often accused of political trickery and insincerity, but never of selfish or unpatriotic motives. The policy of turning from Republican France to form an alliance with the conservative monarchies of central Europe, which was the chief political act of his life, offended the democratic instincts of Italian Liberals, and disappointed the ambitious hopes that were entertained of territorial aggrandizement; yet the country has since accepted the league with Germany and Austria as a safeguard for the security, dignity, and best interests of Italy.

DISASTERS IN 1887. The year's record of disasters is notable for the variety of ways in which life has been cut short and property destroyed. This is due in part to the more rapid means of transit by land and sea, and in part to the increase of telegraphic facilities all over the world. The following list, while far from complete, presents a startling record of the perils that surround every dweller in a civilized land. It is to be observed that the terrible possibilities which seem to threaten mankind from the common use and manufacture of high explosives are not as yet realized; gunpowder is still more destructive than dynamite, and together they fall far short of the railroad and the steamboat.

January 4. Railway: broken axle near West Springfield, Mass., 1 killed, 19 injured; collision near Republic, Ohio, wreck took fire, 13 killed. Explosion in a coal-mine at Mons, Belgium, 37 killed.

8. Shipwreck: German ship Elizabeth, near Cape Henry, 27 lives lost, including 5 of the life-saving crew.

9. Fire: the Alcazar palace at Toledo, Spain, totally destroyed, loss $1,000,000.

11. Railway: train derailed near Dunbar, Nebraska, probably the result of malice, 1 killed, 19 injured.

17. Car-load of cotton burned near Paducah, Ky., bodies of 4 supposed tramps found.

18. False alarm of fire in a London theatre, 17 killed in the panic.

20. Collision at sea: British emigrant ship Kapunda sunk by bark Ada Melmore off Brazilian coast, 300 lives lost.

21. Shipwreck: British steamer Brentford, 23 lives lost. Fire: hotel in New Westminster, B. C., 3 lives lost.

22. Shipwreck: Chinese transport, 100 lives lost.

24. Floods in Queensland, many lives lost. Shipwreck: American schooner C. Graham, on Shad Bay Shoals, all hands lost.

25. Railway: collision at Allandale, Ontario, 5 injured. Explosion: powder-car near Fort Scott, Kansas, many buildings demolished and several lives lost.

31. Explosion: dynamite on American steamer Guyandotte.

February 2. Railway: train derailed by snow near Garrison, Mont., 1 killed, 10 injured.

5. Train derailed near White River Junction, Vt., cars took fire, 30 killed, 37 injured.

7. Train derailed through malice, near Charlotte, N. C., 2 killed.

3. Collision near Dubois, Ga., 2 killed, 2 injured.

12. Collision near Port Huron, Mich., a brakeman was killed while trying to prevent the collision.

18. Fire: 30,000 bales of cotton at Tompkinsville, Staten Island, N. Y. Railway: broken bridge near Mud Lake, Ill., 1 killed, 1 injured.

22. Train derailed near Bloomer, Wis., 4 injured; train derailed by snow near Tamarack, Cal., 1 killed; car-heater exploded near Sidney Station, Ill., fire followed, several passengers injured.

23. Earthquake in Southern Europe, much damage in the Riviera, nearly 400 lives lost. Railway: collision near Red Oak, Iowa, 1 killed, 2 injured.

26. Earthquake in Italy. Railway: collision near Seymour, Iowa, 1 killed, 1 injured.

27. Broken bridge near The Needles, Cal., 3 killed, 4 injured.

28. Collision near Grafton, West Va., 1 killed, 2 injured.

March 1. Explosion in the Beaubrun mines, St. Etienne, France, 86 killed. Fire: steamer W. H. Gardner burned on Tombigbee river near Gainsville, 20 lives lost. Shipwreck: Chinese junk between Hainan and Siam, 600 lives lost. Railway: train buried in snow near Selkirk, Canada, 7 killed. Fire: American steamer Lone Star burned at her wharf in New York city.

5. Explosion: fire-damp in coal-mines near Mons, Belgium, 144 lives lost. Railway: broken bridge near Victoria, Mo., 2 drowned, 2 injured.

8. Railway: train derailed near Hightstown, N. J., 1 killed, 5 injured.

10. Explosion of mélinite in the French arsenal at Belfort, 6 killed, 11 injured.

12. Railway: collision near Wheatland, Dakota, 1 killed, 2 injured.

13. Earthquake in Southern Europe. Train derailed near Hunt's Station, Ohio, several injured.

14. Railway: bridge breaks near Boston, Mass., 24 killed, 115 injured.

16. Railway: collision in Rochester, N. Y., 4 injured; broken bridge near Dunbar, Ohio, 3 killed; train derailed near Park's Station, N. Y., 15 injured, wreck took fire.

18. Fire: Richmond Hotel burned in Buffalo, N. Y., 10 lives lost, many injured.

19. Railway: collision near Toledo, Ohio, 5 injured.

23. Fire: 12 lives lost at Bessemer, Mich. Explosion in colliery near Sidney, New South Wales, 70 killed.

24. Fire: temple burned, China, 260 lives lost (supposed incendiary.)

25. Railway: collision near Leetonia, Ohio, 1 killed, 7 injured.

26. Collision near Rockport, Pa., 1 killed, 2 injured.

31. Explosion: shells fired in target-practice by U. S. S. Omaha, found by Japanese peasants and accidentally exploded, 4 killed.

April 1. Railway: collision near Middleton, Miss., 2 killed, wreck caught fire.

2. Collision near Springfield, Ont., 2 killed.

3. Fall of a church at Linguaglossa, Sicily, 40 killed. Explosion in mine near Venita, Ind. Ter., 18 killed.

6. Fire: 60 horses burned at Buchel, Switzerland.

7. Land-slide at Monte Carlo.

8. Train derailed near Bismarck, Dakota, 2 killed, 8 injured.

12. Collision near Lancaster, Ohio, 1 killed, 6 injured. Fire in St. Augustine, Fla., several historic buildings and two hotels burned.

13. Train derailed near Ravenswood, West Va., 3 killed, 6 injured. Shipwreck: British steamer Victoria, at Dieppe, 12 lives lost.

16. Shipwreck: French steamer Dieu Merci capsized and sank almost instantaneously off Cape Nassau, 3 drowned.

17. Railway: collision near Palatine, Ind., 5 killed.

18. Railway: land-slide near St. Johnsville, N. Y., 1 killed, 1 injured. Collision near Diamond Bluff, Wis., 1 killed, 3 injured. Shipwreck: steamers Tasmania and Volta, in the Mediterranean, about 30 lives lost.

20. Train derailed near Taswell, Ind., 3 killed, 2 injured.

21. Tornado in Missouri and Arkansas, 15 lives lost. Shipwreck: schooner Active, off the coast of Oregon, 33 lives lost. Railway: collision near Chelum, Washington Ter., 6 killed, 18 injured. Earthquake in the island of Jersey.

22. Hurricane off the Australian coast. Pearl-fishing fleet wrecked, 550 lives said to be lost.

23. Railway: broken bridge near Winslow, Arizona, 3 killed. Another broken bridge, near Hoffman, Ind., 3 injured.

24. Fire at Arnaut-Keire, Asia Minor, 500 houses burned, many lives lost.

25. Explosion: an old artillery shell, near Harper's Ferry, Va., burst in the midst of a picnic-party, 6 injured.

27. Railway: train derailed near Timberville, Va., 1 killed, 1 injured. Train derailed by running over two tramps lying on track, both killed.

28. Shipwreck: schooner Flying Scud, in Shalikoff strait, 17 lives lost. Mining accident at Pottsville, Pa., 5 lives lost.

29. Shipwreck: British steamer Benton foundered off Formosa, 150 lives lost; steamer John Knox lost, with all hands, off Cape Ray. Steamer Benhope burned off Tybee island, Georgia.

30. Railway: train derailed near Driscoll, Dakota, 1 killed, 7 injured. Collision near Tamaqua, Pa., 1 killed, 2 injured.

May 1-7. Hot sirocco in Hungary with fires, many lives lost, property destroyed to the value of $2,500,000.

3. Earthquakes in Arizona and Mexico, towns destroyed, and 150 to 200 lives lost. Explosion in a mine near Nanaimo, British Columbia, 126 lives lost.

4. Explosion in Cocoa tunnel, Georgia, 12 killed.

7. Explosion: powder-mill near Pittston, Pa., 1 killed, 2 injured.

8. Collision at sea: 10 Italian emigrants lost from steamer La Champagne off the French coast.

19. Collision at sea between British steamers Britannic and Celtic, 5 killed, 6 injured—cause, fog.

25. Fire: the Opera Comique, in Paris—estimated loss of life nearly 200.

27. Fire: stables of Belt Line Horse-Car Co., New York city, 1,200 horses suffocated.

28. Explosion in a mine, Lanarkshire, Scotland, 75 killed. Explosion in a colliery near Glasgow, Scotland, 75 killed. Shipwreck: British steamer Sir John Lawrence, in a typhoon in the Indian Ocean, 750 lives lost.

June 4. Explosion in Cambria Iron-Works, 9 lives lost.

5. Fire and panic in a circus at Neschen, Germany, many killed, about 300 injured.

8. Explosion: fire-damp in a colliery in Westphalia, 50 killed.

10. News of earthquakes in Turkistan, more than 100 lives lost.

17. Fire: American steamer Champlain burned off Grand Traverse Bay, 22 lives lost.

18. Drowning: nearly 250 pilgrims drowned in the Danube by the upsetting of a boat near Pak.

23. Shipwreck: British ship Dunskeig, off Terra del Fuego, part of the crew perished.

24. Fire in a mine near Virginia City, Nevada, 15 lives lost.

July 2. Railway: collision at Lamonte, Mo., 1 killed, 3 injured; broken axle near St. Thomas, Ont., 3 killed.

3. Train derailed near St. Thomas, Ont., 2 killed.

4. Explosion: dynamite at Jasz-Berény, Hungary, 27 killed. Railway: collisions near Birmingham, Ala., 7 injured; and near Bessemer, Mich., 5 injured, cars caught fire. Accidents and fires, too many for enumeration, caused by fireworks.

5. Explosion of dynamite near Pesth, 27 soldiers killed. Railway: misplaced switch near Galt., Ont., 8 injured, probable carelessness.

6. Train derailed near Loon, Ky., 8 injured. Landslide at Zug, Switzerland, about 100 killed and the town nearly destroyed.

9. Fire: Alcazar theatre at Hurley, Wis., 15 lives lost.

10. Shipwreck: sloop Mystery capsized in Jamaica Bay, N. Y., 24 lives lost; steamer Merrimac lost on Little Hope reef near Halifax.

11. Railway: collision at Lapeer, Mich, 4 injured. Fire in Hurley, Wis., 11 lives lost.

13. Collision near Robinson's, Ky., 1 killed, 5 injured. Explosion: locomotive engine at Crawford's, Pa., 2 killed, 9 injured.

15. Railway: collision near Lincoln, Neb., 2 engines and 13 cars destroyed, no lives lost, but noteworthy because all hands were asleep on one of the engines; another collision at St. Thomas, Ont., between an excursion train and an oil-car, fire followed, 13 killed, more than 100 injured.

16. Railway: engine of the President's special train broke a parallel rod near Glendale, N. Y., engineer killed.

20. Fire: Standard Oil Company's works at Constable Hook, N. J., loss $1,500,000.

21. Eleven railway-laborers run over and killed near Hohokus, N. J.

22. Shipwreck: British ship Firth foundered in a cyclone off the coast of Java.

23. Shipwreck: British steamer Mahratta foundered off Hoogly Point, India, many lives lost.

24. Railway: misplaced switch near Pittsburg, Pa., 8 injured, probable carelessness.

26. Railway: train derailed near Wabash, Ill., 1 killed, 2 injured.

27. Railway: collision near Hopedale, Ill., 9 killed, 15 injured; derailment near Franconia, Ariz., fire resulted, 3 killed.

28. Derailment and broken bridge near Cumberland, Md., 3 killed; collision at Knob Lick Mountain, Mo., 3 killed.

29. Train derailed near Tioga, Tex., 4 injured; broken axle near Cochrane, Ind., 2 killed, 2 injured.

30. Railway: collision at Lawrens, Ohio, 8 injured; another at Hookset, N. H., 2 killed, 5 injured; train derailed near Farmersville, Texas, 7 injured.

31. Car upset at Dedham, Mass., 7 injured.

August 2. Railway: collision near Devil's Lake, Wis., 3 killed, 3 injured.

3. Collision near North Bend, Neb., 2 killed.

4. Train derailed near Greenwood, Va., 1 killed, 8 injured. Tornado in Kansas, 79 houses destroyed in Millbrook.

5. Railway: collision near Milton, Ont., 1 killed.

6. Train derailed near Bangor, Ala., 1 killed, 2 injured.

8. Collision near Chattanooga, Tenn., 2 killed, several injured; misplaced switch near Missouri City, Mo., 2 killed.

9. Train derailed near McCoy's, Ind., 1 killed; collision near White Hill, N. J., 1 killed, 4 injured.

10. Railway: excursion train breaks through a burning bridge near Chatsworth, Ill., 80 killed, from 150 to 250 injured; train derailed near Duff Station, Ind., 5 injured.

11. Fire at sea: British steamer City of Montreal burned, all hands rescued by steamer York City. Railway: train derailed near Albany, Ga., 15 injured. Explosion: Giant Powder Works, near San Francisco, Cal., 1 killed, 10 injured.

12 Fire in Pittsburg, Pa., loss $500,000 Railway: train derailed near Saline City, Ind., 6 injured.

13-20. Run over at grade-crossings in Connecticut, 9 persons.

13. Collision near Greenville, Pa., 3 injured.

15. Wind-storm in France destroyed much property.

17. Four fatal accidents to Alpine tourists reported from Zürich, making 18 within a month. Railway: collision near Ellicott City. Md., 3 killed; train derailed at Washington, D. C., 1 killed, 17 injured.

18. Tornado in Nebraska, houses blown down, 2 persons killed, 6 injured.

20. Railway: collision near Athens, Tenn., 1 killed, 1 injured.

21. Train derailed near Saugus, Cal., 5 injured.

22. Drowning: accident at a regatta on the Thames, England, 17 lives lost.

23. Railway: train derailed near Skelly's Station, Ohio, 1 killed, 3 injured; collision near Culpeper, Va., 2 killed, 4 injured; collision near Round Bay, Md., 1 killed; collision near Woodbine, Md., 1 killed, 1 injured.

24. Collision near Eaton's Siding, W. Va., 2 killed, 17 injured; broken bridge near Denver, Col., 2 killed, 2 injured.

26. Railway: collision near Chattanooga, Tenn., 25 injured.

28. Collision near Port Byron, N. Y., 1 killed, 2 injured.

31. Collision at St. Paul, Minn., 2 injured. Cholera: official returns show 30,780 fatal cases in the Northwestern provinces of India during the month of August.

September 2. Railway: train derailed near Lawrence, Kan., 2 killed, 1 injured; train derailed near Parsons, Kan., 1 killed, several injured.

4. Shipwreck: British ship Falls of Bruar, foundered off Yarmouth, Eng., 24 lives lost.

5. Fire: a theatre burned in Exeter, Eng., 46 lives lost. Railway: collision near Fitchburg, Mass., 2 killed, 1 injured.

6. Explosion of a locomotive engine near Sherman, Texas, 2 killed.

7. Railway: collision near Afton, Ia., 1 killed, 9 injured.

8-9. Heavy rains in Arizona destroyed 25 miles of railroad, and did much damage otherwise.

12. Railway: collision at Peoria, Ohio, 2 killed, 1 injured.

16. Collision near Doncaster, Eng., 28 killed, 70 injured.

19. Collision on elevated road in Brooklyn, N. Y., 7 injured; another collision near Dubuque, Ia., 5 killed, 6 injured; train derailed near Fern, Ind., 2 killed.

20. Collision near Canton, Dak., 3 killed.

21. Hurricane in Texas; many houses and crops destroyed. Shipwreck: steamer Romeo at Villeguier, 13 lives lost.

25 Railway: misplaced switch near Holden, Mo., 2 killed, 1 injured.

26. Collision near Summit, N. J., 2 killed, 6 injured.

27. Train derailed near Jackson, Tenn., 2 killed, 3 injured.

28. Flood: the Yellow River, in the Chinese province of Honan, overflowed its banks and submerged an area of 7,000 square miles, including many populous towns. Many thousand lives lost, and several million people left homeless.

30. Railway: collision near Park Station, Mo., 5 injured.

October 2. Earthquake in Smyrna.

3. Railway: collision near Hillsdale, Pa., wreck took fire, 1 killed; another collision near Dunsmuir, Cal., 1 killed, 4 injured; another collision near Lower Soda Springs, Cal., 1 killed, 8 injured; train derailed near Porter, Ark., 1 killed, 2 injured: another train derailed near Gladstone, Mich., 2 killed. Shipwreck: steamer California, on Lake Michigan, 14 lives lost.

4. Storm on the Great Lakes, 15 lives lost.

9. Shipwreck: British gunboat Wasp, supposed to have been lost at sea with all on board, 80 in number.

10. Railway: collision near Kout, Ind., 10 killed, many injured. Shipwreck: French steamer, in the Bay of Bormes, 22 lives lost.

12. Fire: an asylum for the insane burned at Cleveland, Ohio, 8 women perished.

14. Fire: cotton-mills burned in Baltic, Conn. Estimated loss $1,500,000; 1,000 persons thrown out of work.

17. Fire: at Hankow, China, 2,000 lives lost, 2,000,000 taels' worth of property destroyed.

18. Shipwreck: collision between steamer Upupa and German bark Planteur off Beachy Head, 12 lives lost.

20. Shipwreck: British steamer Cheviot at Port Philip, 12 lives lost. Railway: collision at Green's Station, S. C., 3 killed, 10 injured; train derailed near St. Alban's, W. Va., 26 injured.

21. Collision near Whiteside, Tenn., 2 killed, 1 injured.

22. Fire: town of Kitab, Bokhara, destroyed; nearly half the inhabitants perished.

27. Railway: trains derailed near Florissant, Col., 3 killed; another near Tallahassee, Fla., 5 injured.

28. Train derailed near Morris, Ill., 2 killed, 1 injured. Probably caused by malice.

30. Shipwreck: American steamer Vernon on Lake Michigan, 40 lives lost.

November 3. Railway: derailment and collision in St. Louis, Mo.; circus train wrecked, and a number of wild animals escaped, 1 man killed, several injured.

15. Explosion: locomotive engine near Palatine Station, N. Y., 1 killed, 2 injured. Fire: steamer Wah-Yueng burned in Canton river, China, about 400 lives lost.

17. Fire: 8 locomotives and 150 cars destroyed at Ludlow, Ky.

18. Railway: train derailed near Paducah, Ky., 2 killed, 3 injured.

19. Shipwreck: sunk by collision off Dover, German steamer Scholten, 112 lives lost.

20. Railway: collision near Tunnel Hill, Ill., 4 killed. Fire: winter quarters of Barnum's menagerie burned, many valuable animals lost.

21. Explosion: powder magazine at Amoy, China, 50 soldiers and several hundred civilians reported killed, and a large portion of the town destroyed.

25. Railway: collision near Williams, Ariz., 3 killed, 18 injured; collision near Cochran's Mills, Pa., 3 killed, 5 injured.

December 1. Fire: Strobridge Lithographing Company's buildings burned in Cincinnati. Earthquakes in Sonora, Mexico; much suffering among the inhabitants.

4. Flood: a heavy ocean-wave swept the coasts of Cuba and Porto Rico; many huts and houses destroyed. Earthquake in Calabria.

9. Shipwreck: 20 fishing-smacks lost off the Orkney Islands.

16. Collision between steamer Breakwater and ferry-boat Pavonia in New York harbor, many passengers injured.

18. Shipwrecks: several vessels driven ashore on the North Atlantic coast, 1 life lost.

20. Fire at sea: American steamer San Vincent off San Francisco, 11 lives lost.

22. Explosion: a large quantity of naphtha accidentally discharged into the main sewer in Rochester, N. Y.; explosions and fire followed, several large buildings burned, 4 men killed, 3 missing, and about 20 injured.

23. Explosion: dynamite near Halifax, N. S., 4 killed. Railway: collision near Chicago, 40 injured, 7 of them seriously; collision near Fairfield, Wis., 2 killed, 20 injured.

26. Railway: accidents in Pennsylvania and the District of Columbia, 4 killed.

27. Shipwreck: 25 vessels wrecked in the Gulf of Patras.

29. Shipwreck: scow capsized in New York harbor, 8 men drowned.

31. Explosion in works of Equitable Gas Company, New York city, shock felt throughout the vicinity, cause unexplained, 1 killed. Railway: collision near Greenwood, Ky., 6 killed, 21 injured; the wreck took fire. Another collision near Meadeville, Pa., 5 killed, 11 hurt; several minor accidents occurred, resulting in 3 killed and several injured.

DISCIPLES OF CHRIST. The "Churches of Christ" are not officially represented in any general body, but a considerable proportion of them are in relation through voluntary action by means of the organizations for missionary and benevolent work which meet with the General Christian Missionary Convention.

The twelfth annual General Christian Missionary Convention met in Indianapolis, Ind., October 8. The Convention consists virtually of the annual meetings of three distinct and independent organizations—the Christian Woman's Board of Missions, the Foreign Christian Missionary Society, and the General Christian Missionary Convention, each of which occupies one day of the session in the order in which the names of the bodies are given. The Christian Woman's Board of Missions returned receipts of $26,226, or $5,000 more than the receipts of the previous year: a membership of 12,506 persons; and 870 auxiliaries, bands, and young people's societies. The receipts of the Foreign Missionary Society had been $47,758, and the expenditures had been $47,598. Reports were presented from missions in Turkey (5 stations), Denmark, England (7 churches), India, Japan, and China, in all of which a net gain of 502 members was returned. The whole number of members in Turkey, India, and Japan was 855. The mission in Paris, France, had been discontinued in accordance with the direction of the society at its previous meeting. Complaints made by missionaries of other societies that the agents of this body had interfered with their missions in Turkey were declared not founded in reason, and the explanation was made that there had been no interference with other denominations except of that accidental character which could not be avoided. The receipts of the General Christian Missionary Society, which takes charge of home mission and church extension enter prises, had been $25,772. Under its direct agency 86 new and unorganized places had been visited, 158 churches had been visited and assisted, 25 churches had been organized, and 678 persons had been received by baptism. Several State organizations co-operate with the work of the society through their own agents. They returned in all 179 missionaries, who had visited and assisted 1,204 churches and 811 new and unorganized places, had organized 78 churches, and had received 5,915 members by baptism. The amount of $79,823 was returned as raised by State boards, and about $40,000 as raised by missionaries for local work. The receipts for the church extension fund had been, regular, $937; special, $2,286. Two loans had been made. A favorable report was made of the condition of the Southern Christian Institute, and of the school at New Castle, Ky. Two ministers had been aided from the Ministerial Relief Fund. A reply was adopted to a communication from the Commission of the Protestant Episcopal Church on Christian Unity, inviting a conference on that subject. It expressed gratification that such an invitation had been sent out. The "Churches of Christ," it represented, had been organized in the beginning in 1809, in an effort to restore the faith and discipline of apostolic times, in protest against the sectarian spirit, and were still, with about 800,000 communicants, seeking the same objects. A specification followed of what these churches regarded as essential to Christian unity. First, was the recognition of the Holy Scriptures of the Old and New Testaments as the revealed Word of God and the only authoritative rule of faith—the only one " beyond the reach of compromise or surrender." Second, the restoration of unity demanded a return to New Testament teaching; and this involved the points that the original, inspired creed had but one article, viz.: "Jesus is the Christ, the Son of the living God"; that all who confessed this faith in the Lord Jesus were admitted to

Christian fellowship by an immersion in water in the name of the Father, and of the Son, and of the Holy Spirit, and only such were admitted; and that those who were thus added to the Church were continued in fellowship so long as they walked in the commandments of Jesus. Outside of that which is essential to Christian unity, the answer continued,

There are many things pertaining to growth in knowledge, to methods of working, etc., in reference to which, for the sake of peace and for the preservation of unity, there should be a common agreement. There should, we think, be the largest liberty of opinion, of investigation, and of utterance, on all questions arising out of the study of the Scripture, and no one who holds to Jesus " as God manifest in the flesh," and who keeps his commandments, should be disturbed in his church relations on account of his opinions, *provided* he does not attempt to force his opinions on others, or to make an acceptance of them a test of fellowship. Should he attempt this, he becomes a factionist, to be rejected after the first and second admonition. Many questions unprofitable for discussion in the pulpit, may be profitably, or at least harmlessly, discussed in the schools, to which all speculative questions should be remanded. Then there are practical questions—questions of method in carrying out the work of the Church—which, being left to the discretion of Christians, to be answered according to times and circumstances, should never be made tests of fellowship or occasions of strife.

Finally, the "reply" commended the declaration of the commission that the church which it represented did not seek to absorb other communions, but rather, co-operating with them on the basis of a common faith and order, to discountenance schism, heal the wounds of the Body of Christ, and promote Christian charity; and added, " not what will promote the interests of any denomination, but what will serve the purposes and promote the welfare of the ' one Body ' of Christ, is to be sought. All other communions should adopt this sentiment as their own, as a necessary preliminary to all successful efforts to heal divisions and make manifest that unity which is so prominent a characteristic of the Church of God."

E

EADS, JAMES BUCHANAN, an American engineer, born in Lawrenceburg, Ind., May 23, 1820; died in Nassau, N. P., Bahama Islands, March 8, 1887. He attended school until he was thirteen years of age, and from his earliest youth showed great fondness for machinery, spending his spare moments in visiting places where he could watch the movements of mechanical appliances. In 1833 he accompanied his parents to St. Louis, and, as they reached that place, the steamer took fire, destroying all of their household goods. The boy then obtained a clerkship in the dry-goods house of Williams and Durings, and his evenings during this time were spent in the library of his employer, studying mechanical and civil engineering. In

1838 he became a purser on a Mississippi steamboat. This occupation afforded him the opportunity of studying the details of the construction of steamboats, and while so employed he acquired the title of captain, which clung to him through life. His experience led him to devise means for the saving of wrecks that were found along the river, and in 1842 he built a diving-bell boat for recovering cargoes. This proving successful, he constructed a much larger boat, with novel and powerful machinery for pumping out the sand and water, and lifting the entire hull and cargo. Forming a copartnership with Case and Nelson, he began the business of raising vessels, and soon extended his operations from Balize, La., to

Galena. Ill., and into the tributaries of the Mississippi. While engaged in this business he gained a knowledge of the laws that govern the flow of silt-bearing rivers, and it is said that there was not a stretch in the bed of the

JAMES BUCHANAN EADS.

Mississippi fifty miles long between St. Louis and New Orleans on which he had not stood on the bottom of the stream beneath a diving-bell. In 1845 he disposed of his interest in this business and built the first glass-works in the Mississippi valley. This proved unsuccessful financially, and he resumed the wrecking business. In 1845 twenty-nine steamers were burned at their landings in St. Louis, most of which were raised by him, so that in 1859 he had paid off his losses and acquired a fortune of $500,000. He made a proposition to Congress in 1856 to keep the channels of the Mississippi, Missouri, Ohio, and Arkansas rivers clear of snags, wrecks, and other obstructions for a term of years; but the bill giving him the contract, after passing the House, was not acted on by the Senate. Impaired health led to his retirement from business in 1857, but in 1861, soon after the fall of Fort Sumter, he was summoned to Washington and consulted by the President and his Cabinet relative to the practicability of using light-draught iron-clad vessels on the Mississippi and its tributaries. Almost immediately a contract was given to him for the construction of eight iron clad steamers, fully equipped, to be completed within sixty-five days. The timber to form their hulls was still uncut, the rolls for the manufacture of the armor-plates were not in existence, and the engines were nothing but pig-iron and bars; yet in forty-five days the "St. Louis," the first American iron-clad, was launched. The remainder of the fleet followed in quick succession, and with them the capture

of Fort Henry was accomplished, followed by the conquest of Fort Donelson and Island No. 10. In 1862 he designed and built six turreted iron vessels, all heavily plated. The turrets on these were different from those of Ericsson and Coles, and the guns were worked entirely by steam. In this way the 11- and 15-inch guns could be loaded and discharged every forty-five seconds, and this record stands as the first application of steam in manipulating heavy artillery. These boats proved of great service in the campaigns of Gens. Halleck and Grant. From 1867 till 1874 he was engaged in the construction of the great steel-arch bridge across the Mississippi at St. Louis. In the execution of this work, Mr. Eads had to do with problems that had never before been met by engineers. The bridge consists of three arches, of which the central one has a clear span of 520 feet, and is recognized as "the finest specimen of metal-arch construction in the world," while the side arches are 502 feet each in span. The granite piers all rest upon the bed-rock underlying the river deposits. Two are much deeper than any built at that time, and one, weighing 45,000 tons, was sunk to bed-rock, 136 feet below high-water mark, through 90 feet of sand and gravel, while the other, weighing 40,000 tons, is founded on rock 130 feet below high-water mark. It was opened on July 4, 1874, after an expenditure of exactly $6,536,729.99. Mr. Eads then turned his attention to the deepening of the mouth of the Mississippi by means of jetties. His plans, which were strongly opposed by the engineers of the United States Army, to whom the matter was referred by the Government, were submitted to Congress, and finally a bill was passed granting him permission to attempt the improvement of the South Pass. Work was begun in the summer of 1875, and four years later the inspecting officers reported that a maximum depth of 30 feet had been secured, and the least width of the 26-foot channel was 200 feet, where previously the maximum depth had been but 9 feet. The jetties extend from the land's end at the mouth of South Pass about 2¼ miles out over the bar and into the gulf. They are parallel, and are built of willow mattresses sunken by stone, and capped near the sea-ends with massive concrete blocks, the largest of which weigh 265 tons, and were, at the time they were put in position, the largest blocks ever placed on sea-walls. The character of this work, its great importance to the commercial interests of the country and the world, its successful accomplishment, the continued maintenance of the deep and wide channel that the works created, the difficult engineering problems that were so successfully solved, placed Mr. Eads among the first of hydraulic engineers. Meanwhile, he outlined one of the grandest plans ever undertaken by hydraulic engineering, having for its object the extension of the deep-water from the Gulf of Mexico to the mouth of the Ohio. This magnificent channel was to be made permanent by putting an end to the caving of its banks. In 1879 Congress authorized the creation of the Mississippi River Commission, to consist of seven members, of which Mr. Eads was one. The jetty system was adopted, and two reaches of the Mississippi — Plum Point, twenty miles long, and Lake Providence, thirty-five miles long—were selected for improvement. The low-water depth of the former was only five feet, while the latter, 400 miles farther down the river, had a depth of nearly six feet. Permeable contraction works, similar to those used at the South Pass, were put in position in one season in the period between two floods, and the effect produced by the works during the first flood that followed was marvelous. The depth was increased through the upper reach to twelve feet at low water, and through the lower reach to fifteen feet, and scores of millions of cubic yards of sediment were deposited behind the permeable works, through the checking of the current. New shore-lines of an approximately uniform width were developed; but later Congresses refused to continue sufficient appropriations, although enough had been accomplished to show the entire practicability of the plan. Mr. Eads examined and reported on the bar at the mouth of the St. John's River, Fla., in 1878; on the improvements of Sacramento river in 1880; on the harbor of Toronto, Canada, in 1881; on the ports of Tampico and Vera Cruz, Mexico, in 1882; on the harbor of Galveston, Texas, in 1884; and had been personally consulted by the Emperor of Brazil concerning the harbors of his dominions. During his visits to Europe he inspected the mouths of nearly every river flowing into the Baltic Sea and the German Ocean, and also the river-courses of the Rhone, the Danube, including the works at their mouths, and the Theiss in Hungary, and likewise the Suez, Amsterdam, and Rhone ship canals. On the occasion of the Parliamentary inquiry into the merits of the Manchester Ship Canal, Mr. Eads was retained by the Mersey docks and harbor board of Liverpool, at a fee of £3,500, said to be the largest ever yet paid to an engineer. His evidence caused the rejection of the scheme as it then stood, and the modification by which the canal was laid out along the wide part of the Mersey. The last great enterprise to which Mr. Eads devoted his attention was the ship-railway across the isthmus of Tehuantepec. A valuable concession was obtained from the Mexican Government, and for several years Mr. Eads endeavored to persuade the United States Government to undertake the building of this railway, but he finally gave it up, and formed a private company for its construction. He was elected President of the St. Louis Academy of Sciences in 1872, and held that office for two terms. During the same year he was elected to the National Academy of Sciences. He

addressed the British Association for the Advancement of Sciences, of which he was a member, in 1881, on the improvement of the Mississippi, and also on the Tehuantepec Ship-Railway. In 1884 he received the Albert Medal from the British Society of Arts, which was then for the first time given to an American. He was a member of other scientific societies, and had held the office of Vice-President of the American Society of Civil Engineers in 1882-'83. The State University of Missouri, in 1877, conferred upon him the degree of LL. D. His writings and professional papers appeared variously, but the most important have been collected and published as the "Addresses and Papers of James B. Eads, together with a Biographical Sketch" (St. Louis, 1884).

ECUADOR, an independent republic in South America. (For details relating to area, population, and territorial divisions, see "Annual Cyclopædia" for 1885.)

Government.—The President is Don José Maria Plácido Caamaño, whose term of office will expire on June 30, 1888. The Vice-President is Don Pedro José Cevallos. The Cabinet was composed as follows: Interior, Foreign Affairs, Public Instruction, and Charity, Señor J. Modesto Espinosa; Finance and Public Works, Señor V. L. Salazar; War and Navy, Gen. J. M. Sarasti. The Minister of Ecuador at Washington is Dr. Don Antonio Flores. The Consul-General of Ecuador at New York is Don Domingo L. Ruiz. The American Consul-General at Guayaquil is Owen McGarr.

Finances.—The Government intends soon to pay a great portion of the so-called English debt, which in 1885 amounted to £1,824,000, on which the coupons have remained unpaid since 1867. The interest on this debt is 1 per cent. per annum as long as the duties collected at Guayaquil do not exceed $400,000 per annum, and 25 per cent. of the excess of such revenue at Guayaquil till 6 per cent. per annum interest be reached. This foreign indebtedness arose from the conversion of Ecuador's share in the old Colombian debt. Furthermore, the Government will distribute the state lands that the holders of Ecuador land-warrants are entitled to. The budget for the fiscal year 1886 fixed the income at $2,421,403, and the outlay at the same figure. The Guayaquil custom-house yielded in 1886 a revenue of $1,940,536, being $845,385 more than in 1885. The Banco del Ecuador of Quito declared a dividend of 20 per cent. for the year 1886. The Banco de Crédito Hipotecario has made a contract with the municipality of Guayaquil to advance a considerable sum for water-works.

Navy.—Early in 1887 their arrived at Guayaquil the "Cotopaxi," a new steel transport, which the Government has purchased. This vessel was originally built in 1884 for the Chilian navy. The armament consists of two Armstrong guns. The machinery is very powerful, so that the trip from Valparaiso to Puna was made in less than eight days. Simultaneously a fast gunboat of light draught was bought in Europe, also to be furnished with the best guns. This vessel will be the third of its kind that the navy of Ecuador possesses.

State of the Country.—President Caamaño, in his message to Congress, expressed himself as follows with reference to the progress the republic is making: "Public instruction, considering the difficulties we have had to grapple with, is making most creditable headway; aid is being extended to charitable institutions in a most thorough and liberal manner by assisting with all our might hospitals and asylums; a large amount of money is being spent on the construction of a new lazaretto, and we are building a magnificent lunatic asylum, which will be among the best appointed in South America. Neither the scarcity of money, nor the crippled financial resources of the country, nor the disturbed political status it has suffered from, has prevented us from continuing without interruption the public works undertaken, and from entering upon new ones. Without going into full details I may say that work on the Southern Railroad is proceeding steadily; that the telegraph has been extended to the provinces of Imbabura, Carchi, Bolivar, and Los Rios, and that the lines have begun to be laid in those of Loja, Manabi, and Oro; that the national wagon-road is being repaired in those of Pinchincha, Leon, Tungurahua, and Chimborazo; that an iron bridge is in course of construction over Lita river; that the bridges on the northern and southern wagon-roads are nearly finished; that we are laying out a botanical garden; that all public buildings are being kept in a good state of repair, and a Government edifice is being built at Ohatam; that we have furnished our coast with three additional lighthouses, so that this service of ours may be the best on the Pacific; that we concluded work on our handsome national theatre; that we are laying again the cable at the bottom of Guayaquil river, and that in this matter of telegraphic cables we are attending simultaneously to several enterprises."

Railroads.—In February M. J. Kelly, the contractor for the railway to the interior, had entered into a new contract for extending the line from Yaguachi, the present terminus, to Guayaquil, 22 kilometres. The new line was to be completed, if possible, in 1887, and the Government of Ecuador is to pay Mr. Kelly an interest of 6 per cent. on $500,000 for twenty years. By this arrangement the Government pays interest only, and the contractor furnishes the capital. The new line is believed to be a profitable investment. Surveys were begun in September. The proposal to construct the Bahia de Caráquez and Quito Railroad, on which work was to begin in the autumn of 1887, met with much opposition in Quito, as some of the terms were considered too onerous;

but it met with equally warm support. This road will open up the tropical belt of the coast, and will also pierce the higher and cooler lands, where the products of the temperate zone are found in abundance. The contract made by the Government, and approved by Congress, with Don Ignacio Palan, stipulates that the coast terminus is to be at a point in the Bay of Caráquez where steamers are to connect with it to navigate the bay; that it is to be finished in ten years; and that the Government guarantees 6 per cent. interest on the capital invested in every kilometre from the moment it shall have been constructed. As security for the prompt payment of such interest, the revenue to be collected at the Manabi custom-houses is pledged, such revenue being estimated to produce $100,000 per annum. Valuable land-grants are made on both sides of the line.

Telegraphs.—Early in 1887 the following capitals of provinces were connected by telegraph: Quito, Latecunga, Ambatee, Riobamba, Cañar, Cuenca, Guayaquil, and Daule. There were in course of construction the following lines: Quito, Ibana, Tulcan, Riobamba and Guaranda. The republic is in connection with the world's system by means of a land-line, which connects Guayaquil with Ballanita, thence by cable with New York via the isthmus of Tehuantepec. The number of subscribers to the telephone at Guayaquil was 160 at the close of 1886.

Steam Navigation.—Merchants of Bahía have formed a steamship company for navigating the Chone and Capotillo rivers, and in the autumn the first steamer was being built at San Francisco, Cal., for the service between Motal, Segua, and Bahía, to be followed by another to ply between the two principal ports of Manabí, Manta, and Bahía, touching at Tabuco, Jama, and Pedomales.

Commerce.—The exports in 1885 amounted to $6,680,815, including the precious metals, and 23,227,048 pounds of cocoa, worth $5,080,918; specie and bullion, $688.854; hides, $269,405; coffee, 1,850,088 pounds, worth $249,786; quinine-bark, 298,697 pounds, worth $112,011; India-rubber, 427,254 pounds, worth $102,541; the remainder being straw hats, vegetable ivory, tamarinds, and tobacco. The American trade for the year has been as follows:

Import into the United States from Ecuador..... $1,181,169
Export of domestic goods from the United States to Ecuador................................ 1,049,892

The number of vessels that entered Ecuadorian ports in 1885 was 407, of which 185 entered at Guayaquil alone (117 thereof being steamers). The aggregate tonnage was 131,523.

Cocoa.—There arrived at Guayaquil from the interior for shipment abroad, in 1886, 384,752 quintals of cocoa, against 244,724 in 1885, and 176,955 in 1884. From Jan. 1 to Nov. 8, 1887, 813,000 quintals had been received at Guayaquil. The total consumption of cocoa is 80,000,000 pounds. France heads the list, taking 26,000,000 pounds; Spain comes next with

16,000,000 pounds; then England, 14,000,000 pounds, and the United States, 8,500,000 pounds.

Ivory-Nuts.—There had been shipped abroad from Guayaquil in 1886, 197,808 quintals of ivory-nuts, against 169,000 in 1885, and 107,759 in 1884. From Jan. 1 to Oct. 1, 1887, 237,157 quintals had been shipped.

Earthquake.—The most violent earthquake experienced at Guayaquil since 1868 occurred at twenty minutes past six o'clock A. M. on June 29, 1887. The shock lasted two minutes and twenty seconds, and the direction of the movement was from northeast to southwest. All the clocks in the city were stopped at the moment of the shock, and several buildings were demolished, but without injuring anybody. The great earthquake of Aug. 13, 1868, was most severe on the western flanks of the Peruvian Andes. The immense ocean-wave created by the upheaval of the Peruvian coast was propelled across the Pacific Ocean. On the adjacent South American coasts the sea-wave was very destructive, accomplishing in a few minutes greater havoc than the earthquake had made.

Boundary Dispute.—The Queen-Regent of Spain is to arbitrate in the matter of the limits between Ecuador and Peru.

The Death Penalty.—During the session of Congress that terminated on August 10, the following law was passed, in conformity with Article 136 of the Constitution: "The death penalty is not to be applied in punishment of purely political transgressions of the law, except in cases where a military, armed, and organized rising takes place with the intention of disturbing by force the constitutional order of things. The following are not considered political crimes, although they may have political ends for a pretext: Treason to the country, parricide, assassination, incendiarism, pillage, piracy, and the criminal deeds of military men in active service."

EDUCATION, INDUSTRIAL. The term "industrial education" has come into common use within the past few years, with two distinct meanings. In one sense it is applied to education intended to foster industrial skill and fit the pupil to enter some industrial pursuit on leaving school. But it is used by the most enlightened educators in a totally different sense, synonymous with the terms "new education," "creative method," and "manual training," and is regarded solely as a means of promoting the general education of the pupil by a new system of mental, moral, and physical development The present article will treat the subject of industrial education in the United States in the latter more restricted meaning, viz., the development of the kindergarten principle into a system of general fundamental training, from the beginning to the end of the common-school age.

The Kindergarten was founded in this country by Miss Haines. Its first important branches were established, respectively, in Boston by Miss Elizabeth P. Peabody and her sister, Mrs. Horace Mann; in New York by Mme. Kraus-Bölte; in St. Louis, by Miss Susan E. Blow. To them nearly all the present kindergarten in America can be traced, and the general acceptance of the theories that the development of the child should begin with a guidance of a spontaneous activity by games and recreations, in which practical knowledge for its own sake is ignored. There are about 500 kindergarten institutions, in at least twenty-eight States and Territories, with about 20,000 pupils and 1,000 teachers. The system has been introduced into the first six grades of the common schools in most of our large cities, and is an unquestionable success. The next step in progress, therefore, is the movement to introduce the manual-training school. The kindergarten regards the child as primarily a doer, so as to prepare him to become a knower; so-called industrial education takes him from his recreations to the workshop, and proceeds in the same line of development. The doing goes on, and the knowing begins, by means of a system that neglects none of the faculties that the kindergarten has begun to develop, as does the present common-school system, but proceeds logically to educate evenly the brain, the eye, and the hand.

This system has been advocated as a part of the common-school curriculum for about ten years. Among its first and leading advocates have been Felix Adler and G. von Taube, of New York, Francis A. Walker and John Clark, of Boston, C. M. Woodward, of St. Louis, and James McAlister, of Philadelphia. Since attention has been called to it, the leading educators of the country have begun to study its merits and the practical tests to which it has been put in the industrial training-schools of Europe. By the majority of these men it is warmly approved, as being superior to the old system in its effect on the health, the mind, and the morals, and practically in making the hand a useful instrument. The chief arguments in its favor are: that it is based on a scientific understanding of the physiological development of the child's mental capacity: that in beginning at an early age to give children a knowledge of shape, form, and color, of common materials, their beauty and their usefulness, of tools and how to use them, and to teach them the application of abstract mathematical studies, not only gives them a broader understanding and appreciation of art and mechanics, but also cultivates habits of industry and practical views, accustoms them to exact measurements, to close observation and accuracy in thought as well as work, and at the same time supplies them with some fundamental training for the practical demands of life, while employing the best possible means of developing the reasoning powers, quickening the constructive and inventive faculties, overcoming a growing distaste in the race for purely intellectual work, and raising the grade of general intelligence in the nation. The tendency of this method is to stimulate a desire for excellence for its own sake, to supplant the present want of respect for manual labor, to foster thoroughness, to stimulate Americans to attain a skill in handicraft that shall be equal to that of the Europeans who now almost monopolize the best paying departments of our industrial pursuits, and to turn the attention of the rising generation toward the callings in which there is or will be the greatest demand for workers. From the first the opposition to industrial education has been comparatively small. It is generally approved for special schools, and almost all the opposition to incorporating it into the common-school system arises from a mistaken belief that it is intended to sacrifice some of the present intellectual studies to fit the pupils for immediate practice in certain trades and professions, whereas the soundest advocates of this industrial education are strenuously opposed to any sort or branch of trade-teaching as such, and only accept certain rudiments of certain trades combined with the abstract studies on which they are based, because they provide a better means than any now in use to develop the mental powers and at the same time develop and train manual facility, the latter of which they regard as an essential part of fundamental training.

Cooking has received much attention of late as a branch of industrial education, and in Boston has been made one of the common-school studies. This, also, is practically teaching a trade. Through the liberality of Mrs. Augustus Hemenway, of Boston, a cooking-school, known as the Boston School Kitchen No. 1, was opened in the Tennyson Street Primary-School building, North End, in November, 1885. It was admirably fitted up and placed in charge of a skilled cooking-teacher, who gives instruction in the keeping of the kitchen and care of cooking-utensils, as well as in the making of dishes and the most important facts in the chemistry of foods and their adaptation to the wants of the human body. These pupils, like those in the carpentry classes, are selected by the masters of the schools in the vicinity of the Tennyson Street building. In 1886–'87, there were ten classes of fifteen girls each, each class receiving two hours a week, the sessions of the cooking-school being held the same as in the regular schools. The total cost of such a school is about $900 a year. The Boston School Kitchen No. 2 maintained by the city, under the direction of the Manual-Training Committee, is in the Drake Primary building, South Boston. It was opened in the autumn of 1886. It is modeled after No. 1. Being somewhat larger, it accommodates twenty girls. Much private solicitation has been made for similar schools in various parts of the city, and in the present year the Board of Education has opened one more school in Roxbury, and has arranged for oth-

ers in Charlestown and the South End. One hundred and thirty-four girls attend the private School of Cookery on North Bennett Street, so that all the girls in the schools of the city proper and South Boston have the opportunity to receive a course of twenty lessons in cookery as a part of their common-school education.

Boston.—The first general interest in this subject among Americans was roused by the exhibit at the Centennial Exhibition, in 1876, of the work done at the Imperial Technical School of Moscow, Russia. The School of Mechanic Arts in Boston, established in the same year as a department of the Massachusetts Institute of Technology, was the first direct result of this influence, and was the first attempt in this country to provide for boys a course of study simply preparatory to trade-teaching. It was arranged on a plan similar to those of the Imperial Technical School of Moscow, the Royal Mechanic Art School of Komotau in Bohemia, L'École Municipale d'Apprentis of Paris, and the Ambachtsschoole of the principal cities of Holland, with certain differences adapted to the American student. It has been the pioneer, and, with modifications, the model for nearly all the manual-training schools that have since been established in this country. The hand-work is done without regard to any pecuniary value, but is designed to train and develop the judgment, self-reliance, and executive power of the student. Pieces practically useful are only introduced when this can be done without detriment to the real purposes of the courses. Boys under fifteen years of age are not received for the regular course, and an examination equivalent to that for the ordinary Boston grammar-school graduation is required for admission. The course includes two years of mechanical training and intellectual study, arranged as follows:

FIRST YEAR.—1st term: Shop-work—carpentry; algebra, geometry, English composition, mechanical and free-hand drawing. 2d term: Shop-work—wood-turning, pattern-making, foundry-work; algebra, geometry, metric system, English composition, mechanical and free-hand drawing.

SECOND YEAR.—1st term: Shop-work—forging: algebra, elementary physics, English composition, mechanical and free-hand drawing, French. 2d term: Shop-work—vise-work, machine-tool work; geometry, physics, English composition, French, mechanical and free-hand drawing.

The first attempt to add a manual-training department to any public school was made in Gloucester, Mass., in 1878, with money placed at the disposal of the school trustees for this purpose by the executors of the estate of George O. Hovey. A room was fitted up with twelve benches and all equipments necessary to teach the use of some of the principal tools used in carpentry. With a practical carpenter as teacher, the experiment was begun with four Saturday classes of twelve members each. The pupils were from the two upper grades of the grammar-schools. The course

was of forty lessons, each of which was equivalent to half of a half-day session. In 1880 a
change was made by which pupils did not have
to sacrifice part of their holiday for this instruction, and with it the attendance increased
from thirty to ninety-six. Lessons in carpentry were given during school-hours four afternoons in the week, two classes being taught
each afternoon. Eight classes then received
instruction for one hour each during half the
afternoon session. Two classes and a part of
a third were made up of girls, whose work was
pronounced by the superintendent as equal to
that of the boys, and who seemed to enjoy it
heartily. The superintendent says: "A room
similar to the one we had can be fitted up for
a carpentry class for not more than $500. In
such a shop, thoroughly equipped, one teacher
can efficiently instruct four classes each day—
twenty classes each school-week. Sixteen members may be permitted to attend each class,
without detriment to the progress of each. Allowing forty weeks for the academic year, and
making the salary of the teacher $20 a week,
the annual cost of instruction would be $800.
The cost of stock would not exceed 50 cents
per annum for each pupil. Upon this basis the
per capita cost of instructing 320 pupils would
be about $3 a year." The cost of this experi-
ment during its continuance of about eighteen
months was $742.50. It was discontinued
with the close of the spring term in 1880, because the city government refused to make an
appropriation for it, and the Hovey executors
were not willing to maintain it any longer. It
proved, however, some of the theories on the
effect of such training, and the example was
soon followed in other places.

Upon the offer of the Boston Industrial
School Association, a similar experiment was
tried in the Boston public schools from January to May, 1882. A room in the Dwight
Grammar-School for boys was fitted up as a
carpenter-shop, a practical carpenter was employed as instructor, and two classes of eighteen members each were selected, one being
from the upper or graduating class, the other
from the 2d, 3d, and 4th grades. The boys
selected were of both American and foreign
parentage, and represented the oldest and
largest as well as the youngest and smallest of
their respective classes. The course of instruction was arranged in eighteen progressive lessons, each class receiving practically one two-
hour lesson a week. No pupil could keep on
in this course who did not maintain his rank
in his regular studies. Without any expense
for room-rent and heating, the total cost of these
lessons was $711.95, making the cost per pupil
about $6. The experiment was regarded as a
positive benefit to the students in its influence
on their other school-work.

The second experiment in Boston was the
establishment, in 1884, of another carpentry
class. This was opened in the basement of
the Boston Latin School, and still exists. The

course is similar to that taught in the Dwight
School. The classes come from the different
schools. Each is made up of about twenty
boys, who must be over fourteen years of age,
and who receive one two-hour lesson a week,
for which they are excused from attendance at
their grammar-schools.

Sewing, which is more a branch of trade-
teaching than an element of industrial education, according to the restricted use of that
term, has for many years been a part of the
regular course of instruction for girls from
eight to eleven years of age in the Boston grammar-schools. The cost of materials amounts
to not more than $200 a year for the whole
city; for, as the children become proficient,
parents are glad to have them make and mend
for the family in their school classes. The total
number of articles made in all the Boston
schools in 1887 was 72,721, and, by the skill
there attained, young girls fresh from school
every year find steady, remunerative employment as sewing-women.

New York.—The Free Kindergarten and
Workingman's School of New York city was
the first institution in this country organized
for the purpose of teaching children of all
grades of the school-age according to the
principles of the creative method quoted at the
beginning of this article. It was established
in 1879 by Felix Adler, President of the Society for Ethical Culture, under whose auspices the schools are maintained as a part of
their United Relief Works. In June, 1887, a
class of eight pupils was graduated, the first
that had completed the full course above the
kindergarten. During the past four years the
schools have occupied their present quarters in
the large four-story school-building erected for
them at 109 West Fifty-fourth Street. They
are unsectarian, and receive pupils of both
sexes and all nationalities between the ages of
three and fourteen years, charging no tuition-
fees. At present the pupils are only those
from the poorest classes, since they have the
greatest need of the best education. The
course of study covers six years in the kindergarten and eight years in the Workingman's
School. There are now about 350 children in
both departments. The annual expenses are
about $20,000, and are defrayed by private
contribution. The school receives no aid from
the State. It has been found necessary to
alter the details of the original system many
times, and this year, under the new superintendent of the school and kindergarten, Andrew J. Rickoff, the entire curriculum is to be
thoroughly revised and be made to carry out
more fully and precisely the educational and
humanitarian principles for which the institution was founded. The general plan will still
be the same—parallel work in the shop for
manual training; in the *atelier*, for the development of the artistic and imaginative faculties; and in the recitation-rooms, for the more
intellectual or literary studies. In connection

with the schools there is much home-work in the families of the pupils. Parents' meetings are held regularly, and in summer the superintendent takes his colony of pupils to Sherman, Pa., to give those whose lives are passed in the city certain elementary impressions of nature, without which, as a foundation. the important study of natural history can not be built up.

The College of the City of New York was the second institution in New York to introduce manual training into its curriculum. In 1888 a workshop was opened, in which the students might spend certain hours, and since 1885 there has been a regular mechanical course, including manual training, which extends over the entire three years, and may be taken by any student. For those who are unable to take the full college course of five years, there is a shorter course of three years, called the mechanical course, in which the time is about equally divided between academic studies and drawing and workshop practice. The student, in the five-years' course, can take extra shop-work instruction four and a half hours a week, after the regular exercises of the day. Experience has proved that the additional hours in the shop do not overtax or in any way hamper the student's regular work. It has generally proved beneficial as exercise and recreation. In 1886 there were 185 students in the workshops, their ages ranging from fourteen to twenty-one years. The annual cost of this instruction is about $3,600, about $100 of which is spent for materials. The cost of the plant has been about $8,450, including a steam-engine and boiler, which are used for ventilating and warming the college buildings.

With the exception of the many free, charitable schools that give special training in certain industries, and are in receipt of money from the public-school fund, the college had up to about Jan. 1, 1888, the only manual training-classes under the control of the New York Board of Education. But the kindergarten is established in the first six grades of the primary schools, industrial drawing is taught in the evening schools and in the schools where children of foreign parentage are instructed in the English language; and in October, 1887, the board decided to try experimentally in all the grades above the kindergarten of a few schools the introduction of a new system, combining manual training with the more purely intellectual studies, which, if successful, will be adopted for all the common schools of the city.

Although, with the exception of Prof. Adler's school, New York has been in point of time behind many cities in providing for industrial education, it has now, even before the experiment has yet been put into operation in the public schools, more institutions of this kind than any other place in the country. Besides those already mentioned, it has three corporate schools devoted to this work, viz., the Industrial Education Association, the Hebrew Technical Institute, and the Gramercy Park School and Tool-House. The Industrial Education Association, No. 9 University Place, was organized with its present name and object in 1884. Its devotion to industrial education as defined at the beginning of this article is wholly educational, and not charitable, and is on a broader basis than any other institution in the country. As yet it is no more than started in its actual working, but its purposes are to unite all the work in this direction in the various parts of the city, to influence and educate public opinion in favor of it, to give instruction in the kindergarten and all branches of industrial education, to maintain free courses of lectures on this and other educational topics, and to provide a complete free educational library and reading-room and issue circulars of information on educational topics of the day. In 1886 the association moved into its present quarters, and, with ample room and excellent equipment, entered on its enlarged scale of work, in all branches of which it has, within two years, made a successful beginning. Through its instrumentality industrial drawing, clay-modeling, wood-carving, carpentry, and sewing have been introduced into the public schools of Hoboken and Staten Island, with a fair degree of success. During the summer of 1887 a large part of the work in the association's building was suspended, on account of alterations to provide for more extensive work in the autumn. With the beginning of the second year, a normal college in kindergarten and industrial education was opened, and in connection with it a model school for boys and girls between the ages of three and fifteen years. The schools have begun with 88 normal students, 16 of whom are taking the full course, 85 children in the regular model courses, and 55 others in special instruction.

The Hebrew Technical Institute, at 34 and 36 Stuyvesant Street, is a manual training-school for Jewish boys. It was established in 1884 by the present director, Henry M. Leipziger, for the purpose of turning the attention of the Hebrew youth toward industrial pursuits and giving them a general preparatory education for entering the trades. Instruction, tools, and materials are free. There is an enrollment of about 100 pupils in five classes, averaging 20 pupils each. Pupils are admitted at twelve years of age, and are expected to have reached the fourth grade in the city public schools. The hours are from 9 till 4 o'clock daily, and special instruction in wood-carving is given from 4 to 6 o'clock on Mondays and Thursdays. The course of instruction is made up of common-school studies, drawing and mechanical work. The full course covers three years, during the first two of which the principles of many trades are taught, with a knowledge of materials, use of tools, etc. In the third year, first work in special trades, selected with reference to the aptitudes and preferences of the pupils, is taught.

The Gramercy Park School and Tool-House is a pay-school, in which the theoretical and practical are harmoniously combined in a course of study that is extended over twelve years, and is based on the three essential divisions of culture or education, physical, intellectual, and moral. The course of study, which was originated and developed by Prof. G. von Taube, is adapted to the characteristics shown respectively in the four natural stages of brain development. For the first two of these periods, which comprise six years and take the child up to about thirteen years of age, the course is designated as objective. In the first three years, or junior objective grade, no books are used. Very few are used in the next three years, or senior objective grade, most of the lessons being worked out with the teacher. The course covering the third and fourth stages is more purely intellectual, and is divided into the junior subjective, for the ages of about fourteen to eighteen, and the senior subjective, for the student of the highest grade, whose graduates may be about twenty-one years of age. A course of objective and subjective studies, elaborated on this basis, is held by Mr. von Taube as the true system of education, and aims to provide a complete business and social training, or a thorough preparation for the scientific course in the American colleges or foreign polytechnia. One general course is followed for all in the lower or objective classes, but separate courses for each of the higher or subjective classes. As the school was founded in 1884, there has not been time for a student to complete the full course; but, so far as it has been tested, the system is regarded as eminently successful.

St. Louis.—The Manual Training School of the Washington University at St. Louis, Mo., was the first school established in this country for the sole purpose of providing a graded course of non-technical study for boys of the high-school age, adapted as equally as possible to intellectual and manual training. The plan was in a sense original, and from the first its success has been so great that it has served as a model for many similar schools in various States. It is a non-classical high - school, where, in a three years' course, the essential mechanical principles of all trades are taught, without going into the details of any trade, where articles are not made for sale, and where all shop - work is disciplinary. The school exacts close and thoughtful study with tools as well as with books. By lengthening the usual school-day a full hour, and by abridging somewhat the number of daily recitations, time is found for drawing and tool-work, and a more liberal, intellectual, and physical development. In short, a more symmetrical education is given than can be afforded in the usual high-school. This school was established as an experiment by the Board of Directors of the University, to meet the manifest need of some such education among the growing boys of St. Louis. Under the charge of its present director, Prof. C. M. Woodward, it was opened with about fifty pupils in September, 1880. Sixty-seven pupils were enrolled during the first year, 107 during the second, 176 during the third, at the close of which there were 29 graduates. In the fourth year 201 were enrolled, 29 being graduated in 1884; in the fifth, 218 were enrolled, 39 being graduated in 1885; the sixth year's enrolment was 233, with 45 graduates in 1886; the seventh year's enrolment, 225, with 52 graduates in 1887. The course of instruction covers three years and embraces five parallel lines, three purely intellectual and two both intellectual and manual, and including literary studies, free-hand and mechanical drawing, and mechanical exercises in the shop, together with instruction about tools and their use. Each wood-working shop has uniform accommodations for a class of 24 pupils, and the entire building is admirably equipped with apparatus for the most practical instruction, which is given similarly to laboratory lectures. The school is supported by endowments and by fees paid by its pupils.

Chicago.— The Chicago Manual Training School, which is similar to that of St. Louis, was the second institution of its kind in this country. It was founded as the private enterprise of the Commercial Club of Chicago, which in 1882 subscribed $100,000 "to inaugurate a school for instruction and practice in the use of tools, with such instruction as may be deemed necessary in mathematics, drawing, and the English branches of a high-school course." It is substantially a duplicate of the St. Louis school, but, unlike that, is independent of all other institutions. It was opened in February, 1884, under the charge of its present director, Henry H. Belfield, when 72 pupils, all that could be accommodated, were admitted. In September, 1886, its capacity was increased, and a junior, or first year's class of 96 was admitted. It is supported by the endowment of the Commercial Club and by its tuition fees.

The Chicago Public Training School offering manual training as a part of public-school instruction, was opened in October, 1886. For the first year it was only a school of carpentry. Its plans for the future are not yet definitely arranged, but its work will be upon a broad basis and probably provide a four years' course in combined intellectual and manual training. During the first year the attendance was 72 pupils, whose ages ranged from twelve to sixteen years. It is open to pupils of the first year in the three city high-schools, and the sessions are five afternoons in the week. Attendance is optional, and, by arrangement of the study-hour in the high schools, the pupil loses nothing from his regular studies by taking this additional course.

Toledo.— The Manual Training School of the Toledo University, Toledo, Ohio, also a school of the St. Louis type, was established in February, 1885, as the first department of the Toledo University. It was founded by Mr. and Mrs. Jesup W. Scott and others as the Toledo University of Arts and Trades, but was subsequently deeded to the city, which, in accepting it, passed an ordinance establishing a "university for the promotion of free education of the youth of both sexes within the city," of which this school should be the beginning. The director, Prof. R. H. Smith, is a graduate of the St. Louis school, after which this has been modeled in many respects, but with certain changes. The course is more elaborate than in any of the previously named schools of the West. It covers four years, and includes domestic economy for girls. The lowest age of admission is thirteen years, and no pupil is received who has not reached the senior grade of the grammar-school. Tuition is free to residents of Toledo. During 1886-'87 the attendance was 270, boys and girls. In drawing, girls take much the same course as the boys, modified by a little more of the design and art element. In the first year, girls take simple wood-carving, and enough of carpentry to teach them the manipulation and sharpening of tools. Their work in this department compares favorably with that of the boys. In the second year the girls take cookery. It is proposed hereafter to teach sewing in the second year, and cooking in the third. It is also proposed to add this year a number of senior grammar pupils of the highest grade. The students who enter this school have no election as to particular studies. Each must conform to the course as laid down, and take every branch in its order. But in the evening high-school, opened soon after the day-school, the students can elect such branches as meet their tastes or have direct bearing upon their occupations, although a full course is provided, which is much the same as that of the day-school.

Baltimore.—The Baltimore Manual Training School was the first established by any municipality of the United States as an integral part of its public-school system. The accommodations, fittings, and course of study in this school, as well as its aims and purposes, are similar to those of the St. Louis and Chicago schools. Intellectually, the school is on a level with the city college, from which it differs in affording scientific instruction and actual practice in the care and use of tools, in giving prominence to mechanical drawing, in having more practical methods of teaching book-keeping, physics, and chemistry, and in omitting from its required studies foreign and ancient languages. It was opened in March, 1884, with sixty students, and under the general direction of the present principal, John D. Ford, P. A. E., U. S. N. The enrollment increased to 100 before the close of the year, and to 150 in the following September. In 1886-'87 there were 281 students, of whom 25

were graduated in June after the full three-years' course, while 100 had left before graduation, to take employment as wage-workers. The year 1887-'88 opened with 268 students. A preparatory class has been established since the school was opened, and in Nov., 1887, an unclassified night-school was opened for the winter months, to give as much of the work laid down in the catalogue as possible to those who wish to take these studies but are engaged during the day. In establishing this training-school, the city council provided that admission to it should be regulated by the law governing the ordinary public schools, excepting that the Board of Education should regulate the age of admission and have power to set terms of tuition for pupils outside of the city, and that the use of tools and materials for the city pupils should not exceed $1 for the scholastic quarter.

Philadelphia.—The Manual Training School of Philadelphia provided for boys is one department of an extensive system of industrial education now being developed in the public schools of that city. It was opened in September, 1885, in one of the school-buildings, which was fitted up for the purpose, and is filled to its utmost capacity. Pupils who have finished the grammar-school course are admitted by examination once a year. The course of three years includes systematic manual training similar to that in the Western schools, and in addition a course of instruction in the English language, mathematics, mechanics, elementary science, history, and social science. and free-hand and mechanical drawing. Three hours a day are given to school-work, one hour to drawing, and two hours to manual training in the workshops. The Industrial Art School, which was originally in the hands of a private association, was adopted by the Philadelphia Board of Education in 1882, when, with some important changes in its course of instruction and terms of admission, it was made a free school for boys and girls. Pupils from all grades of the regular grammar-schools and some classes of the secondary schools, have the opportunity, if they wish, to receive class instruction there in free-hand designing, modeling in clay, wood-carving, and metal-work, including hammering, embossing, and chasing. The total attendance is about 600, about 160 pupils being received at once, and each having two hours' instruction a week. Other branches of industrial education in the Philadelphia public-school system consist of the kindergarten, which were adopted Jan. 1, 1887, and of which 30 are in operation this year; of instruction in sewing, which has been in the schools since about 1882, and, thoroughly systematized, now forms a part of the regular school-work of all the grades of the girls' schools, beginning with the third grade, so that 25,000 girls received the instruction in 1887; and the cooking-classes. These were begun as an experiment in the autumn of

1887 in the girls' normal or high school, from which, if successful, it will be extended into the girls' grammar-schools.

The mechanical training department of Girard College, in Philadelphia, is one of the best planned and conducted manual-training schools in this country. The present course of study was adopted in 1886, and has thus far resulted so well that the trustees feel every encouragement to continue and improve it. "Every branch indicated by Mr. Girard is taught, and, although six hours of the week of the thirty-two heretofore devoted to study are now spent in the mechanical shops, we find that, owing to the change of pursuit, the boys get through as much work and as well in the twenty-six hours as they did formerly in thirty-two." The course embraces the whole range of mechanical drawing, carpentry and wood-turning, foundry, forge, and iron-work; but it differs from nearly all other schools of this kind in the arrangement of the plan of instruction. The pupil first makes his drawing from the object—some simple article or piece of machinery. This drawing he takes to the wood-working and turning department and works out a model to scale as a pattern. This, after it is approved, he takes to the molding-room and makes ready for casting, which is done in lead or iron. Then he carries his metal casting to the metal bench, where, with chisel and file, and at an advanced stage with the lathe, he completes his article. He then begins again in the draughting-room with something a little more complicated, and follows the same course as before. The method has proved eminently successful.

Montclair, N. J.—This was one of the first places in the country to introduce manual training into the various grades of the public schools. The experiment of a carpentry-class was first tried, with a plant costing $350, in 1882. Since then it has steadily grown and improved. The teacher is a carpenter and skilled mechanic. The instruction is given to all the grammar-school boys of the fourth, third, and second grades, whose ages are from ten and one half to fourteen years. Girls are instructed in sewing in their class-rooms by their regular class-teachers while the boys of their classes are in the shop. Pupils of the high-school, the highest grade of the grammar-school, and the primary departments do not receive this training.

Cleveland, Ohio.—Here a simple start has been made in a private enterprise which, in view of its almost certain adoption or absorption into the public-school system, is about to be enlarged, and in its control, general course of instruction, etc., will resemble the institution at Toledo. Even in 1887 no pupils were admitted who could not pass an examination equivalent to that required for admission to the local high-school.

Industrial education is also in some way provided for or encouraged in some of the schools

of New Haven, Conn.; Moline and Peru, and Cook County Normal School, Normal Park, Ill.; in Milford and Springfield, Mass.; in the State Normal School at New Britain, Conn.; in Omaha, Neb., Eau Claire, Wis., Barnesville, O., and in San Francisco, Cal.

EGYPT, a principality in northern Africa, tributary to Turkey. The reigning sovereign, called the Khedive, is Mohammed Tewfik, born in 1852, who succeeded to the throne Aug. 8, 1879, on the abdication of his father, the Khedive Ismail. The President of the Council of Ministers and Minister for Foreign Affairs is Nubar Pasha, who is also Minister of Justice. The Minister of the Interior is Mustapha Fehmi Pasha, who is at the same time Minister of War and of the Marine. The Minister of Public Works and Minister of Public Instruction *ad interim* is Abderrahman Rushdi Pasha. The Minister of Finance is Mohammed Zeki Pasha. Mustapha Fehmi Pasha was formerly Minister of Finance, but exchanged that department for the Ministry of the Interior and of War on the retirement of Abd-el-Kader Pasha in March, 1887, being succeeded by Zeki Pasha, previously Minister of the *Wakfs*, or religious estates.

Area and Population.—Egypt proper extends as far south as Wady Halfa, at the second cataract of the Nile. This place has been provisionally agreed upon as the southern boundary of the Egyptian dominions, which formerly extended nearly to the equator.

DIVISIONS.	Area.	Population.
Lower Egypt.		
Governments :		
Cairo	15	374,838
Alexandria.................	150	231,396
Darrietta	11	43,616
Rosetta....................	68	19,378
Moudiriehs :		
Behera	2,418	396,856
Charkieh	2,844	464,855
Dakahieh	2,411	588,082
Gharbieh	6,069	936,276
Kalioubieh	912	271,391
Menoufieh	1,654	646,018
Isthmus of Suez.		
Governments :		
Port Said................}	27	{ 31,296
Suez .... }		{ 11,175
Asia.		
Government :		
El Arish	....	3,923
Upper Egypt.		
Government :		
Kosseir	....	2,490
Moudiriehs :		
Assiout...................	2,174	568,596
Beni Souef...............	1,220	219,573
Fayoum	1,277	234,591
Guizeh	956	326,388
Minieh	1,999	314,816
Esneh	861	237,961
Guerga	1,698	521,411
Kena	1,409	406,556
Oasis :		
Siwa	....	3,346
Total	27,676	6,817,265

The total area of Egypt, not including the still occupied territories of the Soudan, is computed by the general staff to be 1,021,354 square kilometres. Outside of the valley and delta of the Nile, it comprises the Governments of Kosseir, on the Red Sea, El Arish, in Syria, and the isthmus of Suez on the east, and on the west the oases of the Libyan Desert. A great part of the surface is uninhabited, except by nomads. The population of the administrative divisions, with their area in square kilometres, according to the census taken on May 3, 1882, is as shown in the table on the preceding page.

The areas given include only the lands that are surveyed and taxed. The population is divided into 3,401,498 males and 3,415,767 females. There are 246 inhabitants per square kilometre. The sedentary population in 1882 was 6,479,850; the nomadic and semi-nomadic Beduins, 246,529; foreigners, 90,886. The alien population included 37,301 Greeks, 18,665 Italians, 15,716 French, 8,022 Austrians, 6,118 British subjects, 948 Germans, 637 Belgians, 589 Spaniards, 533 Russians, 412 Swiss, 323 Servians, Roumanians, and Montenegrins, 221 Dutch, 65 other Europeans, 188 Americans, and 1,153 Persians and other Asiatics.

The population of the chief cities in 1882 was as follows: Cairo, 374,838, including 21,650 foreigners; Alexandria, 227,064, including 48,672 foreigners; Damietta, 34,044; Tanta, 33,750; Assiout, 31,575; Mehalla-el-Kobra, 27,823; Mansourah, 26,942; Fayoum, 25,799; Damanhour, 23,858; Zagazig, 19,815; Rosetta, 16,666; Port Said, 16,560; Menouf, 16,293; Chibrin-el-Kom, 16,250.

Commerce.—The average annual value of the merchandise imports between 1879 and 1883 was 7,127,152 Egyptian pounds, and the average value of exports 12,488,792 Egyptian pounds (£E1=$5). During that period there was an annual net importation of specie averaging 2,381,596 Egyptian pounds. The commercial movement for the three years following 1883 has been as follows, the values being given in Egyptian pounds:

YEARS.	MERCHANDISE.		SPECIE.	
	Imports.	Exports.	Imports.	Exports.
1884	8,182,709	12,549,080	2,172,596	889,768
1885	8,989,042	11,494,970	3,914,787	1,398,660
1886	7,545,281	10,129,622	1,888,797	2,972,590

Of the total value of the imports in 1886 £E3,552,000 came from Great Britain and her colonies, £E888,000 from France, £E1,898,000 from Turkey, £E445,000 from Russia, £E910,000 from Austria-Hungary, £E270,000 from Italy, and £E460,000 from other countries, including £E83,000 from America. Of the exports £E6,422,000 went to Great Britain, £E907,000 to France, £E878,000 to Turkey, £E1,046,000 to Russia, £E598,000 to Austria-Hungary, £E592,000 to Italy, £E187,000 to other countries, including £E21,000 to America. Of the imports £E6,781,749 and of the exports £E9,866,022 passed through the port of Alexandria. Of the total tonnage entered and cleared there in 1885, which was 1,584,407,

758,324 tons was British, 216,105 Turkish, 186,313 Austrian, 118,800 French, 112,907 Russian, 63,422 Italian, and 48,444 Greek. The English and French, nearly all the Austrian and Russian, the greater part of the Italian, and a large portion of the Turkish, vessels were steamers.

The values imported and exported of the various classes of commodities in 1886 were, in Egyptian pounds, as follow:

MERCHANDISE.	Imports.	Exports.
Cereals	650,000	716,000
Fruits, seeds, etc	816,000	1,925,000
Colonial products	367,000	490,000
Tobacco	293,000	
Fermented beverages	876,000	2,000
Animals, etc	382,000	32,000
Total alimentary articles	2,384,000	3,565,000
Fuel	457,000	
Minerals	80,000	2,000
Metals	260,000	42,000
Hides and skins	48,000	145,000
Textile materials	73,000	7,157,000
Timber, etc	337,000	
Total raw materials	1,290,000	7,876,000
Glass and pottery	96,000	
Metal manufactures and machinery	820,000	41,000
Textile yarns	155,000	12,000
Textile fabrics	2,225,000	83,000
Leather goods	134,000	1,000
Wood manufactures	92,000	16,000
Paper and books	107,000	7,000
Total manufactured articles	3,129,000	110,000
Drugs and chemicals	302,000	33,000
Gums, oils, etc	581,000	15,000
Various articles	302,000	25,000
Total miscellaneous articles	1,185,000	78,000
Total merchandise	7,848,000	10,130,000

Finances.—The normal budget of receipts fixed upon by the international financial convention of March 17, 1885, was as follows:

RECEIPTS.	Egyptian pounds.
Direct contributions	5,116,000
Indirect contributions	1,620,000
Revenues of receipts' administrations	1,580,000
Receipts of administrative services	354,000
Rent of Government property	78,000
Contributions to pension fund	60,000
Total	8,910,000

The expenditure of the Government was limited as follows:

EXPENDITURES.	Egyptian pounds.
Civil list, etc	858,000
Administration and collection of taxes	1,796,000
Cost of receipts' administration	572,000
Public security	597,000
Eastern Soudan	120,000
Pensions	457,000
Tribute and debt	1,057,000
Extraordinary expenditure	
Total	5,287,000

The receipts of the treasury in 1885 amounted to £E9,687,173, and the expenditures to £E9,184,746, including £E417,761 of extraordinary expenditures that were defrayed from the proceeds of the new loan of 1885. In 1886 the receipts amounted to £E9,574,393, and the expenditures to £E9,402,529. The loan of 1885 was drawn on to meet £E616,797 of extraordinary expenditure, and a budget surplus of £E85,012 was applied to the reduction of the debt. The budget estimates for 1887, as sanctioned by the council of ministers on Dec. 1, 1886, make the total revenue £E9,675,247 after deducting £E240,000 for unforeseen deficiencies. The receipts under the various heads were estimated as follows: Direct contributions, £E5,665,883; indirect contributions, £E1,748,069; revenues of the receipts' administration, £E1,864,408; receipts of the administrative services, £E498,940; product of Government property, £E84,152; receipts of the Government of Suakin, £E13,800; retentions of salaries, £E40,000. The expenditures under the various heads were estimated at the following amounts: Civil list, etc., £E358,100; cost of administration and tax-collection, £E1,845,716; expenses of the administration of receipts, £E941,452; public security, £E589,517; the Soudan, £E35,200; pensions, £E500,000; tribute and public debt, £E5,043,976; partial suppression of the corvée, £E250,000; various expenses, £E65,000. The total expenditure amounts to £E9,628,961, leaving an excess of receipts of the amount of £E46,286. The final accounts for 1886-'87 showed a surplus of £177,000, which, added to that of the preceding year, made £578,000, out of which the Government ordered the deduction of 5 per cent. from the coupon, amounting to £437,000, to be refunded. The occurrence of a deficit, which would have entailed an international commission in accordance with the financial convention of 1885, was only avoided by a contribution of £200,000 from the British exchequer. This subsidy was given under pretense of satisfying claims of the Egyptian Government for the transportation of British troops and for the expenses of the Nile expedition and of the defense of the frontier, although previously the British Government had declined to assume these burdens.

The budget for 1887-'88, as finally approved, places the revenue at £9,600,000, and the expenditure at £9,576,000. For the next year the Government will have to meet the expense of defending the Soudan frontier out of the ordinary revenue, as the guaranteed loan has been exhausted. It has therefore determined on increasing the duty on domestic tobacco.

The various classes of the public debt stood on Jan. 1, 1887, at the following amounts in pounds sterling:

Unified debt (4 per cent.)	£55,990,440
Privileged debt (5 per cent)	22,296,800
Guaranteed loan of 1885 (3 per cent.)	9,301,700
Total consolidated debt	£87,588,940
Domains loan	£7,354,240
Daira-Sanieh and Daira-Khassa loans	8,659,500
Total guaranteed loans	£16,013,740
Total public debt	£103,602,650

The Egyptian people have yet to pay for nine years to come the interest on the Khe-

dive's shares of the Suez Canal that were purchased by the British Government, the Khedive Ismail having for that period mortgaged the dividends to his creditors. The Moukabala debt, an internal forced loan, is not included in the above statement. The original Moukabala arrangement was that, if the Egyptians paid for twelve years about 45 per cent. more than the regular land-tax, they would . after that period have to pay only one half the former tax. This agreement was abrogated in 1876 by the Khedive, who promised to return the sums paid in excess of the regular tax. This the foreign creditors would not allow, and, in the final settlement made by the international commission of liquidation, the bulk of the debt, which amounted to £17,000,000, was repudiated, the only return that was promised to the holders of Moukabala certificates being an annuity of £E150,000, to be paid for fifty years, or until 1930.

By the financial convention of 1885 the great powers agreed to guarantee a new loan of £9,000,000, bearing interest at 3 per cent., which was to be applied to the settlement of the Alexandria indemnities and the floating debt, each amounting to about £4,000,000, and to the construction of irrigation works. The sum of £1,000,000 was destined to meet the expense of evacuating the Soudan and defending the frontier, and this appropriation was exhausted by the end of the financial year 1886-'87. The powers at that time sanctioned the suspension of the sinking fund of the other loans and the levying of a tax of 5 per cent. on their coupons, to be repaid if the finances of Egypt permit at any future time, but only for the years 1885 and 1886, unless an international commission shall sanction the continuance of the tax.

The Army.—The Egyptian army has recently been reduced from 17,000 to 11,200 men. It is under the command of an English major-general, Sir Evelyn Wood, and officered partly by Englishmen and partly by Egyptians. It consists of 15 battalions of infantry of about 600 men each, 2 squadrons of cavalry of 180 men each, 1 battery of field-artillery, 2 camel batteries, and 1 battery of heavy artillery.

The gendarmerie and police as organized by Baker Pasha consists of 2 infantry battalions, of which one of 400 men is mounted, and 4 divisions of police troops. The entire force numbers 5,986 men. One of the police divisions, 1,180 strong, is destined for the police service of Cairo.

The British Government in the beginning of 1887 announced the intention of reducing the army of occupation from 11,000 to 5,000. The reduction was begun in January, but was not carried out. In May the force remaining in Egypt was 9,300.

The Suez Canal.—The cost of the original construction of the Suez Canal, and of its subsequent enlargement and other improvements, amounted in the beginning of 1884 to 488,055,019 francs. The receipts during 1886 amounted to 57,730,449 francs. The number of ships that passed through in 1886 was 3,100; the aggregate tonnage was 8,183,313. The English vessels numbered 2,331, of 6,254,418 tons; the French 227, of 699,194 tons; the German 161, of 314,716 tons; the Dutch 127, of 312,965 tons; the Austrian 77, of 191,333 tons; the Italian 69, of 184,960 tons; the Spanish 26, of 86,077 tons; the Russian 24, of 58,289 tons; the Swedish and Norwegian 28, of 47,991 tons; the American, 7 of 9,767 tons; the Japanese 4, of 9,855 tons; the Turkish 10, of 6,419 tons; Portuguese, Belgian, and others 8, of 5,829 tons. The canal has a length from Port Said to Suez of 160 kilometres, a breadth of from 58 to 100 metres at the level of the water and 22 metres at the bottom, and a depth of 8 metres. Further improvements are in progress, to be completed in 1888, and for these a loan of 100,000,000 francs was raised on 3-per-cent. bonds among the shareholders.

Failure of the Anglo-Turkish Convention.—The Conservative Government in England has never repudiated the engagement made by the Gladstone Cabinet to evacuate Egypt as soon as order should be restored. While promising to retire whenever a stable native government should be established, it has taken every practical measure to destroy the authority of the Khedive's government, and has prevented the organization of a native army. The reiterated demands of the Porte and the troublesome insistence of France did not permit the English to ignore their promises. In 1886 Sir Henry Drummond Wolff was sent as a special commissioner to Egypt, and as a special envoy to the Porte, to discuss arrangements for the evacuation of the country. The Ghazi Mukhtar Pasha was sent to Egypt as high commissioner of the Sultan to conduct the necessary inquiries on behalf of the Turkish Government in consultation with Sir Drummond Wolff. In the early part of 1887 negotiations were carried on by the British envoy with the Porte at Constantinople. The Turkish Government demanded before all that a term should be fixed for the evacuation. The English proposed to prolong their occupation for five years more, and then withdraw their troops if the security of the country were not thereby endangered. A proposition for the neutralization of Egypt was considered, the English reserving the right to officer the Egyptian troops, and to march their own forces into the country in case of threatened disturbance. Finally, a convention was drawn up by Sir Drummond Wolff and the Ottoman ministers. The first and second articles confirmed the imperial firmans relative to Egypt, and defined the limits of the Khedive's rights to be such as the firmans prescribe. By the third article the Ottoman Government bound itself to invite the powers to approve a convention for the better regulation of the Suez Canal, which should declare the channel to be neutral and free to the ships of all nations, alike in peace or war. It

was to enjoy immunity from blockade and all acts of war, while the powers were to be asked to agree that no obstacle should be placed in the way of any measures that might be necessary for the defense of Egypt. The fourth article asserted the right of the English Government to maintain troops in Egypt as long as might be necessary for the preservation of order and the protection of the country against internal or external dangers; but by the fifth England bound herself to withdraw her forces within three years from the date of the convention, or, if danger rendered necessary the prolongation of the occupation beyond that period, to evacuate immediately on the disappearance of the danger. Egypt was to enjoy "territorial security," a term that the Sultan considered more consonant with his suzerain rights than the word "neutralization," and the powers were to be invited to sign an act recognizing and guaranteeing inviolability. The fifth article provided also that in the event of external danger or internal disorder at any future time, or of the failure of the Khedive in his duties as a vassal, or in his international obligations, the country might be occupied by Turkish troops, or reoccupied by British troops, each country being bound to notify the other in case of contemplated action, and to withdraw its forces as soon as the reasons for the military intervention should cease to exist. The final article provided that England and Turkey should conjointly invite the powers to approve the convention, and should propose certain modifications in the capitulations and in certain branches of the Egyptian administration which should be especially settled without further discussion. The proposed modification of the capitulations related chiefly to the extension of the jurisdiction of mixed tribunals both in civil and in criminal cases Another protocol had reference to the passage of foreign troops through Egypt in time of war, should communication by way of the Suez Canal be interrupted. In an annex to the convention it was stipulated that the refusal of any Mediterranean power to agree to the convention before the expiration of the three years should be held to constitute a danger from without, justifying postponement of the evacuation. The Turkish negotiators long resisted the right of re-entry, on which point the British Government remained firm. On Jan. 15, 1887, when the negotiations were reopened at Constantinople, Lord Salisbury sent a dispatch declaring that the British Government would never consent to leave Egypt to the danger of renewed anarchy, or accept as an admissible contingency that the void left by the retirement of the British troops should be filled by the forces of any other power. Finally the Turkish plenipotentiaries agreed to recognize the British right of reoccupation on condition that Turkey should have a concurrent right. The convention was signed on May 22. The British and Turkish Governments had promised to keep the French ministry informed of the progress of the negotiations. Both Russia and France had protested from the beginning against the recognition of the right of Great Britain to reoccupy Egypt. When the negotiations approached a conclusion the British Cabinet ceased to hold any communications on the subject with the French Foreign Office. The Ottoman ministers, however, continued to consult with the French minister at Constantinople. The convention was promptly ratified by the Queen of Great Britain, but before finally approving the arrangement the Sultan desired to hear the last word from France. After an interview with the Count de Montebello on June 19, the Sultan was presented by him with a note declaring that the French Government would not accept the situation arising from the ratification of the convention, and if the ratification were given it intended to take measures for safeguarding its interests, prejudiced as they would be by the rupture of the equilibrium in the Mediterranean, while if the ratification were refused it would preserve and guarantee the Sultan against the consequences of the non-ratification. The note concluded with the remark that it is only the disinterested policy of France that can safeguard the Ottoman Empire in view of the encroachments and ambitious desires of England. The Russian Government supported the attitude taken by France, and the Sultan suffered the final date fixed for the ratification, June 22, to go by without confirming the instrument. The British ministry, in compliance with the request of the Porte, directed Sir Henry D. Wolff to remain in Constantinople for a few days longer, and then granted further extensions of the period of ratification, but when he had been kept in attendance on the Sultan for a month, and it became evident that the latter was determined to withhold the ratification, and only wished to prolong the situation indefinitely, he was ordered to return to England, and accordingly sailed from Constantinople on July 17.

The Turkish Commissioner.—Ahmed Mukhtar Pasha, who accompanied Sir Henry D. Wolff to Egypt in 1886, remained after the latter departed to report to his Government on the political situation. His reports were entirely adverse to British rule, which he considered to have greatly retarded instead of advancing the development of Egypt. In March he sent a memorandum complaining that the British occupation had brought a swarm of adventurers to the Nile valley, who only seek to make fortunes, and care nothing for the good of Egypt. The higher officials, he said, are arrogant and tyrannical in their demeanor, and pay little attention to serious work. On the failure of the Wolff negotiations he reported that the result had increased Ottoman prestige, and counseled abstention from further negotiations with England respecting the presence of British troops in Egypt.

Neutralization of the Suez Canal.—The provisions in the Wolff Convention relative to the neutralization of the Suez Canal were made the subject of negotiations between the British and French Governments after the failure of the convention. A convention was concluded in October providing for the inviolability of the canal and its ports, and the free passage of the ships of all nations in time of peace or war. The Khedive and the Sultan are charged with the protection of its neutrality. An International Commission is created, consisting of the consuls-general of the powers in Egypt, which shall meet in time of war, and apprise the Khedive if any danger exists that requires him to take measures for protecting the neutrality of the canal. The commission will determine the ports and territory that shall be included in the neutralized zone. In time of peace it will hold a regular session annually, and formally record the continued observance of the convention. Of the sixteen articles composing the instrument, ten had been accepted by the powers at the Egyptian Conference of 1885. The convention, which is to be submitted to all the powers for ratification, stipulates that the canal is not to be subject to blockade, and that no right of war shall be exercised or act of hostility committed within a radius of three marine miles from its ports of entry. The International Commission will be presided over at each meeting by the senior diplomatic agent present.

Benefits of English Rule.—Under the supervision of Sir Evelyn Baring, the British consul-general and adviser of the Khedive, the administrative methods of India have been introduced into Egypt, the authority of the Khedive has been completely superseded, and the ministry has been reduced to a mere instrument in the hands of the foreign administrators. This process has increased the hatred of the Egyptians for their conquerors, but, on the other hand, it has enabled the latter to carry out reforms and improvements that offset to a considerable extent the additional burdens imposed on the people. The land-taxes were formerly collected at uncertain intervals, and the officials often extorted more than the amount of the tax. Now they are collected monthly in amounts varying according to the times of the crops and the ability of the peasants to pay. There is, consequently, a diminution of debt and usury. The use of the kourbash and the bastinado by the tax-gatherers, once universal, is now interdicted. The diminution of the conscription is felt to be a relief by the peasantry, and the abolition of the corvée where it was most oppressive saves them from much loss and suffering. The barrage has been completed, new canals have been made, and old ones have been dredged out, with the result that the productive area has been enlarged, and expenses for steam-pumping are much lighter. The administration of justice is much improved. The sanitary condition of the prisons has been greatly ameliorated, and prisoners are no longer incarcerated for years without trial. Although the speedy clearing of the criminal dockets is still impossible, prisoners who have been detained for a number of months can demand a hearing in court to determine whether there is ground for holding them longer. The Code Napoléon has been introduced, and a system of procedure adopted, and eleven European judges have been imported to act as guides to the native judges in applying European principles of jurisprudence. These new native courts came into collision, not only with the consular and international tribunals, but with the Mohammedan religious courts. The Sheikh-ul-Islam and the Grand Cadi claimed jurisdiction in all questions of marriage and succession, and also the right to decide any civil dispute that was brought before them. As a consequence, there arose confusion from contradictory decisions. The conflict culminated in the dismissal from office of the Sheikh-ul-Islam, and the issuance of a decree requiring all civil cases to be brought before the lay tribunals.

Abolition of the Corvée.—The condition of the fellaheen has been much improved by the abolition of the forced labor on the canals, in cases where it was most burdensome. The number of men called out for 100 days to clean and repair the irrigation canals was 284,000 in 1882. They were taken away when their labor was necessary for the tillage of their farms, and were often compelled to abandon ripe grain and lose their crops. The English promised to do away with the *corvée*, but were only able to accomplish it by gradual reductions. There were 202,000 summoned for the *corvée* in 1883. In 1886 the number was 95,000. The peasants were not compelled to march from distant places and provide themselves with food away from home, as formerly, but only those living near the works were taken. In 1887 the Government prepared to forego forced labor entirely, but abandoned that purpose, and provided only for the continued partial suppression of the *corvée*. For this the sum of £E250,000 per annum was necessary to pay for cleaning the canals by contract. A similar sum was available from purchases of military exemptions; for so averse are the fellaheen to military service that they will pay £100 or more to escape it. Out of the £5,870,000 to which the administrative expenditures, including the cost of collecting the customs and working the railroads, were limited by the financial convention, it was considered impossible to economize enough to meet the expense of cleaning the canals with paid instead of with forced labor. The decree for the partial substitution of paid labor for another year had been agreed to in principle by the powers in 1886. Yet, when Nubar Pasha in the provisional budget for 1887 proposed to apply the receipts obtained from purchases of military exemption to this object, the French

Government raised a protest, insisting that the revenue from that source should be applied to establishing a native army. The sum of £E180,000 set down in the budget was declared to be palpably inadequate, and the entire budget to be illusory. The protest of France was backed by Russia. The English sought to make the French unpopular by throwing on them the responsibility of preventing the abolition of the *corvée*, and a decree was issued on Feb. 8, 1887, calling out the fellaheen to work on the canals. After further discussion this order was revoked, and the labor was performed by contract. Finally, in August, 1887, an understanding was reached, by which the proceeds of military exemptions should be left intact for the army expenses, but the land-taxes, which in accordance with Lord Northbrook's report were to be reduced by £E420,000, should continue to be levied at the same rates except where they were manifestly too high for the taxpayers to pay them.

The Sarzead Incident.—The International Tribunal of Appeal consisted originally of judges representing each of the great powers of Europe, nominated by the Egyptian authorities, and approved by their several Governments, and one appointed from the United States. In 1884 two additional judges were called up from the lower court, without regard to nationality, one of whom was a Greek, and the other a Frenchman named Bellet. In the spring of 1887, the regular French representative on the tribunal, Martin Sarzeaud, was found to be financially embarrassed, and was accused of having borrowed from attorneys practicing before the court, and of fraudulently selling securities that he had already hypothecated. He fled from his creditors, resigning his post, but the Government refused to accept the resignation, bringing formal charges against him. He then sent word from France that he would withdraw his resignation and meet the charges, but soon afterward was drowned by accident or suicide. The English induced the Egyptian ministry to refrain from nominating a successor, on the ground that an extra number of judges was no longer required, but M. d'Aunay protested that France would then be left without a representative on the tribunal. Nubar Pasha proposed then to make M. Bellet the regular French judge, and to abolish the supernumerary judgeship thus made vacant. The French Government declined to accept him, but finally agreed to allow the post to remain vacant as long as M. Bellet continued to be assistant judge, on condition that the office of procureur-général, which would be vacated by the resignation of M. Vacher, should be filled by a Frenchman during the two years required to complete the latter's term. This office had been for many months a subject of contention between the English and the French. M. Vacher had returned to France on account of ill health, but resumed his duties when the

British decided to sanction the appointment of another Frenchman in his place.

Affray between Natives and British Officers.—A party of British military officers who were shooting quail in March, 1887, near the Pyramids gave offense to the villagers, as had often happened, by trampling their crops, and one of the Englishmen accidentally wounded some natives, who were passing on camels. The Egyptians rushed upon the party, and in a hand-to-hand struggle one of the officers shot and killed a native. The sportsmen were overpowered, taken to the village in bands, and subjected to indignities. A court, consisting of the Mudir of the province, the Egyptian procureur-général, and an English officer, went to the village, and, after holding an investigation, condemned fourteen persons to fines and imprisonment, and nine of them to be flogged, which was done by the English military authorities in the presence of the whole village and of the officials of the district, and the regiment to which the officers belonged, which was drawn up to witness the expiation.

The Soudan.—The Government established by the Mahdi is continued by Abdallah Tashi, who calls himself the Khalifa, and has his seat of government at Omdurman. Khartoum has been abandoned, and the material of the houses has been used as fuel for the steamers that were taken to the Upper Nile by Gen. Gordon. In the spring of 1887 the Khalifa's lieutenant, Nejumi, had a force at Dongola, and incursions of dervishes were feared in Upper Egypt.

Osman Digma, who had been appointed the Khalifa's Emir, was encamped near Galabat, where he was scarcely able to hold his ground against the Kabbabish and other Arabs that were friendly to the Egyptians. Nejumi was also hard pressed at times by the "friendlies," and was reported to have been defeated in a three-days' battle about the 1st of April.

Abdallah sent envoys to Cairo, bearing letters, dated March 15, addressed to the Khedive, the Queen of England, and the Sultan. The letter to the Khedive, which was filled with texts from the Koran, said that God had sent the Mahdi to restore his true religion, and warned the Khedive not to listen to the false sayings, but to embrace the teachings of the Mabdi, or the Khalifa would come and slay him. Abdallah declared that he had no desire for worldly empire, for the Soudan and its riches were his, and that pity alone induced him to send a warning, which, if it were not heeded, would be followed by the occupation of Tewfik's country by the Mahdi's forces. The document was returned to the messengers without an answer, and the Queen's letter was sent back unopened, but that addressed to the Sultan was forwarded by Mukhtar Pasha to Constantinople.

The English troops having been withdrawn from Upper Egypt, the frontier was defended at Wady Halfa by Egyptian soldiers, blacks, and fellaheen, commanded by British officers.

The Soudanese, in the latter part of April, attempted a forward movement, but when they had occupied Sarras, Colonels Chermside and Barrow marched from Halfa on April 28 with 800 black infantry and 200 cavalry, camel corps, and irregulars, with two guns, surrounded their position, and completely routed the 200 dervishes and 800 Dongolese that had been impressed into the Mahdi's service, killing about 200, including the three leaders, though the dervishes fought stubbornly, checking the first attack.

Osman Digma was no longer able to hold the coast region against the Kabbabish, Hadendowah, and other tribes who turned against him, and when he retired to Kassala, he was surrounded with enemies. In Sennaar and other remote provinces the Mahdi's successor was unable to maintain his authority. The friendly tribes were reported as attacking Osman Digma near Kassala in July, and a severe engagement was said to have taken place, in which 1,200 were killed. Another fight of equal magnitude was reported in August between the Kabbabish and the dervishes in the Baggara country. On the southeast the Mahdists were harassed also by the Abyssinians. Abdallah, nevertheless, maintained his power over a large population, and in October his dervishes again intrenched themselves near Sarras, and threatened an inroad into Egypt.

Release of Zebehr Pasha.—Zebehr, who has since 1882 been confined as a state prisoner at Gibraltar, was set at liberty on Aug. 3, 1887. He signed an agreement to remain in the place that should be selected by the Egyptian Government, to submit to surveillance, and to abstain from interference in any political or military question. (See Emin Pasha.)

ELECTIONS, LAWS, CUSTOMS, AND THEORIES OF. The antiquity of the ballot is very great. As soon as men associated into bands or communities, it became necessary to determine the opinions of the associators or of some of them. Different methods of determining the sentiments of the voters were arrived at — the simpler being probably the earliest used — such, for example, as by acclamation (or *viva voce*), by show of hands, by the counting of polls, or by the casting of ballots. At Athens several substances were used as ballots; the Dikasts, in giving their verdict, generally used balls of stone (*psephi*) or of metal (*sponduli*). Of these, the ones pierced in the center, or black, signified condemnation; and those unpierced, or white, signified acquittal. Shells, stones, and beans of different colors were likewise used by the Greeks; marked shells (*ostrakon*) were used to drive persons into exile, and from this custom is derived the word "ostracism." The method of voting at Syracuse was by olive-leaves appropriately marked by the voters. At Rome the ballot (meaning thereby the expression of the voter's will by the casting of a designated substance into a designated receptacle) was regulated by the

Leges Tabellariæ, a collection or series of laws, of which the *Lex Gabiana* (adopted 139 B. C.) related to the election of magistrates; the *Lex Cassia* (adopted 137 B. C.), to the *judicia populi* (or expression of popular judgment); and the *Lex Papiria* (adopted 131 B. C.), to the enactment and repeal of laws. The ballots in Rome were wooden *tabellæ*, or *tabulæ;* in the case of a vote on a proposed statute, these were marked V. R. (*vti rogas*), to express consent to the passage of the statute, and A (*antiquo*), to express a desire to keep the ancient or former law. In the case of an election, *puncta* (holes) were made opposite the names of the candidates. *Tabellæ* were also used by the Roman judges, who expressed their verdict or judgment by the letter A (*absolvo*) if acquitting, and by C (*condemno*) if condemning, and by N. L. (*non liquet*) if not voting. The earliest known instance of the use of a written paper ballot in Great Britain was in 1662. The Scottish Parliament being desirous of banishing certain persons from the realm, each Parliamentary member wrote in a disguised hand on a piece of paper the names of the persons he thought ought to be exiled. The papers were put into a bag, which was afterward opened in the exchequer chamber, and the ballots were then counted and were burned immediately upon the result being known. In modern times the ballot has generally been of paper, appropriately written or printed upon; but up to within fifty years the French imitated the Greeks and used marbles or bullets as their ballots; and small organizations still use the same systems of colored balls—hence the term "black-balls" as a signification of adverse votes. In the United States, the ballots used at elections are pieces of white paper, printed upon as directed by the laws of the several States.

Ballot-Boxes.—Any receptacle may be used to receive the ballots cast at an election or other occasion of voting, yet in different ages the shape and material of the ballot-box have varied. In ancient times the ballot-box was sometimes of metal in the form of an urn. The Greeks used a brass box to receive the ballots cast, and a wooden box to receive the ballots not cast. The Romans used a wicker-woven box or covered basket. The French, until very recently (voting by means of metallic balls), used boxes with tubes connecting with a larger tube, into which latter the voter put his hand until it was hidden from sight, when he dropped his bullet into one small tube for assent and into the other for dissent. The European nations now deposit their paper ballots in wooden boxes, and this was the custom in the United States up to about twenty years ago. Now we have adopted a box that consists of a glass globe with a movable top, having a slit just large enough to admit a folded ballot. This top is locked down during the voting, and only removed when the votes are to be counted. It is easy to detect any attempt to cast two ballots at once.

Suffrage.—The right to vote has seldom been given to all the inhabitants of a country. The United States is the first country to have made the right of suffrage universal to all her male citizens; but even here there are certain States that impose restrictions upon this right—such as Rhode Island, which, in some instances, requires the voter to have been native-born or possessed of a certain amount of property.

Representation.—Under the system of voting now in vogue in most of the States of the Union, the voter has one vote for each candidate. There are several objections to this method, the principal one being that a very large proportion of the people are left without any representation. To obviate this objection, and to afford the minority some representation, many systems have been proposed, the chief of which are known as: 1. Cumulative; 2. Preferential; 3. Limited; 4. Substitutive; 5. Proxy; and 6. List. Cumulative voting permits an elector to give all or any of his votes to a single candidate; thus, if he is to vote for three candidates, he is allowed to give either one vote to each, or to give three votes for one, or two votes for one candidate and one vote for another. This system is in general use in Illinois, and is said to give general satisfaction. The preferential system first ascertains the number of votes necessary to elect a candidate. Thus, if the total of voters be 800,000, and the number of representatives to be chosen 200, the quota of each representative would be 4,000. Then the voter is to deposit a ballot, on which he shall have placed, in the order of his preference, the names of the candidates. Any candidate receiving 4,000 votes is declared elected. On counting these votes, when a candidate has obtained 4,000 votes, the ballots electing him are laid aside, and the remaining votes are counted for the candidates next in order of preference. If there be not 200 persons credited each with 4,000 votes, the deficiency in the number of representatives is made up by taking the candidates who come nearest to the required quota. This system of preferential voting is used in the election of the Board of Overseers of Harvard College, and its practical working in these elections is said to be very satisfactory and far more simple than would at first be surmised. Limited voting is the plan of requiring the votes to be cast for a smaller number of candidates than the whole. Thus, where a district is entitled to three representatives, each voter can vote for only two representatives. This method is prescribed in the Constitution of New York, in the provision that provides—for the first election of the judges of the Court of Appeals, which election is by general ticket of the whole State—that each ticket shall contain the names of only five candidates. Of course there will always be two tickets, each nominated by a party convention; but the minority party will certainly elect two judges. Substitutive voting permits candidates to cast anew the useless votes given them, and substitute a third person in their place. Proxy voting permits every voter to give his vote or proxy to any person he pleases. Proxy voting, it is claimed, will result in each elector's exercising the right of franchise. List voting, in some respects, resembles preferential voting. It was first recommended by M. Naville, of Geneva, Switzerland. It supposes lists of candidates, each containing a number of names equal to the number of representatives to be chosen, ranged in the order of preference, to be deposited with the authorities a certain time before election, and numbered. Each elector gives his vote for a particular list. The whole number of votes for that list is divided by the electoral quotient, and the result gives the number of candidates chosen on that list. For example, if there be 15 representatives to be elected, 15,000 voters, and 5 lists of candidates: list A, receiving 5,000 votes, secures 5 representatives; list B, receiving 4,000 votes, secures 4 representatives; and so on.

Registration.—Registration laws require the electors who desire to vote to register their names, addresses, and, in some cases, other personal information, in books or lists provided for the purpose, several days before voting. The object is to afford an opportunity to investigate the right of each person to vote. In some States, special constitutional provision is made for the enactment of registration laws; such States as Alabama, Colorado, Florida, Georgia, Kansas, Kentucky, Louisiana, Maryland, Michigan, Mississippi, Missouri, Nevada, New York, North Carolina, Oregon, Pennsylvania, Rhode Island, South Carolina, Tennessee, Virginia, and West Virginia. In Arkansas, Nevada, Pennsylvania, and West Virginia some exceptions are made to the application of the registry laws, and in Texas registration laws are forbidden.

Nominations.—Candidates must be nominated before they can be voted for, and while in theory the right to nominate is open to every citizen, yet in practice the nominations are made by party organizations. The voters of each party and each district meet on an appointed evening, and ballot either for the candidate whom they desire to nominate, or for representatives to some nominating convention. Such meetings are known as primary elections, and while the same general procedure is followed all over the country, there are minor details in which one primary election differs from another. In every election district, however, there are men who, for one reason or another, have become leaders: These leaders hold, prior to the primary election, a caucus, at which they decide who shall or shall not be the candidate nominated, and their influence with the majority of the attendants at the primary is usually sufficient to procure such nomination. In order that the people at large may be given a better opportunity to nominate candidates, it

has been proposed to adopt the Australian system of nomination, which, briefly, is as follows: A candidate is nominated in writing (called a "nomination paper"), which must be subscribed by a certain number of electors. During a certain time, a designated public official furnishes the blank forms of nomination to any voter, and at a certain date all nomination papers that are to be of force must be filed with a designated public official. Only those persons whose names are on a nomination paper duly filed and signed by the necessary number of electors can be voted for. This method recommends itself by its extreme simplicity and the thorough opportunity afforded the people for nomination. The form of the Australian nomination paper is as follows:

We, the undersigned, A. B., of ...., in the .... of .... and C. D. of ...., in the .... of ...., being electors for the .... of .... do hereby nominate the following person as a proper person to serve as member for the said .... in Parliament:

Surname.	Other names.	Abode.	Rank, profession, or occupation.
BROWN,	John,	52 George St., Bristol.	Merchant.
JONES,	or William David,	High Elms, Wilts.	Esquire.
MEETON,	or Hon. George Travis, commonly called Viscount,	Swansworth, Berks.	Viscount.
SMITH,	or Henry Sydney,	72 High St., Bath.	Attorney.

(Signed)   A. B.
                    C. D.

We, the undersigned, being registered electors of the ..... do hereby assent to the nomination of the above-mentioned John Brown as a proper person to serve as member for the said .... in Parliament.

(Signed)

Procedure of Elections.—The elections in the different States are conducted under the same general procedure. The polling - places are opened at a designated hour, one or more inspectors are present, each candidate or party has some one present to distribute ballots, the voter drops them into the box in the presence of the inspectors (if a registration system is in force, he first gives his name, and it is verified by the list). The polls close at a certain hour, after which the votes are counted. This system is so well known, and may be so easily seen in practice, that no detailed description is necessary here. It has been found to offer numerous opportunities for bribery and corruption of all kinds. Recently, there has sprung up a movement looking to the adoption in the United States of the election procedure now in vogue in Great Britain, known as the Australian system. Briefly, this system is as follows: The polls being open, the voter enters, and gives his name. His right to vote being ascertained, the chief inspector gives him a ticket or ballot containing all the names of the persons to be voted for. These tickets or ballots are bound in books, which are distributed by an officer designated by law to the several chief inspectors on the morning of election-day. These books are somewhat like the check-books used by the banks, inasmuch as each ballot is connected with a stub (called in England a "counter-foil"), which remains in the book after the ballot is torn out. The following is the form of the ballot:

Counterfoil.		
No.	1	BROWN. (John Brown, of 52 George St., Bristol, Merchant.)
	2	JONES. (William David Jones, of High Elms, Wilts, Esq.)
	3	MERTON. (Hon. George Travis, commonly called Viscount Merton, of Swansworth, Berks.)
NOTE.—The counterfoil is to have a number to correspond with that on the back of the ballot paper.	4	SMITH. (Henry Sydney Smith, of 72 High St., Bath, Attorney.)

Form of Back of Ballot Paper.
No. ....
Election for. ......
18 ..
NOTE.—The number on the ballot paper is to correspond with that in the counterfoil.

Each of these tickets or ballots, when it is handed to the voter, is marked by the chief inspector, either by a stamp specially prepared, or by his initials. Having received his paper, the voter goes into a ballot-room, where a pencil is provided, and marks a cross opposite the name of the candidate he votes for. He then folds the ballot so that none can see his mark, returns to the chief inspector, shows him the initial or stamp, and deposits the folded paper in the box. He then leaves by another door, so that he does not come into contact with voters entering to vote. Each polling-place is provided with six or more ballot-rooms. These ballot-rooms are against the wall, at the side of the inspector. They are mere temporary structures, built of boards, about thirty inches wide, and a curtain hangs in the front. A board about a foot wide is attached to the wall throughout the ballot-room, to serve the voter while marking the names. Each pencil is secured by a strong tape. Red lead is preferred, as it is seen better on black printing-ink, and prevents blotting, which would otherwise be inevitable if ink were used to mark the name. A policeman is placed near the ballot-room to show the voters in, and to take care that one voter only enters the ballot-room at a time, and to show the voter the way out. When the voter can not read or write, he informs the inspector of the fact and for whom

he intends voting. The inspector then goes to the ballot-room with him, and marks the names as directed. The voter then folds the paper and puts it into the ballot-box and retires. If the voter inadvertently spoils a ballot-paper, he can return it to the officer, who will, if satisfied of the inadvertence, give him another paper. Any one who fraudulently forges, defaces, or destroys a ballot-paper, is guilty of a misdemeanor, and the punishment for such misdemeanor is fixed at from six months' to two years' imprisonment. The same punishment is meted out to any person who, without due authority, supplies any one with a ballot-paper, or puts into any ballot-box any other thing than his ballot, or takes any ballot away from the polling-station, or otherwise interferes with the ballot-box. Every officer, clerk, or agent in attendance at the polling-place must take an oath of secrecy. Immediately after the close of the polls, each presiding officer must return the unused and the spoiled ballot-papers, with a statement showing the number of ballot-papers given him, and the number placed in the ballot-box, unused, spoiled, or illegally tendered. Each candidate may appoint one agent to attend at each polling-place. The State or city or county, according to the election, pays all the expense of the ballots, salaries of inspectors, etc. It will be observed that the ballot given above has a number on the stub and on the ballot-paper; this same number is placed on the registration-list opposite the name of the voter, and this is called the open system of voting. The secret system consists in merely leaving off, from both stub and ballot-paper, such numbering, thus preventing the identification of any ballot. When the polls are closed, the votes are counted as under the existing system.

The Crawford County Plan.—This is a system of conducting primary elections which originated and is still in use in Crawford County, Pa. The plan was suggested and adopted at a county convention of Republicans by C. D. Ashley in 1861. This plan nominates candidates directly at the primaries. It compels them to come before the people and have their merits discussed before the nominating machinery is started. Cleveland, Ohio, is the first large city to adopt the plan (1887). The rules in Crawford County are as follow:

1. The candidates for the several offices shall have their names announced in one or more of the county papers at least three weeks previous to the primary meetings, stating the office, and subject to the action of said primary meetings.
2. The voters belonging to the Republican party in each ward, town, or borough, shall meet on the day designated by the Republican party committee at the usual place of holding elections, at 2 o'clock P. M., and proceed to elect one person for judge and two persons for clerks, who shall form a board of election to receive votes and determine who are proper persons to vote, and shall hold open the polls until 7 o'clock P. M. After the polls are opened, the candidates announced as aforesaid shall be balloted for. The name of each person voting shall be written on a list at the time of voting, and no person shall be allowed to vote more

than once for each office. The ballots shall be numbered and the corresponding number written on the poll-list opposite the names of the voters, and said poll-lists and ballots shall be preserved and returned with the return of each district. Every person claiming to be a Republican who voted for the Republican candidate at the last preceding election at which he voted, and declares his intention to support candidates nominated at such primary election, shall be entitled to vote, and every person challenged, or whose vote is doubted by any election officer, shall be sworn as to the qualifications aforesaid and his oath shall be returned with the return of said district. Any person entitled to cast his first vote at the succeeding general election shall be entitled to vote on pledging himself to support the ticket nominated at such primary election.

3. After the polls are closed, the board shall proceed to count the votes that each candidate has received and make out the returns accordingly, to be certified to by the judge and attested by the clerks. It shall be the duty of the persons holding the primary election, as soon as the count is completed in each district, to make a public announcement of the result, and also to post upon the door of the election-house a statement signed by the election officers, showing the votes received by each candidate voted for at said election.

4. The judge, or one of the clerks appointed by the judge of each district, shall meet at the court-house at Meadville, on the same day following the primary meetings, at 1 o'clock P. M., having the certified returns and lists of voters, and the person having the highest number of votes for any office shall be declared the regular nominee of the Republican party. Whenever any return from any district shall show any more votes, exclusive of the number of persons casting their first vote at such election, than were cast by the district for the last preceding Republican candidate for Governor or President, such excess shall be deducted from such return, said deductions to be taken *pro rata* from the vote returned from the district for the respective candidates for each office at said primary election.

5. Any two or more persons having an equal number of votes for the same office, the return judges shall proceed to ballot for a choice, the person having the highest number of votes to be the nominee.

6. The convention of return judges shall have the power to reject all fraudulent votes from the returns of any district, and where frauds have been committed or allowed by the board of election of such a nature and extent that it is impossible to determine the true vote of a district, the convention may reject altogether the return from such district.

7. The return judges shall have power to appoint conferees, senatorial and congressional, or either, as the case may be, who shall be recommended to support the person who shall have received the highest number of votes cast for that office in the county.

8. The return judges may, at any time, change this mode of selecting candidates as they may be instructed by the people at the primary meetings, due notice of such proposed change having been given by the county committee.

9. It shall be the duty of the chairman of the county committee to issue a call for the primary meetings in pursuance of the action of the county committee, to print and distribute blanks for returns, poll-lists, and oaths, as required by the foregoing rules. It shall be the duty of the chairman of the county committee to call a meeting on the request in writing of ten members.

Under the rules printed above, the names of all the candidates for each office who have given due notice of their candidacy are printed on the ticket to be used at the primaries. The blanks include one for a statement of the vote for each candidate at each primary, a tally-sheet for the use of judges and clerks of election, a return-sheet to be sworn to and be forwarded to the return judges, a blank for recording the names of every voter, a blank affidavit to be subscribed by voters whose politics are in doubt, and another for the judges and clerks, and envelopes for forwarding the returns.

The Clarion County Plan.—This is named from Clarion County, Pa. It allows each ward and township represented in a Republican primary one vote for each 50 votes cast at the last election for the Republican candidate for Governor. At the primary elections the voters cast their votes directly for candidates not only for first choice, but for second and third choice also. They elect a delegate to the county convention, who is also the representative of the ward or town on the county central committee. The delegate is required to cast the vote of his constituency as already expressed for the several candidates. For instance, if the ward cast 500 votes for Governor it would be entitled to 10 votes for each office to be filled without regard to the aggregate number of votes or the number of votes for each candidate cast at the primary election. If the convention is to nominate a candidate for Congress, the delegate will cast the 10 votes of his ward or township for the candidate who had the highest number of votes as first choice so long as he remains a candidate. If this candidate is retired, the 10 votes must be cast for the candidate who has the highest number of votes for second choice at the primary election so long as he remains a candidate, etc. At the convention the candidate having the smallest number of votes on the first ballot is dropped and the votes cast for him go to some other candidate, and so on until one has a majority. In this way a nomination is certain to be made on the second or third ballot.

EMERY-WHEELS. A generation ago the uses of emery were confined to the polishing and grinding processes possible with powders of various degrees of fineness. Every woman had in her work-basket a little cushion or bag of powdered emery, to remove particles of rust from her needles. Mechanics used the same powder in various forms, such as emery-paper and emery-cloth, the powder being fixed to the cloth or paper by means of glue. Wheels were made with the periphery covered with emery-powder, and polishing sticks and rods, similarly covered, are still in common use. The new industries and mechanical processes, so universal to-day, are of comparatively recent origin, and have grown out of the obvious advantages resulting from the introduction of solid emery-wheels. Twenty years ago these wheels were few, and were viewed with distrust by most workmen, owing to real or fancied imperfections of manufacture, and consequent danger to the workman. A long series of experiments was tried before even approximate perfection was attained. To secure the best mechanical results, a very high rate of speed was necessary, and immense difficulties lay in the way of securing adequate cohesion of the particles. Rubber, glue, shellac, oxidized linseed-oil, and various metallic and mineral cements were tried, with varying degrees of success. Among the earlier devices was a composition of emery with melted brimstone; but the friable character of this was so effectually demonstrated by frequent accidents, that its use was speedily discontinued, and years passed before the record of precedence was forgotten. The soluble silicates were tried at an early date, and with promising, but not wholly satisfactory, results. Some of the earlier experiments hinged upon the chemical affinities and interchanges of the oxides and chlorides of zinc, magnesium, and other bases, and many failures resulted, owing to the unknown and unexpected changes that went on silently beneath the exterior surface of the wheel, and only made themselves manifest after a lapse of time altogether uncertain in duration.

An instance is mentioned, on good authority, where a manufacturer kept samples of all the wheels sent out from his establishment, and found after a time that they had fallen to pieces on the shelf where they were stored. Another difficulty encountered by the early manufacturers was the warping of wheels, particularly those that were thin. It was found that this was due to turning the sides first and the face last. A reversal of the process corrected the tendency. The main difficulty, however, lay in the composition. Vitrifaction, it was found, was inseparable from a degree of brittleness incompatible with sufficient cohesion, and it appears that upon the whole tanite and vulcanite wheels give the best results. The secret of the details of manufacture of all the best makers is closely guarded to this day; but it is known that success was reached only through a long series of careful experiments. The terrific force of an exploding wheel is little appreciated save by the workmen who are obliged to stand over them, and by the employers who are, or ought to be, responsible for their safety. The testing-room of one of the largest manufactories of emery-wheels is similar to a bomb-proof for strength. Its walls are of stone, 3½ to 4 feet thick, and the roof is made of heavy oaken logs covered with loose stones. The testing-machine is run by a belt, which passes through a narrow slit in the rear wall, and can be thrown into and out of gear by a person outside of the building. The test-speed applied to the wheels is largely in excess of any to which they are likely to be subjected in practice, and when they break in the testing-room they strike the walls and roof with the force of artillery, splintering the stone and penetrating the solid timbers. There is, in fact, no safe-guard except the intrinsic cohesiveness of the wheel. Hoods, cowls, and screens can not be made heavy enough to withstand the shock, and side-flanges can not be so tightly adjusted as to restrain the fragments of a broken wheel, responding to a centrifugal force of 1,500 or 1,600 revolutions a minute.

All this elaboration of experiment and precaution presupposes an enormous demand for a trustworthy manufactured article. In point of fact, the solid emery-wheel has already superseded the file, and all other methods of grinding and polishing on a large scale. An elaborate series of experiments have been instituted to establish the comparative merits of the old and new methods. Perhaps the most striking of the results is found in a table comparing the cost of wearing away one pound of brass, cast-iron, wrought-iron, and steel, respectively, with a file and with an emery-wheel. Skilled workmen were employed accustomed to the use of the file, and they worked as rapidly as possible to wear away the required pound of filings and chippings in the shortest possible time, without regard to the shape in which the metal was left.

COST PER POUND OF REMOVING OR WEARING AWAY METALS.

TOOLS.	Brass.	Cast-iron.	Wrought-iron.	Saw-steel.
	Cents.	Cents.	Cents.	Cents.
Emery-wheel	1·3	5·8	21·2	28·9
File	25·8	85·9	75·	206·4
Hammer and cold-chisel	10·1	5·5	19·6	187·6

A careful comparison of these results shows very largely in favor of the wheels. While every stroke of the file or chisel diminished the cutting power of the instrument, the wheel remained as good as new at the end of the trial. The wheel is in fact a circular file, costing 2½ cents a pound, while files cost about 16 cents apiece. The speed of the wheel during the test-trials was 1,660 revolutions, or about one mile a minute measured at the cutting-edge.

Emery-wheels are made of all sizes, from the size of a shirt-button up to 36 inches in diameter, and of various thicknesses, according to the work required of them, which may be simple saw-gumming, or grinding the treads of car-wheels, evening plate-surfaces, or other heavy work. The mounting of the wheels to secure the utmost durability and immunity from fracture is of the highest importance, and has called for the exercise of much ingenuity in bringing them to their present state of perfection. Vibration has been reduced to a minimum, and the breaking of a good wheel when properly mounted is now a rare occurrence. Wheels when fresh from the factory are, or should be, absolutely true, but the wear of usage is apt to make them somewhat uneven. This is easily corrected by the use of a diamond tool, which is the only instrument that can remove the inequalities and reduce the cutting-face to its normal condition. Wheels are made with edges of various shapes, and they can be cut to all sorts of re-entrant and irregular angles and curves by any mechanic with a diamond tool. So easy is it, indeed, for the workman to shape the wheel according to his needs, that by far the greater proportion of wheels are made with a plain, square face like an ordinary grindstone.

EMIN PASHA. The expedition of Henry M. Stanley for the relief of Emin Pasha, undertaken in the spring of 1887 awakened general public interest. The fact that an able and active explorer, well known to all the geographical societies of Europe, was, so to speak, cast away in Central Africa and unable to return to civilization, was most romantic. Little had been publicly known of the personality of the explorer prior to the general discussion awakened by the organization of this expedition, and even now but few persons are thoroughly informed regarding his career. · Emin Pasha is an Austrian, his real name being Schnitzer, and was born in 1840, at Oppeln. After studying medicine for a time at Breslau, Berlin, and Königsberg, he was appointed in 1868 a surgeon in the Turkish army. It has been said that upon receiving this appointment he embraced Mohammedanism, but there is no positive evidence of it. He was sent to Egypt and was appointed by Gen. Gordon surgeon-general of his army. In 1878 he was made Governor General of the Equatorial Provinces, with the title of Bey (being afterward promoted to Pasha), and immediately set out for the provinces over which he was to rule. Here his remarkable energy and quick grasp of the situation became evident at once. These provinces were at the time of his assumption of authority in a terrible condition. A vast territory, containing six million inhabitants, had been for years overrun by the slave-traders, who did an enormous business in kidnapping or buying the natives and taking them to the nearest slave-market. Within three years Emin had driven the slave-traders out of his dominions, while the provinces, which up to his acquisition of power had cost for their government nearly $200,000 annually, were able to send in 1882 and thereafter a yearly surplus of $40,000 to the Cairo Government after paying all expenses, besides the cost of large public works which had been completed. This change in the financial condition of the territory was brought about, not by increased taxation, but by the exercise of economy and the suppression of abuses, by training the natives to become industrious producers, and by the general exercise of good government. The new Bey devoted himself to the study of the language and customs of the races over whom he ruled, while with wise judgment and a kindly nature he taught the natives to have full confidence in him. Training-stations were established all over his provinces, agriculture was developed, and murder, war, and slavery became things of the past, so that at last, as is said, "the whole country was made so safe that but for the wild beasts in the thickets a man could have gone from one end to the other armed with no more than a walking-stick." Emin's idea of government was to civilize the negroes in as short a time as possible and by the exercise of methods of· kindness and consideration. To this end he appointed the most efficient men he could get as officers, and these enforced a strict discipline, treating the natives as children, but yet gently. Hospitals were built, roads were constructed through the country, the natives were taught how to make wagons, and cotton, coffee, rice, indigo, and wheat were cultivated with success.

In the mean time the country surrounding the territory of Emin remained in its original condition of barbarity, and there the Arab slave-traders carried on their infamous traffic unmolested. These slave-traders had been the bitter enemies of Gordon and were now the most active supporters of the Mahdi, and it was these that created for Emin his greatest difficulties. On first reaching Wadelai he succeeded in forming friendly relations with the kings of Uganda and Unjoro, and the latter continued faithful to him up to the last that was heard of him; but in Uganda a new king came on the throne who was under the influence of the Arab slave-traders and hostile to the missionaries, and he was able, with the assistance of native tribes in various directions, to imprison Emin in his own territory, so that from 1882 he was entirely cut off from communication with the outside world. To the north of him the Egyptian rule had been destroyed, while the hostile King of Uganda prevented assistance reaching him from the south. It was not until October, 1886, that such news came from him in letters which he succeeded in getting through in the hands of negro runners as to set forth clearly the nature of his situation. At that time he had ten fortified stations along the Nile, while his command consisted of 1,500 soldiers, 10 Egyptian and 15 negro officers, and 20 Coptic officials. He expected that his ammunition would last until the end of 1886, and that he would be able to maintain himself still longer if not attacked by the wild tribes; but this latter event he feared as well as that he would be assaulted by the tribes of the Mahdi as soon as it was discovered that he had no more ammunition. Meanwhile, Emin could have escaped on his own account by taking picked men and cutting his way through had he been willing to leave the women and children to their fate and the natives to the mercy of the slave-traders; but this idea seems never to have occurred to him, and in the last letters received from him he made no appeal for assistance, but simply said that if a relief force should be sent to him it would save his life and prevent his provinces from lapsing into barbarism. He kept his men busy in the cultivation of cotton, taught them how to make boots, and established a soap-factory and tobacco plantations, placing his forces toward the Upper Nile, his natural line of retreat, and thus succeeded in retaining his sway over the southern and eastern districts of the ancient province of the equator.

Dr. Junker, the Russian explorer, left Emin Bey on Jan. 1, 1886, and after encountering many dangers reached Europe. It was his account that called the attention of the world to the perilous position of Emin. It was known that in the spring of 1882 Emin went down the Nile to Khartoum to consult in regard to the Mahdi, but was instructed to return to his provinces and defend himself as best he could. This he did, but he was gradually forced to relinquish outlying stations, though losing ground only on compulsion, and at last accounts he was at Wadelai, near Lake Albert Nyanza. His last letter contained the following: "I am glad to be able to tell you that the province is in complete safety and order. It is true that the Bari gave us some little trouble, but I was soon able to restore order in their district. Since I last wrote you all the stations have been busily employed in agricultural work, and at each one considerable cotton has been planted and is doing well. This is all the more important for us, as it enables us to a certain extent to cover our nakedness. I have also introduced the shoemaker's art, and you would be surprised to see the progress we have made. We now make our own soap, and we have at least enough meat and grain, so we have sufficient to keep life going. Such luxuries, however, as sugar, etc., of course we have not seen for many a long day. I forgot to say that we are growing most splendid tobacco. . . . Our relations with Kabrega, King of Unjoro, have still continued friendly. He has also had the goodness to send my letters to Mr. Mackay in Uganda, and has permitted me to buy several necessary articles from the Zanzibar Arabs who live in his country."

Since that period Emin's position has not become any worse, as Dr. Junker succeeded in sending him from Uganda $2,000 worth of cotton goods, and afterward goods were bought by Emin's agents in Uganda, while, under date of Dec. 18, 1886, he wrote to Dr. Junker that King Mwanga allowed him to buy goods from Zanzibar merchants, and that he obtained permission to have ammunition and provisions sent to him from Zanzibar.

This part of the continent forms one of the large plateaus that give Africa its peculiar character. An immense highland occupies the continent south of a line drawn from Abyssinia to the Niger. Its rim is formed by mountain-ranges that fall off in terraces toward the sea. A depression, indicated by the valleys of the Kunene and Zambezi, separates the plateau of South Africa from that of Central Africa. The eastern side of the latter consists of high mountain-ranges and plateaus. This mountainous district contains the sources of all the rivers of Central Africa except the

southern tributaries of the Congo, which come from the water-shed between the Congo and the Zambezi. Emin has explored the greater part of his territory. He made his first excursion in 1876, with Gordon. In 1877 he went from his station of Lado to Lake Mwutan, passing by Dufileh, and returning by way of Unjoro and Rubaga. In 1880 he explored the Makraka country, in 1881 the Lattuka territory east of the Nile, and in 1882 the Uelle. He is a hard worker, passing long hours in his office, gives receptions, makes inspections, and when his official occupations allow him leisure he writes his memoirs and the results of the geographical, physical, ethnographical, and metallurgical observations made during his frequent tours of inspection, transmitting them, whenever some trader passes, to the German scientific reviews. His present stations include Lado, Redjaf, Bedden, Keri, Labos, Dufileh, Fatkio, and Wadelai.

On receiving Dr. Junker's account of the situation of Emin, a great deal of feeling was aroused in England and Germany and in Egypt, and the necessity of fitting out a relief expedition was universally conceded. Different plans were proposed; but, while King Leopold of Belgium and the Khedive of Egypt were both willing to assist, nothing positive was done until a Mr. Mackinnon, of Glasgow, and some other Scotchmen subscribed a fund of $100,000, and called for Henry M. Stanley to take charge of it, and undertake the expedition. Stanley was engaged at that time in a lecturing-tour in the United States, but immediately canceled all his engagements and sailed for England, and in ten days left for Zanzibar by way of the Suez Canal. This was on Feb. 3, 1887. Twenty days after arriving in Zanzibar, the relief expedition sailed in the steamer "Madeira," by way of the Cape of Good Hope, to the mouth of the Congo. The expedition included 61 Soudanese, 13 Somalas, 620 natives of Zanzibar, 8 interpreters, and 40 of Tippoo Tib's followers. With Tippoo Tib, the great Arab slave-trader, Stanley succeeded in making an agreement by which he was to accompany him as second in command, an arrangement that was pronounced by the London "Times" "a master stroke." Tippoo Tib, an ivory- and slave-hunter, is a most powerful factor in Central Africa. In men and means his resources are said to be practically unlimited. His agents are found in all directions throughout the country, while he has factors in Muscat and India, to whom every year he sends vast stores of material for trade. The Stanley expedition arrived at Cape Town on March 9, and proceeded on the following day to the Congo river. In the mean time news had been received at Zanzibar from Emin Pasha, to the effect that in the preceding November he went to Uganda, and that King Mwanga refused to permit him to go through his country. Then Emin tried to effect a passage at Karagwa, on the western shore of Lake Victoria Nyanza; but in this also he failed. He then returned to Wadelai, leaving a detachment of soldiers at Unjoro under the command of Casati, his sole European companion.

There were four routes, any one of which Stanley could take for his expedition: one straight through the hostile Uganda country, the second through the Masai country, a third more southerly by the shores of Lake Alexandra, and the fourth by the Congo. He chose the fourth. The steamer "Navarino" carried his merchandise and ammunition from Graves-end to the starting-point of the expedition, and thence to the mouth of the Congo, where the Belgian steamers, loaned by King Leopold, were to transport everything and everybody to within 250 miles of Wadelai, thus reducing by about three quarters of its distance the march to be made overland—an immense advantage, considering that every article has to be carried on the backs of porters from the sea to the objective point. Stanley took with him a transportable steel boat, about 30 feet long and 6 feet broad, which could be separated and easily carried by two men, and when in use could carry 22 men and 1,000 pounds of baggage. He was also provided with a modern automatic Maxim gun, which can discharge 666 bullets every minute, with a range of about 2,000 yards, and which is provided with an armor-plate as protection against assault by arrows and spears. Altogether the expedition embraced about 1,000 people. Arriving on the Congo, Stanley dispatched couriers overland to the King of Uganda, informing him of the object of the expedition, and to Tippoo Tib at Stanley Pool. He found the latter at Stanley Pool, virtually in command of the whole country, and at once completed the arrangement already mentioned. This was rather forced upon Stanley, as he found that since his absence from the country the power of the Congo Free State had been crippled at most of the outposts. The Belgians, who had everywhere been left in charge, seemed to have proved quite inefficient for the work left in their hands. Stanley Falls Station had been destroyed, and all around that neighborhood the savages were in hostile humor.

The expedition left Bolombo on May 11, and it was expected that it would arrive at the mouth of the Aruwimi the first week in June. At this point Stanley proposed leaving the Congo and pushing on overland through the unexplored territory 350 miles to Wadelai, where Emin Bey was supposed to be encamped. On Dec. 30, 1887, Dr. Schweinfurth, the explorer, wrote from Cairo to Berlin that news of the junction of Stanley with Emin had reached Cairo on Dec. 22, but without further particulars. It should be mentioned that the Egyptian Government gave £10,000 toward the purpose of the expedition, not for the rescue of Emin, but for carrying dispatches and ammunition to him.

The general feeling among experts in Central Africa exploration was that in choosing the Congo route, which has 350 miles of dangerous and difficult unexplored country, Stanley would find that he ran great risks. Sir John Kirk, British Consul-General to Zanzibar, said: "The Congo route by Mobangi or Biyerre is impossible. No one is able to say how many months such an expedition would take. Besides, it would be necessary to bring porters from Zanzibar, for the Congo negroes are not used to that sort of work. The Congo Free State depends even now upon Zanzibar negroes for labor." Gen. Charles P. Stone, formerly chief-of-staff of the Egyptian war establishment, expressed the opinion that "a well-organized expedition, thoroughly prepared with such full information of the route, the obstacles, and the dangers as can be given by Dr. Junker, commanded by such a man as Stanley, who is thoroughly acquainted with these countries and their population, starting in a favorable season, could effect the rescue, provided Emin Pasha could hold out for the necessary time, which Dr. Junker feels he can do." If this expedition should fail, the result would be to hand over to the slave-traders a population of 6,000,000 and a province nearly as large as Europe.

ENGINEERING. Bridge at Poughkeepsie, N. Y.—Ever since the first settlement of North America the Hudson river has been one of the chief arteries of commerce. Forming with its main tributary, the Mohawk, the most direct route from the sea to the Great Lakes and through them to the West, it has for upward of two centuries been the main highway of emigration. The canoe and bateau have been successively superseded by the canal-boat, the steamer, and the railroad. It must ever remain a natural highway for traffic, but with the development of artificial as distinguished from natural highways, it has assumed a new character as an obstacle. A glance at the map will show that it divides New England from the West in a way that does not at all harmonize with the demands of modern economic engineering. For many years it has been bridged at Albany, but there remained a long stretch of 150 miles involving either an indirect course by rail, or the transshipment of freight and passengers at New York.

Several schemes for bridging the river at Peekskill, Fishkill, and Hudson have been proposed, but that at Poughkeepsie is the first that has been pushed to a successful issue. The bridge was designed about 1870. It has four piers of masonry resting upon timber caissons which are dredged to a depth of about 125 feet below high water. The dimensions of these caissons are 60 feet by 100. Twelve pockets were left open for convenience of workmen, and were filled with concrete after the caissons were sunk to their final level. The tops of the caissons proper are 20 feet below high water, and are surmounted by grillage-work 10 feet deep and closely corresponding in area with the caissons themselves. The solid masonry piers are 24 feet thick and 86 feet long, and rise 80 feet above high water, affording support for steel towers 16 feet by 60 at the base, 16 feet by 80 at the top, and 100 feet high to the lower part of the superstructure. The tower construction is shown in the illustration, consisting, in effect, of two pyramidal structures securely braced in every direction. The cantilevers are three in number, of 548 feet each, and two connection spans of 525 feet each. It will be noticed that the two end spans and the central span give a greater clear height above the water—namely, 160 feet — while the connected spans give 180 feet, a plan which facilitated the placing of the cantilevers without staging, and therefore with less obstruction to commerce. The wind-pressures are estimated on the basis of 30 pounds per square foot of surface, including towers, spans, and area of trains. The pressure on the caisson bases is about 8 tons per square foot, and the material upon which they rest is hard gravel.

From end to end, including approaches, the structure is about 1¼ mile long, and it is an excellent example of the latest ideas in bridge construction.

The Tay Bridge.—Some of the ingenious devices for laying the foundations of this grand bridge were described and illustrated in the article on engineering for 1885. The year 1887 saw the completion of the whole structure, and trains were passed over it early in June. Throughout the whole course of construction the ruins of the old bridge, which fell in 1879, were utilized, and the engineers were thus enabled to dispense with

BRIDGE AT POUGHKEEPSIE.

scaffolding more easily than their brethren who are engaged in a similar task on the Firth of Forth. Mr. William Arrol was the supervising engineer of the whole work, and he has discharged his duties so satisfactorily that his place as a bridge engineer is assured. As regards the possible recurrence of such a disaster as startled the civilized world in 1879, all confidence may be felt. A wind-pressure of 55 pounds per

bridge can be opened in five minutes. Capstans are provided for operating the mechanism by hand-power in case of necessity, the time required being seventeen minutes. The structure was opened for public use on May 22, with imposing ceremonies. The distance between the axes of rotation is 220 feet (nearly). The total weight of the iron-work is 526 tons, with a counterbalance of 58½ tons. The clear

LIFTING BRIDGE AT TARANTO, ITALY.

square foot has been provided for, and every part of the foundation has been tested to one third more than the greatest possible load that can be placed upon it.

Bridge at Taranto, Italy.—A strait separates the old and new towns of Taranto, and connects what is known as the Little Sea (Mare Piccolo) with the Gulf of Taranto, both of classic fame and of considerable maritime importance. The bridge recently finished was constructed with a view to the ready passage of large vessels. It consists of two half-arcs meeting above the middle of the strait. Each half is moved by machinery driven by two turbines of 14-horse power. The halves are raised and rotated, the lifting motion being given by four nuts worked by an endless screw, and the rotation effected through large wheels at the end of the abutment. The turbines are driven by water from a reservoir, and the

distance between abutments is 188 feet. A test-load of 280 tons was left for 24 hours upon the bridge, and caused a deflection of less than 3¼ inches, or about half what was allowed in the specifications. On the removal of the load, the deflection disappeared altogether.

Stiffened Suspension Bridges.—A peculiar type of suspension bridge, known as Garson's patent, has been adopted by the British authorities in India, which is believed to secure greater stability with less weight of metal, for small bridges, than any previously adopted plan. The usual plan has been to adopt side girders for small suspension bridges, but this involved too much weight and too great cost. The distribution of stress is stated as follows: *Upper chain.*—Stress at center equal to zero, increases toward piers until it reaches a maximum. *Lower horizontal member.*—Stress at abutments equal to zero, increases toward center, where it

STIFFENED SUSPENSION BRIDGE.—SIDE VIEW.

reaches a maximum. *Diagonal braces.*—Stress horizontal, almost equalized, and of small amount. The bridge is hinged at the center, so that it can rise and fall with changes of temperature. The pins are of wrought-iron or steel, and are hinged at the base and connected at the summit, so that the stress on them is always axial. The stress on the foundations is purely in the nature of a vertical load.

The bridges are built in Glasgow in 70-foot spans complete, and are delivered in Calcutta for $625 each, the weight being 137 cwt.

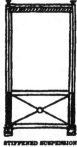

STIFFENED SUSPENSION BRIDGE.—CROSS SECTION.

Other notable bridges are finished or in course of construction, namely, across the Harlem river at 181st Street, New York city, across the Missouri river, near Kansas City, and the Rulo Bridge over the same river. The Hawkesbury river bridge in New South Wales is well under way in charge of American contractors, and it may be said, in conclusion, that American systems of bridge construction are commanding the respectful attention of engineers the world over.

Suspension Foot-Bridge at Oak Park, Ill.—Among the feats of noteworthy amateur engineering is a bridge described by the "Scientific American" as the work of amateurs, young men "just in their twenties." It crosses the Desplaines river with a central span of 125 feet. One bank of the river is a bluff, upon which a concrete tower was erected. On the other bank an elm-tree, having double trunks nearly side by side, was used, the bridge passing between them to a concrete anchorage 75 feet distant. The anchorage on the bluff side is afforded by an oak-tree, to which the cables are made fast near its base. The cables are five eighths of an inch in diameter and are four in number, two of them being merely auxiliary. The footway is about four feet wide, and the whole structure weighs only 2,750 pounds. It has borne a test-strain of fifteen men standing together upon it, and is constantly used by foot-passengers as means of transit.

Dams.—The near completion of the Vyrnwy dam in Wales, for the water-supply of Liverpool, England, and the beginning of work on the great dam at Quaker Bridge, N. Y., for the supply of New York city, are among the largest engineering works of the day. In connection with them it may be well to consider the other great dams of the world, ancient and modern, for the construction of reservoirs dates back to prehistoric times, and bore a conspicuous part in the oldest civilizations. Herodotus describes the lake of Moeris as formed by the Egyptians for husbanding the surplus of the Nile floods, and within a year or two there has been some talk of reconstructing the ancient canals and restoring the lake to its former usefulness. The same writer mentions the reservoir of Nebuchadnezzar at Sippara, which is said to have been 140 miles in circumference—a statement that must be taken with some grains of allowance. Certain it is that in Egypt, Asia, India, Ceylon, and China, vast works were executed for the retention of the surplus rain-fall of the winter months. Some of these ancient earthworks and masonry have wholly disappeared, but traces of others still remain. Conspicuous among them are the reservoirs of Cummum, Kala-Weva, and Horra Bera, in Hindostan. Most of the dams are in ruins now, but have been surveyed, and evince a very creditable degree of engineering skill. The first named, though perhaps the oldest, is still serviceable. The embankment is 102 feet high, with a breadth on top of 76 feet, and a base of about 800 feet. The lake that it created, when perfect, was about 15 square miles in area. The ruins of the dam of Kala-Weva are 12 miles long, and the lake, when full, must have been 40 miles in circumference. That of Horra-Bera is from 50 to 70 feet high, between 3 and 4 miles long, and controlled a lake 8 or 10 miles long and 3 or 4 miles wide.

The advance from earthwork to masonry marks a long step toward theoretical perfection. Most of the great masonry dams have been constructed within the present century. Sections of several of them are shown on the next page in outline, resting upon a common base for ease of comparison, and having a scale in feet at the left.

The Puentes Dam, No. 5, is in Spain, and is almost identical in its elements with the Alicante dam in the same country. Its height is 164 feet, and its width 65 feet at crest. It was built about three centuries ago. The sides of the valley at Puentes were rock, but the bottom was untrustworthy, and a heavy arch of masonry was thrown across, springing from solid rock, and upon this the dam was built, the under space being filled in with walling. The locality was liable to sudden and violent floods, and probably the great width at top was provided in view of unavoidable overflows, covering the entire extent of the dam and calling for great weight, the elements of pressures not being fully understood at that time. It was not practicable to construct side overflows. A very large amount of sand and silt is brought down these streams, and to get rid of it a somewhat primitive method was adopted. Two openings were provided at the base of the dam, the upper end being stopped with loose timber, while the lower end was closed by iron doors. When the accumulation of silt necessitated flushing the dam the iron gates were opened, and workmen sent in to break out the timber screen. If they had good luck it was hoped that the silt would keep back the rush of water long enough for them to escape, but, if not, they must take their chances.

Of modern dams, that at Furens is the most famous of those actually finished. It was built from designs by Messrs. Graiff and Grand-

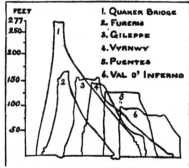

FEET
277
250
200
150
100
50

1. QUAKER BRIDGE
2. FURENS
3. GILEPPE
4. VYRNWY
5. PUENTES
6. VAL D' INFERNO

SECTIONS OF GREAT DAMS.

Champs between the years 1859 and 1866, and was intended partly to protect the town from freshets, and partly to afford a perennial water-supply. Its cross section is shown in the engraving. Its plan is a curve on a radius of 828 feet from a center on the down-stream side. It is founded on compact granite, a trench 8 feet deep having been quarried out to prevent slipping. The material is rubble masonry, laid in courses of 5 feet, and carried up to a height of 184 feet. At the base it is 110 feet thick, and 9 feet 8 inches at the crest. The calculations aimed for a pressure of about 95 pounds to the square inch. The dam contains about 52,000 cubic yards of masonry, and the cost of erection was $180,400. The capacity of the reservoir is 352,000,-000 gallons. The reservoir discharges its surplus water through two tunnels, leading through a hill into an adjacent valley, where such power as is constant is usefully employed.

Another famous structure is the Gileppe Dam at Verviers, Belgium, No. 3. It was finished in 1875, under the supervision of M. Bodson. It differs largely from the Furens section, and, indeed, from the best theories of dam-construction. This was rendered necessary by the anxiety of down-stream residents, who strongly opposed the construction of the dam, on the ground of danger. It is laid on an arc, described by a radius of 1,640 feet, with a length of 771 feet. The reservoir contains 2,701,687,000 gallons, nearly eight times as much as the reservoir at Furens. The foun-

dations are carried down into solid rock. Its total height is 154 feet, and the width of the crest, which carries a roadway, is 49 feet. The base is 216 feet thick. The outlet pipes, always a source of danger, are carried through a hill at some distance from the end of the dam.

Another great Spanish dam is on the river Lozoyera, and supplies water to the city of Madrid. It is known as the Villar Dam. The capacity of its reservoir is 4,400,000,000 gallons, nearly thirteen times that of Furens. It is built on a sharp curve, the radius being 440 feet, and the length of the dam, on the crest, 546 feet. A curve like this probably adds considerably to the strength of a short dam. The material is rubble masonry in hydraulic mortar, costing $402,780.

The Vyrnwy Dam, shown in section in No. 4, crosses the Vyrnwy river in North Wales. The area that will be flooded is, or was, a charming region, largely occupied by villas and country-seats, and, of course, involving a large amount of outlay in property rights. The dam will impound an area of 1,115 acres. It is 1,255 feet long, built of Cyclopean rubble set in mortar, and with the interspaces filled with cement-concrete. The individual masses weigh from 2 to 8 tons each, and it is calculated that this method of construction will give exceptional solidity to the wall. The upper face of the dam is coated with cement. The height is 146 feet, and the breadth at base 117 feet 9 inches.

A large dam is building at San Mateo, Cal.,

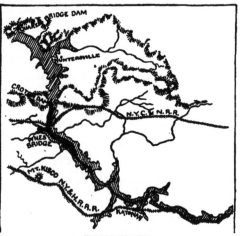

CROTON WATER-SHED.

designed for the water-supply of San Francisco. It is 170 feet high, 176 feet thick at the base, and 20 feet wide, being in shape very much like a truncated pyramid.

No. 6 represents another variety of what may be termed the square-block type of dam, which appears to have been a favorite with Moorish engineers. It is known as the Val d'Inferno, and is in the province of Sarco, Spain.

The dam at Quaker Bridge, N. Y., shown in the diagram, towers above all other structures of the kind, actual or prospective. The lake that will be created will include the present reservoirs, covering the existing dams to a depth of many feet. It will contain something like 40,000,000,000 gallons of water, more or less—a matter of a few million gallons is of small moment where such amounts are concerned. It is estimated that the dam will impound the whole rainfall of the Croton watershed, and will afford an ample supply for the city, even if no rain at all falls for a period of several months. The plans and calculations for this vast structure were drawn by Benjamin S. Church, chief engineer. The estimated strength of the wall is about double what it will ever be called upon to bear. The Croton water-shed, as may be seen from the map, is an irregular valley about 25 miles long by 12 or 15 miles wide.

The dam proper will be 1,350 feet long on the crest, rather more than ¼ of a mile. It will rest in a ditch, quarried out of the solid rock, 216 feet wide at the widest part, and will have an extreme height of 277 feet, decreasing to nothing at the wings. The dam will not be laid on the arc of a circle, that plan being regarded as obsolete for a structure of this size, however it may add to the stability of a short span like that at Furens. The dam is planned to resist by sheer weight any possible pressure that can result from the accumulation of water. The idea that the extent of area increases pressure is wholly erroneous. The pressure of water is due to its depth, not to its extent, as may be readily seen by reference to any authority on hydrostatics. The danger from a large impounded body of water arises, not from the increased pressure upon the restraining dam, but from the cumulative rush of water after a break has occurred. In an earthwork dam, a trifling leak may spread with disastrous rapidity and carry away the whole structure; but a masonry dam, if properly constructed, might be split from crest to base, and would remain in position while the water trickled through the crack.

While the dam is in process of construction, the natural overflow of the Croton river will be confined to an artificial channel running along the side of the valley. An unavoidable danger from freshets must exist while the work is going on, but the habits of the river have long been under close scientific scrutiny, and with existing re-

sources it is unlikely that serious interruptions will occur.

The system of construction is simple. The first work is to lay bare the bed-rock of syenitic gneiss that underlies the whole valley, at a depth of about 90 feet below the river-bed, the width of the trench corresponding with the base of the dam. Two smaller trenches will be made, each 10 feet wide and as many deep, running lengthwise of the dam, and, after all natural fissures in the bed-rock have been filled with hydraulic cement, the trenches will be built in with Cyclopean rubble, as it is termed—namely, large, rough, irregular blocks of stone, laid so as to break joints and filled in with cement, so that the mass becomes as solid as natural rock. All unevenness will be used to anchor the dam beyond the possibility of slipping. Gates and weirs of the best construction will be provided to carry off any overflow during exceptionally wet seasons, and the whole mass of water can be drawn off in case of necessity.

The estimates for the actual cost of construction are $8,000,000, and the contracts contemplate its completion in 1891.

Floating Dock.—An off-shore floating dock for Cardiff, Wales, was constructed at Gray's, near Tilbury, and towed to Cardiff in June. In end elevation the structure resembles the letter L, the horizontal limb, which is in fact the pontoon, being wider than the vertical limb is high. The upright part of the dock is attached to vertical columns on shore by means of booms arranged in pairs, so as to insure parallel motion with the rising or sinking of the dock.

The pontoon, being filled with water, sinks to the desired depth, and the vessel is floated over it with obvious ease, since it can be warped into position broadside on. The keel-blocks and bilge-blocks are all worked by machinery from the top deck, as in all the best modern docks. The pontoon can be held at a level or given an inclination, if a vessel with a considerable list has to be taken up.

Maritime Engineering.—Among the great feats of launching should be noted that of an enormous lumber-raft at Joggins, Nova Scotia. The construction was begun in 1885, the design being to tow the completed raft to New York, and thereby save expense, and at the same time bring to market larger logs than can be handled on ordinary coasting-vessels. The

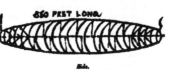
Side.

THE GREAT RAFT.

Cross Section on the Stocks.

first attempt failed, the ways breaking down under the enormous weight; but the designer,

H. R. Robinson, of Nova Scotia, made a second attempt, which proved successful, in November, 1887. The raft was 560 feet long, 50 feet wide, 35 feet deep, and cigar-shaped, as shown in the engraving. A heavy chain-cable ran longitudinally from end to end at the center of the mass, and to this flexible backbone were attached other chains at intervals of ten feet, binding the whole together in a solid, yet more or less elastic mass. Other chains were tightened around the outside, and the swelling of the logs when immersed was counted upon still further to stiffen the whole. No fewer than 25,000 logs were thus lashed together upon launching-ways constructed with the greatest possible strength. In weight the raft largely exceeded any vessel that has ever been launched, and in size nearly equaled the Great Eastern. Its successful management on the ways is certainly a very creditable feat of engineering. The subsequent fate of the raft was not encouraging for a repetition of the experiment. The voyage was undertaken in December, and in tow of an ocean-steamer the raft was towed through several gales and reached a point near Nantucket shoals, when a gale of such violence was encountered that the cables parted and the steamer abandoned her charge. The United States Government at once dispatched vessels to remove such a danger to navigation, and in a few days it was ascertained that the raft had broken up, covering the sea for miles with its fragments.

Under this heading should be mentioned the launching of the Trafalgar (12,000 tons displacement), the largest iron-clad afloat, and the successful raising of the steamers Welles City and Looksley Hall, the first of which was sunk in the Hudson river opposite New York city, and the other in the river Mersey at Liverpool. In both cases wire cables were passed under the sunken vessels, and the rise and fall of the tide utilized in raising them to the surface, so that they could be towed into shoal water for repairs.

Railways.—A few years ago conservative travelers denounced the railway to the summit of Mount Washington as a desecration of nature, and were fond of saying that such outrages would not be permitted in Europe. Since then similar railways have been constructed on Mount Rigi and Mount Pilatus in Switzerland, the last named having been completed within the year. It overcomes steeper grades than any other road of its kind, and such is the rugged character of the mountain that excessive precautions had to be taken to guard against the creeping downward of the rails. The steepest grade of this road is 480 in 1,000. Among the difficulties to be overcome was the provision against expansion and contraction from changes of temperature, which are often abrupt, and in the course of twenty-four hours may cover many degrees. In Russia some of the great government lines are laying double tracks, and the rails are steadily pushing on toward the Asiatic frontier and across Siberia. German contractors have secured a large proportion of the Japanese railways now in course of construction.

In South America the daring schemes of engineers continue to receive encouragement, and the already elaborate system of railways through different regions is being farther extended. It is singular to find at this day that a tramway 200 miles long, with animals for motive power, is under construction in Buenos Ayres. The explanation is, of course, the expensiveness of machinery and the local cheapness of draught-animals.

Transportation by Rail.—The French Government, having recently met with some disasters in sending torpedo-boats from Toulon to Cherbourg by sea, decided to make the attempt to send them by rail. Trucks were constructed for the service. Each had three axles seven feet apart, the end axles having Recour bearings, which enable it to turn readily on a curve of 375 feet radius. The main platform consists of a frame secured to the truck by a main bolt and supported by spherical bearings which rest in guides. On each of the trucks is a large cradle or skid, shaped to correspond with the contour of the boat, and pivoted upon its bed. The two trucks are coupled closely together, forming as it were a single car, with the cradle-pivots about 27 feet apart. To lower the cradles as much as possible the supports are sunk between the wheels, the height of the vessel being, of course, limited by that of the bridges under which it is obliged to pass. The boat selected for the trial was 111 feet long, 11 feet wide, and 9 feet deep, and weighed, when stripped for the journey, 38 tons. Of course all the removable parts were detached before shipment. The line of the keel corresponded always with a line passing through the cradle-pivots, and considerable deflection had to be provided for, since the bow and stern projected, respectively, 44 feet and 38 feet in front and rear of the cradles. There was some danger that this overhang would cause too great a strain, as the iron plates were only three millimetres thick, but the journey of 847 miles was performed with no apparent injury.

The boat occupied the space of about five ordinary cars. The train was moved at a rate of about sixteen miles an hour, except for an experimental test, when the speed was increased to twenty-four miles an hour. It was demonstrated to the satisfaction of the engineers that a boat even larger than the one used could be transported from Toulon to Cherbourg in four days and three nights, and could be ready for service in twenty-four hours after its arrival. This exploit is, beyond doubt, the most considerable feat of ship-transportation by rail ever undertaken, and it goes far to demonstrate the practicability of such transportation, under more favorable conditions, of ships of far greater size.

In this connection may be noticed the shipment from the Krupp gun-foundry at Essen in Westphalia, to Antwerp, of an enormous gun destined for the Italian navy. In this case the inflexibility of the article to be transported simplified the problem, as weight alone had to be considered. This one item, however, was formidable enough. The gun is 45 feet long, 16 inches caliber, and weighs 118 tons. The special truck constructed for the trip weighed 98 tons. It was 75 feet long, and rested on 82 wheels. The trucks were adjusted so that at six different points deflections could take place for passing curves, without disturbing the adjustment-level of the main platform. The transit was effected without accident and the gun transferred to shipboard at Antwerp. It has since reached its destination at Spezzia. It is worth mentioning that this gun has been two years in making, and two others still larger are at present in the works at Essen.

Wells, Artesian.—The great artesian belt, as it is called, in Kern and Tulare counties, California, contains hundreds of flowing wells, and the importance of economizing the water for purposes of irrigation has led to the adoption of various devices, of which storage reservoirs are the simplest and, when all the circumstances favor, are perhaps cheapest and best. Some of the wells deliver 2,500,000 gallons of water every day, and, taking the whole artesian belt, it is probable that 100,000,000 gallons of water run daily to waste. If it found its way promptly into natural water-courses this would not be particularly objectionable, but the conformation of the country is such that it often stays where it is not wanted and rarely goes of its own accord where it is wanted. There is a State law requiring such wells to be capped when not in actual use, but it has heretofore been a dead letter. The nuisance of waste water threatens now to become so serious that the best systems of capping are of prime importance. The illustration shows the cap that controls a large well recently sunk for the Miramonte Colony in Kern County. A is an 8-inch elbow of cast-iron; B is a water-cap or gate of the same diameter; C is the gate-flange; D is a 10-inch casing; E is the small connection and pipe; F is the anchor of concrete; G, the cast-iron flange; H, the 8-inch casing, and I, the sand and cement between the casings. In beginning the work, the 10-inch water-tight casing of galvanized iron was put down forty feet. To the outside of the casing, nine feet below the surface of the ground, was riveted a cast-iron collar and flange, on top of which cement was poured, forming a roughly-circular block, four feet in diameter and a foot thick. When this "set," the earth was filled in above it, and it formed a very secure bar against upward movement. At the upper end of the 10-inch casing is a flange and collar with a water-valve gate, and above it a cast-iron elbow to divert the water. Everything being in place, the well proper was started in-

side the 10-inch casing, well-pieces, 8 inches in diameter, being sunk in the usual manner, and the space between the 8-inch and 10-inch

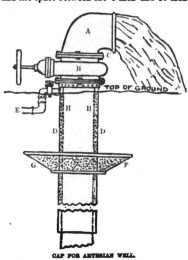

CAP FOR ARTESIAN WELL.

casings filled with sand and cement. The small opening in the side of the casings is intended to connect with a 3-inch pipe to lead the water to houses, barns, etc. When the cap is closed there is, of course, a heavy pressure in the well and all its connections, but it has thus far shown no signs of weakness. The multiplication of artesian wells renders their successful management a matter of considerable moment. Another remarkable well of this character is that recently bored for the new Ponce de Leon Hotel at St. Augustine, Fla. It is 12 inches in diameter, 1,400 feet deep, and flows with a constant volume estimated at 10,000,000 gallons of excellent water daily. It issues from the pipe with sufficient force to rise about 20 feet perpendicularly. The mouth of the well is ten feet above tide-water. The geological formations pierced were sand, small shells, and blue-clay rock, while at a depth of 450 feet a good supply of water was struck. At a depth of 520 feet a large accession of water occurred, and again after, at a depth of 1,100 feet, passing through coral and limestone. The drilling was continued through sandstone and limestone to 1,400 feet, but no advantage was gained thereby. The temperature steadily rose as the depth increased, and reached 86° at the bottom of the boring. Only two months were occupied in the work, the strata being generally easy to penetrate. American engineers have been very successful in sinking artesian wells, but much time and money are annually wasted in ill-advised attempts to sink wells where there is no reason for suspecting the existence of a water supply. The Athletic Club of New York city recently sunk a well under their house and obtained a fine yield of water, but, hoping for still better results, the drill was pushed still farther, when the "bottom dropped out," and the water all went down instead of upward. Such failures must occasionally happen, since at best the location of a well is a matter of uncertainty.

Harbor Improvement.—The port of Ceará, capital of the Brazilian province of the same name,

dragging their anchors and going ashore. The breakwater is placed so as to afford shelter from the prevailing winds, and is of simple construction. The principal quay is of solid concrete, and is connected with the shore by a viaduct of iron and steel 750 feet long. A railway runs the entire length of the structure, alongside of which vessels drawing 19 feet of water can lie even at low tide, the rise and fall being 6 feet. The works are constructed under an imperial concession from the emperor

HARBOR OF CEARÁ, BRAZIL.

has long been one of the principal South American ports at which foreign steamers call, and with which a considerable commerce has sprung up within the last generation. Prior to the erection of the works illustrated herewith, the port hardly deserved the name, since

of Brazil, and it is estimated that the income from port-dues will amount to at least $100,-000 per annum. The fine granite used in the construction of the work and of the adjoining custom-house buildings is quarried about sixteen miles from the port, and brought by rail

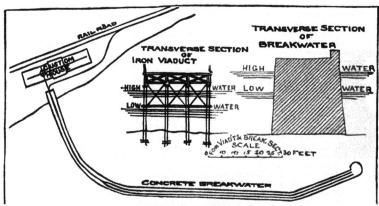

PLAN OF THE CEARÁ BREAKWATER.

the only anchorage was an open roadstead, and all goods and passengers had to pass between ship and shore by means of small boats or lighters. The situation was very dangerous for vessels receiving or discharging cargo, and it was often necessary for large vessels to run out to sea in order to escape the danger of

direct to the works. Railroads already existing afford communication with an inland region rich in all the staples of South American commerce. The engineers in charge are Messrs. R. E. Wilson and R. T. H. Saunders, both of England, and the work is done by a firm of English contractors.

EVANGELICAL ALLIANCE. The American branch of the Evangelical Alliance in March issued an appeal to the public in behalf of a closer and more intelligent co-operation on the part of Christians for defense against the many and great perils with which American institutions and Christian civilization seem to be threatened. Such co-operation, it was believed, would strengthen every denomination and greatly increase the effectiveness of each. Many prominent men of different denominations had expressed the belief that the Evangelical Alliance of the United States was a medium through which the desired co-operation could be naturally sought and easily effected. The alliance therefore would labor to promote this object, by the organization of branch alliances, which, being formed so far as practicable in every community, would afford opportunities for meeting and discussing the situation, and devising plans for the co-operation of the churches; by holding annually great conventions, the discussions of which would be put in print for general distribution; and by making the National Alliance a bureau of information touching religious and reformatory work, in pursuance of which aim carefully prepared tracts, bearing upon different departments of the subject, would be issued at short intervals. In accordance with the motives of this appeal, a National Christian Conference was called by the Alliance, and was held in the city of Washington, December 7, 8 and 9, for the discussion of the following questions: "What are the present perils and opportunities of the Christian Church and of the country?" "Can any of them be met best by a hearty co-operation of all Evangelical Christians, which, without detriment to any denominational interests, will serve the welfare of the whole Church?" "What are the best means to secure such co-operation and to awaken the whole Church to its responsibility?" Mr. William E. Dodge, President of the Evangelical Alliance, made an opening address, in which he dwelt upon the necessity of bringing the truths of Christianity to bear upon the social and economical questions of the day, and insisted upon their power, with the forces which they had in reserve, to meet the perils of the time, and find a solution for its perplexing problems. The several meetings on successive days were presided over in turn by the Hon. John Jay, Mr. Justice Strong, of the United States Supreme Court; Senator Colquitt, of Georgia; Mr. Justice Harlan; President Angell, of the University of Michigan; and Senator Hawley, of Connecticut. Subjects pertaining to the objects of the Conference were discussed in stated papers and addresses, as follows: "The City as a Peril," Rev. Daniel Dorchester, D.D., Rev. S. J. McPherson, D. D., and Rev. Mr. Loomis, of Brooklyn, N. Y.; "Immigration," Professor Hjalmar H. Boyesen, Rev. S. L. Baldwin, and Rev. J. M. Foster; "The Misuse of Wealth," President Gates, of Rutgers College, and Rev. Robert C. Matlack; "Estrangement from the Church," Bishop J. M. Hurst and Rev. Arthur T. Pierson; "Ultramontanism," Bishop A. C. Coxe; "Jesuitism," Rev. J. M. King, D. D.; "The Saloon," Rev. R. S. McArthur, D. D., Rev. A. G. Haygood, D. D.; "Perils to the Family," Rev. S. W. Dike; "The Social Vice," Col. J. L. Greene, Rev. J. C. Thomas, D. D., Prof. S. E. Baldwin; "Illiteracy," Gen. John Eaton and Mr. N. M. Butler; "The Relation of the Church to Capital and Labor," Rev. James McCosh, D. D., Hon. Seth Low, and others; "The Christian Resources of our Country," Rev. J. M. King, D. D.; "Influence of the Universities on the Religious Character of the Nation," President Gilman, of Johns Hopkins University; "The Christian Resources of the South," Rev. N. E. Hatcher, D. D.; "Co-operation of Churches in Christian Work," Bishop Samuel Harris, Rev. Washington Gladden, D. D., and Prof. George E. Post, of Beyrout, Syria; "Methods of Co-operation among Christian Denominations," Rev. Josiah Strong, D. D.; "Methods of Co-operation in Large Cities," Rev. A. F. Schauffler, D. D., with discussion of the general subject of "Christian Co-operation," by other speakers; and "Individual Duty, growing out of Perils and Opportunities," Rev. A. J. Gordon, D. D.

EVANGELICAL ASSOCIATION. The following is a summary of the statistical report of the Evangelical Association, which was made to the General Conference at its meeting in September: Number of itinerant preachers, 1,125; of local preachers, 684; of members, 188,668; of Sunday-schools, 2,348, with 27,210 officers and teachers, and 162,837 pupils; number of churches, 1,836, the value of which was estimated at $4,236,948; number of parsonages, 572, having a probable value of $635,589. The returns show an increase in four years of 18,-487 members, or 15½ per cent, while the increase during the preceding four years (1879 to 1883) amounted to 9½ per cent. The value of church property had increased during the past four years 18⅜ per cent., and the Sunday-schools showed an increase of 20 per cent.

The Charitable Society had a capital fund of $24,822, had received an income during the past four years of $5,948, and had expended, during the same time, $5,852. Its capital had increased $1,048 since 1883. The Ebenezer Orphan Home returned a realized endowment fund of $153,375. Its receipts and expenditures for the year were balanced at $11.920. The Publication House returned the value of its assets at $498.483, and reported a gross profit in four years of $131,749; the net increase in the value of its assets during the same time was $51,681.

The total receipts of the Missionary Society for the year had been $189,448. Of the expenditures, $12,144 had been on account of the "European," and $9,888 of the "heathen," treasury. The total receipts for the past four years had been $496,613, and the total expenditures $520,351. The indebtedness of the society had increased in four years $19,710, and was now $40,819. The society possessed funds and real estate to the value of $112,846. It sustained 542 missions, which were served by 552 missionaries, and returned 45,531 members, with 9,904 officers and teachers, and 63,-788 pupils in Sunday-schools. The conferences in Germany and Switzerland reported a joint net increase of 400 members. The mission in Japan returned 8 itinerant preachers, 2 local preachers, 4 churches with 150 members, 7 Sunday-schools with 33 officers and teachers, and an average attendance of 280 pupils, and 18 baptisms during the year. The Woman's Missionary Society was sustained by 77 auxiliaries, with 2,012 members, and had received during the year $1,825.

The General Conference met in Buffalo, N.Y., September 1. The bishops in their quadrennial address reviewed the condition and growth of the church during the past four years, showing increase in every department, particularly in the building of churches, which, with a few local exceptions, had involved no additional debts, and progress in the cause of higher education. The business transacted related chiefly to the special interests of the funds and benevolent enterprises of the church, and to cases of discipline. A motion to permit an extension of the time during which a preacher may remain on a single charge was disapproved. Resolutions passed by the preceding General Conference respecting changes in certain of the articles of faith were rescinded. Regulations were adopted for procuring more exact statistical returns of the denomination. They include provisions for the appointment of a statistical secretary by each annual conference, and a general statistical secretary by the General Conference, and directions to the ministers, regularly and properly to fill out the statistical blanks, and deliver them to the statistical secretary of their conference. The blanks include tables of membership, property, collections, Sunday-schools, and periodicals, and of financial returns. The sense of the Conference was expressed as in favor of more stringent sanctions of marriage, and ministers were advised "not to marry persons who, in consequence of the existing laxity of the divorce laws of the different States, have been divorced." The formation of a stock company in the Germany Conference for improving the security of the church property was approved.

EVENTS OF 1887. A glance at the following list of the events of the year presents in strong contrast the divided interests of Europe and the comparative harmony of the Western Continent. Riot and bloodshed have marked the history of the "Jubilee" year for Great Britain, and she, perhaps, has less to fear from violence than any of the Continental nations. Repeated attempts to assassinate the Emperor of Russia, almost ceaseless mutterings of war,

and political complications that threaten revolution, have been the lot of nearly all the great powers. In this country our only serious foreign complication has been with Canada, whose interests are after all practically identical with ours. Our elections have been free from undue excitement, and anarchy has received a severe though somewhat tardy lesson. The year's disasters will be found under the appropriate head, and details, as of elections and other important local occurrences, will in general be found in the special articles on the different States and countries.

January 1. The Emperor of Germany celebrated the eightieth anniversary of his entrance into the German army.

3. Stephen H. Mayham appointed Judge of the Supreme Court.

4. The Fitchburg Railroad bought the Hoosac Tunnel for $10,000,000.

6. Pension bill appropriating $76,247,500 passed by the House of Representatives; P. C. Lounsbury (Republican) elected Governor of Connecticut by the Legislature, there having been no choice by popular vote.

10. A new British Ministry appointed. (For details, see article on Great Britain.)

11. Congress passed a bill creating a Department of Agriculture and Labor.

12. William M. Stewart elected United States Senator from Nevada.

14. German Reichstag dissolved on the passage of an amendment to Prince Bismarck's army bill, limiting its duration to three years.

17. Dependent pension bill passed by house (179 to 76); pension bill, appropriating $75,000,000, passed by the Senate.

20. Electoral count bill passed by Senate, having already passed the House.

21. Passage by Congress of the interstate commerce bill.

24. Bill authorizing the President to protect the rights of American fishermen passed by Senate (46 to 1).

27. Dependent pension bill passed by Senate; House rejects resolution to have United States Senators elected by popular vote; the harbor appropriation bill passed the Senate. British Parliament opened by the Queen.

28. Bill appropriating $400,000 for State militia passed the Senate.

29. Post-Office appropriation bill passed the House.

31. Agricultural appropriation bill passed the Senate.

February 4. Congress reassembled after the holiday recess, but adjourned at once out of respect to the memory of General John A. Logan; the President signed the interstate commerce bill.

6. Stanley, the African explorer, set out from Zanzibar in command of an expedition for the rescue of Emin Bey.

7. Appropriation for armament and coast defenses ($21,000,000) passed the Senate; Chinese Indemnity bill ($147,750) passed the House.

8. Italian Ministry resigned because of their doubtful position in the Parliament.

10. Chinese indemnity bill passed the Senate.

11. Mr. Parnell's amendment to the reply to the Queen's speech rejected (352 to 246). Dependent pension bill vetoed by the President.

12. Post-Office appropriation bill passed the Senate; bill to redeem and recoin the trade-dollar passed the Senate.

14. Daniel Manning resigned the secretaryship of the Treasury.

15. In honor of Queen Victoria's Jubilee, 25,000

prisoners were released in India. Municipal election in Philadelphia results in a Republican victory by 23,000 plurality.

16. Bill to increase the naval establishment ($22,-000,000) passed the Senate. Woman suffrage in municipal elections, went into effect in Kansas.

21. Election for German Reichstag resulting as follows: Conservative, 81; Imperialist, 39; National Liberal, 100; Center, 97; New German Liberal, 34; Polish, 15; Protester, 15; Socialist, 11; Guelph, 4.

22. Election in Canada resulting in the choice of 112 Ministerialists, 95 Opposition, 8 doubtful. Senator Ingalls elected (pro tem.) to the presidency of the Senate, vice Sherman resigned.

23. Retaliation bill regarding the fisheries dispute passed the House (252 to 1). Private pensions bill passed over the President's veto.

24. Veto of the dependent pensions bill sustained in the House (175 to 125).

25 and 26. Prolonged engagement between the Italians and Abyssinians near Massowah; Italians defeated.

26. Consular, diplomatic, and agricultural appropriation bills passed the Senate ($1,429,942.14).

March 1. Fisheries retaliatory bill as proposed in the Senate agreed to by the House; legislative and deficiency appropriation bills passed the House. Mr. Parnell twice defeated in the British House of Commons on motions relative to the clôture.

2. Naval appropriation passed by Senate ($25,-753,165.44).

3. Opening of the new German Reichstag (see February 21). Legislative appropriation bill passed by the Senate ($20,701,221.67); Mexican pensions bill passed by the Senate ($6,000,000.96).

4. Sunday civil appropriation bill passed by the Senate ($22,862,490); end of the Forty-ninth Congress; both Houses adjourned.

11. The seven years' army bill passed the Reichstag (227 to 31).

12. Schooner yachts Coronet and Dauntless sailed from New York for an ocean race to Queenstown.

13. An unsuccessful attempt made to assassinate the Czar of Russia; many arrests.

19. Bill for the redemption of trade-dollars passed both Houses.

21. River and harbor appropriation bill passed the Senate.

22. Interstate Commerce Commission appointed by the President. Ninetieth birthday anniversary of the Emperor of Germany.

24. Oscar S. Straus, of New York, appointed Minister to Austria.

27. Schooner yacht Coronet reached Queenstown.

28. Mr. Balfour moved the Irish crimes bill in the House of Commons.

31. The President made an allotment of land to the Warm Spring Indians under the new law; Charles S. Fairchild appointed Secretary of the Treasury vice Manning, resigned.

April 1. The Irish Crimes bill passed its first reading by application of clôture (361 to 253).

4. In Michigan a Constitutional amendment prohibiting the sale of liquor was defeated by about 5,000 majority.

6. John W. Davis, Democrat, elected Governor of Rhode Island.

12. The Governor of New York vetoed the Crosby high license bill.

13. Opening of the Dominion Parliament.

14. The body of Abraham Lincoln removed to its final resting-place at Springfield, Ill.

16. Gen. Alexander R. Lawton appointed Minister to Austria-Hungary.

18. The Irish crimes bill passed its second reading in Parliament of Great Britain.

20. The Queen of Hawaii and suite arrived in San Francisco.

21. A French official, Schnaebeles by name, was arrested as a spy by German police near Pagny-sur-

Moselle, and much excitement followed, but a peaceful solution was at last reached.

26. Resolutions against the Irish coercion bill were passed in the Canadian Parliament. Monument to John C. Calhoun unveiled at Charleston, S. C.

27. The ecclesiastical bill passed the Prussian House (243 to 100).

29. The British House of Commons declined to substitute the word "crime" for "offense" in the coercion bill.

30. Commissary Schnaebeles released by the Germans.

May 1. Convention announced between England and Turkey looking to the evacuation of Egypt in 1890. Turkey cedes to England the island of Cyprus.

11. James W. Hyatt, of Connecticut, appointed Treasurer of the United States vice Conrad N. Jordan, resigned.

12. Monument to James A. Garfield unveiled in Washington. Annexation of Zululand by Great Britain. French crown-jewels sold.

17. The French ministry resigned on the rejection of its financial scheme by the Chamber of Deputies.

19. Samuel Pasco chosen United States Senator from Florida.

June 14. A bill granting a temporary extension of the franchise on a property qualification passed by the Dutch Parliament.

21. Jubilee celebration in honor of the fiftieth anniversary of Victoria's accession to the throne of Great Britain.

27. British House of Commons passed the Irish crimes bill (349 to 262). The French Chamber of Deputies rejects a measure providing for the election of Senators by universal vote. Cutter-yacht Genesta won the Jubilee yacht-race around Great Britain.

29. Jacob Sharp convicted of bribing the Board of Aldermen of New York city.

30. Bloodless revolution in Hawaii. The King forced to grant concessions demanded by citizens of Honolulu.

July 1. Yale won the University boat-race.

3. Meeting of veterans on the battle-field of Gettysburg.

4. Equestrian statue of Gen. Ambrose E. Burnside dedicated at Providence, R. I.

7. Mormon convention at Utah adopted a constitution for a proposed new State, separating Church and State, and forbidding polygamy. Prince Ferdinand, of Saxe-Coburg-Gotha, elected Prince of Bulgaria by the Sobranje. British House of Lords abolished primogeniture in cases of intestacy.

9. Rev. Dr. Edward McGlynn excommunicated by Archbishop Corrigan.

14. Jacob Sharp found guilty of bribing New York Board of Aldermen; sentenced to four years' imprisonment and $5,000 fine.

19. Queen Victoria assented to the Irish crimes bill.

23. Review of the British Navy off Spithead in honor of Queen Victoria's Jubilee.

During the month elections in Hungary resulted in the choice of 224 Liberals, 59 Independents, and 38 Moderate Oppositionists; Otto, King of Bavaria, was officially declared insane; and a bill was passed by the Belgian Chamber of Deputies exempting, with limitations, the pay of clerks and laborers from legal process.

August 1. Election in Kentucky; Gen. S. B. Buckner (Democrat) chosen Governor by 17,000 plurality.

2. An unsuccessful attempt was made to assassinate the Czar of Russia.

4. Election in Texas: vote on Prohibitionist constitutional amendment, 127,273 for, and 221,627 against.

5. Land bill passed to a third reading in the British House of Commons. Conviction in Chicago of eleven city officials for receiving bribes.

9. Fight in Colorado between Ute Indians and State troops; 4 Indians killed. Celebration at Monmouth, England, of the five hundredth anniversary of the birth of Henry V.

14. Prince Ferdinand, of Saxe-Coburg-Gotha, installed ruler of Bulgaria; the ministry resigned at once, and the Sobranje was dissolved.

15. Contracts for new United States cruisers and gun-boats awarded by the Secretary of the Navy.

19. Proclamation of the Irish National League announced in the British House of Lords.

25. Mr. Gladstone, in the British House of Commons, moved an amendment to the Queen, asking the withdrawal of the proclamation; motion lost by 272 to 194.

September 1. Annual meeting of the American Library Association at Round Island, N. Y.

2. New Bulgarian Cabinet announced, with M. Stambuloff as Prime Minister.

3–5. Annual encampment of the Grand Army of the Republic at St. Louis, Mo.

4. Meeting of the Irish National League at Ennis, Ireland, in defiance of the Queen's proclamation.

5. Labor Day, a holiday legalized by the State of New York, and now observed for the first time. The 9th International Medical Congress met in Washington; more than 4,000 physicians in attendance.

15–17. Celebration in Philadelphia of the framing of the United States Constitution.

16. British Parliament prorogued. Mexican Congress opened by President Diaz.

19. Parliament of Holland opened by King William.

21. Launch of the Trafalgar at Portsmouth, England. She is the largest iron-clad ever constructed.

24. William O'Brien, the Irish agitator, found guilty of seditious language and sentenced to three months' imprisonment. A party of French sportsmen fired upon by German guards near the frontier at Raon-sur-Plaine, 1 killed, 1 wounded; much international excitement followed but an amicable arrangement was finally reached.

25. Encounter between the police and the people at Mitchelstown, Ireland.

27–30. International yacht-race between British cutter Thistle and American sloop Volunteer; won by Volunteer.

28. The Jubilee receptions of the Pope began at Rome, Italy.

29. The Hungarian Parliament opened. Election in Tennessee; constitutional amendment in favor of prohibition defeated by 27,893 majority.

October 1. Official scandal in French army circles concerning the alleged sale of decorations; Generals Boulanger and Caffarel involved and placed under arrest.

3. General convention of Knights of Labor at Minneapolis.

9. Elections in Bulgaria; 258 supporters of the Government were elected against 27 Oppositionists.

14–17. Riotous demonstrations in London on the part of the homeless poor.

18. Bronze statue of Gen. George Gordon Meade unveiled in Fairmount Park, Philadelphia. Shakespeare Memorial, presented by George W. Childs of Philadelphia, dedicated at Stratford-upon-Avon, England.

27. Corner-stone of the monument to Gen. R. E. Lee laid at Richmond, Va.

29. Statue of Lief Erikson, the Norse explorer, unveiled at Boston, Mass.

November 8. Elections were held in eleven of the United States (details will be found in the special articles on those States).

12. Four convicted anarchists and rioters hanged in Chicago (the sentences of two others were commuted to imprisonment and another committed suicide in his cell).

16. Bronze statue unveiled at Lexington, Ky., in memory of John C. Breckenridge.

17. John Most, anarchist, arrested for uttering incendiary language.

18. Centennial Anniversary of the Methodist Episcopal Church, held in Brooklyn, N. Y. The Czar and Czarina of Russia made a state visit to Berlin.

24. Yale won the college championship at football, defeating Harvard by a score of 17 to 8.

27. Riotous demonstrations at Limerick, Ireland, on the occasion of a mass meeting to honor the memory of Irish patriots.

29. The Court of Appeals of the State of New York reversed judgment of the lower court in the conviction of Jacob Sharp for bribing the Board of Aldermen of New York city.

December 1. Jacob Sharp released on bail to the amount of $40,000.

2. President Grévy, of France, resigned his office amid great excitement.

3. Marie François Sadi-Carnot chosen President of the French Republic.

5. The Fiftieth Congress of the United States met and organized.

6. The President's message was read to Congress.

7–10. General Conferences of Evangelical Christians in Washington.

8. John Most, the anarchist, sentenced to one year's confinement at hard labor in the penitentiary.

11. Attempted assassination of Jules Ferry in the hall of the Chamber of Deputies by a lunatic.

12. E. L. Harper, lately President of the Fidelity Bank of Cincinnati, sentenced to ten years in the penitentiary for misappropriation of bank funds.

15. National convention of Republican clubs in New York city.

20. Large lumber-raft abandoned at sea while towing from Nova Scotia to New York; raft subsequently broken up by the sea.

21. Steamship Great Eastern sold, to be broken up. Independence of Corea recognized by China.

31. The Pope celebrated the 50th anniversary of his ordination into the priesthood.

F

FINANCIAL REVIEW OF 1887. This year was one of peace and prosperity. Although at intervals political affairs in Europe were in a state of extreme tension, no serious results followed, and the preparations which some of the Continental nations made during the year for offensive or defensive operations may, unless some accident should occur, prevent the collision which has so long been expected. In France the change in the Presidency from M. Grévy to M. Sadi-Carnot was attended with even less friction than sometimes results from a municipal election or a senatorial contest in this country. In Germany the efforts of the nonagenarian Emperor and of his Prime Minister were devoted to the maintenance of peaceful relations with neighboring nations, while at the same time the military and financial strength of the Empire was materially augmented. Russia was restless and apparently continually on the alert for a pretext for war, but at the same time she carefully avoided entanglements with any of the great powers. England enjoyed a season of political repose, broken only by occasional disturbances among some of her Irish subjects.

The trade of European nations appears to have been prosperous, and the financial condition of all, with the exception of Russia, shows an improvement.

In this country nothing of a disturbing character occurred; the laws were enforced, anarchical demonstrations were suppressed, and the growth of socialism was materially checked. The organization of the Knights of Labor was, at the close of the year, less formidable than it was at the beginning. Apparently, members of the association found that their leaders had, in too many instances, been governed more by a desire for personal gain than for the good of the order, and gradually the power of the executive officers lessened, and disintegration of the organization commenced. The most serious blow which the order received was in February, when members of a district association refused to quit work for the purpose of assisting in the strike of the long-shoremen and coal-handlers. The rebellion quickly spread to other districts of the Knights, and then those who had by blind obedience to the demands of their leaders suffered privation, sought to return to their former employment only to find their places filled. The signal failure of this strike encouraged employers to resist unjust demands when made by their workmen, and the result was more peaceful if not harmonious relations between capital and labor. Manufacturing interests revived, and in almost all branches they were active and attended with profitable results. The workmen had steady employment at fair wages in place of the irregular labor from which they suffered during the greater part of the previous year, and, in view of this experience, doubtless the large majority of intelligent laborers decided at the first opportunity to abandon the organization which, while promising so much, resulted in so little real benefit.

That the year was a prosperous one for agriculturists is shown by the fact that our crop of wheat is valued at $419,520,000; that of corn at $917,280,000, and that of cotton at $334,620,000, making a total of $1,671,420,000. The production of anthracite coal is valued at not far from $140,000,000. The construction of nearly 13,000 miles of railroad called for the distribution of about $254,000,000 among the iron and steel manufacturers, land-owners, and men who were employed upon the work. The speculation in lands and town sites West and South brought fortunes to those who were in a position to benefit by the rise in values. The industrial development of the South was in some instances marvelous. Earnings of railroads in almost every section of the country were unprecedentedly great. Capitalists obtained satisfactory returns for the money they had to loan or had invested in banking or other enterprises. Commerce was generally in a flourishing condition, and, although mercantile failures were in excess of those for 1886, doubtless many resulted from the unprofitable operations of previous years.

The silver question, which was a source of anxiety in 1886, had less of a disturbing influence, mainly because of the utilization of the coinage through the issue of silver certificates of small denominations, which, to a considerable extent, satisfied the want for currency, and therefore proved of great public convenience. The report of the Treasurer of the United States shows that during the fiscal year ending June 30, 1887, 27·8 per cent. of the receipts for customs at the port of New York consisted of United States notes, 59½ of gold certificates, and 12 of silver certificates. During the previous fiscal year the percentage of the latter was 13·1, and for the year ending June 30, 1885, it was 35·6 per cent. This is an indication that the withdrawal of small United States notes and the substitution of silver certificates of low denomination was a wise measure, resulting in keeping the latter in active circulation. With a view to prevent the embarrassment which may some time occur from the continued coinage of the standard dollar, the Secretary of the Treasury, in his report to Congress, suggested that the 214,000,000 silver dollars in the Treasury at the date of his report will more than suffice to redeem all the silver certificates that can be issued against all the dollars which will be coined for years to come under the present act, and he therefore advised that the law be so amended as to authorize the Secretary to issue certificates against the coining value of the bullion bought, and to coin only such number of dollars as he might deem expedient.

The constantly accumulating surplus in the Treasury was a source of great anxiety during the last half of the year, and the conviction that the Secretary was unable, without further authority of law, to distribute this surplus, induced bank-officers to pursue a very conservative course, fearing trouble should an emergency arise. The President and the Secretary promptly called the attention of Congress to the subject, and asked for early legislation, at the same time suggesting a remedy for the evil. Toward the close of the year some bankers feared that the action taken by Congress might compel the Secretary to withdraw from the depository banks a large proportion of the funds he had placed therein for the purpose of assisting in relieving the money market; but these fears were partially allayed when it was seen that the withdrawal could be gradually made, and that if the money should be taken for government disbursements it would pass from one bank to another like any other deposit, and thus remain in the channels of trade.

While legitimate business in almost all branches was good and generally profitable during the year, speculation was not attended with satisfactory results. The attempt to corner coffee and wheat in June met with a disastrous failure, and the subsequent manipulation of wheat at San Francisco seriously involved all the parties connected with it. Toward the close of the year there was a very decided rise in copper, caused by the operations of a foreign syndicate who had obtained control of the product. Few, outside the cliques, made money in stocks, and the majority of the non-professional speculators were unfortunate in their ventures.

The following tabular survey of the economical conditions and results of 1887 contrasted with those of the preceding year, is from official returns, and also from the "Commercial and Financial Chronicle":

ECONOMICAL CONDITIONS AND RESULTS.	1886.	1887.
Coin and currency in the United States, November 1	$1,586,271,000	$1,678,009,950
Mercantile failures	114,644,119	167,560,944
Imports of merchandise	666,429,189	708,807,811
Exports of merchandise	718,404,021	715,320,956
Imports of gold and silver	58,592,646	61,661,918
Exports of gold and silver	68,389,196	86,789,414
Railroads constructed, miles	8,648	12,724
Gross earnings, 110 railroads	316,046,287	360,259,567
Wheat raised, bushels	457,000,000	456,000,000
Corn raised, bushels	1,665,000,000	1,456,000,000
Cotton raised, bales	6,412,000	6,650,000
Pig-iron produced, net tons	6,365,328	7,187,206
Anthracite coal produced, tons	32,136,362	34,641,017
Petroleum, barrels	26,043,645	21,570,000
Immigration	386,681	509,281

The prices of leading staples on or about Jan. 1, 1888, compared with prices at the same date in 1887 and 1886, were as follow:

	1886.	1887.	1888.
Cotton, middling uplands, per pound	9¼	9¼	10 3/16
Wool, American XX, per pound	37	34 @ 38	31½ @ 32½
Iron, American pig No. 1, per ton	$18 00 @ $18 50	$20 00 @ $21 00	$21 00 @ $21 50
Steel rails at mills	$34 00 @ $35 00	$37 00	$32 00 @ $33 00
Wheat, No. 2 red winter, per bushel	92½	93½	92
Corn, Western mixed No. 2, per bushel	50½	48½	63
Pork, mess, per barrel	$10 00 @ $10 25	$12 50 @ $12 75	$15 50 @ $16 00

The Money Market.—The range for the year for money on call, represented by bankers' balances, was from 67 per cent., June 30, to 1 per cent., August 18. The highest rate was in part due to manipulation, but mainly to the disturbance resulting from the collapse of the wheat-corner at Chicago and the subsequent failure of the Fidelity National Bank at Cincinnati. The lowest rate simply reflected a temporary absence of demand toward the close of the day's business. During the first quarter of the year the range for bankers' balances was from 8 to 1½ per cent., averaging about 4. For the next quarter the range was from 20 to 2½ per cent., averaging 6. During the third quarter there was a range of from 67 to 1 per cent., the average falling from 10 to 5. Thereafter, for the remainder of the year, bankers' balances ranged from 10 to 2 per cent., averaging 4½. Commercial paper of 60 to 90 days' date, and first class, was comparatively easy during the first quarter at from 4½ to 6 per cent., and at this period time-loans on stock collateral, running from four to five months, gradually became in good request, borrowers anticipating active money and desiring to make early provision. This inquiry for time-loans was so urgent during the next six months that rates advanced from 4 to 6 per cent., and very little could be done in commercial paper; and late in September merchants were unable to obtain discounts except at high rates, and in some cases 9 and even 15 per cent. were paid for the accommodation. For the last quarter of the year the tendency was toward ease for commercial paper, and time-loans were renewed at 5 @ 6 per cent. for 30 days to four and five months, but chiefly by out-of-town institutions, our city banks, during the month of December, preferring to loan on call, thus keeping bankers' balances unusually low for the season. The Comptroller of the Currency, under the act of March 30, 1887, on the application of banks at Chicago and St. Louis, early in the year made those cities central reserve centers, requiring the banks to keep 25 per cent. of their reserve at home. This, to some extent, assisted in the withdrawal of balances held in New York to the credit of institutions in these new reserve cities, and the money thus sent to Chicago and St. Louis was retained. Speculation in farm-lands and real-estate mortgages, extensions of railroads in the Western country, and active business throughout that section and in the South, altogether contributed to drain the banks of New York of the balances owing to interior institutions, and fears that the wild speculation in wheat and in other staples and in mortgages upon farms of uncertain value would some day suddenly collapse, induced our bankers to pursue a very conservative course, which, in many cases, resulted in injury to mercantile interests, especially in the city. The break in the wheat and coffee corners, June 14 and 15, and the disastrous results which followed seemed to justify bank-managers in continuing their conservative course, and appeals were made to the Secretary of the Treasury to relieve, by purchases of bonds, the monetary stringency which threatened all commercial interests. The Secretary had, up to and including May 20, called in $63,612,250 3-per-cent. bonds for redemption, the last call on the above-named date being for $19,717,500 on all the outstanding bonds of this issue, and this call matured July 1. After consideration of the urgent needs of the country, the Secretary, on August 4, directed that the interest due at various dates, to and including January 1, be paid with a rebate of 2 per cent. per annum, and also that 4½-per-cent. bonds be purchased for the sinking-fund each week. After $11,565,300 had been so bought up to September 21, the supply became so limited that further purchases could not be made with profit to the

Government. The money market had been only temporarily relieved by this policy of the Secretary, and therefore he decided, on September 22, to buy 4- as well as 4½-per-cent bonds to the extent of $14,000,000, also for the sinking-fund, and to pay, without rebate, $6,-500,000 interest due October 1. Purchases of about $13,000,000 of these bonds were made, thus completing the sinking-fund requirements for the current fiscal year. This resulted in a little easier feeling, and the market was further relieved by the increase, commencing in October, of the number of the depository banks throughout the country and the augmentation of the amount of public money which each bank was entitled to hold. As this increase in the deposits naturally called for United States bonds as security, no further purchases of them could be profitably made, even if the Secretary had authority of law therefor. Both the President and the Secretary of the Treasury called the attention of Congress, at the opening of the session in December, to the fact that the power of the department further to distribute the almost constantly-increasing surplus was exhausted, and prompt legislation asked for. Summing up the operations of the Treasury for the relief of the money market, we have $63,612,250 3-per-cents. called in for redemption, of which $62,-877,150 were redeemed; $11,565,300 4½-per-cents., and $13,000,000 4-per-cents. bought for the sinking fund, and $25,714,417 public money placed in the designated depositories since July 1. This makes $112,656,867 distributed from the Treasury independent of interest payments. The net gold imports for the year to November 30th were $34,306,111, which, added to the above, makes a total supply of $146,962,978. Notwithstanding this, however, the demand for customs and the drain to the interior kept the reserves of the banks comparatively low. The highest amount of surplus reported was $22,298,450 on January 29, when the banks held an average of $118,038,-900 reserve, consisting of $92,851,600 gold and $25,187,300 legal tenders. The surplus gradually fell to $3,345,900 by June 25, but the gold dropped to $68,120,400 September 10, then recovered to $78,816,600 by October 29, and again fell to $68,146,800 December 3. The demand from the interior for legal tenders reduced the amount to $16,989,500 by April 9. Then came an increase to $24,889,200 by May 28, followed by a fall to $20,328,800, October 1, and then there was a recovery to $27,259,800 by the end of the year. The surplus then stood at $8,559,150, against $11,-962,175, October 29. Discounts were $370,-917,500, April 9, the highest point of the year. Then came a fall to $344,338,900 by September 3, and a recovery to $356,540,000 by the close of December. Deposits were at the maximum $392,771,200, February 12. The fall was gradual to $341,935,900, September 24, and then came a recovery to $358,763,-400, November 4. Bank-clearings showed the highest daily average, $184,794,859, January 9. The lowest average was $84,251,283, August 20, and the highest after that date, $129,-654,229, November 19.

The Comptroller of the Currency reports the failure, during the year, of eight national banks, with an aggregate capital of $1,550,000, and six of these failures resulted from mismanagement or embezzlements. The condition of the New York Clearing-House banks, the rates for money, exchange, and silver, and prices for United States bonds on or about Jan. 1, 1886–8, are shown in the following summary:

BANK RETURNS, ETC.	1886.	1887.	1888.
NEW YORK CITY BANKS:			
Loans and discounts	$339,909,900	$342,687,500	$356,540,000
Specie	89,721,100	82,718,100	71,189,800
Circulation	9,979,800	7,911,500	8,077,800
Net deposits	376,959,300	359,268,600	359,359,800
Legal tenders	28,808,200	19,870,400	27,259,500
Required reserve	94,239,825	89,817,150	89,839,950
Reserve held	118,529,300	102,088,500	98,399,100
Surplus reserve	$24,289,475	$12,271,350	$8,559,150
MONEY, EXCHANGE, SILVER:			
Call-loans	2½ @ 5	4 @ 9	5 @ 6
Prime paper, 60 days	4 @ 5	5 @ 6¼	6 @ 6½
Silver in London, per ounce	46 11/16 *d.*	46½ *d.*	44 7/8 *d.*
Prime sterling bills, 60 days	4 86	4 81½	4 83½
UNITED STATES BONDS:			
6s, currency, 1898	132¾	131¼	125
4½s of 1891, coupon	112¼	110¼	108¼
4s of 1907, coupon	123⅝	127⅜	126⅝

Appended is the New York Clearing-House statement of totals at the beginning of each quarter of 1887 and at the end of the year:

DATE.	Loans.	Specie.	Circulation.	Deposits.	Legal tenders.
January 8	$343,479,900	$85,509,200	$7,896,900	$370,188,900	$21,812,200
March 26	365,408,000	79,602,700	7,647,800	374,702,200	20,259,700
June 25	365,484,400	72,380,700	8,294,100	369,154,400	28,108,800
September 24	346,428,800	70,521,900	8,287,900	341,985,900	20,778,900
December 31	356,540,000	71,189,800	8,077,800	359,359,800	27,259,800

Foreign Exchange.—Imports of merchandise for the year ending Dec. 31, 1887, were $45,378,122 above those for the corresponding period in 1886, and the exports of domestic and foreign goods for the same time were $1,916,985 more. The excess of merchandise exports over imports for the calendar year was $6,513,645 against $49,974,832 for the same time in 1886. There was an excess of imports over exports of specie and bullion amounting to $24,872,499 for the year ending Dec. 31, 1887, against an excess of exports over imports of $9,806,552 for the same time in 1886. The excess of imports over exports of merchandise and specie for the period mentioned was $18,358,854, against an excess of exports over imports of $59,781,384 for the corresponding twelve months of 1886. But, notwithstanding this adverse apparent trade balance, foreign exchange only at infrequent intervals during the year ruled at or near the gold-exporting point.

The banks of England and of France, whenever a drain of gold to America was either threatened or in actual progress, sought to avert or to limit such drain, either by manipulation of the discount market or by an advance in the premium upon gold bars or full-weight coins. At the beginning of the year the bullion in the Bank of England amounted to £19,307,231, and the proportion of reserve to liabilities was 30¾ per cent. The largest amount of bullion held by the bank during the year was £24,770,532 on March 30, and with this sum the bank governors decided a fortnight later to reduce the minimum rate of discount to 2½ per cent., and by the close of April a further reduction was made to 2 per cent., the proportion of reserve to liabilities then being 50¾ per cent. It was not until August 3 that the bank rate was raised, and then it was placed at 3, remaining at that point until the close of the month, when it was further advanced to 4 per cent., at which it stood at the end of the year. But at no time was the open market rate close to the bank minimum, with perhaps the exception of a few days early in the fall, and on two occasions the bank governors sought to sustain the street rate by borrowing for the bank upon consols. The Bank of France opened the year with the equivalent of £49,100,166 gold. This was reduced to £47,494,079 by April 14, and after this the amount fluctuated between this sum and £48,400,182. The gold in the Bank of Germany can not be accurately stated, but the closest estimate places it at about £18,000,000 January 1, advancing to £21,800,000 by June 23, then falling to £19,300,000 October 7, and rising to about £20,159,000 by the end of the year. London and Paris doubtless supplied a large part of Germany's requirements during 1887, and it is known that, while this movement to Germany was in progress, the centers above named were meeting demands for America and the Argentine Republic.

That condition of our foreign exchange market, which enabled importations of gold to be made, was manifestly due neither to trade conditions nor to any plethora of gold in England or France, but mainly to the fact that the rates for money ruled in this country so much higher than they did in London as to induce bankers to employ their foreign balances in our market. These borrowings of foreign capital for temporary use were extended from time to time, as the loan bills matured, and it is estimated that they amounted to at least £5,000,000 sterling. In addition to this there were negotiations of loans upon bonds of new or reorganized roads, or borrowings of capital upon lines in process of reorganization, amounting to as much more; and there were also purchases at intervals of stocks or bonds or both for speculative purposes, which were more or less promptly drawn against. All these transactions furnished a supply of exchange which, while it was plentiful, stimulated imports of gold. Early in January there was a good demand for sterling to remit for stocks sold for European account, and there was also an inquiry for long bills for investment and for speculation. This strong tone carried exchange above the gold-importing point, and the limit at which imports could be made was increased by the Bank of England putting a premium upon bars, and the Bank of France holding full-weight Napoleons at an advance of one franc per 1,000. Toward the close of January the interruption to exports, caused by the strike of longshoremen in New York and vicinity, made commercial bills so scarce as to force rates of bankers' sterling to within a fraction of the gold-exporting point, and by the middle of February gold was shipped to England in moderate amounts. By the end of February the supply of bills increased, in consequence of the free movement of breadstuffs, the partial embargo on the commerce of the port having been raised by the collapse of the longshoremen's strike. Early in the following month liberal sales of short sterling, mainly maturing long bills, bought in January, started selling of commercial sterling, and the market was somewhat affected by activity in money. By the middle of March sales of loan bills had a depressing effect upon the rates of sterling, and then commenced the borrowings of foreign capital, which thereafter had such an important influence upon the market. At the beginning of April the discount rate for sixty-day to three-months' bills in London was 1½ per cent., and at Paris the open market rate was 2, and at Berlin 2½ per cent., while the call-loan rate in New York averaged about 6. This condition of the money markets induced buying of long bills and further borrowings of foreign capital were made later in the month. In May the tone was steadier, although money continued cheap in London and on the Continent, and comparatively dear here, but early in June sterling declined under the influence of offerings of bills against outgoing securities and negotiations of railroad loans, and by the middle of the month the fall in the price of wheat resulted in such free sales of commercial drafts that the market became very weak. Later, active money, due to the feverish condition of the stock market, the break in wheat and coffee, and the failure of the Fidelity Bank at Cincinnati, assisted in unsettling exchange, and in the last few days of the month sterling fell to points which justified gold imports, and about $1,850,000 of the metal was ordered out from London. At the same time Germany drew gold from the British metropolis to assist in floating her new loan of 100,000,000 marks. In July the tone of exchange was heavy, but rates were fractionally above the gold-importing point. Early in August the Bank of England minimum rate of discount was advanced to 3 per cent., partly in consequence of a drain of gold to the Argentine Republic, but this only temporarily affected exchange, and by the middle of the month rates fell so as to justify a renewal of gold imports, the decline being assisted by the negotiation of a railroad loan, and the metal moved hither from London and the Continent in comparatively liberal amounts during the remainder of this month until the middle of September when a rise in sterling checked imports from London, but the movement from Paris was only partiall interrupted, although the Bank of France advanced the premium on gold to 8 francs per 1,000, the highest point recorded in many years. Toward the close of the month a fall in sterling again started gold from London, but it was checked in October, and exchange was strong during this month in response to a demand to remit for stocks sold for European account and in settlement of borrowed capital which was then being returned. Thereafter during the remainder of the year commercial bills were scarce, bankers' sterling in limited supply, and the market gradually advanced so that at the end of December it stood midway between the gold importing and the exporting points.

Manufacturing Industries.—The labor troubles had less influence upon manufacturing enterprises in 1887 than they did in the previous year. The employers seemed to feel more confidence in their ability to resist unjust demands, and the various organizations of the Knights of Labor, probably profiting by the ill-success which attended their efforts in 1886, were less exacting in their requirements. The strike of the coal-handlers in January temporarily unsettled the market for coal, but it only partially checked the operations of the iron-works in Pennsylvania, and after the failure of the strike manufacturing of iron and steel increased. and, under the stimulus of a demand for railroad and structural purposes, the mills were kept at their full capacity for the greater part of the year. The production of these articles was the largest on record, exceeding that of 1886, and the output of pig-iron is estimated at 6,250,000 gross tons against 5,683,329 in the previous

year. The Bessemer steel-rail production was 1,950,000 tons against 1,574,703 in 1886. Iron-ore was produced to the extent of 11,000,000 gross tons. Prices for rails were maintained until after the middle of the year, when they yielded, partly in consequence of the competition of imported rails, but mainly because of the conviction that the phenomenal demand for new railroads could not continue. New iron-mines were developed, principally in the Gogebic region and in Alabama. The industrial growth of the South during the year was most remarkable, covering almost the entire range of manufacturing. Of the fourteen Southern States there were only four in which the capital invested in new enterprises was not double the amount of the previous year. Woolen-goods manufacturers, particularly at the North, probably made less money than they did in 1886, but they worked principally on orders, and, therefore, did not accumulate large stocks to be slaughtered in the auction-rooms. Producers of worsted goods, such as cloths and coatings, turned their attention to cassimeres, chiefly because they could not compete with the foreign fabrics of the same class of material, and, in consequence of the change, they had a prosperous year. The manufacturers of knit-goods were full of orders during the whole of the twelvemonth, the consumption was marvelous, sales were prompt, and prices fair. In cotton and print goods the business of the mills was profitable, with some notable exceptions. New railroad mileage was about 12,724 miles, principally in Kansas, Texas, Nebraska, Michigan, Alabama, Colorado, Montana, Dakota, Georgia, and California. Coal production was vigorously pushed, the demand was good, and prices generally uniform. The total output for the year was 34,641,017 tons against 32,136,862 in 1886.

Railroads.—The most important event of the year affecting the railroad interests of the country was the passage by Congress of the interstate commerce act, which went into operation April 5. While the bill was under discussion, opinions were expressed by prominent railroad-managers that its rigid enforcement would prove injurious, if not disastrous to the transportation interests of the country, and the most objectionable feature of the law, in their estimation, was the fourth section declaring it to be unlawful for any common carrier, subject to the provisions of the act, to charge or receive any greater compensation in the aggregate, for the transportation of passengers or of like kind of property, under substantially similar conditions, for a shorter than for a longer distance over the same line, in the same direction, the shorter being included within the longer distance. Immediately upon the measure taking effect the commissioners appointed under it, acting by authority of the law giving them the power, suspended, for ninety days, the operation of this section on the application of Southern and other roads having competing water-routes or other competitive lines, and before the expiration of the ninety days the commissioners rendered a decision, in substance declaring that the carrier must for himself, and at his own risk, decide the question of his liability under the section. The only judicial decision on this point is the one rendered by Judge Deady, of the United States Circuit Court, sitting at Portland, Oregon, in which the rule was laid down that "freight carried to or from a competitive point is always carried under substantially dissimilar circumstances and conditions from that carried to or from non-competitive points. In the latter case the railway makes its own rates. In the former case the circumstances are altogether different. The power of a corporation to make its own rates is limited to the necessities of the situation. Competition controls the charge. It must take what it can get, or abandon the field and let its trade go to rust." This decision was regarded as practically nullifying the fourth section of the interstate law, and soon after its announcement the

Trunk. At the close of the year amendments to the interstate law were suggested, one of which was the imposition of a duty upon goods transported on Canadian roads from points in the United States to other points in this country, the object being to prevent competition by these lines. By the change in the management of the Baltimore and Ohio, through the retirement of its president, Mr. Garrett, the road was brought into harmony with the other main trunk-lines, thus insuring uniformity of rates. The successful reorganization of the Reading had an important influence upon the anthracite-coal trade, and the reorganization of the Central New Jersey, together with its alliance with the Lehigh Valley, tended to harmonize transportation interests between Philadelphia and New York, which had long been in conflict.

The following table shows gross and net earnings of the principal trunk-roads, the reports, except for the Pennsylvania, being made for fiscal years, and the returns of the New York Central including the operation of the West Shore leased line:

ROADS.	1881-'82.	1882-'83.	1883-'84.	1884-'85.	1885-'86.	1886-'87.
PENNSYLVANIA :						
Gross earnings	$49,079,384	$51,068,259	$48,566,911	$45,615,027	$50,879,066	$55,671,963
Net earnings	18,432,429	19,336,102	18,089,902	16,185,269	17,759,481	18,664,788
NEW YORK CENTRAL :						
Gross earnings	30,623,781	33,770,722	28,146,667	24,429,441	30,506,961	35,297,056
Net earnings	11,282,807	13,030,128	10,299,356	8,110,069	11,995,984	12,906,422
ERIE :						
Gross earnings	19,975,774	22,802,246	21,687,435	18,984,578	22,500,046	24,210,358
Net earnings	6,887,681	7,357,668	5,979,853	4,587,056	6,111,409	6,519,685
BALTIMORE AND OHIO :						
Gross earnings	18,883,875	19,789,587	19,436,607	16,616,642	18,422,488	20,659,086
Net earnings	7,454,562	8,705,823	7,760,800	5,648,057	6,886,696	6,588,905

transcontinental lines of road proceeded to take advantage of it, claiming that they were in competition with the Pacific Mail as a water-route. A few suits were brought during the year by shippers in various sections of the country, who claimed that this and other provisions of the law had been evaded or disregarded, but no judicial decision was reached, the cases not having been brought to trial. The main trunk-lines of the country were not unfavorably affected by the operation of the law, and only a comparatively few local roads suffered. Rates for freight and passengers were advanced by nearly all the lines on or after the passage of the law; the pooling-system was abandoned, this being prohibited by the act; free passes were generally abolished, and other reforms, permitted or required by the act, were instituted, and the result was shown in substantially increased earnings of nearly all the railroads of the country. After the winter-wheat crop was moved, the Granger roads began to cut rates, and this cutting was more or less vigorous at intervals during the latter part of the summer and in the fall. Early in the winter the Grand Trunk, of Canada, commenced a cut upon dressed-beef rates, which was met by the American trunk-lines, and the war was carried on so vigorously that it soon after ended by the abandonment of the contest by the Grand

The Crops.—The yield of wheat for the season of 1887 is reported by the Department of Agriculture as only about 1,000,000 bushels less than that for the previous year, while that of corn is nearly 210,000,000 bushels less. The estimates of cotton vary, but good authorities claim a crop of 6,650,000 bales against 6,513,-620 for 1886. The spring-wheat area was enlarged west of the Mississippi and in the extreme Northwest and particularly in Dakota, where there was a gain in acreage of 24 per cent. The injury to winter wheat by thawing and freezing and the absence of snow was severe in Kansas, and moderate in Missouri, Illinois, Indiana, and in other sections of this belt. The harvest exhibited the results of insect ravages and want of uniformity in the weight of the grain. Drought and insects threatened serious deterioration of spring wheat early in the season, but more favorable conditions followed, and, on the whole, the result of the harvest was better than was expected, owing to the increase of acreage. The Department of Agriculture reports the yield about 456,000,000 bushels. After corn was planted there was an extraordinary development which gave promise of an abundant yield. A high condition was maintained through July, but in the following month and in September the drought was so severe that wide-spread ruin seemed inevitable. Rain came, but too late to repair the damage. The severity of the reduction fell upon Kansas, Illinois, Indiana, and Ohio, and in other of the surplus-producing States. Large quantities of the green corn were cut for fodder in consequence of the destruction by drought of pastures, and therefore a close estimate of the yield of this cereal can not be made, but the Department of Agriculture calculates that the crop will not vary much from 1,456,000,000 bushels. The quality of oats is below the average, but the enlarged area planted will probably bring the crop up to about 659,000,000 bushels. The crop of barley is estimated at 55,000,000, that of rye at 24,000,000, potatoes at 184,000,000 bushels, and cotton at about 6,650,000 bales. At the International Seed and Grain Convention, held in Vienna early in December, the reports received indicated average crops of wheat in the principal exporting countries of the Continent, and a slight deficiency in India. The requirements of Great Britain and France would, it was estimated, be less than those of last year. The corner in wheat, which was the feature of our market in June, carried the price so high that it drew large supplies of the new crop of winter wheat from farmers' hands, and it is probable that all the available surplus was then thrown upon the market. After the collapse of the corner, about the middle of June, the export movement was stimulated, and spring wheat came from the producers rapidly immediately after the harvest. The visible supply of this cereal at the end of the year was about 44,000,000 bushels against a little over 62,000,-000 at the close of 1886. Taking the prices in the New York market on or about the 1st of January in each year and the total yield for the previous season, we have the following aproximate results in quantities and values:

THE CROPS.	Yield.	Price.	Value.
1886.			
Wheat, bushels	457,218,000	$0 98⅝	$428,641,875
Corn, bushels	1,665,441,000	48½	801,498,481
Cotton, bales.........	6,518,623	9⅛	300,783,974
1887.			
Wheat, bushels	456,000,000	92	419,590,000
Corn, bushels	1,456,000,000	63	917,280,000
Cotton, bales.........	6,650,000	10⅟₁₆	334,620,000

The Stock Market.—After an irregular movement in January the course of the stock market was generally upward until June, when a bear combination commenced operations, which were aided by the unsettled feeling resulting from the collapse of the corners in coffee and wheat, and the tendency was downward until early in the fall. Then came a recovery followed by another decline in October, after which the market reacted and gave promise of a decided improvement. Toward the close of the year, however, there was a feverish feeling due to various causes, and the tone was more or less unsettled to the end of the twelvemonth. Comparing closing prices on the 30th of December with those at the opening on

January 3, thirty-three of the active stocks exhibited an average decline of 10 per cent. During the first few days of January, Central New Jersey, Reading, Western Union, and Richmond Terminal were pushed upward by the cliques, and this was the beginning of the movement for a control in the latter which resulted in the deal with the holders of East Tennessee, Virginia, and Georgia preferred stock. The rise in Central New Jersey was also due to purchases for control, as it subsequently appeared, by the Corbin party, who had in view the reorganization of the property on a dividend paying basis. Hocking Valley advanced in consequence of buying for the Vanderbilts, and Reading was favorably influenced by the advice of Mr. Gowen, to holders of junior securities, to accept the plan of reorganization. Raiding of Richmond Terminal followed the announcement of the intended issue of new stock, with which to pay for East Tennessee, Virginia, and Georgia preferred, and thereafter, for the remainder of the month, the bears succeeded in keeping the market in a more or less unsettled condition. The passage by the House of Representatives on the 20th of the interstate commerce bill, and its transmission to the President on the 25th, assisted the bearish demonstrations, and the partial embargo of the commerce of the port of New York through the strike of the longshoremen and coal-handlers also had an unfavorable influence on the market. Stocks were feverish and generally lower during the early part of February, but before the close there was a recovery, and sixty out of sixty-six more or less active properties exhibited a gain, comparing prices at the end with those at the beginning of the month. During the first week the London and Continental markets were unsettled in consequence of war rumors; the threatening attitude of the Knights of Labor on strike in this city excited some apprehensions, and reports that the President would sign the interstate bill were used by the bears to their advantage until the bill was signed on the 4th, and then there were indications that the event had been discounted. The strike of the longshoremen came to an end on the 11th through a refusal of other organizations to assist it by also quitting their employment; the European markets recovered on the subsidence of the war feeling; the Grangers advanced on favorable traffic reports; the coal-shares steadily improved on news that a strike on the Reading had been prevented, and the tendency of the whole market was upward, notwithstanding realizing sales and bearish pressure, for the remainder of the month. The tone was generally strong during March, and only five out of sixty-six stocks recorded declines. The favoring influences were the assurance of the success of the Reading reorganization scheme, as indicated by the prompt deposit of securities; the announcement that an extra session of Congress would be unnecessary, and the news that Mr. Robert Garrett had offered the sale of a controlling interest in the Baltimore and Ohio to a speculator who, it was supposed, would, if he were successful, use it to the advantage of the Richmond Terminal and the Western Union. During the second week the news that the publication of the Baltimore and Ohio scheme was premature started a free-selling movement in Richmond Terminal, Western Union, Central New Jersey, and Reading, which made the whole market unsettled until the last week in the month, when purchases of stocks for European account, manipulation by the bulls in the Grangers and Southwesterns, and a sharp advance in some of the so-called fancy stocks carried prices upward, and the market closed strong. On the 5th of April the interstate law went into effect, but the commissioners immediately suspended for ninety days the operation of the 4th section, relating to the long and short haul, so far as it affected Southern roads in competition with water-routes, and subsequently ordered a suspension on all roads of the country making application. As this section was regarded by the railroads as the most unjust feature of the measure, the action of the commissioners had a favorable effect on the market. One feature early in April was a rise in Central New Jersey on a report that the parties in control were negotiating for an alliance with the Lehigh Valley. The advance in this stock stimulated an improvement in Reading and subsequently in the other coal-shares. Later came good buying of the trunk-line properties, Manhattan Elevated, Richmond Terminal, Union Pacific, Western Union, and the Grangers, and the tendency of the market was generally upward to the close. In May only six of the sixty-six active stocks showed declines, comparing the opening with the close of the month, and some of the advances were important, especially those in the San Francisco's, Duluth, Manitoba, Pullman, and the Grangers. An attack upon New York and New England was one of the features early in the month, but the bulls seemed to combine to resist the assault and the market was advanced more or less rapidly during the next fortnight, the rise being assisted by favorable news, a manipulation of the short interest, and decided increases in railroad earnings, which were regarded as important in view of the fact that these, in some degree, reflected the operation of the interstate commerce law. Toward the close of the month raiding by the bears and realizing sales by many speculators, who had a profit on their holdings, made the market more or less unsettled, but the tone was generally better at the close. Early in June the indications pointed to a further rise in prices of leading stocks, but comparisons at the end of the month showed that, out of fifty-eight stocks, only four had advanced. Reading opened at a price representing the first installment of the assessment, and a few days thereafter the bears commenced to hammer it. The next stock attacked was St. Paul on the news that the directors had decided upon an issue of 100,000 shares of additional stock. Then came on the 14th and the 16th the collapse of the bull movement in coffee and wheat, but after this there was a partial recovery. During the third week rumors of a disquieting character regarding the stability of banks in Chicago, Philadelphia, and Boston, resulting from the failure on the 20th of the Fidelity Bank at Cincinnati, assisted the bearish demonstrations, and then followed a fall of 41¼ points in Manhattan Elevated on June 24, which made the market panicky. In the last week of the month Pacific Mail was broken down, money became active, and persistent attacks by the bears kept the market in a more or less feverish condition to near the close, when there was a sharp upward turn imparting a better feeling. One of the most important events in July was the decision of Judge Deady, sitting in United States Circuit at Portland, Oregon, in the case of the California and Oregon road, whose receiver asked for instructions as to what rates should be established in view of the competition of the water-routes between Portland and San Francisco. The court decided that the road might charge a greater price for a short than for a long haul because of this competition, and then laid down the broad principle that the interstate law was not intended to ruin railroad properties but to foster interstate communication. This was the first judicial decision under the law, and it was, to some extent, subsequently taken advantage of by the transcontinental roads in competition with the Pacific Mail. Another event was the failure of the so-called Baltimore and Ohio deal, the negotiations being declared by Mr. Garrett at an end, because of the inability of the parties proposing to purchase the property to meet their engagements. The course of the stock market was generally downward during July, it being subjected to frequent raids. Western Union was, in the early part of the month, feverishly strong in consequence of rumors of favorable progress toward a consummation of the Baltimore and Ohio deal, which it was expected would result in the transfer of the telegraph line to the Western Union, but on the 18th the announcement that the negotiations were off, and that Mr. Gould did not consider it advisable to buy the Baltimore and Ohio Telegraph property, had an unsettling effect, and one feature was a fall in Cincinnati, Hamilton, and Dayton stock, which was largely held as collateral for a loan to the parties negotiating with Mr. Garrett. The market was feverish during the last week in the month, when Western Union, New England, Richmond Terminal, Reading, St. Paul, and, indeed, nearly all the active stocks were, in turn, attacked, and comparisons of prices at the close with those at the opening of the month showed a fall in every stock on the list with the exception of Northern Pacific common, and the advance in this was only ¼ of 1 per cent. The market was unsettled during the greater part of August. The bear campaign temporarily culminated in the first week, the short contracts being partially covered, and an advance was encouraged on the 4th by the announcement that the Secretary of the Treasury would buy 4½-per-cent. bonds for the Sinking Fund, and would also anticipate interest for the purpose of relieving the stringency in the money market. During the next week the Northern Pacifics and the Grangers were freely sold, but there was a recovery toward the close on the news of gold imports from London. In the early part of the next week the tendency was slightly upward, but later New England, the other active stocks, and Manhattan were freely sold with an unsettling effect. The raiding was continued early in the last week, when Missouri Pacific fell heavily, and the circulation of reports of a disquieting character caused the market to close feverish. One feature was the failure of a house which had borrowed upon unsalable bond collaterals, and this induced lenders to discriminate against securities for which a ready market could not be found. There was a better feeling at the opening of September. The announcement was made that a syndicate of responsible bankers had undertaken to relieve the embarrassments of the Baltimore and Ohio Railroad Company by advancing money with which to pay off the floating debt on condition that the entire property should be managed in harmony with competing lines. One feature was the sale by the Oregon and Transcontinental of about $5,000,000 of its treasury stock, thus giving that company financial relief. On the first day of the month the announcement was made that the Baltimore and Ohio express line had been sold, and, as this was regarded as preliminary to the sale of the telegraph lines, Western Union sharply advanced. The improvement was not sustained, however, and the market was unfavorably affected on the 7th by the refusal of the Acting Secretary of the Treasury to buy bonds at the price at which they were offered. Considering the strained condition of the money market this was regarded as unfortunate, and the bears took advantage of the fear that serious trouble would follow. The market was kept in a feverish state for the remainder of that week and in the next, and it was only temporarily strengthened on the 14th by the purchase of $4,000,000 bonds by the Treasury. Toward the close of that week the discussion of a new policy of financial relief had somewhat of an assuring influence, but the failure of the Secretary to promptly act upon the suggestions made by leading bankers caused a panicky fall in stocks on the 20th, which was checked before the close of the day by supporting orders and by purchases for European account. On the following day the announcement was made that the Secretary had decided to purchase 4

and 4½ per cents. to the extent of $14,000,000, and also to pay the October interest, amounting to $6,500,000, without rebate. This caused a recovery, and, although feverish, the market was generally strong for the remainder of the week and to the close of the month. Pacific Mail rose sharply on news that Mr. Gould had obtained control, and there was also a rapid rise in Central New Jersey on an intimation that the floating stock was very small. One feature early in October was the purchase on the 7th by Mr. Gould, for the Western Union, of the Baltimore and Ohio Telegraph line for 50,000 shares of the stock of the first-named company, and on the 28th it was announced that the Postal and United lines had agreed to an advance in rates to the Western Union tariff, thus settling the telegraph war. Another feature was easier money, the result of the Treasury bond purchases, gold imports, and liberal deposits of public funds in the designated depositories. The bear party devoted their attention early in the month to raids upon Richmond Terminal, New England, and the Grangers, and the fall in the latter was assisted by news of cutting of rates. During the second week Reading, Western Union, the Grangers, Erie, and Missouri Pacific were attacked in turn, and the passing of the quarterly dividend by the Baltimore and Ohio had a disturbing effect, as also did the report of an interview in a St. Louis paper with Mr. Chauncey M. Depew, in which that gentleman was represented as predicting serious disasters as the result of excessive construction of railroads and speculation in Western and Southern lands. This statement caused free selling of the Vanderbilt properties, and the fall in these had a demoralizing effect upon the whole list. During the third week the explanation given by Mr. Depew of his statements to the reporter, good support of the Vanderbilts, buying of stocks for European account, and covering of short contracts by the smaller bears, caused a more or less decided recovery, and the tone was generally stronger until toward the close when the bears renewed their demonstrations, forcing important declines in Missouri, Kansas, and Texas bonds, by the aid of a rumor, subsequently shown to be false, and the market was unsettled at the end of the month. Only ten of the active stocks showed an improvement compared with the opening, and Rock Island fell 11 points. Mr. Gould left for Europe on the 29th, intending to be absent for several months. The bears were apparently content with attacking Missouri Pacific after Mr. Gould's departure, but soon after the opening of November good buying of the coal-shares and of Western Union had a stimulating influence, and subsequently there was an important rise in the trunk-lines and in the Grangers. During the second week the Gould specialties took the lead, followed by Reading, the Vanderbilt properties, and Union Pacific, and the tone was strong for the next fortnight, the impression that the bear campaign was at an end encouraging purchases by non-professional speculators. This resulted in such a wide distribution of stocks that the bears resumed their demonstrations with more or less success, but the market was generally strong to the close, although a little activity in money made the movement irregular in the last days of the month. One feature was the issue of decrees removing the receivers of the Reading and of the Central New Jersey, and another was the negotiation of a third mortgage on the Northern Pacific. Comparisons show a gain for the month in all but eleven of the active stocks, and the most important was 10¼ per cent. in Union Pacific on news of more harmonious relations with the Northern Pacific and the Oregon lines. Stocks were comparatively strong during the first few days in December, the market being affected by the ending of the French political crisis, which imparted a more confident tone to the foreign markets. Then followed a temporary derangement due to the tariff recommendations contained in the President's message, the bears were encouraged to renew their demonstrations, and the decline was assisted by news of unsettled markets abroad caused by the movements of the Russians on the Austrian frontier. The raiding was confined to Richmond Terminal, New England, the coal-shares, and the Grangers, but toward the close of the second week the market was turned upward by news of the restoration of rates for dressed beef, which had been cut by the Grand Trunk, and the tone was generally strong until the last week in the month, although at intervals irregular and fractionally lower. The attempt of the Knights of Labor to force a strike on the Reading on the 25th proved abortive, and on the following day there was a decided advance in this property, the other coal-shares, and indeed in all the active stocks, the market having been oversold in expectation that the strike would succeed. Then came realizing sales and a renewal of bearish pressure based upon rumors regarding the intentions of the Knights, but there was a steadier feeling at the close of the month.

The following is a list of quotations of leading stocks at the beginning of January, 1886, 1887, and 1888:

LEADING STOCKS.	1886.	1887.	1888.
New York Central	106½	118½	107½
Erie	36½	34½	28½
Lake Shore	89	90½	94½
Michigan Central	77	93½	67½
Rock Island	128½	120½	112½
Illinois Central	140	133	118½
Northwestern, common	110½	115½	107½
St. Paul, common	96½	90	75½
Dela., Lackawanna, and Western.	122½	184½	129½
Central New Jersey	44	55½	75

Total sales of all stocks for the year 1887 were 85,291,028 shares against 100,802,050 in 1886; 93,184,478 in 1885; 95,416,368 in 1884; 93,037,905 in 1883; 113,730,665 in 1882; and

113,892,685 in 1881. The transactions in Government bonds during 1887 were $7,110,400, and in railroad and miscellaneous bonds $847,-127,830.

The following is a list of a few of the speculative stocks, the highest prices at which they sold in 1886, and the highest and lowest in 1887:

SPECULATIVE AND OTHER SHARES.	1886.	1887.	
	Highest.	Highest.	Lowest.
Canadian Pacific	73	65½	49½
Canada Southern	71½	64½	49
Central New Jersey	64	86½	55½
Central Pacific	51	43½	25½
Chattanooga	105½	88½	6½
Cleveland, Col., C., and Ind	75½	68	47½
Consolidated Gas	111	89	67
Delaware and Hudson	108½	106½	90½
Dela., Lackawanna, and Western.	144	139½	122½
Erie	38½	35½	24½
Hocking Valley	42½	39½	15
Lake Shore	104½	98½	80
Louisville and Nashville	66	70½	51½
Manhattan Elevated Consol	175	161½	92½
Memphis and Charleston	69½	64½	45
Michigan Central	9¼	95½	80
Minnesota and St. Louis	98½	20½	6½
Minnesota and St. Louis, pref'd.	62½	45½	15
Missouri, Kansas, and Texas	35½	34½	16½
Missouri Pacific	119	112	84½
New York Central	117½	114½	101½
New York and New England	65½	66	34½
Northwestern	121½	127½	104½
Northern Pacific	31½	34½	20
Northern Pacific, preferred	66½	67½	41½
Ohio	35½	32½	21
Omaha	55	54½	34
Omaha, preferred	116½	115½	100
Oregon Transcontinental	38	35½	16
Pacific Mail	67	55½	32½
Reading	58½	71½	34
Richmond Terminal	77½	58	20½
St. Paul	99	95	64½
Texas and Pacific	28½	35½	20
Union Pacific	65½	6½	44
Western Union	80½	81½	67½

FINE ARTS IN 1887. Under this title are treated the principal art events of the past year, ending with December, 1887, including especially the great exhibitions in Europe and the United States, the sales and acquisitions of works of art, and the erection of public statues and monuments.

Paris: Salon.—The exhibition (May 1 to June 30) comprised 5,318 numbers, classified as follow: Paintings, 2,521; cartoons, water-colors, pastels, porcelain pictures, etc., 1,042; sculpture, 1,046; engraving in medals and precious stones, 46; architecture, 187; engraving, 476.

Section of painting: Medal of honor awarded to Fernand Cormon. No first-class medal awarded. Second-class medals: Henri Saintin, Eugène Buland, Lucien Doucet, Pierre Marie Beyle, Albert Fourié, Eugène Carrière, Maurice Francis Auguste Courant, Armand Berton, Joseph Bail, Jean Desbrosses, Arturo Michelena, Félix Lucas, Alexandre Thiollet, Gaston Guignard, Antoine Paul Émile Morlon. Third-class medals: Jules Alexis Muenier, Gabriel Thurner, Léon Tanzi, Louis Auguste Georges Loustaunau, Eugène Henri Alexandre Ohigot, Eugène Claude, Anton Mauve, Prosper Galerne, Maurice Eliot, Mlle. Jeanne Rougier, Mlle. Elizabeth Jane Gardner, Jules Charles

Aviat, Eugène Chaperon, Luis Jimenez, Pierre Louis Léger Vauthier, Julius de Payer, Edmond Picard, Émile Cagniart, Victor Henri Lesur, Jean Jacques Scherrer, Louis Auguste Girardot, Jean André Marty, Stephen Jacob, Mlle. Anna Bilinska, Raoul Arus, Camille Dufour, Georges Busson, Théophile Deyrolle.

Among the "mentions honorables" are the following American artists: C. S. Reinhart, J. Carroll Beckwith, George Hitchcock, and Francis B. Chadwick. Elizabeth Jane Gardner is the only American that received a medal.

Section of sculpture: Medal of honor awarded to Emmanuel Frémiet. First-class medal: Jules Desbois, for his marble statue of "Acis changed into a Flower" (owned by William Schaus, New York). Second-class medals: Jean Sul-Abadie, Félix Charpentier, Henri Peinte, François Roger, Raoul Charles Verlet, Michel Léonard Béguine, Jeanne Marie Mengue. Third-class medals: Édouard Charles Houssin, Émile Louis Truffot, Alphonse Voisin-Delacroix, Virginius Arias, Georges Gardet, —— Cadoux, —— Lequeult, Guillaume Charlier, Charles Joseph Roufosse, Paul Berthet.

Section of engraving: Medal of honor awarded to Charles Courtry. No first-class medal awarded. Second-class medals: Messrs. Boutelier (line engraving), Kœpping, Gaujean, & Mathey (etching), Lepère (wood engraving), Lunois, Vergnes (lithography). Third-class medals: Messrs. Abot (line engraving), Ardail, Kratké (etching), Huyot, Florian (wood engraving), Bahuet (lithography).

Section of architecture: No medal of honor awarded. First-class medal: Charles Wable. Second-class medals: Messrs. Devienne, Deglanne, Bonnier, Esquié, and Monnier. Third-class medals: Messrs. Louzier, Joannis, Debrie, Gontier, Touzet, and Balleyguier.

The *Salon* receipts for the season were 323,190 francs.

Among the noteworthy pictures was Fernand Cormon's "Victors of Salamis," a large work, commissioned by the state, and to which was awarded the medal of honor. On the seashore, with sea and ships in the distance, is a throng of Greek victors, with citizens, women, and children in festal attire, dancing for joy or moving around in a circle, shouting and singing in triumph as they wave aloft weapons and palms of victory. Some hold sistrums, cymbals, and timbrels, many are wounded, and a few are laden with spoil. This, one of the most striking pictures of the season, was always surrounded by admiring crowds.

Another historical picture of large size (30 feet long), by Francis Tattegrain, illustrates a passage in the chronicle of Jean Le Fèvre, "The Surrender of the Casselois to Philippe le Bonn, of Burgundy, in the Marsh of Saint-Omer." In the mid-distance the duke, in armor, with his visor up, and mounted on a handsomely caparisoned horse, is halted with his attendants on a low ridge of land, while in the foreground are the people of Cassel, all

kneeling and bareheaded, with their weapons and shields cast down. A group of soldiers, civic dignitaries, and priests prostrate themselves before the duke's horse, while the pitiless storm, hail and snow mingled with rain, beats on their heads, and nearly blows away their crape-dressed banners.

Alexandre Paul Protais's "Convoy of Wounded" is a fine landscape, with a long line of men and vehicles passing at evening along the edge of a meadow in the shadow of trees, and descending into a valley, where twilight mists are mingled with the rays of the setting sun. Lancers, dragoons, artillerymen, and infantry move slowly along, with here and there an ambulance-wagon or a group of officers directing the march.

Puvis de Chavannes exhibited the cartoon of an immense composition (85 feet x 20 feet), intended for the decoration of the hemicycle of the grand amphitheatre of the Sorbonne, symbolizing the ancient Sorbonne, and Eloquence recounting the struggles and triumphs of the human intellect. The left of the three panels is devoted to Philosophy and History, and the right to Science.

François Flameng's "History of Literature," intended for the decoration of the staircase of the same building, is also a triptych. The first panel represents Saint Louis delivering the charter of the institution to Robert de Sorbon, the second, Abélard and his school, and the third, Jean Heynlin setting up in the cellars of the Sorbonne the first printing-press established in France.

Opposite Puvis de Chavannes's huge work hung another large decorative canvas, "The Evening of Life," by Paul Albert Besnard, intended for the mairie of the first arrondissement. On the threshold of a house are seated an old couple, the wife resting her head on the shoulder of her husband, who, leaning on his staff, looks upward at the stars. Behind them a mother and child represent the earlier stages of life. It is a poetical work, nobly designed and technically fine.

Bouguereau's "L'Amour Vainqueur" shows a Cupid bearing triumphantly through the air a beautiful female child, who clings submissively to her conqueror.

Alexandre Cabanel's "Cleopatra," illustrating a passage in Plutarch's "Life of Antony," represents the Egyptian queen in a vast hall reclining languidly on a lion-skin, with a leopard at her feet and a female slave behind her, watching the effect of poisons on unfortunate wretches selected for experiment. One of her victims rolls in agony on the floor, while two slaves bear away the body of another.

Georges Clairin's "Funeral of Victor Hugo—Evening," is another huge canvas. A long line of cuirassiers, sitting motionless on their horses, hold torches which light up a catafalque covered with flowers, while above, a winged spirit, apparently representing Poetry, shrouds herself in a black veil and holds a golden crown.

Georges Rochegrosse contributed two pictures, "La Curée," a large work illustrating Plutarch's account of the death of Julius Cæsar in the Senate House, and a smaller one, "Salome dancing before Herod." In the former, Cæsar, wounded, lies at the base of Pompey's statue, the center of a knot of assassins, among whom Brutus is prominent, all striving to stab him. In the background, which is all white marble, are many figures in confusion, some flying between the columns of the portico, some hiding their faces, and some rushing forward with drawn daggers. In the smaller picture, the daughter of Herodias dances to the music of a band of negroes and Egyptians seated on the floor in a ring, of which she is the center, before Herod and his companions seated on a dais.

Benjamin-Constant is represented by two pictures, "Orpheus" and "Theodora," the latter a vigorous piece of melodramatic art, magnificent in details. The Empress Theodora, seated on a throne of white marble, rests both her jeweled wrists on its arms. Her robe of dark silk is set with jewels and loaded with gold ornaments, and on her head is a Byzantine crown studded with precious stones, contrasting strongly with the pale bronze of her face and her cruel, snake-like eyes. "Orpheus" represents the singer, entirely nude, advancing through a rocky, dimly lighted gorge into the depths of a mysterious night.

Henry Rachou's "How the Dauphin of France entered Paris" is an illustration of Henri Martin's description of the scene after the revolt of Étienne Marcel. The dead bodies of Marcel and his partisans are stretched upon the steps of the Church of St. Catherine as a long line of knights armed *cap-d-pie*, riding on splendidly caparisoned horses, pick their way among corpses.

Henner was represented by "A Creole" and "Herodias," the latter a young girl with disheveled auburn hair, clad in bright scarlet, standing against a brown wall, holding the charger and head. Carolus Duran's "Andromeda" is a masterly nude figure, with a profusion of blonde hair, against a background of grayish-green rocks. Jules Lefebvre's "Morning-Glory" is an idealized female figure with pale-yellow looks twined with the flowers which give the picture its name.

Among the best of the *genre* pictures was Gaston Mélingue's "Molière and his Company," representing the dramatist reading one of his plays to a small audience.

Of the noteworthy religious pictures, Herr von Uhde's "Last Supper" is as characteristic as his "Christ with the Little Children" of the Salon of 1885. Deschamp's "Sleep of Jesus" and Dinet's "Adoration of the Shepherds" are somewhat similar attempts to excite pathos and religious fervor through eccentricity of treatment.

Julian Story's "Episode of the Massacres of September, 1792," is from Lamartine's "Histoire des Girondins." It represents Mlle. de Sombreuil drinking a goblet of human blood at the dictation of the mob to save her father from the guillotine. It is a powerful picture, and was awarded honorable mention, but its subject is too hideous for art.

American art was also represented in the Salon by Elizabeth Jane Gardner's "Farmer's Daughter" (2d class medal) and "Innocence," James Carroll Beckwith's "Portrait of William Walton" (honorable mention), Charles Sprague Pearce's "St. Geneviève," Frederick A. Bridgman's "On the Terraces, Algiers," Daniel Ridgeway Knight's "In October," Alexander Harrison's "Twilight," Walter Gay's "Petition to Richelieu," and by many others.

The Académie des Beaux-Arts awarded the biennial prize of 20,000 francs, given to the author of the work most creditable to the country, to the sculptor Antonin Mercié for his tomb of Louis Philippe and Queen Amélie, exhibited at the Salon of 1886. The 10,000-franc prize was awarded to Émile Paladilhe, music composer.

London : Royal Academy.—The eighteenth winter exhibition was devoted, like the preceding one, to works of the old masters and deceased British artists, gathered from the collections of Buckingham Palace, the Duke of Wellington, the Earl of Normanton, Lord Leconfield, Lord Carnarvon, Mr. Charles Butler, Mr. R. S. Holford, and many others. Among the old masters represented were Velasquez, Murillo, Raphael, Titian, Tintoretto, Rembrandt, Rubens, Vandyke, Frans Hals, Hobbema, Ruysdael, Cuyp, and, of the more modern schools, Greuze, Sir Joshua Reynolds, Gainsborough, Hogarth, Prout, William Collins, and Turner, the last by a collection of more than a hundred water-color drawings.

The one hundred and nineteenth annual exhibition opened in May, with 1,946 numbers, selected from nearly 5,000 contributions, including oil-paintings, water-colors, works in black and white, architectural drawings, and sculptures.

Among the prominent contributions were "Marianne," by J. W. Waterhouse, representing the wife of Herod the Great going to execution after her trial for the false charges brought against her by Salome and others. By the side of the king, who is seated on his throne at the right, stands Salome, while Marianne stands on a marble staircase in the foreground. In the background are seated the judges.

"The Last Watch of Hero," by Sir Frederick Leighton, exhibits her, in a dark-blue mantle over a rose-colored robe, gazing anxiously forth from between marble columns, just tinted with the sunrise. In a predella below is a smaller picture in brown monochrome, showing the fate of Leander. The picture goes to the Manchester Gallery.

"The Women of Amphissa," by L. Alma-Tadema, represents the market-place of that city with sleeping Bacchantes, with white robes, ivy wreaths, tambourines, and leopard-skins, watched over by the women of the city. Dawn is breaking over the marble pavement and columns of the buildings.

"Mercy," by Sir J. E. Millais, is a scene on St. Bartholomew's Day, 1572, and a companion piece to "A Huguenot." A priest, standing in an open door, is beckoning a soldier, bearing the badge of the cross, to join in the massacre, while a kneeling nun is attempting to restrain him.

"Samson," by S. J. Solomon, is a large canvas (8 feet high × 12 feet), representing the struggle of the strong man with the Philistines after his locks are shorn.

Briton Riviere's "Old World Wanderer" represents a Greek explorer who has landed on the shore of a rocky bay from a galley seen in the distance. He is walking along, spear in hand, his presence unnoticed by the gulls, which have never had 'cause to fear a human being.

"Misery and Mercy," by Frederick Goodall, is the oft-told story of Christ and the adulteress. "The Institution of the Franciscan Order," by Edward Armitage, is a large picture (11 feet, 6 inches × 17 feet) painted for St. John's Catholic church, Islington. "The First Cloud" is one of W. Q. Orchardson's best and most characteristic pictures, representing a handsome drawing-room interior, with a husband standing with his back to the fire, while his wife walks out in graceful anger. It goes to Australia. John S. Sargent's "Carnation, Lily, Lily, Rose," two little girls in a garden, with a foreground of lilies and rose-carnations, has been purchased by the Royal Academy under the Chantry bequest.

Marcus Stone and Luke Fildes were elected full members of the Royal Academy, and Alfred Gilbert, sculptor, an associate member. W. F. Calderon was elected Keeper of the Royal Academy in place of Frederick R. Pickersgill, resigned.

London: Grosvenor Gallery.—The winter exhibition consisted of a collection of 166 works of Sir Anton Van Dyck, principally portraits, including many of the best examples from Windsor and other noble collections throughout England. Among them were the well-known portraits of Charles I, of Henrietta Maria, and of their children, of Van Dyck himself, and of many of the lords and ladies of the time whom he depicted. Other pictures were "Armida and Rinaldo," "The Betrayal of Christ," "Dædalus," "Virgin and St. Catherine," "Christ giving the Keys to Peter," and a "Pieta."

The eleventh summer exhibition of the Grosvenor Gallery contained 420 numbers, including oil-paintings, water-colors, and sculpture. Among the noteworthy pictures were the contributions of Edward Burne-Jones, "The Garden of Pan," representing the youthful god playing to a nude youth and maiden, seated. "The Baleful Head," one of a series illustrative of the story of Perseus and Andromeda, exhibits the former showing the latter the reflection in water of the head of Medusa. By him also were a portrait of a damsel in lapis-lazuli blue seated before a circular mirror; "Katie," a girl lying on a sofa reading; and a memorial tablet. George F. Watts's "Judgment of Paris" represents the three goddesses standing facing the spectator in a golden haze on a floor of clouds. Holman Hunt sent two works, "Amaryllis" (an illustration of Herrick's "Pastoral Song to the King"), and "Master Hilary the Tracer," a boy tracing a picture at a window. E. J. Poynter's "Corner in the Market-Place" represents a young mother seated on a marble bench watching an infant playing on the floor, with a girl seated beside it binding a wreath. W. B. Richmond's "Icarus" depicts him at the moment of starting on his flight from a high rock above the sea. C. E. Halle's "Buondelmonte and the Donati" is an illustration of an incident which led to the war of the Guelphs and the Ghibellines, as related in Machiavelli's "History of Florence." Sir John E. Millais and Hubert Herkomer contributed portraits.

An exhibition of a collection of the works of Basil Vereschagin, the Russian painter, was held in the Grosvenor Gallery in October. Among the pictures were: "After the Battle," "Blowing from Guns in British India," "The Spy," "Skobeleff at Shipka," "The Road of the War Prisoners," "Before the Attack," "The Future Emperor of India" (entrance of Prince of Wales into Jeypore), and " Crucifixion by the Romans."

London: Miscellaneous.—The art sales in 1887 were not as noteworthy as those of the preceding year. One of the most interesting was the famous collection of engravings made by the late Duke of Buccleugh, begun March 8, and lasting twelve days, including the works of Landseer, Sir Joshua Reynolds, Adrian van Ostade, and others, and a nearly full set of Rembrandt's etchings. High prices were obtained for some of the rarer states of fine examples by Rembrandt: The Hundred-Guilder Piece, "Jesus Healing the Sick," first state, £1,800; "Coppenol," large plate, second state, £1,190; "Coppenol," small plate, first state, £320; "Jesus before Pilate," first state, £1,150; "Portrait of Van Tolling," second state, £800; "Abraham Fransz," second state, £510.

On April 2 the collection of Charles H. Rickards, of Manchester, was sold, including 57 pictures and designs by George F. Watts, which realized £15,686. Of these, many of which were replicas, "Love and Death" went at £1,155; "Love and Life," £1,207; "Return of the Dove," £903; "Angel of Death," £577; "Time, Death, and Judgment," £525. The portrait of Herr Joachim was bought for the Chicago Gallery at £441. At the same sale Alma-Tadema's "Emperor Hadrian visiting a Romano-British Pottery" (R. A., 1884) was sold for 750 guineas; Vicat Cole's "Heart of

Surrey" (1874) for 680 guineas; and George H. Boughton's "Music Lesson" (1880) for 800 guineas.

The J. Graham collection, sold April 30, realized a total of £61,847. Among the notable canvases disposed of were: Paul Delaroche, "Christian Martyr," 550 guineas; "Mary Magdalene," 620 guineas; "St. John in Patmos," 580 guineas. Henri Leys, "Antwerp during the Spanish Occupation," 1,400 guineas. J. L. Gérôme, "The Nile Boat," 1,500 guineas. Rosa Bonheur, "Early Morning in Forest of Fontainebleau," 810 guineas; "Highland Raid," 3,900 guineas. Sir Edwin Landseer, "The Shepherd's Bible," 1,020 guineas. Holman Hunt, "Finding of Jesus in the Temple," 1,200 guineas. John Linnell, "Edge of the Wood," 550 guineas; "Christ and the Woman of Samaria," 570 guineas; "Under the Hawthorn-Tree," 1,020 guineas; "The Sheep Drove," 1,850 guineas; "Return of Ulysses," 1,400 guineas; "The Peat-Gatherers" (with Cox), 215 guineas. Sir John E. Millais, "Dream of the Past," 1,300 guineas. D. G. Rossetti, "Venus Verticordia," 450 guineas; "Pandora," 550 guineas. Sir David Wilkie, "The School" (his last work), 1,650 guineas. Edward Burne-Jones, "Fides" (tempera), 440 guineas; "Sperantia" (tempera), 640 guineas. Turner, "Italian Landscape," 1,100 guineas; "The Wreck Buoy," 1,000 guineas; "Van Goyen going about to choose a Subject," 6,500 guineas; "Mercury and Argus," 3,600 guineas. Sir Joshua Reynolds, "The Schoolboys" (Masters Gawler), 2,310 guineas. Gainsborough, "The Sisters" (Lady Day and Baroness de Noailles), 9,500 guineas.

In May Edwin Long's "Christmas at Seville" (1868) sold at Chrystie's for 1,030 guineas; John Linnell's "Storm in Harvest," 1,450 guineas; Holman Hunt's "Scene from 'Two Gentlemen of Verona,'" 1,000 guineas (Birmingham Museum); "The Scapegoat," 1,350 guineas; David Cox's "Going to the Hay-field," 1,805 guineas.

In Mr. Kaye Knowles's collection, sold May 14, which brought £18,343, were: Meissonier, "The Smoker" (water-color), 500 guineas; Alma-Tadema, "A Bacchante—There he is" (1875), 550 guineas; Millais, "Over the Hills and Far Away," 5,000 guineas (G. Glayton).

The collection of the Earl of Lonsdale, sold in June, realized £62,702, of which the pictures brought £28,713. Among the noteworthy canvases were: Reynolds, "Laughing Girl," 240 guineas. J. B. Pater, "The Toilet," 845 guineas. F. Drouais, "Madame du Barri," 950 guineas; "Flower-Gatherers," 1,000 guineas. Gainsborough, "Horses Drinking," 1,620 guineas. Pannini, "Exterior of St. Peter's," 800 guineas; "Interior of St. Peter's," 1,100 guineas. J. B. Santerre, "Mlle. Charlotte Desmares," 2,000 guineas. Boucher, "Madame de Pompadour," 9,900 guineas.

In July, Gainsborough's portrait of the "Hon. Mrs. Henry Fane" (1777), from Fulbeck Hall, Frantham, sold for 4,586 guineas.

Manchester.—In the exhibition in honor of the Queen's Jubilee the fine-art section was an epitome of the history of British art within the Victorian era. The thirteen picture-galleries were painted and decorated under the supervision of Mr. Burne-Jones, who was himself represented by twelve pictures, including the "Wheel of Fortune," the "Chant d'Amour," and the series illustrating the "Story of Pygmalion." Ten works by Dante Rossetti hung in one gallery, among them "Dante's Dream," "Beata Beatrix," "The Blessed Damosel," and "The Blue Bower." Holman Hunt was represented by five examples, including "Claudio and Isabella," "The Scapegoat," and "The Shadow of the Cross"; and Ford Madox Brown by his "Work," "Romeo and Juliet," and "Cromwell on his Farm." Sir John E. Millais had fifteen works, among them "The Vale of Rest," "The Boyhood of Raleigh," "Asleep," "Awake," and the wonderful portrait of "Cardinal Newman." Alma-Tadema's "Painter's Studio," "Sculptor's Studio," "Parting Kiss," "Vintage Festival," "The Apodyterium," and others, nearly filled one room; and George Frederick Watts's twenty-three pictures, including "Love and Death" and many of his portraits, dominated another. Edwin Long's "Diana or Christ" and "Babylonian Marriage-Market," Sir Frederick Leighton's "Daphnephoria," and characteristic works by Sir James Linton and Messrs. Poynter, Fildes, Orchardson, Gow, Vicat Cole, Hook, Miss Montalba, and numerous others, made up a large and most interesting collection.

St. Petersburg.—The Hermitage has been enriched by the collection of Prince Galitzin, acquired by the Government for 800,000 rubles, comprising, besides painting and statuary, porcelain, tapestries, and valuable illuminated books and manuscripts of the fourteenth and fifteenth centuries. The most important picture is a triptych by Raphael, representing Christ on Calvary, surrounded by the Virgin, St. John, and two other persons, formerly presented by the confessor of Pope Alexander VI to the Dominicans of San Gimignano, and acquired by Prince Galitzin in 1840.

United States: Exhibitions, etc.—The National Academy of Design, New York, held its sixty-second annual exhibition (April 4 to May 14), with 503 works. The sales at the close amounted to $33,000. J. Francis Murphy was elected an academician, and Alfred Kappes, Frederick W. Freer, Walter L. Palmer, Thomas W. Dewing, and Walter Shirlaw, associates. The Clarke prize for the best figure-composition was awarded to Thomas W. Dewing for his decorative picture entitled "Days." The first Hallgarten prize, $300, was given to Alfred Kappes for his genre picture, "Buckwheat Cakes"; the second, $200, to Walter L. Palmer for landscape, "January"; the third, $100, to D. W. Tryon, for a landscape. Messrs. Palmer and Tryon being ineligible as to age, their prizes could not be given to them, and they will probably be added to those of next year. The Norman W. Dodge prize of $300, for the best picture painted in the United States by a woman, was awarded to Mrs. Mary Curtis Richardson for her portrait - piece entitled "Lenten Lilies."

At the third annual Prize Fund Exhibition of the American Art Association, held in New York in May, the catalogue contained 242 numbers, including pictures and sculpture. Two prizes of $2,000 each were awarded as follows: Charles H. Davis for his landscape entitled "Late Afternoon"; Edward Gay for a landscape, "Broad Acres." The former belongs to the Union League Club and the latter to the Metropolitan Museum. Ten gold medals of $100 each were distributed as follows: Robert Blum for "Venetian Lacemakers"; W. L. Dodge, "Death of Minnehaha"; Horatio Walker, "Milkmaid"; George W. Maynard, "Sappho"; Carlton Wiggins, "Early Morning"; J. F. Murphy, "September Afternoon"; F. D. Millet, "Difficult Duet"; J. Scott Hartley, "Satan Vanquished" (sculpture); George Hitchcock, "Toilers of the Sea"; D. W. Tryon, "Night."

The Society of American Artists held its ninth annual exhibition at the Yandell Gallery, New York, April 25 to May 14, with 148 entries. A prize of $300, offered to the society by Dr. W. Seward Webb for the best landscape by an American artist under forty years of age, was awarded to J. Francis Murphy for his "Brook and Field."

The American Water-Color Society's twentieth annual exhibition, held in New York (January 31 to February 26), contained 656 works. An exhibition of works by the New York Etching Club was held in one of the rooms of the Academy at the same time.

An exhibition of 223 pictures by French artists was held at the Academy, New York (May 25 to June 30), under the management of M. Durand-Ruel, of Paris. The place of honor was occupied by Eugène Delacroix's great picture, "The Death of Sardanapalus" (Salon, 1827), which marked the transition of the French school from classicism to romanticism. Other noted pictures were ten studies by Puvis de Chavannes, from which were painted the mural decorations of the Pantheon in Paris and the museum at Amiens; Manet's "Death of Maximilian," and examples by Henner, Renoir, Monet, Jules Dupré, and other famed artists.

The Metropolitan Museum has received, by bequest of Miss Catherine L. Wolfe, late of New York, a magnificent collection of about 200 works in oil and water-color, valued at from $400,000 to $500,000. It includes chiefly fine examples of the modern French and German schools. Another noteworthy gift, by George I. Seney, of Brooklyn, consists of about twenty pictures, including Lerolle's "Organ Rehearsal," Julian Dupré's "The

Balloon," and Josef Israel's "Expectation" and "Bashful Suitor." Other works acquired by the museum during the past year are "Christopher Columbus at the Court of Ferdinand and Isabella," by Vaclav Brozik, presented by Morris K. Jesup, who purchased it for $30,000; "The Horse Fair," by Rosa Bonheur, presented by Cornelius Vanderbilt; "1807," by Meissonier, and "The Defense of Champigny," by Detaille, presented by Henry Hilton; "Thusnelda at the Triumph of Germanicus," presented by Horace Russell; "The Vintage," by L'Hermitte, presented by William Schaus; "Trustees of the Earl of Westmoreland," by Sir Joshua Reynolds, presented by Junius S. Morgan, London.

Among the important pictures exhibited in New York during the past year were "The Gilder" (Le Doreur), one of Rembrandt's best works, purchased by William Schaus from the heirs of the De Morny estate; "Christ before Pilate," "Christ on Calvary," and "The Death of Mozart," by Mihail Munkacsy; "Madonna and Child," by Franz Defregger; "Tel-el-Kebir," by Alphonse de Neuville; "Une Bergère—Souvenir de la Picardie," by Charles Sprague Pearce, which won the great medal of honor at Ghent, 1886; "Russian Wedding Feast," and "Choosing the Bride," by Konstantin Makoffsky; "The Wise and Foolish Virgins," by Carl von Piloty; "Diana's Hunting Party," and "The Five Senses," by Hans Makart; "Elaine," by Toby Rosenthal; "The Two Sisters," by Charles Giron. Munkacsy's "Christ before Pilate" has been purchased by John Wannamaker, Philadelphia, for more than $100,000, and his "Last Days of Mozart," for $50,000, by R. A. Alger, Detroit, who has presented it to the Detroit Museum. Benjamin-Constant's "Justinian" (Salon, 1886) has been bought by Robert Mannheimer, St. Paul, Minn.; De Neuville's "Tel-el-Kebir" has been purchased by James Hill, also of St. Paul.

The most important art sale of the year was that of the A. T. Stewart collection, which was exhibited at the American Art Galleries, New York, from February 21 until the sale, March 28, and the following days. An illustrated edition of the catalogue, limited to 500 copies, with etchings of the pictures by prominent artists, was issued. The total amount of the sale, including pictures, sculptures, bronzes, ceramics, books, etc., was $581,938. Among the best prices obtained were: Meissonier, "1807," $66,000, "At the Barracks," $16,000, "Charity," $10,500; Rosa Bonheur, "Horse Fair," $53,000; Auguste Bonheur, "Environs of Fontainebleau," $17,800; Gérôme, "Chariot Race," $7,100, "The Gladiators," $11,000, "Une Collaboration," $8,100; Erskine Nicoll, "The Disputed Boundary," $15,250; Mariano Fortuny, "The Serpent Charmer," $13,100, "Beach at Portici," $10,100; Ludwig Knaus, "The Children's Party," $21,800; Constant Troyon, "Landscape and Cattle," $11,000, "Cattle," $7,150; Bouguereau, "Homer and his Guide," $5,200, "Return from the Harvest," $8,100; Zamacois, "The Begging Monk," $4,400; Piloty, "Triumph of Germanicus," $3,900; F. E. Church, "Niagara Falls from American Side," $7,050 (Edinburgh Gallery); Daniel Huntington. "Lady Washington's Reception," $3,300; Daubigny, "End of Month of May," $7,900; Munkacsy, "Visit to the Baby," $8,700; Benjamin-Constant, "Evening on the Terrace," $4,000. The price paid for Meissonier's "1807" was the highest, and that for Rosa Bonheur's "Horse Fair" the second highest, ever given for a picture at an auction sale in this country.

The collection of Henry Probasco, of Cincinnati, sold in New York, April 18, realized more than $170,000 for 102 works. Among the highest prices obtained were: Rousseau, "Summer Landscape," $21,000, "Forest at Fontainebleau," $7,400; J. F. Millet. "Peasants bringing home a New-born Calf," $18,500; Jules Breton, "Colza Gatherers," $16,600; Troyon, "Landscape with Cattle," $10,000; Schreyer, "Russian Landscape," $6,900; Eugène Delacroix, "Clorinda delivering the Martyrs," $6,000.

A collection of pictures, engravings, art books, etc., belonging to the estate of Asher B. Durand, sold also in New York in April, brought $10,656, of which $9,200 was for eighty studies by the artist.

The Richard H. Halstead collection, sold in New York, January 10, brought $84,820. Works by Bouguereau and by Vibert brought respectively $7,600 and $7,300, and William Bliss Baker's "Woodland Brook," $2,300. At the Robert Graves sale, New York, February 9 to 11, Corot's "Landscape with Figures" brought $10,100; Bouguereau's "Cupid Disarmed," $7,700; "Le Jour," $5,500; "Little Sufferer," $2,525; Rousseau's "Oak Tree in Autumn," $2,000; David Johnson's "On the Unadilla," $1,575.

The Charles F. Haseltine collection of modern French works was sold in New York, February 15 to 17, and realized $107,177.

The fifty-seventh annual exhibition of the Pennsylvania Academy of Fine Arts, Philadelphia (March 10 to April 21), comprised 690 numbers, including oil and water-color pictures, black and whites, and sculptures. Among the black and whites were E. A. Abbey's drawings for "She Stoops to Conquer," first exhibited at the Grolier Club, New York. The endowment fund of $100,000, asked for by the Academy, has been more than filled by the subscriptions of about seventy persons.

A statue of John O. Calhoun, by Harnisch, a Philadelphia sculptor resident in Rome, was unveiled in Charleston, S. C., in April. He is represented seated in a chair, and the work is to be supplemented by accessory statues of Truth, Justice, the Constitution, and History, to be finished next year.

A statue of Gen. Garfield, standing, with arm extended, was unveiled in May in Washington.

Figures on the pedestal represent a studious youth, a warrior, and a statesman, emblematic of periods in his career.

A bronze statue of Nathan Hale, by Carl Gerhardt, was unveiled at Hartford, Conn., in June. The figure, which is of heroic size, represents him standing with his palms open as if addressing the crowd about his place of execution.

A soldiers' and sailors' monument, dedicated to those who fell in the civil war, was also unveiled at Hartford. It is a shaft seventy-five feet high and ten feet in diameter, surmounted by a statue of Peace. The pedestal has five steps, with statues of History, Victory, Prosperity, and Patriotism, at the four corners.

An equestrian bronze statue of Gen. Burnside, by Launt Thompson, was unveiled at Providence, R. I., July 4.

An equestrian bronze statue of Gen. George G. Meade, by Alexander Milne-Calder, was unveiled in Fairmount Park, Philadelphia, October 18.

A bronze statue of Solomon Juneau, the first white settler, mayor, and postmaster of Milwaukee, Wis., was unveiled in Juneau Park, in that city, July 6.

The bronze statue of Lincoln, by Augustus St. Gaudens, was inaugurated in Chicago. The figure, which is eleven and a half feet high, stands on a pedestal of pink granite, forming a long, curved seat approached by steps. The work cost $40,000, and the money was bequeathed for the purpose by Eli Bates, of Chicago.

A bronze statue of Gen. Moses Cleveland, the founder of Cleveland, Ohio, by J. G. C. Hamilton, was unveiled in that city in November.

Montreal.—At an exhibition in April of pictures by native and foreign artists, some noteworthy works were shown, among them Jules Bréton's "Communicants," Benjamin-Constant's "After the Victory," Gabriel Max's "Raising of Jairus's Daughter," Henner's "La Source," Bouguereau's "Crown of Flowers," and choice examples by Millet, Corot, Diaz, Dupré, Berne-Bellecour, Leys, Pettie, Boughton, Jacomin, Van Marcke, Kowalski, and other representative artists.

FISHERY QUESTIONS. One of the minor points at issue in the Revolutionary War was the preservation of the ancient fishery franchises. By the terms of the treaty of peace the Americans were accorded the liberty of fishing both on the banks and within the territorial waters of the maritime provinces, the same as was possessed by British subjects; and also of drying and curing their catch on the unoccupied coasts of Nova Scotia, the Magdalen Islands, and Labrador. The Loyalists who settled Nova Scotia, and whom the States refused to compensate for their confiscated property, raised difficulties in regard to the fishery privileges granted to the Americans. In the war of 1812–'15 Great Britain declared the treaty rights to be abrogated, and when the treaty of peace was concluded refused to accept the restoration of her former right to navigate the Mississippi in return for the fishery. Thus the United States lost the inshore fishing rights, and the use of the uninhabited coasts for drying and curing fish, and were restricted to the limit of three nautical miles from the nearest shore, which has been accepted in international law.

The Fishery Treaty of 1818.—American vessels were seized, and a diplomatic correspondence was opened by John Quincy Adams, who claimed that the treaty of 1783 had recognized an imprescriptible right. The New Englanders had developed and defended the fisheries, and the acknowledgment of their rights was of the same nature as the partition of the territories in North America by the same treaty. The question was settled by the Convention of 1818, whereby the United States gave up the right claimed of fishing and of curing and drying fish within the maritime boundaries except on the southern shore of Newfoundland, from the Rameau Islands westward to Cape Ray, and thence along the whole western and northern shore to Quirpon Island, on the opposite coast of Labrador from Mount Joly northward through the straits of Belle Isle, and on all the shores of the continent and islands farther north; also on the shores of the Magdalen Islands. The right to dry or cure fish on the coasts of Newfoundland and Labrador described was granted for so long a period as those coasts should remain unsettled, and afterward on agreement with the inhabitants or proprietors of the ground. The rights defined in this treaty were to be permanent and not liable to be denounced or to lapse in case of war. The United States renounced the liberty to take, cure, or dry fish on or within three marine miles of the other coasts, bays, or harbors of the British dominions, "provided, however, that the American fishermen shall be permitted to enter such bays or harbors for the purpose of shelter and of repairing damages therein, of purchasing wood, and of obtaining water, and for no other purpose whatever; but they shall be under such restrictions as may be necessary to prevent their taking, drying, or curing fish therein or in any manner abusing the privileges hereby reserved for them." The American commissioners originally inserted bait among the supplies that might be procured, and then suffered it to be stricken out as being a concession of slight value, as was the fact before the mackerel fishery was developed. The inshore mackerel fishery tempted American fishermen to transgress the three-mile limit, while the provincial authorities began to impose novel penalties for infractions of the treaty, and to interpret its provisions in new ways. In 1841 the British legal authorities broached the headlands question, laying down the doctrine that in all bays the three-mile limit should be taken from a line drawn from headland to headland, and that Ameri-

cans therefore possessed no fishery rights in the bays of Fundy and Chaleur; also that they had not the right to land on the shores of the Magdalen Islands or to navigate the Strait of Canso. The Nova Scotian authorities applied the principles thus enunciated, closing to Americans the herring fishery of the Magdalen Islands, and in 1843 seizing a fishing-schooner in the Bay of Fundy. When Edward Everett, the minister at London, demanded an explanation of this act, the British Government offered to admit Americans to the fisheries of the Bay of Fundy; but, on receiving a protest from Nova Scotia, retracted the concession. The question was discussed by a joint commission in 1853, and on the disagreement of the commissioners was decided by an umpire, who held that bays are not territorial waters when the distance from headland to headland exceeds ten marine miles.

The Reciprocity Treaty of 1854.—The fishery question had become involved with negotiations for reciprocity of trade between Canada and the United States, and was used by the politicians of the British provinces as a means of obtaining commercial concessions. In 1854 the Elgin treaty of reciprocity was concluded. Canadian natural products were admitted free of duty into the United States, and the inshore fishing privileges were granted to Americans, as under the treaty of 1783. The maritime provinces objected to this, but the British Government, anxious to obtain for the produce of Canada an outlet to repair the loss of the exclusive market the colonies had enjoyed in Great Britain before the adoption of free trade, paid no attention to them. The provincials had no reason to complain of the operation of the treaty, for the trade that sprang up between them and the neighboring parts of the United States led to the development of neglected resources, and was followed by prosperity such as they had never before known. Even the fisheries partook of the general improvement, and were hardly injured by American competition. By the treaty of 1854 the bounty system came to an end in the United States. The bounties, which had been granted to fishermen by the general Government since 1789, had been one of the chief causes of the jealous and hostile feelings entertained on the fishery question in the maritime provinces. Their removal was the special compensation to the colonial fishing-industry for the admission of Americans to the territorial fishing-grounds. In consequence of unfriendly acts of the British and Canadians during the civil war, the relations between the Government at Washington and the British Government were so strained that neither party was disposed to renew the treaty, which terminated in 1866. The citizens of the maritime provinces now felt aggrieved because the British ministers had not seen a way to perpetuate the commercial relations that had been to them a source of wealth and prosperity.

The President notified the American fishermen by proclamation of the cessation of their fishery rights in Canadian waters, yet they continued to fish within the three-mile limit, as before. Then a license fee was exacted by the provincial authorities, and American fishermen paid it until it was raised from 50 cents to $2 a ton. In 1868 and 1870 the Dominion Parliament passed special acts prohibiting foreign fishermen from poaching on the Canadian grounds, and imposing penalties for their infraction.

The Washington Treaty of 1872.—When the provinces of Nova Scotia and New Brunswick were united to Canada, and the fisheries were placed in charge of a Cabinet minister, that official took measures, not only to protect the Canadian fisheries, but to secure for the fishermen of the Dominion advantages over their American competitors in the open-sea fisheries by reviving the illiberal interpretation that, in periods of tension, had been given to the words of the treaty of 1818. The right of buying bait and other supplies in Canadian ports was called in question. The right of landing fish and shipping them in bond over the railroads to the United States was denied, but the suppression of the practice, as well as the exclusion of Americans from the bay fisheries under the old doctrine that the headlands mark the shore, was left in abeyance pending a satisfactory settlement of the whole question. The Canadian authorities had reason to complain of the New England fishermen, who continued to invade the territorial fishing-grounds without regard to the proclamations of their own Government, or the pains and penalties of the Dominion acts. During 1869-'70 the Canadian Government endeavored to police its fisheries with cruisers, which cost nearly $1,000,000 to maintain. The United States protested at the English court against the exercise of technical rights, such as the prohibition of the purchase of bait. Negotiations were begun for the adjustment of disputes between Great Britain and the United States. The fishery question was complicated with the American claim for damages for the depredations of Confederate cruisers built and fitted out in England. The American Government made an offer of $1,000,000 for the right of the inshore fisheries in perpetuity, but it was declined. The joint commission, which sat at Washington, agreed that the fisheries of Canada and of the United States, north of 39° north latitude, should be thrown open to the citizens of both countries, and that the United States, besides admitting Canadian fish and fish-oil free of duty, should pay in money the value of the rights granted to American fishermen in Canadian waters, with the deduction of the value of the American fishery rights to Canada. The amount was to be fixed by joint commissioners and an umpire. The treaty went into force in 1873. The fishery commission, composed of Messrs. Galt and Kellogg, represent-

ing Canada and the United States, and M. de la Fosse, the Belgian Minister at Washington, as umpire, met at Halifax in 1877. The Canadian counsel claimed that the actual and prospective value of the mackerel fisheries to the United States was $1,000,000 per annum; the American case represented that the commission had nothing to do but to calculate their value from the trade returns, and that the remission of $350,000 of duties, collected annually on fish and oil, was a full equivalent for the Canadian fishery privileges. By its decision, rendered Nov. 23, 1877, the commission fixed the sum due to Canada for the term of treaty at $5,500,000. There was much surprise at the amount of the award, which was compared with the sum awarded to the United States by the "Alabama" commission. Congress authorized the payment only under the proviso that the President should consider that the good faith of the nation demanded it. Mr. Evarts, the Secretary of State, laid before the British Government statistical evidence, showing that the Canadian fisheries were worth to the United States only $25,000 per annum, and that the highest computation would not place their value at more than $125,000, while the duties remitted amounted to $4,200,000 for the twelve years' period of the treaty. Lord Salisbury insisted that the decree of the commission was final, and the award was duly paid.

Some years after the treaty went into operation, the irritation of the Americans was increased by the Fortune Bay dispute. A mob of Newfoundlanders had attacked American fishermen, and driven them out of the bay, for the reason that they were fishing on Sunday, which was forbidden by the local statutes. Lord Salisbury claimed, when the case was presented to him, that the fishery rights were held subject to all local regulations. Lord Granville, who succeeded him, admitted that unreasonable local laws could not act as a restriction of rights granted by treaty. Damages were paid for the Fortune Bay disturbance, and rules for a close season were made the subject of further negotiations. The treaty of Washington was made for ten years, and either party had the right to abrogate it thereafter on two years' notice. The United States promptly renounced the treaty in 1883, and it expired on July 1, 1885.

Recent Fishery Disputes.—As the termination of the fishery rights occurred in the midst of the fishing season, the British Government agreed to prolong them for six months, while the President promised to recommend to Congress the appointment of a joint commission to consider an arrangement for the extension of trade between the United States and British North America. Congress, which even under the Washington Convention had taxed tinned metal cans, now imposed a duty of one cent a pound on preserved fish for the benefit of the Maine canning-establishments. The Canadian authorities proceeded in the spring of 1886 to assert the most inconvenient literal construction of the Convention of 1818, to carry into effect the restrictions that in previous disputes had been only threatened, and to enforce the headlands doctrine in an exaggerated form. They were actuated partly by a desire to extort valuable commercial concessions from the United States and partly by resentment against American fishermen, who, in spite of warnings and penalties, continued to take fish within Canadian jurisdiction, driving the Government to the expense of sending cruisers to patrol the coast. There was an unusual temptation to poach on the Dominion fisheries, because in the season that followed the abrogation of the treaty the run of mackerel was good near the shore but very light outside and on the New England coast. The Canadians sometimes have asserted that the New Englanders, by not observing a close season, have exhausted their own fisheries.

The right to purchase bait, or to land and transship fish, or to enter Canadian ports for any purpose other than the ones specifically mentioned in the treaty of 1818, was strictly inhibited. The United States authorities granted licenses to touch and trade to fishing-vessels, and claimed that, for the purposes of purchasing supplies and transshipping cargoes, they were entitled to all the rights secured to trading-vessels under the treaties. But by a decision of the Canadian customs authorities, no vessel has liberty of commercial intercourse that is manned, equipped, or in any way prepared for taking fish.

During the season of 1886 thirty-two vessels were detained by the Canadian officials, some for buying bait, landing fish, or taking on crews, but in the majority of cases for simply breaking the customs rules by anchoring within the port boundaries or landing persons without regular entry at the custom-house. In no instance was a seizure made for fishing within the three-mile limit, and in only two cases for preparing to fish within the forbidden bounds. In evading the customs and fishery regulations, the fishermen of Gloucester and other New England coast towns were aided by their numerous relatives and business associates in the provincial ports. More than one hundred complaints of illegal interference, arrests, and seizures were made to the United States Government against the Canadian authorities. Some of the arrested fishermen were fined, some were released after being detained and sustaining considerable losses, two vessels were condemned to confiscation, and one of these was fitted out at St. Johns as a cruiser.

The American Case.—In providing fishing-vessels with trading-permits the United States authorities desired to bring cases of seizure and arrest before the British admiralty courts, in order that they be may decided according to international law, and not under acts of the Dominion Parliament that are believed to be in contravention of principles of general application and acceptance between friendly nations. Minister Phelps held that the right to purchase bait and supplies belonged to American vessels by the ordinary usage of international intercourse. The United States Government does not desire to obtain the privilege of the inshore fisheries, which are considered of very little value, since the use of purse-nets has increased the catch of mackerel in the outside waters. The yield of the duty on Canadian fish imports is worth more, and the Americans would be unwilling to remit that duty to secure the inshore fisheries, while the Canadians would desire larger concessions.

Minister Phelps took the ground that the restrictive provisions of the treaty of 1818 were intended to prevent encroachments on the territorial fisheries, and should be interpreted according to their spirit and purpose. Formerly the British Government was guided by the same princi le, and never before had American fishermen been denied the privilege of entering the ports and procuring bait or engaging crews. In a dispatch of Lord Kimberley it was formerly held that, while the exclusion of American fishermen, except for purposes of shelter, repairs, or obtaining wood or water, might be warranted by the letter of the treaty of 1818, it would be "an extreme measure, inconsistent with the general policy of the empire." In reference to the seizure of the "David J. Adams" for purchasing bait in the port of Digby and violating the customs act by not reporting to the authorities, Mr. Phelps, in a communication dated June 2, 1886, called attention to the fact that fishing-vessels had been accustomed for forty years to do as this vessel had done. The seizure and confiscation of vessels for such acts he considered a question apart from the interpretation of the treaty. At the time of the seizure of this and other vessels there was no British or colonial law prohibiting or providing any penalty for the purchase of bait. There had never before been a seizure of an American vessel for the purchase of bait or other supplies, but in every previous case vessels condemned were shown to have been guilty of fishing or preparing to fish within the prohibited limit. On the Canadian side the argument was advanced that the catching of bait is fishing, and that, since it is necessarily caught within the three-mile limit, to come within that limit and buy fish is to be responsible for the fishing. The infliction of severe penalties, amounting even to confiscation of vessels and their contents for technical violations of a treaty, even if the Canadian construction were admitted, was considered by the American minister to be a ground for the recovery of damages.

Retaliatory Legislation.—During the Congressional session of 1886, a bill was introduced in the House of Representatives to close American ports to Canadian vessels, and to forbid the entrance of Canadian fresh or salt fish or other products into the United States by railroad, if the Dominion authorities continued to deny to American fishermen the rights secured to them under the treaty of 1818 and by international law. For this was substituted a bill, which originated in the Senate, giving the President discretionary authority to deny to the vessels of the British Dominions entrance into any or all the ports or waters of the United States, except in cases of distress, and to prohibit the entry of fish or other products from them into the United States.

Diplomatic Arrangements.—In December, 1886, the American minister in London presented to Lord Iddesleigh a proposal for an *ad interim* arrangement, the chief feature of which was to establish a mixed commission in order to "separate the exclusive from the common right of fishing on the coasts and in the adjacent waters of the British North American colonies." The vexed question of the headlands was to be considered as settled by the former decision of a British referee, viz., that bays can only be claimed as territorial waters when the entrance is ten miles wide or less, or from the point where the width does not exceed ten miles. American fishermen were to have the right of purchasing bait and other supplies, and British and American war-vessels were to act as police to prevent poaching on the inshore fisheries. The Canadian Government declined to accept the proposals either as to the headlands or as to provisionally granting commercial privileges to fishing-craft. On March 24, 1887, Lord Salisbury presented a counter-proposition, which was to return for a season to the condition of things as they existed under the Treaty of Washington. The American fishermen were to have the right of buying bait, hiring crews, and shipping fish by railroad, with the privilege of the inshore fisheries, and the Canadians the right of importing fish duty free into the United States. Mr. Bayard had already proposed a mixed commission. After considerable further correspondence, Joseph Chamberlain was sent to Washington in the autumn to endeavor to effect a settlement. The conference began in November, and was continued through December without accomplishing much toward reconciling American and Canadian views. A *résumé* of the diplomatic history of the North Atlantic fisheries from their first discovery is given in "The Fishery Question," by Charles Isham (New York, 1887).

French Fishery Rights.—The French treaty with England in 1783 secured to France fishery rights nearly identical with those accorded to the United States. A large part of the French rights exist at the present day. There has been as much or more hostility to French fishermen in the colonies as was ever felt toward Americans. The right, not only to fish in their waters but to land on their coasts for drying and curing fish, is felt to be a grievance by the Newfoundlanders—the more so because the French have the advantage of a bounty of over $3 a quintal from their Government. The British Government has found it necessary to veto various acts of the colonial Legislature designed to hamper the French fishermen. There were certain open questions between the French and British Governments which, after an intermittent controversy extending over many years, were settled by a new convention on Nov. 14, 1885, which was agreed to notwithstanding its being unacceptable to the colonists. The English Government has not been guided by the same rules in dealing with the French as have governed its recent course toward the United States. In reference to an act passed by the Legislative Council and Assembly of Newfoundland, in regard to the sale of bait, the home Government declared that, in the negotiations that had taken place since 1857, a provision for the sale of bait had always been contemplated.

North Pacific Fishery Dispute.—In 1868, Congress placed Alaska under the jurisdiction of the Treasury Department, and in the same act forbade the killing, except by leave of the department, of any mink, marten, sable, or fur-seal, or other fur-bearing animal within the limits of Alaska Territory, or in the waters thereof, under penalty of fine or imprisonment or both, and the forfeiture of any vessel found in violation of the act. The Pribylov islands of St. Paul and St. George, which are the breeding-grounds of the seal, were leased to the Alaska Commercial Company, of San Francisco, at a rental of $60,000 a year, with $2 royalty for every sealskin shipped. The company is allowed to kill none but young male seals, and only during certain months, and is restricted to the number of 100,-000 in any one year, while the use of firearms, or of any means tending to drive the seals away, is prohibited. These stringent regulations are designed for the preservation of the seals. They have hitherto been more strictly enforced than similar regulations were under the Russian rule, and, consequently, the seals, which had begun to diminish, have become more numerous since the monopoly of the Alaska Company began in 1870. The lack of protective laws has resulted in the disappearance of the fur-bearing seal, which once abounded in the Kerguelen group and other islands of the southern hemisphere, in the Falkland Islands, and on the coasts and islands of South America, from all their known habitats excepting these Alaskan isles. The Indians of the Pribylov Islands are allowed to kill and sell a certain number of seals for their own benefit. The Alaska Company has the monopoly of the fur-trade of Alaska, as well as of the seal-fishery of the islands, and, since other fur-animals besides seals vanish rapidly before the destructive agencies of white men, many obstacles are placed in the way of opening Alaska to traders, settlers, miners, and hunters. With the increase of population on the western coast of North America, the difficulty of preserving the seal-fisheries from destruction becomes greater. Schooners and steamers from British Columbia hover around the seal islands, and find ways of obtaining a share in the profitable seal-trade that the American company can not prevent. American vessels also engage in the business, which may be the main object of the trip, or may be pursued in connection with fishing and walrus-hunting. The seal-hunters have been accustomed to shoot the seals in the waters adjacent to the breeding-places, but this method of obtaining them, though exceedingly destructive, would not be profitable by itself, for only a small proportion of the animals hit are killed instantly and secured while floating on the water. It was more advantageous to land on the islands and shoot the seals on the rocks. In 1876 the United States sent cruisers to put a stop to such depredations, and since then a more or less effective guard has been maintained against poachers on the islands. It has been much more difficult to prevent an illicit traffic in sealskins with the Indians, who stalk and harpoon the seals on the islands, and take the skins out to sea in their boats, exchanging them for money or whisky with the vessels engaged in the traffic. In order to prevent the destructive practices that threatened the extermination of the seals, the Treasury Department in 1886 attempted to enforce a doctrine that it had not previously asserted, viz., that Behring Sea was a *mare clausum*, and that the United States had jurisdiction over one half of it. This right was specifically granted in the treaty ceding Alaska to the United States, yet in 1822, when Russia attempted to claim sovereignty over the sea, the United States, as well as Great Britain, raised a strong protest against the doctrine that a nation could claim territorial jurisdiction over a sea having an entrance a thousand miles wide. The commander of the revenue cutter "Corwin" was instructed to seize all sealers found to the east of a line drawn from between the Diomede Islands in Behring strait in a southwesterly direction to a point equidistant from Copper and Otter islands in the Aleutian group. In 1886 the British schooners "Carolina," "Onward," and "Thornton" were captured and taken to Sitka. A trial was held, the vessels were condemned, the masters fined, and the seal-skins on board confiscated and sent to San Francisco. The vessels were not taken within the three-mile limit. Several American schooners were captured and confiscated. Judge Dawson told the captain of the "Thornton," in sentencing him to a fine of $500 and imprisonment, that it was little better than piracy to go into the waters of another nation and interfere with its industries as he and the other prisoners were doing. The British Government made a demand for the release of the prisoners, and presented a claim of about $160,000 for loss of property and damages for loss of time and probable profits, and for illegal arrest and imprisonment. The first demand for information was made on September 21, and the claim for redress was presented on Oct. 21, 1886. On Jan. 26, 1887, by direction of the President, Attorney-General Garland sent a dispatch to the authorities in Alaska ordering the unconditional release of the imprisoned men, and the surrender of the vessels and other property. The order was not executed, and it was not till September 20 that a letter was received from the United States Marshal at Sitka, explaining that the telegram was supposed to be a fraudulent dispatch. On October 12 the Attorney-General sent another telegram, ordering the vessels to be released, which directions were repeated in a letter dated October 15. Meanwhile, the officials of the Treasury Department had not revoked their instructions, but had sent out the steamer "Rush" with the same orders, which during the summer of 1887 seized the British vessels "Dolphin," "Annie Beck," "W. P. Saywood," "Grace," "Alfred Adams," besides seven American sealers, at distances of from thirty to seventy miles from land.

FLORIDA. State Government.—The following were the State officers during the year: Governor, Edward A. Perry, Democrat; Lieutenant-Governor, Milton H. Mabry; Secretary of State, John L. Crawford; Comptroller, William D. Barnes; Treasurer, Edward S. Crill; Attorney-General, Charles M. Cooper; Superintendent of Public Instruction, Albert J. Russell; Commissioner of Lands and Immigration, Charles L. Mitchell; Chief-Justice of the Supreme Court, George G. McWhorter, succeeded by A. E. Maxwell; Associate Justices, George P. Raney and R. B. Van Valkenburgh.

Legislative Session.—The Legislature assembled on April 5, and continued in session sixty days. Being the first that had met since the adoption of the new Constitution in 1886, it had important work to perform in revising and enlarging the laws to harmonize with or give effect to that instrument. An unusually large amount of legislation was secured, in spite of the fact that much time was taken from the session by a prolonged contest in the Democratic caucus over the succession to United States Senator C. W. Jones. Ex-Gov. Bloxham and Gov. Perry were the leading candidates through nearly 100 ballots, when, upon their withdrawal, Samuel Pasco, Speaker of the House, was chosen as a compromise candidate. The Legislature in joint session elected him Senator by a vote of 84 to 17 for F. S. Goodrich, Republican. As the term of Senator Jones expired in March, before the meeting of the Legislature, the Governor had previously appointed Gen. J. J. Finley to hold the office in the interim.

The legislation adopted embraces a railroad commission act, an act revising the entire method of assessing and collecting State taxes, a new appointment of members of the Legislature according to the census of 1885, and a State militia bill. The last measure provides for the organization of not more than 10 companies of volunteers, to be called the Florida State troops, establishes armories for them, and prescribes their equipment and discipline. Before the passage of this act the State militia was disorganized and almost defunct. New charters were granted to the cities of Jacksonville, Tampa, Fernandina, Palatka, and De Land. The St. John's Conference College (Methodist), and De Land University, in the city of De Land, were incorporated. The regular appropriation for the year 1887 was $470,293; for 1888, $405,900; and for the first quarter of 1889, $51,400. Other acts of the session were as follow:

Appropriating $10,000 to pay the debt of the East Florida Seminary, and $1,000 for each of the next two years for its support.

To repeal all laws or parts of laws that impose a license tax upon commercial agents or " drummers."

To supply deficiencies for the years 1885 and 1886, viz.: for expenses of the Constitutional Convention of 1885, $20,500; for expenses of the census of 1885, $6,000; for contingent expenses of the Supreme Court, $2,600; for jurors and witnesses during 1886 and previous years, $76,000.

To provide, in accordance with the new Constitution, that on petition of one fourth of the electors of any county an election may be had, not oftener than once in two years, to decide whether the sale of intoxicating liquors shall be prohibited therein, and regulating the procedure at such elections.

Fixing the date of elections, the officers to be voted for, and the procedure at such elections under the new Constitution. [By this act a complete set of State officers—legislative, executive, and judicial—are to be chosen on the Tuesday after the first Monday of November, 1888, and a general election is to be held every two years thereafter. Members of the Lower House of the Legislature are elected for two years, Justices of the Supreme Court for six years, one of them retiring every two years; all other State officers hold their places for four years.]

Requiring all railroads in the State to be fenced.

Prohibiting the consolidation of parallel or competing lines of railway in the State.

Giving mechanics, artisans, laborers, and persons furnishing materials, a lien on the property constructed, or upon the property of the contractor for such work or materials.

Forbidding the purchase of seed cotton at night.

To protect the fresh-water fisheries of the State.

Fixing the age of consent in females at 17 years.

To suppress gambling-houses and gambling.

The following new counties were created: Osceola, from portions of Orange and Brevard; Lee, out of Monroe; De Soto, out of Manatee; Lake, from portions of Sumter and Orange; Pasco and Citrus counties, from portions of Hernando.

To authorize the Savannah, Florida, and Western Railway Company to construct and operate a railroad from Tallahassee, and also a railroad from Monticello to the Georgia and Florida State line.

Granting to certain persons the right to dig and mine in the beds of the navigable streams and waters for phosphate rocks and deposits.

To incorporate the Florida Normal School and Business Institute at White Springs.

For the incorporation and regulation of building and loan associations.

To provide for the incorporation of colleges, academies, and other institutions of learning.

To provide for the appointment of a board of examiners, and to regulate the practice of dentistry.

Amending the procedure in taking lands of private individuals or corporations for the use of railroads or canals.

Providing that the county judges shall issue marriage licenses, and that these shall be recorded.

To prescribe the rules of pleading and practice of the county courts of the several counties of this State in civil and criminal cases.

Forbidding free passes or special rates for members of the Legislature or any salaried State officer.

Finances.—The bonded debt of the State, at the beginning of the year, consisted of $350,000 seven-per-cent. bonds of 1871, and $925,000 six-per-cent. bonds of 1873, making a total indebtedness of $1,275,000. Of these bonds, $218,800 are held in the sinking fund of the State, and $625,500 by the various educational funds, leaving only $430,700 in the hands of individuals. No provision being made for refunding them before maturity, the State is unable to take advantage of the lower rates of interest now prevailing. During 1886 the total State expenditures were $407,806, and the income from State tax and licenses $423,679, of which $296,323 was the State tax. In 1887 the same tax was $328,088, an increase caused by a law raising the rate from 4 to 4½ mills. This act was rendered necessary by a provision of the new Constitution, throwing upon the State the cost and expenses of criminal prosecutions, which were heretofore paid by the counties, and which amount to about $100,000 annually. At the same time, the county tax was reduced one mill, making a general reduction of taxes to the people of half a mill. The total county tax in 1886 was $662,067; in 1887, $666,879.

Statistics.—The population of the State, now over 350,000, is increasing more rapidly than at any previous period. In two years from March, 1885, the city of Pensacola gained 3,684 people, increasing her whole population to 14,220. One city, Gainesville, containing 5,088 people, has gained 1,200 in a year. The following figures are taken from the assessment rolls of 1886: number of acres of land assessed, 19,888,091; number improved and cultivated, 709,950; value of city or town lots with improvements, $16,314,568; value of other real property, $41,159,728; number of horses and mules, 40,217; cattle, 464,454; sheep and goats, 111,093; swine, 177,187; value of all animals, $5,466,243; value of all personal property, $18,436,045; total valuation of real and personal property, $76,611,409.

Charities and Prisons.—The superintendent of the State Insane Asylum reports an increase of patients for the two years ending Jan. 1, 1887, from 157 to 192. An additional three-story brick building has been erected. There is a large farm connected with the institution in successful operation. The total cost to the State for the support of its lunatics in 1886 was $44,954.

At the State Blind and Deaf Mute Institute, 15 pupils were in attendance at the beginning of the year.

The convicts are hired out and cared for, without expense to the State, under a four years' contract ending in December, 1889, with an individual who employs them in the manufacture of naval stores. Their number has increased from 197 in 1885 to 236 in 1886, and 313 in 1887. The health of the prisoners and their treatment by the lessee are satisfactory.

Education.—The State superintendent reports for 1886 an increased organization and efficiency in the public schools, and a hopeful prospect. The following table shows their growth and condition as compared with 1885:

ITEMS.	1885.	1886.
Number of schools	1,724	1,919
Number of pupils	67,827	79,887
Number of male teachers	991	1,018
Number of female teachers	782	825
Average daily attendance	45,850	44,813

Estimating the population at 350,000, Florida has a school for every 175 inhabitants. She expends $5 for every child of school age and $7.37 for every average attendant upon the schools. During 1885 and 1886 teachers' institutes were held in twenty-eight counties, bringing under their instruction 795 teachers. Normal departments for instruction of white teachers were conducted in the West and East Florida seminaries, and normal schools for colored teachers organized and conducted at Tallahassee and Gainesville, and continued for two months, giving 275 attendants the benefit of training for their work as educators. These short normal courses were the only instruction the State could offer for the training of teachers, until the Legislature this year provided for the erection of buildings and the maintenance of regularly equipped normal schools at De Funiak Springs and at Tallahassee, the former for white and the latter for colored pupils. The higher institutions, East and West Florida seminaries, and the State Agricultural College are making satisfactory progress.

Railroads.—The Governor, in his message to the Legislature, says: "The two years last past have witnessed the building and equipment of more than 500 miles of new, and the renovation of more than 500 miles of almost worse than useless old road, thus substantially adding to first-class railroad facilities fully 1,000 miles. In no other equal time in the history of our State has such progress been made." The total number of miles of road assessed in 1886 was 1,701, with a total assessment of railroad property amounting to $11,372,016. During 1887 the Legislature granted letters of incorporation to nine new companies, and probably over 150 miles of road were constructed. The assessed value of railroad property for this year rose to $12,752,331, a gain of $1,380,315 over 1886.

By the railroad law passed this year, the duty of supervision was given into the hands of a board of three commissioners, appointed by the Governor, and holding office four years. They have power to make and establish reasonable rates of fare for passengers and freight, and to make any other reasonable regulations applicable to all the railroads of the State. They can require railroads to produce books and papers for inspection, and they may examine such, as well as all agents or employés of the roads. Their decisions may be appealed from. The Governor appointed Ex-Chief-Justice McWhorter, Ex-Circuit Judge Enoch J. Vause, and William Himes as members of the board.

The Okeechobee Drainage.—By a contract made in 1881 between the trustees of the State Internal Improvement Fund and the Atlantic and Gulf Canal and Okeechobee Land Company, it was agreed that the company might drain and reclaim all the overflowed lands in the vicinity of or submerged by Lake Okeechobee or the Kissimmee river, or their tributaries or outlets, by permanently lowering the waters of the lake; and of the lands of the State so reclaimed the company shall be entitled to one half. In pursuance of this agreement the company constructed canals and other works upon a large scale, and by 1884 claimed to have drained a large area. In that year agents of the State sent to inspect the work reported that nearly 2,500,000 acres had been permanently restored to cultivation. The trustees, accordingly, conveyed to the company 1,174,-942 acres as its share. But a committee appointed by the Legislature of 1885 made a report at the session of this year which denies the conclusions arrived at by the trustees, and represents that only 80,000 acres have been actually reclaimed. This report, implying that the company had unfairly obtained title to nearly all of its land, was the subject of extended discussion, and resulted in the passage of a bill giving the trustees power to bring suits to recover the lands so alienated or to enter into any compromise with the company that should seem advisable.

Minerals.—A report upon the geology and mineralogy of the State was made to the Legislature of this year, from which the following facts are gathered: No deposits of the precious metals and but few of the lower metals except iron can be found. The iron-ore is not the best, being of the limonite variety. It is found in the largest quantities in Jackson County, but no attempt has yet been made to utilize it. Rich deposits of phosphates exist in several counties, notably Wakulla, Alachua, Marion, Hillsborough, and Manatee. These are as rich in phosphoric acid as the well-known rocks on the Cooper and Ashley rivers in South Carolina. The largest deposit, in Wakulla County, is a triple phosphate of lime, iron, and alumina. Limestone is found in considerable quantities throughout the State, but is generally too siliceous to produce good lime. Clay suitable for making good brick exists in all parts of the State, the best quality being in Escambia County. A considerable deposit of soft brown or lignite coal has recently been discovered in Santa Rosa County, near the west bank of Blackwater river. The vein lies eight feet below the surface and has an average depth of about thirty inches. There is available building-stone, but none of marked value.

Coast Defense.—In response to a call issued by the Executive Committee of the Coast Defense Association of the coast cities of the South, a convention of delegates from the Southern Atlantic and Gulf States met at De Funiak Springs on February 8 to organize a movement for the better protection of the Southern seaboard. The following memorial to Congress was adopted:

In view of the defenseless condition of the harbors of the Atlantic Gulf States as well as the Pacific and Lake States, we most respectfully memorialize Congress of the United States to take such steps and enact such laws as are necessary to put our coasts in a proper state of defense by building such fortifications as the engineering skill of our army officers may determine to be the best and most important, and, further, by supplying our navy with such ships and armament as modern science renders necessary, and,

Whereas, There is no arsenal south of the Ohio river; and, *whereas,* steel-making ores abound in Tennessee, Alabama, Georgia, and Virginia, as well as other materials for the manufacture of all appliances of war, we recommend to Congress the location of a manufacturing arsenal at some point remote from the sea-board and convenient to the steel-ore belts of the South; and, *whereas,* in our opinion, our navy must be our chief means of defensive and offensive warfare, we recommend that a navy-yard for the construction and armament of the most improved modern ships of war be established in some proper Southern port, believing that, in case of war, our means of building ships and manufacturing the appliances of war should not be confined to one place, but should be widely separated, so that the loss of one would not be the loss of all.

Later in the same month a meeting of the Southern States Forestry Congress was held at the same place, and measures were taken toward insuring the preservation of the timber wealth of the South.

FRANCE, a republic in western Europe. The republican form of government was proclaimed Sept. 4, 1870. Under the act of Feb. 25, 1875, the legislative power is exercised by two chambers. The Senate consists of 300 members, elected by the departments and the colonies in accordance with a special law adopted Dec. 9, 1884. The Chamber of Deputies consists of 584 deputies, or one to every 70,000 inhabitants, elected by universal suffrage for the term of four years. The list of deputies for each department is chosen by all the voters of the department on a single ticket. The President of the republic is elected for seven years by a majority of votes in a Congress or National Assembly, consisting of the Senate and the Chamber of Deputies united. While the ministers are responsible to the Chambers for the general policy of the Government, the President is responsible only on impeachment for high treason.

The President of the republic in the beginning of 1887 was François P. Jules Grévy, born Aug. 15, 1813, who was President of the Chamber of Deputies in 1876-'79, and was elected to the chief magistracy in January,

1879, and re-elected in December, 1885. On his resignation the National Assembly elected as his successor on Dec. 3, 1887, M. Sadi-Carnot, formerly Minister of Finance (see CARNOT, MARIE FRANÇOIS SADI).

Area and Population.—The table on next page gives the area, in square kilometres, and the population of the eighty-six departments of France and the territory of Belfort, according to the census taken on May 30, 1886.

The increase of population between 1881 and 1886, amounting to 766,260, did not extend over all the departments. In thirty-two there was a decrease, the greatest being in Orne, which had 8,878 more inhabitants in 1881 than in 1886.

The population of the cities having over 100,000 inhabitants in 1886 was as follows:

CITIES.	Population.	CITIES.	Population.
Paris	2,344,550	Nantes	127,482
Lyons	401,930	St. Étienne	117,875
Marseilles	376,143	Havre	112,074
Bordeaux	240,582	Rouen	107,163
Lille	188,272	Roubaix	100,299
Toulouse	147,617		

The number of marriages in 1886 was 283,-193, as compared with 283,170 in 1885; the number of births, 956,363, as compared with 966,319; the number of deaths, 908,803, as compared with 880,855; the excess of births, 52,560, as compared with 85,464. The number of emigrants in 1884 was 6,100, of whom 2,564 went to the Argentine Republic, 2,485 to the United States, 886 to Brazil, 833 to Chili, and small numbers to Mexico, Cuba, and other countries.

Commerce.—The value of the special imports in 1885 was 4,088,401,000 francs, and of the special exports, 3,088,145,000 francs. The imports of bullion and specie amounted to 480,-000,000 francs, and the exports to 339,000,000 francs. The returns of the special commerce for 1886 make the total value of merchandise imports 4,234,363,000 francs, and the exports 3,800,230,000 francs. The imports of cereals in 1886 were valued at 297,622,000 francs, and the exports at 52,828,000 francs; imports of wines and liquors, 557,432,000 francs, exports, 350,076,000 francs; imports of sugar, coffee, etc., 192,885,000 francs, of tobacco, 33,569,-000 francs, of vegetables, etc., 342,388,000 francs, of live animals and animal food products, 339,809,000 francs; exports, 252,004,000 francs; total imports of articles of consumption, 1,763,655,000 francs; exports, 822,669,-000 francs. The imports of fuel were 142,-014,000 francs, of hides, etc., 242,286,000 francs, exports, 198,228,000 francs; imports of textile materials, 869,045,000 francs, exports, 306,128,000 francs; imports of timber, 167,723,000 francs; total imports of raw materials, 1,583,640,000 francs; total exports, 578,107,000 francs. The imports of textile fabrics were 216,039,000 francs, exports, 907,-678,000 francs; the exports of pottery and glass, 34,655,000 francs; imports of machinery and metal manufactures, 77,721,000

DEPARTMENTS.	Area.	Population.
Ain	5,796.97	364,408
Aisne	7,352.00	555,925
Allier	7,305.87	424,552
Alpes (Basses-)	6,954.18	129,494
Alpes (Hautes-)	5,559.61	122,024
Alpes-Maritimes	3,916.02	238,057
Ardèche	5,526.65	375,472
Ardennes	5,237.59	332,759
Ariége	4,893.57	237,619
Aube	6,001.89	257,874
Aude	6,313.24	332,080
Aveyron	8,748.33	415,526
Belfort, district of	610.14	79,758
Bouches-du-Rhône	5,104.57	604,857
Calvados	5,530.73	437,267
Cantal	5,741.47	241,742
Charente	5,943.38	366,408
Charente-Inférieure	6,865.69	462,808
Cher	7,199.84	355,849
Corrèze	5,866.09	396,494
Corse	8,747.10	278,501
Côte-d'Or	8,761.16	381,574
Côtes-du-Nord	6,885.02	628,256
Creuse	5,563.80	284,942
Dordogne	9,182.58	492,905
Doubs	5,227.55	310,968
Drôme	6,521.55	314,615
Eure	5,957.65	356,829
Eure-et-Loir	5,874.80	283,719
Finistère	6,721.67	707,520
Gard	5,885.56	417,099
Garonne (Haute-)	6,289.88	481,169
Gers	6,250.81	274,891
Gironde	9,740.82	775,845
Hérault	6,197.99	439,044
Ile-et-Vilaine	6,725.58	621,884
Indre	6,795.80	296,147
Indre-et-Loire	6,113.70	340,921
Isère	8,250.84	581,680
Jura	4,954.01	281,392
Landes	9,321.81	302,266
Loir-et-Cher	6,350.92	279,314
Loire	4,759.62	608,884
Loire (Haute-)	4,962.25	320,063
Loire-Inférieure	6,874.56	643,884
Loiret	6,771.19	374,875
Lot	5,311.74	271,514
Lot-et-Garonne	5,358.96	307,437
Lozère	5,169.73	141,264
Maine-et-Loire	7,120.98	527,690
Manche	5,928.39	520,865
Marne	8,150.44	429,494
Marne (Haute-)	6,219.68	247,781
Mayenne	5,170.68	340,068
Meurthe-et-Moselle	5,282.84	431,698
Meuse	6,227.87	291,971
Morbihan	6,797.51	535,256
Nièvre	6,816.56	347,645
Nord	5,680.87	1,670,184
Oise	5,555.06	406,146
Orne	6,097.29	367,248
Pas-de-Calais	6,605.68	853,526
Puy-de-Dôme	7,950.51	570,964
Pyrénées (Basses-)	7,692.66	482,999
Pyrénées (Hautes-)	4,520.45	234,825
Pyrénées-Orientales	4,122.11	211,187
Rhône	2,790.89	772,912
Saône (Haute-)	5,389.92	290,954
Saône-et-Loire	8,551.74	625,885
Sarthe	6,206.68	436,111
Savoie	5,759.50	267,428
Savoie (Haute-)	4,314.72	275,018
Seine	475.75	2,961,089
Seine-Inférieure	6,035.50	839,386
Seine-et-Marne	5,736.35	355,196
Seine-et-Oise	5,608.64	618,089
Sèvres (Deux-)	5,999.88	353,766
Somme	6,161.20	549,982
Tarn	5,742.16	356,757
Tarn-et-Garonne	3,790.16	214,046
Var	4,027.58	283,649
Vaucluse	3,547.71	241,757
Vendée	6,708.50	484,408
Vienne	6,970.87	342,785
Vienne (Haute-)	5,516.58	363,182
Vosges	5,352.65	413,707
Yonne	7,425.04	355,864
Total	528,571.99	38,218,908

francs, exports, 136,635,000 francs; exports of leather manufactures, 141,113,000 francs; imports of textile yarns, 71,288,000 francs, exports, 45,203,000 francs; exports of jewelry and art objects, 149,032,000 francs; total imports of manufactured articles, 484,871,000 francs; total exports, 1,517,106,000. The imports of drugs, chemicals, and coloring matters were 138,376,000 francs, exports, 100,756,000 francs; imports of gums, fats, and oils, 117,937,000 francs, exports, 68,357,000 francs; total imports of miscellaneous products, 402,223,000 francs; total exports, 382,343,000 francs. The imports of precious metals in 1886 amounted to 443,518,000 francs, and the exports to 333,262,000 francs.

Navigation.—The number of vessels entered at French ports during 1886 was 27,877, of 12,419,848 tons, of which 7,971, of 4,885,258 tons, sailed under the French flag. The number cleared was 21,878; tonnage, 9,024,902. The commercial navy consisted on Jan. 1, 1885, of 14,414 sailing-vessels, of 522,759 tons, and 988 steamers, of 1,083,831 tons.

Railroads.—There were in operation on Dec. 31, 1886, 18,390 miles of railroad, besides 1,165 miles of local roads.

The Post-Office and Telegraphs.—The number of letters and postal-cards transmitted in the mails during 1885 was 679,145,983; circulars, etc., 433,024,173; newspapers, 413,981,838. The receipts of the postal and telegraph service in 1885 were 166,578,653 francs; the expenses, 184,424,285 francs. The length of the state telegraph lines in 1885 was 51,800 miles; the length of wires, 161,800 miles; the number of messages during the year 32,540,780.

Finances.—The financial accounts of 1870 and 1871 showed a surplus. Since then there has been a deficit every year. Ministries have been repeatedly overturned on financial questions, yet the final accounts are never made to balance, though the budget has doubled since 1869. The increased expenditure has been covered chiefly by new indirect taxes, such as customs duties, stamps, the sugar-tax, and duties on wine, salt, and railroad transportation. The accumulated deficits from 1870 to 1885 amount to 481,352,000 francs. Taking account only of the ordinary and normal receipts and expenditures for the same period, it is calculated that there has been really a surplus of receipts amounting to 81,941,802 francs.

The budget for 1887, as adopted on Feb. 17, 1887, makes the total ordinary receipts 2,957,994,090 francs, and the expenditures 2,957,388,964. The expenditure of the Ministry of War is set down as 555,984,529 francs; of the Ministry of Marine and the Colonies, 229,701,863 francs; of the Ministry of Public Instruction, 145,303,435 francs; of the Ministry of Public Works, 121,156,259 francs; the cost of collection, 331,275,175 francs; the expenditure on account of the public debt, 1,286,372,314 francs. The revenue from direct taxes is taken as 440,270,690 francs; from indirect taxes, 1,802,850,300 francs; from domains and forests, 47,560,880 francs; from monopolies and industrial institutions, 580,447,925 francs. The extraordinary expenditures are 191,000,-000 francs for the army, 30,705,000 for the navy, and 54,704,400 for public works. They are provided for by loans. The budget of receipts and expenses from special resources balances with the sum of 467,123,452 francs. Apart from the other accounts is that of special services, viz., the mint, printing establishment, state railroads, and the invalid fund, which shows 79,124,758 francs of expenditures, balanced by the receipts.

The capitalized value of the consolidated debt amounted in 1887 to 21,449,066,123 francs, paying 769,908,038 francs of *rente*. The total debt of the country was calculated by M. Tirard in 1884 at 35,874,736,554 francs. The conversion of the old 4½-per-cent. *rentes*, of the capital amount of 840,000,000 francs, into 3 per cents., was authorized by the Chambers in November, and, notwithstanding the presidential crisis, was successfully effected on November 24.

The Army.—The law of July 25, 1887, increased the number of regiments of the line from 144 to 162, and in the existing regiments suppressed a battalion in each in order to form complementary cadres. The same law authorized the formation of four regiments of dragoons, one of chasseurs, six of hussars, and two of chasseurs d'Afrique. The new infantry regiments are destined to garrison the principal fortresses. The peace effective of the French army is as follows: Infantry, 12,200 officers and 290,000 rank and file; total, 302,-200, with 6,400 horses; cavalry, 3,850 officers and 73,000 men; total, 76,850, with 60,000 horses; artillery, 3,000 officers and 64,600 men; total, 67,600, with 29,600 horses; engineers, 880 officers and 10,300 men; total, 11,-180, with 1,000 horses; military train, 408 officers and 7,720 men; total, 8,128, with 7,672 horses; general staff, 3 marshals, 100 generals of division, 200 generals of brigade, and 33 generals of the *cadres* and reserve; total, 336, with 392 servants and 2,100 horses; employés of the general staff of officers' rank, 3,678; administrative troops, military schools, etc., 18,-474, with 2,470 horses; gendarmerie, 788 officers and 25,024 men; total, 25,812, with 13,-152 horses. Total active army, 25,532 officers and 489,118 men; together, 514,650, with 122,394 horses.

The territorial army numbers 37,000 officers and 579,000 men. The war effective is estimated at 3,759,000 men, of whom 1,887,000 belong to the nine classes of the active army and its reserve, 903,000 to the five classes of the territorial army, and 969,000 to the reserve of that army.

The strength of the active army, as provided for in the budget of 1887, was 523,693 men, including the sick and furloughed, and 130,920 horses. Of these 24,812 men belonged to the gendarmerie and Garde Républicaine, and 52,-708 were quartered in Algeria. All soldiers in the regular army who can read and write and are properly trained in military exercises may be sent on indefinite furloughs at the end of a year.

France is divided into eighteen military regions, each under the command of a general of division, and subdivided into districts, each under a general of brigade. There is a separate service for the strong places. Paris is fortified as a central place of arms. The first-class frontier fortresses are Lille, Dunkirk, Arras, and Douai, on the Belgian frontier; Bellfort, Verdun, and Briançon, on the German; Lyons, Grenoble, and Besançon, on the Italian; the naval harbor of Toulon, on the Mediterranean coast; Perpignan and Bayonne, on the Spanish frontier; Rochefort, Lorient, and Brest, on the Atlantic coast; and Cherbourg, on the Channel coast.

The Navy.—The French navy consists of 410 vessels. There are 52 armor-clads, of which 34 are line-of-battle ships, 21 of the first and 21 of the second class, and 18 are designed for coast defense, comprising 12 coast-guards, 1 gunboat, and 5 floating batteries. The number of cruisers of the first, second, and third classes is 54. There are 22 gunboats of the first and second classes, 57 sloop gunboats, and 64 torpedo-boats. The vessels on the stocks include 9 first-class ironclads, 7 armored gunboats, 4 cruisers, 8 torpedo avisos, and 13 torpedo-boats.

The Goblet Ministry.—After the defeat of the Cabinet of M. Freycinet in December, 1886, on the question of abolishing the sub-prefectures, it was reconstituted by the Minister of Public Instruction in the defeated Cabinet, MM. de Freycinet, Sadi-Carnot, and one or two others going out, and was composed at the beginning of 1887 as follows: President of the Council and Minister of the Interior, René Goblet; Minister of Foreign Affairs, Léopold Émile Flourens; Minister of Finance, H. Albert Dauphin; Minister of Public Instruction, Pierre Eugène Marcelin Berthelot; Minister of Justice, Jean Marie Ferdinand Sarrien; Minister of War, General Boulanger; Minister of Marine and the Colonies, Admiral Aube; Minister of Posts and Telegraphs, Étienne Armand Félix Granet; Minister of Commerce, Edouard Étienne Antoine Simon Lockroy; Minister of Public Works, Edouard B. P. Millaud; Minister of Agriculture, Jean Paul Denelle.

The programme of the new ministry was to balance the budget by reducing the redemption of the debt and to abolish about one sixth of the sub-prefectures. Special military credits of 86,000,000 francs for the new rifles and 30,000,000 francs for the navy were voted without discussion. The Radicals called on the Government to establish as the sole tax a progressive income-tax, but the proposal for a progressive tax was negatived by a vote of 221 to 110, while a resolution for an income tax was agreed to. The Minister of Justice proposed one in the shape of a duty on houses levied on the occupiers, who should pay a percentage of their rent, to be fixed annually according to the financial exigencies of the Government. This scheme, like most of the Government proposals, met with little favor. The Radicals and Reactionaries who demanded the dismissal of the sub-prefects would not accept the Government proposal merely to reduce the number from 360 to 296, and the question was left in abeyance. The Chamber agreed to bills raising the duty on wheat from 3 francs to 5 francs, with a corresponding increase on other cereals andfl our, and the duties on oxen from 25 francs to 38 francs, on cows from 12 francs to 20 francs, on sheep from 8 francs to 5 francs, and on meat from 7 francs to 12 francs per hundred kilos. The last item affects only the United States, since with other countries there are treaties fixing the meat duty at 3 francs. A surtax of 10 francs per 1,000 kilos on sugar was approved. The sale of the crown jewels realized 6,684,000 francs.

The Cabinet had no element of strength, but the question of its displacement was a matter of anxiety on account of the military situation. Gen. Boulanger's efforts to increase the efficiency of the army had been followed by Prince Bismarck's alarming speeches in the Reichstag and the increase of the German army with the sanction of the nation, attested by a general election. A grave situation was thus created, which had passed beyond the ability of statesmen to control. The German authorities forbade the export of horses, called out reservists, and were engaged in military preparations on the French frontier that might portend an invasion in the spring. Gen. Boulanger had constructed barracks, and was planning an experimental mobilization on the German frontier. To forego this test of the army organization, or to dismiss the reorganizer of the military resources of the republic would seem an evidence of fear, and might even precipitate instead of averting an attack. The Radicals, supported by the Monarchists, would not assent to the budget presented by the Minister of Finance, and the budget committee called for a reduction of from 2 to 8 per cent. in each department. The ministry could not see its way to a retrenchment of more than 26,000,000 francs without disorganizing the services. The vote, nominally on the retrenchments demanded by the Radicals, was determined by the military situation, yet it was very uncertain whether, if the Goblet Cabinet were defeated, it would not give place to a Freycinet-Boulanger Cabinet that would probably lead to war. The result of the vote, which was taken on May 17, indicated the perplexity of men's minds, but resulted in a defeat of the Government by a majority of 275, composed of 165 Reactionaries and 110 Republicans, augmented by M. Ferry and 57 other Moderates, less than half of the Extreme Left voting with M. Clémenceau,

while 40, with 60 Radicals and 150 Moderates and Independents, voted to sustain the ministry. M. de Freycinet declined to form a new ministry, while M. Grévy objected firmly to sending for M. Clémenceau. M. Duclerc, M. Rouvier, and others were summoned to the Élysée, and finally M. Floquet, President of the Chamber and a member of the Radical Left, undertook the task, after first declining. A war policy could not be thought of under the premiership of a man who once shouted for Poland in the presence of the Czar. The Opportunists would promise him no support; and, after others had tried and failed, M. Rouvier, who was Minister of Commerce under Gambetta and Ferry, succeeded in forming a cabinet from which—in view of the fact that M. Goblet, who was a Radical, had been overthrown by a part of the Opportunist party joining with the Extremists and the Monarchists—all Radical elements were excluded.

The Rouvier Cabinet.—The new ministry, constituted on May 30, was composed as follows: President of the Council and Minister of Finance and of Posts and Telegraphs, Maurice Rouvier; Minister of the Interior and of Worship, Clément Armand Fallières; Minister of Education, M. Spuller; Minister of Foreign Affairs, L. E. Flourens; Minister of Justice, M. Bousquet; Minister of Public Works, M. de Hérédia; Minister of Agriculture, M. Barbe; Minister of Commerce, M. Dautresme. The portfolio of War was accepted by Gen. Saussier, commandant of Paris, but on his insisting on the withdrawal of the military bill, Gen. Ferron was appointed in his place.

The phrase with which the new ministry introduced itself was "a cabinet of Republican concentration." In the ministerial declaration "all Republicans, all patriots," were invited to help in the work of reconciliation. M. Goblet had offended the Extremists by asserting his independence of them, and invoking support from the moderate section of the Right. During the crisis the Monarchists had received a rebuke from the Comte de Paris for their readiness to combine with Radicals and Socialists for the purpose of upsetting cabinets. The Extremists, who had no representation in the new Cabinet, pressed M. Rouvier to say whether he intended to govern with a Republican majority. This he affirmed, and in the vote, on a motion of want of confidence, he received a majority of ten or twelve among the Republicans, and, with the Right, a majority of 285 against 189 in the Chamber. He promised a reduction of 60,000,000 francs in the expenditure, and expected to make existing taxes suffice by making collections more stringent and repressing fraud.

The Military Bill.—The military organization bill, which Gen. Boulanger had prepared, was adopted by the new ministry, and discussion on it began on June 5. Seminarists, students, and teachers, previously exempt from military conscription, were to be compelled to undergo training, and made liable to serve as reservists. The one-year volunteer system was to be abolished, and a universal obligatory three-year service established, instead of the period of five years. All the Republicans voted in favor of abolishing the exemption of seminarists. The one-year volunteer system, which was adopted after the war of 1870 as a mitigation of the abolition of substitution and in imitation of Germany, permits young men of the upper and middle classes to serve only twelve months, during which they enjoy a privileged position in the army on passing a literary examination and paying 1,000 francs. Under the proposed conscription law, young men, who are liable from the age of twenty, may have the date of their entrance into the army postponed for a year, and the postponement renewed for another year, on proving that their studies, or apprenticeship, or agricultural or commercial occupations would be interrupted to their prejudice. The period may be extended to three or four years in the case of students of the universities and certain technical schools and seminarists. The same privilege was extended to the Catholic colleges that were established in 1875 in opposition to the University. These exceptions, which were adopted during the discussion in spite of the objections of the Radicals, were the only compromise that the upholders of a democratic army system would offer to the advocates of volunteering.

It was originally intended to furlough a considerable part of the conscripts at the end of two years, but the general three-years' service was agreed to at the request of Gen. Ferron, who showed that the aggregate force under the colors would then be 480,000, or only 66,000 more than under the old law, and the extra expense of keeping the whole yearly contingent with the colors only 8,000,000 francs per annum. At this point M. Laisant, the originator of the measure, resigned his post as reporter of the committee, and the bill was abandoned by its friends, who thus put off a reform for which the democracy of France have been clamoring for twelve years, rather than sacrifice a part of the relief from the blood-tax that the working-people would gain. The Chambers authorized the creation of four new cavalry regiments and eighteen infantry regiments, and voted 7,000,000 francs for the experimental mobilization of an army corps, and adjourned on July 23, after a session almost barren of legislative results.

Boulangist Demonstrations.—During the ministerial crisis the Radical populace of Paris became excited over the prospective exclusion of Gen. Boulanger, and when the list of the new ministry was published, it was decried in the Radical journals as a "German Cabinet." On taking leave of office, Boulanger thought it fit, contrary to all precedent, to issue a farewell order of the day to the troops, closing with the words: "I shall be the first to set you the example of that twofold discipline, at once military and republican." The evening of the day on which the ministers appeared before the Chamber, May 31, was the occasion of a grand military festival that had been arranged by the departing Minister of War. He refrained from attending. During the festivities crowds gathered around the Opéra cheering Boulanger and marched to the Ministry of War, shouting for his return. Finally troops appeared, and drove from the Opéra square the clamoring and singing mob.

Gen. Boulanger was assigned to the command of the Clermont-Ferrand Army Corps. His departure for his post was the occasion of noisy demonstrations in the streets of Paris, at the Lyons railroad-station, and in the towns along the route. This was followed on July 11 by a Radical attempt to upset the Government on an interpellation of Tony Révillon, who charged it with an alliance with the Right and an indifference to Royalist intrigues. M. Clémenceau, by whose influence Gen. Boulanger had first been elevated to the ministry, while asserting that the general's popularity was due to his being attacked by the German press and the Right, declared that Gen. Boulanger was now in his right place, and ought to remain in it. M. Laisant, who had just resigned from the army bill committee on the rejection of the two-year service, followed with a defense of Boulanger, declaring that the Rouvier Cabinet had been constituted under foreign pressure. The uproar caused by this remark was such that M. Floquet tendered his resignation as speaker, but it was not accepted. M. Rouvier declared that in case a clear majority of all the Republicans voted against the ministry it would resign. The Right joined their votes to those of the Opportunists in support of the Government, securing a majority of 382 against 120.

The imposing demonstrations that attended Gen. Boulanger's return to the routine of his profession did not occur without some encouragement or connivance on his part. Not long afterward he seized on another opportunity to keep his personality before the public. M. Ferry, in a speech at Épinal, alluded to him in sarcastic terms as a "St. Arnaud of the music-halls," comparing him with the general who carried out Louis Napoleon's *coup d'état*. Gen. Boulanger thereupon sent a challenge to the statesman, which was accepted. Yet when the former, claiming "a serious satisfaction, justified by the gravity of the offense," insisted that the parties should continue firing until one should be struck, or should shoot with deliberate aim at twenty paces, M. Ferry's seconds would not accede to such an encounter, deeming sufficient the customary exchange of shots at twenty-five paces, as in the duel fought a year before between Boulanger and M. de Lareinty, a Royalist senator who had branded as "cowardly" a reference to the exiled Duc d'Aumale. The result of the disagreement of the seconds was that no duel took place. Just before this incident Gen. Boulanger had intimated, in a conversation that was made public, that during the ministerial crisis he had repelled two incitements to a *coup d'état*, one proceeding from the Monarchists, and one approved by ninety-four generals of the army.

Irritation against Germany.—The increase of armaments and greater attention to military precautions in both France and Germany led to acts and incidents that intensified the ill-feeling between the two countries. The Germans expelled a great number of the citizens of Alsace-Lorraine, including a deputy in the Reichstag, named Antoine, and a German official decoyed a French functionary to the frontier, and there had him arrested. (See Germany). Military trials in Germany afforded proof that Gen. Boulanger had elaborated a system of military intelligence that required the services of many paid agents in Germany. The French have cried out against German spies for years, but have not been so successful in detecting their methods. An official in the French War Office was in March detected in giving up documents to the military *attaché* of the German embassy. Several arrests of supposed German spies were made by local officials. The feeling of hostility against Germans was so strong that persons of that nationality were nowhere safe from insult. The provocations on both sides were less frequent, and irritation subsided after the retirement of Boulanger, but in the beginning of August the closing of a factory belonging to a German who had burned a French flag at Embernil was followed by the expulsion of French railroad officials from their homes in a German village.

The Mobilization Experiment.—Gen. Boulanger had planned a mobilization test on the German frontier, but his successor was unwilling to take such a course without an understanding with Germany. After some diplomatic correspondence it was decided to make the experiment on the Spanish frontier, where no fears would be aroused. Four days before the orders were issued the main features of the scheme were divulged by a person who had access to the War Office, and were published in a newspaper. Some changes were made in the plan on this account. The bills for the mobilization were issued on August 30. The 17th Army Corps, including the departments of Arriége, Haute-Garonne, Gers, Lot-et-Garonne, and Tarn-et-Garonne, was ordered to concentrate in the neighborhood of Castelnaudary, in the Aude, to meet a supposed enemy marching on Toulouse. The troops reached the point of concentration in from two to six days, and during the ten days following carried out various manœuvres, ending with a march to the frontier against the putative invader. Serious defects were observed in the administrative services, especially the commissariat, and officers responsible for failures were displaced.

Manifesto of the Comte de Paris.—On September 14 the Comte de Paris published a manifesto in the form of instructions to the representatives of the Royalist party, in which he defined the system of monarchy that he would set up in France. The main features of his scheme are the restoration of the royal prerogative and the re-establishment of an aristocratic senate. He would even deprive the popular representatives of their control over the budget. The restoration of the monarchy might take place by the vote of a constituent assembly or by a *plébiscite*, and preferably by the latter method, which, however, could not be invoked to unseat the king, who would be resuming his historic right and reviving the covenant with the nation which has its sanction in historical tradition. The most important paragraphs of the document are the following:

It is to direct universal suffrage that the choice of deputies ought to belong. Thanks to its early origin and its recent establishment the monarchy will be sufficiently strong to reconcile the custom of universal suffrage with the guarantees of order which the country, disgusted as it is with the republican system of parliamentary government, will demand of it. The country will desire a strong government, because it clearly understands that even the real parliamentary system, which under the monarchy cast so much splendor on the years from 1815 to 1848, is not compatible with an assembly elected by universal suffrage. The method of election must be modified in order to fit it to this new and powerful agent. Under the republic the Chamber governs without control; under the monarchy the king will govern with the concurrence of the Chambers.

By the side of the Chamber of Deputies an equal authority will belong to the Senate, which will be partly elective, and which will unite in itself the representatives of the great forces and interests of society. Between these two assemblies royalty, having its ministers as interpreters and able to lean for support on either the one or the other, will be enlightened and guided, but not enslaved. It needs but a modification of our parliamentary system to maintain this equilibrium and to obviate all exclusive domination of one Chamber or the other. The budget, instead of being voted annually, will be in future an ordinary law, and consequently can only be amended by the agreement of the three powers. Every year the financial project will include only the modifications proposed by the Government on the last budget. If these proposals are rejected all the public services will not be thrown out of gear, nor will private interests be compromised, as they now would be by the rejection of the budget, and meanwhile real constitutional principles will be respected, for no new tax can be imposed, no new expense can be determined on, without the consent of the representatives of the nation.

To these representatives will also fall the task of fully discussing all the subjects which interest the country, of listening to all complaints which the action of the Government can relieve. If these complaints are legitimate, the representatives will be the first to give them utterance, and the adhesion of the other assembly will not fail them. But a caprice of the Chamber of Deputies will no longer be able unexpectedly to paralyze public life and the national policy. The monarchy will have to re-establish economy in finance, order in administration, and independence in the exercise of justice. The monarchy will have to raise by peaceful means our position in Europe, to make us respected and our alliance sought after by our neighbors. The ministers who serve the monarchy in this great undertaking will not be able to persevere in the realization of its views if they are trammeled by the fear that their efforts may be interrupted by a simple parliamentary accident. They will feel themselves set free from such a fear when they find themselves responsible not to one omnipotent chamber only, but to the three estates invested with legislative power. Thus the deputies, being no longer able to raise to power or to overthrow ministries, will not exercise that disastrous influence which is as fatal to the Assembly as to the Administration.

The Royalist pretender promised to guarantee to the clergy the respect that is necessary to insure the adequate pursuit of their calling, and to restore to the districts independence in educational matters and to France freedom of religious education. The army would have a single and immovable head, and thus be sheltered from the fluctuations of politics. The monarchy would satisfy at once the conservative needs of France and her passion for equality. The stability of a monarchical government would enable it to study the problem of industrial conditions and work for the amelioration of the lot of the working-people. Universal suffrage would be preserved for the election of deputies in parliament and for the appointment of mayors by the municipal councils in the rural communes.

The Sale of Decorations.—A disclosure of guilt and dishonor in high places startled the country before the Chambers met again. A woman named Limouzin, who had access to persons of influential position in military and political circles, had offered to procure the cross of the Legion of Honor for certain people in mercantile life, who informed the police. A detective, representing himself to be a silk-merchant who conducted a model establishment at St. Étienne, went first to one of the woman's agents, Baron Kreitmayer, a Bavarian nobleman who had been convicted in Germany of selling military secrets, and was taken by him to Mme. Limouzin, who introduced him to Brig-Gen. Caffarel, sub-chief of the General Staff at the Ministry of War. This officer had been appointed by Gen. Boulanger as a pliable man in the place of Gen. Peaucellier, who criticised some of the plans of the minister. He was retained with the rest of the staff by Gen. Ferron, but had fallen into disgrace by incurring debts on the merit of his official position. Caffarel told the supposed silk-merchant, who agreed to pay Mme. Limouzin 25,000 francs, that he was deserving, and should have the red ribbon of a chevalier that he solicited. Mme. Limouzin and Gen. Caffarel were arrested and the papers in their houses were seized. Mme. Ratazzi, also known as Mme. de la Motte du Portail, Mme. Véron, who called herself Mme. de Courteuil, and a man named Bayle, were arrested as accomplices of the Limouzin woman. On information given by a jeweler, who was approached by Mme. du Courteuil and Bayle, the police proceeded to the house of another general, the Comte d'Andlau, a senator and a man of considerable military and literary reputation. The senator had fled, and in his house were found partly burned letters and account-books with incriminating contents. The Comtesse Despréaux de Saint-Sauveur was also arrested. Gen. Caffarel was brought before a military court of honor, which on October 13 found unanimously that he had been guilty of dishonorable conduct and should be placed on the retired list with half-pay.

Gen. Boulanger, in a newspaper interview, accused the Minister of War of pursuing the Caffarel investigation with a view of entangling him in the scandal. Gen. Ferron demanded an explanation, and, on securing an admission that he had asserted that the Caffarel prosecution was directed solely against himself, ordered Gen. Boulanger to hold himself under an *arrêt de rigueur*, or close confinement to his house, for thirty days.

The persons accused of traffic in decorations, who, besides those already mentioned, included Paul Lorentz and a man named Bary, who committed suicide, were arraigned before the Correctional Tribunal on November 7. There was no evidence that Gen. Caffarel had before procured or engaged to procure decorations for money. It was shown that Gen. d'Andlau had received bribes from different persons on the promise of getting them decorated. The prisoners were condemned to suffer various terms of imprisonment, and some of them to pay fines, on the charge of obtaining money on false pretenses, which was all that could be proved. Senator d'Andlau, who had absconded, was sentenced *in contumaciam.*

The Wilson Scandal.—The two generals were the only persons of official station implicated in the transactions of the decoration agency. Some asserted that the authorities would not have made so much of a simple case of swindling if they had not desired to divert attention from a scandal affecting the detective bureau, two of the chiefs of which had ordered card-cases made from the skin of Pranzini, an executed murderer, whose trial had been the sensation of Paris in an earlier part of the year. Many, however, believed that the chief culprits had escaped detection, if they were not, indeed, shielded by the authorities. This supposition was based on a remark of Mme. Limouzin, who, when arrested, said that the police would find at her house letters from Gen. Thibaudin, MM. Wilson, Delattre, Mackau, and others. M. Wilson, the son-in-law of President Grévy, has for years been subjected to journalistic attacks and popular suspicion. He had been accused of making use of his exceptional sources of political information to gain millions on the bourse. His last stock operations, conducted at the time of the Schnaebele incident, when he speculated for a fall in prices, and spoke of war as imminent, resulted in heavy losses for him, because the affair was arranged more speedily than he had expected; still, he incurred obloquy by his conduct, and popular suspicion began from that time to extend to his father-in-law, with whom he lived. After his name became mixed up in the decoration scandal, his constituents at Tours called on him to appear before them and give an account of his actions. He was received by a crowded assemblage, but, before he had completed his first sentence, his speech was cut short by jeers and cries of execration, and the meeting passed a resolution demanding the resignation of his seat in the House of Deputies. When a committee was appointed by the Chamber to inquire into the scandals that had recently transpired, he demanded an investigation when his case was mentioned, and offered an explanation of his relations with the Limouzin woman, saying that she had once approached him on behalf of her husband, who was one of his constituents. Among the delinquencies now brought to his charge was using the official stamp of the Élysée to forward his private letters and effects through the mails. He confessed the truth of this complaint by paying to the post-office authorities 40,000 francs to cover the amount of postage withheld. When the seized documents were brought into court during Mme. Limouzin's trial, she exclaimed that letters from Gen. Thibaudin and two important ones written to her by M. Wilson in 1884 were missing. The prosecuting attorney and the examining magistrate had three times refused to receive the documents from the police authorities on account of informalities before they were finally delivered, duly sealed and scheduled. When Mme. Limouzin's papers were seized, the prefect of police, M. Gragnon, discovered the two letters, the first of which began by saying that the President of the republic, as well as Wilson, was doing his utmost to have Gen. Thibaudin promoted, though thus far without success. M. Gragnon took them to M. Grévy, who threw them into the fire. When Mme. Limouzin demanded their production, he asked to have them returned. M. Grévy then told his son-in-law to rewrite the letters, which he did, omitting the compromising passages. These substituted letters, with those from Gen. Thibaudin, were then produced in court. The woman declared that they were like the letters that Wilson had written her, but were not the same. No credence was given to this assertion in the face of M. Wilson's denials until it was shown that the forged letters were written on paper bearing a water-mark that was not used till 1885.

The trial of M. Wilson and of the police officials, MM. Gragnon and Geron, for the abstraction of the letters took place in December. The court decided that the case did not fall within the penal code, because Mme. Limouzin was not prejudiced by the suppression of the letters, which act was fastened on M. Gragnon, or the fabrication of substitutes, in which M. Wilson was concerned. The latter could not be held on a charge of forgery, because the contents were similar and the signature his own in the original and the substituted letters.

The Presidential Crisis.—The discovery that M. Wilson and the police had been guilty of the suppression and falsification of judicial evidence, and made away with documents that were so incriminating as to require to be concealed by criminal means, produced a state of political perturbation that led almost to anarchy. M. Gragnon was dismissed from office for his share in the transaction. M. Mazeau, the Minister of Justice, resigned, but was induced to continue in his post. M. Wilson would not resign his seat in the Chamber in order to stand a criminal trial, and therefore a motion was brought to allow the authorities to prosecute. He did not appear before the committee to which the case was referred, and when, on November 17, the vote was taken on the question of waiving his immunity as a deputy from arrest, the Chamber was unanimous in his condemnation. M. Grévy had already threatened to resign if the Chamber voted for prosecution, while in the legislative hall and in the street were heard demands for his resignation, which became gradually more decided.

On November 20 M. Clémenceau demanded a discussion of the general political situation. M. Rouvier declined to enter into a discussion until after the conversion of the debt on the 24th; but the Radical leader ridiculed the idea that the Cabinet could save the financial situation by saying, "Rest in peace till Wednesday, and on Thursday I promise you a crisis such as marks an epoch in parliamentary history"; and continued, "Action is needed. There is no government. Public power is without authority; the administration is disorganized. This infamy can last no longer. You demand time, but the disaster accords none." The Royalists supported the interpellation, and M. Rouvier, being defeated by 328 votes against 242, announced the resignation of the Cabinet.

The vote was directed against the President, but M. Grévy declared that he would not yield to an unconstitutional agitation or to legislative pressure. The retiring prime minister advised him to send for M. Clémenceau, but he first asked M. de Freycinet to form a Cabinet, and, after next consulting M. Floquet, and then M. Goblet, at last appealed to M. Clémenceau, who told him, like the others, that the crisis was of a presidential rather than of a ministerial character. M. Brisson, who was next called, M. Le Royer, the President of the Senate, and M. Ribot likewise intimated that the only solution was his retirement from the presidency. He was told the same thing by several others. He appealed a second time to M. Clémenceau, of whom he said in May that when he entered the Élysée by one door he would leave it himself by the other. When Henri Maret, almost the only journalist that had defended him, declined to attempt to form a ministry, and advised the President that there was no man in the French parliament who had sufficient influence to prevent his retirement, M. Grévy, on November 23, announced his decision to resign. He requested M. Ribot to form a Cabinet, and charged him to convey his message of resignation to the Chamber. M. Ribot consented, but afterward advised him to confer with the retiring ministers, as the message was a political act, requiring the approval of the Cabinet. He recalled M. Rouvier and his colleagues, who consented to continue in office only for the purpose of delivering his message. Although he was told by every responsible politician that his continuance in power was impossible, M. Grévy, with the obstinacy of conviction and vacillation of purpose characteristic of his period of life, after authorizing M. Rouvier again to announce his retirement in a note published on November 26th, recalled the decision in the afternoon. The minister told him that he was at liberty to refrain from laying down his functions, but that the ministers could not continue in office. After another conversation on the following morning, the President authorized him to publish a note requesting the Chambers not to meet till Thursday, Dec. 1, when a message would be communicated to them.

The fears and passions of the French were wrought up by the prolongation of the crisis. The Communists and Socialists of Paris carried on an agitation against M. Ferry, and threatened a rising if he was elected President. His supporters among the moderate Republicans were the more determined to press his claims to the succession. Many of the Radicals, with timorous persons of various parties, and some who, like the President, desired to preserve the constitutional principle of a fixed term for the presidential office, and to keep it beyond the reach of parliamentary attacks and popular clamor, urged M. Grévy to withdraw his resignation. When the Chambers met on December 1 to hear the message, M. Grévy told the ministers that, in view of the danger of insurrection, and of a popular demand from all parts of France that he should defend the Constitution and the prerogatives of his successors, he could not retire. They offered their resignation, which, they said, should be final, and, returning to the Chamber, announced that the President had altered his resolution, and that they had in consequence resigned. The house suspended its sitting for two hours, and the Senate passed a similar resolution, while the ministers informed the President.

When the news of what had happened spread abroad, the streets and squares filled with people. The legislators were agitated by rumors of a *coup d'état* and dread of a revolution, and it would have been possible for a small band of resolute men to gain possession of the hall. The mob, however, had no revolutionary purpose. The troops were vigilant, noisy demonstrations were stopped, and in the evening Louise Michel, the anarchist, and Paul Déroulède, chief of the Patriotic League, were arrested while leading processions. In the even-

ing, meetings at Belleville and in the other faubourgs were addressed by Gen. Eudès, Municipal Councilor Vaillant, Citizen Basly, and other socialist deputies and revolutionary orators. Denunciation of Ferry formed the burden of their speeches. He has incurred the hatred of the democracy, and is decried as "assassin" and "Tonquinese," not so much because he is politically responsible for the Tonquin expedition, but because he is supposed to have made that and other acts, especially his policy toward Germany, the means and the cover of financial speculations, by which he has acquired great wealth. Gen. Boulanger, who, with other corps commanders, was ordered away from Paris, and left for his post, was very little heard of.

The Chamber resumed its sitting only to adopt another resolution of adjournment in expectancy of "the communication which was promised it." On again coming to order, it listened to a statement from M. Rouvier, who announced that the President had no idea of entering into a conflict with the national representatives, and would on the following morning make known his sentiments on the situation. When the House met on December 2, M. Floquet read the message, which was couched in the following terms:

As long as I had only to contend with the difficulties that have accumulated in my path—the attacks of the press, the abstention of the men whom the public voice called to my side, and the increasing impossibility to form a ministry—I struggled on and remained where duty bade me, but at the moment when public opinion, better informed, marked a change which gave me hope of forming a government, the Senate and Chamber of Deputies voted a double resolution, which, under the form of an adjournment to a fixed hour to await the President's promised message, is tantamount to summoning the President to resign. It would be my duty and right to resist, but under the circumstances in which we are placed a conflict between the Executive and Parliament might entail consequences which restrain me. Wisdom and patriotism command me to yield.

I leave to those who assume it the responsibility for such a precedent and for the events that may ensue. I relinquish without regret, but not without sadness, the position of power to which I have been twice raised without solicitation, and in which I feel conscious I have done my duty. To this I call France to witness. She will say that for nine years my government has secured to the country peace, order, and liberty, has made France respected throughout the world, has worked unremittingly to raise her, and surrounded by an armed Europe leaves her in a condition to defend her honor and rights; further, that at home it has been able to maintain the republic in the wise course traced before it by the interest and wishes of the country. She will say that, in return, I have been removed from the post where her confidence placed me. In leaving political life I form but one wish. It is that the republic may not suffer from blows aimed at myself, but that it may issue triumphant from the dangers it is made to incur.

I place on the bureau of the Chamber of Deputies my resignation of the functions of President of the French Republic.

The Congress to elect a new President was summoned to meet at Versailles on the following day.

Street Rioting.—After the resignation of the President riotous demonstrations against Ferry took place in the streets. A crowd that surrounded the Palais Bourbon was driven away by the military and police. The deputies, Camélinat, Duc Quercy, and Basly, marched at the head of a procession toward the Hôtel-de-Ville, and when they attempted to force a passage through a squadron of the Garde Républicaine, the soldiers charged into the crowd, and striking with the flat side of their sabers, soon put the mob to flight. Other crowds were dispersed in like manner. There were revolvers fired and stones thrown at the soldiers, but no one was killed on either side. The Municipal Council met at six o'clock, and passed a resolution expressing the conviction that the election of Jules Ferry would lead to the shedding of blood in the streets of Paris, and civil war throughout France.

The Presidential Election.—The election took place in the great hall of the palace of Versailles, on the afternoon of December 3. The Opportunists were united in favor of M. Ferry, while the Radicals had expected to support M. de Freycinet. The Right had been expected to give their votes to M. Ferry, but they determined to throw them away on Gen. Saussier, who had declined to be a candidate, or on Gen. Appert. In the Republican caucus, M. Sadi-Carnot had been prominently brought forward as a compromise candidate, yet the friends of M. Ferry did not despair of gaining monarchist votes, and electing him yet. The first vote gave Sadi-Carnot 303 ballots; Ferry, 212; Saussier, 148; de Freycinet, 76; Appert, 72; Brisson, 26; Floquet, 5; Anatole de la Forge, Félix Pyat, and Pasteur, 2 each; and Spuller, 1. MM. Ferry and de Freycinet announced their withdrawal in favor of M. Carnot. On the second vote M. Sadi-Carnot was elected by 616 ballots, to 188 cast for Gen. Saussier, 11 for Ferry, 5 for de Freycinet, and 1 for Pyat.

The Tirard Cabinet.—The Rouvier ministry handed in their resignations to the new President, who had much difficulty in finding a statesman who could form a Cabinet. M. Fallières declined to undertake the task. M. Goblet conceived the idea of uniting in the same ministry men from the opposite wings of the party, but gave up the attempt. On December 13 a Cabinet was formed from Opportunist elements, composed as follows: President of the Council and Minister of Finance, Paul Emmanuel Tirard, born in Geneva, of French parents, in 1827, who established a wholesale jewelry establishment in Paris, was a zealous Republican under the Empire, a deputy in 1871, afterward a life-senator. Minister of Agriculture in 1879, and subsequently Minister of Finance; Minister of Foreign Affairs, L. E. Flourens; Minister of Justice, M. Fallières; Minister of the Interior, Jean M. F. Sarrien, who held the same portfolio under M. de Freycinet in 1866; Minister of Education and Worship, M. Faye, a

senator; Minister of Marine and the Colonies, François C. de Mahy, a native of Réunion; Minister of Public Works, M. Loubet; Minister of Agriculture, M. Viette; Minister of Commerce, M. Dautresme; Minister of War, Gen. Logerot, who was a colonel in the war of 1870, distinguished himself in Tunis in 1881, was made general of division, and succeeded Gen. Forgemol in the chief command.

In President Carnot's inaugural message, read in Parliament on December 13, he speaks of himself as "one of the most modest servants of France," and appeals to the patriotism of the deputies to sustain a policy of "progress, reconciliation, and concord."

Attempted Assassination of Jules Ferry.—The agitation against M. Ferry during the presidential canvass prompted a desperate man, who was desirous of notoriety, to attempt his life in the lobby of the Chamber, on December 10. He sent in his card, and when M. Ferry appeared, while engaging him in conversation, fired two shots from a revolver, but inflicted only a slight wound.

The Paris Municipality.—A question underlying the political events of the year was the old one of the right of the communes, notably the city of Paris, to legislative autonomy. The idea of local self-government, which inspires with dread all the conservative elements of French society, and has been resisted and repressed by every means, because the hopes of the Socialists and Revolutionists of every shade are bound up in it, has made great progress in the past two or three years, and has been adopted as a practical issue by a considerable section of the Radical party in parliament. The elections for the Paris Municipal Council in May resulted in a large increase in the Radical and Revolutionary elements in that body. On July 27 the municipality voted to convene a congress of municipal delegates, but the government vetoed the project. The President of the Municipal Council nevertheless issued a circular inviting delegates of all French municipalities to meet on September 22, and the Minister of the Interior again interfered, threatening to annul any resolutions passed in response to the invitation. The fear of a Paris commune and central mayoralty was the main motive that deterred M. Grévy from calling on M. Clémenceau to form a ministry in May, and that governed the selection of the Tirard Cabinet in December.

The Exhibition of 1889.—The Republic received negative replies from the monarchical governments of Europe in response to its invitation to participate in a world's fair at Paris in 1889. The Czar of Russia directed his minister to declare that the Russian Government would take no part in festivities for the glorification of a revolution, and would prohibit Russian merchants and manufacturers from having anything to do with it. The German and Austrian Governments declined to countenance the exhibition by any official action. The Chamber has appropriated the sums necessary for the exhibition. Buildings, including a great iron tower, are being erected in Paris. During the exhibition there will be held, under the direction of committees appointed by the Minister of Commerce, meetings and lectures on literature, art, history and archæology, mathematical science, physics and chemistry, natural science, geography, political economy and legislation, hygiene and sanitation, social economy, education, engineering, agriculture, industry, and commerce.

Algeria.—The area of Algeria is 318,334 square kilometres, not including the territory extending into the Desert of Sahara, which is 349,900 square kilometres in extent. The population on May 30, 1886, was 3,867,465, of which number 3,324,475 are resident in the territories administered by the civil authorities, 492,-990 in the military divisions, and 50,000 in the Algerian Sahara. The number of Arabs and Kabyles is 3,274,354; of French, 261,591; of naturalized Israelites, 28,376. The population of the city of Algiers was 71,199. The budget for 1886 makes the receipts 42,837,628 francs, and the expenditures 52,738,472 francs. The imports in 1884 amounted to 289,800,000 francs, and the exports to 175,900,000 francs. There were 2,065 kilometres of railroad in operation in April, 1887.

Tunis.—The regency of Tunis has an area of about 116,000 square kilometres, and a population of 1,500,000 souls, of which number 35,500 are Christians, 45,000 Israelites, and the rest Mohammedans. Tunis, the capital, has 150,000 inhabitants. The expenditures of the Government amounted in 1886 to 27,145,-000 francs. There is a debt of 142,550,000 francs. The value of imports in 1886 was 30,215,775 francs; of exports, 19,416,475 francs. The chief exports are rye, barley, olive-oil, and esparto-grass. There are 410 kilometres of railroad completed.

Annam.—The kingdom of Annam was taken under the protectorate of France in 1884. A French resident-general represents the republic in the citadel of Hué, with a military escort, and under the treaty European engineers and agents were to direct the customs, public works, and other services. The province of Tonquin was placed more particularly under French control, and is administered by native functionaries under the direction of French residents in all the chief places.

The area of the kingdom is about 275,300 square kilometres. The population of Tonquin is from 10,000.000 to 12,000,000 persons; that of the rest of the kingdom about 2,000,000. The receipts of Annam and Tonquin in 1887 amounted to 44,860,000 francs, including a subvention of 30,000,000 francs. The expenditures were calculated at 44,758,230 francs, of which 20,425,000 francs were for the military, and 10,830,000 francs for the naval expenditure. The imports of Annam in 1883 amounted to 2,860,000 francs, and the exports to 1,200,-

000 francs. The imports of Tonquin for 1885 are reported as 21,679,879 francs, and the exports as 8,079,438 francs.

The fighting in Tonquin still continues. In January, 1887, the French made two unsuccessful attempts to expel a rebel force from Than Hoa, where they were strongly intrenched. A few weeks later Col. Brissaud captured a fort in the same district, which was stubbornly defended by Chinese and Annamites from Thuyet. Columns were sent into the provinces of Phu-Yen and Bin-Dinh. By June the rebels had been driven into the remoter districts. The delimitation of the Chinese frontier had then been nearly completed. By a ministerial decree, issued August 4, the system of protection, exempting from duty French merchandise imported in French ships, and subjecting to the French general tariff all foreign merchandise, was established in Cochin-China, Cambodia, Annam, and Tonquin. Foreign goods in transit pay only one fifth of the regular duty.

Colonies.—The colonies and protectorates of France, including Algeria, Tunis, Madagascar, and Annam, have a combined area of 3,043,-600 square kilometres, and an aggregate population of 28,315,400 souls. The French establishments in India, with an area of 508 square kilometres, had, in 1885, a population of 275,-261. The public expenditure in 1885 was 2,206,000 francs; imports, 8,000,000 francs; exports, 26,500,000 francs. The colony of Cochin-China, is 59,800 square kilometres in extent, and in 1885 contained 1,792,933 inhabitants. The colonial budget was 28,483,000 francs, exclusive of 3,239,000 francs of expenditure assumed by the French Government; imports, 108,700,000 francs; exports, 85,400,-000 francs. The protected kingdom of Cambodia has an area of about 100,000 square kilometres and 1,500,000 inhabitants. The French resident-general was in April, 1887, appointed Prime Minister to King Norodom, and intrusted with the task of reorganizing and directing the finances. The kingdom has an export and import trade of from 10,000,000 to 12,000,000 francs, not reckoning the commercial movement across the frontier of Siam.

The estimated extent of Senegal and its dependencies in 1885 was 667,000 square kilometres, the population, 3,817,465. Protectorates have been proclaimed over the Upper Senegal and the Upper Niger. The warlike natives in these regions frequently attack the French posts. The colonial expenditure in 1885 was 2,861,000 francs, besides 8,897,000 francs which were made a charge on the treasury of the republic. The imports in 1885 were 25,100,000 francs; the exports, 19,500,000 francs. The French possessions on the Gold Coast had, in 1885, an extent of 24,000 square kilometres. The French authorities made treaties with chiefs of an extensive tract on the northern bank of the Gambia river, called the Badiboo territory. The British officials at

Lagos, conceiving the opinion that the region belonged within the sphere of British influence, led a force into the district in April, 1887, and placed a chief in power who was friendly to the English. The French thereupon repelled him, and reinstated their *protegé*, raising the French flag over the districts of Badiboo Saba and Sangally. The officer in command of the troops at Lagos marched into the disputed territory, and pulled down the French flag. The British and French Governments both sent gunboats and higher officials to the spot, and entered into diplomatic correspondence over the question. Sir Samuel Rowe, Governor of the British West African settlements, hoisted the British flag at various points on the Gambia river, but the French remained in practical possession of the Badiboo district. The estimated area of the French possessions at Gaboon and on the Congo is 670,000 square kilometres. On May 27, 1887, a·diplomatic arrangement was concluded between France and Germany, legalizing the importation of spirituous liquors, rifles, gunpowder, and tobacco into their possessions on the Slave Coast, at fixed rates of duty. The expenditure of the colonial government in Gaboon in 1885 was 619,000 francs, and that of the home Government 125,000 francs. The trade is about 1,900,000 francs either way. For the French Congo, M. de Brazza, the Governor, was allowed 1,600,000 francs in the budget of 1887. A convention concluded in April, 1887, between France and the Congo Free State, alters the boundaries indicated in the original treaty in favor of France. The Lecona river and the 17th meridian of east longitude were to mark the eastern boundary of the French possessions. It has since been ascertained that the Lecona is not a favorable route into the interior, and by the new arrangement the boundary will follow the Dubrangi or Mabongi, the right bank of which is to belong to France, and the right bank of the Congo below their junction. The Congo Free State in return acquires the right of having its loan quoted in Paris to the amount of 80,000,-000 francs. France also admits that the preemptive rights acquired in 1883 over the Congo possessions can not be exercised against Belgium, should it desire to acquire the territory of the Free State, but only in respect to other powers, should the founders desire to cede the territory. On the east coast of Africa are the colonies of Réunion, Sainte-Marie de Madagascar, Mayotte, Nossi-Bé, and Obock, besides the recently annexed Comoro Islands, which were occupied without fighting, and the resident installed at Anjouan on March 25, 1887. These islands, which lie between the island of Madagascar and the African continent, are 1,606 square kilometres in extent, and contain 58,000 inhabitants. There occured in the early part of 1887, disputes between French and English authorities on the Somali coast, and a line of demarkation was agreed on, be-

yond which each power engaged not to extend its possessions, after an English officer had hauled down the French flag at a place called Dongareta. The understanding that was arrived at between Lord Salisbury and M. Flourens, recognizes the rights of France over the Obock territory and the Gulf of Tadjourah, Great Britain ceding the island of Mashah, lying in the middle of the gulf. The frontier line of the French territory extends from Cape Djiboujeh to Harrar, and thence westward to Shoa. France acknowledges the rights of England to the territory situate to the east of Cape Djiboujeh, including Dongareta.

The colony of St. Pierre and Miquelon, with an area of 235 square kilometres, had, in 1885, 6,800 inhabitants. The imports were 13,200,-000 francs, and the exports 20,200,000 francs. Guadaloupe and its dependencies have 1,870 square kilometres of territory, and in 1885 contained 181,098 inhabitants, and exported 7,700,000 francs worth of goods, with imports amounting to 4,800,000 francs. Martinique is 988 kilometres in area, with 169,232 inhabitants, and imported 21,900,000 francs, and exported 21,500,000 francs worth of merchandise. French Guiana has an area of 121,413 square kilometres, and 26,502 European inhabitants. The imports in 1885 were 19,500,000 francs, and the exports 18,000,000 francs.

In the Pacific the penal colony of New Caledonia, with the Loyalty Islands, has an area of 19,950 square kilometres, and had a population of 56,453 souls in 1885. The imports amounted to 8,500,000 francs, and the exports to 4,600,-000 francs. The New Hebrides, occupied by French troops, have not yet been definitively annexed. (See NEW HEBRIDES). The other possessions in the Pacific include Tahiti, the Touamotou Archipelago, and the Wallis Islands, which were annexed in 1886. The latter have an area of 96 square kilometres and 8,500 inhabitants. They are situated between the Fiji and Samoa islands, and were occupied, with the intention of making them a coaling-station, by the expedition which went from Noumea in April, 1887. The total expenditure of the French Government on its colonies in 1885 was 82,659,000 francs.

FRIENDS. General Conference of Yearly Meetings.—A General Conference of the yearly meetings of Friends in America, with those of London and Dublin, met in Richmond, Ind., September 22. The meeting was held in pursuance of a call which was made by the Indiana Yearly Meeting in 1886, for such a conference, to consider matters of doctrine, government, and methods of work, and to consult with respect to a closer union of the several bodies of Friends. Thirteen yearly meetings were represented by 108 delegates. The first question discussed after the preliminary matters of organization were disposed of—"Is it desirable that all the yearly meetings of Friends in the world should adopt one declaration of doctrine?"—was answered in the affirmative.

To the second question, "What is the mission of the Society of Friends, and what is its message to the world?" the answers were given in substance: That the mission of the Society is to declare salvation to lost men; to promulgate a pure, sound, full gospel; to hold theology in a living experience, so that the doctrines preached shall be ever fresh and vital; to labor to get men saved and sanctified; to go with Christ into every reform, especially peace, temperance, and purity; to maintain the priesthood of believers and simple worship without priestly intervention; to preach the only saving baptism which is Christ's with the Holy Ghost, and the one Supper of the Lord, which is the spiritual partaking of his flesh and blood. That mission can be best fulfilled and that message declared by Friends being pure, baptized with the Holy Ghost, filled with Christ's love, called to the work, united, and well organized; by preaching, teaching, writing; going to the poor, rich, honored, and unlearned; and by being zealous as missionaries, evangelists, and pastors, according as God bestows gifts. The Conference declared it desirable that there should be a union in missionary work of the yearly meetings, which have now, severally, their own separate missions. The following paper was adopted on the questions of baptism and the Lord's Supper: "A number of suggestions having been made by members of the Conference to the business committee, in reference to the teaching of water baptism and the Supper by those in official position in the Society of Friends, the committee have given careful attention thereto, but believe that the recent official utterances and reaffirmations of eight yearly meetings on this continent have definitely settled that question. They present with the report the minute of the Indiana Yearly Meeting, which is in substantial agreement with the minutes of other yearly meetings, and advise that the subject be not entered upon or debated at this time." The minute referred to declares that: "We believe it to be inconsistent for any one to be acknowledged or retained in the position of a minister or elder among us who continues to participate in or to teach the necessity of the outward rites of baptism and the supper." Concerning the manner of conducting public worship, a general consensus was expressed in favor of preserving the long-established form of silent meetings, having Jesus as the only head, and no minister necessary but much to be desired. The discussion of the question of "The proper relationship of the ministry to the Church, and the duty of the Church toward the ministry, in connection with the liberty of prophesying, and the necessity of maintaining it inviolate in all our meetings," which involved the propriety of recognizing the innovations of revival meetings, with acknowledged leaders, and formal supplies of regular ministers to certain meetings, disclosed a predominance of sentiment in favor of these movements. A declaration of

doctrines was adopted which was compiled from the expressions made at various times by the different yearly meetings. It includes the headings of "God, our Father, Son, and Holy Ghost"; "The Lord Jesus Christ"; "The Holy Spirit"; "The Holy Scriptures"; "Man's Creation and Fall"; "Justification"; "Sanctification"; "Regeneration"; "Baptism"; "The Lord's Supper"; "Worship"; "Ministry, and the Exercise of Spiritual Gifts"; "Prayer and Praise"; "Civil Government"; "Peace"; "Oaths"; "Marriage"; and "The First Day of the Week," upon which, except that the outward rites of baptism and the Lord's Supper, war, fighting, and oaths are specially declared against, the expressions are in general harmony with the doctrines held by the Protestant churches of the Arminian school. A paper was read by Dr. William Nicholson at the Indiana Yearly Meeting, whose session was held after the close of the Conference, advocating the institution of triennial conferences, and of a court of final appeal uniting and binding all the yearly meetings.

London Yearly Meeting.—The statistical reports to the London Yearly Meeting gave the whole number of members of the Society of Friends in England as 15,458, and in Ireland as 2,774. These returns show an increase during the year of 78 members in England, and a decrease of 61 in Ireland. The number of attendants upon meetings not members was 5,803 in England, and 660 in Ireland. The London Yearly Meeting assembled May 18. Though having no official supremacy in the Society, it, being the parent body of all, is recognized by the denomination at large as the leading meeting, and general respect is accorded to its determinations on matters affecting the interests of the Society; and they have usually been influential in pointing out the course to be followed by the other meetings. A question which had already given considerable difficulty came up before the meeting concerning correspondence with the American meetings. Divisions have occurred in several of the yearly meetings of the United States and Canada on questions of divergent practices in meetings. While conservative members still hold to the old order of quiet meetings, and look disparagingly on active movements for spreading the Word, other parties favor active methods, with diversified services, somewhat resembling those employed by other Protestant denominations; and several meetings have been split in two on these divergences. To maintain the even balance, and recognize by correspondence the party representing the English society as it is, has not been an easy task. A conference had been held in London on the subject in the autumn of 1886, but no real change had been made, and the discussion at the present yearly meeting was without result. The Meeting for Sufferings was commissioned to prepare a scheme for simplifying and amending the marriage usages of the society. The committee on education was directed to report to the next yearly meeting respecting the feasibility of establishing a high-class school for young men. The policy followed by the Home Mission Committee in the organization and execution of the work intrusted to it was discussed. On the one side it was feared that the committee was departing from the usages of the Society; on the other side it was shown that the committee represented an almost similar organism that was vital when Friends' principles flourished most in England. The committee was reappointed. The meeting was interested in the discussion of a possible manner in which it might use its influence for the preservation of peace between nations whose relations appear precarious, without becoming involved in political complications. The Meeting for Sufferings was asked "prayerfully and carefully " to watch, and as the way may open, to promote by deputation or otherwise, peaceful solutions. A deputation was appointed to attend the General Conference of yearly meetings to be held in Richmond, Ind., in September.

Friends' Missions.—The annual meeting of the Friends' (English) Foreign Mission Association was held May 23. Mr. Arthur Pease presided. The income of the Association for the year had been £8,587, and the number of missionaries employed 24. A medical missionary academy had been opened in Madagascar, and diplomas had been granted to eight Malagasy students. The mission in that country returned 33,000 adherents, of whom 19,-500 were regular attendants at worship. The work carried on there was chiefly educational. At the Syrian mission 5,121 cases had been treated at the dispensary, and the attending physician had made more than 1,000 visits. A hospital had been opened at Ramleh, Palestine. Favorable reports were also received from the missions in Natal, India, and China. The Friends' Tract Association had expended more than £200, and had a balance of £50. The total issue of tracts had been 130,194, against 108,684 in the previous year, with 28,-000 leaflets in addition. A considerable proportion of these tracts were in foreign languages. The standing committee of the London Yearly Meeting brought in reports from France, Germany, Australasia, Norway, Denmark, Constantinople, Syria and Palestine, Madagascar, India, Natal, and China, representing the work of the agencies of the society as in most places hopeful and well sustained. While enlightened Christian education was everywhere advanced, the military laws of France and Germany were the only hindrances to Friends in those countries. The Friends' Home Mission had expended £1,887 during the year, the most of it in aid of Friends performing missionary labors in various parts of the country.

G

GEOGRAPHICAL PROGRESS AND DISCOVERY.
Africa.—Although not fewer than the usual number of travelers have been in Africa during the year, and the interests of trade have been served to some extent by the increase of topographical knowledge, yet the gain to geographical science is not large. The chief interest has centered on the expedition undertaken by Stanley for the relief of Emin Pasha —not to bring him away, for he has declared that he will not leave his province, but to open a route of communication and relieve him from his position of isolation from the civilized world, beleaguered as he is by jealous tribes ready to fall upon his troops at any moment. Since he has been able to send letters and packages by way of Uganda and Zanzibar, collections of birds, butterflies, and moths, that he has collected, have been received in London, and accounts of short journeys made in the vicinity of his station. In one of these he visited the Albert Nyanza, and found that, since 1879, a low island, about one kilometre in length, has been formed not far south from the former station of Mahagi, by the deposits of rivers flowing into the lake. He thinks the western part of the lake is gradually filling up. He describes the character and customs of the Monbuttu, their weapons and implements of various kinds. In recent letters he reiterates his resolution not to desert his province; he can not abandon the results of his twelve years' work of civilization, and still hopes to restore order in his domain; but he is most anxious to secure some means of regular communication with the outside world. His present facilities depend entirely on the caprice of the despotic sovereigns of Uganda and Unjoro, and it is impossible for him to receive arms and munitions of war. If a free route could be opened for him, he might be able to defend his own province, since he has a force of about 1,400 Egyptians and Soudanese. In February last he met with a serious loss by the burning of Wadelai, his principal station, by which large stores of ivory and provisions, as well as much of his private property, were destroyed. The arms and ammunition were saved with difficulty. Emin was compelled, partly by the difficulty of provisioning, to give up the stations at Lado and Gondokoro, which were important as terminals of the navigation of the Nile; but he has on the other hand extended his sway toward the south, and founded a new station, Ssongo, on an island near the western shore of Albert Lake.

In one of his excursions he discovered a new river flowing from the Usungora mountains to Albert Lake, and called Kakibbi by the Wasongora, and Duera by the Wa-mboga. Near its mouth is a large island. It has a great volume of water, but numerous rapids, making the navigation difficult. He was told by the natives that there is a river to the southwest, on the banks of which lives a colony of the curious dwarf race, or Akkas, called Balia by the Ungoro people, but showing by their speech that they are Betua.

When Mr. Stanley announced his intention of taking the Congo route to Emin's territory, the plan was disapproved by both Junker and Schweinfurth. They thought that at least eighteen months would be required for the journey; and they recommended instead a route from the Red Sea or from Zanzibar.

Mr. Stanley convinced them that the land journey by the Upper Congo would not exceed 400 miles, whereas from Zanzibar to Albert Lake the distance would be 950 miles, and the Masai route would be 925 miles. A strong expedition was determined upon, the cost being defrayed mainly by English contributors to the relief fund with a subsidy from the Egyptian treasury. In Mr. Stanley's own words: "The expedition is non-military—that is to say, its purpose is not to fight, destroy, or waste; its purpose is to save, to relieve distress, to carry comfort. Emin Pasha may be a good man, a brave officer, a gallant fellow deserving of a strong effort of relief; but I decline to believe, and I have not been able to gather from any one in England, an impression that his life, or the lives of the few hundreds under him, would overbalance the lives of thousands of natives and the devastation of immense tracts of country which an expedition strictly military would naturally cause. The expedition is a mere powerful caravan, armed with rifles for the purpose of insuring the safe conduct of the ammunition to Emin Pasha and for the more certain protection of this people during the retreat home; but it also has means of purchasing the friendship of tribes and chiefs, of buying food, and paying its way liberally."

On his arrival at Zanzibar Mr. Stanley found that his agents had already recruited a force of 600 men for the expedition, and that Tippoo-Tip, who had escorted his caravan in 1877 when the first descent of the Congo was made, was waiting for him. Tippoo-Tip was the Zobehr of the Upper Congo, commanding two of the best roads from the river to Wadelai. He agreed to supply 600 carriers at $30 a man, and, as Emin was reported by Dr. Junker to have 75 tons of ivory, the expenses of the expedition might be largely defrayed by the return of the Zanzibaris to the Congo with their precious loads. Tippoo-Tip was also offered the position of Governor at Stanley Falls at a regular salary. He consented to accompany Mr. Stanley on these terms. The steamer set out on February 25 for the mouth of the Congo with about 700 men of the expedition, reaching its destination in four weeks. It was then 1,266 miles from Aruwimi, whence it

was to march 400 miles through an unknown country to Emin's capital. It was as late as April 26 before it could leave Leopoldville, on Stanley Pool, and it was not until the second week in June that the explorer himself was at Aruwimi, much delay having been caused by defective means of transportation. A rear-guard was left at Yambouya, and the advance column of five Europeans and three hundred and eighty natives passed on to the limit of navigation and began the overland march. Few difficulties were encountered apart from the natural obstacles presented by such a country. Meantime, Tippoo-Tip had gone to Stanley Falls to restore to the Congo State the station which was seized by the Arabs, and gather a company of his people to accompany the expedition as carriers. The steamer "Stanley," the largest on the Congo, returned to Bolobo to carry to the Aruwimi station the remaining men and supplies.

By July 25 the advance expedition had ascended the river Aruwimi as far as an elevated tract of country forming a portion of the Mabodi district. Here the river became very narrow, being no longer navigable, and Mr. Stanley was compelled for several days to have all the provisions and munitions for the use of the expedition, as well as those intended for the revictualing of Emin Pasha's garrison, carried on the men's backs. The quantity of rice was so large that each man had to bear a double burden. The rafts which had been employed to convey the heavy baggage were left behind, and only the steel whale-boat brought from the camp at the foot of the Aruwimi Rapids was carried past the narrows and again launched in the river, Mr. Stanley greatly congratulating himself that he had brought it, owing to the amount of water which, according to the inhabitants of that part of the country, the expedition would have to cross before reaching the Albert Nyanza. Mr. Stanley calculated that, once arrived at the summit of the table-lands which shape the basin of the Aruwimi, he would be able to halt for two days in order to rest his men and establish a fresh camp garrisoned like that at Yambouya by twenty men and a European officer. The population of the country through which Mr. Stanley was then traveling was considerable, but the people were much scattered. The district was tranquil, the agitation prevalent in the neighborhood of Stanley Falls not having spread to that part of the country.

At the beginning of August the expedition was reported to be advancing without the ammunition and stores designed for Emin. Provisions were scarce, the officers and men undergoing great privations, and suffering from disease and hunger. Tippoo-Tip had failed to send to Yambouya the 500 carriers who were to convey the stores. This failure was not due to treachery, since he was still at his post and faithful to Mr. Stanley's interests. In consequence of the disturbed state of the country he could not, as had been agreed upon, organize a revictualing caravan to be dispatched direct to the Albert Nyanza by way of the river Mbourou, but he agreed to do so as soon as possible. The agitation continued in the country between Stanley Falls and the confluence of the Aruwimi with the Congo. Several villages on the right bank of the Congo had been pillaged and laid waste, and a large number of the natives had crossed the river to the opposite bank.

The last report was that news had arrived at Cairo, December 22, that Stanley had reached Emin Pasha, and details of the latter part of the journey were expected.

Mr. A. J. Wauters advances the theory that the Muta Nsige, discovered by Stanley in 1876, is not connected with the Albert Nyanza or with the Nile system at all, but is the source of the Aruwimi. He founds his opinion on the difficulty of accounting for the great mass of water in the Aruwimi if it is fed only by the streams and springs of the limited territory that can be drained by it. On the other hand, this leaves unaccounted for the fact that the Nile is twice as great when it issues from the Albert Nyanza as when it enters. Perhaps the return of Stanley's expedition, when it is intended to devote some time to exploration, will answer this question, as well as the still unsettled one as to the identity and final destination of the Welle.

The latest attempt to solve this ever-present problem has come to naught. Capt. Van Gèle, who has made journeys on the Ubangi and Lopuri, had charge of this attempt. He left the station of Bangala July 1, with the steamers "Henry Reed" and "A. J. A.," to ascend the Itimbiri, which is supposed to approach nearest to the Welle. The plan was to go up this river as far as it is navigable, to the Lubi Falls, where he was to leave Lieut. Dhanis behind as the head of a new station, while he himself should proceed northward in as direct a line as possible to the Welle. Here another station was to be left in charge of Lieut. Liénart, while the captain himself was to follow the course of the Welle to its mouth. But when he arrived at the falls he found the country uninhabited, contrary to Mr. Grenfell's descriptions; and, learning from a neighboring petty chief that the land he would have to traverse was covered with primitive forests, he saw no way of provisioning his people or making his journey successfully, and returned as speedily as possible.

Lieut. Wissmann made an extended report of his second journey across the continent of Africa at the November meeting of the Berlin Society for Geographical Research. After starting in a southeasterly direction into the territory of the Baluba, the expedition turned to the northeast toward the Lubi; at the mouth of this river Lake Sankuru was traversed, but here it became apparent that the dense and swampy woodlands would not allow farther progress toward the northeast, and the

project of penetrating to the upper waters of the more northerly tributary of the Congo had to be abandoned. Without passing the Lomami, the lieutenant turned his course to the southward, crossed his route of 1881 in the territory of the Beneki, now laid waste by war, slave-hunting, and pestilence, and reached Nyangwe, whence he crossed by the usual route to Tanganyika. From the southern shore of this lake he went to Nyassa and thence to Mozambique by a new way. He reports the people visited on both his expeditions as having made progress during the four intervening years, and taken the first steps toward civilization. A small lake called Limbi has been discovered southeast from the Schirwa or Kilwa Lake, in the Nyassa territory, having an outlet to the larger lake.

Bishop Smythies's report of his journey to Lake Nyassa and the Magwangwara, undertaken with a view to establishing a mission in their territory, describes them as warlike and lawless, like the Massai to the north and the Masitu to the west. Their land is between Lake Nyassa and the coast. The height of the mountains where the Rovuma has its sources was estimated by the bishop at 1,700 metres.

The German and English governments have at length come to an agreement respecting the boundaries of the territory in Eastern Africa under their influence, and of the Sultanate of Zanzibar. Following are in substance the specifications:

1. Germany and Great Britain recognize the sovereignty of the Sultan of Zanzibar over the islands of Zanzibar and Pemba, and over those smaller islands lying in the vicinity of the former, within a circle of twelve nautical miles, also over the islands Lamu and Mafia. They recognize also as the possession of the sultan a line of coast on the continent, passing from the mouth of the Miningani river on the south to Kipini on the north. This line begins at the south of the Miningani, follows its course five nautical miles, and is then extended on the parallel of latitude to the point where it meets the right bank of the Rovuma river, when it crosses that river and extends along its left bank. This strip has a breadth of ten nautical miles, measured by a straight line inward from the coast at the highest water-mark. The northern boundary includes Kau. The governments acknowledge the right of the sultan to the stations Kismajo, Barawa, Merka, and Magadoxa, with land extending inward about ten nautical miles, and Warsheik with five nautical miles.

2. Great Britain agrees to support those negotiations of Germany with the sultan which have in view the leasing of the harbor dues of Dar-es-Salaam and Pangani to the German East African Company, in consideration of an annual payment to the sultan on the part of the company.

3. Both powers agree to make a boundary-line between their respective spheres of influence, as was previously done with the territory on the Gulf of Guinea.

This territory is to be bounded on the south by the Rovuma river and on the north by a line starting from the mouth of the Tana river, and following its course, or that of its tributaries, to the intersection of the equator and the thirty-eighth degree of east longitude, then passing in a straight line to the intersection of the first degree of north latitude with the thirty-seventh degree of east longitude, where the line ends. The line of demarkation shall begin at the mouth of the Wanga or Umbe river, pass direct to Lake Jipe, along its eastern and northern shores, across the Lumi river, dividing midway the districts of Taveita and Chagga, then along the northern slope of the Kilimandjaro range, and be carried on in a straight line to a point where the first degree of south latitude meets the eastern shore of Victoria Lake. Germany engages to claim no territory north of this line, to assume no protectorate and to make no opposition to the extension of the English influence there; and Great Britain makes the same agreement regarding the territory south of the line.

4. Great Britain will use its influence to forward a friendly agreement concerning the Kilimandjaro territory between the Sultan of Zanzibar and the German East African Company.

5. Both powers recognize as belonging to Witu the coast from Kipini northward to Manda Bay.

6. Germany and Great Britain will conjointly call upon the Sultan of Zanzibar to accede to the general act of the Berlin Conference, the existing rights of his Highness being reserved, according to the specifications of Article I of the act.

7. Germany engages to accede to the declaration made by Great Britain and France, March 10, 1862, regarding the recognition of the independence of the Sultan of Zanzibar.

The private claims of the German East African Company on the territory granted to Great Britain are not affected by this treaty, nor are the acquisitions in Somali Land from Tana to the Gulf of Aden. The German protectorate has heretofore extended only over Useguha, Ukami, Nguru, and Usagara. It is intended to cultivate tobacco, coffee, and cotton in the German territory, and a "Plantation Company" with a large capital has been founded for the purpose. A survey for a railway is soon to be begun.

Germany thus becomes the next neighbor of Portugal on the coast, and a treaty has been made with this power also regarding boundaries. According to this treaty the southern boundary of Angola is marked by the course of the Kunene from its mouth to the second cataract in the Chella or Kanna mountains; thence by the parallel of latitude of the falls to the Kubango; thence by the course of that stream to Andara; then by a straight line to the Zambezi at the Rapids of Katima. The northern boundary of Mozambique is marked by the course of the Rovuma to its junction with the Msinje; thence by the parallel of latitude to Nyassa.

Letters from Lake Tanganyika can now reach England in about three months, the London Missionary Society having established a monthly mail from the lake to Zanzibar.

In the early days of July, Dr. Hans Meyer made the first ascent of Kibo, the westerly and highest peak of Mount Kilimandjaro from the southeast, accompanied for most of the distance by Herr von Eberstein. Passing the highest points reached by Johnston and Count Teleki, he climbed to an immense field strewed with broken ice-blocks, and found himself confronted by a blue wall of ice from thirty-five to forty metres in height, presumably the outer wall of the crater. This barrier is impassable to a single climber without apparatus or help

of any kind, and Dr. Meyer had to content himself with the satisfaction of having reached what should be the edge of the crater without the privilege of looking into it. He thinks it altogether probable that the glacier fills it entirely. Observation showed that the wall of ice surrounds it on the northeast as well as the east and south sides. Dr. Meyer found to his regret afterward that the north side of the mountain was almost entirely free from the snow which stretched in great fields over the route traversed by him and his companion, and added greatly to the hardships of the ascent. The height reached was about 6,050 metres.

The political changes in the lands to the south of Abyssinia have led to several journeys of exploration in the interest of trade and plans for opening the best routes of communication. M. Rimbaud, a French merchant, has made a report of a new and direct route which he followed in returning to Harrar from Entotto. He does not, however, share the views of some earlier travelers as to the commercial value of this region, and doubts whether the railroad which has been planned to Lake Assal for transporting salt, will not meet with such great engineering difficulties as to render it an unprofitable enterprise; neither does he believe in the possibility of navigating the Hawash, even at the season of highest water. He recommends the route from Sela by way of Harrar to Shoa, because it avoids the lands of the lawless Danakil and passes through the more fertile regions to the southward. The country of the Itu-Galla is a plateau about 2,500 metres high, covered with fine pastures and great forests, and is well adapted to European colonization by its fertility and the mildness of its climate.

Italy is gradually extending her sway along the African coast of the Red Sea. She has full possession of the colony on Assab Bay, which was extended northward to Cape Dermah by the annexing of Beilul and Gobbi in 1884. The southern boundary is not definitely settled, but includes the sultanate of Raheita. The stretch of coast from Cape Dermah in the south to the Buri peninsula in the north is under the Italian protectorate, and the Dahlak Islands and the vicinity of Massuah from the Buri peninsula to Emberemi north from Massuah are under Italy's control.

Lake Susi, in the southern part of Shoa, has been supposed to be without an outlet; but it has been visited by Count Antonelli and Dr. Traversi, who discovered an outlet from the southern shore. It is called Shusbaki, and after forming some smaller lakes it flows into Lake Ocah, and leaving that makes its way to the Bhilate, a tributary of the Wabi.

L. Robecchi, an Italian engineer, explored the northeastern part of the Libyan Desert in an adventurous journey begun in the autumn of 1886. The route taken, from Alexandria along the coast to Ras-el-Kanais and over the oasis Garah to Siwah, was not new; but it is said to have afforded some data that will be of use in perfecting the map of that region. Robecchi entered at night the old necropolis of Siwah, and carried away a number of skulls and skeletons. The people of Siwah are fiercely hostile toward Europeans.

A great part of the western Sahara has passed under the Spanish protectorate, and by a government order in the spring that strip of territory along the coast from near Cape Blanco to Cape Bojador, that is, from 20° 51′ north latitude and 10° 56′ east longitude to 26° 8′ north latitude and 8° 17′ east longitude, is placed under the general government of the Canary Islands. The governor will have his capital at Rio del Oro.

A French explorer, C. Douls, gives an account of a remarkable journey made by him in the western Sahara. Disguised as a Mussulman, he landed in a Canary Island fishing-boat at a point on the coast between Cape Bojador and the Rio del Oro. He was suspected and taken prisoner by the first Moors he met, but after some time succeeded in gaining their confidence, and was admitted into their tribe as a "brother." They proved to be a noted robber-band of the Sahara called the Ulad Delim. M. Douls wandered with them five months, going as far as the border of the Desert of Uarau and Djuf, the great depression of the Sahara, making some important observations with his barometer, which, with his compass, had been given back to him by the Moors. Turning to the north he passed near the sebka of Zemmur, determining its exact position and surveying the course of the Saguiat-al-Hamra, which had not before been ascended. At the end of March he was in Tendûf, the great slave-market. Since Dr. Lenz was there in 1880, the oasis, according to this account, has greatly increased in size. Returning, he crossed the plains of the Ketaua and the Takua. Between Tarfaya and Uad Nun the level surface of the desert becomes broken and hilly, and the beds of rivers that have been destroyed by upheavals can be traced. At Glimin he parted from his companions, they passing on south along the steppes, and he north along the Atlas range. Passing the country of the Berbers, and crossing the Atlas, he reached Morocco. Here the sultan, enraged at having his country entered from the south by a European, threw him into a dungeon. But the English embassy, as it happened, reached the city the same day, and upon the representations of Sir Kirby Green the traveler was released. M. Douls has thus traversed a tract of country new to Europeans, and reports that he has brought away important geographical and ethnological information.

Lieut.-Col. Gallieni has sent to Paris a sketch of the work of the French expeditions to the interior of Senegal. The two military columns moved against the marabout Mahmadu Lamine at Diana, who was threatening the forts on the Senegal, and put him speedily to flight. They made surveys of the valley of the Nieriko, the

upper Gambia, and the hitherto unexplored parts of the Faleme. Two companies of officers had quitted Diana; one had surveyed the country between the Faleme and the Tankesso, the other had crossed the Gambia at Badu and the Faleme at Erimina, and had penetrated to Dinguiray, which has never before been visited by a European. The whole region has been placed under the protectorate of France. A most advantageous treaty has been made with the Prophet Samory, who founded an extended empire, Wassulu, in the upper regions of the Niger, from the ruins of Sego and other conquered territory. By the treaty the Niger and the Tankesso from their sources constitute the boundary between the French Sondan and the territory of Samory, who also agreed to place all his possessions on the right bank of the Niger under French protection. This extends the French influence on the right bank of the Niger from Sego to Sierra Leone and the republic of Liberia.

G. A. Krause returned in September from Salaga to the coast after encountering many hardships on the route, the greater part of which has never before been traveled by a European. In going from Sôgede to the slave coast, he turned to the south and went to Atakpáme by way of Beletá or Anguinga, the center of the salt trade in that region, passing twice by boat over the Mono, called the Njéle in the north, and fording its western tributary, Angai or Anai, three times. In Beletá and in Gbeschi opposition was made to his farther progress, and though he saved himself both times by escaping during the night, he was obliged to leave behind at Beletá his baggage and his collections, the latter consisting of from 600 to 800 plants and seeds of various kinds, a number of beetles, butterflies, and other insects, and a few articles from prehistoric settlements between Mosi and Timbuctoo. He discovered in the land of the Gurunsi a remedy for fever which proved efficacious in the thirteen attacks that he suffered after leaving Salaga. He arrived at Accra September 23, having traveled on foot from Little Popo along the strand.

One important result of his journey is the discovery that the Volta rises far inland, northeast of Waga-Dugu, the capital of Mosi. He found also that Timbuctoo had acknowledged the sovereignty of the Sheik Tidshani, although the troops of El Bakai are still in the field against him. Following is a translation of a part of one of Herr Krause's letters: "I left Salaga July 7, 1886, to go to Mosi. The route led by way of the Dagamba city of Kankanga to Wala-Wala, near which we crossed the Volta and entered the eastern part of the country of the tribes called the Gurunsi. After crossing a large tributary of the eastern Volta we entered the land of the Busanga, and then Mosi, where we spent a month in Beri before we went on to Waga-Dugu, the capital. Leaving that place October 26, and passing through the Mosi provinces Tema and Jádega, I arrived at Ban, the first place in the domain of the Sheik Tidshani, a son of that Hadsh Omar who fought so obstinately against the French on the Senegal thirty or more years ago. From Ban I went, November 15, to Duënsa, a depot for the salt trade. Before continuing my journey northward, I crossed a high table-land southwesterly to Ban-Djágara, the seat of the Sheik Tidshani. After two days' sojourn, I was ordered out of the town, but received permission to go to Timbuctoo under the Sheik's protection, though through the dangerous region to the east of the Niger. I returned to Duënsa and started from there for Timbuctoo, but after one day's march received an order, December 8, to go back to Mosi. From Mosi I turned to the southwest and south by way of Sinsani Gasäri in the western territory of the Gurunsi, Funsi, Wa, and Bole, to Kuntampo in northern Ashantee. This was March 30. I had previously crossed the western Volta. From Kuntampo, eight marches brought me to Salaga. As my goods were exhausted, I was obliged to return. If I could have had from 400 to 600 marks I could have gone on with my explorations."

The territory on the lower Congo, secured to Portugal by the treaty of February 14, 1885, with the Congo State and the confirmation by the Berlin Conference, has been united with the colony of Angola as the Fourth Congo District, and is divided into five sub-districts: Oacongo with the capital Landana, and Cabinda, Ambrizette, San Antonio, and San Salvador, with capitals of the same names.

The Swedish traveler, Baron von Schwerin, has discovered the celebrated Pedra Padraõ or inscribed stone, which the Portuguese navigator Diego Cão (Cam) placed at the mouth of the Congo when he discovered it. The baron learned that the natives had been heard to speak of a large "fetich stone" hidden in the jungle. They stood so in awe of it that it was with some difficulty that he persuaded them to show him the way to it. It proved to be the veritable Pedra Padraõ.

In reference to the voyages of Diego Cão, the Visconde de Sanches de Baena has been led by an examination of unpublished documents to the conclusion that he started on his first voyage in 1482 and remained away nineteen months, and that it was during this voyage that he set up the Pedra Padraõ. After his return he was granted a coat of arms, the patent of which is dated April 14, 1484. He started on a second voyage in 1485 and erected similar stones on Cape Agostinho and Cape Cross. This differs from former accounts.

Dr. H. Schinz, the Swiss botanist, made a two years' journey, from October, 1884, to October, 1886, over the German territory in Southwestern Africa. His reports are of importance as showing the extent and quality of the arable lands, and his careful ethnological researches are also of interest. He estimates the number of inhabitants under the German protectorate at 250,000, about 10,000 in Great Namaqualand, 120,000 in Ovaherero, and 120,000 in Ovambo. His observation of Lake Ngami convinced him that the surface of the lake is yearly decreasing.

It is proposed to change the name of the Bay of Angra Pequena to Lüderitz Bay, in memory of Adolph Lüderitz, to whose exertions the colonization movement in Southwestern Africa in 1884 is due, and who lost his life in October, 1886, on his way back from a journey made for the purpose of examining the obstructions to navigation in Orange river. His memory is already honored in the colony by the name Lüderitz Land, which is applied to the stretch of coast between Angra Pequena and the mouth of the Orange.

The New Republic founded by the Boers from the Transvaal, in Zululand, includes, according to the statement of the ministry in Parliament, May 17, 1887, 2,854 square miles (English), or 7,392 square kilometres, a much smaller area than was at first claimed. The republic also failed to secure the direct connection with the sea-coast, which was one of the subjects of negotiation. The remaining part of Zululand, 8,220 square miles, or 21,290 square kilometres, falls under the control of England, and is placed under the administration of the Governor of Natal.

The last census (1886) of the Transvaal gives the native population at 299,743, 62,826 of whom are full-grown men. There is a striking difference between these figures and those of the census of 1879, which gave the native population as 774,930, of whom 154,986 were grown men, a difference not accounted for by the fact that one district was not numbered and one other but incompletely. The white population, according to a church census or estimate, numbers 45,000 adherents of the Dutch churches and about 10,000 belonging to other churches, without counting the fluctuating population of the gold-mining districts.

The first section of the railroad from Delagoa Bay to the South African Republic, 86 kilometres in length, was opened October 31. This is the first step toward making the republic of the Boers independent of Great Britain and her South African colonies.

Asia.—The explorations of this year in Asia are mostly due to Russian and British officers, some of whom have been engaged in defining boundaries, and some in examining the resources of the territory lately acquired and the prospects it offers for business enterprises. Several French explorers have also been in the field, and three of them have made the difficult journey across the Pamir. The French authorities in Cochin-China are improving their possessions by opening the Mekong for navigation. They have already succeeded in removing the rocks causing the rapids between Sambor and Stung-trang, so that the stream can be ascended to the Siamese borders.

Dr. G. J. Radde, Director of the Caucasus Museum and the public library at Tiflis, has published this year his report of the expedition undertaken last year (1886) for the exploration of the Trans-Caspian lands recently acquired by Russia, and the adjoining territory of northern Khorassan, under the auspices of the Russian authorities. The objects of the expedition, which lasted eight months, were: the study of the general physico-geographical conditions of the southwestern part of the former Aral-Caspian basin and the isolated mountains rising from it and connected mountain chains; the study of the geological formations in their general character and in the special features that may be of use in future mining undertakings, such as deposits of salt, sulphur, and naphtha; and the study of the fauna and flora with the gathering of collections for future study. The principal members of the expedition were Dr. Radde, Dr. A. Walker, and A. M. Konschin, an engineer who is well acquainted with the country, having been engaged in mining operations there since 1881, and who has given considerable study to the Oxus question. Many deposits of naphtha, saltpetre, common salt, sulphur, gypsum, Glauber's-salt, and the like have been discovered by him in his various tours, in which he estimates that he has traveled in all about 8,500 kilometres. The Trans-Caspian naphtha-fields lie in the sandy depression at the foot of the Balkan mountains, 30 kilometres west of the stations Bala-ischem and Aidin on the Trans-Caspian railway. The naphtha-bearing hills, of which there are two groups, the Naphtha-dagh and the Buja-dagh, are made up of salty, parti-colored clays and marls, saturated with the naphtha and covered with coarse and fine sand, having a stratified form and also filled with naphtha. As to the value of this product in future, Herr Konschin does not think that its export in either crude or distilled form will ever be profitable. But he thinks it promises to be of great service as fuel for the railroad and the country, which is wholly destitute of forests and of coal. Naphtha is also found on the island of Cheleken, and traces of it have been noticed at Chikishljar and on the mountains of Kelat.

A rich deposit of sulphur was found in the midst of the Desert of Karakum in numerous groups of rounded hills. The place is called by the natives Kyrk-dsubulba, meaning "forty hills." The sulphur, which is in masses and veins amid strata of marl, clay, and sand, is of excellent quality, and in spite of its remote position is worthy the attention of those interested in the sulphur-trade. The railway is at least 200 kilometres distant. The other minerals named exist in good quality and abundance. Great quantities of salt are found along the Caspian on its ancient bed; and the deposits near Akrabad, not far from the Afghan border, supply the inhabitants of the oases of Merv, Pende, and Tejend, as well as those

of the neighboring parts of Afghanistan and Khorassan.

As to the adaptability of the country to agriculture, M. Konschin says scarcely the hundredth part of the surface is fit for cultivation. "All of the remainder bears the typical desolate character of the central Asiatic desert. The greater part of it is covered with vast masses of sand in monotonous wave-like forms. Here and there the sand-hills alternate with bare clay-fields or barren, salt-bearing basins and dried-up lagoon-beds. These three, the salt hills, clay-beds, and dry valleys of salt and gypsum, are the typical features of the physiognomy of Turkomania. Unattractive as the country is, it is of great interest to the geologist. Here must be decided the questions raised by Pallas and Humboldt regarding the history of the ancient Pontic-Aral-Caspian Sea and its division into three great basins, now represented by the Caspian, the Aral, and the Black seas. Was the change made gradually under the influence of dry polar winds, or by an upheaval of the earth's surface causing a sudden outflow of the waters, according to Baer's theory, or were there upheavals at some points with corresponding simultaneous depressions at others, causing the water to settle in the smaller and deeper basins? Here also is the question as to what is called the old beds of the Amu-Darja, known as the Usboi, Ungus, Aktama, etc., all of which traverse the plain between the present Amu and the Caspian Sea. This question is not only of interest to scientists, but its practical importance was recognized even by Peter the Great, and is seen by the Russian Government to-day. The question is whether the Amu-Darja can again be connected with the Caspian, a question of great moment to Russia, politically as well as commercially."

M. Konschin's conclusion is that the dried-up lakes, gulfs, etc., the principal series of which intersects the Karakum steppe from northwest to southeast, are only an ancient shore-line of the Caspian, and not an old bed of the Amu-darja. The Sarakamysh basin when filled with water was in connection with the Aral by means of the Gulf of Abougir and with the Caspian by the Balkan Gulf, and into the basin flowed the Amu-darja from the southeast. The final connection between the Aral and the Caspian was by means of the depression of the western Usboi extending along the Ust-Urt and the Great Balkan. The Usboi, therefore, was not a continuation of the Amu-darja or an old bed of the Oxus. The clear salt water of the Usboi can not be traced to the muddy fresh water of the Amu-darja, and the lack of cut-offs from the latter in the depressed plain of Turkomania and of every trace of life forbids the supposition that it was ever connected with the Caspian in its present limits. The presence of salt in large quantities is a further proof of this view, and traces of the action of flowing water, such as rounded pebbles, pebbly sand, the washing away of banks and the like, are scarcely to be found. Another proof is afforded by the discovery of important traces of the action of marine ice in this depression—a very rare phenomenon in Central Asia.

As to the practical question involved, M. Konschin says: "In order to pass around the Sarakamysh basin from the Amu-darja toward Bala-ischem to the Ust-Urt it would be necessary to construct a canal of at least 300 kilometres through a region of large sand-hills and partly through rock. But to fill the basin again with water seems to me an undertaking not to be thought of, as it would be to form a sea in a place where it would be subjected to the powerful geological agencies there active. Neither would the western Usboi in its present condition, even at high water, afford ship-passage to it. A series of canals would have to be constructed through the Balkan plain, as well as through the swampy tract at Babachodsha, and at other points costly hydrotechnic machinery would be needed. The cost of the undertaking would be out of proportion to the advantages Russia would be likely to gain by this connection with Central Asia.

"In conclusion, it remains to devote a few words to the question: What causes effected the drying up of the Turkomanian plain? In my opinion two causes contributed: first, the action of polar winds; and, second, the upheaval of the earth.

"The latter is evidenced by, first, the high altitude of the more recent Pliocene strata in the ravines of the Kioren-dagh; second, the hooked form of the peninsulas of Krasnovolsk and Darshe, of the island of Cheleken, which is on the way to becoming a peninsula, and of the Great Balkan, which was a peninsula; third, the hooked and finger-form of numerous tongues of land on the northern and western shores of the peninsula Darshe, as on the neighboring shore of the Caspian; fourth, the long, narrow coast-lakes that line the shore of the Caspian between the Khiva and Chikishliar bays; fifth, the many narrow lagoon-beds running parallel to the length of the oasis of Akaltekke and to the Kioren and Kopet-dagh ranges; sixth, the peculiarity of the mouths of the Atrek and Gurgan rivers, showing great marshy stretches, bays, and numerous channels; seventh, the many remains of marine organisms and traces of the dynamic and static action of the sea at elevations considerably above the present sea-level.

"As to the action of polar winds, the effect of the north and northeast winds in Turkomania is well known. They are like powerful pumps continually acting to draw the moisture from the soil and carrying it from east to west. So few showers fall during the warm season that constant diminution of the water would be inevitable.

"From all these considerations it appears that the country is condemned to bear the character of a desolate waste. Nature has given to it only a cloudless sky, barren mountains, rivers without water, clouds of dust and sand, and dead plains of salt."

The boundary between the Russian possessions in Asia and Afghanistan has been settled after three years of negotiation, by a treaty concluded July 22 at St. Petersburg and ratified August 8. Herr H. Wichmann gives an account of the difficulties and the progress of the agreement substantially as follows: As long ago as 1873, England and Russia, whose leading statesmen were convinced of the undesirability of having their possessions meet in Asia, made provisional agreement to maintain the territory of Afghanistan as it then stood, giving that state the position of a bulwark between the two powers. The Amu-darja from the mouth of the Koktsha to Khodsha-Salih was designated as the northern boundary of Afghanistan; the line from there to the Persian borders was not settled, but the districts of Aktsha, Seripul, Maimeneh, Shibagan, and Andkhoi were recognized as belonging to Afghanistan. The western boundary also was left undefined, as this was premised to be already known. There was no anxiety in England about the northwestern boundary, as at that time there was no indication that Russia would advance from that side through the territory of the Turkoman tribes and the Desert of Karakum.

It was not till after the lapse of ten years and more that it became apparent that very little was known of the real extent of the Afghan empire, and that the boundaries laid down so long on the maps between Sarakhs and the Oxus had been drawn at random, without any credible information about the tribes subject to Afghanistan and those that were independent. The question was again agitated in 1881, but nothing came of it. It became more pressing after the surrender of Merv in March, 1885, when the Turkoman tribes, even those most remote, the Sarik Turkomans, who had their pasture-grounds along the middle course of the Murghab and on the lower Kushk, voluntarily subjected themselves to Russia; for this made it evident that Afghan sovereignty did not extend over the territory between the rivers Tejend and Murghab.

The negotiations, taken up again in March, 1884, were delayed, after the appointment of a mixed commission, by the demand on the part of Russia that an understanding should first be had as to the starting-place of the Afghan boundary from Persia, the place of crossing the Murghab, and the direction it should take to the Amu-darja. These questions were settled Sept. 10, 1885, and the commission began its work in November at Zulfikar on the Heri-Rud, the upper course of the Tejend, which forms the boundary between Persia and Russian Turkistan to a little north of Sarakhs. No difficulties were experienced until the question arose as to the ending of the line at the

Oxus. By the agreement of January 31, 1873, the post at Kodsha-Salih had been designated as the most westerly point of Afghanistan. It now appeared that the actual boundary between Bokhara and Afghanistan at the left bank of the Oxus, as it had stood for thirty-six years, took an entirely different course than had been supposed, since it passed between the village of Bossága in Bokhara and the Afghan town of Khamiab. Another difficulty was presented by the fact that there was no town called Kodsha-Salih; the place having most claim to the appellation is the tomb of a Mohammedan saint, called Ziaret Kodsha-Salih. The largest of the four Afghan districts between Bossága and Kilif, Karkin, is frequently called Kodsha-Salih. As the commission could not agree on this point, the governments decided in August, 1886, to declare its work ended, and decide by direct negotiation the terminal of the Afghan boundary at the Oxus.

The matter was resumed in April, 1887, at St. Petersburg. On the side of England it was insisted that the agreement of 1878 had for its object only the maintenance of the then position of the Emir of Afghanistan; and therefore it would be fair not to insist on a boundary drawn in ignorance of some of the facts, but to allow to Afghanistan the whole territory of Khamiab. On the part of Russia it was urged that this principle of the recognition of the boundary of Afghanistan in 1878 was already broken by the treaty of September, 1885, which gave lands on the upper Kushk, the Kashan, and the Murghab, to the Emir of Afghanistan, which had undoubtedly before been the property of the independent tribes of the oasis of Pendjeh.

After tedious debates an understanding was reached by which Russia allowed to Afghanistan the disputed territory on the Oxus, the district of Khamiab, and received in exchange the districts on the Kushk, Kashan, and Murghab previously accorded to Afghanistan. By this arrangement the latter country received about 784 square miles of which 36½ square miles are farming-lands, with about 18,000 inhabitants, while the Turkomans received 824½ square miles of which 6½ square miles are farming-lands, and only 14 square miles are arable.

Great gain to geographical knowledge has resulted from the work of the Russian and British surveyors, who were engaged during the delay in 1885 and 1886 in a thorough examination of great tracts in Central Asia long practically closed to European travelers. The Russian surveyors worked upon the lands of the former independent tribes, the borders toward Persia and the Oxus. The British engineers laid down upon the map a surface of about 120,000 square miles. They measured, besides the new borders, the entire province of Herat, including the heretofore unknown districts of Taimani and Firuzkuhi. Almost the whole of Afghan Turkistan, and a great part of Hazareh land in the vicinity of Bamian,

has been surveyed or at least examined, as well as the Persian province of Khorassan.

The source of the Heri-Rud proved to be at an elevation of 12,000 feet above the level of the sea; it flows 70 or 80 miles under the name of the Ab-i-Sar-i-jangal to Danlalyar, almost due west, and in a direction different from that laid down on the maps. The Chalopdalan or Chahil Abdak peak in Imam Sherif's journey through the Taimani country, was identified, a solitary mountain 12,000 feet high, said to be the Takht of Zohak-i-Maran, the snake-bearing governor of these provinces in the days of Ghur; and it was from here that he built the massive walls and towers of the old forts which surround Taiwara and border the road to Ghur.

The Pamir has been crossed this year by the French travelers MM. Capus, Bonvalot, and Pépin. They were robbed on the way, but succeeded in crossing the Pamir and the Hindu Kush between Samarcand and Chitral, whither help was sent to them from India. Grum Greshimalo also made his third journey to the Pamir, starting this time from Fergana.

In an address before the Royal Geographical Society by E. D. Morgan, giving an account of Gen. Prejevalski's journeys in Central Asia, the following details, with reference to the eastern part of the journey, were specified as having been given to the speaker by the explorer: First, the changes to be made in existing maps are, "(1) the Khoten river makes no bend to the west, but has a nearly meridional course from south to north (our itinerary from Khoten to the confluence of the Khoten-darja with the Tarim measures 327 miles); (2) there is no such lake as Yashil-kul, nor any lakes along the course of the Khoten-darja; (3) thirty miles below the fork of the Kara-Kash and Khoten rivers, a low, narrow, and absolutely barren ridge, having an elevation of only 500 feet, stretches from Fort Maral-bashi in this direction, that is, northeast toward the Khoten-darja."

Further details were: "Forty-three miles below Khoten, following the Khoten-darja, otherwise known as the Yurun-Kash, lies the oasis of Tavek-Kehl, inhabited by about 500 families, not marked on any map. According to native information, the population of the Khoten oasis (including Khoten, Kara-Kash, and Sam-pul) numbers 600,000. In September the Khoten river is an insignificant stream, 70 to 100 feet wide, and from six inches to one foot in depth. After a devious course of seventeen miles below Mazartagh ridge it dries up, only leaving pools here and there along its sandy bed. In summer, however, there is an abundance of water, and the river then reaches the Tarim.

On either side of the Khoten river are driftsands the whole way from Khoten to the Tarim. The valley of the former river is about three miles wide, and indistinctly defined; on the lower river there are no inhabitants. The flora and fauna are extremely poor. Khoten has an elevation of 4,100 feet, and the confluence of the Khoten and the Tarim 2,800, twelve miles below the junction of the Yarkand and Aksu darjas. Here the Tarim has a width of about 200 yards at low water, and a depth of not less than five feet. The whole of the Tarim is navigable for small river-steamers from the confluence of its upper waters to Lob Nor. The first inhabited parts of the Aksu oasis occur on the left bank of its river, eighteen miles from the ford across the Tarim, coming from Khoten, and it is exactly sixty-six miles farther to the town of Aksu. The Aksu oasis has a population of 56,000 families, according to native information, and is the most fertile part of Kashgaria.

Some parts of Thibet not explored by Gen. Prejevalski, seem to have been visited by Mr. A. D. Carey, of the Bombay civil service, who is making a two years' journey through that part of Asia, accompanied by Mr. A. Dalgleish as interpreter. They left India in May, 1885, and marched through the hills to Ladak. The plan was to travel eastward into Northern Thibet as far as the Mangtsa lake, and then turning northward to go on to the plains of Turkistan near Kiria. In carrying out this plan the travelers passed over more than 300 miles believed not to have been previously visited by Europeans. The height of one of the passes crossed was estimated at 19,000 feet. From Khoten the Khoten river was followed to its junction with the Tarim, then that river to Sarik, and from there the travelers crossed the desert to Shâh-yár and Kuchar. Thence the Tarim was followed to a point where it turns southward to Lake Lob, and after some delay the travelers followed it on to the lake, thus exploring its entire course.

The country about is flat and reedy, and the people are poor and destitute. Mr. Carey was everywhere kindly received—a contrast to the treatment encountered by Gen. Prejevalski. After leaving Lob Nor in April, 1886, he crossed the Altyn and Chiman mountains, and reached the foot of a high chain supposed to be the true Kuen-Lun. To the eastward a pass was found leading to the valley of the Machu, the head source of the Yang-tse-kiang. Want of supplies prevented the travelers from following the Machu very far. In the subsequent journey they saw a good deal of the nomadic Kalmuks and Mongols in the valleys of Tsai-dam. Though rather inhospitable, they were not hostile; they often refused to part with food or grain for money. On the way from Chaklik to the point where the Shassa track was struck, a journey of eighty-two days, not a single human being was met with.

Several journeys, undertaken by native explorers to solve the problems of the Sanpo and Lut-se-kiang, have been unsuccessful; but it seems probable from what is known that the Sanpo flows into the Brahmaputra, and that the Lut-se-kiang is the upper part of the Irra-wadi. Col. Woodthorpe has been busied with extensive surveys in Burmah, and Mr. Mac-Carthy has made some explorations in Siam.

Mr. G. N. Potanin returned to St. Petersburg in the spring after his three years' explorations in Mongolia. At the end of 1886 he crossed the Desert of Gobi to Kiakhta and Irkutsk, following the course of the river Ezsin. In its lower part it divides into two streams, the eastern forming the half-dried lake Sugu-nor, while the western flows into the great salt lake Gushun-nor, situated in a desert where neither water nor grass is found for fifty miles. M. Potanin's companion, M. Beresovski, remained behind to increase his already large natural history collection. M. Potanin took home more than 1,500 botanical specimens and 15,000 insects, with photographs and ethnological objects. M. Skassi, a member of the party, surveyed 4,000 miles of country, and determined by astronomical observations the position of more than sixty points.

Three English travelers, Messrs. James, Younghusband, and Fulford, have succeeded in finding the sources of the western Sungari. They started from Mookden for the valley of the Jalu, intending to go to the boundary mountains of Corea and Manchuria. But the way was so difficult that they turned toward the north into a side valley, and, having crossed the mountains by a pass 900 metres high, they followed the He-ho or Black river to the Sungari, the western fork of which they traced to its source in the Peistau or White mountains. The highest point was found to be about 2,500 metres; it has heretofore been estimated at from 3,000 to 4,000. There are no glaciers, but the snow lies in the ravines throughout the year. Near by are the sources of the Jalu and the Tumen, the river on the border of Corea. They attempted to reach it, but finding the mountains impassable turned northward to Kirin, the capital of Chinese Manchuria. They afterward traveled through northern and eastern Manchuria, their whole journey extending over more than 3,000 miles. They found the people civil and kind, but the country is overrun with brigands. The administration is too weak to maintain an efficient police system, and probably order can only be introduced by Chinese authority. The Manchu Tartars are fast losing their language, spoken and written, and adopting the Chinese. This substitution of a complicated hieroglyphic system for a simple alphabet forms an instance of national retrogression unparalleled in modern times. The people, say the travelers, are demoralized with idleness; for every man belonging to the higher classes that can draw a bow receives two taels a month, and land rent free, as compensation for training with the militia twice a year. The country is rich in gold, silver, iron, coal, furs, and silk. Large quantities of opium are raised, which find a market in China.

The English Government has given up its

claim to the little islands near Corea which were to be used as a marine station—Port Hamilton—they having been found unsuitable for the purpose.

Several attempts to sound the depth of the crater of the volcano of Asama-jama northwest of Tokio were made by Mr. Milne some time since. One hundred feet from the edge of the crater the lead reached a depth of 441 feet; at 800 feet from the edge the lead descended more than 700 feet, when the attempt had to be given up on account of the breaking of the line.

In a report to the Geographical Society of Paris, Joseph Martin, the French mining engineer, describes his journeys in Eastern Siberia. He crossed the Stanowoi mountains, a route never before taken by scientific explorers. He was obliged to give up his first plan to cross this watershed between the Lena and Amoor by the two tributaries Aldan and Zea, and to pass again over the watershed between Olekma and Witim, and then the parallel chains of the Stanowoi between the Tungir and Amasar. In this southwestern part the range presents rounded summits covered with forests mostly of larches and birches; its average height is 1,200 metres, while single points rise as high as 1,500 metres.

An attempt made by M. Sibiriakoff to send his steamer " Nordenskiold " to the Yenesei this autumn, by way of the Kara Sea, was unsuccessful. The vessel encountered much drift-ice and fog, but reached the month of the Petchora, where it secured a cargo, and returned to Bremen after a voyage of sixteen days. Another vessel, the " Phœnix," in charge of Captain Wiggins, reached and entered the Yenesei after a voyage of about six weeks, the first since 1880.

Australia.—The central desert of Australia is gradually becoming available for pastureland, as the geography of the country is better understood. Water is conveyed by ditches, and great tracts from which travelers have heretofore been shut out by the want of water are found capable of sustaining vast herds of cattle.

W. J. O'Donnell has found a new route to the Derby gold-fields by the Ord river from West Australia. He discovered a pass through the Leopold II mountains near Mount Leake, whereby the long circuit by way of the Margaret river can be avoided.

The Melbourne section of the geographical society of Australia is planning an expedition into the west Australian desert under the leadership of E. Giles, to penetrate in a northwesterly direction from Lake Amadeus, and cross the unknown portion of the continent.

In an account of his expedition through Central Australia from Lake Nash to the border of Queensland, David Lindsay describes the region traversed as a high table-land, bordered on the south by sandy plains and on the north by the coast mountains; large tracts of it are covered with nutritious grass. In the rainy season it is crossed by the Playford, Buchanan, and other rivers, flowing westward; in the dry season they are lost in the depressions that stretch eastward from the Ashburton range. Water can be conveyed to all parts, and Mr. Lindsay believes that the whole plateau can be made available for sheep-raising. An important discovery made by Mr. Lindsay in the McDonell mountains has drawn there a crowd of adventurers and caused the formation of a mining company in Adelaide. This is the discovery of rubies and garnets. R. Pearson, who made a journey to the place for further search, returned in July with a box of the stones taken from a slight depth at Barrow Creek during the space of a fortnight.

Islands.—An expedition left Sydney in the spring, under the leadership of Theodore F. Bevan, to explore some parts of New Guinea, and met with good success, three new rivers being discovered. Mr. Bevan's ship, the " Victory," entered the Aird river, discovered by Joseph Blackwood in 1845, and, sailing up it, found it to be only one of many subdivisions in the delta of a large river, navigable to the mountains. This was named Douglas river, and a large tributary was called Philip river. Returning, the steamer followed another of the arms of the river to Deception Bay. Near Bald Head, the eastern promontory of this bay, a third large stream was found, and followed a distance of 110 miles, when it became too shallow for farther progress. It was called the Queen's Jubilee, or Jubilee river. It was found to be bordered with forests seemingly uninhabited. The Stanhope river forms a common estuary with the Queen's Jubilee, west of Bald Head, and is navigable for a distance of forty miles. The many branchings of the Queen's Jubilee indicate that this part of the island is a great delta.

Of the people encountered Mr. Bevan writes: " The natives of the few villages found gave indications of Dravidian origin, as well as of both Moluccan and Melanesian characteristics, by dialect, appearance, and customs. From a new tribe beyond Aird Hills, a long screen of lattice-work was obtained, like those used in Siam for stretching across the mouths of creeks to insnare fish. New Guineans likewise use it to form a weir. The war-shields of the Kiva Pori natives resembled not indistinctly those used till lately in New Caledonia. All these tribes wore nose-pencils and distended the lobes of their ears. They smoked sun-dried tobacco (corresponding to the manila leaf) by means of bamboo tubes. The Tumuans, especially, might be described as almost of an intellectual cast. The canoes were dug-outs, with either a bank of mud or a small boy squatting in the prow and opposing his back as an obstacle to the incoming water. All were without outriggers. Some, however, were of unusual dimensions, one Kiva Pori canoe holding twenty-nine men, who all stood up to paddle. Not a few were grotesquely carved and painted outside to represent either inverted turtle-shells or crocodile scales. We were not a little amused at the action of one Moko native, who singly, in his fragile canoe, baled the water out by a motion of his left foot, keeping his balance and paddling vigorously against the choppy sea meanwhile."

The Baron von Schleinitz, in a voyage to the Huon Gulf in New Guinea, made the discovery of eight harbors and nine rivers not heretofore laid down on the maps. He could not ascend the rivers, but he found reason to suppose that some of them, in particular the Markham river, would afford means for exploring the interior, as its broad valley stretches far inland between high mountains. The rocks on the southern coast are primitive and metamorphic, with older sedimentary and volcanic formations; a fact which indicates greater accessibility to the interior, because erosion does not make the harder rocks so broken and impassable as the chalk formations in the vicinity of Finch Bay and other parts of Kaiser Wilhelm's Land. Another voyage was devoted to the coast, from Astrolabe Bay to the mouth of Augusta river, and led to the discovery of many bays, harbors, islands, and rivers not upon the maps, as well as the gathering of information about the country, which will be of value in making plans for its cultivation.

The baron measured 140 nautical miles in Kaiser Wilhelm's Land, and 110 in New Pomerania (New Britain) and Rook Island, and laid down many good harbors and anchoring places. In New Pomerania a low plain of great extent was discovered, having a fertile soil, and traversed by navigable streams. Its area was estimated at 4,000 square kilometres.

The coast between Juno Island and Cape Croisilles was visited in April and May by Dr. Schrader's scientific expedition, to which the discovery of the Empress Augusta river is due. Though lacking in harbors, the region seemed worth cultivating, the land being fertile, and the coast-waters favorable for anchorage.

The Catholic missionaries on Yule Island have discovered, in the course of some excursions to the opposite shore, that the two rivers, Hilda and Ethel, flowing into Hall Sound, are only insignificant streams; but they have found a new and large river, the St. Joseph, rising in Mount Yule and flowing directly southward. In fifteen villages which they visited, the missionaries numbered about 2,000 inhabitants, all of whom seemed very peaceable. They intend to found a new station twenty miles up the river. Dr. Edenfeldt was to accompany them in an ascent of Mount Yule, which is 10,046 feet in height.

Mount Owen Stanley, the highest peak of the range of that name, has at last been ascended by Mr. O. H. Martin, who estimates its height at 13,205 feet. He describes the northern slope of the mountain as a paradise of ferns and palms. The same general character is given to the ridge forming the water-shed between the south and east coasts by the report of Messrs. Harding and Hunter, who ascended it in the summer. It is from five to six thousand feet high. Mount Obree, 10,240 feet high, was ascended by W. R. Cuthbertson. Pines were growing at heights of 6,000 to 8,000 feet, and rhododendrons at the summit.

In an article in Petermann's "Mitteilungen," Dr. Th. Posewitz discusses the Kina-balu Lake in Borneo. This lake, described as lying at the foot of the Kina-balu (Chinese woman) mountain on the south or southeast, has been said by some travelers to be a great body of water, while its existence has been doubted and even wholly denied by others since its first reported discovery in 1812. An examination of the various reports leads him to conclude that the Kina-balu is a swampy depression on the middle course of the Libogu-Labuk river, which was originally a lake like many of those found along the course of the Barito and other streams of Barito; it appears as a level tract or a marshy lowland, according to the time of year it is observed. It is simply now in the course of transformation from a lake to a dry plain. This view is supported by the name given to it on Hatton's map, *Danau-Ebene*, that is, lake-plain, presumably taken from the natives, and embodying the history of the lake. The Kina-balu mountain was lately ascended by Mr. H. M. Little, one of the officials of the Borneo Company, who describes it as a huge volcanic mass, and estimates its height at 11,565 feet.

A visit made by Capt. J. Fairchild to the little islands Antipodes and Bounty, near New Zealand, for the purpose of building on them some little huts as refuges for shipwrecked people, gives some interesting information about those islands. Mount Gallavay on the Antipodes is about 400 metres in height, and is apparently of volcanic origin; the level part of the island is covered with grass of poor quality, and is the home of thousands of the albatross. Capt. Fairchild thinks that, if good grass were sown and sheep and goats placed there, they would thrive well. There are no trees either on these or the Bounty islands, which are fourteen in number, and have neither flowing water nor vegetation, not even lichens and mosses. Millions of penguins and other sea-birds make their nests there, so that shipwrecked men could find enough to eat, and the frequent showers would afford water enough for drinking purposes.

The population of New Zealand, according to a census made March 28, 1886, is 578,482, exclusive of Maoris, of whom there are 41,969, and 2,254 half-castes living with them. The number of Chinese was 4,527.

The Caroline Islands have been divided by the Governor-General of the Philippine Islands into two administration districts, the east and west, divided by the 148th degree of east longitude.

By a treaty of Nov. 19, 1886, the little group

of the Uvea or Wallis Islands was placed under French protection. The territory amounts to only about ninety-six square kilometres with about 3,500 inhabitants; but it is of some political value to France, tending to strengthen French influence in the Pacific and forming a link between the French colonies of New Caledonia and Tahiti.

Mons. A. Marche, after two months of exploration in Saipan, one of the Ladrones or Mariana Islands, says the maps are very incorrect. It has been supposed that a volcano, either active or extinct, was situated on the island, but he found none and no trace of volcanic action. Tapachao, the highest peak, he found to be only 1,345 instead of 2,000 feet high. Other hills were not over 600 or 700 feet. The northern part terminates in a mountain looking like the cliffs at Dieppe, and forming a long, narrow plateau.

Europe.—According to a report of the forest department of Russia, the work of draining the swamps in that country has been very successful. During the years 1883 and 1884, 1,530 square kilometres were drained and opened for cultivation between the Dnieper, Pripet, and Beresina, and about 1,100 between the Pripet, Slutch, and Domanowitch, and the basin of the Ossipovka. During a space of about ten years after the beginning of the work, 2,025 kilometres of canal were made, and 16,600 square kilometres of land drained. The expense was 1,875,000 roubles. In the government of Riazan 420 kilometres of canals were constructed; in the government of Moscow the canalization of the Dubna was finished; and in the northern governments the work of leveling and examining the land was carried on.

The Government of Roumania has ordered a triangulation of the country, a work which will fill a gap in the cartography of Europe. All the maps of Roumania are based on the observations of the Austrian troops in the year 1855.

Travelers and students are turning their attention of late to the Caucasus, which offers a field for research readily accessible to Europeans. Messrs. Dent and Donkin have recently published a report of a tour made last year in the group of the Kasch-tan-tau. They did not succeed in ascending that mountain, because they could not persuade the natives with them to wait for favorable weather or bring fresh supplies to the foot of the Besingi glacier. But they climbed the Tetnuld-tau under great difficulties, ascertaining its height by aneroid measurement to be about 5,040 metres, or 16,550 feet. Notwithstanding the unfavorable weather, they were able to learn something of the orography of the central Caucasus; they found that the Tetnuld and Totonal are not identical, but neighboring peaks of about equal height.

The Tetnuld was again ascended in August of this year by M. Dechy and Mr. D. Freshfield.

The ascent cost thirteen hours walking from a bivouac of 9,000 feet. The views were clear and glorious. Mr. Freshfield describes Tetnuld as the only one of the great peaks standing out on a short southern spur from the Caucasian water-shed, and therefore most favorable for views. A single observation gave the height as 16,700 feet. Four higher summits, 16,900 to 17,200 feet in height, were close at hand. Of the view from Mount Schoda, 11,128 feet in height, he says: "The glacier and forest scenery is in many parts superb. It would be difficult to imagine a more sublime and fantastic landscape than that of Ushkul, the highest community in Suanetia, when behind its fifty towers and two black castles the frozen ridge of Schkara rises 10,000 feet overhead against an unclouded sky. From the valley of the Scena, or western source of the Zenes Skali, the five crests of the same great mountain recall one of the noblest views in the Alps, Monte Rosa from Val Anzasca, and they are seen over virgin forests and fields and flowers which are high enough to conceal a laden horse."

The travelers say there is no danger or difficulty to encounter in travel in the Caucasus district they visited, the one most interesting to mountaineers, except the delay, as in all countries where time is no object. The completion of a railway to Novorossisk, which as a port accessible at all seasons is expected to supersede Taganrog, will open a new route next year to the Caucasus.

Prof. A. Penck describes a journey to the Boehmer Wald with two others for the study of the traces of glaciers. He believes that the walls between the lakes are real moraines, as indicated by the glacier cliffs on the Devil's Lake; but outside of the lake region he finds no trace of glacial phenomena.

An examination of the subterranean watercourses in the Karst district of Austria by W. Putik has led to the discovery of several caves of considerable size, among which the Count Falkenhayn Cave is the largest. The practical result expected from this examination is the prevention of overflows by removal of the masses of débris hindering the regular drainage; so that in a few years great tracts, now swampy, will be ready for cultivation.

The following are the soundings obtained in the Swiss lakes by a recent survey of the Topographical Department: The Bodensee, greatest depth between Uttwil and Friedrichshafen, 838 feet; Lake Geneva, upper part, between Revaz, St. Gingolph, and Villeneuve, 842 feet; in the center, between Ouchy and Evian, 1,017 feet; Lake Lucerne, between Gersan and Rutenen, 700 feet; Lake Zug, between Walchwill and Immensee, 650 feet; Lake Sempach, between Eich and Nottwell, 286 feet; Lake Baldegg, between Rettschwil and Gölpi, 216 feet.

M. Schrader, who has devoted ten years to the study of the orography of the Pyrenees, gives a report of his researches to the French

Association for the Advancement of Science. He says the latest maps are sixty years old, and full of inaccuracies, and no successful corrections have been made since. He made observations with an instrument of his own invention, which he calls an orograph. The mass of the mountains is south of the boundary-line, the water-shed, and they slope gradually into Spain but descend abruptly into France. On the Spanish side the descent is formed by two stages. Starting from the central crests, we find a sort of plateau, a compound mam-millated surface, twelve to twenty miles wide, of a wild and melancholy aspect, contrasting with the beauty of the great crests. At the limit of this region a new chain rises to a height of 1,000 to 1,600 feet. This long belt of sierra, crossed by narrow river gorges, seems to inclose the mass of the Spanish Pyre-nees in a circle of gigantic walls.

In old descriptions the general appearance of the range is compared to a fern-leaf or the dorsal ridge of a fish. But M. Schrader says there are many lines of elevation oblique to the main axis of the chain and generally form-ing an acute angle with it. Certain regions—for example, that of Mont Perdu—present this conformation with almost geometrical regu-larity, while others are less marked. One is struck by the regularity of the meshes of the network shown on the map by the valleys and the elevations, broken in places by gorges of streams that pass from one line of elevation to another, and descend at the first opportunity.

On the side of France, the crests are blunted, having been worn away by the humidity of the atmosphere; but on the side of Spain, the features are much more strongly marked. The hot and cold climate has evaporated the moisture, destroyed the lichens, and preserved the primitive and rugged aspect of the rocks.

North America.—The expedition sent out to survey the boundary-line between Alaska and the British possessions, as fixed by the treaty of 1825, has not yet finished its work. As the Yukon could not be followed to the coast be-fore the close of navigation, Dr. G. M. Daw-son, the leader, after examining the Pelly river, returned to Chilcat, and his companion, Mr. Ogilvie, went into winter-quarters at Fort Reliance, in order to explore next season the country bordering the Mackenzie to its mouth. Dr. Dawson finds that the tract of country be-tween Cassiar and Forty Mile Creek, a tribu-tary of the Yukon, is rich in gold.

It looks as if the hope of opening a regular summer passage through Hudson strait and bay, and thus establishing connection with Manitoba, must be definitely given up. In Lieut. A. R. Gordon's report of the voyage of the Alert in 1886, published this year, he says that the route is not available for ordinary carrying ships, even when they are made specially strong to resist the ice; for it is in such dangerous masses that no ship, not expressly made for polar voyages, can withstand it.

The census report of Manitoba for July, 1886, shows a reduction of its area from 123,-200 to 60,520 square miles since 1881, the re-mainder having been added to the province of Ontario and the district of Keewatin. On the remaining area the population has increased from 62,260 to 108,640 during the five years.

West Indies.—By a series of careful observa-tions Mr. Hall has determined the height of Blue Mountain Peak, Jamaica, to be 7,423 ft.

South America.—Very many explorers have been at work in South America during the year, some of them sent out by their govern-ments to gain data on which to base a settle-ment of boundaries, and others by local scien-tific associations. In Venezuela M. Chaffanjon explored the sources of the Orinoco, following it up from the mouth of the Meta, and giving special attention to the connection between the Orinoco and Amazon by the Cassiquiari. He named the mountains at its source "Ferdi-nand de Lesseps," although they have long borne the name Serra Parime. A commission is at work to settle the boundary between this country and Brazil. In Guiana the Bureau of Education has again sent out H. Condreau, who has been engaged in exploration affecting the boundary between French Guiana and Brazil. He will examine the Tumucuraque mountains, the water-shed between the coast rivers of Guiana and the Amazon branches.

One of the least known parts of Brazil was visited by an expedition, accompanied by Dr. Hassler. Starting from Ouyabá they crossed the water-shed between the La Plata and Ama-zon, and passed several streams entering the upper Xingu, and reached the Rio Mortes, the largest western tributary of the Araguay, and, following it to its mouth, took the main stream to the mouth of the Tocantins. The return was made across the table-land from Matto Grosso to the Rio Lourenço.

A journey on the Rio das Velhas, the largest tributary of the upper Rio San Francisco, was made by Dr. P. de Frontin and F. Paranagua. They passed 200 rapids, but believe that a com-paratively small amount of labor would be suf-ficient to remove them, and make the river a convenient route for the province Minas-Geraes, which needs only better facilities for communication to lead to a much greater de-velopment of its gold-mines, which have already been worked with good success for more than two centuries. It is also the great diamond-field of Brazil.

Dr. von den Steinen's expedition, though not able to carry out its original plan of ex-ploring the upper valley of the Xingu, employed the time in examining the remains of ancient Indian life in the province of Santa Catharina. A great collection of stone implements, human remains, and the like, together with photo-graphs and drawings, were sent to the Berlin Museum of Ethnography.

Richard Payer, whose three years' work on the Amazon was noted last year, is about to return to Europe with large ethnological collections.

The Government of the province of Cordova, in the Argentine Republic, has granted funds for establishing a network of meteorological stations over the province, and appointed Prof. Doering head of the service. The value of the undertaking is enhanced by the great diversity of position among the stations, on pampas, wooded plains, mountains, and salt lakes, and in their varied elevations ranging from 240 to 9,425 feet above the sea.

An international commission is at work surveying the boundary between Brazil and the Argentine Republic; and the question of boundary between the Argentine Republic and Paraguay threatens to come up if it should prove that the Araguay-Guazú is the main lower stream of the Pilcomayo, for the line is defined to be the Great Chaco to the Pilcomayo; and in that case the Argentine Republic would lay claim to the territory between the Pilcomayo and the Araguay-Guazú. According to older Spanish geographers, the latter stream is the largest arm of the lower Pilcomayo, but recent attempts to establish the fact have not been fully carried out.

By an ordinance of March 12, 1887, two new provinces were formed in Chili, Malleco and Cautin, thus bringing what remains of Araucania into administrative relations with the rest of the country. The chief town of Malleco is Angol; it is divided into three departments, Angol, Collipilli, and Traiguen, named by their principal towns. The chief town of Cautin is Temuco, and it is divided into two departments, Temuco and Imperial. These towns have 3,000 to 4,000 inhabitants and will soon be reached by railway.

According to the report of Captain Serrano, who was sent out by the Chilian Government, the Palena is a much larger stream than it has been supposed and represented on the maps, having a breadth in its lower reaches of 800 metres, and being navigable for a long distance. Many new species of plants and a few of insects were found by the expedition. It also confirmed the report that the high chain of the Andes is not here the water-shed between the Atlantic and Pacific; but that this is formed by a table-land about 500 metres in height lying east of the Andes. The streams upon it rise in small lakes and pass through narrow defiles in the Cordilleras, and thus reach the Pacific. The land on the eastern slope of the mountains west of this water-shed is well adapted for grazing. This makes necessary a new settlement of the boundary between Chili and the Argentine Republic, which, according to the treaty of 1881, is to follow the water-shed, and, in case of any difficulties arising from this line being indistinct or not understood, to be settled by a commission appointed by the governments of the two countries.

Lieut. C. Moyano reports to the Argentine authorities the results of a recent journey to the sources of the streams south of the Santa Cruz. He finds that the waters of the Pacific penetrate forty-five nautical miles eastward of the Cordilleras and form harbors in East Patagonia, and that the Argentine lake is connected with the lake lying south of it. This agrees with the observation of Moreno and Moyano in 1877, but was disputed by Rogers and Ibar after their journey in 1880. Lieut. Moyano finds reason to believe that all the Patagonian lakes are connected. As to the fitness of the country for colonization, he says: "The coast region has scanty but peculiar vegetation, which can be utilized for the feeding of cattle, sheep, horses, and goats. A few tracts in the lowlands and river-valleys are adapted for farming. The central region is less suitable for these purposes; for, besides the poverty of vegetation, it seems to be impossible to maintain cattle there during the winter, which is uncommonly severe, owing to the height of the table-lands and the distance from the sea. The mountain region, beginning at the first spurs of the Cordilleras, is marked by vast, dense forests of antarctic beeches, and is rich in plants adapted for grazing. I think it well suited for that purpose; the presence of thousands of wild horses indicates that the protection of the forests offsets the cold produced by the elevation. As to the prospects for mining, though I have found traces of coal and iron at many points, yet they were so far from the highways as not to be of any value at present. I have not found other minerals, but I believe the mountain region is rich in many that a specialist could discover." The lieutenant named three mountains, "Monte Andrade," 5,808 feet high, after the poet of that name; "Monte Guido," 4,200 feet, after the poet and scholar; and "Monte Guerrico," 4,495 feet, for Colonel Martin Guerrico, to whom many young marine officers are greatly indebted for instruction.

Lieut. del Castillo undertook an expedition to examine the harbors mentioned by Moyano. He says that with comparatively little expense the Gallegos can be connected with the harbors of the Pacific; that the pampas of the Gallegos are habitable in winter, and in every respect adapted to the raising of cattle; and that there are coal-beds of immense value in that region.

More favorable views of the fitness of Terra del Fuego, also, for cultivation are expressed by recent travelers—among them Ramon Lista and Julius Popper—and that it is particularly suitable for a grazing country. The discovery of gold on the shore of the Strait of Magellan has awakened a sudden interest in the island. M. Lista says that the mountain-chain in the Argentine part of the island should bear the name of its discoverer, Bartolomé Nodal. The Indians encountered were timid, but not unfriendly when reassured. Some of them were painted, or had their hands and arms colored white with clay, and all had their hair cut and greased with a reddish ointment. They wore cloaks of silver-fox fur. They would not allow themselves to be measured, but were induced to dance at the sound of the trumpet. They keep great numbers of dogs, which they use in hunting. The foxes are greatly prized on account of their fur. The island is infested with great numbers of rodents, and the woods and shores are visited by vast flocks of the wild goose, plover, duck, snipe, ibis, and parrot. Seals and penguins frequent the coast.

Polar Regions.—Dr. Alexander Bunge and Baron E. von Toll report a close examination of the New Siberian Islands begun in April, 1886. The island of Liakov was found to be rich in bone fossils. On the island of New Siberia, Baron von Toll made a special examination of the mountain known to travelers as the "wood-mountain," which was found to be a beautiful tertiary profile, with carbonized tree-trunks and a rich collection of leaf impressions and fruits like the tertiary flora of Greenland and Spitzbergen, as described by Oswald Heer. Besides the fossil remains of the mammoth, rhinoceros, and musk-ox, Dr. Bunge discovered in Liakov remains of two species of oxen, deer, horses, and some smaller animals.

Lieuts. Ryder and Block have closed for the present their survey of the western coast of Greenland for the Danish Government, having carried it as far as from 72° to 74½° north latitude. The winter of 1886–'87 was uncommonly severe, and occasioned destitution among the Greenlanders. Sickness among the dogs and scarcity of food for them prevented much use of sledges. In April an exploration was made of the ice-fiords and glaciers of Augpadlartok, one of the chief parts of the undertaking. Not until the end of June had the ice so far opened that a boat-voyage could be taken northward, and even then it was with difficulty that a point fifteen miles north of the last town of the Danish district could be reached. Seen from a mountain height, the sea presented an unbroken surface of ice, and the summer was so far advanced that a breaking-up of the ice could not be expected in time for anything more to be accomplished, as the travelers were due at Upernavik for the return to Europe. Besides making the coast survey and a close examination of the great ice-fiords and inland lakes, they have made astronomical and physical observations, and gathered anthropologic and natural science collections.

Expeditions were undertaken this summer by Mr. McArthur, a former official of the Hudson Bay Company, who proposed to go north by land to King William Land, winter there, and resume his explorations in the spring so far as the west coast of Grinnell Land, and by Col. Gilder, of New York, whose plan was to go northward by sledge, with Esquimau attendants from Wager River. He expects to reach Fury and Hecla Straits in the spring, and Lancaster Sound by autumn.

An expedition to the antarctic regions has been planned by the Australian colonies, and it is understood that the English Government will contribute £5,000 on condition that an equal amount is raised in Australia.

Atlantic Ocean.—Prince Albert of Monaco took with him this summer Prof. Pouchet and Prof. Guerne, the zoölogist, in his yacht "Hirondelle" for an excursion in the northern Atlantic. They spent three weeks in the Azores, where Prof. Guerne studied the fauna in the lakes of the extinct crater.

The falling-off of the whale-fisheries in antarctic waters threatens the very existence of the people of the solitary island Tristan d'Acunha, who are descendants of the garrison kept there while Napoleon was a prisoner in St. Helena, with a few shipwrecked men that have made their home there since. Their chief means of support—the supplying of whalers with fresh meat and potatoes—is falling off; and, moreover, the island is infested with rats from a wrecked ship, that make the raising of grain impossible, and greatly injure the potato-crop. Relief was sent to them in August, 1886, and it is now proposed to remove the entire population to St. Helena or Cape Colony, though it is to be feared that they will become homesick, like the people removed thirty years ago from Pitcairn to Norfolk Island, and take the first opportunity to return. In August, 1886, the island had 97 inhabitants, of whom only 28 were men.

Observations made by M. J. Thoulet in the Gulf Stream tend toward the conclusion of Mr. Findlay that, after the stream reaches the vicinity of Newfoundland, its volume and depth are no longer great enough to exert any considerable influence on climate, and therefore the causes of the mild climate of Western Europe must be sought elsewhere.

Miscellaneous.—Major-General von Tillo gives the lengths of the longest eight rivers of the world as follows:

	Miles.
1. Missouri Mississippi	4,194
2. Nile	4,030
3. Yang-tse-Kiang	3,158
4. Amazon	3,068
5. Yenesei-Selenga	2,950
6. Amur	2,920
7. Congo	2,833
8. Mackenzie	2,808

At the Brussels International Exhibition next year, a department will be devoted to geography and kindred sciences. It is desired that contributions be sent in of maps and atlases of all kinds, globes and spheres, statistical works and diagrams, general treatises, instruments, and articles for explorers.

Geography in Education.—Prof. Anton Stauber, of the Real Gymnasium of Augsburg, has taken the prize of 25,000 francs offered by the King of the Belgians for the best essay on the means of popularizing geography and improving its position in education of all degrees.

A committee met in England near the beginning of the year to consider the propriety of attempting to have geography placed among the subjects of study in the national universities. In consequence of their efforts it was decided to establish a readership of geography for five years at Oxford, and Mr. H. J. Mackinder, M. A., was appointed. Mr. Mackinder arranged eleven courses, comprising eighty-eight lectures, to be given under the extension scheme from October, 1897, to April, 1888, before about 2,700 students. It is expected that, in view of the growing interest taken in the subject, a similar course will be established at Cambridge.

By a new ordinance of the German Educational Department, the subject of geography has been raised to the first rank in the higher schools of Germany; that is, it may be taken as one of a teacher's two specialties in connection with either a scientific, linguistic, or historical subject. The subjects of examination for a teacher wishing to take the *facultas docendi* in geography are laid down. There are three grades, for lower, middle, and higher classes. For the lower the teacher must have an elementary but exact knowledge of mathematical, physical, and political geography; for the middle, not only this, but acquaintance with the history of exploration and important trade-routes. For the higher, the candidate must have in addition to the foregoing a knowledge of the important geological conditions of the earth's surface, and of the political geography of the present, the politico-historical geography of the chief civilized peoples, and the leading facts of ethnography; also, a readiness in the construction of maps.

It has been decided to found professorships of geography at the Russian Universities, and a chair was to be established at the St. Petersburg University in the autumn of 1887.

GEORGIA. State Government.—The following were the State officers during the year: Governor, John B. Gordon, Democrat; Secretary of State, Nathan B. Barnett; Treasurer, R. U. Hardeman; Comptroller-General, William A. Wright; Attorney-General, Clifford Anderson; Commissioner of Agriculture, J. T. Henderson; Railroad Commissioners, Alexander S. Irwin, O. Wallace, L. N. Trammell; Chief-Justice of Supreme Court, L. E. Bleckley; Associate-Justices, M. H. Blanford and Samuel Hall, succeeded by T. J. Simmons.

Legislative Session.—The session of this year was an adjournment of the November-December session of 1886. It continued from July 6 to October 20, a period of 107 days, which, with the 50 days consumed by the first session, makes the longest legislative record in the history of the State. Fully nine tenths of the legislation was local or special. The principal acts of the first meeting were those fixing the tax-rate and making the regular biennial appropriation. For 1887 the levy is as follows: For general purposes, 2·6 mills; for completing the State capitol, ·85 of a mill; for the sinking fund, ·32 of a mill; total, 3·77 mills. For 1888 the State capitol tax is ·2 of a mill less. A

poll-tax of one dollar per capita is devoted to educational purposes, while a long list of specific taxes upon the professions, traveling agents, peddlers, corporations, and other business enterprises, go into the general fund of the State. Among the specific appropriations are the following: For interest on the public debt, 1887, $509,943; for 1888, $507,575; for work upon the capitol building in 1887, $258,-734; in 1888, $200,000—the last two sums forming a part of $1,000,000 to be expended upon the structure; for the Academy of the Blind, $19,000; for the Deaf and Dumb Asylum, $15,000; for the Lunatic Asylum, $175,-000; for the State universities, $8,000 each—the last three amounts being payable annually.

Other acts passed at this session were as follow:

Authorizing the probate of foreign wills, if the testator was at the time competent to make a will under the laws of Georgia.

Defining the powers of commissioners of pilotage for the ports of the State. [This is a general pilotage law, giving the commissioners power to grant, suspend, or revoke licenses to pilots; to make rules governing those engaged in pilotage; to regulate the fees to be charged; to inflict penalties; and in other ways to supervise the business. All vessels to whom a licensed pilot offers his services are compelled to pay a pilotage fee whether the offer be accepted or not.]

Authorizing the city of Macon to issue $20,000 of bonds and to apply the proceeds of their sale in the construction of a public market-house.

Authorizing the city of Atlanta to issue new bonds at 4½ per cent. or at a lesser rate, to retire certain maturing 6-per-cent. bonds.

At the midsummer session the most notable action was that upon the Glenn bill, so called, prohibiting coeducation of the races. The provisions of this bill, which applied to every public and private educational institution in the State, made it a penal offense for any teacher of a school for colored children to admit white pupils, or for any teacher of white pupils to admit colored children, the penalty being a fine of $1,000, or imprisonment not over six months, or work in the chain-gang not over twelve months. The measure was reported favorably to the lower house by its committee on education, and passed that body almost unanimously, only two votes (those of the only colored members of the body) being recorded against it. The bill was apparently directed against a few white teachers at the Atlanta State University for colored students, who had instructed their own children among the regular pupils of the institution. The Senate yielded to a measure to numerous protests, and amended the bill by restricting its application to schools receiving aid from the State, and by making the only penalty a prohibition of the teacher from receiving any public funds of the State, and of the pupils from ever becoming teachers in the public schools. These amendments the House refused to accept, no compromise was reached, and the bill was dropped. A subject of fruitful discussion at this session was the State road, otherwise known as the Western and Atlantic

Railroad, a lease of which from the State will expire in 1889. Resolutions advising its sale at the end of the lease were rejected, as also those recommending a new lease upon lower terms. The only action taken declares that the State shall not be liable for any betterments made by the lessees, provides for a commission to appraise the road, to ascertain its present condition, to keep it constantly under inspection during the remainder of the lease, and to report promptly to the Governor any attempt of the lessees to depreciate its value, in which case the Governor is authorized to take immediate possession in behalf of the State, and to assume the management of its operations. A bill increasing the number of Supreme Court judges from three to five was among the most meritorious acts of the session. Another bill regulates the business of insurance in the State, making the Comptroller-General an Insurance Commissioner, and requiring companies to secure a license from him before soliciting business. Other acts of this session were as follow:

Providing for the levy and sale of personalty when the title is retained in the vendor.

Authorizing the sale of the Governor's mansion and penitentiary lots in Milledgeville.

Empowering grand jurors to levy a special tax for school purposes.

A bill to prevent the running of excursion trains, steamboats, and sailing-vessels on Sunday.

To rescind and revoke the license of any foreign corporation in this State which shall remove any case from the courts of this State to the United States courts, except to the Supreme Court of the United States.

Amending the practice in equity as to granting injunctions.

Regulating the catching of oysters.

Regulating the inspections and sale of naval stores.

Giving the Methodist Historical Society access to the State records at all times, and directing the Governor to send the secretary of the society copies of the journals of the General Assembly.

Providing payment for maimed Confederate soldiers, so as to conform to the amendments to the Constitution adopted at the last election. The bill includes those who were disabled, though their limbs were not amputated. It makes an annual payment of $30 for an arm or leg above the elbow or knee, and $20 for an arm or leg below elbow or knee.

Codifying and revising all the present common-school laws, and perfecting the machinery of the common-school system.

Authorizing the payment of the six months' interest on the Atlantic and Gulf railroad bonds.

Education.—In 1886 there were enrolled in the public schools 319,724 pupils, 196,852 being white, and 122,872 colored. The per cent. of white youth of school-age enrolled was 74·13, the per cent. of colored youth being 50·52. Of the total number of youths of school-age, white and colored, 62·84 per cent. are enrolled in these schools. The institutions of higher education supported by the State are reported to be doing good work. An extra appropriation, aggregating $17,000, was made by the Legislature of this year for repairs upon the State University buildings at Athens, and at the branch colleges at Dahlonega, Milledgeville, and Thomasville.

Convicts.—Attempts were made this year to improve the condition of the convict camps, and to abolish in part the camp system, but the Legislature took no action except to pass a bill rewarding good behavior by diminishing the length of sentence. It provides that for continuous good conduct on the part of the convict two months shall be deducted from his sentence the second year, and three months each succeeding year to ten, inclusive; after ten, four months each year. An investigation was had by the Governor during the summer into the conduct of the lessees at several of the camps, against whom charges of excessive punishment of convicts and of requiring excessive labor were preferred. The Governor found these charges sustained with respect to penitentiary companies numbered two and three, and imposed a fine of $2,500 upon each.

Railroads and Water-ways.—During the year, eight different lines of railroad were in process of construction, and 231 miles were completed. This is a considerable increase over previous years. The Legislature granted incorporation to more than forty new companies, some of which were prepared to begin construction before the end of the year. The city of Atlanta will reap a large share of the benefit from this new impulse in railroad building, three different lines being already nearly completed to that place, and a fourth and most important one, connecting it with Knoxville, Tenn., and thence with all points in the West, being sure of early construction. At the same time improvements have been made on many of the rivers of the State under the direction of the General Government. On the Ocmulgee a good navigable channel has been obtained between Hawkinsville and the junction of the Oconee. The Oconee is being dredged to secure a uniform depth of three feet at low water as far up as Milledgeville. The work is more than half completed. Nearly $100,000 has been expended on Flint river, resulting in a completed high-water channel from the mouth of the river up to Albany, a completed low-water channel of the projected depth from the mouth to Tea-Cup shoal, and a partially completed high-water channel over the river between Albany and Montezuma. The expenditure on the Chattahoochee has been $188,857, and it has resulted in securing a fair navigable channel between Chattahoochee and Eufaula at all seasons, and between Eufaula and Columbus at all times except during the prevalence of extreme low water. Improvements on Coosa river have cost $417,896, and have opened a good channel from Rome to Greensport. To develop the Coosa coal-fields in the vicinity of Broken Arrow, is the primary object of this work. The Tallapoosa, Oostenaula, and Coosawattee rivers have also been improved.

Prohibition.—As the local-option law permits an election upon this question in any county once in two years, on petition of a sufficient number of voters, contests similar to those of 1885 took place in the autumn of this year in nearly all the large counties. Strenuous efforts were made by the friends of license to recover the ground swept from them by the tide of prohibition sentiment at the previous election, but outside of Atlanta they were attended with only slight success. In that city, after a spirited contest, in which the young men bore a conspicuous part on each side, the Prohibitionists were defeated by 1,122 votes out of a total vote of 9,244. The majority against license in 1885 was 225 out of a total of about 7,000 votes. Of the enforcement and effect of prohibition in the city during the year a local paper says:

In consideration of the small majority with which prohibition was carried, and the large number of people who were opposed to seeing it prohibit, the law has been marvelously well observed. Prohibition has not injured the city financially. According to the assessors' books, property in the city has increased over $2,000,000. Taxes have not been increased. Two streets in the city, Decatur and Peters, were known as liquor streets. Property on them has advanced from 10 to 25 per cent. The loss of $40,000 revenue, consequent on closing the saloons, has tended in no degree to impede the city's progress in any direction. Large appropriations have been made to the waterworks, the public schools, the Piedmont fair, and other improvements. The business men have raised $400,000 to build the Atlanta and Hawkinsville Railroad. The number of city banks is to be increased to five. The coming of four new railroads has been settled during the year.

Farmers' Convention.—There was held at Atlanta in August an important and interesting interstate convention of farmers, at which all the Southern States were represented, and at which the causes and remedies of the existing agricultural depression in that region were discussed at length. Between 200 and 300 delegates were in attendance. The following are some of the resolutions adopted:

Whereas, The cotton States of the South need capital to develop their resources, and the farmers the facilities for borrowing money at a low rate of interest; therefore, be it

Resolved, That in the opinion of this convention it is expedient that the National banking act be so amended as, first, to repeal the tax now existing on the issue of State bank circulation; second, by repealing the clause of said act that prohibits national banks from accepting land as security for the loan of money.

Resolved, That our Senators and Representatives in Washington be requested to use all efforts in their power to advance the Department of Agriculture to the dignity of a Cabinet position.

Whereas, It appears, and really is a fact, that great depression exists throughout the whole cotton-growing region; and, whereas, we believe it to be the duty of this convention to ascertain the cause and to find a remedy; therefore, be it

Resolved, 1. That we believe the cause to be twofold, to-wit: first, undue taxation; second, the raising of too much cotton, thereby neglecting to produce home supplies.

Resolved, 2. That we believe the remedy for the first is the united efforts of our public servants in the Legislatures and in Congress, and this convention earnestly request both these bodies to grant us relief.

Among the many evils under which the agriculture of the South is laboring, and among the serious obstacles to its progress, is the crop-lien and chattel-mortgage system, now being a part of the business methods

of large portions of the States here represented; therefore, be it

Resolved, That this convention urges upon the farmers throughout the South the pressing importance of bringing to bear upon the Legislature of their respective States all legitimate influences which may tend to give speedy relief to our farmers and final abolition to this pernicious and ruinous system.

We desire that Congress shall pass a law returning through the States, to those entitled to the same, the money unjustly collected on what is known as the cotton tax.

Whereas, Certain corporations and individuals have from time to time combined and conspired to destroy or to depreciate the value of some of the agricultural products of the cotton States by such speculation or gambling as that usually termed " dealing in futures," with the prospective cotton-crop as a basis, and by the operations of the American Oil Trust Company in their well-nigh successful effort to crush out all competition either in the purchase of seed, or the sale of the products thereof; therefore

Resolved, That the influence of the entire agricultural population of all the States here convened be brought to bear upon the legislative powers of our respective States to secure the enactment of such laws as will properly define these crimes and furnish commensurate penalties therefor.

The cotton-crop of Georgia for 1887 was estimated at 890,900 bales, raised upon 2,950,000 acres. A severe cold and frost, which visited the State early in March, did great injury to growing fruits, wholly destroying the crop in some sections.

GERMANY, an empire in central Europe, founded on treaties concluded between the North German Confederation and the Grand Duchies of Baden and Hesse on Nov. 15, 1870, the kingdom of Bavaria on Nov. 23, 1870, and the kingdom of Würtemberg on Nov. 25, 1870. The ratifications of the treaties were exchanged on Jan. 29, 1871, at Berlin. For these treaties was substituted, by the decree of April 16, 1871, the Constitution of the German Empire, which went into force on May 4, 1871. The headship of the empire belongs to the Prussian crown. The hereditary dignity of German Emperor was accepted by King William I of Prussia at Versailles on Jan. 18, 1871, in a proclamation addressed to the German people. The confederation of states forming the empire is invested with sovereign imperial power, exercised by the crown of Prussia and by the Federal Council, composed of representatives of the confederated states. The imperial power, in the exercise of certain functions, requires the consent of the Reichstag or parliament, composed of representatives freely elected by the German people. This assembly exercises also in certain regards a right of control.

The Emperor William was born March 22, 1797. The heir-apparent is Prince Frederick William, born Oct. 18, 1831. The next in succession is his son, Frederick William (called Prince William), born Jan. 27, 1859, whose eldest son, named also Frederick William, was born May 6, 1882. (See illustration, page 821.)

The Chancellor of the Empire is Prince Otto von Bismarck, who is also President of the Council of Ministers of State, Minister of Foreign Affairs, and Minister of Commerce in the

Prussian Government. The ministers, who are under the direction of the Chancellor, are as follow : Secretary of State in the Office of Foreign Affairs, Count Herbert von Bismarck-Schönhausen ; Secretary of State in the Imperial Office of the Interior, Herr von Bötticher ; Chief of the Imperial Admiralty, Lieut.-Gen. von Caprivi ; Secretary of State in the Imperial Ministry of Justice, Dr. von Schelling ; Secretary of State in the Treasury of the Empire, Dr. Jacobi ; President of the Imperial Office for Railroads, Herr Maybach ; President of the Court of Audit, Herr von Stuenzner ; President of the Administration of the Invalid Funds, Dr. Michaelis ; Chief of the Imperial Post-Office, Dr. von Stephan.

Area and Population.—The area of the several states of the empire in square kilometres and their population as shown by the final results of the census of Dec. 1, 1885, are as follow :

STATES.	Area.	Males.	Females.	Total population.
Prussia.........	348,347·94	13,896,604	14,424,866	28,318,470
Bavaria	75,859·71	2,649,242	2,780,957	5,420,199
Saxony	14,992·94	1,542,408	1,589,598	3,182,006
Würtemberg	19,508·89	960,510	1,034,375	1,995,195
Baden	15,081·18	782,082	819,216	1,601,285
Hesse	7,681·88	473,740	482,871	956,611
Mecklenburg-Schwerin	13,303·77	284,241	290,911	575,152
Saxe-Weimar	3,594·86	151,996	161,950	313,946
Mecklenburg-Strelitz	2,929·50	48,105	50,963	98,871
Oldenburg	6,422·52	169,048	172,477	341,525
Brunswick	3,690·43	186,175	186,277	372,452
Saxe-Meiningen..	2,468·45	105,061	109,823	214,884
Saxe-Altenburg..	1,323·75	78,572	82,888	161,460
Saxe-Coburg-Gotha	1,956·50	95,581	103,299	198,329
Anhalt	2,347·35	122,676	122,490	245,163
Schwarzburg-Rudolstadt	940·43	40,738	43,108	83,836
Schwarzburg-Sondershausen.	862·11	38,906	37,700	73,626
Waldeck	1,121·05	26,901	29,674	56,575
Reuss (elder line).	316·89	27,307	28,597	55,904
Reuss (cadet line).	825·67	53,947	56,631	110,536
Schaumburg-Lippe	339·71	18,563	19,611	37,204
Lippe	1,215·20	60,776	62,436	123,212
Lübeck	297·70	32,692	34,966	67,658
Bremen	255·56	79,469	86,150	165,623
Hamburg	409·73	252,853	265,767	518,620
Alsace-Lorraine..	14,509·42	771,369	793,086	1,564,355
German Empire	540,596·68	22,933,664	23,922,040	46,855,704

The natural movement of population in the principal states was in 1885 as follows :

STATES.	Marriages.	Births.	Deaths.	Increment.
Prussia	230,707	1,108,760	761,184	347,626
Bavaria	86,496	206,644	160,164	46,480
Saxony	29,286	137,935	95,851	42,084
Würtemberg	13,264	74,582	55,798	18,784
Baden	10,646	54,167	40,029	14,138
Alsace-Lorraine	10,400	50,281	41,095	9,186
Hesse	6,960	31,290	22,898	8,322
Other states...........	30,860	185,148	91,483	48,665
German Empire...	368,619	1,798,687	1,268,460	530,185

The population of the principal cities on Dec. 1, 1885, was as follows : Berlin, 1,315,-287 ; Hamburg, 305,690 ; Breslau, 299,640 ; Munich, 261,981 ; Dresden, 246,086 ; Leipsic, 170,340 ; Cologne, 161,401 ; Frankfort-on-the-

Main, 154,513 ; Königsberg, 151,151 ; **Magdeburg,** including Neustadt, 148,471 ; Hanover, 139,731 ; Stuttgart, 125,901 ; Bremen, 118,-895 ; Dusseldorf, 115,190 ; Nuremberg, 114,-891 ; Dantzic, 114,805 ; Strasburg, 111,987 ; Chemnitz, 110,817 ; Elberfeld, 106,499 ; Altona, 104,717 ; Barmen, 103,068.

The number of foreigners naturalized in 1885 was 4,893 ; the number of Germans who renounced their rights of nationality, 18,877, of whom 18,965 were emigrants to the United States. The total emigration in 1886 was 76,-687, as compared with 103,642 in 1885 and 143,586 in 1884. The emigration to the United States in 1886 was 72,403, as compared with 98,628 in 1885, 139,339 in 1884, 159,894 in 1883, 189,373 in 1882, 206,189 in 1881, 103,-115 in 1880, 30,808 in 1879, and 20,373 in 1878. The total emigration from Germany since 1820 is reckoned at 4,700,000 persons, of whom 3,600,000 settled in the United States.

Commerce.—The Custom-House returns for 1885 and 1886 give the values of the imports and exports of the German Zollverein, in millions of marks and tenths of millions, as follow :

ARTICLES.	IMPORTATION.		EXPORTATION.	
	1885.	1886.	1885.	1886.
Cereals	329·3	206·6	75·0	59·7
Fermented beverages .	47·9	44·4	76·7	69·0
Colonial produce	158·5	172·4	210·2	194·3
Tobacco	66·8	64·7	9·3	5·6
Vegetables, etc	106·0	128·9	21·5	31·6
Animals and meat	278·2	314·5	171·6	145·6
Total articles of consumption	974·7	931·5	564·8	506·5
Fuel...................	42·6	46·7	90·5	94·4
Minerals	106·6	98·7	60·1	38·5
Raw metals	88·3	86·0	54·4	53·2
Hides and leather	192·9	194·7	120·5	127·7
Textile materials	592·9	657·1	145·1	119·1
Timber	185·2	105·7	73·2	54·1
Total raw materials ..	1,098·5	1,188·9	548·8	489·6
Pottery and glass.....	8·1	18·2	56·0	72·5
Partly manufactured metals	7·9	6·9	89·1	74·0
Metal manufactures ...	15·3	15·8	123·9	132·1
Machinery	44·0	89·6	132·5	117·3
Leather goods and furs.	17·0	13·6	127·6	137·9
Yarns	179·7	192·1	76·1	168·0
Textile fabrics and garments	109·9	89·6	627·4	762·3
India-rubber goods ...	5·8	5·1	21·7	21·8
Paper manufactures....	6·3	6·5	72·3	81·3
Wood and straw manufactures	14·4	12·8	87·2	48·4
Jewelry and works of art	36·2	35·0	92·3	99·7
Books	12·9	13·2	53·5	54·7
Total manufactures...	457·0	443·4	1,499·6	1,736·9
Waste materials and fertilizers	27·7	29·4	6·7	12·2
Drugs, dyes, and chemicals	177·4	157·1	186·2	165·7
Gums, fats, and oils.....	209·1	186·1	50·4	74·2
Miscellaneous	......	......	9·5	0·5
Total miscellaneous..	414·2	372·6	252·6	252·6
Total merchandise.....	2,944·4	2,893·4	2,860·3	2,985·6
Coin and bullion......	45·5	56·6	55·0	65·8
Total	2,989·9	2,945·0	2,915·3	3,051·4

Navigation.—The movement of shipping in German ports for the year 1885 was as follows:

FLAG.	Total vessels.	Registered tons.	With cargoes.	Registered tons.	Steamers.	Registered tons.
Entered :						
German.	45,506	5,169,701	37,046	4,650,915	13,750	3,641,570
Foreign..	15,213	5,020,882	12,707	4,598,589	7,877	4,144,545
Total..	60,719	10,190,083	49,758	9,244,504	21,657	7,776,115
Cleared :						
German.	45,421	5,174,522	35,316	4,206,478	13,758	3,645,144
Foreign..	15,218	5,035,089	10,238	3,304,662	7,881	4,131,395
Total..	60,639	10,909,611	45,544	7,513,140	21,639	7,776,569

The merchant marine on Jan. 1, 1886, comprised 4,135 vessels, as compared with 4,257 in 1885 and 4,315 in 1884. The aggregate tonnage was 1,282,449, as compared with 1,294,288 in 1885 and 1,269,477 in 1884. The crews numbered 38,931 men. The steam-vessels were 664 in number, as compared with 650 in 1885 and 608 in 1884. Their tonnage was 420,605, having increased from 413,948 in 1885 and 374,699 in 1884. Of the total fleet, 2,525 vessels belonged to North Sea ports, with an aggregate burden of 861 083 tons; and of the steamers, 337, of 297,808 tons. The vessels of the Baltic ports numbered 1,610, of 421,366 tons, of which 327, of 122,797 tons, were steamers.

Railroads. — The state lines of railroad in operation in April, 1887, had a total length of 38,782 kilometres. The lines belonging to companies had a length of 4,644 kilometres, besides 290 kilometres managed by the Government. The railroads of Germany, Austria, the Netherlands, Luxemburg, Russian Poland, the joint-stock railroads of Roumania, and some of those of Belgium, are under the control of the Union of German Railroads, which has its office in Berlin, and regulates the traffic and arrangements on the 38,146 kilometres of German lines, 23,201 kilometres of Austrian lines, 2,676 kilometres in Holland, and 2,499 kilometres in other countries, making in all 66,522 kilometres.

Posts and Telegraphs.—The telegraph-lines of the empire had in 1886 a total length of 86,-

199 kilometres, inclusive of the 8,551 kilometres of Bavarian and 2,958 kilometres of Würtemberg lines. The total length of wires was 306,038 kilometres. There were 20,510,294 dispatches sent in 1886, of which 18,598,456 were paid, and 974,890 official internal messages, and 2,433,676 departing, 2,783,237 incoming, and 725 transit international messages.

The postal traffic of the Imperial, Bavarian, and Würtemberg post-offices in 1886 was as follows: Letters, 858,587,550; postal-cards, 261,056,660; letters under bands, 245,618,370; circulars, 20,187,170; newspapers, 539,615,480; money-orders, 64,817,455; packages, 98,654,840, of the aggregate weight of 404,255,460 kilogrammes.

PRINCE WILLIAM AND HIS SON.

Bavaria and Würtemberg retain the administration of their telegraphs and postal service. The receipts of the Imperial, Bavarian, and Würtemberg postal and telegraph administrations in the fiscal year 1886–'87 were 202,346,932 marks, and the expenses 175,076,000.

Finances.—The budget of the empire, as approved on March 30, 1887, places the revenue for 1887–'88 at the following amounts in German marks :

SOURCES OF REVENUE.	Receipts.
Customs	945,665,000
Tobacco-tax	8,191,000
Beet-sugar tax	80,420,000
Salt-tax	38,555,000
Spirit-tax	38,188,000
Beer-tax	17,846,000
Customs and excise duties of states not in the Zollverein	8,208,000
Playing-cards	1,040,000
Bill-stamps	6,410,000
Other stamps	19,684,000
Registration	562,000
Posts and telegraphs	99,447,858
Imperial printing-office	1,078,180
Net railroad receipts	14,696,600
Imperial bank	2,106,500
Various administrations	8,429,228
Invalid funds	94,846,098
Construction funds	1,900,000
Extraordinary receipts	72,587,191
Matricular quotas	167,044,406
Total receipts	**745,207,436**

The total expenditure decided on for the year ending March 31, 1888, was 745,207,436 marks. An annex to the law fixed the expenditure on the Imperial Bank at 188,000 marks, and on June 1, 1887, a supplementary credit of 176,085,950 marks was granted, of which 19,408,019 marks were for permanent and 156,677,931 for non-recurring expenditures, the latter to be covered by a loan. Of this 80,225,077 marks is devoted to the army administration, 29,500,000 marks to strengthening fortresses, and 36,314,000 marks to railroads for military purposes.

The debt of the empire, of the nominal amount of 450,000,000 marks, was raised on 4-per-cent. bonds at various times. Issues of 3½-per-cent. bonds have been authorized, and 5,073,500 marks had been emitted on March 31, 1887, while 316,264,473 marks were still to be realized. An imperial decree was issued on June 24, 1887, for the issue of a loan of 238,004,970 marks, the proceeds of which were to be employed in covering the expenses connected with the incorporation of Hamburg and Bremen in the Custom's Union, the construction of the North Sea Canal, the army and navy administration, and the completion of the railroad network in the interests of the national defense. When 100,000,000 marks of these bonds were put on the market on July 5, 1887, they were subscribed for more than seven times over. The currency notes in circulation on April 1, 1887, amounted to 133,868,475 marks.

The invalid fund on March 1, 1887, amounted to 492,719,529 marks, besides 3,671,397 Frankfort florins in securities, and 7,491,884 marks in silver. The fortress construction fund was 20,479,691 marks; the Reichstag-building fund, 19,743,721 marks; the war fund, 120,000,000.

The budget for the Kingdom of Prussia, as adopted for the year ending March 31, 1888, makes the total gross receipts 1,316,717,307 marks, and the net revenue 684,548,761 marks. The ordinary expenditures, including 632,173,-546 marks for financial administration, are calculated at 1,283,120,623 marks, and the total disbursements, including extraordinary and temporary expenditures, are made to balance the estimated revenue. The Saxon budget for 1887 makes the ordinary expenditures 74,-865,542 marks, and the extraordinary 27,603,-690, which sums balance the estimated revenues. The debt of Saxony in January, 1887, was 644,061,400 marks. The budget of Bavaria for each year of the biennial period of 1886-'87 estimates the receipts at 241,491,646 marks, and the expenditures at the same figure. The public debt of Bavaria was 1,354,-681,668 marks on April 1, 1887. The budget of Würtemberg for the year ending March 31, 1887, makes the receipts 56,238,427 marks, and the expenditures the same. The debt on April 1, 1887, was 424,051,519 marks, of which all but 44,717,897 marks was contracted for the construction of railroads. The budget of Alsace-Lorraine for 1887-'88 makes the ordinary gross receipts 40,131,931 marks, and the total expenditures 39,090,195 marks, including 1,662,083 marks for extraordinary purposes. There is, besides, an extraordinary budget of 984,301 marks of receipts, and 2,026,000 marks of expenditure.

The Army.—The peace effective of the German army, under the new army law of 1887, is 19,262 officers, and 468,409 rank and file, with 1,500 guns and 84,077 horses. The general staff numbers 1,972 officers, with 65 soldiers employed; there are 518 battalions of infantry of the line, numbering 10,861 officers and 312,495 men; 21 battalions of Jägers, 446 officers and 11,816 men; Landwehr cadres for 277 battalions, 316 officers and 4,862 men; total infantry, 811 battalions, 11,123 officers, and 329,173 men. There are 465 squadrons of cavalry, numbering 2,358 officers and 64,-590 men, with 62,469 horses. The field artillery, consisting of 365 batteries, with 1,500 guns, counts 1,989 officers and 38,098 men, with 18,232 horses. The fortress artillery is divided into 31 battalions, and numbers 730 officers and 17,226 men. Of pioneers there are 24 battalions, having 558 officers and 12,-285 men; train, 18 battalions, numbering 256 officers and 6,111 men, with 8,360 horses; special corps, 326 officers and 861 men. The rank and file of the army is divided into 55,-447 non-commissioned officers, 19,270 musicians, 378,290 soldiers, 3,704 hospital-attendants, 10,650 workmen, and 848 assistant-paymasters. Not included in these figures are 1,777 surgeons, 641 veterinarians, 840 paymasters, 803 armorers, and 93 saddlers. The horses, as enumerated, do not include the officers' mounts and the work-horses. The Bavarian, Royal Saxon, and Würtemberg armies are independently organized and under the command of the rulers of those states, while all other parts of the empire are under the Prussian military jurisdiction. The Prussian army consisted of 14,937 officers and 362,468 men, with 66,010 horses; the Bavarian army, 2,257 officers and 54,185 men, with 9,004 horses; the Royal Saxon army, 1,261 officers and 31,810 men, with 5,369 horses; the army of the King of Würtemberg, 807 officers and 19,946 men, with 8,694 horses.

The increase in the peace effective of the German army under the septennate law of 1887 is 41,135 men. Of these, 33,298 go to increase the infantry. Of the 81 new battalions are created four new Prussian regiments and one Saxon, while fourth battalions are added to 15 Prussian regiments, and a new battalion of Saxon Jägers is formed. The effective of each Prussian battalion is raised from 569, including 18 officers, to 592. Of the 335,-328 troops in active service, 42,967 are stationed in Alsace-Lorraine. The system of reserve which has been adopted enables Germany to fill the cadres of 166 fourth battalions on the day following mobilization, and thus have 700 battalions available for service. The artillery batteries are increased from 340 to 364, while arrangements are introduced for the formation of 91 more in case of mobilization.

The German army is divided into 18 army corps, viz., 11 Prussian, besides the Guard, which forms a distinct corps; the Saxon, Baden, and Würtemberg corps, which are numbered 12, 13, and 14; the new Alsace-Lorraine corps, which is called the 15th; and 2 Bavarian corps, which have no numbers. A Hessian division is attached to the 11th corps. During the past five years the peace effective of the German army has been increased 65 battalions and 385 guns.

The fortifications on the French frontier, with the railroads, have been designed with reference to a rapid offensive movement. Strong works and strategic railroads have also been built on the Russian frontier, but more of a defensive nature and without the same facilities for rapid concentration. The German troops on the Russian frontier have been increased 21 battalions of infantry, 27 batteries of artillery, and 15 squadrons of cavalry. Since 1878 Germany has built in the eastern provinces 4,850 kilometres of railroads. There are 11 German railroads, by means of which troops can be forwarded to the Russian frontier, and ten junction stations where they can be thrown out of trains and concentrated. Germany has created first-class fortresses at Thorn, Posen, Dantzic, and Königsberg, and is building a similar fortress at Grandenz.

In the autumn session of the Reichstag, bills were introduced for the reorganization of the Landsturm, and the modification of the conditions of service in the Landwehr. Both the Landwehr and the Landsturm will henceforth be divided into two classes. In the first class of the Landwehr the term of service is, as now, five years; while in the second class, in which there is no drill and no periodical roll-call, with liberty to emigrate, the liability to service continues until the men have completed their thirty-ninth year. The first class of the Landsturm consists of persons who have, for some reason, not served in the army, but who remain liable to serve until they have completed their thirty-ninth year. The second class of the Landsturm will only be called out in the last line of defense, and will be composed of men who have already served, or are still liable to service, and are between the ages of thirty-nine and forty-five.

The Navy.—The war fleet on April 1, 1887, consisted of 18 armorclad ships, carrying 148 guns; 14 smaller iron-clads and protected vessels, with 17 guns; 9 frigate cruisers, with 122 guns, 8 corvettes, with 94, and 5 other cruisers with 22; 5 gunboats, with 16 guns; 5 avisos, with 12 guns; 11 school-ships, with 84 guns; and 81 vessels for various purposes, having 9 guns. The aggregate tonnage is 182,-103; the number of men in the crews, 16,581. The military marines, according to the budget of 1887-'88, number 15,256. The "Schwalbe," a new cruiser of 1,300 tons, was launched at Wilhelmshaven in 1887. She is intended for service on the coasts of the African colonies, and has a speed of 18½ knots. The armament consists of 4 Krupp guns of 10½ centimetres' caliber, firing fore and aft, and 4 revolving cannon of the same description.

Dissolution of the Reichstag.—On January 11 the Chancellor made his final appeal to the Reichstag in behalf of an increase of the army by 41,000 men, and a new septennial army budget. "The probability of a French attack on us," he said, "which does not exist to-day, will arise upon the accession to power of another Government than the present, if France has any reason to believe that she can overcome us. Then, I believe, war will be quite certain." If the French, he added, thought that their army was more numerous than that of Germany, their artillery more efficient, or their armament more effective, the resolution to go to war might be taken, for as soon as they believed themselves able to win, they would begin war. That was his firm and irreversible conviction, which he based upon long experience in politics. He had no fear of Germany being worsted, but they must allow for the possibility. Those who pretended that the army needed no strengthening were civilians; but generals and officers who had been in contact with French sabers were of a very different opinion. It would not do to underestimate the strength of France. "France," said Prince Bismarck, "is a great and powerful country, as powerful as we. France has a warlike people, and a brave people, and at all times has possessed skillful generals. It is an accident that the French have succumbed to us. You underestimate the French in a most mistaken way, and it would be vanity to say that France might at once be regarded as beaten if she were opposed to us." Moltke expressed his conviction that if the demands of the Government were refused war would be certain.

Dr. von Stauffenberg, a deputy of the Opposition, moved to fix the peace establishment of the army at 468,409 men, the figure demanded by the Government, but to vote the supplies for three years, beginning April 1, 1887, instead of for seven years. This amendment was carried by 183 votes against 154, the Social Democrats abstaining from voting. The Chancellor, as soon as the vote was announced, read a decree from the Emperor dissolving the Reichstag.

The General Elections.—The new elections were fixed for February 21, the electoral campaign. The Chancellor had made a distinct threat to carry out his military plans, whether the Parliament agreed to them or not. Not only the chief of the general staff, but the Emperor intervened in the question, and appealed to the loyalty and patriotism of the German people to return a willing majority. Official, military, and journalistic agencies were made the most of by the Government in the electoral campaign. Not content with all his ordinary electoral weapons, Prince Bismarck procured the intervention of the Pope. A dispatch was sent on January 21 by Cardinal Jacobini, the Papal Secretary of State, to the Nuncio at Munich, in response to a question addressed to the latter by Baron von Frankenstein, one of the leaders of the Clericals in the Reichstag, who asked whether the Curia considered the Center party as superfluous. Cardinal Jacobini, in the Pope's name, acknowledged the services of the Center party, and expressed the desire that it would still continue to work for the complete removal of exceptional ecclesiastical legislation, the amelioration of the condition of German Catholics, and the improvement of the Pope's position. While admitting that the members of the party have liberty of action in non-ecclesiastical matters, the Pope had the right to express his opinion on the military septennate question, because it involved considerations of moral and religious import. He expected from the conciliatory attitude of the Center on this question a beneficial effect in regard to the final revision of the May laws, and also hoped, through the intermediary of the Center, to work for the maintenance of peace. In conclusion, the Pope expressed his desire to meet the views of the Emperor and Prince Bismarck in order to render the powerful German Empire disposed to a future improvement of the position of the Papacy. There was much speculation throughout Europe on the publication of this note as to whether Prince Bismarck had actually agreed to intervene for the restoration of the temporal power of the Pope.

The National Liberals, who had declared for the septennate, and have returned to the lead of Prince Bismarck, and become identified with the policy previously supported by the two Conservative parties, formed an electoral agreement with the latter to give a united vote in each district for a candidate of the party most numerously represented. This treaty, or cartel, gave the name of "Cartel Brothers" to the members of the three parties. Herr von Bennigsen, who through dissatisfaction with the Chancellor's domestic policy had retired from public life two years before, resumed the leadership of the National Liberals, who, with the help of the cartel, recovered a great part of their former strength, and became the most numerous party in the new Reichstag. Their members were increased from 51 to 104. Their popular vote was 1,658,158, showing an increase of 661,125. The Old Conservatives, who had 77 members in the last Parliament, gained only three seats, though their popular strength increased to 1,194,504, a gain of 383,-441 ballots. The Imperialists polled 693,195 votes, an increase of 305,508, giving them 39 deputies, instead of 28 in the last Parliament. The Cartel Brothers gained votes at the expense of the Deutsche Freisinnigen, or Liberalist party, which was founded from the old Progressive party and seceders from the National Liberals, and follows the lead of Eugen Richter, deputy from Hagen. The popular vote for this fraction fell to 549,302 ballots, and the representation in the Reichstag was reduced from 67 to 31, and would have been still smaller if the Socialists had not come to the aid of the Liberalists in the supplementary elections. The Socialist deputies were again reduced to 11, although the party polled 774,128 votes, showing an increase of 224,192 since 1884. In Alsace-Lorraine the stadtholder, Prince Hohenlohe, had issued a vigorous manifesto, appealing to the people to accept definitely the treaty of 1871. In addition to the covert menaces of the proclamation, military and administrative pressure was exerted to influence the elections, but the result was that 247,654 votes were cast for Protesting candidates, being 82,088 more than in the last elections, again returning a solid phalanx of 15 Alsace-Lorrainers to the Chamber. The Volkspartei, known as the Popularist or Democratic party, was entirely extinguished, losing all of its 8 seats. The Clericals, or Center party, otherwise called the Ultramontanes, or Blacks, came back in undiminished strength, having 99 members in the new Reichstag as in the old, and polling 1,627,095 votes, a gain of 248,701; yet before the electors, in deference to the Pope's appeal, a part of them had changed their attitude toward the septennate bill, and were pledged for its support, while the bulk of the party, following Windhorst and Frankenstein, strongly resented the dictation of the Pope. The Poles in the new Parliament number 13, having lost 3 seats, though the popular vote showed a slight increase. The Independents, or Savages, with the Guelphs and Danes, were reduced in the Reichstag from 12 to 5, though they also received as many ballots as in 1884.

The Social Democratic vote in 1871 was 123,975; in 1874 it had increased to 351,592; and in 1877 to 493,288. In 1878, after the attempts of Hödel and Nobiling, and immediately before the passing of the anti-Socialist law, it was 437,158. In 1881, after the Socialist law had been three years in operation, it fell away to 311,961. In 1884 it increased to about 550,000, and in 1887 showed a further increase of 224,192. In Berlin the number of Socialist voters, which was only 67 in 1867, was about 68,000 in 1884, and in 1887 had grown to 93,000.

The New Reichstag.—Parliament was opened on March 3. The army bill was announced at the head of the Government programme, and in connection with it the budget would have to be promptly voted and new sources of revenue considered. The minor measures heralded in the speech from the throne were the extension of accident insurance to mariners and house-builders, the amplification of the functions of artisans' guilds, the prevention of the use of noxious colors in articles of food and drink, and the establishment of a seminary at Berlin for the teaching of Oriental languages.

The septennate bill was passed on the second reading, March 9, by 247 votes to 20, there being 83 abstentions, mainly on the part of Clericals. A motion to restrict the period to three years was negatived by 222 votes against 23. The army budget, including a provision for a school for non-commissioned officers at Neu-Breisach, which was several times rejected in the former Reichstag, was agreed to on March 21 by a large majority. A bill to impose a tax on brandy was introduced in May. A higher duty on imported and domestic sugar was also demanded. On May 20 the Reichstag passed the supplementary estimates, authorizing within the next few years the expenditure of 860,000,000 marks for altering and perfecting the defensive resources of the empire, providing new equipments for the troops, building barracks and fortresses, laying double tracks on the railroad lines of Alsace-Lorraine, and building new strategic lines, including a railroad to South Germany that will not pass through Switzerland. On May 28 the international treaties for the protection of works of literature and art and for the protection of submarine cables were approved. The seamen's insurance bill was agreed to. A bill relating to the administration of justice in territories under German protection settles the law regarding real estate in the new colonial possessions. The spirit tax, with some amendments, was passed finally on June 17; also a bill prohibiting the use of injurious colors in articles of nourishment, a bill relating to artificial butter, and a workingmen's protection bill.

Amendment of the May Laws.—In April the P.ussian Diet and Herrenhaus repealed important sections of the restrictive ecclesiastical laws. The new amendments to the May laws were first introduced on the basis of an agreement between the Prussian Government and Dr. Kopp, Bishop of Fulda, acting under direct instructions from Rome, and, after undergoing a few modifications, the bill was finally passed in such a shape as caused Monsignor Galimberti, who was in Berlin at the time as

Special Envoy of Leo XIII on the occasion of the Emperor's birthday, to telegraph the result to the Vatican as a cause of gratulation. The fate of the bill was more doubtful in the Upper Chamber. The Chancellor made an important speech in its defense, which he began by pointing out that, with regard to the readmission of religious orders, the chief point to be ascertained was whether Prussian Catholic citizens believed themselves to be in need of such orders. It was his opinion that this need should be satisfied in harmony with the legislation of the country. The state, proceeded the Chancellor, naturally had an interest in the good training of the priests, but such training could just as well be acquired at seminaries as at the universities. The bitterest enemies of the Government came from universities, not from seminaries. Referring next to the law which required the higher ecclesiastics to notify to the state appointments of subordinates, Prince Bismarck observed that he did not attach any special importance to this provision, more particularly in view of the experience gained that clergymen, who had for years exercised their functions under the very eyes of the Government, had changed their disposition as soon as they became bishops. It was unjust to charge the Government with making too large concessions to the Catholics. It had not given up any of its sovereign rights. He had never dreamed of engaging in permanent strife with the Curia. As long ago as 1875 he had called Cardinal Antonelli's attention to the danger which would arise from the formation of a Catholic political party in Prussia. From the moment when the Curia manifested a pacific disposition he had put forward a programme of peace, for the realization of which he had now worked ten years. By the proposals before the House he hoped to obtain a lasting peace. But, should that expectation not be fulfilled, the measures now proposed could at any moment be easily rescinded. It was imperative that the Center, which constantly allied itself with all elements hostile to the state and the empire, should be deprived of any pretext for opposition which the existing state of the law might afford. It was, he added, out of regard for the unity of the nation and the dangers with which that unity was threatened, that he had initiated the present Ecclesiastical Bill, and he did this with a full recognition of his responsibility. Whether the bill would lead to the establishment of religious peace could not yet be known, as the leaders of the Center party had placed themselves in opposition to the Pope. The principles of the Progressist party itself were not less dangerous than the subversive tendencies of the lower clergy, in whose removal the Pope and the Emperor had an equal interest. If the Sovereign Pontiff and the Emperor were at one, the opposition of Herr Windthorst and the Center ceased to have further significance. Prince Bismarck had threatened that if the bill were rejected he would resign the post of Minister-President of the Prussian Cabinet.

Frontier Troubles.—Before the elections, as a part of the policy of alarm adopted by Prince Bismarck in order to secure augmented contingents and septennial supplies for the army, a system of coercion and intimidation was introduced into Alsace-Lorraine. Many persons were arrested, and newspapers were suppressed. When the elections gave an increased majority to the Protesters, repressive measures were applied with greater severity. Social and musical organizations were suppressed, and burgomasters were deposed. The Government announced the intention of taking away all the autonomous institutions that were bestowed on the provinces in 1879. On March 31, M. Antoine, the most ardent of the protesting delegates to the Reichstag, who had been again returned from Metz with a sweeping majority, was expelled from the territory of Alsace-Lorraine, and conducted across the French boundary. Troubles on the frontier, which before were frequent, chiefly on account of the proneness of German soldiers to desert and of young Alsace-Lorrainers to escape from military conscription, were now of constant occurrence. The German authorities were accused in several instances of violating French territory, but the French Government was not disposed to make a diplomatic question of the occasional misbehavior of subordinate officials. The war feeling that was fostered in Germany met with a response from the Patriotic League, but the agitation was discouraged by the French Government, which prosecuted a newspaper for publishing anti-German articles. The German police suspected the existence of secret societies in Alsace-Lorraine which not only were in correspondence with Paul Déroulède's Patriotic League, but which furnished the French War Office with information regarding the fortifications and disposition of troops on the frontier. Several arrests were made, and a warrant was issued for the apprehension, if he appeared on German soil, of M. Schnaebele, the French police commissary of the railroad terminus at Pagny-Sur-Moselle, who was supposed to be an intermediary of the treasonable correspondence. As soon as the German detectives were in receipt of this order, they studied means to carry it out. Herr Gautsch, the police commissary at Ars, on the German side, wrote to Schnaebele, appointing a meeting at the boundary line in relation to the replacing of frontier posts. M. Schnaebele went to the rendezvous, but did not see his German colleague, and, having been warned, did not venture to cross the line. On receiving a second letter, he went again on April 20, and, seeing nobody, stepped a few yards on the other side. A detective disguised as a laborer came out of a ditch and engaged in conversation, and then immediately laid hold of the Frenchman, another disguised policeman coming to his aid from a vineyard. Schnaebele shook off his captors, and ran to the French side, stopping as soon as he had passed the boundary pillar, and pointing to it to indicate to his pursuers that he was safe; but they seized him, dragged him back, bound him, and took him to Metz. The high court at Leipsic, which had issued the order of his arrest, had an indictment against him for treason, on the ground that he was engaged in a movement in Alsace-Lorraine for the subversion of German authority. German, and also French, law sanctions the prosecution of foreigners for high treason, even though the acts have been committed abroad. The French and German Governments both ordered an inquiry into the circumstances of Schnaebele's arrest. Two vine-dressers, who were at work near the spot, swore that he was seized when six or seven yards within the French boundary. German railroad officials, who seem to have witnessed only the latter part of the struggle, made depositions that the whole occurrence took place on German territory. The French authorities found the decoy letters in Schnaebele's desk.

Correspondence was carried on between the German and French Governments, each presenting the testimony that it had collected regarding the circumstances of the arrest, but little was divulged to the public, and intense excitement prevailed in France, where the secrecy and delay were interpreted either as a sign of war or a trick of speculating politicians to make money out of a financial panic. In view of the contradictory evidence, the German Government directed a fresh inquiry, which was completed on April 27. On the following day Prince Bismarck addressed a note to the French ambassador, M. Herbette, affirming that the arrest in all its stages had taken place on German soil, and that it had been ordered on the proved guilt of espionage and treasonable correspondence on the part of Schnaebele, yet the Emperor would command liberation, being "guided in so doing by the doctrine of international law that the crossing of a frontier, when done on the strength of an official agreement between the functionaries of neighboring states, must always be looked upon as carrying with it the tacit assurance of a safe-conduct."

Treason Trials at Leipsic.—The evidence on which the arrest of Schnaebele was made was that of a commercial agent of Strasburg, named Tobias Klein, and of letters of Schnaebele found in the latter's possession. Klein and Martin Grebert, a manufacturer of Schiltigheim, were arrested in February on suspicion of having furnished Col. Vincent, the head of the French bureau of military intelligence, with plans of the fortifications of Strasburg and Metz, and other information. Klein confessed that he had acted as a spy since 1880, receiving 200 marks per month for his services. The letters that he had from Schnaebele were written in disguised terms, having the appearance of correspondence on family subjects. Grebert maintained similar relations with the French commissary of police at Avricourt. Baron Schleinitz, an ex-captain in the German army, was tried by court-martial for treasonable practices, and his sentence of three years' hard labor was confirmed in April. Sarauw, a Danish captain, who had been sentenced to twelve years' imprisonment for high treason, furnished the German with details of the French spy system, and was rewarded for his disclosures by afterward receiving his liberty. At the end of May a chancery clerk at Strasburg, named Cabannes, and another functionary of the name of Brückner, were arrested as spies. An employé in the Government lithographing establishment, August Glausinger, who had furnished Cabannes with secret printed documents, was also arrested.

On June 18 a trial for treason-felony of eight Alsatians, who were charged with belonging to the French Patriotic League, was begun at Leipsic. It was shown that the Ligne des Patriotes, which was founded at Paris in May, 1872, to promote the reacquisition of the provinces, had established rifle clubs and gymnastic and vocal societies in Alsace-Lorraine, and that pamphlets, newspapers, and song-books designed to keep alive French patriotic sentiments had been disseminated. The prisoners confessed to having contributed funds to the League, but denied that it had any treasonable or political object. They were sentenced to several years' confinement, and were consigned to the casemates of the fortresses of Glatz and Magdeburg.

Klein and Grebert were brought to trial on July 4. It was shown that Klein, who was once a mason and architect, and had been a sergeant in the French army in 1870, but afterward adopted German nationality, had forwarded to Paris information regarding the German method of mobilization, the commissariat, the garrisons, armaments, equipments, the dimensions of forts and trenches, and even a complete lan on a large scale of the fortifications at Mayence. He made a complete confession, and gave information against his fellow-prisoner and brother-in law, but was sentenced to six years' imprisonment as a common felon, while Grebert was sentenced for five years, and Erhardt, keeper of a restaurant, who was implicated, was acquitted on the ground of lack of criminal intention. The trial of Cabannes and his accomplices took place in November.

The Raon Incident.—On September 25 M. de Wangen, a sub-lieutenant of French cavalry, and M. Brignon, his game-keeper, while shooting on the former's estate, were fired on by a German soldier who had been detailed to act as a forest guard and prevent poaching on the German side of the boundary at Allarmont, near Vexincourt, in the Vosges, and in the neighborhood of the town of Raon. Lieut. de Wangen was slightly wounded, and his companion was struck in the abdomen, and

died after suffering great agony for five hours. The affair was investigated by the French and German Governments, and, as in the Pagny incident, there was conflicting testimony as to whether the Frenchmen were on the German or French side of the line. Richard Kaufmann, the soldier who fired the shots, mistaking the party for poachers, testified that he summoned them to halt three times before shooting, though M. de Wangen did not hear the command. The incident was closed by the German Government's paying an indemnity of 50,000 marks to the widow of M. Brignon, and promising to prosecute the offending soldier. Negotiations were entered into for the settlement of a better *modus operandi* on the frontier in order to prevent the recurrence of similar painful affairs. After the shooting the French Government found it necessary to adopt stringent regulations to prevent molestation of German officials on French soil.

Illness of the Crown Prince.—Apprehensions in regard to the health of the Crown Prince, which began to be felt in the summer, have caused in Germany, not only sadness, but a feeling of doubt and distress regarding the political future, for high hopes were entertained of his prospective reign by a large section of the German people. Before he attended the Jubilee of the Queen in England a troublesome ailment affected his throat which almost deprived him of the power of speech. His wife persuaded him to place himself in the hands of Dr. Mackenzie, an English specialist, who found a growth on the larynx, which he concluded was of a warty nature, and not cancerous, as was feared by German physicians who had examined his throat. He was confirmed in this opinion by the result of a microscopic examination by Prof. Virchow, of Berlin, of a small portion that was removed. On Dr. Mackenzie's advice the excrescence was cut away, and for a short time the patient was much relieved, but soon the growth reappeared. A second operation had no better result. By the counsel of his physician the prince went to Italy as cool weather approached, in order to have the benefit of a milder climate. When alarming symptoms again showed themselves, Vienna physicians in lectures and medical journals assailed the diagnosis of the English doctor, and condemned his treatment from the beginning, declaring that the malady was cancer, and that an early excision of the larynx might have eradicated it. In this they expressed a common conviction of the German medical profession. The subsequent return of a more favorable condition revived the hope that Dr. Mackenzie had not erred in his diagnosis.

The Session of 1887-'88.—The Reichstag was opened on November 24. The speech from the throne spoke of a gratifying improvement in the finances, which was expected to increase when the new sugar and spirit duties should begin to show their full effect, and produce a surplus for the next year of 50,000,000 marks.

In view of this a beginning would be made with the long-deferred plan of increasing the salaries of certain state functionaries. While other departments of industry were flourishing, agriculture was in a depressed state owing to foreign competition, and consequently a protective duty on grain would be proposed. In continuation of the economic legislation foreshadowed in the Imperial message of Nov. 17, 1881, the Reichstag would be asked to deal with a bill for providing state assistance to old, infirm, and unemployed workingmen, and to extend accident insurance to classes not yet provided for; also to consider a law for the regulation of co-operative societies, and one for applying to the wine-trade the principles adopted in regard to the adulteration of food. The speech concluded with the following allusions to foreign affairs:

The foreign policy of His Majesty the Emperor is successfully endeavoring to strengthen the peace of Europe—the maintenance of which is its object—by cherishing friendly relations to all powers, as well as by treaties and alliances which aim at obviating the dangers of war, and at making common cause against unjust attacks. The German Empire has no aggressive tendencies, and no wants that could be satisfied by victorious wars. The unchristian inclination to fall upon neighboring nations is foreign to the German character, and neither the Constitution nor the military institutions of the empire have been fashioned with a view to disturb the peace of our neighbors by wanton aggression. But for the warding off of such aggression, and for defending our independence, we are strong, and with God's help will become so strong that we can calmly confront every danger.

The Workmen's Insurance Bill.—The new installment in the Chancellor's scheme of social legislation that was promised in the Imperial address, was brought before the Reichstag in December. The bill provides that all workmen who pass the age of seventy, or become permanently and completely incapacitated for work, shall have a pension. Like the previous acts, it affects only workmen, apprentices, servants, and administrative employés having a yearly pay of not more than 2,000 marks. The pension to these is to be due, however, only if contributions, or, in ordinary insurance language, premiums have been paid on their behalf during a certain length of time, which is to be thirty years in case of the pension for old age and five years in case of that for disability. We say contributions must be paid on their behalf, for here, as in the case of the other insurance acts, contributions are paid only in part by the workmen themselves. Not more than one third is paid by them, another third is paid by the employers, and the last third comes from the Imperial Treasury, that is, from taxation of the community at large. The pension in case of old age is 120 marks per year; that for disability varies from a minimum of 120 marks to a maximum of 250 marks, according to the length of time for which contributions have been paid. The sums seem pitiful enough; possibly they have been made small intentionally, in order not to take away

all incentive to independent saving or all occasion for calling on children or other relatives for help. The contributions per workman are fixed for the present at 6 pfennigs per day, or 36 marks per fiscal year. The employers have to advance two thirds of this, or 4 pfennigs per day, but may deduct 2 pfennigs per day from the stipulated wages of the workmen, so that their net charge is 2 pfennigs per day. The rest of the contributions, as was noted above, is paid by the empire. For women the payments are two thirds of those for men, and the pensions correspondingly less. These contributions, or premiums, are, it should be said, merely provisional. Within ten years after the act goes into effect, a new and permanent scale is to be prepared, based on the experience of the workings of the act and of the sums it calls for. The managers of the pension system are the *Berufsgenossenschaften*, or associations of employers, which were organized in order to carry out the system of compulsory insurance against accident. This utilizes the existing machinery and effects an obvious saving of expense. The *Berufsgenossenschaften* are to establish separate accounts for the new system, and the funds are to be kept distinct from those collected for insurance against accident.

The Triple Alliance.—The secret treaty of alliance between Germany, Austria-Hungary, and Italy is supposed to have been renewed and signed by the representatives of the three powers at Vienna, on March 18. The apprehensions of war were directed, in the latter part of the year, more toward Russia than toward France. The tension between Germany and Russia, which the Chancellor had before denied, was revealed by the attitude of the German press, and the interest of Germany in the Balkans was no longer strenuously disavowed. The renewal of the triple alliance was made certain by the visit of Signor Crispi at Friedrichsruhe, where he had a long conference with Prince Bismarck early in November. This visit removed the apprehensions of the Italians regarding the attitude of Germany in the Papal question. The results of the meeting are supposed to be in this respect that Germany admits that the Pope is an Italian subject, under Italian jurisdiction, and therefore outside of the possibility of interference of other nations between the Pope and Italy.

It was feared that the death of Signor Depretis would weaken the bonds uniting Italian policy with that of Germany and Austria; but these bonds have been strengthened under Signor Crispi, who, on his return home, announced that Italy had allied herself with the two empires for the maintenance of European peace. He also intimated that an understanding between Italy and England had secured the *status quo* in the Mediterranean. The German press gave prominence to these statements; and it is generally understood that if Austria should be menaced by Russia or Germany by France, the Italian army will

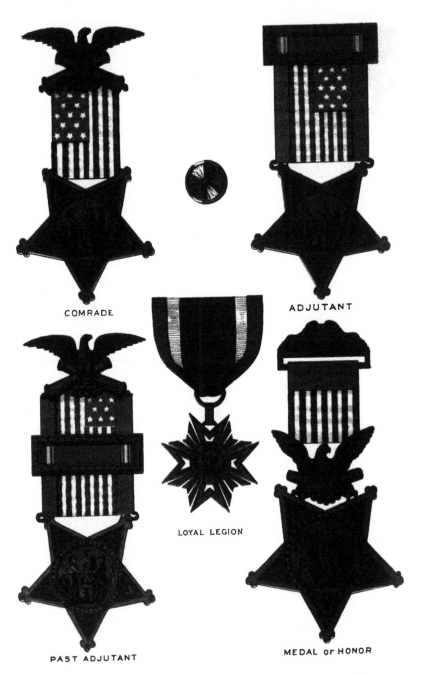

COMRADE

ADJUTANT

LOYAL LEGION

PAST ADJUTANT

MEDAL of HONOR

BADGES OF THE GRAND ARMY OF THE REPUBLIC.
AND LOYAL LEGION AND U S MEDAL OF HONOR

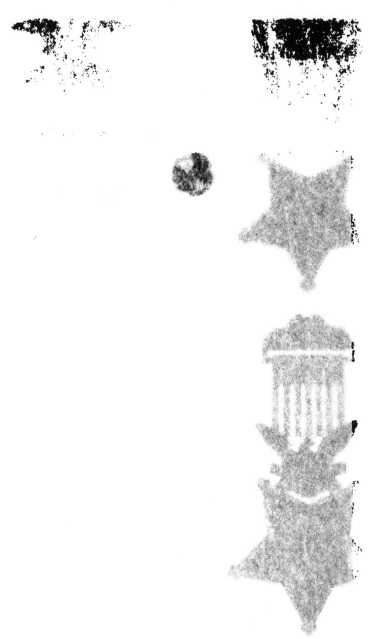

form part of the defensive system, and the English fleet, in conjunction with the Italian navy, will be able to guarantee the coasts and the ports of Italy against a French descent.

Colonies.—There have been taken recently under the protectorate of the Imperial Government the following territories in Africa: (1) The territory of Togo on the Slave Coast, with the districts of Porto Seguro and Little Popo; (2) the territory of Cameroon, bounded on the north by the right bank of the Rio del Rey and on the south by the Campo river; (3) the territory on the west coast of South Africa, bounded by the left bank of the Counene river on the north, and on the south the Orange river, with the exception of Whale Bay, and extending to territories in the interior acquired by treaty; (4) the territories of the negro chiefs of Usagara, Nguru, Useguha, and Ukami, described in the patent of protection issued on February 27, 1885; (5) the territory of Vitou.

On March 28, 1887, the territory of Victoria, which was under the protectorate of Great Britain, was formally handed over to the German authorities to be thenceforth incorporated in the colony of Cameroon, in accordance with an agreement between the two governments.

In the Pacific ocean the protection of the Emperor has been extended over the Marshall Isles, which have an area of 110 square kilometres and 10,000 inhabitants, and over the regions acquired by the Company of New Guinea. The latter comprise King William's Land, situated on the northeast coast of New Guinea, with an area of 179,250 square kilometres, and 109,000 inhabitants; the Bismarck Archipelago, with 52,200 square kilometres of land surface, and 188,000 inhabitants; and the portion of the Solomon Islands that is situated north of the line of demarkation agreed on between Great Britain and Germany on April 6, 1886, having an area of 22,000 square kilometres, and about 80,000 inhabitants.

GRAND ARMY OF THE REPUBLIC. However objectionable secret societies may be on general principles, the fact of their wide-spread existence is an indisputable proof of their popularity. They are found in all nations and under all conditions of civilization and barbarism, and, after an ineffectual struggle to suppress them, even the most conservative of our universities and colleges have been forced to make the best of them and recognize their influence as one of the elements of social life that must be accepted, and, if possible, converted to good and useful ends. No combination of persons can exist, indeed, without some interior affairs of its own which it is not policy to give to the world at large.

It is not strange, therefore, that when the idea of a society of veteran soldiers was first conceived it should have been deemed wise to organize it with a system of signs, grips, and passwords, which may seem very unnecessary to outsiders, but have their uses in strengthening the bond that unites its membership.

Springfield, Illinois, was the birthplace of the Grand Army of the Republic, better known by its initials as the G. A. R. During the winter of 1865-'66, a considerable number of soldiers who had served in the armies of the United States were gathered in the vicinity of Springfield, and Dr. B. F. Stephenson, late surgeon of the Fourteenth Illinois Infantry, was so prominent in perfecting the organization that to him belongs the credit of having founded the now powerful, prosperous, and well-organized association that numbers its members by the hundred thousand.

After much discussion among the original projectors, it was decided that the element of secrecy was best adapted to further the objects of the order, and at the first regular meeting a ritual was adopted, with prescribed oaths and ceremonies of initiation, and the association was launched with a purpose that has been most successfully carried out.

The first post was formed in Decatur, Illinois, on the night of April 6, 1866, and the entire staff of compositors of the Decatur "Tribune" being, as it happened, eligible to membership, was mustered in. This enabled the young fraternity to have its printing done with closed doors, and four hundred copies of the ritual were soon printed and bound for distribution. The town was placarded with notices like the following: "G. A. R., Post No. 1, Decatur, April 6, 1866," and in a short time a large proportion of the veterans in the neighborhood had applied for membership. The objects of the order, as publicly announced, were as follow:

First: To preserve and strengthen those kind and fraternal feelings which bind together the soldiers, sailors, and marines who united to suppress the late rebellion, and to perpetuate the history and memory of the dead.

Second: To assist such former comrades-in-arms as need help and protection, and to extend needful aid to the widows and orphans of those who have fallen.

Third: To maintain true allegiance to the United States of America, based upon a paramount respect for and fidelity to the national Constitution and laws; to discountenance whatever tends to weaken loyalty, incites to insurrection, treason, and rebellion, or in any manner impairs the efficiency or permanency of our free institutions; and to encourage the spread of universal liberty, equal rights, and justice to all men.

The organization of Post No. 1, at Springfield, was soon followed by that of Post No. 2 at the same place, and Dr. Stephenson was recognized as Provisional Commander-in-Chief. In the mean time, other associations having the same general end in view, seeing the advantage of united action, dissolved their organizations, and were duly received into the Grand Army of the Republic.

On October 31, 1866, a call was issued for a National Convention, which was held in Indianapolis November 20, with representatives present from Illinois, Missouri, Kansas, Wisconsin, New York, Pennsylvania, Ohio, Iowa, Kentucky, Indiana, and the District of Columbia. Gen. Stephen A. Hurlbut, of Illinois, was elected Commander-in-Chief, with Dr. Stephenson as his Adjutant-General.

The second general meeting, which was the first officially named an "Encampment," met in the council chambers of Independence Hall, Philadelphia, Jan. 15, 1868, and Gen. John A. Logan was chosen Commander-in-Chief. At this time, owing to various dissensions, the order experienced a period of depression. It was charged with being a secret political organization, and, during the two or three years that followed, its membership was largely reduced by resignation, and the loss was hardly balanced by new recruits. The constitution and by-laws were revised and adapted to the requirements of the case, resulting eventually in renewed vitality, and in its establishment on a basis of assured prosperity. Under the present constitution the following named persons are eligible for membership: Soldiers and sailors of the United States army, navy, or marine corps, between April 12, 1861, and April 9, 1865, in the war for the suppression of the rebellion, and those having been honorably discharged therefrom after such service, and of such State regiments as were called into active service and subject to the orders of United States general officers between the dates mentioned, shall be eligible to membership in the Grand Army of the Republic. No person shall be eligible who has at any time borne arms against the United States.

The order has from the first taken a prominent part in the observance of Decoration Day, or, as it is now more appropriately known, Memorial Day. May 30 of each year has been set apart as a national holiday; banks and public offices are closed, and the survivors of the National armies meet at their respective posts and march together to decorate with flowers and appropriate devices the graves of their former comrades. A simple uniform has been adopted similar to that worn in the service, and the occasion is an impressive one in almost every considerable town and village in the Northern United States.

When on duty, or on occasions of state and ceremony, members of the Grand Army — "comrades" as they are officially termed — wear the badge designated as No. 1 in the illustration. No. 2 is the officers' badge, No. 3 the past or retired officers' badge, and No. 4 the button worn when off duty and in civilian's dress. The cross-bars designate the rank of the wearer according to the insignia of the United States Army, and all the metal-work is of bronze, made from cannon captured during the civil war. The commanders-in-chief of the Grand Army have been as follows, the dates and places of their election corresponding with the annual encampments as indicated:

1. Stephen A. Hurlbut, of Illinois, Indianapolis, Nov. 20, 1866.
2. John A. Logan, of Illinois, Philadelphia, Jan. 15, 1868; re-elected (3) at Cincinnati, May 12, 1869; and again (4) at Washington, May 11, 1870 (died Dec. 26, 1886).
5. Ambrose E. Burnside, of Rhode Island, Boston, May 10, 1871; re-elected (6) at Cleveland, May 8, 1872 (died Sept. 3, 1881).
7. Charles Devins, Jr., of Massachusetts, New Haven, Conn., May 14, 1873; re-elected (8) at Harrisburg, Pa., May 13, 1874.
9. John F. Hartranft, of Pennsylvania, Chicago, May 12, 1875; re-elected (10) at Philadelphia, June 30, 1876.
11. John C. Robinson, of New York, Providence, R. I., June 26, 1877; re-elected (12) at Springfield, Mass., June 4, 1878.
13. William Earnshaw, of Ohio, Albany, N. Y., June 17, 1879.
14. Louis Wagner, of Pennsylvania, Dayton, O., June 8, 1880.
15. George S. Merrill, of Massachusetts, Indianapolis, June 15, 1881.
16. Paul Vandervoort, of Nebraska, Baltimore, June 21, 1882.
17. Robert B. Beath, of Pennsylvania, Denver, July 25, 1883.
18. John S. Kountz, of Ohio, Minneapolis, July 23, 1884.
19. S. S. Burdette, of Washington, D. C., Portland, Me., June 24, 1885.

An organization so powerful in numbers and influence could not but excite animosities based upon supposed political sympathies, and as early in its history as 1869 it was deemed best at the annual encampment, held that year in Cincinnati, to adopt the following rule:

"No officer or comrade of the Grand Army of the Republic shall in any manner use this organization for partisan purposes, and no discussion of partisan questions shall be permitted at any of its meetings, nor shall any nominations for political purposes be made." It is one thing to pass such a resolution, and quite another to carry it out in letter and in spirit. In the nature of things it was unavoidable that members should become candidates for office, and that members already holding public office should be prominent in the conduct of Grand Army affairs, but it is believed that in a remarkable degree unseemly partisanship has been avoided, and certainly no formal action has at any time been taken that can fairly be construed as a deliberate violation of the rule cited. Another charge that has been brought against the organization is that it tends to keep alive the bitter memories of the civil war, but such charges have never come from the soldiers of the Confederacy. Indeed, its relations with similar organizations among veterans of the Confederate service have ever been most friendly, and upon several occasions ex-soldiers of both armies have met and fraternized on the most amicable terms.

The order is constantly active in aiding deserving applicants for pensions, and in exposing unworthy attempts—and they are many— to defraud the Government through unjust claims. During the year more than $253,000 have been officially expended in the relief of families of deceased and dependent soldiers, and probably an equal amount has been contributed by members in a private way calling for no official record. During the sixteen years from 1871 to 1886, the sum of $1,173,-688.60 has been disbursed for charitable purposes. These large sums have been distributed directly to those whose needs were personally known to the donors, and it is probable that very little has gone to unworthy pensioners. Twice within a few years, during the yellow-fever epidemic in the Mississippi Valley and immediately after the Charleston earthquake, it was deemed proper to issue a general call for aid to sufferers, a large majority of whom must have been on the side of the rebellion during the civil war. In both instances the order has promptly and generously responded with pecuniary assistance. The latest accessible figures place the total present membership at 372,674, and the number of recruits during 1887 numbered about 47,000. The order is in fact a supplementary pension bureau. That it should take an active part in making known its sentiments in regard to the Government bureau, is to be expected. Its members are now too far advanced in life ever again to bear arms in defense of the republic, but their influence is still potent for loyalty and good government. (See LOYAL LEGION and MEDAL OF HONOR.)

GREAT BRITAIN AND IRELAND, a monarchy in western Europe. The supreme legislative power is exercised by Parliament. Parliaments hold their sessions annually, meeting about the middle of February. The session is usually closed by prorogation about the middle of August. Parliament is divided into two houses. The House of Lords is composed of hereditary peers; peers created by the sovereign, English bishops, who have seats ex officio, Irish peers, who are elected for life, and Scottish representative peers, who are chosen anew for each Parliament. In 1886 the House of Lords consisted of 549 members, of whom 5 were peers of the blood royal, 2 archbishops, 22 dukes, 20 marquises, 118 earls, 29 viscounts, 24 bishops, 285 barons, 16 Scottish peers, and 28 Irish representative peers. There are 20 Scotch and 65 Irish peers who have no seats in the House of Lords. The House of Commons consists of 670 members, of whom 283 represent county constituencies; 360, boroughs; and 9, universities. For England there are 253 county, 237 borough, and 5 university members; in Scotland, 39 county, 31 borough, and 2 university members; in Ireland, 85 county, 16 borough, and 2 university members.

The elections of 1886 resulted in the return to Parliament of 318 Conservatives, 78 Liberal Unionists, 194 Gladstonian Liberals, and 85 Irish Home Rulers, giving a normal majority to the Conservative government, which was formed in opposition to Mr. Gladstone's scheme of home rule for Ireland, of 112 in a house of 670 members. The metropolis sent 48 Conservatives, 11 Gladstonians, and 3 Liberal Unionists; the rest of England elected 237 Conservatives, 116 Gladstonian Liberals, 49 Liberal Unionists, and 1 Irish Home Ruler, who was returned for one of the divisions of the city of Liverpool; Wales returned 4 Conservatives, 24 Gladstonians, and 2 Liberal Unionists; Scotland returned 12 Conservatives, 43 Gladstonians, and 17 Union Liberals; and in Ireland 17 Conservatives, 2 Liberal Unionists, and 84 Home Rulers were elected. Of the 285 Conservatives elected in England the boroughs returned 98, besides the 48 London members, the county districts 135, and the universities 4. Of the Welsh Conservatives 3 represent boroughs and 1 a county constituency. In Scotland 1 borough, 9 county districts, and both the universities of Edinburgh and Glasgow are represented by Conservatives. In Ireland the universities, 4 boroughs, and 11 county constituencies sent Conservative members to Parliament. Liberal Unionists were elected by 2 of the districts of London, 16 other boroughs, 38 county districts, and 1 university; by 1 borough and 1 county constituency in Wales; by 8 boroughs and 9 county districts in Scotland; and by 2 county divisions in Ireland. Gladstonian Liberals were returned from 11 of the divisions of the metropolis, 50 other borough constituencies, and 66 county constituencies in England; from 7 boroughs and 17 county districts in Wales; and from 22 boroughs and 21 county districts in Scotland. The Irish members were returned from 12 Irish boroughs, 1 English borough, and 72 Irish county districts.

The representation act of 1884, with the redistribution act of 1885, increased the number of voters from 3,152,919 to 5,707,531. The number of county electors was increased in England from 966,719 to 2,536,580; in Scotland, from 99,652 to 325,529; in Ireland, from 165,997 to 681,649. The number entitled to the borough franchise was increased in England from 1,651,782 to 1,840,044; in Scotland, from 210,789 to 285,051; in Ireland, from 58,021 to 106,109. The 32,569 electors who choose the 9 university representatives under the act of 1885 were formerly included in the borough electors. The total number of voters was increased in England from 2,618,451 to 4,391,260; in Scotland, from 810,441 to 574,-358; and in Ireland, from 224,018 to 741,913. An act passed in 1872, requiring parliamentary elections to be by secret vote and by ballot expired in 1880, but has since been continued from year to year. The Parliament which was opened in August, 1886, is the 24th of the United Kingdom and the 12th of the reign of Queen Victoria.

The executive power is exercised, in the name of the sovereign, by the Cabinet. The Prime Minister, who usually holds the office of First Lord of the Treasury, is the representative of the majority in the House of Commons. He selects his colleagues and dispenses all the patronage of the Government.

The reigning sovereign is Queen Victoria I, born May 24, 1819. The heir-apparent is Albert Edward, Prince of Wales, born Nov. 9, 1841. His eldest son, Prince Albert Victor, born Jan. 8, 1864, is next in the order of succession.

The present Cabinet, constituted on Aug. 3, 1886, and reconstructed on Jan. 14, 1887, is composed of the following ministers: Prime Minister, the Marquis of Salisbury, born in 1830, who on Jan. 14, 1887, exchanged the post of First Lord of the Treasury for that of Secretary of State for Foreign Affairs, which he had held when Prime Minister before in 1885-'86; Lord High Chancellor and Keeper of the Great Seal, Baron Halsbury, formerly Sir Hardinge S. Gifford, who filled the same post in Lord Salisbury's former Cabinet; First Lord of the Treasury, W. H. Smith, previously Secretary for War, who received his present appointment on Jan. 14, 1887; Lord President of the Privy Council, Viscount Cranbrook, formerly Gathorne Hardy, who was made a peer in 1878, and was President of the Council in the former Conservative Cabinet; Chancellor of the Exchequer, George Joachim Goschen, who was formerly affiliated with the Liberal party, and more recently with the Liberal Unionists, and who received his appointment on Jan. 14, 1887, succeeding Lord Randolph H. S. Churchill, who had withdrawn from the Cabinet; Secretary of State for the Home Department, Henry Matthews; Secretary of State for War, Edward Stanhope, who was Colonial Secretary before the reconstruction of the Cabinet; Secretary of State for the Colonies, Sir Henry Thurstan Holland, who was transferred from the post of Vice-President of the Council to a Cabinet office on Jan. 17, 1887; Secretary of State for India, Viscount Cross, who was Home Secretary in the last Conservative Cabinet, and was raised to the peerage in 1886, having been previously, Sir Richard Cross; First Lord of the Admiralty, Lord George Hamilton, who held the same appointment under Lord Salisbury before; Lord Chancellor of Ireland, Lord Ashbourne, formerly Edward Gibson, member of Parliament for Dublin University, who was Attorney-General and Lord Chancellor of Ireland under previous Conservative governments, and was created a peer on resuming the latter office in 1886, and given a seat in the Cabinet; Chief Secretary to the Lord Lieutenant of Ireland, Arthur J. Balfour, who received the appointment on the resignation of the office by Sir Michael Hicks-Beach, having previously had a seat in the

Cabinet as Secretary of State for Scotland; Chancellor of the Duchy of Lancaster, Lord John Manners, who was Postmaster-General in 1885; President of the Board of Trade, Lord Stanley de Preston, formerly Sir Frederick Stanley, who was Secretary for the Colonies in 1885; President of the Local Government Board, C. T. Ritchie, who was given a seat in the Cabinet; Minister without a portfolio, Sir Michael Hicks-Beach, who retired from the Irish secretaryship in March, on account of ill-health, but retained a seat in the Cabinet. A. J. Balfour was succeeded as Secretary for Scotland by the Marquis of Lothian, who is not a member of the Cabinet.

Area and Population. — The British Empire covers an area of 8,981,180 square miles, or 23,260,100 square kilometres, and has a population, according to the most recent enumerations, of 310,735,840 persons.

The area of the United Kingdom is 120,832 square miles, exclusive of water areas, but including the Isle of Man and the Norman Islands. The annual computation of the Registrar-General for 1887 makes the population of England 28,247,151, of Scotland, 3,991,499, and of Ireland, 4,852,914. Including the population of the adjacent islands and the soldiers and seamen abroad, as returned in the census of 1881, the total population of the United Kingdom is 37,448,198.

The vital statistics for England for the last five years reported are as follow:

YEARS.	Marriages.	Births.	Deaths.	Surplus of births.
1882	204,405	889,018	516,654	372,364
1883	206,384	890,722	522,997	367,725
1884	204,301	906,750	530,826	375,922
1885	197,745	894,270	522,750	371,520
1886	195,806	903,216	537,078	366,188

The statistics for Scotland were as follow:

YEARS.	Marriages.	Births.	Deaths.	Surplus of births.
1882	26,574	126,182	72,966	53,216
1883	26,555	124,462	76,567	47,595
1884	26,061	129,041	70,129	58,912
1885	25,256	126,110	74,603	51,507
1886	24,469	127,927	73,622	54,305

The returns for Ireland give the following results:

YEARS.	Marriages.	Births.	Deaths.	Surplus of births.
1882	22,029	122,648	88,500	34,148
1883	21,368	118,168	96,233	21,985
1884	22,565	118,875	87,154	31,721
1885	21,177	115,951	90,712	25,239
1886	20,681	118,995	87,376	26,619

The emigration from the United Kingdom to the United States from 1815 to 1886 was 7,486,636; to the British provinces of North America, 1,855,678; to Australia and New Zealand, 1,567,981; to other countries, 433,834, making in all 11,344,079. In 1886 the number of emigrants who left Great Britain, including 94,870 foreigners and 8,531 of unknown origin, was 230,801. There were 83,-066 English and Welsh, 16,786 Scotch, 52,858 Irish, and 85,076 foreign passengers whose destination was the United States. Of the 146,-310 English emigrants, 18,886 sailed for Canada, 33,764 for Australia, and 10,585 went to other countries and colonies, exclusive of those whose destination was the United States. Among the 25,328 Scotch who emigrated, 2,971 were destined for British America, 4,240 for Australia, and 1,326 to other countries. Of the 61,276 Irish emigrants, the number who departed for Canada was 2,888; for Australia, 5,072; and for other countries, 458. The number of immigrants into Great Britain in 1886, including the foreign emigrants passing through, was 108,879.

The population of the chief cities of Great Britain and Ireland, as computed by the Registrar-General in 1885, was as follows: London, 4,083,928; Liverpool, 579,724; Glasgow, 519,-965; Birmingham, 427,769; Dublin, 353,082; Manchester, 337,842; Leeds, 333,189; Sheffield, 305,716; Edinburgh, 250,616; Bristol, 218,169; Bradford, 214,431; Nottingham, 211,424; Salford, 204,075; Hull, 186,292; Newcastle, 153,209.

Commerce.—The total value of the imports of merchandise in 1886 was £349,863,000, as against £370,968,000 in 1885, and £390,019,-000 in 1884. The value of the exports was £268,667,000, as against £271,404,000 in 1885, and £295,968,000 in 1884. The total volume of commerce was £618,530,000 in 1886, as against £642,372,000 in 1885, and £685,987,000 in 1884. The exports of British products amounted to £212,433,000 in 1886, as against £213,-045,000 in 1885, and £233,025,000 in 1884.

The commerce with the principal commercial nations in 1886 was as follows, in pounds sterling:

COUNTRIES.	Imports.	Exports.
United States	81,800,000	26,925,000
France	84,899,000	13,614,000
Germany	21,422,000	15,676,000
Netherlands	25,810,000	8,196,000
Belgium	14,248,000	7,197,000
Russia	13,572,000	4,424,000
China and Hong-Kong	9,597,000	7,560,000
Sweden and Norway	10,227,000	3,271,000
Portugal	9,112,000	1,587,000
Egypt	7,357,000	2,858,000
Turkey	4,155,000	4,905,000

The declared value of the imports of precious metals in 1886 was £20,864,000, of which £18,392,000 were gold and £7,472,000 silver; the exports were £21,007,000, comprising £13,784,000 of gold and £7,223,000 of silver. British colonial possessions participated in the import trade to the extent of £81,884,000, the imports from India amounting to £32,131,000, from Australia and New Zealand to £20,954,-000, from British North America to £10,415,-000, from British South Africa to £4,671,000, from Singapore to £4,878,000, and from other colonies to £9,340,000. The exports to British colonies amounted to £75,507,000, of which

£31,840,000 went to India, £22,383,000 to Australasia, £7,889,000 to British America, £3,304,000 to South Africa, and £10,591,000 to other possessions.

The values of the chief exports of British produce for 1885 and 1886 were as follow:

EXPORTS.	1885.	1886.
Cotton piece goods, white or plain	30,565,477	32,289,614
Cotton prints and dyed goods	17,706,187	17,919,484
Other cotton fabrics	6,589,979	7,194,701
Cotton yarn	11,565,294	11,468,505
Total cotton manufactures	66,976,867	68,842,602
Iron, pig and puddled	2,092,816	2,252,944
Iron, bar, bolt, angle, and rod	1,620,484	1,878,065
Railroad iron	3,905,259	3,858,783
Iron wire	689,238	554,264
Tinned plate	4,437,695	4,689,484
Hoops and plates	3,264,143	3,058,708
Wrought iron	4,018,108	3,879,241
Old iron	261,435	336,876
Steel, wrought and unwrought	1,432,560	1,883,141
Total iron and steel	21,710,788	21,722,951
Cloths and coatings	8,907,320	9,155,491
Flannels, blankets, and baize	986,658	942,216
Worsted stuffs	6,586,810	6,948,261
Carpets and druggets	1,196,492	1,281,961
Other woolen fabrics	1,975,288	1,464,462
Woolen and worsted yarn	4,882,394	4,406,676
Total woolen manufactures	23,239,951	24,144,257
Machinery	11,026,869	10,188,869
Coal	10,693,151	9,886,539
Linen manufactures	4,961,098	5,257,574
Linen yarn	986,588	985,062
Jute manufactures	1,920,599	1,824,718

The values of the principal articles of import, in pounds sterling, were in 1885 and 1886 as follow:

IMPORTS.	1885.	1886.
Grain and flour	56,269,355	48,235,430
Cotton, raw	36,472,612	37,792,413
Wool, sheep and other	21,177,688	23,307,537
Sugar, raw and refined	18,822,382	15,997,867
Wood and timber	15,712,050	12,580,670
Metals	16,295,767	15,089,548
Bacon and hams	8,685,068	8,379,842
Animals	8,930,078	7,143,430
Butter and butterine	11,568,306	10,099,846
Tea	10,606,990	11,360,460
Silk manufactures	10,268,690	10,688,422
Flax, hemp, and jute	8,944,088	7,152,990
Chemicals, etc.	8,797,186	7,952,148
Oils	6,781,921	6,049,148

The quantities of the chief imports in 1885 and 1886, given in hundredweights, except where otherwise designated, were as follow:

IMPORTS.	1885.	1886.
Grain and flour	144,012,466	125,221,898
Bacon and hams	4,068,454	4,199,847
Fish (cured or salted)	784,252	831,655
Refined sugar	5,329,046	5,867,027
Raw sugar	19,416,759	16,141,006
Butter and butterine	2,401,373	2,429,977
Cheese	1,888,050	1,733,197
Beef	1,141,956	901,981
Preserved meat	527,759	430,846
Fresh mutton	571,446	652,259
Sheep and lambs (number)	750,896	1,088,967
Cattle (number)	378,078	319,621
Eggs (great hundreds)	8,356,568	8,613,162

The quantity of grain and flour imported, per head of population, in 1885, was 235·79 pounds, as compared with 155·85 pounds in 1869; of sugar, 74·28 pounds, as compared with 42·56 pounds; of bacon and hams, 11·47 pounds, as compared with 2·68 pounds; of butter, 7·15 pounds, as compared with 4·52 pounds; of cheese, 5·48 pounds, as compared with 3·52 pounds; of tea, 5·02 pounds, as compared with 3·68 pounds.

Navigation.—The total tonnage of vessels engaged in foreign commerce entered at British ports in 1886 was 31,035,618, of which 22,741,061 tons were under the British, and 8,294,557 under foreign flags. The steam tonnage entered was 24,410,809, of which 19,791,481 tons were British and 4,619,328 foreign. The total tonnage cleared was 31,805,459, of which 23,337,238 tons were British. The steam tonnage cleared was 24,992,884, British steamers being represented by 20,250,706 tons. The aggregate burden of vessels entered with cargoes was 24,778,693; cleared, 29,171,079. The aggregate tonnage of vessels in the coasting trade entered in 1886 was 44,005,833; cleared, 37,420,204.

The number of vessels on the registers of the United Kingdom in 1886 was 22,409, of 7,821,000 tons, of which 6,630. of 3,962,000 tons, were steamers. The number of vessels registered in British colonies was 15,143, of 1,924,000 tons. The number of sailing-vessels built in Great Britain in 1885 was 452, of 208,411 tons; the number of steamers, 393, of 196,975 tons.

Railroads.—The number of miles of railroad in operation in the United Kingdom at the end of 1886 was 19,332, of which 13,678 miles were in England and Wales, 3,022 in Scotland, and 2,632 in Ireland. The cost of construction was £828,344,000. The gross receipts in 1886 were £69,592,000, as compared with £69,556,000 in 1885; the net receipts, £33,073,000, as compared with £32,768,000.

Posts and Telegraphs.—The number of letters transmitted by the post-office during the year ended March 31, 1887, was 1,460,000,000; post-cards, 179,000,000; newspapers and printed matter, 520,000,000; parcels, 32,860,000; postal orders for the United Kingdom, 9,800,000, of the aggregate amount of £21,952,000; for foreign countries and the colonies, 300,000, of the amount of £763,000; from foreign countries and British colonies, 700,000, of the amount of £2,218,000.

The length of telegraph lines in April, 1886, was 30,276 miles, with 170,195 miles of wire. The gross receipts from the postal telegraphs in 1886 was £1,758,169, and the net revenue £25,343. The number of inland telegrams forwarded in the year ended March 31, 1887, was 50,243,639, of which 42,320,185 were in England and Wales, 5,106,774 in Scotland, and 2,816,680 in Ireland.

Finances.—The financial year 1886–'87 showed better results than were originally anticipated. The estimates of revenue adopted by Sir William Harcourt, who was Chancellor of the Ex-

chequer at the beginning of the year, amounted to £89,869,000. The actual revenue was £90,773,000. The receipts from customs, which were first estimated at £19,700,000, were £20,155,000; stamps, £11,830,000, exceeding the estimate by £465,000; land-tax and house duty, £2,980,000, which was £60,000 more than the estimate; property and income-tax, £15,900,000, being £145,000 more than the estimate, the 8d. income-tax having been more thoroughly collected than in previous years; the post-office and telegraphs, estimated to yield £8,270,000 and £1,780 000 respectively, produced £8,450,000 and £1,830,000; crown-lands, £370,000; interest on advances, £1,176,000. The excise revenue fell below the estimate, producing £25,250,000 instead of the £25,694,000 that it was expected to yield. The expenditure for 1886–'87 also exceeded the estimates by reason of supplementary rates. The total expenditure was £90,115,000, of which £60,294,000, or £497,000 more than the original estimate, was for the supply services. Mr. Goschen, the Chancellor of the Exchequer, in presenting his financial statement with regard to the revenue, to illustrate its gradual loss of all elasticity, showed how the increased produce of the taxes had fallen from 10·8 per cent. in the five years 1860–'65, and 24 per cent. in 1870–'75, to 1 per cent. in the fiscal year 1886–'87. The most notable features have been a considerable falling off in the alcoholic revenue, showing that the habits of the British people have reformed in respect to the use of spirituous liquors, and the progress of the free breakfast-table movement. Mr. Goschen illustrated the unsatisfactory character of the revenue raised from the higher classes by reference to the falling off in the yield of the different schedules of the income-tax, and drew the general conclusion that the commercial and agricultural depression, while it had touched the two extremes of the social scale severely, had not affected the profits of the middleman.

The revenue for 1887–'88 was estimated by the Chancellor of the Exchequer at £91,155,500, and the expenditure at £90,180,000. He proposed to suppress a part of the sinking fund, reducing the fixed charge of the debt from £28,000,000 to £26,000,000 per annum in order to throw off one penny from the income-tax, which seems to be permanently established at war rates. The proposed relief of local taxes could not yet be taken in hand except to the extent of handing over an amount equal to the proceeds of the carriage-tax to the local authorities. The tobacco duty was lowered from 3s. 6d. to 3s. 2d. per pound, the rate at which it formerly stood.

The Army.—The army estimates for 1887–'88 fix the number of regular troops, exclusive of those serving in India, at 149,391. The total effective strength of the regular army is fixed at 9,939 officers and 211,143 men, making together 221,082, with 25,583 horses. The regular army reserve consists of 57,535 officers and men. The militia and yeomanry number 4,498 officers and 145,906 men, or in all 150,404, with 14,100 horses; the volunteers, 8,251 officers and 245,866 men, making 254,117 altogether. The military police in Ireland is 13,-000 strong. The native army of India numbers 25,757 officers and 785,191 men, or in all 810,948, with 64,243 horses and other animals. There is a military police in India numbering about 190,000 officers and men. The corps of horse artillery which was peculiar to the British army was abolished in 1887, with a view of making the army conform more to Continental models, probably by organizing it into two army corps.

The Navy.—The navy consisted in October, 1887, of 61 armor-clad vessels, including those in process of construction, about 290 steamers, 150 torpedo-boats, and 212 sailing-ships and transports. There were 255 vessels in commission. Of these, 132 were stationed on the coasts of the United Kingdom, comprising 5 large iron-clads and 1 steamer, forming the Channel squadron, 9 iron-clads and 11 steamers in the first reserve, 24 coast-guards, 1 vessel on hydrographic service, 9 without orders, 4 royal yachts, 23 vessels for port service, and 45 school-ships. There were 4 steam cruisers employed as a squadron of instruction. The Mediterranean squadron comprised 6 large iron-clads and 18 other vessels. On the eastern coast of America were stationed one large iron-clad and 12 other vessels; in Brazilian waters, 4 vessels; on the western coast of America, 8 vessels, including 1 large iron-clad; in southern and western Africa, 9 vessels; in India and eastern Africa, 11 vessels; in Chinese waters, 21 vessels, including 2 iron-clads; on the Australian station, 1 large iron-clad and 7 other vessels; on hydrographic service abroad, 2 vessels. The other vessels in the list are 11 transports and 2 cruisers on the return voyage. The 28 iron-clad line-of-battle ships in active service carry 290 guns, and the 160 unarmored steamers carry 790. On July 23 a grand naval review was held at Spithead, in which 114 vessels of all descriptions took part. The last previous pageant of the kind took place in 1856. The antiquated wooden vessels that were present, such as the "Victory," "St. Vincent," and "Duke of Wellington," took no part in the actual review. The vessels of modern type that passed before the Queen were 9 broadside armor-clads, viz., the "Black Prince," "Minotaur," "Agincourt," "Hercules," "Invincible," "Sultan," "Iron Duke," "Shannon," and "Belleisle"; 15 turret-ships, viz., the "Monarch," "Inflexible," "Edinburgh," "Devastation," "Ajax," "Neptune," "Prince Albert," "Conqueror," "Hydra," "Cyclops," "Gorgon," "Hecate," "Glatton," "Rupert," and "Hotspur"; 2 barbette-ships, viz., the "Collingwood" and "Impérieuse"; the "Mersey," a protected vessel; the "Amphion," "Arethusa," and "Calypso," partially protected

vessels; 5 unprotected vessels, viz., the "Inconstant," a frigate, the "Mercury," a dispatch-vessel, and the "Active," "Volage," and "Rover," corvettes; 31 gunboats; and 43 torpedo-craft. While the vessels were assembling, a collision took place between the "Ajax" and "Devastation," followed a few days later by one between the "Agincourt" and "Black Prince," which revealed the difficulty of manoeuvring heavy iron-clads in line of battle in close order without their running each other down. After the review the vessels taking part sailed for various parts of the coast to carry out manoeuvres designed to test the efficiency of the port defenses as well as the offensive power of the navy. The principal test was an attack on a harbor defended by an iron boom and submarine torpedoes, the result of which showed that the huge iron-clads can burst through any obstruction that can be stretched across the mouth of a harbor, but that torpedo-mines are an effective defense. The policy of building monster iron-clads is now condemned by the naval authorities of England as well as of Continental countries. The change in the opinions of naval critics in this regard, and still more the faulty administration, antiquated and defective armaments, and wasteful expenditure of the large sums that have been voted for the navy, as asserted in Parliament and revealed by official inquiries, have, to some extent, lowered the opinion of the formidable character of the British navy held by Continental nations. Lord Randolph Churchill, who has become the political exponent of the critics of the navy, asserted in a speech, delivered before the naval parade, that the ten millions sterling that had been voted for eighteen great ships within a dozen years, in respect to the purposes for which the ships were designed, and for which the money was voted, have been "absolutely misapplied, utterly wasted, and thrown away." A parliamentary inquiry was held regarding the cutlasses and sword-bayonets with which the marines are armed, and which bent and proved worthless when put to use in Egypt. The conclusions reached by the committee were that the design was bad, the workmanship unskillful, and the tests to which the weapons were subjected before acceptance altogether inadequate. The "Camperdown" and the "Anson" were completed and officially tried in the spring of 1887. On April 9 the "Victoria," the heaviest iron-clad yet launched, and one of the largest in the navy, being 340 feet long and 70 broad, with a displacement of 10,500 tons, was launched at the Elswick yard. Her armament will include two 110-ton guns. A still larger iron-clad, the "Trafalgar," was launched at Portsmouth on September 20. Her displacement is 11,-940 tons. There are 5,200 tons of steel and iron in her hull. The length is 345 feet, and the breadth 78 feet. The total cost of the vessel and her equipments is about £900,000.

The armament consists of four 18½-inch 67-ton breech-loading guns, eight 5-inch breech-loaders, six 36-pounder quick-firing guns, and eleven 3 pounder Hotchkiss guns, besides machine-guns, boat and field guns, and twenty-four Whitehead torpedoes. The turret-guns will fire projectiles weighing 1,250 pounds, with a powder charge of 630 pounds, and will train through an angle of 270°. The 5-inch guns will be mounted on the upper deck between the turrets. Of the eight torpedo-tubes, four are above and four below the water-line. A sister ship, the "Nile," is building at Pembroke, and is likely to be the last of the British monster iron-clads.

The Irish Land Commission.—The Tory Government, after assuming power in 1886, appointed a royal commission, under the presidency of Earl Cowper, to take evidence in relation to the working of the land act of 1881, and to make recommendations regarding the removal of the evils existing in Ireland. General Sir Redvers Buller, who had been sent to Ireland to take charge of the constabulary, was examined before the commission on November 11, 1886. He said that in the counties of Kerry, Clare, and a part of Cork, which was the district of which he had special knowledge, rents were fairly well paid, but were not paid in some localities because they were too high. Tenants were anxious to pay when they could get reasonable allowances. In some localities there was an organized stand against existing rents, but it was the pressure of high rent that produced the agitation and intimidation against the payment of rents. Judicial rents were fixed in a summary, general way, and, although they might have been fair at the time, can not be paid now. When asked if he could suggest any remedy, General Buller proposed that the courts should have discretion to withhold orders of eviction, and that a court of assessors should be created for each county which should have power to lower or raise rents at any time according to a sliding scale of prices. The commissioners in their report recognized a fall in agricultural prices which reduced the value of farming capital 18½ per cent. for the last two years, as compared with the four years preceding. The majority of the commissioners recommended a revision of judicial rents every five years, the reduction or enhancement to be determined by the change of prices, and not by a revaluation of the land. Justice O'Hagan and other members of the commission thought that lease-holders ought to be admitted to the benefit of the land act, and have changes made in their rents if the land commission or county court judge should consider that their cases required a modification of the terms of their leases. The commissioners spoke emphatically in favor of emigration for the relief of the congested districts.

The Round Table.—In the spring, when the Conservative ministers were preparing to enter on a new campaign of coercion in Ireland, which the Liberal Unionists of the Radical faction were not ready to support, Mr. Chamberlain repeated the sentiments he had formerly expressed in favor of granting a large measure of home-rule to Ireland. The Liberals, in response to his overtures, intimated that a modification of Mr. Gladstone's scheme was not out of the question. A conference was arranged, and Lord Herschel, Sir William Harcourt, and Mr. Morley, on the part of the Gladstonians, and Mr. Chamberlain and Sir George Trevelyan on the part of the Liberal Unionists, discussed a compromise plan for Ireland. Lord Hartington refused to commit himself beforehand. The "round-table" conferences were held in secret, and went on smoothly, but had not accomplished much toward harmonizing Mr. Gladstone's national plan with Mr. Chamberlain's scheme for local self-government, when the latter, in public speeches and in a letter published in an organ called "The Baptist," declared that reunion was impossible while the Gladstonian Liberals encouraged crime in Ireland and obstruction in Parliament. Sir William Harcourt and his friends thereupon broke off the conferences, throwing the blame of their failure on Mr. Chamberlain. Mr. Gladstone, in a speech made at Swansea, offered to treat every point in his home-rule scheme as open to discussion. The Liberal Unionists replied that they could not be satisfied with vague assurances and undefined concessions which were governed by the condition that the settlement must be satisfactory to the Parnellites.

Sir George Trevelyan, who had before a Unionist meeting at Aberdeen expressed the opinion that the Irish question must be dealt with "radically and remedially," and could be settled only by a reunited Liberal party, was unwilling to follow the Tories in a policy of repression, and after the conferences joined the Gladstonians. In July he was returned to Parliament by one of the divisions of Glasgow.

The Plan of Campaign.—The rejection of Mr. Parnell's bill for the relief of tenants whose condition was still intolerable, notwithstanding the land act, was followed by the adoption by the National League of a "plan of campaign" against rack-renting and tyrannical landlords. It was first published in "United Ireland," on October 23, 1886. Messrs. Dillon, O'Brien, and other members of the Irish party, who explained the plan of campaign and urged its adoption in public speeches during the autumn of 1886, were arrested and tried in Dublin on a charge of conspiracy. The judge's charge declared the plan of campaign to be a criminal conspiracy, yet the trial ended with a disagreement of the jury on February 24, 1887, and the discontinuance of the proceedings. After this result the plan of campaign was widely carried into practice. It consists in the National League's acting as attorney for the tenants. Officers of the local branches receive the rent from the tenants on a rack-rented estate, and notify the agent and landlord that as trustees of the tenants they hold the rent in readiness to be paid over at any time, less the 15, 20, 25, or 30 per cent. abatement, as the case may be, that is demanded. The money thus held is used as a fund for the defense of legal proceedings if the landlord proceeds to eviction. The tenants are advised to dispose of their stock and movable property that might be levied on. The tenantry, when organized under the plan of campaign, have at their command various legal devices and loopholes which enable them to frustrate proceedings that are brought against them. If the landlord takes proceedings in bankruptcy, which he can only in the case of farms let since 1872, it is exceedingly difficult to bring them to a successful termination, and, if the tenant pays at the last moment, he loses his costs. If he proceeds for debt, obtains judgment, and has the tenant's interest in his farm sold at auction, he has to bid it in at the price of the debt and costs, which stops all further proceedings against the tenant, only to find on bringing action for ejectment that the tenant had already mortgaged his interest to other creditors. The third remedy is to proceed by ejectment. The tenant defends, brings the landlord to trial, and raises questions of fact, as, for instance, that his lease was never executed. The landlord finally gets his ejectment decree, and the tenant is evicted after something like a pitched battle. The tenant has then six months within which he can redeem his farm by payment of the amount due, in which case the landlord must pay him the amount of any profit he could have made out of the farm while the tenant was out of possession. The tenant can also claim compensation for improvements, such as unexhausted manures, permanent buildings, and reclamation of waste land. The *onus* is on the landlord to show that the improvements were not done by the tenant; and, as prior to the land act of 1870 there was no necessity for keeping any record, it is not always easy to do so. The landlord can not commence ejectment proceedings until one year's rent is in arrear, the proceedings probably take the best part of another half-year, and the tenant has then six months to redeem. The landlord has, perhaps, to pay a considerable sum for improvements, costs probably amounting to half a year's rent, besides those which he can recover from the tenant, and finally has a boycotted farm thrown on his hands to work as best he can. The remaining remedy is to distrain; but the sheriff invariably has his approach heralded by the blowing of horns and ringing of chapel-bells, the cattle are driven off the land, and this method of recovering rent is in Ireland practically obsolete. The plan of campaign, however, entails great losses on the tenants wherever it is applied, for while the struggle is going on they are compelled to sell their stock and crops and suspend all cultivation.

The essence of the plan is that all the tenants shall stand together, the wealthier putting their money into a common purse with the poor, and all refusing to pay until those who can not pay obtain a fair settlement.

The Court of Queen's Bench decided that the plan of campaign was illegal, and the viceroy issued a proclamation authorizing the summary suppression of all proceedings connected with it, the appropriation of its funds, and the seizure of its documents. In December, 1886, General the Prince of Saxe-Weimar, commander of the forces in Ireland, issued a proclamation against it. After the plan had been enunciated by the Irish leaders, the Government, which had been reluctant to carry out evictions, was urged by the landlords to proceed with more energy. General Buller, in the west of Ireland, was unwilling to turn out tenants who were not able to pay, and interfered to secure a reduction from some landlords, while he declined to evict the tenants of Col. O'Callaghan and others who would grant no abatement. The Chief Secretary, Sir Michael Hicks-Beach, exerted administrative pressure to induce certain landlords to make a reduction, but without success. The exercise of the "dispensing power," as it was called by the Irish Secretary, was remitted as soon as the plan of campaign was developed, and the Government was finally stirred into action by the insistance of the landlords, and made a beginning of the evictions at Glenbergh, Kerry, where three or four hundred families were crowded on land that was so poor that they had not been able to extract from it more than a scanty subsistence. They were from three to five years in arrears, but were not able, as Sir Redvers Buller convinced himself, to pay the half-year's rent and costs that the landlord offered to accept. Early in January the officers of the law ejected them, turning even invalid women and children into the road, and burned their cottages to prevent them from returning. This action on an estate where the plan of campaign had not been applied moved tenants to resort to it on many other estates.

The plan of campaign was first applied on the estates of Lord Clanricarde, on Col. O'Callaghan's property at Bodyke, on the O'Kelly estate in County Kildare, on the Mitchelstown estate, and on the Ponsonby estate of Youghal.

Evictions were ordered on the Bodyke property in County Clare; but the peasantry prepared for a desperate resistance under the leadership of Father Murphy, the parish priest. William O'Brien, the Lord Mayor of Dublin, presided at a meeting held on January 30, and urged them to oppose the execution of the decrees. The authorities found it necessary to postpone the evictions. In the middle of February emergency men and police were fired on in the neighboring village of Ballycar, and one man was killed. Col. O'Callaghan was one of the harshest and most exacting of the Irish landlords, who had raised the rent on the tenants' improvements from 15s. in 1850, when he came into the estate, to 35s. or more per acre in 1880, and who had said, when implored not to turn out his tenants as beggars on the world, that he thought no more of pitching one of them out than of shooting a bird by the roadside. The tenants asked a general reduction of 25 per cent. on the judicial rents that were fixed in 1882, and adopted the plan of campaign. An English gentleman who visited the estate to examine into the facts, was so affected by the condition of the peasants that he subscribed a third of £900 that was contributed to discharge the rent of the poorer tenants. This was offered in satisfaction of claims amounting to £1,500, but was refused. Negotiations were continued for two or three months without leading to a settlement, and finally troops and police were sent into the district to see that the writs of eviction were carried out.

Michael Davitt had been among the people, encouraging them to resistance. The thirty-six families barricaded their houses, and received the bailiffs with stones and with showers of hot water; but by means of crowbars and other instruments the houses were entered, and the inmates ejected. Mrs. Walsh, an old woman of eighty, was struck by a constable, other persons were roughly handled, and when the police were returning they charged into a crowd that hooted and groaned at them.

The Marquis of Lansdowne, Governor-General of Canada, is one of the Whig noblemen who joined the Conservatives on the Unionist issue, and who, in their theoretical adherence to the principle of absolute property in land, have been the only direct and thoroughgoing antagonists of the Irish land reformers. As an Irish landlord he, following the example of his father, has enjoyed an exceptional reputation, having, like a few other English and Scotch land-owners, made expensive improvements on his Irish estates and treated his tenants with the same consideration that is customary in England. When the Irish leaders unfolded their new plan, against which only the wealthy and powerful could effectually contend, he was prompted to take up the challenge in defense of his opinions and of his class. On his property in Kerry he granted a reduction of 20 per cent. on judicial rents, but, when his tenants at Luggacurran in Queen's County asked for the same, he refused on the ground that they were better off than the Kerry tenants and had better land, and that they had refused to improve their breed of cattle and to make silos and build a creamery when he offered to assist them, while the others had accepted his offers. They argued that they were affected by the decline in the price of produce, which bore the same proportion to judicial rents in both districts, and explained their refusal to make the desired improvements by saying that they understood the conditions of farming, and that the new methods would have entailed losses. The principal

tenants adopted the plan of campaign, and when ejectment decrees were issued in January cleared their farms of stock and produce, saying that the land did not yield enough to pay the rent, and that they might better go sooner than later, for their expenses would exhaust their capital in two or three years. One of the largest holders was J. W. Dunne, a justice of the peace, who was deprived of his commission on adopting the plan of campaign; another was Denis Kilbride, a poor-law guardian. Both had erected expensive buildings on their farms. The landlord's improvements on the estate were in part buildings, but mainly consisted of drainage-works, which the tenants declared were unprofitable. For the outlay the tenants were charged about 4 per cent. in increased rents. William O'Brien, in a speech to the tenants, threatened to carry the war against Lord Lansdowne into Canada, saying, "We will meet him at his palace-gates, and will make the air ring with his fame as an evictor and an exterminator. We will track him night and day the wide world over, and from one end of the Dominion of Canada to the other. I promise him, on the part of the Irish in Canada, that wherever he goes he will find Irish hearts and Irish throats that will hoot him and boycott him and hunt him with execrations out of that great and free land." Townsend Trench, the agent, offered an abatement of 15 per cent., but the tenants asserted that the land commissioners were fixing rents on other properties in the neighborhood at 40 and sometimes 60 per cent. below the valuation fixed for them in 1883. The agent in a conference with representatives of the tenants agreed or was on the point of agreeing to their demands. After consultation with the Irish Secretary, however, he broke off the negotiations, and was therefore charged by O'Brien with breach of faith.

The evictions began on March 22 with Kilbride, who farmed 768 acres. He had felled trees to obstruct the road leading to his house. Mr. O'Brien, Father Maher, the assistant parish priest, and a large crowd of hooting peasants watched the sheriff's deputies break down the door and carry out the eviction, which was not accomplished till an entrance was effected through the roof into an upper room which Mr. Kilbride and three companions had barricaded with beams and iron gates. After the ten laborers on this farm had been evicted, the sheriff and his assistants, with the police guard, went on the 24th to John W. Dunne's farm, which was 1,281 acres in extent, and for which he paid £1,367 rent, while Griffith's valuation was £942. He also had felled trees across the carriage-road, but gave up the fine house that he had built as soon as the sheriff forced in the door. In the two days following, all his laborers and sub-tenants were evicted. The friends of Lord Lansdowne's poorer tenants proposed to build for them a row of cottages on the holding of Father Kehoe, their priest, and maintain them until they returned to their homes. Money was subscribed freely for the purpose. The minor tenants on the estate were given some weeks to come to terms, and when they adhered to the plan of campaign were evicted in the latter part of April. William O'Brien carried out his threat to carry the war into Canada, where his speeches against Lord Lansdowne were enthusiastically received by Irish audiences, but were reprobated by other elements in the community. He was mobbed in Toronto, and barely escaped with his life. He afterward delivered speeches in the United States.

A suit brought against Lord Clanricarde, in the latter part of 1887, revealed traits of aristocratic arrogance, injustice, and inhumanity on the part of an Irish landlord that brought additional discredit on the entire class. Disturbances took place on Lord Clanricarde's property at Woodford, in the autumn of 1886, in consequence of the exaction of exorbitant rents. Mr. Joyce, his agent, whose predecessor had been shot, and whose own life was in danger on account of his employer's course of action, wrote to Lord Clanricarde that there was a combination against paying the rents, but that they were more than the land could produce, and that, if he would grant the same abatements that all the other landlords of the district were giving, the country would be quiet. Lord Clanricarde, assuming the *rôle* of a man who was making a struggle for the sake of political principle, ordered the evictions to proceed, but the Irish executive refused to send forces to aid in enforcing the decrees, unless Clanricarde should grant reductions. The facts were laid bare by the press, and the public was horrified. In order to rehabilitate himself, the nobleman sent letters to the newspapers, quoting his agent as saying that there was a combination, but suppressing the other parts of his letter. Mr. Joyce asked to have the entire letter given to the public, but Lord Clanricarde demanded from him a letter denying that he had said that the district would be quiet if abatements were granted. Finally, the agent sent his resignation, giving his reasons in an open letter, to which Lord Clanricarde replied that a scullery-maid might as reasonably give to the public her grounds for quitting a place. Mr. Joyce recovered heavy damages from the employer who had placed him on a pedestal to be shot at and sought to fasten on him the opprobrium of his own actions, presuming on his poverty and dependent position.

Mr. Ponsonby took proceedings in bankruptcy against the tenants on his estate near Youghal without gaining any satisfaction. Father Keller, a priest, was summoned before the court to testify in regard to the bankruptcy of the tenant Patrick O'Brien. He refused to appear as a witness in matters that had been confided to him as a priest, though not in the confessional, and though O'Brien was not one of his parishioners. In this determination he was publicly upheld by Archbishops Croke and Walsh. A warrant was issued for his arrest, producing great excitement among the Catholics of Ireland. Riots attended its execution at Youghal, and a fisherman named Hanlon was killed by a bayonet-thrust, for which the coroner's jury found Ward, the constable, and Somerville, the inspector who ordered the charge, guilty of murder.

Father Keller, an old priest, who had not long been an adherent of the National League, was examined before Judge Boyd in Dublin on March 19, and, on persisting in his refusal to give information regarding O'Brien and the disposal of his assets, was committed to Kilmainham Jail for contempt of court. Rev. Matthew Ryan, president of the Herbertstown branch of the National League, in like manner, refused to attend the Court of Bankruptcy in Dublin to give evidence in the case of Thomas Moroney, a bankrupt, whose assets had disappeared. The police were sent to arrest him on March 27, but were unable to find him. His friends promised that he would appear in court if the police were withdrawn, and a few hours later he was conducted in a great procession to the train at Limerick, and was received by another enthusiastic concourse in Dublin. The tenants of the entire district declared that they would pay no rent until their "general," as they called Father Ryan, should be released. A constable named Dorney refused to take part in the arrest, saying that, when asked to lay hands on a priest of his Church, he would go with the English Government no further. Father Ryan was the leader of the tenantry on the O'Grady estate at Herbertstown, who had barricaded their dwellings, and were evicted with much violence, while Capt. Plunkett, divisional magistrate for the south of Ireland, ordered Father Ryan to be removed, and several times commanded the police to charge into the jeering crowd. The house of Honora Crimmins, a widow, was entered through the roof, and the inmates were handcuffed and taken to jail, Capt. Plunkett refusing to admit them to bail. When the police and military were returning, the people groaned at them from the roadside, whereupon another charge was ordered by Capt. Plunkett, and many were severely beaten, among those who were struck being Mr. Condon, a member of Parliament, and two English gentlemen. Evictions were carried out with violence also on the Brooke property at Coolgreany, in County Wexford, where the tenants were thoroughly united, and the ejectments did not take place without physical resistance and riotous scenes.

Mr. O'Brien was subsequently brought into court on a bench warrant, and was convicted by the magistrates, and sentenced to three months' imprisonment. He appealed under the act, and at quarter sessions the appeal was rejected, and he was imprisoned in Cork jail, and afterward in the prison at Tullamore. He thereby became a hero in Ireland. The efforts of the jailors to subject him to the treatment of a common criminal were chronicled daily, and were vigorously denounced. Even in England it was described as "moral torture" by Mr. Childers and his party associates, although the Liberals in their attempt at coercive government after the Phœnix Park murders had treated Irish members of Parliament in the same way. Mr. O'Brien refused to change his clothes for the prison garb, but by a ruse they were purloined from him while he was bathing. He then went to bed, and refused to rise, although put on bread-and-water diet, until his friends smuggled into the prison another suit. Several other orators were prosecuted and convicted of similar offenses, and all of them appealed to the higher court.

The appointment of Mr. Balfour in the place of Sir Michael Hicks-Beach, the retirement of Sir Redvers Buller, and, finally, the appointment of Col. King-Harman as parliamentary Under-Secretary for Ireland, as well as many minor appointments and the increasing harshness of the authorities, indicated the return to a policy of coercion. Yet, after obtaining the crimes act, the Government hesitated to proclaim the National League. While the bill was under discussion, Archbishop Croke and the priests of the see of Cashel published a formal protest against such a "hateful and insulting measure," which was declared to be causeless and savagely stringent, likely to "lead to the commission of crimes exceeding in number and magnitude those which it is ostensibly designed to check or prevent," and a measure that, "by placing irresponsible power of a repressive and necessarily irritating character in the hands of an unfriendly viceroy and a set of prejudiced, self-seeking, and often sanguinary officials, will bring the administration of the law into still greater contempt than it unfortunately is at present." The agitation against the act in England culminated in a monster meeting in Hyde Park, London, in which nearly 100,000 people took part.

The contest between the Unionists and the advocates of Irish self-government was embittered by a series of articles published in the London "Times" under the title of "Parnellism and Crime," that had no slight effect in rallying the wavering, both among the Liberal Unionists and in the Conservative party, on the side of the Government. These articles showed the connection between the Irish party and its associate organization in America, which was stigmatized as a thoroughly revolutionary society, and sought to connect the Nationalist leaders with the political murders and dynamite plots of the Irish revolutionists. A letter was published on April 18 in fac-simile with the signature of Charles S. Parnell, and supposed to have been addressed to Patrick Egan, in which the denunciations uttered at the time against the murderers of Lord Frederick Cavendish and Mr. Burke are excused as being the

only course open to the Land Leaguers. The letter was declared by Mr. Parnell to be a forgery. The Irish members repelled in Parliament the insinuations made against them. Mr. Dillon was accused in the "Times" of associating with murderers. His refutation was characterized as a "tissue of falsehoods." Sir Charles Lewis, a Tory, called the attention of the House to the breach of privilege. The leader of the House, W. H. Smith, pronounced the statement no breach of privilege, but offered to institute a prosecution against the editor for criminal libel in order to satisfy the Irish members, who now pressed for an inquiry in Parliament. Col. Saunderson, a leader of the north of Ireland Tories, in a speech in Parliament accused the Irish members of associating with men that they knew to be murderers. When the Speaker declined to call him to order for the expression, T. Healy gave Col. Saunderson the lie, and was suspended. Mr. Sexton called him a "willful and cowardly liar," but the Speaker now interfered and compelled Col. Saunderson to retract. The latter, among other statements in support of his assertion, said that Mr. Parnell had partaken of a banquet in America with Patrick Egan, who, he said, was president of the Clanna-Gael. Mr. Egan sent a denial, saying that it was the Irish National League of America of which he was elected president, and that he knew nothing of the Clan-na-Gael. This he followed with an offer to Mr. Balfour to surrender himself for trial on any charges that might be brought against him in connection with the Phœnix Park murders or other crimes, if he were guaranteed that the venue should be in Dublin where the crimes took place. Mr. Balfour replied that no such assurance could be given.

The "unwritten law" of the League was more effectually enforced in 1887 than ever before. Boycotting was more stringently applied against landlords, "land-grabbers," and "grass-grabbers," but the edicts of the League were more faithfully obeyed than formerly. The names of boycotted persons and those who had committed breaches of discipline were openly announced, and the resolutions of censure published in the newspapers. Mr. Balfour, in August, in defending the decision of the Government to proclaim the National League, stated that there were 5,000 boycotted persons in Ireland. He asserted that men were boycotted for not joining the League, but was challenged to cite an instance. Mr. Gladstone in the debate over the crimes bill denied that there was anything unlawful or immoral in "exclusive dealing." The Home-Rulers compared the plan of campaign with trade-unionism, pointing out that the lands which the farmers sought by combined action to secure at a fair rent had been made valuable by their own labor and capital, and that the landlords had for generations, in the form of enhanced rents, confiscated the works of reclamation, the buildings, and the other improvements contributed by the tenants.

The League interfered not only between landlords and tenants, but between the tenant-farmers and their laborers, requiring the farmers to supply garden-plots, or in lieu of them seed and manure. Many persons who had incurred the censure of the local branches of the League published abject apologies for their misconduct. The leaders of the National League could boast, as they have in former years, that never was a similar movement carried on with less violence and fewer excesses. The annual return of agrarian outrages reported to the Government was 1,066 in 1866, against 944 during the previous year. The number of cases in which the offenders were convicted was 64, the number of cases in which they were made amenable, but not convicted, was 87, and the number of cases in which they were neither convicted nor made amenable was 899. The most prevalent offense was sending threatening letters. There were 70 cases of incendiary fires in Munster and 6 murders, in one of which a conviction was obtained. Another murder was reported from Connaught, but none occurred in Ulster or Leinster.

Many of the tenants were unwilling to expose themselves to the danger of eviction by joining their poorer neighbors in refusing to pay rent when the local branch of the League ordered a general reduction. Most of these secretly paid their rent, but regretted it whenever the evictions began, and begged to have it refunded or to be served with judicial notices like the rest.

Proclamation of the National League.—On August 19 a proclamation was issued by the Lord Lieutenant in council declaring the Irish National League to be dangerous, on the ground that it "in parts of Ireland promotes and incites to acts of violence and intimidation and interferes with the administration of the law."

The first notable prosecution under the crimes act was that of William O'Brien, member of Parliament and Lord Mayor of Dublin, for inciting persons to obstruct the sheriff's bailiffs in the discharge of their duty in connection with evictions on the estate of the Countess of Kingston, in speeches delivered at Mitchelstown on the 9th and 10th of August. The Mitchelstown estate is a large one, with 750 tenants besides the people of the town. The agricultural tenants demanded a reduction of 20 per cent., and when it was refused adopted the plan of campaign. John O'Connor, Dr. Tanner, and William O'Brien collected the rents, and Mr. Condon spent several months among the tenants. Proceedings were begun in January against the principal tenants, and in February against the shop-keepers of the town who supported the plan. The farmers cleared their farms and ceased all cultivation and the towns-people suspended trading operations. As on many other estates where

the tenants organized under the plan of campaign, the evictions were not carried out. Mr. O'Brien was cited to appear for trial at Mitchelstown on September 9; but the proceedings were begun without him, while a monster meeting assembled from all the neighboring country, and Irish and English members of Parliament came to utter condemnation of the enforcement of coercion. When the meeting was opened, some policemen demanded a passage through the dense crowd for a Government stenographer, the same who in the court had testified to O'Brien's utterances, such as "I am firmly convinced that if these evictions go on they will end not in the destruction of the tenants, but in the destruction of this system of landlordism," and "There is nobody to oppose except a parcel of broken-down landlord robbers and the base blood-suckers and hirelings that cling to them." The constables attempted to force a way for the police reporter, but the horsemen at the edge of the throng drew closer together. The police then drew their sticks, but received blow for blow. A larger body came up and endeavored with clubs and bayonets to make a passage through the crowd. The peasants resisted, and many were beaten on both sides. Finally, the police retreated to their barracks. Some stones were thrown after them, but no one pursued; yet when safe in the building they mounted to the upper story and fired at persons standing at a distance in the square below. An old man named Riordan, who had already received a blow from the musket of a fleeing constable, was instantly killed by a bullet, while another man named Shinnick and a boy of the name of Casey were mortally wounded. In the investigation before the coroner's jury, Mr. Harrington, member of Parliament, cross-examined witnesses from among the police force, and established the fact that the shooting was wanton and unprovoked. The jury brought in a verdict of willful murder against Inspector Brownrigg who gave the order and the constable who killed Riordan; but the officers of the Government would not place them under arrest or bring them to trial. The outcry raised over the affair in England as well as Ireland, and the rallying word, "Remember Mitchelstown," uttered by Mr. Gladstone to his followers, caused the Government to halt in the policy of terrorism and military violence with which they sought to combat the plan of campaign, and to devise other methods against the National movement. On September 20 the Lord Lieutenant in council issued orders under the crimes act prohibiting and suppressing the National League in the county of Clare and parts of Galway, Kerry, Cork, and Wexford, embracing about two hundred of the eighteen hundred branches of the League. Soon afterward the proclamation was extended over eighteen Irish counties, including the whole of Cork, Kerry, and Wexford, Kings County, and Dublin. Although unable to destroy the organization, the Government made numerous arrests. T. D. Sullivan, the new Lord Mayor of Dublin, was arrested for publishing in the "Nation" a report of the proceedings of suppressed branches of the League. The first case against him was dismissed on the technical point that there was no evidence of the meeting except the report; but the decision was overruled, and he was tried again on a similar charge, sentenced to two months' imprisonment as a first-class misdemeanant, and lodged in Richmond jail on December 2. Some of the Irish orators against whom warrants and summonses were taken out evaded arrest by going to England. Mr. Dillon and some of the other leaders transferred their work of agitation to English soil. Mr. Parnell took no part in the extra-parliamentary action of the party during the year, but hid himself from public notice after the close of the session, as he was an invalid and in need of rest. As a check to the English Radicals, who defiantly engaged in the work in Ireland that Irishmen could not continue without going to prison, Wilfrid Blunt was convicted at Woodford, and incarcerated on a criminal sentence for inciting to resist the law. He had held a meeting to denounce the cruelty of the evictions on Lord Clanricarde's estate in spite of the warnings of the authorities, and when it was roughly broken up by the police not only he and many other men, but his wife, Lady Anne Blunt, was brutally treated.

The Highland Crofters.—The grievances of the crofters and cottars in the Highlands, and disturbances connected therewith, engaged the attention of the Government as well as of the local authorities all through the year. In the last week of 1886 nine men were tried at Inverary for rioting at Easdale, in Argyleshire. Five of the charges were withdrawn, but four were proved, two of the prisoners being sentenced to sixty days' and two others to thirty days' imprisonment. In the first week of January two other sets of rioters were tried. In the case of eight Garalapin prisoners the charges against two were withdrawn, and the other six were acquitted. Seven Herabusta crofters were tried, of whom three were sentenced to two months' and four to one month's imprisonment. At the same time the crofters were encouraged in their resistance to the law and its officers by meetings of their sympathizers both in Edinburgh and Glasgow. Some time afterward a little excitement was caused by the arrest of two Skye crofters when in bed, and after that it was found possible to serve notices in Skye without opposition. The tenants on the Ellore estate, in Aberdeenshire, following the example of Ireland, adopted the plan of campaign, and the speeches of Michael Davitt in Dornoch, Dingwall, and at other places in the Highlands, tended to keep the excitement alive. Further encouragement was given to the malcontents by decisions partially favorable to the crofters in an action for wrongful apprehension raised against Sheriff Ivory. Meantime, a branch of the Land League was established in Skye; and a conference of land law reformers was held at Oban. There was a fresh outbreak in the island of Lewis in November, when an army of discontented and impoverished cottars made a raid on the deerforest of Lochs, and slaughtered a number of deer. The prompt appearance on the scene of disturbance of the gunboat "Seahorse" checked the raiders, and the ringleaders subsequently surrendered themselves. At the same time there was a similar and sympathetic movement on the opposite mainland. Certain pasturelands belonging to the Duke of Sutherland, at Clashmore, in Assynt, were seized by crofters and cottars, who drove their cattle on to them day after day. The crofters claimed the land as theirs, alleging that their forefathers had been unjustly deprived of it. They also objected to the best of the land being rented "to a man of means who had hotels in different parts of the country." Fires occurred at more than one of the Duke's farm-steadings, which aroused suspicions of incendiarism. To bring the offenders to justice in this case was not so easy as in the case of the Lewis cottars. The ringleaders escaped to the hills, and concealed themselves in caves which strangers could not reach. At length the gunboat "Seahorse" was dispatched to Lochinver to protect and support the police in the discharge of their duty, and arrangements were made for vindicating the authority of the law in the disturbed district. The labors of the commissioners under the crofters act of 1886 were continued during the year. In Sutherland and Caithness, in Skye and Uist, rents have been judicially reduced by twenty, thirty, and even fifty per cent., and arrears of rent have been wiped off in even a greater ratio. Yet the crofters are not satisfied, and the discontent continues. In South Uist, Lady Cathcart waived her claim to object to leaseholders demanding the fixing of fair rents, but the leaseholders cared little for the concession. In its latest phase the relief has taken the form of a proposal for the emigration of necessitous crofters to British Columbia with the aid of the Government. The proposal is to advance £150,000 to enable 1,250 families (or about 6,000 persons) to settle on the rich lands of the western continent. It is noteworthy that these disturbances in the Highlands have increased the amount of smuggling in these regions. For the protection of crofters whose cases were under consideration, a short amending act was passed by Parliament. It provided that, where a crofter had applied to the commissioners to fix a fair rent for his holding, his effects could not be seized or sold for rent until his case had been heard and disposed of.

Socialist Agitation.—The misery in London, where the unemployed increased constantly during the year, and great numbers of homeless people from the provinces, as well as the

GREAT BRITAIN AND IRELAND.

metropolis, were obliged to sleep in the streets, gave the Socialists an opportunity to preach their doctrines, and address petitions to the authorities. Trafalgar Square, where the destitute chiefly congregated, was made the scene of several demonstrations, until finally, at the solicitation of the business people of the neighborhood, the police forbade its use for the purpose on the ground that it was the property of the crown, and had never been given to the public as a park or thoroughfare. Mr. Gladstone had shortly before, in connection with the Mitchelstown disturbances, enunciated the doctrine that the people have a right to determine whether the police are justified in interfering with them, and, if there appear to be no justification, may lawfully resist. The Socialists and the unemployed determined to carry out this principle, and hold their meeting in Trafalgar Square in spite of Sir Charles Warren's proclamation. Mr. Gladstone recanted the doctrine that he had upheld in his speech at Nottingham, and counseled the people of London to give way to the police pending the trial of any legal questions that might be raised. On the Sunday set for the meeting, November 13, Sir Charles Warren, using the tactical knowledge that he had gained in warfare, placed strong guards at all the points of approach. The processions attempted to make their way through with no success. In the collisions with the police many persons were hurt. The Socialist leaders and orators, and Cunninghame Graham, a Scotch member of Parliament, in sympathy with them, were arrested and tried on charges of resisting the police or making incendiary speeches. Many of them, including Mr. Graham, were convicted, and sentenced to imprisonment, in most cases for one or two months.

The Parliamentary Session.—The second session of the 12th Parliament of Victoria was opened on January 27. The speech from the throne alluded to the Bulgarian difficulties; to the task undertaken in Egypt "which is not yet accomplished; but substantial advance has been made towards the assurance of external and internal tranquillity"; and to operations conducted in Burmah by the troops "with bravery and skill for the purpose of extirpating brigandage." The condition of Ireland was said to still require serious attention, for though "grave crimes have happily been rarer during the last few months than during a similar period in the preceding year," yet attention would be called to proposals for reforms in legal procedure which seem necessary to secure the prompt and efficient administration of the criminal law, because "the relations between the owners and occupiers of land, which in the early part of the autumn exhibited signs of improvement, have since been seriously disturbed in some districts by organized attempts to incite the latter class to combine against the fulfillment of their legal obligations." The legislative programme comprised, besides the promised coercion act for Ireland, bills for the improvement of local government in England and Scotland, to be followed, if circumstances should render it possible, by a similar measure for Ireland; a bill to cheapen private bill legislation; measures to facilitate the transfer of lands, to secure allotments to small householders, and to provide for the readier sale of glebelands; a bill altering the method of levying tithes in England and Wales; measures for the reform of the universities, defining the powers of the Secretary of State, and amending criminal procedure in Scotland; and measures for the regulation of railway rates and for preventing the fraudulent use of merchandise marks.

As soon as an opportunity occurred Lord Randolph Churchill explained his position in the crisis that preceded the convening of Parliament. He said he was pledged to a policy of retrenchment, and resigned his post as Chancellor of the Exchequer because he was asked to agree to an expenditure of £31,000,000 on the army and navy, which was £6,000,000 more than the average between 1874 and 1884, besides large supplementary estimates. He took exception at the wasteful methods pursued in the army and navy administration, and at the adventurous foreign policy that was sanctioned by the other members of the Cabinet. There were other matters of grave importance, he said, on which he differed from Lord Salisbury, yet they were susceptible of accommodation.

In carrying through the new coercion act the Government had not merely Mr. Parnell and his party to contend with, but Mr. Gladstone and the main division of the Liberal party. After a struggle which lasted over two months, when only six clauses had been considered in committee, closure was applied by a majority of 108, and the bill was passed by the House of Commons without further debate, and in substantially the same form by the House of Lords. The law revives and strengthens the power of the authorities given under the former crimes act to hold preliminary inquiries and examine witnesses though no person be accused. The Attorney-General may direct any resident magistrate to make such inquiries when an offense has been committed in a proclaimed district, and to bind the witnesses to appear at the court of sessions. A witness is not excused from giving evidence tending to criminate himself, but his confessions can not be used against him in criminal proceedings. Summary jurisdiction is given in cases (1) of taking part in a criminal conspiracy to induce any person not to fulfill legal obligations, or not to let, hire, use, or occupy land, or not deal with, work for, or hire any person, or to interfere with the administration of the law; (2) of using violence or intimidation to cause any person to do what he has a legal right to abstain from doing or to abstain from any lawful act, or toward any

GREAT BRITAIN AND IRELAND.

person in consequence of such acts; and (8) of taking part in a riot or unlawful assembly, taking forcible possession of any house or land within twelve months after the execution of any writ of possession, or assaulting, resisting, or obstructing a sheriff, bailiff, constable, or process-server in the execution of his duty. The high court shall order a special jury on the application of the Attorney-General or the defendant. It shall also, on application of the Attorney-General, order the removal of a trial to any county that the Attorney-General may name, but may modify the order on the application of the defendant if it appear that the trial can be most fairly had in another court. The Lord Lieutenant in council may proclaim any specified part of Ireland. The proclamation can be determined by a resolution of either house of Parliament. If the Lord Lieutenant is satisfied that any association exists that is formed for the commission of crime, or of carrying on operations for or by the commission of crime, or of encouraging or aiding persons to commit crime, or of promoting or inciting to acts of violence or intimidation, or of interfering with the administration of the law or disturbing the maintenance of law and order, he may issue a special proclamation declaring such association to be dangerous. Every special proclamation must be laid before Parliament within seven days, or, if Parliament is not sitting, within seven days of its convening, and if either house pass an address that the proclamation shall not remain in force, it shall be deemed to have expired. A proclamation issued when Parliament is not sitting expires in a week, unless a session be called within twenty days. After the issuance of a special proclamation, as long as it continues unrevoked and unexpired, the Lord Lieutenant may issue an order to prohibit or suppress in any specified district the association that he has proclaimed as dangerous. From the date of such order, any one participating in any meeting or proceedings of the unlawful association, publishing its notices, or contributing to its objects may be prosecuted before a court of summary jurisdiction. The term "association" is made to include any combination of persons, whether known by any distinctive name or not. The peace preservation act of 1886 is continued in force for five years, with the modification that under a warrant to search for arms or ammunition any houses in a specified town or municipal ward may be searched without being specified. A criminal case may be removed to a court of assize in any county in England as well as Ireland, or to the English Court of Queen's Bench or Central Criminal Court. The removal may be made before any indictment has been found, and the grand jury of the district to which the trial has been removed may inquire into the case and determine it in the same manner as if the crime had been committed in the county or district of Ireland or England to which the trial has been removed.

Persons convicted of offenses over which summary jurisdiction is exercised are punishable with imprisonment, with or without hard labor, for a term not exceeding six months, and have the right of appeal, which appeal shall be heard by a county court judge, chairman of quarter sessions, or recorder, sitting as a sole judge. A court of summary jurisdiction consists of a district court in Dublin, and elsewhere of two resident magistrates, one of whom must have legal knowledge sufficient to satisfy the Lord Lieutenant. The term "intimidation" is defined as including any words or acts intended or calculated to put any person in fear of an injury or danger to himself, or to any member of his family, or to any person in his employment, or in fear of any injury to or loss of property, business, employment, or means of living.

Besides the coercion act, the only parts of the ministerial programme that passed into legislative shape were the acts for laborers' allotments, the act for the protection of merchandise marks, and the acts for improving Scotch criminal procedure and strengthening the office of Secretary for Scotland. Besides these an act was passed for the regulation of coal-mines. The merchandise-marks act not only gives additional protection to the use of trade-marks and names in Great Britain, but, in pursuance of the stipulations of a treaty lately concluded, empowers the custom-house authorities to detain goods that have forged trade-marks, false trade descriptions, or marks, names, or descriptions that are illegal under the act.

The allotments act empowers the sanitary authorities in any parish, where the laboring population are unable to obtain suitable land at reasonable rents, to lease or purchase land at a price that will be recouped by the rent of the allotments, to be petitioned out among the laborers who desire it. If land can not be obtained otherwise, it can be compulsorily taken at a price to be assessed by arbitration, but no parks or gardens or railroad, canal, or mining lands can be thus taken.

A margarine act was passed, requiring every consignment of artificial butter, whether imported or manufactured in the country, to be made under the name of margarine, every package to be thus marked in durable letters, and every parcel of the substance exposed for retail sale to bear the same label in clear and conspicuous characters. Imitation butter, whether mixed with butter or not, is subject to the act. Food inspectors and medical or police officers may take samples to analyze. Every factory where artificial butter is made must be registered. Offenses under the act are punishable with a fine up to £20 for the first, £50 for the second, and £100 for subsequent convictions. There was a spirited discussion as to whether butter substitutes should be called "butterine," under which name considerable quantities were sold, or "margarine," a name that it was thought would repel buyers, but the wishes of the dairy-farmers and their friends the landlords prevailed.

Sugar Bounties.—The British Government induced the Continental powers to enter into a conference to consider the question of sugar bounties, which was held in London under the presidency of Baron de Worms. The delegates condemned the system of bounties, and reported in favor of a system of refining and manufacturing in London, the Belgian representatives alone objecting. They all agreed to a protocol, signed in December, 1871, recommending their governments to remove the bounties. The governments will inform the British Government before March 1, 1888, whether they accept the proposals and in what manner they propose to carry them into practice. On April 5, 1888, the conference is to reassemble, and exchange ratifications of the convention that was annexed to the protocol. The first article of the convention requires the contracting parties to take or to propose to their respective legislatures such measures as shall constitute an absolute guarantee that no bounty, direct or indirect, shall be paid on the exportation of sugar. The second article specifies the mode in which this principle is to be applied by the imposition of a duty on sugar manufactured in bond. The third article embodies the reserves made by the Belgian delegates, who prefer to retain, with certain modifications, the system in use in Belgium, while making concessions in the direction of an increase of legal yield and a lowering of the tax. The Belgian objection is based on the considerations that a strict excise supervision is expensive to the state and injurious to the industry. The French delegates recorded reserves in regard to the Belgian proposals, on the ground that they did not afford a guarantee for the total suppression of bounties. The German, Austro-Hungarian, Italian, Spanish, Dutch, and Russian delegates recorded their adhesion to these reserves.

GREECE, a constitutional monarchy in southeastern Europe. The present Constitution was framed by a constituent assembly convoked for the purpose in 1864, and was sworn to by the King on Nov. 28, 1864. The legislative authority appertains to a single chamber of deputies. After Delyannis had plunged the country into debt, flooded it with depreciated paper-money, summoned the citizens from their agricultural and commercial pursuits to take their ranks in the army, and disorganized the entire business of the country to carry out a policy of bellicose menace and bravado that injured, rather than benefited, the international position of Greece, his Cabinet was turned out in order to escape European intervention, and Tricoupis formed a ministry on May 21, 1886. The first aim of the new minister was to pay off the debt, restore the currency to a gold basis, and still keep up the army in a state of military efficiency. The necessity of economy and reform furnished a reason for important

changes in the legislative system, which were enacted by the Chamber through dread of an immediate dissolution. The adoption of *scrutin de liste* has rendered the deputies more independent of their constituents in respect to patronage, the expenditure of public money on local improvements, and especially the equalization and thorough collection of taxes. The law of June 24, 1886, fixes the number of deputies at 150, instead of 245, as before.

The ministry is composed of the following members: President of the Council, Minister of Finance, and Minister of War, C. Tricoupis; Minister of Justice, D. S. Voulpiotis; Minister of the Interior, C. Lombardos; Minister of Worship and Public Instruction, P. Manetas; Minister of Foreign Affairs, E. Dragoumis; Minister of Marine, G. Theotokis.

The reigning sovereign is King Georgios I, born Dec. 24, 1845, son of King Christian of Denmark, who was elected by the National Assembly on March 30, 1863, and confirmed by France, Great Britain, and Russia, the three protecting powers. The heir-apparent is Prince Konstantinos, born Aug. 2, 1868.

Area and Population.—The area of Greece is 64,689 square kilometres, or 25,014 miles. The population before the annexation of the district of Arta, Trikkala, and Larissa, in Thessaly and Epirus, under the treaty of June 14, 1881, was in 1879, when the last census was taken, 1,679,775. Adding the population of the annexed districts, as ascertained by an enumeration in 1881, the total population of the kingdom is 1,979,561, inclusive of soldiers, seamen, and citizens abroad. The number of male inhabitants is 1,040,526, and of females 989,085. The civil population is 1,948,174, which is divided into 1,902,800 Orthodox Greek Christians, 14,677 other Christians, 5,792 Israelites, 24,165 Mohammedans, and 740 others. Athens, the capital, contained 84,903 inhabitants in April, 1884.

Finances.—The budget for the year 1887 estimates the total revenue at 94,656,907 drachmas or francs, and the expenditure at 93,288,871 drachmas. The internal debt on Jan. 1, 1887, amounted to 385,776,031 drachmas, and the total public debt to 424,429,713 drachmas, not including 89,814,866 drachmas of paper money. The war preparations of 1886 had added more than 100,000,000 drachmas to the debt. The Chamber in June, 1887, authorized a loan of 150,000,000 drachmas for the liquidation of the floating debt.

The Army and Navy.—The army in 1887 consisted of 1,787 officers, 7,802 non-commissioned officers and musicians, and 18,091 soldiers, making altogether 27,180 men, with 3,509 horses and 120 cannon. The strength of the army for 1888 is fixed at 26,340 men, and the military expenditure at 16,988,500 drachmas, against 18,074,069 drachmas in 1887.

Commerce.—The industry of Greece is largely agricultural. There are 250,000 acres devoted to tobacco, cotton, etc.; 1,000,000 acres to grain-crops; 250,000 acres to vines; 125,000 acres to currants; and 325,000 acres to the olive-culture. The principal imports are cereals and textiles, and the principal exports dried currants, olive-oil, lead, wine, silver-ore, dye and tanning stuffs, and zinc.

The merchant navy on Jan. 1, 1887, comprised 74 steamers, of 33,318 tons, and 8,164 sailing-vessels, of 239,861 tons, exclusive of about 6,000 coasting-vessels. The number of vessels that entered Greek ports in 1885 was 10,597, of 2,431,589 tons; the number that cleared was 10,593, of 2,430,518 tons.

The railroads in operation on Oct. 1, 1887, had a total length of 615 kilometres.

The state telegraphs in 1885 had a total length of 6,603 kilometres, with 7,675 kilometres of wire. The number of internal dispatches was 544,556; of international dispatches, 181,991; the receipts, 1,065,809 drachmas; the expenses, 993,800 drachmas.

The number of letters sent through the post-office in 1885 was 6,182,571; postal-cards, 167,321; registered letters, 381,804; journals and printed matter, 4,792,522. The receipts were 1,034,246 drachmas, and the expenses 695,633 drachmas.

General Election.—In the previous elections, which returned Delyannis to power, Tricoupis, who was then Prime Minister, was censured by his followers for not using the customary official pressure and sending military guards to protect the ministerial candidates and overawe the opposing factions. Elections under the new electoral law were held in January, 1887. The Prime Minister refrained as before from administrative interference, yet so discredited had Delyannis and his party become that 100 ministerial candidates were elected, to only 50 of the opposition.

GUATEMALA, a republic of Central America. (For details relating to area and population, see " Annual Cyclopædia " for 1886.)

Government.—The President is Gen. Manuel Lisandro Barillas. The Cabinet is composed of the following ministers: Foreign Affairs, Don Lorenzo Montúfar; Public Instruction, M. M. A. Herrera; Interior and Justice, F. Anguiano; Public Works, S. Barrutia; Finance, Don Mauricio Rodriguez; War, C. Mendizábal. The Guatemalan Minister at Washington is Don Francisco Lainfiesta, the Consul-General at New York is Jacob Baiz, the Consul at San Francisco, Don José M. Romá. The United States Minister for all Central America, resident at Guatemala, is Hon. Henry C. Hall, and the Consul-General James R. Hosmer.

The strength of the regular army is 2,500 men, and that of the militia is 20,000.

Finances.—Prior to the consolidation of the foreign debt of Guatemala, assented to by the bondholders at their London meeting of Dec. 3, 1887, the national indebtedness was composed of a home debt amounting to $5,504,880, and a foreign debt of $5,702,843, constituting a total indebtedness of $11,207,723. By virtue of the agreement made with the holders of Guatemalan 1856 and 1869 loans, the latter have been consolidated, and, together with accumulated interest, converted into a new 4 per-cent.-bond issue, for which a sinking fund has been provided at the rate of ½ per cent. per annum. Simultaneously it was resolved to convert the home debt into a 6-per-cent.-bond issue, with a sinking fund of 1 per cent. per annum. The customs revenue was pledged as a security for both debts.

The Government received, early in 1887, a proposal from the banking firm of J. P. Nathan & Co., Guatemala, in behalf of the Paris Société de Dépôts et de Comptes-Courants on the one hand, and of the London banking firm of S. S. Thomas, T. Bonar & Co. on the other, for the creation by the two concerns jointly of a national bank in the city of Guatemala, with a share capital of £1,000,000, such national bank to be authorized to issue bank-notes of a face value of $1 to $200, both inclusive.

Postal Service.—There were in operation in 1886 129 post-offices, dispatching altogether 8,400,876 items of mail-matter, the receipts being $56,026 and the expenses $50,597.

Commerce.—The imports and exports for five years have been as follows, in thousands of dollars:

YEARS.	Imports.	Exports.
1882	2,652	3,719
1883	2,421	3,719
1884	3,330	4,988
1885	3,798	6,070
1886	3,587	6,736

The chief articles exported in 1886 were: coffee, $5,883,417; sugar, $352,556; hides and skins, $170,474; India-rubber, $113,807; and there were shipped besides, bananas, sarsaparilla, cocoa, indigo, wool, and some gold-dust; furthermore, silver coin to the amount of $118,261.

The American trade with Guatemala presents the following changes:

FISCAL YEAR.	Import into the United States.	Domestic export to Guatemala.
1886	$1,957,632	$323,840
1887	2,548,713	558,179

The increased import figure is due to the rise in coffee.

Railroads.—There are in running order the Champerico-Retalhulen line of railway from San José to Escuintla, 45 kilometres in length, and the Escuintla-Guatemala line, 71 kilometres. The interoceanic line is being built.

Telegraphs.—The total length of telegraph in operation is 2.905 kilometres, with 77 offices, which in 1886 forwarded 811,976 messages, the receipts being $148,231 and the expenses $115,899. There is direct communication with all Mexican telegraph-offices at minimum rates.

Extradition.—The extradition treaty between

the United States and Guatemala having been ratified by the Senate at Washington, a later convention, styled "an additional article," was the subject of a message of President Cleveland to the latter, accompanied by his recommendation that it be ratified. The additional article reads: "Neither Government shall be required to deliver up its own citizens under the stipulations of this convention."

Mexico and Guatemala.—The substance of a protocol arranged between Mexico and Guatemala in October is that the Government of Guatemala will appoint a minister plenipotentiary to go to the city of Mexico, there to negotiate with the plenipotentiary appointed by the Mexican Government a treaty providing for a mixed commission to decide the claims of citizens of one country against those of the other; also to negotiate a treaty of commerce providing for an absolutely free exchange of the natural products of the two countries.

Events of 1887.—The President of Guatemala on June 29 established a temporary dictatorship by issuing the following decree:

ARTICLE I. The Executive assumes control of the country and suspends the action of the Constitution.

ART. II. The tribunals of the republic will continue to sit under the laws in force on March 1 of the present year.

ART. III. A constituent assembly is hereby convoked to reconsider the reforms in the Constitution decreed on Dec. 11, 1879, and those issued on Oct. 20, 1885, which assembly shall meet on October 1 next.

ART. IV. This decree shall come into force from the moment it is issued.

The decree was signed by President Barillas and all his ministers, and it became the pretext for a rising against the constituted authorities. A revolutionary band formed in Valencia and traversed the departments of Santa Rosa, Jalapa, and Guatemala, but met no sympathizers. Finally, they dispersed and made toward Alzatate for the purpose of thence passing to the Soledad forests. Some, however, came in and surrendered to the Government forces. Of the others, several were captured by the residents, while the remainder made toward Salvador, but were captured before they crossed the frontier. While this news was being received, a telegram arrived saying that Don Vicente Castaneda with a force from Chiantla had attacked Huchuetenango, but was driven off, leaving a lieutenant and three soldiers dead, and carrying away some wounded. Little attention was paid to the affair at the time, but under date of October 30 Gen. Barillas issued a long proclamation. He said he had summoned the Constituent Assembly and reported to it at length all matters of public importance that had occurred, trusting that very shortly the *régime* of the Constitution would again be inaugurated. "But," he added, "on the 28th of September the Government received information that a revolution was being plotted on the frontier of Salvador against the peace of Gua-

temala, and that the leaders were Messrs. Salvador Sandoval, José Aguilar, and Gen. Tinoco, a Nicaraguan officer. The Government was at the same time aware that the movement was backed by many who are averse to the actual political situation. The Government refrained from making investigations, and contented itself by sending a force against those who had appeared with arms in their hands, and who were promptly overthrown by the military commanders at Chiquimula, Jalapa, Zacapa, and Santa Rosa. The Governments of Honduras and Salvador also acted loyally and thus assisted the overthrow of the revolution. The chiefs Pineda, Arzu, Zepeda, and Juarez, were captured, and after trial were condemned and shot. During those same days an attempt was made to capture the barracks at Huchuetenango, and a two hours' fight resulted in the defeat of the rebels after a number had been killed and wounded on both sides. After their defeat a number of the rebels were captured and tried by court-martial, and Col. Vicente Castaneda and Lieuts. Ismail Diaz, José Munoz, Malias Cifuentes, and Francisco Alonzo, have been shot."

While this attempt at revolution had been preparing, the Government on September 8 felt induced to expel from the territory of the republic the Archbishop Don Ricardo Casanova. In 1878 the latter was a lawyer, but decided to become a minister of the Catholic Church. He succeeded at last in securing the archiepiscopal chair, and from that exalted position opened a serious campaign against liberal reforms, pretending that the laws granting liberty of worship, laic and non-sectarian instruction, secular cemeteries, and, in fact, all such legislation that directly or indirectly suppressed the abuses of the Catholic Church against liberty, should be stricken from the Guatemala Constitution. Ignoring the fact that the public schools were established and are controlled and paid for by the Government, the archbishop sought to interfere in their management, by issuing a decree forbidding the perusal of a book entitled "Cartas á Eugenia." Archbishop Casanova even went a step further and declared that he would not obey any authority whatever except God Almighty and the Pope.

Prosperous Condition of the Country.—During 1887 a very healthy tone was observable in business matters in the republic. Agriculturists were jubilant at the abundance of the coffee-crop, which yielded about 600,000 quintals. Money was comparatively cheap, being easily procurable at from 8 to 9 per cent. per annum on good security. The coffee-crops were the main cause of this flourishing condition, and generally a happy state of affairs prevailed.

Privileges of Steamer-Lines.—In August the Government published the following decree, declaring that all foreign merchandise, imported by vessels belonging to companies whose vessels made direct voyages, calling at the Pacific ports of the republic, shall receive a drawback of 8 per cent. on the present customs tariff; but merchandise imported by steamers of lines already established, or that may subsequently be established, between San Francisco and Panama, shall only be allowed a reduction of $2\frac{1}{10}$ per cent. of such import duties.

Central American Union.—On April 15, 1887, the treaty concluded at Guatemala between the five republics of Central America was officially published. The aim of the Diet there assembled was "to establish an intimate relationship between them, and by making the continuance of peace certain, to provide for their future final fusion into one country." The treaty contains thirty-two articles:

The first declares that perpetual peace shall exist between the republics, that all differences shall be arranged, and that in the event of this proving impossible, such differences shall be submitted to arbitration. But should armed disputes arise between two or more of the republics, the others bind themselves to observe the strictest neutrality. All the republics bind themselves to respect the independence of each state, and to prohibit the preparation in any one of armed expeditions against any of the others. Article VI provides that all citizens of the different states shall enjoy similar privileges and rights throughout all of them. The Constitutions of the states which do not contain this proviso will be reformed to make them accord with this article. Article VII stipulates that citizens of any of the Spanish-American republics may become naturalized after one year's residence, and natives of other countries after three years' residence. Under Article VIII, citizens of one republic are exempt from military or naval service in any of the others, and from forced loans or military service or duties, and they shall not be compelled, under any circumstances, to pay either ordinary or extraordinary taxes higher than those paid by the natives of the state. Article XI enables natives of any of the signatory republics to exercise in all of them, but subject to the local laws, their professions or trades without other requisite than the presentation of their documents, with proof of personality and the stamp of the office of the Executive. Article XII permits transport by land or sea between the contracting republics of all articles indigenous to or manufactured in them, and they will be exempt from all customs or taxes. This article will go into force on Sept. 19, 1890. Articles XIII to XVII establish a reciprocal freedom of navigation between the five countries; an equality in port privileges; civil, commercial, and criminal suits are placed on an equality in each state. Article XIX provides that the consular or diplomatic agents of any of the republics must act for a citizen of any of the contracting parties when called upon to do so. Article XX establishes the right of ownership in all literary productions. Article XXI provides for the entrance into the Postal Union of the five republics, and declares all printed matter free of postage. Article XXII provides for the telegraph service between the different states, and for the further reduction of present rates. Article XXIII authorizes the free exchange of official and private publications. Article XXV provides for the establishment of a general system among the five states of coinage, weights, and measures, professional and consular rules, and of the penal and civil codes. Article XXVI provides for the assembling of an international congress every two years. Article XXVII provides that the contracting parties will endeavor peacefully so to frame matters that ultimately the establishment of a Central American confederation may become possible. Consequently members of the conference to meet in 1890 will be fully authorized to act, if present obstructions have ceased

to exist. Article XXX calls upon the Governments of the different states to respect the democratic principles of the several Constitutions, and always refuse to support any second presidential terms. Articles XXX, XXXI, and XXXII provide for the term during which the treaty shall remain in force, its ratification and exchange, and the abrogation of various laws that appear contradictory to it.

GUNS FOR COAST DEFENSE. There has been for many years a discussion among the army and navy authorities of the United States relative to the best kind of guns for the defense of the coast, and also in regard to the best location for making such guns. In 1888 the Military Committee of the House of Representatives agreed to the report in favor of doing away with more than half of the arsenals maintained by the Government. Only three or four of the whole thirteen were declared necessary; and the one at Watervliet, three miles north of Albany, was one of those to be abandoned. It was afterward decided that this particular arsenal should be continued, because its situation is exceptionally fine. A tract of over 100 acres is contained in the triangle, which has a base on the Hudson river, and direct communication with the world by the Erie Canal, which runs through it. Close by there are some of the largest iron and steel mills in the country, from which supplies of raw material can be drawn. As a fortress it is one of the strongest in the country, for it can be guarded by a comparatively small force. For these reasons it is thought better to maintain this arsenal than some other that is more accessible to vessels drawing more water than is afforded by the upper half of Hudson river. Water-power is furnished from a race-way cut from the canal to the river, with a fall of 18 feet. Almost unlimited power is thus close at hand during more than five months of the year. The capacity of the arsenal in time of war was one gun-carriage complete, with limber, per day; but this capacity was often increased. These facts, and other considerations, led to the introduction of a bill by Mr. Cameron, in the United States Senate, in 1885, for the erection of two large gun-factories, one for the army, at Watervliet, and one for the navy, at Washington. This was the first practical measure proposed for the adequate protection of our sea-coast. The bill provided for the erection of the two factories at a cost of about $1,000,000 each, and also for the purchase of about 10,000 pounds of tempered steel from private firms, to be converted into cannon. At that time it was estimated that about 300 or 400 guns of various bores would be required for the forts and ships, some of these to weigh 100 tons. It was expected that each of the proposed factories would be able to turn out in a year twelve fifteen-inch guns, seventeen twelve-inch guns, and fifty six-inch guns, the annual expense being about $2,000,000. This bill did not pass the House of Representatives. Early in 1885 Senator Hawley made a report, founded on the evidence submitted by experts after investigation, recommending that the Government establish two great manufactories or foundries for casting guns for all calibers needed for service at the forts, in the navy, or in the field. It was said that the best locations for the gun-factories were the Washington Navy-yard and the Watervliet Arsenal. It was understood that this bill, as well as Senator Cameron's bill, was recommended by the special Joint Committee of the Army and Navy, who inquired into the manufacture of ordnance abroad. Neither of these bills became law. A small appropriation, however, sustained by the committee detailed by the ordnance department, made it possible for an experiment to be made at Watervliet. The work of preparation was begun in the summer of 1887. An old store-house, 400 feet in length and 60 feet in width, was changed from a two-story building to a one-story building. Foundations of the most solid masonry were laid, upon which were placed the planing, boring, and shrinking machines, the lathes, etc., which had been brought from the arsenals and foundries at West Point, South Boston, Watertown, Frankford, and Fort Monroe. The capacity of the new machinery is only two ten-inch guns, and perhaps eight six-inch guns a year. A more conservative estimate is that it will take over a year to complete one ten-inch gun, the tube being 30 feet long. The carriages for these guns are to be of the best steel instead of wood as formerly. A bill has been introduced in the present Congress which gives a larger appropriation for the work, and provides for new buildings. A rivalry between the Watervliet Arsenal and the arsenal at Frankford has hindered more prompt action in favor of the former. Skilled workmen have been imported from other workshops of the Government. It is thought that the casting of large guns by the Government is impracticable, in view of the improvements that are constantly being made by competitors in the steel trade. The question of casting ingot-steel into the form of guns has been decided by the Government officials in favor of having those who furnish the steel cast it roughly in the shape of guns. It is not likely that cupolas and foundry apparatus will be placed in the Watervliet Arsenal. The buildings will be devoted strictly to assembling and finishing the guns, jackets, rings, and other parts of the guns proper that will be furnished from the outside.

H

HAWAII, a constitutional monarchy, occupying the Hawaiian or Sandwich Islands, in the Pacific Ocean. In former times the various islands were ruled by independent mois or kings, who were absolute in authority, possessing the power of life and death. The chiefs had certain privileges accorded to them for military service, but the mass of the people were in a state of degraded servitude, the taboo system being devised to secure the authority of the chiefs, and keep the common people in subjection. The islands were united into one kingdom under Kamehameha I in 1795. His son and successor, Kamehameha II, on ascending the throne in 1819, abolished the sacred taboo, and thenceforth women occupied a position of social equality with men. The chiefs who clung to the old faith revolted, but were suppressed, and a year later Christianity was first introduced by American missionaries. Roman Catholic missionaries came soon afterward, but they were expelled, and for a time forbidden the kingdom. The King and his Queen died while visiting England in 1823. During the regency that followed, and in the early part of the reign of Kamehameha III, foreign intervention was frequent. The expulsion of Catholic priests and cruelties practiced upon them led to the interference of the French, who threatened to occupy the islands, but were forestalled by the English. The country was taken possession of under an enforced act of cession to Great Britain by Lord George Paulet in February, 1843, but was restored to the King, and independence was officially recognized by England and France on Nov. 28, 1843. Shortly afterward the United States sent a resident commissioner. The absolute power of the sovereign was curtailed by the Constitution granted by Kamehameha III in 1840, which introduced the methods of civilized nations as to courts of justice, juries, tenure of lands, and the definition and punishment of crimes and misdemeanors. The land of the kingdom, which previously had been treated as the absolute property of the King, was divided into three parts, one part being retained as crown lands, one part reserved as a source of revenue for the Government, and the rest apportioned out among the people. Most of the freeholds, by mortgage or purchase, have since passed into the possession of the whites. The Constitution of 1840 was superseded by that of 1852. On the death of Kamehameha III in 1854 he was succeeded by his nephew Alexander Liholiho, who assumed the style of Kamehameha IV. He died in 1863, leaving a widow, the philanthropic Queen Emma, and was succeeded by his brother under the name of Kamehameha V, who in 1864 proclaimed a new Constitution. The legislative power of the three estates was vested in the King and Legislative Assembly. The assembly has power to judge of the qualifications of its members, to punish them for disorderly conduct, and to compel their attendance under penalties. It has the right to make laws with the assent of the King, provided they are not repugnant to the Constitution. The principle of ministerial responsibility has usually been acted upon, though it was not embodied in the organic law. The King appoints a privy council to advise on matters of state, and can dismiss the council at his pleasure. He retained extensive prerogatives under the Constitution of 1864, including the right to make treaties, except such as involved changes in the tariff or the laws of the kingdom, which must be referred to the assembly. All laws to become valid required his assent. He was the fountain of all honors, orders, and distinctions, the commander-in-chief of the military forces, with power to place the country under martial law in case of rebellion or invasion, power to coin money and regulate the currency, and the right of granting pardons. Judges were made irremovable except on impeachment.

In 1873 King Kamehameha V died without heirs and without appointing a successor, as he had power to do under the Constitution. Prince William Charles Lunalilo was elected king by a general vote of the people, as the Constitution directed. He died the following year, leaving his private fortune to found a home for poor, aged, and infirm natives. The High Chief David Kalakaua, his competitor for the throne, was this time elected by a large majority over Queen Emma, and was proclaimed king on Feb. 18, 1874, under the style and title of Kalakaua I. His sister, Princess Liliuokalani, was named heiress-apparent, as defined by the Constitution. King Kalakaua was born Nov. 16, 1836, of pure Hawaiian blood, and related to the royal family, his mother, Keohokalole, having been a niece of Kamehameha I. He was crowned, with his wife, Queen Kapiolani, on Feb. 12, 1883.

Area and Population.—The kingdom consists of eight principal islands and several small isles. Only the islands Hawaii, Maui, Oahu, Kauai, Molokai, Lanai, and Niihau are inhabited, Kahulawe having been abandoned some years ago. The area of the inhabited islands is as follows: Hawaii, 4,850 square miles; Maui, 750 square miles; Oahu, on which is situated Honolulu, the capital, 700 square miles; Kauai, 780 square miles; Molokai, 170 square miles; Lanai, 170 square miles; and Niihau, 110 square miles. The population of the kingdom at the time of the last census, Dec. 27, 1884, was 80,578 persons, divided into 51,539 males and 29,039 females. There were 40,014 natives, 17,939 Chinese, 17,385 whites, 4,218 métis, 116 Japanese, and 956 others. The white po ulation embraced 2,066 Americans, 1,282 English, 1,600 Germans, 192 French, 9,377 Portuguese, 778 of other nationalities, and 2,040 children of foreigners born in the country. The population of Honolulu in 1884 was 20,487. The immigration in 1885 was 5,410 and the emigration 1,805. Of the immigrants 3,108 came from China and 1,961 from Japan, the importation of laborers from the latter country being encouraged at the time by the Government, the Chinese laborers who were formerly brought to cultivate the sugar plantations having proved objectionable.

About 10,000 Portuguese from the islands of St. Michaels and Madeira have been imported for the same purpose. In 1886 there were 8,725 arrivals and 2,189 departures. The passport law is very stringent, no person after a month's residence being permitted to leave the kingdom without a passport, which can not be granted to any one indebted to the Government or to a private individual, or to a defendant in a civil or criminal suit, or to any applicant against whom complaint is made that he is leaving without providing for the maintenance of his family. The native population was probably 200,000 when Capt. Cook discovered the islands in 1778. Within a century the indigenes, who are allied to the Maoris of New Zealand, have decreased to their present number.

The school law compels the attendance at school of every child between the ages of six and fifteen years. The free Government schools are supported by a tax of $2 per capita paid by every male inhabitant of the islands between the ages of twenty and sixty. For the biennial period 1884–'86 the sum spent on the schools for each year was $173,020. Every form of religion is permitted and protected. Nearly all the natives are Christians. There is a bishop of the Episcopal Church, to which the king belongs, and a Roman Catholic bishop. Large sums of money are annually expended by the Government for the cure of the lepers, about 700 in number, who are isolated in hospitals on the island of Molokai. The expenditure under this head in 1885 was $75,000. Father Damien, a Roman Catholic missionary who devoted his life to the welfare of these unfortunates, recently fell a victim to the disease.

Commerce and Agriculture.—The great range of temperature at the different elevations and the variety of soil are conducive to the cultivation of products characteristic of both southern and northern climates. Subtropical plants and shrubs are brought to great perfection on the plains near the sea-level. Sugar is the most valuable product of the kingdom. On higher elevations fruits, cereals, and grasses of the temperate zone grow well. Imported grass has supplanted the native species. The pasture-lands of Hawaii and some of the other islands are favorable for the breeding of cattle. In 1884 there were in the islands 80,140 horses, 117,613 cattle, 121,688 sheep, 21,860 goats, 2,942 mules, and 278 asses, besides hogs and a large quantity of poultry. Wild hogs, goats, and cattle, wild turkeys, pheasants, duck, plover, and quail abound in the forests that clothe the mountains and in other waste places, and excellent food-fish in the rivers of Hawaii and Kauai.

The sugar and rice crops have engaged the entire attention of cultivators until very recently, when the low price of sugar and uncertainty regarding the continuance of the reciprocity treaty with the United States have led to practical attempts to utilize the other natural resources of the country. The sugar-crop of 1886 was the largest ever obtained, amounting to 115,000 tons. The crop of 1887 was estimated at 100,000 tons.

The commerce of the Hawaiian Kingdom is, in proportion to its population, without an equal in the world. The exports for 1885 were about $125 per head of the population, New South Wales coming next in importance with about $60. The imports during 1885 were about $50 per head of the population. The imports and exports for the last four years were valued, in round numbers, as follow:

YEARS.	Imports.	Domestic exports.	Total exports.
1883	$5,624,000	$7,925,000	$8,002,000
1884	4,688,000	8,073,000	8,195,000
1885	3,881,000	8,959,000	9,069,000
1886	4,875,000	10,840,000	10,457,000

The United States monopolizes nearly the whole of the foreign trade. In 1886 94 per cent. of the total foreign commerce was with the United States, the volume of commercial transactions with this country having been $14,414,751. The United States imported merchandise of the value of $4,002,000, while $370,000 of the imports came from Great Britain, $266,000 from China and Japan, $94,000 from Germany, $11,000 from France, and $135,000 from other countries. Of the exports $10,324,000 went to the United States, while Germany took $12,000, and other countries $4,000. The importation of coin and bullion in 1886 was $1,142,946 and the exportation $43,277. The export of sugar has increased from 3,006,000 pounds in 1862 to 142,655,000 pounds in 1884, 171,350,000 pounds in 1885, and 216,223,000 pounds in 1886. The export of rice increased from 111,000 pounds in 1862 to 9,535,000 pounds in 1884, but has since fallen off to 7,867,000 pounds in 1885 and 7,389,000 pounds in 1886. The export of coffee was 146,000 pounds in 1862, but only 4,000 pounds in 1884, 2,000 pounds in 1885, and 6,000 pounds in 1886. The export of wool was 40,000 pounds in 1862, 408,000 pounds in 1884, 474,000 pounds in 1885, and 419,000 pounds in 1886. There were 58,040 bunches of bananas exported in 1884, 60,046 in 1885, and 45,862 in 1886. The number of hides of cattle and skins of calves and goats exported in 1862 was 68,537; in 1884, 49,806; in 1885, 47,636; and in 1886, 61,740. The official returns for 1885 show a sugar production of 171,350,814 pounds, out of which the United States took 171,346,625 pounds. The crop of rice for 1885 was large, though it fell short of the production of the four preceding years. The United States consumed 7,362,200 pounds out of a total production of 7,867,253 pounds. The entire exports of fresh bananas, of goat-skins, 19,782; hides, 19,045; and sheep-skins, 8,783, were consumed by America. The crop of wool, amounting to 474,121 pounds, was exported to England.

Navigation.—The port of Honolulu is the main entrepôt, $4,460,255 of the imports and $8,490,295 of the exports having passed through it in 1886. Among the 810 vessels, of 223,372 tons, that were entered at Honolulu in 1886, there were 226 American vessels, of 132,660 tons; 83 English vessels, of 35,296 tons; 8 German vessels, of 4,278 tons; 35 Hawaiian vessels, of 43,848 tons; and 8 others, of 6,290 tons. The merchant marine in 1886 numbered 58 vessels, of 13,529 tons. Of these, 15 were steamers.

Railroads, Posts, and Telegraphs.—There were 32 miles of railroad in operation in 1887, comprising a line from Mahukona across the district of Kohala, 20 miles in length, and one from Hilo to Waiakea, 5 miles long, both in the island of Hawaii, and another from the port of Kahului to Haiku and Makawao, on the island of Maui, about 7 miles in length. The extension of the line on the island of Hawaii to four times its present length is in contemplation, and a subsidy has been voted by the Legislature.

The post-office, from April 1, 1884, to March 31, 1886, forwarded 1,369,049 letters and cards, and 1,811,470 newspapers and circulars. The receipts were $63,674, and the expenditures $76,347.

The first telegraph line, 40 miles in length, was opened from Wailuku to Lahaina on Maui in 1878, and has since been extended over the entire surface of the island. There are 100 miles of telephone on the island of Oahu and 90 miles between Hilo and Kawaihae on the island of Hawaii, besides lines on the other principal islands. Nearly every house and place of business in Honolulu has a telephone.

The Reign of King Kalakaua.—Kalakaua began his reign with useful acts and benevolent resolves. His policy was declared in a speech that he made shortly after his accession to be "to increase the nation," and measures were taken to promote immigration. The attempt to introduce laborers from other Polynesian islands proved a failure. The Portuguese who were introduced were, however, most useful colonists, capable of performing all kinds of labor, notwithstanding the enervating climate which impairs the energies of men of northern countries. The Chinese poured into the country of their own accord. Although they contributed greatly to develop the productive resources of the country, they soon produced dissatisfaction, because, while remaining a foreign community and being for the major part only temporary residents, they soon acquired property, became planters and traders, and not only obtained possession of the lands of the unthrifty Kanakas, but proved unwelcome competitors to the American and European planters. In 1876, while King Kalakaua was visiting the United States, the reciprocity treaty was concluded, admitting Hawaiian raw sugar into the United States and many American products into the Sandwich islands free of

duty. This arrangement had the effect of
pouring capital into the country, chiefly from
the United States, although English and German capital was invested in plantations and
sugar-mills. Money became plentiful where
it had before been very scarce, and a period of
extravagance in private and public expenditure
began. This has been followed by a period of
depressing reaction. In 1881 Kalakaua made
a tour of the world with the object of promoting immigration. The only practical result of the mission was a convention with
Japan. The tour had the effect, however, of
enlarging the King's ideas of government and
developing his ambition for power and taste
for regal display and military parade, the first
outcome of which was the coronation ceremony of 1883. Since that time extravagance
and waste have run riot in the kingdom, attended with every form of official corruption
and legislative jobbery. The American missionaries, who once controlled a powerful party
and were potent in the affairs of the nation,
had incurred the reproach of avarice and
cruelty, but the politicians who succeeded
them were far less scrupulous. The King
in the beginning of his reign, adopting the
cry of "Hawaii for the Hawaiians," had
dismissed his missionary advisers. He gradually reverted to barbaric customs, revived pagan
dances, and fell under the influence of sooth-
sayers, while his subjects relapsed into their
old habits of sloth and vice. His Government
obtained advances from financial agents without difficulty. A royal palace was built at a
cost of $1,000,000, which was double the origi-
nal estimate. The Government ran into debt
to Claus Spreckles, the San Francisco sugar-
refiner, for money advanced to defray current
expenses to the amount of $750,000. When he
refused to lend a larger sum without security,
a syndicate of London capitalists was formed,
and negotiations for a loan of $10,000,000 were
carried on through an intermediary named
McFarlane with an English banker whose name
was Fruhlung, a member of the syndicate.
The Legislature of 1886 was appealed to for a
loan bill, and one was approved on September
1, authorizing a loan of $2,000,000, of which
$300,000 was to be used in converting 7- and
9-per-cent. bonds, $250,000 for the encour-
agement of immigration, $75,000 for water-
works, and $100,000 for sewerage in Honolulu,
$350,000 for harbor improvements, $250,000
on streets and roads, $75,000 for a highway
across Oahu, $75,000 for a cable between the
islands, $75,000 for bridges, $150,000 to repay
a special loan, $39,000 to purchase a steamer,
and $86,000 to float the loan. The act was not
satisfactory to the agent of the London syndicate, and was not acted upon. An amended
bill was introduced, and subsequently became
law. A proviso limiting the amount of borrowing to $2,000,000 was rejected, which led
to the resignation of the ministry and the formation of a new one by Walter M. Gibson, a

prominent politician, who came to the country
as agent of the Mormons for the purchase of
land when they thought of emigrating from the
United States, became a large land-owner, and
assumed the part of a champion of the rights
and interests of the native race. The loan act
was changed in its main features and was
passed, and on October 15 received the signature of the King. The Legislature, composed
for the most part of Kanakas elected by corrupt means, passed also an appropriation bill
amounting to $4,552,477, the revenue being
estimated at $2,839,924, which was much more
than the probable yield. The Cabinet consisted of Mr. Gibson and three Kanakas. The estimated expenditure was $2,830,809, and the
ministry was twice changed, Mr. Gibson always
remaining in office, before the appropriation
act was passed. The last ministry was composed as follows: Minister of the Interior, W.
M. Gibson; Minister of Foreign Affairs, R. D.
Creighton; Minister of Finance, P. Kanoa;
Attorney-General, J. T. Dare. The Cabinet
and the Legislature were alike subservient to
the King, who is said to have conceived the
ambition of extending his rule to Samoa and
other islands of the Pacific, encouraged by Gibson and by the vaticinations of a female so th-
sayer. Heathen rites were revived, and large
sums were squandered on useless and immoral
objects, while roads, bridges, and all useful
works were neglected. The celebration of the
King's fiftieth birthday consumed $75,000, and
the funeral of a relative $60,000. Places of
trust and emolument were filled with Kanakas
without regard to their character or qualifications. A steamer was bought and fitted out as
a man-of-war at a cost of about $80,000, and
was sent to convey an embassy to the King of
Samoa, to induce him to accept the "tutelage"
of Hawaii. The King bought Gatling guns and
grape cannon to fortify his palace. The appropriation act, besides the civil list of $143,-
000, which does not include $80,000 a year re-
ceived by the King and a large income of the
Queen from crown lands, contained such items
as $35,000 for household expenses, $15,000 for
palace stables, $12,500 for the Board of Gene-
alogy, which went into the pocket of the Queen's
sister in addition to her salary for a sinecure
governorship, $30,000 for the education of
Hawaiian youths abroad. A large proportion of
the appropriations were for fictitious objects,
the money going to the King and his favorites.
The white population, which pays the bulk of
the taxes, protested against these proceedings,
but Mr. Gibson, depending on the support of
the natives, who form the majority of the electors, treated them with contempt. Dissatisfaction grew and finally pervaded all classes,
the natives as well as the whites, excepting those
who profited by the general misgovernment
and corruption. An attempt to divert to the
crown the revenue of lands that had been set
aside for public improvements, and the misappropriation of money that had been voted for

the same purpose, furnished tangible subjects of complaint. International, commercial, and political jealousy was an important element in the situation, as the Americans, who had been instrumental in the development of the country and possessed the main commercial interests there, were suspicious of the English loan. Revolutionary plans were discussed. Many were in favor of proclaiming a republic, and appealing to the United States Government to annex the country. Receiving no encouragement from that quarter, the substantial citizens of Honolulu and the vicinity, representing a large part of the wealth of the kingdom, determined at least to compel the King to lay down the power that he was using to ruin the country. At this stage of affairs a scandal transpired that afforded a pretext for action. The Assembly had passed a bill to license the sale of opium. A Chinese planter and millowner from Ewa, named Tong Kee, and usually called Aki, was approached by another Chinaman and by Junius Kaae, the register of conveyances, a Kanaka, who told him that he could have the license or monopoly if he would bring $60,000 to the King. He declared in an affidavit that he took $20,000 to the palace and placed it in a drawer that the King pointed out, and at another time he and his friends and servants carried $40,000 in bags of gold, and laid it in a trunk as the King requested; and, when more was demanded, raised $11,000 more; but when he had paid it over he learned that another Chinaman had received the license, having agreed, it was supposed, to share the profits with the King. When Aki went to the King to demand his money back, Kalakaua told him that he had made it by smuggling, and it had now come to the right owner.

The Revolution.—The white residents of the capital laid their plans of revolution with deliberation. The movement was conducted by a secret political association called the League, having about 600 members on all the islands, with an executive committee in Honolulu. A volunteer organization, called the Honolulu Rifles, usually about 40 strong, was increased to 300 members, and other military bodies were formed. On June 25, as soon as 1,000 rifles, 70,000 cartridges, and other munitions had arrived from San Francisco, they took possession of the city. Minister Gibson had sent to the agents of the English loan in Australia for arms, but they arrived too late, and fell into the hands of the rebels. Kalakaua's Royal Guards, a native corps, admirably drilled in parade exercises, and costing $80,000 a year, could not be depended on, nor could the native and half-caste volunteers.

On June 30 a large meeting was held in the armory of the Honolulu Rifles, and resolutions were adopted declaring that the administration of the Government had ceased through incompetency and corruption, and calling on the King, 1. To dismiss the ministry, and invite either William L. Green, Henry Waterhouse, Godfrey

VOL. XXVII.—23 A

Brown, or Mark P. Robinson to form a Cabinet; 2. To dismiss Walter M. Gibson from every office held by him; 8. To restore the $71,000 that he had taken as a bribe for the opium license; 4. To dismiss from office Junius Kaae, who was implicated in the transaction; 5. To give a specific pledge that he would not in the future interfere, either directly or indirectly, in the election of representatives, or interfere with or attempt to influence legislation or legislators. The same day the King announced his intention of calling on William L. Green to form a Cabinet. The next morning, however, he summoned the American minister and the British, French, and Portuguese commissioners to a conference, and asked them to take over the Government. They declined the trust, and advised him strongly to choose a Cabinet, and to grant a new Constitution without delay. He denied having received a bribe from Aki, but they counseled him to make the restitution. Gibson, who had tried to escape during the previous night, but had returned to his house through fear of the native populace, and requested a guard of the Honolulu Rifles, was arrested on July 1 by Col. Ashford, the commander of that organization. The King requested the foreign representatives to select a ministry, but they declined, provided he would allow Mr. Green to name the Cabinet. The King consented, and the Cabinet was formed as follows: Premier and Minister of Foreign Affairs, William L. Green; Minister of the Interior, Lorrin A. Thurston; Minister of Finance, Godfrey Brown; Attorney-General, Clarence Ashford. The King returned the following answer to the committee who presented to him the demands of the citizens:

GENTLEMEN: In acknowledging the receipt of resolutions adopted at a mass meeting held yesterday and presented to us by you, we are pleased to convey through you to our loyal subjects, as well as to the citizens of Honolulu, our expressions of good will and our gratification that our people have taken the usual constitutional step in presenting their grievances.

To the first proposition contained in the resolutions passed by the meeting whose action you represent, we reply that it has been substantially complied with by the formal resignation of the ministry, which took place on the 28th of June, and was accepted on that date, and that we had already requested the Hon. W. L. Green to form a new Cabinet on the day succeeding the resignation of the Cabinet.

To the second proposition we reply that Walter M. Gibson has severed all connection with the Hawaiian Government by resignation.

To the third proposition we reply that we do not admit the truth of the matters stated therein, but will submit the whole subject to our new Cabinet, and gladly act according to their advice, and will cause restitution to be made by parties found responsible.

To the fourth proposition we reply, that at our command Mr. J. Onins Kaae resigned his office of Registrar of Conveyances on the 28th of June, and his successor has been appointed.

To the fifth proposition we reply that the specific pledges required of us are each and severally acceded to.

We are pleased to assure the members of the committee and our loyal subjects that we are and shall at all times be anxious and ready to co-operate with our councilors and advisers, as well as with our intelligent and patriotic citizens, in all matters touching the honor, welfare, and prosperity of our kingdom.

Given at our palace the 1st day of July, A. D. 1887, and fourteenth year of our reign.

KALAKAUA REX.

The New Constitution.—Among the resolutions adopted at the meeting of citizens and taxpayers was one declaring that many evils were incurable except by radical changes in the Constitution. An amended Constitution was drawn up by a committee of revision, consisting of the ministers, the judges of the Supreme Court, and a number of citizens. When completed, it was submitted to the King, who affixed his signature to it on July 10, and took the oath to support it before Chief-Justice Judd. The new Constitution establishes the principle of ministerial responsibility, takes away the King's right to nominate the members of the Upper Chamber, and deprives him of all legislative powers. It contains the following chief clauses:

All men may freely speak, write, and publish their sentiments on all subjects, being responsible for the abuse of that right, and no law shall be enacted to restrain the liberty of speech or of the press.

No subsidy or tax of any description shall be levied unless by consent of the Legislature, except when between sessions of the Legislature, the emergencies of invasion, rebellion, pestilence, or other public disaster shall arise, and then not without the concurrence of all the Cabinet, and of a majority of the whole Privy Council, and the Minister of Finance shall render a declared account of such expenditure to the Legislature.

The King is Commander-in-Chief of the army and navy, and of all other military forces of the kingdom by sea and land, but he shall never proclaim war without the consent of the Legislature, and no military or naval force shall be organized except by the authority of the Legislature. The King can not be sued or held to account in any court or tribunal of the kingdom.

The Cabinet shall consist of a Minister of Foreign Affairs, a Minister of Finance, and an Attorney-General, and they shall be his majesty's special advisers in the executive affairs of the kingdom, and they shall be *ex-officio* members of his Council of State that shall be appointed and combined by the King, and shall be removed by him upon a vote of want of confidence passed by the majority of all the elective members of the Legislature, or upon conviction of felony, and no removal shall have effect unless it be countersigned by a member of the Cabinet, who by that signature makes himself responsible.

The legislative power of the kingdom is vested in the King and Legislature, which shall consist of nobles and representatives sitting together. The legislative body will assemble biennially, commencing next May. The Legislature has full power and authority to amend the Constitution, and from time to time to make all manner of wholesome laws not repugnant to the Constitution. Every bill which shall have passed the Legislature shall, before it becomes law, be presented to the King. If he approves, he shall sign it, and it shall thereby become law; but, if he does not, he shall return it, with his objections, to the Legislature, which shall enter the objections at large on their journal, and proceed to reconsider it. If, after such reconsideration, it shall be approved by a two-thirds vote of all the elective members of the Legislature, it shall become law.

The succeeding four clauses provide that a majority of the Assembly shall judge of the qualifications of its members, and provide for the election of twenty-four nobles and twenty-four representatives of the people. The representatives are to be elected biennially. The constitution then reads:

At the first election held under this Constitution the nobles shall be elected to serve until the general election to the Legislature for the year 1890, at which election and thereafter the nobles shall be elected at the same time and place as the representatives. At the election of 1890 one third of the nobles shall be elected for two years, one third for four years, and one third for six years, and electors shall ballot for them for such terms respectively, and at all subsequent general elections they shall be elected for six years. The nobles shall serve without pay.

The judicial power of the kingdom shall be vested in one Supreme Court and in such inferior courts as the Legislature may from time to time establish. All laws now in force in this kingdom shall continue and remain in full effect until altered or repealed by the Legislature, such parts only excepted as are repugnant to this Constitution. All laws heretofore enacted or that may hereafter be enacted which are contrary to this Constitution shall be null and void.

This Constitution shall be in force from the 7th day of July, A. D. 1887, but that there may be no failure of justice or inconvenience to the kingdom from any change, all officers of this kingdom at the time this Constitution shall take effect shall have, hold, and exercise all power to them granted. Such officers shall take oath to support this Constitution within sixty days after promulgation thereof.

The Constitution contains eighty-two sections in all. Article XLIX provides that in voting for nobles electors shall have the following qualifications:

1. That he shall have resided in the country not less than three years and in the district in which he offers to vote not less than three months immediately preceding the election at which he offers to vote.

2. That he shall own and be possessed in his own right of taxable property in this country of the value of not less than $3,000, over and above all encumbrances, or shall have actually received an income of not less than $600 during the year next preceding his registration for such election.

3. That he shall be able to read and comprehend ordinary newspapers printed in either the Hawaiian, English, or some European language. No person shall be eligible as a representative of the people unless he can read Hawaiian, English, or some foreign language, has lived in the kingdom three years, and owns real estate to the value of $500, and has an annual income of $250, acquired from some lawful employment. The electors of representatives must have paid their taxes, but the property qualification is waived. The knowledge to speak and write the Hawaiian language is required, but will not be required of any person residing in the kingdom at the time of the promulgation of the Constitution and who registers and votes at the first election under the new Constitution. A noble shall be a subject of the kingdom who shall have attained the age of twenty-five years and resided in the kingdom three years, and shall be the owner of taxable property of the value of $3,000 or in receipt of an income of not less than $600 per annum.

Although the natives had shown themselves as hostile to the Gibson ministry as the whites, the new Constitution caused much dissatisfaction among them, because, while it made many white residents electors for the House of Nobles who had previously had no votes, the property limitation disqualified the great majority of the Kanakas. The Chinese were also displeased because they were excluded from the franchise, whether owners of property or not.

William L. Green, the head of the new Cabinet, is an American by birth, who served in the Northern army during the war of secession, afterward established himself as a merchant and planter in the Hawaiian Islands, and was formerly premier in 1881 and 1882. Godfrey Brown, the Minister of Finance, is the son of an Englishman who held the office of Register of Accounts. The Attorney-General, C. Ashford, is a Canadian by birth, who was Lieutenant-Colonel of the Honolulu Rifles, and was previous to his appointment a lawyer in private practice. L. A. Thurston, the Chief of the Home Office, was born in the islands of an American missionary family, and was a leader of the Opposition in the Legislature.

Ex-Premier Gibson and his son-in-law, F. H. Hayselden, were charged with the embezzlement of public money. After proceedings had been begun, the Attorney-General withdrew the complaint against Gibson, and on July 13 he was allowed to depart on a steamer for San Francisco. Hayselden was accused of forgery in raising the figures on bills given by the Government for labor in 1888, but the Attorney-General was unable to connect him with the crime. Queen Kapiolani, who had been visiting the United States and England, and had received many attentions in both countries, arrived from San Francisco by steamer in the beginning of August. The American naval steamer "Adams" arrived at Honolulu after the revolution, and was ordered to remain. The British cruisers "Conquest" and "Triumph" were ordered thither from Vancouver before the outbreak, but did not arrive till after the "Adams."

There were many among the natives who considered that the King had been badly treated, and who were strongly attached to the idea of royalty and opposed to the republican sentiments that pervaded the American element, which was most active in the revolution. The partial transfer of political power from the native-born subjects of the King to white residents furnished a grievance which was made much of by the partisans of Kalakaua, who prolonged the crisis by declaring the new Constitution invalid and the King's oath, which had been given under duress, of no binding force. They were sustained in their contention by the law, for the old Constitution defined the manner in which it could be amended, which was by the vote of two successive Legislatures.

The Cabinet was obliged to raise a temporary loan of $200,000 to meet pressing demands on the Government. A dispute arose between the ministers and Fruhlung and McFarlane, the negotiators of the English loan of $2,000,000. On the first $1,000,000 the sum of $200,000 was retained as a commission. The Government refused to pay this. The matter was

brought before the Supreme Court, which decided that the loan was illegal, since the terms of the loan-bill had not been complied with. The British creditors appealed to their consul, who not only protested against the repudiation of the terms of the loan, but threatened to summon a squadron to enforce the rights of his countrymen. The ministry finally gave way, and the Legislature approved the loan by a vote of 88 to 18.

A general election was held in October, and the new Legislature came together on November 8. A bill was passed restricting Chinese immigration to 800 every three months. In December the King vetoed a bill abolishing the office of Governor of Oahu, held by his brother-in-law, John D. Dominis, husband of the heiress-presumptive, and afterward a bill providing for the performance of the duties pertaining to that office. The Ministry denied his right to veto legislation, except by their advice. Fiery speeches were made in the Assembly by the Attorney-General, the Minister of the Interior, and others. The King proposed to submit the question to the Supreme Court, and when the Legislature declined to act with him, passing a resolution denying his right to veto, wrote to the court asking its advice. After a long hearing the judges were unable to agree on a decision, two of them upholding the King, and two sustaining the views of the Cabinet and Legislature. The King vetoed two other bills, one to restrict the sale of liquor, and one relating to the police. He conveyed to trustees all his property, consisting of a life interest in the crown lands, and other real estate that he owned in fee, for the purpose of paying off his debts, which amounted to $250,000, besides the $71,000 that the Chinese merchant claimed to have paid him as a bribe.

Reciprocity Treaty with the United States.—The convention that was concluded between the United States and Hawaii on Jan. 30, 1875, was to continue in force for seven years, after the expiration of which it could be terminated on twelve months' notice by either of the contracting parties. On Dec. 6, 1884, a new treaty was signed at Washington by Frederick T. Frelinghuysen, Secretary of State, and Henry A. P. Carter, the Hawaiian Minister. The United States Senate did not confirm this treaty till Jan. 20, 1887, when it received 43 votes in its favor against 11 contrary votes. The treaty, besides the reciprocity clause, contained an additional article permitting the United States to occupy Pearl river harbor, on the island of Oahu, as a coaling-station. This concession excited the jealousy of the English. The harbor is a deep and capacious one, in which the largest navy in the world could lie in safety. It can never be utilized, however, until a channel is cut through the bar, composed principally of coral rock, which now shuts it off from the ocean. The supplementary convention, renewing the former convention respecting commercial reciprocity and granting the use of Pearl river harbor, consists of the following articles:

ARTICLE I. The high contracting parties agree that the time fixed for the duration of the said convention shall be definitely extended for a term of seven years from the date of the exchange of ratifications hereof, and further until the expiration of twelve months after either of the high contracting parties shall give notice to the other of its wish to terminate the same, each of the high contracting parties being at liberty to give such notice to the other at the end of the said term of seven years or at any time thereafter.

ART. II. His Majesty the King of the Hawaiian Islands, grants to the Government of the United States the exclusive right to enter the harbor of Pearl river, in the island of Oahu, and to establish and maintain there a coaling and repair station for the use of vessels of the United States, and to that end the United States may improve the entrance to said harbor, and do all other things needful to the purpose aforesaid.

ART. III. The present convention shall be ratified, and the ratifications exchanged at Washington as soon as possible.

It was duly ratified, and was made public by a proclamation of President Cleveland, issued on Nov. 9, 1887. The second section was added to the supplementary convention during its discussion in the Senate. The Hawaiian Government would not accede to it without an understanding with the Government at Washington as to its interpretation, and both Governments agreed that it did not involve a transfer of sovereign rights, or a cession in perpetuity, but that at the expiration of the treaty the right of the United States to the coaling and repair station should cease.

HAYDEN, FERDINAND VANDEVEER, an American geologist, born in Westfield, Mass., Sept. 7, 1829; died in Philadelphia, Pa., Dec. 22, 1887. He was graduated at Oberlin College in 1850 (having early in life settled on the Western Reserve, in Ohio), and took his doctor's degree at the Albany Medical College in 1853. During the same year he began his career as a geologist, and was sent by James Hall, State Geologist of New York, to the Bad Lands of Dakota, where he explored one of the remarkable deposits of extinct animals, and returned to Albany with a valuable collection of fossil vertebrates. In 1854 he again went West, and after spending two years in exploring the basin of the Upper Missouri river, returned with a large number of fossils, part of which he deposited in the St. Louis Academy of Science, and the remainder in the Academy of Natural Sciences in Philadelphia. He was employed in February 1856, by Lieut. (afterward General) Gouverneur K. Warren, of the United States Topographical Engineers, to make a report on the district he had just explored. In May, 1856, he was appointed geologist on the staff of Lieut. Warren, who was engaged during 1855-'57 in making a reconnoissance of the Northwest in what is now known as Dakota. Dr. Hayden continued so occupied until May, 1859, when he was appointed naturalist and surgeon to the expedition sent to explore the Yellowstone and Missouri rivers under Capt. William F. Raynolds,

of the United States Engineers. In May, 1862, he was made acting assistant surgeon, and assigned to duty at the Satterlee Military Hospital, in Philadelphia. He was confirmed assistant surgeon and full surgeon on Feb. 19, 1863, and sent to Beaufort, S. C., as chief medical officer. This place he held until February, 1864, when he returned North and was made assistant medical inspector in the department of Washington. In September, 1864, he

FERDINAND VANDEVEER HAYDEN.

was ordered to Winchester, Va., as chief medical officer of the Army of the Shenandoah. He remained with this command until May, 1865, when he resigned from the army and was breveted lieutenant-colonel for meritorious service. In 1865 he was elected Professor of Mineralogy and Geology in the University of Pennsylvania, and held that chair until 1872, when the press of official duties compelled his resignation. He again visited the valley of the Upper Missouri during the summer of 1866 for the Philadelphia Academy of Natural Sciences, and gathered valuable vertebrate fossils. In 1867 Congress provided for the geological survey of Nebraska, then recently admitted to the Union. The direction of the work was assigned to Dr. Hayden, and in 1868 he extended his investigations into the Territory of Wyoming. In April, 1869, this work was reorganized under the title of "The Geological Survey of the Territories of the United States." During the subsequent years, until 1872, Dr. Hayden conducted a series of geological explorations in Dakota, Wyoming, Utah, and Colorado, the scope of investigation including, besides geology, the natural history, climatology, resources, and ethnology of the region. In 1873 geography was added to the work of the survey, and the name became "The Geological and Geographical Survey of the Territories." Meanwhile, in 1871, a portion of the country at the sources of the Yellowstone and Missouri rivers was explored, including the Yellowstone Lake and the geysers and hot springs of Fire-Hole, or Upper Madison river. The wonders of this region soon became known, and as a result of his explorations an act was passed by Congress in 1872 by which the district now known as the Yellowstone Park was "reserved and withdrawn from settlement, occupancy, or sale, under the laws of the United States, and dedicated and set apart as a public park or pleasuring-ground for the benefit and enjoyment of the people." The work of the survey was systematically carried on along the Rocky Mountains, in Colorado and Wyoming, until 1879, when the four surveys then in the field were consolidated into the United States Geological Survey. (See GEOLOGICAL SURVEY, in "Annual Cyclopædia" for 1885.) Dr. Hayden was a candidate for the directorship of the new survey, but Clarence King received the appointment, and he at once invited Dr. Hayden to take charge of the work in the region of the sources of the Mississippi, or the division of Montana, with the rank of geologist. He continued in the active prosecution of the duties of this office until December, 1886, when failing health caused his resignation. Dr. Hayden was a member of scientific societies both in the United States and in Europe, and in 1873 was elected a member of the National Academy of Sciences. The honorary degree of LL. D. was conferred on him by the University of Rochester in 1876, and by the University of Pennsylvania in 1887. His scientific papers were about fifty in number, and appeared in the "American Journal of Science," "The Proceedings of the Philadelphia Academy of Sciences," and in the transactions of other learned societies. His principal publications were issued by the Government, and included annual reports from 1867 to 1879, descriptive of the region surveyed each year, with special reports on the palæontology, natural history, and similar subjects; also "Miscellaneous Publications" designed to give information on subjects of interest connected with the West, and finally a series of quarto volumes entitled "Reports of the United States Geological Survey of the Territories." To most of these volumes he was a contributor, and as United States geologist in charge of the survey, their editor.

HAYTI, a republic in the West Indies, covering the western third of the island of Santo Domingo. (For details relating to territorial divisions, population, etc., see "Annual Cyclopædia" for 1883.)

Government.—The President is Gen. Salomon, re-elected for seven years, dating from May 1, 1887. The Cabinet is as follows: Foreign Affairs and Public Worship, Brutus St. Victor; Justice and Public Instruction, Lechaud; War and Navy, Tirésias S. Sam; Interior and Agriculture, O. Arteaud: and Finance and Commerce, Callisthène Touchard. President of the Senate, Maignan; President of the Chamber, D. Théodore; Director of the National Bank, A. Jung. The United States Minister resident at Port-au-Prince is Dr. John E. W. Thompson; the Haytian Minister to the United States,

Stephen Preston; American Consul at Cape Haytien, Stanislas Goutier; Haytian Consul-General at New York, Ebenezer D. Bassett.

Army and Navy.—The standing army is composed of the guard, 650 strong, and the line, 6,178 strong. The navy comprises 5 men-of-war, 1 of which is armored, the total armament being 80 guns.

Postal Service.—There were in operation in 1885 three general post-offices, which forwarded 212,380 letters and postal-cards, and 144,814 newspapers and sample-packages, the receipts being 67,842 francs, and the expenses 135,860.

Finances.—The public indebtedness in 1886 amounted to $13,500,000, consisting of the foreign loan of 1875, $4,320,000, and the home debt of $9,180,000. The budget for 1887-'88 estimates the expenditure at $4,066,286. During the autumn of 1887 the Minister of Finance submitted to the National Assembly the project of a loan in Europe to the extent of 10,000,000 francs, but that body withheld its authority to issue the loan on the plea that, in view of the good coffee-crop prospects for 1887-'88, there was hope that Haytian finances would get along without such appeal to foreign credit. In consequence of the rise in coffee, Haytian finances have steadily improved, the gold premium declining from its former range of 20 to 30 per cent. to 2 to 6 per cent. The Minister of Finance has meanwhile carried through a notable financial reform. Hitherto the public functionaries and military were paid in treasury notes worth only 15 to 35 per cent. of their face value in the open market. Under authority from the National Assembly the Minister made an arrangement with the Banque Nationale d'Haïti to the effect that for five consecutive years the latter engages to pay all salaries against a commission-charge of 2 per cent. As security for the reimbursement of such outlay, the Government pledges the import duties. In May the National Assembly raised the export duty on coffee $1.20 gold the 100 pounds; added to the $2.16 then in force, this increases the duty to $3.36. In July the Government decided to accept the Mexican dollar on and after October 1 at the value of 80 cents gold, and the dollar of other republics at 75 cents gold.

Island of Tortuga.—In April a definitive settlement was effected between the Haytian Government and the British commissionner, Clement Hill, who had gone to Port-au-Prince accompanied by a naval force, with regard to the Island of Tortuga between Hayti and Cuba, about which a dispute had arisen, and to which maritime nations attach great importance as a strategic station after the Panama Canal shall be completed. The Haytian Government engaged to pay £82,000, in four instalments, as an indemnity for retaining the island as it is. The British Government yields all further claims in the matter of the Maunder brothers. In the event of Hayti failing to meet the instalments as they fall due, she is to pay interest at the rate of 6 per cent. per annum.

Commerce.—In 1886 there were imported into Hayti $4,965,256 worth of merchandise, while the export of Haytian products reached $7,555,996. The chief exports were: Coffee, 58,075,783 pounds; cocoa, 3,939,445 pounds; wool, 2,037,653; hides, 436,579 pounds; orange-peel, 461,768 pounds; raw sugar, 289,354 pounds; cotton-seed, 84,586 pounds; tortoise-shell 906 pounds; wax, 3,619 pounds; honey, 18,001 gallons; cigars, 17,000,000; logwood, 282,620,852 yards, and besides fustic, mahogany, and old copper sheathing. The American trade with Hayti has been as follows:

FISCAL YEAR.	Import into the United States.	Domestic export to Hayti.
1885	$2,471,436	$3,227,059
1886	2,608,999	2,963,147
1887	1,759,587	3,059,818

Real Estate.—In a New-Year's speech delivered by President Salomon on Jan. 1, 1887, it was intimated that the law of section 7 of 1804, prohibiting the holding of real estate by foreigners, might be abolished. As foreigners are debarred from owning real estate in Hayti, structures which they cause to be built for commercial purposes of their own, have to be put under the names of native Haytians, which frequently leads to trouble in cases of inheritance. If this antiquated law were abolished, there would be some inducement for foreign capital to invest in real estate in the republic.

HAZEN, WILLIAM BABCOCK, an American soldier, born in West Hartford, Windham county, Vt., Sept. 27, 1830; died in Washington, D. C., Jan. 16, 1887. In 1833 his father's family re-

WILLIAM BABCOCK HAZEN.

moved to Huron, Portage county, Ohio, where he worked on a farm, enjoying few educational advantages. When twenty-one years old he entered the United States Military Academy, where he was graduated four years later. He was assigned to the army as brevet second lieutenant of the Fourth Infantry, then serving in California and Oregon. For his gallantry in

the Indian war of 1856–'57 he was made second lieutenant in the Eighth Infantry, and shortly after joining his new command distinguished himself in an attack upon and extinction of fifteen lodges of Apaches. He commanded a company in five engagements, and in December, 1859, was severely wounded in a fight with the Comanches. For these services he was complimented in general orders and given a year's leave of absence, and received his brevet of first lieutenant under date of May 6, 1859. Reporting for duty on the expiration of his leave, and still lame from his wounds, he was appointed assistant professor of military tactics at the United States Military Academy in February, 1861. On April 1 he was promoted to be first lieutenant of his company; on May 14, to be captain, and on August 7 was permitted to accept the command of the Forty-first Regiment of Ohio Volunteers. With this he took part in Gen. Buell's operations in Tennessee, being promoted, and assigned to the command of the Nineteenth Brigade of the Army of the Ohio, on June 6, 1862. Under the latter assignment, he participated in the battles of Pittsburg Landing, the siege of Corinth, Perryville, and the pursuit of Gen. Bragg's army out of Kentucky. Later, he was with his brigade in the battle of Stone River, the Middle Tennessee campaign, the Chickamauga contest, the Chattanooga engagement, and the relief of Knoxville in 1863. During Gen. Sherman's march to the sea he commanded a division, which captured Fort McAllister, on Savannah river, thus opening communication between the army and the fleet. He marched through the Carolinas, and was present at the surrender of Gen. Johnston's army. For his gallant services in various actions, he was promoted to be colonel by brevet, Sept. 1, 1864, brigadier-general by brevet, March 13, 1865, and major-general of volunteers, April 20, 1865, to rank from Dec. 13, 1864. In 1866 he was mustered out of the volunteer service and appointed colonel of the Thirty-eighth United States Infantry, from which he was transferred to the Sixth United States Infantry in 1869. He was present with the Prussian army during the investment of Paris in 1871, appointed military attaché to the United States Legation at Vienna in 1877, and while holding this office was detailed by President Hayes to observe the conduct of the Russo-Turkish War. He was appointed Chief Signal Officer of the army, Dec. 6, 1880, held this office till his death, and introduced many new and valuable features in the management of the Weather Bureau.

HITCHCOCK, ROSWELL DWIGHT, an American clergyman, born in East Machias, Me., Aug. 15, 1817; died in South Somerset, Mass., June 16, 1887. He was graduated at Amherst College in 1836, and spent a year in teaching, pursuing at the same time Biblical and other studies under private tutors. In 1838 he entered Andover Theological Seminary, and from 1839 till

1842 served as a tutor in Amherst College, of which he was made a trustee in 1869. After preaching for a year in Waterville, Me., he was ordained pastor of the First Congregational Church in Exeter, N. H., in November, 1845. He retained this charge till 1852, when he resigned it to accept the professorship of Natural and Revealed Religion in Bowdoin College; but before entering upon his new duties he spent a year in study at the universities of Halle and

ROSWELL DWIGHT HITCHCOCK.

Berlin, Germany. In 1855 he was appointed Professor of Church History in Union Theological Seminary. His New England education was supplemented by foreign travel as well as study, and while holding his professorship he found time to engage in literary work. In 1866 he visited Italy and Greece, and in 1869–'70 made a tour of Eg pt, Sinai, and Palestine. From 1863 till 1870 he was one of the editors of the "American Theological Review." In 1871 he was elected President of the Palestine Exploration Society, in the organization of which he had taken an active part. He published a "Life of Edward Robinson" (1863); "A Complete Analysis of the Bible," which was widely circulated (1869); and "Socialism" (1878); and co-operated with Rev. Drs. Eddy and Schaff in the compilation of "Hymns and Songs of Praise" and "Hymns and Songs for Social and Sabbath Worship." Many of his sermons and addresses have been published, and, in addition to his editorial work, he was a frequent contributor of essays to different reviews. On Nov. 9, 1880, Dr. Hitchcock was unanimously elected as the successor of Rev. William Adams, D. D., in the presidency of Union Theological Seminary, and retained the office till his death. The degree of D. D. was conferred upon him by Bowdoin College in 1855, and by the University of Dublin in 1885, and that of LL. D. by Williams College in 1873. During the civil war Dr. Hitchcock was an earnest and effective supporter of the National cause.

HOLLAND. See NETHERLANDS.

HONDURAS, a republic in Central America; area, 39,600 square miles; population, 351,700.

Government.—The President is Gen. Luis Bagrán. whose term will expire on Nov. 27, 1891. The Cabinet is composed of the following ministers: Foreign Affairs, Licenciado Don Jerónimo Zelaya; Justice, Public Works, and War, Señor R. Alvarado; Interior, Señor A. Gomez; Finance, Señor F. Planas; Agriculture, Señor A. Zelaya. The United States Minister is Hon. H. C. Hall, resident at Guatemala; the American Consul at Ruatan and Trujillo is William C. Burchard, and at Tegucigalpa, Daniel W. Herring; the Consular Agent at Yuscaran is Theodore Roehncke. The Consul-General of Honduras at New York is Jacob Baiz; at San Francisco, William V. Wells.

The effective strength of the army is 500 men, and there is besides a militia force of 8,000.

The number of post-offices in 1885 was 88. While the receipts were restricted to $2,280, the expenses reached $40,453.

Finance.—The amount of bonds held in Europe, issued in 1869, usually called the old French loan, is $25,000,000. Congress issued a decree early in 1887, authorizing the receipt of 40 per cent. of the customs duties in Honduranian bonds. The home debt amounts to $700,000, and the floating debt to $200,000.

In February, 1887, the formal opening took place at Trujillo of the Aguan Navigation and Improvement Company's bank. This is the first bank ever established in Honduras. Its stock is owned by New York, Boston, and Milwaukee capitalists. Its bills are similar to the greenbacks of the United States, and are redeemable in silver.

Commerce.—The American trade has developed as follows:

FISCAL YEAR.	Import into the United States.	Domestic export to Honduras.
1886	$730,559	$428,106
1887	557,919	425,741

Soon the new port of San Lorenzo is to be opened, which. in connection with the projected railroad between San Lorenzo and Pespire, 24 miles, will be of incalculable value to Southern Honduras, since ocean-steamers will have easy access to the port.

Railroads.—There is in running order the line from Puerto Cortez to San Pedro-Iula, 47 miles. In July, 1887, Binney & Co., of London, obtained a concession for the construction of 200 miles of railway for the extension and completion of the republic's system. The concession is for 99 years. The contractors are to receive a grant of public lands, the introduction duty free of railroad material, and the privilege of preference for any other railways or for telegraph lines to be constructed hereafter. The *concessionnaires* engage to offer the bondholders of the French loan of 1869 the option of exchanging for the preferred shares of the railroad company to be formed.

Telegraphs.—The number of offices in operation in 1885 was 63; the length of lines, 2,158 kilometres. While the receipts did not exceed $20,000 during the year, the expenses amounted to $51,764. On Feb. 5, 1887, direct telegraphic communication was formally opened between Central America and Mexico by the extension of the Mexican land-lines to Guatemala. The lines in every one of the states thus connected are owned and managed by the Governments, and there is a uniform rate.

In April, telegraphic communication was opened with the new station at San Francisco, in the department of Santa Rosa.

Mining.—Early in 1887 a syndicate of New York and Philadelphia capitalists obtained from the Government of Honduras the exclusive privilege of establishing customs works for the reduction of ores in any part of Tegucigalpa, El Paraiso, and Choluteca. The syndicate owns fifteen mines in the republic, having acquired them under condition that they should be thoroughly developed, and that roads should be constructed from them to the coast.

Boundary Question.—Honduras and Salvador have agreed to fix anew the boundary between the two republics, the line drawn some time ago by Señores Letona and Cruz having been rejected by the Congress of Honduras. Pending the determination of the frontier, the line existing in 1884 is to be adhered to. Meanwhile Señores Zelaya and Castellanos have made an agreement as to the details to be observed in fixing the new line, and the Congress of Honduras has approved it.

Colonization.—Jacob Baiz, Consul-General of Honduras at New York, has petitioned the Government of Honduras for a land grant of 25,000 acres for purposes of colonization between Trujillo and Iriona, including the towns of Limon and Cuzca in the Mosquito territory. American settlers are to be procured, and the land is to be planted with plantains, cocoanut groves, oranges, and other fruit. American capitalists are said to be interested in this project.

Prosperous Condition of the Country.—In 1887 Honduras made rapid strides in progress. The national debt was in course of reduction; schools, colleges, and telegraph lines were established, and high-roads built. Under this favorable condition of affairs, American capital has been flowing into the republic, where it is amply protected by law, and where valuable concessions are granted for public improvements. The frequent visits to the Atlantic coast of Honduras of steamers and sailing-vessels, buying fruit for sale in the United States, has led to a great rise in prices. Cocoanuts, formerly worth from $12 to $14 a thousand, now bring $45 to $48. Bananas, which could be bought for 30 cents a bunch, are now worth $1.30 a bunch.

American Enterprise.—Col. Hurley, Vice-Presi-

dent of the Aguan Navigation and Improvement Company, has proposed to the Government the erection of light-houses on the northern coast of the republic. The company has displayed great activity during the year, not only in the enterprise of canalization, which is to connect the bay of Trujillo with the river Aguan, but also in its banking operations. Colonization of the lands granted to the company, with American settlers, is proposed.

In June, Gen. E. A. Lever, Consul of Honduras at New Orleans, arrived at Trujillo for the purpose of making a contract with the Government in behalf of American capitalists, about the navigation of the river Ulua and the acquisition of tracts of land for settlement.

HOPKINS, MARK, an American clergyman, born in Stockbridge, Mass., Feb. 4, 1802; died in Williamstown, Mass., June 17, 1887. He pursued preparatory studies in the academies at Lenox, Mass., and Clinton, N. Y., and was graduated at Williams College in 1824. Soon

MARK HOPKINS.

afterward he began the study of medicine at the Pittsfield Medical College; but this course was interrupted by his appointment to a tutorship at Williams College, which he held two years, when he resumed his medical studies in New York city. He received the degree of M. D. at Pittsfield in 1829, and in the following year began practicing in New York city. In August, 1830, but a few weeks after opening his office, he was unexpectedly elected Professor of Rhetoric and Moral Philosophy in Williams College, and two years later he was licensed to preach by the Berkshire Association. From 1830 to 1836 he worked steadily at his professorship, lecturing and preaching. In the latter year the presidency of the college became vacant by the resignation of Rev. Dr. Griffin, and Prof. Hopkins, though then only thirty-four years old, was elected to succeed him. He held this office for thirty-six years, resigning its responsibilities in 1872, but retaining the professorship of moral and intellectual philosophy. Thus his connection with Williams

College as student, tutor, professor, and president, covered the long period of sixty-two years; while from 1872 till his death he took an active part in all its affairs, lecturing on his favorite subjects—ethics, metaphysics, and rhetoric—preaching, and making anniversary and commencement addresses. Of his many published writings the best known are: "Evidences of Christianity" (1849); "Moral Science" (1862); "The Law of Love, and Love as a Law" (1869); and "An Outline of the Study of Man" (1874). The last three volumes have been adopted by several colleges as text-books, and translated for similar use abroad. President Hopkins received the degree of D. D. from Dartmouth College in 1837, and from Harvard University in 1841, and that of LL. D. from the Board of Regents of New York in 1857. He became President of the American Board of Commissioners for Foreign Missions in 1857, and held that office till his death.

HOUSES. American Country-Seats.—The present epoch of domestic architecture in the United States, though scarcely more than ten years old, is remarkable in performance and in promise. Twenty years ago the late Andrew J. Downing, an architect of repute, declared that our houses were mainly either of the plainest or most meager description, or, if more ambitious, were frequently shingled palaces of very questionable convenience, and not in the least adapted by their domestic and rural beauty to harmonize with our landscape. Nineteen years ago Mr. E. L. Godkin, in an address before the American Institute of Architects, said that, while their calling was the only one that brought art into contact with busy life—affecting men's imaginations while ministering to their material comfort—the people were only beginning to learn the need of architects. "You have been occupied from the dawn of civilization in the construction of temples and palaces, cathedrals and castles; but it is only in our day that the distribution of property and the arrangements of society have been such as to call your services into requisition for the construction of homes." Eighteen years ago the Rev. Dr. William H. Furness, in an address on a similar occasion, lamented the misfortune of the American architect who lived in a country so young in everything, especially in the fine arts, that architecture was "hardly yet appreciated as an art, or its professors and students deemed anything more than builders and working mechanics. The consequence of this confounding of artists with mechanics is that your art is not only defrauded of its dignity, but is without its rightful authority, and you have incessantly to submit to the humiliation of discussing as questions of taste what are no questions of taste at all, but matters of knowledge, of fact, with persons who have never given a thought to them.

The first private house of the present era of domestic architecture in the United States was designed by the late Mr. H. H. Richardson, and erected in Newport, R. I., near the residences of Mr. Louis L. Lorillard and Mr. Cornelius Vanderbilt, in the year 1870; but it was not until about eight years afterward that Mr. Charles F. McKim designed the Newport Casino, and Mr. Richard M. Hunt the residence of Mr. Henry G. Marquand in the same city, which were speedily followed by other notable structures in various parts of the country. To Newport, therefore, and to the three architects just mentioned, must be awarded especial honor. So rapid and distinguished was the progress of this new American architecture that the British Institute of Architects, a few years later, sent to the United States a delegation of its members with instructions to examine the results obtained by their American brothers. On their return to London these gentlemen reported their surprise and delight at much that they had seen, particularly at the development of the American country-seat. Similar surprise and delight were expressed soon afterward by M. Paul Sédille, the architect of the city of Paris, in a letter to a French journal recounting some impressions of a visit to the United States. Among the best places for studying grouped examples of the new American country-seat are Newport, Lenox, Bar Harbor, Manchester-by-the-Sea, Tuxedo Park, Elberon, the suburbs of Philadelphia, and the Westchester and New Jersey suburbs of New York city. The whole continent of Europe might be searched in vain for a Newport, a Lenox, or a Bar Harbor.

No distinctive American or national style has yet been created, but adaptations of foreign styles and reproductions of our own colonial style are numerous. In the country-houses of the Northwest there is a tendency toward Byzantine effects, bold sometimes to brutality. In New England there is an unmistakable revival of old colonial; five or six colonial houses have been built in Newport alone during the past two years, that belonging to Mr. H. A. C. Taylor being unusually noteworthy for purity of style. Some architects, like Mr. H. Edwards Ficken, Mr. C. C. Haight, and Mr. C. A. Rich, are fond of expressing the domestic sentiment of the lowland counties of England. Mr. W. D. Washburn's house at Minneapolis is called modern Gothic; Mr. R. C. Jefferson's house at St. Paul, modern French; Mr. George Noakes's house on Riverside Drive, New York. Norman Gothic; Col. Andrews's house at Cleveland, Italian Renaissance (see illustration, p. 362); Mr. C. A. Potter's house, near Philadelphia, somewhat Flemish. But architects, as a rule, do not designate their country-houses as specimens of any special styles, and are almost invariably confused when asked such a question as, "What is the style of this house?" Yet it was only ten years ago that an American architect publicly eulogized the "free classic or Queen Anne style," which he described as showing the influence of the Elizabethan, the Jacobean, and the Francis I styles, and which he asserted to be "our vernacular style." The present disposition of our leading architects is expressed in the words of a correspondent of "The American Architect" for February, 1884, who advises his fellow-artists to leave "Queen Anne to the grandmammas of the profession—it goes well with tea and toast."

When Mr. Edward A. Freeman, the historian, was asked to write an article on the more recent achievements of American architecture, he declared that the city of Albany had pleased him most of all; but "What," he asked, "should be the architecture of the United States—i. e., the architecture of an English people settled in a country in the latitude, though not always in the climate, of Italy? Should it be the Gothic of England or the Romanesque of Italy?" To the American architect no such dilemma presents itself. The range of his vision is wider.

The exterior color of country-houses is becoming darker, the aim being to subdue the effect to that of the trees and hills, and to silhouette the edifice against the sky, thus setting

COL. ANDREWS'S HOUSE, CLEVELAND, OHIO.

forth its angles and masses. But old colonial reproductions are, of course, still painted white. In an address before the American Institute of Architects in 1868, Mr. Richard Upjohn said: "Let me speak a word for color, against which our fellow-citizens seem to have had a strong though now happily departing prejudice. Color is the vitalizing principle of architecture, as it is of Nature. Reduce a landscape to a dead uniformity or monotint, and admire the result if you can. Destroy color, and you chill the very life of art. See how the strong yellow tint of a sunset enlivens the most tame and contemptible building. We can not have a permanent sunset; we can not rule the atmospheric laws to our ends; but we can, by choice of material for color and texture on exteriors, and by polychrome and rays of light, stained by their passage through tinted glass, do something toward replacing their effects."

The increasing influence of the architect over his client is a fact of which Mr. Howells made use in writing the story of "The Rise of Silas Lapham," whose idea of a house, it will be remembered, was a brown-stone front, four stories high, and a French roof, with an air-chamber above. Black walnut was to be used in all the rooms, except in the attic, which was to be painted and grained to look like black walnut. The whole was to be very high-studded, and there were to be handsome cornices and elaborate center-pieces throughout. But the architect was skillful, "as nearly all architects are," in playing upon

LODGE OF FREDERICK L. AMES, NORTH EASTON, MASS.

INTERIOR OF SEASIDE COTTAGE, NORTH EAST HARBOR, ME.

that simple instrument, man; and, in the course of a friendly conversation, persuaded Mr. Lapham to have the entrance-story low-studded, with a little reception-room beside the door; to use the whole width of the house frontage for a square hall, with an easy, low-tread staircase, running up three sides of it; to paint the drawing-room white, introducing a little gold here and there, with, perhaps, a painted frieze under the cornice—garlands of roses on a gold ground —and a white-marble chimney-piece, treated in the refined empire style. Lapham "respected a fellow who could beat him at every point, and have a reason ready, as this architect had; and when he recovered from the daze into which the complete upheaval of all his preconceived notions had left him, he was in a fit state to swear by the architect." The most brilliant American example of the possible influence of the architect over his client, was the late Mr. H. H. Richardson, a characteristic specimen of whose genius is seen in the illustration (p. 863) of the lodge of Mr. Frederick L. Ames's house at North Easton, Mass.

For parlors and bedrooms, the most fashionable style of decoration is Louis XVI; there are two French establishments on Fifth Avenue, New York city, which devote themselves entirely to Louis XVI work. For dining-rooms and libraries the fashionable finish is in the styles of Henry II and François I. In city-houses it is not uncommon to sacrifice two feet of the parlor to the hall, in order to give the latter apartment the appearance of a comfortable sitting-room. The styles known to young architects as the "Bloody Mary" and the "Mother Hubbard" have seen their best days. An example of pure Louis XVI is a drawing-room recently renovated by Mr. H. O. Avery, the architect. The wood-work was cleaned with acid, and then subjected to an enamel finish; the walls are a shrimp pink, with Lyons silk in panels decorated with rosettes and intertwined ribbons in relief. The curtains, also of Lyons silk, manufactured after the architect's designs, show a pattern of nosegays held up by ribbons that float over a pink field. On the cream-tinted ceiling are square panels of Louis XVI patterns, surrounded by twined tulip-leaves. The cornice, once a modern classic motive, is now French, with intertwined leaves of ivy. Metal sconces appear between the panels of the walls, at a height of six and a half feet from the floor. All the wood-work has received five coats of paint and three of varnish, and then been rubbed down to its enamel finish with pumice-stone and oil. The old black-walnut furniture, once covered with dark-claret satin, has been painted pink and upholstered with Lyons silk, like that of the panels of the walls; and the general effect of the room is of cream and gold. This revival of Louis XVI decoration began with the Vanderbilt and Goelet houses in New York city. It extends even to the carpet, which in the draw-

room just mentioned is in shrimp and cream—a Louis XVI reflex of the patterns of the ceiling and the walls—manufactured by Templeton Brothers in Scotland, after the architects' designs. A simple and inexpensive method of treating the interior of a seaside cottage, is seen in the illustration of several rooms at North East Harbor, Me., designed by Mr. W. R. Emerson. It may be added that the American architect of to-day desires to have charge of the decoration within the house and the landscape-gardening around it. Both the arrangement of the grounds and the finish of the interior walls are parts of his principal scheme.

To many visitors the most interesting contributions to the third annual exhibition of the Architectural League, in New York city, December, 1887, were the designs for country-houses by William Convers Hazlett, Clarence S. Luce, Charles T. Mott, Charles A. Rich, Rossiter & Wright, Brunner & Tryon, John Calvin Stevens, Wilson Eyre, Jr., and Bruce Price. The object of the league is "the promotion of architecture and the allied fine arts," and among the committees was the Loan Exhibition Committee, which gathered from various private sources nearly two hundred oil paintings, water-color studies, and pieces of sculpture and of furniture. Most of the members have spent years in study in Europe, particularly in Paris, and so great is their confidence in their productive resources that they show freely to one another, twice a month, all their new designs. American architects have hitherto been loath to exhibit their unexecuted designs, for fear that they should be stolen. The league now numbers one hundred and twenty members, residents of New York, Boston, Philadelphia, St. Paul, St. Louis, Albany, Portland, and Buffalo, and is in a highly prosperous condition, its annual exhibitions attracting the best artists and the leading amateurs.

We now proceed to describe in detail some representative country-seats of the new epoch. The late Mr. Charles J. Osborn's house at Mamaroneck, New York (Messrs. McKim, Mead, & White, architects) holds the rank of a modern feudal castle. The plan is L-shaped, the length one hundred and fifty-three feet, and the width one hundred and forty-four feet. The large, round parlor-tower, fifty-three feet high, and twenty-three feet wide at its greatest diameter, is the principal feature of the building as seen from Long Island Sound. The material of the main walls is grayish local stone in the first story, and shingles in the second story, which projects about two feet, and is supported on corbels of rough stone. Through the entire depth of the building is a driveway, fifteen feet wide, under a stone arch, whose keystone is thirteen feet above the ground. The entrance to the house is within this driveway.

Panels of pebbles and cockle-shells, set in gray plastering, appear above the arch. A series of casement windows opens into the

G. M. BLACK'S HOUSE, MANCHESTER-BY-THE-SEA.

JOSEPH E. CHOATE'S HOUSE, STOCKBRIDGE, MASS.

hall, and a circle-headed window into the billiard-room, with ornamental panels in glass and lead-work. The piazza, forty feet by twenty, extends diagonally from the parlor, on a piece of land that overhangs the water. There are four towers, all of the same height, and three of them of stone. (The tower treatment is conspicuous also in Mr. Joseph H. Choate's house, designed by the same architects, at Stockbridge, Mass.; see illustration, p. 367.)

The hall mantel-piece, two stories high, has an enormous fire-opening, and a wind-gauge connected with the weather-vane. The casement windows, above wide seats, overlook the Sound. The paneled wainscoting of English oak is elaborately carved in the moldings, while mahogany has been used in finishing the parlor, and Santo Domingo mahogany in finishing the dining-room. The reception-room is of pine, painted white and gilded. The part of the building at the right of the covered driveway is separate in design, and intended as a winter-quarters, with hall, billiard-room, smoking-room, dining-room, and bedrooms of its own. A gallery extends around three sides of the main hall in the larger part of the structure. Mr. G. N. Black's house at Manchester-by-the-Sea (see illustration, p. 366) also shows a large driveway through the entire depth of the building.

In the beautiful villa of William Simpson, Jr., at Overbrook, near Philadelphia, the architect, Theophilus P. Chandler, Jr, has adopted some features of the old French style. The material is local granite, trimmed with buff Ohio sandstone; the length is one hundred and five feet, and the depth fifty-six feet. As seen in our illustration (p. 369), the north side presents a group of five stained-glass windows, another group of stained-glass windows defining the course of the principal stairs, and a third group lighting the servants' stairs. The oaken hall, twenty-four feet by twenty, has a wainscoting five feet high, a ceiling of open-timber work, and a mantel of carved quarter-oak, with fire-facing of carved English red sandstone. In the reception-room and parlor the trimming is of mahogany; in the library and dining-room, of walnut. Four stained-glass windows on the landing of the principal staircase give access to a balcony with an elaborate wrought-iron railing. The heating is by low-pressure steam indirectly radiated, and each toilet-room is connected with the kitchen flue by a two-inch spiral ventilating pipe of galvanized iron.

Certain French and English features appear in the roof and windows of Travis C. Van Buren's house at Tuxedo Park (see illustration, p. 870), but taken altogether it is as original a piece of work as this country has produced. The architect is Mr. Bruce Price, and attention will be directed, first, to the large central shingled portal, bending inward in a great curve, and strong in contrasts of light and shade; secondly, to the absence of cornices and trimmings,

the shingles running up to the stiles, and the casements hanging directly upon them; thirdly, to the convex, flexible lines of the gables, which, being neither straight nor stiff, give an impression of lightness and of life; and fourthly, to the mechanical excellence of the shingling itself, all the courses correctly meeting one another, and not tolerating defects that might have been hidden by a molding. The interior finish is unostentatious, and the entire cost did not exceed ten thousand dollars.

Chinese and Japanese houses have recently been constructed in California, several of them at great expense. In Florida are five or six important Moorish houses, the most notable of which is that of Franklin W. Smith, called the Villa Zorayda, at St. Augustine, designed by the owner after sketches made in Spain and northern Africa. The material is the French *béton*, or concrete, of a pearly gray tint. Two porches, jutting from the upper stories, show light lattice-work. Over the front entrance of the house is an Arabic inscription in heavy relief, to the effect that "There is no conqueror but God." The court is surrounded by horse-shoe arches, ornamented with an abundance of delicate tracery and supported on slender gray pillars. Many *fac similes* of Arabic inscriptions appear in various places. The staircase is a copy of a pulpit staircase in a Cairo mosque. Divans are placed around the smoking-room, and coffee-cups and a nargileh await the convenience of guests. The fire-place of the dining-room has the shape of an arch well known in Constantinople. In short, this house is thoroughly Moorish without and within.

The feature of the interior of Mr. Robert Goelet's house at Newport is the magnitude and beauty of the two-story hall, its length being forty-four feet, its width thirty feet, and its height twenty-four feet. A gallery supported on columns and arches extends around the second story, its balustrade being of turned spindles of oak. The walls are heavily paneled with the same wood, and hung with immense pieces of old tapestry. Much carving appears in the decoration, especially in the rich leaf-work of the large brackets that support the shelves of the chimney-piece. The ornamental massive brackets of brass are in the form of candelabra, and a curious piece of furniture is an antique carved and canopied bedstead, which serves the purpose of a divan.

One of the largest houses in the suburbs of Philadelphia, on the Pennsylvania Railroad, is divided by the architects, Messrs. G. W. and W. D. Hewitt, into six parts: First, the large *porte-cochère*, with its circular bartizan tower, ten feet in diameter and seventy-two feet high; second, the house proper; third, the servants' hall, kitchen, and laundries; fourth, the carriage-house connected therewith by a covered way; fifth, the covered shed; and, sixth, the stable. The advantages sought by this method of construction are, first, mag-

WILLIAM SIMPSON JR.'S HOUSE, OVERBROOK, NEAR PHILADELPHIA.

nitude of effect; second, preservation of the unity and beauty of the lawn, which thus remains undisfigured by spots; and, third, convenience of the master and mistress.

The present ideal of the American country-seat, as cherished by the more progressive of our architects, was expressed last year by one of their number in the following words: "Among architects orders for city residences are now scarce, while country-houses fill their thoughts and crowd their boards. But the modest cottage, built a few years ago to 'rough

have cottages that would be mansions in England, villas in Italy, or *châteaux* in France. The 'cottage' is an amiable deception, preserved to shield the roof-tree from the prevailing shams and pretenses of nearly everything else in American domestic life. In this one thing at least our countrymen seem to be sincere, above splurge, and to seek the beauties and comforts that wealth can furnish with an honest purpose. This growing taste for country life, coupled with the increased knowledge and higher cultivation of our intelligent people in

TRAVIS C. VAN BUREN'S HOUSE, TUXEDO PARK.

it in' through the hot days of the summer, must be made a more hospitable home for to-day. It must be snug and comfortable, with broad hearth-stones and warm walls, for its tenants, lingering on through the biting days of late autumn and early winter. It is the fashion to call these country-houses cottages; but the cottage exists only in name. The cliffs of Newport, the rocks of Mount Desert, the shores of Shrewsbury, and the beaches of Westchester, Connecticut, and Long Island,

all matters pertaining to art, has given the architect of to-day a great opportunity to raise the structure of an American style. The American country-house is becoming more and more distinctive, its character or plan more developed, and its economics more suited to our habits of life. The great heat of summer demands shady porches and wide verandas; the cold of winter snug corners and sunny rooms—two diametrically opposite conditions, which must be reconciled under the same roof. The rooms must be wide, with through draughts inviting the prevailing winds of summer, yet low-studded and shielded against the blasts of winter. The house must be ample for summer guests and summer hospitality, yet homelike for the family gathering around the winter fireside. These conditions demand original thought and hard study, and fulfilling them brings the architect's reward of facility through training. Facility begets confidence, and with it come new forms in place of the traditions of the studio, dropped one by one. Our distinctive constructive materials call for new lines, masses, and texture in elevations; and, with our national inventiveness fostered by the problem, our work becomes more or less national. Our country-house is already a well-defined school; whether colonial, sixteenth and seventeenth century of England or France, Romanesque from the south of France, or renaissance, the mass is American and typical in handling. The feeling may survive, but the style of the prototype has been bent to the homes we live in, and in bending yields to a new form. This new form will often borrow from a sympathetic type, and the result will be neither of the two, yet good withal. So we are passing through our incipient renaissance, copying less from the masters we studied and revere, and dropping the word 'style' from our practice."

Literature.—" Artistic Country · Seats," five volumes, large folio, one hundred full - page illustrations, (New York, 1887-'8); articles on " American Country-Dwellings," " Century Magazine," 1886; recent numbers of the " American Architect," the " Sanitary Engineer," the " Art Age," " Building," and the " Architects and Builders' Edition " of the " Scientific American "; " Artistic Houses," two hundred large folio views of domestic interiors, (New York, 1886.)

HUNTER, ROBERT MERCER TALIAFERRO, an American lawyer, born in Essex County, Va., April 21, 1809; died there, July 18, 1887. He was educated at the University of Virginia and Winchester Law School, and, after being graduated at both institutions, was admitted to the bar, and began practicing in 1830. In 1833 he entered upon his long and notable political career as a member of the State Legislature, where he served three years. At the close of his last term he was elected a member of Congress, taking his seat in 1838 as a Democrat. He at once took an advanced position by his advocacy of an independent treasury in opposition to the national-bank scheme, and his boldness in combating Henry Clay's protective policy. From that time his free-trade proclivities were intensified, and to his last days he was a most uncompromising supporter of that doctrine. Having been re-elected a Representative, he was chosen Speaker of the

House in 1839, when but thirty years old. In the Polk canvass of 1844 he was an earnest advocate of that candidate's tariff and Texan policies. He was the author of the warehousing system, which was first incorporated in the tariff bill. In 1843 he was defeated for Congress, but in 1845 was re-elected. Before the expiration of his term he was elected to the United States Senate, where he took his seat in December, 1847, and served continuously till his formal expulsion in July, 1861. During the greater part of this period he was Chairman of the Committee on Finance, and was active in the discussion of the great political questions of the day. In 1854 he supported the Kansas-Nebraska bill, in 1858 that provid-

ROBERT MERCER TALIAFERRO HUNTER.

ing for the admission of Kansas under the Lecompton Constitution, and in 1860 received votes upon several ballots as a candidate for the Democratic nomination to the presidency in the Charleston Convention, having for some time the next highest vote to that for Stephen A. Douglas. After the secession of Virginia he was a delegate to the Confederate Provisional Congress, and subsequently he became a Confederate Senator, in which office he was conspicuous for his opposition to Jefferson Davis. He also served for a time as Confederate Secretary of State. In February, 1865, he was associated with Messrs. Stephens and Campbell as commissioners to meet President Lincoln and Secretary Seward at Hampton Roads, to negotiate peace; but the conference was futile. After the close of the war he was arrested, but was released upon his parole, and pardoned in 1867 by President Johnson. In 1875 he was elected State Treasurer of Virginia, retiring to private life on the expiration of his term. His last public office was that of Collector of Customs at the port of Tappahannock, Va., to which he was appointed by President Cleveland in June, 1886, and which he held at the time of his death.

I

IDAHO. Territorial Government.—The following were the Territorial officers during the
year: Governor, Edward A. Stevenson; Secretary, Edward J. Curtis; Controller and Auditor, James L. Onderdonk, succeeded by James
H. Wickersham; Treasurer, Joseph Perrault,
succeeded by Charles Himrod; Attorney-General, D. P. B. Pride, succeeded by Richard Z.
Johnson; Superintendent of Public Instruction, James L. Onderdonk, succeeded by Silas
W. Moody; Chief-Justice of Supreme Court,
James B. Hays; Associate Justices, Norman
Buck and Case Broderick.

Legislative Session.—The Legislature in session
at the beginning of the year adjourned on
February 10, having reached the sixty-day limit.
There was a stubborn contest in the lower
House over the speakership, forty ballots being
necessary for its determination. Among the
important measures passed was an act making
the Superintendency of Public Instruction a distinct office, it having been previously combined
with the controllership. Another act revises
and collates the law regulating corporations.
The commission appointed by the Legislature
of 1885 to revise and compile the General Statutes reported at this session, and its work was
adopted as the Revised Statutes of the Territory. A resolution was adopted opposing the
segregation of Idaho and its annexation to adjoining States or Territories. Other general
acts of the session were as follow:

Providing for the appointment by the Governor of
a board of Capitol trustees, for the custody and maintenance of the new Capitol building and grounds.

Amending the law relating to school trustees.

Authorizing the creation of independent school
districts, if the electors of said district vote to establish such, provided the taxable property of such district amounts to $200,000, and giving the trustees of
the district so created enlarged powers over those exercised by ordinary district trustees.

Empowering the Governor to draw from the Federal
Government arms and equipments for the militia to
the amount of $11,257.58, that being the sum to which
the Territory is entitled from the United States.

Regulating the practice of pharmacy by requiring
every pharmacist to obtain a certificate from, or pass
an examination before, a county board of pharmacy,
providing that the county commisioners of each
county shall appoint three reputable pharmacists or
physicians to act as such board, and prescribing its
duties.

Requiring every practitioner of medicine or surgery
to file with the county recorder a diploma from, some
regularly chartered medical school, and making it
unlawful for any other persons to practice.

Designating the last Monday of April as a legal
holiday, to be known as "Arbor-day."

Revising the law regulating the assessment of taxes.

Providing that the county commissioners may fix
bounties for the destruction of certain wild animals,
and empowering them to levy a special bounty-tax of
not more than one half of one per cent.

Authorizing county commissioners to refund county indebtedness at their discretion.

Providing that all costs in criminal cases, where the

defendant is convicted, shall be taxed against him
and collected, if he is possessed of property.

Giving the conductor or other person in charge of
a railroad train, or a station agent, power to arrest without warrant any person committing an unlawful act
upon any train or in any station, and prescribing the
punishment for such act.

To provide for the registration of electors.

To protect the forests of the Territory from destruction by fire.

Population.—By the census of 1880 the population of the Territory was 32,610. No enumeration has since been made, but careful estimates by county officials, about the middle of
the year, show an increase to 97,250, or three
times as many as in 1880. The most populous
counties were Alturas, with 16,250 people;
Bingham, with 10,500; Ada, with 10,000;
Nez Percé, with 9,600; and Shoshone, with
8,500. At the close of the year the total
population must have exceeded 100,000. There
are at least 3,000 Mormons in the Territory
who are entitled to vote, being about one
seventh of the whole number of voters; but
they are practically disfranchised by a law of
the Territory compelling every voter to take
an oath against polygamy.

There is great need of more extensive surveys of the public lands of the Territory, in
order to open them for settlement. Some of
the best tracts are closed to immigration. In
the Boisé district only 2,500,000 acres out of
10,000,000 are surveyed; in the Blackfoot district there are 3,900,000 acres of surveyed and
5,000,000 of unsurveyed land; in the Hailey
district only one third is surveyed land; in the
Cœur d'Alene district only thirteen townships
are surveyed, and it is estimated that the population of this region would be doubled within
a year if the land were ready for occupation.

Finances.—The following statement shows
the Territorial indebtedness at the 1st of October:

Bonds, act 1877, due Dec. 1, 1891	$46,715 06
Capitol building bonds, due in 1905	80,000 00
Insane asylum bonds, due from 1892 to 1895	20,000 00
Warrants outstanding	54,140 43
Total	$200,855 49

Only the first three items represent the permanent debt. The income of the Territory for
1887 was made up as follows: Property-tax of
3¼ mills, $70,000; poll-tax, $10,000; from
licenses, $7,500; from all other sources, $2,200;
total, $89,700.

Statistics.—The total valuation of taxable
property in 1886 was $17,725,122; in 1887,
$20,741,192. These figures represent only a
fraction of the wealth of the Territory, as the
valuation itself is placed very low, and does not
include the rich mining properties and their
products, on which there is no tax. Growing
crops are also exempt, and, as assessments are
made early in the spring, but little grain, fruit,

hay, or other products of farmers is ever on the assessment rolls.

There are 893·68 miles of railroad in the Territory, owned by the following companies: Oregon Short Line, 550·33 miles; Utah and Northern, 206·49 miles; Idaho Central, 19·5 miles; Oregon Railway and Navigation Company, 8 miles; Northern Pacific, 88 miles; Cœur d'Alene, 13·33; Spokane and Idaho, 13·5 miles.

The grain-crop for 1887 is reported at 2,874,-325 bushels, a considerable increase over former years. The hay-crop was 342,914 tons. There were 132,922 horses, 442,363 cattle, 812,-248 sheep, and 60,411 hogs, reported by the county officers as assessed for this year.

Education.—The Territory supports a system of common schools designed to give all children a knowledge of the elementary branches. The school officers consist of a Territorial Superintendent of Public Instruction, a county superintendent of schools in each county, and a board of three trustees in each district. The following table gives a summary of the reports of the county superintendents for 1887:

School districts	313
School-houses	216
Schools	322
Pupils enrolled	10,607
School libraries	10
Volumes in libraries	1,321
Children of school age	18,506
Received in 1886	$147,258 45
Expended in 1886	$185,818 31
Estimated expenditures for 1887	$170,000 00
Estimated receipts for 1887	$165,000 00
Estimated value of property	$279,500 00

In the past five years the school population has nearly doubled. In addition to the common-school districts, there have been created by special enactment, at Boisé City, Lewiston, and Emmettsburg, independent school-districts, in which graded schools with advanced courses are supported. Several of the larger common schools are also graded. There are 7 sectarian schools, holding property valued at $55,000, and numerous private schools. By an act of the last Legislature, every parent or guardian is required to send his child to school for at least twelve weeks in each school year, eight weeks of which must be consecutive. The act applies only to children between eight and fourteen years of age, who reside within two miles of a school-house. A penalty of not less than $5, or more than $50, is imposed for violation of this law. There are some exceptions, and the board of trustees for each school district is permitted to excuse any parent upon sufficient cause.

Much trouble has been experienced, and more is apprehended, from the attitude of the Mormons toward the school laws of the Territory. These laws require that one of the school trustees of each district shall be elected or appointed in September of each year, and that he shall take the official oath against polygamy before discharging his duties. In portions of Bear Lake, Bingham, Cassia, and Onei-

da counties, there are school districts in which there are no Gentiles eligible either for election or appointment as trustees. The entire community is Mormon. No Mormon can take the official oath. Hence but two trustees remain in office in such districts. Next year there will be but one trustee, and where there is but one trustee the schools can not be carried on. The school superintendents of the above-named counties (except of Bear Lake), have, in the discretion given them by law, held that a person who belongs to an organization that teaches things defined by the statutes to be crimes, is not a law-abiding citizen or a person of good moral character, and therefore they refuse to license any member of that organization to teach in the public schools. The Mormon leaders, on the other hand, have given notice that, where Gentile teachers are employed, they will not permit their children to attend the public school.

Charities and Prisons.—The Territory has recently erected a large three-story building as an asylum for the insane in the town of Blackfoot, Bingham County, and has brought thither the patients it formerly supported at the Oregon Insane Asylum. The asylum opened July 2, 1886, with 26 male and 10 female patients. During the year there were admitted 19 male and 12 female patients. The whole number of patients under treatment during the year was 45 males and 22 females. The daily average was 44. The sum of $34,904 was expended during the first year in furnishing and maintaining the institution.

The prisoners of the Territory are kept at the United States Penitentiary, and about $18,000 annually is paid for their support. There are 64 convicts so supported, of whom 6 are sentenced for life and 19 for periods of from ten to twenty years. The accommodations at this prison are very inadequate.

Capitol.—The Capitol building at Boisé City, for which the Legislature of 1885 appropriated $80,000, was completed and occupied this year. It stands in the center of a large block of land given by the city, and is equipped with the most modern furnishings. Offices are provided not only for the Territorial officials, but for the Governor, Secretary, United States Attorney, United States Marshal, Clerk of the Supreme Court, and United States Surveyor-General and other Federal officials.

Mining.—The product of Idaho's numerous and extensive mines is one of the great reasons of her present growth and prosperity. The production of gold, silver, and lead for the year ending Sept. 30, 1887, is estimated as follows: Gold, $2.417,429; silver, $4,633,160; lead, $2.195,000; making a total of $9,245,-589. The production of the same metals for 1886 was $5,755,602, and for 1885 $5,486,-000. Regarding the effect upon this industry of the alien land law passed by Congress, the Governor says: "The mines in this Territory are mostly undeveloped, and are in the hands of poor men who are not able to make the necessary improvements and work their valuable mines successfully, consequently they are anxious to lease or sell portions of them to capitalists. For this purpose resort must be had to those places where capital is abundant and seeking investment, and rates of interest are low. Several large and important mining transactions were about being consummated by mine-owners in Idaho with foreign capitalists when the act to restrict the ownership of real estate in the Territories to American citizens became a law. I would therefore earnestly recommend that this act may be so amended by Congress as to exclude from its operation mineral lands in this Territory."

Indians.—The Indians in Idaho are peaceable and probably in as prosperous condition as any in the United States. There have been .no murderous outbreaks for several years past; increasing immigration and settlement of the Territory have had their beneficial effect upon them.

There are five reservations, supporting 4,200 Indians, as follow :

RESERVATIONS.	Population.	Acres.
Cœur d'Alene	500	598,500
Fort Hall or Shoshone and Bannocks.	1,500	1,202,880
Nez Percé	1,200	746,651
Leuihi	600	105,960
Western Shoshone	400	181,300

On the Cœur d'Alene reservation valuable mineral discoveries were made late in 1886 and early in 1887, and 300 locations have already been made and recorded.

Annexation.—On this subject the Governor speaks as follows in his annual report: "The desire for annexation to Washington Territory is by no means unanimous in northern Idaho, as is evinced by the protest presented to the last Congress. The inhabitants of the Cœur d'Alene section, in Shoshone County, do not desire to be annexed to Washington at all, but would prefer, if Idaho is to be divided, to be annexed to Montana. It is conceded that the bulk of residents of Kootenai and Idaho counties prefer to remain in Idaho. The principal resource of northern Idaho is mining, and the greater extent of its area is mineral land. Washington is practically non-mineral, and it is very apparent to mining men that mining interests suffer in a State or Territory where the majority of the people are interested in agricultural pursuits. Now that the railroads have connected the two sections of Idaho, one of the standing arguments of annexationists has fallen to the ground."

Climate.—The following meteorological data are furnished by the United States Signal Office at Boisé City, covering the year ending August 31: Amount of rain-fall, 13·18 inches ; average monthly rain-fall, 1·10 inches. There was one inch more of rain-fall during the year above named than during the corresponding period of the previous year. Highest temperature, 100·8° above zero (July 6); lowest temperature, 6·1° above zero (February 25). Average temperature during the year, 50·8° above zero.

ILLINOIS. State Government.—The following were the State officers during the year: Governor, Richard J. Oglesby, Republican; Lieutenant-Governor, John C. Smith; Secretary of State, Henry D. Dement; Auditor, Charles P. Swigert; Treasurer, John R. Tanner; Attorney-General, George Hunt; Superintendent of Public Instruction, Richard Edwards; Railroad and Warehouse Commissioners, John J. Rinaker, B. F. Marsh, and W. T. Johnson; Chief-Justice of the Supreme Court, John M. Scott; Associate Justices, Alfred M. Craig, Benjamin R. Sheldon, Simeon P. Shope, Benjamin D. Magruder, John Scholfield, and John H. Mulkey.

Legislative Session.—The Thirty-fifth General Assembly was in session 172 days, adjourning on June 16. Its first duty was to fill a vacancy in the office of United States Senator, caused by the death of Gen. John A. Logan. The Republican caucus nominated Hon. Charles B. Farwell; the Democrats, Congressman William R. Morrison. Farwell was elected on the first ballot, receiving 78 votes to 61 for Morrison and 8 for Benjamin W. Goodhue, the nominee of the United Labor party, this being a strict party vote. A large amount of useful legislation was secured. Not the least important act was the passage of a bill providing for the organization of savings-banks, and prescribing their management and supervision. Although these institutions at which small deposits may be received have long been a business feature of nearly all the other States, this is the first time that they have been legalized in Illinois. The following stringent act was framed to cover cases similar to those of the Chicago Anarchists:

If any person shall, by speaking to any public or private assemblage of people or in any public place, or shall, by writing, printing, or publishing, or by causing to be written, printed, published, or circulated any written or printed matter, advise, encourage, aid, abet, or incite a local revolution, or the overthrowing or destruction of the existing order of society by force or violence, or the resistance to, and destruction of, the lawful power and authority of the legal authorities of this State, or of any of the towns, cities, or counties of this State, or by any of the means aforesaid shall advise, abet, encourage, or incite the disturbance of the public peace, and by such disturbance [an] attempt at revolution or destruction of public order or resistance to such authorities shall therefore ensue, and human life is taken, or any person is injured or property destroyed, . . . every person so aiding, etc., shall be deemed as having conspired with the person or persons who actually commit the crime, and shall be deemed a principal in the perpetration of the same, and shall be punished accordingly, and it shall not be necessary for the prosecution to show that the speaking was heard, or the written or printed matter was read or communicated to the person or persons actually committing the crime, if such speaking, writing, printing, or publishing is shown to have been done in a public manner.

If two or more persons conspire to overthrow the existing order of society by force and violence . . .

ILLINOIS. 375

and a human being is killed, or person injured, or property destroyed by any of the persons engaged in such conspiracy, or by any one who may participate with them, . . . then all the persons who may have conspired together as aforesaid, together with all persons who may actively participate in carrying into effect their common design, shall be deemed guilty of the crime committed by any one or more of such persons, . . . and shall be punished accordingly; notwithstanding the time and place for the bringing about such revolution . . . had not been definitely agreed upon by such conspirators, but was left to the exigencies of the time or the judgment of co-conspirators, or some one or more of them.

Another law makes "boycotting" a conspiracy, punishable by imprisonment not over five years, or a fine of not over $2,500, or both. Foreigners are forbidden to hold real property in the State by descent, devise, or purchase, except that one who hereafter acquires land by descent or devise may hold it from three to five years after such requisition. Foreigners already owning land in the State are permitted to retain it. Property held contrary to this act will escheat to the State. A question that provoked long discussion was whether the State Fair should be permanently located, and, if so, at what place. The House decided that Springfield should be a permanent location, but the Senate refused to concur, and no legislation was had upon the matter. The commission appointed by the last Legislature to revise the revenue laws and suggest a remedy for the present inefficient method of assessment and collection of taxes, submitted an elaborate report at this session, but no action was taken upon it. The necessity for a change is proved by the fact that, under the present method, the valuation of property in the State is reported to be less than in 1886, and that in the past fifteen years it has decreased over $645,000,000. Other acts of the session were as follow:

To prevent alien landlords from including the payment of taxes in the rent of farm-lands as a part of the rental thereof.

Amending an act relating to the suppression and prevention of contagious diseases among domestic animals, and giving the Live-Stock Commissioners power to suppress such diseases.

To punish false pretenses in obtaining certificates of registration of cattle and other animals, and to punish giving false pedigrees.

Appropriating $20,000 per annum for the next two years for the repairs and running expenses of the Illinois and Michigan Canal.

To create a board of trustees to take and hold the title to the homestead of Abraham Lincoln, in the city of Springfield, in trust for the State of Illinois, and to provide for the care and custody thereof; appropriating $3,800 for the next two years for repairs and for paying a custodian to keep and exhibit said homestead and the relics and curiosities there collected.

Appropriating $10,000 for repairs of the Lincoln Monument near Springfield.

Appropriating $50,000 to erect a monument to Gen. John A. Logan, and providing for its location upon some public park or boulevard.

Appropriating $20,500 for repairs upon the State-House.

To prohibit book-making and pool-selling, except at the grounds of incorporated fair or racing associations during the meetings of such associations.

To suppress "bucket-shops," or dealing upon margins.

To provide for the proper care and management of county cemetery grounds by the appointment of trustees of such by the county commissioners.

Making a residence of two years in the State necessary before admission to the State Soldiers' and Sailors' Home.

To punish the abandonment of children under one year of age.

To provide that the police of any town or city may go into any adjoining town or city to preserve the peace or to protect citizens and property, and making such adjoining towns or cities one police district for such purposes.

To create the office of president of the board of trustees of villages and towns, and to provide for his election annually.

To give power to the city council of cities, and the president and board of trustees in villages and towns, to license, tax, regulate, or prohibit itinerant merchants.

To create, in cities or villages of 50,000 inhabitants or over, having a paid fire department, a firemen's pension fund, which shall be one per cent. of all revenues of such city collected from licenses, to create a board of trustees of such fund, to provide for its distribution for pensions to disabled firemen and to the widows and minor children of deceased firemen, and to authorize the retirement from service upon pensions of members of fire departments in such cities or villages.

To provide a similar pension fund for the police in cities and villages of 50,000 inhabitants or over.

To provide for the incorporation of co-operative associations for pecuniary profit, and defining their powers and duties.

To enable corporations created for that purpose to transact a surety business in this State, and to become surety on bonds required by law.

To provide for and regulate the administration of trusts by organized trust companies.

To prevent the prostitution of females—fixing the age of consent in females at fourteen years.

Defining the offenses and penalties for interfering with or bribing voters.

To regulate the manufacture, transportation, use, and sale of dynamite and other explosives, and to punish an improper use of the same.

Making barbed wire a legal fence.

To regulate the taking of fish in the waters of the State, and to encourage their propagation and cultivation.

Providing that no person shall be imprisoned for debt for a longer period than six months.

Prohibiting the sale of intoxicating liquors outside of incorporated towns, cities, or villages, in less quantities than five gallons.

To organize farmers' county mutual live-stock insurance companies.

To authorize judges of courts of record to appoint, at the request of the electors of the county shown at an election for that purpose, a board of jury commissioners, which shall have charge of the selection of jurors for that county.

Increasing the amount of tax that may be levied in cities of fewer than 100,000 inhabitants to two mills on the dollar.

Ceding the locks and dams in the Illinois river to the United States, on condition that a complete water-way for steam navigation from the Mississippi river to Lake Michigan, by way of the Illinois river, the Des Plaines river, and the Illinois and Michigan Canal, be made by the United States Government.

Prohibiting marriages between cousins of the first degree.

Regulating the practice of medicine and surgery in the State, requiring a certificate from the State Board of Health, and prescribing the powers and duties of the board.

To provide for the greater security and protection of miners.

To indemnify the owners of property for damages occasioned by mobs and riots by making the city (or, if not in the city, the county) liable for three fourths of the damages sustained.

Requiring all grain, mill-stuffs, or seeds delivered by one railroad within the State to another railroad for further transportation, to be weighed in bulk by such roads, unless the shipper, owner, or agent expressly order otherwise.

Amending the railroad law by requiring the Railroad and Warehouse Commissioners to investigate railroad accidents resulting in loss of life, and to report their findings to the Governor, giving them power to investigate at any time the condition of the tracks and bridges of any road, and to make recommendations for repairs or improvements.

To provide for the organization of road districts in counties not under township organization, to regulate the election and duties of road officers therein, and to define the rights of travelers upon the public roads.

Declaring that no prescriptive right to maintain poles, wires, or cables used for telegraph, telephone, electric-light, or other electric purpose, shall be gained by lapse of time over any buildings or land in the State.

Prohibiting the selling, giving, or furnishing of tobacco to minors under sixteen years of age.

Requiring the Governor to designate annually by proclamation a day known as "Arbor-day" to be observed by the planting of trees.

Making employés and laborers preferred creditors to the amount of $50, against judgment creditors of any individual, firm, or corporation.

To provide for special deputy sheriffs, and for calling out and using the militia of the State for the preservation of peace and the protection of property.

Finances.—Two years ago, when the General Assembly met, there was a balance of $1,500,-000 in the State treasury. The tax-levy for 1885-'86 was accordingly reduced to 42 cents, which produced a revenue of about $3,000,000 a year. As the annual expenditures were considerably above this sum, the balance in the treasury at the beginning of 1887 had been reduced to $400,000. For the years 1887-'83 it became necessary to raise the full amount of the legislative appropriation by levy, and the rate was increased to 53 cents, producing an annual revenue of $3,800,000. The total appropriations of the last two General Assemblies have not shown much change, being $7,-776,000 in 1885, and $7,600,000 in 1887. Of these sums, $2,000,000 was in each case devoted to school purposes.

Charities.—The annual report of the State Board for the year ending September 30 shows that the ordinary expenses of the year were $1,014,018; special expenses, $331,850, and expenses of the shoe-factory at the Pontiac Reform School, $16,670. The ordinary expenses were considerably less than for the preceding year, and the cost per capita less.

The average number of inmates in all these institutions for the year was 5,230, against 5,-090 in 1886. The heaviest items of special expense are those for building and repairs, of which $74,847 were at the Eastern Insane Hospital, and $100,989 at the Soldiers' Home at Quincy. The latter institution was opened for the first time during the year. A new

charity, the Industrial Home for the Blind, to be located in Cook County, was established by the Legislature, and $100,000 appropriated for grounds and buildings. The State Prison at Joliet and the Southern Penitentiary received special appropriations for improvements and the completion of buildings.

Railroads.—Eighty-two companies were assessed in 1887 for 8,624 miles of main track and upon property valued at $66,517,748. In 1886, seventy-three companies were assessed for $62,972,101 upon 8,200 miles of track; in 1885 the figures were $60,987,817 upon 8,024 miles. During the past few years the assessed value of railroad and other corporations has steadily increased, while that upon personalty and realty held by individuals has steadily decreased. The total assessment on all kinds of property in the State for this year was $726,-138,163, a decrease in value of $39,968 from 1886. Defective methods of assessment are the cause of this unfavorable showing.

Coal-mining.—For the year ending July 1 the total production of coal in Illinois was 10,278,-890 tons, being 1,000,000 tons in excess of the preceding year, and considerably the largest in the mining history of the State. The miners also realized an improved price for their labor, equivalent to about five cents a ton above the prices of the previous year. The number of mine-operators increased, and the length of active operations was 213.2 days, against 206 days the preceding year. The following additional statistics are given:

Mines and openings of all kinds	817
Value of coal mined	$11,152,596
Employés of all kinds	24,504
Average price per ton for mining	$0.127
Kegs of powder used	152,677
Mules employed under ground	1,474
Men killed	41

The number of producing mines has steadily increased since 1883, when it was 639. Of first-class mines, producing 50,000 tons or more during the year, there are only sixty-four. In fact, only 292 mines in the State are engaged in the coal-shipping trade, the remaining 516 being in the local trade. The most important coal-producing counties are: St. Clair, 915,827 tons; Sangamon, 730,391; Madison, 460,926; La Salle, 657,296; Peoria, 434,900; Macoupin, 914,894; Vermilion, 345,-464; Livingston, 357,600; Fulton, 304,588; Jackson, 311,279; and Perry, 319,552.

The year was remarkably free from interruptions by strikes, the prolonged Grape Creek strike being the most remarkable feature of Illinois coal-fields, standing unsettled at the end of a year and a half of its existence. Yet the business of mining has not been free from difficulties, the most important arising from a scarcity of water, occasioned by a long drought. In some parts of Madison, Macoupin, and St. Clair counties, and even as far north as Minonk, in Woodford County, water was so scarce that many operators were obliged to transport by rail the entire supply for their boilers.

Internal Improvements.—A considerable movement was begun in the latter part of the year to secure improvements upon the water-ways of the State. Two conventions, one at Quincy and the other at Peoria, met in October to promote this object. The Quincy convention urged improvements on the Mississippi from Des Moines, Iowa, to the mouth of the Illinois river, in order to cheapen transportation for the grain-crops of the upper Mississippi region. The purpose of the Peoria convention is seen from the following resolutions:

Whereas, The proper improvement of the Illinois and Des Plaines rivers, with a few miles of wide and deep canal, will connect 1,660 miles of large river navigation with 700 miles of lake navigation, all within the boundaries of the United States, permeating the heart of the republic.

Whereas, The State of Illinois has on the recommendation of the United States engineers, tendered the two locks and dams on Illinois river to the General Government, while the Government has now in course of construction two more locks and dams on the lower Illinois; and the improvement is demanded by the wants of commerce and our national defenses, and have strongly recommended its favorable consideration by Congress, and have

Resolved, That to that end we hereby respectfully urge upon Congress that at the coming session it accept the locks and dams ceded to the General Government by the State of Illinois, and appropriate the amount of money estimated and asked for by the engineers to complete the two locks and dams now under construction on the lower Illinois, and appropriate at least one third of the amount estimated to improve the rivers to Joliet.

That we cordially indorse the proposed canal connecting Lake Michigan with the upper Mississippi river *via* Hennepin to said river, at or near Rock Island, as a national undertaking of great importance to the producers in the West and shippers in the East, and earnestly commend it to Congress and the people of the United States as a national water-way to be promptly acted upon.

Pleuro-Pneumonia.—The discovery in September of last year that this disease had attacked large numbers of cattle in the stock-yards of Chicago, and had existed there for some time, led to strenuous efforts on the part of the Live-Stock Commissioners of the State to prevent its increase, and if possible to eradicate it. The Governor issued a proclamation quarantining the infected district, many of the diseased cattle were slaughtered, and the stables disinfected or destroyed. Up to August of this year over 8,000 animals had been killed by order of the commission. At that time the disease was reported to be fully under control, and, although there were a few chronic cases existing, there was no danger of its communication to other animals. The Governor thereupon requested those States that had issued quarantine regulations against Illinois to modify or revoke them, but it was not till later in the year that the quarantine against any of the Chicago yards was raised. Provision was made by the General Assembly for reimbursing the owners of slaughtered animals, and other action tending to increase the power and efficiency of the Live-Stock Commissioners in similar emergencies was taken.

Chicago.—The municipal election in April resulted in a complete overturn in the political circles of the city. There were only two tickets in the field—Republican and United Labor —the contest being virtually between the friends and opponents of socialistic ideas. Roche, Republican, was elected mayor, receiving 51,089 votes, while his opponent, Nelson, obtained only 22,848. The Democrats largely voted the Republican ticket in preference to allying themselves with the Labor ticket. Only one aldermanic district was carried by the Labor party. In June an election of circuit judges for Cook County was held, in which substantially the same elements were opposed to each other. State-Attorney Grinnell, who was most prominent in the prosecution of the Anarchists, was the principal contestant on the Republican ticket, while the Labor party nominated one of their defenders. The vote was nearly three to one in favor of the Republicans.

Early in the year disclosures were made implicating the County Commissioners of Cook County, and some of the managers of county institutions, notably of the county prison, in a systematic robbery, by approving bills and drawing money for county supplies that were never delivered or consumed. Eleven of the suspected officials were tried in August and convicted.

The Anarchists.—On Sept. 14, 1887, the Supreme Court of Illinois handed in its decision affirming the judgment of the lower court in the case of the condemned Anarchists. The peculiar feature of the action of the court during the trial was the decision that the inciting to murder in general terms, of which the Anarchists had been guilty, followed by their presence at a meeting at which a bomb was thrown and life taken, was evidence of a conspiracy to murder, and that those persons upon whom this was proved were guilty of murder. Application was at once made by counsel to the Supreme Court of the United States for a writ of error. This application was denied by a unanimous decision of the court on Nov. 2, 1887. The decision was very important, and was set forth at great length. The result of the application was evident as soon as the court announced that it was ready to discuss the merits of the case. The court held that its duty was not merely to consider the question of jurisdiction. A writ of error ought certainly not to be allowed against the highest court of a State if it appeared that the action of the State court was so plainly right as not to require argument, and especially if it was evident that the action was in accord with the well-considered judgment of the national Supreme Court in similar cases. The only capital case that had ever been brought before the court—that of Twitchell *vs.* the State of Pennsylvania—had been decided in accordance with this principle. In the case of the Anarchists, while the counsel had not deemed it their duty to go fully into the merits of the questions involved, they had yet shown the court what the decisions were of which they complained, and how the questions arose. In this way the court was able to determine whether the errors alleged were such as to justify it in bringing the case before it for review.

The provisions of the Constitution upon which counsel relied were Articles IV, V, VI, and XIV of the amendments. The first three of these articles secure certain immunities to the people of the United States. Article XIV limits the power of the State governments over the people. The first three were decided more than a half-century ago to be limitations, not upon the State, but upon the national Government, and this decision has always been maintained since. The argument of counsel was that, notwithstanding this construction, the immunities therein conferred pertained to the people of the United States, and could not be abridged under the fourteenth amendment, which declared that no State could enforce a law which affected the "privileges or immunities of the people of the United States." The fourteenth amendment also declares that no State can deprive "any person of life, liberty, or property, without due process of law." It was argued that "due process of law" implied trial by an impartial jury, that being a privilege secured by Article VI.

The particular complaints in this case were (1) that a statute of the State had been so construed as to deprive the petitioners of a trial by an impartial jury; and (2) that Spies was compelled to testify against himself. The decision of the court upon the question of what is "an impartial jury" within the meaning of the Constitution is highly important. The law of Illinois and other States upon this point has been an attempt to harmonize the institution of trial by jury with the conditions of modern life. In a day when everybody reads newspapers it is impossible to get a jury of twelve intelligent men who have formed no opinion with regard to a celebrated case. The statute of Illinois was construed by the Illinois courts to mean that, although a person called as a juryman may have formed an opinion based upon rumor or newspaper statement, but has expressed no opinion as to the truth of the newspaper statement, he is still qualified as a juror if he states that he can fairly and impartially render a verdict thereon in accordance with the law and the evidence. The test question is not whether the juror will have the opinion he has formed from the newspapers changed by the evidence, but whether his verdict will be based only on the account that shall be given by the witnesses under oath. The Supreme Court held that the Illinois statute interpreted in this way is not materially different from that of the Territory of Utah. As that was a Territorial statute, passed by a Territorial Legislature for the govern-

ment of a Territory over which the United States has exclusive jurisdiction, it came directly within the operation of Article VI. This act had been before the Supreme Court, and no doubt had been raised of its constitutionality. The other complaints of the petitioners, viz., that Spies had been compelled to testify against himself, and that Spies and Fielden, the one having been born in Germany and the other in England, had been denied rights guaranteed to them by treaty between the United States and their respective countries, were considered in detail by the court, but are too frivolous to be deserving of more than a mention. The court overruled them. The court unanimously refused to grant the writ of error.

The only recourse of the Anarchists thereafter was to the interference of the Governor of Illinois. Linge, Engel, Fischer, and Parsons refused to join in the application for pardon, and demanded their liberty as a right. A request for pardon was made by Spies, Fielden, and Schwab. On November 10 Linge committed suicide by exploding a cartridge in his mouth with a lighted candle. On the same day Governor Oglesby announced his determination upon the question of the commutation of the condemned men. Fielden and Schwab having joined in the application for pardon, and their guilt being of a somewhat lighter nature than that of the others, had their sentence commuted to imprisonment for life. They had conducted themselves in a less defiant manner than the others during the trial, and the commutation of their sentences was favored by Judge Gary and District-Attorney Grinnell. Spies, Fischer, Engel, and Parsons were hanged on Nov. 11, 1887.

INDIA, an empire in southern Asia, subject to Great Britain. The Secretary of State for India, who is a member of the British Cabinet, exercises almost autocratic powers, as Parliament usually concurs in the decisions of the Government with regard to Indian affairs without serious discussion, yet he is largely guided by the advice of the Governor-General, who is assisted by a council. The Governor-General in council has power to make laws, subject to the approval of the British Government. The Secretary of State for India is Viscount Cross, appointed Aug. 3, 1886. The Viceroy or Governor-General is Frederick Temple-Blackwood, Earl of Dufferin, who succeeded the Marquis of Ripon on Oct. 28, 1884. The Council consists of the commander-in-chief of the forces and six ordinary members appointed by the British Government, who with from six to twelve additional members appointed by the viceroy form a legislative council for making laws and regulations.

Area and Population.—The area of British India is 911,075 square miles, and the population on Feb. 17, 1881, when the last census was taken, was 201,888,897. The feudatory and independent states, all of which are under

British tutelage, have a combined area of 471,-549, and were peopled by 52,002,924 persons, making the aggregate area of India 1,382,624 square miles and the population 253,891,821, divided into 129,941,851 males and 123,949,970 females. The population of the empire was divided in respect to religion into 187,937,450 Hindoos, 50,121,585 Mohammedans, 6,426,511 Nature-worshipers, 3,418,875 Buddhists, 1,-862,684 Christians, 1,853,385 Sikhs, 1,221.896 Jains, 85,350 Parsees, 12,008 Jews, and 952,-127 others. Of the Christians 893,658 were natives, 62,084 Eurasians, 83,330 of British birth, and 59.280 Europeans other than British, while of 764,165 the origin was not specified. The emigration of coolies during nine months ending Dec. 31, 1885, was 6,967 persons, all of whom went to the British West India islands and British Guiana except 540 whose destination was Fiji.

Agriculture.—The total area of British India as shown by surveys is 621,146,297. According to agricultural reports covering 356,017.898 acres there were in 1884–'85 of the latter extent of surface 199,484,230 acres under cultivation, 169,289,983 acres uncultivated, and 38,050,091 acres in forests. Of the cultivated area 180,-458.132 acres were actually cropped, and 19,-026,098 acres were fallow. Of the uncultivated area 82,046,871 were reported as suitable for cultivation, and 75,747,818 acres as not available, exclusive of 11,495,794 acres in Assam, concerning which there was no report as to the character of the soil. In Madras, out of 47,700,000 acres held from the Government, 19,700,000 acres were possessed by peasant proprietors, and 8,500,000 acres by small holders, the average size of both classes of farms being 18 acres, while 16,500,000 acres were owned by zemindaries in estates of the average area of 100,000 acres each and the remainder by smaller zemindaries. In Bombay 29,500,000 acres were divided among peasant proprietors in farms of the average size of 21 acres. In the Northwest Provinces nearly all the land is in the hands of zemindaries whose estates vary from the class paying over 5,000 rupees of revenue or tax to the Government, and averaging 675 acres, to the class paying less than 100 rupees, and 63 acres in average area. In Oudh there are 9,000,000 acres in 440 private estates, and 4,700,000 acres divided among 8,000 village communities. In the Punjab the peasant proprietors own 48,000,000 acres in 30,000 estates, 3,300 communities possess 2,-700,000 acres, one zemindary has an estate of 1,000,000 acres, and 1,500,000 acres are held by zemindaries in estates of 1,000 acres or more. In the Central Provinces 24,500,000 acres are held by zemindaries in estates of an average area of 1,400 acres, 12,900,000 acres in estates of an average area of 1,700 acres, 4,-000.000 acres in estates of an average area of 21,000 acres, and 2,000,000 acres by small holders, the average size of whose farms was 250 acres. In Lower Burmah 3,880,000 acres are

held by peasant proprietors in estates of the average size of 6 acres, the total cultivated area being 4,400,000 acres. In Assam, out of 7,350,-000 acres, the larger zemindaries possess 2,-000,000 acres in estates of the average area of 4,488 acres, small zemindaries hold 1,600,000 acres in estates of the average extent of 82 acres, and peasant proprietors own 2,280,000 acres in estates of the average size of 6 acres.

Of 189,806,225 acres under cultivation in British India in 1884–'85, 58,565,331 acres were devoted to rice, 20,328,254 acres to wheat, 79,523,386 acres to other grain-crops, 9,490,859 acres to oil-seeds, 1,715,009 acres to the sugar-cane, 9,851,970 to fibers, 2,191,470 acres to indigo, and 8,140,116 acres to other crops. Of the rice area 37,500,000 acres were in Bengal, 5,680,106 acres in Madras, 3,630,340 acres in Lower Burmah, and 3,091,625 acres in the Central Provinces. The cultivation of oil-seeds was distributed throughout India. In the Northwest Provinces 670,547 acres were planted to the sugar-cane, and in Bengal and the Punjab about half that area. The indigo-culture occupied 1,300,000 acres of the surface of Bengal. The extent of wheat cultivation in the various provinces was as follows: Punjab, 7,819,509 acres; Central Provinces, 3,745,251 acres; Northwest Provinces, 3,626,225 acres; Bombay, 2,211,459 acres; Oudh, 1,476,946 acres; Bengal, 850,000 acres; Berar, 819,057 acres; Madras, 30,943 acres; Lower Burmah, 2,644 acres. Of the area given up to fiber-crops 8,690,242 acres were devoted to cotton, of which 2,150,000 acres were in Bombay, and 1,500,000 in Madras and the Northwest Provinces. Of the 189,806,225 acres embraced in the crop reports, 7,990,581 acres are twice counted, having borne two crops during the year. The area of crops, excluding Bengal, was 136,113,781 acres, of which 24,720,000 acres were irrigated. Of the total area of wheat cultivation, nearly 5,500,000 acres are irrigated. Of the miscellaneous crop the most important is tobacco, covering over 517,000 acres. About 262,000 acres are devoted to tea, and half that area to coffee. The tea-crop of 1887 was estimated at 82,500,000 pounds.

Commerce.—The following table shows the value of the chief imports and the total value of imports during the fiscal year 1885–'86, in pounds sterling:

IMPORTS.	Value.	IMPORTS.	Value.
Cotton manufactures	24,232,628	Silk (raw and manufactured)	1,680,959
Metals and hardware	5,548,061	Provisions	1,191,681
		Apparel	1,087,209
Machinery	991,558	Salt	596,047
Railway plant and rolling-stock	2,018,065	Spices	715,678
		Oils	961,129
Liquors	1,298,497	Other articles	7,188,451
Woolen goods	1,391,861		
Sugar	1,458,097	Total	51,811,580
Coal	1,308,414		

The following were the leading exports and the total value of exports of domestic products:

EXPORTS.	Value.	EXPORTS.	Value.
Grain and pulse ..	17,506,118	Sugar............	595,419
Raw cotton	10,777,904	Wool	872,231
Opium...........	10,785,518	Raw silk and co-	
Seeds	9,948,850	coons	882,251
Hides and skins ..	5,534,602	Silk, manufactured	829,588
Indigo	8,783,160	Lac	585,128
Jute	4,855,862	Wood, and manu-	
Tea	4,306,183	factures of	611,008
Cotton, manufact-		Oils	895,562
ured	8,685,510	Other articles	£,120,316
Coffee	1,848,895		
Jute manufactures	1,130,808	Total	80,784,781

The imports into Bengal amounted to £22,-
623,418; into Lower Burmah, £3,436,500; into
Madras, £4,552,108; into Bombay and Sind,
£36,577,355; the exports from Bengal, £33,-
211,524; from Lower Burmah, £6,780,819;
from Madras, £8,306,568; from Bombay and
Sind, £36,616,766. The imports of treasure in
the year ending March 31, 1886, £15,477,800,
and the exports to £1,087,837. Of the imports,
£3,091,540 were gold and £12,386,529 silver;
of the exports, £328,606 were gold and £779,-
631 silver. The totals of merchandise and
precious metals do not include the government
stores and treasure, of which the imports were
£3,844,329 and the exports £73,823 in value.

The import and export trade was divided
among foreign nations and Great Britain and
her colonies in 1885–'86, as follows, the imports
and exports of merchandise being given in
pounds sterling:

COUNTRIES.	Imports into India.	Exports from India.
The United Kingdom	41,659,000	84,292,443
China	1,851,860	12,657,459
Straits Settlements...................	1,612,070	8,684,087
United States	833,087	8,047,487
Mauritius.........................	1,105,742	909,212
Ceylon	509,895	1,918,775
Persia	646,188	1,288,021
France	624,079	6,695,528
Australia and New Zealand........ ..	432,079	586,781
Italy	414,545	8,658,590
East Africa	401,565	480,705
Arabia	294,678	901,019
Austria..........................	451,884	2,014,196
Germany.........................	120,000	408,925
Belgium.........................	266,741	8,780,011
Egypt...........................	50,951	8,250,807

In addition to the trade by sea, as given in
the above tables, there is a considerable trade
by way of the land frontiers. The imports
amounted to £5,331,403 in 1885, and the exports to £4,552,996. Of the imports, Upper
Burmah contributed £2,023,933; Nepaul, £1,-
405,519; Cabul, £241,345; and Thibet, £24,-
097. The same countries participated in the
export trade in like proportions.

The imports of American kerosene in 1886–
'87 amounted to over 29,000,000 gallons, exceeding any previous importation.. There were
also received the first consignments of Baku
oil from Batoum, the quantity being 1,500,000
gallons. The Russian oil is said to be safer
than the American kerosene that is shipped
to the East, having a higher flashing-point.
There was a large exportation of wheat to
Italy in 1886–'87, valued at £2,070,000, which
was due to a short crop in Russia. The Indian wheat is adapted for maccaroni and other
pastes, such as are largely manufactured in
Italy. There was an exportation to Hong-
kong of Bombay cotton twist of the value of
£2,360,000, while direct shipments to the
treaty-ports of China amounted to £500,000.
This strong yarn is woven by hand in China
into the cloth that is ordinarily worn by the
men of that country. The exports of articles
of food and of manufactured articles showed
an increase. The exports of wheat were the
largest on record, amounting to 1,113,166 tons,
which was 5·71 per cent. in excess of those of
1885–'86. The exports of cotton amounted to
£18,460,000, and the jute exports to £4,870,-
000.

According to the conclusions reached by Mr.
Smeaton, director of agriculture for the Northwest Provinces in regard to the competition
between Indian and American wheat, it is not
in prime cost that India is at a disadvantage.
For the same outlay she can raise nearly 20
per cent. more grain than America, and of not
much inferior quality; while she has resources
enough in area and labor to raise sufficient
wheat to supply the entire demand of the
British market. India, Mr. Smeaton thinks,
possesses means to compel America to withdraw her hostile tariffs and to open her markets to the products of British industry, but
she is burdened in the struggle with America
by, first, a primary railway freight about 25
per cent. higher; secondly, an extra railway
freight of 5 per cent. on ballast; thirdly, a
further extra freight on bags; fourthly, excessive handling; and, fifthly, she brings into
the English market an article inferior in appearance, though on the whole not much inferior in quality, to the rival one.

Navigation.—The total number of vessels engaged in foreign trade that entered and cleared
at ports of British India with cargoes and in
ballast in 1885–'86 was as follows:

NATIONALITY.	ENTERED.		CLEARED.	
	No.	Tons.	No.	Tons.
British...	2,081	2,895,606	2,055	2,874,566
British Indian	1,075	185,383	1,122	160,211
Native craft...............	1,300	72,271	1,363	76,069
Foreign................	796	587,480	769	584,083
Total.................	5,258	3,640,687	5,369	3,658,909

The number of steam-vessels which entered
Indian ports via the Suez Canal in 1874 was
817, of 434,152 tons; in 1884. 839, of 1,405,-
007 tons; in 1885, 726, of 1,264,105 tons; in
1886, 773, of 1,336,638 tons. Cleared in 1874,
306, of 382,375 tons; in 1884, 1,091, of 1,746,-
785 tons; in 1885, 923, of 1,553,446 tons; in
1886, 1,039, of 1,722,008 tons.

In the coasting-trade 110,348 vessels, of
7,293,462 tons, entered, and 107,963 vessels,
of 7,153,499 tons, cleared in 1884–'85.

Railroads.—The railroad mileage on March
31, 1887, was 13,390. The number of passengers in 1886 was 88,436,318, against 80,864,-
779 in 1885. The number of tons of freight

transported in 1886 was 19,576,365. The receipts were £18,704,586, and the expenses £8,-930,982. There were 1,025 miles constructed during the year, forming part of 16,596 miles of new railroad that had been sanctioned. The profits earned on the capital investment by the traffic of the year was 5·90 per cent. The Bolan Railway to Quetta and portions of the Scinde-Pishin Railway beyond Quetta were opened to the public at the end of March. Work was begun at both ends of the Mandalay Railway, 220 miles in length, which was authorized to be built by the state in November, 1886. The longest new line that was sanctioned was the Bengal-Nagpur Railway, 784 miles, which was intrusted to a guaranteed company. During 1886–'87 the capital expended in railroad construction was £9,740,-000, of which £5,120,000 was on state lines, and £4,620,000 on the lines of guaranteed and subsidized companies. The net loss to the state on the guaranteed railroads in 1886–'87 was £1,177,900, and for 1887-'88 it is estimated at £1,383,700.

The Post-Office.—The number of letters forwarded in the mails in the year ending March 31, 1886, was 216,145,796; the number of newspapers, 20,341,814; the receipts of the post-office were £1,113,086; the expenses, £1,-302,604.

Telegraphs.—The length of the Government telegraph lines in 1886 was 27,510 miles, with 81,480 miles of wires, exclusive of 187 miles of cable. The number of paid dispatches in 1886 was 2,306,876; receipts, £628,484; expenses, £872,761.

The Army.—The European troops quartered in India on March 31, 1885, numbered 3,712 officers and 59,218 rank and file, a total of 62,-980 men. The native army numbered 1,556 officers and 124,388 men, making the total strength of the Indian army 5,268 officers and 183,606 men. The army estimates fix the strength of the European troops for 1886–'87 at 68,196 officers and men. The military budget of the Indian Government for 1887–'88 amounts to £14,010,000, against £14,280,000 in 1886–'87, and provides for an army of 73,552 Europeans and 145,165 natives, making a total of 218,717 men. Returns published in 1884 show that the various Hindu feudatory or independent states of India have armies numbering 275,075 men and 3,372 guns; the Mohammedan states 74,760 men, 865 guns; total, 349,-835 men, 4,237 guns, belonging to the various native armies. The Cashmere army alone numbers 27,000 men; Nepaul, 100,000; Hyderabad, 44,000; Oodeypore, 20,000; Gwalior, 11,000; Baroda, 15,500; Indore, 8,000; Jeypore, 18,-000; Jodhpore, 8,500; Bhurtpore, 11,500. Each army is composed of infantry, cavalry, and artillery.

Finance.—The final accounts for the year ending March 31, 1886, show receipts from the various sources of revenue of the following amounts, in pounds sterling:

SOURCES OF REVENUE.	Receipts.	SOURCES OF REVENUE.	Receipts.
Land revenue	22,592,371	Posts, telegraphs, and mint.......	1,965,860
Opium	8,942,515	Justice	577,709
Salt monopoly....	6,545,128	Police...........	891,011
Stamps	3,663,174	Public works	15,857,948
Excise	4,152,136	War department .	942,672
Provincial rates..	3,980,815	Other ordinary receipts	1,606,495
Customs	1,199,976		
Licenses	508,084		
Forests	1,486,092	Extraordinary receipts	4,194,899
Registration	306,006		
Tributes	689,575		
Interest	698,982	Total	76,660,596

The ordinary receipts and expenditures show a deficit of £2,801,726. The expenditure under the various heads was as follows:

HEADS OF EXPENDITURE.	Disbursements.	HEADS OF EXPENDITURE.	Disbursements.
Interest of the debt	4,580,561	Foreign affairs....	1,150,723
Refunds	1,302,711	Ecclesiastical and medical	911,614
Cost of collection .	8,202,567	Pensions and relief	3,554,523
Posts, telegraphs, and mint.......	2,292,961	Printing	510,696
Civil administration.......	1,732,909	Famine relief.....	1,500,000
		Army.............	20,097,719
Legislation and justice	3,352,284	Public works......	21,836,875
Police...........	2,552,794	Provincial expenses	528,582
Marine	524,700	Miscellaneous	549,374
Public instruction.	1,718,935	Total	77,265,928

The budget estimates for 1886–'87 were disturbed by the fall in exchange and the military expenses in Upper Burmah, which imposed on the Government the necessity of choosing between a deficit, fresh taxation, the withdrawal of grants for railroads, or a reduction of the famine insurance debt. The last expedient was adopted, and thereby £1,049,400 were made available to obviate the deficit. The excess in military expenditures for Upper Burmah amounted to £860,000, while the civil estimates for Upper Burmah were increased by £280,800 for police. The loss by exchange was £474,600 more than the estimate. The revised budget estimates for 1886–'87 make the total receipts £76,081,228 and the expenditures £76,021,150. For 1887–'88 the receipts are estimated at £77,460,200 and the expenditures at £77,443,500. The expenditures in England in 1886–'87 are estimated at £19,661,450, offset by £827,023 of receipts; for 1887-'88 the expenditures in England are reckoned at £20,-309,400 and the receipts at £242,500; the public debt on March 31, 1886, amounted to £174,-524,101, of which £166,510,603 was consolidated debt and £8,013,498 was unfunded; of the consolidated debt £92,703,982 was payable in India and £73,806,621 in England; the amount of paper money in circulation on March 31, 1885, was £14,540,727.

The budget for 1886–'87, besides withholding the promised construction of railroads, canals, and irrigation-works for the prevention of famine, reduces the grants to local administrations for public works in violation of contracts made with the provincial governments. The native press complained that Lord Dufferin had arbitrarily done away with the famine fund, and yet continues the construction of railroads for the advantage of Anglo-Indians and British merchants. The Burmese war, which interfered with a reform that was meant to mitigate the sufferings of starvation in India, was denounced by the vernacular press from the beginning, and sympathy was expressed for the "brave and unhappy people vainly struggling for their birthright." The appropriation of the hoarded treasurer of the late Maharajah Scindia was denounced by the natives. The Gwalior regency was induced to invest 3½ crores of rupees, or £3,500,000 in the securities of the Indian Government, forming part of the public-works loan of 5½ crores to be raised in India in 1887–'88, while no additional loan was raised in England.

In the provisional estimates for 1887–'88 the provincial revenues are again made to contribute £400,000 under the title of a revision of provincial contracts, and the famine insurance fund is suspended more completely than in 1886–'87, indicating its definite suppression. This fund is represented by £6,000,000 which have been expended on the construction of railroads.

The policy of affording facilities for drinking in order to obtain revenue has long been denounced by the natives, and spread of drunkenness has recently attracted attention in England. During the three years ending with 1887, as compared with the ten preceding years, there was an increase in the excise receipts of 16 per cent. in Bengal, 55 per cent. in Bombay, 18 per cent. in Madras, and 74 per cent. in Burmah. Until recently, in Bengal, the right of manufacturing and selling spirits over a tract of country was sold to the highest bidder. Drinking-shops were planted where there were previously none, and the vice was cultivated among the people by the gratuitous distribution of liquor, a practice which is still followed in Ceylon. There is a general demand among the natives for a local control of the liquor-traffic. The Burmese embrace the drinking customs of their conquerors with unusual avidity, and since the annexation of Upper Burmah drunkenness has spread in that country like a pestilence.

Establishment of a Roman Catholic Hierarchy.— India was formally annexed to the spiritual dominions of the papacy by a proclamation read at Bangalore on January 26.

Indian Women.—Reforms in the laws and customs affecting the status of Hindu women have always attracted sympathy among the English, though in India such movements attract little attention or approval except from female reformers of the native race. Lady Dufferin has interested herself in the question of the medical education of Indian women. Female doctors are more necessary in India than elsewhere, because without them persons of their sex are entirely deprived of medical attendance. There are as yet very few of them, and Lady Dufferin headed a subscription for the purpose of establishing a female medical college in the year of the Queen's Jubilee, for which five lakhs was considered necessary, and ten times that sum was desired.

A legal case arising from the custom of early marriages excited much discussion among the English in 1887. A girl named Rukhmabai had been contracted at the age of eleven to a young man of double her years. When he asked her to live with him, some years later, she refused, with the consent of her relatives. He finally brought suit, under a law that had been repealed in England, as far as the enforcement of a judicial decree by imprisonment furnishes it with a sanction, but was still operative in India, for the restitution of conjugal rights. She objected that he was poor, ignorant, indolent, vicious in his habits, and afflicted with an incurable disease, and although he won his case, she still refused to live with him, and appealed the case to the Privy Council, meanwhile publishing her side of the case in the newspapers. He replied in a pamphlet that the quarrel was between himself and her relatives, and had relation to the management of her property, but she declared that the property referred to was not hers, but belonged to her mother. The first judge who heard the case dismissed the suit of Dadaji, the husband, finding no English precedent for compelling a virgin wife to fulfill the marriage contract. He was overruled on the ground that the law of caste governed, while the procedure and penalties were English, although under Hindoo law the decision of the caste could only be enforced by ecclesiastical penalties, such as excommunication. This decision of Justice Farran was regarded with satisfaction by nearly all Hindoos. Rukhmabai, who was well educated in the English language and in Hindoo learning, and was devoted to the reform of the marriage-laws of her people, gained many friends in England by her strong controversial appeals.

Hyderabad.—When the young Nizam was installed at Hyderabad, in 1884, Sir Salar Jung, son of the illustrious statesman who long presided over the government of the state, was made Prime Minister. The relations between the Nizam and the minister became strained, and in April, 1887, the latter was retired with a pension, and on the recommendation of Col. Marshall, who was sent to act as confidential adviser to the Nizam, Nawab-Asman Jah, was selected as his successor. In 1853 the British compelled the then Nizam to hand over the districts in the south of Hyderabad called the Berars to be administered by the Indian Government, on the ground that he was insolvent, and unable to maintain the troops that he was bound to furnish in time of war to aid the British arms. This condition has long ceased to exist, owing to the efficient administration of the late Sir Salar Jung, and for many years the Nizam's Government has been urging the Indian Viceroys to restore those fertile districts, which are still retained in violation of the compact by the British. On August 26 the Nizam sent a letter to the Viceroy, in which he offered a free gift of twenty lakhs a year for three years to the Indian Government, having observed " the persistent advance of another great military power toward India," and the financial burdens assumed by the Government for the purpose of putting the frontier in a state of defense. He expressed the opinion that the Indian princes were deeply concerned in the safety of the empire from invasion, and promised to stand by the British with his sword in the event of war. Although no reference was made to the vexed question of the Berara, the Viceroy was unwilling to accept his offer, and thus place the Government under an obligation to him. A commercial association called the Deccan Company has recently obtained, for 50,000 rupees per annum, a lease of the Singareni coal-fields, for ninety-nine years, and of any other mines of coal, iron, gold, silver, precious stones, or other metals or minerals that may be discovered within the next three years, during which they have the exclusive right of prospecting.

Chinese Suzerainty over Indian States.—China has for centuries claimed suzerain rights over certain of the border states of India, all of which are now under a nominal, and some under an effective British protectorate. Nothing has been done to clear up the question of the Chinese claims, for it was hopeless to expect the Emperor of China to renounce nominal rights of that kind, however shadowy they may be. No practical difficulty arose till 1886, when Mr. Macaulay collected at Darjeeling a commercial mission to Lhassa, that had the appearance and dimensions of an invading army, and was supposed to be one by the Thibetans, who not only blocked all the mountain-passes, but occupied Sikkim, which they declared to be a part of their own territory, carrying off the Rajah to Thibet. In 1887 Mr. Paul went to Darjeeling with a military force for the purpose of re-establishing the normal political conditions and clearing Sikkim and the passes of Thibetans by force, if they refused to withdraw peacefully. The British and Indian chambers of commerce petitioned the Government to carry out the original purpose of sending a mission to Thibet with a view of opening up trade with that country. In the treaty with China regarding the annexation of Burmah the Indian Government had pledged itself not to send such a mission, for which the Chinese authorities had previously given their permission, until the Government at Pekin could exert its influence upon the people of Thibet. After the excitement produced by the Macaulay mission the Government of the Viceroy considered that an opportune moment for urging the concession had not yet arrived.

In 1886, in consequence of disorders in Bhotan, the Chinese residents at Lhassa sent peremptory orders to the Deb Rajah in connection with the troubles, and dispatched troops to the frontier to enforce their orders.

In the early part of 1887 a tribute-bearing mission was sent to Pekin by the King of Nepaul. That state, over which the British have not attempted to exercise dominion of any kind in recent years, though it is the home of the Goorkhas, who are the best soldiers in the Indian army, was conquered in the beginning of the century by a Chinese army. The King promised to send tribute to the Chinese Emperor every five years as an acknowledgement of vassalage. This year the King dispatched an embassy with the full complement of offerings, and with a letter in which he acknowledges, in slavish terms, his subjection to the Emperor of China.

INDIANA. State Government.—The following were the State officers during the year: Governor, Isaac P. Gray, Democrat; Lieutenant-Governor, Robert S. Robertson, Republican; Secretary of State, Charles L. Griffin, Republican; Treasurer, Julius A. Lemcke, Republican; Auditor, Bruce Carr, Republican; Attorney-General, Louis T. Michener, Republican; Superintendent of Public Instruction, Harvey M. La Follette; Justices of the Supreme Court: William E. Niblack, George V. Howk, Allen Zollars, Joseph A. S. Mitchell, and Byron K. Elliott.

Legislative Session.—The meeting of the Legislature on Jan. 6, 1887, began one of the most remarkable political contests in the history of the State. Two questions were at issue, one being the selection of a successor to United States Senator Benjamin Harrison, a Republican; the other involving the right of Robert S. Robertson to exercise the duties of Lieutenant-Governor. Mr. Robertson had been elected at the regular November election, by order of the Governor, to fill a vacancy caused by the resignation of Lieutenant-Governor Munson. The Republicans were successful in this election, at which all the State officers except the Governor were voted for. After the election it was claimed by the Democrats that the voting, so far as related to the Lieutenant-Governor, was illegal and void, no election being possible till 1888. The basis of this claim was the declaration of the statute that the Lieutenant-Governor shall be elected for four years beginning at a fixed time, and the absence of any express statute providing for his election for a shorter period. On the other hand, another statute provides that " a general election shall be held on the first Tuesday after the first Monday in November, in the year 1882, and biennially thereafter on the same day, at which election all existing vacancies in office shall be filled unless otherwise provided by law." The Democrats insisted, further, that there was no vacancy, relying upon the following provision: "Whenever the Lieutenant-Governor shall act as Governor, or shall be unable to attend as President of the Senate, the Senate shall elect one of its own members as President for the occasion." They argued that, as there was a President *pro tem.* of the Senate at the time Munson resigned, that officer became at once the Lieutenant-Governor;

but the statute evidently makes the choice of the Senate nothing more than a President of that body, and it even presupposes that there is an actual Lieutenant-Governor who is performing the other duties of his office. These and other legal questions involved in the case were submitted to the Supreme Court of the State previous to the meeting of the Legislature, but the judges refused to assume jurisdiction. The decision of the dispute had a bearing upon the senatorial contest by reason of the fact that the Lieutenant-Governor, as *ex-officio* President of the Senate, had a right to participate in its deliberations, to vote on all subjects in Committee of the Whole, and to cast a deciding vote in case of a tie at all times. If the election was legal, the Senate, a Democratic body, would have a Republican presiding officer; if invalid, it would elect a Democrat for President. Whether he should be a Republican or a Democrat was important in a closely-divided Legislature like the present one. The Senate was supposed to contain 18 Republicans and 32 Democrats, the House 56 Republicans and 44 Democrats, making on joint ballot 74 Republicans and 76 Democrats. When the Legislature met, the Democrats proceeded to assert their claims by organizing the Senate. Alonzo G. Smith took possession of the chair, called the Senate to order, and resolutions were passed declaring himself the acting Lieutenant-Governor. It was then voted that, as no vacancy existed in that office, the Senate would not attend the joint session for the purpose of declaring the vote in the November election. Nevertheless, the House, controlled by the Republicans, proceeded at the appointed time and in the presence of the Republican members of the Senate, to canvass the votes and to declare Col. Robertson elected. The latter then made a formal demand upon the Senate for possession of the chair by virtue of his office; but this was refused, and Mr. Smith applied to the Circuit Court for an injunction to restrain Robertson from performing any acts as Lieutenant-Governor. After a hearing the application was granted, and the Republicans at once appealed to the Supreme Court of the State. Meanwhile a Democratic caucus had nominated David Turpie as its candidate for United States Senator, while the Republicans renominated Senator Harrison. Neither of these candidates was acceptable to those members of the House who had been elected as special representatives of the Knights of Labor, and they decided to support an independent candidate, Jonas M. Allen. Three votes were thereby drawn from the Republicans and one from the Democrats, making the probable vote in a joint session 75 for Turpie, 71 for Harrison, and 4 for Allen. The number of votes required for an election was 76. At this point the Republicans of the House voted to unseat a Democratic member named Meagher, on the ground that, being a justice of the peace, he was ineligible under the Con-

stitution, and admitted a Republican in his place. The Democrats of the Senate retaliated by unseating a Republican senator, McDonald, and substituting a Democrat. On January 18 the first ballot was taken by each branch separately, 31 senators voting for Turpie and 18 for Harrison; 43 members of the House voting for Turpie, 58 for Harrison, and 4 for Allen. The law requires that after this ballot joint sessions shall be held, presided over by the President of the Senate; but the House refused to recognize any one but Robertson as President, and the Senate declined to enter any convention over which he should preside. A compromise was effected by which the joint convention should be presided over by both Smith and the Speaker of the House, the latter retaining the gavel but allowing Smith to call the assembly to order, neither House surrendering its claims. Each side also protested against a large number of votes of its opponents. Fifteen ballots were taken under this agreement, resulting substantially in 75 for Turpie, 71 for Harrison, and 4 for Allen. On the 16th ballot, Robinson, the Democratic Knight of Labor, who had hitherto voted for Allen, cast his ballot for Turpie, giving him the requisite 76 votes, while Harrison obtained 74, the three other supporters of Allen having changed to Harrison. The Speaker of the House announced no choice, Mr. Smith declared Turpie elected, and the joint session closed amid confusion. The questions at issue were thus left for the U. S. Senate to decide.

About three weeks after the so-called joint session ended, the Supreme Court rendered its decision, dissolving the injunction of the Circuit Court, on the ground that it had no jurisdiction of the case, and that the controversy could only be settled by the Legislature itself. Supported by this decision, Col. Robertson, on February 24, entered the Senate chamber and attempted to take possession of the chair. Mr. Smith ordered the door keeper to remove him from the chamber, and he was ejected amid great excitement and confusion. Although making several attempts subsequently, he was not again allowed to enter the Senate chamber. The House then refused to recognize the Senate, and the Republican Senators refused to act with their colleagues. In this state of affairs the session expired by limitation March 7.

Later in the year, when Col. Robertson attempted to exercise another prerogative of a Lieutenant-Governor by taking part in the work of the Board of Equalization, the contest was still further prolonged by the Democrats entering a protest, through Gov. Gray, the only Democratic member of the board, against Robertson's action in such a capacity. No decision of the conflicting claims of Smith and Robertson was arrived at before the close of the year.

The legislation of the session was extremely meager, only thirty-eight acts being passed. One of the most valuable was an act establishing a School for Feeble-Minded Youth at Fort

Wayne, and appropriating $50,000 for land and buildings. Another act enlarges the Soldiers' Orphans' Home near Knightstown, Rush County, into the Soldiers and Sailors' Orphans' Home, and appropriates $65,000 for the completion of buildings already begun, $25,000 for a building to be used for a literary school, and $20,000 for a shop and tools to equip an industrial school on the premises. The sum of $200,000 was voted for the erection of a State Soldiers and Sailors' Monument in Clyde Park, Indianapolis. No regular appropriation bills were passed, and no provision made for the support of the government for the succeeding two years. The following are some of the principal acts not above referred to:

Requiring all persons or companies of any kind, engaged in mining or manufacturing in the State, to pay their employés semi-monthly, if so requested, in lawful money of the United States; prohibiting the sale of merchandise by such employers to their employés at any higher price than to any other purchasers, and fixing penalties for the violation of this law.

To authorize cities and towns to issue bonds for the purpose of funding their indebtedness, or reducing the rate of interest, or compromising with any creditor, or taking up or canceling bonds, notes, or other obligations, and making it the duty of the Common Council of such cities, and of the Board of Trustees of such towns to levy taxes to pay the interest on such bonds, and for creating sinking-funds to liquidate the principal.

To authorize the Governor to bring a suit in the Supreme Court of the United States to determine the boundary between Indiana and Kentucky, with relation to the ownership of Green River Island, and appropriating $5,000 for such litigation.

Empowering cities and towns to regulate the supply, distribution, and consumption of natural gas within their limits.

To provide for the taxation of building, loan, and savings associations.

To authorize the Hendricks Monument Association to erect and maintain a monument to the memory of the late Thomas A. Hendricks, and the Odd Fellows' Association to erect and maintain a monument to the memory of the late Schuyler Colfax, on State grounds in Indianapolis.

To provide for the organization and perpetuity of voluntary associations for charitable, social, military, or business purposes.

Imposing a penalty for hunting on inclosed lands without consent of the owner.

Providing for the permanent inclosure and preservation of Tippecanoe battle-ground.

Revising the law relating to the practice of dentistry.

Finances.—The annual report of the Treasurer for the fiscal year ending October 31 shows a balance on hand at the beginning of the year of $409,971.73; receipts from all sources, $4,738,198.69; total disbursements, $4,774,226.41; leaving a balance, on October 31, of $373,944.31. Of the receipts, $2,378,043.78 were credited to the general revenue fund; $2,127,946.17 to the school fund for the payment of tuition; and $168,159.51 to the new State House fund. There was also realized $2,103 from the sale of tax-lands, $160 from swamp-lands, $2,385 from escheated lands, and $5,105 from forfeited college lands. Of the total disbursements, $2,351,509.53 was from the general revenue fund, $2,029,410 from the school fund

VOL. XXVII.—25 A

for tuition, and $294,647.06 from the new State House fund, while the only other large amount was $85,400.20 from the permanent endowment fund of the Indiana University. The disbursements from the general fund were as follows: Benevolent institutions, $678,277.57; reformatory, $89,991.73; penal, $196,586.02; State library, $3,648.92; Supreme Court, $32,130; State judiciary, $171,754.50; interest on State debt, $489,394.58; educational institutions, $58.360; State boards, departments, etc., $19,466.67; public printing and stationery, $12,646.47; House of Representatives, $70,985.13; State Senate, $46,028.61; miscellaneous expenditures, $491,635.51.

The failure of the Legislature to pass the regular appropriations produced embarrassment in conducting the financial operations of the State. As the Auditor is forbidden to draw his warrant on the treasury in the absence of an appropriation, the executive and judicial officers not only failed to receive their salaries, but were forced to the alternative of discharging their clerks and employés, or paying them from their own pockets. To meet pressing difficulties, Treasurer Lemcke agreed to pay bills presented to him out of his own funds, if the officers to be accommodated would guarantee him repayment in case the next Legislature failed to make the necessary appropriation. It was deemed useless to call an extra session of the Legislature, which would only result in a reopening of the Smith-Robertson controversy, and a consequent dead-lock. Fortunately, the State charitable institutions were not affected by these difficulties, a statute already providing that in such a contingency the Governor, Secretary, and Treasurer might appropriate each month for their support a sum equal to one twelfth of the last annual appropriation.

The State debt amounted in October to $6,430,608. Of this amount $340,000 was added during the year, being borrowed at 3 per cent. to meet accruing interest.

Prisons.—The annual report of the Northern Prison shows that the number of convicts at the beginning of the year was 697, and at the close 644. The number discharged was 814, against 290 received, while 16 were paroled by the Governor, and 13 died. The warden paid to the State Treasurer during the year $110,245.56, and received from the State $102,245.56. His receipts and earnings amounted to $105,685.42. In the Southern Prison. at Jeffersonville, there were 588 convicts at the close of the year. The disbursements under the new warden were $50,218.40, and the receipts $49,628.25. A change of management in the prison took place early in the year, in consequence of an investigation by a committee of the Legislature. The treatment of convicts, the sanitary arrangements, and the whole system of management was found to be reprehensible, and Warden Howard was discovered to be a defaulter to a large amount. He was deposed, and a new board of management selected. A subject of complaint at both institutions is the necessity of placing young criminals in daily intercourse with older and more hardened convicts. There seems to be no remedy for this state of affairs without some legislation by the Legislature.

The Insane.—Two investigations were had during the year, one by the Senate and one by the House, into the management of the Insane Asylum. The House Committee reported mismanagement and cruel treatment to patients, while the Senate Committee found little to censure. The effect of the investigations was such, however, that Gov. Gray deemed it advisable to supersede Drs. Harrison and Gapen, two of the Board of Directors. They refused to yield the office to their successors, and a legal contest ensued, the outcome of which is not yet determined.

Normal School.—The annual report of this institution for 1887 shows it to be in a flourishing condition. There were 1,343 students enrolled during the year. The necessary expense of a year's course is estimated at $132.-50: The total receipts in the tuition fund for the year were $27,628.82. The disbursements were $22,005, leaving a balance in the treasury of $5,623.82. The incidental fund shows a balance from last year and receipts of $11,-748.28; balance on hand, $4,716.46.

Live-Stock.—For the year ending in June, the following returns are made of the live-stock in the State by the Bureau of Statistics: Total number of horses, 583,257, an increase of 20,-287 over 1886; number of mules, 56,989, a decrease of 294; number of cattle, 1,779,351, an increase of 81,601; number of sheep, 1,-394,045, a decrease of 7,567. The estimated wool-clip was 4,197,000 pounds. In the summer and autumn of 1886, hog cholera prevailed in 72 counties, causing great destruction, the number dying of this disease during the year being 553,692. There were slaughtered for food, 1,245,596. The total number in the State reported for the year was 3,801,248.

Natural Gas.—Great progress was made during the year in utilizing the discoveries of natural gas in many places in the State. The first natural gas company was incorporated March 5, 1886, and from that date till May, 1887, 118 companies had been formed. There were nearly 200 companies by the end of the year.

Election Frauds.—The trial of Simeon Coy and others for altering election-returns at Indianapolis in the congressional election of 1886, by which the result of the election was said to be changed, was held during the year. An indictment was found against them in the United States Court, and the question of the court's jurisdiction was then raised. Justice Harlan decided that in all Congressional elections the United States Courts had the right to review and enforce all rules of procedure, whether made by Congress or by the State law, and to punish any violation of those rules. At the trial upon the merits of the case the prisoners were discharged, sufficient evidence to convict not being offered.

INDIAN EDUCATION. The Indian schools of the United States may be classified as follow: *Day-schools:* 1, established and supported by the Government; 2, supported by contracts with religious societies; 3, mission-schools established and supported by religious societies. *Boarding-schools:* 1, located on reservations and controlled by agents; 2, independent schools; 3, mission-schools established and chiefly supported by religious associations. *State and tribal schools:* 1, Indian schools of New York State; 2, tribal schools of Indian Territory.

For the subsistence of these schools there are five different sources of revenue: 1, appropriations made under the educational provisions of existing treaties; 2, funds, investments of bonds, and other securities held by the Government; 3, proceeds of sales of lands of certain Indian tribes; 4, accumulations of money in the treasury resulting from the sale of lands; and 5, annual appropriations by Congress for Indian school purposes.

The day-schools, established generally at points remote from the agencies, are frequently due to the benevolent efforts of missionaries or the wives of the army officers stationed at the military reservations in the Indian country. These are the primary efforts toward Indian education, and are followed by the boarding schools, in which the Indian children can be more entirely isolated from their savage life, and where also the facilities for instruction can be made greatly superior. The five Indian schools supported by special appropriations are as follow: Carlisle School, Carlisle, Pa.; Chilocco School, Chilocco, Indian Territory; Genoa School, Genoa, Neb.; Haskell Institute, Lawrence, Kan.; and Salem School, Chemawa, Ore. The three schools that are next best known to these, and are under appropriations providing for the education of a certain number of pupils at a specified rate per annum, are Hampton Institute, Hampton, Va., Lincoln Institution, Philadelphia, Pa., and St. Ignatius Mission, Flat Head Reservation, Mon. The table on next page is a general summary of the statistics of the Indian schools from the latest report, that for 1886.

The statistics of all the Indian schools, supported in whole or in part by the Government during the fiscal year ending June 30, 1886, the latest report made, show the following figures, a portion being a recapitulation of the table just given: School population, 38,981; capacity of schools, boarding, 10,021; day, 5,270; number of employés, 708; largest monthly attendance, 12,316; average attendance, boarding, 7,260; day, 2,870; total cost to Government, $997,899.80.

These schools are divided in number among the States and Territories as follow: Alaska, 1; Arizona, 4; California, 15; Colorado, 2; Dakota, 49; Idaho, 3; Illinois, 1; Indiana, 2;

KIND OF SCHOOL.	Number.	No. of employés.	Capacity.	Largest monthly attendance.	Average attendance.	Cost.
Government schools supported by general appropriations...........	154	552	8,231	7,765	5,659	$494,456 52
Government schools supported by special appropriations...........	5	151	1,250	1,425	1,275	216,574 11
Contract schools supported by general appropriations....	52	....	8,852	2,602	2,098	201,992 26
Contract schools supported by special appropriations	3	....	600	524	471	74,576 91
Total...	214	703	18,988	12,316	9,583	$997,599 80

Indian Territory, 14; Iowa, 2; Kansas, 6; Michigan, 10; Minnesota, 9; Nebraska, 10; Nevada, 4; New Mexico, 16; North Carolina, 8; Oregon, 8; Pennsylvania, 3; Utah, 1; Virginia, 1; Washington Territory, 14; Wisconsin, 17; and Wyoming, 1.

As generally illustrating further statistics of special schools we select three, those of Genoa, Neb., Carlisle, Pa., and Hampton, Va. The Indian school at Genoa reports 110 boys and 56 girls, including representatives of the Sioux, Omahas, Winnepegs, Poncas, Arikerees, and Mandans. This school comprises one large building of brick 110 by 40 feet, with two wings 80 by 20 feet, and includes, besides dormitories, school-room, dining-room, sewing-room, officers' apartments, etc. There is also a farm of 320 acres, where, in the last year reported, were raised 1,400 bushels of wheat, 200 bushels of oats, and 3,000 bushels of grain, besides garden-vegetables. There are a few head of stock, and among the industries established here are blacksmithing, horseshoeing, painting, etc.

The Carlisle, Pa., school reports 344 boys and 150 girls, and includes representatives of forty different tribes. This school does more in industrial teaching, covering carpentry, tailoring, shoemaking, tinsmithing, harnessmaking, painting, brickmaking, baking, and printing, besides farming. Added to the Government appropriation for this school the gifts for the year reported amounted to $9,828.11. Religious services and general religious teaching are carried on in all these schools through the co-operation of such clergymen as are accessible, without regard to creed.

The Hampton, Va., school reports 77 boys and 43 girls from sixteen tribes, the average age being about seventeen years. This school, besides the ordinary primary and advanced teaching, has also kindergarten instruction. It is reported that in mathematics the Indians excel, as also in geography. Lessons in vocal and instrumental music are encouraging features in the work of this school, from which developed the colored " Hampton Jubilee Singers," so popular throughout the country a few years ago. The studies and industrial work of the pupils are diversified by various indoor and outdoor amusements, including games, marching, conversation, literary and musical exercises, checkers, etc., within, and outdoor games, such as ball-playing, quoits, rowing, and athletic games. The farm includes 110 acres under cultivation, 43 of which were in vegetables. Of 190 students who left this school and whose record

was afterward followed, 106 were reported as doing very well, 54 as doing fairly, 12 badly, and 6 returned to savage life, while 12 were unaccounted for. There were of the total number 54 in Government employ, of whom 7 were girls.

The Congressional provision for the education of the pupils at Hampton Institute is at the rate of $167 per annum. The cost to the Government was $19,785.89. Besides this, the sum of $13,215.21 was reported as being contributed by friends of the school. In addition to the Indians reported, the Hampton school provides for between 400 and 500 colored pupils.

The schools conducted by the missionary organizations numbered during the year 2,257 Indian pupils, the larger number being under the Home Missions of the Presbyterian Church, the Catholic Indian Missions, the American Missionary Society of the Congregational Church, the Board of Foreign Missions of the Presbyterian Church and the Protestant Episcopal Church, the Government, through the Commissioner of Indian Affairs, contracting to pay a certain sum for each pupil, the sum paid, if insufficient to cover expenses, being supplemented by the religious organizations conducting the schools. The uniform rate of cost per head to the Government of each pupil is $108 per annum, except in New Mexico, Arizona, and California, where $150 per annum is allowed. The schools at Carlisle, Pa., and Lawrence, Kan., are reported to be well adapted for advanced instruction of such pupils as have shown a capacity for higher education, and it is recommended that only graduates of the reservation schools be sent to them. It is also suggested that the schools at Genoa, Chilocco, and Salem should be used for a like purpose.

The annual report of the State Superintendent of Schools of the State of New York for 1885 gives the number of Indian children of school-age in the State as 1,442, the number attending school 1,050, and the average attendance 555. The amount expended by the State in aid of Indian schools was $8,277.53.

What are known as " the five civilized tribes " include the Cherokees, Choctaws, Chickasaws, Creeks, and Seminoles. They occupy a portion of the southern and eastern part of the Indian Territory, and number about 64,000, distributed as follows: Cherokees, 23,-000; Choctaws, 18,000; Chickasaws, 6,000; Creeks, 14,000; Seminoles, 3,000. Each of these tribes manages its own affairs under a constitution modeled upon that of the United

States. Each tribe has a common-school system, and includes schools for advanced instruction. The teachers are generally Indians, and text-books in the Indian language are used. These tribes receive no assistance from the Government in support of their schools. The schools include high, public, and private schools, and male and female seminaries.

As illustrating the progress of Indian education, the following figures are interesting, covering a period between 1882 and 1886, both inclusive:

The increase in the number of boarding-schools was from 71 in the first year to 115 in the last; of day-schools, from 54 to 99; of average attendance at boarding-schools, from 2,755 to 7,260; at day-schools, from 1,311 to 2,870; cost of boarding-schools, from $452,-559 to $941,124; cost of day-schools, from $32,400 to $56,775. The statistics of Government schools supported by general appropriation showed a total number of 154, including 67 boarding- and 87 day-schools; capacity, 8,231; average attendance, 5,689; number of employés, 552; cost, $494,456.52.

It is a curious fact, not commendable to the Government of the United States, that specific treaty agreements with certain tribes by which school-houses and teachers were to be furnished them have never been complied with. Such is the case with regard to the Navajos, to whom the Government is indebted for educational purposes, according to the terms of the treaty of June 1, 1868, in the sum of $792,-000, and the Sioux, to whom is owing $2,500,-000, an indebtedness incurred by solemn treaty of agreement of April 20, 1868.

Provisional training for Indians has been arranged for to a limited extent in the case of Wayland Seminary and Howard University, in the District of Columbia, the Woman's Medical College of Philadelphia, Pa., and the Medical Department of the University of Pennsylvania. At these institutions permission has been given for the professional education of three Indian boys and one Indian girl in the case of each.

The first effort in this direction appears to have been made by the Continental Congress on July 12, 1775, when a bill was passed appropriating $500 for the education of Indian youths at Dartmouth College, N. H. Further effort was made in the same direction, but the Revolutionary War prevented any definite action being taken, and it was not until 1794 that any form of education was mentioned in an Indian treaty, when a provision was inserted in a treaty with the Oneida, Tuscarora, and Stockbridge Indians "to instruct some young men of the three nations in the arts of the miller and sawyer." In 1803 a treaty made with a tribe of Illinois Indians provided for the expenditure on the part of the United States annually for seven years of the sum of $100 toward the support of a Roman Catholic priest to instruct as many Indian children as possible

in the rudiments of English literature. In 1819 $10,000 was appropriated by Congress for a similar purpose, and this appropriation was carried on the books of the Treasury Department until 1873, when so much of the act as provided for the appropriation was repealed. In 1867, what was known as "The Civilization Fund," a re-establishment of the act just mentioned, was arranged for in a treaty with the Great and Little Osage Indian tribe, by which the proceeds of sales of certain lands were to be used under the direction of the Secretary of the Interior for the education and civilization of the Indian tribes residing within the limits of the United States. From 1867 to 1882, under this act, about three quarters of a million dollars were expended in ostensible attempts to fulfill this purpose. Various special treaties were made with Indian tribes from time to time in which education took some part, but so little were such provisions observed by the Government that in 1884 the Secretary of the Interior reported that it would require an appropriation of $4,033,700 to fulfill the educational provisions of eight of our Indian treaties. Requests were accordingly made by the Secretary for appropriations, which, however, were not complied with by Congress. Meanwhile large sums remain in the Treasury Department to the credit of various tribes, the Osage fund, for instance, amounting to $5,000,-000, and drawing interest at the rate of 5 per cent. per annum, which interest may be expended by the President for the benefit of the Osage Indians, in such manner as he may deem proper. The Choctaw school fund in the United States Treasury amounts to $49,472.70, and the Cherokee fund $457,903.72.

The first annual general appropriation for Indian school purposes was made in the Indian bill of 1876, when the sum of $20,000 was appropriated "for the support of industrial schools and other educational purposes for the Indian tribes." This was followed by an appropriation in 1877 of $30,000 for the same purpose, one in 1878 of $60,000, in 1879 and 1880 each of $75,000, in 1881, $85,000, 1882, $471,500. In 1883 Congress appropriated for the fiscal year ending June 30, 1884, for general and special educational purposes among the Indians, the sum of $680,200. In 1884 the appropriations for Indian schools amounted to $992,800, this being for the fiscal year ending June 30, 1885, but of this sum $66,917.50 was not used. The Indian bill of March 3, 1885, appropriated the largest amount ever given up to that time for Indian school purposes, being $1,107,665, and in 1886 Congress increased upon this amount, appropriating $1,211,415.

The machinery of the Indian educational system, which has resulted from Congressional legislation, treaty stipulations, and missionary efforts, includes, first, the day-schools, which are of three kinds: the Government day-schools, being established by the Government and the teachers appointed by the Commissioner of Indian Affairs upon nomination of Indian agents; the contract schools, established by religious organizations, which appoint the teachers; and the mission day-schools, established and conducted by the religious associations. Next are the boarding-schools on reservations, of which the schools are established and conducted by the Government, the contract schools by the religious associations, and the independent schools, appointed by and reporting to the Commissioner of Indian Affairs; the mission, reservation, and boarding-schools being established and conducted by religious societies. Of the boarding-schools not on the reservations, none are Government schools, and they are all independent of the Indian agencies. They report direct to the Commissioner of Indian Affairs. There are also Government training-schools, established by the Government, erected by the Government, and all expenditures paid by the Government out of special appropriations made for the purpose. The Secretary of the Interior appoints the superintendents of these schools, and the employés are appointed by the Commissioner of Indian Affairs. These schools are immediately under the supervision of the Indian Bureau. Some of the Government training-schools are established by educational and religious organizations, and for them Congress makes annually an appropriation for maintaining and educating at each a specified number of Indian pupils. The Hampton Normal and Agricultural Institute, Virginia, and the Lincoln Institution, of Philadelphia, are classed as semi-Government training-schools.

The Hampton school owes its Indian connection to what may be considered a mere accident. In 1875 Capt. R. H. Pratt was put in charge of a number of Indian prisoners at Fort Marion, St. Augustine, Fla. Several of the young men among these captives were, in April, 1878, placed at the Hampton Normal and Agricultural Institute, Va., and subsequently Capt. Pratt was authorized by the Secretary of the Interior to obtain fifty Indian children from the Indian agencies in Dakota, and place them in the Hampton school, to be "instructed in books and manual labor." Under this authority Capt. Pratt placed forty boys and nine girls at the school in November, 1878, and thus the Indian Department of the Hampton Institute was created. At this school Indian cottages are erected at the expense of philanthropic people who make contributions for the purpose, and each of these cottages is occupied by a young Indian and his wife. Some of these married couples attend the school, and others obtain the opportunity of learning housekeeping. In 1884 eleven boys and nine girls spent the summer months with farmers in Massachusetts, the girls doing house-work and sewing, and the boys working on the farms.

The Chilocco school, Indian Territory, has 8,640 acres of good agricultural grazing land. It is about one mile south of the southern line of Kansas, and has suffered a good deal by incursions of Indians and raids of cowboys. This school has extensive buildings, but no shop facilities.

It is to be regretted that the existing system of Indian education was not thoughtfully provided by wise statesmanship, and then deliberately put into operation by a carefully considered Legislature, but was evolved, the schools developing themselves one from another in gradual transition. The school system is in consequence not only imperfect as a whole, but defective in parts. Meanwhile, the co-operation with the Government of religious philanthropic organizations, and religious work among the Indians, is considered desirable. It is reported that the religious organizations together accomplish an amount of education work among the Indians that may well challenge general attention and merits applause. It is not considered desirable, however, on the part of the Government to permit any sect or educational society to use the Government in any effort to proselytize, or to fill its own purse. It is therefore not considered well to permit any religious denomination to make its missionaries, as such, teachers in any of the Government schools.

The affairs of the Indian schools are managed by the Indian School Superintendent, who reports to the Commissioner of Indian Affairs, under whose direction is placed the whole matter of Indian education, which is, in fact, in charge of what is known as the Education Division of the Indian Bureau. Under the existing system, combined with the methods of tuition that have grown out of it, the complaint is made that there is no uniformity in the methods of instruction in Indian schools. "Each school is, in all matters relating to the work to be done by it, a law unto itself." As a result of this absence of uniformity of method in instruction, the text-books of nearly every publisher in the United States are purchased by the Government for use in Indian schools, and it is alleged that thirteen kinds of arithmetics are used, eleven kinds of geographies, eleven kinds of grammars, nine primers, fourteen first readers, fifteen second readers, thirteen third, twelve fourth, six fifth, and twelve spellers. It is also thought that text-books properly used in white schools can not be employed to as good advantage in Indian schools, and the recommendation is made that a set of text-books should be prepared by the Government, and the printing of them done at the Government Printing-Office. On the whole it is shown by experts, long connected with the Indian educational system, that, while good progress has been made, and excellent schools established in many instances, there remain very many opportunities for improvement, some of which, suggested by the Indian School Superintendent in the various official reports of the Commissioner of Indian Affairs, might well be given a fair examination, and if practical carried out.

INTERSTATE COMMERCE LAW, THE. The Federal Government had never undertaken the regulation of railway transportation until the passage of the "act to regulate commerce," which was approved Feb. 4, 1887. Laws had been passed regulating it so far as it was confined to the limits of individual States, some of which were very comprehensive, while others laid down rules of limited application only; and in several of the States there were railroad commissioners or boards of transportation, possessing large powers. But, as the scope of any State law or regulation was necessarily limited to such transportation and traffic as was wholly within the State, the great bulk of the railroad business of the country was left to such imperfect regulation as was afforded by the rules of the common law. Those rules were wholly inadequate: they gave remedies for such distinct wrongs as were known to the common law, but they could not provide for the conditions that new inventions and new methods of doing business had introduced. To a large extent, therefore, the managers of great interstate lines of railway transportation were a law unto themselves, not only as to the methods in which their business was conducted, but as to the charges for the services rendered. Many abuses resulted; those that most attracted public attention being discriminations between persons and places in the facilities furnished and in the charges made. Great numbers of persons were given free transportation; some of them for business reasons, some because they were supposed to possess political or other influence that might be important to railroad companies, some because they occupied public places and claimed free carriage as a perquisite. In the charges for the transportation of property, gross discriminations were made; large customers being given rates that put competition with them on the part of small dealers out of the question, and tended to build up monopolies in particular lines of business. These special rates were often given through the device of secret rebates, and, as both the public and secret rates were changed at pleasure, it was impossible that business should adapt itself to them so that they should have a proper and normal effect upon prices. In many parts of the country, also, the railroad companies made very low charges on long-haul transportation, and very much higher charges in the aggregate for a haul of like property for a distance perhaps not half so great. These were among the abuses that the act to regulate commerce was intended to remedy.

The act provided for five Interstate Commerce Commissioners, and the President appointed Thomas M. Cooley of Michigan, William R. Morrison of Illinois, Augustus Schoonmaker of New York, Aldace F. Walker of Vermont, and Walter L. Bragg of Alabama. The first-named was elected chairman, and the Commission entered upon the performance of its duties April 5, 1887. The passage of the act excited among railroad managers and some classes of shippers great distrust and uneasiness. It was supposed to have been conceived in a spirit of bitter hostility to railroads, and some of its provisions were thought to have been intended to cripple their business and render it unprofitable. Some classes of business men also shared in this distrust, and they discovered grounds for it in the fact that in some quarters it appeared to be taken for granted that the Commission would treat the railroads as public enemies and curb and limit them in every way possible. The result was that business for a time was to some extent paralyzed, and a letter from one of the consular agents in Canada to the Secretary of State probably expressed a general truth when it said: "The result of the act has been most damaging, both as regards imports and exports, and is severely felt both by the buyers and sellers to and from the United States." The immediate effect was most severely felt by those roads which, as to some of their traffic, charged less for the longer than for the shorter haul of the like kind of property. This was forbidden by the act, when the hauls were on the same line in the same direction and under like conditions and circumstances; but the Commission was empowered to make exceptions. The transcontinental roads claimed that a strict application of the statutory rule would ruin very much of their business and be destructive of Pacific coast interests, and the president of one of them telegraphed to the Commission for an order giving immediate relief. The Commission declined to make any order until after a showing, on oath, of its necessity; but, when the showing was produced, orders were made not only for the transcontinental roads, but for many others, permitting a continuance of existing rates for a limited period. This was done as a provisional and prudential measure, that the business of the country might not suffer more than was absolutely indispensable while questions of construction naturally arising under the statute were being considered, and carriers were adapting themselves to the new conditions. On June 15, 1887, the Commission filed an opinion holding that orders of relief were not essential; that the prohibition to charge more for the shorter than for the longer haul only applied when the two were had under circumstances and conditions that were substantially similar; and that every carrier must decide for itself when this was the case, subject to responsibility to the law in case of erroneous action.

Meantime, the railroads of the country had been revising their tariff-sheets in order to bring them more generally into conformity with the "long- and short-haul clause" of the act, and this has now so far been accomplished that, in large sections of the country, no instances occur in which more is charged for a shorter than for a longer haul of the like property over the same line and in the same direction, while in all sections the instances are much less numerous than they were a year ago. The most conspicuous exception of roads that have not come into harmony with the rule the act seeks to establish is seen in the case of the transcontinental roads. How far it is possible for them to do so without serious detriment to their revenues is a question yet to be determined. The Commission now has before it several complaints against these roads, in which the grievance alleged is that the short-haul traffic is subjected to oppressive burdens, and an adjudication of these complaints will, to some extent, involve the general question.

Soon after the act took effect, and when it was seen that the Commission proposed to adopt a cautious and conservative course, confidence returned, and business, not only of the roads but of those who were their principal customers, began to acquire stability and prosperity. Rates were made more generally equal and just than formerly, and were allowed to have a stability unknown before. Discriminations between persons practically ceased, and secret rebates were no longer given. Discriminations between places ceased also, except so far as the managers felt confident of their ability to defend them on the grounds of reason and justice. The giving of free passes for interstate transportation was stopped, except in the few cases allowed by the act, the chief of these being when they were exchange passes between railroads for their officers and employés. The general effect has been that the railroads have had an exceptionally prosperous year, and, at the same time, their business has been transacted much more to the satisfaction of the public than ever before. A great many complaints of violation of law by the railroads have been made to the Commission, a large proportion of which were found on investigation to be grounded in error. Where they have clearly appeared to be just the parties complained of have given redress; where their justice has not been conceded, cases have been brought to a hearing, and an adjudication by the Commission has been had. Whenever an order has been made by the Commission requiring specific action by a railroad company, by way of redressing a grievance, the Commission has been notified that its order has been or will be complied with. The railroad mileage of the United States at the close of the fiscal year 1886 was estimated at 133,606. The number of corporations represented in this mileage was 1,425, and the cost of construction and equipment of roads was computed at $7,254,995,223. It was not to be supposed that a new system could be put in force and a new authority be empowered to regulate so vast an interest without causing considerable disturbance and friction, and perhaps some hardships. But these ill effects have been surprisingly small, and it can safely be said that, almost from the first, the effect of the law has been steadily reformatory and

beneficial. The most serious complaints have come from parties who were specially favored before, and who are now deprived of unfair advantages.

The Commission, in its annual report, recommends a few changes in the act, none of them of considerable moment; it calls attention to the fact that a large business is done by express companies, parlor-car companies, and other organizations not supposed to come under the act, and raises the question whether they ought not to be brought in; it sets forth the difficulties springing from a want of uniform classification of freights, and declares the purpose of the Commission to bring about uniformity as rapidly as possible, and also to keep steadily in view the importance of making rates that, as between long- and short-haul traffic, shall be relatively more equal and just than those that have been made hitherto.

IOWA. State Government.—The following were the State officers during the year: Governor, William Larrabee, Republican; Lieutenant-Governor, John A. T. Hull; Secretary of State, Frank D. Jackson; Auditor, James A. Lyons; Treasurer, Voltaire P. Twombly; Attorney-General, A. J. Baker; Superintendent of Public Instruction, John W. Akers; Railroad Commissioners, Peter A. Dey, Lorenzo S. Coffin, and James W. McDill; Chief-Justice of the Supreme Court, Austin Adams; Associate Justices, James H. Rothrock, Joseph M. Beck, William H. Seevers, and Joseph R. Reed.

Finances.—The Treasurer's report for the two years ending June 30 shows total receipts to the amount of $3,359,110.57, and total expenditures amounting to $3,338,716.62, leaving a balance of $20,393.95. The balance in the treasury at the beginning of this period was $140,151.94. The State debt consists of outstanding warrants to the amount of $455,987.80, of which all but $26,573.42 are interest-bearing. Two years previous the outstanding warrants amounted to $765,524.53. For the past four years the revenue provided has not been sufficient to meet the unusual appropriations made by the Nineteenth and Twentieth General Assemblies for building new State institutions and for extending others, and in consequence a large floating-debt has been created, but it is believed that the increased receipts from taxation for the next two years will be sufficient to pay this indebtedness. The total assessed taxable property for this year was $495,710,241. The rate for State purposes has been 2½ mills for the past six years.

Education.—At the close of the fiscal year 1887, there were 12,444 school-houses in the State, valued at $11,360,472; the number of schools was 14,829, and of teachers 24,675. The permanent school-fund then amounted to $4,187,-893.94, and there were 53,927 acres of school-lands unsold. The total disbursements for schools in 1886 were $6,323,172.42, of which $952,540 came from the school-house fund, $1,-361,749.89 from the contingent fund, and $4,-

008,883.54 from the teacher's fund. In the same year the whole number of children between the ages of five and twenty-one was 638,156, and there were enrolled in the public schools 480,788, with an average attendance of 284,567. The superintendent reports that the law of the Twenty-first General Assembly, requiring instruction in the public schools in relation to the effects of stimulants and narcotics upon the human system, has been generally obeyed. The State Industrial School, since its foundation, had brought under its instruction 1,580 children. On July 1 there were at this school 330 boys and 112 girls, for whom an expenditure of $90,699.14 has been made during the past two years. The Agricultural College, the State Normal School, the College for the Blind, and the Institution for the Deaf and Dumb, are all in successful operation.

State Institutions.—The completion of a substantial and commodious wing to the Hospital for the Insane at Mt. Pleasant, at a cost of $100,000, gives capacity to that institution to accommodate 200 additional patients. Two years ago the number of patients at this hospital was 544; this year there were 707. During the past two years 1,811 patients have been treated, at an aggregate cost of $223,211.66. At the Hospital for the Insane, in Independence, an additional cottage has been completed, and the capacity of the institution thereby increased to accommodate 100 more patients. In July, 1885, there were 694 persons at this place, and this number had increased to 791 at the same time this year. The expenditures during this time were $251,549.68. On July 1, 1887, there were 1,498 patients in the two hospitals for the insane. The foreign-born population of the State is about 17 per cent. of the whole, while the foreign-born patients at the hospitals for the insane are 45 per cent. of the whole number. The new Hospital for the Insane at Clarinda is nearly ready for occupation. At the Institution for Feeble-minded Children there were 259 patients in 1885, and 331 in 1887, an average of 271. The Soldiers' Orphans' Home and Home for Indigent Children, since its opening in 1862, has received 1,496 soldiers' orphans, of whom only 42 remain. Since the institution was opened for indigent children in 1876, there have been received 542 such, of whom 251 remain, making the whole number now in the home 293. The Soldiers' Home at Marshalltown was formally opened on November 30 of this year, and had received over 60 soldiers before the end of December. The number of convicts in the Fort Madison penitentiary two years ago was 412, and on July 1 of this year 360; average number, 390. The total expenditures were $142,245.21. At the Anamosa penitentiary 318 prisoners were confined on July 1, against 255 two years before. The expenditures here for two years were $177,447. The construction of this penitentiary is still in progress. There were only 6 more convicts in both places on July 1 than at

the same time two years ago. This unusually small increase, in comparison with the growth of the State's population during the time, is attributed to the prohibitory liquor law.

Railroads.—The report of the railroad commissioners shows that the number of miles of railway in the State, June 30, 1887, was 7,997, of which the number built last year was 432. The amount of stock representing the roads in Iowa is $147,350,517 and the amount of bonds for the same $150,296,919. The cost of the roads and equipment in Iowa is placed by the commissioners at $261,747,197. At the close of the year the number of miles of road in operation had increased to 8,203. The amount of taxes paid to the State by railroads during the year was $1,011,530, against $962,229 in 1886. In no State have the railroads been more generously aided in their enterprises. They have received as donations 4,393,436 acres of public lands in the State, or about one-eighth of its entire acreage.

Mining.—The number of coal-mines operated in the State at the close of the year was 515. The coal product in 1886 amounted to 3,853,-372 tons; in 1887 it was 4,014,490 tons, an increase of 161,118 tons. The amount of capital invested in this industry is estimated at $9,487,-125. The relations of capital and labor during the year have been harmonious.

Agriculture.—The following table shows the value of the chief farm-products, the quantity produced, and the area cultivated, in 1887:

CROPS.	No. of acres.	Total product, bushels.	Value of product.
Corn	7,287,000	155,570,450	$49,794,784
Wheat	2,491,248	18,141,552	10,340,685
Oats	2,432,696	61,121,336	12,444,672
Rye	107,000	1,765,500	737,096
Barley	172,300	3,801,502	1,571,283
Buckwheat	21,000	315,000	222,100
Flaxseed	265,000	2,186,250	2,055,673
Potatoes	159,880	8,168,785	5,016,608
Hay	3,386,347	2,919,804	23,332,290
Broom-corn	2,500	2,708	311,234
Sorghum	22,560	1,827,360	572,564
Total	16,293,021	... ...	$107,600,585
Against value of 1886	... ...		128,115,096
Loss in 1887, as compared with 1886 ..			$20,514,491

The number and value of live-stock were as follow: horses 973,808, valued at $71,926,052; mules, 48,052, valued at $4,186,822; milch-cows, 1,248,002, valued at $32,541,792; other cattle, 2,116,417, valued at $47,369,232; sheep, 425,498, valued at $1,020,515; hogs, 4,461,087, valued at $23,065,603; total, 9,267,864 head, valued at $180,110,016.

Banks.—The latest returns give the following figures as to the number, capital, and deposits of the State and national banks:

NUMBER.	Capital.	Deposits.
87 savings-banks	$3,128,693 67	$9,969,019 08
65 incorporated banks (not savings)	3,579,843 12	5,747,386 97
128 national banks	10,150,000 00	19,284,697 93
Total	$15,856,586 79	$35,001,008 93

Prohibition.—The Governor says in his message: "Much progress has been made in the enforcement of the prohibitory law. Not only has public sentiment much improved in relation to it, but judicial officers are more disposed to secure its enforcement. Many judges give strong testimony in its favor, showing that, where it has been well executed, there has been a marked reduction in criminal offenses, and also in court expenses. During the last year, and particularly during its latter half, there has been a decided falling off in the penitentiary convicts, and a very large number of county jails have been empty, some of them for the first time in years. There has been a marked improvement in the condition of our poorer people. While there is very little difficulty now in enforcing the law in the rural districts and in a very large majority of the counties, there are still a few portions of the State, particularly some of the larger cities, where the law is not enforced. This, however, does not include all such cities, for in Des Moines, Sioux City, and Cedar Rapids, the prohibitory law is now, and has been for the past year, well enforced." On the other hand, it is claimed by some Republicans that in the large cities the law is openly violated and its operation nullified, while the closing of the saloons has decreased the revenues and the wealth of these communities. These Republicans refuse to support their State ticket in the election of this year.

An important decision was rendered this year by the State Supreme Court in the case of Pearson vs the International Distillery, relative to the right of persons to manufacture liquors in the State, provided that they were not sold within its limits. The defendant held a license to manufacture and sell liquors for mechanical, medicinal, and sacramental purposes, and claimed also the right to export from the State any liquors so manufactured and sell them outside the State for any purpose whatever. The court denied this right, and ordered the distillery closed, as being a public nuisance under the law. Two judges out of five dissented, claiming that, in the absence of an express statute forbidding the export of liquors manufactured legally in the State, the right of export still existed.

Political.—A convention of the Union Labor party, to select candidates for the various State offices, was held on June 8, and resulted in the nomination of the following ticket: For Governor, M. J. Cain; for Lieutenant-Governor, J. R. Sovereign; for Justice of the Supreme Court, M. H. Jones; for Superintendent of Public Instruction, Eugene Hanan. These candidates were adopted by the Greenback party. The following is a part of the Labor platform:

We demand the abolition of the Iowa Railroad Commission, and the enactment of laws limiting the maximum freight charges and reducing the passenger rates to two cents a mile on all first-class roads.

We demand the prompt payment of the State debt, and the reduction of the legal rate of interest.

We denounce the policy which permits large tracts of land to be held unused by individuals or corporations, and insist that foreigners shall not be permitted to acquire title to real estate in Iowa.

We demand that mortgage-owners shall be compelled to pay taxes upon their mortgages where recorded, and that mortgagors be released to that extent.

We arraign the monopolists who controlled the last Legislature for their unscrupulous truculency to corporate interests and their base betrayal of platform pledges.

The Republican Convention was held on August 24, and renominated Governor Larrabee and Lieutenant-Governor Hull. Its choice for Justice of the Supreme Court was G. S. Robinson, and for Superintendent of Public Instruction, Henry Sabin. The platform denounces Southern frauds upon the ballot, favors protection and civil service reform, arraigns the national administration, and speaks as follows upon State issues:

We are opposed to criminal and vicious immigration of all kinds to threaten the public welfare and disturb the social peace, and to all pauper immigration and convict or coolie labor, or to the contract of prison labor by the State, to bring unfair competition to American workingmen. We favor such legislation in the State as will protect miners and all other laborers in their full rights, as to compensation, protection of life, hours of labor, and freedom of trade. All public lands should be held, and all unearned land-grants reclaimed, for actual settlers. Non-resident aliens should not be allowed to acquire titles to land in this country.

The theory of public regulation and control of railways and other corporations, first enacted into law in this State, and by the State carried up to the approval of the Supreme Court of the United States, we maintain with increasing favor. We approve the principles of the interstate commerce law, and favor such amendments thereto as will make it still more protective of the interests of the people, and such State legislation as will apply its principles to this State. We further ask that the next Legislature shall abolish the free pass in all its forms, and that it shall, after thorough and unsparing investigation, so revise and amend the laws forming the railroad code of the State as will secure to the people all possible protection from corporation monopoly and extortion, as will increase the efficiency and the usefulness of the Railway Commission, and as will secure all fair and possible reduction in freights and fares, believing that the first-class roads of the State can afford to reduce passenger fares to two cents a mile. We are opposed to all unjust discriminations between persons and places, and also to any railroad policy or legislation which will tend to injure our agricultural, industrial, or commercial interests, or that will aid in building up outside cities and interests at the expense of the cities and towns of our own State. We are also opposed to granting any form of exclusive rights by which any corporation will be protected from legitimate and honorable competition, and established as a monopoly regardless of public interests. We favor such legislation as will relieve the people of the State from the extortion of the school-book monopoly.

Iowa has no compromise to hold with the saloon. We declare in favor of the faithful and vigorous enforcement in all parts of the State of the prohibitory law. The pharmacy law and county permit law should be so amended as to prevent the drug-store or wholesale liquor-store from becoming in any manner the substitute or successor of the saloon.

We approve of the State administration of public affairs in Iowa, and especially commend Gov. Larrabee for his courageous defense of the people from the extortion of railway monopolies, and for his protest in behalf of Iowa against Cleveland's attempted surrender of the rebel battle-flags.

The Democratic Convention met early in September, and nominated for Governor, T. J. Anderson; for Lieutenant-Governor, J. M. Elder; for Justice of the Supreme Court, Charles F. Fogg; for Superintendent of Public Instruction, H. W. Sawyer. The following is a part of the platform adopted:

We commend the action of the Democratic members of the Twenty-first General Assembly in supporting the Cassatt bill and the bill against the holding of lands by non-resident aliens, and we pledge our candidates to the support of these measures in the next Legislature.

We are opposed to all sumptuary legislation, and in favor of the repeal of the present prohibitory liquor law, and the substitution in its stead of a local option and carefully guarded license law, with a minimum license-fee of five hundred dollars for the better control of the liquor-traffic.

We believe that the railroad companies are public corporations, and therefore subject to public control. We demand such legislation by Congress and the State Legislature as will apply to State and interstate transportation of freights and passengers, the principles of the Reagan bill, viz.: All rates shall be reasonable and shall be made public. No discriminations against individuals or localities. No rebates or drawbacks. The same charge for the same service to all persons and no higher charge for a less than for a greater service. Prohibition of pooling in every form. Equal facilities and opportunities to all shippers. We oppose the free transportation of any and favor the cheap transportation of all. We believe that the first-class roads can profitably carry passengers at two cents per mile, and we demand a law restricting them to such a charge. We are opposed to special tribunals for the settlement of railroad questions, and especially to such tribunals having power to suspend the laws of the land. We therefore favor the abolition of all such tribunals, and believe that the ordinary courts of the country should be vested with full power to enforce the just obligations of the companies and to award adequate damages to persons injured by their violation.

Every citizen of the State is entitled to vote, and his vote should be as effective as the vote of any other citizen. We denounce, as in violation of this inherent right and as a practical disfranchisement of the majority of our people, the infamous gerrymander made by the Republicans in the last General Assembly, by which a small minority of the people were vested with the full control of the law-making power, and we pledge our best endeavors to restore the representation according to population and the right of the majority to rule. We cordially invite the co-operation with us of all persons in accordance with these principles in our endeavor to carry them into effect.

At the election in November, the Republican ticket was successful. Gov. Larrabee received 168,784 votes; Anderson, 152,918; Cain, 11,612; and V. G. Farnham, the Prohibition candidate, 67 votes. The plurality of Gov. Larrabee was 15,866 against 6,979 in 1885. Both houses of the Legislature of 1888 will be strongly Republican, the Senate having 32 Republicans, 17 Democrats, and 1 Independent; the House 63 Republicans, 33 Democrats, and 4 Independents.

ITALY, a kingdom in Southern Europe. On March 17, 1861, the law was promulgated by virtue of which Victor Emanuel II took for himself and his descendants the title of King of Italy. The Constitution of the old kingdom of Sardinia, adopted on March 4, 1848, was extended to the whole of Italy. The executive power is exercised by the King through his ministers, who are responsible to Parliament, which consists of a Senate, nominated by the King, and a Chamber of Deputies, elected by all male citizens over the age of twenty-one, who can read and write, and pay taxes to the amount of 19 lire, or $3.66. In 1886, out of 2,420,000 electors, 1,407,000 actually voted. There are 508 deputies, elected by *scrutin de liste* in 135 electoral districts.

The King is Humbert I, born March 14, 1844, who succeeded to the throne on the death of his father, Victor Emanuel, on Jan. 29, 1878. The heir-apparent is Victor Emanuel, Prince of Naples, the only son of the King, who was born Nov. 11, 1869.

The ministry, at the beginning of 1887, was composed as follows: President of the Council and Minister of the Interior, Agostino Depretis; Minister of Finance and the Treasury, Agostino Magliani; Minister of Foreign Affairs, Gen. Carlo Felice Nicolis di Robilant; Minister of Justice and of Ecclesiastical Affairs, Diego Taiani; Minister of War, Gen. Cesare Ricotti-Magnani; Minister of Marine, Benedetto Brin; Minister of Commerce, Industry, and Agriculture, Bernardino Grimaldi; Minister of Public Instruction, Michele Coppino; Minister of Public Works, Francesco Genala.

Area and Population.—The official estimate of the area of Italy is 296,323 square kilometres, but a more recent computation makes it 286,588 square kilometres. The population on Dec. 31, 1886, was estimated at 29,943,607.

The number of marriages in 1886 was 233,099, against 233,931 in 1885; births, 1,126,464, against 1,165,258; deaths, 882,642, against 826,505; surplus of births, 243,822, against 338,753. The emigration in 1886 was 167,829, against 157,193 in 1885, 147,017 in 1884, 169,101 in 1883, and 161,562 in 1882. The emigrants to European countries numbered 80,406, of whom 35,706 went to France, 19,166 to Austria, 13,181 to Hungary, and 4,346, the next largest number, to Switzerland. There were 4,540 emigrants to Tunis, Algeria, and Egypt, and 717 to other parts of Africa and to Asia and Oceania. The emigration to American countries in 1886 was 82,166, against 72,490 in 1885, 55,467 in 1884, and 63,388 in 1883. The Argentine Republic received 38,588 emigrants in 1886 and 40,054 in 1885, and other parts of South and Central America 15,143 in 1886 and 19,340 in 1884. The emigration to the United States and Canada was 28,640 in 1886, 18,096 in 1885, 10,847 in 1884, 21,837 in 1883, and 18,669 in 1882.

Of the total number of emigrants 85,355 are classed as permanent and 82,474 as temporary or periodical. The emigrants over fourteen years of age numbered 70,098, of whom 44,013 were peasants, 11,426 of these being women. As compared with other countries the emigration from Italy, which was 294·4 out of every

100,000 inhabitants in 1886, was less than in Ireland, where 1,253·7 out of every 100,000 persons emigrated; England, where the proportion was 524·9; Scotland, where it was 641·2; or Denmark, where it was 802·9; but it was greater than in Germany, where it was 163·7.

The most populous cities and their population in 1881, when the last census was taken, are as follow: Naples, 463,172; Milan, 295,-543; Rome, 273,268; Turin, 230,183; Palermo, 205,712; Genoa, 138,081; Florence, 134,992; Venice, 129,445; Bologna, 105,998.

At the time of the census the number of foreigners in Italy was 59,956, of whom 16,092 were Austrians, 12,104 Swiss, 10,781 French, 7,302 English, 5,284 Germans, 1,387 Russians, 1,286 Americans, and the rest mainly Greeks, Spaniards, Turks, Belgians, and Swedes.

The population was divided between the principal conditions and occupations in 1881 as follows: Agriculture, 8,178,382; manufacturing industries, 4,185,461; without occupation, 4,725,681; no occupation stated, 1,580,-975; investors, etc., 962,881; employés and domestics, 713,405; transportation, 313,011; commerce, 279,773; raising of animals, 244,-452; civil administration, 170,652; clothing trades, 151,094; national defense, 160,155; public worship, 131,585; workmen, 129,829; prisoners and paupers, 129,681; instruction, 79,795; horticulture, 73,339; sylviculture, 59,-651; sanitary service, 59,717; mining, 59,512; fishing and hunting, 48,241; fine arts, 35,624; commercial travelers, 34,450; justice, 28,250; literature and science, 19,775. The number of proprietors of land and buildings was 4,183,-432, of whom 1,399,965 were females.

Commerce.—The total value of merchandise imports in 1886 was 1,469,300,000 lire, and of exports 1,066,800,000 lire. The imports of cereals were valued at 240,500,000 lire, an increase of 65,100,000 lire over 1885, while the exports were 86,900,000 lire in value, being 5,800,000 lire less than in 1885. The imports of wines and liquors were 19,000,000 lire, showing a decrease of 9,400,000 lire, and the exports were 90,100,000 lire, an increase of 28,700,000 lire. The imports of sugar and groceries showed a decrease from 101,300,000 to 41,100,000 lire. Tobacco imports increased from 20,800,000 to 31,500,000 lire. The imports of vegetables and fruits were 22,200,000 lire and the exports 61,-200,000 lire; imports of animals and animal food products, 99,700,000 lire; exports, 88,-300,000 lire. The imports of coal amounted to 71,700,000 lire; exports of stone and minerals, 56,500,000 lire; imports of metals, 79,-100,000 lire; imports of hides, hair, and leather, 55,400,000 lire; exports, 14,700,000 lire; imports of textile materials, 182,000,000 lire, as compared with 164,900,000 lire in 1885; exports, 368,400,000 lire, as compared with 310,-300,000 lire. The total imports of raw materials were 457,600,000 lire in value, as compared with 434,400,000 lire in 1885; the total

exports, 463,300,000 lire, as compared with 414,400,000 lire. The imports of manufactured articles fell off from 409,200,000 to 389,-300,000 lire. The imports of textile manufactures were 176,800,000 lire, showing a decrease of 19,400,000 lire, and of yarns 44,000,000 lire, showing a decrease of 6,000,000 lire. The imports of machinery and vehicles, valued at 89,000,000 lire, showed a decrease of 5,800,000. There was a slight decrease in the imports of pottery and glass, while other articles showed an increase, which was greatest under the head of jewelry and art-objects, which were imported to the amount of 28,800,000 lire, against 18,400,000 lire in 1885. The exports of manufactured articles declined from 143,600,000 lire in 1885 to 136,800,000 lire in 1886. There was an increase in the exports of textile fabrics from 26,300,000 to 29,400,000 lire, and in yarns from 11,600,000 to 14,700,000 lire; also in jewelry and objects of art from 30,600,000 to 32,-000,000 lire. All other articles showed a falling off, which was greatest in metal manufactures, which declined from 6,400,000 to 600,000 lire, and in wood manufactures, which declined from 16,700,000 to 9,700,000 lire. The imports of the miscellaneous class fell off from 247,800,-000 to 168,400,000 lire, and the exports from 287,100,000 to 186,500,000 lire, although under the head of oils there was an increase of exports from 52,900,000 lire in 1885 to 83,700,000 lire in 1886, and a slight increase under the head of drugs, dyes, and chemicals, the exports of which amounted to 46,600,000 lire. The imports of coin and bullion amounted to 41,600,-000 lire in 1886, against 27,600,000 lire in the preceding year; the exports to 9,800,000 lire, against 10,300,000 lire. The commerce of 1886 was divided among foreign nations as follows, the values being given in lire or francs:

COUNTRIES.	Imports.	Exports.
France	846,600,000	416,500,000
Austria	224,600,000	160,400,000
England	275,100,000	71,200,000
Germany	129,800,000	108,100,000
Switzerland	94,900,000	49,700,000
Russia	94,800,000	18,100,000
Turkey, Servia, and Roumania	46,300,000	18,800,000
Other European countries	59,500,000	54,800,000
United States and Canada	55,200,000	52,200,000
Other American countries	21,200,000	88,100,000
Asia	108,700,000	21,700,000
Africa	29,600,000	31,800,000
Australia	25,100,000	200,000
Total	1,510,900,000	1,076,100,000

Navigation.—The number of vessels engaged in ocean-commerce entered at Italian ports in 1886 was 16,068, of 6,106,767 tons. Of these, 9,324, of 1,497,003 tons, sailed under the Italian flag, and 6,744, of 4.609,764 tons, under foreign flags. The number of vessels entered with cargoes was 18,670, of 5,842,084 tons. The steamers entered numbered 5,577, of 5,062,812 tons, comprising 983 Italian steamers, of 799,666 tons, and 4,594, of 4,263,146 tons, belonging to other nations. The coasting-vessels entered were 92,504 in number, the tonnage being 12,554,506, and of these 88,898, of 9,497,099 tons, were Italian, and 8,606, of 3,057,407 tons, were foreign. The number of vessels employed in long voyages that were cleared was 15,822, of 6,182,345 tons; the number of coasting-vessels, 92,879, of 12,294,224 tons.

The mercantile navy consisted on Jan. 1, 1887, of 6,992 sailing-vessels, of 801,849 tons, as compared with 7,111, of 828,819 tons, a year before, and of 237 steamers, of 144,328 tons, as compared with 225, of 124,600 tons. The number of inscribed seamen in 1885 was 189,921.

Railroads.—There were 11,625 kilometres of railroad in operation on June 30, 1887. The receipts for the financial year amounted to 225,068,618 lire.

The Post-Office.—The number of letters and post-cards transmitted in 1885 was 195,179,324.

Telegraphs.—The length of telegraph lines at the close of 1884 was 30,021 kilometres, and of wires 106,755 kilometres, not including 188 kilometres of cables. The number of paid internal dispatches in 1885 was 5,896,306; of paid international dispatches, 581,657; of official messages, 469,974; of dispatches connected with the service, 194,384; of international messages in transit, 186,062; total number of telegrams, 7,328,383.

Army.—The permanent army, by virtue of the law of June 29, 1882, modified by the law of June 23, 1887, is organized as follows: Infantry, 96 regiments of the line, and 12 regiments of bersaglieri, each regiment consisting of 3 battalions of 4 companies each and a depot; 7 regiments of Alpine troops, comprising 22 battalions and 75 companies; and 87 military districts, forming 98 companies. Cavalry, 24 regiments, each of 6 squadrons and a depot, besides 6 depots of remount. Artillery, 24 regiments of field artillery, of which 12 are division regiments, each of 8 batteries, 1 company of train, and a depot, and 12 are attached to corps, and have 2 companies of train; 1 regiment of horse artillery, of 6 batteries, with 4 companies of train and a depot; 1 regiment of mountain artillery, having 9 batteries and a depot; 5 regiments of fortress artillery, of which 2 have 16 companies and 3 have 12 companies, each regiment having its depot. Engineers, 4 regiments, of which 2 are sappers, each of 18 companies, 2 companies of train and a depot; 1 regiment contains 7 companies of sappers, 6 companies of telegraphists, and 1 company of specialists having charge of carrier-pigeons, electric lighting, signals, balloon service, etc., with 2 companies of train and a depot; and 1 regiment consists of 8 companies of pontonniers, 4 railroad companies, 2 companies for lagoons, 3 companies of train, and a depot. Carabinieri, 11 legions and 1 legion of élèves. Invalid corps, 4 companies. Sanitary corps, 12 companies. Commissariat, 12 companies. There are, besides, the veterinary corps, artillery and engineer establishments, institutions for instruction, and two military penitentiaries. The mobile militia comprises 48 regiments of infantry of the line, 18 battalions of bersaglieri, 22 companies of Alpine troops, 13 brigades of field artillery, each of 4 batteries, 36 companies of fortress artillery, 3 brigades of mountain artillery, and an engineer corps. The Sardinian militia has a separate organization. The territorial militia is organized as 320 battalions of infantry, 22 battalions of Alpine troops, and 100 companies of fortress artillery, with engineers, a sanitary corps, and a commissariat.

The total strength of the army on the war footing on June 1, 1887, was 2,590,172. There were with the colors 13,864 officers and 252,025 men, while 9,814 officers and 620,768 men of the permanent army were on furloughs. The mobile militia numbered 2,898 officers and 377,110 men, the territorial militia 4,402 officers and 1,308,391 men. The troops serving with the colors were divided as follow: Officers, 13,864; carabinieri, 22,452; infantry, 126.667; bersaglieri, 15,288; Alpine troops, 9,876; military district troops, 9,308; cavalry, 25,501; artillery, 26,800; engineers, 7,753; establishments for instruction, 1,486; sanitary troops, 2,140; administrative troops, 1,866; invalid corps, 407; penitential establishments, 3,081; total, 265,889.

The Navy.—The navy on Jan. 1, 1887, comprised 87 line-of-battle ships, 17 transports, 3 school-ships, 19 vessels for local service, 6 side-wheel gun-boats, 3 sea-going torpedo-boats, 19 first-class and 21 second-class torpedo-boats for coast-defense, and 2 torpedo-vessels. There were 11 armor-clads of the first-class, carrying 89 cannon, with an aggregate displacement of 75,221 tons. The second-class vessels of combat numbered eleven, including three iron-clads. There were under construction 7 iron-clads of the first class, of 87,006 tons' displacement, 4 unarmored cruisers of the second class, 8 of the third class, 2 transports, 2 vessels for port service, 2 torpedo avisos, 44 sea-going torpedo-boats, and 6 torpedo-boats for coast-defense.

Colonial Possessions.—Italy has in part occupied and in part taken under her protectorate the strip of the western coast of the Red Sea which extends from the village of Emberemi, in 16° of north latitude, to the north of the island of Massowah, to the southern limit of the territory of Raheita, in 12° of north latitude, to the south of Assab, with the small islands off the coast, and the Archipelago of Dahlak. The coast-line has a length of about 500 kilometres. Italian sovereignty has been proclaimed over a territory extending about 60 kilometres along the coast from Dermah on the north to Sinthiar on the south. The territory thus far occupied by Italy comprises the island of Massowah, with the neighboring isles and a part of the coast of Emberemi extending to and including the peninsula of Buri, and the Dahlak Islands. The population of the town of Massowah, not including the garrison, was in 1885 about 5,000; of Emberemi, 1,000; of the Dahlak Archipelago, 2,000; Assab contained in 1881 a population of 1,193 persons. A railroad, 20 kilometres in length, has been built from Massowah to Arkiko.

Finances.—The total receipts of the treasury for the year ending June 30, 1886, were 1,745,-515,911 lire, and the expenditures 1,730,598,-335 lire. The budget accounts for 1886–'87 make the ordinary receipts 1,525,412,598, including 92,759,678 lire of *recettes d'ordre* which are entered on both sides of the account. The extraordinary receipts are set down as 193,614,-541 lire, comprising 10,062,644 lire of effective receipts, 41,101,917 lire from sales of property and new debts, and 142,450,000 lire for construction of railroads. The total receipts are 1,719,027,541 lire and the total expenditures 1,700,229,160 lire. The interest on the consolidated debt was 441,679,465 lire, and the total expenses on account of the debt and other fixed charges 639,483,938 lire; the expenses of financial administration, 182,599,112 lire; the ordinary expenditures of the Ministry of Justice and Public Worship, 33,665,-052 lire; of the Ministry of Foreign Affairs, 7,807,242 lire; of the Ministry of Education, 34,736,882 lire; of the Ministry of the Interior, 60,737,184 lire; of the Ministry of Public Works, 78,529,878 lire; of the Ministry of War, 230,106,618 lire; of the Ministry of Marine, 71,815,660 lire; of the Ministry of Agriculture, 13,304,512 lire; total ordinary expenditure, 1,433,916,040 lire. The extraordinary expenditure amounted to 276,313,120 lire, of which 2,207,476 lire were for public instruction, 2,-979,347 lire for the Interior Department, 185,-983,274 lire for public works, 37,185,000 lire for the army, 14,016,000 lire for the navy, 1,182,474 for the Department of Agriculture, and 917,413 for other departments. The budget for 1887–'88 makes the total ordinary revenue 1,452,746,252 lire, exclusive of 91,043,720 lire of *recettes d'ordre*. The ordinary revenue from public property is estimated at 81,492,-142 lire; from direct taxes, 387,126,388 lire; from stamps, registration, etc., 197,270,000 lire; from customs, excise, and tobacco and salt monopolies, 602,077,245 lire; from the lottery, 78,302,000 lire; from posts, telegraphs, and other public services, 74,835,000 lire; from refunds, 25,375,827 lire; from other sources, 6,267,700 lire. The extraordinary revenue is 215,028,272 lire, of which sum 11,184,771 lire effective receipts; 37,443,501 lire the proceeds of the sale of domanial and ecclesiastic property, recovery of debts, and new loans of the amount of 19,040,000 lire; and 166,450,000 are special receipts to be invested in railroad construction. The ordinary expenditure is estimated at 1,486,062,121 lire, which is 57,727,-851 lire less than the ordinary receipts, but extraordinary expenditures to the amount of 315,695,059 lire bring the total up to 1,801,-757,180 lire, leaving a deficit of 42,938,936 lire.

Of the extraordinary expenditures 59,820,856 lire are for amortization and other operations of the treasury, 186,460,300 lire for public works, 47,750,000 lire for the army, and 14,-816,000 lire for the navy. Of the ordinary receipts, 81,492,142 lire were derived from reproductive property, of which 63,657,400 lire were railroad receipts; 387,126,388 lire from direct taxation, of which 106,316,356 lire are from land-taxes, 67,500,000 lire from the house-tax, and 213,309,082 lire from personal-property taxes; 197,270,000 lire from imposts on affairs, of which 33,000,000 lire are derived from succession duties, 63,500,000 lire from registration dues, 58,000,000 lire from stamps, and 17,000,000 lire from a tax on railroad receipts; 602,077,245 lire from duties on consumption, of which 229,000,000 lire are received from customs, 81,577,245 lire from octrois, 196,000,000 lire from the tobacco monopoly, 36,000,000 lire from beer, spirit, sugar, and powder licenses, and 59,500,000 lire from the salt monopoly; 78,-302,000 lire from the state lottery; 74,835,000 lire from public services, the post-office receipts being 44,000,000 lire and the telegraph receipts 13,815,000 lire; 25,375,829 from repayments; and 6,267,700 lire from other sources.

A law for the conversion of the redeemable debt provides that, in order to convert the various issues into a consolidated debt, the 5 per cent. rente shall be replaced by a new rente bearing 4½ per cent. interest. The debt statement for the year 1886–'87 gives the rente of the consolidated debt as 448,748,780 lire; interest due to the Holy See, 3,225,000 lire; debts separately inscribed, 22,815,955 lire, besides 1,091,260 lire for sinking-funds; various debts, 50,623,311 lire, besides 386,851 lire for sinking-funds; interest on the floating debt, 9,840,000 lire; total rentes and interest, 535,-252,996 lire; total sinking-funds, 1,478,111 lire.

Ministerial Crisis.—The disaster at Massowah subjected the ministry to a series of violent attacks in the Chamber. Count Robilant, who minimized the defeat, was made the special object of the assaults. The credit of 5,000,000 lire demanded for the purpose of sending reenforcements was referred to a special committee with Signor Depretis at its head, and was granted, but on a motion which was accepted by the ministers as a vote of confidence, the vote was so close that Count Robilant handed in his resignation. After trying to induce him to withdraw it without success, the ministry on February 7 decided to resign in a body. Signor Depretis desired to retire from public life, but the King was unwilling to lose the services of a minister who had proved himself indispensable, and accordingly he made an attempt to reconstitute his ministry, admitting an element from the hostile groups, but leaving out all the chiefs of the Opposition. When this proved impracticable, he persuaded the King to send for Signor Biancheri, the President of the Chamber, and afterward for Signor

Saracco, a senator, but they were not more successful in forming a ministry than himself. The Chamber adjourned during the crisis, and when it assembled again on March 10 the situation was unchanged, and Signor Depretis announced that, in view of the difficulties of forming a new administration, the King had not accepted the resignation of himself and his colleagues, and that if the Chamber supported them they expected a formal motion of approval. Signor Crispi moved a vote of censure, which was discussed in an animated debate on the following day, and was finally rejected by 214 votes to 194. The session was closed by prorogation on the same day in order to allow time for the settlement of the Cabinet question, which was the more serious on account of the illness of the Prime Minister. A ministry was finally constituted, and was gazetted on April 4. It was composed of the following members: Prime Minister and Minister of Foreign Affairs, Depretis; Minister of the Interior, Crispi; Minister of Justice, Zanardelli; Minister of War, Gen. Bertole Viale; Minister of Finance, Magliani; Minister of Marine, Admiral Brin; Minister of Agriculture, Grimaldi; Minister of Public Works, Saracco; Minister of Public Instruction, Coppino.

Legislation.—Parliament came together again on April 18. Signor Depretis, while affirming that Italy would follow the policy best conforming to her mission, which aimed above all to the maintenance of peace, announced that, since all governments were endeavoring to increase their military power, the Cabinet would apply for fresh credits to augment the country's means of defense. He said that the massacre at Dogali would be avenged, but only after mature deliberation and at the proper moment. The Chamber approved a bill calling to the colors a part of the reserves, numbering about 17,000 men, in order to replace troops sent to Massowah. On May 2 Gen. Bertole Viale introduced the bill for the reorganization of the army, by virtue of which the number of regiments of field artillery was increased from twelve to twenty-four, one regiment being mounted; the mountain artillery was increased to five regiments; and two companies were added to the engineers. The number of infantry officers was increased by 38 colonels, 87 majors, and 100 captains, and two brigade commands were added. The Minister of War asked, moreover, for the establishment of a school at Caserta for the instruction of non-commissioned officers who wished to receive commissions, and for an artillery-school in connection with the existing school of musketry. The Government applied for a credit of 12,000,000 lire for the pay and clothing of the men, and 2,600,000 lire with which to purchase horses. On May 30 the Chamber authorized the expenditure of 85,000,000 lire in the next ten years on the navy, 37,000,000 lire being devoted to the construction of seven second-class ironclads, 25,000,000 lire for torpedoes and machine-guns, and 19,000,000 for fortifications at Spezia, Taranto, and Venice. The budget provided for the expenditure of 7,000,000 lire for the troops in Africa. On June 30 a special credit of 20,000,000 lire for military operations, to be carried on as soon as the season should permit, was voted by a large majority. Signor Crispi had previously explained that the Cabinet simply intended to strengthen Italy's position at Massowah, and had not dreamed of carrying on a war of conquest against Abyssinia. The Government brought in a bill to increase to three lire the duty on grain for the protection of Italian agriculture, since the imports levied by other governments would cause exporting countries to send their cereals to Italy. The reform of the Senate was discussed in that body, and the Government appointed a commission, consisting mainly of senators, to study measures for strengthening the upper Chamber, and promoting the execution of its functions without the sacrifice of its independence.

The Crispi Ministry.—After the death of Signor Depretis, the Cabinet was reconstituted, with Signor Crispi, his old antagonist and recent colleague, at its head. The new ministry, formed on August 7, 1887, is composed as follows: President of the Council of Ministers, Minister of the Interior, and Minister of Foreign Affairs *ad interim*, J. Crispi; Minister of Public Instruction, M. Coppino; Minister of Finance and the Treasury, A. Magliani; Minister of War, E. Bertole Viale; Minister of Marine, B. Brin; Minister of Grace, Justice, and Worship, G. Zanardelli; Minister of Public Works, J. Saracco; Minister of Agriculture, Industry, and Commerce, B. Grimaldi.

Parliament was opened by the King on November 15. In his speech he said:

My heart rejoices that Italy is strong in arms, sure of her alliances, and friendly with all Governments, and that our country continues its forward march in the family of the great powers. Italy is now in the front rank with the leading states, and no longer fears having to recede. Parliament may therefore without anxiety give its careful and prompt attention to internal affairs. There are urgent reforms awaited with impatience by the country. Bills will be submitted to you for the reorganization of the ministerial departments, the reform of the communal and provincial administrations, the establishment of a uniform penal code for the whole of Italy, the radical reform of the prison system, the institution of a sole Court of Cassation, the improvement of the education of youth, the establishment of a sanitary code, and measures for insuring the spontaneity of emigration, and, within possible limits, for supervising emigration, which at present appears to us excessive. Other measures will be brought forward for encouraging thrift among the working and agricultural classes, and in order that credit by the reorganization of the banks of issue and of the paper currency may anticipate the fortune of the future without endangering the present.

A fresh transitory increase in expenditure for the army and railroads is promised in the budget, while for the following year no extraordinary military expenditure is expected to be necessary. Measures for meeting the fresh charges and re-establishing the elasticity of the budget were in preparation, and in the mean time the Government desired to reserve for itself the initiative in proposals involving fresh expenditure. A bill dealing with promotions in the army and navy was promised. The proposed measure for the reorganization of the ministerial departments consisted in a proposal to leave the reorganization in question to the Government itself, to be enacted by a simple decree signed by the King, as it belongs by right to the executive power. This principle was approved by the Chamber, which gave 288 votes against 22 for the bill in that form.

Church and State.—The Pope, in an allocution delivered on May 23, wrote as follows concerning the difficulty between the Papacy and the Italian Government:

God grant that Italy, which is particularly dear to us, may also share the spirit of peace with which we are animated toward all nations. We earnestly desire that Italy may put aside her unhappy difference with the Papacy, whose dignity is violated, and chiefly violated by the conspiracy of the sects. The means of obtaining concord is to establish a state of things under which the Pope would be subject to no power, and would enjoy that full and real liberty which, far from injuring Italy's interests, would powerfully contribute to her prosperity.

Taken in connection with a more conciliatory attitude of the Clerical party, and other indications of the desire of the Vatican for a *modus vivendi*, it was inferred from this that Pope Leo was inclined to abandon his pretensions to the temporal power. It was soon made evident, however, that he had no intention of relinquishing his claim to the sovereignty of the Papal States, or, at least, to the city of Rome, and it is equally impossible for the Italian Government even to allow a European guarantee of the position of the Pontiff under the law of guarantees, much less to yield up the capital of united and indivisible Italy. When Signor Bovio interpellated the Government with regard to the rumors that were current, Signor Crispi said that the Government, at any rate, were not seeking a conciliation. The state was at war with no one. He had no wish to know what was going on in the Vatican, where reigned the Pope, who was not an ordinary man. Time ripened many a question, and might also lead to reconciliation, which would never be detrimental to the national rights.

On June 15, when Cardinal Rampolla assumed the functions of Pontifical Secretary of State, the Pope addressed to him a long letter, in which he expounded his views, and intimated that he would be content with the restitution of the Leonine city. The indispensable condition for pacification in Italy, he declared, was the rendering to the Roman Pontiff a true sovereignty. In the present state of affairs he is in the power, not of himself, but of others, on whom it depends to modify, when and how it pleases them, according to the changes of men and circumstances, the very conditions of his existence. And therefore, during his pon-

tificate, he had insisted on an actual sovereignty, not for purposes of earthly grandeur, but as a true and effective protection to his independence and liberty. He claims, in an especial manner, sovereignty over the city of Rome, to which the steps of the prince of apostles were directed that he might become the shepherd, and transmit in perpetuity the authority of the supreme apostolate, and which bears in every part, deeply engraved, the Papal imprint, and belongs to the pontiffs by such and so many titles as no prince ever had to any city in his kingdom.

Commercial Treaty with Austria-Hungary.—A new treaty of commerce with Austria-Hungary went into effect on January 1, 1888. It remains provisional for six months, at the end of which, when ratified by the Legislature in both countries, it will be signed for ten years. The number of articles of Austrian production which pay duty on entering Italy is diminished from ninety-nine to forty-three, while on the Austrian side the duty has been remitted on twenty-eight articles out of sixty-seven. The articles which are still liable to duty pay higher rates than before, the increase being generally one lire for a certain weight or number of articles. Among the goods relieved of duty are wine, brandy, matches, mirrors, sealing-wax, steam-engines, glass and crystal wares, musical instruments, cattle, meat, butter, and hemp. Among the articles which will henceforth pay a higher duty are beer, leather goods, porcelain, majolica, cheese, and toys.

The New Triple Alliance.—The tripartite treaty by which Italy became a party to the defensive league concluded on October 7, 1879, between Germany and Austria-Hungary was signed for the five years expiring in the autumn of 1887. Although the dominant elements were all in favor of its renewal, the hostility to the compact on the part of Republicans and Irredentists was not dead, and in the early part of the year it manifested itself in the violent and bitter attacks on the ministry in the Chamber, and even in angry demonstrations in the street, for which the military reverse near Massowah served as a pretext. In the spring of 1887 a new alliance was secretly concluded. In October, Signor Crispi went to Friedrichsruhe to arrange with Prince Bismarck a final settlement of details. The points settled were the contingencies which form a *casus belli*, the method of diplomatic action, and the delay to be granted to the offending power before declaring war, the general plan of combined military and naval action, the military and naval forces to be placed in the field and on the sea by each of the three powers, and the territorial modifications and other results to be achieved with a view of securing a lasting peace after a victorious war. Each of the powers agrees not to treat separately for peace, or to desist from war, without the consent of the other two. The original treaty, which Italy accepts in all its parts, was never made public until the winter of 1887–'88, during the debate in the German Parliament over the Landwehr bill. Contrary to the current belief, it contained, so far as is made known, no provision for combined action against France in case of aggression against Germany. The preamble of the treaty declares that "considering the cohesion of the two empires will the more easily secure their own safety, while it can threaten no one, and at the same time is well adapted to consolidate the peace of Europe on the basis of the Berlin Treaty, the two emperors, while giving a mutual and solemn promise never to impart an aggressive tendency in any direction to their purely defensive agreement, resolve to conclude an alliance, and appointed as their plenipotentiaries Count Andrassy and Prince Henry of Reuss." The terms of the treaty follow:

Article I stipulates that, should either of the two countries, contrary to the hope and wish of the contracting parties, be attacked by Russia, each is pledged to assist the other with its entire military force, and only to conclude peace upon such terms as both agree to accept. Article II provides that, should either country be attacked by any other power, the other pledges itself not to support the aggressor, but to maintain an attitude of neutrality. Should Russia assist the aggressor, however, Article I comes into force, and war operations will then be carried on in common and terms of peace be conjointly arranged. Article III sets forth that the treaty, being of a peaceful character, shall, in order to prevent misinterpretation, be kept secret or be communicated to a third power under the consent of the contracting parties. Both parties express the hope, in view of the intentions announced by the Czar at the meeting with Emperor William in September, 1879, at Alexandrowo, that the Russian military preparations may not prove to be in reality menacing to either of them, and may give no cause for them to adopt similar measures. Should this hope, however, contrary to expectation, prove erroneous, both parties recognize it to be their loyal duty to acquaint Emperor Alexander with the fact that an attack upon one country will be regarded as an attack upon both.

J

JAPAN. This empire, consisting of an archipelago in eastern Asia, is officially designated Dai Nihon (great day-root or sunrise). It has had but one line of emperors, who form the oldest dynasty of rulers now existing in the world. The present Mikado, Mutsuhito, is the one hundred and twenty-third of the line. He was born Nov. 3, 1850, assumed power Feb. 3, 1867, married Feb. 10, 1869, made Tokio the national capital Nov. 26, 1868, took an oath before gods and men at Kioto April 6, 1868, which was reaffirmed in public proclamation Oct. 12, 1881, to form two houses of parliament, limit the imperial prerogative, and transform the government into a constitutional monarchy in 1890. He proclaimed his son Haru, born Aug. 31, 1877, heir-apparent to the throne Aug. 31, 1887. With the Mikado is associated a Senate, or Genro-in, of sixty-eight members, a Sanji-in of fifty-five members, and a Council of State consisting of the ministers or heads of departments. The empire, for administrative purposes, is divided into forty-four ken, or prefectures, and three fu, or imperial cities. There are five cities containing over 100,000 people, six containing over 50,000, and seventeen containing over 80,-000. By census of January, 1886, the population numbered 38,151,217 persons, of whom 3,419 were nobles, 1,948,283 gentry, and 36,-199,515 common people. During 1885 there were 259,497 marriages, 1,004,989 births, and 676,369 deaths. Among the foreigners resident in the empire are 4,122 Chinese, and 3,912 Europeans and Americans. There are 410 foreigners in Government employ, and 226 in the Yusen Kaisha, or Ocean Transportation Company, besides many in private Japanese service. Tokio, the capital, has 225,610 houses and 1,132,470 inhabitants, among whom are 485 white aliens who reside in 192 tenements.

Diplomatic Establishment.—Until 1868 the Foreign Office was but a sub-bureau, but not long after the restoration of the Mikado to supreme power, the Gai Mu Shô, or Department of Foreign Affairs, was established, its head outranking the other Cabinet officers. There are now on the staff 18 high native officials, with 2 American, 1 French, and 3 German assistants, the two highest advisory offices being held by Americans. The subalterns number 82. Whereas, in 1868, there was no envoy or consul from Japan abroad, there are now legations at London, Paris, Vienna, St. Petersburg, Washington, Berlin, Rome, the Hague, Pekin, and Séoul, with consulates at London, Lyons, New York, San Francisco, Honolulu, and in China and Corea. The salary of a foreign minister is $11,750 per annum, of consul-general, $5,000. The expense of the Foreign Office is $189,202, and of legations and consulates, $650,026.

Finances.—By the report of Matsukata Masayoshi, rendered March 2, 1887, in the estimates for the twentieth year of Meiji (1887–'88), the total revenue is stated at $79,936,870, and expenditures at $79,955,552.75. An analysis of the sources of income shows that the farmers bear the heaviest burdens, and that after these come the manufacturers of saké (rice-liquor), soy, and tobacco; the taxes on land and these three articles of luxury amounting respectively to $42,559,441; $13,697,723; $1,278,210; $1,-244,002; or, in all, to $58,774,374. The remaining home taxes on banks, shipping, vehicles, confectionery, patent-medicines, marine products, exchanges, and for Government stamps yield only $3,623,196. Customs duties amount to

$2,704,553; fees and licenses, $2,370,183; posts and telegraphs, $3,096,697; forests, $416,783; sales of property, $306,346; or, in all, to $8,348,507. Subscriptions to naval loan bonds, amounting to $6,486,240, form the last item of income. The details of expenditure are reduction of the public debt, $20,000,000; annuities, pensions, and allowances, $885,593.85; imperial household and shrines, $2,751,911.25; Government departments, $55,528,388.52; national buildings, $769,659. The public debt is now $241,491,249.50; national paper currency in circulation, $67,263,274; reserve and special funds in the treasury, $59,645,945. For the second time in her history, Japan's financial exhibit, as officially given, is sanctioned by the Mikado, and shows several old sources of expenditure dried up, and better methods and objects in both collection and disbursement. There are 138 national banks, with a capital of $44,456,100, a reserve fund of $7,923,220, issuing paper money amounting to $34,396,880.

Before the era of Meiji (1868) and the centralization of power in the person of the present Mikado, the various han, or local authorities, issued their own paper scrip, which usually circulated at par only within the boundaries of the provinces, or fiefs, in which the notes were printed. In 1869 the National Government issued its own kin-satsu (gold notes), and called in all the local paper money, assuming also the debts of the extinguished han. For twenty years this national paper has circulated freely, often at a premium as high as 12 per cent., and occasionally falling as low as 20 per cent. discount. There were in circulation, Oct. 1, 1887:

Government paper money	$57,897,619
Exchangeable [for gold or silver] notes	51,788,760
National bank notes	26,757,902

These "exchangeable notes" are presumed to be at any time safely convertible into coin. In June, 1885, the issue amounted to $3,801,830. In two years this had increased to $43,935,696, which was further added to, Oct. 1, 1887, making the total circulation $51,788,760. While the ordinary issue of the Government and national banks decreased, that of these "exchangeable notes" increased from three to thirty millions, that of 1887 amounting to $13,676,927. The total volume of paper money during recent years is as follows: 1880, $143,098,268; 1881, $140,385,578; 1882, $140,032,041; 1883, $132,618,040; 1884, $124,844,639; 1885, $124,267,854; 1887, Oct. 1, $137,944,281.

The Japanese values are those of the yen, nominally worth one dollar, but at present about eighty cents gold. The amount of gold, silver, and copper coinage of the mint at Ozaka from November, 1870, to March, 1887, is $188,044,050.72, of which $137,979,708.82 was put into circulation. The pieces struck are: Gold, 20, 10, 5, 2, and 1 yen pieces; silver, 1 yen, silver trade-dollar, 50, 20, 10, and 5 sen (cent) pieces; copper, 2, 1, ½, 1/10 sen pieces.

The Army.—The peace establishment consists of 59,086 officers and men.

Infantry, 11 regiments, officers and men	45,592
Cavalry, 3 regiments, officers and men	605
Artillery, 7 brigades, officers and men	4,476
Engineers, officers and men	2,148
Transport and commissariat corps, officers and men	3,708
Yeomanry	752
Gendarmes	1,805

The war establishment comprises 188,612 officers and men. The artillery equipment includes 144 field-guns and 72 mountain-guns, both of 7-centimetre bore. The Artillery Body Guard have twenty-four Krupp field-guns, of 7½ centimetre bore. One general, sixteen lieutenant-generals, forty major-generals, and 2,552 commissioned officers, with salaries ranging from $5,000 to $250 per annum, comprise the official staff. The War Department employs five French, one German, and three Italian officers; and 260 officers and clerks in its offices. The expenses of the War Department are $884,848; of the army, $11,321,670; of the gendarmerie, $293,482; total, $11,999,600.

The Navy.—The energies of the nation being especially directed toward fortification of the coast and enlargement of the navy, there are now in course of construction a fleet of torpedo-boats, 2 iron-clad cruisers, 3 corvettes, 4 gunboats, and 2 smaller vessels for coast defense; total, 11 vessels, with 49 guns, having a tonnage of 13,300, and to be manned by 16,600 men. In actual service, afloat, are: 1 powerful iron-clad, 1 frigate, 3 cruisers, 11 corvettes, 1 yacht, 1 dispatch-boat, 5 gunboats, 1 transport; in all, 24 vessels, with a tonnage of 36,790, mounting 172 guns, and manned by 36,790 sailors and officers. In the coast-defense scheme, 153 forts are thought necessary. By popular subscription, to Nov. 19, 1887, $2,115,027.22 had been raised for this purpose. Of the subscribers, 11,985 were officers, 35 nobles, 69 gentry, and the remainder of the common people. Five million dollars in naval loan bonds were issued by the Government in 1887, and taken by the people. The annual expense of the naval establishment is: For the Department, $543,176; navy, $4,345,820; training-schools and aid to disabled, $404,468; total, $5,293,464.

Postal Statistics.—The educative influences of the national system of posts, instituted under the restored Government which began its existence in 1868, is shown by the following figures: The total revenue of this administration for the year ending March 31, 1886, was $1,600,298.86, expenditure $1,720,519.15; carried on in 4,186 post-offices, 659 receiving-agencies, 24,964 stamp-agencies, and 24,823 street letter-boxes; 44,525 miles of mail-routes, with a total transportation of 20,365,704 miles; and handling 87,049,872 covers. Money was sent in 738,639 money-orders, postal-notes, or by telegraph, aggregating in value $5,762,545.51. In the postal saving-banks $7,820,148.29 were deposited, making the amount held on deposit by the Government $14,561,293.88; of which $2,876,494.65 were repaid, including interest amounting to $16,780.55. The number of depositors for the year was 289,990; or, altogether, 463,118; of whom 46,519 withdrew their deposits. The average amount of each deposit was $28.04. The number of postal savings-banks is 4,496. To foreign countries, 330,798 covers were forwarded, and 449,506 were received, the difference being chiefly in newspapers; the excess of letters dispatched *from* Japan is 9,484. Of 497 unclaimed letters sent abroad, 420 were returned to the senders. All letters from foreign countries unclaimed in Japan were sent to the offices of their origin.

Judicial Statistics.—The methods of judicial procedure now in vogue, and based on the reformed codes of law imported from Christendom, are closely approximating the methods of western countries. In 1886, the number of criminal cases tried was 150,252, involving 178,881 persons. Of these cases, 4,088 were grave offenses, 85,173 minor offenses, and 60,991 were violations of rules and ordinances. The sentences were: death, 178; transportation, 2,125; penal servitude, 2,551; confinement, 99,299; fined, 48,256; attachment, 852; fined by the police, 14,284; confiscation, 61; the acquittals numbered 10,995. As compared with 1885, there was an increase of 2,338 cases, and a decrease of 5,291 convictions. This latter item shows the increasing power and influence of the native lawyer, who is now usually educated in one of the schools of law abroad or at home. There are 1,041 licensed practitioners at law; and, in the Law School, Tokio, 1,150 students are in attendance, nearly half of whom study in English.

Productions.—The legendary introduction, A. D. 800, of cotton-seed into Japan by a native of India, is doubted by native scholars, and the historic importation of the seed from China in 1558 was the beginning of a national crop and industry, 38 out of the 44 prefectures now producing it. The seed is sown in the spring in inch-deep drills between the standing wheat or barley, the flowers appearing in August. The yield is about 120 pounds to the acre, the unginned product selling at 4 or 5 cents a pound. The total crop of unginned cotton from 1878 to 1884 was as follows: 1878, 118,-958,000 pounds; 1879, 174,555,000 pounds; 1880, 118,681,000 pounds; 1881, 120,679,000 pounds; 1882, 115,094,000 pounds; 1883, 189,-511,000 pounds; 1884, 129,490,000 pounds. Sixty pounds of uncleansed cotton produce 21 of ginned cotton, or 20 of pure wool. Out of the average crop of 131,000,000 pounds of crude cotton, 44,000,000 pounds of wool are obtained. During the years 1873-'84, 21,500,-000 pounds of raw cotton was imported, or an average of 3,000,000 pounds annually, making the present yearly supply about 47,000,000 pounds. About $\frac{1}{15}$ of native cotton is used for spinning into yarn, of which $\frac{1}{4}$ is made into thread, and $\frac{1}{4}$ into cloth; the remaining $\frac{1}{2}$ is stuffed into quilts, winter clothing, etc. The annual average import of cotton-yarn from 1878 to 1884 was 34,000,000 pounds; during the same time, an average of 28,000,000 pounds of native-made yarn was annually woven into cotton-cloth, making a total annual supply of cotton-yarn in Japan of 62,000,000 pounds. Gin, spindle, and loom, all of the most primitive manufacture, are usually found in one house. A good ginner can clean 10 pounds of raw cotton in ten hours for 4 cents, which is his day's wage. One eighth of the seed yields oil, the remainder being pressed for use as manure. One man in a long day can card from 10 to 20 pounds of cotton, at 2 cents per pound. Most of the weaving is done by women, who can spin 1 pound of yarn a day. Every one of the 38,000,000 of the people wear the products of the plant, and from 1867 to 1885 the Japanese paid $88,800,000 for imported cotton. There are now 23 spinning-mills using foreign machinery (9 of which have steam as a motor), and employing 74,120 spindles, representing a capital of $2,000,000, and producing annually 4,914,847 pounds of yarn. One mill in Osaka, with machinery of the latest pattern, has a capital of $600,000, and declared last year a dividend to shareholders of 18 per cent. All the machinery is imported from England. One mill has 18,000 spindles, but most of them average 2,000 spindles. There is only 1 cotton-weaving mill worked by foreign machinery, the native machine being the rude hand-loom, which turns out a narrow web of cloth about 34 feet long. A careful study of the conditions of the market is the first requisite for what promises to be a good field for American enterprise in this direction.

Mercantile Marine.—Prior to the arrival of Com. M. C. Perry in 1853, the Japanese possessed no steam or sailing vessel for war or peace built on western principles. All her marine consisted of junks of less than 500 koku (3,800 bushels) burden, all over that capacity having been burned by the edict of Iyéyasú in 1609. At the present time, Japan has her own navy and dock yards, and her sons design, construct, launch, equip, and navigate all her own war-ships, and many of her sailing and steam merchantmen. At the Yokoska arsenal (appropriately, though unwittingly, located near the tomb of Will Adams, the English pilot who taught the Japanese the art of foreign ship-building early in the seventeenth century), there have been built twenty-six first-class war or trading ships in wood, steel, iron, or as composite; and four are on the stocks. A number of other ship-yards turn out wooden vessels.

Foreign Trade.—The amount of export and import is now over $80,000,000 annually, and is likely soon to reach $100,000,000. The staple exports are raw silk, tea, marine products, coal, rice, pottery, lacquer-ware, camphor, tobacco, etc., 27 articles covering a value of nearly $49,000,000. The imports consist mainly of yarns, piece goods, kerosene-oil, sugar, and manufactures, 28 articles aggregating in value $30,000,000. China takes $7,600,000 in marine products, the total value of Chinese trade amounting to $12,000,000. England imports goods valued at $12,000,000, taking Japanese products worth $2,400,000. The United States buys $17,000,000 worth of products, but sells only $2,700,000. Trade with Germany is increasing, imports to the amount of $1,700,000 coming to Japan in 1886. With the East Indies trade remains stationary at an average annual value of $3,000,000. Whereas formerly the imports were greatly in excess of exports, the total value of the exports over imports for the past four years is nearly $28,000,000. From 1872 to 1881 the specie and bullion exported showed an excess over imports of about $70,000,000, but the excess in value of imports from 1882 to 1885 inclusive amounts to nearly $8,000,000. The value of imports from the United States was, in 1873, about $1,000,000, and in 1885 nearly $3,000,000. For 1886 the export trade for Japan amounted to $48,870,471, and the import, $32,168,432; total, $81,038,903—an increase over the total trade of 1885 of $16,601,510. The excess of exports over imports for 1886 amounted to $16,702,039. The trade is shown in the following tables:

EXPORTS.

United States and Canada	$19,988,216	Germany	$864,456
France	9,682,902	Corea	829,816
China	9,504,907	East Indies	649,148
Great Britain	4,195,865	Italy, Australia	
		Russia, Austria	1,089,124

IMPORTS.

Great Britain	$12,708,248	France	$1,830,918
China	7,193,851	Corea	568,447
East Indies	3,561,819	Belgium	507,906
United States and Canada	3,368,986	Switzerland, Italy, Australia	473,578
Germany	2,813,650		

The United States consumes nearly the whole of the tea and over one third of the silk of Japan, and one fourth of the whole foreign trade of the empire is with the United States, the imports of which, in 1886, were:

Petroleum	$2,856,497	Drugs and chemicals	$50,642
Leather	149,852	Mercury	44,575
Flour	97,454	Lead-pencils	43,650
Clocks	81,391	Tobacco	29,216
Provisions	60,558	Watches	18,955
Condensed milk	57,102	Iron	16,130
Books	58,230		

For the protection and encouragement of commerce, there are now 58 light-houses, stafflights, and ships—12 of the light-houses being of the first order—17 buoys, and 7 beacons.

JEWS. The organizing of the preparatory class of the Jewish Theological Seminary of New York on January 3, and the incorporation in Chicago, early in January, of a Hebrew Industrial School, were signs of renewed activity in education. The centenary in April of Columbia College was invested with interest, owing to the efforts made by the Rev. Dr. Gottheil, to establish a chair for Hebrew and rabbinical literature, which resulted in a grant of $10,000 by members of the Temple Emanu El of New York and the appointment of Dr. Richard Gottheil to the professorship. On July 1 the annual examination of the Hebrew Union College at Cincinnati was begun, Rev. Drs. Isaacs (New York), Leucht (New Orleans), and Hecht (Montgomery), being examiners Edward Calisch was graduated, and received a call to Peoria, Ill.

The biennial session of the Council of the Union of American Hebrew Congregations was held at Pittsburg July 12. Josiah Cohen, of Pittsburg, was elected permanent chairman, and Lippman Levy, of Cincinnati, secretary. During the year the receipts amounted to $28,516; expenses, $26,874; the sinking fund reached $23,413. It was recommended that an endowment fund of $500,000 be raised to place the college on a firm foundation. The sum of $1,000 was voted to the committee on Sabbath-schools to enable them to prosecute their work. The next session will be held in Detroit, Mich., in July, 1889.

The Jewish Ministers' Association held its spring and autumn conferences in New York city. At the spring conference, April 25 and 26, reports were read on the marriage laws, on ethical teaching in the public schools, and on the publication of a home prayer-book, and resolutions were offered in favor of the Saturday half-holiday, disapproving of funeral display, and expressive of sympathy on the death of Henry Ward Beecher. At the public session Rev. Dr. Szold, of Baltimore, spoke on "How to Extend the Influence of the Congregation in Israel"; Rev. Leon Harrison, of Brooklyn, on "The True Sphere of the Young Men's Hebrew Association." At the autumn conference, November 28 and 29, the publication of the home prayer-book was duly authorized; papers were read by the Rev. Dr. S. Morais, of Philadelphia, on "Two Living Jewish Writers"—Elias Benamozegh, of Leghorn, and Dr. Castelli, of Florence; the Rev. Dr. A. Wise on "Angelogy and Demonology"; the Rev. Dr. Kohut and the Rev. Dr. S. Adler on Talmudic themes; and the Rev. J. Leucht, of Newark, on "Congregational Participation in Public Worship." At the public session the Rev. Dr. Marcus Jastrow, of Philadelphia, gave an address on "The Duty of Congregations to provide Synagogue Privileges to the Poor"; the Rev. Dr. Israel Aaron, of Buffalo, on "The Prophet Jeremiah"; the Rev. M. H. Harris, of New York, on "America, a Favorable Soil for the Development of Judaism."

The third annual conference of Southern Jewish ministers was held at Montgomery, Ala., November 28, the Rev. Dr. Hecht making the opening address. Papers were read by the Rev. Dr. Leucht, of New Orleans, on "The Origin and Development of the Rite of Confirmation in the Synagogue"; "Ritual of Burials," Lowenthal, of San Antonio; "Closer Union of Rabbis," Wechsler, of Meridian; "Advanced Religious Instruction," Heller, of New Orleans. The following were elected for the ensuing year: President, the Rev. Dr. Leucht; Vice-President, the Rev. Max Samfield; Secretary, the Rev. Dr. Berkowitz; Treasurer, the Rev.

Dr. Hecht. The next convention will be held in January, 1889, at New Orleans.

Among the matters of special note during the year were the Beecher memorial service (March 20) at Temple Emanu El, New York, and the great interest taken by Hebrews in the proposed monument to the Brooklyn preacher, one Western synagogue (Rev. Dr. Sonnescheim's, in St. Louis) forwarding $300 to the fund. Further efforts were made to strengthen the Aguilar Free Library in New York, and about $20,000 was given for the purpose. On March 25, Oscar S. Straus was appointed U. S. Minister to Turkey. A pleasant incident was the distribution of the first installment of the Burr bequest ($20,000) to the Mount Sinai Hospital and Hebrew Orphan Asylum of New York —an instance of unsectarian benevolence not often evinced. On Thanksgiving Day, in several places in the West, union services were held by Christian and Jewish congregations. New synagogues were consecrated in San Francisco, Syracuse, Cleveland, Vineland, N. J., Portland, Me., St. Louis, Chicago, New York, Montreal, Boston, Albany and Greenpoint, L. I. The Mount Zion Hospital was incorporated in San Francisco, and steps were taken to lay the corner-stone of a Jewish orphan asylum at Atlanta, Ga., in charge of the Order of Benai Berith.

Among the deaths were those of Prof. Henry G. Wile, of Atlanta Medical College, Hon. Nathaniel Newbergh, of Cincinnati, the Revs. A. Ash and I. Margolies, New York, Jacob Frankel, Philadelphia, B. E. Jacobs, Atlanta, and J. S. Goldammer, Cincinnati. On Nov. 19, Emma Lazarus died (see special article). In literature, the "Jewish Tidings" was established in Rochester, N. Y., on February 1, and the "Jewish Exponent" in Philadelphia, on April 15. Among the publications were "Hymns and Anthems," by Dr. Gottheil (New York), and "The Jews and Moors in Spain," by Dr. Krauskopf (Kansas City), and, apart from scattered sermons and brochures, the following general magazine articles: "Why am I a Jew?" by Rev. Dr. H. P. Mendes, (June "North American Review"); "Race Prejudice against the Jews," by Alice Hyneman Rhine (July "Forum"); "Jewish Progress in the United States," by Dr. A. S. Isaacs (September "American"); "By the Waters of Babylon," by Emma Lazarus (March "Century"); "Religious Liberty in America," by Oscar S. Straus (June "Westminster").

The most important event in English Judaism was the opening of the Anglo-Jewish Exhibition, in Albert Hall, London, on April 1, which contained memorials of the history of the English Jews from the early times, records, books, pictures, seals, coins, synagogue appurtenances, and scrolls of the law, all of unique historic interest. Among the lectures held at the exhibition on Jewish historical topics, that of Prof. Graetz, of Breslau, merits special notice. The Queen's Jubilee, June 14, was marked by services in the synagogues and deputations from Jewish bodies in behalf of Jews of the British Empire. The honor of knighthood was conferred on Sheriff Henry A. Isaacs, August 5. Dr. Moses Gaster, of Bucharest, was elected, March 23, chief rabbi of the Spanish and Portuguese Congregation of British Jews. The subject of foreign immigration excited much discussion, and renewed efforts were made to promote handicrafts among the young and encourage the useful arts, with much success. In literature, mention may be made of "The Moabite Stone a Forgery," by Rev. A. Löwy (April "Scottish Review"); "German Life in London," by Leopold Katscher (May "Nineteenth Century"); and "Schools of Commerce," by Sir Philip Magnus (December "Contemporary").

A quarterly review was projected by Claude Montefiore and I. Abrahams, but did not receive support. The "Jewish Record" was established in Manchester February 1. Frederick H. Cowen's oratorio of "Ruth" was produced September 8 at the Worcester festival. Among the notable deaths were those of Alfred A. Newman (January 21), antiquary and art metal-worker; Sir Barrow H. Ellis (June 20); Lionel Louis Cohen, M. P. (June 26); Rev. S. Lyons (June 27); and Dr. Strauss (September 5).

In British colonial matters is to be noted the appointment of Sir Saul Samuel as representative of New South Wales at the Colonial Conference in London, Hon. Julian E. Salomons as member of the Legislative Council in New South Wales and Vice-President of the Executive Council of Sydney (May), and the election of Benjamin Benjamin as mayor of Melbourne. The Ezra Hospital was opened at Calcutta on January 31. A Jewish bazaar was held at Cape Town, May 3, in aid of the synagogue, and generously supported by the Christian community.

The situation in general throughout Europe showed a favorable activity in religious and educational affairs. There was no renewal of German anti-Semitic disturbances of any great moment, although disastrous fires in Russian and Roumanian towns might be traced to their agency. On July 5 the Union of Rabbis held a session at Breslau, and among other resolutions voted in favor of special services for children, and of elaborating a cyclopædia of the Talmud, as suggested by Prof. Dr. Grætz. The bill to prohibit the Jewish method of slaughtering cattle was rejected in the German Parliament (May). Outrages against the Jews were announced from Morocco, and slight anti Semitic outbreak soccurred in Neutra, Hungary (June 10), and in Kojetein, Moravia (May 6). On January 15 the new rabbinical seminary was opened at Rome, Italy. M. Astruc was elected in June chief rabbi of Bayonne, and Isaac Levy (September 1) chief rabbi of Bordeaux. A new hospital was opened in July at Bassenheim, Germany, by Mme. von Oppenheim, and a free public library given to Frankfort by the family of Baron Carl Rothschild, in addition to many munificent gifts to Jewish and general charities in France and Germany. Baron de Hirsch gave 50,000,000 francs for Jewish educational purposes in Russia — to teach the Jewish youth self-help and aid in raising the masses to a higher level of culture. New synagogues were dedicated in Alexandria (Egypt), Antwerp, Munich, Dantzic, and Vienna. Among the deaths were those of Baron Todesco, of Vienna; Rabbi Marx, of Bayonne; Dr. Asher Samter, author and rabbi. at Berlin; Joseph Ritter v. Wertheimer, of Vienna; Simon Spitzer, author, of Vienna; Baron Lucien de Hirsch, Alexander Sidi, of Smyrna; Meier Goldschmidt, Danish novelist; Charles Wiener, Belgian sculptor and medallist; Baron Elia Todros, of Venice; Rabbi Dr. Pincus F. Frankl, Leopold Freund, journalist, of Breslau; J. E. Kann, Secretary of the Alliance Israelite Universelle, Rabbi Dr. Jacob Auerbach, of Frankfort. The seventieth birthday of Prof. Graetz was celebrated in Breslau in November, and a jubilee work issued by a number of scholars, with articles in Jewish history and research. In literature it is difficult to specify the number of new books and magazine articles, without assuming the dimensions of a bibliography. There was a steady activity in all branches of Oriental lore, by Jewish scholars, old and young, although no great work was produced. It is gratifying to note the continued interest shown in Hebrew studies by Christian students. Schürer,

in Germany, and Stapfer, in France, throw light on the history of Palestine in the early Christian centuries. The year is notable, too. for the movement to erect a monument to Heinrich Heine, at Dusseldorf, his birthplace, the Empress of Austria being a generous contributor.

The latest statistics, as published by the annual of a Paris Jewish weekly, place the Jewish population of the globe, for the year ending Sept. 18, 1887, at 6,800,000. France is said to contain 63,000; Germany, 562,000, of whom 39,000 inhabit Alsace and Lorraine; Austria-Hungary, 1,644,000, of whom 688,000 are in Galicia and 638,000 in Hungary proper; Italy, 40,000; Netherlands, 82,000; Roumania, 165,-000; Russia, 2,552,000 (Russian Poland, 768,-000); Turkey, 105,000; Belgium, 3,000; Bulgaria, 10,000; Switzerland, 7,000; Denmark, 4,000; Spain, 1,900; Gibraltar, 1,500; Greece, 3,000; Servia, 3,500; Sweden, 3,000. In Asia there are 800,000 of the race; Turkey in Asia has 195,000, of whom 25,000 are in Palestine, 47,000 are in Russian Asia, 18,000 in Persia, 14,000 in Central Asia, 1,900 in India, and 1,000 in China. In Africa, 8,000 Jews live in Egypt, 55,600 in Tunisia, 35,000 in Algeria, 60,000 in Morocco, 6,000 in Tripoli, and 200,-000 in Abyssinia. America counts 230,000, and 20,000 more are distributed in other sections of the transatlantic continents, while only 12,000 are scattered through Oceanica. No statistics for England are given. The Jews in the United Kingdom number fully 80,000, and the Jewish population in the United States is about 600,000.

K

KANSAS. The following were the State officers during the year: Governor, John A. Martin, Republican; Lieutenant-Governor, A. P. Riddle; Secretary of State, E. B. Allen; Treasurer, James W. Hamilton; Auditor, Timothy McCarthy; Attorney-General, S. B. Bradford; Superintendent of Public Instruction, J. H. Lawhead; Railroad Commissioners, James Humphrey, L. L. Turner, and Almerin Gillett; Chief Justice of the Supreme Court, Albert H. Horton; Associate Justices, W. A. Johnston and Daniel M. Valentine.

Legislative Session.—The Legislature met on January 11, and adjourned on March 5. The liquor law adopted aims to suppress the so-called "drug-store saloons," which, under the guise of law, in some localities have practically nullified the effect of the prohibitory statutes. It holds the druggist to a rigid accountability for all sales of liquor, each applicant being required to make affidavit that it is wanted for medicinal or mechanical purposes. The blanks for that purpose are issued by the County Clerk in book form, and are numbered, and the druggist's returns must correspond with a record kept jointly by the clerk and probate

judge. The making of a false affidavit becomes perjury, and the signing of a fictitious name forgery. The druggists are also hedged about with pains and penalties to such an extent that any evasion of the law will be difficult and dangerous.

The rate of taxation established for 1887 is as follows: 3¼ mills for State purposes, $\frac{7}{10}$ of a mill to pay interest on the public debt, and a special tax of ¼ mill each year for completing the construction of the main or central building of the State capitol.

The following are some of the specific appropriations for current expenses for the biennial period, 1887-'88: The Deaf and Dumb Asylum at Olathe, $94,000; the Asylum for the Feeble-minded, $40,000; the Soldiers' Orphans' Home, $46,800; the State Reform School, $73,000; the Insane Asylum at Topeka, $288,500; the Insane Asylum at Ossawatomie, $220,500; the Asylum for the Blind, $38,370. The Deaf and Dumb Asylum receive an extra appropriation of $51,000 for the erection of a central building; the Asylum for the Blind, $18,000, to construct a north wing to its main building; and the Normal School at Emporia, $25,000, for additions to the present structure. The sum of $100,000 is appropriated to the Industrial Reformatory at Hutchinson, to complete the construction of that institution.

Two amendments to the Constitution were proposed, to be voted upon at the next general election. The first strikes out a passage that debars colored citizens from joining the militia; the second gives the Legislature express authority to regulate the rights of aliens with reference to the purchase, enjoyment, and descent of property in the State. Other acts of the session were as follow:

To create the counties of Garfield, Gray, Haskell, Grant, Stanton, and Kearney, and to define the boundaries of certain other counties.

To amend an act regarding cities of the first class, by giving the city authorities additional powers.

To authorize cities of the second class to construct and maintain a system of sewerage and drainage.

To provide for the consolidation of adjacent cities, and for the platting of land therein into alleys and lots.

To authorize counties and incorporated cities of the second and third classes to encourage the development of the coal, natural gas, and other resources of their localities, by subscribing to the stock of companies.

To confirm deeds, contracts, and conveyances of private corporations, executed and acknowledged under section 4 of chapter 22, general statutes of 1868, and to repeal said section.

To provide for the organization and incorporation of co-operative societies or companies for promoting or conducting any industrial pursuit.

To provide for the registration of electors at elections for the location of county-seats.

Authorizing county treasurers, in counties of more than 7,000 and fewer than 25,000 inhabitants, to deposit public money in banking institutions.

To provide for the appointment of three commissioners, to be known as Commissioners of the Supreme Court, to aid the court in the performance of its duties. [This act was deemed necessary in consequence of the refusal of the people, at the election in 1886, to approve an amendment to the Constitution increasing the number of supreme judges.]

Raising the age of consent in females to eighteen years.

To legalize abbreviated forms for deeds and mortgages of real estate.

To prevent fraud at elections, and to provide punishment therefor.

Prescribing certain duties of presidential electors.

To establish the office of Commissioner of Forestry.

To encourage the planting and growing of forest-trees and making appropriation therefor.

Making it unlawful for any one to have in his possession, or to use, or sell, or give away, intoxicating liquors within one-half mile of any voting-place at any special or general election.

To secure to laborers in and about coal-mines, and manufactories, and other firms, or corporations, the payment of their wages at regular intervals, and in lawful money of the United States, and to prevent any restrictions upon such laborers as to the place for purchasing their supplies.

Amending the State pharmacy law.

To prohibit grain-dealers, partnerships, companies, corporations, or associations, from combining or entering into any agreement or contract to pool or fix the price to be paid for grain, hogs, cattle, or stock of any kind whatever, and to provide punishment for the same.

For the appointment of a commissioner to examine and audit the Price raid claims.

To provide for the assumption and payment of claims for losses sustained by citizens of Kansas by the invasion of the State by bands of guerillas and marauders during the years 1861 to 1865 inclusive.

Regulating the crossing and intersection of railroads.

Providing a method for the improvement of county roads.

To transfer certain lands to the permanent school fund.

Providing for an assistant Auditor of State.

Appropriating $13,000 for the establishment and maintenance of a silk station in Kansas, appointing three commissioners to assume charge of such station, and to promote the silk-culture in the State.

Regulating the shipment of live-stock and grain.

Granting to women the right to vote in cities of the first, second, and third class, at any election of city or school officers, or for the purpose of authorizing the issue of bonds for school purposes.

To encourage the manufacture of sugar, by offering a bounty of two cents a pound upon all sugar manufactured in the State from beets, sorghum, or other sugar-yielding plants grown therein, the total bounty to be paid in one year not to exceed $15,000.

To authorize townships to provide public parks and cemeteries for the inhabitants thereof, and to levy a tax for the same.

Making counties and townships liable for defects in bridges, culverts, and highways.

To authorize city and township treasurers and treasurers of school districts and boards of education to register all warrants or orders drawn upon them and not paid for want of funds, and providing for the payment of the same in the order of registration.

To authorize the city of Leavenworth to issue bonds and incur indebtedness not exceeding $10,000 for encouraging the development of its coal and natural-gas resources.

Providing that all bonds hereafter issued by county, town, or city authorities to railroads, shall be redeemable at pleasure after ten years.

Providing for the police government of cities of the first class by a board of police commissioners, appointed by the executive council, and for a similar government of cities of the second class in certain contingencies.

The total number of acts was 241, an increase of 84 over the previous regular session.

Prohibition.—The following extract from a public letter by Gov. Martin summarizes the history and the effect of the prohibitory law:

The prohibition amendment to our Constitution was adopted in the autumn of 1880, and the first laws to enforce it went into effect in May, 1881. The war to banish the saloons was for some years only partially successful. The amendment had been adopted by a very meager majority, and public sentiment in all our larger cities was overwhelmingly against it. As late as January, 1885, saloons were open in fully thirty of the larger cities of Kansas, including Topeka, the capital of the State. But steadily and surely the public sentiment against them spread and intensified. The small majority that had voted for the amendment was re-enforced, first by those law-respecting citizens who are always willing to subordinate their personal opinions to the majesty of law; and, second, by an equally large number who, observing the practical results following the abolition of saloons in different cities and towns, became convinced that Kansas would be a more prosperous, happier, and in all respects a better community of people if it had not an open saloon within its borders.

One argument of the whisky interest—viz., that saloons promote the prosperity and growth of communities—has been answered in Kansas by the convincing logic of facts. In 1880 the population of this State, as shown by the census, was 996,096; in March, 1886, as shown by the State census, it was 1,406,738; and it is now fully 1,650,000. In 1880 Kansas had only 3,104 miles of railway within her borders; on the 1st of March last the State Board of Railroad Assessors reported 6,208 miles for taxation, and from 600 to 800 miles will be added to this aggregate before the close of the year.

In 1880 the assessed value of all the real and personal property of the State aggregated only $160,891,-689; on the 1st of March, 1886, the total was $277,-575,363; and for the present fiscal year the returns thus far received indicate a total of $300,000,000. In 1880 there were 5,813 school-houses, 2,514 churches, and 347 newspapers in Kansas. There are now fully 8,500 school-houses, 3,500 churches, and 700 newspapers. In 1880 only fifty-five towns and cities had populations in excess of 1,000 each; in 1887 more than 200 towns have each over 1,000 inhabitants, fully twenty-five have each over 5,000, and four have each over 20,000. In 1880 only 8,868,000 acres were planted in crops; this year the area planted exceeds 16,000,000 acres. In 1880 the value of the farm products of Kansas was only $84,521,000; for 1886 their value was over $264,000,000. For the fiscal year 1880 the percentage of State taxation was 5½ mills; for the present fiscal year the total percentage levied for all State purposes is only 4½ mills.

During the past two years and a half I have organized seventeen counties in the western section of the State, and census takers have been appointed for four other counties, leaving only two counties remaining to be organized. The cities and towns of Kansas, with hardly an exception, have kept pace in growth and prosperity with this marvelous development of the State. Many of them have doubled their population during the past year. And it is a remarkable fact that several cities and towns languished or stood still until they abolished their saloons, and from that date until the present time their growth and prosperity have equaled and in some instances surpassed that of other places with equal natural advantages.

Two cases decided by the United States Supreme Court in December of this year form important landmarks in the history of Kansas prohibition, sustaining, as they do, the right of the State to suppress absolutely the manufacture of intoxicating liquors within its limits. These two cases were Muegler vs. the State of Kansas, and the State of Kansas vs. Zeibold and others, the latter being an appeal from the United States Circuit Court, where Judge Brewer had decided against the contention of the State. The higher court overruled this decision, and sustained the validity of the Kansas law at all points.

Education.—The following is a summary of the work of the public schools for the year ending May 31, 1887:

Number of school-districts	8,164
Population between 5 and 21 years of age	591,091
Number of pupils enrolled	380,341
Number of teachers	10,501
Average salary of male teachers per month	$40 00
Average salary of female teachers per month	$32 96
Average length of school-year in weeks	28
Estimated value of school property, including buildings and grounds	$7,776,746
Number of school buildings	7,751
Number of school-houses built in year ending May 31, 1887	812

The above does not include Sheridan, Wallace, Rush, and Meade counties, from which no report is made. The total cost of maintaining the public schools during the year was $4,-065,466, against $3,849,017 for the previous year, an increase proportionate to the great growth of the State during the year.

Live-Stock.—The following table exhibits the number of head of live-stock assessed in the State, compared with the returns for 1886:

	1886.	1887.
Horses	491,055	558,544
Cattle	2,007,607	2,082,257
Sheep	752,916	670,950
Hogs	1,171,150	1,029,774

The State Capitol.—Considerable progress was made during the year toward the completion of this structure. Up to the end of the year $329,766 had been spent upon the central building, and $313,155 upon the west wing. The east wing is substantially complete. The special tax imposed by the Legislature will enable the work to be forwarded according to the original plans.

KEELY MOTOR, THE. John Worrall Keely, who claims to have discovered a new etheric force, was born in Philadelphia Sept. 3, 1887, of parents who died in his infancy, and has lived and worked ever since in that city. He had attended the common schools of Philadelphia for one or two terms before he was twelve; after that time he had to support himself, learned the carpenter's trade, and worked at it. As an inventor, Keely has been the subject of more controversy than any scientific claimant of the century. He has been ridiculed, perhaps, more than either Galileo or Fulton, while the believers in his alleged discovery of a new force, which he has been so far unable to manage satisfactorily, think the result of his thirty years of study and manipulation has been a discovery greater than Galileo's celestial system or Fulton's steamboat. He says that from his earliest years he was drawn to the study of sound as related to force, and that he began his first systematic investigation when hardly ten years of age, making his first encouraging discovery at thirteen. As a child he observed how windows were often agitated by the heavy tones of an organ, and this led him to suspend glass dishes, and watch for any effect that might be produced by chords he was able to secure by the combination of different tones. He soon found that certain chords invariably resulted in the forcible agitation of objects at a distance. His earliest mechanism for noting the uniform force of sound-vibrations was a steel bar set full of pins of various lengths; while his first "resonator" or "intensifier" consisted of a shingle screwed to two hollow wooden tubes. The first engine was a simple ring of steel, with 300 pins set into it, and this first wheel ran in an open box, into and through which an observer was free to look while the wheel was in motion. For more than sixteen years Keely pursued his investigations in the effort to work out his discovery, using the two elements water and air in connection with sound-vibrations as the media in which to operate his new force. He began with the simplest possible form of vibrator in a shingle screwed to two hollow wooden tubes, recording the vibrations by means of a steel bar studded with pins of various lengths. The result was surprising: the sympathetic flow induced even by this, the first order of vibratory association, being infinitely more tenuous and penetrating than the electric current.

The best idea of what the Keely motor is can probably be obtained from a careful examination made not long since by a disinterested Englishman. He recalls how Tyndall and others have satisfactorily demonstrated that in motion is to be sought the true origin of sound, heat, light, and probably electricity—in a motion that is vibratory, the pulsations of which can be calculated if not explained. The new chemistry goes further and discovers a constant motion of the atoms among themselves. Keely's idea is the liberation of that motion in its primitive or quasi-primitive form,

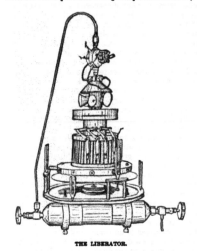

THE LIBERATOR.

and its application to the use of man; the resolution of that ether, so-called—vastly more tenuous and intangible than electricity itself—in which the waves of sound and light are supposed by scientists to be produced. The discovery of the fact that objects composed of a material such as glass could be made to vibrate at a distance only in response to one particular chord to which their mass seemed to respond, led to the discovery on which his work is based —the finding of the so-called "chord of the mass" of any material body, and the application of this discovery to the production of vibrations at will. The utilization of this chord produces disintegration of the body in question, and this disintegration in turn is capable of being converted into motion.

It seems impossible to understand Keely's own language. For an uneducated man he has a surprising command of words. He says:

"All operations of nature have for their sensitizing centers of introductory action triple vacuum evolutions. These evolutions are centered in what I call atomic triple revolutions, highly radiaphonic, and thoroughly independent of all outside forces in their spheres of action. In fact, no conceivable power, however great, can break up their independent centers. So infinitely minute are they in their position that, within a circle that would inclose the smallest grain of sand, hundreds of billions of them perform, to an infinite mathematical precision, their continuous vibratory revolution of inconceivable velocity." In giving a description of the nature of his force and what has been involved in the multitudinous changes necessitated in its development—omitting all thought of the methods of its practical application, which has ever been a problem by itself—Keely says: "The different conditions include the change of the mediums for disturbing equilibrium, under different mediums for intensifying vibration, as associated with them progressively from the molecular to the interetheric : first, percussion; second, undulation ; third, vibratory undulations; fourth, vibratory percussion; fifth, water and air; sixth, air alone." There is not the simplicity of a great truth in these statements, yet they may represent a distinct idea in Keely's mind.

The result of his thirty years of work is a machine popularly known as the "Keely motor," but called a "liberator" by the inventor himself. Its production has "absorbed," he says, a quarter of a million dollars. Yet it is not satisfactory to him, nor has it demonstrated its usefulness to others except by lifting weights on the end of a lever in his workshop. An English writer declares that not long ago, in the presence of several gentlemen interested in mining operations, Mr. Keely bored, with his engine, eighteen feet in eighteen minutes, into the quartz rock of the Catskill mountains. But there is no other evidence of this astounding fact, of which American newspapers would have been only too glad to get hold.

The Keely Motor Company was formed in 1872. The board of directors, seven in number, has been composed for several years past of six residents of New York and one resident of Philadelphia. A few gentlemen have been and are very eager that Mr. Keely shall immediately impart his "secrets" to some one; and in their eagerness, say his defenders, to have this done, they assume that it can be done in a half-hour's time. For twenty-five years Mr. Keely has been exploring a realm of science the most subtile that can be imagined, to wit: the phenomena of acoustics and sound, which embrace the science of music. He has not been content with the construction of machinery for the purpose of utilizing sound-force as a motive power, but has been recording his experiments day by day, and promises shortly to publish the result of his twenty-five years of research in this branch of science.

This will be done at the same time with the application for his letters patent. It is believed by those most conversant with Mr. Keely's work that in a few months he will succeed in securing a commercial engine, since all that remains to be done by him is to control the speed of the engine. The "liberator," which is supposed to liberate the mysterious etheric force and prepare it for application, is represented in its present condition by the illustration on page 408. It is the result of twelve generators, each an improvement, the inventor says, on its predecessors. About four years ago, Mr. Keely discarded the use of water in the production of his force, and this necessitated important changes in the mechanism. The clumsy generator of several tons' weight gave place to the lighter "liberator." Three of these have been constructed, each one slighter than its predecessor, until that at present in his labora-

tory weighs less than 150 pounds, while the inventor has in process of construction the fourth and last one, which "is a perfect machine of its kind," weighing less than seventy-five pounds, with which he expects to produce a greater force than has ever before been shown. Some idea of the wide experimental field that has been covered may be gained by Mr. Keely's statement that "since 1872 there have been over thirty changes in the progressive development of the mechanical to reach the present, and what I call the perfect system." And as many as 124 different machines or engines have been constructed in experiment-

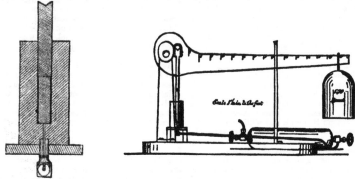

THE LEVER.

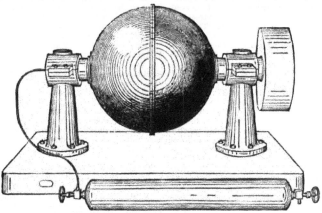

THE ENGINE.

ing with one "liberator." Brass tubes, plates of steel, and tuning-forks, make up the strange machine. The lever, shown in the second illustration, on application of the force generated by the liberator, lifts heavy weights. The third illustration shows the engine, by means of which the new force is to be applied to machinery. The force is applied to the engine in the interior of the hollow sphere. With this engine Mr. Keely says he can attach a common steel wire to a steel bar of the chord of B flat, and associate with it two more bars of the same chord, and, bringing them into contact with a ton of quartz, disintegrate it in fifteen seconds.

KENTUCKY. State Government.—The following were the State officers at the beginning of the year: Governor, J. Proctor Knott, Democrat; Lieutenant-Governor, James R. Hindman; Secretary of State, James A. McKenzie; Treasurer, James W. Tate; Auditor, Fayette Hewitt; Attorney-General, P. W. Hardin; Superintendent of Public Instruction, Joseph D. Pickett; Railroad Commissioners: J. P. Thompson, A. R. Boone, and John D. Young; Chief-Justice of the Court of Appeals: William S. Pryor, Thomas H. Hines; Associate Justices: Joseph H. Lewis and William H. Holt.

Finances.—When the last General Assembly convened in 1885, the receipts of the treasury were insufficient to meet the demands made upon it by existing appropriations, there being a deficiency of $293,185.52. This result was brought about chiefly by a defective system of assessments and collections, under the operations of which great inequalities prevailed in the valuations of property reported for taxation, while a considerable part of the taxable property of the State did not appear on the books of the assessors. The General Assembly of that year responded to the urgent demand for a change in the system by enacting an entirely new revenue law. Under its operation the auditor's report shows that, instead of a deficit, there was a balance in the treasury, on June 30, 1887, of $197,684.88. The total valuation under the new law has been increased to $483,497,690. Two years previously it was $390,827,963. This increase adds $400,000 to the revenue, of which the general expenditure fund receives $180,000 and the school fund $220,000. One of the virtues of the law is that the increase has been gained from personal property which has never before been reached by the tax-gatherer. By a decision of the Court of Appeals, given this year, all acts of the Legislature exempting private property from taxation were declared unconstitutional and invalid. The court held that, since a direct appropriation of public money in support of a private enterprise is forbidden, that support can not be given indirectly by exempting private property from taxation.

Education.—The school population of the year numbered 549,592 white and 107,144 colored children, being an increase over the previous year of 10,623 white and 4,307 colored. The number of school districts was 6,639 white and 1,011 colored, being an increase over the previous year of 66 districts for white children and 8 for the colored. During the year the apportionment of the school fund for white schools was $1,044,224.80, being an increase of $154,925.95 over the previous year; and for colored schools, $203,573.60, being an increase of $33,892.55 over the previous year. The total sum appropriated from the State treasury for school purposes amounted to $1,247,798.40, being a per capita of $1.90. The direct appropriation by the State for school purposes is greater than is devoted by any other State government, with one or two exceptions. A gratifying feature in the educational progress of the State was the completion of the building for the Colored Normal School. It was dedicated during the year and opened under favorable auspices.

Railroads.—The railroad commissioners report that there were 2,341 miles of railroad in operation in the State at the close of the year, 244 miles having been constructed during the past twelve months. The total cost of these roads was $76,513,930. The total assessed value of all railroad property amounted to $35,571,631, an increase over the previous year of $1,924,025. The gross earnings in 1886 were $10,987,177; in 1887, $12,899,724, an increase of over 18 per cent. The Governor recommends that the powers and salaries of the commissioners be increased, and that they be required to maintain a permanent office at the capital.

Mining.—The report of the Inspector of Mines shows a satisfactory growth of the industry. There has been a constant and rapid increase of the out-put of coal, from 1870, when it amounted to only 4,228,000 bushels, to the present time; the yield for the year ending July 1, 1887, amounted to 44,880,000 bushels. When the river improvements now progressing, and the railways under construction and in contemplation, shall have reached the rich beds of coal recently discovered, the out-put will be limited only by the demand.

Public Buildings.—A branch penitentiary at Eddyville was in course of construction during the year, but greater appropriations will be needed for its completion. The commission appointed to construct a building at the Central Lunatic Asylum for the use of colored lunatics was unable to agree upon a site for a structure, and the Legislature will be required to make some changes in the law, in order to forward this work. The Governor, in his message to the Legislature, recommends a complete repair of the Capitol, and the construction of an additional wing.

Rowan County.—Concerning the disturbances in this county during the year and previously, the Governor speaks as follows in his message:

The situation may be summarized by stating that a difficulty has existed between factions in that county since 1884. Though composed of only a small portion of the community, these factions have succeeded by their violence in overawing and silencing the voice of the peaceful element, and in intimidating the officers of the law. Having their origin partially in party rancor, they have ceased to have any political significance, and have become contests of personal ambition and revenge; each party seeking apparently to possess itself of the machinery of justice, in order that it may, under the forms of law, seek the gratification of personal animosities. During the present year the local leader of one of these factions came in possession of the office of police judge of the town of Morehead. Under color of the authority of that office and sustained by an armed band of adherents, he exercised despotic sway over the town and its vicinage. He banished citizens who were obnoxious to him; and, in one instance, after arresting two citizens who seem to have been guilty of no offense, he and his party, attended by a deputy sheriff of the county, murdered them in cold blood. This act of atrocity fully aroused the community. A posse, acting under the authority of a warrant from the county judge, attacked the police judge and his adherents on the 22d of June last, killed several of their number, and put the rest to flight, and temporarily restored something like tranquillity to the community. The proceedings of the Circuit Court, which was held in August, were not calculated to inspire the citizens with confidence in securing justice. The report of the Adjutant General on this subject shows, from information derived "from representative men without reference to party affiliations," that the judge of the Circuit Court seems so far under the influence of the reputed leader of one of the factions as to permit such an organization of the grand juries as will effectually prevent the indictment of members of that faction for the most flagrant crimes.

Political.—A regular biennial election for State officers was held this year. The canvass was opened by the Prohibitionists, who met in convention at Louisville on March 8 and nominated the following ticket: For Governor, Fontaine T. Fox; for Lieutenant-Governor, W. L. Gordon; for Auditor, A. T. Henderson; for Treasurer, R. K. Dyer; for Register of the Land Office, James T. Barbee; for Attorney-General, J. W. Harris; for Superintendent of Public Instruction, D. W. Stevenson. The following resolutions were adopted:

We indorse the National Prohibition party platform. The liquor traffic of this country is a public nuisance, debauching the citizens, corrupting the voter, robbing the laborer, endangering the peace and happiness of society; and we therefore demand the prohibition of the importation, manufacture, sale or traffic, by any and all persons, of all alcoholic, vinous, malt, fermented, distilled, or other intoxicating liquors, except for mechanical or medicinal purposes; and for the consummation of this purpose we further demand a constitutional amendment, State and national, and such congressional and legislative enactment as will be necessary to enforce these provisions.

With regard to the present public affairs in Kentucky, we advocate the call of a sovereignty convention of the people, under and by authority of section 4 of the bill of rights in our present Constitution, to form another Constitution, more in harmony with the changed condition of affairs in the State and of the political advancement of the times.

We advocate the enactment of the following general laws: 1. A law to disfranchise any person who buys or sells a vote. 2. A law to prevent the competition of convict with free labor, or the hiring out the convicts in such a way as to produce such competition, and to brand all articles of every kind made by convict labor as "convict made" when and before the same is put on the market. We indorse Mr. Powderly's opinion that the liquor traffic is the workingman's worst enemy. 3. A law to investigate every ten years the condition of every office connected with the administration of the State government by commissioners selected by the General Assembly.

The Democratic Convention was held on May 4, and resulted in the choice of the following candidates: For Governor, Simon B. Buckner; for Lieutenant-Governor, James W. Bryan; for Auditor, Fayette Hewitt; for Treasurer, James W. Tate; for Attorney-General, P. W. Hardin; for Superintendent of Public Instruction, Joseph D. Pickett; for Register of the Land Office, Thomas H. Corbett. The platform contains very little upon State issues. It declares that convict labor should not be brought into unfair competition with regular lines of business, and that legislation is needed to secure proper ventilation and other safeguards for mines and factories.

One week later the Republicans placed in nomination the following ticket: For Governor, William O. Bradley; for Lieutenant-Governor, Mat. O'Doherty; for Auditor, R. D. Davis; for Treasurer, J. R. Puryear; for Attorney-General, John W. Feland; for Superintendent of Public Instruction, W. H. Childers; for Register of the Land Office, T. J. Tinsley. The platform included the following paragraphs:

That a change is necessary in our State affairs which would curtail offices, reduce expenses, and enable the people of Kentucky to overhaul and examine the books which for nearly twenty years have been virtually sealed against them.

That we condemn the Democratic party of Kentucky for a useless waste of the people's money; for bringing convict labor into competition with that of honest workingmen; for retarding emigration, and for crippling education.

That we approve of and will support a tariff so adjusted as to protect and develop American industries, and also such State legislation as experience has proved to be necessary for the development of the material resources of this commonwealth.

That we favor material aid to internal improvement of our lakes, rivers, and harbors, and disapprove of the course of the President of the United States in refusing to sign a bill which promoted such improvements, causing the work already done to fall into decay.

Believing with the lamented Lincoln that it is the duty of the nation "to care for him who shall have borne the battle, and for his widow and orphans," we hold that the people of the United States owe an ever-living debt of gratitude to the soldiers and sailors who saved the republic, and we hereby disapprove of and condemn the veto of President Cleveland of the bill which provided for their relief.

The nominees of the Union Labor party were: For Governor, A. H. Cardin; for Lieutenant-Governor, O. N. Bradburn; for Auditor, John M. McMurky; for Treasurer, George Smith; for Attorney-General, J. P. Newman; for Superintendent of Public Instruction, R. M. McBeth; for Register of the Land Office, Gaius Henry.

The election was held on the first Monday of August, and resulted in the success of the Democratic ticket, but by a greatly reduced plurality. Official returns for Governor gave Buckner 143,270 votes; Bradley, 126,478; Fox, 8,394; and Cardin, 4,434. Bradley ran 3,000 votes ahead of his ticket. The Democratic plurality at the last gubernatorial election, in 1883, was 44,484, and in 1884 President Cleveland carried the State by a plurality of 34,839. The successful candidates assumed their offices on August 30.

The people also voted at the same election, in accordance with an act of the last Legislature, on the question whether a convention should be called to prepare a new Constitution for the State. The vote from all but 11 counties was 162,557 in favor and 49,795 against; number not voting, 65,956. Should the next Legislature order a similar vote in 1889, and the result be again favorable to a convention, it may then be called to meet in 1890.

KIRCHHOFF, GUSTAV ROBERT, a German physicist, born in Königsberg, Prussia, March 12, 1824; died in Berlin, Oct. 17, 1887. He was graduated at the university of his native city in 1846, where he gave special attention to mathematics and physics. In 1847 he went to Berlin, and a year later began his career at the university as a lecturer on mathematical physics. He was called in 1850 to be Assistant Professor of Experimental Physics at the University of Breslau, and in 1850 accepted the chair of Physics at Heidelberg, passing thence in 1874

GUSTAV ROBERT KIRCHHOFF.

to a similar appointment in the University of Berlin, where he remained until his death. His scientific work began in 1845, a year before he received his degree by the publication of a paper in Poggendorff's "Annalen" "On Electric Conduction in a Thin Plate, and especially in a Circular One," soon followed by other researches on electric questions, among which are those on conduction in curved sheets, on Ohm's law, on the distribution of electricity on two influencing spheres, on the discharge of the Leyden-jar, on the motion of electricity, on the determination of the constants on which depends the intensity of induced currents, and two important papers on induced magnetism. Another series of investigations dealt with the equilibrium and motion of elastic solids, especially in the forms of plates and solids, including also careful experimental determinations of the value of Poisson's ratio for different substances.

Besides these papers he published several noteworthy memoirs on important propositions in the thermo-dynamics of solution and vaporization, on crystalline reflection and refraction, on the influence of heat in a special case of propagation of sound, on the optical constants of aragonite, and on the thermal conductivity of wire. In 1859 he made his discovery of the cause of Fraunhofer's lines in the solar spectrum, and was the first to announce and prove the now-accepted law that "the relation between the power of emission and the power of absorption of one and the same class of rays is the same for all bodies at the same temperature." He associated with himself Robert W. Bunsen, and together they evolved the method of spectrum analysis, and in 1860 perfected it in its essentials. It was at once recognized as a classical discovery, and its great value as an analytical method of investigation in terrestrial and celestial chemistry can not be overestimated. The history of spectrum analysis has from that date been one of unbroken progress. In astronomy the constitution of the heavenly bodies and their motions directly toward or away from the observer, have all been investigated or determined by this method. The atmosphere of a star, comet, or nebula yields its composition to the analyst, who can also approximately determine the temperature and pressure of the glowing gas. In chemistry, new metals have been found by its means. Cæsium and rubidium by Bunsen, thallium by Crookes, gallium by Lecoq de Boisbaudran, and scandium by Nilsen. Were it only for its part in completing the relation of the atomic weights of the elements by Mendelejeff's law, the indebtedness of chemistry to it would be great. His latest work was in electricity, and in 1884–'85 he published papers on the changes and distribution of electricity in certain bodies which he examined for this purpose. Prof. Kirchhoff became in 1870 a member of the Berlin Academy of Sciences, and was an honorary or corresponding member of the leading scientific societies of the world, including his relation as one of the very few foreign associates of the National Academy of Sciences in the United States. His own Government honored him with the title of "geheimrath," or privy councilor, and conferred on him the Prussian order "*Pour la mérite*," the highest honor awarded in Germany. His collected papers were published as "Gesammelte Abhandlungen, von G. Kirchhoff" (Leipsic, 1882). His other works are "Untersuchungen über das Sonnenspectrum und die Spectren des chemischen Elemente" (Berlin, 1861), translated as "Studies of the Solar Spectrum and the Spectra of Simple Bodies" (London, 1862); with Bunsen, "Chemische Analyse durch Spectralbeobachtung" (Vienna, 1861); and his lectures on dynamics, "Vorlesungen über analytische Mechanik, mit Einschluss der Hydrodynamik und der Theorie der Elasticität fester Körper" (Leipsic, 1874).

L

LAW AND ORDER LEAGUE OF THE UNITED STATES, a national organization or alliance of local leagues, which has for its object, as expressed by its constitution, "to maintain the principle that the enforcement of law is essential to the perpetuity of good government, and by promoting the formation of State and local leagues, to secure in all proper ways the enforcement of existing laws relating to the liquor-traffic, and all offenses against morals and the peace and good order of society, and to encourage and assist the authorities in maintaining the same." The honor of precedence in the law-and-order movement is claimed by a "Society for the Prevention of Crime," organized early in 1877 in New York city, under the leadership of Dr. Howard Crosby, which was instrumental in closing many of the saloons of that city. Later in the same year a similar society was formed in Chicago, to which the movement, perhaps, owes its first effective impetus, and which is regarded as the parent of the present national league. It was observed during the railway riots of that year that a large portion of the rioters consisted of half-drunken youths, and subsequent inquiries elicited the information that not fewer than 30,000 such persons habitually frequented the drinking-saloons of Chicago, and were furnished with liquor in defiance of the law against sale to minors. Aroused by these discoveries, a company of energetic men, among whom Frederick F. Elmendorf and Andrew Paxton were prominent, organized on September 25 a "Citizens' League of Chicago for the Suppression of the Sale of Liquor to Minors." The procedure adopted was simple and effective; the prosecuting agent, Mr. Paxton, or his assistants, visited each saloon in order, and whenever a minor was found drinking, a complaint was made before a magistrate, and prosecution and conviction followed. The law, which for seven or eight years had been a dead letter, only two prosecutions and no convictions having been made under it, became at once an effective instrument to eradicate a growing evil. The saloon-keepers were forced to submit, and in the course of a few years fully five sixths of the sale of liquors to minors was effectually suppressed. At the same time the field of labor for the organization was gradually widened till it embraced all forms of legal opposition to the liquor-traffic.

The knowledge of this work and of other similarly successful work by the New York society soon led to the formation of leagues in Cincinnati, Louisville, and other large centers, which became valuable agencies in their separate fields. All these were united into a national league, at a convention held in Boston, Feb. 22, 1883, containing delegates from eight different States, and representing twenty-seven leagues. Mr. Elmendorf, president and founder of the Chicago league, was chosen president of the national organization. This meeting was followed by the formation of a State league in Massachusetts, and of numerous local leagues in other parts of the country. So rapid was the growth of the movement at this time that at the second annual meeting held near Chicago in August, 1884, the number of leagues then in existence was estimated by the secretary at about 500, with an aggregate membership of at least 60,000. Ex-Gov. John D. Long, of Massachusetts, was chosen president of the league by this meeting, Mr. Elmendorf having died in October, 1883. The present incumbent of that office, Hon. Charles C. Bonney, of Chicago, succeeded ex-Gov. Long in 1885.

Although primarily and chiefly an organization to enforce the laws against the liquor-traffic, and though in some States, as in Massachusetts, confined entirely to that work, the constitution of the league does not restrict it to any narrow line of activity, and local clubs have frequently attacked other evils. The league at Cincinnati not only fought the liquor-dealers, but attacked and closed the Sunday theatres of that city. In Louisville a crusade against gamblers was undertaken; they were driven out of the city, and the Kentucky Legislature was induced to make gambling a felony. More recently the league at Seattle, Washington Territory, found an opportunity to work on the side of law and order by protecting the Chinese when they were terrorized and hunted from that place. The work of the league is the aggregate work of its local organizations. No attempt has been made to collect statistics from these, but the efforts of any one are indicative of the character of all. The report of what has been done in Boston is here presented. The Secretary says:

We believe that not less than 15,000 children were patronizing the saloons in the city of Boston when we began our work. It is now a difficult matter to find one of these little children entering a saloon. Most of the saloons were open, doing business on the Lord's day. Hundreds that were then open are now closed. The Sunday arrests for drunkenness were reduced, during the first year of our work, more than one third; during the past year they have been only about half as many as they were during the year before the Law-and-Order League was formed. The members of our association have conducted an agitation for an increase in the license fees of the city with success, and as a result $666,904 has been paid into the treasury in excess of the amount that it would have received from this source if there had been no Law-and-Order League. We found ourselves unable to secure any active work on the part of our police force in the enforcement of this law. We began and carried forward an agitation which culminated in an act of the Legislature taking the power of appointment of the board controlling our police force, and having charge of the administration of the liquor law, from the municipality and investing it in the Governor of the State. We now have a police force with an impulse behind it. which means a faithful performance of duty in respect to this law as well as to others. In consequence of this change, there are 633 fewer places licensed in Boston this year than there were last, and those who have received licenses are held to a more strict compliance with the law which permits them to carry on this business.

At the close of 1887 the number of leagues was estimated at between 700 and 800, with a membership of 100,000 or more, distributed through nearly every State and Territory and in Canada. There are 13 State organizations. Massachusetts leads with 95 societies; Illinois and New York have about 50 each, Pennsylvania about 30, Maine, Michigan, Ohio, Connecticut, and others, from 10 to 20 each. Branches are found in all the large cities, North and South. The present officers of the League are: President, Hon. Charles C. Bonney, Chicago, Ill ; Secretary, L. Edwin Dudley, 28 School Street, Boston, Mass.; Treasurer, John H. Perry; General Agent, Andrew Paxton, Chicago, Ill. The last three meetings of the league have been held in Cincinnati, Albany, and Philadelphia.

LAZARUS, EMMA, an American poet, born in New York city, July 22, 1849; died there, Nov. 19, 1887. She was the daughter of a Jewish merchant. While a mere child, she wrote verses of decided promise, and, still in her teens, she gave to the public a volume (now rare) of original poems and translations from Schiller, Heine, Dumas, and Hugo. In 1871

EMMA LAZARUS.

appeared her "Admetus and Other Poems," dedicated to Ralph Waldo Emerson, who took a warm interest in her literary career. Whatever may have been the influence of this friendship, it did not affect the style of the young writer. Indeed, at this time she seems rather to have assimilated, in such poems in the volume as "Lohengrin" and "Tannhauser," something of the sonorous, limpid rhythm of Tennyson in his Arthurian legends, although she shows a subtlety of thought and vigor of expression, particularly in descriptive passages,

that are quite her own. In the poem that gives its name to the collection, Emma Lazarus may be said to have established her reputation as a writer of originality and power; and to have done this with a theme already successfully treated by some of the most famous of her contemporaries, may well have called forth such eulogiums as were showered on her "Admetus" by English critics. The "Westminster Review" declared that in some points the poem would bear comparison with "Balaustion's Adventure." The "Illustrated London News" considered her "far happier than Mr. Browning in her half adaptation of 'Euripides,'" and that "the conflict between Hercules and Death, and the return to life of Alcestis, are represented with more force as well as grace in this poem than in that of Mr. Browning." The true artist is shown in her withdrawing into the darkness of the night the contending figures in Alcides's awful struggle, which is followed by a gentle calm, thus exquisitely expressed:

> "Through the open casement poured
> Bright floods of sunny light; the air was soft,
> Clear, delicate, as though a summer storm
> Had passed away, and those there standing saw,
> Afar upon the plain, Death fleeing thence,
> And at the door-way, weary, well-nigh spent,
> Alcides, flushed with victory."

These lines, together with the following pretty picture from the same poem, give a fair idea of Miss Lazarus's style at this time:

> "To river pastures of his flocks and herds
> Admetus rode, where sweet-breathed cattle grazed,
> Heifers and goats and kids and foolish sheep,
> Dotted cool, spacious meadows with bent heads,
> And necks' soft wool broken in yellow flakes,
> Nibbling sharp-toothed the rich, thick growing
> blades."

"Alide," a prose romance founded on the story of Goethe's love for Frederika Brion, appeared in 1874, and won for the writer the praise of Tourgéneff. "Lo Spagnoletto," a tragedy, was printed privately in 1876. In 1881 she brought out "Poems and Ballads of Heine," translations that easily surpass previous attempts to put into English the verses of that difficult poet. The rendering of "Donna Clara" is particularly happy, retaining the musical flow of the refrain of the original.

In 1882, when the civilized world stood aghast at the relentless persecutions of the Jews in Russia and Roumania, and thousands of the fugitives were driven to our shores, Emma Lazarus's passive Judaism, fired by this fanatical outburst against her race, found indignant expression in such an indictment as "The Crowing of the Red Cock":

> "When the long roll of Christian guilt
> Against his sires and kin is known,
> The flood of tears, the life-blood spilt,
> The agony of ages shown,
> What oceans can the stain remove
> From Christian law and Christian love?"

and in such stirring lines as the following from "The Banner of the Jew," in which the poet calls to mind the time when

"down poured
The Maccabean clan, who sang
Their battle anthem to the Lord.
Five heroes lead, and following, see,
Ten thousand rush to victory!

"Oh for Jerusalem's trumpet now,
To blow a blast of shattering power,
To wake the sleepers high and low,
And rouse them to the urgent hour!
No hand for vengeance—but to save,
A million naked swords should wave."

These poems, with others in the same vein, are contained in Miss Lazarus's last volume, "Songs of a Semite," in which is also her tragedy in five acts, "The Dance to Death," founded on the burning of thousands of Jews in a German ghetto during the middle ages. Apart from championship of her race through the press, Miss Lazarus labored personally among the refugees in New York, and helped to establish them in manual occupations. Her pen was now devoted solely to Jewish subjects. She learned Hebrew so as to read the Psalms and Isaiah in the original, and studied the poets Solomon Ben Judah Gabirol, Moses Ben Ezra, and Abou Hassan Ben Ha-levi, who, under the mild rule of the Moors, flourished on the Iberian peninsula during the "dark ages" of Christianity. Some of her translations from the Hebrew, from these sources, have been incorporated in the ritual of the New York Temple Emmanuel Congregation. "By the Waters of Babylon," the last of her contributions to the periodical press, appeared in "The Century" during the summer of 1887. It is a series of exquisite little prose poems, recapitulating the persecutions of the Jews from the expulsion from Spain—on the day that Columbus discovered America—up to the present time. A memorial number of "The American Hebrew," to which she had been a contributor, containing tributes to her memory, was issued shortly after her death.

LIBERIA, the Americo-African republic, on the western coast of Africa, occupying what is known as the Grain Coast. It was founded in 1822 by enfranchised negroes from the United States.

Area and Population.—The boundary begins on the north, at the south bank of Manna river, about 6° 80′ north latitude, and runs as far south as San Pedro river, about 4° 20′ south latitude, a distance of about 600 miles. It extends into the interior about 200 miles. The area is about 14,300 square miles. The total population is estimated at 1,068,000, all of the African race, of which number 18,000 are Americo-Liberians, and the remaining aboriginal inhabitants. Monrovia, the capital, had an estimated population in 1884 of 3,400. Other towns are Robertsport, 1,200; Buchanan and Edina, 5,000; and Harper, 3,000, with suburbs, 8,550.

Finances.—For 1883 the revenue was officially returned at £34,802, and expenditure at £31,-493: for 1884, revenue £38,000, expenditure £32,500; and for 1885, revenue £40,000, and expenditure, £32,500. The principal part of the revenue is derived from customs duties, while the expenditure is chiefly the cost of the general administration. In August, 1871, the republic laid the foundation of a public debt by contracting a loan of $500,000 at 7 per cent. interest, to be redeemed in fifteen years. The loan was issued in England, but no interest has been paid on it since 1874, the Government of the republic being bankrupt.

Commerce.—The exports for 1883 were valued at £200,000, and the imports at £150,000. In 1883, 325 vessels, of 260,427 tons, entered and cleared Liberian ports. There are no statistics regarding the extent of the commercial relations of the republic with the United Kingdom, the annual statement of trade and navigation issued by the Board of Trade not mentioning Liberia but only "western coast of Africa (excluding the British and other colonies)." The value of the exports and British imports thus designated was as follows in the five years from 1881 to 1885:

YEAR.	Export from Western Africa to Great Britain.	Imports of British produce into Western Africa.
1881	£1,449,116	£894,287
1882	1,562,988	879,395
1883	1,617,818	1,247,858
1884	1,360,408	1,112,640
1885	1,181,067	779,266

The chief articles of export from Western Africa to Great Britain in 1885 were palm-oil, of the value of £649,147; nuts, £190,988: caoutchouc, £148,297; ivory, £117,824. The British imports into Western Africa consist mainly of cotton manufactures, which were valued at £299,808 in 1885.

New Territory.—The extent of the new territory of Medina is not yet known. The population of Liberia within its former boundaries was estimated at 718,000, and that of Medina at 700,000. The National Legislature in 1884 opened three new ports of entry, San Pedro, Manna, and Niffou. Foreigners have the right to trade at them.

Government.—The Constitution of the republic is modeled on that of the United States. The executive is vested in a president, and the legislative power in a parliament of two houses called the Senate and the House of Representatives. The president and the House of Representatives are elected for two years, and the Senate for four years. There are thirteen members of the lower house and eight of the upper. The president must be thirty-five years of age and have real property to the value of £600. The President in 1884–'86 was Hilary-Richard-Wright Johnson; Vice-President, James M. Thompson. The President's Cabinet was as follows: Secretary of State, E. J. Barclay; Secretary of the Treasury, M. T. Worrell; Secretary of the Interior, B. J. K. Anderson; Postmaster-General, J. Th. Wiles; Attorney-General, W. M. Davis; the commander of the military forces is Brigadier-General R. A. Sherman; the President of the Senate is the Vice-president of the republic. The Speaker of the House of Representatives is J. N. Lewis; the Supreme Judge is C. L. Parsons; the United States Consul at Monrovia died after a few months' service, and C. H. J. Taylor, who was appointed to succeed him, resigned in a short time. There is now no U. S. consul in Monrovia. The republic has concluded treaties with the German Empire, Great Britain, France, Belgium, Denmark, Italy, the United States, the Netherlands, Sweden and Norway, Portugal, Austria-Hungary, and Hayti.

Army.—There is no standing army. Militia service is obligatory upon all citizens from sixteen to fifty years of age. The militia is composed of a brigade of four regiments.

Education.—A fresh impulse has been given to the educational department by the reopening of the Methodist Episcopal seminary in Monrovia, which admits students of all denominations of Christians. At Bassa, a graduate of Liberia College has charge of a school in which the higher branches are pursued. The Alexander High School, now located in Clay Ashland, under the supervision and instruction of another graduate of Liberia College, is also doing good work; and the preparatory school in the college is being carried on with commendable energy and profit. The two schools at Arthington, aggregating seventy-eight pupils, and the school at Brewerville, numbering thirty, supported by the American Colonization Society, are prosperous. The Government schools are instructing as many as will attend them. A compulsory system of education here is impracticable at present.

Religion.—Church and state are separate. All religious beliefs are tolerated. Most of the evangelical denominations are doing missionary work in Liberia. The Presbyterians were the pioneers. The name of Archibald Alexander, first dean of Princeton Seminary, has been commemorated in the Alexander High School of Liberia. The Baptists began their missionary work very early, and with great vigor, and they have the most flourishing churches. The Methodists are largely represented, and their missionary societies of the United States have spent thousands of dollars in evangelical work. The Episcopalians have prosecuted work in Liberia with amazing persistency and great results. Their schools at Cape Palmos and Cape Mount have benefited hundreds of natives. Recently a scholarly and pious colored man was made Bishop of Cape Palmos and parts adjacent. For twenty years or more a board of philanthropists in Boston, and one in New York, have prosecuted missionary educational work in connection with Liberia College; but the condition of the country and the people has not been favorable to great success. It is proposed to establish an industrial department in connection with the college. The Lutherans have sustained for years a manual-labor school and mission near Arthington, and have reached hundreds of natives, converting and enlightening them, and teaching them the art of systematic labor. At Arthington there is also a private missionary school, supported by Edward S. Morris, of Philadelphia. There are several other mission schools; but the educational facilities are few and poor. Of the Americo-African children, not ten per cent. are in school, and of the entire native and Liberia population not one per cent. is receiving any instruction.

Climate.—The climate is somewhat like that of southern Florida. The grass and foliage are always green. The thermometer averages 72° for about six months; for about three months it is from 85° to 90°, and it never remains for any length of time above 95°. The rainy season begins in Liberia in May, and ceases in October. It is dry the remainder of the year. Terrific tornadoes precede and end the rainy season. About the middle of December there is a cold, disagreeable, and dangerous wind, called the "harmattan wind," blowing for from four to six weeks. During these winds the thermometer at sunrise and at sunset averages 66°, and it seldom rises higher than 80° at any time during the day. The harmattan comes from the interior, some say from the Desert of Sahara. It injures vegetation and affects the lower animals, and man does not escape. This is the sickly season. Otherwise, an equable temperature prevails. The Americo-African Republic, like Holland, has a low, flat coast. Marshes and swamps of mangrove-trees abound. These trees thrive in mud. They are found near the mouths of rivers, and form a close, impenetrable thicket. They spread rapidly, and the leaves and branches fall and rot, and form a sickening mass of decayed vegetation. In the dry season particularly, the sun brings out from this bed of putrefaction an extraordinary amount of poison that mingles with the air, and both man and beast inhale disease and receive the seeds of infirmity and death. This malarial coast belt is the great barrier in the way of the growth and development of Liberia. The process of acclimation must be passed through even by colored persons, and for the first six months it is quite as trying to them as to the whites. Back from the Liberian coast, however, are the hills of the Finley and the Kong mountains, with a salubrious climate.

Resources.—The resources of the Americo-African republic are rich and varied. The soil contains gold, silver, and iron in great abundance. The iron-ore yields sixty per cent., and is found near the surface. The natives use gold and iron in certain crude manufactures, and they do not mine for these metals. English capitalists are digging gold at Axim, south of Liberia, and the same rich vein passes through Liberia. Capital is needed to utilize these mines. The resources of the forests are almost inexhaustible, and they are within the reach of simple industry. Palm-trees are found in great abundance, and yield annually an enormous growth of nuts and oil. Cam-wood and rubber-trees also abound, and are very valuable for export. Millions of dollars go annually out of Europe and America to the West Coast; thousands go to Liberia to purchase palm-oil, palm-nuts, cam-wood, and rubber. Added to this is ivory, one of the most valuable articles of trade, which lies around in parts of the interior like common rocks. The forests contain different varieties of valuable timber. Growing almost everywhere are mahogany, oak, hickory, rose-wood, mulberry, and other valuable trees which could be secured easily, and at little cost. There is a great variety of fruit-trees; oranges, limes, guavas, plantains, pine-apples, sour sops, and others grow everywhere, and are remarked for their delicious flavor. The soil is very rich, and may be cultivated with a stick. If it is simply scratched, and the seed dropped in, there is an abundant harvest. Most of the table vegetables may be raised, such as Guinea corn, sweet potatoes, beans, tomatoes, okra, watermelons, cabbages, and turnips. The natives cultivate a vegetable somewhat like the sweet potato, which they call eddoes, and another like the turnip, which they call cassavas.

The Americo-Africans raise and export principally coffee and sugar. They could add to these articles ginger, pepper, ground-nuts, indigo, arrow-root, and cotton, which is found everywhere in a wild state. Enterprise and industry, backed by a little capital, might accomplish great results here. The coffee of Liberia is the best in the world. It is indigenous. Hull, in his work on coffee-culture, gives the Liberian coffee the first place. It is superior to Java and Mocha, both in the size of the berry and the deliciousness of the flavor.

The Natives.—The people are divided into two classes: 1, the aborigines, who are the indigenous tribes, and the slaves recaptured from slave-ships and returned to Africa; and, 2, the colored colonizers from the United States and the West Indies, and their descendants. The natives, as the aborigines are called, are divided into tribes, named Veys, Mandingoes, Kroos, Golahs, Greboes, Pessehs, Bassos, and Deys. They differ in dialect, as do the people of Great Britain even to-day. The Mandingoes are a tall and sinewy race, while the Kroomen are the sailors, navigating all the steamers and ships that do business in African waters. The Krooman was never a slave; he was too useful to the slave-trader as a sailor. Every male Kroo has a blue band tattooed upon his forehead. These tribes dwell in towns, each town having its chief. The houses are neatly constructed of bamboo. The Veys live in conical dwellings, with a porch, in which they usually hang a hammock of their own manufacture. The houses are comparatively neat, and the African wife prides herself on keeping her home tidy and in order. They have their smiths, who work in iron and gold, their

weavers of cloth, and their dyers, carpenters, merchants, teachers, doctors, and farmers, and are engaged in many of the pursuits common to our most advanced civilized life. The food of the natives consists of rice, cassava, beef, mutton, game, fish, palm-oil, and palm-butter; and their drink is water and palm-wine.

Polygamy and Slavery.—Two customs, interwoven with the warp and woof of their social system, are evils that can not be removed except by slow, moral processes—polygamy and slavery. The former evil is not as wide-spread as one would suppose. The man that wants a girl to wife, must first get together the purchase-money in the form of oxen, bullocks, or some other article of trade. A woman has no choice in the matter of marriage. Often she is chosen while still a child. The wife is property, and is in absolute submission to her husband. She never sits down to meals with him, and always treats him as her lord.

Liberia is the fruit of American colonization. The first practical colonizationist was a negro, Paul Cuffee, of Massachusetts. This bold leader, full of zeal for the civilization of Africa, took, in 1815, forty colored persons in his own vessel, at his own expense, from Boston, to Sierra Leone, which was the colony established on the West African Coast by Great Britain, for the reception of slaves taken from the Americans in the Revolutionary War. The emigrants from the United States and the West Indies and their descendants are called "Liberians." They were sent out by the American Colonization Society.

Up to Jan. 1, 1867, 13,180 emigrants had gone to Liberia, and the United States Government had returned to Africa 5,722 captured slaves. But since 1867 there has been a remarkable decrease in the number of colored people who have left America for Africa. The Colonization Society pays the emigrant's passage, and provides for his maintenance for six months. The Government gives every married emigrant twenty-five acres of land, and every single man ten acres. This land is covered with trees and a thick undergrowth, and must be cleared and prepared for planting. Coffee scions must be bought, and set out, and in three or four years the crop matures. There are no horses or oxen in use. The emigrant must build his house, and must struggle hard, if he would enjoy life. But after ten, twenty, it may be thirty years of earnest effort, he settles down under his own vine and fig-tree a happy, contented, and wealthy farmer.

The republic is exclusively a negro state. White persons can not now become citizens or hold property in Liberia. It is seriously argued that the country will not prosper until this obstacle is removed, and citizenship and the rights of property be opened to all. There is a movement on foot to enlarge the privileges of foreigners, so as to encourage them to make investments. It is proposed to allow them: 1. To trade and do business anywhere in the republic. Now they are confined to the sea-ports, and are not allowed to establish factories or stores up the rivers, or in the interior. 2. To lease land for a long term of years, perhaps ninety nine. Now the limitation is twenty years. Such an innovation would certainly encourage the investment of foreign capital and energize the republic. Most of the colored people who have emigrated to Africa were poor and comparatively ignorant, and in this new country and hostile climate they have enjoyed neither the support of large capital, nor the direction of general intelligence. They carried to Africa very little idea of voluntary, systematic labor. They worked in America more from outside than inside influences. The climate is against the people. Their education has been against them, and they have increased their weakness by lying down on native muscle and depending too much on foreign philanthropy. Even after sixty years of opportunity, and thirty-seven years of national existence, there are no railroads, no horses or oxen in use, except at Cape Palmas. See "Liberia," by T. McCants Stewart (New York, 1886).

LIBRARY LEGISLATION. Previous to the Revolution, and for many years after, there appears to have been no legislation in this country for the support of free public libraries from public taxes. The idea of the free public library, as it is known to-day, was not yet evolved. There are in the town records of Boston for 1686 and 1695 notes relating to "the library room in the east end of the town-house," and concerning "all bookes or other things belonging to the library," and in a will of 1674 ten volumes are bequeathed "to the public library in Boston or elsewhere," which prove that such a library existed then, but it was probably destroyed in the town-house in the fire of 1747.

The Assembly of South Carolina passed an act, Nov. 16, 1700, for the preservation of a library which Rev. Thomas Bray, D. D., founder of the Society for the Propagation of the Gospel in Foreign Parts, had sent to Charleston "for the publick use" in that province.

The Philadelphia Library Company was incorporated in 1742, but was started ten years earlier by Benjamin Franklin as a subscription library, "the mother," he called it, "of all the North American subscription libraries," being "imitated by other towns and in other provinces." The Charleston (S. C.) Library Society, organized in 1748, after several failures to secure a charter, was finally incorporated in 1755. The New York Society Library was incorporated in 1754. Many towns in New England had libraries at an early date. Salisbury, Conn., before the Revolution, received a gift of 200 volumes for a library which flourished until the town was nearly a century old; and in 1803 Caleb Bingham presented to the children of the same town a small library which prospered for many years, receiving occasional grants of money from the town without the authority of State law, "the first example, it is believed, of municipal aid to a library in the United States."

The earliest legislation for libraries in the United States took the form of general laws providing for the incorporation of library associations, variously called subscription, proprietary, social, and even public libraries. There is now a general law, providing for the incorporation of such associations, in each of the sixteen States: California, Colorado, Florida, Illinois, Indiana, Maine, Massachusetts, Missouri, New Jersey, New York, Pennsylvania, Rhode Island, Tennessee, Virginia, West Virginia, and Wisconsin.

In twenty-three States and Territories—Alabama, Arizona, California, Colorado, Georgia, Illinois, Indiana, Iowa, Kansas, Maryland, Massachusetts, Minnesota, Mississippi, Montana, Nebraska, Pennsylvania, Rhode Island, Tennessee, Virginia, Vermont, Washington, West Virginia, and Wyoming—the libraries and buildings of these associations are exempted from taxation; and in Alabama, Connecticut, District of Columbia, Illinois, Kansas, Massachusetts, New York, West Virginia, and Wisconsin, private libraries to a certain amount are exempt from taxation or attachment.

In 1835 New York passed a law establishing district libraries, not libraries for schools but for the people, in districts of the size of a school-district, the voters in which were authorized to levy a tax of $20 to start, and $10 annually to continue a library. Another law in 1838 appropriated $55,000 annually to the school districts for the purchase of books, and required them to raise by taxation a similar amount for the same purpose. In 1843 authority was granted school districts to use the library fund for the purchase of school apparatus, and the payment of teachers' salaries, provided the district libraries contained 100 to 125 volumes, according as there were less or more than fifty scholars from five to sixteen years of age in the district. The libraries increased up to 1853, when they contained an aggregate of 1,604,210 volumes. From 1853 to 1886 the State expended $1,195,422 for these district libraries, "and yet they have been steadily running down during this period, and the number of books have decreased more than one half," says the State superintendent in 1886. The number of volumes reported in the libraries in 1886 is 734,506.

Twenty-one States followed New York in passing statutes providing for the establishment of school-district libraries: California, Colorado, Connecticut, Iowa, Indiana, Illinois, Kansas, Maine, Maryland, Massachusetts, Mississippi, Michigan, Minnesota, New York, New Jersey, Ohio, Oregon, Pennsylvania, Rhode Island, Virginia, and Wisconsin. But in all the system has proved a failure, because the unit (the district) was too small; the amount of money annually obtainable in each was too insignificant, and the number of volumes too few to keep up a public interest in the care, circulation, or preservation of the books. From year to year these States have changed their laws or passed statutes providing for public town libraries.

The earliest free public town library, unless we except that of Salisbury named above, was established at Peterborough, N. H., in 1833, is still in existence, but was maintained by the town for nearly seventeen years before the general State law was passed. In March, 1848, the Massachusetts General Court passed an act authorizing the city of Boston to levy a tax of $5,000 for the establishment of a free public library, and in 1851 made the act apply to all the cities and towns of the State. But to the New Hampshire Legislature belongs the credit of passing the first general law, approved July 7. 1849, authorizing towns to maintain libraries free to all inhabitants.

In the following States there has been no legislation except for the State library : Delaware, Kentucky, Louisiana, Nevada, North Carolina, Oregon, and South Carolina. The General Government has provided for Territorial libraries for the use of the legislatures and courts of the Territories.

The following list contains a summary of the legislation with some of the statistics of the several States and Territories.

Arizona in its school law, passed in 1885, permits school trustees in townships where there are 100 school children to use $50 of the school fund, and any donations they may receive, for the purchase of books for school libraries, to be free to teachers and pupils, and to residents on payment of such monthly fee as the trustees may prescribe.

California, in 1854, adopted a district library law, similar to that of New York. In 1878 a full library law on the model of the Illinois statute was passed. There are sixteen public libraries in the State aggregating 131,113 volumes.

Colorado, in 1872, enacted a law based on that of Illinois, but no city or town has taken advantage of its provisions. The only free library in the State, at Denver, was established by contributions made by the Board of Trade.

Connecticut passed a school library law in 1839 ; a town library law in 1869, restricting taxation as in Maine. The public library laws of 1875 and 1876 permitted a city or town to establish a library, but made no provision for its support by taxation. In 1881 a law was passed permitting towns to levy a tax of two mills on the dollar of valuation. Fines for penal offenses may be applied for the support of a public library. There are but sixteen public libraries in the State. aggregating 48,814 volumes.

Dakota in the act of 1883, establishing a common-school system, authorizes the school board of any township to buy a circulating library, of the value of not more than $500 ; the books to be selected from a list approved by the Superintendent of Public Instruction, to include the publications of at least four publishers. Residents of the township may take out books under regulations prescribed by the school board.

Illinois in 1872 enacted a law, with minute details for the establishment, government, and management of public libraries, which has been largely followed in other Western States. It provides a board of nine directors, an independent body nominated by the mayor and approved by the city council, but having the exclusive control of the library and power to

erect or lease library buildings. Towns and villages may levy a tax for libraries not to exceed two mills on the dollar ; cities of less than 100,000 inhabitants, one mill ; and cities of over 100,000 inhabitants, one fifth of a mill. City councils have power to regulate the amount to be appropriated. A special section relates to bequests. There are forty-five public libraries in the State, with an aggregate of 304,584 volumes.

Indiana has the simplest and most concise provision for public libraries in a single paragraph of an act passed in 1871, concerning the election and duties of a board of school commissioners. They are authorized to levy a tax each year of not exceeding one fifth of one mill on each dollar of taxable property for the support of free libraries, to fit up rooms, buy books, pay salaries, make and enforce regulations, and prescribe penalties for their violation. The library associations law was extended, and cities were authorized to have libraries by an act passed in 1873. There are sixty public libraries in the State, with an aggregate of 103,120 volumes ; thirteen of these have 84,-000 volumes ; the others are township libraries with less than 1,000 volumes each, probably the outcome of the old district system. An act passed in 1883 provides that, when the officers of any library incorporated under the law of 1852, and worth $750 or more, shall offer to the trustees of the town where it is located to make it a free public library, the trustees may levy a tax of not less than one quarter nor more than three quarters of a mill on the dollar of assessed valuation, to be paid over to the officers of the library for the purchase of books, and shall continue it annually so long as the money raised is properly applied by the library officers.

Iowa in 1840 enacted a district library law ; in 1873 a town library law of a single short section, authorizing any city or town to levy a tax of one mill on the dollar of assessed valuation, for the support of a public library. There are eight free libraries in the State, with an aggregate of 26,556 volumes.

Kansas passed a free public library law in 1886, having had the general experience with district libraries since 1870.

Maine's statute, passed in 1854, provides that any town may raise by taxation one dollar on each ratable poll for the forming of a public library ; and thereafter twenty-five cents annually for its maintenance. This allowance is so meager that without aid from private individuals no libraries could be formed ; there are but twelve public libraries in the State, aggregating 25,409 volumes. A protection law was passed in 1877.

Massachusetts began in 1851 with a law like that of Maine ; in 1859 allowed a larger tax, and in 1866 adopted the New Hampshire freedom from limitation and authorized a city or town to raise any sum it deemed necessary, also borrowing its provision for the receipt of gifts and bequests. An act of 1870 "for the establishment of districts for maintaining street lamps," grants power "to maintain street lamps, establish and maintain libraries, and maintain sidewalks." A protection law was passed in 1872. There are 192 public libraries, with an aggregate of 1,770,386 volumes, "nearly as many," says Dr. Wm. F. Poole, "as are contained in all the other public libraries of the United States."

Michigan is unique in having in the first Constitution of the State the clause : "The Legislature shall also provide for the establishment of at least one library in every township." In 1859 a school district library law was enacted ; but this plan proving a failure, as in the other States which introduced it, a thorough public library law, like that of Illinois, was enacted in 1877. The State has 157 public libraries, aggregating 231,365 volumes ; thirty-four have 173,944 volumes ; the remainder are township libraries of less than 1,000 volumes each.

Minnesota has a district library law ; in 1867 enacted a law exempting libraries and their buildings from taxation, and in 1875 passed an act for their protection.

Missouri in 1885 enacted a public library law, drafted by Mr. Crunden, of the St. Louis Public Library. It follows the Illinois law, with slight changes.

Montana passed in 1883 a law of the Illinois plan, providing that the municipal authorities of any incorporated town or city may establish a free public library, and may levy a tax for its support not exceeding one mill on the dollar of assessed valuation. But the question of establishing the library must first be submitted to the voters of the town for acceptance or rejection.

Nebraska enacted a library law in 1877 on the Illinois model, and with full details. There are four public libraries, with 17,227 volumes.

New Hampshire enacted the first general free public library law in 1849, so simple in form and effective that it still remains unchanged. Any town may raise and appropriate money for establishing and maintaining a public library, without limitation as to amount or conditions as to management. It allows the receipt of gifts and bequests which may be used in such manner as will best promote the prosperity and utility of the library. There are thirty-five free libraries in the State, with an aggregate of 129,227 volumes. An act of 1877 provides for the protection of public libraries.

New Jersey passed a law in 1884 modeled on that of Illinois. It provides that on the approval of a majority of the voters, at a special election, it shall be the duty of the authorities to lay a tax of one third of a mill on the dollar of assessed valuation, as a free public library fund. The board of trustees is made a corporate body of seven members, the mayor, superintendent of public instruction, and five others to be appointed by the mayor, to serve without compensation. Another act, of the same year, empowers three or more persons to organize a corporation for the purpose of establishing a free public library. An act passed shortly before the two named provides that wherever an incorporated lyceum library now exists, the proper authorities of any town having control of a free library, established and maintained by public moneys, shall have power to lend such free library to such lyceum, and to pay over to the lyceum whatever annual sums the authorities can levy for the free library, provided that the mayor and president of the council be made ex-officio trustees of the lyceum, and that the united library shall be free to the teachers and pupils of the public schools.

New Mexico, in a municipal corporations act of 1884, allows the council or trustees of any city or incorporated town to appropriate money for a public library, provided that the yearly appropriation shall not exceed one mill on the dollar of assessed valuation, and that no appropriation be made until the proposition has been submitted to a popular vote.

New York, in 1872, passed a public library law, providing that upon the written petition of the majority of all the taxable inhabitants of any city, town, or village, its common council, board of trustees, or town auditors may establish and maintain a free public library, with the limitation of one dollar for each legal voter for the foundation, and fifty cents annually for the maintenance; amended, 1885, to include public reading-rooms, with or without libraries. No library is known to have been established under this law. The district library laws are mentioned above. Under a provision of the school law of 1847 there are twenty-two free libraries, indirectly supported by taxation, having an aggregate of 125,811 volumes. In 1886 New York passed a law to encourage the growth of free circulating libraries in the cities of the State. Under it any library association duly incorporated, owning $20,000 worth of real estate and at least 10,000 volumes, and circulating the same as a free library to the number of 75,000 volumes annually, is authorized to apply to the common council or other proper authority for the sum of $5,000, and for a further sum of $5,000 for each additional 100,000 volumes circulated annually. Power is given to such proper authorities to make provision for the payments of such appropriations. An act passed May 13, 1887, provides for towns or cities of less than 30,000 population. Any library association in such a town owning $4,000 worth of real estate or paying $300 annual rent, and also owning at least 5,000 volumes maintained as a free public library, may apply to the common council or other proper authority for $1,000 for each 15,000 volumes circulated annually.

Ohio enacted its first public library law in 1867, and others in 1873 and 1875. Under its school library law of 1853 it had a similar experience to that of New York, and in 1868 the school officers were puzzled what to do with the books. The present law enables cities and towns to raise money by taxation for the purchase of books; provides a board of management for the administration of the library and the purchase of books, but gives to the board of education the control of the library, the providing of funds for the erection of buildings, and all other expenses. It allows school officers to deposit their libraries for use in the town libraries. There are twenty-one public libraries in the State, aggregating 321,071 volumes.

Pennsylvania has a district school library law, passed in 1864, and a general act for incorporating library associations, passed in 1874, but no free public library law. A law passed by the last Legislature enacts that all taxes on dogs may be appropriated for the support and maintenance of public libraries now organized, provided that such library companies shall provide and maintain a free reading room for the use of all inhabitants of the borough where it is established.

Rhode Island, in 1867, gave power to towns to establish libraries; in 1869 authorized two towns to combine and administer a library jointly; and passed a free public library act in 1875. A city or town may lay a tax of 2.5 mills on the dollar of valuation for establishing a library, and two tenths of a mill annually thereafter for its support. The State has thirty public libraries, with 135,834 volumes.

Tennessee and **West Virginia** have general acts for the incorporation and protection of libraries; and Virginia has in addition a district library law.

Texas, in a concise law, enacted in 1874, provides that any incorporated city may establish a free public library, and may make such regulations and grant such part of its revenues for the management and increase thereof as the municipal government of the city may determine. There are two public libraries, that at Galveston having 5,600 volumes.

Vermont, in 1865, adopted a law similar to that of New Hampshire, but changed in 1867 to that of Maine, except that it allows fifty cents per poll for the annual maintenance. A library association law was passed in 1869. In 1884 the law was amended by raising the legal limit of expenditure from one dollar to two dollars upon every poll for establishment, and from fifty cents to one dollar for maintenance. There are fifteen public libraries in the State, aggregating 81,193 volumes.

Wisconsin passed a law in 1868 permitting towns to raise by taxation yearly $150 for the purchase of books. In 1872 a law similar to that of Illinois was enacted, by which cities and towns were authorized to raise a tax of one mill on the dollar for the support of public libraries. The Milwaukee Public Library has a special law which empowers the library board to fix the amount to be raised for the library by taxation. There are nine public libraries in the State, aggregating 62,748 volumes.

LIND (GOLDSCHMIDT), JENNY, a Swedish singer, born in Stockholm, Sweden, Oct. 6, 1820; died in London, England, Nov. 2, 1887. She evinced extraordinary musical talent in her fourth year, and in her ninth year was a pupil in the singing-school attached to the court theatre in Stockholm. In her eighteenth year she made her *début* in opera in that city, and filled an engagement of three years, pleasing the public, but failing to satisfy herself. In 1841 she went to Paris, and placed herself under the instruction of Manuel Garcia, with whom she studied several months, when she secured an engagement at the Berlin opera, where she appeared in Meyerbeer's "Camp of Silesia," the soprano part being specially written for her. From this time (1844) she became known as the "Swedish Nightingale," and the most eminent composers and critics pronounced her the musical miracle of the age. Moscheles said she had "truly enchanted" him. Lablache declared that "every note was like a pearl." Mendelssohn wrote that she was the first artist that "united in the same degree natural gifts, study, and depth of feeling, the combination of the three never existing before." Her first appearance in opera in London was in Her Majesty's Theatre, May 4, 1847, and the critic, Henry F. Chorley, wrote that "the town, sacred and profane, went mad

JENNY (GOLDSCHMIDT) LIND.

about the 'Swedish Nightingale.'" Her last appearance on any operatic stage was in London, March 18, 1849, as Alice in "Robert le Diable." Thereafter she confined herself exclusively to the concert platform, gaining greener and greater laurels than ever before; and here her supremest triumphs were in oratorio. Her voice was a fine soprano, from D to D, especially pure and rich in the upper register, with sweetness, flexibility, and charm of expression; and she had remarkable ventriloquial power, as instanced in her famous bird and echo songs, and in the trio for voice and two flutes, composed for her in "The Camp of Silesia," in which her voice was scarcely distinguishable from the tones of the flutes.

During the whole of 1848 the Lind mania was everywhere epidemic in Europe, and at the close of her engagement in 1849 she went to Lübeck, Germany, where she made her contract for her engagement and remarkable success in the United States. In October, 1849, I conceived the idea of bringing Jenny Lind to America. I felt confident that the finest songstress in the world, having also a world-wide reputation for unstinted benevolence and kindness of heart, would be fully appreciated and liberally patronized by the American people. The agent I sent to Europe to secure, if possible, the engagement of the "Swedish Nightingale" was authorized to give her $1,000 a night, for any number of nights up to 150, with all her expenses, including secretary, servants, carriages, etc., besides engaging such musical assistants as she should select, upon any terms; and I offered to place the entire sum of money mentioned in the contract in the hands of London bankers before she sailed. This sum, amounting in all to $187,000, was so deposited by me, and the contracts were signed Jan. 9, 1850, eight months before the first concert was given in New York. In this interval the merits of the "divine Jenny" as a songstress, and as a woman of unbounded charity, were duly and daily set forth in the American press. When she arrived on our shores, Sept. 1, 1850, the excitement and general desire to see and hear her were intense. Thousands of persons covered the shipping and piers, and other thousands congregated on the wharf at Canal Street to see her land from the steamship "Atlantic." On the wharf was a flag-decorated bower of trees, and farther on two triumphal arches, one bearing the legend "Welcome, Jenny Lind," and the other, surmounted by the American eagle, being inscribed "Welcome to America." My private carriage conveyed her and her party to the Irving House, I myself riding with my coachman on the box as a legitimate advertisement, and within ten minutes of our arrival there were full 20,000 people around the hotel, nor did the throng lessen till late at night. At midnight Miss Lind was serenaded by the 200 members of the New York Musical Fund Society, escorted to the ground by 800 firemen in their red shirts and with torches. The calls for Miss Lind were so vehement that I led her through a window to the balcony, and it was some time before the serenade could go on. Probably no public reception in America ever was more enthusiastic and remarkable. For weeks the excitement was unabated. Her rooms were thronged by visitors, including the magnates of church and state. Presents of all sorts were showered upon her. Milliners, mantua-makers, shopkeepers, and manufacturers, advertised "Jenny Lind" bonnets, riding-habits, gloves, shoes, shawls, robes, mantillas, chairs, sofas, pianos —in fact, everything was "Jenny Lind."

The tickets for the first concert in Castle Garden were sold at auction for $17,864. The first seat was bid off for $225; the first 1,000 seats averaged $10 each, some selling for $25, $40, and $50 each. When I told Jenny Lind what the proceeds for her first concert would be, she seemed horror-struck: "Why, Mr. Barnum," she exclaimed, "this is wicked! the people are mad; I can not accept money which is thrown away in this manner; I shall give my share to public charities." I was as much .elated as she was depressed, and I at once proposed to amend our contract by giving her half of the entire receipts of the first two concerts—not counting those two in our engagement—and also to give her, besides her $1,000 a night, half of the gross receipts of every subsequent concert or oratorio, after deducting $5,500 for general expenses. This voluntary proposition on my part astonished her exceedingly, and caused her tears to flow while she overwhelmed me with compliments and gratitude. From her share of the first two concerts she gave $10,000, which, under the direction of the mayor of New York, by her request, was divided among sundry charities, and the story of her great generosity ran like wild-fire through the country. The third concert, which by agreement we called "the first regular concert," was given Sept. 17, 1850. I had offered a prize of $200 for an ode, "Greeting to America," which was awarded to Bayard Taylor, was set to music by Benedict, and was sung by Miss Lind. The enthusiasm created .by her first concert continued unabated, and whenever and wherever she sang the demand for tickets at the highest prices far exceeded the supply. The concert tour was confined to the following cities: New York, 35 concerts; Philadelphia, 8; Boston, 7; Providence, 1; Baltimore, 4; Washington, 2; Richmond, 1; Charleston, 2; Havana, 3; New Orleans, 12; Natchez, 1; Memphis, 1; St. Louis, 5; Nashville, 2; Louisville, 3; Madison, 1: Cincinnati, 5; Wheeling, 1; Pittsburg. 1; in all 95. The total receipts, except for concerts devoted to charity, were $712,161.34, an average of $7,496.43 for each concert. Of this sum Miss Lind's net avails were $176,675, and as money then had many times the purchasing power it has now, so high a price had never before been paid to a public singer. In our contract, Miss Lind reserved the right of giving charity concerts when she chose, and did so in several cities, thus giving away not less than $50,000. This created a conundrum which ran through the press: "Why will Barnum and Jenny Lind never fall out?"—"Because one is forgetting, and the other for-giving." On reading this, Miss Lind laughed heartily, then, assuming a serious look and tone, she said: "Mr. Barnum, it is not right for me to have so much credit when you give the services of Benedict and Belletti, all the expenses of the company, including the orchestra. hire of halls, attendance, and printing, while I give only my voice."

Our Washington concerts were attended by the President, his Cabinet, and their families; by Clay, Webster, Benton, Cass, Scott, and other prominent people, who, in public and private, paid marked attention to Miss Lind, and the concert party was specially entertained in the White House and at Mount Vernon. Miss Lind was besieged by callers everywhere. At Charleston, S. C., a wealthy young lady, the niece of a distinguished statesman, was so determined to see Jenny Lind in private that she bribed one of the servants to lend her a white cap and apron, and she carried in the tray with Jenny's tea. At Havana we passed a pleasant month in a hired furnished house in the outskirts of the city, where Miss Lind had a visit of several days from her famous countrywoman, Frederika Bremer. After the termination of our contract, Miss Lind gave several concerts, with varied success, and during a visit to Boston she married, Feb. 5, 1852, Mr. Otto Goldschmidt, a German composer and pianist, who had played at several of our concerts, and to whom Miss Lind had long been attached, since she studied music with him in Germany. While she was in Boston, as especially characteristic of her generosity, it is told that a poor working-girl paid $3 for a ticket "to hear that good angel sing," declaring that it was her whole week's wages. This was told to Miss Lind, who exclaimed: "Oh, this must not be! Poor girl! she shall not lose her money; it is wicked!" and she sent her a $20 gold piece. Her natural impulses were more generous than those of any person I ever met. A story of trouble brought tears from her eyes and money from her purse. But she was a woman of strong common sense, and was equally removed from flattery and imposition. She knew herself, and always maintained her rights. Once, on a steamboat journey on the Mississippi from New Orleans to Cairo, she voluntarily sang for the gratification of her fellow-passengers, and so she always was willing to sing on like occasions; but woe to those, however high in social station, who tried to entrap her. Once her New York lawyer invited her, with Benedict and Belletti, to an evening party at his house near Yonkers. She accepted the compliment, as she deemed it, glad to vary the monotony of her public career by mingling socially with refined people, as she had been used to do in Europe. Late in the evening her host gave her his arm, as if for a promenade, and led her to an open piano in a large room, where his expectant guests already were seated, and said: "Now, Miss Lind, you will greatly gratify us by singing some of your favorite selections." Her instant and indignant response was, "Order my carriage immediately." A similar scene occurred in Havana, where, by invitation of a Spanish count, she was at a grand ball attended by the most aristocratic families in that city.

My personal relations with Jenny Lind during our engagement and ever afterward were cordial and unbroken. When she undertook to give concerts on her own account in this country, she always regretted the want of my management, and once said to me, in Bridgeport: "People cheat me and swindle me very much, and I find it very annoying to give concerts on my own account." When I was in

London in 1858, struggling against the Jerome Clock Company's debts, Otto Goldschmidt called upon me and offered, in behalf of his wife, whom to me he always called "Miss Lind," any financial aid I might need, which, of course, I declined. And in all the years since my engagement with Jenny Lind terminated we both were always ready to do each other any possible friendly service. On the day of her death, in response to my message of condolence to her husband, I received from him the following cablegram: "I fully appreciate your condolences, coming from one who well knew my beloved wife, and was always remembered by her with sincere regard." Jenny Lind - Goldschmidt was buried in Malvern Cemetery, near London, Nov. 5, 1887.

LITERATURE, AMERICAN, IN 1887. There is little that is encouraging in a review of American authorship during the past year. The observer's attention is, of course, first directed to the enormous number of reprinted books in comparison with those which are original, and in this connection the opinion on consideration would be pretty general that few among all the works which are republished from English sources or translated from Continental writers are worth the trouble and expense gone to in their reproduction. Doubtless very much of this is done by publishers in order to keep their presses going: but the result is a flood of trash, which is, of course, most comprehensively illustrated in the department of fiction. But neither the fact that a great many foreign books are reprinted in this country nor the other fact that large numbers of these are trashy, frivolous, or harmful, affords any explanation of the paucity of good literary work here. After a thorough examination of the list of books published in this country last year, it is impossible to avoid the conclusion that it hardly contains one really first-class book in science, in botany, in criticism, in fiction, or in history. The selections here given are, as far as is practicable, the best representatives of American literary work for 1887.

Fiction.—In the department of fiction the tendency seems to be in the direction of the purely practical and business-like, novels being written, after feeling the pulse of the public, for the purpose of sale rather than reputation. Very few really imaginative books are written, and among the considerable list of novels and stories by American authors to which we shall refer it is doubtful whether a single one will live as a part of American literature. Mr. W. D. Howells has given us "April Hopes," which is, if anything, a considerable falling off from his other works in point of power, in plot, and character painting. From F. Marion Crawford we have "Marzio's Crucifix," "Paul Patoff," and "Saracinesca," which are not thought equal to his earlier works. From Charles Egbert Craddock we have "The Story of Keedon Bluffs"; Arlo Bates has published

"A Lad's Love" and "Patty's Perversities"; and Albion W. Tourgee "Button's Inn." William H. Bishop gave us "The Golden Justice," which is certainly a bright and clever story: Sidney Luska has written the "Yoke of the Thorah" and "A Land of Love." From Joel Chandler Harris we have "Free Joe, and other Georgian Sketches," a capital collection of tales. Edgar Fawcett has written the "Confessions of Claude"; Harold Frederic "Seth's Brother's Wife"; and Frank R. Stockton "The Hundredth Man," "The Christmas Wreck," and "The Bee-Man of Orn and Other Fanciful Tales." Some of these latter stories are quite up to the best work of this brilliant short story writer. From E. P. Roe we have "The Earth Trembled." The "Van Gelder Papers" and other sketches are bright efforts, something after the style of Irving. Edgar Saltus has published "Mr. Incoul's Misadventure," a work in his customary pessimistic style, which has attracted no little sharp criticism on that account. Augusta Evans Wilson has written "At the Mercy of Tiberius," which is interesting, though in the too inflated style of this writer. "Zorah, a Love Story of Modern Egypt," is by Elizabeth Balch. "Two Gentlemen of Boston" appeared in the "Round Robin Series"; Mrs. G. R. Alden (Pansy) wrote "Eighty-seven"; and the author of the story of "Margaret Kent," a work which attracted a good deal of attention a few years ago, has reappeared in "Sons and Daughters," which is well considered. "Paradise," by Lloyd S. Bryce, "The Fortunes of the Faradays," by Amanda M. Douglass, and "Aunt Tabitha's Trial," by L. O. Cooper, are without special features for criticism. "Happy Dodd," by Rose Terry Cook, is in the usual graceful style of that pleasing writer. In "The Leisure Hour Series" has been published "Pine and Palm," by M. D. Conway. Louisa M. Alcott has written "Agatha and the Shadow"; Blanche Willis Howard published "Tony the Maid," an exceedingly well-written story, and "Aunt Serena." From John Habberton we have "Country Luck," in which there are bits of admirable characterization. Mary J. Holmes has published "Gretchen," and A. C. Gunther has written "Mr. Barnes, of New York," which had the advantage of enormous puffing without presenting any very remarkable reasons for it. "Mahala Sawyer" appears over the initials of D. S. E., and Mrs. Dahlgren is responsible for a novel under the title of "Divorced," while H. S. Cunningham has published "The Coeruleans, a Vacation Idyl." From Mary Cruger we have the "Vanderhyde Manor House"; from Mrs. Schuyler Crowninshield, "The Ignoramuses, a Travel Story"; from Frank H. Converse, "Adventures of Tad"; and from Clara Erskine Clement, "Eleanor Maitland." Bertha M. Clay, a popular writer, wrote "A Woman's Temptation," and Mrs. J. A. Carter "Won by Love." Emily Brodie is the author of "Cousin Dora, or serving the King," Josiah Royce of "The Feud of Oakfield Creek," and Esther B. Carpenter of "South County Neighbors." Mary Greenleaf Darling wrote "Gladys, a Romance," Emily Sarah Holt "Our Little Lady, or Six Years Ago," Miss J. T. Hopkins "Arrowhead Light," Mary Hubbard Howell "Out of the Shadow," and Mrs. Leith Adams "Geoffrey Stirling" and "Madelon Lemoine." Edward Fuller wrote "The Terrace of Mon Desir," Miss E. A. Dillwyn "Jill and Jack," and Rosa N. Carey "Uncle Max" and "Wee Wifee" From Walter L. Campbell we have "Civitas, a Romance of our Nation's Life." Theo. Gift wrote "Victims" for "The Leisure Hour Series," and M. G. McClelland "Jean Monteith" for the same collection. Alice King Hamilton published "One of the Duanes," Maria L. Pool "A Vacation in a Buggy," Melville Philips "The Devil's Hat," and Elizabeth Stuart Phelps "Jack the Fisherman." Henry Peterson gave us an amusing local story entitled "Bessie's Six Lovers, a New York Belle's Summer in the Country." Nora Perry, who is always bright and vivacious and true to nature, published "A Flock of Girls and their Friends." Thomas Nelson Page wrote "In Ole Virginia, or Marse Chan and other Stories," all of which sketches are clever and characteristic. Mrs. Amelia E. Barr manages to bring out her two or three books per annum, and very winning and clever stories they are. They comprised last year "Paul and Christina," "A Border Shepherdess," and "The Squire of Sandal-Side, a Pastoral Romance." Frances Courtenay Baylor published "Behind the Blue Ridge" and "Juan and Juanita"; Howe Benning "One Girl's Way Out," which is instructive as well as interesting to all girls possessed of ambition; Benj. F. Taylor 'Theophilus Trent, Old Times in the Oak Openings"; Florine Thayer McCray "Environment, a Story of Modern Society"; Julia Magruder "A Magnificent Plebeian"; and Grace Livingston "A Chautauqua Idyl," which will doubtless have special interest for the vast number of readers who follow the course of that peculiar institution, the Chautauqua School. Emma Marshall is the author of "Daphne's Decision," and May Agnes Fleming comes to the front with "A Terrible Secret" Martha Livingston Moody wrote "The Tragedy of Brinkwater." Julian Hawthorne, who, considering his father's reputation as well as his own, might really seem to be better employed, is responsible, in company with Inspector Byrnes, for "An American Penman," "A Tragic Mystery," and "The Great Bank Robbery." Bret Harte has written "The Crusade of the Excelsior" and "A Millionaire of Rough and Ready and Devil's Ford." "Bar Harbor Days," by Mrs. Burton Harrison, is a bright book by a bright writer. Sarah Doudney published "Prudence Winterbottom." Christian Reid (Miss Fisher) reappeared with "Miss Churchill," and Edwin L.

Bynner with "Agnes Surriage." "Told at Tuxedo," by A. M. Emory, comprises a collection of short stories. Among anonymous works of fiction are "A Question of Identity," "Cracker Joe," written for the "No-Name Series," "Dethroned, a Story for Girls," "A Child of the Revolution," "After the Failure," and "A Club of One." Among translations, one of the best in the vein of Jules Verne is "The Startling Exploits of Dr. J. B. Quiès," by Paul Célière. A finely illustrated edition of "The Story of Manon Lescaut," by the Abbé Prévost, was published in a translation. Ernest Daudet's "Which? or Between Two Women" and "La Belle Nivernaise," and Henri Gréville's "The Princess Roubine," are the more important modern French novels translated. Of the translations from Balzac we have "The Two Brothers," "The Country Doctor," and "The Alkahest." Tolstoï, who is the present society fad in literature, has been translated in his "Katia," "Ivan Ilyitch and other Stories," "The Invaders and other Stories," and "A Russian Proprietor." From the German of Paul Heyse we have "In Paradise" and "The Romance of the Canoness." Madame Spyri is the author of "Heydi," and any books from her pen are welcome to the child readers of America. Recent translations are "Gritli's Children" and "Swiss Stories for Children."

History.—Works on American history, beginning with the more general, are the following: "Retrospections of America, 1797 to 1811," by J. Bernard, assisted by Lawrence Hutton and Brander Matthews; T. M. Cooley's "The Acquisition of Louisiana"; Arthur Gilman's "The Discovery and Exploration of America, a Book for American Boys and Girls"; W. A. Greene's "Providence Plantations for 250 Years"; "The Kentucky Resolution of 1798," by Ethelbert D. Warfield; "Pioneers of the Western Reserve," by Harvey Rice; "John Anderson's New Grammar-School History of the United States"; "The Pioneer History of Illinois," by J. Reynolds, with a specially complete and valuable index; and Catherine B. Yale's "Story of the Old Willard House of Deerfield, Mass." To the series of "American Commonwealths," Horace E. Scudder has added "New York" and Alexander Johnston "Connecticut." Mr. George Makepeace Towle published "The Nation in a Nutshell; a Rapid Outline of American History." On more local history we have Samuel A. Drake's "The Making of the Great West"; Prof. E. W. Claypole's "The Lake Age of Ohio"; "Annals of Augusta County, Virginia," by Joseph A. Waddell; "A Short History of the City of Philadelphia from its Foundation to the Present Time," by Susan Coolidge; "A Half Century in Salem," by Marianne C. D. Silsbee; and "The History of the Town of Medford (Mass.), 1650 to 1886, with Genealogies of Families, etc.," edited by William S. Tilden. Among the books referring to United States history during and since the war of the rebellion, the following are noteworthy: "The Recent Past from a Southern Standpoint," by R. H. Wilmer, D. D.; "A History of the Negro Troops in the War of the Rebellion, 1861 to 1865," by George W. Williams, LL. D.; "Baltimore and the 19th of April, 1861," by George Wm. Brown; "Drum Beat of the Nation," by Charles Carleton Coffin; "The Great Invasion of 1863, or General Lee in Pennsylvania," by Jacob Hoke; J. S. Mosby's "War Reminiscences and Stuart's Cavalry Campaigns," and a memorial of Gen. Winfield S. Hancock in connection with the "Military Order of the Loyal Legion of the United States." Books upon the Indian tribes include "Mary and I; Forty Years with the Sioux," by Stephen R. Riggs; "The Story of the American Indian," by Elbridge S. Brooks; and Henry S. Welcome's "The Story of Metlakahtla," which gives an account of the expulsion of a tribe of Indians from the British possessions, and which has attracted so much attention as to raise almost a national question concerning it. In history other than American, we have "The Story of Ancient Egypt," by George Rawlinson and Arthur Gilman; "Ancient History," by George Rawlinson; "Modern History," by Arthur St. George Patton; "The Story of Persia," by Hon. S. G. W. Benjamin; "The Story of the Normans; told chiefly in Relation to their Conquest of England," by Sarah Orne Jewett; "The Fall of Maximilian's Empire, as seen from a United States Gunboat," by Seaton Schroeder; a "Young People's History of Ireland," by George Makepeace Towle; "Mediæval History," by George Thomas Stokes, D. D.; "On the Track of Ulysses," by William J. Stillman; "Decisive Battles since Waterloo; the Most Important Military Events from 1815 to 1887," by Thomas W. Knox; "Recollections of a Minister of France," by E. B. Washburne, LL. D.; "The Story of Alexander's Empire" (in "The Nation's Series"), by John P. Mahaffy and Arthur Gilman; "Reminiscences of the Filibuster War in Nicaragua," by O. W. Doubleday; "Brazil; its Condition and Prospects," by C. C. Andrews; and "The Course of Empire," by C. G. Wheeler.

Biography.—Of the making of biographies about Washington there is no end; accordingly we have published last year Virginia F. Townsend's "Life of Washington," and Edward Everett Hale's "The Life of George Washington studied Anew," for which he had previously unpublished resources of no slight value; W. S. Baker's "Character Portraits of Washington, as delineated by Historians, Orators, and Divines"; and John Fiske's "Washington and His Country," which is a reduction from Irving's "Life," with additions. William O. Stoddard has written the "Lives of the Presidents," including Adams, Jefferson, Monroe, John Quincy Adams, Jackson, and Van Buren; and to the series of "American States-

men" Moses Coit Tyler has added "Patrick Henry," Theodore Roosevelt "Thomas H. Benton," and Carl Schurz "Henry Clay." In general biography we have first "Catholic Heroes and Heroines of America," the "Ladies of the White House," by Laura C. Holloway; William Elliott Griffis's "Mathew Galbraith Perry"; E. S. Brooks's "Historic Girls, Stories of Girls who have influenced the History of their Times"; Mrs. M. E. W. Sherwood's "Royal Girls and Royal Courts"; and "Biographical Record of the Officers and Graduates of Rensselaer Polytechnic Institute, 1824 to 1887." The lives of the generals and others who served in the late war include the following: "Memories of the Men who saved the Union," by Donn Piatt; "The Life, Character, and Service of Gen. G. B. McClellan," by George Ticknor Curtis; Oliver Optic's (William T. Adams) "Our Standard Bearer, Gen. U. S. Grant"; "The Personal Memoirs and Military History of U. S. Grant, vs. the Record of the Army of the Potomac," by Carswell McClellan; "Grant as a Soldier," by A. W. Alexander; and John Esten Cooke's "Life of Robert E. Lee," in a new edition. Of autobiographical works and lives of distinguished personages other than warriors, there were published "The Life and Times of John Jay," by William Whitelock; Mrs. Jessie Benton Frémont's "Souvenirs of My Time"; D. Stuart Dodge's "Memorials of William E. Dodge," "Thomas A. Edison," and "S. F. B. Morse" (in the "World's Workers Series"); by Van Buren Denslow and Jane M. Parker, "Letters of Horatio Greenough to his Brother Henry Greenough," edited by Frances B. Greenough; Ben: Perley Poore's "Reminiscences of Sixty Years in the National Metropolis"; C. J. F. Binney's "Binney Family Genealogy"; "Channing's Note Book; Passages from the Unpublished Manuscripts of William Ellery Channing," edited by Grace Ellery Channing. This brings us to the more strictly literary biographies, of which Prof. Charles Eliot Norton's "Reminiscences of Thomas Carlyle" was quite the most important work, and has corrected much of the unpleasant impression produced by Froude's editing of Carlyle's diary, receiving the highest encomiums from both American and English critics. Side by side with this should be placed James Elliot Cabot's "Memoir of Ralph Waldo Emerson," a work of high merit, and one of the few recent American books destined to become authoritative. "John Sevier as a Commonwealth Builder," by James R. Gilmore, is a most interesting biography of the pioneer Governor of the Territory of Tennessee. "Franklin in France," by Edward Everett Hale and his son, strikes the chord of American Colonial history. Mr. Samuel Longfellow published "Final Memoirs of H. W. Longfellow," while Helen Gray Cone and Jeannette L. Gilder edited "Pen Portraits of Literary Women by Themselves and Others," and William H.

Rideing published "The Boyhood of Living Authors." John Bach McMaster added "Benjamin Franklin" to the "American Men of Letters" series; Amanda B. Harris published "American Authors for Young Folks"; David G. Haskins "Ralph Waldo Emerson; his Maternal Ancestors"; and Henry B. Stanton, an old journalist, is to be remembered by his "Random Recollections." Numerous lives and sketches, fair and otherwise, of the late Henry Ward Beecher were published, but the reliable and permanent biography of the great popular preacher is yet to be written. The "Life and Times of Henry Melchior Muhlenberg" was written by W. J. Mann, D. D. Mr. Albert R. Frey, of the Astor Library, published his comprehensive volume on "Sobriquets and Nick-Names." In foreign biography we have W. D. Howells in his charming sketches of "Modern Italian Poets"; "Dante: a Sketch of his Life and Works," by May Alden Ward; and "Madame De Stael," by Bella Duffy in "The Famous Women" series.

Poetry.—This department is perhaps the weakest of any in the literature of the year. A collection of Helen Hunt Jackson's (H. H.) poems and the "Early and Late Poems" of Alice and Phœbe Cary recall the charming talent for versification of three very pleasing writers. Mr. Richard Watson Gilder, one of the very best American lyrical poets, published "The New Day," "The Celestial Passion," and "Lyrics"; Minnie Gilmore, who is a very pleasing writer of verse, wrote a collection of poems entitled "Pipes from Prairie Land and other Places"; Alice Imogen Guiney, one of the more recent Southern writers, published "The White Sail"; Joaquin Miller appeared in "Songs of the Mexican Seas"; while Selina Dolaro, an English actress, did this country the honor to publish here her "Mes Amours: Poems Passionate and Playful," which, indeed, we could have done very well without. Quite a number of writers have grown poetical over places, beginning with A. Bronson Alcott in his "New Connecticut," an autobiographical poem"; and including Belle C. Greene's "A New England Idyl"; Philip Bevan's "Songs of the War for the Union," "The Mystic Isle," etc.; T. J. McMurray's "Legend of the Delaware Valley"; and John J. Piatt's "Idyls and Lyrics of the Ohio Valley." Harriet Prescott Spofford published "Ballads about Authors," and Brander Matthews "Ballads of Books." Ernest Delancey Pierson published "Society Verse by American Writers." Caroline Leslie Field wrote "The Unseen King, and other Verses," and Valeria J. Campbell published "Little Poems for Little Children." Charles Follen Adams gave us "Dialect Ballads," and James Whitcomb Riley "Afterwhiles," a collection of short poems, of which many are also in dialect, and these the best of them. Marietta Holly ("Josiah Allen's Wife") published a volume of "Poems"; Arlo Bates one entitled "Sonnets in Shadow"; Mrs. A. D. T.

Whitney "Daffodils"; and an anonymous writer a volume entitled "The Heart of the Weed."

Criticism and General Literature.—The year presents no important instances of critical writing, and the works included under this head will be rather those in general literature otherwise unclassified. Horace E. Scudder published "Men and Letters: Essays on Characterization and Criticism," and Eleanor Kirke appeared in a volume entitled "Beecher as a Humorist," which gives a very fair representation of the Plymouth Church pastor in that capacity. Louise Chandler Moulton wrote "Ourselves and our Neighbors: Short Chats on Social Topics." The work covers a considerable field of general public interest, and covers it satisfactorily. "How I was Educated" is the title of the autobiographical reminiscences of a number of personages, prominent and otherwise, collected from the pages of the "Forum" Magazine. Robert Collyer published "Talks to Young Men (with Asides to Young Women)"; S. Goodwin brought out his "Sketches and Impressions," and Augusta Larned "Village Photographs." Rose Porter, who is an indefatigable writer and gifted with good taste, published "Thoughts of Beauty and Words of Wisdom: Selections from Ruskin." Griffith A. Nicholas is the responsible author of "The Biddy Club," a work which, if it succeeded in generally promulgatingits theorics, would place the "Biddies" upon a pinnacle of rare delight which would doubtless satisfy even that rather difficult class. Jeannette H. Walworth wrote "Southern Silhouettes," Celia Parker Woolley "Love and Theology," Sarah K. Bolton "Famous American Authors," and Capt. Samuel Samuels an autobiographical work entitled "From the Forecastle to the Cabin." James B. Pond told the story of "A Summer in England with Henry Ward Beecher," and Henry T. Finck published "Romantic Love and Personal Beauty," a work showing great industry and enthusiasm. Henry Giles's "Human Life in Shakespeare" was published in a new edition; E. O. Higginson published his "Life in a Country Village in War Times." Mrs. C. H. Metcalf issued a work entitled "Golden Opportunities in Every-Day Life," and William Mathews his "Men, Places, and Things." R. Osgood Mason, M. D., was the author of "Sketches and Impressions: Musical, Theatrical, and Social." J. Rogers Rees wrote "The Diversions of a Book-Worm," and Margaret J. Preston "A Handful of Monographs, Continental and English." James Porter, D. D., brought out "Self-Reliance encouraged for Young Ladies: indicating the Principles and Possible Measures which will insure Honorable Success Here and Hereafter." Rev. John Philip published "Lights and Shadows of Human Life." S. G. W. Benjamin is the author of "Sea Spray, or Facts and Fancies of a Yachtsman"; Henry A. Beers appeared in "An Outline Sketch of American Literature"; and "The

Sunny Side of Shadow Reveries of a Convalescent" was from the pen of Mrs. S. G. W. Benjamin. Daniel E. Bandmann was the author of "An Actor's Tour, or Seventy Thousand Miles with Shakespeare"; Ingersoll Lockwood published "The Perfect Gentleman"; Rev. J. C. Seymour compiled "Humor, Pith, and Pathos"; while Minot J. Savage brought out "These Degenerate Days." M. Salmonson writes a very comprehensive work entitled "From the Marriage License Window, an Analysis of the Characteristics of the Various Nationalities; Observations made and Incidents told; Facts from Every-Day Life." "The Voice of the Grass" was by Sarah Roberts. "The Vacation Journal, Diary of Outings from May until November," is a very pretty and useful little handbook, containing a list and description of the more common wild-flowers met during such outings. William J. Stoddard brought out "George Washington's Fifty-seven Rules of Behavior"; Helen Erskine Starrell was the author of "Letters to Elder Daughters, Married and Unmarried"; while Mrs. Dora E. W. Spratt wrote "Daylight; or, a Daughter's Duty." Mrs. J. W. Shoemaker brought out a compilation of "Best Things from Best Authors"; Frank Dempster Sherman published "New Waggings of Old Tales"; "Saratoga Chips and Carlsbad Wafers" was by Nathaniel Sheppard; James Morris Whiton published "Turning Points of Thought and Conduct," and A. D. T. Whitney "Bird-Talk: a Calendar of the Orchard and Wild Wood." "Child of the Century" is from the pen of John T. Wheelwright; "Familiar Allusions" was compiled by C. G. and W. A. Wheeler; and "Essays, Reviews, and Discourses" was published by D. D. Whedon. Charles G. D. Roberts is the author of "In Divers Tones." "Breezes from Oak Bluffs" is anonymous; "Modern Viking Stories of Life and Sport in the Norse Laud" is by Hjalmar H. Boyesen; "A Boston Girl at Boston, Bar Harbor, and Paris," appeared anonymously; D. G. Brinton brought out "The Conception of Love in some American Languages"; P. J. Stahl "Her Happy Thoughts"; M. A. P. Ripley "Hidden Homes"; Caroline B. LeRew "English as She is Taught"; and Julian Sturgis "An Accomplished Gentleman."

Political, Social, and Moral Science.—The political and social questions before the country during 1887 being mainly practical, they received more thoughtful attention than those belonging more particularly to morals and manners in the abstract. Thus, J. Watts Kearney published "A Study of American Finance," and John Jay Knox his "United States Notes, a History of the Various Issues of Paper Money." The important question under consideration between Canada and the United States was handled by John Jay under the title of "The Fisheries Dispute," and O. Isham in "The Fishery Question." Charles A. O'Neil wrote on "The American Electoral System," and R. R. Bowker on "Civil Service Examinations." "The Old South and the New, a Series of Letters." is from the pen of Hon. Wm. D. Kelley, the Protectionist leader. Anna Bowman Dodd published "The Republic of the Future," Fremont O. Bennett a study of "Politics and Politicians of Chicago," and Marshal S. Snow an analysis of "The City Government of St. Louis." The temperance question was handled by Rev. G. R. Sikes in "Pen Pictures of Prohibition and Prohibitionists," and by many others. "Antislavery before 1800" is an important historical study by W. F. Poole, the well-known librarian. "Men and Manners One Hundred Years ago" is by H. E. Scudder; and T. W. Higginson published "Women and Men," subjects on which he is fully qualified to write. "Woman First and Last, and What She has Done," is by Mrs. E. J. Richmond. Juliet Corson gave us an economic treatise entitled "Family living on Five Hundred Dollars a Year"; George C. Lorimer, LL. D., published "Studies in Social Life," and Rev. R. Heber Newton his "Problems and Social Studies." Utah was considered by Rev. R. W. Beers in "The Mormon Puzzle, and How to Solve It"; "Social Etiquette of New York" was published anonymously. "Somnambulists and Detectives" was from the pen of the expert, Allan Pinkerton, and Edward A. Rand wrote a deserved tribute in "Fighting the Sea; or, Winter at the Life-saving Station." In moral and intellectual philosophy we have, to begin with, "Morals Versus Art," by Anthony Comstock, a work as to whose importance critics will doubtless differ. Edgar Saltus, the apostle of pessimism, published "The Anatomy of Negation." "A Woman in the Case" was a *brochure* emanating from the pen of Elliott Coues, the Washington theosophist, who adopted this means of warning away the general public from the dangerous study of the occult. Prof. A. P. Peabody published "Moral Philosophy," and Dr. James McCosh "Realistic Philosophy." The questions of capital and labor, and protection and free trade brought into the literary arena numerous writers, beginning with Henry George in the work entitled "Protection or Free Trade," and following with a number of others, bearing critically, more or less severely against or trenchantly in favor of the apostle of anti-poverty. Thus we have R. C. Rutherford in "Henry George *versus* Henry George"; Sister M. Frances Clare with "Anti-Poverty and Progress"; J. B. Miller in "Trade Organizations in Politics," and "Progress and Robbery, and Progress and Justice." L. H. King, D. D., writing upon a side matter, brought out "The Real Issue between the Pope and Dr. McGlynn." Prof. William Oliver Perry published "Capital and Labor; or, the Liquor Traffic considered from a Financial Standpoint." Amos G. Warner wrote "Three Phases of Co-operation in the West"; Giles B. Stebbins came forward with the "American Protectionist's Manual"; and Edward Atkinson brought out "The Margin

of Profit; how it is now Divided; what Part of
the Present Hours of Labor can be spared?"
Henry Wood published a very able and strik-
ingly original work entitled "Natural Law in
the Business World"; and R. S. Hill wrote "A
Chapter on Wall Street, in Four Parts and a
Moral," and Jared Flagg, Jr., "How to take
Money out of Wall Street."

Theology.—There were more books published
on theological subjects than in any other department except that of fiction. A great many
of these were reprints and translations, and a
good many more those dainty little compilations which so many persons affect as suitable and pleasing gifts to the religious minded.
Many of these are published at Easter and
Christmas, which undoubtedly fill their place
and subserve a good moral purpose, but which
need not necessarily be mentioned as forming
any addition to American literature. W. Bacon Stevens, D. D., Bishop of Pennsylvania,
published "The Parables of the New Testament practically unfolded." R. G. Storrs,
D. D., appeared in a work on "The Church of
the Pilgrims"; Dr. Henry Van Dyke, D. D.,
told "The Story of the Psalms"; and "Word
Studies in the New Testament" appeared in its
first volume by Rev. Marvin R. Vincent. Rev.
Charles S. Robinson, D. D., whose hymn and
text books sell between 75,000 and 80,000 a
year, published "The Pharaohs of the Bond-
age and the Exodus"; while from Philip
Schaff, D. D., we had a "Cyclopædia of Living
Divines and Christian Workers of all Denomi-
nations in Europe and America," being a sup-
plement to the Schaff-Herzog "Encyclopædia
of Religious Knowledge." Rev. John Ken,
D. D., published "The Victory of Faith"; J.
A. Broaders, "Commentary on the Gospel of
Matthew"; Rev. Phillips Brooks, "The Little Town of Bethlehem"; and Rev. Arthur
Brooks, "The Life of Christ in the World."
From Daniel D. Buck, D. D., we have "The
Law and Limitations of our Lord's Mira-
cles"; Rev. William Armstrong wrote "Five
Minute Sermons to Children"; James B.
Walker, D. D., published "Philosophy of the
Plan of Salvation; a Book for the Times."
This latter work was from the Chautauqua
press. From Rev. Dr. Theodore D. Woolsey
we have the "Religion of the Present and of
the Future," and from George Dana Board-
man, "The Divine Man." Rev. Samuel Lane
Loomis wrote a book entitled "Modern Cities
and their Religious Problems"; W. W. Everts,
D. D., published "Baptist Layman's Book";
Rev. M. T. Lamb, "The Golden Bible, or the
Book of Mormon; Is it from God?"; Rev. L.
A. Lambert, "Tactics of Infidels"; and "Life's
Problems, Here and Hereafter," was published
anonymously. From Samuel I. Harris, D. D.,
we had "The Self-Revelation of God"; from
Annie S. Swan, "The Gates of Eden"; from
Joseph S. Taylor, "A Romance of Provi-
dence, being a History of the Church of the
Strangers, in the City of New York"; and Rev.

Leighton Parks wrote "His Star in the East."
Rev. Arthur T. Pierson published "Evangelistic Work"; W.C. Prime, "Holy Cross; a History of the Invention, Preservation, and Disposition of the Wood known as the True Cross";
and Rev. W. S. Rainsford published "Sermons preached in St. George's, New York."
W. W. Rand, D. D., issued a "Bible Dictionary." and Daniel March, D. D., "The First
Khedive; Lessons in the Life of Joseph."
Arthur Cleveland Coxe, D. D., Bishop of Western New York, published "Institutes of Chris-
tian History"; J. M. Gibson, D. D., "The
Ages before Moses; a Series of Lectures on
the Book of Genesis"; and Richard G. Greene
wrote "Aids to Common Worship." Rev.
Charles Hale, M. A., wrote a "Manual of the
Book of Common Prayer"; Rev. J. Benson
Hamilton, "Empty Churches and How to Fill
Them"; E. F. Burr, D. D., "Universal Beliefs,
or the Great Concensus"; and James Freeman
Clarke, D. D., published his "Events and
Epochs in Religious History, Illustrated."
Rev. Wilbur F. Crafts published "Talks to
Boys and Girls about Jesus"; R. N. Davies
wrote "Teaching of the Scripture concerning
Wine and Other Liquors"; Rev. Wm. B. Deane
published "Abraham; Life and Times"; Rev.
C. F. Deems, Pastor of the Church of the
Strangers, of New York, published "Christian
Thought; Lectures and Papers on Philosophy,
Christian Evidence, Biblical Elucidation"; and
Daniel Dorchester, D. D., published "The Why
of Methodism." From Rev. Joseph Cook we
had "Current Religious Perils," and from Anna
S. Sadlier, "Gems of Catholic Thought." From
the pen of T. Murphy, D. D., we have "People
and Pastor; Duties involved in their Important
Relations." Rev. Andrew Murray wrote "The
Children for Christ"; Rev. Newman Smyth
published "Christian Facts and Forces"; Rev.
J. F. Spalding issued "The Threefold Ministry of the Church of Christ"; and from Rev.
Sylvanus Stall, a Lutheran clergyman, we
had "Methods of Church Work." Rev. John
Fletcher Hurst, D. D., published "Short History of the Mediæval Church," and Rev. Minot
Judson Savage completes the list, as far as this
class of works is concerned, by "My Creed."

Jurisprudence.—In this department we have
first, in United States law, the "Law of Interstate Commerce," treated by J. C. Harper and
John R. Dos Pasos; Price and Stewart published "American Trade-Mark Cases decided
by the Courts of the United States and by the
Commissioner of Patents between 1879 and
1887." "United States Digests," new series,
reached the seventeenth volume, and B. V.
Abbott published "Patent Laws of all Nations." In State law we have, first, Henry
Hitchcock, LL. D., "On American State Constitutions"; "The New York Excise Law" is
treated by W. E. Bullock; Newton Wyeth
writes on "Essentials of Business Laws of
Illinois"; F. F. Brightly publishes a valuable
compendium under the title of "A Digest of

the Laws and Ordinances of the City of Philadelphia from the Year 1701 to the 21st June, 1887." R. Bach McMaster published an act of the Legislature of New York "To provide for the Organization and Regulation of Certain Business Corporations, with Amendments and Notes." An important work was that issued by Clarence F. Birdseye, "A Table chronologically arranged of the Statutes of the State of New York, Amended, Repealed, Continued, or otherwise Modified or Affected; 1777 to 1886." John D. Works and J. Foster Dillon wrote on "Removal of Causes from State to Federal Courts"; Gustavus Remak, Jr., published "Negotiable Instruments in Pennsylvania"; John A. Hutchison published "Land Titles in Virginia and West Virginia"; Clark D. Knapp wrote "A Treatise on the Laws of the State of New York relating to the Poor, Insane, Idiots, and Habitual Drunkards, with Forms and Digests." Among the more technical works are the following: G. W. Field's "Lawyers' Briefs"; Richard Harris's "Before Trial; What should be done by Client, Solicitor, and Counsel"; C. C. Hine and Walter S. Nichols's "Agent's Hand-Book of Insurance Law"; Alexander M. Burrill writes "A Treatise on the Law and Practice of Voluntary Assignments for the Benefit of Creditors"; E. S. Roe published "Criminal Procedure of the United States Courts"; G. M. Barber furnishes "Guide for Notaries Public and Commissioners"; Charles F. Beach, Jr., wrote "On Receivers." Payne's "Rules of Order and Guide to Parliamentary Law," and "The People's Lawyer and Conveyancer, with Forms," exhibit their purpose in their titles. J. M. Pile wrote "Outline of Commercial Law"; Frederick Pollock, "The Law of Torts"; H. W. May, "Fraudulent Conveyancing"; John B. McPherson, "Competency of Witnesses"; "Legal Hints for Travelers" is by Myron S. Bly, and sets forth the rights of the general public on passenger transportation lines. Lieut.-Col. W. Winthrop published a work on "Military Law," and an abridgment of the same; "The Law of Real Property" was treated by Henry W. Challis, and "The Law of Evidence" by Judge P. Taylor. Emory Washburn published a "Treatise on the American Law of Real Property" (5th edition); Joel Prentiss Bishop wrote "Commentaries on the Law of Contracts. upon a New and Condensed Method." Walter S. Poor published "On Corporations," while "The American Law of Landlord and Tenant" was treated by J. Neilson Taylor. "The Law and Practice as to the Paving of Private Streets" was considered in a small volume by William Spinks; Horace Smith wrote a "Treatise on the Law of Negligence"; R. S. Wright on the "Law of Criminal Conspiracies and Agreements"; and G. Washington Field published "Medico-Legal Guide for Doctors and Lawyers." The subject of marriages and divorces was treated by C. Stewart Welles under the title of "The New Marriage and other Uniform Laws"; by M. S. Robinson in "Marriage and Divorce; giving the Laws of the Various States of the United States, England, and the Continent"; Lloyd A. Parlitt published "A Treatise on the Law of Divorce"; and "A Treatise on Marriage, Divorce, and Legal Rights of Married Women; a Complete Digest of the Statutory Laws of the States and Territories," was published anonymously (Indianapolis, Indiana).

Medicine and Surgery.—This department includes but few important works by experts among the large number of books published on the general topics connected with medical practice during the year. In anatomy, physiology, and hygiene, there were published works by John O. Cutter and Henry G. Chapman. In the treatment of women and children we have: By John M. Keating, M. D., "Maternity, Infancy, Childhood, the Hygiene of Pregnancy"; J. H. Dye "On Painless Childbirth; or Healthy Mothers and Healthy Children"; W. H. Byford on "Diseases of Women"; Rodney Glisan, an authority, "Modern Midwifery"; Dr. J. M. Carnochan on "Operative Surgery and Surgical Pathology" (Parts X, XI); Stephen Smith, M. D., "The Principle and Practice of Operative Surgery"; and A. Hewson, M. D., "Earth as a Topical Application in Surgery." In dentistry there were published works by Eugene S. Talbot, "Irregularities of the Teeth and their Treatment"; J. Taft's "Index of Dental Periodical Literature for 1886"; Wilbur F. Litch, "The American System of Dentistry." Alonzo Clark wrote on "Diseases of the Heart"; Dr. John S. Butler on "The Curability of Insanity"; L. H. Washington on "Headaches"; James Alexander Lindsay on "The Climatic Treatment of Consumption"; E. C. Spitzka "On Insanity." "Massage as a Mode of Treatment" was written by W. Murrell, M. D.; Dr. H. C. Wood wrote on "Nervous Diseases and their Diagnosis"; F. P. Henry, M. D., published a practical treatise on "Anæmia"; Alexander Collie, M. D., issued a work "On Fevers; their History, Diagnosis, etc."; and C. W. Cutler, M. D., "Differential Diagnosis of Diseases of the Skin." Jerome Walker wrote "Health Lessons," a primary book; Albert F. Blaisdell, M. D., issued a work under the title of "How to Keep Well; a Text-Book of Health for Use in the Common Schools"; "A Primer of Physical Training" is by William G. Anderson, M. D., and is one of the Chautauqua text-books; and D. B. St. John Roosa, M. D., an eminent oculist, published an important work entitled "On the Determination of the Necessity for Wearing Glasses." The fourth edition of "The National Dispensatory" was published in Philadelphia; Allen McLane Hamilton published a work on "Medical Jurisprudence"; Henry Thompson, Sr., wrote on "Diet in Relation to Age and Activity"; William Paul Gerhard issued a work on "Notes embodying Recent Practice in the Sanitary Drainage of Buildings."

General Science. — Under this head are included physics, chemistry, the mechanical arts, etc. George Ticknor Curtis published "Creation or Evolution? a Philosophical Inquiry," a work which attracted a good deal of attention as being the presentment by a highly intelligent and cultivated layman of a strictly scientific subject. Probably the most important scientific book of the year—a year remarkable for the absence of any of much importance—was "The New Astronomy," by Prof. S. P. Langley, which appeared first in a magazine, and is indeed rather of a popular form, but is, nevertheless, valuable as exhibiting the condition of advanced knowledge in this important subject. Daniel Kirkwood, LL. D., published "The Asteroids or Minor Planets between Mars and Jupiter"; Edward P. Jackson issued his "Astronomical Geography"; and "Appletons' Physical Geography, prepared on a New and Original Plan," is comprehensive, and forms a useful compendium. In natural history we have "Living Lights; a Popular Account of Phosphorescent Animals and Vegetables," by Charles F. Holder, Fellow of the New York Academy of Sciences. This, although a popular work, affords all essential information concerning the subject on which it treats, and is, moreover, brilliantly and profusely illustrated. The genial John Burroughs writes on "Birds and Bees." Robert Ridgway, a "Manual of North American Birds"; Ellen M. Burnside, "Round Nature's Dial"; and Mrs. Florence Caddy, "Through the Fields with Linnæus." A practical treatise on "Petroleum; together with a Description of Gas-Wells, etc.," by Benjamin G. Crew, and William Burns on "Illuminating and Heating Gas," lead us up to the subject of chemistry. Ira Remsen, M. D., publishes Principles of Theoretical Chemistry" and "The Elements of Chemistry"; Prof. Thomas Egleston, "Metallurgy of Silver, Gold, and Mercury in the United States"; J. Dorman Steele, "Chemistry"; James W. Simmons, "Qualitative Analysis for Use in Schools and Colleges"; Thomas Sterry Hunt, "A New Basis for Chemistry and Chemical Philosophy" and "Mineral Physiology and Physiography"; A. Bromley Holmes came out with "Practical Electric Lighting" in a new edition; and Silvanus P. Thompson with "Dynamo-Electric Machinery." Prof. O. C. Stokes published "Microscopy for Beginners." In the practical arts we have M. H. Ford on "Boiler Making for Boiler Makers"; "The Ventilation and Warmth of School Buildings," by Gilbert B. Morrison; D. H. Mahan on "Permanent Fortifications"; J. B. Johnson on "Theory and Practice of Surveying." "English and American Railroads compared" is by Edward B. Dorsey; "Yachts, Boats, and Canoes," by O. S. Hicks; "Bridge Disasters of America; the Cause and Remedy," by George L. Vose; and C. M. Woodward published "A History of the St. Louis Bridge,"

which completes the list of this class of the arts. "Farm Appliances," a practical manual, is the production of George A. Martin. A. S. Fuller treats of small fruits in a volume entitled "The Illustrated Strawberry Culturist" and in "The Propagation of Plants." Mary Treat writes on "Injurious Insects of the Farm and Garden," a new edition.

Fine Arts.—In this department we have, first, Henry M. Brooks's "Olden Time Music"; A. R. Parsons's "Essay on Music"; James C. Macy's "Young People's History of Music"; "Musical Notation," by Prof. R. M. McIntosh; Langham's "History of Music"; Rev. L. S. Davis's "Studies in Musical History"; "The Musical Year-Book of the United States," compiled by G. H. Wilson; F. C. Mayer's "Essay and Practical Method for Piano or Organ"; and Louis Raymond's "On the Cabinet Organ." Concerning singing, there were published Fulton and Trueblood's "Chart illustrating Principles of Vocal Expression"; Louise G. Courtney's "Hints about my Singing Method"; H. Lottner's "Vocal Calisthenics"; William T. Ross's "Voice Culture and Elocution"; Edmond J. Myer's "The Voice, from a Practical Standpoint"; "How to teach Vocal Music," by Alfred Andrews; and "A Practical Method of Singing," by Josephine Rand. On the subject of painting, Fidelia Bridges issued a second series of her "Studies for Painting"; A. G. Radcliffe published "Schools and Masters of Painting"; M. Louise McLaughlin wrote "Painting in Oil; a Manual for the Use of Students"; Helen M. Knowlton published "Hints for Pupils in Drawing and Painting"; Mary D. Hicks and J. S. Clark published a volume on "The Use of Models"; John D. Champlin, Jr., produced his admirable "Cyclopædia of Painters and Paintings" (4 vols.); and Clara Erskine Clement published "Painting, Sculpture, and Architecture," the three works combined in one volume. Tristram J. Ellis issued "Sketching from Nature; a Hand-Book for Students and Amateurs." Arnold W. Brunner and Thomas Tryon published "Interior Decoration," and Arthur L. Tuckerman wrote "A Short History of Architecture." Among general works of art were "Queens in Art," a lecture by G. W. Chambers; Weldon's "Fancy Costumes"; "Modern Methods of Illustrating Books," by H. T. Wood; "Treasures of Art and Song," arranged by Robert E. Mack; John C. Van Dyke's "Principles of Art"; Sylvester Baxter's "The Morse Collection of Japanese Pottery"; "The Ministry of Fine Arts," by G. Parry; Josephine Pollard and Walter Satterlee's "Artistic Tableaux, containing Diagrams and Text, with Full Description of Necessary Costumes, etc." A superb work was the "Procession of Flowers in Colorado," illustrated in water-colors, in a limited edition of one hundred copies. Lafayette C. Loomis wrote "The Index Guide to Travel and Art Study in Europe"; Edward L. Wilson published "A Quarter Century in Photography";

and Frank M. Gregory "The Photo-Gravure Calendar," with Shakespearean designs.

Voyages and Travels. — Beginning with Europe, we have J. B. Bouton's "Roundabout to Moscow; an Epicurean Journey"; Oliver Wendell Holmes's "Our Hundred Days in Europe"; "Tuscan Cities," by William D. Howells; H. Fry's "London in 1887"; Dr. Rodney Glisan's "Two Years in Europe"; O. J. Butler's "Court Life in Egypt"; S. M. H. Davis's "Norway Nights and Russian Days"; Anna B. Dodd's "Cathedral Days; a Tour through Southern England"; J. M. Buckley's "The Midnight Sun; the Tsar and the Nihilist; Adventures and Observations in Norway, Sweden and Russia"; Francis Wey's "Rome"; and F. Hopkinson Smith's "Well-worn Roads of Spain, Holland, and Italy." Rupert Van Wert also published "Young Folks' Travels in Europe"; William H. Rideing issued "Thackeray's London"; Houghton's "Satchel Guide for the Vacation Tourist in Europe" was issued for 1887; Maturin M. Ballou wrote "Due North; Glimpses of Scandinavia and Russia"; Charles E. Pascoe brought out "London of to-day"; Richard Lovett appeared in "Pictures from Holland"; and Alexander McKenzie published "Some Things Abroad." Lee Meriwether wrote "A Tramp Trip: how to see Europe on Fifty Cents a Day." Of journeys in Asia, around the world, and elsewhere, we have Percival Lowell's "Chosön: the Land of the Morning Calm"; "A Girdle around the Earth," by D. M. Richardson; "Days and Nights in the Tropics," by Felix L. Oswald; De Lancy Floyd Jones's "Letters from the Far East, 1885–1886"; "Wild Tribes of the Soudan," by F. L. James; John L. Stoddard's "Red Letter Days Abroad"; "Around the World on a Bicycle," by Thomas Stevens; Ellen A. Smith's "The Wonderful Cities of the World"; James Harrison Wilson's "China: Travels and Investigations in the Middle Kingdom"; E. Payson Hammond's "Roger's Travels, or Scenes and Incidents connected with the Journey of Two Boys in Foreign Lands"; J. B. Gorman's "Around the World in '84"; A. Feathermann's "The Nigritians" and "The Melanesians"; "Ten Thousand Miles on a Bicycle," by "Kron Karl." Thomas M. Knox's "How to Travel" and "Boy Travelers on the Congo." W. M. Hoyt wrote "A Boy's Adventures in the Wilds of Australia," and Prof. E. S. Morse "Japanese Homes." From the Arctic regions we have Rev. F. E. J. Lloyd's "Two Years in the Region of Icebergs"; Frederick Schwatka's "Children of the Cold"; and W. A. Stearn's "Labrador: its People, its Industries, and its Natural History," new edition. William T. Brigham brought out "Guatemala: the Land of the Quetzal." Concerning the continents and islands of the Western Hemisphere, there were published "Ancient Cities of the New World," by Désiré Charnay; Alice D. Le Plongeon's "Here and There in Yucatan"; Mrs. S. M. Lee's "Glimpses of Mexico and California"; and Thomas A. Janvier's "Mexican Guide," in a new edition. "Capt. Glazier and his Lake; an Inquiry into the History and Progress of Exploration at the Head-waters of the Mississippi since the Discovery of Lake Itasca," and "From the Wabash to the Rio Grande," are descriptive of those sections of the country to which they refer. M. B. Hilliard's "The New South: its Resources and Attractions," and "Explorations on the West Coast of Florida," by Angelo Heilprin, include the principal works of description on the Southern States. Descriptive of American cities and places, we have "The Mormon Metropolis: an Illustrated Guide"; "Charming Bits of Boston Harbor"; "Dictionary of Philadelphia and its Vicinity"; "Album of Cincinnati"; "A Week in Chicago; containing Descriptions of all Points of Interest"; Edwin M. Bacon's "A Dictionary of Boston," new edition, "Philadelphia and its Environs, New Edition for 1887"; "Pleasant Memories of Old Nantucket"; Rev. E. G. Porter's "Rambles in Old Boston, New England"; R. S. Rhodes's "Stories and Sketches of Chicago"; "Appletons' Dictionary of New York and Vicinity" for 1887; and "Appletons' Atlas of the United States, with Maps." Among guide-books were published "Appletons' European Guide-Book"; "General Guide to the United States and Canada"; "Hand-book of Summer Resorts"; and "Hand-book of Winter Resorts." There were also published a "Guide to Europe," by E. C. Stedman; "Cassell's Complete Pocket Guide to Europe"; "Map and Guide to Kansas City, Mo."; M. F. Sweetser's "New England Guide"; "White Mountain Guide"; "Guide to the Maritime Provinces"; and "Brentano's People's Year-Book and Traveler's Companion for 1887."

Educational. — In this department we have, first, the works designed for the use of teachers, of which the following are the most important: T. A. Stecker's "School Tactics for the Use of Schools and Gymnastic Associations"; Southwick's "Handy Helps, Educational"; Arthur Sedgwick's "Stimulus in School." "A Hand-Book for School Trustees" was issued by H. Brownell; Edwin R. Shaw came out with a "National Question Book" and "School Devices"; while there was translated from the Italian by Mrs. William Gray "The Ruling Principle of Method, as applied to Education." "Mistakes in Teaching" is the title of a work by James L. Hughes; Louisa P. Hopkins was the author of "How shall my Child be Taught?"; and J. M. Greenwood appeared in "Principles of Education practically applied," while H. F. Fisk issued a "Teachers' improved Class-book." On elocution and rhetoric there were published, among others, Mrs. J. W. Shoemaker's "Elocutionist's Annual"; John Murray's "Elocution for advanced Pupils"; J. H. Brown's "Common School Educational Selections"; John F. Genung's "Practical Elements of Rhetoric," and "The Study of Rhetoric in the College Course." C. C. Shoemaker appeared in a work entitled "Choice Dialect Recitations"; and there were also published "Young's New Juvenile Speaker," Burdett's "Pathetic Recitations and Readings," and "Little Dialogues for Little People."

Sports and Pastimes.—B. A. Watson is the author of "The Sportsman's Paradise, or The Lake Lands of Canada"; Theodore H. Mead appeared in a volume on "Horsemanship for Women"; and William Edwards wrote on "The Art of Boxing." Concerning angling Seth Green gave us "Home Fishing and Home Waters"; Wakeman Holberton wrote on "The Art of Angling, or How and Where to Catch Fish"; and J. H. Keene published "Fishing Tackle: its Materials and Manufacture." On games of cards, John W. Keller published a work entitled "The Game of Euchre"; "Science in Poker" was issued by the author of "The Thomson Street Poker Club"; "The Game of Draw Poker" was by John W. Keller; "How to Play the Game of Scat" was shown; while "The Whist-Player," by Pole and Cavendish, was reprinted. "Universal Whist" and "The Modern Hoyle; or, How to Play Whist, Chess, Backgammon, Poker, etc.," also appeared.

Housekeeping.—Several works were published on the subject of cooking, of which the following are the best: Hugo Mullert's "How to Cook Fish," the "Universal Cookery Book," by eminent authors, and the "Boston School Cook-Book" by Mrs. D. A. Lincoln. "Family Cook-Book" was the title of a work by J. Whitehead, and the "American Pastry Cook" was by the same author. Lydia Shilaber's "Cook Book; a Practical Guide for Housekeepers," "Mrs. Winchester's Kitchen," and "Canning and Preserving," by Mrs. S. T. Rover, complete the special works on this subject.

Miscellaneous.—Such books as do not come under any particular classification, but are worthy of mention, are given below. The titles will serve somewhat to illustrate the general drift of the great army of writers. Henry B. Carrington published a work on "The Obelisk and its Voices"; John D. Champlin, Jr., brought out "The Chronicle of the Coach"; Rev. Alfred J. Church and Ruth Putnam wrote "The Count of the Saxon Shore"; "Sketch of the History of Yale University" was from the pen of Franklin B. Dexter; "A Bundle of Letters to Busy Girls on Practical Matters" was by Grace H. Dodge; Amanda M. Douglas wrote "Foes of the Household"; Samuel S. Cox published "The Isles of the Princes, or the Pleasures of Prinkipo"; and "Human Faces; what they Mean" was from the pen of Joseph Simms, M. D. A. L Spofford compiled the "American Almanac and Treasury of Facts and Statistics, Financial and Political," for the year 1886; "The Great Image interpreted" was from John Cameron; "Prisoners of Poverty" was contributed by Helen Campbell; Mary E. Bamford was the author of "My Land and Water Friends" and "The Look About Club and the Curious Things they Found"; John Strathesk compiled "The 'Come' and 'Go' Family Text-Book"; "Popular Synonyms; 25,000 Words in Ordinary Use" was anonymous; Charles Remington Talbot wrote "A Midshipman at Large; a Story of Newport and Ocean Yachting"; "Wild Animals in Captivity" was written by J. F. Nott; and Harry Parkes was the author of "The Man who Would Like to Marry" and "The Girl who would not Mind Getting Married." The "Kitchen Companion, a Guide for all who would be Good Housekeepers" was published by the expert Maria Parloa. Emma Louise Parry published "Life among the Germans," and "Two Pilgrims' Progress" was written by Joseph Pennell and Elizabeth Robins. "The American Merino for Wool or for Mutton" was brought out by Stephen Powers; Howard Pyle wrote "The Rose of Paradise"; "The Wonder Clock; or, Four and Twenty Marvelous Tales" was told by Katherine and Howard Pyle; "The World as we see it" was from the pen of Mrs. Amos R. Little; "The Lily and the Cross" was published by E. Mack, and "Under Pine and Palm" was the contribution of Frances L. Mace. "On the Susquehanna" was described by William A. Hammond; "Lights of Two Centuries; Standard Biographies," was edited by Rev. Edward Everett Hale; "Little Flower People" was contributed by Gertrude Elizabeth Hale; and "Satires of Horace" was published by J. B. Greenough. Jesse Bowman Green wrote "Days on the Sea; a Souvenir for an Ocean Voyage"; "Our Party of Four" was by Mrs. H. B. Goodwin; Mrs. Stanley Leathes gave us "Over the Hills and Far Away"; Thomas W. Knox published a work on "Dog Stories and Dog Lore"; "Some Animal Pets" was from Mrs. Oliver Howard; George Fleming published "The Practical Horse Keeper"; and Jessie Fothergill gave us "Border Land," written for the "Leisure Hour Series." "The Monk's Wedding" was the title of a contribution from Sarah H. Adams; "The Emancipation of Massachusetts" was treated by Brooks Adams; and "A Century of Printing; the Issues of the Press in Pennsylvania from 1685 to 1784" (two volumes), was published by C. R. Hildeburn. "Hints on Writing and Speech-Making" was the work of T. W. Higginson; also, by the same author, "The Monarch of Dreams." Mrs. S. J. Higginson wrote "A Princess of Jara"; "It's a Way Love has" is by William Featherstone; and "Fingers and Fortune" was brought out by E. M. Farwell. "The Prince of the Flaming Star" is a fairy operetta by Lydia Hoyt Farmer. Henry Stewart was the author of "The Dairyman's Manual," and "Appletons' Annual Cyclopædia" for 1886, new series, Vol. X, appeared. "Letters to Boys and Girls about the Holy Land, etc.," was published by Theodore Appel, D. D.;

"Arcady; for Better, for Worse," was a work issued by Augustus Jessop, D. D.; "Paradise Almost Lost" was a contribution from D. B. Shaw; "Wild Flowers of the Rocky Mountains" were described by Emma Homan Thayer; the "Seybert" Commission on "Spiritualism" reported; and a "Biographical Record of the Rensselaer Polytechnic Institute from 1824 to 1886" was edited by Henry B. Nason, M. D., LL. D. The second and third volumes of "Appletons' Cyclopædia of American Biography," edited by Gen. James Grant Wilson and Prof. John Fiske, were issued, bringing the work down to "Lockwood." These are illustrated with ten steel portraits in each volume, besides over two hundred engravings in the text, mainly portraits.

LITERATURE, BRITISH, IN 1887. The list of British publications in 1887, while more than usually rich in certain departments, shows a distinct falling off in certain others, notably in fiction and in poetry. The list of publications in theology is also less full than usual, and so is that in science, so far as the number of works is concerned, though the importance of the publications in this department is quite up to recent years; but the celebration of the Victorian half-century has naturally resulted in a very large number of publications in history and biography, which two departments, with that of voyages and travels, will be found the fullest of any.

Fine Arts.—Upon the subject of ornamental art we note first "The Castellated and Domestic Architecture of Scotland from the Twelfth to the Eighteenth Century," by MacGibben and Ross, edited by Boyd, being "Impressions from Copper-Plates and Wood-Blocks Engraved in the Bewick Work-Shop"; an illustrated discussion of "Ornamental Things, Ancient and Modern," by Smith; and a striking and interesting "History of Miniature Art," by Propert, are the principal works in this department. In music we have "History of Musical Instruments," by Hipkins, and Bannister's "Lectures on Musical Analysis." Two works on Greek coins, one being Head's "Manual," and the other, Percy Gardner's "Catalogue," are the only important publications in numismatics. Dr. Doran's "Annals of the Stage" appears in a new edition, and may properly be included here.

History.—The long list of works on the subject of history offers a large number of valuable books from which to make a selection. Mr. Thomas Humphrey's work, "The Reign of Queen Victoria," Capt. Trotter's "History of England under Queen Victoria," the "Third Part of the Greville Memoirs" in two volumes, "A Journal of the Reign of Queen Victoria from 1852 to 1860," Mr. Loftie's "Windsor Castle," Rev. Sir J. W. Cox's "A Concise History of England," Cyril Ransome's "A Short History of England," and Arabella B. Buckley's "A History of England for Beginners," are the more general works on the subject. In its

VOL. XXVII.—28 A

subdivisions we have "Society in the Elizabethan Age," by Hubert Hall, Dr. S. R. Gardiner's "History of the Great Civil War," and "Court and Private Life in the Time of Mrs. Papendiek, Assistant Keeper of Queen Charlotte's Wardrobe and Reader to Her Majesty," by Mrs. Brown Delves Broughton, her granddaughter. The Duke of Argyle published "Scotland as it was and is," and James Taylor "Great Historic Families of Scotland," each work being in two volumes. Mr. Lecky has finished the fifth and sixth volumes of his "History of England in the Eighteenth Century," Dr. E. A. Freeman has printed his Oxford (1885) lectures on "The Chief Periods of European History," and Dr. William Stubbs his eighteen regius professorship "Lectures on the Study of Mediæval and Modern History." The third and fourth volumes have appeared of Mr. Creighton's "History of the Papacy during the Period of the Reformation," and Mr. J. A. Doyle has issued Volume II of his "English Colonies in America," and Mr. George Hopper "The Campaign of Sedan." Mr. C. A. Fyffe presents a second installment of his "History of Modern Europe," in which he traces the European movement from Waterloo to the Paris barricades of 1848. Mr. C. J. Abbey's "English Church and its Bishops" presents a full history of the English Church from the accession of Anne to the close of the last century. The "Rise of British Power in the East," being the continuation of the late Hon. Mountstuart Elphinstone's "History of India," has been edited by Sir Edward Colebrook. "St. Petersburg and London in the Years 1852-'64" contains the reminiscences of the Saxon minister Count Charles Frederick Vitzthum von Eckstoedt.

Essays.—The number of essays proper, though limited in volumes, is strong in the interest of the works, including Sir John Lubbock's "Pleasures of Life," a charming work, which has had already a large popularity; a second series of Mr. Augustine Birrell's "Obiter Dicta," which, while on the same lines as his first pleasing volume and certainly most original, is not quite up to that in acuteness of criticism or interest of subject; and Mr. Ruskin's "Hortus Inclusus," a decidedly Ruskinesque volume, and which can as well be included here as elsewhere. For want of other suitable classification we may note here also Max Müller's "Science of Thought," Andrew Lang's "Myth, Regalia, and Religion," and C. A. Clouston's "Popular Tales and Fictions." Here also may be mentioned Dr. Gaster's "Lectures on Græco-Slavonian Literature and its Relation to the Folk-Lore of Europe during the Middle Ages," and Dr. Augustus Jessop's "Arcady," a charming study of rural life in England. The late Lord Iddesleigh's "Lectures and Essays" are of rather a comprehensive character, including "The Closing of the Exchequer of Charles the Second in 1672," a discourse on "Political Economy," an address on "Desultory Reading," and a good many other equally incongruous topics; and finally among the essays may be mentioned Prof. Veitch's "Feeling for Nature in Scottish Poetry," illustrated by selections, which make it in fact a thoroughly respectable anthology.

Biography.—This subject includes, as usual, men and women of all classes of merit and standing. To begin, we may mention "The Lives of the Sheridans," by Mr. Percy Fitzgerald, a gentleman who has enjoyed access to fresh sources of information. Dowden's "Shelley" and Colvin's "Keats" are two works which have attracted universal attention, and are important contributions to English literature. The new biographical series of "Great Writers" has thus far presented Mr. Knight's sketch of "D. G. Rosetti," Mr. Hall Caine's "Life of Coleridge," and, from Mr. Marzials, an excellent life of "Dickens." Mr. Charles L. Reade and the Rev. Compton Reade have produced what is stigmatized in England as "a rather clumsy compilation made up of hitherto unpublished essays and scraps of letters and diaries," forming what they term "A Memoir of the Late Charles Reade." The book is not attractive as a narrative, and may be properly censured for much of its contents, which should not have been permitted publication. Dr. Charles Mackay's "Through the Long Day" presents a pleasing retrospect of the busy literary life of this one-time popular writer, extending quite through the half-century. A very important biography is the authoritative "Life of Darwin," in two volumes. Lee's "Dorothy Wordsworth" and the "Coleortan Memoirs" are notable for presenting pen-pictures of the literary life of the earlier half of the century. Mr. George Saintsbury has published his "History of Elizabethan Literature," which is exhaustive, and displays remarkable industry and much critical capacity. The "Life and Writings of Ann Gilchrist," by Herbert Gilchrist, the "Life of Agnes Strickland," and the "Life of Rosina, Lady Hamilton," by Miss Louisa Devey, present three important female personages of the century. The last work is a dissection of the character of the late Lord Lytton by the hostile pens of his wife and her literary executrix, and its statements are doubtless to be taken with a very large grain of salt. Still in feminine biography may be mentioned Miss A. Mary F. Robinson's "Margaret of Angoulême," which is her contribution to "Famous Women," and the "Historical Biography of Lady Hamilton and Lord Nelson," in two volumes, by John Cordy Jeaffreson. Prof. Brandl has completed his "Samuel Taylor Coleridge and the English Romantic School," which has been translated by Lady Eastlake. This important work has had the advantage of the use of the family papers referring to its distinguished subject, besides the assistance of many accomplished persons who were able to aid in the accomplishment of a very valuable work. The

story of the short and sad life of the poet Philip Bourke Marston, who was blind from his early youth, has been told in a memoir prefaced to a volume of his sketches entitled "For a Song's Sake, and Other Poems." Many of these stories were published in American periodicals. Mr. Edwin Hodder's "Life of Lord Shaftsbury" is a very incisive and thorough biography. Admiral Hobart Pasha's "Sketches from My Life" presents a pleasant memorial of the deceased English sailor who entered the Turkish services after the American civil war, and remained in high command until his recent death. The "Life of Jabez Bunting," of which the first volume was issued in 1859 by his son, has now been completed by the Rev. G. Stringer Rowe. Of Mr. Leslie Stevens's "The Dictionary of National Biography," twelve volumes have now been published, bringing the articles down to "Craigie." Archibald Ballantyne has published a "Political Biography of Lord Carteret." An entertaining autobiography of Mr. Frith is one of the latest books of the year. Mr. J. H. Lupton's "Life of Dean Colet" is a graceful memoir of the deceased scholar and theologian. The "Life of James Frazier, Bishop of Manchester," by George Thomas Howes, who was one of Frazier's pupils, is a striking biography of a most attractive and genial divine. Other religious biographies are Chase's "Chrysostom," Collette's "Cranmer," and Lee's "Cardinal Pole." Norman's "Corsairs of France." and a biographical volume in Laughton's "Studies in Naval History," complete the list of works to be mentioned in this department.

Poetry.—Mr. Browning has signalized the turning of his third quarter of a century by the production of his quaint but strong "Parleyings with Certain People of Importance in their Day," the said people including personages of a past age, as follows: Bernard de Mandeville, Daniel Bartoli, Christopher Smart, George Bubb Doddington, Francis Furini, Gérard de Lairesse, and Charles Avison. Lord Lytton has published a volume of "After Paradise, and other Poems." Mr. Swinburne has issued no volume, but has contributed to the magazines, his most important work in this direction being "Locrine," which is chiefly notable for having been cabled in full, to the extent of a good many thousand words, to a New York morning paper. Lewis Morris has published "Songs of Britain," and Mr. William Morris his first volume of "The Odyssey" of Homer, which has been sharply criticised by the London literary journals. Lord Carnarvon has also furnished a translation of the same work, both having reached only the first half of it. Robert Louis Stevenson, better known as a writer of fiction, has made his appearance in a volume of poems, entitled "Underwoods," which are pleasing if not remarkable. "Ballads and Poems of Tragic Life," by George Meredith, contains much of the quaint mannerism peculiar to this writer in his prose works, and shows exceeding energy, fire, and poetic insight. Edwin Arnold signalized the last of the year by the publication of a volume of "Oriental Verse," and this completes the rather meager contribution of English poetry for 1887.

Fiction.—The English novels of the year are represented in the first place (first in popularity, certainly) by Mr. Rider Haggard's "She," "Jess," and "Allan Quartermain." Mr. William Black has given us "Sabrina Zembra," which has not added greatly to his fame. Mr. R. D. Blackmore has published "Springhaven," Mr. Thomas Hardy "The Woodlanders," and Mr. Wilkie Collins "Little Novels," none of which are extraordinary efforts. Edna Lyall appears with one new volume, "Knight Errant"; Mr. Baring-Gould has published "Red Spider" and the "Gaverocks"; Grant Allen is represented by "The Beckoning Hand;" Mr. Stevenson by "Merry Men;" Mr. William Westall by the "Phantom City," and "A Queer Race." "Dead Man's Rock" is by a new writer, said to be a young Oxonian. Mr. Hall Caine has published "A Son of Hagar," which is a novel of English jurisprudence, and "The Deemster," both powerful works. Mr. Christie Murray's "Old Blazer's Hero" is a clever mining story; Mr. Westbury offers "Frederick Hazzelden," and Walter Besant has brought out what is considered one of his best novels, "The World went very well Then," in which he displays a large amount of research among the events, customs, and details of life in the middle of the eighteenth century.

Voyages and Travel.—The most important publication in this department is Mr. Jackson's "Dalmatia, the Quarnero, and Istria." The excursion of Messrs. Riley and Owens to "Athos, the Mountain of the Monks," is a very striking and characteristic narrative. Mrs. Craik's "Unknown Country" and Mr. Hamerton's "Saône" are graceful studies, full of personal interest, while "Life in Egypt," by Mr. Butler, and Mr. Laurence Oliphant's "Life in Modern Palestine," are in the same direction, the latter being a collection of letters previously communicated to a New York journal. "Rhodes in Modern Times," by Cecil Torr, completes the list of the more important works on European travel. Three writers have published works on South Africa, namely, Theal, Frelden, and MacKinnon. Capt. C. B. Oliver has published two volumes on "Madagascar," Chalmers has written up "New Guinea," and Messrs. Guillemard and Churchward have chatted about "Formosa and the Navigator Islands." Mr. Julian Thomas has published notes on his personal experiences in the Western Pacific, under the title of "Cannibals and Convicts." The writer is a practiced journalist, and his facts were set down and descriptions written on the spot. Two writers, Rumbold and Simson, have written works on the South American provinces.

Physical, Moral, and Intellectual Science.—There have been few important works in general science, but these include some notable names. Mr. Herbert Spencer has published "The Factors of Organic Evolution," and Mr. E. D. Cope his work entitled "The Origin of the Fittest," which are the contributions of the year on strictly Darwinian subject. Mr. Norman Lockyer is out with a new book entitled "Chemistry of the Century," which is, in fact, a review of the progress of spectroscopy. Huxley has reviewed "Scientific Progress during the Victorian Era," and Sir Henry Roscoe's address before the British Association at Manchester in August was also of that nature. Of the "Scientific Results of the Voyage of H. M. S. 'Challenger,'" four volumes have appeared during the year, three being on Zoölogy and one on Botany. "Railway Problems in Different Countries," by Jeans, and Bucknall Smith's "Cable or Rope Traction as Applied to the working of Street and Other Railways," are important works on transportation. Fowler's "Coleoptera of the British Islands" has appeared in its first volume; the "Dictionary of Plant Names," by Britton-Holland, in its third; and Swainson's "Folk Lore and Provincial Names of British Birds" in its seventeenth. In political science an important work is Sir Charles Dilke's "The Present Position of European Politics." The Irish problem has called forth a great abundance of literary matter, including Prof. Dicey's "England's Case against Home Rule"; Prof. T. D. Ingraham's "History of the Legislative Union of Great Britain and Ireland"; Mr. Shaw-Lefevre's "Peel and O'Connor"; Sir C. Gavan Duffy's "League of the North and South, an Episode of Irish History in 1850–'54"; Mr. J. O'Neil Daunt's "Eighty-five Years of Irish History"; R. Barry O'Brien's "Irish Wrongs and English Remedies"; and Prof. Bryce's "Handbook of Home Rule," which is a collection of articles setting forth a Gladstonian view of the question. Baron E. de Mandat-Grancey's "Paddy at Home" completes the list on Irish subjects. In economics we have Prof. Thorold Rogers in his "First Nine Years of the Bank of England"; Mr. A. M. Smith's "Subjective Political Economy"; Prof. Barrtable's "The Theory of International Trade"; "Common-Sense Socialism," by N. Kempner; and Edward Carpenter's "England's Ideal," and other papers on social problems. Religious writings include Dr. Sayce's Hibbert "Lectures on the Origin and Growth of Religion, as Illustrated by the Religion of the Ancient Babylonians"; Dr. Biggs's "The Christian Platonists of Alexandria"; Dr. Chase's "The Growth of Church Institutions"; Dr. Edwin A. Abbott's "The Kernel and the Husk in Christianity"; Mr. Haweis's completed studies of "Christ and Christianity"; and Dr. Cheyne's "Monograph on Job and Solomon." What is termed by English critics "the most stirring book in the theology of the year," is Mr. J. Cotter Morison's essay toward the religion of the future, entitled "The Service of Man." Something of the same nature is the Rev. Dr. R. T. Smith's "Man's Knowledge of Man and God." The Rev. Mr. Danks has published a volume of sermons entitled "The Church on the Moor"; The Rev. Dr. Hugh Macmillan in "The Olive-Leaf" draws analogies between natural and spiritual laws; and Mr. Arthur Lillie has published "Buddhism in Christendom." In philosophy, we have, first, Part II of Fowler and Wilson's "The Principles of Morals"; then Prof. Sidgwick's "Outlines of the History of Ethics"; Mr. Courtney's volume on "Reconstructive Ethics"; Gurney, Myers, and Podmore, of the Psychical Research Society, on "Phantasms of the Living"; Frith's "Life of Giordano Bruno, the Nolan"; the second and third volumes of Schopenhauer's "The World as Will and Idea," translated by Haldane and Kemp; and Fischer's "Descartes and his School," translated. The total number of new books published in Great Britain last year was 4,410, and of new editions 1,206, being an excess for both of nearly 500 over the previous year. Theology shows an increase of 60 or 70, and there are more than 100 educational works over the product of 1886. Novels, mostly of a very ordinary standard of ability, were up to an average of more than two per diem, Sundays included. In voyages and travels, there are about 50 more than were published in 1886, while in history and biography there are more than 100. Some of the total numbers, as classified by the "Publishers' Circular," are as follow:

CLASSIFICATION.	New books.	New editions
Theology	680	185
Educational	582	102
Juvenile works	459	100
Novels	762	228
Law	73	49
Political and social economy	118	35
Arts and sciences	115	68
Voyages and travels	227	68
History	854	71
Poetry and the drama	82	44
Essays, monographs, etc.	140	285

LITERATURE, CONTINENTAL, IN 1887. As in the preceding year so in this, political troubles and excitement have had a rather depressing effect upon literature. Nevertheless, authors and publishers have been busy to a considerable extent, and in some cases with marked results. In accordance with our usual plan, we give the record in the alphabetical order of countries on the Continent.

Belgium.—History has received a moderate share of attention this year. Protestant martyrology in the sixteenth century is well set forth by M. F. Vander Haeghen, the learned librarian of the University of Ghent, and a like setting forth of Roman Catholic martyrology is promised at an early day. M. Namèche carries forward with spirit his "Cours d'Histoire Nationale," which has reached its eighteenth volume, and includes the history of the Netherlands in the sixteenth century, under the re-

gency of Don John of Austria. Documents and materials of national history have been published by several writers—as by Lettenhove on "Political Relations under Philip II."; by M. L. Devillers, in his "Cartulary of the Counts of Hainault"; by Canon Reusens, in relation to the ancient University of Louvain (1425–1797); by Victor Vander Haeghen, in an "Inventory of the Archives of the City of Ghent," etc. Biography has received a fair share of attention, and to bibliography several valuable additions have been made. The "Bibliographie Nationale" contains a complete catalogue of publications of Belgian authors from 1830 to 1880. A few not very important contributions have been made to philosophical and social sciences, and one fervid Romanist seeks to vindicate the Inquisition, and to prove that the Roman Church has been the founder of liberty of conscience. In the domain of art, M. Rooses's "The Work of P. P. Rubens," a history of this great master's paintings and drawings, with superb phototypes, is very highly praised by the critics, and is a publication of deep interest to all the admirers of that eminent head of the Antwerp school. Educational questions have been ably discussed by Gillet, Keelhoff, Wilmotte, etc., and several interesting works on literary history have appeared. Among these may be named "French Literature of the Seventeenth Century," by the Abbé Stiernet; a short study on "Victor Hugo": a critique on the school of Young Belgium, by M. C. Tilman, under the title "Realism in Contemporary Literature," etc. Flemish literature, properly speaking, has made but indifferent progress during 1887, and seems to be rather on the decline compared with former years. M. F. de Potter is still at work on his elaborate history of "Ghent from Early Times to the Present Day"; the Abbé Am. Joos has brought out "Treasures of the Popular Language," in which several thousands of familiar proverbs and popular modes of speech are given and explained; and M. K. Stallaert has begun the issue of a learned "Glossarium" of terms of jurisprudence during the middle ages, as they are found in the ancient charters and documents of Flanders, Brabant, and Limburg. In light literature there has been the usual amount of production, but nothing of very special moment. We name here only one volume, entitled "Through the Life," by M. E. de Geest, which traces with a powerful realism various scenes in the life of the workmen of Ghent and of the collieries of Hainault. Several new volumes of verse have appeared, and a few dramas have been produced by different authors; among these latter, M. H. Baeldere's historical drama in verse, "Christina Borluut," is deemed to be specially noteworthy.

Denmark.—The loss to Danish literature by death since last year's record has been unusually severe. Just before the close of 1886 the eminent Latin philologist and author, J. N. Madvig, passed away, aged eighty-two. He had been some sixty years professor in the University of Copenhagen, and was known to the world of scholars everywhere. His "Recollections," or Autobiography, and his "Opuscula Academica," posthumous publications, are regarded as no less valuable than interesting. Prof. Johannes Kok, the linguist, died Jan. 20, 1887; Bishop D. G. Mourad, distinguished as an orator and for services to the state in past years, died March 28 at a very advanced age; M. A. Goldschmidt, the great Danish poet and author, died August 15, aged sixty-eight, deeply lamented; and T. Lange, one of the foremost poets and novelists of Denmark, died August 25—he is best known, probably, by his "The Stream and the Ocean," and "Light Nights." In the department of history we note the chief books which have appeared during the year. T. Lund has published Vol. VIII of his valuable "History of Denmark and Norway at the Close of the Sixteenth Century"; Chr. Brunn gives a treatise on "The Establishment of Absolute Government in Denmark"; L. Lund writes in a scholarly manner of the "Real Portraits of Jesus," a volume which has produced quite a sensation in Denmark; and O. H. Aagard has furnished a monogram on Scottish history from 1536 to 1560. In biography, G. Bricka's "Danish Biographical Lexicon" promises to supply a much-felt need; it has reached its sixth part thus far. The popular biography of the great naval hero, Tordenskjold (1691-1720), by W. Carstensen and G. Lütken, with costly illustrations, has been completed. M. Holme and Garde have undertaken to bring out an illustrated record of the recent "Danish Boat Expedition in Greenland"; only the first eight parts have appeared. Galschiot's "Denmark Illustrated" is advancing slowly; part 24 is the latest issued. A. Thorsen has completed his elaborate work on the reign of King Frederick VII. George Brandes, the distinguished critic and *litterateur*, is busy on the sixth volume of his "Main Currents in the Literature of the Nineteenth Century"; he means to publish the work when finished both in Danish and in German. H. Pontoppidan, one of the best among the younger writers of fiction, has brought out two new volumes, viz., "Mimosas, or Sensitive Plants," and "From the Huts," a series of minor tales, in which he depicts powerfully the hard lot of the peasantry. O. Möller furnishes new "Tales and Sketches" of merit, and A. Steenbuch, in his "Rector Lassen," gives evidence of keen observation of provincial life and manners. Mrs. Ina Lange, in a story entitled "A Fate," deals with life a hundred or more years ago. The critics speak in high terms of the book. G. Jensen, in "A Hunting," tells in a lively and pleasant way about the hunter's life and exploits; and the famous poet, H. Drachmann, has just put forth a long story under the name "With the Broad Brush." In the drama, Drachmann, early in the year, wrote a fairy piece, "Once upon a Time," which was well received for its poetic

fervor, and proved a great success at the Royal Theatre. G. Betzonick's "The Soldier" was a still greater success, and roused much enthusiasm by its glorification of the deeds of the army in the first Sleswick war. E. Brandes published a new drama entitled "Love," which met with favor on the stage, and is said to be a work of rare merit. Liebenberg's monumental edition of Holberg's comedies has reached part 37, but it will require nearly double that number to complete the work. In philosophy, H. Höffding has published a large and valuable work on "Ethics," which is regarded as a proper accompaniment to his "Psychology" (1882). Prof. Thomden's "Unity of Matter" is highly praised by the critics. As noted last year, there exists a strong disposition to translate into Danish the writings of American authors, such as Cooper, Ingersoll, Miss Alcott, Henry James, etc. The great poet, Goldschmidt, whose death was noted above, left a number of manuscripts, one of which, "Small Sketches from Fancy and Reality," has been published.

France.—Literary production has been fertile and abundant, and there is no falling off of books published this year. It is simply impossible in our limited space to mention all, or even a tenth part, of the books which have appeared. Hence we shall endeavor to name those only which indicate most fitly the drift or tendency of literature in the several departments. In history, philosophy, and criticism the year's productions are noteworthy; but in great creative or poetic invention there is a marked decline. As one critic phrases it, "there is no doubt that Victor Hugo, Théophile Gautier, and Michelet have carried the most splendid of its radiance to their tombs." Out of the large number of contributions to history we name M. Taine's "Studies respecting Napoleon I"; Renan's "Histoire du Peuple d'Israel," vol. i, which is characterized by all the writer's brilliancy and well-known skepticism; Thureau-Dangin's very able "History of the Monarchy of July," vol. iv; M. A. Sorel's "Europe and the French Revolution"; J. Lichtenberger's "History of Religious Ideas in Germany," from the rise of Wolf and his school to the present epoch of ultra-Romanism and infidelity; G. d'Avenel's third volume of his work on "Richelieu et la Monarchie Absolue"; J. Zeller's second part of his "Entretiens sur l'Histoire du Moyen Age," from Louis I, end of eighth century, to the Crusades; L. Auquez's capital volume on "Henry IV and Germany"; L. Marlot's "Correspondence of Louise de Coligny," which is characterized as fascinating to a high degree; and A. Vandal's narrative of the mission of the Marquis de Villeneuve to Constantinople in 1728-1741. In philosophy, religion, and science, publications have been numerous. M. Ferraz's work on "Spiritualism and Liberalism" is regarded as a valuable and timely, predicting as it does a complete harmony between science and the idealistic philosophy. M. E. de Pressensé continues his vigorous apologetic work in behalf of religion by an interesting volume entitled "Les Antécédents du Christianisme." M. Guyau discourses of "Irreligion and the Future." M. Nourisson opposes evolution in his work "Philosophies of Nature," as exemplified by Bacon, Boyle, Toland, and Buffon. Dr. Paul Regnard says, in a book devoted to this subject, that the epidemic intellectual malady of the seventeenth century was sorcery; of the eighteenth, miracles; of the nineteenth, somnambulism; and that the malady of the twentieth century will be a universal outbreak of carnage. Animal magnetism is treated of fully by A. Binet and C. Féré, and Dr. La Tourette gives a scholarly account of hypnotism and its adjuncts. M. P. Hervieu, in his "L'Inconnu," presents a curious yet interesting study of insanity. A. Laissant, in his book "L'Anarchie Bourgeoise," argues in favor of establishing a great socialist-republican party to overcome the influence of the bourgeoisie, whom he holds to be authors of the ills which have afflicted France since the Revolution; and A. Duruy and E. Maneuvrier discuss freely and pointedly current educational theories. The novels of the year have been much the same as last year's, in quality as well as quantity. The Zola school continues its disgusting work, and seems to find abundance of readers. Paul Bourget's "André Cornélis," a story after the Hamlet type, is highly lauded by the critics, as also are Guy de Maupassant's "Mont-Oriol" and "Pierre et Jean," and M. Prévost's "Le Scorpion." Victor Cherbuliez writes elegantly in his "La Bête," but is held by the critics to have produced a *mélange* less savory than satisfactory. M. de Bonnières gives a good study of a young French girl in "Jeanne Avril"; E. Arène furnishes some gay and pretty stories of the south; and P. Loti presents a series of Japanese romances under the title "Madame Chrysanthème." In poetry the palm is said still to belong to two veterans, M. Sully-Prudhomme and M. François Coppée. The former has given nothing new this year, but M. Coppée has published a charming volume entitled "Arrière-Saison," full of kindliness of heart and genuine sentiment. One of the critics designates him as the French Wordsworth. M. de Rouchaud's "Poèmes de la Mort" are highly commended for artistic execution; M. C. de Pomairols shows delicate sensibility in his "La Nature et l'Art"; M. Henri Guérin's "Pallas Athéné" has been much noticed. He is one of the few young poets who gives promise for the future. M. Samain's "Invitation" is pronounced to be one of the masterpieces of French contemporary literature. Among the essayists who continue to hold high rank are M. Taine, M. Renan, M. Jules Soury, M. Mézières, M. Émile Montégut, etc. The last named has recently published "Choses du Nord et du Midi" and "Mélanges Critiques"; Renan has issued in one volume a collection of his "Discours et Conférences." Two names deserve special mention in this connection, viz., M. J. Darmesteter and M. Eugène M. de Vogüé. The former is characterized as the more intensive and suggestive; the latter more of an artist, more delicately harmonious. His "Souvenirs et Visions," and particularly the pages on the Crimea, testify to his rare talent and skill. The literature of travel is well represented this year. M. Pierre Loti, in his "Propos d'Exil," describes excellently the latest foreign countries visited by him, China, Tonquin, Annam, India, Oboch. Albert Tissandier gives the public "Six Mois aux États-Unis," and C. Bigot tells of his experiences and observations in "De Paris au Niagara." Henri Conti describes "L'Allemagne·Intime"; G. de Molinari furnishes a useful volume made up from letters in the "Débats," on "Panama, La Martinique, Haïti"; Émile Daireaux deals with "La Vie et Les Mœurs à la Plata," a comprehensive work; and Dr. Bernard presents a highly colored picture of primitive conditions in his "L'Algerie qui s'en Va." We may further mention here the "Lettres de Gustave Flaubert," edited by his niece. These cover the period from 1830–'50, and are delightful memorials of a great man. The miscellaneous writings of M. Guizot and his wife have been collected under the title "Le Temps passé." Something also has been done in the way of bringing out new editions of standard works, such as Vol. I of "The Works of Blaise Pascal"; "Select Works of Voltaire," edited by G. Bengesco; "The Works of Cardinal de Retz," in eight volumes, edited by M. R. Chantelauze; and an edition of "Œuvres et Correspondance Inédites de d'Alembert," by Charles Henry.

Germany.—The number of books published this year is very large, amounting in all to nearly 17,000. This includes books of every possible kind, in poetry, fiction, history, biography, the sciences, the fine arts, philosophy, etc. Our record is necessarily confined to a selection from these, which will, however, we hope, give a fair idea of literary culture as well as progress in Germany during 1887. In poetry the publications have not been strikingly good or important. The Westphalian poetess, Annette von Droste-Hülshoff, died prematurely and much lamented. A complete edition of her lyric and epic works has been brought out, and is highly prized. Otto von Leixner, author of "Dämmerungen," makes his first appearance this year, as does also Ernst von Wildenbruch, author of "Lieder und Balladen," in this particular line. The poems of Martin Greif, the Bavarian poet, have reached a fourth edition. Karl Schaeffer and Paul Bähr have brought out two excellent volumes of lyric poetry, under the titles "Heiderosen" and "Neues Buch der Lieder." Several epic productions deserve notice, viz., R. Gottschall's "Merlins Wanderungen," a satire on Parisian life and manners; Johan Fastenrath's "Zwölf Alfonsos von Castilien," a glorification of the Alfonsos of Spain; F. Avenarius's "Die Kinder von Wohldorf," a weird narrative of a fiddler and his doings; Julius Grosse's attractive volume, "Episoden und Epiloge." In dramatic poetry "Vom König," by Paulus Cassel, D. D., pastor of Christ Church, Berlin, is a tragedy of unusual power and effective ethical teaching. E. Bauernfeld, although past four score years, has brought out another volume, "Poetisches Tagebuch," which displays unusual vigor; and M. Bern has made a good collection of German poems from several hundred authors, under the title "Declamatorium." In history, another volume of Ranke's, from manuscripts left by him, has been issued. It contains three long treatises on historical subjects concerning France and Germany. We note only one drama as worthy a place in our record, viz., Ludwig Anzengruber's national drama, "Heimg'-funden"; it obtained the Grillpazer prize this year. The harvest of fiction is unusually large and of a superior quality. Ebers, in his "Nil-braut," opens out a new page in the history of the mysterious Nile country. Though criticised in several respects, this last production of Ebers is evidently a work of great power. Spielhagen's "Was will das werden?" deals with a question of almost universal interest to the human race. The ethical purpose is far-reaching, and worked out with much skill and success. Paul Heyse's "Roman einer Stifts-dame" is admirably told and of noble tendencies; it has appeared in English under the title "Romance of a Canoness"; and his volume of novelettes, "Villa Falconieri und andere Novellen," is praised by the critics. "Arme Mädchen" is the name of a Zolaizing novel by Paul Lindau, much criticised; and a sensational novel with high-flown tendencies, entitled "Die Krankheit des Jahrhunderts," comes from the pen of Max Nordau. Other novels worthy of note are Mrs. F. Lewald's "Die Familie Dar-ner"; H. Heiberg's "Ein Webb"; R. Voss's "Michael Cibula"; E. Marriott's anticlerical stories, "Unter der Tonsur," etc. Numerous short stories, admirably adapted for general reading, have appeared, as also humorous tales and sketches, and a full supply of literature for the young. Among these last are F. Schanz's "Mit Ränzel und Stab," illustrating manners, customs, etc., of the principal nations; V. Blüthgen's "Marchenquell," a collection of the best fairy tales of the Germans; Lina Morgenstern's "Storchstrasse," also a book of fairy tales, etc. In addition to what was said above in regard to Ranke's posthumous treatises, we note that Vol. VII of his "Weltgeschichte" has appeared; it covers the period between Otto II and the death of Henry IV. The great national work of O. H. Am Rhyn, "Kulturgeschichte des Deutschen Volkes," has reached its conclusion; and F. Ratzel's ethnographical book, "Volkerkunde," is completed by the publication of the second part. As to biog-

raphy, we have a number of lives of the famous poet L. Uhland, by A. Rümelin, E. Paulus, H. Fischer, etc. The death of the great gunmaker called forth a volume, "Alfred Krupp und sein Werk"; Prof. Brand has dealt fairly with S. T. Coleridge; and G. Schmeding has published an appreciative life of "Victor Hugo." Three works in literary history deserve to be named here, viz., "Geschichte der Niederländischen Literatur," by Hellwald and Schneider; "Geschichte der Englischen Literatur," by K. Bleibtren; and "Geschichte der Griechischen Literatur," by M. Bender. Eugen Reichel's "Shakespeare Literatur" is an onslaught against the great poet's authorship of his plays; the writer also strangely attacks Bacon's authorship of the "Novum Organon." Two or three other miscellaneous books are all that we have room for. Paul Lanzky furnishes five hundred "Psychologische Betrachtungen," short, aphoristic sentences; M. Seiling has collected some seven hundred utterances of international philosophers on pessimism, under the title "Perlen der pessimistischen Weltanschauung"; and D. Sanders has brought out an excellent anthology of valuable passages from the Bible as well as from the Greek and Roman classics, entitled "Fürs deutsche Haus."

Holland.—Literature in Holland presents little or no improvement over last year's record. In poetry Louis Couperus has given to the public his "Orchideen"; Coens has brought out "Schakeering," a volume of fair merit; and Mrs. Knuttel has favored her readers with a neat and rather attractive little volume. Hardly anything else deserves mention. Few novels have been produced during 1887. No new names have sprung up, and no striking books of fiction have seen the light. For the stage the outlook is better. The dialogues in Mr. Joosten's "Klatergoud" have been deservedly praised; and Mr. Maaldrink's "Jan Masseur" can boast of success too, despite its melodramatic language and situations. In the department of history Captain Vervat has furnished a study on the siege of Amsterdam by the Prussians in 1787, and also an entertaining account of the memorable siege of Ostend by the Spaniards (July, 1601, to September, 1604), the details of which are for the most part taken from the diary of an eye-witness. "Prins Frederik en zijn Tijd," by Major de Bas, of which the first volume has been published, is a work of higher character and claims. It is gotten up in handsome style. "The Calvinists in Holland," by Mr. Geesink, describes the struggle of the Calvinistic Church at Rotterdam (1611-'18), and the energy of the noted preachers, Junius, Plaucius, and Geselius. A monograph, by Rev. F. D. J. Moorrees, on Coornhert, an eminent writer in the time of William the Silent, is regarded as well done. Full justice is meted out to Coornhert as the great champion of absolute freedom in religion, and the defender of the rights of the oppressed. A work from Mr. Krauseman, a prosperous pub lisher retired from business, entitled "Bouw-stoffen voor eene Geschiedenis van den Ned. Boekhandel van 1830–1880," is timely and of real interest to the general reader. It discloses many curious matters in regard to quarrels of authors and publishers, and famous lawsuits about copyrights, etc. Besides "Oud Holland," which continues to furnish many good things respecting the old art and artists, mention should be made of Mr. Bredius's publications about the masterpieces in the Ryks Museum of Amsterdam. The early numbers treat of the predecessors of Rembrandt as well as of the great master himself. Mr. Opzoomer the Younger has brought out a revised edition of the manuscripts of the old nunnery of Diepenveen, and gives many choice specimens of the old vernacular, as well as glimpses of mysticism and life in the cloister and out of it in the days of Brincherink, one of the earliest Dutch humanists (fourteenth century). Mr. B. Hettema is editing specimens of Old, Middle, and Modern Frisian. The second volume is completed. Messrs. Craandyk and Schipperus have undertaken to explore and picture forth the beauties of Holland in a new volume of "Wandelingen." The student, however, will find it well to examine Mr. Beekman's useful books "Nederland als Polderland" and "De Strijd om het Bestaan." The death of Douwes Dekker early in the year is perhaps the greatest event in the Dutch literary world.

Hungary.—Literature in Hungary seems to keep moving at its usual pace. Publications have been comparatively few and not very important. Historical studies have been pursued with zeal, and collections of records and documents have been freely made and carefully annotated by native scholars. Of this sort we note the "Codex Diplomaticus Hungaricus Audagavensis," by Emeric Nagy, the fifth installment of that great work, comprising the period between 1347 and 1352, and filled with the remarkable events of the reign of the House of Anjou in Hungary. Of like value and importance is the "Codex Diplomaticus Comitum Károlyi de Nagy-Károly," edited by Count Tibor Károlyi, aided by M. K. Géresi; Volume IV comprises the seventeenth century, and furnishes a valuable record of history of a great aristocratic family in Hungary. With this may properly be ranked the history of the diplomatic relations of Gabriel Bethlen, a posthumous work of John Mircse, collected in the state archives of Venice, and edited by L. Ovári. Another work, "The Election of Stephen Báthori as King of Poland," is based on documents hitherto unedited and unknown, and is admirably edited by Ludovic Szádeczky. M. K. Thaly's "The History of the Family of Count Bercsényi de Széhes" gives an account of the vicissitudes of one of the richest and most powerful of the Hungarian families until the year 1703. In the way of memoirs we may mention Baron Podmaniczky's "Fragments of a Journal," from 1824 to 1886, containing a large amount of interesting matter relating to social, literary, and political life in Hungary. In bibliography M. Aladár György has done good service by his work on "The Hungarian Private and Public Libraries in 1885," and M. Joseph Ferenczy has sketched for the first time the history of Hungarian journalism. It is very carefully wrought out and highly instructive. The same writer publishes the "Life of Count Aurelius Dessenby," a somewhat famous politician, and the great antagonist of Louis Kossuth. As a contribution to natural science we may put on record the work of M. Otto Hermann, "A Magyar Halászat Könyve," which supplies a valuable history of fishing and its adjuncts in Hungary. It is said to be delightfully written and very reliable as to facts in the line of which it treats. In the *belles lettres* not much is at hand requiring notice. Miss Stephania Wohl's novel "Aranyfüst," or "Goldswobe," is highly praised, and adds to the accomplished writer's reputation. M. G. Csiky (noted in last year's record) has published a new play entitled "A Jó Fülöp," i. e., "The Good Philip," of which the critics speak very favorably. M. Vlassics has given a full exposition of the criminal law in most European countries, under the title, "A Bünkisérlet is a Bevégzett Büncselekvény"; and Mr. R. Rényi has written effectively of "Italian Poetry in the Middle Ages."

Italy.—Literary activity has been of a marked character during 1887, there having been published between eleven and twelve thousand books on the vast variety of topics which occupy attention in Italy. Of this huge number we can of course specify but a small portion at the present time. Ethnology receives attention in Prof. A. Galanti's "I Tedeschi sul versante meridionale delle Alpi." In this able work the writer discusses the question as to the populations of German origin on the Italian slope of the Alps. Pietro Feo's work of five hundred pages, "Narrazione storiche militare" of A. Farnese, Duke of Parma, is highly praised for its thoroughness and for the excellent style in which it is written. Other productions of value and interest are Col. C. B. di Perrero's critical study of Charles Emanuel III of Savoy, and his famous defense of the Alps in the campaign of 1744; Achille Dina's entertaining picture of a youthful Florentine prince, Ludovico il Moro, in the latter part of the fifteenth century; F. Savio's account of the Marchese Guglielmo di Monferrato, influential in Lombard politics in Frederic Barbarossa's time; Prof. Vito Ousumano's documentary history of the private banks of Sicily, a work of real and permanent value, though not yet fully completed. A new work on the Emperor Tiberius, evidencing careful scholarship, and presenting some novel views of that infamous emperor's character and conduct, has been brought out by Prof. I. Gentile, of Padua. One other book on ancient history may be noted, viz., G. Stocchi's "First War of the Romans in Mesopotamia," where Marcus Crassus lost his life, the date being, according to the author, B. C. 54. Prof. Bertolini is busily at work on his " History of the Italian Renaissance," with illustrations; Dr. C. Bertolini displays much ability in researches into Roman jurisprudence and history; E. Natale, in his " Il Ghetto di Roma," gives the result of long and careful study, and presents, as it is said, "a pitiful story of abuses, miseries, and persecutions"; and Prof. G. S. del Vecchio has gathered numerous facts and observations bearing on the family, as regards society and the social problem. E. Checci has written about the great composer, under the title of "Giuseppe Verdi, il Genio e le Opera"; and Prof. A. Favaro is continuing his labors on the life of Galileo. P. d'Ezcola, professor in Turin, has prepared a study of the works of Pietro Ceretti, with a biographical sketch. Ceretti was a Hegelian, and wrote voluminously in Latin on his favorite topic. A. Armetes has contributed a thoughtful production to various sociological questions of the day, under the title, "La Democrazia e la Finanza; Intemperanza e Freni." He advocates strongly reform in several important matters relating to government, constitutional ordinances, etc. Among biographical works may be noted, P. D. Pasolini's "Memorie di Giuseppe Pasolini," noted as a diplomat of high order of ability. Chiola has published the sixth volume of Count Cavour's letters *edite et inédite;* and Ernesto Rossi has brought out his autobiography, in which the great actor gives a picture of the Italian drama during the last forty years. In philosophy we note Luigi Ferri's careful study of the foundation of realism, in which he gives an admirable analysis of both Plato and Aristotle. Prof. G. Touiolo furnishes an interesting study of "Scolastica ed Umanismo," in which he describes fully the two currents of thought, which were contending together at the time of the renaissance in Tuscany. M. Mancini and U. Galeotti have prepared a practical manual of parliamentary usages, which is highly praised and was greatly needed. Two or three good books on political economy have appeared, of which we may specify that of Carlo Cattaneo, which contains portions of a history of Lombardy. Prof. F. Torraca has issued the third and last volume of his "Manuale della Litteratura Italiana," in which are dealt with writers of the seventeenth, eighteenth, and nineteenth centuries. A. Bartoli has brought out the sixth volume of his great history of Italian literature, which covers the period of the "Divine Comedy" of Dante. In fiction may be noted G. Gloria's four *novelle*, under the title, "Spicci d'Amore," Displays of Love; Signora Sperati's "Numeri e Sogni," in which are pleasantly contrasted the ideal and reality in life. A. G. Barilli is author of "The White Blackbird," and three other stories; G. Verga is one of the realists, and writes accordingly about "Vagabondiggio"; and E. Castelnuovo meets with much success in his "Filippo Bossini, Jr." In poetry we must not overlook Dr. D. Ferrari's "History of the Italian Sonnet," which is highly praised. P. Papa, a young poet, has issued a volume of "Madrigali," which are neatly designated as "flowers of field and meadow"; Giuseppi Fracaroli, the translator of Pindar, has published a volume of "Odi" notable for classic flavor and spirit; and Giovanni Franciosi has brought out a book of "Carmi," which justify giving him a suitable position on Mount Parnassus.

Norway.—All the writers of any note seem to have been at rest during the past year. Henrik Ibsen (Björnson's twin brother) has not published anything. He continues to reside in Munich, making only a brief, occasional visit to Norway. Björnstjerne Björnson has simply revised his drama "A Glove," and now, after five years spent in Paris, has resolved, it is said, henceforth to reside in Norway. He has lately been lecturing on the subject of Chastity, and takes the very highest ground. This has led to something of a controversy with Georg Brandes on this rather difficult as well as delicate topic. Alexander Kielland furnishes a drama, "Betty's Guardian," and a story, "St. John's Festivities," which are not deemed of much account by the critics. Jonas Lie has issued a Christmas story for 1887 entitled "A Companionship." It is said that he is gradually approaching Zolaism in his writing, which, if true, is much to be regretted. The two patrons of this abominable naturalism are Hans Jaeger and Christian Krogh. Both these brought out books, but the Government interfered, confiscated the stuff, and fined Krogh and sent Jaeger to prison. Other works of fiction are J. Paulsen's "A Woman of the Future"; L. Dilling's "Gifted," which has attained popularity; C. Flood's "Strong Jansen," a romance based on fact; and K. Glöersen's collection of short stories. Kristofer Kristofersen (who was noted in last year's record) has made his mark in this department. He has published two capital stories, "Leafing" and "Pioneers," both dealing with life in Norway. Th. Klavenås has brought out a drama, "A Forgotten One," and a volume of lyrics and satires comes from the pen of Th. Caspari. The edition of A. Munch's dramatic works (he died in 1884) is not yet completed. In other departments of literature work seems to be advancing slowly. Früs's "Dictionary of the Lappish Language" is about half finished and in type, and Fritzner's "Dictionary of the Old Norse Language" has reached part 2. Bugge's "Researches in Northern Mythology" may soon be expected, and the "Norse Mythology" of Dr. R. B. Anderson (American minister to Denmark) has recently been published in Horn's translation. The "Dictionary of Norwegian Authors," by J. B. Halvorsen, has reached part 16 (Guldberg), and the "Norway Illustrated," of Chr. Tönsberg. has advanced as far as part 17 of the third edition. The account of the North

Sea expedition (1876–'78) is looked for with much interest; only two parts have as yet appeared. Prof. Dietrichsen furnishes a small volume on reform in fashions and clothes; it is said to be marked by good sense and easy application. As a comfort to the doctors, it may be stated that a new edition is under way of Kjaer's "Dictionary of Norwegian Physicians." We close with naming two works of interest and importance, Captain Jacobsen's "Journeys to the Northwest Coast of North America" (1881–'83), and Dr. Carl Lumholtz's "Among the Cannibals," the results of four years' sojourn in Australia.

Russia.—Despite the chronic troubles and excitements in Russian civil and military affairs, literature manifests a good degree of life and activity, as the present brief record will show. Early in the year, January 29, O. S. (i. e., February 12), the semi-centennial of Pushkin's death was celebrated in Russia. This greatest of Russian poetic geniuses foolishly threw away his life in a duel, fifty years ago, at the age of thirty-eight, before he had had full opportunity of serving the interests of literature and humanity in his native land. The anniversary was observed with great enthusiasm by the entire nation, and new editions of his works, as well as biographies, reviews, criticisms, addresses, etc., abounded throughout the empire. We can name now only four or five books called forth by the celebration: P. Ustimovich's "Memoirs," V. A. Yakovief's "Recollections," P. O. Morozof's "Pushkin in Russian Criticism," V. V. Nikolsky's "Pushkin's Ideals," and Archbishop Nikanof's eloquent discourse before the Novo-Rosky University. Count Leo Tolstoi, who has been extravagantly lauded in certain quarters, produced this year his first contribution to the drama. It is entitled "The Power of Darkness"; or, "Tie up the Claw and the Bird is Lost." The critics note with some severity defects in it as regards its tendency and realistic proclivities, yet at the same time pronounce it to be an undoubted work of genius and high art. Much attention has been bestowed upon Tolstoi's other works, such as his profession of faith, "Anna Karenin," etc., and his religious as well as social and political teaching meets with sharp criticism in reviews, pamphlets, and the like. Among dramas which have had good success are Krilof's "The Family," Sumbatov's "The Arkasans," and Kulikov's "The Aunt." Novels and works of fiction have, as in former years, been very abundant. Stchedrin still holds the front rank, and his new series of sketches, entitled "Trifles of Life," furnishes excellent reading. Other writers in this line whom we may note for our readers' benefit are Korolenko, "Sketches and Tales"; Leskov, "Holiday Tales"; Bibikof, "Pure Love"; Madame Vinitski, "Novels and Tales"; Bobourikin, "One of the New School"; Mikhailof, "The Homeless"; and J. A. Goutcharof, who after long silence again

appears before the public; this last holds very high rank among Russian novelists. Prof. Buslaev's "Folk Lore" has been brought out by the Academy of Sciences, and Strakhov has published his "Struggle with the West in the Field of Literature." Prof. Koudakov presents an excellent study of the "Byzantine Churches and Monuments of Constantinople." In history we may note Tcheshikhin's "History of Livonia"; Heyden's "History of Dissent"; Prof. V. C. Nadler's able discussion of the once famous Holy Alliance; I. A. Galaktianof's work in two volumes on the "Reign of Alexander I"; and N. Karéef's "Researches into the History of the Middle Ages." In biography, akin to history, K. K. Zeidlitz furnishes an interesting life of Zhukovsky, tutor of Alexander I"; Shenroch has added to the mass of Gogol literature his "Biographical Remarks"; and Ostrogarsky and Lemenof have written biographical sketches of Pirogof, Ushinsky, and Baron Korff, noted for their devotion to the cause of education in Russia. Here also may be mentioned a work which is under way, on a grand scale, viz., "Critico-Biographical Dictionary of Russian Writers and Savants," by S. A. Vengerof. In the necrology of the year must be noted the death of Mikhail N. Katkof, editor of the "Moscow Gazette," intensely devoted to Slavic unity, and consequently high in favor with the Emperor; the premature passing away of the poet S. Y. Nadson, who, although only twenty-four, had already attained eminence, and the death of P. V. Annenkof, distinguished for critical and biographical work, at the age of seventy-six.

Spain.—Spanish literature in several departments has exhibited more than usual activity, and the number of books published has been large. Secular education seems to be bearing good fruit. Historical and other compilations are on the increase, and the Royal Academy publishes regularly its monthly "Boletin," the tenth volume of which contains several remarkable papers on subjects connected with the history and archæology of the peninsula. Balaquer has brought out the ninth and last volume of his "Historia de Catuloña"; Señor Castelar, the far-famed orator, furnishes a new volume, "Galería Histórica de Mugeres Célebres," highly spoken of by the critics; and Sandoval gives an essay on the middle ages in Spain. Local history, archæology, and numismatics have received a fair share of attention; and geography and travels furnish a few but not important books. Poetry, lyrical and dramatic, prospers as in former years. New devotees of the muse are numerous, and the outlook is encouraging. Among these may be named Don A. C. Y. Navarro, a brilliant writer in prose as well as verse, in his "Literary Pastimes"; Cristino Murciano, in his "Drama of the Cross," a short narrative poem describing the passion of our Saviour; Vincente Colorado, in his light, airy, graceful poems, "Kisses and

Nibbles"; A. Martin, in his "La Extraviada," etc. Novel writing is largely practiced, and seems to be on the increase. Don Luis Alfonso's stories represent the beastly proclivities of the Zola French school. Don Baltasar Ortez de Zárate has published "Los de Gumia," lauded by the critics for its ability, but yet of very doubtful moral tendency. Doña E. P. Bazan, noted last year for her contributions, has not produced any new work. The sixth volume of Don José M. de Pareda's collected works has been issued, under the title "Types and Landscapes"; Pareda is generally acknowledged to be a consummate artist. Other names of less note we pass by. Philology has made some advance, and Señor Echegaray has undertaken to compile an etymological dictionary of the Spanish language. Two parts have already appeared. At Barcelona the issue of new books illustrated by native artists is on the increase. In addition to two more volumes of the "España Monumental" (that splendid work noted in former records), there have been issued Puiggará's "Monografie del Traje," Sala's "Nuevas Fabulas," with one hundred and forty etchings, Cardenas's "El Arte en la Sociedad," and Ixart's "El Año Passado, Letras y Artes en Barcelona." In general literature Zuloaga's treatise, "La Nuevas Ciencia Penal," treats with critical acumen of the genesis of the new school, crime and the criminal, punishment and trial. Señor Rubira has undertaken to prepare a series of biographical studies of selected eminent public men, and Señor Rahola has made a useful contribution to Spanish political economy in the sixteenth and seventeenth centuries. A collection of inedited poetry, chiefly satirical, has been made by Bartolomé and Lupercio Argendolas. The critics regard it as an admirable help to the study of manners and customs in the first half of the seventeenth century.

Sweden.—Literature in Sweden during 1887 presents much the same general characteristics as were noted in last year's records. Strindberg, the representative of the Zola carnalistic school, and a thorough pessimist, has not produced much, for the significant and sufficient reason that no publisher dares to print such books as he is in the habit of writing. One of his works, entitled "The Father," has been dramatized and put upon the stage by the author himself. Two of the best novels of the year are "Marianne," by Ernst Ahlgren, and "Autumn Storms," by Mathilda Ross. Women, it may be noted, show themselves to be specially active in literature in Sweden. Besides Frederika Bremer and others who are known to Americans, a younger generation is making its mark, such as Mrs. Agrell, Mrs. Benedixon, Amalia Fahlstedt, Mrs. Edgren, Hilma Strindberg, etc. A. Fahlstedt has published a collection of stories called "Ears and Straw"; Hilma Strindberg, in her book "From the West," describes life and manners in the western part of Sweden. Georg Nordesvan, a

writer of some note, has brought out a volume of short stories, entitled "Amusements," and G. af Geijerstam, in general of the Strindberg school, has published two stories, "Until Further Notice," and "Pastor Hallin." F. Hedberg is credited with a large volume, in which is described life in Stockholm and its surroundings. His majesty, King Oscar, has issued a new edition of his poems and speeches, and Count Snoilsky has made a charming collection of poems under the title "Swedish Pictures." A. Ahnfelt (noted last year) has brought to a completion his work on the artists of Europe. The "Swedish Encyclopædia" is nearly finished, Vol. XI having recently been published. A. Nyström, the eminent philosopher, has brought out Vol. II of his valuable "General History of Culture." Two or three works of travel may be mentioned in conclusion: S. Hedin's "Journey in Persia, Mesopotamia, and the Caucasus"; G. Bövallins's "Travels in Central America"; and Vol. I of P. Möller's "Three Years in Congo."

LOUISIANA. State Government.—The following were the State officers during the year: Governor, Samuel D. McEnery, Democrat; Lieutenant-Governor, Clay Knobloch; Secretary of State, Oscar Arroyo; Auditor, Ollie B. Steele; Treasurer, Edward A. Burke; Attorney-General, Milton J. Cunningham; Superintendent of Public Education, Warren Easton; Register of Lands, J. L. Lobdell; Commissioner of Agriculture, Thompson J. Bird; Commissioner of Immigration, W. H. Harris; Chief-Justice of the Supreme Court, Edward Bermudez; Associates, Félix P. Poché, Robert B. Todd, Lynn B. Watkins, and Charles E. Fenner.

Finances.—The consolidated debt of the State, bearing 4 per cent. interest, amounts to over $15,000,000, and is constantly increasing, as, in the absence of any provision to meet accruing interest, it is paid by further borrowing. The bonds constituting this debt are quoted at 85. In addition to these there is another class of bonds, called "baby-bonds," amounting to over $1,400,000, on which interest has been unpaid for some time. Another increase in the debt is produced by an excess of annual appropriations over the revenues for the past four years. For 1884 there are unpaid warrants outstanding to the amount of $104,212; for 1885, $162,980; for 1886, $218,148; and a larger sum for 1887. This unfavorable showing is made in spite of the fact that the rate of taxation—6 mills—is higher than in any other Southern State, except Alabama, and that the assessed valuation is constantly increasing, being over $217,000,000 for 1887, or $4,000,000 in excess of 1886.

Education.—The public-school system of the State is acknowledged to be inefficient. Although the number of attendants is increasing, the additions do not keep pace with the growth of the school population. Instruction is given on an average about four months in the year, in inadequate and ill-equipped buildings. The number of illiterate voters has grown from 102,932 in 1880 to 112,411 in 1886; the number that can write has fallen from 113,895 to 105,426 in the same time. Over 80 per cent. of these illiterates belong to the colored population. The State University is declining from lack of financial support. In order to meet expenses, the chair of Ancient Languages was abolished in 1885, and the salaries of the other instructors reduced. The fund available for annual expenses is only about $24,500, of which $10,000 is the annual appropriation of the Legislature. Since 1883 the attendance has diminished from 200 to 69 at the session of this year.

Decisions.—The State Supreme Court was called upon during the year to decide on the constitutionality of a number of important laws of the last General Assembly. The Sunday law, closing all places of business, except certain specified classes, from midnight Saturday till midnight Sunday, was declared to be valid, and an act organizing the northeastern river parishes into the Fifth Levee District, and giving commissioners of the district power to levy a 5-mill tax for levee purposes, was also sustained. Another decision denies that prescription can run against city or State taxes legally assessed. The act of 1884, known as the " iron-clad " act, relating to tax-titles, was likewise upheld. This act provided that the property the State had acquired from tax-sales, its title to which was not considered complete, should be advertised and sold, and that the deed made in conformity with those sales should be conclusive evidence that no defect existed in the procedure by which the State acquired the property. The act applied to property incumbered with taxes prior to the Constitution of 1879, a large amount of which had been bid in by the State. It was contended that this method of curing defects was virtually a taking of property without due process of law, and, therefore, unconstitutional, an opinion that did not prevail. The Sunday law came up for consideration by the court a second time during the year, on the question whether it applied to the public markets of New Orleans and other cities. Among the industries excepted from the operation of the act are enumerated " newspaper-offices, printing-offices, book-stores, drug-stores, apothecary shops, public and private markets, bakeries, dairies, livery-stables, railroads," etc., and it was contended that under this exception any business whatever could be conducted in a public market on Sunday even if forbidden elsewhere. The court, however, decided that the law was intended to confer no special privileges upon any one locality, as that of a public market, and that a grocery stand, or any business not appertaining to an ordinary private market, could not be maintained within the limits of a public market, if forbidden outside of such market.

The ten-hour law, applying to women and children under eighteen years of age, went into operation at the beginning of the year. Its immediate effect was to cause a reduction of wages among the employés of the various mills and manufactories of the State.

Railroads.—Sixty-five miles of new road were constructed during the year upon four different lines. The development of the northern part of the State has been heretofore retarded by insufficient railroad facilities; but plans perfected during the year insure considerable railroad construction in that region in the near future.

Sugar.—The following resolutions, adopted at a meeting of the Louisiana Sugar-Planters Association during the year, represent the position of the State leaders in this industry on the question of protection.

Whereas, the sugar-planters of Louisiana believe that the sugar industry of Louisiana in particular, and of the United States in general, is entitled to protection against the lower forms of labor engaged in the industry elsewhere, and also that all other industries, employing free American laborers, are entitled to like protection ;

Resolved, That we do not propose to be sacrificed to meet any political emergency, and, while holding fast to the tenets of our political faith, shall seek such alliances as may insure us justice.

Resolved, That the internal revenue system of the country, a product of the civil war, and no longer necessary, and contrary to the genius of our free institutions, is the principal cause of surplus revenue, and should be abolished.

Cotton.—The cotton-crop of the State for 1887 is estimated at 464,802 bales, produced from a total acreage of 1,025,000 acres.

Levees.—Through the aid of the Federal Government in its work of improving the navigation of the Mississippi river, Louisiana is in a position to look forward to a complete protection against overflow within the next few years. According to the reports of the State Board of Engineers, the expenditures for levee purposes by the State for the two years ending April 20, 1884, were $756,470. During that time the allotments by the Mississippi River Commission were $750,000 for closing the gaps in the levees between the mouth of Red river and Cypress Creek, the Tensas Basin, and $110,000 for closing gaps in Pointe Coupée parish. During the two years following, the expenditures by the State were $717,493, and the Federal Government expended $262,869.70 on similar work in the State. A further allotment was made of $321,-000 in July for levees in Louisiana by the River Commission, and $400,000 was also allotted out of the unexpended balances prior to that time.

Political.—At the close of the year a lively political contest, which began in August, was still in progress between Governor McEnery and Ex-Governor Francis T. Nichols, to secure the gubernatorial nomination from the Democratic State Convention in January, 1888. A large number of delegates were chosen during December, the majority of whom were claimed to be adherents of Gen. Nichols.

On August 2, Col. E. W. Robertson, representative in Congress from the sixth district, died, and an election was ordered on November 1 to fill the vacancy. Col. R. M. Robertson, a Democrat, was elected at that time over John Yoist, Republican, by 4,156 majority.

LOYAL LEGION. This is an association of officers and honorably discharged officers of the army, navy, marine corps, and volunteers, organized to commemorate the services, perpetuate the memory, and afford relief to those who served in the suppression of the rebellion of 1861–'65 (a roll of honor). Its official title is MILITARY ORDER OF THE LOYAL LEGION OF THE UNITED STATES. It is purely non-sectarian and non-political, and is not secret, although none but Companions are permitted to be present at business meetings. It had its inception in Philadelphia, Pa., in the spring of 1865, the three founders being Brevet-Lieut.-Col. Samuel B. Wylie Mitchell, Surgeon Eighth Pennsylvania Cavalry, Lieut.-Col. Thomas Ellwood Zell, Third Battalion Pennsylvania Infantry, and Capt. Peter D. Keyser, M. D., Ninety-first Pennsylvania Infantry, who were subsequently numbered, respectively, 1, 2, and 3 of the Order. These gentlemen met in the office of Lieut.-Col. Zell on the morning of April 15, 1865, and, after conferring over the awful calamity of the assassination of President Abraham Lincoln, determined to call a meeting of all the officers and ex-officers in the city, to express their horror of the act and sympathy toward the family and country, and to form a society on the plan of the Society of the Cincinnati. The meeting was called, and steps taken for the formation of the society, from which the Order grew. The first regular meeting, at which Companions were elected, was held April 20, and, subsequently, meetings were held July 26 and September 6, and later. The first accredited body, the Commandery of the State of Pennsylvania, was instituted to date April 15, 1865, and a constitution was adopted. Lieut.-Col. Zell was elected Acting-Commander May —, and Brevet-Lieut.-Col. Mitchell, Secretary, May 17, Acting-Recorder July 21, and Recorder November 1. The first Commander, Maj.-Gen. George Cadwalader, United States Volunteers, was elected Nov. 4, 1865. Since April, 1865, Commanderies, one only for a State, located in the principal city thereof, have been instituted, making a total of seventeen, in the order named, as follow:

1. Commandery of the State of Pennsylvania, instituted April 15, 1865. Headquarters, Philadelphia, Pa.

2. Commandery of the State of New York, instituted Jan. 17, 1866. Headquarters, New York city.

3. Commandery of the State of Maine, instituted April 25, 1866. Headquarters, Portland, Me.

4. Commandery of the State of Massachusetts, instituted March 4, 1868. Headquarters, Boston, Mass.

5. Commandery of the State of California, instituted April 12, 1871. Headquarters, San Francisco, Cal.

6. Commandery of the State of Wisconsin, instituted May 15, 1874. Headquarters, Milwaukee, Wis.

7. Commandery of the State of Illinois, instituted May 8, 1879. Headquarters, Chicago, Ill.

8. Commandery of the District of Columbia, instituted Feb. 1, 1882. Headquarters, Washington, D. C.

9. Commandery of the State of Ohio, instituted May 3, 1882. Headquarters, Cincinnati, Ohio.

10. Commandery of the State of Michigan, instituted Feb. 4, 1885. Headquarters, Detroit, Mich.

11. Commandery of the State of Minnesota, instituted May 6, 1885. Headquarters, St. Paul, Minn.

12. Commandery of the State of Oregon, instituted May 6, 1885. Headquarters, Portland, Oregon.

13. Commandery of the State of Missouri, instituted Oct. 21, 1885. Headquarters, St. Louis, Mo.

14. Commandery of the State of Nebraska, instituted Oct. 21, 1885. Headquarters, Omaha, Neb.

15. Commandery of the State of Kansas, instituted April 22, 1886. Headquarters, Leavenworth, Kan.

16. Commandery of the State of Iowa, instituted Oct. 20, 1886. Headquarters, Des Moines, Iowa.

17. Commandery of the State of Colorado, instituted June 1, 1887. Headquarters, Denver, Col.

Commandery-in-Chief, instituted Oct. 21, 1885. Headquarters, Philadelphia, Pa.

These Commanderies have had such eminent Commanders as Admiral David G. Farragut, U. S. N.; Gen. Ulysses S. Grant, U. S. A.; Gen. William T. Sherman, U. S. A.; Maj.-Gen. John M. Schofield, U. S. A.; Maj.-Gen. Henry W. Slocum, U. S. V., and Ex-President, Brevet-Maj.-Gen. Rutherford B. Hayes, U. S. V. At the institution of the Order, the Commandery of the State of Pennsylvania was constituted the Acting Commandery-in-Chief, and had as its only Commanders—

1. Maj.-Gen. George Cadwalader, U. S. V., elected Nov. 4, 1865.

2. Maj.-Gen. Winfield S. Hancock, U. S. A., elected June 5, 1879.

This observance continued until Oct. 21, 1885, when a National Commandery was organized, known as the Commandery-in-Chief, which has had as its only Commanders—

1. Maj.-Gen. Winfield S. Hancock. U. S. A., elected Oct. 21, 1885, and upon his death,

2. Lieut.-Gen. Philip H. Sheridan, U. S. A., elected Oct. 20, 1886.

This is the chief executive and supreme judicial body, and is composed of the Commanders, Senior Vice-Commanders, Junior Vice-Commanders, and Recorders, past and present, of State Commanderies. It assembles once a year, usually in October, at Philadelphia, Pa., the Headquarters of the Order. There is also a Congress of the Order, composed of the Commander-in-chief, Recorder-in-chief, and three representatives from each State Commandery, which assembles once in four years, under the auspices of some one of the State Commanderies. The quadrennial Congresses of the Order have been held as follow:

First, Philadelphia, April 9, 1869; second, Philadelphia, April 15, 1873; second adjourned, New York, December 10, 1873; third, Boston, April 11, 1877; fourth, Philadelphia, April 13, 1881; fifth, Chicago, April 15, 1885. The sixth congress is to be held in Cincinnati, April 10, 1889.

This is a legislative body, having power to revise the constitution and provide for the government of the Order. Members of the Order, called Companions, are of three classes:

First Class.—Commissioned officers and honorably discharged commissioned officers of the United States army, navy, and marine corps, regular or volunteer, including officers of assimilated or corresponding rank by appointment of the Secretary of War or Secretary of the Navy, who were actually engaged in the suppression of the rebellion, whether so engaged as commissioned officers, non-commissioned officers, warrant officers, or enlisted men. Also the eldest direct male lineal descendants, or male heirs in collateral branches, or of officers who died prior to the 31st day of December, 1885, who at the time of death would have been eligible.

Second Class.—The eldest sons, twenty-one years of age, of living original Companions of the First class. Upon the death of their progenitors they become Companions of the First class.

Third Class.—Civilians of eminence, who, during the rebellion, were distinguished for loyalty.

All Companions are elected through Commanderies by ballot, after having been duly announced by printed circular, with their record, and passed upon by a committee of investigation. The admission-fee is at least twenty-five dollars, and the annual assessment at least five dollars, which includes the use of the diploma and insignia. The former is signed both by the Commander and Recorder-in-chief. The insignia is a cross of eight points, gold and enamel, with rays forming a star, and pendant from a silk ribbon of the national colors. In the center, on the obverse side, is the motto, "*Lex Regit Arma Tuentur*" ("Law rules, arms defend"); on the reverse, "M. O. Loyal Legion, U. S., MDCCCLXV." Both the diploma and insignia bear a number corresponding to that of the registered number of the Companion to whom they are issued. When a Companion is not on duty, and as a medium for recognition, a small tricolored silk rosette is

worn on the lapel of the coat. There is no uniform, but on occasions of ceremony Companions may wear the uniform of the rank they held while in service.

The officers of State Commanderies, who are elected annually in May, are: Commander, Senior Vice-Commander, Junior Vice-Commander, Recorder, Registrar, Treasurer, Chancellor, Chaplain, and a Council of five, which officers also constitute a board of officers. There are corresponding officers of the National Commandery, who are styled "in-chief," and are elected every four years. The constitution of the Order provides that State Commanderies shall assemble at least once a year for the election of officers, and as often as prescribed by their respective by-laws, in several monthly meetings, and after the transaction of business either a banquet or a lunch is served, enlivened by the singing of army songs, the recounting of personal reminiscences of the war, and a military paper is usually read. The present membership of the order is 4,800.

As to the matter of relief, some of the Commanderies have accumulated a considerable fund for that purpose, although the *personnel* is such that as yet there has been comparatively little demand for pecuniary assistance. The general Headquarters of the Order are at No. 723 Walnut Street, Philadelphia, Pa., and many of the Commanderies—notably Pennsylvania, New York, Massachusetts, Illinois, Ohio, and Wisconsin—have permanent Headquarters open daily, where may be found valuable military libraries, war relics, and albums of photographs relating to the war, and portraits of Companions. The Order is erroneously considered by some as exclusive; but no worthy and eligible candidate is ever refused admission, the chief object being to maintain a representative body of the best element in the generation that successfully fought the war for the Union. (See colored plate, page 829.)

LUTHERANS. The Evangelical Lutheran Church in America has had an uninterrupted history of more than two hundred and fifty years, and is to-day one of the most rapidly-increasing communions of Protestants in this country. The statistics for 1887 show a larger increase than for several previous years. According to the best authorities the net increase for the year is 193 ministers, 332 congregations, and 47,261 communicant members, the total communicant membership being now nearly if not quite 1,000,000, and the baptized membership not less than three times that number. The rapid increase of the Church is due to the vast immigration of Germans, Swedes, Norwegians, Danes, Finns, and Icelanders, a large majority of whom are Lutherans, as well as to the Church's increased activity in the work of home missions. The Lutheran Church in this country is divided into four general bodies besides eleven independent synods, a statistical summary of which is as follows: 57 synods, 4,188 ministers, 7,478 congregations, and 991,722 members; 23 theological seminaries and theological departments in colleges, 22 colleges, 85 academies and ladies' seminaries, and 48 benevolent institutions. The growth of the Lutheran Church in America by decades during the past sixty-five years is indicated in the following table:

YEAR.	Synods.	Ministers.	Congregations.	Members.
1823	6	175	900	88,086
1833	10	337	1,017	59,828
1843	15	430	1,371	147,000
1853	25	900	1,750	200,000
1863	42	1,421	2,677	265,217
1873	51	2,809	4,115	455,085
1883	54	3,550	5,884	823,296
1887	57	4,186	7,473	991,722

Three of the four general bodies of Lutherans held conventions during the year.

General Synod.—This body, organized in 1821, is composed of twenty-three district synods. The following educational and benevolent institutions exist within the bounds of this body: Five theological seminaries and theological departments at Hartwick Seminary, N. Y., Gettysburg and Selinsgrove, Pa., Springfield, Ohio, and Chicago, Ill., having 66 students, 15 professors and property valued at $100,000; 4 colleges at Gettysburg, Pa., Springfield, Ohio, Carthage, Ill., Atchison, Kan., having 521 students, 32 professors, and property valued at $330,000; besides 3 academies, 2 ladies' seminaries, and 2 orphans' homes. The General Synod held its thirty-third biennial convention in Omaha, Neb., June 1 to 13, 1887. There were present 192 clerical and lay delegates. The Rev. S. A. Ort, D. D., President of Wittenberg College, Springfield, Ohio, was elected president. The Board of Foreign Missions reported concerning the missions in India and Africa. In India there are 4 missionaries, 2 native pastors, 3 evangelists, 7 catechists, 5 Bible and tract colporteurs, 98 village preachers, 2 chapels, 84 prayer-houses, 314 villages containing native Christians, 9,530 baptized members, 5,816 communicants, 2,560 accessions during the two years. Elementary schools, 145; teachers, 147; pupils, 2,178. Luther Mission College: Teachers, 11; students, 416. Sunday-schools, 5; teachers, 27; pupils, 570. In the Muhlenberg Mission at Monrovia, Africa, there are 8 missionaries, 1 native pastor, 122 pupils in schools, 107 communicants, 8 Sunday-school teachers, and 160 pupils. The receipts for two years for both missions were $62,196.19, of which the Woman's Home and Foreign Missionary Society contributed $7,661.28, the Children's Foreign Missionary Society $8,777.90, the United Synod in the South $2,396.83, and sale of coffee received from the African Mission $2,113.35. The total assets of the Board from all sources, including a balance from previous years, were $71,741.22. The expenses for the same period were $63,574.88. The Board of Home Missions received contributions amounting to

$61,091.88, of which the Woman's Society contributed $7,491.66, to which must be added a balance from previous years of $11,673.28, making the total assets of the Board $72,765.06. Their expenditures amounted to $67,384.88. The operations of the Board are in the special charge of two secretaries, who devote their entire time to the interests of home missions. During the two years covered by this report the Board employed 120 missionaries and aided 108 missions, located in the following States and Territories: Canada, 1; New York, 6; Connecticut, 1; Pennsylvania, 19; Maryland, 4; District of Columbia, 1; West Virginia, 1; Ohio, 8; Indiana, 3; Michigan, 1; Illinois, 9; Kentucky, 2; Tennessee, 2; Missouri, 1; Iowa, 1; Nebraska, 18; Dakota, 1; Wyoming, 1; Kansas, 14; Colorado, 8; and California, 2; or 85 English, 8 German, 5 English-German, and 5 Scandinavian. The Board of Church Extension reported receipts for two years amounting to $68,628.88, and expenditures $59,872.84, being loans and donations to weak congregations and other expenses. The total assets of the Board are $189,924.40, and the liabilities $57,040.25. This Board employs a special agent, whose duty it is "to secure desirable and well-located lots for church and parsonage edifices in new and growing towns in Nebraska and adjacent States and Territories." The Board of Publication reported total assets to the amount of $61,946.74. During the two years embraced in this report 18 new publications and 8 new editions of works were issued, also 7 periodicals, of which the number of copies issued in one month aggregated 175,000. Of the surplus funds of the Board, $6,500 were given to the various benevolent operations of the Synod. The publication-house, at 42 North Ninth Street, Philadelphia, was reported too small for the growing business of the Board. The Parent Education Society reported the receipt of $1,579.45 and the expenditure of $1,405 in aiding eight students. The Historical Society reported increased interest in their work from all parts of the Church and the purchase of a valuable collection of books, pamphlets, charts, papers, and synodical minutes. Its library contains 721 volumes, 1,804 pamphlets, and 88 manuscripts of Lutheran authors, together with nearly complete files of the 157 church periodicals and minutes of synods. The Common Order of Service was reported as completed and ready for publication. The committee of the General Synod was instructed to co-operate with the General Council and the United Synod in the preparation of an authorized translation of the Augsburg Confession and Luther's Small Catechism, and in the preparation of orders for ministerial acts.

A pleasant incident connected with this meeting was a free excursion from Omaha to Lincoln and Beatrice, two growing cities in Nebraska, in order to view those cities for the purpose of selecting a place for the location of a Lutheran college. Excellent offers were made by these and other cities. The Board of Education accepted the offer made by the Boards of Trade of the city of Atchison, Kansas, of 25 acres of land, $50,000, and the half-interest in the sale of 600 acres adjoining, and opened Midland College in September, 1887, at this place.

General Council.—This body, organized in 1867, is composed of eleven district synods, two of which, however, the Norwegian and Iowa synods, are not yet in organic connection with the general body, but send delegates to its conventions as advisory members.

There are within the bounds of this general body 5 theological seminaries at Philadelphia, Pa., Rock Island, Ill., Mendota, Ill., Beloit, Wis., and Saginaw, Mich., having 167 students, 14 professors, and property valued at more than $200,000 ; 7 colleges at Rock Island, Ill., Allentown, Pa., Waverly, Iowa, Greenville, Pa., St. Peter, Minn., Rochester, N. Y., and Lindsborg, Kansas, having 828 students, 64 professors and instructors, and property valued at $450,000, besides 5 academies, 1 conservatory of music, 1 ladies' seminary, 1 deaconess institution at Philadelphia, and 24 benevolent institutions. The German Hospital in Philadelphia deserves special mention. The receipts for 1886-'87 amounted to $71,564.03, the expenditures to $64,108.53. During the year nearly 1,500 cases were treated. John D. Lankenau is the efficient president of the board and the munificent benefactor of the institution, having already spent $500,000 or $600,000 on the buildings and grounds. The hospital is under the care of trained nurses and deaconesses. A mother-house of deaconesses is in course of erection which will cost over $300,000, and is the gift of the honored president of the board, called the "Mary J. Drexel Home and Philadelphia Mother-House of Deaconesses," erected in memory of the wife of Mr. Lankenau. The corner-stone of the new building was laid Nov. 11, 1886. The twentieth annual convention of the General Council was held in the Church of the Holy Trinity, Greenville, Mercer County, Pa., Sept. 8 to 13, 1887. The convention was opened with the communion service of the Lutheran Church. The opening sermon was delivered by the President of the Council, the Rev. A. Spaeth, D. D., on the subject, "The Doctrine of the Church as Illustrated by the Life and Teaching of Luther." The district synods were represented by sixty-five clerical and lay delegates, three synods not sending delegates. Prof. Adolph Spaeth, D. D., of the Philadelphia Theological Seminary, was re-elected President. The Council carries on its missionary and benevolent operations through committees, the consideration of whose reports constitutes the important transactions of the convention. The home-mission work is intrusted to three committees—English, German, and Swedish—which have charge of mission-

points not under the care of the district synods. The English committee reported receipts amounting to $5,730.04 and expenditures $5,055.15, with missionaries as follows: Ohio, 1 ; Illinois, 2 ; Minnesota, 2 ; Dakota, 1. The German committee reported receipts to the amount of $5,457.87. Their expenses were $5,454.95 for the support of 15 missionaries and 18 mission congregations in Canada, Michigan, Nebraska, Dakota, Texas, New York, Pennsylvania, and other States and Territories. Fourteen young men were sent to the committee from Rev. Paulsen's institution at Kropp, Germany, which receives support from the German committee and was established some years ago for the special purpose of supplying this committee with German missionaries. Sixty young men have been sent to America during the past six years. The Swedish committee reported receipts and expenditures amounting to $12,200.98, with missions in nearly every State and Territory. Of this large number of missions nineteen were under the special charge of the General Committee ; the others were cared for by the conferences within whose bounds they are located. Efforts were made at this convention to centralize the missionary operations of the district synods and place them under the control of the General Committees ; but no more definite conclusion was reached than that all the committees of the various synods be required to report to the General Council at each meeting, and that the General Committees be authorized at their discretion to appoint traveling missionaries or superintendents of missions in order more efficiently to care for the ever-increasing and widely-scattered members of the Church coming to this country. For the support of the 112 missionaries and 179 missions, under the supervision of the General Council and its district synods, $37,402.43 were expended during the year. The Committee on Foreign Missions reported the following concerning the labors of the missionaries among the Telugus in India. This mission has : Missionaries, 5 ; wives of missionaries, 4 ; native pastors, 2 ; evangelists and catechists (native), 7 ; teachers, 62 ; pupils, 673 ; baptized in 1886, 364 ; baptized from January to June, 1887, 117 ; number of baptized members, 1,912. The expenses for the year were $9,506.30. The German missionary at Castle Garden, New York, reported the care of 10,464 immigrants during the year. Of poor immigrants 457 were lodged and 734 supplied with meals at a cost to the mission of $879.60. The receipts from all sources amounted to $17,329.26, and the expenditures to $16,596.76. In order to impart necessary information to German immigrants, the missionary prepared and published a directory of the Lutheran Church in America, giving in alphabetical order a list of the places in the United States and Canada where Evangelical Lutheran congregations exist. Another pamphlet, prepared by Prof. W. J.

Mann, D. D., entitled "Emigration and the German Emigrant House," was issued in order to facilitate this branch of the Church's work. The Swedish missionary reported: "During the year 1886, 40,349 Scandinavian immigrants landed at Castle Garden; from January to June, 1887, 30,000. "The Scandinavians that arrived this year have been strong, healthy, and good working-people." The Rev. R. Andersen, of the Danish Synod, missionary at the port of New York, co-operates with the two missionaries of the General Council. The missionary on Ward's Island, Rev. L. H. Gerndt, reported the successful continuation of his work among the destitute Germans. This work is sustained by the Council in connection with its emigrant mission. To facilitate the work among immigrants at New York, missionaries are located at the ports at Bremen, Hamburg, and Antwerp.

The Church-Book Committee reported that, in addition to the ministerial acts already adopted (see "Annual Cyclopædia" for 1886, p. 514), they had prepared an order for the solemnization of marriage and rubrics for the orders already adopted. The order of marriage was adopted. There remain orders for the visitation of the sick, burial of the dead, etc., which are to be considered at the next convention. The text of the Common Service was reported as complete for the use of the General Council, the United Synod in the South, and the General Synod, the text of the two former agreeing in all respects, but that of the latter differing in a few points from the others. The committee was authorized to publish, at as early a date as possible, the Common Service, including so much of the ministerial acts and other parts as can be speedily made ready. The three general bodies have also agreed to unite in the preparation of a revised translation of the Augsburg Confession and Luther's Small Catechism. With a view of still further uniting the three general bodies the following resolution was adopted:

That the committee have authority to unite with other bodies in the preparation of orders for ministerial acts, provided the same rule will be applied as in the case of the Common Service, and that the question as to the collection of hymns be referred to the Church-Book Committee, with power to act and report at the next meeting of the General Council.

The Rev. Dr. A. Spaeth, President of the Council, was elected delegate to the General Conference of Lutheran ministers in Germany, held in October at Hamburg. The next convention of the Council will be held in Minneapolis, Minn., Sept. 13, 1888.

Synodical Conference.—This body, organized in 1872 and consisting principally of Germans, embraces four district synods, and the following educational and benevolent institutions are within its bounds: Three theological seminaries at St. Louis, Mo., Springfield, Ill., and Milwaukee, Wis., having 315 students, 13 professors, and property valued at $200,000; 3

colleges at Fort Wayne, Ind., Watertown, Wis., and New Ulm, Minn., 8 academies and 12 benevolent institutions. The Synodical Conference met with a serious loss in the death of Prof. C. F. W. Walther, D. D., which took place on May 7, 1887. The last convention of this body was held in Detroit, Mich., in 1886 (see "Annual Cyclopædia" for 1886, p. 514). The next convention will be held in Milwaukee, Wis., in August, 1888.

United Synod in the South.—This body, organized in 1886, embraces eight district synods, and the following institutions are within its bounds: One theological seminary at Newberry, S. C.; 5 colleges at Salem, Va., Newberry, S. C., Mt. Pleasant, N. C., Mosheim, Tenn., and Conover, N. C., having about 425 students, 32 professors, and property valued at about $150,000; 5 academies, 7 young ladies' seminaries, and 1 orphans' home. The second convention of the United Synod was held in Savannah, Ga., Nov. 24 to 29, 1887. The Rev. E. T. Horn, D. D., of Charleston, S. C., was elected president. The report of the Board of Missions, showing an active interest in the work of home missons, covered the work of the general body only and not that of the district synods. About $2,000 were received during the year and $1,000 expended. The board asked for $4,000 annually to carry on this work. The president in his report spoke in glowing terms of this branch of the synod's work, saying that the field was rapidly widening and new points claimed their attention, especially in Florida and Alabama. The United Synod felt sorely grieved on account of the peculiar actions of the man whom they had sent to labor in the Guntur Mission, in India, under the control of the General Synod: but they did not allow this disappointment to stop their work. They therefore resolved to establish a new mission in China or Japan, according to the judgment of the Board of Missions. The report of the Committee on Common Service which announced the completion of the service and its adoption by the General Council and General Synod was adopted. Much time was devoted to consideration of the subject of establishing a general theological seminary for the synod. The committee appointed at the last convention earnestly urged that the synod at this convention should seriously consider the advisability of establishing such an institution, and gave the following as their reasons:

1. Because several of our district synods, in the exercise of the right of petition, have concurred in urging upon you such action.
2. Because it is an abnormal condition for a church in a settled state to be dependent upon outside resources for means of education.
3. Because a seminary in our own midst would develop a greater interest in the matter of a supply of ministers from within the congregations themselves.
4. Because our present arrangement under which some are educated at Philadelphia, some at Gettysburg, some at Conover, and some at Newberry, can not result otherwise than in a ministry constantly be-

coming more unlike in certain things and impairing practical unity, and besides such a seminary would send out men more truly of one mind and spirit, more surely in sympathy with the common work before them, and possessing in a greater degree an important adaptation for their field of labor.

The committee was instructed to report at the next convention on the feasibility of establishing a general theological seminary. The next convention will be held at Wilmington, N. C., in November, 1889.

Independent Synods.—The following eleven synods carry on their missionary, educational, and benevolent operations independent of the four general bodies, standing aloof from all intercourse with any other synod:

NAME.	Organized.	Ministers.	Congregations.	Members.
Joint Synod of Ohio..........	1818	266	407	56,510
Buffalo (N. Y.)	1845	27	89	5,000
Maryland Synod (German) ...	.....	7	10	1,000
Norwegian Lutheran Synod (three districts)	1853	222	725	74,217
Norwegian-Danish Conference	1870	191	381	90,321
Danish Lutheran Church in America	1872	41	115	5,500
German Augsburg	1875	30	38	9,600
Hauge's Norwegian Synod ...	1876	48	185	8,000
Danish Lutheran Church Society	1884	12	86	4,000
Society of Icelanders in America.	1885	4	15	1,866
Immanuel's Synod..........	1886	16	20	8,225
Without any synodical connection..................	....	64	50	15,000
Total...................	....	840	1,974	218,289

The following is a summary of the statistics of the denomination:

NAME.	Organized.	Synods.	Ministers.	Congregations.	Membership.
General Synod	1821	22	906	1,498	138,679
General Council	1867	11	1,097	2,007	281,846
Synodical Conference...	1872	4	1,165	1,688	322,999
United Synod	1886	8	188	866	80,750
Independent Synods....	....	11	840	1,974	218,289
Grand total	....	57	4,188	7,478	991,722

Muhlenberg Centenary.—Henry Melchior Muhlenberg, D. D., "Patriarch of the Lutheran Church in America," died Oct. 7, 1787, and was buried at Trappe, Montgomery County, Pa., where he had resided for more than forty years. His grave is at the side of the historic church which he built in 1743, and is marked with an ordinary marble slab bearing the following inscription (in Latin): "Sacred be this monument to the memory of the blessed and venerable Henry Melchior Muhlenberg, Doctor of Sacred Theology and Senior of the American Lutheran Ministerium. Born September 6, 1711. Died October 7, 1787. Who and what he was future ages will know without a stone." At the one hundred and forty-first meeting of the Evangelical Lutheran Ministerium of Pennsylvania and adjacent States, the oldest Lutheran synod in the United States and the synod founded by Dr. Muhlenberg in 1748, a resolution was passed to the effect that during the month of October services should be held in every congregation belonging to the synod in commemoration of the sainted Muhlenberg, and that devout thanks be offered to the Head of the Church for the labors of this man of God from 1742 to 1787, and for the blessed and ennobling influence that he exerted on his own and subsequent times, as well as for the blessing that God has showered upon the Lutheran Church in America during the century. It was further resolved that at these memorial services collections be taken in each congregation as thank-offerings to God, and that the money thus collected be given to Muhlenberg College, Allentown, Pa., for the endowment of its German professorship. The movement thus begun by the mother synod was taken up by Lutherans generally in eastern Pennsylvania, and in many congregations were held memorial services, especially in the four hundred and seventeen congregations of the old synod. The chief memorial services, however, were held in the new and commodious Lutheran church at the Trappe, erected near the old and quaint but well-preserved structure on Oct. 7, 1887, attended by several thousand Lutherans from Philadelphia, New York, Allentown, Reading, Lancaster, and many other towns. Many of the descendants of Muhlenberg were present. The centenary discourse was delivered on Friday morning, October 7, by the Rev. G. F. Krotel, D. D., of New York city, President of the Ministerium of Pennsylvania, in which he presented an interesting sketch of the leading facts of his long and useful life and a delineation of his character. In the afternoon of the same day, Revs. W. J. Mann, D. D., and C. W. Schaeffer, D. D., LL. D., in eloquent addresses portrayed his characteristics as a Christian, a scholar, pastor, and missionary, an efficient organizer, a wise master-builder, and a safe leader of the Church in troublous times. Among other memorial services, the services held in Muhlenberg College, Allentown, Pa., and by the Susquehanna Synod at Selinsgrove, Pa, deserve special mention. As a permanent and suitable tribute to the memory of Muhlenberg may be mentioned the interesting volume, "The Life and Times of Henry Melchior Muhlenberg, D. D.," by Wm. J. Mann, D. D., Professor in the Lutheran Theological Seminary (Philadelphia, 1887).

LYONS, RICHARD BICKERTON PEMELL, Lord, English diplomatist, born in Lymington, England, April 26, 1817; died in London, England, Dec. 5, 1887. He was the only son of the first Baron Lyons, who was admiral of the British fleet in the Black Sea during the Crimean war. His ancestors were planters on the island of Antigua, and one of them, Henry Lyons, who resided for some time in Philadelphia, married in 1690 Sarah, daughter of Samuel Winthrop, a grandson of Gov. Winthrop, of Massachusetts. He was educated at Winchester School and Christ Church College,

Oxford, was graduated in 1838, and entered the diplomatic service as *attaché* at Athens in 1839, where his father was minister, becoming a paid *attaché* in 1844, and remaining there until 1852. He was then transferred to Dresden, and in 1853 to Florence, where he was appointed in 1856 secretary of legation, and was promoted in 1858 envoy to Tuscany. On Nov. 23, 1858, he succeeded his father to the barony, and in December of the same year was sent as minister to the United States. When the civil war broke out he had a difficult part to play, and it was in a measure owing to his tact and judgment that war was averted between the United States and Great Britain, in consequence of the seizure of the Confederate commissioners Slidell and Mason on board the British steamship "Trent," in November, 1861. He waited for instructions from Lord Russell, the British Minister of Foreign Affairs, before demanding the release of the prisoners.

RICHARD BICKERTON PEMELL, LORD LYONS.

When the dispatches came he presented the demands of his Government, which were that the commissioners should be given up and an apology made for their capture. Secretary Seward's contention that they were contraband of war was strenuously denied by Lord Lyons and his chief, and the note of the British Government was supported by communications from Austria, France, Italy, Prussia, and Russia. Lord Lyons delivered an ultimatum, and informed Mr. Seward that he would leave Washington in seven days unless the British demands were complied with. After a long diplomatic correspondence, conducted by him in a conciliatory spirit, the two Governments finally arrived at a basis of settlement. Lord Lyons conducted an intricate correspondence with Secretary Seward and with Earl Russell on the subject of the declaration of Paris, and on the question of the blockade of the Southern ports. On April 7, 1862, he concluded at Washington, in behalf of Great Britain, a treaty with the United States for the suppression of the slave-trade, which gave ex-

tensive rights of search to the cruisers of both powers. During the course of the war he conducted a correspondence with his Government in relation to the recognition of the Southern Confederacy, the emancipation proclamation, the "Alabama" question, and other matters of diplomatic moment. In February, 1865, he resigned his post of minister and envoy extraordinary to the United States on account of failing health. In August he was appointed ambassador at Constantinople, and in July, 1867, he was transferred to Paris as British ambassador at the French court. He remained at that important post more than twenty years, through the agitated period of the Franco-Prussian War, the re-establishment of the republic, and the presidencies of Thiers, McMahon, and Grévy. He had several conversations with the Duc de Grammont, the foreign minister of Napoleon III, in relation to the candidature of the Prince of Hohenzollern for the Spanish throne, and endeavored to avert the war, but declined to pledge his Government to bring pressure to bear on Prussia on the question of forbidding the German prince to be a candidate. When the siege of Paris began, he left with all the other principal ministers, except Mr. Washburn. In 1873 he concluded negotiations with the French Government for the renewal of the commercial treaty that the Emperor Napoleon had made with England in 1860, but which had been replaced by a convention with less liberal provisions negotiated by M. Thiers. Through the efforts of Lord Lyons the old treaty was revived provisionally for three years. When Queen Victoria visited the Continent in 1876, Lord Lyons received her at La Villette, and introduced her to Marshal MacMahon. Lord Lyons continued to hold the appointment of minister at Paris until November, 1887. He was created Viscount Lyons of Christ Church, in the county of Southampton, in November, 1881, and on his obligatory retirement from the post of minister at Paris, on reaching the age of seventy, he was advanced to an earldom. The Marquis of Salisbury, in 1886, asked him to join his ministry as Secretary of State for Foreign Affairs, but he declined the office. His sister was the mother of the present Duke of Norfolk, and shortly before his death Lord Lyons joined the communion of the Catholic Church. He had won the gratitude of the Church by first persuading Count Beust, the Austrian ambassador, to object to the expulsion of a convent of German Jesuits in Paris on international grounds, and then, when a precedent had been established, opposing the suppression of the ancient college of the English Benedictines at Douay. Lord Lyons intended to complete a course of theological study before being formally admitted into the Church. When seized with paralysis on November 28, he received the last sacrament at the hands of Rev. Dr. Butt, Bishop of Southwark. The adherents of the English Church, to which he formerly belonged, questioned the completeness of his conversion, or at least the propriety of administering extreme unction to a convert who had not yet changed his religion by formal act, and was probably unconscious during his illness. Lord Lyons was not a brilliant diplomatist, and contributed little to the settlement of important questions of European politics, yet his shrewdness and caution preserved him from errors, while with discretion, patience, and tenacity he labored for and secured many advantages for England in the settlement of diplomatic issues. His aristocratic exclusiveness prevented his becoming popular in republican Paris, though the French people remembered with gratitude that he was one of the first to procure provisions for the famished inhabitants of Paris after the raising of the siege in 1871. As Lord Lyons was a bachelor and had no living brother, the baronetcy and barony that he inherited from his father, as well as the viscounty and earldom that were limited to his own issue, became extinct at his death.

M

MADAGASCAR, an island in the Indian Ocean, opposite the coast of Mozambique, subject to the Queen of the Hovas, who accepted the protectorate of France by the treaty of Dec. 17, 1885. The Government of the French Republic represents Madagascar in all its external relations. A resident-general directs these relations, without interfering in any way in the internal administration, which is reserved to the Queen of Madagascar. He resides at Antananarivo, the capital, with a military escort, and has the right of audience with the Queen. The Hovas engaged to pay a war indemnity of 10,-000,000 francs, and the French Government reserved the right to occupy the Bay of Diego Suarez and make installations there for its convenience. The Hova Queen is Ranavalo Majanka III, born in 1862, who succeeded to the throne in 1882. The Prime Minister and Prince Consort is Rainilaiarivony. The Resident-General of France is M. Le Myre de Vilers, Minister Plenipotentiary of the first class. (For statistics, see "Annual Cyclopædia" for 1886.)

Commerce.— After the French war many English, but few French, went to Madagascar to embark in business. About 60 per cent. of the commerce of 1886 was British and a large proportion American. Rum is the most important article of import, after which come kerosene and American cotton stuffs, which are preferred by the natives to English fabrics. The indemnity for the war was advanced by the Comptoir d'Escompte of Paris to the Hova Government, and was secured on the receipts of ten ports, which are collected by agents of the bank. The British and American importers avoided these ports, taking their goods to the ports still under the control of the Hova authorities, where they have the option of paying the 10 per cent. duty in money or in kind.

Fresh Dispute with France.—The French troops, according to agreement, evacuated Tamatave in January, 1887, and the port was reoccupied by the Malagasy forces on January 25. The French recalled their troops subsequently from all other parts of the island, excepting four companies remaining at Diego Suarez. The French Government appointed an indemnity commission to pass upon the claims that had been brought, chiefly by British subjects, for losses sustained through the war. The French resident demanded that the *exequaturs* of foreign consuls should be presented to him for approval. This the Hova Government refused to do, and was encouraged in this attitude by the British consul. The former British consul, Mr. Pickersgill, had been recalled by his Government at the request of the French Cabinet. His successor, Mr. Haggard, on arriving at Antananarivo, handed his credentials to the Hova official, who granted the *exequatur* without consulting M. Le Myre de Vilers. The French Government immediately represented the matter to the British Government, which admitted the French position, but subsequently Lord Salisbury declared that the question required more study, as it involved serious difficulties. Eventually the French protectorate was formally recognized, Great Britain consenting in principle that its consuls should receive their *exequaturs* from France. The English residents on the island prepared many difficulties for the French representative. The Malagasy Government still persisted in refusing to give up the *exequaturs* of the British and American consuls. Another cause of difference arose from the arrest, trial, and banishment for twenty years of Ravoninahitriniarivo, the Secretary of State for Foreign Affairs, on the charge of having in his possession seals of the Government with treasonable intent, and the appointment to the place of a young son of the Prime Minister. The French resident objected strongly to this appointment, and an under-secretary was provisionally appointed. Mr. Campbell, the American consul, applied to the French representative for his *exequatur*. The Premier demanded the formal recognition of the letter of Admiral Miot explanatory of the treaty, which the Malagasy Government considered a codicil and a part of the treaty, but which the French Government persisted in disavowing. Finally, the relations of M. Le Myre de Vilers with the Hova Government became so strained that on September 19 he hauled down his flag and prepared to leave Antananarivo. This decisive action had the desired effect on the Malagasy Premier, and in October relations between the resident-general and the Hova Government were resumed.

MAINE. State Government.—The following were the State officers during the year: Governor, Joseph R. Bodwell, Republican, who died December 15, and was succeeded by Sebastian S. Marble, President of the Senate; Secretary of State, Oramandal Smith; Treasurer, Edwin C. Burleigh; Attorney-General, Orville D. Baker; Superintendent of Common Schools, Nelson A. Luce; Railroad Commissioners, Asa W. Wildes, John F. Anderson, and David N. Mortland; Chief-Justice of the Supreme Court, John A. Peters; Associate Justices, Charles W. Walton, Charles Danforth, William W. Virgin, Artemus Libbey, Lucilius A. Emery, Enoch Foster, Thomas H. Haskell.

Legislative Session.—The Legislature met on January 5, and adjourned on March 17, being in session 72 days. United States Senator Eugene Hale was re-elected for the term of six years, receiving 114 votes to 26 for the Democratic nominee, William H. Clifford. Senator Hale had no contestant for the Republican nomination.

A compulsory school-law was passed, requiring children between eight and fifteen years of age to attend the public schools at least sixteen weeks in every year, unless physically or mentally incapable, or otherwise provided with instruction, and compelling every town and city to elect truant-officers who shall enforce the law upon both parents and children. Another act abolishes capital punishment in the State. Debtors are, also, freed from liability to imprisonment for their debts, except when fraud is proved against them. Several measures for the relief of labor were adopted. One provides for the fortnightly payment of wages to employés; another prohibits the employment of children under twelve years of age in any manufacturing or mechanical establishment, or of any child under fifteen years, except during vacations of the public schools. Male children under sixteen and women shall not be employed more than ten hours each day, or sixty hours each week, unless by special agreement of the parties, and with the consent of parents or guardians in case of minors. A State bureau of industrial and labor statistics is established, under the management of a commissioner, who is required to submit annual reports.

The liquor law passed at this session is designed to re-enforce former prohibitory legislation. It provides that the penalty for the first offense in selling liquors shall be both fine and imprisonment, instead of a fine or imprisonment or both, thus depriving the judge of discretionary power. The clause permitting sales of over five gallons for certain purposes was repealed, and a fine imposed on railroad or express employés for removing liquor from cars at any places except regular stations. The payment of a United States liquor-tax is made *prima-facie* evidence that the person paying it is a common seller of intoxicating liquors, and guilty of maintaining a liquor nuisance. This provision was designed to strike at a large number of places operated under license from the Internal Revenue Bureau; but by a decision rendered in the Supreme Court, near the close of the year, it was adjudged unconstitutional on the ground of depriving the accused of his right to a judgment of his peers, and to be considered innocent till found guilty.

Provision was made for the payment of the State debt that will become due in June and October, 1889, by authorizing the treasurer to issue three-per-cent. bonds to an amount not exceeding $2,800,000, bearing interest from October of that year. He was also authorized to sell, at his discretion, any or all bonds in the sinking fund, exclusive of State of Maine bonds, and apply the proceeds to the purchase of such outstanding bonds of the State as may be obtained. All State bonds then or thereafter coming into the sinking fund are ordered to be canceled by the Treasurer.

It was voted to submit to the people, at the election in 1888, two amendments to the Constitution, one declaring that the Treasurer shall not be eligible more than six years in succession, the other providing for a return to annual sessions of the Legislature.

Appropriations for 1887 to the amount of $1,262,195 were passed, and for 1888 to the amount of $1,187,389. Other acts of the session were as follow:

Authorizing cities and towns to accept legacies, devises, and bequests when made to them upon conditions, and requiring them to observe such conditions if accepted.

To provide for the descent of intestate estates of and to illegitimate children.

For the protection of the alewife-fishery on Damariscotta river.

Authorizing towns and cities to appropriate money for the observance of Memorial Day.

Establishing a uniform time for the transaction of public affairs.

To provide for the burial expenses of honorably discharged soldiers and sailors.

For the protection of political nominating conventions and primary political meetings or caucuses, from disturbance and fraud.

Regulating the powers and duties of loan and building associations.

Increasing the salaries of the justices of the Supreme Judicial Court to $3,500 a year.

Increasing the exemptions that a debtor may claim against attaching creditors.

Requiring safety-switches and switch-lights after sunset on all railroads, and providing a penalty for tampering with switches.

To establish Arbor Day.

To provide for the permanent location and maintenance of the Madawaska Training-School for the purpose of training teachers in the common schools of Madawaska territory so-called, and appropriating funds for its support.

To protect the breeders of blooded animals against fraudulent registration and misrepresentation.

Amending the insurance law.

To regulate the sale and analysis of commercial fertilizers, by placing the supervision of the business in the control of the Agricultural Experiment Station of the State College.

To carry into effect an act of Congress entitled "An act to establish Agricultural Experiment Stations in connection with colleges in the several States."

To establish local boards of health in cities and

towns, and to protect the people of the State from contagious diseases.

To regulate the sale of opium, morphine, and laudanum.

Raising the age of consent in females from ten to thirteen years.

To prevent indirect preferences of creditors in insolvency.

To create a State Board of Cattle Commissioners, giving them power to investigate and suppress contagious diseases among domestic animals, and providing safeguards against such diseases.

To secure additional protection to the lobster-fisheries.

Authorizing the appointment of special insurance brokers.

Providing that no more than twenty per cent. of the male convicts in the State-prison shall be employed at any time in any industry or manufacture that is carried on at that time in any other place in the State.

Making a copy of a town clerk's record admissible as evidence.

To cede to the United States jurisdiction over certain land in Eastport, as a site for a public building at that place.

To provide for a union railway-station at Portland. Authorizing the Boston and Maine Railroad to purchase certain other railroads in the State.

The legislation of the session consisted of 149 general laws, 288 special laws, and 123 resolves.

Finances.—The following is a summary of the receipts and expenses of the State during the year:

Cash in treasury Jan. 1, 1887 .... $318,851 45
Total receipts for 1887 .... 1,161,980 88

Total $1,480,882 33

Total expenditures for 1887 .... $1,168,544 30
Cash in treasury, Dec. 31, 1887 .... 312,288 03

Total $1,480,882 33

The largest receipts were derived from the State tax of 3½ mills, $743,112.27; from county taxes, $12,964.21; tax on railroads, $89,979.95; tax on insurance companies, $17,294.15; and savings-bank tax, $256,429.88. Among the expenditures are: For interest on the public debt, $240,522.76; for the school fund and mill tax, 1885-'86, $348,877.54; salaries of public officers, $55,056.75; for State institutions, $154,262.96. The bonded debt at the beginning of the year consisted of bonds due June, 1, 1889, $2,330,000, and bonds due Oct. 1, 1889, $2,827,000—total, $5,157,000. At the end of the year it had been reduced to the following figures: Bonds due June 1, 1889, $1,762,000; bonds due Oct. 1, 1889, $2,197,000 —total, $3,959,000. During the same time the amount of securities and cash in the sinking fund had decreased from $2,110,390.57 to $949,-660.64. This decrease of debt and sinking fund is a result of the law requiring the treasurer to destroy all bonds of the State in that fund. Securities to the amount of $1,162,000 were canceled during the year, in compliance with this law, leaving in the fund only securities outside of the State of Maine; $38,479.93 of the interest from these securities was used in the purchase of $36,000 State of Maine bonds which were canceled and deducted from the bonded debt. While the amount with which to pay the bonded debt has decreased $1,160,729.93, the bonded debt has diminished $1,198,000, showing a net reduction during the year of $37,270.07. This reduction is $171.-842.09 less than in 1886—a result caused by the action of the Legislature in making the tax-rate for the year one mill less than before, producing a decrease of $236.902.07 in the annual revenue. The reduced tax-rate is 2½ mills, one mill of which is levied for the support of the common schools. The revenue derived from this tax for this year was $649,497.11.

Prisons.—The number of convicts at the State-prison at Thomastown on December 1 was 165, being fewer than at any report for the past twelve years. One year ago there were 170. All work in the prison is done on the account of the State, instead of by the contract system. An improvement is reported in the condition of the county jails. There has been a decrease also in the prisoners, 33 fewer being reported than in 1886.

Insane.—The Maine Insane Hospital has been in operation forty-seven years, during which time 7,070 patients have been admitted, and 6,518 discharged, leaving at the close of this year 552 patients under treatment. This is an increase of 24 patients over last year. The year has been eventful in the direction of increased demands for accommodations and treatment of patients, resulting in a considerably larger daily average number of inmates than has heretofore existed. The percentage of recoveries during the year, based upon the number of admissions, is 86·28, and 10·87 upon the number under treatment.

Banks.—From the Bank Examiner's report for 1887 it appears that the number of savings-banks in the State on November 1 was 55, or one more than in 1886 at the same time. The number of depositors has increased from 114,-691 in 1886 to 119,229 in 1887, and the aggregate deposits from $37,215,071 to $38,819,643. The amount of dividends paid was $1,366.504. By the appraisement made in May, the banks held assets valued at $5,287,004 in excess of all liabilities. Eight years ago the number of depositors was 75,448, their deposits $20,978,180, and the surplus of the banks above liabilities only $1,057,976.

Shipping.—Complete returns for 1887 show the number of vessels in Maine engaged in the fisheries to be 448; tonnage, 15,857·64—a decrease of about 25 per cent. since 1885. The number of new vessels of all kinds constructed during the year is 38, with a tonnage of 13,-335·57 tons.

Ice.—The total capacity of ice-houses in Maine is as follows: Kennebec river, 1,185,-500 tons; Penobscot river, 238,000 tons; Cathance river, 31,000 tons; coast, 512,000 tons —total, 1,967.000 tons. It is estimated that over 1,000,000 tons of ice was stored in the season of 1887, of which fully 800,000 tons were afterward transported out of the State, chiefly to Southern ports.

MANITOBA, PROVINCE OF. Government.—The Lieutenant-Governor is James Cox Aikins; Premier and President of Council, J. Norquay; Attorney-General, C. E. Hamilton; Minister of Public Works, D. H. Wilson; Provincial Secretary, C. P. Brown; Minister of Agriculture, D. H. Harrison; Provincial Treasurer, A. C. La Rivière.

Population.—By the census taken July 31, 1886, the total population of the province was 108,640. By the census taken April 4. 1881, the population was 65,954, showing an increase of 64·7 per cent. in the five years.

Railway Charters.—The bills passed by the Manitoba Legislature in 1886 to incorporate the Manitoba Central and Winnipeg and Southern Railway companies having been disallowed by the Dominion Government, the Legislature passed an act authorizing the construction of the Red River Valley Railway as a Provincial Government undertaking. This act also being disallowed, the Provincial Government proceeded to build a railway under the public works act. The Dominion Government thereupon applied for and obtained an injunction against the building of the line under the public works act. A threatening agitation followed, the persistence of the Dominion Government in the policy of disallowance being regarded by the people of the province as an unwarrantable interference with provincial rights, and as seriously detrimental to the interests of the province. The right of disallowing Manitoba railway charters is not exercised by the Dominion Government, as is frequently held, by virtue of the Canadian Pacific Railway act, but under the British North America act. which gives the Dominion Government the right of disallowing all provincial legislation. The Canadian Pacific Railway act does indeed provide that for a period of twenty years from Feb. 17, 1870, no line of railway shall be authorized by the Dominion Parliament to be constructed south of the Canadian Pacific Railway, from any point at or near that railway, nor within fifteen miles of the United States unless such line shall run west or west of southwest, boundary. But this provision could not apply to the old province of Manitoba, because under the British North America act the right to legislate with regard to railways entirely within a province appertains to the legislature of that province. Although not compelled by the terms of the Canadian Pacific charter to disallow the railway acts of the Manitoba Legislature, the Dominion Government deemed it in the interests of the Dominion, and particularly of eastern Canada, which has spent so much money in the development of the Northwest, to exercise its veto power in order to protect the Canadian Pacific Railway from American competition, and to prevent the traffic of the Northwest being diverted from the eastern ports of Canada. The Red River Valley Railway was intended to run from Winnipeg to West Lynne on the international boundary, a distance of sixty miles. The line was partly built, but, as the Provincial Government failed to raise the necessary funds (owing. doubtless, to the lack of security offered, through the undertaking being illegal), the contractors abandoned the work.

MARYLAND. State Government.—The following were the State officers during the year: Governor, Henry Lloyd, Democrat; Secretary of State, E. W. Le Compte; Treasurer, Stevenson Archer; Comptroller, J. Frank Turner; Attorney-General, Charles B. Roberts; Secretary of State Board of Education, M. A. Newell; Tax Commissioner, Levin Woolford; Chief-Justice of the Court of Appeals, Richard A. Alvey; Associate Justices, James M. Robinson, John Ritchie, Levin T. H. Irving, William S. Bryan, Frederick Stone, George Yellott, and Oliver Miller.

Finances.—The following statement exhibits the condition of the State treasury during the year:

Total receipts for year ending Sept. 30, 1887 ...	$2,440,363 58
Balance Sept. 30, 1886.........................	616,576 84
Total	$3,056,939 87
Disbursements for the fiscal year	2,374,916 67
Balance Sept. 30, 1887....	$682,023 20

Of the receipts the sum of $463,873 was received on account of the "Exchange Loan of 1886," reducing the income from ordinary sources to $1,976,990.53. While this amount is about $18,000 less than the receipts for the year 1886, the difference is accounted for by the reduction in the cost of marriage licenses from $4 to 50 cents. The amount received in 1886 from this source was $24,226; the amount received in 1887 only $4,491. Of the disbursements the sum of $329,744 was expended in the redemption of State stock. The sum of $301.826 was transferred from the treasury for the purchase of stock for the sinking fund. The further sum of $34,069 surplus revenue was transferred to the free-school fund, and the sum of $20,813 was expended in enlarging the State-house. Deducting these items, it will be seen that the ordinary expenses of the Government for the fiscal year ending Sept. 30, 1887, were $1,689,063. This is a small increase over expenses of the two previous years.

The debt of the State on September 30 aggregated $10,960,535. The State holds stocks and bonds on which interest or dividends are paid, amounting to the sum of $5,299,301. The net debt of the State on Sept. 30, 1886, was $6,113,159, which shows a total reduction during the fiscal year 1887 of $451,925. The total reduction of the last four years has been $1,624,657.

Before the meeting of the next Legislature the sterling debt, payable in gold, amounting to $4,001,111, will fall due. No special tax has ever been laid for the redemption of this, and therefore there is no sinking fund for its payment. The debt was created in 1838 for the purpose of raising money to enable the State to aid in the construction of the Baltimore and Ohio Railroad, and of the Chesapeake and Ohio Canal. The interest that the State holds in these enterprises represents this debt and furnishes ample security to the creditors, without imposing any tax to provide a sinking fund for its ultimate payment.

The sinking fund at the end of the fiscal year amounted to $2,144,215. During the year there was received from investments made on account of the various sinking funds the sum of $95,298, and there was transferred from the treasury proper for the purchase of stock on account of the sinking fund for the redemption of the treasury relief loan the sum of $25,200, and for the redemption of the defense redemption loan the sum of $276,626.

The assessed value of property in the State on September 30 was $485,839,772, an increase of $9,010,161 over 1886. But the assessment in Baltimore city is now over $2,000,000 less than in 1877, and the assessment in the whole State shows only an increase in the past ten years of a fraction over $7,000,000. The amount of tax levied for State purposes for the year was $910,949.50, the rate being 18¼ cents on each $100. Of this rate 10 cents is levied for public-school purposes, producing a revenue of $485,839.

The aggregate assessment of the banks and other corporations upon their shares of stock and assets amounted to $72,706,788. This shows an increase over the corresponding assessments in 1885 of $7,678,786. The amount of assessment of the real property of these corporations for the year was $24,848,255. The total tax assessed upon all corporations was $128,244.

The receipts from the warehouses for tobacco inspection amounted to $84,186, and the disbursements to $76,134, leaving as the net earnings for the year $8,051. The salaries of the inspectors are paid out of the State treasury, and amount to $9,000. Receipts from licenses to trade in 1887 were $122,881, against $127,965 in 1885.

Chesapeake and Ohio Canal.—The claim of the State against this canal, on Sept. 30, 1887, amounted to $25,574,713. Of this sum $7,000,000 is principal, and the balance, $18,574,713, is for interest. Of the general status of the canal the Governor says in his message: "Though intended to connect with the Ohio river, it was never extended beyond Cumberland, and will most probably always remain an unfinished work. It has, however, been, and is now, a most useful water-way for coal seeking shipment from Cumberland, and for the products of the industry of the people of the State living near or along its route. It would seem to be wise to maintain it as a water-way. The canal has had many difficulties to contend with. The repairs, made necessary by repeated freshets, have more than once required expenditures greater than its means or credit could supply." The report

of the operations of the canal for the year shows that it has been unable to meet its regular running expenses, exclusive of interest on bonds or stock. The gross receipts were $129,206, of which all but $13,485 was derived from the transportation of coal ; the expenditures for the same time were $137,007.

The State also owns mortgage bonds of the Susquehanna and Tidewater canals, to the amount of $1,000,000, which have been overdue since January, 1884, and on which interest has been in arrears since July, 1879.

Oysters.—The receipts on account of the fund devoted to the enforcement of the oyster laws of 1886 amounted to $54,961 during the year, while the disbursements for the same period were $67,221. This is $6,067 less than the expenses of 1886. Three steamers and eleven vessels, with 101 men, were engaged in the enforcement of the law during the year. The State force has been resisted and fired upon, and once or twice driven away.

Penitentiary.—The number of convicts in the State Penitentiary at the close of the year was 592, of whom 200 were white men and 359 colored, and 3 were white women and 30 colored. At the close of 1886 the number was 546. The expenses during the year were $67,343, the receipts, $68,004. A small building of twelve rooms for the treatment of insane convicts has been completed. The State is in need of an entirely new structure for its prisoners, or a complete renovation of the old one, which is small, badly ventilated, and ill-suited to modern requirements. Those convicts who are able to work are employed under contract with private individuals, 438 being so engaged at the close of the year.

At the State House of Correction 620 prisoners were received during the year, the daily average being 190. The last Legislature increased the appropriations for this institution from $25,000 to $30,000. Old debts having been paid, good management demonstrates that this institution can be maintained with an appropriation of $25,000, and such profits as are derived from the State farm.

Militia.—Since the act of 1886, making larger appropriations for the support of the militia, providing for biennial encampments, and requiring an enlistment of the men for three years, a marked change in the appearance, bearing, and discipline of the force has followed. There are now in the service 147 commissioned officers and 1,913 enlisted men.

Elections.—On this subject the Governor says in his message: "Our election laws are made up of statutes passed at different periods since 1804. In that long interval of time the population of the State has greatly increased. The simple rules that formerly sufficed for the conduct of elections are now insufficient. Our election laws ought to be completely revised and made adequate in every particular to every requirement of good government. I suggest that sufficient and even liberal compensation be given to those who will act as supervisors of election in Baltimore city."

Mining.—The yield of coal from the George's Creek coal-field for the year was largely in excess of the production of any former year, being not far from 8,000,000 tons. The outlay for labor and transportation within the State to market this product is estimated at over $7,000,000.

Political.—The regular quadrennial canvass for the election of Governor occurred this year. The Democratic Convention met at Baltimore on July 27, and nominated the following ticket: for Governor, Elihu E. Jackson; for Comptroller, Louis Victor Baughman; for Attorney-General, William Pinckney Whyte. A platform was adopted, which approves the national Administration, deprecates civil-service reform, demands a reduction of the tariff, and urges a more stringent law to prevent the importation of foreign paupers. Upon local issues it declares:

That the Democratic party, mindful of its fulfilled pledges to wage-earners to place upon the statute-books of the State laws which would protect their health, their personal safety and welfare, and guarantee to them an equal right with owners of capital to make peaceable combinations for their own protection, renews its pledges to embody in the organic law, upon are vision of the present Constitution, their right to peacefully assemble and organize for their own protection, and now promises to enact such further laws as time and experience may demonstrate to be for their welfare and happiness.

That the Democratic party, recognizing that portions of the present election laws of the State have been upon the statute-books for more than twenty-five years, and are more or less ineffectual to accomplish at the present day absolutely fair elections in districts whose population is dense and shifting, and ever foremost in protecting the purity of the ballot-box and the sanctity of elections, hereby pledges that it will earnestly endeavor at the coming session of the General Assembly to have placed upon the statute-books an election law which will embrace not only all the beneficial provisions of the Tilden act, but will embody, also, all those additional safeguards to guarantee the purity of elections which experience has taught should be incorporated into it.

That inasmuch as the provisions of the present Constitution in providing for a system of taxation and of registration require that they shall be respectively uniform in their operation throughout the State, it is the sense of this convention that the present laws of registration and of taxation are as nearly complete and accurate as they can be made under the present organic law. And the Democratic party now engages that in a revision of the Constitution it will use its best efforts to have embraced within its provisions the requirement of a more thorough system of taxation and of an annual registration of voters in cities whose inhabitants number ten thousand and upward.

The Republican nominations were made at Baltimore, August 24, and were as follow: for Governor, Walter B. Brooks; for Comptroller, Robert B. Dixon; for Attorney-General, Francis Miller. The platform favors the Blair Education bill, civil-service reform in both State and nation, restriction of pauper immigration, and legislation for the protection of labor. Upon local questions it contains the following:

Resolved, That the President of the United States, by his action in regard to the Federal appointments in this State, has given conclusive evidence that his professions of civil-service reform are hollow and delusive, and his failure to call the Federal office-holders to account for their open and shameless disregard of his own declarations that they should not engage in efforts to control the political action of their own party, is a confession of insincerity on his part, or a proof that his will is controlled and dominated by the stronger will of the senior senator from this State.

Resolved, That the colored people of Maryland, in their own separate schools, are entitled to the same provision for the education of their children as is enjoyed by the children of the whites, and we declare the present grossly unjust and unfair discrimination against the colored schools to be a disgrace to the State.

That the enforced system of tobacco inspection, which entails an expense upon the treasury burdensome to the taxpayers, and which in its inefficiency depreciates the value of our products, is a reproach to the State.

Resolved, That we are opposed to the calling of a constitutional convention at this time, and we favor the submission to the public of all questions of constitutional amendment in the manner prescribed by the Constitution when urged by a large portion of our people. The deep-laid schemes of the managers of the Democratic party for the destruction of the Chesapeake and Ohio Canal and its removal as a competitor with railroad monopoly, which are now nearing their consummation, and will result in the impoverishment and ruin of a large number of our fellow-citizens, can only be thwarted by the defeat of their candidates for the Legislature, and the best interests of the people of the whole State demand that this should be done.

We declare ourselves in favor of the following specific measures of reform:

That more efficient laws be passed against bribery and improper use of money in all forms of election, as well as against lobbying, and we pledge ourselves to enforce the present laws upon the subject, without respect to party.

For an equitable system of taxation, so as to relieve the overburdened agricultural interest of the State from its present depressed condition. For a revision of the revenue laws, so as to enforce the prompt payment of public money into the treasury by collectors and other fiscal agents.

For a curtailment of the expenses of legislation, and the correction of the hitherto reckless and extravagant expenditure of public money by the General Assembly in printing, in useless and unnecessary officers and employés, and in appropriations out of the State treasury as a reward for partisan services by the creation of unnecessary commissions, codifications, and contracts.

For revisions of the laws regulating the procedure in our courts, lessening the expense to the taxpayer and to litigants.

For laws preserving the sinking fund inviolate, as demanded by the Constitution.

For using the surplus in the treasury to the extinguishment of the State debt which falls due in 1888 as far as the same will go, instead of expending it in useless conventions and other unnecessary purposes, and the refunding of the balance by offering it in the financial markets of the world, so as to secure the lowest rates of interest, and prevent it from inuring to the benefit of present holders to the prejudice of the taxpayers.

Resolved, That to secure fair elections is the paramount issue before the people of this State. We assert that the following conditions, made effective by law, are absolutely essential if elections are to elect, viz.: Provide registration by non-partisan boards—annual in the city, quadrennial, with annual reviews, in the counties; minority representation not only among the officers of election and registration, but in the boards

458	MASSACHUSETTS.

which appoint these officers; complete publicity at every stage of registration and election procedure, and glass ballot-boxes; and the Republican party of Maryland, speaking for itself and its nominees, pledges it and them to secure all the essentials of a fair election by using its and their best efforts to have the next General Assembly, before it considers other legislative business, enact the Reform League Election Law.

The Prohibitionists nominated Summerfield Baldwin for Governor, Thomas E. Wright for Comptroller, and James Pollard for Attorney-General. At the election on November 8 the Democratic ticket was elected, but the proposition for a constitutional convention failed of adoption. The vote for Governor was: Jackson, 99,038; Brooks, 86,622; Baldwin, 4,416. The Democratic plurality was somewhat reduced from former years owing to the defection of a considerable faction of that party which was opposed to the alleged dictation of Senator Gorman. The official returns of the convention vote were as follow: For the convention, 72,464; against it, 105,735; blank votes, 8,908. A majority of the total vote being necessary, the convention was defeated by 42,179 votes. The State Senate will consist of 22 Democrats and 4 Republicans; the House, of 71 Democrats and 20 Republicans.

Baltimore.—The election for mayor and members of the City Council took place on October 28, and resulted in the success of the Democratic ticket. Gen. F. C. Latrobe, Democrat, received 34,827 votes; David L. Bartlett, Republican, 30,332 votes; scattering, 110; Latrobe's majority, 4,385. The City Council stands 12 Democrats and 8 Republicans in the first branch and 7 Democrats and 3 Republicans in the second branch. The following statement exhibits the financial condition of the city at the close of the year: Amount of funded and guaranteed debt, $36,369,176; total income-producing securities held by the city, $28,661,448; net liability, $7,707,727; increase of total debt during the year, $1,413,886; increase of net debt, $1,878,852; the expenses of the city government for 1886 were $4,643,077; for 1887, $4,541,357; valuation in 1886, $256,-240,655; in 1887, $265,559,952. During the year a number of precinct officers and clerks charged with falsifying election returns at the municipal election in October, 1886, were put on trial, and after considerable delay the conviction of about half of them was secured in June.

MASSACHUSETTS. State Government.—The following were the State officers during the year: Governor, Oliver Ames, Republican; Lieutenant-Governor, John Q. A. Brackett; Secretary of State, Henry B. Peirce; Auditor, Charles R. Ladd; Treasurer, Alanson W. Beard; Attorney-General, Edgar J. Sherman; Railroad Commissioners, Thomas Russell (succeeded by George G. Crocker), Edward W. Kinsley, and Everett A. Stevens; Chief-Justice of the Supreme Court, Marcus Morton; Associate-Justices, Walbridge A. Field, Charles Devens, William Allen, Charles Allen, Oliver W. Holmes,

Jr., and William S. Gardner, succeeded by Marcus P. Knowlton. In September Attorney-General Sherman resigned his office, having been appointed by Governor Ames to the vacancy on the bench of the Superior Court caused by the promotion of Judge Knowlton. Andrew J. Waterman was appointed Attorney-General for the remainder of the term.

Legislative Session.—The first duty of the session was to choose a successor to Henry L. Dawes as United States Senator. A Republican conference failed to agree upon a candidate, and the party entered the contest dividing its support between three aspirants, Senator Dawes, Congressman John D. Long, and ex-Governor George D. Robinson. The Democratic candidate was Congressman Patrick A. Collins. The first joint ballot, as originally cast, gave Collins 92 votes, Dawes 76, Long 53, and Robinson 53. Before its announcement, however, the Democrats, realizing the impossibility of electing their own candidate, determined to decide the Republican quarrel by changing their votes to Senator Dawes. He was therefore re-elected, receiving 181 votes, to 57 for Robinson, 26 for Long, and 11 for Collins. The legislation of the session consisted of 452 acts and 107 resolutions. A large majority of these were special or local measures. Among the important general laws are those securing additional protection and security to employés, abolishing contract labor in prisons, the law exempting veterans from the operation of the civil service act, and the amendments to the Sunday law. The soldiers' exemption act provides that all honorably discharged soldiers and sailors who served in the civil war shall be preferred in appointment for office, without having passed an examination. It is substantially the same measure vetoed by Governor Robinson at the previous session. The Sunday law relieves certain kinds of business from the interdict that the statutes, according to a recent interpretation of the court, place upon all who keep open shop on Sunday. It provides that the law shall not be construed to prohibit "the manufacture and distribution of steam, gas, or electricity for illuminating purposes, heat, or motive power, nor the distribution of water for fire or domestic purposes, nor the use of the telegraph or telephone, nor the retail of drugs and medicines, nor articles ordered by the prescription of a physician, nor mechanical appliances used by physicians and surgeons, nor the letting of horses and carriages, nor the letting of yachts and boats, nor the running of steam ferry-boats on established routes, or street-railway cars, nor the preparation, printing, and publishing of newspapers, nor the sale and delivery of newspapers, nor the retail sale and delivery of milk, nor the transportation of milk, nor the making of butter and cheese, nor the keeping open of public bath-houses, nor the making or selling by bakers of bread or other food before ten o'clock in the morning and between the hours of four and half-past six in the evening."

The most fruitful subject of discussion at this session was the proposed division of the town of Beverly, and the incorporation of the town of Beverly Farms. The measure was opposed by the people of Beverly proper, who derived great benefit from the taxes of their wealthy neighbors. Prolonged hearings took place before the legislative committee, and money was liberally spent by both sides in securing an active lobby. Charges were also made that members of the Legislature had been bribed, and one Senator testified before an investigating committee that he had been corruptly approached by friends of one party. The committee was, however, unable to find any conclusive evidence of bribery. The bill for division finally passed, but was vetoed by the Governor, solely on the ground of the questionable practices attending its passage. He says: "While, of course, no member of the Legislature has taken or would take money for his vote, yet some $20,000 have been spent to indirectly influence the action of the Legislature. It is no excuse that such things, or worse, have happened before without exposure. This time the abuse has been investigated, exposed, and rebuked in scathing terms by the committees of both houses. I regard it as my duty to the Commonwealth, and to the maintenance of a wholesome public sentiment in behalf of legislation which shall be above suspicion, to act upon the reports made by these committees and adopted by their respective houses, and to strike emphatically at the evil thus unearthed."

Another act, passed after a contest, extends for four years the time for the completion of the Cape Cod Ship-Canal across the town of Sandwich, from Cape Cod Bay to Buzzard's Bay. The original company was permitted to retain its franchise, although several others sought earnestly to secure it.

A State tax of $2,250,000 for the year was apportioned among the towns.

An act that promises to be of great value in shortening legislative sessions, gives the Superior Court jurisdiction of all personal claims, either in law or equity, against the Commonwealth, thus removing the necessity for personal-relief bills, of which a large number were passed each year.

Other acts of the session are as follow:

To incorporate the Massachusetts Agricultural Experiment Station at the State Agricultural College.

Regulating the sale and purchase of poisons.

Authorizing the Governor to appoint three directors of the Fitchburg Railroad Company to represent the interest of the State in the stock of that road.

To incorporate the American Pomological Society.

Prohibiting the taking or sale of scallops at certain seasons.

Providing for the appointment of commissioners of wrecks and shipwrecked goods, who shall take charge of such goods and restore them to the owner, or otherwise dispose of them according to the provisions of this act.

Authorizing the city of Boston to issue bonds, not to exceed $2,500,000, for the erection of a new courthouse for Suffolk County.

To secure proper ventilation and sanitary provisions in factories and workshops.

Prohibiting the employment of children in factories to clean machinery in motion.

Providing for the assessment of royalty-paying machines at the place where they are used or operated.

To incorporate the trustees of Clark University in the city of Worcester.

To establish a board of registration in dentistry, and giving it powers to regulate the practice of the profession in the State.

To punish false pretenses in securing the registration of cattle and other animals, or the transfers of such registration, and to punish giving false pedigrees.

To provide for the appointment of a reserve police force in Boston, and that appointments to the regular force be made from such force.

To provide for pensioning members of the Boston police department.

To provide for the free instruction of deaf-mutes or deaf children.

Extending the time for which railroad corporations may issue bonds from 20 to 50 years.

To prohibit the unlicensed selling, distributing, or dispensing of intoxicating liquors by clubs.

To discontinue the Asylum for the Insane at Ipswich.

To accept an annual appropriation of money by Congress for the support of agricultural experiments within the Commonwealth.

To amend and codify the statutes relating to insurance.

To secure uniform and proper meal-hours for children, young persons, or women in factories and workshops.

Exempting corporations whose franchise is subject to taxation from taxation of their shares.

To provide for the appointment of police matrons in cities at the various police stations, and for the establishment of a house of detention for women in Boston.

To co-operate with the United States in the suppression and extirpation of pleuro-pneumonia by giving certain Federal officers the right of inspection, quarantine, and condemnation of diseased animals in the State, and conferring other powers upon them.

To give the boards of health of cities and towns power to suppress contagious diseases among animals.

To make the first Monday of September, known as "Labor's Holiday," a legal holiday.

To extend and regulate the liability of employers to make compensation for personal injuries suffered by employés in their service.

Providing that two hours, after the opening of the polls for any State or national election, shall be allowed an employé, at his request, in which to cast his ballot.

Regulating the taxation of insurance companies.

To authorize a loan of $400,000 by the city of Boston for the payment for lands heretofore acquired for public parks in or near said city.

To provide for the employment by the Commissioners of Prisons of additional agents to aid discharged prisoners.

Enlarging the jurisdiction of the Superior Court by giving it exclusive original jurisdiction over divorces, proceedings for alimony, custody of children, and otherwise, hitherto exercised by the Supreme Judicial Court.

Providing for a more thorough and regular inspection of railroad bridges.

Providing for a change of venue in civil actions in cases tried in the Superior or Supreme Court, whenever it appears, by reason of local prejudice or other cause, that a fair trial can not be had in the county where the action is pending.

To prevent the sale of intoxicating liquors in time of riot or great public excitement.

To provide for the incorporation of churches.

Amending and enlarging the law relative to the State militia.

Providing for the incorporation of the town of North Attleborough, and its separation from Attleborough.

To authorize the West End Street-Railway Company, and other street-railway companies authorized to run cars in the city of Boston, to lease and to purchase and hold the property, rights, and franchises of each other, and to unite and consolidate with each other, and to locate and construct tunnels, and to establish and maintain the cable and electric systems of motive power, and for other purposes.

To authorize the use of the Reformatory Prison for Women at Sherborn, and the State Industrial School for Girls at Lancaster, for the punishment of female offenders convicted in the United States Courts.

To limit and regulate the sale of intoxicating liquors by retail druggists and apothecaries.

Prohibiting the employment of minors who can not read and write in the English language, except during school vacations, if the minor is under fourteen years of age, unless it appears that the work of said minor is necessary for the support of himself or his family.

To provide for the punishment of habitual criminals.

Prohibiting under penalty the admission of any child under thirteen years of age to any licensed show or place of amusement after sunset, unless accompanied by an adult.

The session adjourned June 16, having occupied 162 days.

Finances.—No payment was made upon the funded debt of the State during the year. It amounted, January 1, to $31,429,680.90. The following statement shows the growth of the sinking funds:

Amount of sinking funds, Jan. 1, 1887 .... $18,964,412 62
Amount of sinking funds, Jan. 1, 1888 .... 25,151,516 78

    Increase $6,187,104 16

Actual expenses, 1886 .... $5,275,502 91
Actual expenses, 1887, so far as can be ascertained 5,105,898 85

The large increase in the sinking funds is due to the sale of the Troy and Greenfield Railroad and Hoosac Tunnel, $5,000,000 of Fitchburg Railroad bonds being put into the Troy and Greenfield Railroad loan sinking fund. The State also holds 50,000 shares of common stock in the Fitchburg Railroad Company, par value $5,000,000, which belongs to the Troy and Greenfield Railroad loan sinking fund, but is not included in the above figures. Of the estimated deficit ($1,718,619.89), $464,-922.88 is represented by taxes of 1885, 1886, and 1887, levied upon the stock of national banks, which were paid under protest. This money is held in trust in the State treasury, awaiting the decision of the United States Supreme Court as to the constitutionality of the law under which it was paid.

There has also been collected of these taxes $631,839.45 additional, which has been distributed to the cities and towns. If the law should not be sustained by the court, both of these sums must be refunded.

The receipts of the treasury for 1887 are as follow: Cash on hand, January 1, $2,205,-582.81; securities, $22,860,871.45; from revenue, $11,488,143.95; sinking funds, $25,411,-562.19; trust funds, $611,543.46; trust deposits, $208,496.80; miscellaneous funds, $786,742.81; securities purchased in 1887, $9,608,439.65; total, $73,176,882.62. The disbursements were for actual payments in 1887, $36,963,534.93; securities withdrawn or sold or paid, $4,624,157.75; cash on hand December 31, $3,743,536.59; securities on hand, $27,845,153.35; total, $73,176,882.62.

The taxable property of the Commonwealth is $2,341,555,841.65, divided as follows: Real and personal estate as of May 1, 1887, $1,982,-548,807; amount not included on account of national bank stock held by non-residents, $29,109,821.53: deposits in savings-banks, Nov. 1, 1887, $181,878,137.12; shares in corporations above real estate and machinery locally taxed, $178,109,076. The valuation shows an increase of $132,803,518 over 1886.

Education.—The annual report of the Secretary of the Board of Education gives the following statistics regarding the public schools of the State for 1886–'87: Number of public schools, 6,836; number of pupils, 353,361; average membership, 291,539; average attendance, 262,159; number of children in the State between five and fifteen years on May 1, 1886, 353,052; number of teachers employed, males, 1,038; number of teachers employed, females, 8,696; average wages of male teachers per month, $116.85; average wages of female teachers per month, $44.98.

The number of pupils in the schools has increased by 8,744 during the year, the average membership 2,899, and the average attendance 2,071. The whole amount of money raised by taxation for the support of schools was $5,059,939.43, an increase of $242,510.42 over the previous year. The amount received from all sources and expended, exclusive of money for the erection and repair of school-houses, was $5,857,321, an increase of $180,251.92, and an average of $16.59 for each child of school age. The whole amount expended for all public-school purposes was $7,000,088.52, or $19.82 for each child of school age. The number of private schools in the State is reported at 352 and the attendance for the year 28,941, an estimate far too low, as it is known from official sources that 30,000 pupils attended during the year the schools maintained by the Catholic Church alone.

At the five State normal schools and the Normal Art School, 1,232 pupils received instruction during the school year, and the number of graduates was 250. The Massachusetts School for the Feeble-Minded contained 193 pupils on September 30, of whom 32 were supported at private expense. The cost of maintaining this school during the year was about $41,000. The Legislature of this year appropriated $20,000 for the purchase of a more favorable site for the location of the school-building, and a tract of seventy-two acres was secured for that purpose.

Charities.—The whole number of the State poor who are either fully supported or in some way aided from the State treasury amounts to nearly 20,000 in a year. The number of the in-door poor of the cities and towns is nearly 12,000 in a year, of whom about 8,500 are insane persons. The number of the out-door poor of the cities and towns, as distinct from those of the State, can not readily be given, but is between 80,000 and 40,000 during the year. The valuation of all the establishments in the State for the relief of the poor is $9,000,-000. The valuation of the city and town almshouses, with their personal property (amounting to about $550,000), and their farms of a little less than 21,000 acres, is very nearly $3,000,000. The valuation of the eleven State establishments, including the hospitals and asylums for the insane, has now reached about $6,000,000, of which less than $1,000,000 is personal property, while the number of acres in the State farms but little exceeds 2,800.

At the close of the year the following inmates of the State charitable institutions are reported: Institutions for the insane: Males, 1,782; females, 1,963. Total, 3,695. State Almshouse (excluding the asylum), State Primary School and State Farm (excluding the asylum), 1,410; Lyman School for Boys, State Industrial School and the School for the Feeble-Minded, 402. Aggregate, 5,507.

The Insane.—At the Danvers Insane Hospital 1,209 patients were treated during the year ending September 80. At the beginning of this period there were 768 patients; at its close, 740. The total receipts of the year were $150,874.21; payments, $148,870.09. At the Northampton Hospital 689 cases were treated during the year, there being 491 patients at the beginning and 469 at its close. Total receipts, $96,994.40; payments, $93,-511.38. The Taunton Hospital treated 984 cases, having at the beginning of the fiscal year 663; at its close, 634. The total receipts were $133,836.40; payments, 132,141.80. For the Worcester Hospital the figures are as follow: Total number of cases, 1,078; patients, Sept. 30, 1886, 758; Sept. 30, 1887, 694; total receipts, $187,658.33; total expenses, $162,-801.15. At the Worcester Asylum for Chronic Insane there were 444 cases, 398 at the beginning of the year and 392 at its close. Total receipts, $84,016.82; expenses, $72,833.51. The Westborough Insane Hospital was first opened for patients in December, 1886. It had received from other hospitals and from original commitments up to September 30 of this year 432 patients, of which 123 were discharged, leaving 309 at the end of the year. The total receipts were $70,607.14, and expenditures $65,205.74. In addition to these hospitals there is a department for the insane at the Tewksbury Almshouse, where 444 patients were treated during the year, 849 re-maining at its close. The total number of almshouse inmates at the beginning of the year was 828; at its close, 877.

Prisons.—At the State Prison on December 1 583 prisoners were confined. The Massachusetts Reformatory for men contained 687 convicts, having received during the three years of its existence 2,234 persons. "The work thus far accomplished by the reformatory has been of a high order, and its results are encouraging; but the design of the institution has been seriously interfered with by the fact that to it have been sent men who are wholly unfit to be subjected to its influences." The Reformatory Prison for Women, which contained over 100 inmates at the end of the year, is accomplishing a similar work to that of the Massachusetts Reformatory.

The law abolishing contract labor in the prisons went into effect on November 1. Under its provisions all labor in the prisons must be done for the benefit of the State, and upon such industries as the warden or general superintendent shall direct. Tools, implements, and materials shall be purchased by the State, but no new machinery other than hand or foot-power shall be furnished. A general superintendent of prisons is created, who shall establish and supervise the work in the State Prison, reformatories, and houses of correction, in connection with the superintendents of such institutions. The provisions of this act have proved to be ill-advised in several important particulars. It divides the duty of supervision between the State Superintendent and the wardens or superintendents of each institution without defining their respective powers. The wisdom of State control of county prisons is also doubtful. Prohibition of new machinery operates unfairly against prisons that have not yet used mechanical equipments.

Railroads.—During the year ending September 80 there were constructed 28 miles of main track, making the total length in the State 2,018 miles. There are in addition 740 miles of double track and 964 miles of sidings, making a total of 3,722 miles. The aggregate capital stock of the companies doing business in the State was $150,469,414, an increase of $19,781,445 over 1886. Their gross income was $53,650,438, an increase of $4,834,617. The net income, however, shows a decrease of $195,646 over last year. Dividends were declared to the amount of $7,550,901, or $693,-895 above last year.

Returns from the street-railways in the State show a total length of track, including branches, sidings, and double track, of 507 miles, an increase of nearly 67 miles in a year. The average cost per mile was $34,648 for construction and equipment. The aggregate capital stock was $10,096,800, an increase of $971,155; gross income, $6,459,524, an increase of $580,-941, with a decrease of net income amounting to $107,614. There was an increase of $36,850 in dividends.

Savings-Banks.—There were deposited in savings-banks and other institutions for savings, at the end of their fiscal year, $302,948,483, an increase for the year of $11,750,582. The number of depositors is more than 945,000, or nearly half the number of people in the State. The returns made by savings-banks, in accordance with an act of 1887, of deposits unclaimed for twenty years, and depositors of the same unknown to the banks holding said deposits, or known to be dead, show a very large amount of this class of deposits, aggregating in all the savings-banks several hundred thousand dollars. As all estates, in default of heirs, escheat to the Commonwealth, the State has a large interest in these deposits.

Political.—A convention of the Prohibition party was held at Worcester, September 7, and the following ticket was adopted: For Governor, W. H. Earle; for Lieutenant-Governor, John Blackmer; for Secretary of State, A. E. Hall; for Treasurer, John L. Kilburn; for Auditor, Edmund M. Stowe; for Attorney-General, Allen Coffin. The platform declares:

That the system of licensing the manufacture and sale of liquors, as a professed attempt at restriction, is practically a failure. The consequent diminution of drinking-saloons, even in the case of high license, is scarcely appreciable, while the remainder are abundantly able and entirely willing to make up the deficiency by increased sales.

That the principle of local option, so-called, has been proved by numerous examples to be insufficient to guard any given locality from the inroads of this enemy.

We earnestly warn the sincere temperance reformers of the Commonwealth against the sophistries of the Republican party on the liquor question. Notwithstanding its virtuous professions, we charge it with truckling to the liquor vote. We affirm it to have deceived thousands of Prohibitionists last year by its pledge to submit the amendment to the votes of the people, and by its nomination of a supposed Prohibitionist as a candidate for Governor, while the amendment was not submitted (although it was within the power of the party so to have done), and the gubernatorial candidate, when elected, not only acquiesced in the system of license, but said never a word in advocacy of prohibition. We affirm the Republican party to be responsible for all the drinking-saloons in the city of Boston to-day, since the discretionary licensing power is in the hands of the Governor, or, more directly, in the hands of the Police Commissioners, whom the Governor appoints, a majority of whom are also Republicans.

The Democratic Convention, on September 29, nominated for Governor ex-Congressman Henry B. Lovering; for Lieutenant-Governor, Walter E. Outting; for Secretary of State, John F. Murphy; for Treasurer, Henry C. Thatcher; for Auditor, William F. Cook; for Attorney-General, John W. Corcoran. The platform approves the national Administration, demands a reduction of the tariff, and approves the Federal laws prohibiting the importation of contract labor. Upon State topics it says:

We renew our declaration in favor of an unrestricted ballot. We regard the requirement of the payment of a poll-tax as a qualification to vote as a disgrace to the State, an unjust discrimination against the poor man, demoralizing in its effects, and a fruitful source of political corruption. We demand such an amendment of the Constitution of the State as will make each ballot the representative of a man and not of a dollar. We charge the Republican leaders with deception and double-dealing on this subject, and earnestly recommend that no candidate be voted for who is not unconditionally pledged to support such an amendment.

We acknowledge our obligations to the wage-earners, and pledge to them our earnest efforts in procuring such legislation as will best promote their interests. We cordially approve of the legislative act making Labor Day a legal holiday, and earnestly commend its general observance.

The Republican State Convention, held September 28, renominated Governor Ames, Lieut.-Governor Brackett, Secretary Peirce, Auditor Ladd, and Treasurer Beard. For Attorney-General, Andrew J. Waterman was nominated. The platform favors protection, a reduction of surplus in the national treasury, an honest ballot, and civil service reform. It contains the following upon State issues:

Recognizing in intemperance the most fruitful source of pauperism, crime, corruption in politics, and social degradation, we affirm our belief in the most thorough restriction of the liquor traffic, and the enforcement of law for its suppression. We approve the action of the last Legislature in enacting so many temperance statutes, and demand the continued enactment of progressive temperance measures as the policy of our party. We repeat the recommendation of last year's convention, as follows: "Believing that this great public question now demands settlement, we favor the submission to the people of an amendment to our Constitution prohibiting the manufacture and sale of alcoholic liquors to be used as a beverage." In order to have this matter placed before the people, we call upon all those who are opposed to the political control of the grog-shops to unite with the Republican party in electing Senators and Representatives who will vote for the submission of this amendment.

The elevation and protection of American labor, the increase of its wages, the promotion and security of all its interests, material and moral, are not only a cardinal object of the Republican party, but are the principal purpose for which it was formed, and for which it exists; as witness its protective policy, its demand for a free and fair ballot, and for universal education, and the well-known liberal legislation of republican Massachusetts in behalf of her mechanics and wage-workers. We believe that this end will be defeated by the success of any attempt to array labor against capital, which is the legitimate fruit of industry, skill, and enterprise for all alike, and upon the accumulation of which the employment and prosperity of labor itself largely depends.

The Republican party ever has maintained, and ever will maintain and defend, the common-schools of Massachusetts as the very citadel of her liberties, and the source of her glory, greatness, and happiness. They shall be kept open to all her children, and free from all partisan and sectarian control.

We believe that the Republican administration of the State of Massachusetts is honest, upright, and has earned the confidence of all good citizens. We believe that a Republican Legislature will consider questions outside of party issues more wisely than will a body having a majority of our opponents, and we earnestly recommend to all constituencies that they should select such candidates for Senators and Representatives to the General Court, that the high standard of Massachusetts legislation may not be impaired. We only echo the general opinion of our people in saying that Gov. Ames has performed the duties of his office to the public satisfaction; that the State Government is worthy of indorsement, and that its continuance in office would mean that the voters of Massachusetts are determined not to exhibit in their State affairs the unhappy evidences of public mismanagement which the Democratic leaders have inflicted upon the city of Boston, and would, if in control, repeat upon the State.

A Labor ticket, headed by Charles E. Marks, was also in the field. One notable feature of the campaign was the general refusal of the Independents to support the Democratic ticket. The election on November 8 resulted in the success of the Republicans by an increased plurality over last year. Ames received 136,-000 votes; Lovering, 118,394; Earle, 10,945; and Marks, 595; Republican plurality, 17,606. The plurality of the remainder of the ticket averages about 24,000. The Executive Council will consist of 7 Republicans and 1 Democrat; 30 Republicans and 10 Democrats were elected to the Senate; 164 Republicans, 71 Democrats, and 5 Independents to the House.

Cities.—The annual municipal elections took place on the first and second Tuesdays of December, seventeen cities voting on the former date, and six, including Boston, on the latter. On the license question fifteen cities voted yes, and eight no, a loss of five cities by the prohibitionists, as compared with last year.

Mayor O'Brien was re-elected in Boston for the fourth time, by a plurality of 1,539 over Thomas U. Hart, the Republican candidate, as against a plurality of 4,740 the previous year. O'Brien received 26,640 votes; Hart 25,101. The political complexion of the Board of Alderman was entirely changed, 8 Republicans being elected, and only 4 Democrats and Independent Democrats. The Council is strongly Democratic.

MEDAL OF HONOR, THE UNITED STATES. The one decoration that the Government of the United States gives to those of its soldiers who distinguish themselves by some act of individual gallantry is the Medal of Honor. It is within the reach of the humblest private, and is prized alike by officers and enlisted men. This decoration was authorized as a reward for military service by a joint resolution approved July 12, 1862, as follows:

Resolved, by the Senate and House of Representatives of the United States in Congress assembled, that the President of the United States be, and he is hereby authorized to cause 2,000 medals of honor to be prepared with suitable emblematic devices, and to direct that the same be presented in the name of Congress to such non-commissioned officers and privates as shall most distinguish themselves by their gallantry in action and their soldier-like qualities during the present insurrection.

This was followed. March 3, 1863, by an act to the effect that "the President cause to be struck, from dies recently prepared at the United States mint for that purpose, medals of honor additional to those authorized by the act of July 12, 1862, and present the same to such officers, non-commissioned officers, and privates as have most distinguished, or may hereafter most distinguish themselves in action; and the sum of $20,000 is hereby appropriated out of any money in the Treasury not otherwise appropriated to defray the expenses of the

same." The medal, which is shown on the same page with those of the Grand Army, is a five-pointed star tipped with trefoil, each point containing a crown of laurel and oak; in the middle, within a circle of thirty-four stars, America is personified as Minerva, with her left hand resting on the fasces, while with her right, in which she holds a shield bearing the arms of the United States, she repels Discord. The whole is suspended by a trophy of two crossed cannon and a sword surmounted by the American eagle, and linked with the dependent star. A ribbon of thirteen stripes, palewise, gules and argent, and a chief azure, unites it with a clasp consisting of two cornucopias and the arms of the United States. The metal accessories are of bronze, and no distinction has as yet been made by giving medals of silver or gold where peculiar circumstances would seem to justify some extraordinary recognition of service. Gen. E. D. Townsend, late Adjutant-General of the Army, was especially active in securing the passage of the acts that authorize this coveted reward of distinguished bravery. A large majority of those who received the medal were enlisted men in the volunteer ranks during the civil war, but many have also been conferred upon members of the regular army for acts of self-devotion performed during the civil war or while engaged in fighting hostile Indians in those arduous campaigns that fall to the lot of our little army on its frontier posts. The following is the latest complete list. Opposite each man's name is briefly mentioned the act for which he received the medal. If expanded into paragraphs, this roster would present a record of personal gallantry that can hardly be surpassed in the annals of warfare; and yet, so indifferent are the American public to the patriotism of their bravest soldiers, that this brief record will probably convey to many readers their first knowledge of the existence of this most honorable order of merit. Gen. Theodore F. Rodenbough, has recently published an historic and personal narrative under the title of "Uncle Sam's Medal of Honor" (New York, 1887).

Adams, James F., private, 1st W. Va. Cav., Nineveh, Va., Nov. 12, 1864, capture of flag.
Allen, Abner P., corporal, 39th Ill., gallantry.
Ammerman, Robert W., private, 148th Pa., Spottsylvania, May 12, 1864, capture of flag.
Anderson, Charles W., private, 1st N. Y. Lincoln Cav., Waynesborough, Va., March 2, 1865, capture of flag.
Anderson, Frederic C., private, 18th Mass., Weldon R. R., Aug. 21, 1864, capture of flag.
Anderson, Peter, private, 31st Wis., Bentonville, N. C., March 19, 1865, saving gun from capture.
Anderson, Thomas, corporal, 1st W. Va. Cav., Appomattox Station, April 8, 1865, capture of flag.
Apple, Andrew O., corporal, 12th W. Va., gallantry.
Archer, Lester, sergeant, 96th N. Y., Battery Hudson, near Richmond, Sept. 29, 1864, placing colors on Battery Hudson.
Bacon, Elijah W., private, 14th Conn., Gettysburg, Pa., July 3, 1863, capture of flag.

Barber, James A., corporal, 1st R. I. Art., Petersburg, Va., April 2, 1865, gallantry.

Barnes, William H., private, 38th U. S. C. T., Chaffin's Farm, near Richmond, Va., Sept. 29, 1864, among the first to enter the rebel works, although wounded.

Barry, Augustus, sergeant-major, 16th U. S., 1863 to 1865, gallantry.

Barry, John P., 1st sergeant, 24th V. R. C., April, 1865, acting as escort to remains of President Lincoln.

Bates, Norman F., sergeant, 4th Iowa Cav., Columbus, Ga., April 16, 1865, capture of flag and bearer.

Baybutt, Philip, private, 2d Mass. Cav., Luray, Va.; Sept. 24, 1864, capture of flag.

Beaty, Powhatan, 1st sergeant, 5th U. S. C. T., Chaffin's Farm, near Richmond, Va., Sept. 29, 1864, gallantry.

Bebb, Edward J., private, 4th Iowa Cav., Columbus, Ga., April 16, 1865, capture of flag.

Begley, Terrance, sergeant, 7th N. Y. Hy. Art., Cold Harbor, Va., June 3, 1864, capture of flag.

Belcher, Thomas, private, 9th Me., Chaffin's Farm, near Richmond, Va., Sept. 29, 1864, gallantry.

Benjamin, John F., corporal, 2d N. Y. Cav., Sailor's Creek, Va., April 6, 1865, capture of flag.

Benjamin, Samuel N., 1st lieutenant, 2d U. S. Art., Bull Run to Spottsylvania, Va., July, 1861, to May, 1864, distinguished service as an artillery officer.

Bennett, Orren, private, 141st Pa., Sailor's Creek, Va., April 6, 1865, capture of flag.

Bonsinger, William, private, 21st Ohio, Georgia, 1862, special services under Gen. Mitchel.

Bickford, Henry H., corporal, 8th N. Y. Cav., Waynesborough, Va., March 2, 1865, recapture of flag.

Birdsall, Horatio L., sergeant, 3d Iowa Cav., Columbus, Ga., April 16, 1865, capture of flag and bearer.

Bishop, Francis A., private, 57th Pa., Spottsylvania, Va., May 12, 1864, capture of flag.

Blickensderfer, Milton, corporal, 126th Ohio, Petersburg, Va., April 3, 1865, capture of flag.

Blucher, Charles, corporal, 188th Pa., Fort Harrison, near Richmond, Va., Sept. 29, 1864, planting colors on fortifications.

Bonebrake, Henry G., lieutenant, 17th Pa. Cav., Five Forks, Va., April 1, 1865, capture of flag.

Boon, Hugh P., captain, 1st W. Va. Cav., Sailor's Creek, Va., April 6, 1865, capture of flag.

Bowen, Chester B., corporal, 1st N. Y. Dragoons, Winchester, Va., Sept. 19, 1864, capture of flag.

Bowey, Richard, sergeant, 1st W. Va. Cav., Charlottesville, Va., March 5, 1865, capture of flag.

Box, Thomas J., captain, 27th Ind., Resaca, Ga., May 25, 1864, capture of flag.

Bradbury, James [Jas. Brady], private, 10th N. H., Chaffin's Farm, near Richmond, Va., Sept. 29, 1864, capture of flag.

Brannigan, Felix, private, 74th N. Y., Chancellorsville, Va., May 2, 1863, volunteering on a dangerous service.

Brant, William, lieutenant, 1st N. J. Vet. Batl., Petersburg, Va., April 3, 1865, capture of flag.

Bras, Edgar A., sergeant, 8th Iowa, Spanish Fort, Ala., April 8, 1865, capture of flag.

Brest, Lewis F., private, 57th Pa., Sailor's Creek, Va., April 6, 1865, capture of flag.

Brewer, William I., private, 2d N. Y. Cav., Virginia, April 4, 1865, capture of flag.

Briggs, Elijah A., corporal, 2d Conn. Hy. Art., Petersburg, Va., April 3, 1865, capture of flag.

Bringle, Andrew, corporal, 10th N. Y. Cav., Sailor's Creek, Va., April 6, 1865, gallantry.

Bronson, James H., 1st sergeant, 5th U. S. C. T., Chaffin's Farm, near Richmond, Va., Sept. 29, 1864, gallantry.

Brown, Charles, sergeant, 50th Pa., Weldon R. R., Aug. 19, 1864, capture of flag.

Brown, Jr., Edward, corporal, 62d N. Y., Fredericksburg and Salem Heights, Va., May 3 and 4, 1863, gallantry.

Brown, John H., captain, 12th Ky., Franklin, Tenn., Nov. 30, 1864, capture of flag.

Brown, Jr., Morris, captain, 126th N. Y., Gettysburg, Pa., July 3, 1863, capture of flag.

Brown, Wilson, private, 21st Ohio, Georgia, 1862, special services under Gen. Mitchel.

Brownell, Francis E., private, 11th N. Y., May 24, 1861, shooting the murderer of Col. Ellsworth.

Bruton, Christopher C., captain, 22d N. Y. Cav., Waynesborough, Va., March 2, 1865, capture of Gen. Early's headquarters flag.

Bryant, Andrew S., sergeant, 46th Mass., New Berne, N. C., May 23, 1863, gallantry.

Buchanan, George A., private, 148th N. Y., Chaffin's Farm, near Richmond, Va., Sept. 29, 1864, gallantry.

Buck, F. Clarence, corporal, 21st Conn., Chaffin's Farm, near Richmond, Va., Sept. 29, 1864, capture of flag.

Buckley, Dennis, private, 136th N. Y., Peach Tree Creek, Ga., July 20, 1864, capture of flag.

Buffum, Robert, private, 21st Ohio, Georgia, 1862, special services under Gen. Mitchel.

Bulock, Luther E., 1st sergeant, 9th V. R. C., April, 1865, acting as escort to remains of President Lincoln.

Burk, Michael, private, 125th N. Y., Spottsylvania, Va., May 12, 1864, capture of flag.

Burke, Thomas, sergeant, 5th N. Y. Cav., Hanover C. H., Va., June 30, 1863, capture of flag.

Caldwell, Daniel, sergeant, 13th Pa. Cav., Hatcher's Run, Va., Feb. 6, 1865, capture of flag.

Calkin, Ivers S., 1st sergeant, 2d N. Y. Cav., Sailor's Creek, Va., April 6, 1865, capture of flag.

Callaghan, Patrick, 1st sergeant, 9th V. R. C., April —, 1865, acting as escort to remains of President Lincoln.

Callahan, John H., private, 122d Ill., Blakely, Ala., April 9, 1865, capture of flag.

Capron, Jr., Horace, sergeant, 8th Ill. Cav., Chickahominy and Ashland, Va., June —, 1862, gallantry.

Carey, Frank, 1st sergeant, 12th V. R. C., April —, 1865, acting as escort to remains of President Lincoln.

Carman, Warren, private, 1st N. Y. Lincoln Cav., Waynesborough, Va., March 2, 1865, capture of flag.

Carpenter, Samuel, 1st sergeant, 7th V. R. C., April —, 1865, acting as escort to remains of President Lincoln.

Carr, Augustus E., 1st sergeant, 12th V. R. C., April —, 1865, acting as escort to remains of President Lincoln.

Carr, Franklin, corporal, 124th Ohio, Nashville, Tenn., Dec. 16, 1864, recapture of guidon.

Cart, Jacob, private, 7th Pa. R. C., Fredericksburg, Va., Dec. 13, 1862, capture of flag.

Cary, James L., corporal, 10th N. Y., ——, Va., April 9, 1865, daring bravery and urging the men forward in a charge.

Cayer, Ovila, sergeant, 1st Batl. 14th U. S., Weldon R. R., Va., Aug. 19, 1864, gallantry.

Chambers, Joseph B., private, 100th Pa., Petersburg, Va., March 25, 1865, capture of flag.

Chapman, John, private, 1st Me. Hy. Art., Sailor's Creek, Va., April 6, 1865, capture of flag.

Clancy, James T., sergeant, 1st N. J. Cav., Vaughn Road, Va., Oct. 1, 1864, gallantry.

Clapp, Albert A., 1st sergeant, 2d Ohio Cav., Sailor's Creek, Va., April 6, 1865, capture of flag.

Clopp, John E., private, 71st Pa., Gettysburg, Pa., July 3, 1863, capture of flag.

Coates, Jefferson, sergeant, 7th Wis., Gettysburg, Pa., July 1, 1863, gallantry.

Cohn, Abraham, sergeant-major, 6th N. H., Wilderness, Va., May 6, 1864, gallantry.

Cole, Gabriel, corporal, 5th Mich. Cav., Winchester, Va., Sept. 19, 1864, capture of flag.

Collins, Harrison, corporal, 1st Tenn. Cav., Richland Creek, Tenn., Dec. 24, 1864, capture of flag.

Collins, James, 1st sergeant, 10th V. R. C., April —, 1865, acting as escort to remains of President Lincoln.

Colwell, Oliver, 1st lieutenant, 95th Ohio, Nashville, Tenn., Dec. 16, 1864, capture of flag.

Compson, Hartwell B., major, 8th N. Y. Cav., Waynesborough, Va., March 2, 1865, capture of flag.

Congdon, James, sergeant, 8th N. Y. Cav., Waynesborough, Va., March 2, 1865, recapture of flag.

Connell, Frustrim, corporal, 138th Pa., Sailor's Creek, Va., April 6, 1865, capture of flag.

Connors, James, private, 43d N. Y., Fisher's Hill, Va., Sept. 22, 1864, capture of flag.

Cornwell, Addison, 1st sergeant, 7th V. R. C., April —, 1865, acting as escort to remains of President Lincoln.

Cosgriff, Richard H., private, 4th Iowa Cav., Columbus, Ga., April 16, 1865, capture of flag.

Creed, John, private, 23d Ill., Fisher's Hill, Va., Sept. 22, 1864, capture of flag.

Crocker, Ulric, private, 6th Mich. Cav., Cedar Creek, Va., Oct. 19, 1864, capture of flag.

Crowley, Michael, private, 22d N. Y. Cav., Waynesborough, Va., March 2, 1865, capture of flag.

Cullen, Thomas, corporal, 82d N. Y., Bristow Station, Va., Oct. 14, 1863, capture of flag.

Cumpston, James, private, 91st Ohio, capture of flag.

Cunningham, Francis M., 1st sergeant, 1st W. Va. Cav., Sailor's Creek, Va., April 6, 1865, capture of flag.

Curtis, Josiah M., 2d lieutenant, 12th W. Va., gallantry.

Custer, Thomas W., 2d lieutenant, 6th Mich. Cav., Namozine Church and Sailor's Creek, Va., April 2 and 6, 1865, capture of two flags.

Daly, William T., 1st sergeant, 10th V. R. C., April —, 1865, acting as escort to remains of President Lincoln.

Davidsizer, John A., sergeant, 1st Pa. Cav., Paine's X Roads, Va., April 5, 1865, capture of flag.

Davis, Harry, private, 46th Ohio, Atlanta, Ga., July 28, 1864, capture of flag.

Davis, John, private, 17th Ind. Mtd. Inf., Culloden, Ga., April —, 1865, capture of flag.

Davis, Joseph, corporal, 104th Ohio, Franklin, Tenn., Nov. 30, 1864, capture of flag.

Davis, Thomas, private, 2d N. Y. Hy. Art., Sailor's Creek, Va., April 6, 1865, capture of flag.

De Castro, Joseph H., corporal, 19th Mass., Gettysburg, Pa., July 3, 1863, capture of flag.

Delavie, Hiram A., sergeant, 11th Pa., Five Forks, Va., April 1, 1865, capture of flag.

Dockham, Warren C., private, 121st N. Y., Sailor's Creek, Va., April 6, 1865, capture of flag.

Dolloff, Charles W., corporal, 11th Vt., Petersburg, Va., April 2, 1865, capture of flag.

Donaldson, John, sergeant, 4th Pa. Cav., Appomattox C. H., Va., April 9, 1865, capture of flag.

Dore, George H., sergeant, 126th N. Y., Gettysburg, July 3, 1863, capture of flag.

Dorley, August, private, 1st La. Cav., Mount Pleasant, Ala., April 11, 1865, capture of flag.

Dorsey, Daniel A., corporal, 33d Ohio, Georgia, 1862, special services under Gen. Mitchel.

Dorsey, Decatur, sergeant, 39th U. S. C. T., Petersburg, Va., July 30, 1864, bravery while acting as color-sergeant.

Dow, George P., 1st sergeant, 7th N. H., reconnaissance toward Richmond, Va., Oct. —, 1864, gallantry.

Drake, James M., 1st lieutenant, 9th N. J., 1861 to 1865, gallantry.

Dunlavy, James, private, 3d Iowa Cav., Osage, Kans., Oct. 25, 1864, capturing Gen. Marmaduke.

Durgin, William W., 1st sergeant, 10th V. R. C., April —, 1865, acting as escort to remains of President Lincoln.

Durkee, Joseph H., 1st lieutenant, 7th V. R. C., April —, 1865, acting as escort to remains of President Lincoln.

Edwards, David, private, 146th N. Y., Five Forks, Va., April 1, 1865, capture of flag.

Edwards, John R., 1st sergeant, 7th V. R. C., April —, 1865, acting as escort to remains of President Lincoln.

Elliott, Alexander, sergeant, 1st Pa. Cav., Paine's X Roads, Va., April 5, 1865, capture of flag.

Ellis, Horace, private, 7th Wis., Weldon R. R., Aug. 21, 1864, capture of flag.

Ellis, William, 1st sergeant, 3d Wis. Cav., Dardanelle, Ark., Jan. 14, 1865, gallantry.

Evans, Corren D., private, 3d Ind. Cav., Sailor's Creek, Va., April 6, 1865, capture of flag.

Evans, Thomas, private, 54th Pa., Piedmont, Va., June 5, 1864, capture of flag.

Everson, Adelbert, private, 185th N. Y., Five Forks, Va., April 1, 1865, capture of flag.

Ewing, John C., private, 211th Pa., Petersburg, Va., April 2, 1865, capture of flag.

Falls, Benjamin F., color-sergeant, 19th Mass., Gettysburg, Pa., July 3, 1863, capture of flag.

Fanning, Nicholas, private, 4th Iowa Cav., Selma, Ala., April 2, 1865, capture of flag and two staff officers.

Fasnacht, Charles H., sergeant, 99th Pa., Spottsylvania, Va., May 12, 1864, capture of flag.

Fernald, Albert E., 1st lieutenant, 20th Me., Five Forks, Va., April 1, 1865, capture of flag.

Fesq, Frank, private, 40th N. J., Petersburg, Va., April 2, 1865, capture of flag.

Flanagan, Augustine, sergeant, 55th Pa., Chaffin's Farm, near Richmond, Va., Sept. 29, 1864, gallantry.

Fleetwood, Christian A., sergeant-major, 4th U. S. C. T., Chaffin's Farm, near Richmond, Va., Sept. 29, 1864, gallantry.

Flynn, Christopher, corporal, 14th Conn., Gettysburg, Pa., July 3, 1863, capture of flag.

Ford, George W., 1st lieutenant, 88th N. Y., Sailor's Creek, Va., April 6, 1865, capture of flag.

Forehand, Lloyd D., 1st sergeant, 18th V. R. C., April —, 1865, acting as escort to remains of President Lincoln.

Fox, Henry M., sergeant, 5th Mich. Cav., Winchester, Va., Sept. 19, 1864, capture of flag.

Fox, William R., private, 95th Pa., Petersburg, Va., April 2, 1865, bravery.

Freeman, Archibald, private, 124th N. Y., Spottsylvania, Va., May 12, 1864, capture of flag.

Funk, West, sergeant-major, 121st Pa., Appomattox C. H., Va., April 9, 1865, capture of flag.

Ganse, Isaac, corporal, 2d Ohio, Sept. 5, 1864, escort to stand of colors captured by the 3d Division.

Gardiner, James, private, 36th U. S. C. T., Chaffin's Farm, near Richmond, Va., Sept. 29, 1864, gallantry.

Gardner, Asa B., captain, 22d N. Y. S. M., Maryland and Pennsylvania, June and July, 1863, services during the Gettysburg campaign.

Gardner, Charles N., private, 32d Mass., Five Forks, Va., April 1, 1865, capture of flag.

Gardner, Robert L., sergeant, 34th Mass., gallantry.

Garret, William, sergeant, 41st Ohio, Nashville, Tenn., Dec. 16, 1864, capture of flag.

Gaunt, John C., private, 104th Ohio, Franklin, Tenn., Nov. 30, 1864, capture of flag.

Gerber, Frederick W., sergeant-major, Batl. U. S. Engineers, gallantry.

Gere, Thomas P., 1st lieutenant and adjutant, 5th Minn., Nashville, Tenn., Dec. 16, 1864, capture of flag.

Gibbs, Wesley, sergeant, 2d Conn. Hy. Art., Petersburg, Va., April 2, 1865, capture of flag.

Gifford, Benjamin, private, 121st N. Y., Sailor's Creek, Va., April 6, 1865, capture of flag.

Gion, Joseph, private, 74th N. Y., Chancellorsville, Va., May 2, 1863, bravery when advancing on enemy's line under heavy fire; bringing back valuable information.

Goettel, Philip, private, 149th N. Y., Lookout Mountain, Tenn., Nov. 24, 1863, capture of flag.

Goheen, Charles A., 1st sergeant, 8th N. Y. Cav., Waynesborough, Va., March 2, 1865, capture of flag.

Goodrich, George E., 1st sergeant, 12th V. R. C., April —, 1865, acting as escort to remains of President Lincoln.

Gossou, Richard, sergeant, 47th N. Y., Chaffin's Farm, near Richmond, Va., Sept. 29, 1864, falling dead while planting colors on the enemy's works.

Graul, William, corporal, 188th Pa., Fort Harrison, near Richmond, Va., Sept. 29, 1864, first planting colors on the fortifications.

Gray, John, private, 5th Ohio, Port Republic, Va., June 9, 1862, capture of field-piece in face of the enemy.

Greenwalt, Abraham, private, 104th Ohio, Franklin, Tenn., Nov. 30, 1864, capture of flag.

Gribben, James H., lieutenant, 2d N. Y. Cav., Sailor's Creek, Va., April 6, 1865, capture of flag.

Grube, George, private, 158th N. Y., Chaffin's Farm, near Richmond, Va., Sept. 29, 1864, gallantry.

Gwynne, Nathaniel, private, 13th Ohio Cav.

Ilack, Lester G., sergeant, 5th Vt., Petersburg, Va., April 2, 1865, capture of flag.

Hagerty, Asel, private, 61st N. Y., Sailor's Creek, Va., April 6, 1865, capture of flag.

Hall, Newton H., corporal, 104th Ohio, Franklin, Tenn., Nov. 30, 1864, capture of flag.

Hanford, Edward R., private, 2d U. S. Cav., Woodstock, Va., Oct. 9, 1864, capture of flag.

Hanna, John, 1st sergeant, 14th V. R. C., April —, 1865, acting as escort to remains of President Lincoln.

Ilanscom, Moses C., corporal, 19th Me., Bristow Station, Va., Oct. 14, 1863, capture of flag.

Harbourne, John H., private, 29th Mass., Petersburg, Va., June 17, 1864, capture of flag.

Hardenbergh, Henry M., private, 39th Ill., Deep Run, Va., Aug. 16, 1864, capture of flag.

Harmon, Amzi D., corporal, 211th Pa., Petersburg, Va., April 2, 1865, capture of flag.

Harris, George W., private, 148th Pa., Spottsylvania, Va., May 12, 1864, capture of flag.

Ilarris, James H., sergeant, 38th U. S. C. T., New Market Heights, Va., Sept. 29, 1864, gallantry.

Hart, William E., private, 8th N. Y. Cav., Shenandoah Valley, Va., 1864 and 1865, gallantry and service as scout.

Harvey, Harry, corporal, 22d N. Y. Cav., Waynesborough, Va., March 2, 1865, capture of flag.

Havron, John H., sergeant, 1st R. I. Art., Petersburg, Va., April 2, 1865, gallantry.

Hawken, James M., storekeeper, Q. M. Department, St. Louis, Mo., Sept. 5, 1864, extinguished an incendiary fire in Quartermaster's Department.

Hawkins, Martin J., corporal, 33d Ohio, Georgia, 1862, special services under Gen. Mitchel.

Hawkins, Thomas, sergeant-major, 6th U. S. C. T., Deep Bottom, Va., July —, 1864, rescue of flag.

Haynes, Asbury F., corporal, 17th Me., Sailor's Creek, Va., April 6, 1865, capture of flag.

Hays, John H., private, 4th Iowa Cav., Columbus, Ga., April 16, 1865, capture of flag and bearer.

Hewe, John C., corporal, 8th U. S., San Antonio, Tex., April —, 1861, preserving and bringing away colors after capture of the regiment.

Hickok, Nathan E., corporal, 8th Conn., Chaffin's Farm, near Richmond, Va., Sept. 29, 1864, capture of flag.

Higby, Charles, private, 1st Pa. Cav., Virginia, April —, 1865, capture of flag.

Highland, Patrick, corporal, 23d Ill., gallantry.

Hill, James, sergeant, 14th N. Y. Hy. Art., Petersburg, Va., July 30, 1864, capture of flag.

Hilton, Alfred B., sergeant, 4th U. S. C. T., Chaffin's Farm, near Richmond, Va., Sept. 29, 1864, gallantry as color-bearer.

Hinks, William B., sergeant-major, 14th Conn., Gettysburg, Pa., July 3, 1863, capture of flag.

Hoffman, Henry, corporal, 2d Ohio Cav., Sailor's Creek, Va., April 6, 1865, capture of flag.

Hogan, Franklin, corporal, 45th Pa., front of Petersburg, Va., July 30, 1864, capture of flag.

Holcomb, Daniel J., private, 41st Ohio, Brentwood Hills, Tenn., Dec. 16, 1864, capture of guidon.

Holland, Milton M., sergeant-major, 5th U. S. C. T., Chaffin's Farm, near Richmond, Va., Sept. 29, 1864, gallantry.

Holmes, William T., private, 3d Ind. Cav., Sailor's Creek, Va., April 6, 1865, capture of flag.

Homan, Conrad, color-sergeant, 29th Mass., near Petersburg, Va., July 30, 1864, fighting his way through the enemy's lines with regimental colors.

Hooper, William B., corporal, 1st N. J. Cav., Chamberlain's Creek, Va., March 31, 1865, capture of flag.

Hoppy, Edward, 2d lieutenant, 12th V. R. C., April —, 1865, acting as escort to remains of President Lincoln.

Hotenstine, Solomon J., private, 107th Pa., Petersburg and Norfolk R. R., Aug. 19, 1864, capture of flag.

Hough, Ira, private, 8th Ind., Cedar Creek, Va., Oct. 19, 1864, capture of flag.

Houlton, William, comy. sergeant, 1st W. Va. Cav., Sailor's Creek, Va., April 6, 1865, capture of flag.

Howard, James, sergeant, 158th N. Y., gallantry.

Hudson, Aaron R., private, 17th Ind. Mtd. Inf., Culloden, Ga., April —, 1865, capture of flag.

Hughey, John, corporal, 2d Ohio Cav., Sailor's Creek, Va., April 6, 1865, capture of flag.

Hughs, Oliver, corporal, 12th Ky., capture of flag.

Hunter, Charles A., sergeant, 34th Mass., gallantry.

Jacobson, Eugene P., sergeant-major, 74th N. Y., Chancellorsville, Va., May 2, 1863, bravery in conducting a scouting party in front of the enemy.

James, Isaac, private, 110th Ohio, Petersburg, Va., April 2, 1865, capture of flag.

James, Miles, corporal, 36th U. S. C. T., Chaffin's Farm, Va., Sept. 30, 1864, gallantry.

Jellison, Benjamin H., sergeant, 19th Mass., Gettysburg, Pa., July 3, 1863, capture of flag.

Jennings, James T., private, 56th Pa., Weldon R. R., Va., Aug. 20, 1864, capture of flag.

Johndro, Franklin, private, 118th N. Y., Chaffin's Farm, Va., Sept. 30, 1864, capture of forty prisoners.

Johnston, Samuel, private, 9th Pa. Reserves, capture of flag.

Johnston, Willie, musician, 3d Vt.

Jones, William, 1st sergeant, 73d N. Y., Spottaylvania, Va., May 12, 1864, capture of flag.

Jordan, Absalom, corporal, 3d Ind. Cav., Sailor's Creek, Va., April 6, 1865, capture of flag.

Judje, Francis W., 1st sergeant, 79th N. Y., Fort Sanders, Knoxville, Tenn., Nov. 29, 1863, capture of flag.

Kaiser, John, sergeant, 2d U. S. Art., Richmond, Va., June 27, 1862, gallant and meritorious service during seven days' battle.

Kaltenbach, Luther, corporal, 12th Iowa, Nashville, Tenn., Dec. 16, 1864, capture of flag.

Kane, John, corporal, 100th N. Y., gallantry.

Kappesser, Peter, private, 149th N. Y., Lookout Mountain, Tenn., Nov. 24, 1863, capture of flag.

Karpeles, Leopold, color-sergeant, 57th Mass., Wilderness, Va., May 6, 1864, gallantry.

Karr, John, 1st sergeant, 14th V. R. C., April —, 1865, acting as escort to remains of President Lincoln.

Kauss, Augustus, corporal, 15th N. Y. Hy. Art., Five Forks, Va., April 1, 1865, capture of flag.

Keele, Joseph, sergeant-major, 182d N. Y., 1861 to 1865, service during rebellion.

Kelloy, George V., captain, 104th Ohio, Franklin, Tenn., Nov. 30, 1864, capture of flag.

Kelly, Alexander, 1st sergeant, 6th U. S. C. T., Chaffin's Farm, near Richmond, Va., Sept. 29, 1864, gallantry.

Kelly, Daniel, sergeant, 8th N. Y. Cav., Waynesborough, Va., March 2, 1865, capture of flag.

Kelly, Thomas, private, 6th N. Y. Cav., Front Royal, Va., Aug. 16, 1864, capture of flag.

Kemp, Joseph, 1st sergeant, 5th Mich., Wilderness, Va., May 6, 1864, capture of flag.

Kendig, John M., corporal, 63d Pa., Spottsylvania, Va., May 12, 1864, capture of flag.

Kenyon, Samuel P., private, 24th N. Y. Cav., Sailor's Creek, Va., April 6, 1865, capture of flag.

Keough, John, corporal, 67th Pa., Sailor's Creek, Va., April 6, 1865, capture of flag.

Kimball, Joseph, private, 2d W. Va. Cav., Sailor's Creek, Va., April 6, 1865, capture of flag.

Kline, Henry, private, 40th N. Y., Sailor's Creek, Va., April 6, 1865, capture of flag.

Knight, William, private, 21st Ohio, Georgia, 1862, special services under Gen. Mitchel.

Koogle, Jacob, 1st lieutenant, 7th Md., Five Forks, Va., April 1, 1865, capture of flag.

Kramer, Theodore, private, 188th Pa., Chaffin's Farm, near Richmond, Va., Sept. 29, 1864, taking one of the first prisoners, a captain.

Kuder, Andrew, 2d lieut., 8th N. Y. Cav., Waynesborough, Va., March 2, 1865, capture of flags.

Kuder, Jeremiah, lieutenant, 74th Ind., Jonesborough, Ga., Sept. 1, 1864, capture of flags.

Ladd, George, private, 22d N. Y. Cav., Waynesborough, Va., March 2, 1865, capture of flag.

Laing, William, sergeant, 158th N. Y., Chaffin's Farm, near Richmond, Va., Sept. 29, 1864, being among the first to scale the parapet.

Landis, James P., chief bugler, 1st Pa. Cav., Paine's X Roads, Va., April 5, 1865, capture of flag.

Lane, Morgan D., private, Signal Corps, U. S. A., near Jetersville, Va., April 6, 1865, capture of flag.

Lanfare, Aaron S., 1st lieutenant, 1st Conn. Cav., Sailor's Creek, Va., April 6, 1865, capture of flag.

Larimer, Smith, corporal, 2d Ohio Cav., Sailor's Creek, Va., April 6, 1865, capture of flag.

Leonard, William E., private, 85th Pa., Deep Run, Va., Aug. 16, 1864, capture of flag.

Leslie, Frank, private, 4th N. Y. Cav., Front Royal, Va., Aug. 15, 1864, capture of flag.

Levy, Benjamin, private, 40th N. Y., Glendale, Va., June 30, 1862, saving regimental colors.

Lewis, Rufus W., 1st sergeant, 18th V. R. C., April —, 1865, acting as escort to remains of President Lincoln.

Lewis, Samuel E., corporal, 1st R. I. Art., Petersburg, Va., April 2, 1865, gallantry.

Lilley, John, private, 205th Pa., Petersburg, Va., April 2, 1865, capture of flag.

Little, Henry F. W., sergeant, 7th N. H., near Richmond, Va., Sept. —, 1864, gallantry.

Lohnas, Francis W., private, 1st Nebr. Vet. Cav., Gilman's Ranch, Neb., May 12, 1865, gallantry in defending Government property against Indians.

Lorish, Andrew J., comy. sergeant, 1st N. Y. Dragoons, Winchester, Va., Sept. 19, 1864, capture of flag.

Love, George M., colonel, 116th N. Y., Cedar Creek, Va., Oct. 19, 1864, capture of flag.

Loyd, George, private, 122d Ohio, Petersburg, Va., April 2, 1865, capture of flag.

Lucas, George W., private, 3d Mo. Cav.

Lutes, Franklin W., corporal, 111th N. Y., Petersburg, Va., March 31, 1865, capture of flag.

Luty, Gotlieb, sergeant, 74th N. Y., Chancellorsville, Va., May 3, 1863, bravery.

Lynch, John B., private, 3d Ind. Cav., Fredericksburg, Va., May 6, 1864, carrying dispatch from President to Gen. Grant.

Lyons, Frederick A., corporal, 1st Vt. Cav., Cedar Creek, Va., Oct. 19, 1864, capture of flag.

McCamly, James M., captain, 9th V. R. C., April —, 1865, acting as escort to remains of President Lincoln.

McCarren, Bernard, private, 1st Del., Gettysburg, Pa., July 3, 1863, capture of flag.

McCauslin, Joseph, private, 12th W. Va., gallantry.

McCleary, Charles H., 1st lieutenant, 72d Ohio, Nashville, Tenn., Dec. 16, 1864, capture of flag.

McConnell, Samuel, captain, 119th Ill., Blakely, Ala., April 9, 1865, capture of flag.

McDonald, George E., private, 1st Conn. Art., Fort Stedman, near Petersburg, Va., March 25, 1865, capture of flag.

McElhany, Samuel O., private, 2d W. Va. Cav., Sailor's Creek, Va., April 6, 1865, capture of flag.

McEnroe, Patrick H., sergeant, 6th N. Y. Cav., Winchester, Va., Sept. 19, 1864, capture of flag.

McGraw, Thomas, sergeant, 23d Ill., gallantry.

McKee, George, color-sergeant, 89th N. Y., gallantry.

McKown, Nathaniel A., sergeant, 58th Pa., Chaffin's Farm, near Richmond, Va., Sept. 29, 1864, capture of flag.

McMillan, Francis M., sergeant, 110th Ohio, Petersburg, Va., April 2, 1865, capture of flag.

McVeane, John P., private, 49th N. Y., Fredericksburg, Va., Dec. —, 1862, gallantry.

McWhorton, Walter F., comy. sergeant, 3d W. Va. Cav., Sailor's Creek, Va., April 6, 1865, capture of flag.

Mahoney, Jeremiah, sergeant, 29th Mass., Fort Sanders, Knoxville, Tenn., Nov. 29, 1863, capture of flag.

Mandy, Harry J., 1st sergeant, 4th N. Y. Cav., Front Royal, Va., Aug. 15, 1864, capture of flag.

Manning, Joseph S., private, 29th Mass., Fort Sanders, Knoxville, Tenn., Nov. 29, 1863, capture of flag.

Marquent, Charles, sergeant, 93d Pa., Petersburg, Va., April 2, 1865, capture of flag.

Marsh, Albert, sergeant, 64th N. Y., Spottsylvania, Va., May 12, 1864, capture of flag.

Marsh, Charles H., private, 1st Conn. Cav., Back Creek Valley, Va., July 31, 1864, capture of flag.

Marshall, A. Judson, 1st sergeant, 9th V. R. C., April —, 1865, acting as escort to remains of President Lincoln.

Mason, Elihu H., sergeant, 21st Ohio, Georgia, 1862, special services under Gen. Mitchel.

Matthews, Milton, private, 61st Pa., Petersburg, Va., April 2, 1865, capture of flag.

Mattingly, Henry B., private, 10th Ky., Jonesborough, Ga., Sept. 1, 1864, capture of flags.

May, William, private, 32d Iowa, Nashville, Tenn., Dec. 16, 1864, capture of flag.

Mayberry, John B., private, 1st Del., Gettysburg, Pa., July 3, 1863, capture of flag.

Meach, George E., farrier, 6th N. Y. Cav., Winchester, Va., Sept. 19, 1864, capture of flag.

Meagher, Thomas, 1st sergeant, 158th N. Y., Chaffin's Farm, near Richmond, Va., Sept. 29, 1864, gallantry.

Magee, William, drummer, 33d N. J., Murfreesborough, Tenn., Dec. —, 1864, bravery.

Menter, John W., sergeant, 5th Mich., Sailor's Creek, Va., April 6, 1865, capture of flag.

Merritt, John G., sergeant, 1st Minn., Bull Run, Va., July —, 1861, gallantry.

Miller, Frank, private, 2d N. Y. Cav., Sailor's Creek, Va., April 6, 1865, capture of flag.

Miller, Henry A., captain, 8th Ill., Blakely, Ala., April 9, 1865, capture of flag.

Miller, James P., private, 4th Iowa Cav., Selma, Ala., April 2, 1865, capture of flag.

Miller, John, private, 8th N. Y. Cav., Waynesborough, Va., March 2, 1865, capture of flag.

Miller, John, corporal, 8th Ohio, Gettysburg, Pa., July 3, 1863, capture of two flags.

Mitchell, Theodore, private, 61st Pa., Petersburg, Va., April 2, 1865, capture of flag.

Molbone, Archibald, sergeant, 1st R. I. Art., Petersburg, Va., April 2, 1865, gallantry.

Monaghan, Patrick, corporal, 48th Pa., Petersburg, Va., June 17, 1864, recapture of colors.

Moore, George G., private, 11th W. Va., Fisher's Hill, Va., Sept. 22, 1864, capture of flag.

Moore, Wilbur F., private, 117th Ill., Nashville, Tenn., Dec. 16, 1864, capture of flag.

Morgan, Lewis, private, 4th Ohio, Spottsylvania, Va., May 12, 1864, capture of flag.

Morgan, Richard H., corporal, 4th Iowa Cav., Columbus, Ga., April 16, 1865, capture of flag.

Morris, William, sergeant, 1st N. Y. Lincoln Cav., Sailor's Creek, Va., April 6, 1865, capture of flag.

Mundell, Walter L., corporal, 5th Mich., Sailor's Creek, Va., April 6, 1865, capture of flag.

Munsell, Harvey, M., sergeant, 99th Pa., 1861 to 1865, service during the rebellion; carrying the colors of the regiment.

Murphy, Daniel, sergeant, 19th Mass., Hatcher's Run, Va., Oct. 27, 1864, capture of flag.

Murphy, Edward, 2d lieutenant, 10th V. R. C., April —, 1865, acting as escort to remains of President Lincoln.

Murphy, John P., private, 5th Ohio, Antietam, Md., Sept. 17, 1862, capture of flag.

Murphy, Thomas, corporal, 158th N. Y., Chaffin's Farm, near Richmond, Va., Sept. 29, 1864, capture of flag.

Murphy, Thomas J., 1st sergeant, 146th N. Y., Five Forks, Va., April 1. 1865, capture of flag.

Myers, William H., private, 1st Md. Cav., Appomattox C. H., Va., April 9, 1865, gallantry.

Nelson, Jacob F., 1st sergeant, 9th V. R. C., April —, 1865, acting as escort to remains of President Lincoln.

Nevers, Robert, 2d lieutenant, 8th N. Y. Cav., Waynesborough, Va., March 2, 1865, capture of two flags.

Neville, Edwin M., captain, 1st Conn. Cav., Sailor's Creek, Va., April 6, 1865, capture of flag.

Newman, William H., lieutenant, 86th N. Y., near Amelia Springs, Va., April 6, 1865, capture of flag.

Noble, William H., 1st sergeant, 12th V. R. C., April —, 1865, acting as escort to remains of President Lincoln.

Norton, Elliott M., 2d lieutenant, 6th Mich. Cav., Sailor's Creek, Va., April 6, 1865, capture of two flags.

Norton, John R., lieutenant, 1st N. Y. Lincoln Cav., Sailor's Creek, Va., April 6, 1865, capture of flag.

Norton, Llewellyn P., sergeant, 10th N. Y. Cav., Sailor's Creek, Va., April 6, 1865, gallantry.

O'Brion, Peter, private, 1st N. Y. Lincoln Cav., Waynesborough, Va., March 2, 1865, capture of flag.

O'Connor, Timothy, private, 1st U. S. Cav.

Oliver, Charles, sergeant, 100th Pa., Petersburg, Va., March 25, 1865, capture of flag.

Opel, John N., private, 7th Ind., Wilderness, Va., May 5, 1864, capture of flag.

Orbanski, David, private, 58th Ohio, Shiloh, Tenn., Vicksburg, Miss., etc., 1862 and 1863, gallantry.

Orth, Jacob G., corporal, 28th Pa., Antietam, Md., Sept. 17, 1862, capture of flag.

Pardun, James M., 1st sergeant, 24th V. R. C., April —, 1865, acting as escort to remains of President Lincoln.

Parker, Thomas, corporal, 2d R. I., Petersburg and Sailor's Creek. Va., April 2 and 6, 1865, gallantry.

Parks, James W., corporal, 11th Mo., Nashville, Tenn., Dec. 16, 1864, capture of flag.

Parks, Jeremiah, private, 9th N. Y. Cav., Cedar Creek, Va., Oct. 19, 1864, capture of flag.

Parrott, Jacob, private, 33d Ohio, Georgia, 1862, special services under Gen. Mitchel.

Payne, Irvin C., corporal, 2d N. Y. Cav., Sailor's Creek, Va., April 6, 1865, capture of flag.

Peirsol, James K., sergeant, 13th Ohio Cav., Paine's X Roads, Va., April 5, 1865, capture of flag.

Pentzer, Patrick H., captain, 97th Ill., Blakely, Ala., April 9, 1865, capture of flag.

Phillips, Josiah, private, 148th Pa., Sutherland Station, Va., April 2, 1865, capture of flag.

Pinn, Robert, 1st sergeant, 5th U. S. C. T., Chaffin's Farm, near Richmond, Va., Sept. 29, 1864, gallantry.

Pittenger, William, sergeant, 2d Ohio, Georgia, 1862, special services under Gen. Mitchel.

Pittman, George J., sergeant, 1st N. Y. Lincoln Cav., Sailor's Creek, Va., April 6, 1865, capture of flag.

Plowman, George H., sergeant-major, 3d Md. Batl., Petersburg, Va., June 17, 1864, recapture of the colors.

Plunkett, Thomas, sergeant, 21st Mass., Fredericksburg, Va., Dec. —, 1862, gallantry.

Porter, John R., private, 21st Ohio, Georgia, 1862, special services under Gen. Mitchel.

Porter, William, sergeant, 1st N. J. Cav., Sailor's Creek, Va., April 6, 1865, gallantry.

Potter, Norman F., 1st sergeant, 149th N. Y., Lookout Mountain, Tenn., Nov. 24, 1863, capture of flag.

Ransbottom, Alfred, 1st sergeant, 97th Ohio, Franklin, Tenn., Nov. 30, 1864, capture of flag.

Ratcliff, Edward, 1st sergeant, 38th U. S. C. T., Chaffin's Farm, near Richmond, Va., Sept. 29, 1864, gallantry.

Read, Mort. A., lieutenant, 8th N. Y. Cav., Appomattox Station, Va., April 8, 1865, capture of flag.

Rebmann, George F., sergeant, 119th Ill., Blakely, Ala., April 9, 1865, capture of flag.

Reddick, William H., corporal, 33d Ohio, Georgia, 1862, special services under Gen. Mitchel.

Reed, George W., private, 11th Pa., Weldon R. R., Va., Aug. 21, 1864, capture of flag.

Reed, Thomas, private, 27th N. J., Pennsylvania and Maryland, 1863, offering his services to the Government after expiration of term of service.

Reeder, Charles A., private, 12th W. Va.

Reid, Robert, private, 48th Pa., Petersburg, Va., June 17, 1864, capture of flag.

Reigle, Daniel P., corporal, 87th Pa., Cedar Creek, Va., Oct. 19, 1864, capture of flag.

Reynolds, George, private, 9th N. Y. Cav., Winchester, Va., Sept. 19, 1864, capture of flag.

Richardson, William R., private, 2d Ohio Vet. Cav., Sailor's Creek, Va., April 6, 1865, gallant and meritorious conduct.

Richmond, James, private, 8th Ohio, Gettysburg, Pa., July 3, 1863, capture of flag.

Ricksecker, John H., private, 104th Ohio, Franklin, Tenn., Nov. 30, 1864, capture of flag.

Kiddell, Rudolph, lieutenant, 61st N. Y., Sailor's Creek, Va., April 6, 1865, capture of flag.

Riley, Thomas, private, 1st La. Cav., Blakely, Ala., April 4, 1865, capture of flag.

Roberts, Otis O., sergeant, 6th Me., Rappahannock Station, Va., Nov. 7, 1863, capture of flag.

Robertson, Samuel, private, 33d Ohio, Georgia, 1862, special services under Gen. Mitchel.

Robie, George F. (Frank Robey), sergeant, 7th N. H., Richmond, Va., 1864, bravery.

Robinson, John, private, 19th Mass., Gettysburg, Pa., July 3, 1863, capture of flag.

Robinson, Thomas, private, 81st Pa., Spottsylvania, Va., May 12, 1864, capture of flag.

Rood, Oliver P., private, 20th Ind., Gettysburg, Pa., July 3, 1863, capture of flag.

Ross, Marion A., sergeant-major, 2d Ohio, Georgia, 1862, special services under Gen. Mitchel.

Rought, Stephen, sergeant, 141st Pa., Wilderness, Va., May 6, 1864, capture of flag.

Rounds, Lewis A., private, 8th Ohio, Spottsylvania, Va., May 12, 1864, capture of flag.

Rowand, Archibald H., private, 1st W. Va. Cav., 1861 to 1865, gallant and meritorious services throughout the war.

Rowe, Henry W., private, 11th N. H., Petersburg, Va., June 17, 1864, capture of flag.

Russell, Charles L., corporal, 93d N. Y., Spottsylvania, Va., May 12, 1864, capture of flag.

Ryan, Peter J., private, 11th Ind., Winchester, Va., Sept. 19, 1864, capture of 14 Confederates in severest part of battle.

Savacool, Edwin F., captain, 1st N. Y. Lincoln Cav., Sailor's Creek, Va., April 6, 1865, capture of flag.

Schellenburger, John S., corporal, 85th Pa., Deep Run, Va., Aug. 16, 1864, capture of flag.

Schiller, John, private, 158th N. Y., Chaffin's Farm, near Richmond, Va., Sept. 29, 1864, gallantry.

Schlachter, Philip, private, 73d N. Y., Spottsylvania, Va., May 12, 1864, capture of flag.

Schmal, George W., blacksmith, 24th N. Y. Cav., Paine's X Roads, Va., April 5, 1865, capture of flag.

Schorn, Charles, chief bugler, 1st W. Va. Cav., Appomattox, Va., April 8, 1865, capture of flag.

Scofield, David S., quartermaster sergeant, 5th N. Y. Cav., Cedar Creek, Va., Oct. 19, 1864, capture of flag.

Scott, John M., sergeant, 21st Ohio, Georgia, 1862, special services under Gen. Mitchel.

Scott, John Wallace, captain, 157th Pa., Five Forks, Va., April 1, 1865, capture of flag.

Scott, Julian A., drummer, 3d Vt.

Sedgwick, Irving M., 1st sergeant, 18th V. R. C., April —, 1865, acting as escort to remains of President Lincoln.

Seston, Charles H., sergeant, 11th Ind., Winchester, Va., Sept. 19, 1864, gallant and meritorious services in carrying the colors.

Shahand, Amzi, corporal, 1st W. Va. Cav., Sailor's Creek, Va., April 6, 1865, capture of flag.

Shambaugh, Charles, corporal, 11th Pa. Reserves, Charles City X Roads, Va., June 30, 1862, capture of flag.

Shea, Joseph H., private, 92d N. Y., Chaffin's Farm, near Richmond, Va., Sept. 29, 1864, gallantry in bringing wounded from the field.

Shepherd, William, private, 3d Ind. Cav , Sailor's Creek, Va., April 6, 1865, capture of flag.

Sherman, Marshall, private, 1st Minn., Gettysburg, Pa., July 3, 1863, capture of flag.

Shields, Bernard, private, 2d W. Va. Cav., Appomattox, Va., April 8, 1865, capture of flag.

Shilling, John, 1st sergeant, 3d Del., Weldon R. R., Va., Aug. 21, 1864, capture of flag.

Shipley, Robert F., sergeant, 140th N. Y., Five Forks, Va., April 1, 1865, capture of flag.

Shoemaker, Levi, sergeant, 1st W. Va. Cav., Nineveh, Va., Nov. 12, 1864, capture of flag.

Shopp, George J., private, 191st Pa., Five Forks, Va., April 1, 1865, capture of flag.

Shubert, Frank, sergeant, 43d N. Y., Petersburg, Va., April 2, 1865, capture of two markers.

Simmons, John, private, 2d N. Y. Hy. Art., Sailor's Creek, Va., April 6, 1865, capture of flag.

Simmons, William T., lieutenant, 11th Mo., Nashville, Tenn., Dec. 16, 1864, capture of flag.

Skellie, Ebenezer, corporal, 112th N. Y., Chaffin's Farm, near Richmond, Va., Sept. 29, 1864, gallantry.

Slavens, Samuel, private, 33d Ohio, Georgia, 1862, special services under Gen. Mitchel.

Sloan, Andrew J., private, 12th Iowa, Nashville, Tenn., Dec. 16, 1864, capture of flag.

Smith, Alonzo, sergeant, 7th Mich., Hatcher's Run, Va., Oct. 27, 1864, capture of flag.

Smith, Frank T., 1st sergeant, 10th V. R. C., April —, 1865, acting as escort to remains of President Lincoln.

Smith, James, private, 2d Ohio, Georgia, 1862, special services under Gen. Mitchel.

Smith, John P., 1st sergeant, 14th V. R. C., April —, 1865, acting as escort to remains of President Lincoln.

Smith, Otis W., private, 95th Ohio, Nashville, Tenn., Dec. 16, 1864, capture of flag.

Smith, Richard, private, 95th N. Y., Weldon R. R., Va., Aug. 21, 1864, gallantry.

Southard, David, sergeant, 1st N. J. Cav., Sailor's Creek, Va., April 6, 1865, capture of flag.

Sova, Joseph E., saddler, 8th N. Y. Cav., Virginia, April —, 1865, capture of flag.

Spillane, Timothy, private, 16th Pa. Cav., Hatcher's Run, Va., Feb. 5 and 7, 1865, gallantry.

Sterling, John T., private, 11th Ind., Winchester, Va., Sept. 19, 1864, gallantry.

Stewart, George W., 1st sergeant, 1st N. J. Cav., Paine's X Roads, Va., April 5, 1865, capture of flag.

Stewart, Joseph, private, 1st Md., Five Forks, Va., April 1, 1865, capture of flag.

Stickels, Joseph, sergeant, 83d Ohio, Blakely, Ala., April 9, 1865, capture of flag.

Stokes, George, private, 122d Ill., Nashville, Tenn., Dec. 16, 1864, capture of flag.

Storr, Robert, private, 15th N. Y. Engineers, 1861 and 1862, services during the rebellion.

Strusbaugh, Barnard A., 1st sergeant, 3d Md. Batl., Petersburg, Va., June 17, 1864, recapture of the colors.

Streile, Christian, private, 1st N. J. Cav., Virginia, April —, 1865, capture of flag.

Swan, Charles A., private, 4th Iowa Cav., Selma, Ala., April 2, 1865, capture of flag and bearer.

Sweeney, James, private, 1st Vt. Cav., Cedar Creek, Va., Oct. 19, 1864, capture of flag.

Swinehart, Chester, 1st sergeant, 7th V. R. C., April —, 1865, acting as escort to remains of President Lincoln.

Taggart, Charles A., private, 37th Mass., Sailor's Creek, Va., April 6, 1865, capture of flag.

Taylor, Richard, private, 18th Ind., Cedar Creek, Va., Oct. 19, 1864, capture of flag.

Terry, John D., sergeant, 23d Mass., New Berne, N. C., March 14, 1862, gallantry.

Thompson, Freeman C., corporal, 116th Ohio, gallantry.

Thompson, James B., sergeant, 1st Pa. Rifles, Gettysburg, Pa. July 3, 1863, capture of flag.

Thompson, J. H., brigade surgeon, U. S. Vols., New Berne, N. C., March 14, 1862, gallantry.

Thompson, William P., sergeant, 20th Ind., Wilderness, Va., May 6, 1864, capture of flag.

Tibbets, Andrew W., private, 3d Iowa Cav., Columbus, Ga., April 16, 1865, capture of flag and bearer.

Tilton, William, sergeant, 7th N. H., gallantry.

Titus, Charles, sergeant, 1st N. J. Cav., Sailor's Creek, Va., April 6, 1865, gallantry.

Tompkins, Aaron B., sergeant, 1st N. J. Cav., Virginia, April 5, 1865, gallantry.

Tompkins, George W., corporal, 124th N. Y., near Watkin's House, Petersburg, Va., March 25, 1865, capture of flag.

Truell, Edwin M., private, 12th Wis., near Atlanta, Ga., July 21, 1864, gallantry.

Tucker, Allan, sergeant, 10th Conn., gallantry.

Tucker, Jacob R., corporal, 4th Md., Petersburg, Va., April —, 1865, gallantry.

Tyrrell, George William, corporal, 5th Ohio, Resaca, Ga., May 14, 1864, capture of flag.

Urell, Michael, private, 82d N. Y., Bristow Station, Va., Oct. 14, 1863, gallantry.

Van Matre, Joseph, private, 116th Ohio, gallantry.

Vanwinkle, Edward, corporal, 148th N. Y., Chaffin's Farm, near Richmond, Va., Sept. 29, 1864, gallantry.

Veal, Charles, private, 4th U. S. C. T., Chaffin's Farm, near Richmond, Va., Sept. 29, 1864, gallantry.

Vifquain, Victor, lieutenant-colonel, 97th Ill., Blakely, Ala., April 9, 1865, capture of flag.

Walker, Dr. Mary E., 1861 to 1865, services during the war.

Wall, Jerry, private, 126th N. Y., Gettysburg, Pa., July 3, 1863, capture of flag.

Waller, Francis A., corporal, 6th Wis., Gettysburg, Pa., July 1, 1863, capture of flag.

Walsh, John, corporal, 5th N. Y. Cav., Cedar Creek, Va., Oct. 19, 1864, capture of flag.

Warfel, Henry C., private, 1st Pa. Cav., Paine's X Roads, Va., April 5, 1865, capture of flag.

Weeks, John, private, 152d N. Y., Spottsylvania, Va., May 12, 1864, capture of flag and color-bearer.

Welch, George, private, 11th Mo., Nashville, Tenn., Dec. 16, 1864, capture of flag.

Welch, Richard, corporal, 37th Mass., Petersburg, Va., April 2, 1865, capture of flag.

Wells, Henry S., private, 148th N. Y., Chaffin's Farm, near Richmond, Va., Sept. 29, 1864, gallantry.

Wells, Thomas M., chief bugler, 6th N. Y. Cav., Cedar Creek, Va., Oct. 19, 1864, capture of flag.

Westerhold, William, sergeant, 52d N. Y., Spottsylvania, Va., May 12, 1864, capture of flag.

White, Adam, corporal, 11th W. Va., Hatcher's Run, Va., April 2, 1865, capture of flag.

Whitman, Frank M., private, 35th Mass., Antietam, Md., and Spottsylvania, Va., Sept. 1862, and May, 1864, services in action.

Whitmore, John, private, 119th Ill., Blakely, Ala., April 9, 1865, capture of flag.

Wiley, James, sergeant, 59th N. Y., Gettysburg, Pa., July 3, 1863, capture of flag.

Wilkins, Leander A., sergeant, 9th N. H., Petersburg, Va., July 30, 1864, recapture of colors.

Wilson, Charles E., sergeant, 1st N. J. Cav., Sailor's Creek, Va., April 6, 1865, gallantry as color-bearer.

Wilson, Francis, corporal, 95th Pa., Petersburg, Va., April 2, 1865, gallantry in action.

Wilson, John, sergeant, 1st N. J. Cav., Chamberlain's Creek, Va., March 31, 1865, gallantry.

Wilson, John A., private, 21st Ohio, Georgia, 1862, special services under Gen. Mitchel.

Wilson, Joseph K., sergeant-major, 8th U. S., Texas, 1861, bringing colors out of Texas after capture of the regiment.

Winegar, William W., lieutenant, 1st N. Y. Dragoons, Five Forks, Va., April 1, 1865, capture of flag.

Wiseman, William H., 1st sergeant, 24th V. R. C., April —, 1865, acting as escort to remains of President Lincoln.

Wollam, John, private, 33d Ohio, Georgia, 1862, special services under Gen. Mitchel.

Wood, Mark, private, 21st Ohio, Georgia, 1862, special services under Gen. Mitchel.

Woodall, William H., scout, Gen. Sheridan's headquarters, Virginia, April —, 1865, capture of flag.

Woodbury, Eri D., sergeant, 1st Vt. Cav., Cedar Creek, Va., Oct. 19, 1864, capture of flag.

Woods, Daniel A., private, 1st Va. Cav., Sailor's Creek, Va., April 6, 1865, capture of flag.

Wright, Robert, private, 14th U. S., Chapel House Farm, Va., Oct. 1, 1864, gallantry.

Young, Andrew J., sergeant, 1st Pa. Cav., Paine's X Roads, Va., April 5, 1865, capture of flag.

Young, Calvary M., sergeant, 3d Iowa Cav., Osage, Kan., Sept. 26, 1864, gallantry in capturing Gen. Cabell.

Youngs, Benjamin F., corporal, 1st Mich. S. S., Petersburg, Va., June 17, 1864, capture of flag.

At Gettysburg, July 1, 1863, the 27th Maine Infantry volunteered to remain and take part in the battle, though its term of service had expired. For this the entire regiment received the medal. Their names are as follow:

Abbott, Charles E., private; Abbott, George H., private; Adams, Clement J., sergeant; Adams, John F., private; Adams, John W., musician; Adams, Lucien, private; Adjutant, George W., private; Adlington, Thomas A., private; Allen, Charles H., private; Allen, Jeddiah, private; Allen, Samuel L., private; Allen, Seth G., private; Allen, William A., corporal; Anderson, Amos S., corporal; Anderson, William R., private; Anderson, William A., private; Andrews, Chase, corporal; Andrews, James E., private; Atkins, Charles P., private; Auld, William M., corporal; Ayer, William H. H., private; Bail, William, private; Bailey, Albert, wagoner; Baker, Albert, private; Banfield, Philip, private; Bangs, Willard, private; Barker, William B., corporal; Barnes, Benjamin, private; Barrows, David S., 1st sergeant; Bartlett, Charles S., private; Bartlett, Joseph W., private; Bates, Marcus, private; Bean, Lewis L., private; Bennett, Augustus, private; Benson, James A., private; Berry, Edward M., private; Berry, John, private; Berry, Moses G., private;

Berry, William, private; Berry, William, private; Bisbee, Charles D., private; Bisbee, Orrin S., private; Black, George E., private; Blanchard, Jacob S., private; Blanchard, Stephen, corporal; Blood, Charles H., private; Boody, Sylvester O., private; Boston, Elijah F., private; Bowden, Charles A., private; Boynton, Granville M., private; Bracey, James F., private; Bracey, John, private; Brackett, David H., corporal; Brackett, Lorenzo D., sergeant; Bradbury, Charles W., private; Bradbury, Eben H. C., private; Bradbury, Edward, private; Bradbury, Henry M., private; Bradbury, Joseph F., private; Bradeen, Alcander M., private; Bradeen, Henry, private; Bragdon, Benjamin T., private; Bragdon, Jr., Edmund, 2d lieutenant; Bragdon, James A., private; Bragdon, Sumner, private; Briard, Robert, sergeant; Bridges, Joseph, private; Brooks, Nathaniel, corporal; Brown, Cyrus E., private; Brown, James H., private; Brown, James W., private; Brown, John, private; Brown, John W., private; Brown, Lorenzo T., private; Brown, Philip A., private; Bryant, Frederick S., 1st lieutenant; Bryant, Seth E., captain; Burbank, Arthur C., sergeant; Burbank, Horace H., quartermaster sergeant; Burbank, John P., private; Burbank, Luther S., private; Burbank, Monroe A., corporal; Burbank, Porter M., private; Burnell, Nathaniel A., corporal; Burnes, George, musician; Burnes, James, private; Burnham, Charles L, private; Burnham, Eben, private; Burnham, Elbridge, private; Burnham, Francis M., private; Burnham, Thatcher W., private; Bussell, George, private; Bussell, John C., private; Butland, Nathaniel, private; Butler, Benjamin H., private; Butler, William N., private; Butler, Willis H., sergeant; Butrick, Benjamin, private; Buzzell, Elijah S., private; Buzzell, Jacob L., private; Butland, Francis, 1st sergeant; Call, Nathan, private; Came, Frank, private; Carll, William F., corporal; Carpenter, John R., private; Carpenter, Whitney R., private; Carpenter, William H., private; Carr, William T., private; Cary, Michael, private; Casson, Joseph, private; Center, John W., private; Chancy, Andrew, private; Chaney, Charles H., private; Chaney, Joseph, private; Chapman, Charles, private; Chapman, William, private; Chapman, William W., corporal; Chadbourn, Francis T., private; Chadbourn, James M., private; Chadbourn, Joseph E., 1st lieutenant; Chadbourne, Nathan, corporal; Chadbourne, Henry A., corporal; Chadbourne, Thomas, private; Chadwick, Nathan A., private; Chase, Joseph T., 2d lieutenant; Chase, Jr., Josiah, corporal; Chase, Romanty E., private; Chellis, Albion K. P., private; Chellis, Frank, private; Chellis, Oscar D., private; Chick, Hanson D., private; Chick, Sylvester, private; Chute, Albion, private; Clark, Elisha E., private; Clark, John E., private; Clarvage, Sam. J. C., private; Clements, Henry, private; Clements, James H., private; Clough, Charles, private; Clough, Charles H., private; Clough, George W., private; Clough, Levi, wagoner; Cluff, George W., private; Cluff, Samuel, private; Cobb, Charles, private; Cochran, Adam, private; Coffin, Onsville C., private; Cole, Ai S., wagoner; Cole, Charles E., private; Cole, George C., private; Cole, John G., corporal; Cole, John W., private; Cole, Robert, private; Conner, John, private; Cook, Charles R., sergeant; Cooper, Benjamin F., private; Corson, George M., private; Cottle, Oliver, private; Cotton, Charles, private; Cousins, Francis J., private; Cousins, William A., private; Cousens, William G., private; Crann, Patrick, private; Creanor, George G., private; Cressey, Horace, private; Cribby, George, private; Cross, Charles M., assistant surgeon; Currier, George E., private; Dorman, George R., corporal; Davis, Albert H., corporal; Davis, Charles, corporal; Davis, Charles A., wagoner; Davis, Charles I., private; Davis, Frank M., corporal; Davis, William G., private; Day, Benjamin N., private; Day, Silas, private; Day, Thurston P. M., private; Daymon, George W., private; Dearborn, Charles, private;

Dearborn, Paul C., private; Dearborn, Richard, private; Deooff, Charles, private; Dennett, Alvan A., corporal; Dennett, Reuben, private; Deshon, Elijah S., private; Dillingham, John L., private; Dixon, Edmund A., captain; Dixon, Joseph H., private; Dockham, George A., private; Doe, Joseph D., sergeant; Doieg, Thomas, private; Dow, Simon B., corporal; Downs, Archibald S., private; Downs, Jr, David, private; Doun, Reuben, private; Drew, John, private; Drown, Alonzo J., private; Drown, Orlando, private; Dunn, Alanson, corporal; Dunn, Daniel, private; Dunn, John K., private; Dunn, William S., corporal; Dunnell, Jr., Samuel, 2d lieutenant; Dunnell, Samuel L., private; Dunnells, Loring, private; Dunnella, Mark W., private; Duran, William, private; Durgin, Albion L., sergeant; Durgin, Almon C., corporal; Durgin, George W., private; Dyer, Charles H., private; Dyer, William, private; Eastman, Frank, private; Eaton, Walter, private; Edgerly, George W., private; Edgerly, Samuel H., private; Edwards, George W., private; Eldridge, Edward W., private; Eldridge, Philander, private; Eldridge, William H., private; Elliott, Isaac, private; Elliott, William L., private; Emerson, George W., private; Emery, Franklin, private; Emery, Isaac M., sergeant; Emery, John F., private; Emery, John H., musician; Emery, William R., private; Emmons, D. Taylor, private; Emmons, George, private; Emmons, George W., private; Emmons, John, private; Emmons, John G., private; Emmons, Joseph R., private; Ethridge, Stephen L., private; Fairfield, Lendol N., private; Fall, Henry R., sergeant; Fall, Howard S., private; Fall, Isaac P., captain; Fenderson, Charles W., private; Favour, Horace H., private; Ferguson, George A., private; Fernald, Alonzo, corporal; Fernald, Benjamin, private; Fernald, Simon, private; Fernald, Stephen, private; Fitzgerald, David, private; Flanders, Daniel C., private; Flanders, George W., private; Flood, Ebenezer T., private; Floyd, Daniel, private; Fly, Stephen S., private; Ford, Alvin A., private; Foss, Edward L., private; Foss, Enos L., musician; Foss, James L., private; Foss, Robert, corporal; Foss, William A., corporal; Foster, Charles H., private; Foster, John B. private; Fowler, Edward S., private; Fowler, Frank, private; Foye, Isaac M., private; Freeman, John W., corporal; Frisbee, Josiah P., private; Frost, Harrison T., private; Frost, Hugh A., private; Fuller, Edwin, corporal; Fullerton, David B., captain; Gallagher, Edward H., private; Gallison, Greenleaf W., private; Garland, Albra, private; Garland, Charles E., private; Garland, John, private; Garvin, Paul W., corporal; Garvin, Samuel H., sergeant; Gerrish, Alfred J. W., private; Gerrish, George W., private; Gerrish, Noah W., private; Gerry, Jotham H., corporal; Getchell, Albert F., private; Getchell, Emlus J., sergeant; Getchell, John M., captain; Getchell, Marcus M., private; Getchell, Samuel M., private; Giles, Jesse, corporal; Gilpatrick, William, private; Gooch, Charles W., private; Gooch, Hiram T., private; Gooch, John B., private; Gooch, William H., private; Goodsoe, Horbert, private; Goodwin, Alonzo, private; Goodwin, Charles A., corporal; Goodwin, Charles H., private; Goodwin, Eben M., private; Goodwin, Frank, private; Goodwin, Henry J., 1st lieutenant; Goodwin, Ivory L., private; Goodwin, James M., private; Goodwin, James W., wagoner; Goodwin, John M., private; Goodwin, Joseph B., private; Googins, William H., private; Gordon, Charles S., private; Gordon, George, private; Gordon, Henry, private; Gould, James H. private; Gove, George A., private; Gowell, Benjamin, private; Gowen, Walter A., private; Gowen, William B., corporal; Grace, Hiram M., private; Graffam, Joseph, sergeant; Graffam, Joseph, private; Graffam, William, private; Grant, Daniel W., private; Grant, Elijah M., private; Grant, George W., private; Grant, Nicholas, wagoner; Grant, Jr., Seth, sergeant; Gray, John, sergeant; Gray, Sylvester, private;

vate; Greenleaf, Edgar, sergeant; Guilford, Charles, private; Guptill, John A., private; Guptill, Daniel, private; Gurney, Fred. S., sergeant; Hadlock, Charles H., private; Haley, Albert, private; Haley, James C., private; Haley, Thomas, private; Hall, Freeman, assistant surgeon; Hall, Ivory A., sergeant; Hall, John, 2d lieutenant; Ham, George C., private; Ham, Norris S., private; Ham, Orrin F., private; Hampson, Charles, private; Hanscom, Charles H., private; Hanscom, Elias, private; Hanscom, William L., private; Hanscom, Albert, private; Hanscom, John F., private; Hanscome, Lyman M., private; Hanson, John S., private; Hanson, Lewis B., private; Hanson, Lorenzo S., private; Hardison, Ezra H., private; Harmon, Samuel C., corporal; Harmon, Charles H., private; Harmon, Charles L., private; Harmon, Frank L., 2d lieutenant; Harmon, Frederick M., private; Harmond, Nelson, private; Harriman, Aaron, private; Harvey, Augustus, private; Harvey, Charles A., corporal; Harvey, John W., private; Hasty, Granville, private; Hasty, Winfield F., private; Hatch, Elmore J., private; Hatch, James W., private; Hatch, Joseph E., private; Hayes, Calvin L., sergeant-major; Hayes, Charles E., private; Hayes, Frederick, 2d lieutenant; Hayes, George H., corporal; Hayes, John C., private; Hayes, John M., private; Hayes, John W., 1st sergeant; Hayes, Samuel D., corporal; Henderson, Alvah, private; Hersom, John H., private; Harvey, Henry G., 1st sergeant; Higley, Albert A., private; Higley, Eben N., private; Hill, Albert G., private; Hill, Barnabas R., private; Hill, Daniel, sergeant; Hill, Frederick R., sergeant; Hill, John D., major; Hill, John R., private; Hill, Joseph H., private; Hill, Samuel L., private; Hilton, Charles A., corporal; Hilton, Jr., John, private; Hodgdon, Flanders, private; Hodgdon, Freeman, private; Hodgdon, Hiram, private; Hodsden, David, private; Hogan, Edward W., private; Holt, Otis C., private; Hooper, William H., private; Hooper, Timothy S., private; Hopkins, Jonathan C., private; Hopkinson, James M., private; Horn, Reuben, private; Horn, Rufus A., private; Hubbard, Alonzo, private; Hubbard, Charles S., private; Hubbard, George, private; Huntress, John, private; Hurd, Edwin, private; Hurd, George, private; Hurd, John A., private; Hurd, John H., wagoner; Hurd, Moses S., 1st lieutenant; Hurd, Nathaniel N., 1st sergeant; Hurd, Sylvester, private; Hurd, Thomas S., private; Hussey, Luther G., private; Hussey, Ralph R., 1st lieutenant; Hutchins, Charles L., corporal; Hutchins, Erastus K., private; Hutchins, Ezra, private; Hutchins, Frank A., captain; Hutchins, George, private; Hutchins, Octavus, private; Hutchins, William H., private; Jackson, Anthony, private; Jacobs, Charles, private; Jefferds, Henry, private; Jellison, John W., private; Jellison, Joshua C., private; Jellison, William H., private; Jenkins, Charles W, sergeant; Jennison, Maverick M., sergeant; Jewell, Roscoe, private; Johnson, Daniel E., private; Johnson, David E., private; Johnson, Edward P., private; Johnson, Ivory, private, Johnson, Jr., John, private; Johnson, John O., private; Johnson, Solomon, private; Jordan, George H., sergeant; Jose, Thomas L., private; Judge, Patrick, private; Keay, John F., private; Keays, William W., private; Keen, Hamden C., private; Keene, Harrison M., 1st sergeant; Keen, Josiah E., private; Kennison, Horace, corporal; Kerr, William, private; Kidder, George E., private; Kimball, Alpheus T., private; Kimball, Charles, private; Kimball, John E. L., surgeon; Kimball, Lewis, private; King, Thomas J., private; Kinrick, Eben S., private; Kirwin, James, private; Knight, Edward F., private; Knight, John H., private; Knight, Roscoe G., corporal; Knight, Porter, private; Knox, George F., private; Knox, Hosea B., corporal; Lane, George, private; Lampkin, Gilman H., private; Larrabee, Edward N., private; Lawry, Franklin E., private; Learned, Peter, private; Leavett, Henry, sergeant; Lewis, Gilman, private;

Libby, Aaron R., private; Libby, Arthur, corporal; Libby, Benjamin F., private; Libby, Charles G., private; Libby, Fred W., corporal; Libby, George H., private; Libby, Philander H., corporal; Libby, Samuel H., 1st lieutenant; Littlefield, Charles H., private; Littlefield, Emmerson, private; Littlefield, Franklin, private; Littlefield, George, private; Littlefield, Henry, 2d lieutenant; Littlefield, James H., private; Littlefield, Jedidiah, sergeant; Littlefield, John, private; Littlefield, John T., private; Littlefield, Joseph F., private; Littlefield, Joshua D., private; Littlefield, Josias, private; Littlefield, Ralph, private; Littlefield, Reuben O., private; Littlefield, Thaddeus, private; Locke, Thomas D., private; Lombard, Osbright A., private; Lord, Charles E., private; Lord, Edward, private; Lord, Ezekiel S., private; Lord, George A., private; Lord, John W., private; Lord, Lyman, private; Lord, Timothy H., sergeant; Loud, Elbridge, private; Lowell, John H., private; Lowell, Moses, private; Longee, Lorenzo J., private; Lunt, John W., private; Lydston, Charles, private; Maddox, John F., wagoner; Magrath, George, private; Marr, Cyrus G., comy. sergeant; Manning, George F., private; Manson, Albert, private; Manson, Charles H., sergeant; Manson, Edwin R., private; Manson, Horatio, private; Manson, John S., private; Manson, John W., private; Marriner, James S., private; Marston, Charles N., private; Martin, Frank W., musician; Martin, John, corporal; Martin, Lyman E., private; Mason, Albert D., private; Mason, Joseph T., private; Mealy, John, private; Mildram, Frank S., private; Merrill, Charles H., private; Merrill, Frederick A., private; Merrill, Jonas F., private; Merrill, Samuel, private; Miles, George S., private; Miles, Thomas P., corporal; Miller, Caleb L., private; Miller, Mark, private; Milliken, Charles H., private; Milliken, John S., private; Milliken, Moses S., private; Milliken, Nathaniel M., private; Millerkin, Jr., William, 1st lieutenant; Mills, Elihu J., private; Mitchell, Charles H., private; Mitchell, Deodat, private; Mitchell, Edwin, private; Mitchell, Joseph S., private; Mitchell, Jr., Joseph S., private; Moody, Charles H., private; Moody, James E., private; Moody, William H., 1st sergeant; Moore, George A., private; Moore, John, private; Morgan, William F., private; Morrison, Ivory C., private; Moulton, Alonzo P., private; Moulton, Charles H., private; Moulton, Erastus, sergeant; Mugridge, Samuel, private; Murch, Orrin, private; Murphy, John B., private; Murphy, Joseph W., private; McCulloch, Jr., Adam, private; McGuire, Charles, private; McIntire, Henry, private; McKenney, Abner, private; McKenney, Benjamin R., private; McKenney, Charles F., private; McKenney, Enoch, private; McLaughlin, Dennis, private; Nason, Andrew J., private; Nason, Freeman, private; Nason, Luther, private; Nason, Nathan P., sergeant; Nason, Samuel E., private; Nason, John, private; Nason, Robert, private; Nason, William H., private; Neal, John F., private; Needham, Frank E., private; Newbegin, Luke L., private; Nichols, Franklin, private; Nickolson, Edward P., private; Noble, John M., private; Norman, Charles S., private; Norton, Clark H., private; Norton, Eben H., private; Norton, Leonard, private; Nute, Ivory H., corporal; Okes, George W., private; O'Brion, Lewis, quartermaster; Ordway, Moses, private; Osgood, Henry B., 1st lieutenant; Otis, William M., private; Owen, Elijah J. C., private; Owen, Mark L. H., private; Owen, Melville C., private; Packard, Charles F., private; Page, Amos W., 1st lieutenant; Palmer, James W., private; Parker, Benjamin F., private; Parker, Horace B., private; Parker Joseph D., 1st lieutenant; Parody, John, private; Patch, Jr., John, private; Patterson, Gardiner, private; Patterson, Mark, private; Paul, Elbridge R., corporal; Paul, Henry M., private; Peavey, Chandler, private; Pendexter, Paul, private; Pennell, Horace, private; Perkins, George D., private; Perkins, James G., private; Perkins, John W., 2d lieutenant; Perkins, Otis W., private; Perkins, John, private; Perkins, Samuel, private; Perry, Pharaoh, private; Perry, William R., private; Pettigrew, Colby H., private; Pettigrew, John, corporal; Philbrick, Ira A., private; Philbrick, Robert S., private; Phillips, Rufus, private; Phillips, Trafton, private; Pickernell, Richard, private; Pierce, Charles A., corporal; Pierce, Daniel, private; Pierce, Henry B., corporal; Pierce, Sylvester, private; Pierce, William B., sergeant; Pike, Charles M., private; Pike, George B., private; Pike, William C., corporal; Piper, Horace L., 2d lieutenant; Pitts, George, private; Pillsbury, Woodman, private; Plumer, Jeremiah, captain; Plumer, William, private; Poole, James A., private; Pray, William A., private; Pray, William H., private; Prescott, Roswell, private; Prescott, Alpheus, private; Prescott, Wallace, private; Quinney, James, private; Quimby, Hosea M., sergeant; Ramsdell, Paul E., private; Rand, Edward M., adjutant; Redlon, Gideon W. T., private; Redlon, Isaac, private; Reed, George C., private; Rhodes, Israel K., musician; Richards, Orin E., private; Richardson, Joseph P., private; Ricker, Alonzo F., private; Ricker, Phendeus H., private; Ricker, Timothy F., private; Ridley, Joseph, private; Ridley, Joseph H., private; Ridlon, Henry, private; Ridlon, John, private; Ridlon, William, private; Roberts, Alvah, private; Roberts, Jr., Dimond, corporal; Robert, George H., sergeant; Roberts, John, private; Roberts, Joshua, private; Roberts, Luke H., corporal; Roberts, William F., corporal; Robinson, Edwin A., private; Robinson, Emery S., private; Robinson, George E., private; Robinson, Horace V., corporal; Robinson, Omen W., private; Ross, Albert, private; Ross, Hugh, private; Rounds, Daniel, wagoner; Rounds, Joseph G., private; Rounds, Melville K., private; Rowell, Alexander, private; Rines, George W., private; Russell, Otis F., chaplain; Sadler, Edwin A., private; Sampson, Moses T., 1st sergeant; Sanborn, Charles F., private; Sanborn, Charles F., corporal; Sanborn, Elias, private; Sanborn, John W., private; Sanborn, Nelson, private; Sanborn, Warren G., private; Sawyer, Isaac, private; Sawyer, Joseph R., private; Sawyer, Obediah, private; Scammon, Nicholas, corporal; Scates, David W. C., private; Scriggins, Charles H., private; Seavey, Frank, private; Sewall, Joseph A., private; Shapleigh, Dennis M., 2d lieutenant; Shapleigh, John, private; Shapleigh, Morris G., private; Shapleigh, Roscoe G., private; Shapleigh, William H., private; Shaw, J. Lyman, private; Shehan, George R., private; Shory, Henry W., private; Simpson, Enoch A., private; Skillings, Daniel, musician; Skillins, Lorenzo D., private; Skinner, John B., private; Small, Alfred, corporal; Small, Arthur L., private; Small, John C., private; Small, Lewis L., private; Small, Roland E., private; Smart, Almond O., captain; Smith, Amasa, private; Smith, Atwood F., corporal; Smith, Charles B., private; Smith, Charles F., corporal; Smith, Charles T., private; Smith, George L., 1st sergeant; Smith, James B., private; Smith, James H., private; Smith, James M., private; Smith, Libby H., private; Smith, Milbury S., private; Smith, Ransom E., sergeant; Smith, Rice, private; Smith, Samuel S., private; Smith, Stillman C., sergeant; Smith, William, private; Smith, William M., corporal; Smith, Woodbury, private; Spaulding, Wallis, private; Spencer, Joseph T., private; Spencer, Joshua C., private; Spinney, James P., private; Spinney, Nicholas E., sergeant; Spinney, Stephen S., private; Stacy, Uranus, private; Stanley, John R., private; Staples, Charles F., corporal; Staples, William M., sergeant; Staples, William M., sergeant; Steadfast, Thomas S., private; Stevens, Charles E., private; Stevens, Herrman, private; Stevens, Osgood W., private; Stevenson, William, private; Stillings, Calvin, private; Stimpson, Thomas J., private; Stone, James M., lieutenant-colonel; Stone, Lewis G., private; Stone, Jr., Simon, private;

Stover, Eben, private; Sweetsir, John W., corporal; Sweetair, Stephen E., private; Swett, Augustus D., private; Tufts, John W., private; Tufts, Wilson C., private; Tapley, David G., private; Tapley, William H., private; Tarbox, Alphonso, private; Tarbox, George, private; Tarbox, Thomas B., private; Taylor, Calvin M., private; Taylor, Daniel D., corporal; Taylor, George A., private; Taylor, George W., private; Taylor, Horace, private; Taylor, Oliver G., private; Thompson, Jr., Adrial, private; Thompson, Caleb, private; Thompson, George F., private; Thompson, George W., sergeant; Thompson, Henry C., 1st sergeant; Thompson, William S., private; Thorn, David, private; Thurston, Milton, private; Tibbetts, Charles H., private; Tobey, Samuel A., private; Tobey, William W., sergeant; Tompson, William, private; Trafton, Ham N., private; Trafton, Osborn, private; Trefethern, Horatio W., private; Tripp, Charles D., corporal; Tripp, Pelatiah R., private; Tucker, Charles H., corporal; Tucker, Daniel H., private; Tucker, William H., private; Twombley, Henry W., private; Varney, Aaron, private; Varney, Elijah, private; Wadleigh, Charles H., private; Wadleigh, Elisha, private; Wadsworth, Alexander, private; Wadsworth, Marshall L., corporal; Waitt, John H., private; Wakefield, George W., private; Wakefield, George W., private; Walker, George M., sergeant; Wallingford, Daniel, private; Wells, Thomas, private; Ward, George H., captain; Warren, Chadbourne, private; Warren, Joseph F., captain; Warren, Nathaniel F., private; Watson, Daniel, private; Watson, George W., sergeant; Watson, Seth, private; Webber, Alfred C., private; Webber, Orin B., private; Webber, William C., musician; Weeks, Noah, private; Welch, Charles H., private; Welch, Wentworth, private; Wells, Alexander B., corporal; Wells, Hartley L., private; Wells, Octavus E., private; Wentworth, Albert F., private; Wentworth, Bradford H., private; Wentworth, Enoch J., private; Wentworth, Henry, private; Wentworth, Lewis H., private; Wentworth, Mark F., colonel; Wentworth, Samuel T., private; West, Silas, corporal; Wheelwright, Moses F., private; White, Joseph H., private; Whitehead, John, private; Whitehouse, Harrison, private; Whitehouse, Joseph A., private; Whitten, John G., corporal; Wiggin, George A., private; Wiggin, James E., corporal; Wiggin, John H., corporal; Wiggin, John W., private; Wiggin, Mark N., private; Wilds, Erastus, private; Wilkinson, Steph, private; Willey, Andrew, private; Willey, Frederick L., private; Williams, Joseph B., corporal; Williams, Josiah, private; Wentworth, William, private; Wells, John, private; Wilson, Charles W., private; Wilson, George, private; Wilson, John R., corporal; Wilson, Joseph D., private; Wingate, Jesse B., corporal; Winn, Oliver A., private; Witham, Jr., Josiah W., private; Woodsome, James L., private; Wormwood, John P., private; Worster, Charles H., private; Wright, George C., private; York, Charles E., private; York, Enoch, private; York, George H., private; York, William H., private; Young, Augustus D., private; Young, John, private; Young, Orileas L., private.

The Naval Medal.—No complete list of the sailors who have received the medal of honor for gallant services in the United States Navy has been published. The following is made up from partial lists furnished to us by the Navy Department. In a few cases the medal was forfeited by subsequent bad conduct, and such names are dropped from this list. The last word in each line is the name of the vessel:

Ahearn, Michael, paymaster's steward, Kearsarge.
Anderson, Aaron (colored), landsman, Wyandotte.
Anderson, Robert, quartermaster, Crusader.
Andrews, John, seaman, Benicia.
Angling, John, boy, Pontoosuc.
Arthur, Matthew, signal quartermaster, Carondelet.
Atkinson, Thomas, yeoman, Richmond.
Baldwin, Charles, coal-heaver, Wyalusing.
Barnum, James, boatswain's mate, New Ironsides.
Barter, Gurdon H., landsman, Minnesota.
Barton, Thomas C., seaman, Hunchback.
Bass, David L., seaman, Minnesota.
Bazaar, Philip, seaman, Santiago de Cuba.
Bell, George, captain afterguard, Santee.
Benson, James, seaman, Ossipee.
Betham, Asa, cockswain, Pontoosuc.
Bickford, John F., captain top, Kearsarge.
Bitter, Charles J., gunner's mate, Agawam.
Blagdeen, William, ship's cook, Brooklyn.
Blair, Robert M., boatswain's mate, Pontoosuc.
Blake, Robert (colored), powder boy, Marblehead.
Bob, Frank, quartermaster, Cincinnati.
Bond, William, boatswain's mate, Kearsargo.
Bourne, Thomas, seaman, Varuna.
Bowman, Edward R., quartermaster, Ticonderoga.
Bradley, Alexander, landsman, Wachusett.
Bradley, Amos, landsman, Varuna.
Bradley, Charles, boatswain's mate, Louisville.
Brazell, John, quartermaster, Richmond.
Breene, John, boatswain's mate, Commodore Perry.
Brennen, Christopher, seaman, Colorado.
Brinn, Andrew, seaman, Mississippi.
Brown, Charles, corporal marines, Colorado.
Brown, James, quartermaster, Albatross.
Brown, John, captain forecastle, Brooklyn.
Brown, Robert, captain top, Richmond.
Brown, William H., landsman, Brooklyn.
Brown, Wilson, landsman, Hartford.
Browdell, William P., cockswain, Benton.
Brutsche, Henry, landsman, Tacony.
Buchanan, David M., apprentice, Saratoga.
Buck, James, quartermaster, Brooklyn.
Burns, John M., seaman, Lackawanna.
Burton, Albert, seaman, Wabash.
Butts, George, gunner's mate, Signal.
Byrnes, James, boatswain's mate, Louisville.
Campbell, William, boatswain's mate, Ticonderoga.
Carr, William M., master-at-arms, Richmond.
Cassidy, Michael, landsman, Lackawanna.
Chandler, James B., cockswain, Richmond.
Chaput, Louis G., landsman, Lackawanna.
Charles, Asten, quarter-gunner, Signal.
Clifford, Robert T., master-at-arms, Monticello.
Colbert, Patrick, cockswain, Commodore Hull.
Coleman, John, private marine, Colorado.
Conlan, Dennis, seaman, Agawam.
Connolly, Michael, seaman, Plymouth.
Connor, Thomas, seaman, Minnesota.
Connor, William C., boatswain's mate, Howquah.
Cooper, John, cockswain, Brooklyn.
Cooper, John, quartermaster, Brooklyn.
Corcoran, Thomas E., landsman, Cincinnati.
Corey, William, landsman, Plymouth.
Costello, John, seaman, Hartford.
Cotton, Peter, cockswain, Baron de Kalb.
Crawford, Alexander, fireman, Wyalusing.
Cripps, Thomas, quartermaster, Richmond.
Cronin, Cornelius, quartermaster, Richmond.
Cutter, George W., landsman, Powhatan.
Davis, John, quarter-gunner, Valley City.
Davis, Samuel W., seaman, Brooklyn.
Deakin, Charles, boatswain's mate, Richmond.
Demming, ——, landsman, picket-boat No. 1.
Dempster, John, cockswain, New Ironsides.
Denham, Austin, seaman, Kansas.
Denig, J. Henry, sergeant marines, Brooklyn.
Dennis, Richard, boatswain's mate, Brooklyn.
Densmore, William, boatswain's mate, Richmond.
Ditzenbach, John, quartermaster, Neosho.
Doolen, William, coal-heaver, Richmond.
Dorman, John, seaman, Carondelet.
Dougherty, James, private marine, Benicia.
Dougherty, Patrick, landsman, Lackawanna.
Dow, Henry, boatswain's mate, Cincinnati.

Du Moulin, Frank, apprentice, Sabine.
Duncan, Adam, boatswain's mate, Richmond.
Duncan, J. K. L., seaman, Fort Hindman.
Dunn, William, quartermaster, Monadnock.
Edwards, John, captain top, Lackawanna.
English, Thomas, quartermaster, New Ironsides.
Erickson, John P., captain forecastle, Pontoosuc.
Farley, William, boatswain's mate, Marblehead.
Farrel, Edward, quartermaster, Owasco.
Ferrell, John H., pilot, Neosho.
Fitzpatrick, Thomas, cockswain, Hartford.
Flood, Thomas, boy, Pensacola.
Foy, Charles H., quartermaster, Rhode Island.
Franklin, Frederick, quartermaster, Colorado.
Franks, William J., seaman, Marmora.
Freeman, Martin, pilot, Hartford.
Frisbee, J. B., gunner's mate, Panola.
Fry, Isaac N., sergeant marines, Ticonderoga.
Gardner, William, seaman, Oneida.
Garrison, James R., coal-heaver, Hartford.
Garvin, William, captain forecastle, Agawam.
Giddings, Charles, seaman, Plymouth.
Gile, Frank S., landsman, Lehigh.
Graham, Robert, landsman, Tacony.
Greene, John, captain forecastle, Varuna.
Griffiths, John, captain forecastle, Santiago de Cuba.
Griswold, Luke M., seaman, Rhode Island.
Haffee, Edmund, quarter-gunner, New Ironsides.
Haley, James, captain forecastle, Kearsarge.
Halford, William, cockswain, Saginaw.
Halstead, William, cockswain, Brooklyn.
Hamilton, Hugh, cockswain, Richmond.
Hamilton, Richard, coal-heaver, picket-boat No. 1.
Hamilton, Thomas W., quartermaster, Cincinnati.
Ham, Mark G., carpenter's mate, Kearsarge.
Handran, John, seaman, Franklin.
Harcourt, Thomas, seaman, Minnesota.
Harding, Thomas, captain forecastle. Monticello.
Harley, Bernard, seaman, picket-boat No. 1.
Harrington, Daniel, landsman, Pocahontas.
Harrison, George H., seaman, Kearsarge.
Hawkins, Charles, seaman, Agawam.
Hayden, Cyrus, carpenter, Colorado.
Hayden, John, apprentice, Saratoga.
Hayden, Joseph B., quartermaster, Ticonderoga.
Hayes, John, cockswain, Kearsarge.
Hayes, Thomas, cockswain, Richmond.
Hickman, John, fireman, Richmond.
Hill, John, quarter-gunner, Kansas.
Hinnegan, William, fireman, Agawam.
Holt, George, quarter-gunner, Plymouth.
Hood, Alexander, quartermaster, Ceres.
Horton, James, gunner's mate, Montauk.
Horton, Lewis A., seaman, Rhode Island.
Houghton, Edward J., seaman, picket-boat No. 1.
Howard, Martin, landsman, Tacony.
Howard, Peter, boatswain's mate, Mississippi.
Hudson, Michael, sergeant marines. Brooklyn.
Huskey, Michael, fireman, Carondelet.
Hyland, John, seaman, Signal.
Irlam, Joseph, seaman, Brooklyn.
Irving, John, cockswain, Brooklyn.
Irving, Thomas, cockswain, Lehigh.
Irwin, Nicholas, seaman, Brooklyn.
James, John H., captain top, Richmond.
Jenkins, Thomas, seaman, Cincinnati.
Johnson, Henry, seaman, Metacomet.
Johnson, John, seaman, Kansas.
Johnson, William P., landsman, Fort Hindman.
Jones, Andrew, boatswain's mate, Chickasaw.
Jones, John, landsman, Rhode Island.
Jones, John E., quartermaster, Oneida.
Jones, Thomas, cockswain, Ticonderoga.
Jones, William, captain top, Richmond.
Jordan, Robert, cockswain, Minnesota.
Jordan, Thomas, quartermaster, Galena.
Kane, Thomas, captain hold, Nereus.
Kelley, John, fireman, Ceres.
Kendrick, Thomas, cockswain, Oneida.
Kenna, Barnett, quartermaster, Brooklyn.

Kenyon, Charles, fireman, Galena.
Kersey, Thomas, seaman, Plymouth.
King, Hugh, seaman, Iroquois.
King, R. H., landsman, picket-boat No. 1.
Kinnaird, Samuel W., landsman, Lackawanna.
Laffey, Bartlett, seaman, Petrel.
Lakin, Daniel, seaman, Commodore Perry.
Lann, John S., landsman, Magnolia.
Laverty, John, fireman, Wyalusing.
Lawson, John, landsman, Hartford.
Lear, Nicholas, quartermaster, New Ironsides.
Lee, James H., seaman, Kearsarge.
Leland, George W., gunner's mate, Lehigh.
Leon, Pierre, captain forecastle, Baron de Kalb.
Lloyd, Benjamin, coal-heaver, Wyalusing.
Lloyd, John W., cockswain, Wyalusing.
Logan, Hugh, captain afterguard, Rhode Island.
Lucy, John, boy, Minnesota.
Lukes, William F., landsman, Colorado.
Lyons, Thomas, boatswain's mate, Pensacola.
McClelland, Matthew, fireman, Richmond.
McCloud, James, captain foretop, Colorado.
McCormick, Michael, boatswain's mate, Signal.
McCullock, Adam, seaman, Lackawanna.
McDonald, John, boatswain's mate, Baron de Kalb.
McFarland, James, captain forecastle, Hartford.
McGowan, John, quartermaster, Varuna.
McHugh, Martin, seaman, Cincinnati.
McIntosh, James, captain top, Richmond.
McKenzie, Alexander, boatswain's mate, Colorado.
McKnight, William, cockswain, Varuna.
McNamera, Michael, private marine, Benicia.
McWilliams, George W., landsman, Pontoosuc.
Machon, James, boy, Brooklyn.
Mack, Alexander, captain top, Brooklyn.
Mack, John, seaman, Hendrick Hudson.
Mackie, John, corporal of marines, Galena.
Madden, William, coal-heaver, Brooklyn.
Maddin, Edward, seaman, Franklin.
Martin, Edward, quartermaster, Galena.
Martin, James, sergeant marines, Richmond.
Martin, William, boatswain's mate, Benton.
Martin, William, seaman, Varuna.
Melloy, Hugh, seaman, Fort Hindman.
Melville, Charles, seaman, Hartford.
Merton, James F., landsman, Colorado.
Mifflin, James, engineer's cook, Brooklyn.
Miller, Andrew, sergeant marines, Richmond.
Miller, James, quartermaster, Marblehead.
Milliken, Daniel S., quarter-gunner, New Ironsides.
Mills, Charles, seaman, Minnesota.
Montgomery, Robert, captain afterguard, Agawam.
Moore, Charles, seaman, Kearsarge.
Moore, Charles, landsman, Marblehead.
Moore, George, seaman, Rhode Island.
Moore, William, boatswain's mate, Benton.
Morgan, James H., captain top, Richmond.
Morrison, John G., cockswain, Galena.
Morton, Charles W., boatswain's mate, Benton.
Mullen, Patrick, boatswain's mate, Don.
Naylor, David, landsman, Oneida.
Neil, John, quarter-gunner, Agawam.
Newland, William, seaman, Oneida.
Nibbe, John H., quartermaster, Petrel.
Nichols, William, quartermaster, Brooklyn.
Nugent, Christopher, sergeant marines, Fort Henry.
O'Brien, Oliver, cockswain, Canandaigua.
O'Connell, Thomas, coal-heaver, Hartford.
O'Donoghue, Timothy, seaman, Signal.
O'Neil, John, boatswain's mate, Kansas.
Ortega, John, seaman, Saratoga.
Osborne, John, seaman, Juniata.
Oviatt, Miles M., corporal of marines, Brooklyn.
Owens, Michael, private marine, Colorado.
Parker, Alexander, boatswain's mate, Portsmouth.
Parker, William, captain afterguard, Cayuga.
Parks, George, captain forecastle, Richmond.
Pease, Joachim (colored), seaman, Kearsarge.
Peck, Oscar E., boy, Varuna.
Pelham, William, landsman, Hartford.

Perry, Thomas, boatswain's mate, Kearsarge.
Peterson, Alfred, seaman, Commodore Perry.
Phinney, William, boatswain's mate, Lackawanna.
Pile, Richard, seaman, Kansas.
Poole, William B., quartermaster, Kearsarge.
Powers, John, seaman, Plymouth.
Prance, George, captain maintop, Ticonderoga.
Preston, John, landsman, Oneida.
Price, Edward, cockswain, Brooklyn.
Province, George, seaman, Santiago de Cuba.
Purvis, Hugh, private marine, Alaska.
Pyne, George, seaman, Magnolia.
Ranahan, John, corporal marines, Minnesota.
Read, Charles A., cockswain, Kearsarge.
Read, George E., seaman, Kearsarge.
Reed, Charles, seaman, Magnolia.
Regan, Jeremiah, quartermaster, Galena.
Rice, Charles, coal-heaver, Agawam.
Richards, Lewis, quartermaster, Pensacola.
Ringgold, Edward, cockswain, Wabash.
Roantree, James S., sergeant marines, Oneida.
Roberts, James, seaman, Agawam.
Robinson, Alexander, boatswain's mate, Howquah.
Robinson, Charles, boatswain's mate, Baron de Kalb.
Robinson, John, captain hold, Yucca.
Rogers, Samuel F., quartermaster, Colorado.
Rountry, John, fireman, Montauk.
Rush, John, fireman, Richmond.
Ryan, Richard, seaman, Hartford.
Sapp, Isaac, seaman, Shenandoah.
Saunders, John, quartermaster, Kearsarge.
Savage, Auzella, seaman, Santiago de Cuba.
Schutt, George, cockswain, Hendrick Hudson.
Seanor, James, master-at-arms, Chickasaw.
Sevcarer, Benjamin, seaman, Hatteras Expedition.
Seward, Richard, paymaster's steward, Commodore.
Sharp, Hendrick, seaman, Richmond.
Shepard, L. C., seaman, Wabash.
Sheridan, James, quartermaster, Oneida.
Shipman, William, cockswain, Ticonderoga.
Shivers, John, private marine, Minnesota.
Simkins, Lebbeus, cockswain, Richmond.
Smith, Charles H., cockswain, Rhode Island.
Smith, Edwin, seaman, Whitehead.
Smith, James, first captain forecastle, Richmond.
Smith, James, seaman, Kansas.
Smith, John, captain forecastle, Lackawanna.
Smith, John, second captain top, Richmond.
Smith, Oloff, cockswain, Richmond.
Smith, Thomas, seaman, Magnolia.
Smith, Walter B., seaman, Richmond.
Smith, William, quartermaster, Kearsarge.
Smith, William, seaman, picket-boat No. 1.
Smith, William M., corporal marines, Brooklyn.
Sprowle, David, orderly sergeant marine guard, Richmond.
Stanley, William A., shellman, Hartford.
Sterling, James E., coal-heaver, Brooklyn.
Stewart, James, corporal marine guard, Plymouth.
Stoddard, James, seaman, Marmora.
Stout, Richard, landsman, Isaac Smith.
Strahan, Robert, captain top, Kearsarge.
Sullivan, James, seaman, Agawam.
Sullivan, John, seaman, Monticello.
Sullivan, Timothy, cockswain, Louisville.
Summers, Robert, quartermaster, Ticonderoga.
Swanson, John, seaman, Santiago de Cuba.
Swatton, Edward, seaman, Santiago de Cuba.
Talbott, William, captain forecastle, Louisville.
Tallentine, James, quarter-gunner, Tacony.
Taylor, George, armorer, Lackawanna.
Taylor, Thomas, cockswain, Metacomet.
Taylor, William G., captain forecastle, Ticonderoga.
Thielberg, Henry, seaman, Minnesota.
Thompson, Henry, private marine, Minnesota.
Thompson, William, signal quartermaster, Mohican.
Tobin, Paul, landsman, Plymouth.
Todd, Samuel, quartermaster, Brooklyn.
Tomlin, A. J., corporal marines, Wabash.
Tripp, Othniel, boatswain's mate, Seneca.

Troy, William, seaman, Colorado.
Truett, Alexander H., cockswain, Richmond.
Vantine, Joseph E., fireman, Richmond.
Vaughan, P. R., sergeant marines, Mississippi.
Verney, James W., quartermaster, Pontoosuc.
Wagg, Maurice, cockswain, Rhode Island.
Ward, James, quarter-gunner, Lackawanna.
Warren, David, cockswain, Monticello.
Webster, Henry S., landsman, Susquehanna.
Weeks, Charles H., captain foretop, Susquehanna.
Weisbogel, Albert, captain mizzentop, Benicia.
Wells, William, quartermaster, Richmond.
White, Joseph, cockswain, New Ironsides.
Whitfield, Daniel, quartermaster, Lackawanna.
Wilcox, Franklin L., seaman, Minnesota.
Wilkes, ——, landsman, picket-boat No. 1.
Wilkes, Perry, pilot, Signal.
Williams, Anthony, sailmaker's mate, Pontoosuc.
Williams, Augustus, seaman, Santiago de Cuba.
Williams, John, boatswain's mate, Mohican.
Williams, John, captain maintop, Pawnee.
Williams, John, seaman, Commodore Perry.
Williams, Peter, seaman, Monitor.
Williams, Robert, signal quartermaster, Benton.
Williams, William, landsman, Lehigh.
Willis, Richard, cockswain, New Ironsides.
Wood, Robert B., cockswain, Minnesota.
Woods, Samuel, seaman, Minnesota.
Woon, John, boatswain's mate, Pittsburgh.
Woram, Charles B., seaman, Oneida.
Wright, Edward, quartermaster, Cayuga.
Wright, William, yeoman, Monticello.
Young, Edward B., cockswain, Galena.
Young, Horatio N., seaman, Lehigh.
Young, William, boatswain's mate, Cayuga.

(See colored plate facing page 329.)

MEMORIAL DAY. With the busy Anglo-Saxon race, holidays are of comparatively slow growth. Protestants have few saints of such generally recognized prominence that with common consent days can be set apart to their honor, and, even if they had, popular prejudice against blocking the wheels of commerce would probably check the multiplication of holidays. The more mercurial Latins have a dozen holidays where we have one, and the Mother Church has always stood ready to encourage her children to their observance.

Christmas and New Year's were brought over the ocean from the old country. Thanksgiving grew out of Puritan customs, and was local until after the civil war. Washington's Birthday and the Fourth of July were the natural outgrowth of the war for independence, and with these we were content for the better part of a century.

Memorial Day, or, as it was at first known to the Northern States, "Decoration Day," is the last one added to the list, and it will probably be many years before the number is increased. The observance of this day may be said to have originated at the South before the close of hostilities. It was inaugurated there by Southern women, who, by almost imperceptible degrees, established the custom each year in early spring of decorating with flowers the graves of their dead. When the war closed, the custom had become quite general, and an unwritten law had fixed upon the 30th of May as the day for its observance. At the North, while similar services had been inaugurated, no especial unanimity developed until 1868, when for the first time the same date was adopted, and the daily papers of that year contain the earliest general indications of a popular movement. The Grand Army of the Republic, then in the early days of its organization, naturally took the lead in establishing precedents for the suitable observance of the anniversary that has now become so general.

When it is remembered that probably not a single family fairly naturalized in the United States was wholly exempt from the casualties of war, it may be readily understood how strongly the day and its associations appealed to the popular heart. At first its observance was especially cultivated in rural neighborhoods and in the smaller towns, and for a time it was doubtful if the larger cities would ever adopt the custom. In the course of time, however, with the perfected organization of the Grand Army, it assumed such prominence that business was practically suspended, and the great centers of population recognized the appropriateness of the simple ceremonies.

To the rising generation, of course, the day now carries comparatively small significance. It is welcomed as a holiday and devoted largely to sports and merry-making, and, however inappropriate this may seem to the older generation to whom the realities of war are still a terrible memory, it is inevitable, and must probably increase as time passes. The veterans who march in the ranks to decorate the graves of their former comrades must diminish from year to year, and the interest of the occasion must diminish in a like ratio, but for a generation to come the number of survivors will be strong enough to lend a dignity to the proceedings, and the future of Memorial Day must be governed by circumstances that at present no one can foresee.

The official history of the day is found, for the most part, in the proceedings of the Grand Army of the Republic. It was formally established by Commander-in-Chief John A. Logan, in the following general order:

The 30th day of May, 1868, is designated for the purpose of strewing with flowers or otherwise decorating the graves of comrades who died in defense of their country during the late rebellion, and whose bodies now lie in almost every city, village, and hamlet churchyard in the land. In this observance no form of ceremony is prescribed, but posts and comrades will in their own way arrange such fitting services and testimonials of respect as circumstances may permit.

We are organized, comrades, as our regulations tell us, for the purpose, among other things, " of preserving and strengthening those kind and fraternal feelings which have bound together the soldiers, sailors, and marines who united to suppress the late rebellion." What can aid more to assure this result than by cherishing tenderly the memory of our heroic dead, who made their breasts a barricade between our country and its foes ? Their soldier lives were the reveille of freedom to a race in chains, and their deaths the tattoo of rebellious tyranny in arms. We should guard their graves with sacred vigilance. All that the consecrated wealth and taste of the nation can add to their adornment and security is but a fitting tribute to the memory of her slain defenders.

Let no wanton foot tread rudely on such hallowed ground. Let pleasant paths invite the coming and going of reverent visitors and fond mourners. Let no vandalism of avarice or neglect, no ravages of time, testify to the present or to the coming generations that we have forgotten as a people the cost of a free and undivided republic.

If other eyes grow dull, and other hands slack, and other hearts cold in the solemn trust, ours shall keep it well as long as the light and warmth of life remain.

Let us, then, at the time appointed, gather around their sacred remains and garland the passionless mounds above them with the choicest flowers of springtime; let us raise above them the dear old flag they saved from dishonor : let us in this solemn presence renew our pledges to aid and assist those whom they have left among us, a sacred charge upon a nation's gratitude—the soldier's and sailor's widow and orphan.

It is the purpose of the commander-in-chief to inaugurate this observance with the hope that it will be kept up from year to year, while a survivor of the war remains to honor the memory of his departed comrades. He earnestly desires the public press to call attention to this order, and lend its friendly aid in bringing it to the notice of comrades in all parts of the country in time for simultaneous compliance therewith.

Department commanders will use every effort to make this order effective.

The following resolution was adopted by the National Encampment at Providence, 1877 :

Inasmuch as there have been some differences of opinion as to the intent and meaning of Memorial Day, this encampment hereby calls attention to the language of Chapter V, Article XIV, of the Rules and Regulations, and, therefore, *Resolved*, That the Grand Army of the Republic seeks thus to preserve the memory of those only who fought in defense of the national unity.

The following was adopted at the encampment at Springfield, Mass., June, 1878 : "*Resolved*, That all flags hoisted on Memorial Day, be at half-mast." Among the proceedings is the following under date of April 17, 1878 :

1. Memorial Day—Observance of Memorial Day is obligatory.

2. Private circumstances may excuse a comrade from the observance : but a post that fails or refuses should be subjected to discipline.

3. Where a post fails to observe the day, it is not obligatory on a member of the post.

4. The manner or form of the observance left to the posts.

5. Neither the commander-in-chief nor the department commander has any authority to prescribe a plan for the observance of Memorial Day.

Is it the duty of posts or comrades to observe Memorial Day without any other authorization or direction than that obtained in the Rules and Regulations, Chapter V, Article XIV ?

Is it discretionary with posts and comrades whether they shall observe Memorial Day ?

Would the failure of a post to make arrangements for the observance of Memorial Day as a post, relieve any member of that post from the duty of its observance ?

Do the Rules and Regulations leave the method of the observance of Memorial Day, and the arrangements therefor, to the discretion of posts and comrades ?

Has the commander-in-chief, or a department commander, authority to prescribe any plan of action by posts in the arrangements for the observance of Memorial Day, or to interfere with the arrangement of any post or comrade for its observance, either as a post by itself, or in conjunction with other posts, or as comrades individually ?

1. I answer the first question in general terms in the affirmative. I consider that the Rules and Regulations enjoin upon every post and comrade the duty of observing Memorial Day, and that this provision creates the duty, whether any orders are issued by department or national authority or not.

2. The nature of the duty makes each comrade, necessarily, the judge of how he shall perform it. It is analogous to their obligation which he assumes to relieve the wants of a needy comrade, or his duty to attend the meetings of his post. Each of these duties will be acknowledged by a comrade who feels his responsibility as a member of the order. Yet, from the nature of the case, no post can say what private circumstances are sufficient to excuse a member from giving charity in any particular instance, nor whether he properly waives the obligations to attend a meeting in favor of another duty which seems to him to claim the preference. In all these matters the Grand Army must leave the conduct of each comrade to his own sense of right.

In the case of a post I think somewhat less discretion is allowable. Posts are organized, among other things, for just this purpose. The perpetuation of the memory of our fallen comrades, not only among ourselves, but in the grateful regard of the whole people, whose life they saved, by our annual processions to the resting-places of the heroic dead and the floral decorations of their urns, is one of the most prominent and beautiful objects of our order, none the less important that it was not inaugurated till after the Grand Army had been some time in existence. I think, therefore, that a post which should omit this ceremonial repeatedly, or for a frivolous cause, or which should deliberately pass resolutions of contempt for the observance of it—if such a thing can be imagined—would be amenable to discipline by higher authority as properly as if it should fail for a long period to hold meetings, or in its capacity as a post should commit any other act of insubordination.

3. If the post to which any comrade belongs were to fail to make arrangements for the observance of the day, I think it would not be obligatory upon such comrade to engage in any public ceremonies in its observance. Yet, if inclination prompts him to join with some other post, or to assemble with other comrades, or alone to visit and decorate the graves of the fallen, such voluntary service will be a becoming expression of the sentiments which the Grand Army inculcates and fosters.

4. The Rules and Regulations prescribe the observance of the day by the members of the order. The primary organization of the members is by posts, and, consequently, in the absence of specific orders or regulations, the duty first devolves upon each post. It is generally the case throughout the country that there is only one post in each town or village, and, therefore, the day has been usually observed by each post in its own way. In cities, where there are more posts than one, and where there are, perhaps, different cemeteries to be visited, it has been the custom, and an entirely proper one, for several posts to unite voluntarily in this service.

5. The ordinary duties of a department commander relate to his department as a whole. On occasions when the whole department is ordered out, or assembled for any duty, he takes command. When a post is assembled by itself, or when several posts unite voluntarily, for the purpose of a parade, a reception, or a fair, or any such object, the department commander would hardly assume the direction of affairs. If one post, or any number of posts, were to assemble or combine for an illegal object, or one detrimental to the interests of the order, the department commander would have the right, and it would be his duty, to interfere and stop such proceedings.

Clearly, whatever right a department commander has in his own department, the commander-in-chief has throughout the order, and if the department commander interferes in matters relating to a post in

his jurisdiction, the commander-in-chief may, in his discretion, approve or revoke the order of the department commander.

I may add, in application of the foregoing principles to the facts which suggested the questions submitted, that no department encampment or department commander has the power to order various posts to send delegates to a committee which shall control their action as posts upon any public occasion, because:

1. Such action is in effect forming a new organization, unknown to our Rules and Regulations, and giving it a command which belongs to the senior officer present.

2. Such action, where pecuniary expense is to be incurred under direction of such committee, is giving to an unauthorized body the power to levy a special tax upon the posts concerned.

Of course, any number of posts, conveniently located for the purpose, may voluntarily combine for any lawful object, and may act, through a committee of their own choice, as they see fit, in securing their object, and in collecting the means for defraying the expense incurred.

In spite of these measures the anniversary was still popularly known as Decoration Day at the North, and the following was adopted at the encampment at Baltimore, 1882:

That the commander-in-chief be requested to issue a general order calling the attention of the officers and members of the Grand Army of the Republic, and of the people at large, to the fact that the proper designation of May 30 is Memorial Day, and to request that it may be always so called.

In the constitution of the Grand Army, Article XIV, Chapter V, reads as follows:

The national encampment hereby establishes a Memorial Day, to be observed by the members of the Grand Army of the Republic, on the 30th day of May annually, in commemoration of the deeds of our fallen comrades. When such day occurs on Sunday, the succeeding day shall be observed, except where, by legal enactment, the preceding day is made a legal holiday, when such day shall be observed.

The veterans of New Jersey were, it is believed, the first to make a stated effort to secure legislative action in regard to legalizing the day as a holiday. In their proceedings is found the following resolution, by Comrade Ward:

Whereas, The annual encampment of the Department of New Jersey of 1874, appointed a committee to use every honorable means to have an act passed by the Legislature of the State making the 30th day of May a legal holiday; and

Whereas, The efforts of this committee heretofore put forth to secure the passage of said act have failed; and

Whereas, The evidence of its justice and propriety accumulates as the years roll by; therefore

Resolved, That the committee having this matter in charge be and are hereby instructed to press to the uttermost the passage of a bill that will secure the desired end.

Action on the last two resolutions was deferred until the following morning. No further business being presented, the council adjourned.

On motion, the communication of Comrade Burrows, in reference to having the representatives of this department at the next national encampment of the G. A. R. offer a resolution with the view to ask Congress of the United States to pass resolutions making the 30th day of May a national holiday, was received and adopted.

The committee appointed at the last annual encampment for the purpose of having an act passed by the Legislature of the State of New Jersey, making May 30 a legal holiday, reported as follows:

CHARLES BURROWS, Esq., Dept. Commander.

Comrade : I am sorry to say this bill was defeated in the Senate yesterday. With the assistance of others I got it through the lower house without difficulty. It was introduced at my request by Col. Geo. Patterson, member from Monmouth, who took charge of and advocated it. No serious opposition was made to it. It passed the House day before yesterday. As soon as it got in the Senate yesterday, unexpected opposition was developed there ; before the necessary measures to overcome the opposition could be made effective, and while I was so engaged, it was taken up and lost. Gen. W. J. Sewell, the only soldier in the Senate, had charge of it in that body. It is too late now to get the bill up again with any hope of success, as the Legislature adjourns *sine die* to-day. The matter will have to be deferred until another year. The first assault has carried the first line, the second, if vigorously made, should carry both. I suggest that if the effort be made next year each post should pass a series of resolutions, and send a copy to each member and senator from their respective counties, and also appoint a committee to wait upon them personally at their homes ; then, with a strong lobby committee to visit and work at the State-House, I am convinced it could be made a success.

I beg to be discharged from further duty in this matter. My feelings are very much averse to this business of lobbying ; I have heretofore entirely declined to do such work. Please file this and have it reported, if I am not present, at the next annual encampment.   Your obedient servant,
                        E. L. CAMPBELL, Chairman.
Trenton, March 27, 1874.

On Dec. 8, 1870, James S. Negley, of Pennsylvania, introduced in the U. S. House of Representatives the following resolution, which was referred to the Committee on Printing:

Resolved, That the proceedings of different cities, towns, etc., held on the 29th and 30th days of May, 1869 and 1870, in commemoration of the gallant heroes who sacrificed their lives in defense of the republic, and the record of the ceremonies of the decoration of the honored tombs of the departed, shall be collected, printed, and bound, under the direction of such person as the Speaker shall designate, for the use of Congress.

But this resolution was never reported upon. Feb. 3, 1871, the Senate Committee on Military Affairs reported adversely on a joint resolution introduced in the House by Robert C. Schenck, of Ohio, "to establish the 30th day of May in each year a public holiday." Senator Thayer, of Nebraska, in presenting the report, said : " I do not concur in the report, and am in favor of the resolution, and will call it up at an early day, with a view of taking the sense of the Senate upon it " ; but no record appears of his having done so. June 1, 1872, Mr. Duell, of New York, introduced in the U. S. House of Representatives, a joint resolution to establish the 30th day of May in each year a public holiday, which was referred to Committee on Judiciary. No reference to any subsequent action is to be found in the " Congressional Record."

The U. S. Senate generally, and the House sometimes, adjourned over Memorial Day, and in 1878 both houses adjourned, the Senate, " in order that members might take part in the interesting ceremonies " ; the House, " as a mark of respect to the memory of the illustrious dead." But the law allowing pay for legal holidays to the employés in the Government Printing-Office does not include Memorial Day in the list of such days, nor has Congress ever legalized the day as a holiday, though petitioned by the Grand Army to do so. The Legislature of New York, by Chap. 577 of laws of 1878, (amended in 1881,) designated " the 30th day of May, known as Decoration Day," as one of the "public holidays for all purposes whatsoever as regards the transaction of business in the public offices of the State," or counties of the State, and " in the acceptance and payment of bills of exchange, bank checks, and promissory notes." Rhode Island made the day a legal holiday in 1874, Vermont in 1876, New Hampshire in 1877, Wisconsin in 1879, Massachusetts and Ohio in 1881, and it is believed the same has been done in the other Northern States.

The general sentiment of the victors in the fight is beautifully expressed in one of Thomas Bailey Aldrich's simplest and tenderest poems, " Spring in New England " :

> So let our heroes rest
>   Upon your sunny breast;
> Keep them, O South, our tender hearts and true ;
> Keep them, O South, and learn to hold them dear
>   From year to year !
>   Never forget,
>   Dying for us, they died for you.
> This hallowed dust should knit us closer yet.

MERCUR, ULYSSES, an American lawyer, born in Towanda, Pa., May 28, 1818 ; died in Wallingford, Pa., June 6, 1887. He was graduated at Jefferson College, Canonsburg, Pa., in 1842, read law in the office of Judge William McKennan, of Pittsburg, and began practicing in Towanda in 1843. He rose rapidly in his profession, and, possessing oratorical powers of a high order, soon attracted attention in public and political circles. He was a delegate to the first convention of the Republican party, 1856, casting his vote for John C. Frémont, and four years later a presidential elector on the Lincoln and Hamlin ticket. In 1862 he was appointed judge of the Court of Common Pleas, in Bradford County, by Gov. Curtin, to fill the vacancy caused by the election of Judge Wilmot to the United States Senate, and in the autumn of that year was elected to the office for the full term of ten years. In 1864 he was elected a representative in Congress from the district comprising Montour, Bradford, Sullivan, and Wyoming counties, and in March, 1865, resigned his judgeship. His services in Congress were so appreciated that he was re-elected in 1866, 1868, and 1870. When near the close of the last term, he was elected a justice of the Supreme Court of Pennsylvania. He resigned his seat in Congress in December,

ULYSSES MERCUR.

1872. Upon the expiration of the term of Chief-Justice Sharswood, in January, 1883, Judge Mercur was chosen his successor, and he continued in that office till the day of his death.

METALLURGY. Iron and Steel.—An important contribution to the subject of measuring the endurance of metals has been made by Mr. Henry Adams in a paper on the strength of iron and steel. He remarks, that at first sight the material which would bear the greatest steady stress before breaking would be considered the safest and most reliable; this would be a misleading conclusion; for, in many cases this apparent strength is due to a want of elasticity, and a very slight jerk or sudden application of a small stress would cause fracture. When the failure occurs without much stretching the pull acts through an extremely small distance, and therefore the mechanical value or work done is also small, although the pull itself may be of considerable magnitude. The toughness, which is after all the chief quality sought for structural purposes, depends as much upon the elasticity as upon the ultimate tensile stress. Among the examples presented by the author in illustration of modes of fracture was a piece of wrought-iron known to have been in use as a lever for fifty years, which was remarkable for the very large and perfectly formed crystals appearing over the whole section.

The experiments of Carl Barus and V. Stronhal upon the viscosity of steel and its relations to temperature have led to some interesting results. Abstracting for the moment from the states of temper extreme hard and extreme soft, it appears that the viscosity of steel decreases in proportion as the hardness of the metal increases. Experiments in comparison of the viscosity of glass and steel showed that the torsional viscosity of annealed steel is greater than that of glass. The viscosity of hard steel during the first ten hours of detorsion was very much greater than that of glass; but the curve thereon passed through a maximum for which point the rates of viscous detorsion of glass and of glass-hard steel coincide, after which the viscosity of the steel is decidedly less. The viscosity of iron during the first five or ten hours of detorsion is in a strikingly pronounced manner less than that of steel. As detorsion continues the viscosity of soft iron remains below that of steel, whereas the viscosity of drawn iron grows temporarily greater than that of steel, but finally reaches the same value. These experiments justify the inferences that the viscosity of glass is not uniformly greater than that of glass-hard steel, and that the viscosity of steel is not uniformly greater than that of iron. Again, leaving the extreme states of hardness out of view, it is found that both the viscosity and the moment of linear magnetization per unit of mass, of a permanently saturated steel rod, increase in a marked degree from hard to soft. Hence, permanently saturated linear magnetic intensity and viscosity on the one hand, magnetic stability or coercive force or hardness on the other, seem to belong together. The minimum of permanent linear intensity of saturated steel rods has no viscous equivalent; but the viscosity of extremes of hard steel has not yet been studied minutely by the authors, nor have they as yet sufficiently precise data for determining the relation of the magnetization of very long rods in temper. In the extremely soft region, the occurrence of a unique maximum of magnetization seems to be coincident with the occurrence of maximum velocity, In general, as the ratio of length to diameter increases, the minimum of permanent magnetization shows a tendency to move from soft to hard. The general relations between viscosity and maximum permanent linear intensity of magnetization observed for steel are sustained in iron. Among the chief results of their experiments the authors place the light thrown on the crucial importance of the physical changes which steel undergoes when annealed at high temperatures, that is, when subjected to the action of temperatures between 500° and 1,000°.

In a subsequent paper on "The Effect of Magnetization on the Viscosity and Rigidity of Iron and Steel," Mr. Barus shows that the effect of longitudinal magnetization on either material within the elastic limits is marked detorsion, increasing in amount with the intensity of the magnetic field, increasing also with the rate of twist, at a retarded rate in both instances, toward a maximum. If the sense of the magnetization be reversed, the amount of detorsion is in general unchanged. With steel, the effect of magnetization on rigidity during the first phase of annealing is almost nil, but becomes important during the second phase.

Experiments have been made at the works of the Bethlehem Iron Company in a new system for producing puddle-bar from iron which has been put through the pneumatic process. The melted iron is poured into the puddler, which is a large cylindrical vessel so set that it revolves. Heat from a Stubblebein furnace is turned into the puddler, and as the iron becomes granulated it gradually takes the shape of the vessel. After being puddled the metal is compressed into billet-shape, and is then at once reheated and rolled into bar or other iron.

The magnetic iron-ore of Gellivara, Sweden, according to the report of Mr. John Salt, gives an average yield of 70·55 per cent. of iron. The pig-iron produced by the smelting is very tough and close grained, and appears to the author very suitable for steel-making by the Bessemer process, and for producing the finest quality of forge-iron.

By examining a very thinly-rolled plate of steel from which the iron had been removed by nitric acid, and only the carbon was left, Messrs. Osmond and Worth, of Creusot, France, have found that the carbon is not distributed evenly throughout the mass, but that the steel consists in its inner structure of tiny particles of soft iron inclosed in cells formed by the carbon. These cells are again distributed in the iron either combined or as a collection of cells having considerable open spaces between them, so that a plate or sheet of steel may be rolled till it becomes transparent. These spaces may, in the raw material, be almost noticeable, but are reduced by rolling and hammering.

In the David Brose process for the improvement of steel, which has been satisfactorily tried at Pittsburg, a "purifier"—a substance that is plentiful and cheap—is introduced into the ladle immediately before the steel is run in. The steel is then poured into the ladle upon the purifier, when a violent reaction occurs, setting free the contained gases, and causing a thorough agitation of the metal, with a resultant commingling of the metal and manganese more intimate than can be attained by a mere mechanical mixer. The steel thus rendered is claimed to be more uniform, and the ingots are remarkably free from blow-holes. By this process, steel of excellent quality can be produced, it is said, with from 30 to 40 per cent. less manganese than is ordinarily required.

According to a testing made by Prof. W. F. Barrett on a manganese steel containing from 12 to 14 per cent. of manganese, patented and manufactured by Messrs. Hadfield & Co., of Sheffield, the permanent magnetism of the material was to that of steel of average quality as 20 to 100,000, and the induced magnetism to that of iron as 300 to 100,000. In fact, it is very wonderful, judging by muscular sense, to find no sensible force required to move this steel, even in the most powerful magnetic field that could be obtained. Hence, it is suggested, the use of manganese steel for the bed-plates of dynamos and the plating of iron vessels, is obvious. Ships built of such steel would have no sensible deviation of the compass. Dr.

Hopkinson has reached an accordant result by a different method of interpretation. The electric conductivity is also very low. The hard wire has a tenacity of 110 tons per square inch, and the soft wire of 48 tons per square inch, with an elongation of nearly 20 per cent. The modulus of elasticity was found to be lower than that of wrought-iron; so that, though hard manganese steel-wire has an enormous tenacity, it "gives" more than steel under sudden stress, recovering itself if the limits of elasticity are not passed.

A method of tempering watch-springs by means of the electric current has been applied by the Sedgwick Manufacturing Company, of Chicago. The conductors from the dynamo lead to a bench on which stands an ordinary oil tempering bath. One of the conductors connects with a point within the bath, and the other with a point without. The piece of steel-wire to be tempered is fed first under the contact point on the outside of the bath, and then under the point on the inside. When it has reached the latter the circuit is complete, and the wire at once becomes uniformly heated. Since the variation in the percentage of carbon in different pieces of steel forbids the delicate process of tempering from becoming a purely mechanical piece of work, the color of the steel still has to determine the length of time it shall be heated. The chief advantage claimed for this process is, that the steel not having time to oxidize after it has been heated to the proper color before it is put under cover of the oil, the wire is of the same thickness after it is tempered as it was before it entered the process. The uniformity of the heating throughout the spring, the lessened liability to defective spots, and the rapidity of the heating—four inches of spring per second—are claimed as other advantages.

The report of the first series of experiments performed by the committee appointed by the British Association to investigate the influence of silicon on the properties of steel, has been published. It summarizes the present state of our knowledge on the subject as follows:

1. Ingot iron.—Silicon promotes soundness; it resembles carbon in increasing the tenacity and hardness; it should not exceed 0·15 per cent. if the metal has to be rolled; and in some cases it produces brittleness when cold. 2. In steel-castings.—Silicon promotes soundness; it is, however, regarded as a necessary evil, and excess should be avoided, as tending to brittleness and low extension; about 0·3 per cent. is generally recommended. 3. In crucible steel.— A few hundredths per cent. is necessary to produce soundness. It is generally agreed that considerable quantities of silicon may be present without injury to the material. 4. Manganese appears to be capable of neutralizing the ill effect of silicon.—The first series of experiments was undertaken to determine the effect of silicon on the properties of specially pure iron. The general conclusions were ar-

rived at from the results—that on adding silicon in the form of silicon peg to the purest Bessemer iron, the metal is quiet in the mold even when only a few hundredths per cent. of silicon is added. The metal is originally red-short, especially at a dull-red heat, though it works well at a welding temperature; the red-shortness being increased by silicon. In all cases examined the metal was tough, cold, and welded well, the silicon having little or no influence. Silicon increases the elastic limit and tensile strength, but diminishes the elongation and the contraction of area a few hundredths per cent. The appearance on fracture by tensile force is changed from finely silky to crystalline, while the fracture produced by a blow gradually, as the silicon increases, becomes more like that of tool-steel. The hardness increases with increase of silicon, but appears to be closely connected with the tenacity. With 0·4 per cent. of silicon and 0·2 per cent. of carbon, a steel was obtained difficult to work at high temperature, but tough when cold, capable of being hardened in water, and giving a cutting-edge which successfully resisted considerable hard usage. In some cases silicon was present in the oxidized condition. The effect is then very different, and the mechanical properties of the metal more nearly resemble those of the original Bessemer iron. In the second series of experiments various proportions of silicon have been added to ingot metal, containing manganese and carbon as ordinarily met with in commerce. The results are not yet quite ready for publication, but they show that manganese greatly modifies the effect of silicon in producing redshortness, and hence enables the metal to be rolled and otherwise worked, even in the presence of several tenths per cent. of silicon. The low extension, however, though not nearly so marked as before, is still observed, despite the presence of manganese; and hence, for the majority of the applications of mild steel, silicon does not appear to be advantageous.

In experiments upon the behavior of pigs of iron containing very little silicon and varying proportions of phosphorus and manganese, when heated in wood-charcoal, nine test pieces were packed separately, amid small fragments of charcoal, and heated to about 1,000° C. for 108 hours. On examining the samples it was found that in all the malleable irons the percentage of carbon had increased, while in other specimens there was a diminution in the amount of carbon.

It has been decided by the Supreme Court of Pennsylvania that, in the absence of anything showing the contrary, a grant of the right to mine and carry away iron-ore must be held to apply only to such ore as can be employed in the manufacture of iron as ordinarily carried on; and that it does not necessarily include all substances containing iron, and capable of being made to yield that metal; but only such as are commonly used for that purpose.

An earth containing a percentage of iron too small to be profitably smelted, and suitable only for making paint, did not come within the terms of such an agreement.

Experimental tests have been made with the malleable castings of Messrs. Michaelis and Casparius, of Berlin, to determine the strength of the materials, and of the articles manufactured from them. One series of tests was carried out with pieces in their ordinary condition, 11·81 inches long and 1·58 inch by 0·24 inch in section; while the second was made with welded test pieces, as nearly as possible of the same dimensions as those used in the first series. The results were: in the first series, ultimate tensile stress, 16·88 tons per square inch; contraction, 8·2 per cent.; extension, in a length of 7·87 inches, 2·5 per cent.; limit of elasticity, about 4·44 tons per square inch. Second series; ultimate tensile stress, 19·24 tons per square inch; contraction, 13·3 per cent.; extension, 1·1 per cent. In each case the fracture took place outside the welded part. The experiments with manufactured articles were very severe, but gave satisfactory results, particularly in respect to the strength of the welding.

Aluminum.—The properties of aluminum and the qualities of its alloys have been comprehensively treated in an essay by Edward D. Self. With those properties which promise to make it so valuable in the arts, and which have been described in previous volumes of the "Annual Cyclopædia," it unites a few deficiencies, the most important of which is that it readily unites with oxygen. Hence it is necessary, in casting, to keep the metal covered with charcoal or strongly-burned cryolite, to absorb the oxide that may be formed and at the same time protect the surface. If it absorbs oxygen or becomes alloyed with silicon it is made gray and brittle. The best solders for aluminum are composed of tin and bismuth in proportions varying according to the nature of the solder that may be required. The alloys of aluminum are very numerous and can be usefully formed with very wide variations in the proportions of the several ingredients. In a general way, aluminum may be said to improve the qualities of every metal to which it is added in small quantities. It increases the strength and luster of the soft metals, and renders others much less liable to corrosion. It alloys with nearly all the useful, as well as with the precious metals. The most important alloys are those with copper. They form a striking series, of which the alloy of 10 per cent. of aluminum and 90 per cent. of copper —the original aluminum bronze—is the most prominently known. It possesses a deep-golden color, has a specific gravity of 7·7, can be forged and shaped at a red heat, and hammered till cold without cracking. Its tensile strength has been proved at from 91,463 pounds to 114,514 pounds to the square inch, with elastic limit ranging from 59,815 to 85,084, and elongation from ·05 to 2½ per cent. In the different alloys with copper, a gradual change in properties may be observed as the latter is increased in amount. Aluminum can contain 10 per cent. of copper and still retain most of its malleability. With more than 10 per cent., however, it becomes brittle, but retains its white color up to nearly 80 per cent. A number of remarkable and useful alloys are made by mixing aluminum bronzes with nickel in various proportions. These compositions are said to be very ductile, and to have a tenacity of from 75,000 to 100,000 pounds per square inch, with about 80 per cent. elongation. The addition of a few per cent. of aluminum to common brass greatly increases its tenacity and resistance to corrosion. The alloys of aluminum seem well suited for antifrictional purposes, and are unexcelled for various household uses. The golden color of the 5-per-cent. bronze makes it very suitable for plumbers' and similar fittings, and its resistance to corrosion is greater than that of the materials used. For cooking-utensils and even table-ware, these alloys are unsurpassed in color and durability. The difficulty of soldering the bronzes and the fact that they can not be welded, are drawbacks to using them for small manufactured articles. Pieces can, however, be united by certain jewelers' solders, from which soft solders may be made by adding brass. These bronzes have been made in quantities large enough for testing by melting together the correct proportions of copper and aluminum, but this method is not commercially economical with the ingredients at their present prices. The most economical way seems to be to make the alloys themselves as a first product, and reduce the alumina in the presence of copper. Among the processes employed for this purpose is that of the Cowles Electric Furnace, in which the bronze is produced from a charge of about 25 pounds of corundum, 12 pounds of charcoal and carbon, and 50 pounds of granulated copper. In general, the 10-per cent. bronze works much better and cleaner than copper and takes a more beautiful polish, which it retains longer. The resistance to corrosion in sea and mine water does not seem to be well sustained. For resisting torsion the 10-per-cent. bronze is substantially as good as wrought-iron. The heat conductivity of 5- and 10-per-cent. bronzes is very high, and not much less than that of copper. The friction in journals of bronze is less and the temperature higher, but the heat is very great as compared with box-metal.

The success attending the use of the Cowles Electric Furnace in the production of aluminum and its alloys has induced inventors to turn their attention to that method of obtaining this metal. Dr. Fiertz, of Zürich, has obtained two Swiss patents, in one of which the improvements consist in fusing and decomposing aluminum and other light-metal compounds in an aluminous-lined or other vessel by the direct action of the electric current,

without the aid of external heat; and in the other, they consist mainly in treating cryolite or other metal-bearing substances by the action of an electric current in a vessel provided with a suitable lime cathode, while the anode is formed in the shape of a cylinder or in segments, and is so placed in the inside of the vessel as to be practically excluded from contact with the air. Improvements have been made in the Cowles furnace itself, in the adoption of means by which the varying electrical resistance of the charge in the furnace is made the primary agency in actuating and controlling the feeding of the material to be smelted or reduced, and the discharging of the products.

Dr. Kleiner, of Zürich, has invented a process for producing pure aluminum immediately from the ore by direct electric action. His method differs essentially from that of Mr. Cowles, in that the latter depends upon the heat produced by the application of the electric current, while in the present case the separation is effected by the chemical power of the current. The ore employed is cryolite, a double fluoride of sodium and aluminum. It is ground to a fine powder, and when exposed to the action of the current has its aluminum removed, leaving a double fluoride of sodium which is soluble in water. After the process has been carried as far as is commercially economical, the slag is allowed to cool, and is then broken up and washed. The metal comes out in lumps, the soda-salt is dissolved, and can be saved for conversion into caustic soda, while the unreduced ore, which is insoluble, is dried and returned to the bath.

In a recently patented French process for the extraction of aluminum from its oxide by the combined action of carbon, sulphide of carbon, and heat, aluminous carbon is obtained by mixing powdered alumina with 40 per cent. by weight of powdered charcoal or lampblack; to this mixture is added a sufficient quantity of any oil or tar to form a thick paste. The paste is placed in a closed vessel capable of standing a high temperature, and is calcined to a red heat for the purpose of decomposing the oil or tar, and the coherent mass of aluminous carbon thus obtained is broken up into small pieces. The pieces are placed in a closed vessel provided with pipes, one of which leads a current of gaseous sulphuret of carbon into the mass until the reaction is complete, and the other allows of the escape of the carbonic oxide produced. The sulphuret of aluminum thus obtained is treated at a red heat in a closed vessel having pipes, with a current of carbureted hydrogen. The latter unites with the sulphur, producing sulphureted hydrogen, and leaving the pure aluminum.

For the reduction of alumina, G. A. Faurie makes a paste of two parts of pure and powdered alumina with one part of petroleum, which, having been beaten up, is mixed with one part of sulphuric acid. When the yellow color has become uniform and the mass homogeneous, sulphurous acid begins to escape. The paste is wrapped in paper and thrown into a crucible heated to redness, so as to decompose the petroleum. The flame is allowed to escape and the crucible is cooled. The compact product obtained having been powdered and mixed with an equal weight of a metal in powder, is placed in a graphite crucible, which is well closed and heated to whiteness. In the black powder which is observed when the cooled crucible is opened, are found grains and alloys of aluminum. This process is also applicable to silica, lime, magnesia, etc.

The "Colossus" dynamos of the Cowles works at Lockport, N. Y., the operation and efficiency of which were described in the "Annual Cyclopædia" for 1886, are now at work, and producing the pure metal and its useful alloys and bronzes in large quantities daily.

For electro-plating with aluminum, Mr. Herman Reinhold recommends a mixture consisting of a solution of 50 parts of alum in 800 parts of water, with 10 parts of chloride of aluminum to which, after heating to 200° and cooling, 39 parts of cyanide of potassium are added. The object to be plated, having been cleaned and freed from all forms of grease, is suspended in the bath over the electro-positive anode, while the plate of metallic aluminum is suspended on the negative pole.

In a specimen of what is called aluminum steel, exhibited by the Cowles Electric Smelting and Aluminum Company, a sample bar of iron welded to a band of Siemens-Martin basic steel with 0·2 per cent. of aluminum added, shows no line of weld, and the characteristics of the steel appear to extend far into the iron. Without the aluminum, a clearly defined weld is visible between iron and the same steel.

Alloys.—A number of metallic alloys have been prepared by H. Warren by an electrolytic method which differs slightly from the manner in which mercury combines with other elements by reason of the liquidity of mercury. On substituting for the mercury, iron, copper, zinc, etc., these metals may be readily made to combine with the more oxidizable elements, such as silicon, phosphorus, etc., by so arranging the process that the metal employed for forming the alloy, when in a fluid state, is connected with the negative pole of a voltaic series, and is in direct contact with the substance containing the element with which it is desired to combine it. A silicon bronze was produced by this method by the electric action on metallic copper and silico-fluoride. Phosphor and other bronzes may also be readily formed in a similar manner. For the preparation of silicon-eisen the substitution of iron for copper is all that is required. The silicon-eisen so obtained presents the appearance of hot-blast silicon. Native cryolite may be readily decomposed when in contact with metallic zinc, and by suitable means the zinc may be volatilized, leaving pure aluminum.

It is remarked by Thomas D. West that the difficulties which beset the casting of aluminum bronze are, in some respects, similar to those which were encountered in perfecting methods for casting steel. There is much small work which can be successfully cast by methods used in the ordinary moldings of cast-iron; but in peculiarly proportioned, and in large bronze castings, other means and extra display of skill and judgment will be generally required. In strong metals there appears to be a "redshortness" or degree of temperature, after the material becomes solidified, at which it may be torn apart, if it meets a very little resistance in its contraction; and the separation may be such as can not be detected by the eye, but will be made known only when pressure is put upon the casting. To overcome this evil, and to make allowances for sufficient freedom in contraction, much judgment will often be required, and different modes must be adopted to suit varying conditions. One factor often met with is that of the incompressibility of cores or parts forming the interior portion of castings, while another is the resistance which flanges, etc., upon an exterior surface, oppose to the freedom of contraction of the mass. The author has combated the former difficulty by mixing resin and sand in his cores, or using "green-sand" cores. In castings requiring large round cores, which could be "swept," a hay-rope wound around a core barrel would often prove an excellent backing, and allow freedom for contraction sufficient to insure no rents or invisible strain in the body of the casting. To provide means for freedom in the contraction of exterior portions of castings which may be supposed to offer resistance sufficient to cause an injury, different methods will have to be employed in almost every new form of pattern. One method found to work well is to "gate" a mold so that it can be filled or poured as quickly as possible, and to have the metal as dull as it will flow to warrant a full-run clean casting. Aluminum bronze is free from the "blow-holes" which are liable to exist in strong metals.

The alloy of nickel, copper, and aluminum, known as lechesne, is recommended as combining absolute malleability with an exceptional degree of homogeneity, tenacity, and ductility, and as having less liability to oxidize and act as a heat-conductor than other alloys heretofore in use. Its distinctive feature consists in the addition to the binary alloy (nickel and copper) of a quantity of aluminum, calculated according to the proportion of the nickel. Like gold, silver, and platinum, the lechesne alloy satisfies the conditions of the most difficult processes of hammering, drawing, and deep chasing or punching, especially in ornamental work. It is employed for the production of a superior kind of German-silver.

A new alloy has been discovered by Mr. Reith, of Bockenheim, which practically resists the attack of most acids and alkaline solutions. It is a bronze, with the addition of lead and antimony, and is composed of copper, 15 parts; tin, 2·84 parts; lead, 1·82 part; and antimony 1 part.

Great hardness and ductility are given to red brass by mixing in with the metals a small quantity of green bottle-glass. While the resultant alloy is not easily worked, it is valuable as a mixture in making other qualities of brass, for which purpose borings, filings, etc., can be used with advantage. It is adapted for use in machinery by melting with it one per cent. of oxide of manganese. All sorts of brass made with this alloy are very liquid and close grained.

On account of their power of resisting the corrosion of sulphurous mine-waters, signal ropes made of Delta wire have been found to be much better for use in mines, collieries, etc., than those made of iron. Messrs. Grillo, of Dusseldorf, find them to possess just double the tensile strength of the galvanized-iron wire formerly used by them. This allows the weight of the wire to be reduced one half.

A prize of $750 was offered by the Berlin Union for the Promotion of Industrial Activity for the most exhaustive critical summary of the bronze, red brass, and brass alloys, used or recommended for use in mechanical science. Papers for the competition were required to be sent in by Dec. 31, 1887.

Gold.—The treatment of gold-ores in the arrastra is of interest, because the principle of the apparatus is copied in the new methods that are being devised. The machine is slow, but effective. As used in Mexico, it is built with a circular pavement from six to ten feet in diameter, of the hardest and toughest rock that can be found, which should also be coarse grained and have a rough surface; but all joints should be tightly cemented to prevent waste of gold. In the center of the pavement is fixed a pivoted post, which carries a little above the floor-level two or more arms, to which stone drags are hung, lifted up a little in front, but scraping the ground behind, and weighing from 80 to 300 pounds or more. This machine is moved by such power as is most available. The outside of the pavement is protected by a tight wall, from 18 to 30 inches high. The ore to be treated in the arrastra is broken to the proper size, shoveled or fed in, and mixed with water enough to make a thick pulp. A charge consists generally of from 500 to 1,000 pounds of dry ore. The drags are allowed to act from two to four hours, the limit of time being fixed by testing the fineness of the pulp between the thumb and finger. The principal chemicals used with gold-ore are a little potassium cyanide to "liven" the "quick," or some wood-ashes or lye to neutralize the effect of any grease that may have got into the ore. Generally, no others are employed; but when the ores carry large amounts of silver, copper sulphate (bluestone) and salt are put in solid, in such quantities as seem ne-

cessary. When the pulp has been ground long enough, the mercury is added, in quantities depending on the precious-metal contents of the ore. The time required for the operation is from six to ten hours. The capacity of the simplest arrastra varies with the kind of treatment, and the completeness of the plant, from one to two tons a day. The amount of labor required in this process is extremely small.

"Black gold" has been found by Mr. R. W. E. McIvor's analysis of a specimen from the nuggety reef at Malden, Victoria, to be a natural alloy of gold and bismuth. The ore is crystalline, malleable, of silvery-white luster, when freshly broken, but tarnishing and becoming black on exposure. When roasted, the bismuth is eliminated, and a bead of pure gold is left. The ore contains gold, 64·211; bismuth, 34·378; and silloeous matter, 1·391.

The essential conditions of a successful amalgamation process with gold are to maintain the mercury in a condition of "quickness," so that it may readily take up every atom of gold presented to it, and to keep the pulverized ore in contact with the clean mercury. These conditions are insured in Mr. B. C. Molloy's hydrogen-amalgam process. In this process the mercury is placed, to the thickness of about ½ inch, in a pan, in the center of which is a porous jar having within it a cylinder of lead and a solution of sulphate of soda. The lead cylinder is connected with the positive, and the mercury with the negative pole of a small dynamo. When the current passes, oxygen is evolved from the surface of the lead anode, while hydrogen is evolved from the surface of the mercury. The mercury combines with a portion of the hydrogen, and so forms a hydrogen-amalgam, while the excess of hydrogen passes away. The mercury thus charged with hydrogen can not oxidize, and, no matter how deleterious the ingredients of the ore may be, it is always quick, and its affinity for the gold is manifested by a perfect amalgamation.

Gold has been discovered near Ishpeming, Mich., on the Lake Superior Iron Company's workings. A fairly rich seam of auriferous quartzite lies at a depth of about four feet from the surface; while from twenty feet depth specimens were obtained which would give an average run of $10,000 to the ton in native gold. The gold is said to be so thick that it holds a mass of quartz together after it has been broken with the hammer. The gold-bearing belt seems to extend in a fairly defined line from Marquette to L'Anse, some 60 miles, and is from 2 to 8 miles north of the iron-belt.

Herr M. Dahl, mining engineer, who has been examining northern Norway, on behalf of the Norwegian Government, reports that all the rivers in the interior of Finnmarken, a district of fifty Norwegian square miles, carry gold. The metal is found in sand contained in little hollows, which by their shape prevent its being washed away by the water. Platinum is also found occasionally.

The South African gold-fields have been growing in importance, with the almost daily discovery of new "reefs." The exports of August, 1887, from the district of Johannesberg, were valued at £40,000. The gold region is supposed to extend for 600 miles over the line of country between Kimberly and Delagoa Bay. So far, the gold is mined from the "reef" or rock fountain, and has to be extracted by the aid of crushing-machinery; and, as yet, no large alluvial deposits have been found.

Nickel.—The composition used principally for the electro-deposition of nickel in the process as described by Mr. Thomas T. P. B. Warren, is a double sulphate of nickel and ammonia. The silvery appearance of the deposit depends on the purity of the salt as well as on the anodes. About eight ounces of the double sulphate to each gallon of distilled or rain water, is a good proportion to use when making up a bath. The bath should be neutral, or nearly so, slightly acid rather than alkaline. To produce a bright deposit, the author uses a very small quantity of bisulphide of carbon in his mixture; but if much is used, as in silver plating, the deposit is made very dark, almost black, and can not be buffed or polished bright.

The nickel-mines at Thio, in New Caledonia, are situated on the left bank of the river of that name, and extend over an area of about 6,000 acres. The lodes now being worked vary in thickness from three to seven feet, and are exploited in large open cuts or quarries. The ore contains, on the average, about 10 per cent. of pure nickel. Mr. Croisille, who reports upon the mines, estimates that, with the new machinery and generally increased mining facilities, there will be no difficulty in extracting sufficient ore to provide for the manufacture of two or three thousand tons of the pure metal per annum.

The Ferro-Nickel Society of Paris is making a nickel steel, composed of soft iron, nickel, manganese metal, or an oxide of it, aluminum, and ferro-cyanide of potassium, which requires no hardening. The steel is produced at one melting.

Antimony.—Some of the richest antimony-mines in the world exist within a few miles of Oporto, in Portugal. They have been worked for many years on a small scale. A Portuguese company was lately formed, with a capital of £100,000 to work them; and it has already declared a dividend of 10 per cent., besides adding a very substantial sum to the reserve fund. Adjoining this mine is one that has been worked by English residents of Oporto (the Corgo mine) which, having been bought by English capitalists, is now undergoing development. A lode has been struck which varies from 7 inches to 8 feet 3 inches in thickness, with a metallization of pure antimonial lead. Six distinct lodes in the Corgo mines have been opened and exploited to a considerable extent.

Ores containing a low percentage of sulphide of antimony are treated by Messrs. Parnell and Simpson, of Chester, England, by reducing them to a fine state of division, and agitating with a solution of monosulphide of ammonium, with or without heat. The sulphide of antimony becomes converted into a red sulphide, held in suspension in the liquid, and is separated by drawing off and afterward washing the settlings of gangue and unaffected ore.

Zinc.—Zinc-ores are found in larger or smaller quantities in most of the counties in Missouri south of the Missouri river—generally in conjunction with lead. In Franklin, Crawford, Jefferson, and Washington counties, zinc occurs disseminated along with lead, in immense bodies of barytes. The richest deposits of zinc are on or near the Ozark mountains. The principal part of the mining is done in the southwestern counties. The ores comprise a considerable variety of carbonates, silicates, and sulphurets. Outside of this district, zinc-mining proper may be said to be comparatively unknown; but in Washington and other counties where the ore is exposed to view over large areas, the metal is worked on the surface in the most rudimentary fashion—to a large extent by farmers at times when their proper work is not pressing, who thus find a convenient means for increasing their income. The ores are mined in some of the eastern counties in small quantities, but not profitably, on account of the crudeness and expensiveness of the processes employed, for a furnace in South St. Louis. The oxide of zinc, or zinc-white, an important pigment, was formerly manufactured with profit at works in Washington County. But the works, which consumed about ten tons of ore a day, had to be suspended on account of the difficulty of securing a sufficient supply of ore.

In a new process for extracting zinc from blende, as proposed by Messrs. Hannan and Milburn, of Glasgow, the ores, instead of being roasted, are pulverized, mixed with malleable scrap-iron, and then subjected to distillation in a vertical iron retort attached to a condenser. In this process the lead and copper which zinc-blende frequently contains are obtained in commercially valuable forms.

Processes.—Electricity has been applied efficiently to the treatment of ores at the Douglass Mill, Dayton, Nevada. The method was at first tried on tailings, with a view of recovering the mercury which had been lost; but it has been found still more effective in working ores by preventing loss of mercury and amalgam. The dynamos in use at the Douglass Mills are capable of operating seven settlers. The mill works 185 tons of ore per day. It is represented that the decrease in the cost of chemicals for a silver mill is equivalent to twice the cost of treatment and power when the new process is used; and that in the Douglass Mill it has cut down the cost of chemicals one half, and does better work.

An easy method of cleansing iron from rust is described, by which the article, even if it is much eaten into, is greatly improved in appearance. It is immersed in a nearly saturated solution of chloride of tin, and the duration of the immersion is regulated by the greater or less thickness of the film of rust; in most cases, however, from twelve to twenty-four hours will suffice. The solution of chloride of tin must not contain too great an excess of acid, or it will attack the iron itself. After the articles have been removed from the bath, they should be washed in water, and then with ammonia, and dried as quickly as possible. Articles treated in this manner assume the appearance of dead silver.

Miscellaneous.—A process has been described for casting iron and other metals upon laces, embroidery, fern leaves, and other combustible materials, including even the most delicate fabrics. When this is done, the tissue is not injured or disturbed at all, but is perfectly carbonized into a very refractory carbon, while there is produced on the casting a sharp and accurate mold of the design, which may be used as a die. In one experiment, a piece of lace, having open meshes a little larger than a pin's head, was suspended in the mold, so as to divide it into two equal parts. The molten metal was then poured in on both sides of the lace. When the casting was cold, it was thrown upon the floor of the foundry and separated into two parts, while the lace fell out uninjured. The pattern was reproduced upon each face of the casting. The question naturally arises, why did not the iron run through the holes and run together? The answer is found by Mr. A. E. Outerbridge, in the fact that the thin film of oxide of iron or "skin," which always forms on the surface of molten iron, was caught in the fine meshes, and thus prevented the molten metal from joining through the holes. The author's experiments indicate that to secure this result, the meshes must not be more than about one fiftieth of an inch in diameter. He suggests that the intrusion of particles or globules of particles partly cooled, on which a "skin" has formed, may furnish the explanation for many of the obscure flaws found in castings.

A committee of the Franklin Institute, having examined Mr. Outerbridge's processes, reports that the success of the method of preparation for them consists in first removing the fluid or liquid parts of the structure operated upon, and then so slowly draining off those constituents which are produced by destructive distillation that the carbonaceous parts, which are unaffected by the heat, and the integrity of the fibers or structures of the fabric, shall not be disturbed by the too tumultuous exit of the vapors and gases; the exceedingly high temperature at the close of the treatment insuring the complete expulsion of all volatilizable matter. By this treatment, an easily ignitible material is converted into one exceedingly difficult of ignition, while the method employed in casting at the same time secures the preservation of the structure with but slight diminution of dimensions. The change in the properties of the material permits the use of woven or natural fabrics as molds for the cheap reproduction in metal of designs which could not otherwise be made, except at enormous expense for engraving. The application of the invention in the arts is at present limited to the cheap production of dies for the ornamentation of castings, or to the production of dies for embossing leather, paper, or metallic surfaces, and also for the easy parting or dividing of metal in casting; but new fields of application may be opened when the method is brought into more general use.

Thomas Turner has been led to conclude from the examination of various methods for determining the hardness of metals, that hardness and tenacity are distinct physical properties; that methods for the quantitative determination of hardness, depending on the production of an indentation of considerable size, have the disadvantage that the results are influenced by the tenacity of the metal, and that owing to plasticity they vary according to the time taken to produce the indentation; and that brittle substances are apt to be broken by the pressure; that in substances which are homogeneous in structure, the hardness and tenacity generally vary according to the number of atoms in a given space; but that in substances possessing a definite structure the last rule does not apply.

Having observed that ends of wires were often stuck firmly together after the passage of the electric current, Mr. Elihu Thomson has devised a plan for electric welding, and has constructed suitable apparatus for effecting it. The pieces are prepared for the operation by cleaning those parts with the file or emery, which enter the clamps where the ends are held in place, so that a contact shall be effected. The pieces being placed in the clamps a moderate pressure, tending to hold them in abutment, is applied, and a flux may be added, after which the current is put on. Heating of the abutted ends begins at once, and proceeds with a rapidity depending on the current flow and the size and nature of the pieces treated. With great energy of current, joints on iron bars of over one-half inch diameter have been made in less than three seconds, and with small wires the action is almost instantaneous. The temperature to which the pieces are heated may be kept perfectly under control by employing suitable devices to govern the flow of the current. Consequently, varieties of steel which are easily injured by excessive heating, or which will not bear hammering when hot, may be welded quite readily. Even very fusible metals, such as lead, tin, or zinc, may be welded if resin or tallow or chloride of zinc is used as a flux instead of borax. While ordinarily it has been the exception that metals weld readily, with the electric method no metal or alloy yet tried has failed to unite with pieces of the same metal; and the trials have included most of the metals commonly known. Joints between different metals or alloys are often easily produced, if their physical properties are not too much unlike.

METEOROLOGY. In a lecture on "Popular Errors in Meteorology," Prof. Cleveland Abbe insists that in approaching the study of the science we should recognize that in general the atmosphere is governed by immutable laws, and should seek for the forces that control it. It is folly to pay any attention to the weather-predictions in the old almanacs, which are made up sometimes several years in advance on ancient astrological principles, whereas the plainest teachings of the real science of meteorology go to show that the influence of the moon, the planets, and the stars on our atmosphere is wholly inappreciable. The observations as a whole show it to be probable that the total amount of spottedness, or total frequency of spots, on the sun, is accompanied by a slight change in the general condition of the earth's atmosphere; but these effects are only barely appreciable in the atmosphere as a whole, and it is utterly illogical to conclude that there is any direct connection between special spots on the sun and special localities on the earth. The power of forecasting weather, which has been ascribed to animals, from the observation of some of their habits, is, like many customs of men, simply the result of the accumulated experiences transmitted and increased from generation to generation. The flight of the Rocky Mountain locust, which has been attributed to a seeking for regions where food may be found, is simply the result of the action of a hot, drying air on its wings. Stiffening them, it causes a nervous irritability, which can be gratified best by active flapping of the wings; and thus the insect, without instinct or intention on its part, is carried to the upper, cooler currents, where it is wafted to distant places. In a similar manner nearly all the rules for weather prediction founded on the behavior of plants, or such signs as the gathering of dew on stones, or the falling of soot in the chimney, are simply hygroscopic phenomena; and a well-made hygrometer, such as is used by meteorologists, will give more accurate indications than any of these natural objects. The quotation of such indefinitely known agents as electricity and ozone as active causes of meteorological phenomena, is rated as an error. The supposed cooling of the air by thunder-showers, is just as likely to be the production of the showers by the cooling of the air; or the phenomena may be simply coincident, or the different results of a common cause, and not at all related as cause and effect. Concerning the effect of destruction or restoration of forests and of the extension of railroads and telegraphs on climate, observations have not been long enough continued to justify any definite conclusion whatever. The so-called equinoctial storms are simply those of the several storms likely to occur in the early spring and fall that come nearest to the 21st of March and September.

The discrepancy between the popular names given to meteorological phenomena and their real nature as determined by means of instruments, was discussed at one of the meetings of the Meteorological Society of Berlin. Dr. Schultz remarked that the sirocco wind in Italy is spoken of as "heavy," whereas the barometer indicates a diminished pressure. Summers are spoken of as wet or dry, according as they are accompanied by much or little rain, without taking into account the usually opposed indications of the psychrometers; similarly our sensations of heat and cold are often directly opposed to the indications of the thermometer. Observations made by the speaker in Rome and the Rivièra, showed occasionally, among other things, the anomaly that the temperature in the shade was higher than in the sun, especially when the thermometer in the sun was exposed to a strong wind. Prof. Von Bezold laid stress upon the difference between physical meteorology and the influence of temperature and moisture on the living organism. Alterations of atmospheric pressure have no effect on healthy human beings, although they must have on sickly people, inasmuch as a diminution of pressure must lead to an increased evolution of gases from the soil, and their accompanying miasmas. The idea of sultriness has not yet been defined from a physical point of view; probably in connection with this, it should be borne in mind that the air is occasionally supersaturated with aqueous vapor, and that in this case an incipient condensation may be accompanied by a real evolution of heat. Dr. Sklarek mentioned experiments on the radiation of heat from the human body, which showed, in opposition to the laws of radiation from non-living bodies, that it radiates more heat from exposed parts of its surface which are usually covered with clothes, when the difference of temperature between the skin and the surroundings is less than when it is greater. This anomalous behavior may be explained by the supposition that, when the difference in temperature (between the skin and the surroundings) increases, the physical properties of the skin and its radiating powers undergo some change.

The influence of the moon on the weather has been discussed by J. W. Oliver, in an article in "Longman's Magazine" and the "Popular Science Monthly." The author, considering some of the most important of the popular predictions in which the moon is concerned, deals, first, with the notions that are utterly absurd, and, second, with those that are explicable by the aid of physical principles. While he regards most of the predictions founded upon the changes and aspects of the moon as baseless, he holds it unfair to consider the whole subject as unworthy of serious treatment. For instance, atmospheric tides due to the moon's attraction must exist, although they are generally obliterated by disturbances due to other causes. Sir John Herschel's opinion, that the full moon has a tendency to clear the sky is, apparently, borne out by certain facts, and is supported by the experiments of Melloni and others, which go to show that moonlight contains a minute proportion of dark heat-rays, the effect of which may be in a certain measure to cause the dispersion of the clouds. The lunar halo is an old sign of rainy weather, which is confirmed in a large proportion of instances. Capt. C. Von Bermann, of the Hydrographic Office of Pola, dicussing the same question, reaches the conclusion that, although the moon has an influence on the weather, it is too infinitesimal, compared with other influences, to be appreciable.

Experiments by Prof. E. W. Morley led him to conclude that a diminished amount of oxygen in the atmosphere coincides with a barometric maximum, through the descending current which, in anti-cyclones, brings downward air deficient in oxygen from higher elevations. This is contrary to the conclusion of M. Folly, and has been disputed by Max Schumann as not satisfactory, because the descending air in the region of an anti-cyclone does not proceed from those elevations in which a less amount of oxygen may be expected. There is a certain altitude, indeed, Schumann observes: "and this is certainly greater than that at which these atmospheric processes take place, the combined effect of which is called 'weather,' up to which the amount of oxygen may be regarded as invariable. The air, found by Mr. Morley to contain less oxygen, proceeds from elevations inferior to those, because the air is not sucked down from strata above that limit, but only takes a circular path induced in a region of disturbed air by the ascending current. In consequence of this circular path, which is easily understood by thinking of a ring on a horizontal plain in the center of which the air ascends and is sucked over the upper edge of the ring down along the outer surface and under the lower edge back to the center of the ring, the air descending on a region of high barometrical pressure proceeds at all events only from those elevations in which the amount of oxygen may be regarded as invariable."

The doctrine, formerly prevalent among meteorologists, that watery vapor in the air is more active in absorbing and returning terrestrial radiation than the pure gases of the atmosphere, has been reviewed by W. M. Davis, who concludes, with Magnus and others, that watery vapor as such—that is, water in the gaseous state, possesses very little absorptive power. Still, meteorological observation leaves no question that nocturnal cooling is greater on clear, dry nights than on clear, damp nights. This is because, on the damp nights, we have vapor in a state of incipient temporary condensation to deal with, and instead of uniformly diffused gas, invisible water droplets, which reflect or radiate back the heat that is radiated to them from the earth.

Temperature. — Concerning conditions that may affect temperature in the New England States, the Bulletin of the New England Meteorological Society mentions as worthy of note in the reports for September, 1887, that the maximum temperatures of the 7th of the month were the product of southerly and southwesterly cyclonic winds, importing warmth from the Southern States; while the minimum temperatures of the 24th and 27th were of local origin by nocturnal radiation into the clear, anti-cyclonic sky. Under such conditions the maxima are rather uniform over the greater part of New England except Maine, while the minima are strongly influenced by topography, and are much lower in valleys than on hills.

The results obtained by Mr. John Murray, of the "Challenger" Commission, and himself, in their observations on the temperature of the western lakes and lochs of Scotland, are thus summed up by Dr. H. R. Mill: The eastern fringe of the North Atlantic Ocean, brings between the western islands water at a uniform temperature of 46°. An equal temperature prevails on the surface, except in the vicinity of land, where it is higher. In nearly landlocked sea-lochs and basins the temperature of the mass of water is determined by the configuration, and varies from 47·5° to 43·8°, according to certain definite laws. Fresh-water lakes that are shallow have a temperature of about 45°; those that are deep are colder, their temperatures varying from 43° to 41°, while they show hardly any difference between surface and bottom.

Some details respecting the freezing of the rivers and lakes of Russia are given in a pamphlet published by M. Nikacheff. The times of the earlier frosts vary according to the character of the season in the western and southern parts of the empire, but are more uniform toward the north and east. The first freezing usually takes place about the 1st of September, in a branch of the Kolima. Other rivers follow in due succession, till the Knban, the last to be frozen, is closed about the 18th of January, to open again about the 15th of February. From that time the thawing advances toward the north and east till the end of June, when the great rivers, the Yenesei and the Lena, are open to their mouths, and in July only the rivers of the Taimyr peninsula are partly clogged with ice. The lines of synchronal freezing and thawing trend, like the isothermal lines, as a rule, from west-northwest to east-southeast. In the spring-time, or when the temperature has risen above the freezing-point, the smaller rivers thaw out first, then the larger rivers, next the canals, and finally the lakes. In freezing, the canals are first, next the rivers, small and large, and the lakes last.

Observations were made between 1882 and 1886, by Mr. W. Marriott at the church-tower of Boston, England, of temperatures at 4 feet, 170 feet, and 260 feet above the ground. The results showed that the mean maximum temperature at 4 feet exceeds that at 170 feet in every month of the year, the difference in the summer months amounting to 8°; while the mean minimum temperature at 4 feet differs but little from that at 170 feet, the tendency, however, being for the former to be slightly higher in the winter and lower in the summer than the latter. As indicated by the readings of the electrical thermometer which was depended upon for the observations at the third height, the temperature at 4 feet during the day hours was considerably higher than at 260 feet.

Comparative observations of the ranges of temperature are made under the direction of the New England Meteorological Society at high and low level stations in the White mountain region. The results of those made in June go to show that while the nocturnal mimima in the deep valleys are, during the occurrence of high pressure, almost as low as on Mount Washington, the diurnal maxima are much higher at the lower than at the summit stations, and indeed are, on clear, sunny days, almost as high in the White mountain valleys as anywhere in New England.

In his discussion of the relative capacity of the solid crust of the earth and of the waters to propagate heat, M. Woeikof concludes that a considerable part of the heat of the globe is lost in space by the radiation in the higher latitudes from the surface of the ocean. The loss is manifested by the accumulation of extensive masses of cold water at the bottom of the ocean. Between 20° of north and 20° south latitude, the deep-sea temperature is reduced to 4° C. principally by the influence of under-currents moving slowly from the Antarctic Ocean toward the equator. As the superficial temperature of the ocean is but little changed by this, so the accumulation of cold water in the bottom has but little influence; yet the greatest loss which the earth suffers appears to proceed from the radiation from the seas, particularly from the polar seas.

The examination of the isothermal charts for February and August has led Krummel to the conclusion that two thirds of the surface of the ocean is constantly at a temperature of more than 24° C., and more than half of it above 20°. The waters of the northern hemisphere appear to be decidedly warmer than those of the southern hemisphere.

Clouds.—The phenomenon of iridescence in clouds is presented when—in light cirro-cumulus cloud—the borders of the clouds and their lighter portions are suffused with soft shades of color like those of mother-of-pearl. Usually the colors are distributed in irregular patches, just as in mother-of-pearl; but occasionally they form round the denser patches of cloud a regular colored fringe, in which the several tints are arranged in stripes following the sinuosities of the outline of the cloud. Seeking for an explanation of the phenomenon, G. Johnstone Stoney shows that on account of the low temperature at the elevation in the atmosphere at which these clouds are formed, water can not exist in the liquid state, but the vapor from which the clouds are condensed passes at once to the solid form of tiny crystals of ice. If the vapor has been evenly distributed, and the precipitation has taken place slowly, the crystals in any one neighborhood will be of nearly the same form and size, and from one neighborhood to another they will differ chiefly in number and magnitude. This will give rise to a patched appearance of the clouds. When the conditions prevailing in any one neighborhood of the sky are such as to produce lamellar crystals of nearly the same thickness, these tabular plates will be subsiding through the atmosphere. Although their descent is very slow, the resistance of the air will act upon them, in consequence of their minute size, as it does upon a falling feather, and will cause them, if disturbed, to oscillate before they settle into a horizontal position. If the crystals are plates with parallel faces, since they are also transparent, a part only of the sun's ray that reaches the front face will be reflected from it; the rest will enter the crystal, and, falling on the parallel surface behind, a portion will be there reflected, and, passing out through the front face, will also reach the eye of the observer. These two portions of the ray—that reflected from the front face and that reflected from the back—are precisely in the condition in which they can interfere with one another, so as to produce the splendid colors with which we are familiar in soap-bubbles. The phase of the phenomenon in which the colors form definite fringes around the borders of the cloudlets is accounted for by observing that so long as the cloud is in the process of growth the crystals will keep augmenting. In this case, the patch of cloud may consist of crystals which are largest in its central part, and gradually smaller as their situation approaches the outside; and we have the conditions which will produce one color around the margin of the cloud, and other tints farther in.

In a discussion on the nomenclature of clouds, Prof. Köppen intimates the question whether the same cloud seen from different sides should receive different names, or whether the classification should refer generally to the properties observed in a particular cloud, especially as regards its density and dimensions. The apparent form, which is important in Poey's classification, is shown to lead sometimes to erroneous conclusions. In a report of a conference between the Hon. R. Abercromby and Mr. Hildebrandsson at Upsala, which is embodied in the paper, it is pointed out that the study of the forms of clouds may be undertaken with different objects in view. If the object be weather prediction, a detailed terminology is necessary, and for this purpose, Mr. W. O. Ley's classification is regarded as unsurpassed. One of the principal objects is the determination of the direction of the wind in the higher regions of the atmosphere, and for this it is not necessary to distinguish so many forms; but we must be sure that these forms are, generally speaking, everywhere the same; and their mean heights must be severally determined by direct measurements.

M. Teisserenc de Bort concludes, from his studies of the distribution of cloudiness over the earth, that there is a marked tendency of cloudiness throughout the year to arrange itself in zones parallel to the equator. Aside from perturbations complicating the matter, there may be traced a maximum of cloudiness in the region of the equator; two bands of light cloudiness extending from 15° to 35° of latitude north and south, and two zones of greater cloudiness between 45° and 60°, beyond which, so far as we can judge from appearances in the northern hemisphere, the sky seems to become clearer toward the poles. These zones have a marked tendency to follow the sun in its change of declination, shifting up toward the north in the spring and toward the south in the fall. Further comparisons indicate that the zones of clear sky correspond with the regions of high pressures on either side of the equator, and originate, on one hand, in the trade-winds, and on the other hand, the west winds, which are dominant near the temperate regions of both hemispheres. The zones of more cloudy sky extend above the regions of low pressure; that is, near the equator and near the 60th degrees of latitude. The study of the winds shows that the air, at the surface of the soil, diverges from the zones of high pressure beyond the tropics, and blows toward the regions of low pressure, or toward the equatorial regions, and toward the low pressures near the 60th degrees. Hence, probably, that the winds near the centers of divergence have a descending component, and in the regions toward which they blow, an ascending component, consequently, other things being equal, the cloudiness is light when the wind has a vertical component directed downward, and heavy when the direction is upward. This agrees with the fact that an ascending mass of air cools in expanding, and thus tends to produce a condensation of aqueous vapor, while the contrary takes place with a descending mass. The distribution of cloudiness is a direct consequence of the course of the winds.

The attention of certain observers has been given since 1885 to "the strange effect of bright, silvery-lighted clouds," which have remained visible at times in the northwest sky after sunset till late in the evening. While presenting varieties in structure, they are described as usually exhibiting an opaque, pearly luster, with definite outline. They were first noticed by Mr. D. J. Rowan, of county Dublin,

Ireland, some two or three years previous to 1886, who regards them as sub-auroral and self-luminous, and proposes for them the name nubecula boreales. They are also regarded as auroral by Prof. Piazzi Smith, who has made spectroscopic observations of them, although he admits that their spectrum is that of twilight. Mr. J. W. Backhouse, of Sunderland, England, on the other hand, is of the opinion that they derive their light from direct solar illumination, and points to the fact that they have so far been seen only during a short period before and after the summer solstice, the recorded dates of observations ranging from May 28 to August 12.

Important researches on the motion and height of clouds have been carried on at the University of Upsala, Sweden, under the direction of Prof. Hildebrandsson, with the assistance of Messrs. Ekholm and Hagerström. A peculiar form of altazimuth, which was originally designed for measuring the parallax of the aurora borealis, is used to take the angular measurements. The greatest height of cloud which has yet been measured is 43,800 feet; the highest velocity is 112 miles an hour with a cloud at 28,000 feet. The clouds are not distributed promiscuously at all heights in the air, but have a tendency to form at three definite levels. The mean summer altitude of the three levels has been found to be: low clouds—stratus, cumulus, cumulo-nimbus, from 2,000 to 6,000 feet; middle clouds—strato-cirrus and cumulo-cirrus, from 12,000 to 15,000 feet; and high clouds—cirrus, cirro-stratus, and cirro-cumulus, from 20,000 to 27,000 feet. The velocity observations confirm the results that have been obtained from mountain stations, viz., that, though the general travel of the middle and higher clouds is much greater than that of the surface winds, the diurnal variation of speed at those levels is the reverse of what occurs near the ground. The greatest velocity on the earth's surface is at about 2 o'clock P. M., whereas the lowest rate of the upper currents is at about mid-day. The mean height of all varieties of clouds rises in the course of the day, and is greater at between 6 and 8 o'clock in the evening than either in the early morning or at mid-day.

Rainfall.—The hypothesis suggested by Mr. Norman Lockyer, about 1873, that certain periodical variations of the rainfall at Madras, India, are connected with periods of maxima and minima in the frequency of sunspots, has been re-examined by Mr. Henry F. Blanford in the light of the accumulated data, applying especially to the Carnatic of the last twenty-two years. Comparative tests of the rainfall and of sunspot frequency, year by year, have satisfied the author that, apart from the approximate identity of its period, the oscillation of the rainfall is very different in character from that of the sunspot frequency. Comparisons with the data of other provinces also showed that the apparent periodical variation of the Carnatic rainfall was not representative of a similar variation in that of Southern India generally. A lack of exact correspondence further appeared in the review of the prevalence of droughts and dearths. But while the theory is not sustained, Mr. Blanford would still not "hastily conclude from the facts that there is no relation between the recurrence of drought in Southern India and the periodical variation of the solar photosphere, but merely that the interdependence of the two classes, of phenomena, if real, is far from being simple and direct, and also that other, and, as far as we know, non-periodic causes concur largely in producing drought. If we accept the conclusions . . . as to the highly probable periodicity of the Carnatic rainfall, one must admit that there is, in that province, a recurrent tendency to drought at eleven-year intervals, though it does not always culminate in drought of disastrous intensity; and this epoch anticipates by about two years that of the sunspot minimum. This tendency is much weaker in other parts of the peninsula, and in Northern India there is some indication of a tendency to the recurrence of drought about the time of maximum sunspots."

The exact line of distinction between a clear and a rainy day has never been clearly defined. The Meteorological Congress of Vienna proposed 0·1 mm. as the amount of precipitation that should constitute the minimum for a day to be designated as rainy, while the International Committee in Paris of 1885, and the Prussian Meteorological Institute fixed upon 0·2 mm. E. Brückner has published a memoir in which he proposes that all days be called rainy in which the precipitation exceeds 0·15 mm., or 0·005 of an inch, and this whether it be in the form of rain, snow, hail, drizzle, mist, dew, or hoar-frost. He also recommends, in more exact climatological researches, a classification of the rainy days into several grades according to their varying amounts of precipitation.

The most important feature in the meteorology of the Punjaub, as shown in the report for the financial year 1886-'87, was the failure of the cold-weather rains (January to March). Excluding the exceptional amount of 127·5 inches at Dharmsála (Jullundur), the greatest annual rainfall was 53·3 inches at Abbottabad (Peshawar), and the least 4·3 inches at Mount Zaffargarh (Derajāt). The highest temperature in the sun's rays was 183° at Lahore on April 28, and it ranged from 172° to 175° in the five succeeding months. The maximum reading in the shade was 118° at two stations on the 13th, and the lowest maximum was 79° at Sirsa (Delhi) in January. The absolute minimum in the shade was 29° at Ráwilpindi in February, giving a range of 89° in the shade temperature of the whole province.

Observing during a certain period that the rainfall of Italy was distributed in zones of graduated degrees of intensity parallel with the Apennines, M. Ferrari studied the records of previous years to determine the effect of the mountains upon precipitation. He found that when rain prevailed on the Mediterranean side of the peninsula and not on the Adriatic coast, the center of low pressure was nearly always in the north; but when the rain fell on the Adriatic slope without passing the Apennines, the depression was in the south. In the former case, the winds approach from the Mediterranean side; in the latter from the Adriatic side; and in both cases are drained of their moisture by the summits of the mountains. It is known that the amount of rainfall on mountains increases with the height; but this takes place only up to a certain limit, when a maximum is reached, from which there is a decrease going both up and down. These relations were investigated by Erk on the northern slope of the Bavarian Alps, from November, 1883, to November, 1885. He shows that a seasonal shifting of the zone of maximum precipitation exists, which is dependent on the temperature of the season.

Storms.—The Hon. Ralph Abercromby presented a paper to the Royal Society "On the Relation between Tropical and Extra-tropical Cyclones." All cyclones have a tendency to assume an oval form; the longer diameter may lie in any direction, but has a decided tendency to range itself nearly in a line with the direction of propagation. Tropical cyclones have less tendency to split into two, or to develop secondaries, than those of higher latitudes. A typhoon that has come from the tropics can combine with a cyclone that has been formed outside the tropics, and form a single new, and perhaps more intense, depression. There is much less difference in the temperature and humidity before and after a tropical cyclone than in higher latitudes. The quality of the heat in front is always distressing in every part of the world. The wind rotates counter-clockwise round every cyclone in the northern hemisphere, and everywhere as an ingoing spiral. The amount of incurvature for the same quadrant may vary during the course of the same cyclone. The velocity of the wind always increases as we approach the center in a tropical cyclone. whereas in higher latitudes the strongest winds and steepest gradients are often some way from the center. The general circulation of a cyclone, as shown by the motion of the clouds, appears to be the same everywhere. All over the world unusual coloration of the sky at sunrise and sunset is observed, not only before the barometer has begun to fall at any place, but before the existence of any depression can be traced in the neighborhood. Cirrus appears all round the cloud area of a tropical cyclone, instead of only round the front semicircle as in higher latitudes. Everywhere the rain of a cyclone extends farther in front than in rear. Cyclone rain has a specific character, quite different from that of showers or thunder-storms; and this character is more pronounced in tropical than in extra-tropical cyclones. Squalls are one of the most characteristic features of a tropical cyclone, where they surround the center on all sides; whereas in Great Britain, squalls are almost exclusively formed along that portion of the line of the trough which is south of the center and in the right rear of the depression. The difference is probably due to the different intensities of the two classes of cyclones. A patch of blue sky, commonly known as the "bull's-eye," is almost universal in the tropics, and apparently unknown in higher latitudes. There are reasons for supposing that the formation is dependent on intensity of rotation. The trough phenomena—such as a squall, a sudden shift of wind, and change of cloud character and of temperature, just as the barometer turns to rise, and even far from the center, which are so prominent a feature in British cyclones—have not even been noticed by meteorologists in the tropics; but there are slight indications of these phenomena everywhere. Every cyclone has a double symmetry. One set of phenomena, such as the oval shape, the general rotation of the wind, the cloud-ring, rain area, and central blue space, are more or less related to a central point. Another set, such as temperature, humidity, the general character of the clouds, certain shifts of wind, and a particular line of squalls, are more or less related to the front and rear of the line of the trough of a cyclone. The author's researches show that the first set are strongly marked in the tropics, where the circulating energy of the air is great, and the velocity of propagation small; while the second set are most prominent in extra-tropical cyclones, where the rotational energy is moderate and the translational velocity is great. The first set of characteristics may conveniently be classed together as the rotational, the second set as the translational, phenomena of a cyclone. Tropical and extra-tropical cyclones are identical in character, but differ in certain details due to latitude, surrounding pressure, and the relative intensity of rotation or translation.

Reviewing the state of our knowledge respecting the manner in which thunder-storms are formed, Prof. Hann has remarked that in European latitudes they do not usually break out after the sky has been cloudy for a considerable time; but occasionally the phenomena are observed after a day of persistent rain, and in the midst of dense fog. A thunder-storm frequently marks the end of a longer or shorter period of fair weather. We can then best observe the approach and formation of the storm-clouds, especially if, in a mountainous region, we stand a little above the horizon. The most characteristic sign of the rising storm is the band of cirrus. From the side of the horizon which looks darkest before the appearance of the storm itself, there advances slowly a thick veil of cirrus with fringed edges, which rises to a great height in the sky before the tempestuous masses that follow it are revealed. These masses, the real seat of the electrical phenomena, have characteristic shape and color. Sometimes also the front part of them forms by a perspective effect an arch of clouds well detached from the rest, which is often the foreboding of a violent squall of hail and wind. Under the black, cloudy arch is distinguishable a clearer kind of veil, which is nothing else than the sheet of rain falling from the clouds. In some cases this sheet is covered by a sort of mobile curtain of floating clouds, descending like drapery from the dark, cloudy arch. It also, according to M. Hann, is a certain sign of a violent squall. The cumulus or cumulo-stratus forming the mass of the tempest is usually of a grayish color, verging upon blue or tawny yellow; while the curtain just spoken of takes on more lively hues—white, yellow, or rosy. Lightnings may still be arranged according to Arago's classification. Photography has proved that zigzag lightnings consist not of a single luminous trace, but of several separated by dark lines, the changes of direction of which are made, not at sharp angles, but in curves. Single, undivided traces of lightning are the exception. Surface lightnings present the aspect of a sea of fire visible through the clouds. According to M. Häpke's spectroscopic examinations, they are different from zigzag lightnings. M. Planté has made a study of lightning-balls, and has produced something like them artificially, on a small scale; but much remains to be learned about them. In sparkling lightning the whole trace is broken up into a multitude of sparks, or a zigzag trace terminates in air, when there is usually a fall of a thunder-bolt. Heat-lightnings near the horizon are probably the signs of storms raging beyond them. Sometimes they are seen near the zenith; when they are possibly too far off for the thunder to be heard. In color, lightnings are usually of a dazzling white or bluish violet.

The question of the reality of the supposed equinoctial storms has been examined by Dr. R. Müller, with the aid of the hourly records of the anemometer at Pola for the years 1876–1886, and of observations made upon the German coasts by the "Deutsche Seewarte" for the years 1878–1883. The results of both series are in harmony. The Pola records show that for the Adriatic no important influence in generating gales can be attributed to the equinoctial seasons; and a similar inference is drawn from the German observations. At Pola, 63 per cent., on the German coast, 80 per cent. of the storms occurred during the winter season (October to March). At Pola, after the relative quiet of June and July, a tolerably regular increase in the number of days with stormy winds took place till the end of January. A decrease occurred in February; and March had the greatest number of stormy days. On the German coast, the greatest number of storms occurred in November and December; March had 14 per cent., and September only 8 per cent. of the number.

The cyclonic phenomena of New England have been studied by Prof. Winslow Upton, with especial reference to the distribution of precipitation in the separate storm movements; a term of eighteen months, from January, 1885, to August, 1886, with 41 storms, having been included in the investigation. The storms were classified into those approaching from the great lakes on the west, 22 in number; those approaching from the south or southwest, 13; and 6 special cyclones in which a secondary development was formed on the Atlantic coast, and two movements united. The author concludes that, while the distribution of precipitation in the several storms is very irregular, and each storm seems to be well-nigh individual in this respect, indications of common features are presented in them. The maximum area of precipitation in the northern group of cyclones which entered New England from the west, lies south of their path at an average distance of about 100 miles; in the corresponding southern group, it lies north of their path at an average distance of about 150 miles; the maximum in those cyclones which moved north of New England lies about 300 miles south of their path, in central Massachusetts; in those which entered from the south, it lies approximately along their path. Maximum areas of precipitation in cyclones which have a secondary development, or in combined cyclones, are found near the origin of the secondary development, along the path of each of the component cyclones and near the place of union. The amount of precipitation is greater in storms coming in from the south than from the west, in the proportion of four to three. In double cyclones, it is greater in that component which comes from the south, which, in cyclones having a secondary development is, in the cases examined, the secondary cyclone. The greater amount of precipitation precedes the passage of the cyclonic centers. Finally, the direction in which the rain front and rear advance is not always the same as that of the center of the cyclone. The behavior of the cyclones entering from the west possibly indicates a topographical peculiarity on account of which these storms deposit a greater amount of rain or snow in southern Vermont and New Hampshire and southwestern Maine.

The winds, at altitudes reached by high mountains, are, according to the studies of Mr. William M. Davis, of higher average velocity than those of lower altitude, not only on account of the absence of friction with the ground, but also by reason of the greater steepness of the basic gradients in the upper air, or, in other words, the greater inequality of pressure in a given high-level distance. We may be confident, also, that the winds on the higher mountain-tops are steadier than the lower winds, in both velocity and direction. The winds of the upper levels are prevailingly from some western quarter, even in those latitudes where the surface currents flow from the east, except very close to the equator. The absence at high levels of both the "polar" and "equatorial" currents of the older meteorologists is as significant as the gradual vertical extinction of the lower cyclonic storm-circulation of more recent authors. The general planetary circulation of the winds, resulting from differences of temperature between the equator and the poles, is so far controlled by forces arising from the earth's rotation that the general direction is turned along parallels of latitude rather than meridians. Although the average velocity of the wind increases as we ascend, it is not unusual to find high-mountain winds for a time exceeded by those passing over an exposed seacoast station during periods of storms. A special characteristic of the upper winds is found in the occurrence of their maximum velocity at night instead of in the afternoon, as at the earth's surface. The hills and mountains of New England offer good ground for the study of these diurnal changes. Veerings in direction also take place, corresponding with the changes in velocity. The morning retarded winds incline to the left as their velocity decreases, and the afternoon accelerated winds to the right, as their velocity increases. On lowlands, the change of direction will be reversed. Mountainous regions are often characterized by winds blowing down the valleys at night, and up the valleys in the daytime, thus forming a local current of diurnal period, commonly known as mountain and valley winds. When the mountain-sides are snow-covered, the upcoast wind of the day is reversed into a cold, descending wind. As a consequence of the normal valley and mountain winds, mountain-peaks become covered about noon, and in the afternoon may receive rain condensed from the expanding, ascending current. At night, the cold air collecting in the valleys, often produces lakes of mist there, that melt away under the morning sun. The air on the mountains is clearest and driest during the latter half of the night.

The common weather-cock, or wind-vane, is one of the oldest as well as simplest of meteorological instruments. The fanciful forms which it has assumed in popular use have been replaced, in the application to accurate meteorological observations, by simple plane plates, disks, or arrows, designed solely with regard to the mechanical action of the wind upon them. The form in general use at present is that of an arrow with a double or spread tail. This spread form, when first introduced, consisted of two thin plates joined at one end at an angle of about 45°. Its principle has grown in favor, but the angle of the wings has gradually been reduced to about 22½°, and even less. In practice the surfaces are made with a slight curvature, so that the actual angle made by their tangents increases from zero at the vertex to 30° or more at their extremities. George

E. Curtis has sought to determine what advantages the spread vane possesses, as compared with a straight vane of the same length and shape, and at what angle the wings should be set to secure the greatest efficiency. From calculations based upon the results of experiment, he deduces formulæ showing that the oscillations of both vanes are smaller as the vanes are longer and larger; that the spread vane is always more stable than the straight vane; and that this advantage in stability is greater for long vanes than for short vanes, and is independent of the wind velocity. The analysis obtains for a frictionless bearing. From the discussion of relative sensitiveness, it is found that, with equal friction, a spread vane is more sensitive than a similar straight vane: consequently, for two vanes of equal sensitiveness, the spread vane will have the greater friction, and will come to rest more quickly.

The name of Foehn is applied in Switzerland to the occurrence in mountain-regions, especially in winter-time, of a warm or even hot, dry wind, blowing briskly down the valleys from the high cold passes. The wind is commonly accompanied by a bank of dark clouds over the pass at the head of the valley from which it descends. The effects of the high temperature and aridity are often very marked. Similar phenomena have been observed in New Zealand and in the Andes at San Juan in the Argentine Republic, where the wind is locally called the Zonda; and they are exemplified in the Chinook winds of our western Cordilleras. The Foehn was formerly supposed to be an extension of the dry, hot sirocco which blows into southern Europe from the Desert of Sahara; but investigation, as summarized by Mr. W. M. Davis, has shown that its phenomena are incompatible with this view, and it is now regarded as of local origin. It is, in fact, a result of the changes of temperature which the cyclonic winds undergo in their successive ascent and descent as they cross the tops of the mountains. In rising to the summit these winds are cooled, and precipitate their vapor in the form of rain or cloud. The air, now dried, being compressed as it descends the mountain, becomes warmed more rapidly than it had been cooled in the ascent, and emerges upon the plains below as a warm, drying wind.

Electricity.—Some remarkable phenomena of fire-balls and globular lightning were described at one of the meetings of the Royal Meteorological Society. Both were observed many years ago, but have only now invited scientific attention. Two ladies, walking on a cliff at Ringhead Bay, Dorset, in the afternoon, saw all around them, and from near the surface of the ground to two or three feet over their heads, numerous globes of light, the size of billiard-balls, of various colors, moving independently up and down, sometimes very near them, but always eluding their grasp. They varied in numbers from as few as twenty to thousands. The display was without noise of

any kind. Dr. J. W. Tripe related that, during a thunder-storm in 1874, he saw a ball of fire, of a pale yellow color, rise from behind some houses, at first slowly, then with increasing speed, till its progress became so rapid as to form a continuous line of light, proceeding first east, then west, and rising all the time. At last, after having described several zigzags, it disappeared in a large black cloud to the west, from which flashes of lightning had come. In about three minutes another ball ascended, and in about five minutes afterward a third, both of which behaved like the first one, and disappeared in the same cloud.

The loss of electricity by a conductor in moist air has been studied by Signor Guglielmo. He finds that, with potentials less than 600 volts, moist air insulates as well as dry air, but with higher potentials there is more loss in moist air, and more the moister the air and the higher the potentials. The potential at which the difference becomes perceptible is the same for a ball as for a fine point. It occurs with extremely smooth surfaces, and so can not be attributed to discharges in consequence of roughness of surface. With equal potential the loss of electricity has the same magnitude, whatever the dimensions of the balls used as conductors. In air saturated with vapors of insulating substances, the loss of elasticity of a conductor is nearly the same as in dry air.

The statistics of damage from lightning in Schleswig-Holstein, Baden, and Hesse, show that the danger from lightning in those parts (unlike the experience of other parts of Germany) has been decreasing of late years. Thatched houses are fired about seven times oftener than houses with hard roofs. Windmills and church and clock towers are struck, respectively, fifty-two times and thirty-nine times oftener than ordinary houses with hard roofs. The marshy regions in Schleswig-Holstein are the most dangerous, and the land about inlets of the sea-coast is the safest. With like conditions, the relative danger decreases as the houses are more closely grouped together. The geological nature of the ground, especially its capacity for water, has important influence. Calling the danger on limestone one, that for sand is nine, while for loam it is twenty-two. Four factors affect the danger to buildings from lightning: two physical—unequal frequency of storms, and geological character; and two social—variable population and mode of building. Of all trees, oaks are most frequently damaged, and beeches most rarely, the ratio between the two being as 54 to 1.

As bearing on the extent to which the effect of a lightning-flash may be felt, M. D. Calladon relates an observation of an electric discharge at Schonen, in the Canton Bern, on the 7th of April, which, after striking a large poplar, spread havoc for some hundreds of metres around, with results comparable to those following the explosion of a large powder-magazine.

METHODISTS. I. Methodist Episcopal Church.— The following is a summary of the statistics of this church as compiled from the minutes of the conferences for 1887: Number of traveling preachers, 12,554; of preachers on trial, 1,581; of local preachers, 14,032; of members, 1,860,591; of probationers, 233,344; of members and probationers, 2,093,936; of baptisms, 74,688 of children, and 101,520 of adults; of churches, 20,755, having a probable value of $80,812,702; of parsonages, 7,532, having a probable value of $11,908,047; of Sunday-schools, 24,080, returning 267,447 officers and teachers and 2,016,181 pupils. Amount of collections: for missions, $916,924; for church extension, $127,251; for the Sunday-school Union, $20,848; for the Tract Society, $19,125; for the Freedmen's Aid Society, $83,657; for education, $109,643; for the American Bible Society, $33,589; for the Women's Foreign Missionary Society, $159,844; for the Women's Home Missionary Society, $63,395; for pastors, presiding elders, and bishops, $8,312,052; for conference claimants, $205,128; for building and improvements, $4,381,868.

Church Extension.—The General Committee of Church Extension met in Philadelphia, Pa., November 17. The receipts for the general fund had been, including a balance of $39,965 from the previous year, $198,590; the expenditures to October 31 had been $157,874; the loan fund had received $110,763, and had applied, in loans to churches, $111,650; aid had been afforded, in loans and gifts, to 522 churches, making the whole number of churches aided from the beginning, 6,327; grants had been provided, in loans and donations, to the amount of $69,015, and applications were on file from 112 churches for $62,764; 37 special gifts for frontier churches had been received, representing an aggregate amount of $9,250, of which 29 had been applied to as many churches, representing a valuation of $65,650, with 1,056 members and 2,000 Sunday-school pupils; loans of $8,000 had been added to these gifts. The board fixed the amount to be asked from the conferences for the ensuing year at $236,150.

Freedmen's Aid Society.—The twentieth annual meeting of the Freedmen's Aid Society was held in Chicago, Ill., December 5th. Bishop J. M. Walden presided. The entire receipts for the year had been $184,424, of which $20,957 had been paid by students; the amount of expenditures had been $183,690. The society had since its foundation expended almost $2,000,000 in the work of education in the South, and it now had school property to the value of nearly $1,000,000. The 24 schools and colleges for colored persons in the South were served by 124 teachers, and returned an average attendance of 4,500 pupils; the 15 schools for white persons employed 83 teachers, and had an average attendance of more than 2,000 pupils. Since the institution of the society, more than 100,000 pupils had been taught in its schools,

and more than a million persons had been instructed in other schools by its pupils who had become teachers. Special attention was given to industrial education at Clark University, Atlanta, Ga., where carpentry, agriculture, printing, wagon and carriage building, blacksmithing, and harness-making were taught; Claflin University, Orangeburg, S. C., to which a large farm is attached; Rush University, Holly Springs, Miss.; Central Tennessee College, Nashville; New Orleans University; and Philander Smith College, Little Rock, Ark. At the Gammon School of Theology, Atlanta, Ga., a full course of instruction in that department is given.

Missionary Societies.—The General Missionary Committee met in New York city November 9. The bishops of the Church present presided in their turns at the several sessions. The treasurer reported that the total receipts of the society from all sources for the year ending October 31 had been $1,044,796, being an increase over the previous year's receipts of $52,677; of this sum the conference collections amounted to $982,209, or $95,616 more than the amount of the corresponding collections in the preceding year; but the receipts from legacies had decreased by $98,114. Among the especial gifts was real estate in Indiana valued at $180,000, to be held subject to annuities during the lives of the donors. In addition to these amounts received by the " parent society," the Methodist Episcopal Church had contributed during the year to the Woman's Foreign Missionary Society about $195,000; to the Woman's Home Missionary Society, about $60,000; and to the Transit and Building Fund for Bishop Taylor's missions, $63,079; making the total amount of offerings to the cause of missions, $1,362,875.

The following table gives what an address by the committee to the members of the church describes as an " approximate but inadequate " representation of the condition of the missions in the foreign field:

The number of missionaries, assistant missionaries, helpers, and native workers exceeds	1,300
Members of the Church	42,000
Probationers	14,000
Adherents	40,000
Sunday-schools	1,575
Sunday-school officers and teachers	4,885
Sunday-school scholars	2,400,000
Value of church and school property	$35,000

Appropriations were made for carrying on the missionary work during the ensuing year, as follows:

I. FOREIGN MISSIONS:	
Africa	$16,000
South America	55,500
China	118,855
Germany	85,060
Switzerland	11,440
Scandinavia	54,472
India	188,490
Bulgaria and Turkey	21,054
Italy	52,287
Mexico	59,592
Japan	56,660
Corea	16,266

Total for Foreign Missions $685,628

II. MISSIONS IN THE UNITED STATES, NOT IN ANNUAL CONFERENCES, TO BE ADMINISTERED AS FOREIGN MISSIONS (in Arizona, the Black Hills, Indian Territory, Montana, Nevada, New Mexico, and Utah).......... 71,272

III. DOMESTIC MISSIONS (Welsh, Scandinavian, German, French, Chinese, Japanese, American Indian, Bohemian, and English-speaking)...... 409,921

IV. Miscellaneous appropriations............... 85,000

Total $1,201,819

The Woman's Home Missionary Society met in Syracuse, N. Y., October 27. Mrs. Rutherford B. Hayes presided. The receipts had been $48,124 in money and $35,000 in supplies. Missions had been opened during the year in several new places in the South, among the Indians, among the Mormons, and in New Mexico. Of the missions already in operation, special mention was made of improvements in the industrial departments at Little Rock, Ark., Holly Springs, Miss., and Atlanta, Ga.; of a gift of property for an industrial school at Asheville, N. C.; of buildings for mission schools in Utah; of a purchase of lots in New Orleans for a school of domestic economy; of the evening-school for missionaries and a Deaconnesses' Home at Chicago. A plan for a Home Missionary Reading Circle and Lecture Bureau was approved; appropriations were made for an Immigrants' Home in connection with the Castle Garden Mission, New York; plans were recommended for enlisting young people in behalf of home missions, and arrangements were matured for starting a mission in Alaska. The Woman's Foreign Missionary Society returned 4,388 auxiliary societies, with 103,259 members. Its receipts for the year ending Oct. 1, 1887, had been $191,158. It sustained in Japan, Corea, India, Bulgaria, Italy, South America, and Mexico, at the close of 1886, 70 missionaries, 64 assistants, and 227 Bible women and medical workers; and returned 352 girls in orphanages, 209 day-schools, with 4,808 pupils, 7,000 women under instruction, and 1,286 pupils in boarding-schools. It appropriated for 1888 $228,000.

General Hospital.—A Methodist Episcopal General Hospital was opened in the city of Brooklyn, N. Y., December 15. The plan of the institution was originated by Mr. George R. Seney, who in 1881 appropriated a gift of $250,000 to the founding of a hospital, which, while being under the control of trustees representing the Methodist Episcopal Church, should be open to all sufferers irrespective of their creed or nationality. The corner-stone of the building was laid on Sept. 20, 1882. The sum of $410,000 had been expended by Mr. Seney in the purchase of lots and upon the building, when, in June, 1884, circumstances made a temporary suspension of operations necessary. The work was then resumed with money obtained by subscriptions, of which an additional sum of $70,000 was expended upon the buildings, and $60,000 were secured toward the beginning of a permanent endowment fund. No distinction will be made among patients;

but each one will be permitted the services of ministers of his own creed. The institution was opened free of debt, but with the announcement that subscriptions would be needed.

II. Methodist Episcopal Church South.—The following is a summary of the statistics of this church as they were returned in May, 1887: Number of annual conferences and missions, 42; of bishops, 9; of traveling preachers, 4,434; of local preachers, 5,989; of lay members, 1,055,954, of whom 1,049,816 are white, 658 colored, and 5,485 Indian; of Sunday-schools, 11,177, with which are connected 77,-515 teachers and 612,519 pupils; of churches, 10,951, having a total valuation of $13,685,-149; of parsonages, 2,030, having a total valuation of $2,247,288; number of baptisms during the year, 33,871 of infants, and 74,582 of adults. Amount of contributions: for church extension, $84,682; for conference claimants, $94,089; for foreign missions, $176,-863; for domestic missions, $80,865; total for missions and church extensions, $291,861. The increase of members during the year was 75,809. Appropriations for missions were made in May for the current financial year, as follow: for missions in the Western and border conferences in the United States, $37,455; for missions in Mexico and on the Mexican border, $67,276; for missions and schools in Brazil, $25,101; for the Indian mission conference, $10,975; for the China mission, $21,117; for the Japan mission, $9,930. Including special appropriations applicable to Brazil, Mexico, and China, the whole amount appropriated was $198,416.

III. Methodist Protestant Church.—The statistics of this church, as compiled for 1887, give the following footings: Number of conferences, 44; of itinerant preachers, 1,570; of local preachers, 939; of lay members, 124,638; of probationers, 4,071. Two colleges are sustained under the care of the General Conference, viz., at Westminster, Md., and Adrian, Mich., and theological seminaries at the same places. A foreign mission is supported in Japan, with chief stations at Yokohama and Nagoya, which are served by seven missionaries and several native teachers; while the Woman's Foreign Missionary Society has in addition a school with two teachers at Yokohama.

IV. American Wesleyan Connection.—The General Conference of the Wesleyan Methodist Connection in America met in its twelfth quadrennial session at La Otto, Indiana, October 19. The Rev. N. Wardner presided. Measures were taken for securing the incorporation of the General Conference under the name just given. A committee was appointed to prepare a practical and efficient plan for the organization of missionary societies, the same to be incorporated in the new book of "Discipline." Preparations were making for founding a mission in Africa, for which a missionary was ordained; and the missionary agent was instructed to go, with his family, with the first missionaries when the mission should be begun. The article in the "Discipline" on "Entire Sanctification" was amended, so as to be made more definite; and a minister was designated to preach the doctrine on the Pacific coast. The Rev. Joel Martin was appointed to prepare, subject to the approval of the Book Committee, a new edition of the "Wesleyan Manual," to cover the entire history of the denomination down to the present time. Resolutions were passed reprehending "a deplorably increasing tendency on the part of the professed Christian Church to vanity, extravagance, and show, especially in the matter of furniture and dress"; and the people of the church were invited to rebuke the evil by their example. A vote on the measure favoring the ordination of women resulted in an even division, and it was lost. Attention was called to reports which had been circulated reflecting upon the correctness of the financial report of the Connectional agent of the denominational publishing-house. Upon the report of the committee appointed to investigate the matter, these rumors were condemned.

V. Methodist Church of Canada.—The following is a summary of the statistics of this church, by Conferences, for 1887:

CONFERENCES.	Preach-ers.	Local preachers.	Total members.
Toronto	255	404	83,962
London	178	....	25,829
Niagara	156	199	24,794
Guelph	184	....	26,865
Bay of Quinte	180	254	27,295
Montreal	242	....	29,018
Manitoba and Northwest	72	118	6,192
British Columbia	28	45	1,975
Nova Scotia	106	50	18,208
New Brunswick and Prince Edward's Island	97	43	10,778
Newfoundland	60	54	11,797
Total	1,558	1,169	211,698

The members are classified as probationers (16,847) and lay members (194,701); increase of members during the year, 15,282; number of Sunday-schools, 2,720, with 24,206 officers and teachers, and 191,571 pupils; number of baptisms during the year, 14,315 of infants, and 2,498 of adults.

VI. Wesleyan Methodist Connection.—The whole number of lay members in Great Britain, as returned to the Conference, was 496,623; of whom 412,298 were in society classes, 31,470 on probation, and 52,855 in junior society classes. The number of Sunday-schools was 6,797, with 127,763 officers and teachers, and 895,532 pupils. Number of day-schools, 840, with 178,152 pupils. The receipts to the Connectional funds were returned to the Conference as follows: For foreign missions, £135,260; for theological institutions, £11,161; for the Home Mission and Contingent fund, £34,960; for the General Chapel fund, £9,022; for the Education fund, £9,994; for the Auxiliary fund, £23,827; for the School fund, £21,540; for the Extension fund in Great Britain, £9,258;

for the Sunday-school Union, £21,562; for the Children's Home and Orphan fund, £22,125; for the Metropolitan Chapel fund, £18,470; for the Extension fund in Scotland, £458. The Irish Conference returned a total of 24,988 members, with 864 chapels and 1,892 other preaching-places, and 69,662 "hearers"; and 314 Sunday schools, with 2,857 officers and teachers, and 24,879 pupils.

The Chapel Committee reported to the Conference that it had sanctioned 402 erections and enlargements, with 85 organs, involving a total expenditure of £305,169.

The Committee of the Children's Home reported a debt of £5,000, to meet which a special Jubilee fund was being raised. Land, buildings, and a memorial home had been among the special gifts of the year.

The report of Sunday-schools showed the number of teachers to be 127,763, and of pupils 895,532.

The annual meeting of the Wesleyan Missionary Society was held May 2. Col. Sir Charles Warren presided. Reference was made in the report to the fact that the present Jubilee year of her Majesty's reign coincided with the completion of the first century of the work in the society, its first foreign missionary having landed at Antigua on Christmas-day of 1786. The fifty years of the present reign thus coinciding with the second half-century of the society, an appropriate basis was offered for a comparative review. When the society published its first report in 1818, it had 82 missionaries in charge of 109 stations, with 23,473 enrolled members, and its income from ordinary sources was £18,484. In 1836 it had 306 missionaries, grouped in 180 circuits, with 64,691 members. Its total income was £75,000, and its total expenditure £70,000. Now, the gross income for 1886 had been £143,182, including £7,922 received through the Ladies' Auxiliary fund; the net amount of contributions for ordinary purposes received at the mission-house for the year had exceeded those of 1885 by £1,386; but the debt of the society had grown from £4,000 to £10,863. The missions were represented by 1,959 circuits, 10,919 chapels and preaching-places, 2,592 ministers and missionaries, and (approximately) 430,247 members.

The one hundred and forty-fourth Wesleyan Conference met in Manchester, July 19. The Rev. John Walton was chosen president.

Great interest was attached to the question of the reunion of the Methodist churches, to the discussion of which a special day was assigned, and with reference to which the following resolution was adopted in the Pastoral Conference:

The Conference, with profound thankfulness to the Divine Head of the Church, recognizes and heartily reciprocates the Christian and brotherly feeling expressed in recent resolutions of the Methodist New Connection and of other Methodist Churches (which have appeared in the public press). It expresses the confident hope that our own people will, by all legitimate means, strive to promote the spirit of brotherly kindness among all who hold the Christian faith, as expounded by our venerable founder. While affirming its unabated confidence in the essential principles of the government of the Wesleyan Methodist Church, and while believing that any attempt to promote organic union is not at present desirable, the Conference is of opinion that by mutual forbearance and consideration some at least of the waste of labor and resources caused by the needless multiplication of Methodist Chapels might be prevented. The Conference therefore appoints a committee, which shall meet during the year, to consider and report as to the way by which the waste and friction in the actual working of the various sections of the Methodist Church may be lessened or prevented, and brotherly love promoted.

On the meeting of the Representative Conference, an equal number of laymen were added to the Committee. On the report of a committee on the relation of baptized children to the Church, the Conference, in view of the diversity of opinion on the subject, decided that it would not at present make additional regulations. A series of resolutions were offered, directing that persons attending the Sacrament of the Lord's Supper in connection with the Wesleyan Church, should have their names entered on the class-books, and should be expected to conform to the rules and discipline of the Church; but that attendance at the class-meeting should not be absolutely required as a test of membership. The mover explained that the design of the resolutions was not to impair the class-meeting, but to meet the case of those who for any reason could not meet in class, and yet had on various grounds a claim to be recognized as members of the Methodist Church. The whole subject was referred to a committee to meet during the year. A report of the Home Mission Committee, recommending the extension of the system of employing lay agents, and proposing plans for more active promotion of Methodist work in villages, was approved. A proposal to change the time of the meeting of the Pastoral Session, so that it shall not anticipate the meeting of the representative session of the Conference, was referred to a committee for consideration, lest, if it were passed unadvisedly, the Conference should, by the change, be in future illegally constituted. Proposals for improving the religious education given in the day schools, and for securing a more regular examination in religious knowledge, were ordered to be sent for consideration to the district meetings and school committees. In the matter of help to students in the Theological Institution, it was resolved to encourage those who have means to pay for their education, while still giving aid to poor men who feel called to the work. The Committee on the Preparation of a Catechism of Methodist History and Polity was reappointed.

Colonial Conferences. — The West Indian Conference includes 69 itinerant ministers, 560 local preachers, and 45,124 members.

The South African Conference had, at the time of its meeting in April, 170 itinerant min-

isters, 1,477 local preachers, 60 evangelists, 24,280 full members, 8,002 members on trial, 2,961 in junior society classes; 307 Sunday-schools, with 1,809 teachers and 19,377 pupils; 234 day-schools, with 346 teachers and 15,042 pupils; 102,056 attendants on worship; and 380 churches and chapels, and 1,012 other preaching-places.

The statistical reports made to the New Zealand Conference at its meeting in 1887, showed that during the past four years 2,341 members, 62 churches and preaching-places, and 6,441 attendants on public worship had been added. The Church now numbered 50,-000 adherents. A bequest of £3,000 had been received from a member of the Episcopal Church, and was divided equally between the Loan fund and the Theological Institute. The sum of £2,800 had been raised for home missions. Four Maoris were ordained to the ministry. Resolutions were passed expressing an ardent desire for the union of the Methodist Churches of New Zealand, and for the separation of the New Zealand Conferences from the group of conferences constituting the Australasian Methodist Church. The following action, which, however, has no mandatory force, but merely expresses the feeling of the Conference, was taken with reference to the troubles in Tonga:

1. The Conference deplores the present unhappy divisions which have rent the Methodist Church of Tonga, and trusts that measures may be speedily devised for the restoration of the unity of the church in that district.

2. With a view to the attainment of this desirable end, the Conference recommends the Missionary Committee and the New South Wales and Queensland Conference to make overtures to the Free Church of Tonga for the holding of a friendly conference, composed of representatives of that church, and of the said committee and Conference, for the purpose of discussing the terms and conditions of organic union between the Wesleyan Church and the Free Church of Tonga, the proposed united church to be constituted an annual conference for the Friendly Islands of the Australasian Wesleyan Methodist Church.

VII. Primitive Methodist Church. — Statistics of this church were presented to the Conference in June, of which the following is a summary: Number of members, 191,663; of ministers, 1,088; of local or lay preachers, 16,138; of Connectional and other places of worship, 5,855; of hearers, 552,506; of Sunday-schools, 4,065, with 60,671 teachers and 410,950 pupils; value of Connectional property, £2,999,762.

The income of the Superannuated Ministers, Widows, and Orphans' fund for the year had exceeded £7,400. With this sum the committee had paid £5,150 to superannuated ministers and £1,700 to ministers' widows; a considerable amount had gone to assist orphans. The income of the Book Concern had been, including the small balance from the previous year, £34,000. Out of the profits of its business the Book Committee had given £3,300 to the Superannuated Ministers, Widows, and Orphans' fund, and other sums to various benevolent purposes. The new Book Depot fund had £6,798 toward its new premises. The Insurance Society had accumulated a capital of more than £10,000, and returned clear profits for the year amounting to £1,500. The directors had given £500 to aid distressed chapels, and a large sum had been carried over as a reserve fund.

The sixty-eighth annual Conference of the Primitive Methodist Connection met in Scarborough, June 8. The Rev. Thomas Whitehead was chosen president. A question arose on the filling up of vacancies in the Deed Poll, as to whether the Conference was bound unconditionally by the principle of seniority in choosing members of that body. Being the really legal body of the Connection, its functions are of great importance; and many members of the Conference thought that other than very aged members of the Connection might give it a more efficient character. Counsel who had been consulted had decided that the principle of seniority must be observed. The Conference determined to adhere to the rule of seniority for the present, and reserve the subject for future fuller consideration. A committee was appointed to consider applications for the constitution of new circuits: its chief purpose being to act as a check and to meet apprehensions which were expressed that "inconsiderate and perilous breakings up of large and powerful circuits into small stations might, in some cases, result injuriously." The term during which a Connectional office may be held was extended, in cases of exceptional fitness, from five to seven years. It was decided that legislation enacted by the Conference shall in future take effect at once, without waiting for the interval of a year, heretofore required. A "Primitive Methodist Chapel Aid Association, Limited," was sanctioned. A resolution was adopted condemning the "Coercion Bill" for Ireland. The Conference decided to establish an orphanage at Arlesford, where an eligible estate has been acquired on advantageous terms. The committee was recommended to consider the practicability of opening a new mission in the region of the Zambesi.

Resolutions have been passed by the Moonter Primitive Methodist District Meeting in Australia asking for the organization of a separate Australian Conference, and favoring an organic union of the minor Methodist bodies of the Australian continent; and, to further the latter object, a committee was appointed to consult with committees of other Methodist bodies on the subject.

VIII. United Methodist Free Churches.—The following is a summary of the numerical returns of this Connection as made to the Annual Assembly in July: Number of itinerant ministers, 383; of supernumeraries, 36; of local preachers, 3,313; of leaders, 4,056; of church-members, 76,611; of members on trial, 8,324; of chapels and preaching-rooms, 1,574; of Sunday-schools, 1,357, with 26,612 teachers and 200,706 pupils.

The income of the Chapel Relief fund had been £1,046. The capital of the Chapel Loan fund was £11,405. The sum of £40,748 had been raised during the year for the purposes of the chapel schedule. The capital of the Superannuation and Benevolent fund amounted to £34,845; its income for the year had been £7,750, and 56 annuitants were its beneficiaries. The assets of Asheville College were returned at £18,100 and its liabilities at £7,683. The Theological Institute returned a capital or Endowment fund of £772. The capital of the Book-Room amounted to £6,260; its income for the year had been £9,262 and its disbursements £8,738. The sales had amounted to £6,077. The income on account of the Missionary fund had been £21,946, and the outlay £21,492.

The annual meeting in behalf of the United Methodist Free Churches' Home and Foreign Missions was held April 25. The income for the year had been £22,248, and the expenditure £20,805. The East African Mission had suffered seriously at the beginning of the year by the murder of the Rev. John Haughton and his wife, missionaries, and twenty-one natives belonging to the station at Golbanti, in the Galla country, by the Masai. A net increase of 456 members was reported on the foreign stations (Australia, 848; Jamaica, 151; New Zealand, 22; while East Africa showed no change, and China showed a decrease of 4 and Sierra Leone of 61).

The Annual Assembly of the United Methodist Free Churches met in Louth, July 5. The Rev. James S. Balmer was chosen president. Many memorials had been received on the subject of union of the Methodist bodies, and considered by the Connectional Committee. A resolution was adopted by the Conference expressing satisfaction at the friendly feeling existing among the Methodist bodies, and the hope that this would lead to further co-operation and closer union; and the matter was referred to the Connectional Committee, with authority to take such steps in the matter as it might deem desirable. A favorable report was made of the working of the "Evangelistic Scheme," and modifications of the existing regulations were made, which, it was thought, would promote its greater efficiency.

IX. Methodist New Connection.—The following is a summary of the statistics of this denomination, as they were reported to the Conference in June: Number of chapels, 193; of local preachers, 1,282; of churches, 1,282; of church-members, 30,096; of probationers, 4,603; number of Sunday-schools, 452, with 11,116 teachers and 84,410 pupils.

The income of the Paternal fund was returned as having been above £3,000, and a balance in hand of £780 was reported. The expenditures of the Chapel and Loan fund had been £22,500. The income for missionary purposes had been £6,680; and the debt against the Missionary fund had been reduced from £2,243 to £1,698. The six Connectional funds together returned a gross income of more than £14,000.

The Methodist New Connection Conference met at Stockport, June 13. The Rev. John K. Jackson was chosen president. The subject of Methodist union was considered, in view of the informal correspondence which had taken place respecting it in the previous year (see "Annual Cyclopædia" for 1886), and a resolution was adopted declaring

that this Conference desires to express its devout thankfulness to Almighty God for the spirit of unity and fraternal kindness which, during the past year, he has so graciously poured out upon many Christian churches. It recognizes, with great pleasure, the evident desire for closer communion and intercourse on the part of large numbers of the followers of the Lord Jesus Christ, who have hitherto been content to move within the limits of their own separate organizations. The Conference has special joy in noting the growing spirit of union among the various branches of the Methodist Church, and the kind and friendly references made to the Methodist New Connection by honored brethren connected with the Wesleyan and other Methodist bodies. These various indications inspire the Conference with the hope that events ere long may travel with increasing rapidity toward the more perfect realization of the prayer of Him who is our master—"That they all may be one; as thou, Father, art in me, and I in thee, that they also may be one in us: that the world may believe that thou hast sent me." Believing that the movements toward union are the result of divine leading and influence, the Conference instructs the Annual Committee for the ensuing year to maintain an attitude of friendly observation, and to avail itself of any opportunities which may arise to foster and advance the closer fellowship of the Methodist Churches.

X. Bible Christians.—The statistical reports of the Church, made to the Conference in June, showed an increase of 819 members and 947 pupils in Sunday-schools. The receipts of the Chapel fund had been £25,411. The receipts of the Mission funds had been £7,273 and the disbursements £7,876. The number of home missions was reported to be 38, and these were cared for by 45 ministers, and returned 4,969 members. The amount of £4,404 had been raised on the missions for the support of the ministry and missionary purposes. The Conference directed that the home missions should be visited by the secretary once a year, or oftener, if necessary.

The sixty-ninth annual Conference of the Bible Christian Connection met at Swansea, July 26. The Rev. J. H. Bate was elected president. The following resolution, on the subject of Methodist union, was adopted:

Resolved, That this Conference affirms its conviction that the union of the Methodist bodies in this country, on an honorable basis, would be of incalculable advantage to our common Christianity, and wishes therefore to record its unfeigned satisfaction and thankfulness at the numerous tokens of the manifest growth of the spirit of unity among them, and its desire that the Connectional attitude should be one of sympathetic interest in all well-considered movements to bring these churches into closer fellowship. This Conference further directs the Connectional Commit-

tee to take the necessary steps to join any committees which may be appointed by other Methodist churches in devising a scheme to prevent the present waste which is going on in many parts of the country.

The question of union with the Primitive Methodists and the Methodist New Connection in Australia was deferred.

MEXICO, a confederated republic of North America. (For area and population, see "Annual Cyclopædia" for 1886.)

Government.—The President is Don Porfirio Diaz, whose term of office will expire on Dec. 1, 1888. His Cabinet is composed of the following ministers: Foreign Relations, Señor Ignacio Mariscal; War, Gen. Pedro Hinojosa; Public Works, Gen. Pacheco; Justice, Señor Joaquin Baranda; Finance, Señor Manuel Dublan; Interior, Señor Manuel Romero Rubio. The Minister to the United States is Señor Matias Romero; the United States Secretary of Legation at Mexico is Joseph L. Morgan; the American Consul-General, James W. Porch. The Mexican Consul-General at New York is Señor Juan N. Navarro, and at San Francisco Señor Alejandro K. Coney.

Re-election of the President.—The constitutional amendment permitting election to the presidency for two consecutive terms, after receiving the approval of both houses of Congress, was officially promulgated on October 23. Diaz clubs were organized, and a large number of newspapers proposed the President's candidacy for a second term.

Finance.—On Jan. 1, 1887, the consolidated national indebtedness of Mexico amounted to £14,000,000. Up to Dec. 31, 1890, the Government has reserved the right to redeem at 40 per cent. and later at 50 per cent. The 1 per cent. interest due in 1886 and the 1½ per cent. in 1887 were punctually paid. In 1888 2 per cent. and in 1889 2½ per cent. will fall due. Toward the close of November a settlement of what is known as the English Convention debt of 1851—being bonds issued to pay the claims of British subjects—was effected, the Government to issue a bond for £150 in place of every $500 silver bond, the extra amount being for arrears of interest. The original debt was $4,984,914. A large amount was redeemed between 1851 and 1863, but there remained $2,925,000, all but $95,000 of which has now been converted. On December 8 there was introduced in Congress a bill to permit the Government to contract a loan for £10,500,000 for the purpose of funding the existing national debt. The new issue is to be made in Berlin and London at 5½ per cent. interest per annum, the bankers agreeing to take up the bonds at 84 per cent. of their face value. This will enable the Government to buy up the English debt at 40 per cent., as provided by law, and have in hand over $16,000,000 in gold, with which it will cancel its indebtedness to the National Bank. The maximum rate of interest on the English debt, as recently converted, is 3 per cent., while the new rate of interest would be nearly double; but the Government will save the heavy interest to the National Bank which advanced over $8,000,-000 to the Government; and it is proposed to use what surplus there may be in works of internal improvement. During the last year of President Gonzalez's administration, and the first seven months of President Diaz's term, the custom-house at Vera Cruz collected $7,000,-000, and during the next similar period $9,000,-000. While there was, according to the estimates for the fiscal year just ended, a deficit of $6,000,000, the increased revenues had enabled the Government to meet every expense. In December the banking-house of S. Bleichroder, Berlin, being joined therein by other Berlin and some London firms, succeeded in floating the Mexican 5½ per cent. Government loan to the amount of £10,500,000 at 84. The Government forwarded to Vienna, Austria, in 1887, 4,000 cwts. of old nickel coin.

Army and Navy.—The army of the republic consisted, on June 30, 1886, of 20,806 infantry, with 1,192 officers; 7,658 cavalry, with 672 officers; 2,158 artillery, with 211 officers, and 285 army surgeons: commanded by 20 generals of division and 86 brigadier-generals, who, together with military employés to the number of 1,614, formed a total standing army of 34,-202. The navy consists of 4 gunboats.

Postal Service.—Negotiations for a new postal treaty between the United States and Mexico were concluded on June 21, and the treaty signed by the two Presidents was ratified by the Mexican Senate, going into effect on July 1. Mail communication has been vastly extended thereby between the two republics, and packages weighing four and a half pounds can be sent without delay at the Custom-House. The postal laws of the United States were extended to include mail communications with Mexico, and those of Mexico thenceforward included communication with this country, each country to charge its local rates for transmitting mail matter to the other, retaining all moneys received for postage and overweight charges. The registry systems of the two countries were also made available in the reciprocal services, unclaimed letters to be returned free of charge in accordance with the regulations now in force in the United States.

The number of items of mail matter forwarded by the Mexican post-offices was 8,873,-931 in 1882-'83; in 1885-'86 there had been an increase to 14,057,324. In 1883 the inland postage was still 35 cents the half-ounce, and the amount of postage collected, $842,848; in 1884, with a reduced postage, the amount sank to $622,934; in 1885 it had recovered to $696,-966, and in 1886 to $744,013.

Up to June, 1887, the receipts of the Post-Office Department for the fiscal year were $748,000, against $681,000 for the previous fiscal year. In the fiscal year ending with June, the number of items of mail matter, including packages, carried was 18,000,000.

The international service showed a gain of 20,000 items, mainly arising from increased business with the United States.

Commerce.—The value of imports into Mexico has fluctuated as follows: 1881-'82, $39,020,-000; 1882-'83, $38,951,000; 1883-'84, $84,-025,000; 1884-'85, $35,839,000. The total export in 1884-'85 was $46,670,845; in 1885-'86 it was $48,647,717—the former amount included $33,774,051 specie and bullion, almost exclusively silver, and the latter $29,906,401, the rest in both cases being merchandise. Exportation in 1885-'86 was distributed as follows:

TO—	Silver.	Merchandise.	Total.
Germany	$832,829	$738,770	$1,571,399
Spain	654,287	259,236	913,523
United States	15,496,836	9,983,258	25,439,594
France	8,447,117	489,160	8,936,277
England	9,417,464	2,182,604	11,600,068
Other countries	58,568	138,258	196,556
Total	$29,906,401	$18,741,316	$48,647,717

The customs revenues collected at the port of Vera Cruz for the past ten years amounted to $97,000,000.

Chief among the products exported in 1885-'86 were, in value: Horses, $282,625; indigo, $119,087; sugar, $178,887; coffee, $1,699,724; India-rubber, $108,488; Sisal hemp, $2,844,-356; rope, $528,649; wool, $220,071; mahogany, $901,082; fustic, $110,874; logwood, $670,299; goat-skins, $994,468; hides, $997,-876; deer-skins, $101,089; silver lead, $485,-948; cigars, $316,991; tobacco, $211,578; vanilla-beans, $463,395; sarsaparilla, $119,887; cochineal, $13,850; and other products, $2,876,-992; together, $18,741,316. Aniline colors seem to be doing away with cochineal more and more in Europe and America.

The American trade (merchandise) with Mexico exhibits these figures:

FISCAL YEAR.	Imports into the United States.	Domestic exports from the United States.
1883	$8,177,128	$14,870,992
1884	9,016,486	11,089,608
1885	9,267,021	7,870,599
1886	10,687,972	6,556,077
1887	14,719,840	7,267,129

Railroads.—Probably the most notable change brought about by the era of peace in Mexico has been in the railroad development of the country. Seven years ago there was only the one railroad, from Vera Cruz to the city of Mexico, with a few insignificant branches—in all, less than four hundred miles. Since that date the railroad system has increased tenfold, now approximating 4,000 miles, and rapidly increasing. Some disappointment has been manifested because the railroad construction had not been followed by the same development that marked the extension of railroads in the Western States and Territories of the United States; but the conditions and habits of the two peoples are widely different. The

Mexicans are slow to adopt new methods, and the system of commerce and agriculture there could not be changed in a day or a year, even if it should be found desirable. But a marked advance has already taken place, and the demand for American goods is growing. There is, among others, a Mexican plantation where 250 American plows are in use; there are at times as many as ten railroad cars loaded with American wagons in a single train, and immense quantities of mining and other machinery are daily passing in over the railroads. American investments and interests in Mexico are large and increasing. There are now four American railroads crossing the frontier at widely different points and reaching to the very heart of the republic. The longest and most important of these is that known as the Mexican Central, over whose line travelers now pass from El Paso to the city of Mexico. There has been a great increase in its business of late. In November there were 800 cars loaded with American goods at El Paso awaiting shipment, and to meet the increased business the company ordered 250 new freight-cars and ten locomotives. The International (the Southern Pacific system) completed its connection from Eagle Pass, Texas, to the city of Mexico in December, while the National Railway, crossing the frontier at Laredo, was rapidly constructing the gap-line, which is to give still another international route to the Mexican capital. In September the Mexican Central Railway reduction of freight rates for goods imported into the city of Mexico from Liverpool, via New Orleans and El Paso, caused a reduction in the freight tariff of the Mexican (English) Railway, so as to enable the port of Vera Cruz to maintain its lead over Paso del Norte as a port of entry.

In November a project was set on foot to build a new narrow-gauge railway to run from Patzcuaro, on the line of the National Railway, to a point in the State of Guerrero, on the Pacific Ocean, traversing, in the State of Michoacan, a rich coffee country and gold-placer region, and also penetrating districts where the finest cabinet-woods are to be had. The Government will give the road a subvention, partly in interest-bearing securities. Surveys are to be made immediately for an extension of the Interoceanic Railway from Yantepec to Acapulco. Another project is to build a railway from the city of Mexico to Puebla, crossing the mountains. During the latter part of November the Mexican Central and International railroad companies, through their freight departments, arranged the terms for an interchange of traffic, subject to the approval of the board of directors of the respective companies. In this manner the two companies will act in harmony, and there will be no rate-war. The International Company reached a point on the Mexican Central near Laredo on December 10, in order to begin operations in January, 1888. In January, 1887,

articles of incorporation of the Mexican Pacific Railroad Company were filed at San Francisco. The road is to run from the city of Mexico, through Cuernavaca, to Puente de Ixtla in the State of Morelos, eighty-five miles. The capital stock is $8,000,000.

Under the plan of reorganization adopted almost unanimously by the Mexican National Railroad shareholders in the autumn of 1886, a new corporation was organized in March, 1887, the company issuing $10,500,000 six-per-cent. bonds, having forty-six years to run, to be a first lien on the main line and branches of the old National road, and also upon the lease of the Texas Mexican Railway and upon the bonds and stock of the latter, and also upon bonds of the Corpus Christi road.

In August the contract for the construction of 114 miles of the National Railway, between San Miguel de Allende and San Luis Potosi, was awarded, the work not to begin later than one month from the date of signing the contract, and to be completed within a year.

In December, 1887, the Mexican Chamber of Deputies passed the bill granting a concession to Louis Huller to build railroads in the States of Sinaloa, Sonora, and Chihuahua. In the same month a junction was almost effected between the International Railway and the Central Railway at the Villa Lerdo station, which will reduce the time of travel between the city of Mexico and New York to four days and twelve hours.

The Tehuantepec Ship-Railway.—The directors of the Eads Concession Company held a meeting at Pittsburg, Pa., on July 27, the first since the death of Capt. James B. Eads. It was decided to begin active efforts looking to the opening of the work on the ship-railway at an early date, and also to conduct operations upon a plan entirely different from that mapped out by Capt. Eads. Instead of making new application to Congress for a charter, it was resolved to incorporate a ship-railway company under the laws of one of the States, the property of the Eads Concession Company to be turned over to the ship-railway company, and the stock and bonds of the latter placed on the market. This plan was followed up, and Gov. Hill, of New York, approved, on Nov. 21, 1887, the articles of association of the "Atlantic and Pacific Ship-Railway Company."

Steamer Lines.—On June 30, 1886, the following steamship lines were plying to Mexican Gulf ports : Alexandre & Sons' New York line; Morgan line of Louisiana and Texas steamers; Leandro, Regil & Company Mexican Coasting line; German mail steamers between Hamburg, Havre, and Mexican ports; Harrison line, between Liverpool and Mexican ports; West India and Pacific Steamship Company, between New Orleans, Mexican ports, and the West Indies; Royal Mail Steamship Company's steamers, between Southampton, the West Indies, and Mexican ports. On the Pacific coast of Mexico there were the Californian Steamship Company, San Francisco and Mexican ports; Pacific Mail Steamship Company, Panama, Central American, Mexican ports and San Francisco; Sinaloa and Durango Railroad's steamers, Guaymas, Mazatlan, and other Mexican ports; Sonora Railroad's steamers, Mexican and Central American ports; Mexican Coast line, Guaymas and other Mexican ports. Of the Gulf steamers, the first three lines were subsidized at the time by the Mexican Government, and, of the Pacific steamers, the first two and the last-named line.

In December, 1887, a concession was granted to a steamship company for a line between New York, New Orleans, and Vera Cruz, the vessels to touch at all Mexican ports on the Gulf of Mexico, and carry the mails. The usual rebate of two per cent. on customs duties has been granted, and the line is obliged to carry freight and passengers at lower rates than those hitherto charged. The Government agrees to pay a subsidy of $1,000 a trip.

Education.—In the past few years the Federal and State Governments have done much to encourage and establish a general free-school system. Much opposition has been made by the clergy, but the civil government recognized its duty to provide for the education of the masses, and free schools have been multiplied all over the republic. Congress has latterly been discussing a bill making education in the Federal district compulsory, and such a law is already in force in some of the States.

Immigration.—It was announced in December that the Mexican Government had granted extraordinary concessions to a real estate company to induce immigration to eleven States of Mexico. The company has obtained title to 55,000,000 acres in Chihuahua, Sinaloa, Durango, Coahuila, Zacatecas, Guanajuato, Tamaulipas, Vera Cruz, Michoacan, Jalisco, and Guerrero, and proposes to establish agencies in all the large cities of Europe and America. The Government has granted exemption from taxation to all settlers on those tracts, and insures protection.

A Spanish colony has been founded by Señores Franchi de Alfaro in the State of Guanajuato, and early in 1887 a large amount of plants and seeds was shipped for its use from Barcelona by way of Vera Cruz, the settlers being Catalans and agriculturists from the island of Majorca.

A project is on foot in London for sending 5,000 Jewish colonists to Mexico to be distributed among the agricultural districts. The proposed colonists are victims of Russian persecution. The Government papers in the Mexican capital favor the scheme, but the opposition press is strongly against the introduction into Mexico of Jews or Socialists. Toward the close of 1887 the question of allowing Americans to colonize Lower California was agitated at the Mexican capital, the opposition taking the ground that the administration of

President Diaz, in its cordiality toward Americans, forgets the result of permitting American colonization in Texas. Gen. Pacheco, the Minister of Public Works, replied in a pamphlet, showing that there is no danger from American colonization, and that the Americans are in a minority in the territory.

The Border Country.—Mr. William Gaston Allen, United States Consul at Piedras Negras, while on a visit to Washington, expressed himself, Oct. 30, 1887, as follows: "The condition of affairs along the Rio Grande border has perceptibly improved within the past few years. Much of this is due to the wise and efficient administration of President Diaz of the Mexican Republic. He is an earnest and sincere friend of the United States. Through his efforts smuggling from the Mexican side has been practically stopped. His customs officials, Federal judges, and others are not only men of integrity, but men who reflect his kindly feeling toward this country as well. President Diaz is a strong advocate of closer commercial relations with the United States, and, in furtherance of this desire, has lent the weight of his personal influence wherever it could be advantageously employed. The life and property of foreigners residing in Mexico are quite as secure as those of the natives themselves. The recent murders of Americans in some of the outlying Mexican States were the acts of banditti, whom the Government has thus far been powerless to capture. Where it has been possible to punish the offenders, the Government has not failed to do so."

Relations with Guatemala.—The substance of the protocol arranged in October between Mexico and Guatemala is, that the Government of Guatemala will appoint an envoy extraordinary and minister plenipotentiary to the city of Mexico to negotiate a treaty providing for a mixed commission to decide the claims of citizens of one country against those of the other; also to negotiate a treaty of commerce providing for free exchange of the natural products of the two countries.

Protestantism.—A general assembly of clergymen, representing all the Protestant missions in Mexico, was to be held in the Mexican capital on Jan. 31, 1888. This is the first time that such a union of the Protestant sects carrying on work in Mexico has been possible.

American Enterprise.—On Feb. 16, 1887, the Incorporation Committee of the Connecticut Legislature reported favorably on granting special charters to the Peninsular Railway Company of Lower California, the Gulf of Mexico Guano Company, the Mexican Pacific Pier and Warehouse Company, the Mexican International, the Pacific and Gulf of Mexico Steamship Company, and the Chiapas Railway Company. The committee also reported favorably on a resolution authorizing the International Company of Mexico, which secured a Connecticut charter two or three years ago, to increase its capital to $20,000,000.

Draining the Valley of Mexico.—During the summer the contract for part of the work of draining the valley of Mexico was awarded to a syndicate of Cleveland, Ohio, capitalists, who have formed a company for the purpose of constructing public works in Mexico. The Government proposes to make a tunnel under the mountain, on which work was begun as long ago as the reign of Maximilian.

Insurance.—A new feature in Mexico is the advent of the American life insurance companies. Seven years ago they were almost unknown. Now three American companies have offices in the capital, with agencies throughout the country, and policies to the amount of millions of dollars have been issued.

Telegraphs.—On August 11 telegraphic communication by land-lines was opened between the city of Mexico and Guatemala, the charge per message being twenty-five cents for the first ten words.

Silver-Mining.—The second in importance of the American investments are the mining companies, which are scattered throughout the country, but mainly to be found in the northern and border States. Mining is the chief industry in Mexico, and, notwithstanding the low price of silver, it is just now in a prosperous condition, the product of the mines for 1887 having been greater than in any year since the old Spanish bonanza times. Much of this activity is attributed to the liberal laws recently passed for the encouragement of the industry. A large part of the ores is being shipped over the railroads to works in the United States.

Stock-Raising.—Another important American interest are the land and grazing investments, which have become very considerable in the past three years, and are constantly increasing. These are mainly with a view of stock-raising, for which the table-lands of Mexico are well adapted.

Iridescent Stoneware.—At Patzcuaro true iridescent ware is found, made by the natives. The specimens to be met with are small, round, and rectangular plates. The luster is the true Saracenic, Alhambra, or Gubbio luster. The ware is rude; the makers of it have not the certainty of producing a particular color in a picture, which distinguishes the Gubbio work, and it lacks the elegance and glaze, the solidity and fineness, of the Alhambra tiles. But it is genuine iridescence. The plates are exceedingly thin and brittle. It was said to be made at Santa Fé, a small Indian village on the north shore of Lake Patzcuaro.

Earthquakes.—On May 3 an earthquake occurred in the Sierra Madre mountains of Sonora, accompanied by a terrible volcanic eruption at the pueblo of Bavispe, where 4 persons were killed and 19 injured, and at Opata, where 9 were killed. Both pueblos were destroyed, and the inhabitants of Bavispe, Basarac, Opata, and Guasavas were living in the fields, under trees, and in caves. Repeated shocks occurred subsequently, but they were lighter. There was panic everywhere, and some women died from fright. A wide territory was seamed with crevices and immense chasms. The earth sank in many places, and was flooded with water, making swamps where there never was any water before. In many mountains eruptions were noticed, and continuous smoke indicated volcanic action. The Governor of Sonora, Señor Torres, sent out explorers to ascertain the existence of a volcano, and early in June they returned and reported an active volcano 14 miles southeast of Bavispe. The party could not approach nearer than within 4 miles of the mountains. The crater was pouring forth immense volumes of smoke, fire, and lava. Boiling water issued from the side of the mountain, and lava in vast waves slowly poured down the mountain-side into the cañons, which were being filled up. The boiling water had destroyed all vegetation in the valleys. One peculiar feature of the volcano was its great activity. Bowlders weighing tons were being hurled down from the crater. On June 6 a heavy shock was felt in Tucson, preceded on May 29 by a shock throughout the valley of Mexico, in Jalapa, Córdoba, Esperanza, Tlascala, Tehuacana, Puebla, and Oaxaca.

Bull-Fights.—The Spanish passion for bull-fighting has broken out in Mexico with new zeal of late. After the adoption of the Constitution of 1857, a law had been passed making this amusement unlawful in the Federal District, and the general sentiment of the better class in the various States was in favor of its suppression as a barbarous practice. But there seems to have been a reaction, and the last Congress surprised the outside world by repealing the prohibitory law, and now there are in full operation, in and near the capital, five bull-rings or plazas.

MICHIGAN. State Government.—The following were the State officers during the year: Governor, Cyrus G. Luce, Republican; Lieutenant-Governor, James H. MacDonald; Secretary of State, Gilbert R. Osmun; Auditor-General, Henry H. Aplin; Treasurer, George L. Maltz; Attorney-General, Moses Taggart; Superintendent of Public Instruction, Joseph Estabrook; Railroad Commissioner, John T. Rich; Insurance Commissioner, Henry S. Raymond; Labor Commissioner, Alfred H. Heath; Chief-Justice of the Supreme Court, James V. Campbell; Associate Justices, Thomas R. Sherwood, John W. Champlin, and Allen B. Morse.

Legislative Session.—The session of this year continued from January 5 till June 29. The choice of a successor to United States Senator Omar D. Conger fell upon Francis B. Stockbridge, who received the Republican nomination on the tenth ballot. The vote in the Legislature was as follows: Senate—Stockbridge, 22; George L. Yaple, the Democratic nominee, 9. House—Stockbridge, 45; Yaple, 27; Henry A. Robinson, Labor candidate, 5. The most important legislation of the session relates to the liquor question. A "local option" law

MICHIGAN. 505

was passed, giving the people of each county the right to vote on the question of prohibition or license once in three years, in case one fifth of the voters petition for an election. The people may vote to prohibit not only the sale but the manufacture of liquors within the county. Another act, providing a system of high license, imposes a tax of $500 on each wholesale, and $300 on each retail liquor-dealer. All saloons are required to be closed on Sunday, and at 11 o'clock on every secular night. A State constabulary was created to enforce these laws. Provision was made for the election of an additional judge of the Supreme Court. The tax-levy for 1887 was fixed at $910,312, and for 1888 at $758,750. Among the specific appropriations are the following: for new buildings at the State Reformatory at Ionia, $14,470; for two buildings at the Eastern Michigan Asylum, $26,000; for completing and furnishing the State House of Correction and branch State Prison at Marquette, $75,712; for new buildings and improvements at the State Prison at Jackson, $104,200; for additions to the normal-school building, $60,000; for a building for the use of the mining-school at Houghton, $75,000. Other acts of the session were as follow:

Making an appropriation for the equipment, support, and expenses of a State weather-service.

To punish drunkenness in public places.

To punish registration of cattle and other animals under false pretenses, and giving false pedigrees of such animals.

To provide for the confinement of female prisoners in the Detroit House of Correction.

To prevent the adulteration of candies and confectioneries, and the sale of such adulterated articles.

To abolish the Superior Court of Detroit.

To validate the collection of taxes assessed prior to Act 158 of the session of 1885.

Authorizing the organization of corporations to improve the breed of horses by promoting the interests of the American trotting-turf.

To prevent the taking of bonds, notes, and other evidences of indebtedness, in whole or part consideration of bonds, contracts, and other agreements for the sale of grain, seeds, and other cereals at a fictitious price, and to prevent the sale and transfer of such evidences of indebtedness.

Providing three additional circuit judges for the third judicial district.

To incorporate the Woman's Christian Temperance Unions of the State.

To provide for the appointment of a game and fish warden.

To provide a bounty of one cent for each English sparrow killed in the State.

To authorize the board of supervisors of any county to purchase lots in any cemetery or burial-place for deceased soldiers, sailors, and marines.

To revise the laws providing for the incorporation of co-operative and mutual-benefit associations.

To protect children, and to prevent them from being educated in immorality and crime.

To prevent gambling in stocks, bonds, petroleum, cotton, grain, provisions, and other produce.

Providing for the incorporation of associations for the purpose of supplying water and water-power.

To revise the laws authorizing the business of banking, and to create the office of commission of banking to supervise such business.

To provide for the correction of frauds and mistakes in the canvass and returns made by inspectors of elections.

To provide for the appointment of inspectors of mines and their deputies.

To prevent truancy and the disorderly behavior of youth.

To incorporate engineering societies.

To prevent the sale of impure, unwholesome, or adulterated milk, and to provide for milk inspectors.

To regulate and govern the State House of Correction and branch of the State Prison in the Upper Peninsula.

To provide for an independent forestry commission.

Revising the fish and game laws.

To prohibit railroad companies whose road has been built wholly or in part by public aid or local subscription given as a bonus for such construction, from removing the tracks and abandoning such road.

Making the keeping of houses of ill-fame a felony.

To provide for the incorporation of Arbeiter-bunds.

Providing that all deputy or under sheriffs shall be bona-fide residents of the State.

Providing a means for the settlement of back taxes on vacant or part-paid swamp, school, and other State lands.

To establish a municipal court in the city of East Saginaw.

To provide for the incorporation and regulation of building and loan associations.

To provide for the completion of biographical and historical work relating to early State officials, begun by the Semi-centennial Commission.

To enable the State Agricultural Society to fix a permanent location for the State fair.

To make possession of fish and game out of season prima-facie evidence of the violation of laws protecting the same.

To authorize the incorporation of suburban homestead, villa, park, and summer-resort associations.

To provide for the incorporation of associations for the purpose of constructing, owning, controlling, and leasing buildings for hotels, elevators, or public halls.

To provide for the organization of log and timber insurance companies, to insure against the risk of transportation in towing or carrying logs and timber on the Great Lakes and connected waters.

Permitting the incorporation of societies of reputable pharmacists.

Regulating the testimony of minors.

Providing for the incorporation of lodges of the Ancient Order of United Workmen.

Making all debts for labor preferred claims against the estates of insolvent debtors, and giving them precedence of all debts that were not a lien on such estates prior to the performance of such labor.

For the incorporation of companies for the purpose of buying and selling brood animals.

Changing the termination of the fiscal year of the State from September 30 to June 30.

Regulating the methods of heating railroad trains.

Requiring a civil license in order to marry, and the due registration of the same, and to provide a penalty for violation of these provisions.

To punish the carrying of concealed weapons.

To provide for the punishment of crimes committed by any person confined or before the expiration of his sentence in any penal institution of the State.

Raising the age of consent in women to sixteen years.

Regulating the adoption and change of name of minors.

Requiring railroads to run at least one passenger train each day.

To prohibit the employment of male children under fourteen years, and female children under sixteen years, more than nine hours each day.

To regulate the sale and use of oleomargarine, butterine, and other articles resembling butter, providing a penalty for the sale of such as if genuine butter.

To provide for the change of name of adults.

To provide for keeping clear and open and in good repair all ditches in the State constructed under the authority of the Board of Control having charge of the reclamation of swamp lands.

To require the use of safety-gates upon swing and draw bridges.

To preserve evidence of error and fraud in election returns.

To protect primary elections and conventions of political parties, and to punish offenses committed thereat.

To provide for corporations to carry on the business of printing, publishing, and book-making.

To permit the incorporation of societies to diffuse moral and religious knowledge and instruction.

Three amendments to the Constitution were proposed. Two of them were voted upon at the April election, and the result is given below; the third, providing for an additional judge of the Saginaw County Circuit Court, will be submitted to the people in November, 1888.

Political.—An election was held early in April, for the purpose of choosing two regents of the State University and two justices of the Supreme Court. The justices were to be elected, one for eight years to succeed Chief-Justice Campbell, and one for ten years, the latter being the additional justice provided for by an act of the Legislature passed in February. The Republican candidates were Judge James V. Campbell for justice for the short term, Charles D. Long for justice for the long term, and Roger W. Butterfield and Charles Hebard for regents. The Democrats nominated for these offices respectively: Levi T. Griffin, Charles H. Camp, Christian Vanderveen, and Rufus F. Sprague. A Labor ticket and a Prohibition ticket were also in the field. The vote for judges of the Supreme Court was as follows: For the short term: Campbell, 170,-749; Griffin, 139,940; O'Brien J. Atkinson (Labor), 32,396; Noah W. Cheever (Prohibition), 18,568; for the long term: Long, 174,-024; Camp, 140,315; John C. Blanchard (Labor), 27,658; Lemuel Clute (Prohibition), 18,530. The two amendments to the State Constitution that were voted upon at this time were a prohibitory amendment and one increasing the salaries of State officers. Both were defeated, although the contest over Prohibition was close, 178,636 votes being cast in its favor, and 184,281 against it. The vote upon the salary amendment was 72,718 yeas and 124,888 nays.

Education.—The following is a summary of school statistics for 1886:

School population........................... 605,904
Enrollment 416,751
Number of school-houses 7,237
Estimated value of school property $11,850,971 00
Number of teachers employed............... 15,826
Wages of teachers........... .... $2,842,495 13
Average wages per month, males........... $45 01
Average wages per month, females $31 20
Total revenue $5,684,443 44

Revenue for school purposes is derived from the following sources: 1. The interest on permanent fund in the hands of the State, arising from the sale of primary-school lands, apportioned to the counties by the Superin-

tendent of Public Instruction, upon the number of children in districts having maintained the requisite amount of school. This is used only for the payment of teachers' wages. 2. The one-mill tax levied on each township by the supervisor; used only for school and library purposes, and apportioned to the districts where raised, provided said districts have maintained the requisite amount of school. 3. Local or district taxes, voted by the people for building and other purposes, except for teachers' wages and incidental expenses of the school, which are voted by the district board. 4. The surplus of dog-tax over and above $100, remaining after damages to stock by dogs have been paid. 5. Fines for breaches of the penal laws apportioned to the townships by the county treasurer.

State University.—The following table exhibits the attendance at this institution for the past five years:

YEAR.	From Michigan.	Non-residents.	Total.
1881–'82...........................	686	848	1,534
1882–'83...........................	671	769	1,440
1883–'84...........................	670	707	1,377
1884–'85...........................	644	651	1,295
1886–'87...........................	791	781	1,572

All departments of the university are reported to be in excellent condition. The State appropriation for the year was $108,356.94; for 1888, $46,700. A part of the larger sum is intended to be used in the completion of several laboratories.

Salt.—During the year there were 125 firms in the State engaged in the manufacture of salt, located in nine different counties, and operating 118 steam and 24 pan blocks. The estimated manufacturing capacity of these is 5,265,000 barrels annually. The amount actually manufactured during the year was 4,260,-012 barrels, an increase of 162,079 barrels over any previous year. The State salt inspector examined 8,944,309 barrels during the year. Since the system of State inspection was established in 1869, there have been inspected 38,-014,778 barrels, which with 3,282,117 barrels manufactured prior to that date, makes the total product of the State 41,822,895 barrels. The average price per barrel has decreased from $1.80 in 1869 to 60 cents for this year.

Local Option.—The first elections under the local option law was held in December, ten counties voting at that time, and the result in each case was in favor of Prohibition.

MIND-READING. A phenomenon attributable, it is claimed, to the power of one mind to impress a distinct idea upon another mind without the intervention of the senses. The phenomenon began to be seriously discussed in England in 1882, when the Society of Psychical Research was formed to make a strictly scientific inquiry into this and the kindred subjects of mesmerism, spiritualism, divining-rods, apparitions, etc. On all of these subjects the members of the society threw away their theories and prejudices and agreed to base their subsequent reasoning upon absolute facts demonstrated in their presence. In approaching the subject of mind-reading, Prof. Sidgwick, of Trinity College, Cambridge, declared it to be a scandal that there should still be so much incredulity as to the well authenticated phenomena; and he announced that the basis of all future investigation or theorizing would be the establishing of facts that no one could question. Of course, the element of collusion bars from the investigation any apparent phenomenon. There is no place for the magician who names cards or articles with the assistance of a confederate. Genuine mind-reading may be divided into four forms: 1. Where some action is performed, the hands of the operator being in gentle contact with the subject of the experiment. 2. Where a similar result is obtained with the hands not in contact with the subject. 3. Where a number, name, word, card, or other object has been guessed and expressed in speech or writing without contact, and apparently without possibility of transmission of the idea by the ordinary channels of sensation. 4. Where similar thoughts have simultaneously occurred, or impressions been made, in minds far apart.

The first two forms of the phenomenon are familiar to all as the "willing" games of the drawing-room. A conspicuous example was given by Stuart Cumberland, a professional mind-reader, in Edinburgh, in 1884. He had undertaken to find out by his art a pin secreted anywhere within a radius of a quarter of a mile of the Scott monument. A diamond scarf-pin was handed over for the experiment, and those in the room elected that the pin should be hidden by Mr. Black, and that Mr. Black should be accompanied by a committee. The committee left to secrete the pin, Mr. Cumberland remaining in the hotel with the rest of the company. Mr. Cumberland, blind-folded, then set out in search of the pin. By a thin wire he attached his wrist to that of Mr. Black. At the greenhouse at the foot of the embankment, near Waverly bridge, Mr. Cumberland found the pin pushed into the earth just inside a little wicket-gate. From the moment Mr. Cumberland left the hotel in his search for the pin till his return, only twelve minutes elapsed. Every possible precaution had been taken to preclude the possibility of collusion between Mr. Cumberland and any one else. Mr. Black and the committee pretended to hide the pin in four different places before they actually secreted it; and in this way they drew the attention of onlookers from the actual spot in which the pin was placed. A similar instance took place in Boston recently. Washington Irving Bishop proposed to find a scarf-pin that had been hidden within half a mile of the Vendome Hotel. He left the hotel accompanied by three gentlemen, to whom he was attached by means of twelve or fifteen feet of copper-wire, the thickness of a shoe-lace, which passed from wrist to wrist. This wire, Mr. Bishop had explained, was not supposed to serve as a conductor of thought or magnetic power, but simply as an aid to concentrate the thoughts of the party upon the details of the task they had undertaken. Mr. Bishop and his escort clambered into a carriage, and, taking the reins, the former drove off at a trot. With his head enveloped in a black sack or bag, and with the hand of one companion against the back of his head, and the hand of another now at his forehead, and again above and below the wrists, Mr. Bishop drove through Commonwealth Avenue to Exeter, Marlboro, Gloucester, and Beacon Streets, making two sharp turns, and now and then retracing his route. Suddenly he pulled up his horses on Exeter Street, midway between Marlboro and Beacon Streets, remarking that he knew he was near the spot where the pin was hidden. He dismounted, and led the way to the corner of Marlboro Street, turned to the west, hastened along the sidewalk, and ran up the steps of No. 225 Marlboro Street. He pulled the bell and the party was admitted; Mr. Bishop led the way up the stairs to the parlor on the second floor, and hurried to the fire-place. Stooping, he searched among a pile of shavings, and held up the scarf-pin. It was afterward told that, though the route taken by Mr. Bishop was not exactly that pursued by the committee, the general direction was the same, and that Mr. Bishop had once during the journey driven past the house where the pin was concealed. He, however, soon checked his horses and retraced his steps. Another instance by Mr. Cumberland was closely allied to the phenomenon called Planchette. The Prince of Wales undertook to think of an animal which Mr. Cumberland should endeavor to describe. "I am no artist," said the Prince, "but I will try to do my best to think in the way in which the animal should be drawn." Mr. Cumberland thereupon took the Prince by the hand, and in a few minutes drew upon a piece of paper a rough outline of an elephant, which, it turned out, was the animal that was in the mind of the Prince.

As an example of the third form of mind-reading, which is the most interesting, there may be in the same room three persons, two agents so-called, and one percipient, or mind-reader. The reader sits at a table blindfolded, the ears stopped, and all ordinary means of communication with the agents cut off. The agents then go out, one of them draws a figure of some sort and shows it to the other, the latter fixes the picture in his mind, then, closing his eyes (for concentration), he is led back into the room in which the percipient is seated, but at a distance from him. The agent who has the figure vividly in his mind so impresses the percipient or the percipient so penetrates the mind of the agent, that he (the percipient) draws what he sees with his mind's eye, and often the reproductions are remarkable for accuracy. If the agent forgets certain portions of a figure, or carries a wrong impression, the percipient of course leaves out the portions so forgotten or reproduces the wrong impression. This shows that what is in the agent's mind is read, and what is not there is not read. On one occasion one of the agents drew a ludicrous human figure. The other agent, after looking at it intently, went away forgetting that the figure had eyes; therefore, the percipient reproduced the original figure without eyes. Both Mr. Bishop and Mr. Cumberland are able to give the dates of coins or the numbers on a bank-note if the dates or numbers have been previously examined and retained in the mind of any one who is present in the same room. Another instance is related where Mr. Bishop, blindfolded, seated himself at the piano with his back toward a black-board on which a well-known musician had been requested to write the title of some song or aria. The musician wrote: "Tenor song in the prison scene from 'Il Trovatore.'" Mr. Bishop then called the musician, took his hand, and, after placing it upon his (Bishop's) forehead, strove to strike the first note of the song. First one note came and then another, until he had caught the entire air.

The phenomena of the fourth form of mind-reading relate to the action of one mind upon another at a distance. It is related that a lady of New York was prostrated through grief at the danger of her mother, who was on an eastern-bound vessel, that was twenty-seven days overdue, from Japan to San Francisco. Suddenly all terror and uneasiness left the lady's mind. So sudden was the transition from fear to serenity that she noted the time. The next day a telegram came from her mother, giving the time of the arrival of the ship in port. The two moments—that of the cessation of the daughter's fear and of the arrival of the ship—were identical. There are many instances of this kind of presentiment, where two persons, distant from each other, have been simultaneously impressed with the same idea; as where two daughters are impelled to go to their mother in the belief that she is in distress. Such facts are of too frequent occurrence to require additional examples. The experience of every one will suggest instances in which dreams proved true. But due account should be taken of instances in which the dreams did not prove true. The latest experiments of the Society for Psychical Research include the successful transfer, with and without contact, of (a) visual impressions, actual and imagined, ascending up to complicated pictures; (b) impressions of pains under contact, and (c) impressions of tastes and smells under contact; (d) impressions of names and numbers, with and without contact; (e) willing without contact. Three of the experiments in tastes and pains are given below. The percipient (whose name is mentioned first in every experiment quoted) was isolated and blindfolded:

1. Miss Relph with Mr. H. As agent, citric acid.	"Acid makes the mouth feel rough and the teeth inside. Might be——." Nothing else said.
2. Miss Relph with Mr. G. Cloves.	"A sharp taste, but very pleasant." After a while: "Now it is becoming bitter." N. B.—The taste of cloves changes in the mouth.
3. Miss Relph with Mr. H. Coffee. The sample had no smell, being very old and the aroma all gone.	Miss Relph said, "Tastes rather like coffee."

At this point all the objects for taste were removed from the room; they had been placed behind a screen.

4. Miss Relph and Mr. H. Vinegar.	"Sour and nasty; it isn't vinegar, is it!" (Mr. H. remained silent some time, as if implying a negative.) "Is it some kind of sauce with vinegar in it?" (Another long pause.) "No, I can only taste vinegar."
5. Miss E. and Mr. G. Olive oil.	Nothing perceived.
6. Mr. G. then took Miss Relph's hand.	"Is it oil, like that in sardines?"
7. Miss E. and Mr. H. Mustard.	Described as something hot.
8. Back of neck pinched with scissors.	"Dull pricks back of neck."
9. Tumbler half full of cold water grasped in Mr. H's right hand.	"Is it something in the right hand?" (going through the action of grasping something upright). "A sort of cold feeling."
10. Water dropped in drops upon Mr. H's right hand.	Miss Relph said: "What are you doing with water? I feel some splashes on the left arm." (There were some splashes, and the experiment was abandoned.)
11. Nostrils tickled.	Could not say, but kept putting her hand to her nose as if feeling very uncomfortable.
12. Pricking with two pins between thumb and forefinger of right hand.	"I feel a pricking here," indicating the spot with precision.

The society has a record of 713 experiments. Of these, 318 were successful, 145 partially successful, 148 mis-descriptions, and 109 failures. In submitting this report, Mr. Malcolm Guthrie says: "I do not submit my summary as a basis for calculation of probability. A few successful experiments of a certain kind carry greater weight with them than a large number of another kind; for some experiments are practically beyond the region of guesses. I doubt, indeed, if any amount of calculation of probabilities will help to convince of the trustworthiness of the experiments. One successful evening when the conditions are strict is absolutely convincing; and the simple, genuine truthfulness of the percipients is a better guarantee than any amount of subsequent cross-examination as to the conditions of the trial. I have noticed a falling off in the facility and success of our experiments since our first great results were obtained. I do not know to what cause to attribute this declension. Personally, I find I am not equal to my former self in my power to give off impressions, and if I exert myself to do so I experience unpleasant effects in the head and nervous system. I therefore seldom join in the active experiments, but leave the thinking for the most part for others. Then we have lost one of our percipients; and, as the novelty and vivacity of our séances have departed, there is not the same geniality and freshness as at the outset. The thing has become monotonous, whereas it was formerly a succession of surprises. We have now nothing new to try. I do not know if there is loss of power on the part of the percipient; it is just as likely that the agents are in fault."

With such overwhelming testimony as to the resulting phenomena of thought-transference, there is little denial of their existence. The controversy arises over the media of the transfer. Whether a nervous energy acts by induction across space as well as along the nerve-fibers is a mooted question; although the analogies between electricity and nervous stimuli would readily lead to such an inference. Many of those who once scoffed at the whole subject have "remained to pray." Their answer to a demand for an explanation and a definition of thought-transference is the inquiry, "Can you explain or define life, light, electricity, magnetism, or any other of the forces?" And yet this unsolved problem is championed, or at least looked upon kindly, by Profs. Balfour Stewart, Henry Sidgwick, J. C. Adams, Mr. Gladstone, Mr. Ruskin, Lord Tennyson, Alfred Russel Wallace, and many other men of repute. On the other hand, Prof. Simon Newcomb, of Washington, Prof. G. Stanley Hall, of Johns Hopkins University, and Prof. Josiah Royce, of Harvard, all members of the American Society for Psychical Research, hold that there is no evidence in the reports of the English society, or anywhere else, that justifies a belief in the possibility of mind acting upon mind without the ordinary sense-perceptions. This opinion is based upon examination of the evidence reported by the English committee, and a careful and elaborate study of the conditions that surround the work of the psychic investigator. The late experiments of Mr. Bishop in Boston are also declared to be not a condition of true mind-reading, but of "muscle-reading," because the unconscious action of the muscles of the subject, when his mind is intensely fixed in a given direction, affords Mr. Bishop a clew by which he is able to interpret the former's thought. It is further and more comprehensively said on this side of the question, that thus far the phenomenon has been shown only in regard to unimportant physical objects; that the actual thoughts of another are not read; and that therefore the art, or whatever else it may be called, is of no more practical value than are kindred phenomena in the regions of mesmerism and spiritualism.

Psychical Research Societies.—The initial society of this name was founded in England under the presidency of Prof. H. Sidgwick, of Cambridge, "for the purpose of making an organized attempt to investigate that large group of debatable phenomena designated by such terms as mesmeric, psychical, and spiritualistic." Six committees were appointed to examine (1) the nature and extent of any influence which may be exerted by one mind upon another otherwise than through the recognized sensory channels; (2) hypnotism and mesmerism; (3) obscure relations between living organisms and electric and magnetic forces; (4) haunted houses and ghosts; (5) spiritualism; (6) for the collection of existing evidence in connection with these subjects, and especially in connection with apparitions at the moment of death, or otherwise. A special committee was appointed in 1885 to investigate the abnormal occurrences reported by the Theosophical Society. But these committees were afterward dissolved, and the experimental investigations and collection of evidence were left in the hands of individual members, the result of their inquiry to be embodied in papers and read before the society, and, if approved, to be published in the proceedings thereof. The society has thus published reports containing papers on telepathy, or thought-reading, in its various forms; on mesmerism, with records of valuable experiments; on apparitions of the dead, and haunted houses; on automatic writing, divining-rods, and other subjects. The society has 613 members, it has branches in Cambridge and Oxford, and it publishes a monthly journal. It also possesses a large and growing and valuable library of works, in various languages, on subjects cognate to those enumerated as topics for psychical research. Besides the regular reports of the society, there have been numerous articles contributed by individual members of the organization, notably by Edmund Gurney and Frederic W. H. Myers, to the "Nineteenth Century," the "Fortnightly Review," and other periodicals. These contributions cover a vast amount of ground, being in large part the correspondence and other information obtained by the society or its members on the subjects under consideration. Added to the voluminous collection of narratives of spectral appearances, cases of mind-reading, mesmerism, clairvoyance, etc., reported by the society, they probably include a larger collection of material of this character than was ever before brought together, not excepting Mrs. Crowe's "Night-side of Nature," and Robert Dale Owen's "Foot-falls on the Boundary of Another World." In fact, the society has mainly devoted itself to the collection of "evidences," while its deductions from these have been few and unsatisfactory. This modesty as to declarations of opinion, or the enunciation of any laws to account for the phenomena recorded, may, in a measure, be due to the prevailing skepticism on the subject, concerning which the society's committee on "thought-reading" had the following to say: "The present state of scientific opinion throughout the world is not only hostile to any belief in the possibility of transmitting a single mental concept except through the ordinary channels of sensation, but, generally speaking, it is hostile to any inquiry upon the matter." With a view, therefore, possibly, to creating a favorable public opinion, most of the result of the society's work has been the publication of the usual kind of ghost-stories and narratives of obsession and coincident phenomena of a psychic or seemingly supernatural character. These include "transferred impressions" and telepathy, phantasms of the living, as well as the dead, or spectral aura, the relations of mind and matter, etc. Concerning the difficulties under which the members of the society labor in their investigations, one of them writes as follows: "Such speculations as can now be framed with regard to these obscure phenomena, can hardly be said to differ from the earliest psychical conceptions of Thales and Heraclitus, except in the higher standard of scientific proof which we can now propose to ourselves as our ultimate goal. And the very existence of that standard constitutes a difficulty; the twilight which has, in every department of the endless domain of physics, preceded the illuminating dawn of day, is here made doubly dark and dubious by the advanced daylight of scientific conceptions from which we peer into it. In the second place, like natural history in its early stage, our inquiry is concerned with a variety of sensible phenomena, as such, with forms or sounds simply as they strike the senses of those who come across them; and the isolation of the phenomena, and the absence of any genuine classification, even of the most provisional kind, have a most distinct influence on their *prima-facie* credibility, as compared with the new phenomena of the older sciences, which have the advantage of falling at once under familiar classes."

From the English parent society the movement has spread. In this country there are the American Psychical Research Society, with headquarters in Boston, and branches in Philadelphia and New York, the Anthropological Society in Brooklyn, and the Western Psychical Research Society in Chicago. The founding of this latter society has resulted in the publication of a periodical entitled "Mind and Nature," in which the proceedings of the society are published, and which is otherwise filled with narratives, essays, and disquisitions having relation to psychic subjects. The American Society expressly declines to investigate the physical phenomena usually called "Spiritual," though these are included in the list of subjects covered by the English society. But it does not reject evidence concerning what is known as the "faith-cure."

MINNESOTA. State Government.—The following were the State officers during the year: Governor, Andrew R. McGill, Republican; Lieutenant-Governor, Albert E. Rice; Secretary of State, Hans Mattson; Auditor, W. W. Braden; Treasurer, Joseph Bobleter; Attorney-General, Moses E. Clapp; Superintendent of Public Instruction, D. L. Kiehle; Railroad and Warehouse Commissioners, Horace Austin, John L. Gibbs, and George L. Becker; Chief-Justice of the Supreme Court, James Gilfillan; Associate Justices, John M. Berry, D. A. Dickenson, William Mitchell, and Charles E. Vanderburgh.

Legislative Session.—The Legislature sat from January 4 till March 4. It surpassed in industry all of its predecessors by passing 265 general laws, 399 special laws, and 15 joint resolutions, a total of 679 measures. The choice of a successor to United States Senator S. J. R. McMillan fell upon Ex-Gov. Cushman K. Davis, the Republican nominee. He received 108 votes to 47 for Michael Doran and Ara Barton, the former being the Democratic candidate. Two important subjects of legislation were the sale of liquors and the regulation of railroads. In relation to the former, a system of high license was adopted for those places that do not prohibit liquor-selling under the local-option law. The annual license-fee in cities of 10,000 inhabitants or over was fixed at $1,000, and for other places at half that sum. Liquor-dealers were also required to give a bond for the faithful observance of all liquor laws, and severe penalties were imposed upon unlicensed traffic and upon attempted evasions of the statutes. The payment of a United States revenue-tax is made *prima-facie* evidence of unlicensed selling.

The railroad legislation consisted of a repeal of the railroad commission law and the adoption of a new act embodying many of the features of the old one and adding provisions to prevent rebates and pooling, requiring charges to be equal and reasonable, that facilities shall be ample, that no hindrances to through transportation shall be made, and no undue discrimination for longer or shorter hauls. Other acts were passed requiring all railroads not subject to special-tax laws to pay a percentage of their gross earnings in lieu of taxes; forbidding the sale of watered stock; making companies liable for the negligence of their servants in injuring other servants of the same company; requiring them to build and keep in repair sufficient crossings over their lines; compelling them to transport car-loads of mixed stock without charging a higher rate than for car-loads of any one kind of stock; regulating the heating of passenger-cars; and providing that lands granted to railroads and exempted from taxation shall become liable to assessment as soon as any transfer has been made by the original company.

Contract labor by convicts of the State or any municipality is forbidden after the expiration of existing contracts. It is provided that they shall be employed by the State or municipality, under the direction of the prison authorities, in some form of labor that will avoid competition with the free labor of the State.

The election law was revised by incorporating many features of the New York statute which tend to facilitate the process of voting and of ascertaining the result. No election district is to contain more than 400 voters, and separate ballots and ballot-boxes are required for different classes of officers. Another new provision establishes more stringent rules concerning registration in cities.

The following unique enactment is also found: " Whenever the defendant in any action of garnishment in this State shall make it appear that the sum of money which has been garnished was earned by him or her, as a laboring man or woman, by the actual work of his or her hands, and shall make it appear that the said money is actually necessary to his or her support, it shall be the duty of the court to order the discharge of the garnishment."

Provision was made to re-locate the State Reform School, to create and establish a State Reformatory at St. Cloud, and to create and establish a Soldiers' Home, afterward located at Minnehaha Falls. The sum of $60,000 was appropriated for a new building at the Moorhead Normal School, and $62,500 for additional buildings, land, and improvements at the State Institute for Deaf, Dumb, and Blind.

Honorably discharged soldiers are to be given the preference for public employment over all candidates.

A tax-levy of $800,000 in 1888, and $825,000 in 1889, for State purposes, is provided. The total appropriations for 1887 were $214,405; for 1888, $1,164,315; for 1889, $984,740, to which should be added deficiency bills amounting to $79,630, and miscellaneous appropriations to the amount of $185,892, making an aggregate of $2,628,982. The following are the sums granted for the regular annual expenses of the State institutions:

INSTITUTIONS.	1888.	1889.
State public schools	47,000	50,000
Deaf, dumb, and blind	90,000	95,000
Mankato Normal School	5,500	5,500
Reformatory, St. Cloud	50,000	50,000
Reform School	42,000	42,000
Hospitals for insane, first and second	294,340	344,340
Third hospital for insane	95,000	95,000
State prison	78,000	75,000
Moorhead Normal School	5,000	5,000
University	40,000	40,000
St. Cloud Normal School	5,500	5,500
Winona Normal School	10,000	5,000

Other acts of the session were as follow:

To appoint a State Board of Medical Examiners, who shall examine and license all practitioners of medicine, and to punish all persons practicing without such license.

To provide for the collection of vital statistics, establishing a Bureau of Labor Statistics, and appropriating money for the maintenance thereof.

To provide for the establishment of public-school libraries, and appropriating money to assist the various school districts in the purchase of such.

Requiring instruction in the public schools in physiology and hygiene, with special reference to the effect of stimulants and narcotics on the human system.

Exempting from taxation property of agricultural societies and expositions.

For the relief of persons whose lands have been or may be sold for alleged delinquent taxes, in cases where such taxes have been or may be paid prior to such sale.

To legalize corporations that have filed articles of incorporation and transacted business under a corporate name, but whose proceedings to secure incorporation were, for any reason, defective.

To authorize the consolidation of religious corporations.

Closing barber-shops upon Sunday.

Regulating and confirming the formation of real-estate title-insurance companies.

Providing a penalty to be imposed upon insurance companies that do business without license from the Insurance Commissioner, and authorizing him to sue for and collect such penalties.

To provide for the taxation of telephone companies.

To provide for the taxation of telegraph companies.

To prevent deception in the sale of dairy products, and creating a State Dairy Commissioner to enforce the law.

To secure the better preservation of game.

To encourage the raising and propagation of trout, and to protect streams, ponds, and waters used for that purpose.

To provide a bounty for the destruction of gophers and blackbirds. [Three to five cents for each gopher, and five to ten cents a dozen for blackbirds.]

Providing for a revision and codification of the probate laws of the State.

To establish at the State School Farm an experimental fruit, forest, and ornamental-tree station.

To provide for the compiling, revising, and digesting of the tax-laws of the State.

To exclude minors from court-rooms when trials of an obscene character are being conducted.

To abolish the State Board of Immigration.

To provide for the establishment of permanent funds for the care, maintenance, and improvement of cemeteries.

Giving labor the right of a first lien, and material furnished a second lien, on all property.

To provide for the prosecution, at the expense of the State, of cases in behalf of settlers upon "indemnity lands" in the State.

Requiring landlords and proprietors of eating-establishments using oleomargarine, or any substitute for butter, to print a notice of such fact upon the bill of fare, or to post such notice in their establishments.

To provide necessary crossings for the passage of farm-stock, and for drains over or under railroad-tracks.

To compel employers of females to furnish suitable seats for such employés.

Forbidding the mortgaging of crops before the seed shall have been sown or planted.

To reorganize the State Agricultural Society, and to confer police powers upon the board.

Appropriating $40,000 for the purpose of furnishing seed-grain for distribution in those counties of the State where the crop was destroyed by hail in 1886, and giving the State a lien on the crops of persons so aided till it shall be repaid.

To prevent the practice of fraud by tree-planters and commission-men in the sale of nursery stock.

To prevent contractors of prison labor in the State from manufacturing articles in competition with custom-work done by artisan labor.

To punish false pretenses in obtaining certificates of registration for cattle and other animals, and giving false information concerning them.

Providing that duly authorized surety companies

may be accepted as sufficient sureties on official or other bonds.

To restrict the ownership of real estate in the State to American citizens and those who have lawfully declared their intention to become such, and to limit the quantity of land that corporations may hold or own.

Providing that women shall retain the same legal existence and personality after as before marriage, and sue or be sued in their own names, and possess the same legal rights as their husbands.

Appropriating $40,000 additional for the relief of farmers whose crops were lost in 1886 by hail.

To provide for temporary loans to pay appropriations from the revenue.

To extend the work of the geological and natural-history survey of the State.

To incorporate the city of South St. Paul.

To establish a municipal government for the city of Duluth.

Amending the law of standard weights and measures.

To enable the owners of lands to drain and reclaim them, when the same can not be done without affecting the lands of others, by providing that the county commissioners, upon petition, may order a hearing of parties interested, and, if deemed advisable, may construct said drain and assess the cost upon the properties benefited thereby.

To provide for the formation and organization of county drainage-districts for the drainage of large tracts of wet and overflowed lands.

Enabling the supervisors of towns to construct ditches for drainage purposes.

The following amendments to the Constitution were proposed to be voted upon in 1888:

First. Amending Article IV, by adding the following: Any combination of persons, either as individuals or members or officers of any corporation, to monopolize the markets for food-products in this State, or to interfere with or restrict such markets, is hereby declared to be a criminal conspiracy, and shall be punished in such manner as the Legislature may provide.

Second. Amending section 12 of Article I, relating to exemption, by adding the following proviso: Provided, however, that all property so exempted shall be liable to seizure and sale for any debts incurred to any person for work done or materials furnished in the construction, repair, or improvement of the same; and provided further that such liability to seizure and sale shall extend to all real property for any debt incurred to any laborer or servant for labor or service performed.

Third. Amending section 1 of Article IV so as to increase the length of biennial sessions of the Legislature from sixty to ninety days, and forbidding the introduction of new bills, except in special cases, during the last twenty days of the session.

High License.—The new high-license law went into effect on July 1 throughout the State, but, in those places where the licenses previously granted do not expire till January, 1888, its operation can not yet be fully ascertained. Returns received in September from a majority of the license cities and towns, however, indicate the general result of the change. It appears that in these places one third of the saloons have closed their business, while the revenue derived from the remainder is 50 per cent. greater than the total revenue under the former law. Of 1,650 saloons that flourished under the old license, 550 have been unable to meet the advance. In Minneapolis the saloons have decreased from 334 to 227, though the change there was from a $500 to a $1,000 li-

cense; in Duluth from 113 to 64; in Stillwater from 42 to 32; and in Winona from 93 to 28.

Education.—The number of school-children enrolled this year in the public schools was 243,573, against 232,721 in 1885. The total disbursements for school purposes were $4,565,-395, being an increase of $452,832 over last year, and $1,020,468 over 1885. This increase is due to a greater population, increased number of districts, and higher salaries paid teachers in consequence of a larger average school year. The following items of expenditure are included in the total disbursements:

Teachers' wages...............................	$1,772,485
Wood and school supplies	235,029
Repairs and improving grounds.....	145,696
New school houses and sites	529,059
Bonds and interest ....,................	434,583

Railroads.—Nine lines of railroad were in course of construction during the year, and 196 miles were completed.

Crops.—The following table, compiled from official reports to the Secretary of State, presents the acreage and yield of grain in the State for 1886 and 1887:

GRAINS.	Acres in 1886.	Bushels in 1886.	Acres in 1887.	Bushels in 1887.
Wheat...........	2,949,870	46,795,474	3,046,000	38,085,000
Corn	557,606	17,589,657	631,263	20,208,616
Oats	1,127,390	35,575,135	1,273,000	39,631,000
Barley...........	308,312	6,783,774	374,143	8,305,974
Flax.............	204,147	1,508,772	177,000	1,300,009

In addition to these staples, there were produced this year 468,724 bushels of rye upon 27,572 acres, and 70,632 bushels of buckwheat upon 5,232 acres. The flour-product of the State was as follows: Minneapolis Mills, 6,209,-980 barrels; all other places in the State, 3,500,-000; total, 9,709,980. The wool-clip amounted to 1,460,672 pounds, from 290,196 sheep. Other products were: potatoes, 7,539,332 bushels; beans, 95,500 bushels; sugar, 3,664 pounds.

Iron.—The disclosures of the past few years in St. Louis County place Minnesota among the metal-producing States, but no coal has been found in convenient proximity to the rich iron deposits in the northeastern part of the State, and a great iron-manufacturing industry will be delayed until a substitute is found in natural gas or petroleum or other substance. The Minnesota iron region has not been fully explored. During this year the Minnesota Iron Company mined over 430,000 tons of ore in this region, and shipped 371,642 tons. The increase of business is indicated by the fact that in 1884 its shipments were 62,124 tons; in 1885, 225,484 tons; in 1886, 305,954 tons. The aggregate of shipments of iron-ore from the entire Lake Superior region during this season was over 4,100,000 tons, an increase of 1,000,-000 tons over the aggregate of last year.

Lumber.—The lumber-cut does not equal that of last year by about 200,000,000 feet. Returns from the various lumber districts are as follow:

DISTRICT.	Feet cut.	DISTRICT.	Feet cut.
Minneapolis	230,000,000	Mission Creek	12,000,000
St. Cloud	4,000,000	St. Croix river	150,000,000
Brainerd	12,000,000	Crookston	15,000,000
Gull river	22,000,000	Duluth	25,000,000
Northern Pacific Junction	15,000,000	Total	540,000,000
Cloquet	50,000,000	Valuation, $12.	$6,460,000
Barnham	15,000,000		

The forest wealth of the State is being rapidly destroyed by this immense lumber production, and it is a question of only a few years when this business must be exhausted.

MISSISSIPPI. State Government.—The following were the State officers during the year: Governor, Robert Lowry, Democrat; Lieutenant-Governor, G. D. Shands; Secretary of State, George M. Govan; Auditor, W. W. Stone; Treasurer, W. L. Hemingway; Attorney-general, T. M. Miller; Superintendent of Public Instruction, J. R. Preston; Railroad Commissioners, William McWillie, J. F. Sessions, and J. O. Kyle; Chief-Justice of the Supreme Court, J. A. P. Campbell; Associate Justices, J. M. Arnold and Timothy E. Cooper.

Industrial Condition.—By the census of 1860, Mississippi was shown to be the thirteenth State in the value of her lands, and the eighth state in *per-capita* wealth. In 1870 she had retrograded to be the twenty-sixth State in aggregate wealth; the forty-first State in *per-capita* wealth; and, in 1880, being then the eighteenth State in population, she had retrograded to be only the forty-sixth in *per-capita* wealth, only one of the Territories being behind her in this respect.

The cause of this decline is found in the depression of the agricultural industry, which is practically the sole occupation of the people. The last census shows that of 415,506 persons engaged in gainful occupations, there were engaged in agricultural production and stock-raising 340,651, leaving only 74,955 for all other pursuits. In this occupation the people have not kept pace with modern improvements and methods.

Finances.—The total debt of the State on January 1 was $3,638,057, and on September 1 $3,527,012. The greater part of this debt is "non-payable," consisting of funds that bear interest, but the principal of which need not be paid. These funds and their amount are as follows:

FUNDS.	Jan. 1, 1887.	Sept. 1, 1887.
Chickasaw school fund	$817,360 47	$818,319 12
Common-school fund	817,646 46	817,646 46
Seminary fund, University of Mississippi	544,641 23	544,061 23
Agricultural College bonds	227,150 00	227,150 00
Total	$2,406,918 36	$2,407,176 69

Deducting these amounts, the payable debt on January 1 was $1,231,839, and on September 1, $1,119,835.

The Legislature of 1882 reduced the State tax from 8 to 2½ mills, and so it remained for four years, from 1882 to 1886, making a difference of $50,000 per annum, an aggregate of

$200,000. In addition to this the same Legislature increased the common-school fund $100,000 per annum, while the requirements of the various State institutions have necessitated increasing appropriations for their support. A deficit each year has been the result. The Governor suggests several remedies. He urges a reduction of the interest payable on the Chickasaw school fund. Although a "non-payable" debt, it bears 8 per cent. interest, drawing $65.329 annually from the treasury. A reduction to the rate now prevailing for loans of the State would save $25,000 annually in interest. He also urges the passage of some measure to provide for the collection of delinquent poll-taxes. From $80,000 to $100,000 are lost to the State annually by the inefficiency of the present law, a sum in itself nearly sufficient to wipe out the annual deficiency. He recommends a law making non-payment of this tax a misdemeanor, and the submission to the people of a constitutional amendment making its payment a condition to the right of suffrage. Two other reforms are suggested, relating to the assessment of taxes and to the practice in the State circuit courts. On the former subject the Governor says: "It would be difficult to find a well-informed man in the commonwealth who would hazard his reputation by saying that the wealth of the State is assessed at over one third its value. Upon the present assessment of $128,000,000, less State-tax is levied than almost any Southern, and most of the Northern States." On the latter subject he says: "A large part of the county expenses constitute what is known as the 'Judiciary,' the principal sum of which is fees of witnesses in criminal prosecutions in the circuit courts. Misdemeanors of almost every description find their way to the grand-jury room, become the subjects of indictment, and thereafter for prosecution and trial before a petit jury. The judge, juries, witnesses, and all others having business at court, are detained until the case is concluded, and if it results in a conviction, not unfrequently a fine of one dollar and costs is imposed. The cost bill averages from eighteen to forty dollars, and the State gets one dollar. While the Constitution confers on circuit courts original jurisdiction in all criminal cases, it also provides in section 31, Article I, that the Legislature in cases of misdemeanors may dispense with the inquest of a grand jury and authorize prosecutions before a justice of the peace, or other inferior courts of its creation. Then it may be safely said that, with few exceptions, every misdemeanor could be tried before a justice of the peace, thus saving the counties an immense sum of money. It must be remembered that there are 158 circuit courts held in the State annually, and if they can be relieved of the trial of petty misdemeanors, the cost of holding them will be lessened one half and probably more, thereby reducing the expenses not less than $100,000 or $150,000."

Education.—The average term of the free schools was six days longer in 1887 than in 1885, an increase of nearly 8 per cent. in time, while the total amount expended was $841,-697, being about $1,000 less than in 1885. The total amount collected for free-school purposes for the year 1887 was $967,644, an increase of $100,000 above the collections for 1885.

The expenditures were $126,000 less than the receipts. The laws of 1886 have produced some radical changes in the public-school system. In many counties a gradual disintegration was creeping in, arising from the establishment of many small schools, and to check the disastrous effects of this evil a system of districting the counties was ingrafted on the law, limiting the number of schools by a fixed territorial area and a minimum scholastic population for each district. More than five hundred small schools were discontinued, and the reports from all counties except seventeen show that enough, and in some instances more than enough, schools are now maintained, and in those seventeen counties the superintendents report that all children can be accommodated by establishing a few more districts. To improve the corps of teachers, uniform examinations and institutes were established. Many abuses and inequalities arose under the old salary system based on the per-diem average attendance. The law now bases the salary on the qualifications of the teacher and the kind of work he is capable of doing, and for each grade a maximum and minimum limit is fixed.

The attendance of the State university for the year reaches nearly 250 students, as against 185 for the preceding year. The disbursements for its support amount to $33,791. The Agricultural and Mechanical College, established in 1880, reports an attendance of 260 up to the end of the year. Between two hundred and three hundred applicants were refused admission during the year, on account of the limited size of the dormitory, which is designed to accommodate only 200 students.

The State is in advance of its sister States in providing instruction in agriculture and the mechanical arts for its colored population. At the Alcorn Agricultural and Mechanical College, instruction was given to 209 colored students during the school year 1886–'87, and the institution is reported to be prosperous.

At Tugaloo University additional school and industrial buildings have been erected, thus making all the appointments of the institution excellent and commodious. The university is indebted to the generosity of a private gentleman for the funds necessary for these buildings. The labor of erecting them was performed by the students under the direction of the superintendent of industries. The State Normal School, at Holly Springs, reorganized in 1886 and placed in charge of the State Superintendent of Instruction, reports 107 students matriculated since that time, and the prospect of renewed usefulness for this institu-

tion. The industrial institute and college at Columbus, for the education of white girls, also a beneficiary of the State, has a large attendance, which is limited only by the capacity of the institution.

Insane.—At the Insane Asylum at Jackson the daily average number of patients for the year was 446, or 12 less than in 1886. The appropriation of $60,000 for its annual support was entirely expended. This asylum was established and opened for patients in 1855, and has been enlarged from time to time till its comfortable capacity is 375 patients.

The East Mississippi Insane Asylum, opened for the first time in 1885, has treated 405 patients during the past two years, of whom 234 remained at the close of 1887. The disbursement during the year for support, salaries, and repairs was $80,840.

Penitentiary.—The number of State convicts was 747 in February, a slight decrease from last year. Of these, 189 are employed in and about the State Penitentiary, while the remainder are engaged in railroad and levee construction. They are all leased for a term of years to the Gulf and Ship Island Railroad Company, the State receiving an annual income from their labor. The State superintendent, who is detailed to examine their treatment by the lessees and to correct abuses, reports their general condition to be satisfactory, and that complaints of severe punishment are decreasing. He suggests that a reward should be offered for good behavior by reducing the term of confinement for meritorious convicts, and that a prison hospital be established for the confinement of those who are physically unable to work. The State at present does practically nothing for the reformation of its prisoners, but contents itself with punishing them at the least possible expense to itself. No convicts are now employed on farms or in any mechanical work that would bring them into competition with other occupations. The law of the last Legislature requires their employment on public works or works of internal improvement. The same law provides for the election by the Legislature of a Board of Control to see that the laws relating to convicts are properly enforced.

Levees.—The completion and successful maintenance of the levees on the Mississippi riverfront, from the northern line of the State to Vicksburg, is now fully protecting the Delta from overflow, and has given a great impetus to the settlement and improvement of the districts. Much land is being brought into cultivation, and large tracts, heretofore held without a purchaser, are now eagerly sought after.

State Claims.—The Supreme Court of the United States rendered a decision this year by which a considerable claim of the State arising from the sale of public lands was adjudged valid and payable. Under two acts of Congress of different dates, Mississippi was entitled to five per cent. of the net proceeds of the sale of public lands of the United States, situated in the State. The accumulation of this fund was something over $40,000. This sum was withheld by the General Government, and it was claimed that it should be applied as a credit on what is known as "the war tax of 1861," the apportionment to Mississippi being $413,084. The court refused to permit this set-off.

Political.—At an election held November 6, members of the Legislature of 1888 and the various county officers were chosen. A light vote was cast, there being generally no opposition to the Democratic ticket. The Legislature will be almost solidly Democratic.

MISSOURI. State Government.—The following were the State officers during the year: Governor, John S. Marmaduke, Democrat, who died December 28, and was succeeded by the Lieutenant-Governor, Albert G. Morehouse; Secretary of State, Michael K. McGrath; Treasurer, James M. Siebert; Auditor, John Walker; Attorney-General, D. G. Boone; Superintendent of Public Schools, William E. Coleman; Railroad Commissioners, John B. Breathitt, James Harding, and William G. Downing; Chief-Justice of the Supreme Court, Elijah H. Norton; Associate Justices, Thomas A. Sherwood, Robert D. Ray, Francis M. Black, and Theodore Brace.

Legislative Session.—The regular biennial session of the Legislature began on January 5 and adjourned on March 21. United States Senator Francis M. Cockrell was re-elected for a third term over William Warner, the Republican candidate. The vote in the Senate was: Cockrell, 25; Warner, 8—in the House: Cockrell, 86; Warner, 50; Nicholas Ford (Labor), 2. Two predominant topics of discussion during the session were the railroads and the liquor-traffic. Numerous bills upon these subjects were introduced, but the legislation secured was meager. On the question of regulating the railroads no agreement whatever was reached. The debate on the liquor question resulted in the adoption of a "local option" act, after a proposition to submit to the people a prohibitory constitutional amendment, passed by the House, had been defeated in the Senate. The "local option" act provides that an election to determine whether licenses shall be granted shall be held, on petition of one tenth of the voters of any incorporated town or city or of any county, outside of such town or city, provided such town, city, or county contains 2,500 voters. A second election shall not be held in less than four years thereafter. Another act repeals the law permitting the sale of wine and beer in St. Louis saloons on Sunday, and a third provides a penalty for physicians who write prescriptions of intoxicating liquors for other than strictly medicinal purposes. The road-and-highway act of 1883 was repealed, and a new one, revising and perfecting the former act, was adopted. Another important measure authorizes the incorporation

of mutual savings societies for the accumulation and investment of money, but without general trading or banking powers. The sum of $40,000 was appropriated for the construction and equipment of a State industrial home for girls, and $47,000 for the establishment of a State reform school for boys. The expenditure of $250,000 upon the State capitol was authorized. Provision was made for the payment of $2,500,000 of the State debt, by appropriating that sum out of the sinking fund. Other acts of the session were as follow:

To prevent the keeping of "opium-joints."

To prevent the granting or accepting of free passes or discount tickets by any State, judicial, county, or municipal officer, or by members of the Legislature.

Providing that all actions for recovery of dower shall be begun within ten years after the death of the husband.

To provide for the incorporation and regulation of associations, societies, or companies doing a life or casualty insurance business on the assessment plan.

Providing for the organization of levee districts by the owners of any contiguous body of land bordering on or situate near and subject to overflow by the rivers of the State.

For the promotion of medical science by the distribution of unclaimed human bodies for scientific use through a board created for that purpose.

Enacting a new mining law.

Repealing an act to establish a new State Penitentiary, enacted in 1885.

Authorizing county collectors to pay into the county treasury, pending litigation, moneys in their hands claimed by both the State and county or municipal townships.

Imposing a penalty on bridge, telegraph, and express companies for failure to make an annual statement of their property.

To provide for the collection of personal taxes.

To establish an academic department in connection with Lincoln Institute for the higher education of the negro race.

To prevent diseased stock of any kind from running at large.

To punish false pretenses in obtaining registration of cattle and other animals, and to punish giving false pedigrees.

Defining the duties of circuit and prosecuting attorneys and their assistants in courts having jurisdiction of criminal matters in cities of over 100,000 inhabitants, forbidding their employment in business other than that of the State, and forbidding their accepting, contracting, or bargaining for any fee or gift other than their salary, for any services rendered during their term of office.

Enacting a new law relative to the appointment of a State veterinary surgeon.

To provide for the consolidation of adjoining cities.

Restricting the power of incorporated cities and towns to grant franchises for using streets and alleys for elevated, underground, or other street-railways.

Creating a board of police commissioners, and authorizing the appointment of a permanent police force in cities of the second class.

Enacting a new law for the government of cities of the third class.

Providing for police judges in cities of the fourth class.

Declaring all contracts limiting the time in which suit may be brought null and void.

Making railroads responsible for damages caused by fires communicated from locomotives.

Prohibiting the officers and directors of railroads from furnishing supplies thereto.

Prohibiting the leasing or consolidation of parallel or competing lines of railroad.

Requiring railroads to furnish sufficient stock-cars, and to make no discriminations in rates or in facilities furnished to shippers.

Providing for the incorporation of mutual saving fund, loan, and building associations.

Providing for the appointment of a county counselor in counties containing 75,000 inhabitants or more, and prescribing their qualifications and duties.

Authorizing county courts to pay for bridges, court-houses, jails, and other public buildings contracted for them.

To authorize the funding of county indebtedness.

Punishing attempts to blackmail.

To prevent the use of any substitute for hops, or the pure extract of hops, in the manufacture of ale or beer.

To prevent gambling under the guise of trading in stocks, bonds, petroleum, cotton, grain, provisions, or other commodities, and defining "bucket-shops."

Authorizing the board of regents of Lincoln Institute to sell the institute farms, and to purchase adjoining land.

Providing a penalty for issuing a certificate to an applicant for teaching in the public schools without first examining such applicant.

Granting to the public schools, in townships where saloons may be situated, one third of the county revenue derived from saloon licenses.

To facilitate the collection of statistical data of the productive industries of the State.

To regulate appeals to the circuit court from township boards.

Fixing the weight of flour in barrels and sacks.

As the Legislature adjourned without solving the railroad problem, and also without making appropriations to meet deficiencies for the past two years, the Governor issued a call for an extra session to convene on May 11. The deficiency bill passed at this session appropriates about $150,000, of which $121,000 is required to pay the costs in criminal cases for 1885 and 1886. Several measures relating to railroads were adopted, the most important of which declares all railway lines in the State public highways, prohibits the giving of special rates, rebates, and drawbacks, or the charging of higher proportionate rates for small than for large quantities transported, prohibits discrimination in facilities granted for transportation or in rates for shorter and longer hauls, makes pooling unlawful, requires schedules of rates and fares to be printed and posted, prohibits willful interruption of continuous carriage, and empowers the railroad commissioners to enforce the various provisions of the act. Another law regulates the rights of shippers to build branch tracks from their manufactories or mines to any railroad, and to purchase cars for their own use, while a third relates to the use and protection of switches. The session adjourned on July 2, having passed nine acts.

Finances.—The following are the principal appropriations for ordinary State expenses for 1887 and 1888: for interest on the bonded debt, $1,060,000; for interest on the 6-per-cent. consols held in trust for the school fund, $849,080; interest on other indebtedness, $76,840; for the State asylum at Fulton, $89,-200; the asylum at St. Joseph, $90,200; the asylum at Nevada, $50,000; the asylum at St. Louis, $70,000; the Institution for the Deaf and Dumb, $94,500; the State School for the Blind, $46,000; the State University at Columbia, $65,300; the three State normal schools, $70,000; the Lincoln Institute, $18,000; the State Penitentiary, $140,000. One third of the State revenue is set apart for the support of the public schools.

Penitentiary.—The number of convicts in the State Penitentiary at the beginning of the year was 1,635, an increase of 97 in the past two years. The institution is greatly overcrowded, and the arrangements for classifying and separating the convicts are insufficient. The receipts from convict labor during the two years 1884–'86 were less than the ordinary expenditures by about $100,000. The sum of $110,000 has recently been expended for improvements.

Railroads.—The total railroad construction for the year was 554 miles on 16 different lines.

The Bald-Knobbers.—Efforts were made during the year to destroy the Bald-Knobber organization of Christian County and vicinity, and to bring the principal offenders to justice. The peculiar state of society that permits these night-riding bands of regulators to dispense their own rude law of vengeance, and to burn, whip, and kill in defiance of all authority, has long existed in the southwestern counties of the State, and has had its effect in preventing the development of that region. Ozark, Taney, Douglas, and Christian counties have especially suffered from these bands whose power has been so great as to draw into their number some of the most influential citizens, even judges and ministers of the Gospel being claimed as adherents. Early in March a murder of unusual atrocity by the Knobbers of Christian County led to the arrest of several suspected members of that organization, from whom a confession was obtained concerning the methods and acts of their confederates. Warrants were issued, and about seventy-five persons were brought to Ozark, the county-seat of Christian County, for trial. Indictments were here found against nearly all, the majority being charged with attending unlawful assemblies. Fines varying from $10 to $100 were imposed upon such as confessed their guilt in this regard, while those who were held for murder submitted to trial and were punished with more mercy than they had themselves shown toward their victims. This is said to have crushed out the Christian County organization.

Local Option.—Elections under the new local-option law were held during the autumn in more than half of the 115 counties of the State, and in 16 cities. Fifty of these elections resulted in favor of prohibition, and 28 against it. The total vote polled was 153,180, or about three fourths of the full vote, of which the prohibitionists cast 78,817, a majority of 5,510 against the saloons. The constitutionality of the act was called in question before the State Supreme Court in the case of the State vs. Pond et al., and a decision rendered in December in favor of its validity.

The court, Justice Sherwood dissenting, ruled that it was not a special law, and that it did not delegate legislative power to the people of each county, city, or town, and that it was not in its nature irrepealable.

St. Louis.—An election was held on April 5, to select members of the City Council and House of Delegates, in which the Republicans obtained a partial success. Five out of seven Councilmen were elected by them, and eleven out of twenty-eight members of the House of Delegates. One representative of the Socialist party was elected to the latter body.

MONTANA. Territorial Government.—The following were the Territorial officers during the year: Governor, Samuel T. Hauser, succeeded by Preston H. Leslie; Secretary, William B. Webb; Treasurer, Daniel H. Weston, succeeded by William G. Preuitt; Auditor, Joseph P. Woolman, succeeded by James Sullivan; Superintendent of Public Instruction, William W. Wylie, succeeded by Arthur C. Logan; Chief-Justice of the Supreme Court, Decius S. Wade, succeeded by N. W. McConnell; Associate Justices, Supreme Court, W. J. Galbraith, James H. McLeary, and Thomas C. Bach.

Legislative Session.—The fifteenth Territorial Legislature was in session from January 10 till March 10. It made a decided advance in liquor legislation by passing a local option act in addition to the usual license law. Another feature of the session was the revision of the revenue laws. The existing revenue acts were superseded by an entirely new law, creating a Territorial Board of Equalization and charging it with certain duties, the most important of which are, to assess for the Territory and counties all property belonging to railway corporations; to levy the tax for Territorial purposes upon all the property in the Territory; and, third, "to examine and compare the returns of the assessment of the property in the several counties of the Territory, and to equalize the same, so that all the assessable property in the Territory shall be assessed at its true and full value."

Much discussion was had over the proposed repeal of the so-called "gag laws," which punished as a felony any interference with a contractor, mechanic, or laborer in the performance of any lawful contract or labor, and any interference with individuals or corporations in the control of their business, or in the management of their employés, or in their contracts with them. Attempts and conspiracies to accomplish such interference were also punishable as severely as the crime itself. A proposition to abolish these enactments was voted down, but the sections relating to attempts and conspiracies were repealed, while the rigorous provisions of the other sections were materially softened. Two important measures, providing for the registration of voters and establishing a Territorial asylum for the insane, failed of adoption. Among the acts of the session not above mentioned, are the following:

Creating the county of Park.

Providing for the punishment of persons who bring into the Territory property stolen in another State, Territory, or country, and the punishment of any receiver of such stolen property, and every aider and abettor of a thief bringing in such stolen property.

Providing for a Territorial board of arbitration of three persons to be appointed by the Governor and confirmed by the Council, to settle differences between employers and employés.

Providing for the encouragement of tree-planting and arboriculture by exempting from taxation to a certain amount those who plant fruit and forest trees by the acre, and those who plant and maintain lines of forest-trees along public highways.

Increasing the salaries of Territorial Auditor and Treasurer to $2,500 per annum, and their bonds respectively to $20,000 and $150,000.

Authorizing district courts to change the names of persons, cities, towns, villages, and counties, upon proper application and proof of the desirability of change.

Providing who may and may not adopt children.

Authorizing the Governor and Superintendent of Public Instruction to maintain in schools at the expense of the Territory, for a longer time than has heretofore been allowed by law, any deaf-mutes or blind children who may show unusual ability or great desire to continue their studies, and who might thereby become self-supporting or capable of teaching.

To declare and protect the legal and personal identity of married women.

Providing for municipal incorporations; permitting incorporation as cities of the first class, cities of the second class, and towns; permitting cities and towns already incorporated to incorporate under this law, and permitting incorporated cities and towns to disincorporate.

Authorizing the Governor to restore the rights of citizenship to discharged convicts.

To protect the wages of wage-workers, making wages a first lien on property on which work is done, in cases of assignment, attachment, or death of owner, except in case of liens filed sixty days prior to assignment, attachment, or death.

Amending the fence-law, by taking away that part of the old law making it a misdemeanor to have a barb-wire fence without a pole on top, and making owners of such fences responsible by civil action for any damages to stock.

Prohibiting the circulation of obscene literature through the mails.

Repealing that section of the revised statutes which limits ownership of land by corporations to 640 acres.

Permitting foreign railroad corporations to build into the Territory without organizing under Territorial laws, permitting the consolidation of railroad lines in this Territory under one management and other matters.

Prohibiting the establishing of any saloon or other place for the sale of intoxicating liquors within two miles of any railroad in course of construction or on which track is being laid.

To prevent the sale of intoxicants in variety theatres and in any place where women or minors are employed, or allowed to congregate.

To provide for the registration of voters in incorporated cities and towns.

Amending the law providing bounties for killing certain wild animals.

Providing for the incorporation of private banks under Territorial control.

Punishing persons for employing children under certain ages in certain branches of business.

To punish the making of fraudulent pedigrees of live-stock.

Authorizing county commissioners to build jails.

Raising the age of consent in females from ten to fifteen years.

Amending the school law by providing that the district clerks shall be appointed by the board of trustees instead of elected by the people; that any moneys in the general fund to the credit of any district, after providing for eight months' school, may, on vote of the district, be applied to building purposes; that appointments by county superintendents to fill vacancies shall henceforth only hold until the next annual school election.

To prevent contagious diseases among sheep.

Requiring the use of safety cages and iron bonnets thereon in all mining-shafts of the depth of 300 feet or over.

Making cheating a felony.

Authorizing the county commissioners to issue bonds to redeem outstanding indebtedness.

Regulating the sale of poisonous drugs.

Relieving litigants in civil cases in district courts from the payment of jurors' fees.

Authorizing the commissioners of Lewis and Clarke County to issue $40,000 additional bonds to complete a county court-house.

Preventing diseased animals from running at large on the ranges.

A part of the legislation of this session proved to be so carelessly framed that Gov. Leslie summoned an extra session. Amendments were needed to the revenue law, which had been so drawn that, while all former revenue acts were repealed, the new law could not take effect till the office of attorney-general for the Territory had been created, such an officer being designated as one of the members of the Territorial Board of Equalization therein established. Deprived of a revenue law in this way, and consequently of all means of levying taxes, the Territory at the same time found itself threatened with bankruptcy from another cause. The bounty law, as amended by the legislators of this year, after reducing the bounties formerly fixed, increased the list of bounty animals by offering ten cents for each prairie-dog killed, and five cents for each ground-squirrel. The result was that, while the Territory had previously been paying from $11,000 to $13,000 a year for bounties, it had expended, between January and September of this year, for that purpose, over $48,000, of which over $41,000 was for prairie-dogs and ground-squirrels. "Already, and for several weeks past," says the Governor in his message, "every dollar in the treasury has been paid out, and the Territory is now going in debt every day for killing squirrels, prairie-dogs, wolves, etc., and interest is accumulating upon that indebtedness." At the same time loopholes had been discovered in the license laws, and, as by one act the Legislature had made gambling a felony, and by another provided that it shall be licensed, the attitude of the law-making power upon this subject was not entirely clear. The session continued from August 29 till September 14, and resulted in the entire repeal of the bounty laws, and in the passage of an act creating the office of attorney-general, but nothing was done with the license laws. Other acts were as follow:

Defining the qualifications of voters in cities.

Defining a disturbance of the peace.

To punish interference with railroad-tracks.

To create Cascade County.

Providing for the observance of Arbor Day.

To create a school text-book commission.

Amending the revenue law.

Enabling cities having a valuation of $1,200,000 or over, to incur indebtedness for public improvements to the extent of two per cent. of their valuation.

Population.—The increase of population for this year is placed at 10,000, making the total number of people in the Territory about 130,-000. These are gathered from all quarters of the world, and represent nearly every race and people. The year has witnessed the foundation and growth of many prosperous towns in all parts of the Territory. Increased railroad facilities, which have been recently established, will insure even more rapid development in the next few years.

Finances.—The following statement shows the condition of the treasury at the beginning of the year, and its operations during the last biennial period:

Receipts for the two years ending Dec. 31, 1886. $334,132 61
Balance Jan. 1, 1885............................. 5,237 59

Total $339,370 20
Disbursements for two years ending Dec. 31, 1886................................. 282,101 02

Balance Jan. 1, 1887............................. $57,269 18

The receipts were from the following sources:

Licenses and property-tax $325,889 97
Insurance fees 2,800 00
Fees for recording marks and brands............. 2,065 00
Fees for notaries' commissions, etc............. 874 64

Total $334,132 61

The disbursements were as follow:

Criminal expenses $121,061 19
Insane 86,741 96
Bounty for killing animals...................... 25,439 00
Salaries and other expenses..................... 46,858 93

Total $282,101 02

Warrants outstanding amount to $2,057 00

There is no bonded indebtedness.

Education.—The public schools are supported by direct county and district taxes, and penal fines for violation of Territorial laws. County taxes can not be less than three mills nor more than five mills per dollar on the valuation of all taxable property, but districts may vote additional taxes for building, apparatus, and salaries of teachers. The amount of school-money raised by direct taxation during the last year was $223,871, and from fines in various courts $6,466, making for the public schools $230,337. The number of school-children increased during the past year from 16,626 to 20,193, and twenty-three new districts were organized. But the amount raised for the support of schools did not keep pace with the increase of districts or of pupils, the increase being only $12,461. Still there were forty more teachers employed, and the average length of school in days was increased by ten, and twenty-three new school-houses were erected. The aggregate value of school-buildings is $437,588.

Mining.—This industry continues to be the leading occupation. The product of gold, silver, copper, and lead for 1887 is placed at $26,-000,000. For many years the efforts of miners were directed almost exclusively to the working of the gold and silver only. But additional facilities of transportation have enabled these men to work extensive mines of copper and lead, which are combined with the more valuable precious metals, principally silver. Out of ten different States and Territories having dividend-paying mines, the total amount declared since January 1 was $5,111,894, of which Montana properties furnished nearly one fourth. No State or other Territory approaches Montana in this respect.

Since the completion of the Northern Pacific Railroad, mineral coal has become an important product of the Territory. Extensive beds near the line of that road have been successfully worked. It is now known that beds of good bituminous coal and lignite underlie large areas in nearly every county in the Territory.

Agriculture and Stock-Raising.—The season of 1887 was favorable for the production of all the staple crops. The average yield without irrigation was as high as 80 bushels for oats, 65 for wheat, 40 for corn, and 200 to 300 for potatoes; and there was also an abundant crop of small fruits. An increased rainfall and new canals, together with the severe losses of range-stock, have given a new impulse to regular farming in the Territory.

Prior to the severe winter of 1886–'87, the stock-raising industry was in a flourishing condition. The great losses of cattle then suffered, estimated to reach $25,000,000, were due to excessive cold and deep snows, added to a short grass-crop occasioned by a drought in the preceding summer. The estimated number of domestic animals in the Territory for the year is as follows: Cattle, 1,400,000; horses, 190,-000; sheep, 2,000,000.

Railroads.—During the year the St. Paul, Minneapolis, and Manitoba Railroad entered the Territory, and built upon its soil as far as Great Falls, on Missouri river, a distance of 404 miles of railroad; and the Montana Central has completed its road from Great Falls to Helena, the capital of the Territory, 102 miles, thus furnishing a continuing unbroken line of railroad from the capital of Montana, by way of Great Falls, Benton, Fort Buford, Devil's Lake, and to Saint Paul, a distance of over 1,150 miles. The Montana Central has under contract a continuation of its line of road from Helena to Butte City, about eighty miles, and will be finished in the early months of 1888. The Northern Pacific stretches from Saint Paul on Mississippi river, through the Territory, by way of Helena, to the Pacific waters on Puget Sound. During the year 626 miles of new railroad were built and put in operation.

Public Buildings.—The Territory of Montana has no public buildings. Each county has its court-house and county jail, and a home for the poor within its borders. The United States has built, and now owns and controls, a penitentiary within this Territory, and in that institution are confined the Territorial prisoners. Montana has no asylum for the insane and lunatic, or institutions of learning for the blind, the deaf and dumb, or the feeble-minded, or other eleemosynary institutions; but the legislation of her people has made ample and liberal provisions for the comfort, care, and treatment of all these classes of affliction upon the people.

Militia.—Twenty years ago a general Indian outbreak was threatened in the Territory, to prepare for which there was issued by the Governor, for the use of the militia, arms and ammunition to the value of $67,561, and the Territory thereby became indebted to the General Government in that sum. The yearly appropriation made to the Territory to arm and equip the militia, amounting annually to something less than $1,400, was credited by the ordnance officer to the account of such indebtedness, whereby it was reduced on the books of that office in February, 1887, at the end of twenty years, to $35,436. This balance was, under authority of the act of Congress approved Feb. 17, 1887, credited to the Territory, and the account closed. There are now in the Territory one regiment of infantry, comprising seven companies, and two companies of cavalry, "regularly enlisted, organized, and uniformed active militia," embracing, with the general staff, 473 officers and men.

MUSIC, PROGRESS OF. Belated reports that have appeared in musical periodicals show the following additional novelties in dramatic music brought out during the year 1885:

Operas: "Imilda," by Verhey (Rotterdam, January); "Baldassare," by Gasparo Villate (Madrid, February 18); "Der Trentajäger," by Victor Gluth (Munich, March 26); "Die Königin von Leon," by V. E. Becker (Würzburg); "Der Pomposaner," by Leythäuser (Nuremberg); "St. Johannisnacht," by Albert Eilers (Darmstadt); "Yvonne," by Ernest Lefèvre (Rheims); "Noah," by Halévy, finished by Bizet (Carlsruhe, April 5); "Marco Botzari," by Bonicioli (Valencia); "Il Rinnegato," by Manuel Giro (Barcelona, June 6); "Popelka" (Cinderella), by Rosny (Prague, Czechish Theatre, June); "Der Trompeter von Säkkingen," by Emil Kaiser (Reichenberg, October 31; New York, Thalia Theatre); "Cordelia," Russian opera by Solovieff, the libretto after Sardou's drama "La Haine" (St. Petersburg, November); "Der Schmied von Ruhla," by Lux (Augsburg, November 12); "Frauenlob," by Robert Schwalm (Leipsic, Stadttheater, December 6); "Loreley," by Adolf Mohr (Mentz, Stadttheater); "Ramiro," by Eugen Lindner (Weimar, December 6).

Comic operas: "Fortunato," in three acts, by Adolph Mohr (Berlin and Hamburg);

"Schloss de l'Orme, oder Der blaue Schuh," by Kleinmichel (Dantzic, February 11); "Prinz Dominik," romantic comic opera in four acts, by Otto Fiebach (Dantzic, March 16); "Le joli Gilles," by Ferdinand Poise (Brussels, February); "Toni's Schatz," by Ferdinand Poise (Berlin, December 21).

Operettas: "Prinz und Maurer," by Oelschlegel (Klagenfurt, August); "Das Testament des Herzogs," by G. Seydl (Berlin, Louisenstädtisches Theater); "Rafaela," by Max Wolf (Pesth, Deutsches Theater); "La Fauvette du Temple," by Messager (Paris, Folies-Dramatiques, November 18); "La Béarnaise," by the same (Paris, Bouffes-Parisiens, December 13); "Der Jagdjunker," by Czibulka (Berlin, Walhalla-Theater, December 2); "Pluto," by Triebel (Frankfort, middle of December); "Le Mariage de Tabarin," by Pauline Thys (Rheims, Grand-Théâtre).

The past two years were unusually fertile in the production of new operas. We omit only those that failed at the outset, with the exception of a few, where the prominence of the composer offers sufficient reason for mentioning them.

1884.—Operas: "Dans les Nuages," by Le Rey (Rouen, Théâtre des Arts, January); "Margherita," by Ciro Pinsuti (Florence, Teatro Pergola, January 16); "Les Templiers," by Henry Litolff (Brussels, Théâtre de la Monnaie, January 25); the subject of the opera, which was conducted by the composer and obtained a complete success, is based upon the events during the last years of the reign of Philip IV, of France; "Bianca Capello," by Salomon, libretto by Jules Barbier (Antwerp, February 1), with moderate success; "Andreas Hofer," by Emil Kaiser (Reichenberg, February 5); "Sappho," by Walter Slaughter, libretto by Dr. Harry Lobb (London, Opera Comique, February 10), met with very favorable reception; "Urvasi," by Wilhelm Kienzl, libretto by Alfred Gödel, after a drama of Kalidasa (Dresden, February 20), obtained considerable success, aided by a most brilliant *mise en scène ;* "Leonora," by Serponti (Venice, Teatro Fenice, March); "Der Bravo," by Arthur Könnemann (Münster, Westphalia, in March); "Rioval," by Wiernsberger (Rheims, March); "Dornröschen," by Ferdinand Langer (Hamburg, Stadttheater, March 18), conducted by the composer with signal success; "Das Sonntagskind," by Albert Dietrich, libretto by Bulthaupt (Bremen, Stadttheater, March 21), was well received; the music is of a romantic nature, and the last act of the opera particularly effective; "Palestrina," by M. E. Sachs (Ratisbon, March); "Hirlanda," by Wilhelm Bruch (Mentz, March); "Philips de Schoone," Flemish opera, by G. Van Vlemmeren (Saint-Nicolas, Belgium, March); "Le Roi l'a dit," by Delibes (Monte Carlo, March); "Loreley," by Otto Fiebach, libretto by the same (Dantzic, April 1), conducted by the composer, was fairly successful; "Junker Heinz," by Carl

von Perfall, libretto by G. Franz, after the poem "Heinrich von Schwaben," by Wilhelm Hertz (Munich, April 9), is full of dramatic life, was splendidly mounted, and met with enthusiastic reception; "Gwendoline," by Emanuel Chabrier (Brussels, April 10); "Salambò," by Nicolo Massa (Milan, Scala, April); "Der Geigenmacher von Cremona," by H. Trnecek (Schwerin, April); "La Figlia di Jefte," by Miceli (Naples, Teatro San Carlo, April); "Les Pâques de la Reine," by Paul Mériel (Toulouse, Théâtre du Capitol, April); "Ines di Castiglia," by Seghettini (Nice, April); "La Légende de l'Ondine," by Georges Rosenlecker (Liège Théâtre Royal, April); "Maître Ambros," by Widor, libretto by Coppée and Dorchain (Paris, Opéra-Comique, May 6); the scene is laid in the wars of independence in the Netherlands. The opinions were much divided as to the success of this work: while the Wagnerites praise it as a happy fusion of French manner with Wagner's style, the unbiassed pronounce it heavy and unnecessarily complicated. The *mise en scène* was in every respect excellent and truly artistic. "Flora Mirabilia," by Spiro Samara (Milan, Teatro Carcano, May); "Malawika," by Felix Weingartner (Munich, June 3), conducted by the composer; "The Troubadour," by Mackenzie, libretto by Franz Hüffer, treating the history of the troubadour Guillem de Cabestanh (London, Drury Lane Theatre, June 8), conducted by the composer, with great success; the music shows the influence of Wagner, especially in the abundant use of "Leitmotive"; the instrumentation is very attractive. "Florian," by Ida Walter (London, Novelty Theatre, July 14); "Fornarina," by Paolo Maggi (Barcelona, August); "Don Cesare di Bazan," by Sparapani (Milan, Teatro Manzoni, September 10), succès d'estime; "Glamour," by W. Hutchinson (Edinburgh, Theatre Royal, September), with moderate success; "Fausta," by Primo Bandini (Milan, Teatro dal Verme, September 15), conducted by the composer, and met with deservedly favorable reception; "Marffa," by Johannes Hager (Baron von Hasslinger, Vienna, October 4), although skillfully constructed, the music lacks dramatic power, and sounds antiquated—it was composed twenty-five years ago; "Myrrha," by Stefano Interdonato and Ladislaus Zarstal (Prague, National Theatre, October); "Jean Cavalier," by Anton Langert (Nuremberg, October 14); the scene of the opera is laid in France during the revolt of the Camisards under Louis XIV, of which Jean Cavalier was one of the leaders; the music contains many beautiful details, but on the whole shows a strong leaning toward various models; "Der Goldmacher von Strassburg," by W. Mühldorfer (Hamburg, Stadttheater, November 6); "König Drosselbart," by M. Felix (Dr. Felix Cohn, Altenburg, November 7); "Die Hochzeit des Mönchs," by August Klughardt (Dessau, November 10); "Otto der Schütz," by

Victor Nessler, libretto by Rudolf Bunge after Gottfried Kinkel's epic poem (Leipsic, Stadttheater, November 15); as in his former productions, the composer's intention to be popular is the prevailing feature of the music, but he appears less spontaneous in this work, which met, however, with a favorable reception; "Donna Diana," by Heinrich Hofmann, libretto by Wittkowski after Moreto's comedy (Berlin, November 15); in the merry scenes suggested by the text, the composer is at his best, while the more dramatic parts are less successfully treated; the orchestration is most effective; "Merlin," by Carl Goldmark, libretto by Siegfried Lipiner (Vienna, November 19), was received with much applause, and shows great progress in form and instrumentation compared with his "Queen of Sheba"; the *mise en scène* was most splendid, and the performance exemplary. This was produced in New York at the Metropolitan Opera-house, under Mr. Walter Damrosch's direction, on Jan. 3, 1887. "Harold," dramatic opera in five acts and nine tableaus, by Eduard Nápravnik (St. Petersburg, November 23), met with great success; "Egmont," by Salvayre, libretto by Wolff and Milland (Paris, Opéra-Comique, December 6), failed completely; "Patrie," by Paladilhe, libretto by Sardou (Paris, Opéra, Dec. 16 and 20), was well received; "Jacques Clément," by Grisy (Geneva, Grand-Théâtre, December); "Dalibor," Czechish opera, by Smetana (Prague, National Theatre, December); "Spartacus," by Giuseppe Sinico (Trieste, December).

Comic operas: "Signor Lucifer," by L. Dumack (Berlin, Louisenstädtisches Theater, January 6); "Die Abenteuer einer Neujahrsnacht," by Richard Heuberger, libretto by Franz Schaumann after Zschokke's tale (Leipsic Stadttheater, January 13), was well received; "Die Carabiniers des Königs," by Emil Kaiser (Berlin, Louisenstädtisches Theater, February); "Der Pfarrer von Mendon," by Felix von Woyrsch (Hamburg, Stadttheater); "Le Serment d'Amour," by Edmond Audran (Paris, Théâtre des Nouveautés, February); "Saint-Mégrin," by Paul and Lucien Hillemacher, libretto by Dubreuil and Adenis, very skillfully adapted from Dumas's drama, "Henri III et sa Cour" (Brussels, Théâtre de la Monnaie, March 3); the music contains many exquisite traits, especially in the instrumentation, and the opera was received with much applause; "Plutus," by Lecocq (Paris, Opéra - Comique, March 31), *succès d'estime;* "Die Carabiniers des Königs," oder "Die Mönche," by Gustav Härtel (Breslau); "Frivoli," by Hervé (London, Drury Lane Theatre, June 29); "Die Löwenbraut," by Karl Krafft - Lortzing (Nordhausen, Tivoli-Theater, August); "Dorothy," by Alfred Cellier (London, Gaiety Theatre, September 25); "Rhoda," opera-bouffe, by Antonio Mora (London, Croydon Theatre, September 27); "Auf hohen Befehl," by Carl Reinecke, who also wrote the libretto, after Riehl's novel "Ovid bei Hofe" (Hamburg, Stadttheater, October 1),

with decided success, and well-deserved ovations for the composer, who conducted the opera; "Indiana," by Audran (Manchester, Comedy Theatre, October 4); "La Cigale et la Fourmi," by Audran (Paris, Théâtre Gaîté, October 30); "Die Piraten," by Richard Genée (Berlin, Walhalla-Theater, October 9); "La Femme Juge et Parti," by Missa (Paris, Opéra-Comique, November 17).

Operettas: "Studenten am Rhein," by Josef Goldstein (Pesth, January 7); "Die Novize," by Wilhelm Rab (Vienna, Theater an der Wien, January 31); "Der Botschafter," by Kremser (Vienna, February 13); "La Schiarneto," by Cecoghi (Udine, Teatro Minerva); "Minnekozen," Flemish operetta by De Biozières (Ghent, Théâtre Minard, January); "Les Volontaires de 92," by Felix Boisson (Chalons-sur - Marne, January); "Le Docteur Vieux-temps," by Jules Gontink (Bruges, February); "Der Günstling," by Karl Grau (Hanover, Residenz-Theater); "Josephine vendue par ses Sœurs," by Victor Roger (Paris, Bouffes-Parisiens, March 20); "El Testamento y la Clave," zarzuela by Rubio and Espino (Madrid, Teatro de las Variedades, March); "El Club de las Feas," by the same (ib., December); "Fioretta," by Alfred Straszer and Max von Weinzierl (Prague, Deutsches Landestheater, April 3); "Der schöne Kurfürst," by Josef Hellmesberger, Jr. (Munich, Gärtnerplatz-Theater, May 15); "Aura," by W. Behre (Bremen, Tivoli-Theater, August 15); "Schloss Cailiano," by Victor Holländer (Hamburg, Schultze-Theater, September 8); "Lorraine," by Rudolf Dellinger (Hamburg, October 2); "Der Doppelgänger," by Alfred Zamara, Jr. (Munich, Gärtnerplatz-Theater, September 16); "Der Nachtwandler," by Louis Roth (Berlin, Friedrich-Wilhelm-Theater, September 27); "Adam et Eve," by Gaston Serpette (Paris, Nouveautés, October 8); "Der Vice-Admiral," by Millöcker (Vienna, Theater an der Wien, October 9); "Sataniel," by Adolf Ferron (Dresden, Residenz-Theater, October 17); "Madame Cartouche," by Léon Vasseur (Paris, Folies-Dramatiques, October 19); "Der Cornet," by Emil Kaiser (Leipsic, Carola Theater, October 26); "Der Vagabund," by Karl Zeller (Vienna, Carl-Theater, October 30); "Le Nozze di Figaro," by Antonio Martini (Florence, October); "Der Hofnarr," by Adolf Müller, Jr. (Vienna, Theater an der Wien, November 20); "Farinelli," by Hermann Zumpe (Hamburg, Schultze-Theater, November 27); "Il Telegramma," by R. Matini (Florence, Teatro Pergola, December 30).

1887.—Operas: "Der letzte Abencerage," by Franz Sarosi (Schauer), libretto by Ludwig Bartok, after Chateaubriand's novel (Pesth, Opera House, January 4); the music is melodious and the dramatic effects in the style of Meyerbeer; it was much applauded; "Nordica," by Frederick Corder (Liverpool, Court Theatre, January 26), met with great success; "Las Mugeres que matan," by Fernandez Caballero (Madrid, Teatro de la Princesa, January);

"Le Villi," by Puccini (Genoa, January, Trieste, February 5); "Otello," by Verdi, libretto by Arrigo Boito, after Shakespeare (Milan, Scala, February 5), the great theatrical event, to which the entire operatic world had looked forward for months past, was attended by the *élite* of society, the Italian artists and *literati* of distinction, a great number of foreign musical celebrities, stage directors and managers, journalists, the reporters of all the cosmopolitan papers, and amateurs from every quarter of the globe. The ovations for the venerable master increased after every act, and culminated in the most enthusiastic applause at the close of the performance, when the composer was called forth countless times, and fairly overwhelmed with floral offerings. Outside, the populace unharnessed his horses, and drew the carriage to his hotel, shouting "Evviva Verdi!" The music of this work appears strongly imbued with German, besides specifically Wagnerian influences. The second and fourth acts are the most effective; in the latter the composer evinces the highest inspiration. Desdemona's Willow Song, and Ave Maria are the gems of the entire score. Much is to be said also in praise of the libretto; "I Doria," by Augusto Machado, libretto by Ghislanzoni, after Schiller's "Fiesco" (Lisbon, Teatro San Carlos, January); "Judith," by Karl Götze (Magdeburg, February 17); "Cid," by Willy Böhme (Dessau, February 18); "Quentin Messis," by Karl Göpfarth (Weimar, February 24); "Merlin," by Philipp Rüfer, libretto by Dr. Ludwig Hofmann (Berlin, February 28); "Notte d'Aprile," by Emilio Ferrari (Milan, Teatro dal Verme, February); "Le Tintoret," by Adolf Dietrich (Dijon, Grand-Théâtre, February); "Re Nala," by Antonio Smareglia (Venice, Teatro alla Fenice, February); "Fleur de Lotus," by Georges Fragerolle (Lyons, Casino des Arts, March); "Edelweiss," by Castracane (Verona, Teatro Filarmonico, March); "Proserpine," by Saint-Saëns (Paris, Opéra-Comique, March 16), was a failure; "Giuditta," by Falchi (Rome, Teatro Apollo, March); "La Fiera," by D'Arienzo (Naples, Teatro Nuovo, March); "De Bloemenbruid," Flemish opera, by Franz van Herzeele, libretto by Emil van Goethem (Ghent, Théâtre Minard, March), met with well-deserved success; "Harold," by Karl Pfeffer, libretto by Paul Krone (Vienna, April 3), was well received, and is a skillful work, though lacking in dramatic effect; "Stenio," by De Rey (Rouen, April); "Bluette," by Louis Mayeur (The Hague, April); "Black-eyed Susan," by Meyer-Lutz (Birmingham, April); "Amilda," by Walter Borg (Alexandria, Egypt, April); "Loreley," Finnish opera, by Friedrich Pacius (Helsingfors, Alexandra Theatre, April), met with enthusiastic reception: the composer is seventy-six years old; "Colomba," by Pradeglia (Milan, Teatro dal Verme, May); "Edvardo Stuart," by Cipriano Pantoglio (Milan, Teatro Manzoni, May); "Guerra allo Sposo," by Valentino (Naples,

Teatro Nuovo); "Die Jungfrau von Orléans," by Reznicek, libretto by the same, after Schiller's drama (Prague, Deutsches Landestheater, June 19); "Loreley" (composed twenty-six years ago, but entirely remodeled), by Max Bruch, libretto by Oscar Walther, after Geibel's poem (Leipsic, Neues Stadttheater, September 9); "Alidor," by Janotta, a Neapolitan *maestro* (San Paulo, Brazil); "Sciaroltà," by Enrico Mannheimer (Milan, Teatro dal Verme, September); "Il Conte di Gleichen," by Salvatore Anteri-Manzochi (Milan, October); "L'Agente secreto," by Frangini (Florence, Teatro Alfieri, October); "Robert Macaire," by George Fox (Sydenham, Crystal Palace, October); "Der Sturm," by Ernst Frank, libretto by J. V. Widmann, after Shakespeare's "Tempest" (Hanover, Hoftheater, October 15); "Faust," musical drama in four acts, and a prelude, by Heinrich Zöllner, after Goethe (Munich, October 19), with decided success; "Il Moro di Castiglia," by Masciangelo (Lanciano, in the Abruzzi, October); "Sardanapalo," by Libani (Turin, October 20); "Lanzo," by Michael von Ogarev (Lübeck, Stadttheater, October 20); "Loreley," by Bartholdy, libretto by the same (Copenhagen, October 23); the opera is in the style of Wagner, and was well received; "Tscharodeika" ("The Sorceress"), by Tschaikowski, libretto after the drama of "Schpashinski" (St. Petersburg, November 1), conducted by the composer, who was called out repeatedly after every act; "Schön Rotraut," by Edmund Kretschmer, libretto by Johanna Balz, based on the legend of King Ringang's fair daughter (Dresden, November 6), was received with much applause; "Otto der Schütz," by W. Rudnik (Landsberg an der Warthe, at a concert, November 11), conducted by the composer; "Murillo," by Ferdinand Langer (Mannheim, November 20), conducted by the composer; "Zaïre," by Charles Lefèbvre, libretto by Paul Collin, after Voltaire (Lille, November); "Der wilde Jäger," by A. Schulz, libretto after Julius Wolff's epic poem (Brunswick, November 27); "Stratonice," by Edmond Diet (Paris, Menus-Plaisirs, November); "Fernanda," by Ferruccio-Ferrari (Lucca, November, Pisa, Teatro Rossi, December); "Diana de Spaar," by Adolphe David, libretto by Armand Silvestre (Nantes, Grand-Théâtre, December 3); "La Loi jaune," by Mad. Pauline Thys (Liège, Théâtre des Pavillons-de-Flore, December).

Comic operas: "Ruddygore, or The Witch's Curse," by Arthur Sullivan (London, Savoy Theatre, January 22); "Die Mädchen von Schilda," by Alban Förster (Neustrelitz, February 3), conducted by the composer; "La Belle Etoile," by Henri Vaillard (Rennes, February); "Mynheer Jan," by Jakobovski (London, Comedy Theatre, March); "Le Médecin malgré lui," by Poise (Brussels, February); "Le Carillon," by Julien Bénard (Geneva, Grand-Théâtre, February); "Mondeszauber," romantic comic opera, by Georg Riemenschneider, who also wrote the libretto (Posen,

Stadttheater, March), conducted by the composer; "La Jeunesse de la Tour," by Cieutat (Saint-Quentin, France, March); "Big Pony, or the Gentlemanly Savage," by E. J. Darling (New York, April); "Le Bourgeois de Calais," by André Messager (Paris, Folies-Dramatiques, April); "Le Meunier d'Alcala," by Justin Clérice (Lisbon, Teatro Trinidad, April); "Une Nuit de Trianon," by Prestreau (Rouen, Théâtre des Arts, April); "Prinz Waldmeister," romantic-comic opera, by Adolf Neuendorff, libretto by Heinrich Italiener, after Otto Roquette's "Waldmeisters Brautfahrt" (New York, Thalia-Theater, May 2; Berlin, Walhalla-Theater, September 3); "Der Deutsche Michel," by Adolf Mohr, libretto by the same, after Nötel's drama (Breslau, May 8; Nuremberg, October 28; Magdeburg, December 11; Leipsic, December 14); "Le Roi malgré lui," by Emil Chabrier (Paris, Opéra-Comique, May); "Die Musikanten," posthumous opera, by Flotow, libretto by Richard Genée (Mannheim, June 19); "Rosette," by Antoine Mathieu (Boulogne - sur - Mer, September); "Kérim," by Alfred Bruneau (Paris, Opéra-Populaire); "Surcouf," by Robert Planquette (Paris, Folies-Dramatiques, October 6), won complete success; the subject of the opera is a humorous glorification of the pirate Surcouf, a celebrity of Saint-Malo in Brittany; "L'Ami Pierrot," by Maurice Lefèvre, libretto by the same (Brussels, Flemish Theatre, October 9); "Die sieben Schwaben," by Karl Millöcker (Vienna, Theater an der Wien, October 29), conducted by the composer; "Der Jäger von Soest," by C. A. Raida (Berlin, Walhalla-Theater, November 19); "Der Schatz des Rampsinit," romantic-comic opera, by Albert Kauders, libretto by the same (Prague, Deutsches Landestheater, December 14), met with favorable reception.

Operettas: "Der Hofnarr," by Adolf Müller, Jr. (Berlin, Friedrich-Wilhelmstädtisches Theater, January 7; Frankfort, March 11; Hamburg, June 3; Munich, and Magdeburg); "Les Grenadiers de Mont-Cornette," by Lecocq (Paris, Bouffes - Parisiens, January); "Der liebe Augustin," by Johann Brandl (Vienna, Theater an der Wien, January 15); "Lao Kaï," by Gaston Maynard (Bordeaux, Théâtre des Folies - Bordelaises, January); "Der Inkaschatz," by Karl Müller-Berghaus (Kiel, February); "La Opera Española," by Taboada, "Se afeita á domicilio," by Isidoro Hernandez (Madrid, Alhambra, January); "Cantar da plano," zarzuela by Jimenez and Espino (Madrid, Teatro de las Variedades, January); "L'Amour mouillé," by Varney (Paris, Nouveautés, January 22); "Bellman," by Franz von Suppé (Vienna, Theater an der Wien, February 26), conducted by the composer, who was repeatedly called before the footlights; "La Rivincita di Ricarao," by Viso Redi (Rome, Teatro Quirino, February); "Las Criadas," zarzuela by Hernandez and Blasquez, "Cambiar de rumbo," zarzuela by J. Estarroma, "El Figon de las dedichas,"

zarzuela by Chapi (Madrid, February); "Incognito," by Ludolf Waldmann (Leipsic, Stadttheater, March 27); "Il Ritorno d'America." by Vinaccia (Naples, Teatro Partenope); "La Gamine de Paris," by Gaston Serpette (Paris, Bouffes-Parisiens, March); "La Voce à Nini," by Hervé (Paris, Théâtre des Variétés, March); "Ninon," by Vasseur (Paris, Théâtre des Nouveautés, March); "Un Rapto," by Nicolau (Madrid, Teatro Price, March); "Les Deux Pêcheurs et la Belle-Mère," by Lafage (Angers, April); "Don Pedro di Medina," by Paolo Lanzini (Florence, Teatro Nuovo, April); "Das Ellishorn," by Rudolf Raimann (Munich, Gärtnerplatz-Theater, May 7); "Der Matador," by Adolf Mohr (Hamburg, Schultze - Theater, May); "L'Entr'acte," by André Martinet (Contrexéville and Plombières, France, September); "Don Decubito," by Giuseppe Carboni (Venice, Teatro del Lido, September); "La Corte d'Amore," by Palmieri (Turin, Teatro Balbo, September); "Der Ducatenprinz," by Bernhard Triebel (Leipsic, Altes Stadttheater, September 12); "Les Saturnales," by Lacome (Paris, Nouveautés, September); "Rikiki," by Josef Hellmesberger, Jr. (Vienna, Carltheater, September 27; Berlin, Walhalla-Theater, October 27; then in Munich, and Pesth); "Le Sosie," by Raoul Pugno (Paris, Bouffes-Parisiens, October); "Hannibal," by Otto Schmidt (Stralsund, October 14); "Malajo, der neapolitanische Fischer," by Hugo Schröder (Bunzlau, Stadttheater, October 27); "Die Lieder des Mirza Schaffy," by Louis Roth (Berlin, Friedrich-Wilhelmstädtisches Theater, November 5); "La Fiancée des Verts-Poteaux," by Audran (Paris, Menus-Plaisirs, November 8); "Ali Baba," by Lecocq (Brussels, Alhambra, November 11); "Colombine," by Baron Hans von Zois (Gratz, November 12); "Die Dreizehn," by Richard Genée (Vienna, Carltheater, November 14); "Sposinate per me," by Mascetti, "Fischi per Fiaschi," by Pascucci (Rome, November); "Mirolan," by M. Fall (Linz, Landschaftliches Theater, November 26); "Dix Jours aux Pyrénées," by Varney (Paris, Théâtre Gaîté, November); "Les Délégués," by Banès (Paris, Nouveautés, November); "Les deux Flûtes," by Ch. Joffroy (Paris, Cercle de la Presse, November); "Taquinet," by Mengze (Wesel, November 30); "Die letzte Nacht," by Emil Christiani (Hamburg, Schultze-Theater, December 14); "La Lycaenne," by Serpette (Paris, Nouveautés, December); "Simplicius," by Johann Strauss, libretto by Victor Léon (Vienna, Theater an der Wien, December 17), conducted by the composer, who was the recipient of enthusiastic applause; and "Der Glücksritter," by Alfons Czibulka, libretto by Genée and Mannstädt (Vienna, Carltheater, December 22), which met with great success.

MUTUAL AID SOCIETIES, associations whose members contribute weekly or monthly payments to a common fund, from which a proportionate allowance is promised to them, in case, by sickness or accident, they are rendered for a time incapable of labor. A usual stipulation also provides a sum to defray funeral expenses in case of death. In some cases there is no payment of any kind except a given sum for burial. In others, notably those formed among mechanics, a fund is provided for the loss of tools by accident or otherwise. Their origin dates from an early age, but as a rule the societies are short-lived. The order of Freemasons is probably the oldest, while the guilds of the Anglo-Saxons, and the fraternities and unions formed in trade organizations in Great Britain date from time immemorial. By far the greater number are local. The organization of a society is generally effected under the stress of some difficulty. Some partake of the character of convivial clubs, which meet periodically, make their contributions or pay their fees to the fund, and appoint a committee or officers to manage their affairs. An effort was made in England in 1793, to put the then existing organizations on a firm footing, by giving them a legal status, to wit, permission to hold property, to sue and be sued, and to make investments in a corporate capacity. The act was followed by several amending acts up to the year 1829, when all were repealed, and a new law was passed, which, with slight changes, has remained in force ever since. In the United States there is a very large number of societies having mutual aid for their object. While the great mass are purely local, there are many, like the Knights of Pythias and the Ancient Order of United Workmen, that have grown to national proportions. The national unions have subordinates or branches in various sections of the country, for which they legislate, and give aid and counsel whenever necessary. While the societies are usually composed of men of a single trade or calling, as the Brotherhood of Locomotive Engineers, there are some whose aim is not confined to any particular class. During 1879 and 1880 there was an extraordinary development of organizations in the United States, and, in addition to numerical growth, there was a consolidation of interests that had not before been united, though not discordant. The general aim was to include all the unions and trade societies in the cities or districts where they were formed, and thus become a local parliament of aid and labor. The same thing was developed in England into a trades-union congress, or international union, which sought to bring into its membership all the unions in the country, forming one grand labor congress, which should consider all general questions affecting labor, and endeavor to influence national legislation in a way that small bodies, having only a local constituency, could not hope to do. The largest organization of this kind in the United States is known as the Knights of Labor. While mutual aid societies have usually been formed for the exclusive purpose of affording assistance to their members only in cases of emergency, the consolidation of organizations has brought into existence an aggressive tendency, so that while the sick are relieved, the dead buried, the superannuated cared for, those suffering from accidents protected, and the destitute shielded, provision has also been made on an enlarged scale for providing for those who engage in strikes, or are subjected to lock-outs, or otherwise affected by a conflict between capital and labor. As a rule, the international organization, whether consisting of a single trade or calling, or made up of many, "guarantees its moral and pecuniary support to all its members in difficulties that may arise between them and their employers." The amount of assistance is generally gauged by the interests involved, although it is often gauged only by the amount paid by the member during his paying period. Many mutual aid or benefit societies make no distinction in the amount paid to their members, but guarantee the same sick-pay, etc., to a man of a month's membership as to one of ten years. It is estimated that there are 3,000 mutual aid societies, or benefit guilds, in the United States, and the great majority have had an existence of but a few years. Of the larger national organizations, the International Typographical Union, composed exclusively of compositors, was begun in 1850; the Brotherhood of Locomotive Engineers about 1868; the Cigar-makers' Union in 1864; and the Bricklayers' Union in 1865. These are the oldest of the organizations whose sphere has been enlarged from purely benevolent actions to affording aid in conflicts between employer and employé, or in devising methods to coerce capital. In the matter of securing membership, the rules vary. In some a critical examination is made by a competent physician, as in life-insurance procedure, while in others members are required to pay according to their youth or age, and still others are assessed only in case of certain specified contingencies.

N

NAPHTHA-MOTORS. Within three years a new species of motor has become familiar to all who frequent the navigable waters of the United States. Its peculiar fitness for the propulsion of small boats has led to its most general use in connection with launches of a size suited to the needs of residents in sea-side cottages and the thousand resorts and watering-places along our lakes and rivers. Almost every large yacht now carries one of them as a tender, and the compact little craft, with their neat, upright boilers, sometimes of brass and sometimes of shining nickel-plate, are every-day sights in all the harbors of coastwise and inland waters. They are especially suited to the needs of amateur engineers, from the small space occupied by the machinery, the absence of smoke and odor, and the ease with which they are managed. While they can not compete with the best coal and oil burning engines in actual driving-power, they are efficient for most purposes. Another advantage is that the engine and attachments are so light that they can be placed in the stern-sheets of the boat, leaving the whole forward space available for passengers, while the products of combustion are all

NAPHTHA ENGINE.

aft, and under most conditions of weather pass off astern without the least annoyance to any one on board.

The naphtha used as fuel is stored in a tank in the extreme bow, at the farthest possible remove from the fire, whence the only danger arises, and the possibility of an explosion is very remote. Indeed, the absence of accidents in the record shows that such a mishap is well-nigh impossible. Deodorized naphtha of 76° is used, its vapor supplying the cylinders in place of steam, no water being required. An engine of two-horse power weighs only 200 pounds, and one of four-horse power weighs 800 pounds, less than one-fifth as much as a steam-engine of the same power. The space occupied is only eighteen inches fore and aft for the smaller sizes, and but little more in proportion as the power and size are increased. The three single-action cylinders are contained in a cast-iron casing, the upper part of which forms the valve-seats, the cylinders being suspended below and operated by plain valves connected with one stem reaching from the crank-shaft. On top of the casing is the boiler, consisting of two coils of copper pipe, one within the other, a vertical cylinder being set within the

coils. The coils and cylinder are connected with copper tubing, and the whole is included in a brass casing, above which rises the smoke-stack. The naphtha is carried by a pipe leading from the reservoir in the bow, down through the bottom of the boat, and aft outside the keel to the inner coil of pipe, and thence down and into the outer coil, from the top of which it connects with the vertical cylinder. The heavier gas passes directly to the engine, but the lighter is taken from the cylinder by a pipe and carried to an injector, where it is mixed with air and then delivered to the burner immediately beneath the two coils, which are surrounded with flame as soon as the burner is lighted. That portion of the vapor which passes from the engine is condensed in a tube outside of the keel, and returns to the tank to be used again, the only portion actually expended being that which is burned under the coils. For a two-horse-power engine the consumption is about three quarts an hour. There is no possibility of flame reaching the tank except through the long tube surrounded by water and therefore constantly at a low temperature. Herein lies the safety of the engine, for it is nearly or quite impossible that any circumstances can arise that will force a reverse draught through such a long passage. The engine is shown in detail herewith, exactly as it appears resting upon the bottom of the boat. A is an alcohol lamp, B is the air-valve, E the air-pump, D naphtha-valve, F naphtha-pump, C injector-valve, G governing-wheel, and H safety-valve. To start the engine the alcohol lamp A is lighted and set on the rest-plate, with its tube inserted in the bottom of the retort. The air-valve B is turned from left to right, and with the air-pump E the gas is forced from the tank through the outlet-pipe to the burner, where it is ignited under the retort by the flame of the lamp. The air-pump should be used one or two minutes when the naphtha-valve D may be opened. Five to ten strokes on the pump F will bring the naphtha from the tank to the already heated retort, where it is at once vaporized, and the injector C is opened slowly at first, supplying fuel to the burner, after which the governor G is given a few turns from right to left, until the machinery begins to move. The pressure is increased by a few strokes with the naphtha-pump F, and a gauge shows the amount of pressure. This is opened to increase and closed to reduce speed. The lamp is removed and extinguished as soon as the engine is running, and the pressure is regulated by the injector C so that it will remain stationary.

The air-pump is used to force gas which has generated in the tank through the pipe to the burner, and is also used as a whistle by turning the air-valve B from right to left. The tanks have from 30 to 60 gallons capacity. The engine can be instantly reversed, even when running at full speed, and headway is at once checked and the boat brought to a full stop almost within its own length. When a landing is made, the injector C and the naphtha-valve D are closed, and the boat may be left to itself with perfect safety. An 18-foot boat will carry from six to ten persons, at a speed of six to eight miles an hour, at an expenditure of fuel costing about six cents an hour. No license is required for an engineer, and any person of intelligence can learn all the details of management in one or two lessons. The naphtha-launches are built up to 40 feet in length, but the most popular and useful sizes are from 18 to 25 feet, costing from $600 to $1,200. The naphtha-launches have already made their way to most of the maritime countries of the world, even to India and the Sandwich Islands, and for the present, at least, they seem to be the most perfect vessels of their class in the market.

NEBRASKA. State Government.—The following were the State officers during the year: Governor, John M. Thayer, Republican; Lieutenant-Governor, H. H. Shedd; Secretary of State, George L. Laws; Treasurer, Charles H. Willard; Auditor, H. A. Babcock; Attorney-General, William Leese; Superintendent of Public Instruction, George B. Lane; Chief-Justice of the Supreme Court, Samuel Maxwell; Associates, Amasa Cobb and M. B. Reese.

Legislative Session.—A contest for the seat in the United States Senate, held by Charles H. Van Wyck, occupied the early days of the session. The Senator himself was a candidate for re-election, and enjoyed the earnest support of a considerable number of his own party, but a larger portion were bitterly opposed to his aspirations. Finding himself scarcely able to obtain the caucus nomination, he determined to override party allegiance and to secure a re-election by the aid of Democratic votes as an Independent candidate. In order to accomplish this, it was necessary for him to prevent a Republican caucus by keeping his Republican friends away from such a meeting. He so far succeeded as to postpone the caucus until two joint ballots had been taken, on the last of which he came within 7 votes of the prize. On this second ballot, taken on January 20, Van Wyck received 60 votes, Algernon S. Paddock 18, Adoniram J. Weaver 16, and all others 43. More than two thirds of the Democrats voted for Van Wyck. In the Republican caucus held after this ballot, ex-Senator Algernon S. Paddock was nominated on the fifteenth ballot by a vote of 59 to 36 for N. V. Harlan. Van Wyck was the leading candidate for eleven ballots, receiving on the first 44 votes, only 4 less than a majority. On the following day Paddock was elected by a vote of 93 to 32 for John A. McShane, Democrat.

A compulsory school law was passed at this session which requires children between eight and fourteen years to attend a public or private school at least twelve weeks in each year. The penalty is from ten to fifty dollars for each violation of the law. Another act redistricts the State for members of the Legislature.

Thirty districts are entitled to thirty-three Senators, and sixty-seven districts to one hundred Representatives. Provision was made for the establishment of a State Industrial Home for Women and Girls, and for a State Soldiers' and Sailors' Home, $15,000 being appropriated for the former and $80,000 for the latter. Additional buildings at other State institutions were authorized, among them a new building at the State University to be known as the Grant Memorial Hall, and to be devoted to the uses of the military department of the university and for a gymnasium. A tax of three fourths of a mill is levied for 1887 and 1888, to be used in completing the State Capitol. Other acts are as follow:

Creating a State Board of Live-Stock Agents and defining their powers to exterminate disease among domestic animals.

To authorize counties, precincts, towns, cities, and school districts, to compromise their indebtedness, and to issue new bonds therefor.

Providing for the incorporation of cities of 60,000 inhabitants or over, to be known as cities of the metropolitan class.

To incorporate cities of less than 60,000 and more than 25,000 inhabitants, to be known as cities of the first class.

Revising the powers of cities of over 5,000 and less than 25,000 inhabitants, known as cities of the second class.

Providing special regulations for secret societies and associations.

Creating the counties of Arthur, Grant, McPherson, and Thomas.

Giving county boards the power to borrow money and issue bonds for the construction of necessary county buildings.

Permitting county judges to grant authority to administrators to mortgage real estate of deceased persons in certain cases.

Amending the election laws for metropolitan cities and cities of the first class.

To protect primary elections and conventions of political parties, and to punish offenses committed thereat.

Revising the laws relating to the militia.

Requiring every person who shall hereafter engage in the practice of dentistry to file with the county clerk a diploma from some reputable dental college.

Creating a State Board of Pharmacy to regulate and license the business of druggists.

Providing a new law regarding the duties of the State Inspector of Oils.

Providing the manner in which railroad companies may acquire rights of way over the educational and other lands of the State.

Permitting railroads to purchase, lease, or otherwise control other roads which form a continuous line with the purchasing road or will, when completed, form such.

Fixing the maximum rate of charge by railroads for transportation of passengers and baggage at three cents per mile.

Amending the railroad law by inserting provisions to prevent pooling, relative to longer and shorter hauls and otherwise.

To prohibit non-resident aliens from hereafter acquiring real estate in the State, and providing that when such persons already holding real estate shall die their property shall escheat to the State, shall be appraised, and the appraised value paid to the heirs or other persons entitled to it.

Amending the revenue laws.

To compel railroad corporations and others to make and keep in repair suitable crossings.

Regulating the management of public schools in metropolitan cities.

Providing for a census of all ex-soldiers, sailors, and marines residing in the State.

Providing for the sale of all unsold lands belonging to the State lying in the city of Lincoln.

Extending for ten years from October, 1889, the lease of the State Penitentiary and of the convict labor therein.

Granting telegraph and telephone companies the right of way along public highways, and providing a penalty for interference with the same.

To accept the provisions of an act of Congress establishing agricultural experiment stations in the various States.

Abolishing arrest and imprisonment in civil actions for debt.

Exempting from attachment and levy or sale on execution all pension-money and all property purchased or improved exclusively therewith.

Punishing provocation to assault.

To define and punish the crime of larceny from the person.

Raising the age of consent in females to fifteen years.

To prevent the employment of children under twelve years in workshops, factories, shops, or mines more than four months in each year.

To suppress the circulation, advertising, and vending of obscene and immoral literature and articles of indecent and immoral use, and to confiscate such property.

To prohibit grain-dealers, persons, or corporations of any kind, from combining or entering into any agreement to pool or fix the price to be paid for grain, hogs, cattle, or stock of any kind.

To transfer $125,500 from the University fund to the State General fund, and $86,202.69 from the Insane Hospital fund to the General fund.

Valuation.—The total assessed valuation of the State for the year aggregated $160,506,266.25, as against $148,932,570.51 for 1886. The value of improved land was $37,271,438; of unimproved land, $29,190,115. The assessment also includes 437,450 horses valued at $9,185,101; 1,826,105 cattle valued at $8,789,049, and 1,199,242 hogs valued at $1,351,408.

Railroads.—A total of 3,830 miles of railroad was assessed this year at $23,558,162.25. The assessment for 1886 was upon 2,984 miles valued at $19,458,133.86. The year has been one of unusual activity in railroad construction, 1,101 miles having been completed upon seventeen different lines. Only one State, Kansas, with 2,070 miles constructed, exceeds this.

A decision of importance under the railroad law, passed this year, was rendered by the State Supreme Court in November. The act provides, among other things, that all the charges made for service rendered, or to be rendered, by any railway company in the State, in the transportation of passengers or property, shall be reasonable and just, and gives to the State Board of Transportation power to enforce the act. The court decided that the Board of Transportation had authority to determine, in the first instance, what are just and reasonable charges for the services rendered, or to be rendered, and that the power to decide what is a just rate and charge carried with it the power to fix and establish such rate and charge, although such power was not expressly given by the statute.

Education.—The total number of school children reported for the year was 279,982, against 252,006 for 1886 and 233,060 for 1885. The semi-annual apportionment of income from the State school fund made in December gives to each pupil an average of $1.19. This income is derived as follows:

Interest on United States bonds	$360 00
Interest on State bonds	18,050 09
State tax	98,000 78
Interest on county bonds	28,529 20
Interest on district bonds	50 00
Lease school-lands	64,867 23
Private securities	2,612 00
Total amount	$334,430 83

State Institutions.—The number of convicts at the State Prison on the first day of December was 384, an increase of six since the previous December. The Insane Hospital at the same date contained 399 inmates, of whom 216 were males and 183 females. In the State Industrial School there were 153 boys and 38 girls, a total of 191. Since the establishment of this school there have been confined 238 boys and 61 girls, or 299 in all.

Political.—An election was held in November to choose a justice of the Supreme Court and two regents of the State University. Chief-Justice Maxwell was renominated by the Republicans. The vote for justice was: Maxwell, 86,725; O'Day (Democrat), 56,548; Edgerton (Labor), 2,635; Abbott (Prohibition), 7,359. B. B. Davis and George Roberts (Republicans) were elected regents.

NETHERLANDS, a kingdom in western Europe. According to the Constitution confirmed by royal decree on October 14, and proclaimed on November 3, 1848, the king exercises the legislative power conjointly with the two houses of the States-General. The 39 members of the upper house are elected by the provincial assemblies from the highest taxpayers. The 86 members of the second chamber are chosen by the votes of all Netherlanders of full age who are domiciled and pay a certain amount of direct taxes. The second chamber alone has the initiative of legislation.

The reigning King is Willem III, born Feb. 19, 1817, who succeeded his father, Willem II, March 17, 1849. The King presides at the meetings of the Cabinet.

The Council of Ministers is composed of the following heads of departments: Minister of Foreign Affairs, A. P. G. van Karnebeek; Minister of the Interior, J. Heemskerk Az; Minister of Justice, Baron M. W. du Tour van Bellinchave; Minister of Finance, J. C. Bloem; Minister of the Colonies, J. P. Sprenger van Eyk; Minister of the Waterstaat, Commerce, and Industry, J. N. Brastert, appointed in 1887; Minister of War, Maj.-Gen. A. W. P. Weitzel; Minister of Marine, F. C. Tromp.

Area and Population.—The kingdom has an area of 33,000 square kilometres, and a population which, on Dec. 31, 1886, was computed at 4,390,857, being 133 to the square kilometre, of which 2,174,001 were males and 2,216,856 females. The number of marriages in 1886 was 30,298; births, 158,658; deaths, 103,046; surplus of births over deaths, 55,612. The population in 1879, when the last census was taken, was 4,012,693, and was divided in respect to religion into 2,469,814 Protestants, 1,439,137 Catholics, 81,693 Israelites, and 22,-049 of other faiths. The following are the most populous cities and the number of their inhabitants: Amsterdam, 378,686; Rotterdam, 190,545; the Hague, 143,626; Utrecht, 79,-166; Groningen, 51,821; Haarlem, 48,159; Arnhem, 47,285; Leyden, 45,511.

Commerce.—The total value of the imports for domestic consumption in 1885 was 1,091,-488,000 guilders; of the exports of domestic products, 891,086,000 guilders. The imports from European countries amounted to 873,-481,000 guilders, in which the importations from the German Zollverein are represented by 274,716,000, and those from the Hanseatic cities by 23,188,000 guilders, those from Great Britain by 269,046,000 guilders, those from Belgium by 161,585,000 guilders, those from Russia by 76,803,000 guilders, those from France by 18,875,000 guilders, and those from Spain by 17,826,000 guilders, Sweden and Norway coming next with 9,182,000 guilders, and then Italy with 4,803,000 guilders. Of the exports to European countries, of the total value of 813,095,000 guilders, the exports to the Zollverein made 383,997,000, and those to the Hanseatic cities 17,048,000 guilders, those to Great Britain 229,274,000 guilders, those to Belgium 127,830,000 guilders, those to Italy 14,576,000 guilders, those to France 8,976,000 guilders, those to Sweden and Norway 7,994,-000 guilders, those to Denmark 7,806,000 guilders. Out of the total imports from American countries, amounting to 78,609,000 guilders, those from the United States are represented by 55,609,000 guilders, and out of 27,179,000 guilders of exports of Dutch products to the countries of North and South America 26,899,000 guilders went to the United States. The imports from Asiatic countries amounted to 36,569,000 guilders, to which British India contributed 37,264,000 guilders. The exports to Asia and the trade with all other countries were trifling, excepting the commerce with Java and the Dutch West Indies, which is represented by 98,460,000 guilders of imports and 47,377,000 of exports.

The principal articles of import and export and their values in 1885 were as follow in guilders:

ARTICLES.	Imports.	Exports.
	Guilders.	Guilders.
Iron and steel	186,458,000	92,801,000
Textiles and textile materials	116,988,000	101,828,000
Cereals and flour	183,157,000	65,889,000
Coal	85,00\000	7,414,000
Rice	32,980,000	12,516,000
Mineral oil	19,307,000	374,000
Coffee	45,095,000	31,569,000
Butter	4,948,000	50,864,000
Cheese	62,000	12,051,000

Navigation.—The total number of sailing-vessels entered at the ports of Holland in 1885 was 2,826, of 1,773,542 metric tons, of which 968, of 784,569 tons, sailed under the Netherlands flag. The number cleared was 2,810, of 1,795,854 cubic metres' burden, of which 977, of 784,569 metric tons, were Dutch. The steamers that were entered numbered 5,595, of 9,984,351 metric tons, and of these 1,484, of 2,975,203 tons, were Dutch. The steamers that were cleared numbered 5,604, of 9,778,389 metric tons, of which 1,488, of 2,904,560 tons, were registered in the Netherlands. The commercial marine on Jan. 1, 1885, consisted of 684 sailing-vessels, of the aggregate burden of 550,003 cubic metres, and 106 steamships, of an aggregate measurement of 306,833 cubic metres.

Railroads, Posts, and Telegraphs.—The length of railroads in operation on Dec. 31, 1885, was 2,372 kilometres. The letters conveyed through the post-office in 1885 numbered, with the postal-cards, 87,582,607, and the journals 50,443,168. The telegraphs, which are owned by the state, had a total length of 4,700 kilometres at the end of 1885.

The Army.—The permanent army in 1886 numbered 2,841 officers and 63,230 men, including reserves. The militia, called the Schutteryen, is divided into two classes—the active, organized in 212 companies, and numbering 38,188 men, and the sedentary, of which there are 89 battalions, numbering 77,108 men.

The army of the Dutch East Indies, which is recruited by enlistment in Europe and in the East Indies, numbered 13,680 European and 15,369 natives, making a total of 29,049 soldiers, not including the officers, 1,371 in number. The various bodies of militia in the East Indies numbered 8,704 men, of whom 8,378 were Europeans.

The Navy.—The naval forces of the kingdom in July, 1887, consisted of 24 armor-clads, 27 cruisers, 10 side-wheel steamers, 30 gunboats for coast-defense, 27 torpedo-boats, and 26 other vessels. The iron-clad fleet comprised 6 turret-ships with rams, 7 monitor-rams, 5 other monitors, and 6 vessels for river-defense. The navy was manned by 7,204 sailors and 2,287 marines.

Finances.—The revenue is estimated in the budget for 1887 at 115,978,075 guilders, and the expenditure at 132,257,559 guilders. The yield of direct taxes is reckoned at 26,628,000 guilders; excise, 42,840,000 guilders; stamps, registration, and succession duties, 22,003,500 florins; customs, 4,912,000 guilders; postage 5,550,000 guilders; domains, 2,400,000 guilders; railroads, 2,080,000 guilders; telegraphs, 1,092,100; other receipts, 8,972,475 guilders. The expenditure for the service of the debt is set down at 33,871,314 guilders; for the Waterstaat and public works, 23,666,896 guilders; for the army, 20,386,989 guilders; for the navy, 12,336,000 guilders; for the department of the interior, 10,195,018 guilders;

indemnification of communes for the suppression of the *octroi*, 8,570,000 guilders; financial administration, 7,774,585 guilders; department of justice, 5,108,559 guilders; loss from the demonetization of silver under the law of April 27, 1884, 5,000,000 guilders; public worship, 1,978,660 guilders; foreign affairs, 681,151 guilders; civil list, 650,000 guilders; expenses of the Cabinet, 616,007 guilders; unforeseen expenses, 50,000 guilders.

The amount of the public debt in 1887, including 15,000,000 guilders of paper money, was 1,059,132,450 guilders, and the interest charge was 33,271,304 guilders, as compared with a capital in 1886 of 1,066,322,450 guilders and an interest charge of 34,389,288 guilders. The saving in the annual interest charged was effected by the conversion of 4 per cent. stock into 3½ per cents.

The concession to the Bank of the Netherlands was prolonged in 1887 till 1914. The capital is fixed at 20,000,000 guilders, which must be partly invested in public funds. All profits over 5 per cent. are divided between the stockholders and the Government, except one tenth laid aside as a reserve fund.

Extension of the Franchise.—The Legislature in 1887 adopted a bill introduced by the Ministry that increases the number of electors from 180,000 to 300,000. The principle of the bill was approved by the Chamber on March 23. All soldiers, except commissioned officers, are excluded from the franchise. The electoral law defining the qualifications of voters passed the Chamber on June 14. The franchise is extended to all who pay 10 guilders in personal or land taxes, as well as to lodgers. Amendments aiming at a still wider franchise were resolutely opposed by the Cabinet, and were rejected. Under the former electoral law, enacted in 1878, the limitation was from 20 to 160 guilders of direct taxes. The first Chamber adopted the proposed revision of the Constitution on November 5. After the promulgation of the statute, November 30, the Chambers were dissolved in order that elections might be held under the new law.

Socialist Disturbance.—Domela Nieuwenhuis, a wealthy Socialist and the acknowledged head of the party, was condemned to one year's solitary confinement for lese-majesty in 1886. In January, 1887, the sentence was confirmed by the Court of Cassation. On the King's birthday, the Socialists of Amsterdam, who manifested much indignation at the fate of their leader, held a meeting with closed doors. The police broke open the hall. The persons inside received them with revolver shots, and the police fired back. Twenty-three persons were carried to the hospital, some of whom had received fatal wounds.

Colonies.—Java and Madura, with an area of 131,733 square kilometres, had a population in 1884 of 20,931,654 persons, of whom 20,665,-510 were natives. The other Dutch possessions in the East Indies, embracing Sumatra, Riouw,

Banca, Billiton, Borneo, Celebes, the Moluccas, part of New Guinea, Timor, Bali, and other islands, have a total area of about 1,728,000 square kilometres, and a native population estimated at 8,400,000 souls. The number of Europeans in the Dutch East Indies in 1884 was 46,837, of whom 37,680 were in Java; the number of Chinese, 364,028; the number of Arabs, 16,194; the number of Hindus and others, 8,824. Batavia, the political capital, had a population of 89,401 souls. Other important cities are Soerabaya with 123,177, and Samarang with 68,928 inhabitants. The budget for 1887 estimates the revenue at 133,561,632 guilders and the expenditure at 136,899,953 guilders. The imports of merchandise in 1885 had a total value of 123,869,000 guilders; the exports, 185,129,000 guilders. The imports of specie were 15,499,000 guilders; the exports, 2,942,000 guilders. The value of the exports of coffee in 1884 was 49,152,000 guilders; sugar, 71,807,000 guilders; tin, 8,289,000 guilders; indigo, 8,933,000 guilders; hides and skins, 2,097,000 guilders; cloves and nutmegs, 1,899,-000 guilders; rice, 1,467,000 guilders; tobacco, 16,879,000 guilders; tea, 1,774,000 guilders; gambier, 2,270,000 guilders; gutta-percha, 3,-340,000 guilders; gum, 4,628,000 guilders; pepper, 2,568,000 guilders; rattan, 8,200,000 guilders. The number of vessels engaged in foreign commerce that were entered at the ports of the Netherlandish East Indies in 1885 was 4,749, of the aggregate capacity of 8,201,199 cubic metres. In the beginning of 1887 there were in operation on the island of Java 940 kilometres of railroads. The Government contemplates the construction of a line on the island of Sumatra from Mocara Kalaban through Fort de Hock, the seat of government, to the Bay of Brandewyns, for the purpose of utilizing the coal-fields on the Umbili river. The railroad is expected to be completed in six years at a cost of 16,000,000 guilders. The coal-beds are supposed to contain 200,000,000 tons, and the Government expects to make a profit of 600,000 guilders a year. The receipts of the state lines in 1885 were 4,260,677 guilders, and the expenses 2,355,665 guilders; the receipts of the Netherlands India Railway Company were 3,537,156 guilders, and the expenses 1,486,128 guilders. The length of the state lines of telegraph in 1885 was 5,766 kilometres, with 7,806 kilometres of wires. The lines in Java had a length of 3,629 kilometres, while 2,068 kilometres were on the island of Sumatra. The number of paid messages in 1885 was 370,629, including 91,100 international dispatches.

Surinam or Dutch Guiana has an area of 119,321 square kilometres, and contained 74,132 inhabitants in 1884. The capital is Paramaribo, the population of which was 25,444. There were 98 marriages, 1,962 births, and 1,522 deaths recorded in the colony in 1885. The population, exclusive of Indians and the savage colonies of escaped negro slaves, was reckoned on Dec. 31, 1885, at 57,132 persons, of whom 29,431 were of the male and 27,701 of the female sex. The expenses of the Government in 1887 were estimated in the budget at 1,614,282 guilders, and the revenue at 1,807,143 guilders.

The colony of Curaçao or the Dutch Antilles comprises the islands of Curaçao, Bonaire, Aruba, part of St. Martin, St. Eustatius, and Saba. Their combined area is 1,180 square kilometres, and their population 44,734. On Dec. 31, 1885, the sedentary population was computed to be 44,410 persons, comprising 20,090 males and 24,320 females. The number of marriages in 1885 was 142; of births, 1,640; of deaths, 1,014. The revenue for 1887 is estimated at 635,051 guilders, and the expenditure at the same figure.

NEVADA. State Government.—The following were the State officers during the year: Governor, Christopher C. Stevenson, Republican; Lieutenant-Governor, Henry C. Davis; Secretary of State, John M. Dormer; Treasurer, George Tufly; Comptroller, J. F. Hallock; Attorney-General, John F. Alexander; Superintendent of Public Instruction, W. C. Dovey; Chief-Justice of the Supreme Court, O. R. Leonard; Associate Justices, O. H. Belknap and Thomas P. Hawley.

Legislative Session.—The thirteenth biennial Legislature met on the 3d of January, and continued in session sixty days. Ex-United States Senator William M. Stewart, Republican, was chosen to succeed United States Senator James G. Fair, receiving 43 votes in both houses, to 14 for George W. Cassidy, the Democratic nominee. Stewart was nominated by the Republican caucus without a contest. The legislation of the session embraces an act requiring all voters to take an oath against polygamy, an act authorizing the issue of 4-per-cent. bonds to the amount of $161,000 for the benefit of the general State fund, and the following acts and resolutions:

Providing for the manner of submitting constitutional amendments to the voters of the State.

For the better preservation of titles to mining-claims.

Authorizing county commissioners to bring suit against persons or corporations depositing sawdust in the waters of the State.

Prohibiting and punishing the manufacture and use of dynamite machines or other devices, in destruction of human life and property.

Protecting deer, antelope, mountain-sheep, and elk, from January 1 to September 1.

Releasing insolvent debtors on payment of 50 per cent. of indebtedness.

Providing for a State Immigration Bureau.

Forbidding houses of prostitution within 400 yards of public-school houses, or upon the public thoroughfare of any village.

Changing the legal rate of interest from 10 per cent. to 7 per cent.

Prohibiting the sale of cigarettes, cigars, and tobacco to minors under 18 years.

Fixing the poll-tax at $3.

Constituting the Governor, State Comptroller, and State Treasurer a board of commissioners for the care and maintenance of the State indigent insane.

Prohibiting the sale of ardent spirits to Indians.

To establish a State weather-service station.

To punish false pretenses in obtaining registration of cattle and other animals.

Providing for the observance of Arbor Day in the State.

Authorizing the county of Lincoln to issue bonds to aid in railroad construction.

To establish and provide for an Indian school in Ormsby County.

Granting the consent of the State to the annexation of southern Idaho.

Offering a bounty for the destruction of coyotes, lynxes, and California lions.

Creating a new Capitol Commission.

Providing for the proof of Indian war-claims against the State.

Requiring partners in business to file a certificate of partnership, with the names of each partner.

To prevent the importation and sale of diseased animals.

To encourage the construction of the Nevada and Southwestern Railroad.

To prevent drunkenness in office, and to punish it.

For the preservation of fish in Humboldt river and its tributaries.

Repealing the tax on dogs.

Providing a penalty for driving diseased live-stock, or allowing it to run at large.

Consolidating the offices of county superintendent of schools and district attorney.

To encourage the construction of the Nevada, Idaho, and Montana Railroad.

Consolidating the offices of sheriff and county assessor, and providing for the appointment of assistant assessors.

Enabling the owners of irrigating ditches to construct and maintain waste-ditches or flumes through the land of others, if necessary, in order to carry off surplus waters.

To regulate and license mutual life associations.

Consolidating the offices of county clerk and county treasurer.

Providing for the acceptance of surety companies as sureties on bonds required by law.

To provide for the recording of births and deaths in each county.

Licensing hurdy-gurdy houses and dance-houses or concert-saloons.

Granting convicts six days' commutation of sentence in every month for good behavior, at the discretion of the prison authorities.

Abolishing the office of road supervisor.

Providing a bounty for the sinking of artesian wells.

Giving every person who shall contract to purchase land from the State, and has paid money under such contract, the right to exclusive possession, if no actual adverse possession existed in another at the time of such contract, and the right to defend such possession at law or in equity as if an owner in fee.

Requiring all doors in public buildings to open outward.

Repealing the law making the practice of treating with intoxicating liquors in public places unlawful.

An act to encourage mining declares that "every contract, patent, or deed hereafter made by the State or the authorized agents thereof shall contain a provision expressly reserving all mines of gold, silver, copper, lead, cinnabar, or other valuable minerals; and the State, for itself and its grantees, hereby disclaims any interest in mineral lands selected by the State on account of any grant from the United States. All persons desiring titles to mines upon lands which have been selected by the State must obtain such title from the United States, notwithstanding such selection." It further declares that any citizen may enter upon these selected lands, whether sold or unsold by the State, and explore for minerals and mine them when found, under the laws of miners and of the United States. If improvements have been made upon these lands by purchasers, such improvements may be condemned for the uses and purposes of mining in like manner as private property is condemned and taken for public use. "Mining for gold and other minerals is the paramount interest of the State and is hereby declared to be a public use."

Constitutional Amendments. — Of the three amendments, which were voted upon at the November election in 1886, but were not legally proposed or adopted, owing to defective procedure in the Legislature of 1883 and at the polls, only one, prescribing an easier method of constitutional amendment, was passed again by the Legislature this year. As this amendment was legally passed at the session of 1885, it has now been legally adopted at two successive sessions, as required by the Constitution, and is ready for submission to the people according to the method prescribed by the Legislature. This method, as established by a general law this year, provides for a popular vote at the general election next after the second passage by the Legislature. It will therefore be submitted to the people for the second time in November, 1888. At that election ten other amendments, which received the approval of the Legislature this year for the second time, will be voted upon. These amendments abolish the office of Lieutenant-Governor; provide that the Senate shall elect its own president, who shall succeed to the governorship in case of a vacancy; postpone the meeting of the Legislature to the third Monday of January; revise the power of the Legislature to pass local or special laws; permit an increase of the special school-tax to two mills, if necessary, and give the State, instead of the counties, the duty of providing for infirm and indigent citizens. The Legislature also proposed this year, for the first time, four other amendments, one of which deprives Mormons of the ballot; another authorizes lotteries in the State; another permits the abolition or consolidation of certain county offices; and another makes women eligible for school offices. These amendments can not reach the people before 1890. The Legislature finally reached the conclusion that the whole Constitution would better be revised, and accordingly voted to submit to the people, at the general election in November, 1888, the question of calling a constitutional convention.

Finances. — The total amount of State tax paid into the treasury by the counties during the year was $225,374.33, with the accounts of one county still unsettled. The total assessed valuation of real and personal property, and of the net proceeds of mines during the year, was $27,997,339.23, an increase of more than $1,600,000 over 1886. The State tax of ninety cents upon this amount yields a revenue of $251,976.05 for the year.

Education. — Reports from all but four districts show that the number of attendants on the public schools for the year was 9,828, a gain of 508 over the total from all districts in 1886. The number of white children in the State under the age of 21 is 14,236, and the number of children under the same age, white, colored, and Chinese, is 14,537. During the year over $63,000 was apportioned from the State school fund among the schools of the State. The remainder in this fund at the beginning of the year was $147,632.53.

The State University, which was removed from Elko to Reno by an act of the Legislature of 1885, has been established at the latter place, and was put into full working condition this year. The university building is a substantial brick structure, erected at a cost of over $20,000, a short distance from the town. It was first opened for pupils in March, 1886, and fifty-six had been admitted before the close of that year. The faculty then consisted of two professors, and a president was added during the present year. A preparatory course of two years, a university course, and a normal-school course are established. The legislative appropriation for it in 1887 and 1888 amounts to $22,600, exclusive of the building-fund.

State Prison. — The number of convicts in the State Prison on the first day of the year was 132. The cost of maintaining the prison for 1885-'86 was $75,819.98, or $7,649.89 less than for 1883-'84, and $21,558.98 less than for 1881-'82. A large part of the convicts are engaged in the manufacture of boots and shoes.

Railroads. — The Central Pacific Railroad enters the State at Verdi, on the California line, and traverses it from west to east. It is 450 miles in length, and is the grand trunk line, from which several feeders run into the heart of the country. The Virginia and Truckee Railroad runs from Reno, on the Central Pacific, through Carson City to Virginia City, and is 52 miles in length. The Nevada and Oregon begins at Reno, and runs north into California, having a length of 28 miles in the State. The Nevada Central runs south from Battle Mountain on the Central Pacific to Ledley, 93 miles. From this point the Austin City Railroad runs to Austin, three miles distant. The Carson and Colorado road runs from Mound House, on the Virginia and Truckee route, southerly into California. Its length in the State is 192 miles. The Eureka and Palisade is also a branch of the Central Pacific, running south to Eureka, 90 miles. The Eureka and Ruby Hill is 5 miles in length, and the Lake Tahoe 10. The total length of these lines is 922 miles. There was no new construction during the year.

Mining. — The bullion produced from mines on the Comstock lode in 1887 exceeded $5,000,000. Of that sum above $4,000,000 was the product of the Consolidated California and Virginia mine, out of which $1,800,000 was disbursed in dividends to stockholders. During the year the Ophir, Savage, Hale and Norcross, Potosi, and Alta were added to the list of bullion-yielding mines, and the total product in 1888 will probably exceed $8,000,000, which is within a fraction of the total yield of the State in 1886.

Agriculture.—The number of horses in the State on Jan. 1, 1887, was 44,654, valued at $2,461,449; mules, 1,657, valued at $121,251; milch cows, 17,688, valued at $638,256; oxen and other cattle, 817,059, valued at $6,949,983; sheep, 674,486, valued at $1,153,871; hogs, 14,543, valued at $77,839; making a total of 1,070,082 animals, valued at $11,401,599. The number of animals in the State one year previous was 1,024,425, valued at $11,356,092. The cattle interests of the State are next in importance to its mineral resources. It is estimated that the shipments of beef cattle to San Francisco in 1887 exceeded 200,000 head. The wool product of the State in 1887 was about 3,000,000 pounds. The acreage of alfalfa will be doubled this year. Esparat, a German grass highly recommended for its cattle - fattening properties, is being successfully grown on the rocky, barren hillsides in Douglas County.

State Lands.—There were 1,306 applications to purchase State lands filed during 1887 at the State Land-office, covering 428,788·08 acres. Of this amount there was selected of the Two-Million-Acre-Grant: In the Eureka Land District, 226,504·27; in the Carson City Land District, 156,206·15; total, 382,710·42. Ninety-two contracts were issued in duplicate, covering 16,401·68 acres at $1.25 per acre, and twenty-eight contracts, covering 2,267·08 acres, at $2.50 per acre, representing $22,935.84. State land patents were issued covering 24,006·67 acres. The State received during the year $140,260.63 from the sale of its lands.

Irrigation.—The Surveyor-General reports as follows: "There is no regular system of irrigation or use of water. Every farm is independent of the other, especially along a stream where each irrigator takes the water out through a ditch of his own. When irrigators are supplied through a corporation ditch, a system is made use of and little water is wasted; but even then lawsuits occur from water being run from one farm on to another, to the damage of the latter. In most places a system is very badly needed, as much more land could be cultivated and the present places more easily and profitably handled. There are many places where reservoirs could be created and water stored, and where in flood season the surplus waters from melting snow or falling rains could be turned into and kept for the dry periods of the year. The State might engage in this enterprise of storing this valuable material that annually goes to waste." The Legislature considered the subject at some length this year, but failed to pass any helpful legislation.

NEW BRUNSWICK. Government.—The Provincial Government remains as described in the "Annual Cyclopædia" for 1886, with the exception that A. G. Blair, Attorney-General, has succeeded Mr. Gillespie as Premier.

Commerce.—New Brunswick and Prince Edward Island are the only provinces of Canada whose trade increased in 1886. The following table shows the imports and exports of New Brunswick for five years, including both home and foreign produce:

Year ended 30th June—	IMPORTS.		EXPORTS.	
	Total value.	Value per head.	Total value.	Value per head.
1882	$6,707,944	$20 57	$7,474,407	$22 92
1883	6,973,191	21 14	7,520,107	22 80
1884	6,467,858	19 40	7,768,072	23 26
1885	5,972,886	17 75	6,489,298	19 23
1886	5,849,580	17 22	6,547,096	19 27

The following table shows the trade of New Brunswick with the United States in the same period; the exports including foreign produce:

YEAR.	Imports from United States.	Exports to United States.	Totals.
1882	$2,728,597	$1,935,557	$4,664,154
1883	3,214,333	2,163,196	5,378,029
1884	8,098,292	2,006,527	5,104,819
1885	2,799,440	2,024,469	4,823,909
1886	2,973,765	1,858,996	4,832,761

Legislation.—The twenty-sixth General Assembly of this province met on March 3, 1887, for its first session. Among the most important legislation of the session was the act authorizing the appointment of a Provincial Board of Health, of not more than seven members, to "take cognizance of the interests of health and life among the people of the province." The board is directed to make an intelligent and profitable use of all information available as to deaths and sickness among the people; to make sanitary investigations and inquiries respecting causes of disease, and especially of epidemics; the causes of mortality and the effects of localities, employments, conditions, habits, and other circumstances upon the health of the people; to make suggestions as to the prevention of contagious and infectious diseases; to advise the officers of the Government and local boards of health in regard to public health; to disseminate sanitary literature; to receive evidence on oath in special sanitary investigations; to provide for compulsory vaccination; and to make and enforce quarantine regulations. The act also provides for the appointment of local boards of health by cities, towns, and municipalities, with extensive powers.

Liquor-License Law.—Another important act passed by the General Assembly was the liquor-license act. This provides for the granting of only two kinds of licenses—tavern licenses and wholesale licenses. A tavern license authorizes the licensee to sell in quantities of not more than one quart. The license duties are to be fixed by the councils of the various districts, but must not be more than $200 nor less than $50 in cities and incorporated towns: elsewhere the minimum is $25. Applications for licenses must be supported by one third of the rate-payers in the polling division. Objections may be filed on the ground of the character of the applicant; the condition of the premises; on the score of contiguity to a place of worship, school, or hospital, or simply on the ground that the tavern is not required in the neighborhood. Every tavern is required to provide hotel accommodation, and every tavern-keeper to furnish bonds as security for good behavior. The number of licenses to be granted is restricted; in cities and incorporated towns, to one for every 250 of the first thousand of the population, and one for each 500 additional; in the parishes to one for each four hundred up to 1,200, and one for each 1,000 beyond. One license may be granted in each parish, no matter how small the population. The council of any municipality may, during the month of January, by by-law, prohibit the granting of any licenses during the year, and until the by-law is repealed. The parent, child, master, guardian, or creditor of any person who has contracted the habit of drinking to excess, may require the chief inspector to give notice to any liquor-seller not to supply such person with liquor, under penalty of fifty dollars. Whenever any person comes to his death by suicide, drowning, perishing from cold, or other accident, while intoxicated, the tavern-keepers supplying the liquor that caused the intoxication are held liable to suit for damages from $100 to $1,000 by the legal representatives of the deceased. In case an intoxicated person commits an assault, or damages property, the tavern-keeper who sold him liquor may be held jointly responsible with him.

Registration of Births, Deaths, and Marriages.— An act was passed requiring every clergyman, teacher, minister, or other person authorized by law to baptize, marry, or perform funeral services in the province, to keep a register of the persons whom he has baptized or married, or who have died within his cure; also requiring the father of any child born in the province, or in case of his death or absence the mother, or in case of the inability of both parents, then any person standing in their place, the occupier of the house in which the birth occurs, or the nurse attending, to register the birth of the child within thirty days. In the case of an illegitimate child, it is not lawful to register any person as the father, unless at the joint request of the mother and of the person acknowledging himself to be the father. The penalty for failure to comply with the act by any of the persons referred to is a fine of from one to twenty dollars and costs. The Provincial Secretary is appointed Registrar-General of the Province, and the Lieutenant-Governor in council is authorized to appoint a division registrar in each county.

NEWFOUNDLAND. Government. — Governor, Sir George William Des Dœux, K. C. M. G. Executive Council: Robert Thorburn, Premier; M. Fenelon, Colonial Secretary, William S. Donnelly, Receiver-General; James S. Winter, Q. C., Attorney - General; Augustus F. Goodridge and Charles R. Ayre.

Commerce.—The total imports in 1886 were valued at $6,020,035; the total exports at $4,-862,951. Of the exports, those produced in the colony were valued at $4,833,735. The exports to the United States were valued at $288,453; the imports therefrom at $1,672,810.

The principal article imported is flour; the total value of flour imported in 1886 was $1,-285,758, of which $682,528 was from Canada, and $601,686 from the United States. The principal export is dried cod-fish, the total export of which was valued at $3,481,987.

Shipping.—During the year 1886, 106 vessels were built in Newfoundland, of 8,784 total tonnage; $11,852 bounty being paid thereon. The shipping on the register of the Receiver-General of the colony, on Dec. 31, 1886, was as follows: 2,019 sailing-vessels, 85,588 tons; 25 steam-vessels, 5,291 tons; total, 2,044 vessels, 90,879 tons.

NEW HAMPSHIRE. State Government.—Elections occur biennially in November of even years; legislative sessions bienially in June of odd years. Governor, Charles Henry Sawyer, Republican; Governor's Council—Nathaniel Clark, Republican; John C. Linehan, Republican; Charles Williams, Republican; John B. Smith, Republican; Albert S. Batchellor, Democrat; Secretary, Ai B. Thompson; Editor and Compiler of State Papers, Isaac W. Hammond; Indexer of State Papers, Edward Aiken; Treasurer, Solon A. Carter; Public Printer, John B. Clarke, Manchester; Insurance Commissioner, Oliver Pillsbury; Librarian, William H. Kimball; Superintendent of Public Instruction, James W. Patterson; Adjutant-General, Augustus D. Ayling; Secretary of Board of Health, Irving A. Watson; Secretary of Board of Agriculture, Nahum J. Batchelder. Board of Equalization of Taxes—John M. Hill, Chairman; Charles A. Dole, Secretary. Board of Railroad Commissioners—Henry M. Putney, Chairman; Edward B. S. Sanborn, Edward J. Tenney (succeeded by Benjamin F. Prescott). Board of Bank Commissioners—George E. Gage (succeeded by Alonzo I. Nute), James O. Lyford. Supreme Judicial Court—Chief-Justice, Charles Doe; Associate Justices, Isaac W. Smith, William H. H. Allen, Lewis W. Clark, Isaac N. Blodgett, Alonzo P. Carpenter, and George A. Bingham; Attorney-General, Daniel Barnard; Law Reporter, William S. Ladd.

Political.—Official votes, election of 1886: For Governor, whole vote, 77,394. Charles Henry Sawyer, Republican, had 37,799 votes; Thomas Cogswell, Democrat, 37,338; Joseph Wentworth, Prohibitionist, 2,137; scattering vote, 120. Sawyer's plurality, 461. There being no majority for Governor the choice from the constitutional candidates (the two having the largest number of votes) devolved upon the Legislature of 1887, which, in convention of both houses, voted as follows: Whole vote, 324; Sawyer, 178; Cogswell, 146.

Legislative Session.—Senate, 24 members—15 Republicans and 9 Democrats; President, Frank D. Currier. House of Representatives, 308 members—167 Republicans and 141 Democrats; Speaker, Alvin Burleigh. Both bodies met and organized on June 1, 1887, and were in session till November 5, during which time 279 public acts and 46 joint resolutions were passed, all of which received the Governor's signature. Among the acts and joint resolutions were the following:

To extend the Whitefield and Jefferson Railroad.
To annex Roxbury to Keene.
To amend charter of Concord.
To revive charter of Swift River Railroad.
To incorporate Blackwater Valley Railroad.
For preservation of local histories and financial and other reports of towns, etc.
Incorporating Lake Shore Railroad.
Decree of estates in divorce proceedings.
Relating to New Hampshire National Guard.
Transfer of stock in corporation as collateral security.
Authorizing a railroad between Northfield and Franklin.
Amending chapter 112 of General Laws.
To revive and extend the charter of Littleton and Franconia Railroad.
Incorporating Boston, Concord, and Montreal Railroad.
To make Election-day a legal holiday.
To prevent fraudulent registration of cattle.
Annexing a portion of Wilmot to Danbury.
To provide for weekly payment of wages.
To regulate hours of labor and employment of women and children in manufacturing and mechanical establishments.
Relative to extirpation of pluro-pneumonia and other contagious diseases.
Defining duties of Insurance Commissioner.
Relating to savings-banks deposits.
To annex Crawford's Grant to Carroll.
To revive the charter of the Concord and Rochester Railroad.
To amend the charter of the Windsor and Forest Line Railroad.
Relative to billiard-tables, etc.
In aid of purity of elections.
To record of investments in savings-banks.
To prevent vexatious interference with lawful trades and occupations.
Providing for taxation of fire-insurance companies.
To regulate transportation of intoxicating liquors.
Relative to actions for personal injuries resulting in death.
Fencing canals and water-ways.
Preservation and publication of local vital statistics.
In relation to wild animals.
Amendment of acts concerning preservation of ballots.
In relation to trust funds for support of common schools.
To incorporate the Bartlett and Albany Railroad.
Raising the age of consent in females.
Providing for highways to public waters.
To regulate heating of passenger-cars.
To ratify and confirm the lease of the Manchester and Lawrence to the Boston and Maine Railroad.
In relation to married women, in amendment of chapter 182, General Laws.
In relation to rights of husbands and wives for protection of minor children.
Assessment of taxes upon corporations.
To define and punish the misuse of railroad earnings.
Providing for a convention to revise the Constitution.
To authorize the Boston and Maine to purchase the franchise and property of the Eastern Railroad in New Hampshire.
To insure building the Lake Shore Railroad.
To prevent bribery and corruption.
In relation to interests of the State in the Concord and the Boston and Maine railroads.

Vetoes.—Three important railroad bills were vetoed, as follow:

"An act in amendment of chapter 100 of the laws of 1883, entitled an act providing for the establishment of railroad corporations by general law," "an act to authorize a lease of the Northern Railroad," and "an act regulating freights and fares on railroads and to provide for compensation to dissenting stockholders in case of railroad leases."

Finances.—The Treasurer reports as follows: Cash on hand, June 1, 1886, $84,353.06; receipts during the year, $1,108,044.84; total amount, $1,192,397.90; disbursements for the same time, $951,781.79; cash on hand June 1, 1887, $240,616.11; total, $1,192,397.90. Debt, June 1, 1886, $3,090,577.49; assets, June 1, 1886, $92,035.53; net indebtedness, $2,998,-541.97; liabilities, June 1, 1887, $3,079,161.30; assets at same date, $247,860.51; net indebtedness, $2,831,300.79; decrease of debt in the year, $167,241.18. Revenues—State tax, $400,-000; railroad tax, $101,191.22; insurance tax, $6,563.82; interest, $1,416.81; telegraph tax, $5,806.73; other items, $490.40; total, $516,-226.18. Expenses — ordinary, $142,841,72; extraordinary, $24,805.55; interest, $181,337.-68; total expenses, $348,984.95; excess of revenue over expenses, $167,241.18. Ordinary expenses in detail—salaries, $49,272.99; printers' accounts, $17,215.78; counsel, $1,554; State Library, $500; clerks of Supreme Court, $768.20; indigent insane, $6,000; convict insane, $2,962.10; National Guard, $24,999.51; bounty on wild animals, $1,198.05; fish commissioners, $2,273.59; State-House, $4,578.61; Industrial School, $6,000; Board of Agriculture. $948.51; Board of Equalization, $335.83; Board of Health, $867.30; treasurer's accounts, $200; independent militia, $400; bank commissioners, $4,140; clerk-hire adjutant-general's department, Superintendent Public Instruction, and Board of Health, each $500—$1,500; education of deaf and dumb,$3,997.45; education of blind, $3,600, and feeble-minded youth, $258.-28: Normal School, $5,000; New Hampshire reports, Volume LXIII, $1,050; incidentals, $2,-870.95; other small items, $550.57—$142,841.-72. Extraordinary expenses—abatements of State tax, $219.32; Agricultural College, $3,-000; White Mountain roads, $3,433.26; State Library, $498.19; State Prison, $3,204.74; indexing records, $1,200; dedication of Webster statue, $2,257.32; State-House, $1,279.55; Gettysburg monuments, $1,500; Deaf-Mute mission, $150; publication military records, $1,200; boundary survey, $6,416; other small items, $447.17—$24,805.55.

Constitutional Convention.—The act providing for a convention of delegates for the purpose of revising the Constitution enacts that delegates shall be chosen at the regular biennial election in November, 1888, and that the convention shall meet in Concord on the first Wednesday in January, 1889. The delegates are to be chosen in the same manner and proportion as representatives to the general court. Provision for submitting the amendments to the people and ascertaining their decision, and declaring and publishing it will be made by the convention.

Fire Insurance. — The Commissioner makes his eighteenth annual report, covering the business of 1886, in which he says that the fire-insurance companies organized under the laws of New Hampshire, number eight stock companies, seventeen State companies, and twenty-one town companies. This constitutes the legitimate fire-insurance force in the State; the outside companies, heretofore licensed, having ceased active operations in this State. The home fire companies assumed risks in this State, in 1886, as follows: Stock companies, $31,936,240; State mutual companies, $15,530,194; town mutual companies, $2,609,924; total, $50,076,358. The Governor, in his message to the Legislature, June 1, 1887, said: "As a consequence of the insurance laws enacted by the last Legislature, fifty-eight foreign fire-insurance companies combined and simultaneously withdrew their agencies from the State, refusing to continue to insure New Hampshire property under those laws. This concerted and organized movement of the withdrawing companies justified the charge that it was a deliberate attempt at coercion, by discrediting the laws to make them obnoxious to the people, the understood object being not only to compel a repeal of the laws, but also to intimidate other States from legislating in the same direction. While they had an undoubted right to refuse New Hampshire risks, each company acting in its own capacity and independently of other companies, in banding together and agreeing to act in concert to punish and distress the property and business interests of the State, their course was justly open to censure. It was in effect a strike and a boycott in the accepted meaning of these terms."

The total losses paid by home companies in 1886 was $112,030; by retired companies, $155,487; by manufacturers' mutuals,$388; by outside agency companies, $12,560; total, $280,465.

Life Insurance.—The summary of business for 1886 is as follows: Number of policies issued, 3,841; amount insured, $4,534,356; policies in force, December 31, 7,605; amount insured, $12,694,803; premiums received in 1886, $379,037.55; death losses and other claims paid, $306,263.29.

Savings - Banks. — Herewith is a condensed statement of savings-banks at time of examinations in 1886 and 1887:

ITEMS.	1886.	1887.
Due depositors	$46,681,918 72	$50,292,556 85
Guaranty fund...............	2,149,558 08	2,443,816 68
Surplus	1,671,922 84	1,774,578 18
Miscellaneous indebtedness..	470,569 19	14,222 73
Total...................	$50,923,868 21	$54,524,779 84

Railroads.—The forty-third annual report of the Board of Railroad Commissioners furnishes the following information of the roads in the State: Their value, which depends upon their capacity to earn dividends, as represented by the market value of their securities, is greater than ever, and their physical condition is better. Their rolling-stock has been greatly increased, and is more serviceable. They are doing more business, are operated with greater regularity, speed, and safety, and with more regard to the convenience of the public. The cost of constructing and furnishing these several roads, to the time they may be said to have been finished, is estimated at about $35,000,000. Of this amount about $9,000,000 has never paid any dividends, and is irrecoverably lost. The capital stock of all corporations reporting is $45,691,742.74; funded debt, $25,075,100; floating indebtedness, $8,261,882.10; total liabilities, $79,028,724.84. Total standard-gauge mileage in the State, with branches, 1,041; double track, 66 miles; sidings, 197 miles; total. 1,804 miles.

The taxable property of the State for the present year has been reduced for taxation fifteen per cent. less than its actual value. The valuation of railroads, telegraphs, and telephones, was reduced in like proportion, deducting amounts taxed in and paid to towns. The amount thus obtained is assessed at the rate of other property throughout the State— $1.88 on each $100 of valuation.

The Nashua street-railway was opened for business in the spring of 1886, and its business covers six months in its report. The road is two miles long. An extension of the Manchester street road from Elm Street to Hallsville, a mile, was opened in the autumn of 1885. The earnings of the Manchester, Concord, Dover, (nine months), and Laconia and Lake Village roads in 1885, were $47,801.24, and the operating expenses for the same period was $42,208.28, leaving a net income of $5,593.96. In 1886 the earnings were $62,450.13; expenses, $57,964.68; net income, $4,485.45. These roads in 1885 carried 881,600 passengers, and in 1886 carried 1,105,888.

Board of Health.—The annual reports of the State Board of Health are prepared primarily for the education of the people of the State upon sanitary topics. The most noticeable indications of progress appear in the abandoning of polluted wells for water-supply in villages, and the introduction of an abundance of wholesome water; the sewering of places that had no system of drainage; the demand for local boards of health that will accomplish something; the construction of public buildings upon a thorough sanitary basis; the introduction of hygienic instruction in the public schools; a better knowledge of prevention of zymotic diseases; a more rational view of avoidance of contagious diseases among children, etc. The board has accomplished much in efforts to secure better water for drinking and household purposes. Public water-supplies, from sources of undoubted wholesomeness, have been constructed in many of the larger towns. Much attention has been given to the causes leading to diphtheria and typhoid fever, and their removal; the consideration of influences affecting the quality of milk, from a sanitary standpoint; the sanitary survey of school-houses, and air-supplies; and the disposal of waste matter. The Legislature of 1887 enacted laws in relation to the extirpation of pleuro-pneumonia, and other contagious diseases, and the publication of local vital statistics.

Vital Statistics.—The sixth annual reports of registration of vital statistics comprise returns to Dec. 31, 1885. The marriage-rate in the State for 1885, was 9·16; birth-rate, 18·21; death-rate, 17·87. The marriage-rate appears highest in Hillsborough, Strafford, Rockingham, Carroll, and Coös Counties, in order. The highest birth-rate given is from those counties relatively having the largest number of the laboring-classes. Hillsborough County, with its large number of factory operatives, gives 25·8 per 1,000; Coös, with a large number of lumbermen, foreigners, 24·86; Cheshire, 17·78; Strafford, 17·46. There are reported, for 1885, 6,319 births. There were 56 twin births. In 26 marriages the brides were under fifteen years of age; in 156 cases the man was between fifteen and twenty, and the woman the same in 792 cases; 36 men and 7 women were between seventy and eighty, and 2 men were over eighty. In 459 instances the bride was older than the groom; 553 were widowers, and 419 widows. To the fourth marriage were 3 men and 4 women, and 1 man to the fifth marriage. The oldest couple were eighty-two and seventy-two, and the youngest sixteen and fourteen. The 291 divorces granted were for the following causes: abandonment, 83; adultery, 62; three years' absence, 19; extreme cruelty, 85; habitual drunkenness, 84; treatment injurious to health, 4; impotency, 2; conviction of crime and imprisonment, 2. Of the libellants, 94 were men, and 197 women. Consumption caused more deaths than any single disease—857; 373 males, and 480 females; 4 sex not stated. Other causes of death were: pneumonia, 244 males, 259 females; apoplexy and paralysis, 234 males, 256 females; heart-disease, 241 males, 233 females; old age, 179 males, 240 females; cholera infantum, 110 males, 109 females; cancer, 74 males, 189 females; typhoid fever, 67 males, 74 females; meningitis, 70 males, 64 females; Bright's disease, 70 males, 42 females; brain-diseases, 51 males, 58 females; bronchitis, 41 males, 67 females; debility, 55 males, 52 females; diarrhœa and dysentery, 46 males, 54 females; dropsy, 39 males, 52 females; diphtheria, 37 males, 41 females; convulsions, 31 males, 43 females; croup, 42 males, 31 females; liver-diseases, 32 males, 30 females, scarlatina, 22 males, 31 females.

Fish and Game.—The variety of fish chiefly distributed in 1886 was brook-trout and landlocked salmon. Experience and observation have taught the commissioners that these varieties are the best for the waters of New Hampshire. The work of the commission for the past years has produced favorable and encouraging results in fish-culture, and in restocking the varied waters of the State. The number of brook-trout distributed the past year was over 600,000. Hebron river, a tributary to Newfound lake, is reputed to contain the finest spawning-grounds in the State for the landlocked salmon. The Plymouth and Sunapee hatcheries furnished for distribution in the State 1,300,000 young fish and eggs. Among the different kinds of fish planted for development are the brown trout, rainbow trout, Loch-Levan trout, known as the finest of European species. They were planted in Sunapee lake. The new trout, previously mentioned as inhabiting Sunapee, pronounced to be a variety of the *Oquassa* type, and believed to be a native of this lake, still excites much interest to sportsmen and fish scientists. Good has been accomplished by the enforcement of the game laws, as seen by the increase of deer in the northern portions of the State, where none have been seen for years. These laws have apparently put an end to much of the illegal snaring of the partridge. More than 325 fish and game wardens have been qualified.

Charities.—The State supports and educates its deaf, dumb, and blind in institutions outside of her limits; for its deaf and dumb, $3,997.45; blind, $3,600; idiotic and feeble-minded youth, $258.28; indigent insane at asylum, $6,000; convict insane, $2,962.10; asylum library, $100; Deaf-Mute Mission, $150; total, $11,326.11.

Industrial School.—The number in the school during the year was 150; discharged at expiration of sentence, 14; on probation, 11; honorably discharged, 7; in school, April 1, 1887, 119. Parentage: American, 73; Irish, 42; French, 28; 12 of other nationalities. These are instructed in reading, writing, arithmetic, geography, history, physiology, and philosophy. The State pays $6,000 for the school's support.

State Prison.—The number of convicts was 121; 118 males and 3 females. The earnings for the year were $16,508.17; expenses, $20,-024.85; balance against the institution, $3,-516.68. Commitments for seventeen years have averaged six per cent.; for the last year but four per cent.—a decrease commendable to the State.

Asylum for the Insane.—This has continued self-supporting. The debt of $20,000 incurred in the erection of the Bancroft building has been reduced to $11,000. The past year began with 317 patients; 136 men and 181 women. Admitted during the year 143—83 men and 60 women. Whole number during the year, 471—226 men and 245 women. Discharged, 95—54 men and 41 women. Daily average for the year, 321—137 men and 184 women. Of the

328 patients remaining at the end of the year, only 24 had prospects of cure. There were 38 deaths during the year. A winter work-shop for the patients is in operation, with a promise of good results. This is the first at-tempt at developing skilled labor among the patients of this institution, and the selection of the kind of labor to be done was experimental. The upholstering of mattresses, the manufact-ure of brooms, the reseating of chairs, tailoring, etc., were the most practical forms of industry. Twelve acres of land have been purchased on the shore of Lake Penacook, four miles distant from the asylum, where it is proposed to erect a summer cottage for such patients as are in condition to be benefited thereby. During the summer camping-parties of men visited the place twice a week. An open field furnished a play-ground. The men were permitted to walk to these grounds, cook their meals, fish, play ball, lounge, or indulge in other amuse-ments, and return at night. Women were con-veyed there in barges to spend the day.

Education.—By the report of the Superintend-ent of Instruction it appears that the number of school districts, under the law of 1885, by system of town schools, has been reduced from 1,890 to 275, and that the number of districts organized under special acts is forty-six—six less than the previous year. The schools num-bering twelve pupils or less have decreased from 888 to 640, and those numbering six or less from 359 to 166. Thus 494 small schools have been discontinued, which represented chiefly a wasteful expenditure of money under the old system. By the new system the average length of schools in the State has been 22·39 weeks, against 20·87 weeks last year. This be-comes more markedly noticeable from the ex-penditure of $454,873.92 for teachers under the old law, against $444,095.58 under the new law. The number of enrolled pupils the past year is 59,690, a decrease of 4,529, a result arising from more accurate returns, and the opening of parochial schools. The care of the schools has required 679 fewer teachers than by the old method. The wages of male teach-ers has averaged $41.03, against $40.22 last year. For female teachers, the average has been $24.46 a month, as per $23.56 the pre-vious year. More normal-school teachers were employed last year than before.

A year of more than usual prosperity in the Normal School is reported. The demand for teachers that have had some special preparation for their profession is increasing. There has been an attendance in the several departments as follows: Normal department—graduates, 22; number of different pupils, 68; training de-partment—high-school, 44; grammar-school, 41; intermediate school, 58; primary school, 50: total, 193.

NEW HEBRIDES, a group of islands in the Pacific Ocean. They are 30 in number, ex-tending 400 miles from north to south, and have a population of between 100,000 and 150,000 persons. Scotch Presbyterian mission-aries have made some progress in Christianizing the natives. Laborers have been recruited on the islands both for the Australian colonies and the French colony of New Hebrides. Traf-fic with the natives has been mainly carried on by English traders, while Frenchmen have es-tablished plantations on the islands in recent years. Since 1882 the English interests in the islands have been transferred to French colo-nists, who have purchased 700,000 acres from the former English proprietors, and nearly 1,000,000 acres more from native chiefs. The cultivation of these lands has been carried on to some extent by the labor of the islanders. The French corporation, called the New Heb-rides Company, has attempted more recently to introduce agricultural colonists from France. Several parties were taken out and were set to work on railroads leading to the lands that were to be conceded to them. The majority fell sick from the effects of the climate, many died, most of those who survived returned to Nou-mea, and those who had the means went back to France. The colonists were workmen and peasants who were sent out with their wives and families by the Colonization Society, which has furnished settlers of the same class for New Caledonia and other French islands.

In 1878, when the Australian press was urging the annexation of the New Hebrides by Great Britain, the French ambassador at Lon-don wrote to Lord Derby, saying that, as his Government had no intentions with regard to the group, it would like to have the matter set at rest by a like declaration of the British Government. The British Government an-swered that it had no intention of interfering with the independence of the islands. This agreement was a renewal of an understanding that was come to between the two govern-ments as early as 1840, and took the form of definite promises in 1858. In 1888 the ques-tion of annexation was again agitated in Aus-tralia, and the French Government sent a communication asking whether the declara-tions of 1878 were still adhered to on the part of the English Government, as they were on its own part, because otherwise it would be compelled to insist on the maintenance of the existing state of affairs. Lord Granville, who was then Foreign Minister, replied in a dispatch to Lord Lyons, the British ambassador at Paris, that the agreement of 1878 was consid-ered perfectly valid. A *note verbale* to that effect was handed in at the French Ministry of Foreign Affairs. Lord Derby had assured the Australian colonies that no proposition for the annexation of the New Hebrides by a for-eign power would be entertained without con-sulting the colonies and securing arrangements satisfactory to them. In January, 1886, the French Government offered to relinquish the deportation of relapsed criminals to the Pacific if it were allowed to annex the New Hebrides. Lord Rosebery communicated the proposition

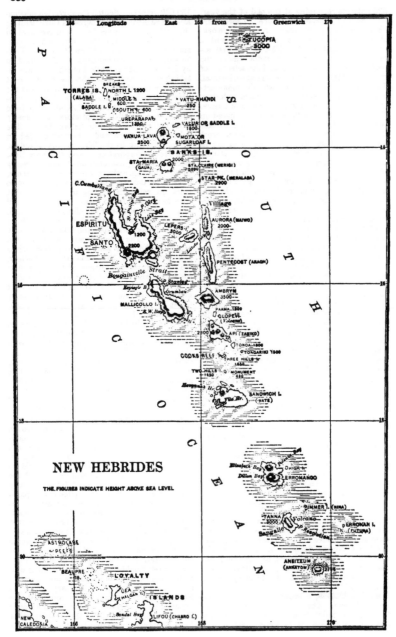

NEW HEBRIDES

THE FIGURES INDICATE HEIGHT ABOVE SEA LEVEL

to the Colonial Office, which laid it before the governments of the Australian colonies. They refused to accede to such an arrangement.

The French Occupation.—In 1885 the natives had attacked French plantations in the New Hebrides, and killed and wounded several persons. On June 1, 1886, a French naval vessel that had been sent by the authorities at Noumea without the knowledge of the Government at Paris, arrived at Havanna Harbor, in the island of Exate, and landed 100 French marines, who established there a military post, and raised the French flag. Immediately afterward another force took possession of Port Sandwich, and established there a similar post. The occupation of the islands by France excited the indignation and anger of the Australians, who were already greatly stirred up over the French recidivist law. The aim of French legislators in regard to their penal settlement in the Pacific was not simply to rid France of habitual malefactors, but, by removing criminals from the associations and conditions which prevented even those who desired to live an honest life from reforming, to give them every opportunity and incentive to become prosperous agriculturists. Quite as baseless as the expectations of the French reformers was the anxiety and dread produced in Australia by the humanitarian legislation of the French Parliament. There have been rare instances of convicts from New Caledonia escaping in open boats, crossing the 700 miles of intervening ocean, and landing on the coast of Queensland. After performing such a feat of daring and endurance, they have sometimes been succored and concealed from the authorities by Queenslanders who admired their courage and pitied their sufferings. Thus a few transported felons have escaped into Australia. The military occupation of the New Hebrides by the French was interpreted in only one way by the Australians, whose minds were filled with the dread of an influx of French criminals kept up by the factitious agitation of the recidivist question. They supposed that, since the land available for reformed criminal settlements in New Caledonia was now occupied, the French Government intended to extend these settlements to the New Hebrides. Such a project was, in fact, entertained by a benevolent society in France. The Imperial Government had declined to annex the various unoccupied islands of the Pacific when urged to do so by the Australian. Recently it had been impelled by the exigencies of European politics to acquiesce in the occupation of the northern coast of Papua by the Germans. Similar motives might now induce it to assent to the French annexation of the New Hebrides, if it had not done so already. The colonial conference that was held in London in the spring of 1887, had two animated debates over the New Hebrides question, in which the feelings of the Australian colonists were so vigorously expressed that the Government omitted this part of the proceedings in the Blue Book containing the minutes of the conference.

The French ministers, in effect, perceiving the awkward situation in which the British Government was placed by the action of the French colonial authorities, which was at first discountenanced, but on inquiry was justified, by the Government at Paris, determined to use the New Hebrides question as a means of obtaining a favorable settlement of the Egyptian question. The French had gone tot he New Hebrides to protect the lives and property of colonists. They remained there in violation of their pledges, as the English had in Egypt, and replied to the representations of the British Foreign Office with the same sort of explanations and assurances that they were used to receiving from London with regard to the British occupation of the Nile valley. M. Flourens assured the English ambassador, after the French military had been quartered in substantial barracks for nearly a year at tho ports of the New Hebrides, that France had no intention of permanently occupying the islands, and no definitive character ought to be attributed to her action. As soon as satisfactory arrangements could be made for policing the islands so that Europeans would be preserved from outrage, he promised that the French troops should be withdrawn. Soon after the French force landed, the British Government sent a naval vessel to the New Hebrides. The English Cabinet, as soon as the French position was explained through diplomatic channels, proposed a system of joint naval protection. To this the French Government replied with a counter-proposal, which was declined on Nov. 26, 1886. The French Government insisted that the negotiations in regard to the New Hebrides and those relating to the neutralization of the Suez Canal should proceed *pari passu*. When asked to name a date for the evacuation of the New Hebrides, M. Flourens replied that he could not give a precise answer so long as England did not make known her intentions regarding Egypt and the Suez Canal. The subject was treated by the French Cabinet in connection with other territorial questions in regard to Pacific islands, and was not finally settled till October, 1887, when the British Government agreed also to the Suez Canal convention.

The New Hebrides Convention.—The convention that was concluded between the British and the French government contains five articles. A joint naval control of the islands was agreed on, and a date was fixed for the withdrawal of the French troops. The English Government agreed to abrogate the treaty made in 1847 between Lord Palmerston and the Comte de Jarnac regarding the neutrality of the Leeward Islands, and allow the French to extend the Tahiti protectorate to the islands of Huahine, Raiatea, and Borabora, and the small islands adjacent thereto. This concession was embodied in the Newfoundland fisheries convention of October, 1885, but that instrument was not yet ratified, having failed to receive the assent of the colonial Legislature. The Australians expected the French Government to refrain from shipping convicts or recidivists to New Caledonia after the New Hebrides question was settled. In December, however, the announcement received at Melbourne that 800 more had embarked created fresh excitement, and the Victoria Government requested the Imperial Government to represent to the French Cabinet the deep feeling prevailing in the colony on the subject.

NEW JERSEY. State Government.—The following were the State officers during the year: Governor, Robert S. Green, Democrat; Secretary of State and Insurance Commissioner, Henry C. Kelsey; Treasurer, John J. Toffey; Comptroller, Edward L. Anderson; Attorney-General, John P. Stockton; Superintendent of Public Instruction, Edwin O. Chapman; Chief-Justice of the Supreme Court, Mercer Beasley; Associate Justices, Manning M. Knapp, Edward W. Scudder, Bennet Van Syckel, David A. Depue, Alfred Reed, Jonathan Dixon, Joel Parker (died in December), and William J. Magie; Chancellor, Theodore Runyon.

Legislative Session.—The Legislature, which met on January 11, was engaged for nearly two months in a bitter contest over the choice of a successor to United States Senator William J. Sewall. The elections of the autumn preceding had resulted in the return of 12 Republicans and 9 Democrats to the Senate, and 26 Republicans, 31 Democrats, and 2 Labor representatives to the Assembly, with one assembly district declared a tie. There was also a contest over the seat held by one of the Democratic assemblymen. Neither party was, therefore, sure of a majority on a joint ballot. Difficulties began when the Democrats of the Assembly entered a caucus to select candidates for Speaker and other Assembly officers. The proceedings of the majority of this caucus were so hostile to the ambition of some of the members from the country districts, that three of them—Messrs. Baird, Wolverton, and Arnwine—withdrew, and refused to join in any further action with their fellow-Democrats. Baird persisted in this course throughout the contest. The caucus, which was held in the Assembly chamber on the morning of the 11th, continued after the withdrawal of these members, and was not finished when the time for formal organization arrived. At that hour the Republican minority demanded entrance to the chamber, and, on being refused, forced the doors. The caucus, however, would not adjourn, but retired after the police had been called in to eject them. Securing the two Labor men and the three disaffected Democrats (which gave them 31 votes and a majority of the Assembly) the Republicans then held a meeting at which it was agreed to support Baird, one of the three Democrats, for Speaker, and a ticket for the minor officers was com-

pleted. This being done, the Democratic caucus was again invaded, and the coalition proceeded, amid great confusion and uproar, to organize and elect Baird as Speaker of the Assembly. A contest for possession of the chair then ensued between Baird and the chairman of the Democratic caucus, in which nearly all the Assembly joined. Baird finally succeeded in gaining the seat, when a motion to adjourn was made and carried. On the following day the election of Baird was conceded, and other Assembly officers were chosen; but the turbulent scenes of the former session were repeated when the question of deciding the rights of claimants in the two contested election cases was reached. In one of these cases, Turley, a Democrat, held a certificate to the seat; in the other a tie had been declared by Chief-Justice Beasley, before whom a recount had been made. A motion to admit Turley to his seat prevailed, but a similar motion to seat Walter, the Democratic claimant in the other case, was not successful. It then was voted to refer the evidence in both cases to the committee on elections when appointed, thus leaving Turley in possession of his seat until ousted by a vote of the Assembly. The committee on elections, as constituted by Speaker Baird, contained a majority of Republicans. On January 19 they reported a tie in the Walter-Jones case, recommending a new election, while the Democratic minority declared Walter entitled to the seat. The Assembly adopted the minority report by a vote of 30 to 29, Speaker Baird and the two Labor men voting with the Republicans, and the other two seceding Democrats joining their own party. The Democrats now had 31 members in the Assembly, a clear majority without the aid of Baird or the Labor men. But they continued to investigate these election cases till February 17, when, upon report of special committees, the rights of Turley and Walter were confirmed.

Meanwhile, on January 25, a Democratic caucus of 36 members nominated Ex-Gov. Leon Abbett for Senator. But Abbett was unable to control the entire strength of his party, and in a so-called joint convention held the next day, at which 8 Senators and 31 Assemblymen were present, he received only 38 votes, 3 less than a majority of the Legislature and 2 less than the total Democratic vote, exclusive of Baird. Conventions similar to this one were held each day by the Democrats till February 15; but they were all irregular for the reason that a majority of the Legislature was never present, and the Senate had not voted to enter a joint convention. In fact, the Senate postponed its organization from day to day till February 1, when officers were chosen, and refused to ballot upon the senatorship at all till February 15. On the 14th, a Republican caucus renominated Senator Sewall, but he, too, was unable to command the united support of his party. When, therefore, after separate balloting on the 15th, a joint convention was held on the 16th, it was

NEW JERSEY. 541

found that neither Abbett nor Sewell was likely to secure the election. Abbett received 85 votes, and Sewell 85, while 11 votes, including the 2 Labor votes, were divided between eight other candidates. Thirteen ballots were taken, with substantially the same result, neither Abbett nor Sewell being able to obtain more than 35 of the 41 votes necessary to a choice. On the fourteenth ballot, the Republicans, seeing the impossibility of electing one of their own party, even with their full vote, united with the anti-Abbett Democrats in the support of Rufus Blodgett, a Democrat, hitherto unmentioned for the office, who was believed to be unfriendly to Abbett. Blodgett received 39 votes on this ballot, and Abbett 38. The fifteenth and decisive ballot, cast on March 2, resulted in the election of Blodgett by a vote of 42, to 36 for Abbett.

The legislation of the session presents no marked features. A State board of agriculture was established, and also a State board of health and bureau of vital statistics. Local boards of health were required to be chosen in each city and township, and their duties were defined. Other acts of the session were as follow:

To incorporate improvement societies in towns, villages, and boroughs.

Authorizing municipal corporations to contract for a supply of water for public use.

Providing for summary arrests for violation of city ordinances.

Accepting the appropriation of money by Congress for the establishment of an agricultural experiment station.

Authorizing the borough governments of seaside resorts to construct and operate water-works.

Allowing camp-meeting associations or seaside resorts to license boats, hacks, and other vehicles, and also hucksters and peddlers of merchandise, within their limits.

Authorizing railroad companies to borrow money and to mortgage their property beyond the limit previously fixed by law, in certain cases.

Giving the boards of chosen freeholders in the several counties the right, at their discretion, to assume the custody and management of the county jails in their respective counties, superseding the county sheriffs in these duties.

Regulating consolidated school districts and the election of the boards of trustees therein.

Validating tax sales and titles under the act of March 27, 1874.

To extend the time for the completion of certain railroads.

That no one who has been convicted or sentenced for crime shall be appointed State detective or State policeman.

To authorize the formation of companies for mutual protection against damage to glass by hail.

To regulate and license pawnbrokers.

To prevent the transportation of dynamite and other explosives on the ponds and lakes of the State.

Prohibiting municipal corporations from issuing bonds after default has been made in the payment of past due bonds or the interest thereon or in the payment of any county or State tax or other legal indebtedness.

To punish false pretenses in obtaining the registration of cattle and other animals, and to punish giving false pedigrees.

To enable cities to elect an assessor for three years.

Providing for the pensioning of police officers and policemen in certain cities of the State.

Regulating the pay of officers and men of paid fire departments in cities.

To protect farmers, gardeners, and fruit-growers against the loss of baskets and other packages.

Regulating settlement for past due taxes.

To authorize the transfer of licenses granted by the excise board of any city.

Regulating the placing of poles and wires by telegraph and telephone companies.

Authorizing the mayor and council of boroughs to order streets to be paved, graded, or otherwise improved, to assess betterments therefor, and to issue certificates of indebtedness for the cost.

Providing a method for the appointment of inspectors of public works in cities.

To authorize cities to erect buildings for fire-department purposes.

To require the payment of debts incurred by counties in constructing or improving roads in such counties.

To provide for the election of chosen freeholders in incorporated boroughs.

Making twelve hours a day's labor on all street-railways and on all elevated railways in the State.

Designating the first Monday of September as a legal holiday, to be known as "Labor Day."

Giving women the right to vote at school-district meetings.

To provide for the transfer of insane criminals from the county prison to the insane asylum.

To authorize police service in townships.

Requiring foreign insurance companies to file annual statements.

Authorizing foreign corporations to acquire as well as hold real property in the State.

Making the purchasers of any railroad, canal, turnpike, bridge, or plank-road of any corporation created by the State, a body politic and corporate succeeding to the rights and duties of the former corporation.

Appropriating $15,000 toward the erection of a monument upon the Trenton battle-ground.

To enable cities to furnish suitable accommodations for the transaction of their business, and also to erect an armory for the use of the National Guard.

Authorizing cities to borrow money, not exceeding $30,000, for the construction and equipment of additional school-buildings.

To provide for the indexing of recorded instruments.

Exempting from taxation buildings for the use of the National Guard.

To provide for sewerage in and by adjoining cities, towns, and townships.

To authorize the boards of chosen freeholders in the respective counties to acquire by condemnation or purchase lands for public use in such counties, and to issue bonds to pay for the same.

To enable surveyors and their assistants to enter upon lands for the purpose of surveying.

To punish fraud in the weighing of live-stock, hay, coal, and grain.

Relating to assignments and mortgages of leasehold estates.

Raising the age of consent in women to sixteen years.

To provide for the assessment of benefits for the construction of sewers in cities.

Appropriating money for the encouragement of industrial education in the school districts of the State.

Regulating the management of street-railways.

Providing that minors and women shall not clean machinery in motion in any workshop or factory, and that fire-escapes shall be provided for such buildings.

Requiring the publication of the public laws of each session in the newspapers of the several counties.

Exempting Union soldiers and sailors from the poll-tax for school purposes.

Finances. — The amount of the State debt outstanding October 31 was $1,356,800, of which $100,000 became payable on Jan. 1, 1888. The reduction during the year amounted to $100,000, paid out of moneys deposited in the sinking fund. This fund has increased during the year from $671,322.60 to $725,422.86. There was received into it $241,197.75 and paid out $187,097.49.

The following statement exhibits the financial condition of the treasury during the year:

RECEIPTS.

State tax on railroad corporations	$1,068,487 24
Tax on miscellaneous corporations	196,701 05
State Prison receipts	71,171 34
From other sources	67,759 91
Total revenue	$1,419,069 54
On hand Oct. 31, 1886	125,404 48

DISBURSEMENTS.

On account of public debt	$90,000 00
Charitable and reformatory institutions	283,960 05
Courts, State Prison, etc	326,045 62
State government, including legislature	316,131 50
Military	109,597 16
Printing, advertising, etc	187,995 27
Other expenses	173,324 99
Total	$1,486,044 59
Balance on hand Oct. 31, 1887	$108,429 43

There are unpaid railroad taxes remaining uncollected for the last three years to the amount of $203,943.68. The greater portion of this sum is involved in cases before the Court of Errors and Appeals, which have been argued, and in which decisions are awaited. During the year the Morris and Essex Railroad Company paid to the Comptroller, in accordance with a joint resolution of the Legislature passed in March, the amount of taxes assessed against that company, under the law of 1884, for the year 1885 for State tax $157,640.19, and for local tax $67,808.45, and for 1886 for State tax $164,719.12, and for local tax $68,437.85, amounting in all to $458,614.11. The joint resolution provided for the submission of all other questions between the company and the State to two arbitrators, one to be appointed by the Governor on the part of the State, and the other to be named by the company. These arbitrators were appointed, but have not yet rendered their decision.

The total receipts from the State school tax for the year were $1,511,820.56 and the disbursements $1,465,268, leaving a balance on October 31 of $46,552.56. The public schools also derive support from the income of the State school fund, which this year amounted to $196,882.29. The principal of this fund consists of $1,089,883.16 of riparian leases, and $2,532,442.50 of United States bonds, real estate mortgages, cash balances, and other securities, a total of $3,22,6275.66.

Riparian Commission.—The following is a summary of the doings of this commission during the year. The grants, leases, and leases converted into grants, amount to $33,178 84. The rentals which have been paid to the State during the past year on leases heretofore made by legislative act and by the commission amount to $61,024.38. The amount that represents the principal for lands disposed of by grant or lease from April 4, 1884, to Oct. 31, 1887, is $3,158,784.56.

Education.—The sum of $2,698,185.17 was expended by the State and local boards for public schools during the last fiscal year, of which the amount expended for building and repairing school-houses was $628,893.57. The school property of the State is valued at $7,486,206. The school census shows that there are 374,011 children between five and eighteen years, and that there were 224,107 children in attendance during the year. The number of male teachers is 825 and of female teachers 3,177. The average monthly salary of male teachers is $64.07, of female teachers, $41.34.

The whole number in attendance at Normal School during the year ending June 30, 1887, was 239; average attendance, 205$\frac{1}{2}$; number graduated from advanced course, 20; number graduated from elementary course, 24. The whole number in attendance in the Model School during the year was 486; average attendance, 396.

Charities.—At the Morristown Insane Asylum there have been under treatment during the year 1,078 patients, and there were remaining on the 31st day of October 873 patients, 743 of whom were public and 130 private. The total receipts for maintenance for the year were $252,359.30; the total expense for the same time, $229,681.54.

The Trenton Insane Asylum cared for 865 patients, of whom 707 remained at the close of the fiscal year. The receipts were $187,192.95, and the expenditures $147,494.86. The Legislature this year made an appropriation of $100.000 for the construction of an additional building at this asylum, for which contracts have been made looking to its completion in November, 1888.

The blind children supported at the expense of the State are placed in the institutions in the cities of New York and Philadelphia, 31 being in the New York and 10 in the Pennsylvania institution. The amount paid during the year to the former was $9,277.18; to the latter, $5,412.51.

There have been 89 feeble-minded children provided for by the State during the year, 78 of these at the Pennsylvania Training-School at Elwyn, 5 at the Connecticut Institution for Imbeciles. The amount expended for the maintenance, support, and care of the children in these two institutions has been $23,491.81.

The State also supports a school for deaf-mutes, containing over 100 pupils.

The Soldiers' Home contained 328 inmates on October 31, the average number during the year being 329. The Home has cared for 14,725 soldiers since its establishment. The total receipts for the year were $3,814.29, and the expenses, $32,592.79. Provision was made by the last Legislature for the establishment of a separate home for disabled soldiers, at a cost not exceeding $125,000. The institution was on the banks of Passaic river, and the necessary buildings have been in process of construction during the year.

State Prison.—There were in confinement at the State Prison, October 31, 877 prisoners; the total number during the year was 1,880, and the daily average 893, of whom 857 were males and 36 females. The total expenditures for the year were $162,858.64, and the earnings $65,617.16, or $97,241.48 less than the expenditures. The labor of nearly all the convicts is employed by the piece-price system instead of by contract. This system has been in operation since June, 1885, but according to the report of the Supervisor it is not successful "either as a revenue measure or as a preventive of undue competition with honest labor." It differs from the contract system only in the fact that under it the State is responsible for both quality and quantity of product, whereas under the old plan it was responsible for neither, the contractor assuming the risk.

In regard to the general condition of the prison the Governor says in his message: "The crowded condition of the State Prison calls for immediate attention; its accommodations are inadequate for the custody of the convicts as required by law, or by the health and morals of the prisoners." He recommends indefinite sentences for hardened criminals.

The State Reform School for Boys, at Jamesburg, had charge of 441 pupils during the year, of whom 269 remained October 31. This is a decrease of 19 from the previous year. The cost of the institution to the State for the year was $42,857.94. At the State Industrial School for Girls there were 67 pupils at the close of the year.

Militia.—From the report of the Inspector-General of the last annual muster and inspection, the strength of the National Guard is shown to be 306 commissioned officers and 3,693 enlisted men. The force now consists of 53 companies of infantry, two gatling companies, and one company of sea-coast artillery organized into seven regiments and three battalions.

In 1885 the Quartermaster-General secured for the State a tract of 119 acres at Sea Girt with an ocean front, in every way adapted to the uses of a camp, rifle-range, and sea-coast battery. It has been occupied under a lease at a rental of $4,000 per annum. An agreement for its purchase was also secured, and an act was passed by which commissioners were appointed on the part of the State for the purpose of completing the purchase, $51,000 being appropriated for that purpose.

On attempting, however, to carry the act into effect during the year, it was ascertained that the sum appropriated was inadequate, and further legislation will be requisite to secure this place as a permanent encampment.

Boundary.—The exact location of the boundary-line between the State of New York and New Jersey, in Raritan and Princes Bays and out to the open sea, has long been a vexed question, and has even led to the arrest and imprisonment of citizens who were following their vocation of taking oysters and clams in what they believed to be the waters of their own State. In pursuance of laws passed by the two States, commissioners were appointed to mark out and designate the boundary-line, which had been settled upon by the agreements between the States in the year 1834. After much labor these commissioners finally fixed a line, which was made the basis of an agreement signed by the representatives of both States. They then proceeded to mark the line so agreed upon, which has been partially done by the placing of eight buoys. The agreement contemplates two permanent monuments, one being the stone beacon on Roamer Shoals, and the other one to be built in Raritan Bay.

Political.—An election was held in November, at which 8 members of the State Senate and all of the Assembly for 1888 were chosen. The Republicans elected 5 Senators and the Democrats 3, making the complexion of the next Senate the same as it was this year. The Assembly will stand 37 Republicans and 23 Democrats, a Republican gain of 11 over 1887.

NEW JERUSALEM CHURCH. The General Convention of the New Jerusalem Church in the United States of America is composed of ten State associations, or similar bodies, comprising 91 societies; 9 separate societies; and 4 members by election. There are connected with it, 8 "general pastors," and 98 pastors and ministers, besides 12 authorized candidates and preachers. The directory of places containing societies includes 128 names of such places. The list of societies in other countries includes 67 societies in England and Scotland, 1 in Austria, 4 in Denmark, 12 in France, 9 in Germany, 1 in Hungary, 9 in Italy, 2 in Norway, 14 in Sweden, 6 in Switzerland, 12 in Australia, 1 in Mauritius, 6 in South Africa, and 5 in the West Indies.

The sixty-seventh annual meeting of the General Convention was held in Detroit, Mich., beginning June 9. The Rev. Chauncey Giles presided. The Treasurer returned the amount of the funds of the convention in his hands, including the General Fund and five special funds, at $16,946. The Board of Publication reported that its income for the year had been $4,726, and its expenditures $1,840, showing a net gain in resources of $2,885. The policy had been adhered to of making the work self-sustaining as far as possible. Editions had been printed of the books, "The Nature of Spirit" (5,000 volumes), "The Last Judgment," "Hosanna," and the "Book of Worship"; the remainder of the fine edition of Martin's "Life of Swedenborg" had been purchased from the former publishers. A translation of the "De Anima," by the Rev. Mr. Sewall; a volume on "The Parables," by the Rev. E. C. Mitchell; and a new and improved edition of the "Compendium" were about to be published. One thousand copies each of "The True Christian Religion" and the "Apocalypse Revealed" had been printed by the trustees of the Iungerich fund for free distribution to the clergy. The income of the Theological School had been $3,778, and its endowment fund amounted to $31,870. Six students had attended the school. To meet the case of faithful students, who are prevented from completing the full course, the president of the school recommended that a formal certificate relating the amount of work actually accomplished, be prepared and presented to such persons. The whole amount of the New Church Building fund was $1,221, of which $971 were at the disposal of the trustees. No loans had been made during the year. The invested funds of the Rice legacy, which is employed for the circulation of New Church literature, amounted to $8,086, and those of the Rotch legacy to $33,786. Arrangements had been made in connection with the administration of the last fund for the revision and retranslation of the "Arcana Cœlestia." The Board of Home and Foreign Missions had received $4,157, and had expended $2,900. Its labors had been carried on in Nebraska, Canada, New Brunswick, and Nova Scotia, Virginia, Tennessee, Georgia, Florida, Texas, and the eastern shore of Maryland. Of foreign missions, reports were received from Italy (where a considerable list of books and tracts had been translated into Italian); Germany, Switzerland, Denmark, and France. The Committee on the Publication of Swedenborg's Manuscripts reported progress in the printing of the "Quatuor Doctrinæ" and the "Apocalypse Revealed," and in the publication of the "Concordance" to the theological writings of Swedenborg. The Sabbath-School Association had prepared graded lessons from the books of Genesis and John, and from two of the works of Swedenborg. The Convention invited the General Conference of Great Britain, and the various American associations, to co-operate in completing the work of photolithographing the manuscripts of Swedenborg, and authorized the collection of funds and the beginning of the work when a sufficient amount should be in hand. The establishment of centers in different parts of the country, whence missionaries of the New Church doctrines should be sent out to the people, was commended. An amendment to the constitution of the convention was proposed and referred, providing for a local or temporary ministry, with limited authority, who should not be regarded as general ministers of the Church.

NEW MEXICO. Territorial Government. — The following were the Territorial officers during the year: Governor, Edmund G. Ross; Secretary, George W. Lane; Treasurer, Antonio Ortiz y Salazar; Auditor, Trinidad Alarid; Attorney-General, William Breeden; Commissioner of Immigration, Henry C. Burnett;

Chief-Justice of the Supreme Court, Elisha Van Long; Associate Justices, William H. Brinker and William F. Henderson. In accordance with an act of Congress providing for a fourth justice of the Supreme Court, President Cleveland in February appointed Judge Reuben A. Reeves, of Texas, to that position.

Legislative Session. — The Legislature, which met on Dec. 27, 1886, continued in session until the last of February, 1887. A law requiring the attendance of children at a public or private school for three months of each year, was passed at this session, but in such a slipshod form as to be practically worthless. Another act establishes a Territorial school for the deaf and dumb, and provides for the support of indigent pupils at such school at the expense of the Territory. The Sunday laws and the gaming laws were made more stringent. The action taken with regard to Territorial finances is discussed below. Other acts of the session were as follow:

To punish cruelty to animals.

Making railroads liable for damages in killing stock.

Creating a sanitary board of the Territory, and providing for the appointment of a Territorial veterinary surgeon to prevent the importation and spread of Texas fever and other cattle-diseases.

To provide for the incorporation of building and loan associations.

To authorize the formation of companies for the purpose of constructing irrigating and other canals, and for the colonization and improvement of lands.

Creating the county of San Juan.

Making it felony to attack railroad trains with the purpose of committing robbery or other felony, and punishing such attacks with death.

Giving persons injured by an intoxicated person a right of action against the one who sold or gave him liquor, after such person has been warned not to sell or give to the person intoxicated.

Providing a penalty for cruel treatment of a wife and for abandonment of her and her family.

To punish bribery and intimidation of witnesses.

To provide additional punishment for crimes against women and children.

To punish the keeping of "opium joints."

To prohibit the unlawful carrying and use of deadly weapons.

Revising the laws of descent and of apportionment of estates.

Requiring all smelting companies to pay the expenses, during sickness, of any employé who has been rendered unable to work by reason of lead-poisoning.

Increasing the list of property exempt from levy and sale under execution.

Providing a salary for justices of the Supreme Court in addition to that paid by the National Government.

Providing that Territorial or county warrants shall be registered by the several treasurers and shall be paid in the order of registry when funds are at hand.

Providing that parties claiming rights in a disputed mine may bring or defend ejectment in the district court of the county where the mine lies during the time the claim is being contested before the United States Land Office.

Giving all parties to an action regarding title or possession of a mining claim the right to enter, inspect, and survey the premises.

Authorizing the Penitentiary authorities to lease or purchase suitable coal-mines, and to employ the convicts therein, and appropriating $25,000 for such lease or purchase, the above sum to be obtained by the issue of 5-per-cent. bonds.

Creating a police force in the county-seat of each county for the protection of lives and property.

To provide for the organization of savings-bank and trust associations.

To authorize the boards of commissioners to re-adjust assessments and taxes at any time before taxes are paid.

To authorize district courts to cancel uncollectable taxes in certain cases.

Adopting an official index of the compiled laws.

Finances.—On February 28 the indebtedness of the Territory was as follows: Capitol bonds, $200,000; Penitentiary bonds, $150,000; warrants outstanding, $174,891, making a total of $524,891. The Legislature provided for the issue of $150,000 of 6-per-cent. bonds to meet a part of these warrants, and such as shall become payable during the next two years.

Public Buildings.—The Territory has but two public buildings—the State-House and a Penitentiary—authorized by the Legislative Assembly of 1884, the first at a cost of $200,000 and the second at $150,000. Five of the counties have commodious court-houses and jails, those of Bernalillo County erected at a cost of $97,-000; San Miguel, $126,000; Socorro, $48,-000; Santa Fé, $50,000; and Grant, $36,000.

Assessment.—The aggregate assessment of taxable property for 1886 was $56,000,000. That amount was increased by the assessment for 1887 to $60,200,000. An exemption of $300 is allowed to every tax-payer. The rate of taxation fixed by statute is, for Territorial purposes, one half of one per cent.; for county purposes, one quarter of one per cent.; and for school purposes, from one quarter to one third of one per cent., the amount to be determined by the school district. For all purposes the rate of taxation is less than two per cent.

Stock-Raising.—The condition of the cattle industry has, in some respects, declined. The number of cattle returned on the last year's (1886) assessment rolls is 916,940, and the average assessed value for taxation is $12 a head, aggregating $11,003,280. The wool-clip for the year, so far as ascertainable, is about 14,000,000 pounds, and the average price per pound 15 cents. The number of sheep returned at the last year's assessment is 1,702,-287. Cattle and sheep constitute mainly the stock industry of the Territory. There are, in addition to sheep and cattle, 91,173 other domestic animals, assessed at $1,278,147. The cattle industry of the Territory is assuming radically changed conditions from those that have heretofore characterized it. The incoming of agriculturists, and the devotion of an increasing area year by year to agricultural product, is gradually restricting the cattle-range, and stockmen are finding themselves forced to the adoption of different methods, more in keeping with the self-sustaining varied industries of civilized communities. The system of great ranches is gradually giving way to that of small farms, and thus people, illustrating the organizing forces of schools, churches, and the

higher forms of civilized life, are taking the place of nomadism peculiar to the cattle-range of the frontier.

Mining.—The output of coal for the year is as follows:

Counties where situated.	Mines.	Tons.
Colfax	Blossburg	101,174
Socorro	San Pedro	68,931
Bernalillo	Gallup	200,000
Rio Arriba	Amargo	1,000
Rio Arriba	Monero	No returns.
Lincoln	White Oaks	1,890
Santa Fé	Cerrillos and Ortiz	11,767

The total value of precious metals mined during the year is officially estimated at $3,-850,000.

Railroads.—The only railroad construction during the year is 38 miles of the Texas, Santa Fé and Northern Narrow Gauge Railroad from Española, in Rio Arriba County, the temporary terminus of the Denver and Rio Grande to Santa Fé, and operated by the latter company, with a prospective continuance southward to the town of Cerrillos, on the line of the Atchison, Topeka, and Santa Fé. The mileage of road operated by the latter company, traversing ten of the fourteen counties, main line and branches, is 670. The mileage of the Denver and Rio Grande in the Territory is 156; of the Arizona and New Mexico, narrow-gauge, from Lordsburg to the Arizona line, 26 miles; of the Southern Pacific, from El Paso to the Arizona line, 160 miles; aggregate mileage of railroad in operation in the Territory, 1,050, traversing twelve of the fourteen counties.

Indians.—The Jicarilla band of the Apaches have, during the past year, been removed from the Mescalero Reservation in the southeast to their former home in the northwest. This band numbers about 700, all peaceable and susceptible of civilization.

There are some disorderly and turbulent elements among the Navajos, but, as a tribe, they are orderly and self-sustaining, having large herds of sheep and horses, and to some extent successfully cultivate the land. They derive considerable revenue from their wool-product, which constitutes a not inconsiderable portion of the wool-clip of the Territory. The Navajos number about 21,000.

The Pueblo Indians are making substantial progress in education. Large numbers of their children are at school on their reservation, and at Albuquerque and Santa Fé. They are self-sustaining, and a simple, peaceable, law-abiding people. They are made by the law of Mexico citizens of that republic, and came under the sovereignty of the United States with all the rights of Mexican citizenship. They hold their lands in fee under patents from the General Government, and therefore occupy a status entirely different from that of all other Indians. These conditions, it is claimed, make them essentially citizens of the United States and of the Territory, and therefore clothed with all the rights and privileges, and subject to all the obligations incident thereto. Their lands have been assessed this year for taxation, and the right of the Territory to tax them will doubtless go to the courts for final adjudication. These people number about 8,000.

The Mescaleros, numbering between 400 and 500, occupy a reservation in the southeast, embracing an area of over 500,000 acres.

Land-Titles.—On this subject the Governor says in his annual report:

I desire to renew the recommendation of my former reports for the passage of some effective measure for the settlement of titles to lands embraced in Spanish and Mexican grants. The investigations of the Surveyor-General have shown that a considerable proportion of these grants are meritorious and ought to be confirmed in accordance with treaty obligations. Those investigations also show that practically the remainder of those grants are either fictitious or greatly expanded, and that the lands they thus embrace should revert to the public domain and become at once subject to disposal under the public-land laws. Both classes of these lands are now practically sealed against settlement and development, simply because no muniments of title thereto can legally pass for want of action by Congress. The owners of *bona-fide* grants can not sell, because an act of Congress is required to enable them to give a legal title, and settlers can not safely go upon the public lands included in the fictitious and expanded grants under the existing condition of conflict of title, which can be finally settled only by Congress, or by some tribunal established for that purpose, and it can not be settled by an act of Congress except by affirmative action. The claimant still has his recourse in the courts, and the fact that former surveyors-general have approved a large number of this class of grants, which approval has had the effect of putting the claimants in possession, with power to eject trespassers, must operate to keep those claimants in possession, and the lands consequently excluded from settlement and development for indefinite years, in the absence of some more effective method of ascertaining and defining titles.

NEW YORK (STATE). State Government.—The following were the State officers during the year: Governor, David B. Hill, Democrat; Lieutenant-Governor, Edward F. Jones; Secretary of State, Frederick Cook; Comptroller, Alfred C. Chapin; Treasurer, Lawrence J. Fitzgerald; State Engineer and Surveyor, Elnathan Sweet; Attorney-General, Denis O'Brien; Court of Appeals, Chief-Justice, William C. Reyer; Associate Judges, Charles Andrews, Theodore Miller, Robert Earl, George F. Danforth, Charles A. Rapallo, and Francis M. Finch. Judge Rapallo died about the close of the year.

Legislative Session.—The Legislature met on the 4th of January and adjourned on the 26th of May. Among the important acts of the session were the following:

To provide for the amicable adjustment of grievances and disputes that may arise between employers and employés, and to authorize the creation of a State board of mediation and arbitration.

For the settlement of territorial disputes in regard to the lands under water in Raritan Bay.

An act to facilitate State commerce by increasing the lockage capacity of the Erie and Oswego canals, and to improve the Oswego, Black river, Champlain, and Cayuga and Seneca canals.

To provide for the appointment of a deputy in the office of the superintendent of public works.

To provide for the purchase and care of the Senate House property at Kingston.

To co-operate with the United States in the suppression and extirpation of pleuro-pneumonia.

To provide for the subpœnaing of witnesses and the production of books and papers in any matter arising before the Governor upon an application for executive clemency.

In relation to health and casualty insurance companies of other States.

In relation to the collection and preservation of the battle-flags, records, and relics of New York volunteers who served in the war of the rebellion.

To provide for the erection of suitable monuments to the memory of the soldiers of the State of New York who were engaged in the battle of Gettysburg.

To establish a fish-hatchery in the Adirondack wilderness.

To encourage the growth of free libraries and free circulating libraries in the villages and smaller cities of the State.

Authorizing the incorporation of fire departments and of fire, hose, and hook and ladder companies in unincorporated villages of this State.

To authorize the incorporation of bar associations in the several counties of this State.

In relation to the labeling and marking of convict-made goods, wares, and merchandise manufactured in States requiring the labeling and marking of such goods, wares, and merchandise.

Regulating the appointment of receivers of life-insurance companies.

To protect the owners of bottles, boxes, syphons, and kegs, used in the sale of soda-waters, mineral or aërated waters, porter, ale, cider, ginger-ale, milk, cream, small beer, lagerbeer, weiss beer, beer, white beer, or other beverages.

In relation to milk-cans.

To prevent the spread of the disease in peach-trees known as the yellows.

Extending to corporations organized under the laws of other States and doing business within this State, the right to hold, purchase, and convey real estate.

To prevent deception and fraud by owner or owners or agent who may have control of any stallion kept for service by proclaiming or publishing fraudulent or false pedigrees, and to protect such owner or owners or agent in the collection of fees for the services of such stallions.

To facilitate State commerce by increasing the lockage of the Erie canal.

Prescribing the period in each year during which and the terms under which racing may take place upon the grounds of the associations incorporated for the purpose of improving the breed of horses, and suspending the operations of certain sections of the penal code.

To enable marine insurance companies to acquire and hold real estate for certain purposes.

For the incorporation of Young Men's Christian Associations.

To authorize the change of location of banks, banking associations, or individual bankers.

To authorize banks, banking associations, and trust companies to change their names.

To regulate the hours of labor in the street surface and elevated railroads chartered by the State in cities of 100,000 inhabitants and over.

For the moral protection of messenger boys.

Defining and securing the rights of riparian owners to ice in the streams of this State.

To authorize and empower a husband to convey directly to his wife and a wife directly to her husband.

To provide for the establishment of evening-schools for free instruction in industrial drawing.

To provide for the organization of trust companies, for their supervision, and for the administration of their affairs.

To provide for the formation of co-operating savings and loan associations.

To promote and protect the cultivation of shell-fish within the waters of this State; for the appointment of an additional commissioner of fisheries; to authorize the grant of franchises for the use of certain lands under water belonging to the State and to make appropriations therefor.

To define pure wines, half wines, made wines, and adulterated wines, and to regulate the manufacture and sale of half wines and made wines, and to prohibit the manufacture or sale of adulterated wines within the State of New York.

To regulate the heating of steam passenger cars and to provide for the placing of guards and guard-posts on railroad bridges and trestles and approaches thereto.

To regulate the licensing and registration of physicians and surgeons, and to codify the medical laws of the State.

In relation to the use of bicycles and tricycles.

An act to provide fire-escapes in hotels.

On January 20 Frank Hiscock, Republican, was chosen United States Senator.

Governor's Message.—The Governor, in his message to the Legislature of 1888, enumerates the following measures, already adopted, as having been previously recommended by him:

General laws have been passed by which much special legislation can be avoided. A general act for the incorporation of trust companies has been enacted.

The powers of the local authorities of villages and towns in the matter of local improvements and expenditures have been enlarged and increased.

Appeals in capital cases have been authorized to be taken from the Court of Oyer and Terminer direct to the Court of Appeals.

Preferences in assignments of insolvent debtors have been regulated and restricted, insuring hereafter a more equitable distribution of the debtor's estate among the creditors.

A State Board of Mediation and Arbitration has been created for the amicable adjustment of labor disputes arising between employers and employés, which board is now in fairly successful operation, and reasonably meeting the expectations of the people.

Additional holidays, including the Saturday half-holiday, have been established by law.

Private bankers, not already engaged in banking-business, have been prohibited from making use of any artificial or corporate name, or other words indicating that their business is that of a bank.

An act has been adopted providing for the preservation of the forests belonging to the State, regulating the control and management thereof, and creating a forest commission for such purpose.

Substantial progress has been made in establishing a complete system for the prevention of adulteration of articles of food and drink. The sale of canned goods has been regulated to a limited extent; the use of certain improper substances in the manufacture of confectionery has been prohibited, as well as the use of any substitute for hops or pure extract of hops in the manufacture of ale or beer; and acts have been passed to prevent the adulteration of vinegar and wines.

The employment of children in various laborious industries has been regulated and beneficially restricted.

The Mechanics' Lien Law has been revised and improved.

The following are the principal recommendations of the message:

The regulation, modification, and restriction of the public account system of prison labor; spring municipal elections in New York City; a special counsel to the Legislature; tax-law revision to place real and personal property on the same footing; a commission to revise the charter of New York City; the abolition of the Board of Regents, most of its duties being transferred to the Department of Public Instruction; abolition of the State Board of Charities and the State Board of Health, the duties of each to be concentrated in one person; specific provision for the free exercise of religion with special reference to penal institutions; further restriction of corporations in the issue of bonds and stocks; taxation of the indebtedness of corporations; creation of a State Gas Commission; increase of damages from a person or corporation for negligence causing death from $5,000 to $10,000; making railroads liable for damages from fires caused by them, without explicit proof of negligence; abolition of the office of State Agent for Discharged Convicts; appointment of a special labor commission; manual training in schools; provision by law for a Constitutional Convention; restrictions upon committals for insanity; that the Court of Appeals be empowered to confirm criminal judgments in spite of the improper admission of unessential evidence; abolition of the power of confirmation by the Senate except where the Constitution requires; a simple enumeration of the inhabitants of the State. To the statement of and argument upon these last two propositions the Governor devotes much space.

He also says:

The Legislature last year passed a concurrent resolution proposing an amendment to section 6 of Article VI of the Constitution, providing for facilitating the determination of causes on the calendar of the Court of Appeals. I recommend the passage of this resolution again at the present session, and the submission of the question of the adoption of this amendment to the electors of the State. The propriety of the adoption of this measure, or some other appropriate plan for the relief of the Court of Appeals in the prompt disposition of its calendar, seems to be very clear.

Financial.—Valuing investments at par, the capital of the more important trust funds upon Sept. 30, 1887, was:

FUNDS.	Securities.	Money in the Treasury.	Total.
Common-school fnd	$3,558,127 88	$72,529 56	$3,930,657 39
U. S. deposit fund	3,949,515 46	67,705 25	4,017,220 71
Literature fund	275,000 00	9,201 30	284,201 30
College land-scrip fund	415,400 00	59,009 12	474,409 12
Total	$8,498,043 29	$208,445 23	$8,706,488 52

The capital of the same funds upon Sept. 30, 1886, was: Securities, $8,514,784.33; money in the treasury, $154,488.65; total, $8,669,-267.98.

The Canal Debt Sinking fund upon Sept. 30, 1887, contained securities and cash to the amount of $4,061,188.84. The total amount, therefore. of cash and securities held by the Comptroller in trust for the principal funds upon Sept. 30, 1887, was $12,767,677.36.

In the report of last year it was estimated that the surplus upon Sept. 30, 1887, would be $2,572,666.39: the actual surplus is $3,714,-907.55, exceeding the estimate by $1,142,241.16. The chief causes of this excess are the prison receipts, the tax upon collateral inheritances, and the tax upon the organization of corporations.

For the current year the State tax is $9,075,-

046.08, the rate being 2 7-10 mills, and the valuation $3,361,128,177, the tax to be devoted as follows:

School purposes	$3,697,240 99
Canals, including canal debt	2,352,789 78
General purposes	3,025,015 36
Total	$9,075,046 08

The direct school-tax for the last fiscal year produced $3,708,384.69. The total expenditure from the State treasury for educational purposes was $4,152,874.65. The total expenditure, State and local, for the maintenance of schools was $14,461,774.94.

Setting aside the General Fund debt for Indian annuities, the principal of which amounts to but $122,694.87, the gross State debt upon Sept. 30, 1887, was $7,444,810, of which sum $800,000 is the amount outstanding of the debt created to provide for the payment of the Niagara Reservation awards in 1885, and which matures at the rate of $100,000 per annum.

The remaining $6,644,810 is the Canal Debt, the last of which matures in October, 1893, and which has been reduced during the fiscal year by the purchase and cancellation of stock to the amount of $223,700, and by the redemption of stock to the amount of $1,436,500, which matured during the year.

The sinking fund Sept. 80, 1886, amounted to	$5,051,073 82
The sinking fund Sept. 30, 1887, amounted to	4,061,188 84
Decrease of sinking fund during the year	$989,884 98

This decrease in the sinking fund is due to the cancellation and redemption of debt as above stated, amounting to $1,660,200, the result for the year being as follows:

ITEMS.	Sept. 30, 1886.	Sept. 30, 1887.
Debt	$9,204,510 00	$7,444,810 00
Sinking fund	5,051,073 82	4,061,188 84
Net debt	$4,153,436 18	$3,383,121 16

The actual surplus on Sept. 30 was $3,714,-907.55. Inasmuch as the actual surplus represents the condition of the State treasury, assuming all valid appropriations to have been liquidated and all collections to have been made, it follows that, if the State had retired from business upon the thirtieth of last September, its available surplus over all current demands would have more than sufficed to extinguish the entire bonded debt not provided for by the sinking fund.

It will be seen that the net debt, that is, the sum not yet provided for by the sinking fund, is barely one tenth of one per cent. of the State's valuation for the current year.

The tax imposed upon corporations for the privilege of organizing or of increasing their capital stock produced during the fiscal year $201,663.99. The collateral inheritance tax produced $561,716.23. The gross amount appropriated from the General fund during the past four years for land purchases and for construction of buildings exceeds eight and one half millions of dollars. Among the more impor-

tant recent appropriations are: An appropriation of $300,000 made by the last Legislature for a new asylum for insane criminals; appropriations of $190,000 for the Hudson River State Hospital (popularly known as the Poughkeepsie Asylum); appropriations of nearly $190,000 for the asylum just projected at Ogdensburg; an appropriation of $120,000 to rebuild the female department of the State Industrial School at Rochester; an appropriation of $300,000 for State-Prison repairs; and an appropriation of $178,000 for additions to the Buffalo Asylum.

Prisons. — The transactions of the prisons during the last fiscal year were peculiar and abnormal, on account of the required change in the method of employing labor in the prisons. By the expiration of contracts during the year, especially in Sing Sing, a large number of prisoners were released from employment, and the duty and work of transferring such men from idleness to new industries was thrown upon the officers in immediate charge and upon the superintendent. The great majority of such prisoners were put at work on the public-account system, the only system for the employment of the convicts in the State prisons, which, under existing laws, is permitted to be operated.

There was a material increase in the prison population during the year. The aggregate number of prisoners in all prisons Sept. 30, 1886, was 3,155; the number in Sept. 30, 1887, was 3,296. The increase is 141, and the rate of increase is very nearly the same as in the preceding year, when it was proximately 6 per centum. There has been an annual increase in prison population since 1883, when the minimum was reached during a period of eleven years. After 1877 there was a constant yearly decrease in the population of the State prisons until 1883; the decline in six years was 739, or more than 20 per centum. In four years the increase has been 468, or 16¼ per centum on the minimum number of 1883. It is a gratifying fact, however, that the total number of convicts in the State prisons is now 271 less than it was in 1877, or something over 7¼ per cent. less, although the population of the State has gained about three quarters of a million. In 1877 there was one prisoner in the State prisons out of each 1,359 persons in the State, while in 1887 there was only one prisoner to each 1,697.

The health of the convicts in all the prisons was generally good. No epidemic diseases prevailed. The death-rate in some prisons was high as compared with some other years in the same prisons, but was not excessive.

The results of the public-account system, so far, afford grounds for confidence in its ultimate success.

Capital Punishment. — The commission to investigate and report the most humane and practical method of carrying into effect the sentence of death in capital cases, transmitted their report to the Legislature at the beginning of 1888. Many pages are occupied with a review of all the different methods of inflicting judicially imposed death sentences from the very earliest down to the present times. These are historically considered, and it is ascertained that there exist in civilized countries at the present time only five different forms of execution. These are the guillotine, used in ten countries; the sword, used in nineteen; the gallows, in three; the musket, in two; and the axe, in one. From their studies the commissioners draw these conclusions:

That the effort to diminish the increase of crime by the indiscriminate application of capital punishment to various offenses, involving different grades of moral turpitude; or, in other words, by the enlarging of the number of offenses to which capital punishment is made applicable, has proved a failure.

That any undue or peculiar severity in the mode of inflicting the death penalty neither operates to lessen the occurrence of the offense, nor to produce a deterrent effect.

That from the long catalogue of various methods of punishment adopted by various nations at different times, only five are now practically resorted to by the civilized world.

To all of the five prevailing methods the commission finds insuperable objections. The American method of hanging is described as fearfully cruel, uncertain, liable to all kinds of mechanical complications, offering more than any method opportunities for suicide and other distressing efforts to cheat justice, or for clumsy and unskillful work on the part of the executioner, as leaving the criminal in a condition that encourages attempts at resuscitation, and as being in the case of women particularly disgusting and horrible. The use of electricity is then urged in these words: " Perhaps the most potent agent known for the destruction of human life is electricity. Death, as a result, is instantaneous upon its application. It is the duty of society to utilize for its benefit the advantages and facilities which science has uncovered to its view. An electric shock of sufficient force to produce death can not produce a sensation which can be recognized. The velocity of the electric current is so great that the brain is paralyzed."

Factory Inspection. — The following are the chief points of the second annual report of the factory inspectors:

The clause prohibiting male minors under eighteen and women under twenty-one years of age from working more than sixty hours a week has been rigidly enforced during the past year, and a number of convictions have been obtained under it. When manufacturers now desire to run overtime they employ an extra set of hands, not necessarily as many as the usual force of the establishment, but a sufficient number to relieve the regular force, and thus keep down the limit to sixty hours. This plan has furnished employment to a large number of people in the aggregate, and is satisfactory to the regular employés of the various factories, very few of whom are willing to work more than the regulation number of hours. Interviews with workingmen and workingwomen all over the State regarding the prohibition of women under twenty-one and minors under eighteen from being employed at labor more than sixty hours a week,

convinces us that the law is popular, and the females especially desire its provisions extended to all women over twenty-one years of age.

Although the law prohibiting the employment of children under thirteen years of age has been in force in this State not quite a year and a half, the resulting benefits are apparent in every manufacturing city and village in the commonwealth. When our report closed last year, we had visited only a small fraction of the manufacturing establishments where children were employed, and a good deal of our time had been previously taken up in preventing the re-employment of the same children in the worst of the places which we had already visited. Gradually the unscrupulous and negligent were made to understand that the law would be impartially enforced, and when the amended act passed, giving us eight deputies, there was no longer any doubt but that, so far as our efforts could be made effective, children under the age of thirteen should not be found in the factories of this State. It is with a feeling of satisfaction that we look back over the work of the year in this direction. Thousands of children who have been driven or drawn into the hard daily grind of mill-life, were set free to enjoy a little sunshine and obtain the rudiments, at least, of an education; manufacturers were required to employ an older class of help, and pay them a higher rate of wages; and worthless fathers were forced to work and support their children, instead of obtaining support from their offspring.

The necessity for truant-schools is obvious. We recommend that a law be passed providing for schools for incorrigible children in all counties of over 125,000 population, with joint schools for counties of smaller population. These schools, in connection with the compulsory-education officers and constables, whom we also recommend to be appointed and empowered, will soon clear the State of the stigma which now rests upon it of having so many ignorant, unlettered children and youths. In this connection, we renew our recommendation, made last year, that the prohibitory age at which children may be employed in manufacturing establishments be increased to fourteen years, and that mercantile houses be included within the provisions of the act. We also recommend that the Compulsory Education Law be amended so as to provide that all children between the ages of eight and fourteen years shall attend school the full scholastic year, instead of for fourteen weeks a year, as at present.

National Guard. — On September 30, the National Guard consisted of 726 officers and 11,909 enlisted men, aggregating 12,635 officers and enlisted men. There was some increase by recruiting subsequently, and the aggregate at the close of the year approximated 13,000 officers and enlisted men. The Inspector-General reports that there were present at the annual inspection and muster 10,444 officers and enlisted men, but that he does not consider the number present at the annual muster a fair indication of the effective or reliable strength of the organizations, for the reason that special efforts are made to bring men out on that occasion. An organization should not be rated, either in strength or efficiency, according to its showing at the annual inspection and muster, but the work done at other times, especially in camp and at its weekly drills, should also be taken into consideration.

The Adjutant-General refers to the need of armories in the city of New York.

Canals. — The annual report of the State Engineer and Surveyor shows that the total amount of freight moved on the canals of the State during the season of navigation was 5,553,805 tons, and was considerably in excess of the average canal tonnage during the past twelve years, and this increased volume of business was done with less detention than ever before known. The canals were opened on the 7th day of May and closed on the 1st day of December, and their navigation was interrupted by no breaks or other serious accidents. The general condition of the towing-path and perishable structures has been improved. This is especially the case with the towing-path, which has been very thoroughly raised and reformed for the greater part of the canals' length during the past three years.

Political.—The United Labor party held its State Convention at Syracuse on the 19th of August. It reaffirmed substantially the platform adopted in New York city on Sept. 23, 1886, with some additional resolutions. The following ticket was nominated: For Secretary of State, Henry George; for Comptroller, Victor A. Wilder, of Kings; for State Treasurer, P. H. Cummins, of Montgomery; for Attorney-General, Denis O. Feeley, of Rochester; for State Engineer and Surveyor, Sylvanus A. Sweet, of Broome.

Mr. Sweet declined, and M. K. Couzens was substituted in his place. The presence of Socialistic delegates from the city of New York caused trouble, but they were finally excluded.

The Prohibition State Convention was held at Syracuse on August 25. Candidates for State offices were nominated, and the following platform was put forth:

We, Prohibitionists of New York, through our representatives in convention assembled, grateful to Almighty God, Sovereign of nations and Guardian of homes, and looking to him for guidance, hereby set forth the following declaration of principles:

1. The government of and by and for the people can be permanent and fit to endure only as the people guard sacredly public morals and private life.

2. That the liquor-traffic being a foe to the individual citizen, a curse to the home, a burden to society, and a crime against God and the State, its entire prohibition is demanded by every interest of social and political economy.

3. That the extermination of this traffic can never be secured through any system which confers license or levies a tax upon it.

4. That to vote for license or tax of the liquor-traffic is to accept, in the name of the State, a bribe from the State's worst enemy, and that he who votes for a corrupt and corrupting system for the revenue it yields is as guilty of a crime against the State as he who sells his vote to a corrupt candidate.

5. That the purity and value of the ballot demand disfranchisement for him who sells a vote and also for him who buys it.

6. That justice and equity alike demand that the ballot should be given to woman, and that we demand the submission by Congress to the several States of a national constitutional amendment guaranteeing her right thereto.

7. That the extermination of the manufacture, importation and sale of intoxicating beverages is the dominant issue before the citizens of both State and nation. It is, therefore, the only test of party fealty.

8. For wage-earners we demand prohibition of the liquor-traffic as the most important reform; that the

health and safety of workers in the performance of their labor should be secured by law; that the laws relating to child-labor and compulsory education should be strictly enforced and their provisions extended; that a just system of profit-sharing between employers and employés should be encouraged; that the establishment of co-operative business enterprises by laboring-men be promoted by wise legislation; that differences relating to the rewards of labor should be settled by arbitration; that equal wages for equal work be paid alike to men and women; that we are opposed to the holding of large tracts of land for speculative purposes by any individual or corporation and demand that the public lands be reserved for actual settlers; that such franchises as street-railroads, stage-routes, ferries, and gas companies should be disposed of to individuals or companies that would agree to serve the public at the lowest rates, and not to the highest bidder; that all men should pay tax upon what they own, and not upon what they owe.

9. And finally, that as proofs of the subserviency of the Republican and Democratic parties to the rum power, we cite the failure of the Republican party for four consecutive years to fulfill its pledge to submit to the people a constitutional amendment and the passage by recent Legislatures of the Mandamus bill, Mooney Excise bill, and the Crosby High-license bill, avowedly to popularize beer and wine; and the Vedder Tax bill, a shameless attempt to bribe citizens; and the Ives Pool bill, by an application of the license principle, thus legalizing gambling and sharing with the gambler his profits; and the Cantor Beer bill, thus increasing the enticements of the saloon by music and song, and by similar acts of party leaders and representatives.

The Republican State Convention was held at Saratoga on September 14. It nominated the following ticket: For Secretary of State, Frederick D. Grant; Comptroller, Jesse S. L'Amoreaux; Treasurer, James H. Carmichael; Attorney-General, James A. Dennison; State Engineer, O. H. P. Cornell. The following is the platform adopted:

1. The Republican party, by all honorable means, seeks restoration to power in the State and in the nation, because of the unchallenged record of history, attesting its administrative success in war-time, in the period of restoration and pacification, in executive, legislative, and financial achievements, in the purity and efficiency of its methods, and in the lasting benefits conferred upon the people, and because, since Democratic ascendancy in the State and nation, the incapacity and inefficiency of that party in administration and legislation, the egregious blunders of the executive and the Democratic branch of Congress, many of whose acts are to the detriment of the public interests, have constantly emphasized the wisdom and necessity of such restoration.

2. Two and a half years of a Democratic President, who has had the co-operation of an overwhelming majority in the House of Representatives, where, under the Constitution, all revenue measures must originate, have exposed the incapacity of the Democratic party and the weakness of the Democratic policy under which so much was promised the people, but from which there have come only broken pledges, failure to promote the people's interests. No plan to reduce the revenues or to retrench expenditures. No purpose to promote a practical civil-service reform, or otherwise to improve the public service; while conspicuous among the many shortcomings of this administration are numberless appointees who have proved faithless and incompetent; the postal service disorganized and its efficiency impaired, and the public business in other departments delayed and obstructed.

3. We adhere firmly to the American policy under whose operation unexampled prosperity and thrift have blessed the land, and hold that any changes to

be made in the tariff laws should be made by the friends of those laws and in the interest of protection of labor on our own soil, and of home markets, not by or in the interests of free-trade propagandists, nor for the benefit of foreign producers and foreign labor. National taxation should be so adjusted as to raise revenue sufficient for an economic and wise administration of the Government, for the payment of the public debt, for the development of national resources, and for national defense; but any reduction should be so made as not to impair the prosperity of home industries. American markets must be preserved to the products of American labor and capital, and protected from foreign encroachments.

4. The principle of the national and State civil-service-reform laws has our hearty approval. These laws should be executed in the spirit in which they were enacted and accepted by the people, and be advanced and be made permanent. The hypocritical pretenses under which both President Cleveland's and Gov. Hill's administration have continually and shamefully violated the law, by systemic perversion to partisan purposes, deserves the popular condemnation.

5. The political rights of all persons throughout the land must be established firmly and beyond controversy. The persecutions of the workingman in the South, and the denial of his civil rights, cause degradation, low wages, and inferior products, which bring into unfair competition the labor of the North, and obstruct that full measure of property and thrift that equal conditions throughout the country would establish and maintain. A fair hearing on all public questions, a free ballot in every citizen's hands, and an honest count of the vote, are just prerogatives of citizenship, to which full respect must be paid, to insure the enjoyment of the freeman's birthright and the maintenance of republican government on a stable foundation.

6. The veterans of the Union armies and navies are entitled to the liberal consideration of this people for all public preferment, and should receive generous care and adequate pensions. The flippant, sneery language of President Cleveland's vetoes of pension bills was insulting to the veterans and degrading to the executive. The subservient spirit displayed in Mr. Cleveland's illegal order to return rebel battle-flags, the precious trophies of the Union troops, deserves only reprobation, and justly excites the resentment of all loyal citizens.

7. Congress should pass laws and establish regulations that will prevent the coming to our shores of disreputable and undesirable persons whose presence here would threaten good government, disturb the peace and order, and depreciate the dignity and rewards of honest labor. Anarchists, communists, polygamists, paupers, fugitives from justice, and insane, vicious, and criminal persons, as also contract labor, should be rigorously excluded; but honest, industrious, well-intended persons, escaping the oppression and degradation of Old World despotisms, and the crushing force of free-trade policies, are welcome as a desirable element in our population.

8. The record of the Republican Legislature for wisdom in general action, for giving labor the legislation it sought, and for efficiency and economy in State expenditure, commands approval. The low rate of State taxation is the best evidence of fidelity and prudence. Had the Democratic Governor given sanction to wise legislative action, the tax list would have been reduced to a minimum, and the people would have cause to rejoice in an era of genuine reform.

9. We heartily indorse the purpose of the Republican majority of the Legislature in passing the bill to limit and restrict the liquor-traffic, and we condemn the vetoes of the Governor as hostile to that purpose. We recommend comprehensive and efficient legislation for giving local option by counties, towns, and cities, and restriction by taxation, on such localities as do not, by their option, exclude absolutely the traffic.

10. The State census under constitutional directions, having been voted by the Republican Legislature, and defeated by the Democratic Governor's veto, the failure to secure an enumeration and reappointment and other benefits of the census is chargeable solely to the executive's nullification of the Constitution's mandate, and his defiance of the co-ordinate branch of the State Government, with which all legislation must originate, and which is accountable therefor; and the Democratic party, in sustaining the Governor's veto, shares with him the responsibility and discredit for the wanton overriding of the Constitution.

11. The veto and defeat, by Gov. Hill, of an improved registry bill, of which the purpose was to promote pure elections, was an outrage upon the rights of lawful electors. The most efficient safeguard should be placed about the primary, the source of all political action, as well as about the ballot-box, so as to secure their purity and inviolability.

12. The people of the State, having voted in favor of a constitutional convention, the Legislature made provision therefor, and the Governor became responsible, by his veto, for the annulment of the popular will.

13. Whatever propositions of legislation will mitigate and equalize taxation should be enacted, and to Republican legislation is due the progress that has been made in this direction in this State. The corporation tax laws and collateral inheritance bill and homestead tax are in the right spirit, and tend to simplify the tax system. We are in favor of further changes in the tax laws as shall equalize the burden, and compel personal property to bear its proper share.

14. We approve the laws, State and national, prohibiting the manufacture and sale of articles of food made in imitation of butter and cheese, and earnestly favor such further legislation as may be necessary for the protection of genuine dairy-products.

15. We recommend to the Legislature a just care of the interest of the people of this State in the maintenance of cheap transportation, through a wholesome competition by the State waterways, and the doing of this without placing unnecessary burdens upon localities beyond the benefits received. National support of the Erie Canal, the great highway for the products of the West to the seaboard, is favored and invited.

16. The cause of Ireland and the efforts in its behalf by Gladstone, Parnell, and their associates, have the earnest sympathy of Republicans, and commend their operation by all peaceful methods to promote an early and complete triumph.

The Democratic State Convention met at Saratoga on September 27, and nominated the following ticket: For Secretary of State, Frederick Cook: Comptroller, Edward Wemple; Attorney-General, Charles F. Tabor; Treasurer, Lawrence J. Fitzgerald: State Engineer and Surveyor, John Bogart. The platform put forth contained the following planks.

Whereas, the unnecessary Federal taxation of the last fiscal year exceeded $100,000,000. Unnecessary taxation is unjust taxation; therefore, the Democracy of New York demand that Federal taxation be straightway reduced by a sum not less than $100,000,-000 a year; and also respectfully urge upon Congress, that a measure shall be adopted which will, in the language of the President's inaugural address, "relieve the people from unnecessary taxation, having a due regard to the interests of capital invested, and workingmen employed in American industries." The taxation to be first reduced, or altogether removed, are those on imported raw material which now assist and promote foreign competition with ourselves in our own markets, and prevent or hinder the sale of our surplus products in foreign markets.

Along with these taxes should be forthwith remitted or reduced the taxation which enriches the cost to our wage-earners of the common necessaries of life and the price of the common daily clothing of all our

people. Besides these there are several hundred articles among the 4,182 articles now taxed which should
be swept off the tax-list into the free list, thereby
diminishing the cost of collecting all our seaport taxes,
and casting away those which are petty, needless, and
vexatious. We also urge the immediate enactment of
the measure prepared by Mr. Manning and Mr.
Hewitt, and reported to the last House by the Committee of Ways and Means, to systematize, simplify,
and economize the machinery for the collection of the
customs revenue, and especially for making correct
appraisement of foreign values on *ad valorem* rates of
duty shall be retained.

To all citizens born in foreign lands, and to the
multitude of our native citizens who desire to obtain
and securely hold their homes, the Democratic party
has rendered inestimable service in reclaiming from
speculative railroad corporations the public lands
which such corporations, by the corrupt aid of Republican administrations, had seized, to be disposed
of for their private gain. Many millions of acres in
these lands have been recovered by the Democratic
administration and returned to the people for the use
of actual settlers.

The Democratic party is the proved friend of all
who have come to our country seeking to be partners
in our welfare and citizens obedient to its laws.
There is in our America bread enough and work
enough for all, and the Federal laws now on the statute-
book for the promotion and protection of foreign emigration do not, in our opinion, if they shall be faithfully executed by the proper Federal and State authorities, require present enlargement or amendment.

The Democracy of New York reiterate their support of the civil-service laws of the United States and
of the State of New York and their purpose to uphold
them both. In view of the radical changes in the
administrative methods which grow out of the civil-
service laws and the differences of opinion which exist in relation thereto, we deem this subject one which
might properly be submitted to the popular vote.

Notwithstanding the decided decrease in the ordinary expenses of the Government, the faithful soldiers, sailors, and their families have been generously
remembered, and the annual pension list under Democratic control shows payments in number and amount
largely in excess of those during the years of Republican administration.

The Democracy of the State of New York deplore
the wrongs inflicted on Ireland by the coercive and
despotic power of the English Government, and express to that suffering people the earnest hope that
they may speedily enjoy the blessings of home-rule
and of self-government.

In order to secure the necessaries of life to our people and raw materials for the employment of our industries and the building up of our towns and cities
at the lowest practicable cost, we favor the continuance of the work of lengthening the locks and of cleaning out channels of the canals upon the plan recommended by the late Governor Seymour and in progress by the State. The State of New York needs and
will accept no Federal aid for such improvements.

We favor a revised excise law applicable without
unjust discrimination throughout the State. We oppose all sumptuary laws grievously interfering with
the personal liberties and reasonable habits and customs of any portion of our citizens. We believe that
excise revenues, like other local revenues, should be
applied in lessening local expenditures.

We assert the right of local self-government for the
cities, and demand that the Legislature shall provide
alike general laws for the exercise of that right.

We heartily approve of such legislation as shall give
the fullest protection against simulated products of the
farm and dairy interests. The oppressive hours of
labor demanded of their employés by many corporations deriving large profits from the use of public
streets, or land accrued for public use, should be so
regulated by law that no more than ten hours shall be
required for a day's work, and all corporations, other
than municipal, should be required to pay their employés whose wages are by the day, once a week, and
in money. The Democratic party, the party of the
people, which in the past has inaugurated and carried
through all legislation of genuine and lasting benefit
to those who work for wages, is always ready to favor
such legislation as may justly be required to promote
their interest and welfare. New York State now enjoys
the benefit of a Democratic State administration,
which has well filled the trust committed to it by the
electors in 1885. In every branch of the State government under Democratic control the laws have been
carried into effect with rigor, with vigor and justice,
and every right of the people has been jealously maintained. Wherefore we heartily indorse the administration of David B. Hill, Governor of New York, and
pledge to him our full confidence and support.

The Democracy of New York approves the administration of Grover Cleveland, President of the United
States. It has won the respect and confidence of all
citizens without regard to party. It has removed that
apprehension of the dangers which would attend a
change of party in Federal administration which had
become a serious obstacle to the maintenance of our
free government dependent upon the popular will. It
has brought back honesty and simplicity to the conduct of affairs. It has checked the waste of public
moneys and insisted upon their devotion to constitutional purposes. It has effected a practical reform
with the civil service. It has maintained the national
character for justice and forbearance in dealing with
foreign countries. Its management of the treasury
has been signally wise and prudent, and it has begun
the reconstruction of our naval establishment with
thoroughness that promises the restoration of our
ancient prestige on the sea. Wherefore, we repeat,
the Democracy of New York, in convention assembled,
again pledge to the President our strong and unwaver-
ing confidence and support.

At the election in November the Democratic
ticket was successful. The vote for Secretary
of State was as follows: Republican, 452,811;
Democratic, 469,888; United Labor, 70,055
(87,477 in New York and 15,685 in Kings
County); Progressive Labor, 7,622 (5,889 in
New York and 1,130 in Kings County); Prohibition, 41,850; all others, 8,149. The lowest
Democratic plurality was 11,026 for Treasurer.
The Legislature consists of 21 Republicans and
11 Democrats in the Senate, and 72 Republicans
and 56 Democrats in the House.

Insurance Legislation.—Perhaps the most important law passed by the Legislature in 1887
was one amending the general acts relative
to the incorporation and regulation of co-
operative or assessment life and casualty associations and societies. After a great struggle between the "old" companies and what
are known as the "people's" companies a
compromise was effected, which requires a
deposit of $100,000 by all the popular compa-
nies before they can commence business in the
State. Another important law is the one continuing for ten years the payment to the exempt firemen of New York city of the two per
cent. on gross receipts exacted from all foreign
companies that do business in that city. The
present force of paid firemen attempted to gain
control of the funds, or, at least, to have one
half of it, but they signally failed. The Governor signed the bill, although he declared that

he did not like such kind of legislation. A law of 1886, enacted for the preservation of policy-holders, required that all fire-insurance policies should be printed in uniform style of type, paper, etc. A new law of the present year amends the former law, so as to except from its provisions all town or town and county operative companies. Another new law authorizes marine companies to hold additional real estate for the purpose of storing wrecked vessels or cargoes. A new provision is to the effect that agents may stamp upon the backs of policies the name and address of themselves or their firms. By another law provision is made that no receiver shall be appointed for a life-insurance company whose general fund equals its outstanding liabilities and a reserve on policies and claims not matured at 4½ per cent., the capital stock not to be considered a liability; and no company to issue new policies if its minimum reserve, with interest at 4 per cent., is impaired, until the impairment is made good. The Governor very promptly signed the bill repealing the law of 1880, relating to the taxation of life companies. This was urged on the ground that the tax is really upon the policy-holders; and, although it will take a million dollars out of the State treasury, the idea seemed to be a popular one. Other new laws are these: Allowing boards of directors of life, fire, casualty, or marine companies to reduce their number to thirteen; enlarging the area of business allotted to credit, guaranty, and indemnity companies; enabling town co-operative companies, by filing a certificate with the county clerk, to extend their business to the entire county. The chief bills that failed to reach the Governor were these: Declaring that fire and marine companies are not exempt from local taxation, as might be inferred from the loosely-drawn act of 1886; extending the time for the payment of the capital stock of corporations organized since May 1, 1884, as limited liability companies; including fidelity companies under the operation of the general act of 1883; amending the title of the co-operative act of 1883, and amending the same relative to the disposition of funds and the exemption from taxation; exempting from State tax all money used in co-operative or assessment life or casualty companies, and providing definitely for the taxation of life companies in this State; repealing the law of 1855 relative to the incorporation of general insurance companies; amending the charter of the Mutual Fire Insurance Company so as to add $200,000 to the capital, and to change the number of trustees to thirteen; amending the life company tax law of 1880 so that the tax shall not apply to premiums of industrial companies, where the premium does not exceed 20 cents a week or the policy $150 in amount; establishing uniform rules for valuing policies in insolvent life companies; authorizing the mayors of New York and Brooklyn to license adjusters of fire losses; forbidding any life

company to discriminate against negroes; providing that every notice to policy-holders looking to a forfeiture shall contain a statement of the value of the policy on the 31st of December preceding; authorizing the incorporation of fidelity companies on the assessment plan; affecting the right of waver so that after two years a policy-holder may at any time demand the amount of premiums paid; allowing any corporation depositing $100,000 with the insurance department for one kind of insurance to transact any kind of life insurance; repealing the laws of 1852 forbidding the publication of statements by foreign fire companies other than the statements of their assets and business. Several very pointed inquiries were directed during the session, but, for the most part, they amounted to nothing. One of them called for a statement from the companies giving reasons for increasing rates on rural property. This was answered by the statement that such companies had not reported to the department, and, therefore, they could not be controlled. Another inquiry asserted that local boards of villages had appointed stamp agents so that they could control the insurance business. This was found to be untrue. A third inquiry was manifestly a " strike," and it was never pressed. Still another inquiry, directed against the receiver of the Universal Life Company, had the effect of closing up the affairs of that concern. The last inquiry requested the insurance superintendent to state whether a fire-insurance company of this State, with $1,000,000 capital, has been refused permission to do business in Massachusetts, what reasons are assigned, are they sufficient or frivolous, and what action is necessary on the part of this State to secure our companies privileges accorded Massachusetts companies in this State, but denied our companies in Massachusetts, and if these privileges are denied, shall not Massachusetts companies be deprived of the right to do business in this State? The company referred to was the Liberty Company, organized in New York in April. The Massachusetts department had refused it admission in that State. This inquiry was withdrawn from the insurance department almost as soon as it was made.

NEW YORK (CITY). Finances.—The total amount of stock and bonds, exclusive of revenue bonds, outstanding on the 31st of December, 1887, was $128,268,719.45. The amount outstanding on the 31st of December, 1886, was $125,982,-735.92. The increase of bonded debt during the year 1887 thus amounts to $2,285,983.53.

Under the operations of the sinking fund and from special funds, there were redeemed and canceled during the year stock and bonds to the amount of $11,326,171.

In addition to the funded debt, however, the amount of revenue bonds outstanding at the close of business was $4,554,346.70, so that the total indebtedness of the city at the close of the year, including revenue bonds, was

$182,823,066.15, against $181.601,103.57 due on the 31st of December, 1886. The net increase of public debt of all kinds during the year, therefore, amounts to $1,221,962.58. Of the total amount there was held by the sinking fund the sum of $38,604,066.15.

The total net bonded debt, including revenue bonds, an Dec. 31, 1887, after deducting the amount on the sinking fund, is $98,300,-581.54, being an increase over the amount due at the close of the year 1886 of $2,904,948.19.

The year 1887 is the first since 1876 which has failed to show a reduction in the net amount of the city indebtedness, after deducting the amount in the sinking fund and the cash in the treasury. The increase, however, is very moderate in view of the large disbursements for new public improvements, which, during the year, were carried on at a cost amounting to $13,612,154.58. But for the expenditures upon the new aqueduct the indebtedness of the city would have been reduced by a larger sum than in any previous year in its financial history.

The credit of the city stands deservedly high. During the year no bonds were issued bearing a higher rate of interest than 3 per cent., and in almost every case the bonds commanded a premium—in some instances as high as 4½ per cent. The bonds paid off during the year bore interest at the rate of 5, 6, and 7 per cent., so that the debt of the city is thus being converted into bonds bearing 3 per cent. interest. The bonds bearing high rates of interest generally mature within the next ten years, so that the burden of interest will be greatly reduced as these bonds are paid off. The debt at this date is in the following condition:

3 per cents	$25,285,150 00
3½ per cents	4,440,000 00
4 per cents	9,786,244 25
5 per cents	17,889,846 42
6 per cents	89,068,778 23
7 per cents	32,404,900 00

Of which the sinking fund holds $34,057,-319.45, distributed as follows:

3 per cents	$4,210,150 00
3½ per cents	
4 per cents	6,986,244 25
5 per cents	7,005,546 42
6 per cents	18,759,378 78
7 per cents	155,000 00

As the result of the work of the Board of Estimate and Apportionment, it is estimated that the taxation for 1888 will be 2·18 as against 2·16 per cent. for 1887.

Insane.—The number of insane in the city asylums of New York, Oct. 1, 1887, was 4,418, as against 4,261 Oct. 1, 1886, of whom 1,903 were men, and 2,515 women. The increase since Oct. 1, 1880, when the insane numbered only 3,018, has been 1,400, or nearly 47 per cent., while the increase of the population of the city, in the mean time, upon the basis of a present population of 1,500,000, as is generally accepted, has been a little less than 25 per cent. The accommodations for the insane by the city have not been extended during the time so as

properly to meet the requirements of this great increase, and, as it sends few, if any, of this class to the State institutions, its asylum buildings are, consequently, all greatly crowded. In 1885 the city purchased a tract of about 1,000 acres of land on Long Island near Central Islip, some forty miles distant, with the intention of erecting buildings thereon and removing its chronic insane, or a part of them at least, to that locality, but until quite recently no positive action in that direction has been taken. In June an investigation was made by the State Board of Charities of the Asylum for Insane Men on Ward's Island. The report of the committee on this investigation says:

The accommodations in the men's asylum are greatly crowded, it then having 1,326 patients in the main building, with proper room for only about 1,000, while there were 590 patients in detached structures, two of which, containing 470 patients, the committee state, "should be condemned as uninhabitable." The food for the insane was found to be generally poor in quality and badly cooked, the attendants were mostly of a low grade of character, and the committee was satisfied that grave abuses and neglect existed in the treatment and care of the patients by them. To remedy these evils, the committee recommend, first, the immediate erection of buildings upon the asylum farm on Long Island, and the removal of patients to that locality, so as to relieve the crowded condition of the present buildings; second, the employment of a more intelligent and better class of attendants, and in greater numbers than at present, the institution and maintenance of a training-school for attendants and nurses, the furnishing of a more generous and varied diet for the patients, and the introduction of proper facilities for their amusement, and for healthful and productive labor, and for their better classification on the wards; and third, the placing of the insane under a department separate from the governing board of the other charitable, penal, and correctional institutions of the city, subject to the appointment, direction, and control of the Mayor.

An appropriation of $60,000 has been set apart by the Board of Estimate and Apportionment for the erection of plain, inexpensive cottage-buildings for 100 male patients on the Long Island farm, and the work of construction has been entered upon.

Health-Office Fees.—From a return made to the Senate it appears that the receipts of the health officers of the port for the past two years have been as follow :

RECEIPTS FOR 1886.

Inspection of vessels from foreign ports	$36,909 71
Disinfection of vessels	6,557 00
Inspection of vessels from domestic ports	4,827 00
Night boarding	1,968 00
Vaccination	699 77
Transporting sick to hospitals	360 00

RECEIPTS FOR 1887.

Inspection of vessels from foreign ports	$36,457 04
Disinfection of vessels	6,764 00
Inspection of vessels from domestic ports	4,699 00
Night boarding	1,810 00
Vaccination	1,649 15
Transportation of sick to hospitals	455 00
Sanitary inspection	40 00

The present fee or specific charge which the health officer collects for each of the services mentioned, is the same as reported to the Senate, March 4, 1886, to wit: Inspection of vessels from foreign ports, $6.50 ; inspection of vessels from domestic ports, vessels under 100 tons $1, vessels over 100 tons and less than

160 tons $2; disinfection of vessels, steamers $8, ships $7. barks $6, brigs $5, schooners $3. Night boarding, $8; transportation of sick to yellow-fever hospital, $5; transporting sick to contagious hospital, Blackwell's Island, $20. The fee for vaccination is 25 cents per capita, less 10 per cent. The disbursements for 1886 were $21,832.14; and for 1887, $21,-118.50.

Assessment and Taxation.—The annual report of the State assessors shows an increase in real and personal property from 1886 of $136,-445,834. The assessment on real estate has increased over $468,000,000 since 1883, while personal property has increased in the same time $21,000,000. A large portion of the report is devoted to the equalization of New York County. The assessors say due complaint comes from the county of New York. New York complains of too high equalization, while fifty-nine counties complain that New York is too low. New York has been largely reduced and pays a much smaller State tax than formerly. In 1873 New York paid its highest per cent. of the State tax, namely, 51·845. In 1877 it paid 44·644, in 1882 it paid 47·150, and in 1887 2¼ per cent. less, while between these years its assessed value increased over $187,000,000. The census of 1870 fixes the value of real estate and personal property in the city at $3,484,000,000. Seventeen years later, after the addition of a large portion of Westchester, the total assessment was $1,381,-000,000, or about 39 per cent. of the census value. Assuming that 50 per cent. of the census value was personal property, the realty owned in 1870 equals $1,742,000,000, or about $361,000,000 more than was assessed in 1887. Not considering the annexed district, the increase in New York since 1870 is estimated at $500,000,000; so that, if the census of 1870 approximately established the value of its realty, the returned assessed value should have been about $700,000,000 more. The increased assessment of real estate from 1883 to 1887 was $168,738,000. In 1887 the equalized value of New York County was $1,323,666,950, in 1874 it was $812,709,047, an increase of $510,857,-903. In 1887 the equalized value of all other counties was $1,701,562,838, in 1874 it was $937,989,871, an increase of $763,572,967. In these years the equalized value of the city was increased by the State board about 62 per cent., while the value of the remaining counties was increased 81 per cent.

Bribery Trials.—The principal criminal trial was that of Jacob Sharp, charged with bribing members of the Board of Aldermen in 1884 to vote for the franchise of the Broadway Surface Railroad. This protracted trial took place in the summer, and resulted in the conviction of Sharp. The conviction was affirmed by the General Term of the Supreme Court on appeal, but in November the Court of Appeals reversed the lower courts and granted a new trial on the ground of errors in admitting testimony.

Political.—The autumn canvass was marked by the advent of the Progressive Labor party, and by a movement of Independent Democrats in combination with the Republicans to elect De Lancey Nicoll District Attorney over John R. Fellows, the regular Democratic nominee. Both were assistants in the office, and Mr. Nicoll was credited, in the public view, with having been the chief agent in the bribery prosecutions. The Progressive Labor party was formed by the Socialists, who had been refused admission to the Syracuse convention that nominated Henry George for Secretary of State. In November the regular Democratic ticket was successful. The vote for City Comptroller was: Democratic, 110,439; Republican, 65,291; United Labor, 33,278; Progressive Labor, 5,636; Prohibition, 1,068. For District Attorney the vote was: Fellows, 99,798; Nicoll, 77,556; United Labor, 32,747; Progressive Labor, 5,276; Prohibition, 709.

The New Croton Aqueduct.—This great public work originated in the following resolutions, adopted by the Senate of the State of New York, Jan. 9, 1883:

Whereas, With the return of business prosperity the rapidly-increasing growth of the city of New York causes a constant increase in the complaints which have prevailed for years past that, by the insufficiency of the city's water-supply, the people are deprived of the ordinary conveniences of domestic life, the public health is endangered, the security of property by fire is diminished, and the pursuit of commerce and manufactures is retarded; and, *whereas*, in a report dated Feb. 22, 1882, the Commissioner of Public Works submitted to the Mayor of said city a plan for a new aqueduct, prepared by the chief engineer of the Croton Aqueduct and other engineers; and, *whereas*, this body may be called upon to consider legislation to secure to said city an additional water-supply; therefore

Resolved, That the Mayor of the city of New York is hereby requested to select and appoint within five days from the passage of this resolution five citizens of said city, who in conjunction with himself shall without delay examine into the said plan and report to this body within twenty days as to the practicability of the proposed plan, the probable cost, the time required for its execution, and such other views and recommendations as they may deem proper.

In accordance with these resolutions, the Mayor, Franklin Edson. appointed the following-named gentlemen as the committee: Orlando B. Potter, John T. Agnew, William Dowd, Amos R. Eno, and Hugh N. Camp, with Mayor Edson, *ex officio*, also as a member. The report of this committee to the Senate of the State of New York, under date of March 7, 1883, presented the following resolutions, unanimously agreed upon:

1. That a new aqueduct should be built immediately of sufficient capacity to carry all the available water in the Croton water-shed, and together with the existing Croton Aqueduct carry any additional supply which the city may hereafter secure in that direction from other sources, and, when practicable, should be built in rock-tunnel.

2. That the work of construction of such an aqueduct and all subsidiary dams and reservoirs should be intrusted to an unprejudiced commission selected from our best citizens.

The committee on March 7, 1883, besides presenting the resolutions already given, made a full report to the State Senate in reference to the matter in their charge, in which the following occurs: "We are of opinion, as well from our own observation and knowledge as from the statements made before us, that the health, security, and growth of this city imperatively require an increased supply of pure and wholesome water, and that such measures should be immediately taken by the Legislature as will enable the city to secure and provide such increased and sufficient supply at the earliest day practicable. . . . The evidence before us leaves no doubt that the Croton water-shed is the best source from which to obtain an increased supply of water, and that the yield of water from this source

DRIVING THE HEADING—DRILLS MOUNTED ON A COLUMN.

will be adequate to meet the wants of the city for at least twenty-five years, or until the consumption of water by the city shall exceed 250,000,000 gallons a day. This water-shed is within the jurisdiction of our own State. It has been more carefully studied and is better known than any other, its water is pure and wholesome, and a supply for a consumption up to 250,000,000 gallons per day can be obtained at less expense from this than from any other source." In reference to the existing water-supply for New York, the report goes on to say that the present Croton Aqueduct is in a condition with proper care to deliver 95,-000,000 to 98,000,000 gallons a day, which it

has done since 1874, but could not be safely relied on to deliver more.

The existing water-supply of New York is drawn from the Croton river, a small stream in Westchester County, about forty miles from the city, and from natural lakes in the vicinity of the sources of the river. The water is brought to the city by means of the Croton Aqueduct, which was completed in 1842. This structure was built of stone, brick, and cement, arched above and below to form a sort of ellipse resembling a horse-shoe in shape, measuring 8½ feet perpendicular and 7½ feet horizontal. It slopes about 13 inches to the mile, and has a capacity of carrying 100,000,-000 gallons a day. Croton Lake, which is at the head of the Croton Aqueduct, was formed by throwing a dam across the river, and so raising the water forty feet. Apart from Croton Lake there are two other artificial storage-reservoirs, while the lakes form such reservoirs naturally. They are known respectively as "Boyd's Corner" and the "Middle Branch" reservoirs. The capacity of all these reservoirs, artificial and natural, is 9,500,000,000 gallons. The aqueduct is carried to New York city across Harlem river on the granite bridge known as High Bridge. In Central Park is the retaining reservoir, capable of holding 1,030,000,000 gallons, and just below this is the receiving reservoir, which holds 150,000,-000 gallons. A distributing reservoir on Fifth Avenue, between Fortieth and Forty-second Streets, has a capacity of 20,000,000 gallons, and is 115 feet above tide-water. Besides these there is a "high service reservoir" holding 11,000,000 gallons at High Bridge, connected with which is a tower containing a powerful pumping-machine, forcing the water into a tank holding 55,000 gallons at the top of the tower. The cost of all these buildings has been between $25,000,000 and $30,000,-000, and the annual water-tax, which is used for repairs, amounts to about $1,500,000.

The committee held thirty-three meetings, at which they had before them many eminent engineers and citizens, and obtained a vast amount of information and evidence concerning the serious question in their charge. The important result of their deliberations was the preparation of an act for the creation of an aqueduct commission, which was subsequently presented to the Legislature, and was the basis of an act finally passed by the Legislature during 1883, known as the "Aqueduct act," whereby the Aqueduct Commission was created. Following is a copy of the title and first section of the act:

An act to provide new reservoirs, dams, and a new aqueduct with the appurtenances thereto, for the purpose of supplying the city of New York with an increased supply of pure and wholesome water. The people of the State of New York, in Senate and Assembly, do enact as follows: SECTION 1. The Mayor, the Comptroller, and the Commissioner of Public Works of the city of New York, and James C. Spencer, George W. Lane, and William Dowd, are hereby authorized, empowered, and directed to carry out the provisions of this act, in the manner hereinafter provided, for the purpose of supplying said city with an increased supply of pure and wholesome water. They shall be known as the Aqueduct Commissioners. Said commissioners (other than the Mayor, the Comptroller, and the Commissioner of Public Works) shall each receive a salary, to be fixed by the Board of Estimate and Apportionment of the city of New York, not to exceed $8,000 per annum. They and their successors shall hold no other Federal, State, or municipal office except the office of notary public or commissioner of deeds.

At the time of the passage of this act, Franklin Edson was the Mayor, Allan Campbell was the Comptroller, and Hubert O. Thompson was the Commissioner of Public Works of the city of New York, and these three gentlemen,

duct, and dams and reservoirs and other appurtenances as contemplated, set forth and described in section 2 of chapter 490 of the act of the Legislature of the State of New York, entitled "An act ,to provide new reservoirs, dams, and a new aqueduct, with the appurtenances thereto, for the purpose of supplying the city of New York with an increased supply of pure and wholesome water, and the said Commissioner of Public Works is hereby directed to include, set forth, and embody in said plan or plans :

1. Such a system or systems of water-supply as will when perfected secure all the water that can be obtained from the Croton Lake and river and its tributaries for the use of the city of New York, with a proper and suitable aqueduct and reservoirs for the same, to the end that an increased storage and supply of water can be provided for the present aqueduct at the earliest time practicable, and for the new aqueduct to be constructed at an early day.

2. A plan for the immediate construction of a res-

A HEAD-HOUSE AT SHAFT.

with James C. Spencer, George W. Lane, and William Dowd, the three citizens named in the law, became by the foregoing section "The Aqueduct Commissioners." The body was permanently organized Aug. 8, 1883, when the Mayor was elected President of the Commission, William Dowd, Vice-President, and Jas. W. McCulloch, Secretary. The following resolution, which was adopted at this meeting, sets forth in a general way the views of the commissioners at the time as to the proposed sources of water-supply, and system and plans, and the line of the aqueduct :

Resolved, That the Commissioner of Public Works be and he is hereby requested to submit to the Aqueduct Commissioners, as soon as practicable, a plan or plans, together with maps, specifications, estimates, and particulars, for the construction of a new aque-

ervoir or reservoirs and dams for the storage and retention of the water-supply of the east branch of the Croton river and its tributaries at a point near Brewster's Station, and known to the said commissioner and the engineer of the Department of Public Works as the Sodom reservoir.

3. A plan and surveys and maps of the proposed line of the aqueduct that will provide for two routes or lines in the northerly portion thereof, one of which will reach or terminate at the Croton river below the Croton Dam and near the proposed site of a dam known as the "Quaker Bridge Dam," and the other route to reach or terminate at the Croton Dam, and near, yet above, the terminus of the present aqueduct.

On Aug. 15, 1883, Benjamin S. Church was unanimously appointed Chief Engineer of the Aqueduct Commission. On the 24th of the same month the Board of Estimate and Apportionment fixed the salaries of Commissioners

Lane, Spencer, and Dowd at $8,000 per annum. The principal work of the commissioners during 1888 included the hearing and consideration of plans and specifications with regard to the work about to be undertaken. The expenditures of the commission at the close of that year amounted to $22,747.90. On December 30 Commissioner George W. Lane died suddenly. The vacancy was filled by the appointment of Christopher C. Baldwin, who entered upon his duties Jan. 9, 1884. On the 23d of January the engineer corps for the aqueduct, as recommended by the chief engineer, was organized, including the following names: Alphonse Fteley, Principal Assistant and Executive Engineer; Henry S. Craven, Engineer of Construction; Edward Wegmann, Jr., and Frederick W. Watkins, Assistant Engineers of Construction; Frederick S. Cook, Assistant Engineer in charge of the Draughting Department; Cæsar Leonhard, Assistant Draughtsman; and Henry M. Patterson, Chief Clerk. Joseph Davis was appointed Consulting Engineer. On Aug. 24, 1884, the Supreme Court appointed E. Ellery Anderson, Henry F. Spaulding, and Robert Murray, Commissioners of Appraisal for property taken for aqueduct purposes within the city and county of New York. On Dec. 3, 1884, the aqueduct work was divided into six divisions, each division in charge of a division engineer, as follows: the first division, commencing at Croton Dam, in charge of Charles S. Gowen; the second division, commencing near Sing Sing and extending southerly, John B. McIntyre; the third division, commencing near Tarrytown and running south, J. M. Wolbrecht; the fourth division, commencing near Irvington, Alfred Craven; the fifth division, commencing north of Yonkers, E. Sherman Gould; and the sixth division, including the Twenty-fourth Ward of the city of New York, in charge of Frederick W. Watkins. Bids for the construction of each section of the aqueduct from Harlem river to the Croton Dam were publicly opened and announced. The work was divided between the following contractors: Heman Clark, O'Brien & Clark, and Brown, Howard & Co. The expenditures for the purposes of the aqueduct commissioners during 1884 amounted to $185,-730.63.

On Jan. 7, 1885, William R. Grace, Mayor, and Rollin M. Squire, Commissioner of Public Works, became aqueduct commissioners, in place of Franklin Edson, late Mayor, and Hubert O. Thompson, late Commissioner of Public Works, and William R. Grace, Mayor, was elected President of the Commission. During 1885 and 1886 the work was laid out and allotted, and decisions reached on plans and specifications, notably in regard to the Sodom and Muscoot dams; also the plan of a siphon tunnel under the Harlem river was adopted, and the construction of the same ordered to be made. The expenditures on account of the aqueduct for 1885 amounted to $2,265,-

147.58. On Jan. 28, 1886, resolutions were adopted fixing the southern terminus of the new aqueduct at the northern side of the Central Park Reservior, and the Commissioner of Public Works was requested to prepare and submit plans for a gate-house at 135th Street and Convent Avenue, and one at the northern side of Central Park Reservoir, and for a pipe-line between said gate-houses. On May 5, 1886, the reservoir previously known as the "Sodom Dam and Reservoir" was ordered to be named and thereafter known as "The East Branch Reservoir," and the following resolution was adopted in regard to the southern terminus of the new aqueduct:

Resolved, That the point in the city of New York to which an additional supply of water shall be brought under the direction of this commission be, and the same is hereby fixed, at a point on the northerly side of the reservoir in Central Park (known as the "New Reservoir"), and adjacent thereto, which point is hereby located as the southern terminus of the "New Aqueduct."

On May 17, 1886, a certified copy of an act (Chap. 337 of the Laws of 1886) amending the act of 1883, under which the commissioners exercised their powers, was received by the commissioners from the Secretary of State, by which amending act Oliver W. Barnes, Edgar L. Ridgway, and Hamilton Fish, Jr., were appointed commissioners, while the Mayor and Comptroller of the city of New York, under this amendment, ceased to be commissioners, and the annual salaries of the commissioners were reduced from $8,000 to $5,000. Commissioner James C. Spencer was then unanimously elected President of the Commission, to fill the vacancy caused by the retirement of the Mayor, and has since been annually elected as such president.

On July 21, 1886, the commissioners determined to divide the work on the line of the new aqueduct into two districts, to be known as the northern and southern districts, and five divisions, to be numbered from one to five respectively, each district to be intrusted to a principal and assistant engineer, and each division to a division and assistant engineer. On July 28, 1886, John C. Sheehan was appointed Secretary of the Commission in the place of James W. McCulloch, the latter being appointed special assistant to the chief engineer. The expenditures of the aqueduct commissioners during the year 1886 amounted to $5,029,-684.21, and the total expenditures from Aug. 8, 1883, to Dec. 31, 1886, amounted to $7,503,-310.32.

The committee appointed by the Senate in 1883, in connection with the portions of their report which formed the basis of the principal proceedings toward the construction of the new aqueduct, included in that report the following statement of their views, and the causes which induced them: "The statistics of rainfall in the Croton water-shed, in connection with the ascertained fall of the river at Croton Dam, show that this water-shed is capable of furnishing at least 250,000,000 gallons a day from the natural Croton water-shed. The flow of Croton water is extremely variable, varying from 10,000,000 to 2,000,000,000 gallons a day, and in order to secure a constant supply at all times it is necessary to impound this water in reservoirs located in the Croton water-shed or elsewhere in the line of the aqueduct. At present there are storage reservoirs as follows: Boyd's Corners, Middle Branch, Lake Mahopac, and other small lakes, representing in all a total capacity of 8,586,000,000 gallons. For such years of drought as 1880 and 1881, in order to be certain of a supply of 100,000,000 gallons of water a day, it is believed that,

city of 82,000,000 gallons of water, is proposed very far down in the Croton valley. By the other plan, smaller reservoirs are proposed on Croton river, and its main branches at and above the present Croton Dam. . . . The plan referred to contemplates the construction of this dam at Quaker Bridge, which, when completed, would be the largest work of the kind in the world."

The act authorizing the expenditures for account of the aqueduct included in section 32 of said act the authorization to issue bonds, to be called "additional water stock." Of the amount already mentioned expended up to Jan. 1, 1887, the sum of $49,057.64 was paid

AN OPEN CUT—TURNING THE ARCH.

in accordance with the plans of the Department of Public Works already made, additional storage reservoirs of a capacity of at least 4,000,000,000 gallons should be built at once. As the city increases in population and manufactures, the supply of 100,000,000 gallons a day will not be sufficient, and it is deemed advisable that further provision should be made, either now or as fast as the same shall be needed, for the storage of such a quantity of water in the Croton water-shed as will secure all the available water therefrom. We have considered two plans for the storage of water, not entirely different, and of which one may serve to supplement the other. By one of these plans a very large reservoir (3,635 acres, including the present Croton Lake), known as the Quaker Bridge Reservoir, and of a capa-

for land and land damages, after having been adjusted by agreement between the aqueduct commissioners and persons interested in the land taken, used, or occupied, and approved by the Board of Estimate and Apportionment. The sum of $202,537.65 was paid on the order of the Supreme Court in proceedings reported from the Commissioners of Appraisal in connection with the acquiring of property and property rights for aqueduct purposes. The aggregate amount of $6,495,324 was paid contractors on the contracts for construction work on the certificates of the aqueduct commissioners. The total expenditures of the aqueduct commissioners during the year 1887 amounted to $7,242,293.75. The total expenditures from August 8, 1883, to January 1, 1888, amounted to $14,745,604.27.

After due consideration, the construction of the proposed Quaker Bridge Dam and Reservoir, and the plan of a tunneled aqueduct, were determined upon by the commission, and, after the completion of soundings for that purpose, plans, etc., for the proposed crossing of the aqueduct by a tunnel under the Harlem river, and its continuance under the north side of "Manhattan valley" at 135th Street, were adopted by the commissioners. The line for the aqueduct, as decided upon, begins at Croton Dam, on Croton river, and runs in a southerly direction along the Pocantico and Saw-Mill River valleys across the Harlem, and thence to the northerly side of Manhattan valley at 135th Street. The general features of the plans comprise the construction of a conduit, beginning at Croton Dam, on Croton river, with its mouth 60 feet below high-water level

iron pipes to the Central Park Reservoir. The length of the tunnel and open cuts from Croton Dam to Harlem river, when completed, will be 28½ miles. From the northeasterly shore of Harlem river to the gate-house at 135th Street and Convent Avenue its length will be 2½ miles. The total length of tunnel, when completed, will be 30¾ miles. The length of pipe-line from the gate-house at 135th Street and Convent Avenue will be 12,525 feet, or about 2¼ miles. The total length of the aqueduct, when completed, will be 33¼ miles. Of the 30¾ miles of tunnel, 22$\frac{41}{100}$ miles were completed by Jan. 1, 1887. At the present time there is about 30½ miles completed.

At the time when the old Croton Aqueduct was completed the population of New York was fewer than 350,000. It is now over 1,800,000. This great increase of population,

POCANTICO GATE-HOUSE—LOOKING EAST.

of the proposed Quaker Bridge Reservoir, at an elevation of 140 feet above tide at the Invert, and to discharge into the Central Park Reservoir, the total fall from the water-level of greatest flow in the aqueduct at Croton Dam to high water in Central Park Reservoir being 33·8 feet for a length of 33¼ miles. The interior of the conduit is to have a cross-sectional area such that its flowing capacity will be equal to that of a circle 14 feet in diameter, and to run mainly in a tunnel built on a uniform grade of $\frac{7}{10}$ of a foot per mile to near shaft No. 20. The tunnel then to run to and under the Harlem river as an inverted siphon, and to continue under flow pressure to 135th Street on the north side of Manhattan valley. From this point the water to be conveyed in

together with the great and increasing demand for water by the rapidly-growing manufactures of the city, has so largely increased the consumption of water, that in many parts of the city where the water was formerly delivered on the highest floors of buildings, it will now often run only on the lowest floors, and sometimes only in the cellars and basements. By the new aqueduct from 80,000,000 to 100,000,-000 gallons a day are reserved for the Twenty-third and Twenty-fourth Wards north of the Harlem to supply a proposed distributing reservoir at or near Jerome Park. Four waste-weir gate-houses have been located, the first at the Pocantico river, near Tarrytown, 9½ miles south of the beginning of the conduit; the second at Saw-Mill river, 6¼ miles farther south, near Ardsley; the third at Tibbets Brook, 5½ miles farther down; and the fourth at Harlem river, 7 miles below. Three gate-houses, for controlling and regulating the water-supply through the aqueduct, were contemplated, the largest and most elaborate one to be located at the Croton Dam entrance, the second at the end of the conduit at 135th Street, where the pipe-lines begin, and the third at the Central Park Reservoir. The gate-house at 135th Street and 10th Avenue is the southern terminus of the tunnel, and from this point the immense volume of water will be carried to its destination by twelve pipes, each four feet in diameter. At the beginning of November, 1887, the excavation for the gate-house had just been completed. It is 25 feet deep, 60 feet long, and 30 feet broad, and is cut in solid rock. Through it there will flow 250,000,000 gallons of water a day. At High Bridge is the deepest and largest shaft on the works, and the largest in the United States. It is 20 by 40 feet, and extends 426½ feet in depth. From its bottom the fourteen foot tunnel is being bored under Harlem river and is now nearly completed. From the north side of the river, from High Bridge to South Yonkers, all the tunneling had been completed at the end of the year, and only a few thousand feet required to be done before that portion of the aqueduct would be ready to carry water. At South Yonkers the aqueduct runs for half a mile on the surface of the ground. Here Tibbets Brook, a stream that swells to considerable size in the spring, is carried under the Croton water-way, and at the point where they cross, a "blow-off," or series of gates, set in massive masonry, for turning the course of the water in the duct out into the brook, has been erected. The bed of the brook has been widened, and the banks walled, preparatory to a sudden increase of its volume should occasion require it. Where Pocantico river intersects the line of the tunnel, the problem whether to carry the river over or under the tunnel was finally solved by making an artificial bed for the river a little south of the natural bed, thus turning it from its course until the aqueduct at that point had been finished, and then turning the river back again to its own course, a remarkable and successful piece of engineering work. An extraordinary instance of engineering skill was also shown in connecting two shafts, each 350 feet deep and 6,250 feet apart. The work was accomplished so accurately that at the point of union the drills met and struck against each other.

The number of accidents reported along the line of the aqueduct up to Jan. 1, 1887, was 166, of which 59 were fatal.

It is believed that the entire work of the aqueduct to 135th Street will be completed before the end of 1888. The East Branch Reservoir and the Muscoot Dam and Reservoir will be completed before the end of 1889,

which will give New York an adequate water-supply until the Quaker Bridge Dam and Reservoir can be constructed, when the whole flow of the Croton river will be utilized as a water-supply.

The present Aqueduct Commissioners are James C. Spencer, President; William Dowd, Vice-President; C. C. Baldwin, Commissioner; John Newton, Commissioner of Public Works, and ex-officio Aqueduct Commissioner; Oliver W. Barnes, Edgar L. Ridgway, and Hamilton Fish, Jr., Commissioners; John C. Sheehan, Secretary. The principal engineers of the Commission are: Benjamin S. Church, Chief Engineer; George S. Rice, Deputy Chief Engineer; Alphonse Fteley, Consulting Engineer; J. Imbrie Miller, Principal Assistant Engineer. Division Engineers: Charles S. Gowan, First Division; H. M. Walbrecht, Second Division; Alfred Craven, Third Division; S. Fisher Morris, Fourth Division; Edward Wegmann, Jr., Fifth Division; George B. Burbank, Sixth Division.

NIAGARA FALLS, UTILIZING THE POWER OF. For many years numerous plans for employing water-power at Niagara, not only for use at hand but also for transmission to other places through the agency of electricity, compressed air, etc., have been discussed. No practical attempt was made to realize this project until 1886, when the Legislature of New York incorporated a company to construct a subterranean tunnel from the water-level below the Falls, about 200 feet under the high bank of the river, extending through the rock to the upper Niagara river, at a point about one mile above the falls, where a head of 120 feet is obtained. The tunnel thence extends parallel with the shore of the river one and a half mile, at an average depth of 100 feet below the surface of the earth, and at a distance of about 400 feet from the navigable waters of the river, with which it is connected by means of conduits, or lateral tunnels. It is thought by electricians that it would be practicable to light the city of Buffalo (distant 20 miles) with power furnished by Niagara Falls. The proposition is, to dig pits at certain distances, so that the water may fall upon turbine wheels. It is said that sufficient land along the river has been secured, surveyed, and apportioned into mill-sites, fronting on the river and on the line of the proposed tunnel, with ample streets and dockage, affording facilities for approach by rail or water, to accommodate 238 mills of 500 horse-power each, or 119,000 horse-power in all. It is said that this total far exceeds the combined available power in use at Holyoke, Lowell, Minneapolis, Cohoes, Lewiston, and Lawrence, and that it can be constructed at an expense not to exceed one tenth of the outlay for the development of the power at the places designated. It is further claimed that the facilities for transportation afforded to the mills are unequaled. The mill-sites are fixed upon the Niagara river at a point above the

Falls where the river is navigable for vessels. Hence, vessels passing through the great western chain of lakes can come down Niagara river with their loads of lumber, grain, coal, etc., and unload them on the wharves and docks of the mills and factories. Canal-boats can also receive and discharge freight at the mills, as Niagara river connects with the Erie Canal at Tonawanda, seven miles distant. The tracks of the New York Central, West Shore, Erie, Grand Trunk, Rome, Watertown and Ogdensburg, Lehigh Valley, and Michigan Central railways adjoin and run parallel with the proposed tunnel, and the entire plot of mill-sites of the company, with provision for sidings to each mill-site.

The estimate of the cost of the tunnel, including lands, docks, conduits, cross-tunnels, etc., is $3,000,000. This represents 238 mill-sites, varying from 75 by 200 to 200 by 400 feet each, with streets 100 feet wide between the rows of lots in the rear of mill-privileges, and also with 100 foot reserve between the rows of lots in the rear, for railway sidings. To each site is allowed 500 horse-power, with conduit and cross-tunnel, bringing the water within 50 feet of each lot.

Another plan, also controlled by a corporation, proposes the building of a large canal from Niagara river to the city of Lockport, where much of the power of the combined locks is already in use. A third plan, which is of local interest to the city of Buffalo, is taking shape under the stimulus of a prize of $100,-000 offered by the business men of that city to the inventor who shall successfully use the power of the nine-mile current that runs past the city. Several designs of wheels and chains, with feathering buckets, have been submitted, but nothing has yet been decided upon. Some of these plans are likely to become of practical use very soon. They are all based upon the proposition that the water-power of the United States heretofore available is steadily diminishing as the country becomes more thickly settled. At many places in the Eastern States it has become necessary to supplement the water-power with steam, in order to be able to run machinery during the entire 24 hours, greatly increasing the cost of production. Nearly all of the water-power in use in various sections of the country has been produced by the construction, at great cost, of dams for storage during the dry season. These devices have at times proved inadequate to supply the water required for manufacturing purposes; and, at other times, when freshets prevailed, the dams have given away. The cost of constructing dams, the unreliability of the water-power, and the isolated location of many establishments on slender lines of railroads where rates are high, owing to a lack of competition, place manufacturers under great disadvantage with those who have the benefit of a steady power and abundant railroad and other shipping facilities. It is said that the power can be rented cheaper than it is in the following places; the figures being for one-horse-power per year: Paterson, N. J., $37.50; Birmingham, Conn., $20; Manayunk, Pa., $56.25; Dayton, O., $38; Lowell, Mass., $20; Lawrence, Mass., $20; Cohoes, N. Y., $20; Holyoke, Mass., $20; Lockport, N. Y., $16.66; Rochester, N. Y., $35.

NICARAGUA, a republic in Central America. Area, 51,600 square miles; population in 1884, 259,794. The capital is Managua, population, 15,000.

Government.—The President is Don Evaristo Carazo, whose term of office will expire on March 1, 1891. The Cabinet was formed of the following ministers: Foreign Affairs, Don Adrian Zavala; Finance, Don Fernando Lacayo; Interior, Don David Osorno; Public Works, Don Ladislas Argüello; War and Navy, Gen. J. Elizondo. The Nicaraguan Minister at Washington is Don Horacio Guzman; the Consul-General at New York is Alexander Cotheal; at San Francisco, Francisco Herrera. The American Consul at Managua is Charles H. Wills, and at San Juan del Norte, William A. Brown.

Finances.—Early in 1887 the Government sent to London Don José Pasos, Director-General of Mails and Telegraphs, with instructions to negotiate a six-per-cent. loan for £285,-000, the proceeds to be spent on public works. This loan was placed by the city bank at 92½. The actual expenditure of the Government, which was $2,191,076 in 1885, amounted to $1,998,667 in 1886. The total amount of Nicaraguan bonds canceled in London, under the contract effected by Mr. Norris with the Government, was $245,260 silver, equivalent to £41,956. Between June 30 and Oct. 6, 1887, there had been withdrawn from circulation and destroyed $158,599 paper money, leaving in circulation at the time $203,553, and in the treasury, $449,270.

Army.—The effective strength of the permanent army is 1,000 men, and there is also a militia 4,227 strong.

Postal Service.—In 1885 the post-offices of the republic forwarded 322,055 letters, 9,781 postal-cards, and 541,878 newspapers.

Railroads.—In December, 1887, a contract was published in the "Official Gazette" of Nicaragua, between the Government and Mr. Jericho for the construction of a railroad which will run from the port of San Juan del Sur, on the Pacific, through the towns of Rivas, San Jorge, and Belan, and terminate either in Masaya or Granada, about fifty-five miles. The districts it will pass through are the richest in Nicaragua. A short branch line will run from the main track to the beach of San Jorge, connecting it with the waters of Lake Nicaragua. Colored or Chinese laborers can not be employed.

In 1886 the eastern section of the Corinto-Granada Railway was finished, connecting Corinto with Managua, on Lake Managua, and thence the latter with Granada. This section is 32 miles long, and, together with the 60 miles of the western section, completes the entire distance of 92 miles, which involved an outlay of $1,942,579, including the rolling-stock.

Steamship Lines.—According to the published interviews with the agents of the Del Campo Spanish Steamship Line at San Francisco, in January, 1888, which line was established three months previous in opposition to the Pacific Mail's new company, it decided to cease operations. The company ordered its four steamships at San Francisco to be tied up until further orders. It is said that the reason for this is found in the fact that the Del Campo line was not afforded any facilities whatever by the Panama Railroad, and that the five-per-cent. rebate granted by the Central American States on all duties on goods shipped by the Del Campo line was not made an exclusive grant to them, but similar concession had been made to the Pacific Mail. For these reasons Marquis del Campo gave orders stopping all the steamers on their way to the Pacific, and ordering steamers there and at Panama to be laid up indefinitely.

The Government, early in 1888, resolved to subsidize, at the rate of $15,000 per annum, the river and lake steamers that are owned by Don T. A. Pellas, in connection with a fortnightly service of coasting steamers between San Juan del Norte, Bluefields, and other Atlantic ports.

Wagon-Roads.—The Government has intrusted an expert with the task of making the necessary surveys for a high-road between the most suitable port of Lake Nicaragua and Bluefields.

Commerce.—The imports into Nicaragua in 1885 amounted to $2,168,426, and to $2,557,590 in 1886. The exports of merchandise reached the sum of $2,286,444 in 1886, as compared with $2,032,883 in 1885. The American trade with Nicaragua has been as follows:

YEARS.	Import into the United States.	Domestic export to Nicaragua.
1887	$1,562,162	$701,151
1886	1,067,902	471,671

The increase of trade between the two countries has been due chiefly to the advance in coffee and India-rubber.

Manufacturing Privileges.—A concession was granted in November to M. E. Salignac, a Frenchman, to introduce during five years, duty and tax free, material for the manufacture of matches, he in return engaging to instruct ten young Nicaraguans in this branch of industry. It granted also a concession to Don Tomás Argüello to manufacture, under an exclusive privilege, cotton cloth, from cotton grown on the spot, in a spinnery and weaving factory to be established by him. A concession was also granted to George A. R. Morris for the exclusive privilege of sinking artesian wells in the republic for a term of ten years.

The Maritime Canal Company.—On Feb. 21, 1887, the United States Senate took up the bill to incorporate the Maritime Canal Company of Nicaragua, and the bill was passed. It incorporates Frederick Billings, Charles P. Daly, H. L. Hotchkiss, Francis A. Stout, W. B. Franklin, Daniel Ammen, William L. Merry, Horace Davis, Edward F. Beale, James H. McMullen, Shepherd Homans, and their associates, as the Maritime Canal Company of Nicaragua, with the principal offices in New York city. The capital stock is to be not less than fifty nor more than one hundred millions. Ten per cent. is to be payable when subscriptions to the capital stock are made, and future payments are to be made as the board of directors may determine. The aggregate of all charges, dues, and towage is to be reasonable, and not to exceed $2.50 a ton weight of the total of all cargo (fuel and supplies included) on board any vessel in transit, or not exceeding $1.25 a ton actual displacement of any steam-vessel and $1.75 a ton actual displacement of any sailing-vessel. The United States is to exercise such control over the canal as provided for by treaty with Nicaragua and not inconsistent with any treaty obligations of the United States with any power, and is to enjoy its unobstructed use (at half rates) for troops, munitions of war, and mails. If stock to the amount of $10,000,000 be not subscribed and 10 per cent. thereof actually paid in within two years, or if the work of construction shall not be actually begun and in progress within four years, the corporation shall be deemed to have expired by limitation and all its franchises to have ceased. The passage is to be entirely through the territory of Nicaragua, excepting in a limited portion of the eastern division, where, by a recent revision of the boundary-lines, Costa Rica is awarded the southern bank of the river at a spot where it will be available for the movement of ships. But, by a convention between these two republics, Costa Rica agrees to accept all the conditions granted to the American Company now engaged in building this canal. The boundary questions in issue have, by common agreement, been left to the arbitration of the President of the United States. The summit-level of the canal above the mean sea-level is 110 feet; the distance from sea to sea is 170 miles, and of this only 40 miles are to be actual cutting or excavation, leaving nearly 130 miles to be navigated on Lake Nicaragua and the river San Juan. The summit-level is to be reached by three or four locks from the Atlantic, and four from the Pacific. The length of the lock-chambers will be 650 feet, and the width 65 feet. No. 8, which will probably be divided into two locks, will be cut out of solid rock, but others are to have timber and concrete foundations, and the cavities, as they may occur, will be filled with concrete. The real question to solve in regard to these locks are the gates, which are of exceptional size. Engineer Peary has invented a rolling gate, combining strength with lightness, as well as facility in opening and shutting. The lower part of the gate consists of a water-tight compartment, in which shifting water-ballast acts to aid both in raising and lowering the gate, while the moving force employed is hydraulic. The gate moves on rails above the floor of the lock. The first division of the canal begins at Greytown, at the mouth of San Juan river, and extends to the valley of the Arroyo de las Cascadas, 19·48 miles. This part consists entirely of excavations, but has lagoons on the line, which will much reduce the labor and expense. At Rio Lajas begins the western division of the canal, which extends 17·27 miles from the western shore of the lake to Brito, on the Pacific. Ships from the Atlantic will here gradually descend by four locks, and arrive in a snug haven. The depths of these locks will be respectively 26·4 feet, 29·7 feet, and 29·7 feet, and for the last one a variable lift of 24·2 to 33·18 feet, in order to meet the state of the tide. Lock No. 4 will rest on solid rock, but the remaining three locks will be cut through strata of clay, gravel, and compact sand, presenting no special difficulties. Several inconsiderable streams intersect this portion of the line. The largest, the Rio Grande, will be deflected into another channel, while it is proposed to carry the others under the canal. When Commodore Hollins shelled the tiled roofs and waving palms of Greytown in 1854, that port was deep enough for the navies of the world. But the silt from the San Juan has reduced the maximum depth to twenty-one feet within the bar. It is proposed to divert the San Juan into another channel near Greytown, and to carry out a jetty over a mile on the east side of the port and anchorage, which must tend to deepen the port as well as serve for a breakwater. At Brito, the western terminus, quite a different formation exists. The shores are bold, and a rocky headland on the east side affords partial protection. It is proposed to build jetties on either side of the little bay, which will afford a good haven, large enough for many ships. The canal is itself a harbor up to the lower lock. It is estimated by Mr. Menocal that the canal can be completed in six years. Owing to the ample supply of water-power, the route can be lighted with electricity at moderate cost. The estimates for this work, based on former surveys, placed the probable cost of the canal at $65,722,147, inclusive of possible contingencies. The latest surveys of Mr. Menocal instead of adding to this amount, have modified the plan of the eastern division to such a degree as to reduce the former estimates $16,921,980. Engineer Menocal secured the canal concessions from Nicaragua, which extend over a period of ninety-nine years, with an expressed option to the company to hold the property as lessees for an additional period of 101 years upon the payment of 25 per cent. of the net profits to the republic. The sum of $100,000 was paid for these concessions. The

first survey expedition of the Nicaragua Canal Construction Company left New York on November 30, Civil Engineer Peary, of the navy, having charge of it under the direction of A. G. Menocal, chief engineer of the company.

NORTH CAROLINA. State Government.—The following were the State officers during the year: Governor, Alfred M. Scales, Democrat; Lieutenant-Governor, Charles M. Stedman; Secretary of State, William L. Saunders; Treasurer, Donald W. Bain; Auditor, William P. Roberts; Attorney-General, Theodore F. Davidson; Superintendent of Public Instruction, Sidney M. Finger; Commissioner of Agriculture, Montford McGlehn; Chief Justice of the Supreme Court, William N. H. Smith; Associate Justices, Thomas S. Ashe,* succeeded by Joseph J. Davis, and Augustus S. Merrimon.

Legislative Session.—The Legislature met on January 5, and adjourned on March 7. It passed 605 laws, nearly all of which are private or special. One of the most important measures adopted provides for a reduction of the the ad-valorem State tax from 25 to 20 cents on each $100. As in Georgia and some other Southern States, a formidable list of special taxes upon all kinds of trades and professions is maintained. The liquor-license tax varies from $20 to $200 a year. Provision was made for the incorporation and establishment of savings-banks within the State, and for regulating their business. The Treasurer is authorized to issue registered four-per-cent. bonds in exchange for coupon bonds issued under the acts of March, 1879, upon surrender of the latter.

An amendment to the State Constitution, increasing the number of Supreme Court judges from three to five, was proposed to be voted upon by the people in 1888. Other acts of the session were as follow:

To prescribe the punishment for waylaying and for poisoning another.

To enable sheriffs and tax-collectors to collect arrears of taxes from 1881 to 1886, inclusive.

Making it unlawful for railroads to collect a larger amount or an equal amount for transportation of freight or passengers a short distance than for a longer distance in the same direction.

Requiring every contractor to furnish to the owner of any building which he is constructing or repairing, before receiving any part of the contract price, an itemized statement of the amounts due laborers upon such building and the furnishers of material therefor, making the debts so set forth a lien on the building, and authorizing the owner to withhold such part of the contract price as is necessary to pay them.

Authorizing the State Board of Education to construct and complete certain roads and canals in eastern North Carolina, and to employ the State convicts thereon.

Constituting the town of Durham a public-school district.

To establish a bureau of labor statistics.

Declaring that the State shall exercise exclusive jurisdiction and control over the shell-fisheries south of Roanoke and Croatan sounds and north of Core sound, and providing for the appointment of a board of shell-fish commissioners, who shall survey all natural beds and proclaim them as public grounds subject

---

* Died February 4.

to the regulation of the board, and who shall, on application, grant licenses to individuals to use exclusively portions of flats outside such public grounds for the private cultivation of shell-fish.

Revising the system of collection of taxes.

Authorizing the owners and agents of vessels to refuse payment to a stevedore until satisfied that all laborers hired by him upon the vessel have been paid, and making such owners or agents who neglect to comply with this statute liable to such laborers for any unpaid wages.

Providing for the employment of convicts upon certain railroads.

Requiring incorporated and private banks in the State to make reports to the State Treasurer.

Providing that appeals to the Supreme Court in criminal cases shall not have the effect of vacating the judgment appealed from, but only of staying execution, and authorizing the sheriff to carry out the judgment at once on receipt of notice from the Supreme Court that the appeal is not sustained.

Making the same provision regarding appeals in civil cases.

Declaring it unlawful to purchase seed-cotton in smaller quantities than what is usually baled, unless a public record of such purchase is kept by the purchaser.

To prohibit the advertisement of lotteries.

Amending the local option law by providing that elections shall not be held oftener than once in two years.

Abolishing free tuition at the State University, and reducing the tuition-fee to $60 per annum.

Requiring marl-pits to be fenced.

To establish a legal oyster measure.

To provide a method for the drainage of low lands.

To prevent the poisoning of cattle.

To provide for the working of convicts upon the public roads of the State.

To establish a reformatory in connection with the State Penitentiary for convicts under fifteen years of age.

Requiring license from the county commissioners in order to sell dynamite and other explosives.

A large number of railroad companies were incorporated.

Increasing the annual appropriation for the Colored Normal Schools from $2,000 to $6,000.

Appropriating $100,000 annually for the State Penitentiary, $37,000 for the School for the Deaf, Dumb, and Blind, $58,000 for the Insane Asylum, and $65,000 in 1887 and $85,000 in 1888 for the Western Insane Asylum.

Finances.—At the close of the fiscal year ending Nov. 30, 1886, there was in the treasury a balance on account of educational fund of $23,223.38; of public fund $172,327.06. During the year ending Nov. 30, 1887, there was received on account of educational fund $6,920.48; on account of public fund $850,177.70, making the total funds of the State for the year ending Nov. 30, 1887, $1,052,648.62. Of this fund there was disbursed during the year on account of educational fund $5,524.21; on account of public fund $885,389.78, making the total disbursements $890,913.99, and leaving a total balance in the treasury on account of educational and public fund on Nov. 30, 1887, of $161,784.63. The valuation of assessed property in the State for 1888 is estimated at $209,000,000.

Banks.—In accordance with the law of this year, requiring incorporated and private banks to report their condition to the State Treasurer, the following summary of the standing of the

incorporated class (twelve in number) and of six private banks has been ascertained. Incorporated banks: total resources $2,492,552,-52, in which is included loans on real estate, $161,636.30; other loans, $1,520,432.51; State bonds, $34,100; gold coin, $47,262; silver, $37,273.18; legal-tender and national-bank notes, $184,788.23. Among the liabilities are: $697,401.94 for capital stock paid in, and $55,-578.38 in undivided profits. The resources and liabilities of the private banks amount to $510,248.47. Their capital stock paid in is $148,770.55, and their undivided profits $15,-908.18.

Cotton.—The first report of the State Bureau of Statistics, published at the close of the year, presents the following facts regarding the cotton-manufactures of the State: In 1880 the number of establishments was forty-nine, with a capital of $2,855,800 and 92,385 spindles. In 1887 the number of mills had increased to about eighty, with a capital of over $4,000,000 and operating over 200,000 spindles. The quantity of cotton consumed annually by these establishments is estimated at 30,000,000 pounds. The average number of hours a day required of operatives is from 10 to 12½. Men get from 50 cents to $1.50 a day; foremen from $1.00 to $2.66; women from 85 cents to $1.00; boys, 25 cents to 65 cents, and girls from 30 cents to 55 cents. The State has need of a law regulating the number of hours that shall constitute a day's labor.

NOVA SCOTIA. Government.—The Lieutenant-Governor is Matthew Henry Richey. Executive Council: President and Provincial Secretary, W. S. Fielding; Attorney-General, J. W. Longley; Commissioner of Works and Mines, Charles E. Church; without portfolio, Thomas Johnson, Angus Macgillivray, and Daniel McNeil.

Commerce.—The following table shows the imports and exports of the province for five years:

YEARS.	IMPORTS.		EXPORTS.	
	Total value.	Value per head.	Total value.	Value per head.
1882	$8,701,589	$19 44	$9,217,295	$20 59
1883	10,088,929	22 12	9,280,882	21 65
1884	9,658,104	20 99	9,509,858	20 87
1885	8,418,826	18 06	8,894,065	19 03
1886	7,840,244	16 60	8,071,518	17 09

EXPORTS OF HOME PRODUCE.

YEARS.	Value.	Value per head.	Percentage of total exports.
1882	$8,580,769	$19 79	9·84
1883	9,492,658	20 92	11·26
1884	9,404,971	20 45	19·19
1885	8,696,686	18 58	11·84
1886	7,818,151	16 55	10·42

Finances.—The total expenditure of the province for 1886 was $656,348.53, and the total revenue was $23,203.10 less. The provincial debt on Dec. 31, 1885, was $700,000. The principal sources of revenue are the Dominion subsidy and interest, and the mining royalties; the former amounting in 1886 to $432,-884.18, and the latter to $127,149.97.

Mining.—The following is the estimated mineral production of Nova Scotia in 1886: Gold, 23,362 ounces; iron-ore, 44,888 tons; manganese-ore, 427 tons; barytes, 230 tons; antimony, 645 tons; coal raised, 1,502,611 tons; gypsum, 123,753 tons; building-stone, 8,000 tons; coke made, 81,604 tons; limestone, 20,-265 tons; grindstones, etc., 1,600 tons.

Legislation.—The Legislature met on March 10, 1887, and the House of Assembly elected Mr. M. J. Power, Speaker. The Hon. Mr. Fielding, Premier, moved the following resolutions:

That the Province of Nova Scotia was on the first day of July, 1867, made a member of the Canadian Confederation with the consent of the Provincial Legislature, but against the well-understood wishes of the people;

That the consummation of the act of union, without the approval of the people of Nova Scotia, was a grave wrong, which produced widespread discontent and marred the future of the Dominion;

That previous to the union of the provinces, the Province of Nova Scotia was in a most healthy financial condition;

That by the terms of the union the chief sources of revenue were transferred to the Federal Government;

That strong objections were taken at the time of the union to the financial terms thereof, relating to the Province of Nova Scotia, as being wholly inadequate to meet the requirements of the various services left under the management of the Provincial Legislature;

That an appeal was made to the Imperial Government and Parliament for a repeal of the union, as far as it related to this province;

That while they refused to assent to such repeal, until a further trial of the union was had, the Imperial Government, in the Colonial Secretary's dispatch of the 10th of June, 1868, to Lord Monck, requested that the Government and Parliament of Canada would modify any arrangement respecting taxation, or respecting the regulation of trade and fisheries, which might prejudice the interests of Nova Scotia;

That the request of the Imperial Government has never been fully complied with by the Government and Parliament of Canada;

That after many years' experience under the union successive governments in Nova Scotia found that the objections which were urged against the terms of union at the beginning applied with greater force than in the first year of the union, and that the feeling of discontent with regard to the financial arrangement was more general and more deeply fixed than before;

That urgent representations on this subject were from time to time made to the Government of the Dominion by the governments of Nova Scotia, representing all shades of political opinion;

That in the year 1884 a joint address of the two branches of the Legislature was unanimously adopted and forwarded to his Excellency the Governor-General, setting forth the absolute necessity of larger allowances to the province from the Federal treasury;

That the advisers of his Excellency, after long delay, replied to the said address in a dispatch dated

December 18, 1885, which was laid before the Legislature in the session of 1886, in which dispatch the claims of the province were rejected;

That the two branches of the Legislature in 1886 reaffirmed their declarations of 1884, as respects the disadvantages under which the province labored;

That on the 10th day of May, 1886, on the motion of the leader of the Government, the House of Assembly adopted a series of resolutions in favor of the withdrawal of the maritime provinces from the Canadian Confederation and the formation of a maritime union, or, in event of such changes being found impracticable, the withdrawal of the Province of Nova Scotia alone, and inviting an expression of the opinion of the people on such proposed change at the general elections then approaching;

That the general election, which took place on the 15th day of June, 1886, resulted in the return of a large majority of members in support of the Government's policy;

That, while the representatives of the people of Nova Scotia in the Provincial Parliament were thus favorable to the policy of separation from the Dominion of Canada, a majority of the representatives of the province in the Federal House of Commons were known to be opposed to such policy;

That the importance of having the representatives of the province in the two Parliaments in harmony on this question was generally recognized;

That on the 22d of February, 1887, a general election for the Parliament of Canada was held throughout the Dominion, affording the people of Nova Scotia an opportunity of electing members of the House of Commons in sympathy with the views of the majority of the representatives in the House of Assembly;

That at the said general election for the House of Commons in February, 1887, the Province of Nova Scotia returned a majority of members opposed to the policy of separation from the Dominion;

That in view of such recent action by the people of the province, an application to the Imperial Government and Parliament for the release of Nova Scotia from the Canadian Confederation could not be favorably received by the Imperial authorities. and it is at present inexpedient to make such application;

That this house strongly reaffirms the declaration of the last house, that Nova Scotia suffers great disadvantages in the union, and declares its opinion that unless a material change takes place in financial affairs and commercial relations, whereby the position of the province is improved, the discontent in Nova Scotia will continue and increase, and it will be necessary to again submit the question of separation from Canada to the people of this province for their decision.

Dr. McKay moved an amendment, which was negatived by 5 to 25. The Premier's resolutions were adopted by 24 to 8. On motion of the Premier, the House of Assembly adopted resolutions in favor of the abolition of the Legislative Council, asking for a conference by committee with the Upper House on the subject. The Legislative Council declined the conference.

An act was passed conferring the right to vote at civil and municipal elections upon widows and spinsters having the same property qualification as men that have the right to vote; also upon married women who hold property under the Married-Women's Property Act of 1884, whose husbands are not qualified to vote.

O

OBITUARIES, AMERICAN. Abbott, Horace, an American manufacturer, born in Worcester County, Mass., July 29, 1806; died in Baltimore, Md., Aug. 8, 1887. He learned the blacksmith's trade, and in 1836 removed to Baltimore, secured the Canton Iron Works, owned by Peter Cooper, and began manufacturing wrought-iron shafts, cranks, and other similar material in iron for steam-vessels. He made the first large steamship shaft of wrought-iron (weighing 26,000 pounds) in this country, for a Russian frigate. In 1850 he added three rolling-mills to his plant, from which he turned out the largest rolled-plate then made in the United States. During the civil war he executed many large contracts with the Government, furnishing among other work the plates for the first monitor, and subsequently the armor-plate for nearly all the vessels of that class built on the Atlantic coast. After the war the plant was sold to a joint stock company, of which he became president. He was identified with many charitable institutions, and was a liberal promoter of religious interests.

Abeel, Gustavus, an American clergyman, born in New York city, June 6, 1801; died in Stamford, N. Y., Sept. 4, 1887. He was a son of the Rev. John Neilson Abeel, for many years pastor of the Collegiate Church in New York city, and a grandson of Col. James S. Abeel, of the Revolutionary army. He was ordained a minister of the Reformed Church in 1824, and after having charges in English Neighborhood and Belleville, N. J., was settled in Geneva, N. Y., for fifteen years. In 1844 he became the first settled pastor of the Second Reformed Church, in Newark, N. J., and remained there till 1864, when his health compelled him to withdraw from active work. He filled many responsible offices in his church organization, and was a member of the New Jersey Historical Society, and the oldest minister of the Reformed classis of Newark.

Adams, James Osgood, an American journalist, born in East Concord, N. H., June 5, 1818; died on his farm in Boscawen, N. H., Feb. 7, 1887. He learned the printing-trade, fitted for college under his brother, Rev. Ezra Eastman Adams, at Lyndon (Vt.) Academy, and was graduated at Dartmouth in 1843. For a time he was principal of Lyndon Academy; afterward at Manchester, N. H., teaching and reading law. Mr. Adams was nine years publisher and editor of the "American." During this time he established and published for six years the "Granite State Farmer." At a later date he was editor of the "Mirror and American." He was clerk of his ward six years, moderator nine years, member of the common council in 1847-'48, and president the last year. He was a member of the Manchester School Board four years, and Superintendent of its schools from 1855 till 1859, and from 1861 till 1867. He became a member of the Legislature in 1852, and was re-elected to the House for nine years, and was the Republican candidate for Speaker of the House in 1871, a year when his party was in a minority. He was five years Secretary of the New Hampshire Agricultural Society, and edited the first five volumes of its reports, and was delegate from that body to the World's Fair, London, in 1851. He was Secretary of the Board of Agriculture from Aug. 23, 1870 till 1887. At his death he was a member of the school board of Boscawen. The fifteen annual reports of the Board of Agriculture which he edited are a valuable contribution to the agricultural literature of the State, and a testimonial to his great interest and labor in that department.

Aiken, David Wyatt, an American agriculturist, born in Winnsboro, Fairfield County, S. C., March 17, 1828; died in Cokesbury, S. C., April 6, 1887. He was educated at the Mt. Zion Collegiate Institute and the South Carolina College, being graduated at the latter in 1849, and directly afterward was appointed Professor of Mathematics in the former. In 1851 he visited Europe, and gave much attention to the study of agricultural science. On his return he established himself on an impoverished farm, where his successful application of science to exhausted nature developed a fondness for agricultural pursuits which was maintained to the close of his life. He conducted costly experiments, and spoke and wrote upon almost every subject connected with farm-life and stock husbandry. In 1860, when his State seceded, he volunteered as a private soldier, but was soon afterward appointed adjutant of the Seventh Regiment of South Carolina Infantry, and a year later was elected its colonel. At the battle of Antietam he was shot through the lungs and left for dead on the field. On recovering he resumed command of his regiment, serving till the close of the Gettysburg campaign, when, his health failing, he was assigned to less laborious duty. He was elected a member of the State Legislature in 1864-'66, and a member of Congress in 1876, 1878, 1880, 1882, and 1884, serving in the latter body on the committees on agriculture and patents, and as chairman of the committee on education. Mr. Aiken was an early and enthusiastic member of the Order of Patrons of Husbandry. He served two years as Master of the State Grange, and fourteen as a member of the executive council of the National Grange.

Aiken, William, an American legislator, born in Charleston, S. C., in 1806; died in Flat Rock, N. C., Sept. 7, 1887. He was graduated at the College of South Carolina, in Columbia, in 1825, and, after spending several years in traveling, became a rice-planter on Jehosse Island, near Charleston. At one time he was the largest slaveholder in the State. From 1838 till 1848 he was a member of the State Legislature, in 1844 Governor, and from 1851 till 1857 a Representative in Congress. He steadily opposed both nullification and secession, and took no active part in politics after leaving Congress, excepting in 1866, when he was again elected Representative, but not admitted to a seat. He was one of the first trustees of the Peabody Education Fund, and contributed liberally to charitable and educational interests.

Alexander, Andrew Jonathan, an American soldier, born in Sherwood, Woodford County, Ky., Nov. 21, 1833 ; died near Utica, N. Y., May 4, 1887. He was appointed second lieutenant of mounted rifles July 26, 1861, and the same day first lieutenant in the Third U. S. Cavalry. During that summer he was on duty in the office of Gen. McClellan. He was present at the battle of Williamsburg, and with the advance of the Army of the Potomac, and in the Seven Days battles, and was afterward on duty with Gen. Banks in the Department of Washington. In September, 1862, he was appointed lieutenant-colonel and assistant adjutant-general Third Army Corps, with which he served in the battle of Fredericksburg. In 1863 he was transferred in the same capacity to the cavalry corps then being organized, and participated in Sherman's raid, the engagements at Beverly Ford, Middleburg, Upperville, Hanover, and the battles of Gettysburg, Boonsboro', and Williamsport. During the winter of 1863-'64, he was on duty at the cavalry bureau, Washington, D. C., and then, being appointed assistant adjutant-general, Seventeenth Army Corps, was engaged in the battles of Kenesaw Mountain, those before Atlanta, and at Jonesboro' and Lovejoy station, in the pursuit of Gen. Hood to Gainesville, Ga. ; and, on being transferred to Gen. Thomas's army, in the battles of Franklin and Nashville, the actions of Spring Hill and Pulaski, and the subsequent pursuit of the Confederates to the Tennessee river. In the spring of 1865 he was placed, on his brevet rank of brigadier-general, in command of the second brigade, fourth division, cavalry corps of the Mississippi, taking part in all the movements in that section, capturing eight pieces of artillery from Gen. Forrest, and after the battle of Columbus, Ga., becoming chief of staff to Gen. Stoneman, commanding the Department of Tennessee. He received several brevets in the regular army for distinguished skill and gallantry in cavalry engagements, and after the war served actively on the frontier till July 3, 1885, when he was retired for disability incurred in the line of duty. He died on a railroad train near Utica, while on his way to his home near Auburn, N. Y.

Anderson, Luther Wilson, an American educator, born in Londonderry, N. H., June 10, 1821 ; died in Quincy, Mass., June 13, 1887. He was graduated at Dartmouth College in 1846, and immediately took charge of an advanced school in East Braintree, where he remained two years, when he was appointed Master of the Winthrop School in Charlestown, Mass. In September, 1852, he became a teacher and usher in the English High School in Boston, and, after passing intermediate grades, was appointed head master in 1867, which office he filled with ability till his death. During his thirty-five years of service in this institution he was absent from his post but six days in all. He was the founder and first head master of the Evening High School in Boston, and an original trustee of the Crane Public Library and Adams Academy in Quincy. Mr. Anderson was considered an expert in matters pertaining to English literature and history, and for several years prior to his death had spent the summer months in giving instruction in his specialties to teachers. He was the lecturer on history at the Saratoga Summer School of Methods in 1885-'86, and, besides performing a large amount of literary work in the direction of criticising and rewriting the works of others, had published school-books on natural history and language.

Ash, Abraham Joseph, an American clergyman, born in Senjatisch, Poland, in 1821 ; died in New York city, May 9, 1887. He came to the United States in 1851 with a mind already well stored with Talmudical and other religious learning, and, settling in New York city, engaged in the humble occupation of a glazier. Gradually making the acquaintance of well-to-do Hebrews, his quiet demeanor and knowledge of the ritualistic and dietary laws of their faith led to the formation of a small congregation, over which he was installed as rabbi. Aided by a wealthy Hebrew, the congregation became incorporated under the name of Beth Hamedrash, and opened a small synagogue on Elm Street. The membership rapidly increased under Rabbi Ash's ministrations, and the congregation sought larger accommodations from time to time, till at length they secured the Episcopal church, on the corner of Norfolk and Broome Streets. For many years no one could kill animals for purposes of food for the Jews in this country without a certificate from Rabbi Ash. He personally instructed several hundred men in the peculiar laws of Judaism relating to the manner of killing animals for food, fitting them to act as inspectors at the slaughter-houses. He was a man of simple habits, extremely modest in all his relations, and possessed of high scholarly attainments.

Ashburner, William, an American mining engineer, born in Stockbridge, Mass., March 28, 1831 ; died in San Francisco, Cal., April 20, 1887. He studied for two years at the Lawrence Scientific School of Harvard, and in 1851 went to the School of Mines, Paris, where he completed his professional studies. In 1854 he returned to the United States and devoted some time to examining the mining region of Lake Superior, and later was engaged in the exploration of a part of Newfoundland. In

1860 he went to California with Josiah D. Whitney, to engage on the geological survey of that State. His services were then retained as mining expert by the Bank of California, and ultimately he devoted his attention exclusively to that branch of work, traveling extensively through the mining districts of the United States, British Columbia, and Mexico, and also in the more distant regions of South America and Asia. He was appointed one of the commissioners of the Yosemite Valley and of the Mariposa Big-tree Grove in 1864, and held that office until 1880. In 1874 he was elected Professor of Mining in the University of California, and after organizing the School of Mines of that institution, was made honorary occupant of the chair, also in 1880 he was appointed one of the Board of Regents of the university. He was chosen by James Lick to be one of the trustees of the California School of Mechanical Arts, and likewise was a trustee of the Leland Stanford Jr., University. Prof. Ashburner was an active member, and for some time a trustee of the California Academy of Sciences, also President of the Microscopical and member of historical and geographical societies of California, and one of the founders of the Harvard Club of San Francisco.

Ashe, Thomas Samuel, an American lawyer, born in Orange County, N. C., July 21, 1812; died in Wadesboro, N. C., Feb. 4, 1887. He received an academic education at the Bingham School, Hillsboro, N. C., and was graduated at the University of North Carolina, Chapel Hill, in 1832. Studying law in the office of the late Chief-Justice Ruffin, he was admitted to the bar, and took up his residence in Wadesboro in 1836. In 1842 he was elected a member of the House of Commons of the Legislature, in 1847 was elected by the Legislature Solicitor of the Fifth Judicial District of the State, in 1854 was elected to the State Senate, and in 1861 was elected a delegate to the State Constitutional Convention, which, however, was not called at that time on account of an adverse popular vote. He was a member of the Confederate House of Representatives, and, while serving his term was elected a member of the Confederate Senate in 1864. Two years later he became a Councilor of State, serving during the administration of Gov. Worth. In 1872 he was elected a member of Congress, and in 1874 was re-elected. At the expiration of his second term, while arranging to resume the practice of law, he was elected an Associate Justice of the Supreme Court of North Carolina, and in 1886 was re-elected.

Astor, Charlotte Augusta, born in New York city, Feb. 27, 1825; died there, Dec. 12, 1887. She was a daughter of Thomas S. Gibbs, an educated man of business and wealth, who had removed from the South to New York, and Miss Vanden Heuval, of an old and rich family. With her two sisters she received all the educational advantages of the day, including thorough instruction in the French, German, and Italian languages, music, and painting. Miss Augusta, as she was usually called in the family, married John Jacob Astor on Dec. 9, 1846, and had one child, William Waldorf, recently U. S. Minister to Italy. To the great fortune of her husband she brought a large personal one derived from her parents, and this, together with her husband's allowances, enabled her to gratify her philanthropic desires. While the range of her benefactions showed a noble catholicity of spirit, she made herself the special promoter of some of the best-known movements in charity. She was particularly interested in the Children's Aid Society, and besides spending a large sum of money annually in gathering little waifs from the streets, and placing them in good homes in the West, she provided, for many years, a grand dinner at the various branches of the society in the holiday season. When her sister, Mrs. Cullone, provided for the founding of the New York Cancer Hospital she gave $225,000 for the erection of the buildings, which were formally opened a few days before her death. For twenty years she supported and personally labored in an industrial school founded by herself, where poor children of German parentage were fed, clothed, and educated. She was also a warm friend of the homeless newsboys, frequently visiting their lodging-house, and caring for their wants. During the past ten years she gave them their Thanksgiving-dinners, and at an expense of $20,000 provided homes in the country for 1,413 of them. From 1872 till her death she was a manager of the Woman's Hospital, giving it liberally of her means and time. Besides these interests, she was actively identified with the Five Points' Mission, St. Barnabas Home, St. Luke's Hospital, and foreign and domestic missionary societies, including the work among the Indians of Dakota and other Territories. She bequeathed $25,000 to the Woman's Hospital, $25,000 to the Young Women's Christian Association, $35,000 to the Children's Aid Society, $25,000 to the Hampton Normal and Agricultural Institute of Virginia, $25,000 to the Domestic and Foreign Missionary Society of the Protestant Episcopal Church, $1,000 to the New York Society for the Prevention of Cruelty to Children, $1,000 to the Orphan's Home and Asylum of the Protestant Episcopal Church in New York, and $1,000 to the Society for the Relief of the Destitute Blind.

Ayres, William Orville, an American physician, born in New Canaan, Conn., Sept. 11, 1817; died in Brooklyn, N. Y., April 30, 1887. He was graduated at Yale University with the class of 1837, and during the ensuing fifteen years was employed as a teacher, his last engagement as such being in Boston, Mass., from 1845 till 1852. In the latter part of this service he began the study of medicine in Boston, finishing his course at Yale and receiving his degree in 1854. Removing directly thereafter to San Francisco, Cal., he was engaged in practice there for twenty years, occupying the chair of Theory and Practice of Medicine in the Toland Medical College of that city during a portion of the time. Shortly before the great fire of 1871 he removed to Chicago, and thence in 1878 returned to New Haven. In the following year he was appointed Lecturer on Diseases of the Nervous System in the Yale Medical School, holding the office till early in 1887, when, on account of failing health, he removed to Brooklyn. While he had made a special study of nervous diseases, he had also given much thought to various branches of natural science, particularly to ichthyology, on which he had published many memoirs in the Proceedings of the Boston Society of Natural History and of the California Academy of Sciences.

Babbitt, Elijah, an American lawyer, born in Providence, R. I., in 1796; died in Erie, Pa., Jan. 9, 1887. He received an academic education in the States of New York and Pennsylvania, studied law, and was admitted to the bar in Erie, Pa., in 1824. He was prosecuting attorney for his county in 1833, a member of the State Legislature in 1836–'37, and a State Senator in 1844–'45. In 1858 he was elected a Representative in Congress, serving as a member of the Committee on Revolutionary Pensions, and in 1860 was re-elected. He was the oldest lawyer in active practice in Pennsylvania, and had survived every judge, attorney, law-officer, physician, and surgeon that lived in Erie when he settled there.

Baldwin, Jesse Garrettson, an American abolitionist, born in Meriden, Conn., March 17, 1804; died in Middletown, Conn., April 5, 1887. In 1827 he engaged in the "Yankeenotion" business in Oxford, Conn., transferring it to Middletown in 1832, and enlarging it by the manufacture of silver spoons, plated ware, and cotton goods. In company with several other capitalists he built and managed a number of coasting-vessels. At the time of his death he had been president of the Central National Bank of Middletown for twenty-nine years, and of the People's Fire Insurance Company for twenty-two, and was also president of the Indian Hill Cemetery Association and the Board of Trustees of the Methodist Church. Mr. Baldwin was specially noted for his early and long activity as an abolitionist. In 1835 his residence was mobbed by 200 men, one of whom was an officer in the U. S. Navy, because an anti-slavery prayer-meeting was being held there. Windows and chairs were broken, the little company were maltreated, and a bucket of water was poured upon Mrs. Baldwin and the babe in her arms. During slavery days Mr. Baldwin would neither use, buy, nor sell any article that he knew to be the product of slave-labor, nor would he permit any vessel in which he held an interest to enter any port in a slave-holding State, because the freight so obtained would have been handled by slaves or been the results of slave-labor. Although he manufactured cotton-goods, he would only buy the raw material that was picked, handled, and owned by free men; and most of his cotton was obtained from a plantation owned and managed by Quakers. He was so grounded in his convictions that when away from home he carried lumps of loaf-sugar in his pockets, that he might not be forced to use the slave holders' production in his tea or coffee. He was once the anti-slavery candidate for Lieutenant-Governor of Connecticut, and after the civil war, besides aiding in forming the National Prohibition party, was its candidate for governor.

Baldwin, Samuel, an American manufacturer, born in South Orange, N. J., April 7, 1808; died in Newark, N. J., April 10, 1887. While a lad he removed to Newark, where he was subsequently engaged for many years in the manufacture of carriages. He was a member of the Common Council in 1855–'56, holding the offices of chairman of the committees on finance and public grounds, and to his energy in the latter the city is indebted for the improvement of South (now Lincoln) Park. He had also served in the Board of Education. More than fifty years ago he joined Engine Company No. 1, and to the hour of his death "Uncle Sammy" remained a fireman in spirit and sympathy. In 1859 he was elected treasurer of the Fire Department Relief Fund, and re-elected at each annual meeting thereafter. Several times during this period he was given costly testimonials of the esteem in which he was held by the firemen. Mr. Baldwin was an active member of the Presbyterian Church from his youth. One of his sons, the Rev. Theodore Baldwin, is now a missionary of that denomination in Syria.

Barnewall, Robert Aylmer, an American publisher, born in County Meath, Ireland, in 1818; died in Philadelphia, Pa., July 14, 1887. He was educated in London, and came to the United States at the age of twenty-one. Settling in New York city, he found employment in several newspaper offices in the publication department, and afterward became publisher of "The Broadway Journal," which was under the editorship of Edgar Allan Poe. From New York he removed to Philadelphia, where he was connected with "The Evening Argus" and other newspapers for several years. In 1865 he was placed in charge of the advertising department of "The Evening Telegraph," remaining there till 1882, when failing health caused him to resign. Mr. Barnewall was well-informed on poetry and the drama, and preserved to the last a keen appetite for gentlemanly sports.

Bartlett, Washington, an American publisher, born in Savannah, Ga., in 1824; died in Oakland, Cal., Sept. 12, 1887. He removed to California in 1850, settling in San Francisco, where he published the first daily newspaper issued in that city. In 1859 he was elected County Clerk, in 1870 appointed Harbor Commissioner, in 1882 and 1884 elected Mayor of San Francisco, and in 1886 elected Governor of the State, holding the latter office at the time of his death.

Bartol, James Lawrence, an American lawyer, born in Havre-de-Grace, Md., June 14, 1813; died in Baltimore, Md., June 23, 1887. In 1828 he went to Baltimore with a view of preparing himself for mercantile life, but soon manifesting an aversion to it, returned home and resumed study under a private tutor. He was graduated at Jefferson College, Philadelphia, in 1832, admitted to the bar in 1836, and began practice in Caroline County. In 1845 he removed to Baltimore, and, after a successful career of twelve years at the bar, was appointed to fill a vacancy on the bench of the Court of Appeals, occasioned by the resignation of Judge J. T. Mason. In the autumn of 1857 he was elected a judge of the Appellate Court, and on the expiration of his term in 1867 was elected Chief-Judge of the Court of Appeals. He held this office till 1883, when failing health compelled him to resign.

Bartow, Mercy Hale, an American genealogist, born in Westchester County, N. Y., April 9, 1831; died in New York city, Dec. 24, 1887. He was a descendant of John Reid, the Surveyor-General of East Jersey, and of Nathan Hale, the New England patriot, who was hanged by the British as a spy, and a great-grandson of Rev. John Bartow, who came to the United States from England as a missionary in 1702, and founded St. Paul's parish, New York city, over which he had charge till 1726. For several years Mr. Bartow was advertising agent of the New York "Observer." He was an earnest worker in genealogy and family history, a member of the New York Genealogical and Biographical, the New York Historical, the American Geographical, and the American Huguenot societies, and a writer on religious, biographical, and genealogical subjects.

Beach, John Sheldon, an American lawyer, born in New Haven, Conn., in 1819: died there, Sept. 12, 1887. He was graduated at Yale College in 1839, admitted to the bar in 1843, and immediately taken into partnership by Gen. D. Kimberly. On the retirement of the latter in 1852, Mr. Beach continued the business alone, and so conducted it that at the time of his death it was the largest practice in the State. While his practice was general, he did much as a patent and corporation lawyer, and as counsel for vast estates, in courts of probate. He was regarded as the father of the New Haven bar, and was credited with having been before the U. S. Supreme Court more frequently than any other lawyer in Connecticut.

Beach, William Morrow, an American physician, born in Amity, Madison County, Ohio, May 10, 1831; died near London, Madison County, Ohio, May 5, 1887. After receiving his education at Ohio Wesleyan University he was graduated at Sterling Medical College, Columbus, Ohio, in 1853, and practiced his profession in Unionville until 1855, when he removed to Lafayette, Ohio, remaining there

until the beginning of the civil war. He entered the service as major-surgeon, and became assistant surgeon in the Seventy-eighth Ohio Volunteers on May 3, 1862, holding this post until May 19, 1864, when he was transferred to the One Hundred and Eighteenth Ohio Volunteers in the Twenty-third Army Corps, Army of the Tennessee, serving until the close of the war. During the Vicksburg campaign he was the hospital director of Gen. John A. Logan's division. He was mustered out in June, 1865, being then division-hospital director of the Second Division, Twenty-third Army Corps, and also one of the surgeons constituting the division operating board. After the war he resided on his farm in Madison County, practicing there until his death. He was a member of the Legislature, and was the Republican candidate for Lieutenant-Governor in 1878. Dr. Beach was a member of the principal medical societies of Ohio, was the first president of the Ohio Sanitary Association, and was president of the State Medical Society in 1885, and served in this capacity for other societies, contributing valuable papers to their proceedings, which were copied extensively in medical journals. Among these was one on "Milk-Sickness," which was read before the American Medical Association and afterward published in the "Reference Hand-Book of Medical Science."

Beers, Henry Newell, an American manufacturer, born in Lexington, N. Y., June 12, 1819; died in Bay Shore, Long Island, July 12, 1887. He received a collegiate education at Amherst College and New York University, being graduated at the latter. Nearly the whole of his life, after that time, was spent in New York city, where he was engaged for many years in the manufacture of glass. He was one of the organizers and most active members of the "Committee of Seventy," which was formed to wrest the control of municipal affairs from the Tweed Ring. Out of that committee grew a more permanent organization, known as the "Council of Municipal Reform," the object of which was to secure a greater efficiency and economy in the city government. Of this body Mr. Beers was an earnest member during the remainder of his life. Among his other labors he was instrumental in procuring the passage of the constitutional amendment limiting the corporate indebtedness of cities, and in having the official conduct of the Park Commissioners investigated by the Supreme Court. He also rendered the city valuable service before the Board of Estimate and Apportionment, and at Albany, in successfully opposing improper and illegal items in tax levies.

Betts, Charles Wyllys, an American lawyer, born in Newburg, N. Y., Aug. 3, 1845; died in New York city, April 27, 1887. He was graduated at Yale in 1867, and directly afterward entered the Law School of Columbia College, where he was graduated two years later. He practiced law in New York city for two years, and then returned to New Haven for the purpose of pursuing graduate studies in history and literature. But before he had completed the course for the degree, he was induced to resume the practice of law with his brother's firm, then Whitney & Betts. In October, 1875, upon the appointment of Mr. Whitney to be Corporation Counsel of New York city, the firm was changed to F. H. and C. W. Betts, and subsequently to Betts, Atterbury & Betts. The specialty of the firm was patent-cases in the United States courts, and in that branch of practice Mr. Betts developed a promising ability. He was a member of the Union, Knickerbocker, and Century Clubs, the New York Bar Association, and the Seawanhaka Yacht Club. At an early age he became interested in the study of numismatics, and during his residence in New Haven gave much time to the arrangement and description of the college coin collection. He bequeathed to the college his own rich collection of coins as well as some valuable specimens of early oak carving.

Blackburn, Luke Pryor, an American physician, born in Fayette County, Ky., June 16, 1816; died in Frankfort, Ky., Sept. 14, 1887. He was graduated in medicine at Transylvania University, Lexington, Ky., in 1834, and began practice in that city. In 1835, when cholera broke out in the town of Versailles, he went there and remained during the prevalence of the plague, giving gratuitous service to the sufferers. He afterward made that town his home, and in 1843 was sent to the Legislature as representative of Woodford County. In 1846 he removed to Natchez, Miss. Two years later, on the outbreak of yellow fever in New Orleans, as health officer of Natchez, he established the first effective quarantine against New Orleans that had ever been known in the Mississippi valley. At the same time he founded at his own expense a hospital for rivermen. He also served through the epidemic of 1854, and after its extinction obtained the passage of an act of Congress establishing the quarantine station below New Orleans. During the civil war he served on the staff of the Confederate General Sterling Price as surgeon, and afterward visited the Bermuda Islands for the relief of sufferers there, at the request of the Governor-General of Canada. In 1867 he retired to his plantation in Arkansas, where he remained till 1873, when he returned to his native State. In 1875, when yellow fever was raging at Memphis and threatened the entire Mississippi valley, he hastened to the city, and organized and directed a corps of physicians and nurses. Again, in 1878, he gave his entire services and time for the relief of yellow-fever sufferers at Hickman, Ky. In 1879 he was elected Governor of the State as a Democrat, and in that office distinguished himself by the large number of pardons issued to convicts, for humane and sanitary reasons.

Blake, Samuel H., an American banker, born in Hartford, Oxford County, Me., in 1807; died in Boston, Mass., April 25, 1887. He was educated in the local schools and at Bowdoin College, and, after being graduated at the latter, studied law, and in 1831 was admitted to the bar. He was a member of the State Senate in 1840-'42, being president during the latter year, and Attorney-General of the State in 1848. In 1854 he unsuccessfully opposed the late Israel Washburn for Congress. Previous to the civil war he acted with the Democratic party, but then became a strong Union man and remained an energetic Republican. Mr. Blake had been president of the Merchants' Bank of Bangor since 1863, when he gave up his law practice to succeed his brother William as the head of the bank. He was very wealthy.

Bodwell, Joseph R., Governor of Maine, born in Methuen, Mass., June 18, 1818; died in Hallowell, Me., Dec. 15, 1887. He worked upon a farm till his seventeenth year, and then learned the shoemaker's trade, which he followed for several years, educating himself in evenings and spare hours. In 1852 he became associated with Moses Webster in quarrying granite at Fox Island, near the mouth of Penobscot river, Me., working an abandoned property, and this venture proved the foundation of his large fortune. At first he drove the single yoke of oxen owned by the firm, but the business soon began to increase, and a joint-stock company was organized with Mr. Bodwell as president. He obtained the contract for furnishing the stone for the building of the War, Navy, and State Departments at Washington, D. C., and, removing in 1866 to Hallowell, organized a second granite company there. From his quarries was taken the stone used in the Yorktown Monument, the Boston Soldiers' Monument, the new Capitol at Albany, N. Y., the public buildings in Chicago, Brooklyn, and New York, and the carved sphinx in Mount Auburn cemetery, Cambridge, Mass. He was an ardent Republican, was twice elected Mayor of Hallowell, and represented for two terms his district in the lower branch of the State Legislature. In 1880 he was a delegate-at-large to the National Republican Convention that nominated Gen. Garfield, in 1884 headed the Maine delegation in the convention that nominated Mr. Blaine, and in 1886 was elected Governor of Maine by a plurality of 12,000. Besides his quarry interests he was largely engaged in lumbering, shipping, and cattle-raising. He was always proud of his early struggles, and made a generous distribution from his fortune among the poor.

Bolingroff, Catherine, an American philanthropist, born in Dublin, Ireland, in April, 1816; died near Emmettsburg, Md., March 18, 1887. She came to the United States when a young girl, became a nun in 1831, entering the novitiate at St. Joseph's Academy, near Emmettsburg, and rose rapidly to the rank of principal teacher in that institution. For several years she was attached to St. Mary's Asylum, Baltimore, but subsequently returned to St. Joseph's Academy, where she was engaged in works of education and mercy till her appointment to be Superioress of the Sisters of Charity of the division of the United States. Her name, in religion, was Mother Euphemia, and during her twenty-five years of humane work she possessed the esteem and sympathy of all with whom she came into contact, irrespective of denominational lines.

Brennan, Margaret, an American educator, born in New York city in 1812; died there, March 24, 1887. She entered a convent of the Order of the Sacred Heart in 1847, and since that time had been constantly engaged in carrying on the work and promoting the interests of the order. She found a congenial mission in instructing the young in the higher branches of study, and to this task she devoted her chief energies. Her rank in the order, that of Mother Superior, entailed upon her labors of considerable magnitude, and called for the exercise of much organizing and executive ability. In carrying out this portion of her duties, she aided in founding many branches of the order throughout the country, and exercised a supervision over the convent at Eaton Hall, near Philadelphia, in Detroit, in Halifax, in Manhattanville, and in New York city.

Brevoort, James Carson, an American bibliophile, born in New York city, July 10, 1818; died in Brooklyn, N. Y., Dec. 7, 1887. He was educated in New York city, at the Model-School in Hofwyl, Switzerland, and the École Centrale des Arts et Manufactures, in Paris, France, being graduated at the latter as a civil engineer. He returned to the United States in 1838, worked for nearly a year in the West Point foundry, and in 1841 accompanied, as surveyor, Prof. James Renwick in the northeastern boundary survey. In 1842 he went abroad as private secretary to Washington Irving, then United States Minister to Spain, and afterward traveled extensively in Europe. In 1844 he returned home, married a daughter of Judge Leffert Lefferts, and settled in Brooklyn. Between 1847 and 1852 he served as a member of the Brooklyn Charter Commission, the Board of Education, and the Constructing Board of Water Commissioners. In the latter year he was elected a trustee of the Astor Library, holding the office for twenty-six years, and acting as superintendent of the institution during the last two. He actively aided in the organization of the Long Island Historical Society, and was its first president, holding the office for ten years. In 1863 he was appointed a regent of the University of New York, and received the degree of LL. D. from Williams College. He was a member of the New York, Massachusetts, and Pennsylvania Historical Societies, of the American Association for the Advancement of Science, the American Geographical Society, and the Academy of Natural Sciences, besides numerous other historical and scientific organizations. Mr. Brevoort was an ardent and critical collector of books, especially rare Americana, of

pamphlets, manuscripts, coins, and medals, and generously distributed choice specimens and collections among institutions of learning.

Brewster, Henry, an American manufacturer, born in New Haven, Conn., May 19, 1824; died in New York city, Sept. 19, 1887. He was prepared for Yale College, but owing to failing health was taken into business with a brother by his father, James Brewster, a carriage-manufacturer of New Haven. After learning the business, Henry removed to New York city to look after the interests of the firm, and subsequently established the firm of Henry Brewster & Co. there. Under his supervision the firm became one of the largest manufacturers in the world. Mr. Brewster was awarded a gold medal and the decoration of the Legion of Honor at the Paris Exposition for his display of carriages and wagons, and on his return home was presented with a gold plate suitably inscribed by the carriage-makers of the United States. He was one of the organizers of the Union League Club of New York.

Brooks, Horatio G., an American manufacturer, born in New Hampshire in 1828; died in Dunkirk, N. Y., April 20, 1887. When sixteen years old he was apprenticed to a machinist in South Boston, when twenty, entered upon railroad service as a fireman, and when twenty-one, was licensed as a locomotive engineer. In 1850 he left Boston on engine No. 90, crossed New York State by way of the Erie Canal, and reached Dunkirk in November, blowing the first locomotive-whistle in the county of Chautauqua. From 1850 till 1856 he did duty on the Erie Railway as an engineer, becoming, in the latter year, master mechanic of the Ohio and Mississippi Railroad. In 1860 he was recalled to Dunkirk to take charge of the Erie shops as master mechanic; in 1862 was appointed superintendent of the western division of the railroad, and in March, 1865, superintendent of the motive power and machinery of the entire road. He resigned his place on the Erie road in October, 1869, to lease on his own account the shops at Dunkirk, which President Gould had ordered closed permanently, and organized the Brooks Locomotive Works, in which a large and prosperous business has since been done. Mr. Brooks was unwearied in his care for the comfort and welfare of his employés. He frequently kept his works open when business was dull, and maintained a good night-school for his men.

Brown, Dyer Date Stanley, an American publisher, born in Richmond, Ontario County, N. Y., June 19, 1819; died in Scottsville, N. Y., Jan. 11, 1887. He received his preliminary education in the district-school, completing his studies in Genesee Wesleyan Seminary, in Lima, in 1839-'40. He taught for four years, and then began studying law in the office of Hon. B. F. Angel, in Geneseo, subsequently reading in that of Judge W. H. Smith, in Caledonia. He was admitted to the bar in Albany, N. Y., in 1846, and immediately settled in

Scottsville for the practice of his profession. His political career began in 1840, when he cast his first vote, a Democratic ticket. In 1847 he was appointed Canal Collector at Scottsville. In the following year he gave his influence to the Barnburner section of his party, supporting the national ticket of Van Buren and Adams, and in 1852 voted for Franklin Pierce, and was appointed Postmaster at Scottsville. He held this office but a short time, resigning because he could not support the national policies of his party chief. On the formation of the Republican party, he cast his political fortunes with it, and in 1858 was its successful candidate for county clerk, holding the office three years and then resuming his practice. In 1860 he was a delegate to the National Republican Convention, and in 1863–'64 a paymaster in the army, with the rank of major. In January, 1865, he bought a controlling interest in the Rochester, N. Y., "Democrat," retaining it till the consolidation of that newspaper with the Rochester "Chronicle," and becoming president of the company that thereafter published the "Democrat and Chronicle." He was one of the four delegates-at-large from New York to the National Republican Convention of 1868, and a delegate to the National Liberal Republican Convention of 1872. He favored the election of Mr. Tilden, from an independent standpoint, in 1876, but afterward acted in the main with the Republican party. Mr. Brown was one of the original promoters of the Buffalo, Rochester, and Pittsburg Railroad, a manager of the State Industrial Home, and, in 1883, by appointment of President Arthur, a commissioner to examine a portion of the Northern Pacific Railroad.

Buffum, James N., an American abolitionist, born in North Berwick, Me., May 16, 1807; died in Lynn, Mass., June 12, 1887. He was of Quaker parentage. Removing to Salem, he learned the carpenter's trade, but became acquainted with William Lloyd Garrison, and was soon recognized as one of the most fearless and active workers in the anti-slavery cause. Many a fugitive from slavery in the South was encouraged and aided on his road to freedom by Mr. Buffum. In 1845 he accompanied Frederick Douglass on his memorable visit to England, and with him stirred large audiences by his eloquent abolition speeches. He was first elected to public office in 1868, when he was chosen a Presidential Elector from Massachusetts. In the following year he was elected Mayor of Lynn, in 1872 was re-elected Mayor, and in 1874 was sent to the Legislature. During his first mayoralty he was largely instrumental in securing the introduction of water into Lynn. He subsequently united with the Greenback party, and was an unsuccessful candidate for Congress.

Bunzl, Julius, an American philanthropist, born in Prague, Austria, April 30, 1838; died in New York city, July 4, 1887. He came to the United States when nineteen years old, forming a partnership with Henry Dormitzer, and engaging in the tobacco business in New York city. The operations of the firm were so successful, that by 1884, when Mr. Dormitzer retired, both partners had acquired considerable fortunes. While Mr. Bunzl was well-known through his long connection with the New York Chamber of Commerce, and the Metropolitan Museum of Art, he will be longer remembered by reason of the active interets he took in the strictly secular charitable organizations of the city; for with none other would he identify himself. Among those with which he was connected, and to which he gave liberal support, were the St. John's Guild, German Hospital, Hebrew Orphan Asylum, Home for the Aged and Infirm, Hebrew's Fund Society, United Hebrew Charities, German Society, German Society for the Protection of Widows and Orphans, and the Fresh Air Fund. His heart and purse were alike open to various other charities whose work of benefaction was in harmony with his fixed principle of support.

Burtis, Divine, an American ship-builder, born in Huntsville, L. I., in 1811; died in Brooklyn, N. Y., Sept. 5, 1887. While a boy working in a carpenter-shop in Brooklyn, he attracted the attention of the firm of Smith & Dimond, boat-builders, and in its employ learned ship-building. With the aid of borrowed capital he set out in business for himself, and by 1840 had constructed most of the ferry-boats plying on the waters of New York. He then turned his attention to larger vessels, building the "South America," "Columbia," "Roger Williams," and other fast boats for the Hudson river service. An evidence of the thorough workmanship of that time is found in the fact that the "South America," forty years ago, made twenty-six miles in one hour on a trip from New York to Albany, a record never exceeded till about twelve years ago, when the "Chauncy Vibbard" made the distance in sixteen minutes' less time.

Burton, Nathaniel J., an American clergyman, born in Trumbull, Conn., Dec. 17, 1824; died in Hartford, Conn., Oct. 18, 1887. He was graduated at Wilbraham Academy, Wesleyan University, and Yale Theological School, ordained in 1853, and settled as pastor of the Second Congregational Church in Fairhaven, Conn., remaining there four years. From 1857 till 1870 he was pastor of the Fourth Congregational Church in Hartford, going to the Park Church in the latter year and holding that pastorate till his death. He was a member of the Yale College corporation, and occupied for one year the Lyman Beecher lectureship. A week before his death he was selected by the American Board of Commissioners for Foreign Missions to deliver the annual sermon in Cleveland, Ohio, at the meeting of 1888. He received the degree of D. D. from Wesleyan University in 1870, and was ranked among the first pulpit orators of the State.

Cain, Richard Harvey, an American clergyman, born in Greenbrier County, Va., April 12, 1825, died in Washington, D. C., Jan. 18, 1887. In 1831 his father removed to Gallipolis, Ohio, where, till after his marriage, Richard's education was confined exclusively to the instructions of the Sunday-school. He entered the ministry at an early age, and became a student at Wilberforce University, Xenia, Ohio, in 1860. In 1861 he became a pastor in Brooklyn, N. Y., and in 1865 his congregation sent him to South Carolina as a missionary to the freedmen. He was a member of the Constitutional Convention of 1868, and for two years a member of the State Senate from the city of Charleston. In 1872, he was elected Congressman-at-Large as a Republican, and in 1876 member of Congress from the Second District of South Carolina. On the expiration of his second term he was elected fourteenth bishop of the African Methodist Episcopal Church, and thereafter devoted himself to its interests.

Carnochan, John Murray, an American surgeon, born in Savannah, Ga., July 4, 1817; died in New York city, Oct. 28, 1887. He was educated in the high-school and the University of Edinburgh, and after taking his degrees in the latter, returned to the United States, and at the age of seventeen began the study of medicine and surgery in the office of Dr. Valentine Mott in New York City. In 1841 he went to Paris, entered the École de Medicine, and for six years worked in the hospitals and attended clinical lectures. He then returned to New York and began to practice as a surgeon. In 1850 he was placed in charge of the newly established hospital for immigrants on Ward's Island, and gave it a thorough organization. The same year he was appointed Professor of Surgery in the Medical College of the University of New York. He was also health officer of the port of New York for two years, under the administration of Gov. Hoffman. Dr. Carnochan was the author of a number of professional books, among which "A Treatise on the Etiology, Pathology, and Treatment of Congenital Dislocation of the Head of the Femur" (1850), and "Contributions to Operative Surgery" (begun in 1877 and incomplete at his death), being an account of his own practice, are standard authorities throughout the world.

Carpenter, Henry, an American physician, born in Lancaster, Pa., in 1820; died there July 9, 1887. Springing from a long race of physicians on both the paternal and maternal sides, his early education was directed with a view of maintaining in him the distinctive profession of the family. After studying five years in the office of Dr. Samuel Humes, he headed, in 1839, the first seven students that entered the Pennsylvania Medical College, then just opened. He was graduated in 1841, and at once began a practice in Lancaster which was continued till his last illness, becoming in the mean time one of the most noted physicians and surgeons in the State. Dr. Carpenter was one of the founders and officers of the Lancaster County Medical Society, an officer of the State Medical Society, and one of the censors for the eastern district of Pennsylvania. Among his best-known patients were ex-President Buchanan and Thaddeus Stevens, both of whom he attended for many years. He rendered valuable services during the civil war, being at various periods surgeon-in-charge of the Eckington Hospital at Washington and of the State Hospital at Hagerstown.

Cartter, David Kellogg, an American jurist, born in Rochester, N. Y., June 22, 1812; died in Washington, D. C., April 16, 1887. He received a thorough preparatory education, studied law, was admitted to the bar, and began practicing in Massillon, Ohio. He served two terms in the State Legislature, and was elected a member of Congress in 1848–'50, as a Democrat. Shortly before the civil war he removed to Cleveland, Ohio. He took an active part in the presidential canvass of 1860, giving his time, voice, and influence to the Republican cause. In 1861 he was appointed U. S. Minister to Bolivia, and served till March, 1862. On his return he was appointed chief-justice of the newly organized Supreme Court of the District of Columbia, and he held the office till his death.

Chetwood, George Ross, an American physician, born in Elizabeth, N. J., in 1802; died there, April 24, 1887. He was a son of Dr. John Chetwood, who died from exposure and overwork during the epidemic of cholera in 1832. In early life he was educated for a mercantile career in New York city, but subsequently adopted his father's profession and was graduated as a physician in time to succeed to his father's practice upon his death. In 1824 he formed one of the troop of cavalrymen that escorted Lafayette over New Jersey's Revolutionary battle-fields, and he was the last survivor of the company. He was for many years active in the public affairs of his city and state, serving as a member of the State Senate from 1854 till 1857, and being an early director of the old State bank, one of the first directors of the Elizabeth Mutual Insurance Company, and a large stockholder of the old New Jersey Railroad and Transportation Company, now the New York Division of the Pennsylvania Railroad Company. Dr. Chetwood practiced his profession for seven years in Paris, France.

Christian, William Henry, an American soldier, born in Utica, N. Y., April 9, 1825; died there, May 8, 1887. In August, 1846, he enlisted in Col. J. D. Stevenson's regiment as a private for service in California during the Mexican War, and was afterward promoted to be lieutenant. Returning to Utica, he engaged in business till the outbreak of the civil war. He was the first volunteer in the State, if not in the country, as he offered his services to the Secretary of War some time before the firing on Sumter, coupled with a proposition to raise a regiment of volunteers. On May 13, 1861, he organized the 26th Regiment of New York

Volunteers, which was mustered in at Elmira eight days later, when he was elected colonel. The regiment was attached to the Army of the Potomac, in which Col. Christian won the reputation of being an excellent drill-master and a strict disciplinarian. He commanded the regiment in the engagements at Cedar Mountain, Rappahannock Station, Thoroughfare Gap, Gainesville, the second Bull Run, Chantilly, South Mountain, and Antietam. His experience as a civil engineer made him invaluable in military councils, and his advice was often sought by superior officers. He was brevetted brigadier-general after the second Bull Run, and resigned his commission shortly after the battle of Antietam. On his return to Utica he resumed his occupation of civil engineering, and continued it till he developed such marked evidences of mental troubles that his friends were compelled to place him in the Insane Asylum, where he died. He was one of the founders, and for years an active member of the Oneida Historical Society

Cilley, Joseph, an American lawyer, born in Nottingham, N. H., Jan. 4, 1791; died there, Sept. 16, 1887. He was a grandson of Gen. Joseph Cilley, a Revolutionary hero and an officer on Washington's staff. He entered the army as an ensign in 1812, and took part in the battles of Sackett's Harbor, Chippewa, and Lundy's Lane. In the latter battle, while acting as captain of the company of which he was lieutenant, he was struck by a solid shot during a charge and suffered a fracture of his left thigh, which produced a permanent lameness. At Detroit he lost the sight of an eye by an explosion of powder in a magazine. He resigned from the army in 1816, studied law, and was admitted to the bar in his native State. In 1827 he was appointed an aide on the staff of Gov. Pierce, by which office he obtained the title of colonel. In 1846 he was nominated for Governor by the Whigs, but declined. The same year he was elected by the Legislature United States Senator, to fill the vacancy caused by the resignation of Levi Woodbury. He was an abolitionist from his youth, and was the first of that party to hold a seat in the United States Senate. While there he presented the first petition for the abolition of slavery. At the close of his brief term he retired to a farm, and he died in a house that he built in 1824, the oldest ex-United States Senator.

Clark, Patrick, an American inventor, born in Roscommon, Ireland, April 2, 1818; died in Rahway, N. J., March 5, 1887. His father emigrated to the United States with his family in 1827. Within a few years Patrick lost both parents and all of his brothers and sisters by death. As he was thus left alone in the world, he determined to learn a trade, and, walking to Rahway, N. J., apprenticed himself as fireman's boy in Vreeland's iron-mill, where he remained till 1840, becoming proficient in the various branches of the industry. In 1847 he

established an iron-foundry in partnership with E. G. Scisco, subsequently conducting it alone till induced to engage in the manufacture of pasteboard. This venture led to his financial embarrassment. He then studied land-surveying and civil engineering. In 1857, when the gas-works were projected, he superintended the erection of the buildings and the construction of the machinery, retaining a connection with the works till his death. Mr. Clark was the inventor of many useful mechanical appliances, the most noted being a damper regulator for steam-boilers, in almost universal use to-day, for which he received the only gold medal of the American Institute in 1852; a multiple fan-blower; a machine for manufacturing paper; an improved packing for pistons; a dryer for pasteboards; a dryer for oakum; and a dynometer for preventing explosions in boilers, which was patented in 1885. He was frequently engaged by inventors to argue interference cases before the Commissioner and Examiners in Washington.

Clark, William Audley, an American banker, born in Newport, R. I., in 1803; died there, March 26, 1887. His father was Audley Clark, well-known in financial circles for his connection with the Bank of Rhode Island from its organization in 1795 till his death in 1844. The son was placed at work in the bank when fifteen years old. He became cashier in 1839 president in 1862, holding the latter office at the time of his death. Mr. Clark was also president of the first telegraph company that ever stretched wires in Newport, and of the Rhode Island Bridge Company; a director, with a life interest, of the Newport Library; a leading Unitarian, and one of the largest contributors to the fund for the erection of the Channing Memorial Church. He furnished the money for the second Liberty Tree erected at the head of Thames Street, and inclosed it with an iron fence. He was unmarried, and in person and surroundings was exceedingly old-fashioned, clinging to the bank furniture that his father had purchased, and using to the last a box of black sand in preference to blotting-paper.

Cleveland, Chauncey Fitch, an American lawyer, born in Hampton, Conn., in 1799; died there, June 6, 1887. He received a public-school education, studied law, and was admitted to the bar in 1819. In 1826 he was elected a member of the General Assembly, and served as such twelve years, during the period of 1826-'66, being elected Speaker in 1836, 1838, and 1863. He was appointed Attorney for the State in 1832; elected Governor in 1842-'43, being chosen by the Legislature both years because of indecisive popular votes; and elected a member of Congress in 1849, serving till 1853. In 1851 he was a Free-Soil Democrat, and afterward was one of the founders of the Republican party. He was a presidential elector in 1860, and a member of the Peace Congress of 1861. During the past twenty years he led a life of retirement, although taking a deep interest in public affairs. Yale College gave him the degree of LL. D.

Coates, Benjamin, an American abolitionist, born in Philadelphia, Pa., Feb. 16, 1808; died there, March 7, 1887. He was the eldest son of George M. Coates, whose ancestors followed William Penn from England in 1682, and of Rebecca Horner, whose grandfather settled in New Jersey in 1683. In early manhood he entered the dry-goods business, and became a member of the firm of Wurtz, Musgrave & Wurtz. He was afterward senior partner successively in the firms of Coates & Anstie, Coates & Brown, and later in that of Coates Brothers, as well as silent partner in the publishing-house of Porter & Coates. Mr. Coates was one of the founders of the Union Benevolent Association of Philadelphia, and of the Penn Mutual Life Insurance Company, one of the first institutions of its kind organized in the United States. He became an abolitionist in early life, and, as vice-president of the Abolition Society, he was untiring in his efforts for its success by constitutional means. The scheme of colonization had from the first his warm sympathy. He was a most active laborer in the establishment of the republic of Liberia, and in obtaining the recognition of its independence from Great Britain in 1848 and the United States in 1861. After the solution of the slavery question by the proclamation of emancipation, his attention was turned to the education of the freedmen, the establishment of Indian schools, and other philanthropic movements. He lived and died a member of the Society of Friends.

Cobb, Sylvanus, Jr., an American novelist, born in Waterville, Me., in 1823; died in Hyde Park, Mass., July 20, 1887. He was a son of the Rev. Sylvanus Cobb, a Universalist clergyman, author of several religious books, and editor for many years of "The Christian Freeman." When about seventeen years old, young Cobb ran away from home and enlisted in the navy; but, soon afterward repenting of the act, sent for his father, who, after a consultation with the officers of the man-of-war, took their advice and allowed him to make the Mediterranean trip. The lad was made private secretary to the captain, who had desires for literary renown, and in the cabin of the war-ship Cobb received his earliest insight into story-writing while attempting to correct the captain's manuscript. On his release from the navy, he began his career as a writer of novelettes, and continued it with large pecuniary success till his last illness, confining himself almost exclusively to the "New York Ledger," wherein his "Gun-Maker of Moscow" gave both author and publication a wide-spread reputation. He performed military service in the civil war as captain of the Norway Light Infantry, and was a man of many accomplishments.

Cogswell, Elliot Colby, an American author, born in Tamworth, N. H., June 11, 1814; died

at Rye Beach, N. H., Aug. 31, 1887. He was fitted at Gilmanton Academy, and was graduated at Dartmouth in 1838. He was principal of Gilmanton Academy two years, studied theology in Gilmanton Theological Seminary, and was ordained pastor of the Congregational Church in Northwood, Nov. 3, 1842, which pastorate lasted six years. He was pastor of the church in Newmarket seven years, and at New Boston ten years. He returned to Northwood, and was engaged in pastoral labors there for eleven years, and all that time was principal of Coe Academy. He was author of a history of New Boston, a history of Nottingham, Deerfield, and Northwood, a memoir of the Rev. Samuel Hidden, of Tamworth, together with miscellaneous sermons and addresses. At the time of his death he was writing a history of Tamworth. He was postmaster of Northwood Center several years.

Collins, Jennie, an American philanthropist, born in Amoskeag, N. H., in 1828; died in Brookline, Mass., July 20, 1887. Her parents died when she was a little girl, and she went to live with her grandmother, a Quakeress. When she was fourteen years old the death of her grandmother forced her to seek means to support herself, and for several years she was employed in the mills at Lawrence and Lowell, subsequently going to Boston, working as a nurse in the family of Judge Lowell, and finally becoming a vest-maker. In the early part of the civil war she began speaking in favor of the abolition of slavery, and organized a soldiers' relief association among her shop-mates, the pioneer organization of that character in Boston. She then gave two years of her time to the patriotic duty of raising funds to support the soldiers' homes, and to provide artificial limbs for those inmates who had left their own on the field of battle. Her necessities then forced her to resume her needle, but even in this condition she took upon herself the duty of educating the children of deceased soldiers. In 1868 she made her first appearance as a public speaker, taking for her subject the grievances of workingwomen. In the mean time she had been devoting her time to self-culture, and attached herself to the evening-classes of the Church of the Unity, where she was appointed to lead the class in English history. In 1869 the first eight-hour convention of workingmen was held in Boston, and this was the occasion of her first appearance as a speaker at a gathering of public importance. During the political campaign of that year she was called upon for active work in nearly all the manufacturing towns in the State. In January, 1870, she delivered an impressive address at a meeting of the Woman's Suffrage Association at Washington, D. C., and during the same year frequently occupied pulpits, lecturing to large audiences. In the summer of 1870 she began a series of meetings on Boston Common, with the intention of advocating the provision of cheap and rational amusement for workingwomen. This effort led to the establishment of the famous "Boffin's Bower" on July 25, 1870, through the means cheerfully granted her by the large employers of female labor and the wealthy merchants. She provided food, clothing, and lodging when necessary, and found employment for hundreds of needy women every year. At the time of the great fire the utility of the "Bower" was so thoroughly demonstrated, that thereafter she had no difficulty in obtaining all the money necessary to carry on her humane work.

Conner, James Madison, an American manufacturer, born in New York city in 1825; died there, July 14, 1887. At an early age he entered his father's type-foundry, and, displaying a marked aptitude for the business, was rapidly advanced till he occupied a place of much responsibility in the mechanical department. At the death of his father, the founder of the establishment, his elder brother, William, assumed charge, while James remained at the bench, where from time to time he devised a number of the most important inventions now known to the trade. He succeeded to the charge of the business on the death of his brother William, but clung to his bench and inventive study to the last. His excellence as a designer of new faces for type was well known throughout this country and in Europe. Among his most noted inventions is what is known in the trade as dropped type. For many years he was a popular member of the old Volunteer Fire Department, being connected with "Honey Bee" engine, No. 5.

Conway, Thomas William, an American clergyman, born in County Clare, Ireland, March 25, 1840; died in Brooklyn, N. Y., April 6, 1887. He was brought to the United States when a child, and paid for his education by his own labor, being graduated at Madison University, and ordained a minister of the Baptist Church when only twenty-one years of age. His first pastorate was in Tottenville, Staten Island, where he remained till the war broke out, when he accompanied the Ninth Regiment of New York Volunteers to the front as chaplain. He remained with this regiment two years, and was then commissioned as chaplain of the Seventy-Ninth Regiment United States Colored Infantry, and in this capacity served under Gen. Butler in New Orleans. For his gallant action in leading a brigade to victory, he was promoted to the rank of brigadier-general, and appointed Assistant Commissioner of Freedmen for Louisiana, subsequently becoming State Superintendent of Education. He remained in Louisiana nearly eleven years, during which time he established 1,500 schools for the education of the freedmen. While on Roanoke Island he administered the rites of Christian burial to the first contraband of the war, and in the interests of civilization and morality, instituted and insisted upon the performance of the marriage ceremony among the colored people. Gen. Conway returned North in 1878, and, after a brief pastorate in Vineland, N. J., became assistant to Rev. Justin D. Fulton, D. D., in the Centennial Baptist Church, Brooklyn, N. Y. He served there for two years, and then devoted himself almost wholly to labor in the cause of temperance, organizing the New York Anti-Saloon League, and working and speaking vigorously for the establishment of high license. At the time of his death he was secretary of the State Temperance Republican League, and had just organized a temperance insurance company.

Cooke, Phineas Baldwin, an American pioneer, born in Litchfield, Conn., Nov. 24, 1803; died in New York city, Feb. 7, 1887. On attaining his majority he removed to Rochester, N. Y., and was a resident of that city till 1856. He was actively employed in the temperance and anti-slavery movements in Western New York for many years. In 1825 he was one of the party that went through the Erie Canal with De Witt Clinton on its completion, carrying the waters of Lake Erie to mingle with those of the Atlantic Ocean. In 1857 he removed to New York city, and entered the employ of the post-office department, retaining his place till within a year of his death. He survived the celebration of his golden wedding six years. To his last days he felt great pride in having been one of the early settlers of Rochester, and his interest in the prosperity of that city never abated.

Cornell, John Black, an American manufacturer, born in Far Rockaway, Long Island, N. Y., Feb. 7, 1821; died in Lakewood, N. J., Oct. 26, 1887. He was brought up on his father's farm, but at the age of fifteen left home under an apprenticeship to learn the foundry trade. In 1847 he opened a factory in New York, in connection with his brother, for the general manufacture of articles in iron, and their success was such that within a few years the iron-works of J. B. and W. W. Cornell were among the largest in the country. As their business increased, the brothers constantly sought methods of doing good with their large means. Both had united in boyhood with the Methodist Episcopal Church, and in prosperous days found a large but not exclusive field for benevolent effort in the many societies of that denomination. They devoted a fixed percentage of their annual income to religious and charitable purposes, and the annual contribution of John to the interests of the Methodist Episcopal Church, exclusive of schools and missions, frequently amounted to $50,000. The brothers founded the New York City Mission and Sunday-School Society, and each in turn held the presidency of it, while the Cornell Memorial Church, though named in honor of W. W. Cornell, was practically erected by his brother John. At the time of his death John was erecting a fire-proof library building for Drew Theological Seminary in Madison, N. J., at an expense of

$30,000. It is believed that he gave in all for charitable and religious purposes $1,000,000. Mr. Cornell was a member of the American Bible Society, the City Church Extension Society, General Missionary Society, Methodist Episcopal Church Home, Board of Managers of St. Christopher's Home for Children, president of the board of trustees of Drew Theological Seminary, member of the Union League Club, and the only Christian member of the Hebrew Society for the Improvement of Deaf Mutes.

Cornly, James Madison, an American journalist, born in Perry County, Ohio, March 6, 1832; died in Toledo, Ohio, July 26, 1887. When ten years old he removed to Columbus, where he was apprenticed to the printing business, working in the offices of "The Cross and Journal" and "The Ohio State Journal." While learning his trade, he attended school at intervals, obtaining the necessary means by working at night, and availing himself of the opportunities of the State Library for profitable reading. He was graduated at the high-school in 1848, and shortly afterward began studying law in the office of Attorney-General Wolcott, from which he was admitted to the bar in 1859. Soon after the firing on Fort Sumter he enlisted as a private in an independent company, which for several months was charged with the duty of guarding the Marietta and Cincinnati Railroad from Virginia raiders. He entered the U. S. service in June, 1861, and in August following was commissioned lieutenant-colonel of the Forty-Third Ohio Regiment. In October of the same year, having asked a reduction in rank in consideration of being transferred to a regiment actually in the field, he was mustered as major of the Twenty-Third Regiment of Ohio Infantry, succeeding Rutherford B. Hayes, who had been promoted to lieutenant-colonel. He was successively promoted to be lieutenant-colonel and colonel of this famous regiment, commanding it in all of the fights in which it took part, and winning the rank of brevet brigadier-general. At the close of the war, Gen. Cornly resumed the practice of law in Columbus, but soon abandoned it for journalism, and purchased a controlling interest in "The Ohio State Journal." He was postmaster at Columbus from 1872 till 1876, and United States Minister to the Sandwich Islands from 1877 till 1883. On his return to Ohio he removed to Toledo, where he purchased the "Commercial," which he edited till within a short time of his death. He was considered one of the strongest and best-informed Republican editors in the country, and was equally effective with speech and pen.

Craven, Thomas Tingey, an American naval officer, born in Portsmouth, N. H., Dec. 30, 1808; died in Charleston, S. C., Aug. 23, 1887. He entered the navy as midshipman in 1822, was promoted to past midshipman, 1828, commissioned lieutenant in 1830, commander in 1852, captain in 1861, commodore in 1862, and

rear-admiral in 1866, and placed on the retired list in 1869. He was in command of the steam-sloop "Brooklyn" during the attack and passage of forts Jackson and St. Philip, and at the capture of New Orleans and Vicksburg. In the attack upon the forts his vessel became entangled in the obstructions in the river, and received a severe fire from Fort St. Philip, besides being attacked by two vessels, one a ram; but he got his ship clear without material injury. At Vicksburg he was engaged with the enemy's batteries nearly three hours. He commanded the steam-frigate "Niagara" on special service in European waters in 1864-'65, was commandant of the Mare Island Navy-yard, San Francisco, Cal., in 1867-'68, and commanded the North Pacific squadron, 1869.

Crocker, Uriel, an American publisher, born in Marblehead, Mass., Sept. 13, 1796; died near Cohasset, Mass., July 19, 1887. He went to Boston in 1811, and was apprenticed to the printing business in the office of Samuel T. Armstrong. On Nov. 1, 1818, shortly after he and his fellow-apprentice, Osmyn Brewster, became of age, Mr. Armstrong took them into partnership with him, and in 1825 the young men bought out their employer's interest, continuing the business in the same place from that time till 1865, when they removed to an adjoining building, remaining there till 1875, when they retired from business. The firm passed safely through the financial crises of 1837 and 1857, and their reputation was continental. They made a specialty of religious and educational books, and their six-volume edition of "Scott's Family Bible," published shortly after Mr. Armstrong took his apprentices into partnership, was at the time the largest work that had ever been stereotyped in this country. Mr. Crocker was for over fifty years an active promoter of the Bunker Hill Monument project, and was concerned in other large enterprises besides publishing. He was an original organizer of the Old Colony Railroad, and for forty years one of its directors; a director of the Concord Railroad; a director, vice-president, and president of the Atlantic and Pacific and St. Louis and San Francisco railroads, and director and president of the United States Hotel Company, and of the Revere House Association. In November, 1886, a reception was held at Mr. Crocker's residence in Boston, at which the families and friends of the venerable partners celebrated with them the seventy-fifth anniversary of their first meeting in Mr. Armstrong's office.

Curry, Daniel, an American clergyman, born near Peekskill, N. Y., Nov. 26, 1809; died in New York city, Aug. 17, 1887. He was graduated at Wesleyan University, Middletown, Conn., in 1827 and the same year appointed Principal of the Troy Conference Academy, New York. He entered the ministry of the Methodist Episcopal Church in Macon, Ga., in 1841, and occupied pulpits in that city, Athens, Savannah, and Columbus, till the separation of his denomination on the slavery question, when he returned North, and joined the New York Conference. In 1848 he was elected a representative in the General Conference of the Church, and from 1860 held a seat in that body without interruption. He was three years president of the Indiana Wesleyan University. He was appointed editor of the "Christian Advocate" in 1864, and held the office till 1876. He was subsequently editor of "The Methodist," "The National Repository" (1877–'80), and, at the time of his death, of "The Methodist Magazine." Besides his editorial work and contributions to other religious periodicals, he was the author of a "Life of Wesley" (1847), a "Life of Bishop Clark," "Platform Papers," "Fragments," "The Metropolitan City of America," and other works, editor of Southey's "Life of Wesley," and reviser of Clarke's "Commentaries on the New Testament."

Dana, Alexander Hamilton, an American lawyer, born in Owego, N. Y., July 4, 1807; died in Montclair, N. J., April 27, 1887. His father was Eleazer Dana, a jurist of high repute throughout New York State. At the age of fifteen Alexander entered Union College, Schenectady, and at seventeen was graduated second in his class. He studied law under his father's direction, and was admitted to the bar in 1828. Shortly after beginning practice he became head of the firm of Dana, Woodruff, and Leonard, maintaining his connection till 1854, when he took offices with the late Clarkson N. Potter, subsequently practicing alone, or in connection with his son, Francis E. Dana. His last noted appearance, professionally, was in the controversy of the Stewart estate with the Lelands, in which he was successful. During the last few years of his life he did scarcely any legal work. Besides being an effective pleader and possessing the advantages of a good voice and fluent speech, Mr. Dana was a pleasing writer on legal and other thoughtful subjects. He was a contributor to "The National Quarterly Review" from 1879, his most noticeable articles being "The Republic of Athens, from Alcibiades to Demosthenes," and "Problems, Physical and Metaphysical." He also wrote for the "Sanitarium," and prepared the legal articles in the first six volumes of the "New American Cyclopædia." His published books are: "Ethical and Physiological Enigmas" (1862); "Inquiries in Physiology, Ethics, and Ethnology" (1873); and "Enigmas of Life and Death" (1882).

Danenhower, John Wilson, an American naval officer, born in Chicago, Ill., Sept. 30, 1849; died in Annapolis, Md., April 20, 1887. He entered the United States Naval Academy in 1866, was graduated in 1870, commissioned as ensign in 1871, master in 1873, and lieutenant in 1879; was attached to the "Portsmouth," on surveying duty in the North Pacific, 1873–'74; to the "Vandalia," during her cruise in the Mediterranean when Gen. Grant with his

family was on board, and visited the Holy Land, 1876–'77, and to the "Jeannette," as a volunteer officer for the Arctic expedition fitted out by James Gordon Bennett, in 1879. This vessel was crushed in the ice on June 11, 1880, in latitude 77°, longitude 157°. The crew embarked in three boats, but were soon separated by wind and fog. Two boats made a landing at distant points of the Lena river, in September, one containing Lieut.-Com. De Long, Surgeon Ambler, and twelve men; the other, Chief-Engineer Melville, Lieut. Danenhower, and ten men. The loss of the third boat, under command of Lieut. Chipp, and the death of all of De Long's party from exposure and starvation, left Messrs. Melville and Danenhower the sole surviving officers of the expedition. On his return to the United States in 1882, Mr. Danenhower was placed on waiting orders during the official inquiry into the loss of the "Jeannette," and at its conclusion was granted a year's leave of absence. During this time he delivered lectures in different parts of the country. In September, 1884, he was assigned to duty at the Naval Academy as assistant commandant of cadets, holding the office till his death.

Davie, Winston Jones, an American agriculturist, born in Christian County, Ky., April 3, 1824; died in Hopkinsville, Ky., May 24, 1887. He was graduated at Yale in 1845, and returning to his native State became a cotton and tobacco planter, with several large plantations and numerous slaves. In 1849 he was elected a member of the State Legislature, as a Democrat, and in 1853 failed of election as a member of Congress by only a few votes. From that time till the outbreak of the civil war, he was also engaged as a banker and dealer in real estate in Memphis, Tenn. He identified himself with the interests of the South during the war, and lost all his property by its results. In 1865 he removed to Hopkinsville, in his native county; in 1876 was appointed State Commissioner of Agriculture; and, from the expiration of his term of office till his death, was engaged in the manufacture of chemical fertilizers in Louisville. Mr. Davie was regarded throughout the South as an expert in the various details of the cultivation of cotton and tobacco.

Dearborn, Frederick M., an American physician, born in Malden, Mass., in 1842; died in New York city, April 24, 1887. He received a common-school education in his native city, was graduated at Harvard Medical School, and appointed an assistant surgeon in the United States Navy on Sept. 15, 1864. He was attached to the receiving-ship at Boston, 1864–'65; steamer "Estrella," 1865–'67; promoted to past assistant-surgeon, 1867; assigned to the Navy-Yard at Washington, D. C., 1868; the "Wasp," on the South Atlantic Station, 1869–'72; the "Franklin" flag-ship of the European squadron, 1873–'75; and promoted to full surgeon, May 21, 1875. In 1876 he was on duty on the receiving-ship "Sabine"; from 1877 till 1879 at the Naval Hospital at New York, whence he was transferred to the training-ship "Constitution," and from 1880 till 1888 in charge of the hospital at the Navy-Yard, Brooklyn. About ten years ago Surgeon Dearborne contracted the Chagres fever, while on duty in Panama, and never recovered, although he traveled extensively in the hope of restoration. He was accounted in the service one of its ablest surgeons.

De Pauw, Washington C., an American manufacturer, born in Salem, Ind., Jan. 4, 1822; died in New Albany, Ind., May 5, 1887. His grandfather came from France to the United States with Lafayette, and his father was a lawyer in Indiana. He received a liberal education, found employment in the office of the county-clerk when nineteen years old, and became county-clerk himself by election just after passing his majority. A brief service in office-work proving too confining for his health, he resigned the place, and interested himself in the saw-mill and grist-mill business, to which he added farming and banking. These interests prospered greatly and led him to increase the number of his mills, by doing which at a fortunate time he was enabled to amass considerable wealth by providing largely for the Government's need of supplies for troops during the civil war. After the war he began to concentrate his chief enterprises in New Albany, Ind., till he had a capital of $2,000,000 invested in manufactories there, the principal establishment being the American Plate-Glass Works, one of the largest of its kind in the world. His investments in New Albany and in real estate, banking, railroad, and other interests elsewhere, brought to him a fortune, estimated at his death to amount to $7,000,-000. Besides being the wealthiest citizen of Indiana, he was the most philanthropic. He took hold of the Indiana Asbury University at a time when not only the usefulness but the existence of the institution was imperiled, met all its immediate wants, provided for its future on a magnificent scale, and enabled it to be at once reorganized and expanded into a university in fact. At the solicitation of the board of trustees, he consented that the university should bear his name, and on May 5, 1884, the change of name was legally effected. The university is at Greencastle, Ind., and received from Mr. De Pauw during his lifetime the sum of $1,500,000. He established the De Pauw College at New Albany, Ind., for the education of young women, giving it a handsome sustentation fund, and was proportionately liberal to the various religious, educational, and charitable enterprises of his State. His will disposed of his entire fortune among members of his family and religious and educational organizations, and as a special offer of thanksgiving for the prosperity that had attended his business career, he minutely provided for the erection of a building in New Albany with accommodations for an industrial school, infirmary, hospital, lying-in-hospital, home for the friendless,

free reading-room, drug-store, and fancy store, all for the free use of the worthy poor.

Detmold, Christian E., an American civil engineer, born in Hanover, Germany, in 1809; died in New York city, July 2, 1887. He was educated in a military school in his native country, and on removing to the United States in 1835 adopted the profession of a civil-engineer. In this career he became very successful, and had charge of the construction of important works, notably the Charleston and Hamburg Railroad in South Carolina, several canals in Pennsylvania and Maryland, and the famous Crystal Palace in New York city, in 1853. He subsequently became the owner of a large coal-mine in Pennsylvania, to which he gave close attention, and from which he gained an independent fortune. He spent much of the latter part of his life in Paris, France, returning at regular periods to look after his business interests. He was a Republican in politics, a member of the Union League and Century clubs, and one of the committee appointed to investigate the Tweed frauds.

Detwiller, Henry, an American physician, born in Basle, Switzerland, Dec. 18, 1795; died in Easton, Pa., April 21, 1887. He came to the United States in 1817, and settled in the Lehigh valley, where he remained a few years, and then returned to Europe. While abroad he became intimate with Hahnemann, the father of homœopathy, by whom he was induced to study medicine according to the new school. He followed this course, returned to the United States, and became one of the first members of the American Institute of Homœopathy in New York, having been the first physician to administer homœopathic medicines in America, beginning their use in 1828. Quite early in his medical career an unusual epidemic broke out in the Lehigh valley, which for a time baffled the skill of the oldest practitioners. With others he attempted an investigation, and, while it was in progress, his treatment of the sick was so uniformly successful as to excite widespread comment. He had satisfied himself that the lining in earthen vessels in common use in housekeeping contained poison, and was the cause of the mysterious malady, and to this conclusion he owed his remarkable success and subsequent large fortune. He was an enthusiastic student of botany and ornithology.

Dix, Dorothea Lynde, an American philanthropist, born in Worcester, Mass., in 1805; died in Trenton, N. J., July 19, 1887. She was the daughter of a physician, was left an orphan in early life, and, having received a good education, supported herself by teaching, in Boston, meanwhile indulging a naturally practical mind in the preparation of juvenile and devotional books. She inherited a considerable sum of money in 1830, and at once consecrated herself and her fortune to the amelioration of suffering humanity. With a rare courage she espoused the cause of the most uninviting classes, beginning her self-imposed labor in the State

Prison at Charlestown, Mass. Her early aim was to effect a moral improvement of the convicts, for which purpose she established a school within the prison. After four years of such teaching she became restless for a larger field. In 1834 she sailed for Europe, and spent the succeeding three years in investigating the methods of treatment for the pauper, insane, and criminal classes. On her return in 1837, she applied herself to ascertaining the condition of the insane in the prisons and the poorhouses of the United States, beginning her work in the institutions of her native State. She traveled from State to State, lodging among the objects of her solicitude, examining the sanitary condition of poor-houses, prisons, and asylums, noting the methods of treatment, and suggesting such improvements as her European travels had impressed her as being advantageous, and collecting a mass of statistical information remarkable alike in detail and extent. Legislatures were appealed to by her for a more humane treatment of the insane. Her arguments, accompanied by a wealth of irresistible and indisputable facts, aroused the attention and sympathy of the public, and invariably led to the erection of asylums for the insane in accordance with her views. To her efforts more than to those of any other person, are due the costly, commodious, and scientifically conducted institutions for this class of unfortunates that now exist in every part of the country. For many years she toiled without success to secure from the General Government an allotment of 10,000,000 acres of land among the several States for the relief of the indigent insane, but accomplished what was more immediately practical within the States themselves. Upon the breaking out of the civil war she volunteered her services to the Government, and while awaiting acceptance went to Baltimore in April, 1861, and nursed the Massachusetts soldiers wounded in the mob attack. On June 10 she was appointed Superintendent of Female Nurses by the Secretary of War, and held the office till several months after the close of the war, when she resumed her mission for the insane. She defrayed her entire expenses from her private means, never received a cent of pay, and died among her wards in the New Jersey State Asylum for the Insane at Trenton.

Doniphan, Alexander W., an American lawyer, born near Maysville, Mason County, Ky., July 9, 1808; died in Richmond, Mo., Aug. 8, 1887. He was graduated at Augusta College, Kentucky, in 1826, and two years later was admitted to practice in the Supreme Court of Ohio. In 1830 he removed to Missouri, settling in Lexington and beginning his long and brilliant legal career. In 1836 he was elected a member of the State Legislature, and in 1838 appointed brigadier-general of Missouri militia, his brigade being the one selected by the Governor to drive the Mormons from the State. In 1846, when a requisition was made on the Governor for volunteers to join Gen. Kearny in his expedition to Mexico, Doniphan was appointed colonel of the First Regiment of Missouri Mounted Volunteers, and with his regiment marched 900 miles across a treeless desert and over lofty mountains, dispersed the Mexican forces defending Santa Fé, entered that ancient capital, and declared all New Mexico annexed to the United States. He then received orders to reduce the Navajo Indians on the western slope of the Rocky mountains to submission, and after accomplishing that he turned his horses' heads toward the city of Mexico. On Christmas-day, 1846, he was attacked by a superior Mexican force, which he routed with great loss, and on the last day of the month defeated 4,000 Mexicans near Chihuahua, of which city he took possession on March 1, 1847. Then, by a march of 700 miles, he joined Gen. Wool at Saltillo on May 21. After the war he resumed the practice of law, returning to western Missouri in 1869, and living quietly in Richmond till his death.

Duffield, Samuel Willoughby, an American clergyman, born in Brooklyn, N. Y., Sept. 24, 1843; died in Bloomfield, N. J., May 12, 1887. He was a son of the Rev. George Duffield, D. D., for many years pastor of the old Presbyterian Church in Bloomfield. He was graduated at Yale in 1863, and after teaching a short time in Adrian, Mich., began the study of theology under his father's direction. In 1866 he was licensed to preach, and assigned to the charge of a mission enterprise in Chicago, and on Nov. 12, 1867, was ordained and installed as pastor of the Kenderton Presbyterian Church in Philadelphia. In 1871 he became pastor of the First Presbyterian Church, Ann Arbor, Mich.; in 1874, of the Eighth Presbyterian Church, Chicago, Ill.; in 1876, of the Central Presbyterian Church, Auburn, N. Y.; in 1878, of the Second Presbyterian Church, Altoona, Pa.; and in 1881, of the Westminster Presbyterian Church, Bloomfield, N. J., where he remained until his death. In 1886 he ruptured a blood-vessel of the heart, and was compelled to cease active pastoral labor, but occupied his period of illness with literary work, preparing poems and essays on religious topics for publication in "The Independent." His publications include "Warp and Woof," a book of verse (New York, 1870), and an elaborate work on "English Hymns, their Authors and History" (1886).

Dulles, John Welsh, an American clergyman, born in Philadelphia, Pa., Nov. 4, 1823; died there April 13, 1887. He was graduated at Yale in 1844, and for two years pursued the study of medicine in the University of Pennsylvania; then entered Union Theological Seminary, New York city, in 1846, and completed the course there in 1848. He was ordained October 2 by the Fourth Presbytery of Philadelphia, and eight days later sailed for Madras, India, as a missionary of the American Board. A loss of voice led to his return home in 1853, when, being otherwise in good health, he entered the service of the American Sunday-School Union, of which his father, Joseph H. Dulles, was one of the founders, and for three years was its secretary for missions. In 1857 he was given charge of the affairs of the Presbyterian Publication Committee as its secretary and editor of its publications, and in 1870, on the reunion of the Old School and New School branches of that church, he became editorial secretary of the united board, editing its books and periodicals till the close of his life, and serving for a time as corresponding secretary. In this congenial relation he was the author of many publications, of which "Life in India" and "The Ride through Palestine" are best known.

Duncan, Thomas, an American soldier, born in Kaskaskia, Ill., April 14, 1819; died in Washington, D. C., Jan. 7, 1887. He served as a private in the Illinois Mounted Volunteers during the Black Hawk War in 1832, and for some time thereafter was connected with military expeditions. In 1846 he was appointed first lieutenant in the United States Mounted Rifles (now the Third Cavalry), and served during the war with Mexico, being engaged in the siege and surrender of Vera Cruz. Subsequently, he was on recruiting duty, and then served in various garrisons until 1856, having meanwhile been promoted captain in March, 1848. He was with his regiment in New Mexico until 1862, had command successively of Forts Burgwin, Massachusetts, Garland, and Union, participated in the Navajo expedition of 1858, defeated the Comanche Indians in the action at Hatch's Ranch in May, 1861, and was advanced to major of his regiment in June, 1861. During the civil war he had command of Fort Craig, N. M., was in charge of the cavalry forces at the battle of Valverde, N. M., and commanded his regiment in the action at Albuquerque, N. M., where a portion of his skull was removed by a cannon-ball. In 1863–'66 he was assistant provost-marshal of Iowa, and in July, 1866, he became lieutenant-colonel of the Fifth United States Cavalry, after which, until September, 1868, he had command of the District of Nashville. He was then ordered to the Department of the Platte, where he was stationed successively at Forts McPherson and D. A. Russell, and then, until November, 1871, he had charge of the construction of Sidney barracks. His wound compelled him to obtain sick-leave, and he resided in Baltimore until his retirement in January, 1873. He received for his services during the civil war the successive brevets, including, on March 13, 1865, that of brigadier-general.

Dunn, William McKee, an American lawyer, born in the Territory of Indiana, Dec. 12, 1813; died in Maplewood, Fairfax County, Va., July 24, 1887. He was graduated at Indiana State College in 1832, and, after teaching for two years, at Yale in 1835. He studied law, and began practicing in his native State. In 1848 he was elected a member of the State House of Representatives, in 1850 of the State Constitutional Convention, and in 1858 a Representative in Congress, serving on the committees on Manufactures, Roads and Canals, and the Special Committee of "Thirty-three." Two years later he was re-elected, and served as chairman of the Committee on Patents. While still a member of Congress he served as an aide on Gen. McClellan's staff in the western Virginia campaign. In March, 1863, he was commissioned as a major and judge-advocate of United States volunteers; in June, 1866, was promoted to be a colonel and assistant judge-advocate-general in the regular army; and in December, 1875, was appointed judge-advocate-general, with the rank of brigadier-general. He held this office till Jan. 21, 1881, when he was placed on the retired list by reason of his age. He was brevetted a brigadier-general in March, 1865, for faithful, meritorious, and distinguished services in his department, and was a delegate to the Loyalists' Convention in Philadelphia in 1866.

Eaton, Hosea Ballou, an American physician, born in Plymouth, Me., March 24, 1822; died in Rockport, Me., April 19, 1887. He was educated at St. Alban's Academy, and graduated in medicine at the medical college, Brunswick, Me., in 1845, beginning his practice at Rockport. About 1855 he adopted the principles of homœopathy, and was thereupon expelled from his medical society. In 1870 he was elected President of the Homœopathic Medical Society of Maine, and at the time of his death was a senior of the American Institute of Homœopathy. Dr. Eaton was several times elected a member of the State Legislature, and there exposed the mismanagement of the institutions for the insane, opposed the law of imprisonment for debt, and favored legislation tending to suppress intemperance. He served as an army surgeon during the greater part of the civil war.

Elder, Robert, an American musician, born in Edinburgh, Scotland, in 1825; died in New York city, June 21, 1887. He came to the United States with his father, a ship-builder, while a mere boy, the family settling in New York city. At the age of ten years, while playing with a group of children, he fell and injured his eyes so severely that he became totally blind. After recovering from this accident he entered the New York Institution for the Blind, where he applied himself to his studies with unusual diligence. While a bright scholar in the general branches there taught, he developed a passion for music so noticeable that the faculty encouraged his efforts to become a thorough instrumentalist. He was graduated when twenty years old, and came before the public as an organist. He gave concerts on the organ in New York city and elsewhere, and had been giving lessons on his favorite instrument a few months when he was appointed organist in the Sixteenth Street

Baptist Church, New York city, which place he held continuously till the day of his death, a period of forty-three years. He was considered the most skillful reader of raised type in the country, and was widely known as the blind organist. He left a wife and two children whom he had never seen.

Eliot, William Greenleaf, an American educator, born in New Bedford, Mass., Aug. 5, 1811; died in Pass Christian, La., Jan. 28, 1887. He was graduated at Columbian College, Washington, D. C., in 1831, and at Harvard Divinity School in 1834. In the latter year he removed to St. Louis, Mo., where he became pastor of the Unitarian Church of the Messiah, maintaining that relation till 1872. During this period he established a reputation for scholarship and led an active career as a promoter of educational and reformatory enterprises. In 1854, on the organization of the Board of Directors of Washington University of St. Louis, he was unanimously elected president, and in 1872 was induced to resign his pastorate and accept the office of chancellor of the institution. He was an energetic, self-denying, and zealous officer, faithfully discharging his duty till within a short time of his death, despite extreme feebleness.

Embree, Effingham, an American manufacturer, born in New York city in 1817; died in Westfield, N. J., April 28, 1887. His connection with the paper business began when he was fourteen years old, as clerk in the office of Caleb Bartlett. Soon after attaining his majority he established a book and stationery business in connection with his brother, under the firm-name of A. & E. Embree. Subsequently he was associated with E. B. Clayton & Sons in Burling Slip, and was a partner in the firm of Jackson, Embree & Co., in the rag and paper business. About 1867 he was appointed New York manager of the American Wood-Paper Company, whose pulp-works are in Manayunk and Royer's Ford, Pa., and was engaged in that business at the time of his death. Mr. Embree was the pioneer in the industry of making paper from wood-fiber. For several years he met great opposition, both in the paper-trade and in the line of mechanical manipulation of the pulp; but his energy, persistence, and inventive ability enabled him to overcome obstacles and build up a large business. He felt pride in the progress of the town of Westfield, and contributed in many ways to its advancement. He had been treasurer of the Town Committee, a member of the Board of Health, and a supporter of the public-school system, and was treasurer of the Congregational Church and of Fairview Cemetery.

Emory, William Helmsley, an American soldier, born in Poplar Grove, Md., in 1811; died in Washington, D. C., Dec. 1, 1887. He was graduated at the United States Military Academy in 1831, and assigned to service as a lieutenant in the Fourth Artillery, serving in garrisons at Fort McHenry, Fort Severn, and in Charles-

ton harbor during the nullification excitement. He resigned his commission in 1836, and spent two years in civil engineering, being reappointed to the army as first lieutenant in the corps of topographical engineers, July 7, 1837. From this date till 1846 he was employed in surveys on coast fortifications and in establishing the boundary between the United States and the British provinces. In 1846–'47 he was acting assistant adjutant-general on Gen. Kearny's staff during the expedition to California. He was brevetted captain for meritorious conduct at San Pasqual, Dec. 6, 1846, and major for services at San Gabriel and the Plains of Mesa, Jan. 9, 1847. After this campaign he surveyed the new boundary-line between the United States and Mexico, for which he was promoted to be lieutenant-colonel. In 1855 he was appointed major of the Second Cavalry and transferred to the First, serving on the frontier till the opening of the civil war, when he declined overtures to surrender his command and join the Confederate forces, captured a body of Texas troops raised for the Confederacy at Fort Arbuckle, and took them—the first prisoners of war—and his command to Fort Leavenworth, Kan. He was appointed lieutenant-colonel of the Sixth United States Cavalry in 1861, and promoted to be brigadier-general of volunteers in 1862, serving under Gens. Stoneman and McClellan in the Army of the Potomac, and having command of a brigade of cavalry at Harrison's Landing. For his services in the siege of Yorktown, the battle of Williamsburg, and the action at Hanover Court-House, he was brevetted colonel in the regular army. On the landing of a secret expedition at New Orleans, which he had organized in Baltimore in December, 1862, he was assigned to the command of the Nineteenth Army Corps, and in the following spring was with the column in the attack on Port Hudson, which movement covered the passage of the fort by Admiral Farragut's fleet. While in command of New Orleans, he repelled attacks by the Confederate Gen. Taylor at Donaldsonville and the La Fourche Crossing. He took part in the Red River campaign, was in command at Morganzia, and for his services in the Shenandoah campaign was brevetted a brigadier-general in the regular army. In October, 1864, he was brevetted a major-general; in September, 1865, placed in command of the Department of West Virginia; and in January, 1866, mustered out of the volunteer service. After the war he was in command of the Department of Washington, succeeded Gen. Sheridan in New Orleans, and was a member and president of the Retiring Board till July 1, 1876, when he was placed on the retired list with the rank of brigadier-general U. S. Army.

Ezzard, William, an American lawyer, born near Athens, Clarke County, Ga., June 12, 1798; died in Atlanta, Ga., March 24, 1887. He removed to the site of the present city of Atlanta in 1824, was admitted to the bar, and was elected intendant on the incorporation of the village, and Mayor on the incorporation of the city, holding the latter office through five terms. He served one term as a member of Congress. While in Washington he frequently appeared before the Supreme Court of the United States in important suits, being associated in several with Daniel Webster and Henry Clay, by both of whom he was spoken of as one of the most promising lawyers in the country. At the close of his congressional service he returned to Atlanta, and was elected Judge of the Superior Court, occupying his seat on the bench for ten years, and then resuming practice, to which he applied himself, with the exception of a term in the State Senate, till 1877.

Fairfield, Francis Gerry, an American clergyman, physician, and author, born in Stamford, Conn., Aug. 18, 1844; died in New York city, April 4, 1887. He was graduated at Gettysburg at an early age, and, after spending some time in scientific researches, entered Hartwick Theological Seminary, where he astonished his teachers by his remarkable aptitude for religious study and investigation. On receiving his degree of D. D. from the Lutheran Church, he was assigned to a mission in Waterloo, N. Y. Removing to New York city to avail himself of larger facilities for scientific study, he relinquished preaching, and applied himself to the study of medicine and surgery in the office of Dr. Worcester. The natural rapidity with which he acquired information, especially of a complex character, enabled him to complete his course in half the usual time. He was graduated at the New York College of Physicians and Surgeons with a distinguished record, but never practiced this profession to any extent. In 1867 he married Josephine Griswold, who had already won a reputation by her literary work. After this Mr. and Mrs. Fairfield devoted themselves to literature, contributing to newspapers, magazines, and reviews. Mr. Fairfield's articles inclined to the discussion of scientific and other questions of current interest, displaying the evidences of a scholarship far beyond his years. For ten or twelve years they worked with much industry, and their joint income enabled them to live in circumstances of affluence. They were familiar figures at the various publishing-houses, always arm-in-arm. Then a cloud began to creep over their lives, talent and intellect slowly gave way in husband and wife before the opium-habit, and both were reduced to physical and mental wrecks. For several months nothing had been seen of them on their accustomed routes. A messenger notifying Coroner Levy on the night of March 31, 1887, that the body of a dead woman had just been found in a designated house, led to the discovery of all that was mortal of the accomplished and once beautiful Mrs. Fairfield. Four days later her husband was found dead in another part of the city. Mr. Fairfield received the degrees of

A. M. and Ph. D. from Gettysburg, that of D. D. from the Lutheran Theological Seminary, and M. D. from the New York College of Physicians and Surgeons. He published in book-form "The Clubs of New York" (1873) and "Ten Years with Spiritual Mediums" (1875).

Fellows, John F., an American banker, born in Salem, Mass., in 1815; died in Chelsea, Mass., July 6, 1887. In early life he removed to Boston, became financial manager of the daily "Atlas," and subsequently publisher and proprietor of the "Courier." At the outbreak of the civil war he sold out his newspaper interests, and went to the front as lieutenant-colonel of the Seventeenth Regiment of Massachusetts Volunteers. He performed meritorious services in North Carolina, being in command of his regiment most of the time. He was taken prisoner in action, sent to Libby Prison in Richmond, and kept in close confinement there till he was selected as one of the company of 100 Union soldiers to be placed in Charleston, S. C., within range of the guns of Fort Wagner during the bombardment of that city. At the end of the siege he procured an exchange, and returned home. He was shortly afterward appointed Superintendent of the Chelsea Savings-Bank, which office he retained till within two months of his death. Mr. Fellows was a member of the Salem Glee Club, famous many years ago, and for a long time captain of the Chelsea Light Infantry, which he brought up to a high standard of military perfection.

Foster, Abby Kelly, an American reformer, born in Pelham, Mass., Jan. 15, 1811; died in Worcester, Mass., Jan. 14, 1887. She was of Quaker parentage, and received her chief education in a Sunday-school in Providence, R. I. She taught for several years in Worcester and Millbury, but in 1837 became interested in the anti-slavery movement, and thenceforward gave her time and energy to the advancement of that cause. She was reputed to have been the first woman that addressed a mixed audience on the subject, and suffered many indignities because of her freedom of speech. On Dec. 21, 1845, she married Stephen S. Foster, an equally vigorous laborer in the cause, after which they continued their work together. In 1850 they began speaking in advocacy of woman suffrage, Mrs. Foster participating in the agitation till her health compelled her to cease from public speaking. She was also an earnest worker in the cause of prohibition, and a sturdy opponent of the practice of taxation without representation, carrying her views to such an extreme that she allowed her cows to be levied upon and sold, and her farm to be seized and offered for sale rather than pay her taxes without being permitted to vote or hold public office.

Fowler, Orson Squire, an American phrenologist, born in Cohocton, Steuben County, N. Y., Oct. 11, 1809; d. in Sharon Station, N. Y., Aug. 18, 1887. He was graduated at Amherst in 1834, in the class with Henry Ward Beecher.

He had entered college with the intention of preparing for the ministry, but while a student he became interested in the system of mental philosophy expounded by Spurzheim and Combe, and put its principles to practice. His success, in class-room lectures and in examining the heads of his fellow-students, led him to pursue phrenology as a profession. Taking his brother Lorenzo in partnership, he removed to New York city, established an office in old Clinton Hall, on Nassau Street, and began the publication of "The Phrenological Journal" in 1838. He wrote books rapidly, was active in works of reform and progress, an opponent of slavery, intemperance, and other evils, and became the recognized founder of practical phrenology in the United States. In 1843 the Fowler brothers admitted Samuel R. Wells into the firm, which then took the name of Fowler & Wells. Orson Fowler remained with the firm, lecturing, writing books, and editing "The Phrenological Journal," till 1865, when he withdrew to devote himself to lectures and examinations exclusively. From that time till within a month of his death he spent ten months of the year in lecture-tours through the United States. His most important books are: "Memory and Intellectual Improvement"; "Self-Culture and Perfection of Character"; "Physiology, Mental and Animal"; "Matrimony"; "Hereditary Descent"; "Phrenology Proved, Illustrated, and Applied"; and "Self-Instructor in Phrenology."

Francis, Charles Stephen, an American publisher, born in Boston, Mass., June 9, 1805; died in Tarrytown, N. Y., Dec. 1, 1887. He was a son of David Francis, of the Boston book-publishing house of Monroe & Francis, and learned the printing-trade and book-selling business under his father. When twenty-one years of age he removed to New York city, and engaged in book-selling on Broadway, near Dey Street. In 1838 his brother, David G. Francis, entered into partnership with him, and later they moved up Broadway nearly to Spring Street. This partnership was kept up till 1860, and Charles carried on the business till about 1877, when he retired and passed the remainder of his life in Tarrytown. His Broadway store was headquarters for men of letters and bibliophiles from all parts of the country. He was the publisher of Audubon's "Birds of America," and the works of William Ellery Channing, William Ware, Rev. Orville Dewey, Rev. Henry W. Bellows, Mrs. Kirkland, and others, and was the first publisher in this country of Mrs. Browning's works.

Geddes, James, an American agriculturist, born in Camillus, Onondaga County, N. Y., Nov. 10, 1831; died in Syracuse, N. Y., May 16, 1887. He was educated at Homer and Cazenova academies, N. Y., and, at the age of seventeen, began work as a civil engineer. Having inherited his father's love of agriculture, after the latter's death, he devoted himself more particularly to the development of the farming interests of the State, taking his father's place in the operations of the Agricultural Society. For many years he was a member of its executive committee, and general manager of its exhibitions. In 1882 he was elected a member of the Legislature, and re-elected the following year. During this service he secured important amendments to the game laws of the State, and guided all agricultural questions that appeared before the Assembly. When the New York Agricultural Experimental Station was established at Geneva, Gov. Cornell appointed Mr. Geddes to be its general manager. Personally, he developed one of the largest and finest farms in the State, contributed largely to the agricultural literature of the day, and, in leisure moments, acquainted himself fully with the latest advances in pisciculture.

Germer, Edward, an American physician, born in Altsbrisach, Baden, Germany, in 1830; died in Erie, Pa., Aug. 22, 1887. He was graduated at the Vienna University of Medicine, and, having taken part in the Revolution of 1849, came to the United States upon its suppression. Settling in Erie, Pa., he rapidly rose to prominence in local, State, and national medical circles. He served the city as health officer for fifteen years, was president of the State Board of Health under Gov. Pattison, and, at the time of his death, was the elected representative of Pennsylvania to the International Sanitary Convention, held in Vienna a month later. It was through Dr. Germer's efforts that the grave of Gen. Anthony Wayne was discovered, and marked by the State Legislature with a block-house patterned after the original fort.

Gillespie, Elvia, an American educator, born in Brownsville, Pa.; died in South Bend, Ind., March 4, 1887. She was a niece of Thomas Swing, Secretary of State under President Harrison, and a cousin of James Gillespie Blaine and of the wife of Gen. William T. Sherman. She was educated with the latter at the Georgetown Convent, and during her residence in the national capital was a leader in society, noted for her learning. When twenty-six years old she withdrew from worldly associations, joined the Order of the Sisters of the Holy Cross, and, removing to South Bend, Ind., where the Very Rev. Father Sorin had already founded the University of Notre Dame, established St. Mary's Academy. Under her administration this academy became one of the best-known educational institutions in the country. During the war she devoted most of her time to establishing hospitals and overseeing the care of sick and wounded soldiers. In 1870 she was appointed Mother Superior of the Order of the Sisters of the Holy Cross for the United States, and, as such, founded many female academies throughout the country. Her name in religion was Mother Angelia.

Goodall, Albert Gallatin, an American engraver, born in Montgomery, Ala., Oct. 31, 1826; died in New York city Feb. 19, 1887. He entered the navy of the republic of Texas when but fifteen years old, and served as a midshipman three years. On his discharge he went to Havana, Cuba, and took a course of instruction in copper-plate engraving. Thence he removed to Philadelphia to study engraving on steel, subsequently establishing himself in New York city as a bank-note engraver, in connection with a firm that afterward became the American Bank-Note Company, and advancing till he reached the office of president of the corporation. He personally made contracts for the production of bank-notes and bonds with many foreign governments, and received costly tokens of royal and imperial favor. He was a thoughtful, conservative man, with a fondness for domestic retirement.

Goodwin, Eliza Weathersby, an American actress, born in London, England, in 1849; died in New York city March 24, 1887. She was one of four sisters, all of whom have made reputations in the theatrical profession. She made her first appearance on the stage in Bradford, England, in 1865, and her first American appearance in Chestnut Street Theatre, Philadelphia, Pa., in the burlesque of "Lucretia Borgia," April 12, 1869. After the return of the Lydia Thompson troupe, with which she had been playing, to England, she joined Rice's Evangeline company, and appeared in the principal rôle, Gabriel, with much success. At this time Nat C. Goodwin was playing the part of the Dutch policeman, and an attachment sprang up between them, which resulted in their marriage on June 24, 1877. The same year she joined Willie Edouin's company in Boston, reappearing in the plays in which she had won general popularity. After leaving this company she and her husband formed one of their own, and appeared in the large cities in "Cruets and Hobbies." Mrs. Goodwin was highly esteemed socially.

Green, Charles, an American naval officer, born in New London, Conn., Oct. 17, 1812; died in Providence, R. I., April 7, 1887. He entered the navy May 1, 1826, and was ordered to the receiving-ship "Independence," at Boston, the same year. He was on duty on the "Erie," West India squadron, 1827-'28; sloop "Peacock," West Indies, 1829-'31; promoted to passed midshipman April 28, 1832; New York station, 1831-'34; frigate "Brandywine," Pacific squadron, 1834-'37; commissioned as lieutenant March 8, 1837; sloop "Levant," West Indies, 1838; receiving-ship at New York, 1839-'40; sloop "Falmouth," home squadron, 1841-'43; steamer "Union," Norfolk, 1847; steamer "Michigan," on the lakes, 1848-'50; steamer "Fulton," 1852; receiving-ship "Ohio," at Boston, 1853-'55; commissioned as commander Sept. 14, 1855; navy-yard at New York, 1857-'58; light-house inspector at Buffalo, 1858-'61. On July 16, 1862, he was commissioned as captain while in command of the "Jamestown," and subsequently took part in the blockade off Savannah, Fernandina, and Wilmington, N. C. At Fernandina he sent his small-boats with a picked crew, and destroyed the bark "Alvarado" under the guns of the fort, and while on blockade duty captured and either sent in port or destroyed six prizes. He was in command of the receiving-ship "Ohio," at Boston, 1863-'65; light-house inspector at New Orleans 1865-'67; commissioned as commodore March 12, 1867; and retired Nov. 15, 1862.

Green, William Mercer, an American clergyman, born in Wilmington, N. C., May 2, 1798; died in Sewanee, Tenn., Feb. 13, 1887. He was descended from the Bradley and Sharpless families of Quakers, was early prepared for the service of the Church, and was graduated at the University of North Carolina in 1818. He was admitted to deacon's orders in the Protestant Episcopal Church in 1821, and to those of the priesthood two years later. During the first four years of his ministry he was in charge of a church in Williamsborough, N. C., acting in the mean time also as chief missionary of the diocese. In 1826 he removed to Hillsborough, and founded St. Matthew's Church, where he labored till 1837, when he was appointed chaplain and Professor of Belles-lettres in the University of North Carolina. After a congenial and fruitful service of twelve years in this institution, he was unexpectedly elected first bishop of the diocese of Mississippi in 1849, and on Feb. 24, 1850, was consecrated in St. Andrew's Church, Jackson. The degree of D. D. was conferred upon him in 1845 by the University of Pennsylvania, and afterward that of LL. D. by the University of North Carolina.

Greene, Theodore P., an American naval officer, born in Montreal, Canada, in 1809; died in Jaffrey, N. H., Aug. 30, 1887. He was appointed a midshipman in the United States navy from Vermont Nov. 1, 1826, promoted to passed-midshipman in 1832, commissioned as lieutenant Dec. 20, 1837, commander Sept. 14, 1855, captain July 16, 1862, commodore July 24, 1867, rear-admiral May 24, 1872, and placed on the retired list Nov. 1, 1871. During the Mexican War he was a lieutenant on the frigate "Congress," of the Pacific squadron, and for six months had command of the land forces at Mazatlan. In 1864, while in command of the "San Jacinto," he was left in command of the Eastern Gulf squadron, on the return of Rear-Admiral Bailey to the United States, and in 1865, while commanding the "Richmond," of the Western Gulf squadron, protected the troops that were being landed for the attack upon Mobile. He commanded the Pensacola Navy-yard in 1868-'70.

Greenwood, John, an American lawyer, born in Providence, R. I., Nov. 6, 1798; died in Brooklyn, N. Y., Dec. 11, 1887. In 1810 his father removed to New York city, and two years afterward placed John in the office of Aaron Burr, where he studied law for five years. In 1819 he was admitted to the bar, practicing in New York city till 1823, when he settled in Brooklyn. In 1837 he was appointed a Judge in the Court of Common Pleas, and afterward an examiner in Chancery and a Supreme Court commissioner. When the City Court of Brooklyn was organized, in 1849, he was elected the first judge, holding the office for five years, when he declined a renomination and resumed his practice. He drew up the original charter of the city, and was largely instrumental in securing the appointment of a commission to license ferries between New York and Brooklyn. Judge Greenwood was one of the founders and the first vice-president of the Long Island Historical Society, a founder of the Brooklyn Academy of Music, and an incorporator of the Philharmonic Society

Griffin, Samuel P., an American navigator, born in Savannah, Ga., in 1826; died in Aspinwall, Isthmus of Panama, July 4, 1887. He was graduated at the United States Naval Academy first in a class of sixty, and served throughout the Mexican War on the United States frigate "Savannah," then attached to the Pacific squadron, which took possession of California and held it till the close of the war. His skill as a navigator being recognized at an early age, an extra hazardous duty was assigned to him in 1849, when he was appointed to command the United States brig "Rescue," which, with the "Advance," formed the first United States Arctic expedition, fitted out at the expense of the late Moses H. Grinnell, to search for Sir John Franklin. This expedition secured the first traces of the lost English explorer, and both Capt. Griffin and Lieut. De Haven were personally decorated by Queen Victoria for their services. During the civil war he was detailed, at New Orleans, to collect a fleet for Gen. Banks's Red River expedition, and rendered other efficient service to the national military and naval commanders in that section. He subsequently entered the employ of the Pacific Mail Steamship Company, and commanded, as commodore, successive steamers of their fleet till 1882, taking the palatial steamer "City of Tokio" around Cape Horn to San Francisco. During the last four years of his life he was employed at Aspinwall, superintending a large contract on the Panama Canal.

Guerin, Thomas J., an American manufacturer, born in Davenport, Devonshire, England, in 1799; died in New York city, Jan. 31, 1887. He came to the United States in 1822, and soon afterward was engaged as a publisher in New York city, reprinting, in the cheap form of his "Republic of Letters," the works of many of the noted novelists of Europe, including those of Sir Walter Scott. This occupation led him to become interested in type-founding, and it was he who furnished the elder Bennett the type used on the first "New York Herald." His foundry, on Gold Street, was sold to James Conner, and became the nucleus of a large establishment. Mr. Guerin

erected the first type-foundry in Canada, and supplied the funds to establish one in the city of Mexico, but his plans and capital were stolen by the Mexican consul in New York, to whom he had intrusted them. He was also interested in several foundries in England.

Hague, William, clergyman, born in Pelham, Westchester Co., N. Y., Jan. 4, 1808; died in Boston, Mass., Aug. 1, 1887. He was graduated at Hamilton in 1826, and, after studying at Princeton Theological Seminary for a year, was graduated at Newton Theological Institution in 1829. On Oct. 20, 1827, he was ordained pastor of the Second Baptist Church in Utica, N. Y., and in 1831 entered upon the pastorate of the First Baptist Church in Boston. In 1837 he became pastor of the First Baptist Church in Providence, R. I., but returned to Boston in 1840 to the charge of the Federal Street Church. He subsequently held pastorates in Jamaica Plain, Mass. (1848-'50); Newark, N. J. (1850-'53); Albany, N. Y. (1853-'58); New York city (1858-'62), returning thence to Boston, where he remained for seven years. He was elected in 1869 Professor of Homiletics in the Baptist Theological Seminary, Chicago, occupying that chair about one year, and then accepting a charge in Orange, N. J. His last pastorate was on Wollaston Heights, near Boston, where he was in 1876-'87, making the aggregate duration of his several charges in that city and its suburbs nearly thirty-five years. He received the degree of D. D. from Brown in 1849, and from Harvard in 1863. Dr. Hague was a trustee of the former university from 1837 until his death, also of Vassar College from its incorporation, and of Columbian University in Washington, D. C. Besides numerous occasional addresses and orations, including discourses on the life and character of John Quincy Adams (1848), Adoniram Judson (1851), and John Overton Choules (1856), he published "Historical Discourse on the Two Hundredth Anniversary of the First Baptist Church, Providence, R. I., November 7, 1889" (Boston, 1889); "Guide to Conversation, on the Gospel of John" (Boston, 1840); "Eight Views of Baptism" (1841); "The Baptist Church transplanted from the Old World to the New" (New York, 1846); "Conversational Commentaries on the Gospel of Matthew" (1851); "Acts of the Apostles" (1851); "Christianity and Statesmanship" (1855), enlarged edition, Boston, 1865); "Home Life" (1855); "The Self-sustaining Character of the New-Testament Christianity" (Philadelphia, 1871); and "Christian Greatness in the Minister" (Boston, 1880). His latest work, completed a few days before his death, was issued posthumously as "Life Notes; or, Fifty Years' Outlook" (Boston, 1887), and is a volume of reminiscences.

Harrington, Henry F., an American educator, born in Roxbury, Mass., in 1813; died in Keene, N. H., Sept. 19, 1887. He was graduated at Harvard in 1834, became a Unitarian minister, and filled pastorates in Lawrence and Cambridge, Mass. He took an active interest in the educational systems of those cities, and, while preaching regularly, served as a member of both school boards, and also as superintendent of schools in the latter city. In 1864 he was appointed superintendent of public schools in New Bedford, Mass., and held the office continuously until his death. He began contributing to magazines early in life, confining himself almost wholly to educational topics, and, when he accepted the superintendency at New Bedford, he had established a national reputation by his writings on that subject. Shortly before his death he published a spelling-book, and completed a school history.

Harris, John Wesley, an American lawyer, born in Virginia in 1808; died in Galveston, Texas, April 1, 1887. He was educated for the bar in his native State, and removed to Texas in 1837, settling in Brazoria, the most populous county at that time. He achieved distinction in his profession during the existence of the republic of Texas, and when it was organized as a State of the Federal Union was appointed its first attorney-general, serving a second term by reappointment. He was a member of the Legislature several times, and served on the commission that revised the State laws and formulated the present penal code and the code of criminal and civil procedure of the State.

Harris, William Logan, an American clergyman, born in Mansfield, O., Nov. 4, 1817; died in New York city, Sept. 2, 1887. He united with the Methodist Episcopal Church in 1834, was licensed to preach in 1836, and joined the Michigan Conference, which then included the northern part of Ohio, in 1837. Having received a thorough training at Norwalk Seminary in the classic languages and mathematics, he was appointed a tutor in the Ohio Wesleyan University in 1845, and principal of Baldwin Institute in 1848. In 1852 he was elected Professor of Chemistry and Natural History in Ohio Wesleyan University, and in 1860 Assistant Corresponding Secretary of the Methodist Missionary Society, holding the latter office till 1872, when he was elected bishop. After his elevation to the episcopate he visited Japan, China, India, Turkey, Italy, Switzerland, Germany, and Scandinavia, inspecting and directing the Methodist missions in those countries. He traveled through every State and Territory in the Union, and circumnavigated the globe. Bishop Harris received the degree of D. D. from Allegheny College in 1856, and that of LL. D. from Baldwin University in 1870.

Harvey, William Street, an American journalist, born in London, England, Dec. 11, 1834; died in Brooklyn, N. Y., April 8, 1887. He was educated for the Church, but after graduation at Oxford his mind changed and he became a writer for the press and a teacher in Birmingham. In 1865 he came to the United States, settling in San Francisco, Cal., where he re-ceived an editorial appointment on "The San Francisco News-Letter." He attracted the attention of the Rev. T. De Witt Talmage during a lecturing tour of the latter in California, and was induced to remove to Brooklyn, N. Y., where he became an editorial writer and book-reviewer for the Brooklyn "Eagle." His writings revealed a wide familiarity with English literature and the theological thought of the day. Among his literary remains is the manuscript of a book entitled "Six Modern Humorists," which he completed in 1881.

Hassinger, David Stanley, an American soldier, born in Philadelphia, Pa., Dec. 24, 1842; died there, April 5, 1887. At the outbreak of the civil war he entered the National service, and he was continually in the field till the close of the war, participating in many of the battles in which the Army of the Potomac was engaged. At the battle of the Wilderness all the officers of his company were killed or wounded, and four color-bearers were successively shot down. While the engagement was at its height he was assigned to the command of the color company, and at great peril preserved the flags. He was wounded in a charge at Spottsylvania Court-House in May, 1864, and upon his recovery was detailed as adjutant of his regiment, continuing in that office till the close of the war. In 1873 Gov. Hartranft appointed him Assistant Adjutant-General of Pennsylvania, and he occupied the office through all the changes of administration till his death.

Hathorn, Henry H., an American hotel-keeper, born in Greenfield, N. Y., Nov. 28, 1813; died in Saratoga, N. Y., Feb. 20, 1887. He received an academic education, and, removing to Saratoga, was engaged in mercantile business from 1839 till 1849. He was among the first to take advantage of the mineral springs, and to engage in the hotel business, becoming one of the owners of the old Congress Hall, which was burned in 1865, and replaced with the present structure, opened in 1868. In the latter year, while workmen were digging for the foundation of a business block, a new spring was discovered, which has since been known as the Hathorn Spring, and owned and managed by Mr. Hathorn and his family. He was supervisor of Saratoga four years, elected sheriff of the county in 1858 and 1862, and member of Congress in 1872–'74.

Hayes, John Lord, lawyer, born in South Berwick, Me., April 18, 1812; died in Cambridge, Mass., April 18, 1887. He was graduated at Dartmouth in 1831, and then studied law at the Harvard Law School. In 1835 he was admitted to the bar and settled in Portsmouth, Me., where he followed his profession, and for a time was Clerk of the United States Courts for the District of New Hampshire. He was called in 1846 to become general manager of the Katahdin Iron Works, but the British free-trade tariff of that year ruined the project. In 1851 he moved to Washington, where he was employed by the Canadian Government as its counsel in the advocacy of the reciprocity treaty. He organized and was Secretary of the Mexican, Rio Grande, and Pacific Railway Company, and in 1854 obtained a charter from the Mexican Government that authorized the construction of a railroad across that country. Mr. Hayes was one of the marshals that rode beside the carriage of Abraham Lincoln at his first inauguration, and in 1861 was appointed Chief Clerk of the Patent-Office. This place he held until 1865 when, on the organization of the National Association of Wool Manufacturers, he became its secretary, and continued so until his death. In 1822 he was appointed president of the Tariff Commission. Mr. Hayes collected and mounted a cabinet of birds, made a herbarium, and studied geology in the library and field. In 1848 he read a paper before the American Association of Geologists and Naturalists, of which he was a member, on "Glaciers," which was regarded as the most important contribution, up to that time, on glacial phenomena in relation to geology. He was elected a member of the Boston Society of Natural History in 1845, and was connected with other scientific bodies both at home and abroad. In 1860 he received the degree of LL.D. from Dartmouth. He edited the "United States Industrial Directory" and the "Bulletin of the National Association of Wool Manufacturers," of which he was also the principal contributor. His writings, which are both scientific and political, include nearly one hundred titles, among which are "Report on North American Indians"; "Jackson's Vindication as the Discoverer of Anæsthetics"; "Sketch of Maryland Geology"; "Sheep Industry in the South"; and very many papers on wool-growing and wool-manufacture, as well as on its relations to the tariff issues. He also published "Reminiscences of the Free-soil Movement in New Hampshire" (1845), that attracted much attention, he himself drawing up the call for the first convention of Independent Democrats, when Senator John P. Hale withdrew from the Democratic party; also, "Corolla Hymnorum Sacrorum," a selection of Latin hymns of the early and middle ages (Boston, 1887).

Henne, Antonia, an American singer, born in Cincinnati, Ohio, in 1850; died in New York city, July 18, 1887. While yet a child she distinguished herself by singing in concerts and operas in her native city, where her father was employed as a teacher of languages in the public schools, appearing in "Der Freischütz" as early as her twelfth year. In 1865 she removed to New York city for the purpose of vocal study, and, while under the tuition of Signor Muzio, sang in Theodore Thomas's symphony soirees in the season of 1866. In 1869 she went to Europe, studying two years in Florence, and returning to New York in 1871, having been engaged as contralto for the choir of Madison Square Presbyterian Church, where she sang till two months previous to her death. During this engagement she took part

in many of the Philharmonic concerts and in the classical concerts of Thomas and Damrosch, and appeared in all the concerts of the Church Music Association, besides those of other societies. Latterly she had given much of her time to the musical instruction of young ladies, and was winning a high reputation as a teacher when she was bitten by a dog in the summer of 1886, and her nervous system sustained a shock from which she never recovered. Abandoning all else, she sang with the choir till she became too feeble to leave her house, and passed away in an attack of apoplexy.

Holliday, Ben, an American pioneer, born in Bourbon County, Ky., in 1819; died in Portland, Ore., July 8, 1887. While a mere youth he removed to Leavenworth, Kan., and became a leader in the rugged life of that section. At the outbreak of the civil war he established himself as a contractor, purchasing the various materials required by the subsistence, military, and Indian departments. With the proceeds of this business he opened mercantile houses in Salt Lake City and San Francisco, and bought out the Brigham Young express, with which the Federal authorities had refused to renew a contract for mail transportation after the Mormon war of 1857-'58. Mr. Holliday had no difficulty in securing a valuable contract with the Government, and his mail and overland express was for the next ten years the connecting-link between the frontier States of the West and the Pacific coast. To facilitate the speedy delivery of important business letters and newspapers, he organized the "pony express," for which stations were opened at regular intervals over an uninhabited stretch of country 2,000 miles across, relays of horses were kept at each station, and daring riders at every third station. The trip from San Francisco to St. Joseph, Mo., was thus made in ten days. Mr. Holliday's mail pay from the Government on the overland route soon amounted to $150,000 a year, and the income from his stages to $1,500 a day. He invested largely in cattle-raising, was one of the owners of the famed Ophir mine in Nevada, and established steamship-lines between San Francisco and Portland, Oregon, the Sandwich Islands, and Australia. By 1866 his wealth was estimated at $10,000,000. In 1868 he sold his overland mail route to Wells, Fargo & Co. for $850,-000, removed to Portland, and began building the Oregon and California Railroad. With his income from the Ophir mine he purchased a farm in Westchester County, N. Y., to which he gave the name of Ophir, and expended about $1,000,000 on the erection of a stately castle and the beautifying of the grounds. He met with serious losses in the panic of 1873, abandoned Ophir farm, and retired to Portland. One of his daughters became the Comtesse de Pourtales, and another the Baroness de Bussière.

Homes, Henry Augustus, an American librarian, born in Boston, Mass., March 10, 1812; died in

Albany, N. Y., Nov. 3, 1887. He was graduated at Amherst in 1830, and, after a two-years' course in theology in the Andover Theological Seminary, he took a two-years' course in medicine at Yale. He went to Paris, France, in 1835, began the study of Arabic under De Say, and was ordained as a missionary of the Eglise Reformee, being assigned to the Turkish field. In the following year he joined the American Board in Constantinople, laboring there till 1850. He was then appointed assistant dragoman in the American Legation to the Porte, holding the office for three years, and acting as *chargé d'affaires* for one year. In 1858 he returned to the United States, in 1854 was appointed assistant librarian of the New York State Library at Albany, and in 1862, upon the death of Alfred B. Street, the librarian, succeeded to the head of the library staff. He was the author of numerous books on oriental and historical subjects, edited the papers of Govs. Clinton and Tompkins and Sir William Johnson, translated important Arabic and Persian works, and saw the library increase from 30,000 to 185,000 volumes during his connection with it. He received the degree of LL. D. from Columbia College in 1873.

Hope, James Barron, an American journalist, born in Norfolk, Va., March 23, 1827; died in Norfolk, Va., Sept. 15, 1887. He was a grandson of Commodore James Barron and a nephew of Commodore Samuel Barron, and was educated for the profession of law, which he followed for several years, leaving it for a service of three years as secretary to his uncle just previous to the civil war. In 1861 he enlisted in the Confederate army, in which he attained the rank of captain. Immediately after the war he became a newspaper editor, and was connected with the Norfolk "Day-Book" and the Norfolk "Virginian," till 1879, when he established the Norfolk "Landmark," which he published and edited until his death. Besides his editorial labors, Mr. Hope had made a reputation as a poet. He wrote the ode for the unveiling of the statue of Washington in Richmond, Va., in 1858, and that for the Yorktown Centennial in 1881. A few days before his death he finished a poem, written at the request of Gov. Lee, to be read at the laying of the corner-stone of the Robert E. Lee monument in Richmond on Oct. 27, 1887.

Hovey, Charles M., an American pomologist, born in Cambridge, Mass., in October, 1810; died there Sept. 1, 1887. He began his active work in the interest of pomology and floriculture when but twenty-one years old, and founded the "Horticultural Magazine," of which he was editor for thirty-five years. In 1838, by means of hybridization, he secured the seeds from which he afterward raised "the Boston pine" and "Hovey's seedling" strawberries; in 1835 he began the hybridization of camellias; in 1838 that of Indian azalias; and in 1845 that of Japanese lilies, for all of which he obtained prizes from the Massachusetts Horticultural Society. He began the collection in 1844 of all kinds of cherry, plum, peach, apple, and pear trees that were attainable, and in time the whole numbered over 1,500 of proved fertility. He was a member of the Massachusetts Horticultural Society for fifty-five years, an authority on fruits, flowers, and agriculture generally, and the author of "The Fruits of America" (begun in 1847), the illustrations for which were made from his own sketches.

Howland, Robert Southworth, an American clergyman, born in New York city Nov. 9, 1820; died in Morristown, N. J., Feb. 3, 1887. He received a primary education in France, was graduated at St. Paul's College, Long Island, N. Y., in 1840, and took a partial course in the General Theological Seminary of the Protestant Episcopal Church, New York city, which he left to assist Bishop Kerfoot, of the diocese of Western Pennsylvania, in the organization of St. James College, Maryland. He was employed in this task nearly a year, and then, on being released by the bishop, went abroad, spending a year and a half in travel, much of it in the Holy Land. On his return he resumed his theological studies, and was graduated in 1845. Soon after this he was ordered a deacon and in the following year a priest, and became assistant to the Rev. Dr. Forbes, New York. The congregation of the Church of the Holy Apostles sprang from a Sunday-school held in a private residence, its growth attracted friends by whom a church-edifice was erected in 1847, and Mr. Howland was called to the rectorship. Under his guidance during the ensuing twenty years the number of communicants increased from 20 to over 400, and the Sunday-school attained a membership of 450 children. In 1868 he was called to the rectorship of the Church of the Heavenly Rest, then being organized. The church edifice and the adjoining houses were built under his supervision, and largely from his personal means, as he desired to have the architecture of the latter harmonize with that of the church. The new church was dedicated in 1869, with himself as rector, and the Rev. J. K. Conrad as assistant. A few years ago a stroke of paralysis admonished him to withdraw from active pastoral work, and from that time till his second and fatal attack he sought to recover his strength by travel and recreation. He received the degree of D. D. from Columbia College, New York city, in 1863.

Hussey, John, an American life-saver, born in Castle Murtha, Ireland, in 1824; died in New York city, June 21, 1887. He emigrated to New York city in 1847, and, after following several humble occupations for three years, became a longshoreman. From 1850 till within a few days of his death he was constantly on duty along the water-front of New York city. On April 17, 1852, he saved from drowning Miss Ellen Dooney, whom he afterward married. This was his first feat as a life-saver. Up to Sept. 10, 1886, he had an official record of having saved thirty-four lives, although it was claimed for him that the actual number was much larger. He received nearly thirty medals for his heroism, one of which was awarded by Congress, three were presented by South Street merchants, and one by the Society for the Prevention of Cruelty to Animals, for rescuing two horses from the North river. In 1886, while Sir Alfred Goolis was visiting the United States, he became acquainted with John Hussey, and, impressed with his record as a life-saver, endeavored to secure for him the medal of the Royal Humane Society of England. But in this he was unsuccessful, owing to the fact, as communicated to Mr. Hussey in April, 1887, that he had renounced his allegiance to the Queen, and had not saved the life of a British subject. On June 2 he was shot by a policeman, and he died from the effects of the wound nineteen days afterward.

Hutchison, Joseph C., an American physician, born in Old Franklin, Howard County, Mo., Feb. 22, 1827; died in Brooklyn, N. Y., July 17, 1887. He was educated in the University of Missouri and the University of Pennsylvania, being graduated at the latter as a physician in 1848. He practiced his profession in Missouri till 1853, when he settled in Brooklyn, where he resided thereafter. During the cholera epidemic of 1854 he was in charge of the cholera hospital in Brooklyn, on the disappearance of which he resumed practice in his special field, operative surgery, and soon attained high rank among American surgeons. In 1860 he was appointed Professor of Surgery in the Long Island College Hospital, occupying the chair till 1867. He founded the Brooklyn Orthopedic Hospital, and was its surgeon-in-chief for several years. He was appointed a Health Commissioner of Brooklyn in 1873, and served for three years, devoting his skill to the sanitary improvement of the city. Dr. Hutchison was a member of the Kings County Medical Society and its president in 1864, a member of the New York Medical Society, of the New York Pathological Society, and a Fellow of the New York Academy of Medicine, and had been a delegate to the International Medical Congresses in Philadelphia, 1867, and London, 1881. In 1880 the University of Missouri conferred upon him the degree of LL. D.

Ingersoll, Elihu Parsons, an American clergyman, born in Lee, Mass., Sept. 20, 1804; died in Springfield, Clay County, Kan., March 29, 1887. He was graduated at Yale in 1832, studied for a year in Auburn Theological Seminary and for a year in the Yale Divinity School, and was ordained as pastor of the Congregational Church in Woonsocket, R. I., Dec. 22, 1834. The following year he accepted a call to Oberlin College, remaining there nearly five years, in part engaged as Professor of Sacred Music. In 1840 he removed to Michigan, with

the intention of founding an institution similar to Oberlin College, but in this he was unsuccessful, owing to the general financial depression. The ensuing thirteen years he passed in home-missionary work at his own expense, becoming regularly settled in May, 1853, as pastor of the Congregational Church in Bloomington, Ill. He resigned this charge two years later, and went to Kansas to labor in aid of the anti-slavery cause. He was engaged in this service at his own expense till 1861, when he was induced to return to pastoral work in Illinois, where he officiated for one year in Elmwood, and five in Malden, returning to Kansas in 1868. Of his published works "Lost Israel Found" (1886) is best known.

Jewell, James Stewart, an American physician, born in Galena, Ill., Sept. 8, 1837; died in Chicago, Ill., April 18, 1887. He was graduated at Chicago Medical College in 1860, and two years later settled in Chicago, where he continued in practice till his death. In 1864 he was appointed Professor of Anatomy in Chicago Medical College, serving as such till 1869, when he resigned to devote his time wholly to practice. In 1872, however, he accepted the professorship of nervous and mental diseases in the college. His practice was constantly increasing, and he was subject to many calls from the courts as an expert witness, yet, notwithstanding this and his own physical weaknesses, he occupied the professor's chair till his death, conducted a quarterly medical journal, the columns of which were devoted to the discussion of his specialties, and maintained corresponding membership in many literary and scientific societies.

Johnston, Archibald, an American composer, born in New York city in 1831; died there Aug. 31, 1887. In early life he was a merchant tailor. On the outbreak of the civil war he raised a company and went to the field as a captain in the Sixty-Second New York Volunteers, serving under Gen. McClellan, and taking part in the battle of Fair Oaks. On his return from the army he established himself in the business of selling horses and carriages at auction. He was well known as a musical composer, many of his songs and compositions obtaining wide celebrity. Among his most popular works were the words and music of "Alone, and Oh! So Lonely!" and "The Toilers," the cantata "Ossian's Address to the Sun," the musical score of a "Te Deum," and the music of that famous song "Baby Mine." He was treasurer of the New York Harmonic Society for many years, and vice-president of the Metropolitan Musical Club.

Kolloch, Isaac S., an American clergyman, born in Rockland, Me., in 1832; died in New Whatcom, Washington Territory, Dec. 9, 1887. He was a son of the Rev. Amariah Kalloch, who established and officiated in the First Baptist Church in Rockland, Me., for seventeen years, and died near San Francisco in 1851. Isaac was educated by his father for the ministry of the Baptist Church, and was ordained in Rockland. He became pastor of the Temple Society in Boston, Mass., in 1855, identified himself with the Know-Nothing movement, and, after bearing a conspicuous part in a noted scandal case, resigned his charge, removed to Kansas, and entered into a law-partnership. He preached in New York city in 1861-'64, again went to Kansas, and, shortly before Denis Kearney started his sand-lots movement, settled in San Francisco. His activity in this movement led the De Young brothers to attack his moral character in their newspaper, the San Francisco "Chronicle," after he had received the sand-lots nomination for Mayor of the city, and on Aug. 23, 1879, he was shot by Charles De Young for slandering the mother of the De Young brothers. Notwithstanding the excitement that followed, Mr. Kalloch was elected Mayor. Subsequently his son, the Rev. Isaac M. Kalloch, shot and killed Charles De Young, and was acquitted of the charge of murder after a sensational trial.

Kellogg, Albert, botanist, born in New Hartford, Conn., Dec. 6, 1813; died in Alameda, Cal., March 31, 1887. He was educated at the Wilbraham Academy, Mass., and then studied medicine at the medical department of the Transylvania University. Dr. Kellogg was one of the first botanists to visit the far West, and the earliest scientific description of the big trees of California was made by him and published by John C. Frémont in his "Report of the Exploring Expedition to the Rocky Mountains in 1842, and to Oregon and North California in the years 1843-'44" (Washington, 1845). He was also associated with John J. Audubon in his exploration of Texas at the time of the annexation of that country to the United States. Subsequently, he made botanical explorations along the western coast of the American continent from Terra del Fuego to Alaska in the north. In 1867 he was chosen botanist of the expedition sent in June of that year on a geographical reconnoissance of Alaska under Prof. George Davidson. He began his work at the northern end of Vancouver's Island and continued through the Alexander Archipelago, then on part of Kadiak Island, and finally at Unalaska Island. His collection embraced more than 500 species of plants, from which he furnished complete collections to the Smithsonian Institution, the Philadelphia Academy of Sciences, and the California Academy of Sciences. Dr. Kellogg was one of the founders of the California Academy of Sciences and a member of other learned bodies. He contributed largely to scientific periodicals and also to State and National reports. Dr. Kellogg was exceedingly skillful with his pencil and brush, and up to nearly the last moment was occupied in making drawings of the floral and sylvan species of the Pacific States, particularly the sylva, with the intention of illustrating a work on the indigenous trees of California. Over 500 large

drawings of elaborate and accurate execution as well as of exquisite beauty had already been completed at the time of his death.

Kemen, Mary Josephine, an American educator, born in Prum, Germany, in 1824; died in Lockport, N. Y., July 20, 1887. She received a superior education in her native town, becoming proficient in several languages. In 1844 she entered the convent of the Sisters of St. Mary in Namur, Belgium, and through her keen business tact and intellectual qualities was given the management of important official trusts there and in Brussels. In 1863 she founded the order in the United States, erecting the home convent at Lockport, N. Y., and subsequently established other houses in various parts of the country, three in New York State, and ten altogether. Under the name in religion of Mother Emilie, she was appointed Superior of the Order of Sisters of St. Mary in America, soon after settling in Lockport, holding that office at the time of her death.

Kennedy, Joseph C. G., an American lawyer, born in Meadville, Pa., in 1813; died in Washington, D. C., July 13, 1887. He was a son of Samuel Kennedy, a surgeon in the Revolutionary War, and a grandson of Andrew Ellicott, who, at the request of President Washington, surveyed and planned the National capital in 1791. He was educated at Allegheny College, and afterward was admitted to the bar. His public career began in 1849, when he was invited to Washington and appointed secretary of the Census Board. From that time till his murder by a demented outcast, he was one of the best-known residents of Washington, esteemed in all quarters for his scholarly attainments and familiarity with the archives of American independence. Mr. Kennedy drafted the bill that created the Census Bureau, and was its chief in 1850 and 1860. In 1851 he visited Europe on official business connected with cheap postage and other public measures, and in 1862 was a commissioner to the International Exhibition in London. His labor in establishing the Census Bureau and superintending its operations in the years mentioned led to the bestowal upon him of high honors by learned men and societies of Europe. He was a voluminous writer on national statistics and other subjects, and directed for many years a great mass of official publications. During the latter part of his life he was employed as an attorney and real-estate agent. He contributed liberally to local charities.

Kinloch, Eliza, an American actress, born in London, England, March 6, 1796; died in Long Branch, N. J., Aug. 11, 1887. She made her first appearance in the United States at the Walnut Street Theatre, Philadelphia, as Margaretta in "No Song, no Supper," in July, 1827. In 1828 she married Mr. Kinloch, an English actor, then playing in Philadelphia, and in the same year made her first appearance in New York city as Diana Vernon in "Rob Roy" at the Chatham Theatre. In 1831 she retired from the stage on account of her husband's failing health, and accompanied him to Jamaica, where he died. She then returned to the stage in Philadelphia, playing in light comedy *rôles* and bringing out her daughter, subsequently Mrs. John Drew, whose first appearance was as the Duke of York in the Richard III of Junius Brutus Booth. She finally retired from the stage in 1825, and had since lived with Mrs. Drew. On her ninety-first birthday Mrs. Drew gave her mother a reception in Philadelphia, at which four generations of children were present.

Krzyzanowski, Wladimir, an American soldier, born in Raznova, Polish Prussia, July 8, 1824; died in New York city Jan. 31, 1887. He took an active part in the uprising of the Poles in 1846, and upon the suppression of the revolution fled to the United States, where he was engaged in civil engineering till the outbreak of the civil war, much of his work being in connection with the extension of railroads in the Western States. When the news of the attack on Fort Sumter reached New York, he canceled all his engagements, organized the Turner Rifles, of which he was appointed captain on May 9, 1861, aided the formation of the Fifty-eighth Regiment of New York Volunteers, and in September accompanied the troops to the front as their colonel. He served with distinction through the war, mainly with the Army of the Potomac, and when mustered out held the brevet rank of brigadier-general. For some time after the war he held a Government office in California, and was then appointed Governor of the newly-acquired Territory of Alaska. At the close of the latter service he was transferred to the custom-department, performing inspector's duty at various South American ports and on the Isthmus of Panama till 1883, when he was appointed a special agent of the treasury department in the New York Custom-House. He was removed from this office soon after the inauguration of President Cleveland, but his eminent military services led to his speedy reinstatement, and he remained in office till his death.

Leighton, Albert, an American poet, born in Portsmouth, N. H., Jan. 8, 1829; died there Feb. 6, 1887. He was educated in a private school, and during the past twenty years was teller of the Rockingham National Bank, Portsmouth. From early manhood he was a frequent contributor to the poetical literature of the country. In 1859 the first edition of his "Poems" was published in Boston. Its chief feature was the poem entitled "Beauty," which he had read before the literary societies of Bowdoin College in August, 1858. An enlarged edition was published in 1879. His best-known poems are: "Beauty," "Found Dead," "The Missing Ships," "Joe," "The Song of the Skaters," and the one in memory of Gen. Grant. President Peabody, of Harvard University, in an article in "The North American Review," criticising Mr. Leighton's

poems, pronounced them "choice and polished, yet without conceit or mannerism in diction, rich and glowing in imagery, and lofty, while unexaggerated in sentiment."

La Motte, Charles E., an American lawyer, born in Lenni Mills, Delaware County, Pa., in 1839; died in Wilmington, Del., May 24, 1887. He took a preparatory course of study in the Military Academy in Oxford, Md., and was graduated at the University of Pennsylvania in 1858. He removed to Wilmington, Del., and studied in the office of Judge Bradford till the outbreak of the civil war, when he threw aside his books, raised a company of volunteers and took the field as a captain in the First Regiment of Delaware Volunteers. At the expiration of the three months' term of this regiment, he was appointed colonel, and was subsequently brevetted brigadier-general, and served on the staff of Gen. Ayres, Second Division, Fifth Army Corps, to the end of the war. After being mustered out of the service, he went to Cincinnati, where he practiced his profession till 1882, when a neuralgic affection of the heart, caused by exposures on the field, compelled him to retire from active life. He returned to his home in Wilmington, and passed the remainder of his life in severe suffering.

Lawrence, Albert Gallatin, an American soldier, born in New York city, April 14, 1836; died there Jan. 12, 1887. He was a son of William Beach Lawrence, Governor of Rhode Island. He pursued a preliminary course of instruction in New York city and Vevay, Switzerland, and was graduated at Harvard in 1857 and at the Cambridge Law School in 1858. After his admission to the bar he was appointed Secretary of the United States Legation at Vienna, and served there till the outbreak of the civil war, when he resigned the office, returned home, and entered the volunteer army as second lieutenant in the Fifty-fourth Regiment of New York Infantry. He was soon transferred to Gen. Butler's staff, and when that officer detached a force under Gen. Ames to assist Gen. Terry in the reduction of Fort Fisher, Capt. Lawrence accompanied the re-enforcements as aide-de-camp to Gen. Ames. In the memorable assault upon that stronghold Capt. Lawrence behaved most gallantly, and received three wounds, one of which resulted in the loss of his left arm. For his services on that occasion, he received the thanks of Gen. Terry and the Legislature of Rhode Island, and four brevets and a pension from the Government. Shortly after the close of the war he returned to diplomatic service, being appointed Minister to Costa Rica by President Johnson. While holding this office, he challenged an *attaché* of the Prussian Legation to a duel for having spoken disrespectfully of the American flag. The Prussian fired and missed, and then Gen. Lawrence fired in the air, after which the principals declared themselves satisfied. This affair led to considerable official correspondence, which caused Gen. Lawrence to resign his office.

His only subsequent public service was as a member of the commission appointed to investigate the troubles with Sitting Bull and his tribe, and other Indian difficulties. He spent the greater part of his last years in literary pursuits, social enjoyment, and the care of his property in New York city and Newport, R. I. Gen. Lawrence was a member of the Union, New York, and Newport Reading clubs, and of the Military Order of the Loyal Legion.

Laws, Charles Alfred, an American engineer, born in Philadelphia in 1848; died in New York city Jan. 12, 1887. He was one of the first volunteers in Philadelphia in 1860, and for two years was a sergeant in Anderson's famous cavalry regiment. Soon after his discharge from the army he studied engineering, passed the examination for service in the navy, and was appointed assistant engineer on the gunboat "Itaska," which was ordered to the Gulf squadron under Admiral Farragut. He was present at the battle of Mobile Bay, where he rendered services for which he was officially complimented. At the close of the war he entered the United States Revenue Marine service, and was on duty along the Gulf and Atlantic coasts till 1878, when he was ordered to San Francisco as engineer of the "Corwin," then about to sail in search of the missing Arctic steamer "Jeannette." He was also engineer of the expedition sent out in search of the "Rodgers," also in arctic waters. In 1885 he was appointed first assistant engineer of the United States revenue cutter "Washington," and was on duty off the coast of North Carolina till the following summer, when he was ordered to New York. Mr. Laws was a general favorite in the service, and stood first on the list for promotion to the rank of chief engineer.

Layton, Caleb Rodney, an American soldier, born in Germantown, Pa., in 1821; died in Rehoboth, Del., Aug. 20, 1887. He joined the army as a captain in the First Regiment of Delaware Volunteers May 16, 1861; became major July 1, following; was appointed captain in the Seventh United States Infantry Aug. 5, 1861; brevetted major July 2, 1863, for gallant conduct at Gettysburg, and promoted to rank of major and assigned to the Twentieth Infantry March 4, 1879. He retired in 1884, and had since lived in Georgetown, Delaware.

Leavenworth, Elias Warner, an American lawyer, born in Canaan, N. Y., Dec. 20, 1803; died in Syracuse, N. Y., Nov. 25, 1887. He received an academic education in Great Barrington, Mass., was graduated at Yale in 1824, and, after studying law in the office of the late William Cullen Bryant and the Litchfield, Conn., Law School, was admitted to the bar in 1827. Settling in Syracuse he practiced his profession till 1850, when failing health forced him to abandon it. In 1835 he was elected a member of the State Assembly, and in the following year was appointed brigadier-general, and placed in command of the State artillery. He was president of the village of Syracuse in 1839–'41 and 1846–'47, and Mayor from 1849 till 1859, and served continuously as a member of the Assembly from 1850 till 1857, with the exception of the years 1854–'55, when he was Secretary of State. In 1861 he was chosen a regent of the State University, the same year appointed by President Lincoln the commissioner to adjust claims against New Grenada, in 1872 elected a member of the State Constitutional Commission, and in 1875 a Representative in Congress. He received the degree of LL. D. from Hamilton College in 1872.

Lee, Alfred, an American clergyman, born in Cambridge, Mass., Sept. 9, 1807; died in Wilmington, Del., April 12, 1887. He first studied law, and was admitted to the bar in New London, Conn., where he practiced for two years, and then studied theology. In 1837 he was graduated at the General Theological Seminary of the Protestant Episcopal Church, New York city; in May of that year was ordered deacon; and on June 12, 1838, was ordained priest by Bishop Brownell, in Christ Church, Hartford, Conn. He officiated a few months in St. James's Church, Poquetannock, Conn., and in September, 1838, became rector of Calvary Church, Rockdale, Pa. In 1841 a convention was held in Georgetown, Del., for the purpose of electing a bishop for the diocese, which had previously been under the supervision of the bishop of Pennsylvania, and the choice fell upon him. He was consecrated as first bishop of Delaware in St. Paul's Church, New York city, on Oct. 12, 1841, being the youngest of the twenty-one members of the House of Bishops, and the thirty-eighth in succession of American bishops. In 1842 he became rector of St. Andrew's Church, Wilmington, Del., and on May 31, 1884, by the death of the Rt. Rev. Benjamin Bosworth Smith, presiding bishop of the American Church. Bishop Lee received the degree of S. T. D. from Trinity College, Hartford, Conn., and Hobart College, Geneva, N.Y., in 1841, and from Harvard in 1860, and that of LL. D. from Delaware College, Newark, Del., in 1877. In 1881, in a sermon before the Diocesan Convention, Bishop Lee said that, during his forty years of service as bishop, twenty-four churches had been built within the diocese, he had confirmed 4,327 persons, and 10,082 baptisms had been reported to him. The number of active clergymen had increased from 4 to 29, the parishes from 7 to 37, and the communicants from 339 to 2,282. He published a "Life of the Apostle Peter, in a Series of Practical Discourses," a "Life of St. John," a "Treatise on Baptism," "A Memoir of Miss Susan Allibone," "The Harbinger of Christ," "A Voice in the Wilderness," and "Eventful Nights in Bible History," besides many charges, special sermons, and addresses. He was a member of the committee of bishops that had charge of the missionary work of the Church in Mexico, and bore an influential part in the establishment of the Anglican Church in the capital city. He was also a member of the American commission that, conjointly with the English committee, revised the translation of the Bible, and of the Pan-Anglican council that met in London, England, in 1873.

Lent, Lewis Benjamin, an American showman, born in Somers, Westchester County, N. Y., in 1814; died in New York city May 26, 1887. He entered the show business at the age of nineteen, his father having bought "Bett," believed to be the first elephant exhibited in the United States, and several trick-horses, and formed a company to take the wonders about the country. Lewis accompanied the show for two seasons, and then, anxious for a larger field, induced his father to buy him an interest in Brown & Fogg's Circus. This circus soon became known as the Zoölogical Institute, other shows being consolidated with it, but under the new title it met with failure. Young Lent then formed the firm of Sands & Lent, and took his show all over the United States, and subsequently to England. In 1852 he purchased an interest in Franconi's Hippodrome, located where the Fifth Avenue Hotel now stands, with which Messrs. P. T. Barnum and Avery Smith were connected, and later joined Mr. Barnum in the management of his traveling managerie. At the beginning of the war, Mr. Lent went with E. P. Christy to the West Indies with the National Circus, and exhibited there for two seasons. On his return to New York city, he took Wallack's old theatre, and used it as a circus till October, 1865, when he opened a circus in the "Hippotheatron," on Fourteenth Street, opposite the Academy of Music. He managed this successfully till August, 1872, when he sold out to Mr. Barnum, and went on the road with the traveling New York Circus. During the season of 1873 he managed a circus and menagerie in Madison Square Garden, New York city. In 1882 Mr. Lent closed his career as a showman, with Frank A. Robbins's circus and managerie, and from that time led a comparatively quiet life. He had been connected, as partner, director, or manager, with every circus of note in the United States since 1833, and, though he accumulated and lost several fortunes, died rich.

Leray, Francis Xavier, an American clergyman, born near Rennes, Brittany, France, April 20, 1825; died there in September, 1887. He was educated by the Eudist fathers, and accompanied a missionary party of that order to the United States in 1843, settling with them in Vincennes, Ind. After nine years of missionary work, he completed his theological course in St. Mary's Seminary, Baltimore, Md. and was ordained priest at Natchez, Miss., March 19, 1852. On the death of Bishop Chauche he was sent to Jackson, Miss., where he labored with great zeal during the yellow-fever epidemics of 1853 and 1854, administering to the comfort of the victims in Vicksburg and Brandon as well in the latter year. He was sent to Vicksburg in 1857, and was just getting his large parish into effective working order when

the civil war began. Shortly after its close the city was visited by cholera, and for two years the priest labored among his stricken flock with little save his sense of duty to encourage him. On the death of the Rt. Rev. Dr. Martin, he was selected to succeed him as bishop of Natchitoches. He was consecrated in the cathedral of Rennes April 23, 1877. In October, 1879, he was transferred to the see of Janopolis, and made coadjutor of New Orleans, retaining also the care of the diocese of Natchitoches as administrator-apostolic, and in December, 1883, on the death of Archbishop Perché, he became apostolic administrator of the diocese of New Orleans, being thus invested with the care of the whole State of Louisiana. Soon afterward he was appointed Archbishop of New Orleans. At the time of his death he was visiting relatives at his birthplace.

Linsly, Jared, an American physician, born in Branford, Conn., Oct. 30, 1803; died in Northford, Conn., July 12, 1887. He was educated at Bacon Academy, Colchester, Conn., and at Yale, being graduated in 1826. In 1827 he removed to New York city, and began the study of medicine in the office of Dr. John C. Cheesman, also entering the College of Physicians and Surgeons, from which he received his degree in 1829. During the next two years he served in the surgical department of the New York Hospital, and throughout the cholera epidemic of 1832 was attached to the Cholera Hospital. He first formed a partnership with Dr. William Miner, and in 1834 with Dr. William Baldwin, which continued till the latter's death in 1841. During his long practice he was seldom absent from New York city, except for occasional visits to his homestead, and during the year 1853, when he and his wife were guests of the late Cornelius Vanderbilt on the noted trip of the steam-yacht "North Star" to England, Russia, and the Mediterranean. He was Mr. Vanderbilt's physician, and attended him till death. Dr. Linsly was a trustee of the College of Physicians and Surgeons, and of the New York Ophthalmic and Aural Institute, physician of the charity committee of the New England Society of the City of New York, and consulting physician of the New York Asylum for Lying-in Women, of the New York Dispensary, and of the Lenox Presbyterian Hospital. From his student days Dr. Linsly took a keen interest in the welfare of Yale College. An uncle, Noah Linsly, who was graduated there in 1791, and died in 1814, made a bequest to the college for its general purposes; this endowment was increased by Dr. Linsly, and is now known as "The Noah and Jared Linsly Fund." The income from the sum is applied, at Dr. Linsly's desire, to the purchase of books for the department of modern languages in the college library.

Lord, Jarvis, an American banker, born in Rallston, Saratoga County, N. Y., Feb. 10, 1816; died in Pittsford, N. Y., July 24, 1887. He received a common-school education, and became a farmer. In 1858 he was elected a member of the Assembly, as a Democrat, when the district went Republican by a majority of several hundreds, and in 1866 was re-elected by a majority of fifteen over a strong opponent, his district then giving Gov. Fenton a majority of 600. He was presented as the Democratic candidate for Speaker in 1867, but was defeated by Edward L. Pitts, Republican. In 1869 he was elected a State Senator and appointed chairman of the finance committee, and he was re-elected in 1871–'73. For many years he was the heaviest contractor for building canals in the interior of the State; but, after Gov. Tilden's attack upon the "canal ring" in 1875, Mr. Lord devoted himself wholly to his stock-farm and the interests of the Bank of Monroe, in Rochester, of which he was president.

Lall, Edward Phelps, an American naval officer, born in Windsor, Vt., Feb. 20. 1836; died in Pensacola, Fla., March 5, 1887. He entered the United States Naval Academy in 1851, was graduated in 1855, commissioned past-midshipman April 15, and master Nov. 4, 1858, and lieutenant in 1860. He was appointed assistant professor of English studies and sword-master at the Naval Academy in 1860, and, after taking part in the engagement with the forts at Hatteras Inlet on board the "Roanoke" in July, 1861, became instructor of gunnery and infantry tactics. From October, 1861, till December, 1863, he was in command of the school-ship "Constitution," and from the latter date till August, 1864, was executive officer of the "Brooklyn." He continued on sea-service till the close of the civil war, was assistant professor of mathematics at the Naval Academy in 1866–'67, assistant professor of Spanish in 1867–'68, professor of drawing in 1868–'69, commandant of the "Girard" in the Darien exploring expedition in 1870–'71, in command of the Nicaragua surveying expedition in 1872–'73, and of the Panama surveying expedition in 1875, and hydrographic inspector, Coast and Geodetic Survey in 1875–'80. He was promoted to lieutenant-commander July 16, 1862, and to commander June 10, 1870.

Manning, Daniel, an American journalist, born in Albany, N. Y., Aug. 16. 1831; died there Dec. 24, 1887. At the age of ten years he found employment in the office of the Albany "Atlas," and, on the subsequent consolidation of that paper with the "Argus," was apprenticed to the printer's trade. He soon became foreman of the composing-room and manager of the mechanical department of the paper, and from this work was transferred to the editorial department as a reporter. Subsequently he was appointed legislative reporter, and under the guidance of William Cassidy (*q. v.*) became thoroughly informed on the minutiæ of State politics. In 1865 he was made associate editor with Mr. Cassidy, and on the death of the latter he obtained a part ownership of the paper. In 1876 he was a member of the Democratic State Committee. By his influence in party councils and the editorial chair, he greatly advanced Gov. Tilden's reform measures, and established such a degree of personal intimacy with Mr. Tilden that the latter addressed to him his noted letter declining to be a candidate for renomination for the presidency before the convention of 1880. In 1881 Mr. Manning was elected chairman of the Democratic State Committee, and served until the close of 1885. In this office he exerted a most potent influence during the gubernatorial canvass of 1882, and the presidential canvass of 1884. When President Cleveland selected his Cabinet, Mr. Manning was called to the Secretaryship of the Treasury, and he held this office till failing health forced him to tender his resignation on Feb. 4, 1887, which, however, was not accepted till the President became convinced that Mr. Manning could no longer stand the strain of office. After a brief visit to England, Mr. Manning appeared so much improved that he was induced to accept the presidency of the Western National bank, of New York city, but the physical gain was temporary, and in December he was taken to Albany that he might die in his own home.

Manning, Thomas Courtlandt, an American lawyer, born in Edentown, N. C., in 1831; died in New York city Oct. 11, 1887. He was graduated at the University of North Carolina, admitted to the bar, and practiced in his native town. In 1855 he removed to Alexandria, La., and when the civil war broke out had built up an extensive practice and established a large plantation between New Orleans and Baton Rouge. He was elected a member of the Secession Convention of 1861 as a States'-rights Democrat, and at the close of the sitting entered the Confederate army as a lieutenant. Shortly afterward he was transferred to the staff of Gov. Moore. with the rank of lieutenant-colonel. and in 1863 was appointed Adjutant-General of the State. In 1864 he became associate judge of the Supreme Court of Louisiana. From the close of the war he devoted himself to his practice, declining a nomination for Governor. till January. 1877, when he was appointed Chief-Justice of the Supreme Court of Louisiana. In November, 1880, he was appointed United States Senator to fill the vacancy caused by the death of Senator Spofford, and on Aug. 31, 1886, was appointed United States Minister to Mexico. He was nominated for the same office Jan. 6, 1887, and confirmed February 22. Judge Manning was a member of the Board of Trustees of the Peabody Education Fund, and died while on a special trip to New York to attend a meeting of the board.

Marcy, Randolph Barnes, an American soldier, born in Greenwich, Mass., April 9, 1812; died in Orange, N. J., Nov. 22, 1887. He was graduated at the United States Military Academy, West Point, in July, 1832, brevetted second lieutenant in the Fifth United States Infantry, promoted to first lieutenant June 22, 1837, captain May 18, 1846, and brevetted brigadier-general for meritorious services in the civil war March 13, 1865. He served on frontier duty during the Black Hawk expedition, and from 1838 till 1845 was on recruiting and frontier service. At the opening of the Mexican War he was a captain in the Fifth United States Infantry, and with it took part in the battles of Palo Alto and Resaca de la Palma. He remained on frontier duty in the Southwest till 1857, took part in the operations against the Seminole Indians in Florida, and, after a brief service as inspector-general of the Department of Utah in 1858, was paymaster of the Northwestern posts from 1859 till 1861. In the latter year he was appointed chief of staff to Gen. McClellan, his son-in-law, holding the office till Nov. 5, 1863, and taking part in the West Virginia, Peninsula, and Maryland campaigns. From the latter part of 1863 till September, 1865, he was on inspection duty in the departments of the Northwest, Missouri, Arkansas, Mississippi, and the Gulf. He was inspector-general of the military division of the Missouri in 1866, and retired at his own request Jan. 2, 1881. Gen. Marcy was the author of "Exploration of the Red River in 1852" (1853); "The Prairie Traveler," a handbook for overland expeditions, prepared under instructions from the War Department (1859); and "Thirty Years of Army Life on the Border" (1866).

Marmaduke, John Sappington, an American soldier, born in Saline County, Mo., March 14, 1833; died in Jefferson City, Mo., Dec. 28, 1887. He studied for two years at Yale, then for a time at Harvard, and was then appointed to a cadetship at West Point, where he was graduated in 1857, and commissioned as a lieutenant in the Seventh United States Infantry, then forming a part of Gen. Albert S. Johnston's force engaged in the operations against the Mormons. In 1860 he resigned his commission, returned to Missouri, and raised a company for the Confederate service. Soon afterward he was given a lieutenant's commission and assigned to Gen. Hardee's staff. In the latter part of 1861 he was appointed colonel of the Third Confederate Infantry, in 1862 was promoted to brigadier-general for his services at Shiloh, and in 1864 to major-general for gallantry at Jenkins's Ferry and in the campaign against Gen. Steele. In October of the latter year he was taken prisoner, and held till August, 1865. After the war he spent a year in Europe, and on his return to Missouri was engaged in various pursuits, including journalism, till 1873, when he was appointed secretary of the Missouri State Board of Agriculture. He was a State railroad commissioner from 1875 till 1884, was an unsuccessful candidate for Governor in 1880, and a successful one in 1884, for the term ending in 1889.

McAllister, Julian, an American soldier, born in New York city in 1824; died on Governor's Island, New York harbor, Jan. 3, 1887. He was graduated at the United States Military Academy, West Point, in 1847; immediately assigned to the Second Artillery, with the rank of second lieutenant, and served with his company throughout the Mexican War. In 1848 he was transferred to the ordnance department, and served two years as assistant ordnance officer at Watervliet Arsenal, N. Y., and the same length of time at the St. Louis arsenal, Mo., being promoted to the rank of first lieutenant of ordnance in 1853. He subsequently served at Fort Monroe Arsenal and at the Richmond, Va., foundry, and was assistant ordnance officer at Benicia Arsenal, Cal., 1858-'60, and in command 1861-'64, receiving his commission as captain on July 1, 1861. During the civil war he served as chief of ordnance. In 1865 he received the brevets of major and lieutenant-colonel for faithful and meritorious duty in his department, and at the same time that of colonel for zeal, ability, and faithfulness as senior ordnance officer in the Department of the Pacific. He received the full rank of major in 1866, lieutenant-colonel in 1874, and colonel in 1881. At the time of his death the Governor's Island arsenal and the Sandy Hook proving-grounds for ordnance were in his charge, and he was the senior officer of his rank in the ordnance corps.

Meyrowitz, Alexander, an American educator, born in Wilna, Poland, Aug. 1, 1816; died in New York city Aug. 18, 1887. He was educated for the office of rabbi, and began preaching when only fourteen years old. A few years later, becoming dissatisfied with Judaism, he went to Leipsic, put himself under the instruction of Franz Delitsch, and accepted the tenets of Christianity. He completed his studies under Prof. Fleischer, the Orientalist, and then went to London, where he was graduated at Brasenose College, with the degree of A. B. Next he attended the lectures of Fathers Perona and Modena in Rome, Italy, and, returning to England, was appointed tutor in Bristol College in 1843. From 1844 till 1869 he was engaged in teaching in Edinburgh, St. Petersburg, and several German cities, removing to the United States in October of the latter year. Soon after his arrival in New York city he was appointed Professor of Hebrew Language and Semitic Literature in the University of New York, and in 1876 to a similar chair in the State University of Missouri.

Mills, Zophar, fireman, born in New York city Sept. 23, 1807; died there Feb. 28, 1887. He began his career as a fireman in 1820 by running with Eagle Company No. 13, and in 1835 was made its foreman. In 1838 he became assistant engineer of the entire city fire department, and in 1854 he was active in the organizing of Exempt Engine Company, of which he was elected foreman, and continued so until the volunteer fire department was abolished. Meanwhile Mr. Mills established himself as a commission merchant of naval stores in 1838, and followed that business until his retirement in 1884. He had a high reputation as a fireman, and many testimonials to that effect had been presented to him. For nearly twenty-five years he was vice-president of the Lorillard Fire Insurance Company, and was president of the Exempt Firemen's Association until his death. The fire-boat of the present department was named in his honor.

Miles, Pierre Solider, an American musician, born in Nice, France, Nov. 10, 1787; died in Philadelphia, Pa., March 16, 1887. He served in the French army from July 4, 1806, till Dec. 12, 1817, rising from the ranks to the grade of lieutenant, and being appointed a chevalier of the Legion of Honor for bravery in action. Two years after his retirement from the army he came to the United States, and within a few months was sent by Joseph Bonaparte on a secret mission through Mexico. While so employed he was arrested for criticising a painting of Christ, and put into prison. On his release he continued his mission, extending it into several of the South American states. Returning to the United States he spent several years in teaching languages and music, finally settling in Philadelphia in 1859, where he was employed for many years as a violin-player in the Walnut and Arch Street theatres. He was the father of sixteen children by two wives.

Mitchell, Alexander, an American banker, born in the parish of Ellow, Aberdeenshire, Scotland, Oct. 17, 1817; died in New York city April 19, 1887. He was educated in the parish schools, and early in life became a clerk in a local banking-house. He attracted the attention of George Smith, also of Aberdeenshire, who practically owned the Wisconsin Marine and Fire Insurance Company, with headquarters in Milwaukee, and was induced to remove to the United States and take charge of the business as secretary. In May, 1839, he took up his residence in Milwaukee, and entered upon his notable career as a financier, the company being in all essentials a banking institution. From the capital he brought with him he slowly accumulated wealth, and engaged in different enterprises, till he became the owner of the business in which he had begun as secretary, and had identified himself with almost every improvement of note in Milwaukee, and Wisconsin as well. His attention had been strongly engaged in railroad matters, and in 1848 he became a director in the Milwaukee and Waukesha road. From this time he rapidly acquired an interest in the different roads in the State. He was elected president of the Milwaukee and St. Paul road in 1864, consolidated the Milwaukee and La Crosse, Milwaukee and Prairie du Chien, and Milwaukee and Watertown roads with it, forming the Chicago, Milwaukee, and St. Paul Railroad, and was president of the consolidated road till death. In 1869 he was elected president of the Chicago and Northwestern road, but resigned a year later to give all his time to the other road. Mr. Mitchell was elected to Congress as a Democrat in 1870, re-elected in 1872, and de-

clined a renomination in 1874; declining also the nomination of the Democratic State Convention for Governor in 1879. He was considered the wealthiest man in the Northwest, and was exceedingly liberal in his benefactions and charities. Among his bequests the following have been made public: Protestant Orphan Asylum, $10,000; Catholic Orphan Asylum, $5,000; Milwaukee Hospital, $10,000; St. Mary's Catholic Hospital, $5,000; Young Men's Christian Association, $10,000; Episcopal Theological Seminary, in Nashotah, Wis., $5,000; and Racine College, $5,000.

Moody, Granville, an American clergyman, born in Portland, Me., Jan. 2, 1812; died in Mount Vernon, Iowa, June 4, 1887. He was educated in his father's school in Baltimore, Md., received into the Methodist Episcopal Church in 1830, licensed to preach March 4, 1832, ordained deacon by Bishop Andrew in 1835, and elder by Bishop Roberts in 1837. He was an active preacher of the Gospel, chiefly in Ohio, for half a century, held several presiding elderships, and took part in the great forensic contests that marked the anti-slavery struggle in the General Conference of the Methodist Church. On Dec. 10, 1861, he was appointed colonel of the Seventy-fourth Regiment of Ohio Volunteers, serving with it till May 16, 1863. He was painfully wounded four times, and a horse was killed under him in the battle of Stone River. These injuries compelled his resignation, but he was brevetted a brigadier-general for meritorious services on March 13, 1865. He was a warm personal friend of President Lincoln, and to him the latter gave his pledge to issue the Emancipation Proclamation some days before it was acted upon by the Cabinet. In 1882 he removed to Mount Vernon, Iowa, settling upon a farm, but passing most of his time in literary work. On May 29, 1887, while on his way to deliver the memorial sermon in Jefferson, for George H. Thomas Post, G. A. R., he was thrown from his carriage, sustaining injuries from which he died.

Morley, Thomas, an American pilot, born in Fermoy, Ireland, in Sept., 1826; died in Brooklyn, N. Y., July 12, 1887. He came to the United States when a boy, and served throughout the Mexican War, enlisting in the artillery, and winning a handsome record by his bravery. At the close of that war he removed to New York city and became a pilot, being first attached to the "Moses H. Grinnell." At the opening of the civil war he enlisted in the Fourth New York Artillery, with which he served during the war, attaining the rank of captain, and receiving several wounds. During the past twenty years he had been attached to the pilot-boat "Hope," of which he was part owner. Mr. Morley was regarded in maritime circles as one of the most efficient of Sandy Hook pilots.

Merrill, Anson P., an American legislator, born in Belgrade, Me., June 10, 1803; died in Augusta, Me., July 4, 1887. Both he and his brother, the late Lot M. Morrill, were given a common-school education, and Anson then devoted himself to mercantile pursuits in Belgrade. In 1838 he was elected to the State Legislature as a Democrat. His next office was that of sheriff of Somerset County, to which he was appointed in 1839, holding it one year. In 1850 he was made land agent. The Democratic Convention in 1853 had a formidable struggle over the subject of prohibition, and the opponents of prohibitory legislation prevailed. Believing that the leaders of his party were about making an alliance with the liquor-dealers at home and the slaveholders at the South, Mr. Morrill withdrew from the party and became the candidate on the Prohibition and Free-soil tickets for Governor, but failed of election. In the following year he was again a candidate; there was no choice by the people, and he was chosen by the Legislature. He served the term of 1855 as the first Republican Governor of Maine, his supporters having adopted the party name that year, and was a candidate for re-election, but was defeated in the Legislature (there being no choice by the people) by a combination of the Whig and Democratic members. In 1860 he was elected a Representative in Congress, but served only one term, declining a re-election through aversion to congressional labor. In his stead, the Republicans elected James G. Blaine. On his retirement from Congress, Gov. Morrill became interested in railroad work. He removed to Augusta in 1876, making that city his home until death. In 1881 he was elected a member of the State Legislature, and with that term closed his public career, though he maintained his interest in temperance, prohibition, and the success of the Republican party.

Morrison, Pitcairn, an American soldier, born in New York city in 1795; died in Baltimore, Md., Oct. 5, 1887. He was appointed a second lieutenant in the artillery corps of the regular army in 1820, transferred to the Fourth Regiment of Artillery June 1, 1821, promoted to first lieutenant in 1826, and captain in 1836. He was actively engaged through the Mexican War, winning the brevet of major by his gallantry in the battles of Palo Alto and Resaca de la Palma, May 8, 9, 1846, and being promoted to the full rank of major and assigned to the Eighth United States Infantry in 1847. In 1853 he became lieutenant-colonel of the Seventh Infantry, in June, 1861, colonel of the Eighth, and on Oct. 20, 1863, was retired with the brevet rank of brigadier-general for long and faithful services.

Morrison, Robert Francis, an American lawyer, born in Illinois in 1826; died in San Francisco, Cal., March 2, 1887. He was educated in the public schools of his native State. When the Mexican War broke out he joined the regiment commanded by his brother, Col. Don Morrison, of St. Louis, Mo., as a non-commissioned officer, distinguishing himself at the battle of Buena Vista. In 1852 he

went to California, studied law, and was admitted to the bar. After practicing for several years in Sacramento he removed to San Francisco, where he became associated with James T. Boyd. Again returning to Sacramento, ho was elected and served one term as district attorney. Subsequently, he again removed to San Francisco, where he formed a partnership with Judge Delos Lake. When the latter was appointed United States Attorney Mr. Morrison accepted the office of assistant. In 1869 he was elected district judge of the Fourth District of the State, embracing a portion of the city of San Francisco, and after serving a term of six years was re-elected in 1875. In 1879 he was elected Chief-Justice of the Supreme Court of California, when he resigned his district appointment.

Morse, Charles Walker, an American civil engineer, born in New Haven, Conn., March 17, 1823; died in Saybrook, Conn., April 16, 1887. He was the eldest son of Prof. Samuel Finley Breese Morse, received a collegiate education, and in early life assisted his father in his numerous experiments with the electric telegraph. His father was the first to introduce photography into the United States, and he was the first to sit for a picture, the operation requiring an exposure of thirty minutes in a glare of sunlight. He crossed the plains in 1857, and spent several years on the frontier as a civil engineer, laying out a large part of Georgetown, Central City, and other Colorado settlements. While pursuing this profession he rendered valuable service to the Federal Government in the protection of its property on the Upper Minnesota river during the trouble with the Sioux Indians at the Spirit Lake massacre. Mr. Morse was attached to the United States Navy during the civil war, and during Commodore Paulding's administration at the Brooklyn Navy-yard was his private secretary. In 1888 the decoration of the "Bust of the Liberator" was conferred upon him by the Venezuelan Government in appreciation of his services in furthering the advance of the Morse system of telegraphy in that country. During the last few years of his life he was connected with the Western Union Telegraph Company, in New York.

Mullany, James Robert Madison, an American naval officer, born in New York city Oct. 26, 1818; died in Bryn Mawr, Pa., Sept. 17, 1887. He entered the United States Navy as a midshipman Jan. 7, 1832, and was promoted to passed midshipman in June, 1838, lieutenant in February, 1844, commander in October, 1861, captain in July, 1866, commodore in August, 1870, and rear-admiral in June, 1874. He served throughout the Mexican War, distinguishing himself in the capture of Tabasco. During the civil war he commanded the sailing-ship "Supply" and the steamers "Wyandotte," "Oneida," and "Bienville." While in command of the "Bienville," off Charleston, S. C., in 1862, he captured eleven heavily-laden blockade-runners, all under English colors, and with the "Oneida" played a gallant part in the naval battle in Mobile Bay on Aug. 5, 1864, at the cost of his left arm. As rear-admiral he commanded the North Atlantic station from June, 1874, till February, 1876, and during that period co-operated with Gens. Emory and Sheridan at New Orleans, and protected American interests on the Isthmus when they were menaced by the revolution in Panama. He was governor of the naval asylum and station at Philadelphia, Pa., from March 1, 1876, till Oct. 26, 1879, when he was retired.

Newberry, John Stoughton, an American lawyer, born in Waterville, Oneida County, N. Y., Nov. 18, 1826; died in Detroit, Mich., Jan. 2, 1887. He was a descendant of Thomas Newberry, who, early in the seventeenth century, emigrated from England and settled at Dorchester, Mass. In his early boyhood he removed with his parents to Detroit, and thence to Romeo, Mich., where he prepared for college and was graduated at Michigan University in 1845, being valedictorian. For two years afterward he followed the profession of civil engineer, assisting in the laying out and construction of the Michigan Central Railroad west of Kalamazoo. He subsequently studied law, and entered upon the practice of this profession in 1853 in Detroit. That city being one of the most important of the ports of the Great Lakes, he soon found himself engaged in a large practice in admiralty and maritime law in the United States courts, and eventually he made a specialty of admiralty practice. He compiled "Reports of Admiralty Cases in the Several District Courts of the United States" (1859), which was the first compilation of admiralty cases pertaining to the commerce of the inland lakes. In 1864 Mr. Newberry, in company with James McMillan, of Detroit, who was subsequently associated with him in all business enterprises, organized the Michigan Car Company, which began the manufacture of freight-cars. They gradually enlarged their business, until they became the most extensive car-builders in the country, controlling also large car-manufactories in St. Louis, Mo., and London, Ont. They also embarked in various other manufacturing, mining, railroad, and steamboat enterprises, Mr. Newberry holding the office of president, vice-president, or director in more than a score of incorporated companies, which gave employment to 5,000 men, and materially aided in the development of various portions of the State of Michigan. Among the more important of these were the Detroit, Mackinaw, and Marquette Railroad Company (now the Duluth, South Shore, and Atlantic Railroad Company), the Detroit, Bay City, and Alpena Railroad Company, the Detroit and Cleveland Steam Navigation Company, and the Detroit Transportation Company. His attention to these vast business interests led Mr. Newberry gradually out of the practice of law, and resulted in his accu-

mulating a vast fortune, a portion of which he has given for various charitable and philanthropic purposes. One of the last public acts of his life was to join with his partner Mr. McMillan in each giving $100,000 for the building of a large hospital in Detroit. His bequests to charitable institutions, missionary societies, and for religious and philanthropic purposes amount to about $600,000 more. In politics he was a Republican. He was appointed by President Lincoln Provost-Marshal for Michigan in 1862, and served for two years, during which time he had charge of two drafts and the forwarding of conscripts and enlisted soldiers to the field. In 1878 he received the Republican nomination for Congress in the First District of Michigan, and was elected by a plurality of 1,800 over Gen. A. S. Williams, Democrat, who had already served two terms. After serving his term of two years in Congress he refused a renomination in order to give his attention to his business enterprises. He was an active member of the Presbyterian Church, and during all his life contributed largely toward the maintenance of church, missionary, and charitable enterprises.

Nicholson, James William Augustus, an American naval officer, born in Dedham, Mass., March 10, 1821; died in New York city, Oct. 28, 1887. He entered the United States Navy from New York as midshipman, Feb. 10, 1838, was promoted to passed-midshipman in 1844, lieutenant in 1852, commander in 1862, captain in 1866, commodore in 1873, and rear-admiral in 1881, and retired in 1883. He served on the "Vandalia" in the Japanese expedition of Com. Perry in 1853-'55, was engaged in suppressing the slave-trade on the coast of Africa in 1857-'60, volunteered to accompany the "Pocahontas" for the relief of Fort Sumter, and arrived off Charleston within a few moments of the surrender, April 13, 1861. He took part in the actions with the Confederate fleet, November 5, 6. and the battle of Port Royal. Nov. 7, 1861, the capture of Jacksonville, Fernandina, and St. Augustine, Fla., the engagement with Confederate infantry in St. John's river, and that with the flotilla in Savannah river in February, 1862, and rendered highly meritorious service in the battle of Mobile Bay and the capture of the Confederate ram "Tennessee," Aug. 5. 1864. He was commandant of the Brooklyn Navy-yard in 1876-'80. In October, 1881, he was placed in command of the European station, and in June, 1882, arrived at Alexandria, Egypt. Receiving an official notification from Admiral Seymour, commanding the British naval forces, on July 10, that hostilities might occur within twenty-four hours, he gathered the archives of the United States Consulate in that city, received all American citizens who desired protection, and moved his squadron to the lower harbor, pending the expected attack upon the city. After the cessation of the bombardment he re-established the consulate, and, landing

100 marines, rendered timely service in extinguishing the fires and burying the dead lying about the streets.

Olney, Edward, an American mathematician, born in Morean, Saratoga County, N. Y., July 24, 1827; died in Ann Arbor, Mich., Jan. 16, 1887. His father removed to Oakland County, Mich., in 1833, but finally settled in Weston, Wood County, Ohio. Although bred to a farm-life, and having merely the educational advantages of a log school-house, the son developed an early passion for mathematics and natural history. The only blackboards used in his schooling were the plow-beam and the cylinder of a fanning-mill, yet with these he mastered Day's "Algebra" in six weeks. When nineteen years old he began teaching in the district school, devoting his evenings to the study of Latin. At twenty-one he engaged to teach in a school in Perryville, the county-seat, and a year later became principal of the newly established union graded school. As he had to teach Latin as well as the higher English branches, the greatest diligence in private studies accompanied his work in the school-room. He remained with this school as principal and superintendent over five years. In the autumn of 1858 he was called to the professorship of Mathematics in Kalamazoo College, where he taught till September, 1863, when he entered upon similar duty in the academic department of the University of Michigan, and remained until death. He was the author of a complete series of mathematical text-books in general use, and one of the best-known educators in the West.

Palmer, Alonzo B., an American physician, born in Richfield, Otsego County, N. Y., Oct. 4, 1815; died in Ann Arbor, Mich., Dec. 23, 1887. He was educated in medicine in New York city and Philadelphia, and became connected with the medical department of the University of Michigan in 1852, when he was appointed Professor of Anatomy. In 1854 he was appointed Professor of Materia Medica, and in 1860 Professor of Pathology and the Practice of Medicine, holding the latter chair continuously till his death. He was elected vice-president of the American Medical Association in 1860, and president of the United States Medical Society in 1872. He received the degree of A. M. from the University of Nashville in 1855, and that of LL. D. from the University of Michigan in 1873.

Palmer, George Washington, an American lawyer, born in Ripley, Chautauqua County, N. Y., in 1835; died in New York city, Jan. 2, 1887. He was graduated at the Albany, N. Y., Law-School in 1857, and had just established himself in practice when the civil war broke out. Hastening to Washington, he volunteered his services, received a commission, and was employed in the field, at the national capital, and in the West till the close of the war, retiring from the army with the rank of brigadier-general. From 1865 till 1868 he was Commis-

sioner-General of Ordnance of New York State. He was appointed Appraiser of the Port of New York by President Grant, and Deputy-Collector, in charge of the seventh or law division of the Custom-House, in March, 1879, holding the latter office till after the appointment of Collector Hedden by President Cleveland. He then resumed the practice of law in New York city.

Palmer, Ray, an American clergyman, born in Little Compton, R. I., Nov. 12, 1808; died in Newark, N. J., March 29, 1887. He began life as a clerk in Boston, Mass., at the age of thirteen, but attended school at the same time. Two years later he went to Phillips Academy, Andover, to prepare for college, and in 1826 entered Yale College, where he was graduated in 1830. His first occupation after leaving college was that of teaching in a fashionable private school on Fulton Street, New York city. In the latter part of 1831 he returned to New Haven, and was associated with Prof. E. A. Andrews in founding the New Haven Young Ladies' Institute. Ever since he left Yale he had looked longingly toward pastoral work, and been preparing for it by theological study. His desire was fulfilled in 1832, when he was licensed to preach by the New Haven West Association of Congregational Ministers. Shortly afterward he accepted a call to the Central Congregational Church of Bath, Me., and was ordained there in 1835. Fifteen years of earnest pastoral labor followed, and he then made a tour of England, Scotland, and the Continent. On his return he accepted a call from the First Congregational Church of Albany, N. Y., and, removing to that city in 1850, he remained there fifteen years and a half. At the end of this period he was urged by his ministerial brethren to accept the office of Secretary of the Congregational Union, and he performed its responsible duties for twelve years, during which time six hundred Congregational churches were built by the aid of the association. While thus actively engaged as a pastor and in official work he produced numerous works, besides pamphlets and contributions to religious periodicals. Among his books are: "Spiritual Improvement; or, Aid to Growth in Grace" (1839); "Closet Hours" (1851); "Remember Me" (1855); "Hints on the Formation of Religious Opinions" (1860); "Hymns and Sacred Pieces" (1865); "Hymns of My Holy Hours" (1866); "Home; or, The Unlost Paradise" (1868); "Earnest Words on True Success in Life" (1873); "Complete Poetical Works" (1876); and "Voices of Hope and Gladness" (1880). While teaching in New York city he composed a poem of four stanzas, which has been translated into more than twenty languages and sung the world over, beginning with, "My faith looks up to Thee, Thou Lamb of Calvary." Next to this, his chief productions in hymnology were: "Fount of Everlasting Love" (1832); "Thou who roll'st the Year around" (1832); "Away from Earth my Spirit turns" (1833);

"Stealing from the World away" (1834); "Before Thy Throne, with Tearful Eyes" (1834); "Wake thee, O Zion, thy Mourning is ended" (1834); "When downward to the Darksome Tomb" (1842); "And is there, Lord, a Rest?" (1843); "O, sweetly breathe the Lyres above" (1843); "Eternal Father, Thou hast said" (1860); "Jesus, Lamb of God, for me" (1863); "Take me, O my Father, take me" (1864); "Wouldst thou Eternal Life obtain" (1864); "Thou, Saviour, from Thy Throne on high" (1864); "Lord, Thou on Earth didst love Thine own" (1864): and "Lord, Thou wilt bring the Joyful Day" (1864). These are but a portion of Dr. Palmer's hymns and poems, and may be found in most evangelical hymn-books. About two years ago he was stricken with paralysis, and till the second and fatal stroke lived in retirement, preserving his cordial manners and charming simplicity to the last.

Perkins, William, an American merchant, born in Boston, Mass., Oct. 4, 1804; died there, June 13, 1887. He first came into notice about fifty years ago as a partner of Robert G. Shaw, then one of the most widely known merchants as well as one of the wealthiest citizens of Boston. The firm was dissolved about 1842 by the retirement of Mr. Perkins, who established a business of his own, and for years thereafter his name was associated with the commercial interests of Boston, particularly with the India and China trade. He was also the owner and builder of some of the finest ships sailing from that port. His large experience caused him to be elected president of the China Insurance Company, which office he held until his death. With one exception, he was the only survivor of the original occupants of Commercial Wharf when it was first opened for business. Mr. Perkins was a member and, at times, an officer of the Massachusetts Humane Society, and had been treasurer of, and a liberal contributor to, several of the relief funds for the benefit of sufferers by conflagrations in Boston and distant cities having commercial interests with it. He never held public office.

Perry, William, an American physician, born in Norton, Mass., in 1788; died in Exeter, N. H., Jan 11, 1887. He was graduated at Harvard in 1811, and became one of the most successful and skillful physicians of his day in New Hampshire, being particularly noted for his familiarity with the phenomena of insanity. With a lady friend he rode from Albany to Kingston on the celebrated steamboat "Clermont," on Aug. 10, 1807, that being Robert Fulton's first venture in steam navigation. At the time of his death he was the oldest person in Exeter, the oldest graduate of Harvard, and the second survivor of the class of 1811.

Pettingell, John Hancock, an American clergyman, born in Manchester, Vt., May 11, 1815; died in New Haven, Conn., Feb. 27, 1887. He was graduated at Yale in 1837, and for six years was a teacher in the Institution for the Deaf and Dumb, New York city, pursuing, in the mean time, a course in Union Theological Seminary. He was ordained, Dec. 6, 1848, as pastor of the Congregational Church in South Dennis, Mass., and remained there four years. From April, 1849, till October, 1852, he was settled over the Congregational Church in Essex, Conn., and from 1853 till 1860 served as district-secretary of the American Board of Commissioners for Foreign Missions, with residence in Albany, N. Y. After filling pastorates in Saxonville, Mass., and Westbrook, Conn., he went to Antwerp in 1866, as chaplain under the Seaman's Friend Society, returning to the United States in 1872, and residing alternately in New York city and Philadelphia, passing the remainder of his life in the preparation of volumes for the press, in advocacy of the doctrine of conditional immortality. Among his works, many of which have been translated into German, Italian, and other European languages, are "Homiletical Index," "Theological Trilemma," "Platonism es. Christianity," "Bible Terminology," "The Life Everlasting," "The Unspeakable Gift," and "Views and Reviews in Eschatology."

Pierce, Thomas Prescott, an American soldier, born in Chelsea, Mass., Aug. 30, 1820; died in Nashua, N. H., Oct. 14, 1887. He was an ornamental painter, employed in Manchester, N. H., 1840-'46, then enlisted, and was appointed second lieutenant in the Ninth Regiment of United States Infantry. He was brevetted first lieutenant Aug. 29, 1847, for gallant and meritorious conduct in the battles of Contreras and Churubusco, Mexico, under Gen. Franklin Pierce. Returning to the State, he was aide-de-camp on Gov. Dinsmore's staff, with the rank of colonel. He resumed his previous vocation, but in 1852 Gen. Pierce procured his appointment as post-master of Manchester, which office he filled eight years. On the breaking out of the civil war he was selected colonel of the Second New Hampshire Regiment of three-months' troops. He declined the appointment when the term of enlistments was extended to three years, and organized the Twelfth New Hampshire Regiment as temporary commander. In 1866 he removed to Nashua, and became a director and official in the Card and Glazed Paper Company, a director of the Second National and of the Mechanics' Savings banks. He was a member of the State Senate in 1875-'76, and sheriff of Hillsborough County.

Poland, Luke P., an American lawyer, born in Westford, Chittenden County, Vt., Nov. 1, 1815; died in Waterville, Vt., July 2, 1887. He received a common-school and academic education, and was admitted to the bar in 1836. In 1839-'40 he was register of probate for Lamoille County, in 1843 a member of the State Constitutional Convention, and in 1844-'45 prosecuting attorney for the county. Three years later he was elected by the Legislature one of the judges of the Supreme Court of Vermont, an office he continued to hold by annual elections till November, 1865, when he was appointed United States Senator to fill the vacancy caused by the death of Jacob Collamer, whose term would have expired in 1867. Just before this appointment he had been re-elected to the Supreme Court, of which he was chief-justice, by virtue of promotion in 1860. During his brief term as United States Senator he served on the committees on judiciary, patents, and the Patent-Office. He was an uncompromising Republican, and while in the Senate was a delegate to the Loyalists' Convention in Philadelphia. Before his term as Senator expired, he was elected a Representative in Congress, stepping from the higher to the lower House on March 4, 1867. He was re-elected in 1868, 1870, 1872, and 1882. Judge Poland was chairman of the committee on revision of the laws of the United States, had charge of the revision of the United States statutes, and was chairman of the select committee on Crédit Mobilier. During the interval of his service in Congress he accepted a term in the State Legislature.

Poore, Ben: Perley, an American journalist, born in Newburyport, Mass., Nov. 2, 1820; died in Washington, D. C., May 29, 1887. His parents took him to the national capital when he was seven years old, and four years later he accompanied them to Europe. On their return he was placed in a military school to prepare for admission to the United States Military Academy, but, disliking the choice, ran away and apprenticed himself to a printer in Worcester, Mass. After he had served his time, his father purchased the "Southern Whig" newspaper in Atlanta, Ga., and sent him South to edit and manage it. He remained there two years, when, on returning to Washington, he was appointed an *attaché* of the American legation in Belgium. While abroad he visited nearly every portion of Europe, the Holy Land, and Lower Egypt, and wrote many letters to the Boston "Atlas" about Europe and the East. He also made a valuable collection of historical manuscripts for the State of Massachusetts from the French archives. In 1854 he became Washington correspondent of several newspapers, notably the Boston "Journal," to which he contributed periodical letters, under the signature of "Perley," on the advance news, social happenings, and political and diplomatic gossip of the day till 1884. He served in the national army during the civil war. Among his published works are "Rise and Fall of Louis Philippe" (1848); "Life of General Taylor" (1848); "Early Life of Napoleon" (1851); "The Political Register and Congressional Directory" (1878); and "Perley's Reminiscences of Sixty Years in the National Metropolis" (1886). He edited the volumes of the "Conspiracy Trials" in 1865, and, for many years, as clerk of printing records, compiled the "Congressional Directory" for each session of Congress. His summer home, Indian Hill Farm, near Newburyport,

was a veritable museum of art and antiquity, and a favorite resort of historians.

Potter, Horatio, an American clergyman, born in Beekman (now La Grange), Dutchess County, N. Y., Feb. 9, 1802; d. in New York city, Jan. 2, 1887. He was the youngest of ten children of Joseph and Ann (Knight) Potter, the ninth being Alonzo, who became bishop

of the Protestant Episcopal diocese of Pennsylvania. Horatio received an academic education in Poughkeepsie, N. Y., and was graduated at Union College in 1826. He was made a deacon July 15, 1827, and priest Dec. 14, 1828. From the date of his ordination till 1833 he was Professor of Mathematics and Natural Philosophy in Washington (now Trinity) College, Hartford, Conn., and in 1833 he declined the presidency of the college, and became rector of St. Peter's Church, Albany, N. Y., where he remained till 1854. On the death of Rev. Dr. Jonathan Wainwright, provisional bishop of the diocese of New York, in the latter year, Dr. Potter was chosen to succeed him, and was consecrated in Trinity Church, New York city, on Nov. 22, 1854, by Bishops T. C. Brownell, of Connecticut; J. H. Hopkins, of Vermont; G. W. Doane, of New Jersey; S. A. McCoskry, of Michigan; W. R. Whittingham, of Maryland; H. W. Lee, of Iowa; and F. Fulford, of Montreal, Canada. Although consecrated as "provisional" bishop, he was invested with all the functions of the episcopate, the canon providing for the election of a "provisional bishop" having been passed in 1850 to obviate the evil of the diocese being virtually without a bishop, Bishop Benjamin T. Onderdonk being still alive but under suspension from the episcopal office since 1844. Bishop Onderdonk died early in 1861, and Dr. Potter then became bishop of the diocese in name as he had been in fact. It was a curious coincidence that the Potter brothers—Alonzo, in Pennsylvania, and Horatio, in New

York — succeeded the Onderdonk brothers, after each of the latter had been suspended from their sacred offices. In 1867 and again in 1877, Bishop Potter attended the Lambeth Palace conferences in England, and during his episcopate he welcomed several English bishops and clergymen to the diocesan conventions of New York. On Nov. 29, 1879, a notable reception was held at the Academy of Music, New York city, for the purpose of presenting to Bishop Potter a testimonial commemorative of the completion of twenty-five years of his episcopate. The testimonial took the form of a casket modeled after the ancient Ark of the Covenant, and was composed of gold, silver, and steel, exquisitely chased and inlaid. The following inscription appeared on the base: "To the Right Reverend Horatio Potter, D. D., LL. D., D. O. L., Bishop of New York, from his diocese, with love and gratitude for twenty-five years of faithful service." In 1888 the cares of his office bore so heavily upon his failing strength that he felt constrained to ask relief, and the annual convention elected his choice, his nephew Rev. Dr. Henry C. Potter, as assistant bishop, with practically full episcopal authority. Bishop Potter received the degree of D. D. from Trinity College, Hartford, Conn., in 1838; that of LL. D. from Hobart College, Geneva, N. Y., in 1856; and that of D. O. L. from the University of Oxford, England, in 1860. During his episcopate he saw the church in New York multiply from two dioceses to five, those of Long Island, Albany, and Central New York being erected after his consecration. From 1854 till 1881 he performed 78,092 confirmations and over 150,000 baptisms (of which number 18,358 were adults); consecrated 117 churches and laid more than 100 corner-stones; ordered 450 deacons, ordained 864 priests, and instituted 47 rectors; received 614 clergymen into the diocese and transferred 688 to other stations. His published writings, which are very numerous, consist chiefly of sermons, pastoral letters, and addresses on special occasions.

Potter, Robert B., an American soldier, born in Boston, Mass., in 1829; died in Newport, R. I., Feb. 19, 1887. He was a son of the Right Rev. Alonzo Potter, bishop of the Protestant Episcopal diocese of Pennsylvania, and brother of the Right Rev. Henry C. Potter, the present bishop of the diocese of New York. He was graduated at Union College, studied law, and established himself in chamber practice. On the organization of the Fifty-first Regiment of New York Volunteers he was commissioned its lieutenant-colonel, and was shortly afterward attached to Gen. Burnside's army, his regiment being brigaded under Gen. Reno. At Roanoke Island, he led three companies to the assault of the batteries, and was the first to enter the Confederate works. At New Berne he stormed the intrenchments on the left of the lines, receiving a bullet in the groin. His regiment next served under Gen. McClellan,

and soon afterward under Gen. Pope in the second Bull Run campaign, and under his command broke the enemy's line that was advancing on Pope's retreating army. At South Mountain, and again at Antietam, Col. Potter displayed high soldierly instincts. Seizing the flag of his regiment, he headed a dash over the bridge, secured a desired position, and, as Gen. McClellan declared, saved the day. He was again wounded in this action. After that campaign the regiment was detailed to Gen. Burnside's army, Col. Potter being given an independent command by order of Gen. Grant. He took part in the siege of Knoxville, and with his division checked the advance of Longstreet, who was hastening to the relief of the besieged. In the Wilderness campaign he was often under fire, and in the assault after the explosion of the mine at Petersburg was wounded a third time and severely. He had matured plans for destroying the bridge over Appomattox river, with a view of preventing a retreat of the Confederates, and had just mounted his horse in front of Fort Sedgwick to lead his division, when he was struck by a ball. In his "Memoirs," alluding to this assault, Gen. Grant says: "In fact, Potter and Wilson were the only division commanders Burnside had who were equal to the occasion." After the war he was assigned to the command of the Connecticut and Rhode Island Division of the Military Department of the East, with headquarters in Newport. In 1865 he was commissioned a major-general of volunteers, and in the following year appointed colonel of the Forty-first United States Infantry (colored), but never assumed the command.

Powell, Thomas, an American journalist, born in London, England, in 1809; died in Newark, N. J., Jan. 14, 1887. Early in life he studied law, but soon abandoned the idea of becoming a barrister, and allowed his pen and fancies free sway. He was equally happy in prose and verse, and, besides editing the "Lantern" and managing the "Figaro," in London, published twenty-seven volumes, including "Lives of English Authors" and "Lives of American Authors." In 1849 he came to the United States with Frank Leslie, and made a business connection with him. He was the first editor of "Frank Leslie's Illustrated Newspaper," and a frequent contributor to all Mr. Leslie's publications. For a year before his death he had devoted himself to the preparation of a series of sketches of the large number of literary and dramatic persons he had known intimately, and several of these, "Leaves from My Life," appeared in "Frank Leslie's Sunday Magazine."

Pratt, Daniel, an American adventurer, born in Chelsea, Mass., in 1809; died in Boston, Mass., June 20, 1887. He was apprenticed to the carpenter's trade, and followed it for some years, but disappeared suddenly and was not seen at home again for ten or twelve years. When he returned, his mind was unbalanced, and from that time he led a wandering life, be-

ing known all over the country as "General
Pratt, the Great American Traveler." For
nearly fifty years he thus went from place to
place, often making long journeys and subsisting on what was given him in charity as a return for the amusement that his eccentricities
afforded. He made regular tours of the colleges, especially of those in New England, and
his arrival was always the signal for uproarious
merriment on the part of the students. He
was usually attired in semi-military garb, and
wore enormous shoes filled in with straw,
while his breast displayed a curious array of
burlesque decorations. His lectures, which
usually treated of some gigantic invention he
had just perfected, were an interminable string
of high-sounding but meaningless sentences.

Pratt, James T., an American politician, born
in Middletown, Conn., in 1805; died in Wethersfield, Conn., April 11, 1887. He was bred
a farmer, and subsequently engaged in the dry-
goods business in Hartford. He served in the
State Legislature in 1850 from Rocky Hill, and
represented the First Senatorial District, which
included Hartford, in 1852. In the autumn of
that year he was elected a member of Congress from the First Connecticut District, and
was an earnest advocate of Franklin Pierce in
the national canvass. In 1859 he was an unsuccessful candidate for Governor against
William Buckingham. He was a delegate to
the Peace Congress in 1861, and a staunch supporter of the Union cause during the civil war,
and served a second term in the State Legislature in 1870-'71, designating himself an "old-
school" Democrat. At one time he was in
command of the State militia, and he obtained
his title of general from that service.

Preston, David, an American banker, born
in Harmony, N. Y., Sept. 20, 1826; died in
Detroit, Mich., April 24, 1887. He was a son
of the Rev. David Preston, a Methodist clergyman, and was educated at Westfield Academy.
In 1848 he removed to Detroit and entered the
employ of a banker, with whom he remained
for four years. He then established himself in
similar business as David Preston & Co., and
soon afterward extended his relations by opening a branch establishment in Chicago. During
the panic of 1873 he was compelled to close
his doors for two days, and, although advised
to make an assignment for the benefit of his
creditors, he refused to do so, and public confidence in him was so great that he was permitted to manage his own affairs. His business increased with great rapidity, and at the
time of his death he was head of the Preston
Bank of Detroit, and was a large stockholder
in the Metropolitan National Bank of Chicago.
He was prominent in the formation of the
United States Christian Commission, organized
during the civil war, and his name stood first
among the directors. Mr. Preston was likewise active in the Methodist Episcopal Church.
Through his influence a large sum of money
was raised as an endowment fund for Albion

College, toward which he gave $60,000, and
he was a trustee of that institution from 1862
until his death. He expended upward of
$200,000 in various charities during his life-
time. In 1876 he was a delegate to the General Conference of the Methodist Church, and
also in 1884 a delegate to the Centenary Conference of Methodism held in Baltimore. He
was president of the Detroit Young Men's
Christian Association in 1869-'70, and was an
active member of the Prohibition party, by
which he was nominated for Governor in 1884.
A collection of his letters, written for various
papers during his travels in Europe in 1881
and 1886, has been privately printed.

Preston, John, an American centenarian, born
in England Dec. 20, 1782; died near Brown-
town, Madison Township, N. J., May 23, 1887.
He came to the United States in 1797 with his
parents, and lived in New York city for many
years, removing thence to Philadelphia, where
he remained till 1837, when he settled on the
farm in New Jersey. He attended to all the
business of the farm when he was over one
hundred years old, and was frequently seen, as
late as three years ago, miles away from home,
on horseback, looking after his affairs with all
the vigor of a man of fifty. Two years before
his death he cut a cord of wood, as an exhibition of his strength. He was a superior horse-
man. In politics he was first a Whig and then
a Republican, and never missed an election
after he became a citizen.

Preston, William, an American lawyer, born
near Louisville, Ky., Oct. 16, 1816; died in
Lexington, Ky., Sept. 21, 1887. He was educated in St. Joseph's College, Kentucky, and at
Yale and Harvard, and was graduated from the
law-school of the latter in 1838. Two years
later he began the practice of his profession in
Louisville, remaining there till the opening of
the Mexican War, when he went to the field as
a lieutenant-colonel of Kentucky Volunteers.
He was elected a member of the Legislature in
1850-'51, presidential elector in 1852, and a
Representative in Congress in 1852 for the unexpired term of Humphrey Marshall, resigned,
and in 1853 for a full term. He was a member
of the Cincinnati Convention of 1856, which
nominated James Buchanan, and was appointed
United States Minister to Spain in 1858. On
his return to Kentucky in 1861, he was appointed colonel on the staff of his brother-in-
law, Gen. Albert Sidney Johnston, in the Confederate service, and took part in the Kentucky
campaign, and in the actions at Bowling
Green, Nashville, Fort Donelson, Corinth,
Shiloh (where Gen. Johnston died in his arms),
and Murfreesboro'. After the war he returned
to his home, was again elected a member of
the Legislature in 1867, and a delegate-at-large
to the convention that nominated Gen. Hancock for the presidency.

Quinn, William, an American clergyman, born
in the County Donegal, Ireland, May 21, 1821;
died in Paris, France, April 15, 1887. He was

educated in the diocese of Derry, and, coming to the United States in 1841, was among the first students at the newly-established college in Fordham, N. Y. After completing the course of study there, he was ordained priest in St. Patrick's Cathedral on Dec. 14, 1845. He was assigned to duty in St. Joseph's Church, as assistant priest to the Rev. Michael McCarron, remained there four years, then after a brief term at Rondout, N. Y., took charge of St. Peter's Church, in Barclay Street, then overwhelmed with debt. He labored in this field during a period of twenty-four years, in the face of grave difficulties; but his enthusiasm, ingenious plans, and rare business abilities enabled him in that time to pay off a debt of $100,000, mainly due to poor people in the parish, and reduce the large mortgage debt to $7,000, besides providing for all the current expenses of his parish. He took part in the First Provincial Council, held by Archbishop Hughes in 1854; in the Second Plenary Council of Baltimore, held by Archbishop Spalding in 1866, as delegate apostolic; and in the Third New York Synod in September, 1868, as one of the procurators of the clergy. On the death of the Very Rev. William Storrs in May, 1873, he was appointed the successor of that clergyman, both as pastor of St. Patrick's Cathedral and as Vicar-General of the Diocese. In 1882 he was made a domestic prelate of the Pope's household, with the title of monsignor. Mgr. Quinn, who was suffering from general debility, had spent the winter of 1886–'87 in Nice, and was on his way home, when he had a fatal relapse in Paris.

Randal, Alanson Merwin, an American soldier, born in Newburg, N. Y., Oct. 23, 1837; died in New Almaden, Cal., May 7, 1887. He was graduated at the United States Military Academy, West Point, in 1860, and made brevet second lieutenant of artillery. In October following he was transferred to the ordnance corps, and, being ordered to California, served for several months at the ordnance depot in Benicia. He was appointed second lieutenant, First United States Artillery, Nov. 22, 1860, and ordered to join his regiment in the East. In May, 1861, he was promoted first lieutenant, and from August 1 till December 20 served in Gen. Frémont's operations in Missouri, organizing artillery, and in command of a battery of the First Missouri Light Artillery. He served through the Peninsula campaign of 1862, participating in the most important battles and skirmishes. He was promoted captain, Oct. 11, 1862, for gallantry in the action at Newmarket, Va., and in December was appointed chief of artillery of Humphreys's Division, Fifth Army Corps, taking part in the battles of Fredericksburg and Chancellorsville, where he commanded the artillery of the Fifth Corps. In 1863 he was in command of a battery of horse-artillery attached to Gen. Gregg's Cavalry Division, and in June of that year was pursuing Stuart's Cavalry

through Maryland and Pennsylvania. At the battles of Gettysburg, a month later, he took an active part, and for gallant and meritorious services in those actions received the brevet rank of major. On March 13, 1865, he received the brevet of lieutenant-colonel, United States Army, for his services at the battle of Five Forks, Va., and of colonel, United States Army, and on June 24 following, that of brigadier-general, United States Volunteers, the last two being in recognition of his services during the war. At the close of the war he returned to his battery, and served with it at various military posts in Texas, Connecticut, Delaware, New York, South Carolina, Florida, Louisiana, Massachusetts, Pennsylvania, and California. He was promoted major, Third United States Artillery, April 19, 1882, and transferred to the First in the following month.

Rapallo, Charles Anthony, an American lawyer, born in New York city Sept. 15, 1823; died there Dec. 28, 1887. He was educated wholly by his father, never going to school nor to college, and at the age of twenty-one was admitted to the bar. The following year he formed a partnership with J. Blunt, and in 1848 another with H. F. Clark, maintaining the latter relation till 1867. In 1870 he was elected an associate judge of the Court of Appeals, as a Democrat, in 1880 was defeated by Charles J. Folger in the election for chief-justice of the court, and in 1884 was re-elected associate judge. This election was remarkable because of the great vote cast. Two vacancies were to be filled, for which Judges Andrews and Rapallo were nominated; they had no party opposition, and the official returns gave 1,089,896 votes for Judge Andrews, and 1,089,414 (or 18 more) for Judge Rapallo.

Rau, Charles, an American archæologist, born in Verviers, Belgium, in 1826; died in Philadelphia, Pa., July 25, 1887. He was educated in Germany, principally at the University in Heidelberg, and came to the United States in 1848, where he taught first in Belleville, Ill., and then in New York city. In 1875 he was invited to become curator in the department of antiquities in the United States National Museum at Washington, D. C., which office he held until his death. He early devoted his attention to archæology, and in 1859 began writing for "Die Natur" on the subject of American antiquities. His contributions to the publications of the Smithsonian Institution first appeared in 1863, and thereafter his articles were published in nearly every annual report of that institution. These papers gained for him a world-wide reputation as an authority, and he ranked high among the pioneers of American archæology. It is said that he was better known in Europe than any other American scholar devoted to that subject. In 1882 he received the degree of Ph. D. from the University of Freiburg, in Baden, for his researches. His published papers exceed fifty in number, among which were a series on the Stone Age in Europe, originally contributed to "Harper's Magazine," which were issued in book-form as "Early Man in Europe" (New York, 1876). Dr. Rau also published "The Archæological Collection of the United States National Museum" (Washington, 1876); "The Palenque Tablet in the United States National Museum" (1879); and his collected "Articles on Anthropological Subjects, 1853–'87" (1882); besides which he left in process of publication a work on the types of North American implements, and a still larger work, nearly finished, designed to cover the entire subject of archæology in America. He bequeathed his library and collections to the United States National Museum in Washington, D. C.

Raymond, Israel Ward, an American pioneer, born in New York city in April, 1811; died in San Francisco, Cal., Jan. 14, 1887. He was a son of Eliakim Raymond, who turned out the first machine-made hats in the United States, and brother of the late John H. Raymond, first president of Vassar College. In early life Mr. Raymond was employed as a furrier, but when the gold-fever broke out in 1848 he went in the "Crescent City," the first steamship that sailed for California with passengers from New York, and remained in San Francisco. He became identified with various New York shipping interests, associating himself at different times with the Pacific Mail Steamship Company, the Panama Railroad Company, and the Nicaraguan line of steamers owned by William H. Webb. He declined all public office, contenting himself with the care of the large interests intrusted to him.

Raymond, John T., an American actor, born in Buffalo, New York, April 5, 1836; died in Evansville, Ind., April 10, 1887. He received a business education, but adopted the profession of the stage, making his first appearance June 27, 1853, in Rochester, N. Y., in the part of Lopez in "The Honeymoon." In 1854 he filled an engagement in the Chestnut Street Theatre, Philadelphia, as Timothy Quaint in "The Soldier's Daughter," and then traveled through the South for several seasons, playing in Charleston, Savannah, Mobile, and New Orleans. In 1861, as a member of Laura Keene's company, he made a great hit in the part of Asa Trenchard in "Our American Cousin," and for several years this was his most popular characterization. He went to England in 1867, and after appearing as Asa Trenchard joined E. A. Sothern's company, prolonging his trip more than a year. Returning in the latter part of 1868, he appeared as Toby Twinkle in "All that Glitters is not Gold" in the Theatre Comique, New York city, and on the burning of that house went to the California Theatre, San Francisco, appearing as Graves in "Money," Jan. 18, 1869. In 1874 he produced a dramatization of Mark Twain's "Gilded Age," taking the part of Colonel Sellers, which proved immensely popular. Between 1876 and 1882 Mr. Raymond appeared in "Risks," "Wolfert's Roost," "Fresh, the American," "For Congress," and "In Paradise," and played an engagement in the Gaiety Theatre, London, where his Colonel Sellers, not being understood, was not appreciated. At the time of his death he was at the height of a successful Western tour, producing "A Gold Mine," "A Woman-Hater," "For Congress," and "Colonel Sellers." Mr. Raymond's original name was O'Brien, but he adopted that of Raymond on the stage, and legally assumed it in 1881.

Ricketts, James Brewerton, an American soldier, born in New York city in 1816; died in Washington, D. C., Sept. 22, 1887. He was graduated at the United States Military Academy, West Point, July 1, 1839, and appointed second lieutenant in the First United States Artillery. In 1846 he was promoted to the rank of first lieutenant, and in 1852 to that of captain, the latter being for gallant services in the Mexican War, during which he had taken part in the capture of Monterey, and held the Rinconada Pass throughout the battle of Buena Vista. He commanded a battery in the first battle of Bull Run July 21, 1861, from which date he was made a brigadier-general, and was severely wounded, captured, and held a prisoner till January, 1862. After his release he took part in the operations in the Shenandoah Valley, the Northern Virginia campaign, and the battles of Cedar Mountain, the second Bull Run, Chantilly, and Antietam, commanding a division at Chantilly. In 1864 he was in command of a division, leading it in the actions at Monocacy, Opequan, Fisher's Hill, and Cedar Creek. He was brevetted successively from lieutenant-colonel to major-general for gallantry, and retired on the full rank of major-general, for disability from wounds, Jan. 3, 1867.

Ripley, Roswell Sabin, an American soldier, born in Ohio in 1824; died in New York city March 29, 1887. He was graduated at the U. S. Military Academy, and commissioned a brevet second lieutenant of artillery in 1843. He served with distinction throughout the Mexican War, winning the brevets of captain and major for special gallantry at the battle of Chapultepec. At the close of that war he resigned his commission in the army, and engaged in business in Charleston, S. C. In April, 1861, he entered the Confederate army, and was placed in command of the battery on Sullivan's Island, which opened the fire on Fort Sumter. After Major Anderson's surrender, Gen. Ripley was appointed Confederate commander of that sea-coast district, with headquarters at Charleston. In November, 1861, he arrived at Hilton Head just before the memorable action there began, and, retiring to Coosawhatchie, advised that the region be abandoned to the National forces, as further resistance would be useless. Subsequently he took part in the Antietam campaign, receiving a wound. The remainder of his service was mainly within the limits of South Carolina. He published a "History of the War with Mexico" (New York, 1849).

Robertson, John, an American soldier, born in Scotland in 1814; died in Detroit, Mich., March 19, 1887. While a boy he took passage in a sailing-vessel for the United States, and on his arrival in New York he inquired for the nearest recruiting-station and promptly enlisted in the regular army, serving a term of seven years. When his time was out his regiment was stationed in Detroit, and there he engaged in the commission business. In 1861 Gov. Blair commissioned him Adjutant-General of the State, an office he held under every administration since. He rendered invaluable service in raising and equipping troops for the field, and after the war he charged himself with the duty of collecting all available statistics that would illustrate the part borne by the State of Michigan in the great struggle.

Rochester, Thomas Fortescue, an American physician, born in Rochester, N. Y., Oct. 8, 1823; died in Buffalo, N. Y., May 24, 1887. He was descended from colonial English settlers of Virginia, and grandson of Nathaniel Rochester, deputy commissary-general in the Continental army, after whom the city of Rochester is named. He was graduated at Geneva College in 1845, and received the degree of M. D. from the University of Pennsylvania in 1848, continuing his medical studies in different countries of Europe. Returning to the United States in 1851 he established himself in New York city, where he continued two years, or till June, 1853, when he removed to Buffalo, N. Y., to take the chair of principles and practice of medicine in the University of Buffalo. Since 1861 he had been consulting physician to the Buffalo General Hospital, and from 1858 till 1888 was attending or consulting physician at the Sisters of Charity Hospital. He was elected a member of the New York Pathological Society in 1848, president of the Erie County Medical Society in 1860, president of the New York State Medical Society in 1875, and its delegate to the International Medical Congress at Philadelphia in 1876. During the civil war he was appointed by President Lincoln an inspector of Union field-hospitals. Among his works are: "The Winter Climate of Malaga," "The Medical Society of Buffalo," "The Army Surgeon," "The Modern Hygeia," and "Medical Men and Medical Matters in 1876."

Ross, William Henry Harrison, an American lawyer, born in Laurel, Del., June 2, 1814; died in Philadelphia, Pa., June 29, 1887. He commanded a regiment of cavalry in the Mexican War, was Governor of Delaware from 1851 till 1855, and represented the State in the National Democratic Conventions of 1844, 1848, 1856, and 1860.

Rouquette, Adrien, an American clergyman, born in New Orleans, La., Feb. 26, 1813; died there, July 15, 1887. He came of one of the oldest and wealthiest creole families in Louisiana, and was brought up in luxury and the enjoyment of the best society in New Orleans and Paris. Most of his boyhood days were

passed among the Indians on Bayou Lacombe. He was educated in the preparatory school of Transylvania University, in Kentucky, the College Royal of Paris, the College Royal of Nantes, and at Rennes, receiving his baccalaureate in the latter place March 26, 1833. To gratify his family, who were eager to separate him from his Indian associates, he agreed to study law, and returned to Paris for the purpose, making frequent trips, however, to New Orleans and Bayou Lacombe. The law proved distasteful to him at the start, and instead of pursuing its study he abandoned it for literature and poetry, till about 1842, when he resolved to enter the priesthood of the Catholic Church. Faithful to early associations he passed his probation at Bayou Lacombe, and his novitiate in the seminary of Assumption Parish. He was ordained as subdeacon in 1844, and as priest by Monsignor Blanc, Archbishop of New Orleans, in 1845. For fourteen years he was attached to the cathedral as *prédicateur*, and then, in the spring of 1859, took the step that had been his dream for years. This was to establish a mission in the Indian village at the headsprings of Bayou Lacombe, where the remnant of the Chahtas, or Choctaws, had mainly settled. On September 8, as a priest of the Catholic Church, he first gathered his Indians around him at Ravine aux Cannes, which he had placed under the protection of Catherine Tegebkwitha, the Indian saint of Canada. From this time till within a year of his death he lived and worked among the Indians, establishing several mission stations in St. Tammany Parish, to which he had gathered the Choctaws, and acting as their temporal as well as spiritual head, their devoted Chahta-Ima. Father Rouquette possessed a thorough knowledge of French, Italian, Spanish, English, and Choctaw, besides the dead languages, and had published books, the best known of which are: "Les Savanes" (Paris, 1843); "Wild Flowers"; "La Thébaïde," a prose poem in French; "L'Antoniade"; "St. Catherine Tegebkwitha"; and "La Nouvelle Atalá" (1879.

Rowett, Richard, an American soldier, born in Cornwall, England, in 1830: died in Chicago, Ill., July 13, 1887. He came to the United States in 1851, and established himself on a large farm near Carlinville, Ill., as a breeder of thorough-bred horses. The success of his farm and his connection with the turf gave him an early reputation. At the outbreak of the civil war he entered the service as a captain in the Seventh Regiment of Illinois Infantry, and was commissioned successively as major, lieutenant-colonel, and colonel, and brevetted brigadier-general for special gallantry at the battle of Allatoona in 1864. He served throughout the war, receiving wounds in the battles of Shiloh, Corinth, and Allatoona, and will be popularly remembered as the "hero" of the latter engagement. At the close of the war he returned to his stock-farm, and also began

to take an active interest in politics, being a
warm friend and earnest supporter of Gen.
Logan, through whose influence he was appointed canal commissioner, and in 1871 a
member of the Board of Penitentiary Commissioners. In 1876 he was elected a member of
the State Legislature, and in the early part of
President Arthur's administration was appointed collector of internal revenue at Quincy, Ill., retaining the office till the consolidation of that district with another under the
administration of President Cleveland. Gen.
Rowett dropped dead on the Washington Park
race-track with heart-disease.

Ryle, John, an American manufacturer, born
in Bollington, England, Oct. 22, 1817; died
there Nov. 6, 1887. At the age of five years
he was set to work in a silk-mill in Maccles-
field, near his home, and when his two brothers engaged largely in silk manufacturing he
served them for several years as superintendent. He came to the United States in 1839,
beginning business as an importer of silk goods
in New York city. While so employed he
made the acquaintance of George W. Murray,
who was seeking an investment in the silk industry, and the two bought the old Colt fire-
arms factory in Paterson, N. J., put in it a
few looms, and began weaving silk. In 1846
Mr. Ryle bought out his partner's interest,
continuing the business alone for some years,
and accumulating a handsome fortune. In
1864 he organized the firm of John Ryle &
Co., which built the large mill near the depot,
and on March 10, 1869, was left nearly penni-
less by the destruction of the uninsured works
by fire. He rebuilt the mill on credit, organized the Ryle Silk Manufacturing Company,
which in 1878 was renamed the Pioneer Silk
Company, and, though holding the majority
of stock and the office of president, gradually
withdrew from the active management of the
works. He was a strong protection Democrat,
a member of the various silk associations of
this country, and their stanch representative
in Washington during the sessions of Congress.
He wove the silk flag which floated over the
Crystal Palace in New York city, was one of
the originators of the Paterson water-works
system, Mayor of the city in 1870-'71, and the
beautifier of the grounds about the Passaic
Falls. He was visiting his old home at the
time of his death.

Rumsey, Henry Barlow, an American naval
officer, born in Fort Wayne, Ind., Nov. 22,
1841; died in Buffalo, N. Y., March 19, 1887.
He was appointed from Indiana an acting
midshipman in the navy Oct. 25, 1859; transferred to the "St. Lawrence" from the Naval
Academy in 1861: ordered to the "Clifton"
in 1862; Feb. 24, 1863, appointed ensign;
April 27, 1864, commissioned a lieutenant;
Aug. 9, 1866, a lieutenant-commander; and
resigned from the navy in March, 1871. In
his nine years and nine months of naval service Mr. Rumsey was eight years and six

months on sea-service, his last sea-service being on the "Quinnebaug," of which he was
executive officer. He served on that ship,
and on the flag-ship "Guerriere," in the
South Atlantic squadron, from July 22, 1867,
till July 18, 1870. He served throughout the
civil war, being present at the bombardment
of Forts Jackson and St. Philip, Mississippi
river, April, 1861; at Vicksburg, June 29,
1862; capture of Galveston, Oct. 4, 1862;
recapture of Galveston, Jan. 1, 1863; Mata-
gorda, Texas, November, 1862; and at both
attacks on Fort Fisher. After resigning he
was engaged in business at Laramie City, Wyoming Territory, and at Sidney and Omaha,
Neb. On the night of March 18, 1887, he was
a guest of the Richmond Hotel in Buffalo
when it was burned. Waked from sleep by
the flames, he found a way for escape, but as
he was about to leap from the burning building he heard the appealing cry of a child who
had become separated from her parents. He
went back to save her, following her even to
the room into which in her fright she had
rushed and closed the door. Seizing the child,
and sheltering her in his arms as best he could,
he ran back to the window through which he
had planned his escape, but the flames enveloped him and his little charge before he could
again reach it. He jumped with her to a roof
below, from which both were soon rescued,
but they were so badly burned that he died
the next morning, and the child a day or two
later. Mr. Rumsey was a man of superior
mental ability, of extensive reading and varied
knowledge.

Sargent, Aaron A., an American legislator,
born in Newburyport, Mass., Sept. 28, 1827;
died in San Francisco, Cal., Aug. 14, 1887.
He learned the printer's trade in early life, and
when twenty years old was a newspaper reporter in Washington, D. C. In 1849 he removed to California, where he engaged in mining, and established the "Nevada Journal."
While editing his paper he studied law, was
admitted to the bar in 1854, and elected district attorney of Nevada County two years
later. In 1860 he was vice-president of the
Republican National Convention; in 1861 was
elected Representative in Congress, and in
that session was the author of the first Pacific
Railroad act passed by that body; in 1869
was returned to Congress, and on the expiration of the term re-elected; and in 1872 elected
United States Senator for the term of six years,
serving on the committees on Naval Affairs,
Mines and Mining, and Appropriations. In
March, 1882, he was appointed United States
Minister to Germany by President Garfield,
and held the office till the action of the German
authorities in excluding American pork from
the empire made his incumbency personally
distasteful. President Arthur offered him the
Russian mission, but he declined it.

Scott, Robert N., an American soldier, born in
Winchester, Tenn., in 1836; died in Washing-

ton, D. C., March 5, 1887. He was graduated at the United States Military Academy, and commissioned second lieutenant in the Fourth United States Infantry in 1857. Previous to the civil war he was stationed on the Pacific coast, and had at one time under his charge the steamer "Massachusetts" during the San Juan troubles. He served with the volunteer forces of the Union during the war, and was brevetted major, June 27, 1862, for gallant services in the battle of Gaines's Mill, Va., and lieutenant-colonel, March 13, 1865, for meritorious services in connection with the volunteer army. In the regular army he was commissioned major March 20, 1878, and lieutenant-colonel March 22, 1885. He was appointed military secretary to the Joint Commission of Congress on the reorganization of the army under the Burnside bill in 1878, and the same year became chief of the Publication Office of War Records of the Rebellion. He was thoroughly impartial in this important public work, a remarkably strong master of details, and a persistent searcher of records bearing on disputed points in the history of the war. For these reasons, if none other, his death before the completion of the immense historical work he had in hand was a public calamity.

Scroggs, Gustavus A., an American lawyer, born in Darlington, Beaver County, Ky., Aug. 8, 1820; died in Buffalo, N. Y., Jan. 24, 1887. He was a lineal descendant of Sir William Scroggs, the English judge, who died in 1683. He removed to Buffalo, N. Y., in 1848, studied law, and was admitted to the bar of Erie County. Previous to the civil war he was sheriff of Erie County, a United States commissioner, and an officer in the National Guard. At the outbreak of the war he organized the Twenty-first Regiment of New York Volunteers. In 1862 he was appointed by President Lincoln provost-marshal of the Thirtieth District of New York, and after holding the office two years resigned it to take command of the Twenty-fifth Regiment of United States Colored Infantry, under Gen. Banks. He was a Republican from the organization of that party, but was once the candidate of the American Party for the office of Lieutenant-Governor. Mr. Scroggs was very popular, and successful as an instructor of students in law, and was proud of the fact that the late Emory Storrs, of Chicago, was one of his pupils.

Shaw, Aaron, an American lawyer, born in Orange County, N. Y., in 1811; died in Olney, Ill., Jan. 8, 1887. He held the office of State's Attorney in the Fourth Judicial District of Illinois for two terms of four years each, was a member of the State House of Representatives in 1849-'50, and a Representative in Congress in 1857-'59, serving as a member of the committee on the militia. He also held the office of Judge of the Circuit Court.

Sheldon, James, an American lawyer, born in Buffalo, N. Y., Sept. 6, 1821; died there May 1, 1887. In 1837 he entered Hobart College,

Geneva, N. Y., subsequently studying law, and being admitted to the bar in 1843. He became successively city attorney, county judge from 1853 till 1864, United States commissioner, supervisor for the Eleventh Ward of Buffalo, Judge of the Superior Court in 1871 for the term of fourteen years, and Chief Judge in 1878. He was connected with many educational and charitable organizations, and was a fluent and scholarly writer.

Sill, Edward Rowland, an American educator, born in Windsor, Conn., April 29, 1841; died in Cleveland, O., Feb. 27, 1887. He was graduated at Yale University in 1861. Owing to failing health he set out with a classmate on a voyage around Cape Horn to California after graduation, remaining on the Pacific coast till July, 1866, when he returned to the East. In the following spring he studied theology in the Harvard Divinity School; but, believing his strength to be inadequate for the exactions of an active clerical life, he abandoned these studies, and for nearly two years was engaged in literary work in New York city. After teaching for three years in Medina County and in Cayahoga Falls, Ohio, he accepted the office of principal of the High-School at Oakland, and returned to California in 1871. Three years later he was appointed Professor of English in the University of California. He occupied that chair for a period of eight years, attracting marked attention by his fine scholarship, his devotion to his work, his rare power of stimulating pupils, and his intelligent and persistent advocacy of the cause of higher education. He resigned his professorship in March, 1882, to resume literary work, and returned to Cayahoga Falls. He died in the Cleveland Hospital after undergoing a surgical operation. He published "The Hermitage, and other Poems" (New York, 1867).

Smith, Francis S., an American author, born in New York city Dec. 29, 1819; died there Feb. 1, 1887. In 1833 he was apprenticed to the printer's trade in the office of "The Albion," and subsequently worked as a compositor on Porter's "Spirit of the Times," the "New York Tribune," the "New York Globe," and the "Sunday Dispatch." In the latter establishment he became a reporter, and began his career as a story-writer. A dramatization of his "Eveleen Wilson" proved the foundation of Maggie Mitchell's fame as an actress. Mr. Smith was soon advanced to the editor's chair. The influence of his stories upon the circulation of the paper induced the proprietors to start a weekly literary periodical with Mr. Smith as editor. In 1859 the paper, then known as "The New York Weekly," was sold by its owner to Francis S. Smith, his editor, and Francis S. Street, his book-keeper, by whom it was personally conducted till the death of Mr. Street a few years ago. This event laid additional burdens on Mr. Smith in the direction of the periodical, under which his constitution began to fail, and he sought relief by

612 OBITUARIES, AMERICAN.

placing the active management of his business in the hands of his sons, and retiring to a privacy, which was clouded by the death of his wife in July, 1885.

Smith, Thomas Kilby, an American soldier, born in Dorchester, Mass., Sept. 23, 1820; died in New York city Dec. 14, 1887. In 1825 his parents removed to Cincinnati, O., where he studied at the Military and Engineering School of Prof. O. M. Mitchell, and, after spending some time in civil engineering, read law in the office of the late Chief-Justice Chase, and was admitted to the bar, where he had for associates such men as George Hoadly, Stanley Matthews, Edward Marshall, and George Pugh. In 1861 he volunteered to raise a brigade of troops for the national service at his own expense, and Gov. Denison appointed him lieutenant-colonel of the Fifty-fourth Regiment of Ohio Volunteers, and promoted him to the colonelcy before he left the State. His regiment was part of Gen. Sherman's division in the battle of Shiloh, and when Gen. Stuart, commanding the brigade, was wounded, the command was given to Col. Smith, who held it till the siege of Vicksburg. When Gen. Grant assumed the direction of the siege, Col. Smith was promoted to the rank of brigadier-general, and acted for some time as chief of Gen. Grant's staff. After the capitulation of Vicksburg, Gen. Smith was given command of a division of the Army of the Tennessee to assist Gen. Banks in the Red River expedition, and succeeded in protecting Admiral Porter's fleet while withdrawing down the river after the disaster of Sabine Cross Roads. He assisted in the reduction of Mobile, and was then placed in command of the district of Southern Alabama and Florida, which was his last military service. He was brevetted Major-General of volunteers for distinguished services in the war, and on being mustered out was appointed by President Johnson United States Consul at Panama, holding the office till after the inauguration of President Grant.

Smith, William, an American lawyer, born in King George County, Va., Sept. 6, 1797; died in Warrenton, Va., May 18, 1887. He was educated in Plainfield Academy, Connecticut, and private classical schools in Virginia, studied law in Fredericksburg and Warrenton, Va., was admitted to the bar in 1818, and began practicing in Culpeper. At the same time he entered the political field as a Democrat, pledged to a strict construction of party doctrines, frugality in public expenditures, and honesty in the public servant. For eighteen years he took an active part in all political campaigns without being a candidate for office. In 1830 he was elected a member of the State Senate for four years, and was re-elected for a second term, but resigned after serving its first year. In 1841 he was elected a representative in Congress and served the term, but at its close found that a reapportionment had made his district strongly Whig. He then removed to Fauquier County, where in December, 1845, having just returned from one of his courts, he was saluted as "Governor Smith," and informed that the Legislature had elected him Governor for three years from Jan. 1, 1846, without even consulting him. In 1850 he removed to California, and was chosen president of the first Democratic Convention held in that State. Within a year he was back in Virginia, and in 1853 was returned to Congress, where he served till 1861. In June of that year he was commissioned colonel of the Forty-seventh Regiment of Virginia Volunteers, and afterward was elected a representative in the Confederate Congress, from which he resigned a year later to return to the field. He was promoted to the rank of major-general, and received a serious wound at Antietam. He was again elected Governor in 1863, and after the war served one term in the Legislature. In early life he established a line of post-coaches through Virginia, the Carolinas, and Georgia, and secured a contract for carrying the mails. His demand for extra compensation gave him the name of "Extra Billy" Smith.

Spencer, Charles S., an American lawyer, born in Ithaca, N. Y., Feb. 13, 1824; died in New York city Aug. 12, 1887. He was graduated at Williams College in 1844, and in 1847 was admitted to the bar. In 1850 he removed to New York city to take an office in the United States Custom House, but soon resigned and began the regular practice of his profession. Though his practice embraced a wide range, his chief reputation was achieved by his ability and successes as a criminal lawyer. Previous to 1856 he was a Whig in politics, but in that year united with the Republican party, and continued in it through all its mutations till his death. He was elected a member of the New York Assembly in 1859, and again in 1878, serving through both sessions on the Committee on Judiciary, and was an unsuccessful candidate for representative in Congress in 1866 and 1868. He represented his district in the Republican State Conventions for sixteen successive years, and was twice a delegate to the National Conventions of his party. He was also for ten years colonel of the Fifth Regiment N. G., S. N. Y.

Spooner, Lysander, an American lawyer, born in Athol, Mass., Jan. 19, 1808; died in Boston, Mass., May 14, 1887. He studied law in Worcester, Mass. In 1844 he established an independent mail from Boston to New York, carrying letters at the uniform rate of five cents. The prosecution of the Government soon compelled him to retire from this undertaking, but not until he had shown the possibility of supporting the post-office department by a lower rate of postage. His efforts resulted in an act of Congress reducing the rates, followed in 1851 and subsequent years by still further reductions. He was called the "father of cheap postage in America." Mr. Spooner was an active abolitionist, and contributed to the literature of that subject by his "Unconstitutionality of Slavery" (1845), the tenets of which were supported by Gerritt Smith, Elizur Wright, and others of the Liberty party, but were opposed by the Garrisonians. He defended Thomas Drew, who, in 1870, declined to take his oath as a witness before a legislative committee on the ground that in the matter they were investigating they had no rightful authority to compel him to testify. The case was adversely decided on the ground of precedent, but the principles of Mr. Spooner's argument were afterward sustained by the United States Supreme Court. His writings include: "A Deistic Reply to the Alleged Supernatural Evidences of Christianity" and "The Deistic Immortality, and an Essay on Man's Accountability for his Belief" (1836); "Credit, Currency, and Banking" (1848); "Poverty, Causes and Cure" (1846); "A Defense for Fugitive Slaves" (1856); "A New System of Paper Currency" (1861); "Considerations on United States Bonds" (1866); "No Treason" (1867); "A New Banking System; the Needful Capital for Rebuilding the Burnt District" (1878); "Our Financiers, their Ignorance, Usurpations, and Frauds" (1877); "The Law of Prices; Demonstration of the Necessity of an Indefinite Use of Money" (1877); "Gold and Silver as Standards of Value" (1878); and "Letter to Grover Cleveland, on his False Inaugural Address" (1886).

Standeford, Elisha D., an American capitalist, born in Jefferson County, Ky., Dec. 28, 1831; died in Louisville, Ky., July 26, 1887. He received a common-school education, studied medicine, and was graduated in 1858. He was by turns a banker, farmer, and manufacturer, and became actively identified with political and railroad affairs. In 1868–'71 he was elected a State Senator, and in 1872 a representative in Congress, serving through the term on the committee on the Pacific Railroad, and declining a re-election. Dr. Standeford was ex-president of the Louisville and Nashville Railroad, vice-president of the Jeffersonville, Madison, and Indianapolis Bridge Company, a director of the Farmers and Drovers' Bank, and a farmer on a very extensive scale in several counties. His fortune was estimated at upward of $3,000,000.

Stanton, Henry Brewster, an American lawyer and journalist, born in Pachaug, New London County, Conn., June 27, 1805; died in New York city Jan. 14, 1887. He was liberally educated, and when twenty-one years old removed to Rochester, N. Y., where he began writing for Thurlow Weed's newspaper, "The Monroe Telegraph," which was advocating the election of Henry Clay to the presidency. Attracted by the excitements of political life, he took the stump, making his first political speech in Rochester. Afterward he was appointed deputy-clerk of Monroe County, holding the office three years. In 1832 he removed to Cincinnati to complete his studies in

Lane Theological Seminary. While there he entered upon his anti-slavery career by making a stirring speech on the "Nat Turner insurrection," and at the anniversary of the American Anti-Slavery Society, held in New York city in 1834, he faced the first of the many mobs he encountered in his fearless advocacy of human freedom. In 1840 he married Miss Elizabeth Cady, and on May 12 sailed with her for London to attend a convention for the promotion of the anti-slavery cause. At the close of the convention they extended their tour through the principal cities of England, Scotland, Ireland, and France, speaking and working for the relief of the slaves at every opportunity. In 1847 he established his home in Seneca Falls, N. Y., was admitted to the bar, and soon acquired reputation as a successful lawyer in patent cases. He was one of the founders of the Republican party, and maintained an active connection with the daily press for nearly half a century, his contributions consisting in the main of scholarly articles on current political topics, and of elaborate biographies of public men. Mr. Stanton published "Sketches of Reforms and Reformers in Great Britain and Ireland" soon after his first trip abroad, and at the time of his death was engaged on a volume of personal reminiscences.

Stearns, Charles W., an American physician, born in Springfield, Mass., in 1818; died in Longmeadow, Mass., Sept. 8, 1887. He was graduated at Yale College in 1837, and took his medical degree at the University of Pennsylvania in 1840. He practiced for a while in Springfield, Mass., and then entered the army as a surgeon. Subsequently he spent several years in travel and study in Europe, re-entering the army at the outbreak of the civil war as surgeon of the Third Regiment of New York Volunteers, and serving at Fort McHenry, Baltimore, Suffolk, Va., Fortress Monroe, and in the field. Dr. Stearns was most widely known as an enthusiastic Shakespearean student and writer, although he published several surgical and physiological works previous to 1860, and a "Concordance and Classified Index to the Constitution of the United States," which is an authority among lawyers and legislators. The most noted of his later works are "Shakespeare's Medical Knowledge" (New York, 1865), and "The Shakespeare Treasury of Wisdom and Knowledge" (New York, 1869).

Stevens, Aaron Fletcher, an American lawyer, born in Londonderry, N. H., Aug. 9, 1819; died in Nashua, N. H., May 10, 1887. He was engaged in mechanical pursuits in early life, but was admitted to the bar in 1845. On the outbreak of the civil war he assisted in organizing the First Regiment of New Hampshire Volunteers, and went to the field with the rank of major, subsequently attaining the grade of brevet brigadier-general in recognition of his meritorious conduct while under fire. Gen. Stevens was well known in political circles. He represented the Whig party in the State Legislature in 1849 and 1854, and was a delegate in 1852 to the Baltimore convention that nominated Gen. Scott for the presidency. In 1856 he united with the newly-formed Republican party, and as its candidate was re-elected to the Legislature in that and the following years. He was elected a representative in Congress in 1866 and 1869, and defeated by a few votes in 1871, and from 1876 till 1884 was a member of every State Legislature.

Stewart, Isaac Dalton, an American clergyman, born in Warner, N. H., Dec. 23, 1817; died in Dover June 7, 1887. He was educated at Hopkinton and Henniker Academies, and taught in Ohio, New Jersey, and New Hampshire several years. In 1841 he studied in the Biblical School at Parsonsfield, Me., and later in the New Hampton Theological School. In 1842 he became principal of Henniker Academy. Mr. Stewart was ordained to the Free Baptist ministry at Meredith Feb. 2, 1843. He held pastorates at Meredith and Laconia, and was teacher, preacher, and financial manager at the New Hampton Institution. In 1867 he became pastor of the Free Baptist church, Dover, N. H., to 1873, when he became agent of the "Morning Star" newspaper, and its denominational printing establishment for the country. This office he held until the paper and office were moved to Boston in 1885. He represented New Hampshire twice in the Legislature of the State. In conjunction with Rev. Silas Curtis, he prepared the first volume of "Minutes of the General Conference" for publication, collected the material for, and wrote the first volume of the "History of the Free Baptists" and the "Minister's Manual," also chapters for the "Centennial Record." He prepared many reports, papers, and addresses of value.

Stone, Charles P., an American soldier, born in Greenfield, Franklin County, Mass., in 1826; died in New York city Jan. 24, 1887. He entered the United States Military Academy in 1841 and was graduated in 1845, immediately thereafter being appointed a brevet second lieutenant of ordnance. A month later he was appointed acting assistant professor of ethics in the Military Academy, an office he held till January, 1846, when he was ordered to duty in Mexico. He distinguished himself in several battles under Gen. Scott, was brevetted first lieutenant Sept. 8, 1847, for gallant and meritorious conduct in the battle of Molino del Rey, and captain five days later for similar conduct at Chapultepec, and commissioned first lieutenant in the regular army in February, 1853. In 1851 he was sent to California, where he constructed the Benicia Arsenal and acted as chief of ordnance for the Pacific coast, and resigned from the army in 1856. He was engaged in the banking business in San Francisco for a year, and then undertook a survey of Sonora and Lower California under a commission from the Mexican President. Just before the inauguration of President Lincoln, Mr. Holt, the Secretary of War, called Lieut.

Stone to Washington, appointed him a captain in the army, and assigned him to the duty of inspector-general of all the militia in the District of Columbia then organizing for the protection of the national capital. On May 14, 1861, he was appointed colonel of the Fourteenth Regiment of United States Infantry, and on May 17 a brigadier-general of volunteers. He served in the Shenandoah valley under Gen. Patterson during July, and, when after the battle of Bull Run Gen. McClellan was appointed to the command of the Army of the Potomac, Gen. Stone was selected to command a division, which was directed to occupy the valley of the Potomac above Washington as a corps of observation. In October following occurred the disastrous battle of Ball's Bluff, in which the National troops were defeated. The event produced a profound excitement in Congress and throughout the country, in which Gen. Stone was bitterly accused of having risked the battle without due preparation. On Jan. 5, 1862, he appeared before the congressional committee on the conduct of the war, and was rigidly examined as to every detail of the battle. His responses were given frankly and seemed to satisfy the committee; but in February he was arrested and imprisoned in Fort Lafayette, New York harbor, and kept in confinement there seven months without any charges having been preferred against him, and despite his appeals to Gen. McClellan, Secretary Stanton, and President Lincoln for such a hearing as the military code provided for every accused officer. To the day of his death he was never informed of the cause of his arrest and imprisonment. After his release he served in the siege of Port Hudson and was one of the commissioners to receive its surrender, and as chief of staff of Gen. Banks was engaged in the skirmish of Bayou Teche and the battles of Sabine Cross-roads and Pleasant Hill, April 8 and 9, 1864. He was mustered out of the volunteer service the same month, and remained unemployed till August, when he was assigned to the command of a brigade in the Army of the Potomac, retaining it till after the surrender of Petersburg, then resigning from the army. He was engineer and superintendent of the Dover Mining Company of Virginia from 1865 till 1869, and in 1870 entered the service of the Khedive of Egypt, becoming chief of the general staff or practically commander-in-chief of the entire army. For his valuable services in command, organization, and administration, he was decorated commander of the Order of Osmanieh Oct. 10, 1870, grand officer of the Order of Medjii Jan. 24, 1875, and raised to the dignity of a pasha in 1873. Early in 1883 Gen. Stone resigned his commission in the Egyptian service, and, returning to the United States, was appointed engineer-in-chief of the construction of the pedestal for Bartholdi's statue of Liberty in the harbor of New York, which proved his last work.

Stone, Della Charlotte Hall, an American philanthropist, born in Wallingford, Conn., Jan. 10, 1818; died in Brooklyn, N. Y., Oct. 19, 1887. Her father was a wealthy farmer who educated her for practical work in life. In 1841 she married David M. Stone, editor of the New York "Journal of Commerce," and, as no children came from the union, she consecrated herself to the labor of relieving human suffering. For nearly thirty-eight years she was connected with the Old Ladies' Home in Brooklyn, twenty-five years as its treasurer, and the remainder as its president. She was president of the Congregational Church's Benevolent Association and of its Foreign Missionary Society, an official in the chief charitable and benevolent organizations of the city, and notably active in the church work and charities of her parish. It is believed that for many years she had distributed not less than $10,000 annually to institutions of charity and among the deserving poor.

Sullivan, Algernon Sydney, an American lawyer, born in Madison, Ind., in 1827; died in New York city Dec. 4, 1887. He was a son of Jeremiah Sullivan, the first judge of Indiana by appointment after it was admitted into the Union. He was graduated at Miami University in 1850, was admitted to the bar, and practiced till 1855, when he removed to Cincinnati. In the spring of 1859 he settled in New York city, where he quickly attracted attention by his legal and oratorical abilities. Shortly after the opening of the civil war he was engaged by a number of privateersmen who had been captured and taken to New York to defend them in the courts, and his acceptance of the cases drew upon him the suspicions of the authorities, by whom he was arrested and confined in Fort Lafayette for three months. He was Assistant District Attorney of New York for three years, and Public Administrator from 1875 till 1885, resigning each to attend to private practice, and refusing all other public offices. Mr. Sullivan was president of the Southern Society, and was identified with many charitable and other associations.

Sutherland, Josiah, an American lawyer, born in Stamford, Dutchess County, N. Y., in 1807; died in New York city May 25, 1887. He was graduated at Union College, Schenectady, N. Y., and, after his admittance to the bar, entered into partnership with Robert H. Morris in Johnston, Columbia County. Soon afterward he was appointed district attorney of the county, and held the office twelve years. In 1850 he was elected a representative in Congress, declining a second term, as he had concluded to remove to New York city. There he formed a partnership with Claudius L. Monell, and, upon the retirement of James R. Whiting from the bench of the Supreme Court, was elected his successor for the unexpired term of six years. In 1863 he was re-elected for the full term of eight years, and in 1872 he was elected City Judge for six years. After his retirement he engaged in practice with Francis M. Scott.

Talcott, John Ledyard, an American lawyer, born in Williamstown, Mass., Sept. 2, 1812; died in Buffalo, N. Y., Jan. 20, 1887. He was educated at the Albany Academy, New York, and the Pittsfield Institute, Massachusetts, and studied law in New York city with his father, Samuel Austin Talcott, and in Utica, N. Y., with William H. Maynard and Joshua A. Spencer. On his admission to the bar he made his permanent home in Buffalo, N. Y., and began practicing there. In 1869 he was elected a judge of the Supreme Court of New York, and took his seat Jan. 1, 1870, to fill the vacancy caused by the resignation of Judge Noah Davis. His partial term expired Dec. 31, 1873, but by his election for a full term he served altogether about fourteen years. In May, 1870, he was appointed one of the associate justices of the General Term of the Fourth Department by Gov. Hoffman, was transferred to the Second Department by Gov. Dix, and appointed presiding justice of the Fourth Department by Gov. Cornell in 1881.

Tarbox, John Kemble, an American lawyer, born in Methuen, Mass., May 6, 1838; died in Boston, Mass., May 28, 1887. He was educated for college in the public schools and academy at Lawrence, Mass., but ill health prevented him taking the full collegiate course, and he applied himself to the study of law. He was admitted to the bar in 1860, and practiced his profession in Lawrence till 1883, acting for some time as political editor of the "Lawrence Sentinel," and serving through the civil war as a line officer of the Fourth Regiment of Massachusetts Volunteers. In 1868, 1870, and 1871 he was a member of the Massachusetts House of Representatives, and in 1872 of the State Senate. He was elected Mayor of Lawrence in 1873; a representative in Congress, as a Democrat, in 1874; and defeated for a second term in Congress in 1876, when Gen. Butler succeeded to his seat. After his retirement from Congress he held no public office till April 11, 1883, when Gov. Butler appointed him State Insurance Commissioner, an office he held through three administrations to the day of his death.

Taylor, John, president of the Mormons, born in Milnthorp, Westmoreland County, England, Nov. 1, 1808; died in Salt Lake City, Utah, July 25, 1887. His parents were members of the Church of England, and he was brought up in that faith, but when fifteen years old joined the Methodist Church and was shortly afterward appointed a local preacher. He emigrated to Toronto, Canada, in 1832, following his parents who had preceded him two years. He continued his Methodist connection but a short time, owing to some difficulty with his superiors. In 1835 he was baptized into the Mormon Church during the Canadian "missionary" tour of Porley P. Pratt, and in 1837 was ordained a high priest by Joseph Smith, who prevailed upon him to remove to Kirkland, Ohio, by alleging that he had been designated by revelation for the apostleship and even higher honor in the new church. In the following year Smith announced that it had been revealed to him that Taylor and several others had been chosen to constitute a quorum of the twelve apostles to fill vacancies, upon which Taylor was sent on a mission to England, reaching Liverpool in January, 1840. After preaching Mormonism in Ireland and on the Isle of Man, he made a brief trip to Scotland, and returned to the new Mormon community at Nauvoo, Ill., in January, 1841. In the early part of 1844, charges of sedition and disloyalty having been made against the community, the Smith brothers, John Taylor, and William Richards voluntarily surrendered themselves, at the suggestion of Gov. Ford, to stand trial on the charges. They were placed in the Carthage jail for protection against the fury of the populace, but on the night of June 27 the jail was attacked, the guard overpowered, and the Mormons fired upon; Joseph and Hyrum Smith were killed, John Taylor was struck by four bullets, and Richards made his escape. In 1846 Taylor was again sent to England as a missionary, remaining less than a year, and on his return going direct to the new settlement in Salt Lake City, Utah. He was elected one of the associate judges of the Mormon state of Deseret in March, 1849, and in the following October went on a mission to France, where he translated the "Book of Mormon" into French. He then went to Hamburg and had the work translated into German and published, returning to Salt Lake City in 1852, where two years later he was elected a member of the legislative council. In 1855 he began a mission in New York city, published "The Mormon," and assumed charge of the Mormons in the Eastern States. He was President of the Twelve Apostles in 1877, when Brigham Young died, and as such remained at the head of the church till October, 1880, when he organized the first presidency of the church anew, taking the chief place himself. In March, 1885, he was indicted with others by a Federal grand jury under the Edmunds law, but being warned of the intentions of the authorities secreted himself, and remained in hiding till his death.

Thacher, George Hornell, an American manufacturer, born in Hornellsville, Steuben County, N. Y., June 4, 1818; died in St. Augustine, Fla., Feb. 15, 1887. He was a descendant of Rev. Thomas Thacher, first pastor of the old South Church, Boston, and, on the maternal side, of the founder of Hornellsville. He was graduated at Union College, Schenectady, N. Y., in 1843, and Princeton Theological Seminary a few years later. As a Democrat, he was elected Mayor of the city of Albany, N. Y., shortly before the opening of the civil war, and by re-elections served throughout four terms. He was the first chief magistrate to permit the Abolitionists to exercise the right

of free speech. They had been mobbed in nearly every city where they had attempted to have a public hearing; but he enforced their rights as citizens to free speech, at the head of the entire police forces, and personally introduced Frederick Douglass. His coolness and determined preparations effectually overawed the rough element that went from New York to break up the meeting. Mr. Thacher was vice-president of the Albany City Bank, and president of the Thacher Car-Wheel Company. His son, John Boyd Thacher, was Mayor of Albany in 1887.

Therington, James, an American consul, born in North Carolina in 1816; died in Santa Fé, N. M., June 13, 1887. He removed to Iowa in early life, and, after holding many political trusts, was a representative in Congress from 1855 till 1859, and United States Consul at Aspinwall from 1871 till 1883.

Tousey, Sinclair, an American newsdealer, born in New Haven, Conn., Jan. 18, 1815; died in New York city June 16, 1887. He received a common-school education, and up to his eighteenth year was engaged in various occupations. In 1833 he went to New York city with a large quantity of quinces in which he had invested his savings, and, selling them advantageously, became a newspaper carrier, delivering the "Evening Star" and the morning "Jeffersonian" to subscribers, and later being the first regular carrier of the "Herald." In 1836 he was appointed general agent in all the States bordering on the Mississippi for a large patent-medicine concern. He resided in Louisville, Ky., establishing agencies in various cities, and founding the "Louisville Daily Times," the first penny paper published west of the Alleghany mountains. In 1840 he returned to New York State and engaged in farming till 1853, when he became a partner with Messrs. Ross and Jones, wholesale newsagents and booksellers, on Nassau Street. In May, 1860, Mr. Tousey bought out his partners, and on Feb. 1, 1864, the American News Company was organized. Mr. Tousey became the first president, and held the office till death. He was an active anti-slavery man, one of the first members of the Republican party, a frequent writer for the press, a member of the Union League Club, the Society for the Prevention of Cruelty to Animals, and the Society for the Prevention of Cruelty to Children, vice-president of the Hahnemann Hospital Association, and for many years chairman of the executive committee of the New York Prison Association, devoting a large part of his time to the work of the latter.

Travers, William Priggin, an American financier, born in Baltimore, Md., in 1819; died in Hamilton, Bermuda, March 19, 1887. When he was about sixteen years old the family removed to New York city, from which he entered the United States Military Academy. At the expiration of two years his father induced him to abandon the idea of a military career, ·

and prepare himself for business life. He therefore entered Columbia College, New York city, was graduated in 1838, and upon the return of the family to Baltimore became partner in a commission house dealing with the West Indies and South America, in 1840. In 1843 he married Mary, a daughter of Hon. Reverdy Johnson. His firm prospered till 1853, when, through reverses, they were forced to discontinue business. The partnership was dissolved, and Mr. Travers again removed to New York. In 1854 he formed a partnership with Edmund H. Muller, and they began business in Wall Street as stock-brokers. In July, 1856, he was admitted to membership in the New York Stock Exchange. On the expiration of his partnership in 1857, Mr. Travers became associated with Leonard Jerome, and it is believed that each partner was worth over $1,000,000 when their partnership was dissolved by limitation. Mr. Travers was afterward associated with C. Kowalsky, Van Schaik & Masset, Plume & Van Emburgh, and, as silent partner, with French & Travers, J. D. Prince & Co., Prince & Whitely, Travers & Hackman, and Moale, Armstrong & Co., of Baltimore. In 1880 Mr. Travers began building the picturesque village of Lyndhurst, in New Jersey, about fifty minutes' ride from New York, to provide domiciles for people in moderate circumstances, leasing the buildings at a small rent, and giving tenants the option of buying them by easy installments. This is now a thriving community, with several factories, also built by him. He was a man of much original wit, which an impediment in his speech greatly sharpened, popular in every circle, and lavishly generous.

Treat, Samuel H., an American lawyer, born in Otsego County, N. Y., in 1812; died in Springfield, Ill., March 27, 1887. He was admitted to the bar in his native State, and, removing to Springfield in 1834, formed a law partnership with George Forquer, formerly attorney-general of Illinois, and subsequently register of the land-office in Springfield. The death of Mr. Forquer left Mr. Treat in sole possession of a large and growing law practice. In 1839 a new State judicial circuit was formed, and Stephen T. Logan appointed judge. After serving about three months he resigned, and Gov. Carlin appointed Mr. Treat to fill the vacancy. He was afterward elected to the same bench, serving till 1841, when he was transferred to the Supreme Court of the State. He held this office continuously till 1855. On the division of the former United States Judicial District of Illinois into the northern and southern districts, Judge Treat was appointed to the latter by President Pierce, and at the time of his death had held the office over thirty years.

Truxtun, William Talbot, an American naval officer, born in Philadelphia, Pa., March 11, 1824; died in Norfolk, Va., Feb. 25, 1887. He was appointed midshipman in the United States Navy Feb. 9, 1841, and, after a service of five years at sea and one at the United States Naval Academy, passed the examination Aug. 10, 1847, and received the warrant of passed-midshipman. He was attached to the flag-ship "Brandywine" and brig "Perry" on the Brazilian station 1847–'48; returned from Brazil as acting master on the slaver "Independence," captured by the "Perry" off Rio de Janeiro, January, 1848; and served on the "Dolphin" in 1853 when the bank on which the first transatlantic cable was laid was discovered, and the first specimens of the bottom brought up. In 1854 he was detailed to special duty with the Strain expedition to survey a route for a ship-canal across Darien; in 1855 promoted to the grades of master and lieutenant; in 1855–'57 on coast-survey duty, and in 1861 attached to the sloop "Dale" as executive officer. In the following year that vessel was assigned to the North Atlantic blockading squadron, and he was placed in command, with the grade of lieutenant-commander. He remained attached to that squadron till the close of the war, taking part in the capture of Plymouth, N. C., 1864, the two attacks and capture of Fort Fisher, N. C., 1864–'65, and in various engagements with Confederate batteries along the coast of North Carolina. He was promoted to the grade of commander in 1866, and in that and the following years was on special duty at the Philadelphia Navy-yard. He had command of the "Jamestown," of the Pacific squadron, in 1868–'70; was inspector of ordnance at the Boston Navy-yard 1871–'73; commanded the "Brooklyn" 1873–'75; was a member of the Board of Inspectors 1876; and in command of the Brooklyn Navy-yard 1879–'80. After his promotion to the grade of commodore he was in command a second time of the Brooklyn Navy-yard, and of that at Norfolk, Va. His nomination by the President for promotion to the grade of rear-admiral was held back so long by the Senate Naval Committee that he had to be retired on the grade of commodore.

Tulane, Paul, an American philanthropist, born in Princeton, N. J., about 1800; died there March 28, 1887. He received a common-school education, and when eighteen years old rode to New Orleans on horseback, and opened a store there for the sale of general merchandise, from which he realized a fortune of over $150,000 by 1828. He continued in this business for nearly forty years, engaging at the same time in cotton and real-estate transactions. In 1867 he retired with a large fortune, making his home in Princeton. For many years it was known to a few of his most intimate friends that he was regularly and liberally assisting several of the charitable institutions of New Orleans, but it was not till 1882 that he made the gift that will perpetuate his name among the grand philanthropists of the United States. In that year he transferred to a board of trustees all the property he possessed in New Orleans, which was then appraised at $2,000,000, for the founding of Tulane University, an institution he designed for the promotion of intellectual, moral, and industrial education among young white people of Louisiana. Between this time and his death he added a large sum in stock securities to the endowment of the university. Mr. Tulane never married, was eccentric in his manner and habits, and would never give information about his age, or the amount of his fortune.

Upchurch, John Jordan, an American engineer, born in Franklin County, N. C., March 26, 1822; died in Steelville, Mo., Jan. 18, 1887. As a boy he showed mechanical skill, and, being obliged to support himself at an early age, invariably sought employments requiring the handling of machinery of various kinds. As a young man he supplemented his mechanical knowledge by a practical one of engineering, working for several years on various railroads, and superintending the construction of a number of large saw and flour mills. In 1873 he removed to Missouri under appointment as master mechanic of the car-shops of the St. Louis, Salem and Little Rock Railroad, superintended the building of the shops, and purchased and erected all the machinery. Mr. Upchurch was most widely known as the founder of the American Order of United Workmen, a benevolent institution with lodges in nearly every city, town, and village in the United States. He instituted the first lodge in Meadville, Pa., Oct. 27, 1868.

Vanderpoel, Aaron J., an American lawyer, born in Kinderhook, N. Y., in October, 1825; died in Paris, France, Aug. 22, 1887. He was a son of Dr. John Vanderpoel, the family physician and intimate friend of Martin Van Buren, and was named after his uncle Aaron, the "Kinderhook Roarer" in Congress and politics. Young Aaron was called Aaron Vanderpoel, Jr., till his uncle married, when he changed the Jr. into a middle initial, and thenceforth called himself Aaron J. Vanderpoel. He took the preparatory course of study at the Kinderhook Academy, and was graduated at the University of New York in 1842. He studied law in Kinderhook and New York city, and, after being admitted to the bar, formed a partnership with J. Bryce Smith under the firm name of Smith & Vanderpoel. In 1858 the firm was reorganized in consequence of the death of Mr. Blunt and the withdrawal of Mr. Smith, by the admission of Messrs. A. L. Brown and A. Oakey Hall, the latter a college friend of Mr. Vanderpoel, and the name became Brown, Hall & Vanderpoel, and in this form remained till 1878. During this period Mr. Hall was twice Mayor, and for several years district-attorney, and the firm were the recognized counsel of the sheriff, the metropolitan boards of health and police, many street railways, and corporations of a public and private character. In 1875 the firm became Vanderpoel, Green & Cumming, and since that time has mainly engaged in vast cor-

poration work. Mr. Vanderpoel was a member of the council of the University of New York, president of its alumni, and its senior law professor; was also a member of the Manhattan Club and St. Nicholas Society, and vice-president of the New York Bar Association. He received the degree of LL. D. from the University of New York in 1880.

Varick, Theodore Romeyn, an American physician, born in Dutchess County, N. Y., June 24, 1825; died in Jersey City, N. J., Nov. 23, 1887. In 1846 he was graduated at the medical department of New York University, and, after practicing for two years in New York, he removed in 1848 to Jersey City, where he resided until his death. He was eminent both as a physician and a surgeon, but it is by his successes in the latter field of practice that he is most widely known. He was a vigorous and original thinker, and made many valuable additions to medical and surgical knowledge. He was the first to prove the usefulness of cocaine in capital amputations, and he introduced into America Trendelenberg's method of amputating at the hip-joint. Being dissatisfied with the results of the Lister method of dressing open wounds, he perfected a system for the employment of hot water in surgery, and thereby secured the largest percentage of successful operations known, but three deaths resulting from fifty-four capital amputations. He also was the first to use hot water to control oozing in laparotomy. Among the records of his cases which were read before medical societies, or contributed to medical journals, are monographs on "Urticaria produced by Hydrocyanic Acid," "Complete Luxation of the Radius and Ulna to the Radial Side," "Subperiosteal Resection of the Clavicle," "Distal Compression in Inguinal Aneurism," "The Causes of Death after Operations and Grave Injuries." "The Use of Hot Water in Surgery," "The Protective Treatment of Open Wounds," and "Railroad Injuries of the Extremities of the Human Body." Dr. Varick was an incorporator of the District Medical Society of Hudson County, president of the New Jersey State Medical Society, surgeon-general of New Jersey, president of the New York Medical Society, director of Morris Plains Hospital for the Insane, director of St. Francis's Hospital, surgeon of Jersey City Hospital, and a member of the New York Academy of Medicine, of the New York State Medical Society, of the New York Neurological Society, and of the American Medical Association.

Vincent, Mary Anne Farley, an American actress, born in Portsmouth, England, Aug. 18, 1818; died in Boston, Mass., Sept. 4, 1887. She made her first appearance on the stage in Cowes, Isle of Wight, playing the part of Lucy in "The Review; or, the Wags of Windsor," in 1835, and in the same year married James R. Vincent, a noted comedian of the day. After winning high praise in England, Scotland, and Ireland, Mr. and Mrs. Vincent were engaged to appear in Boston, Mass., in September, 1846, which they did in "Popping the Question." Mr. Vincent died in 1850, and his widow, after a brief retirement, resumed her profession. She joined the stock company of the Boston Museum in 1858, and remained a member of it till her death. During these thirty-four years she had appeared in 450 different characters. Her most popular parts were Mrs. Hardcastle, Dame Cashfield, Lucretia McTubb, Lady Duberby, The Widow Green, and Mrs. Malaprop.

Walcott, Charles F., an American lawyer, born in Cambridge, Mass., in 1836; died in Gooseberry Island, Salem harbor, Mass., June 11, 1887. He was graduated at Harvard University in 1857, and immediately began practicing law in Boston. At the breaking out of the war he enlisted, and in July, 1861, was commissioned captain in the Twenty-first Regiment of Massachusetts Volunteers. With this regiment he served with distinguished honor in North Carolina and Virginia, and, after the regiment was transferred to Kentucky in April, 1863, he resigned his commission and returned home. He was then appointed military secretary to Gov. Andrew, and served as such until October, 1864, when he was commissioned lieutenant-colonel of the Sixty-first Regiment. On his arrival at the front he was promoted to the rank of colonel, and for gallant services during the attack on Fort Stedman to that of brevet brigadier-general. After the war he published a history of the Twenty-first Regiment, attended all its annual reunions, and resumed the practice of law in Boston. His death occurred immediately after rowing to his summer-resort in Salem harbor.

Walter, Thomas Ustick, an American architect, born in Philadelphia, Pa., Sept. 4, 1804; died there Oct. 30, 1887. He was for many years professor of architecture in the Franklin Institute, Philadelphia, one of the founders of the American Institute of Architects, and, at the time of his death, its president. Mr. Walter was the designer of the Philadelphia County Prison, 1831; Girard College, 1833; the extension and dome of the United States Capitol at Washington, D. C., 1851-'65; the wing of the United States Patent-Office, 1851; the reconstructed Congressional Library building, and the extensions of the United States Treasury and Post-Office buildings, 1855.

Walther, Carl Ferdinand Wilhelm, an American educator, born in Langenchursdorf, Saxony, Oct. 25, 1811; died in St. Louis, Mo., May 7, 1887. He received a preparatory education at Hohenstein and Schneesberg, and entered the University of Leipsic with the intention of studying medicine. The reading of a biography of Oberlin changed his views as to a profession and led him to apply himself to theology. He was graduated at the university in 1833, and entered upon the work of the ministry at Braeunsdorf in 1686. In the latter year he joined a company of Saxon Lutheran emigrants, under the leadership of Martin Stephan, and with

them settled in Perry County, Mo., subsequently becoming their spiritual director. In 1841 he was called to the pastorate of the Lutheran church in St. Louis; in 1847, on the organization of the Lutheran Synod of Missouri, Ohio, and adjacent States, was elected its first president; and in 1849, on the removal of Concordia College and Theological Seminary from Perry County to St. Louis, was chosen Professor of Theology, which office, together with the pastorate of the First Lutheran Church, he held till death. He was a prolific writer for the periodicals of his denomination, while of his numerous books, two postils, a treatise on the Church and the ministry, a hand-book of pastoral theology, and an edition of Beyer's "Theological Compend," with annotations, are particularly deserving of mention.

Ward, George Cabot, an American financier, born in Boston, Mass., in 1825; died in New York city May 4, 1887. He removed to New York city while a young man, and was educated for the banking business. Subsequently, he established the firm of S. G. & G. C. Ward, who represented the London banking-house of Baring Brothers. Mr. Ward's abilities and high standing as an executive officer and financier induced many of the large charitable and financial institutions to seek his co-operation in their management; and he thus became an original member of the association which formed the Union League Club in 1863, and a member of the executive committee on its organization; treasurer of the New York Hospital and of the New York Geographical Society; trustee of the Bloomingdale Lunatic Asylum; promoter of the Newsboys' Lodging-house; secretary of the Bleecker Street Savings-Bank; and director of the Union Trust Company and of the Bank of Commerce.

Washburn, William Barrett, an American manufacturer, born in Winchendon, Mass., Jan. 31, 1820; died in Springfield, Mass., Oct. 5, 1887. He was graduated at Yale in 1844. Soon afterward he engaged in a manufacturing business in Greenfield, Mass., continuing it till his death. He entered political life in 1850, when he was elected a State Senator. At the close of this term he was elected a member of the House of Representatives. He became a Republican on the organization of the party in 1856, and afterward remained an active member of it. In 1862 he was elected a representative in Congress, and was returned every succeeding term till his election to the chief magistracy of the State in 1871. He was re-elected Governor in 1872-'73, and on May 1, 1874, was elected United States Senator by the State Legislature to fill the unexpired term of Charles Sumner. His senatorial term expired March 3, 1875, since when he had held no political office. He was president of the Greenfield National Bank, trustee of Smith College at Northampton, director of the Connecticut River Railroad, corporate member of the American Board of Commissioners of Foreign Missions, alumni trustee of Yate College from 1872 till 1881, first president of the Connecticut Valley Congregational Club, 1882, trustee of the Massachusetts Agricultural College, and member of the board of overseers of Amherst College. He built a free library for his townspeople, and received the degree of LL. D. from Harvard College in 1872.

Wasson, David Atwood, an American author, born in Brooksville, Me., May 14, 1823; died in West Medford, Mass., Jan. 21, 1887. In 1845 he entered Bowdoin College, but withdrew before completing the course, and began studying law in Sedgwick, Me. This course proving uncongenial was abandoned in 1849, when he entered the Bangor Theological Seminary with a view of preparing for the ministry, completed the course, and accepted a pastorate in Groveland, Mass. While attending the seminary he gave much offense to the faculty by his extremely liberal views, and he had been settled over his church but a short time when his ideas caused the congregation to dismiss him. He then devoted himself to literature, and became widely known as a poet and essayist, contributing to the "Atlantic Monthly," the "Radical," the "North American Review," among other publications. In 1865 he resumed pastoral work in Boston, preaching to the Parker congregation, but within a year his health failed, and he was obliged to cease from all work.

Watkins, Alice, an American actress, born in Nashville, Tenn., Sept. 22, 1849; died in Philadelphia, Pa., Jan. 10, 1887. About 1865 she married James A. Oates, who put her upon the stage in Cincinnati when she was twenty years of age. Her first appearance was in the part of "Earl Darnley" in the burlesque of "The Field of the Cloth of Gold," in which she achieved such a success that after the first week she was billed as a star. She played an entire year in Chicago without a change of bill, and then produced the piece for over 200 nights in Philadelphia. After this she appeared in comic opera wholly, her most distinguished performance being the dual role of the two sisters in "Girofla-Girofle." Her husband died in 1868, and in November, 1872, she married Tracey W. Titus, from whom she was divorced in 1875. On May 17, 1879, she married Samuel P. Watkins, a non-professional, at whose father's house she passed away.

Weaver, Archibald J., an American lawyer, born in Dundaff, Susquehanna County, Pa., April 15, 1844; died in Falls City, Neb., April 18, 1887. He worked on a farm from his ninth till his seventeenth year, and was then educated in Wyoming Seminary, Pennsylvania, of which institution he served as a member of the faculty from 1864 till 1867. He then studied law at Harvard University, was admitted to the bar in Boston, Mass., in January, 1869, and, removing at once to Falls City, Neb., soon established himself in practice and took an active part in political affairs. In 1871 he was elected a member of the Nebraska Constitutional Convention; in 1872, district-attorney for the First District of the State; in 1875, a member of the new State Constitutional Convention; and the same year judge of the First Judicial District of Nebraska. He was re-elected in 1879, and held the office till 1883, when he was elected a representative in Congress from the First District, and resigned from the bench. He was re-elected to Congress in 1885, serving on the Committee on Commerce. At the expiration of his second term he resumed the practice of law.

Webb, George James, an American composer, born in Wiltshire, England, June 24, 1803; died in Orange, N. J., Oct. 7, 1887. He came to the United States in 1830, settled in Boston. Mass., and was one of the founders of the Academy of Music in that city in 1836. Shortly afterward he was elected president of the Handel and Haydn Society. He was one of the earliest conductors of symphony and oratorio concerts in New England, and for many years one of the most popular teachers of vocal and instrumental music in Boston. In 1871 he removed to New York city and was organist of the Swedenborgian Church for a long time. He compiled hymnals and wrote popular hymns and secular songs, of which "The Morning Light is Breaking" is the best known.

Weld, Mason Cogswell, an American agriculturist, born in Philadelphia, Pa., in 1829; died near Closter, N. J., Sept. 25, 1887. He was graduated at Yale College in 1852, with the degree of Ph. B., and then spent two years studying chemistry under Prof. Silliman in New Haven. He afterward studied at Munich and Leipsic under Professors Liebig and Bunsen, principally the chemistry of agriculture, and on his return to the United States became connected with "The American Agriculturist." In 1868 he followed his two brothers into the army, going out as captain in the Twenty-fifth Regiment of Connecticut Volunteers, and returning with the rank of lieutenant-colonel, gained by meritorious services in the southwest under Gen. Banks. After the war he devoted himself to scientific agriculture, resumed his connection with the agricultural press, and became noted as a breeder and expert judge of fine cattle, particularly Jerseys and Guernseys.

Whitall, Henry, an American astronomer, born near Thoroughfare, Gloucester County, N. J., April 28, 1819; died in London, England. June 3, 1857. He was educated at the Friends' boarding-school at Westtown, N. J., and began studying astronomy at an early age. He taught school for some time near Paulsboro', and then came before the public as a lecturer on astronomical phenomena and an inventor of charts and mechanical apparatus to illustrate the movements, positions, and laws governing the heavenly bodies. His movable planispheres and valuable improvements of the heliotellus, as well as the extent of his researches and calculations, made him famous in astronomical circles throughout the world. He contributed a vast amount of technical information to the Smithsonian Institution, made the astronomical calculations for many of the best-known almanacs in this country and in Europe, and at the time of his death was professor of astronomy in Belvidere (N. J.) Seminary. He had traveled over nearly the whole habitable globe.

Wilder, Royal G., an American clergyman, born in Bridgeport, Vt., in 1816; died in New York city Oct. 10, 1887. He was graduated at Andover Theological Seminary in 1843, and with six of his classmates sailed for India, for missionary work under the American Board of Commissioners, in 1845. His missionary labors covered a period of thirty years, during which he preached in upward of 3,000 cities, towns, and villages, distributed over 3,000,000 pages of the Scriptures and tracts, and taught 3,200 boys and 800 girls in his school. For twelve years he conducted his mission at Kolapoor independent of any board, its expenses being supplied by voluntary gifts; but in 1871 he placed it under the control of the Presbyterian Board. In 1875 he returned to the United States, and had since been editor of "The Missionary Review." He was the author of "Mission Schools in India," and of the only original commentary on the three first Gospels in the Marathi language, besides having translated a large number of books into that tongue.

Woods, William Burnham, an American lawyer, born in Newark, Licking County, Ohio, Aug. 3, 1824; died in Washington, D. C., May 14,

1887. He studied at the Western Reserve College, but was graduated at Yale College in 1845, and two years later was admitted to the Ohio bar and formed a partnership with G. D. King. He was elected Mayor of Newark in 1856-'57, and a member of the Legislature and Speaker in the latter year. After serving two terms in the Legislature he accepted a commission as lieutenant-colonel of the Seventy-sixth Regiment of Ohio Infantry, in September, 1861, and from that time till the close of the war was in constant service, and, with the exception of three months, was all the time in the field at the front and in command of troops. He participated in the battles of Fort Donelson, Shiloh, Chickasaw Bayou, Arkansas Post—in which fight he was wounded—Resaca, Dallas, Atlanta, Jonesboro', Lovejoy Station, the sieges of Vicksburg and Jackson, and in many minor affairs. He was promoted to the rank of colonel after the siege of Jackson, and to those of brigadier-general and brevet major-general after the Atlanta campaign, his military career closing with Gen. Sherman's march to the sea, in which he was in command of a division. After the war he settled in Alabama, engaging in cotton-planting and practicing law. In 1869 he was appointed by President Grant judge of the Fifth United States Circuit, comprising the States of Georgia, Florida, Alabama, Mississippi, Louisiana, and Texas, having then served two years as chancellor of the Middle Chancery Division of Alabama. In October, 1877, he removed to Atlanta, Ga., and on Dec. 15, 1880, was appointed by President Hayes an associate-justice of the United States Supreme Court, to fill the vacancy caused by the retirement of Justice Strong. His familiarity with the old Spanish and French forms of law, which still prevail in many sections of the South, made him very valuable on the Supreme Bench.

Wootten, Edward, an American lawyer, born in Laurel, Del., in September, 1805; died in Georgetown, Del., Feb. 1, 1887. He was reared on his father's farm and educated at Laurel Academy. In 1823 he entered the office of the late Thomas Cooper, a noted lawyer and former member of Congress, and began the study of law, but, on the death of Mr. Cooper, soon after, he went to the office of James Rogers, of Newcastle, and completed his course of reading. He was admitted to the bar in 1830, and, removing to Georgetown, began practicing. In 1845 he received the nomination for Congress by the unanimous vote of the Democratic Convention, but declined the honor, although the nomination was equivalent to election. In 1848 he was appointed an associate-justice of the Superior Court of Delaware, to succeed Judge David Hazzard, and held the office continuously till his death.

OBITUARIES, FOREIGN. Agiar, Antonio Augusto, a Portuguese statesman, born in 1837; died in Lisbon, Portugal, Sept. 4, 1887. He was a professor of the Polytechnic School in Lisbon, contributed much to the advancement of commerce and industry in Portugal, and became Minister of Public Works. He projected extensive dock and street improvements in Lisbon that were begun a month after his death. He was President of the Portuguese Geographical and Agricultural Societies, and one of the most active members of the House of Peers.

Baker, Valentine, an English soldier and pasha

iu the service of the Khedive of Egypt, born in Gloucestershire, England, in 1830; died in Tel el Kebir, Egypt, Nov. 17, 1887. He was the brother of Sir Samuel White Baker, the distinguished explorer, and entered the British army as cornet in the Ceylon forces in 1848. He served with distinction in the Kaffir War of 1852-'53, and in the Crimean War he led one of the storming parties in the final assault in the desperate battle of Tchernaya. In 1859 he was appointed colonel of the Tenth Hussars, the regiment in which the Prince of Wales was placed for military education. He was present as a spectator in the Austro-Prussian and Franco-German Wars. In 1872 he made an unsuccessful attempt to reach Khiva, and this was made the subject of a book called "Clouds in the East," which added to his reputation. In 1875 he was one of the most popular officers in the English army, when, by a disgraceful escapade, for which he was cashiered and for a time imprisoned, he clouded his future career. On the breaking out of the Russo-Turkish War in 1877, he resolved to retrieve his reputation by gallant conduct, and entered the Turkish service, where, after first organizing the Ottoman gendarmerie, he was appointed by Mehemet Ali to an important command on the Lom, where he was decorated with the Osmanieh for his bravery in storming and capturing the heights of Yenikoi, with only 200 foot and 50 cavalry, in the face of two batteries of Russian guns and more than 8,000 troops. Toward the end of 1887 he was appointed to the command of a division in the Balkans, and for the brilliant generalship in covering the retreat of Chakir Pasha's army on Adrianople and Constantinople, he received the decoration of the Medjidyeh. He commanded half the second line of defense before Constantinople, after the surrender of the troops of the first line, and distinguished himself by his energy in constructing defensive works. At the close of this campaign he carried out various reforms in the gendarmerie of Asia Minor. At the end of the Egyptian campaign that followed the siege of Alexandria Baker Pasha resigned his post as aide-de-camp of the Sultan to accept the task of reorganizing the Egyptian army. When he arrived at Cairo the British authorities refused to allow him to organize an army, and instead of that he was given the task of creating a gendarmerie force. Nevertheless, after the defeat of the Egyptian forces under Hicks Pasha, during the insurrection of the Mahdi, he was the main support of the Khedive's authority. In February, 1884, with an army of 35,000 men, he met with disastrous defeat at the hands of the Mahdi's forces in the battle of El Teb, fifty miles south of Suakim, near the Red Sea. In the second battle at the same place he was severely wounded. After this campaign he continued to hold his commission in the Egyptian army until his death. Numerous attempts were made at various times by his friends to obtain

his reinstatement in the English army, and their efforts were about to be crowned with success when his death occurred, hastened, it is supposed, by chagrin and disappointment. Besides the work already mentioned, Col. Baker was the author of "Army Reform" (London, 1869), and other military treatises, including a history of the "War in Bulgaria."

Baldwin, Professor, one of the sub-commissioners appointed under the Irish land act, died in Dublin, Ireland, Aug. 31, 1887. He was manager of an agricultural establishment at Glasnevin, maintained by the National Board of Education, before his appointment on the Land Commission. In this body he was one of those who showed most sympathy for the tenants. He was an advocate of the policy of creating a peasant proprietary, and of encouraging tillage instead of stock-raising, and teaching improved methods of agriculture.

Ballantine, William, an English lawyer, born in London, England, Jan. 3, 1812; died in Margate, England, Jan. 19. 1887. He was the son of a police magistrate, and was called to the bar on June 6, 1834. He achieved early success in practice, and became a sergeant in 1856. He was appointed by the House of Commons, in 1869, to conduct the legal proceedings against the Mayor of Cork, Mr. O'Sullivan, for eulogizing the Fenian O'Farrell, who had attempted to assassinate the Duke of Edinburgh in Australia. He was retained by the Tichborne claimant in his suit to establish his title to the baronetcy in 1871, but in the midst of the proceedings threw up his brief, perceiving the hopelessness of the case. The cases with which his name is more closely associated are the Müller murder-trial in 1864, and the case of the Galkwar of Baroda, who was tried for poisoning the British Resident in 1875. Sergeant Ballantine was famous both for his eloquence in addressing juries and for his skill in the cross-examination of witnesses. He was frequently retained in divorce cases. In one famous suit of this character, when the Prince of Wales took the stand, the sergeant declined to cross-examine him. He retired several years before his death. In 1882 he wrote "Experiences of a Barrister's Life."

Bathie, Anselm Polycarpe, a French jurist, born in Seissan, France, May 31, 1828; died in Paris, France, June 13, 1887. He was appointed Auditor of the Council of State in 1849, and received the degree of Doctor from the law faculty of Paris in 1850. After holding assistant professorships at Dijon, Toulouse, and Paris, he was appointed, in 1860, by the Minister of Public Instruction, to visit the universities of Belgium, Holland, and Germany, in order to study the mode of giving instruction in public and administrative law in those countries. In 1862 he became Professor of Administrative Law in the University of Paris. In February, 1871, he was elected senator for his native department of Gers, and voted with the Right Center. He was the author of a number of works on public law and political economy, among which were "The Forum Judicum of the Visigoths," " Essay on the Life and Works of Turgot" (1860); "Traité théorique et pratique du droit public et administratif" (1861); also essays on "Public Credit" and "Interest-bearing Loans."

Baynes, Thomas Spencer, an English logician, born in Wellington, Somersetshire, England, in 1823; died in London, England, May 30, 1887. He was educated at Bath and Bristol, and at the University of Edinburgh. From 1851 to 1855 he was assistant to Sir William Hamilton in Edinburgh University, and in 1851 published a translation of the "Port Royal Logic." In 1852 he published an "Essay on the New Analytic of Logical Forms." He was appointed assistant editor of the London "Daily News" in 1857, and filled this post till 1864. From 1857 to 1863 he was Examiner in Logic and Mental Philosophy in the University of London. In 1860 he published "The Song of Solomon in the Somersetshire Dialect," and in 1861 produced "The Somersetshire Dialect: its Pronunciation." He was appointed Professor of Logic, Rhetoric, and Metaphysics in the University of St. Andrews in 1864. Numerous articles from his pen appeared in the "Edinburgh Review," "North British Review," "Saturday Review," and "Fraser's Magazine." His greatest work was the ninth edition of the "Encyclopædia Britannica," of which he was principal editor. The publication of this edition was begun in 1875, and was almost completed at the time of his death. His most notable contribution to the work is the article on "Shakespeare."

Beckx, Pierre Jean, Superior-General of the Jesuits, born in Sechem, in Brabant, in 1794; died in Rome, Italy, March 3, 1887. He began his education in a school at Testelt. After it was closed by Napoleon in 1812 he pursued his classical studies by himself, and in 1815 entered the Mechlin Seminary. In 1819 he was ordained, but having decided to become a Jesuit he entered Hildesheim College, and on completing his theological studies was employed in important missions. The Duke of Anhalt-Köthen, who had become converted to Catholicism, engaged him as chaplin and superior of a Catholic mission. In 1846 he effected the readmission of the Jesuits into Venetia, and in 1850 was appointed rector of the Jesuit College at Louvain. He became head of the Austrian province of the order in 1852, and in 1853 succeeded Roothaan as Superior-General. Only one of his predecessors as General of the Jesuits held the office for a longer period. During the time that he was their chief the number of Jesuits more than doubled, and they were re-established in France, Spain, Portugal, and American countries, but subsequently he saw them expelled from Germany, France, and a great part of Italy. On the union of Rome with Italy he withdrew to a country-house near Florence, from which he continued

to direct the order till 1883. On retiring from active duty, he took up his residence in the Jesuit building in Rome occupied by the American Seminary.

Béclard, Jules, a French physiologist, born in Paris, France, in 1818; died there in July, 1887. He was the son of a celebrated anatomist, was educated in Paris, and received the degree of Doctor at Charenton in 1842. He edited his father's "Elements of General Anatomy" in 1851, with copious notes. In 1872 he became Professor of Physiology in the faculty at Paris. He was the author of elementary works on physiology and hygiene, and of a "Précis de histologie" (Paris, 1865).

Beresford-Hope, A. J. B., an English scholar and statesman, born in England, Jan. 25, 1820; died in Bedgebury, England, Oct. 20, 1887. He was educated at Harrow and at Trinity College, Cambridge, where he was graduated in 1841. He early evinced an interest in archæological questions, Gothic art, and ecclesiastical antiquities. He purchased St. Augustine's Abbey at Canterbury in 1844, and fitted it up as a college for missionary clergy. He entered Parliament as member for Maidstone in 1841, and represented that borough till 1852, when he retired, and remained out of Parliament until, in 1857, he was re-elected by Maidstone. In 1859, and when it reappeared in subsequent sessions, he was the most conspicuous opponent of the bill to legalize marriage with a deceased wife's sister, and spoke against every measure encroaching on the rights and immunities of the Established Church. In 1868 he was elected member for the University of Cambridge in Parliament, and continued to represent it until his death. When Mr. Disraeli introduced his reform bill he was taunted by Mr. Beresford-Hope with "outbidding Liberals in a Liberal market," to which he retorted by calling attention to the "Batavian grace" of the latter's oration. Mr. Beresford-Hope was created a Privy Councilor in 1880. He was president of the Society of British Architects in 1865–'67, and frequently lectured on art-subjects. In 1843 he published a volume of "Poems," which was followed by a translation of the "Hymns of the Church" for popular use (London, 1844). Subsequently appeared "Letters on Church Matters," signed "D. C. L.," "The English Cathedral of the Nineteenth Century," and "Worship in the Church of England." Among his treatises and lectures on art subjects are "The Art Workman's Position" (1853); "The Common Sense of Art"; "Church Art" (1863); and "The World's Debt to Art." During the American war he delivered three lectures entitled "A Popular View of the Civil War," "England, the North, and the South," and "The Results of the American Disruption." He contributed many caustic essays to the "Saturday Review," and late in life published two satirical novels entitled "Strictly Tied Up" and "The Brandreths."

Bernhardi, Theodor, a German historian, born in Berlin, Prussia, in 1802; died in March, 1887. His father, August Ferdinand Bernhardi, was one of the founders of the science of comparative philology. His mother, Sophie, a sister of Ludwig Tieck, was divorced from her husband, gained a reputation as a poetess, and married Baron von Knorring, a wealthy Esthonian nobleman. The son was educated at Heidelberg, and after a sojourn in Italy made St. Petersburg his residence, where he was equally at home in courtly and in literary circles. In 1838, when the St. Petersburg Academy of Sciences hesitated between stultifying itself by awarding a prize to Gen. Danileffski, whose fulsome flatteries had gained him the favor of the Czar Nicholas, for a "History of the War of 1812," or offending the autocrat, Bernhardi wrote a critique on the work which was laid before a commission of generals, to whom the academy had referred the question, as the production of a general officer who wished to keep the authorship secret, and formed the basis of the report on which the academy acted in refusing the prize. About 1846 Bernhardi settled on the estate that he purchased near Berlin, and wrote a treatise on "Property in Land," in which he controverted the views of Ricardo. As literary executor of Count Toll, he published that Russian general's "Reminiscences" (1852). In 1854 appeared an essay on "The Russian Army," and in 1859 one on the "Abolition of Serfdom in Russia," which was followed by a disquisition on the "Prussian Military Question." After the publication of the first volume of his "History of Russia and European Politics from 1815 to 1831," he then entered the diplomatic service of Prussia, accompanying the Italian army in the campaign of 1866 against Austria, and subsequently residing at the Florentine court, and then at the court of Madrid, as Secretary of Legation and Military Plenipotentiary, till he was retired at the age of seventy. Resuming his literary labors, he published in rapid succession three more volumes of his history (1874-'77), a work on "Frederick the Great as a General," and two volumes of "Miscellaneous Essays" (Berlin, 1879). He was engaged, when death overtook him, on the last part of the "History of Russia." The three parts that have appeared are filled with introductory matter and digressions covering the entire field of modern political history, and bring the proper subject of the work down only to 1881.

Boussingault, Jean Baptiste Joseph Dieudonné, a French chemist, born in Paris, France, Feb. 2, 1802; died there May 12, 1887. He was educated at the Mining School in Saint Étienne and was sent, on completing his course, to Venezuela by an English company to reopen certain silver-mines known to the ancients. His researches attracted the attention of Alexander von Humboldt, who warmly commended his work. The war for the independence of the republic of Colombia soon broke out and Boussingault became scientific aid to Gen. Simon Bolivar with the rank of colonel. He succeeded in exploring Venezuela and all the regions between Cartagena and the mouths of the Orinoco, as well as Peru and Ecuador. On his return to France, a few years later, he received the appointment of Professor of Chemistry and Dean of the Faculty of Sciences at Lyons. In 1839 he settled in Paris where he was made Professor of Agriculture in the Conservatory of Arts and Industry, and was elected a member of the Academy of Sciences. He devoted much attention to the conditions of soil and air necessary for the best results in grazing, the rearing of domestic animals, and the acclimatization of useful animals from foreign countries. The value of fertilizers according to the proportions of nitrogen which they contain is chiefly due to his researches, and in conjunction with Jean Baptiste André Dumas, he first measured the exact proportions of the constituent elements of atmospheric air. He also discovered a simple method of preparing oxygen by means of baryta. In 1848 he was elected to the National Assembly as a moderate Republican from the department of Bas-Rhin, where he owned chemical works and was chosen a member of the Council of State in which he retained a seat until the *coup d'état* of Dec. 2, 1851, after which he withdrew from political life. Boussingault was made commander of the Legion of Honor in March, 1857, and promoted to the supreme grade of grand officer in August, 1876. He was a prominent member of the four World's Fairs held in Paris, and at that held in Vienna in 1873, and was appointed in August, 1876, a member of the special commission for the formation of an Agronomic Institute in Paris. Many of his monographs from the "Annales de Physique et de Chimie," of which he was one of the editors, and from the "Comptes Rendus," of the Academy of Sciences, were collected into a volume entitled "Memoirs on Agricultural Chemistry and Physiology" (Paris, 1854). His chief work was a "Treatise on Rural Economy" (2 vols., 1844, English translation, London, 1845) republished with the title "Agronomy, Agricultural Chemistry, and Physiology" (8 vols., 1861-'64).

Bove, an Italian explorer, died in Verona, Italy, Aug. 9, 1887. He was a lieutenant in the Italian service, and accompanied Prof. Nordenskjöld in his voyage through the northeast passage to Siberia. In 1882 he conducted the exploration of the southern coast of Patagonia and the shores of Terra del Fuego. He was a sufferer from ill-health, and died by his own hand.

Brinz, Alois von, a German educator and politician, born in 1820; died in Munich, Bavaria, Sept. 19, 1887. He studied law at Munich and Berlin, became a writer of the Romantic school, and in 1851 was appointed to a professorship at Erlangen. In 1857 he was called to the chair of Roman Law at the University of

Prague. He entered with ardor into the conflict with the rising national sentiment of the Czechs, and became the leading exponent of the German idea in Bohemia. He was elected to the Diet, and afterward to the Reichsrath, where his passionate advocacy of Germanic supremacy placed him in the front rank of politicians. When the federalistic principle gained the upper hand after the wars of 1866 and 1870, he withdrew from politics, left Austria, and resumed literary work. At the time of his death he was acting as a professor at the University of Munich.

Brown, Sir Thomas Gore, English administrator, born July 3, 1807; died in London, England, April 18, 1887. He entered the army at the age of sixteen, and served with distinction in the Afghan War of 1836. In 1851 he was made governor of St. Helena; from St. Helena he was transferred to the governorship of New Zealand, where he inaugurated responsible government, and conducted the Maori war with such severity that he incurred much odium, though supported by the colonial minister and by the Imperial Government. He was knighted in 1860. On the completion of his term of office in 1861, he became governor of Tasmania, where he remained until 1869. In 1870-'71 he was governor of Bermuda, after which he retired from public life.

Brüggemann, Karl Heinrich, a German journalist, born in Hopsten, Westphalia, Aug. 20, 1810; died in Cologne, Rhenish Prussia, July 2, 1887. While a student of law and political science at Bonn and Heidelberg he was a member of the patriotic student societies, and in May, 1832, came before the public as an orator at a celebrated meeting at Hambach, where he was one of those who demanded the promised constitution and the union of the German states. He was arrested, delivered up to the Prussian authorities, and after an examination that lasted two years, was condemned to death on the wheel as a traitor. The sentence was commuted to imprisonment for life, and when Friedrich Wilhelm IV became King in 1840 a general amnesty gave him freedom. He settled in Berlin, where he wrote for the press and published works on political and economical subjects, but was refused permission to lecture at the university. In 1845 he became editor of the " Cologne Gazette." This paper was an influential organ of the Constitutionalists, and after the revolution of 1848 the editor received many reprimands and warnings from the Goverment, until finally in 1855, in order to avert the threatened suppression of the journal, he retired from its management. He continued to write for the paper, however, and remained on its staff till two years before his death.

Buddicom, William Barber, an English engineer, born in Liverpool, England, in 1816; died in Flintshire, England, Aug. 11, 1887. At an early age he was apprenticed to an engineering firm. After serving as engineer on some of the

first railroads that were constructed in England, he was called to France, in 1841, to take charge of shops for making the rolling-stock for the Paris and Rouen Railway, and he held the contract for working that railway till 1860. He was connected with Thomas Brassey and others in making the Bellegarde tunnel on the Lyons and Geneva line, and also in constructing and working the temporary Mont Cenis Mountain railway, the southern railways, and Maremma railways of Italy. He retired from business in 1864.

Cantagrel, Félix François Jean, a French engineer and deputy, born in Amboise, France, Jan. 27, 1810; died in Paris, France, Feb. 27, 1887. He first acquired note by a pamphlet published in 1841 entitled " Le fou du Palais-Royal." In 1848 he was conspicuous as an ardent adherent of Fourier. He was a member of the National Assembly in 1849, and for participation in the insurrection of June 18 was sentenced to transportation, but escaped to Belgium, where he married a German, with whom he traveled extensively. They lived for several years in Texas, where, with other Fourierists, they established a phalanstery, and attempted to carry out the ideal of communism. After the amnesty of 1859 Cantagrel returned to France, and advocated his socialistic principles in the press. In 1871 he was elected a municipal councillor of Paris, and in 1876 a representative of the Seine Department in the Chamber of Deputies, where he was president by seniority of the group of the Extreme Left.

Caro, Elme Marie, a French philosophical writer, born in Poitiers, France, March 4, 1826; died in Paris, France, July 13, 1887. After completing his studies at the Stanislas College he entered the Normal School. In 1848 he discharged the duties of Professor of Philosophy in several provincial colleges, and in 1858 became master of conferences at the Normal School. He became Professor of Philosophy to the Faculty of Letters at Paris in July, 1864, and in 1869 was admitted to the Academy of Moral and Political Sciences. He was a member of the French Academy, and a member of the Legion of Honor. He early made his reputation as a brilliant lecturer and elegant writer. In 1849 he gained the prize of the Academy for a eulogy on Madame de Staël. His lectures in Paris, which had for their main burden the defense of Christianity against the rationalistic and materialistic philosophies, were especially attractive to women.

Ciparia, Timotee, a Roumanian philologist, born in Panade, Transylvania, Feb. 21, 1805; died in Bucharest, Roumania, Sept. 14, 1887. He studied at the high-school at Blasin, became a teacher in the gymnasium there in 1825, and was afterward Professor of Philosophy and Oriental Languages in the Theological Institute. He was president of the Academia Romana, and editor of the Roumanian "Archives of Philology and History," and was a frequent contributor to the periodicals of Roumania.

He was the author of works on the Roumanian language, among them "Elements of the Rouman Tongue" (1854), and a "Roumanian Grammar" (1877); also "Elements of Poetry" (1860), and "Elements of Philosophy" (1863).

Clam-Martinitz, Count **Heinrich,** a Bohemian politician, born in 1826; died in Prague, Bohemia, June 5, 1887. He was the representative of a German feudal family in Bohemia, and while the Liberal German Party was dominant in Austrian politics he was a prominent figure in the Clerical Opposition. After the Franco-German War the Czech party under Count Clam's leadership attained to a position of power and influence in the affairs of the empire, and, although in more recent times the national movement has become dissociated from the interests of the aristocratic and Ultramontane section of the party, he was still the acknowledged leader of the Czechs at the time of his death. Count Clam entered the Reichsrath with the other Czechs when Count Taafe became Austrian prime minister, and was the chief of the Czech Club and the most influential member of the committee or caucus of the Government party until 1885, when severe illness compelled him to be less active.

Comber, T. J., an English missionary, born about 1844; died at sea in June, 1887. He was one of the most courageous and energetic of the Baptist missionaries on the Congo. After having lived for many years in Africa, he was seized with malarial fever about the middle of June at Matadi, and died on board a German steamer while on the route to Europe. Not long before his sister and his brother had died from the effects of the African climate while engaged in mission work.

Cearcy, Roussel de, a French general, born in Orleans in 1827; died in Paris, France, Nov. 9, 1887. He served, in the Crimea, Italy, and Mexico, was with the Metz garrison which was surrendered in 1870, and fought against the Paris Communards. He was a general of recognized ability, and, after the fall of the Ferry Cabinet in 1885, he was sent out to take command of the French forces in Tonquin. There he came into conflict with the civil authorities, and in a few months was called upon to resign. In 1886 General Boulanger intrusted him with a secret mission to the German frontier.

Cuvillier-Fleury, Alfred Auguste, a French journalist, born in 1802; died in Paris, Oct. 18, 1887. He was a student in the College of Louis-le-Grand, and won in 1819 the annual prize for a Latin essay open to the competition of all the schools of Paris. For two years he was Secretary to Louis Bonaparte, King of Holland, and shared with him his exile at Rome and Florence. In 1827 Louis Philippe intrusted him with the education of his son, the Duc d'Aumale, with whom he afterward remained as secretary. He became one of the editors of the "Journal des Débats" in 1834. He was chief editor of that paper until the fall of the empire, and devoted his literary talents

to upholding in politics the doomed cause of Orleanism, and in literature the losing side of the Classicists against the Romantic school. While remaining a stanch Orleanist, he offended the Duc d'Aumale in 1872 by publishing a letter in which he deprecated the efforts of the deputies of the right to constrain President Thiers to declare for the monarchy. The biographical and critical essays which make up his published works are reprints of articles that were written for the "Journal des Débats." In 1866 he was chosen a member of the French Academy. He published "Political and Revolutionary Portraits" (Paris, 1851); "Historic and Literary Studies" (1854); "Voyages and Voyagers" (1854); and "Illustrious Poets and Romancers" (1863).

Dancer, John Benjamin, an English optician, born in London in 1812; died in Manchester, Dec. 6, 1887. He settled in Manchester in 1835, and soon made his mark in scientific circles. His services in connection with electricity and photography were important, and he was the first to suggest the application of photography in connection with the magic lantern. He made the first thermometer in England with any pretensions to accuracy. During the later years of his life he was totally blind.

Dupin, Jean Henri, a French dramatist, born in Paris, France, Sept. 1, 1791; died there, April 8, 1887. He produced his first play, "Le Voyage à Chambord," in 1808. He wrote about fifty pieces in collaboration with Scribe, as many more with Armand Dartois, a large number with other playwrights, and some twenty that were produced under his own name. Among these the most successful were "La fête de famille" (1831); "L'Amour vient après" (1838); "Le chat noir" (1839); and "L'orphelin de la Chine" (1867).

Duruy, Albert, a French journalist, born in 1844; died in Paris, Aug. 12, 1887. He was the son of Victor Duruy, the historian who was Louis Napoleon's Minister of Education in 1863. In 1869 he began writing for "Le Peuple Français" under the pen-name of "Albert Villeneuve," and for "La Liberté" under his own name. He served in the Franco-Prussian War and was wounded at Sedan. In 1875 he wrote a Bonapartist pamphlet entitled "Comment les Empires reviennent," which created considerable stir. In 1876 he established "La Nation," which was soon absorbed in "Le Petit Caporal."

Duval, Raoul, a French politician, born in 1833; died in Monte Carlo, Feb. 10, 1887. He was an active and eloquent member of the French Chamber, in which he first sat with the Moderate Republicans, but became one of the foremost champions of Bonapartism, and afterward of the united Conservative party. In 1886 he endeavored to effect an alliance between Moderate Conservatives who were prepared to accept the republic and the sections of the Republican party, who were equally opposed to the Radical programme. He was a grandson of Jean Baptiste Say, and remained steadfast to free trade when his political associates supported the duties on grain.

Faris, Ahmed, Effendi, an Arab scholar and Turkish publicist, died Sept. 23, 1887. He was a member of a Maronite family which embraced Protestantism in consequence of what they deemed the perversion of Mohammedanism. To escape imprisonment he fled to Egypt where he became a teacher in the Christian schools at Cairo, studied Arabic under the sheikhs of the Yamant Aghar, and translated the Bible into Arabic. Reverting to Mohammedanism, he became secretary to the Bey of Tunis, and in 1860 went to reside at Constantinople, where he started the newspaper "El Jewaib," through which he exerted a wide influence throughout Islam.

Farre, Arthur, an English surgeon, born in London, England, March 6, 1811; d. there, Dec. 17, 1887. He was a pupil at the Charterhouse School in London, and was graduated from Caius College, Cambridge, in 1833, studied medicine at St. Bartholomew's Hospital, and received his degree of M. D. in 1841. He lectured on comparative anatomy at St. Bartholomew's Hospital in 1836–'37 and on forensic medicine from 1838 to 1840. From 1841 to 1862 he was Professor of Obstetric Medicine at King's College, as well as physician *accoucheur* to King's College Hospital, and was recognized as the head of the profession in obstetric science and surgery. He was at different times censor, examiner, and councilor in the Royal College of Physicians, and was for twenty-four years examiner in midwifery in the Royal College of Surgeons. He had a large obstetrical practice, numbering among his clients the Princess of Wales and other members of the royal family. He was the author of "The Uterus and its Appendages," and also of numerous physiological papers.

Fäustle, Johann, a Bavarian minister of justice, born in Augsburg, Bavaria, in 1828; died in Munich, Bavaria, April 18, 1887. He was the son of a school-teacher, rose rapidly to high posts in the judiciary, entered the ministry about 1865, and took a prominent part in legislation. In 1871 he was appointed Minister of Justice in the Cabinet of Count Hegnenberg-Dux, although a Liberal, and was retained in office till his death. He secured the King's signature in 1878 to the law accepting the jurisdiction of the imperial courts, and was instrumental in effecting changes in the municipal law in order to bring it into conformity with the code of the empire.

Fontes, Periera de Mello, A. M. de, a Portuguese statesman, died in Lisbon, Portugal, Jan. 23, 1887. He was a soldier by profession, holding the rank of general in the army, and was for many years the chief of the Conservative party in Portugal. First becoming Prime Minister in 1872, he kept his party and himself in power by the use of patronage and of official pressure in elections until the country was almost ripe for revolution, when the King in 1886 insisted on calling a ministry from the Monarchical Liberals.

Gallait, Louis, a Belgian painter, born in Tournay, Belgium, May 10, 1810; died in Brussels, Belgium, Nov. 20, 1887. He was one of the foremost representatives of the modern Dutch school. Among his noted paintings are "Montaigne visiting Tasso in Prison" (1886); "Battle of Cassel," painted for the Versailles gallery; "Temptation of St. Anthony" (1848); "Last Moments of Count Egmont," exhibited at the World's Fair of 1862 and purchased for the Berlin Museum; "Queen Joanna and her Dead Husband"; "The Taking of Antioch"; "Counts Egmont and Horn listening to their Death Sentence"; and "Count Baldwin crowned at Jerusalem." His most important work is "The Plague in Turnay."

Ganetzky, Johann Stephanovitch, a Russian soldier, died in St. Petersburg, Russia, May 7, 1887. He was one of the heroes of the last Russo-Turkish War, in which he commanded the corps of grenadiers before Plevna, and victoriously repulsed the last desperate sortie of Osman Pasha. At the time of his death he was governor of the fortress of St. Petersburg.

Genast, Wilhelm, a German politician and author, born in Leipsic, Saxony, July 30, 1822; died in January, 1887. He studied jurisprudence at Jena and Heidelberg, entered on the practice of law, and in 1848 first appeared in the political arena as a champion of constitutionalism. He was one of the most active members of the Weimar Diet and a favorite speaker in the North German Parliament and afterward in the German Reichstag, where he acted with the National Liberals. Genast advanced in his profession to high official posts, and was instrumental in legal reforms. He was the author of romances entitled "Der Köhlergraf" and "Im hohen Hause," and of the dramas, "Bernhard von Weimar" and "Florian Geyer."

Goldschmidt, Meyer Aaron, a Danish journalist, born in Vordinborg, in the Island of Jutland, Oct. 26, 1819; died Aug. 15, 1887. He was of Israelitish origin, and was educated at the University of Copenhagen. In 1840 he founded the "Corsair," a weekly satirical journal, and in 1843 was sentenced to a term of imprisonment for his attacks on the ministry. In 1848 he took control of a periodical entitled "North and South." He was the author of "The Jew," a romance which was translated into German and English; "The Heir" which was also translated into English; and "The History of Love in Divers Countries." He also published several poems and dramas.

Gozzadini, Count Giovanni, an Italian archæologist, born in 1810; died in Bologna, Italy, Sept. 14, 1887. In early life he was a soldier in the Italian army. He began the pursuit of archæology by making a collection of weapons, which he afterward presented to the city of Bologna. In 1871 he was elected to preside at the International Congress of Prehistoric Anthropology and Archæology, the proceedings of which he opened with an address on Etruscan remains. He was the author of a large number of works, among which are "La vita di Armanciotto de Ramazzatti" (1835); "Memorie per la vita di Giovanni II. Bentivogli" (1839); "Di ulteriori scorperte nella Necropoli a Marzabotto" (1870); "Il conte Giovanni Pepoli e Sixto V" (1878).

Grant, James, a Scottish novelist, born in Edinburgh, Scotland, Aug. 1, 1822; died in London, England, May 5, 1887. He was the son of a captain in the British army. After spending seven years with his father in British America, he returned to England in 1839, and was commissioned as ensign, but in 1843 he resigned, and devoted himself to literature. Many of his novels treat of modern military life, with which his early barrack experiences made him familiar, others are the fruit of studies in Scottish history and antiquities. In 1875 Mr. Grantt embraced the Roman Catholic faith. His first work, "The Romance of War, or the Highlanders in Spain," was published in 1846, and in the next year the companion volume, "The Highlanders in Belgium." Among his numerous works are the following: "The Adventures of an Aide-de-camp" (London, 1848); "Memoirs of Kirkcaldy of Grange" (1849); "Walter Fenton" (1850); "Edinburgh Castle" (1850); "Bothwell, or the Days of Mary Queen of Scotts" (1851); "Memoirs of Sir John Hepburn, Marshal of France and Colonel of the Scots Brigade" (1851); "Jane Seton" (1853); "Philip Rollo" (1854); "Frank Hilson, or the Queen's Own" (1855); "The Yellow Frigate" (1855); "The Phantom Regiment" (1856); "Harry Ogilvie" (1856); "Laura Everingham" (1857); "Memoirs of the Marquis of Montrose" (1858); "Arthur Blane" (1858); "The Cavaliers of Fortune" (1858); "Lucy Arden" (1859); "Legends of the Black Watch" (1859); "Mary of Loraine" (1860); "Olliver Ellis" (1861); "Dick Rodney" (1861); "The Captain of the Guard" (1862); "The Adventures of Rob Roy" (1863); "Letty Hyde's Lovers" (1863); "Second to None" (1864); "The King's Own Borderers" (1865); "The Constable of France" (1866); "The White Cockade" (1867); "First Love and Last Love" (1868); "The Secret Dispatch" (1868); "The Girl He Married" (1869); "Jack Manly, his Adventures" (1870); "Lady Wedderburn's Wish" (1870); "Only an Ensign" (1871); "Under the Red Dragon" (1871); "British Battles on Land and Sea" (1873-'75); "Shall I Win Her?" (1874); "Fairer than a Fairy" (1874); "One of the Six Hundred" (1875); "Morley Ashton" (1876); "Old and New Edinburgh" (1880-'83); "Lady Glendonwynd" (1882); "Jack Chaloner" (1883); "Miss Cheyne of Essilmont" (1883); "The Master of Aberfeldie" (1884); and "History of the War in the Soudan" (1885).

Greig, Samuel Alexeivich, a Russian statesman, born in 1827; died in Berlin, Germany, March 22, 1887. His father and grandfather were well-known Russian admirals of Scotch extraction. He was educated for the army, served in the guards, rose to the rank of general, and was wounded at Sebastopol. His first civil post was in the Ministry of Marine. He held for seven years the second place in the Ministry of Finance, was for the next four years Comptroller-General, and in 1878 became Minister of Finance. He had to settle the expenses of the Turkish War, and concluded two internal loans of 300,000,000 rubles each. In 1880 he contracted a metallic loan without resorting to the assistance of foreign syndicates. He devised five new taxes yielding 21,000,000 annually, and was pursuing fiscal reform and retrenchment when a court intrigue deprived him of office. His last six years were passed in retirement.

Hadji, Loja, a Bosnian chieftain, died in Mecca, Aug. 16, 1887. Taking advantage of the interregnum between the retirement of the Turks from Serajevo, and the entry of the Austrians, he placed himself at the head of the National party, organized a guerilla insurrection, and harassed the Austrian army of occupation for several months. At last he was taken prisoner, tried by court-martial, and sentenced to five years' imprisonment in the Bohemian fortress of Theresienstadt. On being pardoned and granted a small pension on condition that he would never return to Bosnia, he took up his residence in the holy city of Islam and spent the rest of his life in religious contemplation.

Hauser, Miska, a Hungarian violinist and composer, born in Pressburg, Hungary, in 1822; died Dec. 17, 1887. At an early age he manifested a remarkable taste for music, and was taught the violin by Conradin Kreutzer. He first appeared in public at the age of eleven. He studied at the Vienna Conservatorium under Mayseder and Sechter, and then made a musical tour through nearly all of the civilized countries of the world. The notes of his tour were published as "Traveling Diary of an Austrian Virtuoso" (Leipsic, 1859). Some of his "Lieder ohne Worte" and his arrangements of Schubert's "Lieder" are still popular.

Hennequin, Alfred Nicolas, a French dramatist, born in Liége, Belgium, Jan. 13, 1842; died in St. Mandé, France, Aug. 6, 1887. He was originally a railroad engineer, but on attaining a success with a play that was brought out at Brussels in 1869, was encouraged to write others. His reputation was made with "Le Procés Veauradieux," which was produced in 1875. This was followed by "Les Dominos Roses" and other pieces, most of them written in conjunction with other dramatists.

Herrmann, Herr, a German juggler, born in Hanover in 1815; died in Carlsbad, Jan. 8, 1887. He exhibited his performances of sleight-of-hand through all the countries of Europe and America, and gained a large fortune, of which he made a generous use. His performances were distinguished, not only for skillful prestidigitation, in which art he was without an equal, but for original delusive tricks of his invention and witty impromptu variations. Herrmann acquired such control over his facial muscles that he could alter his features so as to be unrecognizable. He delighted to puzzle strangers in hotels and public places by transforming objects before their eyes, and other tricks of legerdemain. He once, before giving a performance at the palace of Abdul Aziz, provided himself with a duplicate of a watch of unique design that was usually worn by the Sultan. In the course of his exhibition he threw the Sultan's valuable time-piece into the Bosporus, and then allayed the consternation of the courtiers by conjuring the replica from the monarch's pocket.

Hunt, Robert, an English scientist, born in Devonport, England, Sept. 1, 1807; died in Chelsea, England, Oct. 17, 1887. He discovered several photographic processes, and largely contributed to a more perfect knowledge of the influences of light, heat, and the chemical action of the solar rays upon the growth of plants. The results of these researches were printed in the "Transactions" of the British Association and of the Royal Society. He was the originator of the publication of statistical returns of the mineral produce of the United Kingdom, and was made keeper of the mining records. In 1866, he was one of the Royal Commissioners appointed to inquire into the quantity of coal left unworked in the British coal-fields. He was the first appointed Professor of Mechanical Sciences to the Government School of Mines. When the Mining Record office was abolished in 1883, he was retired with a pension. His first book was a treatise on "Photography." His other publications are "Researches on Light" (1844); "The Poetry of Science" (1849); "Panthea, or the Spirit of Nature" (1849); "Elementary Physics" (1851); "Manual of Photography" (1852); three editions of "Ure's Dictionary of Arts, Manufactures, and Mines"; the "Synopsis" and "Hand-book" of the exhibitions of 1851 and 1862; and a comprehensive work on "British Mining" (1884).

Husband, William, an English mechanical engineer, born at Mylor, near Falmouth, England, Oct. 12, 1823; died in Clifton, England, May 3, 1887. He became an apprentice in the Hayle foundry, and in 1844 was sent to erect the pumping-engines used to drain Haarlem Lake, Holland. He entered the service of the Dutch Government, and was employed to superintend the drainage-works, which were completed in seven years. He then returned to England, and eventually became a partner in the Hayle foundry. He was the inventor of an oscillating cylinder ore-stamping machine, a balance-valve for water-works, a four-beat pump-valve, and a safety plug for the prevention of accidents.

Iddesleigh, Sir Stafford Henry Northcote, Earl of, an English statesman, born in London, England, Oct. 27, 1818; died there, Jan. 12, 1887. He came of an ancient Devonshire family, and was educated at Eton, and at Balliol College, Oxford. After his graduation he returned to London, and in 1841 was chosen by Mr. Gladstone, who was then President of the Board of Trade, as his private secretary. He remained in this position until Mr. Gladstone retired from the Government of Sir Robert Peel in 1845. In 1847 he was admitted to the bar, and the same year he became Legal Secretary of the Board of Trade. His pamphlet on the "Navigation Laws" attracted much attention at this time. He succeeded his grandfather in 1851 in the baronetcy, which had belonged to his family for several generations, and in the same year he officiated as one of the secretaries of the World's Fair. In 1853–'54 he was associated with Sir Charles Trevelyan in an inquiry into the condition of the civil establishments of the Crown, and their report presented in 1854 eventually led to the establishment of the Civil Service Commission, and to the throwing open of the Civil Service generally to public competition. He first entered the House of Commons in 1855 as the Conservative member for Dudley. From 1858 to 1866 he sat in the House as member for Stamford, and in 1866 he first became a member for his native constituency of North Devon, which he represented until 1885. In 1856 he was appointed Financial Secretary to the Treasury, but went out of office with his party in 1859. In 1866, on the formation of Lord Derby's third Administration, he became President of the Board of Trade, but resigned this office in the following year for that of Secretary of State for India, in which post he remained till 1868. Sir Stafford Northcote was by this time recognized as one of the leaders of the Conservative party. In 1871 he was nominated by Mr. Gladstone as one of the Special Commissioners for the negotiation of the Treaty of Washington, which had for its main object the final settlement of the "Alabama" Claims. In 1874, after the resignation of Mr. Gladstone and the return of Mr. Disraeli to power, Sir Stafford Northcote was appointed Chancellor of the Exchequer. His financial policy is remarkable for the final extinction of the sugar duties, counterbalanced by a slight increase in the tax on tobacco; for the temporary reduction of the income-tax to 2d. in the pound; and for the establishment and maintenance of a really effective sinking fund, which has been maintained intact by his successors. From 1876, when Mr. Disraeli entered the upper House, till 1880, Sir Stafford Northcote was Conservative leader of the House of Commons. In 1885 he was elevated to the House of Lords as Earl of Iddesleigh, and became First Lord of the Treasury in Lord Salisbury's first Government. In 1886, when Lord Salisbury again became Prime Minister he was appointed Secretary of State for Foreign Affairs. As Chancellor of the Exchequer, Sir Stafford Northcote, who was trained in the Gladstonian school of finance, inspired more confidence than any other Tory who had held that office in recent times. His urbanity in debate and conciliatory disposition pleased every one except the aggressive section of his own party, which, by a political combination enforced his retirement from the position of leader of the House, which was made easy for him by making him a peer. He is succeeded in the earldom by his eldest son, Viscount St. Cyres.

Ideville, Henri, Comte d', a French diplomatist, born in Saulnat, in the Puy-de-Dôme, July 16, 1830; died July 3, 1887. At an early age he entered the diplomatic service, and in 1859 was appointed Secretary of the French Embassy at Turin. In 1862 he was sent to Rome where he remained five years, and subsequently he was stationed at Dresden and Athens. In 1873 he was made Prefect of Algiers, but only occupied the post for a year. He was the author of the following works : "Journal of a Diplomatist in Italy in 1859-'66"; "Notes for a History of the Second Empire" (1872-"78); "Journal of a Diplomatist in Germany and Greece" (1875); "The Piedmontese in Rome" (1867-'70); "Flemish Letters" (1876); "Gustave Courbet" (1878); "Victor Emmanuel" (1878); and a "Life of Rossi."

Jacobini, Cardinal **Ludovico,** Pontifical Secretary of State, born in Genzano, Italy, Jan. 6, 1832; died in Rome, Italy, Feb. 28, 1887. He was sprung from a family possessing estates at Genzano, studied theology at the University of Rome, and in 1862 was selected by Pius IX as one of his domestic chaplains, and made a referendary of the Segnatura. Soon afterward he was appointed secretary of the Propaganda for the Eastern churches, and then a consultor of the society. He took part in the preliminary arrangements for the Œcumenical Council of 1867, and during the proceedings served as an under-secretary. In 1874 he was appointed nuncio to the court of Austria and made Archbishop of Thessalonica *in partibus infidelium.* While at Vienna he carried on negotiations with Austria and Russia in regard to ecclesiastical arrangements for Bosnia and the Herzegovina, and began the negotiations with Bismarck aiming at a settlement of the disputes with Prussia. He received a cardinal's hat from Leo X on Sept. 19, 1879, and was recalled to Rome to take the office of Secretary of State in succession to Cardinal Nina. He was in feeble health for two years before he died, and aggravated his condition by his application to the questions relating to the Church in France, Prussia, Switzerland, Bavaria, Russia, and Turkey. At the time of his death, besides being Papal Secretary of State, he was administrator of the estates of the Holy See, prefect of the Laurentani Congregation, and secretary of the Propaganda.

Jauréguiberry, Jean Bernard, a French naval officer, senator, and minister, born in Bayonne, France, Aug. 26, 1815; died, Oct. 21, 1887.

He was descended from a Basque family of Protestants, was educated in the naval school at Brest, and was commissioned as ensign in 1839, lieutenant in 1845, commander in 1850, captain in 1860, rear-admiral in 1869, and vice-admiral in 1870. He commanded vessels in Senegal and Cayenne in 1852, in the Black Sea in 1855-'56, and in the China seas in 1857-'60. He was fleet-major at Toulon in the Franco-Prussian War. Gambetta appointed him to the command of a division in the Army of the Loire, and made him a corp commander on the elevation of Chanzy to the chief command. He was elected a deputy as a Republican in February, 1871, resigned his seat in the following December, was for some time president of the Board of Naval Construction, and became Minister of Marine under Waddington on Feb. 4, 1879. He was chosen a life-senator in the following May, retained his portfolio in the Freycinet Cabinet, and in 1882 was again selected by M. de Freycinet for the same post.

Jefferies, Richard, an English author, died at Goring, Aug. 14, 1887. He was the son of a farmer, but in early life went to London, where he began to write books and contributed to magazines. His writings treated of rural life and kindred subjects, and he dealt with nature in a picturesque and graphic style. Among his principal works are "The Gamekeeper at Home" (London, 1876); "Wild Life in a Southern County," "Round About a Great Estate," "Hodge and his Masters," "Nature near London," "The Life of the Fields," "Red Deer," and "The Open Air" (1885). He also wrote works of fiction, among which are "The Scarlet Shawl," "Restless Human Hearts," "World's End," and "Amaryllis at the Fair" (1887). He also published an interesting autobiography entitled "The Story of My Heart" (London, 1883).

Katkoff, Michel Nikipherovich, a Russian journalist, born in Moscow in 1821; died at St. Petersburg, Aug. 1, 1887. His family belonged to the higher nobility, and no pains were spared in his rearing and education. He was graduated in 1839 from the University of Moscow with high scholastic honors, and subsequently studied at the German universities of Königsberg and Berlin, in which latter institution he was the student of the philosopher Schelling. After his return to Russia he accepted the chair of Philosophy in the University of Moscow, where he made a reputation as a teacher of the progressive ideas of the popular German school and an advocate of national progress toward a constitutional government. When Russia was stirred by the revolutionary movement of 1848, and rigorous restrictions were placed by the Government of the Czar Nicholas on academical teaching and all expression of opinions, Katkoff fell under the suspicion of the authorities, and was placed under police surveillance. Finally, in 1849, his professorship was abolished. He made several journeys to England in the next few years, spending much time on the Isle of Wight, where in friendly intimacy with Englishmen he familiarized himself with the principles and working of the British Constitution. In 1856 he returned to Moscow and founded the "Russky Vestnik" ("Russian Messenger"), in which he ventilated his ideas, arguing that national advancement should keep pace with the march of European civilization, and especially advocating a system of self-government on the model of the English Constitution. In his paper Turgenieff and other famous writers were first introduced to the public. Katkoff opposed radicalism as well as reaction, and vigorously combated the revolutionary projects of the Socialists in their intrigues against the established government of the Empire. In this contest he won the hearty commendation of the Czar. He founded, in association with his former fellow-student, Prof. Leontieff, the Moscow "Gazette," of which he became editor in 1861. Katkoff's political opinions underwent a radical change. The revolution in Poland and the force lent by that event to revolutionary doctrines in Russia itself hastened the transmutation in his political views. He became the apostle of national Russia, and in this position he appeared an ardent admirer of autocracy, of the classical system of education, and of the orthodox Church, and a bitter foe to anything in the shape of freedom on the part of the people. Katkoff preached a crusade against Western civilization and learning that had been cultivated in Russia since Peter the Great's time, and which he declared to have worked as a debasing and corrupting influence, while the elements of a nobler Slavic civilization were neglected and the national genius was stifled. He urged the forcible Russification of the Baltic Provinces and Poland. In the latter country the spirit of revolution was rife, and the Government sought to allay discontent by a conciliatory policy. The doctrines enunciated by Katkoff found an echo in the hearts of untraveled Russians, who were continually outstripped in every line of advancement by foreigners and their denationalized countrymen. The Government ordered Katkoff to publish a sharp reprimand for his articles on Poland, or pay a fine of 2,000 rubles for every day of delay. Refusing to print the "vile prose," he paid the fine for eleven days. The situation in Poland became more critical, and the Government refunded the fines that the popular and prophetic journalist had paid, and withdrew its warning. When the revolt of 1863 finally broke out in Poland he urged in the "Gazette," the most energetic measures for its suppression, and this now accorded well with the temper of Alexander II. Following the reactionary principles that he had adopted, Katkoff made a vigorous onslaught upon the educational theories he had taught when he held the chair of Philosophy in the Moscow University. In conjunction with other Panslavist champions he founded in Moscow the

Nicolai Alexandrovich Institute, where, under his supervision, by a strictly classical and military pedagogism, the sons of wealthy and noble Russians were taught the ultra tenets of unchecked imperialism. It was upon the model of this school that Count Tolstoi reorganized the whole educational sytem of the Empire, so that now the reactionary doctrines of Katkoff are the formative principle of all Russian youth. On account of the influence of Katkoff over Czar Alexander II, this school was the recipient of large sums from the national treasury. The articles that he published in the "Gazette" against Nihilism were so frantic that opinion was divided as to whether he was cleverly rendering autocracy hateful by an overdisplay of zeal, or suffering from aberration of intellect. He became an advocate of the Panslavist idea, urging the union of the Slav populations of Europe in one empire. The present Emperor in his early youth became very strongly attached to Katkoff, who, after the death of Alexander II, became the head of the National party, and it was due to his influence that the proposed summoning of a parliament of provincial delegates was abandoned. He was then offered, but refused, the portfolio of Minister of Instruction, accepting, however, the dignity of a privy councilor. By this time his views on educational matters had been modified by his political leanings to such an extent that he used his influence with the minister Delyanoff, to procure the abandonment of the liberal university statutes of 1863, which he had been himself instrumental in procuring. Katkoff was throughout the greater part of his career anti-German in everything except the system of education, yet in 1884 he caused it to be made known that he regarded the alliance with Germany as useful to Russia, and that he saw no reason why she should not live on good terms with Austria-Hungary. Katkoff's name was again brought into great prominence in 1886 and 1887 by bitter attacks on Germany and an undisguised polemic against the ministry in relation to the influence which Bismarck was said to have in controlling the foreign policy of the Empire. This led to a spirited protest on the part of M. de Giers, the Russian Foreign Minister, and an appeal to the Czar to silence the Moscow editor. Katkoff will always be remembered in Russia as the eloquent exponent of Russian instincts. During the reign of Alexander III his influence over that monarch, who had discredited his ministers by often concealing or capriciously altering his policy, caused the utterances of Katkoff to be examined with the closest interest throughout the world. The peculiar conditions of the Russian Government afforded an example that is singular in modern times of a philosopher and enthusiast exercising a potent and irresponsible influence in the policy of a mighty military power.

Kirchbach, Hugo Ewald von, a Prussian soldier, born in 1809; died in October, 1887. In the campaign of 1866, as a general of division, he performed brilliant services at Nachod, Skalitz, and Schweinschädel. As commander of the Fifth Army Corps during the Franco-Prussian War, he took part in the battles of Weissenburg, Wörth, and Sedan. During the siege of Paris his duty was to cover the headquarters of the Emperor and Crown-Prince. He retired from active service in 1880.

Kraszewski, Joseph Ignatius, a Polish author, born in Warsaw, July 26, 1812; died at Dresden, March 20, 1887. He entered Wilna University in 1825. In the insurrection of 1830 he was one of the most active students, and was prominent in their councils. He was arrested, and after being tried was sentenced to death, but influential friends obtained his pardon. Retiring to the country, he began a literary career, and wrote a great number of novels, painting Polish life of every period and every phase. He removed to Warsaw in 1860, and became editor of the "Tagblatt." Although he did his utmost to restrain the people from insurrection, he was exiled from Poland in consequence of the disturbances of 1862-'63, and took up his residence in Dresden. He was, perhaps, the most prolific writer of modern times, and, besides novels, produced works of history, criticism, and philosophy. His published volumes number almost five hundred.

Kriker, Odian Effendi, a Turkish statesman, born in 1834; died in Paris, France, Aug. 30, 1887. He was of Armenian birth, and long held the post of Under-Secretary in the Ministry of Public Works at Constantinople. He was much consulted by Midhat Pasha, Ali Pasha, and other Turkish ministers, and was more than once offered a Cabinet office. Through his instrumentality the organic law of the Armenian nation was in 1862 enacted as a law of the Ottoman Empire. The Turkish Constitution that was promulgated in 1876 was in its original form elaborated by him, and in the same year Midhat Pasha sent him on a special mission to England, and again in 1877 to implore the aid of the British Government in the impending war with Russia. In 1879 the Sultan deprived him of his office and dignities, and after that he lived in exile.

Krupp, Alfred, a German engineer, born in Essen, Germany, April 26, 1812; died there, July 14, 1887. He was the son of Friedrich Krupp, the proprietor of a small foundry. He extended the business with his brother, and in 1848 became sole owner of the works which were still called by his father's name, in the course of time developing the greatest steel-casting industry in the world. After many experiments he succeeded in making steel in large blocks. At the London exhibition he showed an ingot weighing twenty centners, which was more than double the size that had previously been achieved. When cast-steel became the approved metal for cannon he became the purveyor of ordnance, not only to Germany, but to most of the governments of the world. In Europe, only France and England have not provided themselves with Krupp guns. The factory had, up to 1885, furnished thirty-four states with artillery of various calibers, numbering in all two hundred thousand pieces. The Krupp breech-loaders, which are made of all sizes, some of them rivaling the largest guns of Armstrong and Whitworth in England, surpass all others in durability, accuracy, and range, owing partly to the purity, fineness, and strength of the metal employed, and partly to peculiarities of construction. Besides cannon and shells, the works at Essen turn out steel rails, axles, wheels, and machinery of various kinds. The firm employs more than twenty thousand persons. There are seventy-seven steam-hammers constantly at work in the factories, which cover a thousand acres, besides mining and smelting works elsewhere. Private railroads connect Essen with the railroad system of Germany, and four steamers are employed in bringing metal from the mines owned by the Krupps in northern Spain.

Langenbeck, Bernhard von, a German surgeon, born in Hanover, Germany, in 1810; died in Wiesbaden, Germany, Sept. 30, 1887. He was a member of a noted medical family, began his career as a professor at Kiel, and in 1848 received a call to Berlin, where he taught and practiced with brilliant success until 1882, when he retired from active practice. He had the reputation of being the best operator in Germany, though he represented the conservative or non-amputating school of surgery. He paid special attention to the subject of gunshot and stab wounds, and as surgeon-general of the Prussian army did conspicuous work in the campaigns of 1866 and 1870.

Langer, Karl, an Austrian anatomist, born in 1819; died at Vienna, Dec. 17, 1887. He studied at Vienna and Prague, and in 1842 obtained an assistant professorship in Vienna. In 1850 he was promoted to a professorship, and in 1856 became Professor of Zoölogy at the Buda-Pesth University. Returning to Vienna in 1870, he was appointed Professor of Anatomy at the Josefinum and the university. A few years before his death he was created a privy councilor, with the title of Ritter von Edenberg. He was a voluminous writer, and, although he belonged to the older school of anatomists, he was esteemed for his learning and experimental researches. His "Manual of Anatomy" (Vienna, 1865) has been translated into almost every European language.

Langiewicz, Marian, a Polish patriot, born in Krotoszin, Posen, Aug. 5, 1827, died in Constantinople in May, 1887. He was prominent in the Polish insurrection of 1863. He defeated the Russians in several engagements in February and March of that year, and assumed a dictatorship, but was soon afterward overpowered by force of numbers, taken prisoner, and confined in Bohemia. In 1865 he was released at the request of the Swiss Government, and took up his residence at Scutari.

Laurent, Francis, a Belgian historian, born in Luxemburg, July 8, 1810; died in Brussels, Belgium, Feb. 12, 1887. He attended classes in his native city, after which he studied philosophy at Louvain and law at Liége, where he was graduated in 1832. After practicing as an advocate for two years at Luxemburg, he became, in 1834, chief of the division of legislation in the ministry of justice at Brussels. In 1835 he was named Professor of Civil Law in the University of Ghent. A collected edition of his writings was issued under the title of "Studies in History and Humanity." He was the author also of an important work in thirty-two volumes entitled "Principles of the French Civil Law" and of controversial letters and pamphlets presenting the Liberal side of the question of church and state in Belgium.

Lawson, James Anthony, an Irish jurist, born in Waterford, Ireland, in 1817, died in Dublin, Ireland, Aug. 10, 1887. He was educated at Trinity College, Dublin, where he was graduated in 1838. In 1840 he was called to the Irish bar, after which he was appointed to the Whateley Professorship of Political Economy at the University of Dublin. He was made Solicitor-General for Ireland in 1859, and Attorney-General in 1865. In the exercise of this office he instituted vigorous proceedings against the Irish revolutionary party, suppressing the "Irish People" newspaper, and causing the arrest of prominent men on suspicion of their being connected with the Fenian Society. In 1868 he was elevated to the bench. He was selected by Mr. Gladstone as Chief Commissioner to carry out the provisions of the Church Act, while still retaining his seat on the bench, and in 1882 was transferred to the Queen's Bench division, where he applied the principles of the criminal law against the Land Leaguers with such arbitrary severity that he incurred the hatred of his countrymen. It was in this year that an attempt was made upon his life by one of the Phœnix Park murderers. He entered the House of Commons as member for the borough of Portarlington in 1866, and was active in carrying through the Irish Church Act and the land act of 1870.

Le Flô, Adolphe Emmanuel Charles, a French soldier and diplomatist, born in Garlin, in the department of the Basses Pyrénées, March 2, 1809; died at Nechoat, near Morlaix, France, Nov. 16, 1887. He entered the army in 1828, distinguished himself in Algeria, became brigadier-general in 1848, was appointed by Cavaignac ambassador to Russia, returned in 1849, and was elected to the Assembly. He was one of the deputies captured in their beds after the *coup d'état*, and was expelled from France. He resided in Belgium and England, and was allowed to return in 1857. During the siege of Paris he became Minister of War, and retained this office until the Commune was suppressed, when he was appointed to the St. Petersburg embassy, which he resigned in 1879. In 1887 he created a political sensation by publishing letters of Alexander II, Prince Gortchakoff, and the Duc Decazes which showed that Germany intended to declare war against France in 1875, and was only restrained by pressure that Russia brought to bear at the request of the French minister.

Lemaire, Pierre Auguste, a French philologist, born at Briancourt, in the department of the Meuse, in 1802; died there, Dec. 17, 1887. After brilliant university studies, he was appointed Professor of Rhetoric successively at the Saint Louis, Buonaparte, and Louis Le Grand colleges at Paris. He retired from the active work of teaching in 1847. He was a nephew of the philologist, Nicholas Lemaire, and first collaborated with him, and afterward continued, the "Bibliotheca Classica Latina." To this he contributed annotated editions of the "Pharsalia" of Lucan (1830), "Terence," "Velleius Paterculus," "Pliny the Younger," "Lucretius," and "Silius Italicus." Among his other works are "Athenarum Panorama" (1822); "On History, with special reference to Titus Livius" (1828); "The Liberation of the Greeks," a poem, (1827), and several revised editions of the "Grammaire des Grammaires."

Lequesne, Eugène Louis, a French sculptor, born in Paris, France, Feb. 15, 1815; died June 12, 1887. He was educated for the bar, but in 1841 entered the School of Fine Arts as the pupil of Pradier. In 1844 his "Death of Priam" won the grand prize for sculpture. He spent some years in Rome where he executed a copy of Barberini's "Faun," and in 1850 he sent to the *salon* a model of his own "Dancing Faun." He executed a bust of "Stephen" for the *foyer* of the Opera, and finished Pradier's "Victories," for the tomb of Napoleon in the Hôtel des Invalides. Among his other works are "Lesbia," "The Bather," "The Roman Slave," "The Dying Soldier," "The Priestess of Bacchus," "The Dreams of Youth," and busts of Philippe de Commines, Marshal St. Armand, General Dumas, Hippolyte Guérin, Visconti, and Adelina Patti.

Macgregor, Sir Charles Metcalfe, an English soldier, born in 1840; died in Cairo, Egypt, Feb. 5, 1887. He received his education at Marlborough, and in 1856 entered the Indian artillery service in which his father was a distinguished officer. The son was present at many of the battles of the Indian mutiny, and was thrice wounded. In 1860 he went with Sir Hope Grant on the China expedition, and in the march to Pekin received two severe wounds. In 1864–'66 he was employed with the expeditionary force sent into Bhotan, and in this war was twice severely wounded. In 1867 he joined the Abyssinian expedition, in which he served with the rank of lieutenant-colonel. For the next seven years he was engaged in the compilation of information relating to the countries west of India, and produced gazetteers of the northwest frontier, giving full accounts of the tribes of Afghanistan, Persia, Asiatic Turkey, and Caucasia. In 1875 he started on a tour in

Northwestern Persia, and made an attempt to enter Herat, but found the Afghan officials unfriendly. The journey to Meshed, Serakhs, and along the frontier of Khorassan furnished the material for his "Travels in Khorassan" (London, 1878). He next made a tour through the deserts of Beloochistan, and in 1882 published an account of his journey. In the first campaign of the Afghan War of 1878 he acted as chief of staff to Sir Samuel Browne, and after the Cabul massacre became chief of staff to Sir Frederick Roberts. He took a prominent part in the operations around Cabul, and in the battle of Candahar he commanded a brigade. He was knighted for his services in this campaign. After the Afghan War he served for five years as quartermaster-general in India, and was then given command of the Punjaub frontier force, which he was compelled to resign a year later on account of ill health. He prepared reports on the military aspect of the Russian advance towards India, on which subject he was the most decided alarmist. Most of these works are treated as confidential hand-books, and preserved in the greatest possible official secrecy, although the Russian Government is known to possess copies of them.

Marsegg, Herrman Maltner von, an Austrian soldier, born at Bielitz, Silesia, in 1829; died, Dec. 16, 1887. He was educated for a legal career, but entered the army in 1848, where, an account of his *bourgeois* origin and lack of influence, his advancement was slow. He at length received a staff appointment, in which his talents were soon recognized, and promotion was rapid. He served in the campaign against Italy in 1859, and on the re-establishment of peace was employed by the Austrian Foreign Office on several military and diplomatic missions. In the War of 1866 he executed a dashing charge at Custozza, and he was soon made a general of brigade. His health was seriously impaired by the labors and anxieties of the post at Banjaluka, Bosnia, where he commanded the force that occupied the Sanjak in 1878. He attained to the rank of lieutenant-field-marshal.

Mayhew, Henry, an English author, born in 1812; died in London, England, July 25, 1887. He left Westminister School to go on a voyage to Calcutta. On his return he was articled to his father, a solicitor, for three years. He began his literary career by writing, in conjunction with Gilbert A'Beckett, a farce called "The Wandering Minstrel." In 1841 he was one of the original promoters of "Punch," and was the first editor of that journal, from which he shortly afterward withdrew. He was the author of "London Labor and the London Poor," which was long an authority on the condition of the laboring classes. Among his other works may be mentioned "The Mormons, or Latter Day Saints" (London, 1852); "The Wonders of Science" (1855); and "The Greatest Plague of Life," "Tricks of Trade," and other humorous works of fiction, which,

as well as farces and fairy stories, he wrote with his brothers, Augustus and Horace.

Michel, Francisque Xavier, a French antiquarian, born in Lyons, France, Feb. 18, 1809; died in Paris, France, May 11, 1887. He finished his education in Paris, and in 1880 edited the "Chronique de Duguesclin." In 1832 he published two novels. After investigating French manuscripts in English libraries for the Government, he was appointed Professor of Foreign Literature at Bordeaux in 1839. His works on Anglo-Norman history are very numerous. A visit to Scotland interested him in Franco-Scottish relations, and in 1862 he published "Les Écossais en France et les Français en Écosse." His latest work appeared in English, and was devoted to French words in the Scottish vocabulary.

Monrad, Ditlev Gothard, a Danish prelate and statesman, born in Copenhagen, Denmark, Nov. 24, 1811; died there, March 28, 1887. He embraced the clerical profession, acquired a reputation as a political writer, and, as a chief of the National Liberal party, entered the ministry of Orla Lehmann in 1848. A year later he was installed as bishop of the diocese of Laaland-Falster. In 1854 he was appointed director of the school system of Denmark. In 1859 he was Minister of Ecclesiastical Affairs, and in 1863 he became Prime Minister. The responsibility of the hopeless war with Prussia had to be borne by Bishop Monrad, and after the peace of 1864 he resigned and went into voluntary exile, emigrating with his family to New Zealand. His estate there was devastated during the Maori war, and in 1869 he returned to Denmark, and was reappointed to his former bishopric. He recently tried to make his voice heard again in Danish politics, but without attracting much attention.

Newdegate, Charles Newdigate, an English politician, born in Warwickshire, England, in 1816; died there, April 10, 1887. He was educated at Eton, at King's College, London, and at Christ Church, Oxford. He was elected to Parliament in 1843 to represent the old county division of North Warwickshire, and he continued to represent this constituency until it disappeared in the electoral changes of 1885, when he withdrew. A Conservative of the old school, he was a vigorous opponent of the Romish Church. He repeatedly brought forward motions in the House for the investigation of convents and monasteries, and collected with indefatigable zeal a long array of facts to show the existence of abuses in such institutions. His exertions in the No-Popery cause made him a ridiculous figure in Parliament, yet did not deter him from expending his energy in endeavoring to revive other buried issues. He was first elected as a Protectionist, and to the last he lost no opportunity for urging the reimposition of the corn-tax. He was the foremost opponent of the admission to Parliament of Mr. Bradlaugh, who brought action against him for malicious maintenance, and the case was decided in Mr. Bradlaugh's favor by Chief-Justice Coleridge, Mr. Newdegate being held responsible in damages for the entire loss Mr. Bradlaugh had suffered in the action.

Nordman, Johannes, an Austrian novelist, born in Krems, Lower Austria, in 1820; died in Vienna, Aug. 21, 1887. His real name was Rumpelmaier, and he was originally an actor. In 1847 he published a volume of poems and a novel entitled "Aurelie," after which he took long voyages, the results of which enriched his later works. He settled in Vienna and became a contributor of tales to the principal journals. Among his most important romances are "Zwei Frauen" (1850); "Carrara" (1851); "Ein Wiener Bürger" (1860); and "Frühlingsnächte in Salamanca" (1880). He was also the author of dramatic pieces.

O'Sullivan, William Henry, an Irish politician, born in 1827; died in Kilmallock. Ireland, April 27, 1887. He was once an advocate of revolutionary methods to secure Irish independence. Previously to the suppression of the "Irish People" newspaper he was under police surveillance, and on the night before the Fenian outbreak of 1867 was arrested and detained for several months in Limerick Jail, from which he was eventually discharged without a trial. He became an ardent supporter of the constitutional party of Home Rule while Isaac Butt was its leader, and in 1874 was elected to represent Limerick in Parliament, retaining the seat until 1885. He was one of the first to adopt Mr. Parnell's policy in preference to Mr. Butt's less aggressive tactics, yet in late years he gave only a qualified support to the Irish leader.

Oude, Wadjid Ali Shah, ex-King of, born in Lucknow in 1822; died in Calcutta, Sept. 23, 1887. He ascended the throne in 1847. His state had been denounced before his accession by Indian administrators, who had its annexation in view, as a sink of anarchy and misrule. He was immediately warned and given two years of grace in which to retrieve the evil reputation of his house. Other conquests in Burmah and the Punjaub, engaged the attention of the Government, and it was not till February, 1856, that the decree for his deposition was issued. He was asked to sign a treaty resigning all his powers in consideration of his remaining in possession of his palace with an allowance of twelve lakhs a year. He indignantly refused, and declared his intention to go to England and lay his wrongs before the throne. His mother went in his stead, and was so harshly received that she died in Paris from her sufferings and disappointment. The Indian Government allotted the dethroned King a residence on the river Hooghly and granted him the promised pension of £120,000 per annum. When the mutiny broke out, however, he was placed under arrest, and remained immured until the rebellion was suppressed. He was then allowed to return to Garden Reach, where, within his walled in-

closure, he kept up all the pomp of an Oriental court. He refused to hold any intercourse with the court of the Viceroy. Within the square mile of land that was granted for his residence he maintained a miniature army, a ministry, orders of nobility, and the entire semblance of royal power. His harem contained one hundred and fifty women. Parks and gardens, the largest menagerie in the world, dancing nautch girls, and other kingly pleasures contributed to his amusement. He was an accomplished musician and poet, and composed songs that are popular throughout India.

Panofka, Heinrich, a German musician and composer, born in Breslau, Prussia, Oct. 2, 1807; died in Carlsruhe, Dec. 4, 1887. From his earliest years he was taught singing and the use of the violin. After studying under Mayseder and Hoffman, he gave a series of concerts in Vienna, Munich, and Berlin in 1827. He then went to Paris, where he became associated with Berlioz. He removed to London in 1844, and was the musical director of the Opera Company there, which included Fraschini, Lablache, and Jenny Lind. In 1852 he returned to Paris and became attached to the staff of several musical journals. He was also very successful as a teacher, and in 1858 he published "The Art of Singing." He was the author of fantasies, studies for the violin called "Reveries," a vocal "Abecedaire," an elegy, a caprice, and a number of religious pieces that were published under the title of "Hours of Devotion."

Pasaglia, Carlo, an Italian theologian, born in Pieve di San Paolo, near Lucca, in 1814; died, March 17, 1887. He was educated at Rome, and, after taking orders, became a member of the Society of Jesus. He was appointed Professor of Theology in the Roman University, and was the author of several theological works, among which were "A Commentary on the Prerogatives of St. Peter, the Chief of the Apostles" (Ratisbon, 1850) and "The Eternity of Future Punishment." He also edited and annotated the treatise of Petavius on "Dogmatic Theology." In 1861 he published a work in Latin, addressed to the Pope, in which the abandonment of the temporal power of the papacy was advocated, and thereby drew upon himself the censure of the ecclesiastical authorities. The book was placed upon the "Index Expurgatorius," and its author was compelled to leave Rome. In 1862 he was appointed, at the instance of Victor Emanuel, Professor of Theology at the University of Turin, and in 1863 was elected a member of the Italian Parliament. His chief aim was to form a party that should be at once liberal and catholic.

Pellegrini, Antonio, an Italian prelate, born in Rome, Italy, Aug. 11, 1812; died there, Nov. 2, 1887. He was one of the last cardinals created by Pius IX, and was one of those who, on receiving assurances of protection from Signor Crispi, then Italian Minister of the

Interior, voted in favor of holding the conclave for the election of a new Pope in 1878 within the city of Rome.

Phillips, John Arthur, a British mining engineer, born in Cornwall in 1823; died in Kensington, London, Jan. 4, 1887. He received his technical education at the École des Mines in Paris, where he acquired a fondness for investigation which never deserted him and which for the most part had reference to the application of chemistry to mineralogical and petrological questions. The results of his investigations were published in the proceedings of the Chemical or Geological societies of which he was a fellow or in the "Philosophical Magazine." Mr. Phillips was also a Fellow of the Royal Society and a member of the Institute of Civil Engineers. Besides the article "Metallurgy" in the "Encyclopædia Metropolitana," he was the author of "The Mining and Metallurgy of Gold and Silver" (1867); "Elements of Metallurgy" (1874); "A Treatise on Ore Deposits" (1884), and at the time of his death was, with Prof. H. Bauerman, preparing a new edition of his "Metallurgy."

Pott, August Friedrich, a German philologist, born in Nettelrede, Hanover, Nov. 14, 1802; died in Halle, Prussia, July 12, 1887. He was, with Grimm and Bopp, an originator of the study of comparative philology, and made important discoveries in that science. For many years he filled a professorship at Halle. He was the author of "Die Zigeuner in Europa" (1844); "Die quinare und vigesimale Zählmethode by Völkern aller Welttheile" (1847); "Die Ungleichheit der menschlichen Rassen" (1856); "Etymologische Forschungen auf dem Gebiete der Indogermanischen Sprachen" (2d ed., 1867-'70); and "Die Sprachverschiedenheiten in Europa an den Zahlwörtern nachgewiesen" (1868).

Ramée, Daniel, a French architect, born in 1806; died in Hamburg, Germany, Oct. 15, 1887. Among his most important works were the restoration of the Palais de Justice at Beauvais and the churches at Noyon, Abbeville, and Senlis. He was the author of a "Histoire générale de l'architecture," "Monumens anciens et modernes," "Dictionnaire général de termes d'architecture en quatre langues," and numerous essays on architecture.

Randi, Lorenzo, an Italian prelate, born in 1817; died in Rome, Italy, Dec. 30, 1887. He was the Minister of Police to Pope Pius IX, and during the last few years of the temporal power of the papacy his name was a source of terror. He persecuted Liberal politicians, exercised the most rigorous censorship over the press, and organized a spy system so complete that no native or stranger dared utter an opinion without fear of arrest. He was made a cardinal in 1875, and during his last years was prefect of the congregation of the Propaganda.

Rousseau, Philippe, a French painter, born in Paris in 1816; died at Acquigny, Dec. 4, 1887. He early displayed a genius for art, and studied under Gros, Bertin, and the marine painter Hippolyte Garneray. His first appearance at the *Salon* was in 1831 with a landscape from Auvergne. This was followed each year till 1838 by similar works. He then occupied himself for several years with painting panoramas. In 1845 he exhibited in the *Salon* "The City Rat and the Field Rat," which won a medal. Among his other works are: "The Cat and the Old Rat" (1846); "The Mole and the Rabbit" (1847); "Interior of a Farm-House" (1850); "Recreation" (1857); "The Gala Day" (1859); "Home of Walter Scott" (1868); "Spring" and "Autumn" (1869); "The First Plums and the Last Cherries" (1870); and "The Wolf and the Lamb" (1875).

Saint-Hilaire, Émile Marco de, a French author, born in Versailles, France, in 1793; died Nov. 3, 1887. He was a page to Napoleon I, and after the fall of the First Empire began writing little books on such trivialities as the art of adjusting cravats, and the art of succeeding in love. When, after 1830, works in defense of the Empire were in vogue, he published "Mémoires d'un page de la cour impériale," and similar Napoleonic works. Napoleon III gave him a librarianship at Strassburg, which he held until 1870.

Sayn-Wittgenstein, Caroline, Princess von, a Russian author, born in Poland in 1819; died in Rome, Italy, March 9, 1887. She was the daughter of a Prince Ivanoffska, a wealthy Polish landowner, and in 1836 married, at the command of the Emperor Nicholas, the German Prince Nicholas von Sayn-Wittgenstein, who was in the military service of Russia. She left Russia in 1848, and for twelve years lived at Weimar in the closest intimacy with Franz Liszt, chapel-master there, with whom she had first become acquainted in St. Petersburg in 1847. The Czar granted her a divorce from her husband in 1855, but this had no validity in the Roman Catholic Church, to which she belonged, and in which she could not obtain the annulment of her marriage in order to wed Liszt without illegitimating her daughter. The Czar commanded the princess to resume her residence in Russia, and when she refused to obey confiscated her estates, which he afterward restored to her daughter, who married the Prince of Hohenlohe-Schillingsfürst. In 1860 the Princess Wittgenstein took up her residence in Rome, to be followed a year later by Liszt, who in 1865 took holy orders in the Catholic Church. When the composer died in 1886 he made the princess his heiress, and intrusted to her the task of arranging for publication his artistic remains, which she was unable to complete. Her life in Rome was mainly devoted to literary composition. The books that were issued under her name treat for the most part of religious and theological subjects. The more important ones are "Christianisme et Buddhisme" and "Religion et monde." She also wrote anonymously on controversial themes.

Schirmer, Heinrich Ernst, a German architect, born at Leipsic in 1814; died at Giessen in December, 1887. Early in life he entered the service of the Norwegian Government, and was employed in the designing and erection of public buildings. Many of the most beautiful edifices in Norway are due to him. His principal work was the restoration of the Drontheim Cathedral in 1869–'71.

Schmidt, Wilhelm Adolf, a German historian, born in Berlin, Prussia, Sept. 26, 1812; died in Jena, April 10, 1887. He entered the university at Berlin in 1831, studied history under Ranke, giving attention also to philology, and after teaching in different gymnasia became tutor in ancient history at Berlin in 1840. In 1842 he published a pamphlet on the Greek papyrus manuscripts in the Berlin Library. He became extraordinary professor in 1844, and began a highly successful course of lectures on modern history. He also founded a magazine of historical science, which was continued till 1848, when he took his seat in the Frankfort Parliament. He was an earnest advocate of a German union under Prussian supremacy, and published a *brochure* on "Prussia's German Policy," the arguments of which were supported by citations from the secret archives of Berlin in a fuller work entitled "Prusso-German Unionist Aims since the Time of Frederick the Great." The triumph of absolutism drove him to Zürich in 1851, where his professional duties were more exacting. There he published a work entitled "Contemporary History" (1859), and when war was threatened between France and Prussia in 1859 he wrote a book on "Elsass and Lothringen," recounting the circumstances of their annexation to France. He began at Zürich the revision of Becker's "Universal History." In 1860 Schmidt was called to Jena to take the chair that Droysen had left vacant. He published a work on "Paris in the Time of the Revolution" (3 vols., Jena, 1874–'76) and a volume of historical parallels entitled "Epochs and Catastrophes," and afterward devoted himself exclusively to Greek history. Two volumes dealing with "The Age of Pericles" were issued, and a third volume was partly printed.

Schröder, Karl, a German physician, born in 1838; died in Berlin, Prussia, Feb. 7, 1887. He was a professor in the University of Berlin, and was surgeon of a hospital for women which attracted students and patients from all parts of the world. The strain of his professional work brought on fatal brain-fever.

Simpson, John Palgrave, an English dramatic author, born in Norfolk, England, in 1809; died in London, England, Aug. 19, 1887. He was educated at Corpus Christi College, Cambridge, and was intended for the Church, but abandoned the idea of a clerical profession. After traveling for several years on the Continent he entered the literary profession, and for many years contributed to "Fraser," "Blackwood," and "Bentley's Miscellany." He published: "Second Love, and Other Tales" (1846); "Gisella, a Novel" (1847); "Letters from the Danube" (1847); "The Lily of Paris, or the King's Nurse" (1848); and "Pictures from Revolutionary Paris" (1848). In 1850 he began writing for the stage. His dramatic works consist of about sixty plays and farces, among which are "World and Stage," "Second Love," "Sybilla, or Step by Step," "A Scrap of Paper," "Alone," "Time and the Hour," "All for Her," and "Court Cards, a School for Coquettes." In 1865 he wrote a "Life of Weber," and more recently published "For Ever and Never," a novel.

Stewart, Balfour, an English physicist, born in Edinburgh, Scotland, Nov. 1, 1828; died in Balrath, Ireland, Dec. 19, 1887. He was educated at the universities of St. Andrews and Edinburgh where he showed special ability as a mathematician. After graduation he spent four years in a mercantile house in compliance with the wishes of his father and then passed several years in Australia, but finally determined to devote his attention to physical sciences. On his return home during 1856–'58 he assisted James D. Forbes, then Professor of Natural Philosophy at the University of Edinburgh. In 1859 he was appointed director of the Magnetic Observatory at Kew, and in 1867 to the secretaryship of the meteorological committee. These offices he resigned in 1870 to accept the chair of Natural Philosophy in Owens College, Manchester, which place he held until his death. In 1868 he received the Rumford medal from the Royal Society of London for his discovery of the law of equality between the absorptive and radiative powers of bodies, and the degree of LL. D. had been conferred on him by the University of Edinburgh. Besides being a Fellow of the Royal Society of London, the Astronomical and the Meteorological Societies of London, he was a member of learned bodies, both in the United States and on the Continent, and at the time of his death was president of the Physical Society and of the Society for Psychical Research in London, also a member of the committee appointed to advise the Government on solar physics. In addition to many papers on subjects connected with various branches of physics among which are: with Warren De la Rue and others "Researches on Solar Physics," and with Peter G. Tait researches on the "Heating Produced by Rotation in Vacuo"; on "Meteorology and Magnetism"; and a recent article "Terrestrial Magnetism," for the "Encyclopædia Britannica," in which he advocates a working hypothesis. Prof. Stewart published an "Elementary Treatise on Heat"(1871); "Lesson in Elementary Physics" (1871); a science primer on "Physics" (1872); "The Conservation of Energy" (1874); in the "International Scientific Series," with Peter G. Tait, "The Unseen Universe"(1875), of which twelve editions have been issued, and "Practical Physics" (1885).

Strakosch, Maurice, operatic manager, born in Lemberg, Poland, 1823; died in Paris, Oct. 8, 1887. He first introduced to the American and European musical public Patti, Nilsson, and many other celebrated singers. Not long before his death he published "Memoirs of an Impresario."

Strangford, Emily Anne, Viscountess, an English philanthropist, born about 1834; died at sea, March 24, 1887. She was a daughter of Admiral Beaufort. After his death in 1857 she traveled with her sister in the East, and described her travels in "Egyptian Sepulchres and Syrian Shrines" (London, 1860), a work which obtained great popularity and led to her acquaintance with Percy, the last Viscount Strangford, distinguished as a philologist and Orientalist, whom she married in 1862. After his death in 1869 she secluded herself from society and devoted her attention to philanthropic works. Taking a special interest in hospital nursing, she went through a course of training in one of the London hospitals in order to acquire a practical knowledge of the subject. She founded the National Association for providing nurses for the sick poor and many similar institutions. When the Bulgarian atrocities were published to the world, she collected £80,000 sterling for the aid of the suffering peasantry of Bulgaria. In 1877 she founded a fund for the relief of Turkish sick and wounded in the war between Turkey and Russia, and went with a staff of nurses to the front, where she opened field-hospitals. She was taken prisoner by the Russians, and underwent hardships from which she never recovered. In 1882 Lady Strangford went to Cairo and opened the Victoria Hospital, in which many sick and wounded English officers and soldiers were nursed. With other ladies she established the Women's Emigration Society in London in 1882. She died while on the journey to Port Said to organize there a hospital for British sailors.

Stromeyer, August, a German chemist, born in Bad Limmer, Hanover, July 7, 1807; died in Hanover, Nov. 21, 1887. He entered the University of Göttingen as a student of jurisprudence in 1825, but soon abandoned this branch for the study of natural science, especially chemistry. In 1825 he went to Paris and there studied under Dumas, Gay Lussac, and Thénard. A year later he returned to Hanover, but in 1832 was appointed to a college assistantship in Aberdeen. In 1834 he was called to the charge of a factory in Drontheim, Norway, where until 1853 he was engaged in the making of chromium preparations, principally the potassium bichromate from the chromic iron of Röraas. Failing health then compelled his return to Hanover, where he spent the remainder of his life in investigations in applied chemistry, many of which he carried on in the university laboratory in Göttingen. He was a member of scientific societies, and the results of his various investigations are given in papers that appeared chiefly in the "Annalen der Chemie und Pharmacie."

Uhrich, Jean Jacques Alexis, a French soldier, born in Pfalsburg, Feb. 15, 1802; died in Paris, France, Oct. 11, 1887. He was educated at St. Cyr, and took part in the campaign of 1823 in Spain, became a captain in 1831, was transferred to the African army, and remained in that service for twenty years. He rose to the rank of brigadier-general in 1852, and was a general of division during the Crimean War. In the Italian campaign he commanded an infantry division. After having been transferred to the reserve in 1867, he resumed active service when the Franco-Prussian War broke out in 1870, commanding a division of Alsatian troops. After the battle of Worth he became commandant of Strasburg, and defended the fortress during the bombardment, lasting seven weeks, but finally capitulated. For this he was severely censured in the report of the committee appointed to investigate the capitulations during the war.

Vassalli Bey Luigi, an Italian revolutionist and Egyptologist, born in 1812; died in Rome, Italy, June 18, 1887. He possessed talents and inclination for an artistic career, but entered the Austrian army at the age of seventeen. He resigned his commission on account of a wound received in a frontier affray with Prussian soldiers. Already a member of a secret political society, he was soon afterward forced to flee from the police to Lugano and thence to Geneva, where he became a friend of Mazzini, and took part in the expedition into Savoy in 1834, after which they resided in Paris until the Austrian amnesty enabled Vassali to go to Milan as agent of the Mazzinians. He was soon discovered, tried for treason, and sentenced to death. The sentence was commuted to banishment for life. For the next nine years he traveled through various countries, supporting himself by the sale of his paintings. In 1848 he returned to Italy to fight for the independence of his country, and when again driven into exile after the fall of Rome, went to Egypt, where he became the most zealous and capable coadjutor of Mariette in the discovery and interpretation of antiquities. The events of 1859 again summoned him to Italy, and in the following year he fought with Garibaldi in Sicily, returning after the close of the campaign to Egypt. He held the rank of colonel in the service of the Khedive. His last years were passed in Rome. He was a sufferer from a painful disease, and took his own life in a fit of depression. A public funeral was given him by the Italian Government.

Viel-Castel, M. de, a French diplomatist and historian, born in Paris, France, Oct. 11, 1800; died there, Oct. 6, 1887. In 1821 he was appointed *attaché* to the Spanish Embassy, of which he afterward became secretary. He was removed to Vienna in 1828, and the following year became a sub-director at the Ministry of Foreign Affairs, a post that he occupied to the end of 1848, when he was made director. He tendered his resignation at the *coup d'état*, yet in 1853 he obtained his retiring allowance, and devoted himself to historical studies. He wrote a "History of the Restoration," which appeared in twenty volumes. He was the oldest member of the French Academy, of which he was elected a member in 1873.

Vischer, Friedrich Theodor, a German philosopher, born in Ludwigsburg, Würtemberg, June 30, 1807; died in Gmunden, Sept. 15, 1887. He was educated at the Stuttgart Gymnasium, studied theology at Tübingen, and visited the principal German cities for the examination of their artistic treasures. After teaching theology for three years at Tübingen, he became extraordinary professor of philosophy there in 1837, traveled in Italy and Greece, and was made full professor in 1844, but was dismissed from that post in 1846 on account of his opinions as a free thinker. Shortly after his restoration to his post in 1848, the revolution broke out, and he was elected deputy to the National Parliament. In 1855 he was made professor at the cantonal high-school, and at the Federal Polytechnic School of Zürich, Switzerland, but in 1866 returned to Würtemburg as Professor of Æsthetics and German Literature both at Tübingen at the Stuttgart Polytecnic School. His principal works were a treatise on "Æsthetics, or Science of the Beautiful" (6 vols., 1847-'57), "The Sublime and the Comic" (1857); "Faust; the Third Part of the Tragedy" (1862); "Epigrams from Baden-Baden" (1862); "The German War of 1870-'71" a heroic poem; and "Fashion and Cynicism" (1879). His great work on "Æsthetics" presents an analysis of the metaphysical sources of the sense of the beautiful, and had for its basis a philosophical system that was idealistic, and yet diverged from the methods of thought that had been taught by his master, Hegel.

Volckmar, Wilhelm, a German organist and composer, born in Hersfeld, Hesse, in 1812; died in Homburg, Sept. 3, 1867. He was the son of a musician, and was early taught the piano, organ, violin, and other instruments. He was organist and teacher of music in various places, and about 1836 became Professor of Music at the Homburg Seminary in Hesse. He composed fantasias, fugues, quartets for strings, and vocal pieces, a collection of which was published in London in 1881. He also published a series of collections of German choral melodies from the time of the Reformation, with valuable historical notes, of which three volumes were issued (1845-'65).

Vulpian, Edme Félix Alfred, a French physiologist, born in France, Jan. 5, 1826; died in Paris, May 18, 1887. He was the son of a distinguished lawyer, and was graduated in medicine in 1854. Soon after he was appointed to the Museum of Natural History, where he conducted a series of investigations on the nervous system. In 1867 he was appointed Professor of Pathological Anatomy to the Faculty of Medicine in Paris, and in 1872 was transferred to the chair of Comparative and Experimental Pathology, becoming in December, 1875, Dean of the Medical Faculty. He was accused during the empire of holding materialistic views, but was called in to attend the Comte de Chambord, when the latter was dying at Frohsdorf. Dr. Vulpian was an ardent champion of the Pasteur treatment, and taxed his colleagues for lack of patriotism in questioning the safety of the intensive treatment, which has since been abandoned. In 1869 he was elected to the Academy of Medicine, and in 1876 to the Academy of Sciences. He was given the Cross of the Legion of Honor in 1869, and was made an officer in 1878. Dr. Vulpian was the author of various medical works, among which are: "Des Pneumonies Secondaires" (1860); "Leçons sur la Physiologie Générale et comparée du Système Nerveux" (1866); "Leçons sur l'Appareil vasomoteur" (1874); "Clinique médicale de l'Hôpital de la Charité" (1878); and "Maladies du Système nerveux" (1879).

Wagner, Moritz Friedrich, a German ethnologist, born in Bayreuth, Bavaria, Oct. 13, 1813; died in Munich, Bavaria, in May, 1887. In early youth he entered a counting-house at Marseilles, whence he visited Algeria, and acquired such a taste for travel that he made it thenceforth the business of his life. After studying the natural sciences, especially zoölogy, at Paris, he returned to Algeria, and traveled for two years in all parts of the colony, after which he published "Travels in the Regency of Algiers from 1836 to 1838" (3 vols., Augsburg, 1841). In 1843-'46 he made long explorations in the Caucasus and Armenia, and in Persia and Kurdistan in 1851-'52. He spent three years in North America with Karl von Scherzer, then three years in South America, giving special attention to Panama, Chiriqui, and the Ecuadorian Andes. In 1860 he returned to Munich, and was made honorary Professor of Geography at the university and keeper of the new Ethnographical Museum. He there devoted himself to prehistoric archæology, and discovered abundant lacustrine habitations in the Starnberg See and other Bavarian lakes. His books include: "The Caucasus and the Cossack Country" (1847); "Travels in Persia and Kurdistan" (1852-'53); "Travels in North America" (3 vols., 1854); "The Republic of Costa Rica" (1856); "On the Origin of Lacustrine Habitations in Bavaria" (1867); "The Topography, Object, and Age of Lacustrine Habitations" (1867); "The Darwinian Theory and the Law of the Migration of Organisms" (1868); "The Influence of Geographical Isolation and Colonization on the Morphological Variations of Organisms" (1871); "New Contributions to the Darwinian Controversy" (1871); "The Natural Process of Species-Formation" (1875); and a great work entitled "Natural History Travels in Tropical America" (1870).

Werder, August Carl Leopold, Count von, a German soldier, born at Schlossberg, East Prussia, Sept. 12, 1808; died in Pomerania, Sept. 13, 1887. He was descended from an ancient and noble family, and was the son of a lieutenant of dragoons. Educated in the military schools of Glogau and Berlin, he became an officer of the Topographical Corps, and was sent as a commissioner with the Russian army, then in conflict with the mountain tribes of the Caucasus, and was wounded at Kefar. He was rapidly advanced in rank, becoming a lieutenant-general in 1866, when he bore a conspicuous part in the Bohemian campaign of Prince Frederick Carl, and in the victories of Gitchin and Sadowa. In the Franco-Prussian War of 1870–'71, Gen. Werder was the virtual commander-in-chief of the Third German Army, nominally under the direction of the Crown-Prince of Germany, and took part in the battle of Wörth. He directed the siege of Strasburg, and when the garrison capitulated he was made a full general of infantry. He then formed the Fourteenth German Army Corps, and completed the conquest of Alsace. He was next ordered to oppose the Army of the East under Bourbaki. He captured that general's headquarters by storm, Jan. 9, 1871, and in a three days' battle, January 15 to 17, completely defeated the French, who fled to Switzerland. After the war he was definitely appointed commander-in-chief of the Fourteenth Corps of the German Army.

Werner, Gustav, a German philanthropist, born in Zwiefalten, Würtemberg, March 12, 1809; died in Reutlingen, Würtemberg, Aug. 2, 1887. He was educated for the Protestant ministry, and for six years was curate of a village church. He established a children's asylum, and, besides practicing, he preached the doctrine of self-sacrificing benevolence with such eloquence that he excited envy and vexation among the regular pastors of the towns and villages in which he appeared by drawing away all their hearers. Having been dismissed by the consistory. the churches were thenceforth closed to him, yet he continued his appeals in work-shops and beer-houses. He went to Reutlingen, and, purchasing on credit the water-power of a mountain·brook in the neighboring village of Dettingen, established a paper-factory for the purpose of giving employment to the helpless, and educating paupers and outcasts to work. He interested others in his objects, and in the course of time founded an iron·foundry and mechanical workshops in Reutlingen in which the blind, the crippled, and the destitute were taught to do useful work, and were maintained in comfort in a lodging-house.

Werthheimer, Joseph Ritter von, a Jewish philanthropist and author, born in 1800; died in Vienna, Austria, March 19, 1887. He was for more than thirty years president of the Jewish community in Vienna. As an author he is best known by "The Jews in Austria," and "The Taking of an Oath."

Whitworth, Sir Joseph, a British mechanical engineer, born in Stockport, England, Dec. 21, 1803; died in Monte Carlo, Italy, Jan. 22, 1887. He was taught by his father, who kept a school, until he was fourteen years old, when he was placed with his uncle, a cotton-spinner in Derbyshire, where he became familiar with the machinery of the factory and ultimately its practical managing engineer. In 1821 he went to Manchester and spent four years in acquiring a knowledge of the manufacture of cotton-machinery. He then went to London and sought employment in the best shops of that city During off hours he worked at his own devices, and in this way completed the true plane, an instrument which conferred the power of making perfectly true surfaces for all kinds of sliding tools, by which the resistance arising from friction was reduced to its smallest figure. Among other things he was employed on the manufacture of Babbage's calculating machine, in which he was always a firm believer. In 1833 he returned to Manchester and established himself as a maker of tools. Through his efforts a uniform system of screw-heads was introduced, and has since been employed not only through the United Kingdom and its colonies, but in Russia, Italy, and Germany. By this reform nuts and screws have been made interchangeable wherever the Whitworth thread is used. The manufacture of appliances for accurate measurements followed. His standard gauges, taps, and dies, and improved forms of tools grew steadily in public favor. At the World's Fair held in London in 1851 he exhibited an assortment of machine-tools and also his machine for measuring differences of one millionth of an inch, for which he received the Council medal. In 1853 he was appointed a Royal Commissioner to the World's Fair held in New York, and prepared a report on "American Manufacturing Industries" which attracted much attention. He was requested by the British Government in 1854 to design and produce machinery for the manufacture of rifles for the army. He determined the effects of every pitch and kind of rifling, and of every length of projectile, from the sphere to a missile having a length of twenty times its diameter, and the principles determined upon have resulted in the production of the Whitworth rifle now extensively used. These same principles were applied to the Whitworth cannon, said to be "the most enduring, the most accurate, the most powerful in penetration, and the longest in range." In the search for a proper material for the construction of these guns he introduced the use of the fluid-pressed steel now largely employed for many purposes. He founded in 1868 the Whitworth Scholarships, by means of which £3,000 are annually awarded to students in engineering. Each scholarship has a value of £100, and is tenable for three years. In 1875 he added to this benefaction by the foundation of a number of Whitworth exhibitions. He was awarded one of the five *grands prix* given to England at the World's Fair held in Paris in 1867, and a year later received the Cross of the Legion of Honor from Napoleon III. In 1878 his firm received three *grands prix* and a gold medal for their exhibit at the World's Fair held in Paris during that year. He also received the Albert medal from the Society of Arts in London in 1858. The degree of D. C. L. was conferred on him by Oxford, and that of LL. D. by the universities of Dublin and Edinburgh. He was elected a Fellow of the Royal Society of London in 1857, and in 1869 was created a baronet. His writings include papers which have been collected as "Miscellaneous Papers on Mechanical Subjects" (1858); "Papers on Practical Subjects: Guns and Steel" (1873); and "Essays on Mechanical Subjects" (1882).

Wittich, Ludwig von, a Prussian soldier, born in Münster, Oct. 15, 1818: died in Coburg, Dec. 7, 1887. He received his early education at the Collegium Fredericianum, Königsberg, and then proceeded to the cadet school at Berlin, after which he entered the army. He rose rapidly, becoming a lieutenant-colonel in 1861. In the war of 1866, the brigade that he commanded was prominently connected with the series of victories at Nachod, Skalitz, Schweinschädel, Gradlitz, and Königgratz. He was promoted major-general in 1868. In the Franco-Prussian War, at the head of the Forty-ninth Brigade of Infantry, he was a conspicuous contributor to the successes of Mars-le-Tour, Gravelotte, and Roisseville. On Sept. 27, 1870, he was promoted to the command of the Twenty-second Infantry Division, with which he took part in the siege of Paris, marched on the Loire, fought on October 10, at Artenay, and on the following day at Orleans, stormed Chateaudun on October 18, occupied Chartres on the 21st, assisted the Grand Duke of Mecklenburg-Schwerin in several engagements, and contributed substantially to the reduction of Le Mans and Alençon. On May 23, 1871, he was appointed a general of division, and on August 18 a lieutenant-general. He published a "Diary" relating his experience in the French war (1872).

Wolverton, George Grenfell Glyn, Baron, an English politician, born in London, England, in 1824; died in Brighton, England, Nov. 6, 1887. He was the son of George Carr, the first Lord Wolverton, and after receiving his education at Rugby school was admitted as a partner in the banking-house of Glyn, Mills, Currie and Co. He was elected to Parliament as member for Shaftesbury in 1857, and represented that borough till he succeeded to his father's title in 1873. When Mr. Gladstone first became Prime Minister Mr. Glyn was chosen as whip of the Liberal party. He filled that position with great zeal till he entered the upper House, was a thorough-going party man, and spent his money freely for party purposes. In the Gladstone Cabinet of 1886 Lord Wolverton was Postmaster-General.

Wood, Mrs. Henry, an English authoress, born in Worcestershire, England, about 1820; died Feb. 8, 1887. Her maiden name was Ellen Price. Her early life was passed in the city of Worcester, where she obtained familiarity with the phases of cathedral life which have formed the subject of many of her stories. Shortly after her marriage she went to live abroad. Her first efforts at fiction were short stories, which appeared in "Bentley's Miscellany" and "Colburn's Magazine." In 1861 "East Lynne" was published. This romance proved so popular that up to the time of her death 140,000 copies had been sold in England, and it had been translated into most Continental languages, and into some Eastern tongues, besides being dramatized. "The Channings" and "Mrs. Halliburton's Troubles" appeared in quick succession. In 1867 she became associate editor of the "Argosy," in which many of her later stories were first published. One of her stories, "A Life's Secret," dealt with the evil tendencies of strikes and trades unions, was published anonymously, and caused a riot in front of the premises of the Religious Tract Society, which brought it out. Another, "Danesbury House," gained the prize of the Scottish Temperance Society. She wrote much under the pen-name of "Johnny Ludlow." After the death of her husband she returned to England. Mrs. Wood's other stories are: "Anne Hereford," "Bessy Rane," "Court Netherleigh," "Dene Hollow," "Edina," "Elster's Folly." "George Canterbury's Will," "Johnny Ludlow" (first and second series), "Lady Adelaide," "Lord Oakburn's Daughters," "Master of Greylands," "Mildred Arkell," "Orvill College," "Oswald Cray," "Parkwater," "Pomeroy Abbey," "Red Court Farm," "Roland Yorke," "Shadow of Ashlydyat," "St. Martin's Eve." "Trevelyn Hold," "Verner's Pride," "Within the Maze," "Danesbury House," "Bessy Wells," and "Lady Grace."

OHIO. State Government.—The State officers during 1887 were: Governor, Joseph B. Foraker, Republican; Lieutenant-Governor, S. A. Conrad; Secretary of State, James S. Robinson; Auditor, Emil Kiesewetter; Treasurer of State, John C. Brown; Attorney-General, Jacob A. Kobler; Board of Public Works: William M. Hahn, C. A. Flickinger, Wells S. Jones; Commissioner of Common Schools, Eli T. Tappan; Judges of Supreme Court: Selwyn N. Owen, Marshall G. Williams, William T. Spear, Thaddeus A. Minshall, Franklin J. Dickman; Clerk of Supreme Court, Urban H. Hester.

Finances.—The balances in the treasury to the credit of the several funds at the close of the fiscal year 1886 were as follow: General revenue, $272,794.73; sinking fund, $96,236.92; State common-school fund, $87,189.59; total, $456,221.24. The receipts into the treasury during the year from all sources amounted to $6,055.868.53. The disbursements during the same period were $6,289,-

811.04, leaving the cash balance in the treasury, November 15, 1887, to the credit of the following funds: General revenue, $65,864.09; sinking fund, $102,294.08; State common-school fund, $54,620.56; making a total of $222,278.73. The State Auditor, in his report for 1887, estimated the total income of the State for the fiscal year 1888 at $5,555,-413.99, and the expenditures at $7,071,466.49.

The grand duplicate for 1887 showed the taxable value of property as follows: Lands, $720,329,294; real estate in cities, towns, and villages, $464,681,331; chattel property, $520,-172,094: total value, $1,705,182,719. On this the total levy for State purposes was two and nine tenths mills on the dollar, producing $32,-235,067.93, excluding delinquent taxes and also a $1 per-capita tax on dogs, which produced $202,772. On the same valuation the total taxes of the county and minor organizations amounted to $27,292,620.70.

State and Local Debts.—The total funded debt of the State is $3,416,465, and the irreducible debt of the State (trust funds) $4,526,716.65. The local debts are as follow: Debts of counties, $6,892,745.26; debts of cities, $43,193,-963.34; debts of incorporated villages, $1,743,-772.98; debts of townships, $557,883.71; debts of special school-districts, $2,455,330.71; total State and local debts, $54,843,696.

Railroads.—The report of the Railroad Commissioner gives the following statistics for 1887: Total mileage of standard gauge railroad in Ohio, 6,725; double-track railroad, 620; total mileage of narrow gauge railroads, 619; mileage in hands of receivers, 1,067; miles of steel rail, 6,702; miles of fencing of all kinds, 9,965; proportion of stock and debt of lines in Ohio, $536,189,882; stock and debt per mile-line in Ohio, $72,335; average cost per mile-line in Ohio, $73,272. These figures include depot buildings, wood and water stations, and sidings. The statistics show the following gross earnings: Passenger transportation, $25,495,-598; per cent. of total earnings, 22·65; freight transportation, $78,889,473; per cent. of total earnings, 70·09; mail service, $2,826,679; per cent. of total earnings, 2·51; express, $2,119,-892; other sources, $3,215,100; proportion of gross earnings in Ohio, $56,785,652; earnings per mile, $7,415; proportion of operating expenses in Ohio, $37,980,580; operating expenses per mile in Ohio, $4,960; net earnings per mile in Ohio, $2,455; number of passengers carried, 34,378,926; average amount received per passenger per mile, 2·179 cents; number of tons of freight hauled, 85,739,801; rate received per ton per mile, 7·07 cent.

Coal and Gas.—The State Mine Inspector's report shows a larger production than ever before, and claims for the State the second place among coal-producing States, a position hitherto held by Illinois. The introduction of natural gas from Pennsylvania and the discovery of large supplies of the gas at Findlay, Lima, and other places in the northern part

of the State, so far from having a bane fect upon the coal-trade of the State, on the contrary, to be beneficial by forc coal-product upon localities hitherto und of and which have proved to be of a co tive capacity beyond expectation. The show the product to have been 10,8 tons. The number of miners employed ported as 22,237.

Political.—The first of the State conv of the political parties was that of th hibitionists, held in Delaware June 8 nominated for Governor, Morris Sha Washington Court-House, and for Lieut Governor, Walter T. Mills, of Wooster, County. The platform adopted comm the work of the Women's Christian T ance Union, denounced the Dow law, ex sympathy for the wage-earners, declare personal and corrupt motives had no p politics, expressed indignation at the of anarchy, which was declared to be shoot of the saloon, opposed sudden and changes in the tariff system, demanded safeguards for the Christian Sabbatt asked that a law be passed compelling i tion in the public schools as to the eff alcohol and narcotics on the human syst

The State Convention of the Union party was held in Columbus July 4 John Seitz, of Tiffin, was nominated fo ernor, and F. McDonald, of Springfie Lieutenant-Governor. The platform a favored the abolishment of the fee sys paying public officials, demanded the e ment of laws against bribery, asked f revocation of the charters of corpo which violate the laws, asked for the of a law taxing mortgages and granting responding exemption to mortgagor manded that school-books be printed State and furnished to pupils at cost, den that banks be required to give security State, denounced the courts for not en the laws against gambling in stocks an products, asked that discrimination by e ers against associations of workingmen b a felony, and demanded that railroads b on their capitalization.

The Democratic State Convention wi in Cleveland July 20 and 21. Thor Powell, of Delaware, was nominated fo ernor, and D. C. Coolman, of Raven Lieutenant-Governor. The platform der a judicious reduction of the tariff, ask the public domain be reserved for act tlers, expressed sympathy with the pe Ireland, demanded protection for lab vored a restriction of immigration, den the Republican State administration as nesslike and partisan, demanded saf for the ballot, declared for home rule nicipalities, indorsed Cleveland's adm tion, declared that there should be no d ination by common carriers, and asked regulation of the liquor-traffic by a lice

The Republican State Convention was held in Toledo July 27 and 28. J. B. Foraker was renominated for Governor, and W. C. Lyon, of Newark, was nominated for Lieutenant-Governor. The platform declared in favor of protection to American industries and labor, favored the restriction of pauper and criminal immigration, asked Congress to supervise the election of congressmen in the South to the end that a full vote and a fair count might be secured, demanded the restoration of the tariff of 1867 on wool, favored liberal pensions for Union veterans and the making of public improvements as a means of disposing of the Treasury surplus, demanded that the public domain be reserved for actual settlers, condemned the false pretenses of President Cleveland on the civil-service question, and demanded the enforcement of the law, expressed sympathy for Ireland, condemned the action of President Cleveland in vetoing pension bills, asked for the passage of laws to protect the users of patents, approved the administration of Gov. Foraker and his action regarding the rebel flags, condemned the election crimes perpetrated by the Democrats in Cincinnati and Columbus, sustained the Dow law, favored the passage of laws to prevent discrimination by railroads, and recommended John Sherman to the consideration of the Republicans of the nation as a candidate for President in 1888.

Each of the conventions nominated a full State ticket in addition to the candidates for Governor and Lieutenant-Governor. The canvass was very bitter between the Republican and Democratic leaders, national questions being mingled with several State and local questions, on which feeling was high. The excitement was increased toward the close of the campaign by the introduction of Gov. Gordon, of Georgia, to speak for Mr. Powell. The election, Nov. 8, resulted in the following vote for Governor: Foraker, Republican, 356,534; Powell, Democrat, 333,205; Seitz, Union Labor, 24,711; Sharp, Prohibition, 29,700; Foraker's plurality, 23,329. For the other offices the Republican candidates had pluralities ranging from 28,000 to 31,000. A Legislature was also elected, the result being as follows:

PARTY.	Senate.	House.	Joint ballot.
Republicans	25	64	89
Democrats	11	44	55
Republican majority	14	20	34

The Legislature.—The adjourned session of the sixty-seventh General Assembly began January 4, and ended March 21. Very few measures of general importance were passed. The most important were an act repealing the so-called black laws, an act amending the Dow law so as to prevent the sale of liquor in quantities of one gallon or more by the agent of the manufacturer without paying the tax, an act providing for the relief of indigent Union soldiers and sailors, their widows and minor children, an act giving wives the right to buy and sell property without the consent of their husbands and more clearly defining the property-rights of the husband and wife, and an act extending the provisions of the registration law to the cities of Toledo, Columbus, and Dayton.

The Liquor Question.—At the first session of the sixty-seventh General Assembly in 1886, a law was passed known as the Dow law, imposing special taxes on manufacturers and dealers in intoxicating liquors. The constitutionality of the law was assailed on the ground that it violated the provision of the Constitution prohibiting the licensing of the liquor-traffic. The Supreme Court decided the law constitutional in two cases before it, January 5, the following being the syllabus of the decisions:

Mary F. Anderson *vs.* Joseph W. Brewster *et al.* Error to the Circuit Court of Hamilton County. Dickman, J.

1. Under the second section of the statute of May 14, 1886, known as the Dow law (83 Ohio L., 157), a valid lien is created upon the real property when the tenant holds under a lease, written or parol, made after the passage of the statute.

2. The assessment imposed by the first section of the statute is not in conflict with the second section of the twelfth article of the Constitution.

3. The statute, so far as it provides for an assessment or tax upon the business of trafficking in intoxicating liquors is not, in effect, a license law, and not within the inhibition of the eighteenth section of the schedule to the Constitution.

Judgment affirmed. Owen, C. J., and Follett, J., dissent.

Leo Adler *et al vs.* H. N. Whitbeck, Treasurer. Error to the Circuit Court of Cuyahoga County. Minshall, J.

1. It is competent to the General Assembly of the State to impose a tax on the business of trafficking in intoxicating liquors as a means of providing against evils resulting therefrom.

2. Neither the tax so imposed, nor a provision that the same shall attach as a lien on the property in which it is conducted, constitutes a license within the meaning of section 9 of Article XV of the Constitution.

3. The statute imposing the tax may provide for its collection by the treasurer of the county as other taxes are collected, may impose penalties for its non-payment, and for the refusal of a person engaged in the business, on the demand of the assessor, to sign and verify the statement of the return; and, for an injury done him in his property, such provisions do not deprive the citizen of the due course of law secured to him by section 16 of the bill of rights, nor are they inhibited by the fourteenth amendment to the Constitution of the United States.

4. The Legislature may, in providing against evils resulting from the traffic in intoxicating liquors, levy a tax upon such forms of the traffic as in its wisdom it may seem best without infringing the constitutional requirements (section 26, Article II), that all laws of a general nature shall be uniform in their operation throughout the State.

5. The act of the General Assembly passed May 14, 1886, providing against the evils resulting from the traffic in intoxicating liquors (83 Ohio L., 157) is not in any of these respects in conflict with the Constitution of the State nor of the United States, and is a valid law.

The judgment is affirmed, without prejudice to the right of any of the plaintiffs to prosecute a separate action for relief against any erroneous or wrongful return that may have been made by the assessor as to his business. Owen, C. J., and Follett, J., dissent.

OLD CATHOLIC CHURCH. The Old Catholic Church originated in the dissent of a portion of the Roman Catholic clergy of Germany from the decree asserting the infallibility of the Pope when speaking *ex cathedra*, which was promulgated in accordance with the resolution passed by the Vatican Council of 1870. About two hundred of the 744 bishops who attended the Council refused to vote for the decree, and a number of them asserted for a time a determination not to abide by it. They were all, however, ultimately won to obedience; and it devolved upon Dr. Döllinger, of the University of Munich, who had gained eminence as a theological writer, to give voice to the sentiment of opposition within the Church to the "Vatican decrees," and to lead the revolt against the imposition of the dogma. He was supported by his fellow professors in the theological faculty at Munich, and by their action a large list of signatures was obtained to a protest against the enforcement of the decree, which was presented to the King of Bavaria. A conference, attended by five hundred members, prepared a plan of action, the effect of which was to cut the participants off from all relations with the Roman Catholic hierarchy. Their professed object was to restore the Church to the simplicity which characterized the earlier centuries of its history, as well as to separate it from political influences. The organization of the Old Catholic Church was completed in 1873, when articles of faith were agreed upon, and the first bishop, Bishop Reinkens, was chosen, and afterward consecrated by the Jansenist bishop of Utrecht. This bishop was recognized by the Prussian Government, and the Church received its moral support for several years. The Old Catholic Church now has a regularly organized existence in the Rhine provinces of Germany and in Switzerland and Austria; and it is represented in France by the Gallican Church, of which Henry Lascelles Jenner is bishop *pro tem.*, and Père Hyacinthe is an active clergyman. Friendly relations and correspondence are maintained with the latter branch of the Old Catholic Church by the bishops of the Protestant Episcopal Church in the United States. The Old Catholics have ceased to enforce the celibacy of the clergy, oral confessions to the priest, prayers for deliverance from purgatory, fasting, and penance, although they believe the last two services to be Christian duties. They have disused the service of the mass in the Latin language, although some of the German clergy still prefer it. At the last meeting of the synod in Germany, it was decided to prepare a mass-book in the German language, the use of which is left optional with individual congregations. The clergy of Baden have unanimously resolved to introduce this book, but in Prussia a division of opinion prevails on the subject. The Holy Communion is administered in both kinds to the laity. The incomes of the clergy are fixed, and fees—including those for the services of marriage, baptism, and burial—are dispensed with. The Virgin Mary is adored only as an example and as the mother of the Lord, in a service that is so modified as to exclude the idea of worship. The Old Catholic Church was legally recognized in Austria in 1878, and now numbers in Vienna between 2,000 and 8,000 members, of whom 700, above twenty years of age, are contributing members. It has recently been making great progress in northern Bohemia.

The Anglican Bishops of Salisbury and Lichfield, by the request of the Archbishop of Canterbury, visited the principal communities and most influential divines of this Church in October, bearing a commission to consider with them the relations between the Church of England and the Old Catholics. At Bonn they had a conference with Bishop Reinkens and Dr. Von Schulte, at which, it is represented, such an agreement of views touching the constitutions and creeds of their respective churches appeared to exist as to encourage hopes for the ultimate success of the mission. At Freiburg, in Breisgau, they attended a confirmation service performed by Bishop Reinkens. At Olten, in Switzerland, they conferred with Bishop Herzog, and other prominent men of the Swiss churches, and at Munich with Dr. Döllinger and Prof. Friedrich. At Vienna, October 23, they attended, in their canonical robes, the Old Catholic service, held in the church which had been given to the community by the municipal council in commemoration of the foundation of the society, sixteen years previously, and witnessed the baptism of an infant according to the Old Catholic rite. On the next day they conferred with representative members of the Church in Austria, among whom were the president of the synod, Herr Sinnek, and Prof. Reudel, a member of the Austrian Parliament.

ONTARIO. Government.—Lieutenant-Governor, Sir Alexander Campbell; Executive Council: Premier and Attorney-General, Oliver Mowatt; Commissioner of Crown Lands, T. B. Pardee; Commissioner of Public Works, C. F. Fraser; Provincial Secretary and Registrar, A. S. Hardy; Provincial Treasurer and Commissioner of Agriculture, A. M. Ross; Minister of Education, G. W. Ross.

Finances.—The revenue for the year 1886 was $4,811,876.96, and the expenditure $4,-860,642.62.

Commerce.—The following table shows the imports and exports of the province for a period of five years:

Year ending 30th June—	IMPORTS		EXPORTS	
	Total value.	Value per head.	Total value.	Value per head.
1882	$41,690,760	$21 22	$40,765,921	$20 75
1883	44,666,445	22 35	32,590,019	16 46
1884	41,967,215	20 66	26,591,017	18 24
1885	89,928,084	19 80	28,484,781	18 78
1886	89,069,475	18 64	27,088,868	19 99

The exports of home produce and manufacture for the same period were as follow:

YEAR.	Total value.	Value per head.	Percentage of total exports.
1882	$36,770,168	$15 71	40·84
1883	29,657,681	14 84	35·19
1884	23,785,055	11 68	30·77
1885	25,471,992	12 84	33·43
1886	24,092,581	11 49	33·13

Legislation.—The sixth Legislature of the province met for its first session on Feb. 10, 1887, the Mowatt Government (Liberal) being supported by a majority of about 22. The Hon. Jacob Baxter, member for Haldimand, was elected Speaker. The following resolution was adopted by the Legislative Assembly:

That in the opinion of this House it is unjust to other classes of the community who are taxed on their incomes that the salaries of officials holding office under the Government of Canada should be exempt from municipal taxation, and this House regrets that the Dominion Parliament, in the exercise of its jurisdiction under the B. N. A. Act, has not passed any act placing, or purporting to place, such salaries on the same footing in that respect as this Legislature has placed the salaries of officials holding office under the Provincial Government.

An act was passed to amend the provincial law of libel (Revised Statutes of Ontario, Ch. 56, Sec. 4). The act provides that no action for libel shall lie, unless the plaintiff has given the defendant written notice complaining of the libel; and damages are restricted to actual damages, provided the article complained of is published in good faith; if there is reasonable ground for believing it was for the public benefit; if it did not involve a criminal charge; if the publication took place in mistake or misapprehension of facts, and if a full and fair retractation is made within three days after the receipt of the plaintiff's notice, in as conspicuous a place and type as the article complained of. The provisions of this act are not to apply to a libel against any candidate for public office in the province, unless the retractation is made five days before the election. Reports of public meetings are privileged, and also reports of proceedings in courts of justice, unless defendant has refused to publish a reasonable letter of explanation by plaintiff. Defendants may, under certain circumstances, demand security for costs, and unless otherwise directed by a judge, a libel suit must be entered in the county wherein the chief office of the newspaper or the residence of the plaintiff is situated.

An act was passed exempting from seizure, under any writ in respect of which the province has legislative authority, the bedding and wearing-apparel of the debtor and his family. Also furniture specified, not exceeding in value $150; fuel and provisions for the family for thirty days, not exceeding $40 in value; one cow, six sheep, four hogs, and twelve hens, not exceeding $75 in value; food therefor for thirty days, and one dog. Also the tools, chattels, or implements used in the debtor's occupation, to the value of $100; and bees to the extent of fifteen hives.

Acts were also passed appointing commissioners for the "Queen Victoria Niagara Falls Park," etc., extending the provisions of the Land Titles Act (Torrens System) to any county, city, or town, if adopted by the municipal council thereof; and providing for the federation of the University of Toronto and University College with other universities and colleges in the province.

OREGON. State Government.—The following were the State officers during the year: Governor, Sylvester Pennoyer; Secretary of State, Auditor, and Lieutenant-Governor ex officio, George W. McBride; Treasurer, George W. Webb; Superintendent of Public Instruction, E. B. McElroy; Chief-Justice of the Supreme Court, William P. Lord; Associate Justices, William W. Thayer and R. S. Strahan. Except the Governor and Justice Strahan these officers are all Republicans.

Legislative Session.—The Legislature was in session through January and February. It passed an act redistricting the State for its own members, an act creating a railroad commission of two members, with power to investigate and regulate the management of railroads and to enforce the laws relating to them, and resolutions proposing three constitutional amendments to be voted upon in November. These amendments, which were first proposed at the session of 1885, are given below with the vote thereon. The appropriations include $80,000 for finishing and furnishing the State Capitol, $55,550 for additions and repairs at the Insane Asylum, $150,000 for current expenses of the asylum, and $89,480 for general expenses of the State Prison. A compulsory school bill was vetoed by the Governor. Other acts were as follow:

Authorizing county courts to build armories in cities of over 10,000 inhabitants and to provide for the use thereof.

Requiring publication of reports of county finances.

Settling the title to, and the method of sale of, swamp and overflowed lands held by the State.

Defining the duties of directors of school-districts and of district clerks.

Providing for the appointment of a State Fish Commission to preserve and propagate salmon and other food-fishes.

Refunding to the counties taxes paid by them on account of a tax on mortgages assessed by the State, which tax has been declared illegal.

To prevent frauds in obtaining registration of cattle and other animals, and to punish giving false pedigrees.

To protect live-stock and to compel railroads to pay for stock killed or injured on any unfenced railroad track.

Providing a method of procedure for ascertaining and establishing disputed boundary-lines.

Authorizing county courts to construct county roads.

Defining vagrancy and providing a punishment therefor.

Creating the office of recorder of conveyances in the counties of Linn, Marion, Washington, and Yamhill.

Declaring that the irreducible school fund of the State shall consist of proceeds from the sale of the sixteenth and thirty-sixth sections of every township, the proceeds of all escheats and forfeitures to the State, all moneys paid as exemptions from military duty, all gifts to the State for common-school purposes, and all gifts the purpose of which is not stated, and the proceeds of the 500,000-acre grant of 1841.

Providing a new law relative to escheats and forfeitures to the State.

To provide for the maintenance of kindergarten schools as a part of the public-school system.

Fixing the price and the method of sale of school, university, Capitol building, internal improvement, and Agricultural College lands.

Enacting a new bounty law for killing wild animals.

Revising the powers and duties of county superintendents of schools.

Declaring the first Saturday in June of each year a public holiday, to be known as "Labor Day."

Prohibiting the sale or gift of opium, morphine, eng-she or cooked opium, and hydrate of chloral or cocaine, by any but regularly qualified and licensed physicians and druggists, and only for the cure of disease.

Regulating the practice of dentistry by creating a State board of examiners and requiring all practitioners hereafter beginning business to obtain a certificate from such board.

Providing for the appointment of an inspector of stock in each county and giving him power to suppress infectious diseases among domestic animals and to exercise supervision over stock in the county.

Providing a new law for the organization and discipline of the State militia.

To license and regulate the insurance business in the State and making the Secretary of State *ex-officio* Insurance Commissioner.

Creating the county of Malheur.

Creating the county of Wallowa.

Finances.—The balance in the State treasury at the close of the fiscal year 1887 was $71,755.83. The estimates for 1888 anticipate an expenditure of $482,709.37 for general purposes, which, after deducting the sum now in the treasury, will require a tax levy of four and nine tenth mills. An additional tax of two tenths of a mill for the State militia and one tenth of a mill for the university will increase the rate to five and two tenths mills. The total assessed value of property in the State for 1887 was over $84,000,000; in 1885 it was $78,776,011.

Education.—The following is an abstract of school statistics for the school year ending March 7, 1887:

Persons over four and under twenty years of age—males, 44,691; females, 42,526; total, 87,217.

Number enrolled during the year in the public schools—males, 27,183; females, 25,842; total, 53,025.

Average daily attendance—males, 18,973; females, 18,433; total, 37,406.

Number of teachers employed during the year—males, 919; females, 1,170; total, 2,089.

Number of pupils enrolled in private schools—males, 2,505; females, 2,429; total, 4,934.

Number of school-houses built during the year, 88; previously erected, 1,236; total, 1,324.

Average salaries paid teachers per month—males, $45.78; females, $34.79.

Number of colleges, 8; teachers employed, 44; pupils attending, 809.

Receipts: In school-clerks' hands at beginning of the year, $100,223.26; received during the year from district tax, $165,446.65; four-mill county tax, $286,877.83; State fund, $85,625.90; rate bills, $213,075.79; other sources, $19,187.81; total receipts, $669,935.54.

At the State University 184 pupils were enrolled in all departments during the year ending June 30, the average enrollment being 110, of which 68 were males and 42 females. A law-school and a school of music are connected with the university. The total expenses for the year were $18,285.87, and the income $21,511.50. The latter sum is derived from lands given by the Federal Government, private donations, and the State tax of one tenth of a mill for university purposes.

In August the corner-stone of a new building for the State Agricultural College was laid at Corvallis. This building is erected by the citizens of Benton County upon State land and given to the State. The Agricultural College has been in existence since 1870, when by an act of the Legislature it was located at and made a part of Corvallis College. Since that time the State has appropriated biennially a fixed amount which has been expended by the trustees of Corvallis College, under the direction of a State board, in giving instruction in agricultural subjects at that institution. But in 1885 the Methodist Conference, which founded and maintained Corvallis College, finding itself unable to raise money for new buildings, offered to transfer the whole institution to the State for the uses of the State Agricultural College free from all sectarian control. The Legislature of that year accepted the offer on condition that the friends of the State institution should construct the building which is now being erected. During the present year, however, the Methodists have preferred a claim that the offer to the State was not made by their duly authorized agents or with their consent, and that they still own the Corvallis property with the new building included. The question is not yet decided. The number of students at the State institution in 1885-'86 was 52, and the expenses $8,470.37.

Penitentiary.—At the close of September there were 267 prisoners confined in the State Penitentiary. Of these, 165 were engaged under contract in foundry work, 30 in the manufacture of bricks, and the remainder in various useful employments. Their labor repays about half the cost of maintenance.

The Salmon-Fishery.—The fishing-season of 1887 on Columbia river was not a success, and the decreased catch is taken as an indication that the resources of the river are being exhausted. Only 356,000 cases were packed during the season, 92,500 fewer than in 1886, and 197,800 fewer than in 1885. The value of the product is estimated at $2,124,000. There are engaged in this business on the river 40 canneries valued at $800,000, 1,400 fishing-boats worth $245,000, 1,400 nets worth $440,000, and other apparatus worth $200,000 more, making the total investment over $1,500,000. In the season 6,000 persons are employed.

Statistics.—The following figures show the shipments of grain and other agricultural products from Portland for the year ending in August as compared with the preceding year:

	1885–'86.	1886–'87.
Wheat, centals	5,321,496	3,754,188
Flour, barrels	541,689	590,781
Wool, pounds	14,100,718	11,589,283
Hops, pounds	4,916,819	5,422,291
Oats, centals	898,151	151,787
Barley, centals	127,763	16,814
Flaxseed, sacks	62,400	65,215

The number of sheep in the State at the last assessment was 2,593,029.

Constitutional Amendments.—The amendments to be voted upon in November prohibited the manufacture, sale, or giving away of intoxicating liquors, changed the date of State elections from June to November, and gave the Legislature power to fix the salaries of State officers, these being now established by the Constitution. Neither of these propositions were successful. The prohibitory amendment, in spite of all efforts in its behalf, failed by 7,985 votes, 19,973 votes being cast in its favor and 27,958 against it. The election amendment obtained 19,947 affirmative and 22,760 negative votes, while the salary amendment found only 5,998 supporters to 35,628 opponents.

P

PAPUA, or NEW GUINEA, a large island in the Pacific Ocean, lying north of Australia. The southern coast is separated from the northernmost point of Queensland by the Torres Strait, about 90 miles wide. The area is estimated at 300,000 square miles. The Netherlands Government claims the western part of the island as far as the 141st meridian east from Greenwich. The area of Dutch New Guinea is 150,755 square miles. The German Government proclaimed a protectorate over the northern coast east of the Dutch line and over New Britain and other islands constituting the Bismarck Archipelago on Dec. 17, 1884. The area of Kaiser Wilhelm's Land in Papua is 70,300 square miles, and that of the islands of the Bismarck Archipelago 18,150 square miles. Both are under the administration of the German New Guinea Company. The population of German New Guinea is 109,000; that of Bismarck Archipelago, which embraces all the islands lying between 141° and 154° east longitude and between 8° south latitude and the equator, is 188,000. By virtue of the Delimitation Convention concluded between England and Germany on April 6, 1886, a part of the Solomon Islands are also included in the German boundaries. The German islands of the group have an area of 8,460 square miles and contain about 80,000 inhabitants. The southern coast of Papua was formerly annexed by Great Britain on Nov. 18, 1884. The eastern extremity of Papua and the Luisiad group and other islands were annexed to the British dominions in January, 1885. The area of the British possessions in Papua and the adjacent islands is 88,460 square miles, and the population 229,100.

British New Guinea.—The British Government, after the protectorate was proclaimed over Southeastern New Guinea, appointed Sir Peter Scratchley High Commissioner. He spent several months in endeavoring to induce the governments of the Australian colonies to contribute to the expenses of the administration. They finally agreed to raise £15,000 per annum for the purpose. As soon as he arrived in Papua the Commissioner was attacked with coast fever, and died. John Douglas was appointed temporarily to the post of High Commissioner. After the death of Sir Peter Scratchley, the South Australian Government withdrew from the agreement to contribute to the expense of the administration. This was followed by similar action on the part of Tasmania, New Zealand, and Western Australia. The premier of Queensland drew up a plan by which he undertook to organize the administration. The premiers of Victoria and New South Wales met him at Sydney in the beginning of May, 1886, and agreed to his plan. The sum of £15,000 annually is contributed by the three colonies in equal shares, and will be guaranteed by the Government of Queensland, which will direct the administration. The legislative and executive powers are to be concentrated in the hands of a crown administrator. No purchase of land is allowed to be made by private persons except from the Government or from persons who have obtained their titles from the Government. Trading with the natives in arms, ammunition, or intoxicating liquors is prohibited. The enlistment of laborers is allowed only under Government supervision. The administrator will act under the instructions of the governor of Queensland. The arrangement whereby Queensland guarantees the expenses is to remain in force five years.

German New Guinea.—The New Guinea Company in Berlin fitted out an expedition, which sailed from Hamburg on Feb. 3, 1886, for the thorough exploration of Kaiser Wilhelm's Land and the Bismarck Archipelago, and for the establishment of plantations and factories. The leader of the expedition was Dr. Schrader, of Hamburg. In the German, as well as in the English possessions, the sale of fire-arms, ammunition, and spirituous liquors is forbidden.

The Russian naturalist Nicholas de Miklouho Maclay has resided many years on the shore of Astrolabe Bay, northwest of the district which the Germans intend immediately to colonize, and within the territory conceded to Germany in the arrangement with Great Britain. The natives of the coast between Cape Croisilles and Cape King William looked upon Maclay as their protector, and obeyed him as a ruler. When he returned to St. Petersburg, in the summer of 1886, he endeavored to induce the Russian Government to assert a claim to this district on the ground of prior possession. It had been visited by Russian men-of-war, which surveyed the two harbors, Port Alexis and Port Constantine, and the islands off the coast in 1871 and 1883. A project for the colonization of this region was discussed in Russia, and many young men were desirous of embarking in the enterprise, but the Russian Government refrained from interference with the rights asserted by Germany.

PARAGUAY, a republic in South America. According to the census of 1886, the white population was 300,000—170,000 females and 130,000 males. There are besides, 60,000 semi-civilized Indians and 70,000 wild Indians. The number of foreigners permanently settled in the country was shown to be about 9,000, of whom 1,500 were Italians, 5,000 Argentines, 600 Brazilians, 300 French, 550 Germans, and 100 Englishmen. The German population increases rapidly. In 1886 Asuncion, the capital, had 25,000 inhabitants; Villa Rica had 11,000; Caazapa, 9,000; Villa Concepcion, 8,000; Villa San Pedro, 8,000; Luque, 8,000; Carapegua, 8,000; San Estanislas, 7,000; Ita-guá, 6,000; Ita, 5,000; Paraguari, 5,000; Villa Ilumaitá, 4,205; Villa Pilar, 3,621; and Ja-guaron, 3,106.

Government.—The President is Gen. P. Esco-bar, elected Nov. 25, 1886. His Cabinet was composed of the following ministers: Secretary of the Interior, Col. Mesa; Foreign Affairs, Dr. B. Aceval; Finance, A. Cañete; Justice and Public Worship, M. Maciel; and War, Col. Duarte. The United States *Chargé d'Affaires* for Paraguay and Uruguay, resident at Montevideo, is John E. Bacon; the American Consul at Asuncion is Frank D. Hill. The Paraguayan Consul-General at New York is Rafael R. Barthold; Consul at San Francisco, Petrus J. Van Loben Sels; Consul-General in the United States, John Stewart.

Army and Navy.—The effective strength of the permanent army is reduced to 500 men; in an emergency the National Guard is enrolled. The navy consists of three small steamers.

Finances.—On Jan. 1, 1887, the home debt had been reduced to $179,435 through the operations of a sinking fund, created by sales of public lands and the levying of 10 per cent. additional customs duties. The converted foreign debt, bearing successively 2, 3, and 4 per cent. interest, amounts to $4,250,000. In exchange for unpaid coupons of the old foreign indebtedness, a 145-acre land-warrant is delivered for every £100 in coupons.

The income of the republic in 1886 was $1,-531,802, and the outlay, $1,377,756. The revenue derived from customs was $844,218, as compared with $769,000 in 1885.

During the summer the Government issued

a decree admitting for circulation, on a par with Paraguayan silver dollars, the silver dollars of the Argentine Republic, Chili, Bolivia, Peru, and Mexico, and also the five-franc pieces of France, Belgium, and Italy that weigh 25 grains and are 900 fine.

Postal Service.—The number of items of mail-matter reached 304,617 in 1886, 130,740 being forwarded in the interior, 81,030 having been received from abroad, and 92,847 sent abroad. The receipts were $7,778, and the expenses, $14,521.

Telegraphs.—A telegraph-line runs beside the track of the Asuncion-Villa Rica Railroad, a distance of 152 kilometres, and *via* Paso de la Patria, Paraguay is linked to the world's cable system.

Commerce.—The merchandise imported into Paraguay in 1886 was valued at $1,621,000 worth, compared with $1,524,000 the previous year, while the exports were $1,571,000 and $1,493,000 respectively. Chief among the products exported in 1886 were: Tobacco, 5,-306,000 kilogrammes; yerba maté, or Paraguay tea, 4,508,000 kilogrammes; hides, 81,000; oranges, 25,000,000; and cabinet-wood, 151,281 metres.

Railroads.—In November the Paraguayan Legislature passed a bill empowering the Government to sell to William Stewart the Asuncion-Villa Rica Railway for $2,100,000 gold. The purchaser engages to extend the line to Villa Encarnacion, and on the cost of construction of this extension, at the rate of $30.000 per kilometre, the Government is authorized to guarantee 6 per cent. interest for twenty years. When this extension is in running order, the operating expenses are estimated to amount to 55 per cent. of the gross earnings.

The remarkably prosperous condition of the country has encouraged the Legislature to authorize the Government to push railway enterprise, and a bill was passed, on September 28, decreeing that a railroad and telegraph line be constructed, which, starting from the right bank of Paraguay river, are to traverse the Chaco, and have their terminus at a point of junction on the northwestern frontier of Paraguay and Bolivia; plans to be submitted to the Government within two years from the date of passage of the bill. The law establishes the principle of absolute right of expropriation of all the land necessary on the line.

German-Paraguayan Treaty.—A treaty of commerce and navigation was signed between Germany and Paraguay in 1887, containing, similar to the one concluded with Great Britain in 1886 and with Spain and Portugal previously, the " most-favored-nation " clause, with this reservation, however, that Germany waives the privileges conceded to the Brazilian province of Matto Grosso by treaty as long as they are not granted to a third nation. Furthermore, Article III of the treaty grants German consuls the right to perform the ceremony of marriage within their district in cases in which both the applicants are German. The treaty has been made for ten years, and if, upon its termination, neither party should have signified its wish of non-renewal, it is to remain operative for another twelvemonth.

Colonization. — Dr. Bernhard Forster, who emigrated to Paraguay some years ago, invites German emigration to a tract of land secured by him, containing about 580 square kilometres. The settlement is named New Germania. Under the title of New Bordeaux, a French colony is about to be founded between the rivers Paraguay and Bermejo, in the region known as the Chaco Alto Peruano. The following is one of the clauses of the contract that has to be signed in France before the emigrant receives his passage: "I bind myself, on arriving at my destination, to labor and cultivate the ground that shall be given to me by deed, although it will not pass definitively into my posession until I shall have returned to the Government of Paraguay, from my crops, the cost of my passage [$56 in silver], and the seeds, instruments, cattle, etc., that may be advanced to me." The Government of Paraguay, at the same time, binds itself to furnish a house, tools, seeds, etc., and provisions for at least eight months. The amount so advanced will bear no interest, and the colonists will pay no taxes. Only in the event of their possessions being menaced will they be called upon to assist in their defense.

PATENTS. Statistics. — The following statistics show the extent of the business of the United States Patent-Office for the year 1887:

Total receipts (net) $1,144,509 80
Total expenditures 994,472 22

Receipts over expenditures $150,037 88

Amount in treasury to credit of office January 1, 1888.. .... $3,257,490 91
Expenditures for salaries..................... 689,124 85

The following is a summary of the business of the Patent-Office: Number of applications for patents for inventions, 34,420; number of applications for patents for designs, 1,041; number of applications for reissues of patents, 152; total number of applications relating to patents, 35,613. Number of caveats filed, 2,622; number of applications for registration of trade-marks, 1,282; number of applications for registration of labels, 686; number of disclaimers filed, 9; number of appeals on the merits, 941; total, 5,540; total number of applications requiring investigation and action, 41,-153. Number of patents issued, including designs, 21,378; number of patents reissued, 99; number of trade-marks registered, 1,133; number of labels registered, 380; total, 22,990. Number of patents expired during the year, 12,157; number of patents withheld for non-payment of final fee, 8,044; number of patents issued to foreigners, 1,466; number of patents issued to citizens of the United States, 19,912.

Among the States, Connecticut leads the list in inventiveness with one patent to every 790

inhabitants; the District of Columbia comes next with one to 845 inhabitants; Massachusetts is next with one to 950 inhabitants, and Mississippi brings up the rear with one patent to every 25,146 inhabitants. Of foreign countries, England took out 500 patents; Germany, 291; France, 122, while Corea, Finland, Japan, Luxemburg, the Argentine Republic, Newfoundland, Syria, Victoria, and the West Indies are credited with but one apiece.

Annual Report. — The Commissioner of Patents issued his annual report under the date of Jan. 31, 1888; it appears in the "Official Gazette" of Feb. 7. It is of rather greater length than usual, and embodies many suggestions for amendments of the statutes. It is interesting to note that he states that he needs no additional force to do the work; he only appeals for more room and better office facilities.

The International Union for the Protection of Industrial Property. — The Senate of the United States on March 2, 1887, agreed that this country should become a member of the Industrial Union. Later, on June 11, 1887, the convention was proclaimed by the President. The idea of the Union is analogous to that of the Postal Union; to secure a uniformity of patent practice among nations, and to do away with interfering clauses and statutes. It includes nineteen articles, affecting inventions and trade-marks. It so happens that the present statutes of the United States are such as to prevent any, except the most trivial effect, from following upon the adoption of the treaty. The subject will be found discussed at length in "History of the International Union for the Protection of Industrial Property," by Patent-Office Examiner F. A. Seeley, published under the direction of the Commissioner of Patents. Washington, Government Printing-Office, 1887. Reference may also be made to the "Official Gazette," xl, 447; xli, 355, which publish the treaty and comments thereon.

The Commissionership. — The office of Patent Commissioner becoming vacant by the resignation of the Hon. Martin V. Montgomery, the President in April, 1887, appointed to the position the Hon. Benton J. Hall, of Iowa. The new incumbent was born at Mount Vernon, Ohio, in 1835, and graduated at Miami University in 1855. He commenced the practice of law in the office of his father, Mr. J. C. Hall, of Burlington, Iowa, in his day regarded as one of the best lawyers of the State. Mr. Hall is the second commissioner from that State. Mr. Montgomery, his predecessor in office, was appointed Associate Justice of the Supreme Court of the District of Columbia to succeed Justice MacArthur, who retired. This court has jurisdiction over patents on appeal from the Commissioner's decisions.

Litigation. — Various important decisions have been reached in the Federal courts. The Government has met with two reverses in a suit brought by the Attorney-General of the United States to annul the Bell telephone patent of

1876. Both were on demurrer. See "Official Gazette," xxxvii, 1,287; and xli, 123, for text of decisions. Meanwhile no decision has been rendered by the United States Supreme Court in the five appealed cases in which arguments from all points of attack were made against the same patent. The patent expires by natural limitation in the beginning of 1893. The corresponding patent has been canceled in Austria as far as reference to telephones is concerned. The court found that it embodied scientific principles which are unpatentable by the Austrian law. A decision handed down by the United States Supreme Court on Nov. 14 declares the famous driven-well patent, granted to Nelson W. Green, to be invalid on account of prior use, and the decision was confirmed on a later motion for a rehearing of the case. A Circuit Court decision by Judge Shiras in Iowa, rendered about the beginning of January, 1888, declares the equally famous barbed-wire-fence patent, No. 157,124, granted to J. F. Glidden, invalid on account of prior use. The latter case has been appealed to the Supreme Court. These two decisions mark the extinction of very important interests. Immense sums of money had been spent on litigating them, and, although they are now annulled practically, they have in their life filled an important place in the history of inventions. An important action in extending a patent has been taken by Congress. The Forty-ninth Congress granted a petition of Mrs. Henrietta H. Cole, of New York, authorizing an extension of her patent for a fluting-machine, dated June 12, 1866. It had expired in 1883. The Commissioner of Patents, after hearing evidence, granted an extension of seven years from June 12, 1883. This is a very rare grant under the present system. When the term of patents was extended from a limit of fourteen to one of seventeen years, it was thought that extensions, formerly provided for in the statutes, would no longer be needed.

Revised Classification of Inventions.—The revised classification of inventions will be found summarized in the supplement to the "Official Gazette" of Jan. 4, 1887, xxxvii, 1. It also gives the names of the chief examiners.

Court Decisions.—Below will be found a few points made in court decisions during the year 1887. The references are to volume and page of the "Official Gazette" of the United States Patent-Office:

Construction of Patents.—There may be many ways of effecting a desired result, but every patent must rest upon its mechanical devices therefor. Steam Gauge and Lantern Company vs. St. Louis Railway Supplies Manufacturing Company, xxxviii, 107.

Matter Excluded by Amendment.—A patentee having, in compliance with the requirements of the Patent-Office, excluded by amendment certain matter from his original specification, is not at liberty to insist upon a construction of his patent, which will include what he was expressly required to abandon and disavow in it. (In Supreme Court). Sutter vs. Robinson, xxxviii, 230.

Effect of English Patent on Duration of United States Patent.—Fourteen years is the term of an English patent, and, although said patent ceases to be in force after three years from its date, if the stamp-duty is not paid, it only operates by limitation upon an after-granted United States patent as a patent for fourteen years. Pallard vs. Bruno, xxxviii, 900.

Combination Claims to be valid must cover Operative Constructions.—Where a claim in a patent is for a combination of several elements, and it appears in evidence that the combination is inoperative without the addition of another element, such claim is void. Tarrant vs. Duluth Lumber Company, xxxix, 1.425.

Public Use.—A use of an invention prior to application can not be considered experimental when the subsequent completion of the invention added nothing to its patentable quality. International Tooth-Crown Company vs. Richmond et al., xxxix, 1,550.

Construction of Claims.—Claims must be construed by the language which the patentee has employed in his specification, not by that which he might have employed. Patent Clothing Company vs. Glover, xl, 1,155.

Evidence to prove Priority of Invention.—To antedate a patent by evidence of an earlier machine such evidence must be very clear and precise to overcome the presumptions arising from the grant of the patent. Osborn vs. Glazier, xl, 1,137.

Description of Process in Application.—Description of a process in an application for a machine patent does not constitute an abandonment or dedication to the public of such process, so as to estop the inventor from subsequently obtaining a patent for the process if applied for in two years. Eastern Paper Bag Company vs. Standard Paper Bag Company, xli, 231.

Effect of Limitation Imposed by Patent-Office.—It is wholly irrelevant to inquire whether the patentee was obliged to limit himself by the ruling of the Patent-Office. It is enough to say that he did so limit himself. Toepfer vs. Goetz, xli, 933.

Inventions.—The following list comprises a few of the improvements that have been devised for the more homely and familiar walks of life. Few persons appreciate the enormous number of patents that are annually issued. A list even of one-tenth of those really deserving mention would far exceed available space. The following, therefore, should be regarded as suggestive rather than comprehensive. Those who are interested will find in the "Patent-Office Gazette" a full descriptive list which presents an adequate idea of American fertility of invention.

Coffee-making.—Among the new inventions that may prove of advantage to housekeepers is a contrivance known as a "percolator," though the term does not accurately describe its operation. It consists of a small cage or basket of perforated tin or of fine wire-gauze attached to an air-tight tin float. The float forms a sort of cover for the cage and is easily detachable therefrom. A bent wire at the top of the float serves as a handle. The finely-ground coffee, as much as required, is placed in the cage, and the whole is then lowered into the water. The float keeps the coffee near the surface of the water where the ebullition is most violent, and the strength is very quickly extracted. Fig. 1 shows a common tin coffee-pot with the side cut away and the percolator floating in the water. Coffee-makers have from time immemorial resorted to methods similar in principle, tying the coffee loosely in thin cambric or placing it in the familiar little spherical wire-gauze receptacles that are to be found in every hardware shop. These, however, have the disadvantage of sinking as soon as the coffee becomes water-soaked, while the percolator floats till the process is completed, and can be easily lifted out of the water before

the beverage reaches the stage of bitterness. By means of this device coffee can be made as well in a covered tin cup, pail, or a stew-pan as in a regular strainer. Those who object to boiled coffee need perhaps to be told that it is objectionable only when improperly boiled. If rightly done, as is easy with this contrivance, the beverage is equal to the best filtered coffee.

Heat Regulator.—Several devices have been introduced within a few years designed to maintain at an even temperature the air of houses heated by furnaces. Some of them are adjustable by a thermometer suspended perhaps in the sitting-room of the house and operated by electric connection with the draught of the furnace. The most simple and practical appears to be an automatic governor which is operated by direct mechanical action resulting from the expansion and contraction of a brass tube passing just above the fire-box of the furnace. It can be readily placed in any heater, fixed or portable. The upper part of a portable furnace is shown in Fig. 2 as being easy of illustration. The outer jacket being cut away the tube, about an inch and a quarter in diameter, is seen extending across the interior space. At the front it is fitted with a small register for the admission of more or less air, and the rear end extends beyond the jacket toward the smoke-pipe. Just outside the jacket it connects with a small iron box containing nicely adjusted multiplying wheels, so that a slight alteration

of the length of the tube acts upon a lever, which in turn opens or closes a valve or damper in the smoke-pipe. The necessary result is obvious. When the fire is burning fiercely the tube expands to its greatest length, a small fraction of an inch, but enough almost or quite to close the damper according to adjustment. As the heat moderates the tube contracts, and the damper opens increasing the draught and tending to maintain the temperature. An ingenious and simple contrivance renders it easy to adjust the connections so that the machinery will act when a certain desired temperature is reached. Of course such a device can only approximate perfection. No furnace will give out an unvarying amount of heat for an indef-

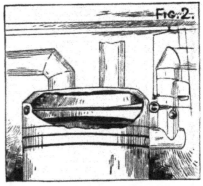

inite time without personal care, but such an attachment as this reduces to a minimum the necessity of constantly watching the fire and frequently altering the draughts and dampers.

Oil Fuel.—Another really admirable invention of the year was the fuel-cartridge, so called. As supplied to the dealers it is packed in a small tin pail holding perhaps about a pint and a half, and fitted with a cover. The cartridge itself as shown in Fig. 8 is a cylinder of rather coarse and heavy iron-wire netting, the meshes being perhaps one fourth of an inch square. The ends of the cylinder are closed by circular disks of cast-iron, perforated with small holes, and the upper one fitted with raised handles into which an ordinary stove-poker can be hooked for convenience of lifting. The inside of the cylinder is closely packed with a fibrous material, presumably asbestos. The cartridge can be used in any stove that has a damper in the smoke-pipe. When a fire is wanted the cartridge is placed in the little tin pail in which it came, or one of like size if that has been lost, and kerosene-oil of good quality is poured in until the cartridge is covered. In two or three minutes the material inside of the cartridge will have absorbed all the kerosene. A piece of paper is then placed in the stove, the cartridge is taken up with the poker and placed upon the paper, and the latter is lighted with a match. In a few seconds the oil will ignite and burn with vigor for a full hour. After it is fully ignited the front draughts of the stove are closed, and the fire regulated by means of the damper in the smoke-pipe. If the latter is closed too tightly smoke will issue through the cracks of the stove and at once notify the attendant that more draught is required. The cartridge can not be recharged with oil until it has cooled off, so that if a continuous fire is to be maintained two or more cartridges must be used, so that while one is burning the others

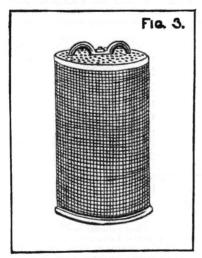

Fig. 3.

may be cooling. Apparently there is no possibility of explosion or of other danger from the use of oil in this shape, unless indeed some hopelessly stupid domestic should attempt to refill the cartridge by pouring oil upon it while it is lighted, as is her frequent custom in quickening the kitchen-fire. It is proper to say that some cartridges are in the market which are filled with an absorbent of inferior grade. Where good material is used the cartridge is practicably indestructible, and its usefulness wherever or whenever continuous heat is not required, is evident.

Improved Gas-Burners.—In these days, when the introduction of electric lights threatens to supersede the ordinary use of gas, improvements in burners are important. The burner shown in Fig. 4 is of foreign origin, the invention of Dr. Auer Von Welsbach. It is an improvement on the well-known Bunsen burner, consisting of a mantle or case passed over the burner and suspended by a wire frame shown in the illustration. The mantle is woven upon a stocking-loom and impregnated with a solution whose precise constituents are kept secret but which

contains oxides of zirconium and lanthanum. The excess liquid is removed by pressure and the cotton burned out, leaving a fragile incombustible mantle of a pure white substance, which becomes highly incandescent when the gas is lighted, and maintains this property indefinitely and without any apparent loss. Ex-

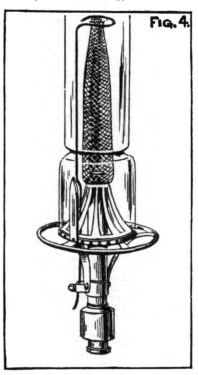

Fig. 4.

periments show an illuminating power of 16·5 candles per cubic foot of gas under a pressure involving an expenditure of 2·25 cubic feet of gas per hour (about 0·90 of an inch), and yielding a light equal to 7·82 candles per cubic foot of gas.

Improved Oil-Burner.—In the same direction is the Lucigen, successfully exhibited in the Crystal Palace, London. The method of producing this light lies in forming an intimate mixture of air and minutely divided oil-particles yielding a flame of extraordinary brightness. It requires the aid of a simple mechanism worked by a small supply of compressed air, and the flame is controlled by means of a tap or faucet. The light is produced by the combustion of crude and waste oils, costing by measurement from one tenth to one twelfth as much as gas, and about one twentieth as much as electric light of the same candle-power. It was estimated as the result of the Crystal Palace experiments that an area of one half of a square mile could be brilliantly illuminated at a cost of less than twenty-five cents an hour. The quality of the light it is claimed is greatly superior to that of electricity, owing to its greater diffusiveness, rendering it less trying to the eye, and therefore better for all practical purposes. The carbon particles are raised to an intense white heat, and the form of the flame is such that they are retained in that condition for a longer period than is the case with any other system. The lucigen has been adopted with satisfactory results at the works of the great bridge over the Frith of Forth and at a large number of manufacturing establishments in Great Britain.

Improved Curtain Fixture.—Persons who are partionlar about the quantity and direction of the light falling through a window will be interested in a device which uncovers at will either the whole of a window, or the upper or lower half, or any part thereof. The roller (A, Fig. 5) is provided with a longitudinal slot through which the curtain passes as shown in section at B. At the left the whole appliance is shown in position for use. The roller is fixed at a middle point of the sash and a cord ascends over a pulley above the window. By pulling this upper cord the curtain unwinds and the whole window is covered. Continuing the hoisting operation the lower

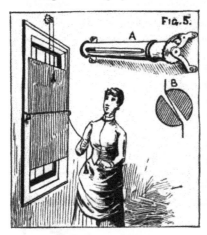

half is exposed. By lowering and partially rolling the curtain, the central portion of the window will be screened, and by lowering it to the floor and then pulling the side cord, the lower half of the window is covered, and by a slightly different manipulation the upper half is covered if the room is not high enough to hoist the curtain by the upper cord. The tas-

sels are weighted so that they balance in any position, and a very complete adjustable shade is thus provided for any conditions of light.

A Gravity Latch.—The liability of springs to wear out or become useless through rust or mechanical complications in connection with door-latches has, in the course of time, given

rise to innumerable annoyances, and a latch-lock operating by gravity has many claims to consideration. The one shown in Fig. 6 is very simple in construction. The diagram at the left presents a front view, and that at the right an edge. The casing has a central channel and side-flanges for attachment to the door at an angle of forty-five degrees. A bolt having its lower end obliquely beveled rests in the channel riding upon an anti-friction wheel and projecting when the door is open like the catch of an ordinary knob-latch. When the door is closed it engages a beveled striking plate, and the bolt slides upward in the channel, slipping at once into the mortise when the door is shut, and automatically locking itself in its lowest position by a shoulder near its upper end. A pawl is provided at the upper end, which drops into a notch, affording additional security. A knob on one side of the door and a key on the other afford an easy means of sliding the bolt upward when the door is to be opened. The key acts through the door upon the pawl and disengages it from the other side. A set screw, however, locks the bolt permanently, so that it can not be opened by means of the key.

A Self-Closing Gate.—The accompanying sketch shows a simple device for closing a gate by means of a weight and pulleys without the usual post and chain which occupy space, and are generally in the way. An arm is attached to the upper cross-bar of the gate, and from its end a line passes around a horizontal and over a vertical pulley, the action being direct and the rise and fall of the weight perpendicular and close to the fence. The cut (Fig. 7) explains the principle, which is so simple that any one with moderate ingenuity can render himself liable to prosecution for infringement of the patent which has been secured for the invention.

FIG. 7.

Gate for Railway-Crossings. — Numerous accidents at grade-crossings have recently led to the passage of laws in several of the States framed with a view to prevent such casualties in future, and the device shown herewith is intended to simplify the problem. The invention includes a shaft journaled transversely to the track at some distance from the crossing. A crank-arm is connected with this shaft and joined to an elbow operating a gear-wheel in the post at the crossing. The wheels of an approaching engine engage trip-arms, sound a gong, lower the barriers, and the wheels of the train, passing over tread-bars, keep the barriers depressed until the last car has passed. The operation is the same in whichever direction the train is moving, and it would seem that the invention should prevent many accidents if generally introduced.

An Improved Car-Starter. — The problem of utilizing the momentum of a moving car to accumulate power for starting it again after it has been stopped has received much attention from inventors. The illustration (Fig. 8) shows one of the latest attempts in this direction: 1 is a perspective, partly in section, of the car with its mechanical attachments; 2 shows the parts in detail; and 3, the connection of the spring tension band with the barrel on one of the friction-wheel shafts; 4 is a vertical section, in elevation, of the starter-spring, with its barrel and ratchet-wheel. A friction drum, A, is attached to the car-axle, and friction-wheels B and C bear against this, being fixed in a frame so pivoted that either of the wheels may be brought in contact with the drum. On the shaft of C there is fixed a barrel, D, to which is attached a band whose other end extends to a spring-case, G, within which is a powerful, coiled spring. This case is supported by a hanger fixed to the bottom of the car. One end of the spring is fixed to the hanger-shaft, and the other to the case. Ratchets are fitted to prevent the release of the spring when wound, until it is properly disengaged, and the connection is such that, the

FIG. 8.

band may wind in either direction on the barrel. Connecting rods, E, F, extend to each end of the car, where they are attached to levers shown in 1. In stopping the car, the driver moves the lever, carrying the lower wheel B against the friction-drum. This revolves the barrel D, and through the band revolves the case G, coiling the spring, the friction-wheel B also operating on the axle as a brake to stop the car. When the car is to be started, the driver presses with his foot upon a foot-plate, which, acting through the chain K, releases the ratchet. At the same time he pulls back the lever and brings the upper wheel C in contact with the friction-drum A, so that, as the spring expends its force in starting the car, the band is rewound and is again ready for service on the outside of the spring-case G. A different manipulation, unnecessary to describe here, applies the force of the spring to backing the car, if desired.

Construction of Propeller Screws.—The draughting and making of models of propeller screws has hitherto been one of the most difficult of the mechanical problems, but M. G. Trouve has so simplified the process that any mechanic can make a model of any desired pitch. A cylinder (B, Fig. 9), the size of the boss of the intended screw, is placed in an ordinary gear lathe, and helicoidal grooves are cut in it of

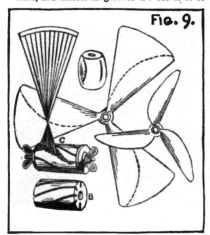

FIG. 9.

the desired pitch, and of a width and depth corresponding with a series of metallic rods. Retaining plates are fastened to the ends of the cylinder by means of thumb-screws, and the rods are then placed in the grooves and crowded closely together (C, Fig. 9). They arrange themselves, of necessity, divergently in a perfect helicoid of easily determined pitch, and only need to be connected at the top, and have the interspaces filled with some suitable material to form a complete model of a screw

from which castings can be made. The blades, once formed, can be cut to any desired shape.

Washing Photograph Plates.—A simple device whereby a large number of developed plates can be submitted to a gentle flow of water or other fluid is shown herewith. The main sup-

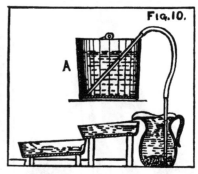

FIG. 10.

ply of fluid is placed in a vessel, A, and set on an elevated support. Below, any number of pans are arranged, slightly tilted, one overlapping another, and a pitcher standing so that its lip overhangs the uppermost pan. Two glass tubes and a short length of India-rubber tubing furnish a siphon, which only needs to be put in operation to set the current in motion, when it will run until the pail is empty. If the overflow from the lowermost pan is received in another suitable vessel, the fluid can be retransferred to A, and made to do duty repeatedly. If no pitcher is procurable having a sufficiently depressed lip, a bit of bent wire, or a bent glass rod, laid in the channel of the lip, and hanging downward toward the upper pan, will serve to guide the overflow. By this means some of the most tedious operations of photography may be greatly expedited. A number of small blocks of wood may serve as adjustable supports for the pans.

A Simple Fire-Escape.—In view of several terrible warnings, the best hotels are providing fire-escapes for their guests, and it is to be hoped that laws will be passed making it obligatory upon all hotel proprietors to follow their example. A rope is the most simple means of escape from the window of a burning building, but only an athlete can descend a rope safely without aid. The device shown herewith seems to make it possible for any one to perform this otherwise difficult feat with ease. Fig. 12 shows with sufficient distinctness the arrangement of the rope, clutch, and belt. Fig. 11 shows the practical operation. The upper end of the rope is made fast near the window, and the lower end is thrown out. The rope, it will be seen, takes a turn around a pin in the clutch, and then passes between two handles. Grasping these handles with one hand, the operator sits on the window-ledge, and, pressing the handles together simply by closing the fingers, swings himself clear of the ledge. Slightly loosening his grip, he begins to descend, and can regulate the speed of descent at will. Even if presence of mind forsakes him, the turn of the rope around the pin

FIG. 11.

FIG. 12.

Body Belt

Web Seat

will check the downward movement sufficiently to prevent serious injury on reaching the ground, and, if a person on the ground holds the lower end of the rope, he can regulate the rate of descent without any aid from the clutch by merely bearing more or less weight on the rope, and thus tightening the turns.

PENNSYLVANIA. State Government.—The following were the State officers during the year: Governor, James A. Beaver, Republican; Lieutenant-Governor, William T. Davies; Secretary of State, Charles W. Stone; Treasurer, Matthew S. Quay (elected United States Senator); Auditor-General, Jerome B. Niles, succeeded by A. Wilson Norris; Secretary of Internal Affairs, J. Simpson Africa, succeeded by Thomas J. Stewart; Attorney-General, W. S. Kirkpatrick; Superintendent of Public Instruction, E. E. Higbee; Chief-Justice of the Supreme Court, Ulysses Mercur,* succeeded by Isaac G. Gordon; Associate Justices, Edward M. Paxson, John Trunkey, James P. Sterrett, Henry Green, and Silas M. Clark. In August Governor Beaver appointed Henry W. Williams to fill the vacancy on the Supreme bench caused by the death of Chief-Justice Mercur until a successor should be elected in November. Judge Williams then became his own successor.

Legislative Session.—The Legislature met on January 4, and adjourned May 19, having been in session 135 days. State Treasurer Matthew S. Quay was chosen to succeed United States Senator John J. Mitchell, receiving 88 votes in the Senate and 133 in the House. Fourteen votes in the Senate and 66 in the House were cast for Simon P. Wolverton, the Democratic candidate. In the Republican caucus, Jan. 4, Quay received 154 votes to 9 for Galusha A. Grow.

The Legislation adopted includes an act fixing the number of members in the lower House of the Legislature at 204, and rearranging the districts from which they shall be elected; an act reorganizing and defining the congressional districts; an act providing for the semi-monthly payment of wages by employers; a " married women's property act," and a high license act.

The property act declares that every married woman shall have the same right to acquire, hold, control, and dispose of her property as if she were a *feme sole*, without the intervention of any trustee, and free from the control of her husband, except that the latter must join in any mortgage or conveyance of real estate made by her. She may contract upon the basis of her separate property, may sue or be sued alone on such contracts, and for torts committed to or by her, and her separate property is alone liable. The license act fixes the amount to be paid by wholesale and retail dealers in cities of the first, second, and third class at $500, in all other cities $300, in boroughs $200 for wholesale, and $150 for retail dealers, and in townships half of the last mentioned sums respectively. It further provides that the sale or gift of liquor to any person, whether by a licensed dealer or not, shall be unlawful on election-days and on Sundays, and at all times when the person receiving it

---

* Died June 6.

is a minor or known to be intemperate, or is already under the influence of liquor.

Special appropriations were made to complete the Industrial Reformatory at Huntingdon ($273,750), to complete buildings at the Insane Hospital at Norristown ($45,000), for buildings of the Normal School at Lockhaven ($15,000), for additions to the Soldiers' and Sailors' Home at Erie ($120,000), for the erection of a State hospital for injured persons at Luzerne ($60,000), and for the erection of other hospitals for the injured at points in the bituminous coal-fields ($60,000). Many items providing for improvements at public institutions were vetoed by the Governor. An elaborate revenue act, though much debated, failed of passage. Other acts of the session were:

Establishing four additional magistrate courts for the trial of minor civil and criminal causes in Philadelphia.

Requiring employers of females to furnish suitable seats for their use.

Providing for the incorporation and regulation of motor-power companies for operating passenger railways by cables, electrical appliances, or other means.

Constituting twelve hours a day's work for drivers and other employés of street-railway companies.

Permitting the Federal Government to acquire lands for the use of the Carlisle Indian Industrial School.

Establishing a uniform standard of time throughout the State.

Enacting a new law for the organization, discipline, and regulation of the National Guard.

To authorize chattel mortgages upon iron-ore, pig-iron, blooms, steel and iron nails, steel ingots and billets, rolled or hammered steel in sheets, bars, or plates, and all steel and iron castings.

To provide for the better collection of collateral-inheritance taxes.

To prevent and punish the making and dissemination of obscene literature and other immoral and indecent matter.

To prevent the mutilation and destruction of show-bills, placards, etc.

Prohibiting the issue of "watered" stock by railroads and other corporations.

To establish a State weather service to disseminate forecasts of the weather, and to maintain meteorological stations for observation in each county.

To abolish all taxes heretofore laid upon watches, household furniture, and pleasure-carriages.

Providing for the sale of the eastern and western farms belonging to the State college.

Repealing the bounty law upon foxes, minks, hawks, weasels, and owls, and offering a bounty for the pelts of wolves and wild-cats only.

Giving mechanics and those who furnish materials the same lien on buildings that have been repaired, altered, or enlarged, as upon those newly erected.

Declaring drunkenness on the part of election officers and assessors of poll taxes a misdemeanor, and requiring elections to be held in rooms where liquor is not sold.

Raising the age of consent in females from ten to sixteen years.

To punish false pretenses in obtaining registration of cattle and other animals, and to punish giving false pedigrees.

Providing a punishment for refusing accommodation or admittance to persons on account of their race or color, at any restaurant, hotel, public conveyance, theatre, concert, or other place of entertainment.

Giving honorably discharged soldiers and sailors the preference in public appointment and employment.

Providing for the preservation of monuments marking the boundary-line of the State.

Extending the minimum school term to six months.

To prevent the adulteration of candy or confectionery.

Revising and consolidating the law relating to evidence in legal proceedings.

Providing that equity proceedings may be begun by foreign attachment, when payment of money is involved in the case.

Appropriating the dog-tax to the support of public libraries.

Authorizing the abandonment of burying-grounds.

Requiring detectives to be licensed, and otherwise regulating their business.

Making it a felony to break and enter a car, or any part of a railroad train, with felonious intent.

Creating a State board of pharmacy, to license and regulate the sale of medicines, prescribing its duties, and making regulations to prevent the adulteration of drugs and the indiscriminate sale of poisons.

Dividing the cities of the State into seven classes, prescribing general regulations relative to the passage of ordinances, the giving of contracts, the management of finances, the terms and duties of officers, and the punishment of offenses, and providing for the incorporation and government of cities of the fourth, fifth, sixth, and seventh classes.

Authorizing cities of the first class to maintain juvenile reformatories.

Authorizing the formation of associations for the prevention of cruelty to children and aged persons.

Abolishing all distinctions, so far as relates to procedure, between the various kinds of actions ex contractu, and providing one form of action, the "action of assumpsit" therefor; abolishing the distinction between the various actions ex delicto, and providing one form, the "action of trespass" therefor, and abolishing all forms of special pleading.

Permitting the stockholders of corporations to determine the number of directors and the time for holding annual elections.

Prohibiting the employment of children under twelve years old in any mill, manufactory, or mine.

To encourage the planting of forests, by remitting a part of the taxes on land so planted, and to punish the injury and destruction of forests.

Authorizing county courts, on petition of persons interested, to take and condemn for public use, free from tolls, any highway upon which tolls have before been charged, first compensating the owners of such tolls for the loss thereof.

Appropriating money for the protection and propagation of fish.

To confirm the boundary-lines between Pennsylvania and the States of New York, Ohio, and West Virginia, as resurveyed by the joint commissions appointed for that purpose, and to ratify the agreement of the Commissioners of the State and of New York relative to the boundary between said States.

To encourage and authorize the formation of co-operative associations, productive and distributive.

Providing for the incorporation of expositions of artistic, mechanical, agricultural, and horticultural products, and giving them the right of eminent domain.

Directing councils of cities of the second class to provide for the improvement of streets, lanes, sewers, and sidewalks, and defining their powers in this regard.

Requesting the Governor annually to designate a day to be known as "Arbor Day," appropriating money for tablets and monuments of Pennsylvania troops upon the Gettysburg battle-field.

Giving mechanics, laborers, and others a lien upon personal property and upon leasehold estates.

Two amendments to the Constitution were proposed for adoption, the ratification of the succeeding Legislature being necessary before their submission to the people. The first of these changes the qualifications of voters by abolishing the requirement of paying a State or county tax within two years, and by reducing the length of residence necessary to vote in any election district from two months to thirty days. The second declares that "the manufacture, sale, and keeping for sale of intoxicating liquor, to be used as a beverage, is hereby prohibited, and any violation of this prohibition shall be a misdemeanor punishable as shall be provided by law."

Finances.—The report of the Auditor-General shows the total receipts of the treasury for the year to be $7,646,147.37, and the total expenditures $7,366,763.47. The balance on hand November 30, 1886, was $2,101,457.57, and at the same time in 1887, $2,380,841.47. The principal receipts are from the following sources: from taxes on corporation stock, $1,702,057.04; gross receipts, corporations, $766,388.12; gross premiums, $42,619.89; banks, safe deposits, etc., $431,628.14; net earnings, $81,596.92; loans, $161,054.75; personal property, $864,-855.36; writs, wills, deeds, etc., $117,495.89; collateral inheritance, $763,871.57; foreign insurance companies, $377,571.63; tavern licenses, $565,163.67; eating-house licenses, $90,989.01; wholesale liquor licenses, $39,-821.29; brewers' licenses, $15,446.69; bottlers' licenses, $9,140.25; retailers' licenses, $405,-105; billiard licenses, $29,845.98; broker licenses, $20,893.38; auctioneers' licenses, $9,-004.67; peddlers' licenses, $3,064.76; theatre and circus licenses, $14,025.37; bonus on charters, $148,624.56; Allegheny Valley Railroad, $212,500; United States Government, $172,-000; commutation of tonnage tax, $460,000. The expenditures included expenses for State government, $1,938,619.20; loans redeemed, $1,418,511; interest on loans, $720,277; premiums on loans redeemed, $223,384.50; Pennsylvania State College, $17,750; charitable institutions, $780,219.11; penitentiaries, $188,-974; Huntingdon Reformatory, $125,000; House of Refuge, Philadelphia, $75,000; Morganza Reform School, $30,040.03; Second Geological Survey, $80,500; Soldiers' Home, $70,-000; Soldiers' Orphans' Schools, $351,964.19; Common Schools, $1,171,811.55; National Guard of Pennsylvania, $204,605.22.

The following statement shows the condition of the public debt at the beginning and end of the fiscal year:

Total public debt, Nov. 30, 1886	$17,258,962 26
Assets in the sinking fund	10,180,746 46
Leaving unprovided for	$7,078,285 82

PUBLIC DEBT STATEMENT, NOV. 30, 1887.

Non-interest bearing debt	$113,657 00
Overdue loans upon which interest has been stopped	34,213 36
Debt bearing interest	15,692,800 00
Total debt	$15,840,741 28
Total assets in sinking fund	10,684,862 43
Balance	$5,156,198 85
Debt unprovided for Nov. 30, 1886	$7,078,285 82
Debt unprovided for Nov. 30, 1887	5,156,108 85
Amount of reduction of debt in 1887	$1,925,126 97

Education.—The State Superintendent of Public Schools reports an increase in the number of pupils during the last school year, exclusive of Philadelphia, of 9,235. The total number of pupils enrolled is now over 1,000,000. Fifteen new school districts formed during the year have increased the total number to 2,281. The number of schools is 21,062, an increase of 379, of which 9,444 are graded, an increase of 357. Four superintendents have been added to the work of school supervision, making the present number 115. The increase in the number of teachers has been 519; male teachers 340, and female teachers 179, making the present total 23,822. The average monthly salary of male teachers is $38.53, and of female teachers $29.86. The length of the school term is steadily advancing, being now 7.75 months.

Decisions.—The United States Supreme Court in May delivered an opinion, declaring that part of the State tax-law unconstitutional which imposed a tax upon the gross receipts of companies engaged in interstate transportation, the ground being that such an act was a regulation of interstate commerce. But this decision is not considered as invalidating the tax upon the capital stock or property of such companies organized in the State.

The constitutionality of the oleomargarine law of 1885 was also passed upon during the year, and sustained by a majority of the State Supreme Court.

Political.—The only State officers to be voted for at the November election were a treasurer and a judge of the Supreme Court. The Republican Convention at Harrisburg, on August 17, nominated William B. Hart for the former office and Henry W. Williams for the latter. A platform was adopted favoring protection, enlargement of the Federal pension-list, and Federal aid for American shipping, condemning Southern outrages, and urging the nomination of James G. Blaine by the National Convention in 1888. It also declares:

That they [the Republicans] reaffirm their declaration of 1886 in favor of submitting to a vote of the people the prohibitory constitutional amendment. We also indorse the action of the last Legislature in the submission of the amendment making suffrage free by abolishing the tax-qualification for a vote.

We approve the action of the Legislature touching the revenue of the Commonwealth in diverting a large portion of the direct State tax and the receipts from licenses to the treasuries of the different cities and counties, and especially indorse that part of the general revenue bill which continued to impose the support of the State government upon the corporations of the Commonwealth, and brought within the purview of the law for taxation a large amount of moneys at interest in the hands of corporations not previously reached. We believe that a new bill, perfecting these features, should be matured by the commission charged with that duty, with a view of having it submitted to the present Legislature for enactment in time to meet the assessment of next year, provided the Governor shall deem the calling of an extra session for this purpose such an extraordinary occasion as is contemplated by the twelfth section of the fourth article of the Constitution.

We give unqualified indorsement to the Republican State administration. By careful and conscientious

PENNSYLVANIA.

discharge of duty it has reflected high credit upon the party which called it into power, and gives assurance to the people of an economical and wise administration of the affairs of the Commonwealth.

On August 24, at Harrisburg, the Prohibitionists nominated Col. Dallas C. Irish for State Treasurer, and Simeon B. Chase for Supreme Judge. The following is a part of the platform:

We denounce the hypocrisy of the Republican party in pretending to favor the prohibition of the drink traffic by the passage of a resolution for the submission of a constitutional amendment prohibiting the manufacture and sale of intoxicating liquor, and then nullifying the same law by the passage of a high-license law, with the approval, as we believe, of the liquor interest of the State, in and by which they seek by a division of the license fees to make the citizens of the Commonwealth in every county, city, and borough, partners in the profits of the liquor-traffic, and thereby secure the defeat of the amendment if finally submitted to a vote of the people.

The Democratic Convention was held at Allentown on August 31, and resulted in the nomination of Bernard J. McGrann for Treasurer, and J. Ross Thompson for Supreme Judge. Its platform approves the national Democratic platform of 1884, and the national administration, favors the restriction of pauper immigration, and a liberal pension-list, and continues as follows:

The failure of the State revenue bill, after it had been carefully perfected and nearly unanimously passed by both branches of the Legislature, was a crime against the majority of the Commonwealth, whereby the people must pay a million dollars annually that should and would have been paid by the corporations, and the failure of the State administration to attempt any correction of the wrong-doing or exposure of the fraud or criminal neglect condoned a crime against both authority and people, and confessed the supremacy of ring-rule in Pennsylvania.

We reaffirm our declaration in favor of the passage of such legislation as will properly enforce the provisions of act seventeen of the Constitution, relative to corporations to previous improper discrimination, and to equalize taxation.

We denounce the action of the last Republican Legislature in the defeat of the bill for the relief of producers and refiners of oil in the oil-district of the State, known as the Billingsley bill, as being in the interest of monopoly and against the interest of the people of that large section of the State.

The nominees of the Union Labor and Greenback party were, H. L. Banker for Treasurer, and Charles S. Keyser for Judge. The former having declined the nomination, the name of John Q. A. Kennedy was substituted before the election. The vote for Treasurer was: Hart, 885,514; McGrann, 340,269; Irish, 18,471; Kennedy, 8,900.—Republican plurality, 45,245. Williams, for Supreme Judge, received 883,257 votes; Thompson, 343,042; Chase, 16,921; Keyser, 8,477—Republican plurality, 40,215.

The American Party.—A convention of delegates from various States met at Philadelphia on September 16 and 17, for the purpose of organizing a new American party, having for its object to maintain the power and supremacy of American-born citizens. The time and place for holding the convention were chosen to coincide with the centennial celebration of the ratification of the Constitution. In the following resolutions adopted by the convention the object of the new party are fully set forth:

Whereas, We Americans hold that a longer continuance of our present system of immigration and naturalization of foreigners is detrimental to the welfare of our beloved country, and that the time is fast approaching when rigid restriction of immigration will be necessary in order to preserve the peace and prosperity of our people and the stability of our institutions, and that the time has arrived when a new departure must be taken by the Government of the American people, looking to the elimination and restriction of all evil-disposed foreigners from landing on our shores or becoming citizens of the United States;

Whereas, the past has demonstrated that hordes of foreign immigrants whom we have welcomed to our land, and to whom we have given the right of citizenship, without regard to character or qualification, are the refuse subjects of European nations, who, by teaching and training, are unfit subjects to become American citizens; banding together in societies for the destruction of private property and personal liberty; becoming the political and social agitators of every cause looking to the destruction of private rights, heading and encouraging all disturbances of labor, seeking to array labor against capital, setting themselves up as the judges of the rights of the American people, committing murder, arson, and other crimes by means of secret organizations, thrusting aside the American citizen and wage-worker to make place for themselves, preventing by threats the children of American citizens from apprenticeship to trades, the enemies of all free government by the people; and,

Whereas, Both the Republican and Democratic parties are unwilling to adopt an adequate policy on this question, and have in recent elections pandered to the worst element of foreign-born citizens, giving them prominence as the balance of voting power, offering offices as a reward for their political labor, and setting up new parties composed of foreigners to accomplish their selfish ends, having no issue save the issue of office; therefore,

Resolved, That we, the representatives of the American party, in convention assembled, in discharge of the duty we owe to our constituents and our country, and in order to perpetuate the sentiment of "America for Americans," unite in the following declaration:

1. That our present system of immigration and naturalization of foreigners is detrimental to the welfare of the United States, and we pledge ourselves to its restriction and regulation; to that end we demand the establishment of a department of immigration by Congress, the head of which shall be appointed by the President of the United States, and who shall be a member of his Cabinet.

2. We demand a revision of the naturalization laws, making a continued residence of fourteen years an indispensable requisite for citizenship, and excluding all communists, socialists, nihilists, anarchists, paupers, and criminals from naturalization as American citizens; but no interference with the vested rights of foreigners.

3. To protect and promote the American free common-school system, we recommend that the several States and Territories establish, by law, a system of free common schools for the universal and enforced education of our children.

4. That the safety of the republic rests largely with her citizens who have small holdings of her soil, and any attempt at the destruction of ownership thereof is revolutionary and in violation of the guarantees of our Constitution. We hold that American lands should be reserved for American citizens; that no alien nonresident should be permitted to own real estate in the United States, and that the real-estate possessions of resident aliens should be limited in area and value;

we condemn the system of donating public lands to private corporations, and all lands heretofore donated to railroad corporations by the Government on conditions which have not been complied with, should be reclaimed and opened for settlement by American citizens.

5. The vast sums of money accumulated in the treasury from the taxation of the people in excess of the necessities of the Government should be released to the people; and we demand a judicial system of internal improvements; and favor the construction of suitable fortifications and the building up of a navy compatible with our station among the nations of the earth.

6. We reassert the American principle of absolute freedom of religious worship and belief, the permanent separation of Church and State, and we oppose the appropriation of money and property of the people to any church or institution administered by a church.

7. We recognize the right of labor to organize for its protection, and by all lawful and peaceable means to secure to itself the greatest reward for its thrift and industry.

8. We demand and advocate a firm and consistent foreign policy and a vigorous assertion of our national dignity and respect to our flag on land and sea; especially do we demand the assertion and vindication of the rights of our citizens to an equal participation in the fisheries in the North Atlantic ocean; and we view with alarm the aims and purposes of European powers to absorb and establish protectorates over the islands adjacent to our Pacific coast; and we demand an emphatic reassertion and vigorous maintenance of the American doctrine as handed down to us by our fathers, excluding European governments from all interference with the practical affairs of the western world.

9. The American party declares that it recognizes no North, no South, no East, and no West in these United States, but one people pledged to our liberty and independence.

PERSIA, an empire in Asia. The government is an absolute monarchy, tempered by the precepts of the Koran. The administration is carried on under the Shah by a ministry, consisting of the Vizier, the Treasurer, and five subordinate ministers. The empire is divided into fifteen provinces, over each of which is a governor with extensive powers, who is usually a prince of the royal family. The towns and villages elect their own magistrates. The reigning Shah is Nassr-ed-Din. The heir-apparent is Muzaffer-ed-Din Valiahd, the eldest son of the Shah, who is governor of Azerbaijan. The Vizier is Mirza-Ali Khan. The Minister of War is Kamran Mirza, called Naïb-es-Sultaneh, the third son of the Shah. The Minister of Foreign Affairs is Yahia Khan, brother-in-law of the Shah; Treasurer, Ali Asghar Khan. The second son of the Shah Zil-es-Sultan, is governor of Ispahan and the adjacent provinces, while his brother Naïb-es-Sultaneh is governor of Teheran and other provinces, and also commander-in-chief of the army. The Minister of Foreign Affairs was formerly Minister of the Interior and of Justice. He was educated in Paris, and is versed in European culture. His appointment in 1886 was supposed to indicate a policy favorable to Russia.

Area and Population.—The empire is about 610,000 square miles in extent. A recent esti-

mate makes the population not over 7,000,000, including 2,500,000 Nomads. The capital, Teheran, has 210,000 inhabitants; the city of Tabreez or Tauris, 170,000; Ispahan, 90,000; Meshed, 70,000.

Commerce.—The value of the imports in 1884–'85 was 125,800,000 francs; that of the exports, 72,200,000 francs. The leading imports are cottons, glassware, paper, iron, copper, sugar, and tea. The principal articles of export are silk, tobacco, skins, carpets, and opium. The number of letters that passed through the Post-Office in 1885 was 1,468,984. The length of the telegraph lines in 1885 was 5,185 kilometres, with 9,846 kilometres of wire.

Finances.—The receipts of the Treasury are about 43,750,000 francs per annum, of which 6,600,000 proceed from customs. The expenditure amounts to 40,750,000 francs, of which 21,250,000 francs are for the army and 7,500,000 francs for the royal household.

PERU, a republic in South America. (For details relating to area, population, etc., see "Annual Cyclopædia" for 1883.)

Government.—The President, since June 2, 1886, is Gen. Nadres Avelino Cáceres. The Cabinet is composed of the following ministers: President of the Council and Minister of the Interior, Señor Aurelio Denegri; Minister of Foreign Affairs, Dr. Alberto Elmore; Minister of the Treasury, Señor Antonio Aspillaga; Minister of War and Marine, Señor Elias Mujica, and Minister of Justice, Dr. Adolfo Garcia. The United States Minister at Lima is Charles W. Buck. The American Consul at Callao is Henry May Brent. The Peruvian Consul at New York is Señor José Cárlos Tracy; at San Francisco, George Duval.

Army and Navy.—The effective strength of the permanent Peruvian army has been fixed for 1887–'88 at 4,000 men, comprising six battalions of infantry, two regiments of horse, two brigades of artillery, and one battery of mitralleuses. There is also a police force of 3,371 men, of whom 848 are mounted. The naval force, once the pride of the country, has been reduced to two transports of a carrying capacity of 1,300 tons each.

Finance.—On July, 1, 1886, the Peruvian national indebtedness stood as follows:

FOREIGN DEBT.	Interest an coupons unprovided for since July 1, 1875.	Total.
6 p. c. loan of 1869.. $1,828,400.	$694,765	$2,018,165
6 p. c. loan of 1870.. 55,707,900.	35,095,975	90,803,875
5 p. c. loan of 1892..107,788,700.	56,560,080	164,298,880
Total........$164,765,000.	$92,850,940	$257,115,940
Home debt, consolidated with unpaid interest since 1880		$7,900,000
Paper money		79,000,000
Paper money, Incas issued in 1880, Dictator Piérola's administration		9,541,800
Grand total.............................		$373,456,940

The paper money has depreciated uninterruptedly. In August, 1886, 19 paper dollars equaled $1 in silver; a year later, 29 paper dollars were necessary to obtain a silver dollar, and at this exchange the various branch offices of the national treasury admitted payment in paper to the extent of fifty per cent. The public and railroads insisted on $30 paper for one silver dollar. Damaged or partially torn paper money is refused everywhere; the loss on mutilated $100 and $500 notes is comparatively heavier than on small notes. The Government has caused $14,675,000 of fractional notes to be printed and circulated, in order to facilitate current dealings. In December there was intense excitement in Lima and Callao, owing to the paper currency continuing to decrease in value. Disorders resulted in the market-places and the streets, and a panic occurred. The streets had to be patroled in Lima, and squads of soldiers stationed in the markets to prevent acts of violence against those who refused to sell for paper money. The money-changers in Lima kept their places closed in consequence of the violent manner in which they were spoken of at a meeting in the plaza. When a crowd formed around the palace, President Cáceres spoke from a balcony, and assured all present that the Government was doing everything possible to remove the causes of alarm and re-establish confidence. In the main market in Lima there are 1,800 stalls. Of this number 1,300 were closed on December 15. The steeples of the churches were occupied by pickets to prevent the rioters making a call to arms with the bells, and all liquor-shops and hotels were closed by the police. The banks were also closed. While a meeting was held in the main square, pickets of armed police were stationed at the four corners of the square. One of these pickets was molested by boys and drunken men, and the police fired, wounding several boys. Two days prior to these events not a single money-changer or business house in Lima was selling silver dollars for paper money. In Ascope, in the north of Peru, trouble was feared, as the business houses all refused to sell for paper money. In Trujillo holders of notes were in a panic. Nearly all the retail stores were closed, and the bakers stopped baking because the holders of flour refused to sell except for silver dollars, while the bakers only held notes, and the greater part of these were in halves. The prefect exercised great vigilance, and succeeded in borrowing $40,000 gold notes with which he was changing the half-notes for the poor people. Business men in Cerro de Pasco rejected bank-notes, doing all their business in private notes payable on presentation. Disorders occurred in Huancavelica, and the acting prefect and the treasurer were murdered.

The budget for 1887-'88 estimates the revenue at $16,183,674, and the expenditure at $13,632,886.

During the first six months of 1887 the revenue from customs was $2,300,000 short of the estimate, and the cash collected was absorbed by the expense of maintaining the army in a state of efficiency. At Callao the amount of duties collected only reached $1,216,728, while $2,000,000 had been calculated upon. Salaries of Peruvian consuls were reduced to fifty per cent. of the fees collected, except that of the consul at Panama.

In December the import duties were raised five per cent. ad valorem, the product to be applied to a gradual withdrawal of the paper currency.

Another decree, simultaneously issued, ordered that Peruvian consuls issuing or viséing bills of health be allowed to charge only one cent a ton up to 500 tons, at the port of departure, and half a cent at the large ports where the ship may call.

The silver exportation to Hamburg through the port of Callao amounted in 1886 to 5,789,-276 kilograms, and in September, 1887, there were indications that it would be considerably exceeded.

In November opium was declared a Government monopoly, and the right to import and sell it was offered for sale.

Boundary Question.—In September an understanding was arrived at with reference to the settlement of the boundary question between Peru and Ecuador. The Peruvian minister at Quito signed an agreement with the Minister of Foreign Affairs of Ecuador, subsequently ratified by the Congress of the latter, submitting the difference to the arbitration of the Queen-Regent of Spain. In the event of her declining, either France, Belgium, or Switzerland is to be requested to assume the task.

A Military Revolt.—At 11 P. M. on September 27, a mutiny broke out at Trujillo, in the barracks of the Zepita battalion, and two companies escaped, after mortally wounding the captain of the guard, and killing the sentry. It was said that the soldiers mutinied because they received only two paper dollars a day as ration-money. The movement was led by a sergeant known to have been a criminal of the worst kind. The mutineers went to the barracks, but the lieutenant on duty stood bravely to his post and resisted a heavy fire with great skill, until he was re-enforced by the subprefect of police. During this time some of the mutineers had also attacked the hospital, but they were driven off. These two defeated parties subsequently went to the mountains. The authorities followed them about three leagues into the country, where a fight took place in which several were killed. In the square at Trujillo fifteen or twenty persons were killed or wounded. It was said that the mutiny would not have taken place if the soldiers had been paid regularly. Their pay was in arrears, and no one would trust them. The taxes are paid in silver dollars; this the soldiers see, and therefore they object to being paid in paper money. The sergeant who led the mutiny was caught, tried by court martial, and shot. He confessed having committed fourteen murders, and gave the names of his victims. Fourteen of the mutineers were shot.

Posts and Telegraphs.—In 1885 the Peruvian post-offices forwarded 865,823 letters and postal cards, and 386,141 newspapers and sample packages. There were in operation in the republic 2,211 kilometres of telegraph line, the number of offices being 34, dispatching 94,214 private, and 16,455 Government messages.

Railroads.—There are in operation 2,600 kilometres. Two railroads run from Lima to the higher Andes. One line begins at the coast at Mollendo, south of Callao, and, running by Arequipa, crosses the crest of the Andes, and terminates at Lake Titicaca, 12,800 feet above the sea. The other starts from Lima itself. It was projected with the intention of piercing the crest of the Cordilleras at an elevation of 15,645 feet above the sea, and thence descending to Oroya, a plateau between the main ranges. Its ultimate object was to afford a route to the fertile districts on the eastern slopes of the Andes. As yet it has only reached a village called Chicla, 12,200 feet above the sea, its progress having been stopped by the war between Peru and Chili. In November it became apparent that the congressional action respecting the southern railways, and those of Chimbote and Salaverry would probably give rise to serious complications. According to stipulations with the Government, the southern roads, when completed, were to be turned over to the State by the contractor, Henry Meiggs, or by his successors and executors. The roads have not been completed, the contractor alleges, from the fact that the necessary money has not been furnished by the Government, and it was also said that a large sum for freight and passages was due from the Government. In spite of the arguments and proofs adduced, Congress, led by the deputies from the south, ordered the executive to assume the administration of these roads, as well as those connecting Salaverry with Trujillo, and leading from Chimbote to the interior. Prior to the promulgation of this law, the American, British, and German legations at Lima energetically protested against such an assumption of dictatorial power by Congress, basing their protest on the fact that, as the contracts were legal and bilateral, there are two parties to be heard, and that such hearing must be given before the proper legal tribunals. Despite these formal protests, the Government adopted vigorous measures to carry out the orders of Congress. The railway from Salaverry to Trujillo, and the fine wharf at the first-named place, constructed for the Government under contract, since under the control of E. C. Dubois, an American citizen, by virtue of a concession granted by the Government of Iglesias, were in December declared forfeited. The State is also to assume possession of the southern lines.

Early in October a commission of engineers and mining experts appointed by the Peruvian bondholders in London, arrived at Callao. They were to examine the railways, and make a report regarding the capacity of the lines in question, and the probable increase of business in case of their being extended as originally planned. In December the commission had concluded its labors on the Oroya Railroad and at the Cary de Pasco mining district. The commission next proceeded to examine the Pacasmayo and Chimbote railroads, and to travel through the rich sugar-producing country in the immediate neighborhood of those lines. After this work is accomplished, an inspection will be made of the southern railroads, and the bondholders will be thoroughly informed as to the prospects of reimbursement from all of these undertakings in which their money has been employed so liberally.

The Grace-Aranibar Contract.—Toward the close of 1886, Mr. Grace, of New York, as the representative of the European bondholders of the Peruvian debt, made a proposal to the Government of Peru for the cancellation of part of the latter and the extension of the railroads. In March, 1887, Mr. M. P. Grace, of the firm of W. R. Grace & Co., New York, in pursuance of this plan, arrived from Lima and left for London, accompanied by Dr. Aranibar, the Peruvian Commissioner. The result of the trip was an arrangement with the committee of bondholders in June, since accepted by the Government at Lima, but still awaiting ratification by the Peruvian Congress. The chief clauses of the contract that are likely to be ratified with some modifications are the following: The Peruvian Government relinquishes to its creditors for sixty-six years 768 miles of its railroads, which the latter engage to extend as stipulated. It furthermore relinquishes to them all the guano the Government still owns on the coast, and all that may be discovered, for a term of sixty-six years. As long as the railroads and guano do not net, together, the sum of £420,000 during two consecutive years, the Government agrees to set aside the annual sum of £120,000 out of the customs revenue of the ports of Mollendo and Payta to cover the deficiency. Peru also granted the creditors forever the coal along the Chimbote-Huaraz Railway, but while doing so retains 15 per cent. of the net profit that those coal deposits shall produce. Another concession grants them the exclusive right of exploitation for fifty years of the Huancavelica cinnabar-mines, 15 per cent. to be paid the Government out of the net profits while the grant lasts. Next, the perpetual privilege is conceded the creditors to work all the gold, silver, copper, and lead mines, and other mineral deposits, the Government only to collect the usual tax of $30 per annum, to which every mine in Peru is subject. A grant is made them of 1,800,000 hectares of arable land, and each family of settling immigrants is besides to receive 180 hectares under contracts with the creditors' representatives. The Government finally concedes them the privilege of free navigation on the rivers and lakes of the republic. The creditors are to have the right of at once founding a bank of issue at Lima, with the exclusive privilege for twenty-five years of issuing bank-notes, this circulation to be backed by 33⅓ per cent. cash. The syndicate obtains 75 per cent. of the net profits of the bank, after paying its shareholders 9 per cent. per annum. The bank is to manage the home indebtedness of Peru, to secure which the Government agrees to set aside annually 8 per cent. of the customs revenue collected at Callao, other revenue designated in section 22 of the agreement, and its share of 25 per cent. of the net profits of the bank after payment of the 9 per cent. Certain privileges exempting the property of creditors from taxation are stipulated in addition to those enumerated. In return, the bondholders agree to carry out the railroad repairs and constructions stipulated, to pay the Government 20 per cent. of the net earnings of the railways, and 25 per cent. of those of the guano deposits, after the representatives or committee shall have received therefrom the sum of £420,000. The bondholders agree to surrender 50 per cent. of the bonds they hold, the total outstanding debt amounting to £82,000,000; the remaining 50 per cent. the committee take their chances to recover from Chili as the owner of the ceded province of Tarapacá. The bondholders further agree to advance the Government at once £400,000, payable in thirty consecutive monthly installments, out of which the Government engages to pay £6,000 a month toward defraying interest on the internal debt, and transportation over the railroads of military and civil officers, material, and mails. When the terms of this agreement were made known in London, the secretary of the Chilian Legation in that city wrote a letter to the "London Times," in which he warned Peruvian bondholders against any illusions in connection with the one half of the Peruvian bonded debt and the conquered province of Tarapacá, so far as Chili was concerned. He referred to the treaty of peace between Chili and Peru, by the terms of which the conquered province of Tarapacá was ceded without Chili's assuming any responsibilities whatever that might be construed as if Chili had considered, or ever would consider, them pledged to Peruvian bondholders. He also reminded the latter that the highest English and French courts of law have declared that the bonds, however worded, constitute no lien whatever on the territories acquired by Chili by conquest, or on the stocks of guano and nitrate. Considerable opposition also came from southern Peru, and neither the Government nor Congress felt prepared to advance further in the matter, which was left in abeyance pending a modification of the terms so as to satisfy Chili, and the report from engineers sent out by the bondholders upon the actual state and value of the Government railroad system.

Commerce.—The import of merchandise into Peru in 1884 amounted to $11,064,744, while the export of products reached $7,958,625. The exports to Peru from England in 1885 were valued at $3,426,751; from France, $1,899,492; and from Germany, $498,184. The American trade with Peru has been as follows:

FISCAL YEAR.	Import from Peru.	Domestic export to Peru.
1883	$2,596,918	$487,860
1884	2,077,645	1,048,902
1885	1,764,800	755,979
1886	963,480	796,577
1887	461,796	717,968

The South American Sanitary Congress.—Early in July, 1887, the Peruvian Government addressed a note to those of Chili, Brazil, the Argentine Republic, Uruguay, Paraguay, Bolivia, Ecuador, Colombia, Venezuela, Mexico, and Central America, inviting them to send medical representatives to a Sanitary Congress to be held at Lima, and to open its sessions on Jan. 2, 1888. The purpose of the meeting was to prepare measures of protection against the introduction and propagation of epidemics, which for the first time invaded the western coast of South America during 1886, and, if possible, arrive at an understanding on the subject of quarantine regulations. All the governments addressed promised to send representatives. The idea which prompted this action is all the more commendable as international passenger traffic, trade, and mail service suffered severely from the restrictions resorted to in 1886 and 1887. The Congress opened on January 2, although only the delegates from Peru, Ecuador, and Bolivia were present. Meanwhile, a Sanitary Convention had been signed in December at Rio de Janeiro by the Sanitary Convention composed of delegates from Brazil, Uruguay, and the Argentine Republic. The main causes agreed upon were the following:

Yellow fever, cholera morbus, and the plague are the three exotic pestilences treated of, and the articles considered pestiferous are clothing, cloth, rags, mattresses, and objects of personal use, also the boxes containing them, and fresh hides. No other articles are to be considered as suspected. Each party undertakes to found a lazaretto and to establish in time of pestilence at least one floating hospital. Quarantines or other sanitary measures undergone in the lazaretto of any of the three powers are valid for all the others. The closing of ports to vessels from abroad is prohibited, and no vessel is to be driven away, no matter what disease prevails aboard. Packets and other steamers carrying emigrants must have a doctor and be supplied with a steam disinfector, medicines, and disinfectants, keeping, besides, regular books of record. A corps of ship sanitary inspectors is to be established by each power, to embark in vessels, fiscalize the execution of the sanitary provisions, and report on all occurrences during the voyage. Strict quarantine is limited to ten days for yellow fever, eight for cholera, and twenty for Eastern plague, and the time may be counted from the date of last case on board, if duly verified.

A Charitable Bequest.—A worthy old Peruvian, José Sevilla, during the last years of his life spent most of his time in the city of New

York. By a will executed on March 20, 1885, in New York, he left the bulk of his estate, valued at nearly $4,000,000, for the foundation of a charitable educational institution for children. Mr. Sevilla authorized the executors to locate the home anywhere in the United States, but if they found it impossible to incorporate such an institution in this country the gift was to be transferred to France. The institution was to be for the benefit of American and Peruvian children.

PHARMACY. The continual enactment of more stringent laws requiring the selection of competent persons for the dispensing of medicines is shown by the increased demands for pharmaceutical education. The publication of new and better journals likewise indicates an improved condition of the art.

Colleges.—The trustees of Cornell founded a School of Pharmacy on March 7, 1887, in connection with the University at Ithaca, N. Y. About the same time a Department of Pharmacy was added to the University of Kansas in Kansas City. During the year special schools for this branch have been inaugurated at Howard University, Washington, D. C.; Purdue University, Lafayette, Ind.; and at Vanderbilt University, Nashville, Tenn. A Pharmaceutical Department has recently been established in connection with the Minnesota Hospital College at Minneapolis, Minn.

Legislation.—Acts regulating the sale of poisons in Alabama, Georgia, and New York have come into force before the first of the year, also pharmaceutical laws have been enacted in Alabama, Colorado, Dakota, Idaho, Montana, Nebraska, and Pennsylvania. So that at present proper measures regulating the practice of pharmacy are in active operation in all of the States excepting the following: Arkansas, California, Florida, Indiana, Louisiana, Mississippi, Nevada, Oregon, Tennessee, Texas, and Vermont. Certain of the Territories are still without laws.

Associations.—The thirty-fifth annual meeting of the American Pharmaceutical Association was held in Cincinnati, Ohio, on September 5, and continued four days. Several hundred members were present and upward of seventy new members were elected. In order to expedite the work of the Association and render it more efficient, it was reorganized and formed into four sections as follows: 1, scientific papers; 2, commercial interests; 3, pharmaceutical education; 4, legislation—each of which elects its own chairman and secretary. Subsequent to this action, the National Retail Druggists' Association, no longer being necessary, was merged into the parent organization. The admission-fee was abolished and hereafter only annual dues will be required. Besides the scientific papers read and discussed, various reports were accepted, notably that on the "National Formulary," which provided for the speedy publication of the manual containing the accepted formulas. John U. Lloyd of Cincinnati, Ohio, was elected president, and John M. Maisch, of Philadelphia, Pa., continued as secretary. Detroit, Mich., was chosen for the meeting-place in 1888, and the date September 3. The Florida State Pharmaceutical Association was organized at Jacksonville on June 8, 1887, and local associations at Fort Worth and San Antonio, Texas, during the year.

Trade Associations.—The twelfth annual meeting of the Wholesale Druggists' Association was held in Boston, Mass., beginning its sessions on August 23. Reports on adulterations, credits and collections, paints, oils, and glass, the drug market, commercial travelers, transportation, and fraternal relations were presented by the committees appointed to consider those subjects and discussed by the members. The special committee on mutual fire insurance reported that under the auspices of the Association there had been established "The Druggists' Mutual Fire Insurance Company," which was organized in June, under the laws of Pennsylvania, at Philadelphia. Offerings of nearly $1,000,000 insurance were received almost immediately, and success is assured. It will afford an enormous saving to the wholesale druggists of the country, and the maintenance of an important competitor of the old-line companies, and some exemption from their tyranny. E. Waldo Cutter, of Boston, Mass., was chosen president, and A. B. Merriam retained as secretary for the year. Saratoga Springs, N. Y., was selected as the meeting-place for 1888.

Trade Relations.—Under the direction of the National Wholesale Druggists' Association the contract plan between manufacturers and jobbers is becoming more perfect, while among the retailers the entire absence of any concerted action is shown by the increasing tendency among pharmacists, especially in large cities, to cut prices on proprietary articles.

Literature.—The books of the year include "Text Book of Therapeutics and Materia Medica," by Robert T. Edes (Philadelphia); "Manual of Pharmacy and Pharmaceutical Chemistry," by Charles F. Heebner (New York); "Handbook of Pharmacy and Therapeutics," by James E. Lilly (Indianapolis); "Drug Eruptions," by P. A. Morrow (New York); "Pharmaceutical Problems and Exercises in Metrology, Chemistry, and Pharmacy," by Oscar Oldberg, and "A Laboratory Manual of Chemistry," by Oscar Oldberg and John H. Long (Chicago); "Handbook of Materia Medica, Pharmacy, and Therapeutics," by S. O. L. Potter (Philadelphia); and "The Principles of Pharmacognosy," translated from the German of Flückiger and Tschirch by Frederick B. Power; also, new editions of C. L. Lochman's "Dose and Price Labels of all the Drugs and Preparations of the United States Pharmacopœia" (Philadelphia); John M. Maisch's "Organic Materia Medica"; and F. E. Stewart's "Quiz-Compend of Pharmacy."

"The Pharmaceutical Era," under the editorship of Dr. Albert B. Lyons, began in Detroit with the January issue. This journal, one of the best that has yet appeared, is most valuable on account of its "Index Pharamaceuticus" published in each, giving reference to all books and original papers of interest to pharmacists that appear in the English, French, German, and Italian languages. "The American Drug-Clerks' Journal," whose scope is indicated by its title, issued its first number in June at Chicago.

PHOTO-ENGRAVING, photo-gravure, photozincography, and process-engraving are different terms applied to various methods of reproducing pictures without the aid of an engraver. In ordinary zincography the picture is laid down on a zinc-plate with lithographic ink from "transfer-paper." Those portions of the plate which are to be protected are then prepared by using an ink or varnish which will resist acid, after which the plate is subjected to a bath of dilute nitrous acid; this is continued through successive baths of acid of increased strength, until the biting-in is sufficient, when the plate is dried, and the ink removed by benzine. There is another process, in which brass plates are used, which are covered with white wax, when the picture is drawn on the wax with an etching-point. This plate is afterward used as a mold from which an electrotype is obtained. In photo-zincography the drawing is photographed to the size required, and an ordinary negative on glass is taken. This is then laid on a sensitized zinc plate, on which the picture is printed by the action of light. The coating of the zinc-plate is known by its French name of *bitumen de Judée*, four parts of which are dissolved in one hundred parts of benzine. After the picture is printed, so much of the bitumen as has not been made insoluble by the action of light is dissolved off by using a wash of turpentine. To obtain gradations of light a specially prepared enameled paper, or a gray-tinted lined paper is used, by scraping away which, leaving the white paper beneath exposed, the artist is able to obtain his high lights. In Hentschel's photographic etching process the negative is printed on sensitized carbon paper. This is laid face down on a polished zinc plate, which being placed in a bath, all the carbon paper, except that holding the lines of the drawing, is washed away. The plate is then bitten in an acid bath. The Ives (Philadelphia) process is accomplished by applying the negative to a gelatine plate sensitized with bichromate of potash. The plate is then swollen in water, and a cast taken of it in plaster-of-Paris, in which the highest parts represent the blacks and the lowest the whites. The Meisenbach process is thus described: "A transparent plate is hatched or stippled in parallel lines. A transparent positive is made of the object. The two plates are joined, preferably face to face, and from the combined plates a definite negative is photographed in the usual way. In order to cross-hatch and break the lines of the shading, the hatched or stippled plate may be shifted once or twice during the production of the negative. The photographic negative thus obtained may be either applied direct to a zinc-plate, or a lithographic transfer may first be made in the usual manner, and the plate bitten by acid to form a block in relief."

A process for yielding plates in *intaglio* has recently been employed in London. A copper-plate is covered with a film of sensitized gelatine, on which a picture is printed from a photographic negative. The film is now desensitized in a water-bath, and a mixture of camphor and resin dissolved in chloroform is washed over the surface. On heat being applied to the plate, the gelatine breaks into a delicate grain, and the resin is left in minute particles on the surface. The plate is then bitten in an acid bath where the soluble portions of the gelatine have been removed. Those parts which have been rendered insoluble by photographic printing carry the lines of the drawing, and resist the mordant. The rule for mordants is to use nitrous oxide for copper and nitric acid for zinc.

Electrotypes from process blocks are found to be weaker than the original, yielding poorer and paler impressions: stereotypes from process blocks hardly ever print well. The best results are usually obtained by reducing the original drawing one third by photography before printing it on the zinc plate. Process work has not been well adapted to newspaper illustration in any degree of perfection, owing to the impracticability of applying the blocks to rotary presses. Some methods of doing this have been patented, without giving much satisfaction, the best being claimed to be that of Mr. Le Sage, manager of the London "Daily Telegraph."

PHYSICAL TRAINING. From the earliest ages a system of diet and exercise beneficial to the strength, speed, and stamina has been carefully studied. For many centuries the body was carefully cultivated at the expense of the mind, and then for a long period this state of things was almost exactly reversed. The old systems of physical training were severe, the object in view being to secure great strength and endurance, the idea of speed not being much thought of. The Isthmian games were first instituted by Sisyphus, King of Corinth, 1326 B. C. The winners received a simple garland of leaves for their great and long-continued exertions. The Olympic games were held every four years at Olympia, and the same prize was held out to recompense a man for months of hard work and suffering such as would now suffice for a man to endure during life's whole battle.

The ancient system of physical training was terribly thorough, and if a man could stand the preparation he need never fear the contest or conflict, whether with man or beast. The ancient Greek system called for nine or ten months of severe work in the gymnasium. The athlete's flesh was rubbed and scrubbed several times every day with the strigil, a sort of curry-comb, after baths that were merely douches of cold salt water thrown over the athlete while he was standing naked after severe exercise. His diet was restricted to nearly raw meat and almost no vegetables, his exercise was of the hardest and most laborious, and consisted of running in heavy clothing, lifting heavy weights, severe bouts at boxing and wrestling, horse-backriding, and vaulting, much of the work being done with more or less of the accoutrements of the ancient soldier. This system tended to produce big, showy muscles and soundness of wind and limb, but it made a man simply large and strong, not quick or graceful, or at all clever; it had much the same effect that the work of a blacksmith at the present day has upon the followers of that trade.

In the ancient games a subdivision of labor, such as is now in vogue at the games of our modern athletic clubs, was not known. A man had to be what is now known as an all-round athlete or nothing, unless he competed only at such military exercises as casting javelins or weights, or shooting in the archery contests, or was a slinger. There was no knowledge of the advantages of developing one man's legs for running and another man's arms, shoulders, and back for weight-putting or lifting. The old Greek and Roman systems of physical training were in very many ways radically different from the modern French school of calisthenics, which, though they place rather too much dependence on lightness and quickness in all their exercises, are rapidly finding favor with the best modern thinkers on athletic subjects.

About all we know of the old English systems of physical training is their method of preparing prize-fighters and runners for their contests. A great change has surely taken place in the past thirty years. As the present system has, we are quite sure, produced a more rapid and effective class of fighters, and has, we know, lowered even the sometimes more than doubtful records of the old English foot-runners and walkers, we must accept it as being at least considerably nearer the mark. Two hundred years ago in England the science of boxing, as it got to be a century later, was but little understood. Though the nobility and even royalty patronized the ring, only one or two men had a much better idea of fighting scientifically, as it is now understood, than to toe a scratch, round after round, and see which could take the most punishment in the shape of broken noses, jaws, and teeth, and closed-up eyes. The idea of getting in, administering punishment, and getting away without a blow, was almost unknown. A hundred years ago an English prize-fighter was taken from his haunts for a match gotten up for him by his backers—members of the no-

bility, very likely—and put in training. The old-time trainers must have thought a man in anything like a natural state to be in a very foul condition from the number of purges and physics they prescribed for his stomach, the first thing to be attended to. Black draughts and other strong physics were given, and a man would sometimes lose as much as thirty pounds by physicking alone before he was allowed to have any exercise. It sometimes required two weeks to get over the weakness and sickness that this occasioned. The weakness partially over, he was put upon a diet in which the rarest of meats was the principal part. Wines and spirits were quite freely indulged in, but vegetables were forbidden until the battle was over. The exercise or work given a man in training at this time was entirely wrong, according to modern ideas. He was required to be up, in summer, as early as four o'clock, and exercise with clubs and dumb-bells and take a long walk, all before breakfast, a practice now universally acknowledged to be wrong. Of several essays lately submitted to a committee for a prize in a London competition, only one advocated exercise of any kind, save perhaps a few minutes' walk or five minutes' work of the lightest description with a three-pound pair of dumb-bells, before breakfast. An hour after breakfast the man in training was walked out to a track for a morning sweat, and here, enveloped in heavy flannels, he ran ten or twenty miles. Then he punched a heavy sand-bag for an hour, and put up heavy dumb-bells, and swung heavy clubs, all this being done not only in heavy flannels, but oftentimes in a suit of ordinary or perhaps winter clothes as well, and broad-soled shoes with lead in the bottoms. As he walked or ran he either carried a pair of one-pound dumb-bells or twirled a stout stick, to strengthen the hands and forearms and keep the small bones of both from being in as much danger of breaking. After about three or four hours of hard work he was stripped, sponged off, and rubbed down, then wet down with whisky, and, after dressing in a clean suit of flannel underclothes, would stroll home for dinner. In the afternoon the work, but not quite as much of it, was repeated. After supper came a walk till bed-time. In most prize-fighting matches in the olden time the men were not allowed to exceed a stipulated weight, which doubtless caused much of the severity of the training. If a man, on the day of fighting, was overweight, his backers would lose their money, just as if he lost by being defeated. Particular care was taken to harden the skin of the hands, face, and feet, and for this many decoctions were in use. About the best and almost the only harmless things to use are rock salt and water and a little lemon and whisky. A pail of water with a large lump of rock salt in the bottom should be used to soak the feet in every morning and night for a week or two before and during training.

This will prevent painful blisters. Another pail of salt and water should be kept for the face and hands, the lemon (care being taken to keep it out of the eyes) should with the whisky be well rubbed into the skin of the face, neck, hands, and forearms. There can hardly be too much of good hard hand-rubbing of these parts. There was much in this old system of training that was terribly demoralizing, and it is no wonder that the lives of those who went through it more than once or twice were much shortened. Water for drinking was almost entirely cut off. No man in training felt much like talking.

In modern physical training all is changed; the number of events for which persons go into more or less strict training is daily increasing, and the increased gymnasium facilities give almost all, even ladies and children, a chance to reap some of the benefits to be derived from even a slight consideration of so important a subject. It is no longer necessary for a man that wishes to prepare for an athletic contest to go to some remote country-place. Provided only his will be strong enough to withstand the city temptation, he would much better remain where he can have all the advantages of a city home and the improved appliances of a modern gymnasium. In considering modern physical training it might not be entirely incorrect to take for an example a specimen of the same class of athletes, and we will look at the manner in which a modern pugilist would now train. The science of boxing has now perhaps reached perfection. A clever boxer can, with no weapons but Nature's, and even with the effects of them partially neutralized by soft boxing-gloves, stand face to face with a man who, if not clever, may be pounds over his weight, and often without getting struck at all administer punishment that will entirely deprive his opponent of his senses, and lay him on the ground apparently dead for from five minutes to half an hour.

A modern pugilist, if out of practice and not expecting any encounter, would want about three months' notice to fit himself. If he had trained before, and was intelligent and careful and knew his own system, he would only require the services of a professional trainer to rub him down. He would know how much exercise he could stand and the amount of food and drink he would need. The first two weeks would be spent in trying to get the system into a proper condition to stand a severe strain. The bowels would have to be cleared out and got into regular and easy working order, as there should be at least two evacuations in a day. When a person is training this would be accomplished by gentle physics, and the face, hands, and feet should be soaked as before described and faithfully rubbed to guard against the pain and great inconvenience of blisters from running, walking, or punching the bag, and to keep the face from swelling

and the eyes from closing during the contest, which would otherwise be likely to occur. A little work in the gymnasium and on the cinder-path would be done in order to stretch the muscles and plenty of good walking to keep them from getting stiff. During the first two weeks a man such as described would lose in his weight from five to fifteen pounds; the latter figure would be reached only in case he were very large and extremely fat. About the beginning of the third week the real work would begin. The pugilist would retire every night about ten o'clock and rise at half-past six or seven in the morning. His breakfast half an hour later would be light, consisting, perhaps, of a little oatmeal with little or no milk or sugar, one, two, or three eggs poached or raw if desired, and a cup of tea, little or no milk and sugar, with a slice or two of toast. The eggs should only be used occasionally to vary the rare or well-done (as taste dictates) broiled steak or chop. An hour or an hour and a half after breakfast a walk of a mile in the pleasant air and into the gymnasium, where exercises of all kinds would be tried for perhaps an hour, light dumb-bells and Indian clubs being freely used. Dumb-bells of different shapes and weights and sizes have been in use almost as long as athletics have been known. The old Greek dumb-bells were heavy, flat, generally diagonal pieces of iron, with holes large enough for the hands. The ancients believed in lifting heavy weights, and had bells weighing as much as two hundred pounds. This theory is now exploded. Not many dumb-bells are now in use for active work, even for strong men, weighing over ten pounds apiece; and there is one exercise, not generally known but of the greatest benefit, at which the strongest man can be tired in less than a minute, just as a sprint runner is as tired at the end of his one hundred and fifty yards' dash at tremendous speed, as a six-day walker is at the end of his one hundred and forty-two hours' effort. This exercise consists of first placing both hands on the chest, holding in each a one-pound dumb-bell, and then striking out as if at a foe as hard and as rapidly as possible with each of the hands alternately. If it is done properly, twenty seconds of this work will tire more than an hour's slow work with heavy bells, and it will be found equal to sprinting as an exercise to increase the wind, and far superior to anything in developing the muscles of the back, arms, and chest. In some suitable part a large ball or bag should be swung up at a suitable height, and at this bag, armed with light one-pound dumb-bells and with hands incased in dogskin driving-gloves, the pugilist should punch for from thirty to fifty minutes, three or four minutes at a time, letting go every blow as if life depended upon its being squarely and forcibly delivered. One minute's rest should be taken at the end of each round, and during this time a short walk should be indulged in.

The tendency of modern athletics is toward light but extremely quick movements. One old-time bruiser would have used a twenty or even a forty-pound bag of sand suspended from a beam. The heaviest bag a modern boxer would dare to use would not weigh over eight pounds, and several new punching-bags have been invented of late, the particular object of which is to impart quickness and precision, although the hard hitting part is by no means forgotten. It is claimed that the present champion of the world, John L. Sullivan, whose terrible powers of hitting probably go far beyond anything ever seen before, got the ability to deliver his quick and powerful blows from practicing first on a blown-up beef's-bladder suspended from a ceiling in such a manner as to rebound toward him very quickly after each blow, and afterward on an inflated Rugby foot-ball hung in the same manner. Practice on these light bags or on footballs certainly conduces very greatly to quickness and precision, and forms, perhaps, without exception the best exercise for general development of speed and power and for the precision of hand and eye. Any one can try it without fear of injury from overexertion, and in a short time will perceive its many and great benefits.

After the bag-work is done an adjournment should be had to the yard and a few miles run on the track, after which the clothing should be quickly removed, and, after a short rubbing over with a coarse towel while the perspiration was still pouring off, a shower-bath should be turned on and the man should stand under it for a moment, vigorously rubbing himself meanwhile, and thoroughly wilting and cleansing as well all parts. Care must be taken not to remain in the bath more than a very few minutes, as a severe cold and great weakness is apt to follow too long an exposure. Many athletes will not train in summer without the use of ice in their bathing-water. As soon as the bath is over the towel is again put in use and the man wiped dry. After that a short and not over-severe hand-rub should be given, clean clothes put on, and a stroll of a mile or so taken before dinner, which should be about five hours after the morning meal. A rest of at least half an hour should be taken before this meal, which may be quite heavy unless a man is very fat and is trying to get rid of his flesh. Dinner may consist of roast beef or mutton with vegetables; but, though now partaken of rather freely, they should be sparingly indulged in. A good glass of old, mixed, or Bass's ale may also be taken, and, if very dry, a few swallows of water. Water may be often used to rinse the mouth, but little should be drunk, as it is fattening. A pebble carried in the mouth the first few days of training will reduce the thirst. A little cup-custard and plum-pudding may be taken for dessert. A good rest of an hour or two will be well earned and the need of it

much felt by the time dinner is over. About three or four o'clock in the afternoon a walk may be taken to some near-by athletic club-ground, and there in sprinter's costume a thousand yards in dashes of seventy-five to one hundred yards each may be run off. This will be found to be one of the best of exercises for the wind.

The evening like the morning meal should be rather light, and consist mainly of toast, mutton-chops, and eggs, with a few vegetables and a little tea. After supper a stroll may be taken for a mile or two and a rest till an early bed-time arrives. Great care should be used not to catch cold. The scales should be used every day and the weight under the same bodily conditions carefully recorded. The weight should be gradually rising from about the middle to the end of training, and all work except moderate strolling should be discontinued two or three days before the contest.

Physical training is now a subject of consideration not only in our numerous athletic clubs and among professionals of the different branches, but is carefully dwelt upon by all that have anything to do with the instruction of the youth of either sex, and almost all schools have a system of light gymnastics or calisthenics. Any new game, such as lawn-tennis, that compels light and active out-door exercise under the disguise of sport, always meets with favor among young ladies and gentlemen. It is only within the past few years that the importance of physical training for women has begun to receive the attention it deserves. There are now two gymnasiums in New York for the fair sex alone, and their influence will surely be felt in the next generation. The importance of a careful system of physical training can hardly be overestimated in its relations to the proper enjoyments of a long and vigorous life.

PHYSIOLOGY. The originating causes of the various forms and modifications of structure, characteristic of plant and animal life, that become transmitted and perpetuated, are discussed by Herbert Spencer in his "Factors of Organic Evolution." Accepting the inheritance of useful variations fortuitously arising, and along with the inheritance of effects produced by use and disuse, as real factors, there still remain classes of organic phenomena unaccounted for and certain cardinal traits of animals and plants at large that are still unexplained. Hence a further factor must be recognized. The words "natural selection" do not express a cause in the physical sense, but a mode of co-operation, or the effect of it, among causes. The cause is to be found in the operation of the environment, in special amounts and combinations of agencies therein, but in a more important degree in the general and constant operation of those agencies. We infer that organisms have certain structural characters in common which are consequent on the action of the medium in which they exist, including under the term medium all physical forces falling upon them, as well as matters bathing them; and we may conclude that from the primary characters thus produced there must result secondary characters. When the respective effects of gravitation, heat, light, etc., are studied, as well as the respective effects, physical and chemical, of the matters forming the media, water and air, it will be found that while more or less operative on all bodies, each modifies *organic* bodies to an extent immensely greater than the extent to which it modifies *inorganic* bodies. The most general trait of such effects is the greater amount of change wrought by them on the outer surface than in the inner mass of the bodies affected. The matters composing the medium must act more on the parts directly exposed to them than on the parts sheltered from them; and the forces pervading it, except gravity, which affects outer and inner parts indiscriminately, must exert the larger share of their actions upon the outer parts. Hence, the primary and almost universal effect of the converse between the body and its medium is to differentiate its outside from its inside. This differentiation is exemplified and exhibited in all cell-organisms, beginning with the unicellular, in the cell-envelope, which is an outside, differentiated by the influence of the environment from the cell-content. The operation of this same force producing this effect in primary organisms has predetermined the universal cell-structure of all embryos, plant and animal, and the consequent cell-composition of adult forms arising from them. The differentiation of outer from inner reappears in the aggregations of cell-units which constitute living organisms. In its simplest and most unmistakable form we see this in the early changes of an unfolding ovum of primitive type. The original fertilized single cell having multiplied into a cluster of cells, then begins to show itself a contrast between periphery and center; and presently there is formed a sphere consisting of a superficial layer unlike its contents. In another class of organisms—as in leaves—from the thallus of a seaweed up to the leaf of a highly developed phænogam, we find, at all stages, a contrast between the inner and outer parts of these masses of flattened tissue. Then, in the outsides of the leaves a differentiation appears dependent on exposure to the light. In the frond of *Marchantia polymorpha* the side which happens to fall uppermost and is exposed to the light, forms stomata, while the under and dark side produces root-hairs and leafy processes. In roots, while in darkness and surrounded by moist earth, the protective coats are comparatively thin; but when the accidents of growth entail permanent exposure to light and air, roots acquire coverings allied in character to the coverings of branches. Similar modifications of the integument by the environment are seen in men in the hardening and roughening of the skin by exposure and usage, and the healing of wounds. So in all animal life, the outer surface, with the in-foldings and ingrowings to which it conforms, is the part which is modified by contact with the environment, and in which are initiated the various instrumentalities for carrying on intercourse with it. Clearly, organization could not but begin on the surface; and, having thus begun, its subsequent course could not but be determined by its superficial origin. Doubtless, natural selection soon came into action, but it could operate only under subjection; it could do no more than take advantage of those structural changes which the medium and its contents had initiated. Thus this primordial factor of the influence of the environment by causing the first differentiations of those clusters of units out of which visible animals in general arose, fixed the starting-place for organization, and therefore determined the course of organization; and doing this, gave indelible traits to embryonic transformations and to adult structures.

Prof. Rudolf Virchow defines acclimatization by saying that when a person goes to a different climate from that to which he has been accustomed, he feels at first uncomfortable, but after some weeks finds his system regaining its equilibrium. He has then accommodated himself to the new conditions; his organs have endured material change. Two kinds of effects accompany the course of acclimatization; simple discomfort or climatic indisposition, and disease or climatic illness, which differs from the former by possessing the element of danger as distinguished from simple inconvenience. Much has been published by the French and English on the subject, yet researches are entirely wanting upon the special changes which precede the onset of disease. On the other hand, the clinical study of tropical disease itself has been very much advanced. Whoever studies acclimatization must do so with a view to establish certain geographical limits of ethnological provinces analogous to botanical and zoölogical provinces. Comparing the capability of the different white races for acclimatization, the Semitic race is found to be superior to the Aryan. Among Aryan races, those of the south (Portuguese, Spanish, and Maltese) are superior to those of the north. Races, with a strong Semitic admixture, are more easily acclimatized than the pure Aryan stock. A population transplanted into a distant country often remains apparently stationary, though its new latitude may not be greatly different from that in which it flourished at home. It suffers from a decrease of fecundity and an arrest of development which may go to the end of the complete elimination of its posterity. Such is the case, among other instances, with the British in India, whose life never exceeds three generations, and all attempts by sanitary measures to perpetuate it have failed. Medical officers of the navy and mercantile service and others should study these conditions in the light of physiology. What is it that is most at fault? Is tropical anæmia a diminished formation or an increased destruction of blood? It is found, not only where malaria, pernicious relapsing fever, dysentery, or yellow fever prevail, but it occurs apart from those diseases. This increase of blood disintegration excites a great tendency to disorders of the liver, which is the main point of attack for diseases of acclimatization. The study of the particular disorders induced by acclimatization in individual organs, is a duty that is imposed upon the science of the colonizing nations.

A paper on the "Physiology of Shorthand Writing," by Dr. Gowers, excited considerable interest at the Shorthand Congress of 1887. Shorthand being only a variety of writing, the paper was mainly occupied with the cerebral physiology of writing. It was explained that the arm-center of the cortex is merely concerned in producing the movements for the written symbols, and that the word-processes are arranged in the motor speech-center on the left side, as is shown by the fact that disease of this center abolishes the power of writing as well as of speech. Thus, in the work of the reporter, so far as is at present known, there is no direct transfer of the nerve-processes from the auditory to the arm-center; they must go through the motor speech-center. The fact that it is the activity of the latter center which excites the arm-center and the movements for the written symbols, affords a strong theoretical justification for the phonetic element in shorthand, in which the written symbols are uniform for the same speech-processes. The non-phonetic systems, in so far as they do not adopt the phonetic principle, proceed on a re-symbolizing of the ordinary longhand signs; there are two steps to the process, whereas in the phonetic systems the symbols replace the longhand signs, and are placed at once on their permanent footing in direct relation to the speech-processes. It was mentioned that many persons, perhaps all persons, read by means of the motor speech-center, so that if this is destroyed the power of reading is lost; and illiterate persons actually move the lips in reading. This affords another justification for the phonetic principle—i. e., for the uniformity of relation between the written symbols and the motor processes.

Mr. A. R. Wallace accounts for the white color of Arctic animals by his theory of protective adaptation or mimicry. The validity of this explanation is disputed by Mr. R. Meldola, who has mentioned some Arctic animals that are not white, and regards that color as having some relation to the radiation or absorption of heat. Mr. Wallace, in defending his own view, says that "if the white coloration of Arctic animals stood alone, it might be thought necessary to supplement the protective theory by some physical explanation, but we have to take account of the parallel cases of the sand-colored desert animals, and the green-colored denizens of the ever-verdant tropical forests; and, though in both these regions there are numerous exceptional cases, we can almost always see the reason of these, either in the absence of the need of protection, or in the greater importance of conspicuous covering. In the Arctic regions the exceptions are particularly instructive, because the reason of them is obvious." The Arctic wolf does not turn white, because he hunts in packs, and concealment is not necessary; the musk-sheep, yak, moose, caribou, and reindeer are able to take care of themselves, and need no protection or concealment. The glutton and sable are dark colored because they live in trees, and must look like them. The raven, living on carion, requires no concealment, and continues black. Mr. Wallace is of the opinion that color has very little to do with the absorption or radiation of heat, because those matters are largely determined by the structure and surface-texture of the colored substances.

Lanoline is the name given by Prof. Liebreich to a new fat, composed of sebacic acid and cholesterine, which he has found in sheep's wool. It appears to reside exclusively in the hairs and the epidermis skin. The author had found it in the epidermis, the hairs, and the nails of men, in the hairs of all mammalia he had examined, in the hoofs of horses and swine, the horns of cattle, the prickles of the hedgehog, the feathers of fowls, geese, and other birds, and in the plated sheaths of the tortoise; in short, in all horned textures which he had examined. Also in the kidneys and the liver of mammalia. It would probably be found generally where epithelial cells occur. The constant presence in all epithelial formations of a particular fat, which was there formed in the keratine cells, rendered it highly probable that the hairs of mammalia and the feathers of birds owe their elasticity and pliancy not exclusively to the secretion of the sebaceous or caudal glands, but to the cholesterine fat generated in the horn cells themselves. The quality possessed by cholesterine fat of not oxidizing, or of oxidizing only under very rare conditions, renders it peculiarly adapted for lubricating the skin and feathers. Beyond the property of not becoming rancid, lanoline possesses a series of other advantages distinguishing it peculiarly as a salve constituent. It absorbs, for example, 100 per cent. of water, and by so doing becomes a soft substance, pleasant to the touch, penetrating the skin with extraordinary facility, and disappearing from view after a short rubbing of the cutis.

Nervous System.—In discussing the question of the nature of nerve-force, Dr. H. P. Bowditch has presented as important facts, forbidding the identification of that force with electricity, the absence of an insulating sheath on the nerve-fiber, the slow rate at which the force is transmitted, and the effect of a ligature on a nerve in preventing the passage of nerve-force, while not interfering with the flow of electricity. The electrical phenomena connected with the activity of nerves appear, therefore, to be secondary in their character, and not to constitute the essential process in nerve action. In studying the nature of nerve-force, two alternatives present themselves. We may conceive the impulse to be conducted through the nerve-fiber by a series of retrograde chemical changes in the successive molecules of the nerve substance, or we may suppose it to be transmitted from molecule to molecule by some sort of vibratory action. As the former theory involves the supposition of a using up of organic material and the consequent discharge of potential energy in the successive portions of the nerve, it may be called "the discharging hypothesis." The second theory, implying simply the transferring of motion, may be called "the kinetic hypothesis." If the discharging hypothesis be correct, we may reasonably expect to find in the active nerve-fiber evidences of chemical decomposition and of heat-production; and, as under it the organic substances are used up faster than they are replaced or their products of decomposition removed, we may expect to observe a diminution of nerve-action during the continuance of the stimulation, or the phenomena of fatigue. Experiments indicate that none of these phenomena show consumption of organic substance. They are, therefore, so far not favorable to a discharging theory, and are, by implication, more favorable to the kinetic theory.

An electric chronometer has been employed by Dr. D'Arsonval for the direct measurement of the speed with which nervous impressions are conveyed. On application of the instrument to the body, circuit is broken, and a pointer begins to travel. On feeling the sensation the patient touches a button, which restores circuit and stops the pointer. The interval can then be determined within hundredths of a second. Experiments with the instrument show that different sensations are transmitted with different velocities, and that different diseases abolish some while exalting others.

Remarking on the degeneration of nerves resulting from sectional injury, Dr. Prause says that, according to Waller, when a nerve is cut through the peripheral parts degenerate, whereas the central remain intact. The result of a thorough investigation of the nerves in cases of amputation, which the author had carried on some years ago in conjunction with Dr. Friedländer, had, however, shown that the central parts of the divided nerves had degenerated up to the spinal cord. In a case where, on account of gangrene of the foot, the leg had been amputated close below the knee, the degeneration of the nerves, having started from the gangrenous parts and progressed centripetally, had extended up to and probably beyond the surface of amputation. Side by side, however, with the larger number of degenerated

fibers a few normal fibers were found. From experiments on animals in which nerves of very different kinds, both sensory and mixed, were cut through, it appeared that in the peripheral parts by far the larger number of the fibers degenerate, while at the same time a not inconsiderable number remain unaltered. Similarly degenerated and normal fibers were found in the central part of the nerve, only in this case the relative number of each kind is an inverse proportion to that in which they are found in the peripheral part. It follows from the above that, starting from the point of section of a nerve, one set of fibers degenerates toward the periphery, the other toward the center. It seemed right to assume that those fibers which degenerate toward the periphery have their trophic center in the spinal cord or brain, as the case may be, while those which degenerate centripetally are dependent for their nutrition on some center at the periphery, such as, presumably, the tactile corpuscles of Meissner. Were this not so, Waller's law would again hold good, since only those parts of a nerve degenerate which are cut off from their trophic center; only sensory nerves degenerate centripetally.

Experiments have been made by Dr. Raske with the co-operation of Dr. Kossel, on the chemical composition of the brains of the embryos of horned cattle, in order to determine whether it or morphological structure is primary during the process of development. The values found in two brains were compared with the results of the chemical investigation of brains which had been carried out in the laboratory of Prof. Hoppe Seyler, whose investigations had shown that the gray substance of the brain of full-grown cattle differs essentially from the white substance, by containing but little, if any, cerebrine, a less amount of cholesterine, and a greater quantity of albumen and extractives than the latter. In these particulars, the brains of the embryos of horned cattle hold exactly the same position as does the gray substance of grown-up brains. It was only in the quantity of lecithine and of salts that the embryonal brains demonstrated any difference from the gray substance. The embryonal brain is, therefore, very essentially distinguished from the white substance —a phenomenon which is in harmony with the fact that, in the embryonal brain medullated nerve-fibers were not met with.

From an investigation of the histology and function of the mammalian cervical ganglion, in which a large number of specimens—human, other mammalian, and fetal—were examined, W. Hale White concludes that human adult ganglia vary as much in size as do the largest and smallest of other mammals, and that the size of the ganglion in other mammals varies directly as the size of the animal; that human superior cervical ganglia present granular pigmented atrophied cells much more frequently than those of other mammals; that this condition, though present to some degree in monkeys, diminishes regularly as we descend lower in the mammalian scale, till at last it is not seen at all; and that human fetal ganglia do not show any of these changes in their nerve-cells. These facts, the author adds, "seem to show that the superior cervical ganglion is becoming less and less functionally important the higher we ascend in the animal scale, till in the human adult its minimum of importance is reached. It is, in fact, an atrophied degenerate organ, like the coccyx or the appendix cæci. So that, although I do not pretend to have discovered whatever function the superior cervical ganglion may have in the lower mammalia, it is probably dying out in us."

In demonstrating the structure of the epidermis, Dr. Blaschko remarked that, starting with the assumption that the final endings of the nerves of feeling must be sought in the layer of the epidermis, and not in the cutis, he had studied the structure of the upper skin at the boundary between epidermis and cutis. He distinguished the main parts of direct feeling (the hairless parts of the skin) from the parts of indirect feeling (the hairy parts of the skin). The former possessed on the under side of the epidermis very beautifully developed grooves (*Leisten*), forming a reticular system with spiral longitudinal and transverse lines. The hairy parts of the skin were influenced in their structure by the hairs, which likewise stood in spiral series, and had but very indistinct reticulations in the intermediate spaces.

Researches made by Dr. Joseph on the physiology of the spinal ganglia show that there are a number of nerve-fibers which simply pass through the ganglion without being connected with its cells; that the ganglion is the trophic center for the large number of sensory nerves; and that the ganglionic cells are bipolar.

Experiments by J. W. Warren upon the effect of pure alcohol on the reaction time, warrant the conclusions that the changes in this time, after taking varying amounts of pure alcohol, are, on the whole, more considerable than those occurring in equally long experiments without alcohol; that there is no obvious and unquestionable relation of the effect, in quality or in quantity, either to the amount of alcohol taken, or to the time during which its influence has been exerted; and that where the normal observations are subject to great variations from day to day, the alcohol appears to lessen these variations and to bring the observations to a common mean.

Special Senses. — "The Muscular Sense; its Nature and Cortical Localization" has been made the subject of a discussion in the Neurological Society of London, which was opened by H. Charlton Bastian, M. D. Recognizing the inherent difficulties of the subject and the unsettled state of opinion on it, the author premised that the discussion might do good, if not by leading to the immediate settlement of the many points still in dispute, at least by serving to bring out into clearer light the nature of the problems to be settled by future workers and thinkers. The subject, he adds, is eminently one of those on which observation and experiment alone will not suffice, especially observations and experiments conducted upon lower animals. Dr. Bastian expresses the opinion that the evidence in our possession points very strongly to the conclusion that Ferrier's so-called "motor centers" are in reality kinæsthetic centers in which "muscular sense" impressions in particular have been registered. As reasons supporting this conclusion, he adduces that all the effects resulting from the stimulation or destruction of these centers are in accordance with it; and that the view that "motor centers" exist in the cerebral cortex can not be correct, unless it can be shown that there is in the cortex of each hemisphere another totally distinct set of centers, the stimulation of which evokes definite movements, and the destruction of which involves an inability to execute the same movements. But both experimental physiology and clinical medicine support the fact that there is but one set of areas (Rolandic and marginal) in which irritation or destruction leads to any such results.

The Rev. J. L. Zabriskie observes of the vision of the honey-bee, that it sees, as it were, through the woods. The ocelli are situated on the top of the head, arranged as in an equilateral triangle, so that one is directed to the front, one to the right, and one to the left. "Long, branching hairs on the crown of the head stand thick, like a miniature forest, so that an ocellus is scarcely discernible except from a particular point of view;" and then the observer remarks an opening through the hairs —a cleared pathway, as it were, in such a forest—and notes that the ocellus, looking like a glittering globe half immersed in the substance of the head, lies at the inner end of the path. The opening connected with the front ocellus expands forward from it like a funnel with an angle of about fifteen degrees. The side ocelli have paths more narrow, but opening more vertically, so that the two together command a field which, though hedged in anteriorly and posteriorly, embraces in a plane transverse to the axis of the insect's body, an angle of nearly one hundred and eighty degrees.

Color perception, as explained by Dr. Charles A. Oliver, in his "Correlation Theory" upon the subject, is not dependent upon specialization of nerve-fibers, but takes place through each and every optical nerve-filament. "It consists in the passive separation of a specific nerve-energy equal to the exposed natural color, from a supposed 'energy equivalent' resident in the peripheral nerve tip, by an active chemico-vital process of the impinging natural color vibration upon the sensitized nerve terminal. The separated nerve-energy is transmitted to the central terminus of the filament in the cerebral retina, where it is fully evolved into such a condition as to be transferred into an automatic form of perception by an action upon some unknown contiguous perceptive nerve-elements." Suppose the nerve-points to be exposed to a beam of light of, say five hundred trillion beats per second, the average response to the sensation thus produced upon healthy tissue would be what is known as red. Each impinged point would excite a sensation equal to a specific energy equivalent to red. If the undulations are six hundred trillions to the second, the sensation would produce a specific energy giving the response of green. And if a beam of light of, say seven hundred and thirty-three trillions of vibrations per second be thrown upon the same sentient points, violet would be given as the answer. "Each and every optic-nerve fiber tip has a receiving power equal to its individual strength. Each and every healthy optic-nerve filament transmits to the color center for recognition nerve-energies equal to as many special sensations as its peripheral tip is capable of receiving. The innumerable quantities of nerve-filaments placed side by side on a sheet or membrane serve to give a greater field and allow many colors to be seen at one and the same time, thus making our every-day and momentary pictures."

The feeling of cold produced in the forehead on the application of menthol for relief from headache has been assumed to be a result of the cooling of the skin consequent on evaporation. On the other hand, the feeling of cold produced in the mouth by mouth-washes containing mentha has been supposed to be due to an astringent effect of this substance. Not believing that these explanations were correct, Dr. Goldschneider experimented with a solution of menthol in lanoline, which was rubbed into circumscribed places of the skin. Measured with the thermometer, those places showed an increase of temperature after the rubbing, yet there was a decided feeling of cold; and this feeling was also observed when the place where the solution was rubbed in was protected against evaporation by a watch-glass. The feeling in question could therefore proceed only from a direct stimulation of the nerves conveying the sensation of cold. If of two places on the forehead exactly corresponding to one another, the author observed, the one were rubbed with menthol salves and the other not, bodies which before had produced no impression, being indifferent, would now be felt as cold by the part of the skin where the rubbing was made, whereas there would be no perceptible impression on the other part. Hence Dr. Goldschneider concludes that menthol produces a specific influence on the nerves of cold which are distributed with especial copiousness on the forehead.

Circulation.—Experiments on the relation between the curve of distention of elastic tubes

and the rate of the pulse-wave in the same, have been made by Dr. Grunmach with various gutta-percha tubes and with the aorta of horses. The internal pressure being varied from 0 to 200 mm. of mercury, the alteration of volume of the tubes, and the rate of transmission of the pulse-wave were measured. The results showed that the rate of the pulse-wave is most markedly dependent upon the distention-curve or coefficient of elasticity of the tube. This coefficient is, however, very variable with different tubes. The behavior of a horse's aorta approximated to that of an India-rubber tube wrapped with linen. The thickness of the walls of the tubes and the size of their lumen was very slightly, if at all, altered by the varying pressure, and their influence upon the relationship of pressure and rate of pulse-wave was quite subordinate.

The specific gravity of the blood in health, according to the investigations of Mr. E. Lloyd Jones, is highest at birth, reaches a minimum between the second week and the second year, and rises gradually to a point attained in the male between the ages of thirty-five and forty-five; and in the female after the climacteric. As a rule, it tends to be higher in the male than in the female; and in the female the child-bearing period is marked by a fall. In pregnancy it is slightly diminished, though it still remains well within healthy limits. The immediate effect of mixed food is to cause a fall; if alcohol is taken this fall is not observed. Exercise, if gentle and not too prolonged, causes a fall; if perspiration becomes well marked the specific gravity rises, as it does when violent exercise is taken. The conditions of the circulation in the affected part modify the specific gravity of the blood circulating through it. It is always high in a passively congested part. It varies also in different parts of the body. It exhibits a certain diurnal variation, tending to fall during the day and to rise at night.

The influence of extremes of temperature on the color of the blood has been described by Prof. Falk, who found that temperatures of 0° C. and below lead to the color of the blood becoming bright red by causing the oxygen of the air to be more readily fixed and more stably retained by the corpuscles than is the case at ordinary temperatures. If, however, the blood has stood exposed to the air until putrefactive changes have set in, the action of cold no longer makes it brighter in color. Other experiments have shown that in animals killed by low temperatures, the blood is bright red, not only in the peripheral parts, but also in the heart and great vessels. Also in human beings frozen to death the blood even in the heart is sometimes observed to be bright red, although in most cases only the blood of the peripheral parts presents this appearance; probably death has ensued from freezing only in cases presenting the first of these two appearances.

The researches of Brücke and Lacken indicated that contact with foreign bodies causes blood to coagulate; while Grünhagen found that blood when received into glycerine, and so long as it did not mix, remained liquid. A reconciliation of these contradictory results seems to have been found by Ernst Fresend, whose comparative experiments with blood in contact with substances of different characters show that coagulation depends on adhesion; the lack of adhesion preventing it, while its presence gives the impulse to the change.

From experiments upon the eel's heart and the skeletal muscles of the frog, S. Ringer and D. W. Buxton conclude that contractions can not be maintained when the heart is supplied with a circulation composed of simple saline, or saline plus potassium chloride, or saline plus sodium bicarbonate, or saline plus both these salts; that phosphate of calcium added to saturation to saline can sustain contractility, but leads to great delay of dilatation with persistent spasm and fusion of the beats; that these effects are completely obviated by the addition of potassium chloride; that we have in phosphate of calcium saline with potassium chloride an excellent circulating fluid capable of maintaining the heart for several hours; and that calcium chloride solution is inferior to the phosphate in its powers of supporting contractility.

The heart of the toad-fish, *Batrachus tau*, has been studied by Prof. T. Wesley Mills, with especial reference to determining the order of the beats and the effect of various drugs upon it. The normal order of the beats is sinus, auricle, venticle, but the heart of this fish is distinguished from that of all animals above it in the scale of life by the great ease with which its natural order of beat may be disturbed. Of drugs, pilocarpine tends to slow the rhythm, while atropine quickens it, and increases the force of the beat. Sodium carbonate quickens rhythm, diminishes diastolic relaxation, and hardens cardiac excitability, but to a less extent than atropine. Potassium carbonate diminishes excitability, weakens the heart's action, and tends to arrest it in diastole. Lactic acid in five-per-cent. solution is a rapid poison, while in solution of one per cent. it depresses the heart and gradually kills it in diastole. Digitalin produces gradually increasing systolic contraction, while the diastolic relaxation gets less and less till the heart is finally arrested in most pronounced systolic tetanus. Nicotine produces variable effects, from which the heart has the power of recovering rapidly. The principal action of veratria is on the diastole, which it renders more sluggish, while the effect on the systole is slight. The rhythm is slowed, but want of harmony between the different parts of the heart and different fibers of the same part is liable to manifest itself. Undiluted chloroform is a cardiac depressor, acting most readily on the auricle proper, and capable of arresting the heart in diastole. The organ has considerable ability to recover from the effects of this agent. Acetate of strychnia has the power of shortening the diastole, lengthening the systole, and slowing the rhythm.

Experiments by Augustus D. Waller show that each beat of the human heart is accompanied by an electrical variation which is proved, by the method of investigation adopted, to be physiological and not due to any mechanical or accidental conditions. But the character and direction of the variations are not yet so clear as to enable the author to attempt an interpretation of them.

The distribution of the blood-vessels in the retinæ of mammals has been studied by James W. Barrett with the aid of the hardened eyes of men and children and of wild animals. The term "internuclear layer" in the catalogued arrangement of the layers of the retina was found to be wanting in accurate definition, and in many animals appeared susceptible of further, more precise, division; as in the retinæ of man and some other animals, it seems to be divided into "fibrous" and "reticulated" layers. Blood-vessels were seen in the outer reticular layer of the internuclear layer or in the undivided internuclear layer of most of the animals examined, and generally in the inner part of the layer only; but in no case was a blood-vessel seen in the outer nuclear layer of a mammalian retina or crossing the membrane dividing the nerve from the epithelial layers. The author's observations therefore go to confirm the supposition that the epithelial layers of the retina are extra-vascular. The retinæ of ruminants appear to be exceedingly vascular.

Respiration.—The question whether an increased absorption of oxygen takes place when the tension is increased, has been investigated by Dr. Lukjanow through experiments on various animals exposed to an atmosphere containing larger proportions of oxygen and of higher pressure than the normal. The mean result of all the experiments was a slight increase, of four per cent. in volume, of oxygen absorption. Dr. Herter, who presented the subject before the Physiological Society of Berlin, was of the opinion that this small increase could not be regarded as a consequence of increased oxygen tension, because, in individual animals, the means of oxygen absorption sometimes fell below, and sometimes exceeded the normal amounts, and, further, because they did not vary proportionately with the increased tension of the oxygen of the air. The increase must be referred to other causes, such as the movements of the animals during the experiments. No increase of the temperature was observed under the increased pressure of oxygen; the conclusion was drawn that the absorption of oxygen is not an ordinary combustion process, and that the normal composition of the atmosphere contains the most suitable percentage of oxygen.

An experiment carried out by Zuntz and Wolff goes to show that any one can diminish his weight by taking a deep inspiration. The experiment is most striking when the subject is standing on a decimal balance, which is so arranged that it can only give a kick upward. In this case the pan with the weights in it sinks when the inspiration is taken. The phenomenon is explained as being the result of the sudden straightening of the spinal column and elevation of the head which occurs in taking the inspiration. The head, by its momentum, carries the lower part of the body slightly with it, so that the latter presses less forcibly on its support.

Experiments by Dr. Loewy indicate that the respiratory center in the medulla oblongata is able to maintain the rhythm of the respiratory movements after the nerve is separated from both the brain and the peripheral parts of the vagi. Moreover, the center when thus isolated was found to be equally susceptible to stimuli, whether applied directly or arriving from the periphery, as when it was still connected with the brain and lungs.

Sydney Ringer, investigating the action on fish of distilled water alone and of distilled water holding inorganic salts in solution, found that the fish soon died when placed in distilled water, not because of the absence of air, but of the absence of salts in the water. To ascertain in what manner the destruction of the fish is brought about, the author tested the action on the gill-edges of fresh-water mussels of distilled water alone and of distilled water containing various proportions of salts. Distilled water soon destroyed ciliary action, causing the cells to swell often to quadruple their natural size, so that many burst and liberated their nuclei. The distilled water also separated the cells, and caused complete disintegration of the tissue, separating them from one another, and seeming to induce swelling of the cement material which united them. It was therefore evident that distilled water, in part at least, will destroy life by disorganizing the gills and impeding respiration. Further experiments made it probable that this disintegration of the structure and the consequent death of the fish were caused by both osmosis of the cells and imbibition by the material uniting the cells to one another. The swelling and other effects were checked by the addition of minute quantities of various salts to the water.

Digestion.—R. H. Chittenden and Herbert E. Smith, having studied quantitatively the modifications, under various conditions, of the diastatic action of saliva, conclude that such action can be taken as a definite measure of the amount of ferment present only when the dilution of the saliva in the digestive mixture is 1 to 50 or 100. The limit of dilution at which decisive diastatic action will manifest itself with formation of reducing bodies is 1 to 2,000 or 3,000. The diastatic action of neutralized saliva is greater than that of normally alkaline saliva. The difference is particularly noticeable where the dilution is as 1 to 50 or 100, and is apparently out of all proportion to the amount of alkalinity. Sodium carbonate retards the diastatic action of ptyaline in proportion to the amount of alkaline carbonate present; but its destructive action is modified materially by the dilution of the saliva, becoming greater the more the fluid is diluted. Neutral peptone has a direct stimulating effect on the diastatic action of neutral saliva. The presence of small percentages of that agent tends to raise the diastatic action of normally alkaline saliva to a point beyond the action of the neutralized fluid. Peptone tends likewise to diminish the retarding action of the various percentages of sodium carbonate. It tends to prevent the destructive action of dilute sodium carbonate on salivary ptyaline, thus giving proof of the probable formation of an alkaline-proteid body. Saliva, with its proteid matter saturated with acid, appears to have a greater diastatic action than when simply neutralized, except when the acid-proteids thus formed are above a certain percentage. Small percentages of peptone saturated with acid similarly increase the diastatic action of neutralized saliva up to a certain point. Increasing the percentage of acid-proteids may cause almost a complete destruction of the ferment. The most favorable condition for the diastatic action of ptyaline, under most circumstances, appears to be a neutral condition of the fluid, together with the presence of more or less proteid matter. The addition of hydrochloric acid, however, to dilute solutions of saliva, giving thereby a small percentage of alkaline proteids, appears still further to increase diastatic action. Three thousandths per cent. of free hydrochloric acid almost completely stops the amylolotic action of ptyaline. The larger the amount of saturated proteids, the more pronounced becomes the retarding action of free acids. The retarding effect of the smaller percentages of free acid are not wholly due to destruction of the ferment. Pronounced destruction takes place with from 0.005 to 0.010 per cent. of free hydrochloric acid. Proteid matter, in influencing the diastatic activity of salivary ptyaline, acts not only by combining with acids and alkalies, but apparently also by direct stimulation of the ferment.

Mr. Schneitzer, of Kansas City, has found that pancreatine and pepsine act with perfect ease and freedom in presence of each other. When digested together they do not destroy one another, nor do they lessen each other's digestive activity in whatever proportion they may be digested. Long-continued exposure to heat and moisture injures their original activity. Digested in acid or alkaline solutions the injury is increased. Pancreatine, when digested for some hours in an acid solution, becomes permanently injured or destroyed, and pepsine, when digested in an alkaline solution for some hours, is also permanently destroyed. But such a state as prevails in the healthy natural secretion of the salivary glands of the stomach or the pancreas, is not such as to interfere with any of their digestive functions.

In experiments upon the relative digestibility of various feeding-stuffs, adopting Stutzen's method, E. F. Ladd employed as a menstruum a solution of scale pepsine. The substances experimented with were classified as "hay and coarse fodders," "by-products," and "grains." Of the feeds examined in per cent. of digestibility of the albuminoids, he reports, bean-meal stands the highest, linseed-meal (old process) next, and pea-meal but little less, while mixed hay of rather inferior quality, but similar to much hay fed, stands lowest. The old-process linseed-meal shows a higher per cent. of digestibility than the new process, a difference which is due, very likely, to the partial cooking of the meal by steam during the process of oil-extraction and preparation of the meal for feed. Cotton-seed meal, much the richest substance examined, gives a high coefficient for digestibility. A marked difference existed between different qualities of hay, showing the effects of the manner of curing. Of the raw and cooked foods examined, in every instance the higher digestion coefficients were obtained for the raw foods, and an examination of the table of analysis shows an actual loss in albuminoids by cooking, and a change in the fat rendering it insoluble in ether, and unacted upon by acids or alkalies of the strength used for fiber determinations.

The influence of hot drinks on digestion has been investigated by V. E. Nyeshel on the persons of twenty hospital surgical patients. When not more than three tumblerfuls of hot tea had been swallowed, digestion was found to have proceeded just as well as without it, but a larger quantity of hot tea retarded the process. As between hot and cold food no difference was found.

Three hypotheses have been advanced to account for the structure of the "edible bird's-nest"; the first, that it is partly, at least, of vegetable origin, and consists of pieces of alga fastened together by the bird's saliva; the second, that the material is made by the bird from fish-spawn, or is collected from mollusca; the third, which was advanced by Sir Everard Home, and sustained by Bernstein in the "Journal für Ornithologie," is that the material consists entirely of an animal secretion, and is essentially the product of some peculiar glands possessed by the bird. Mr. J. R. Green, of Trinity College, has subjected some of the material to a microscopic examination in order to ascertain whether any evidences of vegetable structure can be detected. None were found, and this fact was regarded as bearing adversely to the theory of a vegetable origin. The results of the chemical tests bore in the same direction. Mr. Green concludes from these facts, combined with the more positive indications afforded by his experiments, that the substance is an animal product so closely allied to mucine that it may be said to be a variety of it, and that there can be little doubt that it is the result of the activity of certain glands described by Bernstein as being remarkably developed in the nest-building season, and as atrophying immediately afterward.

Zweifel, of Zürich, has made some observations on the rate of absorption through the stomach, using iodide of potassium, which was introduced inclosed in gelatine capsules. When so given, in doses of three grains, the time taken for the appearance of the salt in the saliva, in the case of the healthy individual, varies from eight to ten minutes; this rate of absorption remaining much the same on different days. The salt appears in the urine and the saliva at about the same time, although on the whole somewhat earlier in the latter than in the former. Absorption is always much delayed when the stomach is full. In almost all diseases of the stomach absorption tends to be delayed, this tendency being most marked in dilatation and cancer, and least so in chronic catarrh. In ulcer of the stomach the delay is only slight, but in ulcer of the stomach with extensive recent ulceration of the mucous membrane, it may be considerable. If in the empty condition of the stomach absorption is longer delayed than twenty minutes, there is every reason to believe that we have to deal either with dilatation of the stomach or with cancer of the pylorus, or both together, provided always that the existence of any fresh ulceration has been excluded. A differential diagnosis between cancer, ulcer, and chronic catarrh of the stomach is not always possible from the rate of absorption alone. The differences between the rates of absorption in the empty and full conditions of the stomach are less marked in diseases of the stomach than in health. During fever the rapidity of absorption is diminished, but it is not affected by the height of the fever.

Muscular System.— Drs. Mosso and Maggiora have reported to the Accademia dei Lincei concerning experiments which they have recently made on the laws of fatigue. They employed a mechanism, by means of which they could observe the variations of the efforts put forth by a finger in lifting a weight until entire exhaustion had set in. The mechanism was then readjusted in such a way that the operator's whole arm remained motionless with the exception of the muscle corresponding to the finger in action. From the tracings of the variations of the muscular effort it was shown that every individual under experiment gave a special characteristic trace, which at once distinguished his effort from those of the others. Resistance to fatigue was seen to be different at different hours of the day, and to be variously affected by the influence of food. Studies were also made of the problem of the disposing of the pauses, so as to make the outlay of force as economical and effective as possible. According to the experimenters, the resulting fatigue is twofold—the fatigue of nervous failure and the fatigue of muscular failure. In certain cases the fatigue comes from the collapse of the muscular tissue only, while in others it happens that the brain suspends the supplies necessary to keep the muscles active. Some experiments showed that if a fatigued finger bore a weight with difficulty, the moment the weight was withdrawn the finger would recoil backward with force, a proof that while the muscular energy had run out, the nervous energy was striving to compensate it by imposing on the muscle an effort much stronger than necessary. Other experiments were made on the influence of the weight to be lifted, as well as on that of anæmia. When the arteries of the arm under experiment were constricted or it was made wholly bloodless, the muscle was found capable of continuous effort, but only through nervous excitation; and it was observed how the muscular energy revived gradually as the blood returned into the arm. The effects of fasting, and the duration of the time that must elapse after the taking of food to re-establish the conditions of normal muscular labor; the influence of respiration and of those processes of training whereby the organism is inured to bear the heaviest fatigue; and the influence of certain aliments in the production of labor, were the subjects of further series of investigations. On the last point the induction was confirmed by novel methods that alcohol, instead of augmenting muscular energy, positively diminishes it.

The influence of gases on the intestinal movements has been investigated by Bokai, who finds that while such inert gases as hydrogen and nitrogen are without effect either in inducing or allaying peristaltic contractions, others — notably carbonic acid, carbureted hydrogen, and sulphureted hydrogen — increase these movements to a very marked degree. The violent peristalsis induced by the injection of carbonic acid into any portion of the intestine can at once be stopped by passing a stream of oxygen into the part, as well as by the injection of lime-water. The mere absence of oxygen has the same effect as the presence of carbonic acid, in both cases the action being entirely a peripheral one, limited to the portion of the intestine affected. Carbureted hydrogen or marsh gas and sulphureted hydrogen also produce marked peristaltic movements when injected into the intestine, which can similarly be allayed, although not completely, by the subsequent injection of oxygen. These observations serve to throw some light on the mode of action of sulphur as a purgative, and of subnitrate of bismuth as an astringent and sedative. The latter substance is found to be a useful remedy, in cases of diarrhœa, from its power of combining with sulphureted hydrogen and with other gases developed in the intestinal tract as the result of fermentation and decomposition.

The action of hot and cold water on the muscular walls of the uterus and on the blood-vessels has been partially investigated by Dr. Milne Murray, of Edinburgh. The main results arrived at after experimenting with three grades of temperature, viz.: Water at from 32° F. to 60° F., from 60° F. to 110° F., and from 110° F. to 120° F., are: 1. That the application of the low temperature water produces a marked latent period; a slow contraction period of from one to five minutes; and a period of a gradual relaxation—a very important one for arrest of hæmorrhage—lasting for about three times the contraction period, namely, for from three to fifteen minutes; 2. That the application of water at the high temperature produces a very short latent period, or even obliterates it; the contraction period developes rapidly (thirty-five seconds); and the period of gradual relaxation occupies from six to fifteen minutes. In the case of the arteries water at temperatures of from 110° F. to 120° F., constricts blood-vessels and arrests hæmorrhage from small arteries; at temperatures of from 60° F. to 100° F. it dilates small vessels, and promotes hæmorrhage; at temperatures of from 30° F. to 50° F. it checks hæmorrhage by temporarily constricting the vessels; but this is followed by intense reaction. These experiments, though needing to be repeated with greater care for scientific purposes, give results of great practical value to those who have to deal with the arrest of hæmorrhage.

A new method and apparatus for obtaining graphic records of the various kinds of movements of the hand and its parts and for enumerating such movements and their combinations have been devised by Dr. Francis Warner. The apparatus consists of an arrangement of India-rubber tubes to be fitted upon the fingers or moving parts, with which adaptations for electrical registration are so connected that every movement is correspondingly marked. By the method of investigation which this apparatus is intended to assist, tracings may be obtained of muscular movements due to the action of the central nerve-mechanism, from which some evidence can be derived concerning the effects of brain action in its different parts as indicated by muscular movements. Thus, in infancy, spontaneous movements of the fingers are usual while the child is awake and spontaneous muscular movements are occurring all over the body. These movements can be arrested by light and probably by sound. In studying the mental development of infants we mainly judge of the rapidity and stage of their growth by observing the amount, kind, and co-ordination of their motions. Tracings could be given of these motions; separate movements might be enumerated; and possibly we might enumerate the special combinations of movement, showing whether such combinations occur more commonly at one time than at another, or more commonly under any particular set of circumstances.

Glandular System.—For the more complete investigation of the action of diuretics, O. D. F. Phillips and J. Rose Bradford have studied the effects of certain drugs upon the general blood-pressure; upon the renal circulation (as measured by changes in the volume of the kidney); and upon the renal secretion. Citrate of caffeine, studied in its action on the general blood-pressure, was found to produce, first a diminution in the force of the heart-beats, with or without a slight acceleration of the rhythm; and, second, an increase in the force of the heart and a distinct slowing of the rhythm, which is occasionally followed by a slight but persistent acceleration. During the first stage there is a fall of arterial pressure, which regains, or may slightly exceed, its normal height during the second stage. In the second phase of the experiments, a contraction of the peripheral vessels of the kidney and spleen took place, which lasted longer than the fall of general blood-pressure, and was followed by a persistent and marked expansion, greater relatively in the kidney than in the spleen; which expansion in the case of the kidney was accompanied by a very marked increase in the amount of urine secreted. While the action of caffeine on the circulation was undoubtedly peripheral, it was not clear whether the drug acts on the peripheral nerve structures or on the muscular elements directly. The diuretic effect, as shown by other observers, is complex, and is not entirely dependent on the vascular dilatation. The injection of digitaline was followed by a contraction of the kidney, which was usually, but not always, more slow in its course than that described as following the injection of caffeine. The peculiarity of the contraction is its extreme persistence, it enduring frequently for a half an hour, or to the end of the experiment; and it is not followed by any expansion. While both digitaline and caffeine produce constriction of the kidney vessels, this is the sole effect of digitaline, and the initiatory effect of caffeine. The two drugs exhibit a marked difference in their action on the secretion. During the contraction produced by caffeine the flow is either diminished or frequently arrested; whereas, with the contraction of digitaline, it is certainly not diminished, and is generally slightly increased. Hence with digitaline we have an example of a drug producing a diuretic effect at the same time that the renal vessels are constricted.

The researches of De Burgh Birch and Harry Spong, on the secretion of the gall-bladder —which is described as a clear and somewhat viscid fluid, in constant flow—lead them to infer that the secretion can not be regarded as having any important part to play in digestion, the small diastatic action it possesses on starch being shared by many fluids in the economy upon which it does not confer any special digestive value. Its use is probably confined to lubricating the walls of the gall-bladder, and it adventitiously adds some mucus to the bile.

The question whether the secretion of the kidneys normally varies on each side has been studied by Buelzer in a case of vesical ectopia. Iodide of potassium, given by the mouth, appeared in the urine from one ureter at a different time from that of the other side; salicylic acid showed the same difference. Chemical analysis also proved that the proportions of urea, phosphoric acid, and sulphuric acid differed on the two sides. Great differences were observed in the quantity and density of the urine discharged from the two sides respectively. This difference leads Buelzer to think that the composition of the blood in the aorta is far from being uniform.

Peiper concludes, after an elaborate research, that the perspiration is more concentrated on the right-hand side of the body. The palm of the hand sweats four times more than the skin of the chest, and the cheeks one and a half time as much. A slow increase in the sweat is felt in the afternoon, which is especially obvious from 8 to 12 o'clock at night, after which the amount diminishes. Feeling has but little influence in this direction. Elevation of the surrounding temperature increases the perspiration, and variations of the hygrometric state of the atmosphere have an immense influence on the function. The quantity of water evaporated in a quarter of an hour from a cutaneous surface 25 centimetres square, in a normal individual is about ·176 of a grain. In infants the quantity is generally less than in adults. The weight of the body and sex have no marked influence on the perspiration.

The results of Dr. Stabrovski's experiments to determine the effects of massage on pulmonary and cutaneous exhalation have been discordant. In five out of the fourteen cases experimented upon there was an increase in the pulmono-cutaneous exhalation and a diminution in the amount of urine; in three cases the massage increased the amount of urine and diminished the pulmono-cutaneous exhalation; and in the remaining six cases both the urine and the pulmono-cutaneous exhalation were increased. The general effect on the pulse was to lower it some ten or fifteen beats. No alteration appeared to be produced in the rate of respiration.

Action of Poisons.—The supposition has been advanced by Dr. B. W. Richardson that various forms of mental and nervous affection may depend for their development on the presence in the body of organic chemical compounds, formed and distilled through an unnatural chemical process carried on in the body itself. Amylene, a substance easily formed in vital chemical changes, produces phenomena identical with those of somnambulism, and with some of those of hysteria. Another organic product, called *mercaptan* or sulphur-alcohol, causes, when inhaled, symptoms of profound melancholy; and in the process of being eliminated by the breath, it gives to the breath an odor which is identical with that evolved in the breath of many patients who are suffering from the disease called melancholia. Dr. Richardson has also shown that lactic acid, diffused through the body by the blood, acts as a direct irritant upon the lining membrane of the heart, and all the fibro-serous membranes of the body, so that a synthesis of heart-disease and rheumatism can be established by means of it. It is also the most copious product thrown out in rheumatic fever; and considerable evidence is collected to indicate that this acid, the product of a fermentative change going on in the body during acute rheumatism, is the cause of the secondary structural affections which so frequently follow that disease. The breath of diabetic patients is characterized by an odor of acetone, which may be likened to a brewery smell; and it is believed that the symptoms originate in the decomposition of the diabetic sugar which is in the body, producing acetone, a volatile ethereal fluid which has been discovered in the blood and secretions of certain affected persons.

Charles Ludeking, of St. Louis, having obtained reactions for chloroform in the viscera of a murdered man twelve days after death, made experiments upon dogs for the purpose of determining how long evident traces of that drug would remain in the body. He deduced the conclusions that by the process of decomposition no substances are generated which could vitiate the tests for chloroform by the Ragsky method; and that chloroform, when it has caused death by inhalation, can with certainty be detected in the body four weeks after death, and, notwithstanding its volatility, is certainly retained in the viscera in large amount during this time. The persistency of the substance is explained by the observation of Dubois, that the vapor of chloroform penetrates into the interior of the tissues, and becomes substituted for normal water. This is not a phenomenon of desiccation or osmose, but results from the play of a true affinity, by which the protoplasm absorbs the vapor of the anæsthetic which replaces a certain quantity of water. The powerful preservative qualities of chloroform are also, probably, a factor in the matter.

Drs. S. Weir Mitchell and Reichert have made careful physiological analyses of the proteids which have been determined to be the active principle of the venoms of snakes. The venoms closely resemble the salivary secretions of other vertebrates; and their active principle, which can be maintained in the dried state or in such preserving fluids as glycerine and alcohol, is contained in the fluid part of the venom only. This active principle is divisible into globulines and peptones, of which the former may consist of several distinct principles. If taken into the stomach during the intervals of digestion the poisons may prove fatal, whereas during digestion they are rendered harmless. The chief local antidotes are permanganate of potash, ferric chloride, and tincture of iodine. The venom has a powerful effect upon the liv-

ing tissue, on which it induces more rapid nervous changes than any other known organic substance. It renders the blood incapable of coagulation, and exerts a local effect on the capillaries, so that extravasation occurs—sometimes into the substance of organs. The effects upon the respiratory and nervous systems, and on blood-pressure, depend upon antagonistic factors. Death may occur through the paralysis of the respiratory centers, or cardiac paralysis, or hæmorrhage in the medulla, or from the widespread destruction of the red blood-corpuscles. The authors conclude that, because of the proteid nature of the venom and its close relation in composition to the blood, it is almost futile to look for a chemical antidote to it—for what would destroy the poison would have a similar action on the blood itself. A physiological antagonist, rather than a chemical antidote, should be sought for.

Dr. Dudley Buxton describes the effects of the inhalation of nitrous oxide on the mammalian organism as: 1, a condition of anæsthesia; 2, an emotional state, provoking a sensation of exhilaration; 3, modifications of the respiratory, and 4, of the circulatory systems; and 5, muscular movements, which may be classed as rigidity and jactitation. The anæsthesia produced by nitrous oxide is not dependent upon analgesia, or loss of sensation of painful impressions of the sensory end-organs, such as is produced by cocaine, etc., or upon failure of the conducting sensory nerves, for sensation is retained until the perceptive powers themselves cease to receive; moreover, there is immediately anterior to the loss of consciousness a hyperæsthetic stage, whence it may be concluded that the nerve-centers are acted upon. The heart's action appears to be but little interfered with. The dose of nitrous oxide required to produce insensibility varies considerably in different persons; and this fact supports the view that a specific action is exerted upon the nerve-centers.

Considerable additions have been made to our knowledge of the chemical products of the action of bacteria upon the animal body, called ptomaines. The composition of the best known of them, cadaverine, is shown by Dr. Ladenburg to be identical with artificially prepared penta-methylene-diamine. Dr. Bocklish has published the results of his researches upon the products of the action of Finkler's bacillus, *Vibrio proteus*, upon sterilized flesh. They show that this bacillus decomposes flesh with the formation of the alkaloid cadaverine, which is non-poisonous, and ammonia. But in repeating his experiments in presence of the ordinary putrefactive germs in addition to the Finkler bacilli, the author made the remarkable discovery that an entirely different base, methyl-guanidine, of intensely poisonous properties, was the chief product. Hence the symptoms of particular diseases may be due to the poisonous alkaloids formed by the joint action of specific bacilli and ordinary putrefaction germs. Bocklisch made several analyses of the cadaverine which he obtained in the first series of experiments from the action of pure cultivations of the *Vibrio proteus*, and showed that its hydrochloride forms a crystalline compound with mercuric chloride; and as this differed somewhat from the composition formerly assigned to the artificial preparation by Ladenburg the subject was involved in some doubt. But Ladenburg has made fresh and purer preparations of his penta-methylene-diamine, and finds that its compound with mercuric chloride has precisely the composition assigned to the double chloride of mercury and cadaverine by Bocklisch. Hence cadaverine is conclusively proved to be none other than penta-methylene-diamine, and consequently must be added to the list of products of animal life which have been synthesized. The formation of these alkaloids, during disease or after death, has a most important bearing upon the treatment of cases of suspected poisoning, inasmuch as, whether poisonous or not, their reactions differ very little from those of the deadly alkaloids; and in the interest of justice it is to be hoped that our knowledge respecting them may soon be rendered as complete as possible.

The experiments of M. Dumoulin upon the poisonous properties of the salts of copper indicate that these qualities have been exaggerated. Doses of from 62 to 93 grains of the sulphate were administered to rabbits and dogs without serious results. The subacetate (verdigris) caused vomiting at first, but the animals soon became used to it. The carbonate, oxide, and oleopalmitate also gave negative results. One animal was cured of impetigo by the administration of the copper salt, and the remedy was afterward successfully applied to children for scrofulous and skin diseases.

POLO. Since the introduction of the English equestrian game of polo in the United States, a new game has been evolved from it, entitled "polo," which is played exclusively in the roller-skating rinks of the country. Like lacrosse this skating game of polo is very similar to the English sports of "hockey" and "shinny,"—that is, they are all based upon the same plan of making the capture of "goals" the object in view of the contesting sides of the game. Unlike the old British sports of golf, hockey, shinny, and foot-ball, the new rink game of polo has an American authorship attached to it, which greatly adds to its chances for popularity. Roller-skating is a distinctively American sport, and rink polo belongs to roller-skating. In taking the title of "polo" from the English equestrian game of that name, it may be said that that is the only English part of the game which has been naturalized, as it were. Polo proper can never become a popular sport in this country, as it is far too expensive to be indulged in except by the wealthy, and only by those of that class who excel as equestrians. On the other hand, what we may rightly call the American game of polo bids fair to out-rank all the older sports of its kind in American public favor, judging from its rapid growth within the past three years. The origin of this American skating game illustrates a national characteristic of our people, and that is their peculiar *penchant* for adapting all sports and pastimes to the demands of the period; and for Americanizing games that, in their original form, do not suit our progressive ideas. The English equestrian game of polo was introduced to the fashionable summer residents of Newport, R. I., about the same time that a *furore* for roller-skating set in, and when the English game became somewhat familiar to the Newport public, the idea occurred to a few of the skaters of the town that it would be a good game to play, in a modified form, on roller-skates. The experiment was tried, and it proved so successful that within a year the new game was played at all the skating-rinks in the Eastern States, but especially so at the rinks of Boston and Providence. During the decade following the introduction of polo on skates in Newport in 1874, the new game, greatly improved in its details and rules, became the established skating-rink sport, and not long afterwards it began to flourish to a still greater extent under the auspices of a league of polo clubs, the first authorized code of playing rules emanating from the New England League. Of course, the game, in its original form, as played at Newport, was governed by rules somewhat crude and incomplete; but the materials then used in the game—comprising a comparatively light ball and light sticks —were far better adapted for the development of skillful strategy in playing the game than were the large heavy ball and heavy sticks that subsequently came into use, which until recently formed a serious barrier to the progress of the new game in popularity, the polo of 1883 and 1884 proving to be a decidedly rough and dangerous sport, not to mention its great tendency to promote disputes among the clubs. But these difficulties were partially removed through the medium of the more perfect code of rules adopted by the Massachusetts League in 1885, which tended to rid the game of most of its objectionable features.

How the Game is Played.—The game of polo is played by twelve men, six on each side, though it can be played by ten on a side. One player of the six on a side guards the goal, while two others—"point" and "cover point"—assist him, and the other three form the attacking force as "rushers." The referee governs the contest, he calling "play" and "time" when the game is begun or suspended, and also deciding what constitutes foul play. The ball is placed in the center, and at the referee's call the contesting sides strive to get possession of it and force it into their opponents' goal, in which case they win a game, and so many won games constitute a match, such as best two out of three goals, or best three out of five. The goal is in the form of a net cage, which retains possession of the ball the moment it passes the entrance to the cage. By this means all dispute in regard to the passage of the ball between goal-posts is removed. The ball used in the game is made of cork and yarn, and is covered with a coating of rubber. It weighs from four to five ounces, and is from eight to nine inches in circumference. The polo-stick weighs from ten to twelve ounces, and measures from three to four feet in length. It is "foul" play whenever a player strikes or stops the ball while any part of his person touches the floor of the rink; or if he touches the ball with his hands or arms, or kick the ball with his foot or skate, or if he strike down the stick of an opposing player, or if he trips or strikes an opponent, or if he runs into his opponent's goal. The goal-keeper, however, may defend his goal by kicking the ball away with his skate. Three fouls give a goal to the opposite side.

PORPOISE-HUNTING.—The abundance of the common porpoise, variously known as "puffer," "herring hog," "snuffer," and "snuffing pig," has from the earliest times tempted fishermen to pursue and capture him for profit; but his habits are so uncertain, his strength, speed, and intelligence so great, that until recently attempts to establish a successful business have failed. The porpoise is hunted for his hide, which, when properly cured, makes perhaps the most durable of leathers for shoe-uppers, and lacings, and for harness. Like his larger cousins of the whale tribe, he is covered with "blubber" or fat, which yields three to eight gallons of excellent oil for each porpoise. This quantity of oil is greatly exceeded in the larger species of the family. The common porpoise rarely grows larger than seven feet long, while the white whale of the St. Lawrence attains fourteen to sixteen feet in length, and often weighs from 700 to 1,000 pounds. The Indians of the North Atlantic coast were the first to hunt porpoises, and to this day the survivors of the Passamaquoddy tribes along the coasts of Maine and Nova Scotia keep up the practice, fire-arms having for the most part taken the place of the aboriginal bow and spear. Two Indians put out to sea in a birch canoe, and on reaching the feeding-grounds one of them stands up in the bow and fires at or spears the game as it rises to "blow." To be a successful hunter, especially in the winter season along that tempestuous coast, calls for a high degree of daring and coolness. Yet these Indians venture out in their bark canoes in almost any weather, and handle them with wonderful dexterity. A good hunter counts 200 porpoises a fair season's work, as this may represent to him several hundred dollars.

After being shot or harpooned, the porpoise is taken on board the canoe, and when a full cargo is obtained they are taken ashore, and stripped of their fat. At intervals along the beaches frequented by the hunters there are gallows-like structures from which the try-pots are suspended over fires built within circles of stones. The stones become hot, and so economize fuel in the later stages of the process. Pure porpoise-oil is worth from 90 cents to $1 a gallon; but the arts of civilization are not wholly unknown to the coast Indians, and the product is sometimes adulterated with seal-oil. Until recently the oil was largely used by the light-houses, being without offensive smell and retaining its fluidity even in cold weather. From the head is obtained a small quantity of very superior lubricant, known to commerce as "porpoise-jaw oil," which is much sought for by watch-makers and others requiring a perfect lubricant. The aboriginal method of trying out this precious head-oil is to hang up the jaws in the sun, with a receptacle underneath, into which the oil slowly drips. Porpoise-meat is used for food by the Indians, and fishermen are often ready to secure a change of diet by trading fresh fish for it.

These slow aboriginal methods do not suit the more grasping Anglo-Saxon, and from the earliest settlement of the country attempts have

A PORPOISE.

been made to secure the porpoises in large numbers. The first Swedish settlers along Delaware Bay engaged to some extent in porpoise-hunting. Certain portions of the coast seem to offer especial attractions to porpoises. This is true of the eastern coast of Long Island, of Cape May, and of the coast of North Carolina. Seines of great length and about twenty-five feet deep are made of twine or small rope about one fourth of an inch in diameter, and with meshes about one foot square. The intelligence and wariness of the porpoise are such that the greatest caution has to be exercised in surrounding a "school" on the feeding-grounds. The seine is sometimes cast from a silently-running steam-launch, or from a seine-boat pulled with muffled oars, or perhaps from both working together. After the school is surrounded the greatest caution has to be exercised, because if once the quarry starts for the open sea, no net can hold them. A smaller and still stronger net is therefore provided, and a few porpoises at a time are separated from the main school and captured, hauled ashore by main strength, or harpooned, as may be most convenient. The oil is tried out on ship-board or in rough sheds on the beach, special care being taken to secure every drop of the precious head-oil. The hides are salted and sent north to be cured. An excellent fertilizer has been made from the refuse of the porpoise after the hide and the blubber have been removed, and an attempt has been made, not attended as yet with any marked success, to introduce the preserved flesh as an article of food. The hunting season off Cape Hatteras begins in November and ends in the latter part of May. About 2,000 porpoises are reported so have been captured during a single season.

Recent researches and observations have thrown new light upon the history and habits of the different species. Whales, porpoises, and seals were reckoned as fish in the early days, and were permitted for Lenten diet; but after the 14th century they were pronounced by royal edict too dainty a dish for the million, and even in Elizabeth's time they were among the *pisces regales.* The tongue was, and indeed is still in some quarters, considered an especial dainty. In Roger's "History of Agriculture and Prices in England," A. D. 1200 to 1582, it is said that "porpoise was much bought. The Duke of Bucks gave 7s 10d for a quarter of one in 1444, while Sion Abbey paid 10s for the same delicacy in 1502. In 1530–'33, at Durham, their price varied from 15s to 6s 8d; in 1531, from 4s to 13s; in 1532, 9s; in 1533 one whole porpoise cost 1s 8d." In "Via Recta ad Vitam Longam" (1650) it is said that "the tunie, porpoise, and such like great bestial fish are of very hard digestion, noisome to stomach, of a very gross excremental and naughty juice," from which it appears either that the digestive powers of the English race had deteriorated in the interim or else that public opinion was all wrong two hundred years before. Considered as variants from the mammalian type found in seals, having mere paddles for hind legs, it is found that porpoises retain only a remnant of the hip-girdle. The neck has disappeared altogether, and the vertebræ of that region are united in a mass. The external ear and the hairy coat have disappeared, but in the young of all the species there is a trace of whiskers, and often an ear-like appendage that disappears with maturer years.

Common or harbor porpoises are found all along both coasts of North America, varying slightly in the Atlantic and the Pacific Ocean. They ascend rivers far above brackish water, but do not venture far off soundings. The species encountered at sea are distinct. Speci-

mens of the white whale have been captured as far south as Cape Cod, but their recognized habitat is north of the Bay of Fundy. The brain of all porpoises is far more highly developed than that of true fishes, and their behavior in captivity shows that they are possessed of an interesting degree of intelligence. Some of the European species, which is closely allied to, if not identical with, that of the American coast, have for several years been domesticated in the Aquarium at Brighton, England, and in this country a large specimen of the white whale was exhibited for a time in the New York Aquarium.

PORTUGAL, a constitutional monarchy in southwestern Europe. The *carta de ley*, or fundamental law, was accorded by Dom Pedro IV in 1826, and revised in 1852, and again in 1885 by the Cortes. The Cortes, or Representative Assembly, is composed of a Chamber of Peers and a Chamber of Deputies. The law of July 24, 1885, provides for the gradual extinction of hereditary peerages. The King will appoint life-peers, but can only appoint one for every three vacancies that occur until their number is reduced to 100, after which a new peer will be nominated to fill every vacancy. The hereditary peers now living, and their immediate successors, will continue to have seats in the Chamber. Princes of the blood royal and the 12 bishops of the Continental dioceses are official members. There will be 50 elective peers, who must be chosen from the class from which the King may select life-members under the law of May 3, 1878. Of these, 5 are to be chosen by delegates of the University of Coimbra and certain scientific bodies, 4 by delegates of the city of Lisbon, 3 by delegates of Oporto, and 2 each by delegates from 19 other districts. The members of the Chamber of Deputies are elected directly by the citizens of full age who can read or write and possess an income of 100 milreis, and by heads of families. The King has the right of veto, but a vetoed act that is passed again by both houses becomes law. The reigning King is Luis I, born Oct. 31, 1838. The heir-apparent is Prince Carlos, Duke of Braganza, born Sept. 28, 1863. The Cabinet, constituted Feb. 20, 1886, is composed of the following ministers: President of the Council and Minister of the Interior, Lucianno de Castro Pereira Corte Real; Minister of Justice, F. A. da Veiga Beirão; Minister of Public Works, E. J. Navarro; Minister of Finance, M. Cyrillo de Carvalho; Minister of Foreign Affairs and Minister of Marine and the Colonies, *ad interim,* H. de Barros Gomes; Minister of War, Viscount de San Januario.

Area and Population.—The area of Continental Portugal, according to the latest calculations of the geodetic survey, is 88,872 square kilometres; its population in 1881 was 4,306,554. The Azores have an area of 2,388 square kilometres, and contained 269,401 inhabitants in 1881, while the island of Madeira, with an area of 815 square kilometres, had a population of 132,223 persons, making the area of the islands 3,203 square kilometres, and their population 401,624 persons.

Finances.—The revenue is estimated in the budget for 1887-'88 at 34,409,891 milreis, of which sum 6,290,410 milreis are derived from the land-tax, licenses, and other direct imposts, 3,341,700 milreis from registration duties and stamped paper, 18,173,110 milreis from customs and excise duties, 1,138,000 from supplemental imposts under the law of April 27, 1882, and 3,528,613 milreis from national property, while 1,938,058 milreis are *recettes d'ordre*. The total expenditure is estimated at 39,307,316 milreis, the charge of the public debt being 14,886,963 milreis, the disbursements of the Ministry of Finance 8,087,717 milreis, of the Ministry of the Interior 2,020,-527 milreis, of the Ministry of Justice and Worship 727,697 milreis, of the Ministry of War 4,963,583 milreis, of the Ministry of Marine and the Colonies 2,013,563 milreis, of the Ministry of Foreign Affairs 332,685 milreis, of the Ministry of Public Works 4,074,581 milreis, extraordinary expenditure 2,200,000 milreis.

The public debt on June 30, 1886, amounted to 490,301,599 milreis, consisting of internal 3-per-cent. bonds of the amount of 261,694,054 milreis, and a sterling loan amounting to 228,-607,545 milreis. The interest to be paid during the financial year 1887-'88 is 14,044,777 milreis, while 5,389,106 milreis of the interest remains unpaid, and is added to the debt. The Government has proposed the optional conversion of the perpetual exterior debt into redeemable obligations, and of the internal debt, as far as the financial condition will allow, into annuities.

The Army.—By virtue of the military law of 1884 the army will consist of 24 regiments of infantry, 12 regiments of chasseurs, 10 regiments of cavalry, 3 regiments of mounted artillery, 1 brigade of mountain artillery, 1 regiment and 4 companies of garrison artillery, and 1 regiment of engineers. The time of service is 12 years, of which 3 are spent in the active army and 5 in the first and 4 in the second reserves. The war effective, as fixed by the budget of 1886, was 3,862 officers and 125,057 men, with 7,821 horses, 4,870 mules, and 264 guns. The peace establishment on Aug. 30, 1887, consisted of 1,952 officers and 23,566 men, with 2,243 horses. Including the municipal guard and the fiscal guards, the total strength was 32,120 officers and men. This does not include the colonial troops, consisting of a regiment of infantry, numbering 1,193 officers and men, and native troops of the first line, 7,683 in number, besides the first and second native reserves.

The Navy.—The naval forces include 1 iron-clad corvette, 6 other cruisers, 17 gun-boats, 7 armed steamers, and 4 torpedo-boats.

The Post-Office.—The number of letters carried in the mails during the year 1885 was 20,104,526 ; of postal cards, 2,289,600 ; of journals and circulars, 16,418,660.

Railroads.—There were 1,674 kilometres of railroad in the principal lines in September, 1887, while 480 kilometres were in process of construction ; and in the subsidiary lines there were 144 kilometres in operation and 22 kilometres under way.

Telegraphs.—The length of the state lines at the end of 1884 was 4,978 kilometres ; the length of wires, 11,732 kilometres. The number of paid messages sent during the year was 460,841, exclusive of 87,192 foreign dispatches and 159,771 in transit ; the number of messages exempt from the tax was 506,607, 432,-265 were in transit and 74,342 official. The receipts for 1884 were 220,684,941 reis.

Commerce.—The imports and exports of the various classes of commodities and the total value of the foreign commerce in 1886 were as follow, the values being given in milreis :

CLASSES OF ARTICLES.	Imports.	Exports.
Cereals	5,092,000	258,000
Vegetables and fruits	1,013,000	1,564,000
Colonial produce	3,346,000	93,000
Wines and liquors	165,000	16,956,000
Animals and animal food-products	5,313,000	2,220,000
Minerals	2,699,000	215,000
Metals	11,658,000	159,000
Hides and leather	3,272,000	192,000
Timber	1,290,000	2,757,000
Pottery and glass	345,000	16,000
Textiles and textile materials	6,364,000	134,000
Various manufactures	4,722,000	366,000
Drugs, etc	582,000	388,000
Total	46,594,000	25,334,000

Navigation.—The number of sailing-vessels entered at the ports of the kingdom in 1886 was 2,400, of 462,000 tons ; and the number of steamers was 3,272, of 3,014,000 tons ; not including 4,510 sailing-vessels, of 285,000 tons, and 1,122 steamers, of 595,000 tons, that were engaged in the coasting trade. The sailing-vessels employed in ocean commerce that were cleared numbered 2,546, of 474,000 tons ; the steamers, 3,252, of 2,975,000 tons. The merchant navy in 1886 consisted of 36 steamers, of an aggregate burden of 16,583 cubic metres, and 433 sailing-vessels, of 67,515 cubic metres, not including coasting vessels.

Dissolution of the Cortes.—The Chamber of Deputies on January 4, 1887, elected a member of the Opposition as its president. In consequence of this action the Chamber and the elective portion of the House of Peers were dissolved on January 6. The new Chamber was elected on February 27, and elections for the House of Peers were held in March. The new Cortes, in which the ministry have a strong majority, met on April 7. The Conservative minority enacted violent scenes in the Chamber. On May 8 a deputy, who was a lieutenant-colonel of marines, named Ferriera d'Almeida, actually assaulted the Minister of Marine, Henrique de Macedo, who resigned his post in consequence, while the officer was arrested and confined on board a vessel-of-war for his act of insubordination. He was tried before the House of Peers in August, and was sentenced to four months' imprisonment. The session was closed on August 18 after the passage of a new military bill and a bill for the taxation of tobacco. The Cortes also approved treaties with France and Germany for the delimitation of the territories of the three powers in Africa.

Colonies. — The Portuguese possessions in Africa, comprising the Cape Verde Islands, Bissao, and other stations on the Guinea coast, Prince's Island and St. Thomas, Ajuda, Angola, and Mozambique, have an aggregate area of 1,805,550 square kilometres, and about 4,136,700 inhabitants. The possessions in Asia and Oceanica, comprising Goa in India, Daman and Diu, Timor, and other islands in the Indian Archipelago, and Macao off the coast of China, are 16,666 square kilometres in extent, and have 848,500 inhabitants. The colonial budget for 1885–'86 makes the revenues of all the colonies 2,746,663 milreis, and the expenditures 3,405,936 milreis. There were 62 kilometres of railroad in India, while 20 kilometres were under construction and 82 kilometres authorized. In Angola 410 kilometres were authorized, and in Mozambique 152.

A protocol that was signed at Lisbon in 1887 contains a preliminary arrangement or basis of a treaty, by which China agrees to cede full rights of sovereignty over Macao to Portugal, the latter agreeing on her side to aid the Chinese custom-house authorities in the prevention of smuggling from Macao by an arrangement similar to that made with the British in respect to Hong-Kong. For two centuries Portugal has been in full possession of Macao, but has recognized Chinese suzerainty by the payment of an annual tribute of 500 taels until about 1850, when she refused to continue the payments. There was much opposition at Pekin to the proposed treaty, as is invariably the case in regard to the abandonment of any claims of China to suzerain rights. A treaty was at last concluded at Pekin.

In the beginning of March, 1887, Lieut. Maia, the governor of the Island of Timor, was murdered by the natives, and gunboats were sent from Macao to restore order. After the Sultan of Zanzibar had taken possession of Tungi Bay, and his rights to that district had received recognition from England and Germany, Portugal asserted a claim to the territory. The Portuguese squadron and a detachment of troops were sent from Mozambique, which captured the Sultan's posts. The corvette "Affonso d'Albuquerque" and the gunboat "Douro" on February 15, 1887, bombarded the fortress of Tungi and the village of Massingane, after which two detachments of infantry were landed, which took possession of the fortress, capturing flags and three guns, and burned the village. The natives of Mozambique, taking advantage of the absence of the military forces, revolted against the Portuguese authority, and

sacked several villages on the mainland opposite the town of Mozambique.

In April the Portuguese garrison in Tungi was attacked and driven out by the Sultan's former governor, who raised the flag of Zanzibar. Negotiations were subsequently entered upon for the delimitation of the territories of Portugal and Zanzibar, but the Sultan and the Portuguese commissioners failed to come to an agreement. The recommendation of England and Germany that the dispute should be referred to the King of the Netherlands for arbitration was not accepted. The Sultan subsequently consented to abide by the decision of a conference of the English, German, and Portuguese representatives that was held at Lisbon in October.

Portuguese political agents negotiated for a protectorate over the kingdom of Dahomey, and supposed that they had secured a treaty to that effect. When the King of Dahomey heard of it in June, he not only denied that he had accepted a protectorate, but gave orders to have every Portuguese settler in his dominions arrested.

POSTAL FACILITIES, RECENT IMPROVEMENTS IN. A fully equipped postal-car, traveling at the rate of forty miles an hour, with a full complement of clerks to receive and distribute the mail *en route*, is the best illustration of the advancement made in recent years in postal progress. The mails are no longer taken by the railways as so much freight, to be handled only at certain specified "distributing-offices," when, after the customary sorting and resorting, they were again turned into freight and boxed up until the destination was reached. The first railway-post-office journey in England was made on July 1, 1887, on the completion of the line between Liverpool and Birmingham. Although its success was demonstrated at once, nothing was done in the United States until 1860, when a vague experimental effort was made to run a mail-train from New York to Boston, *via* Hartford and Springfield, by which the southern mails arriving in New York could be forwarded promptly instead of lying over in New York until the following day. In 1861 similar facilities were secured on the railway between New York and Washington, and ten years afterward a plan was suggested by Col. George B. Armstrong, at that time assistant postmaster at Chicago, for putting post-office cars on the principal railroads, in which mails could be made up by clerks, while in transit, for offices at the termini and along the lines. The first experiment on Col. Armstrong's plan was made on the route between Chicago and Clinton on the morning of Aug. 28, 1864. The initial trip proving successful, the work was enlarged by the distribution of mail-matter at stations along the route. This was the inauguration proper of the railway-post-office system in the United States in its present form. and differs materially from the plan proposed and partially carried into execution in 1860. In October, 1864, a post-office car was used between New York and the National capital. During November, the Chicago-Davenport, Ia., and the Chicago-Dunleith, Ill., lines were equipped. On Jan. 17, 1865, the Chicago-Burlington, and Galesburg-Quincy lines were established. On May 22, the Philadelphia-Pittsburg was established. During the summer all the principal railway lines leading out of Chicago were fitted with post-offices on wheels. The New York Central came next, and ran postal-cars between New York, Albany, and Buffalo. Aside from the two routes above specified, no new lines were established in the eastern part of the country for two years. The growth of the project was at the West, and it is on the Western lines that the railway post-office is .to be found in its completest form. The United States postal-car is divided into sections, and pigeon-holed and pouched and labeled to its fullest extent. The car has a head clerk and a corps of assistants, each one with specific duties. Skilled workers only are employed, and accuracy of eye and hand, and steady nerves are all-important. Stops are not made at way-stations, but as the express goes by, and a pouch containing the mail for that station is hurled out with force enough to carry it beyond the suck of the whirlwind created by the speeding train, a "catcher" is let down, and a sack of mail, hanging like an hour-glass from the arm of the gibbet-like mail-crane near the track, is deftly caught and whirled within the door, and the assorting of the new lot of matter received is added to the work already in progress. The catcher in use on the railways is known as "Ward's Catcher." It consists simply of a large V-shaped iron, fastened securely to the inner part of the car, and controlled by a strong handle fitted at right angles near the apex. One arm of the V is longer than the other, and when not in use, the V hangs close against the side of the car-door. The mail-pouch to be secured is tied in hour-glass form and hung on a light "mail-crane" built near the track, and so adjusted as to be readily removed. An approach to a hanging pouch is signalled to the postal-car by the engineer with a peculiar whistle, when the attendant seizes the lever, the short arm of the catcher is turned in its bearings, the long arm projects from the side of the car at an acute angle, and the pouch is caught with a jerk around the middle, the lever turned, and the pouch secured. The catcher was first used on the Baltimore-Washington line in 1865, and worked satisfactorily from the outset. In the British postal-cars a net is attached to the side, which, by some complicated mechanism, is supposed to open out and secure the pouches, but it misses frequently.

Prior to July 1, 1879, there was no separate appropriation for railway post-office cars, the cost for that branch of the service being included with the cost of transportation; but so great and rapid was its growth, that appropriations for steadily increasing amounts were annually made, until $1,924,793 was required in 1886. The great benefit that has accrued from the introduction of the railway postal service is shown by the fact that at the close of the fiscal year ending June 30, 1886, there were 871 railway post-office lines, 4,512 railway clerks, 485 whole cars, and 1,769 apartment cars. During the year the total number of letters and pieces of ordinary mail matter handled amounted to 5,329,521,475 pieces. To this must be added 15,525,998 registered packages, and 798,571 through registered pouches, making a total of 5,845,846,044 pieces, large and small, handled while the trains were moving and at high speed.

Distributing Post-Offices.—In the days of stage-coach and steamer traffic, the necessity for prominent points where the mail for given geographical areas could be reassorted, was obvious. Central cities were selected, and all mail for a given section was sent to the main office, where the reassorting was done. For all mail thus handled and passing through the office, a commission of 5 per cent. (afterward increased to 7 per cent., and then to 12½) was paid to the postmaster. The system led to great abuses. For instance, a package of 100 letters, on which the postage amounted to $3, sent from towns in Ohio and destined for New England, was first sent to Pittsburg for distribution. They were subject to the commission of 12½ per cent., as well as delay, and when the package reached New York, it was subject to a second commission and delay, and when it reached Boston, to a third, thus costing in the way of commission alone, the sum of $2.25 out of the original $3. With the advent of the railway post-office a remedy was found, and the legend "D. P. O." was officially superseded by another legend, "Dis.," when distributing post-offices disappeared, Jan. 26, 1880.

Distribution.—In order to facilitate the distribution of large quantities of mail-matter, especially that intended for distant points, General Superintendent George S. Bangs, in 1871, devised the method of distributing the mail by "States." In the accomplishment of this desirable object, the mail for each entire State is made up by itself, and dispatched direct to the railway post-office line that can dispose of it *en route*. For example, the mail for West Virginia would be distributed in the New York-Washington railway post-office car; the mail for Mississippi in the Cairo-New Orleans railway post-office car. So convenient had this system proved that in 1872 Mr. Bangs sent a special agent to the principal New York publishers and sought their co-operation in the handling of newspaper mail. This was cheerfully given in the majority of instances, though it frequently caused the inconvenience of an entire change in the system of bookkeeping. The enormous newspaper mail is now made up in the publishers' offices, special bags being provided, and the mail weighed in bulk.

Nearly 50 per cent. of the newspaper mail passes through the office with the bags unopened until they reach their appropriate line.

The Fast Mail of 1875.—The crowning act of Mr. Bangs's administration was the fast mail in 1875. The first equipment was twenty cars, four on a train, and the trains were composed exclusively of mail-cars. The terminal points were New York and Chicago, and the run was made in 26 hours and 40 minutes, over the New York Central. On the same day a limited mail between the same points was established over the line of the Pennsylvania Central, which left New York 15 minutes later. Connections were made with roads running in every direction, so that every State and Territory felt the benefit. The existence of the fast mail and the limited mail was terminated by the action of Congress in the reduction of 10 per cent. in the pay of all railway companies, and after a life of ten months and six days it became a thing of the past. But it has been reproduced in the most perfect form yet attainable in the present railway post-office system.

Stamped Envelopes.—In 1823 a Swedish artillery officer, Lieut. Frekenbar, petitioned the Chamber of Nobles to propose to the Government to issue stamped paper, specially destined to serve as envelopes for letters. The proposition, duly recorded on the minutes of the Chamber for March 23 of that year, was favorably considered, on the ground that it would be convenient both to the public and to the post-office, but was finally rejected by a large majority. Stamped envelopes are now regarded almost as a necessity, and in the United States alone there were issued for the fiscal year 1886, no fewer than 354,008,100, having an aggregate value of $6,932,055.02. Those issued by the Government are of three qualities, and are made in sizes ranging from "small note," designated as No. 1, to "large baronial," designated as No. 11.

Special-Request Envelopes.—To facilitate the prompt return of undelivered matter, and avoid the trouble and expense of transmission to the Dead-Letter Office in Washington, and the opening of letters and parcels to learn the name of the sender, the Government adopted, in 1876, the plan of printing without charge on the upper left-hand corner of the envelope the name and address of the sender. This procedure was a convenience in two ways: if the postage was insufficient, the sender was notified; and if the letter was not duly delivered to the person addressed, it was returned directly to the sender. These envelopes were furnished in lots of not less than 500 each. In the first year after their adoption, 64,874,500 were issued, while by steady advances the number in 1886 had reached 152,742,250. These figures, however, give but a faint idea of the matter of "return," for the reason that the Government declines to put anything on the envelope besides the request and the address. Business men prefer to incur the extra

expense involved in printing a few additional words designating their calling, and the number of letters bearing a return mark is probably tenfold the figures given in the Postmaster-General's report.

Letter-Sheet Envelopes.—An effort was made by Postmaster-General Howe in 1882 for the introduction of a stamped sheet of paper that would combine letter and envelope in one, and a contract was attempted with the owner of one of the many patents known. The contractor failed to perform his part, and no steps were taken to provide the letter-sheet until October, 1884, when a contract was entered into with the United States Sealed Postal-Card Company, and a new article of postal stationery, combining a letter-sheet and a stamped envelope, was introduced and designated a "letter-sheet envelope." The issue was begun Aug. 18, 1886, and in three months nearly 3,000,000 were sold. The envelopes are furnished in separate sheets, or put up in pads or tablets of 25, 50, or 100. They are made of a single sheet of unruled white paper, with a writing surface of about $5\frac{1}{2}$ by 9 inches, and of such pattern as readily to suggest the manner in which they are to be used.

Reduction of Postage.—The charges on postage for first-class matter were in effect reduced by the act of March 3, 1885, which provided that on and after July 1 of that year, the rate should be two cents for each ounce or fraction of an ounce, instead of two cents for each half ounce. By the same act, newspaper postage was reduced from two cents a pound to one cent a pound, when issued direct from publishing-offices in bulk. When papers or other matter belonging to the second class are put into the mail by other than publishing-offices with their regular issue, the charges are one cent for each four ounces.

Stamp Agencies.—On March 1, 1884, to accommodate the public, agencies for the sale of stamps were established. The place usually selected is a drug-store or stationer's, where ladies and children can go to make purchases with perfect freedom. A contract is entered into between the Government and the individual, whereby a notice is to be displayed, and stamps, stamped envelopes, postal cards, and letter-sheet envelopes are to be had in any quantity desired, up to the limit of two dollars. The agent in turn receives the nominal sum of two dollars a month as salary, the Government considering that the indirect benefit accruing to him will further repay his trouble. Of these agencies there are one hundred in the city of New York, and they exist in about the same proportion in other cities.

Special Delivery.—On March 3, 1885, a stamp was authorized by Congress, which, when affixed to any letter or registered parcel, would require a delivery by special messenger, within the carrier-delivery limit of any free-delivery office, and within one mile of any other post-office specially designated, in advance of the regular delivery. On Oct. 1, 1886, the privileges of the system were extended to all post-offices in the United States, and covered all classes of mail-matter. Postmasters open all mails at once upon their arrival, and immediately separate the matter bearing special-delivery stamps, and stamp or write on the envelope or wrapper the name of the office, and the day and hour when the matter arrived. Next, the matter is numbered, and entered according to number in a record, after which it must be delivered without loss of time. The same attention is given to drop or local matter bearing special-delivery stamps, from the time it is deposited in the post-office.

Matter held for Postage.—An important change in the mode of treating held-for-postage matter was made on May 11, 1882, by which, instead of its being sent to the Dead-Letter Office, the postmaster at the office where received at once notifies the writer by a card delivered through the mail, of the existence of the letter and the deficiency, in order that the proper amount may be forwarded and the letter sent on its way. The system has resulted in a material reduction of letters and parcels sent to the Dead-Letter office. The plan was at first confined to the larger offices, but on May 19, 1883, an order was issued, going into effect on July 1 of that year, whereby it was put into operation throughout the United States.

Money-Orders.—The postal money-order system is older than is generally supposed, having existed in one form or another since 1792. In its present form in England it dates from 1859, and there have been constant extensions and improvements since that time. As to certainty of payment in transmission, there seems to be no question. The applicant for a money-order fills up a small blank form, gives it, with the proper amount of money plus the fee, to the clerk, receives his order, and mails it to his correspondent. The post-office sends to the postmaster at the paying station an "advice note" or "advice letter," which contains a few words of information known only to the immediate persons interested, to wit, the name of the sender and his address. The payee receives his letter, containing the required order in which the amount is named, from his correspondent, and presents it at the money-order department of the post-office. One or two questions are asked, and if they are answered according to the tenor of the "advice letter," and the applicant is properly identified, the money is paid. In 1859 when the system was established in Great Britain, Mr. Robert B. Minturn, of New York, was in Europe and observed its workings. He satisfied himself that it would be a great boon to the United States, and securing the necessary blank forms, visited the Postmaster-General on his return. After a consultation on the subject, the Postmaster-General admitted the value of the system, but said "it was not feasible on account of the want of ability of postmasters."

Postal Notes.—One of the outgrowths of the money-order system, as well as a substitute for fractional currency produced by the exigencies of the civil war, is the postal note. Its aim is the utmost convenience in the payment of sums of less than $5 through the agency of the mails. The law by which the postal note was authorized was signed by the President March 3, 1883, and the issue was begun simultaneously at all money-order officers on Sept. 3, 1883. The postal note was not designed to take the place of the money-order. In the money-order the Government is responsible for the payment to the true payee, while in the case of the postal note it assumes no responsibility whatever, but pays the money to the holder, who by his possession of it is *prima facia* owner. A note is issued for any sum from one cent to $4.99 inclusive, and the uniform fee is three cents. The postmaster who is called upon to issue a postal note enters in the body of the note the name of the office drawn upon, and the amount. In every instance he is required to write out the full number of dollars, but may insert figures for the number of cents; and his signature must be written, not stamped. With a plyer-punch the requisite figures are canceled, and the note is ready for the sender. The postmaster must also enter in the stub of his book the amount in figures, the date of issue, and the name of the money-order office drawn upon. On April 25, 1884, a circular was sent out by the post-office department, giving notice of a new design known as the coupon order, which was issued to supersede the note of 1883. The popularity of the postal note is shown by the following statement of its growth up to the end of the fiscal year, June 30, 1886.

FISCAL YEAR.	Number issued.	Value.
1884	3,689,287 (10 mos.)	$7,411,992 46
1885	5,058,257	9,996,274 87
1886	5,999,428	11,718,010 05

Post-Office Savings-Bank.—This institution has been greatly developed of late years in Great Britain and her colonies, and in Italy, but has not as yet been established in the United States. In Great Britain deposits are received of any sum not less than a shilling (25 cents), nor more than £30 ($150), in one year. Where the deposits amount to one pound ($5), interest is allowed at the rate of 2½ per cent. per annum. The late Postmaster-General of Great Britain, the Right Hon. Henry Fawcett, introduced in September, 1880, an improvement that consisted in giving to every applicant at any post-office in the United Kingdom, free of charge, blank forms upon which twelve penny-postage stamps could be affixed. Any person desiring to invest in a stamp, made his purchase, and when the card was full, it was re-receivable at any post-office savings-bank as a deposit of one shilling. The system of post-office savings depositories has been agitated for some years in the United States, but has taken no practical form.

Extension of the Registration Privilege.—Previous to Oct. 1, 1878, the registration system had been confined to letters and matter chargeable with first-class rates of postage. On that date it was extended to all classes of matter entitled to admission in the mails, at the uniform registration fee of ten cents a package. The fees of registration have always been greatly in excess of the cost of conducting the labor, and thus afforded an inducement for adding to the volume of business while adding nothing to the weight of the mails, and consequently nothing to the cost of transportation. The burden consists solely in giving and taking receipts and making the necessary records. It has proved a safe and regular means of transmitting small articles of value to remote points not reached by ordinary means of conveyance, and not least among its benefits to the public was the reduction to which it led in the rates of the express companies. In its present state it scarcely retains a vestige of the plan upon which it was originally founded. There has been developed the through-pouch system, introduced in 1875; the establishment of the brass-lock system on star routes; a combination of the sending and return letter bill; the adoption of the combined tag and envelope for inconveniently shaped parcels, containing a pocket for bill and receipt; and the adoption of a card form of registered bill and return receipt, thus greatly simplifying the labor.

Registered-Package Tag-Envelopes.—The ordinary registered-package envelope is useful for everything but irregularly shaped packages. Various expedients were considered with a view to supply a remedy, and resulted in the adoption in 1879 of a registered-package-tag envelope. It is a small envelope made of tough manilla, and only large enough to admit the registry bill and the return registry receipt. It is open at the top, and midway across is furnished with eyelets, through which it is fastened with twine to the package, thus becoming a tag. One side contains the address and registered number, the other the instructions and space for the record of transit. By its use the rewrapping of packages is entirely done away with, as well as the clumsy readjustment of the older style envelopes, which was required for their preservation.

The Combination Lock.—A new lock for through pouches was put into use on Jan. 1, 1882. It was fitted with a combination of numbers, the order of which was changed by turning the key. The pouch is billed at the dispatching office under a given number corresponding with the lock, and receipted for under this number, from point to point, until it reaches its destination. Any improper interference will be readily detected by a disagreement between the number on the lock and that on the bill, and the responsibility readily located.

Post-Office Equipments.—Post-office equipments gauged to given populations and requirements, have come into existence. Two large houses

have been established in the United States, and for prices ranging from $100 upward will send a complete outfit for a post-office, on the most approved principles, to any part of the country. This outfit consists of an entire room arranged in complete form and order with tables, call-boxes, lock-boxes, alphabetical cases for general-delivery letters, numbers, name clips, tags, stamps, inks, pads, scales, direction-plates, etc., and can be erected in the end or corner of a room or store, as occasion requires. They have become extremely popular, because of their attractiveness, and the ease with which they can be erected.

Post-Office Letter-Boxes.—One of the best systems of post-office boxes is that designed by Henry G. Pearson, postmaster of New York city. Though originally intended for the railway postal-car service, the boxes designed by him were quickly adopted, and have been used extensively, not only in postal-cars, but in post-offices throughout the United States. The peculiar feature of the invention is a wire bottom to the box. No dust can accumulate; the boxes are always neat and clean, which was never the case before; and a clerk looking for mail in an upper tier, can readily see through the wires whether the boxes have been properly cleared, without being obliged to stand on tiptoe, or climb up on the table. Prior to the introduction of metallic boxes in 1868, post-offices had used a wooden box or drawer with a lock. In that year an improvement was introduced by making a metal frame, to which was hinged a metal door. It was the invention of Linus Yale, Jr., and was first tested by Gen. Burt in the Boston post-office. The introduction was purely a private enterprise, but so great security was obtained that it came largely into use, and was finally adopted by the post-office department to the exclusion of all other styles. The first departure from the old style pigeon-hole set in a window-glass frame was also in the Boston post-office, where the pigeon-hole receptacle was fitted with a glass panel across the front, occupying about half the space. It was strengthened by two wire rods, fixed horizontally and parallel to each other, but an open space was left, through which a few robberies having been perpetrated, they were superseded by a metallic lattice work cast into the frame, covering the whole glass. This, in turn, was at a recent date improved by removing the metal work from the lower front altogether, and substituting heavy plate-glass.

The Silicate Tablet.—When bulky mail, either of papers, packages, or books, too large to be put into the ordinary box, is received, a little device has been provided whereby attention is called to the fact, and the article held in reserve in another receptacle, is procured. The idea was first put into practical use by a village postmaster in a small office in Indiana. His plan was to use old envelopes, on which he wrote the name of the person addressed, and the name of the article in hand. This crude card, on being presented, secured the delivery of the package or the book to the proper person. The idea was improved upon by Mr. Keating, of the Yale Lock Manufacturing Company, in 1880, and he produced a silicate card, the size of an ordinary envelope, ruled in blank, and labeled with the words: "Date," "Name," "Papers," "Packages," "Books," arranged in proper form. When a parcel is received, the date of reception is indicated, the name written in, and a figure placed under the appropriate heading. This card is then deposited in the letter-box.

Mail-Bags.—These are manufactured in different forms and colors, according to the service required, and are the result of a close study of the question by Postmaster-General Marshall Jewell and Thomas L. James, while the latter was postmaster in New York. For the convenience of the various services they devised the following classes: Leather mail-pouches, brown; leather horse mail-bags, brown; through registered mail-pouches, scarlet and white duck; mail-carrier pouch, striped blue and white duck; mail-sacks, made of jute canvas; mail-sacks, cotton canvas with thirteen blue stripes, for foreign mails; registered foreign mail-sacks, with twelve red stripes; coin-sacks, made of jute; inter-registered mail-sacks, with vermilion stripes.

Sealing Bags.—The system of sealing mail-bags originated in Great Britain about 1875. After the bag was bound and tied, the ends of the cord were passed through holes in a little block of wood, depressed into a cup hollowed in the side of the block, and the cup filled with wax, on which the seal was impressed. Any accident by which the wood became wet resulted in its swelling and injuring the seal. An improvement was made by Henry G. Pearson, of the New York city post-office, whereby a piece of tin about the size of a fifty-cent piece, but deeper, was struck out in form of a cup, and substituted for the wood. Its expense was merely nominal, and it was not patented. Its benefit, however, caused its rapid introduction in all directions.

Bag-Distributing Rack.—This is a light framework made of gas-piping, and fitted with hooks for holding mail-bags, designed for the rapid sorting of mail-matter. The rack is constructed with segments and angles, rather than circles, the obvious advantage being that the eye of the distributor more readily locates each bag, as there is too much sameness in a circle. The hooks are made of malleable iron, and adjust themselves to any sized sack or pouch, and by the movement of a finger-piece, the bag when filled can be removed without lifting. The racks are built singly or in sections, and mounted on casters, so as to be conveniently adjustable to any light or position. Their introduction has diminished much of the labor devolving on clerks, and the ease with which the bags can be reached enables a ready cor-

VOL. XXVII.—44 A

rection of any error in the throwing of letters or papers. This frame is the invention of Gen. La Rue Harrison, of Washington, D. C.

Lamp-post Boxes.—Since the octagonal form, which was held in place by having the lamp-post pass through it, was replaced by the square box with the rounded top, but little improvement has been made, except at a very recent date. In the box, as ordinarily constructed, a little door is opened at the side by being let down, and the mail removed. In 1881 a new box was devised by Henry G. Pearson, which opens at the front, the hinging of the door being at the side. At the bottom of the door is a shelf, which follows the door outward in the opening, and prevents the contents of the box from falling. Just within the door, at its upper edge is a series of compartments for holding checks, to be put by the collector in a small receptacle in the upper right-hand corner, which specify the time of the next gathering. These checks are renewed every evening, are gathered one at a time during the day, and serve as an indication of the visit of a collector to his box. On his return to the office from making his rounds, he is obliged to hang up his check on one of a series of numbered hooks, and any failure is immediately noticed by the absence of the check. Of these new boxes only 250 have been manufactured, and these are used exclusively in the down-town territory in New York city.

Canceling-Machines.—For five or six years an effort has been made, both in Europe and America, to perform automatically the canceling of stamps, and the stamping of the name of the post-office from which a letter is sent, but on account of the great diversity in shape and size, as well as thickness of envelopes, no automatic means has yet been found successful. Postal cards can be more readily massed and subjected to mechanical work than letters. Two instruments, designed by Mr. Leavitt of of Boston, were submitted for trial in the Boston post-office about 1880, and one invented by Leonard Tilton of Brooklyn is now on trial in the New York post-office, but up to the present date nothing superior to hand movement has been found except in the case of postal cards.

Postal Union.—An international convention, which originated in a meeting of delegates from different counties, held at Berne, Switzerland, in September and October, 1874. An agreement was entered into and signed Oct. 9, 1874, to go into effect July 1, 1875. The Congress included authorized representatives from the following countries, all of whom signed the treaty which was there formed and adopted: Germany, Austria, Hungary, Belgium, Denmark, Spain, Great Britain, Greece, Italy, Luxemburg, Norway, Sweden, Netherlands, Portugal, Roumania, Servia, Russia, Switzerland, Turkey, United States, and Egypt. The delegate from France declined to sign, the French Government not feeling itself at liberty to give in its adhesion to the Union until it had been approved by the National Assembly. France, however, afterward joined, with a stipulation that the treaty should not come into operation in France until Jan. 1, 1876. The substance of the Convention is as follows: The countries comprised will form a single postal territory, and letters not exceeding 15 grammes in weight will be forwarded from any part of it to another for 25 centimes. As a transitional measure and for fiscal and other reasons, any country may raise to 32 centimes or reduce to 20. Letters exceeding the weight specified to be charged for proportionally, and if not prepaid the rate to be doubled. Sea transportation of more than 300 marine miles of 1,852 metres each, to be charged an extra rate, not to be more than one half the original rate. Newspapers, samples, and prints or lithographic matter to be charged 7 centimes for 50 grammes, with the option for each country of raising to 11 centimes or lowering to 5, and like provisions as to sea transportation. The weight of samples limited to 250 grammes, and other packages to 1,000. The charge for registry not to exceed the inland rate of the country whence dispatched, and, if lost, a compensation of 50 francs will be paid, unless in the country where lost compensation be not allowed by the post-office. Stamps current in the country where posted to be used in all cases. Newspapers insufficiently stamped not to be forwarded, and letters charged double, minus the rate paid. On letters reforwarded no extra charge unless sent from one country to another, when the charge shall be the latter's internal rate. Official correspondence on postal business to be free, but in no other case. Mails to be forwarded by the quickest means of transport. Two francs per kilo for letters, and 25 centimes per kilo for newspapers, etc., will be paid to the state through which they pass, or, if transit be in excess of 570 metres, the rate may be doubled. The Government which arranges for transportation of letters by sea for more than 300 marine miles will have a right to be recouped but not to the extent of more than 5½ francs per kilo for letters, and 50 centimes per kilo for newspapers. The Indian mails and the railway mails between New York and San Francisco are not included in the treaty. Letters sent beyond the limits of the Union are liable to whatever additional rate is fixed by existing conventions. The central office of the Union was established at Berne, and to be conducted at the joint expense of the members. From this bureau a very interesting journal is issued every month, containing articles and notices of postal matters in all countries, printed in French, German, and English. The list of members of the Union has been added to since its organization, until now nearly every country in the world having postal facilities belongs to it. The treaty made provision for triennial Congresses to be held by appointment, and at these various modifica-

tions and improvements of the original Convention have been made. The last of these Congresses was held in Lisbon in 1885, and the design has been to hold one every five years.

PRESBYTERIANS. I. Presbyterian Church in the United States of America.—The following is the summary of the statistics of this Church as they were reported to the General Assembly in May, 1887. The statistics for 1886 and 1883 are appended for comparison, and to show the rate of growth of the Church:

ITEMS.	1883.	1886.	1887.
Synods	28	26	28
Presbyteries	182	199	201
Candidates	678	906	966
Licentiates	262	387	357
Ministers	5,216	5,546	5,654
Elders	18,968	21,212	21,885
Deacons	5,876	6,676	7,065
Churches	5,858	6,281	6,437
Added on examination....	32,182	51,177	58,567
Total communicants	600,695	666,909	698,827
No. of adults baptized	10,897	18,474	20,115
No. of infants baptized	17,728	21,616	28,470
Sabbath-school members..	668,765	743,518	771,899
CONTRIBUTIONS.			
Home Missions	$569,860	$760,947	$785,075
Foreign Missions	501,578	651,160	669,908
Education	187,254	97,954	117,900
Publication *	89,178	84,789	82,439
Church erection	150,891	243,016	286,690
Relief fund	75,249	99,479	110,942
Freedmen	84,012	91,373	108,406
Aid for colleges	......	119,730	127,627
Sustentation	21,275	21,750	26,419
General Assembly	46,847	60,812	62,380
Congregational	7,189,904	7,640,655	7,902,485
Miscellaneous	883,444	771,116	860,726
Total	$9,661,492	$10,592,331	$11,092,892

The resources for the year of the Board of Church Erection amounted to $102,830, and the full amount of its appropriations for churches and manses had been $104,816. The board had aided, by appropriations and the transmission of special gifts, in the erection of 186 churches and chapels and 47 manses.

The receipts of the Board of Relief were $136,323. Its permanent fund amounted to $365,588. The whole number of beneficiaries upon its roll was 532, consisting of 220 ministers, 284 widows of ministers, and 28 orphan families; besides which, 30 families had been accommodated at the Ministers' House, in Perth Amboy, N. J.

The twelve theological seminaries returned to the General Assembly an aggregate valuation of $3,082,994 in real estate; general endowment funds amounting to $3,169,631; other funds of $916,252; income of $272,076, with expenditures of $286,987; 55 professors and 18 other teachers, and 709 students.

The Board of Home Missions had received from all sources $653,456. An indebtedness of $21,681 was returned. Fourteen hundred and sixty-five missionaries had been employed, with 215 missionary teachers, who returned totals of 87,294 church members, 138,590 members of congregations, 2,182 Sabbath-schools with 142,-246 members, 3,974 baptisms of adults, 4,658

---

* To be known hereafter as Sabbath-school work.

baptisms of infants, 10,812 additions by profession of faith, and 175 churches and 392 Sabbath-schools organized during the year. The work of the board among the "exceptional populations" of the land—in which are included Indians, Mexicans, Mormons, and Southern whites —was represented by 83 schools, with 215 teachers. The Board of Education had aided 696 candidates, of whom 32 were Germans, 4 Bulgarians, 104 negroes, 1 Indian, 1 Mexican, 1 Corean, 1 Japanese, and 1 Brazilian. It was indebted to the amount of $15,000.

The Board of Publication had received $236,-637 from sales and $46,386 from contributions for missionary and Sabbath-school work. It had employed 51 colporteurs, and had published 18,266,618 copies of books and periodicals. The General Assembly ordered that it should hereafter be called the "Board of Publication and Sabbath-school Work," and directed that special prominence be given to the latter branch of its functions.

The receipts of the Board of Aid for Colleges had been $29,681. It had since its institution in 1883 aided 16 colleges and 19 academies, at which 2,950 students were attending, in the total sum of $70,139.

The Board of Missions for Freedmen had received $115,204. It had employed 280 preachers, catechists, and teachers, of whom 111 were ordained ministers, and 198 were colored. It returned 217 churches under its care with 15,880 communicants, and 220 Sunday-schools with 15,689 pupils. Twelve churches had been organized during the year, 1,923 members had been admitted on examination, and 744 adults and 879 children had been baptized. The 88 schools returned 195 teachers and 1,748 pupils, and 15 night-schools were attended by 98 pupils. The six colleges and schools, viz., Biddle University, Charlotte, N. C.; Scotia Seminary (for girls), Concord, N. C.; Wallingford Academy, Charleston, S. C.; Brainerd Institute, Chester, S. C.; Fairfield Institute, Winnsboro, S. C.; and Mary Allen Seminary (for girls), Crockett, Texas, returned an enrollment of 1,800 students.

The receipts of the Board of Foreign Missions had been $784,157, and its expenditures $780,-348. The missionary work had been carried on on the American Continent among eleven tribes of Indians and there resident Japanese and Chinese in the United States; in Mexico, Guatemala, the United States of Colombia, Brazil, and Chili; in Africa, among the inhabitants of Liberia and those of the Gaboon and Corisco region; and in Asia, in India, Siam, China, Japan, Corea, Persia, and Syria. The Board had also assisted evangelistic work in Roman Catholic countries in Europe through approved societies on the Continent. It had had in commission during the year 173 ordained missionaries, 30 laymen (mostly physicians), and 296 women; together with 184 native ordained ministers, 154 licentiates, and 756 Bible-readers, catechists, etc., making a total force in its em-

ploy of 1,543 laborers. Three hundred and ten organized churches were on the roll, with 21,420 communicants, of whom 2,791 had been added during the year. These churches reported contributions to the amount of $28,552. The aggregate attendance on schools of all grades was 23,329. The restrictions imposed by the French Government in the territory occupied by the Gaboon and Corisco Mission had become so severe as virtually to tie the hands of the missionaries and drive them from the field. After efforts to secure modifications of these restrictions had failed, the board had been constrained to take measures to transfer that mission to another evangelical body, and to secure foothold, if possible, within German territory.

General Assembly.—The General Assembly met in Omaha, Nebraska, May 19. The Rev. Joseph T. Smith, D. D., of Baltimore, Md., was chosen moderator. The following action was unanimously adopted respecting the relations of this church with the Presbyterian Church in the United States (Southern Presbyterian Church):

Whereas, The Synod of Missouri, in connection with the General Assembly of the Presbyterian Church of the United States of America, at its meeting in Fulton, Mo., in October, 1886, unanimously adopted the following paper and declaration of principles, to wit:

It has come to the knowledge of this Synod that many brethren belonging to the Synod in connection with the General Assembly of the Presbyterian Church in the United States, are under misapprehension with regard to the position of this body touching the spiritual or non-political character of the Church, and also touching the rights of individuals under the constitution of the Church. Owing to this misapprehension, and to the continued separation of the two Synods, many of the congregations on both sides are greatly weakened, our educational institutions are partially paralyzed, and all of our interests are seriously crippled. With the hope of healing for ever the breach between us, we once more affectionately extend the hand of fellowship to our separated brethren, and cheerfully reaffirm the action unanimously taken by the Synod in 1873, as follows:

(1) We affirm the spiritual character of the Church as separated from the kingdoms of this world, and having no other head but the Lord Jesus Christ, as entitled to speak only where he has spoken, and to legislate only where he has legislated; we also recognize the rights of conscience, and the right of respectful protest on the part of the humblest member of the Presbyterian household of faith, and declare the obligation of all our judicatories to be subject to the authority and to follow the doctrines of our ecclesiastical constitution.

(2) We distinctly and particularly affirm our belief in the following principles and statements found in our standards, to wit: "Synods and councils are to handle or conclude nothing but that which is ecclesiastical, and are not to intermeddle with civil affairs, which concern the commonwealth, unless by way of humble petition in cases extraordinary, or by way of advice for the satisfaction of conscience, if they be thereunto required by the civil magistrate" ("Confession of Faith," chap. 31, sec. 4). "That God alone is Lord of the conscience, and hath left it free from the doctrines and commandments of men, which are in anything contrary to his word, or beside it in matters of faith or worship. . . . that all church power, whether exercised by the body in general, or in the way of representation by delegated authority, is only ministerial

or declarative—that is to say, the Holy Scriptures are the only rule of faith and practice : that no church judicatory ought to pretend to make laws to bind the conscience in virtue of their own authority, and that all their decisions should be founded upon the revealed will of God ("Form of Government," chap. 1, secs. 1, 7); and that process against a Gospel minister should always be entered before the presbytery of which he is a member" ("Book of Discipline," chap. 5, sec. 2).

(8) In order to give the strongest possible ground of confidence to those of our brethren in the other Synods, who desire organic union with us, we do hereby express confidence in the soundness of doctrine, and in the Christian character of these brethren, and can not doubt that a more intimate communion would lead to the speedy removal of the barriers that now separate those of like precious faith, and to increase mutual affection and esteem.

Now, therefore, be it

Resolved, That this General Assembly heartily approves the action of the Synod of Missouri in adopting said paper, and the declaration of principles therein set forth.

A delegate was received bearing the fraternal greetings of the Council of the Protestant Episcopal Church in the Diocese of Nebraska to the General Assembly, to which the Assembly responded by a like fraternal greeting and the appointment of delegates to visit the Council. A letter was received from the Commission on Christian Unity of the General Convention of the Protestant Episcopal Church in the United States, transmitting a declaration of the House of Bishops on Christian Unity, with the action of the General Convention upon the same, and expressing the readiness of the commission to enter into brotherly conference on the subject, with the trust that the General Assembly might be "numbered among those Christian bodies that are seeking the restoration of the organic unity of the Church." To this the Assembly replied:

To the Commission of Conference on Church Unity of the House of Bishops and of the House of Deputies of the Protestant Episcopal Church convened in the city of Chicago, October, 1886.

Dear Brethren: The General Assembly of the Presbyterian Church in the United States of America, now in session at Omaha, Nebraska, have received with sincere gratification the "declaration" of your House of Bishops, and your request under it for a brotherly conference with us and with other branches of the Church of Christ, "seeking the organic unity of the Church, with a view to the earnest study of the conditions under which so priceless a blessing might happily be brought to pass."

The General Assembly are in cordial sympathy with the growing desire among the Evangelical Christian Churches for practical unity and co-operation in the work of spreading the Gospel of our Lord Jesus Christ throughout all the earth; and they respond to your invitation with the sincere desire that the conference asked for may lead, if not to a formal oneness of organization, yet to such a vital and essential unity of faith and spirit and co-operation as shall bring all the followers of our common Lord into hearty fellowship, and to mutual recognition, affection, reciprocity of ministerial service in the membership of the one visible Church of Christ, and workers together with him in advancing his kingdom upon earth.

Without entering here into consideration of any of the principles which your House of Bishops lay down "as essential to the restoration of unity among the divided branches of Christendom," but leaving the consideration of them to the conference which you request, the General Assembly have appointed from our ministers and ruling elders a committee to confer with you and with any similar commissions or committees that may be appointed by any other Christian churches for conference, with instructions to report to the next General Assembly the results of their deliberations.

Very truly and fraternally yours,
JOSEPH T. SMITH, Moderator,
WM. H. ROBERTS, Stated Clerk.
OMAHA, Neb., May 27, 1887.

A committee appointed by the previous General Assembly to consider the ecclesiastical relations of foreign missionaries, particularly in view of the formation of Union Presbyteries in the foreign fields, reported, recommending:

That, in order to build up independent national churches, holding to the Reformed doctrine and the Presbyterian polity, on foreign fields, the more general and complete identification of our missionaries with the native ministers and churches and other foreign missionaries in those fields is of the most vital importance, and needs to be pushed forward as rapidly as is consistent with a due regard to the interests of all parties to those unions; that in countries where it is possible satisfactorily to form union presbyteries, the further organization of presbyteries in connection with this General Assembly is discouraged, and in countries where there are now presbyteries in connection with this General Assembly, but where it is possible satisfactorily to form union presbyteries, it is strongly urged that the steps be taken as rapidly as this can wisely be done, to merge the membership in union presbyteries, and to dissolve the presbyteries of this General Assembly.

The report further recommended that ordained foreign missionaries be urged to become full members of the union presbyteries where they are residing, upon which they will be dismissed from the presbyteries of which they are members at home; or that, if they do not choose to do this, their reasons for declining to do so be considered by the presbyteries; that the home presbyteries keep lists from year to year of all foreign missionaries sent out from them who have become members of the union presbyteries; and that each mission of the General Assembly's Board represented in the union presbyteries (when there are no presbyteries in connection with the General Assembly) be authorized to send a delegate to the General Assembly, to sit as an advisory member, and to speak, under the rules, on all questions.

A programme was adopted for the celebration of the one hundredth year of the General Assembly, to be held at the meeting in Philadelphia in May, 1888, which embraces the raising of contributions for endowments for buildings for Presbyterian colleges and academies and other institutions of learning in the United States and foreign lands; and for home mission and evangelistic work under the care of Synods and presbyteries; the raising of $1,000,000 for the endowment of the Board of Relief; the holding of two series of memorial and historical meetings in Philadelphia on the fourth Thursday of May, 1888; and the holding of popular meetings in the interest of theological education on two evenings during the session of the Assembly.

An overture sent down by the previous General Assembly for an amendment to the Confession of Faith by striking out from the rule in reference to marriage the prohibition, "the man may not marry any of his wife's kindred nearer in blood than he may of his own, nor the woman of her husband's kindred nearer in blood than of her own," having been approved by the majority of the presbyteries, the clause was stricken out. An overture proposing an amendment to the form of government making ruling elders eligible to the office of moderator was lost on the vote of the presbyteries. It was decided that, where the statutes of individual States did not forbid, the right of succession to the property of defunct churches should vest in the presbyteries with which those churches were connected; and with a view to securing the titles to such property, the presbyteries were advised to become incorporated. The President of the United States was requested by resolution to modify the army and navy regulations with reference to inspections and parades on the Lord's day, and secular studies in the academies, so that they shall interfere as little as possible with the Sabbath rest and worship of the officers and men.

II. Presbyterian Church in the United States (Southern).—The following is the summary of the statistics of this Church as they were reported to the General Assembly in May, 1887. The statistics for 1886 and 1888 are appended for comparison, and to show the rate of growth of the Church:

ITEMS.	1883.	1886.	1887.
Synods	18	18	18
Presbyteries	67	69	69
Candidates	199	269	267
Licentiates	45	67	57
Ministers	1,079	1,065	1,116
Churches	2,040	2,193	2,236
Number of ruling elders ..	6,290	6,827	6,981
Number of deacons	4,220	4,814	5,070
Added on examination	6,684	11,644	12,145
Total communicants	127,017	143,743	150,899
No. of adults baptized ...	1,719	3,790	4,214
No. of infants baptized	4,465	5,121	5,090
No. of baptized non-communicants	83,474	84,805	84,168
Teachers in Sunday-school and Bible-classes	7,706	10,702	12,021
Scholars in Sunday-school and Bible-classes	76,725	88,968	98,906
CONTRIBUTIONS.			
Sustentation	$49,155	$45,676	$42,944
Evangelistic	32,750	42,054	42,484
Invalid fund	10,798	11,677	11,921
Foreign missions	52,885	67,685	67,204
Education	32,147	38,704	39,250
Publication	9,458	8,347	9,054
Tuscaloosa Institute......	2,724	3,505	4,152
Presbyterial	13,034	18,649	18,754
Pastors' salaries	568,618	591,896	614,588
Congregational	440,870	420,097	458,977
Miscellaneous	62,982	81,104	114,015
Total	$1,269,416	$1,324,874	$1,415,818

The Committee of Publication reported that its assets exceeded its liabilities by $64,099.

The receipts of the Committee of Home Missions were, for the year, for the Sustentation Department, $26,951; for the Evangelistic fund, $18,132; for the Invalid fund, $12,158. The ministers supported in part from the Sustentation and Evangelistic Funds, had supplied between 600 and 700 of the weaker churches, and had preached at some 300 destitute points. About 60 new church-buildings had been erected, nearly half of them without asking aid of the Central Committee. One hundred and seven cases of infirm ministers, widows, and children of ministers had been aided from the Invalid fund in the amount of $10,702. The Central Committee had had charge of the collections for the work of colored evangelization, which had yielded $4,495. One white minister, and 17 colored ministers, licentiates, and students had been supported from this fund. The work of the institution for training colored ministers at Tuscaloosa, Ala., was reported upon favorably. Aid had been given to 17 colored ministers, licentiates, and students.

The Committee of Education had received $18,688, and returned 158 candidates aided.

The receipts of the Board of Foreign Missions had been $84,072. The report reviewed the condition and progress of the missions in Mexico, China, Northern (Pernambuco) and Southern (Campinas), Brazil, the Indian Territory, Italy Greece, and Japan.

General Assembly.—The General Assembly met in St. Louis, Mo., May 19. The Rev. G. B. Strickler, of Atlanta, Ga., was chosen moderator. The most prominent subject of discussion was the question of organic union with the Presbyterian Church in the United States of America, or the Northern Presbyterian Church, the debate upon which occupied several days. Upon it the Assembly adopted the following report:

Whereas, A number of overtures in reference to closer relations to the Northern Presbyterian Church have come up to this Assembly; and

Whereas, The Northern Assembly has just adopted the deliverance of the Northern and Southern Synods of Missouri on the spirituality of the Church; and

Whereas, The Northern and Southern Presbyterian Churches ought to labor together for the accomplishment of the great object which they have in view if they are sufficiently agreed in their principles to make them more efficient in their work united than they now are divided; and,

Whereas, The recent action of the Northern Assembly, apparently different from their former action as to the spirituality of the Church, makes the impression on the minds of many of our people that one obstacle to closer relations to that Church has been or soon may be removed. Therefore, be it

Resolved, That a committee of four ministers and four ruling elders, and the moderator as *ex-officio* chairman, be appointed to meet with a similar committee of the Northern Assembly, if such a committee shall be appointed. for the sole purpose of inquiring into and ascertaining the facts as to the point above mentioned, and as to the position that Assembly proposes to maintain as to the colored churches, ecclesiastical boards, and any other subjects now regarded as obstacles in the way of united effort for the propagation of the Gospel, and report these facts to the next General Assembly for such action as they may warrant.

The Committee appointed in accordance with this resolution consists of the Rev. Dr. G. B. Strickler, chairman: the Rev. Drs. M. D. Hoge, J. R. Wilson, T. D. Witherspoon, and W. F. Junkin; and elders Dr. W. P. McPheeters, of St. Louis, Mo.; T. H. Carter, of Texas; R. T. Simpson, of Alabama; and W. S. Primrose, of North Carolina.

Several matters were acted upon in relation to the "Centennial Celebration" of Presbyterianism in the United States, to be held in Philadelphia in May, 1888. The Assembly replied to invitations from the Presbytery and from the Second Church of Philadelphia to hold its next meeting in that city, that it was not deemed judicious "to appoint a meeting of the body outside our own bounds, or to depart from the invariable custom of meeting within the limits of one of our own churches." Also:

That the General Assembly adjourn to meet next year in the Franklin Street Church, Baltimore, tendered to the Assembly by the pastor, so as to secure the fullest co-operation in this celebration.

That on Memorial Day, the fourth Thursday of May, 1888, the Assembly shall suspend its usual sessions, allowing all its members to participate in this reunion.

That the following be appointed as the speakers who shall represent this Assembly in the centennial celebration: Dr. B. M. Palmer, Dr. M. D. Hoge, Dr. J. L. Girardeau, Dr. M. H. Houston, Dr. W. W. Moore, Dr. Jerry Witherspoon, Hon. J. Randolph Tucker of Virginia, Hon. W. C. P. Breckenridge of Kentucky, Hon. J. S. Cothran, of South Carolina, and Hon. Clifford Anderson, of Georgia.

That the matter of raising a memorial fund be left to the different portions of the Church which may choose to embark in it.

That the Assembly recommend to the Presbyteries to collect historical material within their bounds, and forward the same to the Assembly of 1888.

Assignment of subjects for speakers : 1, "History of Presbyterianism—Its Work for the Future," Dr. Girardeau; 2, "Calvinism and Religious Liberty," Mr. Breckenridge; 3, "Adaptation of Presbyterianism to the Masses," Mr. Tucker; 4, "City Evangelization," Dr. Hoge; 5, "Calvinism and Human Progress," John Cothran; 6, "Lay Effort among the Masses," Mr. Anderson; 7, "Foreign Missions," Dr. Houston; 8, "Home Missions," Dr. Moore; 9, "Children of the Covenant," Dr. Palmer; 10, "Closing Address," Dr. Witherspoon.

A fraternal answer was returned to the declaration of the General Convention of the Protestant Episcopal Church (see "Annual Cyclopædia" for 1886) concerning Christian unity; but further action on the subject was remanded to the General Assembly of 1888. Continued interest was expressed in the "Alliance of the Reformed Churches holding the Presbyterian system," and approval of its efforts to promote closer fellowship and co-operation among these churches.

In answer to overtures touching the acts of the last Assembly respecting the theory of evolution, and the power of the General Assembly over theological seminaries and their instructors, the Assembly "declined to formulate any detailed explanation of the acts of the last Assembly, as any such statement, however expressed, could only be regarded as a

new deliverance on the same subjects which this Assembly does not feel called upon to make."

Approval was given to the formation of a Synod in Brazil, to be composed of the presbyteries which shall be separated from both the Assemblies in the United States, to constitute in Brazil a distinct and independent Church, free from foreign control; and it was further advised that the missionaries of this Church in Brazil, "as soon as these native Presbyteries can be safely left, push forward as rapidly as possible into the destitute regions beyond."

The eligibility of ruling elders to the moderatorship having been affirmatively decided upon by the vote of the presbyteries, such amendments of the "Book of Church Order" as would bring the other provisions of the book into harmony with the change were proposed and referred to a special committee. The presbyteries were directed to take the matter of Sabbath observance under presbyterial supervision, and to adopt measures to discourage and stop unnecessary riding by ministers and members in Sunday trains and steamboats.

Conference of Northern and Southern Presbyteries.—The Committees of Conference of the Northern and Southern Presbyterian General Assemblies met in Louisville, Ky., December 14, for the discussions of questions concerning the relations of the two bodies; but no report of their proceedings or conclusions will be authoritatively published till the meeting of the General Assemblies in May, 1888.

III. United Presbyterian Church in North America. —The summary of the statistics of this Church, as they were presented to the General Assembly in 1887, gives the following footings: Number of synods, 10; of presbyteries, 60; of ministers, 786, of whom 523 were pastors and stated supplies, and 213 were without charge; of licentiates, 46; of students of theology, 55; of ruling elders, 3,515; of congregations, 885, of which 609 were provided with pastors and stated supplies, and 276 were "vacant"; of pastoral charges, 678; of mission stations, 144; of new stations during the year, 22; of members, 94,641; of members received during the year on profession, 7,408; of baptisms during the year, 2,840 of adults and 4,316 of infants; of Sabbath-schools, 937, with 9,220 officers and teachers and 83,617 pupils. Amount of contributions: For salaries of ministers, $482,020; for congregational purposes, $274,602; for the boards, $167,010; for general purposes, $49,-609; for quarter-centennial, $4,619; total, $977,860; average per member, $11.51; average salary of pastors, $935.

The receipts of the Board of Church Extension for the year had been $25,658. Appropriations had been made for the ensuing year of $13,600, of which $10,400 were to be in the form of donations and $3,200 of loans.

The receipts of the Board of Home Missions had been $39,964. The board had granted aid to 217 stations, with which were connected 11,208 communicants—an average of 17,318 attendants on worship—and 1,296 teachers and 13,077 pupils in Sabbath-schools. An increase of 887 members by profession was returned. Sixteen stations were designated as special missions.

Four ministers and 31 assistants were serving among the Freedmen, and 168 colored teachers, who had been educated in the Assembly's institutions, were employed in the public schools. The institutions returned 1,693 pupils.

The following is a statement of the condition of the missions in India and Egypt: Missions, 2; stations, 121. Foreign missionaries, 16; married women, 16; single, 20; physicians, 2. Total of foreign laborers, 54. Native ordained ministers, 20; licentiates, 9; other native laborers, 346. Total of native laborers, 375; total of all laborers, 429. Churches, 31; average Sabbath attendance, 7,759; communicants, 6,161. Increase past year, 2,341. Baptisms, 2,881. Sabbath-schools, 188; Sabbath-school pupils, 5,625; other schools, 192; pupils, 9,219. Contributions, $5,587. Appraised value of property, £235,701.

General Assembly.—The twenty-ninth General Assembly met in Philadelphia May 25. The Rev. Dr. M. M. Gibson, of San Francisco, was chosen moderator. A number of cases of appeal came up from the decisions of lower judicatories, in which the question of the use of instrumental music in worship was involved. All were decided in favor of the principle of liberty of action by each congregation which has been allowed by recent General Assemblies. In one case, an organ having been introduced into the church, the appellant had demanded that the presbytery order its removal, and also prohibit the use of the instrument in worship in other congregations, Sabbath-schools, and families under its inspection. The case having been brought through the successive courts to the Assembly, a decision was here given that, inasmuch as there is no law of the Church on the subject of instrumental music, there could be no violation of law in the present case. In considering the report on home missions, a motion that no part of the general fund should be used when an instrument of music is employed in worship was rejected by a vote of 60 to 128. A protest was entered against this action.

To the question, sent up in a memorial presented to the Assembly, Does the declaration of our "Testimony on Psalmody," Art. XVIII, permit members of the United Presbyterian Church to join in the singing of compositions of uninspired men, in connection with religious services held anywhere, or under any circumstances? a negative answer was returned. The action of a previous General Assembly, recommending the sessions of churches to provide unfermented wine for the service of the communion, was reaffirmed. A memorial, asking whether a member is in good standing who urges an alteration in the confession and votes for it, was answered by saying that the constitution confers on communicants the liberty which would be restrained by prohibiting such a course. A delegate from the Associate Reformed Synod of the South represented that the agitation on the subject of instrumental music and the article of the "Testimony on Slavery" operated as objections to the immediate union of the two bodies. In consequence of objections in the Synod, the consideration of the question of organic union had been postponed. A committee was appointed to confer with a committee of the Reformed Presbyterian Church on the subject of union. Further action concerning participation in the Council of the Presbyterian Alliance was omitted, on the ground that no guarantee had been given that the "Scripture Psalmody" alone would be used in future meetings of the Council.

IV. Reformed Presbyterian Church, Synod.—This body comprises 11 presbyteries, 103 ministers, 10,832 communicants, and 12,102 members of Sunday-schools. The invested funds of the Synod on the 1st day of May, 1887, amounted to $171,829, having increased during the year by $24,165. A sufficient net surplus had been earned during the year to permit a dividend of 5 per cent., the amount of which had been divided and credited to the Foreign and Domestic Missions, Theological Seminary, and other funds entitled to share in the proceeds of the investments.

The Synod met in Newburgh, N. Y., June 1. Prof. D. B. Wilson, of Allegheny Seminary, was chosen moderator. The total contributions for the year were reported to have been $201,197, or $78.75 per member. The contributions for missions had been $17,000. The election to office of any member of the Church who uses tobacco was prohibited. Membership in secret societies was condemned. A delegate was appointed to the Council of the Presbyterian Alliance. A resolution was adopted declaring that violation of Sunday by the Post-Office Department is one of the greatest sins of the Government as well as one of the greatest causes of Sunday desecration throughout the whole country.

V. Reformed Presbyterian Church, General Synod.—This Church has 6 presbyteries, 25 ministers, 7 licentiates, about 6,500 communicants, and 4,000 Sunday-school pupils.

The General Synod of the Reformed Presbyterian Church in North America met in Philadelphia May 18. The Rev. John H. Kendall was chosen moderator. Seven presbyteries, including 45 congregations and the mission in India, were represented. Reports were made of the condition of the funds and missionary and educational enterprises of the Synod, as follow: Theological Seminary fund—receipts, $2,284; value of the Lamb estate, $11,200; amount of the Endowment fund, $35,197; receipts of the Educational fund, $545; receipts of the Church Extension fund, $2,295; receipts of the Disabled Ministers' fund, $99; receipts of the Sustentation fund, $6,418; receipts of the Domestic Mission fund, $2,590; receipts of the Board of Foreign Missions, $9,808. The mission is at Roorkee and surrounding villages, in Northern India. It returned 7 families, 14 communicants, 50 members of congregation, 26 persons under Christian instruction, and 24 baptisms of adults and 4 of infants and children during the year. The Committee on a Literary Institution had been incorporated under the laws of Ohio, and had organized Cedarville College, at Cedarville, in that State. The delegates appointed to attend a "Pan-Psalmody Council," to be held in Kampen, Holland, reported that the place of meeting of the Council had been changed to Glasgow, Scotland, and that it met on the 15th of October, 1886. The delegates had not been able to attend, but had sent letters in which were included suggestions for making changes in the version of the Psalms, such as the elimination of obsolete words and the introduction of some additional versions, particularly of the Messianic Psalms. At the meeting an association was formed which was designated "The Psalmody Alliance," the objects of which were defined to be "to sustain and promote the exclusive use of the Psalms in the praise of God," and in the membership of which the exclusively psalm-singing churches and associations, "formed in connection with other churches that fully approve of the objects of the alliance," should be represented. A delegate was appointed to represent the General Synod in this council. A minute was adopted alleging that the Presbyterian Alliance of the Reformed Churches, "which was founded upon the consensus of the Reformed Confessions, appears to have shifted its ground by admitting into its councils those who are not sound in the faith, and by departing from the original position of the Alliance as understood by the Synod—the brotherly covenant respecting the sole use of the Psalms of inspiration in the devotional exercises of the council." It was therefore resolved that the Synod withdraw at present from the Alliance. In reply to a communication of the General Assembly of the Presbyterian Church of the United States of America regarding a closer Christian fellowship and intercommunion among those who bear the name of Presbyterians, and are represented in the Alliance, the Synod, expressing its sympathy with all movements for the advance of unity in the Church, declared itself ready and willing to correspond with the General Assembly, or with any other Presbyterian body, "upon such terms as may be acceptable to the parties concerned." A paper which was adopted upon the observance of the Lord's day urged the members of the Church to give the day a careful, conscientious respect, abstaining from seeking their own pleasure or doing their work upon it, and warning them "against the reading of

secular books and papers, and indulging in pleasure walks or rides or vain conversation." The objects of the National Christian Association, which opposes secret societies, and of the National Reform Association, which aims to secure the incorporation of a "Religious Amendment" in the Constitution of the United States, were approved.

A fraternal letter was received from the Eastern Synod of Ireland, which mentioned an effort to effect a union with a sister Synod in the same country. The movement had failed, although all the other circumstances were favorable to its success, because the Eastern Synod refused, with its present information on constitutional questions, to say that it would censure its members for voting for members of Parliament.

VI. Cumberland Presbyterian Church. — This Church, according to its statistical returns, includes 22 Synods, 119 presbyteries, 2,546 churches, 1,547 ministers, and 138,564 communicants, with 78,000 pupils in Sabbath-schools. The Cumberland Presbyterian Church, colored, a separate body, but allied to it in doctrine and form of government, has 4 Synods, 21 presbyteries, 300 ordained ministers, 250 licentiates, and 225 candidates, and reports 40,000 members.

The receipts of the Board of Foreign Missions had been $44,766. The work of the mission in Japan was represented in the reports as having been attended with much success. A work in Mexico had "opened favorably," and the mission among the Indians "was gradually developing." The policy had been adopted in home missions of concentrating energy and funds on important places until self-supporting congregations are established.

The General Assembly of the Cumberland Presbyterian Church met at Covington, Ohio, May 19. Chancellor Nathan Green, of Cumberland University, a ruling elder, was chosen moderator. The report of the Committee on Organic Union with the Methodist Protestant Church, which had been presented to the previous General Assembly, and by it postponed for action at the present meeting, was considered. The minute adopted upon the subject expressed gratification that a spirit favorable to union had marked the action of the committees of both churches at their conferences, and that the doctrinal differences between the two bodies had been found unimportant and "not essential to Christian unity," but with the reservation of an expression of "unwillingness to omit from our system of faith a doctrine so precious for us as that of the 'preservation of believers.'" A commission of seven members was appointed, with power "to confer with any commission or committee appointed by the Methodist Protestant Church upon this subject, and with them to argue, subject to the approval and ratification of the General Assembly, upon such terms of organic union as to them may seem right and proper." On the question whether probationers (licentiates) were authorized to solemnize the rites of matrimony, the Assembly, without making a special enactment, decided to leave the matter of qualification of such persons to be determined by the laws of the State in which the marriage is to take place. To a question whether a presbytery has the power to depose a ruling elder, answer was returned that, "as a general rule, the session is the only Church court that has original jurisdiction to hear charges, and try and depose a ruling elder; but where, from any cause, a fair and impartial trial can not be had before the session; or where the trial of the cause, for sufficient reasons, is referred by the session to the presbytery; or where the case is removed by appeal from the session to the presbytery, and is there heard and determined, the presbytery may depose an elder, but not otherwise." A committee of legal members of the Church was appointed to examine the laws of the different States concerning titles to church property, and to make such regulations as shall secure Cumberland Presbyterian titles in conformity with them. The minutes of the Oregon Synod showing that that body had invited women to sit in council, and given them the right to speak in the meetings of the Synod, such action was declared to be a departure from the rules of the Church. To a memorial asking that the connection of this Church with the Presbyterian Alliance be dissolved, the Assembly replied that its connection with that body had called the attention of the world to the doctrinal position of the Church, and was a means of bringing churches into closer fraternity, and of securing co-operation in foreign missionary work; and it was therefore of the opinion that the relation should be continued. The appointment of delegates to the council of the Alliance was relegated to the next meeting of the General Assembly. To a protest, which was entered against the election of a ruling elder to the office of moderator, for the reason that the protestants believed it to be a violation of the fundamental principles of Presbyterianism, the Assembly replied, declaring that "there is nothing, either in the spirit or genius of Presbyterianism, violated by such action, and nothing in our "Form of Government" that forbids the election of a ruling elder to this position." The subject of establishing a training-school for women in Biblical and medical knowledge for special missionary work, at home and abroad, was commended to the consideration of the Board of Missions and the Trustees of Cumberland University, with authority, if they judge best, to found and organize such a school at Lebanon, Tenn. Reiterating its former expressions on the subject of temperance, the Assembly declared in addition that "the failure or refusal of any follower of our Divine Master to use his profession in favor of, to pray for, labor for, such legislation as will free the country and God's Church, from this drink curse, is inconsistent with the teachings of Holy Scripture and the example of our Saviour"; and it approved all organizations "looking to, and laboring for, the prohibition of the liquor-traffic by every lawful means." The use of unfermented wine in the Lord's Supper was advised. The Assembly advised the enforcement, by legal and moral means, of a strict observance of the Lord's day.

The General Assembly of the Cumberland Presbyterian Church, colored, met in Chattanooga, Tenn., May 19. The Rev. W. L. Clark was chosen moderator. The Church sustains a school at Bowling Green, Ky., to which the General Assembly of the Cumberland Presbyterian Church contributed at its session $2,700 for the removal of debt.

VII. Presbyterian Church in Canada.—The following is a summary of the statistics of this Church as they were presented to the General Assembly in June: Number of presbyteries, 42; of pastoral charges, 775; of mission stations or groups, 309; of ministers, 823; of churches and stations supplied, 1,778; of communicant members, 136,598; of families connected with the churches, 76,226; of Sunday-school teachers, 12,070; of pupils in Sabbath-schools and Bible-classes, 108,284; of baptisms, 10,264 of infants and 1,051 of adults. Amount of contributions: For stipends, $667,218; for congregational objects, $1,242,910; for schemes of the Church, $193,458.

The payments to the Home Mission fund were $32,204. One hundred and eighty-nine missionaries had been employed in the western section in the service of 714 preaching stations, and 1,562 stations had been served in the eastern section.

The contributions to the Aged and Infirm Minister's fund had been $7,926; to the Widows and Orphans' fund, $5,782. The income of the College funds amounted to $92,860.

The receipts of the French Evangelization fund had been $19,884. Twenty-five churches, including 78 preaching stations, had been served under the auspices of this board, with which were connected 1,268 church-members, 1,016 families, and an average attendance of 2,650 persons. The twenty-nine schools returned an enrollment of 905 pupils. The principal schools were at Pointe aux Trembles, where six teachers were employed, and 120 pupils enrolled. The school at St. Anne, Illinois, returned 136 pupils.

The receipts of the Foreign Mission Committees had been $55,981. The Woman's Foreign Missionary Society (Western Division) had contributed $18,581 to the purposes of this work. The missions are in the New Hebrides; the West Indies and Demerara, where 1,675 pupils were enrolled in the schools; the Indians of the Northwest; China (Northern Formosa), where 38 stations are sustained, and 2,546 members are enrolled, and 8,448 patients were treated in the hospital at Tam-Sui; and Central India (Indore, Mhow, etc.), where ten missionaries and eleven teachers, catechists, etc., nine of whom are natives, were employed.

General Assembly.—The thirteenth General Assembly of the Presbyterian Church in Canada met in Winnipeg, Manitoba, June 9. The Rev. Robert Ferrier Burns, D. D., was chosen moderator. A message was received from the Provincial Synod of the Church of England in Canada announcing the appointment of a committee of the two houses constituting that body to confer with committees representing other Christian bodies "for the purpose of ascertaining whether there is any possibility of honorable union with such bodies." To this the Assembly responded by the appointment of a corresponding committee with a resolution reciting that, "deeply sensible of the evils of disunion in the Church of Christ, and their contrariety to the ideal of the Church, as presented in Scripture," it had heard with lively gratification of the action respecting union of the Provincial Synod. Another message from the Provincial Synod invited the co-operation of the Assembly in measures for obtaining legislation that would insure the daily and reverent use of the Holy Scriptures and the teaching of the elements of Christian truth in the public schools. The response to this was a resolution that "the General Assembly, deeply sensible of the importance of the subject of religious instruction in the public schools of the country, appoints a committee to consider the whole matter carefully during the ensuing year, to ascertain the state of the law and the actual practice in the different provinces of the Dominion, and report to the next General Assembly." A remit of the previous General Assembly respecting the rule concerning marriage with a deceased wife's sister having been approved by a majority of the presbyteries, the remit—directing that "the discipline of the Church shall not be exercised in regard to marriage with a deceased wife's sister or a deceased wife's niece"—was passed into an *ad interim* act. The Assembly also resolved to send down to the presbyteries, under the Barrier act, a remit for amending the fourth section of the twenty-fourth chapter of the "Confession of Faith" by striking out the words "the man may not marry any of his wife's kindred nearer in blood than he may of his own, nor the woman of her husband's kindred nearer in blood than of her own." A committee was appointed to submit to the next General Assembly some suitable way in which to celebrate the two hundredth anniversary of the Revolution of 1688. It was resolved to obtain signatures in all the congregations to a petition to be presented to the Dominion Legislature for the total prohibition of the liquor-traffic.

VIII. Church of Scotland.—The report to the General Assembly of this Church of its Committee on Presbyterial Superintendence showed that there were now in the Church 535 preaching stations, or 58 more than in 1885, with 571,029 members in communion. The number admitted during the year as young communicants was 25,676, and the number admitted by baptism was 48,272. The Statistical Committee reported that the contributions for religious and charitable purposes, exclusive of seat-rents, had been £343,595. The income of the Aged and Infirm Ministers' fund was returned as £8,450, and the total amount of capital, having been augmented by £2,203, was about £22,000. The Committee on Home Missions had voted £1,650 to 64 mission churches. The income of the Committee on Patronage Compensation had been £1,231, while £1,511 had been paid for compensations. The committee had £800 on hand. The Committee on Missions to the Jews had received £6,190, of which £4,941 were available for the ordinary purposes of the mission, while it had expended £4,971. In the schools at all the stations — Alexandria, Beyrout, Smyrna, Salonica, and Constantinople—898 Jewish boys and girls were enrolled. Twelve Jews, of whom 10 were adults, had been baptized during the year.

The General Assembly of the Church of Scotland met in Edinburgh May 19, and was opened by Lord Hopetoun as Lord High Commissioner. The Rev. Dr. George Hutchison was chosen moderator. The Lord High Commissioner having read the Queen's letter said that he was commanded to assure the Assembly of her Majesty's determination to maintain the Presbyterian form of church government in Scotland. Her Majesty's gift of £2,000 for the promotion of the Gospel in the Highlands was transmitted, with the provision that a part of it should be appropriated to the encouragement of young men to preach in the Gaelic language. The report of the Committee on Church Interests related the failure of the conference which was proposed to be held with the Free Church on the subject of reunion. The Established Church had wished the Conference to consider the present state of Scotland "in the light of the standards common to both Churches, of the claims of right, and of the recent abolition of patronage," while the Free Church would not go into conference unless the subject of disestablishment and endowment was left an open question." The Committee profoundly regretted that the difficulties in the way of arranging any basis upon which a conference could usefully take place had proved insurmountable, and admitted that the reply of the Assembly Arrangements Committee of the Free Church seemed to leave no ground on which it could recommend the Assembly to continue any correspondence on the subject at the present time. As there was evidence that an organized and deliberate attempt would be made to force the question of disestablishment and disendowment into the domain of practical politics, it behooved all the friends of the Church to be active and watchful. The Assembly, expressing regret at the failure of the present effort, reappointed the committee with instructions to watch for any opportunity of kindly co-operation and intercourse with other Scottish Churches. A deputation from the Synod of the Presbyterian Church in England in connection with the Church of Scotland was received, and the Assembly, in answer to the appeal made to it, resolved to allow the Synod to be represented in future Assemblies. This Synod was endeavoring to secure an Aged and Infirm Ministers' fund of £8,000, of which it was hoped that a half would be contributed by the Church of Scotland. The report on Patronage Compensation showed that several patrons had not claimed compensation for parishes formerly in their hands. An overture in favor of rescinding the acts requiring elders to sign the Confession of Faith was considered, after which the whole matter was referred to a committee to report upon in the next year. The subject of providing a better method than the present system of superintending ministers in the discharge of their parochial duties by means of schedules of questions to be answered, was remitted to a committee. The Committee on Temperance expressed satisfaction that that cause had made marked progress during the year. The Church of Scotland did not, however, take that place in the promotion of temperance that it might take. A Jubilee address to the Queen was adopted, and a day of thanksgiving for the prosperous continuance of Her Majesty's reign was appointed. The Assembly decided to send a delegate to attend the jubilee celebration of the Belgian Presbyterian Church.

IX. Free Church of Scotland.—The statistical reports made to the General Assembly showed that there were in this Church 1,019 regular charges, of which 100 were collegiate, with 16 professorships and 1,144 ministers. The number of members had increased by 778 during the year, and was now 331,242.

The total income of the Church for the year, exclusive of the widows' and orphans' schemes, had been £564,442, showing a decrease of £29,-607. The whole amount of the widows' fund was £249,114, and the amount of the orphans' fund £65,115. There were upon these funds 232 widows entitled to £46 a year each, 129 children entitled to £24 each, and 12 receiving £36 each. The year's contributions to the Sustentation fund had been £172,125. Eight hundred and seven ministers were receiving the equal dividend. The Church Extension Building fund had made grants of £4,011 for building, rebuilding, and enlargement to 17 churches, and had on hand for future distribution a little less than £30,000. The expenditure of the Aged and Infirm Ministers' fund had exceeded the income by £2,000. The whole amount obtained by the ten collections appointed to be made throughout the Church by the last Assembly was £17,931. The gross income for the year for foreign missions had been £81,588.

The mission fields were in India, South Africa, Syria, and the New Hebrides.

The General Assembly of the Free Church of Scotland met in Edinburgh May 19. The Rev. Dr. Robert Rainy, Principal of New College, Edinburgh, was chosen moderator. In his inaugural address the moderator presented a review of the social and religious progress during the last half-century. A report on religion and morals was submitted, which represented that great improvement had taken place throughout the Church in regard to Church attendance, temperance, and social purity. An address to the Queen on the occasion of her Jubilee was adopted. A communication from the Established Church committee on Church interests to the Assembly Arrangements Committee was taken up. In it, the former committee refused to meet in conference on the questions of establishment and endowment, but suggested a conference on the basis of the claim of right and the recent abolition of patronage. The Arrangements Committee had replied that it could not accept a conference on the grounds proposed. The Assembly approved the report of its Arrangements Committee, and, while recognizing the friendly intentions of the Established Church Assembly, declared that any proposal to the Free Church excluding from consideration the solution—namely, disestablishment and disendowment—declared by the Free Church to be necessary, must be regarded as totally unfitted to promote a worthy, intelligent, and harmonious settlement of the subject. The Assembly further declared on the direct question of disestablishment that, "continuing to adhere to the grounds of separation from the state which were embodied in the disruption of 1843, and impressed with the strong and various public grounds which point to disestablishment as the only solution of the Scottish Church question, it resolves again to petition in favor of disendowment and disestablishment in Scotland." The committee on federal relations between the Free Church and the Presbyterian Church in England reported favoring such arrangements as should make ordained ministers of the latter Church open to calls on the same terms as those of the Free Church, and attendance at a divinity hall of the English Presbyterian Church to be held equivalent to attendance at a Free Church college; and that in missionary operations each Church should conduct its own work, but aim at combined efforts in regard to the same missionary enterprise. The Assembly approved of this report, declared it desirable to federate with the English Church as recommended, and ordered a committee appointed to prepare an overture on the subject for submission to the presbyteries, and to communicate with the Presbyterian Church in England. A measure was approved giving to the presbyteries the power, in case of continued inefficiency of a minister, to dissolve the pastoral tie; and making five years, instead of three, the period for visitation of congregations. A committee appointed to inquire into the treatment of members of non-established churches in country districts, reported that some instances of attempts prejudicial to such churches had come to their knowledge, while many church sessions had represented that they had no difficulties of the kind to encounter.

X. United Presbyterian Church of Scotland.—The Synod of the United Presbyterian Church of Scotland met May 2. The Rev. John B. Smith, of Greenock, was chosen moderator. The statistical reports showed increase in the number of baptisms and of members, although the increase in the latter item was less than it had been in the two previous years—and improvement in the financial condition. The capital of the Aged and Infirm Ministers' fund was returned at £48,399, with an excess of expenditure over income during the year of £439. Complaints being made of want of caution in the administration of the fund, the Home Mission Board was requested to consider whether the rules regulating the admission of annuitants required amendment. The report of the stipend augmentation fund showed a slight decrease in income.

The Committee on Temperance and Morals was directed to open communication with other churches in order to secure harmony and co-operation. The Synod declared itself in favor of the Local Option bill then before Parliament, and decided to address a memorial to the Government on the subject of the drink-traffic in India and its rapid development in Africa. The Ecclesiastical Assessment (Scotland) Bill was disapproved of. A proposal to permit a session to elect as its representative in the higher courts of the Church an acting member of another session, concerning which the presbyteries and sessions had expressed considerable diversities of opinion, was remitted. A report bearing on the supervision of the Church's work and the tenure of the pastorate was laid over for another year. The subject of the organization of a fund for the widows and orphans of ministers was remitted to the committee having it in charge, with instructions to consider if the proposed scheme could not be grafted upon some of the already existing friendly societies of the Church. A report on the formation of guilds for the young of both sexes was left to lie on the table for another year. An address was ordered drafted to the Queen on the occasion of her Jubilee.

XI. Presbyterian Church in England.—The following is a summary of the statistics of this Church for 1887: Number of congregations, 286; of communicants, 61,781; number of sittings in churches, 146,742; number of pupils in Sabbath-schools, 75,794; of teachers in the same, 7,210; total income of the Church for the year, £206,533.

The Synod of the Presbyterian Church in England met in Manchester April 24. The Rev. William Sutherland Swanson, a returned missionary from China, was chosen moderator. Reports were presented from the committees on the Church's relation to the Confession of Faith and on public worship. The former committee, not being prepared to make a final report, was continued, and instructed to proceed with the Compendium of Doctrine and to consider the legal bearing of the declaratory statement. The Committee on Public Worship reported progress in the work of examining the "Westminster Directory" and of determining what abridgments and modifications were needed to adapt it to the condition and wants of the Church at the present day, and was continued. The Home Mission Committee reported growth in the northern presbyteries. A proposal to ordain missionaries for home work was remitted back to the committee, and it was instructed to inquire into the spiritual needs of the classes who habitually absent themselves from public worship. Favorable reports were made of the foreign missions in China and in India. In China there were returned 16 ordained, 6 medical, and 8 woman missionaries, 84 native evangelists, 46 students, 100 mission stations, and 3,553 communicants; and 840 adult members had been added during the year. A "dutiful address" was adopted to be presented to the Queen on the occasion of her Jubilee, in which mention was made of the "immense development of religious and philanthropic activity" that had taken place during her reign. During the discussion of this paper, satisfaction was expressed that her Majesty had continued to show an intelligent appreciation of the simple worship of the Presbyterian Church. During her reign, the English Presbyterian Church had grown about sevenfold. The churches were recommended to hold a special service on "Jubilee day," June 21st. Overtures were adopted on the strict observance of the Sabbath, as well as petitions against the Marriages Bill and the opium-traffic, and in favor of the Sunday closing of public-houses. Six delegates were appointed to attend the meeting of the Presbyterian Alliance to be held in London in 1888. Upon the report that the temperance societies of the Church comprised 23,884 members, gratification was expressed at the measure of interest taken by the Church in this work. In view of the proposals for a settlement of a contending claim with the Congregationalists for the possession of a church in Tooting, it was resolved that all such cases be submitted in future to arbitration.

XII. Presbyterian Church in Ireland.—The statistical summaries of this Church, as presented to the General Assembly in June, showed that the number of families in connection with the congregations had increased by 528; of communicants, by 645; of stipend-payers, by 535; of Sabbath-school teachers, by 142; and of pupils in Sabbath-schools, by 1,074.

The number of Sabbath-schools was now 1,107, with 8,939 teachers, and 101,280 pupils.

The contributions from these schools for the year amounted to £2,951. The total congregational income for the year was £159,550, or £2,721 more than in the previous year. The commutation trustees returned a capital account of £587,735, the same as in the previous year. The income for Foreign Missions had been £12,728, showing an increase of £700. The Aged and Infirm Ministers' fund secured a retiring allowance of £100 to each minister.

The General Assembly met in Belfast June 6. The Rev. Dr. Orr was chosen moderator. The business transacted was chiefly of a routine character, without questions to excite active discussion. The "Revised Book of the Constitution and Government of the Church and Directory for the Administration of Ordinances" was adopted. The subject of raffling at bazaars, which was brought up in the report on the State of Religion and Evangelization, was referred to a committee for consideration. The erection of a Victoria Jubilee Assembly Hall was decided upon. Deputies were appointed to attend the Presbyterian Alliance and the Centennial Celebration of Presbyterianism in America.

XIII. Welsh Calvinistic Methodists.—Statistics of this Church were presented to the General Assembly, of which the following is a summary: Number of congregations, 1,224; of ministers, 619 ordained, and 370 not ordained; of deacons, 4,505; of communicants, 128,401; of adherents, 278,039; of teachers in Sunday-schools, 23,898; of pupils in Sunday-schools, 186,740; amount of contributions during the year, £172,012. The amount contributed for missions was £6,080. Of 1,252 chapels belonging to the connection, 652 were freehold and 600 leasehold. The General Assembly met in Liverpool in May. Rev. Owen Thomas, D. D., was chosen moderator. Gains of 363 members and 827 adherents were reported in the English churches. The subject of dealing with the chapel debts, which had grown from £202,000 in 1871 to £325,000, was referred to the provincial synods. A proposition for the union of the colleges at Bala and Trevecca was relegated to the committee appointed to consider the question of union between the two provinces of Wales. The object of the Intermediate Education Bill recently introduced into Parliament was commended, but the bill was declared "both inadequate and unsuitable to the requirements of the principality."

XIV. Original Secession Church of Scotland.—At the meeting of the Synod, a committee was appointed to consider the condition of the Church and report to the next meeting. The mover of the motion for appointing the committee said that, if affairs continued to go on as they had been going, there would be great danger of the Church losing its identity. The present number of members was shown by the reports to be only 3,475.

XV. Federal Assembly of Australia.—The Presbyterian Federal Assembly of Australia is a body, the purpose of which is to promote the organic unity of the Presbyterian Church throughout the Australian colonies. At its second meeting, held in 1887, steps were taken to perfect the machinery for federal action. A scheme was advanced for the common training and uniform examination of theological candidates; and additional measures were instituted for securing a uniform directory of worship, with a view as was understood, not of destroying individual liberty in the conduct of public worship, but of protecting the order of worship from undue caprice.

PRISON REFORM. Prison reform during the past quarter of a century has been almost entirely experimental; and it is only within the past decade that the science of penology has shaped for itself a body of principles and precepts that are likely to be permanent. Prior to the enunciation of the indeterminate-sentence principle by the Hon. Frederick Hill and its modified application in the prisons of Ireland under Sir Walter Crofton, with its more complete realization in the New York State Reformatory, the protection of society by mere incarceration of law-breakers was the dominant idea of most of the prison systems. Prison discipline, from the earliest records to the beginning of the present century, had in it the following principles: 1. Retribution for injury done to society. 2. Protection to society by incarceration or banishment or death. 3. Protection to society by deterrent example of punishments. The practical working of these principles resulted in such a state of the prisons as called forth the labors of John Howard and Elizabeth Fry in England, and of the Philadelphia Society for the Alleviation of the Miseries of Public Prisons in America. The malefactor was regarded as an enemy of society, and an effort was made to mete out to him a degree of retributive justice such as should make him suffer for the injury he had done, not with a view to the uplifting of the culprit, but to inflict punishment for the sake of the pain—to get the criminal out of sight, out of the temporary possibility of doing harm; to make the pain of his punishment a popularly recognized sequence of his wrongdoing. The practical result was, that men were treated in prison as outcasts, were returned to society with enmity in their hearts, unfitted to cope with the forces of society, branded as criminals, and at the same time the principle of deterrence was found to be almost wholly inoperative either upon the imprisoned malefactor or the class from which he came. It was not until the early part of the present century that better statistics made the world aware how little had been accomplished by the prevailing prison systems. The great work of Beccaria on "Crimes and Punishments" (1764) laid down principles that at once arrested the respectful attention of social scientists. But there were at that time no general statistics and no collated information. There came afterward the published works of John Howard, whose philanthropic labors found their best fruitage in the information that he collected and arranged. But Howard's suggestions only pointed to a remedy in external conditions, to greater cleanliness and better ventilation, to the better classification of criminals, and to the abolishment of fees for jail-delivery. His work called the attention of European governments to the condition of prisons, and during the first half of the present century more information as to the actual state of the prisons was gathered than during the whole preceding history of the world. The writings of the Hon. Matthew Davenport Hill, the masterly reports of the Hon. Frederick Hill, and the works of Buxton in England, with the works of Livingston and Dr. Francis Lieber in America, of Wichern in Germany, and of De Tocqueville in France, all showed an intelligent view of the real prison question. Each suggested some new and radical change. The solitary system had been tried, and the severities of entire and idle isolation had been found wanting in efficiency and productive of grave evils. Transportation had been tried for more than a century, and its evils were becoming more apparent. Then the key-note of the most conspicuous reform known to practical penology was struck in an utterance of the Hon. Frederick Hill, Inspector of the Scottish Prisons. He boldly declared himself for the principle of indefinite or indeterminate sentences. The sentence that Pope Clement XI had written over the door of the Roman prison of St. Michele, "*Parum est improbus coercere pœnd, nisi bonos efficias disciplina,*" was becoming a generally recognized axiom of penology, but so firmly were the old methods of treatment grounded in custom that it had little practical application. When the attempt was made to apply it, it was found to be inconsistent with existing systems. The length of sentence having been determined by the court, there was no incentive to improvement in the possibility of an earlier liberation. The retributive idea being dominant in the old system, there was an unwillingness to make an incentive by the introduction of any special privileges that would ameliorate the condition of the prisoner.

Statistics show that by the old system the primary object of imprisonment, protection of society, was not efficiently promoted. It was found, moreover, that the deterrent influences of severe punishments had been vastly overrated. In spite of the vast machinery of criminal courts, prisons, capital punishments, and police organization, the world's criminal class was increasing. The rotation of prisoners in the prisons was noted. It came to be a popular adage, "Once a criminal, always a criminal." There seemed to be something radically wrong in the whole system of penal procedure. By the system of time-sentences, men were kept in the prisons long after they were fitted to take their places as self-supporting and self-respecting members of society, while criminals were released on the expiration of time-sentences who were as much members of the criminal class as they were on the first day of their incarceration. The remedy for this condition of things, as suggested by Frederick Hill, was to transfer the decision as to the length of sentence from the court to the managers and keepers of the prisons—the duration of the sentence to depend on the evidences given by the prisoner of his ability and intention to earn an honest living and lead a law-abiding life. The moment the indefinite - sentence principle was broached, a storm of discussion arose as to whether the primary end of punishment was the reformation of the criminal or the protection of society. Until the experiment was tried, of purely reformatory prisons conducted on the graded and indefinite-sentence plan, there were no data to prove what has since been most clearly demonstrated, that the highest protection to society was effected by the largest reformation of criminals. In "The State of the Prisons," by Rev. E. C. Wines, a view of this discussion is afforded in the following words: "Archbishop Whately entered the discussion, saying: 'We can not admit that the reformation of the convict is an essential part of punishment; it may be joined to it incidentally, but can not belong essentially and necessarily to a penal system.' Abstractly, this may be true; but prison discipline is a very concrete thing. The real question is, What class of agencies — the reformatory or the deterrent—will be found most effective in preventing crime, and so in protecting society? Mr. Clay, of Preston jail, maintained with earnestness that reformation is a more essential element than even punishment, in any system directed to these ends. He looked upon the mass of prisoners as (to use his own phrase) 'incidental offenders,' men who broke the law on sudden impulse, and generally as the effect of drink. These incipient criminals he considered the very men whom it was most possible to reform through a firm but kindly discipline, and especially through the regenerative and purifying influences of religion. The real problem (he contended) was to devise some method of treatment that would combine deterrence and moral amendment, punishment and reformation; always, however, in view of the protection of society through the prevention of crime. This is the view now generally held by the soundest students of penitentiary science." The reformation of the offender as a protection to society is now the aim of the best penal systems. To keep him a ward of the State till such reformation has taken place, and to release him as soon as it has taken place, is the practical problem involved. The solution of this problem has occupied the attention of the master minds of penological science. No one has perhaps done more toward this end than Sir Walter Crofton, who devised and organized the Irish penitentiary system. This system, sometimes called the Crofton System and sometimes the Irish System, has three stages: 1. A penal stage of cellular separation continuing eight months, which may be prolonged to nine months by misconduct. 2. A reformatory stage, where the progressive principle comes into play, of unequal duration according to length of sentence. 3. A probationary stage to verify the reformatory action of the preceding discipline. 4. A stage of conditional liberation, on the ticket-of-leave plan; the convict, though at large, still remaining a ward of the state and subject to the friendly surveillance of the police. Dr. Wines, in describing the Crofton system, says: "It may be shortly defined as an adult reformatory, in which, through moral agencies, the will of the prisoner is brought into accord with the will of the keeper, and held there so long that virtue becomes a habit." After visiting one department of the Irish system, the same author says: "The progress toward liberation is the great force, but there are other manifold motives besides to exertion, self-control, and self-conquest. With every advance there is an increase of privilege, of gratuity, of liberty. The great point is, to induce the prisoner to become an agent in his own reformation." The result of the Irish system was so satisfactory that its principles have come to be the dominant force in all the British prisons. In a report on the English prisons, made by a committee of the Prison Association of New York, we learn that the principal characteristics of the system in vogue are: 1. The gradual progress made in the disuse of short terms of imprisonment. 2. The thorough classification of convicts under penal sentence. 3. The public-account system of labor on public work. 4. The rules of civil-service selection and protection, rigidly applied to prison officers. 5. The supervision of the prisons by the Government and by local authorities. By three similar acts of Parliament, passed in 1877, all the prisons of the kingdom came under the supervision of the Home Office; but special supervisory powers are vested in the local authorities, in so far as local prisons are concerned. This is the last remnant of the borough prison system. The convict prisons have not to any great degree been affected by the law of 1877, having previously been under the charge of the Home Office. The result of this centralization and the creation of a system looking first to the protection of society by the reformation of the criminal, has been most instructive. In a recent work by Sir Edmund F. Du Cane, Chairman of Directors of Convict Prisons, we find that, notwithstanding the steady increase in the population of England and Wales, there was an actual decrease in the number of criminals sentenced. And from statistics obtained elsewhere it is shown that the ratio of prisoners to the population of the entire kingdom is steadily decreasing.

The advantages derived from making the release conditional upon behavior are so patent that in some modification the plan has been adopted in all civilized countries. In the United States the principle finds recognition in what is known as the commutation plan. Commutation laws are on the statute-books of nearly all the States. By these the prisoner earns a diminution of his sentence by good behavior. The managers of prisons are unanimous in their testimony of the good effect of these laws. The lesson learned from this partial application of the indeterminate-sentence principle has prompted another step in practical penology, in the establishment of the State Reformatory at Elmira, N. Y., a prison for felons from sixteen to thirty years of age, under their first sentence. Here the indeterminate sentence is still further applied, and no limit is fixed to the sentence other than that fixed by the maximum term of the statute-book. The burglar may earn his way to respectability in one year or he may remain twenty years under the discipline of the prison. The Elmira Reformatory was established in 1877, and was for five years regarded as an experiment. It is now regarded as a success. In addition to an indeterminate period of incarceration, there is a period of conditional liberation called the parole period. The prisoner, on the decision of the warden and managers, is allowed to go out into the world to test his ability to make his own way in an honest life. He is still a ward of the State, and may remain so during the maximum term that the statute imposes for his crime if there is any doubt as to his reformation. If, on the other hand, he gives satisfactory evidence of a complete change of life, he may at any time receive his absolute release at the hands of the managers. The claim is made by the managers of the reformatory that more than 80 per cent. of those who enter the institution give satisfactory evidences of reformation. This is a larger claim than has ever been made under the old system of penal discipline. The results of the Elmira system have been so startling that other States have regarded them with doubt, and have sent commissions to verify them. Massachusetts, Ohio, and Pennsylvania have already established similar reformatory prisons, and other States are preparing to follow. The Elmira Reformatory has been from its establishment under the charge of Z. R. Brockway, who had earned a prominent place as a practical penologist before he was called to this special work.

The tendency during the last quarter of a century in all matters of prison discipline in civilized countries is to a more complete organization and centralization of authority. The jail system in the United States, and all local-prison systems elsewhere, have been universally condemned in all councils of penology. In England the borough prisons have been abolished, and in France the departmental prisons of all classes are now little more than prisons

for detention of witnesses and those awaiting
trial. In Austria, in Belgium, and in Italy,
the cellular system of imprisonment prevails,
but with considerable modification. In Russia
the newer prisons, under the intelligent direction of Count Solluhab, were built on the sepa-
rate-cell plan, with the intention of working
certain classes of prisoners together. Under
the present direction of M. Galkine-Wroskoi
an effort is being made to form a complete
system of such prisons for all classes of prisoners. The improvements in Russian prisons
and in the prison-stations of Siberia has been
very marked during the past twenty-five years,
and the Government has shown a hearty desire to effect a complete reform. In Spain,
through the efforts of Donna Concepcion
d'Arenal and her colaborers, there has been a
complete *exposé* of the atrocious system of
contracting out the prisons. They have been
greatly improved, the congregate system prevailing. In Italy the new prisons are among
the best in the world, and through the efforts
of Signor Beltrani - Scalia, late Director of
Prisons, a new model prison has been built on
the site of the ancient prison of Regina Cœli,
which is in harmony with the latest developments of penological science. In Germany, in
Switzerland, in Denmark, and in Brazil, a
strong effort is made to carry out a progressive
and classified system. In the United States
prevails what is known as the Auburn system
—cellular separation by night and on Sunday,
and association during the working hours of
the day. The one exception to this is the
solitary-cellular system as shown at the Eastern Penitentiary of Pennsylvania. Here the
prisoners are supposed to be kept in complete
isolation, working in their cells, and never
leaving them until the term of their imprisonment expires. As there is a much larger number of prisoners in this prison than of cells,
the system can not be carried out perfectly;
but this prison is generally regarded as typical
of the solitary-cellular plan. In the Southern
States, the peculiar conditions resulting from
the late war made the establishment of con-
vict-camps a necessity. There were no prisons, and the States were too poor to build
prisons. Stockades were made, huts were
erected in the vicinity of mines, railroads, or
other similar works, and the convicts hired to
contractors, who virtually assumed complete
control of them. Very great abuses grew up
under this system, which have become known
through official reports and through investigations made by individuals. Several of the
Southern States are now building prisons, and
all of them are taking measures to remedy the
evils that have been pointed out.

The United States Government has no prisons
of its own, with the exception of the Military
Prison at Fort Leavenworth, Kansas. It has
several jails at its military posts, all of which
are in wretched condition. Those convicted
for offenses against the United States Govern-

ment are sent to various State-prisons or county penitentiaries where contracts have been
made for their care. This plan has been condemned by the National Prison Association,
and efforts have been unsuccessfully made to
establish one or more prisons for United States
prisoners. The agitation for a more unified
system of prisons in the United States has been
continuous since 1885, and much has been accomplished in this direction through the efforts
of volunteer prison associations.

Prison Associations. — Volunteer associations
for amelioration of the condition of prisoners,
for improvement of prison discipline, and for
assistance of discharged prisoners, have exercised great influence in promoting prison reform. They exist in France, England, Ireland,
Scotland, Belgium, Spain, Germany, the United
States, and other countries. In several cases
they have been granted powers of inspection
and supervision by the Government, and have
thus become a part of the system for the care
of criminal and delinquent classes. The oldest
association of the kind in the United States,
and one of the oldest in the world, is the Pennsylvania Prison Society, organized as "The
Philadelphia Society for Alleviating the Miseries of Public Prisons." It has recently celebrated its centennial. Similar organizations
have been long established in the older States,
notably in Massachusetts, Maryland, and New
York. In 1872, through the efforts of E. C.
Wines, then corresponding secretary of the
Prison Association of New York, the National
Prison Association of the United States was
organized. It was designed to harmonize all
the elements of prison reform in the country,
and was doing much in that direction when Dr.
Wines died in 1879. Before his death the National Prison Association had brought about an
organization of the International Prison Com-
mission, made up of delegates from several of
the most important governments of the world.
This organization grew directly out of the International Prison Congress at London in 1872.
It is the body under which two International
Prison Congresses have since been held—that of
Stockholm in 1878, and that of Rome in 1886.
It is now making arrangements for the fourth
Prison Congress, to be held in St. Petersburg,
Russia, in 1890. At the last Prison Congress,
at Rome, the members numbered 234, of whom
about one third were official delegates, appointed to represent their governments. The
National Prison Association of the United
States was reorganized at Saratoga in 1885,
with Rutherford B. Hayes, ex-President of the
United States, at its head. It has held congresses in Saratoga, Detroit, Atlanta, and Toronto (Canada). These have been the largest
prison-reform meetings ever known, and have
done much to unify the various plans of prison
discipline in North America. The National
Prison Association is in full affiliation and correspondence with the principal prison associations of the world, and valuable reports and

documents have been published. There are in the United States and Canada fourteen prison associations or prisoners' aid associations, and in the whole world the number exceeds two hundred.

PROPHETIC CONFERENCE. A Bible and Prophetic Conference was held in Chicago, Ill., from November 16 to 21, 1886. It was the second meeting of the kind that has been held, the first one having met in New York city in 1878. The call for the present conference was signed by more than two hundred ministers, and various denominations were represented among those who participated in its proceedings. The conference was devoted to the reading of papers and discussions upon topics connected with the prophecies and the doctrine of the second coming of Christ. Papers were read on "The Return of the Lord, Literal, Personal, Visible," by the Rev. Dr. Goodwin; "The Second Coming to be premillennial," by Prof E. F. Stroeter; "Premillennial Motives to Evangelism," by the Rev. Dr. A. T. Pearson; "Objections to the Doctrine of Christ's Premillennial Coming answered," by Elder J. M. Orrock; "The Times of the Gentiles," by Dr. George S. Bishop; "Christ's Prophecies," by Prof. Lummis; "The Fullness of the Gentiles," by the Rev. W. J. Erdman; "Spiritualism, Ritualism, and Theosophy," by the Rev. Dr. A. J. Gordon; "The Practical Influence and Power of "Christ's Second Coming," by the Rev. Dr. J. C. Kennedy; "Judgments and Rewards," by the Rev. Henry M. Parsons; "Eschatology, as taught by our Lord," by Prof. D. C. Marquis; "Contending earnestly for the Faith," by the Rev. Dr. Albert Erdman; "The Antichrist," by Prof. W. G. Moorhead; "The Judgment," by the Rev. Dr. J. F. Kendall; "The Priesthood of Christ," by the Rev. Dr. William Dinwiddie; "Prophecy and Israel," by the Rev. Dr. Nathaniel West; and "Messiah's Kingly Glory," by Bishop W. R. Nicholson. Letters of sympathy with the objects of the Conference were read from Mr. Dwight L. Moody, the Rev. Dr. Andrew Bonar, Canon Faussett, Prof. Godet, Prof. Volck, of Dorpat, Russia; and Dr. F. Delitzsch, of Leipsic. Prof. Delitzsch avowed himself a chiliast, but not in the sense that the glorified Christ will come to the unglorified earth to dwell a thousand years in flesh and blood; but rather in the sense that the saints will rule with him a thousand years from heaven.

PROTESTANT EPISCOPAL CHURCH IN THE UNITED STATES. This Church has continued its steady course during the year 1887. It adheres to its usual methods, avoiding excitements and spasmodic efforts, and is at the same time fully alive to all the great questions that are stirring the heart of Protestant Christendom in this latter part of the nineteenth century. The proposed enrichment of the Liturgy, by enlarging and improving for congregational use the public services of the Church, has met with more or less favor, while

final settlement of debated and doubtful points has been postponed to the meeting of the General Convention in 1889. The sources of information in preparing this article are the published journals of conventions, reports and documents of church societies and corporations, Pott's "Church Almanac," and Whitaker's "Protestant Episcopal Almanac." The following table presents a summary of statistics of the Church during 1887:

DIOCESES AND MISSIONS.

DIOCESES.	Clergy	Parishes	Baptisms	Confirmations	Communicants
Alabama................	80	42	489	865	4,652
Albany	181	111	1,816	1,049	15,455
Arkansas	15	29	180	148	1,418
California.............	76	26	1,001	906	5,987
Central New York	101	110	1,581	1,008	13,283
Central Pennsylvania ..	108	91	1,346	1,082	8,542
Chicago...............	74	47	1,484	1,492	10,974
Connecticut...........	194	157	2,072	1,166	22,744
Delaware	28	29	206	98	2,055
East Carolina	18	34	819	258	2,528
Easton	88	86	441	186	2,768
Florida	45	55	450	848	2,422
Fond du Lac...........	82	51	800	856	2,988
Georgia...............	40	59	577	466	4,582
Indiana...............	86	41	655	499	4,928
Iowa	55	58	696	516	5,748
Kansas	82	64	258	187	2,167
Kentucky	49	42	478	466	5,714
Long Island	118	69	2,427	1,449	19,174
Louisiana.............	85	42	597	512	4,445
Maine	30	84	894	249	2,829
Maryland	170	180	2,888	2,351	24,596
Massachusetts	179	111	2,890	1,684	28,418
Michigan	80	66	1,486	994	11,486
Milwaukee	66	87	668	549	5,481
Minnesota	88	104	1,016	717	7,895
Mississippi	29	54	856	298	2,810
Missouri..............	80	98	829	717	6,944
Nebraska.............	40	24	297	229	2,400
Newark	91	80	1,742	979	12,221
New Hampshire	87	81	221	257	2,456
New Jersey	104	74	1,084	921	10,369
New York.............	888	196	5,766	8,605	46,066
North Carolina.......	57	75	611	806	5,492
Ohio	06	71	1,549	756	5,751
Pennsylvania	234	128	2,918	2,156	32,200
Pittsburg............	68	59	1,220	766	7,852
Quincy	24	28	190	160	2,066
Rhode Island	60	42	950	488	8,204
South Carolina.......	46	50	571	857	5,188
Southern Ohio	94	60	565	478	6,108
Springfield..........	40	58	845	229	3,148
Tennessee	45	67	584	847	3,718
Texas	25	58	498	264	2,978
Vermont	85	51	820	268	3,926
Virginia.............	154	181	1,625	1,496	15,892
Western Michigan.....	24	27	427	888	8,456
Western New York	114	110	1,809	1,264	13,805
West Virginia	22	27	271	227	2,719
MISSIONARY JURISDICTIONS.					
Oregon...............	17	27	220	184	1,224
North Dakota.........	12	48	154	51	668
Colorado	85	52	457	260	2,159
Utah	6	7	126	61	518
Nevada...............	4	2	156	58	402
South Dakota	82	75	598	196	1,628
Northern Texas	12	21	191	120	1,541
Western Texas	14	41	205	2	1,850
Northern California ..	16	21	811	128	824
New Mexico and Arizona..	6	21	106	81	192
Montana..............	12	24	158	98	1,005
Washington.......... ..	12	15	188	79	661
Wyoming and Idaho ..	10	17	175	59	577
West Africa	14	..	97	82	472
China	24	..	106	..	874
Japan	11	..	847	67	429
Total...	3,906	3,200	58,569	35,871	487,328

Number of dioceses......................................	49
Number of missionary jurisdictions (including Africa, China, and Japan)........................	17
Bishops..	68
Candidates for orders...............................	342
Deacons ordained.....................................	126
Priests ordained.....................................	100
Priests and deacons..................................	3,533
Whole number of clergy.............................	3,906
Whole number of parishes (about).................	3,200
Baptisms, infant.....................................	41,903
Baptisms, adult......................................	9,979
Baptisms, not specified.............................	1,707
Total..	53,589
Confirmed, number of...............................	35,871
Communicants..	437,328
Marriages...	14,875
Burials..	28,158
Sunday-school teachers.............................	38,400
Sunday-school scholars..............................	349,500
Contributions for church purposes................	$9,776,314

Domestic and Foreign Missions.—The Missionary Council, as constituted by the General Convention of 1886, consists of all the bishops, an equal number of presbyters, and an equal number of laymen. It meets annually (except in the years when the Board of Missions meets), and is charged with taking all necessary action in regard to the missionary work of the Church. The Council met in Philadelphia, Oct. 25, 1887, and continued in session for two days. It was largely attended by bishops, clergy, and laity, and disposed of its work with rapidity. The Annual Report of the Board of Managers was received, with accompanying documents; also, the Report of the Commission for Work among the Colored People, the Report (informal) of the Work of the Church Building Fund Commission, and the Sixteenth Annual Report of the Woman's Auxiliary. Appropriate action was discussed and outlined, and was urgently pressed upon the attention of the Church at large. The Board of Missions divides its work between a Domestic Committee and a Foreign Committee, which have their headquarters in New York city.

Domestic Missions.—Sept. 1, 1886 to Sept. 1, 1887. Missionaries (14 missionary jurisdictions and 30 dioceses): bishops, 12; other clergy (white, colored, Indian), 488; teachers, other helpers, etc., 78; total, 556. The financial condition was as follows:

Cash in hand (September, 1886)................	$24,885 08
Offerings, etc.........................	159,894 12
Legacies for domestic missions..................	21,244 00
Legacies for investment.........................	1,000 00
Specials..................................	47,996 40
Total.................................	$254,519 60

Expenditures (14 missionary jurisdictions and 32 dioceses)......................................	$102,597 33
Missions among Indians and colored people........	59,247 40
Specials.................................	47,634 75
Office and other expenses......................	19,281 21
Balance in hand........................	25,468 92
Total.................................	$254,519 60

Foreign Missions.—From Sept. 1, 1886, to Sept. 1, 1887, the number of missionary bishops was 3; the number of other clergy (white and native), 49; teachers, physicians, helpers, etc., 165; total, 217. The financial condition was as follows:

Cash in hand (September, 1886)............	$20,789 51
Offerings, legacies, etc.....................	133,327 16
Specials.................................	21,731 79
Total.................................	$175,848 46

Expenditures on account of missions, etc., in West Africa, China, and Japan........	$101,179 82
Specials.................................	11,413 05
Salaries, rent, printing, etc...............	18,281 21
Balance in hand.........................	44,974 38
Total.................................	$175,848 46

The mission property at foreign stations is estimated to be worth, in Africa, $21,400; in China (about), $170,000; in Japan (about), $50,000; total, $241,400.

The Woman's Auxiliary to the Board of Missions renders important and efficient aid in all the departments by means of parochial, city, county, and diocesan associations of ladies, formed for the purpose of raising money, preparing and forwarding boxes to missionaries and mission stations, and in various other ways giving help to the missions of the Church.

Money raised for domestic, foreign, and other mission work...................	$97,340 35
Boxes for the same (2,848 in number), value....	154,362 55
Total.................................	$251,702 90

The American Church Missionary Society (also auxiliary to the Board of Missions) has employed during the year, in 18 dioceses and missionary jurisdictions, 28 missionaries. The financial condition was as follows:

Balance in treasury Sept. 1, 1886..............	$8,720 84
Receipts from parishes, etc...............	9,055 44
Receipts from foreign missions...........	799 95
Balance in treasury Sept. 1, 1887.............	6,479 18
Total.................................	$25,058 41

A number of boxes of clothing was sent to the missionaries, in value....	$2,500 00
The society has also in property, securities, etc..	104,675 00

Church Work in Mexico was aided by the appointment of a presbyter (on nomination of the presiding bishop) in March, 1887, to whom was "assigned the duty of counseling and guiding the work of those presbyters and readers in Mexico who have asked for the fostering care of this Church to be extended to them as a mission." The clergyman appointed arrived in the city of Mexico June 2, and entered at once upon his work. An advisory committee for the work in Mexico have in charge all offerings for this field. "The Mexican League," it may be noted, is still in existence, as an independent association, consisting of ladies, for aid in missionary work in Mexico. It has no further connection with the Board of Missions. **The American Church Building-Fund Commission,** established in 1880, is gradually enlarging its usefulness. It hopes ere long to create a fund of not less than $1,000,000, so as to be able to give effective aid in all parts of the land toward building new churches. The permanent fund (Sept. 1, 1887) reached only the sum of $81,875.93; but the attention of wealthy members of the Church has been aroused, and the prospect of raising the fund to its proposed height grows brighter. During the year about twenty churches have been helped by loans, varying in amount from $300 to $1,500.

The Society for Promoting Christianity among the Jews (auxiliary to the Board of Missions) reports steady and, on the whole, encouraging progress. The society has missionaries at work in seven of the large cities, as well as in a number of populous towns. About $20,000 have been received by the Board of Managers, and expended in paying missionaries, supporting schools, etc. There are five missionary schools and five industrial schools, and over 250 of the parochial clergy co-operate in local activities. The entire work reaches the Jews in 254 cities and towns in the United States. Of publications, 13,300 copies have been issued during the year, and Bibles, Testaments, Scripture portions, and prayer-books have been circulated in English, Hebrew, German, and other languages.

Balance in hand, Sept. 1, 1886	$7,731 67
Contributions, specials, etc	12,373 92
Total	$20,105 59
Expenditures for schools, salaries, publications, etc.	$11,121 40
Real estate account	1,137 24
Balance to new account	7,846 95
Total	$20,105 59

General Condition of Church Affairs.—During the year five of the bishops have died, viz., Bishop Alfred Lee, of Delaware, presiding bishop; Bishop W. M. Green, of Mississippi; Bishop W. B. Stevens, of Pennsylvania; and Bishop R. W. B. Elliott, missionary bishop of Western Texas. Two presbyters have been consecrated bishops, viz., E. S. Thomas, assistant bishop of Kansas, and E. Talbot, missionary bishop of Wyoming and Idaho. Bishop W. F. Adams, formerly missionary bishop of New Mexico, has accepted the episcopate of the diocese of Easton. Three are on the list of retired bishops, viz., H. Southgate, C. C. Penick, S. I. J. Schereschewsky. In addition

to those above named, nearly sixty of the clergy have died during the year.

The important question of a more liberal support of the clergy, and more generous and considerate provision for aged and infirm servants of the Church's ministry, has been agitated to a considerable extent; but no special result of moment has yet been reached. In regard to the great lack of candidates for orders, there is little or no improvement. The bishops utter the same complaint as heretofore. The greatly superior attractions of business and other positions render it almost impossible to induce young men of ability and character to consider the claims which the ministry offers for their acceptance, and the high honor of serving the Lord in preaching his gospel. Hence, in view of the steady passing away of the older clergy, and of the vacancies that must necessarily be filled, the prospect becomes alarming, and calls for vigorous effort and fervent prayer that the Lord will send forth laborers into his harvest. The Society for the Increase of the Ministry is doing all that lies in its power, but it by no means succeeds in meeting the grave difficulty of the case. Numerous other societies (including a large number of sisterhoods) are striving to do good service to the cause of the Master and his Church, and have accomplished much in their respective fields of labor.

The action taken by the bishops of the Protestant Episcopal Church, in regard to a reunion of Protestant Christendom in the United States, has produced much discussion, as looked at from the various standpoints of Protestant denominations. The discussions have done good, in bringing out the sentiments and views of leading representative men among the larger bodies, Presbyterians, Baptists, Methodists, etc. No definite result has been reached thus far.

PSYCHICAL RESEARCH SOCIETIES. See MIND-READING.

Q

QUEBEC, PROVINCE OF. Government.—The Lieutenant-Governor is L. F. R. Masson. The Executive Council consists of: Premier and Attorney-General, H. Mercier; Commissioner of Crown Lands, Pierre Garneau; Treasurer, Joseph Shehyn; Commissioner of Agriculture and Public Works, James McShane; Provincial Secretary, C. A. E. Gagnon; Solicitor-General, George Duhamel; without portfolio, D. A. Ross and A. Turcotte.

Finances.—The gross public debt of the province on June 80, 1885, was $18,871,592, with assets amounting to $13,833,403. During the session of 1887 the Legislature passed an act to consolidate the floating debt, which amounts to $3,763,434.32, and to issue a new loan of three and a half million dollars at 4 per cent.

The floating debt has been largely increased by the putting into force of an act passed in 1886, authorizing the conversion of land-subsidies granted to certain railways into cash-subsidies.

Commerce.—The following table shows the imports and exports of the province for a period of five years:

YEAR.	IMPORTS.		EXPORTS.	
	Total value.	Value per head.	Total value.	Value per head.
1882	$56,105,257	$38 44	$38,972,121	$28 21
1883	55,909,571	39 95	42,642,956	30 47
1884	49,122,472	34 68	42,029,878	29 67
1885	46,738,088	32 61	39,604,451	27 64
1886	45,001,694	31 04	38,171,389	26 83

The exports of home produce and manufacture for the same period were as follow:

YEAR.	Total value.	Value per head.	Percentage of total exports.
1882	$32,157,451	$28 27	35·71
1883	33,389,549	28 89	39·56
1884	32,424,707	22 89	42·04
1885	31,152,169	21 74	40·89
1886	32,622,066	22 50	43·51

Legislation.—The first session of the Sixth Legislature of the province opened on Jan. 27, 1887. The Government (Conservative) was defeated by a vote of 36 to 27 upon a motion by the Attorney-General, Mr. Taillon, that Mr. Faucher de Saint Maurice be elected Speaker, and Felix Gabriel Marchand was elected to that office upon an amendment moved by the leader of the Opposition, Mr. Mercier, who subsequently formed the ministry described at the beginning of this article. On April 26, a motion being made to go into Committee of Supply, Mr. Taillon moved an amendment setting forth that the House is prepared to vote the supplies to her Majesty for the requirements of the public service, but regrets that the Government persists in condemning the policy of progress followed in this province since 1867; that the House is of opinion that this policy deserved and in fact obtained the approval of a majority of the electors; that this policy has brought about the construction of a vast network of railways; that several members of the new Government are responsible for this broad policy, and that the House is of opinion that the debt contracted in subsidizing these railways has been contracted in the interests of the public; that the new Government has admitted that the creation of the greater part of the provincial debt is due to this liberal railway policy; that the previous Government efficiently and economically administered the affairs of the province, without having recourse to a permanent loan; and, finally, that the House regrets that the Honorable Treasurer has submitted statements that are incorrect and calculated to injure the credit of the province. This resolution was defeated by a vote of 35 to 27.

Incorporation of the Jesuits.—An act was passed, after considerable opposition from Cardinal Taschereau and other Roman Catholic bishops, to incorporate the Society of Jesus, with the right to acquire and hold movable and immovable property, provided that the revenue from immovable property held by the society for revenue in any diocese shall not exceed $30,000 per annum.

Corrupt Practices at Elections.—A short but stringent act was passed, providing that, if it be proved upon the trial of an election petition that the successful candidate has employed as canvasser or agent any person who has, to his knowledge, been within three years proved guilty of any corrupt practice, the election shall be void. The act further provides for the disqualification for seven years of any person, other than a candidate, who shall be found guilty of corrupt practices.

R

REFORMED CHURCHES. I. Reformed Church in America.—The statistical reports of this Church, as made to the General Synod in June, 1887, give the following footings: Number of Particular Synods, 4; of classes, 34; of churches, 547; of ministers, 547, with 8 licentiates; of families, 48,064; of persons received during the year on confession, 5,524. Total number in communion, 85,543; number of baptisms during the year, 4,669 of infants and 1,347 of adults; whole number of baptized non-communicants, 29,623; of catechumens, 31,173; of Sabbath-schools, 767, with 95,717 enrolled members. Amount of contributions: for religious and benevolent purposes, $232,202; for congregational purposes, $913,734.

The Board of Direction returned the whole amount of the funds, endowments, and investments in the hands of its treasurer as $746,-294. The total amount of the Endowed Scholarship funds of the Theological Seminary at New Brunswick, N. J., was $113,109. The invested funds of Hope College were $112,-658, from which an income of 5½ per cent. had been derived. The whole amount of the Widows' fund was $70,399, and the receipts in its behalf had been $10,883. The Disabled Ministers' fund amounted to $53,817; it had received $9,-115, and 38 cases of beneficiaries had been assisted from it. The Board of Publication had received $16,676 from sales, and returned a cash balance of $4,173. The Board of Domestic Missions had received $61,378, and had expended $61,380. It returned 107 assisted churches, with 82 missionary pastors, 4,633 families, 6,891 members, and 685 additions on confession. Seven new Sabbath-schools had been organized, making the whole number of schools 101, with which 9,922 pupils were connected. The sum of $12,357 had been contributed to the Church-Building fund. The Woman's Executive Committee of Home Missions returned $5,956 of collections for the year. The total receipts of the Board of Foreign Missions had been $86,487. The missions in China, India, and Japan comprised 11 stations, 101 out-stations and preaching-places, 28 missionaries, 29 assistant missionaries, with 6 missionaries and assistants under appointment, 7 native ordained missionaries, 207 native helpers, 31 churches, 2,471 communicants, 11 seminaries, with 431 pupils, 3 theological schools or classes, with 28 students, and 101 day-schools with 2,622 pupils. The tables do not, however, include the ordained ministers and other helpers, churches, and communicants in Japan, as they are connected with the Union Church and the Council of Ministers, and are represented in the reports of those bodies.

The General Synod of the Reformed Church in America met in Catskill, N. Y., June 1. The Rev. Charles J. Shepherd was chosen moderator. A number of communications were received on the subject of union with the Presbyterian Church. After consideration of them by committee and debate in the Synod, it was unanimously resolved:—

1. That the indications of Providence are not of such a nature as to make the present effort of some in this direction wise or hopeful of good to the Church. From all present appearances it would only be detrimental to our peace, unity, and prosperity.

Resolved (2), That the present duty of the Reformed Church, its ministers and elders, is not to agitate and probably disrupt itself with vain questions, but, with evidently much work to do, to do its duty as God has given and gives to us loyally and faithfully till such time as the workings of his Spirit shall indicate much more manifestly than at present that our denominational work is done.

The Committee on Union with the Reformed Church in the United States reported that formal movements on the subject were waiting the action of the General Synod of the latter body, which met only triennially, and was at this time in session. The committee had therefore been restricted to obtaining information by correspondence and the observation of public utterances. It had found a general feeling prevalent in favor of a closer union of some kind between the bodies. The committee was continued.

A report was made by the Rev. R. Randal Hoes, chaplain in the United States Navy, concerning researches which he had made in Holland of documents and historical memoranda affecting the Reformed Church. He represented that the books of the Classis of Amsterdam, which had been supposed to be lost, were in a good state of preservation, and that he had had free access to them. He had also seen and had arranged for the transcription of some four hundred original letters and other documents, which would probably complete the historic records of the Church. He was ready to place all these papers in charge of the Synod without cost to the Church, and Mr. B. Fernow, of the New York State Library, had offered to translate them and prepare them for use. The Synod made provision for obtaining possession of the documents, and appointed a committee of custodians to take charge of them and see that they were translated and published. A question arose concerning the status of a church in the Classis of Cayuga, which, it was represented, had been transferred by the consistory to an adjoining presbytery without taking the vote of the members upon the subject, and contrary to the advice of the

Classis. A special committee was appointed to consider what steps could be taken in the matter, in order that, though the congregation be lost, the property of the church might be recovered to the Reformed Church. A report was received from the committee which had been appointed two years previously to formulate the plan of the Theological School at New Brunswick, N. J. It was ordered to be printed as a circular, copies of which should be sent to every Reformed minister, while the subject should be reserved for the action of the next General Synod. An overture asking that the Particular Synods be made final courts of appeal in all cases except questions of doctrine was denied, on the ground that sufficient provision on the subject already existed in the constitution of the Church. A motion was ordered sent down to the Classes for approval, directing that "no text-books known as catechisms, and designed for the instruction of the children and youth in Christian doctrine, shall be used in the Sabbath-schools of the Reformed (Dutch) Church except such as are approved and recommended by the General Synod." A proposition for forming a Sustentation fund to raise all salaries of pastors to $1,000 a year, which was presented to the Synod of the previous year, and had been under the consideration of a special committee, was taken up and negatived.

II. Reformed Church in the United States.—The following is a summary of the statistics of this church for 1887, as they were reported to the General Synod in June. Comparison with the appended statistics for 1878 will serve to show the growth of the Church in nine years:

ITEMS.	1878.	1887.
Synods	6	7
Classes	45	54
Ministers	719	862
Congregations	1,369	1,481
Members	147,788	182,950
Members unconfirmed	90,996	108,724
Baptisms, infants	12,328	14,159
Baptisms, adults	880	1,711
Confirmed	8,456	10,783
Communed	120,681	146,436
Sunday-schools	1,237	1,422
Sunday-school pupils	89,982	192,695
Students for the ministry	157	186
Benevolent contributions	$61,797	$141,122
Contributions for congregational purposes	$581,929	$904,821

The report of the Board of Home Missions embraces the work of the several Boards of the Synods of the United States, Pittsburg, and the Potomac; of the Synod of Ohio; of the Synod of the Northwest, and the Central Synod —German; of the German Synod of the East, and the mission department of Ursinus Union. The total receipts for the past three years had been $89,541; number of missions 111, and number of members, 10,519. The receipts of three years for church extension had been $15,-497. The combined receipts for home missions and church extension were shown to have been $27,048 in excess of those of the preceding three years. The sum of $2,313 had been spent in the service of the Harbor Mission at New York, where one missionary had been employed. The appointment of a General Superintendent of Home Mission Work was authorized. The three Orphans' Homes—Bethany, at Womelsdorf, Pa.; St. Paul's, at Butler, Pa.; and Fort Wayne, Ind., returned about two hundred children as under their care. The Society for the Relief of Ministers and Ministers' Widows—the oldest charitable institution of the Church, being now a hundred years old—was commended by the Synod, and collections were directed to be taken up annually for its benefit. The receipts of the Board of Foreign Missions for three years had been $38,989; seven missionaries were employed in the mission at Sendai, in Japan, in connection with which 14 stations were returned, with 705 members, a ministerial training-school, with seven students, and a girls' school, with 41 pupils.

The Triennial General Synod of the Reformed Church in the United States met at Akron, Ohio, June 1. The Rev. George W. Welker, D. D., of Lamont, N. C., was chosen president. A report was adopted on the subject of a closer union between the Reformed Churches holding the Presbyterian polity, and on subjects relating to church union in general, in which the Synod declared:

If any should ask what we think of unity among Christians, and what we may stand ready to do in favor of a closer union between not only churches known by the distinctive name Reformed, but all evangelical churches, we might simply point to the history of the Church of which we are the oldest branch, and to the testimony of its general course during the past three centuries in regard to the relations of amity and fraternization between different parts of the communion of saints. We may never have indulged in loud proclamations of our love of liberty and union, but it may be affirmed without boasting that from the great conference at Marburg onward the Reformed Church has shown a willingness to do more and suffer more in the interest of a true, consistent Christian union than any other. Had her spirit, wishes, and counsel prevailed in other days, there would be fewer divisions in the great household of faith than now exist. And now that they do exist, it is believed she will be found ready to go any length short of sacrificing vital, fundamental principles and doctrines to heal the divisions. We may, indeed, not magnify the facts or evils of sects, or be willing to stigmatize all as sects whom some superciliously despise and condemn as such. Some of the divisions now maintained sprang not from schismatic agitations, but from social and national causes naturally leading to such diversity of organizations. This holds, indeed, of almost every branch of the Reformed Church. They are, in fact, one in everything but formal union, and some less vital usages.

With regard to the action proposed particularly by the House of Bishops of the Protestant Episcopal Church, the Synod expressed itself as cordially holding what it had always held and pleaded for, viz.: That the Church, as the 'General Assembly' of the truly chosen and regenerated of the Lord has no doubt been often greatly afflicted with needless divisions and dissensions. . . . And holding this, the desirableness of purging the Church of this evil

is unhesitatingly admitted. For this we should labor, pray, and hope. And accordingly we ... welcome the advance made in the direction of such a union, and declare our willingness to meet them and any other fellow-Christians of the common apostolic faith, on some equal ground or platform of conference, for the purpose of furthering such a union. As between the several families of the distinctively Reformed Church, the Synod would, above all, declare that either a closer spiritual or possibly formal union might be effected. It could not now see clearly enough into the future to anticipate union under one organization and government, although that was to be hoped and prayed for. " But as to some closer fellowship, and some method of evangelizing general work, there seems to be no reason why a movement should not be inaugurated at once looking to such co-operation. And to make a modest beginning in the movement, the Synod would suggest that instead of taking any steps involving the entire Church it represents, it be left to the district synods to begin the work, if occasion offers and justifies it, within their several bounds by co-operative evangelistic efforts." A committee was appointed to confer with a similar committee of the Reformed Church in America on the subject of union. The Council of the Alliance of the Reformed Churches held in Belfast, Ireland, in 1884, had been attended by eight of the appointed delegates from this body, who reported that they had been impressed with the pleasant conviction that, under divine favor the Alliance is proving an efficient means of promoting the vital evangelical principles and interests which it represents." A committee, appointed by the previous General Synod to consider and report upon revision of the Constitution of the Church, submitted a draft of the Constitution embodying the amendments suggested, which was approved by the General Synod and referred to the classes for their decision upon it. The Directory of Worship, having been submitted to the classes for their approval or rejection, was found to have been approved by the majority of the members, and was declared to be constitutionally adopted. In reply to an inquiry from a classis concerning the form of receiving persons into the Church by re-profession, the Synod directed that " all persons applying for admission into the Church, having no valid certificate of church-membership, shall be strictly examined as to their moral and spiritual qualifications before they are admitted by the spiritual council, and that their reception thereafter be accomplished formally by the pastor, in the presence of either the congregation or the spiritual council "; and a suitable formula was ordered prepared for the service. A committee on a digest of the decisions of the several synods of the Church, having appellate jurisdiction on questions of doctrine, morals, customs, and constitutional interpretations, not being prepared to report, was reorganized to report to the next General

Synod. Provision was made for the revision of all existing formulas, and the preparation of other formulas necessary for the use of pastors, congregations, judicatories, and institutions. A General Sunday-School Board was instituted, to have charge of the Sunday-school interests of the Church. Co-operation with the several State and the International Sunday-School Associations was recommended. Synods, classes, and churches were invited to unite in efforts for the extermination of intemperance. The proceedings and documents of the Synod are published in both the English and the German languages.

Meeting of Committees on Union.—A meeting of the union committees of the Reformed Church in America and the Reformed Church in the United States was held in the city of New York in December, to consider the question of a closer union of the two churches. Without reaching any conclusions on the subject of their deliberations, the committees adjourned, to meet again in March, 1888.

III. Reformed Churches in Germany.—The Reformed Churches of Germany, while they hold to the Heidelberg Catechism as a common standard of faith, are separated into several bodies by their various relations to the different states. Differences also exist among them in respect to the doctrine of predestination. A movement for a closer union among them was begun in 1884, after the meeting of the Presbyterian Alliance at Belfast, which was expressed in a preliminary consultation held at Marburg in that year. This was followed by the first conference of the Alliance of the Reformed Churches in Germany, which was held at Elberfeld in 1885. The plan of the conferences includes discussions of questions bearing upon the welfare of the churches, but without vote, except upon those points on which full agreement is evident. The second meeting of the Alliance was held at Detmold in August, 1887. More than one hundred and fifty delegates were present, who came principally from northern and eastern Germany. Prof. John Cairns, of Edinburgh, attended as a representative of the Presbyterian Alliance. Among the subjects considered were "The Condition of the Reformed Church in Germany and the Alliance Organization"; "The Means by which Theological Representation for the Reformed Church in the Universities and Seminaries"—where, it was complained, Lutheran influence has become predominant—"can be better secured"; "The Support of Reformed Churches in other Lands" (the churches in America being had chiefly in view); "The Presbyterian Church Polity, particularly in the French Reformed Church" (with especial reference to the French Reformed churches in Berlin); "The Mission to the Hebrew People," and the situation of the Church in the capital city of the empire (where the increase of church buildings was regarded as not at all commensurate with the growth of the population).

The conference provided for having an expression of its views on theological representation of the Church in the universities and seminaries carried up through the proper synods to the Supreme State Consistory.

IV. Reformed Church in Hungary.—The Reformed Church in Hungary has 1,980 regularly organized congregations, with 1,909 pastors, 2,278 teachers, 202,898 pupils in schools, and 300 students in theological colleges. In addition, services in behalf of scattered Protestants are occasionally held in some 8,261 places.

REFORMED EPISCOPAL CHURCH. The following is a summary of the statistics of this Church as they were reported to the General Council in May, 1887. The statistics of 1885, when the last previous General Council was held, are appended for comparison:

ITEMS.	1885.	1887.
Sunday-school pupils	10,256	11,720
Sunday-school teachers	846	999
Baptisms	776	907
Confirmations	521	916
Received otherwise	849	519
Communicants	7,210	8,249
Expenses and offerings	$142,747	$155,869
Value of property unencumbered	$972,067	$1,077,758

The treasurer of the Council reported the following as the amounts at which the funds under his charge were balanced: General and Missionary fund, $18,026; Martin College fund, $971; Theological Seminary Endowment fund, including pledges uncollected, $17,562.

The trustees of the Sustentation fund reported that their receipts for two years had been $10,254. The chief part of this amount had, however, been received from the proceeds of an annuity, but one congregational contribution having been offered. As the annuity is of limited duration, the trustees recommended that a part of the proceeds from it be regularly retained for investment, and that means be taken to encourage the churches to contribute to the fund. The amount of the Widows' and Orphans' fund was returned at $6,181. Its receipts during the past two years had been $2,636, and the actual increase of the fund had been $1,624. Return was made of the Special Missionary fund, $5,000; the income of which, $276, had been applied to the work among the freedmen; the Eleanor H. Stroud fund of $5,000, devoted to the support of the rector of a particular church; and of legacies in which the Church is interested, to the total amount of $28,395, with two unvalued legacies, and an annuity fund of $4,000 for twenty years.

The Co-operative Committee on Work among the Freedmen had received and applied $199. Bishop Stevens, of the special jurisdiction of the South, who is in charge of the work among the freedmen of South Carolina, returned as connected with his diocese, 36 churches, with 18 pastors, 1,584 members, and 851 Sunday-school pupils. The contributions of these churches had amounted in all to $4,815. He had received for the purposes of the work

RHODE ISLAND.

$4,895, and had expended $4,716. The work is mainly in the country, among the laborers in the rice and cotton fields. The jurisdiction owns 32 lots with 31 church-buildings, valued in all at about $17,000, which are free of debt except to their own people.

The Foreign Mission Committee had received $2,755, all of which had been applied toward the support of the station of the Woman's Union Missionary Society at Cawnpore. India.

The eleventh General Council of the Reformed Episcopal Church met in Philadelphia, May 25. Presiding Bishop James A. Latané, D. D., presided. The bishops made reports of the condition and work of the several jurisdictions under their charge, viz.: Bishop Cheney, of the Synod of Chicago; Bishop Nicholson, of the Synod of New York and Philadelphia; Bishop Cridge, of the jurisdiction of the Pacific; Bishop Fellows, of the jurisdiction of the Northwest and West; Bishop Stevens, of the special jurisdiction of the South; Bishop Latané, of the missionary jurisdiction of the South; and Bishop Wilson, of the Synod of Canada. On the subject of marriage and divorce, the Synod resolved "that the Reformed Episcopal Church recognizes adultery as the only scriptural ground for divorce: that this Church forbids its ministers to perform the marriage ceremony for any divorced party, unless the person from whom that party is divorced, has been guilty of or is living in adultery"; and "that nothing in these resolutions forbids the remarriage of a former husband and wife." Evangelistic services were recognized as a potent factor in the aggressive work of the Church, and evangelistic unions were approved as useful, wherever practicable, for the more systematic and efficient conduct of such services. Collections were ordered taken regularly in the churches every year for the Board of Missions and the current expenses of the theological seminary. The Council declared, by resolution, "that all Christian men and women should, both by precept and example, uphold the cause of temperance, and do all in their power to suppress the liquor-traffic; that no Christian can consistently engage in this traffic, or profit by it, either by leasing or letting the building in which to carry it on, or otherwise; and that no Christian can consistently aid this traffic by signing petitions for license to engage in the same."

The General Synod of Great Britain and Ireland of this Church has a separate and independent existence, which was granted by a resolution of the General Council of 1888.

RHODE ISLAND. State Government.—The following were the State officers during the year: Governor, George P. Wetmore, Republican, succeeded by John W. Davis, Democrat; Lieutenant-Governor, Lucius B. Darling, succeeded by Samuel R. Honey; Secretary of State, Joshua M. Addeman, succeeded by Edwin D. McGuinness; Treasurer, Samuel Clark, succeeded by John G. Perry; Auditor and Insurance Commissioner, Samuel H. Cross, succeeded by E. W. Bucklin; Attorney-General, Edwin Metcalf, succeeded by Ziba O. Slocum; Railroad Commissioner, Walter R. Stiness; Chief-Justice of the Supreme Court, Thomas Durfee; Associate Justices, Pardon E. Tillinghast, Charles Matteson, John H. Stiness, and George A. Wilbur.

Legislative Sessions.—The adjourned session of the Legislature of 1886 continued from January 18 to May 6. A woman-suffrage amendment to the Constitution, proposed by the preceding Legislature, was approved, and provision made for its submission to the people in April. Considerable changes were made in the liquor law passed at the May session, with the object of removing difficulties and defects preventing its complete enforcement. The chief of State police may now designate as his assistants ten members of the State police, for service outside of their usual jurisdiction. Any officer may, without warrant, seize liquor, or arrest persons illegally selling or handling liquor, provided a warrant be sworn out within twenty-four hours in case of arrest. Except on railroads and steamships, there can be no transportation of liquor by night, and all receptacles containing it must be fully marked, to show the contents and destination. The dispensing of liquor at clubs is made a common nuisance, punishable by a heavy fine or imprisonment. Annual reports from the various local sheriffs and from the chief of State police are required.

Other acts of the session were as follow:

Making additional regulations for the treatment of diseased cattle.

Amending the election laws, to prevent fraud and irregularity.

Regulating the powers of orphanages.

Establishing the boundary-line between this State and Connecticut from the mouth of Ashaway river through the waters of the Pawcatuck river and the waters of the sea.

Establishing "Arbor-day" as a holiday.

To punish false pretenses in securing the registration of cattle and other animals, and to punish giving false pedigrees.

Annexing a part of the town of Cranston to the city of Providence.

Amending and revising the truant law.

The new Legislature elected in April met at Newport on May 31, for its first session, and adjourned June 17 to meet in January, 1888, at Providence. Only six public laws were passed, among them the following:

Authorizing the city of Providence to borrow $300,-000, to be expended on highways.

Giving the Secretary of State full control and management of the State-House at Providence.

Prohibiting the sale of liquors or merchandise within one mile of out-door religious meetings or associations without consent of such religious society.

Authorizing the town of Woonsocket to issue $300,-000 of bonds.

Before the end of the year, it was found that the appropriation for paying jurors in the county courts had been exhausted, as well as the miscellaneous fund. The Governor therefore called an extra session. This session met at Providence November 15, and continued four days. The amendment relative to qualifications of voters was the only one discussed, but, the houses failing to agree upon a time for its submisson, it was deferred to the January session. The only important legislation effected was the passage of appropriation bills, amounting in all to $23,665. An appropriation of $5,000 was made for completion and equipment of the new insane asylum at Cranston.

Finances.—The State indebtedness at the close of the year consisted of $609,000 in bonds, due in July, 1893, and $732,000 in bonds due in August, 1894, a total of $1,341,000. The amount in the sinking-fund at the same time was $701,504.40, reducing the actual indebtedness to $639,495.60. The actual debt twelve months previous was $781,834.05. The total expenditures of the State for the year were $852,704.12, and the receipts $737,751.29. The cash in the treasury on January 1 was $250,-410 99; on December 31, $135,458.16. There has been a deficiency in revenue for the past two years amounting to $208,066.83, caused by the falling off in receipts from licenses since the prohibitory law came into force. The State received in 1885 from licenses of all kinds $112,870.59, while in 1886 and 1887 only $5,500 accrued from this source.

Charities and Prisons.—The total annual appropriation for the State charitable and penal institutions for 1887 was $135,000. There was also received from the earnings of these institutions $39,740.87, making the total income $174,740.87. The cost of support during the year was $162,015.21. At the State Prison on December 31 there were 92 inmates, 89 males and 3 females; at the Workhouse and House of Correction, about 150; at the Providence County Jail, 235; and at the Sockanosset School for Boys, 214.

Prohibition.—Varying opinions are entertained regarding the success of the prohibitory amendment in accomplishing its object. Chief-of-Police Brayton, in his letter of resignation, in May, says: "Statistics of arrests in the city of Providence show a decrease in the number of arrests for drunkenness of more than 40 per cent. during the nine months under prohibition, ending March 31, 1887, as compared with the corresponding period under license. Commitments to the State Workhouse—the result almost wholly of the use of intoxicating liqors—show a decrease of more than 51 per cent., resulting in an actual saving to the State in board alone of more than $22,800."

On the other hand, the "Providence Journal," in July, speaking of the result of one year's enforcement, says: "During the first few months after the law went into effect, uncertainty and fear closed many bar-rooms; the result was promptly seen in the police records, and materially diminishes the year's arrests. But now the case is far different. Drunkenness fell off considerably last summer, but since then it has been increasing throughout the State. The use of intoxicants is as extensive now as it ever was; prohibition at the present

time is doing nothing to raise the moral tone of the community." The arrests for drunkenness in Newport and Providence, for the last twelve months of license, and the first twelve months of prohibition, ending July 1, are as follows: Newport, under license, 375; under prohibition, 245; Providence, under license, 4,670; under prohibition, 2,947. During the first three months of prohibition the arrests in these two places were 725; during the last three months, 945.

Political.—On February 23, the Prohibitionists met in State Convention, and nominated the following candidates: Governor, Thomas H. Peabody; Lieutenant-Governor, Anthony M. Kimber; Secretary of State, Frederick A. Warner; Treasurer, John G. Perry; Attorney-General, Edwin Metcalf. Among the resolutions adopted is the following:

Resolved, That in conjunction with the temperance voters of all parties, the Prohibitionists of this State aided in securing the triumph of the prohibitory amendment of the Constitution, and rejoice in the victory thus achieved over the desolating, debauching, and destructive influence of the saloon; but neither as citizens nor prohibitionists are we responsible for the chronic weakness of any provision of the law enacted by a Republican Legislature for the enforcement of the Constitution as thus amended, nor for the machinery created to carry such law into effect. We approve that which has proved itself effective in the law, but we decline any responsibility for acts performed by other parties in furtherance of their own party interests and ends.

The Democratic State Convention met in Providence on March 9, and nominated the following ticket: Governor, John W. Davis; Lieutenant-Governor, Samuel R. Honey; Secretary of State, Edwin D. McGuinness; Treasurer, John G. Perry; Attorney-General, Ziba O. Slocum. The platform contains the following declarations:

We declare that the abuses, irregularities, and corruptions now existing are largely due to defects in, and departures from, our fundamental law, and that the true interests of the State demand such revision and amendment of the Constitution as shall—

1. Abolish the registry-tax now imposed upon native-born citizens, and which for the last thirty-five years has been the source of political corruption, making money the qualification for office, instead of intelligence, capacity, and character.

2. Abolish all discriminations now made against naturalized citizens, and place them on an equal basis with native-born citizens.

3. Forbid members of the judiciary department of the State from holding other offices, either legislative or administrative.

Also that the laws of the State should be so amended as—

1. To provide reasonable rules for the acquirement and exercise of the right of the elective franchise.

2. To prevent and severely punish bribery.

3. To provide schools for the education of children, particularly those engaged in labor, including those speaking a foreign language.

4. For the enforcement of laws limiting the hours of labor, preventing truancy, and protecting the employed.

5. To establish a Bureau of Industrial Statistics similar to those already in successful operation in other States.

6. To protect the whole people by just, necessary, and prudent laws.

The Republican Convention, held on March 16, at Providence, renominated the State officers. Its platform declarations favor protection, civil-service reform, and a national bankrupt act, and contain the following upon State issues:

We recognise the fact that the adoption of the fifth amendment to our State Constitution was not a partisan measure, and that such amendment has become a part of our fundamental law in obedience to the will of the constitutional majority. We demand the enactment of laws adequate to carry this amendment into effect, and that such laws shall be rigidly enforced, recognising at the same time the right of the people to agitate for the repeal of this or any other constitutional provision which time may prove to be unwise or ineffectual.

We believe that the General Assembly should submit to the people a proposition for a constitutional amendment providing for the abolition of the registry-tax as a prerequisite for voting, and that the adoption of such amendment would conduce to the welfare of the State. We also favor the enactment of strict laws to prevent and punish fraudulent voting and bribery at elections.

The canvass developed a wide-spread feeling of discontent among Republicans with the character and purposes of their party leaders, and at the polls on April 6 the number of disaffected ones proved sufficient to give the victory to the Democrats. For Governor, Davis received 18,095 votes, Wetmore 15,111, and Peabody 1,895. No one having received a majority of votes for Secretary of State or for Lieutenant-Governor, the choice of these officers devolved upon the Legislature, which elected the Democratic candidates. The political character of the Legislature chosen at the same election is as follows: Senate, 20 Republicans, 16 Democrats; House, 29 Republicans, 41 Democrats, 1 Prohibitionist. A constitutional amendment, giving women the right to vote in the election of all civil officers, and on all questions in town, district, and ward meetings, subject to the same conditions as men, was voted upon at this time, and was defeated by a vote of 6,889 to 21,957.

A special election was held February 21, in the Second Congressional District, to fill a vacancy in the Forty-ninth Congress caused by the House declaring William A. Pirce not entitled to a seat. Pirce was again the Republican candidate, but was defeated by Charles H. Page, Democrat, the vote being Pirce, 5,495; Page, 5,790; Chadsey, Prohibition, 466. A second special election in the same district on November 8, to fill a vacancy in the Fiftieth Congress, caused by failure to hold an election in 1886, resulted in the choice of Warren O. Arnold, Republican, by a vote of 8,099, over Charles S. Bradley, Democrat, who received

7,252 votes, and Thomas H. Peabody, Prohibitionist, who had 299 votes.

RIFLES, REPEATING. The advantages possessed by a rifle that could be fired several times without stopping to reload, over a single-loader, have always been recognized by sportsmen, and latterly by soldiers, and many attempts have been made to produce such a weapon. When rifles were loaded with a ball and loose powder, it was found practically impossible to produce a really good repeating-rifle. The Colt, in which six charges were contained in a revolving cylinder in the rear of the barrel (as in a revolving pistol) was the only one that was used to any extent. But this admitted the escape of gas between the cylinder and the barrel, which burned the left arm when the hand was placed in front of it in firing.

Since the introduction of metallic cartridge-cases, the number of rifles of this description that have been invented has been great. The first to come into general use in America was the Henry, which has been improved into the Winchester and the Bullard. These rifles have been extensively used for sporting-arms. In them the cartridges are contained in a cham-

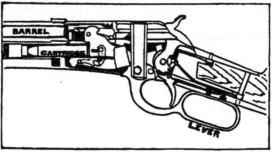

NEW WINCHESTER REPEATER.

ber, which is underneath the barrel and parallel with it. By throwing down a lever (A, Fig. 1), which constitutes a part of the trigger-guard, the cartridge in the barrel is ejected, the gun is cocked, a carrier-block is thrown down to the level of the cartridge-chamber, and a cartridge from the latter is thrown into it by the pressure of a spring. When the lever is pulled back, the carrier-block raises the cartridge and pushes it into the barrel, which is closed by the breech-block, and the gun is ready to fire.

With the usual conservatism of army authorities, the introduction of repeating-rifles for military purposes has been very slow, great apprehension being felt that troops armed with them would waste their ammunition—the same objection that retarded the adoption of the breech-loader. Although the use of the Henry rifle was common among sportsmen, no attempt was made to introduce them into the United States Army during the civil war. In the latter part of that war the Spencer was issued to a few organizations, mostly cavalry. In this rifle

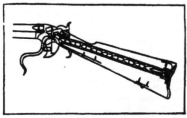

ORIGINAL SPENCER REPEATING-RIFLE.

the cartridges were contained in a tube, which was inserted in the butt, extending from the heel-plate to the rear of the barrel. Although the gun was clumsy and difficult to load, it was

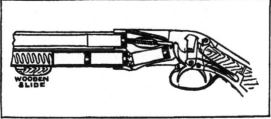

NEW MODEL SPENCER REPEATING SHOT-GUN.

found to increase very greatly the efficiency of the troops that were armed with it. During the Turco-Russian War, the Turks armed some · of their troops, usually the cavalry, with Winchesters. They were also used by the infantry at Plevna with great effect in repelling the Russian attacks. The Swiss were the first European nation to adopt a repeater for their troops. Germany, within the past year, suddenly equipped its army with the repeating Mauser, and since then there has been a race between the different nations as to which shall first provide a magazine-gun for their troops. The different rifles may be divided as follow:

1. Those in which the cartridges are contained in a tube under the barrel, as in the Winchester (Am.), Bullard (Am.), Henry (Am.), Ward Biviton (Am.), Spencer (new model, Am.), Colt (new model, Am.), Mauser

(Ger.), Lobel (Fr.), Jarmen (Swd.), Vetterli .(Swiss), and Kropatschech (Fr. and Port.). The objection to this style of gun is, that its balance alters as the magazine is emptied.

2. Where they are contained in the stock, as in the Spencer (old style), Meigs (all Am.), Evans (Am. and Russian), Hotchkiss, Chaffee-Reece, and others.

3. Where they are contained in a chamber behind the barrel, as in the Schulhoff (Russian), where they revolve around a central pin as in a revolver (which is complicated).

4. Where they are contained in a magazine (fixed or detachable) attached to the rear of the barrel, as in the Lee (Am.), Elliott (Am.), Mannlicher (Aus.), Vitali (It.), Burton (Am.), Lee Burton (Am.), Owen Jones (Eng.), which seems to be generally preferred for military purposes.

The new Spencer (shot-gun and rifle) and Colt are operated by the pulling back and pushing forward of a knob under the center of the barrel, which is held in the left hand when the piece is being aimed. Like the Winchester, they can be fired without taking them from the shoulder. Most of the others (especially the European) are bolt guns—i. e., instead of a lever, the rifle is operated by a bolt, which is actuated by a short handle. When this handle is turned to the left and drawn back, the old cartridge is ejected, the gun cocked, and a new cartridge thrown opposite the cartridge-chamber. When it is pushed forward and turned down, the cartridge is forced into the chamber, and the breech is closed and locked. In the Mannlicher (Aus.) the bolt is drawn straight back-

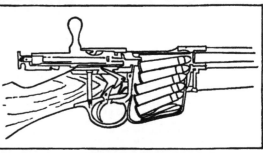

LEE MAGAZINE GUN.

ward, so that the gun need not be taken from the shoulder. The more modern repeaters have a device by which the magazine may be closed and the rifle used as a single loader.

In the Lee (Am.), Vitali (It.), and others,

small detachable magazines, carrying from four to six cartridges, are slipped into position under the breech-opening when it is desired to use the magazine, the soldier carrying several. The cartridges are pressed up one at a time by a spring in the magazine.

The first repeating-rifles were only adapted to light charges. They are now made to carry as heavy ones as are needed, the Winchester Express using ninety grains of powder. The general opinion of experts is, that the coming military rifle will be a repeater, with a caliber of about ·31, using 90 to 100 grains of compressed and (if possible) smokeless powder, and a long composite bullet—i. e., a steel shell with a lead center, weighing about 340 grains. Such a rifle will sweep the ground for 600 yards, without any elevation of the sights, will give a range of 2,000 yards, and in emergencies will render it possible to produce a hail of fire that would be irresistible. The cartridges are so light that the soldier can carry a much larger number of them than he can of those now in use.

ROACH, JOHN, an American ship-builder, born in Mitchellstown, County Cork, Ireland, Dec. 25, 1813; died in New York city Jan. 10, 1887. The death of his father when he was twelve years old threw him upon his own resources, and he supported himself until he was sixteen, when he came to the United States.

JOHN ROACH.

After varying fortunes he found work in James Allaire's iron-foundry, where he served an apprenticeship and was a journeyman machinist. At the age of twenty-one he had saved $1,500, $500 of which he then invested in Illinois prairie-land, leaving the remainder in Mr. Allaire's hands and losing it in his subsequent failure. He resumed work as a machinist, learning also to make castings for marine engines and ship-work. When he had saved $100 he joined three other mechanics in buying the Ætna Iron Works, then in the hands of a receiver, subsequently buying out their interest and possessing a prosperous business

at the age of thirty-six. At the height of his first prosperity his foundry was destroyed by a boiler explosion, and he experienced great difficulty in obtaining money to rebuild on a larger scale; but after he had established himself again his success was rapid. In his new works he constructed the engines of the "Dunderberg," "Bristol," and "Providence," the largest ever built in this country, and, becoming a ship-builder as well as an iron-founder, increased his plant by the purchase of the Morgan Iron Works in 1867, the Neptune Works in 1868, the Franklin Forge and the Allaire Works in 1870, and the ship-yards at Chester, Pa., in 1871. In the latter year he began building iron vessels, and completed in all sixty-three during the next twelve years under contracts with the United States Government, corporations, and private individuals. Ninety per cent. of the iron vessels sailing under the American flag were built by him, mostly for the merchant marine. For the Government he built six of the great monitors ordered during President Grant's administration, and more recently the three cruisers "Chicago," "Atlanta," and "Boston," and the dispatch-boat "Dolphin," besides repairing many old vessels. The refusal of the Government to accept the "Dolphin" in 1885 led to his suspension, but the vast works were reopened soon afterward upon the acceptance of the ship. From 1871 till his death he built in all 114 iron vessels, and in the latter part of his life his possessions were so extensive that he could draw from his own property every article that entered into the construction of a complete sea-going vessel.

ROMAN CATHOLIC CHURCH. The year 1887–'88 was remarkable for momentous events in the history of the Roman Catholic Church. During the year 1887 constant preparations were made for the celebration of the Golden Jubilee, or the fiftieth anniversary of the ordination of Leo XIII to the priesthood. This anniversary was signalized by the presentation of gifts from all the rulers of Europe, with the exception of King Humbert of Italy. President Cleveland sent through His Eminence, Cardinal Gibbons, an appropriately bound copy of the Constitution of the United States. It was received by His Holiness with marked distinction. The present Pope was ordained on the last day of the year 1837. He celebrated mass in honor of the great event in his life on January 1, 1888. Rome was crowded with pilgrims, strangers, and the halls of the Vatican were hardly large enough to hold the innumerable gifts sent from all parts of the world. Among them were Hebrew Bibles from Jewish rabbis, a magnificent present from the Sultan, and a gold basin from the Queen of England.

On January 30, Cardinals Gibbons and Taschereau started for Rome. During their stay in Rome, Cardinal Gibbons presented his celebrated letter against the condemnation of the Knights of Labor. Dr. McGlynn, late rector of St. Stephen's Church, New York city, who had been suspended by the Most Rev. Archbishop Corrigan for insisting on publicly preaching that private property in land is a crime, was excommunicated for refusing to go to Rome when summoned by the Prefect of the Propaganda. In France no change—except a slightly favorable movement—took place in the relations of the Government to the Church. In Germany an *entente cordiale* was arranged between the Pope and Prince Bismarck. His Holiness advised the Catholics of Germany to support the Septennat bill in the interests of the peace of Europe. Herr Windhorst and the Center did not at first sympathize with the policy of Rome in thus by a concession mitigating the tyranny of the Kulturkampf. But the matter was settled by firm protests of loyalty and reverence to the Holy Father on the part of the ex-Hanoverian Chancellor. In Italy some commotion was occasioned by the rumors of a coming triumph of the party of Conciliation. Padre Tosti printed a pamphlet favoring a *modus vivendi* between the Vatican and the Quirinal. Several Italian deputies were in favor of it, and the tenor of "Le Moniteur de Rome," the semi-official organ of the Vatican, did not disapprove of it. Numerous articles and pamphlets were written on the subject of the possibility of the restoration of Rome to the Holy See; but apparently nothing practical came of them. In England, particularly among the Tories, a movement to establish diplomatic relations between the Court of St. James and the Vatican seemed to have some force. Catholic opinion in Ireland had become so crystallized in favor of Home Rule, that it was felt that some attempt must be made to counterbalance its influence at Rome. Mgr. Persico, formerly Bishop of Savannah, was, with Mgr. Gualdi, sent to Ireland. But his utterances seemed to show that he was satisfied that the archbishops and bishops of Ireland were right in their championship of the cause of the people. The Duke of Norfolk, the head of the Catholic family of the Howards, is looked upon as the leader of the Catholic anti-Home-Rule party in England, while Lord Ripon, an equally devout Catholic and a convert, is one of the chiefs of the pro-Irish movement in the Liberal party. In Venezuela a struggle between the Catholic and Radical parties resulted in the exile of the archbishop to San Francisco. On January 30, 1887, Cardinal Ferrieri died at Rome. On February 17 Rt. Rev. Pfraengle was installed as abbot of St. Mary's Monastery, Newark, N. J. On January 26 Cardinal Jacobini died at Rome. On March 4 Father Beckx, General of the Society of Jesus for thirty-three years, died in Rome. On March 17 Cardinals Gibbons and Taschereau received their hats in consistory; and on March 25 Cardinal Gibbons took formal possession of his titular church of Santa Maria in Trastevere. On March 27 was published the brief of the Holy Father addressed to Bishop Ireland in favor of

the total abstinence movement. On March 29 the Holy Father, as a mark of his approbation of the Most Rev. Archbishop Corrigan's management of the McGlynn revolt, conferred on him the rank of bishop-assistant at the Pontifical throne. On April 10 the Holy Father sent out a brief relating to the founding of the Catholic University. On April 12 the ancient cathedral at St. Augustine, Fla., was almost totally destroyed by fire. On April 15 the Rt. Rev. Matthew Haskins was consecrated Bishop of Providence, R. I., to succeed Bishop Hendrickin—by the Most Rev. Archbishop of Boston. On May 1 the Rt. Rev. P. D. Ludden was consecrated Bishop of Syracuse, N. Y., by the Most Rev. Archbishop Corrigan, D. D. On May 22 the first church in New York dedicated to St. Thomas Aquinas, the saint and philosopher, whose doctrines Leo VIII has specially promulgated, was blessed by Bishop Loughlin in Brooklyn. On June 3 the grand cathedral at Providence, R. I., was formally opened. On May 21, during Queen Victoria's Jubilee celebration, Mgr. Ruffo-Scilla, the first Papal envoy to enter the English court since the Reformation was received. On May 27 the Rt. Rev. Lawrence Scanlan was consecrated Bishop by the Most Rev. Archbishop Riordan. On July 8 was published in "The Catholic Review" the circular of the Most Rev. Archbishop Corrigan, in which was announced the excommunication of Dr. McGlynn. On August 2 the Redemptorists celebrated with reverent splendor the centenary of the death of St. Alphonsus Liguori. On September 2 the abbey of St. Meinrad (Benedictine) at Indiantown, Ind., was destroyed by fire. On September 17 the centenary celebration of the Constitution of the United States was closed with prayer by Cardinal Gibbons. On October 2 St. Michael's church, Newark, was consecrated by Bishop Wigger. On September 28 Most Rev. Z. X. Leroy, Archbishop of New Orleans, died in France. On October 9 the pallium was conferred on the Most Rev. Archbishop Gross, of Portland, Ore., by Cardinal Gibbons. On October 17 the Rev. Dr. Kerner, who had come from England to serve the Italians, was killed in New York by the falling of his unfinished school-house. On October 28 the Rt. Rev. Maurice F. Burke was consecrated Bishop of Cheyenne, W. T., by Archbishop Feehan. On the same day Rt. Rev. Nicholas Matz, coadjutor of the Bishop of Denver, was consecrated by Archbishop Salpointe. On November 2 Cardinal Pellegrini died. On November 30 Rt. Rev. Thomas Bonacum was consecrated Bishop of Lincoln, Neb., at St. Louis by Archbishop Kenrich. On the same day the Rt. Rev. Richard Scannell was consecrated Bishop of Concordia, La., by Archbishop Feehan at Nashville. Archbishop Lamy, of Santa Fé, died in that city on February 14. It was announced early in February that the new Bishops of Alton, Ill., and Belleville, Ill., were the Very Rev. Father Janssens and Rev. James Ryan, of Ottawa, Ill. On February 25 Rt. Rev.

D. M. Blanchet, D. D., Bishop of Nesqualy, died. On March 11, Rt. Rev. Bishop McGovern was consecrated at Harrisburg. Among the other important deaths were Bishop-elect James O'Reilly, appointed to the see of Wichita, Kan.; Isidor Robert, O. S. B.; Arch-Abbot Wimmer; Rev. John J. Riordan, of Castle Garden; and Rev. Dr. Moriasty, the well-known author, and Père Rouquette.

ROUMANIA, a kingdom in Eastern Europe. Independence was proclaimed on May 22, 1877, and recognized by the powers at the Berlin Congress on June 13, 1878. The principality of Roumania was erected into a kingdom on March 26, 1881. The fundamental laws are embodied in the Constitution, elaborated in 1866 by a Constituent Assembly, and modified in 1884 by the chambers convoked for the purposes of revision. It delegates the national representation to two chambers, a Senate consisting of 120 members and a Chamber of Deputies, having 183 members. Both classes of representatives are elected by electoral colleges in each district. The reigning sovereign is Carol I, son of Prince Hohenzollern-Sigmaringen, who was born April 20, 1839, and was elected Prince of Roumania in 1886. He married in 1869 the Princess Elizabeth of Wied. In default of heirs to his body, the King in 1886 chose his nephew, Prince Ferdinand of Hohenzollern, to be his successor. The heir-apparent is the second son of Leopold, hereditary Prince of Hohenzollern, and was born at Sigmaringen, Aug. 24, 1865.

The ministry is composed of the following members: President of the Council and Minister of the Interior. Joan C. Bratiano; Minister of Foreign Affairs, M. Phere Kyde; Minister of Public Instruction and Worship, D. Sturdza; Minister of Justice, Eugene Statesco; Minister of Agriculture, Commerce. Industry, and Domains, V. Gheorghian; Minister of Finance, C. Nacu; Minister of Public Works, P. S. Aurelian; Minister of War, Gen. A. Angelesco, successor to M. Falcojano, who resigned his post on Jan. 24, 1886.

Area and Population.—The area of the kingdom is 48,307 square miles. The population is estimated at 5,376,000. The number of marriages in 1885 was 39,586; of births, 215,-776; of deaths, 126,010; excess of births over deaths, 89,766. In 1886 there were 77,976 marriages, 215,209 births, and 136,755 deaths, making the natural increment 78,454. The number of Israelites in Roumania was estimated at the time of the Treaty of Berlin at 400,000 souls, the Bohemians at 200,000, the Slavs at 85,000, the Germans at 39,000, the Hungarians at 29,500, the Armenians at 8,000, the Greeks at 5,000, the French at 2,000, and the English at 1,000. The population of Bucharest, the capital, is 221,000. Jassy has about 90,000 inhabitants, and Galatz 80,000.

Finances.—The receipts of the treasury during the year ending March 30, 1885, were 127,-359,220 lei; the disbursements, 130,852,265 lei. The receipts for 1885–'86 were 124,478,-398 lei, and the expenditures 129,971,646 lei. The budget for 1886–'87 made the receipts 138,237,695 lei, and the expenditures 134,244,-650 lei. The expenditure for the public debt was estimated at 57,546,959 lei; for the army, 28,552,760 lei; for education and worship, 13,-120,294 lei. The nominal amount of the debt outstanding on April 1, 1886, was 724,171,624 lei. At the same date in 1887 it was 835,815,-342 lei, having been increased by 16,170,000 lei of treasury warrants and other sums raised through the Government savings-bank. In 1887 a loan of 80,000,000 lei was raised in Berlin, at 4½ per cent. interest.

The Army and Navy.—The effective strength of the regular army on the peace footing is 1,249 officers, 31,627 rank and file, 5,558 horses, and 312 guns. The territorial army numbers 1,213 officers and 124,000 men, with 11,897 horses. The kingdom is divided into four districts, besides the district of the Dobrudja, where an active division is permanently stationed. The permanent army and the Dorobantzi, or territorial troops number on the peace footing about 95,000 men, which can be increased to 225,000 on the outbreak of war. There are besides about 150,000 militia and depot troops, without reckoning the Landsturm. The average expenditure on the army is only about 30,000,000 lei.

The number of men of the age of twenty-one drawn for service in the permanent army for 1887 was 14,000. Every recruit who possesses and can maintain a suitable horse, or who will pay 300 lei into the military chest, is assigned to the calarashi or cavalry. The infantry serve three years in the permanent army and five in the reserve, after which they are enrolled in the militia till they become thirty-six years of age.

The fortifications of Bucharest, on plans approved by General Brialmont, the Belgian military engineer, were rapidly constructed and nearly completed before the close of 1887. The plans were modified in important particulars on the advice of German officers. The Parliament, on Feb. 3, 1887, voted 5,000,000 lei for completing the fortifications.

The navy consists of two avisos, two gun-boats, a torpedo-vessel, and two torpedo-boats. There are besides three launches for the police service of the Danube, which was confided to the Government of Roumania by the European Congress.

Commerce.—The total value of the imports in 1884 was 294,986.000 lei or francs, against 359,907,000 lei in 1883; the value of the exports, 184,116,000 lei, against 220,650,279 lei. The imports from Austria were 129,867,000 lei in value; from Great Britain, 58,223.000 lei; from Germany, 43,384,000, lei; from France, 23,804,000 lei. The exports to Austria amounted to 70,392,000 lei; to Great Britain, 61,783,000 lei; to France, 17,417,000 lei. The imports and exports of the principal classes were in 1884 as follow, the values being given in lei:

CLASSES.	Imports.	Exports.
Cereals..........................	5,900,000	186,200,000
Fruits and vegetables...........	18,900,000	5,500,000
Beverages.......................	2,100,000	400,000
Animals and animal products....	8,000,000	10,700,000
Fuel............................	9,800,000	2,400,000
Minerals, glass, and pottery......	11,400,000	800,000
Metals and metal manufactures ..	47,800,000	1,100,000
Skins and leather	85,000,000	10,800,000
Timber and manufactures of wood	17,100,000	6,900,000
Textiles and textile materials	100,800,000	6,500,000
Drugs, etc......................	6,200,000	900,000
Oils, etc	9,700,000	900,000
Other articles	92,800,000	3,400,000
Total	295,000,000	184,100,000

In 1885 the imports fell off to 268,539,150 lei, while the exports increased to 247,968,201.

The European Commission of the Danube.—The number of vessels entered at the Roumanian ports on the Danube during 1884 was 20,478; the tonnage, 8,711.143; the number cleared, 20,650; tonnage, 8,678,849. The exports of grain from the ports of the Lower Danube were 6,461,889 quarters, against 6,070,157 quarters in 1885 and 4,441,039 quarters in 1884. Of 872 steamers of 866,763 tons that entered the Sulina mouth of the Danube during 1886, 564, of 622,201 tons, were English; 61, of 63,140 tons, Greek; 84, of 62,836 tons, Austrian; and 49, of 55,772 tons, French. Of 1,879 sailing-vessels, of 950,567 tons, 568, of 628,470 tons, were British; 262, of 102,599 tons, Greek; 91, of 64,828 tons, Austrian; and 50, of 57,025 tons, French.

The receipts of the Danube Commission in 1885 were 1,430,958 francs from taxes, and 1,196,400 francs from special resources. The expenditures were 1,805,824 francs. The only remaining debt of the commission was 583,782 francs advanced by the Porte. The assets were 1,821,534 francs, not including a pension fund.

Railroads, Posts, and Telegraphs.—The length of the railroads in operation in 1886 was 1,682 kilometres, of which 1,458 kilometres belong to the state. There were 900 kilometres building, and 454 kilometres more surveyed.

The post-office during the year 1885 forwarded 18,830,367 letters and postal-cards and 528,992 packets.

The telegraphs in 1886 had a length of 5,319 kilometres, with 9,674 kilometres of wires. The internal paid dispatches during the year numbered 814,880; the international dispatches, 272,858. The receipts of the postal and telegraph service were 4,530,468 francs; the expenses, 3,653,730 francs.

Politics and Legislation.—The Chamber on Feb. 7, 1886, voted a Government project for the fortification of Bucharest, and authorized the emission of a loan of 6,000,000 francs for covering the first part of the cost. The works are to be completed in 1890. Models of armor-plated towers were submitted by German and

French engineers. After a series of tests the French design was selected. The Minister of War, M. Falcojano, resigned on Jan. 23, 1886. The Prime Minister took the portfolio provisionally, and on February 25 Gen. Angelesco was appointed to the post.

Attempted Assassination of the Prime Minister.—While M. Bratiano was returning from a Cabinet council on Sept. 16, 1886, he was fired at by a hotel-keeper named Alexandrescu. The bullet, which was fired from a revolver, struck a deputy named Robesco, who was walking with the minister. For some time previous the Prime Minister had been the object of virulent attacks in the Opposition press, similar to those that preceded the former attempt on his life, in 1880. The assassin was immediately arrested, and confessed that he was led to the crime by political motives. In his possession was found a check for 5,000 francs, signed by Oroveanu, an Opposition deputy. The next day an attempt was made to lynch Alexandrescu. The same evening on which the shot was fired a mob surrounded the office of the "Epoca," the only paper in Bucharest that opposed the Government, blamed the editor for inciting the deed by his inflammatory articles, broke up the furniture and fittings, wounded two of the staff, and would have destroyed the building if the police had not succeeded in gaining the upper hand. Alexandrescu was sentenced to twenty years' imprisonment at hard labor. All the suspected accomplices were acquitted, except Muscal, a non-political offender.

The Government commanded a large majority in the Chamber, 110 against 37, and had an equal preponderance of votes in the Senate. Yet among the people there was a very bitter feeling against Bratiano on account of his despotic party government.

Foreign Relations.—Several important commercial treaties expired in 1886. A new general tariff was adopted, which subjects to light imposts raw material and manufactured articles not produced in Roumania, exempts from duty raw materials that it is in Roumania's interest to obtain as cheaply as possible, and imposes protective duties on articles entering into competition with Roumanian products. The protective principle was followed in the English treaty and in the negotiations for reciprocity treaties with other powers.

The expired ten-years' treaty with Austria-Hungary hindered the development of Roumanian industries by admitting Austrian manufactures at the lowest rates of duty. The reciprocal concession of permitting the free importation of Roumanian cattle and swine into Austria-Hungary was rendered futile by the Hungarians, who on various pretexts stopped the imports on the border, and finally prohibited them altogether. The result was that, in the winter of 1885–'86, the Roumanian farmers had more cattle than they could feed, and oxen were sold for thirty francs a pair.

The Austrians suffered from the selfish policy of the Hungarians scarcely less than the Roumanians, for meat rose to famine prices in Vienna, and in Galicia the distress of a long winter was so severe that many peasants died of hunger. The crisis in Ronmania caused the imports of Austrian goods to fall away as much as 100,000,000 francs in a single year. The tariff war that followed the rupture of negotiations for a new treaty renders the cost of living exorbitantly dear for the classes in Roumania who consume imported products. The indignation against Hungary was heightened by the attempt to Magyarize the 2,825,000 Roumanians of Transylvania. The irritating policy of the Hungarian Government lends strength to the pro-Russian party in Roumania, which desires an alliance with Russia in the event of a war between Russia and Austria in order to annex Transylvania to Roumania. The Government gives no countenance to the Irredentist agitation, which is fostered by Russian agents, yet constant complaints are made by the Hungarian authorities at the license which the free-press laws allow to the ventilation of this scheme. In the main body of the Roumanian population, on the other hand, there is a strong dread of the extension of Russian power in the Balkan Peninsula, and a deep feeling of resentment against Russians for requiting the aid given by Roumania in the last Turkish war, by robbing her of the fruitful province of Bessarabia.

The boundary disputes of long standing between Roumania and Austria-Hungary were settled by a mixed commission, which concluded its labors in April, 1887. The adjustment of the frontier added about thirty-two square miles to Roumania's territory.

A convention with Great Britain, continuing the existing commercial treaty in a revised form till 1891 was signed at Bucharest on Nov. 26, 1886. The duties on textile fabrics and on most other imports are fixed at considerably higher rates than under the former treaty. In 1887 a favorable reciprocity treaty was concluded with Turkey, through which the Roumanians hoped to regain the prosperity that was lost through the rupture of the commercial relations with Austria, and for that reason they were the less anxious to resume negotiations for a treaty.

The German Government concluded a consular treaty with Roumania in Berlin on June 5, 1886. It abandons the right of extra-territorial jurisdiction, which was exercised under treaties with Turkey as the suzerain power over Moldavia and Wallachia, and was not formally abolished when the Treaty of Berlin extinguished the relation of vassalage, but was left to be dealt with in treaties with the powers regulating consular relations. Although legally still in force, no power has exercised the right of consular jurisdiction in Roumania since her independence was conceded in 1878.

RUSSIA, an empire in northeastern Europe and northern Asia. The Emperor exercises autocratic power and is the head of the national Church. There are four bodies through which the functions of government are usually exercised, viz., the Council of the Empire, consisting in 1886 of sixty-two members, exclusive of the ministers, who have seats by virtue of their offices; the Senate, which combines legislative, executive, and judicial functions; the Holy Synod, which has the direction of ecclesiastical affairs; and the Committee of Ministers. The reigning Emperor is Alexander III, born Feb. 26, 1845, who succeeded to the throne on the assassination of his father, March 13, 1881, and was crowned at Moscow on May 27, 1883. The heir-apparent is the Grand Duke Nicholas, the eldest son of the Emperor, born May 18, 1868. The Cabinet is composed of the following ministers: President, M. Bunge; Minister of the Imperial Household, Lieutenant-General Count Vorontzoff Dashkoff; Minister of Foreign Affairs, Nicholas Carlovich de Giers; Minister of War, General P. Vannovski; Minister of the Navy, Vice-Admiral Shestakoff; Minister of the Interior, Count Tolstoi; Minister of Public Instruction, M. Delianoff; Minister of Finance, M. Vishnegradski; Minister of Domains, M. Ostrovski; Minister of Roads and Communications, Admiral O. Possiet.

Area and Population.—The area of the different divisions of the empire, in square kilometres, and the population according to the latest returns, are as follow:

GEOGRAPHICAL DIVISIONS.	Area.	Population.
Russia in Europe	4,888,718	78,269,114
Kingdom of Poland	127,319	7,884,100
Grand Duchy of Finland	373,608	2,208,858
The Caucasus	472,666	6,654,017
Trans-Caspian territory	551,524	480,000
Central Asia	3,083,016	5,210,946
Siberia	12,495,110	4,148,226
Sea of Aral	66,998	....
Caspian Sea	439,418	....
Total	22,448,660	104,785,761

The number of marriages registered in European Russia in 1883 was 782,750; births, 3,880,857; deaths, 2,879,265; excess of births, 1,001,582. In Poland the marriages in 1880 numbered 62,771; births, 294,021; deaths, 189,514; excess of births, 104,507. The number of marriages in Finland in 1884 was 16,585; births, 80,411; deaths, 47,468; excess of births, 32,948. The number of marriages in Siberia in 1880 was 32,952; births, 180,802; deaths, 131,-793; excess of births, 49,009. The population of St. Petersburg is 929,093. Moscow had 753,469 inhabitants in 1884; Warsaw, 431,864 in 1885; Riga, 169,329 in 1881; Kharkov, 166,921 in 1884; Odessa, 154,240 in 1885; Kasan, 140,726 in 1883; Kishinev, 130,000; Kiev, 127,251; Lodz, 113,146 in 1884; Saratov, 112,428 in 1883.

The Army.—The peace effective of the regular army in the beginning of 1887 was 659,274 men, comprising 1,890 officers of the general staff, 336,960 infantry in Europe, 25,636 riflemen, 21,318 infantry in Asia, 47,920 cavalry, 84,925 artillery, 17,977 engineers, 57,834 reserves of all arms, 17,290 local troops, 47,000 auxiliary troops, and 1,024 depot and instruction troops. The war effective of the regular army is approximately 1,689,000 men, including 36,600 officers, with 3,776 cannon and 204,390 horses. The Cossack troops are in part incorporated in the regular army. Their strength is 47,150 in peace, and 140,083 on the war footing. The irregular troops number 5,769 men. The total war effective of the Russian army is about 2,000,000, not including the militia, which, it is supposed, could add as many more men.

The Navy.—In the beginning of 1887 the Russian fleet in the Baltic comprised 28 ironclads, of which 13 were for coast defense, 1 unarmored frigate, 6 corvettes, 2 transports, 95 torpedo-boats, including 12 of the first class, 4 cruisers, 9 clippers, 15 gunboats, 6 imperial yachts, and 57 other steamers. In the Black Sea fleet there were 2 Popoffka ironclads, 2 armored gunboats, 8 corvettes, 26 steamers, and 26 torpedo-boats, of which 12 were of the first class. The flotilla in the Caspian Sea contained 9 armed steamers; the White Sea flotilla, 7 armed steamers and 6 torpedo-boats. The "Catherine II," having 16-inch plates at the water line and a pear-shaped redoubt with a shield 12 to 14 inches thick, with a displacement of 10,180 tons and engines of 9,000 horsepower, was launched in the spring of 1887. Two other vessels, the "Sinope" and the "Tchesma," of the same type and proportions, are under construction. The "Sinope" was launched on June 1, 1887. Each of these vessels will carry six 12-inch or 50-ton guns and seven 6-inch guns, besides pieces of smaller caliber and mitrailleuses. The "Alexander II," plated with 14 inches of armor and 8,440 tons' displacement, was launched on the Neva on July 26, 1887, and the "Nicholas I," a sister ship, later in the year. Each is designed to carry two 2-inch, four 9-inch, and eight 6-inch guns. With the three vessels mentioned above, they complete the list of the great ironclads comprised in the twenty-years' plan that was adopted for the establishment of a modern navy.

Finances.—The budget estimates of the Russian Ministry of Finance are invariably made to balance, but the final accounts always show a deficit, owing to extraordinary expenditures, mainly for military purposes. The accounts for 1885 show a revenue from ordinary sources of 762,282,000 rubles, which was augmented by extraordinary receipts to 887,028,861 rubles. The ordinary expenditures were 806,614,346 rubles and the extraordinary expenditures 106,523,822 rubles, making a total of 913,138,168 rubles, and leaving a deficit of 76,109,307 rubles. The budget for 1887 makes the ordinary receipts 798,118,046 rubles, and the total receipts 881,341,672 rubles. The

ordinary expenditures are set down as 826,676,680 rubles, and the total expenditures are made to balance the estimated receipts by applying the difference to extraordinary expenditures on railroads and harbors. The sum appropriated for the service of the debt is 278,591,694 rubles, including 36,117,536 rubles for the proposed conversion of 5-per-cent. metallic bonds into 4½ per cents. The sum devoted to military expenditure is 208,466,551 rubles, while 39,247,488 rubles are devoted to the navy. In the budget estimates for 1888 the income from all sources is placed at 960,429,550 rubles, and the expenditure at 945,023,281 rubles. The ordinary revenue is estimated at 783,000,000 rubles, while the ordinary expenditures will exceed 832,000,000 rubles.

The public debt on Jan. 1, 1887, amounted to 894,144,015 rubles, payable in specie, and 3,185,653,497 rubles, due in paper currency, besides Dutch loans amounting to 68,695,000 florins, sterling loans of £123,046,620, and the bonds of the Nicholas Railroad, amounting to 553,959,500 francs. The other railroad debts included in this summary were £82,644,400 borrowed in England and 166,139,253 metallic rubles. The amount of paper currency in circulation on Jan. 1, 1887, was 716,433,349 rubles.

A new iron duty, which went into force in the summer of 1887, has a prohibitory effect on the heretofore very large imports of iron and iron wares from Germany. This and other protective duties, in conjunction with the suppression of iron-mills and other factories in Poland and other border provinces that were owned by Germans and that employed German workmen, the expulsion of German citizens, the expropriation of foreign land-owners, and other hostile measures produced a feeling of exasperation and resentment in Germany that had a profound effect on Russian credit. During the existence of the Three Emperors' League the German bankers negotiated loans, and large sums were lent to the Russian Government by Germans when London and other money markets were no longer available. Sustained by the Berlin bankers, the price of Russian 5 per-cent. securities rose from 80 to 95. In 1887, when the Czar's Government desired to raise a new loan, the German bankers refused to involve their countrymen in further risks. An attempt was made to raise money in Paris; but there also the influence of the German bankers was powerful, and the project was abandoned. A loan of 100,000,000 rubles, bearing interest at 4 per cent., was successfully issued at the price of 84 per cent. in St. Petersburg in April, 1887. The German holders sold during the year a considerable part of their Russian securities, their action causing a fall in prices. A large proportion of the bonds that were sold went to Paris, where previously there were very few holders of Russian securities. The gold ruble was worth 1·50 in credit rubles in 1886, while in August, 1887, the exchange value had risen to 1·67 credit ruble.

The adoption of prohibitive duties against German products in the interest of the manufacturers of central Russia was a triumph of the Panslavist party of M. Katkoff, who openly attacked Ministers Bunge and De Giers in the "Moscow Gazette." M. Bunge on Jan. 13, 1887, retired from the Ministry of Finance, which was placed under the charge of M. Vishnegradski, a high protectionist and the first man in mercantile life who has held a ministerial post in Russia during recent times. When M. Katkoff continued his attacks on the foreign office and his efforts to displace M. de Giers also, he was finally warned to desist. The iron duties that were adopted range from 30 to 70 copecks per pood, which is equivalent to from $13.25 to $31 per ton for pig, plate, and bar iron, while for manufactured articles they are fixed at 140 copecks, except locomotives, which pay 200 copecks.

Commerce.—The value of the imports in 1885 was 433,800,000 rubles, as compared with 538,000,000 rubles in 1884, 557,300,000 rubles in 1883, and 566,800,000 rubles in 1882. The imports from Europe in 1885 were of the value of 379,800,000 rubles, as compared with 486,-300,000 rubles in 1884; from Finland, 14,500,-000 rubles, as compared with 15,400,000 rubles; from Asia, 39,500,000 rubles, as compared with 36,300,000 rubles. The total exports in 1885 amounted to 538,600,000 rubles, as compared with 589,900,000 rubles in 1884, 640,300,000 rubles in 1883, and 617,700,000 rubles in 1882. The exports across the European frontiers were of the value of 497,900,000 rubles in 1885, as compared with 550,500,000 rubles in 1884; to Finland, 17,100,000 rubles, as compared with 14,700,000 rubles; to Asiatic countries, 23,600,-000 rubles, as compared with 24,700,000 rubles. The following table shows the proportions in which different foreign countries participated in the foreign trade in 1885, the values of the imports and exports being given in rubles:

COUNTRIES.	Imports.	Exports.
Germany	144,170,000	142,467,000
Great Britain	96,401,000	157,480,000
France	14,641,000	87,217,000
Austria-Hungary	22,001,000	27,957,000
Netherlands	5,054,000	82,506,000
Belgium	8,234,000	28,138,000
Italy	6,477,000	26,346,000
China	12,288,000	17,036,000
Turkey	23,857,000	1,556,000
Sweden and Norway	5,214,000	18,781,000
United States	24,627,000	481,000
Persia	8,951,000	8,981,000
Greece	836,000	8,959,000
Denmark	1,415,000	7,955,000
Roumania	2,948,000	8,824,000
Other countries	55,281,000	28,648,000
Total	433,780,000	538,552,000

The exports of cereals to European countries in 1885 were valued at 280,050,000 rubles, against 310,381,000 rubles in 1884. The exports of textile materials declined from 96,346,000 to 81,400,000 rubles; the exports of timber from 35,156,000 to 26,470,000 rubles. There was a falling off also in the exportation of sugar and other natural products. The imports of precious metals in 1885 amounted to 6,407,000 rubles and the exports to 8,549,000 rubles. The imports and exports of the different classes of merchandise and of specie by way of the European frontiers in 1886 were of the following values:

CLASSES OF ARTICLES.	Imports.	Exports.
Articles of food	89,024,451	252,572,215
Raw materials	221,407,002	160,889,144
Animals	616,286	11,830,403
Manufactures	71,851,508	11,773,454
Precious metals	5,802,000	14,186,000
Total	388,701,192	450,651,216

Navigation.—The number of vessels entered at the Baltic ports in 1885 was 5,833, of which 3,528 were with cargoes; the number entered at the ports of the Black Sea and the Sea of Azov was 5,016, of which 1,862 had cargoes, while of 5,004 that were cleared, 4,227 were laden. The returns of the Caspian and White Sea ports swell the total number of vessels entered to 12,944, of which 2,837 were Russian, 3,063 English, 1,671 German, 1,448 Swedish and Norwegian, 588 Turkish, 971 Greek, 919 Danish, 778 Austrian, and 200 Dutch. The number of steamers entered was 8,100. The total number of vessels cleared was 12,939, of which 8,130 were steamers. The number of coasting voyages recorded was 39,086, of which 18,861 were made by steam-vessels.

The merchant marine on Jan. 1, 1884, numbered 4,411 sailing-vessels, of 401,340 tons, and 379 steamers, of 199,214 tons.

Railroads.—The railroad network on Jan. 1, 1887, comprised 26,145 kilometres of completed lines, exclusive of the railroads of Finland and without reckoning the Trans-Caspian line, which had a length of 1,072 kilometres. The gross receipts of the railroads in 1885 amounted to 280,171,000 rubles. The Government has approved plans for the building, within five years, of a line from St. Petersburg, through the whole length of Siberia, to Vladivostock, the naval port on the Pacific. The section between the capital and Ekaterinburg is already in existence, and its extension to Tiumen is in progress, to be soon continued to Tomsk, the capital of West Siberia. The Council of State, on the recommendation of the War Department, which urged the need of arrangements for the transport of troops to the Chinese frontier and the Pacific, approved the construction of lines from Tomsk to Irkutsk, near Lake Baikal, and to Stretinsk, a settlement on a branch of the Amoor, whence communication may be continued by water to Lake Khanka, which will be connected by a line of railroad with Vladivostock.

The Post-Office.—The number of letters forwarded in 1885 was 139,103,194; post-cards, 11,642,962; registered letters, 12,030,224; money letters, 10,423,649; newspapers, 102,-515,895; circulars, 17,508,609. The receipts were 66,112,720 francs.

Telegraphs.—The state lines in 1884 had a length of 101,697 kilometres, with 189,816 kilometres of wires. Including the railroad lines, the Anglo-Indian line and others, the total length of telegraphs in the empire was 109,778 kilometres, with 248,470 kilometres of wires. The number of dispatches in 1884 was 10,471,084, of which 8,599,295 were paid internal messages, 595,774 official dispatches, and the remainder international messages. The receipts in 1884 were 85,871,696 francs; the expenses, 12,848,720 francs, exclusive of 2,400,000 francs expended in the construction of new lines.

Revolutionary Plots.—In January, 1887, a band of conspirators was discovered among the cadets of the naval-school at St. Petersburg and young officers of the navy who had recently been students in the school. Within a few weeks many arrests were made among the students of the military academies and officers in the army who had received their commissions within a year or two and were posted in various parts of the empire. The trials that had taken place recently showed that Nihilism had spread to an alarming extent among the officers of the army and navy. In February and March a large number of persons of the middle class were arrested; also a general in the army, a nobleman of high rank, and several large land-owners, while others of his class fled the country to escape arrest. These arrests were made in consequence of what was called a Constitutionalist conspiracy, which had wide ramifications among the provincial nobility and among army officers. The organ of the conspirators was a lithographed periodical called the "Constitutional," which contained extracts from famous writers on constitutional law and political economy. The statutes of the organization bound all the members at a given signal to do their utmost to subvert the existing Government and establish constitutional forms. The motto of the society was "The people, with the Czar or against the Czar." Within a few weeks of the discovery of the society and the wholesale arrest of its members occurred the anniversary of the murder of Alexander II, March 13, on which the Czar with the imperial family intended to assist at religious services at the tomb of his father. Extraordinary precautions were taken by Gen. Gresser, who had charge of the police arrangements for the safety of the Czar, because the German police agents in Zürich had learned of an intended plot, and the Berlin police had warned the St. Petersburg authorities. The detectives of Gen. Gresser observed three suspicious characters in a tea-house, one of whom carried a book, one a traveling-bag, and one a paper parcel. These men, who were students in the St. Petersburg University, were followed, while the Czar was warned to take a circuitous route to the cathedral of the Neva fortress, where the services were performed. In the crowd that gathered on the Nevsky Prospect to see the Czar pass by were the three suspected persons, who were arrested with three other students, who also carried bombs disguised as opera-glasses and rolls of music. Two of the suspicious articles were found in their possession, and proved to contain a large quantity of dynamite and some bullets filled with strychnine. Before night more than one hundred suspected persons were taken into custody. The names of the students who first incurred the suspicions of the detectives were Andrejushkin, Graboff, and Generaloff. Many students of the Women's Higher Educational Institute in St. Petersburg were arrested, and the institution was closed. Two women, one the wife of a general and the other a doctor's wife, who had long been under police espionage, were arrested for their suspected complicity in the plot. The rector of the university, in an address to the students, spoke of the connection of the conspirators with the university as a disgrace, and the remark was received with hisses. For taking part in this demonstration about 300 students were placed under arrest. Many of the officers and others who had been lately arrested are supposed to have been summarily tried and executed. Of this band of conspirators, who called themselves by the name of "Bleeding Russia," some fifty were arrested. They had their bomb-factory in the cellar of a house on the Neva, where they worked at night, and a larger establishment at Paulovka, on the Finland Railroad. The plot was concocted in Vilna, from which place a part of the chemicals were brought. A man of Polish origin, disguised as an officer, is said to have fired at the Czar while he was walking in the park at Gatshina, about April 1, and when the guard instantly shot this man, another, who was a military officer, is said to have fired from another spot, and to have wounded the Czar slightly in the arm. On April 6, when Alexander again was driving through the streets of the capital, a man and a woman were seized by the police, presumably in the act of throwing grenades at the Emperor's carriage, which had been stopped by a man who stood in the road waving a petition in his hand, and who is supposed to have been a confederate. In April 482 officers of the army were transported to Siberia for complicity in the attempts on the Czar's life. On April 27 the trial of 15 persons who were accused of active participation in the plot of March 13 was begun in St. Petersburg. Of the three bomb-carriers who were first arrested, two were Cossacks from the Kuban and one a native of Tomsk, Siberia. Two of the accused were Polish noblemen named Pilzousky and Lukashevich, three were women, of whom two were graduates of the St. Petersburg College of Midwifery, and the third a school-teacher named Sered Yukora. The other prisoners, except one who was a pharmacist, were students of the university, one of whom had received the gold medal of his class, and had sold it to procure money to enable an accomplice to leave the country. Among the prisoners were two Jews, and among those who evaded arrest a much larger proportion. There was evidence given during the trial of four centers of revolutionary activity—one in St. Petersburg, one in Vilna, a third either at Kiev or Kharkov, and a fourth in Siberia. One of the Poles from Vilna had contributed large sums of money toward the revolutionary cause. All of the prisoners pleaded guilty, and some made speeches in justification of their action. Seven of them were condemned to death, and the others to long terms of imprisonment. Five of the condemned, named Generaloff, Andrejushkin, Ossipanoff, Shevireff, and Uljanoff, were executed on May 20. In June twenty-one Nihilists were tried before a military court. The chief prisoner was Hermann Alexander Lopatin, the organizer of the scheme for killing Col. Sudeikin, which was carried out on Dec. 28, 1883, by Starodvorsky and Konashevich, two others of the prisoners, and by Degaieff, alias Jaklonsky, who escaped to the United States. Lopatin, with a young woman named Saloff, the daughter of a staff-officer, and Sookhomlin, an official's son, established a branch of the central revolutionary organization in 1884, which Lopatin directed until, in the same year, he was arrested in connection with the Sudeikin murder. Jakobovich, a student, who had set on foot the Young Party of the Will of the People and advocated a system of industrial and agrarian terrorism, succeeded Lopatin as head of the St. Petersburg group. With these were tried Ivanoff and Peter Elko, who directed revolutionary operations in the south of Russia, and their subordinates and agents who helped them to make bombs and conduct a secret printing-office and who committed various mail-robberies and other crimes. Of the accused, fifteen were sentenced to be hanged, but the punishment was changed by the Czar to imprisonment for life or for long terms. In the beginning of November eighteen officers, five of the navy and the rest belonging mostly to regiments stationed in the neighborhood of Kiev, were tried by a secret military tribunal at St. Petersburg on the charge of forming circles in which the members pledged themselves in case of a revolutionary outbreak to render clandestine aid to the revolutionists and to take no part in suppressing them if it could be avoided. Most of them were condemned to deportation to Siberia.

Restrictions on Education.—The attempted assassination of the Czar in March followed upon the adoption of harsher regulations in the universities. The Government, in consequence of the fermentation that was discovered among the student class, closed the Institution for Midwifery and other schools that seemed to be most infected. In August a circular was issued by the Minister of Education ordering the district managers to refuse to enter children of humble parentage on the rolls of the gymnasia and pro-gymnasia, which are the only preparatory schools for the universities. Formerly the Government encouraged the expansion of education of the approved classical kind among the children of small tradesmen, and received them into the public service, expecting thus to create a counterpoise to the disaffected aristocratic class that has hitherto engrossed all higher education and public employment. The discovery that the educated proletarians are as open to revolutionary teachings as the aristocracy has led to the reversal of this policy, and henceforth, unless they reveal exceptional promise, the sons of shopkeepers or persons in humble employment will not be admitted to the preparatory schools, since long experience has shown that such youth "should not be raised from the circle to which they belong, and be thereby led to despise their parents, to become discontented with their lot, and irritated against the inevitable inequalities of existing social positions." The directors of the schools are furthermore ordered to exclude students the moral character of whose family-life is such as to exercise a pernicious influence upon their school companions. Severe regulations were adopted in July regarding the admission of students to the St. Petersburg University. Restrictions are placed in the way of Jews entering, and all students must bring certificates as to their moral character and loyalty as well as in regard to their competency, and while at the university must reside either with their parents or with guardians who will be responsible for their conduct.

In December the University of Moscow was closed in consequence of a serious disturbance, during which the Government inspector was attacked and the rector, Count Kapnist, was hissed. Finally the Cossacks were called out, and order was restored by means of the knout. Several hundred students were arrested and expelled.

Laws against Foreigners.—On March 26, 1887, a ukase was issued prohibiting Poles of other nationalities or other foreigners from acquiring, leasing, or farming land in Russian Poland or in other western provinces of the empire. This decree is in direct contravention of the act signed at the Congress of Vienna in 1815, which secured to Poles the property rights that they possessed or might acquire in any part of their divided kingdom, and granted to them the right to own land in all of the territories of Russia. It affected many Austrian Poles and aristocratic families in Austria and other countries of Europe, and although the German Government did not demur, notwithstanding the fact that many German subjects were prejudiced in their property rights, the Austrian Government, at the instance of Polish deputies, protested against the violation of treaty obligations. The regulations under which foreigners are allowed to carry on business in Russia were made more restrictive, and were enforced with such severity that many German manufacturers and merchants and some Englishmen were forced to abandon their business. The law prohibiting foreign Jews from trading within the confines of the Russian empire was extended to Poland, where many merchants were expelled on short notice, although provided with the requisite guild certificates. In order to prevent Russians from traveling or residing abroad, a duty of 150 rubles was imposed on passports, and 10 rubles a quarter during absence from Russia, while foreigners living in Russia were compelled to pay 30 rubles a month for the privilege. A statistical investigation showed that 1,900,000 acres in Russian Poland were owned by foreigners, 29,370 of whom were Prussians, including 900 large landholders and 550 manufacturers, 3,040 were Austrians, and more than 700 belonged to other nationalities.

The Czar's Visit to the Cossacks.—In May the Emperor and Empress, with the heir-apparent, visited the country of the Don Cossacks. A continuous line of sentinels guarded the 1,150 miles of railway over which the imperial party traveled from St. Petersburg. The object of the journey was the formal investiture of the Czarevich as Chief Ataman or Hetman of the Cossacks, a dynastic ceremonial that is gone through in every reign, unless omitted for special reasons, as in the case of the present Emperor. The installation took place on May 18, and, after a second day was spent in other ceremonies and parades, the party returned in haste to St. Petersburg. The Nihilists have gained a footing within two or three years even among the Cossacks, who have been hitherto the most devoted of the Czar's subjects in return for the favors and immunities that they enjoy.

S

SALT-MINING IN NEW YORK. The great advantage of mining salt over evaporating the brine has made the discovery of beds of rock-salt a most desirable thing. Several experiments have been made on the New York State salt reservation at Syracuse. The first, directed by the Legislature of 1838, passed through the blue and red shales and the Niagara limestone, into the Clinton group, terminating in fresh water at a depth of 600 feet. The second was made by the Salt Company of Onondaga, at Liverpool, in 1867. The first limestone encountered, "a dark-colored, hard, gypseous, bituminous shale-limestone," was 394 feet from the surface and 31 feet in thickness. It is not known whether this limestone belongs to the Niagara epoch. The underlying strata were softer limestone, similar in character, 11 feet; hard, bluish, gypseous, and bituminous limestone, 64 feet; followed by soft, bluish-gray gypseous, non-bituminous, clayish shale, 112 feet; hard shale of similar order, 1 foot; light-gray shale rock, frequently interlaid with harder shale, 72 feet; and, finally, hard, green-colored shale, 80 feet; total depth of the well, 715 feet. The third attempt to find saturated brine, or rock-salt, was made in 1867, at Canastota, twenty-two miles east of Syracuse. Two wells were sunk. One of them, after passing through red and blue clays for 300 feet, followed by cemented gravel, and this by loose gravel and sand, to a total depth of 648 feet, was abandoned on encountering a hard rock. The brine was very bitter, containing 4·820 per cent. of chloride of calcium, 0·928 of chloride of magnesium, 15·228 of salt, 0·015 of carbonate of iron, and only 0·0058 of sulphate of lime. The second well gave no more satisfactory results. The fourth attempt was made in 1881, by the Solvay Process Company, south of Jamesville, near Syracuse. The first red-

dish appearing material, shale, was struck at 587 feet. The failure was due to the accidental losing of tools at 1,040 feet. The fifth attempt, made by the same company, in the Onondaga valley, near Cardiff, about twelve miles south of Syracuse, was abandoned in consequence of the bending of the well-tube. The material passed through was similar to that met with when sinking wells on the State reservation—diluvial drift in masses. The sixth attempt was undertaken by the same company in 1882, about eight miles southwest of Syracuse, at Cedar Vale. The materials passed through after reaching a depth of 795 feet were: mixed shales, green shale, red shale, green shale, red shale, green shale, shale and sand, red shale, green shale, and red shale. The brine obtained by pumping this well from a depth of 500 feet (the length of the pump) stood 90° on the salometer, or 10° within the saturation point. In 1884 a seventh attempt was made, by the enterprise of a private individual, to answer the question: "Does rock-salt lie under the reservation?" The location was three miles west of Syracuse, north of the Oswego Canal and Onondaga Lake. The total depth of the well was 1,600 feet. Nearly all of these samples contained carbonates, the greater part being magnesian; some in abundance, others only in traces. The limestones were, with few exceptions, bituminous. The sands were hard quartz or sandstones. The result showed that the Niagara limestone was first touched at 527 feet, and that at 517 feet the material was red shale only; disproving the oft-repeated assertion that the red shales are only 400 feet thick at Syracuse. It was also proved that the Medina group was reached shortly below 1,000 feet. An analysis of the brine showed that while sulphate of lime disappeared as the depth increased, and while the chlorides of calcium and magnesium grew less as the proportions of pure salt increased, yet the chlorides were so deliquescent as to make the brine unavailable for the manufacture of good salt. Although this was a disappointing end, yet it was resolved to give an eighth and final test by boring to a depth of 2,000 feet. The new boring was known as the "State Well," and the result was the finding of the same bitter and useless brine at a depth of 1,600 or 1,700 feet below the old wells of the reservation. This proved the statement that the Hudson river group is the lowest formation that contains springs or brine. In the State well the Niagara limestone was reached at 578 feet; the true limestone at 650 feet; the Clinton ore at 995 feet; and the first quartz rock at 1,005 feet. The Medina sandstone appeared at 1,075 feet; after 1,815 feet gray sandstone alone was encountered for 25 feet, followed at 1,840 feet by a mixture of gray sandstone and black slate in various proportions, to the end of the well, except 4 feet of bluish-black slate at a depth of 1,854 feet. The total depth of the well, 1,969 feet, is greater than that of any other salt-boring in America.

All the indications based upon scientific research were in favor of the success of the experiments. Nearly fifty years ago thorough surveys in the central and western parts of the State of New York showed salt-springs in many localities that served for the salting of cattle. These springs were along the northern edge of the great basin of salt deposits that lay, as was afterward found, with a dip toward the south. The similarity of the salt deposits of New York, Michigan, and Canada, and their origin from evaporation of overflows by an inland salt-water sea, have been often recorded. The theory of Prof. Goessmann — advanced nearly twenty years ago—was that "the brines of Onondaga issue from rocks of the Upper Silurian age: they indicate with great probability, by their composition and copiousness, a close connection with quite an extensive salt deposit of that age." In 1865 a thirty-foot bed of rock-salt was found at the depth of 964 feet near Goderich, Canada. Soon afterward, in the same locality, a bed of rock-salt was found at the depth of 997 feet, succeeded by five more—the total thickness of the beds being 126 feet. To show that the best of geologists may be at fault in regard to these matters, it may be said that, in commenting upon this, Prof. T. Sterry Hunt said: "The discovery in Ontario of rock-salt in solid masses, interstratified with the base of the Onondaga formation, leaves, however, but little doubt of the correctness of the views long maintained by the New York geologists, that the source of the brine is to be found in this formation. Borings like those of Goderich will probably one day show the existence in the vicinity of Syracuse of similar beds of rock-salt, which now yield to the action of infiltrating waters the brines that accumulate in the gravel-beds occupying the reservoirs just described." Rock-salt had also been discovered at Manistee, Mich., at a depth of 1,930 feet. The succession of materials and the number of feet were as follow: Surface, sand, etc., 570; lime, 45 shale; and lime, 85; shale, 105; black slate, 25; yellow marl, 15; black slate, 5; lime, 5; black slate, 95; lime, 575; brown shale (caves), 100; rock-salt, 34.

In consequence of the failure to find rock-salt at Syracuse, the State began to experiment, with the object of finding the localities where the strongest brine could be found. A large appropriation from the Legislature for ten new wells, together with the necessary pipes, engines, etc., led to an increased supply of brine that is of a better quality than hitherto. New iron pipes, in place of the old wooden ones, have also had their part in placing the salt reservation of the State of New York upon as good a footing as it ever had. And yet, while the brine at Syracuse was growing weaker, it was still obliged to pay a duty to the State. The desirable thing, for many years, was therefore, to find brine of better quality away from the State reservation. The several experiments noted above were undertaken to meet, if possible, the objection of weak brine with the solid salt itself. The failure to do this led not only to the furnishing of better brine at Syracuse, but also to the development of the deep borings in the valleys of the Oatka, the Genesee, and the Wyoming.

The central and western parts of the State of New York had always given evidence of the presence of immense beds of salt. Over forty years ago extensive surveys were made from Oswego to Niagara, and salt-springs were found in many places. In the hollows toward Lake Ontario the brine was discovered in such quantities as to make unnecessary any additional salting of the cattle that were pastured in the vicinity. It was discovered that salt might be found south of this belt; but not without considerable boring. No one, however, suspected that the valley would yield salt as far as Warsaw. Therefore, when the Vacuum Oil Company, of Rochester, began to bore for oil at Wyoming, just north of Warsaw, the enterprise was thought to be only a natural extension of the oil-fields of Pennsylvania, which lie fifty to seventy-five miles southward. The man that directed the boring had been a boy in the Wyoming valley He had faith enough in the existence of oil to lease the neighboring farms for ninety-nine years, with the agreement that he would put down a test-well, and, if successful, a well should go down on every man's farm, the owner to have one eighth of the product in every case. Oil was not found, but brine came in sufficient quantities to show that salt was there. It is evident that the average depth of the salt-bed thereabout is eighty feet, and that the depth required to reach the bed becomes less as the prospector travels north. This southern dip has given hopes to the dwell ers about Rochester that the bed will be found much nearer the surface at the point mentioned —a fact that would lead to cheaper production even if the thickness of the bed were less. Then, too, the dwellers to the east and west of the "meridian-line," upon which are located most of the wells bored thus far, are confident that salt will be found many miles away from that line. They have started "pointers," after the manner of the oil country, to mark the limits of the territory. The best geologists affirm that all the salt of Syracuse, Warsaw, Saginaw, and even of Wisconsin and Iowa, belongs to the Onondaga salt-group, and that it is deposited all over this extensive tract in a chain of land-locked lakes, fed by an occasional overflow of the ocean, and depositing their saline qualities by evaporation. A similar process is now going on at the Runn of Crutch, of which Sir Charles Lyell says: "That successive layers of salt might be thrown down, one upon another, over a thousand square miles, is undeniable. The supply of water from the ocean would be as inexhaustible as the supply of heat from the sun for its evaporation." This theory may explain why the dip of the salt-strain of Western New York, added to the natural rise of the ground, makes a boring of 1,500 feet necessary at Warsaw, while at Salina a depth of only 200 feet is required.

The outward appearance of a salt-well in the Wyoming or Warsaw valley does not differ from that of a well in the oil district, except that vats are added to the derricks. The stratum of salt having been once pierced, a saturated solution of the saline matter frequently rises in the boring to within eighty feet of the surface. This, however, can not always be depended on, and here center the increased difficulty and expense. When a few dozen feet have been drilled, an iron pipe is inserted as a "casing," inside of this a two-inch pipe, also of iron, is placed. The casing-head has two openings, one for pure water from a neighboring spring into the larger pipe, at the lower end of which it becomes saturated with saline matter; the other, at the end of a smaller pipe, to allow the expulsion of the brine. After the brine has once reached the surface, it is forced into large reservoirs, whence it is drawn off through "string" after string of "covers," until solar evaporation has left the coarser grades of salt. The covers, or vats, are usually 16x16 feet, and the product of each one in a year is estimated at 150 bushels, while the product at Syracuse is about half that quantity. It is also claimed that the slope of the valley at Warsaw is peculiarly adapted to rapid evaporation by the sun. When the finer grades of salt are wanted, the brine is led from the reservoirs to an evaporating-pan, where a gentle heat is applied. Similar treatment in another pan completes the process. The residuum of salt is raked upon a shelf at the side of the evaporator. After a slight draining it is taken to the bins, where a more thorough draining is al-

lowed for a space of two or three weeks. The heat is applied to the evaporating-pans through steam-pipes. Among the more recent wells in this region are two at Piffard, Livingston County, of 856 and 845 feet in depth, respectively In the former wells the succession of materials and the depth of feet are as follow : Blue clay, 64 ; slate and gravel, 46 ; blue limestone, 186 ; corniferous limestone, 150 ; black slate, 64 ; gray limestone and shale, 416 ; rock-salt, 18 ; saline shales, 40 ; rock-salt, 53. In the one well they are : Clay and gravel, 64 ; corniferous limestone, 186 ; corniferous limestone, 142 ; slate, 3 ; slate and gray limestone, 813 ; black slate and shales, 24 ; rock-salt, 18 ; slate and shales, 24 ; rock-salt, 6 ; shale, 7 ; rock-salt, 58 ; black slate, 4. Salt water was first obtained in the one well at 708 feet, and in the other well at 709 feet. Analyses of the layers of salt show that the percentage of pure salt is from 97·038 to 98·280, the obnoxious chlorides being found in very small quantities.

Although the original purpose of all the new wells in the Wyoming and Genesee valleys was to force water into the layers of salt, and then pump the brine to the surface for evaporation, yet the project of mining the salt directly proved more attractive and promised a greater reward for the outlay. The new "Empire" mine, also near Piffard, is a conspicuous example. Two drifts, running east and west, were begun at the shaft in the upper vein, and large quantities of salt have been brought up. It is clearer and more free from shale than the salt through which the shaft had been sunk.

Exports of mined salt from western New York have now (1887) been made for about two years. The salt is of a strong quality, but not of the finer grade. Much of the output is sent to Syracuse to strengthen the brine on the State reservation. The prospects are that as the brine at Syracuse grows weaker, as it must, still more of the mined salt will be sent to re-enforce its strength. The quantity of salt that can be mined in Western New York is estimated to be enough to supply the United States for from seven hundred to one thousand years. That the product is still in its earlier stages of development is shown by the fact that the whole State of New York now furnishes only one fifth of the 10,000,000 barrels of salt annually consumed in the United States.

SALVADOR, a republic of Central America. Area, 18,720 square kilometres; population, Oct. 30, 1886, 612,787. The most populous department is Santa Ana, counting 68,781 inhabitants; the least populous, Cabañas, which has 30,733.

Government.—The President is Gen. Francisco Menendez, whose term of office will expire in 1891. His Cabinet is composed of the following ministers: Public Instruction and Charitable Institutions, Dr. Hermogenes Alvarado; Finance, Señor E. Perez; Foreign Affairs, Justice, and Public Worship, Dr. Manuel Delgado; Interior, Dr. Rafael Reyes; War, Gen.

Valentin Amaya. The United States Minister to nearly all Central American republics is Henry C. Hall, residing at Guatemala. The Minister Resident from Salvador at Washington is Señor Don Miguel Velasco y Velasco. The American Consul at San Salvador is Louis J. Du Pré. The Salvador Consul at New York is Mariano Pomáres; New Orleans, Emiliano Martinez; San Francisco, José Mariano Roma.

Finances.—Salvador has practically no foreign debt. The home indebtedness is $5,000,000, acknowledged by the Junta de Clasificacion y Liquidacion, under provisions of the decree of March 24, 1886, for which a like amount of treasury-notes was distributed among the creditors of the state. The income of the latter in 1885 was $3,685,251, and the outlay $3,556,469, leaving a balance in the Treasury on Jan. 1, 1886, of $78,782. The liquor-tax alone produced $605,523 in 1885, being $85,488 less than the previous year. when it netted $691,011. During the ensuing two years it yielded a surplus of $188,658. The amount of duties collected on imports in 1886 was $2,547,615. During the latter half of 1887 a project was set on foot for canceling the home debt, which, as stated above, amounts to $5,000,-000. It was suggested that the Government be allowed 19 per cent. of the nation's income for administrative purposes and the entire public service, while the remaining 81 per cent. is set aside to buy up the internal indebtedness. The Government owes abroad only £200,000 advanced on the Salvador Railroad.

Postal Service.—The number of offices in 1885 was 38. The receipts in 1883-'84 were $12,700, and the expenses $19,000.

Railroads.—A concession has been applied for to build an extension of the railroad, now in working order, which runs from Acajutla, in the interior, to Sonsonate, Armenia, and Amate Marin, to within 34½ miles of the coast. It is now proposed to extend it from San Salvador to Ahuachapan. European capitalists made the Government acceptable proposals to that effect during the summer of 1887.

Telegraphs.—The number of offices in 1885 was 68; length of wire, 1624 kilometres: receipts in 1883-'84, $58,941; expenses, $73,648. All the cities and towns are united by telegraph, and the submarine cable at La Libertad places Salvador in communication with the world's system. In May, 1886, the Government made a contract with Don Florentin Souza for the establishment of communication by telephone in San Salvador and Santa Tecla as well as between these cities. The duration of the privilege is to be for fifteen years, the Government to have a separate line.

Steamship Communication.—A contract was made by the Goverment in June, 1886, with the Kosmos line of German steamers, by virtue of which the latter engage to call regularly at La Union, and receive in compensation a subsidy of $500 for every round trip.

Commerce.—In 1886 the amount of coffee exported was 210,000 quintals, worth $3,150,000; that of indigo 8,001 serroons, worth $1,209,000. The United States imported from Salvador, during the fiscal year 1886, $1,261.275 worth of goods, and exported thither $470,541 worth of domestic merchandise. In the fiscal year 1887 the amounts were $1,059,841 and $477,125 respectively.

Mining.—In February, 1886, the Government made a contract with Dr. Francisco E. Galindo and Mr. John Moffat, representing Mr. E. Reade and John Drummond, respectively, for exploiting the mines in the Departments of Santa Ana and Chalatenango, and the construction of a railway in connection therewith between Santa Ana and Metapan.

Education.—In 1885 the number of public schools was 524, attended by 18,970 pupils.

Commercial Treaties.—By virtue of an agreement, signed June 28, 1886, the treaty of commerce and navigation between Salvador and Great Britain was renewed. In November, 1887, a treaty was concluded with Spain.

Adoption of the Metric System.—Beginning with 1886, Salvador adopted the metric system of weights and measures.

Agricultural Implements.—The only agricultural implements used or understood by the natives are the large hoe, the bill-hook, and the long knife or machete, as they term it. With these they work very cleverly. The native plow is merely a triangular piece of iron, about four inches broad at the base, fastened to a pole, and with oxen the point of this rude implement is run through the land to the depth of about three inches. Such labor-saving machines as seed-sowers, harrows, rakes, plows, etc., are almost unknown.

SAMOAN (OR NAVIGATORS') ISLANDS. The year 1886 left King Malietoa in control of the Samoan Islands, and the German Imperial Government on record officially and conjointly with the French and English Governments through their several consuls to sustain the King as against the opposing chief Tamesese. The importance that has been universally attached to the action of the German Government in connection with these islands in the year 1887 renders it desirable in this place to afford such information concerning the history of the islands as is possible, to be taken in connection with the account given in the volume of this work for 1886. The interest of the United States in these islands may be said to have begun in the year 1872, when Commander Meade, United States Navy, made a treaty with Maunga, the great chief of the island of Tutuila, one of the Samoan group, by which the port of Pango-Pango was given up to the Americans on condition that a friendly alliance be made between that island and the United States. In accordance with this treaty President Hayes sent a naval vessel to the Samoan Islands "to make surveys and to take possession of the privileges conceded to the United States by Samoa in the harbor of Pango-Pango." A United States coaling-station was also established there for the convenience and use of the United States.

These acts, and the obtaining of special privileges in Samoa for the United States, proved very mortifying to the German Government, and were made the subject of discussions on the part of Herr von Bülow and Prince Bismarck in the German Reichstag. Prior to this treaty the German land claims in Samoa were officially stated to comprise 232,000 acres, while British subjects claimed not less than 857,000 acres. But the terrible animosities and the series of wars which ensued between 1869 and 1872 gave the Germans their opportunity, when the natives being anxious to procure firearms, German traders would only sell them for land. The consequence was that between the years named more than one hundred thousand acres passed into the hands of Germans, and at a virtual cost of but a few pence per acre.

President Grant, in his message committing the treaty of 1872 to the Senate, said: "The advantages of the concessions which it professes to make are so great, in view of the advantageous position of Tutuila seaport as a coaling-station for steamers between San Francisco and Australia, that I should not hesitate to recommend its adoption but for the obligation of protection on the part of the United States which it seems to imply." This "obligation of protection" was modified by the Senate, which then ratified the treaty.

Under this agreement the chief had promised that he would not grant a like privilege to any other foreign power or potentate. This undertaking it was which disturbed the German and English statesmen, who have never since ceased their machinations to break up the advantage which the United States thus had over Great Britain and Germany in Samoa.

On the basis of the facts concerning German interference with King Malietoa up to the close of 1886, President Cleveland in his annual message at that time said: "Civil perturbations in the Samoan Islands have during the past four years been a source of extreme embarrassment to three governments, Germany, Great Britain, and the United States, whose relations and extra-territorial rights in that important sea group are granted by treaties. The weakness of the native administration and the conflict of opposing interests in the islands had led King Malietoa to seek alliance or protection in some one quarter, regardless of the distinct requirement that no one of the three treaty powers may acquire any permanent or exclusive interest. In May last Malietoa offered to place Samoa under the protection of the United States, and the late consul, without authority, assumed to grant it. This proceeding was promptly disavowed and the overzealous official recalled. Special agents of the three governments having been deputed to examine the situation in the islands, with a change in the representatives of all the powers and a harmonious understanding among them, the business prosperity of the autonomous administration and the neutrality of Samoa can hardly fail to be secured."

In the mean time even the Sandwich Islands became interested in the questions agitating the Samoan group, and King Kalakaua, having elected to support Malietoa sent a half-breed named Bush to Apia as ambassador, accompanied by a suite, to draw up a treaty as between the two sovereigns. Malietoa, however, did not seem to take kindly to the proposition, not even being influenced thereunto by the presence of the Hawaiian naval steamer "Kamoa," which followed Bush three months later. The ambassador was not only unsuccessful, but, as is alleged, brought to himself no credit for his manner of conducting his commission, and an order for his recall was sent down by the late Minister Gibson from Honolulu. Rough weather prevented the landing of this dispatch at Apia, and it was carried on to Australia. A new ministry being formed, a second recall was sent to Apia, and after some difficulty in finding the ambassador he was discovered and brought back to the Sandwich Islands.

Early in the year, the United States Government, being without a representative at Apia, the President appointed and the Senate confirmed Mr. Harold Sewall, of Maine, a young gentleman who had been trained in the diplomatic service, as American consul at Apia. Meanwhile, steamers arriving at San Francisco brought the news of continued movements on the part of the Germans in the Samoan Islands, which gave rise to considerable discussion and some uneasiness, as it was feared that the fact of several German men-of-war having sailed for the Samoan Islands indicated that that Government designed to assume a protectorate over the group.

On September 8 it was announced in the British House of Commons, by the Secretary to the Foreign Office, that the Government had received advices that the Germans had deposed the King of Samoa, and that the English and American consuls at Apia had protested against the action of the Germans. A newspaper interview with ex-Consul Greenebaum, in San Francisco, extracted from that gentleman the statement that Prince Bismarck was largely interested in the German Commercial Company of the South Seas, and that this fact to some extent accounted for the movement which had been announced in the British House of Commons and cabled to the United States. It was pointed out at this time that the treaty of 1878 between England, Germany, and the United States, contained the following article: "In the event of the Government of Samoa being at any time in difficulty with powers in amity with the United States the Samoan Government then reserves to itself the right to claim the protection of the American flag."

It was not until the beginning of October

that the detailed facts of the interposition of Germany in the affairs of the Samoan Islands reached the United States. It then appeared that during the months of June and July the German war-ship "Adler" visited Apia, and that the rebel chief Tamesese was publicly entertained on board of her, and his banner floated at her maintop, although the ship was anchored not three hundred yards from Malietoa's house. In fact, the king was frequently insulted, and his patience severely tried, but through the intercessions of the representatives of the United States and Great Britain he remained in a state of quietude, although his followers were clamorous for war. Their strength was then as eight to one, as a large portion of Tamesese's forces had come under the influence of J. E. Bush, the ambassador of the Hawaian Government already mentioned, and were making overtures to join the party of Malietoa against his opponent.

But in the middle of August a German squadron arrived, and on August 23 the German consul-general wrote to King Malietoa as follows:

GERMAN CONSULATE, APIA, SAMOA,
Aug. 23, 1887.

To His Majesty Malietoa, the King, at Afega:

YOUR MAJESTY: I am commanded by the Government of Germany to inform you as follows:

1. That your people attacked German people on the night and day of celebrating the anniversary of the birthday of his Majesty the Emperor on the 22d day of March of the present year. This action has caused great offense and much disturbance of mind to the Emperor and all the German people.

I now inform you to become on friendly terms with the Government of Germany in this wise; you will be quick in punishing the above offenders, and do so at once. You will also pay the sum of $1,000 to those who are wounded, and you are to make an abject apology (to Germany).

2. From one year to another year in the past your people have stolen animals and produce from plantations belonging to the Germans, and have injured their lands to the extent of more than $3,000 each year.

I now inform you that you are to pay quickly for all the above done by your people.

3. For many years past your judges have been unable by themselves to protect Germans (among you), and this is the reason your people have been abusing these Germans.

I now tell you that it is a law of Germany that the Government should be more severe in their trials and judgments, in order that they may be able to protect Germans in the future.

It is my opinion that there is nothing just or correct in Samoa in all the days you have ruled or while you are at the head of the Government.

(Signed)   BECKER, Consul-General.

To this letter the King made the following reply:

APIA, SAMOA, Aug. 24, 1887.

To Becker, Esq., German Consul at Apia.

SIR: I have to acknowledge the receipt of your letter of yesterday's date. It will be obvious to you that it is essential for me to consult my Government and chiefs before replying to the grave charges and heavy demands contained in your communication; and the time within which an answer is required does not enable me to do so. I shall, however, at once convene a meeting for the purpose of considering your letter, and will send you a reply on Saturday, the 27th inst.

I regret that it is impossible for me to comply with your demands for an answer this morning, and trust you will be satisfied with a reply on the date mentioned. I am, etc.,

(Signed)   MALIETOA, *King of Samoa.*

This answer was sent aboard the flag-ship of the squadron at 7 o'clock, A. M., the morning of the 25th. Malietoa, fearing treachery, having left the town and retreated into the interior with a number of his followers during the night. At 8 o'clock launches left the German war-ships crowded with men, and in less than fifteen minutes a force of nine hundred armed marines landed at Apia, and instantly began a search of the houses for Malietoa. It is alleged by eye-witnesses that, in making this search numerous outrages were committed, furniture was tossed about, doorways were broken in, and pistols were drawn and presented at the heads of inoffensive persons. No consideration was shown regarding the nationalities of the persons thus attacked, even Americans being abused, and the American and British consuls denied the right to pass along the main road.

The United States consul wrote to Mr. Becker, the German representative, demanding an explanation, and entering his protest against the action of the German naval authorities. In reply the German consul stated that war had been declared against Chief Malietoa.

The German flag was raised over the Malietoa government house, and continued to fly there until even the followers of Tamesese arrived in Apia and demanded that it should be taken down, and be replaced by their flag, or they would desert the Germans. Meanwhile the war-ship Olga was dispatched for Tamesese, and on his arrival at Apia he was saluted with twenty-one guns. Martial law was now proclaimed in the following notice:

PROCLAMATION.

CITIZENS OF APIA: By order of his Majesty the Emperor of Germany, war has been declared against the chief Malietoa. The neutrality of the municipal district will be respected as long as the security of the German troops is not injured by agitators within the municipal district.

I call upon the inhabitants of Apia to assist me in the maintenance of peace and good order in Apia.

(Signed)   HEUSNER,
Commodore and Commander of the German Squadron.
APIA, *August 27, 1887.*

The following proclamation was issued by the United States Consul as a matter of precaution:

PROCLAMATION.

Whereas, War has been declared by his Imperial Majesty the Emperor of Germany, against his Majesty Malietoa, King of Samoa:

I hereby caution all those entitled to the protection of the Government of the United States of America to offer no opposition to the German forces, but to immediately report to me any molestation of person or property.

(Signed)   HAROLD MARSH SEWALL,
Consul-General of the United States of America
APIA, SAMOA, *August 25, 1887.*

PROCLAMATION.

To all who are under the Protection of the Government of the United States of America.

Whereas, The commander of the German squadron has proclaimed "Martial Law":

Now, therefore, take notice that the sentries are commanded to shoot until dead men who do not stop when challenged, but attempt to run away.

(Signed) HAROLD MARSH SEWALL,
Consul-General of the United States.
APIA, SAMOA, *August* 27, 1887.

A joint proclamation was now issued by the American and English consuls, as follows:

PROCLAMATION.

(*Translation.*)

Whereas, The Government of Germany has this day proclaimed Tamesese King of Samoa:

Now, therefore, we, the undersigned representatives of the United States of America and Great Britain, hereby give notice that we and our governments do not and never have recognized Tamesese as King of Samoa, but continue as heretofore to recognize Malietoa.

We advise all Samoans to submit quietly to what they can not help, not to fight, whatever the provocation, but to await peaceably the result of the deliberations now in progress, which alone can determine the future of Samoa.

(Signed) HAROLD MARSH SEWALL,
Consul-General of the United States of America.
(Signed) W. H. WILSON, *British Pro-Consul.*
APIA, SAMOA, *August* 25, 1887.

In the mean time, Malietoa, with two thousand men, having made a successful retreat to the mountains, remained hidden there, awaiting some action on the part of the American Government. The situation in Apia and in the other native towns was described as exciting and dangerous in the extreme. The natives were exasperated, and in some towns tore down Tamesese's proclamation, whereupon the German fleet visited these towns, plundered them, and reduced them to ashes.

The action of Germany, in thus violently and on a trumped up charge seizing upon King Malietoa's sovereignty, was viewed with as much annoyance and irritability in Great Britain as in the United States. It appearing that Germany suggested that she should have Upolu and Apia, the best land and harbors of the Samoan group, and England and the United States should take Savaii and Tubereti, the London "Morning Post" remarked that "the Washington conference would be exceedingly ill-advised if it accepted this suggestion." The "Post" strongly advised "the appointment of a native government with advisers chosen in behalf of the great powers, but who should be men who have no interest in or connection with the trading-houses of the countries involved."

King Malietoa remained in hiding for some weeks, during which time negotiations to a certain extent were going on between him and the Germans. At length, upon being promised security of person and a pension, the King gave himself up, and upon being placed on the German man-of-war "Adler," was transported, first to Cooktown, and from there transferred to the German man-of-war "Albatross," and

taken to the German possessions in New Guinea. It was stated that had the King remained in concealment a few days longer, until the arrival of the American man-of-war "Adams," he would have been protected. Four German men-of-war were stationed at the Samoan Islands at this time, including the flag-ship "Bismarck," and the "Olga," "Corona," and "Sophie."

In the mean time the British consul had been instructed by his Government not to interfere with any thing that the Germans might do, and the American consul, Mr. Sewall, while doing all in his power for the natives, stated that if the United States did not take the matter in hand and support his action he would resign his office. After King Malietoa had thus been successfully deposed and extradited, it is stated that the German naval commander demanded a large sum from King Tamesese for the assistance which the Germans had given him against King Malietoa. It was believed at Apia that this movement on the part of the Germans was probably only a *ruse* to obtain an available excuse, on account of his inability to make any such payment, for deposing Tamesese and establishing a German protectorate over the islands.

The latest date from Samoa was November 30, when it was stated that the Germans continued to occupy the islands, that Apia was quiet, and that the position of Tamesese was extremely weak. The majority of the natives had paid a poll tax, demanded of them by the Germans. An interview with Mr. Goward in Washington, who was sent to the Samoan Islands to arrange for the treaty with the United States already referred to, brought out the following statement: "The present landed and commercial interest of the United States in Samoa is very great. The Samoan commerce is principally on the Pacific coast. The harbor of Pango-Pango is to all intents and purposes the possession of the United States, secured after years of exertion and expense, and for ten years occupied as a coaling-station. The capacity of this harbor is sufficient for the accommodation of large fleets; land-locked, it is safe from hurricanes and storms, and could easily be defended from land or sea attack at a small expense. In a naval point of view, it is the key position to the Samoan group, and likewise Central Polynesia, and is eminently located for the protection of American commerce. The Samoan Archipelago is now, by reason of its geographical position in Central Polynesia, lying in the course of vessels from San Francisco to Auckland, from Panama to Sydney, and from Valparaiso to China and Japan, and from being outside the hurricane track, the most valuable group in the South Pacific. Situated half-way between Honolulu and Auckland, Pango-Pango would be a most convenient stopping-place or coaling-station for vessels or steamers either for supplies or the exchange of commodities. With the Pacific mail steamers making it a port for coaling, it would necessarily become the controlling commercial place in that part of Polynesia.

The American interests at Samoa are probably larger than is generally believed. Ten years ago the Germans were all-powerful in Samoa. They controlled all the trade and had numerous large plantations in working order. About this time a few Americans and Englishmen were attracted to the country, and finding openings, commenced business. From small beginnings they grew strong, until to-day it is stated that the bulk of the trade is in their hands. The American Land Company purchased lands in Samoa amounting in all to two hundred thousand acres. Subjects of Great Britain were also not only purchasers of large tracts of land, but started and maintained several large plantations, so that although the investments of the Germans slightly exceed in value the investments of either the citizens of the United States or those of Great Britain, still, when the investments of these two nations are combined, they vastly exceed those of the subjects of Germany. The trade of the United States with Samoa has been steadily increasing for the past ten years, at which time one small schooner visited the islands but three times a year. At present six or seven large vessels are required in the trade, and considerable quantities of American goods are purchased in the Australian markets and shipped to Apia either direct or via New Zealand, whose government subsidizes a steamer to visit the islands ten times yearly.

Although, as stated, the situation at the Samoan Islands at the time when the latest news came from there was that all was quiet, there was nevertheless a feeling of insecurity in Apia, which boded ill for the future. It was feared that a fierce and bloody war might be inaugurated, in which old and young would be indiscriminately massacred, much property destroyed, and the American trade ruined. Among the British and American residents the following conditions had been agreed upon as in their judgment offering the best plan on which to effect a settlement of the existing difficulty:

1. That the Governments of the United States and Great Britain demand that Germany instantly withdraw her troops and her squadron and depart from Samoan waters, leaving one vessel only to protect her subjects, who have rendered themselves obnoxious to the natives.

2. That the United States and Great Britain at once dispatch each a war-ship to Samoa to protect the lives and property of their subjects there.

3. That arrangements be made in Samoa, under the auspices of the consuls and the commanders of the war-ships, for a popular vote to be taken in Samoa as to who shall be the future ruler, and that the person so selected shall be maintained in his position.

4. That a scheme of government be formulated by the contracting powers which shall guarantee the independence of Samoa, that an impartial land court shall be established, and that three or four offices of importance in the government be filled by white men of mixed nationalities, who shall be paid fair salaries from the public fund.

5. That a war-ship belonging to at least two of the contracting parties be kept in Samoan waters continuously for the next twelve months, or until the new government is established and in good working order.

Although these conclusions were sent forward from Apia to the United States, and there published, no attention was paid to them, nor was anything done by the American or British governments, at least to which publicity was given, in the way of any interference with the proceedings of the German Government at Samoa. For map of the Samoan Islands, see "Annual Cyclopædia" for 1886, page 793.

SANTO DOMINGO. A republic, occupying the eastern portion of the West Indian island of that name, the western portion being Hayti. The population of the republic is 350,000; that of the capital, Santo Domingo, 20,000. A current of immigration has set in during late years from Cuba, Jamaica, Porto Rico, and the United States.

Government.—The President is Gen. Ulysses Heureaux, whose term of office will expire on Sept. 1, 1888. His Cabinet was composed of the following ministers: Interior and Police, Gen. Wenceslao Figuereo; Foreign Affairs, Don Manuel Maria Gautier; War and Navy, Gen. Miguel A. Pichardo; Finance and Commerce, Don Julio Julia; Justice, Public Works, and Instruction, Don Juan Tomás Mejía. The Dominican Consul at New York is Don Carlos Julien. The American Minister at Santo Domingo and Hayti, resident at Port-au-Prince, is John E. W. Thompson.

Finances.—On Jan. 1, 1886, the public indebtedness stood as follows: home debt, (gradually being canceled through the operations of a sinking fund, which consists of 15 per cent. of the import duties) $1,499,982; foreign debt, consolidated in June, 1886, £357,150. The Government, in the autumn of 1887, sent to Paris a commissioner, to raise, if possible, a small loan. Santo Domingo has still a claim against Hayti for $824,878. A decree appeared in October, 1887, abolishing the two-per-cent. extra export duty. A decree dated in March, 1886, prohibits the introduction into the country of fractional South American and Mexican coin.

On June 22, 1886, Congress sanctioned the new tariff. Simultaneously, the export duty on sugar was fixed on the basis of 60 pounds for every 100 pounds shipped, and on molasses of 40 pounds for every 100 pounds. In March, 1887, Congress passed a bill admitting, duty free, manures, both in a natural state and chemically treated.

Postal Service.—The mail service of the republic, in 1885, was carried on through the medium of 44 offices, forwarding 226,535 letters and postal cards, and 92,077 newspapers, the receipts being 85,100 francs, and the expenses, 87,264 francs.

Railroads.—The suppression of the rebellion in the summer of 1886 was so swift, and pacification so prompt and thorough, that work on the railroads was not interrupted. On June 10, 1886, the Samaná and Santiago Railway went into operation from the newly-created port of Las Cañitas to Almacen, thirty-seven miles. In May, 1886, a concession was given Messrs. Horatio C. King and Henry L. Bean, of New York, to build a railroad from the Calderas, Puerto Viejo, or Barabona, in the south of the republic, terminating in the north at Manzanillo Bay. The city of Santo Domingo took, in October, 1887, the necessary steps to procure capital sufficient for the construction and equipment of a line from the port of Barahona to Neyba, fifty miles. The railroad between Sanchez and La Vega went into operation in August, 1887.

Harbor Improvements.—For the past three years the work, undertaken by Engineer Thomassett, of improving the harbor of the capital has been proceeding steadily.

Sugar.—In spite of the low price of sugar, sugar production, by virtue of the introduction of central sugar-houses and improved methods and machinery, combined with the high degree of saccharine matter in Dominican cane, has been rapidly on the increase, enabling Puerto Plata to export in 1885 4,665,874 pounds, whereas the preceding year the export had not exceeded 2,961,778 pounds.

Commerce.—The imports into the ports of the republic in 1885 amounted to $2,104,869, and the exports to $2,544,408. There were exported from Puerto Plata, during the year: Leaf-tobacco, 10,493,524 pounds; beeswax, 118,752 pounds; cocoa, 268,680 pounds; sugar, 4,065,847 pounds; coffee, 84,776 pounds; dividivi, 36,795 pounds; turtle shell, 99 pounds; mahogany, 440,952 feet; cotton, 600 pounds; fustic, 235 tons; logwood, 246 tons; lignum vitæ, 237 tons; molasses, 85,048 gallons, and honey, 7,310 gallons; hides, 21,115, and goatskins, 3,595 dozen.

Rebellion.—The presidential election took place during the last three days of June, and the defeated candidate, Gen. Casimiro N. de Moya rebelled against its result in July in La Vega and Monte Cristy. On the 24th the country was put under martial law, and in a series of bloody encounters the rebels were defeated in August. The number of casualties on both sides exceeded 1,100 dead and wounded.

SAXE, JOHN GODFREY, an American poet, born in Highgate, Franklin County, Vt., June 2, 1816; died in Albany, N. Y., March 31, 1887. He was educated in the local district schools, the grammar school in St. Albans, Vt., Wesleyan University in Middletown, Conn., and Middlebury college, Vt., taking the degree of A. B. in 1839, and that of A. M. in 1843. He

then studied law, was admitted to the bar in 1843, and practiced in St. Albans from that year till 1850. It was during this period that he began to give rein to his poetic gifts, his first verses appearing in "The Knickerbocker Magazine." In 1846 he published "Progress: a Satire"; in 1847, "The New Rape of the Lock"; in 1848, "The Proud Miss McBride"; and in 1849, "The Times." In 1850 he entered the profession of journalism, taking charge of "The Burlington Sentinel," and in 1856 was Attorney-General of the State. Subsequently he was a candidate for Governor, but, being defeated by the Whig nominee, re-

JOHN GODFREY SAXE.

nounced politics, and thereafter devoted himself to literature and lecturing, in which fields he was eminently popular and successful. In 1859 he published "The Money King, and other Poems"; in 1864, "Clever Stories of Many Nations rendered in Rhyme"; in 1866, "The Masquerade and other Poems"; in 1872, "Fables and Legends in Rhyme"; and in 1875, "Leisure-Day Rhymes." Up to 1874 he contributed frequently to "Harper's Magazine," "The Atlantic Monthly," and other periodicals, lecturing in the mean time to large audiences in all parts of the country. He settled in Albany, N. Y., in 1872, and became one of the editors of the "Evening Journal." In 1874, while on a lecturing tour in Virginia, he met with a railroad accident, and barely escaped with his life. Soon after this he lost his wife, three daughters, and a son, and the combined shock brought on extreme spells of melancholy, from which nothing could arouse him. He shrank from the world, and in his retirement became almost forgotten. Mr. Saxe will be best remembered as a writer of humorous and satirical verse, although many of his serious poems, like "Jerry, the Miller," "I'm Growing Old," "The Old Church Bell," "Treasures in Heaven," and "Boyhood," will keep his name alive for generations to come.

SERVIA, a kingdom of Eastern Europe. The Legislature consists of a single Chamber, called the Skupshtina, containing 178 members, of whom three fourths are elected by the people, every tax-payer having a vote, and the remaining fourth are nominated by the King. The reigning sovereign is Milan I, born in 1854, who succeeded to the throne in 1868. Servia was formerly a principality, and was erected into a kingdom in 1882. The ministry in the beginning of 1887 was composed of the following members: President of the Council and Minister of the Interior, M. Garashauin; Minister of War, G. Horvatovich; Minister of Finance, T. Mijatovich; Minister of Agriculture and Commerce, T. Mijatovich; Minister of Justice, D. Marinkovich; Minister of Foreign Affairs, D. Franassovich; Minister of Public Works, P. Topalovich; Minister of Education and Worship, M. Kuyundchich.

Area and Population.—The area of Servia is 18,800 square miles. The population, as determined by the census of 1884, is 1,903,350, comprising 973,910 males and 929,440 females. The bulk of the population are Servians, professing the Greek Orthodox religion. There are 150,103 speaking the Roumanian, and 30,000 the Bohemian language. The population of Belgrade, the capital, is 35,726. The number of marriages in 1885 was 17,093; of births, 91,813; of deaths, 53,565; natural increment, 38,248. In 1886 there were 23,311 marriages, 84,351 births, and 60,818 deaths; natural increment, 23,533. The population of the kingdom at the close of 1886 was reckoned at 1,970,032 persons.

The Army.—The reorganization of the army was completed in 1882. In time of peace the standing army numbers 13,213 men, with 132 guns. In case of mobilization there are 60 battalions of infantry, 24 squadrons of cavalry, 46 batteries of field artillery, a battalion of fortress artillery, 11 companies of engineers, 6 trains of pontoons, and the train. The total effective is about 70,000 fighting men, with 264 guns. The reserve army, comprising the men of the second ban, numbers 58,415 men.

Finance.—The budget for the fiscal year 1884-'85 makes the total receipts 37,365,000 dinars, and the expenditures 37,291,000 dinars. The receipts from direct taxes were 20,000,000 dinars; from customs, 5,500,000 dinars; from duties on tobacco, salt, and spirits, 5,080,000 dinars. The expenditure on the debt was 11,583,824 dinars; on the army, 16,211,276 dinars. The public debt on Jan. 1, 1886, amounted to 213,000,000 dinars, of which 130,000,000 dinars were borrowed for railroad construction. The amount raised on loans in 1885 for the mobilization of the troops was 35,000,000 dinars. In January, 1886, a loan of 40,000,000 dinars was taken by a French syndicate which obtained the tobacco monopoly as a guarantee. In the autumn session of 1886 the Skupshtina appointed a committee to investigate the finances, which recommended that the tobacco

concession should be recalled, but the Minister of Finance declared that the arrangement could not be canceled without an agreement with the company. A new tax law increased the direct taxes, suppressed taxes bearing on the poorer classes, and removed the retail license tax on the sale of wine and spirits. Earlier in the year bills were passed authorizing a loan of 20,000,000 dinars to cover the floating debt, imposing duties on petroleum and matches, and removing the export duties on wine and brandy. A syndicate of German bankers contracted in November, 1887, to take the loan of 20,000,000 dinars at the price of 74·25 per cent. The consolidated debt on Jan. 1, 1887, amounted to 254,123,466 dinars, and the floating debt to 32,063,762, not including the deficit of 1886-'87, which exceeds 26,000,000.

Commerce.—The total value of the imports in 1886 was 42,029,379 dinars or francs, against 40,472,989 dinars in 1885, and 43,898,859 in 1884. The value of the exports was 40.-718,677 dinars, against 37,615,299 dinars in 1885, and 39,968,706 dinars in 1884. The chief articles of export are swine, dried prunes, skins, sheep and goats, cereals, and wine. The principal part of the foreign commerce is with Austria-Hungary, which imported into Servia in 1884 goods valued at 32,717,000 dinars, and received 32,859,000 of the Servian exports.

Railroads.—There were 427 kilometres of railroads in operation at the close of 1886, comprising the line, 354 kilometres in length, from Belgrade through Nish to Vranja, and the roads connecting Lapovo and Kragwievatz and Velika Plana with Smederevo. The section of the international line between Nish and Zaribrod, 90 kilometres in length, was completed in 1887, and the junction with the Turkish railroad to Salonica effected according to agreement. The railroad between Nish and Pirot was finished in July, leaving only the 150 kilometres of Bulgarian line between Pirot and Tatar Bazardjik to be completed to afford continuous railroad communication between Paris and Constantinople.

Telegraphs.—The length of telegraph lines at the end of 1886 was 2,841 kilometres; the length of wires, 4,130 kilometres. The number of messages sent over the wires in 1886 was 478,110, of which 383,851 were internal, 85,220 international, 1,447 official, and 7,592 dispatches forwarded in transit. The receipts were 687,098 francs, and the expenses 526,782.

Politics and Legislation.—The result of the general election that was held in May, 1886, was a defeat of the Government. The ministers, however, proceeded to nullify the popular vote by declaring many of the elections invalid, redoubling the pressure on the voters in the supplementary elections, and casting in prison many politicians of the Opposition. By such measures they secured as many of the elective seats as their opponents, and with the forty members nominated by the crown possessed a large apparent majority.

Gen. Horvatovich, who after the Servian war was recalled from the St. Petersburg mission to take the chief command of the army, and given the portfolio of the Ministry of War in order to develop a scheme for the complete reorganization of the military forces, resigned his seat in the Cabinet in February, 1887, because M. Garashanin objected to his plans as being too costly. Another cause of difference was that the Prime Minister insisted on controlling appointments to high commands in the army. Gen. Topalovich succeeded Gen. Horvatovich as Minister of War. The Minister of Public Works tendered his resignation at the same time, and was succeeded by Gen. Michael Bogitchevich, the burgomaster of Belgrade. In April the Cabinet was weakened by the retirement of M. Mijatovich, the Minister of Finance, on account of difficulties arising out of the tobacco monopoly. M. Garashanin proposed the entire reconstruction of the Cabinet, but the King insisted that the ministers should remain in office. At length M. Garashnin found it impossible to continue longer his unpopular administration, and in the beginning of June the whole Cabinet resigned. The King did not send for M. Theodorovich, the chief of the Radical party which had gained the victory in the elections of the preceding year, but first called on Nikola Cristich to form a Cabinet, and when he declined intrusted the task to Jovan Ristich, the representative of the pro-Russian party with which Queen Natalie was identified, and who had been the chief antagonist of King Milan and his policy. On June 18 a ministry was formed which was composed as follows: President of the Council and Minister of Foreign Affairs, Ristich; Minister of the Interior, Milojlovich; Minister of Public Instruction and Worship, Vasiljevich; Minister of Justice. Avakumovich; Minister of Agriculture and Commerce, Molosavljevich; Minister of Finance, Vujich; Minister of Public Works, Velimirovich; Minister of War ad interim, Gen. Bogitchevich. Col. Gruich was subsequently appointed to the Ministry of War, returning from St. Petersburg where he was Servian minister to assume the duties of the office. The new Prime Minister hastened to give assurances that the change of government did not signify the inauguration of a policy hostile to Russia. He announced a programme embracing four points: (1) the revision of the Constitution; (2) the maintenance of good relations with all foreign states; (3) economy in the public expenditure; (4) the honorable fulfillment of all engagements entered into with other countries. On June 15 the Skupshtina was dissolved, and new elections were appointed for September. The anti-Austrian sentiment which had much to do with the political crisis was aggravated by the vexatious restrictions placed upon Servian exports of cattle and swine to the dual monarchy in the interest of the Hungarian stock-breeders, who were accused by an Austrian member of the Delegations of discovering cattle-disease in Servia whenever the Hungarian cattle-market was overstocked. The cession of the tobacco monopoly to Austrian capitalists had contributed to the unpopularity of the Garashanin Cabinet by adding to the prevalent jealousy of the economical domination of Austria. In order to smooth over the difficulties that might arise from the return of the old enemy of Austria to the head of the Government, King Milan, after the constitution of the new Cabinet paid a visit to the Emperor at Vienna. Queen Natalie, who had separated from her husband for reasons partly domestic and partly political, had gone to Russia with her son, the Crown Prince, previously to the change of government. One of the last diplomatic acts of the Garashanin ministry was to follow the similar proceeding of the Roumanian Government in presenting a remonstrance or inquiry at St. Petersburg in regard to the action of the Russian minister at Belgrade, M. Persiani, in interfering in Servian politics and encouraging anti-dynastic movements. The retiring Cabinet had also adopted the sharp retaliatory measure against Turkey of prohibiting from May 13 the trading operations of Turkish subjects in Servia because the Porte had not been willing to conclude a commercial treaty. Incursions of Arnauts into Servian territory gave occasion for a menacing note from M. Ristich to the Government at Constantinople. In the early part of June the Servian frontier post at Dabishevsky was attacked by Albanian marauders, who killed the commanding officer of the Servians. A few days later 400 Arnauts plundered the village of Dabinovac and killed two Servians before they were driven back by the frontier guards, who killed a number of the raiders and captured two flags.

M. Ristich gave orders that there should be no official interference in the elections, which took place in the latter part of September. The result was again a victory for the Radicals, who elected 85 members out of 156, while the Liberal or Ministerial party elected only 44 members. The remaining seats went to neutrals or independents, the Progressists, who followed M. Garashanin and formed his majority in the late Skupshtina, having retired altogether from the electoral contest. The Radicals demanded that the 52 seats that were to be filled by appointment should be divided between the Liberals and themselves, and the King was inclined to nominate 26 members from each of the two parties, but M. Ristich insisted on retiring at once if that were done, since it would leave him without a majority. The matter was compromised by giving 36 seats to Ministerialists and 16 to Radicals.

The Skupshtina was opened on December 4. The King in the speech from the throne dwelt on the good relations that existed with all the powers, especially the neighboring states, and their recognition of the correctness of Servia's attitude, which left her the opportunity to bestow her attention on internal reforms and the revision of the Constitution. The address of the Skupshtina in reply to the royal speech, censured the foreign and domestic policy of the late ministry, and demanded a general amnesty and greater freedom of the press. King Milan refused to receive the address, declaring that if he accepted it in that form, Austria-Hungary would demand explanations, pointing out that the granting of amnesties was a prerogative of the crown, and asserting that the press in Servia enjoyed an ample measure of freedom. He admitted that the royal power was disproportionate to that of the Legislature, and said he would gladly see the Constitution revised in a way that would divide the power more equally between the King and the Skupshtina, but said that he would exercise the authority that was his under the existing laws, and threatened to call other ministers if the address were not modified.

Arrangement with Bulgaria.—When a treaty of peace with Servia was concluded, under pressure from the powers, in March, 1886, the Servian Government refused to resume friendly relations until the Bregova matter and other disputes were settled. After the expulsion of Prince Alexander a common dread of Russia engendered a sympathy between all the Balkan nations. On Oct. 27, 1886, Dr. Stransky was received by King Milan as the representative of the Bulgarian regency. An agreement had previously been signed, October 13, whereby Bregova was evacuated by the Bulgarians, and remained in the hands of a mixed commission pending the decision on the claims of the two states to the district. A treaty of commerce was to be concluded within six months; Bulgaria promised to keep the Servian refugees from settling within sixty kilometres of the frontier; also, to build the Vakarel-Sofia-Zaribrod section of the international railway by the time when the Servian section shall have been completed. This latter stipulation was not fulfilled owing to the financial difficulties of the Bulgarian Government, and the Servians felt much resentment in consequence, because, in accordance with the decision of the Conférence à Quatre, their line, which had made pecuniary sacrifices to build within the stipulated time, could not be opened to traffic until the Bulgarian branch of the International Railroad was also ready for operation.

The mixed Servian and Bulgarian commission to whom the frontier delimitation was referred, decided, in December, 1886, that the district near Bregova belonged to Servia, and that the old bed of the Timok river should at this point mark the boundary. An act embodying this decision was signed by the delegates of the two governments on April 12, 1887.

SOMALI-LAND. The fact, that in February, 1886, this country was formally taken under the protection of Germany, the German Government declaring a protectorate over the whole promontory, has brought this portion of Africa under public notice. Somali-land is an extensive maritime tract in eastern Africa, having the Gulf of Aden on the north, the Indian Ocean on the south, and the Jub river as its southwestern boundary. From this latter point to Cape Guardafui is about 900 miles, and the entire area of the country is estimated at 300,000 square miles, but a great portion of the interior is unexplored, and its population unknown. The land is elevated and mountainous in the north, but slopes in terraces toward the south. The river Jub finds its source in the mountains of southern Abyssinia, its mouth being on the northern frontier of Zanzibar. This country was but little known until explored by Mr. F. L. James, whose report upon it was published in London, in the " Proceedings of the Royal Geographical Society," in 1885. An English protectorate of the north coast was declared in that year, and since then the ports of Zeilah and Berbera, on the Gulf of Aden have been occupied by British soldiers. The Somalis are a Hamite race, akin to the ancient Egyptians, and closely related to the Gallas, who live south of Abyssinia, with whom, however, they are at perpetual feud. They are a pastoral people, but are none the less warlike on that account. They are divided into tribes, each tribe having its own sultan, and are not altogether barbarous. About the center of the promontory lies the country of Ogadayn, and south of it is the rich valley of the Webbe Shebeyli ("Leopard river"). About 175 miles south of Zeilah, lies the town of Harar, with about 35,000 inhabitants, protected by walls, and surrounded by fields and orchards. Burton visited it in 1856. It was the capital of Hadiyeh, one of the seven provinces of the Arab empire of Zeilah, founded in the seventh century. In 1875 it was occupied by Egyptian troops. It sends slaves, ivory, tobacco, gums, tallow, and other produce to Berbera. The Somali people breed enormous quantities of camels, mainly for the sake of their flesh, and the price of a camel in the markets is from eighteen to twenty-five dollars. Off Cape Guardafui, lies the island of Socotra, comprising 1,810 square miles, its capital, Tamarida. It is mostly rocky and barren, but possesses fertile valleys and plains. This island belongs to the Sultan of Oman, but was taken under British protection by treaty in 1876. The German protectorate covers the territory to the north beyond the land covered by British claims (Berbera) and as far south as Warsheikh, where the Zanzibar claims begin. Treaties have been effected with the various Somali native rulers. These natives have hitherto had very little dealings with white traders, but a short time since, an enterprising firm in Aden, undertook to build up a regular communication and traffic. They accordingly dispatched agents along the coast to inform the natives that if they would make their appearance at certain points on the coast at specified periods, trade would be opened with them. The Aden firm then purchased a small steamer, and entered upon the commerce, which succeeded beyond their hopes. The natives were found at the appointed times and places, supplied with their products. The steamer would anchor off the coast, trading-boats were sent ashore, and a lively market was opened. They brought ivory, hides, palm-oil, etc., and were found to prefer in exchange Venetian glassware and American cotton-shirtings. They conducted their trade on very fair principles, and it was soon found that their taste improved, and in place of the cheap and flimsy stuffs with which they were at first satisfied, they demanded a better quality of goods.

SOUTH CAROLINA. State Government.—The following were the State officers during the year: Governor, John P. Richardson, Democrat; Lieutenant-Governor, William L. Mauldin; Secretary of State, William Z. Leitner; Treasurer, Isaac S. Bamberg; Comptroller-General, William E. Stoney; Attorney-General, Joseph H. Earle; Superintendent of Public Instruction, James H. Rice; Commissioner of Agriculture, A. P. Butler; Chief-Justice of the Supreme Court, W. D. Simpson; Associates, Henry McIver and Samuel McGowan.

Finances.—The following is a statement of the State debt on Oct. 31, 1887, the close of the fiscal year: Brown consuls, all valid, $5,304,-936.83; valid green consuls, $205,953.26; deficiency bonds and stocks, $420,287.91; Agricultural College scrip, $191,8?0; ante-bellum and post-bellum bonds, not exchanged, estimated, $276,814.54; total, $6,399,742.54. During the year the commissioners of the sinking fund canceled $32,517.50 of deficiency bonds. The remaining deficiency bonds and stocks become payable in July, 1888. The apparent reduction of the debt during the year is over $124,000 instead of $32,517.50, owing to the fact that interest on consols, due and unpaid, to and including 1878, and amounting to (estimated) $91,698.65, has heretofore been exchangeable for consol bonds, and was included in the debt statement. By act of 1886 this interest was made payable in cash. Only $24,822.58 of old ante-bellum and post-bellum bonds have been exchanged for consols at 50 per cent. during the year. Nearly all the debt bears interest at 6 per cent. The report of the Treasurer shows receipts during the year of $995,551.18; cash on hand Oct. 31, 1886, $96,808.70; total, $1,092,359.88. The expenditures amount to $987,974.88, leaving a cash balance Oct. 31, 1887, of $104,385,-05. The total value of taxable property, as assessed for the year, is $141,074,347, a loss of $5,444,623 as compared with the valuation of 1886. The State tax of 4½ mills upon this sum yields a revenue of $599,566.11.

Education.—The following statistics represent the condition of the public schools for the school year 1886-'87: Number of districts, 568; number of public schools, 3,760; number of school-houses, 3,531; valuation of property,

$360,504.63; white pupils enrolled, 82,416; colored pupils enrolled, 92,601; average attendance (white) 59,824; (colored) 65,697. The number of schools shows an increase of 100 over 1886. At the State University 188 pupils were enrolled during 1886-'87. The appropriation for support of the institution for this year was $28,000. There were 113 pupils at the Military Academy. The usual appropriation for this school is $20,000.

Charities.—At the State Lunatic Asylum there were 647 patients at the beginning of the fiscal year, of whom 304 were males and 343 females. There were under treatment during the year 894 people, and at its close, October 31, there remained 649. The cost of maintenance during the year was $94,142.24, and $4,251.71 was expended for repairs. The Institute for the Deaf, Dumb, and Blind, at Cedar Springs, enrolled 96 pupils during the year, and supported them at an average cost of $152 per capita.

Penitentiary.—The prison officials report that the total number of convicts has increased from 985 at the beginning to 1,006 at the close of the fiscal year. Of these 78 are white males, 2 white females, 876 colored males, and 50 colored females. Some of these are leased to individuals outside the prison, some work under contract within the prison, and others are employed on the State farms. The income from their labor during the year has made the prison more than self-sustaining.

State Capitol.—Various appropriations for the completion of this building have been made to the amount of $211,600, of which $196,578.97 has already been expended. The stone work and roofing of the two wings is finished according to the original design, and the two halls of legislation are ready for use.

State Canal.—No progress was made upon this enterprise during the year, owing to the failure of the Legislature of 1886 to provide an appropriation. The sum of $130,705.68 has already been expended, $53,130.71 in cash and $77,574.97 in the labor of convicts. More than $160,000 additional will be needed. The work thus far has been paid for in cash out of the surplus earnings of the Penitentiary or is the result of the labor of the prisoners.

Forfeited Lands.—On this subject the Governor says in his message: "There were on the forfeited land list, at the end of the fiscal year 1886, 954,287 acres. During the present fiscal year new forfeitures have been incurred, which amount to 100,045 acres, the whole amounting to 1,054,282 acres. During the present fiscal year 45,298 acres of land have been sold or redeemed, and 94,131 acres have been stricken from the forfeited list as erroneous entries, and still there remains on this list a net acreage of 914,853 acres."

Legislative Session.—The Legislature met on November 22, and adjourned December 23, having passed 236 acts and 32 joint resolutions. More than two thirds of these are private

or special. Two joint resolutions proposing
amendments to the State Constitution were
passed, and will be submitted to the people in
November, 1888. One is to strike out the provision for the election of a school commissioner
by the people, every two years, in each county.
The other proposes to make the term of office
of the probate judge four years instead of two.
The more important new laws are as follow:

To regulate the delivery of warehousemen's receipts.
To provide for the redemption of the State deficiency bonds by the issue of new bonds, running forty
years and bearing four and one half per cent interest.
To amend the law against discrimination by railroads,
so as to give them the power to make special rates for
the purpose of developing manufacturing, mining,
milling, and internal improvements in the State.
To submit the question of license or no license to
the voters of Abbeville and Greenville counties.
To declare the law relating to the separate estate
of a married woman, so that she may convey or charge
her separate estate, and so that all her earnings and
income shall be her own separate estate.
To provide for scholarships for one young woman
from each county in the State in the Winthrop Training School for Teachers.
To require the railroads to carry merchandise by
the route designated by the shippers, and to deliver
it promptly.
To restore to the tax lists unimproved lands that
have been allowed to remain forfeited, because the
taxes amount to more than the land is worth.
To change the time of listing property for taxation.
To prevent cock-fighting within three miles of any
institution of learning.
To provide for obtaining lists of all persons who are
disqualified from voting by reason of their conviction
of disqualifying offenses.

Different propositions looking to a provision for
disabled Confederate soldiers and sailors, and their
widows, were discussed. It was not considered advisable to establish a system of pensions and a soldiers'
home as well. The result was the passage of a law
providing for a pension of $5 a month to every dis-
abled soldier or sailor who is incapable of earning his
own livelihood, and is without means. The law applies equally to the widows of the disabled soldiers or
sailors. The sum of $50,000 was appropriated for this
purpose for 1888.

A bill for the reorganization of the South Carolina
University was debated, in connection with a proposition for the establishment of a separate college. Under its new organization the university will consist
of the College of Agriculture and Mechanic Arts, the
College of Liberal Arts and Sciences, and the College
of Pharmacy, together with a normal-school and law-
school.

Provision was made for the transfer of the State
canal to a board of trustees, and the city of Columbia
was authorized to guarantee the interest on such bonds
as the trustees should issue to insure its completion.

The State tax-rate for 1888 was fixed at five and
one half mills, an increase of one and one quarter mill
over 1887.

Industrial Statistics.—The following comparison of the products of the State in 1880 and
1887 is made by the State Department of Agriculture:

INDUSTRIES.	1880.	1887.
Farm products	$41,969,749	$46,968,292
Manufactures	16,788,008	31,975,108
Live-stock	12,279,412	19,781,098
Mineral products	1,371,989	2,093,028
Fruits and vegetables	168,297	865,009
Total	$72,582,405	$101,582,580

The yield of cotton, estimated at 605,000
bales grown upon 1,714,937 acres, is larger
than in any year since 1882; the corn-crop
was above the average, and the minor crops
show the effect of a favorable season. The
value of the cotton-crop is placed at $23,476,-
828, and that of the corn-crop at $11,543,855.
About 54,000,000 pounds of rice were raised,
valued at $1,080,000. The value of wheat
raised was $1,166,299.

In manufactures there has been an increase
in seven years of 1,198 establishments, giving
employment to more than twice as many hands
as were employed in 1880, and both the capital and production of these establishments have
been nearly doubled in the seven years.

Granite is quarried at Winnsboro in Fairfield County. Phosphate mining is one of the
most valuable industries of the State. During
the year twelve companies were engaged in
mining land rock, with a capital of about $2,-
000,000; and twenty companies and individuals in mining river rock, with a capital of
$1,500,000.

Railroads.—In the two years from November,
1885, to November, 1887, 176 miles of railroads
were constructed in the State. Since 1880, 387
miles of railroad have been completed. The
number of miles in the State is 1,813.

SPAIN, a monarchy in southwestern Europe.
The legislative authority is vested by the Constitution of June 30, 1876, in two bodies, forming the Cortes. The Senate is composed of (1)
princes of the blood and grandees of Spain,
who are senators in their own right, and certain high functionaries, who are senators by
virtue of their offices; (2) senators appointed
for life; (3) senators elected by communal and
provincial states, religious bodies, universities,
and other corporate institutions. The number
in the first two classes taken together must not
exceed 180, and the elective members are limited to the same number. The Chamber of
Deputies is composed of members elected for
five years by electoral colleges in the proportion of one to every 50,000 inhabitants.

The present King is Alfonso XIII, born May
17, 1886, the posthumous child of Alfonso
XII. The royal power is exercised during his
minority by his mother, the Queen-Dowager
Maria Christina, born July 21, 1858, daughter
of the Archduke Carl Ferdinand, of Austria,
who was elected Regent by the Cortes.

The ministry, constituted Oct. 9, 1886, is
composed as follows: President of the Council, Praxedes Mateo Sagasta; Minister of Foreign Affairs, Segismundo Moret; Minister of
Finance, Maquin Lopez Puigcerver; Minister
of Grace and Justice, Manuel Alonso Martinez;
Minister of the Interior, Albereda; Minister of
Commerce and Agriculture, Carlos Navarro
Rodrigo; Minister of War, Lieut.-Gen. Cassola; Minister of Marine, Admiral Rafael Rodriguez de Arias; Minister of the Colonies, Victor Balaguer. Albereda, who had been ambassador at Paris since Jan. 22, 1886, succeeded

Fernando Leon y Castillo as Minister of the Interior in November, 1887. Gen. Cassola on March 8, 1887, replaced Gen. Ignacio de Castillo in the Ministry of War.

Area and Population.—The area of Continental Spain is 492,230 square kilometres, and the population at the end of 1885 was 16,609,295. The Balearic Islands have an area of 5,014 square kilometres and 309,216 inhabitants; the Canaries are 7,272 square kilometres in extent, and contain 307,743 inhabitants; and the Spanish territory on the north coast of Africa, exclusive of Ceuta, which is attached to the province of Cadiz, is 85 square kilometres in extent, with 2,532 inhabitants; making the total area of the kingdom 504,551 square kilometres and the total population 17,228,776.

The principal cities of the kingdom and their population, as computed in December, 1885, are as follow: Madrid, 387,080; Barcelona, 243,077; Valencia, 140,382; Sevilla, 131,209; Malaga, 110,478; Murcia, 91,948; Saragossa, 81,012; Carthagena, 75,908 (1877); Granada, 67,895; Jerez, 64,533 (1877); Palma, 59,586; Cadiz, 58,042.

The Army.—The peace effective of the Spanish army is fixed by the law of April 14, 1887, at 131,400 men, of whom 100,000 serve in the peninsula, 19,000 in Cuba, 8,700 in the Philippines, and 3,700 in Porto Rico. The number of horses is 16,495, and the number of cannon 416. In time of war the strength of the army is 869,353 men, with 23,467 horses and 484 cannon. (For statistics of the navy see the "Annual Cyclopædia" for 1886.)

Finances.—The budget for the year ending June 30, 1888, estimates the revenue at 850,-596,753 pesetas, approximately equivalent to $170,119,000, of which sum 263,293,362 pesetas are derived from direct taxation, 184,723,-000 pesetas from indirect taxation, 135,000,-000 pesetas from customs, 217,262,950 pesetas from stamps and régies, 38,662,441 pesetas from national property, and 66,655,000 pesetas from receipts of the treasury. The total expenditure is estimated at 855,753,015 pesetas, of which the following are the items: Public debt, 274,861,752 pesetas; Ministry of War, 158,343,267 pesetas; Ministry of Public Works, 103,912,367 pesetas; Ministry of Justice, 59,-680,656 pesetas; indemnities and pensions, 50,209,728 pesetas; Ministry of Finance, 22,-801,620 pesetas; collection of taxes, 89,023,-511 pesetas; Ministry of Marine, 44,572,322 pesetas; Ministry of the Interior, 31,985,529 pesetas; civil list, 9,350,000 pesetas; Ministry of Foreign Affairs, 5,396,658 pesetas; legislation, 2,299,205 pesetas; judicial expenses, 2,167,441 pesetas; Presidency of the Council of Ministers, 1,148,959 pesetas.

The capital of the public debt in the beginning of 1886 amounted to 6,324,070,926 pesetas, paying 237,161,098 pesetas of interest in that year.

The principal financial measure of the Government in 1887 was the lease of the tobacco monopoly for the price of 90,000,000 pesetas per annum. The bill received the royal sanction on April 2. The lease was taken by the Bank of Spain, which contracted to pay the stated sum for three years and thereafter half the profits in addition to the same annual price. The deterioration of Spanish wines through adulteration with inferior grades of alcohol impelled the Government to study measures for the exclusion of the deleterious potato brandy known as Hamburg spirits. Since, however, this might be construed by the German Government as a violation of the favored-nation clause, it was decided to subject all distilled liquors, domestic as well as imported, to a thorough inspection, and by suitable means to so destroy the nature of all except the absolutely pure as to render them useless for the manufacture of beverages.

Commerce.—The total value of the import trade in 1885 was 764,757,664 pesetas, equivalent to about $152,950,000, against 779,643,-866 pesetas in 1884; the value of the export trade, 698,003,042 pesetas, against 619,192,389 pesetas. The proportions in which foreign countries participated in the foreign trade of 1885 are shown in the following table, giving in round numbers the import and export trade with each in pesetas:

COUNTRIES.	Imports.	Exports.
France	198,600,000	315,600,000
Great Britain	118,600,000	162,000,000
Germany	94,700,000	13,000,000
Belgium	39,900,000	8,560,000
Portugal	8,800,000	22,100,000
Sweden and Norway	24,500,000	4,500,000
Russia	16,500,000	2,400,000
Italy	17,300,000	10,100,000
Turkey	11,600,000	....
Netherlands	1,500,000	16,100,000
Other European countries	11,400,000	7,700,000
America	178,900,000	130,600,000
Asia and Australia	32,700,000	4,000,000
Africa	20,300,000	8,400,000
Other countries	400,000	....
Total	764,200,000	698,000,000

The following were the values of the principal imports in 1885: Cotton and cotton manufactures, 83,798,100 pesetas; spirits, 57,454,-250 pesetas; wool and woolen manufactures, 41,588,500 pesetas; timber, 36,747,475 pesetas; fish, 29,975,000 pesetas; sugar, 28,236,-600 pesetas; coal, 26,344,925 pesetas; wheat and flour, 26,198,750 pesetas; machinery, 21,-898,505 pesetas; hides and skins, 20,397,700 pesetas; silk manufactures, 20,300,000 pesetas, iron and iron manufactures, 19,417,575 pesetas; hemp and flax, 17,875,450 pesetas.

The values of the leading exports were as follow: Wine, 270,923,000 pesetas; fruit, 47,-068,925 pesetas; lead and lead ores, 41,702,450 pesetas; oil, 35,968,350 pesetas; iron-ore, 84,-055,875 pesetas; copper-ore, 23,576,750 pesetas; cattle, 19,393,675 pesetas; cork, 15,617,-800 pesetas; esparto grass, 8,148,050 pesetas. The wine exports amounted to 152,778,000 gallons, of which 117,000,000 gallons went to France.

Navigation.—The number of vessels entered at Spanish ports in 1885 was 17,055, of 2,673,-269 tons, of which 7,421, of 708,211 tons sailed under the Spanish flag. The number of clearances was 15,240; the tonnage, 5,767,728.

The mercantile marine in 1884 comprised 1,902 vessels of over 50 tons burden, including 426 steamers.

Railroads, Posts, and Telegraphs.—The railroads in operation at the close of 1885 had a total length of 9,185 kilometres.

The post-office, in the course of the financial year 1883-'84, transmitted 118,394,708 domestic and 84,343,456 foreign letters and circulars.

The telegraph lines in 1884 had a total length of 17,853 kilometres, with 43,446 kilometres of wires. The number of dispatches was 3,281,885, of which 483,581 were official, 2,048,459 private internal, and 749,845 international messages. The receipts were 5,881,-767 pesetas.

Politics and Legislation.—The Sagasta ministry took office under pledges to carry out an extensive programme of liberal reforms. Personal ambitions and party policy have interfered with the fulfillment of the ministerial promises, and it was not till 1887 that a beginning was made by the introduction of a bill for the establishment of trial by jury, one of the less important of the reforms that were promised. The bill, which was a compromise measure, passed the Chamber of Deputies on May 14. Civil marriage formed a part of the programme, and in the early part of the year the terms of a convention were arranged with the Vatican sanctioning a law of civil marriage under certain restrictions.

In the early summer Gen. Salamanca through the influence of Gen. Martinez Campos and at the express desire of Queen Christina, was appointed Governor-General of Cuba. When on the point of leaving for his post he uttered a sharp criticism of the colonial policy of the Government, and attacked Balaguer, the Colonial Minister, in a public speech. The immediate party of Sagasta, when Salamanca declined to resign the office to which he had been regularly appointed, insisted that the appointment should be canceled. After some hesitation the Prime Minister advised the Queen to revoke the nomination, and a decree to that effect was issued on August 22. Gen. Salamanca threatened to assail the colonial administration in the Cortes, and call attention particularly to immoral and corrupt practices of the officials in Cuba. Sagasta endeavored in vain to secure his neutrality by inducing him to accept the governorship of the Philippine Islands or the post of military governor of Catalonia.

A section of the Liberals joined the regular Opposition in objecting to a bill proposed by the Government for granting a subsidy of 8,250,000 pesetas to the Transatlantic Steamship Company. Although there was no prospect of the defeat of the bill, Sagasta declared that it would be considered a Cabinet question, and by this tactical mistake incurred much criticism. Gen. Cassola introduced bills for the reorganization of the army, introducing territorial military divisions, modifying the system of captain-generalships, abolishing substitution except in the case of recruits who are assigned to the colonial service, and requiring those who secure exemption from such service to perform active duty in the peninsula army. Lopez Dominguez, Salamanca, Martinez Campos, and other military generals who were ambitious of sharing the credit of military reforms opposed the plans with all their influence. They first raised a technical objection to Cassola's project, on the ground that bills presented by Jovellar and Castillo, the former Liberal Ministers of War, were still before the Cortes. This difficulty was arranged, and Gen. Cassola, who repeatedly announced his intention to resign, was persuaded by his colleagues to retain his post, but the action of the Committee of the Chamber in altering essential features of his scheme rendered his continuance in office uncertain.

Popular Discontent.—While the floating debt of the Government is rapidly increasing, and a crushing burden of taxes presses upon the people and discourages enterprise, agriculture, commerce, and manufacturing are depressed in all the provinces of Spain, and lack of employment has produced a dangerous discontent among the working classes. In the autumn months of 1887 from 3,000 to 4,000 persons emigrated from the provinces of Galicia, and more than 15,000 from Catalonia, where, in November, there were 20,000 laborers seeking work. On April 2 a dynamite cartridge was found concealed in the legislative chamber, and one was exploded in the courtyard of the finance ministry. Three days later a powder magazine was exploded at Cañete in the province of Cuenca. Arms and explosives were seized in some shops in Madrid by the police. The fear of popular outbreaks impelled the Government to take rigorous measures to repress democratic agitation in the press or on the platform.

Foreign Relations.—In 1887 the long-desired recognition of Spain as a great power, which had previously been accorded by France, was given by Germany, Austria, and Italy, through the elevation of their ministers at the court of Madrid to the rank of ambassadors. This act was supposed to signify the adhesion of Spain to Prince Bismarck's league of peace in some qualified manner, like that in which England joined the alliance about the same time.

The Colonies.—The colonial possessions of Spain, comprising Cuba and Porto Rico, the Philippine, Caroline, and Sulu islands, and Fernando Po, Corisco, Elobey, and other territory on the Guinea coast, have a combined area of 429,120 square kilometres, and contain 8,023,-300 inhabitants. Spain also possesses sovereign rights over the territory of Ifni on the west coast of Africa, and the coast of the Desert of Sahara between Cape Bojador and Cape Blanco, possessions of undetermined extent. A royal decree, placing this Saharan territory under the governorship of the Captain-General of the Canary Islands, was published on April 7. It was acquired by virtue of treaties with the Sheikhs of Adarer, whose dominions lie back of the annexed territory, which has a coast-line of about 500 miles, and extends 150 miles into the interior. There is only one harbor—the Rio de Oro—which is shallow, but is capable of improvement. The Spanish Government, in the spring of 1887, purchased of some native chiefs a strip of land on the Red Sea coast, south of Massowah, and within the limits of the Italian protectorate, where, by arrangement with the Government of Italy, it intends to establish a coaling-station.

Abuses in the administration of the Caroline and Palaos led to a catastrophe in July, 1887. The islands were insufficiently garrisoned, and the Governor of the Philippines, General Terrero, neglected to send the regular supplies and re-enforcements. Captain Posadillo, Governor of the Carolines, exasperated the natives by his tyrannical and arbitrary conduct, and when he decided to expel their friends, the American missionaries, and suppress the mission-schools, they rose in revolt. Mr. Deane, a missionary, was arrested and carried in chains to Manila. Soon afterward a native force collected and marched on Ponape, a Spanish settlement on the island of Asuncion, and the capital of the eastern Carolines. Captain Posadillo sent out a squad of twenty soldiers to watch the rebels, and an engagement took place in which the Spanish force was annihilated. The women and Capuchin missionaries took refuge on the corvette "Maria de Molina," while Ponape was fortified, and stood a siege, until, on July 5, the ammunition became exhausted. The Spaniards then attempted to retreat to the corvette, but the greater part of the garrison and some of the civil officials were killed on the way. The natives for forty days made efforts to capture the corvette. At length a vessel arrived from Manila, and took away the remaining Europeans. The captain-general sent a force to put down the rebellion. In the mean time the United States Government had made reclamations in regard to the suppressed Protestant mission and the maltreated missionary, and the Madrid authorities took action to compel the colonial administration to respect treaty rights.

A large military expedition was sent out from Manila on Jan. 10, 1887, to subjugate the natives of the Mindanao islands and the Sulu Archipelago. The operations in the Mindanao group were concluded in the early part of March, when the Sultan of Bahagan and other chiefs submitted to the Spanish forces on terms that were considered satisfactory. The expedition then sailed for Sulu. The Governor, Col.

Arolas, in April, won a victory over the rebels, capturing and burning the town of Maiburg. About a month later 800 troops of the expeditionary force captured a fortified village on the island of Tapula, after severe fighting and heavy losses on both sides, and the inhabitants submitted to the authority of the Sultan of Sulu, and accepted the Spanish dominion.

SPEED, JAMES, an American statesman, born near Louisville, Ky., March 11, 1812; died there, June 25, 1887. He was graduated at St. Joseph's College, Bardstown, Ky., and then devoted his attention to the law, being employed for a time in the office of the clerk of the circuit and county courts, and completing his legal study in Transylvania University. After his admission to the bar, he removed to Louisville, and began practice in 1833. In 1847 he was elected to the State Legislature, but

served one term only. In 1849 he was the unsuccessful candidate of the Emancipation party for a seat in the State Constitutional Convention. He was elected to the State Senate in 1861. At the outbreak of the civil war he was an uncompromising Union man, standing with Gen. Rousseau, Judge Harland, and others in determined opposition to the neutral position forced upon his State by the conduct of her authorities. It is said that next to Gen. Rousseau's establishment of a Union recruiting-camp opposite Louisville, the firm attitude of Mr. Speed was the most effective step taken by the loyalists of Kentucky to keep the State in the Union. When President Lincoln issued the call for 75,000 men, in April, 1861, Mr. Speed was placed in charge of the recruiting stations in Kentucky, and devoted his whole time and influence to the service of his country. In November, 1864, President Lincoln appointed him Attorney-General of the United States, and he was retained in office by President Johnson till July, 1866, when he resigned on account of dissatisfaction with the reconstruction policy of the President. On the assembling of the loyalist convention in Philadelphia, in 1866, Mr. Speed was elected its presiding officer. He resumed his legal practice in Louisville on his retirement from the Cabinet; was a delegate to the National Convention of 1868, which nominated Gen. Grant for the presidency, and also to that of 1876, but supported Gov. Cleveland in the canvass of 1884. He was a professor in the law department of the University of Louisville in 1856-'58 and 1875-'79.

STRIKES. Strikes are by no means new products of industrial discontent. They have, it is true, increased numerically as the laboring-classes have grown in organization and numbers; for, as capital has become more powerful, labor has become more rebellious. There can be, however, no strike without previous organization among the strikers, and such organization among men of Anglo-Saxon descent almost invariably takes the form of a guild or trades-union. History teaches us that guilds, or unions of the different trades, have existed in Europe for many centuries, and this system of organization (or at least a tradition of it) was, no doubt, brought to this country by those mechanics who immigrated hither prior to the Revolution. It is easy to imagine that at first the conditions of society were such that every worker could dictate the terms upon which he would labor, without the intervention or interference of others of his craft, but the need or convenience of organization must have been felt at an early date, for we find a "Calkers' Club" existing in Boston a score of years prior to our national independence, and a trades-union of boot and shoe makers vigorously flourishing in Philadelphia in 1792. The first-mentioned society is remembered because from it we have derived the word "caucus," and the latter organization has not been forgotten because the early law reports have considerable to say about the doings of its members.

There were strikes that created much comment in Philadelphia in 1798 and 1805; there was trouble between the master and the journeymen cordwainers in Pittsburg as early as 1810; and New York witnessed the trial of a score or more of strikers in 1809. Space does not permit more than a reference to these cases, but it is interesting to note that the term *scab* was in constant use by the strikers in 1798, that there were then *walking delegates* (then called *tramping committee*), and that the word *turnout* was used instead of *strike*. It may be also noted, for the benefit of those curious in philological matters, that the word "scab" is used by Shakespeare in "Coriolanus," Act I., Sc. 1; "Troilus and Cressida," Act II., Sc. 1.; "King Henry IV.," Part 2, Act. III., Sc. 2.

Strikes during 1886 greatly outnumbered those during 1885. The reason of this is problematical. The former year was peculiarly noted for the organization or combination of labor; and possibly this may, to an extent, account for the result. During the same year there was also much political organization on the part of laborers, and it is not improbable that the resultant agitation was productive of strikes among the industrial classes.

The following is a list of the recent strikes in the United States, as nearly complete as it is practicable to make it:

Agricultural-Machinists.—*Chicago.*—Feb. 16, 1886. About 1,300 employés of McCormick Reaper Works strike for discharge of all non-union hands.
Feb. 17. Switchmen on Chicago, Burlington and Quincy Railroad refuse to switch cars laden with McCormick goods or supplies.
March 1. Disorder among strikers, and 500 policemen guard works. The strike failed, and strikers gradually returned to work.
May 5, 1886. About 2,000 employés of Deering Harvester Works strike for eight hours and 20 per cent. advance in wages.
May 16. Settled by employers granting eight hours and 15 per cent. advance.

Bakers.—*New York City.*—April 14, 1886. Bohemian bakers employed by Mrs. Landgraf strike for higher pay and discharge of non-union bakers. Boycott declared.
April 21. Newspapers open subscriptions for Mrs. Landgraf.
May 5. Seventeen strikers and boycotters indicted.
June 28. Mrs. Landgraf's horses and wagons sold to pay debts.
July 9. Mrs. Landgraf sells out her business.
Pittsburg, Pa.—May 3, 1886. Bakers at Pittsburg strike for shorter hours.
May 11. Fears of bread-famine. 190 out of 160 bakeries closed.
July 30. Strike ended; employers yield to demands of the workmen.
Basket-Makers.—*Petersburg, Va.*—June 18, 1887. Employés in basket-factories strike for more pay. Strike settled by mutual concessions.
Boatmen.—*New York City.*—July 7, 1886. Owners of 86 vessels refuse to lighter coal except at advanced rates.
Jan. 27, 1887. (See *Coal-Handlers.*)
Box-Makers.—*Brooklyn, N. Y.*—Sept. 4, 1886. 200 employés in Smith's box-factory strike for advance of $2 a week; they had been getting $13 a week.
Chicago.—Sept. 27, 1886. 700 box-makers strike for 25 per cent. and 15 per cent. advance in fourteen out of 16 factories.
Brass-Workers.—*Chicago.*—April 30, 1886. 350 employés of the Union Brass Manufacturing Company strike for the eight-hour system.
New Haven, Conn.—April 17, 1886. Having asked for and obtained an advance of 10 per cent. wages, and relinquishment of the contract system, employés of Peck & Co. struck because of discharge of one union man.
April 27. Strikers return to work unconditionally.
New York City.—Oct. 4, 1886. Employés of four firms strike against increase in the hours of labor.
Nov. 15, 1886. Brass-workers strike for Saturday half-holiday.
Jan. 7, 1887. Strike settled by mutual concessions.
Brooklyn, N. Y.—Sept. 24. 1887. 5,000 brass-workers strike for Saturday half-holiday.
Nov. 5, 1887. Strike settled by mutual concessions.
Cincinnati, O.—May 2, 1887. Employés of Hesterborg & Co. strike for shorter hours.
Brewers.—*Milwaukee, Wis.*—May 1, 1886. About 2,000 brewers strike for eight-hour system.
New York City.—July 19, 1886. Drivers for Herman Brewery strike because of discharge of one union man. He was reinstated and strike ended.
Philadelphia.—Dec. 29, 1886. General strike of employés in lager-beer breweries for higher wages. About 3,000 men go out.
St. Louis.—Sept. 1, 1886. Strike of employés of

breweries in resistance to demand that they resign from Knights of Labor.

Baltimore, Md.—May 15, 1887. General strike of employés in the breweries for higher wages. Demands granted and strike settled in a few days.

Buffalo, N. Y.—May 2, 1887. Employés in 20 breweries strike for more wages. Demands granted same day.

Detroit, Mich.—Jan. 22, 1887. Strike by employés in several breweries. Settled by mutual concessions.

Bricklayers.—*Boston.*—May 3, 1886. Bricklayers join in a general strike of all the building-trades for eight-hour system.

Chicago.—May 4, 1886. Bricklayers join in the general strike for eight hours.

Cincinnati.—Aug. 3, 1886. Bricklayers' Union refuse to work where non-union hod-carriers are employed, and master-builders stop work, making idle 3,000 men in the other building-trades.

Detroit.—Aug. 10, 1886.—In consequence of general strike of the building-trades, brickyards shut down, making idle 2,500.

Malden, Mass.—May 3, 1886. Bricklayers strike for nine hours.

Mobile, Ala.—May 3, 1886. Bricklayers strike for nine hours.

Newburg, N. Y.—May 3, 1886. 200 bricklayers strike for eight hours, but compromise on nine.

Pittsburg, Pa.—May 3, 1886. Bricklayers and masons strike for nine hours.

Troy, N. Y.—May 3, 1886. Bricklayers strike for work to begin at 7 A. M. The eight-hour system had previously been granted by bosses.

Washington, D. C.—May 3, 1886. Bricklayers strike for eight-hour system.

Cincinnati.—April 4, 1887. Fifteen hundred men engaged in the building-trades strike for nine hours and $2.80 per day. Strike settled by mutual concessions.

Chicago.—May 1, 1887. Strike of employés in the building-trades for more pay.

July 1. Arbitration agreed upon and strike settled by mutual concessions.

Newark, N. J.—May 10, 1887. General strike of masons and bricklayers to assist striking stone-cutters.

Orange, N. J.—May 2, 1887. Three hundred masons and bricklayers strike for higher wages.

Rochester, N. Y.—June 27, 1887. Bricklayers on the sewers strike for more pay. Rioting followed, and strike finally settled by mutual concessions.

Brickmakers.—*Verplanck, N. Y.*—July 27, 1886. Nine hundred men employed in eleven brickyards strike for more wages and abolition of pluck-me-store system.

Chicago.—May 18, 1887. Seven thousand brick-makers locked out by closing of brickyards on account of general strike of the building-trades employés.

Kingston, N. Y.—May 16, 1887. Five hundred brickmakers strike for more pay. Strike settled by mutual concessions.

Builders.—*St. Louis.*—June 9, 1886. Master-builders decide to return to the ten-hour system. (See also *Bricklayers, Carpenters*, etc.)

Butchers.—*Chicago.*—Aug. 4, 1886. Eight hundred men employed in the Hately Packing-house strike for the eight-hour system.

Aug. 6. Strike settled. Forty men in Fowler Packing-house strike for the eight-hour system.

Aug. 5, 1886. Pork-packers resolve to return to ten-hour system.

Aug. 12, 1886. About 300 meat-handlers of Robert Warren & Co. strike rather than load Lake Shore cars switched by scabs.

Oct. 8, 1886. General strike of employés of packing-houses against return to the ten-hour system. The packing-yards were put in charge of Pinkerton's guards.

Oct. 15, 1886. Twelve hundred beef-butchers employed by Armour & Co. strike. 20,000 men out.

Oct. 19, 1886. Pinkerton men while removing

scabs are surrounded by a mob and fire into it with deadly effect.

Nov. 5, 1886. All the beef-killers (about 6,000) strike to aid striking beef-killers in two packing-houses.

Nov. 4, 1886. Beef-packers still out, bosses getting a few new hands.

Nov. 19, 1886. Five thousand packers taken back on the same terms as existed before the strike.

East Cambridge, Mass.—Aug. 4, 1886. Serious rioting by strikers at Squire's pork-packing establishment; several scabs assaulted.

Aug. 9. Settled by arbitration of the Mayor of Cambridge.

Hackensack, N. J.—Nov. 4, 1886. Hog-butchers in Central Stock-Yards strike for discharge of non-union men.

New York City.—June 13, 1886. General strike of sheep-killers employed by butchering-houses in New York, Brooklyn, and Jersey City, for advance in pay of 2½ cents per sheep. Thirty-nine out of forty employers yield, but strikers refuse to return to work until all yield.

June 17. Strike ended; the recusant butcher being boycotted.

Nov. 8, 1886. Hog-butchers strike for uniform rate of $18 per week.

Nov. 9. Conference held with employers who offer $18 per week to a few and lower rates to others.

Buttonhole-Makers.—(See *Cloak-Makers*.)

Can-Makers.—*Baltimore, Md.*—May 3, 1886. Can-makers strike for eight-hour system.

Cap-Makers.—*New York City.*—Sept. 5, 1886. Cap-makers strike against reduction in wages. (See also *Hatters*.)

Carpenters.—*Baltimore, Md.*—May 3, 1886. Carpenters strike for eight-hour system.

Boston.—May 3, 1886. Carpenters strike for eight-hour system.

Chicago.—July 21, 1886. Carpenters on strike assault workmen on California Avenue.

Malden, Mass.—May 3, 1886. Carpenters strike for nine hours.

New York.—March 19, 1886. Carpenters strike for $3.50 and nine hours per day. Granted by all employers except twenty shops.

Pittsburg, Pa.—May 3, 1886. Carpenters strike for nine hours.

Troy, N. Y.—May 3, 1886. Carpenters strike for working-day to begin at 7 A. M.—eight-hour system had been previously granted by bosses.

Washington, D. C.—May 3, 1886. Carpenters strike for eight-hour system.

Chicago, Ill.—April 5, 1887. Six thousand five hundred carpenters strike for eight hours.

April 7.—Bosses agree to demand for eight hours, but refuse to recognize union.

April 16.—Settled—all demands granted.

Newburgh, N. Y.—June 13, 1887. Carpenters strike for nine hours a day. Settled by mutual concessions.

Carpet-Weavers.—*New York City.*—April 17, 1887. Employés of Higgins & Co. strike for more pay. Strike fails, and men gradually return to work.

Carriage-Makers.—*Cincinnati, Ohio.*—May 3, 1886. Sixteen hundred carriage-makers strike for eight-hour system.

New Haven, Conn.—April 26, 1886. General strike of carriage-makers for the eight-hour system.

New York.—May 3, 1886. General strike of the carriage-makers for eight-hour system.

Cigar-Makers.—*Buffalo, N. Y.*—May 22, 1886. International Cigar-makers' Union strike for increased wages.

July 22. Strike settled: manufacturers concede advance of $1.00 per thousand cigars.

New York City.—Jan. 6, 1886. Employés of Lozano, Pendas & Co. strike, demanding additional sanitary arrangements.

April 8. Strikers gradually return upon slight improvements being made.

Jan. 14, 1886. Four hundred employés in Lovy Brothers' factory and 500 in factory of Brown & Earle strike for increased wages.

Jan. 15. Manufacturers' Association resolve to close all factories if strikers do not return to work.

Jan. 16. Cigar-packers strike to aid strikers.

Jan. 18. Kerbs & Spies retire from Manufacturers' Association, and settle with their employés.

Jan. 19. Hirsch & Co. resign from Manufacturers' Association, and settle with their employés.

Jan. 20. Manufacturers close their factories, and lock out 1,200 persons.

Jan. 21. Manufacturers propose arbitration. Proposal refused.

Jan. 29. Conference between manufacturers and committee of Cigar-makers' Union. Compromise agreed upon but rejected by strikers. Some disorder, and police called upon to guard factories.

Feb. 7. New compromise agreed upon.

Feb. 13. All but 400 strikers return to work.

Feb. 15. New strike at Stahl & Fletcher's factory because compromise is not kept.

Feb. 20. Strike at Stahl & Fletcher's factory ended.

July 30, 1886. Numerous strikes in the cigar-trade, owing to contest between Knights of Labor and Cigar-makers' Progressive Union.

July 31. Knights of Labor make contract with cigar manufacturers to furnish 5,000 cigar-makers on condition that no members of International and Progressive Cigar-makers' Union are employed.

Aug. 13. Trouble between Knights and Cigar-makers' Union practically settled. Employers yield to demands of cigar-makers.

Jan. 11, 1887. Three thousand five hundred workers in Lorillard's factory strike for more pay.

May 6, 1887. Employés of Lozano, Pendas & Co. strike for more pay. Strike settled by mutual concessions.

Philadelphia.—Sept. 13, 1886. General strike of cigar-makers to procure discharge of all men who are not Knights of Labor.

Reading, Pa.—Aug. 29, 1886. Collapse of the cigar-makers' strike for recognition of Knights of Labor. It had lasted about sixteen weeks.

Syracuse, N. Y.—Jan. 5, 1886. General strike of employés in cigar-factories for higher wages. About 1,000 men and many girls affected.

Boston, Mass.—Sept. 12. 1887. One thousand cigar-makers locked out to anticipate strike to reduce number of apprentices.

Cloak-Makers.—*New York City.*—March 17, 1886. About 3,000 cloak-makers strike for higher pay and to abolish the system of middlemen, who give out work and contract with dealers.

March 22. Dealers suggest a compromise.

March 23. Compromise declined by strikers. Four firms yield.

March 25. Buttonhole-makers stop work to aid strikers.

March 26. Two more firms yield.

March 30. Buttonhole-makers return to work. Strikers suggest compromise.

March 31. Cloak-Makers' Association (dealers) decline to compromise.

April 1. About 2,000 strikers return to work.

April 5. Remainder of strikers return to work. Strike officially declared off.

Coal-Handlers.—*New Jersey.*—Jan. 4, 1887. One thousand coal-handlers on docks between Hoboken and Perth Amboy strike against reduction of wages.

Jan. 5. Men at Port Richmond and Weehawken join strikers.

Jan. 21. Pinkerton's detectives fire into a crowd of boys skating and kill one.

Jan. 27. Thirty thousand coal-handlers, longshoremen, boatmen, and kindred workers strike to help the New Jersey strikers. Prominent Labor leaders are arrested.

Feb. 12. Strike ended by mutual concessions and arbitration. This strike closed the Lehigh and Wilkesbarre mines, and it is estimated threw, at one time, 60,000 men out of work.

Coal-Workers.—*Pennsylvania and Ohio.*—Jan., 1886. Coke-burners and miners in the Pennsylvania and Ohio coal-regions were on strike when the year began. In the Connellsville district there were 766 ovens idle; in Mt. Pleasant district, 1,094; in Stonerville district, 397; in Scottdale district, 758; in Bradford district, 148. Mines and buildings generally protected by armed guards. Strikers numbered over 6,000.

Jan. 20. Rioting, accompanied by some loss of life, broke out in various localities.

Jan. 21. Convention of coke-workers held in Pittsburg, and decide to continue strike. Citizens of Confluence, on the Baltimore & Ohio Railroad, stop and send back car-loads of Hungarians procured in New York, and intended to replace strikers.

Jan. 25. The Austro-Hungarian consul visits Mt. Pleasant and tries to effect a settlement.

Feb. 2. Mine-owners prevent strikers from securing fuel for their homes.

Feb. 3. Beginning of a general system of eviction of strikers from houses owned by coke-companies.

Feb. 5. Sheriffs in many regions refuse to evict. Several iron-mills close down for lack of fuel.

Feb. 8. Serious riot at Henry Clay Coke-Works near Bradford; several men shot and $4,000 worth of property burned.

Feb. 13. Another convention of coke-workers held at Scottdale, and decide to continue strike.

Hocking Valley.—Jan. 18, 1886. Judge Thurman, who had been arbitrator between miners and mine-owners, decides in favor of increased wages as demanded.

Pennsylvania.—Oct. 2, 1886. Order for general strike issued unless employers restore the 10 per cent. reduction made in 1885.

Coalton, Ohio.—Dec. 1, 1886. About 3,000 miners strike for advance of 5 cents per ton.

Dubois, Pa.—July 30, 1886. Four hundred miners at Hampton and Duquesne mines strike for 11 cents per ton.

July 30. Five hundred miners, who for nearly twenty weeks had been on strike for higher wages, return to work at employers' terms.

Hazleton, Pa.—Aug. 5, 1886. One thousand miners employed by Pardee & Co. strike for increased wages and decrease in price of mining supplies.

Mt. Carmel, Pa.—Nov. 4, 1886. Five hundred miners in Excelsior Colliery strike for advance of 10 per cent.

Pennsville, Pa.—July 30, 1886. Strike of employés at the coke-works for increased pay.

Pittsburg, Pa.—July 30, 1886. Employés at Hecla Works strike to secure discharge of obnoxious yard-boss.

Pottsville, Pa.—July 21, 1886. Miners employed by Elmwood Colliery were discharged for inspecting cards of employés. Reinstated when Knights threatened to strike.

Scott Haven, Pa.—July 24, 1886. Miners employed in five mines strike for reinstatement of discharged union men.

Shamokin, Pa.—Dec. 11, 1886. Six hundred miners of Philadelphia & Reading Coal Co. strike against reduction of 10 per cent. in wages.

March —. Colliers strike for more pay.

May 3. Strikers return to work on the eight-hour system.

May 26. Colliers return to work in the Clearfield region on terms of a compromise.

Oct. 7. Miners at Peerless Colliery strike for increased facilities in removing coal.

Dec. 6. Strike of miners at Excelsior Colliery ended by employers granting demands of the strikers.

St. Louis.—Sept. 1, 1886. General strike of miners in the St. Louis region for advance of 27½ cents per ton.

Gogebic, Wis.—Sept. 5, 1887. Five hundred miners

strike for arrears of pay. Strike settled by mutual concessions.

Hazleton, Pa.—Sept. 12, 1887. Twenty thousand laborers and miners in the Lehigh district strike for more pay.

Sept. 15. Reading Coal and Iron Company grants increase of pay and strike declared off.

Pittsburg, Pa.—May 2, 1887. General strike among the miners and laborers in the coke region.

June 12. Strike ended by mutual concessions

June 14. Strike declared on again.

July 15. Serious rioting following attempt to import new laborers.

Vincennes, Ind.—Sept. 24, 1887. Miners in the Indiana coal-fields strike for more pay.

Oct. 31. Strike settled by mutual concessions.

Coopers.—Cincinnati, O.—Nov. 23, 1886. About 1,000 coopers strike for an advance of 10 to 25 per cent.

Coppersmiths.—Brooklyn, N. Y.—May 3, 1887. One hundred and seventy-five coppersmiths strike for more pay. Demands granted in a few hours.

Cornice-Makers.—New York City.—May 2, 1887. Four hundred cornice-makers strike for more pay. Demands granted same day.

Cotton-Pressers.—New Orleans. —March 24, 1887. Nine thousand laborers at the cotton-presses strike for recognition of the union and exclusion of scab labor.

Cotton-Spinners. — Augusta, Ga. — July 30, 1886. Seven hundred hands in Sibley Cotton Mills are thrown out of employment by the strike of the strippers for advanced wages.

Aug. 11. Strike of employés in cotton-mills results in closing all cotton-factories ; 2,738 hands out.

Aug. 17. Officers of Knights of Labor visit Augusta to investigate strike.

Sept. 8. Mills endeavor to start up under police protection.

Sept. 9. Considerable rioting.

Nov. 4. Strike settled ; employés gaining nearly all that they demanded.

Cincinnati, O.—May 3, 1886. General strike of cotton-spinners for advance in wages. They are granted increase of 10 per cent.

Fall River, Mass.—Jan. 14, 1886. General strike of cotton-spinners for a return to the rate of wages which had existed prior to a recent reduction.

Jan. 26. Attempt made to keep the King Philip Mill in operation ; scabs assaulted and considerable rioting.

Feb. 3. Mill-owners offer compromise ; wages to be increased after March 1.

Feb. 6. Strike declared off. Employés return to work.

July 28. Two hundred weavers at Durfee Mills Nos. 1 and 3 strike because of poor material given to them for piece-work.

Aug. 10. Strike of spinners at Barnard Cotton Mill settled after a conference.

July 16, 1887. Employés at the Pocassett Mills strike against a reduction of wages.

Dec. 25, 1887. Spinners at Stafford Mills strike because of defective sizing of yarn.

Dec. 27. Upon promise of arbitration strike declared off.

Dec. 28. Promise being repudiated strike is renewed.

Frankford, Pa.—Sept., 1886. Strike of weavers at Wingohocking Gingham Mill.

Oct. 2, 1886. Manufacturers' Association decide to close all mills, throwing 3,000 hands out of work, if strike is not ended.

Oct. 18. Strikers resume work on employers' terms, but strike when they learn that their committee-men have been refused work.

Nov. 4. Strike settled after conference between Knights and manufacturers ; grievances of employés to be settled by arbitration.

Manchester, N. H.—Feb. 15, 1886. About 5,000 employés of Amoskeag Manufacturing Company strike for advance in wages ; 171,096 spindles and 6,246 looms stopped ; noticeable as first large strike in Manchester since 1865.

Mar. 4. Strike practically settled by company making some concessions. Nearly all the employés return to work.

New Bedford, Mass.—Sept. 13, 1886. Employés strike because one of them is required to do extra work.

Norwich, Conn.—March 10, 1886. Strike of 1,000 hands at Baltic Mill for shorter hours and better wages ; their present hours being 11, and wages 58 cents.

Philadelphia.—Sept., 1886. Strike at Troth's mills.

Oct. 20. Manufacturers' Association resolve to close the 100 mills represented by them if strike is not ended.

Oct. 26. Wm. V. McKean, editor of " The Public Ledger," consents to act as arbitrator.

Salmon Falls, N. H.—Aug. 10, 1886. Strike of cotton-weavers for revision of rules governing blemished cloth.

Aug. 16. Strike settled.

Cohoes, N. Y.—July 1, 1887. Two thousand cotton-spinners strike for fewer hours of work.

Norwich, Conn.—March 30, 1887. One hundred children, mostly under fifteen years of age, strike for higher wages.

Putnam, Conn.—July 11, 1887. One hundred and fifty spinners strike for shorter hours. Six hundred persons thrown out of employment.

Schuylerville, N. Y. — April 24, 1887. " Mule " boys at the Victory Mills strike for more pay.

April 26.—Mills shut down, locking out 600 employés.

Furniture-Makers.—Detroit.—June 7, 1886. Furniture factory owners return to ten-hour system and several strikes follow as a consequence.

Fort Plain, N. Y.—May 6, 1886. General strike of furniture-makers for eight-hour system.

Indianapolis, Ind.—March 11, 1886. Strike for increased pay by employés of Indianapolis Chair Company. Settled by employers agreeing upon co-operation.

Pittsburg, Pa.—June 9, 1886. Furniture-workers return to work at old rates.

Furriers.—New York City. May 3, 1886. Eight hundred and seventy-five furriers strike for increased wages

Gas-Fitters.—New York City. Nov. 9, 1886. Gas-fitters strike to aid striking plumbers.

Glass-Workers.—Baltimore.—Nov. 28, 1886. Glass-blowers strike for reduction in number of apprentices.

Binghamton.—Nov. 23, 1886. Glass-blowers strike to reduce number of apprentices.

Brooklyn, N. Y.—March 20, 1886. Boys at Empire State Glass Works strike for increased pay.

Dec. 1, 1886. Glass-blowers and helpers strike for reduction in number of employés.

Philadelphia.—Sept. 27, 1886. At conference between manufacturers and workers, wage question was amicably settled. The strike ended. Settlement affects all union factories in New Jersey, Maryland, New York, and in Pennsylvania east of the Alleghanies.

Sept. 3, 1887. Two thousand employés in window-glass factories strike for more pay. Strike settled in a few days by mutual concessions.

Pittsburg, Pa.—Aug. 17, 1886.—Employers and employés hold a conference to determine rate of wages.

Aug. 27. Employés demand 8 per cent. advance in wages. Two thousand six hundred men out.

Sept. 10. Conference between manufacturers and workmen.

Sept. 25. Strike ended ; workmen return on employers' terms.

April 27, 1887. One hundred and ninety-six mixers and teasers strike for more pay. One thousand employés thrown out of work.

Dec. 9, 1887. Flint glass workers strike against reduction of wages.

Sandwich, Mass.—Aug. 4, 1886. Strike at Boston and Sandwich Glass Works.

Aug. 10. Strike settled.

St. Louis.—Nov. 27, 1886. Great Western Glass Company shut down to anticipate strike of glass-blowers to reduce number of apprentices.

Harness-Makers.—*Newark, N. J.*—April 13, 1886. Harness-makers strike for revision of schedule of wages.

Hatters.—*Norwalk, Conn.*—Aug. 30, 1886. Employés of hat-factories strike for higher pay.

Sept. 2. Employers yield to demands of the workmen, and strike ends.

Hod-Carriers.—*Chicago.*—May 2, 1887. Five thousand hod-carriers strike for more pay. One hundred and two out of 185 employers yield within forty-eight hours.

Horse-Shoers.—*Hartford, Conn.*—May 3, 1886. Journeymen horse-shoers strike for higher wages. Strike immediately settled by joint concessions.

Boston.—July 11, 1887. Horse-shoers on street-railroads strike for more pay and shorter hours. Strikers' demands granted.

Hosiery-Makers.—*Philadelphia.*—Oct. 19, 1886. General strike of employés of hosiery and woolen mills, affecting about 2,000 men.

Nov. 9. Four hosiery firms grant the demands of the strikers, who return to work. (See also *Knitters*.)

Ice-Men.—*New York.*—Jan. 15, 1887. General strike of ice-cutters along the Hudson river.

Jan. 22. Both sides submit to arbitration, and strike ended.

July 11, 1887. Employés of ice-companies in New York city strike for more pay. Demands granted same day.

Iron-Workers.—*Bath, Me.*—Sept. 13, 1886. Employés of iron-works strike to aid striking ship-builders.

Bridgewater, Mass.—July 16, 1886. Employés of Bridgewater Iron Company strike for higher wages.

July 21. Company fails from losses occasioned by strike.

Brooklyn.—May 3, 1886. General strike of iron-molders for ten per cent. increase of wages.

Sept. 10. Seventy mechanics at Hecla Iron Works strike for discharge of scabs.

Harrisburg, Pa.—Aug. 30, 1886. Puddlers at Barley's mills strike for increase of 50 cents per ton; about 500 men and boys made idle.

Lancaster, Pa.—Aug. 4, 1886. Strike for higher wages by puddlers in the iron-works extends to the other employés.

Aug. 13. Strike settled by mutual concessions.

Sept. 5. Strikers at Columbia Rolling Mill propose to return to work for $3.85 per ton. Employers offer $3.75, which strikers refuse to accept.

Nov. 4. Mills have about half force.

Lebanon, Pa.—Aug. 30, 1886. Puddlers at Lights', East End, and Kapp's rolling-mills, strike for increased wages.

Sept. 18. General strike of employés in rolling-mills for advance in wages.

New York City.—May 4, 1886. Employés of Malleable Iron Works, who had struck for eight-hour system, return to work with their demand granted.

June 24. Four hundred employés of Mott Iron Works strike for advance in wages of ten per cent.

July 24. Strike for advance of ten per cent. wages, by employés of Jordan L. Mott Iron Works, after lasting for five weeks, settled by arbitration.

Northeast, Del.—Sept. 5, 1886. Strike at McCullough Iron Works ended by mutual concessions.

Sept. 9. Strike renewed because employers break their agreement.

Nov. 27. McCullough's rolling mill. Strike ended; employers granting all the demands of the strikers.

Paterson, N. J.—Aug. 13, 1886. Molders in J. C. Todd's machine-shop strike for higher wages. Molders at Rogers Locomotive Works strike to aid them.

Sept. 6. General strike of molders at mills and locomotive works; strike for higher wages.

Philadelphia.—June 30, 1886. Fifteen hundred men employed in rolling-mills strike for advance in wages.

New Haven, Conn.—July 20, 1886. One hundred employés of Sargent's South Foundry strike because of employment of non-union men.

Reading, Pa.—Aug. 4, 1886. Employés in Philadelphia and Reading Foundry strike for discharge of non-union employés.

Aug. 5. Strike settled; employers yield.

Nov. 4. Puddlers in Naomi Mill strike for advance of five cents per ton.

St. Louis.—May. 3, 1886. Employés of Vulcan Iron Works return to work after strike of several months' duration, mutual concessions having been made.

Troy, N. Y.—July 14, 1886. Employés in steel and iron works strike for advance of wages of from thirty-five per cent. to fifty per cent. About 2,000 men affected.

July 16. Employers propose arbitration.

New York City.—July 2, 1887. Employés of Delamater Iron Works strike for reinstatement of discharged employés.

July 14. Strike declared off. Strikers defeated.

Pittsburg, Pa.—Sept. 15, 1887. Two thousand five hundred roll-turners strike for more pay. Strike settled by mutual concessions.

Reading, Pa.—June 24, 1887. Two thousand men locked out to anticipate strike for more pay.

July 22. Employers grant more pay, and employés return to work.

Jute-Workers.—*New York City.*—March 25, 1886. Employés of Chelsea Jute Mills strike for higher wages.

March 31. Twenty of the strikers return to work. After some disorderly conduct, strikers gradually return, and strike fails.

Knitters.—*Amsterdam, N. Y.*—Sept. 6, 1886. Strike of employés of Schuyler and Blood Knitting Mill for discharge of obnoxious employé.

Sept. 13. Strike extends to all mills, affecting about 6,000 persons.

Cohoes, N. Y.—Oct. 2, 1886. Manufacturers' Association threatens to close all mills if Amsterdam strike is not ended.

Oct. 11. Manufacturers' Association at Cohoes and Waterford close their mills, 28 in number, until end of strike at Amsterdam.

Oct. 11. Manufacturers' Association of Hudson threatens to close their mills if strike at Amsterdam is not settled.

Oct. 26. Knit-goods manufacturers refuse to recognize arbitration committee of the Knights of Labor.

Nov. Several delays prevent settlement of strike. Refusal to discharge scabs, etc.

Nov. 11. Manufacturers' Association decides to allow individual owners to make the best terms they can with the strikers.

Knights at Amsterdam refuse to go to work until employés of all the mills are taken back.

Nov. 13. Strikers go to work in seven mills, their terms having been granted by employers.

Dec. 5. More trouble owing to manufacturers not keeping their promises. Mills closed.

Dec. 12. Several mills open under private arrangement with Knights of Labor.

Laborers.—*Mobile, Ala.*—Sept. 5, 1886. Laborers employed on West Mobile and Alabama Railroad strike for $2 a day.

New York City.—March 31, 1886. Laborers on the new aqueduct strike for more pay and better precautions against danger.

June 21. About 2,000 men employed on the new aqueduct strike because of removal of a manager.

June 24. Strikers return to work upon request of manager.

Shenandoah, Pa.—July 26, 1886. Italian laborers

on Schuylkill Valley Road strike for advance in wages. The refusal of Hungarian laborers to join in the strike led to considerable rioting and bloodshed.

West Virginia.—July 9, 1886. Laborers along line of Grafton and Greenbrier Railroad strike for day of ten hours.

Sterling, Kan.—Jan. 19, 1887. Tracklayers on a branch of the Missouri Pacific Railroad strike for higher wages.

Sharon, Pa.—June 20, 1887. Laborers on the Sharon Valley Railroad strike for more pay, and become riotous.

Marquette, Mich.—March 10, 1887. Strike of laborers on Duluth, South Shore and Atlantic Railroad for more pay. Some rioting.

Laundrymen.—*Troy, N. Y.*—May 3, 1886. Laundrymen in collar and cuff factories strike for eight-hour system. Seven thousand employés are thrown out of work.

June 21. Employés return to work upon promise of employers to arbitrate.

Lock-Makers.—*New Haven, Conn.*—Sept. 29, 1886. Employés of Sargent's Lock Factory strike against adoption of half-day system.

Longshoremen.—*New York City.*—March 17, 1886. Longshoremen who had replaced union men on certain North River piers strike for more wages.

Jan. 10, 1887. Strike at Old Dominion Steamship docks for more pay.

Newport News, Va.—Jan. 11. Longshoremen strike against Old Dominion Steamship Line. Considerable rioting. State troops called out.

Lumbermen.—*Chicago.*—April 30, 1886. Twelve thousand lumbermen strike for increased pay ; making idle about eight hundred vessels, each with an average crew of seven men.

April 18. Strike collapsed, and strikers generally return to work. Estimated loss to strikers, $250,000.

Machinists.—*Dover, N. H.*—Aug. 10, 1886. Employés in bobbin-factory of Somersworth Machine Company strike for reduction of hours of labor.

Messengers.—*New York City.*—Nov. 20, 1886. Boys employed by Mutual District Messenger Company strike for six days' work and ten hours a day.

Nov. 24. Strike settled by allowing every other Sunday.

Morocco-Workers.—*Wilmington, Del.*—April, 1886. Morocco-workers strike because of refusal of employers to recognize Knights.

Aug. 27. About one half of the strikers replaced by colored men.

Sept. 13. Strike ended. Employés return on employers' terms.

Nail-Makers.—*Pittsburg, Pa.*—Aug. 27, 1886. Employés of nail-mills offer to resume work on a compromise scale of wages. Strike lasted several weeks.

Aug. 30. Strike resumed owing to disagreement.

Oil-Refiners.—*Philadelphia, Pa.*—June 24, 1887. Six hundred refiners at the Atlantic Refinery strike against scab labor. The strike was shortly afterward settled by mutual concessions.

Painters.—*Boston.*—May 3, 1886. About 1,200 painters strike for eight-hour system. Bosses yield quickly.

Brooklyn, N. Y.—April 15, 1886. Journeymen painters strike for eight-hour system. Bosses yield during the next few days.

Newark, N. J.—April 5, 1886. Painters strike for $3.00 per day. Bosses yield after one hour's delay.

New York City.—Nov. 26, 1886. Painters strike against reduction of pay to $3.10 from $3.50.

Washington, D. C.—May 3, 1886. Painters strike for eight-hour system.

Paint-Makers.—*New York City.*—April 22, 1887. Employés of Devoe & Co. strike for revision of schedule of wages. Strike settled by mutual concessions.

Paper-Rulers.—*New York City.*—Jan. 7, 1887. Five hundred paper-rulers strike for more pay.

Jan. 10. Demands granted and strike declared off.

Pattern-Makers.—*New York.*—May 3, 1886. Pattern-makers strike for nine-hour system.

Piano-Makers.—*New York City.*—May 3, 1886. About 1,500 employés in piano-factories strike for eight-hour system.

May 9. Strike officially declared off; strikers return on employers' terms.

Plasterers.—*Pittsburg, Pa.*—May 3, 1886. Plasterers strike for eight-hour system.

Plaster-Makers.—*Orange, N. J.*—March 29, 1886. Strike of hands at Seabury & Johnson's factory because of discharge of nine union hands.

Plate-Millers.—*Harrisburg, Pa.*—Sept. 4, 1886. Employés in plate-mill of Bailey & Co. strike for increased wages.

Plumbers.—*Boston.*—May 3, 1886. Plumbers join in general strike of building-trades for eight-hour system.

Brooklyn, N. Y.—Aug. 14, 1886. Fifty plumbers employed by J. Manneschmidt strike for discharge of non-union workmen.

Buffalo, N. Y.—May 3, 1886. Union plumbers strike for advance of fifty cents per day.

Jersey City.—Sept. 20, 1886. Plumbers strike for shorter hours on Saturday.

New York City.—Aug. 24, 1886. General strike of all plumbers to resist reduction in wages.

Nov. 1886. To aid the striking plumbers, members of the building-trades unions generally refuse to work on buildings where scab plumbers are employed.

Washington, D. C.—May 3, 1886. Plumbers strike for eight-hour system.

Pocketbook-Makers.—*New York City.*—April 14, 1886. Employés of Binswanger & Sons strike because of discharge of one union man.

Printers.—*Cleveland, O.*—Aug. 11, 1886. Strike of printers for increase of rates of typesetting. Settled within twenty-four hours ; employers grant advance except the "Leader."

Indianapolis, Ind.—July 9, 1887. Printers on the daily newspapers strike for recognition of the union.

July 11. Strike fails, and is declared off.

New York City.—Sept. 27, 1886. Strike of printers in some of the printing-offices for increased wages.

Oct. 11, 1887. General strike of printers for recognition of the union.

Oct. 27. Strike settled by mutual concessions.

Rochester, N. Y.—Nov. 2, 1887. Two hundred printers strike for more pay.

St. Louis, Mo.—Nov. 2, 1887. Employés of twenty-one offices strike for more pay.

Pump-Makers.—*Cincinnati, O.*—May 3, 1886. Employés in pump-factories strike for eight-hour system ; but compromise at ten hours, and ten per cent. advance in wages.

St. Louis.—Sept. 18, 1886. Molders at Belleville Pump Works strike for advance of ten per cent.

Quarrymen.—*Lamont.*—July 14, 1886. Four hundred quarrymen strike against reduction in wages which had been granted on May 1.

Railroads (Street-Car Employés).—*Brooklyn, N. Y.*—Feb. 22, 1886. Employés on Hamilton Avenue and Smith Street lines demand more pay ; granted at once by companies.

March 3, 1886. Drivers and conductors on seven lines strike for twelve hours and $2 per day.

March 4. There being symptoms of disorderly conduct the police force is all called out.

March 5. Companies yield to demands of strikers, and strike declared off.

March 6, 1886. Stablemen on Brooklyn City Railroad threaten to strike for increased pay, but company immediately grants the demand.

March 15, 1886. Railroad commissioner reports to Legislature severely condemning "Deacon" Richardson's management.

March 26, 1886. Drivers and conductors of four lines strike for twelve hours and $2 per day.

March 27. Companies yield to demands, and strike ends.

April 1. Committee of employés submit list of twenty-two grievances to president of Brooklyn City Railroad.

April 2. Company reforms these grievances.

Dec. 22, 1886. Strike of drivers and conductors on eleven lines for twelve hours' work and regular wages. Settled December 24 by the companies yielding to all demands.

April 10, 1886. Drivers and conductors on Franklin Avenue line strike for shorter hours and more pay. This strike is settled after one half-hour by company yielding all demanded.

Columbus, O.—March 18, 1886. The drivers and conductors of all the lines struck, demanding wages proportionate to the number of hours of service, which were fifteen hours and twenty minutes one day and seventeen hours and ten minutes the next. The strike was ended by a compromise.

Dayton, O.—March 20, 1886. Strike by drivers of the Third Street line demanding twelve hours and $1.75 per day.

March 23. An attempt to run a car was made, and it was attacked by strikers, who completely wrecked it.

New York City.—Feb. 3, 1886. General dissatisfaction among the employés of horse-car lines at the hours of labor and rate of wages. Numerous conferences held between railroad officials and Knights of Labor.

Feb. 4. Drivers and conductors on Fourth and Sixth Avenue lines strike, but upon promise of companies to grant demands resume work before night.

Feb. 16. Fourth Avenue road, having failed to keep its promise, strike is renewed, but settled before night.

Feb. 17, 1886. Employés of Eighth and Ninth Avenue lines strike for twelve hours and increased wages.

Feb. 18. Strike settled, roads yielding to all demands.

March 2, 1886. Strike of employés on the four lines of the Dry Dock Railroad for twelve hours and increased wages.

March 3. Attempts to run cars under police protection, and some rioting in Grand Street.

March 4. Railroad commissioners warn the road that failure to run cars will forfeit charter.

March 5. General strike on all the other lines in the city—15,000 men idle. The Dry Dock Company, however, settled with its men before night, and strike ended.

March 11. The companies form an association for mutual aid against strikers.

March 11. Employés on Twenty-third Street, Thirty-fourth Street, and Bleecker Street lines strike for regular hours and pay.

March 16. Strike settled by intervention of railroad commissioners. Companies grant demands.

April 16. Drivers and conductors on Third Avenue line strike against employment of non-union men.

April 17. Railroad commissioners have a hearing of both sides.

April 19. General tie-up on all other lines in the city, because of aid furnished by the railroad companies to Third Avenue Company. Considerable rioting along Third Avenue. Company offers to arbitrate, but strikers refuse.

April 20. General strike ended, other roads promising not to aid Third Avenue.

May 6. Agreement reached by company and committee of Knights of Labor, but strikers refuse to accept it.

Aug. 19. Financial report of Third Avenue Railroad for quarter ending June 30 shows deficiency of $60,620 against net earnings of $25,544 last year.

June 5. General tie-up, or strike, for one day, of all the lines in New York, Brooklyn, and Long Island City, to aid Third Avenue strikers.

May 5. Strike declared off; strikers defeated.

Aug. 23, 1886. Strike of employés of Broadway and Seventh Avenue lines to prevent reduction of wages and increase of hours of work.

Aug. 29. Compromise between strikers and railroad companies effected, and strike ended.

Aug. 25, 1886. Strike of employés on Belt Line Railroads to prevent reduction in wages and increase in hours of work.

Sept. 1. Strike ended by railroads yielding to strikers' demands.

Pittsburg, Pa.—March 29, 1886. Strike of conductors and drivers for more pay and fewer hours of work.

April 3. Strike settled by mutual concessions.

San Francisco.—July 16, 1886. Two hundred drivers and conductors on North Beach and Mission and City Railroad lines strike for shorter hours. Considerable rioting.

Dec. 27. Considerable rioting and use of dynamite.

Toronto, Can.—March 10, 1886. Street-car companies lock out men because they have organized, and agree not to employ organized labor.

March 12. Considerable rioting, which the police are hopeless to quell.

March 13. Strike ends—men taken back—no questions asked.

Troy, N. Y.—March 9, 1886. Employés of street-car companies in Troy strike; demands granted same day.

Boston.—Jan. 10, 1887. Drivers and conductors strike for more pay. Demands granted in a few hours.

Feb. 7. Employés of South Boston and Cambridge companies strike for more pay.

Feb. 13. Considerable rioting. Strikers mob a horse-car. Strike subsequently settled by mutual concessions.

Brooklyn, N. Y.—July 2, 1887. Drivers and conductors strike for longer times for meals. Demands granted same day.

Cincinnati.—Sept. 18. Gripmen and conductors on the cable-roads strike for reinstatement of discharged men.

Nov. 17, 1887. Strike of drivers and conductors for discharge of superintendent.

Indianapolis, Ind.—May 28, 1887. Drivers strike for more pay.

Lockport, N. Y.—Jan. 14, 1887. Drivers strike for more pay.

Railroads (Steam)—*Chicago.*—April 18, 1886. Strike of switchmen in yards of Lake Shore Railroad. Considerable disorder.

April 20. Gov. Oglesby visits yards, and advises strikers to arbitrate.

April 22. Conference between Knights and railroad companies, and after mutual concessions men return to work.

April 30, 1886. Freight-handlers and yardmen in railroad yards strike for eight-hour system.

May 3. Considerable rioting and some bloodshed.

May 4. Serious riot about midnight. Police attempted to break up anarchist meeting, and dynamite bomb was exploded, which killed or wounded thirty-three policemen and several other persons.

May 9. Strikers very generally return to work on old terms.

April 30, 1886. The Chicago and Northwestern Railroad settle with 1,800 striking shopmen by granting nine hours and full pay.

June 23, 1886. Switchmen in yards of Lake Shore Railroad strike because company has failed to keep promises made to men to induce them to return in April.

June 28. Yards put under protection of body of armed men known as Pinkerton's guards.

Dec. 15, 1886. Difficulty between Lake Shore Railroad and strikers has been settled. The company will take back all the old men, except those who engaged in acts of violence against the corporation, and will abolish the black list.

Cleveland, Ohio.—Oct. 6, 1886. Brakemen on New

York, Pennsylvania and Ohio Railroad strike for higher pay.

Corning, N. Y.—Oct. 2, 1886. Brakemen on Fall Brook Railroad strike against new rules of the company.

Denison, Tex.—Dec. 10, 1886. Switchmen in yards of the Missouri Pacific strike for shorter hours.

Detroit.—May 3, 1886. Three thousand shopmen in car-works strike for eight-hour system.
May 27. Strike collapses; men return to work.

Erie, Pa.—April 24, 1886. Yard-men of Philadelphia and Erie Railroad strike for more wages.

Galveston, Tex.—Jan., 1886. When the year began, a strike and boycott were in force against the Mallory Steamship Line. The difficulty originated in October, 1885, when the company began to fill places of white Knights of Labor who had struck for higher wages. The railroad strikes of the Southwest were largely due to this trouble.

Jackson, Tenn.—Dec. 29, 1886. Strike of employés at Baltimore and Ohio Railroad Company's yards settled by mutual concessions.

Louisiana.—Feb. 16, 1886. Attempt made to run trains on Southern Pacific Railroad, but prevented by strikes. The strike extends to the division between Lafayette and Houston.
Feb. 17. Railroad issued general order to refuse freight at points of strike.
Feb. 19. Strike settled by yielding to the demands of the strikers.

Lafayette, Ind.—Dec. 13. 1886. Freight conductors on Louisville, New Albany and Chicago Railroad strike for an advance in pay of two and a half to three cents per mile and allowance for lost time.

Minneapolis, Minn.—Oct. 14, 1886. General strike of switchmen in yards of the Chicago, Milwaukee and St. Paul Railroad.

Nebraska.—May 3, 1886. Brakemen on the Nebraska division of the Union Pacific Railroad struck against a new schedule of mileage and pay—demanding old schedule and $65 per month.

New Orleans, La.—Feb. 15, 1886. Freight-handlers strike to assist strikers on Southern Pacific Railroad.

New York City.—Jan. 2, 1886. Engineers on Elevated Railroad ask for revision of hours of work and rates of pay.
Jan. 4. Trains on City Hall branch and on Ninth and Second Avenue lines stopped by the company.
Jan. 5. Railroad commissioner notifies the company that failure to run trains will forfeit charter.
Jan. 7. Conference between P. M. Arthur and railroad officials.
Jan. 8. Strike settled; company yielding to all demands of the engineers.

Port Richmond, N. J.—Dec. 27, 1886. General dissatisfaction among Knights of Labor on the Reading road at reduction of wages. Switch engineers and firemen strike.
Dec. 28. Settled by company yielding to demands.

Pullman, Ill.—May 4, 1886. Four thousand shopmen in car-works strike for eight-hour system.
May 27. Strike collapses; men return to work.

Texas.—March 5, 1886. General strike of freight-handlers on railroads in Texas against handling freight consigned to or from the Mallory line.

Youngstown, Ohio.—Sept. 8, 1886. Yard brakemen and conductors employed on Pittsburg and Western Railroad strike for increase of 20 per cent. wages.
Sept. 9. Strike ended; demands conceded by the companies.
Sept. 16. Conductors and brakemen on New York, Pennsylvania and Ohio Railroad and Ohio and Pittsburg Railroad strike for increase of ten cents per day. Advance granted after six hours. Strike ended. Employés of Cleveland and Pittsburg strike for same cause.
Nov. 22. Strike of employés of Cleveland and Pittsburg Railway Company settled by company yielding to all demands.

St. Louis.—May 5, 1886. Mechanics and shopmen of Missouri-Pacific Railroad strike. Nominal cause, the discharge of one union man ; but the trouble had been growing for several months.
May 6. Engineers, firemen, brakemen, and switchmen join in the strike.
May 10. Hoxie discharges many employés who had not struck.
May 17. Knights of Labor ask for conference, but H. M. Hoxie, Vice-President, refuses to recognize Knights.
May 21. Powderly asks for interview with Hoxie, but it is refused. Govs. Marmaduke, of Missouri, and Martin, of Kansas, act as mediators between Hoxie and the Knights. Hoxie proposes a settlement which Knights declare meaningless, and accuse Hoxie of purposely exciting trouble.
May 22. Switchmen at Kansas City and vicinity join in the strike.
May 24. Considerable rioting at St. Louis. Gov. Marmaduke issues proclamation.
May 25. Govs. Hughes, of Arkansas, and Ireland, of Texas, issue proclamations.
May 26. Yardmen at North St. Louis Wabash yards go out.
May 27. Correspondence between Powderly and Gould.
May 28. Powderly, McDowell, and Gould have conference, which only results in a misunderstanding.
May 30. Hoxie offers to arbitrate if men return to work.
April 1. Strike declared off. Hoxie refuses to arbitrate with Knights of Labor, but only with strikers individually.
April 5. Strike renewed.
April 28. Five hundred men in Missouri Car Foundry Company join the strike.
May 1. From this date the strike gradually collapsed, men going back to work on company's terms. This strike, probably the largest which every occurred in the United States, extended over the States of Texas, Louisiana, Missouri, Kansas, Arkansas, and portions of some neighboring States.

Brooklyn, N. Y.—July 11, 1887. Engineers and firemen of the Brooklyn Elevated Railroad strike for reinstatement of discharged employés. Strike settled in a few days by mutual concessions.

Cleveland, Ohio.—March 12, 1887. Conductors, brakemen, and switchmen of the Pennsylvania and Ohio Railroad strike for higher wages.
June 14. Considerable rioting.
June 17. Demands granted.

Huntsville, Ala.—Aug. 16, 1887. Freight conductors on the Memphis and Charleston Railroad strike for more pay.

Montgomery, Ala.—Sept. 4, 1887. Brakemen on the Louisville & Nashville Railroad strike for more pay.

Reading, Pa.—July 19, 1887. Eleven hundred men on the Reading Railroad coal-trains strike for reinstatement of discharged employés. Demands granted same day.

Port Richmond, N. J.—Dec. 23, 1887. Freight-handlers of Reading Railroad strike against scabs.
Dec. 24, 1887. General strike of employés of the Reading Railroad against reduction of wages ; 60,000 men idle.

Waukesha, Wis.—Sept. 1, 1887. Strike of switchmen on the Wisconsin Central Railroad for more pay.
Sept. 7. Strike fails and is declared off.

Youngstown, Ohio.—Feb. 10, 1887. Conductors, brakemen, and firemen on railroads centering at Youngstown strike for more pay.

Ribbon-Weavers.—*New York City.*—July 19, 1886. Ribbon-weavers at Samuel Bernstein's factory strike for privilege of drinking beer during working-hours.
July 24. Strike ended by weavers voluntarily relinquishing their demand.

Roofers.—*New York City.*—May 3, 1886. Tin and slate roofers strike for more wages and eight hours.

Cincinnati, Ohio.—May 2, 1887. Five hundred roofers strike for more wages.

Rope-Walkers.—*Brooklyn, N. Y.*—March 16, 1886. Girls at Waterbury's Rope-Walk strike against reduction of 20 per cent. in wages.

March 29. Strike fails and girls return on employer's terms.

Rubber-Workers.—*New Haven, Conn.*—Aug. 13, 1886. Fifty girls employed in the Candee Rubber-Shop strike for better ventilation.

South Framingham, Mass.—Aug. 2, 1886. Seven hundred employés in the Para Rubber Shoe Company strike for reinstatement of union man.

Aug. 9. Strike settled by mutual concessions.

Akron, Ohio.—April 18, 1887. Rubber-turners of the Goodrich Company strike for more pay.

Rag-Weavers.—*Philadelphia.*—July 13, 1886. Four hundred striking rug-weavers return to work; they had been out only a few days.

July 16, 1887. Employés of Arianna Mills strike for dismissal of apprentices. Strike settled by mutual concessions.

Sailors.—*Oswego, N. Y.*—Aug. 9, 1886. Sailors prevent scabs from working on shipboard.

Salesmen.—*New York City.*—June 28, 1886. Salesmen employed by Singer Manufacturing Company (sewing-machines) strike for increase of commissions on sales.

Salt-Workers.—*Natrona, Pa.*—April 17, 1887. Employés of Pennsylvania Salt Company strike for more pay.

May 29. Considerable rioting. Three strikers wounded by armed scabs.

July 1. Two car-loads of imported salt-workers arrive but refuse to work. Strike settled by mutual concessions.

Sateen-Weavers.—*New Bedford, Mass.*—Sept. 9 1886. Weavers at Potomska Mills strike against heavy fines imposed by new overseer.

Sept. 11. Strike settled by mutual concessions.

Saw-Makers.—*Tacony, Pa.*—Oct. 8, 1886. About 1,200 employés at saw-works strike.

School-Children.—*Boston.*—April 20, 1886. Sixty pupils of South Boston public school strike for one single, continuous session. They adopt picket-system. Dispersed by police, they obtain flags and parade through the streets.

April 20, 1886. Pupils of Frothingham Grammar School petition for shorter hours. Being refused they lock the school-gates, hide keys, and adopt picket-system.

Brooklyn, N. Y.—March 18, 1886. Pupils of St. Anne's Parochial School were required to pay 10 cents weekly. Being economically inclined they demand that fee to be reduced to 5 cents, and on refusal of school authorities to grant the reduction the pupils stay away from school. The police and parents are called upon, and strike lasts but one day.

April 12, 1886. Boys at Public School 34 strike for half-hour recess in morning session, and half-holiday on Friday. They adopt a picket system, and prevent scholars approaching school-house until police are called upon.

Goshen, N. Y.—Oct. 19, 1886. Scholars of Free Colored School strike because the whole of the morning is devoted to study.

Troy, N. Y.—April 12, 1886. Boys at Public School, Eleventh Ward, strike for single school-session from 8 to 12; adopt picket-system, and attack scholars approaching school-house. Police and parents intervene, and strike collapses.

Ship-Builders.—*Bath, Me.*—Sept. 4, 1886. New England Ship-Building Company reduce wages, and employés refer the matter to Knights of Labor, and strike.

Oct. 4. End of strike; mutual concessions. Three hundred men—ship-carpenters, joiners, blacksmiths, boiler-makers, and machinists—return to work.

Detroit.—Aug. 12, 1886. Ship-carpenters strike because of refusal of employers to recognize Knights of Labor.

Shirt-Makers.—*New Bedford, Mass.*—Nov. 9, 1886. Employés in Denham's shirt-factory strike to prevent reduction in wages.

New York City.—Nov. 9, 1886. Shirt-cutters of Herman & Co. strike against the employment of boys.

July 19, 1887. Two hundred and fifty employés of Davies & Co. strike against reduction of wages.

Shoemakers.—*Athol, Mass.*—Aug. 2, 1886. Shoe-manufacturers employing about 500 hands give notice that all employés must sign notice that they do not belong to any labor association.

Aug. 30. Strike of about 500 hands at Lee's Factory upon demand that they resign from Knights of Labor.

Brockton, Mass.—July 31, 1886. Employés of J. B. Reynolds strike for dismissal of non-union man. The Manufacturers' Union voted to shut down their factories, 42 in number, until trouble is settled.

New York City.—March 20, 1886. Strike at and boycott of Pingree & Smith's shoe-factory settled. It had lasted about a year. Employers yielded to all demands, and discharged all non-union men.

Sept. 7, 1886.—Three hundred employés of Hanan & Co. strike for increased wages.

Sept. 9. Strike off; strikers return on old rates.

Pittsfield, Mass.—July 23, 1886. Lasters employed at Cheshire Shoe-shop strike for reinstatement of discharged union man.

Pittsburg, Pa.—Dec. 6, 1886. About 500 employés of Breed's shoe-factory strike for increased wages.

Port Jervis, N. Y.—July 20, 1886. Lasters and finishers in Buckley Shoe Factory strike against proposed reduction in wages.

Rochester, N. Y.—Sept. 1, 1886. Strike of hands in factory of Williams & Hoyt for higher wages.

Sept. 10. Strike settled by mutual concessions.

Nov. 2, 1887. Two hundred shoe-cutters strike for more pay. Demands granted same day.

Sheboygan, Mo.—Dec. 10, 1886. Knights of Labor employed by Keene Brothers strike for discharge of non-union men.

Stoughton, Mass.—July 30, 1886. Hand-sewers strike for advance of wages.

Worcester, Mass.—Jan. 25, 1886. Shoemakers at Worcester strike for higher wages. A conference between employers and a committee of the Knights of Labor resulted in the compromise offered by the former being rejected by the latter. On Feb 3 the employers yielded to all the demands, and employés returned to work.

Feb. 3. Strike of employés of 90 factories against attempt of manufacturers to break the labor-unions.

June 30. Strike declared off. Men return to work on employers' terms.

Beverley, Mass.—July 16, 1887. General strike against reduction of wages.

Dover, N. H.—Feb. 10, 1887. Four hundred and twenty employés strike for reinstatement of discharged employé.

Philadelphia.—Oct. 5, 1887. Five thousand employés locked out to anticipate strike for more wages.

Nov. 14. Employés return to work, on former wages.

St. Louis, Mo.—June 13, 1887. Employés of St. Louis Shoe Company strike against scab labor.

Silk-Dyers.—*Paterson, N. J.*—April 12, 1886. Dyers in silk-mills strike for a new schedule of wages.

April 23. Strike settled by mutual concessions.

Silk-Weavers.—*Paterson, N. J.*—Jan 25, 1887. Silk-weavers strike for more pay.

March 30. Strike settled by arbitration.

Phillipsburg, N. J.—Jan. 6, 1887. General strike for more pay.

Silversmiths.—*New York City.*—April 21, 1887. General strike for reduction of number of apprentices.

June 16. Strike settled by mutual concessions.

Steam-Workers.—*New York City.*—March 2, 1886. Employés of New York Steam Company strike because of discharge of union men.

March 3. Coal-handlers refuse to handle coal for Steam Company; police called upon for protection.

March 5. Carts carrying coal are upset by strikers.

March 8. Conference between Steam Company and committee of strikers, but no result reached.

March 10. Steamboat men refuse to remove Steam Company's ashes.

March 16. Strikers defeated, non-union men having filled their places.

Stone-Cutters.—Washington, D. C.—May 3, 1886. Stone-cutters strike for eight-hour system.

Chicago.—Dec. 19, 1887. One hundred and thirty-three stone-cutters strike for more pay.

Philadelphia.—May 26, 1887. Three hundred stone-cutters strike against scab labor.

New Jersey.—May 3, 1887. General strike by the stone-cutters of the State for more pay.

Stone-Rubbers.—New York City.—Sept. 25, 1886. About 500 stone-rubbers strike for discharge of a non-union man.

Store-Men.—Brooklyn.—April 15, 1886. Over 2,000 store-men on the water-front strike for increased pay.

April 29. Strike ended. Warehousemen having yielded all that strikers demanded.

Stove-Workers.—Philadelphia.—Sept. 13, 1886. Conference between Knights of Labor and Stove Manufacturers' Union. Knights demand 10 per cent. advance in wages. That being refused, they demand 5 per cent. advance; refused. Strike.

Oct. 26, 1886. Stove-workers return to work, after five weeks' strike, on terms of employers.

Pittsburg, Pa.—Sept. 9, 1886. General strike of about 3,000 stove-molders for increase of 10 per cent.

Reading, Pa.—Aug. 19, 1886. Strike of several hundred molders at Mt. Penn Stove-Works settled, after duration of some months, by strikers returning to work voluntarily.

Troy, N. Y.—Feb. 15, 1886. About 2,000 molders in stove-factories strike for more wages.

June 21. Stove-molders return to work, their demands being granted.

St. Louis, Mo.—April 11, 1887. Five thousand stove-molders strike because required to cast patterns for a shop at which there is a strike. The strike becomes general throughout the country.

April 18. The strike spreads to Pittsburg, Sharon, Louisville, Cincinnati, and Akron.

April 26. The strike extends to Oswego, Syracuse, Albany, Troy, Peekskill, Lancaster, Reading, Wilkesbarre, and Philadelphia.

June 1. Nearly all shops outside of St. Louis refuse patterns from St. Louis, and men return to work.

Sept. 5. Strike settled on mutual concessions.

Sugar-Refiners.—Brooklyn, N. Y.—April 16, 1886. Havermeyer & Elder warn their employés not to join Knights of Labor.

April 20. Committee of Knights present list of grievances, and demand 25 per cent. increase of pay and ten hours a day. Employers refuse to recognize Knights.

April 21. Two thousand five hundred men go on strike.

April 22. Considerable rioting and some bloodshed. Police and rioters both injured.

May 3. Employers make some small concessions, and strikers begin to return. Strike gradually collapses.

Louisiana.—Oct. 5, 1887. General strike throughout the State for more pay.

Nov. 23. Fatal rioting. Twelve men shot.

Tailors.—Newark, N. J.—Sept. 4, 1886. Cutters and trimmers strike to assist strikers in New York city.

New York City.—April 16, 1886. Cutters and trimmers employed by Cavanagh, Sandford & Co. go on strike.

April 28. Forty-seven of the strikers are indicted for conspiracy.

May 18. Three hundred journeymen tailors strike for ten hours on five days and nine hours on the sixth.

May 24. Strike extends to all the shops of the Contractor Tailors' Association, affecting about 8,000 employés.

May 27. Conference between bosses and journeymen.

June 13. Strike settled by mutual concessions.

Aug. 25, 1886. General strike of union cutters to compel masters to employ no non-union men, and to take only such apprentices as union allows.

Sept. 7, 1886. Arbitration committee of Knights offer to send men back to work if scabs are discharged. Employers refuse.

Sept. 9. Men return on employers' terms.

Philadelphia.—May 10, 1886. One thousand cutters and trimmers strike for the adoption of eight-hour system.

Feb. 5, 1887. Ten thousand tailors employed by members of the Clothing Exchange are locked out to anticipate strike.

May 28. Men return to work on their own terms.

Tanners.—Salem and Peabody, Mass.—July 14, 1886. General strike for day of ten hours.

Aug. 6. Considerable rioting.

Aug. 9. Police from other towns placed on guard.

Aug. 11. Considerable rioting.

Aug. 12. One tanner yields to demands of the strikers but resumes his former opposition next day.

Nov. 25. Considerable rioting. Several scab tanners beaten and one striker shot. Strike declared off.

Woburn, Mass.—Sept. 9, 1886. Employés in Duncan's Leather Factory strike against increase in day's work.

Newark, N. J.—Jan. 7, 1887. Employés at Newark strike for revival of wages schedule.

Aug. 10, 1887. General strike for recognition of the Union.

Sept. 7. Strike settled by mutual concessions.

Telegraph-Operators.—Omaha, Neb.—July 12, 1886. Telegraph-operators strike for increase of wages.

Terra-Cotta Makers—New Brunswick, N. J.—Aug. 19, 1886. Strike of employés of Perth Amboy Terra-Cotta Works to secure reinstatement of discharged union man. Settled; employers yield.

Tinsmiths.—Memphis, Tenn.—Sept. 10, 1886. Journeymen tinkers strike for recognition of rules of trades-union.

Sept. 13. Bosses yield. Strike ended.

Toy-Makers.—Chicago.—April 30, 1886. Employés of St. Nicholas Toy Company strike for eight hours.

Tube-Makers.—Chicago.—April 30, 1886. Employés of Crane Brothers strike for eight-hour system—1,100 men affected.

Harrisburg, Pa.—July 30, 1886. Strike of employés of American Iron Tube Company declared off—strikers being defeated.

McKeesport, Pa.—March 18, 1886. Strike by employés of one department for an advance of fifteen per cent. of wages.

March 20. Extended to all employés—about 4,000.

Middletown, Pa.—July 21, 1886. Five hundred employés of American Tube and Iron Company strike for rate of wages prevailing in 1883 and for reinstatement of two discharged union men.

Millville, N. J.—Aug. 8, 1886. Employés of R. D. Wood's foundry strike for reduction in piece-work.

Aug. 13. Employers offer to make reduction if men will leave Knights of Labor; offer refused.

Youngstown, O.—April 17, 1887. Three hundred workmen in American Tube Company strike for reinstatement of discharged employé.

Wire-Workers.—Norwalk, Conn.—April 26, 1886. Wire-workers strike for advance in wages.

May 30. Strikers return on employers' terms.

Wool-Workers.—Louisville, Ky.—July 27, 1887. Strike for more pay.

Sept. 27. Strikers return to work on employers' terms.

Marlboro, Mass.—April 21, 1887. Five hundred employés of Chapin & Co. strike for shorter hours.

Philadelphia, Pa.—Sept. 4, 1887. Employés of Star Mills strike for more pay.

SWEDEN AND NORWAY, two kingdoms in the north of Europe possessing separate constitutions, but united in the person of the sovereign by the act of union promulgated in 1814. The King of both countries is Oscar II, born Jan. 21, 1829, who succeeded his brother, Carl XV, Sept. 18, 1872. The common affairs are decided upon by a Council of State composed of Swedes and Norwegians.

SWEDEN.—The fundamental laws are the law on the form of government of June 6, 1809, the law on national representation of June 22, 1866, the law of succession, enacted Sept. 26, 1810, and the law on the liberty of the press of July 16, 1812. The national Parliament or Diet consists of two elective Chambers. The first Chamber has 142 members, who are elected by 25 provincial bodies and the municipalities of Stockholm, Göteborg, Malmö, and Norrköping. The second Chamber consists of 214 members, of whom 69 are elected by the towns and 145 by the rural districts by limited suffrage. The ministry consists of seven members with portfolios and three with a consultative voice, and is composed as follows: Oscar R. Themptander, Minister of State, appointed May 16, 1884; Count Albert Carl August Lars Ehrensvärd, Minister of Foreign Affairs, appointed Sept. 25, 1885; Nils Henrik Vult von Steyern, Minister of Justice; Baron Carl Gustaf von Otter, Minister of Marine; Major-General Baron G. O. de Peyron, Minister of War, appointed Oct. 4, 1887; Julius Edvard von Krusenstjerna, Minister of the Interior; Baron Claes Gustaf Adolf Tamm, Minister of Finance, appointed Nov. 30, 1886; Carl Gustaf Hammarskjöld, Minister of Education and Ecclesiastical Affairs; Johan Henrik Lovén; Johan C. Emil Richert.

Area and Population.—The area of the kingdom is 450,574 square kilometres. The population on Dec. 31, 1886, was computed at 4,717,189 persons, of whom 2,290,340 were males and 2,426,849 females. The number of marriages in 1885 was 30,911; births, 141,316; deaths, 86,789; excess of births, 54.527. The number of emigrants in 1885 was 23,493, against 23,560 in 1884, 31,605 in 1883, 50,178 in 1882, and 45,992 in 1881. The population of the chief cities in 1886 was as follows: Stockholm, 228,063; Göteborg, 92,805; Malmö, 45,346; Norrköping, 28,993.

Finances.—The budget for 1888 makes the total ordinary receipts 18,954,000 kronor, the surplus from previous budgets 8,493,000 kronor, extraordinary receipts, comprising the receipts from customs, the post-office, stamps, spirit-tax, sugar-tax, and income-tax, 55,700,000 kronor, the surplus from the postal receipts 300,000 kronor, and the net receipts from the Bank of Sweden 1,250,000 kronor, giving a total sum of 84,697,000 kronor. The total expenditures are estimated at the same figure, the chief items being 19,685,500 kronor for the army, 11,129,994 kronor for public instruction, 14,412,600 kronor for finan-

cial administration, and 10,820,700 for the public debt. The debt on Jan. 1, 1887, amounted to 245,808,228 kronor.

The Army.—The Swedish military system is an antiquated one that was established by Charles XI. The soldiers are supported by the land-owners, who furnish them with cottages and allotments of land. There are also enlisted troops, constituting the guards, the engineers, and the artillery, and the German conscription system has been introduced to some extent. A thorough military reorganization, substituting modern conscription for the old and ineffective militia system, has been under discussion for twenty years. In 1885 a further step was taken in this direction, the land-owners obtaining a remission of 30 per cent. of their military taxes. The burden resting on the farming class in consequence of the indelta or distributive military system was reckoned at 10,000,000 kronor per annum, but of this 3,000,000 kronor were removed by the military law of 1885, which made the annual periods of drill considerably longer. The Agrarian party is strongly opposed to reorganization on the plan of universal obligatory service unless the farmers are entirely relieved of their exceptional military taxes. The enrolled troops in 1887 numbered 9,874 and the indelta or cantoned troops 27,198, exclusive of officers. The total strength of the Swedish army was reported as 174,440, consisting of 40,146 troops of the line and 134,294 conscription troops.

The Navy.—The navy, as well as the army, has hitherto been organized largely on the indelta system. In 1887 the Diet agreed to the total abolition of the indelta in the navy, which pressed severely upon the land-owners on the coast, and furnished 7,000 badly-trained sailors, who by no means supplied the actual need of from 4,000 to 6,000 capable men. The navy will henceforth be manned by 1,100 men who remain permanently in the service, and 2,900 who are enlisted for eight years, and are required to serve three years and five months under the flag. The effective strength of the crews under the new organization is 2,550 men in summer and 2,187 in winter, while in case of war 1,450 trained furloughed men can be called out to increase the personnel to 4,000. The Minister of Marine in 1876 asked for a credit of 55,000,000 kronor, to be expended in twelve years in the creation of an iron-clad fleet. The proposition was rejected, and he has since sought to build up a navy with whatever means the Diet would grant from time to time. In 1887 the lower Chamber refused to vote 3,000,000 kronor for an iron-clad, yet in the upper Chamber the bill passed with a majority sufficient to carry it through in joint session.

The navy in 1887 contained 1 small turret-ship, 4 monitors, 10 iron-clad gun-boats, 17 torpedo-boats, and 31 unarmored steamers.

Commerce.—The total value of the imports in 1885 was 340,003,000 kronor, equivalent to

$91,800,000; the value of the exports, 246,-271.000 kronor, equivalent to $66,492,000. Of the imports 100,718,000 kronor came from Germany, 84,650,000 kronor from Great Britain, 50,470.000 kronor from Denmark, 29,870,-000 kronor from Russia, and 28,786,000 kronor from Norway. Of the total value of the exports 121,796.000 kronor went to Great Britain, 30,856,000 kronor to Denmark, 24,479,000 kronor to France, 19,122,000 kronor to Germany, and 10,311,000 kronor to Norway. The imports from the United States were valued at 8,644,000 kronor and the exports to the United States at 822,000 kronor. The principal imports are textile manufactures, grain and flour, sugar, coffee, coal, and metal goods. The principal article of exports is timber, the export amounting to 103,452.000 kronor in 1884, after which come iron, live animals and animal food, and grain.

Navigation.—The number of vessels entered at the ports of Sweden in 1885 was 28,761, of 4,536,000 tons. Of these, 14,256, of 1,653,000 tons, were Swedish; 2,276, of 551,000 tons, Norwegian; and 12,229, of 2,332,000 tons, foreign vessels. The number of steamers entered was 11,174, tonnage 2,917.000. The total number of clearances was 26,890, tonnage 4,481,000. The vessels entered with cargoes numbered 11,782, of 2,273,000 tons; cleared, 18,985, of 3,394,000 tons.

The merchant navy on Jan. 1, 1886, numbered 3,163 sailing-vessels, of 486,437 tons, and 898 steam vessels, of 109,566 tons.

Railroads.—The length of railroads open to traffic at the close of 1886 was 7,277 kilometres, of which 2,469 kilometres belonged to the state and 4,808 kilometres to companies.

The Post-Office.—The number of letters and post-cards forwarded in 1885 was 50,007,058; circulars and printed matter, 5,272,895; newspapers, 36,435,449. The receipts were 6,013,-641 kronor. and the expenses 5,753,062 kronor.

Telegraphs.—The length of the state telegraph lines in 1886 was 8,512 kilometres; length of wires, 21,351 kilometres. There were transmitted 560,764 internal. 448,664 international, and 162,314 transit dispatches. The receipts were 1,246,528 kronor and the expenditures 1,242,545 kronor.

Politics and Legislation. — The Thempander ministry has received its principal support from the Farmer party; yet it resisted a demand for a duty on grain, and, when it was defeated by a vote of 111 to 101 in the lower Chamber on this question, it dissolved the Chamber on March 5, 1887. In the newly-elected Chamber there was a large majority against protection. The position of the ministry, however, was precarious, because it had broken with the party with which it was in a large measure identified. The result of the regular elections, which took place in the autumn, rendered the position of the ministry more insecure. In the first Chamber the Protectionists obtained the majority, and in the

lower Chamber the Free-Traders lost so many seats that on a joint vote the Government could count on a majority of ten votes only. The twenty-two members for Stockholm, who supported the Government on the tariff question, stood in danger of losing their seats, as their election was annulled by the civic authorities, and the matter had to be decided by the supreme court.

Norway.—The Grundlov, or Constitution, adopted Nov. 4, 1814, and modified by various amendments, the last of which was passed in 1884, vests the legislative authority in the Storthing, or Great Court, over the acts of which the King possesses a limited right of veto. The Storthing contains 114 members, two thirds of whom represent rural districts, and the other third towns. One fourth of the members separate from the others to form the Lagthing, which passes upon laws that have originated in the larger Chamber, called the Odelsthing. When the two houses do not agree, the matter is decided by a joint vote. The ministry is composed of two Ministers of State, one of whom resides at Stockholm, and seven concoilors, two of whom sojourn at the Swedish capital, alternating every year. Since July, 1884, the ministers and councilors of state are required to answer interpellations in the Storthing and may take part in its proceedings. The present ministry, constituted June 26, 1884, is composed as follows: Minister of State residing at Christiania, Johan Sverdrup; Education and Ecclesiastical Affairs, Elias Blix; Justice and Police, Hans Georg Jakob Stang; Revision of Public Accounts, Jakob Liv Rosted Sverdrup; Interior, Sofus Anton Birger Arctander; Customs and Finance, Bard Madsen Hauegland; Public Works, Birger Kildal; Minister of State residing at Stockholm, Ole Richter; Councilors of State at Stockholm, Hans Rasmus Astrup, appointed Aug. 3, 1885; and Aimar August Sörenssen. The Department of National Defense is presided over by Johan Sverdrup, the Prime Minister.

Area and Population.—The area of Norway is 325,422 square kilometres. The population at the last decennial census, taken in 1875, was 1,806,900, divided into 876,762 males and 930,138 females. The population at the end of 1880 was estimated at 1,913,000. The number of marriages in 1885 was 13,024; births, 61,052; deaths, 32,111; excess of births, 28,941. The number of emigrants in 1886 was 15,158, as compared with 13,981 in 1885, 14,-776 in 1884, 22,167 in 1883, 28,804 in 1882, 25,976 in 1881, 20,212 in 1880, 7,608 in 1879, 4,863 in 1878, 3,206 in 1877, and 4,355 in 1876. The population of Christiania in 1885 was 128,302. Bergen, the next largest city, had 46,552 inhabitants.

Finances.—The receipts of the Government for the year ended June 30, 1885, were 43,540,-800 kronor, of which 20,117,500 kronor were derived from customs, and 6,000,200 kronor from railroads. The expenditure amounted to 42,500,300 kronor. The budget for the year 1886–'87 estimated the revenue at 43,450,000 kronor, and the expenditure at an equal amount. The national debt, which was contracted for the construction of public works, chiefly railroads, amounted, on June 30, 1886, to 105,329,500 kronor, while the value of the railroads and other assets was 139,919,600 kronor.

The Army.—The troops of the line number 750 officers and 18,000 soldiers, which number must not be exceeded even in time of war without the consent of the Storthing. The landvaern and landstorm are democratic organizations, which can only be called on for the defense of the country.

The Navy.—The fleet in July, 1887, consisted of 4 monitors, 42 other steamers, and 50 sailing-vessels.

Commerce.—The total value of the imports in 1886 was 185,169,000 kronor, equivalent to $36,495,000; the value of the exports, 102,844,000 kronor, equivalent to $27,567,000. Of the imports 38,039,000 kronor came from Germany, 34,472,000 kronor from Great Britain, 16,691,000 kronor from Sweden, and 11,933,000 kronor from Russia. Of the exports, 34,021,000 kronor went to Great Britain, 14,255,000 kronor to Sweden, and 12,818,000 kronor to Germany. The imports from the United States were valued at 5,950,000 kronor, and the exports to the United States at 540,000 kronor.

Navigation.—The number of vessels entered at Norwegian ports in 1885 was 11,049 of 2,359,600 tons, of which 5,732 of 1,334,160 tons had cargoes. The number cleared was 11,911, of 2,878,149 tons, of which 10,462, of 1,883,575 tons, were with cargoes. The number entered that carried the Norwegian flag was 6,887, of 757,271 tons; the number cleared, 6,408, of 1,524,008 tons.

The mercantile marine, in the beginning of 1886, comprised 7,664 vessels, of 1,563,020 tons, employing 58,624 men. The steam-vessels numbered 510, of the aggregate burden of 114,108 tons.

Railroads, Posts, and Telegraphs.—The length of the railroad lines in operation in 1887 was 1,562 kilometres.

The post-office in 1886 forwarded 20,776,622 letters and 20,718,555 newspapers. The receipts were 2,258,936 kronor; expenses, 2,310,263 kronor.

The state telegraph lines at the close of 1886 had a total length of 7,487 kilometres, with 13,933 kilometres of wires. The number of internal dispatches was 479,091, and the total number of dispatches 850,959. The receipts were 888,155 kronor, and the expenses 1,062,233 kronor. The railroad companies possessed 1,588 kilometres of lines, and 2,531 kilometres of wires.

Ministerial Crisis.—The Democratic Prime Minister, Sverdrup, has not satisfied by his course a great section of his party, although, by in-

sisting on a compromise measure giving to Norway more of a voice and more representation in the common diplomacy of the two kingdoms, he offended the governing circles in Stockholm. The defection of Democratic members of the Storthing was made up by the adherence of the Conservatives, who supported Sverdrup in order to avert a more radical *régime* under Judge Qvam and Prof. Sars. The rejection of an ecclesiastical bill that was presented by Jakob Sverdrup, while he was Minister of Worship, brought on a protracted Cabinet crisis. The opponents of the Prime Minister demanded the resignation of his nephew, but Sverdrup declared that the question was not of a nature to require the retirement of the defeated minister, and that the whole Cabinet would retire if the matter were pressed to an issue, and his view should not be sustained. Besides his nephew, only Councilors Haugland and Stang among the members of the Cabinet supported the Premier on this question. The members who held the opposite view were not entirely true to the principle of parliamentarism which they championed, because Councilor Blix, the actual chief of the Department of Ecclesiastical Affairs, who belonged to the opposition clique in the Cabinet, was as fully committed to the rejected project of church reform as Jakob Sverdrup. The question of diplomatic administration was settled by an agreement that foreign affairs should be brought before a council composed of Swedish and Norwegian representatives, in which the King should be the presiding officer, and the Swedish Foreign Minister should have the initiative. This was far from satisfactory to the Norwegian Democrats, who insisted on Sverdrup's original demands. In the Storthing a resolution was offered by Qvam in favor of the creation of a separate Norwegian Ministry of Foreign Affairs, a proposition which has been adopted by the Democratic party in its programme for the elections of 1888. The question of the viceroyalty has been brought forward by Björnstjerne Björnson and other upholders of the parity of Norway. The articles of union provide that a viceroy of Norway shall be appointed, who must be a Swede. This dignity has been uniformly conferred on either the crown prince or his eldest son. The Norwegians now complain that the office is a badge of subjection, and that it should either be abolished or filled by a Norwegian.

SWITZERLAND, a federal republic in central Europe. The legislative authority of the confederacy is vested in the State Council, in which each of the twenty-two cantons is represented by two members, and the National Council, chosen by direct suffrage in the proportion of one member to every 20,000 inhabitants. The executive authority is in the hands of the Federal Council. The members of this body, elected on Dec. 15, 1886, are as follow: Numa Droz, President for 1887; W. F. Hertenstein, Vice-President for 1887 and President for 1888;

Dr. A. Schenck; Dr. E. Welti; L. Ruchonnet; Dr. Adolph Deucher; B. Hammer.

Area and Population.—The area of Switzerland is 41,346 square kilometres. The population in 1880 was 2,846,102, comprising 1,394,626 males and 1,451,476 females. The number of marriages in 1886 was 20,080, against 20,105 in 1885; the number of births, 84,142, against 88,579; the number of deaths, 63,440, against 64,778; excess of births over deaths, 20,702, against 18,801. The population of Geneva in 1886 was 52,819 without, and 72,819 with the suburbs. Zürich and its suburbs had 89,804 inhabitants; Basle had 72,304, and Bern 49,410. Emigration beyond seas amounted in 1886 to 6,342 individuals, against 7,588 in 1885, 9,608 in 1884, and 18,502 in 1882. Of the emigrants 4,863 went to North America.

Finances.—The financial account for 1886 makes the total revenue 61,097,496 francs, and the expenditure 58,067,506 francs. The budget for 1888, approved by the National Council on Dec. 9, 1887, estimates the revenue at 56,066,000 francs, and the expenditure at 56,866,000 francs. The assets of the Confederation amounted to 65,966,173 francs, and the debt to 36,670,616 francs on Jan. 1, 1887. A bill to establish a spirit monopoly was passed in 1886 by the National and State Councils, and on the demand of 48,255 citizens was submitted in 1887 to the popular vote, which confirmed the law. The Federal Council in August, 1887, authorized a loan of 10,000,000 francs to carry the measure into effect.

The Army.—The Federal army is composed of the regular troops or Bundesauszug, composed of citizens from twenty to thirty-two years of age; the Landwehr, which comprises all the men from thirty-three to forty-five years old; and the Landsturm, organized under a law that went into force in 1887. The latter category includes retired officers under fifty-five years old, retired non-commissioned officers and soldiers up to the age of fifty, and all other citizens between forty and fifty years of age who are not enrolled in the Landwehr, as well as young men between the ages of seventeen and twenty. The effective strength of the regular army on Jan. 1, 1887, was 120,398 officers and soldiers; that of the Landwehr, 81,485 men. The Landsturm is expected to add 300,000 men to the fighting strength of the republic. A credit of 840,000 francs was granted by the National Council in June, 1887, for the purpose of supplying 12 batteries with new cannon. The Swiss artillery possesses 400 field-pieces and 400 siege-guns.

Commerce.—The special imports of merchandise in 1886 were of the total value of 758,608,000 francs; the special exports 637,633,000 francs.

Railroads.—The length of railroad lines in operation in 1885 was 2,784 kilometres, exclusive of 63 kilometres of mountain railroad operated by foreign companies. The cost of construction was 1,048,627,602 francs. The

receipts in 1885 were 78,787,412 francs and the expenses of operation 39,577,625 francs.

The Post-Office.—The number of letters and post-cards forwarded in 1886 was 58,381,144, not including 31,477,056 international letters; the number of journals, 63,215,302.

Telegraphs.—The length of telegraph lines in 1886 was 7,025 kilometres; the length of wires, 17,063 kilometres. There were 3,184,470 messages sent over the wires in 1886, of which 1,798,938 were paid internal dispatches, 956,981 were foreign dispatches, 326,993 were forwarded in transit, and 106,508 were official. The receipts were 3,293,264 francs and the expenses 2,799,855 francs.

International Copyright.—The ratifications of the treaty for the creation of an international union for the protection of literary and artistic property, which was signed at Bern on Sept 9, 1886, were exchanged at the same place on Sept. 5, 1887, by the representatives of Germany, England, Belgium, Spain, France, Hayti, Italy, Liberia, Switzerland, and Tunis. Other states may be admitted into the union at any time on giving their adhesion to the treaty. Authors, painters, engravers, composers, and dramatists enjoy in all the countries forming the union the same protection for their works that each country gives to its own citizens, subject to the conditions and formalities which are prescribed in the country where the work is first published. The duration of copyright can not exceed in other countries the limit of time established in the country of origin of the work. Authorized translations are protected as original works, and authors possess for the term of ten years the right of making or authorizing translations of their productions. Articles from newspapers and magazines may be protected by international copyright, with the exception of articles of political discussion and of news of the day and current topics. The publication of extracts from copyrighted works for educational or scientific purposes or in chrestomathics is governed by the laws existing in the several countries, or by special arrangements that may be made between the contracting parties. Plays and musical dramas are protected, whether published or not, and if published, their representation on the stage is interdicted whenever the author prints a warning to that effect on the title-page or in the beginning of the work. Literary adaptations, arrangements of music, and similar appropriations are forbidden unless the alterations are sufficient to confer the character of a new original work. An international office is established at Bern under the name of the Office of the International Union for the Protection of Literary and Artistic Works. The expenses will be borne by the governments composing the union, but must not exceed 60,000 francs per annum. The office is placed under the authority of the superior administration of the Swiss Confederation. The functions of the office are prescribed in a special protocol, and include the collection and publication of information relative to the protection of authors' rights, the consideration of general questions of utility likely to be of interest to the union, and the publication of a periodical. Photographic reproductions of protected works are forbidden, and countries in which photographs are protected extend the same protection to citizens of the other states of the international union. The same is true of ballet dances. The protection of musical works does not extend to automatic arrangements of airs in mechanical instruments. The treaty went into force three months from the date of the exchange of ratifications. It was concluded for an indefinite period, any of the contracting governments being at liberty to withdraw on twelve months' notice.

T

TARPON. The largest and most important of the *Clupeidæ*, specifically *Megolops thrissoides* (Gunther), a salt-water fish occurring in the western Atlantic and the Gulf of Mexico, and ranging from the coast of South America northward as far as Cape Cod. In the higher latitudes it is comparatively rare, though the specimen in the National Museum at Washington was captured off the coast of New Jersey. It is quite abundant among the West Indies, and has rarely been found as far eastward as the Bermudas. In the summer it frequently ascends the southern rivers in large numbers it with the rod and line. It has long been known that it would take bait, but its wonderful activity enabled it to break away with such certainty that few sportsmen cared to risk their tackle in the encounter. So recently as 1883, S. C. Clarke, author of "Fishes of the East Florida Coast," wrote somewhat incredulously of the alleged capture of a tarpon with rod and reel in Indian River, Florida, and pronounced it one of the greatest angling feats on record. "No man," he says "is strong enough to hold a large tarpon unless he is provided with a drag or buoy, in the shape

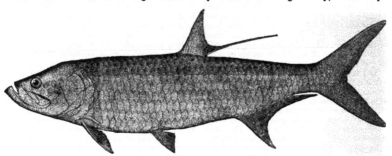

in pursuit of small fish, its natural food. The tarpon not infrequently attains a length of 6 feet and a weight of 150 pounds. The whole body is covered with large circular scales, sometimes as much as 2½ inches in diameter, and of a beautiful silvery luster, darker on the back. These scales are, to some extent, an article of trade, being sought for as curiosities and used for decorative purposes.

The commonly-accepted name is tarpon, but it was formerly written tarpom and tarpum. It is sometimes called "Jew-fish," especially in Georgia and Florida, and elsewhere "silver-fish" and "silver king." Farther west among the French-speaking people of the gulf coast it is the "grand-écaille" (great scale), and in Texas the "savanilla." It is edible, though not especially prized as an article of food.

Within a few years the tarpon has become famous among sportsmen as a game-fish, owing to its great beauty, strength, and endurance, and the extreme difficulty of capturing of an empty keg attached to the line, which may retard or even stop the fish after a while." With the aid of such a drag the fish may be harpooned. Such was the usual method of capture until within a few years, and similar methods are still followed for purposes of trade, for the tarpon makes light of any net or snare, leaping over or breaking through, as may best suit his convenience.

It has been demonstrated by skillful sportsmen that the tarpon can be taken with the tackle used for bass, but successful captures are still so rare that they are regarded as evidence of great skill. At Charlotte Harbor, according to "Forest and Stream," 78 tarpon were taken during the winter of 1886–'87. The writer, who signs himself "Al Fresco," recommends a stout two-joint split-bamboo, lancewood, or greenheart rod, from seven to eight feet six inches in length, and a strong reel to carry 600 feet of 15, 18, or 21 thread Cuttyhunk line. For hooks 10-0 O'Shaughnessy or 13-0 Limerick, and for snoods heavy cotton or silk or jointed piano-wire. The bait is usually mullet or some common fish. The tarpon season may be said to last all winter in Florida, though it is best toward spring. It is the habit of the fish when struck to make a rapid rush of 50 or 60 yards, and then leap from the water, opening his immense mouth and gills to their widest extent, and shaking himself with such violent contortions that the hook is often torn out, and he swims away, none the worse for his adventure and probably none the wiser. By experienced fishermen the tarpon is regarded as a far more difficult antagonist than the salmon, and he must no doubt take rank as the king of American game-fishes. Very little has as yet been published about the tarpon outside of the bare scientific details, or in the letters of newspaper correspondents, but the time is no doubt at hand when sportsmen will come from across the sea to test their skill against his strength and endurance.

TAYLOR, BENJAMIN FRANKLIN, an American author, born in Lowville, N. Y., July 19, 1819; died in Cleveland, O., Feb. 24, 1887. He was graduated at Madison University, Hamilton, N. Y., of which his father, Stephen W. Taylor, was president, in 1839, and at the age of twenty-one he became literary editor of the Chicago "Evening Journal," and subsequently its war correspondent. He also appeared frequently before literary associations and the general public as a lecturer. Among his published writings are "Attractions of Language" (New

BENJAMIN FRANKLIN TAYLOR.

York, 1845); "January and June" (Chicago, 1853); "Pictures in Camp and Field" (1871); "The World on Wheels" (1873); "Old-Time Pictures and Sheaves of Rhyme" (1874); "Songs of Yesterday" (1877); "Summer Savory, Gleaned from Rural Nooks" (1879); "Between the Gates," pictures of California life (1881); "Dulce Domum, the Burden of Song" (1884); and a complete collected edition of his poems (1887). Shortly before his

death he delivered to his publishers the manuscript of his first novel, entitled "Theophilus Trent." Much of Mr. Taylor's prose is very fine. Although his fancy was exuberant and untrained, it was also picturesque, sympathetic, and earnest. The London "Times" called him the Oliver Goldsmith of America. His letters from the seat of war were among the most vivid and notable that filled the newspapers at that tragic period. His "Battle above the Clouds," a description of the engagement on Lookout mountain in November, 1863, was especially famous. Like his prose, Mr. Taylor's verse is somewhat embarrassed by conceits and cadenced syllables, but he has left a few poems that pass from one anthology to another, and constantly find their way into scrap-books and newspaper corners. Among these are notably "The Isle of the Long Ago," which begins—

"Oh! a wonderful stream is the river Time,
   As it flows through the realm of Tears,"

"Rhymes of the River," of which the opening is—

"Oh river, far flowing,
   How broad thou art growing,
And the sentinel headlands wait grimly for thee,"

and "The Old Village Choir." A fine specimen of Mr. Taylor's work, both as to conception and style, is found in a fragment entitled "The Northern Lights":

"To claim the Arctic came the sun,
   With banners of the burning zone;
Unrolled upon their airy spars,
   They froze beneath the light of stars;
And there they float, those streamers old,
   Those Northern Lights, for ever cold!"

Personally, Mr. Taylor was genial and responsive, but he was so sensitive and shrinking that he invented methods to avoid meeting strangers, and to account for his late appearances before and sudden disappearances after his lectures. To the chairman who was to introduce him, he would say: "Do it quickly! I would rather chop a cord of wood than sit here five minutes." In his later years Mr. Taylor traveled extensively in California, Mexico, and the islands of the Pacific. The University of California gave him the degree of LL. D.

TENNESSEE. State Government.—The following were the State officers during the year: Governor, Robert L. Taylor, Democrat; Secretary of State, John Allison; Treasurer and Insurance Commissioner, J. W. Thomas; Comptroller, P. P. Pickard; Attorney-General, B. J. Lea; Superintendent of Public Instruction, T. H. Paine, succeeded by Frank M. Smith; Commissioner of Agriculture, Statistics, and Mines, A. J. McWhirter, succeeded by B. M. Hord; Chief-Justice of the Supreme Court, Peter Turney; Associate Justices, W. C. Tolkes, W. C. Caldwell, B. L. Snodgrass, and W. H. Lurton.

Legislative Session.—The session of this year extended from January 3 to March 29. On

January 18 Hon. Washington C. Whitthorne, who was then holding under appointment from the Governor, was elected United States Senator for the term ending March 3. The choice of his successor for the next full term of six years also devolved upon this Legislature, and was the cause of a prolonged contest in the Democratic caucus. Sixty-eight ballots were taken, on the last of which ex-Governor William B. Bate received 78 votes, all but 5 of the votes cast. Before this result had been reached, five joint ballots had been taken in the Legislature without a choice. On the sixth ballot Bate received 81 votes, and Archibald M. Hughes (Republican) 45. Two important results of the session were a new law regulating the assessment and collection of revenue, and a resolution in favor of the prohibitory constitutional amendment as passed by the Legislature of 1885. The revenue act seeks to secure a more equitable valuation of property, more complete assessment, and more efficient collection of taxes. Coupled with it, an act was passed raising the State tax to forty-five cents, and revising the system of special taxes. Specific appropriations were made for the completion of the West Tennessee Insane Hospital ($150,000) and the completion and equipment of a similar hospital in East Tennessee ($50,000). Other acts of the session were as follow:

To enable counties, cities, and towns to subscribe to the capital stock of any railroad company incorporated under the laws of the State.

To punish false pretenses in obtaining the registration of cattle and other animals, and to punish giving false pedigrees.

To prevent the adulteration of candy.

Increasing the pension granted to disabled Confederate soldiers and to disabled Federal soldiers, not pensioned by the Federal Government, from ten to twenty-five dollars a month, and extending the act to those who have lost both arms or both legs in the service.

To permit parties defendant in criminal causes to testify in their own behalf.

To provide a more just and equitable mechanics' lien law.

To relieve druggists of all taxes that have accrued against them as liquor-dealers under the revenue laws of 1881-'82, 1883-'84, and 1885-'86.

To create a board of public works for the city of Chattanooga.

Authorizing the funding of coupons that have been detached from State bonds, and not heretofore funded.

For the protection of fish between March 15 and June 1.

Making it unlawful for any firm, corporation, or other employer who owns or controls a store for the sale of general merchandise to force or attempt to force employés to trade at such store.

To organize the militia of the State, and to provide for its government.

Accepting the gift to the State of the Randall-Cole Industrial School, and organizing it as the Tennessee Industrial School.

Making it unlawful to sell intoxicating liquors within four miles of any school-house outside of an incorporated town.

Giving land-owners a lien on the crops raised on their land by share-croppers, for supplies, implements, and work-stock.

Providing for the observance of "Arbor Day" by the public schools.

Taxing and regulating the business of mutual or assessment insurance.

Authorizing cities of over 32,000 inhabitants to issue bonds for water-works.

To permit the consolidation of non-competing railroad lines.

Prohibiting corporations from influencing the votes or dictating the place for trading of their employés.

Incorporating the town of Newburn.

To establish a uniform standard of weights and measures in the State.

Allowing guardians to loan money of their wards on real estate.

Providing for the appointment of a State mine inspector.

Finances.—At the beginning of the year the treasury statement showed a considerable deficit; at its close there was a cash balance of $225,752.81. For the last three months of the year the receipts were $448,101.87, and the expenditures $230,602.03. In 1887 the increase in assessed values over 1886 was $14,640,402.

Industrial School.—The Tennessee Industrial School for Boys at Nashville, founded by private enterprise and given to the State, was first opened for the reception of pupils at the beginning of the year. Fifty-two boys were admitted during the year, of whom forty-three remained at its close. Of these, thirty-five were white and eight colored. The expense of constructing and furnishing the institution was over $18,000.

Peanuts.—The entire commercial supply of peanuts for the country comes from Virginia and Tennessee, with small exports from North Carolina. The Virginia crop for this year is estimated at 1,800,000 bushels, and the Tennessee production at 750,000 bushels. For the past two years there has been a gradual decrease in the Tennessee production, while that of Virginia shows a considerable increase.

Coal and Iron.—The estimated production of coal in the State for the year was 2,000,000 tons, and of pig-iron, 250,344 tons.

Election.—The prohibitory constitutional amendment, having been adopted by two successive Legislatures, was submitted to the people for ratification in August. Out of a total vote of 252,701, which is nearly equal to the presidential vote of 1884, the friends of prohibition polled 117,504 votes, and its opponents 145,197 against the amendment.

TEXAS. State Government.—The following were the State officers during the year: Governor, Lawrence S. Ross, Democrat; Lieutenant-Governor, T. B. Wheeler; Secretary of State, J. W. Baines, succeeded by J. M. Moore; Comptroller, John D. McCall; Treasurer, Frank R. Lubbock; Attorney-General, James S. Hogg; Superintendent of Public Instruction, Oscar H. Cooper; Commissioner of the Land Office, R. M. Hall; Chief-Justice of the Supreme Court, Asa H. Willie; Associate Justices, John W. Stayton and R. R. Gaines.

Legislative Session.—The Legislature met January 11, and was in session three months. Its early days were occupied with a contest for the seat held by United States Senator Samuel B.

Maxey. As both houses were almost unanimously Democratic, the contest, which continued through thirty joint ballots, was entirely between Democratic leaders. The principal candidates were Senator Maxey, Congressman John H. Reagan, and Judge Ireland. On the last ballot February 1, Reagan was elected by a vote of 101 to 25 for Maxey and 10 scattering. The legislation of the session includes the following acts:

To create the county of Brewster.

Repealing the law of March, 1881, granting to veterans certificates of 1,280 acres of land in the State.

Increasing the punishment for carrying concealed weapons.

Creating six new counties out of Tom Green County, viz., Ector, Winkler, Loving, Upton, Crane, and Ward.

To prohibit and punish dealing in futures.

Making it a penal offense to prevent or attempt to prevent any person from engaging or continuing in any lawful employment.

Punishing abuse and profanity toward another, and abuse of his relatives in his presence.

Making the conversion of property by borrowers or bailees punishable as theft.

Requiring railroad companies to give their employés thirty days' notice of a reduction of wages.

To provide a more expeditious method of ascertaining the results of elections.

Prohibiting the taking of fish by use of poisons or explosives.

To create the county of Mills.

To provide for the sale of all lands set apart and surveyed for the benefit of the public schools, the University, and the several asylums, and the lease of such lands and of the public lands of the State, and to prevent the unlawful occupation and inclosure of the same. [A new land law].

Authorizing the formation of corporations to construct, own, and operate deep-water channels and docks.

To create the counties of Sutton and Schleicher from the county of Crockett.

To create a bureau of agriculture.

To regulate the time and manner of taking and catching fish, oysters, crabs, and shrimp within the bays and tributaries of the State up to tide-water, and in the waters of the Gulf of Mexico.

To protect live-stock by offering a bounty for the destruction of wolves, panthers, Mexican lions, tigers, leopards, and wildcats.

Accepting the act of Congress providing for agricultural experiment stations.

Requiring all railroads to furnish reasonable and equal facilities to all express companies.

Requiring foreign corporations to file their articles of incorporation with the Secretary of State, and imposing certain conditions on such corporations.

To create the counties of Buchel, Foley, and Jeff Davis out of the county of Presidio.

Increasing the penalty for bigamy.

Authorizing cities and towns to levy and collect taxes for the construction or purchase of public buildings, water-works, sewers, streets, and other permanent improvements, and to issue bonds therefor.

Authorizing wills and testaments that have been probated in other States and Territories to be recorded as muniments of title to real property in this State.

Authorizing cities and towns to compromise existing indebtedness.

To provide for the sale of such appropriated public lands in the organized counties of the State as contain not more than 640 acres.

To punish the keeping of "opium-joints."

Making it an offense to detain or prevent the running of railroad trains by force, threats, or intimidation of any kind.

Punishing persons who divulge the secrets of grand juries.

Requiring railroads to furnish a sufficient number of cars for the shipment of freight upon the application of any person therefor.

To create the county of Glascock out of Tom Green County.

Authorizing incorporated cities and towns to hire out their convicts.

Providing a penalty for the attempted consolidation of parallel or competing lines of railroad.

Provision was made for the creation of a commission of appeals, consisting of three persons, to which the Supreme Court might refer cases brought before it. The Governor appointed as members of the commission under this act Walter Acker, W. E. Collard, and Richard Maltby.

Three new public institutions were established—a house of correction and reformatory for youthful convicts, to cost $50,000; an asylum for indigent orphans, to cost $7,500; and a deaf, dumb, and blind asylum for colored youth, to cost $50,000. These were in process of construction at the close of the year. For the sufferers by the great drouth of 1886 the sum of $100,000 was appropriated, which was distributed among 28,750 persons living in 37 different counties. The school laws were amended so as to create the office of county superintendent of schools, and otherwise to render school management more efficient. A more stringent law for the enforcement of prohibition in places under a prohibitory régime was also adopted.

Finances.—The annual report of the Comptroller for the fiscal year ending August 31 shows that the annual revenue exceeded the expenditures by $325,507.44, leaving a balance of $888,970.44 in the treasury at the close of the period. This balance had increased to $1,210,596 on December 31, and will probably reach $1,500,000 before the meeting of the next Legislature. No change has been made in the bonded debt, which remains at $4,237,780. The school fund and other special funds hold the greater part of this, only $1,245,831 being beyond State and county control.

Education.—According to the school census for the year ending August 31, the total school population was 508,041, an increase of 44,489 over 1886. Of this number 85,484 were in cities and towns having special school districts. There was apportioned out of the school fund during the year $2,326,526.25, or nearly $4.70 for each child of school age. This apportionment being greater than the actual revenues of the school fund during the year, a deficit of $228,000 was found at the end of the period. The State University at the close of the year contained 256 students.

Charities.—There were 155 pupils at the State Deaf and Dumb Asylum at Austin during the fiscal year, and 131 at its close. The annual expenses were $27,548. The Institution for the Blind at the same place contained over 100 pupils for the year. At the Austin Lunatic Asylum 691 patients were cared for during the year, 556 remaining at the end. The Terrell Lunatic Asylum contained 601 patients during the year, and 872 at its close.

Penitentiary.—There were at the Penitentiary and the various convict camps of the State, 3,033 prisoners on December 31. A part of these were leased to individuals, a part employed on State plantations in raising cotton and sugar-cane, others were engaged in brick-making, and the remainder worked within the walls of the prisons at Huntsville and Rusk.

Constitutional Amendments.—Six amendments to the Constitution, proposed by the Legislature in March, were submitted to the people at an election held on the first Thursday in August. The first and most important of these provided that "the manufacture, sale, and exchange of intoxicating liquors, except for medical, mechanical, sacramental, and scientific purposes," should be prohibited in the State. An aggressive campaign was made by the friends of this measure, but it was defeated by a vote of 129,270 yeas to 220,627 nays. The other five amendments proposed an increase in the pay of members of the Legislature, an enlargement of the list of securities in which the University fund may be invested, a provision by which the Legislature should regulate the assessment of taxes in unorganized counties, a repeal of the provision forbidding the registration of voters, and a reorganization of the judicial system, which should include an increase in the number of Supreme Court judges. All of these amendments were defeated by majorities varying from 60,000 to nearly 150,000, that increasing the pay of legislators being most unpopular.

Greer County.—Jurisdiction over this territory, which lies between the North and Prairie Dog forks of the Red River, has long been a subject of dispute between the State and the United States, the difficulty arising out of some doubt as to which fork of the river was intended to be the boundary between it and Indian Territory. As early as 1860 the State gave the name of Greer County to the region, and it has since exercised numerous acts of jurisdiction over it, chiefly for judicial purposes. Three years ago it was surveyed by State officials, a county organization perfected, and locations of veteran land-scrip made within it by the State. These locations have, however, been adjudged invalid by the State Supreme Court. For several years negotiations have been in progress looking toward a settlement of the question, and a boundary commission created by Congress has passed upon the conflicting claims. The majority of the commission, in their report to Congress, reject the claims of Texas, while the Texas members of the commission report favorably for their own State. The matter awaits the decision of Congress, but meanwhile a complication has arisen by the action of the State Land Commissioner, who, upon the ad-vice of Attorney-General Hogg, announced in the latter part of the year that the Greer County lands were open for sale by the State on the same terms as other State land. This was met by a proclamation of the President, issued on Jan. 3, 1888, forbidding any exercise of authority by the State over this region, and claiming it, in accordance with the majority report of the commission, as a part of Indian Territory.

Political.—In April an election was held in the Second Congressional District, to choose a successor to John H. Reagan, Senator-elect. Hon. William H. Martin, the only candidate, was elected.

TREATY-MAKING POWER OF THE UNITED STATES. This was the subject of an important opinion rendered by the United States Supreme Court. What are the scope of and limitations on the authority vested by the Constitution in the President and Senate? what are the powers of Congress or the prerogative of the House of Representatives? what is the effect of a treaty or an act of Congress when the two are in conflict? are questions which have been periodically discussed since the foundation of the Government. The provisions in the Federal Constitution bearing directly and indirectly on the treaty-making power are as follow:

He [the President] shall have power, by and with the advice and consent of the Senate, to make treaties, provided two thirds of the Senators present concur. Art. II, sec. 2, cl. 2.

No State shall enter into any treaty, alliance, or confederation. Art. I, sec. 10, cl. 1.

This Constitution, and the laws of the United States which shall be made in pursuance thereof, and all treaties made, or which shall be made, under the authority of the United States, shall be the supreme law of the land; and the judges in every State shall be bound thereby, anything in the Constitution or laws of any State to the contrary, notwithstanding. Art. VI, cl. 2.

The judicial power shall extend to all cases in law and equity arising under this Constitution, the laws of the United States, and treaties made, or which shall be made, under their authority. Art. III, sec. 2, cl. 1.

The Congress shall have power: To regulate commerce with foreign nations, and among the several States, and with the Indian tribes. Art. I, sec. 8, cl. 3.

All bills for raising revenue shall originate in the House of Representatives; but the Senate may propose or concur with amendments as on other bills. Art. I, sec. 7, cl. 1.

The powers not delegated to the United States by the Constitution, nor prohibited by it to the States, are reserved to the States respectively, or to the people. Amendment X.

The scope of the treaty-making power as compared with the legislative power of the Government, and the effect of treaties as compared with acts of Congress, are not defined by the Constitution, but they have been considered in numerous cases by the Federal courts and with no diversity in the decisions. As early as 1829, Chief Justice Marshall, delivering the opinion of the United States Supreme Court, in Foster vs. Neilson (2 Peters's Reports, 314), thus expounded the law:

A treaty is in its nature a contract between two nations, not a legislative act. It does not generally effect, of itself, the object to be accomplished, especially so far as its operation is infra-territorial, but is carried into execution by the sovereign power of the respective parties to the instrument. In the United States a different principle is established. Our Constitution declares a treaty to be the supreme law of the land. It is, consequently, to be regarded in courts of justice as equivalent to an act of the Legislature, whenever it operates of itself, without the aid of any legislative provision. But when the terms of the stipulation import a contract, when either of the parties engages to perform a particular act, the treaty addresses itself to the political, not the judicial department: and the Legislature must execute the contract before it can become a rule for the court.

In Taylor *vs.* Morton (2 Curtis's Reports, 454), heard by the United States Circuit Court in Massachusetts, in 1855, it was decided that the duty on Russian hemp was to be determined by the Tariff Act of 1842, and not by the Russian treaty of 1832. Justice Curtis held that the act of Congress was to rule, because it was the later expression of the legislative will. He said:

The foreign sovereign between whom and the United States a treaty has been made has a right to expect and require its stipulations to be kept with scrupulous good faith; but through what internal arrangements this shall be done is exclusively for the consideration of the United States. Whether the treaty shall itself be the rule of action of the people as well as the Government, whether the power to enforce and apply it shall reside in one department or another neither the treaty itself nor any implication drawn from it gives him any right to inquire. If the people of the United States were to repeal so much of their Constitution as makes treaties part of their municipal law, no foreign sovereign with whom a treaty exists could justly complain, for it is not a matter with which he has any concern. . . .

The second section of the fourth article of the Constitution is: "This Constitution and the laws of the United States, which shall be made in pursuance thereof, and all treaties made, or which shall be made, under the authority of the United States, shall be the supreme law of the land." There is nothing in the language of this clause which enables us to say that in the case supposed, the treaty, and not the act of Congress, is to afford the rule. Ordinarily treaties are not rules prescribed by sovereigns for the conduct of their subjects, but contracts, by which they agree to regulate their own conduct. This provision of our Constitution has made treaties part of our municipal law. But it has not assigned to them any particular degree of authority in our municipal law, nor declared whether laws so enacted shall or shall not be paramount to laws otherwise enacted. No such declaration is made even in respect to the Constitution itself. It is named in conjunction with treaties and acts of Congress, as one of the supreme laws, but no supremacy is in terms assigned to one over the other.

In 1861 Congress imposed a duty of forty dollars a ton on Russian hemp. It was contended that under a prior treaty with Russia no higher duty than twenty-five dollars a ton could be exacted. The United States District Court in New York held in 1871 that the act of Congress superseded the treaty. (Ropes *vs.* Clinch, 8 Blatchford's "Reports," 304.) In the case of Bartram *vs.* Robertson. (15 "Federal Reporter," 212) the United States Circuit Court for the Southern District of New York held in 1883 that the duty on Danish sugar imported

into the United States was to be determined by the acts of Congress of 1870 and 1875, and not by the treaty made with Denmark in 1870. "That Congress," said Judge Wallace, "had the power to annul this treaty, so far as it might have validity as a rule of municipal law, is not disputed. Both treaties and acts of Congress are, under the Constitution, the supreme law of the land, and each are of equal authority within the sphere of the constitutional power of the respective departments of the Government by which they are adopted; therefore, the treaty or the act of Congress is paramount, according as it is the latest expression of the will of the law-making power." Similar views were expressed by Justice Field in the opinion of the United States Circuit Court in California in the case of Ah Lung (18 Federal Reporter, 28) decided September 24, 1883. The question had reference to an alleged conflict between the Chinese exclusion law passed by Congress and the treaty with China. Justice Field said:

A treaty is in its nature a contract between two nations, and by writers on public law is generally so treated, and not as having of itself the force of a legislative act. The Constitution of the United States, however, places both treaties and laws made in pursuance thereof in the same category, and declares them to be the supreme law of the land. It does not give to either a paramount authority over the other. So far as a treaty operates by its own force, without legislation, it is to be regarded by the courts as equivalent to a legislative act, but nothing further. If the subject to which it relates be one upon which Congress can also act, that body may modify its provisions or supersede them entirely. The immigration of foreigners to the United States, and the conditions upon which they shall be permitted to remain, are appropriate subjects of legislation as well as of treaty stipulation. No treaty can deprive Congress of its power in that respect. As said by Mr. Justice Curtis, in the case of Taylor *vs.* Morton: "Inasmuch as treaties must continue to operate as part of our municipal law, and be obeyed by the people, applied by the judiciary, and executed by the President, while they continue unrepealed; and inasmuch as the power of repealing these municipal laws must reside somewhere, and nobody other than Congress possesses it, then legislative power is applicable to such laws whenever they relate to subjects which the Constitution has placed under that legislative power." (2 Curtis's Circuit Court Reports, 459). An act of Congress, then, upon a subject within its legislative power, is as binding upon the courts as a treaty upon the same subject. Both are binding, except as the later one conflicts or interferes with the former. If the nation with whom we have made the treaty objects to the action of the legislative department, it may present its complaint to the executive department, and take such other measures as it may deem that justice to its own citizens or subjects requires. The courts can not heed such complaint, nor refuse to give effect to a law of Congress, however much it may seem to conflict with the stipulations of the treaty. Whether a treaty has been violated by our legislation, so as to be the proper occasion of complaint by the foreign government, is not a judicial question. To the courts it is simply the case of conflicting laws, the last modifying or superseding the earlier.

In the Cherokee Tobacco case (11 Wallace's Reports, 616) the United States Supreme Court in 1870 sustained the power of Congress to tax certain tobacco in the territory of the Cherokee nation in the face of a prior treaty between that nation and the United States, stipulating that such tobacco should be exempt from taxation. Justice Swayne said: "A treaty may supersede a prior act of Congress (Foster *es.* Neilson, 2 Peters's Reports, 314), and an act of Congress may supersede a prior treaty (Taylor *es.* Morton, 2 Curtis's Reports, 454, Clinton Bridge case, 1 Walworth's Reports, 155). In the cases referred to these principles were applied to treaties with foreign nations. Treaties with Indian nations within the jurisdiction of the United States, whatever considerations of humanity and good faith may be involved and require their faithful observance, can not be more obligatory. They have no higher sanctity, and no greater inviolability or immunity from legislative invasion can be claimed for them. The consequences in all such cases give rise to questions which must be met by the political department of the Government. They are beyond the sphere of judicial cognizance." These decisions were cited with approval, and the principles laid down in them were reaffirmed by the United States Supreme Court in the case of Edye *es.* Robertson, decided Dec. 8, 1884. In this case the constitutionality of the Immigration Act of Congress was under consideration. It was contended on one side that the act was in violation of existing treaties with friendly foreign powers. The Court remarked that "we are not satisfied that this act of Congress violates any of these treaties, or any just construction of them," but held that, "so far as the provisions in that act may be found to be in conflict with any treaty with a foreign nation, they must prevail in all the judicial courts of this country." Justice Miller, who delivered the opinion, then expounded the law on this point as follows:

A treaty is primarily a compact between independent nations. It depends for the enforcement of its provisions on the interest and the honor of the governments which are parties to it. If these fail, its infraction becomes the subject of international negotiations and reclamations, so far as the injured party chooses to seek redress, which may in the end be enforced by actual war. It is obvious that with all this the judicial courts have nothing to do, and can give no redress. But a treaty may also contain provisions which confer certain rights upon the citizens or subjects of one of the nations residing in the territorial limits of the other, which partake of the nature of municipal law, and which are capable of enforcement as between private parties in the courts of the country. An illustration of this character is found in treaties which regulate the mutual rights of citizens and subjects of the contracting nations in regard to rights of property by descent or inheritance, when the individuals concerned are aliens. The Constitution of the United States places such provisions as these in the same category as other laws of Congress by its declaration that "this Constitution and the laws made in pursuance thereof, and all treaties made or which shall be made under authority of the United States, shall be the supreme law of the land." A treaty, then, is a law of the land as an act of Congress is, whenever its provisions prescribe a rule by which the rights of the private citizen or subject may be determined. And when such rights are of a nature to be enforced in a court of justice, that court

resorts to the treaty for a rule of decision for the case before it, as it would to a statute.

But even in this aspect of the case there is nothing in this law which makes it irrepealable or unchangeable. The Constitution gives it no superiority over an act of Congress in this respect, which may be repealed or modified by an act of a later date. Nor is there anything in its essential character, or in the branches of the Government by which the treaty is made, which gives it this superior sanctity. A treaty is made by the President and the Senate. Statutes are made by the President, the Senate, and the House of Representatives. The addition of the latter body to the other two in making a law certainly does not render it less entitled to respect in the matter of its repeal or modification than a treaty made by the other two. If there be any difference in this regard, it would seem to be in favor of an act in which all three of the bodies participate. And such is, in fact, the case in a declaration of war, which must be made by Congress, and which, when made, usually suspends or destroys existing treaties between the nations thus at war.

In short, we are of opinion that, so far as a treaty made by the United States with any foreign nation can become the subject of judicial cognizance in the courts of this country, it is subject to such acts as Congress may pass for its enforcement, modification, or repeal.

At the session beginning in October, 1879, the same court rendered an opinion in the case of Hauenstein *es.* Lynham (100 United States Reports. 483) that a treaty giving subjects of a foreign country the right to hold lands in the United States supersedes any State laws in conflict with it. "It must always be borne in mind," said Justice Swayne in the opinion of the Court, "that the Constitution, laws and treaties of the United States are as much a part of the law of every State as its own local laws and constitution. This is a fundamental principle in our system of complex national polity." The same principle was laid down by the Supreme Court as early as 1796—only seven years after the Federal Constitution took effect—in the case of Ware *es.* Hylton, (3 Dallas's Reports 286). The opinion delivered by Judge Chace contains this passage:

A treaty can not be the supreme law of the land, that is of all the United States, if any act of the State Legislature can stand in its way. If the Constitution of a State (which is the fundamental law of the State, and paramount to its Legislature) must give way to a treaty and fall before it, can it be questioned whether the less power, an act of the State Legislature, must not be prostrate? It is the declared will of the people of the United States that every treaty made by the authority of the United States shall be superior to the Constitution and laws of any individual State, and their will alone is to decide. If a law of a State contrary to a treaty is not void but voidable only, by a repeal or nullification by a State Legislature, this certain consequence follows—that the will of a small part of the United States may control or defeat the will of the whole.

From this review it will be seen that from the earliest time to the present both the Supreme and the lower Federal courts have given a uniform construction to the Constitution on the questions that have been brought before them touching the treaty-making power. By these decisions, certain principles may be regarded as settled. The power of the President and Senate to make a treaty of any kind or for any purpose within the scope of the treaty-making power is as independent and absolute as is the power of Congress to legislate within its sphere. A treaty when made is a supreme law of the land, and supersedes any prior act of Congress in conflict with it. An act of Congress is a supreme law of the land, and abrogates any earlier treaty inconsistent with it. Supremacy turns wholly on the question of date. The later does not necessarily supersede the earlier as a whole, but only to the extent of conflict. The courts deal with the question as one of purely municipal law. It is their duty to determine whether a treaty and an act of Congress are inconsistent, and, if so, to declare which is the supreme law. It is a recognized rule that a treaty stipulation should not be annulled by the courts unless a later act of Congress clearly overrides it. "It must appear that the later provision is certainly and clearly in hostility to the former. If by any reasonable construction the two can stand together they must so stand. If harmony is impossible, and only in that event, the former is repealed in part, or wholly, as the case may be." This rule was applied by the United States Supreme Court as recently as December, 1884, when on the point in question it construed the Chinese Exclusion Act in harmony, rather than conflict, with the Chinese treaty. But when it is clear that a later act of Congress is contrary to a treaty stipulation, the courts do not hesitate to declare the former the law of the land. In such case the responsibility for abrogation of the treaty or breach of the national faith rests not upon the judiciary, but the political department of the Government.

A treaty, just as an act of Congress, must conform with the Constitution of the United States. "It need hardly be said," remarked Justice Swayne, of the United States Supreme Court, in the Cherokee Tobacco case (11 Wallace's Reports, 620), "that a treaty can not change the Constitution or be held valid, if it be in violation of that instrument." The subject matter of a treaty must be within the jurisdiction or proper scope of the treaty-making power, just as an act of Congress must be within the constitutional powers of that body. The courts have held, as will be seen by reference to the above review of cases, that a treaty may supersede a State law as well as an act of Congress. But it does not follow from such decisions that a treaty will supersede a State law in a matter that is left by the Constitution to the exclusive jurisdiction of the States. Treaties and acts of Congress are put by the courts on the same footing. Acts of Congress have repeatedly been set aside on the ground of invading State sovereignty. Does not the same principle apply to treaties?

A treaty may be an executed or an executory contract, a completed compact or one requiring legislation to complete it. Some treaties are completed by the action of the treaty-making power, the President and Senate, alone. Such a treaty is a law without the concurring action of Congress or the House of Representatives. It may at any time be nullified by an act of Congress approved by the President or passed over his veto; or it may be abrogated by another treaty made by the President and Senate. But while it remains a law it is like every other supreme law binding upon the general Government, the States, the courts, and the people. Other treaties are dependent for their completion on legislation. Of this kind are treaties requiring an appropriation of money which can be made only by Congress, and, in short, all treaties which by their express terms and conditions are concluded subject to legislative acts to be passed. Such treaties are not recognized as laws by the courts until they are completed by the needed legislation (Foster vs. Neilson, 2 Peters' Reports, 314).

It has long been contended by some public men that the treaty-making power does not extend to matters involving revenue, and that the making of commercial or reciprocity treaties is not within the constitutional scope of the power. This claim is based on the theory that every revenue measure must originate in the House, and that absolute control over commerce is vested by the Constitution in Congress. As recently as January, 1885, Senator Justin S. Morrill, of Vermont, argued in the Senate that "any treaty which encroaches upon the power to regulate commerce, or upon that to originate revenue bills involves a plain, open, and palpable violation of the Constitution." Like objections were raised by certain members of Congress against the Spanish and other commercial treaties negotiated by President Arthur, and laid before Congress at the session beginning in December, 1884. To these objections Secretary Frelinghuysen, in a communication to Hon. John F. Miller, of California, chairman of the Senate Committee on Foreign Relations, dated December, 26, 1884, replied as follows:

Another line of adverse argument remains to be considered. It is said that this class of treaties is an infringement upon the constitutional rights of Congress, in that they change duties prescribed by law. This argument is advanced against all, including the convention with Mexico, which, having been already ratified, awaits legislation to carry it into effect. The claim that the Mexican treaty is unconstitutional because it affects the revenue and did not originate in the House of Representatives is singularly untenable. It did so originate. The first action of this Government toward its negotiation was the appropriation by Congress "for the salaries and expenses of a commission to negotiate a commercial treaty with Mexico, a sum not exceeding $20,000 to be expended under the direction of the President of the United States," [Sundry Civil Appropriation Act, Aug. 7, 1882,] and under this authority Gen. Grant and Mr. Trescot were appointed Commissioners and negotiated the treaty. The Senate introduced an amendment that the legislation of Congress should be necessary to give it force. This rule, the precedent for which is found in previous treaties of this character, has been followed in the subsequent treaty negotiations, and the steps taken thereto have been conducted under the sanction given by Congress to the general policy of fostering intimate trade with the neighboring countries.

I observe that a constitutional amendment has been introduced in Congress that the Senate and House of Representatives shall be joined to the Executive as the treaty-making power. Such amendment would not avoid the necessity of the Executive conducting the negotiations for a treaty, subject, of course, to the ratification of the co-ordinate branch. The prerogative of the House of Representatives has in all these treaties been abundantly secured by a provision that they should not take effect until a bill originating in the House had made the laws affecting the revenue conform thereto. The precedents are against the position that negotiations of this class are unconstitutional. From the foundation of the Government, beginning with the time when the administration was in the hands of the men who framed the Constitution itself, and may, therefore, be assumed to have best understood its import and scope, public treaties affecting the revenues have been concluded by the President and carried into effect by the legislation of Congress without admission of a doubt as to the entire constitutionality of the proceeding. A few examples among many may be cited. First in order comes the treaty of 1794 with Great Britain, which stipulated for commercial privileges and exemptions from duty, and set limitations upon the imposition of tonnage dues on British vessels by Congress. The treaty of 1803 with France for the acquisition of Louisiana stipulated for special favors to French and Spanish goods and vessels in the ceded territory during a term of twelve years, notwithstanding any general regulations as to trade and navigation which Congress might make. The treaty of 1815 with Great Britain, changed existing legislation as to discriminating duties. The treaty of 1831 with France contains special tariff provisions. The Canadian reciprocity treaty with Great Britain of 1854, and the reciprocity treaty of 1875 with the Hawaiian Islands both contained the provision that they should not become operative until the necessary laws to carry them into effect should have been enacted by Congress. In response to all these treaties the required legislation was passed. In short, the precedents are in favor of the constitutional negotiation of treaties affecting the revenues by the President, subject to approval by the Senate and to the legislative co-operation of Congress in carrying out their provision.

These questions do not appear to have been expressly decided by the Supreme or any lower Federal court. The practice has been in framing commercial treaties as explained by Secretary Frelinghuysen in the passage above quoted, to insert in them a stipulation that they were not to take effect until sanctioned by Congress, and hence that they were concluded subject to this condition. Thus the reciprocity convention negotiated with Spain in 1884 contains the following provision in Article XXVI:

This treaty shall be ratified by the President of the United States, by and with the advice and consent of the Senate thereof, and by Spain, in accordance with the law which authorizes its Government to celebrate it; and it shall go into effect thirty days after having been officially published by the two governments by mutual agreement on the same day. The publication shall not be made, however, until after the Congress of the United States shall have passed the laws necessary to carry it into effect, and both governments shall have adopted regulations accordingly, which shall take place within six months from the date of signature.

This sanction has usually been given by Congress to treaties that have become laws, and so the constitutional objection, if any existed,

may be deemed to have been removed. But on the other hand it is maintained that the President and the Senate alone have the power to make a commercial treaty, and that while it may be desirable or expedient to have the concurrent action of Congress, such action is not constitutionally essential when no appropriation of money is needed to carry out the provisions of the treaty.

The treaty-making power, it is maintained, is granted in the most general terms. It is not expressly limited to any class of subjects. It extends to all relations between this and foreign nations, to all matters that usually fall within the province of treaties. In his commentaries on the Constitution Story says: "The power to make treaties is, by the Constitution, general, and of course it embraces all sorts of treaties, for peace or war; for commerce or territory; for alliance or succors; for indemnity for injuries or payment of debts; for the recognition and enforcement of principles of public law; and for any other purposes which the policy or interests of independent sovereigns may dictate in their intercourse with each other" (fourth edition, vol. ii, sec. 1508, p. 825). The same authority further says: "It is difficult to circumscribe the power within any definite limits, applicable to all times and exigencies, without impairing its efficacy or defeating its purposes. The Constitution has therefore made it general and unqualified." (Id., sec. 1,509). When the Constitution was framed, commercial treaties were, and long had been, one of the commonest kinds of international agreements. From this it is argued that if the makers of that instrument had intended not to embrace such treaties within the scope of the power they would have made an express proviso or exception to that effect. The argument that the power is impliedly limited by the grant to Congress of power to regulate commerce was thus met in the Senate by Senator Lapham, of New York, in his reply to Mr. Morrill in January, 1885:

By the same article Congress has power to establish post-roads, and yet by treaty we have postal conventions with many nations, and could not have obtained them in any other way. Congress has the power to give to authors and inventors the exclusive right to their discoveries; yet we have treaties on the subject of trade-marks with most of the nations with whom we have other treaty relations. Congress has power to declare war, but before a gun is fired or any other hostile act performed the treaty-making power may intervene and stop the contest, without bloodshed, by a treaty of peace.

Congress has power to dispose of and make all needful rules and regulations respecting the Territories of the United States. But the treaty-making power may be exercised on the subject, and territory be alienated or acquired, as the best interests of the country may demand. Congress has power to establish a uniform rule of naturalization; still, foreigners resident in the Territories, when acquired, have been declared to be clothed with the rights of citizens. In Alaska the treaty for its cession admitted foreigners to all such rights.

Commercial and reciprocity treaties have been before the Federal courts in numerous cases, and though the question under consideration has never been expressly decided, or raised, the courts do not appear to have doubted the constitutionality of such treaties. A more doubtful question is the one whether the making of a commercial treaty by the President and Senate is an infringement of the constitutional right of the House to originate revenue bills. It may be argued on the one hand that this clause of the Constitution is in the nature of a proviso or limitation to the the treaty-making power. It may be maintained on the other that the grant of the treaty-making power is absolute, and not subject to such proviso. It may be further contended that a commercial treaty which does not materially increase customs duties, or one which lowers or abolishes them, or one which does not seriously affect them, is not, within the meaning of the Constitution, such a "bill for raising revenue" as must originate in the House; that the making of such a treaty does not impose any limitation or check upon the power of the House to raise revenue. This question has not been expressly decided by any Federal court. If the making of a treaty which touches the revenue is a violation of the constitutional right of the House, then legislation is necessary to complete and give effect to the treaty, and the legislation must originate in the House. If such legislation is not constitutionally essential, the President and Senate alone, independently of Congress or the House, may conclude a commercial treaty removing or imposing customs duties, and make the treaty a law which will take effect by its own operation. It will supersede, by its own force, any existing revenue law in conflict with it. Congress may not prevent the making of the treaty nor its going into effect as a law; but it may nullify it by only passing a law overriding it.

It is the opinion of some writers on law that Congress is bound to pass the laws necessary to carry a treaty into effect. (See Kent's "Commentaries," twelfth edition, vol. i, p. 236, and Wheaton's "International Law," § 266, and authorities there cited.) In a note to Wheaton's text, Mr. Dana says: "In the United States, it is settled that Congress is under an obligation to execute all treaties. A refusal by Congress to pass the necessary legislative acts, is a national breach of the treaties, and may be so regarded by the other party." Similar views were held by Washington in his message to the House of Representatives in March, 1796. (See Kent's Commentaries, as cited above; also Story, on the Constitution, vol. ii, §§ 1841, 1842.) Jefferson and Randolph seem to have been of a different opinion. In a letter to William B. Giles under date of December, 1795, Jefferson wrote:

Randolph seems to have hit upon the true theory of our Constitution—that when a treaty is made, involving matters confided by the Constitution to the three branches of the Legislature conjointly, the Representatives are as free as the President and the Senate were to consider whether the national interest requires

or forbids their giving the forms and force of law to the articles over which they have the power.

The doctrine that Congress or the House is bound to give its consent to a treaty has not been sanctioned or favored by the courts. On the contrary, it does not appear to be consistent with the principles they have affirmed and the views they have expressed. While the question has not been directly decided—the opinion given below is on this point an *obiter dictum*—the decisions of the courts on other points have proceeded on the theory that the treaty-making and the legislative powers are coequal and independent within their respective spheres; that it is discretionary with Congress or the House, being a deliberative body, whether it will co-operate with the President and Senate to complete a treaty by providing the legislation necessary to give the treaty effect; and that this is a condition of municipal law of which every foreign nation which makes a treaty with the United States must be presumed to have knowledge. On this point, Justice McLean, in the case of Turner *vs.* the American Baptist Missionary Union, decided in the Michigan Circuit (United States Court) in 1852 and reported in 5 McLean's Reports, said:

A treaty under the Federal Constitution is declared to be the supreme law of the land. This unquestionably applies to all treaties where the treaty-making power, without the aid of Congress, can carry it into effect. It is not, however, and can not be, the supreme law of the land, where the concurrence of Congress is necessary to give it effect. Until this power is exercised, as where the appropriation of money is required, the treaty is not perfect. It is not operative, in the sense of the Constitution, as money can not be appropriated by the treaty-making power. This results from the limitations of our Government. The action of no department of the Government can be regarded as a law until it shall have all the sanctions required by the Constitution to make it such. As well might it be contended that an ordinary act of Congress, without the signature of the President, was a law, as that a treaty which engages to pay a sum of money, is in itself a law. And in such a case the Representatives of the people and the States exercise their own judgments in granting or withholding the money. They act upon their own responsibility, and not upon the responsibility of the treaty-making power. It can not bind or control the legislative action in this respect, and every foreign Government may be presumed to know that so far as the treaty stipulated to pay money the legislative sanction is required.

TREE-PLANTING. The planting of trees has become so general that there are now seventeen States in which a particular day, at the season of the year when trees are just starting into life, is celebrated as Arbor Day. The credit of inventing this day is due to Governor Morton, of Nebraska, who contrived it as a means of raising up a barrier of trees against the fierce blizzards of the West and the scorching blasts of the South. States where trees were once so abundant as to be considered by the agriculturist as worthy only to be cut down and burned—that being the quickest method of getting rid of them—are now welcoming Arbor Day as a promise that they may be restored to that condition which they lost by the destruction of their forests. Thus Michigan, lately a wilderness of forest, and sending even yet annually to market more lumber than any other State, has become sensible of the need of trees for other purposes than to be converted into lumber, and, in 1886, made the experiment of Arbor Day, designated, by a proclamation of Governor Alger, as the 11th of April.

A noticeable and important development of the Arbor Day movement is its connection with the public schools. This may be said to date from the memorable tree-planting by the pupils of the public schools of Cincinnati, on the occasion of the meeting of the American Forestry Congress, in that city, in the spring of 1882. Then, on a lovely May day, more than 20,000 school-children, marshaled by their teachers, formed a part of the grand procession, which, with the accompaniment of military battalions and bands of music, while flags and banners fluttered from the house-tops and windows along the streets, went out to Eden Park, and there planted trees in memory of the most eminent authors and statesmen of our own and other lands. The example set by the schools of Cincinnati was speedily followed elsewhere. Michigan had its Arbor Day on April 11, 1886, but the most recent adoption of the celebration or anniversary was by California, on Nov. 27, 1886. The latter was a popular movement carried out by private munificence and endeavor, and was first suggested by Mr. Joaquin Miller, in the "Golden Era," and pressed by Messrs. Harr Wagner, Adolph Sutro, W. E. Adams, and S. W. Forman. November 27 was a clear, charming day. Thousands of school-children from San Francisco and Oakland were ferried over to Yerba Buena Island, where the principal planting occurred, while the Government steamer, "Gen. McDowell," brought over the committee and invited guests. Numerous private organizations, among which may be mentioned the Oakland Canoe Club, participated in the exercises. Through the liberality of Mr. Adolph Sutro 40,000 young trees were supplied for the occasion. The space chosen for planting at Yerba Buena Island was marked out in the shape of a Greek cross, the longer part 300 feet long by 80 feet wide, and the transverse part, 150 feet long by 30 feet wide, lying toward the south, on the hill-slope, its foot touching the waters of the bay, its head reaching the crown of the island, and its arms extending east and west. The trees selected for the occasion were the marine pine (*Pinus maritimus*), the Monterey cypress, and the eucalyptus, with the *Acacia latifolia* or *Lophanta malva* for protection. At the Presidio Reservation many thousands of trees were planted, principally along the roadway leading up the hill to Cemetery Avenue. Holes and trenches had been previously dug along the side of this road, and the labor of planting was thus greatly reduced. At Fort Mason over 12,000 trees were planted.

Considerable interesting literature on the subject of tree-planting has been published by the Forestry Division of the Department of Agriculture at Washington, including a series of reports on forestry, embodying the results of much investigation and experiment, and the Bureau of Education, Department of the Interior, has also published information about the planting of trees in school-grounds and by school-children, suggestions as to the manner of celebrating the day of planting, and a collection of extracts, from the poets and prose-writers, suitable for declamation at the celebration. The United States are but just beginning to recognize the importance of protecting their forests; but, as yet, there is no accepted standard by which to determine what shall be classed as forest land, how abundant the trees must be, or in what proximity to each other, in order to bring them within the classification of forest in distinction from waste, or pasture land. The following table, compiled from the State and national records, is, therefore, not minutely accurate, but it is more closely approximate to a correct representation of our forest-area than any which have been given in the past:

STATES AND TERRITORIES.	Total land-area in acres.	Forest-area in acres.	Farm-area in acres.	Percentage of forest to total area.
Alabama	32,985,600	17,500,000	6,500,000	58·1
Arizona	72,268,800	10,000,000	100,000	18·8
Arkansas	33,948,800	20,000,000	4,000,000	58·9
California	99,827,200	20,000,000	11,000,000	20·0
Colorado	66,882,800	10,000,000	700,000	15·1
Connecticut	3,100,600	650,000	1,700,000	21·0
Dakota	94,528,000	3,000,000	3,700,000	3·2
Delaware	1,254,400	300,000	800,000	28·9
Florida	34,718,600	90,000,000	1,500,000	57·6
Georgia	37,747,200	18,000,000	6,500,000	47·7
Idaho	53,945,600	10,000,000	200,000	18·5
Illinois	35,840,000	3,500,000	26,500,000	9·8
Indiana	22,982,400	4,500,000	14,000,000	19·6
Iowa	35,504,000	2,800,000	20,000,000	12·7
Kansas	52,288,000	3,500,000	11,000,000	6·7
Kentucky	25,600,000	12,800,000	11,000,000	50·0
Louisiana	29,068,800	13,000,000	3,000,000	44·6
Maine	19,132,800	12,000,000	8,500,000	62·7
Maryland	6,810,400	2,000,000	8,400,000	31·7
Massachusetts	5,145,600	1,000,000	2,200,000	19·6
Michigan	36,755,200	14,000,000	7,500,000	38·1
Minnesota	50,591,200	30,000,000	7,800,000	59·8
Mississippi	29,657,600	13,000,000	5,800,000	44·0
Missouri	43,990,400	16,000,000	17,000,000	36·4
Montana	92,993,400	25,000,000	1,400,000	26·9
Nebraska	48,758,600	1,500,000	6,000,000	3·1
Nevada	70,283,600	2,000,000	500,000	2·8
New H'mpshire	5,763,200	3,000,000	3,250,000	52·0
New Jersey	4,771,200	2,330,000	2,100,000	48·8
New Mexico	78,374,400	8,000,000	300,000	10·2
New York	30,476,800	8,000,000	18,000,000	26·2
North Carolina	31,091,200	18,000,000	7,000,000	57·9
Ohio	26,046,400	4,500,000	18,300,000	17·3
Oregon	60,518,400	20,000,000	3,000,000	33·0
Pennsylvania	28,790,400	7,000,000	18,500,000	24·3
Rhode Island	694,400	200,000	300,000	28·8
South Carolina	19,305,800	9,000,000	4,500,000	46·6
Tennessee	26,720,000	11,000,000	8,500,000	41·2
Texas	167,565,600	40,000,000	13,000,000	23·2
Utah	52,501,600	4,000,000	500,000	7·6
Vermont	5,846,400	1,900,000	3,800,000	32·5
Virginia	25,680,000	13,000,000	9,000,000	50·6
Washington	42,808,200	20,000,000	500,000	44·8
West Virginia	15,772,800	9,000,000	4,000,000	57·0
Wisconsin	34,545,000	17,000,000	10,000,000	48·8
Wyoming	62,448,000	7,800,000	100,000	10·9
United States	1,856,070,400	489,280,000	284,780,000	26·4

The yearly demand for railroad ties is one of the principal causes of the deforesting of the country. It has been estimated that there is annually required for this one purpose alone the available timber on 565,714 acres, and that, allowing that a growth of 30 years is requisite to produce trees of proper dimensions for ties, it would require 16,971,420 acres of woodland to be held as a sort of railroad reserve to supply the annual demands of the existing roads, to say nothing of those not yet built. This is between three and four per cent. of the woodland of the United States, exclusive of Alaska. In view of the importance of this question, several of the large land-grant railroad companies have, on tracts of land specially adapted for the purpose, planted trees in sufficient quantities to supply the future needs of the railroad. The Kansas City, Fort Scott, and Gulf Railroad has already nearly 700 acres of finely growing timber, 2,000 trees to the acre, as the result of its forethought.

It would not be proper to dismiss this subject without calling attention to the production of maple-trees in the States of Ohio and Vermont. The former produces annually about 591,432 gallons of maple sirup, and 1,807,701 pounds of sugar, valued at $617,762; while Vermont annually produces sugar and sirup at the rate of about 36 pounds for each of her inhabitants, or a total production of more than 12,000,000 pounds per year. The census of 1880 showed that the annual value of the products of industries using wood or other forest products entirely was $469,073,165; and that the value of the materials from which such products were made was $233,983,030.

TURF, TEN YEARS' RECORD OF THE. No decade in the history of horse-racing, in this or any other country, has witnessed such a remarkable growth as that, which has taken place in the United States during the past ten years. New driving associations have been organized all over the country, new race-tracks have been opened near almost every important city. The number of horses in training has doubled, tripled, quadrupled. New breeding-farms have been established and stocked, and the prices of thoroughbred yearlings have greatly increased. The number of races has been augmented from year to year, until now, from April to November each season, they are held on at least three days in each week and during a considerable portion of the time, every day in the week, with no breathing-spell except on Sunday, and the attendance has grown from year to year as the interest in the sport has increased and intensified. This growth had begun in 1876 with a slight recovery from the set-back due to the financial panic of 1873 and the subsequent business depression, but in the succeeding five years it went on with accelerating speed, especially in the Northern States, where horse-racing had not attained as much popularity as in the South, before the civil war. Prior to 1881

the Monmouth Park Association, having passed under the control of some of the most honored gentlemen connected with the turf, so improved its course and so added to the attractions of its programmes as to collect crowds, such as had not been seen at a race-track for ten years before. The American Jockey Club was roused to new life and activity, and its meetings were made more interesting and important. Some of its most prominent members resolved on forming a new association, which should give races at the seaside, at a time when the heat made Jerome Park a place to be shunned rather than sought. The Coney Island Jockey Club, with its really admirable grounds, was the result. Unfortunately, the management of the races there have of late fallen into disrepute, a belief having gotten abroad that the races are not always honestly contested, but are won or lost to suit the purposes of book-makers, who themselves own horses and make books upon races in which their own horses contend. At St. Louis, at Chicago, at Cincinnati, and other Western cities, as well as in the East, at Hartford and Boston, the racing-meetings became more successful than ever before. At Saratoga, in 1881, and since, races have been given week after week with only Sundays intervening, with no apparent flagging of interest. It used to be thought that no first-class race-horse could be bred in this country at any great distance from the blue-grass of Kentucky. The theory has been that the best stock follows the limestone formation; and it is a theory that has not been disproved. For the glories of the Southern turf have by no means departed. At Louisville, the racing is still of the highest order, and Lexington and Nashville keep up the old traditions. Kentucky still brings forth her annual brood of sons and daughters of sires famous on both sides of the Atlantic. But it is no longer necessary, as it once was, to go to the blue-grass region to see a great breeding-farm. Chestnut Hill, Rancocas, Meadowbrook, and Westbrook have compared well, during the past five years, with the best the South can show, while, for completeness and perfection of appointment, for care and thoroughness of management, and for high character of racing, even Louisville is equaled by Jerome Park, Gravesend, Monmouth, and Saratoga. The increased interest in breeding is shown by the organization in almost every State where thoroughbreds are raised at all, of breeders' associations and by the large attendance upon their meetings. Within the last year or two racing has been carried to such an extent as actually to alarm the more judicious devotees of the turf. Great as has been the increase in the number of horses in training, it has not been sufficient to supply the demand, and the natural consequence has been that the horses actually on the turf have been called upon for much more work than they could safely perform. Many have been broken down when they ought to have been in their prime, or worn and jaded, have given very inferior exhibitions of speed. The prices of race-horses have also been unduly inflated. The prevalence of gambling in some of its worst forms, at many of the parks, and the too intimate connection of book-makers with the management of races, is another cause of anxiety among judicious turfmen, some of whom look for a disastrous revulsion in the near future.

Trotting.—The trotting-horse of to-day is distinctively the product of American breeding, and the speed of those now on the turf of the United States, or which have made the best records, can not be approached by the animals of any other country. " It has been attained," to quote from Hiram Woodruff's book, "by our method of breeding, training, and driving trotting-horses, aided by the enterprise and ingenuity which provide vehicles, harness, and all the paraphernalia of that combination of lightness with strength which is modeled upon the plan of the best trotting-horse himself. The high-bred American trotter differs in many important respects from the English thoroughbred. He is not as finely drawn out and whalebone-like as the latter, and, to use a turf expression, he does not "stand over as much ground." He has a more compact and stocky build, more sloping pasterns, and a shorter and wider neck through which the full, deep chest is supplied with an ample amount of air. By some it is thought that there is still dead weight forward which will be bred off in generations to come. The American trotter has a fine, intelligent face, wide between the eyes, rather low withers, powerful hind-quarters, and especially powerful hocks, the initial points from which his great bursts of speed proceed. Given a horse with such a structure, and if he is low-going, gets a long reach with his hind-legs by overlapping those in front, which should play between, he may be set down as fast, possibly great. The English thoroughbred Messenger was the progenitor of the best trotters the world has ever seen. The wonderful stock of the blue-grass region of Kentucky are his descendants through his son Mambrino, his two best grandsons, Mambrino Chief and Rysdyk's Hambletonian, and Alexander's Abdallah, another descendant. Mambrino Chief, sire. among others, of Lady Thorne, was the sire of a remarkable family of mothers of trotters. At his death there were of his descendants in the direct male line seventy-four trotters with records of 2.30 or better. Among Alexander's Abdallah's descendants at his death were thirty-nine trotters with records of 2.30 or better, one being Goldsmith Maid, whose record was 2.14. Nearly all the trotters that have made records of 2.30 or better belong to this family, and, in the last few years their number has increased with remarkable rapidity. As the test of speed is increased, a larger and larger proportion are found to be descendants of Rysdyk's Hambletonian. The trotter and the

runner require an entirely different system of education and training. The latter is put upon the turf at a much earlier age than the former, and generally retires when the trotter would be winning his first victories, or at most would no more than have attained his maximum speed. The runner is brought on by the forcing system, and is expected to do his best at the age of two or three years, and shortly after is good for little or nothing on the race-course. The trotter, on the other hand, is developed much more slowly and lasts much longer. Dexter, for instance, did not begin his racing career until he was six years of age, Lady Thorne not until she was eight, and Goldsmith Maid not until she was nine, and the last-mentioned made her best record of a mile in 2.14 at the advanced age of seventeen. The most wonderful product of the trotting-turf in the last ten years is Mr. Robert Bonner's Maud S., whose fastest time, a mile in 2.08¾, at Cleveland, Ohio, in 1885, in harness, against time, has not yet been approached. Maud S. is a lightish red chestnut mare, with a small blaze in her face, and one foot behind, white. She is 15·2½ hands high, and in excellent form. Her gait is even, low, and smooth; she has little knee action, her fore-legs going low and reaching far out, and her fore-feet coming down easily on the ground. Her hind-quarters are powerful, with great thighs and bocks. Her action behind is close and in line and reaches far forward, and she has a rare power behind to propel, and as rare a one in front to extend the fore-legs and take advantage of the power and reach behind. Her movement is the symmetry of trotting motion. Maud S. is a Kentucky blue-grass horse, having been bred by Mr. A. J. Alexander, of Woodburn Farm, Woodford County, and foaled March 28, 1874. Her sire was Harold, dam Miss Russell; Pilot, Jr.; second dam Sally Russell, by Boston; third dam Maria Russell, by Thornton's Rattler; fourth dam Miss Shepherd, by Stockholder; fifth dam Miranda, by Top Gallant (of Tennessee); sixth dam by imported Diomed; seventh dam by imported Medley; eighth dam by imported Juniper. In her veins, therefore, commingle a double inbred Messenger cross, enriched by the blood of imported Bellfounder, strengthened by the stout lineage of Old Boston, and enlivened by the infusion of Pilot Jr., blood. This is a combination of Messenger, thoroughbred, and pacing strains that satisfies all the varied schools of writers on the make up of the perfect trotter of the period. At Mr. Alexander's sale of yearlings, Maud S. was purchased by the late Capt. James Bugher, of Cincinnati, for $325, and in her three-year old form she was sold by his son, as his residuary legatee, for $350, to Capt. G. N. Stone, President of the Chester Driving Park Association. In October, 1878, Capt. Stone made a conditional sale of her to the late Mr. William H. Vanderbilt for $20,000, the condition being that she should show a speed of 2.20. Mr. Vanderbilt admired her quite as much for her beauty and excellent disposition as for her ability to trot a fast mile. October 26, at Lexington, Ky., she trotted a mile in 2.17½, making the first quarter in 33½ seconds, the second quarter in 32¾ seconds, the third quarter in 35 seconds, and the fourth quarter in 36½ seconds. This was better than any previous four-year-old record by 3¾ seconds. She was driven by Bair, and at the close of the trial showed some signs of fatigue, but entirely recovered in half an hour. Mr. Vanderbilt paid $21,000 for Maud S., the additional $1,000 having been promised to Bair by Capt. Stone if he drove the mare during the season of 1878 in 2.18 or less. In 1880 Maud S. and St. Julian met at Rochester, and each trotted a mile on the same afternoon, in 2.11¾. St. Julian had made a record of 2.12¾ the previous year, at Oakland Park, San Francisco, Cal., the time of the quarters being 33, 32½, 34¾ and 32¾ seconds respectively. He has been one of the best trotting-horses of the decade—a bay gelding, sired by Volunteer, after Rysdyk's Hambletonian, and his dam by Sayer's Harry Clay. He was foaled in 1869, and was, in 1879, when he made his record, ten years old. He was 15·3 hands high, had a white patch upon his face, and his off hind-foot and near fore-foot were white. He was purchased, when four years old, by James Galway, for $600. He began his career as a trotter in 1875, and made a good record. He was bought by Orrin A. Hickok, and taken to the Pacific coast, where he became famous by beating all previous trotting records. Two weeks after the Rochester meeting, in 1880, St. Julian lowered the record at Hartford, to 2.11¼, but in September Maud S., at Chicago, trotted a mile in 2.10¾, thus closing the season as "Queen of the Turf." In 1881 Maud S. opened the season by trotting a mile at Pittsburg in 2.10½, and followed it up in August, at Rochester, by reducing the record to 2.10¼. This latter time she also subsequently made at Chicago, where she also trotted the fastest second heat on record—2.11½—and the fastest third heat—2.11. This was also the record of the fastest two consecutive heats. At Belmont Park, Philadelphia, the same season, she also trotted the fastest three consecutive heats—2.12, 2.13½, 2.12½. During this year no rival appeared to dispute her supremacy. In 1883 Maud S. and Aldine trotted a double-team mile in 2.15½, driven by an amateur, and drawing more than 400 pounds of weight—an unapproached performance in all the annals of trotting. During the same season Jay Eye See trotted a mile in 2.10¾, the fastest time that had then been made, except by Maud S., and a performance that led many turfman to look upon him as a possible successful rival of the "Queen" the next season. In 1884, August 1, at Providence, Jay Eye See trotted a mile in 2.10, a quarter of a second better than the fastest mile made by Maud S. up to that time. But this wonderful son of Dictator, full brother to Dexter, by Rysdyk's Hambletonian, dam Clara, by American Star, was able to hold the first place on the American turf but a single day; for, August 2, at Cleveland, Maud S. made a mile in 2.09¾, and Jay Eye See, after making several ineffectual attempts to reduce his Providence time, gave it up and retired from the contest. Two weeks after the Cleveland performance Mr. Vanderbilt surprised the country by selling Maud S. to Mr. Robert Bonner for $40,000. The reason he gave to the public for parting with the "Queen of the Turf" was, that after her wonderful trotting at Cleveland he received so many letters in regard to her, and was importuned to such an extent to allow her to make attempts to reduce her record still further, that he became tired of it. He kept Maud S. solely for his own pleasure, and parted with her when he could no longer retain possession of her in peace. He was offered $100,000 for her, but preferred that she should pass into Mr. Bonner's hands at the price named. In November, at Lexington, Ky., she closed the season by reducing her former time one half a second—to 2.09¼—a speed that has never yet been attained by any other trotter. But Maud S. was still to score her greatest triumph. On July 30, 1885, at Cleveland, over a heavy track, she trotted a mile in 2.08¾! The first quarter was made in 32¼ seconds, the half-mile in 1.04½, the three quarters in 1.35½, and the last quarter in 33¼ seconds. This closes the record thus far of the fastest trotting-horses the world has ever seen. Competent judges believed, in 1885, that under favorable circumstances, Maud S. might have reduced her own unapproached time by at least two seconds. But the strain upon her at Cleveland was about all that she could bear. It is still an unsolved problem—the ultimate limit of the speed of the trotting-horse. The following is a list of the horses that have gone a mile in 2.15 or better: Maud S., 2.08¾; Jay Eye See, 2.10; St. Julian, 2.11¼; Maxey Cobb, 2.13¼; Rarus, 2.13¼; Harry Wilkes, 2.13½; Phallas, 2.13¾; Belle Hamlin, 2.13¾; Clingstone, 2.14; Goldsmith Maid, 2.14; Trinket, 2.14; Patron, 2.14¼; Hopeful, 2.14¾; Majolica, 2.15; Lulu, 2.15. The past decade has produced a great number of trotters, which, in their several classes, have made remarkable records; almost every one, however, has been reduced the succeeding season. Among the more noted may be mentioned Woodford Chief, Great Eastern, Phil. Thompson, Judge Fullerton, Lucile, Golddust, Frank Reeves, Smuggler, So So, Elaine, Hopeful, Jewett, Santa Claus, Steve Maxwell, Bonita, and Aldine. The value of a trotting-horse depends largely upon the disposition of the seller and purchaser. One with a record of 2.30 may be estimated in a general way to be worth $10,000. From 2.30 down to 2.20 $1,000 may be added for each second. Below that there is no standard by which to estimate a horse's value. One hundred thousand dollars, the price offered Mr.

Vanderbilt for Maud S., when her record was 2.09¼, was not considered too great.

Running.—While trotting is distinctively an American sport, the breeding and training of runners has not been neglected in the United States during the past ten years. Indeed, the achievements of our thoroughbreds, both at home and in Europe, have been almost as remarkable as those of our trotters. And this is not surprising. They have been bred from the best English stock, and our soil and climate have been proved to be equally favorable to improvement of the breed. Early in the decade Ten Broeck scored a series of most brilliant performances, beating all previous records of running one mile, two miles, and four miles. This horse was of the purest blood, being by imported Phaeton (son of King Tom, who was by the great Irish race-horse Harkaway, dam Pocahontas, the dam of Stockwell, Rataplan, etc., by Glencoe), dam Fanny Holton (Lyttleton's dam), by Lexington. He was bred by the late John Harper, near Midway, Ky., and in 1876 started eight times, winning seven times, and coming in second once. The horses that he ran against were the best in the country. His greatest performance of the year was at Louisville, Ky., where, in a four-mile race against time, he scored in 7.15¼, the fastest previous time being that of Fellowcraft, 7.19¾. The same season and the next Ten Broeck ran a mile at Louisville, Ky., in 1.39¾, two miles in 3.27½, and three miles in 5.26¼, the time in neither case having been equaled before. Ten Broeck died in Midway, Ky., June 28, 1887. Some of the greatest triumphs of American running-horses have been won on the English turf. In 1877 Mr. H. M. Sanford crossed the Atlantic with American horses. Brown Prince (by Lexington out of imported Britannia IV by the Flying Dutchman) won his first race at the Newmarket Craven meeting as a three-year-old, beating four at even weights; but his best record was made in the two thousand guineas stakes, where he ran second to Chamant, beating Silvio, and showing sufficient form to call public attention to his chances for the Derby. This race was the best comparison of high-class horses of the two countries that had then occurred; for, though Brown Prince never after showed form, he was a good representative American horse in that day, and he met horses of equally good rating in England. In 1879 Mr. Pierre Lorillard's venture was more successful. His six-year-old gelding, Parole (by imported Leamington, dam Maiden by Lexington, grand-dam by imported Glencoe), won four handicaps and one weight-for-weight race (the Epsom cup) out of seven starts. His opponents do not seem to have been of the highest class, but from favorable weights at first, he was compelled to take up the top weight in the Ascot stakes in which he was defeated, possibly owing to the heaviness of the course, which made the extra weight tell doubly against his chances. His two-year-old sister, Papoose, also won her maiden race, a sweepstakes, at Newmarket. In 1881 Mr. Lorillard's Iroquois eclipsed the performances of all previous American horses in England. This horse was a sturdy American colt, bright brown in color, and standing 15¼ hands high. He was not elegant in appearance nor symmetrical in shape as some racers are, but he had all the qualities that mark a high-bred race-horse. His sire was Leamington, the famous sire of Parole, Harold, Sensation, and other noted horses, and his dam the American mare Maggie B. B. He was bred by Mr. Aristides Welch, at Chestnut Hill farm, near Philadelphia, and was sold to Mr. Lorillard, when a yearling, for $7,000. He was sent to England in 1879, and in 1880 started in twelve races, winning four. In 1881 he unfortunately missed the two thousand guineas stake, but won the Derby by half a length (the first time an American horse ever did it, and the third instance only in which it was won by horses of foreign birth), and the St. Leger, over a longer course, by a length. In both races he was ridden by the famous jockey, Fred. Archer. Between the two great events he won the Prince of Wales's stakes at Ascot, giving nine pounds. The success of Iroquois, aside from his admitted high qualities, was to be attributed in no small degree to his American trainer, Pincas, who, as a well-informed sporting correspondent wrote at the time, "took a lame horse from the hands of his predecessor and won the great event of the year." How great a horse Iroquois was is proved by the fact that since the establishment of the two races, only nine double victories had been gained. The effect of this unexpected victory upon the English people was thus told by a veteran correspondent: "Nothing we could have done—not the victory of the America, nor winning the international rifle match—no, nor the sewing machine, nor the telegraph, nor the telephone, nor any exploit in all our long list, has ever brought us that kind of renown that goes with the Derby." The same year (1881) Mr. Keen's Foxhall won the Grand Prix de Paris. This was a bay colt with black points, and the near hind pastern white. He had a clean head, light neck, a back a trifle long, but a good barrel, and shoulders of admirable power. He was bred by Mr. A. J. Alexander at Woodburn Farm, Ky., and was bought by Mr. Keen's agent in 1879 for $650. His sire was King Alphonso, son of the imported Phaeton. King Alphonso's dam was Capitola, a daughter of Vandal. Foxhall's dam was Jamaica, a daughter of Lexington by Fanny Ludlow. He won his first race at Newmarket in 1880. Foxhall was the first American colt that ever ran in France, and his finish for the Grand Prix was magnificent. Fred. Archer was riding the French colt Tristan, and as they came along the home-stretch, rode his very best, and lifted his horse almost even with Foxhall. A shout of "Tristan! Tristan!" was rending the air from thousands of excited Frenchmen, the horses were almost past the Jockey Club stand, when Fordham, for the first time, raised his whip. A cut on the shoulder of Foxhall was answered by a grand leap forward, and the Grand Prix de Paris, with its 160,000 francs, was won by Mr. Keen. He did not do well at Ascot, but in the Cesarewitch he carried 110 pounds, and won in a common canter. In the Select stakes, with 127 pounds, he again defeated with the utmost ease his old French rival, Tristan. In the Cambridgeshire, with 126 pounds on his back, he defeated Lucy Glitters, carrying 91 pounds, by a head, while Tristan came in third, with 107 pounds. Among the horses not placed by the judges in this last race was the Derby victor of 1880, Bend Or, carrying 134 pounds. In the Champion stakes, ten days before the Cambridgeshire, Bend Or, with 130 pounds, had defeated Iroquois with only 116 pounds on his back. Foxhall's double victory in the two great Newmarket handicaps had had only one parallel, the victory of Rosebery, in 1876. The Cesarewitch course is 2¼ miles in length, and Foxhall came in 10 lengths ahead of Chippendale — an exploit of which the greatest horses in the annals of the turf might well be proud. But Iroquois and Foxhall were not conceded to be by any means the best American runners at the time they won their laurels abroad. There was Hindoo, the winner of the Kentucky Derby and Clark stakes at Louisville and the Blue Ribbon stakes at Lexington. There was the grand filly, Thora, who, in 1881, defeated both Hindoo and Crickmore, but was beaten in 1882 at Jerome Park by Sly Dance, having to concede a year and six pounds. There was Parole, whose brilliant performance in the Manhattan handicap, with 120 pounds, aroused great enthusiasm. There was the steeple-chaser, Trouble, who, at Jerome Park, in 1882, won the handicap steeple-chase, carrying 157 pounds. There was Glenmore that achieved the unparalleled performance of running the four miles in the last two heats for the Bowie stakes in the time of 7.30½ and 7.31 respectively. With his easy action and great staying-powers, he was a wonderful horse. In the Coney Island cup race he defeated Luke Blackburn, Monitor, Parole, and Uncas, winning in 3.58¾. Among the other successful American running-horses of the past ten years may be mentioned Fiddlestick, Belle of the Meade, Brother to Harry Bassett, Rhadamanthus, Aristides, Harkaway, Himyar, Lottery, Bushwhacker, Mistake, Beatitude, Lord Murphy, Pontiac, Winfred, and Dew Drop. This latter horse was purchased in February, 1886, by the Dwyer Brothers at the sale of Mr. Pierre Lorillard's stock at Rancocas, for $29,000, but his performances during the succeeding season were disappointing.

By Teams.—Maud S. and Aldine were driven in New York by W. H. Vanderbilt one mile to a road-wagon (not a record) in 2.15½. Maxey Cobb and Neta Medium were driven one mile in New York to a skeleton-wagon, not in a race, but against time, for a record, by John Murphy, in 2.15¾. Arab and Conde were driven by O. A. Hickok three straight mile-heats over the Bay District track, San Francisco, Nov. 26, 1887, and won the race from Jane L. and Palatina in 2.30½, 2.23, 2.18½. The third heat is the best time ever made in a team-race —first half, 1.13; second half, 1.05½.

Pacing. — A number of good pacing-horses have been bred and trained in America during the past ten years, the most noted of which are Sweetser, not of distinguished pedigree, but who paced in Cleveland, in 1877, three heats in 2.16, 2.16, 2.16½, the slowest of which was faster than any previous record; Little Brown Jug, who reduced the record still further in 1879 by pacing three heats in 2.11¾, 2.11¾, 2.12½, and Johnson, who paced a heat in 1883 in 2.10, and one in 1884 in 2.06¼.

Steeple-Chasing.—This class of racing has not yet become very popular in the United States, although a few good steeple-chase trials are run. The most important event in the history of the American turf during 1886 was the retirement of Mr. Pierre Lorillard and the sale of a large part of his stock at Rancocas. In the latter 27 horses brought $149,050. Besides Dew Drop, already mentioned as having been sold for $29,000, Pontiac, winner of the Suburban handicap in 1885, brought $17,500, and Winfred, brother of the great Wanda, $18,000.

The Turf in England.—The English breeding-farms have continued to supply the stock from which the best horses are obtained in all other European countries, and, during the past ten years interest in the thoroughbreds and in the great national races has been increased. The high character of the horses that have participated in the principal handicaps has been maintained. The racing associations of England, and especially the Jockey Club, are stronger than ever before, and important improvements have been made in their grounds. The number of horses in training has been increased and several new handicaps have been established, the most important being the £10,000 Eclipse stakes, established in 1886, and won that year by Bendigo. In 1886, also, Fred. Archer, the "Centaur of the Century," died.

The Continent.—In France interest in the great national race, the Grand Prix de Paris, has increased since 1876, and there has been a marked improvement in the character of the horses that contend for it. For the systematic encouragement of horse-breeding, France is divided into twenty-seven districts in which three classes of stallions are employed—Government stallions, horses owned by private individuals that have received premiums, and inferior horses employed for want of better ones. It is a penal offense for a private individual to employ a stallion not belonging to one of these classes, except for his own mares. Statistics of the production of horses, horse-rearing, and pastures in each district are published. The Agricultural Department maintains the stud establishments, supplies fit stallions to the country, institutes races in the breeding districts, offer premiums for the best animals exhibited, and diffuses sound information. The fact that thoroughbred animals raised by the Government carried off all the national prizes until, on account of the remonstrances of the Jockey Club, the breeding-studs at Le Pin and Pompadour were suppressed, is evidence of the excellence of the breeding. While French-bred horses were once allowed several pounds on the English race-course, they now compete on equal terms with the best bred animals of England. In Prussia there are at least a score of private studs of English thoroughbred stock, more than one half as many Government stallion depots, and three great Government breeding establishments, at Trakehuen, Graditz, and Neustad. German horses are, upon the whole, inferior, owing to the poor pasturage; when well-bred they are soft and without bottom. The principal Government stud in Austria is at Lipitza, and is devoted to the breeding of a race of pure Spanish blood, and of a cross between Spanish and Arab horses. The private stud of the Emperor, at Kladrup, in Bohemia, breeds for the turf, but the pasturage is poor, and no very superior horses are produced. In Hungary, the stud at Mezöhegyes has 45,000 acres of excellent herbage and produces thoroughbreds, Arabs, Norfolk trotters, Normans, and stud-bred horses. The Kisber stud, also in Hungary, is devoted entirely to English thoroughbreds and half-bred stock. The most interesting feature of this stud is that in selecting the best models to breed from, and in aiming at a combination of the three great qualities of substance, speed, and endurance, none but sound animals, uninjured by early struggles upon the turf, are employed.

TURKEY, an empire in southeastern Europe and western Asia. The Government is an absolute monarchy. Constitutional limitations were proclaimed by Sultan Abdul Medjid on Feb. 18, 1856, and a representative system by Abdul Hamid II, in November, 1876, but these reforms have not been carried into effect. The reigning Sultan is Abdul Hamid II, born Sept. 22, 1842. who succeeded to the throne on the deposition of his brother, Murad V, Aug. 31, 1876. The Grand Vizier is Kisamil Pasha.

Area and Population.—The area of the territory under the direct rule of the Sultan in Europe and Asia is 8,088,400 square kilometres, and its population 21,633,000 souls. The area of the tributary states and protectorates in Europe, Asia, and Africa is 1,182,000 square kilometres, and their population is 11,345,000. The population of Constantinople, the capital, was 873,565 in 1885. Salonica has from 60,000 to 80,000 inhabitants, and Adrianople from 60,000 to 62,000. In Asiatic Turkey the chief cities are Smyrna, with 186,510 inhabitants; Damascus, with about 150,000; Bagdad, with 100,000; and Aleppo, with 70,000.

Finances.—In the budget for the year ended Feb. 28, 1884, the receipts were reckoned at 1,631,800,600 piasters, and the expenditures at 1,622,301,600 piasters. No official budget has since been published. The revenue for the financial year 1887–'88 is estimated at 1,750,-000,000 piasters, equal to $77,000,000.

By an arrangement with the creditors for the conversion of the Ottoman debt into a unified and consolidated debt, the Sultan, in an irade of December, 1881, decreed the emission of new bonds of the amount of £92,225,827 sterling. The amount of the Roumelian railroad bonds added to this makes the sum of £106,437,284, in lieu of £190,997,980 sterling, the figure at which the debt stood before the compromise. Up to March 1, 1887, £1,978,528 had been paid off, leaving a debt of £101,-458,706.

Commerce.—The total value of the imports in 1885–'86 was 2,000,867,000 piasters, against 2,063,764,000 in the preceding year; the value of the exports 1,207,626,000 piasters, against 1,279,817,000 piasters. The imports from Great Britain were 876,843,000 piasters in value; from Austria-Hungary, 391,984,000 piasters; from France, 231,689,000 piasters; from Russia, 175,850,000 piasters; from Italy, 60,621,000 piasters; from Persia, 54,493,000 piasters. The exports to Great Britain were valued at 455,567,000 piasters; to France, 872,499,000 piasters; to Austria-Hungary, 118,220,000 piasters; to Egypt, 100,889,000 piasters; to Greece, 53,530.000 piasters. The values in piasters of the leading exports in 1885–'86 as compared with the preceding year are shown in the following table:

EXPORTS.	1884–'85.	1885–'86.
Raisins	164,408,000	145,906,000
Silk	79,895,000	77,039,000
Cocoons	83,686,000	97,678,000
Other textile materials	189,188,000	159,392,000
Opium	58,825,000	90,300,000
Coffee	45,022,000	39,717,000
Tropical fruits	47,897,000	62,421,000
Other fruits and seeds	28,018,000	29,154,000
Skins	81,616,000	50,375,000
Minerals	12,000,000	14,995,000
Drugs and colors	68,670,000	59,570,000
Gums and oils	67,580,000	57,695,000
Carpets	15,949,000	12,678,000
Timber	11,876,000	11,711,000

The chief article of import is cotton manufactures. There were fabrics of the value of 412,777,000 piasters, and yarns of the value of 125,718,000 piasters, imported in 1885–'86, as compared with 446,362,000 and 138,988,000 piasters respectively in 1884–'85.

Navigation.—There were entered at Constantinople in 1886–'87, 15,519 vessels, of 7,099,012 tons; of which, 7,817, of 6,212,055 tons, were steamers. The tonnage entered at Smyrna in 1885 was 1,232,686; at Salonica, 579,847; at Trebizond, 446,327; at Beyrut in 1886, 618,699. The estimated tonnage of the merchant navy is 181,500.

Railroads.—The railroads in operation on Dec. 31, 1885, had a total length of 1,170 kilometres, including 810 kilometres in Eastern Roumelia. In Asia Minor there were four lines of the total length of 462 kilometres in the neighborhood of Smyrna, a line 98 kilometres long, between Haidar Pasha and Ismid, and one of 85 kilometres running from Mersina to Tarsus. The extension of the Ismid railroad to Diarbekir was sanctioned in August, 1887, and plans have been approved for the continuation of the main line through Angora to Bagdad, and the completion of an Asiatic network. English and French capitalists were rival bidders for the concessions, the former proposing to build broad-gauge roads and the latter a narrower track. The broad-gauge of 1·44 metre was adopted, and the concession for the trunk line was given to the English syndicate. The entire scheme for Asiatic railroads embraces the purchase and extension of the existing lines and the building of others, involving the expenditure of $150,000.000 altogether. The railroads will not only subserve strategical and commercial purposes, but will help to prevent the periodical famines that periodically decimate the brave and virtuous race of peasantry inhabiting the plains of Anatolia.

The Army.—The active army numbers about 12,000 officers and 170,000 men, with 30,000 horses and pack-animals, 1,188 field-guns, and 2,374 fortress guns. The army is organized into 80 regiments of infantry, 89 regiments of cavalry, 198 batteries of field artillery, 8 battalions of fortress artillery, and 6 battalions of engineers. There are besides 96 regiments of Redifs, and 48 regiments of Mustafiz. The new conscription law requires all Mussulman subjects to be enrolled between the ages of seventeen and forty. Notwithstanding the financial straits of the Government the War Department has begun to arm and equip the army on an extensive scale of expenditure. The Government ordered 500,000 rifles of the new Mauser pattern, besides 60,000 carbines. A part of these were delivered and distributed among the soldiers in 1887.

Palace Intrigues.—A plot to dethrone the Sultan in favor of one of his nephews, either Selim or Sala Eddin, was discovered or suspected in May, 1887. There were many officials disgraced, and the cabal of politicians that obtained the credit of revealing the conspiracy, had, as usual, an opportunity to remove their rivals and enemies. Among the persons who fell into disgrace were the chief eunuch, and Osman Pasha, the victor of Plevna.

The Œcumenical Patriarchate.—After an exciting contest, the Bishop of Adrianople was on Feb. 4, 1887, elected Greek Patriarch over the other candidates. He was the most popular of them on account of his liberal tendencies, and was supported by the influence of the Greek Government, but was strongly opposed by Russian diplomacy.

Crete.—The Christian population of Crete in 1886 made a demand that two thirds of the customs revenue should be ceded to the autonomous legislature. The Porte then refused to consider such a proposition. In March, 1887, the assembly again raised the question, and Costaki Pasha, the new governor, reported that the Cretans would not cease to agitate till the point had been settled. It was thereupon referred to a commission at Constantinople, and Savas Pasha, the former governor, was sent to Crete to study the situation. The Christians in the Assembly presented an address to the Ottoman Government, asking, in addition to two thirds of the customs duties the entire stamp duties, as well as the salt and tobacco monoplics, and demanding that laws should be enacted by an absolute, instead of by a two-thirds majority, and that the Sultan should forego his right of veto, and exercise only a suspensive veto for the period of three months; also that deputies should be elected in proportion to the population of each religious community. At the end of April disturbances broke out in the island. French and English ironclads were sent to Suda Bay. A conflict took place in the outskirts of Canea between Turks and Christians, in which several persons were killed. Order was restored, and the Porte sent a circular note to the powers denying that this incident had any serious political significance. Troops and war-ships were ordered to the island. When the Assembly met, May 11, the Christian deputies refused to take part in the proceedings until their grievances had been redressed. Collisions took place between troops, some of whom could not be restrained by their officers, and armed bands of Christians, who were finally driven into the mountains. The deputies voted a resolution declaring that tithes should not be paid by the people until one half of the customs receipts for the past year should be paid into the local treasury, according to agreement. The Greek Government, some time before, had solicited the support of the great powers in demanding new concessions for the Cretans, but its representations had been coldly received. Some of the cabinets not only refused to interfere in the internal affairs of Turkey, but intimated that the Hellenic Government could put a stop to the Cretan agitation. The revenue which the Cretans demanded for their own uses barely sufficed for the maintenance of the Turkish garrison on the island. A Cretan deputation conferred with the Grand Vizier, and with the Ottoman commission. The Greek Government was seconded by the powers in asking that the demands of the deputation should be treated with moderation. Mahmoud Pasha president of the legislative section of the Council of State, was appointed an extraordinary commissioner, with power to settle the question on the spot. He went to Crete in the early part of July, accompanied by the Christian deputation and a Mohammedan deputation of Cretans that had come to Constantinople to present the side of the town population, for whose sake alone the Ottoman Government felt constrained to retain so expensive and troublesome a dependency. The Imperial Government insisted that the proclamation against paying tithes should be withdrawn before concessions could be discussed, and this was done by the Christian members of the Assembly. The Government had declared that it could not go further than the Khalepa convention of 1879 without endangering the sovereignty of the Sultan over the island; yet under pressure from the powers it agreed to a compromise. On July 19, Mahmoud Pasha issued a proclamation definitely ceding to Crete one half of the customs revenue, promising that deficits in bad years should be made up from the surplus revenue of good years, granting to the Christians a larger share in the local administration, and binding the Imperial Government to sanction all acts of the local legislature within three months of their passage. After accepting this favorable settlement, the Cretan Assembly was closed on July 30. The agitation did not cease immediately, and Mahmoud Pasha was ordered back to the island, but threats of military and naval action convinced the unruly Candiotes that they could gain nothing by further disturbances.

The Montenegrin Boundary.—The still unsettled Montenegrin frontier was the occasion of some fighting between Albanians and Montenegrins in the summer of 1887. · A mixed commission came to an agreement in July concerning the delimitation of certain pasture-lands in the Berana district that were still in dispute. The suspicious conduct of Prince Nicholas of Montenegro in increasing his troops and armaments created alarm in Constantinople, as well as in Belgrade, Vienna, and other capitals. The provocative acts of his subjects impelled the Ottoman Government to strengthen its garrisons on the frontier, and to ask the good offices of Russia in averting trouble, besides remonstrating directly with the Montenegrin Government. The convention for the delimitation of the frontier was signed on November 7, and all differences were believed to have been adjusted to the satisfaction of the Montenegrins. It simply carried out provisions of the Berlin Treaty which the Turkish authorities were slow in fulfilling because they entailed the handing over to Montenegro of districts that were inhabited and owned by Albanians.

Famine in Asia Minor.—A severe drought in Anatolia, extending over the southern part of the vilayet of Broussa and the vilayets of Angora, Konieh, and Adana, and with less severity through parts of Smyrna, northern Broussa, and Sevas, occurred in the summer of 1887. The price of barley, which is the principal food-product, rose to twenty times the ordinary rate. Through the liberality of the Sultan and other charitable persons American wheat and other food was sent into the district, and the suffering of the people was alleviated to some extent. Even drinking-water was very scarce. Sheep, goats, and horses perished in great numbers. To add to the misfortune, after the grain, opium, and other crops were dried up, there came heavy rains which destroyed the grapes.

U

UNITARIANS. The "Year-Book of the Unitarian Congregational Churches" for 1888 gives lists of 384 Unitarian societies and 482 ministers in the United States and Canada; and in foreign countries, of Unitarian churches and societies "in fellowship and habitual association with Unitarians," in England, 277; in Wales, 33; in Ireland, 45; in Scotland, 9; in Hungary, 108; in Australia, 3; in Italy, (1 at Milan); in India, 3; and in Japan, 1. The minutes connected with the Protestant Unions of Germany and Holland, and the Free Christian Union of Switzerland, hold opinions which approximate to those of Unitarians. The independent "Church of the People" (Dr. Kalthoff), in Berlin, is a body of advanced Unitarian principles. Liberal Protestant services are conducted regularly by M. J. Hocart in Brussels, Belgium.

The oldest representative Unitarian body in the United States, though a wholly voluntary one, is the American Unitarian Association, which was founded in 1825 and incorporated in 1847. Its objects are to collect and diffuse information respecting the state of Unitarian Christianity in America, to promote union, sympathy, and co-operation among liberal Christians; to publish and distribute books and tracts inculcating the religious doctrines believed by Unitarians; to supply missionaries; and to help in the support of clergymen and in building churches, when aid is needed. The National Conference of Unitarian and other Christian Churches was organized under the auspices of the American Unitarian Association in 1865. Its purpose is to promote the spread of Unitarian doctrines and the unity and harmony of the churches, by means of conferences held regularly, at which every Unitarian church, association or conference, theological, academic, and benevolent institution may be represented. It meets every two years; and its last meeting was held at Saratoga Springs, N. Y., in September, 1886. The Unitarian Church Building Loan fund has been formed by the American Unitarian Association and the National Conference co-operating with each other to aid Unitarian societies in erecting churches. There are also connected, or in sympathy with these bodies, the

Woman's Auxiliary Conference, the Woman's Western Unitarian Conference, the Western Unitarian Conference, the Western Unitarian Association, the Southern Conference and the Pacific Coast Conference, of Unitarian and other Christian Churches, and a considerable number of local bodies of similar character, and associations of ministers and of persons engaged in Sunday-school work. The Divinity School of Harvard University is Unitarian in the general tendencies of its teaching, and the Meadville Theological School, Meadville, Pa., is controlled by Unitarians. The Unitarian Church Temperance Society was formed in 1886, "to work for the cause of temperance in whatever ways may seem to it wise and right; to study the social problems of poverty, crime, and disease in their relations to the use of intoxicating drinks, and to diffuse whatever knowledge may be gained; to discuss methods of temperance reform; to devise, and so far as possible, to execute plans for practical reform," etc.

The sixty-second annual meeting of the American Unitarian Association was held in Boston, Mass., May 24. The Rev. James de Normandie presided. The treasurer reported that the receipts for the year for the general objects of the Association had been $73,519, and the total receipts, including all those for special and other funds, $220,829. The report of the Board of Directors represented that the year just past had been the most successful year that the Unitarian body in America had known since the association came into existence. While in each of the two preceding years eight new Unitarian societies had been formed, the number of new organizations in this year was twenty-one. The amount of contributions this year, and also the number of contributing churches (246) were considerably in excess of those of preceding years. The Post-Office Mission, by which tracts setting forth Unitarian doctrines were sent to all who applied for them, had been active and successful. The trustees of the Church Building Loan fund reported the total amount of the fund as $46,742, of which $38,235 were in the form of unpaid loans, and $8,517 available for investments. The receipts for the year had been $3,202 in contributions, and $1,465 in payment of loans. The work of the association in behalf of Southern and Indian education was administered by a special commission, with funds expressly contributed for the purpose. In the matter of Southern education, it was not intended to establish new schools, but to select and recommend to the churches and people some of the schools already established. The committee had recommended the Hampton Institute, Virginia; the Tuskegee Normal School, Alabama; and the Channing School, Barnwell, S. C. The enterprise of education of Indians was represented by the Montana Industrial School among the Crows, where a tract of two hundred acres of land had been granted by the Government, suitable log buildings had been erect-

ed upon it, and eighteen pupils were enrolled, with the expectation that the number would be increased to fifty as soon as the equipment of the school was completed.

The executive officers of the Association were requested to prepare and publish for the information of the churches, a statement of the business principles and methods by which aid is given to missionary societies. A resolution advising, in the case of applications for assistance from the funds of the association from societies which retain the private ownership of pews, that efforts be made to induce such societies to acquire ownership of pews by the society, was referred to a special committee for consideration.

British Unitarian Association.—The British and Foreign Unitarian Association met in London, May 31. Mr. Frederick Nettlefold presided. The report of the secretary traced the progress of the Association during the past fifty years. In 1837 the expenditure was £871; in 1886, £4,122. The grants made were for the two years, respectively, £52 and £1,626, while the assisted congregations had increased from seven to fifty-two. About £2,500 still remained of the debt on Essex Hall, toward the extinction of which £23,000 had been raised. Dr. M. A. N. Rovers, of Arnheim, as representative of the Protestantenbond of Holland, said that his society, though only seventeen years old, consisted of 18,000 members, who were called "moderns." Resolutions were passed affirming the desirability of holding people's services and of increased missionary exertions, and expressing a desire for the complete triumph of civil and religious liberty before the close of the Queen's Jubilee.

Unitarian Church in Hungary.—Unitarianism has existed in Transylvania since 1568. The Unitarian Church in Hungary was founded by Francis David about 1568. The churches, which numbered 108 in 1888, are superintended by a bishop (Joseph Ferencz), with eight rural deans, and an ecclesiastical council of 350 members. The quadrennial meeting of the Synod was held in 1887, when 15 young ministers were ordained. The whole number of registered Unitarians in the country is 57,516, and of Unitarian children in the public elementary schools, 6,975. The higher education is provided for by the college or high school at Klausenburg (848 students), and the middle schools at Thorda (183 pupils), and Szekely Kereztur (152 pupils).

UNITED STATES. The Administration.—Early in the year Secretary Manning, of the Treasury, resigned his portfolio. (See article on Mr. Manning, page 597.) The President thereupon nominated the Assistant Secretary, Charles S. Fairchild, to the vacant place. His commission dated from April 1.

Charles Stebbins Fairchild was born in Cazenovia, N. Y., April 30, 1842. He was graduated at Harvard College in 1863, and, after studying at the law school of that university, was admitted to the bar in 1865. In 1874 he was Deputy Attorney-General of New York, and in 1876 was elected to the attorney-generalship. He served in that capacity for two

CHARLES STEBBINS FAIRCHILD.

years, and then spent some time in travel abroad. From 1880 till 1885 he was engaged in the practice of his profession in New York city. Upon the entrance of President Cleveland into office, he was appointed Assistant Secretary of the Treasury. Owing to the illness of Secretary Manning, he had been Acting Secretary for some time before his promotion.

The death of Justice Woods of the Supreme Court in May (see page 621) left a vacancy on the bench. No nomination of a successor was made till December, when Secretary L. Q. C. Lamar, of the Interior Department, was selected by the President. This appointment was followed by the transfer of Postmaster-General Vilas to the Interior Department, and the nomination of Don M. Dickinson, of Michigan, to be Postmaster-General. These nominations were not acted upon by the Senate till early in 1888, when they were confirmed.

Donald McDonald Dickinson was born in Port Ontario, Oswego County, N. Y., Jan. 17, 1846. He was graduated at the University of Michigan in 1867, studied law, and in the same year was admitted to the bar. Among the important cases with which he has been connected professionally are the Ward and Campan will cases, the ship-canal case, the telephone cases (in which he made the leading argument for Drawbaugh), the Paris, Allen & Co. liquor case, and a series of cases that resulted in the setting aside of the claim and exercise of jurisdiction by the Federal *nisi-prius* courts under the bankruptcy laws to enjoin proceedings in State courts. He was chairman of the Democratic State Committee in 1876, and in 1880 was a delegate-at-large and chairman of the Michigan delegation in the Democratic National Convention. Since 1884 he has represented Michigan on the Democratic National

Committee. He was nominated for Postmaster-General on Dec. 6, 1887, and confirmed by the Senate on Jan. 17, 1888. He has been noted for his personal devotion to President Cleveland; and in the Michigan Democratic Convention of 1886, when the chaplain in his opening prayer failed to mention Mr. Cleveland, Mr. Dickinson rose at once to protest against the omission, and thereupon offered a supplementary prayer in which he invoked a blessing for the President considered as a "Democrat of Democrats, the noblest of them all."

Five new appointive offices were created early in the year by Congress, under the provisions of the interstate commerce bill, passed in January. These offices, constituting the Interstate Commerce Commission, were filled late in March by the appointment of Thomas M. Cooley, of Michigan, for the term of six years; William R. Morrison, of Illinois, for five years; August Schoonmaker, of New York, for four years; Aldace F. Walker, of Vermont, for three years; and Walter A. Bragg, of Alabama, for two years. Two members of the commission, Messrs. Cooley and Walker, were Republicans. (See INTERSTATE COMMERCE COMMISSION.) The more important appointments of subordinate administrative officials during the year were the following: James S. Rives, of New York, to be Assistant Secretary of State, *vice* James D. Porter, resigned; Hugh S. Thompson, of South Carolina, to succeed Mr. Fairchild as Assistant Secretary of the Treasury; James W. Hyatt, of Connecticut, to be Treasurer, *vice* Conrad N. Jordan, resigned; Sigourney Butler, of Massachusetts, to be Second Comptroller; Benton J. Hall to

DONALD M'DONALD DICKINSON.

be Commissioner of Patents, *vice* M. V. Montgomery; and Lieut. A. W. Greely to be brigadier-general and chief signal officer, succeeding Gen. W. B. Hazen, deceased. Early in February the Senate took action upon the second nomination of James C. Matthews, of New York, to be Recorder of Deeds in the District of Columbia, and rejected it by substantially the same vote as at the preceding session. The President then named James M. Trotter, of Massachusetts, who was confirmed without difficulty. In November Commissioner William A. J. Sparks tendered his resignation as head of the General Land-Office, in consequence of difficulties arising between him and Secretary Lamar. S. M. Stockslager, of Indiana, was nominated to succeed him.

In the diplomatic service an understanding was reached with Austria regarding her refusal to receive Minister Keiley, and Gen. Alexander R. Lawton, of Georgia, was appointed in April to the post at Vienna, which had been vacant for over a year in consequence of this refusal. About the same time the vacancy at the court of Turkey, caused by the resignation of Samuel S. Cox, was filled by the appointment of Oscar S. Strauss, of New York. New ministers resident and consuls - general were appointed to Liberia and Corea during the year.

But little outside of the ordinary routine occurred in the general administration during the year. One Executive act, however, aroused much discussion. This was the order directing the return to the States of flags captured from the Confederates during the war which are now stored in the War Department at Washington. The order was made upon the suggestion of the Adjutant-General, and with the concurrence of the officers of the War Department. No sooner had it been published than indignant protests arose throughout the Northern States from the men whose bravery and toil had won these trophies, and to whom they were invested with peculiar value. The action so exasperated some of the veterans of the Grand Army of the Republic as to provoke intemperate threats against the Executive. But it was soon discovered that these flags had become, by capture, public property, which could not be disposed of by Executive decree, but required an act of Congress. Finding, therefore, that his act was not only ill-advised but nugatory, the President hastened to recall it, and to assure the country that it had been prompted only by patriotic motives, and in the hope that it would accord with the general feelings of conciliation hitherto expressed between the two sections.

In the department of foreign relations, new postal conventions were arranged during the year with Mexico and Jamaica, and an agreement was reached with Spain by which each country abolished the discriminating duties against the commerce of the other. The President's proclamation abolishing these duties was issued on September 26. On the 29th of the same month the President appointed R. B. Angell, of Michigan, and W. L. Putnam, of Maine, commissioners, with the Secretary of State, to meet representatives of England and Canada, for the purpose of settling the Canadian fisheries dispute. (See FISHERIES.) The

representatives of England were Hon. Joseph Chamberlain and Sir Lionel Sackville West, British Minister at Washington; the Canadian representative was Sir Charles Tupper. The commission began its session in Washington late in November, and, after deliberations lasting over a month, perfected a new treaty, the provisions of which had not been published at the close of the year.

Public Lands.—The number of acres of land disposed of during the fiscal year, under the various acts of Congress authorizing sales, entries, and selections, aggregates 25,111,400 84, of which 746,637·29 acres were Indian lands, 5,511,807·88 railroad selections, and 2,109,481·-43 selections under other grants; the aggregate amount showing an increase of 4,862,524·-55 acres as compared with the previous year. The receipts from disposal of the public lands were $10,783,921.72; from sales of Indian lands, $1,484,302.30; a total of $12,268,224.02; an increase over the previous year of $3,247,-727.08.

During the year the Secretary of the Interior instituted special investigations into the status of the various grants of indemnity lands to railroads under different acts of Congress, with a view to restoring to the public domain such lands as had been forfeited by non-compliance with the conditions of the grant. He found that, notwithstanding these indemnity withdrawals were made exclusively for the interests of the company, few of these, if any of them, constructed their roads within the time prescribed in the granting act. Maps of "probable," "general," "designated," and "definite" routes of the roads were filed with rapidity in the department, and withdrawals thereunder asked and almost invariably granted, until the public-land States and Territories were gridironed over with railroad granted and indemnity limits; and in many instances the limits of one road overlapped and conflicted with other roads. Accordingly, on May 28, the Secretary issued orders to various companies to show cause before a certain date why grants to them should not be revoked. The objections of such remonstrants as appeared were considered, and a decision given by the department on August 13. Two days later orders were issued revoking grants made to about thirty different companies, restoring to the Government and opening for settlement an area estimated at 21,823,600 acres, or equal in size to the State of Maine. In addition to this, there was canceled for various causes, from March 4, 1885, to Oct. 1, 1886, a total of 24,339,794 acres of entries or grants. The work of destroying unlawful inclosures of the public land by cattle owners upon the plains also progressed successfully during the year, about 5,000,000 acres being thus reclaimed.

Indians.—The statistics compiled from the annual reports of the various Indian agents represent that, of the remaining 173,600 Indians under their supervision, about 58,000 wear citizens' clothes wholly; that 16,477 houses are occupied by them; that about 25,000 can speak English; that more than 10,500 of their children are in schools receiving educational and industrial training, for whom 227 schools are in operation; and that over 31,000 families are engaged in industrial pursuits. They have cultivated over 288,000 acres, built over 295,000 rods of fencing, produced over 750,000 bushels of wheat, 950,000 bushels of corn, 402,000 bushels of oats, 68,000 bushels of barley and rye, 514,000 bushels of vegetables, and 83,000 pounds of butter. They own over 392,000 horses, 8,000 mules, 118,000 cattle, 46,000 swine, and 1,120,000 sheep. During the year a beginning was made in the allotment of land in severalty among members of the Sioux tribe in Dakota, the Winnebagos in Nebraska, the Pottawattomies and Absentee Shawnees in Indian Territory, the Crows of Montana, and small tribes in Oregon. The commission appointed to negotiate with the various tribes has, during the year, provided for cession to the United States by the Indians of nearly 22,000,000 acres of territory, besides the surrender by certain tribes of claims to large areas of territory, the quantities and limits of which are rather indefinite. For the lands ceded and the claims covered by the negotiations the total money obligation involved amounts to about $5,800,000. The total expenditure for the Indian service during the year amounted to $5,996,824.43, and the income $7,869,249.47, leaving a balance on hand, June 30, of $1,872,925.04. The appropriation by Congress for the year was $5,561,252.84. There have been no Indian outbreaks during the year, and no hostilities have occurred, except in Colorado, where a band of Utes, numbering about sixty, under Colarow, who were wandering about outside of their reservation, were pursued and attacked by a sheriff's party sent to arrest some of their number for horse-stealing and for violating the game laws. Their horses, cattle, sheep, and supplies were seized, and five Indians killed and seven wounded, and they retreated to the reservation.

The Army.—The latest compiled returns from the army show that there were 2,200 officers and 24,286 enlisted men in the service. The general condition of the troops is reported to be satisfactory, and their efficiency increasing. Several new military posts have been established in the West, and the accommodations of others enlarged. The last Congress authorized appropriations during the last fiscal year for seventy-one new buildings for army purposes in nineteen States and Territories. The military prison at Fort Leavenworth has been increased by the construction of a building of three stories, 200 feet in length by 40 in width. The number of inmates on June 30 was 496, or 81 fewer than in the previous year. The number of trials by general courts-martial during the year decreased 848, and by inferior courts-martial 729. At the Military Academy

at West Point an attendance of 304 cadets was reported on September 1. The total expenditures for the army and the Military Academy, during the year ending June 30, were $24,184,458.48. The only emergencies arising during the year requiring the presence of military force, were the Ute difficulties in Colorado, the riotous conduct of the Crow Indians upon their reservation, leading to an attack on the agent's house, and the usual minor quarrels between settlers and Indians regarding lands. A patrol has also been maintained over the Oklahoma country in Indian Territory, for the purpose of keeping out intruders.

The Navy.—The number of war-vessels in commission at the date of the Secretary's report for this year was 6 in the North Atlantic squadron, 8 in the South Atlantic squadron, 2 in European and 6 in Asiatic waters, 8 on the Pacific coast, and 4 in special service, besides 4 recently put in commission and not assigned to any squadron. This is exclusive of training-ships. The "Tennessee" and six other condemned vessels were sold at auction during the year, and $125,705 derived therefrom. There are now in course of construction 11 unarmored steel vessels, viz.: 6 cruisers, 4 gunboats, and 1 torpedo-boat, of which 2 cruisers and 2 gunboats were authorized by act of Congress in March of this year. Plans for the two armor-clad vessels authorized by the act of August, 1886, were submitted and passed upon during the year, and the construction of one of them is already undertaken. The present strength of the navy, including all vessels completed, is 18 single-turreted monitors, now of little use against modern armaments, 12 unarmored steel and iron vessels, constituting the real strength of the navy, 28 wooden steam-vessels, 10 wooden sailing-vessels, used only as training and receiving ships, and 12 iron and wood tug-boats. There are no armored vessels yet completed fit for defense. The total number of enlisted men and apprentices in the naval service on June 30 was 8,342. The number of enlisted men allowed by law, 7,500, has not been exceeded. When the last annual report of the department was made the country lacked three manufactories necessary to the construction and armament of a modern war-vessel, viz., that of steel forgings for the heavier guns, that of armor for iron-clad vessels, and that of the secondary batteries (machine and rapid-fire guns), an essential portion of the armament. Now all three manufactories are in process of construction under contracts with the department, the two former at the Bethlehem Iron-Works in Pennsylvania, the latter at Washington. The financial report of the department shows that the total appropriations for the fiscal year 1887 were $13,189,153.72, from which there had been expended up to June 30, the close of the year, $10,835,102.25, leaving a balance of $2,354,051.47. On the last of October this balance had been reduced to $185,338 26.

At the Naval Academy at Annapolis, Md., there were 237 cadets on Oct. 1, 1886, and 229 at the same date this year. The graduating class in June contained 44 members. The total appropriations for the fiscal year ending June 30 were $189,031.97, and the expenditures $179,964.91.

Postal Service.—The business of this department shows a gratifying increase during the year, which justifies the expectation that it will soon become self-supporting again, notwithstanding the recent reduction of rates. The operations of the first two years, 1885 and 1886, in which this reduction took effect, resulted in a cash deficiency of nearly $7,000,-000 each year. For the fiscal year 1887, the deficiency has been reduced to $4,000,000. The total revenue for 1887 was $48,837,609.39, against $48,948,422.95 for 1886, and $42,560,-848.88 for 1885. The expenditures in the same time have increased from $49,584,788.65 in 1885, to $50,854,109.12 in 1886, and $52,-814,113.61 in 1887.

The increase of post-offices filled by presidential appointment during the year ending July 1 was 92, making the total number 2,386. Between July 1 and Oct. 1 there were 45 added to the list. The fourth-class offices on July 1 numbered 52,821, an increase of 1,543 for the year; on Oct. 1 there were 53,053. The appointments of postmasters numbered altogether during the fiscal year 13,079, of which 6,863 were to fill vacancies upon the expiration of commissions or by resignations; 2,584 upon removals or suspensions; 589 by death; and 3,043 to newly established offices. Of these the presidential appointments numbered 893, as follows: By expiration of commission, 350; by resignation, 122; by removal or suspension, 237; by death, 39; and upon the assignment of fourth-class offices to a presidential class, 145. The total changes in presidential offices existing March 4, 1885, has been 86·6 per cent., and in fourth-class offices 61 per cent. The free-delivery service was extended during the fiscal year to 8 additional cities, making the total number 189. This and the growth of business necessitated an increase of 469 carriers, making the total number 5,810. The act of Jan. 3, 1887, which authorizes the discretionary extension of the service to cities having 10,000 inhabitants or collecting $10,000 of gross postal revenue, first became operative on July 1. Under its provisions free delivery was established, up to October 1, in 140 additional cities, and other applications were on file.

The money-order service continued to increase during the year, the amount of domestic orders issued reaching $117,462,660.89, and of international orders $9,035,530.31. The aggregate of postal-notes issued was $11,768,824.81, an increase of but $50,814.76 In the special delivery service there has been but slight increase during the year, the number of articles delivered being about one million and a half. A considerable saving in the cost of domestic mail transportation was made during the year. (See POSTAL FACILITIES.)

Pensions.—During the year, 55,194 new pensions were granted, besides 2,707 names restored to the rolls, making the total number of pensioners at the close of the year 406,007. Old names were dropped from the rolls to the number of 17,677. The new pensions granted numbered more than in any previous year. The aggregate annual value of all pensions on June 30 was $52,824,641, an increase for the year of $8,116,638. The amount paid for pensions during the year was $73,465,581, an increase over the previous year of $9,669,750. There was paid to 44,019 new pensioners during the year upon first payment $25,166,990.

Public Building.—The State, War, and Navy Building at Washington, was substantially completed at the close of the year. It was begun by the construction of the south wing, now occupied by the State Department, which was erected at a cost of $3,873,939, between June 21, 1871, and Dec. 31, 1875. The eastern wing, now occupied by the Navy Department, was built at a cost of $2,672,287, between July 14, 1872, and April 16, 1879. The northern wing, now occupied by the War Department, cost $1,914,501, and was built between May 22, 1879, and Dec. 28, 1882. The western and central wings, the erection of which was begun Feb. 18, 1884, are substantially completed at the present time, and will be ready for occupation early in 1888. The cost of these two wings will not exceed $2,-163,478. Under the legislative bill approved March 3, 1887, these two wings are to be occupied entirely by the War Department.

Alaska.—The Territorial officers for the year were as follow: Governor, Alfred P. Swineford; United States District Judge, Lafayette Dawson; Clerk of the Court and ex-officio Secretary and Treasurer, Henry E. Haydon; District Attorney, M. D. Ball, succeeded by Whitaker M. Grant. The total population of the Territory is estimated to be about as follows: Whites, 5,000; Creoles (practically white), 1,800; Aleuts, 3,000; natives (civilized, and more or less educated), 2,500; natives (uncivilized), 27,500; total, 39,800.

There are no fee-simple titles in the whole Territory, except in the cases of twenty small lots or parcels of land in the town of Sitka, and one in Saint Paul, Kadiak Island, the absolute ownership of which was vested in the occupants at the time of the transfer by the protocol executed by the American and Russian commissioners, Oct. 18, 1867. In all other cases the occupants and claimants of lands, except mining claims, are simply squatters.

During the year considerable progress has been made in the development of the gold-bearing ledges of southeastern Alaska, though as yet the Territory can boast of but one paying quartz-mine. This last is the great Paris mine, on Douglas Island, which, together with its 120-stamp mill, has been in continuous operation the past year, turning out a monthly product of over $100,000.

The commerce for the year is estimated as follows: Fur-trade, $2,500,000; gold (bullion and dust), $1,350,000; fisheries, $3,000,000; lumber and ivory, $100,000; total, $6,950,000.

There are now in operation in the Territory 15 Government day-schools, the cost of maintaining which must be paid from the appropriation of $25,000 made at the last session of Congress. The salaries of teachers aggregate $15,000; $5,000 is being expended in the erection of new school buildings at Sitka and Juneau and in the repair of an old Government building for the school at Wrangell.

Until this year there has been practically no local supervision of these schools, their management being in the hands of a Commissioner of Education residing at Washington. On June last, the Secretary of the Interior appointed a board of local management, consisting of the Governor, the judge of the district court, and the general agent.

The Centennial Anniversary of the Constitution.—The celebration of this event at Philadelphia, on September 15, 16, and 17, was attended with brilliant and imposing ceremonies. The exercises of each day were arranged and conducted by the Constitutional Centennial Commission, composed of members from each of the States and Territories appointed for this purpose early in the year by the respective Governors. There were present the President and other members of the Federal Government, the Governor and other officers of all the States and Territories, foreign ministers, and official dignitaries. On the first day the principal feature of the celebration was a grand industrial parade, designed to show the progress of the arts and sciences during the century just completed. This was participated in by over 12,000 persons. The evening was devoted to public receptions by Gov. Beaver and other people of note. On the second day, members of the Federal and State military organizations to the number of over 30,000 joined in a parade, passing in review before President Cleveland. In the evening the public reception given by the President at the Academy of Music was attended by thousands, including some of the most distinguished people of the land. On the third day occurred the literary exercises commemorative of the framing of the Constitution. This was the actual memorial day, being the same month and day on which the members of the convention of 1787 completed and signed their work and sent it forth to the thirteen colonies for ratification. The exercises took place in Independence Square, before a vast concourse. Ex-Minister John A. Kasson, President of the Centennial Commission, delivered the opening address, at the close of which he introduced the President of the United States. The concluding words of the President's address, given below, reflect the spirit of the occasion:

As we look down the past century to the origin of our Constitution, as we contemplate its trials and triumphs, as we realize how completely the principles upon which it is based have met every national peril and every national need, how devoutly should we confess with Franklin, "God governs in the affairs of men"; and how solemn should be the reflection that to our hands is committed this ark of the people's covenant, and that ours is the duty to shield it from impious hands. We receive it sealed with the tests of a century. It has been found sufficient in the past; and in all the future years it will be found sufficient, if the American people are true to their sacred trust. Another Centennial day will come, and millions yet unborn will inquire concerning our stewardship and the safety of their Constitution. God grant that they may find it unimpaired; and as we rejoice in the patriotism and devotion of those who lived a hundred years ago, so may others who follow us rejoice in our fidelity and in our jealous love for constitutional liberty.

The memorial oration that followed was delivered by Hon. Samuel F. Miller, Justice of the Supreme Court of the United States. The recital of a new national hymn, written for the occasion by Francis Marion Crawford, completed the exercises of the day and closed the celebration.

UNITED STATES, FINANCES OF THE. In reviewing the financial operations of the Government for the year 1887, the chief features that attract attention are: The increasing sums derived from all sources of revenue, the large decrease in national-bank circulation, the continued coinage of silver, and the heavy decrease of the public debt, which includes the redemption of the remainder of the 8-per-cent. bonds issued in 1882 in exchange for 3½-per-cent. bonds. The evil consequences from the withdrawal of money from the channels of business by the large accumulations in the national Treasury, which at one time threatened to be serious, both in themselves and as furnishing a theme for political contention, were happily averted by the judicious measures adopted by the Secretary of the Treasury. The following statements exhibit in detail the transactions of the Treasury during the year:

Receipts and Expenditures.—The ordinary revenues of the Government, from all sources, for the fiscal year ending June 30, 1887, were: Customs, $217,286,893.13; internal revenue, $118,823,391.22; sales of public lands, $9,254,286.42; profits on coinage, $8,929,252.83; tax on national banks, $2,385,851.18; consular, land, and patent fees, $3,801,647.16; customs fees, fines, etc., $1,053,087.86; sales of Indian lands, $1,479,028.81; Soldiers' Home fund, $1,226,259.47; Pacific Railroad sinking fund, $1,364,435.87; Pacific Railroad interest, $914,793.13; sales of old buildings, $624,882.20; sales of other Government property, $262,882.32; immigrant fund, $258,402.50; tax on sealskins, $317,452.75; deposits for surveying public lands, $94,289.76; revenues of District of Columbia, $2,367,869.01; miscellaneous, $1,458,672.04; total $371,403,277.66. The ordinary expenditures for same period were: Civil list, $22,072,436 27; foreign intercourse, $7,104,-

490.47; Indian service, $6,194,522.69; pensions, $75,029,101.79; military establishment, $88,561,025.85; naval establishment, $15,141,126.80; miscellaneous, including public buildings, light-houses, and collecting the revenue, $52,002,647.46; District of Columbia, $4,085,251.39; interest on the public debt, $47,741,577.25; total, $267,982,179.97; leaving a surplus of $103,471,097.69; which, with $24,455,720.46, drawn from the cash balance in the Treasury, made $127,926,818.15. This was applied as follows: To the redemption of bonds for the sinking fund, $47,903,248.15; to the redemption of 3-per-cent. bonds, $79,864,100; to the redemption of other securities, $159,470; total, $127,926,818.15.

The receipts for the year ending June 30, 1887, were $371,403,277.66, while the expenditures, including $5,789,265.29 for payment of judgments of the Court of Alabama Claims, were $267,932,179.97. This shows an excess of revenue of $103,471,097.69 during the year, or $9,514,509.13 more than that collected during the year ending June 30, 1886. Last year the customs receipts were $192,905,023.44. For the year 1887 the receipts from the same source were $217,286,893.13, or $24,381,869.69 greater than for the preceding year. The receipts from internal revenue also increased enough to show that there was a material growth in all the branches of business that contribute to the support of Government by special tax. In 1886 the internal revenue receipts were $116,805,986.48; for 1887 they were $118,823,391.22, showing an increase of $2,017,454.74. The other items of increase in 1887 were: Sales of public lands, $3,628,287.08; profits on coinage, $3,024,633.57, and miscellaneous, $2,774,023.41. There was a decrease of $857,717.89 in registers' and receivers' fees, tax on national banks, steamboat fees, deposits for surveying public lands, sales of Indian lands, shipping fees, fees on letters-patent, and sales of condemned naval vessels, making a net increase of revenue for the year of $34,963,550.60. The surplus revenue of $108,471,097.69 was accumulated in spite of the fact that the expenditures for the various branches of the public service were all, excepting for interest on the public debt, greater than they were for the same objects last year. The expenditures for civil and miscellaneous purposes have been greater by $11,097,895.74 than for the year 1886. The expenditures for the military establishment were $4,236,873.11 greater; those for the naval establishment were $1,238,239.06 greater; the Indian service $95,364.52, and the outlay for pensions was $11,624,237.76 more than in the preceding fiscal year. The decrease in expenditures for interest on the public debt was $2,838,568.72, making a net increase in all expenditures over the previous year of $25,449,041.47. The revenue derived from the various objects of internal taxation during the last two fiscal years is shown in the following table:

OBJECT.	1886.	1887.
Spirits	$69,092,266 00	$65,829,321 71
Tobacco	27,907,362 58	30,108,067 18
Fermented liquors	19,676,731 29	21,922,187 49
State banks and bankers		4,238 87
Oleomargarine		723,948 04
Miscellaneous	226,509 62	249,488 82
Total	$116,902,869 44	$118,837,301 06

The receipts from customs and internal revenue by quarter-years during 1886-'87 were:

QUARTERS.	1886.	1887.
Customs:		
First	$52,203,858 12	$59,177,566 50
Second	48,541,187 28	48,176,846 55
Third	49,564,788 89	57,200,270 26
Fourth	47,595,199 20	52,792,189 82
Total	$192,905,023 44	$217,286,893 13
INTERNAL REVENUE:		
First	$28,600,281 06	$28,980,043 94
Second	29,912,390 27	28,604,844 81
Third	25,990,668 74	26,422,825 02
Fourth	32,302,596 41	34,866,177 95
Total	$116,805,986 48	$118,823,891 22

State of the Treasury. — The following is a statement of the condition of the public treasury on Dec. 31, 1886, and Dec. 31, 1887:

ITEMS.	Dec. 31, 1886.	Dec. 31, 1887.
ASSETS:		
Gold coin	$187,196,596 81	$168,618,948 88
Gold bullion	80,951,421 66	122,728,223 19
Standard silver dollars	186,506,238 00	218,917,589 00
Silver bullion	4,739,376 81	3,352,686 64
Trade-dollar bullion		6,729,229 54
United States notes	29,679,325 78	22,409,424 94
National-bank notes	227,065 00	164,096 00
Deposits in national-bank depositaries	18,183,929 65	52,199,917 54
Fract'nal and minor coin	26,792,857 78	24,588,299 70
National-bank notes in process of redemption	2,785,270 02	4,755,840 74
Miscellaneous items	6,106,907 98	4,006,542 09
Total	$544,094,782 40	$642,640,200 28
LIABILITIES:		
Gold certificates outstanding	$97,215,605 00	$96,734,057 00
Silver certificates outstanding	117,246,670 00	176,555,428 00
Currency certificates outstanding	6,510,000 00	6,985,000 00
Reserve for redemption of United States notes	100,000,000 00	100,000,000 00
Funds for retirement of bank circulation	90,509,782 60	102,584,767 50
Five per cent. redemption fund	9,599,415 22	7,578,699 48
Disbursing officers' balances	28,818,596 88	37,766,835 79
Transfer ch'cks and drafts	4,045,217 74	2,519,738 88
Post-Office Department account	4,782,084 10	4,246,478 82
Matured debt and interest	20,980,269 64	15,844,944 50
Miscellaneous items	1,978,189 76	2,346,092 04
Balance	67,986,990 55	94,226,168 81
Total	$544,094,782 49	$642,640,200 28

The gold coin and bullion on hand increased from $268,128,018.47 to $305,342,187.07, or $37,214,168.60. There was a decrease of $481,548 in the gold certificates outstanding, making an increase in the net gold actually belonging to the Government of $37,695,716.60. The standard silver dollars on hand increased from $188,506,238 to $218,917,539, and the silver certificates outstanding increased from $117,246,670 to $176,855,428, or $59,608,753. The silver dollars not represented by certificates in circulation fell off from $71,259,568 to $42,062,116. The United States notes owned by the Treasury in excess of outstanding certificates decreased from $23,169,325.78 to $15,424,424.94; and the total assets increased from $544,094,782.49 to $642,640,200.28, or a gain of $98,545,417.79. The total liabilities increased from $476,105,791.94 to $548,414,031.47, or $72,308,239.53, the principal items of increase being in silver certificates outstanding and in the fund held for redemption of notes of national banks "failed," "in liquidation," and "reducing circulation." The available balance in the Treasury increased from $67,988,090.55 to $94,226,168.81.

The Public Debt. — During the year ending Dec. 31, 1887, the last of 3-per-cent. bonds issued under the act of July 12, 1882, were redeemed. In 1865, when the public debt of the United States was at its maximum, about $1,281,000,000 of the bonded debt was in 6 per cents., and $1,100,000,000 in all other forms, $830,000,000 being in 7·3 per cents. The first step after the war was to consolidate this indebtedness, and by 1868 the amount of 6-per-cent. debt had reached its maximum at $1,878,000,000, the aggregate interest-bearing debt being at that time $2,202,000,000. The next important step was the gradual substitution of 5 per cents. for 6-per-cent. bonds, which continued until 1876, when the amount of 6 per cents. was reduced below $1,000,000,000, and the amount of 5 per cents. rose to $711,000,000. At that time over $670,000,000 of the original debt had been paid in about eleven years, and the aggregate of interest-bearing debt was but $1,710,000,000. Then came the issue of $250,000,000 of 4½ per cents., and within three years thereafter, under the refunding operations so magnificently accomplished by the Treasury, the 6 per cents. were reduced to less than $300,000,000, the 5 per cents. to about $500,000,000, the 4½ per cents. remaining at $250,000,000, while $740,000,000 of the 4 per cents. were placed on the market. During the past six years the amount of the 4 and 4½ per cents. has but slightly decreased, while the 6 per cents. and 5 per cents. have been exchanged for 3½ and 3 per cent. bonds, while they in turn have been called in and redeemed. At the close of the year there remained outstanding less than $1,000,000,000 of interest-bearing debt, of which the 4½ per cents. run until 1891, and the 4 per cents. until 1907.

It thus appears that in about twenty-two years the country has paid off a bonded indebtedness exceeding $1,380,000,000, and reduced the annual interest charge from over $150,000,000 to less than $41,000.000; all of which has been accomplished with a develop-

ment of industries and of trade in all their branches, to a degree never before witnessed in the history of the country.

The following table shows the changes in the various denominations of United States legal-tender notes in circulation during the fiscal years 1886-'87:

DENOMINATIONS.	June 30, 1886.	June 30, 1887.
One dollar	$17,632,922 40	$8,197,876 50
Two dollars	18,904,369 50	9,005,579 00
Five dollars	85,629,219 00	95,064,850 50
Ten dollars	66,636,661 00	80,871,471 00
Twenty dollars.........	55,078,579 00	68,929,361 00
Fifty dollars	25,291,265 00	21,905,985 00
One hundred dollars	31,359,700 00	29,643,400 00
Five hundred dollars	12,424,000 00	7,704,500 00
One thousand dollars	87,361,500 00	81,197,500 00
Five thousand dollars ...	60,000 00	45,000 00
Ten thousand dollars ...	10,000 00	10,000 00
Total	$347,681,016 00	$347,681,016 00
Deduct for unknown denominations destroyed.	1,000,000 00	1,000,000 00
In circulation	$346,681,016 00	$346,681,016 00

The Coinage. — The value of the gold deposited at the mints and assay-offices during the fiscal year 1887, not including re-deposits, was $68,223,072.87 (3,666,990·17 standard ounces), against $44,909,749.23 in the preceding year, an excess of $23,313,323.64 over the fiscal year 1886. In addition there were re-deposits of the value of $15,193,706.53. Of the re-deposits of gold $3,517,523.15 represents the value of imported bars sent in for refining and coinage. The remainder, $11,676,183.38 was fine bars, of which $7,933,743.98 had been exported and subsequently imported into the United States, and re-deposited during the year. The value of the total deposits of gold, including all re-deposits as above cited, was $83,416,779 40 against $49,606,534.65 in 1886, an excess in the year 1887 of $33,810,244.75. The value of the silver deposited and purchased, not including re-deposits, was $47,756,618.75 (41,041,102·21 ounces) against $35,491,183.24 in the preceding year, an excess of $12,262,785.51. In addition, there were re deposits of silver amounting to $462,113.19. Of these re-deposits $169,514.91 consisted of fine bars, and $292,598.28 of imported bars, being the value of the silver contained in gold bullion originally deposited at the minor assay-offices. This total, calculated at coining rate in standard silver dollars, was $48,219,031.94 against $37,917,026.36 in the preceding year, an excess of $10,302.905.58. The total value of both gold and silver deposited and purchased at the mints of the United States during the fiscal year 1887, not including re-deposits, was $115,979,991.62, and including re-deposits, $131,635,811.34. The value of the gold and silver received at the mints and assay-offices during the fiscal year 1887, was greater than in any previous year since 1881. Of the gold deposited at the mints and assay-offices during the year, $82,973,027.41 was classified as of domestic production, against almost the same amount in 1886. The value of the foreign gold bullion deposited was $22,-

571,828.70, against $4,317,068.27 in 1886. The value of the foreign gold coin received and melted was $9,896,512.28, against $5,673,565.- 04, and the value of such coin deposited for re- coinage was $516,984,68, against $393,545.28 in the preceding year. In addition to the gold bullion, both of domestic and foreign produc- tion, and the foreign and domestic gold coin deposited, old material in the form of jewelry, bars, old plate, etc., was received, containing gold of the value of $2,265,219.85.

Of the silver bullion deposited and purchased at the mints and assay-offices during the year, $37,874,259.61 (32,548,191·98 standard ounces), was classified as of domestic production. The value of silver bullion of foreign extraction, classified as such, deposited during the year, was $1,457,406.01 (1,252,458·80 standard ounces). The value of foreign silver coin de- posited was $350.598.86 against $812,664.50 in the preceding year. The value of United States silver coin deposited, not including trade- dollars, was $768,739.32 (660,635·86 standard ounces), most of which consisted of worn and uncurrent coins transferred from the Treasury for recoinage. Trade-dollars were received mostly by transfer from the Treasury, and melted. The bullion contained 5,837,791·87 standard ounces, of the coinage value in stand- ard silver dollars of $6,793,066.89. In addition to the foreign and domestic bullion and coin deposited at the mints, silver, consisting of plate, jewelry, and old material generally, of the value of $512,848.06, was deposited during the year, against $467,156.86 in the preceding year.

The coinage of the fiscal year 1887 consisted of 98,122,517 pieces, of the value of $57,708,- 413.40. The gold coinage consisted of 3,724,- 720 pieces, of the value of $22,398,279, of which $22,280 was in double eagles, $7,560,670 in eagles, $14,800,375 in half-eagles, $3,501 in three-dollar pieces, $260 in quarter-eagles, and $6,193 in dollars. The silver coinage during the year consisted of 44,231,288 pieces, of the coinage value of $34,866,483.75, of which $33,- 266,831 was in silver dollars, and $1,095,279.- 50 in dimes. A very large minor coinage was executed during the year, consisting of 50,166,- 509 pieces, of the nominal value of $943,650.65. Of this coinage 11,047,523 pieces consisted of five cent nickels, 4,232 of three-cent nickel pieces, and 30,114,754 pieces of bronze cents. While the *value* of the coinage executed during the year 1887 was not so great as that of the preceding year, the number of pieces struck largely exceeded the coinage of that year, being 98,122,517 pieces, against 88,884,622 pieces in 1886. The act of Congress of Feb. 12, 1873, which revised the laws relative to the mints and coinage, provided for the coinage of a trade-dollar of 420 grains Troy, which should be a legal tender for any amount not exceed- ing five dollars in any one payment. By joint resolution of July 22, 1876, Congress provided that the trade-dollar should not thereafter be

a legal tender, and the Secretary of the Treas- ury was authorized to limit its coinage to such an amount as might be necessary to meet ex- port demand. By the act of March 3, 1887, Congress provided that for a period of six months thereafter, trade-dollars, not defaced, mutilated, or stamped, should be received at the Treasury in exchange for a like amount, dollar for dollar, of standard silver dollars, or of subsidiary coins of the United States, and that the trade-dollars so received should not be paid out, but recoined into silver dollars or subsidiary coin. By the same act the provision of law authorizing the coinage of trade-dollars was repealed. The total number of trade-dol- lars coined at the mints of the United States from 1878 to the date of the suspension of the coinage was 35,965,924, and the number re- deemed by the Treasury under the provisions of the act, was 7,689,036.

The coinage of gold the past year was smaller than in any previous year since 1850. The year 1885, with gold coinage of $24,861,123, and 1884, with a coinage of $27,932,924, were the smallest on record previously. The coin- age of silver dollars, on the other hand, ex- ceeds that of any previous year. A notable record was made in the matter of minor coin also, the aggregate coinage for the year being 51,000,000 pieces, of a total value of $934,000.

The increase in the coin and paper money in general circulation during the past two years and eight months was $73,345,456; while the total circulation of the country was greater on Nov. 1, 1887, than at any previous time in the history of the country.

National Banks.—Under the act of Feb. 25, 1863, establishing the national banking system, national banking associations are required to deposit with the Treasurer of the United States bonds to the amount of one third of their paid-in capital. In 1864 this provision was amended by fixing $30,000 as the minimum amount to be deposited. The act of June 20, 1874, permitted associations to withdraw any bonds they might have on deposit in excess of $50,000. The act of July 12, 1882, specified that banks of which the capital does not ex- ceed $150,000 should be required to keep on deposit bonds to the amount of one fourth of their capital, and by a special provision of law, banks and banking corporations having State charters may be converted into national banks.

The whole number of State banks converted into national banking associations from 1863 to Nov. 1, 1887 was 586, with a capital of $152,423,800, of which number 498, with a capital of $166,442,600, are still in existence. The whole number of national banks of pri- mary organization under the national - bank laws, from 1863 to November 1, 1887, was 3,219 with a capital of $347,216,500, of which number 2,568 with a capital of $412,474,100 are now in existence, making a grand total ex- isting on Nov. 1, 1887, of 3,061.

The act of July 12, 1882, contains the only provision made for the extension of the corporate existence of national banks, and 1,234, with a capital of $340,069,505 have availed themselves of the privilege. All of the banks organized under the act of 1863 have either ceased to exist or have had their corporate existence extended, while of those organized prior to 1882 under the national-bank act of 1864, 1,760 are still in operation under their original certificates of organization, 717 of which, with a capital of $96,915,550 will reach the expiration of their corporate existence from 1888 to 1901, inclusive.

During the year ending November 1, 1887, 225 national banks, with an aggregate capital of $30,546,000, to which $4,690,375 in circulating notes were issued, were organized. Of these banks 5, with a capital of $400,000, were located in the Eastern States; 33, with a capital of $7,525,000, were located in the Middle States; 50, with a capital of $6,199,000, were located in the Southern States; 107, with a capital of $14,012,000, were located in the Western States; 17, with a capital of $1,510,-000, were located in the Pacific States; and 13, with a capital of $900,000, were located in the Territories. Eight national banks, with an aggregate capital of $1,550,000, failed and were placed in the hands of receivers during the year.

On Oct. 31, 1883, national banks had on deposit to secure circulation bonds exceeding by 72·9 per cent. the minimum amount required by law. In 1884 the minimum was exceeded by only 35·3 per cent., in 1885 by 42 per cent., in 1886 by 4·1 per cent., and on Oct. 31, 1887, by 0·72 per cent.

UNITED WORKMEN, ANCIENT ORDER OF, an American co-operative fraternal beneficiary society, founded at Meadville, Pa., by Father J. J. Upchurch, a philanthropic mechanic, Oct. 27, 1868. The principles and objects of the order are officially stated as follow :

To embrace in its membership and give equal protection to all classes and kinds of labor, mental and physical; to strive earnestly to improve the moral, intellectual, and social condition of its members. To endeavor, by wholesome precepts, fraternal admonitions, and substantial aid, to inspire a due appreciation of the stern realities and responsibilities of life. To create and disburse a fund to the beneficiaries of its deceased members, as they may while living direct; thus enabling them to protect their families against want. The adoption of such secret work and means of recognition as will insure the protection of its members wherever the order may exist. To listen to lectures, read essays, discuss new inventions and improvements, encourage research in art, science, and literature, and maintain libraries for the use of members.

The requirements for membership (for white males only, between the ages of twenty-one and fifty years) are physical health, and freedom from hereditary disposition to disease; good moral character, belief in a Supreme Being the Creator of the universe, the ability to earn a livelihood, and a willingness to live without political, religious, sectarian, or social prejudices. A medical examination of the "first rank," equally rigid with those of the old-line life insurance companies, is made of all applicants by a local examiner, and this is subject to correction or rejection by the grand medical examiner.

The governing bodies of the order consist of a supreme lodge, grand lodges, and subordinate lodges. The supreme lodge has the following officers: past supreme master workman, supreme master workman, supreme foreman, supreme overseer, supreme recorder, supreme receiver, supreme guide, supreme watchman, supreme medical examiner, three supreme trustees, and all representatives elected by the various grand lodges composing the organization. To this may be added members of certain standing committees of the supreme lodge. Each grand lodge is entitled to elect three representatives, whose votes are cast in the proportion of one vote for each thousand members under its jurisdiction, whenever such a vote shall be demanded by five members, and also in case of election.

The powers of the supreme lodge extend to the exercise of the right to pass laws pertaining to the general welfare of the society. It exercises appellate jurisdiction from the decision of grand lodges, has sole power to regulate and control the unwritten or secret work of the order, and to make assessments for revenue to defray its expenses. Meetings of the supreme lodge are held annually at such times and places as may be determined at the preceding regular meeting. The particular time of holding the meetings has heretofore depended upon the latitude of the place selected, and has varied from March to June, as the place of meeting changed from south to north.

Grand lodges have grand officers having the same titles as those of the supreme lodge, together with duly elected representatives of the subordinate lodges under its jurisdiction, and of members of such standing committees as the several grand lodges may determine. Each grand lodge is permitted to fix the time and place of its meeting. Each is also empowered to adopt for its government a constitution, by-laws, rules and regulations, as also a constitution, by-laws, and rules for the government of subordinate lodges. It is provided that these laws shall have no binding force until approved by the supreme lodge. Grand lodges are permitted to establish subordinate lodges within their territorial jurisdiction, and to reprove and punish their misconduct; to make assessments for promoting the welfare of the order; to prescribe the duties of its officers and committees; to hear and determine all matters of controversy brought before it by appeal subject to the appellate jurisdiction of the supreme lodge; to establish a board of arbitration; to settle disputed questions arising between it and the beneficiaries of its deceased members, and between rival beneficiary claimants, and generally to do all things right and proper for promoting the honor, welfare, and perpetuity of the order within its bounds, subject also to the paramount authority of the supreme lodge. There are at present twenty-three grand lodges, which were instituted in the order named: Pennsylvania, Ohio, Kentucky, Indiana, Iowa, New York, Illinois, Missouri, Minnesota, Wisconsin, Tennessee, Michigan, California, Georgia, Alabama and Mississippi, Kansas, Ontario, Oregon and Washington, Massachusetts, Maryland, New Jersey and Delaware, Texas, Nevada, Colorado, New Mexico and Arizona Territory, Nebraska.

The subordinate lodge is the unit of organization. Its officers have similar titles to those of the supreme and grand lodges; and through the lodge organizations the beneficiary business of the membership is conducted with the grand lodge officers having its general control. The fees for admission to membership are fixed by each subordinate lodge within a certain minimum limit provided for by the grand lodge, which, according to the supreme lodge constitution, can not be less than two dollars. The payment of sick benefits is also left to the discretion of subordinate lodges, although the principles and teachings of the order enforce the mutual assistance and encouragement of a member or his family in misfortune; and the tendency of the organization is to unite the membership under a common bond of sympathy and fraternal allegiance. The subordinate lodge may punish offenses committed against the laws of the order or flagrant violation by the member of his duty to society.

The beneficiary system or insurance plan of this order is as follows: Each person, on obtaining full membership, pays one dollar into the beneficiary fund of his lodge. When death occurs in the order, and on the first day of any month there is not $2,000 on hand in the beneficiary fund of the grand lodge, the grand recorder issues an assessment of one dollar on each member, which is served by the financier of the several lodges, payment being required by the tenth day of the following month. The amount paid to the beneficiaries of each member is $2,000, with no divisions or classes, all benefits being equal. Collections from assessments to pay death-losses, are used for that purpose only, all other expenses of management, etc., being paid from the annual dues of members. All receiving or disbursing officers of the order are required to give bond for the faithful discharge of their duties, to keep separate accounts of the beneficiary and general funds, and to keep the moneys of the order distinct from all other moneys in their possession. The beneficiary business of the order is made public each month to the membership of the jurisdiction affected by it, through assessment notices sent to each member. Each grand lodge having a membership of two thousand or upward (with

the exception of certain grand lodges), is set apart as an independent beneficiary jurisdiction, and is permitted to manage its own beneficiary affairs. Most of the grand lodges have thus been organized under a separate beneficiary jurisdiction; but from the manner in which the order has grown, the grand lodges of Indiana, Tennessee, Georgia, Alabama, Mississippi, Texas, and some others, are included in one beneficiary jurisdiction known as that of the supreme lodge, and their beneficiary affairs are governed by that body. It results from the system of independent beneficiary jurisdictions, that each grand lodge managing its own beneficiary affairs is called upon to pay only death-losses occurring within itself.

The foregoing, however, must be taken subject to the provisions of what is known as the relief law. Under this law it is provided that whenever the death-rate in any beneficiary jurisdiction of the order may have been increased by exigencies to a point that would make the payment of assessments burdensome to its membership, the entire membership may be called upon to contribute to the relief of such overburdened jurisdiction. The maximum rate of assessments to be paid by each jurisdiction is fixed by the supreme lodge under the relief law, which is based upon the experience of the order, and other orders, as to the death-rate in various States. At present, the maximum annual rate of assessments to be paid by each jurisdiction before being entitled to relief from the entire order varies from 42 assessments in Kentucky, 37 in Ohio, 35 in Tennessee and other States, to 19 in Ontario and Iowa.

The early regalia of the order comprehended collars and aprons, bearing emblematic devices, with official jewels appropriate to each station. These have been supplanted by a badge, which is a circular medal of the diameter of two inches, bearing sun's rays, anchor, and shield, with the letters A. O. U. W. suspended from a cross-bar 1¼ inch in length, connected with a pin-bar 2¼ inches long and ¼ inch wide, by a ribbon 2¼ inches long and 1¼ inch wide; the pin-bar to have displayed upon it the letters C. H. P., being the initial letters of the motto of the order, which is "Charity, Hope, and Protection." These badges are worn alike by officers and members, but the officers' badges are distinguished by appropriate jewels of office suspended from the pin-bar. The color of the ribbon worn upon the badge is scarlet in the subordinate lodge, blue in the grand lodge, and purple in the supreme lodge. The ritual of the order is under the control of the supreme lodge. It teaches by impressive lessons the duties attaching to membership.

The Select Knights, a uniformed auxiliary body, composed of members in good standing of the Ancient Order of United Workmen, has a distinct organization and beneficiary system, the governing powers being vested in a supreme legion, in grand legions, and in subordinate legions. The principles and workings of this body are almost identical with those of the parent order. The latest official returns give the total membership in the United States and Canada at 187,000.

UNIVERSALISTS. The following is a summary of the statistics of the Universalist Church as given in the "Universalist Register" for 1888: Number of parishes, 988; of families, 39,338; of churches, 730; of church members, 37,807; of Sunday-schools, 657, having 54,636 members; of church edifices, 796; value of church property, $7,591,550. The returns show an apparent gain over the previous year of 43 parishes, 909 families, 35 churches, 2,257 church-members, 23 Sunday-schools, 1,083 members of Sunday-schools, 7 church edifices, and $97,-623 in valuation of church property. The returns include several places from which no reports had been previously received for many years. The educational institutions of the Church—Tuft's College, with its Divinity School, Medford, Mass.: St. Lawrence University, with its Theological School, Canton, N. Y.; Lombard University, with its theological department, Galesburg, Ill.; Buchtel College, Akron, Ohio; Clinton Liberal Institute, Port Plain, N. Y.; Westbrook Seminary, Deering, Me.; Dean Academy, Franklin, Mass.; Goddard Seminary, Barre, Vt.; and Green Mountain Perkins Academy, South Woodstock, Vt.; returned 110 professors and teachers, 1,284 students, and property, the value of which was estimated at $2,716,500.

The Universalist Historical Society has a library of 2,800 volumes, about 1,000 pamphlets, and many important manuscripts and papers.

The Brevoort Mission, New York, was founded as a school in 1858, and as a society in 1869. It has a fund which was founded by the mission school, and has been increased from various sources, and has been invested in the purchase of Brevoort Hall, from the rentals of which all expenses are fully met.

The General Convention of Universalists in the United States met in New York city October 19. The Rev. Dr. E. C. Sweetser presided. The Board of Trustees returned the total value of the church property, including churches, colleges, homes, and convention endowments at $11,128,410; and reported the amount of funds under the control of the convention to be $177,726, with a corresponding amount of securities. The receipts for the year had been $23,736, and the expenditures $17,985; besides which $47,598 had been applied to missionary and other church work, and an expenditure had been made for ministerial relief. The aggregate increase of the Convention funds for the year had been $6,808. The Committee on Foreign Missions reported in favor of organizing a mission in Japan. A resolution was adopted, which, to be valid, has to be approved by another meeting of the Convention, for holding the sessions of the Convention bien-

nially instead of annually. The committee appointed by a previous General Convention to prepare a new formula for the profession of faith reported a series of articles which, after discussion and modifications, were accepted to be referred to the next General Convention. They are as follow:

1. I believe that the Holy Scriptures of the Old and New Testaments contain a revelation from God to mankind.

2. I believe in one God, the Father Almighty, Maker of heaven and earth: in Jesus Christ his Son, who is the revealer of God and the Saviour of the world from sin, and in his Holy Spirit the Comforter, through which all disciples of Christ are united in one spiritual body.

3. I believe in the forgiveness of sins; in the certainty of retribution; in the immortality of the human soul, and in the final holiness and happiness of all mankind.

4. I believe that the opportunities, obligations, and rewards of religion are in their nature eternal, and that I ought to strive earnestly for salvation by repenting of my sins and diligently using the means of grace which God has provided for me.

The following resolutions were approved as expressing the sense of the Convention on the subjects to which they severally refer:

1. That the position of the Convention in favor of total abstinence be reasserted.

2. That the Convention be recorded as opposed to any legislation looking to a relaxation of the Sunday liquor laws.

3. That the board of trustees, in consultation with the faculties of the theological schools, be directed to consider the feasibility of educating young men at their homes by means of correspondence.

4. That the convention is opposed to making the public schools sectarian.

The report of the committee appointed to consider the reports of the Board of Trustees recommended the establishment of young people's missionary societies; that all means be taken to promote an increase of the ministry; that Sunday-school children should be encouraged to become members of the Church; and that the title to church property should be vested in the State Conventions, in order that the property may be secured to the Universalist denomination.

It was represented at the meeting of the Woman's Centenary Association that since its institution that society had raised $200,000, and had expended all of it except $10,000, which was held as a permanent fund in the promotion of the objects of the Association, which are chiefly the aid of poor parishes, infirm ministers, and struggling students. The year's receipts of the Association had been $4,149, and its disbursements $1,586. Its permanent fund amounted to $7,467.

URUGUAY, a republic in South America. Area, 69,835 square miles. In 1885 the population was 582,858, showing an increase of 62,322 since 1883.

Government.—The President is Gen. Máximo Tajes. The Cabinet is composed of the following ministers: Prime Minister and Interior, Dr. Herrera y Obes; Foreign Affairs, Señor J. G. Lagos; Finance, Dr. A. M. Marquez;

Justice, Dr. D. Terra; War and Navy, Col. de Leon. The American Consul at Montevideo is Edward J. Hill, and the Uruguayan Consul-General at New York is Señor E. M. Estrázulas, and the Consul at San Francisco J. G. Grace.

Army and Navy.—The standing army was increased to 3,323 men early in 1886. There is also a police force of 3,200 men and a national guard of 20,000.

The navy is composed of three small steamers and three gunboats, the latter including the former French gunboat "Tactique," purchased in 1886.

Postal Service.—The number of post-offices in 1886 was 438. Ordinary private letters increased from 2,635,980 in 1884 to 2,911,969 in 1885; registered from 92,850 to 103,746; Government dispatches from 116,543 to 131,656; postal-cards declined from 32,217 to 28,611; newspapers rose from 8,689,269 to 8,876,805, and samples from 103,316 to 150,394; money-orders from $2,743,697 to $2,854,589; the receipts decreased from $170,559 to $163,459.

Finances.—The amount of paper money in circulation on Jan. 1, 1885, was $1,327,778. In October, 1886, the Chamber of Representatives passed the Senate bill authorizing the issue of $4.700,000 consolidated bonds of the second series and abrogating the law authorizing the issue of a further amount of treasury notes. In this manner the amount of consolidated bonds created in 1886 reached the sum of $12,700,000, bearing 8 per cent. interest. On Jan. 1, 1887, the combined home and foreign indebtedness aggregated $72,205,721. In the autumn the Government resolved to consolidate this debt out of part of the proceeds of a £20,000,000 loan, to run thirty-three years, during which it is to be canceled by a sinking fund and to pay 6 per cent. interest per annum. The amount required being about £14,000,000, the proceeds of the remaining £6,000,000 were set aside for expenditure on public works.

New Press Law.—The new press law, passed in 1886, contains a clause providing that foreign residents not naturalized are prohibited from criticising in public prints the politics of the country, the penalty being an exile of two years and fines, for the payment of which the printer and his establishment will be held responsible.

Extradition Treaty.—During 1886 an extradition treaty between Uruguay and Spain was negotiated and ratified.

Commercial Travelers' License.—Early in 1886 a decree appeared making it obligatory on all commercial travelers, non-residents of the country and not representatives of firms there established, to take out a license for one year at a cost of $2.500, to be annually renewed, payable in advance.

Railroads.—There were in running order, on July 1, 1887, 556 kilometres of railway, comprising the Central Railroad of Uruguay, in operation between Montevideo and Paso de los Toros, 274 kilometres in length; the North-western, 176 kilometres, connecting Salto with Cuareim, on the Brazilian frontier, where it joins the system of Brazil; the Eastern of Uruguay, from Montevideo to Barra de Santa Lucia, a distance of 21 miles, and finally the 85 kilometres from El Paso to Salto via Paysandu.

Telegraphs.—The length of land lines of telegraph in operation in 1884 was 1,492 kilometres, and there was besides a cable of 160 kilometres. The number of offices was 29; of operators, 96: inland messages forwarded, 35,-348; messages sent abroad, 26,790; in transit, 11,530; aggregate telegrams forwarded, 78,-663.

Commerce.—Uruguayan commerce generally suffered from the attempt at revolution in 1886 and subsequently from the cholera. Instead of the usual 1,000,000 head of cattle slaughtered, only 400,000 were killed. The American trade was as follows:

FISCAL YEAR.	Imports into the United States.	Domestic export to Uruguay.
1887	$3,518,761	$1,898,725
1886	4,925,848	1,110,545

The maritime movement at Montevideo showed in 1886 2,951 sea-going vessels entered, with a joint tonnage of 2,707,066. The British flag was represented by 1,000,000 tons, France coming next with 726,000 tons, then Italy with 403,000, Sweden with 126,000, and Belgium with 116,000.

Invasion.—An unsuccessful attempt at invading Uruguay and overthrowing its Government was made by the revolutionary Gen. Arredondo from Argentine territory early in April, 1886. He began by encamping near Salto, thence proceeded to Concordia, seized the river steamers, and debarked at Guavizo at the head of 2,000 men; but after reaching Quebracho he was defeated by a strong force under the command of Gen. Tajes.

Assassination.—On Aug. 17, 1886, an attempt was made to kill President Santos while he was entering the theatre, and he was wounded in the face, the would-be assassin having fired a revolver at his head. An infuriated crowd attacked the assassin and injured him so terribly that he soon died. Although the wound appeared slight the President suffered from it, and on November 18 resigned the presidency and embarked for Europe. Gen. Tajes, then Minister of War and the Navy, became his successor. On his return from Europe early in 1887, ex-President Santos was not allowed to land, having been exiled by the National Legislature. He consequently went to Rio de Janeiro.

UTAH. Territorial Government.—The following were the Territorial officers during the year: Governor, Caleb W. West; Secretary, William C. Hall; Treasurer de facto, James Jack; Auditor de facto, Nephi W. Clayton. (The last two officials claim to hold office by virtue of an election by the people, although the organic act of the Territory requires their appointment by the Governor with the consent of the Council.) Chief Justice of the Supreme Court, Charles S. Zane; Associate Justices, Jacob S. Boreman and H. P. Henderson. The office of Superintendent of Public Schools was abolished by the Edmunds-Tucker law of Congress, which came into force March 3, and the office of Commissioner of Schools substituted. The Territorial Supreme Court appointed P. L. Williams to the new office in April. Previous to March the office of Superintendent of Schools was claimed by Williams under an executive appointment and by L. G. Nuttall through election by the people.

Population.—No enumeration has been made since 1880, but estimates place the number of people in the Territory at 200,000. During the year 1,500 Mormon emigrants, chiefly English and Scandinavian, were added to the population. A total of 4,158,743 acres of public land had been taken for settlement up to June 30 out of 11,711,118 acres surveyed.

Finances.—The Territory has no public debt, but, owing to the veto by Gov. Murray of the appropriation bills passed by the last Legislature, the expenses of the Government for nearly four years are unpaid, and a large amount of outstanding warrants are in existence, which can not be redeemed till the Legislature of 1888 makes the necessary appropriations. For the year ending Jan. 1, 1886, the Territorial receipts were $193,628.56, and the expenditures $129,445.94. The surplus had increased before the end of 1887 to over $200,000.

Education.—The number of children of school age in the Territory for the school year 1886–'87 was as follows: Of non-Mormon parents, 6,868; of Mormon parents, 46,225; total, 53,093. The University of Deseret, which is supported by the Territory, contained at the close of the year 231 pupils in all departments, 149 males and 82 females. There is a normal department connected with the university, to which the Commissioner of Schools annually appoints forty students, and a department for the instruction of deaf-mutes established in 1884. A new building has been in process of construction since 1881, when $20,000 was appropriated therefor. This sum and over $35,000 additional obtained from private subscriptions has been expended, but a further sum of $30,000 will be needed.

Insane Asylum.—This institution, at Provo, greatly needs enlarged accommodations. The number of inmates during 1886 averaged 63 daily, the cost of support was 70 cents per capita each day, and $16,028.75 for the whole institution for the year. The number of inmates in April, 1887, had increased to 78.

Penitentiary.—The sum of $50,000 was appropriated by the Forty-eighth Congress for a Federal penitentiary at Salt Lake City, the construction of which was not begun till late in 1887. The penitentiary buildings now at that place are inadequate. On the last of Oc-

tober they contained 215 prisoners, nearly half of whom were confined for polygamy and similar offenses.

Manufactures.—The aggregate annual value of the manufactured products of the Territory amounts to $8,726,500, giving employment to 3,573 persons, and capital amounting to $4,468,350. There are 120 flour-mills, 8 woolen-mills, 75 brick-making firms, 43 wood-working establishments, and five knitting-factories, besides breweries, tanneries, shoe-shops, foundries, salt-manufactories, and other industries.

Agriculture.—A careful estimate shows that the wheat-crop of 1887 was about 3,250,000 bushels. The crop of oats is estimated at 1,250,000 bushels, some farms yielding 85 bushels to the acre. About 600,000 bushels of barley were raised, and 500,000 bushels of corn.

Mining.—The following is a summary of the mineral product of the Territory for 1886: 2,407,550 pounds of copper, at 6 cents per pound, $144,453; 208,800 pounds of refined lead, at 4·63 cents per pound, $9,667.44; 48,456,260 pounds of unrefined lead, at $58 per ton, $1,405,281.54; 5,918,842 ounces of fine silver, at $0.9902 per ounce, $5,860,837.34; 10,577 ounces of fine gold, at $20 per ounce, $211,540; total export value, $7,631,729.32. The total for 1887 is almost exactly the same. The coal product for 1886 was 161,439 tons, valued at $347,134 at the mine; for 1887 there was a slightly increased output.

Constitutional Convention.—Early in June a call was issued by the leaders of the People's (Mormon) party for the election of delegates to a constitutional convention at Salt Lake City, to assemble on the last day of the month. In this movement, designed to inaugurate an agitation for the admission of Utah as a State, an effort was made to enlist the aid of the Gentile population, but without success, and the Convention remained, as it originated, entirely a Mormon affair. It continued in session seven days, and drafted a Constitution, of which the following provisions, in view of their authorship, are the most noteworthy features:

SECTION 3 (of Article I). There shall be no union of church and state, nor shall any church dominate the state.

SEC. 12 (of Article XV).. Bigamy and polygamy being considered incompatible with a "republican form of government," each of them is hereby forbidden and declared a misdemeanor. Any person who shall violate this section shall, on conviction thereof, be punished by a fine of not more than one thousand dollars and imprisonment for a term of not less than six months nor more than three years, in the discretion of the court. This section shall be construed as operative without the aid of legislation, and the offenses prohibited by this section shall not be barred by any statute of limitation within three years after the commission of the offense; nor shall the power of pardon extend thereto until such pardon shall be approved by the President of the United States.

It is further provided that section 12 shall not be amended or changed unless such amendment or change "be reported to the Congress of the United States, and shall be by Congress approved and ratified, and such approval and ratification be proclaimed by the President of the United States."

The Constitution was submitted to the people on the first Monday of August, and ratified by a vote of 13,195 to 502, the non-Mormons generally not voting. In December it was submitted to Congress by Delegate Caine, accompanied by a memorial from the Convention praying for the admission of Utah to the Union.

Political.—In accordance with section 22 of the Edmunds-Tucker act, which abolishes the existing legislative districts of the Territory and provides for a redistricting and reapportionment of the members of the Legislature by a commission consisting of the Governor, Secretary, and Board of Utah Commissioners, a meeting of these officials was held at Salt Lake City in May, at which the Territory was divided into twenty-four representative and twelve councilor districts, giving approximately one representative to every 7,000 inhabitants, and one councilor to every 14,000. Elections were held in these new districts on August 1 for members of the Legislature of 1888. The Mormons elected ten of the twelve councilors, and twenty-one of the twenty-four representatives. This is the first time that the anti-Mormon party has elected as many as five of its candidates. Three of these were chosen in Salt Lake City.

The Edmunds-Tucker Act.—In addition to the provisions already referred to, this law enacts that every marriage in the Territory shall be duly recorded in the Probate Court; that the judge of each Probate Court shall be a pointed by the President, with the advice and consent of the Senate; that all laws of the Territory recognizing the capacity of illegitimate children to inherit shall be annulled; that every widow shall have a dower of one third of her husband's estate; that females shall not be allowed to vote; that in prosecutions for bigamy or polygamy the husband or wife may testify with the consent of the other, and persons desired as witnesses may be arrested by order of the Court, in order to insure their attendance, if it is thought they will not obey a subpœna; that prosecutions for adultery may be begun by persons other than the husband or wife; that every voter shall be required to state on oath whether he is married or single, and, if married, the name of his lawful wife, and shall promise to support the Constitution and obey the laws, especially those against polygamy: that the corporation known as the Mormon Church and the corporation called the Perpetual Emigrating Fund Company are hereby abolished, and that the Attorney-General of the United States shall take measures to secure the forfeit and escheat of their property to the United States, the proceeds thereof to be invested for the benefit of the common schools of the Territory. In pursuance of this act, the Attorney-General in August instituted suits in the Territorial Supreme Court against the above-named corporations, praying for a decree of dissolution and for the appointment of receivers of their property. The amount owned by the Church is estimated at $3,000,000, and that of the Fund Company at $1,000,000. In November the prayer of the bill was granted, and a receiver appointed, who proceeded to take possession of such property as could be found. These proceedings are regarded merely as preliminary to the real issue upon the constitutionality of the act authorizing this confiscation.

Under the various acts of Congress, 160 convictions for polygamy and unlawful cohabitation were obtained during the year; 71 in the First, 26 in the Second, and 63 in the Third District Court of the Territory. Sentence was suspended as to 15, upon their promising to obey the law in the future.

V

VENEZUELA, a republic in South America; area, 1,689,898 square kilometres. The population on Jan. 1, 1886, was 2,198,320. The cities having over 20,000 inhabitants were: Carácas, the capital, 70,509; Valencia, 36,145; Maracaybo, 31,921; Barquisimeuto, 28,918.

The sum of 5,000,000 francs has been set aside for facilitating immigration, and two agricultural settlements have been founded.

Government.—The President is Gen. Don Hermógenes Lopez, whose term of office expires on Feb. 20, 1888. His Cabinet was composed of the following ministers: Foreign Affairs, Dr. D. B. Urbaneja; Interior and Justice, Dr. F. Gonzalez Guinan; Public Works, Gen. T. C. de Castro: Public Credit, Señor A. A. Herrera; Public Instruction, Gen. T. M. Ortega Martinez; Finance, Dr. T. P. Rojas Paul: War and Navy, Gen. F. Carabaño. The United States Minister Resident at Carácas is Charles L. Scott. The American consul at La Guayra is Winfield Scott Bird. The Venezuelan *chargé d'affaires* in Washington is Señor José Antonio Olavarria. The Venezuelan Consul-General at New York, is Señor Francisco Antonio Silva.

Army and Navy.—The effective strength of the permanent army is 1,842 men. The national militia numbers 265,000 men, who can easily be formed into an active army of 100,000, for which there are in the arsenal the necessary arms and material.

The navy is composed of 8 steamers, 1 schooner, and 1 schoolship, manned by 7 officers, 8 marine guards, 8 naval cadets, 8 second officers, 27 boatsmen, 6 machinists, and 102 marines.

Postal Service.—There are in operation in the

republic 162 post-offices, which in 1886 forwarded 2,911,400 items of mail matter, against 2,673,404 in 1888. The annual expenditure is 583,868 francs.

Railroads and Telegraphs.—In 1887 there were in the country 232 kilometres of railway open to traffic, with 407 more in course of construction. Besides, several contracts have been made for the construction of 1,982 kilometres, which will give a total of 2,622 kilometres. On Jan. 1, 1888, the telegraphic lines of Venezuela made an extension of 4,179 kilometres. During the fiscal year of 1885-'86, the offices transmitted 68,066 official messages and 174,320 private telegrams. The Venezuelan Government has granted a concession for two submarine cables between that country and the United States. The concession will carry with it a liberal subsidy for a term of years, and will last seventy years.

Finances.—On Jan. 1, 1887, the public indebtedness included a home debt amounting to 39,285,692 francs, and a foreign debt of 67,-016,250 francs. The budget estimate for 1887-'8 was 27,695,000 francs income, the expenditure being the same.

Tariff Changes.—An important change in the tariff, effectually prohibiting the importation of foreign lumber, was promulgated in January, 1887. The custom heretofore observed has been to admit, free of duty, all classes of machinery. But admission upon such terms, must hereafter depend upon the pleasure of the President.

In February a decree was issued abolishing the discriminating duty of 30 per cent. on European and American goods coming from the West Indies. In May the duty on maccaroni and vermicelli was raised from 15 cents to 25 cents a kilogramme, and on the flour for making them from 2 to 5 cents a kilogramme.

Education.—In the fourteen years from 1872 to 1886, there was an increase in the public schools of 1,565 schools and 84,385 pupils. There are in the country 2 universities, 6 first-class federal colleges, 14 second class, 4 normal schools, 24 private colleges, 9 national colleges for girls, 1 polytechnic school, 1 of arts and trades, 1 naval and 1 telegraphic school. The libraries and public collections that existed in the public offices and suppressed convents were consolidated in 1874 into the Library of the University of Caracas, which now contains 28,895 volumes. The library is open daily to the public. The National Museum, founded also in 1874, contains numerous collections of natural history and national history, which, after the exhibition of Bolivar's Centennial in 1883, were enriched with ethnographical, zoölogical, and geological specimens and valuable samples of all the natural products of the country.

Commerce.—The imports for 1885-'86 were valued at 47,168,277 francs, and the exports at 82,304,289 francs. Among the imports were 15,296,873 francs from the United States; from England, 9,690,105 francs; from France, 9,272,-879 francs; from Germany, 8,949,085 francs; and from the West Indies, 1,680,691 francs. The chief articles exported were coffee, 35,-733,423 francs, worth; Cocoa, 8,447,986 francs; hides, 3,695,312 francs; skins, 2,877,746 francs; ore, 3,263,900 francs; cattle, 834,366 francs. The export of gold amounted to 21,230,800 francs, and there was also specie to the amount of 4,442,707 francs.

The American trade was as follows:

FISCAL YEAR.	Import into the United States.	Domestic export to Venezuela.
1887	$8,261,286	$2,827,010
1886	5,791,021	2,695,488

Survey of Lake Maracaybo.—Early in 1887 the United States Government sent to Maracaybo the dispatch boat "Dolphin," for the purpose of surveying the lake and port of Maracaybo, with their approaches, the charts in use being old and unreliable. Lake Maracaybo has never been surveyed, and it is uncertain what kind of vessel may be placed on it. The lake is 180 miles long, by 70 miles wide. The lands about it are rich, producing India-rubber, coffee, and articles of food.

VERMONT. State Government.—The following were the State officers during the year: Governor, Ebenezer J. Ormsbee, Republican; Lieutenant-Governor, Levi K. Fuller; Secretary of State, Charles W. Porter; Treasurer, William H. DuBois; Auditor, E. Henry Powell; Inspector of Finance, Carroll S. Page; Commissioner of Taxes, W. P. Dillingham; Railroad Commissioner, Thomas O. Seaver; Superintendent of Public Instruction, Justus Dartt; Chief-Justice, Homer E. Royce; Associate Justices, Jonathan Ross, H. Henry Powers, Wheelock G. Veazey, Russell S. Taft, John W. Rowell, and William H. Walker. There was no general election and no legislative session during the year.

Finances.—For the year ending July 31, 1887, the Treasurer reports receipts amounting to $426,797.14; cash on hand at the beginning of the year, $160,974.97; total, $587,772.11. The expenditures during the same period were $566,295.84, leaving a balance of $21,476.77 in the treasury on July 31. The largest receipts were derived from the tax on corporations, which amounted to $220,702.05. The convict labor of the State yielded an income of $10,-385.50, and the courts and judges of probate paid into the treasury $45,083.08. The liabilities of the State on July 31 amounted to $234,165. The Legislature of 1886 provided for the assessment for the year 1887-'88 of a property-tax which will yield a revenue of $210,017 in addition to the ordinary income for that year, and will enable the Treasurer to cancel the floating debt.

Education.—The following statistics exhibit the condition of the public schools for the year ending March 31, 1887: Number of districts, 2,116; number of schools, 2,547; number of pupils between five and twenty years of age enrolled, 71,402; average daily attendance, 45,-705; number of male teachers, 555; number of female teachers, 3,644; average wages per week of male teachers, $8.45; average wages per week of female teachers, $5.22; total revenue for school purposes, $607,382.37; total expenditure, not including supervision for school purposes, $602,800.20; appropriations to normal schools, $7,908. Not more than seventy-five per cent. of children of school age are enrolled in the public schools, and only about sixty-five per cent. of those enrolled are regularly in attendance. A recent writer remarks concerning the school system:

The greatest obstacle to the improvement of the public schools of Vermont is the district system, which should give place to the more efficient town system. The changed condition of the population in the rural districts by Western emigration of the old Puritan stock and the immigration of foreigners from Canada and other countries has left the country districts at the mercy of local mismanagement, which has starved out the once flourishing district school. To revive it under its old forms and conditions is out of the question. The subject of the adoption of the town system of schools has been before the people of the State for over twenty years.

Banks.—The savings-banks of Vermont, June 30, 1887, showed 53,810 depositors, credited with $15,587,050, an increase of 4,357 depositors, and $1,833,087 over last year. The average amount to the credit of one individual was $289.67, an increase of $1.44 over 1886. Three banks paid five-per-cent. dividends to depositors; two, four and three fourths; eight, four and one half; and four, four per cent. Of the ten trust companies in the State, two have passed dividends to stockholders; one has paid fourteen, two eight, three six, one five, and one three per cent. The total accumulations, including the surplus, undivided earnings, and interest, amount to $106,665.43 more than last year. New trust companies have organized at St. Albans and St. Johnsbury and a savings-bank at White River Junction.

VICTORIAN JUBILEE. Victoria was proclaimed Queen of Great Britain and Ireland, June 21, 1837. The occurrence of the fiftieth anniversary of her accession to the throne, June 21, 1887, was accordingly celebrated throughout her kingdom and colonies, and by English people the world over, as the "Queen's Jubilee." The festival so named originated among the Israelites, but was borrowed for the Roman Catholic Church by Pope Boniface VIII, by whom it was instituted as a centennial festival. Clement VI abridged the period to fifty years, and this time has been generally observed ever since his celebration of it in 1350 as "the year of jubilee."

Great preparations were made throughout the British Empire for an appropriate celebration of Queen Victoria's Jubilee, the most solemn and most notable ceremonies taking place in London. The chief function in observance of the day was the great procession of royal persons and others, which accompanied the Queen in her state progress to Westminster Abbey on June 21. This procession was guarded by nearly 10,000 troops, besides the entire police force of London and its suburbs. The royal *cortège* included a number of Indian princes and the King of Denmark, King and Queen of the Belgians, King of Saxony, King and Crown-Prince of Greece and Prince George of Greece, Crown-Prince of Portugal, Crown-Prince and Crown-Princess of Austria, and the Grand Duke of Mecklenburg-Strelitz. The princesses of the blood royal of England, with their attendants, occupied five carriages, preceding the state coach, drawn by eight cream-colored horses, in which were the Queen, the Princess of Wales, and the Princess Royal, Victoria, Crown-Princess of Germany. Accompanying the state coach as escort, on horseback, were the Grand Duke Sergius of Russia, Prince Albert Victor of Wales, Prince William of Prussia, Prince Henry of Prussia, Prince George of Wales, the hereditary Prince of Saxe-Meiningen, Prince Christian Victor of Schleswig-Holstein, Prince Louis of Battenberg, Prince Christian of Schleswig-Holstein, the Crown-Prince of Germany, and the Grand Duke of Hesse. After them came Prince Henry of Battenberg and the Marquis of Lorne, the Prince of Wales and the Duke of Connaught, and the Duke of Edinburgh riding alone. The streets through which the procession passed were crowded with people, in number said to exceed any similar occasion in the history of England, excepting, perhaps, the funeral of the Duke of Wellington. The ceremonies in Westminster Abbey were solemn and impressive, and were witnessed by the Queen, throned in state, dressed in her royal robes, and surrounded by the members of the royal family. London was profusely decorated, and at night was generally illuminated. On the 22d the Queen received addresses and gifts at Buckingham Palace, the latter being a vast number of articles of great value, from all parts of the world, and including the sum of £75,000 presented by "the women of England." On the same day, her Majesty, with the Prince and Princess of Wales, was present at a grand *fête* in Hyde Park, where she was received and welcomed by 30,-000 children. The Queen on this occasion presented a memorial cup to a little girl chosen to represent the children present. On the same day her Majesty unveiled at Windsor, in the presence of an enormous gathering of people, a statue of herself. The day was celebrated in Paris by a Jubilee garden-party at the British Embassy, and in the cities of India, Australia, New Zealand, and Canada, by appropriate and enthusiastic ceremonies. Addresses, telegrams, and letters of congratulation from potentates and high officials of all the powers were received at court, and British citizens in various parts of the United States sent addresses and resolutions recognizing the event. On June 28 the Queen's Jubilee was celebrated at St. Paul's Cathedral, London, by religious ceremonies of thanksgiving. On the 25th there was held a state banquet at Windsor Castle, and on the 27th the Queen received there numerous deputations bearing congratulatory addresses. On the 28th a Jubilee ball took place at the Mansion House, at which were present four kings, members of the royal family, and many foreign princes. On the 29th the Queen gave a grand garden-party at Buckingham Palace, and there reviewed, on July 2, 28,000 volunteers. On July 4 the Queen laid the first stone of the Imperial Institute at South Kensington. On the 6th, by royal command, a state ball was given at Buckingham Palace. The ceremonies and functions of the Jubilee were closed by a review at Aldershot, by the Queen, on July 9, of 60,000 regulars, militia, and volunteers. On November 4 the Queen caused to be made public the proclamation of her thanks for the loyal demonstrations of her subjects.

VIRGINIA. State Government.—The following were the State officers during the year: Governor, Fitzhugh Lee, Democrat; Lieutenant-Governor, John E. Massey; Secretary of State, H. W. Flournoy; Treasurer, A. G. Harmon; Auditor, Morton Marye; Second Auditor, Frank G. Ruffin; Attorney-General, Rufus A. Ayers; Superintendent of Public Instruction, James L. Buchanan; Railroad Commissioner, H. G. Moffett; President of the Supreme Court, Lunsford L. Lewis; Judges, T. T. Fauntleroy, Robert A. Richardson, Benjamin T. Lacy, and Drury A. Hinton.

The Legislature and the Debt.—On March 16 the Governor convened the Legislature in extra session. His reasons therefor, as expressed in his message, were as follow:

1. To call your attention to the present condition of the debt of the Commonwealth and to the recent decision of the Supreme Court of the United States in reference to the law imposing tax upon sample merchants.

2. To ask that you receive and, if proper, adopt the work of the revisers of the code.

3. To request that you make proper provision for the insane confined in jails because of insufficient accommodations at the regular asylums.

With reference to the debt, the Governor made two suggestions, one for the appointment of a committee to confer with the foreign bond-holders regarding a settlement, the other detailing an amendment to the law regulating the reception of past-due coupons in payment of taxes. In accordance with the first suggestion, a joint committee of ten members was chosen on March 29, and directed to confer with a committee of the bond-holders at a date not later than April 20. The Legislature then adjourned from the 6th to the 28th of April, to await the result of the conference. Two representatives of the bond-holders appeared, and sessions were held for several weeks, but without reaching an agreement. The final proposal

of the English representatives, requiring the State to assume a debt of $24,909,919, and the payment of $922,508 in annual interest, was far beyond what the State was willing to concede.

The second suggestion of the Governor was made in view of the recent decisions of the United States Supreme Court, regarding the validity of the act of Jan. 14, 1882, which required that all debt coupons tendered in payment of taxes should be proved to be genuine before being received. The requirements of the act were decided by the Supreme Court to be reasonable in the case of Antoni *vs.* Greenhow; but in Poindexter *vs.* Greenhow it was held that the tender of *genuine* coupons was payment, and that the collecting officer, if he subsequently levies, is a trespasser and liable for damages. In view of these decisions, the collecting officers were unwilling to subject themselves to the danger of a suit by levying upon the property of those who had tendered their coupons, but who refused to surrender them for identification or to prove them, and the Attorney-General finally declined to advise collecting officers to execute the law. As no penalty was imposed for its non-enforcement, it had therefore become almost a dead letter at the beginning of the year. Meanwhile, the act of 1882 being found inapplicable to taxes payable for licenses, an act had been passed in March, 1886, practically extending its provisions to those cases. The constitutionality of this law was brought before the State Supreme Court in January, 1887, and affirmed in the case of the Commonwealth *vs.* Jones. Soon afterward the same question was brought before Judge Bond of the Federal Circuit Court in another case, and an opposite decision was reached on February 2, when the judge released on *habeas corpus* the violators of the law. An appeal was taken to the Supreme Court from this decision. Under both of these acts, the tax-payer was first required to pay in money, surrender his coupons, and then file a petition to prove them in the local court. If he was successful, his money was refunded by the State. Upon refusal to make this proof after tender, the collecting officer was authorized to collect the taxes as if no tender had been made. The suggestion offered by the Governor and adopted by the Legislature was that, after a tender, the State, instead of the individual, should take the initiative by instituting a suit against the tax-payer and giving him a day in court to prove his coupons according to law. This lifted the burden of the law from the collectors, and placed it upon the State where it belonged. No sooner had it been passed, however, than the foreign bond-holders, through their attorney, applied to Judge Bond for an injunction restraining the State officers from obeying the law. After a hearing, a perpetual injunction was granted, on the ground that, like its predecessors, the act violated the obligation of the contract by which the State agreed to receive coupons for taxes. No heed was taken of the injunction order by the Attorney-General and other officials, whereupon Judge Bond fined them for contempt of court. Refusing to pay the fine, they were imprisoned, but were at once released upon *habeas corpus* returnable before the United States Supreme Court. In that court, on December 5. their application was granted, and Judge Bond's decision was reversed on the ground that the injunction proceedings were in violation of that article of the Constitution which forbids any suit against a State by citizens of another State, or by citizens or subjects of any foreign state. "The Coupon Crusher," as the new act was called, remained, therefore, at the close of the year, unimpaired.

Other legislation of the session, suggested by the Governor, included an act imposing a penalty on officers of the State for receiving coupons for taxes except for identification or verification ; an act adopting the code as submitted by the code commission and providing for an index; an act repealing part of the tax on drummers; and an act giving the Governor authority to provide for the insane in jails till they could be transferred to asylums. The following bills were also passed :

To provide for the care of the colored insane, and to enlarge for that purpose the Central Lunatic Asylum.

Appropriating $72,000 to pay the claims allowed disabled soldiers and marines under an act approved Feb. 24, 1884.

To provide for the payment of Virginia's due proportion of the joint expense of re-running and re-marking a portion of the boundary-line between Virginia and North Carolina under the act of March 6, 1836.

To punish persons fraudulently using coupons.

To secure to operatives and laborers engaged in and about coal-mines, manufactories of iron and steel, and all other manufactories the payment of their wages at regular intervals and in lawful money of the United States.

To direct a sale of the State's interest in the Alexandria Canal Company.

To provide for the keeping of a record of coupons purporting to have been clipped from bonds of the State, tendered for taxes, and to impose a penalty for twice tendering the same coupons.

To appropriate $6,000 to the Western Lunatic Asylum for improvements.

To protect the crab industry.

To provide for the removal of obstructions from the Chickahominy river.

To provide for the appointment and removal of district school trustees.

To co-operate with the United States in the suppression and extirpation of pleuro-pneumonia and other contagious diseases among domestic animals.

To punish false pretenses in obtaining the registration of cattle and other animals, and to punish giving false pedigrees.

Requiring insurance companies upon the assessment plan to obtain a license from the State to do business, and otherwise regulating them.

The session adjourned finally on May 24, having passed 480 bills and joint resolutions, nine tenths of them being local or special. In December the new Legislature, elected in November, began its regular session, which was not concluded at the close of the year. On December 20, it elected Congressman John S. Barbour United States Senator, from March 4, 1889, to succeed Harrison H. Riddleberger. Barbour, who was the unanimous nominee of the Democratic caucus, received 87 votes to 48 for ex-Senator William Mahone, the Republican candidate.

Finances.—The balance on hand in the treasury Oct. 1, 1887, was $352,181.22. The receipts during the fiscal year, ending September 30, amounted to $2,569,338.73, and the disbursements to $2,637,138.25, being $67,799.52 more than the revenue ; but included in the expenditures is $143.070.84 advanced under the act of April 6, 1887, to the treasurers of the counties for the support of the public schools until the taxes could be collected for that purpose. Of that amount $107,015.82 has been returned. These disbursements also embrace special appropriations to the building funds of the Eastern, Western, Southwestern, and Central Lunatic Asylums, and to the Colored Normal School, also $52,200 paid to Washington and Lee University, being the last arrears of interest due on bonds held by it, and $25,000 used by the commissioners of the sinking fund in purchase of Riddleberger bonds. It also comprises the interest paid on Riddleberger bonds and coupons forced into the treasury, which, being redeemed, represent interest on the public debt.

The number of tax-receivable coupons outstanding at the end of the last fiscal year was $4,278,696.50. The number of tax-receivable coupons that found their way into the treasury on judgments for taxes during the year was $81,620.50.

Of the new 3-per-cent. bonds $2,280,643.60 are held by the sinking fund, and $1,342,327.28 by other State funds, leaving $19,572,526.89 as the actual liability of the State. Nearly one third of the whole debt has been refunded under the Riddleberger act.

Education.—The report of the State Superintendent of Education for the year ending July 31, presents the following statistics regarding public schools: School population (white), 345,022 ; (colored), 265,249. Number of pupils enrolled (white), 206,638 ; (colored), 115,546. Average attendance (white), 121,571 ; (colored), 69,949. Number of schools (white), 5,047; (colored), 2,093. Number of teachers (white), 5,305 : (colored), 1,856. Average monthly salary (male), $31.20 ; (female), $26.62. Value of school property, $1,907,775.

The average length of the school year increased from 5·92 months in 1886 to 6·01 in 1887. There were 202 new school-houses built during the year the increase of schools was 377, and of teachers 376. There was also an increase of 16,888 in the total enrollment for the year. The total expenditures for all school purposes amounted to $1,535,289. The percentage of school population enrolled and in average attendance shows a slight advance over the previous year. There has been a largely increased attendance at all the higher educational institutions. At the State University the enrollment increased from 287 students on Dec. 1, 1886, to 361 at the same date this year. The increase at the State Military Institute was from 135 to 166 pupils. At the Virginia Agricultural and Mechanical College on Dec. 1, 1886, there were 87 students. At the corresponding date this year there were 136. The Female Normal School at Farmville has 215 students. At the Virginia Normal and Collegiate Institute Dec. 1, 1886, there were 162 academic students. On Dec. 1, 1887, the number of academic students was 187. The annual appropriations to these institutions aggregate about $100,000.

Charities.—During the fiscal year ending Sept. 30, 1887, 420 applications were received at the Eastern, Western, and Southwestern Asylums for admission, and 317 were admitted. In the Eastern Asylum the average number of patients was 401; in the Western Asylum on October 1 there were 589; in the Southwestern, 139; in the Central Asylum the daily average was 470. The number of pupils at the Deaf, Dumb, and Blind Institute is 334. The additional building to the Central Asylum, for which the Legislature of 1886 appropriated $22,500, was ready for use at the close of the year, and will accommodate 200 patients.

Penitentiary.—On December 1 the State convicts numbered 960, 190 being white and 770 colored, or 185 white males and 706 colored males, 5 white females and 64 colored females. Of these, 807 are in the prison, 115 on the South Atlantic and Ohio Railroad, and 38 in Russell County. The total earnings of the institution for the year ending September 30 were $42,826, an excess over expenditures of $7,657.56.

Political.—The November election for members of the Legislature of 1887–'88, which met in December, resulted in favor of the Democrats, a light vote being cast. The Republicans elected 14 Senators and 38 members of the House; the Democrats, 26 Senators and 61 members of the House, with one member Independent.

VOLAPÜK. The inconvenience caused by the diversity of human speech has long been deplored, and many projects have been formed for remedying the evil. Of these, the earliest recorded is that of John Wilkins, Bishop of Chester, who published in 1668 "The Essay toward a Real Character and a Philosophical Language." We have recently heard of the existence of a work entitled "Logopandecteision; or an Introduction to the Universal Language," by Sir Thomas Urquhart, of Cromartie, said to have been published in 1653 at London. Many similar attempts have been made; among the latest and most widely known are those of Sinibaldo de Mas (Ideography, 1863), and Stephen Pearl Andrews (Alwato, 1877). But, with the exception of Volapük, no such attempt has ever advanced beyond

mere experiment. Volapük has steadily gained ground during the nine years of its existence, and is now understood and used in correspondence by a large number of persons in all parts of the civilized world.

The Inventor.—Johann Martin Schleyer, the inventor, or, as he expresses it, "excogitator" (datikel) of Volapük, was born at Oberlauda, Baden, in 1831. He was educated for the Catholic priesthood, which he entered in 1856. He had a love for linguistic studies, and lost no opportunity of acquiring from the numerous foreigners with whom he came in contact a speaking knowledge of their several languages. He had studied about fifty languages and dialects. His studies were, it would seem, directed rather to the comparison of languages as to their relative merits for practical use, than to researches into the history and origin of speech. In 1879 the idea of a universal, or rather neutral, language possessed his mind, and during March of that year he constructed its entire grammar. He published his first book, "Entwurf einer Weltsprache," in the same year, and followed it with a grammar and dictionary. Father Schleyer now resides in Constance, having been retired on a pension. He devotes his energies entirely to the propagation of the Volapük idea, and is the author of numerous writings on the subject.

Structure of the Language.—1. *Phonetics and Alphabet.* The Roman letters are used to the following extent: a, ä, b, c, d, e, f, g, h, i, j, k, l, m, n, o, ö, p, r, s, t, u, ü, v, x, y, z. Schleyer's arrangement of the alphabet is as follows: a, e, i, o, u; ä, ö, ü; b, p; d, t; v, f; h, y, g, k; l, r, m, n; s, j, c, x, z. The dotted vowels, ä, ö, ü, have their German sounds. The introduction of these three letters has been more severely criticised than any other feature of the system, and they are certainly a serious obstacle to the races speaking English, Spanish, and Italian. The vowels, a, e, i, o, u, have their usual "Continental" sounds, as in German, Italian, or Spanish, or as in the English words father, they, pique, go, rude (rood). The following consonants have peculiar sounds: j like sh in English; *jip* being sounded exactly like its equivalent sheep; c like j in joy; z like ts; y as in yet. The accent is invariably on the last syllable. There are two unaccented enclitics, -li and -la, always united by a hyphen to the preceding word, which retains its accent on the last syllable—e. g., *golóm*, he goes; *golóm-li?* does he go? There are no diphthongs; two vowels coming together divide the syllables between them; as *geil*, pronounced like the English words *gay eel*.

2. *Selection of Radicals.*—The radicals, or root-words, are mostly monosyllabic. Using v as a symbol for vowel and c for consonant, the usual form of a root is cvc, as *man*, man; *dom*, house; *köm*, come; *log*, eye; *lam*, arm. The sibilants, s, c, j, x, z, seldom or never occur at the end of a root. There are also radicals of the forms covc, as *sten*, stain; *pled*, play;

and ovoo as *kost*, coat. Both of these classes are fewer in number than ovo, because many combinations of two consonants are unpronounceable. In dissyllabic roots the formulas are ovovo, oovovo; as, *vikod*, victory; *plisip*, principle. These represent more complex ideas than the single roots. There are even some trisyllabic roots, but they can usually be better expressed by a compound word, as *lotogaf*, orthography; better, *tonabav*.

As to meaning the radical is always, when standing by itself, as noun, either concrete or abstract.

The process of selection seems to have been as follows: English being the most important of the civilized languages, the root is taken from an English word, provided there be one within the limits of the rules, which is unobjectionable. If there be no such word suitable, recourse is had to the Latin and the Romance languages, with the endeavor to find a word which shall be somewhat familiar to as wide a public as possible. German is drawn upon if necessary, and some few other languages sparingly. The letters *r* and *h* are avoided.

Thus, for the idea *man* the English word is unobjectionable, and it is retained as to spelling, but with a slight change of pronunciation. As pronounced it is immediately recognized by all the Teutonic races. The Latin peoples must learn it, for their *homin-* has degenerated into *om* and has not sufficient body. But for the word *house* the English word will not do, as it begins with *h*, contains a diphthong, and ends in *s*. Therefore the Latin *dom* is the next choice. The Romance languages have lost it (strangely), and have replaced it by *mansion* and *cabin* (*maison*, *casa*); but they as well as the English are familiar with it in *domestic*. *Hand* is objectionable not only because of the *h*, but of the two consonants at the end, which would make it difficult in the plural for some nations. We can not use *man* (manus, mano, main) because it has been used for man. As a last resort it is transposed, and *nam* (not being required for any other purpose) is adopted. Frequently the sound and not the spelling of the English word is followed, as *jip*, sheep; *kip* (keep), hold. R is often changed into l, as *flen*, friend; *Yulop*, Europe.

Where an English or other word has dwindled down to less than the formula ovo, it is sometimes filled out by prefixing or affixing a letter, usually l or n. Pay becomes *pel*, do[ing] becomes *dun*, purchase (em-ere) is *lem*.

It is necessary that a root should begin and end with consonants in order to receive the signs of inflection, which are vowels joined at the beginning or end.

The numerals are not borrowed from any existing language, but are made after a pattern which brings in the vowels in regular order:

bal	tel	kil	fol	lul	mäl	vel	jöl	zül.
1	2	3	4	5	6	7	8	9.

The object in the selection of roots is to aid the memory, and there is not any attempt, as in former systems, to suggest metaphysical or classificatory relations of ideas.

3. *Derivation.* — Words are derived from roots, very much as in Greek and other Aryan languages, by the three processes of composition, prefixing, and suffixing. In compounding, the modifying word is placed first and the sound *a* connects the two parts — *volapük*, world-language, ·from *vol*, world, *pük*, language; *yagadog*, hunting-dog. The prefixes are frequently prepositions, unchanged, as *selän*, foreign country, from *se*, out; or abbreviated as *bi-* from *bifü*, before; *bisiedel*, president, fore-sitter. Some prefixes are shortened forms of adjectives or nouns of quality, as *gle-*, principal, chief, from *glet*, greatness, *gletik*, great; *blä-*, black, *blägik*.

The suffixes *-el*, *-ik*, *-am* are so regularly applicable to all roots that they are almost a part of the inflectional system. *El* forms a noun indicating the do-er, ac-tor. *Tid*, instruction; *tidel*, teacher; *pükel*, speaker. *El* sometimes denotes an inhabitant, as *Deut*, Germany; *deutel*, a German. *Ik* is the adjective termination; all adjectives except numeral adjectives have it.

Am is a sort of gerund, like the German noun in -ung or the English verbal noun in -ing. It frequently corresponds to nouns in -tion. The terminations *o*, *ü*, and *ö*, are also regarded as rather inflectional than derivational, although this line of distinction is difficult to draw. *O* forms adverbs: From adjectives, *gudik*, good; *gudiko*, well. From other parts of speech, as *neit*, night; *neito*, at night; *flen*, a friend; *flenik*, friendly; *fleniko* or *fleno*, in a friendly manner. *Ü* forms prepositions, as from *kod*, cause, *kodü*, by reason of; from *sesum*, exception, *sesumü*, except; *tef*, relation, *tefü*, relating to. *Ö* forms interjections — *bafö!* bravo! *spidö!* hasten!

4. *Inflection.* — The modifications to which words are subject in Volapük are number, gender, case, person, tense, voice, mood, degree. (1) *Number.* — The singular is the simple form of the word. There is no dual. The plural is invariably formed by adding s to the singular, no matter what the part of speech, noun, pronoun, verb, or (exceptionally) adjective. *Man, mans; mana, munas; golob*, I go, *golobs*, we go. The numerals *bal*, 1; *tel*, 2; etc., with the *s* added, form the tens, as *bals*, 10; *tels*, 20; *kils*, 30. (2) *Gender.* — In the pronouns of the third person there are three forms, *om*, *of*, *os*, called the masculine, feminine, and neuter. In referring to a noun which is the name of a female being, *of* is used, both as a pronoun standing alone and as a verb termination. Referring to a male being, *om* is used similarly. We should naturally expect, then, that for lifeless or sexless things *os* would be used; but this is not the case. The pronoun and verb termination for a lifeless thing is *om* — that is, things are *he*. *Os* is used only impersonally or abstractly, as it thunders, *tötos*; it is said, *pasagos*. This certainly seems

a defect, that the masculine forms should be
used for things without sex. It would be impossible to remedy it without replacing *os* by
some other termination capable of forming the
plural. In nouns denoting persons, the prefix
ji forms a feminine derivative, while the simple form is understood to be masculine, as
ciudel, widower; *jiciudel*, widow. In case of
animals the simple form represents the species
irrespective of sex. The distinctively masculine form begins with *om*, the distinctively
feminine form with *ji*; *jeval*, horse; *omjeval*,
stallion; *jijeval*, mare. *Os* is used as a neuter
adjective termination: *gudikos*, the good; *das
Gute*, τὸ ἀγαθόν. (3) *Cases.*—The simple form
of the word is the nominative. To form the
genitive, dative, and accusative, add the three
vowels *a*, *e*, *i*, plural *as*, *es*, *is*. Nom., *fat*
(father); gen., *fata*; dat., *fate*; acc., *futi*.
Plural: Nom., *fats*; gen., *fatas*; dat., *fates*;
acc., *fatis*. These cases are often designated by
the Volapük names *kimfal*, *kimafal*, *kimefal*,
kimifal—that is, "who-case," "whose-case,"
etc. The vocative is the nominative preceded
by the interjection *o*; *si, o söl*, yes, sir. The
omission of *o* is permitted and is habitual with
some writers. The nominative is the subject.
Prepositions govern the nominative except
when they denote motion, and then govern
the accusative. *Binob in gad*, I am in the
garden; *golob in gadi*, I go into the garden.
The latter may also be expressed *golob ini
gad*, the ending *i* placed after the preposition
instead of after the noun. Besides nouns and
pronouns, adjectives and participles may be
declined. This usually occurs when they are
separated from the nouns which they qualify,
so that it is necessary to make them agree in
case in order to show the relation. Verbs in
the infinitive are declined by Schleyer, although
writers of the "simplifying" school disuse
this. (4) *Person.*—The person-endings of verbs
and the personal pronouns are the same series
of syllables—*ob, ol, om, of, os, on*. First person, *ob*, I; *obs*, we. Second person, *ol*, thou;
ols, you. In the third person there are forms,
as explained under genders, for masculine-
neuter, *om*; feminine, *of*; neuter-impersonal,
os; besides there is the indefinite "one,"
"people," *on* (French *on*, German *man*). *Om*
and *of* have the plurals *oms* and *ofs*. These
syllables are attached to the root to form verbs
in the indicative: *Penob*, I write; *penol*, thou
writest; *penom* [he or it], writes; *penof* [she],
writes; *penos*, it (indef.) writes; *penon*, one
writes, "they" write. *Penobs*, we write;
penols, you write; *penoms, penofs*, they write.
(5) *Tenses.*—The tense-signs are vowels prefixed
to the stem, *a* for the present, *ä* for the imperfect, *e* for the perfect, *i* for the pluperfect,
o for the future, *u* for the future perfect. But
the present tense-sign *a* is always omitted in
the active tenses, as in the above conjugation
of *penob* (instead of *apenob*). This is a little
anomalous. *Äpenob*, I wrote; *epenol*, thou
hast written; *ipenom*, he had written; *openof*,

she will write; *upenon*, one will have written.
(6) *Passive voice.*—The tense-vowel preceded
by the letter *p* makes the verb passive. *Palö-
fob*, I am loved; *pälöfol*, thou wast loved;
man pelöfom, the man has been loved; *com
pilöfof*, the woman had been loved; *polöfobs*,
we shall be loved; *pulöfols*, you will have
been loved. (7) *Moods and Special Forms.*—
The conditional and conjunctive words are
formed by adding another syllable, *-öv* and *-la*
respectively, after the person-endings. *Äbino-
böv labik, if äbinob-la liegik*, I would be happy
if I were rich. The imperative adds *-öd* after
the person-ending: *gololöd*, go [thou]! *golol-
söd*, go [ye]! There is also *-ös*, a softened form
of the imperative, denoting a wish or request,
and a harsh form, *-ös*. *-Öz* (seldom used) is a
potential ending, "may possibly." The infinitive ends in *-ön*, and the participle in *öl*. These
have the tense-vowels: *ebinön*, to have been;
ebinöl, having been; *pefinöl*, about to be finished. They may even take the person-sylla-
bles: *binobön*, for me to be; *ebinoföl*, she having been. The continuous or habitual form
inserts *-i-* next after the tense-vowel. *Äipenob*,
I am in the habit of writing; *äipenob*, I used
to write. The reflexive form adds *-ok* to the
active voice: *vatükob*, I wash; *vatükobok*, I
wash myself. The interrogative form is de-
noted by *li*, prefixed, or suffixed as an enclitic.
Li-penol? Do you write? *Penom-li?* Does
he write? (8) *Degree.*—The comparative degree adds *-um* to the positive; the superlative
adds *-ün*. *Gletik*, great; *gletikum*, greater;
gletikün, greatest; *vifiko*, swiftly; *vifikumo*,
more swiftly; *vifiküno*, most swiftly.

5. *Order of Words.*—The normal order of
words in a sentence is, broadly: 1. Subject; 2.
Predicate; 3. Object; and each of these principal parts is followed by its modifiers. For
instance, a noun is followed by the adjective
qualifying it or by another noun in the kimafal (genitive) or by a preposition with a noun.
The adverb follows the verb which it modifies.
In fact, the object is a modifier of the predicate, so that its position is in accordance with
the rule. But adverbs, when they modify adjectives or other adverbs, precede, not follow,
those words, the connection being so close
that the phrase is almost a compound word;
and the negative *no* also precedes the verb
which it negates. Schleyer authorized deviation from this natural "word-placement"
(*vödatopam*) whenever emphasis, and in some
cases euphony, demanded it. At first German
writers took advantage of this liberty to place
sentences in the complex and inverted order
of their own language. They were specially
addicted to setting the verb at the very end of
a subordinate sentence, conforming to a German idiom which is one of the greatest obstacles to other nations in studying German. It
is noticeable that this peculiarity is disappearing, partly through the raillery of Prof. Kerckhoffs, who has not ceased to ridicule this Ger-
manism and to insist upon the natural word-

placement being retained except for extraordinary reasons; and it is rare now that a German volapükist commits the solecism of putting the accusative before the verb.

Characteristics.—It is the nature of all language to be regular and symmetrical; but various historical causes have produced irregularities and anomalies interesting to the philologist and not troublesome to those who learn them as part of a mother-tongue. In learning a second language, however, these irregularities present an obstacle which for many is insuperable, so that if one of the national languages were by any possibility adopted for international use, all the other nations would be under a double disadvantage: first, because of having to learn a second idiom; second, because no reasonable amount of study would ever place them on an absolute equality with its native speakers as to dexterity. This characteristic of Volapük, that it is modeled upon the evolutionary languages, is, in our opinion, the reason of its success. Former systems had attempted too much or too little. Some of them, like Wilkins's and De Mas's, endeavored to classify all ideas and thus became too metaphysical. Others, like Alwato, professed to be revelations of an inner harmony between sound and meaning, and thus to be the vehicles of a universal science. Some of them had no phonetic form, but were mere codes of symbols. Naturally, the reader would translate into his own language instead of deriving the knowledge directly through the new medium. Most of these languages were insufficiently worked out, their authors leaving them as sketches only. This was fatal to any hopes of their employment. But Schleyer neither presented something beyond language nor something falling short of the requirements of language. He made simply a complete, regular, facile language, selecting material and form with rare practical sense. His system has its blemishes; but, to its credit, it may be said that these blemishes always arise from a deviation from the principles laid down by him.

Adoption of Volapük.—Schleyer's adherents were for some time few and mostly in South Germany. The idea was ignored by the scientific and literary world. In 1882 it awakened considerable interest in Austria, and in that year the first society for its propagation was organized at Vienna; but until 1884 its adherents, outside of the German-speaking countries, were few and scattered. In 1884 it invaded Holland and Belgium, and numerous societies were formed in those countries. In 1885, Dr. Auguste Kerckhoffs, professor in the École des Hautes Études Commercielles at Paris, introduced it to the French nation through several articles and addresses, creating a great sensation. He wrote excellent textbooks on the subject, much more attractive and clear than those of the inventor. Unfortunately, he permitted himself to deviate in some points from the system as published by the inventor. In themselves these changes were for the most part decided improvements, but to make them without consultation was dangerous to the unity of the movement, on which everything depended. Still, Prof. Kerckhoffs did more than any other to advance the language, and the system has been to some extent modified to harmonize with his views. The other Latin races received an impetus from him, and first Spain, then Italy and Portugal, were aroused to enthusiasm. During 1885 and 1886 Sweden, Denmark, and Russia were also awakened. Thus the extension of Volapük over the Continent of Europe was geographical. England has as yet shown but little activity in the matter.

In the United States there were some learners of Volapük as early as 1882, mostly of German origin. Their number gradually increased, but there was little general interest in the matter until June, 1887, when an article on the subject, written by Z. L. White, under the pseudonym of Richmond Walker, appeared in the "American Magazine." This attracted attention, and was commented upon by the press. Since that time the interest in the subject has constantly increased, numerous articles and paragraphs in periodical literature have appeared, societies or classes have been formed in several towns (Chicago, New Orleans, Milwaukee, Walla Walla, Alma, etc.) and various textbooks have already appeared or are announced for early publication.

Organization.—A convention or meeting of representatives from the various Volapük societies was held at Friedrichshafen, in August, 1884. No very important action was taken, but the dissemination of the language was discussed, and a committee appointed with power to call the next convention, which took place at Munich, in August, 1887. A large number of delegates were present, the Germans greatly preponderating; in fact, the Latin races were scarcely represented. This congress was very zealous and active. In advance of the organization of an academy, certain urgent linguistic matters were discussed and settled, generally in the direction of the simplifications which Prof. Kerckhoffs had not only recommended, but had somewhat arbitrarily introduced. One of the most curious of these, and worthy of note, was the abolition of the ceremonial pronoun *ons*. This *ons* represented the *you* of politeness, the German *Sie*, Spanish *Usted*. The use of *Sie* had led the Germans, apparently, to consider the second person singular *thou* as disrespectful, a purely conventional and fictitious idea. Therefore Schleyer provided a special word for it, a word which violated several canons. It has the plural form, although usually singular in meaning; it is incapable of forming a plural when several are addressed; it should logically be the plural of *on*, the indefinite pronoun. As the use of this form *ons* was optional, many volapükists rejected it, employing *ol*. The conservatives combated this usage, claiming that *ol*, except between intimates, was impolite, subversive, socialistic. In the congress a warm debate took place, but finally *ons* was abolished by a decisive vote, making the second person singular always *ol*.

The most important action of the congress was the establishment of a General Society or Federation of Clubs (Volapükaklub Valemik) and of an academy (Kadem Volapüka). Father Schleyer was made permanent head (*cifal*) of both of these organizations. The academy begins its functions with the year 1888. It consists of the *cifal*, the *dilekel*, twenty *kademals*, and of *kademels* and *kademans*. There are twenty language groups, and twenty-five technical groups. A section is composed of the specialists in one technical group, belonging to the same language: thus, the French geological section, the Spanish mathematical section. The twenty geological sections form the geological group; the French language-group is made up of twenty-five technical sections. Thus, there are in all 500 sections. Each section is presided over by a *kademel*, and its members are *kademans*. The director (*dilekel*) is vice-chief and working head of the academy. Seventeen *kademals* were elected, who were to organize the academy and to choose its remaining members.

Bibliography.—Over one hundred books had been published in or upon Volapük up to July, 1887, all in Europe. This was exclusive of periodicals, leaflets, and contributions to periodicals. These books were in the following languages: Volapük, German, French, Spanish, Italian, English, Portuguese, Danish, Swedish, Dutch, Russian, Hungarian, Croatian, Bohemian, Roumanian. They consisted mostly of text-books and translations. In Great Britain the only book thus far published is W. A. Seret's "Grammar and Vocabularies" (Glasgow), a translation very imperfectly made from Schleyer's works. In America the following books have appeared in 1887: "Volapük Grammar for Beginners," by O. J. Stilwell (Alma, Mich.); "Hand-Book of Volapük," by Charles E. Sprague, kademal (New York); "Volapük," by Prof. J. Hanno Deiler, of Tulane University (New Orleans); "Volapük, a Guide to the Universal Language," by Samuel Huebsch (New York); "Volapük: an Easy Method of Acquiring the Universal Language," by Klas August Linderfelt (Milwaukee). The following works are in preparation: "Practical Volapük-English and English-Volapük Dictionary," by Dr. M. W. Wood, U. S. A.; "Essentials of Volapük," by Prof. Henry Cohn; "Volapük Reading-book," by Mrs. J. H. Bauer. In periodical literature, Volapük especially abounds. The following periodicals are now published: Weekly—"Volapükisten" (Stockholm). Monthlies—"Volapükabled Zenodik," official organ (Constance); "Le Volapük" (Paris); "Volapük" (Guadalajara and Madrid); "Volapükaklubs" (Breslau); "Volapükagased" (Vienna); "Cogabled Volapükelas," humorous, illustrated (Munich); "Volapükabled Dānik" (Aabybro); "Il Volapük" (Milan); "Nogan Volapükik plo Beljän e Nedän" (Antwerp). To these may be added, "Volaspodel, lābled gaseda konodik The Office" (New York).

W

WASHBURNE, ELIHU BENJAMIN, an American lawyer, born in Livermore, Oxford County, Me., Sept. 23, 1816; died in Chicago, Ill., Oct. 22, 1887. He received a public-school education, was a printer's apprentice in the office of the "Christian Intelligencer," and assistant editor of the "Kennebec Journal," Augusta, studied law in Kent's Hill Seminary and the office of John Otis, in Augusta, and in 1839 was graduated at the Cambridge Law-School, and admitted to the bar. He settled in Galena, Ill., in 1840, and slowly obtained practice. In 1844 he was a delegate to the Baltimore Whig Convention, in 1852 to the convention that nominated Gen. Scott for the presidency, and the same year a Representative in Congress, where he occupied a seat continuously for sixteen years. He was the senior member of the House during the civil war, won the appellation of "watch-dog of the Treasury" by his opposition to jobbery, introduced the first postal-telegraph bill and the bill to establish national cemeteries, was chairman of the Committee on Commerce for ten years, and chairman of the joint committee of the whole on the impeachment of President Johnson. He was the steadfast friend of Gen. Grant during and after the civil war. In 1869 President Grant appointed him Secretary of State, and, resigning a few days afterward, he was appointed United States Minister to France. On the declaration of the Franco-Prussian War he was asked to protect with the American flag the diplomatic headquarters of the various German states in Paris and the records they contained, as well as the persons and property of German residents in the city. He remained in Paris throughout the siege, and was the only foreign minister that continued at his post during the terrible days of the Commune, giving protection not only to the Germans but to all other foreigners abandoned by their ministers. At the close of the war he was offered the decoration of the Order of the Red Eagle by the German Emperor, which he was obliged by law to decline; but he subsequently accepted from his Majesty two large oil-portraits, one of the Emperor, the other of Prince Bismarck. He served as minister till 1877, and on his return to the United States made his home in Chicago, refusing further political honors, although his admirers endeavored to secure for him the presidential nomination in 1880. During the past few years he delivered addresses before historical

ELIHU BENJAMIN WASHBURNE.

societies on the Franco-Prussian War, and published several magazine articles on that event. While his remains were lying in state the German flag was displayed at the foot of the catafalque by the express desire of the Emperor.

WASHINGTON TERRITORY. Territorial Government.—The following were the Territorial officers during the year: Governor, Watson C. Squire, succeeded by Eugene Semple; Secretary, N. H. Owings; Treasurer, T. M. Ford; Auditor, T. M. Reed; Superintendent of Public Instruction, J. C. Kerr, succeeded by J. C. Lawrence; Chief-Justice of the Supreme Court, Richard A. Jones; Associate Justices, William G. Langford, George Turner, and Frank Allyn. The Legislature met on Dec. 5, and was in session at the close of the year.

Finances.—The total valuation of assessed property for 1887 was $56,177,458, against $50,484,427 for 1885. This does not include the property of railroads, which pay a percentage of their gross earnings in lieu of taxes. The assessment includes 5,138,967 acres of land valued at $28,205,658, with improvements thereon amounting to $8,739,628, and personal property valued at $19,041,663.

The report of the Auditor for two years ending September 30 shows that at the beginning of the period there was a surplus in the treasury of $81,101.10, while at the close there was a deficit of $75,000, over two thirds of which was in the form of unpaid warrants bearing 10 per cent. interest. This deficiency is due to extraordinary expenses incurred in building a penitentiary at Walla Walla and a new asylum building at Steilacoom. The sources of Territorial revenue are a tax of two and a half mills on all property, and one third of the sum collected from railroad companies under the gross earnings law.

Population.—The census returns for 1887 present the following figures:

COUNTIES.	Males.	Females.
Adams	585	405
Asotin	947	715
Chehalis	1,981	1,261
Clallam	610	362
Clarke	3,829	3,236
Columbia	3,106	2,651
Cowlitz	1,778	1,424
Douglas	541	297
Franklin	188	61
Garfield	1,919	1,580
Island	677	393
Jefferson	2,308	995
King	9,258	6,694
Kitsap	2,254	584
Kittitass	3,773	1,673
Klikitat	8,016	2,229
Lewis	2,927	2,509
Lincoln	3,359	2,257
Mason	7C8	382
Pacific	1,441	871
Pierce	6,970	5,024
San Juan	689	456
Skagit	2,826	1,360
Skamania	447	278
Snohomish	1,967	1,164
Spokane	6,514	4,801
Stevens	806	472
Thurston	2,751	1,894
Wahkiakum	974	549
Walla Walla	5,147	3,752
Whatcom	1,776	1,428
Whitman	7,201	5,691
Yakima	1,654	1,266
Total	84,470	59,199

Of the total population, 137,480 are whites, 254 blacks, 69 mulattoes, 2,584 Chinese, 3,288 Indian half-breeds, and 44 Kanakas. The total population in 1888 was 99,508, and in 1885, 127,292. The increase since 1885 is 16,377, or less than half what it was during the preceding two years.

Education.—The following statistics for 1887 regarding the public schools are presented: Number of school-houses, 868; number of districts maintaining schools, 885; average number of months of school, 4½; number of male teachers, 479; number of female teachers, 752; average salary paid male teachers, $44.86; average salary paid female teachers, $36.87; number of children enrolled, 29,992; total disbursements for schools, $305,365.

The Territorial University at Seattle has a faculty of 7 professors and an attendance of 168 pupils, of whom 94 are males and 74 females. The Legislature appropriates $5,000 annually toward its support.

Charities.—A school for the deaf and dumb has been established at Vancouver. The cost of the grounds and the buildings was $5,000; the Legislative grant for the year, $3,000; and the cost of maintenance during that period, $3,500. There are eighteen inmates.

The Territorial Asylum for the Insane, at Steilacoom, was established in 1871, and is supported by an annual appropriation of about $30,000. During the year an entirely new structure has been completed at a cost of $100,000. There are 215 inmates.

Penitentiary.—The new Penitentiary building at Walla Walla, provided for by the Legislature of 1886, was completed during the year at an expense of $60,000, and the Territorial prisoners have been transferred to it. Their number in October was 103.

Mining.—Until recently no considerable deposits of the precious metals were known to exist in the Territory. Since 1883 discoveries have been made of gold, silver, and copper ores in three localities in eastern Washington, and companies are now working mines with success. The Colville district is the largest, and extends along Columbia river in the eastern central part of the Territory. The most important discovery in this district was made in 1885, about six miles east of Colville, which led to the opening of the Old Dominion mine. The ore here found is chloride and galena. Shipments of over $100,000 have been made from this place. The Kettle river district is near the British Columbia boundary. A high grade of copper-ore, gold-quartz, placer, and galena, with carbonates is found here. Some of the mines have already been worked for three years. The Salmon river or Okanagan district is east of the Colville district. In May, 1886, the first mines were discovered on Salmon river, thirty miles from the Columbia. In September, 1886, additional discoveries were made four miles south of the first ores, and these two groups, called, respectively, Salmon City and Ruby City, are the present centers of attraction. Galena, gray copper, and silver-bearing quartz have been discovered here.

The principal known deposits of iron-ore are in the eastern county of Kittitass and the western counties of Jefferson, King, and Pierce. The total shipment of coal for the year ending June 30 was 525,705·15 tons, and the total product of the Territory since coal-mining began is estimated at 2,461,108 tons. The approximate acreage of coal-lands in the various counties is: King, 70,000; Pierce, 40,000; Kittitass, 50; Lewis, 5,000; Thurston, 5,000; Whatcom, 10,000; total, 180,000.

Timber.—The timber-trees are the yellow and red fir, white and red cedar, spruce, larch, white pine, white fir, hemlock, bull pine, tamarack, alder and maple, ash and oak, cherry and laurel, and cotton woods. By far the largest article of export is the yellow and red fir. which is generally classed as " Oregon pine." The trees from which this product is obtained reach 12 feet in diameter and 300 feet in height, in exceptional cases, but the ordinary saw-logs range from 24 to 60 inches in diameter. Nearly all the timber wealth of the Territory is found west of the Cascade mountains. About 5,000 people are engaged in the lumber industry, and the annual product is estimated at about 645,000,000 feet.

Hops.—The hop-crop of 1881 was 6,098 bales; of 1883, 9,301; of 1885, 20,000; of 1887, according to present estimates, 25,000. The last crop is estimated to bring $1,125,000. The vines are universally free from pests, and as the yield is large, averaging 1,600 pounds to the acre, growers find the business profitable on an average price of twelve cents a pound.

Railroads.—The total mileage of railroads in the Territory, on October 1, was as follows: Northern Pacific, 564·2 miles; Oregon Railway and Navigation Company, 289·9; Mason County lines, 41; Puget Sound Shore, 23; Spokane and Palouse, 48; Seattle, Lake Shore. and Eastern, 40; Columbia and Puget Sound, 44·5; Olympia and Chehalis Valley, 15; total, 1,-060·6 miles. The total mileage at the same time last year was 924 miles.

Exports.—The value of goods exported from the Puget Sound district for the year ending June 30 was as follows: Coal, $1,549,652; lumber, $3,090,696; miscellaneous and produce, $2,527,000; total coastwise, $7,167,348; foreign exports, $1,769,209; total exports, 8,-936,557. There were twenty-six new vessels built, and three rebuilt, during the year, of which twelve were steam-vessels and seventeen sailing-vessels.

Indians.—The total acreage in Indian reservations for the Territory is 4,086,148. Of this, 3,753,000 acres are east of the Cascade mountains, and 333,148 acres west of the mountains. The total Indian population, not including that of the Colville agency (of which there is no report), is 5,895, of which 1,741, besides the Colville, are east of the mountains and 4,156 are west of the mountains.

WEST INDIES. British. *Barbadoes.*— This island is the most easterly of the Caribbee group; it is nearly twenty-one miles long by fourteen in breadth, with an area of 166 square miles. Bridgetown, the chief town and port, has a population of 20,947, and the whole island 171,860, only 16,560 of whom are white. The island is almost encircled by coral reefs, and has the appearance of a well-kept garden. The Governor is Sir Charles O. Lees. The colony possesses representative institutions, but not responsible government. The island forms the headquarters of her Majesty's forces in the West Indies. The public debt amounts to £15,700. The revenue in 1885 was £145,-758, and the expenditure £146,134. There is a college and also a good grammar-school in Bridgetown. A lunatic asylum and a lazaretto are kept up at the public expense, and there is a general hospital in Bridgetown. A railway from Bridgetown to the parish of St. Andrew, twenty-three miles, was completed in 1882. There is a station of the West India and Panama Telegraph Company at Barbadoes. The chief industry is sugar-planting. There are over 500 sugar-works in operation, and the annual product is over 50,000 hogsheads of sugar, and over 33,000 puncheons of molasses.

British Guiana.—The population on Dec. 31, 1885, was 270,042, including 7,487 aborigines and 92,005 East Indians, besides 3,474 Chinese. The capital is Georgetown, population, 60,000. The Governor is Sir Henry Turner Irving. The American Consul at Demerara is David T. Bunker. There is a good network of roads, and there are small canals in connection with Demerara river. There is a railway from Georgetown to Berbice, twenty-one miles. The telegraph system owned and worked by the Government now comprises about 260 miles of line, with seven cables covering a distance of twelve miles. A telephone exchange is established at Georgetown in connection with the Government telegraph; length of telephone lines, thirty-two miles. The regular mail leaves Southampton every alternate Thursday. The public debt on Dec. 31, 1885, amounted to £162,000, the revenue was £434,813 in 1885, and the expenditure was respectively £463,942. There were 105 sugar estates in active operation in 1885, having an aggregate of sugar-cane cultivation of 75,844 acres, and of plantain cultivation of 8,777 acres. The sugar-crop of 1885 was 107,028 hogsheads. The American trade in 1886 was: imports into the United States, $1,864,596; domestic exports, $1,544,726. The schools are denominational, except the estates schools. The number of schools receiving aid in 1885 was 166, with 17,793 pupils, and the aid granted amounted to £15,963. There is a Government college in Georgetown, in which a course of instruction is given similar to that of a public school or first grammar-school in England.

Jamaica is the largest of the British West India Islands; area, about 4,193 square miles. The Cayman Islands are dependencies of Jamaica. The population, in 1881, was 580,804; 14,433 being whites, 109,946 colored, 444,186 black, and 12,240 East Indians. The Governor is Sir H. W. Norman. The American Consul at Kingston is Louis D. Beylard. There are in operation 64 miles of Government railways, constructed at a cost of £775,000. A line of telegraphs connects all the principal towns, having 48 stations. There is also telegraphic communication with Europe. The public debt amounts to £1,257,916. The revenue in 1885 was £595,156. The imports in 1885 amounted to £1,487,833; the exports to £1,413,722. Elementary education is left to private enterprise, aided since 1867 by a system of grants from the colonial revenue. The number of schools is 663, with 57,557 pupils. The Colonial Government maintains a system of inspection, and has provided two training colleges for teachers, which are wholly supported from public funds.

The Leeward Islands—The Leeward Islands, comprising the colonies of Antigua, Montserrat, St. Kitts, Nevis, Dominica, and the Virgin Islands, were constituted a single Federal Colony by an act of Parliament in 1871. The total population in 1886 was 116,050. The Governor is Lord Gormanstown. The white population in 1881 was 1,795; black, 27,219; colored, 5,950; total, 34,964. The crop of 1885 consisted of 14,080 hogsheads of sugar, 6,059 puncheons of molasses, and 20 puncheons of rum. The island of Montserrat is about 12 miles long and 8 miles broad. It is considered the most healthful in the Antilles. Instead of

a legislative assembly, the island has had, since Feb. 26, 1867, a legislative council. Montserrat is a presidency; the President is the resident district magistrate, and a Commissioner of the Supreme Court. The population in 1881 was 10,087. The principal export is sugar. For some years past a valuable export has been lime-juice, raw and concentrated. There are about 650 acres planted in lime-trees, and the cultivation is extending. The twin islands, St. Christopher (also called St. Kitts), and Nevis, are separated by a strait about two miles wide at its narrowest part. They are traversed by a range of rugged mountains, which attains its greatest height at Mount Misery, 4,100 feet above the sea. The area of St. Kitts is 68 square miles. Since Jan. 1, 1883, the presidencies of Saint Christopher, Nevis, and Anquilla, with their respective dependencies, have formed the presidency of Saint Christopher and Nevis. There is an Executive Council for the United Presidency, appointed by the queen, and there is also a legislative body of twenty members. The acting President is F. Spencer Wigley.

The island of Anquilla is about sixty miles northwest of St. Christopher, and has an area of 35 square miles. The population is computed at 2,500, of whom 100 are white. Beside cattle, ponies, and garden stock, the productions are phosphate of lime and salt. The chief magistrate is J. L. Lake. The Virgin Islands are a cluster of rocks. The largest island in the group belonging to Great Britain is Tortola; population in 1881, 5,287. The President is F. A. Pickering. A small quantity of sugar is made, and recently many of the landed proprietors have planted cotton, which grows luxuriantly, and appears likely to prove remunerative. Dominica is in the center of the Caribbean Sea; it is 29 miles long, 16 miles broad, and very mountainous; population in 1881, 22,211. The local government is administered by a President, aided by an Executive Council of seven members. The Legislative Assembly was reduced in 1865 to fourteen members. The imports in 1885 were £56,205; exports, £52,486.

Trinidad.—This island lies eastward of Venezuela, being separated from the continent by the Gulf of Paria. Its area is 1,754 square miles. Sugar and cocoa are the staple products. The climate is healthful; the average rainfall during the past 19 years has been 66·39 inches. The mean temperature during the same period was lowest at 76° Fahr. in January, and highest at 79° in September and October. The population of the island in 1881 was 153,128. The chief town and principal port is Port of Spain; population, 31,858. The next town and port is San Fernando, population, 6,335, about 30 miles south from Port of Spain. The harbor is the finest in the West Indies. There is a lake of pitch, 90 acres in extent, about 30 miles from Port of Spain; it has considerable value on account of the asphaltum it furnishes for export, and yields a slight revenue to the island. Coolie immigration from India is conducted under Government control. Under this head, £41,526 was expended in 1883, besides the fixed establishment of the department, the cost of which is about £3,350. The number of Indian immigrants was as follows: in 1882, 2,629; in 1883, 1,960; in 1884, 3,147; in 1885, 1,706. The Governor of the island is Sir W. Robinson, who is assisted in the administration by an Executive Council of three members. The legislative body is a Council, including the Governor, 6 official, and 8 unofficial members, all of whom are appointed by the Crown. Education has made considerable progress. The schools are of two kinds: one secular, supported entirely by the Government, the other denominational, aided by the Government. For higher education there are the Queen's Royal College (secular), and its affiliated Roman Catholic institution, the College of the Immaculate Conception. The primary schools now number 108, of which 50 are secular and 58 denominational. The railway from the Port of Spain to Arima, 16 miles, was opened in 1876. The Conva line—18 miles from the junction at St. Joseph, 24 miles in all from Port of Spain—was opened in 1880. An extension of 4½ miles was opened to Clayton's Bay on Jan. 1, 1881, and the further extension to San Fernando—7 miles—was opened in April, 1882. There are also 7 miles of tramways between San Fernando and Sabana Grande, and a short line at Chaguanas, used chiefly for the conveyance of sugar. The Guaracara Valley Extension Railway, from San Fernando to Prince's Town, was opened in 1884. * The imports in 1885 were £2,241,478; the exports, £2,246,664. The sugar shipments in 1887 included 30,617 hogsheads, 13,614 tierces, and 331,237 bags and barrels. The cocoa shipments were 70,556 bags.

The Windward Islands.—These form a group comprising Grenada, St. Vincent, Tobago, and St. Lucia. Grenada is about 21 miles long, and 12 miles in its greatest breadth; population on Dec. 31, 1884, 45,495. The chief productions are cocoa, spices, and sugar. On March 17, 1885, Grenada was made the headquarters of the group, with an Executive and a Legislative Council, Walter J. Sendall being the Governor in-Chief. The imports in 1885 were £138,105; the exports, £178,178. St. Vincent is 18 miles in length, and 11 in breadth, containing 85,000 acres; population in 1881, 40,548. Kingstown, the capital, has a population of 5,593. The most striking feature of St. Vincent is its *soufrière*, or volcanic mountain, celebrated for the violence of its eruption in 1812. This mountain is about 3,000 feet above the level of the sea. St. Vincent received the first cargo of coolie laborers in 1861. There are about 500 of these on the sugar plantations. There are 17 churches and chapels belonging to the Established Church,

8 Roman Catholic, 11 Wesleyan, and 1 Presbyterian. The imports declined from £158,056, in 1875, to £101,032, in 1885, and the exports from £207,616 to £130,342. Tobago is the most southerly of the Windward group. It has an area of 114 square miles. The formation of the island is volcanic. The Government is administered by a resident Administrator, subordinate to the Governor-in-Chief at Grenada. The present Administrator is Robert B. Llewelyn. The population in 1881 was 18,051. Scarborough, the principal town, has a population of about 1,370. Sugar, rum, and molasses form the principal articles of export. The imports declined from £46,435, in 1874, to £30,758, in 1885, and the exports from £45,887 to £38,436.

St. Lucia.—This island is 24 miles southeast of Martinique. Its area is 158,620 acres. The population in 1884 was 40,532; Castries, the capital, has a population of 4,555. The government is conducted by an Administrator—at present Edward Laborde—aided by an Executive Council. The legislature consists of the Administrator and a Council composed as the queen may direct. Probably no climate in the world is more suitable as a winter resort for invalids suffering from chest complaints. The temperature from December to April seldom exceeds 80° Fahr. The imports declined from £150,740, in 1875, to £93,739, in 1884; and the exports from £159,468 to £121,262.

Spanish.—*Porto Rico* is the lesser of the Spanish Antilles, Cuba being the greater. (For area and population, see "Annual Cyclopædia" for 1885.) The Captain-General is Juan Contreras. The American Consul at St. John's is Edward Conroy. The strength of the garrison in the island in 1887 was 3,700 men. Primary instruction being deplorably deficient, the home Government has applied to Porto Rico the royal decree of June 15, 1882, ordering that a portion of the direct local taxation be spent henceforward on gratuitous popular education. A decree of Feb. 13, 1886, instituted a "mercantile register," that is, the registering of all tradesmen, to date from May 1, one register's office being opened at St. John's and one at Ponce, thus completing the adoption of the commercial code recently introduced into the Spanish Antilles. Another reform is the formation of agricultural colonies and villages in the island, the rural population on the plateau, mostly small planters and farmers, living so isolated that it was impossible to get them to send their children to school regularly. Henceforward "juntas" are to be formed among this scattered population, whose duty will be to see that the adults attend divine service and the children attend school. The low price of sugar in 1886 and the first quarter of 1887 caused great distress through the districts in which the cultivation of the cane is the chief or only resource, and 30,000 field-hands were deprived of their daily wages for several months, because planters, rather than ruin themselves, were compelled to reduce production. The rise in coffee, on the contrary, restored planters of that product to a more prosperous condition than they had seen for five years. The Spanish Antilles being flooded with Mexican and other foreign fractional coins, the home Government resolved to provide a special circulating medium in the shape of new silver money, to show on its face the stamp "Antillas Españolas." The commercial *modus vivendi* between Spain and the United States relating to Cuba and Porto Rico was by mutual agreement prolonged to July 1, 1888. The colonial budget estimate for 1887-'88 fixed the revenue of the island at $3,550,372, and the expenditure at $3,551,841. The peninsular and foreign trade movement in Porto Rico for two years was: In 1885, imports, $11,745,022; exports, $14,048,639. In 1884, imports, $13,182,293; exports, $11,618,-883. The chief articles exported during 1885 were: Sugar, 88,959 tons, valued at $5,782,-846; coffee, 21,669 tons valued at $6,067,-185; molasses, 30,646 tons, valued at $735,-494; tobacco, 3.495 tons, valued at $1,139,-498. The American trade with Porto Rico has been as follows:

FISCAL YEAR.	Imports into the United States.	Domestic exports from the United States.
1886	$4,594,514	$1,676,929
1887	4,861,690	1,707,941

The custom-houses of the island collected in 1886 a revenue of $2,087,928. There entered Porto Rican ports in 1885, 1,648 vessels, with a joint tonnage of 108,896, while the departures were 1,544, registering together 147,195 tons.

WEST VIRGINIA. State Government.—The following were the State officers during the year: Governor, E. Willis Wilson; Secretary of State, Henry S. Walker; Treasurer, William T. Thompson; Auditor, Patrick F. Duffey; Attorney-General, Alfred Caldwell; Superintendent of Free Schools, Benjamin S. Morgan; President of the Supreme Court of Appeals Okey Johnson; Judges, Thomas C. Green, Adam C. Snyder, and Samuel Woods.

Legislative Session.—The Legislature was in session from January 12 to February 25. It was charged with the duty of electing a successor to United States Senator Johnson N. Camden, but after repeated ballotings it adjourned without a decision. Senator Camden was a candidate for re-election, but failed to command the united support of his party. At a caucus on January 19, attended by 38 of the 51 Democrats in the Legislature, he was nominated with only two dissenting votes; but in the legislative balloting, which began on January 25, he failed to secure a majority. The Republicans made no nomination, but cast their 35 votes as a compliment to various party leaders. There were six Greenback-Labor members, who first voted for Samuel C. Burdett, and then joined their strength with the Republicans.

The legislation of the session included a general act permitting the incorporation of savings-banks, an act to secure to laborers in mines and manufactories the fortnightly payment of wages in lawful money, and an act revising and consolidating the license and tax laws. The last measure raises the tax-rate on real and personal property for general purposes from 20 to 25 cents, leaving the rate for school purposes unchanged, and increases the liquor-tax on brewers and dealers. The former now pay from $50 to $550, and the latter, whether wholesale or retail, $350. Dealers in domestic wines, ale, and beer pay $100. Other license taxes were also revised.

Three amendments to the Constitution were proposed to be voted upon by the people in 1888. One prohibits the manufacture and sale of liquor; another strikes out the following clause: "No fact tried by a jury shall be otherwise re-examined than according to the rules of the common law"; the third extends the regular legislative session from 45 to 60 days and longer, if two thirds of each house agree to such further extension. Other acts of the session were as follow:

To provide for the study of the nature and effect of alcoholic drinks and narcotics in the public schools of the State.

To prevent the employment of minors under twelve years that can not read and write in any factory, workshop, manufactory, or mine.

Imposing a tax on collateral inheritances, distributive shares, and legacies.

Providing for the removal of mill-dams and all other dams from the lower part of the Elk and Guyandotte rivers.

Revising the game laws.

To regulate the working, ventilation, and drainage of coal-mines, and to provide for the appointment of two mine-inspectors.

Changing the name of the State "Institution for the Deaf and Dumb and Blind" to the "West Virginia Schools for the Deaf and the Blind."

Revising the election laws.

Providing for the appointment of a State board of Examiners, who shall conduct stated examinations of candidates for teachers in the public schools and shall grant certificates.

The Legislature having adjourned without electing a successor to Senator Camden, Hon. Daniel B. Lucas was appointed by the Governor on March 5 to hold office until the next meeting of the Legislature having authority to fill the vacancy. There had also been a failure at this session to pass the usual appropriation bills, and important measures relating to the courts and to railroads had been untouched. The Governor, therefore, issued a call for an extra session, to meet on April 20. The Constitution provides that at special sessions only such business shall be acted upon as the Governor in his proclamation shall direct. The subjects for legislation as set forth by the Governor included the appropriations, regulating the costs in criminal cases, limiting the allowance for maintenance of lunatics in jail, the regulation of railroad traffic, the prohibition of free passes to public officers or to members of political conventions, the punishment of corruption and bribery at elections, and the establishment of the boundary between the State and Pennsylvania, Maryland, and Virginia. No mention was made regarding the election of a United States Senator, and the session apparently had no authority to act upon that question. Nevertheless, on May 3 both houses voted to ballot for United States Senator, and W. H. H. Flick received 9 votes and Camden 10 in the Senate, with 4 votes scattering, and Flick 23 and Camden 29 in the House, with 18 votes scattering. Seven joint ballots were taken thereafter, with no choice, but on the eighth Charles J. Faulkner obtained 48 votes, and Flick 31, with 10 scattering, and Faulkner was declared elected by the presiding officer. Governor Wilson refused to sign the certificate of his election, but his claim to the office was presented to the Senate on the meeting of Congress in December, and that body decided in his favor. While the Senatorial contest was pending, the Legislature passed the regular appropriation bills, accepted and adopted the acts of the several commissions appointed to establish the Pennsylvania, Maryland, and Virginia boundaries, fixed the allowance for lunatics in prison at not over 60 cents a day, and limited the liability of the State in criminal prosecutions to payment for five witnesses in its behalf in ordinary cases.

State Institutions. — The following appropriations for the year ending Sept. 30, 1887, were made: State Normal School, $18,200; State University, $28,086; Institution for the Deaf, Dumb, and Blind, $25,000; Insane Asylum, $100,000. For the care of lunatics in jail, $20,000 was appropriated, and $90,000 for the costs of criminal prosecutions.

WHEELER, WILLIAM ALMON, an American legislator, born in Malone, Franklin County, N. Y., June 30, 1819; died there, June 4, 1887. He prepared himself for college, entered the University of Vermont, in 1838, and pursued his studies there for two years, when he began studying law in the office of Asa Hascall, in Malone. In 1845 he was admitted to the bar, and in the following year, when Mr. Hascall, who had held the office of district-attorney of Franklin County for several years, was compelled by failing health to resign it, Mr. Wheeler was appointed his successor for the remainder of the term. His brief conduct of this office was so satisfactory that in 1847, at the first election by popular vote under the Constitution of 1846, he was chosen to fill the office for the full term of three years. At this time his political sympathies were with the Whig party, as whose candidate he was elected a member of the State Assembly in 1849–'50; but in the early part of the Frémont campaign, in 1856, he gave his support to the newly-formed Republican party, and remained in unswerving allegiance to it till the close of his life. In 1851 an affection of the throat threatened to impair his practice as an advocate, and

he abandoned the law. The same year a bank was organized in Malone, of which he became cashier, continuing in charge of its financial interests for fifteen years. About the same time, also, he was elected president of the

WILLIAM ALMON WHEELER.

Northern New York Railroad Company, and for twelve years he was the supervisory manager of the line from Rouse's Point to Ogdensburg. He was a member and president pro tem. of the State Senate in 1858–'59, and displayed special aptitude for the duties of presiding officer of a deliberative body. He was elected a Representative in Congress from the Sixteenth District in 1860, and returned to his railroad and banking interest at the close of the term. In 1867 he was again called to public service, being elected a member, and then president, of the State Constitutional Convention, and in 1868 was returned to Congress. From March 4, 1869, till March 4. 1877, he served continuously, holding at various times the chairmanship of the Committee on the Pacific Railroad, and membership in the committees on Appropriations and Southern Affairs. He was the first member in either House to cover his back pay into the Treasury after the passage of the back-salary act, and was the author of the famous "compromise" in the adjustment of the political disturbances in Louisiana, by which Mr. Kellogg was recognized as Governor, while the State Legislature became Republican in the Senate and Democratic in the House. In 1876 he received the nomination for Vice-President of the United States in the Republican National Convention, and after the declaration by the Electoral Commission of the election of the Republican candidates, took his seat as presiding officer of the Senate, March 4, 1877. On the expiration of the term, March 4, 1881, he returned to his home in Malone, and passed the remainder of his life in retirement.

WHITE CROSS SOCIETY. An organization for the promotion of personal purity among men. It is sometimes called the White Cross Army, and its members are known as Knights of the White Cross, because the order is in the nature of a crusade not only for the improvement of men, but also for the elevation of women. The first White Cross Society was formed in England, by the Bishop of Durham, in his own diocese. To Miss Ellice Hopkins the bishop ascribes the honor of giving the inspiration for the movement. In speaking of the aims of the order, he says: "The obvious hopelessness of attacking the degradation of women and children from one side only, is at length forcing itself on the recognition of the Church. The weary hammering away at degraded women, while leaving all the causes that make them degraded untouched, is beginning to be recognized as not a very fruitful method. We must strike at the root of the evil. A more wholesome and righteous public opinion must be created in the matter of social purity. Not until it is generally recognized that the man who has wrought a woman's degradation is at least as great an offender against society as the man who has robbed a till, or the man who has forged a check—nay, much greater, for he has done a far more irreparable wrong—not until society is prepared to visit such an offender with the severest social penalties, will there be any real change for the better. So long as the violation of purity is condoned in the one sex, and visited with shame in the other, our unrighteousness and unmanliness must continue to work out its own terrible retribution. Is it beyond hope that, by involving widely the principle of association on a very simple religious basis, this end of creating a healthy public opinion may be obtained?" In regard to the machinery employed to reach this end the same authority says: "The White Cross movement has the advantage of flexibility. It may be worked as a parochial or a town organization, or both. It may be grafted on some existing guild or society, or it may be worked independently, as is found convenient. It may be connected with the Church of England Purity Society, or it may be erected on a narrower or a broader religious basis, as its promoters desire. The one characteristic that we regard as distinctive of White Cross fellowship is the adherence to the fivefold pledge." The pledge alluded to is as follows: "I, ———, promise by the help of God—1. To treat all women with respect, and endeavor to protect them from wrong and degradation. 2. To endeavor to put down all indecent language and coarse jests. 3. To maintain the law of purity as equally binding upon men and women. 4. To endeavor to spread these principles among my companions, and to try and help my younger brothers. 5. To use every possible means to fulfill the command 'Keep thyself pure.'" The age at which boys are permitted to join the society is placed at sixteen years. It is announced that a White Cross league may be organized in a church, a Bible-class, a secular school, or in a manufacturing establishment where men are employed; that any mother may form a society in her home with her own boys and their companions; and that if a league be formed in a church, the pastor, Sunday-school superintendent, and teachers, the older and prominent men, as well as the younger, in a word, all the men and all the boys over sixteen years of age in the congregation should be asked to unite. The first efforts of the Bishop of Durham were made in 1883, and the work spread rapidly over England, men of all classes and professions enrolling themselves. The movement is said to have made special headway at Cambridge and Oxford. Immense gatherings of pitmen, clerks, and others, held to gain recruits, were addressed by ministers and laymen, and often with great effect by Miss Hopkins. Organizations were soon formed in England's colonies, in India, Africa, Australia, and Canada. The first society in America, formed in February, 1884, in New York city, now numbers over one thousand members. Branches have also been established in all the larger cities of the United States. While this work has received the countenance of the Church of England, and of the Episcopal Church in America, in so marked a degree, it has also been taken up by special organizations, and earnest men and women in all denominations. At the annual meeting of the National White Cross T. U. in Philadelphia, in November, 1885, that society created a department for social purity, with the intent that it should include efforts to organize White Cross leagues. Other vehicles for the spread of the organization have been formed in the Young Men's Christian Associations throughout the United States.

WISCONSIN. State Government.—The following were the State officers during the year: Governor, Jeremiah M. Rusk, Republican; Lieutenant-Governor, George W. Ryland; Secretary of State, Ernst G. Timme; Treasurer, Henry B. Harshaw; Attorney-General, C. E. Estabrook; Superintendent of Public Schools, Jesse B. Thayer; Railroad Commissioner, Atley Peterson; Insurance Commissioner, Philip Cheek; Chief-Justice of the Supreme Court, Arasmus Cole; Associate Justices, William P. Lyon, Harlow S. Orton, David Taylor, and John B. Cassody.

Legislative Session.—The Legislature met on January 12, and adjourned on April 16, after a session of ninety-four days. U. S. Senator Philetus Sawyer, who was unanimously nominated by the Republican caucus, was re-elected. The Democratic candidate was John Winans. A bill reapportioning the State for members of the Legislature was passed at this session; also bills prohibiting aliens from acquiring or holding more than 320 acres of land, unless by inheritance or for debt, providing for the levy in

1888 or 1889 of a special tax of $200,000, if the Governor shall deem it necessary, to meet the appropriation for new buildings at the State University, and authorizing the prison officials in their discretion to purchase machinery for the State Prison, and begin the business of manufacturing therein by the State on its own account. Special appropriations were made of $65,000 for buildings at the School for Dependent Children, and of $175,000 for the construction of Science Hall and other buildings at the State University. The State also agreed to pay three dollars a week to the Veteran's Home, established by the Grand Army, for the support of each inmate thereof. A constitutional amendment, passed at the session of 1885, giving to the Legislature power to prescribe the qualifications and duties of the State Superintendent of Schools and other school officers, and to fix the superintendent's salary, was again adopted; and a new amendment, making the oldest member of the Supreme Court in point of service *ex-officio* chief-justice, was proposed for the first time. Other acts of the session were as follow:

Abolishing the State Board of Immigration.
Providing that all factories and public buildings shall be erected with fire-escapes and outward-swinging doors.
Appropriating money for the erection of monuments on the Gettysburg battlefield.
To incorporate the city of Onalaska, the city of Juneau, the city of Richland Center, the city of Marinette, the city of Ashland, the city of Reedsburg, and eight others.
To punish the taking and carrying away by trespass of things annexed to the realty.
To provide for the formation of mutual or co-operative associations for carrying on any trade or engaging in any business.
Punishing the issue of bank checks by persons having no money on deposit.
Requiring dealers and consumers of imitation butter to post a notice of such sale or use in their establishments.
To provide for the partition of personal property owned by tenants in common.
Raising the age of consent in females from ten to fourteen years.
For the confinement of habitual drunkards in an inebriate or insane asylum.
To punish the abduction of unmarried women for purposes of prostitution.
To prevent the holding of elections in saloons or rooms adjoining saloons.
To punish false pretenses in obtaining the registration of cattle and other animals, and to punish giving false pedigrees.
To prevent deception in the sale of cheese.
Punishing the sale of land which the seller knows to be encumbered, without informing the purchaser in regard thereto.
Authorizing railway companies to appoint police officers to protect their property.
Making the conversion of property by a bailee punishable as larceny.
Punishing by fine or imprisonment any conspiracy to "boycott" or otherwise injure a person in his reputation or business.
Authorizing the board of supervisors of each county to levy a tax, not exceeding one fifth of a mill, for the relief of indigent soldiers, sailors, and marines, and their wives and children, and providing a county commission for the distribution of the fund raised by this tax.

Authorizing and regulating the organization of local fire insurance companies.
Requiring owners of land to destroy all Canada thistles, daisies, and other noxious weeds growing on their land, before such time as they shall bear seed, and creating an officer in each town and city to enforce this act.
To provide for the construction of levees to protect bottom lands from overflow.
Authorizing town officers to suppress or license the keeping of billiard and pool tables and bowling-alleys.
To prevent employers from blacklisting employés.
Enacting a new game law and a new fish law.
To provide for the burial of honorably discharged soldiers.
To prevent the killing of birds for millinery purposes.
Authorizing the use of one twentieth of its portion of the school fund income by each school district for the purchase of a school library.
To punish interference with persons employed at lawful labor, and with the use or operation of machinery.
Extending the lien law to architects, civil engineers, and surveyors.
To appropriate a fund for the prevention and suppression of Asiatic cholera and other dangerous diseases.
To provide for the appointment of four game wardens.
Authorizing the Governor to prosecute and settle the claims of the State against the United States.
Providing that temporary aid may be granted to veterans or their wives and children, without removing them to an almshouse.
To punish the counterfeiting of election tickets.
Making the keeping of a house of ill-fame or the leasing of property for immoral purposes punishable by a maximum fine of $1,000 or maximum imprisonment of one year.
Requiring railroad companies to carry live-stock in mixed car-loads, provided the different kinds be separated by partitions.
Authorizing the city of Milwaukee to issue bonds aggregating a million dollars or more for parks, viaducts, intercepting sewers, public bathing-places, and other purposes.

Finances.—The report of the Treasurer for the year ending September 30 shows cash on hand at the beginning, $485,689.85; general receipts, $1,021,963.86; educational fund receipts, $783,-158.90; total, $2,290,812.61. The disbursements for the same time were $755,777.82 from the educational fund, and $1,415,423.97 from other funds; total, $2,171,201.79, leaving a surplus of $119,610.82 on September 30. The largest item of receipts, $763,994.56, is derived from a tax on railroad companies. The only tax levied upon individual property is a small rate for educational purposes. The total debt of the State, $2,252,000, bearing interest at 7 per cent., is all held by the State trust funds. The amount of these trust funds on September 30 was $4,738,465.99, distributed as follows: School-fund, $2,893,986.26; University fund, $194,488.47; Agricultural College fund, $228,882; Normal School fund, $1,416,903.26; drainage fund, $4,756.

Charities.—The number of inmates of the several State asylums on December 31, was as follows: State hospital, 504; Northern hospital, 643; Milwaukee hospital, 338; total, 1,485. There were in county asylums at the same date 1,220 more, making a total of 2,705 cared for at public institutions. The State School for the Deaf contained 213 pupils at the close of the year, the School for the Blind 85 pupils, and the public School for Dependent Children 97 pupils. At the new Veterans' Home, at Waupaca, 12 inmates had been received before the year ended.

Prisons.—There were 446 convicts at the State Prison on December 31. The State hires their labor to a manufacturer, at a fixed rate per day for each man, and pays all the prison expenses. By this arrangement the actual cost of the prison is $10,000 annually. The industrial school for boys contained 349 inmates when the year closed.

Agriculture.—About half of the population of the State is engaged in agriculture upon 150,-000 farms having an area of 16,000,000 acres, 8,000,000 of which are in cultivation. The acreage of corn last year was 1,000,000, producing 32,000,000 bushels. The pasturage and grasses of Wisconsin amount annually to $45,000,000, of which the hay-crop represents $15,000,000. Farm-lands and farm-products for 1886 were valued at $600,000,000, which is $200,000,000 more than all other industries in the State.

Political.—At the State election in April, the only officer to be chosen was a justice of the Supreme Court. Justice Harlow S. Orton was re-elected without opposition, receiving 127,944 votes out of a total of 128,308.

WOLFE, CATHERINE LORILLARD, an American philanthropist, born in New York City, March 8, 1828; died there, April 4, 1887. She was the youngest and only surviving child of John David Wolfe, a rich hardware merchant, and Dorothea Ann, youngest daughter of Peter Lorillard the elder. She received an excellent education, and in early life was a leader in society. On the death of her mother, in 1867, she withdrew from social life and devoted herself to her father, who died in 1872. Both parents were noted for their many deeds of charity and their ardent love of the Protestant Episcopal Church. Her father was a warden for many years of Grace Church, with which she united in early life, and to which she gave the chantry at the south side and Grace House at the north, the grand organ, the reredos, and a large stained-glass window (regarded as the most beautiful and costly in the United States) at the back of the transept. Her father survived the rest of Mr. Lorillard's heirs, and at his death left her sole heiress to a fortune estimated at $12,000,000 from the two estates, much of which consisted of securities and real estate. From that time till her death she gave away about $2,000,000 for religious, educational, and charitable purposes, averaging over $200,000 a year. During the last year of her life she gave $50,000 to purchase a church for the Italian mission in New York; $30,000 to the trustees of Grace Church to purchase a building on Fourth Avenue in the rear of the church, which she desired torn down, that nothing should ever obscure the light from the stained-glass window; $170,000 for the purchase of a lot and the erection of a diocesan house in Lafayette place; $25,000 to the Virginia Seminary; $40,000 to the American Church in Rome, Italy; $20,000 to the American school in Athens, Greece; $30,000 for educational purposes in Iowa, besides endowing the chair of English Literature and Belles Lettres in Griswold College; over $100,000 to home and foreign missionary societies; and corresponding amounts to sev-

CATHERINE LORILLARD WOLFE.

eral churches and schools in Nevada, California, Colorado, Georgia, Kansas, and Minnesota. She had previously given $50,000 to Union College, $50,000 to St. Johnsland College, and $30,000 toward purchasing the site on which the Home for Incurables, at Fordham, N. Y., is built, and a large sum for the endowment of the Wolfe Fund for Infirm Clergymen, besides establishing the Newsboys' Lodging House, and supporting the Wolfe expedition to Asia Minor in 1884. She had a house and lot, valued with the furniture at over $300,000, in New York City, and an estate at Newport, R. I., the lot, house, and furniture of which represented an outlay of $500,000. In her will she gave her entire collection of oil-paintings and water-color drawings to the Metropolitan Museum of Art, bequeathing $200,000 for their preservation, and gave the corporation of Grace Church $350,000 for the care of the edifice and the buildings she had previously provided, and the promotion of worship according to the rites of the Protestant Episcopal Church.

WYOMING TERRITORY. Territorial Government.—The following were the Territorial officers during the year: Governor, Thomas Moonlight; Secretary, Elliott S. N. Morgan, succeeded by Samuel D. Shannon; Auditor, Mortimer N. Grant; Treasurer, William P. Gannett; Attorney-General, Hugo Donzelman; Superintendent of Public Instruction, John Slaughter; Chief-Justice of the Supreme Court, William L. Maginnis; Associate Justices, Jacob P. Blair and Samuel T. Corn.

Population.—The number of people in the Territory at the close of the year is estimated at 85,000, an increase of 10,000 since 1886.

Finances.—The Territory has no public debt, except to a very limited amount. The last session of the Legislature in 1886 authorized the issuing of $280,000 in bonds, divided as follows: For a capitol building to be erected at Cheyenne, $150,000; a university at Laramie City, $50,000; and an insane asylum at Evanston, $30,000. These bonds, payable in fifteen to thirty-five years, with six per centum annual interest, were sold at an average premium of over five cents on the dollar. The valuation of assessed property for the year was $32,-089,613.12, of which $5,741,715.46 was the estimate for railroad property. The total valuation is $1,068,829 higher than that of last year, an increase caused chiefly by an act of the Legislature in 1886 taxing all railroad lands. A tract of twenty miles wide on each side of the Union Pacific Railroad was thus placed upon the rolls. The tax-levy was 2¼ mills for the general fund, one quarter of a mill each for the university fund and the bond tax fund, and one hundredth of a mill for the insane asylum fund. A tax of one hundredth of a mill is also imposed on cattle, horses, mules, and sheep, for the stock indemnity fund.

Education.—The following figures present the condition of the public schools in 1866, the date of the latest report: Number of schoolhouses, 111; schools taught, 180; male pupils, 2,572; female pupils, 2,416; teachers, 210. In September the Territorial University provided for by the Legislature of 1886 was formerly opened at Laramie City.

Charities.—The building for the Territorial Insane Asylum, at Evanston, was nearly completed at the close of the year, and will afford accommodations for the insane who are now cared for by the different counties and by individuals. The Institute for the Education of Deaf-mutes has been located at Cheyenne, and was ready at the close of the year.

The Capitol.—The Capitol is the fourth public building in course of erection by the Territory during the year, all of them being provided for by the Legislature of 1886. It is of cut and dressed stone, and is of ample proportions. At the close of the year it was sufficiently completed for use by the incoming Legislature.

Mining.—Gold, silver, copper, and iron are found in the mountainous sections of the Territory, but not in quantities sufficiently rich to make mining profitable; some mines are worked on a limited scale, but their total annual product is not known. Deposits of coal underlie a large part of the Territory.

Stock-Raising.—The interests of cattle-growers have suffered during the year from low prices, and from losses during the severe winter of 1886-'87. The number of cattle returned as assessed for the year, 753,608, shows a large decrease from the assessment of 1886. Their assessed value, $10,186,860, is nearly one third of the entire valuation of the Territory. More horses and sheep were assessed in 1887 than ever before.

Oil.—Large developments have been made during the past few years, in the oil-fields.

Railroads.—The number of miles of railroad assessed in 1887 was 669·64, of which 498·54 miles were owned by the Union Pacific Railroad, 92·34 by the Oregon Short Line, and 78·76 by the Wyoming Central. The last line is in process of construction westward through the central part of the Territory.

Y

YOUMANS, EDWARD LIVINGSTON, an American scientist, born at Coeymans, Albany County, N. Y., June 3, 1821; died in New York city, Jan. 18, 1887. His father was a farmer and wagon-builder, whose independence and gifts of clear, incisive expression made him one of the leading men in the neighborhood. His mother, a woman of energy and capacity, had been a teacher before marriage. In her blood was a Celtic strain, which came out distinctly in the vivacity and enthusiasm of her son. To pay the subscription to the local circulating library he planted a potato-patch in a corner of his father's farm. This local library contained not more than four hundred volumes, of which the only work of science was Buffon's "Natural History," which young Youmans read and reread. In his fourteenth year he was attacked with a malady of the eyes, which afflicted him more or less throughout his life. He persisted in reading and study until his eyes demanded rest, and his imprudence resulted in so serious an aggravation of his case that at seventeen his vision was almost totally lost. He was obliged to relinquish his post as teacher in a common school and his purpose of entering college. Until he was thirty he remained practically blind. Finding the services of the local oculist of no avail, in 1840 he went to the metropolis for treatment in the eye infirmary. He remained there several weeks without improvement, when he was informed by the physician in charge that his case was hopeless. He left the infirmary only to go from one oculist to another for examination. Among these, Dr. Elliott gave him most encouragement, and to the care of this skillful physician he committed himself, and the first moderate fee was the only one the doctor ever accepted during years of constant treatment. Until 1851 Mr. Youmans did not measurably recover his vision; short intervals of improved sight alternated with long periods of total blindness. The mental depression incident to this experience was deepened by the severity of his struggle for bread. He managed to pay his way by assiduous literary toil in various fields; but the incidental hardships of his lot did much to retard his recovery of sight. Friendship, however, won by his intelligence, courage, and address, he enjoyed in many useful quarters. To the end of his life he recalled with feeling kind services rendered him in days of poverty and blindness. In 1845, the sixth year of his residence in New York, his sister, Miss Eliza Ann Youmans, came to live with him and aid him in his work.

While earning a livelihood with his pen, Mr. Youmans prosecuted a course of scientific

EDWARD LIVINGSTON YOUMANS.

study, centering his interest in the chemistry of agriculture. His blindness made it impossible for him to see chemical experiments, much less perform them, so that he could form clear conceptions of chemical fact and law only by asking many questions and applying himself perseveringly to study of the information he received. His difficulties as a student, faithfully overcome, enabled him, when he took up the task of exposition, to make clear and interesting to others the knowledge he had with so much pains first made clear to himself. While occupied one day with the subject of presenting chemistry attractively and intelligibly to those uninformed about it, he planned a graphical method of picturing to the eye the principal compounds of chemistry and their component atoms. His "Chemical Chart" resulted. It won acceptance at once as a valuable aid in teaching chemistry, and from educators throughout the country came requests that the author should prepare a book to go with it. Mr. Youmans then applied himself to this task, his sister acting as reader and

amanuensis. Carefully studying the standard chemical text-books of the day, he found them technical, abstract, and diffuse—quite unsuited for such common schools as he had attended when a boy. Keeping in mental view such pupils as he himself had been, he dictated his "Class-Book of Chemistry." Its style was so simple and clear, its presentation so animated by an evident love of the subject, its illustrations from every-day matters so well chosen, that the volume sprang into popularity at once. With its two subsequent and rewritten editions, the "Class-Book" has found more acceptance than any other work on chemistry ever issued. In 1854 Mr. Youmans published a "Chemical Atlas," an extension of the method employed in the "Chart." It presented pictorially the chemical changes involved in combustion, respiration, fermentation, and the solar influences exerted on the earth. The atlas was accompanied by text as lucid as that of the "Class-Book."

His success as author of these publications determined his career. Debarred from adding to science by original research, he decided to devote himself to the work of making science known and appreciated by the common people. His remarkable gifts in conversation soon led to his being asked to lecture on the topics that so much interested him. His talents in elucidation and enthusiasm of manner filled the halls wherever he appeared. His lectures, delivered throughout the United States, comprised courses on the "Relations of the Living World to the Atmosphere," the "Chemistry of the Sunbeam," and the "Dynamics of Life." In 1856, the year after its publication, Mr. Youmans read Mr. Herbert Spencer's "Psychology," and was so much impressed with its ability that a correspondence with the author ensued, resulting in the publication in New York of Mr. Spencer's essays on education. The acquaintance with Mr. Spencer soon ripened into a friendship which lasted to the end of Mr. Youmans's life, and largely determined his course as the chief popularizer in America of the philosophy of evolution. In 1866, when Mr. Spencer's losses from his works had compelled him to suspend publication, Mr. Youmans raised a subscription of $7,000 among the American admirers of the English philosopher, enabling him to resume his plans.

Convinced that one of the principal fields for science was in its application to household economy, Mr. Youmans published in 1857 his "Hand-Book of Household Science." It was characterized by the same good style as the "Class-Book," and proved very successful. In 1864 he published the "Correlation and Conservation of Forces," a collection of expositions by eminent scientists of the new theory of the relations of forces. His introduction to the volume set forth the work done in America toward establishing the new philosophy. Three years later he issued the "Culture demanded by Modern Life," presenting the views of the foremost modern physicists, chemists, and other scientific specialists regarding the value of science, not only as knowledge for guidance of life, but as affording the best mental discipline. Mr. Youmans's contributions to the volume were on "Scientific Study of Human Nature" and on "Mental Discipline in Education." Not only as author and lecturer did Mr. Youmans do much for the diffusion of science in America, but also by causing the republication in New York of the most valuable English scientific works as they appeared in London. On his advice Messrs. D. Appleton & Co. produced American editions of Bagehot, Buckle, Carpenter, Darwin, Huxley, Lubbock. Lyell, Roscoe, Spencer, Tyndall, Whewell, and others. In every case the author was paid exactly as much as if he were an American enjoying copyright. In 1871 Mr. Youmans gave further extension to this enterprise by planning the "International Scientific Series," the volumes to appear simultaneously in New York, London, Paris, Leipsic, Milan, and St. Petersburg. The project gave all the effect of international copyright to the authors concerned. By judicious selection of eminent specialists in whatever land they were to be found, the whole civilized world had popular expositions of interesting scientific topics from the most competent sources rendered into the reader's own tongue.

In 1872 Mr. Youmans was appointed editor of "The Popular Science Monthly," a magazine established, at his suggestion, by the Messrs. Appleton. Its purpose was to present the constant advances of science in all departments, and to discuss the larger relations of science to history, education, the state, and the problems of life. His editorials on current topics were crisp, forcible, and characteristic, often widely quoted, and sometimes combated, and served to maintain his influence as an educator. In the winter of 1880–'81 he was attacked by pneumonia, and his constitution, early impaired by lack of exercise through blindness, never recovered. He married in 1861 the widow of William L. Lee, who survives him.

Z

ZANZIBAR, a monarchy on the eastern coast of Africa. The reigning sovereign is Seyid Burgash ben Said, who succeeded his brother in 1870. The area of the sultanate is 23,960 square kilometres. The island of Zanzibar contains about 200,000 inhabitants. The population of the continental possessions of the Sultan is not known. His annual revenue is about $1,250,000, derived chiefly from customs duties, which are regulated by a treaty of commerce concluded with Germany on Aug. 19, 1886. The principal products are cloves, gum-copal and other gums, red pepper, and cocoanuts. The transit trade in elephants' tusks amounts to $1,500,000 per annum.

Anglo-German Agreement.—The Sultan of Zanzibar formerly held dominion over the island only. He acquired and garrisoned points on the mainland for the purpose of keeping open and guarding trade-routes into the interior. Under compulsion from England he suppressed the slave-trade. His continental possessions were not defined, and, when the German East African Company acquired territory in the region, disputes arose. In 1886 a joint commission, representing Great Britain, Germany, and France, fixed the boundaries of his dominions, and England and Germany entered into an agreement as to their respective spheres of influence. The work of the commission was embodied in a formal agreement by Germany to recognize the sovereign rights of the Sultan over Zanzibar and Pemba, with adjacent islands, Lamu, Mafia, and a strip of coast of 10 nautical miles' breadth extending from the mouth of the Miningani River in the Bay of Tunghi as far as Kipini. North of Kipini the Sultan has the stations Kismaju, Barawa, Merka, and Makdishu, each with a radius of 12 nautical miles, and Warsheik with 5 nautical miles of territory. Great Britain agreed to use her influence to induce the Sultan to allow the Germans to have possession of the ports of Dar-es-Salaam and Pangani, paying over the customs receipts to the Sultan; also to promote a friendly agreement with Germany in regard to conflicting claims to districts in the Kilimandjaro mountains. The authority of the Sultan of Vitu, who stands under German protection, was recognized over a strip of coast including Manda Bay. The sphere of influence of England and Germany in the region lying between the Rovuma and Tana rivers is divided by a line beginning at the mouth of the river Wanga or Umbe, running to Lake Jipe, then along its eastern and northern banks, across the river Lumi, so as to bisect the districts of Taveta and Dshagga, and then along the northern slope of the Kilimandjaro mountain to a point on the eastern bank of the Victoria Nyanza, where it is intersected by the first parallel of south latitude.

INDEX TO THIS VOLUME.

A complete index to the twelve volumes of the series is issued separately.

Abeel, Gustavus, obit., 567.
Absorption of liquids through stomach, 676.
Abyssinia, 1.
Acclimatization, 669.
Adams, James Osgood, obit., 567.
Adventists, Seventh-Day, 3.
Afghanistan, 4.
Agiar, Antonio Augusto, obit., 621.
Aiken, David Wyatt, obit., 567.
Aiken, William, obit., 567.
Alabama, 8.
Alcohol, effect of, 672.
Alexander, Andrew Jonathan, obit., 568.
Algeria, 298.
Allaire, James, 716.
Allentown, 118.
Alloys, new, 483.
Aluminum, alloys of, 481; production of, 482; steel, 483.
Amatongaland, 93.
American Literature, 423.
American Party, organized in Pennsylvania, 659.
Amsterdam, 119.
Anarchists, trials in Austria, 52; in Illinois, 377; act to punish, 374.
Anderson, Luther Wilson, obit., 568.
Andover Cases, 146.
Anglican Churches, 10.
Annam, 298.
Antimony, 485.
Aqueduct, New Croton, 555.
Arbor-day, 765.
Archæology, 14.
Argentine Republic, 26.
Arizona, 28.
Arkansas, 30.
Artesian Wells, 259.
Ash, Abraham Joseph, obit., 568.
Ashburner, William, obit., 568.
Ashe, Thomas Samuel, obit., 569.
Associations for the Advancement of Science, 31.
Asteroids discovered, 42.
Astor, Charlotte Augusta, obit., 569.
Astronomical Progress and Phenomena, 35; Prizes, 45.

Astrophotographic Congress, 37.
Atlantic City, 119.
Atomic Weights, 110.
Australasia, 45.
Austria-Hungary, 49.
Ayres, William Orville, obit., 569.
Ayub Khan, 7.

Babbitt, Elijah, obit., 570.
Baird, Spencer Fullerton, sketch and portrait, 54.
Baker, Valentine, obit., 621.
Bald-knobbers, 516.
Baldwin, Prof., obit., 622.
Baldwin, Jesse Garrettson, obit., 570.
Baldwin, Samuel, obit., 570.
Ballentine, William, obit., 622.
Baptists, 55.
Barbadoes, 800.
Barnewall, Robert Aylomer, obit., 570.
Bartlett, Washington, obit., 570.
Bartol, James Lawrence, obit., 571.
Bartow, Morey Hale, obit., 571.
Batbie, Anselm Polycarpe, obit., 622.
Baynes, Thomas Spencer, obit., 623.
Beach, John Sheldon, obit., 571.
Beach, William Morrow, obit., 571.
Beckx, Pierre Jean, obit., 623.
Béclard, Jules, obit, 623.
Beecher, Henry Ward, sketch and portrait, 60.
Beers, Henry Newell, obit., 571.
Belgium, 64.
Beresford-Hope, A. J. B., obit., 623.
Bernhardi, Theodor, obit., 624.
Betts, Charles Wyllys, obit., 571.
Bible Societies, 67.
Blackburn, Luke Pryor, obit., 572.
Blake, Samuel H., obit., 572.
Blood, temperature of, 673; specific gravity of, 673; color of, 673.
Bodwell, Joseph R., obit., 572.
Bolingsoff, Catherine, obit., 572.
Bolivia, 68.
Boundaries, between Honduras and Salvador, 360; between Peru and Ecuador, 661; between

Roumania and Austria-Hungary, 720; between New York and New Jersey, 543; between Bulgaria and Servia, 736; Montenegrin, 774.
Boussingault, Jean Baptiste Joseph Dieudonné, obit., 624.
Bove, explorer, obit., 624.
Bradford, 119.
Brassey, Lady Annie, obit. and portrait, 70.
Bratiano, M., attempted assassination of, 719.
Brazil, 71.
Breakwater at Ceará, 260.
Brennan, Margaret, obit., 573.
Brevoort, James Carson, obit., 573.
Brewster, Henry, obit., 573.
Bridges, at Poughkeepsie, 252; Tay, 253; at Taranto, 254; Stiffened Suspension, 254; at Oak Park, 255.
Brinz, Aloiz von, obit., 624.
Brooks, Horatio G., obit., 573.
Brown, Dyer Date Stanley, obit., 573.
Brown, Sir Thomas Gore, obit., 625.
Brüggemann, Karl Heinrich, obit., 625.
Bubastis, Temple of, 19.
Buddicom, William Barber, obit., 625.
Buffalo, or Bison, Extermination of the, 74.
Buffum, James N., obit., 574.
Bulgaria, 76; election of Ferdinand, 80; new cabinet, 80.
Bunzl, Julius, obit., 574.
Burmah, 81.
Burtis, Divine, obit., 574.
Burton, Nathaniel J., obit., 574.

Cain, Richard Harvey, obit., 575.
California, 85.
Canada, Dominion of, 88.
Canals, Cape Cod ship, 459; Nicaragua maritime, 563; Panama, 138; Suez, 240; Chesapeake and Ohio, 456.
Cantagrel, Félix François Jean, obit., 625.

Cape of Good Hope, 91.

Capital Punishment, commission to decide on Method of, 548.

Carnochan, John Murray, obit., 575.

Carnot, Marie François Sadi, sketch and portrait, 93.

Caro, Elmo Marie, obit., 625.

Carpenter, Henry, obit., 575.

Carriers, Mechanical, 94.

Cartter, David Kellogg, obit., 575.

Ceará Breakwater, 260.

Chemistry, 99 ; New Substances, 104 ; New Processes, 106.

Chetwood, George Ross, obit., 575.

Chicopee, 120.

Chili, 118 ; contract with Peru, 114.

China, 115 ; opium traffic, 200; suzerainty over Indian states, 388.

Cholera in Chili, 114.

Christian, William Henry, obit., 575.

Christian Churches, 118.

Churches, building-fund commission, 706 ; work in Mexico, 706; documents affecting the Reformed Church, 709 ; Unitarian, 774.

Cilley, Joseph, obit., 576.

Cinchona-Bark, 69, 140.

Ciparin, Timoteo, obit., 625.

Cities, American, Recent Growth of, 118 et seq.

Clam-Martinitz, Count Heinrich, obit., 626.

Clark, Alvan, sketch and portrait, 137.

Clark, Patrick, obit., 576.

Clark, William Audley, obit., 576.

Cleveland, Chauncey Fitch, obit., 576.

Coates, Benjamin, obit., 577.

Cobb, Sylvanus, Jr., obit., 577.

Cocoa, 231.

Coggswell, Elliot Colby, obit., 577.

Cohoes, 120.

Collins, Jennie, obit., 577.

Colombia, 137.

Colorado, 140.

Columbus's remains, burial of, in Genoa, 217.

Comber, T. J., obit., 626.

Comets, 42.

Commerce, bill on Interstate, 173 ; and Navigation, of the United States, 143.

Confederate Monument, 9.

Congregationalists, 145.

Congress of the United States, 153.

Congress, Sanitary, 663.

Connecticut, 208.

Conner, James Madison, obit., 578.

Constitution, California's amended, 86 ; convention to change, in

Delaware, 221 ; U. S. Centennial Anniversary of, 780.

Contract, Grace-Aranibar, 562.

Convention, New Hebrides, 539.

Conway, Thomas William, obit., 578.

Cooke, Phineas Baldwin, obit., 578.

Cooking-schools, 238.

Copyright, International, 755.

Cornell, John Black, obit., 578.

Cornly, James Madison, obit., 579.

Corvée, Abolition of, in Egypt, 243.

Costa Rica, 210.

Cotton, cultivation of, in Japan, 402.

Cotton, large yield in South Carolina, 738.

Couroy, Roussel de, obit., 626.

Court of Claims bill, 189.

Cox, Mr. Bell, case of, 13.

Craik, Dinah Maria Mulock, sketch and portrait, 212.

Craven, Thomas Tingey, obit., 579.

Crawford, County plan for elections, 247.

Crete, 773.

Crotia, 54.

Crocker, Uriel, obit., 579.

Crofters, Highland, 342.

Cuba, 214.

Curry, Daniel, obit., 579.

Cuvillier-Fleury, Alfred Auguste, obit., 626.

Dakota, 217.

Dams, famous, 255.

Dana, Alexander Hamilton, obit., 580.

Dancer, John Benjamin, obit., 626.

Danenhower, John Wilson, obit., 580.

Davis, Winston Jones, obit., 580.

Dearborne, Frederick M., obit., 580.

Death Penalty in Ecuador, 232.

Decorations, Sale of, in France, 294.

Delaware, 220.

Denmark, 221.

De Pauw, Washington C., obit., 581.

Deprétris, Agostino, 223.

Detmold, Christian E., obit., 581.

Detwiller, Henry, obit., 581.

Dhuleep Singh, 7.

Dickinson, Donald McDonald, sketch and portrait, 776.

Diet, while in training, 668.

Digestibility of various substances, 676.

Disasters in 1887, 294.

Disciples of Christ, 227.

Dix, Dorothea Lynde, obit., 581.

Dock, Floating, 257.

Doniphan, Alexander W., obit., 582.

Duffield, Samuel Willoughby, obit., 582.

Dulles, John Welsh, obit., 582.

Duncan, Thomas, obit., 583.

Dunn, William McKee, obit., 583.

Dupin, Jean Henri, obit., 626.

Duruy, Albert, obit., 626.

Duval, Raoul, obit, 626.

Eads, James Buchanan, sketch and portrait, 228.

Earthquake at Guayaquil, 232; in Mexico, 504.

Eaton, Hosea Ballou, obit., 583.

Ecuador, 230.

Edmunds-Tucker act, 789.

Education, attitude of Mormons toward, in Idaho, 372 ; compulsory, in Hawaii, 350 ; in Nebraska, 526 ; in New Mexico, 544 ; geography in, 316 ; industrial, 232 ; institution, bequest of José Sevilla, 663 ; of Indians, 386 ; medical, of women, in India, 382 ; technical, in Massachusetts, 233 ; in New York, 234 ; in Missouri, 236 ; in Illinois, 236 ; in Ohio, 236 ; in Maryland, 237 ; in Pennsylvania, 237 ; in New Jersey, 238.

Egypt, 238.

Elder, Robert, obit., 583.

Elections, contested in Indiana, 384 ; frauds in Indiana, 386 ; of Greek Patriarch, 773 ; special, in Rhode Island, 714 ; Crawford County plan of, 247 ; Clarion County plan of, 248 ; Laws, Customs, and Theories of, 244.

Electrical phenomena, 494.

Electro-plating with aluminum, 483.

Eliot, William Greenleaf, obit., 584.

Emancipation in Brazil, 73 ; in Cuba, 215.

Embree, Effingham, obit., 584.

Emery-wheels, 248.

Emin Pasha, 250.

Emory, William Helmsley, obit., 584.

Engineering, 252.

Erie, 190.

Evangelical Alliance, 261.

Evangelical Association, 261.

Evansville, 121.

Events of 1887, 262.

Extradition Treaty, Spain and Uruguay, 787.

Ezzard, William, obit., 584.

Fairchild, Charles Stebbins, sketch and portrait, 775.

Fairfield, Francis Gerry, obit., 585.

Famine in Asia Minor, 774.

Faris, Ahmed Effendi, obit., 627.

Farre, Arthur, obit., 627.
Fäustle, Johann, obit., 627.
Fellows, John F., obit., 585.
Ferry, Jules, Attempted Assassination of, 297.
Financial Review of 1887, 264.
Fine arts in 1887, 274.
Fisheries Questions, 280; Riots, 66; bill to protect, 178.
Florida, 285.
Fontes, Periera de Mello, A. M. de, obit., 627.
Foster, Abby Kelly, obit., 585.
Fowler, Orson Squire, obit., 585.
France, 288.
Francis, Charles S., obit., 586.
Frederick William (crown prince), portrait, frontispiece; illness of, 327.
Frederick William (prince), portrait, 321.
Friends, 299.

Gallait, Louis, obit., 627.
Ganetzky, Johann S., obit., 627.
Geddes, James, obit., 586.
Genast, Wilhelm, obit., 627.
Geographical Progress and Discovery, 301.
Geography in Education, 316.
Georgia, 317.
Germany, 319.
Germer, Edward, obit., 586.
Ghilzai Revolt, 4.
Gillespie, Elvia, obit., 586.
Gloucester, 121.
Gold. treatment of ore, 484; discovery of, in Michigan, 484.
Goldschmidt, Meyer A., obit., 627.
Goodall, Albert Gallatin, obit., 586.
Goodwin, Eliza Weathersby, obit., 587.
Gozzadini, Count Giovanni, obit., 627.
Grace-Aranibar Contract, 662.
Grand Army of the Republic, 329.
Grand-écaille, 756.
Grand Rapids, 122.
Grant, James, obit., 628.
Great Britain and Ireland, 331.
Greece, 345.
Green, Charles, obit., 587.
Green, William Mercer, obit., 587.
Greene, Theodore P., obit., 587.
Greenwood, John, obit., 587.
Greer County, Texas, claimed by United States, 760.
Greig, Samuel Alexeivich, obit., 628.
Griffin, Samuel P., obit., 588.
Guatemala, 346.
Guerin, Thomas J., obit., 588.
Guiana, British, 600.
Guns for Coast Defense, 348.

Hadji, Loja, obit., 628.

Hague, William, obit., 588.
Hall, Benton J., sketch, 649.
Hamilton, 122.
Harrar, Conquest of, 2.
Harrington, Henry F., obit., 588.
Harris, John Wesley, obit., 589.
Harris, William Logan, obit., 589.
Harvey, William Street, obit., 589.
Hassinger, David Stanley, obit., 589.
Hathorn, Henry H., obit., 589.
Hauser, Miska, obit., 628.
Hawaii, 349; Revolution in, 353; New Constitution of, 354.
Hayden, Ferdinand Vandeveer, sketch and portrait, 356.
Hayes, John Lord, obit., 589.
Hayti, 357.
Hazen, William Babcock, sketch and portrait, 358.
Heat, radiation of, from human body, 487.
Henne, Antonia, obit., 590.
Hennequin, Alfred Nicoclès, obit., 628.
Herrmann, Herr, obit., 628.
High License in Minnesota, 512.
Hitchcock, Roswell Dwight, sketch and portrait, 358.
Hittite Inscriptions, 25.
Holland. See NETHERLANDS, 359.
Holliday, Ben, obit., 590.
Homes, Henry Augustus, obit., 590.
Honduras, 359.
Hope, James Barron, obit., 591.
Hopkins, Mark, sketch and portrait, 360.
Hops, in Washington Territory, 800.
Horses, racing, 767; running, 770; trotting, 768.
Hot Water, effect of, on uterus, 677.
Houses, 361.
Hovey, Charles M., obit., 591.
Howland, Robert Southworth, obit., 591.
Hudson, 122.
Hungary. See AUSTRIA, 53.
Hunt, Robert, obit., 629.
Hunter, Robert Mercer Taliaferro, sketch and portrait, 371.
Husband, William, obit., 629.
Hussey, John, obit., 591.
Hutchison, Joseph C., obit., 522.
Hyderabad, 382.
Hyksos, the, 21.

Iceland, 223.
Idaho, 372.
Iddesleigh, Sir Stafford Henry Northcote, obit., 629.
Ideville, Henri, obit., 630.
Illinois, 374.
India, 376.
Indiana, 383.

Indianapolis, 122.
Indians, Education, 386; Reservations in Dakota, 219; attack upon, 143; in New Mexico, 545; Pueblo, 545; Reports of Agents, 777.
India Rubber, 140.
Industrial Union, International, 649.
Ingersoll, Elihu Parsons, obit., 592.
Inscriptions, Ancient, 17, 25.
Interstate Commerce Law, The, 173, 390.
Iowa, 391.
Iridescent Stoneware, 504.
Irish Land Commission, 336.
Iron and Steel, 479; malleable, 481.
Italy, 394; Changes in Ministry, 397, 398.

Jacobini, Cardinal Ludovico, obit., 630.
Jamaica, 801.
Japan, 400.
Jauréguiberry, Jean Bernard, obit., 630.
Jeffries, Richard, obit., 630.
Jewell, James Stewart, obit., 592.
Jew-fish, 756.
Jews, 403.
Johnston, Archibald, obit., 592.
Jupiter Olympius, Temple of, 21.
Jurisdiction, Disputed, of Greer County, Texas, 760.

Kalakana, Reign of, 351.
Kansas, 405.
Katkoff, Michel Nikiphorovich, obit., 630.
Keely Motor, The, 407.
Kellogg, Albert, obit., 593.
Kemen, Mary Josephine, obit., 593.
Kennedy, Joseph C. G., obit., 593.
Kentucky, 410.
Kerki, Russian Occupation of, 7.
Kindergarten, 232.
Kingston, 123.
Kinloch, Eliza, obit., 593.
Kirchhoff, Gustav Robert, sketch and portrait, 412.
Knoxville, 123.
Kolloch, Isaac S., obit., 592.
Kraszewski, Joseph Ignatius, obit., 632.
Krikor, Odian Effendi, obit., 632.
Krupp, Alfred, obit., 632.
Krzyzanowski, Wladimir, obit., 594.
Labor, Foreign Contract, 207; Legislation in Belgium, 66; in the United States, 85, 444; Strikes, in Belgium, 66; in Illinois, 376. See also STRIKES.
Leighton, Albert, obit., 594.
La Motte, Charles E., obit., 594.

Land-Grant Railroads, 202.
Langenbeck, Bernhard von, obit., 632.
Langer, Karl, obit., 632.
Langiewicz, Marian, obit., 632.
Lanoline, 670.
L'Argar, discoveries at, 23.
Laurent, Francis, obit., 633.
Law and Order League of the United States, 413.
Lawrence, Albert Gallatin, obit., 594.
Laws, Charles Alfred, obit., 595.
Laws against Foreigners in Russia, 724.
Lawson, James Anthony, obit.,633.
Layton, Caleb Rodney, obit., 595.
Lazarus, Emma, sketch and portrait, 414.
Leavenworth, Eliza Warner, obit., 595.
Lee, Alfred, obit., 595.
Leeward Islands, The, 801.
Le Flô, Adolphe Emmanuel Charles, obit., 633.
Legislature, extra session in Montana, 518.
Lemaire, Pierre Auguste, obit., 633.
Lent, Lewis Benjamin, obit., 596.
Lequesne, Eugène Louis, obit., 633.
Leray, Francis Xavier, obit., 596.
Liberia, 416.
Library Legislation, 418.
Lind (Goldschmidt), Jenny, sketch and portrait, 490.
Linsly, Jared, obit., 596.
Liquor Question, in Ohio, 643.
Literary Property, 140.
Literature, American, in 1887, 423.
Literature, British, in 1887, 433.
Literature, Continental, in 1887, 436.
Lord, Jarvis, obit., 596.
Los Angeles, 123.
Lotteries, in Brazil, 71.
Louisiana, 443.
Loyal Legion, 445.
Lull, Edward Phelps, obit., 597.
Lutherans, 446.
Lynchburgh, 124.
Lyons, Richard Bickerton Pemoll, sketch and portrait, 450.

McAllister, Julian, obit., 598.
Macgregor, Sir Charles Metcalfe, obit., 633.
Madagascar, 452.
Mail-matter, Distribution of, 685.
Maine, 453.
Manitoba, province of, 455.
Manitou, 124.
Manning, Daniel, obit., 597.
Manning, Thomas Courtlandt, obit., 597.
Manuscripts, Decipherment of Mexican, 16.

Maracaybo, Lake, Survey of, 790.
Marcy, Randolph Barnes, obit., 597.
Marmaduke, John Sappington, obit., 598.
Marsegg, Herrman Mallner von, obit., 634.
Maryland, 455.
Massachusetts, 458.
Massowah, Italians at, 1.
Maté, exportation of, 72.
Mayhew, Henry, obit., 634.
Medal of Honor, the United States, 463.
Medina, Territory of, 415.
Memorial Day, 475.
Menthol, influence of, 673.
Mercur, Ulysses, sketch and portrait, 478.
Metallurgy, 479; new processes, 485; to weld by electricity, 486.
Meteorology, 487.
Methodists, 495.
Meuse, Fortification of the Valley of the, 64.
Mexico, 500.
Meyrowitz, Alexander, obit., 598.
Michel, Francisque Xavier, obit., 634.
Michigan, 504.
Mills, Zophar, obit., 598.
Milon, Pierre Solidor, obit., 599.
Mind-Reading, 506.
Mines in Bolivia, 69; in Colorado, 142; in Dakota, 219; in Idaho, 373; in Montana, 519; nickel in New Caledonia, 485; Antimony in Portugal, 485; ruby in Burmah, 84; salt in New York, 735.
Minnesota, 510.
Missionaries, expelled from Caroline Islands, 741.
Mississippi, 513.
Missouri, 515.
Mitchell, Alexander, obit.,599.
Monrad, Ditlev Gothard, obit., 634.
Montana, 517.
Montenegrin Boundary, 774.
Montreal, 124.
Moody, Granville, obit., 599.
Moon, influence of, on weather, 487.
Morley, Thomas, obit., 599.
Morrill, Anson P., obit., 599.
Morrison, Pitcairn, obit., 600.
Morrison, Robert Francis, obit., 600.
Morse, Charles Walker, obit., 600.
Mound-Builders, Funeral rites of Certain, 16.
Moya, Gen. Casimiro N. de, 733.
Muhlenberg Centenary, 450.
Mullany, James Robert Madison, obit., 600.
Music, Progress of, 519.

Naphtha-Motors, 524.
National Banks, 783.
National League Proclamation, 341.
Natural Gas in Indiana, 386.
Natural selection, 668.
Navigators' Islands. See SAMOA.
Nebraska, 526.
Nervous System, 670.
Netherlands, 527.
Nevada, 530.
Newberry, John Stoughton, obit., 601.
New Brunswick, 532.
Newdegate, Charles Newdigate, obit., 634.
Newfoundland, 533.
New Guinea, British, 48. See also PAPUA.
New Hampshire, 533.
New Hebrides, 537.
New Jersey, 540.
New Jerusalem Church, 543.
New Mexico, 544.
Newport, 124.
New substance, 670.
New York (city), 553.
New York (State), 546.
New Zealand, 48.
Niagara Falls, utilizing the Power of, 561.
Nicaragua, 562.
Nicholson, James William Augustus, obit., 601.
Nickel-plating, 485; nickel-steel, 485.
Nordman, Johannes, obit., 635.
Norristown, 126.
North Carolina, 564.
Nova Scotia, 565.

Oakland, 126.
Obituaries, American, 567, et seq.
Ohio, 641.
Okeechobee Drainage bill, 287.
Old Catholic Church, 644.
Olney, Edward, obit., 602.
Ontario, 644.
Oregon, 645.
O'Sullivan, William Henry, obit., 635.
Oude, Wadjid Ali Shah, obit., 635.
Oysters, application to plant, in Chili, 115.

Pacific Railroad Investigation, 193.
Palmer, Alonzo B., obit., 602.
Palmer, George Washington, obit., 602.
Palmer, Ray, obit., 602.
Panama Canal, 138.
Pango-Pango, 731.
Panofka, Heinrich, obit., 635.
Papua, or New Guinea, 647.
Paraguay, 648.
Pasadena, 126.
Pasaglia, Carlo, obit., 635.

Patents, 649; amendment of law, 204.
Patriarchate, Œcumenical, 778.
Pawtucket, 126.
Peanuts, 758.
Pellegrini, Antonio, obit., 635.
Pennsylvania, 656.
Pensions, bill in United States, 183; in Germany, 328; increase in number of, 779.
Perkins, William, obit., 603.
Perry, William, obit., 603.
Persia, 660.
Peru, 660.
Petroleum, in Argentine Republic, 28; in Burmah, 84.
Pettingell, John Hancock, obit., 603.
Pharmacy, 664.
Phillips, John Arthur, obit., 636.
Photo-Engraving, 665.
Photography, Astronomical, 35.
Photometry, Stellar, 43.
Physical Training, 665.
Physiology, 668.
Pierce, Thomas Prescott, obit., 603.
Plants, New, 73.
Plot to dethrone Sultan, 778.
Poisons, Action of, 678.
Poland, Luke P., obit., 603.
Polo, 680.
Polygamy, bill to prevent, 168.
Poore, Ben: Perley, obit., 604.
Porpoise-Hunting, 681.
Port Hamilton, Retrocession of, 118.
Portland, 127.
Porto Rico, 802.
Portugal, 682.
Postal Facilities, Improvement in, 684, et seq.
Pott, August Friedrich, obit., 636.
Potter, Horatio, obit. and portrait, 604.
Potter, Robert B., obit., 605.
Powell, Thomas, obit., 605.
Pratt, Daniel, obit., 605.
Pratt, James T., obit., 606.
Presbyterians, 690.
Preston, David, obit., 606.
Preston, John, obit., 606.
Preston, William, obit., 606.
Prisons, Associations, 704; Reform, 701; U. S. Government, 704.
Prohibition, in Iowa, 393; in Kansas, 406; in Kentucky, 411; in Maine, 453; in Michigan, 506; in Missouri, 516; in Rhode Island, 713; in Tennessee, 758.
Prophetic Conference, 705.
Protestant Episcopal Church in the United States, 705.

Quebec, 127; Province of, 707.
Quincy, 127.
Quinn, William, obit., 606.

Racine, 128.
Raft, great lumber, 257.
Railroads, in China, 116; Investigation, Pacific, 193; Interstate Commerce act, 269; Trans-Caspian, 6; British Strategic, 6; in Mexico, 502, 503; Tehuantepec Ship, 502.
Ramée, Daniel, obit., 636.
Randal, Alanson Merwin, obit., 607.
Randi, Lorenzo, obit., 636.
Rapallo, Charles Anthony, obit., 607.
Rau, Charles, obit., 607.
Raymond, Israel Ward, obit., 608.
Raymond, John T., obit., 608.
Rebellion of Caroline Islands against Spain, 741; military in Peru, 661.
Record of the Turf, 767.
Reformed Churches, 708.
Reformed Episcopal Church, 711.
Reunion of Protestant Christendom, action in regard to, 707-710.
Revolutionary Plots in Russia, 723; effect of, upon education, 724.
Rhode Island, 712.
Ricketts, James Brewerton, obit., 608.
Rifles, Repeating, 714.
Rights of married women in Alabama, 8; in Pennsylvania, 656.
Ripley, Roswell Sabin, obit., 608.
Roach, John, sketch and port., 716.
Robertson, John, obit., 609.
Rochester, Thomas Fortescue, obit., 609.
Roman Catholic Church, 716; hierarchy established in India, 382.
Rosewood, exportation from Costa Rica, 211.
Ross, William Henry Harrison, obit., 609.
Roumania, 718; Attempted Assassination of Prime Minister, 719; tariff-war in, 790.
Rouquette, Adrien, obit., 609.
Rousseau, Philippe, obit., 636.
Rowett, Richard, obit., 609.
Rumsey, Henry Barlow, obit., 610.
Russia, 720.
Ryle, John, obit., 610.

Saint-Hilaire, Émile Marco de, obit., 636.
Saint John, 128.
St. Lucia, 802.
Salt-Mining in New York, 725.
Salvador, 727.

Samoan Islands, 728; American interests at, 732; Germany declares war on, 730; King Malietoa deposed, 731.
San Diego, 128.
Sandusky, 129.
Sanitary Congress in Peru, 663.
San José, 129.
Santo Domingo, 732; rebellion in, 733.
Sargent, Aaron A., obit., 610.
Sarzeaud Incident, 243.
Savanilla, 756.
Savings-Bank, Post-Office, 687.
Saxe, John Godfrey, sketch and portrait, 733.
Sayn-Wittgenstein, Caroline, obit., 636.
Schenectady, 129.
Schirmer, Heinrich Ernst, obit., 637.
Schleyer, Johann Martin, inventor of Volapük, 794.
Schmidt, Wilhelm Adolf, obit., 637.
Schröder, Karl, obit., 637.
Scott, Robert N., obit., 610.
Scroggs, Gustavus A., obit., 611.
Senatorial, election contested in Texas, 758.
Servia, 734; defeat of Government of, 735.
Sevilla, José, bequest of, 663.
Shaw, Aaron, obit., 611.
Sheldon, James, obit., 611.
Sherbrooke, 130.
Short-hand writing, 670.
Sidon, Tombs at, 24.
Sill, Edward Rowland, obit., 611.
Silver fish, 756.
Silver king, 756.
Simpson, John Palgrave, obit., 637.
Smith, Francis S., obit., 611.
Smith, Thomas Kilby, obit., 612.
Smith, William, obit., 612.
Socialists, Agitation in London, 342; Disturbance in the Netherlands, 529.
Societies, Mutual Aid, 523; of Jesus, Incorporation of, in Quebec, 706; Psychical Research, 509.
Somali-Land, 736.
Soudan, The, 244.
South Carolina, 737.
Spain, 738; Popular Discontent in, 740; recognized as a great power, 740.
Speed, James, obit. and port., 741.
Spencer, Charles S., obit., 612.
Sphinx, The, 18.
Spooner, Lysander, obit., 612.
Standeford, Elisha D., obit., 613.
Stanton, Henry Brewster, obit., 613.
Stars, Discoveries of, 43.
Stearns, Charles W., obit., 613.

Steeple-Chasing, 771.
Stevens, Aaron Fletcher, obit., 613.
Stewart, Balfour, obit., 637.
Stewart, Isaac Dalton, obit., 614.
Stockton, 180.
Stone, Charles P., obit., 614.
Stone, Delia Charlotte Hall, obit., 615.
Strakosch, Maurice, obit., 638.
Strangford, Emily Anne, obit., 638.
Strikes, 742, et seq.
Stromeyer, August, obit., 638.
Suez Canal, 240; Neutralization of, 242.
Sullivan, Algernon Sydney, obit., 615.
Sun, parallax, 40; total eclipse, 41.
Sutherland, Josiah, obit., 615.
Swaziland, 93.
Sweden and Norway, 752; Ministerial Crisis in, 754.
Switzerland, 754.

Talcott, John Ledyard, obit., 615.
Tarbox, John Kemble, obit., 615.
Tariff-war in Roumania, 720.
Tarpom, 756.
Tarpon, 756.
Tarpum, 756.
Tasmania, 48.
Taylor, Benjamin Franklin, obit. and portrait, 755.
Taylor, John, obit., 615.
Temperature, conditions that affect, 488; effect of, on blood, 673.
Temple of Bubastis, 19.
Temple of Jupiter Olympius, 21.
Tennessee, 757.
Texas, 759.
Textile Fiber, New, 140.
Thacher, George Hornell, obit., 616.
Thasos, Ruins at, 22.
Thorington, James, obit., 616.
Tiberias, City of, 25.
Timor, island of, revolt in, 684.
Toronto, 180.
Tortuga, 357.
Tousey, Sinclair, obit., 616.
Trade - Dollars, Redemption of, 201.
Travers, William Priggin, obit., 616.
Treat, Samuel H., obit., 617.
Treaties, between Germany, Austria-Hungary, and Italy, 328, 399; Central American republics with Guatemala, 348;

China with France and Portugal, 117; China with Portugal, 684; Costa Rica with Guatemala, 210; with Nicaragua, 210; Germany with Paraguay, 648; literary, 140: power of United States, 760; Russia with Austria, 51; United States with Guatemala, 346; United States with Hawaiian Islands, 355; United States with Spain, 215.
Tree-Planting, 765.
Trenton, 182.
Trials, for bribery in New York, 555; for treason in Germany, 326.
Trinidad, 801.
Triple Alliance, 328, 399.
Truxtun, William Talbot, obit., 617.
Tucson, 132.
Tulane, Paul, obit., 617.
Tunis, 298.
Turf, Ten Years' Record of, 767.
Turkey, 772.

Uhrich, Jean Jacques Alexis, obit., 638.
Unitarians, 774.
United States, 775; claims Greer County, Texas, 760; Finances of, 780.
United Workmen, Ancient Order of, 784.
Universalists, 786.
Upchurch, John Jordan, obit., 618.
Uruguay, 786.
Utah, 787; Constitutional Convention, 788.
Utes, in Colorado, 143.

Vanderpool, Aaron J., obit., 618.
Varick, Theodore Romeyn, obit., 618.
Vassali Bey Luigi, obit., 634.
Venezuela, 789.
Vermont, 790.
Victorian Jubilee, 791.
Viel-Castel, M. de, obit., 638.
Vincent, Mary Anne Farley, obit., 618.
Virginia, 792.
Virginia City, 133.
Vischer, Friedrich Theodor, obit., 639.
Volapük, 794.
Volckmar, Wilhelm, obit., 639.
Vulpian, Edme Felix Alfred, obit., 639.

Wagner, Moritz Friedrich, obit., 639.
Walcott, Charles F., obit., 619.
Walter, Thomas Ustick, obit., 619.
Walther, Carl Ferdinand Wilhelm, obit., 619.
Ward, George Cabot, obit., 619.
Washburn, William Barrett, obit., 619.
Washburne, Elihu B., sketch and portrait, 798.
Washington, 133.
Washington Territory, 799; Census of, 799.
Wasson, David Atwood, obit., 620.
Watkins, Alice, obit., 620.
Weaver, Archibald J., obit., 620.
Webb, George James, obit., 620.
Weld, Mason Coggswell, obit., 620.
Werder, August Carl Leopold, obit., 640.
Werner, Gustav, obit., 640.
Werthheimer, Joseph Ritter von, obit., 640.
West Indies, 800.
West Virginia, 803.
Wheeler, William A., sketch and portrait, 804.
Whitall, Henry, obit., 620.
White Cross Society, 805.
Whitworth, Sir Joseph, obit., 640.
Wilder, Royal G., obit., 621.
Wilmington, 135.
Wilson Scandal, in France, 294.
Windward Islands, The, 802.
Wisconsin, 805.
Wittich, Ludwig von, obit., 641.
Woburn, 135.
Wolfe, Catherine L., sketch and portrait, 807.
Wolverton, George Grenfell Glyn, obit., 641.
Women, in India, 382.
Wood, Mrs. Henry, obit., 641.
Woods, William B., obit. and portrait, 621.
Woonsocket, 135.
Wootten, Edward, obit., 621.
Worcester, 136.
Wyoming Territory, 807.

York, 136.
Youmans, Edward L., sketch and portrait, 808.

Zanzibar, 810; treaties concerning, 810.
Zebehr Pasha, 244.
Zinc-mining, 485.
Zululand, Annexation of, 92.

Lightning Source UK Ltd.
Milton Keynes UK
UKHW020907260119

336226UK00009B/379/P